The
Greek-English
NEW TESTAMENT

- **King James Version**
- **New International Version**
- **Greek Text**
- **Literal Interlinear**

The

Greek-English
NEW TESTAMENT

- **King James Version**
- **New International Version**
- **Greek Text**
- **Literal Interlinear**

CHRISTIANITY TODAY
Washington Building
Washington, D.C. 20005

First Printing   1975
Second Printing   1975

Copyright © 1975
The Iversen-Norman Associates
175 Fifth Avenue, N.Y. 10010
Library of Congress Catalog Card Number: 75-4148
Printed in the United States of America

CONTENTS

INTRODUCTION

The purpose of this volume is to promote the comparative reading and study of the Scriptures. By placing the Interlinear Greek-English text alongside the classic King James and the newly translated New International Version of the New Testament, we have attempted to create a valuable resource for all students of the Word.

The Nestle's Greek New Testament used herein is one of the most reliable available today. This widely used edition was prepared by Eberhard Nestle seventy-seven years ago. It was Nestle's intention to offer the results of the scientific investigations of the nineteenth century. The text is based on a comparison of the texts edited by Tischendorf (1869-72), by Westcott and Hort (1881), and by Bernhard Weiss (1894-1900). Where two of these editions agree, this reading is printed by Nestle.

In connection with the sesquicentennial celebration of the British and Foreign Bible Society, a revised edition of Eberhard Nestle's 1904 text was edited by G. D. Kilpatrick, Erwin Nestle and several other scholars in London during 1958.

The King James Version is the product of the best Bible scholars of the 16th century. It is still highly regarded for its accuracy and beauty. The New International Version is the most recent translation made by scholars working directly from the Greek. Hence, you have in this volume two excellent translations to compare with the literal Greek translation.

It is hoped that you will find using this book to be both an inspiration as well as enhancing your knowledge of the New Testament.

THE IVERSEN-NORMAN ASSOCIATES

THE

NEW TESTAMENT

OF OUR LORD AND SAVIOUR
JESUS CHRIST

Translated out of the original Greek and with the former
translations diligently compared and revised

Set forth in 1611
And commonly known as the

KING JAMES VERSION

THE EPISTLE DEDICATORY

TO THE MOST HIGH *and* MIGHTY PRINCE JAMES *by the Grace of God*
KING OF GREAT BRITAIN, FRANCE, *and* IRELAND, DEFENDER OF THE
FAITH, &C. *The Translators of this Bible wish Grace, Mercy, and*
Peace, through JESUS CHRIST *our Lord*

Great and manifold were the blessings, most dread Sovereign, which
Almighty God, the Father of all mercies, bestowed upon us the people
of England, when first he sent Your Majesty's Royal Person to rule and
reign over us. For whereas it was the expectation of many, who
wished not well unto our Sion, that upon the setting of that bright
Occidental Star, Queen Elizabeth of most happy memory, some thick
and palpable clouds of darkness would so have overshadowed this
Land, that men should have been in doubt which way they were to
walk; and that it should hardly be known, who was to direct the unsettled State; the appearance of Your Majesty, as of the Sun in his
strength, instantly dispelled those supposed and surmised mists, and
gave unto all that were well affected exceeding cause of comfort; especially when we beheld the Government established in Your Highness,
and Your hopeful Seed, by an undoubted Title, and this also accompanied with peace and tranquillity at home and abroad.

But among all our joys, there was no one that more filled our
hearts, than the blessed continuance of the preaching of God's sacred
Word among us; which is that inestimable treasure, which excelleth
all the riches of the earth; because the fruit thereof extendeth itself,
not only to the time spent in this transitory world, but directeth and
disposeth men unto that eternal happiness which is above in heaven.

Then not to suffer this to fall to the ground, but rather to take it up,
and to continue it in that state, wherein the famous Predecessor of
Your Highness did leave it: nay, to go forward with the confidence and
resolution of a Man in maintaining the truth of Christ, and propagating
it far and near, is that which hath so bound and firmly knit the hearts
of all Your Majesty's loyal and religious people unto You, that Your
very name is precious among them: their eye doth behold You with
comfort, and they bless You in their hearts, as that sanctified Person,
who, under God, is the immediate Author of their true happiness.
And this their contentment doth not diminish or decay, but every day
increaseth and taketh strength, when they observe, that the zeal of
Your Majesty toward the house of God doth not slack or go backward, but is more and more kindled, manifesting itself abroad in the

farthest parts of Christendom, by writing in defence of the Truth, (which hath given such a blow unto that man of sin, as will not be healed,) and every day at home, by religious and learned discourse, by frequenting the house of God, by hearing the Word preached, by cherishing the Teachers thereof, by caring for the Church, as a most tender and loving nursing Father.

There are infinite arguments of this right Christian and religious affection in Your Majesty; but none is more forcible to declare it to others than the vehement and perpetuated desire of accomplishing and publishing of this work, which now with all humility we present unto Your Majesty. For when Your Highness had once out of deep judgment apprehended how convenient it was, that out of the Original Sacred Tongues, together with comparing of the labours, both in our own, and other foreign Languages, of many worthy men who went before us, there should be one more exact Translation of the Holy Scriptures into the English Tongue; Your Majesty did never desist to urge and to excite those to whom it was commended, that the work might be hastened, and that the business might be expedited in so decent a manner, as a matter of such importance might justly require.

And now at last, by the mercy of God, and the continuance of our labours, it being brought unto such a conclusion, as that we have great hopes that the Church of England shall reap good fruit thereby; we hold it our duty to offer it to Your Majesty, not only as to our King and Sovereign, but as to the principal Mover and Author of the work: humbly craving of Your most Sacred Majesty, that since things of this quality have ever been subject to the censures of illmeaning and discontented persons, it may receive approbation and patronage from so learned and judicious a Prince as Your Highness is, whose allowance and acceptance of our labours shall more honour and encourage us, than all the calumniations and hard interpretations of other men shall dismay us. So that if, on the one side, we shall be traduced by Popish Persons at home or abroad, who therefore will malign us, because we are poor instruments to make God's holy Truth to be yet more and more known unto the people, whom they desire still to keep in ignorance and darkness; or if, on the other side, we shall be maligned by selfconceited Brethren, who run their own ways, and give liking unto nothing, but what is framed by themselves, and hammered on their anvil; we may rest secure, supported within by the truth and innocency of a good conscience, having walked the ways of simplicity and integrity, as before the Lord; and sustained without by the powerful protection of Your Majesty's grace and favour, which will ever give countenance to honest and Christian endeavours against bitter censures and uncharitable imputations.

The Lord of heaven and earth bless Your Majesty with many and happy days, that, as his heavenly hand hath enriched Your Highness with many singular and extraordinary graces, so You may be the wonder of the world in this latter age for happiness and true felicity, to the honour of that great GOD, and the good of his Church, through Jesus Christ our Lord and only Saviour.

NEW INTERNATIONAL VERSION

OF THE

NEW TESTAMENT

ZONDERVAN BIBLE PUBLISHERS
Grand Rapids, Michigan

PREFACE

This New Testament is the first portion of The New International Version of the Holy Bible. It is a completely new translation made by many scholars working directly from the Greek.

The New International Version had its beginning in 1965, when, after many years of exploratory study, a group of biblical scholars met in Chicago and concurred in the need for a new translation of the Holy Scriptures. This group, though not made up of official church representatives, was nevertheless transdenominational in character. Their conclusion was subsequently endorsed by a large gathering of Christian leaders from many denominations in North America. Final responsibility for the new version was delegated to a body of fifteen, the Committee on Bible Translation, composed for the most part of biblical specialists from universities, colleges and theological seminaries. In 1967 the New York Bible Society International generously undertook financial sponsorship of the project—a sponsorship that has made it possible to enlist the help of many distinguished scholars. The fact that participants from the United States, Canada, England, Australia and New Zealand are working together gives the project its international scope. That they come from various denominations, including Baptist, Brethren, Church of Christ, Episcopal, Lutheran, Mennonite, Methodist, Nazarene, Presbyterian, and Reformed churches, safeguards it from sectarian bias.

Because the distinctive nature of the New International Version is derived so largely from the working procedures, an explanation of these is in order. The translation of each book was assigned to a team of scholars. Next, an Intermediate Editorial Committee revised the initial translation, with constant reference to the Greek. Their work then went to a General Editorial Committee, which rechecked it in relation to the Greek and made another thorough revision. This revision in turn was carefully reviewed by the Committee on Bible Translation, which made further changes and then issued the final version. In this way the entire New Testament underwent three revisions, during each of which the translation was examined for its faithfulness to the original Greek and for its English style.

A sensitive feeling for style does not always go with scholarship in biblical languages. Accordingly the Committee on Bible Translation submitted the developing version to a number of literary consultants. Two of them read every word of the completed New Testament twice—once before the last major revision and once afterward—making invaluable suggestions. During the process, it was also tested for clarity and idiom by various kinds of people—young and old, educated and uneducated, ministers and laymen.

The Greek text used in the work of translation was an eclectic one. No other piece of ancient literature has so much manuscript support as does the New Testament. Where existing texts differ, the translators made their choice of readings in accord with sound principles of textual criticism. Footnotes call attention to places where there is uncertainty about what constitutes the original text. These have been introduced by the phrase "Some MSS add (*or* omit *or* read)."

As in all translations of the Scriptures, the precise meaning of the original text could not in every case be determined. In important instances of this kind, footnotes introduced by "Or" suggest an alternate rendering of the text. In the translation itself, brackets are occasionally used to indicate words or phrases supplied for clarification.

Certain convictions and aims have guided the translators. They are all committed to the full authority and complete trustworthiness of the Scriptures, which they believe to be God's Word in written form. They are agreed that the Bible contains the answer to man's deepest needs and sets forth the way to his eternal well-being. Therefore their first concern has been the accuracy of the translation and its fidelity to the thought of the New Testament writers. While they have weighed the significance of the lexical and grammatical details of the Greek text, they have striven for more than a word-for-word translation. Because thought patterns and syntax differ from language to language, faithful communication of the meaning of the writers of the New Testament demands frequent modifications in sentence structure and constant regard for the contextual meanings of words.

Concern for clarity of style—that it should be idiomatic without being idiosyncratic, contemporary without being dated—has also motivated the translators and their consultants. They have consistently aimed at simplicity of expression, with sensitive attention to the connotation and sound of the chosen word. At the same time, they have endeavored to avoid a sameness of style in order to reflect the varied styles and moods of the New Testament writers. These aims the translators and consultants have tried to embody in language that will speak not only to people today but also to those of future decades. And they trust that the wide use of the New International Version will encourage the wholesome practice of memorizing Scripture.

Among the languages of the world, English stands first in international use. The translators of this version, coming as they do from major English-speaking nations, have sought to recognize the world-wide character of the language by avoiding overt Americanisms on the one hand and overt Anglicisms on the other hand.

As for the omission of the pronouns "thou," "thee," and "thine" in reference to the Deity, the translators remind the reader that to retain these archaisms (along with the strange verb forms, such as *doest, wouldest* and *hadst*) would have violated their aim of faithful translation. The Greek text uses no special pronouns to express reverence for God and Christ. Scripture is not enhanced by keeping, as a special mode of addressing Deity, forms that in the days of the King James Bible were simply the regular pronouns and verbs used in everyday speech, whether referring to God or to man.

Like all translations of the Bible, made as they are by imperfect men, this one undoubtedly falls short of its aims. Yet we are grateful to God for the extent to which he has enabled us to realize our aims and for the strength he has given us to complete this part of our task. We offer this version of the New Testament to him in whose name and for whose glory it has been made. We pray that it will lead many into a better understanding of the Holy Scriptures and a fuller knowledge of Jesus Christ the Incarnate Word, of whom the Scriptures so faithfully testify.

The Committee on Bible Translation
Names of the translators and editors may be secured
from the New York Bible Society International,
5 East 48th Street, New York, New York 10017

THE INTERLINEAR

GREEK-ENGLISH

NEW TESTAMENT

**The Nestle Greek Text
with a Literal English Translation
by**

The Reverend Alfred Marshall D. Litt.

and a Foreword by

The Reverend Prebendary J. B. Phillips M.A.

ZONDERVAN PUBLISHING HOUSE
A DIVISION OF THE ZONDERVAN CORPORATION
Grand Rapids, Michigan

First Edition 1968
Published by special arrangement with
Samuel Bagster & Sons, Ltd.
London
Printed in the United States of America

FOREWORD

THE REVEREND PREBENDARY J. B. PHILLIPS M.A.

There is undoubtedly a revived interest in the reading of the New Testament today. The sales of modern versions have, I think, surprised everybody while the demand for the Authorized Version continues as before. It seems that a great many people are turning again to these inspired documents to see for themselves the foundations on which the Christian Faith is built. Naturally, to any Christian these are the most important documents in the world. If we believe with our adult minds that we live on a planet visited by God Himself in human form, the record of His life and teaching and that of the movement which He began are of supreme importance to the entire human race. Anything therefore which makes the significance and relevance of the Personal Visit clearer to the reader is to be welcomed with open arms.

As a modern translator I am delighted to see this new Interlinear Greek-English New Testament. By no means everybody knows of the quiet patient work of the textual critics who, with the utmost care and reverence, compare and revise Greek texts so that we may possess Greek as near as possible to the original documents, none of which, alas, survives. In this book we have the Greek text in its most modern revised form; it is the fruit of many years of diligent scholarship and, to my mind, should be accepted with the respect it deserves. A lot has been learned and a good deal of fresh material has been discovered since the Authorized Version was made in 1611 and indeed since the issue of the Revised Version in 1881. Here, interlined with probably the most accurate Greek that we can arrive at, is a literal English version. Dr. Marshall has obviously done this work of putting the nearest English equivalents to the Greek words with great care and skill and his work should prove of the highest value to any student of the New Testament.

It need hardly be said that this giving of verbal equivalents is not a full translation, but it is an essential stage in that process. The art of translation itself is not only the transferring of words from one language to another but also the accurate transmission of thought, feeling, atmosphere and even of style. But no translator can do his work properly without the transitional stage which Dr. Marshall exhibits so brilliantly in this book. Anyone with even a small knowledge of Greek will be able to see how and why the Authorized Version translators did their work as they did, and will also see how and why a modern translator produces a vastly different verbal result. The intelligent reader cannot fail to find this transitional stage, which is here so clearly shown, both fascinating and revealing. And if, with only a small knowledge of Greek, he should try to make his own translation, so much the better! He will at least be saved from over-familiarity with extremely meaningful words and sayings; and the chances are that the Truth will break over him afresh, as it does over any translator, ancient or modern, professional or amateur.

Although I consider that Dr. Marshall has done his work supremely well, it is a good thing to bear in mind that you cannot always either give an English equivalent for a Greek word or expression, or even always render the same Greek word by the same English one. May I take one word, the Greek verb *ΕΚΒΑΛΛΩ* with its basic meaning of "throwing out". Dr. Marshall renders this word variously: it is "pluck out" (Matthew *ch.* 7, *v.* 5), "cast out" (Matthew *ch.* 8, *v.* 12), "put out" (Matthew *ch.* 9, *v.* 25), "expel" (Matthew *ch.* 12, *v.* 24), "puts forth" (Matthew *ch.* 12, *v.* 35), and "take out" (Luke *ch.* 6, *v.* 42)! And of course there are many other cases where absolute consistency is impossible; for words are not static things but expressions of thought which are inevitably modified by their context. But we must not expect impossibilities and I for one am grateful for an alert and intelligent literal translation wedded to the latest and most reliable Greek Text. I am glad, for example, to see that Dr. Marshall has not missed the peculiar Greek construction in Matthew *ch.* 16, *v.* 19, where Jesus tells Peter that "what he binds on earth" will be "what has been bound" in Heaven. There is a world of difference between guaranteeing celestial endorsement of the Apostle's actions and promising that his actions guided by the Holy Spirit will be in accordance with the Heavenly pattern! Again, since I know there are many who imagine that the Authorized Version is a particularly literal and accurate translation of the Greek, it is refreshing to turn to Matthew *ch.* 27, *v.* 44 and see that not one single word of the expression "cast the same in his teeth" is in fact in the Greek! It is further made clear that the "bottles" of Matthew *ch.* 9, *v.* 17, were in reality wineskins, and that in Jesus' time people did not "sit at meat" so much as recline! (Luke *ch.* 7, *v.* 36), and naturally there are scores of further examples which are both interesting and important.

It would be unwise to omit reading Dr. Marshall's Introduction; for in it he not only explains some peculiarities of Greek construction, of which the ordinary reader may be quite unaware, but also clearly shows the rules he has set for himself in making this literal translation. Moreover, his Notes on Particular Passages are well worth our attention. In all, I have the greatest pleasure in recommending this book. It is timely because of the great contemporary interest in the New Testament. And it is profoundly interesting because we have here, combined in the most intimate fashion, the results of a great deal of textual research and the interpretation of a scholar thoroughly familiar with New Testament Greek.

INTRODUCTION

The Reverend Alfred Marshall d.litt

The Greek Text

The text of the Greek New Testament has come down to us in various manuscripts, printing not being invented until the 15th century (Erasmus published his Greek New Testament in 1516). Some of these manuscripts are more important than others (age is not necessarily determinative of importance). The study of the various manuscript copies, and the assessment of their individual value in attempting to reconstruct the original as nearly as possible, constitutes the science of Textual Criticism. For those who wish to study this seriously there are many books available; it is sufficient to say here that, after Erasmus, a great number of scholars have, over a long period, applied themselves to the task of constructing a reliable text out of the mass of various readings which have arisen from copying and making copies from copies of the old manuscripts: such scholars as Mill, Stephens, Griesbach, Lachmann, Tischendorf, Tregelles, Alford, and many more.

The Revised Standard Version of the New Testament is an authorized revision of the American Standard Version, published in 1901. This was a revision of the King James Version, published in 1611, itself more a revision of older versions than a new translation.

The Greek text used in this book is that of the 21st edition of Eberhard Nestle's *Novum Testamentum Graece*, based on the study and critical research of generations of scholars, except that the passage John 7. 53, 8. 1-11 is not in that text but is relegated to the foot of the page as a critical note. It is here retained in the text. The critical notes of Nestle's work, which enable students to follow the reasons for variations in the text, have been omitted as being outside the scope of this publication. The student who requires these critical notes is referred to the Greek edition published in this country by the British and Foreign Bible Society and in Germany (Stuttgart) by Privilegierte Württembergische Bibelanstalt, by whose permission this recension is used.

In certain places in the Greek text square brackets are found; these indicate only that, according to Nestle, some editors include and others omit the word or words so enclosed. Translation has been made here in the usual way.

Avoiding interpretation, then, we give some details of how we have proceeded in the matter of a literal translation. These should be studied and understood if proper use is to be made of this attempt to promote an intelligent reading of the Greek New Testament.

THE ENGLISH TRANSLATION

The relationship between the Greek text and the interlinear English is as follows: Greek words not required in the translation into English are (*a*) represented by a short dash, as for example the definite article with proper names. Alternatively (*b*) italic type is used to show that words or even in some cases letters are not really needed for an idiomatic English rendering. 'Man' is sometimes redundant (see Matthew *ch.* 20, *v.* 1 and Acts *ch.* 2, *v.* 22) and so on. On the other hand, words supplied in English for which there is no Greek equivalent are placed in square brackets [. . .]. Naturally, there will be differences of judgment as to this practice in the passages involved.

In the interlinear translation, a comma has in a number of places been introduced after "Behold". The reason for this is as follows: the Greek ἰδού (or other form), properly an imperative of the defective verb ὁράω, is used as an exclamation, as is its English equivalent; that is to say, it is not then an active verb taking a direct object in the accusative case, but is simply exclamatory and is followed by a noun in the nominative, with its predicate or complement understood.

For example, in John *ch.* 1, *v.* 29, there is not a command to behold the Lamb of God, but, as it might be said (and as in fact a preacher was recently heard to say), "Look! [there goes] . . . " The position is different in such passages as Matthew *ch.* 28, *v.* 6 and Romans *ch.* 11, *v.* 22, where there is a command. Strangely enough, the Authorized Version inserts a comma in I. John *ch.* 3, *v.* 1, where it is not required. There is here a command as in the two passages just cited: "See what manner of love . . . ".

The modern form for the third person singular of verbs (present indicative) has been used (loves) in place of the now obsolete -(e)th (loveth); but the older 'ye' has been retained for the nominative ('you' for the oblique cases) of the second person plural pronoun; and 'thou' (thee), not 'you', for the second person singular. It is a loss that in modern English these differences have disappeared; so unaccustomed are we now to them that even the average reader of the Authorized Version misses the point of Luke *ch.* 22, *v.* 31. The loss is even more to be regretted when God is addressed as 'You'.

The subjunctive mood is dying out in English, and no attempt has been made to represent consistently the Greek mood, except by the use of the analytic form "I may . . . ", with its related optative (of which latter there are only 37 examples in the New Testament, 15 of these being the familiar γένοιτο =may it be). But such words as ἵνα and compounds of ἄν (ὅταν, ἐάν), etc., introducing a subjective or hypothetical element into a verbal idea, require to be followed by the subjunctive mood.

The Greek perfect can generally be taken as represented by an English present: a past action continuing in its effect down to the present, in contrast to an action wholly in the past. But in a literal translation the English perfect has been retained. In John *ch.* 11, *v.* 27, the Authorized Version is idiomatically correct but the Revised Version is literally so (πεπίστευκα =I have believed); *cf.* II. Timothy *ch.* 1, *v.* 12, where the Authorized Version adopts the literal equivalent. So, *e.g.*, τετέλεσται =it has been finished =it is finished. In participles, italics show that the auxiliary verbs may be dispensed with in English.

Where some word other than the strictly literal one seems to be needed in the translation, the former is printed in parentheses immediately after the latter; *e.g.*, Matthew *ch.* 10, *v.* 17, "beware from(of) men."

Occasionally it is not feasible to give a literal rendering without undue explanation; some idiomatic word or phrase has to be used. There are only a few of such passages and they are indicated by the mark †.

There are a number of Greek phrases, other than where † is used, which are not to be taken word for word, but as a whole:

ἐπὶ τὸ αὐτό =on the same =together
διὰ τοῦτο =because-of this =therefore
ἵνα μή =in-order-that not =lest
καθ' ὑπερβολήν =by-way-of excess =excessively

In familiar proper names there will appear some inconsistency, a compromise between the actual spellings preferred by Nestle and the Authorized Version; but this is of no great importance.

Εὐαγγελίζω. This and its cognate noun have been anglicized (evangelize, evangel). But while we can 'evangelize' a city, we do not 'evangelize' a person or a subject; so we must speak of 'preaching (good tidings) to' a person or of 'preaching' a subject. We can of course speak of 'evangelizing' absolutely, as in I. Corinthians *ch.* 1, *v.* 17. Ellicott on I. Thessalonians *ch.* 3, *v.* 6 has some useful information for the student.

There are five idiomatic Greek constructions which, being of frequent occurrence, call for explanation.

a. The *genitive absolute*. This is made up of a participle and a noun or pronoun, both in the genitive case and agreeing otherwise as well, but having no grammatical relation to the context. It is used to indicate time during or at which something takes place, or in some circumstances connected therewith. The close of such a Greek phrase is shown by the superior letter [a]; see Luke *ch*. 3, *v*. 1. There are variations of this. In Luke *ch*. 12, *v*. 36, two participles are used with no noun—it has to be supplied from the context. So also II. Corinthians *ch*. 7, *v*. 15, and see the note on Romans *ch*. 9, *v*. 11 under "Notes on Particular Passages" below.

b. The *accusative* (or other case) *and infinitive*. Here what is in English the subject of the verb (the doer of the action) is put in the accusative (or other) case and the verb itself in the infinitive. A superior letter [b] closes such a phrase; see Luke *ch*. 1, *v*. 21.

c. The *dative of possession*. The possessor is put in the dative case. The idea may be grasped by comparing our English way of saying that a thing 'belongs to so-and-so'. The superior letter [c] shows this idiom; see Luke *ch*. 1, *v*. 5, 7, 14.

d. The *genitive of purpose* or *result*. The infinitive of a verb is in the genitive case, as shown by the preceding definite article. The article itself can be ignored. Again the appropriate letter [d] shows the existence of the idiom; see Matthew *ch*. 2, *v*. 13. The same idea can be shown without any article; see Matthew *ch*. 4, *v*. 1.

e. The *dative of time*. A point of time 'in' or 'at' which a thing happens is thus shown (ἐν may or may not be used). The letter [e] shows this; see Luke *ch*. 2, *v*. 43, and *ch*. 18, *v*. 35.

The constructions b and e can sometimes be combined; see Luke *ch*. 1, *v*. 8.

There is no indefinite article in Greek. The use of it in translation is a matter of individual judgment. The numeral 'one' is sometimes found; whether this means that just one, and no more, is to be understood is again open to argument. See Matthew *ch*. 21, *v*. 19 and *ch*. 26, *v*. 69. We have inserted 'a' or 'an' as a matter of course where it seems called for.

The definite article must sometimes be rendered by a pronoun or a possessive adjective. This is particularly so where parts of the body are indicated; *e.g.*, Matthew *ch*. 8, *v*. 3. Sometimes it is used 'pronominally'—that is, it must be rendered 'he' (or otherwise according to the gender) or 'they'; see Mark *ch*. 10, *v*. 4.

The ending of a Greek verb normally indicates the person (1st, 2nd, or 3rd, sing. or pl.). If the pronoun is separately expressed, this can be clearly seen in the interlinear translation.

μέν ... δέ. These two particles, in contrasted clauses, are not translatable literally, unless "indeed ... but" be used, as we have done in some places. But by adopting the phrases "on one hand ... on the other" the contrast is brought out. These particles are, in fact, somewhat elusive as to their force. See John *ch.* 19, *v.* 24 and 32, where μέν has been left untranslated—an example of the difficulty of rendering it satisfactorily in a literal translation.

It has not been considered necessary always to indicate the order of a noun and its adjective; a knowledge of English is sufficient for this. But where there is any risk of ambiguity small superior figures indicate the order in which the words should be read.

A number of Greek particles are said to be 'post-positive'—that is to say, they cannot stand as the first word in a sentence, but are found in the second, third, or even in the fourth place. Such words must of course be taken first in English; but it has not been thought necessary to show this, as the construction is sufficiently obvious. They include γάρ (for), δέ (and, but, now), οὖν (therefore; "therefore" can be post-positive in English), τις (a certain), μέν (indeed), γε (really—generally too subtle to be reproduced in English).

ὅτι as a conjunction, when meaning "that", is used to introduce spoken words as recorded; it is then known as the 'recitative ὅτι'. In English the original present tense of any verb would in such a construction ('indirect speech') be changed to the past: He said that the man was a liar. But Greek retains the original tense as actually used. What the speaker really said was "The man is a liar". The conjunction thus becomes superfluous and the reported words would in modern usage be put within quotation marks, as above. These, however, are not used in this translation. See Matthew *ch.* 21, *v.* 3.

ἵνα is, strictly, a 'telic' particle—*i.e.*, it denotes purpose (τέλος, an end); hence a full translation is "in order that". But inasmuch as in New Testament times there was a tendency to use it where ὅτι would be expected, it sometimes means no more than the conjunction "that"; see Matthew *ch.* 5, *v.* 29. Sometimes, then, where there may be room for difference of opinion as to its precise force, or even where there is none, "*in order* that" will be found in the literal translation.

A peculiarity of Greek construction is that a neuter plural subject may take a singular verb; but this is by no means invariable, and there appears to be no rule to go by. In translating, the position is sometimes shown by the use of an italic letter for the ending of the verb ([they] commits); at other times the alternative is given in parenthesis (is(are)). But there are places where neither course is possible without taking up too much space, and the matter is left to the intelligence of the reader.

Where there is more than one subject of a verb, Greek will often put the verb in the singular to agree with the nearest subject. This is not in accordance with English grammar, which requires a plural verb if there is more than one subject. In Revelation *ch.* 9, *v.* 2, "sun" and "air" call for the plural "were darkened", as in the Authorized Version. But the Greek verb is in the singular. It is sometimes typographically possible to indicate the difference of grammatical usage, but not always.

In Greek, gender belongs to the word and not necessarily to what is indicated by the word; whereas of course in English we keep the ideas of masculine, feminine, and neuter to men, women, and inanimate things respectively. (English, by the way, is the only great modern language to do so.) Allowance must be made for this in translating: sometimes it is possible to transfer the idea from one language to another, but not always. The note to Revelation *ch.* 13, *v.* 1, may be consulted.

The construction of the demonstrative adjectives is peculiar in Greek. The definite article is used as well as the demonstrative adjective in one of two possible positions: either—

οὗτος ὁ οἶκος
this *the* house

or—

ὁ οἶκος οὗτος
the house this

The definite article is of course not wanted in English, and the proper translation of the phrase is obvious—"this house". ἐκεῖνος (that) similarly. It is sometimes possible typographically to treat the three-word phrase as a whole, with the idiomatic translation underneath.

Similarly, the definite article is used in Greek with a possessive adjective, as in Matthew *ch.* 18, *v.* 20—

εἰς τὸ ἐμὸν ὄνομα
in *the* my name

or, alternatively again, the construction may be, say—

εἰς τὸ ὄνομα τὸ ἐμόν
in *the* name *the* my

This remark applies only to the first and second persons, singular and plural, but not to the third, where the only possible construction in this respect would be "in the name of him/her/them". This has been followed literally, as the reader can always make the needful English construction for himself. Occasionally such a construction as "in the name of me" will be found, meaning the same thing.

The neuter form of an adjective may be used as an adverb. ἀληθῆ in John *ch.* 19, *v.* 35, is the neuter of ἀληθής (true) and must be rendered "truly". So πρῶτον (firstly), though "first" is quite often used in English as an adverb. Conversely, an adverb may be used as an adjective; *e.g.* νῦν, now=present.

ταῦτα=these things (neuter plural) might be rendered by the singular "this", as in the common phrase μετὰ ταῦτα=after this; but this liberty has not been taken in the present literal translation.

The gender of an adjective may demand 'man', 'woman', or 'thing' to be supplied; *e.g.* Matthew *ch.* 9, *v.* 27—"two blind men".

Greek will often use a preposition in a compound verb and then repeat it (or use one similar) before a noun in the same sentence; in such passages the preposition would not be used twice in English. But in such a phrase as εἰσέρχεσθαι εἰς οἶκον we can say 'to enter into a house' (this has a counterpart in French—*entrer dans une maison*). We can indeed say simply 'to enter a house'. Another exception would be ἀπέρχεσθαι ἀπό =to go away from. But διαφέρειν διὰ τοῦ ἱεροῦ= to carry *through* through the temple (see Mark *ch.* 11, *v.* 16).

As the negatives οὐ(κ) (categorical) and μή (hypothetical) are easily recognizable, it has not been thought necessary always to render them separately, but they are included with any verb with which they may be used. But whereas in English the negative follows the verb, in Greek it precedes; see Matthew *ch.* 3, *v.* 11. If such a phrase happens to be broken at the end of a line this course has not been feasible.

The double negative οὐ μή has been consistently rendered "by no means".

Incidentally, though of importance, these two negative particles, or their compounds, when introducing questions, expect different answers. οὐ appeals to the fact, anticipating 'Yes, it is so'; *e.g.* John *ch.* 11, *v.* 9, "Are there not twelve hours of the day?" The answer would be 'Yes, there are'. μή, on the contrary, denies the suggestion and expects the reply 'No, it is not so'; or, if not so explicit as that, doubts whether it is so; *e.g.* John *ch.* 18, *v.* 35. The form of the question in the Authorized Version and the Revised Version indicates that Pilate was asking for information, whereas he was rejecting the idea with scorn and contempt—'I am not a Jew [am I]?' The answer, if any, would be—'No, certainly not.' This distinction is largely overlooked in the English Versions.

To assist to the correct nuance of thought, in such places the latter negative in the interlinear translation is italicized, and the reader must read into the original what is intended; the result is sometimes surprising.

An article in *The Bible Translator* for January, 1953, may be consulted.

While on the subject of negatives, Greek favours the use of two such, one strengthening the other. In such sentences the second negative has to be replaced in English by a positive; *e.g.* Matthew *ch.* 22, *v.* 46.

There is the *genitive of quality*, of which there are many examples in the New Testament. If in English we say "a man of courage" or "an act of kindness", this is equivalent to "a courageous man" or "a kind act" respectively. We have translated literally, with an occasional footnote where this construction is not generally recognized. The Authorized Version itself is not consistent—*cf.* Philippians *ch.* 3, *v.* 21, with Colossians *ch.* 1, *v.* 22, where surely the distinction is between "his glorious body" and "his fleshly body".

Necessity or compulsion is most frequently expressed by the use of an impersonal verb (or a verb used impersonally), with the person concerned in the accusative as the object of the verb: δεῖ με=it behoves me=I must.

As 'first' is used as an adverb as well as 'firstly' it has not been thought necessary always to print 'first*ly*'; the matter is of no great importance.

Finally, but certainly not least in importance, there are the Greek participles, to which we now give special attention.

Greek is "a participle-loving language", said the late A. T. Robertson, and it uses this part of speech much more frequently than we do, and in different ways.

To begin with, it is absolutely essential to grasp the distinction between *continuous*, *momentary*, and *completed* action. The first is commonly, but wrongly, spoken of as a present participle; the second as an aorist (which does not mean "past"); and the third as a perfect. (There is a rare future participle—continuous in the future.) Now—

1. A participle may be used as an adjective qualifying a noun, just as in English; *e.g.* I. Thessalonians *ch.* 1, *v.* 9—"a living God"; Hebrews *ch.* 7, *v.* 8—"dying men". This is so simple as not to need further remark.

2. A participle may be used, again as in English, as a verb to

describe some action; *e.g.* Acts *ch.* 9, *v.* 39—"all the widows stood by . . . weeping and showing . . .".

3. A participle may be used, with the definite article, with, say, "one" understood, where we should use a noun or a relative phrase; *e.g.*, frequently, ὁ πιστεύων=the [one] believing=the believer *or* he who believes. Here the participle is continuous; in Luke *ch.* 1, *v.* 45, it is momentary (and, naturally, feminine in gender as referring to Mary's one act of faith at the Annunciation). If two participles are used with but one definite article, as in John *ch.* 5, *v.* 24, the meaning is that one person is doubly described, not two persons doing two things. This feature has been preserved in our translation.

4. Very frequently indeed, where in English we use two or more finite verbs to describe associated actions, Greek will use participles and only one finite verb for the main action. But here judgment is necessary to distinguish two (or more) simultaneous actions from consecutive ones; and as we have no aorist participle in English the matter is not always free from difficulty. In Acts *ch.* 10, *v.* 34, "Peter opening his mouth said", the two actions were obviously simultaneous! So in Acts *ch.* 1, *v.* 24—"praying they said". But sometimes one action must be completed before another could begin; *e.g.* Luke *ch.* 22, *v.* 17—"having given thanks, he said . . .". Here the act of giving thanks to God would be complete before Jesus addressed His disciples; therefore the aorist participle must be represented in English by the analytic "having given thanks". That this is not unimportant is shown by Matthew *ch.* 26, *v.* 30—"having sung a hymn they went out". To translate the aorist participle here by "singing a hymn" would certainly convey the idea that the singing occurred as they went out. In Acts *ch.* 21, *v.* 14, it is not easy to see how the keeping silence and the saying could be contemporaneous: "Having said, The will of the Lord be done, we kept silence." These few examples should, we think, suffice to show the principles involved.

NOTES ON PARTICULAR PASSAGES

Mark *ch.* 10, *v.* 11.—An article by Dr. Nigel Turner in *The Bible Translator* for October, 1956, gives good reasons for understanding the verse thus, αὐτήν referring to the last woman mentioned (ἄλλην).

Mark *ch.* 14, *v.* 6.—The use of ἐν here is somewhat puzzling. The parallel in Matthew (*ch.* 26, *v.* 10) has εἰς, which would mean 'to', 'toward', or 'for'; and Mark's ἐν must then be taken as equivalent in meaning to εἰς. This may throw light on I John *ch.* 4, *v.* 16.

Luke *ch*. 7, *v*. 14.—ἐγέρθητι. It does not seem right to insist here on the passive voice; compare with *ch*. 8, *v*. 54, and, in another connection, *ch*. 11, *v*. 8. But our Lord "was raised", as are the dead generally (they do not "rise"). See I. Corinthians *ch*. 15, etc.

John *ch*. 8, *v*. 25.—"The answer of Jesus is one of the most disputed passages in the Gospel" (Godet). Nestle punctuates as a question; hence we have given what appears to be a reasonable rendering interrogatively.

Acts *ch*. 7, *v*. 46.—οἴκῳ is a manuscript variant for θεῷ. There is some uncertainty as to how this reading arose; see the Authorized Version. Has Psalm 24, *v*. 6, text and margin, any bearing on the matter?

Acts *ch*. 18, *v*. 10.—λαὸς πολύς must not be understood as meaning "many persons". λαός is the regular word for the chosen people, Israel (almost without exception). Here in Corinth was to be a new community, taking the place of the Jewish population. Translate—"a great people".

Romans *ch*. 1, *v*. 12.—That is, their faith (=confidence) in one another—Paul and his readers. "Mutual" is correct in A.V., but is generally misunderstood as being equivalent to "common", which it is not.

Romans *ch*. 9, *v*. 11.—There is no noun agreeing with the two participles. But it is nevertheless a 'genitive absolute' construction. The Authorized Version supplies the subject.

II. Corinthians *ch*. 11, *v*. 28.—There is another view of Paul's words here. ἐπίστασις occurs in the New Testament only here and in Acts *ch*. 24, *v*. 12. The related noun ἐπιστάτης (one standing over, superintendent, master) is peculiar to Luke (six times in his gospel). Then there is a variant reading in our verse, μου instead of μοι. So the meaning may be—"my daily superintendence *or* attention". This would bring it into line with the remainder of the verse.

Philippians *ch*. 3, *v*. 16.—This is, according to Burton, the only certain use in the New Testament of the 'imperatival infinitive', Romans *ch*. 12, *v*. 15 being a probable example. Moulton thinks it highly probable in Titus *ch*. 2, *v*. 1-10. The epistolary χαίρειν (Acts *ch*. 15, *v*. 23, *ch*. 23, *v*. 26; James *ch*. 1, *v*. 1) is said to be the same in origin, though a verb of bidding may be assumed, as in fact we do find in II. John *vs*. 10, 11. *Cf*. the French warning in railway carriages—*Ne pas se pencher au dehors*. In English we have such a full expression as "You are 'to do' so and so"; see II. Thessalonians *ch*. 3, *v*. 14. If Nestle's text is accepted here, it is an additional instance to those given under Philippians *ch*. 3, *v*. 16 above, though with a negative as a prohibition. (Textus Receptus, etc., give a plain imperative.) But perhaps we may insert "so as" —"mark this man, so as not to mix with him."

II. Timothy *ch.* 4, *v.* 3.—The construction of the last three words of this verse is difficult. "Having itching ears" may be a workable paraphrase, but it cannot be said to represent literally the actual Greek. There is no word for "having"; and there is nothing corresponding to "itching" as a participial adjective qualifying "ears". τὴν ἀκοήν is accusative singular, the object of a verb—and the only verb is the participle which precedes. This is masculine plural, agreeing with διδασκάλους, and, while this latter is accusative, whereas the participle is nominative, this must be taken as an example of rational rather than grammatical concord. It is the teachers who "tickle" the ears of those concerned.

Hebrews *ch.* 2, *v.* 10.—That is, it is God who perfected Jesus Christ (the author, or captain, of our salvation) by means of sufferings, whose work it is to lead many sons to glory. This is not what the Authorized Version nor the Revised Version says, but it is demanded by the grammar: ἀγαγόντα (leading) agrees with ἀρχηγόν not with αὐτῷ (=God). Besides, there is a parallel between Joshua and Jesus, as both leaders of their peoples. (The Berkeley version adopts this view, though we were not aware of it until our own order of words had been adopted.) In fine, it is the function of a captain to lead, and Jesus is the leader here.

Hebrews *ch.* 9, *vs.* 16-17.—We are aware of the problem in regard to διαθήκη in this passage; but this translation is no place for purporting to settle a question that has divided commentators. It must suffice to say that we have translated the word consistently as 'covenant'; the idea of a legatee receiving something on the death of a testator by reason of the latter's having made a 'testament' or 'will' is, so far as we can see, quite non-biblical. The covenant victim, then, is 'the one making covenant', unless the person establishing the covenant is to be understood as identifying himself with it; and the covenant is in fact ratified over the dead body or bodies. But other views are taken of the matter.

James *ch.* 2, *v.* 1.—There are other instances of such a construction—two genitives in apposition. Colossians *ch.* 1, *v.* 18: the meaning must be 'of the body (,) *of* the Church'—the body is the Church, as verse 24 says. Colossians *ch.* 2, *v.* 2: 'of God, of Christ'. Romans *ch.* 11, *v.* 17: see note at that place. John *ch.* 8, *v.* 44: 'of the father (,) *of* the devil'—their father was the devil.

Revelation *ch.* 16, *v.* 14: 'Almighty' is not an adjective but another noun in apposition.

NOTE on Mat. 16. 3, 27. 65; Luke 12. 56; Acts 21. 37; I. Thes. 4. 4; I. Tim. 3. 5; Jas. 4. 17; II. Pet. 2. 9.

As in French, so in the Greek of the N.T., we have the idea of "to know (how) to do" a thing as being the same as "to be able to do" it. But while *savoir* only is used in this way, not *connaître*, both γινώσκω and οἶδα are found in the N.T. In fact it is the former in Mat. 16. 3 and the latter in the parallel in Luke (12. 56). So, in French, *Savez-vous nager?* = Know you to swim? = Can you swim? In all the above passages this seems to be the meaning. It may be noted that the A.V. so renders the verbs in some passages, in others giving "know how". The James instance may be arguable. Phil. 4. 12 also may be considered, and Mat. 7. 11 = Luke 11. 13.

THE GREEK ALPHABET

A α	Alpha	a	
B β	Beta	b	
Γ γ	Gamma	g	hard, as in be*g*in[1]
Δ δ	Delta	d	
E ε	Epsilon	e	short, as in m*e*t
Z ζ	Zeta	z	
H η	Eta	e	long, as in sc*e*ne
Θ θ	Theta	th	as in *th*in
I ι	Iota	i	
K κ	Kappa	k	
Λ λ	Lambda	l	
M μ	Mu	m	
N ν	Nu	n	
Ξ ξ	Xi	x	
O ο	Omicron	o	short, as in l*o*t
Π π	Pi	p	
P ρ	Rho	r	
Σ σ, *final* s	Sigma	s[2]	
T τ	Tau	t	
Y υ	Upsilon	u	
Φ φ	Phi	ph	
X χ	Chi	ch	hard, as in lo*ch*
Ψ ψ	Psi	ps	
Ω ω	Omega	o	long, as in thr*o*ne

[1] Except that before κ, χ or another γ it is nasal—ng, as in a*n*chor.
[2] Sharp as in thi*s*, but flat before β or μ, as in a*s*bestos, di*s*mal.

The

Greek-English
NEW TESTAMENT

- **King James Version**
- **New International Version**
- **Greek Text**
- **Literal Interlinear**

King James Version

New International Version

THE GOSPEL

ACCORDING TO

SAINT MATTHEW

MATTHEW

The genealogy of Jesus

1 The book of the generation of Jesus Christ, the son of David, the son of Abraham. 2Abraham begat Isaac; and Isaac begat Jacob; and Jacob begat Judas and his brethren; 3And Judas begat Phares and Zara of Thamar; and Phares begat Esrom; and Esrom begat Aram; 4And Aram begat Aminadab; and Aminadab begat Naasson; and Naasson begat Salmon; 5And Salmon begat Booz of Rachab; and Booz begat Obed of Ruth; and Obed begat Jesse; 6And Jesse begat David the king; and David the king begat Solomon of her *that had been the wife* of Urias; 7And Solomon begat Roboam; and Roboam begat Abia; and Abia begat Asa; 8And Asa begat Josaphat; and Josaphat begat Joram; and Joram begat Ozias; 9And Ozias begat Joatham; and Joatham begat Achaz; and Achaz begat Ezekias; 10And Ezekias begat Manasses; and Manasses begat Amon; and Amon begat Josias; 11And Josias begat Jechonias and his brethren, about the time they were carried away to Babylon: 12And after they were brought to Babylon, Jechonias begat Salathiel; and Salathiel begat Zorobabel; 13And Zorobabel begat Abiud; and Abiud begat Eliakim; and Eliakim begat Azor; 14And Azor begat Sadoc; and Sadoc begat Achim; and Achim begat Eliud; 15And Eliud begat Eleazar; and Eleazar begat Matthan; and Matthan begat Jacob; 16And Jacob begat Joseph the husband of Mary, of whom was born Jesus, who is called Christ. 17 So all the generations from Abraham to David *are* fourteen generations; and from David until the carrying away into Babylon *are* fourteen generations; and from the carrying away into Babylon unto Christ *are* fourteen generations.

1 A record of the genealogy of Jesus Christ, son of David, son of Abraham:
2 Abraham was the father of Isaac,
  Isaac the father of Jacob,
  Jacob the father of Judah and his brothers,
  3 Judah the father of Perez and Zerah, whose mother was Tamar,
  Perez the father of Hezron,
  Hezron the father of Ram,
  4 Ram the father of Amminadab,
  Amminadab the father of Nahshon,
  Nahshon the father of Salmon,
  5 Salmon the father of Boaz, whose mother was Rahab,
  Boaz the father of Obed, whose mother was Ruth,
  Obed the father of Jesse,
  6 and Jesse the father of King David.
David was the father of Solomon, whose mother had been Uriah's wife,
  7 Solomon the father of Rehoboam,
  Rehoboam the father of Abijah,
  Abijah the father of Asa,
  8 Asa the father of Jehoshaphat,
  Jehoshaphat the father of Joram,
  Joram the father of Uzziah,
  9 Uzziah the father of Jotham,
  Jotham the father of Ahaz,
  Ahaz the father of Hezekiah,
  10 Hezekiah the father of Manasseh,
  Manasseh the father of Amon,
  Amon the father of Josiah,
  11 and Josiah the father of Jeconiah and his brothers at the time of the exile to Babylon.
12 After the exile to Babylon:
  Jeconiah was the father of Shealtiel,
  Shealtiel the father of Zerubbabel,
  13 Zerubbabel the father of Abiud,
  Abiud the father of Eliakim,
  Eliakim the father of Azor,
  14 Azor the father of Zadok,
  Zadok the father of Achim,
  Achim the father of Eliud,
  15 Eliud the father of Eleazar,
  Eleazar the father of Matthan,
  Matthan the father of Jacob,
  16 and Jacob the father of Joseph, the husband of Mary, of whom was born Jesus, who is called Christ.
17 Thus there were fourteen generations in all from Abraham to David, fourteen from David to the exile to Babylon, and fourteen from the exile to the Christ.[a]

[a] Or Messiah. "The Christ" (Greek) and "the Messiah" (Hebrew) both mean "the Anointed One."

ΚΑΤΑ   ΜΑΘΘΑΙΟΝ

Chapter 1

Βίβλος   γενέσεως   Ἰησοῦ   Χριστοῦ
[The] book of [the] generation of Jesus   Christ
υἱοῦ Δαυὶδ υἱοῦ Ἀβραάμ.
son of David son of Abraham.

2 Ἀβραὰμ ἐγέννησεν τὸν Ἰσαάκ, Ἰσαὰκ δὲ
Abraham   begat   -   Isaac,   and Isaac
ἐγέννησεν τὸν Ἰακώβ, Ἰακὼβ δὲ ἐγέννησεν τὸν
begat   -   Jacob,   and Jacob begat   -
Ἰούδαν καὶ τοὺς ἀδελφοὺς αὐτοῦ, 3 Ἰούδας δὲ
Judas and the   brothers   of him,   and Judas
ἐγέννησεν τὸν Φάρες καὶ τὸν Ζάρα ἐκ τῆς
begat   -   Phares and -   Zara out of -
Θαμάρ, Φάρες δὲ ἐγέννησεν τὸν Ἐσρώμ,
Thamar, and Phares begat   -   Esrom,
Ἐσρὼμ δὲ ἐγέννησεν τὸν Ἀράμ, 4 Ἀρὰμ δὲ
and Esrom begat   -   Aram,   and Aram
ἐγέννησεν τὸν Ἀμιναδάβ, Ἀμιναδὰβ δὲ
begat   -   Aminadab,   and Aminadab
ἐγέννησεν τὸν Ναασσών, Ναασσὼν δὲ ἐγέννησεν
begat   -   Naasson, and Naasson begat
τὸν Σαλμών, 5 Σαλμὼν δὲ ἐγέννησεν τὸν Βόες
-   Salmon,   and Salmon begat   -   Booz
ἐκ τῆς Ῥαχάβ, Βόες δὲ ἐγέννησεν τὸν Ἰωβὴδ
out of -   Rachab, and Booz begat   -   Obed
ἐκ τῆς Ῥούθ, Ἰωβὴδ δὲ ἐγέννησεν τὸν Ἰεσσαί,
out of -   Ruth, and Obed begat   -   Jesse,
6 Ἰεσσαὶ δὲ ἐγέννησεν τὸν Δαυὶδ τὸν βασιλέα.
and Jesse   begat   -   David the king.
Δαυὶδ δὲ ἐγέννησεν τὸν Σολομῶνα ἐκ τῆς
And David   begat   -   Solomon out of the
τοῦ Οὐρίου, 7 Σολομῶν δὲ ἐγέννησεν
[one who had been the wife]– of Uriah, and Solomon begat
τὸν Ῥοβοάμ, Ῥοβοὰμ δὲ ἐγέννησεν τὸν
-   Roboam,   and Roboam begat   -
Ἀβιά, Ἀβιὰ δὲ ἐγέννησεν τὸν Ἀσάφ, 8 Ἀσὰφ
Abia, and Abia begat   -   Asaph,   and Asaph
δὲ ἐγέννησεν τὸν Ἰωσαφάτ, Ἰωσαφὰτ δὲ
begat   -   Josaphat,   and Josaphat
ἐγέννησεν τὸν Ἰωράμ, Ἰωρὰμ δὲ ἐγέννησεν τὸν
begat   -   Joram,   and Joram begat   -
Ὀζίαν, 9 Ὀζίας δὲ ἐγέννησεν τὸν Ἰωαθάμ,
Ozias,   and Ozias begat   -   Joatham,
Ἰωαθὰμ δὲ ἐγέννησεν τὸν Ἀχάζ, Ἀχὰζ δὲ
and Joatham begat   -   Achaz,   and Achaz
ἐγέννησεν τὸν Ἐζεκίαν, 10 Ἐζεκίας δὲ
begat   -   Hezekias,   and Hezekias

ἐγέννησεν τὸν Μανασσῆ, Μανασσῆς δὲ ἐγέννησεν
begat   -   Manasses,   and Manasses begat
τὸν Ἀμώς, Ἀμὼς δὲ ἐγέννησεν τὸν Ἰωσίαν,
-   Amos,   and Amos begat   -   Josias,
11 Ἰωσίας δὲ ἐγέννησεν τὸν Ἰεχονίαν καὶ
and Josias   begat   -   Jechonias and
τοὺς ἀδελφοὺς αὐτοῦ ἐπὶ τῆς μετοικεσίας
the brothers   of him at the   deportation
Βαβυλῶνος. 12 Μετὰ δὲ τὴν μετοικεσίαν
of Babylon.   And after the   deportation
Βαβυλῶνος Ἰεχονίας ἐγέννησεν τὸν Σαλαθιήλ,
of Babylon Jechonias begat   -   Salathiel,
Σαλαθιὴλ δὲ ἐγέννησεν τὸν Ζοροβαβέλ,
and Salathiel begat   -   Zorobabel,
13 Ζοροβαβὲλ δὲ ἐγέννησεν τὸν Ἀβιούδ,
and Zorobabel   begat   -   Abiud,
Ἀβιοὺδ δὲ ἐγέννησεν τὸν Ἐλιακίμ, Ἐλιακὶμ δὲ
and Abiud begat   -   Eliakim,   and Eliakim
ἐγέννησεν τὸν Ἀζώρ, 14 Ἀζὼρ δὲ ἐγέννησεν
begat   -   Azor,   and Azor begat
τὸν Σαδώκ, Σαδὼκ δὲ ἐγέννησεν τὸν Ἀχίμ,
-   Sadoc,   and Sadoc begat   -   Achim,
Ἀχὶμ δὲ ἐγέννησεν τὸν Ἐλιούδ, 15 Ἐλιοὺδ δὲ
and Achim begat   -   Eliud,   and Eliud
ἐγέννησεν τὸν Ἐλεαζάρ, Ἐλεαζὰρ δὲ ἐγέννησεν
begat   -   Eleazar,   and Eleazar begat
τὸν Ματθάν, Ματθὰν δὲ ἐγέννησεν τὸν Ἰακώβ,
-   Matthan,   and Matthan begat   -   Jacob,
16 Ἰακὼβ δὲ ἐγέννησεν τὸν Ἰωσὴφ τὸν ἄνδρα
and Jacob   begat   -   Joseph the husband
Μαρίας, ἐξ ἧς ἐγεννήθη Ἰησοῦς ὁ λεγόμενος
of Mary, of whom was born Jesus the [one] called
Χριστός.
Christ.

17 Πᾶσαι οὖν αἱ γενεαὶ ἀπὸ Ἀβραὰμ
Therefore all the generations from Abraham
ἕως Δαυὶδ γενεαὶ δεκατέσσαρες, καὶ ἀπὸ
until David   generations fourteen,   and from
Δαυὶδ ἕως τῆς μετοικεσίας Βαβυλῶνος γενεαὶ
David until the deportation of Babylon generations
δεκατέσσαρες, καὶ ἀπὸ τῆς μετοικεσίας Βαβυ-
fourteen,   and from the deportation of Baby-
λῶνος ἕως τοῦ Χριστοῦ γενεαὶ δεκατέσσαρες.
lon until the Christ generations fourteen.

King James Version

18 Now the birth of Jesus Christ was on this wise: When as his mother Mary was espoused to Joseph, before they came together, she was found with child of the Holy Ghost. 19 Then Joseph her husband, being a just *man*, and not willing to make her a public example, was minded to put her away privily. 20 But while he thought on these things, behold, the angel of the Lord appeared unto him in a dream, saying, Joseph, thou son of David, fear not to take unto thee Mary thy wife: for that which is conceived in her is of the Holy Ghost. 21 And she shall bring forth a son, and thou shalt call his name JESUS: for he shall save his people from their sins. 22 Now all this was done, that it might be fulfilled which was spoken of the Lord by the prophet, saying, 23 Behold, a virgin shall be with child, and shall bring forth a son, and they shall call his name Emmanuel, which being interpreted is, God with us. 24 Then Joseph being raised from sleep did as the angel of the Lord had bidden him, and took unto him his wife: 25 And knew her not till she had brought forth her firstborn son: and he called his name JESUS.

New International Version

The birth of Jesus Christ

18 This is how the birth of Jesus Christ came about. His mother Mary was pledged to be married to Joseph, but before they came together, she was found to be with child through the Holy Spirit. 19 Because Joseph her husband was a righteous man and did not want to expose her to public disgrace, he had in mind to divorce her quietly.
20 But after he had considered this, an angel of the Lord appeared to him in a dream and said, "Joseph son of David, do not be afraid to take Mary home as your wife, because what is conceived in her is from the Holy Spirit. 21 She will give birth to a son, and you are to give him the name Jesus, because he will save his people from their sins."
22 All this took place to fulfill what the Lord had said through the prophet: 23 "The virgin will be with child and will give birth to a son, and they will call him Immanuel" [b]—which means, "God with us."
24 When Joseph woke up, he did what the angel of the Lord had commanded him and took Mary home as his wife. 25 But he had no union with her until she gave birth to a son. And he gave him the name Jesus.

The visit of the Magi

2 Now when Jesus was born in Bethlehem of Judea in the days of Herod the king, behold, there came wise men from the east to Jerusalem, 2 Saying, Where is he that is born King of the Jews? for we have seen his star in the east, and are come to worship him. 3 When Herod the king had heard *these things,* he was troubled, and all Jerusalem with him. 4 And when he had gathered all the chief priests and scribes of the people together, he demanded of them where Christ should be born. 5 And they said unto him, In Bethlehem of Judea: for thus it is written by the prophet, 6 And thou Bethlehem, *in* the land of Juda, art not the least among the princes of Juda: for out of thee shall come a Governor, that shall rule my people Israel. 7 Then Herod, when he had privily called the wise men, inquired of them diligently what time the star appeared. 8 And he sent them to Bethlehem, and said, Go and search diligently for the young child; and when ye have found *him,* bring me word again, that I may come and worship him also. 9 When they had heard the king, they departed; and, lo, the star, which they saw in the east, went before them, till it came and stood over where the young child was. 10 When they saw the star, they rejoiced with exceeding great joy.
11 And when they were come into the house, they saw the young child with Mary his mother, and fell down, and worshipped him: and when they had opened their treasures, they presented

2 After Jesus was born in Bethlehem in Judea, during the time of King Herod, Magi from the east came to Jerusalem 2 and asked, "Where is the one who has been born king of the Jews? We saw his star in the east[c] and have come to worship him."
3 When King Herod heard this he was disturbed, and all Jerusalem with him. 4 When he had called together all the chief priests and teachers of the law, he asked them where the Christ[d] was to be born. 5 "In Bethlehem in Judea," they replied, "for this is what the prophet has written:
6 'And you, Bethlehem, in the land of Judah,
      are by no means least among the rulers of Judah;
   for out of you will come a ruler
      who will be the shepherd of my people Israel.' [e] "
7 Then Herod called the Magi secretly and found out from them the exact time the star had appeared. 8 He sent them to Bethlehem and said, "Go and make a careful search for the child. As soon as you find him, report to me, so that I too may go and worship him."
9 After they had heard the king, they went on their way, and the star they had seen in the east[f] went ahead of them until it stopped over the place where the child was. 10 When they saw the star, they were overjoyed. 11 On coming to the house, they saw the child with his mother Mary, and they bowed down and worshiped him. Then they opened their treasures and presented

[b] Isaiah 7:14. [c] Or *star when it rose.* [d] Or *Messiah.* [e] Micah 5:2. [f] Or *seen when it rose.*

Greek Interlinear

18 Τοῦ δὲ Ἰησοῦ Χριστοῦ ἡ γένεσις
\- Now   *of Jesus   *Christ   ¹the   *birth

οὕτως ἦν. μνηστευθείσης τῆς μητρὸς αὐτοῦ
*thus   *was. Being betrothed   the   mother   of him
= When his mother Mary was betrothed

Μαρίας τῷ Ἰωσήφ, πρὶν ἢ συνελθεῖν αὐτοὺς
Mary*   -   to Joseph, before to come together them^b
= before they came together

εὑρέθη ἐν γαστρὶ ἔχουσα ἐκ πνεύματος
¹she was found ²in   *womb   *having of(by) [the] Spirit
= she was pregnant

ἁγίου. **19** Ἰωσὴφ δὲ ὁ ἀνὴρ αὐτῆς,
Holy.   Now Joseph   the   husband   of her,

δίκαιος ὢν καὶ μὴ θέλων αὐτὴν δειγμα-
³just   ¹being ²and   not   wishing   her to hold up as an

τίσαι, ἐβουλήθη λάθρα ἀπολῦσαι αὐτήν.
example, resolved   secretly   to dismiss   her.

20 ταῦτα δὲ αὐτοῦ ἐνθυμηθέντος, ἰδοὺ
But these things   him   thinking on,*   behold
= while he thought on these things,

ἄγγελος κυρίου κατ᾽ ὄναρ ἐφάνη
an angel   of [the] Lord   by   a dream   appeared

αὐτῷ λέγων· Ἰωσὴφ υἱὸς Δαυίδ, μὴ
to him   saying: Joseph   son   of David, *not

φοβηθῇς παραλαβεῖν Μαρίαν τὴν
¹fear thou   to take   Mary   the

γυναῖκά σου· τὸ γὰρ ἐν αὐτῇ γεννηθὲν
wife   of thee: for the thing   in   her   begotten

ἐκ πνεύματός ἐστιν ἁγίου. **21** τέξεται δὲ
²of *[the] Spirit   ¹is   *Holy.   And she will bear

υἱόν, καὶ καλέσεις τὸ ὄνομα αὐτοῦ
a son,   and   thou shalt call   the   name   of him

Ἰησοῦν· αὐτὸς γὰρ σώσει τὸν λαὸν
Jesus;   for he   will save   the   people

αὐτοῦ ἀπὸ τῶν ἁμαρτιῶν αὐτῶν. **22** Τοῦτο δὲ
of him from   the   sins   of them.   Now *this

ὅλον γέγονεν ἵνα πληρωθῇ τὸ ῥηθὲν
¹all has occurred in order that might be fulfilled the [thing] spoken

ὑπὸ κυρίου διὰ τοῦ προφήτου λέγοντος·
by   [the] Lord through   the   prophet   saying:

23 ἰδοὺ ἡ παρθένος ἐν γαστρὶ ἕξει
Behold the   virgin   ²in   *womb ¹will have

καὶ τέξεται υἱόν, καὶ καλέσουσιν τὸ
and   will bear   a son,   and   they will call   the

ὄνομα αὐτοῦ Ἐμμανουήλ, ὃ ἐστιν
name   of him   Emmanuel,   which   is

μεθερμηνευόμενον μεθ᾽ ἡμῶν ὁ θεός.
being interpreted   with   us   -   God.

24 ἐγερθεὶς δὲ [ὁ] Ἰωσὴφ ἀπὸ τοῦ
Then *being raised   -   ¹Joseph   from the(his)

ὕπνου ἐποίησεν ὡς προσέταξεν αὐτῷ ὁ
sleep   did   as   bade   him   the

ἄγγελος κυρίου, καὶ παρέλαβεν τὴν
angel   of [the] Lord,   and   took   the

γυναῖκα αὐτοῦ· **25** καὶ οὐκ ἐγίνωσκεν
wife   of him;   and   knew not

αὐτὴν ἕως [οὗ] ἔτεκεν υἱόν· καὶ ἐκάλεσεν
her   until   she bore a son;   and   he called

τὸ ὄνομα αὐτοῦ Ἰησοῦν.
the   name   of him   Jesus.

Chapter 2

Τοῦ δὲ Ἰησοῦ γεννηθέντος ἐν Βηθλέεμ
\- Now Jesus   having been born* in   Bethlehem
= when Jesus was born

τῆς Ἰουδαίας ἐν ἡμέραις Ἡρώδου τοῦ
\- of Judæa   in   [the] days   of Herod   the

βασιλέως, ἰδοὺ μάγοι ἀπὸ ἀνατολῶν
king,   behold   magi   from   [the] east

παρεγένοντο εἰς Ἱεροσόλυμα **2** λέγοντες·
arrived   in   Jerusalem   saying:

ποῦ ἐστιν ὁ τεχθεὶς βασιλεὺς τῶν
Where   is   the [one]   born   king   of the

Ἰουδαίων; εἴδομεν γὰρ αὐτοῦ τὸν ἀστέρα
Jews?   for we saw   of him   the   star

ἐν τῇ ἀνατολῇ, καὶ ἤλθομεν προσκυνῆσαι
in   the   east,   and   came   to worship

αὐτῷ. **3** ἀκούσας δὲ ὁ βασιλεὺς Ἡρώδης
him.   Now hearing [this] the   king   Herod

ἐταράχθη, καὶ πᾶσα Ἱεροσόλυμα μετ᾽
was troubled,   and   all   Jerusalem   with

αὐτοῦ, **4** καὶ συναγαγὼν πάντας τοὺς
him,   and   having assembled   all   the

ἀρχιερεῖς καὶ γραμματεῖς τοῦ λαοῦ
chief priests   and   scribes   of the   people

ἐπυνθάνετο παρ᾽ αὐτῶν ποῦ ὁ χριστὸς
he inquired   from   them   where   the   Christ

γεννᾶται. **5** οἱ δὲ εἶπαν αὐτῷ· ἐν
is being born.   And they   told   him: In

Βηθλέεμ τῆς Ἰουδαίας· οὕτως γὰρ
Bethlehem   -   of Judæa;   for thus

γέγραπται διὰ τοῦ προφήτου· **6** καὶ
it has been written   through   the   prophet: And

σὺ Βηθλέεμ, γῆ Ἰούδα, οὐδαμῶς ἐλαχίστη
thou   Bethlehem,   land   of Juda, ²not at all   ¹least

εἶ ἐν τοῖς ἡγεμόσιν Ἰούδα. ἐκ σοῦ γὰρ
¹art among the   governors   of Juda.   For out of thee

ἐξελεύσεται ἡγούμενος, ὅστις ποιμανεῖ
will come forth   a governor,   who   will shepherd

τὸν λαόν μου τὸν Ἰσραήλ.
the   people   of me   -   Israel.

7 Τότε Ἡρώδης λάθρα καλέσας τοὺς
Then   Herod   secretly   calling   the

μάγους ἠκρίβωσεν παρ᾽ αὐτῶν τὸν
magi   inquired carefully   from   them   the

χρόνον τοῦ φαινομένου ἀστέρος, **8** καὶ
time   of the   appearing   star,   and

πέμψας αὐτοὺς εἰς Βηθλέεμ εἶπεν·
sending   them   to   Bethlehem   said:

πορευθέντες ἐξετάσατε ἀκριβῶς περὶ τοῦ
Going   question ye   carefully   concerning   the

παιδίου· ἐπὰν δὲ εὕρητε, ἀπαγγείλατέ
child;   and when   ye find,   report

μοι, ὅπως κἀγὼ ἐλθὼν προσκυνήσω αὐτῷ.
to me, so that   I also   coming   may worship   him.

9 οἱ δὲ ἀκούσαντες τοῦ βασιλέως ἐπορεύθησαν·
So they   hearing   the   king   went;

καὶ ἰδοὺ ὁ ἀστήρ, ὃν εἶδον ἐν τῇ
and   behold   the   star,   which   they saw   in   the

ἀνατολῇ, προῆγεν αὐτοὺς ἕως ἐλθὼν
east,   went before   them   until   coming

ἐστάθη ἐπάνω οὗ ἦν τὸ παιδίον. **10** ἰδόντες
it stood   over   where was the   child.   *seeing

δὲ τὸν ἀστέρα ἐχάρησαν χαρὰν μεγάλην
¹And the   star   they rejoiced   [with] a joy   great

σφόδρα. **11** καὶ ἐλθόντες εἰς τὴν οἰκίαν
exceedingly.   And   coming   into   the   house

εἶδον τὸ παιδίον μετὰ Μαρίας τῆς μητρὸς
they saw the   child   with   Mary   the   mother

αὐτοῦ, καὶ πεσόντες προσεκύνησαν αὐτῷ,
of him,   and   falling   they worshipped   him,

καὶ ἀνοίξαντες τοὺς θησαυροὺς αὐτῶν
and   opening   the   treasures   of them

King James Version

unto him gifts; gold, and frankincense, and myrrh. 12And being warned of God in a dream that they should not return to Herod, they departed into their own country another way. 13And when they were departed, behold, the angel of the Lord appeareth to Joseph in a dream, saying, Arise, and take the young child and his mother, and flee into Egypt, and be thou there until I bring thee word: for Herod will seek the young child to destroy him. 14When he arose, he took the young child and his mother by night, and departed into Egypt: 15And was there until the death of Herod: that it might be fulfilled which was spoken of the Lord by the prophet, saying, Out of Egypt have I called my son.

16 Then Herod, when he saw that he was mocked of the wise men, was exceeding wroth, and sent forth, and slew all the children that were in Bethlehem, and in all the coasts thereof, from two years old and under, according to the time which he had diligently inquired of the wise men. 17 Then was fulfilled that which was spoken by Jeremy the prophet, saying, 18 In Rama was there a voice heard, lamentation, and weeping, and great mourning, Rachel weeping *for* her children, and would not be comforted, because they are not.

19 But when Herod was dead, behold, an angel of the Lord appeareth in a dream to Joseph in Egypt, 20 Saying, Arise, and take the young child and his mother, and go into the land of Israel: for they are dead which sought the young child's life. 21And he arose, and took the young child and his mother, and came into the land of Israel. 22 But when he heard that Archelaus did reign in Judea in the room of his father Herod, he was afraid to go thither: notwithstanding, being warned of God in a dream, he turned aside into the parts of Galilee: 23And he came and dwelt in a city called Nazareth: that it might be fulfilled which was spoken by the prophets, He shall be called a Nazarene.

3 In those days came John the Baptist, preaching in the wilderness of Judea, 2And saying, Repent ye: for the kingdom of heaven is at hand. 3 For this is he that was spoken of by the prophet Esaias, saying, The voice of one crying in the wilderness, Prepare ye the way of the Lord, make his paths straight. 4And the same John had his raiment of camel's hair, and a leathern girdle about his loins; and his meat was locusts and wild honey. 5 Then went out to him Jerusalem, and all Judea, and all the region round about Jordan, 6And were baptized of him in Jordan, confessing their sins.

New International Version

him with gifts of gold and of incense and of myrrh. 12And having been warned in a dream not to go back to Herod, they returned to their country by another route.

The escape to Egypt

13 When they had gone, an angel of the Lord appeared to Joseph in a dream. "Get up," he said, "take the child and his mother and escape to Egypt. Stay there until I tell you, for Herod is going to search for the child to kill him."
14 So he got up, took the child and his mother during the night and left for Egypt, 15 where he stayed until the death of Herod. And so was fulfilled what the Lord had said through the prophet: "I called my son out of Egypt." *g*
16 When Herod realized that he had been outwitted by the Magi, he was furious, and he gave orders to kill all the boys in Bethlehem and its vicinity who were two years old and under, in accordance with the time he had learned from the Magi. 17 Then what was said through the prophet Jeremiah was fulfilled:
18 "A voice was heard in Ramah,
    weeping and great mourning,
Rachel weeping for her children
    and refusing to be comforted,
because they were no more." *h*

The return to Nazareth

19 After Herod died, an angel of the Lord appeared in a dream to Joseph in Egypt 20 and said, "Get up, take the child and his mother and go to the land of Israel, for those who were trying to take the child's life are dead."
21 So he got up, took the child and his mother and went to the land of Israel. 22 But when he heard that Archelaus was reigning in Judea in place of his father Herod, he was afraid to go there. Having been warned in a dream, he withdrew to the district of Galilee, 23 and he went and lived in a town called Nazareth. So was fulfilled what was said through the prophets: "He will be called a Nazarene."

John the Baptist prepares the way

3 In those days John the Baptist came, preaching in the desert of Judea 2 and saying, "Repent, for the kingdom of heaven is near." 3 This is he who was spoken of through the prophet Isaiah:
"A voice of one calling in the desert,
'Prepare the way for the Lord,
    make straight paths for him.'" *i*
4 John's clothes were made of camel's hair, and he had a leather belt around his waist. His food was locusts and wild honey. 5 People went out to him from Jerusalem and all Judea and the whole region of the Jordan. 6 Confessing their sins, they were baptized by him in the Jordan River.

Greek Interlinear

προσήνεγκαν   αὐτῷ   δῶρα,   χρυσὸν   καὶ
they offered   to him   gifts,   gold   and

λίβανον   καὶ   σμύρναν.   12 καὶ χρηματισθέντες
frankincense and   myrrh.   And having been warned

κατ' ὄναρ   μὴ   ἀνακάμψαι   πρὸς   Ἡρῴδην,
by a dream   not   to return   to   Herod,

δι'   ἄλλης   ὁδοῦ   ἀνεχώρησαν   εἰς   τὴν
by   another   way   they departed   to   the

χώραν   αὐτῶν.
country   of them.

13 Ἀναχωρησάντων   δὲ   αὐτῶν,   ἰδοὺ
   Now having departed   them,ᵃ   behold
   = when they had departed,

ἄγγελος   κυρίου   φαίνεται   κατ'   ὄναρ   τῷ
an angel   of [the] Lord   appears   by   a dream   -

Ἰωσὴφ   λέγων·   ἐγερθεὶς   παράλαβε   τὸ
to Joseph   saying: Rising   take thou   the

παιδίον   καὶ   τὴν   μητέρα   αὐτοῦ,   καὶ   φεῦγε
child   and   the   mother   of him,   and   flee

εἰς   Αἴγυπτον,   καὶ   ἴσθι   ἐκεῖ   ἕως   ἂν   εἴπω
into   Egypt,   and   be   there   until   I tell

σοι·   μέλλει γὰρ   Ἡρῴδης   ζητεῖν   τὸ   παιδίον   τοῦ
thee;   for ⁵is about   ¹Herod   to seek   the   child

ἀπολέσαι   αὐτό.   14 ὁ δὲ   ἐγερθεὶς   παρέλαβεν
to destroyᵈ   him.   So he   rising   took

τὸ   παιδίον   καὶ   τὴν   μητέρα   αὐτοῦ
the   child   and   the   mother   of him

νυκτὸς   καὶ   ἀνεχώρησεν   εἰς   Αἴγυπτον,
of(by) night   and   departed   to   Egypt,

15 καὶ   ἦν   ἐκεῖ   ἕως   τῆς   τελευτῆς   Ἡρῴδου·
and   was   there   until   the   death   of Herod;

ἵνα   πληρωθῇ   τὸ   ῥηθὲν   ὑπὸ   κυρίου
in order that might be fulfilled the [thing] spoken   by [the] Lord

διὰ   τοῦ   προφήτου   λέγοντος·   ἐξ
through   the   prophet   saying: Out of

Αἰγύπτου   ἐκάλεσα   τὸν   υἱόν   μου.
Egypt   I called   the   son   of me.

16 Τότε   Ἡρῴδης   ἰδὼν   ὅτι   ἐνεπαίχθη
Then   Herod   seeing   that   he was mocked

ὑπὸ   τῶν   μάγων   ἐθυμώθη   λίαν,   καὶ
by   the   magi   was angered   exceedingly,   and

ἀποστείλας   ἀνεῖλεν   πάντας   τοὺς   παῖδας
sending   killed   all   the   boy-children

τοὺς   ἐν   Βηθλέεμ   καὶ   ἐν   πᾶσι   τοῖς
-    in   Bethlehem   and   in   all   the

ὁρίοις   αὐτῆς   ἀπὸ   διετοῦς   καὶ   κατωτέρω,
districts   of it   from   two years   and   under,

κατὰ   τὸν   χρόνον   ὃν   ἠκρίβωσεν   παρὰ   τῶν
according to the   time   which he strictly inquired from   the

μάγων.   17 τότε   ἐπληρώθη   τὸ   ῥηθὲν   διὰ
magi.   Then   was fulfilled the [thing] spoken   through

Ἰερεμίου   τοῦ   προφήτου   λέγοντος·   18 φωνὴ
Jeremiah   the   prophet   saying: A voice

ἐν   Ῥαμὰ   ἠκούσθη,   κλαυθμὸς   καὶ   ὀδυρμὸς
in   Rama   was heard,   weeping   and   mourning

πολύς·   Ῥαχὴλ   κλαίουσα   τὰ   τέκνα   αὐτῆς,
much;   Rachel   weeping for   the   children   of her,

καὶ   οὐκ   ἤθελεν   παρακληθῆναι,   ὅτι
and   would not   to be comforted,   because

οὐκ   εἰσίν.
they are not.

19 Τελευτήσαντος   δὲ   τοῦ   Ἡρῴδου,   ἰδοὺ
   But dying   -   Herod,ᵃ   behold
   = Herod having died,

ἄγγελος   κυρίου   φαίνεται   κατ'   ὄναρ   τῷ
an angel   of [the] Lord   appears   by   a dream   -

Ἰωσὴφ   ἐν   Αἰγύπτῳ   20 λέγων·   ἐγερθεὶς
to Joseph   in   Egypt   saying: Rising

παράλαβε   τὸ   παιδίον   καὶ   τὴν   μητέρα
take thou   the   child   and   the   mother

αὐτοῦ,   καὶ   πορεύου   εἰς   γῆν   Ἰσραήλ·
of him,   and   go   into [the] land   of Israel;

τεθνήκασιν   γὰρ   οἱ   ζητοῦντες   τὴν   ψυχὴν
for have died   the [ones]   seeking   the   life

τοῦ   παιδίου.   21 ὁ δὲ   ἐγερθεὶς   παρέλαβεν
of the   child.   So he   rising   took

τὸ   παιδίον   καὶ   τὴν   μητέρα   αὐτοῦ   καὶ
the   child   and   the   mother   of him   and

εἰσῆλθεν   εἰς   γῆν   Ἰσραήλ.   22 ἀκούσας   δὲ
entered   into [the] land   of Israel.   But hearing

ὅτι   Ἀρχέλαος   βασιλεύει   τῆς   Ἰουδαίας
that   Archelaus   reigns over   the   Judæa

ἀντὶ   τοῦ   πατρὸς   αὐτοῦ   Ἡρῴδου   ἐφοβήθη
instead of   the   father   of him   Herod   he feared

ἐκεῖ   ἀπελθεῖν·   χρηματισθεὶς   δὲ   κατ'
there   to go;   and being warned   by

ὄναρ   ἀνεχώρησεν   εἰς   τὰ   μέρη   τῆς
a dream   he departed   into   the   parts   -

Γαλιλαίας,   23 καὶ   ἐλθὼν   κατῴκησεν   εἰς
of Galilee,   and   coming   dwelt   in

πόλιν   λεγομένην   Ναζαρέθ·   ὅπως   πληρωθῇ
a city   called   Nazareth;   so that   was fulfilled

τὸ   ῥηθὲν   διὰ   τῶν   προφητῶν   ὅτι
the [thing] spoken   through   the   prophets[,]   -

Ναζωραῖος   κληθήσεται.
A Nazarene   he shall be called.

Chapter 3

Ἐν   δὲ   ταῖς   ἡμέραις   ἐκείναις   παραγίνεται
Now in   -   the   days   those   arrives

Ἰωάννης   ὁ   βαπτιστὴς   κηρύσσων   ἐν   τῇ
John   the   Baptist   proclaiming   in   the

ἐρήμῳ   τῆς   Ἰουδαίας,   2 λέγων·   μετανοεῖτε·
wilderness   -   of Judæa,   saying: Repent ye;

ἤγγικεν   γὰρ   ἡ   βασιλεία   τῶν   οὐρανῶν.
for has come near   the   kingdom   of the   heavens.

3 οὗτος γάρ   ἐστιν   ὁ   ῥηθεὶς   διὰ   Ἡσαΐου
For this   is   the [one] spoken [of] through   Isaiah

τοῦ   προφήτου   λέγοντος·   φωνὴ   βοῶντος
the   prophet   saying: A voice   of [one] crying

ἐν   τῇ   ἐρήμῳ·   ἑτοιμάσατε   τὴν   ὁδὸν
in   the   wilderness: Prepare ye   the   way

κυρίου,   εὐθείας   ποιεῖτε   τὰς   τρίβους
of [the] Lord,   straight   make   the   paths

αὐτοῦ.   4 Αὐτὸς   δὲ   ὁ   Ἰωάννης   εἶχεν
of him.   Now ⁵himself   -   ¹John   had

τὸ   ἔνδυμα   αὐτοῦ   ἀπὸ   τριχῶν   καμήλου
the   raiment   of him   from   hairs   of a camel

καὶ   ζώνην   δερματίνην   περὶ   τὴν   ὀσφὺν
and   a girdle   leathern   round   the   loin[s]

αὐτοῦ·   ἡ   δὲ   τροφὴ   ἦν   αὐτοῦ   ἀκρίδες
of him;   and the   food   ⁸was ¹of him   locusts

καὶ   μέλι   ἄγριον.   5 Τότε   ἐξεπορεύετο   πρὸς
and   honey   wild.   Then   went out   to

αὐτὸν   Ἱεροσόλυμα   καὶ   πᾶσα   ἡ   Ἰουδαία
him   Jerusalem   and   all   -   Judæa

καὶ   πᾶσα   ἡ   περίχωρος   τοῦ   Ἰορδάνου,
and   all   the   neighbourhood   of the   Jordan,

6 καὶ   ἐβαπτίζοντο   ἐν   τῷ   Ἰορδάνῃ   ποταμῷ
and   were baptized   in   the   Jordan   river

ὑπ'   αὐτοῦ   ἐξομολογούμενοι   τὰς   ἁμαρτίας
by   him   confessing   the   sins

7

King James Version

7 But when he saw many of the Pharisees and Sadducees come to his baptism, he said unto them, O generation of vipers, who hath warned you to flee from the wrath to come? 8 Bring forth therefore fruits meet for repentance: 9And think not to say within yourselves, We have Abraham to *our* father: for I say unto you, that God is able of these stones to raise up children unto Abraham. 10And now also the axe is laid unto the root of the trees: therefore every tree which bringeth not forth good fruit is hewn down, and cast into the fire. 11 I indeed baptize you with water unto repentance: but he that cometh after me is mightier than I, whose shoes I am not worthy to bear: he shall baptize you with the Holy Ghost, and *with* fire: 12 Whose fan *is* in his hand, and he will thoroughly purge his floor, and gather his wheat into the garner; but he will burn up the chaff with unquenchable fire.

13 Then cometh Jesus from Galilee to Jordan unto John, to be baptized of him. 14 But John forbade him, saying, I have need to be baptized of thee, and comest thou to me? 15And Jesus answering said unto him, Suffer *it to be so* now: for thus it becometh us to fulfil all righteousness. Then he suffered him. 16And Jesus, when he was baptized, went up straightway out of the water: and, lo, the heavens were opened unto him, and he saw the Spirit of God descending like a dove, and lighting upon him: 17And lo a voice from heaven, saying, This is my beloved Son, in whom I am well pleased.

New International Version

7 But when he saw many of the Pharisees and Sadducees coming to where he was baptizing, he said to them: "You brood of vipers! Who warned you to flee from the coming wrath? 8 Produce fruit in keeping with repentance. 9And do not think you can say to yourselves, 'We have Abraham as our father.' I tell you that out of these stones God can raise up children for Abraham. 10 The ax is already at the root of the trees, and every tree that does not produce good fruit will be cut down and thrown into the fire.

11 "I baptize you with[j] water for repentance. But after me will come one who is more powerful than I, whose sandals I am not fit to carry. He will baptize you with the Holy Spirit and with fire. 12 His winnowing fork is in his hand, and he will clear his threshing floor, gathering the wheat into his barn and burning up the chaff with unquenchable fire."

The baptism of Jesus

13 Then Jesus came from Galilee to the Jordan to be baptized by John. 14 But John tried to deter him, saying, "I need to be baptized by you, and do you come to me?"

15 Jesus replied, "Let it be so now; it is proper for us to do this to fulfill all righteousness." Then John consented.

16 As soon as Jesus was baptized, he went up out of the water. At that moment heaven was opened, and he saw the Spirit of God descending on him like a dove. 17And a voice from heaven said, "This is my Son, whom I love; with him I am well-pleased."

The temptation of Jesus

4 Then was Jesus led up of the Spirit into the wilderness to be tempted of the devil. 2And when he had fasted forty days and forty nights, he was afterward a hungered. 3And when the tempter came to him, he said, If thou be the Son of God, command that these stones be made bread. 4 But he answered and said, It is written, Man shall not live by bread alone, but by every word that proceedeth out of the mouth of God. 5 Then the devil taketh him up into the holy city, and setteth him on a pinnacle of the temple, 6And saith unto him, If thou be the Son of God, cast thyself down: for it is written, He shall give his angels charge concerning thee: and in *their* hands they shall bear thee up, lest at any time thou dash thy foot against a stone. 7 Jesus said unto him, It is written again, Thou shalt not tempt the Lord thy God. 8Again, the devil taketh him up into an exceeding high mountain, and sheweth him all the kingdoms of the world, and the glory of them; 9And saith unto him, All these things will I give thee, if thou wilt fall

4 Then Jesus was led by the Spirit into the desert to be tempted by the devil. 2After fasting forty days and nights, he was hungry. 3 The tempter came to him and said, "If you are the Son of God, tell these stones to become bread."

4 Jesus answered, "It is written:
'Man does not live on bread alone,
but on every word that comes from the mouth of God.'[k]"

5 Then the devil took him to the holy city and had him stand on the highest point of the temple. 6 "If you are the Son of God," he said, "throw yourself down. For it is written:
'He will command his angels concerning you,
and they will lift you up in their hands,
so that you will not strike your foot against a stone.'[l]"

7 Jesus answered him, "It is also written: 'Do not put the Lord your God to the test.'[m]"

8 Again, the devil took him to a very high mountain and showed him all the kingdoms of the world and their splendor. 9 "All this I will give you," he said, "if you will bow down and worship me."

[j] Or *in*. [k] Deut. 8:3. [l] Psalm 91:11, 12. [m] Deut. 6:16.

Greek Interlinear

αὐτῶν. 7 Ἰδὼν δὲ πολλοὺς τῶν
of them.   And seeing many of the

Φαρισαίων καὶ Σαδδουκαίων ἐρχομένους
Pharisees and Sadducees coming

ἐπὶ τὸ βάπτισμα εἶπεν αὐτοῖς· γεννήματα
to the baptism he said to them: Offspring

ἐχιδνῶν, τίς ὑπέδειξεν ὑμῖν φυγεῖν ἀπὸ
of vipers, who warned you to flee from

τῆς μελλούσης ὀργῆς; 8 ποιήσατε οὖν
the coming wrath? Produce therefore

καρπὸν ἄξιον τῆς μετανοίας· 9 καὶ
fruit worthy - of repentance; and

μὴ δόξητε λέγειν ἐν ἑαυτοῖς· ¹[as] πατέρα
think not to say among [your]selves: ¹[as] father

ἔχομεν τὸν Ἀβραάμ· λέγω γὰρ ὑμῖν ὅτι
¹We have - ¹Abraham; for I tell you that

δύναται ὁ θεὸς ἐκ τῶν λίθων τούτων
¹is able - ¹God out of - stones these

ἐγεῖραι τέκνα τῷ Ἀβραάμ. 10 ἤδη δὲ
to raise children - to Abraham. And already

ἡ ἀξίνη πρὸς τὴν ῥίζαν τῶν δένδρων
the axe at the root of the trees

κεῖται· πᾶν οὖν δένδρον μὴ ποιοῦν
is laid; therefore every tree not producing

καρπὸν καλὸν ἐκκόπτεται καὶ εἰς πῦρ
fruit good is cut down and into [the] fire

βάλλεται. 11 ἐγὼ μὲν ὑμᾶς βαπτίζω
is cast. I indeed you baptize

ἐν ὕδατι εἰς μετάνοιαν· ὁ δὲ
in water to repentance; but the [one]

ὀπίσω μου ἐρχόμενος ἰσχυρότερός μού
after me coming ²stronger ³[than] ⁴I

ἐστιν, οὗ οὐκ εἰμὶ ἱκανὸς τὰ ὑποδήματα
¹is, of whom I am not worthy the sandals

βαστάσαι· αὐτὸς ὑμᾶς βαπτίσει ἐν πνεύματι
to bear; he ²you ¹will baptize in [the] Spirit

ἁγίῳ καὶ πυρί· 12 οὗ τὸ πτύον ἐν τῇ
Holy and fire; of whom the fan [is] in the

χειρὶ αὐτοῦ, καὶ διακαθαριεῖ τὴν ἅλωνα
hand of him, and he will thoroughly cleanse the threshing-floor

αὐτοῦ, καὶ συνάξει τὸν σῖτον αὐτοῦ
of him, and will gather the wheat of him

εἰς τὴν ἀποθήκην, τὸ δὲ ἄχυρον κατα-
into the barn, but the chaff he will

καύσει πυρὶ ἀσβέστῳ.
consume with fire unquenchable.

13 Τότε παραγίνεται ὁ Ἰησοῦς ἀπὸ τῆς
Then arrives - Jesus from -

Γαλιλαίας ἐπὶ τὸν Ἰορδάνην πρὸς τὸν
Galilee at the Jordan to -

Ἰωάννην τοῦ βαπτισθῆναι ὑπ᾽ αὐτοῦ.
John - to be baptized by him.

14 ὁ δὲ διεκώλυεν αὐτὸν λέγων· ἐγὼ
But he forbade him saying: I

χρείαν ἔχω ὑπὸ σοῦ βαπτισθῆναι, καὶ σὺ
¹need ¹have ⁴by ³thee ²to be baptized, and thou

ἔρχῃ πρὸς μέ; 15 ἀποκριθεὶς δὲ ὁ
comest to me? But answering -

Ἰησοῦς εἶπεν αὐτῷ· ἄφες ἄρτι· οὕτως γὰρ
Jesus said to him: Permit now; for thus

πρέπον ἐστὶν ἡμῖν πληρῶσαι πᾶσαν
²fitting ¹it is to us to fulfil all

δικαιοσύνην. τότε ἀφίησιν αὐτόν.
righteousness. Then he permits him.

16 βαπτισθεὶς δὲ ὁ Ἰησοῦς εὐθὺς ἀνέβη
And having been baptized - Jesus immediately went up

ἀπὸ τοῦ ὕδατος· καὶ ἰδοὺ ἠνεῴχθησαν
from the water; and behold ²were opened

οἱ οὐρανοί, καὶ εἶδεν πνεῦμα θεοῦ
¹the ³heavens, and he saw [the] Spirit of God

καταβαῖνον ὡσεὶ περιστεράν, ἐρχόμενον ἐπ᾽
coming down as a dove, coming upon

αὐτόν· 17 καὶ ἰδοὺ φωνὴ ἐκ τῶν
him; and behold a voice out of the

οὐρανῶν λέγουσα· οὗτός ἐστιν ὁ υἱός
heavens saying: This is the son

μου ὁ ἀγαπητός, ἐν ᾧ εὐδόκησα.
of me the beloved, in whom I was well pleased.

Chapter 4

Τότε ὁ Ἰησοῦς ἀνήχθη εἰς τὴν
Then - Jesus was led up into the

ἔρημον ὑπὸ τοῦ πνεύματος πειρασθῆναι
wilderness by the Spirit to be tempted

ὑπὸ τοῦ διαβόλου. 2 καὶ νηστεύσας ἡμέρας
by the devil. And having fasted days

τεσσεράκοντα καὶ τεσσεράκοντα νύκτας
forty and forty nights

ὕστερον ἐπείνασεν. 3 καὶ προσελθὼν ὁ
afterward he hungered. And approaching the

πειράζων εἶπεν αὐτῷ· εἰ υἱὸς εἶ τοῦ
tempting [one] said to him: If Son thou art -

θεοῦ, εἰπὲ ἵνα οἱ λίθοι οὗτοι ἄρτοι
of God, say in order that - stones these ²loaves

γένωνται. 4 ὁ δὲ ἀποκριθεὶς εἶπεν·
¹may become. But he answering said:

γέγραπται· οὐκ ἐπ᾽ ἄρτῳ μόνῳ ζήσεται
It has been written: Not on bread only shall live

ὁ ἄνθρωπος, ἀλλ᾽ ἐπὶ παντὶ ῥήματι
- man, but on every word

ἐκπορευομένῳ διὰ στόματος θεοῦ. 5 Τότε
proceeding through [the] mouth of God. Then

παραλαμβάνει αὐτὸν ὁ διάβολος εἰς τὴν
takes him the devil into the

ἁγίαν πόλιν, καὶ ἔστησεν αὐτὸν ἐπὶ τὸ
holy city, and stood him on the

πτερύγιον τοῦ ἱεροῦ, 6 καὶ λέγει αὐτῷ·
wing of the temple, and says to him:

εἰ υἱὸς εἶ τοῦ θεοῦ, βάλε σεαυτὸν
If Son thou art - of God, cast thyself

κάτω· γέγραπται γὰρ ὅτι τοῖς ἀγγέλοις
down; for it has been written[,] - To the angels

αὐτοῦ ἐντελεῖται περὶ σοῦ καὶ ἐπὶ χειρῶν
of him he will give command concerning thee and on hands

ἀροῦσίν σε, μήποτε προσκόψῃς πρὸς
they will bear thee, lest thou strike against

λίθον τὸν πόδα σου. 7 ἔφη αὐτῷ ὁ
a stone the foot of thee. Said to him -

Ἰησοῦς· πάλιν γέγραπται· οὐκ ἐκπειράσεις
Jesus: Again it has been written: Not overtempt shalt thou

κύριον τὸν θεόν σου. 8 Πάλιν παρα-
[the] Lord the God of thee. Again

λαμβάνει αὐτὸν ὁ διάβολος εἰς ὄρος
takes him the devil to a mountain

ὑψηλὸν λίαν, καὶ δείκνυσιν αὐτῷ πάσας
high exceedingly, and shows him all

τὰς βασιλείας τοῦ κόσμου καὶ τὴν
the kingdoms of the world and the

δόξαν αὐτῶν, 9 καὶ εἶπεν αὐτῷ· ταῦτά
glory of them, and said to him: These things

σοι πάντα δώσω, ἐὰν πεσὼν προσκυνήσῃς
to thee all I will give, if falling thou wilt worship

9

King James Version

down and worship me. 10 Then saith Jesus unto him, Get thee hence, Satan: for it is written, Thou shalt worship the Lord thy God, and him only shalt thou serve. 11 Then the devil leaveth him, and, behold, angels came and ministered unto him.

12 Now when Jesus had heard that John was cast into prison, he departed into Galilee; 13And leaving Nazareth, he came and dwelt in Capernaum, which is upon the sea coast, in the borders of Zabulon and Nephthalim: 14 That it might be fulfilled which was spoken by Esaias the prophet, saying, 15 The land of Zabulon, and the land of Nephthalim, *by* the way of the sea, beyond Jordan, Galilee of the Gentiles; 16 The people which sat in darkness saw great light; and to them which sat in the region and shadow of death light is sprung up.

17 From that time Jesus began to preach, and to say, Repent: for the kingdom of heaven is at hand.

18 And Jesus, walking by the sea of Galilee, saw two brethren, Simon called Peter, and Andrew his brother, casting a net into the sea: for they were fishers. 19And he saith unto them, Follow me, and I will make you fishers of men. 20And they straightway left *their* nets, and followed him. 21And going on from thence, he saw other two brethren, James *the son* of Zebedee, and John his brother, in a ship with Zebedee their father, mending their nets; and he called them. 22And they immediately left the ship and their father, and followed him.

23 And Jesus went about all Galilee, teaching in their synagogues, and preaching the gospel of the kingdom, and healing all manner of sickness and all manner of disease among the people. 24And his fame went throughout all Syria: and they brought unto him all sick people that were taken with divers diseases and torments, and those which were possessed with devils, and those which were lunatic, and those that had the palsy; and he healed them. 25And there followed him great multitudes of people from Galilee, and *from* Decapolis, and *from* Jerusalem, and *from* Judea, and *from* beyond Jordan.

5 And seeing the multitudes, he went up into a mountain: and when he was set, his disciples came unto him: 2And he opened his mouth, and taught them, saying, 3 Blessed *are* the poor in spirit: for theirs is the kingdom of heaven. 4 Blessed *are* they that mourn: for they shall be comforted. 5 Blessed *are* the meek: for they shall inherit the earth. 6 Blessed *are* they which do hunger and thirst after righteousness: for they

New International Version

10 Jesus said to him, "Away from me, Satan! For it is written: 'Worship the Lord your God, and serve him only.' [n] "
11 Then the devil left him, and angels came and attended him.

Jesus begins to preach

12 When Jesus heard that John had been put in prison, he returned to Galilee. 13 Leaving Nazareth, he went and lived in Capernaum, which was by the lake in the area of Zebulun and Naphtali—14 to fulfill what was said through the prophet Isaiah:
15 "Land of Zebulun and land of Naphtali,
　　the way to the sea, along the Jordan,
　　Galilee of the Gentiles—
16 the people living in darkness
　　have seen a great light;
　on those living in the land of the shadow
　　of death
　a light has dawned." [o]
17 From that time on Jesus began to preach, "Repent, for the kingdom of heaven is near."

The calling of the first disciples

18 As Jesus was walking beside the Sea of Galilee, he saw two brothers, Simon called Peter and his brother Andrew. They were casting a net into the lake, for they were fishermen. 19 "Come, follow me," Jesus said, "and I will make you fishers of men." 20At once they left their nets and followed him.

21 Going on from there, he saw two other brothers, James son of Zebedee and his brother John. They were in a boat with their father Zebedee, preparing their nets. Jesus called them, 22 and immediately they left the boat and their father and followed him.

Jesus heals the sick

23 Jesus went throughout Galilee teaching in their synagogues, preaching the good news of the kingdom, and healing every disease and sickness among the people. 24 News about him spread all over Syria, and people brought to him all who were ill with various diseases, those suffering severe pain, the demon-possessed, the epileptics and the paralytics, and he healed them. 25 Large crowds from Galilee, the Decapolis,[p] Jerusalem, Judea and the region across the Jordan followed him.

The beatitudes

5 Now when he saw the crowds, he went up on a mountainside and sat down. His disciples came to him, 2 and he began to teach them, saying:
3 "Blessed are the poor in spirit,
　　for theirs is the kingdom of heaven.
4 Blessed are those who mourn,
　　for they will be comforted.
5 Blessed are the meek,
　　for they will inherit the earth.
6 Blessed are those who hunger and thirst for
　　righteousness,
　　for they will be filled.

[n] Deut. 6:13. [o] Isaiah 9:1, 2. [p] That is, *the Ten Cities.*

Greek Interlinear

μοι. **10** τότε λέγει αὐτῷ ὁ Ἰησοῦς·
me.   Then says   to him – Jesus:

ὕπαγε, σατανᾶ· γέγραπται γάρ· κύριον
Go,   Satan;   for it has been written: [The] Lord

τὸν θεόν σου προσκυνήσεις καὶ αὐτῷ
the God of thee thou shalt worship and him

μόνῳ λατρεύσεις. **11** Τότε ἀφίησιν αὐτὸν
only thou shalt serve. Then leaves   him

ὁ διάβολος, καὶ ἰδοὺ ἄγγελοι προσῆλθον
the devil,   and behold angels approached

καὶ διηκόνουν αὐτῷ.
and ministered to him.

12 Ἀκούσας δὲ ὅτι Ἰωάννης παρεδόθη
Now hearing that John was delivered up

ἀνεχώρησεν εἰς τὴν Γαλιλαίαν. **13** καὶ
he departed to – Galilee.   And

καταλιπὼν τὴν Ναζαρὰ ἐλθὼν κατῴκησεν
leaving   – Nazareth coming he dwelt

εἰς Καφαρναοὺμ τὴν παραθαλασσίαν ἐν
in Capernaum – beside the sea in [the]

ὁρίοις Ζαβουλὼν καὶ Νεφθαλίμ· **14** ἵνα
districts of Zebulon and Naphthali; in order that

πληρωθῇ τὸ ῥηθὲν διὰ Ἠσαΐου
might be fulfilled the [thing] spoken through Isaiah

τοῦ προφήτου λέγοντος· **15** γῆ Ζαβουλὼν
the prophet   saying: Land of Zebulon

καὶ γῆ Νεφθαλίμ, ὁδὸν θαλάσσης,
and land of Naphthali, way of [the] sea,

πέραν τοῦ Ἰορδάνου, Γαλιλαία τῶν ἐθνῶν,
beyond the Jordan,   Galilee of the nations,

16 ὁ λαὸς ὁ καθήμενος ἐν σκοτίᾳ φῶς
the people – sitting in darkness ²light

εἶδεν μέγα, καὶ τοῖς καθημένοις ἐν
¹saw ²a great, and to the [ones] sitting in

χώρᾳ καὶ σκιᾷ θανάτου, φῶς ἀνέτειλεν
a land and shadow of death, light sprang up

αὐτοῖς.
to them.

17 Ἀπὸ τότε ἤρξατο ὁ Ἰησοῦς κηρύσσειν
From then began – Jesus to proclaim

καὶ λέγειν· μετανοεῖτε· ἤγγικεν γὰρ
and to say: Repent ye;   for has drawn near

ἡ βασιλεία τῶν οὐρανῶν.
the kingdom of the heavens.

18 Περιπατῶν δὲ παρὰ τὴν θάλασσαν
And walking beside the sea

τῆς Γαλιλαίας εἶδεν δύο ἀδελφούς, Σίμωνα
– of Galilee he saw two brothers, Simon

τὸν λεγόμενον Πέτρον καὶ Ἀνδρέαν τὸν
– called   Peter and Andrew the

ἀδελφὸν αὐτοῦ, βάλλοντας ἀμφίβληστρον εἰς
brother of him, casting   a net   into

τὴν θάλασσαν· ἦσαν γὰρ ἁλεεῖς. **19** καὶ
the sea;   for they were fishers.   And

λέγει αὐτοῖς· δεῦτε ὀπίσω μου, καὶ
he says to them: Come after me,   and

ποιήσω ὑμᾶς ἁλεεῖς ἀνθρώπων. **20** οἱ
I will make you fishers of men.   ²they

δὲ εὐθέως ἀφέντες τὰ δίκτυα ἠκολούθη-
¹And immediately leaving the nets fol-

σαν αὐτῷ. **21** Καὶ προβὰς ἐκεῖθεν εἶδεν
lowed him.   And going on thence he saw

ἄλλους δύο ἀδελφούς, Ἰάκωβον τὸν τοῦ
other two brothers, James the [son] –

Ζεβεδαίου καὶ Ἰωάννην τὸν ἀδελφὸν
of Zebedee and John the brother

αὐτοῦ, ἐν τῷ πλοίῳ μετὰ Ζεβεδαίου τοῦ
of him, in the boat with Zebedee the

πατρὸς αὐτῶν καταρτίζοντας τὰ δίκτυα
father of them mending   the nets

αὐτῶν· καὶ ἐκάλεσεν αὐτούς. **22** οἱ δὲ
of them; and he called them.   And they

εὐθέως ἀφέντες τὸ πλοῖον καὶ τὸν
immediately leaving the boat and the

πατέρα αὐτῶν ἠκολούθησαν αὐτῷ.
father of them followed   him.

23 Καὶ περιῆγεν ἐν ὅλῃ τῇ Γαλιλαίᾳ,
And he went about in all – Galilee.

διδάσκων ἐν ταῖς συναγωγαῖς αὐτῶν
teaching in the synagogues of them

καὶ κηρύσσων τὸ εὐαγγέλιον τῆς βασιλείας
and proclaiming the gospel of the kingdom

καὶ θεραπεύων πᾶσαν νόσον καὶ πᾶσαν
and healing   every disease and every

μαλακίαν ἐν τῷ λαῷ. **24** καὶ ἀπῆλθεν ἡ
illness among the people. And wen¹ the

ἀκοὴ αὐτοῦ εἰς ὅλην τὴν Συρίαν· καὶ
report of him into all – Syria; and

προσήνεγκαν αὐτῷ πάντας τοὺς κακῶς
they brought to him all [the ones] ¹ill
= those who were ill

ἔχοντας ποικίλαις νόσοις καὶ βασάνοις
¹having ²various ²diseases ²and ¹tortures

συνεχομένους, δαιμονιζομένους καὶ σεληνιαζ-
¹suffering from, demon-possessed and luna-

ομένους καὶ παραλυτικούς, καὶ ἐθεράπευσεν
tics and paralysed, and he healed

αὐτούς. **25** καὶ ἠκολούθησαν αὐτῷ ὄχλοι
them.   And ²followed   ⁴him ²crowds

πολλοὶ ἀπὸ τῆς Γαλιλαίας καὶ Δεκαπόλεως
¹many from – Galilee and Decapolis

καὶ Ἱεροσολύμων καὶ Ἰουδαίας καὶ πέραν
and Jerusalem and Judæa and beyond

τοῦ Ἰορδάνου.
the Jordan.

Chapter 5

Ἰδὼν δὲ τοὺς ὄχλους ἀνέβη εἰς
And seeing the crowds he went up into

τὸ ὄρος· καὶ καθίσαντος αὐτοῦ προσῆλθαν
the mountain; and sitting him³ ⁴approached
= when he sat

αὐτῷ οἱ μαθηταὶ αὐτοῦ· **2** καὶ ἀνοίξας τὸ
²to him ¹the ²disciples ³of him; and opening the

στόμα αὐτοῦ ἐδίδασκεν αὐτοὺς λέγων·
mouth of him he taught them saying:

3 Μακάριοι οἱ πτωχοὶ τῷ πνεύματι,
Blessed [are] the poor – in spirit,

ὅτι αὐτῶν ἐστιν ἡ βασιλεία τῶν οὐρανῶν.
for of them is the kingdom of the heavens.

4 μακάριοι οἱ πενθοῦντες, ὅτι αὐτοὶ
Blessed [are] the mourning [ones], for they

παρακληθήσονται. **5** μακάριοι οἱ πραεῖς,
shall be comforted. Blessed [are] the meek,

ὅτι αὐτοὶ κληρονομήσουσιν τὴν γῆν.
for they shall inherit the earth.

6 μακάριοι οἱ πεινῶντες καὶ διψῶντες
Blessed [are] the hungering and thirsting [ones] [after]

τὴν δικαιοσύνην, ὅτι αὐτοὶ χορτασ-
– righteousness, for they shall be

King James Version

shall be filled. 7 Blessed *are* the merciful: for they shall obtain mercy. 8 Blessed *are* the pure in heart: for they shall see God. 9 Blessed *are* the peacemakers: for they shall be called the children of God. 10 Blessed *are* they which are persecuted for righteousness' sake: for theirs is the kingdom of heaven. 11 Blessed are ye, when *men* shall revile you, and persecute *you*, and shall say all manner of evil against you falsely, for my sake. 12 Rejoice, and be exceeding glad: for great *is* your reward in heaven: for so persecuted they the prophets which were before you.

13 Ye are the salt of the earth: but if the salt have lost his savour, wherewith shall it be salted? It is thenceforth good for nothing, but to be cast out, and to be trodden under foot of men. 14 Ye are the light of the world. A city that is set on a hill cannot be hid. 15 Neither do men light a candle, and put it under a bushel, but on a candlestick; and it giveth light unto all that are in the house. 16 Let your light so shine before men, that they may see your good works, and glorify your Father which is in heaven.

17 Think not that I am come to destroy the law, or the prophets: I am not come to destroy, but to fulfil. 18 For verily I say unto you, Till heaven and earth pass, one jot or one tittle shall in no wise pass from the law, till all be fulfilled. 19 Whosoever therefore shall break one of these least commandments, and shall teach men so, he shall be called the least in the kingdom of heaven: but whosoever shall do and teach *them,* the same shall be called great in the kingdom of heaven. 20 For I say unto you, That except your righteousness shall exceed *the righteousness* of the scribes and Pharisees, ye shall in no case enter into the kingdom of heaven.

21 Ye have heard that it was said by them of old time, Thou shalt not kill; and whosoever shall kill shall be in danger of the judgment: 22 But I say unto you, That whosoever is angry with his brother without a cause shall be in danger of the judgment: and whosoever shall say to his brother, Raca, shall be in danger of the council: but whosoever shall say, Thou fool, shall be in danger of hell fire. 23 Therefore if thou bring thy gift to the altar, and there rememberest that thy brother hath aught against thee; 24 Leave there thy gift before the altar, and go thy way; first be reconciled to thy brother, and then come and offer thy gift. 25 Agree with thine adversary quickly, while thou art in the way with him; lest at any time the adversary deliver thee to the judge, and the judge deliver thee to the officer, and thou be cast into prison. 26 Verily I say unto thee, Thou shalt by no means come out thence, till thou hast paid the uttermost farthing.

New International Version

7 Blessed are the merciful,
  for they will be shown mercy.
8 Blessed are the pure in heart,
  for they will see God.
9 Blessed are the peacemakers,
  for they will be called sons of God.
10 Blessed are those who are persecuted because of righteousness,
  for theirs is the kingdom of heaven.

11 "Blessed are you when people insult you, persecute you and falsely say all kinds of evil against you because of me. 12 Rejoice and be glad, because great is your reward in heaven, for in the same way they persecuted the prophets who were before you.

Salt and light

13 "You are the salt of the earth. But if the salt loses its saltiness, how can it be made salty again? It is no longer good for anything, except to be thrown out and trampled by men.
14 "You are the light of the world. A city on a hill cannot be hidden. 15 Neither do people light a lamp and put it under a bowl. Instead they put it on its stand, and it gives light to everyone in the house. 16 In the same way, let your light shine before men, that they may see your good deeds and praise your Father in heaven.

The fulfillment of the Law

17 "Do not think that I have come to abolish the Law or the Prophets; I have not come to abolish them but to fulfill them. 18 I tell you the truth, until heaven and earth disappear, not the smallest letter, not the least stroke of a pen, will by any means disappear from the Law until everything is accomplished. 19 Anyone who breaks one of the least of these commandments and teaches others to do the same will be called least in the kingdom of heaven, but whoever practices and teaches these commands will be called great in the kingdom of heaven. 20 For I tell you that unless your righteousness surpasses that of the Pharisees and the teachers of the law, you will certainly not enter the kingdom of heaven.

Murder

21 "You have heard that it was said to the people long ago, 'Do not murder,*q* and anyone who murders will be subject to judgment.' 22 But I tell you that anyone who is angry with his brother*r* will be subject to judgment. Again, anyone who says to his brother, 'Raca,'*s* is answerable to the Sanhedrin. But anyone who says, 'You fool!' will be in danger of the fire of hell.

23 "Therefore, if you are offering your gift at the altar and there remember that your brother has something against you, 24 leave your gift there in front of the altar. First go and be reconciled to your brother; then come and offer your gift.

25 "Settle matters quickly with your adversary who is taking you to court. Do it while you are still with him on the way, or he may hand you over to the judge, and the judge may hand you over to the officer, and you may be thrown into prison. 26 I tell you the truth, you will not get out until you have paid the last penny.

[q] Exodus 20:13. [r] Some MSS add *without cause.* [s] An Aramaic term of contempt.

Greek Interlinear

θήσονται. **7** μακάριοι οἱ ἐλεήμονες, ὅτι
satisfied. Blessed [are] the merciful, for

αὐτοὶ ἐλεηθήσονται. **8** μακάριοι οἱ καθαροὶ
they shall obtain mercy. Blessed [are] the clean

τῇ καρδίᾳ, ὅτι αὐτοὶ τὸν θεὸν ὄψονται.
- in heart, for they - ²God ¹shall see.

9 μακάριοι οἱ εἰρηνοποιοί, ὅτι [αὐτοὶ]
Blessed [are] the peacemakers, for they

υἱοὶ θεοῦ κληθήσονται. **10** μακάριοι οἱ
sons of God shall be called. Blessed [are] the [ones]

δεδιωγμένοι ἕνεκεν δικαιοσύνης, ὅτι αὐτῶν
having been persecuted for the sake of righteousness, for of them

ἐστιν ἡ βασιλεία τῶν οὐρανῶν. **11** μακάριοί
is the kingdom of the heavens. Blessed

ἐστε ὅταν ὀνειδίσωσιν ὑμᾶς καὶ διώξωσιν
are ye when they reproach you and persecute

καὶ εἴπωσιν πᾶν πονηρὸν καθ' ὑμῶν
and say all evil against you

ψευδόμενοι ἕνεκεν ἐμοῦ. **12** χαίρετε
lying for the sake of me. Rejoice

καὶ ἀγαλλιᾶσθε, ὅτι ὁ μισθὸς ὑμῶν
and be glad, because the reward of you [is]

πολὺς ἐν τοῖς οὐρανοῖς· οὕτως γὰρ
much in the heavens· for thus

ἐδίωξαν τοὺς προφήτας τοὺς πρὸ
they persecuted the prophets - before

ὑμῶν.
you.

13 Ὑμεῖς ἐστε τὸ ἅλας τῆς γῆς· ἐὰν δὲ
Ye are the salt of the earth; but if

τὸ ἅλας μωρανθῇ, ἐν τίνι ἁλισθήσεται;
the salt be tainted, by what shall it be salted?

εἰς οὐδὲν ἰσχύει ἔτι εἰ μὴ βληθὲν ἔξω
for nothing is it strong longer except being cast out

καταπατεῖσθαι ὑπὸ τῶν ἀνθρώπων. **14** Ὑμεῖς
to be trodden down by - men. Ye

ἐστε τὸ φῶς τοῦ κόσμου. οὐ δύναται
are the light of the world. ²Not ¹can

πόλις κρυβῆναι ἐπάνω ὄρους κειμένη·
¹a city ¹to be hid ²on ¹a mountain ²set;

15 οὐδὲ καίουσιν λύχνον καὶ τιθέασιν
nor do they light a lamp and place

αὐτὸν ὑπὸ τὸν μόδιον, ἀλλ' ἐπὶ τὴν
it under the bushel, but on the

λυχνίαν, καὶ λάμπει πᾶσιν τοῖς ἐν τῇ
lampstand, and it lightens all the [ones] in the

οἰκίᾳ. **16** οὕτως λαμψάτω τὸ φῶς ὑμῶν
house. Thus let shine the light of you

ἔμπροσθεν τῶν ἀνθρώπων, ὅπως ἴδωσιν
before - men, so that they may see

ὑμῶν τὰ καλὰ ἔργα καὶ δοξάσωσιν
of you the good works and may glorify

τὸν πατέρα ὑμῶν τὸν ἐν τοῖς οὐρανοῖς.
the Father of you - in the heavens.

17 Μὴ νομίσητε ὅτι ἦλθον καταλῦσαι
Think not that I came to destroy

τὸν νόμον ἢ τοὺς προφήτας· οὐκ ἦλθον
the law or the prophets· I came not

καταλῦσαι ἀλλὰ πληρῶσαι. **18** ἀμὴν γὰρ
to destroy but to fulfil. For truly

λέγω ὑμῖν, ἕως ἂν παρέλθῃ ὁ οὐρανὸς
I say to you, until pass away the heaven

καὶ ἡ γῆ, ἰῶτα ἓν ἢ μία κεραία οὐ
and the earth, iota one or one point by no

μὴ παρέλθῃ ἀπὸ τοῦ νόμου, ἕως ἂν
means shall pass away from the law, until

πάντα γένηται. **19** ὃς ἐὰν οὖν λύσῃ
all things come to pass. ²Whoever ¹therefore breaks

μίαν τῶν ἐντολῶν τούτων τῶν ἐλαχίστων
one - commandments of these the least

καὶ διδάξῃ οὕτως τοὺς ἀνθρώπους, ἐλάχιστος
and teaches thus - men, least

κληθήσεται ἐν τῇ βασιλείᾳ τῶν οὐρανῶν·
he shall be called in the kingdom of the heavens;

ὃς δ' ἂν ποιήσῃ καὶ διδάξῃ, οὗτος
but whoever does and teaches, this [one]

μέγας κληθήσεται ἐν τῇ βασιλείᾳ τῶν
great shall be called in the kingdom of the

οὐρανῶν. **20** λέγω γὰρ ὑμῖν ὅτι ἐὰν μὴ
heavens. For I tell you that except

περισσεύσῃ ὑμῶν ἡ δικαιοσύνη πλεῖον
shall exceed of you the righteousness more [than] [that]

τῶν γραμματέων καὶ Φαρισαίων, οὐ μὴ
of the scribes and Pharisees, by no means

εἰσέλθητε εἰς τὴν βασιλείαν τῶν οὐρανῶν.
shall ye enter into the kingdom of the heavens.

21 Ἠκούσατε ὅτι ἐρρέθη τοῖς ἀρχαίοις·
Ye heard that it was said to the ancients:

οὐ φονεύσεις· ὃς δ' ἂν φονεύσῃ,
Thou shalt not kill; and whoever kills,

ἔνοχος ἔσται τῇ κρίσει. **22** ἐγὼ δὲ
liable shall be to the judgment. But I

λέγω ὑμῖν ὅτι πᾶς ὁ ὀργιζόμενος τῷ
tell you that everyone being angry with the

ἀδελφῷ αὐτοῦ ἔνοχος ἔσται τῇ κρίσει·
brother of him liable shall be to the judgment;

ὃς δ' ἂν εἴπῃ τῷ ἀδελφῷ αὐτοῦ ῥακά,
and whoever says to the brother of him[,] Raca,

ἔνοχος ἔσται τῷ συνεδρίῳ· ὃς δ' ἂν εἴπῃ
liable shall be to the council; and whoever says[,]

μωρέ, ἔνοχος ἔσται εἰς τὴν γέενναν
Fool, liable shall be to the gehenna

τοῦ πυρός. **23** ἐὰν οὖν προσφέρῃς τὸ
- of fire. Therefore if thou bringest the

δῶρόν σου ἐπὶ τὸ θυσιαστήριον κἀκεῖ
gift of thee to the altar and there

μνησθῇς ὅτι ὁ ἀδελφός σου ἔχει τι
rememberest that the brother of thee has something

κατὰ σοῦ, **24** ἄφες ἐκεῖ τὸ δῶρόν σου
against thee, leave there the gift of thee

ἔμπροσθεν τοῦ θυσιαστηρίου, καὶ ὕπαγε
before the altar, and go

πρῶτον διαλλάγηθι τῷ ἀδελφῷ σου, καὶ
first be reconciled to the brother of thee, and

τότε ἐλθὼν πρόσφερε τὸ δῶρόν σου.
then coming offer the gift of thee.

25 ἴσθι εὐνοῶν τῷ ἀντιδίκῳ σου
Be well disposed to the opponent of thee

ταχὺ ἕως ὅτου εἶ μετ' αὐτοῦ ἐν τῇ
quickly while thou art with him in the

ὁδῷ· μήποτέ σε παραδῷ ὁ ἀντίδικος τῷ
way; lest ⁴thee ³deliver ¹the ²opponent to the

κριτῇ καὶ ὁ κριτὴς τῷ ὑπηρέτῃ, καὶ
judge and the judge to the attendant, and

εἰς φυλακὴν βληθήσῃ· **26** ἀμὴν λέγω
into prison thou be cast; truly I say

σοι, οὐ μὴ ἐξέλθῃς ἐκεῖθεν ἕως ἂν
to thee, by no means shalt thou come out thence until

ἀποδῷς τὸν ἔσχατον κοδράντην.
thou repayest the last farthing.

King James Version

27 Ye have heard that it was said by them of old time, Thou shall not commit adultery: 28 But I say unto you, That whosoever looketh on a woman to lust after her hath committed adultery with her already in his heart. 29And if thy right eye offend thee, pluck it out, and cast *it* from thee: for it is profitable for thee that one of thy members should perish, and not *that* thy whole body should be cast into hell. 30And if thy right hand offend thee, cut it off, and cast *it* from thee: for it is profitable for thee that one of thy members should perish, and not *that* thy whole body should be cast into hell. 31 It hath been said, Whosoever shall put away his wife, let him give her a writing of divorcement: 32 But I say unto you, That whosoever shall put away his wife, saving for the cause of fornication, causeth her to commit adultery: and whosoever shall marry her that is divorced committeth adultery.

33 Again, ye have heard that it hath been said by them of old time, Thou shalt not forswear thyself, but shalt perform unto the Lord thine oaths: 34 But I say unto you, Swear not at all; neither by heaven; for it is God's throne: 35 Nor by the earth; for it is his footstool: neither by Jerusalem; for it is the city of the great King. 36 Neither shalt thou swear by thy head, because thou canst not make one hair white or black. 37 But let your communication be, Yea, yea; Nay, nay: for whatsoever is more than these cometh of evil.

38 Ye have heard that it hath been said, An eye for an eye, and a tooth for a tooth: 39 But I say unto you, That ye resist not evil: but whosoever shall smite thee on thy right cheek, turn to him the other also. 40And if any man will sue thee at the law, and take away thy coat, let him have *thy* cloak also. 41And whosoever shall compel thee to go a mile, go with him twain. 42 Give to him that asketh thee, and from him that would borrow of thee turn not thou away.

43 Ye have heard that it hath been said, Thou shalt love thy neighbour, and hate thine enemy. 44 But I say unto you, Love your enemies, bless them that curse you, do good to them that hate you, and pray for them which despitefully use you, and persecute you; 45 That ye may be the children of your Father which is in heaven: for he maketh his sun to rise on the evil and on the good, and sendeth rain on the just and on the unjust. 46 For if ye love them which love you, what reward have ye? do not even the publicans the same? 47And if ye salute your brethren only, what do ye more *than others?* do not even the publicans so? 48 Be ye therefore perfect, even as your Father which is in heaven is perfect.

New International Version

Adultery

27 "You have heard that it was said, 'Do not commit adultery.' [t] 28 But I tell you that anyone who looks at a woman lustfully has already committed adultery with her in his heart. 29 If your right eye causes you to sin, gouge it out and throw it away. It is better for you to lose one part of your body than for your whole body to be thrown into hell. 30And if your right hand causes you to sin, cut it off and throw it away. It is better for you to lose one part of your body than for your whole body to go into hell. 31 "It has been said, 'Anyone who divorces his wife must give her a certificate of divorce.' [u] 32 But I tell you that anyone who divorces his wife, except for marital unfaithfulness, causes her to commit adultery, and anyone who marries a woman so divorced commits adultery.

Oaths

33 "Again, you have heard that it was said to the people long ago, 'Do not break your oath, but keep the oaths you have made to the Lord.' 34 But I tell you, Do not swear at all: either by heaven, for it is God's throne; 35 or by the earth, for it is his footstool; or by Jerusalem, for it is the city of the great King. 36And do not swear by your head, for you cannot make even one hair white or black. 37 Simply let your 'Yes' be 'Yes,' and your 'No,' 'No'; anything beyond this comes from the evil one.

An eye for an eye

38 "You have heard that it was said, 'An eye for an eye, and a tooth for a tooth.' [v] 39 But I tell you, Do not resist an evil person. If someone strikes you on the right cheek, turn to him the other also. 40And if someone wants to sue you and take your tunic, let him have your cloak as well. 41 If someone forces you to go one mile, go with him two miles. 42 Give to the one who asks you, and do not turn away from the one who wants to borrow from you.

Love for enemies

43 "You have heard that it was said, 'Love your neighbor [w] and hate your enemy.' 44 But I tell you, Love your enemies [x] and pray for those who persecute you, 45 that you may be sons of your Father in heaven. He causes his sun to rise on the evil and the good, and sends rain on the righteous and the unrighteous. 46 If you love those who love you, what reward will you get? Are not even the tax collectors doing that? 47And if you greet only your brothers, what are you doing more than others? Do not even pagans do that? 48 Be perfect, therefore, as your heavenly Father is perfect.

[t] Exodus 20:13. [u] Deut. 24:1. [v] Exodus 21:24; Lev. 24:20; Deut 19:21. [w] Lev. 19:18. [x] Some late MSS and *bless those who curse you. do good to those who hate you.*

Greek Interlinear

27 Ἠκούσατε ὅτι ἐρρέθη·   οὐ   μοιχεύσεις.
Ye heard that it was said: Thou shalt not commit adultery.

28 ἐγὼ δὲ λέγω ὑμῖν ὅτι πᾶς ὁ βλέπων
But I tell you that everyone seeing

γυναῖκα πρὸς τὸ ἐπιθυμῆσαι [αὐτὴν]
a woman with a view –   to desire   her

ἤδη ἐμοίχευσεν αὐτὴν ἐν τῇ καρδίᾳ
already committed adultery with her in the heart

αὐτοῦ. 29 εἰ δὲ ὁ ὀφθαλμός σου ὁ δεξιὸς
of him.   So if the ²eye ³of thee – ¹right

σκανδαλίζει σε, ἔξελε αὐτὸν καὶ βάλε
¹causes ⁶to stumble ⁵thee, pluck out it   and cast

ἀπὸ σοῦ· συμφέρει γάρ σοι ἵνα ἀπόληται
from thee; for it is expedient for thee that ⁵perish

ἐν τῶν μελῶν σου καὶ μὴ ὅλον τὸ
¹one ²of the ⁵members ⁴of thee and not all   the

σῶμά σου βληθῇ εἰς γέενναν. 30 καὶ
body of thee be cast into gehenna.   And

εἰ ἡ δεξιά σου χεὶρ σκανδαλίζει σε, ἔκκοψον
if the ¹right ³of thee ²hand ⁴causes ⁶to stumble ⁵thee, cut out

αὐτὴν καὶ βάλε ἀπὸ σοῦ· συμφέρει γάρ
it and cast from thee; for it is expedient

σοι ἵνα ἀπόληται ἐν τῶν μελῶν σου
for thee that ⁵perish ¹one ²of the ⁴members ³of thee

καὶ μὴ ὅλον τὸ σῶμά σου εἰς γέενναν
and not all the body of thee into gehenna

ἀπέλθῃ. 31 Ἐρρέθη δέ· ὃς ἂν ἀπολύσῃ
go away.   And it was said: Whoever dismisses

τὴν γυναῖκι αὐτοῦ, δότω αὐτῇ ἀποστάσιον.
the wife of him, let him give her a bill of divorce.

32 ἐγὼ δὲ λέγω ὑμῖν ὅτι πᾶς ὁ ἀπολύων
But I tell you that everyone dismissing

τὴν γυναῖκα αὐτοῦ παρεκτὸς λόγου
the wife of him apart from a matter

πορνείας ποιεῖ αὐτὴν μοιχευθῆναι,
of fornication makes her to commit adultery,

καὶ ὃς ἐὰν ἀπολελυμένην γαμήσῃ,
and whoever ¹a dismissed [woman] ¹marries,

μοιχᾶται. 33 Πάλιν ἠκούσατε ὅτι ἐρρέθη
commits adultery. Again ye heard that it was said

τοῖς ἀρχαίοις· οὐκ ἐπιορκήσεις, ἀποδώσεις
to the ancients; Thou shalt not perjure, ²shalt repay

δὲ τῷ κυρίῳ τοὺς ὅρκους σου. 34 ἐγὼ δὲ
¹but to the Lord the oaths of thee.   But I

λέγω ὑμῖν μὴ ὀμόσαι ὅλως· μήτε ἐν τῷ
tell you not to swear at all; neither by the

οὐρανῷ, ὅτι θρόνος ἐστὶν τοῦ θεοῦ·
heaven, because [the] throne it is of God;

35 μήτε ἐν τῇ γῇ, ὅτι ὑποπόδιόν
nor by the earth, because footstool

ἐστιν τῶν ποδῶν αὐτοῦ· μήτε εἰς
it is of the feet of him; nor by

Ἱεροσόλυμα, ὅτι πόλις ἐστὶν τοῦ μεγάλου
Jerusalem, because city it is of the great

βασιλέως· 36 μήτε ἐν τῇ κεφαλῇ σου
King;   nor by the head of thee

ὀμόσῃς, ὅτι οὐ δύνασαι μίαν τρίχα
swear, because thou canst not one hair

λευκὴν ποιῆσαι ἢ μέλαιναν. 37 ἔστω
white to make or black.   ⁵let ⁶be

δὲ ὁ λόγος ὑμῶν ναὶ ναί, οὖ οὔ·
¹But ²the ⁴word ³of you Yes yes, No no;

τὸ δὲ περισσὸν τούτων ἐκ τοῦ πονηροῦ
for the excess of these of – evil

ἐστιν. 38 Ἠκούσατε ὅτι ἐρρέθη· ὀφθαλμὸν
is.   Ye heard that it was said: An eye

ἀντὶ ὀφθαλμοῦ καὶ ὀδόντα ἀντὶ ὀδόντος.
instead of an eye and a tooth instead of a tooth.

39 ἐγὼ δὲ λέγω ὑμῖν μὴ ἀντιστῆναι
But I tell you not to oppose

τῷ πονηρῷ· ἀλλ' ὅστις σε ῥαπίζει εἰς
–   evil;   but who thee strikes on

τὴν δεξιὰν σιαγόνα [σου], στρέψον αὐτῷ
the right cheek of thee, turn to him

καὶ τὴν ἄλλην· 40 καὶ τῷ θέλοντί
also the other;   and to the [one] wishing

σοι κριθῆναι καὶ τὸν χιτῶνά σου λαβεῖν,
thee to judge and the tunic of thee to take,

ἄφες αὐτῷ καὶ τὸ ἱμάτιον· 41 καὶ
allow him also the [outer] garment;   and

ὅστις σε ἀγγαρεύσει μίλιον ἕν, ὕπαγε
who thee ¹shall impress ²mile ¹one, go

μετ' αὐτοῦ δύο. 42 τῷ αἰτοῦντί
with him two.   To the [one] asking

σε δός, καὶ τὸν θέλοντα ἀπὸ σοῦ
thee give, and the [one] wishing from thee

δανείσασθαι μὴ ἀποστραφῇς. 43 Ἠκούσατε
to borrow turn not away.   Ye heard

ὅτι ἐρρέθη· ἀγαπήσεις τὸν πλησίον σου
that it was said: Thou shalt love the neighbour of thee

καὶ μισήσεις τὸν ἐχθρόν σου. 44 ἐγὼ
and thou shalt hate the enemy of thee.   ²I

δὲ λέγω ὑμῖν· ἀγαπᾶτε τοὺς ἐχθροὺς
¹But tell you: Love ye the enemies

ὑμῶν καὶ προσεύχεσθε ὑπὲρ τῶν
of you and pray ye for the [ones]

διωκόντων ὑμᾶς· 45 ὅπως γένησθε υἱοὶ
persecuting you;   so that ye may become sons

τοῦ πατρὸς ὑμῶν τοῦ ἐν οὐρανοῖς,
of the Father of you the – in heavens,

ὅτι τὸν ἥλιον αὐτοῦ ἀνατέλλει ἐπὶ
because the sun of him he makes to rise on

πονηροὺς καὶ ἀγαθοὺς καὶ βρέχει ἐπὶ
evil men and good and rains on

δικαίους καὶ ἀδίκους. 46 ἐὰν γὰρ
just men and unjust.   For if

ἀγαπήσητε τοὺς ἀγαπῶντας ὑμᾶς, τίνα
ye love the [ones] loving you, what

μισθὸν ἔχετε; οὐχὶ καὶ οἱ τελῶναι τὸ
reward have ye? ²not ³even ⁴the ¹tax-collectors ⁵the

αὐτὸ ποιοῦσιν; 47 καὶ ἐὰν ἀσπάσησθε
⁵same ¹do?   and if ye greet

τοὺς ἀδελφοὺς ὑμῶν μόνον, τί περισσὸν
the brothers of you only, what excess

ποιεῖτε; οὐχὶ καὶ οἱ ἐθνικοὶ τὸ αὐτὸ
do ye? ²not ³even ⁴the ¹gentiles ⁵the ⁵same

ποιοῦσιν; 48 Ἔσεσθε οὖν ὑμεῖς τέλειοι
¹do?   Be therefore ye perfect

ὡς ὁ πατὴρ ὑμῶν ὁ οὐράνιος τέλειός
as the ²Father ³of you – ¹heavenly perfect

ἐστιν.
is.

King James Version

6 Take heed that ye do not your alms before men, to be seen of them: otherwise ye have no reward of your Father which is in heaven. 2 Therefore when thou doest *thine* alms, do not sound a trumpet before thee, as the hypocrites do in the synagogues and in the streets, that they may have glory of men. Verily I say unto you, They have their reward. 3 But when thou doest alms, let not thy left hand know what thy right hand doeth: 4 That thine alms may be in secret: and thy Father which seeth in secret himself shall reward thee openly.

5 And when thou prayest, thou shalt not be as the hypocrites *are:* for they love to pray standing in the synagogues and in the corners of the streets, that they may be seen of men. Verily I say unto you, They have their reward. 6 But thou, when thou prayest, enter into thy closet, and when thou hast shut thy door, pray to thy Father which is in secret; and thy Father which seeth in secret shall reward thee openly. 7 But when ye pray, use not vain repetitions, as the heathen *do:* for they think that they shall be heard for their much speaking. 8 Be not ye therefore like unto them: for your Father knoweth what things ye have need of, before ye ask him. 9 After this manner therefore pray ye: Our Father which art in heaven, Hallowed be thy name. 10 Thy kingdom come. Thy will be done in earth, as *it is* in heaven. 11 Give us this day our daily bread. 12 And forgive us our debts, as we forgive our debtors. 13 And lead us not into temptation, but deliver us from evil: For thine is the kingdom, and the power, and the glory, for ever. Amen. 14 For if ye forgive men their trespasses, your heavenly Father will also forgive you: 15 But if ye forgive not men their trespasses, neither will your Father forgive your trespasses.

16 Moreover when ye fast, be not, as the hypocrites, of a sad countenance: for they disfigure their faces, that they may appear unto men to fast. Verily I say unto you, They have their reward. 17 But thou, when thou fastest, anoint thine head, and wash thy face; 18 That thou appear not unto men to fast, but unto thy Father which is in secret: and thy Father which seeth in secret shall reward thee openly.

19 Lay not up for yourselves treasures upon earth, where moth and rust doth corrupt, and where thieves break through and steal: 20 But lay up for yourselves treasures in heaven, where neither moth nor rust doth corrupt, and where thieves do not break through nor steal: 21 For where your treasure is, there will your heart be

New International Version

Giving to the needy

6 "Be careful not to do your 'acts of righteousness' before men, to be seen by them. If you do, you will have no reward from your Father in heaven.
2 "So when you give to the needy, do not announce it with trumpets, as the hypocrites do in the synagogues and on the streets, to be honored by men. I tell you the truth, they have received their reward in full. 3 But when you give to the needy, do not let your left hand know what your right hand is doing, 4 so that your giving may be in secret. Then your Father, who sees what is done in secret, will reward you.

Prayer

5 "When you pray, do not be like the hypocrites, for they love to pray standing in the synagogues and on the street corners to be seen by men. I tell you the truth, they have received their reward in full. 6 But when you pray, go into your room, close the door and pray to your Father, who is unseen. Then your Father, who sees what is done in secret, will reward you. 7 And when you pray, do not keep on babbling like pagans, for they think they will be heard because of their many words. 8 Do not be like them, for your Father knows what you need before you ask him.
9 "This is how you should pray:
'Our Father in heaven,
  hallowed be your name,
10 your kingdom come,
  your will be done
    on earth as it is in heaven.
11 Give us today our daily bread.
12 Forgive us our debts,
  as we also have forgiven our debtors.
13 And lead us not into temptation,
  but deliver us from the evil one.' *y*
14 For if you forgive men when they sin against you, your heavenly Father will also forgive you. 15 But if you do not forgive men their sins, your Father will not forgive your sins.

Fasting

16 "When you fast, do not look somber as the hypocrites do, for they disfigure their faces to show men they are fasting. I tell you the truth, they have received their reward in full. 17 But when you fast, put oil on your head and wash your face, 18 so that it will not be obvious to men that you are fasting, but only to your Father, who is unseen; and your Father, who sees what is done in secret, will reward you.

Treasures in heaven

19 "Do not store up for yourselves treasures on earth, where moth and rust destroy, and where thieves break in and steal. 20 But store up for yourselves treasures in heaven, where moth and rust do not destroy, and where thieves do not break in and steal. 21 For where your treasure is, there your heart will be also.

[y] Or *from evil.* Som late MSS add *for yours is the kingdom and the power and the glory forever. Amen.*

Greek Interlinear

Chapter 6

Προσέχετε δὲ τὴν δικαιοσύνην ὑμῶν
And take ye heed   the   righteousness   of you

μὴ ποιεῖν ἔμπροσθεν τῶν ἀνθρώπων πρὸς
not to do   in front of -   men   with a view to

τὸ θεαθῆναι αὐτοῖς· εἰ δὲ μή γε, μισθὸν
- to be seen   by them;   otherwise,   reward

οὐκ ἔχετε παρὰ τῷ πατρὶ ὑμῶν τῷ
ye have not   with   the   Father of you -

ἐν τοῖς οὐρανοῖς. 2 Ὅταν οὖν ποιῇς
in the heavens.   ²When ¹therefore thou doest

ἐλεημοσύνην, μὴ σαλπίσῃς ἔμπροσθέν σου,
alms,   sound not a trumpet   before   thee,

ὥσπερ οἱ ὑποκριταὶ ποιοῦσιν ἐν ταῖς
as the   hypocrites   do   in   the

συναγωγαῖς καὶ ἐν ταῖς ῥύμαις, ὅπως
synagogues   and in the   streets,   so that

δοξασθῶσιν ὑπὸ τῶν ἀνθρώπων· ἀμὴν
they may be glorified by   the   men;   truly

λέγω ὑμῖν, ἀπέχουσιν τὸν μισθὸν αὐτῶν.
I tell   you,   they have   the   reward   of them.

3 σοῦ δὲ ποιοῦντος ἐλεημοσύνην μὴ
But thee   doing*   alms   not
= when thou doest

γνώτω ἡ ἀριστερά σου τί ποιεῖ ἡ
let know the left [hand] of thee what does the

δεξιά σου, 4 ὅπως ᾖ σου ἡ ἐλεημοσύνη
right of thee,   so that ⁴may be ²of thee ¹the   ³alms

ἐν τῷ κρυπτῷ· καὶ ὁ πατήρ σου
in -   secret;   and   the   Father of thee

ὁ βλέπων ἐν τῷ κρυπτῷ ἀποδώσει σοι.
the [one] seeing in -   secret   will repay   thee.

5 Καὶ ὅταν προσεύχησθε, οὐκ ἔσεσθε
And   when   ye pray,   be not ye

ὡς οἱ ὑποκριταί· ὅτι φιλοῦσιν ἐν ταῖς
as the   hypocrites: because they love   in   the

συναγωγαῖς καὶ ἐν ταῖς γωνίαις τῶν
synagogues   and in the   corners   of the

πλατειῶν ἑστῶτες προσεύχεσθαι, ὅπως
open streets   standing   to pray,   so that

φανῶσιν τοῖς ἀνθρώποις· ἀμὴν λέγω
they may appear -   to men;   truly   I tell

ὑμῖν, ἀπέχουσιν τὸν μισθὸν αὐτῶν. 6 σὺ
you,   they have   the   reward   of them.   ²thou

δὲ ὅταν προσεύχῃ, εἴσελθε εἰς τὸ ταμιεῖόν
¹But ³when ⁴prayest,   enter   into the private room

σου καὶ κλείσας τὴν θύραν σου πρόσευξαι
of thee and having shut the   door   of thee   pray

τῷ πατρί σου τῷ ἐν τῷ κρυπτῷ·
to the Father of thee the [one] in -   secret;

καὶ ὁ πατήρ σου ὁ βλέπων ἐν τῷ
and   the   Father of thee the [one] seeing   in   -

κρυπτῷ ἀποδώσει σοι. 7 Προσευχόμενοι δὲ
secret   will repay   thee.   But praying

μὴ βατταλογήσητε ὥσπερ οἱ ἐθνικοί·
do not utter empty words   as   the   gentiles:

δοκοῦσιν γὰρ ὅτι ἐν τῇ πολυλογίᾳ αὐτῶν
for they think that in the   much speaking   of them

εἰσακουσθήσονται. 8 μὴ οὖν ὁμοιωθῆτε
they will be heard.   Not therefore   be ye like

αὐτοῖς· οἶδεν γὰρ [ὁ θεὸς] ὁ πατὴρ
them;   for ²knows - ¹God ³the ⁴Father

ὑμῶν ὧν χρείαν ἔχετε πρὸ τοῦ ὑμᾶς
⁵of you of what things ⁷need ⁶ye have before -   you

αἰτῆσαι αὐτόν. 9 οὕτως οὖν προσεύχεσθε
to ask[b] him.   ²Thus ¹therefore   pray

ὑμεῖς· Πάτερ ἡμῶν ὁ ἐν τοῖς οὐρανοῖς·
ye: Father of us the [one] in the   heavens:

Ἁγιασθήτω τὸ ὄνομά σου· 10 ἐλθάτω
Let it be hallowed the   name of thee;   let it come

ἡ βασιλεία σου· γενηθήτω τὸ θέλημά σου,
the kingdom of thee; let it come about the will   of thee,

ὡς ἐν οὐρανῷ καὶ ἐπὶ γῆς· 11 Τὸν
as in   heaven also on earth;   The

ἄρτον ἡμῶν τὸν ἐπιούσιον δὸς ἡμῖν
¹bread ²of us -   ³daily   give to us

σήμερον· 12 καὶ ἄφες ἡμῖν τὰ ὀφειλή-
to-day;   and forgive us   the   debts

ματα ἡμῶν, ὡς καὶ ἡμεῖς ἀφήκαμεν
of us,   as indeed   we   forgave

τοῖς ὀφειλέταις ἡμῶν· 13 καὶ μὴ εἰσενέγκῃς
the debtors of us;   and not   bring

ἡμᾶς εἰς πειρασμόν, ἀλλὰ ῥῦσαι ἡμᾶς ἀπὸ
us into temptation,   but rescue   us   from

τοῦ πονηροῦ. 14 Ἐὰν γὰρ ἀφῆτε τοῖς
-   evil.   For if   ye forgive

ἀνθρώποις τὰ παραπτώματα αὐτῶν, ἀφήσει
men   the   trespasses   of them, will forgive

καὶ ὑμῖν ὁ πατὴρ ὑμῶν ὁ οὐράνιος·
also you the ¹Father ²of you -   ³heavenly;

15 ἐὰν δὲ μὴ ἀφῆτε τοῖς ἀνθρώποις,
but if   ye forgive not -   men.

οὐδὲ ὁ πατὴρ ὑμῶν ἀφήσει τὰ παραπτώ-
neither the Father of you will forgive the   tres-

ματα ὑμῶν. 16 Ὅταν δὲ νηστεύητε,
passes of you.   And when   ye fast,

μὴ γίνεσθε ὡς οἱ ὑποκριταὶ σκυθρωποί·
be not   as the   hypocrites   gloomy;

ἀφανίζουσιν γὰρ τὰ πρόσωπα αὐτῶν
for they disfigure   the   faces   of them

ὅπως φανῶσιν τοῖς ἀνθρώποις νηστεύοντες·
so that they may appear -   to men   fasting;

ἀμὴν λέγω ὑμῖν, ἀπέχουσιν τὸν μισθὸν
truly   I tell   you,   they have   the   reward

αὐτῶν. 17 σὺ δὲ νηστεύων ἄλειψαί σου
of them.   But thou   fasting   anoint   of thee

τὴν κεφαλὴν καὶ τὸ πρόσωπόν σου νίψαι,
the   head   and   the   face   of thee   wash,

18 ὅπως μὴ φανῇς τοῖς ἀνθρώποις νηστεύων
so that thou appearest not -   to men   fasting

ἀλλὰ τῷ πατρί σου τῷ ἐν τῷ κρυφαίῳ·
but to the Father of thee the [one] in -   secret;

καὶ ὁ πατήρ σου ὁ βλέπων ἐν τῷ
and   the   Father of thee the [one] seeing   in   -

κρυφαίῳ ἀποδώσει σοι.
secret   will repay   thee.

19 Μὴ θησαυρίζετε ὑμῖν θησαυροὺς
Do not lay up *treasure*   for you   ¹treasures

ἐπὶ τῆς γῆς, ὅπου σὴς καὶ βρῶσις
on the   earth,   where moth   and   rust

ἀφανίζει, καὶ ὅπου κλέπται διορύσσουσιν
removes,   and where   thieves   dig through

καὶ κλέπτουσιν· 20 θησαυρίζετε δὲ ὑμῖν
and   steal;   but lay up *treasure* for you

θησαυροὺς ἐν οὐρανῷ, ὅπου οὔτε σὴς
treasures in   heaven,   where   neither   moth

οὔτε βρῶσις ἀφανίζει, καὶ ὅπου κλέπται
nor   rust   removes,   and   where   thieves

οὐ διορύσσουσιν οὐδὲ κλέπτουσιν· 21 ὅπου
do not dig through   nor   steal;   ¹where

γὰρ ἐστιν ὁ θησαυρός σου, ἐκεῖ
¹for   is   the   treasure of thee,   there

King James Version

also. 22 The light of the body is the eye: if therefore thine eye be single, thy whole body shall be full of light. 23 But if thine eye be evil, thy whole body shall be full of darkness. If therefore the light that is in thee be darkness, how great *is* that darkness!

24 No man can serve two masters: for either he will hate the one, and love the other; or else he will hold to the one, and despise the other. Ye cannot serve God and mammon. 25 Therefore I say unto you, Take no thought for your life, what ye shall eat, or what ye shall drink; nor yet for your body, what ye shall put on. Is not the life more than meat, and the body than raiment? 26 Behold the fowls of the air: for they sow not, neither do they reap, nor gather into barns; yet your heavenly Father feedeth them. Are ye not much better than they? 27 Which of you by taking thought can add one cubit unto his stature? 28 And why take ye thought for raiment? Consider the lilies of the field, how they grow; they toil not, neither do they spin: 29 And yet I say unto you, That even Solomon in all his glory was not arrayed like one of these. 30 Wherefore, if God so clothe the grass of the field, which to day is, and to morrow is cast into the oven, *shall he* not much more *clothe* you, O ye of little faith? 31 Therefore take no thought, saying, What shall we eat? or, What shall we drink? or, Wherewithal shall we be clothed? 32 (For after all these things do the Gentiles seek:) for your heavenly Father knoweth that ye have need of all these things. 33 But seek ye first the kingdom of God, and his righteousness; and all these things shall be added unto you. 34 Take therefore no thought for the morrow: for the morrow shall take thought for the things of itself. Sufficient unto the day *is* the evil thereof.

7 Judge not, that ye be not judged. 2 For with what judgment ye judge, ye shall be judged: and with what measure ye mete, it shall be measured to you again. 3 And why beholdest thou the mote that is in thy brother's eye, but considerest not the beam that is in thine own eye? 4 Or how wilt thou say to thy brother, Let me pull out the mote out of thine eye; and, behold, a beam *is* in thine own eye? 5 Thou hypocrite, first cast out the beam out of thine own eye; and then shalt thou see clearly to cast out the mote out of thy brother's eye.

6 Give not that which is holy unto the dogs, neither cast ye your pearls before swine, lest they trample them under their feet, and turn again and rend you.

7 Ask, and it shall be given you; seek, and ye shall find; knock, and it shall be opened unto

New International Version

22 "The eye is the lamp of the body. If your eyes are good, your whole body will be full of light. 23 But if your eyes are bad, your whole body will be full of darkness. If then the light within you is darkness, how great is that darkness!

24 "No one can serve two masters. Either he will hate the one and love the other, or he will be devoted to the one and despise the other. You cannot serve both God and Money.

Do not worry

25 "Therefore I tell you, do not worry about your life, what you will eat or drink; or about your body, what you will wear. Is not life more important than food, and the body more important than clothes? 26 Look at the birds of the air; they do not sow or reap or store away in barns, and yet your heavenly Father feeds them. Are you not much more valuable than they? 27 Who of you by worrying can add a single hour to his life? [z] 28 "And why do you worry about clothes? See how the lilies of the field grow. They do not labor or spin. 29 Yet I tell you that not even Solomon in all his splendor was dressed like one of these. 30 If that is how God clothes the grass of the field, which is here today and tomorrow is thrown into the fire, will he not much more clothe you, O you of little faith? 31 So do not worry, saying, 'What shall we eat?' or 'What shall we drink?' or 'What shall we wear?' 32 For the pagans run after all these things, and your heavenly Father knows that you need them. 33 But seek first his kingdom and his righteousness, and all these things will be given to you as well. 34 Therefore do not worry about tomorrow, for tomorrow will worry about itself. Each day has enough trouble of its own.

Judging others

7 "Do not judge, or you too will be judged. 2 For in the same way you judge others, you will be judged, and with the measure you use, it will be measured to you.

3 "Why do you look at the speck of sawdust in your brother's eye and pay no attention to the plank in your own eye? 4 How can you say to your brother, 'Let me take the speck out of your eye,' when all the time there is a plank in your own eye? 5 You hypocrite, first take the plank out of your own eye, and then you will see clearly to remove the speck from your brother's eye.

6 "Do not give dogs what is sacred; do not throw your pearls to pigs. If you do, they may trample them under their feet, and then turn and tear you to pieces.

Ask, seek, knock

7 "Ask and it will be given to you; seek and you will find; knock and the door will be

[z] Or *single cubit to his height.*

Greek Interlinear

ἔσται καὶ ἡ καρδία σου. 22 Ὁ λύχνος
will be also the heart of thee. The lamp

τοῦ σώματός ἐστιν ὁ ὀφθαλμός. ἐὰν οὖν
of the body is the eye. ²If ¹therefore

ᾖ ὁ ὀφθαλμός σου ἁπλοῦς, ὅλον τὸ σῶμά
⁴be ¹the ²eye ³of thee single, all the body

σου φωτεινὸν ἔσται· 23 ἐὰν δὲ ὁ
of thee shining will be; but if the

ὀφθαλμός σου πονηρὸς ᾖ, ὅλον τὸ σῶμά
eye of thee evil be, all the body

σου σκοτεινὸν ἔσται. εἰ οὖν τὸ φῶς
of thee dark will be. ²If ¹therefore the light

τὸ ἐν σοὶ σκότος ἐστιν, τὸ σκότος
- in thee darkness is, the darkness

πόσον. 24 Οὐδεὶς δύναται δυσὶ κυρίοις
how great. No one can two lords

δουλεύειν· ἢ γὰρ τὸν ἕνα μισήσει καὶ
to serve; for either the one he will hate and

τὸν ἕτερον ἀγαπήσει, ἢ ἑνὸς ἀνθέξεται
the other he will love, or one he will hold to

καὶ τοῦ ἑτέρου καταφρονήσει. οὐ δύνασθε
and the other he will despise. Ye cannot

θεῷ δουλεύειν καὶ μαμωνᾷ. 25 Διὰ
God to serve and mammon. There-

τοῦτο λέγω ὑμῖν· μὴ μεριμνᾶτε τῇ
fore I say to you: Be not anxious for the

ψυχῇ ὑμῶν τί φάγητε [ἢ τί πίητε],
life of you[,] what ye may eat or what ye may drink,

μηδὲ τῷ σώματι ὑμῶν τί ἐνδύσησθε.
nor for the body of you[,] what ye may put on.

οὐχὶ ἡ ψυχὴ πλεῖόν ἐστιν τῆς τροφῆς καὶ τὸ
²not ³the ⁴life ⁵more ¹Is [than] the food and the

σῶμα τοῦ ἐνδύματος; 26 ἐμβλέψατε εἰς
body [than] the raiment? Look ye at

τὰ πετεινὰ τοῦ οὐρανοῦ, ὅτι οὐ σπείρουσιν
the birds - of heaven, that they sow not

οὐδὲ θερίζουσιν οὐδὲ συνάγουσιν εἰς
nor reap nor gather into

ἀποθήκας, καὶ ὁ πατὴρ ὑμῶν ὁ οὐράνιος
barns, and the ²Father ³of you - ¹heavenly

τρέφει αὐτά· οὐχ ὑμεῖς μᾶλλον διαφέρετε
feeds them; do not ye more excel

αὐτῶν; 27 τίς δὲ ἐξ ὑμῶν μεριμνῶν
them? But who of you being anxious

δύναται προσθεῖναι ἐπὶ τὴν ἡλικίαν αὐτοῦ
can to add to the stature of him

πῆχυν ἕνα; 28 καὶ περὶ ἐνδύματος τί
cubit one? and concerning clothing why

μεριμνᾶτε; καταμάθετε τὰ κρίνα τοῦ ἀγροῦ,
be ye anxious? consider the lilies of the field,

πῶς αὐξάνουσιν· οὐ κοπιῶσιν οὐδὲ
how they grow; they labour not nor

νήθουσιν· 29 λέγω δὲ ὑμῖν ὅτι οὐδὲ Σολομὼν
spin; but I tell you that not Solomon

ἐν πάσῃ τῇ δόξῃ αὐτοῦ περιεβάλετο ὡς
in all the glory of him was clothed as

ἓν τούτων. 30 εἰ δὲ τὸν χόρτον τοῦ
one of these. But if the grass of the

ἀγροῦ σήμερον ὄντα καὶ αὔριον εἰς
field to-day being and to-morrow into

κλίβανον βαλλόμενον ὁ θεὸς οὕτως
an oven being thrown - God thus

ἀμφιέννυσιν, οὐ πολλῷ μᾶλλον ὑμᾶς,
clothes, not much more you,

ὀλιγόπιστοι; 31 μὴ οὖν μεριμνήσητε
little-faiths? Therefore be ye not anxious

λέγοντες· τί φάγωμεν; ἤ· τί
saying: What may we eat? or: What

πίωμεν; ἤ· τί περιβαλώμεθα; 32 πάντα
may we drink? or: What may we put on? ²all

γὰρ ταῦτα τὰ ἔθνη ἐπιζητοῦσιν· οἶδεν
¹for these things the nations seek after; ²knows

γὰρ ὁ πατὴρ ὑμῶν ὁ οὐράνιος ὅτι
¹for ²the ³Father ⁴of you - ⁵heavenly that

χρῄζετε τούτων ἁπάντων. 33 ζητεῖτε δὲ
ye need these things of all. But seek ye

πρῶτον τὴν βασιλείαν καὶ τὴν δικαιοσύνην
first the kingdom and the righteousness

αὐτοῦ, καὶ ταῦτα πάντα προστεθήσεται
of him, and these things all shall be added

ὑμῖν. 34 μὴ οὖν μεριμνήσητε εἰς τὴν
to you. Therefore be ye not anxious for the

αὔριον, ἡ γὰρ αὔριον μεριμνήσει
morrow, for the morrow will be anxious

ἑαυτῆς· ἀρκετὸν τῇ ἡμέρᾳ ἡ κακία αὐτῆς.
of itself; sufficient to the day the evil of it.

Chapter 7

Μὴ κρίνετε, ἵνα μὴ κριθῆτε· 2 ἐν ᾧ
Judge not, lest ye be judged; ²with ³what

γὰρ κρίματι κρίνετε κριθήσεσθε, καὶ
¹for judgment ye judge ye shall be judged, and

ἐν ᾧ μέτρῳ μετρεῖτε μετρηθήσεται ὑμῖν.
with what measure ye measure it shall be measured to you.

3 τί δὲ βλέπεις τὸ κάρφος τὸ ἐν
And why seest thou the chip - in

τῷ ὀφθαλμῷ τοῦ ἀδελφοῦ σου, τὴν
the eye of the brother of thee, ²the

δὲ ἐν τῷ σῷ ὀφθαλμῷ δοκὸν οὐ κατα-
¹but ⁴in - ³thine ⁵eye ⁶beam thou consider-

νοεῖς; 4 ἢ πῶς ἐρεῖς τῷ ἀδελφῷ σου·
est not? or how wilt thou say to the brother of thee:

ἄφες ἐκβάλω τὸ κάρφος ἐκ τοῦ ὀφθαλμοῦ
Allow [that] I may pluck out the chip out of the eye

σου, καὶ ἰδοὺ ἡ δοκὸς ἐν τῷ ὀφθαλμῷ
of thee, and behold the beam in the eye

σου; 5 ὑποκριτά, ἔκβαλε πρῶτον ἐκ τοῦ
of thee? hypocrite, pluck out first out of the

ὀφθαλμοῦ σου τὴν δοκόν, καὶ τότε
eye of thee the beam, and then

διαβλέψεις ἐκβαλεῖν τὸ κάρφος ἐκ
thou wilt see clearly to pluck out the chip out of

τοῦ ὀφθαλμοῦ τοῦ ἀδελφοῦ σου. 6 Μὴ
the eye of the brother of thee. not

δῶτε τὸ ἅγιον τοῖς κυσίν, μηδὲ βάλητε
Give the holy to the dogs, neither cast

τοὺς μαργαρίτας ὑμῶν ἔμπροσθεν τῶν
the pearls of you before the

χοίρων, μήποτε καταπατήσουσιν αὐτοὺς
pigs, lest they will trample them

ἐν τοῖς ποσὶν αὐτῶν καὶ στραφέντες
with the feet of them and turning

ῥήξωσιν ὑμᾶς. 7 Αἰτεῖτε, καὶ δοθήσεται
may rend you. Ask, and it shall be given

ὑμῖν· ζητεῖτε, καὶ εὑρήσετε· κρούετε,
to you; seek, and ye shall find; knock,

King James Version

you: 8 For every one that asketh receiveth; and he that seeketh findeth; and to him that knocketh it shall be opened. 9 Or what man is there of you, whom if his son ask bread, will he give him a stone? 10 Or if he ask a fish, will he give him a serpent? 11 If ye then, being evil, know how to give good gifts unto your children, how much more shall your Father which is in heaven give good things to them that ask him? 12 Therefore all things whatsoever ye would that men should do to you, do ye even so to them: for this is the law and the prophets.

13 Enter ye in at the strait gate: for wide *is* the gate, and broad *is* the way, that leadeth to destruction, and many there be which go in thereat: 14 Because strait *is* the gate, and narrow *is* the way, which leadeth unto life, and few there be that find it.

15 Beware of false prophets, which come to you in sheep's clothing, but inwardly they are ravening wolves. 16 Ye shall know them by their fruits. Do men gather grapes of thorns, or figs of thistles? 17 Even so every good tree bringeth forth good fruit; but a corrupt tree bringeth forth evil fruit. 18 A good tree cannot bring forth evil fruit, neither *can* a corrupt tree bring forth good fruit. 19 Every tree that bringeth not forth good fruit is hewn down, and cast into the fire. 20 Wherefore by their fruits ye shall know them.

21 Not every one that saith unto me, Lord, Lord, shall enter into the kingdom of heaven; but he that doeth the will of my Father which is in heaven. 22 Many will say to me in that day, Lord, Lord, have we not prophesied in thy name? and in thy name have cast out devils? and in thy name done many wonderful works? 23 And then will I profess unto them, I never knew you: depart from me, ye that work iniquity.

24 Therefore whosoever heareth these sayings of mine, and doeth them, I will liken him unto a wise man, which built his house upon a rock: 25 And the rain descended, and the floods came, and the winds blew, and beat upon that house; and it fell not: for it was founded upon a rock. 26 And every one that heareth these sayings of mine, and doeth them not, shall be likened unto a foolish man, which built his house upon the sand: 27 And the rain descended, and the floods came, and the winds blew, and beat upon that house; and it fell: and great was the fall of it. 28 And it came to pass, when Jesus had ended these sayings, the people were astonished at his doctrine: 29 For he taught them as *one* having authority, and not as the scribes.

New International Version

opened to you. 8 For everyone who asks receives; he who seeks finds; and to him who knocks, the door will be opened.

9 "Which of you, if his son asks for bread, will give him a stone? 10 Or if he asks for a fish, will give him a snake? 11 If you, then, though you are evil, know how to give good gifts to your children, how much more will your Father in heaven give good gifts to those who ask him! 12 In everything do to others what you would have them do to you, for this sums up the Law and the Prophets.

The narrow and wide gates

13 "Enter through the narrow gate. For wide is the gate and broad is the road that leads to destruction, and many enter through it. 14 But small is the gate and narrow the road that leads to life, and only a few find it.

A tree and its fruit

15 "Watch out for false prophets. They come to you in sheep's clothing, but inwardly they are ferocious wolves. 16 By their fruit you will recognize them. Do people pick grapes from thornbushes, or figs from thistles? 17 Likewise every good tree bears good fruit, but a bad tree bears bad fruit. 18 A good tree cannot bear bad fruit, and a bad tree cannot bear good fruit. 19 Every tree that does not bear good fruit is cut down and thrown into the fire. 20 Thus, by their fruit you will recognize them.

21 "Not everyone who says to me, 'Lord, Lord,' will enter the kingdom of heaven, but only he who does the will of my Father who is in heaven. 22 Many will say to me on that day, 'Lord, Lord, did we not prophesy in your name, and in your name drive out demons and perform many miracles?' 23 Then I will tell them plainly, 'I never knew you. Away from me, you evildoers!'

The wise and foolish builders

24 "Therefore, everyone who hears these words of mine and puts them into practice is like a wise man who built his house on the rock. 25 The rain came down, the streams rose, and the winds blew and beat against that house; yet it did not fall, because it had its foundation on the rock. 26 But everyone who hears these words of mine and does not put them into practice is like a foolish man who built his house on sand. 27 The rain came down, the streams rose, and the winds blew and beat against that house, and it fell with a great crash."

28 When Jesus had finished saying these things, the crowds were amazed at his teaching, 29 because he taught as one who had authority, and not as their teachers of the law.

Greek Interlinear

καὶ ἀνοιγήσεται ὑμῖν. **8** πᾶς γὰρ ὁ αἰτῶν
and it shall be opened to you. For every asking [one]

λαμβάνει, καὶ ὁ ζητῶν εὑρίσκει, καὶ
receives, and the seeking [one] finds, and

τῷ κρούοντι ἀνοιγήσεται. **9** ἢ τίς ἐστιν
to the knocking [one] it shall be opened. Or ¹what ²is there

ἐξ ὑμῶν ἄνθρωπος, ὃν αἰτήσει ὁ υἱὸς
⁴of ⁵you ³man, whom ⁴will ask ¹the ²son

αὐτοῦ ἄρτον, μὴ λίθον ἐπιδώσει αὐτῷ;
³of him ⁶a loaf, not a stone he will give him?

10 ἢ καὶ ἰχθὺν αἰτήσει, μὴ ὄφιν ἐπιδώσει
or also a fish he will ask, not a serpent he will give

αὐτῷ; **11** εἰ οὖν ὑμεῖς πονηροὶ ὄντες
him? If therefore ye ¹evil ¹being

οἴδατε δόματα ἀγαθὰ διδόναι τοῖς τέκνοις
know gifts² good² to give¹ to the children

ὑμῶν, πόσῳ μᾶλλον ὁ πατὴρ ὑμῶν ὁ
of you, how much more the Father of you -

ἐν τοῖς οὐρανοῖς δώσει ἀγαθὰ τοῖς
in the heavens will give good things to the [ones]

αἰτοῦσιν αὐτόν. **12** Πάντα οὖν ὅσα ἐὰν
asking him. All things therefore as many soever as

θέλητε ἵνα ποιῶσιν ὑμῖν οἱ ἄνθρωποι,
ye wish that may do to you - men,

οὕτως καὶ ὑμεῖς ποιεῖτε αὐτοῖς· οὗτος
thus also ye do to them; ¹this

γάρ ἐστιν ὁ νόμος καὶ οἱ προφῆται.
¹for is the law and the prophets.

13 Εἰσέλθατε διὰ τῆς στενῆς πύλης
Enter ye in through the narrow gate;

ὅτι πλατεῖα [ἡ πύλη] καὶ εὐρύχωρος
because wide the gate and broad

ἡ ὁδὸς ἡ ἀπάγουσα εἰς τὴν ἀπώλειαν,
the way - leading away to - destruction,

καὶ πολλοί εἰσιν οἱ εἰσερχόμενοι δι'
and many are the [ones] going in through

αὐτῆς· **14** ὅτι στενὴ ἡ πύλη καὶ τεθλιμ-
it; because strait the gate and made

μένη ἡ ὁδὸς ἡ ἀπάγουσα εἰς τὴν ζωήν,
narrow the way - leading away to - life,

καὶ ὀλίγοι εἰσὶν οἱ εὑρίσκοντες αὐτήν.
and few are the [ones] finding it.

15 Προσέχετε ἀπὸ τῶν ψευδοπροφητῶν,
Beware from(of) - false prophets,

οἵτινες ἔρχονται πρὸς ὑμᾶς ἐν ἐνδύμασι
who come to you in clothes

προβάτων, ἔσωθεν δέ εἰσιν λύκοι ἅρπαγες.
of sheep, but within are wolves greedy.

16 ἀπὸ τῶν καρπῶν αὐτῶν ἐπιγνώσεσθε
From the fruits of them ye will know

αὐτούς. μήτι συλλέγουσιν ἀπὸ ἀκανθῶν σταφυλὰς
them. They do not gather from thorns grapes

ἢ ἀπὸ τριβόλων σῦκα; **17** οὕτως πᾶν
or from thistles figs? So ¹every

δένδρον ἀγαθὸν καρποὺς καλοὺς ποιεῖ,
²tree ²good ⁵fruits ⁴good ⁴produces,

τὸ δὲ σαπρὸν δένδρον καρποὺς πονηροὺς
but the corrupt tree fruits evil

ποιεῖ. **18** οὐ δύναται δένδρον ἀγαθὸν
produces. ²Cannot ²tree ¹a good

καρποὺς πονηροὺς ἐνεγκεῖν, οὐδὲ δένδρον
⁴fruits ⁵evil ¹to bear, nor ¹tree

σαπρὸν καρποὺς καλοὺς ἐνεγκεῖν. **19** πᾶν
¹a corrupt ⁴fruits ⁵good ²to bear. Every

δένδρον μὴ ποιοῦν καρπὸν καλὸν ἐκκόπτεται
tree not producing fruit good is cut down

καὶ εἰς πῦρ βάλλεται. **20** ἄρα γε ἀπὸ
and into fire is cast. Therefore from

τῶν καρπῶν αὐτῶν ἐπιγνώσεσθε αὐτούς.
the fruits of them ye will know them.

21 Οὐ πᾶς ὁ λέγων μοι κύριε κύριε,
Not everyone saying to me Lord[,] Lord,

εἰσελεύσεται εἰς τὴν βασιλείαν τῶν οὐρανῶν,
will enter into the kingdom of the heavens,

ἀλλ' ὁ ποιῶν τὸ θέλημα τοῦ πατρός
but the [one] doing the will of the Father

μου τοῦ ἐν τοῖς οὐρανοῖς. **22** πολλοὶ
of me - in the heavens. Many

ἐροῦσίν μοι ἐν ἐκείνῃ τῇ ἡμέρᾳ· κύριε
will say to me in that - day· Lord[,]

κύριε, οὐ τῷ σῷ ὀνόματι ἐπροφητεύσαμεν,
Lord, not - in thy name we prophesied,

καὶ τῷ σῷ ὀνόματι δαιμόνια ἐξεβάλομεν,
and - in thy name demons we expelled,

καὶ τῷ σῷ ὀνόματι δυνάμεις πολλὰς
and - in thy name mighty works many

ἐποιήσαμεν; **23** καὶ τότε ὁμολογήσω
did? and then I will declare

αὐτοῖς ὅτι οὐδέποτε ἔγνων ὑμᾶς· ἀπο-
to them[,] - Never I knew you; de-

χωρεῖτε ἀπ' ἐμοῦ οἱ ἐργαζόμενοι τὴν
part from me the [ones] working -

ἀνομίαν.
lawlessness.

24 Πᾶς οὖν ὅστις ἀκούει μου τοὺς
Everyone therefore who hears of me -

λόγους τούτους καὶ ποιεῖ αὐτούς,
words these and does them,

ὁμοιωθήσεται ἀνδρὶ φρονίμῳ, ὅστις ᾠκοδό-
shall be likened man to a prudent, who built

μησεν αὐτοῦ τὴν οἰκίαν ἐπὶ τὴν πέτραν.
of him the house on the rock.

25 καὶ κατέβη ἡ βροχὴ καὶ ἦλθον οἱ
And came down the rain and came the

ποταμοὶ καὶ ἔπνευσαν οἱ ἄνεμοι καὶ
rivers and blew the winds and

προσέπεσαν τῇ οἰκίᾳ ἐκείνῃ, καὶ οὐκ
fell against - house that, and not

ἔπεσεν· τεθεμελίωτο γὰρ ἐπὶ τὴν
it fell; for it had been founded on the

πέτραν. **26** καὶ πᾶς ὁ ἀκούων μου
rock. And everyone hearing of me

τοὺς λόγους τούτους καὶ μὴ ποιῶν
- words these and not doing

αὐτοὺς ὁμοιωθήσεται ἀνδρὶ μωρῷ, ὅστις
them shall be likened man to a foolish, who

ᾠκοδόμησεν αὐτοῦ τὴν οἰκίαν ἐπὶ τὴν
built of him the house on the

ἄμμον. **27** καὶ κατέβη ἡ βροχὴ καὶ
sand. And came down the rain and

ἦλθον οἱ ποταμοὶ καὶ ἔπνευσαν οἱ
came the rivers and blew the

ἄνεμοι καὶ προσέκοψαν τῇ οἰκίᾳ ἐκείνῃ,
winds and beat against - house that,

καὶ ἔπεσεν, καὶ ἦν ἡ πτῶσις αὐτῆς
and it fell, and was the fall of it

μεγάλη.
great.

28 Καὶ ἐγένετο ὅτε ἐτέλεσεν ὁ Ἰησοῦς
And it came to pass when finished - Jesus

τοὺς λόγους τούτους, ἐξεπλήσσοντο οἱ
- words these, were astounded the

ὄχλοι ἐπὶ τῇ διδαχῇ αὐτοῦ· **29** ἦν γὰρ
crowds at the teaching of him; for he was

διδάσκων αὐτοὺς ὡς ἐξουσίαν ἔχων, καὶ
teaching them as authority having, and

οὐχ ὡς οἱ γραμματεῖς αὐτῶν.
not as the scribes of them.

21

King James Version

8 When he was come down from the mountain, great multitudes followed him. 2And, behold, there came a leper and worshipped him, saying, Lord, if thou wilt, thou canst make me clean. 3And Jesus put forth *his* hand, and touched him, saying, I will; be thou clean. And immediately his leprosy was cleansed. 4And Jesus saith unto him, See thou tell no man; but go thy way, shew thyself to the priest, and offer the gift that Moses commanded, for a testimony unto them.

5 And when Jesus was entered into Capernaum, there came unto him a centurion, beseeching him, 6And saying, Lord, my servant lieth at home sick of the palsy, grievously tormented. 7And Jesus saith unto him, I will come and heal him. 8 The centurion answered and said, Lord, I am not worthy that thou shouldest come under my roof: but speak the word only, and my servant shall be healed. 9 For I am a man under authority, having soldiers under me: and I say to this *man*, Go, and he goeth; and to another, Come, and he cometh; and to my servant, Do this, and he doeth *it*. 10 When Jesus heard *it*, he marvelled, and said to them that followed, Verily I say unto you, I have not found so great faith, no, not in Israel. 11And I say unto you, That many shall come from the east and west, and shall sit down with Abraham, and Isaac, and Jacob, in the kingdom of heaven: 12 But the children of the kingdom shall be cast out into outer darkness: there shall be weeping and gnashing of teeth. 13And Jesus said unto the centurion, Go thy way; and as thou hast believed, *so* be it done unto thee. And his servant was healed in the selfsame hour.

14 And when Jesus was come into Peter's house, he saw his wife's mother laid, and sick of a fever. 15And he touched her hand, and the fever left her: and she arose, and ministered unto them.

16 When the even was come, they brought unto him many that were possessed with devils: and he cast out the spirits with *his* word, and healed all that were sick: 17 That it might be fulfilled which was spoken by Esaias the prophet, saying, Himself took our infirmities, and bare *our* sicknesses.

18 Now when Jesus saw great multitudes about him, he gave commandment to depart unto the other side. 19And a certain scribe came, and said unto him, Master, I will follow thee whithersoever thou goest. 20And Jesus saith unto him, The foxes have holes, and the birds of the air *have* nests; but the Son of man hath not

New International Version

The man with leprosy

8 When he came down from the mountainside, large crowds followed him. 2A man with leprosy[a] came and knelt before him and said, "Lord, if you are willing, you can make me clean."
3 Jesus reached out his hand and touched the man. "I am willing," he said. "Be clean!" Immediately he was cured[b] of his leprosy. 4 Then Jesus said to him, "See that you don't tell anyone. But go, show yourself to the priest and offer the gift Moses commanded, as a testimony to them."

The faith of the centurion

5 When Jesus had entered Capernaum, a centurion came to him, asking for help. 6 "Lord," he said, "my servant lies at home paralyzed and in terrible suffering."
7 Jesus said to him, "I will go and heal him."
8 The centurion replied, "Lord, I do not deserve to have you come under my roof. But just say the word, and my servant will be healed. 9 For I myself am a man under authority, with soldiers under me. I tell this one, 'Go,' and he goes; and that one, 'Come,' and he comes. I say to my servant, 'Do this,' and he does it."
10 When Jesus heard this, he was astonished and said to those following him, "I tell you the truth, I have not found anyone in Israel with such great faith. 11 I say to you that many will come from the east and the west, and will take their places at the feast with Abraham, Isaac and Jacob in the kingdom of heaven. 12 But the subjects of the kingdom will be thrown outside, into the darkness, where there will be weeping and grinding of teeth."
13 Then Jesus said to the centurion, "Go! It will be done just as you believed it would." And his servant was healed at that very hour.

Jesus heals many

14 When Jesus came into Peter's house, he saw Peter's mother-in-law lying in bed with a fever. 15 He touched her hand and the fever left her, and she got up and began to wait on him.
16 When evening came, many who were demon-possessed were brought to him, and he drove out the spirits with a word and healed all the sick. 17 This was to fulfill what was spoken through the prophet Isaiah:
"He took up our diseases
     and carried our illnesses." [c]

The cost of following Jesus

18 When Jesus saw the crowd around him, he gave orders to cross to the other side of the lake. 19 Then a teacher of the law came to him and said, "Teacher, I will follow you wherever you go."
20 Jesus replied, "Foxes have holes and birds of the air have nests, but the Son of Man has no place to lay his head."

[a] The Greek word probably designated other related diseases also. [b] Greek *made clean*. [c] Isaiah 53:4.

22

Greek Interlinear

Chapter 8

Καταβάντος δὲ αὐτοῦ ἀπὸ τοῦ ὄρους
And coming down him* from the mountain
= as he came down

ἠκολούθησαν αὐτῷ ὄχλοι πολλοί. 2 καὶ
followed him crowds many. And

ἰδοὺ λεπρὸς προσελθὼν προσεκύνει αὐτῷ
behold a leper approaching worshipped him

λέγων· κύριε, ἐὰν θέλῃς, δύνασαί με
saying: Lord, if thou art willing, thou art able me

καθαρίσαι. 3 καὶ ἐκτείνας τὴν χεῖρα
to cleanse. And stretching out the(his) hand

ἥψατο αὐτοῦ λέγων· θέλω, καθαρίσθητι.
he touched him saying: I am willing, be thou cleansed.

καὶ εὐθέως ἐκαθαρίσθη αὐτοῦ ἡ λέπρα.
And immediately was cleansed of him the leprosy.

4 καὶ λέγει αὐτῷ ὁ Ἰησοῦς· ὅρα μηδενὶ
And says to him - Jesus: See to no one

εἴπῃς, ἀλλὰ ὕπαγε σεαυτὸν δεῖξον τῷ
thou tellest, but go thyself show to the

ἱερεῖ καὶ προσένεγκον τὸ δῶρον ὃ
priest and offer the gift which

προσέταξεν Μωϋσῆς, εἰς μαρτύριον αὐτοῖς.
commanded Moses, for a testimony to them.

5 Εἰσελθόντος δὲ αὐτοῦ εἰς Καφαρναοὺμ
And entering him* into Capernaum,
= as he entered

προσῆλθεν αὐτῷ ἑκατόνταρχος παρακαλῶν
approached to him a centurion beseeching

αὐτὸν 6 καὶ λέγων· κύριε, ὁ παῖς μου
him and saying: Lord, the boy of me

βέβληται ἐν τῇ οἰκίᾳ παραλυτικός,
has been laid [aside] in the house a paralytic.

δεινῶς βασανιζόμενος. 7 λέγει αὐτῷ·
terribly being tortured. He says to him:

ἐγὼ ἐλθὼν θεραπεύσω αὐτόν. 8 ἀποκριθεὶς
I coming will heal him. answering

δὲ ὁ ἑκατόνταρχος ἔφη· κύριε, οὐκ εἰμὶ
But the centurion said: Lord, I am not

ἱκανὸς ἵνα μου ὑπὸ τὴν στέγην εἰσέλθῃς·
worthy that of me under the roof thou mayest enter;

ἀλλὰ μόνον εἰπὲ λόγῳ, καὶ ἰαθήσεται ὁ παῖς
but only say in a word, and will be healed the boy

μου. 9 καὶ γὰρ ἐγὼ ἄνθρωπός εἰμι
of me. *also ¹For ²I *a man *am

ὑπὸ ἐξουσίαν, ἔχων ὑπ᾽ ἐμαυτὸν στρατιώτας,
under authority, having under myself soldiers,

καὶ λέγω τούτῳ· πορεύθητι, καὶ πορεύεται,
and I say to this: Go, and he goes,

καὶ ἄλλῳ· ἔρχου, καὶ ἔρχεται, καὶ τῷ
and to another: Come, and he comes, and to the

δούλῳ μου· ποίησον τοῦτο, καὶ ποιεῖ.
slave of me: Do this, and he does [it].

10 ἀκούσας δὲ ὁ Ἰησοῦς ἐθαύμασεν
And hearing - Jesus marvelled

καὶ εἶπεν τοῖς ἀκολουθοῦσιν· ἀμὴν λέγω
and said to the [ones] following: Truly I tell

ὑμῖν, παρ᾽ οὐδενὶ τοσαύτην πίστιν ἐν τῷ
you, from no one such faith in -

Ἰσραὴλ εὗρον. 11 λέγω δὲ ὑμῖν ὅτι
Israel I found. And I tell you that

πολλοὶ ἀπὸ ἀνατολῶν καὶ δυσμῶν ἥξουσιν
many from east and west will come

καὶ ἀνακλιθήσονται μετὰ Ἀβραάμ καὶ
and will recline with Abraham and

Ἰσαὰκ καὶ Ἰακὼβ ἐν τῇ βασιλείᾳ τῶν
Isaac and Jacob in the kingdom of the

οὐρανῶν· 12 οἱ δὲ υἱοὶ τῆς βασιλείας
heavens; but the sons of the kingdom

ἐκβληθήσονται εἰς τὸ σκότος τὸ ἐξώτερον·
will be cast out into the darkness - outer:

ἐκεῖ ἔσται ὁ κλαυθμὸς καὶ ὁ βρυγμὸς
there will be the weeping and the gnashing

τῶν ὀδόντων. 13 καὶ εἶπεν ὁ Ἰησοῦς τῷ
of the teeth. And said - Jesus to the

ἑκατοντάρχῃ· ὕπαγε, ὡς ἐπίστευσας γενη-
centurion: Go, as thou believedst let it

θήτω σοι. καὶ ἰάθη ὁ παῖς ἐν τῇ
be to thee. And was healed the boy in -

ὥρᾳ ἐκείνῃ.
hour that.

14 Καὶ ἐλθὼν ὁ Ἰησοῦς εἰς τὴν οἰκίαν
And coming - Jesus into the house

Πέτρου εἶδεν τὴν πενθερὰν αὐτοῦ βεβλη-
of Peter he saw the mother-in-law of him having been

μένην καὶ πυρέσσουσαν· 15 καὶ ἥψατο
laid [aside] and fever-stricken; and he touched

τῆς χειρὸς αὐτῆς, καὶ ἀφῆκεν αὐτὴν ὁ
the hand of her, and left her the

πυρετός· καὶ ἠγέρθη, καὶ διηκόνει αὐτῷ.
fever; and she arose, and ministered to him.

16 Ὀψίας δὲ γενομένης προσήνεγκαν
And evening coming* they brought
= when evening came

αὐτῷ δαιμονιζομένους πολλούς· καὶ ἐξέβαλεν
to him being demon-possessed many; and he expelled

τὰ πνεύματα λόγῳ, καὶ πάντας τοὺς
the spirits with a word, and all the [ones]
= those

κακῶς ἔχοντας ἐθεράπευσεν· 17 ὅπως
ill having he healed; so that
who were ill

πληρωθῇ τὸ ῥηθὲν διὰ Ἡσαΐου τοῦ
was fulfilled the [thing] spoken through Isaiah the

προφήτου λέγοντος· αὐτὸς τὰς ἀσθενείας
prophet saying: He the weaknesses

ἡμῶν ἔλαβεν καὶ τὰς νόσους ἐβάστασεν.
of us took and the diseases he bore.

18 Ἰδὼν δὲ ὁ Ἰησοῦς ὄχλον περὶ
But ²seeing ¹Jesus a crowd around

αὐτὸν ἐκέλευσεν ἀπελθεῖν εἰς τὸ πέραν.
him commanded to go away to the other side.

19 Καὶ προσελθὼν εἷς γραμματεὺς εἶπεν
And approaching one scribe said

αὐτῷ· διδάσκαλε, ἀκολουθήσω σοι
to him: Teacher, I will follow thee

ὅπου ἐὰν ἀπέρχῃ. 20 καὶ λέγει αὐτῷ
wherever thou mayest go. And says to him

ὁ Ἰησοῦς· αἱ ἀλώπεκες φωλεοὺς ἔχουσιν
- Jesus: The foxes holes have

καὶ τὰ πετεινὰ τοῦ οὐρανοῦ κατα-
and the birds of the heaven nests,

σκηνώσεις, ὁ δὲ υἱὸς τοῦ ἀνθρώπου
but the Son of man

οὐκ ἔχει ποῦ τὴν κεφαλὴν κλίνῃ.
has not where the(his) head he may lay.

King James Version

where to lay *his* head. 21And another of his disciples said unto him, Lord, suffer me first to go and bury my father. 22 But Jesus said unto him, Follow me; and let the dead bury their dead.

23 And when he was entered into a ship, his disciples followed him. 24And, behold, there arose a great tempest in the sea, insomuch that the ship was covered with the waves: but he was asleep. 25And his disciples came to *him*, and awoke him, saying, Lord, save us: we perish. 26And he saith unto them, Why are ye fearful, O ye of little faith? Then he arose, and rebuked the winds and the sea; and there was a great calm. 27 But the men marvelled, saying, What manner of man is this, that even the winds and the sea obey him!

28 And when he was come to the other side into the country of the Gergesenes, there met him two possessed with devils, coming out of the tombs, exceeding fierce, so that no man might pass by that way. 29And behold, they cried out, saying, What have we to do with thee, Jesus, thou Son of God? art thou come hither to torment us before the time? 30And there was a good way off from them a herd of many swine feeding. 31 So the devils besought him, saying, If thou cast us out, suffer us to go away into the herd of swine. 32And he said unto them, Go. And when they were come out, they went into the herd of swine: and, behold, the whole herd of swine ran violently down a steep place into the sea, and perished in the waters. 33And they that kept them fled, and went their ways into the city, and told every thing, and what was befallen to the possessed of the devils. 34And, behold, the whole city came out to meet Jesus: and when they saw him, they besought *him* that he would depart out of their coasts.

9 And he entered into a ship, and passed over, and came into his own city. 2And, behold, they brought to him a man sick of the palsy, lying on a bed: and Jesus seeing their faith said unto the sick of the palsy; Son, be of good cheer; thy sins be forgiven thee. 3And, behold, certain of the scribes said within themselves, This *man* blasphemeth. 4And Jesus knowing their thoughts said, Wherefore think ye evil in your hearts? 5 For whether is easier, to say, *Thy* sins be forgiven thee; or to say, Arise, and walk? 6 But that ye may know that the Son of man hath power on earth to forgive sins, (then saith he to the sick of the palsy,) Arise, take up thy bed, and go unto thine house. 7And he arose, and departed to his house. 8 But when the multi-

New International Version

21 Another man, one of his disciples, said to him, "Lord, first let me go and bury my father." 22 But Jesus told him, "Follow me, and let the dead bury their own dead."

Jesus calms the storm

23 Then he got into the boat and his disciples followed him. 24 Without warning, a furious storm came up on the lake, so that the waves swept over the boat. But Jesus was sleeping. 25 The disciples went and woke him, saying, "Lord, save us! We're going to drown!"
26 He replied, "You of little faith, why are you so afraid?" Then he got up and rebuked the winds and the waves, and it was completely calm.
27 The men were amazed and asked, "What kind of man is this? Even the winds and the waves obey him!"

The healing of two demon-possessed men

28 When he arrived at the other side in the region of the Gadarenes,[d] two demon-possessed men coming from the tombs met him. They were so violent that no one could pass that way. 29 "What do you want with us, Son of God?" they shouted. "Have you come here to torture us before the appointed time?"
30 Some distance from them a large herd of pigs was feeding. 31 The demons begged Jesus, "If you drive us out, send us into the herd of pigs."
32 He said to them, "Go!" So they came out and went into the pigs, and the whole herd rushed down the steep bank into the lake and died in the water. 33 Those tending the pigs ran off, went into the town, and reported all this, including what had happened to the demon-possessed men. 34 Then the whole town went out to meet Jesus. And when they saw him, they pleaded with him to leave their region.

Jesus heals a paralytic

9 Jesus stepped into a boat, crossed over and came to his own town. 2 Some men brought to him a paralytic, lying on a mat. When Jesus saw their faith, he said to the paralytic, "Take heart, son; your sins are forgiven."
3 At this, some of the teachers of the law said to themselves, "This fellow is blaspheming!"
4 Knowing their thoughts, Jesus said, "Why do you entertain evil thoughts in your hearts? 5 Which is easier: to say, 'Your sins are forgiven,' or to say, 'Get up and walk'? 6 But so that you may know that the Son of Man has authority on earth to forgive sins. . . ." Then he said to the paralytic, "Get up, take your mat and go home." 7And the man got up and went home. 8 When the crowd saw this, they were

[d] Some MSS read *Gergesenes*; others read *Gerasenes*.

Greek Interlinear

21 ἕτερος   δὲ   τῶν   μαθητῶν   εἶπεν
And another   of the   disciples   said

αὐτῷ·   κύριε,   ἐπίτρεψόν   μοι   πρῶτον
to him: Lord,   allow   me   first

ἀπελθεῖν   καὶ   θάψαι   τὸν   πατέρα   μου.
to go away   and   bury   the   father   of me.

22 ὁ   δὲ   Ἰησοῦς   λέγει   αὐτῷ·   ἀκολούθει
– But   Jesus   says   to him: Follow thou

μοι,   καὶ   ἄφες   τοὺς   νεκροὺς   θάψαι   τοὺς
me,   and   leave   the   dead   to bury   the

ἑαυτῶν   νεκρούς.
of themselves   dead.

23 Καὶ   ἐμβάντι   αὐτῷ   εἰς   τὸ   πλοῖον,
And   embarking   him*   in   the   ship,
                *= as he embarked

ἠκολούθησαν   αὐτῷ   οἱ   μαθηταὶ   αὐτοῦ.
followed   him   the   disciples   of him.

24 καὶ   ἰδοὺ   σεισμὸς   μέγας   ἐγένετο   ἐν
And   behold   storm   a great   there was   in

τῇ   θαλάσσῃ,   ὥστε   τὸ   πλοῖον   καλύπτ-
the   sea,   so as   the   ship   to be en-

εσθαι   ὑπὸ   τῶν   κυμάτων·   αὐτὸς   δὲ   ἐκάθευδεν.
veloped   by   the   waves;   but he   was sleeping.

25 καὶ   προσελθόντες   ἤγειραν   αὐτὸν   λέγοντες·
And   approaching   they roused   him   saying:

κύριε,   σῶσον,   ἀπολλύμεθα.   26 καὶ   λέγει
Lord,   save,   we are perishing.   And   he says

αὐτοῖς·   τί   δειλοί   ἐστε,   ὀλιγόπιστοι;
to them: Why   fearful   are ye,   little-faiths?

τότε   ἐγερθεὶς   ἐπετίμησεν   τοῖς   ἀνέμοις   καὶ
Then   rising   he rebuked   the   winds   and

τῇ   θαλάσσῃ,   καὶ   ἐγένετο   γαλήνη   μεγάλη.
the   sea,   and   there was   calm   a great.

27 οἱ   δὲ   ἄνθρωποι   ἐθαύμασαν   λέγοντες·
And the   men   marvelled   saying:

ποταπός   ἐστιν   οὗτος,   ὅτι   καὶ   οἱ   ἄνεμοι
Of what sort   is   this [man],   that   even   the   winds

καὶ   ἡ   θάλασσα   αὐτῷ   ὑπακούουσιν;
and   the   sea   him   obey?

28 Καὶ   ἐλθόντος   αὐτοῦ   εἰς   τὸ   πέραν   εἰς
And   coming   him*   to   the other side   into
         = when he came

τὴν   χώραν   τῶν   Γαδαρηνῶν   ὑπήντησαν
the   country   of the   Gadarenes   met

αὐτῷ   δύο   δαιμονιζόμενοι   ἐκ   τῶν   μνημείων
him   two   demon-possessed   out of the   tombs

ἐξερχόμενοι,   χαλεποὶ   λίαν,   ὥστε   μὴ
coming out,   dangerous   exceedingly,   so as   not

ἰσχύειν   τινὰ   παρελθεῖν   διὰ   τῆς   ὁδοῦ
to be able   anyone*   to pass   through   –   way

ἐκείνης.   29 καὶ   ἰδοὺ   ἔκραξαν   λέγοντες·
that.   And   behold   they cried out   saying:

τί   ἡμῖν   καὶ   σοί,   υἱὲ   τοῦ   θεοῦ;   ἦλθες
What to us   and   to thee,   Son   –   of God?   camest thou

ὧδε   πρὸ   καιροῦ   βασανίσαι   ἡμᾶς;   30 ἦν
here before [the]   time   to torture   us?   there was

δὲ   μακρὰν   ἀπ᾽   αὐτῶν   ἀγέλη   χοίρων
Now   far off   from   them   a herd   pigs

πολλῶν   βοσκομένη.   31 οἱ   δὲ   δαίμονες
of many   feeding.   And the   demons

παρεκάλουν   αὐτὸν   λέγοντες·   εἰ   ἐκβάλλεις
besought   him   saying: If   thou expellest

ἡμᾶς,   ἀπόστειλον   ἡμᾶς   εἰς   τὴν   ἀγέλην
us,   send   us   into   the   herd

τῶν   χοίρων.   32 καὶ   εἶπεν   αὐτοῖς·
of the   pigs.   And   he said   to them:

ὑπάγετε.   οἱ   δὲ   ἐξελθόντες   ἀπῆλθον   εἰς
Go ye.   So the   coming out [ones]   went away   into

τοὺς   χοίρους·   καὶ   ἰδοὺ   ὥρμησεν   πᾶσα   ἡ
the   pigs;   and   behold   rushed   all   the

ἀγέλη   κατὰ   τοῦ   κρημνοῦ   εἰς   τὴν   θάλασσαν,
herd   down   the   precipice   into   the   sea,

καὶ   ἀπέθανον   ἐν   τοῖς   ὕδασιν.   33 οἱ
and   died   in   the   waters.   the

δὲ   βόσκοντες   ἔφυγον,   καὶ   ἀπελθόντες
But   feeding [ones]   fled,   and   going away

εἰς   τὴν   πόλιν   ἀπήγγειλαν   πάντα   καὶ
into   the   city   reported   all things   and

τὰ   τῶν   δαιμονιζομένων.   34 καὶ   ἰδοὺ
the [things]   of the   demon-possessed [ones].   And   behold

πᾶσα   ἡ   πόλις   ἐξῆλθεν   εἰς   ὑπάντησιν
all   the   city   came out   with a view to   a meeting [with]

τῷ   Ἰησοῦ,   καὶ   ἰδόντες   αὐτὸν   παρεκάλεσαν
–   Jesus,   and   seeing   ¹him   ¹besought

ὅπως   μεταβῇ   ἀπὸ   τῶν   ὁρίων   αὐτῶν.
so that   he might remove   from   the   borders   of them.

Chapter 9

Καὶ   ἐμβὰς   εἰς   πλοῖον   διεπέρασεν,
And   embarking   in   a ship   he crossed over,

καὶ   ἦλθεν   εἰς   τὴν   ἰδίαν   πόλιν.   2 Καὶ
and   came   into   the(his)   own   city.   And

ἰδοὺ   προσέφερον   αὐτῷ   παραλυτικὸν   ἐπὶ
behold   they brought   to him   a paralytic   on

κλίνης   βεβλημένον.   καὶ   ἰδὼν   ὁ   Ἰησοῦς
a mattress   having been laid.   And   ¹seeing   –   ¹Jesus

τὴν   πίστιν   αὐτῶν   εἶπεν   τῷ   παραλυτικῷ·
the   faith   of them   said   to the   paralytic:

θάρσει,   τέκνον,   ἀφίενταί   σου   αἱ   ἁμαρτίαι.
Be of good cheer,   child,   are forgiven of thee the   sins.

3 καὶ   ἰδού   τινες   τῶν   γραμματέων   εἶπαν
And   behold   some   of the   scribes   said

ἐν   ἑαυτοῖς·   οὗτος   βλασφημεῖ.   4 καὶ
among themselves: This [man]   blasphemes.   And

εἰδὼς   ὁ   Ἰησοῦς   τὰς   ἐνθυμήσεις   αὐτῶν
¹knowing   –   ¹Jesus   the   thoughts   of them

εἶπεν·   ἱνατί   ἐνθυμεῖσθε   πονηρὰ   ἐν   ταῖς
said: Why   think ye   evil things   in   the

καρδίαις   ὑμῶν;   5 τί   γάρ   ἐστιν   εὐκοπώ-
hearts   of you?   for which   is   easier,

τερον,   εἰπεῖν·   ἀφίενταί   σου   αἱ   ἁμαρτίαι,   ἢ
to say: ¹are forgiven ²of thee ¹The   ³sins,   or

εἰπεῖν·   ἔγειρε   καὶ   περιπάτει;   6 ἵνα   δὲ
to say: Rise   and   walk?   But in order that

εἰδῆτε   ὅτι   ἐξουσίαν   ἔχει   ὁ   υἱὸς   τοῦ
ye may know that   authority   has   the   Son   –

ἀνθρώπου   ἐπὶ   τῆς   γῆς   ἀφιέναι   ἁμαρτίας
of man   on   the   earth   to forgive   sins—

τότε   λέγει   τῷ   παραλυτικῷ·   ἔγειρε   ἆρόν
then   he says to the   paralytic: Rise[,]   take

σου   τὴν   κλίνην   καὶ   ὕπαγε   εἰς   τὸν   οἶκόν
of thee the   mattress   and   go   to   the   house

σου.   7 καὶ   ἐγερθεὶς   ἀπῆλθεν   εἰς   τὸν
of thee.   And   rising   he went away   to   the

οἶκον   αὐτοῦ.   8 ἰδόντες   δὲ   οἱ   ὄχλοι
house   of him.   But seeing   the   crowds

25

King James Version

tudes saw *it*, they marvelled, and glorified God, which had given such power unto men.

9 And as Jesus passed forth from thence, he saw a man, named Matthew, sitting at the receipt of custom: and he saith unto him, Follow me. And he arose, and followed him.

10 And it came to pass, as Jesus sat at meat in the house, behold, many publicans and sinners came and sat down with him and his disciples. 11And when the Pharisees saw *it*, they said unto his disciples, Why eateth your master with publicans and sinners? 12 But when Jesus heard *that*, he said unto them, They that be whole need not a physician, but they that are sick. 13 But go ye and learn what *that* meaneth, I will have mercy, and not sacrifice: for I am not come to call the righteous, but sinners to repentance.

14 Then came to him the disciples of John, saying, Why do we and the Pharisees fast oft, but thy disciples fast not? 15And Jesus said unto them, Can the children of the bridechamber mourn, as long as the bridegroom is with them? but the days will come, when the bridegroom shall be taken from them, and then shall they fast. 16 No man putteth a piece of new cloth unto an old garment; for that which is put in to fill it up taketh from the garment, and the rent is made worse. 17 Neither do men put new wine into old bottles: else the bottles break, and the wine runneth out, and the bottles perish: but they put new wine into new bottles, and both are preserved.

18 While he spake these things unto them, behold, there came a certain ruler, and worshipped him, saying, My daughter is even now dead: but come and lay thy hand upon her, and she shall live. 19And Jesus arose, and followed him, and *so did* his disciples.

20 And, behold, a woman, which was diseased with an issue of blood twelve years, came behind *him*, and touched the hem of his garment: 21 For she said within herself, If I may but touch his garment, I shall be whole. 22 But Jesus turned him about, and when he saw her, he said, Daughter, be of good comfort; thy faith hath made thee whole. And the woman was made whole from that hour. 23And when Jesus came into the ruler's house, and saw the minstrels and the people making a noise, 24 He said unto them, Give place: for the maid is not dead, but sleepeth. And they laughed him to scorn. 25 But when the people were put forth, he went in, and took her by the hand, and the maid arose. 26And the fame hereof went abroad into all that land.

27 And when Jesus departed thence, two blind men followed him, crying, and saying, *Thou*

New International Version

filled with awe; and they praised God, who had given such authority to men.

The calling of Matthew

9 As Jesus went on from there, he saw a man named Matthew sitting at the tax collector's booth. "Follow me," he told him, and Matthew got up and followed him.

10 While Jesus was having dinner at Matthew's house, many tax collectors and "sinners" came and ate with him and his disciples. 11 When the Pharisees saw this, they asked his disciples, "Why does your teacher eat with tax collectors and 'sinners'?"

12 On hearing this, Jesus said, "It is not the healthy who need a doctor, but the sick. 13 But go and learn what this means: 'I desire mercy, not sacrifice.' * For I have not come to call the righteous, but sinners."

Jesus questioned about fasting

14 Then John's disciples came and asked him, "How is it that we and the Pharisees fast, but your disciples do not fast?"

15 Jesus answered, "How can the guests of the bridegroom mourn while he is with them? The time will come when the bridegroom will be taken from them; then they will fast.

16 "No one sews a patch of unshrunk cloth on an old garment, for the patch will pull away from the garment, making the tear worse. 17 Neither do men pour new wine into old wineskins. If they do, the skins will burst, the wine will run out and the wineskins will be ruined. No, they pour new wine into new wineskins, and both are preserved."

A dead girl and a sick woman

18 While he was saying this, a ruler of the synagogue came and knelt before him and said, "My daughter is at the point of death. But come and put your hand on her, and she will live." 19 Jesus got up and went with him, and so did his disciples.

20 Just then a woman who had been subject to bleeding for twelve years came up behind him and touched the edge of his cloak. 21 She said to herself, "If I only touch his cloak, I will be healed."

22 Jesus turned and saw her. "Take heart, daughter," he said, "your faith has healed you." And the woman was healed from that moment.

23 When Jesus entered the ruler's house and saw the flute-players and the noisy crowd, 24 he said, "Go away. The girl is not dead but asleep." But they laughed at him. 25After the crowd had been put outside, he went in and took the girl by the hand, and she got up. 26 News of this spread through all that region.

Jesus heals the blind and dumb

27 As Jesus went on from there, two blind men followed him, calling out, "Have mercy on us, Son of David!"

[e] Hosea 6:6.

Greek Interlinear

ἐφοβήθησαν   καὶ   ἐδόξασαν   τὸν   θεὸν   τὸν
feared   and   glorified   -   God   the [one]

δόντα   ἐξουσίαν   τοιαύτην   τοῖς   ἀνθρώποις.
giving ¹authority ¹such   -   to men.

9 Καὶ   παράγων   ὁ   Ἰησοῦς   ἐκεῖθεν   εἶδεν
And ²passing by -   ¹Jesus   thence   saw

ἄνθρωπον   καθήμενον   ἐπὶ   τὸ   τελώνιον,
a man   sitting   at   the custom house.

Ματθαῖον   λεγόμενον,   καὶ   λέγει   αὐτῷ·
Matthew   named,   and   says   to him:

ἀκολούθει   μοι.   καὶ   ἀναστὰς   ἠκολούθησεν
Follow   me.   And   rising up   he followed

αὐτῷ.   **10** Καὶ   ἐγένετο   αὐτοῦ   ἀνακει-
him.   And   it came to pass him   reclin-
= as he was reclining

μένου   ἐν   τῇ   οἰκίᾳ,   καὶ   ἰδοὺ   πολλοὶ
ing²   in   the house,   and   behold   many

τελῶναι   καὶ ἁμαρτωλοὶ ἐλθόντες   συνανέκειντο
tax-collectors and sinners   coming reclined at table with

τῷ   Ἰησοῦ   καὶ   τοῖς   μαθηταῖς   αὐτοῦ.
-   Jesus   and   the   disciples   of him.

11 καὶ   ἰδόντες   οἱ   Φαρισαῖοι   ἔλεγον   τοῖς
And ²seeing ¹the ²Pharisees   said   to the

μαθηταῖς   αὐτοῦ·   διὰ   τί   μετὰ   τῶν   τελωλῶν
disciples of him: Why   with - tax-collectors

καὶ   ἁμαρτωλῶν   ἐσθίει   ὁ   διδάσκαλος   ὑμῶν;
and   sinners   eats   the teacher   of you?

12 ὁ   δὲ   ἀκούσας   εἶπεν·   οὐ   χρείαν
But he hearing   said: Not   need

ἔχουσιν   οἱ   ἰσχύοντες   ἰατροῦ   ἀλλ'   οἱ
have   the [ones] being strong of a physician but the [ones]
= those

κακῶς   ἔχοντες.   **13** πορευθέντες   δὲ   μάθετε
ill   having.   But going   learn ye
who are ill.

τί   ἐστιν·   ἔλεος   θέλω   καὶ   οὐ   θυσίαν·   οὐ
what it is: Mercy I desire and not sacrifice; not

γὰρ   ἦλθον   καλέσαι   δικαίους   ἀλλὰ
for   I came   to call   righteous [people]   but

ἁμαρτωλούς.
sinners.

14 Τότε   προσέρχονται   αὐτῷ   οἱ   μαθηταὶ
Then   approach   to him   the   disciples

Ἰωάννου   λέγοντες·   διὰ   τί   ἡμεῖς   καὶ   οἱ
of John   saying: Why   we   and   the

Φαρισαῖοι   νηστεύομεν,   οἱ   δὲ   μαθηταὶ
Pharisees   fast,   but the   disciples

σου   οὐ   νηστεύουσιν;   **15** καὶ   εἶπεν
of thee   fast not?   And   said

αὐτοῖς   ὁ   Ἰησοῦς·   μὴ   δύνανται   οἱ
to them   -   Jesus: not   Can   the

υἱοὶ   τοῦ   νυμφῶνος   πενθεῖν,   ἐφ'   ὅσον
sons of the bridechamber to mourn, so long as

μετ'   αὐτῶν   ἐστιν   ὁ   νυμφίος;   ἐλεύσονται
with   them   is   the   bridegroom? ²will come

δὲ   ἡμέραι   ὅταν   ἀπαρθῇ   ἀπ'   αὐτῶν   ὁ
¹but ²days when is taken away from them the

νυμφίος,   καὶ   τότε   νηστεύσουσιν.   **16** οὐδεὶς
bridegroom, and   then   they will fast.   no one

δὲ   ἐπιβάλλει   ἐπίβλημα   ῥάκους   ἀγνάφου
Now   puts on   a patch   cloth   of unfulled

ἐπὶ   ἱματίῳ   παλαιῷ·   αἴρει   γὰρ   τὸ
on   garment   an old;   for takes away   the

πλήρωμα   αὐτοῦ   ἀπὸ   τοῦ   ἱματίου,   καὶ
fullness   of it   from   the   garment,   and

χεῖρον   σχίσμα   γίνεται.   **17** οὐδὲ
a worse   rent   becomes.   Neither

βάλλουσιν   οἶνον   νέον   εἰς   ἀσκοὺς
do they put   wine   new   into   wineskins

παλαιούς·   εἰ   δὲ   μή   γε,   ῥήγνυνται
old;   otherwise,   are burst

οἱ   ἀσκοί,   καὶ   ὁ   οἶνος   ἐκχεῖται   καὶ
the   wineskins, and the   wine   is poured out   and

οἱ   ἀσκοὶ   ἀπόλλυνται.   ἀλλὰ   βάλλουσιν
the   wineskins   are destroyed.   But   they put

οἶνον   νέον   εἰς   ἀσκοὺς   καινούς,   καὶ
wine   new   into   wineskins   fresh,   and

ἀμφότεροι   συντηροῦνται.
both   are preserved.

18 Ταῦτα   αὐτοῦ   λαλοῦντος   αὐτοῖς,
These things   him   speaking³   to them,
= As he was speaking these things

ἰδοὺ   ἄρχων   [εἷς]   προσελθὼν   προσ-
behold   ruler   one   approaching   wor-

εκύνει   αὐτῷ   λέγων   ὅτι   ἡ   θυγάτηρ
shipped   him   saying[,]   -   The   daughter

μου   ἄρτι   ἐτελεύτησεν·   ἀλλὰ   ἐλθὼν
of me   just now   died;   but   coming

ἐπίθες   τὴν   χεῖρά   σου   ἐπ'   αὐτήν,
lay on   the   hand   of thee   on   her,

καὶ   ζήσεται.   **19** καὶ   ἐγερθεὶς   ὁ   Ἰησοῦς
and   she will live.   And   rising   -   Jesus

ἠκολούθει   αὐτῷ   καὶ   οἱ   μαθηταὶ   αὐτοῦ.
followed   him[,]   also   the   disciples   of him.

20 Καὶ   ἰδοὺ   γυνὴ   αἱμορροοῦσα
And   behold   a woman   suffering from a flow of blood

δώδεκα   ἔτη   προσελθοῦσα   ὄπισθεν   ἥψατο
twelve   years   approaching   behind   touched

τοῦ   κρασπέδου   τοῦ   ἱματίου   αὐτοῦ·
the   fringe   of the   garment   of him;

21 ἔλεγεν   γὰρ   ἐν   ἑαυτῇ·   ἐὰν   μόνον
for she was saying   in   herself: If   only

ἅψωμαι   τοῦ   ἱματίου   αὐτοῦ,   σωθήσομαι.
I may touch   the   garment   of him,   I shall be healed.

22 ὁ   δὲ   Ἰησοῦς   στραφεὶς   καὶ   ἰδὼν
-   And   Jesus   turning   and   seeing

αὐτὴν   εἶπεν·   θάρσει,   θύγατερ·   ἡ
her   said: Be of good cheer,   daughter;   the

πίστις   σου   σέσωκέν   σε.   καὶ   ἐσώθη
faith   of thee   has healed   thee.   And   was healed

ἡ   γυνὴ   ἀπὸ   τῆς   ὥρας   ἐκείνης.   **23** Καὶ
the woman   from   -   hour   that.   And

ἐλθὼν   ὁ   Ἰησοῦς   εἰς   τὴν   οἰκίαν   τοῦ   ἄρχοντος
coming   -   Jesus   into   the   house of the   ruler

καὶ   ἰδὼν   τοὺς   αὐλητὰς   καὶ   τὸν   ὄχλον
and   seeing   the   flute-players   and   the   crowd

θορυβούμενον   **24** ἔλεγεν·   ἀναχωρεῖτε·   οὐ
terrified   he said: Depart ye;   not

γὰρ   ἀπέθανεν   τὸ   κοράσιον   ἀλλὰ   καθεύδει.
for   died   the   girl   but   sleeps.

καὶ   κατεγέλων   αὐτοῦ.   **25** ὅτε   δὲ
And   they ridiculed   him.   But when

ἐξεβλήθη   ὁ   ὄχλος,   εἰσελθὼν   ἐκράτησεν
was put out   the   crowd,   entering   he took hold of

τῆς   χειρὸς   αὐτῆς,   καὶ   ἠγέρθη   τὸ   κορά-
the   hand   of her,   and   was raised   the   girl.

σιον.   **26** καὶ   ἐξῆλθεν   ἡ   φήμη   αὕτη
And   went out   -   report   this

εἰς   ὅλην   τὴν   γῆν   ἐκείνην.   **27** Καὶ
into   all   -   land   that.   And

παράγοντι   ἐκεῖθεν   τῷ   Ἰησοῦ   ἠκολούθησαν
passing by   thence   -   Jesus³   followed
= as Jesus passed by thence

δύο   τυφλοὶ   κράζοντες   καὶ   λέγοντες·   ἐλέησον
two blind men   crying out   and   saying: Pity

King James Version

Son of David, have mercy on us. 28And when he was come into the house, the blind men came to him: and Jesus saith unto them, Believe ye that I am able to do this? They said unto him, Yea, Lord. 29 Then touched he their eyes, saying, According to your faith be it unto you. 30And their eyes were opened; and Jesus straitly charged them, saying, See *that* no man know *it*. 31 But they, when they were departed, spread abroad his fame in all that country.

32 As they went out, behold, they brought to him a dumb man possessed with a devil. 33And when the devil was cast out, the dumb spake: and the multitudes marvelled, saying, It was never so seen in Israel. 34 But the Pharisees said, He casteth out devils through the prince of the devils. 35And Jesus went about all the cities and villages, teaching in their synagogues, and preaching the gospel of the kingdom, and healing every sickness and every disease among the people.

36 But when he saw the multitudes, he was moved with compassion on them, because they fainted, and were scattered abroad, as sheep having no shepherd. 37 Then saith he unto his disciples, The harvest truly *is* plenteous, but the labourers *are* few; 38 Pray ye therefore the Lord of the harvest, that he will send forth labourers into his harvest.

10 And when he had called unto *him* his twelve disciples, he gave them power *against* unclean spirits, to cast them out, and to heal all manner of sickness and all manner of disease. 2 Now the names of the twelve apostles are these; The first, Simon, who is called Peter, and Andrew his brother; James *the son* of Zebedee, and John his brother; 3 Philip, and Bartholomew; Thomas, and Matthew the publican; James *the son* of Alpheus, and Lebbeus, whose surname was Thaddeus; 4 Simon the Canaanite, and Judas Iscariot, who also betrayed him. 5 These twelve Jesus sent forth, and commanded them, saying, Go not into the way of the Gentiles, and into *any* city of the Samaritans enter ye not: 6 But go rather to the lost sheep of the house of Israel. 7And as ye go, preach, saying, The kingdom of heaven is at hand. 8 Heal the sick, cleanse the lepers, raise the dead, cast out devils: freely ye have received, freely give. 9 Provide neither gold, nor silver, nor brass in your purses; 10 Nor scrip for *your* journey, neither two coats, neither shoes, nor yet staves:

New International Version

28 When he had gone indoors, the blind men came to him, and he asked them, "Do you believe that I am able to do this?"

"Yes, Lord," they replied.

29 Then he touched their eyes and said, "According to your faith will it be done to you"; 30 and their sight was restored. Jesus warned them sternly, "See that no one knows about this." 31 But they went out and spread the news about him all over that region.

32 While they were going out, a man who was demon-possessed and could not talk was brought to Jesus. 33And when the demon was driven out, the man who had been dumb spoke. The crowd was amazed and said, "Nothing like this has ever been seen in Israel."

34 But the Pharisees said, "It is by the prince of demons that he drives out demons."

The workers are few

35 Jesus went through all the towns and villages, teaching in their synagogues, preaching the good news of the kingdom and healing every kind of disease and sickness. 36 When he saw the crowds, he had compassion on them, because they were harassed and helpless, like sheep without a shepherd. 37 Then he said to his disciples, "The harvest is plentiful but the workers are few. 38Ask the Lord of the harvest, therefore, to send out workers into his harvest field."

Jesus sends out the twelve

10 He called his twelve disciples to him and gave them authority to drive out evil *f* spirits and to cure every kind of disease and sickness.

2 These are the names of the twelve apostles: first, Simon (who is called Peter) and his brother Andrew; James son of Zebedee, and his brother John; 3 Philip and Bartholomew; Thomas and Matthew the tax collector; James son of Alphaeus, and Thaddaeus; 4 Simon the Zealot and Judas Iscariot, who betrayed him.

5 These twelve Jesus sent out with the following instructions: "Do not go among the Gentiles or enter any town of the Samaritans. 6 Go rather to the lost sheep of Israel. 7As you go, preach this message: 'The kingdom of heaven is near.' 8 Heal the sick, raise the dead, cleanse those who have leprosy,*g* drive out demons. Freely you have received, freely give. 9 Do not take along any gold or silver or copper in your belts; 10 take no bag for the journey, or extra tunic, or sandals or a staff; for the worker is worth his keep.

[f] Greek *unclean*. [g] The Greek word probably designated other related diseases also.

Greek Interlinear

ἡμᾶς, υἱός Δαυίδ.   28 ἐλθόντι δὲ εἰς
us, son of David.   And coming* into
= when he came

τὴν οἰκίαν προσῆλθον αὐτῷ οἱ τυφλοί,
the house approached to him the blind men,

καὶ λέγει αὐτοῖς ὁ Ἰησοῦς· πιστεύετε
and says to them - Jesus: Believe ye

ὅτι δύναμαι τοῦτο ποιῆσαι; λέγουσιν
that I can this to do? They say

αὐτῷ· ναί, κύριε.   29 τότε ἥψατο τῶν
to him: Yes, Lord.   Then he touched the

ὀφθαλμῶν αὐτῶν λέγων· κατὰ τὴν
eyes of them saying: According to the

πίστιν ὑμῶν γενηθήτω ὑμῖν.   30 καὶ
faith of you let it be to you.   And

ἠνεῴχθησαν αὐτῶν οἱ ὀφθαλμοί. καὶ
were opened of them the eyes. And

ἐνεβριμήθη αὐτοῖς ὁ Ἰησοῦς λέγων·
sternly admonished them - Jesus saying:

ὁρᾶτε μηδεὶς γινωσκέτω.   31 οἱ δὲ
See ²no one ¹let ³know.   But they

ἐξελθόντες διεφήμισαν αὐτὸν ἐν ὅλῃ
going out spread about him in all

τῇ γῇ ἐκείνῃ.   32 Αὐτῶν δὲ ἐξερχομένων,
- land that.   And them going out,*
= as they were going out,

ἰδοὺ προσήνεγκαν αὐτῷ κωφὸν δαι-
behold they brought to him a dumb man being

μονιζόμενον.   33 καὶ ἐκβληθέντος τοῦ
demon-possessed.   And being expelled the
= when the demon was expelled

δαιμονίου ἐλάλησεν ὁ κωφός. καὶ ἐθαύμασαν
demon* spoke the dumb man. And marvelled

οἱ ὄχλοι λέγοντες· οὐδέποτε ἐφάνη οὕτως
the crowds saying: Never it appeared thus

ἐν τῷ Ἰσραήλ.   34 οἱ δὲ Φαρισαῖοι
in - Israel.   But the Pharisees

ἔλεγον· ἐν τῷ ἄρχοντι τῶν δαιμονίων
said: By the ruler of the demons

ἐκβάλλει τὰ δαιμόνια.
he expels the demons.

35 Καὶ περιῆγεν ὁ Ἰησοῦς τὰς
And went about - Jesus the

πόλεις πάσας καὶ τὰς κώμας, διδάσκων
cities all and the villages, teaching

ἐν ταῖς συναγωγαῖς αὐτῶν καὶ κηρύσσων
in the synagogues of them and proclaiming

τὸ εὐαγγέλιον τῆς βασιλείας καὶ θεραπεύων
the gospel of the kingdom and healing

πᾶσαν νόσον καὶ πᾶσαν μαλακίαν.
- every disease and every illness.

36 Ἰδὼν δὲ τοὺς ὄχλους ἐσπλαγχνίσθη
And seeing the crowds he was filled with tenderness

περὶ αὐτῶν, ὅτι ἦσαν ἐσκυλμένοι καὶ
concerning them, because they were distressed and

ἐρριμμένοι ὡσεὶ πρόβατα μὴ ἔχοντα
prostrate as sheep not having

ποιμένα.   37 τότε λέγει τοῖς μαθηταῖς
a shepherd.   Then he says to the disciples

αὐτοῦ· ὁ μὲν θερισμὸς πολύς, οἱ δὲ
of him: Indeed the harvest [is] much, but the

ἐργάται ὀλίγοι·   38 δεήθητε οὖν τοῦ κυρίου
workmen few; pray ye therefore the Lord

τοῦ θερισμοῦ ὅπως ἐκβάλῃ
of the harvest so that he may thrust forth

ἐργάτας εἰς τὸν θερισμὸν αὐτοῦ.   10 Καὶ
workmen into the harvest of him.   And

Chapter 10

προσκαλεσάμενος τοὺς δώδεκα μαθητὰς
calling forward the twelve disciples

αὐτοῦ ἔδωκεν αὐτοῖς ἐξουσίαν πνευμάτων
of him he gave to them authority of(over) spirits

ἀκαθάρτων ὥστε ἐκβάλλειν αὐτά, καὶ
unclean so as to expel them, and

θεραπεύειν πᾶσαν νόσον καὶ πᾶσαν μαλα-
to heal every disease and every ill-

κίαν.   2 Τῶν δὲ δώδεκα ἀποστόλων
ness.   Now of the twelve apostles

τὰ ὀνόματά ἐστιν ταῦτα· πρῶτος Σίμων
the names is(are) these: first Simon

ὁ λεγόμενος Πέτρος καὶ Ἀνδρέας ὁ
the [one] named Peter and Andrew the

ἀδελφὸς αὐτοῦ, καὶ Ἰάκωβος ὁ τοῦ
brother of him, and James the [son] -

Ζεβεδαίου καὶ Ἰωάννης ὁ ἀδελφὸς αὐτοῦ,
of Zebedee and John the brother of him,

3 Φίλιππος καὶ Βαρθολομαῖος, Θωμᾶς
Philip and Bartholomew, Thomas

καὶ Μαθθαῖος ὁ τελώνης, Ἰάκωβος
and Matthew the tax-collector, James

ὁ τοῦ Ἀλφαίου καὶ Θαδδαῖος, 4 Σίμων
the [son] - of Alphæus and Thaddæus, Simon

ὁ Καναναῖος καὶ Ἰούδας - Ἰσκαριώτης
the Cananæan and Judas - Iscariot

ὁ καὶ παραδοὺς αὐτόν.   5 Τούτους
the [one] also betraying him.   These

τοὺς δώδεκα ἀπέστειλεν ὁ Ἰησοῦς
- twelve sent forth - Jesus

παραγγείλας αὐτοῖς λέγων·
giving charge to them saying:

Εἰς ὁδὸν ἐθνῶν μὴ ἀπέλθητε, καὶ
Into [the] way of [the] nations go ye not, and

εἰς πόλιν Σαμαριτῶν μὴ εἰσέλθητε·
into a city of Samaritans not enter not;

6 πορεύεσθε δὲ μᾶλλον πρὸς τὰ πρόβατα
but go rather unto the sheep

τὰ ἀπολωλότα οἴκου Ἰσραήλ.   7 πορευ-
the lost of [the] house of Israel.   And

όμενοι δὲ κηρύσσετε λέγοντες ὅτι ἤγγικεν
going proclaim ye saying[,] - has drawn near

ἡ βασιλεία τῶν οὐρανῶν.   8 ἀσθενοῦντας
The kingdom of the heavens.   Ailing [ones]

θεραπεύετε, νεκροὺς ἐγείρετε, λεπροὺς
heal ye, dead [ones] raise, lepers

καθαρίζετε, δαιμόνια ἐκβάλλετε· δωρεὰν
cleanse, demons expel; freely

ἐλάβετε, δωρεὰν δότε.   9 Μὴ κτήσησθε
ye received, freely give.   Do not provide

χρυσὸν μηδὲ ἄργυρον μηδὲ χαλκὸν εἰς
gold nor silver nor brass in

τὰς ζώνας ὑμῶν,   10 μὴ πήραν εἰς ὁδὸν
the girdles of you, not a wallet for [the] way

μηδὲ δύο χιτῶνας μηδὲ ὑποδήματα μηδὲ
nor two tunics nor sandals nor

ῥάβδον· ἄξιος γὰρ ὁ ἐργάτης τῆς
a staff; for worthy [is] the workman of the

29

King James Version

for the workman is worthy of his meat. 11And into whatsoever city or town ye shall enter, inquire who in it is worthy; and there abide till ye go thence. 12And when ye come into a house, salute it. 13And if the house be worthy, let your peace come upon it: but if it be not worthy, let your peace return to you. 14And whosoever shall not receive you, nor hear your words, when ye depart out of that house or city, shake off the dust of your feet. 15 Verily I say unto you, It shall be more tolerable for the land of Sodom and Gomorrah in the day of judgment, than for that city.

16 Behold, I send you forth as sheep in the midst of wolves: be ye therefore wise as serpents, and harmless as doves. 17 But beware of men: for they will deliver you up to the councils, and they will scourge you in their synagogues; 18And ye shall be brought before governors and kings for my sake, for a testimony against them and the Gentiles. 19 But when they deliver you up, take no thought how or what ye shall speak: for it shall be given you in that same hour what ye shall speak. 20 For it is not ye that speak, but the Spirit of your Father which speaketh in you. 21And the brother shall deliver up the brother to death, and the father the child: and the children shall rise up against *their* parents, and cause them to be put to death. 22And ye shall be hated of all *men* for my name's sake: but he that endureth to the end shall be saved. 23 But when they persecute you in this city, flee ye into another: for verily I say unto you, Ye shall not have gone over the cities of Israel, till the Son of man be come. 24 The disciple is not above *his* master, nor the servant above his lord. 25 It is enough for the disciple that he be as his master, and the servant as his lord. If they have called the master of the house Beelzebub, how much more *shall they call* them of his household? 26 Fear them not therefore: for there is nothing covered, that shall not be revealed; and hid, that shall not be known. 27 What I tell you in darkness, *that* speak ye in light: and what ye hear in the ear, *that* preach ye upon the housetops. 28And fear not them which kill the body, but are not able to kill the soul: but rather fear him which is able to destroy both soul and body in hell. 29Are not two sparrows sold for a farthing? and one of them shall not fall on the ground without your Father. 30 But the very hairs of your head are all numbered. 31 Fear ye not therefore, ye are of more value than many sparrows. 32 Whosoever therefore shall confess me before men, him will I confess also before my Father which is in heaven. 33 But whosoever shall deny me before men, him will I also deny before my Father which is in heaven.

New International Version

11 "Whatever city or village you enter, search for some worthy person there and stay at his house until you leave. 12As you enter the home, give it your greeting. 13 If the home is deserving, let your peace rest on it; if it is not, let your peace return to you. 14 If anyone will not welcome you or listen to your words, shake the dust off your feet when you leave that home or town. 15 I tell you the truth, it will be more bearable for Sodom and Gomorrah on the day of judgment than for that town.

16 "I am sending you out like sheep among wolves. Therefore be as shrewd as snakes and as innocent as doves. 17 But be on your guard against men; they will hand you over to the local councils and flog you in their synagogues. 18 On my account you will be brought before governors and kings as witnesses to them and to the Gentiles. 19 But when they arrest you, do not worry about what to say or how to say it. At that time you will be given what to say, 20 for it will not be you speaking, but the Spirit of your Father speaking through you.

21 "Brother will betray brother to death, and a father his child; children will rebel against their parents and have them put to death. 22All men will hate you because of me, but he who stands firm to the end will be saved. 23 When you are persecuted in one place, flee to another. I tell you the truth, you will not finish going through the cities of Israel before the Son of Man comes.

24 "A student is not above his teacher, nor a servant above his master. 25 It is enough for the student to be like his teacher, and the servant like his master. If the head of the house has been called Beelzebub,[h] how much more the members of his household!

26 "So do not be afraid of them. There is nothing concealed that will not be disclosed, or hidden that will not be made known. 27 What I tell you in the dark, speak in the daylight; what is whispered in your ear, proclaim from the housetops. 28 Do not be afraid of those who kill the body but cannot kill the soul. Rather, be afraid of the one who can destroy both soul and body in hell. 29Are not two sparrows sold for a penny? Yet not one of them will fall to the ground apart from the will of your Father. 30And even the very hairs of your head are all numbered. 31 So don't be afraid; you are worth more than many sparrows.

32 "Whoever acknowledges me before men, I will also acknowledge him before my Father in heaven. 33 But whoever disowns me before men, I will disown him before my Father in heaven.

[h] Greek MSS *Beelzeboul* or *Beezeboul*.

τροφῆς αὐτοῦ. 11 εἰς ἣν δ᾽ ἂν πόλιν
food of him. And into whatever city

ἢ κώμην εἰσέλθητε, ἐξετάσατε τίς ἐν
or village ye may enter, inquire who in

αὐτῇ ἄξιός ἐστιν· κἀκεῖ μείνατε ἕως ἂν
it worthy is; and there remain until

ἐξέλθητε. 12 εἰσερχόμενοι δὲ εἰς τὴν
ye may go out. And entering into the

οἰκίαν ἀσπάσασθε αὐτήν· 13 καὶ ἐὰν μὲν
house greet it; and if indeed

ᾖ ἡ οἰκία ἀξία, ἐλθάτω ἡ εἰρήνη ὑμῶν
be the house worthy, let come the peace of you

ἐπ᾽ αὐτήν· ἐὰν δὲ μὴ ᾖ ἀξία, ἡ εἰρήνη
on it; but if it be not worthy, the peace

ὑμῶν πρὸς ὑμᾶς ἐπιστραφήτω. 14 καὶ
of you unto you let return. And

ὃς ἂν μὴ δέξηται ὑμᾶς μηδὲ ἀκούσῃ
whoever may not receive you nor hear

τοὺς λόγους ὑμῶν, ἐξερχόμενοι ἔξω
the words of you, going out outside

τῆς οἰκίας ἢ τῆς πόλεως ἐκείνης ἐκτινά-
house or city that shake

ξατε τὸν κονιορτὸν τῶν ποδῶν ὑμῶν.
off the dust of the feet of you.

15 ἀμὴν λέγω ὑμῖν, ἀνεκτότερον ἔσται
Truly I tell you, more tolerable it will be [for]

γῇ Σοδόμων καὶ Γομόρρων ἐν ἡμέρᾳ κρίσεως
[the] land of Sodom and Gomorra in [the] day of judgment

ἢ τῇ πόλει ἐκείνῃ. 16 Ἰδοὺ ἐγὼ
than [for] city that. Behold I

ἀποστέλλω ὑμᾶς ὡς πρόβατα ἐν μέσῳ
send forth you as sheep in [the] midst

λύκων· γίνεσθε οὖν φρόνιμοι ὡς οἱ
of wolves; be ye therefore prudent as the

ὄφεις καὶ ἀκέραιοι ὡς αἱ περιστεραί.
serpents and harmless as doves.

17 Προσέχετε δὲ ἀπὸ τῶν ἀνθρώπων·
And beware from (of) - men;

παραδώσουσιν γὰρ ὑμᾶς εἰς συνέδρια,
for they will deliver up you to councils,

καὶ ἐν ταῖς συναγωγαῖς αὐτῶν μαστιγώ-
and in the synagogues of them they will

σουσιν ὑμᾶς· 18 καὶ ἐπὶ ἡγεμόνας δὲ καὶ
scourge you; and before leaders and also

βασιλεῖς ἀχθήσεσθε ἕνεκεν ἐμοῦ, εἰς
kings ye will be led for the sake of me, for

μαρτύριον αὐτοῖς καὶ τοῖς ἔθνεσιν.
a testimony to them and to the nations.

19 ὅταν δὲ παραδῶσιν ὑμᾶς, μὴ μεριμνή-
But when they deliver up you, do not be

σητε πῶς ἢ τί λαλήσητε· δοθήσεται
anxious how or what ye may say; it will be given

γὰρ ὑμῖν ἐν ἐκείνῃ τῇ ὥρᾳ τί λαλήσητε·
for to you in that - hour what ye may say;

20 οὐ γὰρ ὑμεῖς ἐστε οἱ λαλοῦντες,
for not ye are the [ones] speaking,

ἀλλὰ τὸ πνεῦμα τοῦ πατρὸς ὑμῶν τὸ
but the Spirit of the Father of you the [one]

λαλοῦν ἐν ὑμῖν. 21 παραδώσει δὲ
speaking in you. And ⁵will deliver up

ἀδελφὸς ἀδελφὸν εἰς θάνατον καὶ πατὴρ
¹brother brother to death and father

τέκνον, καὶ ἐπαναστήσονται τέκνα ἐπὶ
child, and will stand up children against

γονεῖς καὶ θανατώσουσιν αὐτούς. 22 καὶ
parents and put to death them. And

ἔσεσθε μισούμενοι ὑπὸ πάντων διὰ
ye will be being hated by all men on account of

τὸ ὄνομά μου· ὁ δὲ ὑπομείνας εἰς
the name of me; but the [one] enduring to

τέλος, οὗτος σωθήσεται. 23 ὅταν δὲ
[the] end, this will be saved. But when

διώκωσιν ὑμᾶς ἐν τῇ πόλει ταύτῃ,
they persecute you in - city this,

φεύγετε εἰς τὴν ἑτέραν· ἀμὴν γὰρ
flee ye to - [an]other; for truly

λέγω ὑμῖν, οὐ μὴ τελέσητε τὰς πόλεις
I tell you, by no means ye will complete the cities

[τοῦ] Ἰσραὴλ ἕως ἔλθῃ ὁ υἱὸς τοῦ ἀν-
of Israel until comes the Son - of

θρώπου. 24 Οὐκ ἔστιν μαθητὴς ὑπὲρ
man. not is A disciple above

τὸν διδάσκαλον οὐδὲ δοῦλος ὑπὲρ τὸν
the teacher nor a slave above the

κύριον αὐτοῦ. 25 ἀρκετὸν τῷ μαθητῇ
lord of him. Enough for the disciple

ἵνα γένηται ὡς ὁ διδάσκαλος αὐτοῦ,
that he be as the teacher of him,

καὶ ὁ δοῦλος ὡς ὁ κύριος αὐτοῦ. εἰ
and the slave as the lord of him. If

τὸν οἰκοδεσπότην Βεεζεβοὺλ ἐπεκάλεσαν,
the housemaster Beelzebub they called,

πόσῳ μᾶλλον τοὺς οἰκιακοὺς αὐτοῦ.
how much more the members of [the] household of him.

26 μὴ οὖν φοβηθῆτε αὐτούς· οὐδὲν γὰρ
Therefore fear ye not them; for nothing

ἐστιν κεκαλυμμένον ὃ οὐκ ἀποκαλυφ-
is having been veiled which will not be un-

θήσεται, καὶ κρυπτὸν ὃ οὐ γνωσθήσεται.
veiled, and hidden which will not be made known.

27 ὃ λέγω ὑμῖν ἐν τῇ σκοτίᾳ, εἴπατε
What I say to you in the darkness,

ἐν τῷ φωτί· καὶ ὃ εἰς τὸ οὖς ἀκούετε,
in the light; and what in the ear ye hear,

κηρύξατε ἐπὶ τῶν δωμάτων. 28 καὶ
proclaim on the housetops. And

μὴ φοβεῖσθε ἀπὸ τῶν ἀποκτεννόντων
do not fear - the [ones] killing

τὸ σῶμα, τὴν δὲ ψυχὴν μὴ δυναμένων
the body, but the soul not being able

ἀποκτεῖναι· φοβεῖσθε δὲ μᾶλλον τὸν
to kill; but fear ye rather the [one]

δυνάμενον καὶ ψυχὴν καὶ σῶμα ἀπολέσαι
being able both soul and body to destroy

ἐν γεέννῃ. 29 οὐχὶ δύο στρουθία ἀσσα-
in gehenna. Not two sparrows of (for) a

ρίου πωλεῖται; καὶ ἓν ἐξ αὐτῶν οὐ
farthing are sold? and one of them not

πεσεῖται ἐπὶ τὴν γῆν ἄνευ τοῦ πατρὸς
will fall on the earth without the Father

ὑμῶν. 30 ὑμῶν δὲ καὶ αἱ τρίχες τῆς
of you. But of you even the hairs of the

κεφαλῆς πᾶσαι ἠριθμημέναι εἰσίν. 31 μὴ
head all having been numbered are. not

οὖν φοβεῖσθε· πολλῶν στρουθίων διαφέρετε
Therefore fear ye; ³many ⁴sparrows ²excel

ὑμεῖς. 32 Πᾶς οὖν ὅστις ὁμολογήσει
¹ye. Everyone therefore who shall confess

ἐν ἐμοὶ ἔμπροσθεν τῶν ἀνθρώπων,
- me before - men,

ὁμολογήσω κἀγὼ ἐν αὐτῷ ἔμπροσθεν
will confess I also - him before

τοῦ πατρός μου τοῦ ἐν τοῖς οὐρανοῖς·
the Father of me - in the heavens;

33 ὅστις δ᾽ ἂν ἀρνήσηται με ἔμπροσθεν
and whoever denies me before

τῶν ἀνθρώπων, ἀρνήσομαι κἀγὼ αὐτὸν
- men, will deny I also him

ἔμπροσθεν τοῦ πατρός μου τοῦ ἐν
before the Father of me - in

King James Version

34 Think not that I am come to send peace on earth: I came not to send peace, but a sword. 35 For I am come to set a man at variance against his father, and the daughter against her mother, and the daughter in law against her mother in law. 36 And a man's foes *shall be* they of his own household. 37 He that loveth father or mother more than me is not worthy of me: and he that loveth son or daughter more than me is not worthy of me. 38 And he that taketh not his cross, and followeth after me, is not worthy of me. 39 He that findeth his life shall lose it: and he that loseth his life for my sake shall find it.

40 He that receiveth you receiveth me; and he that receiveth me receiveth him that sent me. 41 He that receiveth a prophet in the name of a prophet shall receive a prophet's reward; and he that receiveth a righteous man in the name of a righteous man shall receive a righteous man's reward. 42 And whosoever shall give to drink unto one of these little ones a cup of cold *water* only in the name of a disciple, verily I say unto you, he shall in no wise lose his reward.

11 And it came to pass, when Jesus had made an end of commanding his twelve disciples, he departed thence to teach and to preach in their cities. 2 Now when John had heard in the prison the works of Christ, he sent two of his disciples, 3 And said unto him, Art thou he that should come, or do we look for another? 4 Jesus answered and said unto them, Go and shew John again those things which ye do hear and see: 5 The blind receive their sight, and the lame walk, the lepers are cleansed, and the deaf hear, the dead are raised up, and the poor have the gospel preached to them. 6 And blessed is *he,* whosoever shall not be offended in me.

7 And as they departed, Jesus began to say unto the multitudes concerning John, What went ye out into the wilderness to see? A reed shaken with the wind? 8 But what went ye out for to see? A man clothed in soft raiment? behold, they that wear soft *clothing* are in kings' houses. 9 But what went ye out for to see? A prophet? yea, I say unto you, and more than a prophet. 10 For this is *he,* of whom it is written, Behold, I send my messenger before thy face, which shall prepare thy way before thee. 11 Verily I say unto you, Among them that are born of women there hath not risen a greater than John the Baptist: notwithstanding, he that is least in the kingdom of heaven is greater than he. 12 And from the days of John the Baptist until now the kingdom of heaven suffereth violence, and the violent take it by force. 13 For all the prophets and the law prophesied until John. 14 And if ye will re-

New International Version

34 "Do not suppose that I have come to bring peace to the earth. I did not come to bring peace, but a sword. 35 For I have come to turn

'a man against his father,
    a daughter against her mother,
    and a daughter-in-law against her mother-in-law.

36   A man's enemies will be the members of his own household.' [i]

37 "Anyone who loves his father or mother more than me is not worthy of me; anyone who loves his son or daughter more than me is not worthy of me; 38 and anyone who does not take his cross and follow me is not worthy of me. 39 Whoever finds his life will lose it, and whoever loses his life for my sake will find it.

40 "He who receives you receives me, and he who receives me receives the one who sent me. 41 Anyone who receives a prophet because he is a prophet will receive a prophet's reward, and anyone who receives a righteous man because he is a righteous man will receive a righteous man's reward. 42 And if anyone gives a cup of cold water to one of these little ones because he is my disciple, I tell you the truth, he will certainly not lose his reward."

Jesus and John the Baptist

11 After Jesus had finished instructing his twelve disciples, he went on from there to teach and preach in the towns of Galilee. [j]

2 When John heard in prison what Christ was doing, he sent his disciples 3 to ask him, "Are you the one who was to come, or should we expect someone else?"

4 Jesus replied, "Go back and report to John what you hear and see: 5 The blind receive sight, the lame walk, those who have leprosy [k] are cured, the deaf hear, the dead are raised, and the good news is preached to the poor. 6 Blessed is the man who does not fall away on account of me."

7 As John's disciples were leaving, Jesus began to speak to the crowd about John: "What did you go out into the desert to see? A reed swayed by the wind? 8 If not, what did you go out to see? A man dressed in fine clothes? No, those who wear fine clothes are in kings' palaces. 9 Then what did you go out to see? A prophet? Yes, I tell you, and more than a prophet. 10 This is the one about whom it is written:

'I will send my messenger ahead of you,
    who will prepare your way before you.' [l]

11 I tell you the truth: Among those born of women there has not risen anyone greater than John the Baptist; yet he who is least in the kingdom of heaven is greater than he. 12 From the days of John the Baptist until now, the kingdom of heaven has been forcefully advancing, and forceful men lay hold of it. 13 For all the Prophets and the Law prophesied until John. 14 And if you are willing to accept it, he is the

[i] Micah 7:6. [j] Greek *in their towns.* [k] The Greek word probably designated other related diseases also. [l] Mal. 3:1.

Greek Interlinear

τοῖς   οὐρανοῖς.   34 Μὴ   νομίσητε   ὅτι
the   heavens.   Do not suppose   that

ἦλθον βαλεῖν εἰρήνην ἐπὶ τὴν γῆν· οὐκ ἦλθον
I came to bring   peace   on   the earth;   I came not

βαλεῖν εἰρήνην ἀλλὰ μάχαιραν. 35 ἦλθον γὰρ
to bring   peace   but   a sword.   For I came

διχάσαι   ἄνθρωπον κατὰ   τοῦ   πατρὸς
to make hostile   a man   against   the   father

αὐτοῦ   καὶ   θυγατέρα κατὰ   τῆς   μητρὸς
of him   and   a daughter   against   the   mother

αὐτῆς   καὶ   νύμφην κατὰ   τῆς   πενθερᾶς
of her   and   a bride   against   the   mother-in-law

αὐτῆς,   36 καὶ   ἐχθροὶ   τοῦ   ἀνθρώπου οἱ
of her,   and [the] enemies   -   of a man   the

οἰκιακοὶ   αὐτοῦ. 37 Ὁ φιλῶν πατέρα
members of [the] household of him.   The [one] loving   father

ἢ   μητέρα ὑπὲρ ἐμὲ   οὐκ   ἔστιν   μου   ἄξιος·
or   mother   beyond   me   is not   of me   worthy;

καὶ   ὁ   φιλῶν   υἱὸν   ἢ   θυγατέρα   ὑπὲρ
and   the [one] loving   son   or   daughter   beyond

ἐμὲ   οὐκ   ἔστιν   μου   ἄξιος· 38 καὶ   ὃς
me   is not   of me   worthy;   and [he] who

οὐ   λαμβάνει   τὸν   σταυρὸν   αὐτοῦ   καὶ
takes not   the   cross   of him   and

ἀκολουθεῖ   ὀπίσω   μου,   οὐκ   ἔστιν   μου
follows   after   me,   is not   of me

ἄξιος. 39 ὁ   εὑρὼν   τὴν   ψυχὴν   αὐτοῦ
worthy.   The [one] finding   the   life   of him

ἀπολέσει   αὐτήν,   καὶ   ὁ   ἀπολέσας   τὴν
will lose   it,   and   the [one] losing   the

ψυχὴν αὐτοῦ ἕνεκεν ἐμοῦ εὑρήσει αὐτήν.
life   of him   for the sake of   me   will find   it.

40 Ὁ   δεχόμενος ὑμᾶς ἐμὲ   δέχεται,   καὶ
The [one] receiving   you   me   receives,   and

ὁ   ἐμὲ   δεχόμενος   δέχεται   τὸν
the [one] me   receiving   receives   the [one]

ἀποστείλαντά   με. 41 ὁ δεχόμενος προ-
having sent   me.   The [one] receiving   a pro-

φήτην   εἰς   ὄνομα   προφήτου   μισθὸν
phet   in   [the] name   of a prophet   [the] reward

προφήτου   λήμψεται,   καὶ   ὁ   δεχόμενος
of a prophet   will receive,   and   the [one]   receiving

δίκαιον   εἰς   ὄνομα   δικαίου   μισθὸν
a righteous man   in   [the] name of a righteous man   [the] reward

δικαίου   λήμψεται. 42 καὶ ὃς ἐὰν   ποτίσῃ
of a righteous man will receive.   And whoever gives to drink

ἕνα   τῶν   μικρῶν   τούτων   ποτήριον ψυχροῦ
one   -   of these little [ones]   a cup   of cold water

μόνον   εἰς   ὄνομα μαθητοῦ, ἀμὴν λέγω ὑμῖν,
only   in   [the] name of a disciple,   truly   I tell   you,

οὐ   μὴ   ἀπολέσῃ   τὸν   μισθὸν   αὐτοῦ.
on no account   will he lose   the   reward   of him.

Chapter 11

Καὶ   ἐγένετο   ὅτε   ἐτέλεσεν   ὁ
And   it came to pass   when   ended   -

Ἰησοῦς διατάσσων τοῖς δώδεκα μαθηταῖς
Jesus   giving charge   to the   twelve   disciples

αὐτοῦ,   μετέβη   ἐκεῖθεν   τοῦ   διδάσκειν
of him,   he removed   thence   -   to teach[d]

καὶ   κηρύσσειν   ἐν ταῖς   πόλεσιν   αὐτῶν.
and   to proclaim[d]   in   the   cities   of them.

2 Ὁ   δὲ   Ἰωάννης   ἀκούσας   ἐν   τῷ
-   But   John   hearing   in   the

δεσμωτηρίῳ   τὰ   ἔργα   τοῦ   Χριστοῦ,
prison   the   works   -   of Christ,

πέμψας διὰ τῶν μαθητῶν αὐτοῦ 3 εἶπεν
sending through   the   disciples   of him   said

αὐτῷ·   σὺ   εἶ   ὁ   ἐρχόμενος,   ἢ   ἕτερον
to him·   Thou art   the   coming [one],   or   another

προσδοκῶμεν;   4 καὶ   ἀποκριθεὶς   ὁ
may we expect?   And   answering   -

Ἰησοῦς   εἶπεν   αὐτοῖς·   πορευθέντες   ἀπαγ-
Jesus   said   to them·   Going   report

γείλατε Ἰωάννη ἃ ἀκούετε καὶ βλέπετε·
ye   to John [the things] which   ye hear   and   see·

5 τυφλοὶ   ἀναβλέπουσιν   καὶ   χωλοὶ
blind men   see again   and   lame men

περιπατοῦσιν, λεπροὶ καθαρίζονται καὶ κωφοὶ
walk,   lepers   are cleansed   and deaf men

ἀκούουσιν,   καὶ   νεκροὶ   ἐγείρονται   καὶ
hear,   and   dead men   are raised   and

πτωχοὶ   εὐαγγελίζονται· 6 καὶ   μακάριός
poor men   are evangelized;   and   blessed

ἐστιν   ὃς   ἐὰν   μὴ   σκανδαλισθῇ   ἐν ἐμοί.
is   whoever   is not offended   in   me.

7 Τούτων   δὲ   πορευομένων   ἤρξατο   ὁ
And these   going[a]   began   -
= as these were going

Ἰησοῦς   λέγειν   τοῖς   ὄχλοις περὶ   Ἰωάννου·
Jesus   to say   to the   crowds concerning   John:

τί   ἐξήλθατε   εἰς   τὴν   ἔρημον   θεάσασθαι;
What went ye out   into   the   wilderness   to see?

κάλαμον ὑπὸ ἀνέμου σαλευόμενον; 8 ἀλλὰ
a reed   by   wind   being shaken?   But

τί   ἐξήλθατε   ἰδεῖν;   ἄνθρωπον ἐν μαλακοῖς
what went ye out   to see?   a man   in   soft material

ἠμφιεσμένον; ἰδοὺ οἱ   τὰ   μαλακὰ
having been clothed?   Behold[.]   the [ones]   -   soft material

φοροῦντες ἐν τοῖς οἴκοις τῶν βασιλέων. 9 ἀλλὰ
wearing [are]   in   the   houses   -   of kings.   But

τί   ἐξήλθατε;   προφήτην   ἰδεῖν;   ναὶ   λέγω
why   went ye out?   a prophet   to see?   Yes[,]   I tell

ὑμῖν,   καὶ   περισσότερον   προφήτου. 10 οὗτός
you,   and   more [than]   a prophet.   This

ἐστιν   περὶ   οὗ   γέγραπται·   ἰδοὺ ἐγὼ
is he   concerning whom   it has been written·   Behold[,]   I

ἀποστέλλω τὸν ἄγγελόν μου πρὸ προσώπου
send forth   the   messenger   of me   before [the] face

σου,   ὃς   κατασκευάσει   τὴν   ὁδόν   σου
of thee,   who   will prepare   the   way   of thee

ἔμπροσθέν   σου. 11 ἀμὴν   λέγω   ὑμῖν,
before   thee.   Truly   I tell   you,

οὐκ   ἐγήγερται   ἐν γεννητοῖς   γυναικῶν
there has not arisen   among [those] born   of women

μείζων   Ἰωάννου τοῦ   βαπτιστοῦ·   ὁ   δὲ
a greater [than] John   the   Baptist;   but the

μικρότερος ἐν τῇ   βασιλείᾳ τῶν   οὐρανῶν
lesser   in   the   kingdom   of the   heavens

μείζων   αὐτοῦ   ἐστιν. 12 ἀπὸ δὲ   τῶν
greater [than]   he   is.   And from   the

ἡμερῶν   Ἰωάννου τοῦ   βαπτιστοῦ   ἕως
days   of John   the   Baptist   until

ἄρτι ἡ   βασιλεία τῶν   οὐρανῶν   βιάζεται,
now   the   kingdom   of the   heavens   is forcibly treated,

καὶ   βιασταὶ   ἁρπάζουσιν   αὐτήν. 13 πάντες γὰρ
and   forceful men   seize   it.   For all

οἱ   προφῆται   καὶ   ὁ   νόμος   ἕως
the   prophets   and   the   law   until

Ἰωάννου ἐπροφήτευσαν· 14 καὶ εἰ θέλετε
John   prophesied;   and if ye are willing

King James Version

ceive *it*, this is Elias, which was for to come.
15 He that hath ears to hear, let him hear.

16 But whereunto shall I liken this generation? It is like unto children sitting in the
markets, and calling unto their fellows, 17And
saying, We have piped unto you, and ye have
not danced; we have mourned unto you, and ye
have not lamented. 18 For John came neither
eating nor drinking, and they say, He hath a
devil. 19 The Son of man came eating and drinking, and they say, Behold a man gluttonous, and
a winebibber, a friend of publicans and sinners.
But wisdom is justified of her children.

20 Then began he to upbraid the cities wherein most of his mighty works were done, because
they repented not: 21 Woe unto thee, Chorazin!
woe unto thee, Bethsaida! for if the mighty
works, which were done in you, had been done
in Tyre and Sidon, they would have repented
long ago in sackcloth and ashes. 22 But I say
unto you, It shall be more tolerable for Tyre and
Sidon at the day of judgment, than for you.
23And thou, Capernaum, which art exalted unto
heaven, shalt be brought down to hell: for if the
mighty works, which have been done in thee,
had been done in Sodom, it would have remained until this day. 24 But I say unto you,
That it shall be more tolerable for the land of
Sodom in the day of judgment, than for thee.

25 At that time Jesus answered and said, I
thank thee, O Father, Lord of heaven and earth,
because thou hast hid these things from the wise
and prudent, and hast revealed them unto babes.
26 Even so, Father; for so it seemed good in thy
sight. 27All things are delivered unto me of my
Father: and no man knoweth the Son, but the
Father; neither knoweth any man the Father,
save the Son, and *he* to whomsoever the Son
will reveal *him*.

28 Come unto me, all *ye* that labour and are
heavy laden, and I will give you rest. 29 Take my
yoke upon you, and learn of me; for I am meek
and lowly in heart: and ye shall find rest unto
your souls. 30 For my yoke *is* easy, and my
burden is light.

12 At that time Jesus went on the sabbath
day through the corn; and his disciples
were a hungered, and began to pluck the ears of
corn, and to eat. 2 But when the Pharisees saw
it, they said unto him, Behold, thy disciples do
that which is not lawful to do upon the sabbath
day. 3 But he said unto them, Have ye not read
what David did, when he was a hungered, and
they that were with him; 4 How he entered into
the house of God, and did eat the shewbread,
which was not lawful for him to eat, neither for
them which were with him, but only for the
priests? 5 Or have ye not read in the law, how

New International Version

Elijah who was to come. 15 He who has ears,
let him hear.

16 "To what can I compare this generation?
They are like children sitting in the marketplaces
and calling out to others:

17 'We played the flute for you, and you did
not dance;

we sang a dirge, and you did not mourn.'
18 For John came neither eating nor drinking,
and they say, 'He has a demon.' 19 The Son of
Man came eating and drinking, and they say,
'Here is a glutton and a drunkard, a friend of
tax collectors and "sinners." ' But wisdom is
proved right by her actions."

Woes on unrepentant cities

20 Then Jesus began to denounce the cities
in which most of his miracles had been performed, because they did not repent. 21 "Woe to
you, Chorazin! Woe to you, Bethsaida! If the
miracles that were performed in you had been
performed in Tyre and Sidon, they would have
repented long ago in sackcloth and ashes. 22 But
I tell you, it will be more bearable for Tyre and
Sidon on the day of judgment than for you.
23And you, Capernaum, will you be lifted up to
the skies? No, you will go down to the depths.ᵐ
If the miracles that were performed in you had
been performed in Sodom, it would have remained to this day. 24 But I tell you that it will
be more bearable for Sodom on the day of
judgment than for you."

Rest for the weary

25 At that time Jesus said, "I praise you,
Father, Lord of heaven and earth, because you
have hidden these things from the wise and
learned, and revealed them to little children.
26 Yes, Father, for this was your good pleasure.

27 "All things have been committed to me by
my Father. No one knows the Son except the
Father, and no one knows the Father except the
Son and those to whom the Son chooses to
reveal him.

28 "Come to me, all you who are weary and
burdened, and I will give you rest. 29 Take my
yoke upon you and learn from me, for I am
gentle and humble in heart, and you will find
rest for your souls. 30 For my yoke is easy and
my burden is light."

Lord of the Sabbath

12 At that time Jesus went through the grainfields on the Sabbath. His disciples were
hungry and began to pick some heads of grain
and eat them. 2 When the Pharisees saw this,
they said to him, "Look! Your disciples are
doing what is unlawful on the Sabbath."

3 He answered, "Haven't you read what
David did when he and his companions were
hungry? 4 He entered the house of God, and he
and his companions ate the consecrated bread—
which was not lawful for them to do, but only
for the priests. 5 Or haven't you read in the Law

Greek Interlinear

δέξασθαι, αὐτός ἐστιν Ἠλίας ὁ μέλλων
to receive [it or him], he is Elias the [one] about

ἔρχεσθαι. 15 ὁ ἔχων ὦτα ἀκουέτω.
to come. The [one] having ears let him hear.

16 Τίνι δὲ ὁμοιώσω τὴν γενεὰν ταύτην;
But to what shall I liken the generation this?

ὁμοία ἐστὶν παιδίοις καθημένοις ἐν ταῖς
Like it is to children sitting in the

ἀγοραῖς ἃ προσφωνοῦντα τοῖς ἑτέροις
marketplaces who calling to the others

17 λέγουσιν· ηὐλήσαμεν ὑμῖν καὶ οὐκ
say: We piped to you and not

ὠρχήσασθε· ἐθρηνήσαμεν καὶ οὐκ ἐκόψασθε.
ye did dance; we lamented and ye did not mourn.

18 ἦλθεν γὰρ Ἰωάννης μήτε ἐσθίων μήτε
For came John neither eating nor

πίνων, καὶ λέγουσιν· δαιμόνιον ἔχει.
drinking, and they say: a demon He has.

19 ἦλθεν ὁ υἱὸς τοῦ ἀνθρώπου ἐσθίων καὶ
Came the Son - of man eating and

πίνων, καὶ λέγουσιν· ἰδοὺ ἄνθρωπος
drinking, and they say: Behold[.] a man

φάγος καὶ οἰνοπότης, τελωνῶν φίλος καὶ
gluttonous and a wine-drinker, of tax-collectors a friend and

ἁμαρτωλῶν. καὶ ἐδικαιώθη ἡ σοφία ἀπὸ
of sinners. And was(is) justified - wisdom from(by)

τῶν ἔργων αὐτῆς.
the works of her.

20 Τότε ἤρξατο ὀνειδίζειν τὰς πόλεις
Then he began to reproach the cities

ἐν αἷς ἐγένοντο αἱ πλεῖσται δυνάμεις
in which happened the very many powerful deeds

αὐτοῦ, ὅτι οὐ μετενόησαν· 21 οὐαί σοι,
of him, because they repented not: Woe to thee,

Χοραζίν· οὐαί σοι, Βηθσαϊδά· ὅτι εἰ
Chorazin; woe to thee, Bethsaida; because if

ἐν Τύρῳ καὶ Σιδῶνι ἐγένοντο αἱ δυνάμεις
in Tyre and Sidon happened the powerful deeds

αἱ γενόμεναι ἐν ὑμῖν, πάλαι ἂν
- having happened in you, long ago -

ἐν σάκκῳ καὶ σποδῷ μετενόησαν.
in sackcloth and ashes they would have repented.

22 πλὴν λέγω ὑμῖν, Τύρῳ καὶ Σιδῶνι
However I tell you, For Tyre and for Sidon

ἀνεκτότερον ἔσται ἐν ἡμέρᾳ κρίσεως ἢ
more tolerable it will be in [the] day of judgment than

ὑμῖν. 23 καὶ σύ, Καφαρναούμ, μὴ
for you. And thou, Capernaum, not

ἕως οὐρανοῦ ὑψωθήσῃ; ἕως ᾅδου
as far as heaven wast thou exalted? as far as hades

καταβήσῃ· ὅτι εἰ ἐν Σοδόμοις ἐγενήθησαν
thou shalt descend; because if in Sodom happened

αἱ δυνάμεις αἱ γενόμεναι ἐν σοί,
the powerful deeds - having happened in thee,

ἔμεινεν ἂν μέχρι τῆς σήμερον. 24 πλὴν
it would have remained until - to-day. However

λέγω ὑμῖν ὅτι γῇ Σοδόμων ἀνεκτότερον
I tell you that for [the] land of Sodom more tolerable

ἔσται ἐν ἡμέρᾳ κρίσεως ἢ σοί.
it will be in [the] day of judgment than for thee.

25 Ἐν ἐκείνῳ τῷ καιρῷ ἀποκριθεὶς
At that - time answering

ὁ Ἰησοῦς εἶπεν· ἐξομολογοῦμαί σοι,
- Jesus said: I give thanks to thee,

πάτερ, κύριε τοῦ οὐρανοῦ καὶ τῆς γῆς,
Father, lord of the heaven and of the earth,

ὅτι ἔκρυψας ταῦτα ἀπὸ σοφῶν καὶ συνε-
because thou hiddest these things from wise and intel-

τῶν, καὶ ἀπεκάλυψας αὐτὰ νηπίοις·
ligent men, and didst reveal them to infants:

26 ναί, ὁ πατήρ, ὅτι οὕτως εὐδοκία
yes, - Father, because thus good pleasure

ἐγένετο ἔμπροσθέν σου. 27 Πάντα μοι
it was before thee. All things to me

παρεδόθη ὑπὸ τοῦ πατρός μου, καὶ
were delivered by the Father of me, and

οὐδεὶς ἐπιγινώσκει τὸν υἱὸν εἰ μὴ ὁ
no one fully knows the Son except the

πατήρ, οὐδὲ τὸν πατέρα τις ἐπιγινώσκει
Father, neither the Father anyone fully knows

εἰ μὴ ὁ υἱὸς καὶ ᾧ ἐὰν βούληται ὁ
except the Son and [he] to whom if wills the

υἱὸς ἀποκαλύψαι. 28 Δεῦτε πρός με
Son to reveal. Come unto me

πάντες οἱ κοπιῶντες καὶ πεφορτισμένοι,
all the [ones] labouring and having been burdened,

κἀγὼ ἀναπαύσω ὑμᾶς. 29 ἄρατε τὸν
and I will rest you. Take the

ζυγόν μου ἐφ' ὑμᾶς καὶ μάθετε ἀπ'
yoke of me on you and learn from

ἐμοῦ, ὅτι πραΰς εἰμι καὶ ταπεινὸς τῇ
me, because meek I am and lowly -

καρδίᾳ, καὶ εὑρήσετε ἀνάπαυσιν ταῖς
in heart, and ye will find rest to the

ψυχαῖς ὑμῶν· 30 ὁ γὰρ ζυγός μου
souls of you; for the yoke of me

χρηστὸς καὶ τὸ φορτίον μου ἐλαφρόν
gentle and the burden of me light

ἐστιν.
is.

Chapter 12

Ἐν ἐκείνῳ τῷ καιρῷ ἐπορεύθη ὁ
At that - time went -

Ἰησοῦς τοῖς σάββασιν διὰ τῶν σπορίμων·
Jesus on the sabbath through the cornfields;

οἱ δὲ μαθηταὶ αὐτοῦ ἐπείνασαν, καὶ
and the disciples of him hungered, and

ἤρξαντο τίλλειν στάχυας καὶ ἐσθίειν.
began to pluck ears [of corn] and to eat.

2 οἱ δὲ Φαρισαῖοι ἰδόντες εἶπαν αὐτῷ·
But the Pharisees seeing said to him:

ἰδοὺ οἱ μαθηταί σου ποιοῦσιν ὃ οὐκ
Behold[,] the disciples of thee are doing what not

ἔξεστιν ποιεῖν ἐν σαββάτῳ. 3 ὁ δὲ
it is lawful to do on a sabbath. And he

εἶπεν αὐτοῖς· οὐκ ἀνέγνωτε τί ἐποίησεν
said to them: Did ye not read what did

Δαυίδ, ὅτε ἐπείνασεν καὶ οἱ μετ'
David, when he hungered and the [ones] with

αὐτοῦ; 4 πῶς εἰσῆλθεν εἰς τὸν οἶκον
him? how he entered into the house

τοῦ θεοῦ καὶ τοὺς ἄρτους τῆς προ-
- of God and the loaves of the set-

θέσεως ἔφαγον, ὃ οὐκ ἐξὸν ἦν αὐτῷ
ting forth ate, which not lawful it was for him

φαγεῖν οὐδὲ τοῖς μετ' αὐτοῦ, εἰ μὴ
to eat neither the [ones] with him, except

τοῖς ἱερεῦσιν μόνοις; 5 ἢ οὐκ ἀνέγνωτε
for the priests only? or did ye not read

King James Version

that on the sabbath days the priests in the temple profane the sabbath, and are blameless? 6 But I say unto you, That in this place is *one* greater than the temple. 7 But if ye had known what *this* meaneth, I will have mercy, and not sacrifice, ye would not have condemned the guiltless. 8 For the Son of man is Lord even of the sabbath day. 9And when he was departed thence, he went into their synagogue:

10 And, behold, there was a man which had *his* hand withered. And they asked him, saying, Is it lawful to heal on the sabbath days? that they might accuse him. 11And he said unto them, What man shall there be among you, that shall have one sheep, and if it fall into a pit on the sabbath day, will he not lay hold on it, and lift *it* out? 12 How much then is a man better than a sheep? Wherefore it is lawful to do well on the sabbath days. 13 Then saith he to the man, Stretch forth thine hand. And he stretched *it* forth; and it was restored whole, like as the other.

14 Then the Pharisees went out, and held a council against him, how they might destroy him. 15 But when Jesus knew *it*, he withdrew himself from thence: and great multitudes followed him, and he healed them all; 16And charged them that they should not make him known: 17 That it might be fulfilled which was spoken by Esaias the prophet, saying, 18 Behold my servant, whom I have chosen; my beloved, in whom my soul is well pleased: I will put my Spirit upon him, and he shall shew judgment to the Gentiles. 19 He shall not strive, nor cry; neither shall any man hear his voice in the streets. 20A bruised reed shall he not break, and smoking flax shall he not quench, till he send forth judgment unto victory. 21And in his name shall the Gentiles trust.

22 Then was brought unto him one possessed with a devil, blind, and dumb: and he healed him, insomuch that the blind and dumb both spake and saw. 23And all the people were amazed, and said, Is not this the Son of David? 24 But when the Pharisees heard *it*, they said, This *fellow* doth not cast out devils, but by Beelzebub the prince of the devils. 25And Jesus knew their thoughts, and said unto them, Every kingdom divided against itself is brought to desolation; and every city or house divided against itself shall not stand: 26And if Satan cast out Satan, he is divided against himself; how shall then his kingdom stand? 27And if I by Beelzebub cast out devils, by whom do your children cast *them* out? therefore they shall be your judges. 28 But if I cast out devils by the Spirit of God, then the kingdom of God is come unto you. 29 Or else, how can one enter into a strong man's house, and spoil his goods, except he first bind the strong man? and then he will spoil his house. 30 He that is not with me is against me; and he that gathereth not with me scattereth abroad.

New International Version

that on the Sabbath the priests in the temple desecrate the day and yet are innocent? 6 I tell you that one greater than the temple is here. 7 If you had known what these words mean, 'I desire mercy, not sacrifice,' [n] you would not have condemned the innocent. 8 For the Son of Man is Lord of the Sabbath."

9 Going on from that place, he went into their synagogue, 10 and a man with a shriveled hand was there. Looking for a reason to accuse Jesus, they asked him, "Is it lawful to heal on the Sabbath?"

11 He said to them, "If any of you has a sheep and it falls into a pit on the Sabbath, will you not take hold of it and lift it out? 12 How much more valuable is a man than a sheep! Therefore, it is lawful to do good on the Sabbath."

13 Then he said to the man, "Stretch out your hand." So he stretched it out and it was completely restored, just as sound as the other. 14 But the Pharisees went out and plotted how they might kill Jesus.

God's chosen servant

15 Aware of this, Jesus withdrew from that place. Many followed him, and he healed all their sick, 16 warning them not to tell who he was. 17 This was to fulfill what was spoken through the prophet Isaiah:

18 "Here is my servant whom I have chosen,
    the one I love and in whom I delight;
I will put my Spirit on him,
    and he will proclaim justice to the nations.
19 He will not quarrel or cry out;
    no one will hear his voice in the streets.
20 A bruised reed he will not break,
    and a smoldering wick he will not quench,
till he leads justice to victory.
21   In his name the nations will put their hope." [o]

Jesus and Beelzebub

22 Then they brought him a demon-possessed man who was blind and mute, and Jesus healed him, so that he could both talk and see. 23All the people were astonished and said, "Could this be the Son of David?"

24 But when the Pharisees heard this, they said, "It is only by Beelzebub, [p] the prince of demons, that this fellow drives out demons."

25 Jesus knew their thoughts and said to them, "Every kingdom divided against itself will be ruined, and every city or household divided against itself will not stand. 26 If Satan drives out Satan, he is divided against himself. How then can his kingdom stand? 27And if I drive out demons by Beelzebub, [p] by whom do your people drive them out? So then, they will be your judges. 28 But if I drive out demons by the Spirit of God, then the kingdom of God has come upon you.

29 "Or again, how can anyone enter a strong man's house and carry off his possessions unless he first ties up the strong man? Then he can rob his house.

30 "He who is not with me is against me, and

[n] Hosea 6:6. [o] Isaiah 42:1-4. [p] Greek MSS *Beelzeboul* or *Beezeboul*.

Greek Interlinear

ἐν τῷ νόμῳ ὅτι τοῖς σάββασιν οἱ
in the law that on the sabbaths the

ἱερεῖς ἐν τῷ ἱερῷ τὸ σάββατον βεβηλοῦ-
priests in the temple the sabbath pro-

σιν καὶ ἀναίτιοί εἰσιν; 6 λέγω δὲ
fane and guiltless are? And I tell

ὑμῖν ὅτι τοῦ ἱεροῦ μεῖζόν ἐστιν ὧδε.
you that [than] the temple a greater [thing] is here.

7 εἰ δὲ ἐγνώκειτε τί ἐστιν· ἔλεος
But if ye had known what it is: Mercy

θέλω καὶ οὐ θυσίαν, οὐκ ἂν κατε-
I desire and not sacrifice, ye would not have

δικάσατε τοὺς ἀναιτίους. 8 κύριος γάρ
condemned the guiltless. For Lord

ἐστιν τοῦ σαββάτου ὁ υἱὸς τοῦ ἀνθρώπου.
is of the sabbath the Son of man.

9 Καὶ μεταβὰς ἐκεῖθεν ἦλθεν εἰς τὴν
And removing thence he came into the

συναγωγὴν αὐτῶν. 10 καὶ ἰδοὺ ἄνθρωπος
synagogue of them. And behold[,] a man

χεῖρα ἔχων ξηράν· καὶ ἐπηρώτησαν αὐτὸν
[his] hand having withered; and they questioned him

λέγοντες· εἰ ἔξεστιν τοῖς σάββασιν
saying: If it is lawful on the sabbaths

θεραπεῦσαι; ἵνα κατηγορήσωσιν αὐτοῦ.
to heal? in order that they might accuse him.

11 ὁ δὲ εἶπεν αὐτοῖς· τίς ἔσται ἐξ
So he said to them: ¹What ²will there be ³of

ὑμῶν ἄνθρωπος ὃς ἕξει πρόβατον ἕν,
¹you ²man who will have sheep one,

καὶ ἐὰν ἐμπέσῃ τοῦτο τοῖς σάββασιν
and if ²fall in ¹this on the sabbaths

εἰς βόθυνον, οὐχὶ κρατήσει αὐτὸ καὶ
into a ditch, will he not lay hold of it and

ἐγερεῖ; 12 πόσῳ οὖν διαφέρει ἄνθρωπος
raise? By how much then surpasses a man

προβάτου. ὥστε ἔξεστιν τοῖς σάββασιν
a sheep. So that it is lawful on the sabbaths

καλῶς ποιεῖν. 13 τότε λέγει τῷ ἀνθρώπῳ·
well to do. Then he says to the man:

ἔκτεινόν σου τὴν χεῖρα. καὶ ἐξέτεινεν,
Stretch forth of thee the hand. And he stretched forth,

καὶ ἀπεκατεστάθη ὑγιὴς ὡς ἡ ἄλλη.
and it was restored healthy as the other.

14 ἐξελθόντες δὲ οἱ Φαρισαῖοι συμβούλιον
And going out the Pharisees counsel

ἔλαβον κατ' αὐτοῦ, ὅπως αὐτὸν ἀπολέ-
took against him, so as him they might

σωσιν. 15 Ὁ δὲ Ἰησοῦς γνοὺς ἀνε-
destroy. But Jesus knowing de-

χώρησεν ἐκεῖθεν. καὶ ἠκολούθησαν αὐτῷ
parted thence. And followed him

πολλοί, καὶ ἐθεράπευσεν αὐτοὺς πάντας,
many, and he healed them all,

16 καὶ ἐπετίμησεν αὐτοῖς ἵνα μὴ φανερὸν
and warned them that ²not ³manifest

αὐτὸν ποιήσωσιν· 17 ἵνα πληρωθῇ τὸ
⁴him ¹they ⁴should ⁴make; that might be fulfilled the [thing]

ῥηθὲν διὰ Ἡσαΐου τοῦ προφήτου
spoken through Isaiah the prophet

λέγοντος· 18 ἰδοὺ ὁ παῖς μου ὃν
saying: Behold[,] the servant of me whom

ᾑρέτισα, ὁ ἀγαπητός μου ὃν εὐδόκησεν
I chose, the beloved of me [with] whom was well pleased

ἡ ψυχή μου· θήσω τὸ πνεῦμα μου ἐπ'
the soul of me; I will put the spirit of me on

αὐτόν, καὶ κρίσιν τοῖς ἔθνεσιν ἀπαγγελεῖ.
him, and judgment to the nations he will announce.

19 οὐκ ἐρίσει οὐδὲ κραυγάσει, οὐδὲ
He will not strive nor will shout, nor

ἀκούσει τις ἐν ταῖς πλατείαις τὴν
will hear anyone in the streets the

φωνὴν αὐτοῦ. 20 κάλαμον συντετριμμένον
voice of him. A reed having been bruised

οὐ κατεάξει καὶ λίνον τυφόμενον οὐ
he will not break and flax smoking not

σβέσει, ἕως ἂν ἐκβάλῃ εἰς νῖκος τὴν
he will quench, until he put forth to victory -

κρίσιν. 21 καὶ τῷ ὀνόματι αὐτοῦ ἔθνη
judgment. And in the name of him nations

ἐλπιοῦσιν.
will hope.

22 Τότε προσηνέχθη αὐτῷ δαιμονιζ-
Then was brought to him a demon-

όμενος τυφλὸς καὶ κωφός· καὶ ἐθεράπευσεν
possessed man blind and dumb; and he healed

αὐτόν, ὥστε τὸν κωφὸν λαλεῖν καὶ
him, so as the dumb to speak and

βλέπειν. 23 καὶ ἐξίσταντο πάντες οἱ
to see. And were astonished all the

ὄχλοι καὶ ἔλεγον· μήτι οὗτός ἐστιν ὁ
crowds and said: not This is the

υἱὸς Δαυίδ; 24 οἱ δὲ Φαρισαῖοι ἀκού-
son of David? But the Pharisees hear-

σαντες εἶπον· οὗτος οὐκ ἐκβάλλει τὰ
ing said: This man does not expel the

δαιμόνια εἰ μὴ ἐν τῷ Βεελζεβοὺλ ἄρχοντι
demons except by Beelzebub ruler

τῶν δαιμονίων. 25 εἰδὼς δὲ τὰς ἐνθυμήσεις
of the demons. But knowing the thoughts

αὐτῶν εἶπεν αὐτοῖς· πᾶσα βασιλεία
of them he said to them: Every kingdom

μερισθεῖσα καθ' ἑαυτῆς ἐρημοῦται,
divided against itself is brought to desolation,

καὶ πᾶσα πόλις ἢ οἰκία μερισθεῖσα καθ'
and every city or house divided against

ἑαυτῆς οὐ σταθήσεται. 26 καὶ εἰ
itself will not stand. And if

ὁ σατανᾶς τὸν σατανᾶν ἐκβάλλει, ἐφ'
- Satan - ²Satan ¹expels, against

ἑαυτὸν ἐμερίσθη· πῶς οὖν σταθή-
himself he was(is) divided; how therefore will

σεται ἡ βασιλεία αὐτοῦ; 27 καὶ εἰ
stand the kingdom of him? And if

ἐγὼ ἐν Βεελζεβοὺλ ἐκβάλλω τὰ δαιμόνια,
I by Beelzebub expel the demons,

οἱ υἱοὶ ὑμῶν ἐν τίνι ἐκβάλλουσιν;
the sons of you by what do they expel?

διὰ τοῦτο αὐτοὶ κριταὶ ἔσονται ὑμῶν.
therefore they judges shall be of you.

28 εἰ δὲ ἐν πνεύματι θεοῦ ἐγὼ
But if by [the] Spirit of God I

ἐκβάλλω τὰ δαιμόνια, ἄρα ἔφθασεν
expel the demons, then came

ἐφ' ὑμᾶς ἡ βασιλεία τοῦ θεοῦ. 29 ἢ
upon you the kingdom - of God. Or

πῶς δύναταί τις εἰσελθεῖν εἰς τὴν
how can anyone to enter into the

οἰκίαν τοῦ ἰσχυροῦ καὶ τὰ σκεύη αὐτοῦ
house of the strong man and the vessels of him

ἁρπάσαι, ἐὰν μὴ πρῶτον δήσῃ τὸν
to seize, if not first he binds the

ἰσχυρόν; καὶ τότε τὴν οἰκίαν αὐτοῦ
strong man? and then the house of him

διαρπάσει. 30 ὁ μὴ ὢν μετ' ἐμοῦ
he will plunder. The [one] not being with me

κατ' ἐμοῦ ἐστιν, καὶ ὁ μὴ συνάγων μετ'
against me is, and the [one] not gathering with

37

King James Version

31 Wherefore I say unto you, All manner of sin and blasphemy shall be forgiven unto men: but the blasphemy *against* the *Holy* Ghost shall not be forgiven unto men. 32And whosoever speaketh a word against the Son of man, it shall be forgiven him: but whosoever speaketh against the Holy Ghost, it shall not be forgiven him, neither in this world, neither in the *world* to come. 33 Either make the tree good, and his fruit good; or else make the tree corrupt, and his fruit corrupt: for the tree is known by *his* fruit. 34 O generation of vipers, how can ye, being evil, speak good things? for out of the abundance of the heart the mouth speaketh. 35A good man out of the good treasure of the heart bringeth forth good things: and an evil man out of the evil treasure bringeth forth evil things. 36 But I say unto you, That every idle word that men shall speak, they shall give account thereof in the day of judgment. 37 For by. thy words thou shalt be justified, and by thy words thou shalt be condemned.

38 Then certain of the scribes and of the Pharisees answered, saying, Master, we would see a sign from thee. 39 But he answered and said unto them, An evil and adulterous generation seeketh after a sign; and there shall no sign be given to it, but the sign of the prophet Jonas: 40 For as Jonas was three days and three nights in the whale's belly; so shall the Son of man be three days and three nights in the heart of the earth. 41 The men of Nineveh shall rise in judgment with this generation, and shall condemn it: because they repented at the preaching of Jonas; and, behold, a greater than Jonas *is* here. 42 The queen of the south shall rise up in the judgment with this generation, and shall condemn it: for she came from the uttermost parts of the earth to hear the wisdom of Solomon; and, behold, a greater than Solomon *is* here. 43 When the unclean spirit is gone out of a man, he walketh through dry places, seeking rest, and findeth none. 44 Then he saith, I will return into my house from whence I came out; and when he is come, he findeth *it* empty, swept, and garnished. 45 Then goeth he, and taketh with himself seven other spirits more wicked than himself, and they enter in and dwell there: and the last *state* of that man is worse than the first. Even so shall it be also unto this wicked generation.

46 While he yet talked to the people, behold, *his* mother and his brethren stood without, desiring to speak with him. 47 Then one said unto him, Behold, thy mother and thy brethren stand without, desiring to speak with thee. 48 But he answered and said unto him that told him, Who

New International Version

he who does not gather with me scatters. 31And so I tell you, every sin and blasphemy will be forgiven men, but the blasphemy against the Spirit will not be forgiven. 32Anyone who speaks a word against the Son of Man will be forgiven, but anyone who speaks against the Holy Spirit will not be forgiven, either in this age or in the age to come.

33 "Make a tree good and its fruit will be good, or make a tree bad and its fruit will be bad, for a tree is recognized by its fruit. 34 You brood of vipers, how can you who are evil say anything good? For out of the overflow of the heart the mouth speaks. 35 The good man brings good things out of the good stored up in him, and the evil man brings evil things out of the evil stored up in him. 36 But I tell you that men will have to give account on the day of judgment for every careless word they have spoken. 37 For by your words you will be acquitted, and by your words you will be condemned."

The sign of Jonah

38 Then some of the Pharisees and teachers of the law said to him, "Teacher, we want to see a miraculous sign from you."

39 He answered, "A wicked and adulterous generation asks for a miraculous sign! But none will be given it except the sign of the prophet Jonah. 40 For as Jonah was three days and three nights in the belly of a huge fish, so the Son of Man will be three days and three nights in the heart of the earth. 41 The men of Nineveh will stand up at the judgment with this generation and condemn it; for they repented at the preaching of Jonah, and now one greater than Jonah is here. 42 The Queen of the South will rise at the judgment with this generation and condemn it; for she came from the ends of the earth to listen to Solomon's wisdom; and now one greater than Solomon is here.

43 "When an evil *q* spirit comes out of a man, it goes through arid places seeking rest and does not find it. 44 Then it says, 'I will return to the house I left.' When it arrives, it finds the house unoccupied, swept clean and put in order. 45 Then it goes and takes with it seven other spirits more wicked than itself, and they go in and live there. And the final condition of that man is worse than the first. That is how it will be with this wicked generation."

Jesus' mother and brothers

46 While Jesus was still talking to the crowd, his mother and brothers stood outside, wanting to speak to him. 47 Someone told him, "Your mother and brothers are standing outside, wanting to speak to you." *r*

48 He replied, "Who is my mother, and who

Greek Interlinear

ἐμοῦ σκορπίζει. **31** Διὰ τοῦτο λέγω
me scatters. Therefore I tell

ὑμῖν, πᾶσα ἁμαρτία καὶ βλασφημία
you, all sin and blasphemy

ἀφεθήσεται τοῖς ἀνθρώποις, ἡ δὲ τοῦ
will be forgiven - to men, but the of the

πνεύματος βλασφημία οὐκ ἀφεθήσεται.
Spirit blasphemy will not be forgiven.

32 καὶ ὃς ἐὰν εἴπῃ λόγον κατὰ τοῦ
And whoever speaks a word against the

υἱοῦ τοῦ ἀνθρώπου, ἀφεθήσεται αὐτῷ·
Son of man, it will be forgiven to him;

ὃς δ' ἂν εἴπῃ κατὰ τοῦ πνεύματος
but whoever speaks against the Spirit

τοῦ ἁγίου, οὐκ ἀφεθήσεται αὐτῷ
- Holy, it will not be forgiven to him

οὔτε ἐν τούτῳ τῷ αἰῶνι οὔτε ἐν τῷ
neither in this - age nor in the [one]

μέλλοντ:. **33** Ἢ ποιήσατε τὸ δένδρον
coming. Either make the tree

καλὸν καὶ τὸν καρπὸν αὐτοῦ καλόν,
good and the fruit of it good,

ἢ ποιήσατε τὸ δένδρον σαπρὸν καὶ τὸν
or make the tree bad and the

καρπὸν αὐτοῦ σαπρόν· ἐκ γὰρ τοῦ
fruit of it bad; for of(by) the

καρποῦ τὸ δένδρον γινώσκεται. **34** γεννή-
fruit the tree is known. Off-

ματα ἐχιδνῶν, πῶς δύνασθε ἀγαθὰ λαλεῖν
spring of vipers, how can ye good things to speak

πονηροὶ ὄντες; ἐκ γὰρ τοῦ περισ-
'evil **'**being? for out of the abund-

σεύματος τῆς καρδίας τὸ στόμα λαλεῖ.
ance of the heart the mouth speaks.

35 ὁ ἀγαθὸς ἄνθρωπος ἐκ τοῦ ἀγαθοῦ
The good man out of the good

θησαυροῦ ἐκβάλλει ἀγαθά, καὶ ὁ πονηρὸς
treasure puts forth good things, and the evil

ἄνθρωπος ἐκ τοῦ πονηροῦ θησαυροῦ
man out of the evil treasure

ἐκβάλλει πονηρά. **36** λέγω δὲ
puts forth evil things. But I tell

ὑμῖν ὅτι πᾶν ῥῆμα ἀργὸν ὃ λαλήσουσιν
you that every word idle which will speak

οἱ ἄνθρωποι, ἀποδώσουσιν περὶ αὐτοῦ
- men, they will render concerning it

λόγον ἐν ἡμέρᾳ κρίσεως· **37** ἐκ γὰρ
account in [the] day of judgment; for of(by)

τῶν λόγων σου δικαιωθήσῃ, καὶ ἐκ
the words of thee thou wilt be justified, and of(by)

τῶν λόγων σου καταδικασθήσῃ.
the words of thee thou wilt be condemned.

38 Τότε ἀπεκρίθησαν αὐτῷ τινες τῶν
Then answered him some of the

γραμματέων καὶ Φαρισαίων λέγοντες·
scribes and Pharisees saying:

διδάσκαλε, θέλομεν ἀπὸ σοῦ σημεῖον ἰδεῖν.
Teacher, we wish from thee a sign to see.

39 ὁ δὲ ἀποκριθεὶς εἶπεν αὐτοῖς·
But he answering said to them:

γενεὰ πονηρὰ καὶ μοιχαλὶς σημεῖον
generation An evil and adulterous a sign

ἐπιζητεῖ, καὶ σημεῖον οὐ δοθήσεται
seeks, and a sign shall not be given

αὐτῇ εἰ μὴ τὸ σημεῖον Ἰωνᾶ τοῦ
to it except the sign of Jonas the

προφήτου. **40** ὥσπερ γὰρ ἦν Ἰωνᾶς
prophet. For as was Jonas

ἐν τῇ κοιλίᾳ τοῦ κήτους τρεῖς ἡμέρας
in the belly of the sea monster three days

καὶ τρεῖς νύκτας, οὕτως ἔσται ὁ υἱὸς
and three nights, so will be the Son

τοῦ ἀνθρώπου ἐν τῇ καρδίᾳ τῆς γῆς
- of man in the heart of the earth

τρεῖς ἡμέρας καὶ τρεῖς νύκτας. **41** ἄνδρες
three days and three nights. Men

Νινευῖται ἀναστήσονται ἐν τῇ κρίσει
Ninevites will stand up in the judgment

μετὰ τῆς γενεᾶς ταύτης καὶ κατα-
with - generation this and will

κρινοῦσιν αὐτήν· ὅτι μετενόησαν εἰς τὸ
condemn it; because they repented at the

κήρυγμα Ἰωνᾶ, καὶ ἰδοὺ πλεῖον Ἰωνᾶ
proclamation of Jonas, and behold a greater thing [than] Jonas

ὧδε. **42** βασίλισσα νότου ἐγερθήσεται
[is] here. [The] queen of [the] south will be raised

ἐν τῇ κρίσει μετὰ τῆς γενεᾶς ταύτης
in the judgment with - generation this

καὶ κατακρινεῖ αὐτήν· ὅτι ἦλθεν ἐκ
and will condemn it; because she came out of

τῶν περάτων τῆς γῆς ἀκοῦσαι τὴν σοφίαν
the limits of the earth to hear the wisdom

Σολομῶνος, καὶ ἰδοὺ πλεῖον Σολομῶνος
of Solomon, and behold a greater thing [than] Solomon

ὧδε. **43** Ὅταν δὲ τὸ ἀκάθαρτον πνεῦμα
[is] here. Now when the unclean spirit

ἐξέλθῃ ἀπὸ τοῦ ἀνθρώπου, διέρχεται δι'
goes out from - a man, he goes through

ἀνύδρων τόπων ζητοῦν ἀνάπαυσιν, καὶ
dry places seeking rest, and

οὐχ εὑρίσκει. **44** τότε λέγει· εἰς τὸν
finds not. Then he says: Into the

οἶκόν μου ἐπιστρέψω ὅθεν ἐξῆλθον·
house of me I will return whence I came out;

καὶ ἐλθὸν εὑρίσκει σχολάζοντα [καὶ]
and coming he finds [it] standing empty and

σεσαρωμένον καὶ κεκοσμημένον. **45** τότε
having been swept and having been furnished. Then

πορεύεται καὶ παραλαμβάνει μεθ' ἑαυτοῦ
he goes and takes with himself

ἑπτὰ ἕτερα πνεύματα πονηρότερα ἑαυτοῦ,
seven other spirits more evil [than] himself,

καὶ εἰσελθόντα κατοικεῖ ἐκεῖ· καὶ
and entering dwells there; and

γίνεται τὰ ἔσχατα τοῦ ἀνθρώπου ἐκείνου
becomes the last things - man of that

χείρονα τῶν πρώτων. οὕτως ἔσται
worse [than] the first. Thus it will be

καὶ τῇ γενεᾷ ταύτῃ τῇ πονηρᾷ.
also - **'**generation **'**to this - **'**evil.

46 Ἔτι αὐτοῦ λαλοῦντος τοῖς ὄχλοις,
Yet him speaking**ª** to the crowds,
= While he was still speaking

ἰδοὺ ἡ μήτηρ καὶ οἱ ἀδελφοὶ αὐτοῦ
behold the mother and the brothers of him

εἱστήκεισαν ἔξω ζητοῦντες αὐτῷ λαλῆσαι.
stood outside seeking to him to speak.

47 [εἶπεν δέ τις αὐτῷ· ἰδοὺ ἡ μήτηρ
And said someone to him: Behold[,] the mother

σου καὶ οἱ ἀδελφοί σου ἔξω ἑστήκασιν
of thee and the brothers of thee outside are standing

ζητοῦντές σοι λαλῆσαι.] **48** ὁ δὲ
seeking to thee to speak.] And he

ἀποκριθεὶς εἶπεν τῷ λέγοντι αὐτῷ· τίς
answering said to the [one] saying to him: Who

ἐστιν ἡ μήτηρ μου, καὶ τίνες εἰσὶν οἱ
is the mother of me, and who are the

King James Version

is my mother? and who are my brethren? 49And he stretched forth his hand toward his disciples, and said, Behold my mother and my brethren! 50 For whosoever shall do the will of my Father which is in heaven, the same is my brother, and sister, and mother.

13 The same day went Jesus out of the house, and sat by the sea side. 2And great multitudes were gathered together unto him, so that he went into a ship, and sat; and the whole multitude stood on the shore. 3And he spake many things unto them in parables, saying, Behold, a sower went forth to sow; 4And when he sowed, some *seeds* fell by the way side, and the fowls came and devoured them up: 5 Some fell upon stony places, where they had not much earth: and forthwith they sprung up, because they had no deepness of earth: 6And when the sun was up, they were scorched; and because they had no root, they withered away. 7And some fell among thorns; and the thorns sprung up, and choked them: 8 But other fell into good ground, and brought forth fruit, some a hundredfold, some sixtyfold, some thirtyfold. 9 Who hath ears to hear, let him hear. 10And the disciples came, and said unto him, Why speakest thou unto them in parables? 11 He answered and said unto them, Because it is given unto you to know the mysteries of the kingdom of heaven, but to them it is not given. 12 For whosoever hath, to him shall be given, and he shall have more abundance: but whosoever hath not, from him shall be taken away even that he hath. 13 Therefore speak I to them in parables: because they seeing see not; and hearing they hear not, neither do they understand. 14And in them is fulfilled the prophecy of Esaias, which saith, By hearing ye shall hear, and shall not understand; and seeing ye shall see, and shall not perceive: 15 For this people's heart is waxed gross, and *their* ears are dull of hearing, and their eyes they have closed; lest at any time they should see with *their* eyes, and hear with *their* ears, and should understand with *their* heart, and should be converted, and I should heal them. 16 But blessed *are* your eyes, for they see: and your ears, for they hear. 17 For verily I say unto you, That many prophets and righteous *men* have desired to see *those things* which ye see, and have not seen *them;* and to hear *those things* which ye hear, and have not heard *them.* 18 Hear ye therefore the parable of the sower. 19 When any one heareth the word of the kingdom, and understandeth *it* not, then cometh the wicked one, and catcheth away that which was sown in his heart. This is he which received seed by the way side. 20 But he that received the

New International Version

are my brothers?" 49 Pointing to his disciples, he said, "Here are my mother and my brothers. 50 For whoever does the will of my Father in heaven is my brother and sister and mother."

The parable of the sower

13 That same day Jesus went out of the house and sat by the lake. 2 Such large crowds gathered around him that he got into a boat and sat in it, while all the people stood on the shore. 3 Then he told them many things in parables, saying: "A farmer went out to sow his seed. 4As he was scattering the seed, some fell along the path, and the birds came and ate it up. 5 Some fell on rocky places, where it did not have much soil. It sprang up quickly, because the soil was shallow. 6 But when the sun came up, the plants were scorched, and they withered because they had no root. 7 Other seed fell among thorns, which grew up and choked the plants. 8 Still other seed fell on good soil, where it produced a crop, a hundred, sixty or thirty times what was sown. 9 He who has ears, let him hear."

10 The disciples came to him and asked, "Why do you speak to the people in parables?"

11 He replied, "The knowledge of the secrets of the kingdom of heaven has been given to you, but not to them. 12 Whoever has will be given more, and he will have an abundance. Whoever does not have, even what he has will be taken from him. 13 This is why I speak to them in parables:

"Though seeing, they do not see;
    though hearing, they do not hear or understand.

14 In them is fulfilled the prophecy of Isaiah:

'You will be ever hearing but never understanding;
    you will be ever seeing but never perceiving.
15 For this people's heart has become calloused;
    they hardly hear with their ears,
    and they have closed their eyes.
Otherwise they might see with their eyes,
    hear with their ears,
    understand with their hearts
and turn, and I would heal them.' *s*

16 But blessed are your eyes because they see, and your ears because they hear. 17 For I tell you the truth, many prophets and righteous men longed to see what you see but did not see it, and to hear what you hear but did not hear it.

18 "Listen then to what the parable of the sower means: 19 When anyone hears the message about the kingdom and does not understand it, the evil one comes and snatches away what was sown in his heart. This is the seed sown along the path. 20 What was sown on rocky places is

Greek Interlinear

ἀδελφοί μου; **49** καὶ ἐκτείνας τὴν
brothers of me? And stretching forth the

χεῖρα [αὐτοῦ] ἐπὶ τοὺς μαθητὰς αὐτοῦ
hand of him on the disciples of him

εἶπεν· ἰδοὺ ἡ μήτηρ μου καὶ οἱ ἀδελφοί
he said: Behold[,] the mother of me and the brothers

μου. **50** ὅστις γὰρ ἂν ποιήσῃ τὸ θέλημα
of me. For whoever does the will

τοῦ πατρός μου τοῦ ἐν οὐρανοῖς, αὐτός
of the Father of me – in heavens, he

μου ἀδελφὸς καὶ ἀδελφὴ καὶ μήτηρ ἐστίν.
of me brother and sister and mother is.

Chapter 13

Ἐν τῇ ἡμέρᾳ ἐκείνῃ ἐξελθὼν ὁ
On – day that ²going out of –

Ἰησοῦς τῆς οἰκίας ἐκάθητο παρὰ τὴν
¹Jesus of the house sat beside the

θάλασσαν· **2** καὶ συνήχθησαν πρὸς αὐτὸν
sea; and were assembled to him

ὄχλοι πολλοί, ὥστε αὐτὸν εἰς πλοῖον
crowds many, so as him in a ship
= so that embarking in a ship he sat,

ἐμβάντα καθῆσθαι, καὶ πᾶς ὁ ὄχλος
embarking to sit[b], and all the crowd

ἐπὶ τὸν αἰγιαλὸν εἱστήκει. **3** καὶ ἐλάλησεν
on the beach stood. And he spoke

αὐτοῖς πολλὰ ἐν παραβολαῖς λέγων·
to them many things in parables saying:

Ἰδοὺ ἐξῆλθεν ὁ σπείρων τοῦ σπείρειν.
Behold went out the [one] sowing – to sow[d].

4 καὶ ἐν τῷ σπείρειν αὐτὸν ἃ μὲν
And in the to sow him[e] some indeed
= as he sowed

ἔπεσεν παρὰ τὴν ὁδόν, καὶ ἐλθόντα τὰ
fell beside the way, and coming the

πετεινὰ κατέφαγεν αὐτά. **5** ἄλλα δὲ
birds devoured them. But others

ἔπεσεν ἐπὶ τὰ πετρώδη ὅπου οὐκ
fell on the rocky places where not

εἶχεν γῆν πολλήν, καὶ εὐθέως ἐξανέτειλεν
it had earth much, and immediately it sprang up

διὰ τὸ μὴ ἔχειν βάθος γῆς· **6** ἡλίου
on account of the not to have depth of earth; [the] sun
= because it had not

δὲ ἀνατείλαντος ἐκαυματίσθη, καὶ διὰ
But having risen[a] it was scorched, and on account of
= when the sun rose ~ because

τὸ μὴ ἔχειν ῥίζαν ἐξηράνθη. **7** ἄλλα δὲ
the not to have root it was dried up. But others
it had not

ἔπεσεν ἐπὶ τὰς ἀκάνθας, καὶ ἀνέβησαν
fell on the thorns, and came up

αἱ ἄκανθαι καὶ ἀπέπνιξαν αὐτά. **8** ἄλλα δὲ
the thorns and choked them. And others

ἔπεσεν ἐπὶ τὴν γῆν τὴν καλὴν καὶ
fell on the earth – good and

ἐδίδου καρπόν, ὃ μὲν ἑκατόν, ὃ δὲ
gave fruit, the one a hundred, the other

ἑξήκοντα, ὃ δὲ τριάκοντα. **9** ὁ ἔχων
sixty, the other thirty. The [one] having

ὦτα ἀκουέτω. **10** Καὶ προσελθόντες οἱ
ears let him hear. And approaching the

μαθηταὶ εἶπαν αὐτῷ· διὰ τί ἐν παρα-
disciples said to him: Why in par-

βολαῖς λαλεῖς αὐτοῖς; **11** ὁ δὲ
ables speakest thou to them? And he

ἀποκριθεὶς εἶπεν· ὅτι ὑμῖν δέδοται
answering said: Because to you it has been given

γνῶναι τὰ μυστήρια τῆς βασιλείας τῶν
to know the mysteries of the kingdom of the

οὐρανῶν, ἐκείνοις δὲ οὐ δέδοται. **12** ὅστις
heavens, but to those it has not been given. [he] who

γὰρ ἔχει, δοθήσεται αὐτῷ καὶ περισ-
For has, it will be given to him and he will

σευθήσεται· ὅστις δὲ οὐκ ἔχει, καὶ
have abundance; but [he] who has not, even

ὃ ἔχει ἀρθήσεται ἀπ᾽ αὐτοῦ. **13** διὰ
what he has will be taken from him. There-

τοῦτο ἐν παραβολαῖς αὐτοῖς λαλῶ, ὅτι
fore in parables to them I speak, because

βλέποντες οὐ βλέπουσιν καὶ ἀκούοντες
seeing they see not and hearing

οὐκ ἀκούουσιν οὐδὲ συνιοῦσιν. **14** καὶ
they hear not neither understand. And

ἀναπληροῦται αὐτοῖς ἡ προφητεία Ἠσαΐου
is fulfilled in them the prophecy of Isaiah

ἡ λέγουσα· ἀκοῇ ἀκούσετε καὶ οὐ μὴ
– saying: In hearing ye will hear and by no means

συνῆτε, καὶ βλέποντες βλέψετε
understand, and seeing ye will see

καὶ οὐ μὴ ἴδητε. **15** ἐπαχύνθη γὰρ
and by no means perceive. For waxed gross

ἡ καρδία τοῦ λαοῦ τούτου, καὶ τοῖς
the heart – people of this, and with the

ὠσὶν βαρέως ἤκουσαν, καὶ τοὺς ὀφθαλμοὺς
ears heavily they heard, and the eyes

αὐτῶν ἐκάμμυσαν· μήποτε ἴδωσιν τοῖς
of them they closed; lest they see with the

ὀφθαλμοῖς καὶ τοῖς ὠσὶν ἀκούσωσιν
eyes and with the ears hear

καὶ τῇ καρδίᾳ συνῶσιν καὶ ἐπιστρέψωσιν,
and with the heart understand and turn back,

καὶ ἰάσομαι αὐτούς. **16** ὑμῶν δὲ μακάριοι
and I will heal them. But of you blessed

οἱ ὀφθαλμοὶ ὅτι βλέπουσιν, καὶ τὰ
the eyes because they see, and the

ὦτα [ὑμῶν] ὅτι ἀκούουσιν. **17** ἀμὴν
ears of you because they hear. truly

γὰρ λέγω ὑμῖν ὅτι πολλοὶ προφῆται καὶ
For I say to you that many prophets and

δίκαιοι ἐπεθύμησαν ἰδεῖν ἃ
righteous men desired to see [the things] which

βλέπετε καὶ οὐκ εἶδαν, καὶ ἀκοῦσαι
ye see and did not see, and to hear

ἃ ἀκούετε καὶ οὐκ ἤκουσαν.
[the things] which ye hear and did not hear.

18 Ὑμεῖς οὖν ἀκούσατε τὴν παραβολὴν
²Ye ³therefore ¹hear the parable

τοῦ σπείραντος. **19** Παντὸς ἀκούοντος
of the sowing [one]. Everyone hearing[a]
= When anyone hears

τὸν λόγον τῆς βασιλείας καὶ μὴ συνιέντος
the word of the kingdom and not understanding[a]
= does not understand

ἔρχεται ὁ πονηρὸς καὶ ἁρπάζει τὸ
comes the evil one and seizes the [thing]

ἐσπαρμένον ἐν τῇ καρδίᾳ αὐτοῦ· οὗτός
having been sown in the heart of him; this

ἐστιν ὁ παρὰ τὴν ὁδὸν σπαρείς. **20** ὁ
is the [word] by the way sown. the [word]

41

King James Version

seed into stony places, the same is he that heareth the word, and anon with joy receiveth it; 21 Yet hath he not root in himself, but dureth for a while: for when tribulation or persecution ariseth because of the word, by and by he is offended. 22 He also that received seed among the thorns is he that heareth the word; and the care of this world, and the deceitfulness of riches, choke the word, and he becometh unfruitful. 23 But he that received seed into the good ground is he that heareth the word, and understandeth *it;* which also beareth fruit, and bringeth forth, some a hundredfold, some sixty, some thirty.

24 Another parable put he forth unto them, saying, The kingdom of heaven is likened unto a man which sowed good seed in his field: 25 But while men slept, his enemy came and sowed tares among the wheat, and went his way. 26 But when the blade was sprung up, and brought forth fruit, then appeared the tares also. 27 So the servants of the householder came and said unto him, Sir, didst not thou sow good seed in thy field? from whence then hath it tares? 28 He said unto them, An enemy hath done this. The servants said unto him, Wilt thou then that we go and gather them up? 29 But he said, Nay; lest while ye gather up the tares, ye root up also the wheat with them. 30 Let both grow together until the harvest: and in the time of harvest I will say to the reapers, Gather ye together first the tares, and bind them in bundles to burn them: but gather the wheat into my barn.

31 Another parable put he forth unto them, saying, The kingdom of heaven is like to a grain of mustard seed, which a man took, and sowed in his field: 32 Which indeed is the least of all seeds: but when it is grown, it is the greatest among herbs, and becometh a tree, so that the birds of the air come and lodge in the branches thereof.

33 Another parable spake he unto them; The kingdom of heaven is like unto leaven, which a woman took, and hid in three measures of meal, till the whole was leavened. 34 All these things spake Jesus unto the multitude in parables; and without a parable spake he not unto them: 35 That it might be fulfilled which was spoken by the prophet, saying, I will open my mouth in parables; I will utter things which have been kept secret from the foundation of the world. 36 Then Jesus sent the multitude away, and went into the house: and his disciples came unto him, saying, Declare unto us the parable of the tares of the field. 37 He answered and said unto them, He that soweth the good seed is the Son of man; 38 The field is the world; the good seed are the children of the kingdom; but the tares are the children of the wicked one; 39 The enemy that

New International Version

the man who hears the word and at once receives it with joy. 21 But since he has no root, he lasts only a short time. When trouble or persecution comes because of the word, he quickly falls away. 22 What was sown among the thorns is the man who hears the word, but the worries of this life and the deceitfulness of wealth choke it, making it unfruitful. 23 But what was sown on good soil is the man who hears the word and understands it. He produces a crop, yielding a hundred, sixty or thirty times what was sown."

The parable of the weeds

24 Jesus told them another parable: "The kingdom of heaven is like a man who sowed good seed in his field. 25 But while everyone was sleeping, his enemy came and sowed weeds among the wheat, and went away. 26 When the wheat sprouted and formed heads, then the weeds also appeared.

27 "The owner's servants came to him and said, 'Sir, didn't you sow good seed in your field? Where then did the weeds come from?'

28 " 'An enemy did this,' he replied.

"The servants asked him, 'Do you want us to go and pull them up?'

29 " 'No,' he answered, 'because while you are pulling the weeds, you may root up the wheat with them. 30 Let both grow together until the harvest. At that time I will tell the harvesters: First collect the weeds and tie them in bundles to be burned, then gather the wheat and bring it into my barn.' "

The parables of the mustard seed and the yeast

31 He told them another parable: "The kingdom of heaven is like a mustard seed, which a man took and planted in his field. 32 Though it is the smallest of all your seeds, yet when it grows, it is the largest of garden plants and becomes a tree, so that the birds of the air come and perch in its branches."

33 He told them still another parable: "The kingdom of heaven is like yeast that a woman took and mixed into a large amount[t] of flour until it worked all through the dough."

34 Jesus spoke all these things to the crowd in parables, and he did not say anything to them without using a parable. 35 So was fulfilled what was spoken through the prophet:

"I will open my mouth in parables;
　I will utter things hidden since the creation
　　of the world."[u]

The parable of the weeds explained

36 Then he left the crowd and went into the house. His disciples came to him and said, "Explain to us the parable of the weeds in the field."

37 He answered, "The one who sowed the good seed is the Son of Man. 38 The field is the world, and the good seed stands for the sons of the kingdom. The weeds are the sons of the evil one, 39 and the enemy who sows them is the

---

[t] Greek *Three satas* (about a bushel.) [u] Psalm 78:2.

Greek Interlinear

δὲ ἐπὶ τὰ πετρώδη σπαρείς, οὗτός ἐστιν
And on the rocky places sown, this is

ὁ τὸν λόγον ἀκούων καὶ εὐθὺς μετὰ
the [one] ⁴the ³word ¹hearing and immediately with

χαρᾶς λαμβάνων αὐτόν· 21 οὐκ ἔχει δὲ
joy receiving it; but he has not

ῥίζαν ἐν ἑαυτῷ ἀλλὰ πρόσκαιρός ἐστιν,
root in himself but short-lived is,

γενομένης δὲ θλίψεως ἢ διωγμοῦ
and occurring tribulation or persecution³
= when tribulation or persecution occurs

διὰ τὸν λόγον εὐθὺς σκανδαλίζεται.
on account of the word immediately he is offended.

22 ὁ δὲ εἰς τὰς ἀκάνθας σπαρείς, οὗτός
But the [word] in the thorns sown, this

ἐστιν ὁ τὸν λόγον ἀκούων, καὶ ἡ
is the [one] ²the ³word ¹hearing, and the

μέριμνα τοῦ αἰῶνος καὶ ἡ ἀπάτη
anxiety of the age and the deceit

τοῦ πλούτου συμπνίγει τὸν λόγον, καὶ
— of riches chokes the word, and

ἄκαρπος γίνεται. 23 ὁ δὲ ἐπὶ τὴν
unfruitful it becomes. And the [word] on the

καλὴν γῆν σπαρείς, οὗτός ἐστιν ὁ
good earth sown, this is the [one]

τὸν λόγον ἀκούων καὶ συνιείς, ὃς
⁴the ⁵word ¹hearing ²and ³understanding, who

δὴ καρποφορεῖ καὶ ποιεῖ ὁ μὲν ἑκατόν,
indeed bears fruit and produces one indeed a hundred,

ὁ δὲ ἑξήκοντα, ὁ δὲ τριάκοντα.
the other sixty, the other thirty.

24 Ἄλλην παραβολὴν παρέθηκεν αὐτοῖς
Another parable he set before them

λέγων· ὡμοιώθη ἡ βασιλεία τῶν
saying: was(is) likened The kingdom of the

οὐρανῶν ἀνθρώπῳ σπείραντι καλὸν σπέρμα
heavens to a man sowing good seed

ἐν τῷ ἀγρῷ αὐτοῦ. 25 ἐν δὲ τῷ
in the field of him. But in the
= while men slept

καθεύδειν τοὺς ἀνθρώπους ἦλθεν αὐτοῦ
to sleep - men* came of him

ὁ ἐχθρὸς καὶ ἐπέσπειρεν ζιζάνια ἀνὰ μέσον
the enemy and oversowed tares in between

τοῦ σίτου καὶ ἀπῆλθεν. 26 ὅτε δὲ
the wheat and went away. But when

ἐβλάστησεν ὁ χόρτος καὶ καρπὸν
sprouted the grass and fruit

ἐποίησεν, τότε ἐφάνη καὶ τὰ ζιζάνια.
produced, then appeared also the tares.

27 προσελθόντες δὲ οἱ δοῦλοι τοῦ οἰκο-
So approaching the slaves of the house-

δεσπότου εἶπον αὐτῷ· κύριε, οὐχὶ καλὸν
master said to him: Lord, not good

σπέρμα ἔσπειρας ἐν τῷ σῷ ἀγρῷ;
seed sowedst thou in - thy field?

πόθεν οὖν ἔχει ζιζάνια; 28 ὁ δὲ ἔφη
whence then has it tares? And he said

αὐτοῖς· ἐχθρὸς ἄνθρωπος τοῦτο ἐποίησεν.
to them: An enemy man this did.

οἱ δὲ δοῦλοι αὐτῷ λέγουσιν· θέλεις
So the slaves to him say· Willest thou

οὖν ἀπελθόντες συλλέξωμεν αὐτά; 29 ὁ
then going away we may collect them? he

δέ φησιν· οὔ, μήποτε συλλέγοντες τὰ
But says: No, lest collecting the

ζιζάνια ἐκριζώσητε ἅμα αὐτοῖς τὸν
tares ye should root up together with them the

σῖτον. 30 ἄφετε συναυξάνεσθαι ἀμφότερα
wheat. Leave to grow together both

ἕως τοῦ θερισμοῦ· καὶ ἐν καιρῷ τοῦ
until the harvest; and in time of the

θερισμοῦ ἐρῶ τοῖς θερισταῖς· συλλέξατε
harvest I will say to the reapers: Collect ye

πρῶτον τὰ ζιζάνια καὶ δήσατε αὐτὰ
first the tares and bind them

εἰς δέσμας πρὸς τὸ κατακαῦσαι αὐτά,
in bundles - - to burn them,

τὸν δὲ σῖτον συναγάγετε εἰς τὴν ἀποθήκην
but the wheat gather ye into the barn

μου. 31 Ἄλλην παραβολὴν παρέθηκεν
of me. Another parable he set before

αὐτοῖς λέγων· ὁμοία ἐστὶν ἡ βασιλεία
them saying: Like is the kingdom

τῶν οὐρανῶν κόκκῳ σινάπεως, ὃν
of the heavens to a grain of mustard, which

λαβὼν ἄνθρωπος ἔσπειρεν ἐν τῷ ἀγρῷ
⁴taking ¹a man sowed in the field

αὐτοῦ· 32 ὃ μικρότερον μὲν ἐστὶ
of him; which less indeed is

πάντων τῶν σπερμάτων, ὅταν δὲ
[than] all the seeds, but when

αὐξηθῇ, μεῖζον τῶν λαχάνων ἐστὶν
it grows, greater [than] the herbs it is

καὶ γίνεται δένδρον, ὥστε ἐλθεῖν τὰ
and becomes a tree, so as to come the

πετεινὰ τοῦ οὐρανοῦ καὶ κατασκηνοῦν
birds of the heaven and dwell

ἐν τοῖς κλάδοις αὐτοῦ. 33 Ἄλλην
in the branches of it. Another

παραβολὴν ἐλάλησεν αὐτοῖς· ὁμοία
parable he spoke to them: Like

ἐστὶν ἡ βασιλεία τῶν οὐρανῶν ζύμῃ,
is the kingdom of the heavens to leaven,

ἣν λαβοῦσα γυνὴ ἐνέκρυψεν εἰς ἀλεύρου
which ²taking ¹a woman hid in ³of meal

σάτα τρία, ἕως οὗ ἐζυμώθη ὅλον.
²measures ¹three, until was leavened [the] whole.

34 Ταῦτα πάντα ἐλάλησεν ὁ Ἰησοῦς ἐν
These things all spoke - Jesus in

παραβολαῖς τοῖς ὄχλοις, καὶ χωρὶς παραβολῆς
parables to the crowds, and without a parable

οὐδὲν ἐλάλει αὐτοῖς· 35 ὅπως πληρωθῇ
nothing he spoke to them; so that was fulfilled

τὸ ῥηθὲν διὰ τοῦ προφήτου λέγοντος·
the [thing] spoken through the prophet saying:

ἀνοίξω ἐν παραβολαῖς τὸ στόμα μου,
I will open in parables the mouth of me,

ἐρεύξομαι κεκρυμμένα ἀπὸ καταβολῆς.
I will utter things having been hidden from [the] foundation.

36 Τότε ἀφεὶς τοὺς ὄχλους ἦλθεν
Then sending away the crowds he came

εἰς τὴν οἰκίαν. Καὶ προσῆλθον αὐτῷ
into the house. And approached to him

οἱ μαθηταὶ αὐτοῦ λέγοντες· διασάφησον
the disciples of him saying: Explain thou

ἡμῖν τὴν παραβολὴν τῶν ζιζανίων τοῦ
to us the parable of the tares of the

ἀγροῦ. 37 ὁ δὲ ἀποκριθεὶς εἶπεν· ὁ
field. And he answering said: The [one]

σπείρων τὸ καλὸν σπέρμα ἐστὶν ὁ
sowing the good seed is the

υἱὸς τοῦ ἀνθρώπου· 38 ὁ δὲ ἀγρός
Son of man; and the field

ἐστιν ὁ κόσμος· τὸ δὲ καλὸν σπέρμα,
is the world; and the good seed,

οὗτοί εἰσιν οἱ υἱοὶ τῆς βασιλείας· τὰ δὲ
these are the sons of the kingdom; and the

ζιζάνιά εἰσιν οἱ υἱοὶ τοῦ πονηροῦ, 39 ὁ
tares are the sons of the evil [one], the

King James Version

sowed them is the devil; the harvest is the end of the world; and the reapers are the angels. 40As therefore the tares are gathered and burned in the fire; so shall it be in the end of this world. 41 The Son of man shall send forth his angels, and they shall gather out of his kingdom all things that offend, and them which do iniquity; 42And shall cast them into a furnace of fire: there shall be wailing and gnashing of teeth. 43 Then shall the righteous shine forth as the sun in the kingdom of their Father. Who hath ears to hear, let him hear.

44 Again, the kingdom of heaven is like unto treasure hid in a field; the which when a man hath found, he hideth, and for joy thereof goeth and selleth all that he hath, and buyeth that field.

45 Again, the kingdom of heaven is like unto a merchantman, seeking goodly pearls: 46 Who, when he had found one pearl of great price, went and sold all that he had, and bought it:

47 Again, the kingdom of heaven is like unto a net, that was cast into the sea, and gathered of every kind: 48 Which, when it was full, they drew to shore, and sat down, and gathered the good into vessels, but cast the bad away. 49 So shall it be at the end of the world: the angels shall come forth, and sever the wicked from among the just, 50And shall cast them into the furnace of fire: there shall be wailing and gnashing of teeth. 51 Jesus saith unto them, Have ye understood all these things? They say unto him, Yea, Lord. 52 Then said he unto them, Therefore every scribe *which is* instructed unto the kingdom of heaven, is like unto a man *that is* a householder, which bringeth forth out of his treasure *things* new and old.

53 And it came to pass, *that* when Jesus had finished these parables, he departed thence. 54And when he was come into his own country, he taught them in their synagogue, insomuch that they were astonished, and said, Whence hath this *man* this wisdom, and *these* mighty works? 55 Is not this the carpenter's son? is not his mother called Mary? and his brethren, James, and Joses, and Simon, and Judas? 56And his sisters, are they not all with us? Whence then hath this *man* all these things? 57And they were offended in him. But Jesus said unto them, A prophet is not without honour, save in his own country, and in his own house. 58And he did not many mighty works there because of their unbelief.

New International Version

devil. The harvest is the end of the age, and the harvesters are angels.

40 "As the weeds are pulled up and burned in the fire, so it will be at the end of the age. 41 The Son of Man will send out his angels, and they will weed out of his kingdom everything that causes sin and all who do evil. 42 They will throw them into the fiery furnace, where there will be weeping and grinding of teeth. 43 Then the righteous will shine like the sun in the kingdom of their Father. He who has ears, let him hear.

The parables of the hidden treasure and the pearl

44 "The kingdom of heaven is like treasure hidden in a field. When a man found it, he hid it again, and then in his joy went and sold all he had and bought that field.

45 "Again, the kingdom of heaven is like a merchant looking for fine pearls. 46 When he found one of great value, he went away and sold everything he had and bought it.

The parable of the net

47 "Once again, the kingdom of heaven is like a net that was let down into the lake and caught all kinds of fish. 48 When it was full, the fishermen pulled it up on the shore. Then they sat down and collected the good fish in baskets, but threw the bad away. 49 This is how it will be at the end of the age. The angels will come and separate the wicked from the righteous 50 and throw them into the fiery furnace, where there will be weeping and grinding of teeth."

51 "Have you understood all these things?" Jesus asked.

"Yes," they replied.

52 He said to them, "Therefore every teacher of the law who has been instructed about the kingdom of heaven is like the owner of a house who brings out of his storeroom new treasures as well as old."

A prophet without honor

53 When Jesus had finished these parables, he moved on from there. 54 Coming to his home town, he began teaching the people in their synagogue, and they were amazed. "Where did this man get this wisdom and these miraculous powers?" they asked. 55 "Isn't this the carpenter's son? Isn't his mother's name Mary, and aren't his brothers James, Joseph, Simon and Judas? 56 Aren't all his sisters with us? Where then did this man get all these things?" 57And they took offense at him.

But Jesus said to them, "Only in his home town and in his own house is a prophet without honor."

58 And he did not do many miracles there because of their lack of faith.

Greek Interlinear

δὲ ἐχθρὸς ὁ σπείρας αὐτά ἐστιν ὁ
and enemy the [one] sowing them is the

διάβολος· ὁ δὲ θερισμὸς συντέλεια
devil; and the harvest [the] completion

αἰῶνός ἐστιν, οἱ δὲ θερισταὶ ἄγγελοί
of [the] age is, and the reapers angels

εἰσιν. **40** ὥσπερ οὖν συλλέγεται τὰ
are. As therefore are collected the

ζιζάνια καὶ πυρὶ κατακαίεται, οὕτως
tares and with fire are consumed, thus

ἔσται ἐν τῇ συντελείᾳ τοῦ αἰῶνος·
it will be at the completion of the age;

41 ἀποστελεῖ ὁ υἱὸς τοῦ ἀνθρώπου
will send forth the Son - of man

τοὺς ἀγγέλους αὐτοῦ, καὶ συλλέξουσιν
the angels of him, and they will collect

ἐκ τῆς βασιλείας αὐτοῦ πάντα
out of the kingdom of him all

τὰ σκάνδαλα καὶ τοὺς ποιοῦντας
the things leading to sin and the [ones] doing

τὴν ἀνομίαν, **42** καὶ βαλοῦσιν αὐτοὺς εἰς
- lawlessness, and will cast them into

τὴν κάμινον τοῦ πυρός· ἐκεῖ ἔσται ὁ
the furnace - of fire; there will be the

κλαυθμὸς καὶ ὁ βρυγμὸς τῶν ὀδόντων.
wailing and the gnashing of the teeth.

43 τότε οἱ δίκαιοι ἐκλάμψουσιν ὡς ὁ
Then the righteous will shine forth as the

ἥλιος ἐν τῇ βασιλείᾳ τοῦ πατρὸς
sun in the kingdom of the Father

αὐτῶν. ὁ ἔχων ὦτα ἀκουέτω.
of them. The [one] having ears let him hear.

44 Ὁμοία ἐστὶν ἡ βασιλεία τῶν
Like is the kingdom of the

οὐρανῶν θησαυρῷ κεκρυμμένῳ ἐν τῷ
heavens to treasure having been hidden in the

ἀγρῷ, ὃν εὑρὼν ἄνθρωπος ἔκρυψεν, καὶ
field, which ²finding ¹a man hid, and

ἀπὸ τῆς χαρᾶς αὐτοῦ ὑπάγει καὶ πωλεῖ
from the joy of him goes and sells

ὅσα ἔχει καὶ ἀγοράζει τὸν ἀγρὸν
what things he has and buys the field

ἐκεῖνον. **45** Πάλιν ὁμοία ἐστὶν ἡ
that. Again like is the

βασιλεία τῶν οὐρανῶν ἐμπόρῳ ζητοῦντι
kingdom of the heavens to a merchant seeking

καλοὺς μαργαρίτας· **46** εὑρὼν δὲ ἕνα πολύτιμον
beautiful pearls; and finding one valuable

μαργαρίτην ἀπελθὼν πέπρακεν πάντα
pearl going away sold all things

ὅσα εἶχεν καὶ ἠγόρασεν αὐτόν.
what he had and bought it.

47 Πάλιν ὁμοία ἐστὶν ἡ βασιλεία τῶν
Again like is the kingdom of the

οὐρανῶν σαγήνῃ βληθείσῃ εἰς τὴν θάλασσαν
heavens to a net cast into the sea

καὶ ἐκ παντὸς γένους συναγαγούσῃ·
and of every kind gathering;

48 ἣν ὅτε ἐπληρώθη ἀναβιβάσαντες ἐπὶ
which when it was filled bringing up onto

τὸν αἰγιαλὸν καὶ καθίσαντες συνέλεξαν
the shore and sitting collected

τὰ καλὰ εἰς ἄγγη, τὰ δὲ σαπρὰ ἔξω
the good into vessels, but the bad out

ἔβαλον. **49** οὕτως ἔσται ἐν τῇ συντελείᾳ
cast. Thus it will be at the completion

τοῦ αἰῶνος· ἐξελεύσονται οἱ ἄγγελοι καὶ
of the age: will go forth the angels and

ἀφοριοῦσιν τοὺς πονηροὺς ἐκ μέσου
will separate the evil men from [the] midst

τῶν δικαίων, **50** καὶ βαλοῦσιν αὐτοὺς
of the righteous, and will cast them

εἰς τὴν κάμινον τοῦ πυρός· ἐκεῖ
into the furnace - of fire; there

ἔσται ὁ κλαυθμὸς καὶ ὁ βρυγμὸς τῶν
will be the wailing and the gnashing of the

ὀδόντων. **51** Συνήκατε ταῦτα πάντα;
teeth. Did ye understand ²these things ¹all?

λέγουσιν αὐτῷ· ναί. **52** ὁ δὲ εἶπεν
They say to him: Yes. So he said

αὐτοῖς· διὰ τοῦτο πᾶς γραμματεὺς
to them: Therefore every scribe

μαθητευθεὶς τῇ βασιλείᾳ τῶν οὐρανῶν
made a disciple to the kingdom of the heavens

ὅμοιός ἐστιν ἀνθρώπῳ οἰκοδεσπότῃ,
like is to a man a housemaster,

ὅστις ἐκβάλλει ἐκ τοῦ θησαυροῦ
who puts forth out of the treasure

αὐτοῦ καινὰ καὶ παλαιά.
of him new and old things.

53 Καὶ ἐγένετο ὅτε ἐτέλεσεν ὁ
And it came to pass when ended -

Ἰησοῦς τὰς παραβολὰς ταύτας, μετῆρεν
Jesus - parables these, he removed

ἐκεῖθεν. **54** καὶ ἐλθὼν εἰς τὴν πατρίδα
thence. And coming into the native town

αὐτοῦ ἐδίδασκεν αὐτοὺς ἐν τῇ συνα-
of him he taught them in the syna-

γωγῇ αὐτῶν, ὥστε ἐκπλήσσεσθαι αὐτοὺς
gogue of them, so as to be astounded them
= so that they were astounded

καὶ λέγειν· πόθεν τούτῳ ἡ σοφία αὕτη
and to say[b]: Whence to this man - wisdom this
and said:

καὶ αἱ δυνάμεις; **55** οὐχ οὗτός ἐστιν
and the powerful deeds? not this man is

ὁ τοῦ τέκτονος υἱός; οὐχ ἡ μήτηρ
the of the carpenter son? not the mother

αὐτοῦ λέγεται Μαριὰμ καὶ οἱ ἀδελφοὶ
of him called Mary and the brothers

αὐτοῦ Ἰάκωβος καὶ Ἰωσὴφ καὶ Σίμων
of him James and Joseph and Simon

καὶ Ἰούδας; **56** καὶ αἱ ἀδελφαὶ αὐτοῦ
and Judas? and the sisters of him

οὐχὶ πᾶσαι πρὸς ἡμᾶς εἰσιν; πόθεν
not all with us are? Whence

οὖν τούτῳ ταῦτα πάντα; **57** καὶ
then to this man these things all? And

ἐσκανδαλίζοντο ἐν αὐτῷ. ὁ δὲ Ἰησοῦς
they were offended in him. - But Jesus

εἶπεν αὐτοῖς· οὐκ ἔστιν προφήτης
said to them: ²not ¹is ¹A prophet

ἄτιμος εἰ μὴ ἐν τῇ πατρίδι καὶ
unhonoured except in the (his) native town and

ἐν τῇ οἰκίᾳ αὐτοῦ. **58** καὶ οὐκ ἐποίησεν ἐκεῖ
in the house of him. And not he did there

δυνάμεις πολλὰς διὰ τὴν ἀπιστίαν αὐτῶν.
powerful deeds many because of the unbelief of them.

45

King James Version

14 At that time Herod the tetrarch heard of the fame of Jesus, 2And said unto his servants, This is John the Baptist; he is risen from the dead; and therefore mighty works do shew forth themselves in him.

3 For Herod had laid hold on John, and bound him, and put *him* in prison for Herodias' sake, his brother Philip's wife. 4 For John said unto him, It is not lawful for thee to have her. 5And when he would have put him to death, he feared the multitude, because they counted him as a prophet. 6 But when Herod's birthday was kept, the daughter of Herodias danced before them, and pleased Herod. 7 Whereupon he promised with an oath to give her whatsoever she would ask. 8And she, being before instructed of her mother, said, Give me here John Baptist's head in a charger. 9And the king was sorry: nevertheless for the oath's sake, and them which sat with him at meat, he commanded *it* to be given *her.* 10And he sent, and beheaded John in the prison. 11And his head was brought in a charger, and given to the damsel: and she brought *it* to her mother. 12And his disciples came, and took up the body, and buried it, and went and told Jesus.

13 When Jesus heard *of it*, he departed thence by ship into a desert place apart: and when the people had heard *thereof*, they followed him on foot out of the cities. 14And Jesus went forth, and saw a great multitude, and was moved with compassion toward them, and he healed their sick.

15 And when it was evening, his disciples came to him, saying, This is a desert place, and the time is now past; send the multitude away, that they may go into the villages, and buy themselves victuals. 16 But Jesus said unto them, They need not depart; give ye them to eat. 17And they say unto him, We have here but five loaves, and two fishes. 18 He said, Bring them hither to me. 19And he commanded the multitude to sit down on the grass, and took the five loaves, and the two fishes, and looking up to heaven, he blessed, and brake, and gave the loaves to *his* disciples, and the disciples to the multitude. 20And they did all eat, and were filled: and they took up of the fragments that remained twelve baskets full. 21And they that had eaten were about five thousand men, beside women and children.

22 And straightway Jesus constrained his disciples to get into a ship, and to go before him unto the other side, while he sent the multitudes away. 23And when he had sent the multitudes away, he went up into a mountain apart to pray: and when the evening was come, he was there alone. 24 But the ship was now in the midst of

New International Version

John the Baptist beheaded

14 At that time Herod the tetrarch heard the reports about Jesus, 2 and he said to his attendants, "This is John the Baptist; he has risen from the dead! That is why miraculous powers are at work in him."

3 Now Herod had arrested John and bound him and put him in prison because of Herodias, his brother Philip's wife, 4 for John had been saying to him: "It is not lawful for you to have her." 5 Herod wanted to kill John, but he was afraid of the people, because they considered him a prophet.

6 On Herod's birthday the daughter of Herodias danced for them and pleased Herod so much 7 that he promised with an oath to give her whatever she asked. 8 Prompted by her mother, she said, "Give me here on a platter the head of John the Baptist." 9 The king was distressed, but because of his oaths and his dinner guests, he ordered that her request be granted 10 and had John beheaded in the prison. 11 His head was brought in on a platter and given to the girl, who carried it to her mother. 12 John's disciples came and took his body and buried it. Then they went and told Jesus.

Jesus feeds the five thousand

13 When Jesus heard what had happened, he withdrew by boat privately to a solitary place. Hearing of this, the crowds followed him on foot from the towns. 14 When Jesus landed and saw a large crowd, he had compassion on them and healed their sick.

15 As evening approached, the disciples came to him and said, "This is a remote place, and it's already getting late. Send the crowds away, so they can go to the villages and buy themselves some food."

16 Jesus replied, "They do not need to go away. You give them something to eat."

17 "We have here only five loaves of bread and two fish," they answered.

18 "Bring them here to me," he said. 19And he directed the people to sit down on the grass. Taking the five loaves and the two fish and looking up to heaven, he gave thanks and broke the loaves. Then he gave them to the disciples, and the disciples gave them to the people. 20 They all ate and were satisfied, and the disciples picked up twelve basketfuls of broken pieces that were left over. 21 The number of those who ate was about five thousand men, besides women and children.

Jesus walks on the water

22 Immediately Jesus made the disciples get into the boat and go on ahead of him to the other side, while he dismissed the crowd. 23After he had dismissed them, he went up into the hills by himself to pray. When evening came, he was there alone, 24 but the boat was already a con-

Greek Interlinear

Chapter 14

Ἐν   ἐκείνῳ   τῷ   καιρῷ   ἤκουσεν
At   that   -   time   heard

Ἡρώδης   ὁ   τετραάρχης   τὴν   ἀκοὴν   Ἰησοῦ,
Herod   the   tetrarch   the   report   of Jesus,

2 καὶ   εἶπεν   τοῖς   παισὶν   αὐτοῦ·   οὗτός
and   said   to the   servants   of him: This

ἐστιν   Ἰωάννης   ὁ   βαπτιστής·   αὐτὸς
is   John   the   Baptist;   he

ἠγέρθη   ἀπὸ   τῶν   νεκρῶν,   καὶ   διὰ   τοῦτο
was raised   from   the   dead,   and   therefore

αἱ   δυνάμεις   ἐνεργοῦσιν   ἐν   αὐτῷ.
the   powerful deeds   operate   in   him.

3 Ὁ   γὰρ   Ἡρώδης   κρατήσας   τὸν   Ἰωάννην
-   For   Herod   seizing   -   John

ἔδησεν   καὶ   ἐν   φυλακῇ   ἀπέθετο   διὰ
bound   and   in   prison   put away   on account of

Ἡρωδιάδα   τὴν   γυναῖκα   Φιλίππου   τοῦ
Herodias   the   wife   of Philip   the

ἀδελφοῦ   αὐτοῦ·   4 ἔλεγεν   γὰρ   ὁ   Ἰωάννης
brother   of him;   for said   -   John

αὐτῷ·   οὐκ   ἔξεστίν   σοι   ἔχειν   αὐτήν.
to him: It is not lawful   for thee   to have   her.

5 καὶ   θέλων   αὐτὸν   ἀποκτεῖναι   ἐφοβήθη
And   wishing   him   to kill   he feared

τὸν   ὄχλον,   ὅτι   ὡς   προφήτην   αὐτὸν
the   crowd,   because   as   a prophet   him

εἶχον.   6 γενεσίοις   δὲ   γενομένοις   τοῦ
they had.   Now on the birthday   occurring   -

Ἡρώδου   ὠρχήσατο   ἡ   θυγάτηρ   τῆς
of Herod   danced   the   daughter   -

Ἡρωδιάδος   ἐν   τῷ   μέσῳ   καὶ   ἤρεσεν
of Herodias   in   the   midst   and   pleased

τῷ   Ἡρώδῃ,   7 ὅθεν   μεθ'   ὅρκου   ὡμολόγησεν
-   Herod,   whence   with   an oath   he promised

αὐτῇ   δοῦναι   ὃ   ἐὰν   αἰτήσηται.   8 ἡ   δὲ
her   to give   whatever   she might ask.   So she

προβιβασθεῖσα   ὑπὸ   τῆς   μητρὸς   αὐτῆς·
being instructed   by   the   mother   of her:

δός   μοι,   φησίν,   ὧδε   ἐπὶ   πίνακι   τὴν
Give   me,   she says,   here   on   a platter   the

κεφαλὴν   Ἰωάννου   τοῦ   βαπτιστοῦ.   9 καὶ
head   of John   the   Baptist.   And

λυπηθεὶς   ὁ   βασιλεὺς   διὰ   τοὺς
being grieved   the   king   on account of   the

ὅρκους   καὶ   τοὺς   συνανακειμένους
oaths   and   the [ones] reclining at table with [him]

ἐκέλευσεν   δοθῆναι,   10 καὶ   πέμψας
he commanded   to be given,   and   sending

ἀπεκεφάλισεν   Ἰωάννην   ἐν   τῇ   φυλακῇ.
beheaded   John   in   the   prison.

11 καὶ   ἠνέχθη   ἡ   κεφαλὴ   αὐτοῦ   ἐπὶ
And   was brought   the   head   of him   on

πίνακι   καὶ   ἐδόθη   τῷ   κορασίῳ,   καὶ
a platter   and   was given   to the   maid,   and

ἤνεγκεν   τῇ   μητρὶ   αὐτῆς.   12 καὶ
she brought [it]   to the   mother   of her.   And

προσελθόντες   οἱ   μαθηταὶ   αὐτοῦ   ἦραν   τὸ
approaching   the   disciples   of him   took   the

πτῶμα   καὶ   ἔθαψαν   αὐτόν,   καὶ   ἐλθόντες
corpse   and   buried   him,   and   coming

ἀπήγγειλαν   τῷ   Ἰησοῦ.   13 Ἀκούσας   δὲ
reported   -   to Jesus.   And hearing

ὁ   Ἰησοῦς   ἀνεχώρησεν   ἐκεῖθεν   ἐν
-   Jesus   departed   thence   in

πλοίῳ   εἰς   ἔρημον   τόπον   κατ' ἰδίαν·
a ship   to   a desert   place   privately;

καὶ   ἀκούσαντες   οἱ   ὄχλοι   ἠκολούθησαν
and   hearing   the   crowds   followed

αὐτῷ   πεζῇ   ἀπὸ   τῶν   πόλεων.   14 Καὶ
him   afoot   from   the   cities.   And

ἐξελθὼν   εἶδεν   πολὺν   ὄχλον,   καὶ
going forth   he saw   a much   crowd,   and

ἐσπλαγχνίσθη   ἐπ'   αὐτοῖς   καὶ
was filled with tenderness   over   them   and

ἐθεράπευσεν   τοὺς   ἀρρώστους   αὐτῶν.
healed   the   sick   of them.

15 ὀψίας   δὲ   γενομένης   προσῆλθον   αὐτῷ
Now evening   coming on   approached   to him
-- when evening came on

οἱ   μαθηταὶ   λέγοντες·   ἔρημός   ἐστιν   ὁ
the   disciples   saying: Desert   is   the

τόπος   καὶ   ἡ   ὥρα   ἤδη   παρῆλθεν·
place   and   the   hour   already   passed;

ἀπόλυσον   οὖν   τοὺς   ὄχλους,   ἵνα   ἀπελθόντες
dismiss   therefore   the   crowds,   that   going away

εἰς   τὰς   κώμας   ἀγοράσωσιν   ἑαυτοῖς
into   the   villages   they may buy   for themselves

βρώματα.   16 ὁ   δὲ   Ἰησοῦς   εἶπεν   αὐτοῖς·
foods.   -   But   Jesus   said   to them:

οὐ   χρείαν   ἔχουσιν   ἀπελθεῖν·   δότε
Not   need   they have   to go away;   give

αὐτοῖς   ὑμεῖς   φαγεῖν.   17 οἱ   δὲ   λέγουσιν
them   ye   to eat.   But they   say

αὐτῷ·   οὐκ   ἔχομεν   ὧδε   εἰ   μὴ   πέντε
to him: We have not   here   except   five

ἄρτους   καὶ   δύο   ἰχθύας.   18 ὁ   δὲ   εἶπεν·
loaves   and   two   fishes.   And he   said:

φέρετέ   μοι   ὧδε   αὐτούς.   19 καὶ   κελεύσας
Bring   to me   here   them.   And   having commanded

τοὺς   ὄχλους   ἀνακλιθῆναι   ἐπὶ   τοῦ   χόρτου,
the   crowds   to recline   on   the   grass,

λαβὼν   τοὺς   πέντε   ἄρτους   καὶ   τοὺς   δύο
taking   the   five   loaves   and   the   two

ἰχθύας,   ἀναβλέψας   εἰς   τὸν   οὐρανὸν
fishes,   looking up   to   -   heaven

εὐλόγησεν,   καὶ   κλάσας   ἔδωκεν   τοῖς
he blessed,   and   breaking   gave   to the

μαθηταῖς   τοὺς   ἄρτους,   οἱ   δὲ   μαθηταὶ
disciples   the   loaves,   and the   disciples

τοῖς   ὄχλοις.   20 καὶ   ἔφαγον   πάντες   καὶ
to the   crowds,   And   ate   all   and

ἐχορτάσθησαν·   καὶ   ἦραν   τὸ   περισσεῦον
were satisfied;   and   they took   the   excess

τῶν   κλασμάτων,   δώδεκα   κοφίνους   πλήρεις.
of the   fragments,   twelve   baskets   full.

21 οἱ   δὲ   ἐσθίοντες   ἦσαν   ἄνδρες   ὡσεὶ
And the [ones]   eating   were   men   about

πεντακισχίλιοι   χωρὶς   γυναικῶν   καὶ
five thousand   apart from   women   and

παιδίων.   22 Καὶ   [εὐθέως]   ἠνάγκασεν
children.   And   immediately   he constrained

τοὺς   μαθητὰς   ἐμβῆναι   εἰς   τὸ   πλοῖον
the   disciples   to embark   in   the   ship

καὶ   προάγειν   αὐτὸν   εἰς   τὸ   πέραν,
and   to go before   him   to   the   other side,

ἕως   οὗ   ἀπολύσῃ   τοὺς   ὄχλους.   23 Καὶ
until   he should dismiss   the   crowds.   And

ἀπολύσας   τοὺς   ὄχλους   ἀνέβη   εἰς   τὸ
having dismissed   the   crowds   he went up   into   the

ὄρος   κατ' ἰδίαν   προσεύξασθαι.   ὀψίας
mountain   privately   to pray.   evening
-- And when

δὲ   γενομένης   μόνος   ἦν   ἐκεῖ.   24 τὸ   δὲ
And   coming on   alone   he was   there.   But the
evening came on

47

King James Version

the sea, tossed with waves: for the wind was contrary. 25 And in the fourth watch of the night Jesus went unto them, walking on the sea. 26 And when the disciples saw him walking on the sea, they were troubled, saying, It is a spirit; and they cried out for fear. 27 But straightway Jesus spake unto them, saying, Be of good cheer; it is I; be not afraid. 28 And Peter answered him and said, Lord, if it be thou, bid me come unto thee on the water. 29 And he said, Come. And when Peter was come down out of the ship, he walked on the water, to go to Jesus. 30 But when he saw the wind boisterous, he was afraid; and beginning to sink, he cried, saying, Lord, save me. 31 And immediately Jesus stretched forth *his* hand, and caught him, and said unto him, O thou of little faith, wherefore didst thou doubt? 32 And when they were come into the ship, the wind ceased. 33 Then they that were in the ship came and worshipped him, saying, Of a truth thou art the Son of God.

34 And when they were gone over, they came into the land of Gennesaret. 35 And when the men of that place had knowledge of him, they sent out into all that country round about, and brought unto him all that were diseased; 36 And besought him that they might only touch the hem of his garment: and as many as touched were made perfectly whole.

15 Then came to Jesus scribes and Pharisees, which were of Jerusalem, saying, 2 Why do thy disciples transgress the tradition of the elders? for they wash not their hands when they eat bread. 3 But he answered and said unto them, Why do ye also transgress the commandment of God by your tradition? 4 For God commanded, saying, Honour thy father and mother: and, He that curseth father or mother, let him die the death. 5 But ye say, Whosoever shall say to *his* father or *his* mother, *It is* a gift, by whatsoever thou mightest be profited by me; 6 And honour not his father or his mother, *he shall be free.* Thus have ye made the commandment of God of none effect by your tradition. 7 *Ye* hypocrites, well did Esaias prophesy of you, saying, 8 This people draweth nigh unto me with their mouth, and honoureth me with *their* lips; but their heart is far from me. 9 But in vain they do worship me, teaching *for* doctrines the commandments of men.

10 And he called the multitude, and said unto them, Hear, and understand: 11 Not that which goeth into the mouth defileth a man; but that which cometh out of the mouth, this defileth a man. 12 Then came his disciples, and said unto him, Knowest thou that the Pharisees were of-

New International Version

siderable distance from land, buffeted by the waves because the wind was against it.

25 During the fourth watch of the night Jesus went out to them, walking on the lake. 26 When the disciples saw him walking on the lake, they were terrified. "It's a ghost," they said, and cried out in fear.

27 But Jesus immediately said to them: "Take courage! It is I. Don't be afraid."

28 "Lord, if it's you," Peter replied, "tell me to come to you on the water."

29 "Come," he said.

Then Peter got down out of the boat and walked on the water to Jesus. 30 But when he saw the wind, he was afraid and, beginning to sink, cried out, "Lord, save me!"

31 Immediately Jesus reached out his hand and caught him. "You of little faith," he said, "why did you doubt?"

32 And when they climbed into the boat, the wind died down. 33 Then those who were in the boat worshiped him, saying, "Truly you are the Son of God."

34 When they had crossed over, they landed at Gennesaret. 35 And when the men of that place recognized Jesus, they sent word to all the surrounding country. People brought all their sick to him 36 and begged him to let the sick just touch the edge of his cloak, and all who touched him were healed.

Clean and unclean

15 Then some Pharisees and teachers of the law came to Jesus from Jerusalem and asked, 2 "Why do your disciples break the tradition of the elders? They don't wash their hands before they eat!"

3 Jesus replied, "And why do you break the command of God for the sake of your tradition? 4 For God said, 'Honor your father and mother,' *v* and, 'Anyone who curses his father or mother must be put to death.' *w* 5 But you say that if a man says to his father or mother, 'Whatever help you might otherwise have received from me is a gift devoted to God,' 6 he is not to 'honor his father' *x* with it. Thus you nullify the word of God for the sake of your tradition. 7 You hypocrites! Isaiah was right when he prophesied about you:

8 'These people honor me with their lips,
    but their hearts are far from me.
9 They worship me in vain;
    their teachings are but rules made by
        man.' *y* "

10 Jesus called the crowd to him and said, "Listen and understand. 11 What goes into a man's mouth does not make him 'unclean,' but what comes out of his mouth, that is what makes him 'unclean.' "

12 Then the disciples came to him and asked, "Do you know that the Pharisees were offended when they heard this?"

[v] exodus 20:12; Deut. 5:16. [w] Exodus 21:17. [x] Some MSS add *or his mother.* [y] Isaiah 29:13.

Greek Interlinear

πλοῖον ἤδη σταδίους πολλοὺς ἀπὸ τῆς
ship now furlongs many from the

γῆς ἀπεῖχεν, βασανιζόμενον ὑπὸ τῶν
land was away, being distressed by the

κυμάτων, ἦν γὰρ ἐναντίος ὁ ἄνεμος.
waves, ⁴was ¹for ⁵contrary ²the ³wind.

25 τετάρτῃ δὲ φυλακῇ τῆς νυκτὸς
Now in [the] fourth watch of the night

ἦλθεν πρὸς αὐτοὺς περιπατῶν ἐπὶ τὴν
he came toward them walking on the

θάλασσαν. 26 οἱ δὲ μαθηταὶ ἰδόντες
sea. And the disciples seeing

αὐτὸν ἐπὶ τῆς θαλάσσης περιπατοῦντα
him on the sea walking

ἐταράχθησαν λέγοντες ὅτι φάντασμά
were troubled saying[,] – A phantasm

ἐστιν, καὶ ἀπὸ τοῦ φόβου ἔκραξαν.
it is, and from – fear they cried out.

27 εὐθὺς δὲ ἐλάλησεν [ὁ Ἰησοῦς]
But immediately spoke – Jesus

αὐτοῖς λέγων· θαρσεῖτε, ἐγώ εἰμι·
to them saying: Be of good cheer, I am;

μὴ φοβεῖσθε. 28 ἀποκριθεὶς δὲ αὐτῷ ὁ
do not fear. And answering him –

Πέτρος εἶπεν· κύριε, εἰ σὺ εἶ, κέλευσόν
Peter said: Lord, if thou art, command

με ἐλθεῖν πρὸς σὲ ἐπὶ τὰ ὕδατα. 29 ὁ
me to come to thee on the waters. he

δὲ εἶπεν· ἐλθέ. καὶ καταβὰς ἀπὸ τοῦ
And said: Come. And going down from the

πλοίου Πέτρος περιπάτησεν ἐπὶ τὰ ὕδατα
ship Peter walked on the waters

καὶ ἦλθεν πρὸς τὸν Ἰησοῦν. 30 βλέπων δὲ
and came toward – Jesus. But seeing

τὸν ἄνεμον ἐφοβήθη, καὶ ἀρξάμενος
the wind he was afraid, and beginning

καταποντίζεσθαι ἔκραξεν λέγων·
to sink he cried out saying:

κύριε, σῶσόν με. 31 εὐθέως δὲ ὁ
Lord, save me. And immediately –

Ἰησοῦς ἐκτείνας τὴν χεῖρα ἐπελάβετο
Jesus stretching out the(his) hand took hold

αὐτοῦ, καὶ λέγει αὐτῷ· ὀλιγόπιστε,
of him, and says to him: Little-faith,

εἰς τί ἐδίστασας; 32 καὶ ἀναβάντων
why didst thou doubt? And going up
= as they went up

αὐτῶν εἰς τὸ πλοῖον ἐκόπασεν ὁ ἄνεμος.
them* into the ship ceased the wind.

33 οἱ δὲ ἐν τῷ πλοίῳ προσεκύνησαν αὐτῷ
And the [ones] in the ship worshipped him

λέγοντες· ἀληθῶς θεοῦ υἱὸς εἶ. 34 Καὶ
saying: Truly of God Son thou art. And

διαπεράσαντες ἦλθον ἐπὶ τὴν γῆν εἰς
crossing over they came onto the land to

Γεννησαρέτ. 35 καὶ ἐπιγνόντες αὐτὸν
Gennesaret. And recognizing him

οἱ ἄνδρες τοῦ τόπου ἐκείνου ἀπέστειλαν
the men – place of that sent

εἰς ὅλην τὴν περίχωρον ἐκείνην, καὶ
into all – neighbourhood that, and

προσήνεγκαν αὐτῷ πάντας τοὺς κακῶς
brought to him all the [ones] ill
= those who were ill,

ἔχοντας, 36 καὶ παρεκάλουν αὐτὸν ἵνα
having, and besought him that

μόνον ἅψωνται τοῦ κρασπέδου τοῦ
only they might touch the fringe of the

ἱματίου αὐτοῦ· καὶ ὅσοι ἥψαντο διεσώθησαν.
garment of him; and as many as touched were completely
healed.

Chapter 15

Τότε προσέρχονται τῷ Ἰησοῦ
Then approach – to Jesus

ἀπὸ Ἱεροσολύμων Φαρισαῖοι καὶ γραμματεῖς
from Jerusalem Pharisees and scribes

λέγοντες· 2 διὰ τί οἱ μαθηταί σου
saying: Why the disciples of thee

παραβαίνουσιν τὴν παράδοσιν τῶν
transgress the tradition of the

πρεσβυτέρων; οὐ γὰρ νίπτονται τὰς χεῖρας
elders? for not they wash the(ir) hands

ὅταν ἄρτον ἐσθίωσιν. 3 ὁ δὲ ἀπο-
whenever bread they eat. And he answer-

κριθεὶς εἶπεν αὐτοῖς· διὰ τί καὶ ὑμεῖς
ing said to them: Why indeed ye

παραβαίνετε τὴν ἐντολὴν τοῦ θεοῦ
transgress the commandment – of God

διὰ τὴν παράδοσιν ὑμῶν; 4 ὁ γὰρ
on account of the tradition of you? – For

θεὸς εἶπεν· τίμα τὸν πατέρα καὶ τὴν
God said: Honour the father and the

μητέρα, καί· ὁ κακολογῶν πατέρα
mother, and: The [one] speaking evil of father

ἢ μητέρα θανάτῳ τελευτάτω. 5 ὑμεῖς δὲ
or mother by death let him die. But ye

λέγετε· ὃς ἂν εἴπῃ τῷ πατρὶ ἢ
say: Whoever says to the(his) father or

τῇ μητρί· δῶρον ὃ ἐὰν ἐξ ἐμοῦ
to the(his) mother: A gift whatever by me

ὠφεληθῇς, 6 οὐ μὴ τιμήσει τὸν
thou mightest be owed, by no means shall he honour the

πατέρα αὐτοῦ ἢ τὴν μητέρα αὐτοῦ·
father of him or the mother of him;

καὶ ἠκυρώσατε τὸν λόγον τοῦ θεοῦ
and ye annulled the word – of God

διὰ τὴν παράδοσιν ὑμῶν. 7 ὑποκρι-
on account of the tradition of you. Hypocrites,

ταί, καλῶς ἐπροφήτευσεν περὶ ὑμῶν
well prophesied concerning you

Ἠσαΐας λέγων· 8 ὁ λαὸς οὗτος τοῖς
Isaiah saying: This people with the

χείλεσίν με τιμᾷ, ἡ δὲ καρδία αὐτῶν
lips me honours, but the heart of them

πόρρω ἀπέχει ἀπ' ἐμοῦ· 9 μάτην δὲ
far ᴸ away from me; and vainly

σέβονται με, διδάσκοντες διδασκαλίας
they worship me, teaching teachings

ἐντάλματα ἀνθρώπων. 10 Καὶ προσκαλε-
ordinances of men. And calling

σάμενος τὸν ὄχλον εἶπεν αὐτοῖς·
forward the crowd he said to them:

ἀκούετε καὶ συνίετε· 11 οὐ τὸ εἰσερχ-
Hear ye and understand: Not the[thing] enter-

όμενον εἰς τὸ στόμα κοινοῖ τὸν ἄνθρωπον,
ing into the mouth defiles the man,

ἀλλὰ τὸ ἐκπορευόμενον ἐκ τοῦ στόματος,
but the [thing] coming forth out of the mouth,

τοῦτο κοινοῖ τὸν ἄνθρωπον. 12 Τότε
this defiles the man. Then

προσελθόντες οἱ μαθηταὶ λέγουσιν αὐτῷ·
approaching the disciples say to him:

οἶδας ὅτι οἱ Φαρισαῖοι ἀκούσαντες τὸν
Dost thou know that the Pharisees hearing the

King James Version

fended, after they heard this saying? 13 But he answered and said, Every plant, which my heavenly Father hath not planted, shall be rooted up. 14 Let them alone: they are blind leaders of the blind. And if the blind lead the blind, both shall fall into the ditch. 15 Then answered Peter and said unto him, Declare unto us this parable. 16And Jesus said, Are ye also yet without understanding? 17 Do not ye yet understand, that whatsoever entereth in at the mouth goeth into the belly, and is cast out into the draught? 18 But those things which proceed out of the mouth come forth from the heart; and they defile the man. 19 For out of the heart proceed evil thoughts, murders, adulteries, fornications, thefts, false witness, blasphemies: 20 These are *the things* which defile a man: but to eat with unwashen hands defileth not a man.

21 Then Jesus went thence, and departed into the coasts of Tyre and Sidon. 22And, behold, a woman of Canaan came out of the same coasts, and cried unto him, saying, Have mercy on me, O Lord, *thou* Son of David; my daughter is grievously vexed with a devil. 23 But he answered her not a word. And his disciples came and besought him, saying, Send her away; for she crieth after us. 24 But he answered and said, I am not sent but unto the lost sheep of the house of Israel. 25 Then came she and worshipped him, saying, Lord, help me. 26 But he answered and said, It is not meet to take the children's bread, and to cast *it* to dogs. 27And she said, Truth, Lord: yet the dogs eat of the crumbs which fall from their masters' table. 28 Then Jesus answered and said unto her, O woman, great *is* thy faith: be it unto thee even as thou wilt. And her daughter was made whole from that very hour. 29And Jesus departed from thence, and came nigh unto the sea of Galilee; and went up into a mountain, and sat down there. 30And great multitudes came unto him, having with them *those that were* lame, blind, dumb, maimed, and many others, and cast them down at Jesus' feet; and he healed them: 31 Insomuch that the multitude wondered, when they saw the dumb to speak, the maimed to be whole, the lame to walk, and the blind to see: and they glorified the God of Israel.

32 Then Jesus called his disciples *unto him,* and said, I have compassion on the multitude, because they continue with me now three days, and have nothing to eat: and I will not send them away fasting, lest they faint in the way. 33And his disciples say unto him, Whence should we have so much bread in the wilderness, as to fill so great a multitude? 34And Jesus saith unto them, How many loaves have ye? And they said, Seven, and a few little fishes. 35And he commanded the multitude to sit down on the ground. 36And he took the seven loaves and the fishes,

New International Version

13 He replied, "Every plant that my heavenly Father has not planted will be pulled up by the roots. 14 Leave them; they are blind guides.[z] If a blind man leads a blind man, both will fall into a pit."

15 Peter said, "Explain the parable to us."

16 "Are you still so dull?" Jesus asked them. 17 "Don't you see that whatever enters the mouth goes into the stomach and then out of the body? 18 But the things that come out of the mouth come from the heart, and these make a man 'unclean.' 19 For out of the heart come evil thoughts, murder, adultery, sexual immorality, theft, false testimony, slander. 20 These are what make a man 'unclean'; but eating with unwashed hands does not make him 'unclean.'"

The faith of the Canaanite woman

21 Leaving that place, Jesus withdrew to the region of Tyre and Sidon. 22A Canaanite woman from that vicinity came to him, crying out, "Lord, Son of David, have mercy on me! My daughter is suffering terribly from demon-possession."

23 Jesus did not answer a word. So his disciples came to him and urged him, "Send her away, for she keeps crying out after us."

24 He answered, "I was sent only to the lost sheep of Israel."

25 The woman came and knelt before him. "Lord, help me!" she said.

26 He replied, "It is not right to take the children's bread and toss it to their dogs."

27 "Yes, Lord," she said, "but even the dogs eat the crumbs that fall from their masters' table."

28 Then Jesus answered, "Woman, you have great faith! Your request is granted." And her daughter was healed from that very hour.

Jesus feeds the four thousand

29 Jesus left there and went along the Sea of Galilee. Then he went up into the hills and sat down. 30 Great crowds came to him, bringing the lame, the blind, the crippled, the dumb and many others, and laid them at his feet; and he healed them. 31 The people were amazed when they saw the dumb speaking, the crippled made well, the lame walking and the blind seeing. And they praised the God of Israel.

32 Jesus called his disciples to him and said, "I have compassion for these people; they have already been with me three days and have nothing to eat. I do not want to send them away hungry, or they may collapse on the way."

33 His disciples answered, "Where could we get enough bread in this remote place to feed such a crowd?"

34 "How many loaves do you have?" Jesus asked.

"Seven," they replied, "and a few small fish."

35 He told the crowd to sit down on the ground. 36 Then he took the seven loaves and

[z] Some MSS add *of the blind.*

50

Greek Interlinear

λόγον ἐσκανδαλίσθησαν; 13 ὁ δὲ ἀπο-
saying were offended? And he answer-

κριθεὶς εἶπεν· πᾶσα φυτεία ἦν οὐκ
ing said: Every plant which not

ἐφύτευσεν ὁ πατήρ μου ὁ οὐράνιος ἐκριζω-
planted the Father of me - heavenly shall be

θήσεται. 14 ἄφετε αὐτούς· τυφλοὶ εἰσιν
uprooted. Leave them; blind they are

ὁδηγοὶ τυφλῶν· τυφλὸς δὲ τυφλὸν
leaders of blind; ᵃa blind man ᵃand ᵃa blind man

ἐὰν ὁδηγῇ, ἀμφότεροι εἰς βόθυνον πεσοῦνται.
ᵃif ᵃleads, both into a ditch will fall.

15 Ἀποκριθεὶς δὲ ὁ Πέτρος εἶπεν αὐτῷ·
And answering - Peter said to him:

φράσον ἡμῖν τὴν παραβολήν. 16 ὁ δὲ
Explain to us the parable. So he

εἶπεν· ἀκμὴν καὶ ὑμεῖς ἀσύνετοί
said; Thus also ye unintelligent

ἐστε, 17 οὐ νοεῖτε ὅτι πᾶν τὸ
are? Do ye not understand that everything

εἰσπορευόμενον εἰς τὸ στόμα εἰς τὴν
entering into the mouth into the

κοιλίαν χωρεῖ καὶ εἰς ἀφεδρῶνα ἐκβάλλεται;
stomach goes and into a drain is cast out?

18 τὰ δὲ ἐκπορευόμενα ἐκ τοῦ
but the things coming forth out of the

στόματος ἐκ τῆς καρδίας ἐξέρχεται,
mouth out of the heart comes forth,

κἀκεῖνα κοινοῖ τὸν ἄνθρωπον. 19 ἐκ
and those defiles the man. out of

γὰρ τῆς καρδίας ἐξέρχονται διαλογισμοὶ
For the heart come forth thoughts

πονηροί, φόνοι, μοιχεῖαι, πορνεῖαι, κλοπαί,
evil, murders, adulteries, fornications, thefts,

ψευδομαρτυρίαι, βλασφημίαι. 20 ταῦτά
false witnessings, blasphemies. These things

ἐστιν τὰ κοινοῦντα τὸν ἄνθρωπον·
is(are) the [ones] defiling the man;

τὸ δὲ ἀνίπτοις χερσὶν φαγεῖν οὐ
- but with unwashed hands to eat not

κοινοῖ τὸν ἄνθρωπον.
defiles the man.

21 Καὶ ἐξελθὼν ἐκεῖθεν ὁ Ἰησοῦς
And going forth thence - Jesus

ἀνεχώρησεν εἰς τὰ μέρη Τύρου καὶ
departed into the parts of Tyre and

Σιδῶνος. 22 καὶ ἰδοὺ γυνὴ Χαναναία
Sidon. And behold woman a Canaanite

ἀπὸ τῶν ὁρίων ἐκείνων ἐξελθοῦσα
from - borders those coming forth

ἔκραζεν λέγουσα· ἐλέησόν με, κύριε
cried out saying: Pity me, Lord[,]

υἱὸς Δαυίδ· ἡ θυγάτηρ μου κακῶς
son of David; the daughter of me badly

δαιμονίζεται. 23 ὁ δὲ οὐκ ἀπεκρίθη
is demon-possessed. But he answered not

αὐτῇ λόγον. καὶ προσελθόντες οἱ μαθηταὶ
her a word. And approaching the disciples

αὐτοῦ ἠρώτων αὐτὸν λέγοντες· ἀπόλυσον
of him besought him saying: Dismiss

αὐτήν, ὅτι κράζει ὄπισθεν ἡμῶν. 24 ὁ
her, because she is crying out behind us. he

δὲ ἀποκριθεὶς εἶπεν· οὐκ ἀπεστάλην
But answering said: I was not sent

εἰ μὴ εἰς τὰ πρόβατα τὰ ἀπολωλότα
except to the sheep - lost

οἴκου Ἰσραήλ. 25 ἡ δὲ ἐλθοῦσα
of [the] house of Israel. But she coming

προσεκύνει αὐτῷ λέγουσα· κύριε, βοήθει
worshipped him saying: Lord, help

μοι. 26 ὁ δὲ ἀποκριθεὶς εἶπεν· οὐκ
me. But he answering said: not

ἔστιν καλὸν λαβεῖν τὸν ἄρτον τῶν τέκνων
It is good to take the bread of the children

καὶ βαλεῖν τοῖς κυναρίοις. 27 ἡ δὲ
and to throw to the dogs. And she

εἶπεν· ναί, κύριε· καὶ γὰρ τὰ κυνάρια
said: Yes, Lord; but even the dogs

ἐσθίει ἀπὸ τῶν ψιχίων τῶν πιπτόντων
eats from the crumbs - falling

ἀπὸ τῆς τραπέζης τῶν κυρίων αὐτῶν.
from the table of the masters of them.

28 τότε ἀποκριθεὶς ὁ Ἰησοῦς εἶπεν αὐτῇ·
Then answering - Jesus said to her:

ὦ γύναι, μεγάλη σου ἡ πίστις· γενηθήτω
O woman, great of thee the faith; let it be

σοι ὡς θέλεις. καὶ ἰάθη ἡ
to thee as thou desirest. And was healed the

θυγάτηρ αὐτῆς ἀπὸ τῆς ὥρας ἐκείνης.
daughter of her from - hour that.

29 Καὶ μεταβὰς ἐκεῖθεν ὁ Ἰησοῦς
And removing thence - Jesus

ἦλθεν παρὰ τὴν θάλασσαν τῆς Γαλιλαίας,
came by the sea - of Galilee,

καὶ ἀναβὰς εἰς τὸ ὄρος ἐκάθητο ἐκεῖ.
and going up into the mountain he sat there.

30 καὶ προσῆλθον αὐτῷ ὄχλοι πολλοὶ ἔχοντες
And approached to him crowds many having

μεθ᾽ ἑαυτῶν χωλούς, κυλλούς, τυφλούς,
with themselves lame, maimed, blind,

κωφούς, καὶ ἑτέρους πολλούς, καὶ ἔρριψαν
dumb, and others many, and cast

αὐτοὺς παρὰ τοὺς πόδας αὐτοῦ· καὶ
them at the feet of him; and

ἐθεράπευσεν αὐτούς· 31 ὥστε τὸν ὄχλον
he healed them; so as the crowd
=so that the crowd marvelled

θαυμάσαι βλέποντας κωφοὺς λαλοῦντας,
to marvelᵇ seeing dumb men speaking,

κυλλοὺς ὑγιεῖς καὶ χωλοὺς περιπατοῦντας
maimed whole and lame walking

καὶ τυφλοὺς βλέποντας· καὶ ἐδόξασαν
and blind seeing; and they glorified

τὸν θεὸν Ἰσραήλ. 32 Ὁ δὲ Ἰησοῦς
the God of Israel. - And Jesus

προσκαλεσάμενος τοὺς μαθητὰς αὐτοῦ
calling forward the disciples of him

εἶπεν· σπλαγχνίζομαι ἐπὶ τὸν ὄχλον,
said: I am filled with tenderness over the crowd,

ὅτι ἤδη ἡμέραι τρεῖς προσμένουσίν
because now days three they remain

μοι καὶ οὐκ ἔχουσιν τί φάγωσιν·
with me and have not anything they may eat;

καὶ ἀπολῦσαι αὐτοὺς νήστεις οὐ θέλω,
and to dismiss them without food I am not willing,

μήποτε ἐκλυθῶσιν ἐν τῇ ὁδῷ. 33 καὶ
lest they fail in the way. And

λέγουσιν αὐτῷ οἱ μαθηταί· πόθεν
say to him the disciples: Whence

ἡμῖν ἐν ἐρημίᾳ ἄρτοι τοσοῦτοι ὥστε
to us in a desert loaves so many so as

χορτάσαι ὄχλον τοσοῦτον; 34 καὶ λέγει
to satisfy a crowd so great? And says

αὐτοῖς ὁ Ἰησοῦς· πόσους ἄρτους ἔχετε;
to them - Jesus: How many loaves have ye?

οἱ δὲ εἶπαν· ἑπτά, καὶ ὀλίγα ἰχθύδια.
And they said: Seven, and a few fishes.

35 καὶ παραγγείλας τῷ ὄχλῳ ἀναπεσεῖν
And having enjoined the crowd to recline

ἐπὶ τὴν γῆν 36 ἔλαβεν τοὺς ἑπτὰ
on the ground he took the seven

<table>
<tr><td>

King James Version

and gave thanks, and brake *them,* and gave to his disciples, and the disciples to the multitude. 37And they did all eat, and were filled: and they took up of the broken *meat* that was left seven baskets full. 38And they that did eat were four thousand men, beside women and children. 39And he sent away the multitude, and took ship, and came into the coasts of Magdala.

</td><td>

New International Version

the fish, and when he had given thanks, he broke them and gave them to the disciples, and they in turn to the people. 37 They all ate and were satisfied. Afterward the disciples picked up seven basketfuls of broken pieces that were left over. 38 The number of those who ate was four thousand, besides women and children. 39After Jesus had sent the crowd away, he got into the boat and went to the vicinity of Magadan.

</td></tr>
</table>

The demand for a sign

<table>
<tr><td>

16 The Pharisees also with the Sadducees came, and tempting desired him that he would shew them a sign from heaven. 2 He answered and said unto them, When it is· evening, ye say, *It will be* fair weather: for the sky is red. 3And in the morning, *It will be* foul weather to day: for the sky is red and lowering. O *ye* hypocrites, ye can discern the face of the sky; but can ye not *discern* the signs of the times? 4A wicked and adulterous generation seeketh after a sign; and there shall no sign be given unto it, but the sign of the prophet Jonas. And he left them, and departed. 5And when his disciples were come to the other side, they had forgotten to take bread.

6 Then Jesus said unto them, Take heed and beware of the leaven of the Pharisees and of the Sadducees. 7And they reasoned among themselves, saying, *It is* because we have taken no bread. 8 *Which* when Jesus perceived, he said unto them, O ye of little faith, why reason ye among yourselves, because ye have brought no bread? 9 Do ye not yet understand, neither remember the five loaves of the five thousand, and how many baskets ye took up? 10 Neither the seven loaves of the four thousand, and how many baskets ye took up? 11 How is it that ye do not understand that I spake *it* not to you concerning bread, that ye should beware of the leaven of the Pharisees and of the Sadducees? 12 Then understood they how that he bade *them* not beware of the leaven of bread, but of the doctrine of the Pharisees and of the Sadducees.

13 When Jesus came into the coasts of Cesarea Philippi, he asked his disciples, saying, Whom do men say that I, the Son of man, am? 14And they said, Some *say that thou art* John the Baptist; some, Elias; and others, Jeremias, or one of the prophets. 15 He saith unto them, But whom say ye that I am? 16And Simon Peter answered and said, Thou art the Christ, the Son of the living God. 17And Jesus answered and said unto him, Blessed art thou, Simon Bar-jona: for flesh and blood hath not revealed *it* unto thee, but my Father which is in heaven. 18And I say also unto thee, That thou art Peter, and upon this rock I will build my church; and the gates of hell shall not prevail against it. 19And I will give unto thee the keys of the kingdom of

</td><td>

16 The Pharisees and Sadducees came to Jesus and tested him by asking him to show them a sign from heaven.

2 He replied,*a* "When evening comes, you say, 'It will be fair weather, for the sky is red,' 3 and in the morning, 'Today it will be stormy, for the sky is red and overcast.' You know how to interpret the appearance of the sky, but you cannot interpret the signs of the times. 4A wicked and adulterous generation looks for a miraculous sign, but none will be given it except the sign of Jonah." Jesus then left them and went away.

The yeast of the Pharisees and Sadducees

5 But when they went across the lake, the disciples forgot to take bread. 6 "Be careful," Jesus said to them. "Be on your guard against the yeast of the Pharisees and Sadducees."

7 They discussed this among themselves and said, "It is because we didn't bring any bread."

8 Aware of their discussion, Jesus asked, "You of little faith, why are you talking among yourselves about having no bread? 9 Do you still not understand? Don't you remember the five loaves for the five thousand, and how many basketfuls you gathered? 10 Or the seven loaves for the four thousand, and how many basketfuls you gathered? 11 How is it you don't understand that I was not talking to you about bread? But be on your guard against the yeast of the Pharisees and Sadducees." 12 Then they understood that he was not telling them to guard against the yeast used in bread, but against the teaching of the Pharisees and Sadducees.

Peter's confession of Christ

13 When Jesus came to the region of Caesarea Philippi, he asked his disciples, "Who do people say the Son of Man is?"

14 They replied, "Some say John the Baptist; others say Elijah; and still others, Jeremiah or one of the prophets."

15 "But what about you?" he asked. "Who do you say I am?"

16 Simon Peter answered, "You are the Christ,*b* the Son of the living God."

17 Jesus replied, "Blessed are you, Simon son of Jonah, for this was not revealed to you by man, but by my Father in heaven. 18And I tell you that you are Peter,*e* and on this rock I will build my church, and the gates of Hades will not overcome it.*d* 19 I will give you the keys of

</td></tr>
</table>

[a] Some early MSS omit the rest of verse 2 and all of verse 3. [b] Or *Messiah.* [c] *Peter* means *rock.* [d] Or *not prove stronger than it.*

Greek Interlinear

ἄρτους καὶ τοὺς ἰχθύας καὶ εὐχαριστήσας
loaves and the fishes and giving thanks
ἔκλασεν καὶ ἐδίδου τοῖς μαθηταῖς, οἱ δὲ
he broke and gave to the disciples, and the
μαθηταὶ τοῖς ὄχλοις. 37 καὶ ἔφαγον πάντες
disciples to the crowds. And ate all
καὶ ἐχορτάσθησαν, καὶ τὸ περισσεῦον τῶν
and were satisfied, and the excess of the
κλασμάτων ἦραν, ἑπτὰ σπυρίδας πλήρεις.
fragments they took, seven baskets full.

38 οἱ δὲ ἐσθίοντες ἦσαν τετρακισχίλιοι
And the [ones] eating were four thousand
ἄνδρες χωρὶς γυναικῶν καὶ παιδίων.
men apart from women and children.
39 Καὶ ἀπολύσας τοὺς ὄχλους ἐνέβη εἰς
And having dismissed the crowds he embarked in
τὸ πλοῖον, καὶ ἦλθεν εἰς τὰ ὅρια Μαγαδάν.
the ship, and came into the borders of Magadan.

Chapter 16

Καὶ προσελθόντες οἱ Φαρισαῖοι καὶ
And approaching the Pharisees and
Σαδδουκαῖοι πειράζοντες ἐπηρώτησαν αὐτὸν
Sadducees tempting asked him
σημεῖον ἐκ τοῦ οὐρανοῦ ἐπιδεῖξαι
a sign out of the heaven to show
αὐτοῖς. 2 ὁ δὲ ἀποκριθεὶς εἶπεν αὐτοῖς·
to them. But he answering said to them:
[ὀψίας γενομένης λέγετε· εὐδία,
Evening coming on* ye say: Fair weather,
=When evening comes on
πυρράζει γὰρ ὁ οὐρανός· 3 καὶ πρωΐ·
for is red the heaven(sky); and in the morning:
σήμερον χειμών, πυρράζει γὰρ στυγνάζων
To-day stormy weather, for is red being overcast
ὁ οὐρανός. τὸ μὲν πρόσωπον τοῦ
the heaven(sky). The face of the
οὐρανοῦ γινώσκετε διακρίνειν, τὰ δὲ
heaven(sky) ye know* to discern, but the
σημεῖα τῶν καιρῶν οὐ δύνασθε;] 4 γενεὰ
signs of the times can ye not? A generation
πονηρὰ καὶ μοιχαλὶς σημεῖον ἐπιζητεῖ,
evil and adulterous a sign seeks,
καὶ σημεῖον οὐ δοθήσεται αὐτῇ εἰ μὴ
and a sign shall not be given to it except
τὸ σημεῖον Ἰωνᾶ. καὶ καταλιπὼν αὐτοὺς
the sign of Jonah. And leaving them
ἀπῆλθεν. 5 Καὶ ἐλθόντες οἱ μαθηταὶ εἰς
he went away. And coming the disciples to
τὸ πέραν ἐπελάθοντο ἄρτους λαβεῖν.
the other side they forgot loaves to take.
ὁ δὲ Ἰησοῦς εἶπεν αὐτοῖς· 6 ὁρᾶτε καὶ
- And Jesus said to them: Beware and
προσέχετε ἀπὸ τῆς ζύμης τῶν Φαρισαίων
take heed from the leaven of the Pharisees
καὶ Σαδδουκαίων. 7 οἱ δὲ διελογίζοντο
and Sadducees. But they reasoned
ἐν ἑαυτοῖς λέγοντες ὅτι ἄρτους οὐκ
among themselves saying[:] - Loaves not
ἐλάβομεν. 8 γνοὺς δὲ ὁ Ἰησοῦς εἶπεν·
we took. But knowing - Jesus said:
τί διαλογίζεσθε ἐν ἑαυτοῖς, ὀλιγόπιστοι,
Why reason ye among yourselves, little-faiths,
ὅτι ἄρτους οὐκ ἔχετε; 9 οὔπω νοεῖτε,
because loaves not ye have not? Do ye not understand,
οὐδὲ μνημονεύετε τοὺς πέντε ἄρτους τῶν
neither remember ye the five loaves of the
πεντακισχιλίων καὶ πόσους κοφίνους
five thousand and how many baskets
ἐλάβετε; 10 οὐδὲ τοὺς ἑπτὰ ἄρτους τῶν
ye took? Neither the seven loaves of the
τετρακισχιλίων καὶ πόσας σπυρίδας
four thousand and how many baskets
ἐλάβετε; 11 πῶς οὐ νοεῖτε ὅτι οὐ
ye took? How do ye not understand that not

περὶ ἄρτων εἶπον ὑμῖν; προσέχετε δὲ ἀπὸ
concerning loaves I said to you? But take heed from
τῆς ζύμης τῶν Φαρισαίων καὶ Σαδ-
the leaven of the Pharisees and Sad-
δουκαίων. 12 τότε συνῆκαν ὅτι οὐκ
ducees. Then they understood that not
εἶπεν προσέχειν ἀπὸ τῆς ζύμης [τῶν
he said to take heed from the leaven of the
ἄρτων], ἀλλὰ ἀπὸ τῆς διδαχῆς τῶν
loaves, but from the teaching of the
Φαρισαίων καὶ Σαδδουκαίων.
Pharisees and Sadducees.
13 Ἐλθὼν δὲ ὁ Ἰησοῦς εἰς τὰ μέρη
And coming - Jesus into the parts
Καισαρείας τῆς Φιλίππου ἠρώτα τοὺς
of Cæsarea - of Philip he questioned the
μαθητὰς αὐτοῦ λέγων· τίνα λέγουσιν οἱ
disciples of him saying: Whom say -
ἄνθρωποι εἶναι τὸν υἱὸν τοῦ ἀνθρώπου;
men to be the Son - of man?
14 οἱ δὲ εἶπαν· οἱ μὲν Ἰωάννην τὸν
And they said: Some indeed John the
βαπτιστήν, ἄλλοι δὲ Ἠλίαν, ἕτεροι δὲ
Baptist, and others Elias, and others
Ἱερεμίαν ἢ ἕνα τῶν προφητῶν. 15 λέγει
Jeremias or one of the prophets. He says
αὐτοῖς· ὑμεῖς δὲ τίνα με λέγετε εἶναι;
to them: But ²ye ¹whom *me ²say to be?
16 ἀποκριθεὶς δὲ Σίμων Πέτρος εἶπεν·
And answering Simon Peter said:
17 σὺ εἶ ὁ χριστὸς ὁ υἱὸς τοῦ θεοῦ
Thou art the Christ the Son - of God
τοῦ ζῶντος. ἀποκριθεὶς δὲ ὁ Ἰησοῦς
of the living. And answering - Jesus
εἶπεν αὐτῷ· μακάριος εἶ, Σίμων
said to him: Blessed art thou, Simon
Βαριωνᾶ, ὅτι σὰρξ καὶ αἷμα οὐκ ἀπεκά-
Barjonas, because flesh and blood did not
λυψέν σοι ἀλλ' ὁ πατήρ μου ὁ ἐν
reveal to thee but the Father of me - in
τοῖς οὐρανοῖς. 18 κἀγὼ δέ σοι λέγω
the heavens. And I also to thee say[,]
ὅτι σὺ εἶ Πέτρος, καὶ ἐπὶ ταύτῃ τῇ
- Thou art Peter, and on this -
πέτρα οἰκοδομήσω μου τὴν ἐκκλησίαν,
rock I will build of me the church,
καὶ πύλαι ᾅδου οὐ κατισχύσουσιν
and [the] gates of hades will not prevail against
αὐτῆς. 19 δώσω σοι τὰς κλεῖδας τῆς
it. I will give thee the keys of the

---

* See note on page xxxviii. Note the use in the next
line of δύνασθε.

King James Version

heaven: and whatsoever thou shalt bind on earth shall be bound in heaven; and whatsoever thou shalt loose on earth shall be loosed in heaven. 20 Then charged he his disciples that they should tell no man that he was Jesus the Christ.

21 From that time forth began Jesus to shew unto his disciples, how that he must go unto Jerusalem, and suffer many things of the elders and chief priests and scribes, and be killed, and be raised again the third day. 22 Then Peter took him, and began to rebuke him, saying, Be it far from thee, Lord: this shall not be unto thee. 23 But he turned, and said unto Peter, Get thee behind me, Satan: thou art an offence unto me: for thou savourest not the things that be of God, but those that be of men.

24 Then said Jesus unto his disciples, If any *man* will come after me, let him deny himself, and take up his cross, and follow me. 25 For whosoever will save his life shall lose it: and whosoever will lose his life for my sake shall find it. 26 For what is a man profited, if he shall gain the whole world, and lose his own soul? or what shall a man give in exchange for his soul? 27 For the Son of man shall come in the glory of his Father with his angels; and then he shall reward every man according to his works. 28 Verily I say unto you, There be some standing here, which shall not taste of death, till they see the Son of man coming in his kingdom.

New International Version

the kingdom of heaven; whatever you bind on earth will be bound in heaven, and whatever you loose on earth will be loosed in heaven." 20 Then he warned his disciples not to tell anyone that he was the Christ.[b]

Jesus predicts his death

21 From that time on Jesus began to explain to his disciples that he must go to Jerusalem and suffer many things at the hands of the elders, chief priests and teachers of the law, and that he must be killed and on the third day be raised to life.

22 Peter took him aside and began to rebuke him. "Perish the thought, Lord!" he said. "This shall never happen to you!"

23 Jesus turned and said to Peter, "Out of my sight, Satan! You are a stumbling block to me; you do not have in mind the things of God, but the things of men."

24 Then Jesus said to his disciples, "If anyone would come after me, he must deny himself and take up his cross and follow me. 25 For whoever wants to save his life[e] will lose it, but whoever loses his life for me will find it. 26 What good will it be for a man if he gains the whole world, yet forfeits his soul? [e] Or what can a man give in exchange for his soul? 27 For the Son of Man is going to come in his Father's glory with his angels, and then he will reward each person according to what he has done. 28 I tell you the truth, some who are standing here will not taste death before they see the Son of Man coming in his kingdom."

The transfiguration

17 And after six days Jesus taketh Peter, James, and John his brother, and bringeth them up into a high mountain apart, 2 And was transfigured before them: and his face did shine as the sun, and his raiment was white as the light. 3 And, behold, there appeared unto them Moses and Elias talking with him. 4 Then answered Peter, and said unto Jesus, Lord, it is good for us to be here: if thou wilt, let us make here three tabernacles; one for thee, and one for Moses, and one for Elias. 5 While he yet spake, behold, a bright cloud overshadowed them: and behold a voice out of the cloud, which said, This is my beloved Son, in whom I am well pleased; hear ye him. 6 And when the disciples heard *it,* they fell on their face, and were sore afraid. 7 And Jesus came and touched them, and said, Arise, and be not afraid. 8 And when they had lifted up their eyes, they saw no man, save Jesus

17 After six days Jesus took with him Peter, James, and John the brother of James, and led them up a high mountain by themselves. 2 There he was transfigured before them. His face shone like the sun, and his clothes became as white as the light. 3 Just then there appeared before them Moses and Elijah, talking with Jesus.

4 Peter said to Jesus, "Lord, it is good for us to be here. If you wish, I will put up three shelters[f]—one for you, one for Moses and one for Elijah."

5 While he was still speaking, a bright cloud enveloped them, and a voice from the cloud said, "This is my Son, whom I love; with him I am well-pleased. Listen to him!"

6 When the disciples heard this, they fell face down to the ground, terrified. 7 But Jesus came and touched them. "Get up," he said. "Don't be afraid." 8 When they looked up, they saw no one except Jesus.

[b] Or *Messiah.* [e] The Greek word means either *life* or *soul.* [f] Or *sanctuaries.*

54

Greek Interlinear

βασιλείας τῶν οὐρανῶν, καὶ ὃ ἐὰν
kingdom   of the heavens,   and whatever

δήσῃς ἐπὶ τῆς γῆς ἔσται δεδεμένον ἐν τοῖς
thou bindest on the earth shall be *having been* bound in the

οὐρανοῖς, καὶ ὃ ἐὰν λύσῃς ἐπὶ τῆς
heavens,   and whatever thou loosest on the

γῆς ἔσται λελυμένον ἐν τοῖς οὐρανοῖς.
earth shall be *having been* loosed in the heavens.

20 τότε ἐπετίμησεν τοῖς μαθηταῖς ἵνα
Then he warned   the disciples that

μηδενὶ εἴπωσιν ὅτι αὐτός ἐστιν ὁ
to no one they should tell that he is the

χριστός.
Christ.

21 Ἀπὸ τότε ἤρξατο Ἰησοῦς Χριστὸς
From then began Jesus Christ

δεικνύειν τοῖς μαθηταῖς αὐτοῦ ὅτι δεῖ
to show to the disciples of him that it behoves

αὐτὸν εἰς Ἰεροσόλυμα ἀπελθεῖν καὶ
him to Jerusalem to go and

πολλὰ παθεῖν ἀπὸ τῶν πρεσβυτέρων καὶ
many things to suffer from the elders and

ἀρχιερέων καὶ γραμματέων καὶ ἀποκτανθῆναι
chief priests and scribes and to be killed

καὶ τῇ τρίτῃ ἡμέρᾳ ἐγερθῆναι. 22 καὶ
and on the third day to be raised. And

προσλαβόμενος αὐτὸν ὁ Πέτρος ἤρξατο
taking him Peter began

ἐπιτιμᾶν αὐτῷ λέγων· ἵλεώς σοι,
to rebuke him saying: Propitious to thee,
= May God help thee,

κύριε· οὐ μὴ ἔσται σοι τοῦτο. 23 ὁ δὲ
Lord: by no means shall be to thee this. But he

στραφεὶς εἶπεν τῷ Πέτρῳ· ὕπαγε ὀπίσω
turning said to Peter: Go behind

μου, σατανᾶ· σκάνδαλον εἶ ἐμοῦ,
me, Satan; an offence thou art of me,

ὅτι οὐ φρονεῖς τὰ τοῦ θεοῦ
because thou thinkest not the things - of God

ἀλλὰ τὰ τῶν ἀνθρώπων. 24 Τότε ὁ
but the things - of men. Then -

Ἰησοῦς εἶπεν τοῖς μαθηταῖς αὐτοῦ· εἰ
Jesus said to the disciples of him: If

τις θέλει ὀπίσω μου ἐλθεῖν, ἀπαρνησάσθω
anyone wishes after me to come, let him deny

ἑαυτὸν καὶ ἀράτω τὸν σταυρὸν αὐτοῦ,
himself and let him take the cross of him,

καὶ ἀκολουθείτω μοι. 25 ὃς γὰρ ἐὰν
and let him follow me. For whoever

θέλῃ τὴν ψυχὴν αὐτοῦ σῶσαι, ἀπολέσει
wishes the life of him to save, he will lose

αὐτήν· ὃς δ᾽ ἂν ἀπολέσῃ τὴν ψυχὴν
it; and whoever loses the life

αὐτοῦ ἕνεκεν ἐμοῦ, εὑρήσει αὐτήν. 26 τί
of him for the sake of me, he will find it. what

γὰρ ὠφεληθήσεται ἄνθρωπος, ἐὰν τὸν
For will be benefited a man, if the

κόσμον ὅλον κερδήσῃ, τὴν δὲ ψυχὴν
world whole he should gain, but the soul

αὐτοῦ ζημιωθῇ; ἢ τί δώσει ἄνθρωπος
of him loses? or what will give a man

ἀντάλλαγμα τῆς ψυχῆς αὐτοῦ; 27 μέλλει
an exchange of the soul of him? is about

γὰρ ὁ υἱὸς τοῦ ἀνθρώπου ἔρχεσθαι ἐν τῇ
For the Son - of man to come in the

δόξῃ τοῦ πατρὸς αὐτοῦ μετὰ τῶν ἀγγέλων
glory of the Father of him with the angels

αὐτοῦ, καὶ τότε ἀποδώσει ἑκάστῳ
of him, and then he will reward *to* each man

κατὰ τὴν πρᾶξιν αὐτοῦ. 28 ἀμὴν λέγω
according to the conduct of him. Truly I say

ὑμῖν ὅτι εἰσίν τινες τῶν ὧδε ἑστώτων
to you[.] - There are some of the [ones] here standing

οἵτινες οὐ μὴ γεύσωνται θανάτου ἕως ἂν
who by no means may taste of death until

ἴδωσιν τὸν υἱὸν τοῦ ἀνθρώπου ἐρχόμενον
they see the Son - of man coming

ἐν τῇ βασιλείᾳ αὐτοῦ.
in the kingdom of him.

Chapter 17

Καὶ μεθ᾽ ἡμέρας ἓξ παραλαμβάνει ὁ
And after days six takes -

Ἰησοῦς τὸν Πέτρον καὶ Ἰάκωβον καὶ
Jesus - Peter and James and

Ἰωάννην τὸν ἀδελφὸν αὐτοῦ, καὶ ἀναφέρει
John the brother of him, and leads up

αὐτοὺς εἰς ὄρος ὑψηλὸν κατ᾽ ἰδίαν. 2 καὶ
them to mountain a high privately. And

μετεμορφώθη ἔμπροσθεν αὐτῶν, καὶ
he was transfigured before them, and

ἔλαμψεν τὸ πρόσωπον αὐτοῦ ὡς ὁ ἥλιος,
shone the face of him as the sun,

τὰ δὲ ἱμάτια αὐτοῦ ἐγένετο λευκὰ ὡς
and the garments of him became white as

τὸ φῶς. 3 καὶ ἰδοὺ ὤφθη αὐτοῖς Μωϋσῆς
the light. And behold was seen by them Moses

καὶ Ἡλίας συλλαλοῦντες μετ᾽ αὐτοῦ.
and Elias conversing with him.

4 ἀποκριθεὶς δὲ ὁ Πέτρος εἶπεν τῷ
And answering - Peter said -

Ἰησοῦ· κύριε, καλόν ἐστιν ἡμᾶς ὧδε
to Jesus: Lord, good it is us here

εἶναι· εἰ θέλεις, ποιήσω ὧδε τρεῖς
to be; if thou willest, I will make here three

σκηνάς, σοὶ μίαν καὶ Μωϋσεῖ
tents, for thee one and for Moses

μίαν καὶ Ἡλίᾳ μίαν. 5 ἔτι αὐτοῦ
one and for Elias one. Yet him
= While he was yet

λαλοῦντος, ἰδοὺ νεφέλη φωτεινὴ ἐπεσκίασεν
speaking*, behold cloud a bright overshadowed
speaking,

αὐτούς, καὶ ἰδοὺ φωνὴ ἐκ τῆς νεφέλης
them, and behold a voice out of the cloud

λέγουσα· οὗτός ἐστιν ὁ υἱός μου ὁ
saying: This is the son of me the

ἀγαπητός, ἐν ᾧ εὐδόκησα· ἀκούετε
beloved, in whom I was well pleased; hear ye

αὐτοῦ. 6 καὶ ἀκούσαντες οἱ μαθηταὶ
him. And hearing the disciples

ἔπεσαν ἐπὶ πρόσωπον αὐτῶν καὶ
fell on [the] face[s] of them and

ἐφοβήθησαν σφόδρα. 7 καὶ προσῆλθεν ὁ
feared exceedingly. And approached -

Ἰησοῦς καὶ ἁψάμενος αὐτῶν εἶπεν·
Jesus and touching them said:

ἐγέρθητε καὶ μὴ φοβεῖσθε. 8 ἐπάραντες δὲ
Rise and do not fear. And lifting up

τοὺς ὀφθαλμοὺς αὐτῶν οὐδένα εἶδον εἰ
the eyes of them no one they saw ex-

55

King James Version

only. 9And as they came down from the mountain, Jesus charged them, saying, Tell the vision to no man, until the Son of man be risen again from the dead. 10And his disciples asked him, saying, Why then say the scribes that Elias must first come? 11And Jesus answered and said unto them, Elias truly shall first come, and restore all things. 12 But I say unto you, That Elias is come already, and they knew him not, but have done unto him whatsoever they listed. Likewise' shall also the Son of man suffer of them. 13 Then the disciples understood that he spake unto them of John the Baptist.

14 And when they were come to the multitude, there came to him a *certain* man, kneeling down to him, and saying, 15 Lord, have mercy on my son; for he is lunatic, and sore vexed: for ofttimes he falleth into the fire, and oft into the water. 16And I brought him to thy disciples, and they could not cure him. 17 Then Jesus answered and said, O faithless and perverse generation, how long shall I be with you? how long shall I suffer you? bring him hither to me. 18And Jesus rebuked the devil; and he departed out of him: and the child was cured from that very hour. 19 Then came the disciples to Jesus apart, and said, Why could not we cast him out? 20And Jesus said unto them, Because of your unbelief: for verily I say unto you, If ye have faith as a grain of mustard seed, ye shall say unto this mountain, Remove hence to yonder place; and it shall remove: and nothing shall be impossible unto you. 21 Howbeit this kind goeth not out but by prayer and fasting.

22 And while they abode in Galilee, Jesus said unto them, The Son of man shall be betrayed into the hands of men: 23And they shall kill him, and the third day he shall be raised again. And they were exceeding sorry.

24 And when they were come to Capernaum, they that received tribute *money* came to Peter, and said, Doth not your master pay tribute? 25 He saith, Yes. And when he was come into the house, Jesus prevented him, saying, What thinkest thou, Simon? of whom do the kings of the earth take custom or tribute? of their own children, or of strangers? 26 Peter saith unto him, Of strangers. Jesus saith unto him, Then are the children free. 27 Notwithstanding, lest we should offend them, go thou to the sea, and cast a hook, and take up the fish that first cometh up; and when thou hast opened his mouth, thou shalt find a piece of money: that take, and give unto them for me and thee.

New International Version

9 As they were coming down the mountain, Jesus instructed them, "Don't tell anyone what you have seen, until the Son of Man has been raised from the dead."

10 The disciples asked him, "Why then do the teachers of the law say that Elijah must come first?"

11 Jesus replied, "To be sure, Elijah comes and will restore all things. 12 But I tell you, Elijah has already come, and they did not recognize him, but have done to him everything they wished. In the same way the Son of Man is going to suffer at their hands." 13 Then the disciples understood that he was talking to them about John the Baptist.

The healing of an epileptic boy

14 When they came to the crowd, a man approached Jesus and knelt before him. 15 "Lord, have mercy on my son," he said. "He is an epileptic and is suffering greatly. He often falls into the fire or into the water. 16 I brought him to your disciples, but they could not heal him."

17 "O unbelieving and perverse generation," Jesus replied, "how long shall I stay with you? How long shall I put up with you? Bring the boy here to me." 18 Jesus rebuked the demon, and it came out of the boy, and he was healed from that moment.

19 Then the disciples came to Jesus in private and asked, "Why couldn't we drive it out?"

20 He replied, "Because you have so little faith. I tell you the truth, if you have faith as small as a mustard seed, you can say to this mountain, 'Move from here to there' and it will move. Nothing will be impossible for you." *g*

22 When they came together in Galilee, he said to them, "The Son of Man is going to be betrayed into the hands of men. 23 They will kill him, and on the third day he will be raised to life." And the disciples were filled with grief.

The temple tax

24 After Jesus and his disciples arrived in Capernaum, the collectors of the two-drachma tax came to Peter and asked, "Doesn't your teacher pay the temple tax*h* ?"

25 "Yes, he does," he replied.

When Peter came into the house, Jesus was the first to speak. "What do you think, Simon?" he asked. "From whom do the kings of the earth collect duty and taxes—from their own sons or from others?"

26 "From others," Peter answered.

"Then the sons are exempt," Jesus said to him. 27 "But so that we may not offend them, go to the lake and throw out your line. Take the first fish you catch; open its mouth and you will find a four-drachma coin. Take it and give it to them for my tax and yours."

Greek Interlinear

μὴ αὐτὸν Ἰησοῦν μόνον. 9 Καὶ κατα-
cept himself Jesus only. And com-
=as

βαινόντων αὐτῶν ἐκ τοῦ ὄρους ἐνετείλατο
ing down them⁰ out of the mountain enjoined
they were coming down

αὐτοῖς ὁ Ἰησοῦς λέγων· μηδενὶ εἴπητε
them - Jesus saying: To no one tell

τὸ ὅραμα ἕως οὗ ὁ υἱὸς τοῦ ἀνθρώπου
the vision until the Son - of man

ἐκ νεκρῶν ἐγερθῇ. 10 Καὶ ἐπηρώτησαν
out of dead be raised. And questioned

αὐτὸν οἱ μαθηταὶ λέγοντες· τί οὖν
him the disciples saying: Why then

οἱ γραμματεῖς λέγουσιν ὅτι Ἠλίαν δεῖ
the scribes say that ¹Elias ¹it behoves

ἐλθεῖν πρῶτον; 11 ὁ δὲ ἀποκριθεὶς εἶπεν·
to come first? And he answering said:

Ἠλίας μὲν ἔρχεται καὶ ἀποκαταστήσει
Elias indeed is coming and will restore

πάντα· 12 λέγω δὲ ὑμῖν ὅτι Ἠλίας
all things; but I tell you that Elias

ἤδη ἦλθεν, καὶ οὐκ ἐπέγνωσαν
already came, and they did not recognize

αὐτόν, ἀλλ' ἐποίησαν ἐν αὐτῷ ὅσα
him, but did by him whatever things

ἠθέλησαν· οὕτως καὶ ὁ υἱὸς τοῦ ἀνθρώπου
they wished; thus also the Son - of man

μέλλει πάσχειν ὑπ' αὐτῶν. 13 τότε
is about to suffer by them. Then

συνῆκαν οἱ μαθηταὶ ὅτι περὶ
understood the disciples that concerning

Ἰωάννου τοῦ βαπτιστοῦ εἶπεν αὐτοῖς.
John the Baptist he spoke to them.

14 Καὶ ἐλθόντων πρὸς τὸν ὄχλον προσ-
And [they] coming to the crowd ap-

ῆλθεν αὐτῷ ἄνθρωπος γονυπετῶν αὐτὸν
proached to him a man falling on knees to him

15 καὶ λέγων· κύριε, ἐλέησόν μου τὸν
and saying: Lord, pity of me the

υἱόν, ὅτι σεληνιάζεται καὶ κακῶς ἔχει·
son, because he is moonstruck and ill has;
=is ill;

πολλάκις γὰρ πίπτει εἰς τὸ πῦρ καὶ
for often he falls into the fire and

πολλάκις εἰς τὸ ὕδωρ. 16 καὶ προσήνεγκα
often into the water. And I brought

αὐτὸν τοῖς μαθηταῖς σου, καὶ οὐκ
him to the disciples of thee, and not

ἠδυνήθησαν αὐτὸν θεραπεῦσαι. 17 ἀπο-
they were able him to heal. an-

κριθεὶς δὲ ὁ Ἰησοῦς εἶπεν· ὦ γενεὰ
swering And - Jesus said: O generation

ἄπιστος καὶ διεστραμμένη, ἕως πότε
unbelieving and having been perverted, until when

μεθ' ὑμῶν ἔσομαι; ἕως πότε
with you shall I be? until when

ἀνέξομαι ὑμῶν; φέρετέ μοι αὐτὸν
shall I endure you? bring to me him

ὧδε. 18 καὶ ἐπετίμησεν αὐτῷ ὁ Ἰησοῦς,
here. And rebuked it - Jesus,

καὶ ἐξῆλθεν ἀπ' αὐτοῦ τὸ δαιμόνιον,
and came out from him the demon,

καὶ ἐθεραπεύθη ὁ παῖς ἀπὸ τῆς ὥρας
and was healed the boy from the hour

ἐκείνης. 19 Τότε προσελθόντες οἱ μαθηταὶ
that. Then ²approaching ¹the ³disciples

τῷ Ἰησοῦ κατ' ἰδίαν εἶπον· διὰ
- to Jesus privately said: Why

τί ἡμεῖς οὐκ ἠδυνήθημεν ἐκβαλεῖν αὐτό;
we were not able to expel it?

20 ὁ δὲ λέγει αὐτοῖς· διὰ τὴν ὀλιγο-
And he says to them: Because of the little

πιστίαν ὑμῶν· ἀμὴν γὰρ λέγω ὑμῖν, ἐὰν
faith of you; for truly I say to you, if

ἔχητε πίστιν ὡς κόκκον σινάπεως,
ye have faith as a grain of mustard,

ἐρεῖτε τῷ ὄρει τούτῳ· μετάβα
ye will say - mountain to this: Remove

ἔνθεν ἐκεῖ, καὶ μεταβήσεται, καὶ οὐδὲν
hence there, and it will be removed, and nothing

ἀδυνατήσει ὑμῖν. ‡
will be impossible to you.

22 Συστρεφομένων δὲ αὐτῶν ἐν τῇ
And strolling them⁰ in -
=as they were strolling

Γαλιλαίᾳ εἶπεν αὐτοῖς ὁ Ἰησοῦς· μέλλει
Galilee said to them - Jesus: is about

ὁ υἱὸς τοῦ ἀνθρώπου παραδίδοσθαι εἰς
The Son - of man to be delivered into

χεῖρας ἀνθρώπων, 23 καὶ ἀποκτενοῦσιν
[the] hands of men, and they will kill

αὐτόν, καὶ τῇ τρίτῃ ἡμέρᾳ ἐγερθήσεται.
him, and on the third day he will be raised.

καὶ ἐλυπήθησαν σφόδρα.
And they were grieved exceedingly.

24 Ἐλθόντων δὲ αὐτῶν εἰς Καφαρναοὺμ
And coming them⁰ to Capernaum
=when they came

προσῆλθον οἱ τὰ δίδραχμα λαμβάνοντες
approached the [ones] the didrachmæ receiving

τῷ Πέτρῳ καὶ εἶπαν· ὁ διδάσκαλος
- Peter and said: The teacher

ὑμῶν οὐ τελεῖ δίδραχμα; λέγει· ναί.
of you not pays drachmæ? He says: Yes.

25 καὶ ἐλθόντα εἰς τὴν οἰκίαν προ-
And ²coming ³into ⁴the ⁵house ¹pre-

έφθασεν αὐτὸν ὁ Ἰησοῦς λέγων· τί σοι
ceded ²him - ¹Jesus saying: What to thee

δοκεῖ, Σίμων; οἱ βασιλεῖς τῆς γῆς
seems it, Simon? the kings of the earth

ἀπὸ τίνων λαμβάνουσιν τέλη ἢ κῆνσον;
from whom do they take toll or poll-tax?

ἀπὸ τῶν υἱῶν αὐτῶν ἢ ἀπὸ τῶν ἀλλοτρίων;
from the sons of them or from - strangers?

26 εἰπόντος δέ· ἀπὸ τῶν ἀλλο-
and [he] saying⁰: From the strangers,
=when he said:

τρίων, ἔφη αὐτῷ ὁ Ἰησοῦς· ἄρα γε
said to him - Jesus: Then

ἐλεύθεροί εἰσιν οἱ υἱοί. 27 ἵνα δὲ μὴ
free are the sons. But lest

σκανδαλίσωμεν αὐτούς, πορευθεὶς εἰς
we should offend them, going to

θάλασσαν βάλε ἄγκιστρον καὶ τὸν
[the] sea cast a hook and the

ἀναβάντα πρῶτον ἰχθὺν ἆρον, καὶ ἀνοίξας
²coming up ¹first ³fish take, and opening

τὸ στόμα αὐτοῦ εὑρήσεις στατῆρα·
the mouth of it thou wilt find a stater;

ἐκεῖνον λαβὼν δὸς αὐτοῖς ἀντὶ ἐμοῦ καὶ
that taking give them for me and

σοῦ.
thee.

‡ Verse 21 omitted by Nestle

King James Version

18 At the same time came the disciples unto Jesus, saying, Who is the greatest in the kingdom of heaven? 2And Jesus called a little child unto him, and set him in the midst of them, 3And said, Verily I say unto you, Except ye be converted, and become as little children, ye shall not enter into the kingdom of heaven. 4 Whosoever therefore shall humble himself as this little child, the same is greatest in the kingdom of heaven. 5And whoso shall receive one such little child in my name receiveth me. 6 But whoso shall offend one of these little ones which believe in me, it were better for him that a millstone were hanged about his neck, and *that* he were drowned in the depth of the sea.

7 Woe unto the world because of offences! for it must needs be that offences come; but woe to that man by whom the offence cometh! 8 Wherefore if thy hand or thy foot offend thee, cut them off, and cast *them* from thee: it is better for thee to enter into life halt or maimed, rather than having two hands or two feet to be cast into everlasting fire. 9And if thine eye offend thee, pluck it out, and cast *it* from thee: it is better for thee to enter into life with one eye, rather than having two eyes to be cast into hell fire. 10 Take heed that ye despise not one of these little ones; for I say unto you, That in heaven their angels do always behold the face of my Father which is in heaven. 11 For the Son of man is come to save that which was lost. 12 How think ye? if a man have a hundred sheep, and one of them be gone astray, doth he not leave the ninety and nine, and goeth into the mountains, and seeketh that which is gone astray? 13And if so be that he find it, verily I say unto you, he rejoiceth more of that *sheep,* than of the ninety and nine which went not astray. 14 Even so it is not the will of your Father which is in heaven, that one of these little ones should perish.

15 Moreover if thy brother shall trespass against thee, go and tell him his fault between thee and him alone: if he shall hear thee, thou hast gained thy brother. 16 But if he will not hear *thee, then* take with thee one or two more, that in the mouth of two or three witnesses every word may be established. 17And if he shall neglect to hear them, tell *it* unto the church: but if he neglect to hear the church, let him be unto thee as a heathen man and a publican. 18 Verily I say unto you, Whatsoever ye shall bind on earth shall be bound in heaven; and whatsoever ye shall loose on earth shall be loosed in heaven. 19Again I say unto you, That if two of you shall agree on earth as touching any thing that they shall ask, it shall be done for them of my Father which is in heaven. 20 For where two or three

New International Version

The greatest in the kingdom of heaven

18 At that time the disciples came to Jesus and asked, "Who is the greatest in the kingdom of heaven?"

2 He called a little child and had him stand among them. 3And he said: "I tell you the truth, unless you change and become like little children, you will never enter the kingdom of heaven. 4 Therefore, whoever humbles himself like this child is the greatest in the kingdom of heaven. 5And whoever welcomes a little child like this in my name welcomes me.

6 "But if anyone causes one of these little ones who believe in me to sin, it would be better for him to have a large millstone hung around his neck and to be drowned in the depths of the sea. 7 Woe to the world because of the things that cause people to sin! Such things must come, but woe to the man through whom they come! 8 If your hand or your foot causes you to sin, cut it off and throw it away. It is better for you to enter life maimed or crippled than to have two hands or two feet and be thrown into eternal fire. 9And if your eye causes you to sin, gouge it out and throw it away. It is better for you to enter life with one eye than to have two eyes and be thrown into the fire of hell.

The parable of the lost sheep

10 "See that you do not look down on one of these little ones. For I tell you that their angels in heaven always see the face of my Father in heaven.[i]

12 "What do you think? If a man owns a hundred sheep, and one of them wanders away, will he not leave the ninety-nine on the hills and go to look for the one that wandered off? 13And if he finds it, I tell you the truth, he is happier about that one sheep than about the ninety-nine that did not wander off. 14 In the same way your Father in heaven is not willing that any of these little ones should be lost.

A brother who sins against you

15 "If your brother sins against you, go and show him his fault, just between the two of you. If he listens to you, you have won your brother over. 16 But if he will not listen, take one or two others along, so that 'every matter may be established by the testimony of two or three witnesses.'[j] 17 If he refuses to listen to them, tell it to the church; and if he refuses to listen even to the church, treat him as you would a pagan or a tax collector.

18 "I tell you the truth, whatever you bind on earth will be bound in heaven, and whatever you loose on earth will be loosed in heaven.

19 "Again, I tell you that if two of you on earth agree about anything you ask for, it will be done for you by my Father in heaven. 20 For

[i] Some MSS add verse 11: *The Son of the Man came to save what was lost.* [j] Deut. 19:15.

58

Greek Interlinear
Chapter 18

Ἐν ἐκείνῃ τῇ ὥρᾳ προσῆλθον οἱ
In that - hour approached the

μαθηταὶ τῷ Ἰησοῦ λέγοντες· τίς ἄρα
disciples - to Jesus saying: Who then

μείζων ἐστὶν ἐν τῇ βασιλείᾳ τῶν οὐρανῶν;
greater is in the kingdom of the heavens?

2 καὶ προσκαλεσάμενος παιδίον ἔστησεν
And calling forward a child he set

αὐτὸ ἐν μέσῳ αὐτῶν **3** καὶ εἶπεν· ἀμὴν
him in [the] midst of them and said: Truly

λέγω ὑμῖν, ἐὰν μὴ στραφῆτε καὶ
I say to you, except ye turn and

γένησθε ὡς τὰ παιδία, οὐ μὴ
become as - children, by no means

εἰσέλθητε εἰς τὴν βασιλείαν τῶν
may ye enter into the kingdom of the

οὐρανῶν. **4** ὅστις οὖν ταπεινώσει ἑαυτὸν
heavens. [he] who ¹Therefore will humble himself

ὡς τὸ παιδίον τοῦτο, οὗτός ἐστιν ὁ
as - child this, this [one] is the

μείζων ἐν τῇ βασιλείᾳ τῶν οὐρανῶν.
greater in the kingdom of the heavens.

5 καὶ ὃς ἐὰν δέξηται ἐν παιδίον
And whoever receives one child

τοιοῦτο ἐπὶ τῷ ὀνόματί μου, ἐμὲ δέχεται·
such on(in) the name of me, me receives;

6 ὃς δ' ἂν σκανδαλίσῃ ἕνα τῶν
and whoever offends one -

μικρῶν τούτων τῶν πιστευόντων εἰς ἐμέ,
little [ones] of these - believing in me,

συμφέρει αὐτῷ ἵνα κρεμασθῇ μύλος
it is expedient for him that be hanged an upper

ὀνικὸς περὶ τὸν τράχηλον αὐτοῦ καὶ
millstone round the neck of him and

καταποντισθῇ ἐν τῷ πελάγει τῆς θαλάσσης.
he be drowned in the depth of the sea.

7 Οὐαὶ τῷ κόσμῳ ἀπὸ τῶν σκανδάλων·
Woe to the world from - offences;

ἀνάγκη γὰρ ἐλθεῖν τὰ σκάνδαλα, πλὴν
for [it is] a necessity to come - offences, but

οὐαὶ τῷ ἀνθρώπῳ δι' οὗ τὸ σκάνδαλον
woe to the man through whom the offence

ἔρχεται. **8** Εἰ δὲ ἡ χείρ σου ἢ ὁ
comes. Now if the hand of thee or the

πούς σου σκανδαλίζει σε, ἔκκοψον αὐτὸν
foot of thee offends thee, cut off it

καὶ βάλε ἀπὸ σοῦ· καλόν σοί ἐστιν
and cast from thee; good for thee it is

εἰσελθεῖν εἰς τὴν ζωὴν κυλλὸν ἢ χωλόν,
to enter into - life maimed or lame,

ἢ δύο χεῖρας ἢ δύο πόδας ἔχοντα βληθῆναι
than two hands or two feet having to be cast

εἰς τὸ πῦρ τὸ αἰώνιον. **9** καὶ εἰ ὁ
into the fire - eternal. And if the

ὀφθαλμός σου σκανδαλίζει σε, ἔξελε αὐτὸν
eye of thee offends thee, pluck out it

καὶ βάλε ἀπὸ σοῦ· καλόν σοί ἐστιν
and cast from thee; good for thee it is

μονόφθαλμον εἰς τὴν ζωὴν εἰσελθεῖν, ἢ
one-eyed into the life to enter, than

δύο ὀφθαλμοὺς ἔχοντα βληθῆναι εἰς
two eyes having to be cast into

τὴν γέενναν τοῦ πυρός. **10** Ὁρᾶτε μὴ
the gehenna - of fire. See [that] not

καταφρονήσητε ἑνὸς τῶν μικρῶν τούτων·
ye despise · one - little [ones] of these;

λέγω γὰρ ὑμῖν ὅτι οἱ ἄγγελοι αὐτῶν
for I tell you that the angels of them

ἐν οὐρανοῖς διὰ παντὸς βλέπουσι τὸ
in heavens always see the

πρόσωπον τοῦ πατρός μου τοῦ ἐν οὐρανοῖς.‡
face of the Father of me - in heavens.‡

12 Τί ὑμῖν δοκεῖ; ἐὰν γένηταί τινι
What to you seems it? if there be to any
=any man has

ἀνθρώπῳ ἑκατὸν πρόβατα καὶ πλανηθῇ
man a hundred sheep and wanders

ἐν ἐξ αὐτῶν, οὐχὶ ἀφήσει τὰ ἐνενήκοντα
one of them, will he not leave the ninety-

ἐννέα ἐπὶ τὰ ὄρη καὶ πορευθεὶς ζητεῖ τὸ
nine on the mountains and going seeks the

πλανώμενον; **13** καὶ ἐὰν γένηται
wandering [one]? And if he happens

εὑρεῖν αὐτό, ἀμὴν λέγω ὑμῖν ὅτι
to find it, truly I say to you that

χαίρει ἐπ' αὐτῷ μᾶλλον ἢ ἐπὶ τοῖς
he rejoices over it more than over the

ἐνενήκοντα ἐννέα τοῖς μὴ πεπλανημένοις.
ninety-nine - not having wandered.

14 οὕτως οὐκ ἔστιν θέλημα ἔμπροσθεν
So it is not [the] will before

τοῦ πατρὸς ὑμῶν τοῦ ἐν οὐρανοῖς ἵνα
the Father of you - in heavens that

ἀπόληται ἓν τῶν μικρῶν τούτων.
should perish one - little [ones] of these.

15 Ἐὰν δὲ ἁμαρτήσῃ ὁ ἀδελφός σου,
Now if sins the brother of thee,

ὕπαγε ἔλεγξον αὐτὸν μεταξὺ σοῦ καὶ
go reprove him between thee and

αὐτοῦ μόνου. ἐάν σου ἀκούσῃ, ἐκέρδησας
him alone. If thee he hears, thou gainedst

τὸν ἀδελφόν σου· **16** ἐὰν δὲ μὴ
the brother of thee; but if not

ἀκούσῃ, παράλαβε μετὰ σοῦ ἔτι ἕνα ἢ
he hears, take with thee more one or

δύο, ἵνα ἐπὶ στόματος δύο μαρτύρων
two, that on(by) [the] mouth of two witnesses

ἢ τριῶν σταθῇ πᾶν ῥῆμα· **17** ἐὰν δὲ
or three may be established every word; but if

παρακούσῃ αὐτῶν, εἰπὸν τῇ ἐκκλησίᾳ·
he refuses to hear them, tell to the church;

ἐὰν δὲ καὶ τῆς ἐκκλησίας παρακούσῃ,
and if even the church he refuses to hear,

ἔστω σοι ὥσπερ ὁ ἐθνικὸς καὶ
let him be to thee as the gentile and

ὁ τελώνης. **18** Ἀμὴν λέγω ὑμῖν,
the tax-collector. Truly I say to you,

ὅσα ἐὰν δήσητε ἐπὶ τῆς γῆς ἔσται
whatever things ye bind on the earth shall be

δεδεμένα ἐν οὐρανῷ, καὶ ὅσα ἐὰν
having been bound in heaven, and whatever things

λύσητε ἐπὶ τῆς γῆς ἔσται λελυμένα
ye loose on the earth shall be having been loosed

ἐν οὐρανῷ. **19** Πάλιν [ἀμὴν] λέγω
in heaven. Again truly I say

ὑμῖν ὅτι ἐὰν δύο συμφωνήσωσιν ἐξ
to you that if two agree of

ὑμῶν ἐπὶ τῆς γῆς περὶ παντὸς πράγ-
you on the earth concerning every

ματος οὗ ἐὰν αἰτήσωνται, γενήσεται
thing whatever they ask, it shall be

αὐτοῖς παρὰ τοῦ πατρός μου τοῦ ἐν
to them from the Father of me - in

οὐρανοῖς. **20** οὗ γὰρ εἰσιν δύο ἢ τρεῖς
heavens. For where are two or three

‡ Ver. 11 omitted by Nestle

King James Version

are gathered together in my name, there am I in the midst of them.

21 Then came Peter to him, and said, Lord, how oft shall my brother sin against me, and I forgive him? till seven times? 22 Jesus saith unto him, I say not unto thee, Until seven times: but, Until seventy times seven.

23 Therefore is the kingdom of heaven likened unto a certain king, which would take account of his servants. 24And when he had begun to reckon, one was brought unto him, which owed him ten thousand talents. 25 But forasmuch as he had not to pay, his lord commanded him to be sold, and his wife, and children, and all that he had, and payment to be made. 26 The servant therefore fell down, and worshipped him, saying, Lord, have patience with me, and I will pay thee all. 27 Then the lord of that servant was moved with compassion, and loosed him, and forgave him the debt. 28 But the same servant went out, and found one of his fellow servants, which owed him a hundred pence: and he laid hands on him, and took *him* by the throat, saying, Pay me that thou owest. 29And his fellow servant fell down at his feet, and besought him, saying, Have patience with me, and I will pay thee all. 30And he would not: but went and cast him into prison, till he should pay the debt. 31 So when his fellow servants saw what was done, they were very sorry, and came and told unto their lord all that was done. 32 Then his lord, after that he had called him, said unto him, O thou wicked servant, I forgave thee all that debt, because thou desiredst me: 33 Shouldest not thou also have had compassion on thy fellow servant, even as I had pity on thee? 34And his lord was wroth, and delivered him to the tormentors, till he should pay all that was due unto him. 35 So likewise shall my heavenly Father do also unto you, if ye from your hearts forgive not every one his brother their trespasses.

New International Version

where two or three come together in my name, there am I with them."

The parable of the unmerciful servant

21 Then Peter came to Jesus and asked, "Lord, how many times shall I forgive my brother when he sins against me? Up to seven times?"

22 Jesus answered, "I tell you, not seven times, but seventy-seven times.[k]

23 "Therefore, the kingdom of heaven is like a king who wanted to settle accounts with his servants. 24As he began the settlement, a man who owed him ten thousand talents[i] was brought to him. 25 Since he was not able to pay, the master ordered that he and his wife and his children and all that he had be sold to repay the debt.

26 "The servant fell on his knees before him. 'Be patient with me,' he begged, 'and I will pay back everything.' 27 The servant's master took pity on him, canceled the debt and let him go.

28 "But when that servant went out, he found one of his fellow servants who owed him a hundred denarii.[m] He grabbed him and began to choke him. 'Pay back what you owe me!' he demanded.

29 "His fellow servant fell to his knees and begged him, 'Be patient with me, and I will pay you back.'

30 "But he refused. Instead, he went off and had the man thrown in prison until he could pay the debt. 31 When the other servants saw what had happened, they were greatly distressed and went and told their master everything that had happened.

32 "Then the master called the servant in. 'You wicked servant,' he said, 'I canceled all that debt of yours because you begged me to. 33 Shouldn't you have had mercy on your fellow servant just as I had on you?' 34 In anger his master turned him over to the jailers until he should pay back all he owed.

35 "This is how my heavenly Father will treat each of you unless you forgive your brother from your heart."

Divorce

19 And it came to pass, *that* when Jesus had finished these sayings, he departed from Galilee, and came into the coasts of Judea beyond Jordan; 2And great multitudes followed him; and he healed them there.

3 The Pharisees also came unto him, tempting him, and saying unto him, Is it lawful for a man to put away his wife for every cause? 4And he answered and said unto them, Have ye not read, that he which made *them* at the beginning made them male and female, 5And said, For this cause shall a man leave father and mother, and shall cleave to his wife: and they twain shall be one

19 When Jesus had finished saying these things, he left Galilee and went into the region of Judea to the other side of the Jordan. 2 Large crowds followed him, and he healed them there.

3 Some Pharisees came to him to test him. They asked, "Is it lawful for a man to divorce his wife for any and every reason?"

4 "Haven't you read," he replied, "that at the beginning the Creator 'made them male and female,'[n] 5 and said, 'For this reason a man will leave his father and mother and be united to his wife, and the two will become one flesh'[o]?

[k] Or *seventy time seven.* [i] That is, several million dollars. [m] That is, a few dollars. [n] Gen. 1:27. [o] Gen. 2:24.

60

Greek Interlinear

συνηγμένοι　εἰς τὸ ἐμὸν ὄνομα, ἐκεῖ εἰμι
having been assembled in　-　my　name,　there I am
ἐν μέσῳ　αὐτῶν.
in [the] midst　of them.

21 Τότε　προσελθὼν ὁ　Πέτρος　εἶπεν
Then　approaching　-　Peter　said
αὐτῷ·　κύριε, ποσάκις　ἁμαρτήσει εἰς
to him:　Lord,　how often　will sin　against
ἐμὲ ὁ ἀδελφός μου καὶ ἀφήσω αὐτῷ;
me　the brother of me and I will forgive him?
ἕως ἑπτάκις; 22 λέγει αὐτῷ ὁ Ἰησοῦς·
until seven times?　says to him　-　Jesus:
οὐ λέγω σοι ἕως ἑπτάκις, ἀλλὰ
I tell not　to thee until　seven times,　but
ἕως ἑβδομηκοντάκις ἑπτά. 23 Διὰ τοῦτο
until seventy times seven.　Therefore
ὡμοιώθη ἡ βασιλεία τῶν οὐρανῶν
was(is) likened the kingdom of the heavens
ἀνθρώπῳ βασιλεῖ, ὃς ἠθέλησεν συνᾶραι
to a man　a king, who wished to take
λόγον μετὰ τῶν δούλων αὐτοῦ. 24 ἀρξα-
account with the slaves of him.　beginning
μένου δὲ αὐτοῦ συναίρειν, προσήχθη
beginning　him　to take, *was brought forward
= as he began
εἷς αὐτῷ ὀφειλέτης μυρίων ταλάντων.
¹one *to him　-　³debtor　⁵of ten thousand　⁴talents.
25 μὴ ἔχοντος δὲ αὐτοῦ ἀποδοῦναι, ἐκέλευσεν
And not having him⁸ to repay,　commanded
= as he had not
αὐτὸν ὁ κύριος πραθῆναι καὶ τὴν
him the lord to be sold and the(his)
γυναῖκα καὶ τὰ τέκνα καὶ πάντα ὅσα
wife and - children and all things whatever
ἔχει, καὶ ἀποδοθῆναι. 26 πεσὼν οὖν ὁ
he has, and to be repaid.　Falling therefore the
δοῦλος προσεκύνει αὐτῷ λέγων· μακρο-
slave did obeisance to him saying:　Defer
θύμησον ἐπ' ἐμοί, καὶ πάντα ἀποδώσω
anger over me, and all things I will repay
σοι. 27 σπλαγχνισθεὶς δὲ ὁ κύριος τοῦ
thee.　And filled with tenderness the lord　-
δούλου ἐκείνου ἀπέλυσεν αὐτόν, καὶ τὸ
slave of that released him, and the
δάνειον ἀφῆκεν αὐτῷ. 28 ἐξελθὼν δὲ
loan forgave him.　But going out
ὁ δοῦλος ἐκεῖνος εὗρεν ἕνα τῶν
- slave that found one of the
συνδούλων αὐτοῦ, ὃς ὤφειλεν αὐτὸν ἑκατὸν
fellow-slaves of him, who owed him a hundred

δηνάρια, καὶ κρατήσας αὐτὸν ἔπνιγεν
denarii, and seizing him throttled
λέγων· ἀπόδος εἴ τι ὀφείλεις.
saying:　Repay if something thou owest.
29 πεσὼν οὖν ὁ σύνδουλος αὐτοῦ παρε-
Falling therefore the fellow-slave of him be-
κάλει αὐτὸν λέγων· μακροθύμησον ἐπ'
sought him saying:　Defer anger over
ἐμοί, καὶ ἀποδώσω σοι. 30 ὁ δὲ οὐκ
me, and I will repay thee.　But he not
ἤθελεν, ἀλλὰ ἀπελθὼν ἔβαλεν αὐτὸν εἰς
wished, but going away threw him into
φυλακὴν ἕως ἀποδῷ τὸ ὀφειλόμενον.
prison until he should repay the thing owing.
31 ἰδόντες οὖν οἱ σύνδουλοι αὐτοῦ τὰ
Seeing therefore the fellow-slaves of him the things
γενόμενα ἐλυπήθησαν σφόδρα, καὶ
having taken place they were grieved exceedingly, and
ἐλθόντες διεσάφησαν τῷ κυρίῳ ἑαυτῶν
coming explained to the lord of themselves
πάντα τὰ γενόμενα. 32 τότε προσ-
all the things having taken place.　Then ¹call-
καλεσάμενος αὐτὸν ὁ κύριος αὐτοῦ λέγει
ing ²forward ³him the lord of him says
αὐτῷ· δοῦλε πονηρέ, πᾶσαν τὴν ὀφειλὴν
to him: ²Slave ¹wicked, all - debt
ἐκείνην ἀφῆκά σοι, ἐπεὶ παρεκάλεσάς με·
that I forgave thee, since thou besoughtest me·
33 οὐκ ἔδει καὶ σὲ ἐλεῆσαι τὸν
did it not behove also thee to pity the
σύνδουλόν σου, ὡς κἀγὼ σὲ ἠλέησα;
fellow-slave of thee, as I also thee pitied?
34 καὶ ὀργισθεὶς ὁ κύριος αὐτοῦ
And being angry the lord of him
παρέδωκεν αὐτὸν τοῖς βασανισταῖς ἕως οὗ
delivered him to the tormentors until
ἀποδῷ πᾶν τὸ ὀφειλόμενον αὐτῷ.
he should repay all the thing owing to him.
35 Οὕτως καὶ ὁ πατήρ μου ὁ οὐράνιος
Thus also the Father of me - heavenly
ποιήσει ὑμῖν, ἐὰν μὴ ἀφῆτε ἕκαστος
will do to you, unless ye forgive each one
τῷ ἀδελφῷ αὐτοῦ ἀπὸ τῶν καρδιῶν
the brother of him from the hearts
ὑμῶν.
of you.

Chapter 19

Καὶ ἐγένετο ὅτε ἐτέλεσεν ὁ
And it came to pass when ended -
Ἰησοῦς τοὺς λόγους τούτους, μετῆρεν
Jesus - words these, he removed
ἀπὸ τῆς Γαλιλαίας καὶ ἦλθεν εἰς τὰ
from the Galilee and came into the
ὅρια τῆς Ἰουδαίας πέραν τοῦ Ἰορδάνου.
borders of Judæa across the Jordan.
2 καὶ ἠκολούθησαν αὐτῷ ὄχλοι πολλοί,
And followed him crowds many,
καὶ ἐθεράπευσεν αὐτοὺς ἐκεῖ.
and he healed them there.
3 Καὶ προσῆλθον αὐτῷ Φαρισαῖοι
And approached to him Pharisees
πειράζοντες αὐτὸν καὶ λέγοντες· εἰ ἔξεστιν
tempting him and saying: If it is lawful

ἀπολῦσαι τὴν γυναῖκα αὐτοῦ κατὰ πᾶσαν
to dismiss the wife of him for every
αἰτίαν; 4 ὁ δὲ ἀποκριθεὶς εἶπεν· οὐκ
cause?　And he answering said: not
ἀνέγνωτε ὅτι ὁ κτίσας ἀπ'
Did ye read that the [one] creating from
ἀρχῆς ἄρσεν καὶ θῆλυ ἐποίησεν αὐτούς;
[the] beginning male and female made them?
5 καὶ εἶπεν· ἕνεκα τούτου καταλείψει
And he said: For the sake of this shall leave
ἄνθρωπος τὸν πατέρα καὶ τὴν μητέρα
a man the(his) father and the(his) mother
καὶ κολληθήσεται τῇ γυναικὶ αὐτοῦ,
and shall cleave to the wife of him,
καὶ ἔσονται οἱ δύο εἰς σάρκα μίαν·
and ²shall be ¹the ²two ⁴in ⁵flesh ³one;

King James Version

flesh? 6 Wherefore they are no more twain, but one flesh. What therefore God hath joined together, let not man put asunder. 7 They say unto him, Why did Moses then command to give a writing of divorcement, and to put her away? 8 He saith unto them, Moses because of the hardness of your hearts suffered you to put away your wives: but from the beginning it was not so. 9And I say unto you, Whosoever shall put away his wife, except *it be* for fornication, and shall marry another, committeth adultery: and whoso marrieth her which is put away doth commit adultery.

10 His disciples say unto him, If the case of the man be so with *his* wife, it is not good to marry. 11 But he said unto them, All *men* cannot receive this saying, save *they* to whom it is given. 12 For there are some eunuchs, which were so born from *their* mother's womb: and there are some eunuchs, which were made eunuchs of men: and there be eunuchs, which have made themselves eunuchs for the kingdom of heaven's sake. He that is able to receive *it*, let him receive *it*.

13 Then were there brought unto him little children, that he should put *his* hands on them, and pray: and the disciples rebuked them. 14 But Jesus said, Suffer little children, and forbid them not, to come unto me; for of such is the kingdom of heaven. 15And he laid *his* hands on them, and departed thence.

16 And, behold, one came and said unto him, Good Master, what good thing shall I do, that I may have eternal life? 17And he said unto him, Why callest thou me good? *there is* none good but one, *that is,* God: but if thou wilt enter into life, keep the commandments. 18 He saith unto him, Which? Jesus said, Thou shalt do no murder, Thou shalt not commit adultery, Thou shalt not steal, Thou shalt not bear false witness, 19 Honour thy father and *thy* mother: and, Thou shalt love thy neighbour as thyself. 20 The young man saith unto him, All these things have I kept from my youth up: what lack I yet? 21 Jesus said unto him, If thou wilt be perfect, go *and* sell that thou hast, and give to the poor, and thou shalt have treasure in heaven: and come *and* follow me. 22 But when the young man heard that saying, he went away sorrowful: for he had great possessions.

23 Then said Jesus unto his disciples, Verily I say unto you, That a rich man shall hardly enter into the kingdom of heaven. 24And again I say unto you, It is easier for a camel to go through the eye of a needle, than for a rich man to enter into the kingdom of God. 25 When his disciples heard *it*, they were exceedingly amazed, saying, Who then can be saved? 26 But Jesus beheld *them*, and said unto them, With men this is impossible; but with God all things are possible.

27 Then answered Peter and said unto him, Behold, we have forsaken all, and followed thee;

New International Version

6 So they are no longer two, but one. Therefore what God has joined together, let man not separate."

7 "Why then," they asked, "did Moses command that a man give his wife a certificate of divorce and send her away?"

8 Jesus replied, "Moses permitted you to divorce your wives because your hearts were hard. But it was not this way from the beginning. 9 I tell you that anyone who divorces his wife, except for marital unfaithfulness, and marries another woman commits adultery."

10 The disciples said to him, "If this is the situation between a husband and wife, it is better not to marry."

11 Jesus replied, "Not everyone can accept this teaching, but only those to whom it has been given. 12 For some are eunuchs because they were born that way; others were made that way by men; and others have renounced marriage[p] because of the kingdom of heaven. The one who can accept this should accept it."

The little children and Jesus

13 Then little children were brought to Jesus for him to place his hands on them and pray for them. But the disciples rebuked those who brought them.

14 Jesus said, "Let the little children come to me, and do not hinder them, for the kingdom of heaven belongs to such as these." 15 When he had placed his hands on them, he went on from there.

The rich young man

16 Now a man came up to Jesus and asked, "Teacher, what good thing must I do to get eternal life?"

17 "Why do you ask me about what is good?" Jesus replied. "There is only One who is good. If you want to enter life, obey the commandments."

18 "Which ones?" the man inquired.

Jesus replied, " 'Do not murder, do not commit adultery, do not steal, do not give false testimony, 19 honor your father and mother,'[q] and 'love your neighbor as yourself.'[r] "

20 "All these I have kept," the young man said. "What do I still lack?"

21 Jesus answered, "If you want to be perfect, go, sell your possessions and give to the poor, and you will have treasure in heaven. Then come, follow me."

22 When the young man heard this, he went away sad, because he had great wealth.

23 Then Jesus said to his disciples, "I tell you the truth, it is hard for a rich man to enter the kingdom of heaven. 24 Again I tell you, it is easier for a camel to go through the eye of a needle than for a rich man to enter the kingdom of God."

25 When the disciples heard this, they were greatly astonished and asked, "Who then can be saved?"

26 Jesus looked at them and said, "With man this is impossible, but with God all things are possible."

27 Peter answered him, "We have left everything to follow you! What then will there be for us?"

[p] Or *have made themselves eunuchs.* [q] Exodus 20:12-16; Deut. 5:16-20. [r] Lev. 19:18.

Greek Interlinear

6 ὥστε οὐκέτι εἰσὶν δύο ἀλλὰ σὰρξ μία.
so as no longer are they two but flesh one.

ὃ οὖν ὁ θεὸς συνέζευξεν, ἄνθρωπος
What therefore - God yoked together, ε man

μὴ χωριζέτω. 7 λέγουσιν αὐτῷ· τί οὖν
let not separate. They say to him: Why then

Μωϋσῆς ἐνετείλατο δοῦναι βιβλίον ἀπο-
¹Moses ¹did ²enjoin to give a document of

στασίου καὶ ἀπολῦσαι; 8 λέγει αὐτοῖς·
divorce and to dismiss? He says to them:

ὅτι Μωϋσῆς πρὸς τὴν σκληροκαρδίαν
- Moses in view of the obduracy

ὑμῶν ἐπέτρεψεν ὑμῖν ἀπολῦσαι τὰς
of you allowed you to dismiss the

γυναῖκας ὑμῶν· ἀπ' ἀρχῆς δὲ οὐ
wives of you; but from [the] beginning not

γέγονεν οὕτως. 9 λέγω δὲ ὑμῖν ὅτι
it has been so. But I say to you that

ὃς ἂν ἀπολύσῃ τὴν γυναῖκα αὐτοῦ
whoever dismisses the wife of him

μὴ ἐπὶ πορνείᾳ καὶ γαμήσῃ ἄλλην,
not of(for) fornication and marries another,

μοιχᾶται. 10 λέγουσιν αὐτῷ οἱ μαθηταί·
commits adultery. Say to him the disciples:

εἰ οὕτως ἐστὶν ἡ αἰτία τοῦ ἀνθρώπου
If so is the cause of the man

μετὰ τῆς γυναικός, οὐ συμφέρει γαμῆσαι.
with the wife, it is not expedient to marry.

11 ὁ δὲ εἶπεν αὐτοῖς· οὐ πάντες χωροῦσιν
And he said to them: Not all men grasp

τὸν λόγον τοῦτον, ἀλλ' οἷς δέδοται.
- saying this, but [those] to whom it has been given.

12 εἰσὶν γὰρ εὐνοῦχοι οἵτινες ἐκ κοιλίας
For there are eunuchs who from [the] womb

μητρὸς ἐγεννήθησαν οὕτως, καὶ εἰσὶν
of a mother were born so, and there are

εὐνοῦχοι οἵτινες εὐνουχίσθησαν ὑπὸ τῶν
eunuchs who were made eunuchs by -

ἀνθρώπων, καὶ εἰσὶν εὐνοῦχοι οἵτινες
men, and there are eunuchs who

εὐνούχισαν ἑαυτοὺς διὰ τὴν
made eunuchs themselves on account of the

βασιλείαν τῶν οὐρανῶν. ὁ δυνάμενος
kingdom of the heavens. The [one] being able

χωρεῖν χωρείτω.
to grasp [it] let him grasp.

13 Τότε προσηνέχθησαν αὐτῷ παιδία,
Then were brought to him children,

ἵνα τὰς χεῖρας ἐπιθῇ αὐτοῖς καὶ
that the(his) hands he should put on them and

προσεύξηται· οἱ δὲ μαθηταὶ ἐπετίμησαν
pray; but the disciples rebuked

αὐτοῖς. 14 ὁ δὲ Ἰησοῦς εἶπεν· ἄφετε
them. - But Jesus said: Permit

τὰ παιδία καὶ μὴ κωλύετε αὐτὰ ἐλθεῖν
the children and do not prevent them to come

πρός με· τῶν γὰρ τοιούτων ἐστὶν ἡ
unto me; - for of such is the

βασιλεία τῶν οὐρανῶν. 15 καὶ ἐπιθεὶς
kingdom of the heavens. And putting on

τὰς χεῖρας αὐτοῖς ἐπορεύθη ἐκεῖθεν.
the(his) hands on them he went thence.

16 Καὶ ἰδοὺ εἷς προσελθὼν αὐτῷ εἶπεν·
And behold one approaching to him said:

διδάσκαλε, τί ἀγαθὸν ποιήσω ἵνα
Teacher, what good thing may I do that

σχῶ ζωὴν αἰώνιον; ὁ δὲ εἶπεν αὐτῷ·
I may have life eternal? And he said to him:

17 τί με ἐρωτᾷς περὶ τοῦ ἀγαθοῦ;
Why me questionest thou concerning the good?

εἷς ἐστιν ὁ ἀγαθός· εἰ δὲ θέλεις εἰς
one is the good; but if thou wishest into

τὴν ζωὴν εἰσελθεῖν, τήρει τὰς ἐντολάς.
- life to enter, keep the commandments.

18 λέγει αὐτῷ· ποίας; ὁ δὲ Ἰησοῦς
He says to him: Which? - And Jesus

ἔφη· τὸ οὐ φονεύσεις, οὐ μοιχεύσεις,
said: - Thou shalt not kill, Thou shalt not commit adultery,

οὐ κλέψεις, οὐ ψευδομαρτυρήσεις,
Thou shalt not steal, Thou shalt not bear false witness,

19 τίμα τὸν πατέρα καὶ τὴν μητέρα,
Honour the(thy) father and the(thy) mother,

καὶ ἀγαπήσεις τὸν πλησίον σου ὡς
and Thou shalt love the neighbour of thee as

σεαυτόν. 20 λέγει αὐτῷ ὁ νεανίσκος·
thyself. Says to him the young man:

ταῦτα πάντα ἐφύλαξα· τί ἔτι ὑστερῶ;
¹These things ¹all I kept; what yet do I lack?

21 ἔφη αὐτῷ ὁ Ἰησοῦς· εἰ θέλεις τέλειος
Said to him - Jesus: If thou wishest perfect

εἶναι, ὕπαγε πώλησόν σου τὰ ὑπάρχοντα
to be, go sell of thee the belongings

καὶ δὸς πτωχοῖς, καὶ ἕξεις
and give to [the] poor, and thou shalt have

θησαυρὸν ἐν οὐρανοῖς, καὶ δεῦρο ἀκολούθει
treasure in heavens, and come follow

μοι. 22 ἀκούσας δὲ ὁ νεανίσκος τὸν
me. But hearing the young man the

λόγον [τοῦτον] ἀπῆλθεν λυπούμενος·
word this went away grieving;

ἦν γὰρ ἔχων κτήματα πολλά. 23 Ὁ
for he was having possessions many.

δὲ Ἰησοῦς εἶπεν τοῖς μαθηταῖς αὐτοῦ·
So Jesus said to the disciples of him:

ἀμὴν λέγω ὑμῖν ὅτι πλούσιος δυσκόλως
Truly I tell you that a rich man hardly

εἰσελεύσεται εἰς τὴν βασιλείαν τῶν
will enter into the kingdom of the

οὐρανῶν. 24 πάλιν δὲ λέγω ὑμῖν,
heavens. And again I tell you,

εὐκοπώτερόν ἐστιν κάμηλον διὰ τρήματος
easier it is a camel through [the] eye

ῥαφίδος εἰσελθεῖν ἢ πλούσιον εἰς τὴν
of a needle to enter than a rich man into the

βασιλείαν τοῦ θεοῦ. 25 ἀκούσαντες δὲ
kingdom of God. And hearing

οἱ μαθηταὶ ἐξεπλήσσοντο σφόδρα
the disciples were astounded exceedingly

λέγοντες· τίς ἄρα δύναται σωθῆναι;
saying: Who then can to be saved?

26 ἐμβλέψας δὲ ὁ Ἰησοῦς εἶπεν
And looking upon - Jesus said

αὐτοῖς· παρὰ ἀνθρώποις τοῦτο ἀδύνατόν
to them: With men this impossible

ἐστιν, παρὰ δὲ θεῷ πάντα δυνατά.
is, but with God all things [are] possible.

27 Τότε ἀποκριθεὶς ὁ Πέτρος εἶπεν αὐτῷ·
Then answering - Peter said to him:

ἰδοὺ ἡμεῖς ἀφήκαμεν πάντα καὶ
Behold we left all things and

ἠκολουθήσαμέν σοι· τί ἄρα ἔσται
followed thee; what then shall be
=shall we have?

63

King James Version

what shall we have therefore? 28And Jesus said unto them, Verily I say unto you, That ye which have followed me, in the regeneration when the Son of man shall sit in the throne of his glory, ye also shall sit upon twelve thrones, judging the twelve tribes of Israel. 29And every one that hath forsaken houses, or brethren, or sisters, or father, or mother, or wife, or children, or lands, for my name's sake, shall receive a hundredfold, and shall inherit everlasting life. 30 But many *that are* first shall be last; and the last *shall be* first.

20 For the kingdom of heaven is like unto a man *that is* a householder, which went out early in the morning to hire labourers into his vineyard. 2And when he had agreed with the labourers for a penny a day, he sent them into his vineyard. 3And he went out about the third hour, and saw others standing idle in the marketplace, 4And said unto them; Go ye also into the vineyard, and whatsoever is right I will give you. And they went their way. 5Again he went out about the sixth and ninth hour, and did likewise. 6And about the eleventh hour he went out, and found others standing idle, and saith unto them, Why stand ye here all the day idle? 7 They say unto him, Because no man hath hired us. He saith unto them, Go ye also into the vineyard; and whatsoever is right, *that* shall ye receive. 8 So when even was come, the lord of the vineyard saith unto his steward, Call the labourers, and give them *their* hire, beginning from the last unto the first. 9And when they came that *were hired* about the eleventh hour, they received every man a penny. 10 But when the first came, they supposed that they should have received more; and they likewise received every man a penny. 11And when they had received *it*, they murmured against the goodman of the house, 12 Saying, These last have wrought *but* one hour, and thou hast made them equal unto us, which have borne the burden and heat of the day. 13 But he answered one of them, and said, Friend, I do thee no wrong: didst not thou agree with me for a penny? 14 Take *that* thine *is*, and go thy way: I will give unto this last, even as unto thee. 15 Is it not lawful for me to do what I will with mine own? Is thine eye evil, because I am good? 16 So the last shall be first, and the first last: for many be called, but few chosen.

17 And Jesus going up to Jerusalem took the twelve disciples apart in the way, and said unto them, 18 Behold, we go up to Jerusalem; and the Son of man shall be betrayed unto the chief priests and unto the scribes, and they shall condemn him to death, 19And shall deliver him to

New International Version

28 Jesus said to them, "I tell you the truth, at the renewal of all things, when the Son of Man sits on his throne in heavenly glory, you who have followed me will also sit on twelve thrones, judging the twelve tribes of Israel. 29And everyone who has left houses or brothers or sisters or father or mother or children or fields for my sake will receive a hundred times as much and will inherit eternal life. 30 But many who are first will be last, and many who are last will be first.

The parable of the workers in the vineyard

20 "The kingdom of heaven is like a landowner who went out early in the morning to hire men to work in his vineyard. 2 He agreed to pay them a denarius for the day and sent them into his vineyard.

3 "About the third hour he went out and saw others standing in the marketplace doing nothing. 4 He told them, 'You also go and work in my vineyard, and I will pay you whatever is right.' 5 So they went.

"He went out again about the sixth hour and the ninth hour and did the same thing. 6About the eleventh hour he went out and found still others standing around. He asked them, 'Why have you been standing here all day long doing nothing?'

7 " 'Because no one has hired us,' they answered.

"He said to them, 'You also go and work in my vineyard.'

8 "When evening came, the owner of the vineyard said to his foreman, 'Call the workers and pay them their wages, beginning with the last ones hired and going on to the first.'

9 "The workers who were hired about the eleventh hour came and each received a denarius. 10 So when those came who were hired first, they expected to receive more. But each one of them also received a denarius. 11 When they received it, they began to grumble against the landowner. 12 'These men who were hired last worked only one hour,' they said, 'and you have made them equal to us who have borne the burden of the work and the heat of the day.'

13 "But he answered one of them, 'Friend, I am not being unfair to you. Didn't you agree to work for a denarius? 14 Take your pay and go. I want to give the man who was hired last the same as I gave you. 15 Don't I have the right to do what I want with my own money? Or are you envious because I am generous?'

16 "So the last will be first, and the first will be last."

Jesus again predicts his death

17 Now as Jesus was going up to Jerusalem, he took the twelve disciples aside and said to them, 18 "We are going up to Jerusalem, and the Son of Man will be betrayed to the chief priests and the teachers of the law. They will condemn him to death 19 and will turn him

Greek Interlinear

ἡμῖν; **28** ὁ δὲ Ἰησοῦς εἶπεν αὐτοῖς·
to us^e?   - And Jesus said to them:

ἀμὴν λέγω ὑμῖν ὅτι ὑμεῖς οἱ ἀκολουθή-
Truly I tell you that ye the [ones] having

σαντές μοι, ἐν τῇ παλιγγενεσίᾳ, ὅταν
followed me, in the regeneration, when

καθίσῃ ὁ υἱὸς τοῦ ἀνθρώπου ἐπὶ θρόνου
sits the Son - of man on [the] throne

δόξης αὐτοῦ, καθήσεσθε καὶ αὐτοὶ ἐπὶ
of glory of him, ye will sit also [your]selves on

δώδεκα θρόνους κρίνοντες τὰς δώδεκα
twelve thrones judging the twelve

φυλὰς τοῦ Ἰσραήλ. **29** καὶ πᾶς ὅστις
tribes - of Israel. And everyone who

ἀφῆκεν οἰκίας ἢ ἀδελφοὺς ἢ ἀδελφὰς ἢ
left houses or brothers or sisters or

πατέρα ἢ μητέρα ἢ τέκνα ἢ ἀγροὺς
father or mother or children or fields

ἕνεκεν τοῦ ἐμοῦ ὀνόματος, πολλαπλα-
for the sake of - my name, mani-

σίονα λήμψεται καὶ ζωὴν αἰώνιον
fold will receive and life eternal

κληρονομήσει. **30** Πολλοὶ δὲ ἔσονται πρῶτοι
will inherit. But many ²will be ¹first

ἔσχατοι καὶ ἔσχατοι πρῶτοι.
²last and last first.

Chapter 20

Ὁμοία γάρ ἐστιν ἡ βασιλεία τῶν
For like is the kingdom of the

οὐρανῶν ἀνθρώπῳ οἰκοδεσπότῃ, ὅστις
heavens to a man a housemaster, who

ἐξῆλθεν ἅμα πρωῒ μισθώσασθαι
went out early in the morning to hire

ἐργάτας εἰς τὸν ἀμπελῶνα αὐτοῦ. **2** συμ-
workmen in the vineyard of him. And

φωνήσας δὲ μετὰ τῶν ἐργατῶν ἐκ δηναρίου
agreeing with the workmen out of(for) a denarius

τὴν ἡμέραν ἀπέστειλεν αὐτοὺς εἰς τὸν
the day he sent them into the

ἀμπελῶνα αὐτοῦ. **3** καὶ ἐξελθὼν περὶ
vineyard of him. And going out about

τρίτην ὥραν εἶδεν ἄλλους ἑστῶτας
[the] third hour he saw others standing

ἐν τῇ ἀγορᾷ ἀργούς, **4** καὶ ἐκείνοις
in the marketplace idle, and to those

εἶπεν· ὑπάγετε καὶ ὑμεῖς εἰς τὸν
said: Go also ye into the

ἀμπελῶνα, καὶ ὃ ἐὰν ᾖ δίκαιον δώσω
vineyard, and whatever may be just I will give

ὑμῖν. οἱ δὲ ἀπῆλθον. **5** πάλιν [δὲ]
you. And they went. And again

ἐξελθὼν περὶ [the] ἕκτην καὶ ἐνάτην ὥραν
going out about [the] sixth and [the] ninth hour

ἐποίησεν ὡσαύτως. **6** περὶ δὲ τὴν
he did similarly. And about the

ἑνδεκάτην ἐξελθὼν εὗρεν ἄλλους ἑστῶτας,
eleventh going out he found others standing,

καὶ λέγει αὐτοῖς· τί ὧδε ἑστήκατε
and says to them: Why here stand ye

ὅλην τὴν ἡμέραν ἀργοί; **7** λέγουσιν αὐτῷ·
all the day idle? They say to him:

ὅτι οὐδεὶς ἡμᾶς ἐμισθώσατο. λέγει αὐτοῖς·
Because no one us hired. He says to them:

ὑπάγετε καὶ ὑμεῖς εἰς τὸν ἀμπελῶνα.
Go also ye into the vineyard.

8 ὀψίας δὲ γενομένης λέγει ὁ κύριος
And evening having come^a says the lord
= when evening had come

τοῦ ἀμπελῶνος τῷ ἐπιτρόπῳ αὐτοῦ·
of the vineyard to the steward of him:

κάλεσον τοὺς ἐργάτας καὶ ἀπόδος τὸν
Call the workmen and pay the

μισθόν, ἀρξάμενος ἀπὸ τῶν ἐσχάτων
wage, beginning from the last ones

ἕως τῶν πρώτων. **9** ἐλθόντες δὲ οἱ
until the first. And coming the [ones]

περὶ τὴν ἑνδεκάτην ὥραν ἔλαβον ἀνὰ
about the eleventh hour received each

δηνάριον. **10** καὶ ἐλθόντες οἱ πρῶτοι
a denarius. And coming the first

ἐνόμισαν ὅτι πλεῖον λήμψονται· καὶ
supposed that more they will receive; and

ἔλαβον τὸ ἀνὰ δηνάριον καὶ αὐτοί.
they received the ²each ¹denarius also [them]selves.

11 λαβόντες δὲ ἐγόγγυζον κατὰ τοῦ
And receiving they grumbled against the

οἰκοδεσπότου λέγοντες· **12** οὗτοι οἱ ἔσχατοι
housemaster saying: These - last

μίαν ὥραν ἐποίησαν, καὶ ἴσους αὐτοὺς
one hour wrought, and equal them

ἡμῖν ἐποίησας τοῖς βαστάσασι τὸ
to us thou madest the [ones] having borne the

βάρος τῆς ἡμέρας καὶ τὸν καύσωνα.
burden of the day and the heat.

13 ὁ δὲ ἀποκριθεὶς ἑνὶ αὐτῶν εἶπεν·
But he answering to one of them said:

ἑταῖρε, οὐκ ἀδικῶ σε· οὐχὶ
Comrade, I do not injure thee; not

δηναρίου συνεφώνησάς μοι; **14** ἆρον
of(for) a denarius thou didst agree with me? take

τὸ σὸν καὶ ὕπαγε· θέλω δὲ
the thine and go; but I wish
= that which is thine

τούτῳ τῷ ἐσχάτῳ δοῦναι ὡς καὶ
to this - last man to give as also

σοί· **15** οὐκ ἔξεστίν μοι ὃ θέλω
to thee; is it not lawful to me what I wish

ποιῆσαι ἐν τοῖς ἐμοῖς; ἢ ὁ
to do among the my things? or the

ὀφθαλμός σου πονηρός ἐστιν ὅτι ἐγὼ
eye of thee evil is because I

ἀγαθός εἰμι; **16** Οὕτως ἔσονται οἱ ἔσχατοι
good am? Thus will be the last [ones]

πρῶτοι καὶ οἱ πρῶτοι ἔσχατοι.
first and the first last.

17 Μέλλων δὲ ἀναβαίνων Ἰησοῦς εἰς
And being about to go up Jesus to

Ἰεροσόλυμα παρέλαβεν τοὺς δώδεκα κατ'
Jerusalem he took the twelve private-

ἰδίαν, καὶ ἐν τῇ ὁδῷ εἶπεν αὐτοῖς·
ly, and in the way said to them:

18 ἰδοὺ ἀναβαίνομεν εἰς Ἰεροσόλυμα, καὶ
Behold we are going up to Jerusalem, and

ὁ υἱὸς τοῦ ἀνθρώπου παραδοθήσεται τοῖς
the Son - of man will be delivered to the

ἀρχιερεῦσιν καὶ γραμματεῦσιν, καὶ κατα-
chief priests and scribes, and they will

κρινοῦσιν αὐτὸν εἰς θάνατον, **19** καὶ
condemn him to death, and

65

King James Version

the Gentiles to mock, and to scourge, and to crucify *him:* and the third day he shall rise again.
20 Then came to him the mother of Zebedee's children with her sons, worshipping *him,* and desiring a certain thing of him. 21And he said unto her, What wilt thou? She saith unto him, Grant that these my two sons may sit, the one on thy right hand, and the other on the left, in thy kingdom. 22 But Jesus answered and said, Ye know not what ye ask. Are ye able to drink of the cup that I shall drink of, and to be baptized with the baptism that I am baptized with? They say unto him, We are able. 23And he saith unto them, Ye shall drink indeed of my cup, and be baptized with the baptism that I am baptized with: but to sit on my right hand, and on my left, is not mine to give, but *it shall be given to them* for whom it is prepared of my Father. 24And when the ten heard *it,* they were moved with indignation against the two brethren. 25 But Jesus called them *unto him,* and said, Ye know that the princes of the Gentiles exercise dominion over them, and they that are great exercise authority upon them. 26 But it shall not be so among you: but whosoever will be great among you, let him be your minister; 27And whosoever will be chief among you, let him be your servant: 28 Even as the Son of man came not to be ministered unto, but to minister, and to give his life a ransom for many. 29And as they departed from Jericho, a great multitude followed him.
30 And, behold, two blind men sitting by the way side, when they heard that Jesus passed by, cried out, saying, Have mercy on us, O Lord, *thou* Son of David. 31And the multitude rebuked them, because they should hold their peace: but they cried the more, saying, Have mercy on us, O Lord, *thou* Son of David. 32And Jesus stood still, and called them, and said, What will ye that I shall do unto you? 33 They say unto him, Lord, that our eyes may be opened. 34 So Jesus had compassion *on them,* and touched their eyes: and immediately their eyes received sight, and they followed him.

21 And when they drew nigh unto Jerusalem, and were come to Bethphage, unto the mount of Olives, then sent Jesus two disciples, 2 Saying unto them, Go into the village over against you, and straightway ye shall find an ass tied, and a colt with her: loose *them,* and bring *them* unto me. 3And if any *man* say aught unto you, ye shall say, The Lord hath need of them; and straightway he will send them. 4All this was done, that it might be fulfilled which was spoken by the prophet, saying, 5 Tell ye the daughter of Sion, Behold, thy King cometh unto thee, meek, and sitting upon an ass, and a colt the foal of

New International Version

over to the Gentiles to be mocked and flogged and crucified. On the third day he will be raised to life!"

A mother's request

20 Then the mother of Zebedee's sons came to Jesus with her sons and, kneeling down, asked a favor of him.
21 "What is it you want?" he asked.
She said, "Grant that one of these two sons of mine may sit at your right and the other at your left in your kingdom."
22 "You don't know what you are asking," Jesus said to them. "Can you drink the cup I am going to drink?"
"We can," they answered.
23 Jesus said to them, "You will indeed drink from my cup, but to sit at my right or left is not for me to grant. These places belong to those for whom they have been prepared by my Father."
24 When the ten heard about this, they were indignant with the two brothers. 25 Jesus called them together and said, "You know that the rulers of the Gentiles lord it over them, and their high officials exercise authority over them. 26 Not so with you. Instead, whoever wants to become great among you must be your servant, 27 and whoever wants to be first must be your slave—28 just as the Son of Man did not come to be served, but to serve, and to give his life a ransom for many."

Two blind men receive sight

29 As Jesus and his disciples were leaving Jericho, a large crowd followed him. 30 Two blind men were sitting by the roadside, and when they heard that Jesus was going by, they shouted, "Lord, Son of David, have mercy on us!"
31 The crowd rebuked them and told them to be quiet, but they shouted all the louder, "Lord, Son of David, have mercy on us!"
32 Jesus stopped and called them. "What do you want me to do for you?" he asked.
33 "Lord," they answered, "we want our sight."
34 Jesus had compassion on them and touched their eyes. Immediately they received their sight and followed him.

The triumphal entry

21 As they approached Jerusalem and came to Bethphage on the Mount of Olives, Jesus sent two disciples, 2 saying to them, "Go to the village ahead of you, and at once you will find a donkey tied there, with her colt by her. Untie them and bring them to me. 3 If anyone says anything to you, tell him that the Lord needs them, and he will send them right away."
4 This took place to fulfill what was spoken through the prophet:
5 "Say to the daughter of Zion,
　'See, your king comes to you,
　gentle and riding on a donkey,
　　on a colt, the foal of a donkey.' " *s*

[s] Zech. 9:9.

Greek Interlinear

παραδώσουσιν αὐτὸν τοῖς ἔθνεσιν εἰς
they will deliver him to the nations for

τὸ ἐμπαῖξαι καὶ μαστιγῶσαι καὶ
- to mock and to scourge and

σταυρῶσαι, καὶ τῇ τρίτῃ ἡμέρᾳ ἐγερθή-
to crucify, and on the third day he will be

σεται.
raised.

20 Τότε προσῆλθεν αὐτῷ ἡ μήτηρ τῶν
Then approached to him the mother of the

υἱῶν Ζεβεδαίου μετὰ τῶν υἱῶν αὐτῆς
sons of Zebedee with the sons of her

προσκυνοῦσα καὶ αἰτοῦσά τι ἀπ' αὐτοῦ.
doing obeisance and asking something from him.

21 ὁ δὲ εἶπεν αὐτῇ· τί θέλεις; λέγει
And he said to her: What wishest thou? She says

αὐτῷ· εἰπὲ ἵνα καθίσωσιν οὗτοι οἱ
to him: Say that may sit these the

δύο υἱοί μου εἷς ἐκ δεξιῶν καὶ εἷς
two sons of me one on [the] right and one

ἐξ εὐωνύμων σου ἐν τῇ βασιλείᾳ
on [the] left of thee in the kingdom

σου. **22** ἀποκριθεὶς δὲ ὁ Ἰησοῦς
of thee. And answering - Jesus

εἶπεν· οὐκ οἴδατε τί αἰτεῖσθε.
said: Ye know not what ye ask.

δύνασθε πιεῖν τὸ ποτήριον ὃ ἐγὼ
Can ye to drink the cup which I

μέλλω πίνειν; λέγουσιν αὐτῷ· δυνάμεθα.
am about to drink? They say to him: We can.

23 λέγει αὐτοῖς· τὸ μὲν ποτήριόν μου
He says to them: Indeed the cup of me

πίεσθε, τὸ δὲ καθίσαι ἐκ δεξιῶν
ye shall drink, - but to sit on [the] right

μου καὶ ἐξ εὐωνύμων οὐκ ἔστιν
of me and on [the] left is not

ἐμὸν τοῦτο δοῦναι, ἀλλ' οἷς ἡτοί-
mine this to give, but to whom it has

μασται ὑπὸ τοῦ πατρός μου. **24** καὶ
been prepared by the Father of me. And

ἀκούσαντες οἱ δέκα ἠγανάκτησαν περὶ
hearing the ten were incensed about

τῶν δύο ἀδελφῶν. **25** ὁ δὲ Ἰησοῦς
the two brothers. - So Jesus

προσκαλεσάμενος αὐτοῖς εἶπεν· οἴδατε
calling forward them said: Ye know

ὅτι οἱ ἄρχοντες τῶν ἐθνῶν κατακυριεύουσιν
that the rulers of the nations lord it over

αὐτῶν καὶ οἱ μεγάλοι κατεξουσιάζουσιν
them and the great ones have authority over

αὐτῶν. **26** οὐχ οὕτως ἐστὶν ἐν ὑμῖν·
them. Not thus is it among you;

ἀλλ' ὃς ἐὰν θέλῃ ἐν ὑμῖν μέγας γενέσθαι,
but whoever wishes among you great to become,

ἔσται ὑμῶν διάκονος, **27** καὶ ὃς ἂν
will be of you servant, and whoever

θέλῃ ἐν ὑμῖν εἶναι πρῶτος, ἔσται ὑμῶν
wishes among you to be first, he shall be of you

δοῦλος· **28** ὥσπερ ὁ υἱὸς τοῦ ἀνθρώπου
slave; as the Son - of man

οὐκ ἦλθεν διακονηθῆναι, ἀλλὰ διακο-
came not to be served, but to

νῆσαι καὶ δοῦναι τὴν ψυχὴν αὐτοῦ
serve and to give the life of him

λύτρον ἀντὶ πολλῶν.
a ransom instead of many.

29 Καὶ ἐκπορευομένων αὐτῶν ἀπὸ Ἰεριχὼ
And going out them* from Jericho
= as they were going out

ἠκολούθησεν αὐτῷ ὄχλος πολύς. **30** καὶ
followed him crowd a much. And

ἰδοὺ δύο τυφλοὶ καθήμενοι παρὰ τὴν
behold two blind men sitting beside the

ὁδόν, ἀκούσαντες ὅτι Ἰησοῦς παράγει,
way, hearing that Jesus is passing by,

ἔκραξαν λέγοντες· κύριε, ἐλέησον ἡμᾶς,
cried out saying: Lord, pity us,

υἱὸς Δαυίδ. **31** ὁ δὲ ὄχλος ἐπετίμησεν
son of David. But the crowd rebuked

αὐτοῖς ἵνα σιωπήσωσιν· οἱ δὲ μεῖζον
them that they should be silent; but they more

ἔκραξαν λέγοντες· κύριε, ἐλέησον ἡμᾶς,
cried out saying: Lord, pity us,

υἱὸς Δαυίδ. **32** καὶ στὰς ὁ Ἰησοῦς
son of David. And standing - Jesus

ἐφώνησεν αὐτοὺς καὶ εἶπεν· τί θέλετε
called them and said: What wish ye

ποιήσω ὑμῖν; **33** λέγουσιν αὐτῷ· κύριε,
I may do to you? They say to him: Lord,

ἵνα ἀνοιγῶσιν οἱ ὀφθαλμοὶ ἡμῶν.
that may be opened the eyes of us.

34 σπλαγχνισθεὶς δὲ ὁ Ἰησοῦς ἥψατο
And being filled with tenderness - Jesus touched

τῶν ὀμμάτων αὐτῶν, καὶ εὐθέως ἀνέβλεψαν
the eyes of them, and immediately they saw again

καὶ ἠκολούθησαν αὐτῷ.
and followed him.

Chapter 21

Καὶ ὅτε ἤγγισαν εἰς Ἰεροσόλυμα
And when they drew near to Jerusalem

καὶ ἦλθον εἰς Βηθφαγὴ εἰς τὸ ὄρος τῶν
and came to Bethphage to the mount of the

ἐλαιῶν, τότε Ἰησοῦς ἀπέστειλεν δύο
olives, then Jesus sent two

μαθητὰς **2** λέγων αὐτοῖς· πορεύεσθε εἰς
disciples telling them: Go ye into

τὴν κώμην τὴν κατέναντι ὑμῶν, καὶ εὐθὺς
the village - opposite you, and at once

εὑρήσετε ὄνον δεδεμένην καὶ πῶλον μετ'
ye will find an ass *having been* tied and a colt with

αὐτῆς· λύσαντες ἀγάγετέ μοι. **3** καὶ ἐάν
her/it; loosening bring to me. And if

τις ὑμῖν εἴπῃ τι, ἐρεῖτε ὅτι ὁ
anyone to you says anything, ye shall say[.] - The

κύριος αὐτῶν χρείαν ἔχει· εὐθὺς δὲ
Lord of them need has; and immediately

ἀποστελεῖ αὐτούς. **4** Τοῦτο δὲ γέγονεν
he will send them. Now this has happened

ἵνα πληρωθῇ τὸ ῥηθὲν διὰ τοῦ
that might be fulfilled the thing spoken through the

προφήτου λέγοντος· **5** εἴπατε τῇ θυγατρὶ
prophet saying: Tell ye the daughter

Σιών· ἰδοὺ ὁ βασιλεύς σου ἔρχεταί σοι
of Zion: Behold[,] the king of thee comes to thee

πραΰς καὶ ἐπιβεβηκὼς ἐπὶ ὄνον καὶ ἐπὶ
meek and having mounted on an ass and on

King James Version

an ass. 6And the disciples went, and did as Jesus commanded them, 7And brought the ass, and the colt, and put on them their clothes, and they set *him* thereon. 8And a very great multitude spread their garments in the way; others cut down branches from the trees, and strewed *them* in the way. 9And the multitudes that went before, and that followed, cried, saying, Hosanna to the Son of David: Blessed *is* he that cometh in the name of the Lord; Hosanna in the highest. 10And when he was come into Jerusalem, all the city was moved, saying, Who is this? 11And the multitude said, This is Jesus the prophet of Nazareth of Galilee.

12 And Jesus went into the temple of God, and cast out all them that sold and bought in the temple, and overthrew the tables of the money changers, and the seats of them that sold doves, 13And said unto them, It is written, My house shall be called the house of prayer; but ye have made it a den of thieves. 14And the blind and the lame came to him in the temple; and he healed them. 15And when the chief priests and scribes saw the wonderful things that he did, and the children crying in the temple, and saying, Hosanna to the Son of David; they were sore displeased, 16And said unto him, Hearest thou what these say? And Jesus saith unto them, Yea; have ye never read, Out of the mouth of babes and sucklings thou hast perfected praise?

17 And he left them, and went out of the city into Bethany; and he lodged there. 18 Now in the morning, as he returned into the city, he hungered. 19And when he saw a fig tree in the way, he came to it, and found nothing thereon, but leaves only, and said unto it, Let no fruit grow on thee henceforward for ever. And presently the fig tree withered away. 20And when the disciples saw *it*, they marvelled, saying, How soon is the fig tree withered away! 21 Jesus answered and said unto them, Verily I say unto you, If ye have faith, and doubt not, ye shall not only do this *which is done* to the fig tree, but also if ye shall say unto this mountain, Be thou removed, and be thou cast into the sea; it shall be done. 22And all things, whatsoever ye shall ask in prayer, believing, ye shall receive.

23 And when he was come into the temple, the chief priests and the elders of the people came unto him as he was teaching, and said, By what authority doest thou these things? and who gave thee this authority? 24And Jesus answered and said unto them, I also will ask you one thing, which if ye tell me, I in like wise will tell you by what authority I do these things.

New International Version

6 The disciples went and did as Jesus had instructed them. 7 They brought the donkey and the colt, placed their cloaks on them, and Jesus sat on them. 8A very large crowd spread their cloaks on the road, while others cut branches from the trees and spread them on the road. 9 The crowds that went ahead of him and those that followed shouted,

"Hosanna[t] to the Son of David!

Blessed is he who comes in the name of the Lord![u]

Hosanna[t] in the highest!"

10 When Jesus entered Jerusalem, the whole city was stirred and asked, "Who is this?"

11 The crowds answered, "This is Jesus, the prophet from Nazareth in Galilee."

Jesus at the temple

12 Jesus entered the temple area and drove out all who were buying and selling there. He overturned the tables of the money-changers and the benches of those selling doves. 13 "It is written," he said to them, " 'My house will be called a house of prayer,'[v] but you are making it a 'den of robbers.'[w] "

14 The blind and the lame came to him at the temple, and he healed them. 15 But when the chief priests and the teachers of the law saw the wonderful things he did and the children shouting in the temple area, "Hosanna[t] to the Son of David," they were indignant.

16 "Do you hear what these children are saying?" they asked him.

"Yes," replied Jesus, "have you never read,

'From the lips of children and infants

you have raised up praise'[y] ?"

17 And he left them and went out of the city to Bethany, where he spent the night.

The fig tree withers

18 Early the next morning, as he was on his way back to the city, he was hungry. 19 Seeing a fig tree by the road, he went up to it but found nothing on it except leaves. Then he said to it, "May you never bear fruit again!" Immediately the tree withered.

20 When the disciples saw this, they were amazed. "How did the fig tree wither so quickly?" they asked.

21 Jesus replied, "I tell you the truth, if you have faith and do not doubt, not only can you do what was done to the fig tree, but also you can say to this mountain, 'Go, throw yourself into the sea,' and it will be done. 22 If you believe, you will receive whatever you ask for in prayer."

The authority of Jesus questioned

23 Jesus entered the temple courts, and, while he was teaching, the chief priests and the elders of the people came to him. "By what authority are you doing these things?" they asked. "And who gave you this authority?"

24 Jesus replied, "I will also ask you one question. If you answer me, I will tell you by

[t] A Hebrew expression meaning "Save!" which became an exclamation of praise. [u] Psalm 118:26. [v] Isaiah 56:7. [w] Jer. 7:11. [y] Psalm 8:2.

Greek Interlinear

πῶλον υἱὸν ὑποζυγίου. 6 πορευθέντες δὲ
a colt son(foal) of an ass. And going

οἱ μαθηταὶ καὶ ποιήσαντες καθὼς συνέταξεν
the disciples and doing as directed

αὐτοῖς ὁ Ἰησοῦς 7 ἤγαγον τὴν ὄνον καὶ
them - Jesus they brought the ass and

τὸν πῶλον, καὶ ἐπέθηκαν ἐπ' αὐτῶν
the colt, and put on on them

τὰ ἱμάτια, καὶ ἐπεκάθισεν ἐπάνω αὐτῶν.
the(ir) garments, and he sat on on them.

8 ὁ δὲ πλεῖστος ὄχλος ἔστρωσαν ἑαυτῶν
And the very large crowd strewed of themselves

τὰ ἱμάτια ἐν τῇ ὁδῷ, ἄλλοι δὲ ἔκοπτον
the garments in the way, and others cut

κλάδους ἀπὸ τῶν δένδρων καὶ ἐστρών-
branches from the trees and strewed

νυον ἐν τῇ ὁδῷ. 9 οἱ δὲ ὄχλοι
in the way. And the crowds the [ones]

προάγοντες αὐτὸν καὶ οἱ ἀκολουθοῦντες
going before him and the [ones] following

ἔκραζον λέγοντες· ὡσαννὰ τῷ υἱῷ Δαυίδ·
cried out saying: Hosanna to the son of David;

εὐλογημένος ὁ ἐρχόμενος ἐν ὀνόματι
blessed the [one] coming in [the] name

κυρίου· ὡσαννὰ ἐν τοῖς ὑψίστοις. 10 καὶ
of [the] Lord; hosanna in the highest [places]. And

εἰσελθόντος αὐτοῦ εἰς Ἱεροσόλυμα ἐσείσθη
entering him[a] into Jerusalem was shaken
= as he entered

πᾶσα ἡ πόλις λέγουσα· τίς ἐστιν οὗτος;
all the city saying: Who is this?

11 οἱ δὲ ὄχλοι ἔλεγον· οὗτός ἐστιν ὁ
And the crowds said: This is the

προφήτης Ἰησοῦς ὁ ἀπὸ Ναζαρὲθ τῆς
prophet Jesus the [one] from Nazareth -

Γαλιλαίας.
of Galilee.

12 Καὶ εἰσῆλθεν Ἰησοῦς εἰς τὸ ἱερὸν
And entered Jesus into the temple

καὶ ἐξέβαλεν πάντας τοὺς πωλοῦντας καὶ
and cast out all the [ones] selling and

ἀγοράζοντας ἐν τῷ ἱερῷ, καὶ τὰς τραπέζας
buying in the temple, and the tables

τῶν κολλυβιστῶν κατέστρεψεν καὶ τὰς
of the money-changers he overturned and the

καθέδρας τῶν πωλούντων τὰς περιστεράς,
seats of the [ones] selling the doves,

13 καὶ λέγει αὐτοῖς· γέγραπται· ὁ οἶκός
and says to them: It has been written: The house

μου οἶκος προσευχῆς κληθήσεται, ὑμεῖς
of me a house of prayer shall be called, [b]ye

δὲ αὐτὸν ποιεῖτε σπήλαιον λῃστῶν. 14 Καὶ
[1]but [4]it [3]are making a den of robbers. And

προσῆλθον αὐτῷ τυφλοὶ καὶ χωλοὶ ἐν τῷ
approached to him blind and lame [ones] in the

ἱερῷ, καὶ ἐθεράπευσεν αὐτούς. 15 ἰδόντες
temple, and he healed them. [3]seeing

δὲ οἱ ἀρχιερεῖς καὶ οἱ γραμματεῖς τὰ
[1]But [2]the [2]chief priests [4]and [5]the [6]scribes the

θαυμάσια ἃ ἐποίησεν καὶ τοὺς παῖδας
marvels which he did and the children

τοὺς κράζοντας ἐν τῷ ἱερῷ καὶ λέγοντας·
- crying out in the temple and saying:

ὡσαννὰ τῷ υἱῷ Δαυίδ, ἠγανάκτησαν, 16 καὶ
Hosanna to the son of David, they were incensed, and

εἶπαν αὐτῷ· ἀκούεις τί οὗτοι λέγουσιν;
said to him: Hearest thou what these are saying?

ὁ δὲ Ἰησοῦς λέγει αὐτοῖς· ναί· οὐδέποτε
- And Jesus says to them: Yes; never

ἀνέγνωτε ὅτι ἐκ στόματος νηπίων καὶ
did ye read[,] - Out of [the] mouth of infants and

θηλαζόντων κατηρτίσω αἶνον; 17 Καὶ
sucking [ones] thou didst prepare praise? And

καταλιπὼν αὐτοὺς ἐξῆλθεν ἔξω τῆς
leaving them he went forth outside the

πόλεως εἰς Βηθανίαν, καὶ ηὐλίσθη ἐκεῖ.
city to Bethany, and lodged there.

18 Πρωῒ δὲ ἐπαναγαγὼν εἰς τὴν πόλιν
Now early going up to the city

ἐπείνασεν. 19 καὶ ἰδὼν συκῆν μίαν ἐπὶ τῆς
he hungered. And seeing fig-tree one on the

ὁδοῦ ἦλθεν ἐπ' αὐτήν, καὶ οὐδὲν εὗρεν
way he went up(to) it, and nothing found

ἐν αὐτῇ εἰ μὴ φύλλα μόνον, καὶ λέγει
in it except leaves only, and says

αὐτῇ· οὐ μηκέτι ἐκ σοῦ καρπὸς γένηται
to it: Never of thee fruit may be

εἰς τὸν αἰῶνα. καὶ ἐξηράνθη παραχρῆμα
to the age. And was dried up instantly

ἡ συκῆ. 20 καὶ ἰδόντες οἱ μαθηταὶ
the fig-tree. And seeing the disciples

ἐθαύμασαν λέγοντες· πῶς παραχρῆμα
marvelled saying: How instantly

ἐξηράνθη ἡ συκῆ; 21 ἀποκριθεὶς δὲ ὁ
was withered the fig-tree? And answering -

Ἰησοῦς εἶπεν αὐτοῖς· ἀμὴν λέγω ὑμῖν,
Jesus said to them: Truly I say to you,

ἐὰν ἔχητε πίστιν καὶ μὴ διακριθῆτε,
If ye have faith and do not doubt,

οὐ μόνον τὸ τῆς συκῆς ποιήσετε, ἀλλὰ
not only the[a] of the fig-tree ye will do, but

κἂν τῷ ὄρει τούτῳ εἴπητε· ἄρθητι
also if - mountain to this ye say: Be thou taken

καὶ βλήθητι εἰς τὴν θάλασσαν, γενήσεται·
and cast into the sea, it shall be;

22 καὶ πάντα ὅσα ἂν αἰτήσητε ἐν τῇ
and all things whatever ye may ask in -

προσευχῇ πιστεύοντες λήμψεσθε.
prayer believing ye shall receive.

23 Καὶ ἐλθόντος αὐτοῦ εἰς τὸ ἱερὸν
And coming him[a] into the temple
= as he came

προσῆλθον αὐτῷ διδάσκοντι οἱ ἀρχιερεῖς
approached to him teaching[a] the chief priests
= while he taught

καὶ οἱ πρεσβύτεροι τοῦ λαοῦ λέγοντες·
and the elders of the people saying:

ἐν ποίᾳ ἐξουσίᾳ ταῦτα ποιεῖς; καὶ
By what authority these things doest thou? and

τίς σοι ἔδωκεν τὴν ἐξουσίαν ταύτην;
who thee gave the authority this?

24 ἀποκριθεὶς δὲ ὁ Ἰησοῦς εἶπεν αὐτοῖς·
And answering - Jesus said to them:

ἐρωτήσω ὑμᾶς κἀγὼ λόγον ἕνα, ὃν
will question you I also word one, which

ἐὰν εἴπητέ μοι, κἀγὼ ὑμῖν ἐρῶ ἐν ποίᾳ
if ye tell me, I also you will tell by what

* Some such word as 'sign' must be supplied.

King James Version

25 The baptism of John, whence was it? from heaven, or of men? And they reasoned with themselves, saying, If we shall say, From heaven; he will say unto us, Why did ye not then believe him? 26 But if we shall say, Of men; we fear the people; for all hold John as a prophet. 27And they answered Jesus, and said, We cannot tell. And he said unto them, Neither tell I you by what authority I do these things.

28 But what think ye? A *certain* man had two sons; and he came to the first, and said, Son, go work to day in my vineyard. 29 He answered and said, I will not; but afterward he repented, and went. 30And he came to the second, and said likewise. And he answered and said, I *go*, sir; and went not. 31 Whether of them twain did the will of *his* father? They say unto him, The first. Jesus saith unto them, Verily I say unto you, That the publicans and the harlots go into the kingdom of God before you. 32 For John came unto you in the way of righteousness, and ye believed him not; but the publicans and the harlots believed him: and ye, when ye had seen *it*, repented not afterward, that ye might believe him.

33 Hear another parable: There was a certain householder, which planted a vineyard, and hedged it round about, and digged a winepress in it, and built a tower, and let it out to husbandmen, and went into a far country: 34And when the time of the fruit drew near, he sent his servants to the husbandmen, that they might receive the fruits of it. 35And the husbandmen took his servants, and beat one, and killed another, and stoned another. 36Again, he sent other servants more than the first: and they did unto them likewise. 37 But last of all he sent unto them his son, saying, They will reverence my son. 38 But when the husbandmen saw the son, they said among themselves, This is the heir; come, let us kill him, and let us seize on his inheritance. 39And they caught him, and cast *him* out of the vineyard, and slew *him*. 40 When the lord therefore of the vineyard cometh, what will he do unto those husbandmen? 41 They say unto him, He will miserably destroy those wicked men, and will let out *his* vineyard unto other husbandmen, which shall render him the fruits in their seasons. 42 Jesus saith unto them, Did ye never read in the Scriptures, The stone which the builders rejected, the same is become the head of the corner: this is the Lord's doing, and it is marvellous in our eyes? 43 Therefore say I unto you, The kingdom of God shall be taken from you, and given to a nation bringing forth the fruits thereof. 44And whosoever shall fall on this stone shall be broken: but on whomsoever

New International Version

what authority I am doing these things. 25 John's baptism—where did it come from? Was it from heaven, or from men?"

They discussed it among themselves and said, "If we say, 'From heaven,' he will ask, 'Then why didn't you believe him?' 26 But if we say, 'From men'—we are afraid of the people, for they all hold that John was a prophet."

27 So they answered Jesus, "We don't know."

Then he said, "Neither will I tell you by what authority I am doing these things.

The parable of the two sons

28 "What do you think? There was a man who had two sons. He went to the first and said, 'Son, go and work today in the vineyard.'

29 " 'I will not,' he answered, but later he changed his mind and went.

30 "Then the father went to the other son and said the same thing. He answered, 'I will, sir,' but he did not go.

31 "Which of the two did what his father wanted?"

"The first," they answered.

Jesus said to them, "I tell you the truth, the tax collectors and the prostitutes are entering the kingdom of God ahead of you. 32 For John came to you to show you the way of righteousness, and you did not believe him, but the tax collectors and the prostitutes did. And even after you saw this, you did not repent and believe him.

The parable of the tenants

33 "Listen to another parable: There was a landowner who planted a vineyard. He put a wall around it, dug a wine press in it and built a tower. Then he rented the vineyard to some farmers and went away on a journey. 34 When the harvest time approached, he sent his servants to the tenants to collect his fruit.

35 "The tenants seized his servants; they beat one, killed another, and stoned a third. 36 Then he sent other servants to them, more than the first time, and the tenants treated them the same way. 37 Last of all, he sent his son to them. 'They will respect my son,' he said.

38 "But when the tenants saw the son, they said to one another, 'This is the heir. Come, let's kill him and take his inheritance.' 39 So they took him and threw him out of the vineyard and killed him.

40 "Therefore, when the owner of the vineyard comes, what will he do to those tenants?"

41 "He will bring those wretches to a wretched end," they replied, "and he will rent the vineyard to other tenants, who will give him his share of the crop at harvest time."

42 Jesus said to them, "Have you never read in the Scriptures:

" 'The stone the builders rejected
　　has become the capstone;
the Lord has done this,
　　and it is marvelous in our eyes' [z] ?

43 "Therefore I tell you that the kingdom of God will be taken away from you and given to a people who will produce its fruit. 44 He who falls on this stone will be broken to pieces, but he on whom it falls will be crushed." [a]

[z] *Psalm 118:22, 23.* [a] Some MSS omit verse 44.

Greek Interlinear

ἐξουσίᾳ ταῦτα ποιῶ· **25** τὸ βάπτισμα
authority these things I do: The baptism

τὸ Ἰωάννου πόθεν ἦν; ἐξ οὐρανοῦ ἢ
- of John whence was it? from heaven or

ἐξ ἀνθρώπων; οἱ δὲ διελογίζοντο ἐν
from men? And they reasoned among

ἑαυτοῖς λέγοντες· ἐὰν εἴπωμεν· ἐξ οὐρανοῦ,
themselves saying: If we say: From heaven,

ἐρεῖ ἡμῖν· διὰ τί οὖν οὐκ ἐπιστεύσατε
he will say to us: Why then believed ye not

αὐτῷ; **26** ἐὰν δὲ εἴπωμεν· ἐξ ἀνθρώπων,
him? But if we say: From men,

φοβούμεθα τὸν ὄχλον· πάντες γὰρ ὡς
we fear the crowd: for all as

προφήτην ἔχουσιν τὸν Ἰωάννην. **27** καὶ
a prophet have - John. And

ἀποκριθέντες τῷ Ἰησοῦ εἶπαν· οὐκ
answering - Jesus they said: We do

οἴδαμεν. ἔφη αὐτοῖς καὶ αὐτός· οὐδὲ
not know. said to them also he: Neither

ἐγὼ λέγω ὑμῖν ἐν ποίᾳ ἐξουσίᾳ ταῦτα
I tell you by what authority these things

ποιῶ. **28** Τί δὲ ὑμῖν δοκεῖ; ἄνθρωπος
I do. But what to you seems it? A man

εἶχεν τέκνα δύο· προσελθὼν τῷ πρώτῳ
had children two: approaching to the first

εἶπεν· τέκνον, ὕπαγε σήμερον ἐργάζου ἐν
he said: Child, go to-day work in

τῷ ἀμπελῶνι. **29** ὁ δὲ ἀποκριθεὶς εἶπεν·
the vineyard. But he answering said:

ἐγὼ κύριε, καὶ οὐκ ἀπῆλθεν. **30** προσ-
I [go], lord, and went not. And

ελθὼν δὲ τῷ δευτέρῳ εἶπεν ὡσαύτως.
approaching to the second he said similarly.

ὁ δὲ ἀποκριθεὶς εἶπεν· οὐ θέλω, ὕστερον
And he answering said: I will not, later

μεταμεληθεὶς ἀπῆλθεν. **31** τίς ἐκ τῶν δύο
repenting he went. Which of the two

ἐποίησεν τὸ θέλημα τοῦ πατρός; λέγουσιν·
did the will of the father? They say:

ὁ ὕστερος. λέγει αὐτοῖς ὁ Ἰησοῦς· ἀμὴν
The latter. Says to them - Jesus: Truly

λέγω ὑμῖν ὅτι οἱ τελῶναι καὶ αἱ πόρναι
I tell you[,] - The tax-collectors and the harlots

προάγουσιν ὑμᾶς εἰς τὴν βασιλείαν τοῦ
are going before you into the kingdom

θεοῦ. **32** ἦλθεν γὰρ Ἰωάννης πρὸς ὑμᾶς
of God. For came John to you

ἐν ὁδῷ δικαιοσύνης, καὶ οὐκ ἐπιστεύσατε
in a way of righteousness, and ye believed not

αὐτῷ· οἱ δὲ τελῶναι καὶ αἱ πόρναι
him; but the tax-collectors and the harlots

ἐπίστευσαν αὐτῷ· ὑμεῖς δὲ ἰδόντες οὐδὲ
believed him; but ye seeing not

μετεμελήθητε ὕστερον τοῦ πιστεῦσαι αὐτῷ.
repented later - to believe[d] him.
=so as to believe

33 Ἄλλην παραβολὴν ἀκούσατε. Ἄνθρωπος
Another parable hear ye. A man

ἦν οἰκοδεσπότης ὅστις ἐφύτευσεν ἀμπελῶνα,
there was a housemaster who planted a vineyard,

καὶ φραγμὸν αὐτῷ περιέθηκεν καὶ ὤρυξεν
and 'a hedge 'it 'put round and dug

ἐν αὐτῷ ληνὸν καὶ ᾠκοδόμησεν πύργον,
in it a winepress and built a tower,

καὶ ἐξέδοτο αὐτὸν· γεωργοῖς, καὶ ἀπεδή-
and let it to husbandmen, and departed.

μησεν. **34** ὅτε δὲ ἤγγισεν ὁ καιρὸς τῶν
And when drew near the time of the

καρπῶν, ἀπέστειλεν τοὺς δούλους αὐτοῦ
fruits, he sent the slaves of him

πρὸς τοὺς γεωργοὺς λαβεῖν τοὺς καρποὺς
to the husbandmen to receive the fruits

αὐτοῦ. **35** καὶ λαβόντες οἱ γεωργοὶ
of it. And 'taking 'the 'husbandmen

τοὺς δούλους αὐτοῦ ὃν μὲν ἔδειραν, ὃν
the slaves of him this one they flogged, that

δὲ ἀπέκτειναν, ὃν δὲ ἐλιθοβόλησαν. **36** πάλιν
one they killed, another they stoned. Again

ἀπέστειλεν ἄλλους δούλους πλείονας τῶν
he sent other slaves more [than] the

πρώτων, καὶ ἐποίησαν αὐτοῖς ὡσαύτως.
first [ones], and they did to them similarly.

37 ὕστερον δὲ ἀπέστειλεν πρὸς αὐτοὺς
But later he sent to them

τὸν υἱὸν αὐτοῦ λέγων· ἐντραπήσονται
the son of him saying: They will reverence

τὸν υἱόν μου. **38** οἱ δὲ γεωργοὶ ἰδόντες
the son of me. But the husbandmen seeing

τὸν υἱὸν εἶπον ἐν ἑαυτοῖς· οὗτός ἐστιν
the son said among themselves: This is

ὁ κληρονόμος· δεῦτε ἀποκτείνωμεν αὐτὸν
the heir: come[,] let us kill him

καὶ σχῶμεν τὴν κληρονομίαν αὐτοῦ·
and let us possess the inheritance of him:

39 καὶ λαβόντες αὐτὸν ἐξέβαλον ἔξω τοῦ
and taking 'him 'they cast out outside the

ἀμπελῶνος καὶ ἀπέκτειναν. **40** ὅταν οὖν
vineyard and killed. When therefore

ἔλθῃ ὁ κύριος τοῦ ἀμπελῶνος, τί ποιήσει
comes the lord of the vineyard, what will he do

τοῖς γεωργοῖς ἐκείνοις; **41** λέγουσιν αὐτῷ·
- husbandmen to those? They say to him:

κακοὺς κακῶς ἀπολέσει αὐτούς, καὶ τὸν
Bad men badly he will destroy them, and the

ἀμπελῶνα ἐκδώσεται ἄλλοις γεωργοῖς,
vineyard he will give out to other husbandmen,

οἵτινες ἀποδώσουσιν αὐτῷ τοὺς καρποὺς
who will render to him the fruits

ἐν τοῖς καιροῖς αὐτῶν. **42** λέγει αὐτοῖς ὁ
in the seasons of them. Says to them -

Ἰησοῦς· οὐδέποτε ἀνέγνωτε ἐν ταῖς
Jesus: Did ye never read in the

γραφαῖς· λίθον ὃν ἀπεδοκίμασαν οἱ
scriptures: A stone which rejected the

οἰκοδομοῦντες, οὗτος ἐγενήθη εἰς κεφαλὴν
building [ones], this became - head

γωνίας· παρὰ κυρίου ἐγένετο αὕτη, καὶ
of [the] corner; from [the] Lord became this, and

ἔστιν θαυμαστὴ ἐν ὀφθαλμοῖς ἡμῶν; **43** διὰ
it is marvellous in [the] eyes of us? There-

τοῦτο λέγω ὑμῖν ὅτι ἀρθήσεται ἀφ' ὑμῶν
fore I tell you[,] - will be taken from you

ἡ βασιλεία τοῦ θεοῦ καὶ δοθήσεται
The kingdom - of God and will be given

ἔθνει ποιοῦντι τοὺς καρποὺς αὐτῆς.
to a nation producing the fruits of it.

44 [καὶ ὁ πεσὼν ἐπὶ τὸν λίθον τοῦτον
And the [one] falling on - stone this

συνθλασθήσεται· ἐφ' ὃν δ' ἂν πέσῃ,
will be broken in pieces; but on whomever it falls,

King James Version

it shall fall, it will grind him to powder. 45And when the chief priests and Pharisees had heard his parables, they perceived that he spake of them. 46 But when they sought to lay hands on him, they feared the multitude, because they took him for a prophet.

22 And Jesus answered and spake unto them again by parables, and said, 2 The kingdom of heaven is like unto a certain king, which made a marriage for his son, 3And sent forth his servants to call them that were bidden to the wedding: and they would not come. 4Again, he sent forth other servants, saying, Tell them which are bidden, Behold, I have prepared my dinner: my oxen and *my* fatlings *are* killed, and all things *are* ready: come unto the marriage. 5 But they made light of *it*, and went their ways, one to his farm, another to his merchandise: 6And the remnant took his servants, and entreated *them* spitefully, and slew *them*. 7 But when the king heard *thereof*, he was wroth: and he sent forth his armies, and destroyed those murderers, and burned up their city. 8 Then saith he to his servants, The wedding is ready, but they which were bidden were not worthy. 9 Go ye therefore into the highways, and as many as ye shall find, bid to the marriage. 10 So those servants went out into the highways, and gathered together all as many as they found, both bad and good: and the wedding was furnished with guests.

11 And when the king came in to see the guests, he saw there a man which had not on a wedding garment: 12And he saith unto him, Friend, how camest thou in hither not having a wedding garment? And he was speechless. 13 Then said the king to the servants, Bind him hand and foot, and take him away, and cast *him* into outer darkness; there shall be weeping and gnashing of teeth. 14 For many are called, but few *are* chosen.

15 Then went the Pharisees, and took counsel how they might entangle him in *his* talk. 16And they sent out unto him their disciples with the Herodians, saying, Master, we know that thou art true, and teachest the way of God in truth, neither carest thou for any *man*: for thou regardest not the person of men. 17 Tell us therefore, What thinkest thou? Is it lawful to give tribute unto Cesar, or not? 18 But Jesus perceived their wickedness, and said, Why tempt ye me, *ye* hypocrites? 19 Shew me the tribute money. And they brought unto him a penny. 20And he saith unto them, Whose *is* this image and superscription? 21 They say unto him, Cesar's. Then saith he unto them, Render therefore unto Cesar the things which are Cesar's;

New International Version

45 When the chief priests and the Pharisees heard Jesus' parables, they knew he was talking about them. 46 They looked for a way to arrest him, but they were afraid of the crowd because the people held that he was a prophet.

The parable of the wedding banquet

22 Jesus spoke to them again in parables, saying: 2 "The kingdom of heaven is like a king who prepared a wedding banquet for his son. 3 He sent his servants to those who had been invited to the banquet to tell them to come, but they refused to come.

4 "Then he sent some more servants and said, 'Tell those who have been invited that I have prepared my dinner: My oxen and fattened cattle have been butchered, and everything is ready. Come to the wedding banquet.'

5 "But they paid no attention and went off— one to his field, another to his business. 6 The rest seized his servants, mistreated them and killed them. 7 The king was enraged. He sent his army and destroyed those murderers and burned their city.

8 "Then he said to his servants, 'The wedding banquet is ready, but those I invited did not deserve to come. 9 Go to the street corners and invite to the banquet anyone you find.' 10 So the servants went out into the streets and gathered all the people they could find, both good and bad, and the wedding hall was filled with guests.

11 "But when the king came in to see the guests, he noticed a man there who was not wearing wedding clothes. 12 'Friend,' he asked, 'how did you get in here without wedding clothes?' The man was speechless.

13 "Then the king told the attendants, 'Tie him hand and foot, and throw him outside, into the darkness, where there will be weeping and grinding of teeth.'

14 "For many are invited, but few are chosen."

Paying taxes to Caesar

15 Then the Pharisees went out and laid plans to trap him in his words. 16 They sent their disciples to him along with the Herodians. "Teacher," they said, "we know you are a man of integrity and that you teach the way of God in accordance with the truth. You aren't swayed by men, because you pay no attention to who they are. 17 Tell us then, what is your opinion? Is it right to pay taxes to Caesar or not?"

18 But Jesus, knowing their evil intent, said, "You hypocrites, why are you trying to trap me? 19 Show me the coin used for paying the tax." They brought him a denarius, 20 and he asked them, "Whose portrait is this? And whose inscription?"

21 "Caesar's," they replied.

Then he said to them, "Give to Caesar what is Caesar's, and to God what is God's."

Greek Interlinear

λικμήσει αὐτόν.] **45** Καὶ ἀκούσαντες οἱ
it will crush to powder him. And hearing the

ἀρχιερεῖς καὶ οἱ Φαρισαῖοι τὰς παραβολὰς
chief priests and the Pharisees the parables

αὐτοῦ ἔγνωσαν ὅτι περὶ αὐτῶν λέγει·
of him they knew that concerning them he tells;

46 καὶ ζητοῦντες αὐτὸν κρατῆσαι ἐφοβήθησαν
and seeking him to seize they feared

τοὺς ὄχλους, ἐπεὶ εἰς προφήτην αὐτὸν εἶχον.
the crowds, since for a prophet him they had.

Chapter 22

Καὶ ἀποκριθεὶς ὁ Ἰησοῦς πάλιν
And answering - Jesus again

εἶπεν ἐν παραβολαῖς αὐτοῖς λέγων·
spoke in parables to them saying·

2 ὡμοιώθη ἡ βασιλεία τῶν οὐρανῶν
Was(is) likened the kingdom of the heavens

ἀνθρώπῳ βασιλεῖ, ὅστις ἐποίησεν γάμους
to a man a king, who made a wedding feast

τῷ υἱῷ αὐτοῦ. **3** καὶ ἀπέστειλεν τοὺς
for the son of him. And he sent the

δούλους αὐτοῦ καλέσαι τοὺς κεκλημένους
slaves of him to call the [ones] having been invited

εἰς τοὺς γάμους, καὶ οὐκ ἤθελον ἐλθεῖν.
to the feast, and they wished not to come.

4 πάλιν ἀπέστειλεν ἄλλους δούλους λέγων·
Again he sent other slaves saying·

εἴπατε τοῖς κεκλημένοις· ἰδοὺ τὸ
Tell the [ones] having been invited: Behold[,] the

ἄριστόν μου ἡτοίμακα, οἱ ταῦροί μου
supper of me I have prepared, the oxen of me

καὶ τὰ σιτιστὰ τεθυμένα, καὶ πάντα
and the fatted beasts having been killed, and all things

ἕτοιμα· δεῦτε εἰς τοὺς γάμους. **5** οἱ δὲ
[are] ready; come to the feast. But they

ἀμελήσαντες ἀπῆλθον, ὃς μὲν εἰς τὸν
not caring went off, one to the(his)

ἴδιον ἀγρόν, ὃς δὲ ἐπὶ τὴν ἐμπορίαν
own field, another on the trading

αὐτοῦ· **6** οἱ δὲ λοιποὶ κρατήσαντες
of him; and the rest seizing

τοὺς δούλους αὐτοῦ ὕβρισαν καὶ ἀπέκτειναν.
the slaves of him insulted and killed.

7 ὁ δὲ βασιλεὺς ὠργίσθη, καὶ πέμψας
So the king became angry, and sending

τὰ στρατεύματα αὐτοῦ ἀπώλεσεν τοὺς
the armies of him destroyed -

φονεῖς ἐκείνους καὶ τὴν πόλιν αὐτῶν
murderers those and the city of them

ἐνέπρησεν. **8** τότε λέγει τοῖς δούλοις
burned. Then he says to the slaves

αὐτοῦ· ὁ μὲν γάμος ἕτοιμός ἐστιν, οἱ δὲ
of him: Indeed the feast ready is, but the [ones]

κεκλημένοι οὐκ ἦσαν ἄξιοι· **9** πορεύεσθε
having been invited were not worthy; go ye

οὖν ἐπὶ τὰς διεξόδους τῶν ὁδῶν, καὶ
therefore onto the partings of the ways, and

ὅσους ἐὰν εὕρητε καλέσατε εἰς τοὺς
as many as ye find call to the

γάμους. **10** καὶ ἐξελθόντες οἱ δοῦλοι
feast. And going forth - slaves

ἐκεῖνοι εἰς τὰς ὁδοὺς συνήγαγον πάντας
those into the ways assembled all

οὓς εὗρον, πονηρούς τε καὶ ἀγαθούς·
whom they found, both bad and good;

καὶ ἐπλήσθη ὁ νυμφὼν ἀνακειμένων.
and was filled the wedding chamber of(with) reclining [ones].

11 εἰσελθὼν δὲ ὁ βασιλεὺς θεάσασθαι
But entering the king to behold

τοὺς ἀνακειμένους εἶδεν ἐκεῖ
the reclining [ones] he saw there

ἄνθρωπον οὐκ ἐνδεδυμένον ἔνδυμα γάμου·
a man not having been dressed[in] a dress of wedding;

12 καὶ λέγει αὐτῷ· ἑταῖρε, πῶς
and he says to him: Comrade, how

εἰσῆλθες ὧδε μὴ ἔχων ἔνδυμα γάμου;
enteredst thou here not having a dress of wedding?

ὁ δὲ ἐφιμώθη. **13** τότε ὁ βασιλεὺς
And he was silenced. Then the king

εἶπεν τοῖς διακόνοις· δήσαντες αὐτοῦ
said to the servants: Binding of him

πόδας καὶ χεῖρας ἐκβάλετε αὐτὸν
feet and hands throw out him

εἰς τὸ σκότος τὸ ἐξώτερον· ἐκεῖ ἔσται
into the darkness - outer; there will be

ὁ κλαυθμὸς καὶ ὁ βρυγμὸς τῶν
the wailing and the gnashing of the

ὀδόντων. **14** Πολλοὶ γάρ εἰσιν κλητοί,
teeth. For many are called,

ὀλίγοι δὲ ἐκλεκτοί.
but few chosen.

15 Τότε πορευθέντες οἱ Φαρισαῖοι συμ-
Then going the Pharisees coun-

βούλιον ἔλαβον ὅπως αὐτὸν παγιδεύσωσιν
sel took so as him they might ensnare

ἐν λόγῳ. **16** καὶ ἀποστέλλουσιν αὐτῷ
in a word. And they send to him

τοὺς μαθητὰς αὐτῶν μετὰ τῶν Ἡρω-
the disciples of them with the Hero-

διανῶν λέγοντας· διδάσκαλε, οἴδαμεν
dians saying· Teacher, we know

ὅτι ἀληθὴς εἶ καὶ τὴν ὁδὸν τοῦ
that truthful thou art and the way -

θεοῦ ἐν ἀληθείᾳ διδάσκεις, καὶ οὐ
of God in truth thou teachest, and not

μέλει σοι περὶ οὐδενός, οὐ γὰρ
it concerns to thee about no one(anyone), ²not ¹for

βλέπεις εἰς πρόσωπον ἀνθρώπων·
¹thou lookest to face of men;

17 εἰπὸν οὖν ἡμῖν, τί σοι δοκεῖ;
tell therefore us, what to thee seems it?

ἔξεστιν δοῦναι κῆνσον Καίσαρι ἢ οὔ;
is it lawful to give tribute to Cæsar or no?

18 γνοὺς δὲ ὁ Ἰησοῦς τὴν πονηρίαν
But knowing - Jesus the wickedness

αὐτῶν εἶπεν· τί με πειράζετε, ὑποκριταί;
of them said: Why me tempt ye, hypocrites?

19 ἐπιδείξατέ μοι τὸ νόμισμα τοῦ κήνσου.
Show me the money of the tribute.

οἱ δὲ προσήνεγκαν αὐτῷ δηνάριον. **20** καὶ
And they brought to him a denarius. And

λέγει αὐτοῖς· τίνος ἡ εἰκὼν αὕτη
he says to them: Of whom - image this

καὶ ἡ ἐπιγραφή; **21** λέγουσιν· Καίσαρος.
and - superscription? They say: Of Cæsar.

τότε λέγει αὐτοῖς· ἀπόδοτε οὖν τὰ
Then he says to them: Render then the things

Καίσαρος Καίσαρι καὶ τὰ τοῦ θεοῦ
of Cæsar to Cæsar and the things - of God

King James Version

and unto God the things that are God's. 22 When they had heard *these words,* they marvelled, and left him, and went their way.

23 The same day came to him the Sadducees, which say that there is no resurrection, and asked him, 24 Saying, Master, Moses said, If a man die, having no children, his brother shall marry his wife, and raise up seed unto his brother. 25 Now there were with us seven brethren: and the first, when he had married a wife, deceased, and, having no issue, left his wife unto his brother: 26 Likewise the second also, and the third, unto the seventh. 27 And last of all the woman died also. 28 Therefore in the resurrection, whose wife shall she be of the seven? for they all had her. 29 Jesus answered and said unto them, Ye do err, not knowing the Scriptures, nor the power of God. 30 For in the resurrection they neither marry, nor are given in marriage, but are as the angels of God in heaven. 31 But as touching the resurrection of the dead, have ye not read that which was spoken unto you by God, saying, 32 I am the God of Abraham, and the God of Isaac, and the God of Jacob? God is not the God of the dead, but of the living. 33 And when the multitude heard *this,* they were astonished at his doctrine.

34 But when the Pharisees had heard that he had put the Sadducees to silence, they were gathered together. 35 Then one of them, *which was* a lawyer, asked *him a question,* tempting him, and saying, 36 Master, which *is* the great commandment in the law? 37 Jesus said unto him, Thou shalt love the Lord thy God with all thy heart, and with all thy soul, and with all thy mind. 38 This is the first and great commandment. 39 And the second *is* like unto it, Thou shalt love thy neighbour as thyself. 40 On these two commandments hang all the law and the prophets.

41 While the Pharisees were gathered together, Jesus asked them, 42 Saying, What think ye of Christ? whose son is he? They say unto him, *The son* of David. 43 He saith unto them, How then doth David in spirit call him Lord, saying, 44 The Lord said unto my Lord, Sit thou on my right hand, till I make thine enemies thy footstool? 45 If David then call him Lord, how is he his son? 46 And no man was able to answer him a word, neither durst any *man* from that day forth ask him any more *questions.*

23 Then spake Jesus to the multitude, and to his disciples, 2 Saying, The scribes and the Pharisees sit in Moses' seat: 3 All therefore

New International Version

22 When they heard this, they were amazed. So they left him and went away.

Marriage at the resurrection

23 That same day the Sadducees, who say there is no resurrection, came to him with a question. 24 "Teacher," they said, "Moses told us that if a man dies without having children, his brother must marry the widow and have children for him. 25 Now there were seven brothers among us. The first one married and died, and since he had no children, he left his wife to his brother. 26 The same thing happened to the second and third brother, right on down to the seventh. 27 Finally, the woman died. 28 Now then, at the resurrection, whose wife will she be of the seven, since all of them were married to her?"

29 Jesus replied, "You are in error because you do not know the Scriptures or the power of God. 30 At the resurrection people will neither marry nor be given in marriage; they will be like the angels in heaven. 31 But about the resurrection of the dead—have you not read what God said to you, 32 'I am the God of Abraham, the God of Isaac, and the God of Jacob'[b]? He is not the God of the dead but of the living."

33 When the crowds heard this, they were astonished at his teaching.

The greatest commandment

34 Hearing that Jesus had silenced the Sadducees, the Pharisees got together. 35 One of them, an expert in the law, tested him with this question: 36 "Teacher, which is the greatest commandment in the Law?"

37 Jesus replied: " 'Love the Lord your God with all your heart, with all your soul and with all your mind.'[c] 38 This is the first and greatest commandment. 39 And the second is like it: 'Love your neighbor as yourself.'[d] 40 All the Law and the Prophets hang on these two commandments."

Whose son is the Christ?

41 While the Pharisees were gathered together, Jesus asked them, 42 "What do you think about the Christ?[e] Whose son is he?"

"The son of David," they replied.

43 He said to them, "How is it then that David, speaking by the Spirit, calls him 'Lord'? For he says,

44 " 'The Lord said to my Lord:
    Sit at my right hand
        until I put your enemies under your
        feet.'[f]

45 If then David calls him 'Lord,' how can he be his son?" 46 No one could say a word in reply, and from that day on no one dared to ask him any more questions.

Seven woes

23 Then Jesus said to the crowds and to his disciples: 2 "The teachers of the law and the Pharisees sit in Moses' seat. 3 So you must

[b] Exodus 3:6. [c] Deut. 6:5. [d] Lev. 19:18. [e] Or *Messiah.* [f] Psalm 110:1.

74

Greek Interlinear

τῷ   θεῷ.   22 καὶ   ἀκούσαντες   ἐθαύμασαν,
-    to God.   And   hearing   they marvelled,

καὶ   ἀφέντες   αὐτὸν   ἀπῆλθαν.
and   leaving   him   went away.

23 Ἐν   ἐκείνῃ   τῇ   ἡμέρᾳ   προσῆλθον
On   that   -   day   approached

αὐτῷ   Σαδδουκαῖοι,   λέγοντες   μὴ   εἶναι
to him   Sadducees,   saying   not   to be

ἀνάστασιν,   καὶ   ἐπηρώτησαν   αὐτὸν
a resurrection,   and   questioned   him

24 λέγοντες·   διδάσκαλε,   Μωϋσῆς   εἶπεν·
saying: Teacher,   Moses   said:

ἐάν   τις   ἀποθάνῃ   μὴ   ἔχων   τέκνα,
If   any man   dies   not   having   children,

ἐπιγαμβρεύσει   ὁ   ἀδελφὸς   αὐτοῦ   τὴν
shall take to wife after   the   brother   of him   the

γυναῖκα   αὐτοῦ   καὶ   ἀναστήσει   σπέρμα
wife   of him   and   shall raise up   seed

τῷ   ἀδελφῷ   αὐτοῦ.   25 ἦσαν   δὲ   παρ'
to the   brother   of him.   Now there were   with

ἡμῖν   ἑπτὰ   ἀδελφοί·   καὶ   ὁ   πρῶτος
us   seven   brothers;   and   the   first

γήμας   ἐτελεύτησεν,   καὶ   μὴ   ἔχων
having married   died,   and   not   having

σπέρμα   ἀφῆκεν   τὴν   γυναῖκα   αὐτοῦ   τῷ
seed   left   the   wife   of him   to the

ἀδελφῷ   αὐτοῦ·   26 ὁμοίως   καὶ   ὁ   δεύτερος
brother   of him;   likewise   also   the   second

καὶ   ὁ   τρίτος,   ἕως   τῶν   ἑπτά.   27 ὕστερον
and   the   third,   until   of the   seven.   last

δὲ   πάντων   ἀπέθανεν   ἡ   γυνή.   28 ἐν   τῇ
And   of all   died   the   woman.   In   the

ἀναστάσει   οὖν   τίνος   τῶν   ἑπτὰ   ἔσται
resurrection   then   of which   of the   seven   will she be

γυνή;   πάντες   γὰρ   ἔσχον   αὐτήν.   29 ἀπο-
wife?   for all   had   her.   an-

κριθεὶς   δὲ   ὁ   Ἰησοῦς   εἶπεν   αὐτοῖς·
swering   And   -   Jesus   said   to them:

πλανᾶσθε   μὴ   εἰδότες   τὰς   γραφὰς   μηδὲ
Ye err   not   knowing   the   scriptures   nor

τὴν   δύναμιν   τοῦ   θεοῦ.   30 ἐν   γὰρ   τῇ
the   power   -   of God.   For in   the

ἀναστάσει   οὔτε   γαμοῦσιν   οὔτε   γαμίζονται,
resurrection   neither   they marry   nor   are given in marriage,

ἀλλ'   ὡς   ἄγγελοι   ἐν   τῷ   οὐρανῷ   εἰσιν.
but   as   angels   in   the   heaven   are.

31 περὶ   δὲ   τῆς   ἀναστάσεως   τῶν   νεκρῶν
But concerning   the   resurrection   of the   dead

οὐκ   ἀνέγνωτε   τὸ   ῥηθὲν   ὑμῖν   ὑπὸ
did ye not read   the thing   spoken   to you   by

τοῦ   θεοῦ   λέγοντος·   32 ἐγώ   εἰμι   ὁ   θεὸς
-    God   saying: I   am   the   God

Ἀβραὰμ   καὶ   ὁ   θεὸς   Ἰσαὰκ   καὶ   ὁ   θεὸς
of Abraham   and   the   God   of Isaac   and   the   God

Ἰακώβ;   οὐκ   ἔστιν   [ὁ]   θεὸς   νεκρῶν
of Jacob?   He is not   the   God   of dead men

ἀλλὰ   ζώντων.   33 καὶ   ἀκούσαντες   οἱ   ὄχλοι
but   of living [ones].   And   hearing   the   crowds

ἐξεπλήσσοντο   ἐπὶ   τῇ   διδαχῇ   αὐτοῦ.
were astounded   over(at)   the   teaching   of him.

34 Οἱ   δὲ   Φαρισαῖοι   ἀκούσαντες   ὅτι
But the   Pharisees   hearing   that

ἐφίμωσεν   τοὺς   Σαδδουκαίους,   συνήχθησαν
he silenced   the   Sadducees,   were assembled

ἐπὶ   τὸ   αὐτό,   35 καὶ   ἐπηρώτησεν   εἷς
together,   and   'questioned   'one

ἐξ   αὐτῶν   νομικὸς   πειράζων   αὐτόν·   36 δι-
'of   'them   'a lawyer   'tempting   him: Teach-

δάσκαλε,   ποία   ἐντολὴ   μεγάλη   ἐν   τῷ
er,   what   commandment [is]   great   in   the

νόμῳ;   37 ὁ   δὲ   ἔφη   αὐτῷ·   ἀγαπήσεις
law?   And he   said   to him: Thou shalt love

κύριον   τὸν   θεόν   σου   ἐν   ὅλῃ   τῇ   καρδίᾳ
[the] Lord   the   God   of thee   with   all   the   heart

σου   καὶ   ἐν   ὅλῃ   τῇ   ψυχῇ   σου   καὶ   ἐν
of thee   and   with   all   the   soul   of thee   and   with

ὅλῃ   τῇ   διανοίᾳ   σου.   38 αὕτη   ἐστὶν   ἡ
all   the   understanding   of thee.   This   is   the

μεγάλη   καὶ   πρώτη   ἐντολή.   39 δευτέρα
great   and   first   commandment.   [The] second

ὁμοία   αὐτῇ·   ἀγαπήσεις   τὸν   πλησίον   σου
[is] like   to it: Thou shalt love   the   neighbour   of thee

ὡς   σεαυτόν.   40 ἐν   ταύταις   ταῖς   δυσὶν   ἐντολαῖς
as   thyself.   In(on)   these   -   two   commandments

ὅλος   ὁ   νόμος   κρέμαται   καὶ   οἱ   προφῆται.
all   the   law   hangs   and   the   prophets.

41 Συνηγμένων   δὲ   τῶν   Φαρισαίων[a]
And having assembled   the   Pharisees
= when the Pharisees were assembled

ἐπηρώτησεν   αὐτοὺς   ὁ   Ἰησοῦς   42 λέγων·   τι
questioned   them   -   Jesus   saying: What

ὑμῖν   δοκεῖ   περὶ   τοῦ   χριστοῦ;   τίνος
to you   seems it concerning   the   Christ?   of whom

υἱός   ἐστιν;   λέγουσιν   αὐτῷ·   τοῦ   Δαυίδ.
son   is he?   They say   to him: -   Of David.

43 λέγει   αὐτοῖς·   πῶς   οὖν   Δαυὶδ   ἐν
He says   to them: How   then   David   in

πνεύματι   καλεῖ   αὐτὸν   κύριον   λέγων·
spirit   calls   him   Lord   saying:

44 εἶπεν   κύριος   τῷ   κυρίῳ   μου·
Said   [the] LORD   to the   Lord   of me:

κάθου   ἐκ   δεξιῶν   μου   ἕως   ἂν   θῶ   τοὺς
Sit   on [the] right   of me   until   I put   the

ἐχθρούς   σου   ὑποκάτω   τῶν   ποδῶν   σου;
enemies   of thee   underneath   the   feet   of thee?

45 εἰ   οὖν   Δαυὶδ   καλεῖ   αὐτὸν   κύριον,   πῶς
If   then   David   calls   him   Lord,   how

υἱὸς   αὐτοῦ   ἐστιν;   46 καὶ   οὐδεὶς   ἐδύνατο
son   of him   is he?   And   no one   was able

ἀποκριθῆναι   αὐτῷ   λόγον   οὐδὲ   ἐτόλμησέν
to answer   him   a word   nor   dared

τις   ἀπ'   ἐκείνης   τῆς   ἡμέρας   ἐπερωτῆσαι
anyone from   that   -   day   to question

αὐτὸν   οὐκέτι.
him   no(any) more.

Chapter 23

Τότε   ὁ   Ἰησοῦς   ἐλάλησεν   τοῖς   ὄχλοις
Then   -   Jesus   spoke   to the   crowds

καὶ   τοῖς   μαθηταῖς   αὐτοῦ   2 λέγων·   ἐπὶ
and   to the   disciples   of him   saying: On

τῆς   Μωϋσέως   καθέδρας   ἐκάθισαν   οἱ
the   of Moses   seat   sat   the

γραμματεῖς   καὶ   οἱ   Φαρισαῖοι.   3 πάντα
scribes   and   the   Pharisees.   All things

King James Version

whatsoever they bid you observe, *that* observe and do; but do not ye after their works: for they say, and do not. 4 For they bind heavy burdens and grievous to be borne, and lay *them* on men's shoulders; but they *themselves* will not move them with one of their fingers. 5 But all their works they do for to be seen of men: they make broad their phylacteries, and enlarge the borders of their garments, 6And love the uppermost rooms at feasts, and the chief seats in the synagogues, 7And greetings in the markets, and to be called of men, Rabbi, Rabbi. 8 But be not ye called Rabbi: for one is your Master, *even* Christ; and all ye are brethren. 9And call no *man* your father upon the earth: for one is your Father, which is in heaven. 10 Neither be ye called masters: for one is your Master, *even* Christ. 11 But he that is greatest among you shall be your servant. 12And whosoever shall exalt himself shall be abased; and he that shall humble himself shall be exalted.

13 But woe unto you, scribes and Pharisees, hypocrites! for ye shut up the kingdom of heaven against men: for ye neither go in *yourselves*, neither suffer ye them that are entering to go in. 14 Woe unto you, scribes and Pharisees, hypocrites! for ye devour widows' houses, and for a pretence make long prayer: therefore ye shall receive the greater damnation. 15 Woe unto you, scribes and Pharisees, hypocrites! for ye compass sea and land to make one proselyte; and when he is made, ye make him twofold more the child of hell than yourselves. 16 Woe unto you, *ye* blind guides, which say, Whosoever shall swear by the temple, it is nothing; but whosoever shall swear by the gold of the temple, he is a debtor! 17 *Ye* fools and blind: for whether is greater, the gold, or the temple that sanctifieth the gold? 18And, Whosoever shall swear by the altar, it is nothing; but whosoever sweareth by the gift that is upon it, he is guilty. 19 *Ye* fools and blind: for whether *is* greater, the gift, or the altar that sanctifieth the gift? 20 Whoso therefore shall swear by the altar, sweareth by it, and by all things thereon. 21And whoso shall swear by the temple, sweareth by it, and by him that dwelleth therein. 22And he that shall swear by heaven, sweareth by the throne of God, and by him that sitteth thereon. 23 Woe unto you, scribes and Pharisees, hypocrites! for ye pay tithe of mint and anise and cummin, and have omitted the weightier *matters* of the law, judgment, mercy, and faith: these ought ye to have done, and not to leave the other undone. 24 *Ye* blind guides, which strain at a gnat, and swallow a camel. 25 Woe unto you, scribes and Pharisees, hypocrites! for ye make clean the outside of the cup and of the platter, but within they are full of extortion and excess. 26 *Thou* blind Pharisee, cleanse first that *which is* within the cup and platter, that the outside of them may be clean also. 27 Woe unto you, scribes and Pharisees, hypocrites! for ye are like unto whited

New International Version

obey them and do everything they tell you. But do not do what they do, for they do not practice what they preach. 4 They tie up heavy loads and put them on men's shoulders, but they themselves are not willing to lift a finger to move them.

5 "Everything they do is done for men to see: They make their phylacteries[g] wide and the tassels of their prayer shawls long; 6 they love the place of honor at banquets and the most important seats in the synagogues; 7 they love to be greeted in the marketplaces and to have men call them 'Rabbi.'

8 "But you are not to be called 'Rabbi,' for you have only one Master and you are all brothers. 9And do not call anyone on earth 'father,' for you have one Father, and he is in heaven. 10 Nor are you to be called 'teacher,' for you have one Teacher, the Christ.[h] 11 The greatest among you will be your servant. 12 For whoever exalts himself will be humbled, and whoever humbles himself will be exalted.

13 "Woe to you, teachers of the law and Pharisees, you hypocrites! You shut the kingdom of heaven in men's faces. You yourselves do not enter, nor will you let those enter who are trying to.[i]

15 "Woe to you, teachers of the law and Pharisees, you hypocrites! You travel over land and sea to win a single convert, and when he becomes one, you make him twice as much a son of hell as you are.

16 "Woe to you, blind guides! You say, 'If anyone swears by the temple, it means nothing; but if anyone swears by the gold of the temple, he is bound by his oath.' 17 You blind fools! Which is greater: the gold, or the temple that makes the gold sacred? 18 You also say, 'If anyone swears by the altar, it means nothing; but if anyone swears by the gift on it, he is bound by his oath.' 19 You blind men! Which is greater: the gift, or the altar that makes the gift sacred? 20 Therefore, he who swears by the altar swears by it and by everything on it. 21And he who swears by the temple swears by it and by the one who dwells in it. 22And he who swears by heaven swears by God's throne and by the one who sits on it.

23 "Woe to you, teachers of the law and Pharisees, you hypocrites! You give a tenth of your spices—mint, dill and cummin. But you have neglected the more important matters of the law —justice, mercy and faithfulness. You ought to have practiced the latter, without neglecting the former. 24 You blind guides! You strain out a gnat but swallow a camel.

25 "Woe to you, teachers of the law and Pharisees, you hypocrites! You clean the outside of the cup and dish, but inside they are full of greed and self-indulgence. 26 Blind Pharisee! First clean the inside of the cup and dish, and then the outside also will be clean.

27 "Woe to you, teachers of the law and Pharisees, you hypocrites! You are like white-

[g] That is, boxes containing Scripture verses, which were worn on the forehead and arms. [h] Or *Messiah*. [i] Some MSS add verse 14: *Woe to you, teachers of the law and Pharisees, you hypocrites! You devour widows' houses and for a show make lengthy prayers. Therefore you will be punished more severely.*

Greek Interlinear

οὖν ὅσα ἐὰν εἴπωσιν ὑμῖν ποιήσατε
therefore whatever they may tell you do ye

καὶ τηρεῖτε, κατὰ δὲ τὰ ἔργα αὐτῶν
and keep, but according to the works of them

μὴ ποιεῖτε· λέγουσιν γὰρ καὶ οὐ ποιοῦσιν.
do ye not; for they say and do not.

4 δεσμεύουσιν δὲ φορτία βαρέα καὶ
And they bind burdens heavy and

ἐπιτιθέασιν ἐπὶ τοὺς ὤμους τῶν ἀνθρώπων,
put on on the shoulders - of men,

αὐτοὶ δὲ τῷ δακτύλῳ αὐτῶν οὐ
but they with the finger of them not

θέλουσιν κινῆσαι αὐτά. 5 πάντα δὲ
are willing to move them. But all

τὰ ἔργα αὐτῶν ποιοῦσιν πρὸς τὸ θεαθῆναι
the works of them they do for - to be seen

τοῖς ἀνθρώποις· πλατύνουσιν γὰρ τὰ
- by men; for they broaden the

φυλακτήρια αὐτῶν καὶ μεγαλύνουσιν τὰ
phylacteries of them and enlarge the

κράσπεδα, 6 φιλοῦσιν δὲ τὴν πρωτο-
fringes, and they like the chief

κλισίαν ἐν τοῖς δείπνοις καὶ τὰς πρωτο-
place in the suppers and the chief

καθεδρίας ἐν ταῖς συναγωγαῖς 7 καὶ τοὺς
seats in the synagogues . and the

ἀσπασμοὺς ἐν ταῖς ἀγοραῖς καὶ
greetings in the marketplaces and

καλεῖσθαι ὑπὸ τῶν ἀνθρώπων ῥαββί.
to be called by - men rabbi.

8 ὑμεῖς δὲ μὴ κληθῆτε ῥαββί· εἷς γὰρ
But ye be not called rabbi; for one

ἐστιν ὑμῶν ὁ διδάσκαλος, πάντες δὲ ὑμεῖς
is of you the teacher, and all ye

ἀδελφοί ἐστε. 9 καὶ πατέρα μὴ καλέσητε
brothers are. And father call ye not

ὑμῶν ἐπὶ τῆς γῆς· εἷς γάρ ἐστιν
of you on the earth; for one is

ὑμῶν ὁ πατὴρ ὁ οὐράνιος. 10 μηδὲ
of you the Father heavenly. Neither

κληθῆτε καθηγηταί, ὅτι καθηγητὴς
be ye called leaders, because leader

ὑμῶν ἐστιν εἷς ὁ Χριστός. 11 ὁ δὲ
of you is one the Christ. And the

μείζων ὑμῶν ἔσται ὑμῶν διάκονος.
greater of you shall be of you servant.

12 Ὅστις δὲ ὑψώσει ἑαυτὸν ταπεινωθήσεται,
And [he] who will exalt himself shall be humbled,

καὶ ὅστις ταπεινώσει ἑαυτὸν ὑψωθήσεται.
and [he] who will humble himself shall be exalted.

13 Οὐαὶ δὲ ὑμῖν, γραμματεῖς καὶ Φαρισαῖοι
But woe to you, scribes and Pharisees

ὑποκριταί, ὅτι κλείετε τὴν βασιλείαν
hypocrites, because ye shut the kingdom

τῶν οὐρανῶν ἔμπροσθεν τῶν ἀνθρώπων·
of the heavens before - men;

ὑμεῖς γὰρ οὐκ εἰσέρχεσθε, οὐδὲ τοὺς
for ye do not enter, nor the [ones]

εἰσερχομένους ἀφίετε εἰσελθεῖν.‡ 15 Οὐαὶ
entering do ye allow to enter. Woe

ὑμῖν, γραμματεῖς καὶ Φαρισαῖοι ὑποκριταί,
to you, scribes and Pharisees hypocrites,

ὅτι περιάγετε τὴν θάλασσαν καὶ τὴν
because ye go about the sea and the

ξηρὰν ποιῆσαι ἕνα προσήλυτον, καὶ ὅταν
dry [land] to make one proselyte, and when

γένηται, ποιεῖτε αὐτὸν υἱὸν γεέννης διπλό-
he becomes, ye make him a son of gehenna twofold

τερον ὑμῶν. 16 Οὐαὶ ὑμῖν, ὁδηγοὶ τυφλοὶ
more [than] you. Woe to you, leaders blind

οἱ λέγοντες· ὃς ἂν ὀμόσῃ ἐν τῷ ναῷ,
the [ones] saying: Whoever swears by the shrine,

οὐδέν ἐστιν· ὃς δ' ἂν ὀμόσῃ ἐν τῷ χρυσῷ
nothing it is; but whoever swears by the gold

τοῦ ναοῦ, ὀφείλει. 17 μωροὶ καὶ τυφλοί,
of the shrine, he owes. Fools and blind,

τίς γὰρ μείζων ἐστιν, ὁ χρυσὸς ἢ ὁ ναὸς
for which greater is, the gold or the shrine

ὁ ἁγιάσας τὸν χρυσόν; 18 καί· ὃς ἂν
- sanctifying the gold? And: whoever

ὀμόσῃ ἐν τῷ θυσιαστηρίῳ, οὐδέν ἐστιν·
swears by the altar, nothing it is;

ὃς δ' ἂν ὀμόσῃ ἐν τῷ δώρῳ τῷ ἐπάνω
but whoever swears by the gift - upon

αὐτοῦ, ὀφείλει. 19 τυφλοί, τί γὰρ μεῖζον,
it, he owes. Blind, for which [is] greater,

τὸ δῶρον ἢ τὸ θυσιαστήριον τὸ
the gift or the altar the

ἁγιάζον τὸ δῶρον; 20 ὁ οὖν ὀμόσας
sanctifying the gift? Therefore the [one] swearing

ἐν τῷ θυσιαστηρίῳ ὀμνύει ἐν αὐτῷ καὶ
by the altar swears by it and

ἐν πᾶσι τοῖς ἐπάνω αὐτοῦ· 21 καὶ ὁ
by all the things upon it; and the [one]

ὀμόσας ἐν τῷ ναῷ ὀμνύει ἐν αὐτῷ
swearing by the shrine swears by it

καὶ ἐν τῷ κατοικοῦντι αὐτόν· 22 καὶ
and by the [one] inhabiting it; and

ὁ ὀμόσας ἐν τῷ οὐρανῷ ὀμνύει ἐν τῷ
the [one] swearing by the heaven swears by the

θρόνῳ τοῦ θεοῦ καὶ ἐν τῷ καθημένῳ
throne - of God and by the [one] sitting

ἐπάνω αὐτοῦ. 23 Οὐαὶ ὑμῖν, γραμματεῖς
upon it. Woe to you, scribes

καὶ Φαρισαῖοι ὑποκριταί, ὅτι ἀποδεκατοῦτε
and Pharisees hypocrites, because ye tithe

τὸ ἡδύοσμον καὶ τὸ ἄνηθον καὶ τὸ
the mint and the dill and the

κύμινον, καὶ ἀφήκατε τὰ βαρύτερα
cummin, and ye [have] left the heavier things

τοῦ νόμου, τὴν κρίσιν καὶ τὸ ἔλεος
of the law, - judgment and - mercy

καὶ τὴν πίστιν· ταῦτα δὲ ἔδει ποιῆσαι
and - faith; but these things it behoved to do

κἀκεῖνα μὴ ἀφεῖναι. 24 ὁδηγοὶ τυφλοί,
and those not to leave. Leaders blind,

οἱ διϋλίζοντες τὸν κώνωπα, τὴν δὲ ²τὴν
the [ones] straining the gnat, but ²the

κάμηλον καταπίνοντες. 25 Οὐαὶ ὑμῖν,
²camel ¹swallowing. Woe to you,

γραμματεῖς καὶ Φαρισαῖοι ὑποκριταί, because
scribes and Pharisees hypocrites, because

καθαρίζετε τὸ ἔξωθεν τοῦ ποτηρίου καὶ
ye cleanse the outside of the cup and

τῆς παροψίδος, ἔσωθεν δὲ γέμουσιν ἐξ
the dish, but within they are full of

ἁρπαγῆς καὶ ἀκρασίας. 26 Φαρισαῖε τυφλέ,
robbery and intemperance. Pharisee blind,

καθάρισον πρῶτον τὸ ἐντὸς τοῦ ποτηρίου
cleanse thou first the inside of the cup

ἵνα γένηται καὶ τὸ ἐκτὸς αὐτοῦ καθαρόν.
that may be also the outside of it clean.

27 Οὐαὶ ὑμῖν, γραμματεῖς καὶ Φαρισαῖοι
Woe to you, scribes and Pharisees

ὑποκριταί, ὅτι παρομοιάζετε τάφοις κεκονια-
hypocrites, because ye resemble graves having been

---

‡ Ver. 14 omitted by Nestle

King James Version

sepulchres, which indeed appear beautiful outward, but are within full of dead *men's* bones, and of all uncleanness. 28 Even so ye also outwardly appear righteous unto men, but within ye are full of hypocrisy and iniquity. 29 Woe unto you, scribes and Pharisees, hypocrites! because ye build the tombs of the prophets, and garnish the sepulchres of the righteous, 30And say, If we had been in the days of our fathers, we would not have been partakers with them in the blood of the prophets. 31 Wherefore ye be witnesses unto yourselves, that ye are the children of them which killed the prophets. 32 Fill ye up then the measure of your fathers. 33 *Ye* serpents, *ye* generation of vipers, how can ye escape the damnation of hell?

34 Wherefore, behold, I send unto you prophets, and wise men, and scribes: and *some* of them ye shall kill and crucify; and *some* of them shall ye scourge in your synagogues, and persecute *them* from city to city: 35 That upon you may come all the righteous blood shed upon the earth, from the blood of righteous Abel unto the blood of Zacharias son of Barachias, whom ye slew between the temple and the altar. 36 Verily I say unto you, All these things shall come upon this generation. 37 O Jerusalem, Jerusalem, *thou* that killest the prophets, and stonest them which are sent unto thee, how often would I have gathered thy children together, even as a hen gathereth her chickens under *her* wings, and ye would not! 38 Behold, your house is left unto you desolate. 39 For I say unto you, Ye shall not see me henceforth, till ye shall say, Blessed *is* he that cometh in the name of the Lord.

24 And Jesus went out, and departed from the temple: and his disciples came to *him* for to shew him the buildings of the temple. 2And Jesus said unto them, See ye not all these things? verily I say unto you, There shall not be left here one stone upon another, that shall not be thrown down.

3 And as he sat upon the mount of Olives, the disciples came unto him privately, saying, Tell us, when shall these things be? and what *shall be* the sign of thy coming, and of the end of the world? 4And Jesus answered and said unto them, Take heed that no man deceive you. 5 For many shall come in my name, saying, I am Christ; and shall deceive many. 6And ye shall hear of wars and rumours of wars: see that ye be not troubled: for all *these things* must come to pass, but the end is not yet. 7 For nation shall rise against nation, and kingdom against kingdom: and there shall be famines, and pestilences, and earthquakes, in divers places. 8All these *are*

New International Version

washed tombs, which look beautiful on the outside but on the inside are full of dead men's bones and everything unclean. 28 In the same way, on the outside you appear to people as righteous but on the inside you are full of hypocrisy and wickedness.

29 "Woe to you, teachers of the law and Pharisees, you hypocrites! You build tombs for the prophets and decorate the graves of the righteous. 30And you say, 'If we had lived in the days of our forefathers, we would not have taken part with them in shedding the blood of the prophets.' 31 So you testify against yourselves that you are the descendants of those who murdered the prophets. 32 Fill up, then, the measure of the sin of your forefathers!

33 "You snakes! You brood of vipers! How will you escape being condemned to hell? 34 Therefore I am sending you prophets and wise men and teachers. Some of them you will kill and crucify; others you will flog in your synagogues and pursue from town to town. 35And so upon you will come all the righteous blood that has been shed on earth, from the blood of righteous Abel to the blood of Zechariah son of Berachiah, whom you murdered between the temple and the altar. 36 I tell you the truth, all this will come upon this generation.

37 "O Jerusalem, Jerusalem, you who kill the prophets and stone those sent to you, how often I have longed to gather your children together, as a hen gathers her chicks under her wings, but you were not willing. 38 Look, your house is left to you desolate. 39 For I tell you, you will not see me again until you say, 'Blessed is he who comes in the name of the Lord.' *j* "

Signs of the end of the age

24 Jesus left the temple and was walking away when his disciples came up to him to call his attention to its buildings. 2 "Do you see all these things?" he asked. "I tell you the truth, not one stone here will be left on another; every one will be thrown down."

3 As Jesus was sitting on the Mount of Olives, the disciples came to him privately. "Tell us," they said, "when will this happen, and what will be the sign of your coming and of the end of the age?"

4 Jesus answered: "Watch out that no one deceives you. 5 For many will come in my name, claiming, 'I am the Christ,*k*' and will deceive many. 6 You will hear of wars and rumors of wars, but see to it that you are not alarmed. Such things must happen, but the end is still to come. 7 Nation will rise against nation, and kingdom against kingdom. There will be famines and earthquakes in various places. 8All these are the beginning of birth pains.

[*j*] Psalm 118:26. [*k*] Or *Messiah*.

78

Greek Interlinear

μένοις,   οἵτινες   ἔξωθεν   μὲν   φαίνονται
whitewashed, who(which) outwardly indeed appear

ὡραῖοι,   ἔσωθεν   δὲ   γέμουσιν   ὀστέων
beautiful,   but within   they are full   of bones

νεκρῶν   καὶ   πάσης   ἀκαθαρσίας.   28 οὕτως
of dead men and   of all   uncleanness.   Thus

καὶ   ὑμεῖς   ἔξωθεν   μὲν   φαίνεσθε   τοῖς
also   ye   outwardly   indeed   appear   -

ἀνθρώποις   δίκαιοι,   ἔσωθεν   δὲ   ἐστε   μεστοὶ
to men   righteous,   but within   ye are   full

ὑποκρίσεως   καὶ   ἀνομίας.   29 Οὐαὶ   ὑμῖν,
of hypocrisy   and   of lawlessness.   Woe   to you

γραμματεῖς   καὶ   Φαρισαῖοι   ὑποκριταί,
scribes   and   Pharisees   hypocrites,

ὅτι   οἰκοδομεῖτε   τοὺς   τάφους   τῶν   προφητῶν
because ye build   the   graves   of the   prophets

καὶ   κοσμεῖτε   τὰ   μνημεῖα   τῶν   δικαίων,
and   adorn   the   monuments   of the   righteous,

30 καὶ   λέγετε·   εἰ   ἤμεθα   ἐν   ταῖς   ἡμέραις
and   say: If   we were   in   the   days

τῶν   πατέρων   ἡμῶν,   οὐκ   ἂν   ἤμεθα
of the   fathers   of us,   we would not have been

αὐτῶν   κοινωνοὶ   ἐν   τῷ   αἵματι   τῶν   προ-
of them   partakers   in   the   blood   of the   pro-

φητῶν.   31 ὥστε   μαρτυρεῖτε   ἑαυτοῖς   ὅτι
phets.   So   ye witness   to [your]selves   that

υἱοί   ἐστε   τῶν   φονευσάντων   τοὺς   προφήτας.
sons   ye are   of the [ones]   having killed   the   prophets.

32 καὶ   ὑμεῖς   πληρώσατε   τὸ   μέτρον   τῶν
And   ²ye   ¹fulfil   the   measure   of the

πατέρων   ὑμῶν.   33 ὄφεις,   γεννήματα   ἐχιδνῶν,
fathers   of you.   Serpents,   offspring   of vipers,

πῶς   φύγητε   ἀπὸ   τῆς   κρίσεως   τῆς   γεέννης;
how   escape ye   from   the   judgment   -   of gehenna?

34 διὰ   τοῦτο   ἰδοὺ   ἐγὼ   ἀποστέλλω   πρὸς
Therefore   behold   I   send   to

ὑμᾶς   προφήτας   καὶ   σοφοὺς   καὶ   γραμ-
you   prophets   and   wise men   and   scribes;

ματεῖς·   ἐξ   αὐτῶν   ἀποκτενεῖτε   καὶ
of   them   ye will kill   and

σταυρώσετε,   καὶ   ἐξ   αὐτῶν   μαστιγώσετε
will crucify,   and   of   them   ye will scourge

ἐν   ταῖς   συναγωγαῖς   ὑμῶν   καὶ   διώξετε
in   the   synagogues   of you   and   will persecute

ἀπὸ   πόλεως   εἰς   πόλιν·   35 ὅπως   ἔλθη
from   city   to   city;   so   comes

ἐφ'   ὑμᾶς   πᾶν   αἷμα   δίκαιον   ἐκχυννόμενον
on   you   all   blood   righteous   being shed

ἐπὶ   τῆς   γῆς   ἀπὸ   τοῦ   αἵματος   Ἀβελ   τοῦ
on   the   earth   from   the   blood   of Abel   the

δικαίου   ἕως   τοῦ   αἵματος   Ζαχαρίου   υἱοῦ
righteous   until   the   blood   of Zacharias   son

Βαραχίου,   ὃν   ἐφονεύσατε   μεταξὺ   τοῦ   ναοῦ
Barachias,   whom ye murdered   between   the   shrine

καὶ   τοῦ   θυσιαστηρίου.   36 ἀμὴν   λέγω
and   the   altar.   Truly   I tell

ὑμῖν,   ἥξει   ταῦτα   πάντα   ἐπὶ   τὴν
you,   will come   all these things   on   the

γενεὰν   ταύτην.   37 Ἰερουσαλὴμ   Ἰερουσαλήμ,
generation   this.   Jerusalem   Jerusalem,

ἡ   ἀποκτείνουσα   τοὺς   προφήτας   καὶ
the [one]   killing   the   prophets   and

λιθοβολοῦσα   τοὺς   ἀπεσταλμένους   πρὸς   αὐτήν,
stoning   the [ones]   sent   to   her,

ποσάκις   ἠθέλησα   ἐπισυναγαγεῖν   τὰ   τέκνα
how often   I wished   to gather   the   children

σου,   ὃν   τρόπον   ὄρνις   ἐπισυνάγει   τὰ
of thee,   as   a bird   gathers   the

νοσσία   [αὐτῆς]   ὑπὸ   τὰς   πτέρυγας,   καὶ
young   of her   under   the(her)   wings,   and

οὐκ   ἠθελήσατε.   38 ἰδοὺ   ἀφίεται   ὑμῖν   ὁ
ye wished not.   Behold   is left   to you   the

οἶκος   ὑμῶν.   39 λέγω   γὰρ   ὑμῖν,   οὐ   μὴ
house   of you.   For I tell   you,   by no means

με   ἴδητε   ἀπ'   ἄρτι   ἕως   ἂν   εἴπητε·
me   ye see   from   now   until   ye say:

εὐλογημένος   ὁ   ἐρχόμενος   ἐν   ὀνόματι
Blessed   the [one]   coming   in   [the] name

κυρίου.
of [the] Lord.

Chapter 24

Καὶ   ἐξελθὼν   ὁ   Ἰησοῦς   ἀπὸ   τοῦ
And   going forth   -   Jesus   from   the

ἱεροῦ   ἐπορεύετο,   καὶ   προσῆλθον   οἱ   μαθηταὶ
temple   went,   and   ⁴approached   ¹the   ³disciples

αὐτοῦ   ἐπιδεῖξαι   αὐτῷ   τὰς   οἰκοδομὰς
²of him   to show   him   the   buildings

τοῦ   ἱεροῦ.   2 ὁ   δὲ   ἀποκριθεὶς   εἶπεν
of the   temple.   And he   answering   said

αὐτοῖς·   οὐ   βλέπετε   ταῦτα   πάντα;   ἀμὴν
to them: See ye not   all these things?   Truly

λέγω   ὑμῖν,   οὐ   μὴ   ἀφεθῇ   ὧδε   λίθος   ἐπὶ
I tell   you,   by no means will be left   here   stone   on

λίθον   ὃς   οὐ   καταλυθήσεται.   3 Καθημένου
stone   which   shall not be overthrown.   sitting

δὲ   αὐτοῦ   ἐπὶ   τοῦ   ὄρους   τῶν   ἐλαιῶν
and   him   on   the   mount   of the   olives
= And as he sat

προσῆλθον   αὐτῷ   οἱ   μαθηταὶ   κατ'   ἰδίαν
approached   to him   the   disciples   privately

λέγοντες·   εἰπὲ   ἡμῖν,   πότε   ταῦτα   ἔσται,
saying: Tell   us,   when these things   will be,

καὶ   τί   τὸ   σημεῖον   τῆς   σῆς   παρουσίας
and   what   the   sign   -   of thy   presence

καὶ   συντελείας   τοῦ   αἰῶνος;   4 καὶ   ἀπο-
and   of [the] completion of the   age?   And   answer-

κριθεὶς   ὁ   Ἰησοῦς   εἶπεν   αὐτοῖς·   βλέπετε
ing   -   Jesus   said   to them: See ye

μή   τις   ὑμᾶς   πλανήσῃ.   5 πολλοὶ   γὰρ
not(lest) anyone   ²you   ¹cause   ³to err.   For many

ἐλεύσονται   ἐπὶ   τῷ   ὀνόματί   μου   λέγοντες·
will come   on(in)   the   name   of me   saying:

ἐγώ   εἰμι   ὁ   χριστός,   καὶ   πολλοὺς   πλανή-
I   am   the   Christ,   and   ²many   ¹will cause

σουσιν.   6 μελλήσετε   δὲ   ἀκούειν   πολέ-
³to err.   But ye will be about   to hear   [of]

μους   καὶ   ἀκοὰς   πολέμων·   ὁρᾶτε   μὴ
wars   and   rumours   of wars;   see   not

θροεῖσθε·   δεῖ   γὰρ   γενέσθαι,   ἀλλ'
ye are disturbed;   for it behoves   to happen,   but

οὔπω   ἐστὶν   τὸ   τέλος.   7 ἐγερθήσεται   γὰρ
not yet   is   the   end.   For will be raised

ἔθνος   ἐπὶ   ἔθνος   καὶ   βασιλεία   ἐπὶ   βασιλείαν,
nation against nation   and   kingdom   against   kingdom,

καὶ   ἔσονται   λιμοὶ   καὶ   σεισμοὶ
and   there will be   famines   and   earthquakes

κατὰ   τόπους·   8 πάντα   δὲ   ταῦτα   ἀρχὴ
throughout places;   but all these things   [are]   beginning

King James Version

the beginning of sorrows. 9 Then shall they deliver you up to be afflicted, and shall kill you: and ye shall be hated of all nations for my name's sake. 10And then shall many be offended, and shall betray one another, and shall hate one another. 11And many false prophets shall rise, and shall deceive many. 12And because iniquity shall abound, the love of many shall wax cold. 13 But he that shall endure unto the end, the same shall be saved. 14And this gospel of the kingdom shall be preached in all the world for a witness unto all nations; and then shall the end come. 15 When ye therefore shall see the abomination of desolation, spoken of by Daniel the prophet, stand in the holy place, (whoso readeth, let him understand,) 16 Then let them which be in Judea flee into the mountains: 17 Let him which is on the housetop not come down to take any thing out of his house: 18 Neither let him which is in the field return back to take his clothes. 19And woe unto them that are with child, and to them that give suck in those days! 20 But pray ye that your flight be not in the winter, neither on the sabbath day: 21 For then shall be great tribulation, such as was not since the beginning of the world to this time, no, nor ever shall be. 22And except those days should be shortened, there should no flesh be saved: but for the elect's sake those days shall be shortened. 23 Then if any man shall say unto you, Lo, here *is* Christ, or there; believe *it* not. 24 For there shall arise false Christs, and false prophets, and shall shew great signs and wonders; insomuch that, if *it were* possible, they shall deceive the very elect. 25 Behold, I have told you before. 26 Wherefore if they shall say unto you, Behold, he is in the desert; go not forth: behold, *he is* in the secret chambers; believe *it* not. 27 For as the lightning cometh out of the east, and shineth even unto the west; so shall also the coming of the Son of man be. 28 For wheresoever the carcass is, there will the eagles be gathered together. 29 Immediately after the tribulation of those days shall the sun be darkened, and the moon shall not give her light, and the stars shall fall from heaven, and the powers of the heavens shall be shaken: 30And then shall appear the sign of the Son of man in heaven: and then shall all the tribes of the earth mourn, and they shall see the Son of man coming in the clouds of heaven with power and great glory. 31And he shall send his angels with a great sound of a trumpet, and they shall gather together his elect from the four winds, from one end of heaven to the other. 32 Now learn a parable of the fig tree; When his branch is yet tender, and putteth forth leaves, ye know that summer *is* nigh: 33 So likewise ye, when ye shall see all these things, know that it is near, *even* at the doors.

New International Version

9 "Then you will be handed over to be persecuted and put to death, and you will be hated by all nations because of me. 10At that time many will turn away from the faith and will betray and hate each other, 11 and many false prophets will appear and deceive many people. 12 Because of the increase of wickedness, the love of most will grow cold, 13 but he who stands firm to the end will be saved. 14And this gospel of the kingdom will be preached in the whole world as a testimony to all nations, and then the end will come.

15 "So when you see standing in the holy place 'the abomination that causes desolation,' [l] spoken of through the prophet Daniel—let the reader understand—16 then let those who are in Judea flee to the mountains. 17 Let no one on the roof of his house go down to take anything out of the house. 18 Let no one in the field go back to get his cloak. 19 How dreadful it will be in those days for pregnant women and nursing mothers! 20 Pray that your flight will not take place in winter or on the Sabbath. 21 For then there will be great distress, unequaled from the beginning of the world until now—and never to be equaled again. 22 If those days had not been cut short, no one would survive, but for the sake of the elect those days will be shortened. 23At that time if anyone says to you, 'Look, here is the Christ! [m]' or, 'There he is!' do not believe it. 24 For false Christs and false prophets will appear and perform great signs and miracles to deceive even the elect—if that were possible. 25 See, I have told you ahead of time.

26 "So if anyone tells you, 'There he is, out in the desert,' do not go out; or, 'Here he is, in the inner rooms,' do not believe it. 27 For as the lightning comes from the east and flashes to the west, so will be the coming of the Son of Man. 28 Wherever there is a carcass, there the vultures will gather.

29 "Immediately after the distress of those days,

'the sun will be darkened,
    and the moon will not give its light;
the stars will fall from the sky,
    and the heavenly bodies will be shaken.' [n]

30 "At that time the sign of the Son of Man will appear in the sky, and all the nations of the earth will mourn. They will see the Son of Man coming on the clouds of the sky, with power and great glory. 31And he will send his angels with a loud trumpet call, and they will gather his elect from the four winds, from one end of the heavens to the other.

32 "Now learn this lesson from the fig tree: As soon as its twigs get tender and its leaves come out, you know that summer is near. 33 Even so, when you see all these things, you

---

[l] Daniel 9:27; 11:31; 12:11. [m] Or *Messiah*. [n] Isaiah 13:10; 34:4.

Greek Interlinear

ὠδίνων.　9 τότε παραδώσουσιν ὑμᾶς
of birth-pangs.　Then they will deliver you

εἰς θλῖψιν καὶ ἀποκτενοῦσιν ὑμᾶς,
to affliction and will kill you,

καὶ ἔσεσθε μισούμενοι ὑπὸ πάντων
and ye will be being hated by all

τῶν ἐθνῶν διὰ τὸ ὄνομά μου.
the nations because of the name of me.

10 καὶ τότε σκανδαλισθήσονται πολλοὶ καὶ
And then will be offended many and

ἀλλήλους παραδώσουσιν καὶ μισήσουσιν
one another will deliver and they will hate

ἀλλήλους· 11 καὶ πολλοὶ ψευδοπροφῆται
one another; and many false prophets

ἐγερθήσονται καὶ πλανήσουσιν πολλούς·
will be raised and will cause to err many;

12 καὶ διὰ τὸ πληθυνθῆναι τὴν
and because of - to be increased the

ἀνομίαν ψυγήσεται ἡ ἀγάπη τῶν
lawlessness will grow cold the love of the

πολλῶν. 13 ὁ δὲ ὑπομείνας εἰς τέλος,
many. But the [one] enduring to [the] end,

οὗτος σωθήσεται. 14 καὶ κηρυχθήσεται
this will be saved. And will be proclaimed

τοῦτο τὸ εὐαγγέλιον τῆς βασιλείας
this - gospel of the kingdom

ἐν ὅλῃ τῇ οἰκουμένῃ εἰς μαρτύριον
in all the inhabited earth for a testimony

πᾶσιν τοῖς ἔθνεσιν, καὶ τότε ἥξει τὸ
to all the nations, and then will come the

τέλος. 15 Ὅταν οὖν ἴδητε τὸ
end. When therefore ye see the

βδέλυγμα τῆς ἐρημώσεως τὸ ῥηθὲν διὰ
abomination - of desolation - spoken through

Δανιὴλ τοῦ προφήτου ἑστὸς ἐν τόπῳ
Daniel the prophet stand in place

ἁγίῳ, ὁ ἀναγινώσκων νοείτω,
holy, the [one] reading let him understand,

16 τότε οἱ ἐν τῇ Ἰουδαίᾳ φευγέτωσαν
then the [ones] in - Judæa let them flee

εἰς τὰ ὄρη, 17 ὁ ἐπὶ τοῦ δώματος μὴ
to the mountains, the [one] on the housetop let him

καταβάτω ἆραι τὰ ἐκ τῆς οἰκίας αὐτοῦ,
not come down to take the things out of the house of him,

18 καὶ ὁ ἐν τῷ ἀγρῷ μὴ ἐπιστρεψάτω
and the [one] in the field let him not turn back

ὀπίσω ἆραι τὸ ἱμάτιον αὐτοῦ. 19 οὐαὶ
behind to take the garment of him. woe

δὲ ταῖς ἐν γαστρὶ ἐχούσαις καὶ ταῖς
And to the women in womb having and to the [ones]
= the pregnant women

θηλαζούσαις ἐν ἐκείναις ταῖς ἡμέραις.
giving suck in those - days.

20 προσεύχεσθε δὲ ἵνα μὴ γένηται ἡ
And pray ye lest happen the

φυγὴ ὑμῶν χειμῶνος μηδὲ σαββάτῳ·
flight of you of(in) winter nor on a sabbath;

21 ἔσται γὰρ τότε θλῖψις μεγάλη, οἵα οὐ
for will be then affliction great, such as not

γέγονεν ἀπ' ἀρχῆς κόσμου ἕως
has happened from [the] beginning of [the] world until

τοῦ νῦν οὐδ' οὐ μὴ γένηται. 22 καὶ
- now neither by no means may happen. And

εἰ μὴ ἐκολοβώθησαν αἱ ἡμέραι ἐκεῖναι,
except were cut short - days those,

οὐκ ἂν ἐσώθη πᾶσα σάρξ· διὰ δὲ τοὺς
not - was saved all flesh; but on account of the
= no flesh would be saved;

ἐκλεκτοὺς κολοβωθήσονται αἱ ἡμέραι ἐκεῖναι.
chosen will be cut short - days those.

23 τότε ἐάν τις ὑμῖν εἴπῃ· ἰδοὺ ὧδε
Then if anyone to you says: Behold here

ὁ χριστός, ἤ· ὧδε, μὴ πιστεύσητε·
the Christ, or: Here, do not believe;

24 ἐγερθήσονται γὰρ ψευδόχριστοι καὶ
for will be raised false Christs and

ψευδοπροφῆται, καὶ δώσουσιν σημεῖα μεγάλα
false prophets, and they will give signs great

καὶ τέρατα, ὥστε πλανῆσαι, εἰ δυνατόν,
and marvels, so as to cause to err, if possible,

καὶ τοὺς ἐκλεκτούς. 25 ἰδοὺ προείρηκα
even the chosen. Behold I have before told

ὑμῖν. 26 ἐὰν οὖν εἴπωσιν ὑμῖν· ἰδοὺ
you. If therefore they say to you: Behold

ἐν τῇ ἐρήμῳ ἐστίν, μὴ ἐξέλθητε· ἰδοὺ
in the desert he is, go not ye forth; Behold

ἐν τοῖς ταμείοις, μὴ πιστεύσητε·
in the private rooms, do not ye believe;

27 ὥσπερ γὰρ ἡ ἀστραπὴ ἐξέρχεται ἀπὸ
for as the lightning comes forth from

ἀνατολῶν καὶ φαίνεται ἕως δυσμῶν,
[the] east and shines unto [the] west,

οὕτως ἔσται ἡ παρουσία τοῦ υἱοῦ
so will be the presence of the Son

τοῦ ἀνθρώπου· 28 ὅπου ἐὰν ᾖ τὸ
- of man; wherever may be the

πτῶμα, ἐκεῖ συναχθήσονται οἱ ἀετοί.
carcase, there will be assembled the eagles.

29 Εὐθέως δὲ μετὰ τὴν θλῖψιν τῶν
And immediately after the affliction of those

ἡμερῶν ἐκείνων ὁ ἥλιος σκοτισθήσεται,
days of those the sun will be darkened,

καὶ ἡ σελήνη οὐ δώσει τὸ φέγγος
and the moon will not give the light

αὐτῆς, καὶ οἱ ἀστέρες πεσοῦνται ἀπὸ τοῦ
of her, and the stars will fall from -

οὐρανοῦ, καὶ αἱ δυνάμεις τῶν οὐρανῶν
heaven, and the powers of the heavens

σαλευθήσονται. 30 καὶ τότε φανήσεται
will be shaken. And then will appear

τὸ σημεῖον τοῦ υἱοῦ τοῦ ἀνθρώπου ἐν
the sign of the Son - of man in

οὐρανῷ, καὶ τότε κόψονται πᾶσαι αἱ
heaven, and then will bewail all the

φυλαὶ τῆς γῆς καὶ ὄψονται τὸν υἱὸν
tribes of the land and they will see the Son

τοῦ ἀνθρώπου ἐρχόμενον ἐπὶ τῶν
- of man coming on the

νεφελῶν τοῦ οὐρανοῦ μετὰ δυνάμεως καὶ
clouds - of heaven with power and

δόξης πολλῆς· 31 καὶ ἀποστελεῖ τοὺς
glory much; and he will send the

ἀγγέλους αὐτοῦ μετὰ σάλπιγγος μεγάλης,
angels of him with trumpet a great,

καὶ ἐπισυνάξουσιν τοὺς ἐκλεκτοὺς αὐτοῦ
and they will assemble the chosen of him

ἐκ τῶν τεσσάρων ἀνέμων ἀπ' ἄκρων
out of the four winds from [the] extremities

οὐρανῶν ἕως [τῶν] ἄκρων αὐτῶν. 32 Ἀπὸ
of [the] heavens unto the extremities of them. from

δὲ τῆς συκῆς μάθετε τὴν παραβολήν·
Now the fig-tree learn ye the parable:

ὅταν ἤδη ὁ κλάδος αὐτῆς γένηται ἁπαλὸς
When now the branch of it becomes tender

καὶ τὰ φύλλα ἐκφύῃ, γινώσκετε ὅτι
and the leaves it puts forth, ye know that

ἐγγὺς τὸ θέρος· 33 οὕτως καὶ ὑμεῖς
near [is] the summer; so also ye

ὅταν ἴδητε πάντα ταῦτα, γινώσκετε ὅτι
when ye see all these things, know that

81

King James Version

34 Verily I say unto you, This generation shall not pass, till all these things be fulfilled. 35 Heaven and earth shall pass away, but my words shall not pass away.

36 But of that day and hour knoweth no *man*, no, not the angels of heaven, but my Father only. 37 But as the days of Noe *were,* so shall also the coming of the Son of man be. 38 For as in the days that were before the flood they were eating and drinking, marrying and giving in marriage, until the day that Noe entered into the ark, 39And knew not until the flood came, and took them all away; so shall also the coming of the Son of man be. 40 Then shall two be in the field; the one shall be taken, and the other left. 41 Two *women shall be* grinding at the mill; the one shall be taken, and the other left.

42 Watch therefore; for ye know not what hour your Lord doth come. 43 But know this, that if the goodman of the house had known in what watch the thief would come, he would have watched, and would not have suffered his house to be broken up. 44 Therefore be ye also ready: for in such an hour as ye think not the Son of man cometh. 45 Who then is a faithful and wise servant, whom his lord hath made ruler over his household, to give them meat in due season? 46 Blessed *is* that servant, whom his lord when he cometh shall find so doing. 47 Verily I say unto you, That he shall make him ruler over all his goods. 48 But and if that evil servant shall say in his heart, My lord delayeth his coming; 49And shall begin to smite *his* fellow servants, and to eat and drink with the drunken; 50 The lord of that servant shall come in a day when he looketh not for *him,* and in an hour that he is not aware of, 51And shall cut him asunder, and appoint *him* his portion with the hypocrites: there shall be weeping and gnashing of teeth.

25 Then shall the kingdom of heaven be likened unto ten virgins, which took their lamps, and went forth to meet the bridegroom. 2And five of them were wise, and five *were* foolish. 3 They that *were* foolish took their lamps, and took no oil with them: 4 But the wise took oil in their vessels with their lamps. 5 While the bridegroom tarried, they all slumbered and slept. 6And at midnight there was a cry made, Behold, the bridegroom cometh; go ye out to meet him. 7 Then all those virgins arose, and trimmed their lamps. 8And the foolish said unto the wise, Give

New International Version

know that it[o] is near, right at the door. 34 I tell you the truth, this generation[p] will certainly not pass away until all these things have happened. 35 Heaven and earth will pass away, but my words will never pass away.

The day and hour unknown

36 "No one knows about that day or hour, not even the angels in heaven, nor the Son,[q] but only the Father. 37As it was in the days of Noah, so it will be at the coming of the Son of Man. 38 For in the days before the flood, people were eating and drinking, marrying and giving in marriage, up to the day Noah entered the ark; 39 and they knew nothing about what would happen until the flood came and took them all away. That is how it will be at the coming of the Son of Man. 40 Two men will be in the field; one will be taken and the other left. 41 Two women will be grinding with a hand mill; one will be taken and the other left.

42 "Therefore keep watch, because you do not know on what day your Lord will come. 43 But understand this: If the owner of the house had known at what time of night the thief was coming, he would have kept watch and would not have let his house be broken into. 44 So you also must be ready, because the Son of Man will come at an hour when you do not expect him.

45 "Who then is the faithful and wise servant, whom the master has put in charge of the servants in his household to give them their food at the proper time? 46 It will be good for that servant whose master finds him doing so when he returns. 47 I tell you the truth, he will put him in charge of all his possessions. 48 But suppose that servant is wicked and says to himself, 'My master is staying away a long time,' 49 and he then begins to beat his fellow servants and to eat and drink with drunkards. 50 The master of that servant will come on a day when he does not expect him and at an hour he is not aware of. 51 He will cut him to pieces and assign him a place with the hypocrites, where there will be weeping and grinding of teeth.

The parable of the ten virgins

25 "At that time the kingdom of heaven will be like ten virgins who took their lamps and went out to meet the bridegroom. 2 Five of them were foolish and five were wise. 3 The foolish ones took their lamps but did not take any oil with them. 4 The wise, however, took oil in jars along with their lamps. 5 The bridegroom was late, and they all became drowsy and fell asleep.

6 "At midnight the cry rang out: 'Here's the bridegroom! Come out to meet him!'

7 "Then all the virgins woke up and trimmed their lamps. 8 The foolish ones said to the wise,

[o] Or *he.* [p] Or *race.* [q] Some MSS omit *nor the Son.*

Greek Interlinear

ἐγγύς ἐστιν ἐπὶ θύραις. **34** ἀμὴν λέγω
near   it is on(at) [the] doors.   Truly   I tell

ὑμῖν ὅτι οὐ μὴ παρέλθῃ ἡ γενεὰ
you   that by no means passes away - generation

αὕτη ἕως ἂν πάντα ταῦτα γένηται.
this until all these things happens.

35 ὁ οὐρανὸς καὶ ἡ γῆ παρελεύσεται, οἱ
The heaven and the earth will pass away, ²the

δὲ λόγοι μου οὐ μὴ παρέλθωσιν. **36** Περὶ
¹but words of me by no means may pass away. concerning

δὲ τῆς ἡμέρας ἐκείνης καὶ ὥρας οὐδεὶς
But - day that and hour no one

οἶδεν, οὐδὲ οἱ ἄγγελοι τῶν οὐρανῶν
knows, neither the angels of the heavens

οὐδὲ ὁ υἱός, εἰ μὴ ὁ πατὴρ μόνος.
nor the Son, except the Father only.

37 ὥσπερ γὰρ αἱ ἡμέραι τοῦ Νῶε, οὕτως
For as the days - of Noah, so

ἔσται ἡ παρουσία τοῦ υἱοῦ τοῦ ἀνθρώπου.
will be the presence of the Son - of man.

38 ὡς γὰρ ἦσαν ἐν ταῖς ἡμέραις
For as they were in - days

[ἐκείναις] ταῖς πρὸ τοῦ κατακλυσμοῦ
those the [ones] before the flood

τρώγοντες καὶ πίνοντες, γαμοῦντες καὶ
eating and drinking, marrying and

γαμίζοντες, ἄχρι ἧς ἡμέρας εἰσῆλθεν
being given in marriage, until which day entered

Νῶε εἰς τὴν κιβωτόν, **39** καὶ οὐκ ἔγνωσαν
Noah into the ark, and knew not

ἕως ἦλθεν ὁ κατακλυσμὸς καὶ ἦρεν
until came the flood and took

ἅπαντας, οὕτως ἔσται καὶ ἡ παρουσία
all, so will be also the presence

τοῦ υἱοῦ τοῦ ἀνθρώπου **40** τότε ἔσονται
of the Son - of man. Then will be

δύο ἐν τῷ ἀγρῷ, εἷς παραλαμβάνεται
two men in the field, one is taken

καὶ εἷς ἀφίεται· **41** δύο ἀλήθουσαι
and one is left; two women grinding

ἐν τῷ μύλῳ, μία παραλαμβάνεται καὶ
in(at) the mill, one is taken and

μία ἀφίεται. **42** γρηγορεῖτε οὖν, ὅτι
one is left. Watch ye therefore, because

οὐκ οἴδατε ποίᾳ ἡμέρᾳ ὁ κύριος
ye know not on what day the lord

ὑμῶν ἔρχεται. **43** Ἐκεῖνο δὲ γινώσκετε
of you is coming. And that know ye

ὅτι εἰ ᾔδει ὁ οἰκοδεσπότης ποίᾳ
that if knew the housemaster in what

φυλακῇ ὁ κλέπτης ἔρχεται, ἐγρηγόρησεν
watch the thief is coming, he would have

ἂν καὶ οὐκ ἂν εἴασεν διορυχθῆναι
watched and would not have allowed to be dug through

τὴν οἰκίαν αὐτοῦ. **44** διὰ τοῦτο καὶ
the house of him. Therefore also

ὑμεῖς γίνεσθε ἕτοιμοι, ὅτι ᾗ οὐ δοκεῖτε
ye be ready, because ¹in which ²ye think not

ὥρᾳ ὁ υἱὸς τοῦ ἀνθρώπου ἔρχεται. **45** Τίς
²hour the Son - of man comes. Who

ἄρα ἐστὶν ὁ πιστὸς δοῦλος καὶ φρόνιμος
then is the faithful slave and prudent

ὃν κατέστησεν ὁ κύριος ἐπὶ τῆς οἰκετείας
whom appointed the lord over the household

αὐτοῦ τοῦ δοῦναι αὐτοῖς τὴν τροφὴν ἐν
of him - to give to them the food in

καιρῷ; **46** μακάριος ὁ δοῦλος ἐκεῖνος ὃν
season? blessed [is] - slave that whom

ἐλθὼν ὁ κύριος αὐτοῦ εὑρήσει οὕτως
coming the lord of him will find so

ποιοῦντα· **47** ἀμὴν λέγω ὑμῖν ὅτι ἐπὶ
doing; truly I tell you that over

πᾶσιν τοῖς ὑπάρχουσιν αὐτοῦ καταστήσει
all the goods of him he will appoint

αὐτόν. **48** ἐὰν δὲ εἴπῃ ὁ κακὸς δοῦλος
him. But if says - wicked slave

ἐκεῖνος ἐν τῇ καρδίᾳ αὐτοῦ· χρονίζει
that in the heart of him· Delays

μου ὁ κύριος, **49** καὶ ἄρξηται τύπτειν
of me the lord, and begins to strike

τοὺς συνδούλους αὐτοῦ, ἐσθίῃ δὲ καὶ
the fellow-slaves of him, and eats and

πίνῃ μετὰ τῶν μεθυόντων, **50** ἥξει ὁ
drinks with the [ones] being drunk, will come the

κύριος τοῦ δούλου ἐκείνου ἐν ἡμέρᾳ ᾗ
lord - slave of that on a day on which

οὐ προσδοκᾷ καὶ ἐν ὥρᾳ ᾗ οὐ
he does not expect and in an hour in which not

γινώσκει, **51** καὶ διχοτομήσει αὐτόν,
he knows, and will cut asunder him,

καὶ τὸ μέρος αὐτοῦ μετὰ τῶν
and the portion of him with the

ὑποκριτῶν θήσει· ἐκεῖ ἔσται ὁ
hypocrites will place; there will be the

κλαυθμὸς καὶ ὁ βρυγμὸς τῶν ὀδόντων.
wailing and the gnashing of the teeth.

Chapter 25

Τότε ὁμοιωθήσεται ἡ βασιλεία
Then shall be likened the kingdom

τῶν οὐρανῶν δέκα παρθένοις, αἵτινες
of the heavens to ten virgins, who

λαβοῦσαι τὰς λαμπάδας ἑαυτῶν ἐξῆλθον
taking the lamps of them* went forth

εἰς ὑπάντησιν τοῦ νυμφίου. **2** πέντε δὲ
to a meeting of the bridegroom. Now five

ἐξ αὐτῶν ἦσαν μωραὶ καὶ πέντε φρόνιμοι.
of them were foolish and five prudent.

3 αἱ γὰρ μωραὶ λαβοῦσαι τὰς λαμπάδας
For the foolish [ones] taking the lamps

οὐκ ἔλαβον μεθ' ἑαυτῶν ἔλαιον.
did not take with them oil.

4 αἱ δὲ φρόνιμοι ἔλαβον ἔλαιον ἐν
But the prudent [ones] took oil in

τοῖς ἀγγείοις μετὰ τῶν λαμπάδων ἑαυτῶν.
the vessels with the lamps of them.

5 χρονίζοντος δὲ τοῦ νυμφίου ἐνύσταξαν
But delaying the bridegroom* slumbered
= while the bridegroom delayed

πᾶσαι καὶ ἐκάθευδον. **6** μέσης δὲ
all and slept. And of(in) [the] middle

νυκτὸς κραυγὴ γέγονεν· ἰδοὺ ὁ
of [the] night a cry there has been: Behold[,] the

νυμφίος, ἐξέρχεσθε εἰς ἀπάντησιν. **7** τότε
bridegroom, go ye forth to a meeting. Then

ἠγέρθησαν πᾶσαι αἱ παρθένοι ἐκεῖναι
were raised all - virgins those

καὶ ἐκόσμησαν τὰς λαμπάδας ἑαυτῶν.
and trimmed the lamps of them.

8 αἱ δὲ μωραὶ ταῖς φρονίμοις εἶπαν·
So the foolish [ones] to the prudent said:

*Here, and in the three following occurrences, as elsewhere, the
strict meaning is emphatic or reflexive—'of themselves'; but this
cannot be insisted on.

King James Version

us of your oil; for our lamps are gone out. 9 But the wise answered, saying, *Not so;* lest there be not enough for us and you: but go ye rather to them that sell, and buy for yourselves. 10And while they went to buy, the bridegroom came; and they that were ready went in with him to the marriage: and the door was shut. 11Afterward came also the other virgins, saying, Lord, Lord, open to us. 12 But he answered and said, Verily I say unto you, I know you not. 13 Watch therefore; for ye know neither the day nor the hour wherein the Son of man cometh.

14 For *the kingdom of heaven is* as a man travelling into a far country, *who* called his own servants, and delivered unto them his goods. 15And unto one he gave five talents, to another two, and to another one; to every man according to his several ability; and straightway took his journey. 16 Then he that had received the five talents went and traded with the same, and made *them* other five talents. 17And likewise 'he that *had received* two, he also gained other two. 18 But he that had received one went and digged in the earth, and hid his lord's money. 19After a long time the lord of those servants cometh, and reckoneth with them. 20And so he that had received five talents came and brought other five talents, saying, Lord, thou deliveredst unto me five talents: behold, I have gained beside them five talents more. 21 His lord said unto him, Well done, *thou* good and faithful servant: thou hast been faithful over a few things, I will make thee ruler over many things: enter thou into the joy of thy lord. 22 He also that had received two talents came and said, Lord, thou deliveredst unto me two talents: behold, I have gained two other talents beside them. 23 His lord said unto him, Well done, good and faithful servant; thou hast been faithful over a few things, I will make thee ruler over many things: enter thou into the joy of thy lord. 24 Then he which had received the one talent came and said, Lord, I knew thee that thou art a hard man, reaping where thou hast not sown, and gathering where thou hast not strewed: 25And I was afraid, and went and hid thy talent in the earth: lo, *there* thou hast *that is* thine. 26 His lord answered and said unto him, *Thou* wicked and slothful servant, thou knewest that I reap where I sowed not, and gather where I have not strewed: 27 Thou oughtest therefore to have put my money to the exchangers, and *then* at my coming I should have received mine own with usury. 28 Take therefore the talent from him, and give *it* unto him which hath ten talents. 29 For unto every one that hath shall be given, and he shall have abundance: but from him that hath not shall be taken away even that which he hath. 30And cast ye the unprofitable servant into outer darkness: there shall be weeping and gnashing of teeth.

New International Version

'Give us some of your oil; our lamps are going out.'

9 " 'No,' they replied, 'there may not be enough for both us and you. Instead, go to those who sell oil and buy some for yourselves.'

10 "But while they were on their way to buy the oil, the bridegroom arrived. The virgins who were ready went in with him to the wedding banquet. And the door was shut.

11 "Later the others also came. 'Sir! Sir!' they said. 'Open the door for us!'

12 "But he replied, 'I tell you the truth, I don't know you.'

13 "Therefore keep watch, because you do not know the day or the hour.

The parable of the talents

14 "Again, it will be like a man going on a journey, who called his servants and entrusted his property to them. 15 To one he gave five talents[r] of money, to another two talents, and to another one talent, each according to his ability. Then he went on his journey. 16 The man who had received the five talents went at once and put his money to work and gained five more. 17 So also, the one with the two talents gained two more. 18 But the man who had received the one talent went off, dug a hole in the ground and hid his master's money.

19 "After a long time the master of those servants returned and settled accounts with them. 20 The man who had received the five talents brought the other five. 'Master,' he said, 'you entrusted me with five talents. See, I have gained five more.'

21 "His master replied, 'Well done, good and faithful servant! You have been faithful with a few things; I will put you in charge of many things. Come and share your master's happiness!'

22 "The man with the two talents also came. 'Master,' he said, 'you entrusted me with two talents; see, I have gained two more.'

23 "His master replied, 'Well done, good and faithful servant! You have been faithful with a few things; I will put you in charge of many things. Come and share your master's happiness!'

24 "Then the man who had received the one talent came. 'Master,' he said, 'I knew that you are a hard man, harvesting where you have not sown and gathering where you have not scattered seed. 25 So I was afraid and went out and hid your talent in the ground. See, here is what belongs to you.'

26 "His master replied, 'You wicked, lazy servant! So you knew that I harvest where I have not sown and gather where I have not scattered seed? 27 Well then, you should have put my money on deposit with the bankers, so that when I returned I would have received it back with interest.

28 " 'Take the talent from him and give it to the one who has the ten talents. 29 For everyone who has will be given more, and he will have an abundance. Whoever does not have, even what he has will be taken from him. 30And throw that worthless servant outside, into the darkness, where there will be weeping and grinding of teeth.'

[r] A talent was worth more than a thousand dollars.

Greek Interlinear

δότε ἡμῖν ἐκ τοῦ ἐλαίου ὑμῶν, ὅτι
Give us of the oil of you, because

αἱ λαμπάδες ἡμῶν σβέννυνται. 9 ἀπεκρί-
the lamps of us are being quenched. But

θησαν δὲ αἱ φρόνιμοι λέγουσαι· μήποτε
answered the prudent saying: Lest

οὐ μὴ ἀρκέσῃ ἡμῖν καὶ ὑμῖν·
by no means it suffices to us and to you;

πορεύεσθε μᾶλλον πρὸς τοὺς πωλοῦντας
go ye rather to the [ones] selling

καὶ ἀγοράσατε ἑαυταῖς. 10 ἀπερχομένων
and buy for [your]selves. And going
= as they

δὲ αὐτῶν ἀγοράσαι ἦλθεν ὁ νυμφίος,
away them to buy came the bridegroom,
were going away

καὶ αἱ ἕτοιμοι εἰσῆλθον μετ᾽ αὐτοῦ
and the ready [ones] went in with him

εἰς τοὺς γάμους, καὶ ἐκλείσθη ἡ
to the wedding festivities, and was shut the

θύρα. 11 ὕστερον δὲ ἔρχονται καὶ αἱ
door. Then later come also the

λοιπαὶ παρθένοι λέγουσαι· κύριε κύριε,
remaining virgins saying: Lord[,] Lord,

ἄνοιξον ἡμῖν. 12 ὁ δὲ ἀποκριθεὶς εἶπεν·
open to us. But he answering said:

ἀμὴν λέγω ὑμῖν, οὐκ οἶδα ὑμᾶς.
Truly I say to you, I know not you.

13 Γρηγορεῖτε οὖν, ὅτι οὐκ οἴδατε
Watch ye therefore, because ye know not

τὴν ἡμέραν οὐδὲ τὴν ὥραν. 14 Ὥσπερ
the day nor the hour. as

γὰρ ἄνθρωπος ἀποδημῶν ἐκάλεσεν
For a man going from home called

τοὺς ἰδίους δούλους καὶ παρέδωκεν αὐτοῖς
the(his) own slaves and delivered to them

τὰ ὑπάρχοντα αὐτοῦ, 15 καὶ ᾧ μὲν ἔδωκεν
the goods of him, and to one he gave

πέντε τάλαντα, ᾧ δὲ δύο, ᾧ δὲ
five talents, to another two, to another

ἕν, ἑκάστῳ κατὰ τὴν ἰδίαν δύναμιν,
one, to each according to the(his) own ability,

καὶ ἀπεδήμησεν. 16 εὐθέως πορευθεὶς
and went from home. Immediately going

ὁ τὰ πέντε τάλαντα λαβὼν ἠργάσατο
the [one] the five talents receiving traded

ἐν αὐτοῖς καὶ ἐκέρδησεν ἄλλα
in them and gained other

πέντε· 17 ὡσαύτως ὁ τὰ δύο ἐκέρδησεν
five; similarly the [one] the two gained
[receiving]

ἄλλα δύο. 18 ὁ δὲ τὸ ἓν λαβὼν
other two. But the [one] the one receiving

ἀπελθὼν ὤρυξεν γῆν καὶ ἐκρύψεν
going away dug earth and hid

τὸ ἀργύριον τοῦ κυρίου αὐτοῦ.
the silver of the lord of him.

19 μετὰ δὲ πολὺν χρόνον ἔρχεται ὁ
Then after much time comes the

κύριος τῶν δούλων ἐκείνων καὶ συναίρει
lord – slaves of those and takes

λόγον μετ᾽ αὐτῶν. 20 καὶ προσελθὼν
account with them. And approaching

ὁ τὰ πέντε τάλαντα λαβὼν προσ-
the [one] the five talents receiving brought

ἤνεγκεν ἄλλα πέντε τάλαντα λέγων· κύριε,
other five talents saying: Lord,

πέντε τάλαντά μοι παρέδωκας· ἴδε ἄλλα
five talents to me thou deliveredst; behold other

πέντε τάλαντα ἐκέρδησα. 21 ἔφη αὐτῷ
five talents I gained. Said to him

ὁ κύριος αὐτοῦ· εὖ, δοῦλε ἀγαθὲ καὶ
the lord of him: Well, slave good and

πιστέ, ἐπὶ ὀλίγα ἦς πιστός,
faithful, over a few things thou wast faithful,

ἐπὶ πολλῶν σε καταστήσω· εἴσελθε
over many thee I will set; enter thou

εἰς τὴν χαρὰν τοῦ κυρίου σου. 22 προσ-
into the joy of the lord of thee. Ap-

ελθὼν καὶ ὁ τὰ δύο τάλαντα
proaching also the [one] the two talents
[having received]

εἶπεν· κύριε, δύο τάλαντά μοι
said: Lord, two talents to me

παρέδωκας· ἴδε ἄλλα δύο τάλαντα
thou deliveredst; behold other two talents

ἐκέρδησα. 23 ἔφη αὐτῷ ὁ κύριος αὐτοῦ·
I gained. Said to him the lord of him:

εὖ, δοῦλε ἀγαθὲ καὶ πιστέ, ἐπὶ
Well, slave good and faithful, over

ὀλίγα ἦς πιστός, ἐπὶ πολλῶν
a few things thou wast faithful, over many

σε καταστήσω· εἴσελθε εἰς τὴν
thee I will set; enter thou into the

χαρὰν τοῦ κυρίου σου. 24 προσ-
joy of the lord of thee. ap-

ελθὼν δὲ καὶ ὁ τὸ ἓν τάλαντον
proaching And also the [one] the one talent

εἰληφὼς εἶπεν· κύριε, ἔγνων σε
having received said: Lord, I knew thee

ὅτι σκληρὸς εἶ ἄνθρωπος, θερίζων
that a hard thou art man, reaping

ὅπου οὐκ ἔσπειρας, καὶ συνάγων
where thou didst not sow, and gathering

ὅθεν οὐ διεσκόρπισας· 25 καὶ φοβηθεὶς
whence thou didst not scatter; and fearing

ἀπελθὼν ἔκρυψα τὸ τάλαντόν σου
going away I hid the talent of thee

ἐν τῇ γῇ· ἴδε ἔχεις τὸ σόν.
in the earth; behold thou hast the thine.

26 ἀποκριθεὶς δὲ ὁ κύριος αὐτοῦ εἶπεν
And answering the lord of him said

αὐτῷ· πονηρὲ δοῦλε καὶ ὀκνηρέ,
to him: Evil slave and slothful,

ᾔδεις ὅτι θερίζω ὅπου οὐκ ἔσπειρα,
thou knewest that I reap where I sowed not,

καὶ συνάγω ὅθεν οὐ διεσκόρπισα;
and I gather whence I did not scatter?

27 ἔδει σε οὖν βαλεῖν τὰ ἀργύριά
it behoved thee therefore to put the silver pieces

μου τοῖς τραπεζίταις, καὶ ἐλθὼν ἐγὼ
of me to the bankers, and coming I

ἐκομισάμην ἂν τὸ ἐμὸν σὺν τόκῳ.
would have received the mine with interest.

28 ἄρατε οὖν ἀπ᾽ αὐτοῦ τὸ τάλαντον
Take therefore from him the talent

καὶ δότε τῷ ἔχοντι τὰ δέκα τάλαντα·
and give to the [one] having the ten talents;

29 τῷ γὰρ ἔχοντι παντὶ δοθήσεται καὶ
for to having everyone will be given and

περισσευθήσεται· τοῦ δὲ μὴ ἔχοντος
he will have abundance; but from the [one] not having

καὶ ὃ ἔχει ἀρθήσεται ἀπ᾽ αὐτοῦ.
even what he has will be taken from him.

30 καὶ τὸν ἀχρεῖον δοῦλον ἐκβάλετε εἰς
And the useless slave cast ye out into

τὸ σκότος τὸ ἐξώτερον· ἐκεῖ ἔσται ὁ
the darkness – outer; there will be the

κλαυθμὸς καὶ ὁ βρυγμὸς τῶν ὀδόντων.
wailing and the gnashing of the teeth.

King James Version

31 When the Son of man shall come in his glory, and all the holy angels with him, then shall he sit upon the throne of his glory: 32And before him shall be gathered all nations: and he shall separate them one from another, as a shepherd divideth *his* sheep from the goats: 33And he shall set the sheep on his right hand, but the goats on the left. 34 Then shall the King say unto them on his right hand, Come, ye blessed of my Father, inherit the kingdom prepared for you from the foundation of the world: 35 For I was a hungered, and ye gave me meat: I was thirsty, and ye gave me drink: I was a stranger, and ye took me in: 36 Naked, and ye clothed me: I was sick, and ye visited me: I was in prison, and ye came unto me. 37 Then shall the righteous answer him, saying, Lord, when saw we thee a hungered, and fed *thee?* or thirsty, and gave *thee* drink? 38 When saw we thee a stranger, and took *thee* in? or naked, and clothed *thee?* 39 Or when saw we thee sick, or in prison, and came unto thee? 40And the King shall answer and say unto them, Verily I say unto you, Inasmuch as ye have done *it* unto one of the least of these my brethren, ye have done *it* unto me. 41 Then shall he say also unto them on the left hand, Depart from me, ye cursed, into everlasting fire, prepared for the devil and his angels: 42 For I was a hungered, and ye gave me no meat: I was thirsty, and ye gave me no drink: 43 I was a stranger, and ye took me not in: naked, and ye clothed me not: sick, and in prison, and ye visited me not. 44 Then shall they also answer him, saying, Lord, when saw we thee a hungered, or athirst, or a stranger, or naked, or sick, or in prison, and did not minister unto thee? 45 Then shall he answer them, saying, Verily I say unto you, Inasmuch as ye did *it* not to one of the least of these, ye did *it* not to me. 46And these shall go away into everlasting punishment: but the righteous into life eternal.

New International Version

The sheep and the goats

31 "When the Son of Man comes in his glory, and all the angels with him, he will sit on his throne in heavenly glory. 32All the nations will be gathered before him, and he will separate the people one from another as a shepherd separates the sheep from the goats. 33 He will put the sheep on his right and the goats on his left.

34 "Then the King will say to those on his right, 'Come, you who are blessed by my Father; take your inheritance, the kingdom prepared for you since the creation of the world. 35 For I was hungry and you gave me something to eat, I was thirsty and you gave me something to drink, I was a stranger and you invited me in, 36 I needed clothes and you clothed me, I was sick and you looked after me, I was in prison and you came to visit me.'

37 "Then the righteous will answer him, 'Lord, when did we see you hungry and feed you, or thirsty and give you something to drink? 38 When did we see you a stranger and invite you in, or needing clothes and clothe you? 39 When did we see you sick or in prison and go to visit you?'

40 "The King will reply, 'I tell you the truth, whatever you did for one of the least of these brothers of mine, you did for me.'

41 "Then he will say to those on his left, 'Depart from me, you who are cursed, into the eternal fire prepared for the devil and his angels. 42 For I was hungry and you gave me nothing to eat, I was thirsty and you gave me nothing to drink, 43 I was a stranger and you did not invite me in, I needed clothes and you did not clothe me, I was sick and in prison and you did not look after me.'

44 "They also will answer, 'Lord, when did we see you hungry or thirsty or a stranger or needing clothes or sick or in prison, and did not help you?'

45 "He will reply, 'I tell you the truth, whatever you did not do for one of the least of these, you did not do for me.'

46 "Then they will go away to eternal punishment, but the righteous to eternal life."

The plot against Jesus

26 And it came to pass, when Jesus had finished all these sayings, he said unto his disciples, 2 Ye know that after two days is *the feast of* the passover, and the Son of man is betrayed to be crucified. 3 Then assembled together the chief priests, and the scribes, and the elders of the people, unto the palace of the high priest, who was called Caiaphas, 4And consulted that they might take Jesus by subtilty, and kill *him.* 5 But they said, Not on the feast *day,* lest there be an uproar among the people.

26 When Jesus had finished saying all these things, he said to his disciples, 2 "As you know, the Passover is two days away—and the Son of Man will be handed over to be crucified."

3 Then the chief priests and the elders of the people assembled in the palace of the high priest, whose name was Caiaphas, 4 and they plotted to arrest Jesus in some sly way and kill him. 5 "But not during the feast," they said, "or there may be a riot among the people."

Greek Interlinear

31 Ὅταν δὲ ἔλθῃ ὁ υἱὸς τοῦ ἀνθρώπου
And when comes the Son - of man

ἐν τῇ δόξῃ αὐτοῦ καὶ πάντες οἱ ἄγγελοι
in the glory of him and all the angels

μετ' αὐτοῦ, τότε καθίσει ἐπὶ θρόνου
with him, then he will sit on a throne

δόξης αὐτοῦ· 32 καὶ συναχθήσονται
of glory of him; and will be assembled

ἔμπροσθεν αὐτοῦ πάντα τὰ ἔθνη, καὶ
before him all the nations, and

ἀφορίσει αὐτοὺς ἀπ' ἀλλήλων, ὥσπερ
he will separate them from one another, as

ὁ ποιμὴν ἀφορίζει τὰ πρόβατα ἀπὸ
the shepherd separates the sheep from

τῶν ἐρίφων, 33 καὶ στήσει τὰ μὲν
the goats, and will set the -

πρόβατα ἐκ δεξιῶν αὐτοῦ, τὰ δὲ ἐρίφια
sheep on [the] right of him, but the goats

ἐξ εὐωνύμων. 34 τότε ἐρεῖ ὁ
on [the] left. Then will say the

βασιλεὺς τοῖς ἐκ δεξιῶν αὐτοῦ·
king to the [ones] on [the] right of him:

δεῦτε οἱ εὐλογημένοι τοῦ πατρός μου,
Come the [ones] blessed of the Father of me,

κληρονομήσατε τὴν ἡτοιμασμένην ὑμῖν
inherit ye the ²having been prepared ³for you

βασιλείαν ἀπὸ καταβολῆς κόσμου.
¹kingdom from [the] foundation of [the] world.

35 ἐπείνασα γὰρ καὶ ἐδώκατέ μοι
For I hungered and ye gave me

φαγεῖν, ἐδίψησα , καὶ ἐποτίσατέ με,
to eat, I thirsted and ye gave ²drink ¹me,

ξένος ἤμην καὶ συνηγάγετέ με,
a stranger I was and ye entertained me,

36 γυμνὸς καὶ περιεβάλετέ με, ἠσθένησα
naked and ye clothed me, I ailed

καὶ ἐπεσκέψασθέ με, ἐν φυλακῇ ἤμην
and ye visited me, in prison I was

καὶ ἤλθατε πρός με. 37 τότε ἀποκριθή-
and ye came to me. Then will

σονται αὐτῷ οἱ δίκαιοι λέγοντες· κύριε,
answer him the righteous saying: Lord,

πότε σε εἴδομεν πεινῶντα καὶ ἐθρέψαμεν,
when thee saw we hungering and fed,

ἢ διψῶντα καὶ ἐποτίσαμεν; 38 πότε δέ
or thirsting and gave drink? and when

σε εἴδομεν ξένον καὶ συνηγάγομεν,
thee saw we a stranger and entertained,

ἢ γυμνὸν καὶ περιεβάλομεν; 39 πότε δέ
or naked and clothed? and when

σε εἴδομεν ἀσθενοῦντα ἢ ἐν φυλακῇ καὶ
thee saw we ailing or in prison and

ἤλθομεν πρὸς σέ; 40 καὶ ἀποκριθεὶς ὁ
came to thee? And answering the

βασιλεὺς ἐρεῖ αὐτοῖς· ἀμὴν λέγω
king will say to them: Truly I tell

ὑμῖν, ἐφ' ὅσον ἐποιήσατε ἑνὶ τούτων
you, inasmuch as ye did to one of these

τῶν ἀδελφῶν μου τῶν ἐλαχίστων, ἐμοὶ
- brothers of me the least, to me

ἐποιήσατε. 41 τότε ἐρεῖ καὶ τοῖς ἐξ
ye did. Then he will say also to the [ones] on

εὐωνύμων· πορεύεσθε ἀπ' ἐμοῦ κατ-
[the] left: Go from me having been

ηραμένοι εἰς τὸ πῦρ τὸ αἰώνιον
cursed [ones] into the fire - eternal

τὸ ἡτοιμασμένον τῷ διαβόλῳ καὶ τοῖς
- having been prepared for the devil and the

ἀγγέλοις αὐτοῦ. 42 ἐπείνασα γὰρ καὶ
angels of him. For I hungered and

οὐκ ἐδώκατέ μοι φαγεῖν, ἐδίψησα
ye gave not me to eat, I thirsted

καὶ οὐκ ἐποτίσατέ με, 43 ξένος
and ye ¹gave ²not ⁴drink ³me, a stranger

ἤμην καὶ οὐ συνηγάγετέ με, γυμνὸς
I was and ye entertained not me, naked

καὶ οὐ περιεβάλετέ με, ἀσθενὴς καὶ ἐν
and ye clothed not me, ill and in

φυλακῇ καὶ οὐκ ἐπεσκέψασθέ με. 44 τότε
prison and ye visited not me. Then

ἀποκριθήσονται καὶ αὐτοὶ λέγοντες· κύριε,
will answer also they saying: Lord,

πότε σε εἴδομεν πεινῶντα ἢ διψῶντα ἢ
when thee saw we hungering or thirsting or

ξένον ἢ γυμνὸν ἢ ἀσθενῆ ἢ ἐν φυλακῇ
a stranger or naked or ill or in prison

καὶ οὐ διηκονήσαμέν σοι; 45 τότε
and did not minister to thee? Then

ἀποκριθήσεται αὐτοῖς λέγων· ἀμὴν λέγω
he will answer them saying: Truly I tell

ὑμῖν, ἐφ' ὅσον οὐκ ἐποιήσατε ἑνὶ
you, inasmuch as ye did not to one

τούτων τῶν ἐλαχίστων, οὐδὲ ἐμοὶ
of these - least [ones], neither to me

ἐποιήσατε. 46 καὶ ἀπελεύσονται οὗτοι εἰς
ye did. And will go away these into

κόλασιν αἰώνιον, οἱ δὲ δίκαιοι εἰς
punishment eternal, but the righteous into

ζωὴν αἰώνιον.
life eternal.

Chapter 26

Καὶ ἐγένετο ὅτε ἐτέλεσεν ὁ
And it came to pass when ended -

Ἰησοῦς πάντας τοὺς λόγους τούτους,
Jesus all the words these,

εἶπεν τοῖς μαθηταῖς αὐτοῦ· 2 οἴδατε
he said to the disciples of him: Ye know

ὅτι μετὰ δύο ἡμέρας τὸ πάσχα γίνεται,
that after two days the passover occurs,

καὶ ὁ υἱὸς τοῦ ἀνθρώπου παραδίδοται εἰς
and the Son - of man is delivered -

τὸ σταυρωθῆναι. 3 Τότε συνήχθησαν οἱ
- to be crucified. Then were assembled the

ἀρχιερεῖς καὶ οἱ πρεσβύτεροι τοῦ λαοῦ
chief priests and the elders of the people

εἰς τὴν αὐλὴν τοῦ ἀρχιερέως τοῦ
in the court of the high priest -

λεγομένον Καϊαφᾶ, 4 καὶ συνεβουλεύ-
named Caiaphas, and con-

σαντο ἵνα τὸν Ἰησοῦν δόλῳ κρατή-
sulted that - Jesus by guile they might

σωσιν καὶ ἀποκτείνωσιν· 5 ἔλεγον δέ·
seize and might kill; but they said:

μὴ ἐν τῇ ἑορτῇ, ἵνα μὴ θόρυβος
Not at the feast, lest a disturbance

γένηται ἐν τῷ λαῷ.
occurs among the people.

King James Version

6 Now when Jesus was in Bethany, in the house of Simon the leper, 7 There came unto him a woman having an alabaster box of very precious ointment, and poured it on his head, as he sat at meat. 8 But when his disciples saw *it*, they had indignation, saying, To what purpose *is* this waste? 9 For this ointment might have been sold for much, and given to the poor. 10 When Jesus understood *it*, he said unto them, Why trouble ye the woman? for she hath wrought a good work upon me. 11 For ye have the poor always with you; but me ye have not always. 12 For in that she hath poured this ointment on my body, she did *it* for my burial. 13 Verily I say unto you, Wheresoever this gospel shall be preached in the whole world, *there* shall also this, that this woman hath done, be told for a memorial of her.

14 Then one of the twelve, called Judas Iscariot, went unto the chief priests, 15 And said *unto them*, What will ye give me, and I will deliver him unto you? And they covenanted with him for thirty pieces of silver. 16 And from that time he sought opportunity to betray him.

17 Now the first *day* of the *feast of* unleavened bread the disciples came to Jesus, saying unto him, Where wilt thou that we prepare for thee to eat the passover? 18 And he said, Go into the city to such a man, and say unto him, The Master saith, My time is at hand; I will keep the passover at thy house with my disciples. 19 And the disciples did as Jesus had appointed them; and they made ready the passover. 20 Now when the even was come, he sat down with the twelve. 21 And as they did eat, he said, Verily I say unto you, that one of you shall betray me. 22 And they were exceeding sorrowful, and began every one of them to say unto him, Lord, is it I? 23 And he answered and said, He that dippeth *his* hand with me in the dish, the same shall betray me. 24 The Son of man goeth as it is written of him: but woe unto that man by whom the Son of man is betrayed! it had been good for that man if he had not been born. 25 Then Judas, which betrayed him, answered and said, Master, is it I? He said unto him, Thou hast said.

26 And as they were eating, Jesus took bread, and blessed *it*, and brake it, *and* gave *it* to the disciples, and said, Take, eat; this is my body. 27 And he took the cup, and gave thanks, and gave *it* to them, saying, Drink ye all of it; 28 For this is my blood of the new testament, which is shed for many for the remission of sins. 29 But I say unto you, I will not drink henceforth of this fruit of the vine, until that day when I drink it

New International Version

Jesus anointed at Bethany

6 While Jesus was in Bethany in the home of a man known as Simon the Leper, 7 a woman came to him with an alabaster jar of very expensive perfume, which she poured on his head as he was reclining at the table.

8 When the disciples saw this, they were indignant. "Why this waste?" they asked. 9 "This perfume could have been sold at a high price and the money given to the poor."

10 Aware of this, Jesus said to them, "Why are you bothering this woman? She has done a beautiful thing to me. 11 The poor you will always have with you, but you will not always have me. 12 When she poured this perfume on my body, she did it to prepare me for burial. 13 I tell you the truth, wherever this gospel is preached throughout the world, what she has done will also be told, in memory of her."

Judas agrees to betray Jesus

14 Then one of the Twelve—the one called Judas Iscariot—went to the chief priests 15 and asked, "What are you willing to give me if I hand him over to you?" So they counted out for him thirty silver coins. 16 From then on Judas watched for an opportunity to hand him over.

The Lord's Supper

17 On the first day of the Feast of Unleavened Bread, the disciples came to Jesus and asked, "Where do you want us to make preparations for you to eat the Passover?"

18 He replied, "Go into the city to a certain man and tell him, 'The Teacher says: My appointed time is near. I am going to celebrate the Passover with my disciples at your house.' " 19 So the disciples did as Jesus had directed them and prepared the Passover.

20 When evening came, Jesus was reclining at the table with the Twelve. 21 And while they were eating, he said, "I tell you the truth, one of you will betray me."

22 They were very sad and began to say to him one after the other, "Surely not I, Lord?"

23 Jesus replied, "The one who has dipped his hand into the bowl with me will betray me. 24 The Son of Man will go just as it is written about him. But woe to that man who betrays the Son of Man! It would be better for him if he had not been born."

25 Then Judas, the one who would betray him, said, "Surely not I, Rabbi?"

Jesus answered, "Yes, it is you." *s*

26 While they were eating, Jesus took bread, gave thanks and broke it, and gave it to his disciples, saying, "Take and eat; this is my body."

27 Then he took the cup, gave thanks and offered it to them, saying, "Drink from it, all of you. 28 This is my blood of the *t* covenant, which is poured out for many for the forgiveness of sins. 29 I tell you, I will not drink from this fruit of the vine from now on until that day when I drink it anew with you in my Father's kingdom."

[s] Or *You yourself have said it.* [t] Some MSS add *new.*

Greek Interlinear

6 Τοῦ δὲ Ἰησοῦ γενομένου ἐν Βηθανίᾳ
　 - And Jesus being* in Bethany
　　　　　　　　 = when Jesus was

ἐν οἰκίᾳ Σίμωνος τοῦ λεπροῦ,
in [the] house of Simon the leper,

7 προσῆλθεν αὐτῷ γυνὴ ἔχουσα ἀλάβαστρον
approached to him a woman having an alabaster phial

μύρου βαρυτίμου καὶ κατέχεεν ἐπὶ
of ointment very expensive and poured [it] on

τῆς κεφαλῆς αὐτοῦ ἀνακειμένου. 8 ἰδόντες
the head of him reclining. And see-

δὲ οἱ μαθηταὶ ἠγανάκτησαν λέγοντες·
ing the disciples were angry saying:

εἰς τί ἡ ἀπώλεια αὕτη; 9 ἐδύνατο γὰρ
To what - waste this? for could

τοῦτο πραθῆναι πολλοῦ καὶ δοθῆναι
this to be sold of:(for) much and to be given

πτωχοῖς. 10 γνοὺς δὲ ὁ Ἰησοῦς εἶπεν
to poor. And knowing - Jesus said

αὐτοῖς· τί κόπους παρέχετε τῇ γυναικί;
to them: Why trouble ye the woman?

ἔργον γὰρ καλὸν ἠργάσατο εἰς ἐμέ·
for work a good she wrought to me;

11 πάντοτε γὰρ τοὺς πτωχοὺς ἔχετε μεθ'
for always the poor ye have with

ἑαυτῶν, ἐμὲ δὲ οὐ πάντοτε ἔχετε·
yourselves, but me not always ye have;

12 βαλοῦσα γὰρ αὕτη τὸ μύρον τοῦτο
for ¹putting ²this woman ⁴ointment ³this

ἐπὶ τοῦ σώματός μου πρὸς τὸ ἐνταφιάσαι
on the body of me for - to bury

με ἐποίησεν. 13 ἀμὴν λέγω ὑμῖν, ὅπου
me she did. Truly I tell you, wher-

ἐὰν κηρυχθῇ τὸ εὐαγγέλιον τοῦτο ἐν
ever is proclaimed - gospel this in

ὅλῳ τῷ κόσμῳ, λαληθήσεται καὶ ὃ
all the world, will be spoken also what

ἐποίησεν αὕτη εἰς μνημόσυνον αὐτῆς.
did this woman for a memorial of her.

14 Τότε πορευθεὶς εἷς τῶν δώδεκα, ὁ
Then going one of the twelve, the [one]

λεγόμενος Ἰούδας Ἰσκαριώτης, πρὸς
named Judas Iscariot, to

τοὺς ἀρχιερεῖς 15 εἶπεν· τί θέλετέ μοι
the chief priests he said: What are ye willing me

δοῦναι, κἀγὼ ὑμῖν παραδώσω αὐτόν;
to give, and I to you will deliver him?

οἱ δὲ ἔστησαν αὐτῷ τριάκοντα ἀργύρια.
And they weighed him thirty pieces of silver.

16 καὶ ἀπὸ τότε ἐζήτει εὐκαιρίαν ἵνα
And from then he sought opportunity that

αὐτὸν παραδῷ.
him he might deliver.

17 Τῇ δὲ πρώτῃ τῶν ἀζύμων
Now on the first [day] - of unleavened bread

προσῆλθον οἱ μαθηταὶ τῷ Ἰησοῦ
approached the disciples - to Jesus

λέγοντες· ποῦ θέλεις ἑτοιμάσωμέν
saying: Where willest thou we may prepare

σοι φαγεῖν τὸ πάσχα; 18 ὁ δὲ
for thee to eat the passover? So he

εἶπεν· ὑπάγετε εἰς τὴν πόλιν πρὸς
said: Go ye into the city to

τὸν δεῖνα καὶ εἴπατε αὐτῷ· ὁ
such a one and say to him: The

διδάσκαλος λέγει· ὁ καιρός μου
teacher says: The time of me

ἐγγύς ἐστιν· πρὸς σὲ ποιῶ τὸ πάσχα
near is; with thee I make the passover

μετὰ τῶν μαθητῶν μου. 19 καὶ ἐποίησαν
with the disciples of me. And did

οἱ μαθηταὶ ὡς συνέταξεν αὐτοῖς ὁ
the disciples as enjoined them -

Ἰησοῦς, καὶ ἡτοίμασαν τὸ πάσχα. 20 Ὀψίας
Jesus, and prepared the passover. evening

δὲ γενομένης ἀνέκειτο μετὰ τῶν δώδεκα
And coming* he reclined with the twelve
　 = when evening came

[μαθητῶν]. 21 καὶ ἐσθιόντων αὐτῶν εἶπεν·
disciples. And eating them* he said:
　　　　　　 = as they were eating

ἀμὴν λέγω ὑμῖν ὅτι εἷς ἐξ ὑμῶν παρα-
Truly I tell you that one of you will

δώσει με. 22 καὶ λυπούμενοι σφόδρα
betray me. And grieving exceedingly

ἤρξαντο λέγειν αὐτῷ εἷς ἕκαστος·
they began to say to him *one ¹each:

μήτι ἐγώ εἰμι, κύριε; 23 ὁ δὲ ἀποκριθεὶς
Not I am, Lord? And he answering
= It is not I,

εἶπεν· ὁ ἐμβάψας μετ' ἐμοῦ τὴν
said: The [one] dipping with me the(his)

χεῖρα ἐν τῷ τρυβλίῳ, οὗτός με παρα-
hand in the dish, this man me will

δώσει. 24 ὁ μὲν υἱὸς τοῦ ἀνθρώπου
betray. Indeed the Son - of man

ὑπάγει καθὼς γέγραπται περὶ αὐτοῦ,
goes as it has been written concerning him,

οὐαὶ δὲ τῷ ἀνθρώπῳ ἐκείνῳ δι'
but woe - man to that through

οὗ ὁ υἱὸς τοῦ ἀνθρώπου παραδίδοται·
whom the Son - of man is betrayed;

καλὸν ἦν αὐτῷ εἰ οὐκ ἐγεννήθη
good were it for him if was not born

ὁ ἄνθρωπος ἐκεῖνος. 25 ἀποκριθεὶς δὲ
- man that. And answering

Ἰούδας ὁ παραδιδοὺς αὐτὸν εἶπεν·
Judas the [one] betraying him said:

μήτι ἐγώ εἰμι, ῥαββί; λέγει αὐτῷ·
Not I am, rabbi? He says to him:
= It is not I,

σὺ εἶπας. 26 Ἐσθιόντων δὲ αὐτῶν
Thou saidst. And eating them*
　　　　　　 = as they were eating

λαβὼν ὁ Ἰησοῦς ἄρτον καὶ εὐλογήσας
taking - Jesus a loaf and blessing

ἔκλασεν καὶ δοὺς τοῖς μαθηταῖς εἶπεν·
he broke and giving to the disciples said:

λάβετε φάγετε· τοῦτό ἐστιν τὸ σῶμά
Take ye[,] eat ye; this is the body

μου. 27 καὶ λαβὼν ποτήριον καὶ εὐχαρι-
of me. And taking a cup and giving

στήσας ἔδωκεν αὐτοῖς λέγων· πίετε ἐξ
thanks he gave to them saying: Drink ye of

αὐτοῦ πάντες· 28 τοῦτο γάρ ἐστιν τὸ
it all; for this is the

αἷμά μου τῆς διαθήκης τὸ περὶ πολλῶν
blood of me of the covenant the [blood] concerning many

ἐκχυννόμενον εἰς ἄφεσιν ἁμαρτιῶν. 29 λέγω
being shed for forgiveness of sins. I tell

δὲ ὑμῖν, οὐ μὴ πίω ἀπ' ἄρτι ἐκ
And you, by no means will I drink from now of

τούτου τοῦ γενήματος τῆς ἀμπέλου ἕως
this - fruit of the vine until

τῆς ἡμέρας ἐκείνης ὅταν αὐτὸ πίνω μεθ'
- day that when it I drink with

ὑμῶν καινὸν ἐν τῇ βασιλείᾳ τοῦ πατρός
you new in the kingdom of the Father

μου.
of me.

89

King James Version

new with you in my Father's kingdom. 30And when they had sung a hymn, they went out into the mount of Olives. 31 Then saith Jesus unto them, All ye shall be offended because of me this night: for it is written, I will smite the Shepherd, and the sheep of the flock shall be scattered abroad. 32 But after I am risen again, I will go before you into Galilee. 33 Peter answered and said unto him, Though all *men* shall be offended because of thee, *yet* will I never be offended. 34 Jesus said unto him, Verily I say unto thee, That this night, before the cock crow, thou shalt deny me thrice. 35 Peter said unto him, Though I should die with thee, yet will I not deny thee. Likewise also said all the disciples.

36 Then cometh Jesus with them unto a place called Gethsemane, and saith unto the disciples, Sit ye here, while I go and pray yonder. 37And he took with him Peter and the two sons of Zebedee, and began to be sorrowful and very heavy. 38 Then saith he unto them, My soul is exceeding sorrowful, even unto death: tarry ye here, and watch with me. 39And he went a little further, and fell on his face, and prayed, saying, O my Father, if it be possible, let this cup pass from me: nevertheless, not as I will, but as thou *wilt*. 40And he cometh unto the disciples, and findeth them asleep, and saith unto Peter, What, could ye not watch with me one hour? 41Watch and pray, that ye enter not into temptation: the spirit indeed *is* willing, but the flesh *is* weak. 42 He went away again the second time, and prayed, saying, O my Father, if this cup may not pass away from me, except I drink it, thy will be done. 43And he came and found them asleep again: for their eyes were heavy. 44And he left them, and went away again, and prayed the third time, saying the same words. 45 Then cometh he to his disciples, and saith unto them, Sleep on now, and take *your* rest: behold, the hour is at hand, and the Son of man is betrayed into the hands of sinners. 46 Rise, let us be going: behold, he is at hand that doth betray me.

47 And while he yet spake, lo, Judas, one of the twelve, came, and with him a great multitude with swords and staves, from the chief priests and elders of the people. 48 Now he that betrayed him gave them a sign, saying, Whomsoever I shall kiss, that same is he; hold him fast. 49And forthwith he came to Jesus, and said, Hail, Master; and kissed him. 50And Jesus said unto him, Friend, wherefore art thou come? Then came they, and laid hands on Jesus, and took him. 51And, behold, one of them which were with Jesus stretched out *his* hand, and

New International Version

30 When they had sung a hymn, they went out to the Mount of Olives.

Jesus predicts Peter's denial

31 Then Jesus told them, "This very night you will all fall away on account of me, for it is written:

'I will strike the shepherd,
　and the sheep of the flock will be scattered.' ᵘ

32 But after I have risen, I will go ahead of you into Galilee."

33 Peter replied, "Even if all fall away on account of you, I never will."

34 "I tell you the truth," Jesus answered, "this very night, before the rooster crows, you will disown me three times."

35 But Peter declared, "Even if I have to die with you, I will never disown you." And all the other disciples said the same.

Gethsemane

36 Then Jesus went with his disciples to a place called Gethsemane, and he said to them, "Sit here while I go over there and pray." 37 He took Peter and the two sons of Zebedee along with him, and he began to be sorrowful and troubled. 38 Then he said to them, "My soul is overwhelmed with sorrow to the point of death. Stay here and keep watch with me."

39 Going a little farther, he fell with his face to the ground and prayed, "My Father, if it is possible, may this cup be taken from me. Yet not as I will, but as you will."

40 Then he returned to his disciples and found them sleeping. "Could you men not keep watch with me for one hour?" he asked Peter. 41 "Watch and pray so that you will not fall into temptation. The spirit is willing, but the body is weak."

42 He went away a second time and prayed, "My Father, if it is not possible for this cup to be taken away unless I drink it, may your will be done."

43 When he came back, he again found them sleeping, because their eyes were heavy. 44 So he left them and went away once more and prayed the third time, saying the same thing.

45 Then he returned to the disciples and said to them, "Are you still sleeping and resting? Look, the hour is near, and the Son of Man is betrayed into the hands of sinners. 46 Rise, let us go! Here comes my betrayer!"

Jesus arrested

47 While he was still speaking, Judas, one of the Twelve, arrived. With him was a large crowd armed with swords and clubs, sent from the chief priests and the elders of the people. 48 Now the betrayer had arranged a signal with them: "The one I kiss is the man; arrest him." 49 Going at once to Jesus, Judas said, "Greetings, Rabbi!" and kissed him.

50 Jesus replied, "Friend, do what you came for." ᵛ

Then the men stepped forward, seized Jesus and arrested him. 51 With that, one of Jesus' companions reached for his sword, drew it out

[u] Zech 13:7. [v] Or *"Friend, why have you come?"*

Greek Interlinear

30 Καὶ ὑμνήσαντες ἐξῆλθον εἰς τὸ
And having sung a hymn they went forth to the

ὄρος τῶν ἐλαιῶν. **31** Τότε λέγει αὐτοῖς ὁ
mount of the olives. Then says to them –

Ἰησοῦς· πάντες ὑμεῖς σκανδαλισθήσεσθε
Jesus: All ye will be offended

ἐν ἐμοὶ ἐν τῇ νυκτὶ ταύτῃ· γέγραπται
in me to-night; it has been written

γάρ· πατάξω τὸν ποιμένα, καὶ δια-
for: I will strike the shepherd, and will

σκορπισθήσονται τὰ πρόβατα τῆς ποίμνης·
be scattered the sheep of the flock;

32 μετὰ δὲ τὸ ἐγερθῆναί με[b] προάξω
but after the to be raised me[b] I will go before
= I am raised

ὑμᾶς εἰς τὴν Γαλιλαίαν. **33** ἀποκριθεὶς
you to – Galilee. answering

δὲ ὁ Πέτρος εἶπεν αὐτῷ· εἰ πάντες
And – Peter said to him: If all men

σκανδαλισθήσονται ἐν σοί, ἐγὼ οὐδέποτε
shall be offended in thee, I never

σκανδαλισθήσομαι. **34** ἔφη αὐτῷ ὁ Ἰησοῦς·
will be offended. Said to him – Jesus:

ἀμὴν λέγω σοι ὅτι ἐν ταύτῃ τῇ νυκτὶ
Truly I tell thee that in this to-night

πρὶν ἀλέκτορα φωνῆσαι τρὶς ἀπαρνήσῃ
before a cock to crow[b] three times thou wilt deny

με. **35** λέγει αὐτῷ ὁ Πέτρος· κἂν
me. Says to him – Peter: Even if

δέῃ με σὺν σοὶ ἀποθανεῖν, οὐ μή σε
it behoves me with thee to die, by no means thee
= I must die with thee,

ἀπαρνήσομαι. ὁμοίως καὶ πάντες οἱ
I will deny. Likewise also all the

μαθηταὶ εἶπαν.
disciples said.

36 Τότε ἔρχεται μετ᾽ αὐτῶν ὁ Ἰησοῦς
Then comes with them – Jesus

εἰς χωρίον λεγόμενον Γεθσημανί, καὶ λέγει
to a piece of land called Gethsemane, and says

τοῖς μαθηταῖς· καθίσατε αὐτοῦ ἕως οὗ
to the disciples: Sit ye here until

ἀπελθὼν ἐκεῖ προσεύξωμαι. **37** καὶ παρα-
going away there I may pray. And tak-

λαβὼν τὸν Πέτρον καὶ τοὺς δύο υἱοὺς
ing – Peter and the two sons

Ζεβεδαίου ἤρξατο λυπεῖσθαι καὶ ἀδημονεῖν.
of Zebedee he began to grieve and to be distressed.

38 τότε λέγει αὐτοῖς· περίλυπός ἐστιν
Then he says to them: Deeply grieved is

ἡ ψυχή μου ἕως θανάτου· μείνατε
the soul of me unto death; remain ye

ὧδε καὶ γρηγορεῖτε μετ᾽ ἐμοῦ. **39** καὶ
here and watch ye with me. And

προελθὼν μικρὸν ἔπεσεν ἐπὶ πρόσωπον
going forward a little he fell on [the] face

αὐτοῦ προσευχόμενος καὶ λέγων· πάτερ
of him praying and saying: Father

μου, εἰ δυνατόν ἐστιν, παρελθάτω ἀπ᾽
of me, if possible it is, let pass from

ἐμοῦ τὸ ποτήριον τοῦτο· πλὴν οὐχ
me the cup this; yet not

ὡς ἐγὼ θέλω ἀλλ᾽ ὡς σύ. **40** καὶ
as I will but as thou. And

ἔρχεται πρὸς τοὺς μαθητὰς καὶ εὑρίσκει
he comes to the disciples and finds

αὐτοὺς καθεύδοντας, καὶ λέγει τῷ Πέτρῳ·
them sleeping, and says – to Peter:

οὕτως οὐκ ἰσχύσατε μίαν ὥραν
So were ye not able one hour

γρηγορῆσαι μετ᾽ ἐμοῦ; **41** γρηγορεῖτε καὶ
to watch with me? Watch ye and

προσεύχεσθε, ἵνα μὴ εἰσέλθητε εἰς
pray, lest ye enter into

πειρασμόν· τὸ μὲν πνεῦμα πρόθυμον,
temptation: indeed the spirit [is] eager,

ἡ δὲ σὰρξ ἀσθενής. **42** πάλιν ἐκ
but the flesh weak. Again –

δευτέρου ἀπελθὼν προσηύξατο λέγων·
second [time] going away he prayed saying:

πάτερ μου, εἰ οὐ δύναται τοῦτο παρελθεῖν
Father of me, if cannot this to pass away

ἐὰν μὴ αὐτὸ πίω, γενηθήτω τὸ θέλημά
except it I drink, let be done the will

σου. **43** καὶ ἐλθὼν πάλιν εὗρεν αὐτοὺς
of thee. And coming again he found them

καθεύδοντας, ἦσαν γὰρ αὐτῶν οἱ ὀφθαλμοὶ
sleeping, for were of them the eyes

βεβαρημένοι. **44** καὶ ἀφεὶς αὐτοὺς πάλιν
having been burdened. And leaving them again

ἀπελθὼν προσηύξατο ἐκ τρίτου, τὸν
going away he prayed a third [time], the

αὐτὸν λόγον εἰπὼν πάλιν. **45** τότε ἔρχεται
same word saying again. Then he comes

πρὸς τοὺς μαθητὰς καὶ λέγει αὐτοῖς·
to the disciples and says to them:

καθεύδετε λοιπὸν καὶ ἀναπαύεσθε·
Sleep ye now and rest;

ἰδοὺ ἤγγικεν ἡ ὥρα καὶ ὁ υἱὸς τοῦ
behold has drawn near the hour and the Son

ἀνθρώπου παραδίδοται εἰς χεῖρας
of man is betrayed into [the] hands

ἁμαρτωλῶν. **46** ἐγείρεσθε, ἄγωμεν· ἰδοὺ
of sinners. Rise ye, let us be going; behold

ἤγγικεν ὁ παραδιδούς με.
has drawn near the [one] betraying me.

47 Καὶ ἔτι αὐτοῦ λαλοῦντος, ἰδοὺ
And still him speaking,[a] behold
= while he was still speaking,

Ἰούδας εἷς τῶν δώδεκα ἦλθεν, καὶ μετ᾽
Judas one of the twelve came, and with

αὐτοῦ ὄχλος πολὺς μετὰ μαχαιρῶν καὶ
him crowd a much with swords and

ξύλων ἀπὸ τῶν ἀρχιερέων καὶ πρεσβυτέρων
clubs from the chief priests and elders

τοῦ λαοῦ. **48** ὁ δὲ παραδιδοὺς αὐτὸν ἔδωκεν
of the people. Now the [one] betraying him gave

αὐτοῖς σημεῖον λέγων· ὃν ἂν φιλήσω
them a sign saying: Whomever I may kiss

αὐτός ἐστιν· κρατήσατε αὐτόν. **49** καὶ
he it is; seize ye him. And

εὐθέως προσελθὼν τῷ Ἰησοῦ εἶπεν· χαῖρε,
immediately approaching – to Jesus he said: Hail,

ῥαββί, καὶ κατεφίλησεν αὐτόν. **50** ὁ
rabbi, and affectionately kissed him. –

δὲ Ἰησοῦς εἶπεν αὐτῷ· ἑταῖρε,
But Jesus said to him: Comrade, [do that]

ἐφ᾽ ὃ πάρει. τότε προσελθόντες ἐπέβαλον
on what thou art here. Then approaching they laid on

τὰς χεῖρας ἐπὶ τὸν Ἰησοῦν καὶ ἐκράτησαν
the(ir) hands on – Jesus and seized

αὐτόν. **51** καὶ ἰδοὺ εἷς τῶν μετὰ
him. And behold one of the [ones] with

Ἰησοῦ ἐκτείνας τὴν χεῖρα ἀπέσπασεν
Jesus stretching out the(his) hand drew

τὴν μάχαιραν αὐτοῦ, καὶ πατάξας τὸν
the sword of him, and striking the

King James Version

drew his sword, and struck a servant of the high priest, and smote off his ear. 52 Then said Jesus unto him, Put up again thy sword into his place: for all they that take the sword shall perish with the sword. 53 Thinkest thou that I cannot now pray to my Father, and he shall presently give me more than twelve legions of angels? 54 But how then shall the Scriptures be fulfilled, that thus it must be? 55 In that same hour said Jesus to the multitudes, Are ye come out as against a thief with swords and staves for to take me? I sat daily with you teaching in the temple, and ye laid no hold on me. 56 But all this was done, that the Scriptures of the prophets might be fulfilled. Then all the disciples forsook him, and fled.

57 And they that had laid hold on Jesus led *him* away to Caiaphas the high priest, where the scribes and the elders were assembled. 58 But Peter followed him afar off unto the high priest's palace, and went in, and sat with the servants, to see the end. 59 Now the chief priests, and elders, and all the council, sought false witness against Jesus, to put him to death; 60 But found none: yea, though many false witnesses came, *yet* found they none. At the last came two false witnesses, 61 And said, This *fellow* said, I am able to destroy the temple of God, and to build it in three days. 62 And the high priest arose, and said unto him, Answerest thou nothing? what *is it which* these witness against thee? 63 But Jesus held his peace. And the high priest answered and said unto him, I adjure thee by the living God, that thou tell us whether thou be the Christ, the Son of God. 64 Jesus saith unto him, Thou hast said: nevertheless I say unto you, Hereafter shall ye see the Son of man sitting on the right hand of power, and coming in the clouds of heaven. 65 Then the high priest rent his clothes, saying, He hath spoken blasphemy; what further need have we of witnesses? behold, now ye have heard his blasphemy. 66 What think ye? They answered and said, He is guilty of death. 67 Then did they spit in his face, and buffeted him; and others smote *him* with the palms of their hands, 68 Saying, Prophesy unto us, thou Christ, Who is he that smote thee?

69 Now Peter sat without in the palace: and a damsel came unto him, saying, Thou also wast with Jesus of Galilee. 70 But he denied before *them* all, saying, I know not what thou sayest. 71 And when he was gone out into the porch, another *maid* saw him, and said unto them that were there, This *fellow* was also with Jesus of Nazareth. 72 And again he denied with an oath, I do not know the man. 73 And after a while came unto *him* they that stood by, and said to Peter, Surely thou also art *one* of them; for thy speech bewrayeth thee. 74 Then began he to curse and to swear, *saying,* I know not the man. And im-

New International Version

and struck the servant of the high priest, cutting off his ear. 52 "Put your sword back in its place," Jesus said to him, "for all who draw the sword will die by the sword. 53 Do you think I cannot call on my Father, and he will at once put at my disposal more than twelve legions of angels? 54 But how then would the Scriptures be fulfilled that say it must happen in this way?"

55 At that time Jesus said to the crowd, "Am I leading a rebellion, that you have come out with swords and clubs to capture me? Every day I sat in the temple courts teaching, and you did not arrest me. 56 But this has all taken place that the writings of the prophets might be fulfilled." Then all the disciples deserted him and fled.

Before the Sanhedrin

57 Those who had arrested Jesus took him to Caiaphas, the high priest, where the teachers of the law and the elders had assembled. 58 But Peter followed him at a distance, right up to the courtyard of the high priest. He entered and sat down with the guards to see the outcome.

59 The chief priests and the whole Sanhedrin were looking for false evidence against Jesus so that they could put him to death. 60 But they did not find any, though many false witnesses came forward.

Finally two came forward 61 and declared, "This fellow said, 'I am able to destroy the temple of God and rebuild it in three days.'"

62 Then the high priest stood up and said to Jesus, "Are you not going to answer? What is this testimony that these men are bringing against you?" 63 But Jesus remained silent.

The high priest said to him, "I charge you under oath by the living God: Tell us if you are the Christ,[w] the Son of God."

64 "Yes, it is as you say," Jesus replied. "But I say to all of you: In the future you will see the Son of Man sitting at the right hand of the Mighty One and coming on the clouds of heaven."

65 Then the high priest tore his clothes and said, "He has spoken blasphemy! Why do we need any more witnesses? Look, now you have heard the blasphemy. 66 What do you think?"

"He is worthy of death," they answered.

67 Then they spit in his face and struck him with their fists. Others slapped him 68 and said, "Prophesy to us, Christ.[w] Who hit you?"

Peter disowns Jesus

69 Now Peter was sitting out in the courtyard, and a servant girl came to him. "You also were with Jesus of Galilee," she said.

70 But he denied it before them all. "I don't know what you're talking about," he said.

71 Then he went out to the gateway, where another girl saw him and said to the people there, "This fellow was with Jesus of Nazareth."

72 He denied it again, with an oath: "I don't know the man!"

73 After a little while, those standing there went up to Peter and said, "Surely you are one of them, for your accent gives you away."

74 Then he began to call down curses on himself and he swore to them, "I don't know the man!"

[w] Or *Messiah.*

Greek Interlinear

δοῦλος τοῦ ἀρχιερέως ἀφεῖλεν αὐτοῦ τὸ
slave of the high priest cut off of him the

ὠτίον. **52** τότε λέγει αὐτῷ ὁ Ἰησοῦς·
ear. Then says to him - Jesus:

ἀπόστρεψον τὴν μάχαιράν σου εἰς τὸν
Put back the sword of thee into the

τόπον αὐτῆς· πάντες γὰρ οἱ λαβόντες
place of it; for all the [ones] taking

μάχαιραν ἐν μαχαίρῃ ἀπολοῦνται. **53** ἢ
a sword by a sword will perish. Or

δοκεῖς· ὅτι οὐ δύναμαι παρακαλέσαι
thinkest thou that I cannot to ask

τὸν πατέρα μου, καὶ παραστήσει μοι
the Father of me, and he will provide me

ἄρτι πλείω δώδεκα λεγιῶνας ἀγγέλων;
now more [than] twelve legions of angels?

54 πῶς οὖν πληρωθῶσιν αἱ γραφαὶ ὅτι
how may be fulfilled the scriptures that

οὕτως δεῖ γενέσθαι; **55** Ἐν ἐκείνῃ τῇ ὥρᾳ
thus it must be? In that - hour

εἶπεν ὁ Ἰησοῦς τοῖς ὄχλοις· ὡς ἐπὶ
said - Jesus to the crowds: As against

λῃστὴν ἐξήλθατε μετὰ μαχαιρῶν καὶ
a robber came ye forth with swords and

ξύλων συλλαβεῖν με; καθ᾽ ἡμέραν ἐν
clubs to take me? daily in

τῷ ἱερῷ ἐκαθεζόμην διδάσκων, καὶ οὐκ
the temple I sat teaching, and not

ἐκρατήσατέ με. **56** τοῦτο δὲ ὅλον
ye seized me. But this all

γέγονεν ἵνα πληρωθῶσιν αἱ γραφαὶ
has come to pass that may be fulfilled the scriptures

τῶν προφητῶν. Τότε οἱ μαθηταὶ πάντες
of the prophets. Then the disciples all

ἀφέντες αὐτὸν ἔφυγον.
leaving him fled.

57 Οἱ δὲ κρατήσαντες τὸν Ἰησοῦν
But the [ones] having seized - Jesus

ἀπήγαγον πρὸς Καϊάφαν τὸν ἀρχιερέα,
led [him] away to Caiaphas the high priest,

ὅπου οἱ γραμματεῖς καὶ οἱ πρεσβύτεροι
where the scribes and the elders

συνήχθησαν. **58** ὁ δὲ Πέτρος ἠκολούθει
were assembled. - And Peter followed

αὐτῷ [ἀπὸ] μακρόθεν ἕως τῆς αὐλῆς
him from afar up to the court

τοῦ ἀρχιερέως, καὶ εἰσελθὼν ἔσω ἐκάθητο
of the high priest, and entering within sat

μετὰ τῶν ὑπηρετῶν ἰδεῖν τὸ τέλος.
with the attendants to see the end.

59 Οἱ δὲ ἀρχιερεῖς καὶ τὸ συνέδριον
And the chief priests and the council

ὅλον ἐζήτουν ψευδομαρτυρίαν κατὰ τοῦ
whole sought false witness against -

Ἰησοῦ ὅπως αὐτὸν θανατώσωσιν, **60** καὶ
Jesus so as him they might put to death, and

οὐχ εὗρον πολλῶν προσελθόντων
did not find[,] many approaching
= when many false witnesses approached.

ψευδομαρτύρων. ὕστερον δὲ προσελθόντες
false witnessesᵃ. But later approaching

δύο **61** εἶπαν· οὗτος ἔφη· δύναμαι κατα-
two said: This man said: I can to de-

λῦσαι τὸν ναὸν τοῦ θεοῦ καὶ διὰ τριῶν
stroy the shrine - of God and through(after) three

ἡμερῶν οἰκοδομῆσαι. **62** καὶ ἀναστὰς
days to build. And standing up

ὁ ἀρχιερεὺς εἶπεν αὐτῷ· οὐδὲν
the high priest said to him: Nothing

ἀποκρίνῃ, τί οὗτοί σου κατα-
answerest thou, what these men thee give

μαρτυροῦσιν; **63** ὁ δὲ Ἰησοῦς ἐσιώπα.
evidence against? - But Jesus remained silent.

καὶ ὁ ἀρχιερεὺς εἶπεν αὐτῷ· ἐξορκίζω
And the high priest said to him: I adjure

σε κατὰ τοῦ θεοῦ τοῦ ζῶντος ἵνα ἡμῖν
thee by - God the living that us

εἴπῃς εἰ σὺ εἶ ὁ χριστὸς ὁ υἱὸς τοῦ
thou tell if thou art the Christ the Son -

θεοῦ. **64** λέγει αὐτῷ ὁ Ἰησοῦς· σὺ εἶπας·
of God. Says to him - Jesus: Thou saidst;

πλὴν λέγω ὑμῖν, ἀπ᾽ ἄρτι ὄψεσθε τὸν
yet I tell you, from now ye will see the

υἱὸν τοῦ ἀνθρώπου καθήμενον ἐκ
Son - of man sitting on [the]

δεξιῶν τῆς δυνάμεως καὶ ἐρχόμενον
right [hand] of the power and coming

ἐπὶ τῶν νεφελῶν τοῦ οὐρανοῦ. **65** τότε
on the clouds - of heaven. Then

ὁ ἀρχιερεὺς διέρρηξεν τὰ ἱμάτια αὐτοῦ
the high priest rent the garments of him

λέγων· ἐβλασφήμησεν· τί ἔτι χρείαν ἔχομεν
saying: He blasphemed; what yet need have we

μαρτύρων; ἴδε νῦν ἠκούσατε τὴν βλασφη-
of witnesses? behold now ye heard the blas-

μίαν· **66** τί ὑμῖν δοκεῖ; οἱ δὲ ἀπο-
phemy; what to you seems it? And they answer-

κριθέντες εἶπαν· ἔνοχος θανάτου ἐστίν.
ing said: Liable of(to) death he is.

67 Τότε ἐνέπτυσαν εἰς τὸ πρόσωπον αὐτοῦ
Then they spat in the face of him

καὶ ἐκολάφισαν αὐτόν, οἱ δὲ
and violently maltreated him, and they

ἐρράπισαν **68** λέγοντες· προφήτευσον ἡμῖν,
slapped [him] saying: Prophesy thou to us,

χριστέ, τίς ἐστιν ὁ παίσας σε;
Christ, who is it the [one] having struck thee?

69 Ὁ δὲ Πέτρος ἐκάθητο ἔξω ἐν
- And Peter sat outside in

τῇ αὐλῇ· καὶ προσῆλθεν αὐτῷ μία
the court; and approached to him one

παιδίσκη λέγουσα· καὶ σὺ ἦσθα μετὰ
maidservant saying: Also thou wast with

Ἰησοῦ τοῦ Γαλιλαίου. **70** ὁ δὲ ἠρνήσατο
Jesus the Galilæan. But he denied

ἔμπροσθεν πάντων λέγων· οὐκ οἶδα
before all saying: I know not

τί λέγεις. **71** ἐξελθόντα δὲ εἰς τὸν
what thou sayest. And ²going out ¹into ³the

πυλῶνα εἶδεν αὐτὸν ἄλλη καὶ λέγει
⁴porch ²saw ³him ¹another and says

τοῖς ἐκεῖ· οὗτος ἦν μετὰ Ἰησοῦ τοῦ
to the [ones] there: This man was with Jesus the

Ναζωραίου. **72** καὶ πάλιν ἠρνήσατο
Nazarene. And again he denied

μετὰ ὅρκου ὅτι οὐκ οἶδα τὸν ἄνθρωπον.
with an oath[,] I know not the man.

73 μετὰ μικρὸν δὲ προσελθόντες οἱ
And after a little approaching the [ones]

ἑστῶτες εἶπον τῷ Πέτρῳ· ἀληθῶς καὶ
standing said - to Peter: Truly also

σὺ ἐξ αὐτῶν εἶ, καὶ γὰρ ἡ λαλιά σου
thou of them art, for indeed the speech of thee

δῆλόν σε ποιεῖ. **74** τότε ἤρξατο καταθε-
manifest thee makes. Then he began to

ματίζειν καὶ ὀμνύειν ὅτι οὐκ οἶδα τὸν
curse and to swear[,] I know not the

ἄνθρωπον. καὶ εὐθὺς ἀλέκτωρ ἐφώνησεν
man. And immediately a cock crowed.

King James Version

mediately the cock crew. 75And Peter remembered the word of Jesus, which said unto him, Before the cock crow, thou shalt deny me thrice. And he went out, and wept bitterly.

27 When the morning was come, all the chief priests and elders of the people took counsel against Jesus to put him to death: 2And when they had bound him, they led *him* away, and delivered him to Pontius Pilate the governor.

3 Then Judas, which had betrayed him, when he saw that he was condemned, repented himself, and brought again the thirty pieces of silver to the chief priests and elders, 4 Saying, I have sinned in that I have betrayed the innocent blood. And they said, What *is that* to us? see thou *to that.* 5And he cast down the pieces of silver in the temple, and departed, and went and hanged himself. 6And the chief priests took the silver pieces, and said, It is not lawful for to put them into the treasury, because it is the price of blood. 7And they took counsel, and bought with them the potter's field, to bury strangers in. 8 Wherefore that field was called, The field of blood, unto this day. 9 Then was fulfilled that which was spoken by Jeremy the prophet, saying, And they took the thirty pieces of silver, the price of him that was valued, whom they of the children of Israel did value; 10And gave them for the potter's field, as the Lord appointed me. 11And Jesus stood before the governor: and the governor asked him, saying, Art thou the King of the Jews? And Jesus said unto him, Thou sayest. 12And when he was accused of the chief priests and elders, he answered nothing. 13 Then said Pilate unto him, Hearest thou not how many things they witness against thee? 14And he answered him to never a word; insomuch that the governor marvelled greatly. 15 Now at *that* feast the governor was wont to release unto the people a prisoner, whom they would. 16And they had then a notable prisoner, called Barabbas. 17 Therefore when they were gathered together, Pilate said unto them, Whom will ye that I release unto you? Barabbas, or Jesus which is called Christ? 18 For he knew that for envy they had delivered him.

19 When he was set down on the judgment seat, his wife sent unto him, saying, Have thou nothing to do with that just man: for I have suffered many things this day in a dream because of him. 20 But the chief priests and elders persuaded the multitude that they should ask Barabbas, and destroy Jesus. 21 The governor answered and said unto them, Whether of the twain will ye that I release unto you? They said, Barabbas. 22 Pilate saith unto them, What shall I do then with Jesus which is called Christ? *They* all say unto him, Let him be crucified.

New International Version

Immediately a rooster crowed. 75 Then Peter remembered the word Jesus had spoken: "Before the rooster crows, you will disown me three times." And he went outside and wept bitterly.

Judas hangs himself

27 Early in the morning, all the chief priests and the elders of the people came to the decision to put Jesus to death. 2 They bound him, led him away and handed him over to Pilate, the governor.

3 When Judas, who betrayed him, saw that Jesus was condemned, he was seized with remorse and returned the thirty silver coins to the chief priests and the elders. 4 "I have sinned," he said, "for I have betrayed innocent blood."

"What is that to us?" they replied. "That's your responsibility."

5 So Judas threw the money into the temple and left. Then he went away and hanged himself.

6 The chief priests picked up the coins and said, "It is against the law to put this into the treasury, since it is blood money." 7 So they decided to use the money to buy the potter's field as a burial place for foreigners. 8 That is why it has been called the Field of Blood to this day. 9 Then what was spoken by Jeremiah the prophet was fulfilled: "They took the thirty silver coins, the price set on him by the people of Israel, 10 and they used them to buy the potter's field, as the Lord commanded me." *x*

Jesus before Pilate

11 Meanwhile Jesus stood before the governor, and the governor asked him, "Are you the king of the Jews?"

"Yes, it is as you say," Jesus replied.

12 When he was accused by the chief priests and the elders, he gave no answer. 13 Then Pilate asked him, "Don't you hear how many things they are accusing you of?" 14 But Jesus made no reply, not even to a single charge—to the great amazement of the governor.

15 Now it was the governor's custom at the Feast to release a prisoner chosen by the crowd. 16At that time they had a notorious prisoner, called Barabbas. 17 So when the crowd had gathered, Pilate asked them, "Which one do you want me to release to you: Barabbas, or Jesus who is called Christ?" 18 For he knew it was out of envy that they had handed Jesus over to him.

19 While Pilate was sitting on the judge's seat, his wife sent him this message: "Don't have anything to do with that innocent man, because I have suffered a great deal today in a dream on account of him."

20 But the chief priests and the elders persuaded the crowd to ask for Barabbas and to have Jesus executed.

21 "Which of the two do you want me to release to you?" asked the governor.

"Barabbas," they answered.

22 "What shall I do, then, with Jesus who is called Christ?" Pilate asked.

They all answered, "Crucify him!"

[x] Zech. 11:12, 13: Jer. 32: 6-9.

Greek Interlinear

75 καὶ   ἐμνήσθη   ὁ   Πέτρος   τοῦ   ῥήματος
And   remembered   -   Peter   the   word

'Ιησοῦ   εἰρηκότος   ὅτι   πρὶν   ἀλέκτορα
of Jesus   having said[,]   -   Before   a cock

φωνῆσαι   τρὶς   ἀπαρνήσῃ   με·   καὶ
to crow⁵   three times   thou wilt deny   me;   and

ἐξελθὼν   ἔξω   ἔκλαυσεν   πικρῶς.
going forth   outside   he wept   bitterly.

Chapter 27

Πρωΐας   δὲ   γενομένης   συμβούλιον
And early morning   coming*   counsel
= when early morning came

ἔλαβον   πάντες   οἱ   ἀρχιερεῖς   καὶ   οἱ
took   all   the   chief priests   and   the

πρεσβύτεροι   τοῦ   λαοῦ   κατὰ   τοῦ
elders   of the   people   against   the

'Ιησοῦ   ὥστε   θανατῶσαι   αὐτόν·   **2** καὶ
Jesus   so as   to put to death   him;   and

δήσαντες   αὐτὸν   ἀπήγαγον   καὶ   παρ-
having bound   him   they led away   and   de-

έδωκαν   Πιλάτῳ   τῷ   ἡγεμόνι.   **3** Τότε
livered   to Pilate   the   governor.   Then

ἰδὼν   'Ιούδας   ὁ   παραδοὺς   αὐτὸν
⁵seeing   ¹Judas   ²the [one]   ³having betrayed   ⁴him

ὅτι   κατεκρίθη,   μεταμεληθεὶς   ἔστρεψεν   τὰ
that   he was condemned,   repenting   returned   the

τριάκοντα   ἀργύρια   τοῖς   ἀρχιερεῦσιν
thirty   pieces of silver   to the   chief priests

καὶ   πρεσβυτέροις   **4** λέγων·   ἥμαρτον
and   elders   saying: I sinned

παραδοὺς   αἷμα   ἀθῷον.   οἱ   δὲ   εἶπαν·
betraying   blood   innocent.   But they   said:

τί   πρὸς   ἡμᾶς;   σὺ   ὄψῃ.   **5** καὶ   ῥίψας
What to   us?   thou shalt see [to it].   And   tossing

τὰ   ἀργύρια   εἰς   τὸν   ναὸν   ἀν-
the   pieces of silver   into   the   shrine   he

εχώρησεν,   καὶ   ἀπελθὼν   ἀπήγξατο.   **6** οἱ
departed,   and   going away   hanged himself.   the

δὲ   ἀρχιερεῖς   λαβόντες   τὰ   ἀργύρια   εἶπαν·
But   chief priests   taking   the   pieces of silver   said:

οὐκ   ἔξεστιν   βαλεῖν   αὐτὰ   εἰς   τὸν
It is not lawful   to put   them   into   the

κορβανᾶν,   ἐπεὶ   τιμὴ   αἵματός   ἐστιν.
treasury,   since   price   of blood   it is.

7 συμβούλιον   δὲ   λαβόντες   ἠγόρασαν   ἐξ
So counsel   taking   they bought of(with)

αὐτῶν   τὸν   ἀγρὸν   τοῦ   κεραμέως   εἰς   ταφὴν
them   the   field   of the   potter   for   burial

τοῖς   ξένοις.   **8** διὸ   ἐκλήθη   ὁ   ἀγρὸς
for the   strangers.   Wherefore   was called   -   field

ἐκεῖνος   ἀγρὸς   αἵματος   ἕως   τῆς   σήμερον.
that   Field   of blood   until   -   to-day.

9 τότε   ἐπληρώθη   τὸ   ῥηθὲν   διὰ
Then   was fulfilled   the [thing]   spoken   through

'Ιερεμίου   τοῦ   προφήτου   λέγοντος·   καὶ
Jeremiah   the   prophet   saying: And

ἔλαβον   τὰ   τριάκοντα   ἀργύρια,   τὴν
they took   the   thirty   pieces of silver,   the

τιμὴν   τοῦ   τετιμημένου   ὃν   ἐτιμήσαντο
price   of the [one] *having been* priced   whom   they priced

ἀπὸ   υἱῶν   'Ισραήλ,   **10** καὶ   ἔδωκαν
from [the]   sons   of Israel,   and   gave

αὐτὰ   εἰς   τὸν   ἀγρὸν   τοῦ   κεραμέως,   καθὰ
them   for   the   field   of the   potter,   as

συνέταξέν   μοι   κύριος.   **11** Ὁ   δὲ
directed   me   [the] Lord.   -   And

'Ιησοῦς   ἐστάθη   ἔμπροσθεν   τοῦ   ἡγεμόνος·
Jesus   stood   before   the   governor;

καὶ   ἐπηρώτησεν   αὐτὸν   ὁ   ἡγεμὼν   λέγων·
and   questioned   him   the   governor   saying:

σὺ   εἶ   ὁ   βασιλεὺς   τῶν   'Ιουδαίων;   ὁ   δὲ
Thou art   the   king   of the   Jews?   - And

'Ιησοῦς   ἔφη·   σὺ   λέγεις.   **12** καὶ   ἐν
Jesus   said: Thou   sayest.   And   in

τῷ   κατηγορεῖσθαι   αὐτὸν   ὑπὸ   τῶν
the   to be accused   himᵉ   by   the
= as he was accused

ἀρχιερέων   καὶ   πρεσβυτέρων   οὐδὲν
chief priests   and   elders   nothing

ἀπεκρίνατο.   **13** τότε   λέγει   αὐτῷ   ὁ   Πιλᾶτος·
he answered.   Then   says   to him   -   Pilate:

οὐκ   ἀκούεις   πόσα   σου   κατα-
Hearest thou not   what things   ⁴thee   ¹they

μαρτυροῦσιν;   **14** καὶ   οὐκ   ἀπεκρίθη   αὐτῷ
²give evidence against?   And   he answered not   him

πρὸς   οὐδὲ   ἓν   ῥῆμα,   ὥστε   θαυμάζειν
to   not   one   word,   so as   to marvel
= so that the governor marvelled

τὸν   ἡγεμόνα   λίαν.   **15** Κατὰ   δὲ   ἑορτὴν
the   governorᵇ   exceedingly.   Now at   a feast

εἰώθει   ὁ   ἡγεμὼν   ἀπολύειν   ἕνα   τῷ   ὄχλῳ
was accustomed   the governor   to release   ³one ¹to the ²crowd

δέσμιον   ὃν   ἤθελον.   **16** εἶχον   δὲ   τότε
⁴prisoner   whom   they wished.   And they had   then

δέσμιον   ἐπίσημον   λεγόμενον   Βαραββᾶν
prisoner   a notable   named   Barabbas.

17 συνηγμένων   οὖν   αὐτῶν   εἶπεν   αὐτοῖς
Therefore having assembled   them*   said   to them
= when they were assembled

ὁ   Πιλᾶτος·   τίνα   θέλετε   ἀπολύσω
-   Pilate: Whom   do ye wish   I may release

ὑμῖν,   [τὸν]   Βαραββᾶν   ἢ   'Ιησοῦν   τὸν
to you,   -   Barabbas   or   Jesus   -

λεγόμενον   χριστόν;   **18** ᾔδει   γὰρ   ὅτι
called   Christ?   for he knew   that

διὰ   φθόνον   παρέδωκαν   αὐτόν.   **19** Καθη-
because of   envy   they delivered   him.   sit-

μένου   δὲ   αὐτοῦ   ἐπὶ   τοῦ   βήματος
ting   Now   him*   on   the   tribunal
= Now as he sat

ἀπέστειλεν   πρὸς   αὐτὸν   ἡ   γυνὴ   αὐτοῦ
sent   to   him   the   wife   of him

λέγουσα·   μηδὲν   σοὶ   καὶ   τῷ   δικαίῳ
saying: Nothing   to thee   and   -   just man

ἐκείνῳ·   πολλὰ   γὰρ   ἔπαθον   σήμερον   κατ’
to that;   for many things   I suffered   to-day   by

ὄναρ   δι’   αὐτόν.   **20** Οἱ   δὲ   ἀρχιερεῖς
a dream   because of   him.   But the   chief priests

καὶ   οἱ   πρεσβύτεροι   ἔπεισαν   τοὺς
and   the   elders   persuaded   the

ὄχλους   ἵνα   αἰτήσωνται   τὸν   Βαραββᾶν,
crowds   that   they should ask   the   Barabbas,

τὸν   δὲ   'Ιησοῦν   ἀπολέσωσιν.   **21** ἀπο-
-   and   Jesus   should destroy.   So

κριθεὶς   δὲ   ὁ   ἡγεμὼν   εἶπεν   αὐτοῖς·
answering   the   governor   said   to them:

τίνα   θέλετε   ἀπὸ   τῶν   δύο   ἀπολύσω
Which   do ye wish   from   the   two   I may release

ὑμῖν,   οἱ   δὲ   εἶπαν·   τὸν   Βαραββᾶν.
to you?   And they   said: -   Barabbas.

22 λέγει   αὐτοῖς   ὁ   Πιλᾶτος·   τί   οὖν
Says   to them   -   Pilate: What then

ποιήσω   'Ιησοῦν   τὸν   λεγόμενον   χριστόν;
may I do   [to] Jesus   the   called   Christ?

King James Version

23 And the governor said, Why, what evil hath he done? But they cried out the more, saying, Let him be crucified.

24 When Pilate saw that he could prevail nothing, but *that* rather a tumult was made, he took water, and washed *his* hands before the multitude, saying, I am innocent of the blood of this just person: see ye *to it.* 25 Then answered all the people, and said, His blood *be* on us, and on our children.

26 Then released he Barabbas unto them: and when he had scourged Jesus, he delivered *him* to be crucified. 27 Then the soldiers of the governor took Jesus into the common hall, and gathered unto him the whole band *of soldiers.* 28 And they stripped him, and put on him a scarlet robe.

29 And when they had platted a crown of thorns, they put *it* upon his head, and a reed in his right hand: and they bowed the knee before him, and mocked him, saying, Hail, King of the Jews! 30 And they spit upon him, and took the reed, and smote him on the head. 31 And after that they had mocked him, they took the robe off from him, and put his own raiment on him, and led him away to crucify *him.* 32 And as they came out, they found a man of Cyrene, Simon by name: him they compelled to bear his cross. 33 And when they were come unto a place called Golgotha, that is to say, a place of a skull,

34 They gave him vinegar to drink mingled with gall: and when he had tasted *thereof,* he would not drink. 35 And they crucified him, and parted his garments, casting lots: that it might be fulfilled which was spoken by the prophet, They parted my garments among them, and upon my vesture did they cast lots. 36 And sitting down they watched him there; 37 And set up over his head his accusation written, THIS IS JESUS THE KING OF THE JEWS. 38 Then were there two thieves crucified with him; one on the right hand, and another on the left.

39 And they that passed by reviled him, wagging their heads, 40 And saying, Thou that destroyest the temple, and buildest *it* in three days, save thyself. If thou be the Son of God, come down from the cross. 41 Likewise also the chief priests mocking *him,* with the scribes and elders, said, 42 He saved others; himself he cannot save. If he be the King of Israel, let him now come down from the cross, and we will believe him. 43 He trusted in God; let him deliver him now, if he will have him: for he said, I am the Son of God. 44 The thieves also, which were crucified with him, cast the same in his teeth. 45 Now from the sixth hour there was darkness over all the land unto the ninth hour. 46 And about the ninth hour Jesus cried with a loud voice, saying, Eli, Eli, lama sabachthani? that is to say, My God, my God, why hast thou forsaken me?

New International Version

23 "Why? What crime has he committed?" asked Pilate.

But they shouted all the louder, "Crucify him!"

24 When Pilate saw that he was getting nowhere, but that instead an uproar was starting, he took water and washed his hands in front of the crowd. "I am innocent of this man's blood," he said. "It is your responsibility!"

25 All the people answered, "Let his blood be on us and on our children!"

26 Then he released Barabbas to them. But he had Jesus flogged, and handed him over to be crucified.

The soldiers mock Jesus

27 Then the governor's soldiers took Jesus into the Praetorium and gathered the whole company of soldiers around him. 28 They stripped him and put a scarlet robe on him, 29 and then wove a crown of thorns and set it on his head. They put a staff in his right hand and knelt in front of him and mocked him. "Hail, king of the Jews!" they said. 30 They spit on him, and took the staff and struck him on the head again and again. 31 After they had mocked him, they took off the robe and put his own clothes on him. Then they led him away to crucify him.

The crucifixion

32 As they were going out, they met a man from Cyrene, named Simon, and they forced him to carry the cross. 33 They came to a place called Golgotha (which means The Place of the Skull). 34 There they offered him wine to drink, mixed with gall; but after tasting it, he refused to drink it. 35 When they had crucified him, they divided up his clothes by casting lots.[y] 36 And sitting down, they kept watch over him there. 37 Above his head they placed the written charge against him: THIS IS JESUS, THE KING OF THE JEWS. 38 Two robbers were crucified with him, one on his right and one on his left. 39 Those who passed by hurled insults at him, shaking their heads 40 and saying, "You who are going to destroy the temple and build it in three days, save yourself! Come down from the cross, if you are the Son of God!"

41 In the same way the chief priests, the teachers of the law and the elders mocked him. 42 "He saved others," they said, "but he can't save himself! He's the king of Israel! Let him come down from the cross, and we will believe in him. 43 He trusts in God. Let God rescue him now if he wants him, for he said, 'I am the Son of God.'" 44 In the same way the robbers who were crucified with him also heaped insults on him.

The death of Jesus

45 From the sixth hour until the ninth hour darkness came over all the land. 46 About the ninth hour Jesus cried out in a loud voice, *"Eloi, Eloi, lama sabachthani?"*—which means, "My God, my God, why have you forsaken me?"[z]

[y] A few late MSS add *that the word spoken by the prophet might be fulfilled: "They divided my garments among them and cast lots for my clothing"* (Psalm 22:18). [z] Psalm 22:1.

Greek Interlinear

λέγουσιν πάντες· σταυρωθήτω. **23** ὁ δὲ
They say all: Let him be crucified. But he

ἔφη, τί γὰρ κακὸν ἐποίησεν; οἱ δὲ
said: Why what evil did he? But they

περισσῶς ἔκραζον λέγοντες· σταυρω-
more cried out saying: Let him be

θήτω. **24** ἰδὼν δὲ ὁ Πιλᾶτος ὅτι οὐδὲν
crucified. And seeing – Pilate that nothing

ὠφελεῖ ἀλλὰ μᾶλλον θόρυβος γίνεται,
is gained but rather an uproar occurs,

λαβὼν ὕδωρ ἀπενίψατο τὰς χεῖρας
taking water he washed the(his) hands

κατέναντι τοῦ ὄχλου λέγων· ἀθῷός
in front of the crowd saying: Innocent

εἰμι ἀπὸ τοῦ αἵματος τούτου· ὑμεῖς
I am from the blood of this man; ye

ὄψεσθε. **25** καὶ ἀποκριθεὶς πᾶς ὁ λαὸς
will see [to it]. And answering all the people

εἶπεν· τὸ αἷμα αὐτοῦ ἐφ' ἡμᾶς καὶ
said: The blood of him on us and

ἐπὶ τὰ τέκνα ἡμῶν. **26** τότε ἀπέλυσεν
on the children of us. Then he released

αὐτοῖς τὸν Βαραββᾶν, τὸν δὲ Ἰησοῦν
to them – Barabbas, – but Jesus

φραγελλώσας παρέδωκεν ἵνα σταυρωθῇ.
having scourged he delivered that he might be crucified.

27 Τότε οἱ στρατιῶται τοῦ ἡγεμόνος
Then the soldiers of the governor

παραλαβόντες τὸν Ἰησοῦν εἰς τὸ πραιτώ-
having taken – Jesus into the præ-

ριον συνήγαγον ἐπ' αὐτὸν ὅλην τὴν
torium assembled against him all the

σπεῖραν. **28** καὶ ἐκδύσαντες αὐτὸν χλαμύδα
band. And stripping him cloak

κοκκίνην περιέθηκαν αὐτῷ, **29** καὶ
a purple they placed round him, and

πλέξαντες στέφανον ἐξ ἀκανθῶν ἐπέθηκαν
having plaited a crown of thorns they placed [it] on

ἐπὶ τῆς κεφαλῆς αὐτοῦ καὶ κάλαμον
on the head of him and a reed

ἐν τῇ δεξιᾷ αὐτοῦ, καὶ γονυπετή-
in the right [hand] of him, and bowing

σαντες ἔμπροσθεν αὐτοῦ ἐνέπαιξαν αὐτῷ
the knee in front of him mocked at him

λέγοντες· χαῖρε, βασιλεῦ τῶν Ἰουδαίων,
saying: Hail, king of the Jews,

30 καὶ ἐμπτύσαντες εἰς αὐτὸν ἔλαβον
and spitting at him took

τὸν κάλαμον καὶ ἔτυπτον εἰς τὴν κεφαλὴν
the reed and struck at the head

αὐτοῦ. **31** καὶ ὅτε ἐνέπαιξαν αὐτῷ,
of him. And when they mocked at him,

ἐξέδυσαν αὐτὸν τὴν χλαμύδα καὶ ἐνέδυσαν
they took off him the cloak and put on

αὐτὸν τὰ ἱμάτια αὐτοῦ, καὶ ἀπήγαγον
him the garments of him, and led away

αὐτὸν εἰς τὸ σταυρῶσαι. **32** Ἐξερχόμενοι
him – – to crucify. going forth

'δὲ εὗρον ἄνθρωπον Κυρηναῖον, ὀνό-
And they found a man a Cyrenian, by

ματι Σίμωνα· τοῦτον ἠγγάρευσαν ἵνα
name Simon; this man they impressed that

ἄρῃ τὸν σταυρὸν αὐτοῦ. **33** Καὶ
he should bear the cross of him. And

ἐλθόντες εἰς τόπον λεγόμενον Γολγοθά,
coming to a place called Golgotha,

ὃ ἐστιν κρανίου τόπος λεγόμενος·
which is ²of a skull ²A place ¹called,

34 ἔδωκαν αὐτῷ πιεῖν οἶνον μετὰ
they gave him to drink wine with

χολῆς μεμιγμένον· καὶ γευσάμενος οὐκ
gall having been mixed; and tasting not

ἠθέλησεν πιεῖν. **35** σταυρώσαντες δὲ
he would to drink. And having crucified

αὐτὸν διεμερίσαντο τὰ ἱμάτια αὐτοῦ
him they divided the garments of him

βάλλοντες κλῆρον, **36** καὶ καθήμενοι ἐτήρουν
casting a lot, and sitting they guarded

αὐτὸν ἐκεῖ. **37** καὶ ἐπέθηκαν ἐπάνω
him there. And they placed on above

τῆς κεφαλῆς αὐτοῦ τὴν αἰτίαν αὐτοῦ
the head of him the charge of him

γεγραμμένην· ΟΥΤΟΣ ΕΣΤΙΝ ΙΗΣΟΥΣ
having been written: THIS IS JESUS

Ο ΒΑΣΙΛΕΥΣ ΤΩΝ ΙΟΥΔΑΙΩΝ. **38** Τότε
THE KING OF THE JEWS. Then

σταυροῦνται σὺν αὐτῷ δύο λῃσταί,
are crucified with him two robbers,

εἷς ἐκ δεξιῶν καὶ εἷς ἐξ εὐωνύμων.
one on [the] right and one on [the] left.

39 Οἱ δὲ παραπορευόμενοι ἐβλασφήμουν
And the [ones] passing by blasphemed

αὐτὸν κινοῦντες τὰς κεφαλὰς αὐτῶν
him wagging the heads of them

40 καὶ λέγοντες· ὁ καταλύων τὸν ναὸν
and saying: The [one] destroying the shrine

καὶ ἐν τρισὶν ἡμέραις οἰκοδομῶν,
and in three days building [it],

σῶσον σεαυτόν, εἰ υἱὸς εἶ τοῦ θεοῦ,
save thyself, if Son thou art – of God,

καὶ κατάβηθι ἀπὸ τοῦ σταυροῦ. **41** ὁμοίως
and come down from the cross. Likewise

[καὶ] οἱ ἀρχιερεῖς ἐμπαίζοντες μετὰ
also the chief priests mocking with

τῶν γραμματέων καὶ πρεσβυτέρων ἔλεγον
the scribes and elders said:

42 ἄλλους ἔσωσεν, ἑαυτὸν οὐ δύναται
Others he saved, himself he cannot

σῶσαι· βασιλεὺς Ἰσραὴλ ἐστιν,
to save; King of Israel he is,

καταβάτω νῦν ἀπὸ τοῦ σταυροῦ καὶ
let him come down now from the cross and

πιστεύσομεν ἐπ' αὐτόν. **43** πέποιθεν
we will believe on him. He has trusted

ἐπὶ τὸν θεόν, ῥυσάσθω νῦν εἰ θέλει
on – God, let him rescue now if he wants

αὐτόν· εἶπεν γὰρ ὅτι θεοῦ εἰμι υἱός.
him; for he said[.] – of God I am Son.

44 τὸ δ' αὐτὸ καὶ οἱ λῃσταὶ οἱ συσταυρω-
And the same also the robbers – crucified

θέντες σὺν αὐτῷ ὠνείδιζον αὐτόν. **45** Ἀπὸ
with him reproached him. from

δὲ ἕκτης ὥρας σκότος ἐγένετο ἐπὶ
Now [the] sixth hour darkness occurred over

πᾶσαν τὴν γῆν ἕως ὥρας ἐνάτης.
all the land until hour [the] ninth.

46 περὶ δὲ τὴν ἐνάτην ὥραν ἀνεβόησεν ὁ
And about the ninth hour cried out –

Ἰησοῦς φωνῇ μεγάλῃ λέγων· ἠλὶ ἠλὶ
Jesus voice with a great saying: Eli Eli

λεμὰ σαβαχθάνι; τοῦτ' ἔστιν· θεέ μου
lema sabachthani? this is: God of me[,]

King James Version

47 Some of them that stood there, when they heard *that,* said, This *man* calleth for Elias. 48And straightway one of them ran, and took a sponge, and filled *it* with vinegar, and put *it* on a reed, and gave him to drink. 49 The rest said, Let be, let us see whether Elias will come to save him.

50 Jesus, when he had cried again with a loud voice, yielded up the ghost. 51And, behold, the vail of the temple was rent in twain from the top to the bottom; and the earth did quake, and the rocks rent; 52And the graves were opened; and many bodies of the saints which slept arose, 53And came out of the graves after his resurrection, and went into the holy city, and appeared unto many. 54 Now when the centurion, and they that were with him, watching Jesus, saw the earthquake, and those things that were done, they feared greatly, saying, Truly this was the Son of God. 55And many women were there beholding afar off, which followed Jesus from Galilee, ministering unto him: 56Among which was Mary Magdalene, and Mary the mother of James and Joses, and the mother of Zebedee's children. 57 When the even was come, there came a rich man of Arimathea, named Joseph, who also himself was Jesus' disciple: 58 He went to Pilate, and begged the body of Jesus. Then Pilate commanded the body to be delivered. 59And when Joseph had taken the body, he wrapped it in a clean linen cloth, 60And laid it in his own new tomb, which he had hewn out in the rock: and he rolled a great stone to the door of the sepulchre, and departed. 61And there was Mary Magdalene, and the other Mary, sitting over against the sepulchre.

62 Now the next day, that followed the day of the preparation, the chief priests and Pharisees came together unto Pilate, 63 Saying, Sir, we remember that that deceiver said, while he was yet alive, After three days I will rise again. 64 Command therefore that the sepulchre be made sure until the third day, lest his disciples come by night, and steal him away, and say unto the people, He is risen from the dead: so the last error shall be worse than the first. 65 Pilate said unto them, Ye have a watch: go your way, make *it* as sure as ye can. 66 So they went, and made the sepulchre sure, sealing the stone, and setting a watch.

New International Version

47 When some of those standing there heard this, they said, "He's calling Elijah." 48 Immediately one of them ran and got a sponge. He filled it with wine vinegar, put it on a stick, and offered it to Jesus to drink. 49 But the rest said, "Leave him alone. Let's see if Elijah comes to save him."

50 And when Jesus had cried out again in a loud voice, he gave up his spirit.

51 At that moment the curtain of the temple was torn in two from top to bottom. The earth shook and the rocks split. 52 The tombs broke open and the bodies of many holy people who had died were raised to life. 53 They came out of the tombs, and after Jesus' resurrection they went into the holy city and appeared to many people.

54 When the centurion and those with him who were guarding Jesus saw the earthquake and all that had happened, they were terrified, and exclaimed, "Surely he was the Son[a] of God!"

55 Many women were there, watching from a distance. They had followed Jesus from Galilee to care for his needs. 56Among them were Mary Magdalene, Mary the mother of James and Joseph, and the mother of Zebedee's sons.

The burial of Jesus

57 As evening approached, there came a rich man from Arimathea, named Joseph, who had himself become a disciple of Jesus. 58 Going to Pilate, he asked for Jesus' body, and Pilate ordered that it be given to him. 59 Joseph took the body, wrapped it in a clean linen cloth, 60 and placed it in his own new tomb that he had cut out of the rock. He rolled a big stone in front of the entrance to the tomb and went away. 61 Mary Magdalene and the other Mary were sitting there across from the tomb.

The guard at the tomb

62 The next day, the one after Preparation Day, the chief priests and the Pharisees went to Pilate. 63 "Sir," they said, "we remember that while he was still alive that impostor said, 'After three days I will rise again.' 64 So give the order for the tomb to be made secure until the third day. Otherwise, his disciples may come and steal the body and tell the people that he has been raised from the dead. This last deception will be worse than the first."

65 "Take a guard," Pilate answered. "Go, make the tomb as secure as you know how." 66 So they went and made the tomb secure by putting a seal on the stone and posting the guard.

[a] Or *a son.*

98

Greek Interlinear

θεέ μου, ἱνατί με ἐγκατέλιπες; **47** τινὲς
God of me, why me didst thou forsake? some

δὲ τῶν ἐκεῖ ἑστηκότων ἀκούσαντες
And of the [ones] there standing hearing

ἔλεγον ὅτι ᾽Ηλίαν φωνεῖ οὗτος.
said[,] - ᵃElias ᵇcalls ¹this man.

48 καὶ εὐθέως δραμὼν εἷς ἐξ αὐτῶν καὶ
And immediately running one of them and

λαβὼν σπόγγον πλήσας τε ὄξους καὶ
taking a sponge and filling of (with) vinegar and

περιθεὶς καλάμῳ ἐπότιζεν αὐτόν.
putting [it] round a reed gave to drink him.

49 οἱ δὲ λοιποὶ εἶπαν· ἄφες ἴδωμεν
But the rest said: Leave[,] let us see

εἰ ἔρχεται ᾽Ηλίας σώσων αὐτόν. **50** ὁ
if comes Elias saving him.

δὲ ᾽Ιησοῦς πάλιν κράξας φωνῇ
And Jesus again crying out voice

μεγάλῃ ἀφῆκεν τὸ πνεῦμα. **51** Καὶ
with a great released the(his) spirit. And

ἰδοὺ τὸ καταπέτασμα τοῦ ναοῦ ἐσχίσθη
behold the veil of the shrine was rent

[ἀπ'] ἄνωθεν ἕως κάτω εἰς δύο, καὶ ἡ
from above to below in two, and the

γῆ ἐσείσθη, καὶ αἱ πέτραι ἐσχίσ-
earth was shaken, and the rocks were

θησαν, **52** καὶ τὰ μνημεῖα ἀνεῴχθησαν
rent, and the tombs were opened

καὶ πολλὰ σώματα τῶν κεκοιμημένων
and many bodies of the having fallen asleep

ἁγίων ἠγέρθησαν· **53** καὶ ἐξελθόντες
saints were raised; and coming forth

ἐκ τῶν μνημείων μετὰ τὴν ἔγερσιν
out of the tombs after the rising

αὐτοῦ εἰσῆλθον εἰς τὴν ἁγίαν πόλιν καὶ
of him entered into the holy city and

ἐνεφανίσθησαν πολλοῖς. **54** Ὁ δὲ ἑκατόν-
appeared to many. And the centu-

ταρχος καὶ οἱ μετ' αὐτοῦ τηροῦντες
rion and the [ones] with him guarding

τὸν ᾽Ιησοῦν ἰδόντες τὸν σεισμὸν καὶ
- Jesus seeing the earthquake and

τὰ γινόμενα ἐφοβήθησαν σφόδρα,
the things happening feared exceedingly,

λέγοντες· ἀληθῶς θεοῦ υἱὸς ἦν οὗτος.
saying: Truly ᵃof God ᵇSon ᵇwas ¹this man.

55 ᾽Ησαν δὲ ἐκεῖ γυναῖκες πολλαὶ
Now there were there women many

ἀπὸ μακρόθεν θεωροῦσαι, αἵτινες ἠκολού-
from afar beholding, who followed

θησαν τῷ ᾽Ιησοῦ ἀπὸ τῆς Γαλιλαίας
- Jesus from - Galilee

διακονοῦσαι αὐτῷ· **56** ἐν αἷς ἦν
ministering to him; among whom was

Μαρία ἡ Μαγδαληνή, καὶ Μαρία ἡ
Mary the Magdalene, and Mary the

τοῦ ᾽Ιακώβου καὶ ᾽Ιωσὴφ μήτηρ, καὶ ἡ
- of James and of Joseph mother, and the

μήτηρ τῶν υἱῶν Ζεβεδαίου.
mother of the sons of Zebedee.

57 ᾽Οψίας δὲ γενομένης ἦλθεν ἄνθρωπος
Now evening having come* came man
= when evening had come

πλούσιος ἀπὸ ᾽Αριμαθαίας, τοὔνομα ᾽Ιωσήφ,
a rich from Arimathæa, the name Joseph,

ὃς καὶ αὐτὸς ἐμαθητεύθη τῷ ᾽Ιησοῦ·
who also himself was discipled - to Jesus;

58 οὗτος προσελθὼν τῷ Πιλάτῳ ᾔτήσατο
this man approaching - to Pilate asked

τὸ σῶμα τοῦ ᾽Ιησοῦ. τότε ὁ Πιλᾶτος
the body - of Jesus. Then - Pilate

ἐκέλευσεν ἀποδοθῆναι. **59** καὶ λαβὼν
commanded [it] to be given [him]. And taking

τὸ σῶμα ὁ ᾽Ιωσὴφ ἐνετύλιξεν αὐτὸ [ἐν]
the body - Joseph wrapped it in

σινδόνι καθαρᾷ, **60** καὶ ἔθηκεν αὐτὸ ἐν
sheet a clean, and placed it in

τῷ καινῷ αὐτοῦ μνημείῳ ὃ ἐλατό-
the new of him tomb which he

μησεν ἐν τῇ πέτρᾳ, καὶ προσκυλίσας
hewed in the rock, and having rolled to

λίθον μέγαν τῇ θύρᾳ τοῦ μνημείου
stone a great to the door of the tomb

ἀπῆλθεν. **61** ᾽Ην δὲ ἐκεῖ Μαριὰμ
went away. And there was there Mary

ἡ Μαγδαληνὴ καὶ ἡ ἄλλη Μαρία,
the Magdalene and the other Mary,

καθήμεναι ἀπέναντι τοῦ τάφου. **62** Τῇ
sitting opposite the grave. on the

δὲ ἐπαύριον, ἥτις ἐστὶν μετὰ τὴν παρα-
And morrow, which is after the prepara-

σκευήν, συνήχθησαν οἱ ἀρχιερεῖς
tion, were assembled the chief priests

καὶ οἱ Φαρισαῖοι πρὸς Πιλᾶτον **63** λέ-
and the Pharisees to Pilate say-

γοντες· κύριε, ἐμνήσθημεν ὅτι ἐκεῖνος
ing: Sir, we remembered that that

ὁ πλάνος εἶπεν ἔτι ζῶν· μετὰ τρεῖς
- deceiver said yet living: After three

ἡμέρας ἐγείρομαι. **64** κέλευσον οὖν
days I am raised. Command therefore

ἀσφαλισθῆναι τὸν τάφον ἕως τῆς
to be made fast the grave until the

τρίτης ἡμέρας, μήποτε ἐλθόντες οἱ μαθηταὶ
third day, lest coming the disciples

κλέψωσιν αὐτὸν καὶ εἴπωσιν τῷ λαῷ·
may steal him and may say to the people:

ἠγέρθη ἀπὸ τῶν νεκρῶν, καὶ ἔσται
He was raised from the dead, and will be

ἡ ἐσχάτη πλάνη χείρων τῆς πρώτης.
the last deceit worse [than] the first.

65 ἔφη αὐτοῖς ὁ Πιλᾶτος· ἔχετε κου-
Said to them - Pilate: Ye have a

στωδίαν· ὑπάγετε ἀσφαλίσασθε ὡς οἴδατε.
guard; go ye make fast as ye know*.

66 οἱ δὲ πορευθέντες ἠσφαλίσαντο τὸν
And they going made fast the

τάφον σφραγίσαντες τὸν λίθον μετὰ τῆς
grave sealing the stone with the

κουστωδίας.
guard.

---

* can. See note on page xxxviii.

King James Version

28 In the end of the sabbath, as it began to dawn toward the first *day* of the week, came Mary Magdalene and the other Mary to see the sepulchre. 2And, behold, there was a great earthquake: for the angel of the Lord descended from heaven, and came and rolled back the stone from the door, and sat upon it. 3 His countenance was like lightning, and his raiment white as snow: 4And for fear of him the keepers did shake, and became as dead *men*. 5And the angel answered and said unto the women, Fear not ye: for I know that ye seek Jesus, which was crucified. 6 He is not here: for he is risen, as he said. Come, see the place where the Lord lay. 7And go quickly, and tell his disciples that he is risen from the dead; and, behold, he goeth before you into Galilee; there shall ye see him: lo, I have told you. 8And they departed quickly from the sepulchre with fear and great joy; and did run to bring his disciples word.

9 And as they went to tell his disciples, behold, Jesus met them, saying, All hail. And they came and held him by the feet, and worshipped him. 10 Then said Jesus unto them, Be not afraid: go tell my brethren that they go into Galilee, and there shall they see me.

11 Now when they were going, behold, some of the watch came into the city, and shewed unto the chief priests all the things that were done. 12And when they were assembled with the elders, and had taken counsel, they gave large money unto the soldiers, 13 Saying, Say ye, His disciples came by night, and stole him *away* while we slept. 14And if this come to the governor's ears, we will persuade him, and secure you. 15 So they took the money, and did as they were taught: and this saying is commonly reported among the Jews until this day.

16 Then the eleven disciples went away into Galilee, into a mountain where Jesus had appointed them. 17And when they saw him, they worshipped him: but some doubted. 18And Jesus came and spake unto them, saying, All power is given unto me in heaven and in earth. 19 Go ye therefore, and teach all nations, baptizing them in the name of the Father, and of the Son, and of the Holy Ghost: 20 Teaching them to observe all things whatsoever I have commanded you: and, lo, I am with you alway, *even* unto the end of the world. Amen.

New International Version

The resurrection

28 After the Sabbath, at dawn on the first day of the week, Mary Magdalene and the other Mary went to look at the tomb.

2 There was a violent earthquake, for an angel of the Lord came down from heaven and, going to the tomb, rolled back the stone and sat on it. 3 His appearance was like lightning, and his clothes were white as snow. 4 The guards were so afraid of him that they shook and became like dead men.

5 The angel said to the women, "Do not be afraid, for I know that you are looking for Jesus, who was crucified. 6 He is not here; he has risen, just as he said. Come and see the place where he lay. 7 Then go quickly and tell his disciples: 'He has risen from the dead and is going ahead of you into Galilee. There you will see him.' Now I have told you."

8 So the women hurried away from the tomb, afraid yet filled with joy, and ran to tell his disciples. 9 Suddenly Jesus met them. "Greetings," he said. They came to him, clasped his feet and worshiped him. 10 Then Jesus said to them, "Do not be afraid. Go and tell my brothers to go to Galilee; there they will see me."

The guards' report

11 While the women were on their way, some of the guards went into the city and reported to the chief priests everything that had happened. 12 When the chief priests had met with the elders, they devised a plan. They gave the soldiers a large sum of money, 13 telling them, "You are to say, 'His disciples came during the night and stole him away while we were asleep.' 14 If this report gets to the governor, we will satisfy him and keep you out of trouble." 15 So the soldiers took the money and did as they were instructed. And this story has been widely circulated among the Jews to this very day.

The great commission

16 Then the eleven disciples went to Galilee, to the mountain where Jesus had told them to go. 17 When they saw him, they worshiped him; but some doubted. 18 Then Jesus came to them and said, "All authority in heaven and on earth has been given to me. 19 Therefore go and make disciples of all nations, baptizing them in[b] the name of the Father and of the Son and of the Holy Spirit, 20 and teaching them to obey everything I have commanded you. And surely I will be with you always, to the very end of the age."

[b] Or *into.* See Acts 8:16; 19:5; Rom. 6:3; ICor. 1:13, 10:2; Gal. 3:27.

Greek Interlinear

Chapter 28

'Οψὲ δὲ σαββάτων, τῇ ἐπιφωσκούσῃ
But late of [the] sabbaths, at the drawing on

εἰς μίαν σαββάτων, ἦλθεν Μαριὰμ ἡ
toward one of [the] sabbaths, came Mary the
= the first day of the week,

Μαγδαληνὴ καὶ ἡ ἄλλη Μαρία θεωρῆσαι
Magdalene and the other Mary to view

τὸν τάφον. 2 καὶ ἰδοὺ σεισμὸς ἐγένετο
the grave. And behold earthquake occurred

μέγας· ἄγγελος γὰρ κυρίου καταβὰς
a great; for an angel of [the] Lord descending

ἐξ οὐρανοῦ καὶ προσελθὼν ἀπεκύλισεν
out of heaven and approaching rolled away

τὸν λίθον καὶ ἐκάθητο ἐπάνω αὐτοῦ.
the stone and sat upon it.

3 ἦν δὲ ἡ εἰδέα αὐτοῦ ὡς ἀστραπή,
And was the appearance of him as lightning,

καὶ τὸ ἔνδυμα αὐτοῦ λευκὸν ὡς χιών.
and the dress of him white as snow.

4 ἀπὸ δὲ τοῦ φόβου αὐτοῦ ἐσείσθησαν
And from the fear of him were shaken

οἱ τηροῦντες καὶ ἐγενήθησαν ὡς
the [ones] guarding and they became as

νεκροί. 5 ἀποκριθεὶς δὲ ὁ ἄγγελος
dead. And answering the angel

εἶπεν ταῖς γυναιξίν· μὴ φοβεῖσθε ὑμεῖς·
said to the women: Fear not ye;

οἶδα γὰρ ὅτι Ἰησοῦν τὸν ἐσταυρω-
for I know that Jesus the [one] having been

μένον ζητεῖτε· 6 οὐκ ἔστιν ὧδε·
crucified ye seek; he is not here;

ἠγέρθη γὰρ καθὼς εἶπεν· δεῦτε ἴδετε τὸν
for he was raised as he said; come see ye the

τόπον ὅπου ἔκειτο. 7 καὶ ταχὺ πορευθεῖσαι
place where he lay. And quickly going

εἴπατε τοῖς μαθηταῖς αὐτοῦ ὅτι ἠγέρθη
tell the disciples of him that he was raised

ἀπὸ τῶν νεκρῶν, καὶ ἰδοὺ προάγει ὑμᾶς
from the dead, and behold he goes before you

εἰς τὴν Γαλιλαίαν, ἐκεῖ αὐτὸν ὄψεσθε.
to - Galilee, there him ye will see.

ἰδοὺ εἶπον ὑμῖν. 8 καὶ ἀπελθοῦσαι ταχὺ
Behold I told you. And going away quickly

ἀπὸ τοῦ μνημείου μετὰ φόβου καὶ χαρᾶς
from the tomb with fear and joy

μεγάλης ἔδραμον ἀπαγγεῖλαι τοῖς
great they ran to announce to the

μαθηταῖς αὐτοῦ. 9 καὶ ἰδοὺ Ἰησοῦς
disciples of him. And behold Jesus

ὑπήντησεν αὐταῖς λέγων· χαίρετε. αἱ δὲ
met them saying: Hail. And they

προσελθοῦσαι ἐκράτησαν αὐτοῦ τοὺς πόδας
approaching held of him the feet

καὶ προσεκύνησαν αὐτῷ. 10 τότε λέγει
and worshipped him. Then says

αὐταῖς ὁ Ἰησοῦς· μὴ φοβεῖσθε· ὑπάγετε
to them - Jesus: Fear ye not; go ye

ἀπαγγείλατε τοῖς ἀδελφοῖς μου ἵνα
announce to the brothers of me that

ἀπέλθωσιν εἰς τὴν Γαλιλαίαν, κἀκεῖ
they may go away into - Galilee, and there

με ὄψονται. 11 Πορευομένων δὲ αὐτῶν
me they will see. And going them
= as they were going

ἰδού τινες τῆς κουστωδίας ἐλθόντες εἰς
behold some of the guard coming into

τὴν πόλιν ἀπήγγειλαν τοῖς ἀρχιερεῦσιν
the city announced to the chief priests

ἅπαντα τὰ γενόμενα. 12 καὶ συν-
all the things having happened. And being

αχθέντες μετὰ τῶν πρεσβυτέρων συμβούλιόν
assembled with the elders ²counsel

τε λαβόντες ἀργύρια ἱκανὰ ἔδωκαν τοῖς
¹and ²taking silver enough gave to the

στρατιώταις, 13 λέγοντες· εἴπατε ὅτι οἱ
soldiers, saying: Say ye that the

μαθηταὶ αὐτοῦ νυκτὸς ἐλθόντες ἔκλεψαν
disciples of him of (by) night coming stole

αὐτὸν ἡμῶν κοιμωμένων. 14 καὶ ἐὰν
him we sleeping. And if
= while we slept.

ἀκουσθῇ τοῦτο ἐπὶ τοῦ ἡγεμόνος,
be heard this before the governor,

ἡμεῖς πείσομεν καὶ ὑμᾶς ἀμερίμνους
we will persuade and you free from anxiety

ποιήσομεν. 15 οἱ δὲ λαβόντες ἀργύρια
we will make. And they taking silver

ἐποίησαν ὡς ἐδιδάχθησαν. Καὶ διεφη-
did as they were taught. And was spread

μίσθη ὁ λόγος οὗτος παρὰ Ἰουδαίοις
about - saying this by Jews

μέχρι τῆς σήμερον [ἡμέρας]. 16 Οἱ δὲ
until the to-day. So the

ἔνδεκα μαθηταὶ ἐπορεύθησαν εἰς τὴν
eleven disciples went to -

Γαλιλαίαν, εἰς τὸ ὄρος οὗ ἐτάξατο
Galilee, to the mountain where appointed

αὐτοῖς ὁ Ἰησοῦς, 17 καὶ ἰδόντες αὐτὸν
them - Jesus, and seeing him

προσεκύνησαν, οἱ δὲ ἐδίστασαν. 18 καὶ
they worshipped, but some doubted. And

προσελθὼν ὁ Ἰησοῦς ἐλάλησεν αὐτοῖς
approaching - Jesus talked with them

λέγων· ἐδόθη μοι πᾶσα ἐξουσία ἐν
saying: was given to me All authority in

οὐρανῷ καὶ ἐπὶ [τῆς] γῆς. 19 πορευθέντες
heaven and on the earth. Going

οὖν μαθητεύσατε πάντα τὰ ἔθνη, βαπτίζ-
therefore disciple ye all the nations, baptiz-

οντες αὐτοὺς εἰς τὸ ὄνομα τοῦ πατρὸς
ing them in the name of the Father

καὶ τοῦ υἱοῦ καὶ τοῦ ἁγίου πνεύματος,
and of the Son and of the Holy Spirit,

20 διδάσκοντες αὐτοὺς τηρεῖν πάντα
teaching them to observe all things

ὅσα ἐνετειλάμην ὑμῖν· καὶ ἰδοὺ ἐγὼ
whatever I gave command to you; and behold I

μεθ᾽ ὑμῶν εἰμι πάσας τὰς ἡμέρας ἕως
with you am all the days until

τῆς συντελείας τοῦ αἰῶνος.
the completion of the age.

King James Version   New International Version

THE
GOSPEL ACCORDING TO
SAINT MARK

MARK

John the Baptist prepares the way

King James Version

1 The beginning of the gospel of Jesus Christ, the Son of God; 2As it is written in the prophets, Behold, I send my messenger before thy face, which shall prepare thy way before thee. 3 The voice of one crying in the wilderness, Prepare ye the way of the Lord, make his paths straight. 4 John did baptize in the wilderness, and preach the baptism of repentance for the remission of sins. 5And there went out unto him all the land of Judea, and they of Jerusalem, and were all baptized of him in the river of Jordan, confessing their sins. 6And John was clothed with camel's hair, and with a girdle of a skin about his loins; and he did eat locusts and wild honey; 7And preached, saying, There cometh one mightier than I after me, the latchet of whose shoes I am not worthy to stoop down and unloose. 8 I indeed have baptized you with water: but he shall baptize you with the Holy Ghost. 9And it came to pass in those days, that Jesus came from Nazareth of Galilee, and was baptized of John in Jordan. 10And straightway coming up out of the water, he saw the heavens opened, and the Spirit like a dove descending upon him: 11And there came a voice from heaven, *saying,* Thou art my beloved Son, in whom I am well pleased. 12And immediately the Spirit driveth him into the wilderness. 13And he was there in the wilderness forty days tempted of Satan; and was with the wild beasts; and the angels ministered unto him. 14 Now after that John was put in prison, Jesus came into Galilee, preaching the gospel of the kingdom of God, 15And saying, The time is fulfilled, and the kingdom of God is at hand: repent ye, and believe the gospel. 16 Now as he walked by the sea of Galilee, he saw Simon and Andrew his brother casting a net into the sea: for they were fishers. 17And Jesus said unto them, Come ye after me, and I will make you to become fishers of men. 18And straightway they forsook their nets, and followed him. 19And when he had gone a little further thence, he saw James the *son* of Zebedee, and John his brother, who also were in the ship mending their nets. 20And straightway he called them: and they left their father Zebedee in the ship with the hired servants, and went after him.

New International Version

1 The beginning of the gospel about Jesus Christ, the Son of God.*a*
2 It is written in Isaiah the prophet:
"I will send my messenger ahead of you,
who will prepare your way" *b*—
3 "a voice of one calling in the desert,
'Prepare the way for the Lord,
make straight paths for him.' *c* "
4And so John came, baptizing in the desert region and preaching repentance and baptism for the forgiveness of sins. 5 The whole Judean countryside and all the people of Jerusalem went out to him. Confessing their sins, they were baptized by him in the Jordan River. 6 John wore clothing made of camel's hair, with a leather belt around his waist, and he ate locusts and wild honey. 7And this was his message: "After me will come one more powerful than I, the thongs of whose sandals I am not worthy to stoop down and untie. 8 I baptize you with water, but he will baptize you with the Holy Spirit."

The baptism and temptation of Jesus

9 At that time Jesus came from Nazareth in Galilee and was baptized by John in the Jordan. 10As Jesus was coming up out of the water, he saw heaven torn open and the Spirit descend on him like a dove. 11And a voice came from heaven: "You are my Son, whom I love; with you I am well-pleased."
12 At once the Spirit sent him out into the desert, 13 and he was in the desert forty days, being tempted by Satan. He was with the wild animals, and angels attended him.

The calling of the first disciples

14 After John was put in prison, Jesus went into Galilee, proclaiming the good news of God. 15 "The time has come," he said. "The kingdom of God is near. Repent and believe the good news!"
16 As Jesus walked beside the Sea of Galilee, he saw Simon and his brother Andrew casting a net into the lake, for they were fishermen. 17 "Come, follow me," Jesus said, "and I will make you fishers of men." 18At once they left their nets and followed him.
19 When he had gone a little farther, he saw James son of Zebedee and his brother John in a boat, preparing their nets. 20 Without delay he called them, and they left their father Zebedee in the boat with the hired men and followed him.

[a] Some MSS omit *the Son of God.* [b] 2 Mal. 3:1. [c] Isaiah 40:3.

ΚΑΤΑ ΜΑΡΚΟΝ

Chapter 1

Ἀρχὴ τοῦ εὐαγγελίου Ἰησοῦ Χριστοῦ.
[The] beginning of the gospel of Jesus Christ.

2 Καθὼς γέγραπται ἐν τῷ Ἠσαΐᾳ τῷ
As it has been written in - Isaiah the

προφήτῃ· ἰδοὺ ἀποστέλλω τὸν ἄγγελόν μου
prophet: Behold[,] I send the messenger of me

πρὸ προσώπου σου, ὃς κατασκευάσει τὴν ὁδόν
before [the] face of thee, who will prepare the way

σου· **3** φωνὴ βοῶντος ἐν τῇ ἐρήμῳ· ἑτοιμάσατε
of thee; a voice of [one] crying in the desert: Prepare ye

τὴν ὁδὸν κυρίου, εὐθείας ποιεῖτε τὰς τρίβους
the way of [the] Lord, straight make the paths

αὐτοῦ, **4** ἐγένετο Ἰωάννης ὁ βαπτίζων ἐν τῇ
of him, came John the [one] baptizing in the

ἐρήμῳ κηρύσσων βάπτισμα μετανοίας εἰς
desert proclaiming a baptism of repentance for

ἄφεσιν ἁμαρτιῶν. **5** καὶ ἐξεπορεύετο πρὸς
forgiveness of sins. And went out to

αὐτὸν πᾶσα ἡ Ἰουδαία χώρα καὶ οἱ Ἱεροσο-
him all the Judæan country and the Jerusa-

λυμῖται πάντες, καὶ ἐβαπτίζοντο ὑπ᾽ αὐτοῦ
lemites all, and were baptized by him

ἐν τῷ Ἰορδάνῃ ποταμῷ ἐξομολογούμενοι τὰς
in the Jordan river confessing the

ἁμαρτίας αὐτῶν. **6** καὶ ἦν ὁ Ἰωάννης
sins of them. And was - John

ἐνδεδυμένος τρίχας καμήλου καὶ ζώνην
having been clothed [in] hairs of a camel and girdle

δερματίνην περὶ τὴν ὀσφὺν αὐτοῦ, καὶ ἔσθων
a leathern round the loin[s] of him, and eating

ἀκρίδας καὶ μέλι ἄγριον. **7** καὶ ἐκήρυσσεν
locusts and honey wild. And he proclaimed

λέγων· ἔρχεται ὁ ἰσχυρότερός μου ὀπίσω
saying: Comes the [one] stronger of me after
=than I

[μου], οὗ οὐκ εἰμὶ ἱκανὸς κύψας λῦσαι
me, of whom I am not competent stooping to loosen

τὸν ἱμάντα τῶν ὑποδημάτων αὐτοῦ. **8** ἐγὼ
the thong of the sandals of him. I

ἐβάπτισα ὑμᾶς ὕδατι, αὐτὸς δὲ βαπτίσει ὑμᾶς
baptized you in water, but he will baptize you

πνεύματι ἁγίῳ.
Spirit in [the] Holy.

9 Καὶ ἐγένετο ἐν ἐκείναις ταῖς ἡμέραις
And it came to pass in those - days

ἦλθεν Ἰησοῦς ἀπὸ Ναζαρὲθ τῆς Γαλιλαίας
came Jesus from Nazareth - of Galilee

καὶ ἐβαπτίσθη εἰς τὸν Ἰορδάνην ὑπὸ
and was baptized in the Jordan by

Ἰωάννου. **10** καὶ εὐθὺς ἀναβαίνων ἐκ τοῦ
John. And immediately going up out of the

ὕδατος εἶδεν σχιζομένους τοὺς οὐρανοὺς
water he saw being rent the heavens

καὶ τὸ πνεῦμα ὡς περιστερὰν καταβαῖνον
and the Spirit as a dove coming down

εἰς αὐτόν· **11** καὶ φωνὴ [ἐγένετο] ἐκ τῶν
to him; and a voice there was out of the

οὐρανῶν· σὺ εἶ ὁ υἱός μου ὁ ἀγαπητός,
heavens: Thou art the Son of me the beloved,

ἐν σοὶ εὐδόκησα. **12** Καὶ εὐθὺς τὸ
in thee I was well pleased. And immediately the

πνεῦμα αὐτὸν ἐκβάλλει εἰς τὴν ἔρημον.
Spirit him thrusts forth into the desert.

13 καὶ ἦν ἐν τῇ ἐρήμῳ τεσσεράκοντα
And he was in the desert forty

ἡμέρας πειραζόμενος ὑπὸ τοῦ σατανᾶ, καὶ
days being tempted by - Satan, and

ἦν μετὰ τῶν θηρίων, καὶ οἱ ἄγγελοι
was with the wild beasts, and the angels

διηκόνουν αὐτῷ.
ministered to him.

14 Καὶ μετὰ τὸ παραδοθῆναι τὸν
And after the to be delivered -
= after John was delivered

Ἰωάννην ἦλθεν ὁ Ἰησοῦς εἰς τὴν Γαλιλαίαν
John came - Jesus into - Galilee

κηρύσσων τὸ εὐαγγέλιον τοῦ θεοῦ **15** [καὶ
proclaiming the gospel - of God and

λέγων], ὅτι πεπλήρωται ὁ καιρὸς καὶ
saying, - Has been fulfilled the time and

ἤγγικεν ἡ βασιλεία τοῦ θεοῦ· μετανοεῖτε
has drawn near the kingdom - of God; repent ye

καὶ πιστεύετε ἐν τῷ εὐαγγελίῳ. **16** Καὶ
and believe in the gospel. And

παράγων παρὰ τὴν θάλασσαν τῆς Γαλιλαίας
passing along beside the sea - of Galilee

εἶδεν Σίμωνα καὶ Ἀνδρέαν τὸν ἀδελφὸν
he saw Simon and Andrew the brother

Σίμωνος ἀμφιβάλλοντας ἐν τῇ θαλάσσῃ·
of Simon casting [a net] in the sea;

ἦσαν γὰρ ἁλεεῖς. **17** καὶ εἶπεν αὐτοῖς
for they were fishers. And said to them

ὁ Ἰησοῦς· δεῦτε ὀπίσω μου, καὶ ποιήσω
- Jesus: Come after me, and I will make

ὑμᾶς γενέσθαι ἁλεεῖς ἀνθρώπων. **18** καὶ
you to become fishers of men. And

εὐθὺς ἀφέντες τὰ δίκτυα ἠκολούθησαν
immediately leaving the nets they followed

αὐτῷ. **19** Καὶ προβὰς ὀλίγον εἶδεν
him. And going forward a little he saw

Ἰάκωβον τὸν τοῦ Ζεβεδαίου καὶ Ἰωάννην
James the [son] - of Zebedee and John

τὸν ἀδελφὸν αὐτοῦ καὶ αὐτοὺς ἐν τῷ
the brother of him even them in the

πλοίῳ καταρτίζοντας τὰ δίκτυα. **20** καὶ
ship mending the nets. And

εὐθὺς ἐκάλεσεν αὐτούς· καὶ ἀφέντες τὸν
immediately he called them; and leaving the

πατέρα αὐτῶν Ζεβεδαῖον ἐν τῷ πλοίῳ
father of them Zebedee in the ship

μετὰ τῶν μισθωτῶν ἀπῆλθον ὀπίσω αὐτοῦ.
with the hired servants they went after him.

103

King James Version

21And they went into Capernaum; and straightway on the sabbath day he entered into the synagogue, and taught. 22And they were astonished at his doctrine: for he taught them as one that had authority, and not as the scribes. 23And there was in their synagogue a man with an unclean spirit; and he cried out, 24 Saying, Let *us* alone; what have we to do with thee, thou Jesus of Nazareth? art thou come to destroy us? I know thee who thou art, the Holy One of God. 25And Jesus rebuked him, saying, Hold thy peace, and come out of him. 26And when the unclean spirit had torn him, and cried with a loud voice, he came out of him. 27And they were all amazed, insomuch that they questioned among themselves, saying, What thing is this? what new doctrine *is* this? for with authority commandeth he even the unclean spirits, and they do obey him. 28And immediately his fame spread abroad throughout all the region round about Galilee. 29And forthwith, when they were come out of the synagogue, they entered into the house of Simon and Andrew, with James and John. 30 But Simon's wife's mother lay sick of a fever; and anon they tell him of her. 31And he came and took her by the hand, and lifted her up; and immediately the fever left her, and she ministered unto them. 32And at even, when the sun did set, they brought unto him all that were diseased, and them that were possessed with devils. 33And all the city was gathered together at the door. 34And he healed many that were sick of divers diseases, and cast out many devils; and suffered not the devils to speak, because they knew him. 35And in the morning, rising up a great while before day, he went out, and departed into a solitary place, and there prayed. 36And Simon and they that were with him followed after him. 37And when they had found him, they said unto him, All *men* seek for thee. 38And he said unto them, Let us go into the next towns, that I may preach there also: for therefore came I forth. 39And he preached in their synagogues throughout all Galilee, and cast out devils. 40And there came a leper to him, beseeching him, and kneeling down to him, and saying unto him, If thou wilt, thou canst make me clean. 41And Jesus, moved with compassion, put forth *his* hand, and touched him, and saith unto him, I will; be thou clean. 42And as soon as he had spoken, immediately the leprosy departed from him, and he was cleansed. 43And he straitly charged him, and forthwith sent him away; 44And saith unto him, See thou say nothing to any man: but go thy way, shew thyself to the priest, and offer for thy cleansing those things which Moses commanded, for a testimony unto them. 45 But he went out, and began to publish *it* much, and to blaze abroad the matter, insomuch that Jesus could no more openly enter into the city, but was without in desert places: and they came to him from every quarter.

New International Version

Jesus drives out an evil spirit

21 They went to Capernaum, and when the Sabbath came, Jesus went into the synagogue and began to teach. 22 The people were amazed at his teaching, because he taught them as one who had authority, not as the teachers of the law. 23 Just then a man in their synagogue who was possessed by an evil [d] spirit cried out, 24 "What do you want with us, Jesus of Nazareth? Have you come to destroy us? I know who you are—the Holy One of God!"

25 "Be quiet!" said Jesus sternly. "Come out of him!" 26 The evil [d] spirit shook the man violently and came out of him with a shriek.

27 The people were all so amazed that they asked each other, "What is this? A new teaching —and with authority! He even gives orders to evil [d] spirits and they obey him." 28 News about him spread quickly over the whole region of Galilee.

Jesus heals many

29 As soon as they left the synagogue, they went with James and John to the home of Simon and Andrew. 30 Simon's mother-in-law was in bed with a fever, and they told Jesus about her. 31 So he went to her, took her hand and helped her up. The fever left her and she began to wait on them.

32 That evening after sunset the people brought to Jesus all the sick and demon-possessed. 33 The whole town gathered at the door, 34 and Jesus healed many who had various diseases. He also drove out many demons, but he would not let the demons speak because they knew who he was.

Jesus prays in a solitary place

35 Very early in the morning, while it was still dark, Jesus got up, left the house and went off to a solitary place, where he prayed. 36 Simon and his companions went to look for him, 37 and when they found him, they exclaimed: "Everyone is looking for you!"

38 Jesus replied, "Let's go somewhere else— to the nearby villages—so I can preach there also. That is why I have come." 39 So he traveled throughout Galilee, preaching in their synagogues and driving out demons.

A man with leprosy

40 A man with leprosy[f] came to him and begged him on his knees, "If you are willing, you can make me clean."

41 Filled with compassion, Jesus reached out his hand and touched the man. "I am willing," he said. "Be clean!" 42 Immediately the leprosy left him and he was cured.

43 Jesus sent him away at once with a strong warning: 44 "See that you don't tell this to anyone. But go, show yourself to the priest and offer the sacrifices that Moses commanded for your cleansing, as a testimony to them." 45 Instead he went out and began to talk freely, spreading the news. As a result, Jesus could no longer enter a town openly but stayed outside in lonely places. Yet the people still came to him from everywhere.

[d] Greek *unclean*. [f] The Greek word probably designated other related diseases also.

Greek Interlinear

21 Καὶ   εἰσπορεύονται   εἰς   Καφαρναούμ·
    And   they enter   into   Capernaum;
καὶ   εὐθὺς   τοῖς   σάββασιν   εἰσελθὼν
and   immediately on the   sabbaths   entering
εἰς   τὴν   συναγωγὴν   ἐδίδασκεν.   22 καὶ
into   the   synagogue   he taught.   And
ἐξεπλήσσοντο ἐπὶ   τῇ   διδαχῇ   αὐτοῦ·   ἦν
they were astounded on(at) the teaching of him; ¹he was
γὰρ   διδάσκων   αὐτοὺς   ὡς   ἐξουσίαν   ἔχων,
¹for   teaching   them   as   authority   having,
καὶ   οὐχ   ὡς   οἱ   γραμματεῖς.   23 Καὶ   εὐθὺς
and   not   as   the   scribes.   And immediately
ἦν   ἐν   τῇ   συναγωγῇ   αὐτῶν   ἄνθρωπος
there was in the   synagogue   of them   a man
ἐν   πνεύματι   ἀκαθάρτῳ,   καὶ   ἀνέκραξεν
in   spirit   an unclean,   and   he cried out
24 λέγων·   τί   ἡμῖν   καὶ   σοί,   Ἰησοῦ
    saying: What to us and   to thee,   Jesus
Ναζαρηνέ;   ἦλθες   ἀπολέσαι   ἡμᾶς;   οἶδά
Nazarene? camest thou to destroy   us ?   I know
σε   τίς   εἶ,   ὁ   ἅγιος   τοῦ   θεοῦ.   25 καὶ
thee who thou art, the holy [one]   -   of God.   And
ἐπετίμησεν   αὐτῷ   ὁ   Ἰησοῦς   [λέγων]·
rebuked   him   -   Jesus   saying:
φιμώθητι   καὶ   ἔξελθε   [ἐξ   αὐτοῦ].   26 καὶ
Be quiet   and   come out   out of   him.   And
σπαράξαν   αὐτὸν   τὸ   πνεῦμα   τὸ   ἀκάθαρτον
throwing   him   the   spirit   the   unclean
καὶ   φωνῆσαν   φωνῇ   μεγάλῃ   ἐξῆλθεν   ἐξ
and   shouting   voice   with a great   he came out out of
αὐτοῦ.   27 καὶ   ἐθαμβήθησαν   ἅπαντες,   ὥστε
him.   And   were astounded   all,   so as
συζητεῖν   αὐτοὺς   λέγοντας·   τί   ἐστιν   τοῦτο;
to debate   them[b]   saying·   What   is   this ?
they debated
διδαχὴ   καινὴ   κατ’   ἐξουσίαν·   καὶ   τοῖς
teaching   a new   by   authority;   and   the
πνεύμασι   τοῖς   ἀκαθάρτοις   ἐπιτάσσει,   καὶ
spirits   -   unclean   he commands,   and
ὑπακούουσιν   αὐτῷ.   28 καὶ   ἐξῆλθεν   ἡ
they obey   him.   And   went forth   the
ἀκοὴ   αὐτοῦ   εὐθὺς   πανταχοῦ   εἰς   ὅλην
report   of him   immediately   everywhere   into   all
τὴν   περίχωρον   τῆς   Γαλιλαίας.   29 Καὶ
the   neighbourhood   -   of Galilee.   And
εὐθὺς   ἐκ   τῆς   συναγωγῆς   ἐξελθόντες   ἦλθον
immediately out of the   synagogue   going forth they came
εἰς   τὴν   οἰκίαν   Σίμωνος   καὶ   Ἀνδρέου
into   the   house   of Simon   and   Andrew
μετὰ   Ἰακώβου   καὶ   Ἰωάννου.   30 ἡ   δὲ
with   James   and   John.   Now the
πενθερὰ   Σίμωνος   κατέκειτο   πυρέσσουσα,
mother-in-law of Simon   was laid [aside] fever-stricken,
καὶ   εὐθὺς   λέγουσιν   αὐτῷ   περὶ   αὐτῆς.
and   immediately   they tell   him   about   her.
31 καὶ   προσελθὼν   ἤγειρεν   αὐτὴν   κρατήσας
    And   approaching   he raised   her   holding
τῆς   χειρός·   καὶ   ἀφῆκεν   αὐτὴν   ὁ   πυρετός,
the(her) hand;   and   left   her   the   fever,
καὶ   διηκόνει   αὐτοῖς.   32 Ὀψίας   δὲ   γενο-
and   she served   them.   And evening   com-
                                            = when evening
μένης,   ὅτε   ἔδυσεν   ὁ   ἥλιος,   ἔφερον   πρὸς
ing,[a]   when   set   the   sun,   they brought   to
came,
αὐτὸν   πάντας   τοὺς   κακῶς   ἔχοντας   καὶ
him   all   the [ones]   ill   having   and
                                        = those who were ill
τοὺς   δαιμονιζομένους·   33 καὶ   ἦν   ὅλη   ἡ
the   being demon-possessed;   and   was   all   the

πόλις   ἐπισυνηγμένη   πρὸς   τὴν   θύραν.
city   having been assembled   at   the   door.
34 καὶ   ἐθεράπευσεν   πολλοὺς   κακῶς   ἔχοντας
    And   he healed   many   ill   having
                                                 = who were ill
ποικίλαις   νόσοις,   καὶ   δαιμόνια   πολλὰ
with various   diseases,   and   demons   many
ἐξέβαλεν,   καὶ   οὐκ   ἤφιεν   λαλεῖν   τὰ   δαιμόνια,
he expelled,   and   did not allow to speak the   demons,
ὅτι   ᾔδεισαν   αὐτόν.   35 Καὶ   πρωῒ   ἔννυχα
because they knew   him.   And ²early ⁴in the night
λίαν   ἀναστὰς   ἐξῆλθεν   καὶ   ἀπῆλθεν   εἰς
⁵very   ³rising up   he went out   and   went away   to
ἔρημον   τόπον,   κἀκεῖ   προσηύχετο.   36 καὶ
a desert   place,   and there   prayed.   And
κατεδίωξεν   αὐτὸν   Σίμων   καὶ   οἱ   μετ’
hunted down   him   Simon   and the [ones] with
αὐτοῦ,   καὶ   εὗρον   αὐτὸν   καὶ   λέγουσιν
him,   and   found   him   and   say
αὐτῷ   37 ὅτι   πάντες   ζητοῦσίν   σε.   38 καὶ
to him[.]   -   All   are seeking   thee.   And
λέγει   αὐτοῖς·   ἄγωμεν   ἀλλαχοῦ   εἰς   τὰς
he says   to them: Let us go   elsewhere   into   the
ἐχομένας   κωμοπόλεις,   ἵνα   καὶ   ἐκεῖ
neighbouring   towns,   that   also   there
κηρύξω·   εἰς   τοῦτο   γὰρ   ἐξῆλθον.   39 καὶ
I may proclaim; for for this [purpose] I came forth.   And
ἦλθεν   κηρύσσων   εἰς   τὰς   συναγωγὰς   αὐτῶν
he came   proclaiming   in   the   synagogues   of them
εἰς   ὅλην   τὴν   Γαλιλαίαν   καὶ   τὰ   δαιμόνια
in   all   -   Galilee   and   the   demons
ἐκβάλλων.
expelling.
40 Καὶ   ἔρχεται   πρὸς   αὐτὸν   λεπρὸς
    And   comes   to   him   a leper
παρακαλῶν   αὐτὸν   καὶ   γονυπετῶν   λέγων
beseeching   him   and falling on [his] knees saying
αὐτῷ   ὅτι   ἐὰν   θέλῃς   δύνασαί   με   καθαρίσαι.
to him[.] -   If thou art willing thou art able me   to cleanse.
41 καὶ   σπλαγχνισθεὶς   ἐκτείνας   τὴν
    And being filled with tenderness stretching forth the(his)
χεῖρα   αὐτοῦ   ἥψατο   καὶ   λέγει   αὐτῷ·   θέλω,
hand   ¹him   ¹he touched   and   says   to him: I am willing,
καθαρίσθητι.   42 καὶ   εὐθὺς   ἀπῆλθεν   ἀπ’
be thou cleansed.   And   immediately   departed   from
αὐτοῦ   ἡ   λέπρα,   καὶ   ἐκαθαρίσθη.   43 καὶ
him   the   leprosy,   and   he was cleansed.   And
ἐμβριμησάμενος   αὐτῷ   εὐθὺς   ἐξέβαλεν   αὐτόν,
sternly admonishing   him   immediately he put out   him,
44 καὶ   λέγει   αὐτῷ·   ὅρα   μηδενὶ   μηδὲν
    and   says   to him: See   no one no(any)thing
εἴπῃς,   ἀλλὰ   ὕπαγε   σεαυτὸν   δεῖξον   τῷ
thou tellest, but   go   thyself   show   to the
ἱερεῖ   καὶ   προσένεγκε   περὶ   τοῦ   καθαρισμοῦ   σου
priest   and   offer   concerning the   cleansing   of thee
ἃ   προσέταξεν   Μωϋσῆς,   εἰς   μαρτύριον
[the things] which commanded Moses,   for   a testimony
αὐτοῖς.   45 ὁ   δὲ   ἐξελθὼν   ἤρξατο   κηρύσσειν
to them.   But he going out   began   to proclaim
πολλὰ   καὶ   διαφημίζειν   τὸν   λόγον,   ὥστε
many things and to spread about   the   matter,   so as
                                                    = so that
μηκέτι   αὐτὸν   δύνασθαι   φανερῶς   εἰς   πόλιν
no longer   him   to be able[b]   openly   into   a city
he was no longer able
εἰσελθεῖν,   ἀλλ’   ἔξω   ἐπ’   ἐρήμοις   τόποις
to enter,   but   outside on(in)   desert   places
ἦν·   καὶ   ἤρχοντο   πρὸς   αὐτὸν   πάντοθεν.
he was; and   they came   to   him   from all directions.

105

King James Version　　　　　　　　　　　　New International Version

Jesus heals a paralytic

2 And again he entered into Capernaum after *some* days; and it was noised that he was in the house. 2And straightway many were gathered together, insomuch that there was no room to receive *them*, no, not so much as about the door: and he preached the word unto them. 3And they come unto him, bringing one sick of the palsy, which was borne of four. 4And when they could not come nigh unto him for the press, they uncovered the roof where he was: and when they had broken *it* up, they let down the bed wherein the sick of the palsy lay. 5 When Jesus saw their faith, he said unto the sick of the palsy, Son, thy sins be forgiven thee. 6 But there were certain of the scribes sitting there, and reasoning in their hearts, 7 Why doth this *man* thus speak blasphemies? who can forgive sins but God only? 8And immediately, when Jesus perceived in his spirit that they so reasoned within themselves, he said unto them, Why reason ye these things in your hearts? 9 Whether is it easier to say to the sick of the palsy, *Thy* sins be forgiven thee; or to say, Arise, and take up thy bed, and walk? 10 But that ye may know that the Son of man hath power on earth to forgive sins, (he saith to the sick of the palsy,) 11 I say unto thee, Arise, and take up thy bed, and go thy way into thine house. 12And immediately he arose, took up the bed, and went forth before them all; insomuch that they were all amazed, and glorified God, saying, We never saw it on this fashion. 13And he went forth again by the sea side; and all the multitude resorted unto him, and he taught them. 14And as he passed by, he saw Levi the *son* of Alpheus sitting at the receipt of custom, and said unto him, Follow me. And he arose and followed him. 15And it came to pass, that, as Jesus sat at meat in his house, many publicans and sinners sat also together with Jesus and his disciples; for there were many, and they followed him. 16And when the scribes and Pharisees saw him eat with publicans and sinners, they said unto his disciples, How is it that he eateth and drinketh with publicans and sinners? 17 When Jesus heard *it*, he saith unto them, They that are whole have no need of the physician, but they that are sick: I came not to call the righteous, but sinners to repentance. 18And the disciples of John and of the Pharisees used to fast: and they come and say unto him, Why do the disciples of John and of the Pharisees fast, but thy disciples fast not? 19And Jesus said unto them, Can the children of the bridechamber fast, while the bridegroom is with them? as long as they have the bridegroom with them, they cannot fast. 20 But the days will come, when the bridegroom shall be taken away

Jesus heals a paralytic

2 A few days later, when Jesus again entered Capernaum, the people heard that he had come home. 2 So many gathered that there was no room left, not even outside the door, and he preached to them. 3 Some men came, bringing to him a paralytic, carried by four of them. 4 Since they could not get him to Jesus because of the crowd, they made an opening in the roof above Jesus and having dug through, lowered the mat the paralyzed man was lying on. 5 When Jesus saw their faith, he said to the paralytic, "Son, your sins are forgiven."

6 Now some teachers of the law were sitting there, thinking to themselves, 7 "Why does this fellow talk like that? He's blaspheming! Who can forgive sins but God alone?"

8 Immediately Jesus knew in his spirit that this was what they were thinking in their hearts, and he said to them, "Why are you thinking these things? 9 Which is easier: to say to the paralytic, 'Your sins are forgiven,' or to say, 'Get up, take your mat and walk'? 10 But that you may know that the Son of Man has authority on earth to forgive sins . . . ." He said to the paralytic, 11 "I tell you, get up, take your mat and go home." 12 He got up, took his mat and walked out in full view of them all. This amazed everyone and they praised God, saying, "We have never seen anything like this!"

The calling of Matthew

13 Once again Jesus went out beside the lake. A large crowd came to him, and he began to teach them. 14As he walked along, he saw Levi son of Alphaeus sitting at the tax collector's booth. "Follow me," Jesus told him, and Levi got up and followed him.

15 While Jesus was having dinner at Levi's house, many tax collectors and "sinners" were eating with him and his disciples, for there were many who followed him. 16 When the teachers of the law who were Pharisees saw him eating with the "sinners" and tax collectors, they asked his disciples: "Why does he eat with tax collectors and 'sinners'?"

17 On hearing this, Jesus said to them, "It is not the healthy who need a doctor, but the sick. I have not come to call the righteous, but sinners."

Jesus questioned about fasting

18 Now John's disciples and the Pharisees were fasting. Some people came and asked Jesus, "How is it that John's disciples and the disciples of the Pharisees are fasting, but yours are not?"

19 Jesus answered, "How can the guests of the bridegroom fast while he is with them? They cannot, so long as they have him with them. 20 But the time will come when the bridegroom

Greek Interlinear

Chapter 2

Καὶ   εἰσελθὼν πάλιν εἰς Καφαρναοὺμ
And   entering   again   into   Capernaum
δι' ἡμερῶν ἠκούσθη ὅτι ἐν οἴκῳ ἐστίν.
through days   it was heard that   at home   he is(was).
= after [some] days

2 καὶ   συνήχθησαν πολλοί, ὥστε μηκέτι
And   were assembled   many,   so as   no longer
χωρεῖν μηδὲ τὰ πρὸς τὴν θύραν, καὶ
to have room not   -   at   the   door,   and
ἐλάλει αὐτοῖς τὸν λόγον. 3 καὶ ἔρχονται
he spoke   to them   the   word.   And   they come
φέροντες πρὸς αὐτὸν παραλυτικὸν αἱρόμενον
carrying   to   him   a paralytic   being borne
ὑπὸ τεσσάρων. 4 καὶ μὴ δυνάμενοι
by   four [men].   And   not   being able
προσενέγκαι αὐτῷ διὰ τὸν ὄχλον
to bring   to him   because of   the   crowd
ἀπεστέγασαν τὴν στέγην ὅπου ἦν, καὶ
they unroofed   the   roof   where   he was,   and
ἐξορύξαντες χαλῶσι τὸν κράβατον ὅπου ὁ
having opened up they lower   the   mattress   where   the
παραλυτικὸς κατέκειτο. 5 καὶ ἰδὼν ὁ
paralytic   was lying.   And   seeing   -
Ἰησοῦς τὴν πίστιν αὐτῶν λέγει τῷ
Jesus   the   faith   of them   he says   to the
παραλυτικῷ· τέκνον, ἀφίενταί σου αἱ
paralytic: Child,   are forgiven   of thee   the
ἁμαρτίαι. 6 ἦσαν δέ τινες τῶν γραμματέων
sins.   Now there were   some   of the   scribes
ἐκεῖ καθήμενοι καὶ διαλογιζόμενοι ἐν ταῖς
there   sitting   and   reasoning   in   the
καρδίαις αὐτῶν· 7 τί οὗτος οὕτως λαλεῖ;
hearts   of them: Why this [man]   thus   speaks?
βλασφημεῖ· τίς δύναται ἀφιέναι ἁμαρτίας
he blasphemes: who   can   to forgive   sins
εἰ μὴ εἷς ὁ θεός; 8 καὶ εὐθὺς ἐπιγνοὺς
except   one[,]   -   God?   And immediately knowing
ὁ Ἰησοῦς τῷ πνεύματι αὐτοῦ ὅτι οὕτως
-   Jesus   in the   spirit   of him   that   thus
διαλογίζονται ἐν ἑαυτοῖς, λέγει αὐτοῖς·
they reason   among   themselves,   he says   to them:
τί ταῦτα διαλογίζεσθε ἐν ταῖς καρδίαις
Why these things   reason ye   in   the   hearts
ὑμῶν, 9 τί ἐστιν εὐκοπώτερον, εἰπεῖν
of you?   What   is   easier,   to say
τῷ παραλυτικῷ· ἀφίενταί σου αἱ ἁμαρτίαι,
to the   paralytic: are forgiven of thee   the   sins,
ἢ εἰπεῖν· ἔγειρε καὶ ἆρον τὸν κράβατόν
or   to say: Rise   and   take   the   mattress
σου καὶ περιπάτει; 10 ἵνα δὲ εἰδῆτε
of thee   and   walk?   But that   ye may know
ὅτι ἐξουσίαν ἔχει ὁ υἱὸς τοῦ ἀνθρώπου
that   authority   has   the   Son   of man
ἀφιέναι ἁμαρτίας ἐπὶ τῆς γῆς,—λέγει τῷ
to forgive   sins   on   the   earth,—he says   to the
παραλυτικῷ· 11 σοὶ λέγω, ἔγειρε ἆρον
paralytic: To thee   I say,   rise[,]   take
τὸν κράβατόν σου καὶ ὕπαγε εἰς τὸν
the   mattress   of thee   and   go   to   the
οἶκόν σου. 12 καὶ ἠγέρθη καὶ εὐθὺς
house   of thee.   And   he arose   and immediately
ἄρας τὸν κράβατον ἐξῆλθεν ἔμπροσθεν
taking   the   mattress   he went forth   before
πάντων, ὥστε ἐξίστασθαι πάντας καὶ
all,   so as   to be astonished   all   and
= so that they were all astonished and glorified

δοξάζειν τὸν θεὸν λέγοντας ὅτι οὕτως
to glorify[b]   -   God   saying[.]   -   Thus
οὐδέποτε εἴδαμεν.
never   we saw.

13 Καὶ ἐξῆλθεν πάλιν παρὰ τὴν θάλασσαν·
And he went forth   again   by   the   sea;
καὶ πᾶς ὁ ὄχλος ἤρχετο πρὸς αὐτόν,
and   all   the   crowd   came   to   him,
καὶ ἐδίδασκεν αὐτούς. 14 Καὶ παράγων
and   he taught   them.   And   passing along
εἶδεν Λευὶν τὸν τοῦ Ἀλφαίου καθήμενον
he saw   Levi   the [son]   -   Alphæus   sitting
ἐπὶ τὸ τελώνιον, καὶ λέγει αὐτῷ· ἀκολούθει
on(in or at)the custom house,   and   says   to him: Follow
μοι. καὶ ἀναστὰς ἠκολούθησεν αὐτῷ.
me.   And   rising up   he followed   him.
15 Καὶ γίνεται κατακεῖσθαι αὐτὸν ἐν τῇ
And it comes to pass   to recline   him[b]   in   the
= he reclines
οἰκίᾳ αὐτοῦ, καὶ πολλοὶ τελῶναι καὶ
house   of him,   and   many   tax-collectors   and
ἁμαρτωλοὶ συνανέκειντο τῷ Ἰησοῦ καὶ
sinners   reclined with   -   Jesus   and
τοῖς μαθηταῖς αὐτοῦ· ἦσαν γὰρ πολλοί,
the   disciples   of him;   for there were   many,
καὶ ἠκολούθουν αὐτῷ. 16 καὶ οἱ γραμματεῖς
and   they followed   him.   And the   scribes
τῶν Φαρισαίων ἰδόντες ὅτι ἐσθίει
of the   Pharisees   seeing   that   he eats(ate)
μετὰ τῶν ἁμαρτωλῶν καὶ τελωνῶν ἔλεγον
with   -   sinners   and   tax-collectors   said
τοῖς μαθηταῖς αὐτοῦ· ὅτι μετὰ τῶν
to the   disciples   of him: -   With   -
τελωνῶν καὶ ἁμαρτωλῶν ἐσθίει; 17 καὶ
tax-collectors   and   sinners   does he eat?   And
ἀκούσας ὁ Ἰησοῦς λέγει αὐτοῖς [ὅτι] οὐ
hearing   -   Jesus   says   to them[,]   -   Not
χρείαν ἔχουσιν οἱ ἰσχύοντες ἰατροῦ ἀλλ'
need   have   the [ones] being strong of a physician but
οἱ κακῶς ἔχοντες· οὐκ ἦλθον καλέσαι
the [ones] ill   having;   I came not   to call
= those who are ill;
δικαίους ἀλλὰ ἁμαρτωλούς. 18 Καὶ ἦσαν
righteous men but   sinners.   And   [7]were
οἱ μαθηταὶ Ἰωάννου καὶ οἱ Φαρισαῖοι
[1]the [2]disciples [6]of John [3]and [4]the [5]Pharisees
νηστεύοντες. καὶ ἔρχονται καὶ λέγουσιν
[8]fasting.   And   they come   and   say
αὐτῷ· διὰ τί οἱ μαθηταὶ Ἰωάννου καὶ
to him: Why   the   disciples   of John   and
οἱ μαθηταὶ τῶν Φαρισαίων νηστεύουσιν,
the   disciples   of the   Pharisees   fast,
οἱ δὲ σοὶ μαθηταὶ οὐ νηστεύουσιν; 19 καὶ
-   but   thy   disciples   do not fast?   And
εἶπεν αὐτοῖς ὁ Ἰησοῦς· μὴ δύνανται οἱ
said   to them   -   Jesus: not   can   the
υἱοὶ τοῦ νυμφῶνος, ἐν ᾧ ὁ νυμφίος
sons   of the   bridechamber,   while†   the   bridegroom
μετ' αὐτῶν ἐστιν, νηστεύειν; ὅσον χρόνον
with   them   is,   to fast?   what   time
ἔχουσιν τὸν νυμφίον μετ' αὐτῶν, οὐ
they have   the   bridegroom   with   them,   not
δύνανται νηστεύειν. 20 ἐλεύσονται δὲ ἡμέραι
they can   to fast.   But will come   days
ὅταν ἀπαρθῇ ἀπ' αὐτῶν ὁ νυμφίος, καὶ
when   taken away   from   them   the   bridegroom,   and

King James Version

from them, and then shall they fast in those days. 21 No man also seweth a piece of new cloth on an old garment; else the new piece that filled it up taketh away from the old, and the rent is made worse. 22And no man putteth new wine into old bottles; else the new wine doth burst the bottles, and the wine is spilled, and the bottles will be marred: but new wine must be put into new bottles. 23And it came to pass, that he went through the corn fields on the sabbath day; and his disciples began, as they went, to pluck the ears of corn. 24And the Pharisees said unto him, Behold, why do they on the sabbath day that which is not lawful? 25And he said unto them, Have ye never read what David did, when he had need, and was a hungered, he, and they that were with him? 26 How he went into the house of God in the days of Abiathar the high priest, and did eat the shewbread, which is not lawful to eat but for the priests, and gave also to them which were with him? 27And he said unto them, The sabbath was made for man, and not man for the sabbath: 28 Therefore the Son of man is Lord also of the sabbath.

New International Version

will be taken from them, and on that day they will fast.
21 "No one sews a patch of unshrunk cloth on an old garment. If he does, the new piece will pull away from the old, making the tear worse. 22And no one pours new wine into old wineskins. If he does, the wine will burst the skins, and both the wine and the wineskins will be ruined. No, he pours new wine into new wineskins."

Lord of the Sabbath

23 One Sabbath Jesus was going through the grainfields, and as his disciples walked along, they began to pick some heads of grain. 24 The Pharisees said to him, "Look, why are they doing what is unlawful on the Sabbath?"
25 He answered, "Have you never read what David did when he and his companions were hungry and in need? 26 In the time of Abiathar the high priest, he entered the house of God and ate the consecrated bread, which is only lawful for priests to eat. And he also gave some to his companions."
27 Then he said to them, "The Sabbath was made for man, not man for the Sabbath. 28 So the Son of Man is Lord even of the Sabbath."

3 And he entered again into the synagogue; and there was a man there which had a withered hand. 2And they watched him, whether he would heal him on the sabbath day; that they might accuse him. 3And he saith unto the man which had the withered hand, Stand forth. 4And he saith unto them, Is it lawful to do good on the sabbath days, or to do evil? to save life, or to kill? But they held their peace. 5And when he had looked round about on them with anger, being grieved for the hardness of their hearts, he saith unto the man, Stretch forth thine hand. And he stretched it out: and his hand was restored whole as the other. 6And the Pharisees went forth, and straightway took counsel with the Herodians against him, how they might destroy him. 7 But Jesus withdrew himself with his disciples to the sea: and a great multitude from Galilee followed him, and from Judea, 8And from Jerusalem, and from Idumea, and *from* beyond Jordan; and they about Tyre and Sidon, a great multitude, when they had heard what great things he did, came unto him. 9And he spake to his disciples, that a small ship should wait on him because of the multitude, lest they should throng him. 10 For he had healed many; insomuch that they pressed upon him for to touch him, as many as had plagues. 11And unclean spirits, when they saw him, fell down before him, and cried, saying, Thou art the Son of God. 12And he straitly charged them that they should

3 Another time he went into the synagogue, and a man with a shriveled hand was there. 2 Some of them were looking for a reason to accuse Jesus, so they watched him closely to see if he would heal him on the Sabbath. 3 Jesus said to the man with the shriveled hand, "Stand up in front of everyone."
4 Then Jesus asked them, "Which is lawful on the Sabbath: to do good or to do evil, to save life or to kill?" But they remained silent.
5 He looked around at them in anger and, deeply distressed at their stubborn hearts, said to the man, "Stretch out your hand." He stretched it out, and his hand was completely restored. 6 Then the Pharisees went out and began to plot with the Herodians how they might kill Jesus.

Crowds follow Jesus

7 Jesus withdrew with his disciples to the lake, and a large crowd from Galilee followed. 8 When they heard all he was doing, many people came to him from Judea, Jerusalem, Idumea, and the regions across the Jordan and around Tyre and Sidon. 9 Because of the crowd he told his disciples to have a small boat ready for him, to keep the people from crowding him. 10 For he had healed many, so that those with diseases were pushing forward to touch him. 11 Whenever the evil *g* spirits saw him, they fell down before him and cried out, "You are the Son of God." 12 But he gave them strict orders not to tell who he was.

[g] Greek *unclean*.

Greek Interlinear

τότε νηστεύσουσιν ἐν ἐκείνῃ τῇ ἡμέρᾳ.
then they will fast in that - day.

21 Οὐδεὶς ἐπίβλημα ῥάκους ἀγνάφου ἐπιράπτει
No one a patch cloth of unfulled sews

ἐπὶ ἱμάτιον παλαιόν· εἰ δὲ μή, αἴρει
on garment an old; otherwise, ²takes

τὸ πλήρωμα ἀπ' αὐτοῦ τὸ καινὸν τοῦ
⁴the ⁵fulness ⁶from ⁷itself ¹the ⁸ new ³the

παλαιοῦ, καὶ χεῖρον σχίσμα γίνεται. 22 καὶ
⁹old, and a worse rent occurs. And

οὐδεὶς βάλλει οἶνον νέον εἰς ἀσκοὺς παλαιούς·
no one puts wine new into wineskins old;

εἰ δὲ μή, ῥήξει ὁ οἶνος τοὺς ἀσκούς,
otherwise, ²will burst ³wine the wineskins,

καὶ ὁ οἶνος ἀπόλλυται καὶ οἱ ἀσκοί.
and the wine perishes and the wineskins.

[ἀλλὰ οἶνον νέον εἰς ἀσκοὺς καινούς.]
But wine new into wineskins fresh.

23 Καὶ ἐγένετο αὐτὸν ἐν τοῖς σάββασιν
And it came to pass him on the sabbaths
= as he passed on the sabbath

παραπορεύεσθαι διὰ τῶν σπορίμων, καὶ
to pass^b through the cornfields, and

οἱ μαθηταὶ αὐτοῦ ἤρξαντο ὁδὸν ποιεῖν
the disciples of him began way to make

τίλλοντες τοὺς στάχυας. 24 καὶ οἱ Φαρισαῖοι
plucking the ears of corn. And the Pharisees

ἔλεγον αὐτῷ· ἴδε τί ποιοῦσιν τοῖς σάββασιν
said to him: Behold[,] why do on the sabbaths

ὃ οὐκ ἔξεστιν; 25 καὶ λέγει αὐτοῖς·
what is not lawful? And he says to them:

οὐδέποτε ἀνέγνωτε τί ἐποίησεν Δαυίδ,
never read ye what did David,

ὅτε χρείαν ἔσχεν καὶ ἐπείνασεν αὐτός
when need he had and hungered he

καὶ οἱ μετ' αὐτοῦ; 26 [πῶς] εἰσῆλθεν
and the [ones] with him? how he entered

εἰς τὸν οἶκον τοῦ θεοῦ ἐπὶ 'Αβιαθὰρ
into the house - of God on(in the days of) Abiathar

ἀρχιερέως καὶ τοὺς ἄρτους τῆς προθέσεως
high priest and the loaves of the setting forth

ἔφαγεν, οὓς οὐκ ἔξεστιν φαγεῖν εἰ μὴ
ate, which it is not lawful to eat except

τοὺς ἱερεῖς, καὶ ἔδωκεν καὶ τοῖς σὺν
the priests, and gave also to the [ones] with

αὐτῷ οὖσιν; 27 καὶ ἔλεγεν αὐτοῖς·
him being? And he said to them:

τὸ σάββατον διὰ τὸν ἄνθρωπον ἐγένετο,
The sabbath on account of - man was,

καὶ οὐχ ὁ ἄνθρωπος διὰ τὸ σάββατον·
and not - man on account of the sabbath;

28 ὥστε κύριός ἐστιν ὁ υἱὸς τοῦ ἀνθρώπου
so as Lord is the Son - of man

καὶ τοῦ σαββάτου.
also of the sabbath.

Chapter 3

Καὶ εἰσῆλθεν πάλιν εἰς συναγωγήν.
And he entered again into a synagogue.

καὶ ἦν ἐκεῖ ἄνθρωπος ἐξηραμμένην ἔχων
And there was there a man ⁴having been withered ¹having

τὴν χεῖρα. 2 καὶ παρετήρουν αὐτὸν εἰ
²the ³hand; and they watched carefully him if

τοῖς σάββασιν θεραπεύσει αὐτόν, ἵνα
on the sabbaths he will heal him, that

κατηγορήσωσιν αὐτοῦ. 3 καὶ λέγει τῷ
they might accuse him. And he says to the

ἀνθρώπῳ τῷ τὴν χεῖρα ἔχοντι ξηράν·
man - the hand having dry:

ἔγειρε εἰς τὸ μέσον. 4 καὶ λέγει αὐτοῖς·
Rise into the midst. And he says to them:

ἔξεστιν τοῖς σάββασιν ἀγαθὸν ποιῆσαι
Lawful on the sabbaths good to do

ἢ κακοποιῆσαι, ψυχὴν σῶσαι ἢ ἀποκτεῖναι;
or to do evil, life to save or to kill?

οἱ δὲ ἐσιώπων. 5 καὶ περιβλεψάμενος
But they were silent. And looking round

αὐτοὺς μετ' ὀργῆς, συλλυπούμενος ἐπὶ
[on] them with anger, being greatly grieved on(at)

τῇ πωρώσει τῆς καρδίας αὐτῶν, λέγει
the hardness of the heart of them, he says

τῷ ἀνθρώπῳ· ἔκτεινον τὴν χεῖρα. καὶ
to the man: Stretch forth the hand. And

ἐξέτεινεν, καὶ ἀπεκατεστάθη ἡ χεὶρ αὐτοῦ.
he stretched forth, and was restored the hand of him.

6 καὶ ἐξελθόντες οἱ Φαρισαῖοι εὐθὺς μετὰ
And going forth the Pharisees immediately with

τῶν 'Ηρωδιανῶν συμβούλιον ἐδίδουν κατ'
the Herodians counsel gave against

αὐτοῦ, ὅπως αὐτὸν ἀπολέσωσιν.
him, that him they might destroy.

7 Καὶ ὁ 'Ιησοῦς μετὰ τῶν μαθητῶν
And - Jesus with the disciples

αὐτοῦ ἀνεχώρησεν πρὸς τὴν θάλασσαν·
of him departed to the sea;

καὶ πολὺ πλῆθος ἀπὸ τῆς Γαλιλαίας
and a much(great) multitude from the Galilee

ἠκολούθησεν· καὶ ἀπὸ τῆς 'Ιουδαίας 8 καὶ
followed; and from - Judæa and

ἀπὸ 'Ιεροσολύμων καὶ ἀπὸ τῆς 'Ιδουμαίας
from Jerusalem and from the Idumæa

καὶ πέραν τοῦ 'Ιορδάνου καὶ περὶ Τύρον
and beyond the Jordan and round Tyre

καὶ Σιδῶνα, πλῆθος πολύ, ἀκούοντες ὅσα
and Sidon, multitude a much(great), hearing what things

ποιεῖ, ἦλθον πρὸς αὐτόν. 9 καὶ εἶπεν
he does, came to him. And he told

τοῖς μαθηταῖς αὐτοῦ ἵνα πλοιάριον προσκαρτερῇ
the disciples of him that a boat should remain near

αὐτῷ διὰ τὸν ὄχλον, ἵνα μὴ θλίβωσιν
him because of the crowd, lest they should press upon

αὐτόν· 10 πολλοὺς γὰρ ἐθεράπευσεν, ὥστε
him; for many he healed, so as

ἐπιπίπτειν αὐτῷ ἵνα αὐτοῦ ἅψωνται
to fall upon him that him they might touch

ὅσοι εἶχον μάστιγας. 11 καὶ τὰ πνεύματα
as many as had plagues. And the spirits

τὰ ἀκάθαρτα, ὅταν αὐτὸν ἐθεώρουν, προσέπιπτον
- unclean, when him they saw, fell before

αὐτῷ καὶ ἔκραζον λέγοντα ὅτι σὺ εἶ ὁ
him and cried out saying[,] - Thou art the

υἱὸς τοῦ θεοῦ. 12 καὶ πολλὰ ἐπετίμα
Son - of God. And much he warned

αὐτοῖς ἵνα μὴ αὐτὸν φανερὸν ποιήσωσιν.
them that not him manifest they should make.

King James Version

not make him known. 13And he goeth up into a mountain, and called *unto him* whom he would: and they came unto him. 14And he ordained twelve, that they should be with him, and that he might send them forth to preach, 15And to have power to heal sicknesses, and to cast out devils: 16And Simon he surnamed Peter; 17And James the *son* of Zebedee, and John the brother of James; and he surnamed them Boanerges, which is, The sons of thunder: 18And Andrew, and Philip, and Bartholomew, and Matthew, and Thomas, and James the *son* of Alpheus, and Thaddeus, and Simon the Canaanite, 19And Judas Iscariot, which also betrayed him: and they went into a house. 20And the multitude cometh together again, so that they could not so much as eat bread. 21And when his friends heard *of it*, they went out to lay hold on him: for they said, He is beside himself.

22 And the scribes which came down from Jerusalem said, He hath Beelzebub, and by the prince of the devils casteth he out devils. 23And he called them *unto him*, and said unto them in parables, How can Satan cast out Satan? 24And if a kingdom be divided against itself, that kingdom cannot stand. 25And if a house be divided against itself, that house cannot stand. 26And if Satan rise up against himself, and be divided, he cannot stand, but hath an end. 27No man can enter into a strong man's house, and spoil his goods, except he will first bind the strong man; and then he will spoil his house. 28 Verily I say unto you, All sins shall be forgiven unto the sons of men, and blasphemies wherewith soever they shall blaspheme: 29 But he that shall blaspheme against the Holy Ghost hath never forgiveness, but is in danger of eternal damnation: 30 Because they said, He hath an unclean spirit.

31 There came then his brethren and his mother, and, standing without, sent unto him, calling him. 32And the multitude sat about him, and they said unto him, Behold, thy mother and thy brethren without seek for thee. 33And he answered them, saying, Who is my mother, or my brethren? 34And he looked round about on them which sat about him, and said, Behold my mother and my brethren! 35 For whosoever shall do the will of God, the same is my brother, and my sister, and mother.

New International Version

The appointing of the twelve apostles

13 Jesus went up into the hills and called to him those he wanted, and they came to him. 14 He appointed twelve—designating them apostles[h]—that they might be with him and that he might send them out to preach 15 and to have authority to drive out demons. 16 These are the twelve he appointed: Simon (to whom he gave the name Peter); 17 James son of Zebedee and his brother John (to them he gave the name Boanerges, which means Sons of Thunder); 18Andrew, Philip, Bartholomew, Matthew, Thomas, James son of Alphaeus, Thaddaeus, Simon the Zealot, 19 and Judas Iscariot, who betrayed him.

Jesus and Beelzebub

20 Then Jesus entered a house, and again a crowd gathered, so that he and his disciples were not even able to eat. 21 When his family heard about this, they went to take charge of him, for they said, "He is out of his mind."

22 And the teachers of the law who came down from Jerusalem said, "He is possessed by Beelzebub![i] By the prince of demons he is driving out demons."

23 So Jesus called them and spoke to them in parables: "How can Satan drive out Satan? 24 If a kingdom is divided against itself, that kingdom cannot stand. 25 If a house is divided against itself, that house cannot stand. 26And if Satan opposes himself and is divided, he cannot stand; his end has come. 27 In fact, no one can enter a strong man's house and carry off his possessions unless he first ties up the strong man. Then he can rob his house. 28 I tell you the truth, all the sins and blasphemies of men will be forgiven them. 29 But whoever blasphemes against the Holy Spirit will never be forgiven; he is guilty of an eternal sin."

30 He said this because they were saying, "He has an evil[j] spirit."

Jesus' mother and brothers

31 Then Jesus' mother and brothers arrived. Standing outside, they sent someone in to call him. 32A crowd was sitting around him, and they told him, "Your mother and brothers are outside looking for you."

33 "Who are my mother and my brothers?" he asked.

34 Then he looked at those seated in a circle around him and said, "Here are my mother and my brothers! 35 Whoever does God's will is my brother and sister and mother."

The parable of the sower

4 And he began again to teach by the sea side: and there was gathered unto him a great multitude, so that he entered into a ship, and sat in the sea; and the whole multitude was

4 On another occasion Jesus began to teach by the lake. The crowd that gathered around him was so large that he got into a boat and sat in it out on the lake, while all the peo-

[h] Some MSS omit *designating them apostles.* [i] Greek MSS *Beelzeboul* or *Beezeboul.* [j] Greek *unclean.*

Greek Interlinear

13 Καὶ ἀναβαίνει εἰς τὸ ὄρος, καὶ
And he goes up into the mountain, and
προσκαλεῖται οὓς ἤθελεν αὐτός, καὶ
calls to [him] [those] whom wished he, and
ἀπῆλθον πρὸς αὐτόν. 14 καὶ ἐποίησεν δώδεκα
they went to him. And he made twelve
ἵνα ὦσιν μετ᾽ αὐτοῦ, καὶ ἵνα ἀποστέλλῃ
that they might be with him, and that he might send
αὐτοὺς κηρύσσειν 15 καὶ ἔχειν ἐξουσίαν
them to proclaim and to have authority
ἐκβάλλειν τὰ δαιμόνια· 16 καὶ ἐποίησεν
to expel the demons; and he made
τοὺς δώδεκα, καὶ ἐπέθηκεν ὄνομα τῷ
the twelve, and he added· a name
Σίμωνι Πέτρον· 17 καὶ Ἰάκωβον τὸν τοῦ
to Simon[,] Peter; and James the [son] -
Ζεβεδαίου καὶ Ἰωάννην τὸν ἀδελφὸν τοῦ
of Zebedee and John the brother
Ἰακώβου, καὶ ἐπέθηκεν αὐτοῖς ὄνομα
of James, and he added to them a name[.]
Βοανηργές, ὅ ἐστιν υἱοὶ βροντῆς· 18 καὶ
Boanerges, which is sons of thunder; and
Ἀνδρέαν καὶ Φίλιππον καὶ Βαρθολομαῖον
Andrew and Philip and Bartholomew
καὶ Μαθθαῖον καὶ Θωμᾶν καὶ Ἰάκωβον
and Matthew and Thomas and· James
τὸν τοῦ Ἀλφαίου καὶ Θαδδαῖον καὶ
the [son] - of Alphæus and Thaddæus and
Σίμωνα τὸν Καναναῖον 19 καὶ Ἰούδαν
Simon the Cananæan and Judas
Ἰσκαριώθ, ὃς καὶ παρέδωκεν αὐτόν.
Iscariot, who indeed betrayed him.
20 Καὶ ἔρχεται εἰς οἶκον· καὶ συνέρχεται
And he comes into a house; and comes together
πάλιν [ὁ] ὄχλος, ὥστε μὴ δύνασθαι
again the crowd, so as not to be able
= so that they were not able
αὐτοὺς μηδὲ ἄρτον φαγεῖν. 21 καὶ ἀκούσαντες
them[b] not bread to eat. And hearing
οἱ παρ᾽ αὐτοῦ ἐξῆλθον κρατῆσαι αὐτόν·
the[ones] with him went forth to seize him;
= his relations
ἔλεγον γὰρ ὅτι ἐξέστη. 22 καὶ οἱ
for they said[,] - He is beside himself. And the
γραμματεῖς οἱ ἀπὸ Ἱεροσολύμων καταβάντες
scribes - from Jerusalem coming down
ἔλεγον ὅτι Βεελζεβοὺλ ἔχει, καὶ ὅτι ἐν
said[,] - Beelzebub he has, and[,] - By
τῷ ἄρχοντι τῶν δαιμονίων ἐκβάλλει τὰ
the ruler of the demons he expels the
δαιμόνια. 23 καὶ προσκαλεσάμενος αὐτοὺς
demons. And calling to [him] them
ἐν παραβολαῖς ἔλεγεν αὐτοῖς· πῶς δύναται
in parables he said to them: How can
σατανᾶς σατανᾶν ἐκβάλλειν; 24 καὶ ἐὰν
Satan ¹Satan ¹to expel ? and if
βασιλεία ἐφ᾽ ἑαυτὴν μερισθῇ, οὐ δύναται
a kingdom against itself be divided, cannot
σταθῆναι ἡ βασιλεία ἐκείνη· 25 καὶ ἐὰν
stand - kingdom that; and if
οἰκία ἐφ᾽ ἑαυτὴν μερισθῇ, οὐ δυνήσεται
a house against itself be divided, will not be able
ἡ οἰκία ἐκείνη στῆναι. 26 καὶ εἰ ὁ
- house that to stand. And if -
σατανᾶς ἀνέστη ἐφ᾽ ἑαυτὸν καὶ ἐμερίσθη,
Satan stood up against himself and was divided,
οὐ δύναται στῆναι ἀλλὰ τέλος ἔχει.
he cannot to stand but an end has.
27 ἀλλ᾽ οὐ δύναται οὐδεὶς εἰς τὴν οἰκίαν
But cannot no(any)one into the house
τοῦ ἰσχυροῦ εἰσελθὼν τὰ σκεύη αὐτοῦ
of the strong man entering the goods of him
διαρπάσαι, ἐὰν μὴ πρῶτον τὸν ἰσχυρὸν
to plunder, unless first the strong man
δήσῃ, καὶ τότε τὴν οἰκίαν αὐτοῦ διαρπάσει.
he bind, and then the house of him he will plunder.
28 Ἀμὴν λέγω ὑμῖν ὅτι πάντα ἀφεθήσεται
Truly I tell you that all will be forgiven
τοῖς υἱοῖς τῶν ἀνθρώπων τὰ ἁμαρτήματα
to the sons - of men the sins
καὶ αἱ βλασφημίαι, ὅσα ἐὰν βλασφημήσωσιν·
and the blasphemies, whatever they may blaspheme;
29 ὃς δ᾽ ἂν βλασφημήσῃ εἰς τὸ πνεῦμα
but whoever blasphemes against the Spirit
τὸ ἅγιον, οὐκ ἔχει ἄφεσιν εἰς τὸν αἰῶνα,
- Holy, has not forgiveness unto the age,
ἀλλὰ ἔνοχός ἐστιν αἰωνίου ἁμαρτήματος.
but liable is of an eternal sin.
30 ὅτι ἔλεγον· πνεῦμα ἀκάθαρτον ἔχει.
Because they said: spirit an unclean he has.
31 Καὶ ἔρχονται ἡ μήτηρ αὐτοῦ καὶ οἱ
And come the mother of him and the
ἀδελφοὶ αὐτοῦ, καὶ ἔξω στήκοντες ἀπέστειλαν
brothers of him, and outside standing sent
πρὸς αὐτὸν καλοῦντες αὐτόν. 32 καὶ
to him calling him. And
ἐκάθητο περὶ αὐτὸν ὄχλος, καὶ λέγουσιν
sat round him a crowd, and they say
αὐτῷ· ἰδοὺ ἡ μήτηρ σου καὶ οἱ ἀδελφοὶ
to him: Behold[,] the mother of thee and the brothers
σου καὶ αἱ ἀδελφαί σου ἔξω ζητοῦσίν σε.
of thee and the sisters of thee outside seek thee.
33 καὶ ἀποκριθεὶς αὐτοῖς λέγει· τίς ἐστιν
And answering them he says: Who is
ἡ μήτηρ μου καὶ οἱ ἀδελφοί; 34 καὶ
the mother of me and the brothers ? And
περιβλεψάμενος τοὺς περὶ αὐτὸν κύκλῳ
looking round [at] the [ones] round him in a circle
καθημένους λέγει· ἴδε ἡ μήτηρ μου
sitting he says: Behold[,] the mother of me
καὶ οἱ ἀδελφοί μου. 35 ὃς ἂν ποιήσῃ τὸ
and the brothers of me. Whoever does the
θέλημα τοῦ θεοῦ, οὗτος ἀδελφός μου
will - of God, this one brother of me
καὶ ἀδελφὴ καὶ μήτηρ ἐστίν.
and sister and mother is.

Chapter 4

Καὶ πάλιν ἤρξατο διδάσκειν παρὰ τὴν
And again he began to teach by the
θάλασσαν· καὶ συνάγεται πρὸς αὐτὸν ὄχλος
sea; and is assembled to him crowd
πλεῖστος, ὥστε αὐτὸν εἰς πλοῖον ἐμβάντα
a very large, so as him in a ship embarking
= so that embarking in a ship he sat
καθῆσθαι ἐν τῇ θαλάσσῃ, καὶ πᾶς ὁ
to sit[b] in the sea, and all the

King James Version

by the sea on the land. 2And he taught them many things by parables, and said unto them in his doctrine, 3 Hearken; Behold, there went out a sower to sow: 4And it came to pass, as he sowed, some fell by the way side, and the fowls of the air came and devoured it up. 5And some fell on stony ground, where it had not much earth; and immediately it sprang up, because it had no depth of earth: 6 But when the sun was up, it was scorched; and because it had no root, it withered away. 7And some fell among thorns, and the thorns grew up, and choked it, and it yielded no fruit. 8And other fell on good ground, and did yield fruit that sprang up and increased, and brought forth, some thirty, and some sixty, and some a hundred. 9And he said unto them, He that hath ears to hear, let him hear. 10And when he was alone, they that were about him with the twelve asked of him the parable. 11And he said unto them, Unto you it is given to know the mystery of the kingdom of God: but unto them that are without, all *these* things are done in parables: 12 That seeing they may see, and not perceive; and hearing they may hear, and not understand; lest at any time they should be converted, and *their* sins should be forgiven them. 13And he said unto them, Know ye not this parable? and how then will ye know all parables?

14 The sower soweth the word. 15And these are they by the way side, where the word is sown; but when they have heard, Satan cometh immediately, and taketh away the word that was sown in their hearts. 16And these are they likewise which are sown on stony ground; who, when they have heard the word, immediately receive it with gladness; 17And have no root in themselves, and so endure but for a time: afterward, when affliction or persecution ariseth for the word's sake, immediately they are offended. 18And these are they which are sown among thorns; such as hear the word, 19And the cares of this world, and the deceitfulness of riches, and the lusts of other things entering in, choke the word, and it becometh unfruitful. 20And these are they which are sown on good ground; such as hear the word, and receive *it*, and bring forth fruit, some thirtyfold, some sixty, and some a hundred.

21 And he said unto them, Is a candle brought to be put under a bushel, or under a bed? and not to be set on a candlestick? 22 For there is nothing hid, which shall not be manifested; neither was any thing kept secret, but that it should come abroad. 23 If any man have ears to hear, let him hear. 24And he said unto them, Take heed what ye hear. With what measure ye mete, it shall be measured to you; and unto you that hear shall more be given. 25 For he that hath, to him shall be given; and he that hath not, from him shall be taken even that which he hath.

26 And he said, So is the kingdom of God, as if a man should cast seed into the ground; 27And should sleep, and rise night and day, and

New International Version

ple were along the shore at the water's edge. 2 He taught them many things by parables, and in his teaching said: 3 "Listen! A farmer went out to sow his seed. 4As he was scattering the seed, some fell along the path, and the birds came and ate it up. 5 Some fell on rocky places, where it did not have much soil. It sprang up quickly, because the soil was shallow. 6 But when the sun came up, the plants were scorched, and they withered because they had no root. 7 Other seed fell among thorns, which grew up and choked the plants, so that they did not bear grain. 8 Still other seed fell on good soil. It came up, grew and produced a crop, multiplying thirty, sixty, or even a hundred times."

9 Then Jesus said, "He who has ears to hear, let him hear."

10 When he was alone, the Twelve and the others around him asked him about the parables. 11 He told them, "The secret of the kingdom of God has been given to you. But to those on the outside everything is said in parables 12 so that,

'they may be ever seeing but never perceiving,
   and ever hearing but never understanding;
otherwise they might turn and be forgiven!' [k] "

13 Then Jesus said to them, "Don't you understand this parable? How then will you understand any parable? 14 The farmer sows the word. 15 Some people are like seed along the path, where the word is sown. As soon as they hear it, Satan comes and takes away the word that was sown in them. 16 Others, like seed sown on rocky places, hear the word and at once receive it with joy. 17 But since they have no root, they last only a short time. When trouble or persecution comes because of the word, they quickly fall away. 18 Still others, like seed sown among thorns, hear the word; 19 but the worries of this life, the deceitfulness of wealth and the desires for other things come in and choke the word, making it unfruitful. 20 Others, like seed sown on good soil, hear the word, accept it, and produce a crop—thirty, sixty, or even a hundred times what was sown."

A lamp on a stand

21 He said to them, "Do you bring in a lamp to put it under a bowl or a bed? Instead, don't you put it on its stand? 22 For whatever is hidden is meant to be disclosed, and whatever is concealed is meant to be brought out into the open. 23 If anyone has ears to hear, let him hear."

24 "Consider carefully what you hear," he continued. "With the measure you use it will be measured to you—and even more. 25 Whoever has will be given more; whoever does not have, even what he has will be taken from him."

The parable of the growing seed

26 He also said, "This is what the kingdom of God is like. A man scatters seed on the ground. 27 Night and day, whether he sleeps or gets up,

---

[k] Isaiah 6:9, 10.

Greek Interlinear

ὄχλος πρὸς τὴν θάλασσαν ἐπὶ τῆς γῆς
crowd toward the sea on the land

ἦσαν. 2 καὶ ἐδίδασκεν αὐτοὺς ἐν παραβολαῖς
were. And he taught them in parables

πολλά, καὶ ἔλεγεν αὐτοῖς ἐν τῇ διδαχῇ
many things, and said to them in the teaching

αὐτοῦ· 3 ἀκούετε. ἰδοὺ ἐξῆλθεν ὁ σπείρων
of him: Hear ye. Behold[,] went out the [one] sowing

σπεῖραι. 4 καὶ ἐγένετο ἐν τῷ σπείρειν
to sow. And it came to pass in the to sowᵉ
= as he sowed

ὃ μὲν ἔπεσεν παρὰ τὴν ὁδόν, καὶ ἦλθεν
some fell by the way, and came

τὰ πετεινὰ καὶ κατέφαγεν αὐτό. 5 καὶ
the birds and devoured it. And

ἄλλο ἔπεσεν ἐπὶ τὸ πετρῶδες ὅπου οὐκ
other fell on the rocky place where not

εἶχεν γῆν πολλήν, καὶ εὐθὺς ἐξανέτειλεν
it had earth much, and immediately it sprang up

διὰ τὸ μὴ ἔχειν βάθος γῆς·
on account of the not to have depth of earth;
= because it had no depth of earth;

6 καὶ ὅτε ἀνέτειλεν ὁ ἥλιος ἐκαυματίσθη, καὶ
and when rose the sun it was scorched, and

διὰ τὸ μὴ ἔχειν ῥίζαν ἐξηράνθη. 7 καὶ
on account of the not to have root it was withered. And
= because it had no root

ἄλλο ἔπεσεν εἰς τὰς ἀκάνθας, καὶ ἀνέβησαν
other fell among the thorns, and came up

αἱ ἄκανθαι καὶ συνέπνιξαν αὐτό, καὶ
the thorns and choked it, and

καρπὸν οὐκ ἔδωκεν. 8 καὶ ἄλλα ἔπεσεν
fruit it gave not. And others fell

εἰς τὴν γῆν τὴν καλὴν καὶ ἐδίδου καρπὸν
into the earth - good and gave fruit

ἀναβαίνοντα καὶ αὐξανόμενα καὶ ἔφερεν
coming up and growing and bore

εἰς τριάκοντα καὶ ἐν ἑξήκοντα καὶ ἐν
in thirty and in sixty and in

ἑκατόν. 9 καὶ ἔλεγεν· ὃς ἔχει ὦτα
a hundred. And he said: Who has ears

ἀκούειν ἀκουέτω. 10 Καὶ ὅτε ἐγένετο
to hear let him hear. And when he was

κατὰ μόνας, ἠρώτων αὐτὸν οἱ περὶ
alone,† asked him the [ones] round

αὐτὸν σὺν τοῖς δώδεκα τὰς παραβολάς.
him with the twelve the parables.

11 καὶ ἔλεγεν αὐτοῖς· ὑμῖν τὸ μυστήριον
And he said to them: To you the mystery

δέδοται τῆς βασιλείας τοῦ θεοῦ· ἐκείνοις δὲ
has been given of the kingdom - of God; but to those

τοῖς ἔξω ἐν παραβολαῖς τὰ πάντα
the [ones] outside in parables - all things

γίνεται, 12 ἵνα βλέποντες βλέπωσιν καὶ
is(are), that seeing they may see and

μὴ ἴδωσιν, καὶ ἀκούοντες ἀκούωσιν καὶ
not perceive, and hearing they may hear and

μὴ συνιῶσιν, μήποτε ἐπιστρέψωσιν καὶ
not understand, lest they should turn and

ἀφεθῇ αὐτοῖς. 13 καὶ λέγει αὐτοῖς·
it should be forgiven them. And he says to them:

οὐκ οἴδατε τὴν παραβολὴν ταύτην, καὶ πῶς
Know ye not - parable this, and how

πάσας τὰς παραβολὰς γνώσεσθε; 14 ὁ
all the parables will ye know? The [one]

σπείρων τὸν λόγον σπείρει. 15 οὗτοι δέ εἰσιν
sowing ²the ³word ¹sows. And these are

οἱ παρὰ τὴν ὁδόν, ὅπου σπείρεται ὁ
the [ones] by the way, where is sown the

λόγος, καὶ ὅταν ἀκούσωσιν, εὐθὺς ἔρχεται
word, and when they hear, immediately comes

ὁ σατανᾶς καὶ αἴρει τὸν λόγον τὸν
- Satan and takes the word -

ἐσπαρμένον εἰς αὐτούς. 16 καὶ οὗτοί εἰσιν
having been sown in them. And these are

ὁμοίως οἱ ἐπὶ τὰ πετρώδη σπειρόμενοι,
likewise the [ones] on the rocky places being sown,

οἳ ὅταν ἀκούσωσιν τὸν λόγον εὐθὺς
who when they hear the word immediately

μετὰ χαρᾶς λαμβάνουσιν αὐτόν, 17 καὶ
with joy receive it, and

οὐκ ἔχουσιν ῥίζαν ἐν ἑαυτοῖς ἀλλὰ
have not root in themselves but

πρόσκαιροί εἰσιν, εἶτα γενομένης θλίψεως
shortlived are, then happening affliction
= when affliction or persecution happens

ἢ διωγμοῦ διὰ τὸν λόγον εὐθὺς
or persecutionᵃ on account of the word immediately

σκανδαλίζονται. 18 καὶ ἄλλοι εἰσὶν οἱ εἰς
they are offended. And others are the [ones] among

τὰς ἀκάνθας σπειρόμενοι· οὗτοί εἰσιν οἱ
the thorns being sown; these are the [ones]

τὸν λόγον ἀκούσαντες, 19 καὶ αἱ μέριμναι
the word hearing, and the cares

τοῦ αἰῶνος καὶ ἡ ἀπάτη τοῦ πλούτου
of the age and the deceitfulness - of riches

καὶ αἱ περὶ τὰ λοιπὰ ἐπιθυμίαι
and ¹the ²about ⁴the ³other things ²desires

εἰσπορευόμεναι συμπνίγουσιν τὸν λόγον, καὶ
coming in choke the word, and

ἄκαρπος γίνεται. 20 καὶ ἐκεῖνοί εἰσιν
unfruitful it becomes. And those are

οἱ ἐπὶ τὴν γῆν τὴν καλὴν σπαρέντες,
the [ones] on the earth - good sown,

οἵτινες ἀκούουσιν τὸν λόγον καὶ παραδέχονται
who hear the word and welcome [it]

καὶ καρποφοροῦσιν ἐν τριάκοντα καὶ ἐν
and bear fruit in thirty and in

ἑξήκοντα καὶ ἐν ἑκατόν. 21 Καὶ ἔλεγεν
sixty and in a hundred. And he said

αὐτοῖς ὅτι μήτι ἔρχεται ὁ λύχνος ἵνα
to them[,] - not Comes the lamp that

ὑπὸ τὸν μόδιον τεθῇ ἢ ὑπὸ τὴν
under the bushel it may be placed or under the

κλίνην; οὐχ ἵνα ἐπὶ τὴν λυχνίαν
couch? not that on the lampstand

τεθῇ; 22 οὐ γάρ ἐστίν τι κρυπτόν,
it may be placed? For there is not anything hidden,

ἐὰν μὴ ἵνα φανερωθῇ· οὐδὲ ἐγένετο
except that it may be manifested; nor became

ἀπόκρυφον, ἀλλ' ἵνα ἔλθῃ εἰς φανερόν.
covered, but that it may come into [the] open.

23 εἴ τις ἔχει ὦτα ἀκούειν ἀκουέτω.
If anyone has ears to hear let him hear.

24 Καὶ ἔλεγεν αὐτοῖς· βλέπετε τί
And he said to them: Take heed what

ἀκούετε. ἐν ᾧ μέτρῳ μετρεῖτε
ye hear. With what measure ye measure

μετρηθήσεται ὑμῖν, καὶ προστεθήσεται ὑμῖν.
it will be measured to you, and it will be added to you.

25 ὃς γὰρ ἔχει, δοθήσεται αὐτῷ· καὶ ὃς
For [he] who has, it will be given to him; and who

οὐκ ἔχει, καὶ ὃ ἔχει ἀρθήσεται ἀπ'
has not, even what he has will be taken from

αὐτοῦ. 26 Καὶ ἔλεγεν· οὕτως ἐστὶν ἡ
him. And he said: Thus is the

βασιλεία τοῦ θεοῦ, ὡς ἄνθρωπος βάλῃ
kingdom - of God, as a man might cast

τὸν σπόρον ἐπὶ τῆς γῆς, 27 καὶ καθεύδῃ
the seed on the earth, and might sleep

King James Version

the seed should spring and grow up, he knoweth not how. 28 For the earth bringeth forth fruit of herself; first the blade, then the ear, after that the full corn in the ear. 29 But when the fruit is brought forth, immediately he putteth in the sickle, because the harvest is come.

30 And he said, Whereunto shall we liken the kingdom of God? or with what comparison shall we compare it? 31 *It is* like a grain of mustard seed, which, when it is sown in the earth, is less than all the seeds that be in the earth: 32 But when it is sown, it groweth up, and becometh greater than all herbs, and shooteth out great branches; so that the fowls of the air may lodge under the shadow of it. 33 And with many such parables spake he the word unto them, as they were able to hear *it.* 34 But without a parable spake he not unto them: and when they were alone, he expounded all things to his disciples. 35 And the same day, when the even was come, he saith unto them, Let us pass over unto the other side. 36 And when they had sent away the multitude, they took him even as he was in the ship. And there were also with him other little ships. 37 And there arose a great storm of wind, and the waves beat into the ship, so that it was now full. 38 And he was in the hinder part of the ship, asleep on a pillow: and they awake him, and say unto him, Master, carest thou not that we perish? 39 And he arose, and rebuked the wind, and said unto the sea, Peace, be still. And the wind ceased, and there was a great calm. 40 And he said unto them, Why are ye so fearful? how is it that ye have no faith? 41 And they feared exceedingly, and said one to another, What manner of man is this, that even the wind and the sea obey him?

5 And they came over unto the other side of the sea, into the country of the Gadarenes. 2 And when he was come out of the ship, immediately there met him out of the tombs a man with an unclean spirit, 3 Who had *his* dwelling among the tombs; and no man could bind him, no, not with chains: 4 Because that he had been often bound with fetters and chains, and the chains had been plucked asunder by him, and the fetters broken in pieces: neither could any *man* tame him. 5 And always, night and day, he was in the mountains, and in the tombs, crying, and cutting himself with stones. 6 But when he saw Jesus afar off, he ran and worshipped him, 7 And cried with a loud voice, and said, What have I to do with thee, Jesus, *thou* Son of the most high God? I adjure thee by God, that thou torment me not. 8 (For he said unto him, Come out of the man, *thou* unclean spirit.) 9 And he asked him, What *is* thy name? And he answered,

New International Version

the seed sprouts and grows, though he does not know how. 28 All by itself the soil produces grain —first the stalk, then the head, then the full kernel in the head. 29 As soon as the grain is ripe, he puts the sickle to it, because the harvest has come."

The parable of the mustard seed

30 Again he said, "What shall we say the kingdom of God is like, or what parable shall we use to describe it? 31 It is like a mustard seed, which is the smallest seed you plant in the ground. 32 Yet when planted, it grows and becomes the largest of all garden plants, with such big branches that the birds of the air can perch in its shade."

33 With many similar parables Jesus spoke the word to them, as much as they could understand. 34 He did not say anything to them without using a parable. But when he was alone with his own disciples, he explained everything.

Jesus calms the storm

35 That day when evening came, he said to his disciples, "Let's go over to the other side." 36 Leaving the crowd behind, they took him along, just as he was, in the boat. There were also other boats with him. 37 A furious squall came up, and the waves broke over the boat, so that it was nearly swamped. 38 Jesus was in the stern, sleeping on a cushion. The disciples woke him and said to him, "Teacher, don't you care if we drown?"

39 He got up, rebuked the wind and said to the waves, "Quiet! Be still!" Then the wind died down and it was completely calm.

40 He said to his disciples, "Why are you so afraid? Have you still no faith?"

41 They were terrified and asked each other, "Who is this? Even the wind and the waves obey him!"

The healing of a demon-possessed man

5 They went across the lake to the region of the Gerasenes.[*l*] 2 When Jesus got out of the boat, a man with an evil [*m*] spirit came from the tombs to meet him. 3 This man lived in the tombs, and no one could bind him any more, not even with a chain. 4 For he had often been chained hand and foot, but he tore the chains apart and broke the irons on his feet. No one was strong enough to subdue him. 5 Night and day among the tombs and in the hills he would cry out and cut himself with stones.

6 When he saw Jesus from a distance, he ran and fell on his knees in front of him. 7 He shouted at the top of his voice, "What do you want with me, Jesus, Son of the Most High God? Swear to God that you won't torture me!" 8 For Jesus was saying to him, "Come out of this man, you evil [*m*] spirit!"

9 Then Jesus asked him, "What is your name?"

[*l*] Some MSS read *Gadarenes;* others read *Gergesenes.* [*m*] Greek *unclean.*

Greek Interlinear

καὶ ἐγείρηται νύκτα καὶ ἡμέραν, καὶ ὁ
and rise night and day, and the

σπόρος βλαστᾷ καὶ μηκύνηται ὡς οὐκ
seed sprouts and lengthens as not

οἶδεν αὐτός. 28 αὐτομάτη ἡ γῆ καρποφορεῖ,
knows he. Of its own accord the earth bears fruit,

πρῶτον χόρτον, εἶτεν στάχυν, εἶτεν πλήρης
first grass, then an ear, then full

σῖτος ἐν τῷ στάχυϊ. 29 ὅταν δὲ παραδοῖ
corn in the ear. But when permits

ὁ καρπός, εὐθὺς ἀποστέλλει τὸ δρέπανον,
the fruit, immediately he sends(puts) forth the sickle,

ὅτι παρέστηκεν ὁ θερισμός. 30 Καὶ ἔλεγεν·
because has come the harvest. And he said:

πῶς ὁμοιώσωμεν τὴν βασιλείαν τοῦ θεοῦ,
How may we liken the kingdom of God,

ἢ ἐν τίνι αὐτὴν παραβολῇ θῶμεν; 31 ὡς
or by ¹what ⁴it ³parable ²may we place? As

κόκκῳ σινάπεως, ὃς ὅταν σπαρῇ ἐπὶ τῆς
a grain of mustard, which when it is sown on the

γῆς, μικρότερον ὂν πάντων τῶν σπερμάτων
earth, smaller being [than] all the seeds

τῶν ἐπὶ τῆς γῆς, 32 καὶ ὅταν σπαρῇ,
- on the earth, and when it is sown,

ἀναβαίνει καὶ γίνεται μεῖζον πάντων τῶν
comes up and becomes greater [than] all the

λαχάνων, καὶ ποιεῖ κλάδους μεγάλους,
herbs, and makes branches great,

ὥστε δύνασθαι ὑπὸ τὴν σκιὰν αὐτοῦ τὰ
so as to be able under the shade of it the
= so that the birds of heaven are able to dwell under its shade.

πετεινὰ τοῦ οὐρανοῦ κατασκηνοῦν. 33 Καὶ
birds - of heaven to dwell.ᵇ And

τοιαύταις παραβολαῖς πολλαῖς ἐλάλει αὐτοῖς
³such ²parables ¹in many he spoke to them

τὸν λόγον, καθὼς ἠδύναντο ἀκούειν·
the word, as they were able to hear:

34 χωρὶς δὲ παραβολῆς οὐκ ἐλάλει αὐτοῖς,
and without a parable he spoke not to them,

κατ' ἰδίαν δὲ τοῖς ἰδίοις μαθηταῖς ἐπέλυεν
but privately to the(his) own disciples he explained

πάντα.
all things.

35 Καὶ λέγει αὐτοῖς ἐν ἐκείνῃ τῇ
And he says to them on that -

ἡμέρᾳ ὀψίας γενομένης· διέλθωμεν εἰς τὸ
day evening having comeᵃ: Let us pass over to the
= when evening had come:

πέραν. 36 καὶ ἀφέντες τὸν ὄχλον
other side. And leaving the crowd

παραλαμβάνουσιν αὐτὸν ὡς ἦν ἐν τῷ
they take him as he was in the

πλοίῳ, καὶ ἄλλα πλοῖα ἦν μετ' αὐτοῦ.
ship, and other ships were with him.

37 καὶ γίνεται λαῖλαψ μεγάλη ἀνέμου,
And occurs storm a great of wind,

καὶ τὰ κύματα ἐπέβαλλεν εἰς τὸ πλοῖον,
and the waves struck into the ship,

ὥστε ἤδη γεμίζεσθαι τὸ πλοῖον. 38 καὶ
so as now to be filled the ship.ᵇ And

αὐτὸς ἦν ἐν τῇ πρύμνῃ ἐπὶ τὸ
he was in the stern on the

προσκεφάλαιον καθεύδων. καὶ ἐγείρουσιν
pillow sleeping. And they rouse

αὐτὸν καὶ λέγουσιν αὐτῷ· διδάσκαλε, οὐ μέλει
him and say to him: Teacher, matters it not

σοι ὅτι ἀπολλύμεθα; 39 καὶ διεγερθεὶς
to thee that we are perishing? And being roused

ἐπετίμησεν τῷ ἀνέμῳ καὶ εἶπεν τῇ
he rebuked the wind and said to the

θαλάσσῃ· σιώπα, πεφίμωσο. καὶ ἐκόπασεν
sea: Be quiet, be muzzled. And dropped

ὁ ἄνεμος, καὶ ἐγένετο γαλήνη μεγάλη.
the wind, and there was calm a great.

40 καὶ εἶπεν αὐτοῖς· τί δειλοί ἐστε
And he said to them: Why fearful are ye

οὕτως; πῶς οὐκ ἔχετε πίστιν; 41 καὶ
thus? how have ye not faith? And

ἐφοβήθησαν φόβον μέγαν, καὶ ἔλεγον πρὸς
they feared fear a great, and said to

ἀλλήλους· τίς ἄρα οὗτός ἐστιν, ὅτι καὶ
one another: Who then this man is, that both

ὁ ἄνεμος καὶ ἡ θάλασσα ὑπακούει αὐτῷ;
the wind and the sea obeys him?

Chapter 5

Καὶ ἦλθον εἰς τὸ πέραν τῆς θαλάσσης
And they came to the other side of the sea

εἰς τὴν χώραν τῶν Γερασηνῶν. 2 καὶ
into the country of the Gerasenes. And

ἐξελθόντος αὐτοῦ ἐκ τοῦ πλοίου, [εὐθὺς]
coming out himᵃ out of the ship, immediately
= as he came out

ὑπήντησεν αὐτῷ ἐκ τῶν μνημείων ἄνθρωπος
met him out of the tombs a man

ἐν πνεύματι ἀκαθάρτῳ, 3 ὃς τὴν κατοίκησιν
in(with) spirit an unclean, who the(his) dwelling

εἶχεν ἐν τοῖς μνήμασιν, καὶ οὐδὲ ἁλύσει
had among the tombs, and not with a chain
= no one any more

οὐκέτι οὐδεὶς ἐδύνατο αὐτὸν δῆσαι, 4 διὰ
no longer no one was able him to bind, on account of
was able to bind him with a chain = because

τὸ αὐτὸν πολλάκις πέδαις καὶ ἁλύσεσιν
the him often with fetters and chains
he had often been bound with fetters and chains, and . . .

δεδέσθαι, καὶ διεσπάσθαι ὑπ' αὐτοῦ τὰς
to have been bound, and to be burst by him the

ἁλύσεις καὶ τὰς πέδας συντετρίφθαι, καὶ
chains and the fetters to have been broken, and

οὐδεὶς ἴσχυεν αὐτὸν δαμάσαι· 5 καὶ
no one was able him to subdue; and

διὰ παντὸς νυκτὸς καὶ ἡμέρας ἐν τοῖς μνήμασιν
always of(by) night and day among the tombs

καὶ ἐν τοῖς ὄρεσιν ἦν κράζων καὶ
and in the mountains he was crying out and

κατακόπτων ἑαυτὸν λίθοις. 6 καὶ ἰδὼν
cutting himself with stones. And seeing

τὸν Ἰησοῦν ἀπὸ μακρόθεν ἔδραμεν καὶ
- Jesus from afar he ran and

προσεκύνησεν αὐτόν, 7 καὶ κράξας φωνῇ
worshipped him, and crying out with a voice

μεγάλῃ λέγει· τί ἐμοὶ καὶ σοί, Ἰησοῦ
great(loud) he says: What to me and to thee, Jesus

υἱὲ τοῦ θεοῦ τοῦ ὑψίστου; ὁρκίζω σε
Son - of God the most high? I adjure thee

τὸν θεόν, μή με βασανίσῃς. 8 ἔλεγεν
- by God, not me thou mayest torment. he said

γὰρ αὐτῷ· ἔξελθε τὸ πνεῦμα τὸ ἀκάθαρτον
For to him: Come out the spirit - unclean

ἐκ τοῦ ἀνθρώπου. 9 καὶ ἐπηρώτα αὐτόν·
out of the man. And he questioned him:

τί ὄνομά σοι; καὶ λέγει αὐτῷ· λεγιών
What name to thee?ᵉ And he says to him: Legion
= What name hast thou? = My

King James Version

saying, My name *is* Legion: for we are many. 10And he besought him much that he would not send them away out of the country. 11 Now there was there nigh unto the mountains a great herd of swine feeding. 12And all the devils besought him, saying, Send us into the swine, that we may enter into them. 13And forthwith Jesus gave them leave. And the unclean spirits went out, and entered into the swine; and the herd ran violently down a steep place into the sea, (they were about two thousand,) and were choked in the sea. 14And they that fed the swine fled, and told *it* in the city, and in the country. And they went out to see what it was that was done. 15And they come to Jesus, and see him that was possessed with the devil, and had the legion, sitting, and clothed, and in his right mind; and they were afraid. 16And they that saw *it* told them how it befell to him that was possessed with the devil, and *also* concerning the swine. 17And they began to pray him to depart ˙out of their coasts. 18And when he was come into the ship, he that had been possessed with the devil prayed him that he might be with him. 19 Howbeit Jesus suffered him not, but saith unto him, Go home to thy friends, and tell them how great things the Lord hath done for thee, and hath had compassion on thee. 20And he departed, and began to publish in Decapolis how great things Jesus had done for him: and all *men* did marvel. 21And when Jesus was passed over again by ship unto the other side, much people gathered unto him; and he was nigh unto the sea. 22And, behold, there cometh one of the rulers of the synagogue, Jairus by name; and when he saw him, he fell at his feet, 23And besought him greatly, saying, My little daughter lieth at the point of death: *I pray thee,* come and lay thy hands on her, that she may be healed; and she shall live. 24And *Jesus* went with him; and much people followed him, and thronged him. 25And a certain woman, which had an issue of blood twelve years, 26And had suffered many things of many physicians, and had spent all that she had, and was nothing bettered, but rather grew worse, 27 When she had heard of Jesus, came in the press behind, and touched his garment. 28 For she said, If I may touch but his clothes, I shall be whole. 29And straightway the fountain of her blood was dried up; and she felt in *her* body that she was healed of that plague. 30And Jesus, immediately knowing in himself that virtue had gone out of him, turned him about in the press, and said, Who touched my clothes? 31And his disciples said unto him, Thou seest the multitude thronging thee, and sayest thou, Who touched me? 32And he looked round about to see her that had done this thing. 33 But the woman fearing and trembling, knowing what was done in her, came and fell down before him, and told him all the truth. 34And he said unto her, Daughter, thy faith hath made thee whole; go in peace, and be whole of thy plague. 35 While he yet spake, there came from the ruler of the synagogue's *house certain*

New International Version

"My name is Legion," he replied, "for we are many." 10And he begged Jesus again and again not to send them out of the area.

11 A large herd of pigs was feeding on the nearby hillside. 12 The demons begged Jesus, "Send us among the pigs; allow us to go into them." 13 He gave them permission, and the evil [m] spirits came out and went into the pigs. The herd, about two thousand in number, rushed down the steep bank into the lake and were drowned.

14 Those tending the pigs ran off and reported this in the town and countryside, and the people went out to see what had happened. 15 When they came to Jesus, they saw the man who had been possessed by the legion of demons, sitting there, dressed and in his right mind; and they were afraid. 16 Those who had seen it told the people what had happened to the demon-possessed man—and told about the pigs as well. 17 Then the people began to plead with Jesus to leave their region.

18 As Jesus was getting into the boat, the man who had been demon-possessed begged to go with him. 19 Jesus did not let him, but said, "Go home to your family and tell them how much the Lord has done for you, and how he has had mercy on you." 20 So the man went away and began to tell in the Decapolis [n] how much Jesus had done for him. And all the people were amazed.

A dead girl and a sick woman

21 When Jesus had again crossed over by boat to the other side of the lake, a large crowd gathered around him. While he was by the lake, 22 one of the synagogue rulers, named Jairus, came there. Seeing Jesus, he fell at his feet 23 and pleaded earnestly with him, "My little daughter is dying. Please come and put your hands on her so that she will be healed and live." 24 So Jesus went with him.

A large crowd followed and pressed around him. 25And a woman was there who had been subject to bleeding for twelve years. 26 She had suffered a great deal under the care of many doctors and had spent all she had, yet instead of getting better she grew worse. 27 When she heard about Jesus, she came up behind him in the crowd and touched his cloak, 28 because she thought, "If I just touch his clothes, I will be healed." 29 Immediately her bleeding stopped and she felt in her body that she was freed from her suffering.

30 At once Jesus realized that power had gone out from him. He turned around in the crowd and asked, "Who touched my clothes?"

31 "You see the people crowding against you," his disciples answered, "and yet you can ask, 'Who touched me?'"

32 But Jesus kept looking around to see who had done it. 33 Then the woman, knowing what had happened to her, came and fell at his feet and, trembling with fear, told him the whole truth. 34 He said to her, "Daughter, your faith has healed you. Go in peace, and be freed from your suffering."

35 While Jesus was still speaking, some men came from the house of Jairus, the synagogue

---

[m] Greek *unclean.* [n] That is, *the Ten Cities.*

Greek Interlinear

ὄνομά μοι, ὅτι πολλοί ἐσμεν. 10 καὶ
name to me,° because many we are. And
name is Legion,

παρεκάλει αὐτὸν πολλὰ ἵνα μὴ αὐτὰ
he besought him much that not them

ἀποστείλῃ ἔξω τῆς χώρας. 11 ἦν δὲ
he would send outside the country. Now there was

ἐκεῖ πρὸς τῷ ὄρει ἀγέλη χοίρων μεγάλη
there near the mountain herd of pigs a great

βοσκομένη· 12 καὶ παρεκάλεσαν αὐτὸν
feeding; and they besought him

λέγοντες· πέμψον ἡμᾶς εἰς τοὺς χοίρους,
saying: Send us into the pigs,

ἵνα εἰς αὐτοὺς εἰσέλθωμεν. 13 καὶ ἐπέτρεψεν
that into them we may enter. And he allowed

αὐτοῖς. καὶ ἐξελθόντα τὰ πνεύματα τὰ
them. And coming out the spirits the

ἀκάθαρτα εἰσῆλθον εἰς τοὺς χοίρους, καὶ
unclean entered into the pigs, and

ὥρμησεν ἡ ἀγέλη κατὰ τοῦ κρημνοῦ εἰς
rushed the herd down the precipice into

τὴν θάλασσαν, ὡς δισχίλιοι, καὶ ἐπνίγοντο
the sea, about two thousand, and were choked

ἐν τῇ θαλάσσῃ. 14 καὶ οἱ βόσκοντες
in the sea. And the [ones] feeding

αὐτοὺς ἔφυγον καὶ ἀπήγγειλαν εἰς τὴν
them fled and reported in the

πόλιν καὶ εἰς τοὺς ἀγρούς· καὶ ἦλθον
city and in the fields; and they came

ἰδεῖν τί ἐστιν τὸ γεγονός. 15 καὶ
to see what is the thing having happened. And

ἔρχονται πρὸς τὸν Ἰησοῦν, καὶ θεωροῦσιν τὸν
they come to - Jesus, and see the

δαιμονιζόμενον καθήμενον ἱματισμένον καὶ
demon-possessed man sitting having been clothed and

σωφρονοῦντα, τὸν ἐσχηκότα τὸν λεγιῶνα,
being in his senses, the man having had the legion,

καὶ ἐφοβήθησαν. 16 καὶ διηγήσαντο αὐτοῖς οἱ
and they were afraid. And related to them the [ones]

ἰδόντες πῶς ἐγένετο τῷ δαιμονιζομένῳ
seeing how it happened to the demon-possessed man

καὶ περὶ τῶν χοίρων. 17 καὶ ἤρξαντο
and about the pigs. And they began

παρακαλεῖν αὐτὸν ἀπελθεῖν ἀπὸ τῶν ὁρίων
to beseech him to depart from the territory

αὐτῶν. 18 καὶ ἐμβαίνοντος αὐτοῦ εἰς τὸ
of them. And embarking him° in the
= as he embarked

πλοῖον παρεκάλει αὐτὸν ὁ δαιμονισθεὶς
ship besought him the [one] demon-possessed

ἵνα μετ᾽ αὐτοῦ ᾖ. 19 καὶ οὐκ ἀφῆκεν
that with him he might be. And he permitted not

αὐτόν, ἀλλὰ λέγει αὐτῷ· ὕπαγε εἰς τὸν
him, but says to him: Go to the

οἶκόν σου πρὸς τοὺς σούς, καὶ ἀπάγγειλον
house of thee to the thine, and report
= thy people,

αὐτοῖς ὅσα ὁ κύριός σοι πεποίηκεν καὶ
to them what things the Lord to thee has done and

ἠλέησέν σε. 20 καὶ ἀπῆλθεν καὶ ἤρξατο
pitied thee. And he departed and began

κηρύσσειν ἐν τῇ Δεκαπόλει ὅσα ἐποίησεν
to proclaim in - Decapolis what things did

αὐτῷ . ὁ Ἰησοῦς, καὶ πάντες ἐθαύμαζον
to him - Jesus, and all men marvelled.

21 Καὶ διαπεράσαντος τοῦ Ἰησοῦ° ἐν τῷ
And crossing over - Jesus° in the
= when Jesus had crossed over

πλοίῳ πάλιν εἰς τὸ πέραν συνήχθη ὄχλος
ship again to the other side was assembled crowd

πολὺς ἐπ᾽ αὐτόν, καὶ ἦν παρὰ τὴν θάλασσαν.
a much(great) to him, and he was by the sea.

22 Καὶ ἔρχεται εἰς τῶν ἀρχισυναγώγων,
And comes one of the synagogue chiefs,

ὀνόματι Ἰάϊρος, καὶ ἰδὼν αὐτὸν πίπτει
by name Jairus, and seeing him falls

πρὸς τοὺς πόδας αὐτοῦ, 23 καὶ παρακαλεῖ
at the feet of him, and beseeches

αὐτὸν πολλὰ λέγων ὅτι τὸ θυγάτριόν μου
him much saying[.] - The daughter of me

ἐσχάτως ἔχει, ἵνα ἐλθὼν ἐπιθῇς
is at the point of death,† that coming thou mayest lay on

τὰς χεῖρας αὐτῇ, ἵνα σωθῇ καὶ ζήσῃ.
the(thy) hands on her, that she may be healed and may live.

24 καὶ ἀπῆλθεν μετ᾽ αὐτοῦ. καὶ ἠκολούθει αὐτῷ
And he went with him. And followed him

ὄχλος πολύς, καὶ συνέθλιβον αὐτόν. 25 Καὶ
crowd a much(great), and pressed upon him. And

γυνὴ οὖσα ἐν ῥύσει αἵματος δώδεκα
a woman being in a flow of blood twelve
= having

ἔτη, 26 καὶ πολλὰ παθοῦσα ὑπὸ πολλῶν
years, and many things suffering by many

ἰατρῶν καὶ δαπανήσασα τὰ παρ᾽ αὐτῆς
physicians and having spent the with her

πάντα, καὶ μηδὲν ὠφεληθεῖσα ἀλλὰ μᾶλλον
all things, and nothing having been profited but rather

εἰς τὸ χεῖρον ἐλθοῦσα, 27 ἀκούσασα τὰ
to the worse having come, hearing the things

περὶ τοῦ Ἰησοῦ, ἐλθοῦσα ἐν τῷ ὄχλῳ
about - Jesus, coming in the crowd

ὄπισθεν ἥψατο τοῦ ἱματίου αὐτοῦ· 28 ἔλεγεν
behind touched the garment of him; she said[,]

γὰρ ὅτι ἐὰν ἅψωμαι κἂν τῶν ἱματίων
for - If I may touch even the garments

αὐτοῦ, σωθήσομαι. 29 καὶ εὐθὺς ἐξηράνθη
of him, I shall be healed. And immediately was dried up

ἡ πηγὴ τοῦ αἵματος αὐτῆς, καὶ ἔγνω
the fountain of the blood of her, and she knew

τῷ σώματι ὅτι ἴαται ἀπὸ τῆς
in the(her) body that she is(was) cured from the

μάστιγος. 30 καὶ εὐθὺς ὁ Ἰησοῦς ἐπιγνοὺς ἐν
plague. And immediately - Jesus knowing in

ἑαυτῷ τὴν ἐξ αὐτοῦ δύναμιν ἐξελθοῦσαν,
himself ¹the °out of °him °power ³going forth,

ἐπιστραφεὶς ἐν τῷ ὄχλῳ ἔλεγεν· τίς μου ἥψατο τῶν
turning in the crowd said: Who of me touched the

ἱματίων; 31 καὶ ἔλεγον αὐτῷ οἱ μαθηταὶ
garments? And said to him the disciples

αὐτοῦ· βλέπεις τὸν ὄχλον συνθλίβοντά σε,
of him: Thou seest the crowd pressing upon thee,

καὶ λέγεις· τίς μου ἥψατο; 32 καὶ
and thou sayest: Who me touched? And

περιεβλέπετο ἰδεῖν τὴν τοῦτο ποιήσασαν.
he looked round to see the [one] this having done.

33 ἡ δὲ γυνὴ φοβηθεῖσα καὶ τρέμουσα,
And the woman fearing and trembling,

εἰδυῖα ὃ γέγονεν αὐτῇ, ἦλθεν καὶ προσέ-
knowing what has happened to her, came and fell

πεσεν αὐτῷ καὶ εἶπεν αὐτῷ πᾶσαν τὴν ἀλήθειαν.
before him and told him all the truth.

34 ὁ δὲ εἶπεν αὐτῇ· θυγάτηρ, ἡ πίστις
And he said to her: Daughter, the faith

σου σέσωκέν σε· ὕπαγε εἰς εἰρήνην, καὶ
of thee has healed thee; go in peace, and

ἴσθι ὑγιὴς ἀπὸ τῆς μάστιγός σου. 35 Ἔτι
be whole from the plague of thee. Still
= While

αὐτοῦ λαλοῦντος ἔρχονται ἀπὸ τοῦ
him speaking° they come from the
he was still speaking

117

King James Version

which said, Thy daughter is dead; why troublest thou the Master any further? 36As soon as Jesus heard the word that was spoken, he saith unto the ruler of the synagogue, Be not afraid, only believe. 37And he suffered no man to follow him, save Peter, and James, and John the brother of James. 38And he cometh to the house of the ruler of the synagogue, and seeth the tumult, and them that wept and wailed greatly. 39And when he was come in, he saith unto them, Why make ye this ado, and weep? the damsel is not dead, but sleepeth. 40And they laughed him to scorn. But when he had put them all out, he taketh the father and the mother of the damsel, and them that were with him, and entereth in where the damsel was lying. 41And he took the damsel by the hand, and said unto her, Talitha cumi; which is, being interpreted, Damsel, (I say unto thee,) arise. 42And straightway the damsel arose, and walked; for she was *of the age* of twelve years. And they were astonished with a great astonishment. 43And he charged them straitly that no man should know it; and commanded that something should be given her to eat.

And he went out from thence, and came **6** into his own country; and his disciples follow him. 2And when the sabbath day was come, he began to teach in the synagogue: and many hearing *him* were astonished, saying, From whence hath this *man* these things? and what wisdom *is* this which is given unto him, that even such mighty works are wrought by his hands? 3 Is not this the carpenter, the son of Mary, the brother of James, and Joses, and of Juda, and Simon? and are not his sisters here with us? And they were offended at him. 4 But Jesus said unto them, A prophet is not without honour, but in his own country, and among his own kin, and in his own house. 5And he could there do no mighty work, save that he laid his hands upon a few sick folk, and healed *them*. 6And he marvelled because of their unbelief. And he went round about the villages, teaching.

7 And he called *unto him* the twelve, and began to send them forth by two and two; and gave them power over unclean spirits; 8And commanded them that they should take nothing for *their* journey, save a staff only; no scrip, no bread, no money in *their* purse: 9 But *be* shod with sandals; and not put on two coats. 10And he said unto them, In what place soever ye enter into a house, there abide till ye depart from that place. 11And whosoever shall not receive you, nor hear you, when ye depart thence, shake off the dust under your feet for a testimony against them. Verily I say unto you, It shall be more tolerable for Sodom and Gomorrah in the

New International Version

ruler. "Your daughter is dead," they said. "Why bother the teacher any more?"

36 Ignoring what they said, Jesus told the synagogue ruler, "Don't be afraid; just believe."

37 He did not let anyone follow him except Peter, James and John, the brother of James. 38 When they came to the home of the synagogue ruler, Jesus saw a commotion, with people crying and wailing loudly. 39 He went in and said to them, "Why all this commotion and wailing? The child is not dead but asleep." 40 But they laughed at him.

After he put them all out, he took the child's father and mother and the disciples who were with him, and went in where the child was. 41 He took her by the hand and said to her, *"Talitha koum!"* (which means, "Little girl, I say to you, get up!"). 42 She stood right up and walked around (she was twelve years old). At this they were completely astonished. 43 He gave strict orders not to let anyone know about this, and told them to give her something to eat.

A prophet without honor

Jesus left there and went to his home town, **6** accompanied by his disciples. 2 When the Sabbath came, he began to teach in the synagogue, and many who heard him were amazed.

"Where did this man get these things?" they asked. "What's this wisdom that has been given him, that he even does miracles! 3 Isn't this the carpenter? Isn't this Mary's son and the brother of James, Joses, Judas and Simon? Aren't his sisters here with us?" And they took offense at him.

4 Jesus said to them, "Only in his home town, among his relatives and in his own house is a prophet without honor." 5 He could not do any miracles there, except lay his hands on a few sick people and heal them. 6And he was amazed at their lack of faith.

Jesus sends out the Twelve

Then Jesus went around teaching from village to village. 7 Calling the Twelve to him, he sent them out two by two and gave them authority over evil ° spirits.

8 These were his instructions: "Take nothing for the journey except a staff—no bread, no bag, no money in your belts. 9 Wear sandals but not an extra tunic. 10 Whenever you enter a house, stay there until you leave that town. 11And if any place will not welcome you or listen to you, shake the dust off your feet when you leave, as a testimony against them."

[o] Greek *unclean.*

Greek Interlinear

ἀρχισυναγώγου λέγοντες ὅτι ἡ θυγάτηρ
synagogue chief　saying[,]　 - 　The 　daughter
σου ἀπέθανεν· τί ἔτι σκύλλεις τὸν διδάσκαλον;
of thee died;　 why still troublest thou the 　teacher ?
36 ὁ δὲ Ἰησοῦς παρακούσας τὸν λόγον
- But 　Jesus　 overhearing 　the 　word
λαλούμενόν λέγει τῷ ἀρχισυναγώγῳ· μὴ
being spoken 　says 　to the 　synagogue chief:　 not
φοβοῦ, μόνον πίστευε. **37** καὶ οὐκ ἀφῆκεν
Fear,　 only 　believe.　 And 　he allowed not
οὐδένα μετ᾽ αὐτοῦ συνακολουθῆσαι εἰ μὴ
no(any)one with 　him 　to accompany 　except
τὸν Πέτρον καὶ Ἰάκωβον καὶ Ἰωάννην
- 　Peter 　and 　James 　and 　John
τὸν ἀδελφὸν Ἰακώβου. **38** καὶ ἔρχονται
the 　brother 　of James.　 And 　they come
εἰς τὸν οἶκον τοῦ ἀρχισυναγώγου, καὶ
into 　the 　house 　of the 　synagogue chief,　 and
θεωρεῖ θόρυβον, καὶ κλαίοντάς καὶ
he sees 　an uproar,　 and 　[men] weeping 　and
ἀλαλάζοντας πολλά, **39** καὶ εἰσελθὼν λέγει
crying aloud 　much,　 and 　entering 　he says
αὐτοῖς· τί θορυβεῖσθε καὶ κλαίετε; τὸ
to them: 　Why make ye an uproar and 　weep ? 　the
παιδίον οὐκ ἀπέθανεν ἀλλὰ καθεύδει.
child 　did not die 　but 　sleeps.
40 καὶ κατεγέλων αὐτοῦ. αὐτὸς δὲ ἐκβαλὼν
And 　they ridiculed 　him.　 But he 　putting out

πάντας παραλαμβάνει τὸν πατέρα τοῦ
all 　takes 　the 　father 　of the
παιδίου καὶ τὴν μητέρα καὶ τοὺς μετ᾽
child 　and 　the 　mother 　and the [ones] with
αὐτοῦ, καὶ εἰσπορεύεται ὅπου ἦν τὸ
him,　 and 　goes in 　where 　was 　the
παιδίον. **41** καὶ κρατήσας τῆς χειρὸς
child.　 And 　taking hold of 　the 　hand
τοῦ παιδίου λέγει αὐτῇ· ταλιθὰ κοῦμ, ὃ
of the 　child 　he says to her:　 Talitha 　koum, which
ἐστιν μεθερμηνευόμενον· τὸ κοράσιον, σοὶ
is 　being interpreted:　 - 　Maid,　 to thee
λέγω, ἔγειρε. **42** καὶ εὐθὺς ἀνέστη τὸ
I say,　 arise.　 And immediately 　rose up 　the
κοράσιον καὶ περιεπάτει· ἦν γὰρ
maid 　and 　walked;　 for she was
ἐτῶν δώδεκα. καὶ ἐξέστησαν εὐθὺς
[of the age] twelve.　 And they were astonished immediately
of years 　=immediately they were exceedingly astonished.
ἐκστάσει μεγάλη. **43** καὶ διεστείλατο
astonishment 　with a great.　 And 　he ordered
αὐτοῖς πολλὰ ἵνα μηδεὶς γνοῖ τοῦτο, καὶ
them 　much 　that no one should know this,　 and
εἶπεν δοθῆναι αὐτῇ φαγεῖν.
to!d 　to be given to her 　to eat.
=[them] to give her [something] to eat.

Chapter 6

Καὶ ἐξῆλθεν ἐκεῖθεν, καὶ ἔρχεται εἰς
And he went forth thence,　 and 　comes 　into
τὴν πατρίδα αὐτοῦ, καὶ ἀκολουθοῦσιν
the 　native place 　of him,　 and 　follow
αὐτῷ οἱ μαθηταὶ αὐτοῦ. **2** καὶ γενομένου
him 　the 　disciples 　of him.　 And 　coming
= when
σαββάτου ἤρξατο διδάσκειν ἐν τῇ συναγωγῇ·
a sabbath 　he began 　to teach 　in 　the 　synagogue:
a sabbath came
καὶ οἱ πολλοὶ ἀκούοντες ἐξεπλήσσοντο
and 　the 　many 　hearing 　were astonished
λέγοντες· πόθεν τούτῳ ταῦτα, καὶ τίς ἡ
saying:　 Whence to this man these things, and 　what the
σοφία ἡ δοθεῖσα τούτῳ; καὶ αἱ δυνάμεις
wisdom - 　given 　to this(him) ? And 　the 　powerful deeds
τοιαῦται διὰ τῶν χειρῶν αὐτοῦ γινόμεναι;
such 　through 　the 　hands 　of him 　coming about?
3 οὐχ οὗτός ἐστιν ὁ τέκτων, ὁ υἱὸς
[2]Not [3]this man [1]is 　the 　carpenter,　 the 　son
τῆς Μαρίας καὶ ἀδελφὸς Ἰακώβου καὶ
- 　of Mary 　and 　brother 　of James 　and
Ἰωσῆτος καὶ Ἰούδα καὶ Σίμωνος; καὶ
Joses 　and 　Judas 　and 　Simon ?　 and
οὐκ εἰσὶν αἱ ἀδελφαὶ αὐτοῦ ὧδε πρὸς
[2]not [3]are 　the 　sisters 　of him 　here 　with
ἡμᾶς; καὶ ἐσκανδαλίζοντο ἐν αὐτῷ. **4** καὶ
us ?　 And 　they were offended in(at) 　him.　 And
ἔλεγεν αὐτοῖς ὁ Ἰησοῦς ὅτι οὐκ ἔστιν
said 　to them 　- 　Jesus[,]　 - [2]not [1]is
προφήτης ἄτιμος εἰ μὴ ἐν τῇ πατρίδι
[1]A prophet unhonoured except 　in 　the 　native place
αὐτοῦ καὶ ἐν τοῖς συγγενεῦσιν αὐτοῦ
of him 　and 　among 　the 　relatives 　of him
καὶ ἐν τῇ οἰκίᾳ αὐτοῦ. **5** καὶ οὐκ
and 　in 　the 　house 　of him.　 And 　not
ἐδύνατο ἐκεῖ ποιῆσαι οὐδεμίαν δύναμιν,
he could 　there 　to do 　no(any) 　powerful deed,

εἰ μὴ ὀλίγοις ἀρρώστοις ἐπιθεὶς τὰς
except 　on a few 　sick [ones] 　laying on the(his)
χεῖρας ἐθεράπευσεν. **6** καὶ ἐθαύμασεν διὰ
hands 　he healed.　 And 　he marvelled because of
τὴν ἀπιστίαν αὐτῶν.
the 　unbelief 　of them.

Καὶ περιῆγεν τὰς κώμας κύκλῳ
And 　he went round 　the 　villages 　in circuit
διδάσκων. **7** Καὶ προσκαλεῖται τοὺς δώδεκα,
teaching.　 And he calls to [him] 　the 　twelve,
καὶ ἤρξατο αὐτοὺς ἀποστέλλειν δύο δύο,
and 　began 　them 　to send forth 　two [by] two,
καὶ ἐδίδου αὐτοῖς ἐξουσίαν τῶν πνευμάτων
and 　gave 　them 　authority 　the 　spirits
τῶν ἀκαθάρτων, **8** καὶ παρήγγειλεν αὐτοῖς
- 　of(over) unclean,　 and 　charged 　them
ἵνα μηδὲν αἴρωσιν εἰς ὁδὸν εἰ μὴ ῥάβδον
that nothing they should take in [the] way 　except 　a staff
μόνον, μὴ ἄρτον, μὴ πήραν, μὴ εἰς τὴν
only,　 not 　bread,　 not a wallet,　 not 　in the
ζώνην χαλκόν, **9** ἀλλὰ ὑποδεδεμένους σανδάλια,
girdle copper [money],　 but 　having had tied on 　sandals,
καὶ μὴ ἐνδύσησθε δύο χιτῶνας. **10** καὶ
and 　do not put on 　two 　tunics.　 And
ἔλεγεν αὐτοῖς· ὅπου ἐὰν εἰσέλθητε εἰς
he said 　to them:　 Wherever 　ye enter 　into
οἰκίαν, ἐκεῖ μένετε ἕως ἂν ἐξέλθητε
a house,　 there 　remain 　until 　ye go out
ἐκεῖθεν. **11** καὶ ὃς ἂν τόπος μὴ δέξηται
thence.　 And 　whatever 　place 　receives not
ὑμᾶς μηδὲ ἀκούσωσιν ὑμῶν, ἐκπορευόμενοι
you 　nor 　they hear 　you,　 going out
ἐκεῖθεν ἐκτινάξατε τὸν χοῦν τὸν ὑποκάτω
thence 　shake off 　the 　dust 　the - 　under
τῶν ποδῶν ὑμῶν εἰς μαρτύριον αὐτοῖς.
the 　feet 　of you 　for 　a testimony 　to them.

King James Version

day of judgment, than for that city. 12And they went out, and preached that men should repent. 13And they cast out many devils, and anointed with oil many that were sick, and healed *them*. 14And king Herod heard *of him;* (for his name was spread abroad;) and he said, That John the Baptist was risen from the dead, and therefore mighty works do shew forth themselves in him. 15 Others said, That it is Elias. And others said, That it is a prophet, or as one of the prophets. 16 But when Herod heard *thereof,* he said, It is John, whom I beheaded: he is risen from the dead. 17 For Herod himself had sent forth and laid hold upon John, and bound him in prison for Herodias' sake, his brother Philip's wife; for he had married her. 18 For John had said unto Herod, It is not lawful for thee to have thy brother's wife. 19 Therefore Herodias had a quarrel against him, and would have killed him; but she could not: 20 For Herod feared John, knowing that he was a just man and a holy, and observed him; and when he heard him, he did many things, and heard him gladly. 21And when a convenient day was come, that Herod on his birthday made a supper to his lords, high captains, and chief *estates* of Galilee; 22And when the daughter of the said Herodias came in, and danced, and pleased Herod and them that sat with him, the king said unto the damsel, Ask of me whatsoever thou wilt, and I will give *it* thee. 23And he sware unto her, Whatsoever thou shalt ask of me, I will give *it* thee, unto the half of my kingdom. 24And she went forth, and said unto her mother, What shall I ask? And she said, The head of John the Baptist. 25And she came in straightway with haste unto the king, and asked, saying, I will that thou give me by and by in a charger the head of John the Baptist. 26And the king was exceeding sorry; *yet* for his oath's sake, and for their sakes which sat with him, he would not reject her. 27And immediately the king sent an executioner, and commanded his head to be brought: and he went and beheaded him in the prison, 28And brought his head in a charger, and gave it to the damsel; and the damsel gave it to her mother. 29And when his disciples heard *of it,* they came and took up his corpse, and laid it in a tomb. 30And the apostles gathered themselves together unto Jesus, and told him all things, both what they had done, and what they had taught. 31And he said unto them, Come ye yourselves apart into a desert place, and rest a while: for there were many coming and going, and they had no leisure so much as to eat. 32And they departed into a desert place by ship privately. 33And the people saw them departing, and many knew him, and ran afoot thither out of all cities, and outwent them, and came together unto him. 34And Jesus, when he came out, saw much people, and was moved with compassion toward them, because they were as sheep not having a shepherd: and he began to

New International Version

12 They went out and preached that people should repent. 13 They drove out many demons and anointed many sick people with oil and healed them.

John the Baptist beheaded

14 King Herod heard about this, for Jesus' name had become well-known. Some were saying,[p] "John the Baptist has been raised from the dead, and that is why miraculous powers are at work in him."
15 Others said, "He is Elijah."
And still others claimed, "He is a prophet, like one of the prophets of long ago."
16 But when Herod heard this, he said, "John, the man I beheaded, has been raised from the dead!"
17 For Herod himself had given orders to have John arrested and put in prison. He did this because of Herodias, his brother Philip's wife, whom he had married. 18 For John had been saying to Herod, "It is not lawful for you to have your brother's wife." 19 So Herodias nursed a grudge against John and wanted to kill him. But she was not able to, 20 because Herod feared John and protected him, knowing him to be a righteous and holy man. When Herod heard John, he was greatly puzzled;[q] yet he liked to listen to him.
21 Finally the opportune time came. On his birthday Herod gave a banquet for his high officials and military commanders and the leading men of Galilee. 22 When the daughter of Herodias came in and danced, she pleased Herod and his dinner guests.
The king said to the girl, "Ask me for anything you want, and I'll give it to you." 23And he promised her with an oath, "Whatever you ask I will give you, up to half my kingdom."
24 She went out and said to her mother, "What shall I ask for?"
"The head of John the Baptist," she answered.
25 At once the girl hurried in to the king with the request: "I want you to give me right now the head of John the Baptist on a platter."
26 The king was greatly distressed, but because of his oaths and his dinner guests, he did not want to refuse her. 27 So he immediately sent an executioner with orders to bring John's head. The man went, beheaded John in the prison, 28 and brought back his head on a platter. He presented it to the girl, and she gave it to her mother. 29 On hearing of this, John's disciples came and took his body and laid it in a tomb.

Jesus feeds the five thousand

30 The apostles gathered around Jesus and reported to him all they had done and taught. 31 Then, because so many people were coming and going that they did not even have a chance to eat, he said to them, "Come with me by yourselves to a quiet place and get some rest."
32 So they went away by themselves in a boat to a solitary place. 33 But many who saw them leaving recognized them and ran on foot from all the towns and got there ahead of them. 34 When Jesus landed and saw a large crowd, he had compassion on them, because they were like sheep without a shepherd. So he began teaching them many things.

[p] Some early MSS read *He was saying.* [q] Some early MSS read *he did many things.*

Greek Interlinear

12 Καὶ ἐξελθόντες ἐκήρυξαν ἵνα μετανοῶσιν,
And going forth they proclaimed that men should repent,

13 καὶ δαιμόνια πολλὰ ἐξέβαλλον, καὶ
and demons many they expelled, and

ἤλειφον ἐλαίῳ πολλοὺς ἀρρώστους καὶ
anointed with oil many sick [ones] and

ἐθεράπευον.
healed.

14 Καὶ ἤκουσεν ὁ βασιλεὺς Ἡρώδης,
And heard the king Herod,

φανερὸν γὰρ ἐγένετο τὸ ὄνομα αὐτοῦ, καὶ
for manifest became the name of him, and

ἔλεγον ὅτι Ἰωάννης ὁ βαπτίζων ἐγήγερται
they said[,] - John the baptizing [one] has been raised

ἐκ νεκρῶν, καὶ διὰ τοῦτο ἐνεργοῦσιν αἱ
from [the] dead, and therefore operate the

δυνάμεις ἐν αὐτῷ. 15 ἄλλοι δὲ ἔλεγον
powerful deeds in him. But others said[,]

ὅτι Ἡλίας ἐστίν· ἄλλοι δὲ ἔλεγον ὅτι
- Elias it/he is; and [yet] others said[,] -

προφήτης ὡς εἷς τῶν προφητῶν. 16 ἀκούσας δὲ
A prophet as one of the prophets. But hearing

ὁ Ἡρώδης ἔλεγεν· ὃν ἐγὼ ἀπεκεφάλισα
- Herod said: [2]whom [3]I [4]beheaded

Ἰωάννην, οὗτος ἠγέρθη. 17 Αὐτὸς γὰρ ὁ
[1]John, this was raised. For [1]himself -

Ἡρώδης ἀποστείλας ἐκράτησεν τὸν Ἰωάννην
[1]Herod sending seized - John

καὶ ἔδησεν αὐτὸν ἐν φυλακῇ διὰ Ἡρωδιάδα
and bound him in prison because of Herodias

τὴν γυναῖκα Φιλίππου τοῦ ἀδελφοῦ αὐτοῦ,
the wife of Philip the brother of him,

ὅτι αὐτὴν ἐγάμησεν· 18 ἔλεγεν γὰρ ὁ
because her he married; for said -

Ἰωάννης τῷ Ἡρώδῃ ὅτι οὐκ ἔξεστίν
John - to Herod[,] It is not lawful

σοι ἔχειν τὴν γυναῖκα τοῦ ἀδελφοῦ σου.
for thee to have the wife of the brother of thee.

19 ἡ δὲ Ἡρωδιὰς ἐνεῖχεν αὐτῷ καὶ
- Now Herodias had a grudge against him and

ἤθελεν αὐτὸν ἀποκτεῖναι, καὶ οὐκ ἠδύνατο·
wished [2]him [1]to kill, and could not;

20 ὁ γὰρ Ἡρώδης ἐφοβεῖτο τὸν Ἰωάννην,
- for Herod feared - John,

εἰδὼς αὐτὸν ἄνδρα δίκαιον καὶ ἅγιον, καὶ
knowing him a man just and holy, and

συνετήρει αὐτόν, καὶ ἀκούσας αὐτοῦ πολλὰ
kept safe him, and hearing him much
= was

ἠπόρει, καὶ ἡδέως αὐτοῦ ἤκουεν. 21 καὶ
was in difficulties, and gladly him heard. And
in great difficulties,

γενομένης ἡμέρας εὐκαίρου ὅτε Ἡρώδης
coming day a suitable[a] when Herod
= when a suitable day came

τοῖς γενεσίοις αὐτοῦ δεῖπνον ἐποίησεν τοῖς
on the birthday festivities of him a supper made for the

μεγιστᾶσιν αὐτοῦ καὶ τοῖς χιλιάρχοις καὶ
courtiers of him and the chiliarchs and

τοῖς πρώτοις τῆς Γαλιλαίας, 22 καὶ
the chief men of the of Galilee, and

εἰσελθούσης τῆς θυγατρὸς αὐτῆς τῆς
entering the daughter [2]of herself -
= when the daughter of Herodias herself entered and danced,

Ἡρωδιάδος καὶ ὀρχησαμένης, ἤρεσεν τῷ
[1]of Herodias and dancing,[a] she pleased -

Ἡρώδῃ καὶ τοῖς συνανακειμένοις. ὁ δὲ
Herod and the [ones] reclining with [him]. And the

βασιλεὺς εἶπεν τῷ κορασίῳ· αἴτησόν με
king said to the girl: Ask me

ὃ ἐὰν θέλῃς, καὶ δώσω σοι· 23 καὶ
whatever thou wishest, and I will give thee; and

ὤμοσεν αὐτῇ ὅτι ὃ ἐὰν αἰτήσῃς δώσω
he swore to her[,] - Whatever thou askest I will give

σοι ἕως ἡμίσους τῆς βασιλείας μου.
thee up to half of the kingdom of me.

24 καὶ ἐξελθοῦσα εἶπεν τῇ μητρὶ αὐτῆς·
And going out she said to the mother of her:

τί αἰτήσωμαι; ἡ δὲ εἶπεν· τὴν κεφαλὴν
What may I ask? And she said: The head

Ἰωάννου τοῦ βαπτίζοντος. 25 καὶ
of John the [one] baptizing. And

εἰσελθοῦσα εὐθὺς μετὰ σπουδῆς πρὸς τὸν
entering immediately with haste to the

βασιλέα ᾐτήσατο λέγουσα· θέλω ἵνα ἐξαυτῆς
king she asked saying: I wish that at once

δῷς μοι ἐπὶ πίνακι τὴν κεφαλὴν Ἰωάννου
thou mayest give me on a dish the head of John

τοῦ βαπτιστοῦ. 26 καὶ περίλυπος γενόμενος
the Baptist. And deeply grieved becoming

ὁ βασιλεὺς διὰ τοὺς ὅρκους καὶ τοὺς
the king because of the oaths and the [ones]

ἀνακειμένους οὐκ ἠθέλησεν ἀθετῆσαι αὐτήν.
reclining did not wish to reject her.

27 καὶ εὐθὺς ἀποστείλας ὁ βασιλεὺς
And immediately [2]sending [1]the [1]king

σπεκουλάτορα ἐπέταξεν ἐνέγκαι τὴν κεφαλὴν
an executioner gave order to bring the head

αὐτοῦ. καὶ ἀπελθὼν ἀπεκεφάλισεν αὐτὸν
of him. And going he beheaded him

ἐν τῇ φυλακῇ, 28 καὶ ἤνεγκεν τὴν κεφαλὴν
in the prison, and brought the head

αὐτοῦ ἐπὶ πίνακι καὶ ἔδωκεν αὐτὴν τῷ
of him on a dish and gave it to the

κορασίῳ, καὶ τὸ κοράσιον ἔδωκεν αὐτὴν
girl, and the girl gave it

τῇ μητρὶ αὐτῆς. 29 καὶ ἀκούσαντες οἱ
to the mother of her. And hearing the

μαθηταὶ αὐτοῦ ἦλθαν καὶ ἦραν τὸ πτῶμα
disciples of him went and took the corpse

αὐτοῦ καὶ ἔθηκαν αὐτὸ ἐν μνημείῳ.
of him and put it in a tomb.

30 Καὶ συνάγονται οἱ ἀπόστολοι πρὸς
And assemble the apostles to

τὸν Ἰησοῦν, καὶ ἀπήγγειλαν αὐτῷ πάντα
- Jesus, and reported to him all things

ὅσα ἐποίησαν καὶ ὅσα ἐδίδαξαν. 31 καὶ
which they did and which they taught. And

λέγει αὐτοῖς· δεῦτε ὑμεῖς αὐτοὶ κατ'
he says to them: Come ye [your]selves pri-

ἰδίαν εἰς ἔρημον τόπον καὶ ἀναπαύσασθε ὀλίγον.
vately to a desert place and rest a little.

ἦσαν γὰρ οἱ ἐρχόμενοι καὶ οἱ
For [2]were [3]the [ones] [4]coming [5]and [6]the [ones]

ὑπάγοντες πολλοί, καὶ οὐδὲ φαγεῖν
[7]going [1]many, and not to eat

εὐκαίρουν. 32 καὶ ἀπῆλθον ἐν τῷ πλοίῳ
they had opportunity. And they went away in the ship

εἰς ἔρημον τόπον κατ' ἰδίαν. 33 καὶ
to a desert place privately. And

εἶδον αὐτοὺς ὑπάγοντας καὶ ἐπέγνωσαν
[2]saw [3]them [1]going [4]and [5]knew

πολλοί, καὶ πεζῇ ἀπὸ πασῶν τῶν πόλεων
[1]many, and on foot from all the cities

συνέδραμον ἐκεῖ καὶ προῆλθον αὐτούς.
ran together there and came before them.

34 Καὶ ἐξελθὼν εἶδεν πολὺν ὄχλον, καὶ
And going forth he saw a much(great) crowd, and

ἐσπλαγχνίσθη ἐπ' αὐτοὺς ὅτι ἦσαν ὡς
had compassion on them because they were as

πρόβατα μὴ ἔχοντα ποιμένα, καὶ ἤρξατο
sheep not having a shepherd, and he began

King James Version

teach them many things. 35And when the day was now far spent, his disciples came unto him, and said, This is a desert place, and now the time *is* far passed: 36 Send them away, that they may go into the country round about, and into the villages, and buy themselves bread: for they have nothing to eat. 37 He answered and said unto them, Give ye them to eat. And they say unto him, Shall we go and buy two hundred pennyworth of bread, and give them to eat? 38 He saith unto them, How many loaves have ye? go and see. And when they knew, they say, Five, and two fishes. 39And he commanded them to make all sit down by companies upon the green grass. 40And they sat down in ranks, by hundreds, and by fifties. 41And when he had taken the five loaves and the two fishes, he looked up to heaven, and blessed, and brake the loaves, and gave *them* to his disciples to set before them; and the two fishes divided he among them all. 42And they did all eat, and were filled. 43And they took up twelve baskets full of the fragments, and of the fishes. 44And they that did eat of the loaves were about five thousand men. 45And straightway he constrained his disciples to get into the ship, and to go to the other side before unto Bethsaida, while he sent away the people. 46And when he had sent them away, he departed into a mountain to pray. 47And when even was come, the ship was in the midst of the sea, and he alone on the land. 48And he saw them toiling in rowing; for the wind was contrary unto them: and about the fourth watch of the night he cometh unto them, walking upon the sea, and would have passed by them. 49 But when they saw him walking upon the sea, they supposed it had been a spirit, and cried out: 50 For they all saw him, and were troubled. And immediately he talked with them, and saith unto them, Be of good cheer: it is I; be not afraid. 51And he went up unto them into the ship; and the wind ceased: and they were sore amazed in themselves beyond measure, and wondered. 52 For they considered not *the miracle* of the loaves; for their heart was hardened. 53And when they had passed over, they came into the land of Gennesaret, and drew to the shore. 54And when they were come out of the ship, straightway they knew him, 55And ran through that whole region round about, and began to carry about in beds those that were sick, where they heard he was. 56And whithersoever he entered, into villages, or cities, or country, they laid the sick in the streets, and besought him that they might touch if it were but the border of his garment: and as many as touched him were made whole.

New International Version

35 By this time it was late in the day, so his disciples came to him. "This is a remote place," they said, "and it's already very late. 36 Send the people away so they can go to the surrounding countryside and villages and buy themselves something to eat."

37 But he answered, "You give them something to eat."

They said to him, "That would take eight months of a man's wages! [r] Are we to go and spend that much on bread and give it to them to eat?"

38 "How many loaves do you have?" he asked. "Go and see."

When they found out, they said, "Five—and two fish."

39 Then Jesus directed them to have all the people sit down in groups on the green grass. 40 So they sat down in groups of hundreds and fifties. 41 Taking the five loaves and the two fish and looking up to heaven, he gave thanks and broke the loaves. Then he gave them to his disciples to set before the people. He also divided the two fish among them all. 42 They all ate and were satisfied, 43 and the disciples picked up twelve basketfuls of broken pieces of bread and fish. 44 The number of the men who had eaten was five thousand.

Jesus walks on the water

45 Immediately Jesus made his disciples get into the boat and go on ahead of him to Bethsaida, while he dismissed the crowd. 46After leaving them, he went into the hills to pray.

47 When evening came, the boat was in the middle of the lake, and he was alone on land. 48 He saw the disciples straining at the oars, because the wind was against them. About the fourth watch of the night he went out to them, walking on the lake. He was about to pass by them, 49 but when they saw him walking on the lake, they thought he was a ghost. They cried out, 50 because they all saw him and were terrified.

Immediately he spoke to them and said, "Take courage! It is I. Don't be afraid." 51 Then he climbed into the boat with them, and the wind died down. They were completely amazed, 52 for they had not understood about the loaves; their minds were closed.

53 When they had crossed over, they landed at Gennesaret and anchored there. 54As soon as they got out of the boat, people recognized Jesus. 55 They ran throughout that whole region and carried the sick on mats to wherever they heard he was. 56And everywhere he went, into villages, towns or countryside, they placed the sick in the marketplaces. They begged him to let them touch even the edge of his cloak, and all who touched him were healed.

[r] Greek *take 200 denarii.*

Greek Interlinear

διδάσκειν αὐτοὺς πολλά. 35 Καὶ ἤδη ὥρας
to teach them many things. And now an hour
= it being

πολλῆς γενομένης προσελθόντες αὐτῷ οἱ
much coming* approaching to him the
late

μαθηταὶ αὐτοῦ ἔλεγον ὅτι ἔρημός ἐστιν
disciples of him said[,] - Desert is

ὁ τόπος καὶ ἤδη ὥρα πολλή· 36 ἀπόλυσον
the place and now hour a much; dismiss
= it is late;

αὐτούς, ἵνα ἀπελθόντες εἰς τοὺς κύκλῳ
them, that going away to the round about

ἀγροὺς καὶ κώμας ἀγοράσωσιν ἑαυτοῖς τί
fields and villages they may buy for themselves what

φάγωσιν. 37 ὁ δὲ ἀποκριθεὶς εἶπεν αὐτοῖς·
they may eat. But he answering said to them:

δότε αὐτοῖς ὑμεῖς φαγεῖν. καὶ λέγουσιν
Give them ye to eat. And they say

αὐτῷ· ἀπελθόντες ἀγοράσωμεν δηναρίων
to him: Going away may we buy *of(for) ⁴denarii

διακοσίων ἄρτους, καὶ δώσομεν αὐτοῖς
*two hundred ¹loaves, and shall we give them

φαγεῖν; 38 ὁ δὲ λέγει αὐτοῖς· πόσους
to eat? And he says to them: How many

ἔχετε ἄρτους; ὑπάγετε ἴδετε. καὶ γνόντες
have ye loaves? Go see. And knowing

λέγουσιν· πέντε, καὶ δύο ἰχθύας. 39 καὶ
they say: Five, and two fishes. And

ἐπέταξεν αὐτοῖς ἀνακλιθῆναι πάντας συμπόσια
he instructed them to recline all companies

συμπόσια ἐπὶ τῷ χλωρῷ χόρτῳ. 40 καὶ
companies on the green grass. And

ἀνέπεσαν πρασιαὶ πρασιαὶ κατὰ ἑκατὸν
they reclined groups groups by a hundred

καὶ κατὰ πεντήκοντα. 41 καὶ λαβὼν τοὺς
and by fifty. And taking the

πέντε ἄρτους καὶ τοὺς δύο ἰχθύας,
five loaves and the two fishes,

ἀναβλέψας εἰς τὸν οὐρανὸν εὐλόγησεν καὶ
looking up to - heaven he blessed and

κατέκλασεν τοὺς ἄρτους καὶ ἐδίδου τοῖς
broke the loaves and gave to the

μαθηταῖς ἵνα παρατιθῶσιν αὐτοῖς, καὶ
disciples that they might set before them, and

τοὺς δύο ἰχθύας ἐμέρισεν πᾶσιν. 42 καὶ
the two fishes he divided to all. And

ἔφαγον πάντες καὶ ἐχορτάσθησαν, 43 καὶ
they ate all and were satisfied, and

ἦραν κλάσματα δώδεκα κοφίνων πληρώματα
they took fragments twelve *of baskets ¹fullnesses

καὶ ἀπὸ τῶν ἰχθύων 44 καὶ ἦσαν οἱ
and from the fishes. And were the

φαγόντες τοὺς ἄρτους πεντακισχίλιοι ἄνδρες.
[ones] eating the loaves five thousand males.

45 Καὶ εὐθὺς ἠνάγκασεν τοὺς μαθητὰς
And immediately he constrained the disciples

αὐτοῦ ἐμβῆναι εἰς τὸ πλοῖον καὶ προάγειν
of him to embark in the ship and to go before

εἰς τὸ πέραν πρὸς Βηθσαϊδάν, ἕως αὐτὸς
to the other side to Bethsaida, until he

ἀπολύει τὸν ὄχλον. 46 καὶ ἀποταξάμενος
dismisses the crowd. And having said farewell

αὐτοῖς ἀπῆλθεν εἰς τὸ ὄρος προσεύξασθαι.
to them he went away to the mountain to pray.

47 καὶ ὀψίας γενομένης ἦν τὸ πλοῖον ἐν
And evening coming on* was the ship in
= when evening came on

μέσῳ τῆς θαλάσσης, καὶ αὐτὸς μόνος ἐπὶ
[the] midst of the sea, and he alone on

τῆς γῆς. 48 καὶ ἰδὼν αὐτοὺς βασανιζομένους
the land. And seeing them being distressed

ἐν τῷ ἐλαύνειν, ἦν γὰρ ὁ ἄνεμος ἐναντίος
in the to row, ⁴was ¹for ²the ³wind contrary
= rowing,

αὐτοῖς, περὶ τετάρτην φυλακὴν τῆς νυκτὸς
to them, about [the] fourth watch of the night

ἔρχεται πρὸς αὐτοὺς περιπατῶν ἐπὶ τῆς
he comes toward them walking on the

θαλάσσης· καὶ ἤθελεν παρελθεῖν αὐτούς.
sea; and wished to go by them.

49 οἱ δὲ ἰδόντες αὐτὸν ἐπὶ τῆς θαλάσσης
But they seeing him on the sea

περιπατοῦντα ἔδοξαν ὅτι φάντασμά ἐστιν,
walking thought that a phantasm it is(was),

καὶ ἀνέκραξαν· 50 πάντες γὰρ αὐτὸν εἶδαν
and cried out; for all him saw

καὶ ἐταράχθησαν. ὁ δὲ εὐθὺς ἐλάλησεν
and were troubled. But he immediately talked

μετ᾽ αὐτῶν, καὶ λέγει αὐτοῖς· θαρσεῖτε,
with them, and says to them: Be of good cheer,

ἐγώ εἰμι· μὴ φοβεῖσθε. 51 καὶ ἀνέβη
I am; be ye not afraid. And he went up

πρὸς αὐτοὺς εἰς τὸ πλοῖον· καὶ ἐκόπασεν
to them into the ship, and ceased

ὁ ἄνεμος· καὶ λίαν ἐκ περισσοῦ ἐν ἑαυτοῖς
the wind; and very much exceedingly in themselves

ἐξίσταντο. 52 οὐ γὰρ συνῆκαν ἐπὶ
they were astonished; for they did not understand concerning

τοῖς ἄρτοις ἀλλ᾽ ἦν αὐτῶν ἡ καρδία
the loaves, but was of them the heart

πεπωρωμένη. 53 Καὶ διαπεράσαντες ἐπὶ
having been hardened. And crossing over ²onto

τὴν γῆν ἦλθον εἰς Γεννησαρὲτ καὶ
²the ⁴land ¹they came to Gennesaret and

προσωρμίσθησαν. 54 καὶ ἐξελθόντων αὐτῶν
anchored. And coming out them*

ἐκ τοῦ πλοίου εὐθὺς ἐπιγνόντες αὐτὸν
out of the ship immediately knowing him
= as they came

55 περιέδραμον ὅλην τὴν χώραν ἐκείνην
they ran round all - country that

καὶ ἤρξαντο ἐπὶ τοῖς κραβάτοις τοὺς
and began on the pallets the [ones]
= those

κακῶς ἔχοντας περιφέρειν, ὅπου ἤκουον
ill having to carry round, where they heard
who were ill

ὅτι ἐστίν. 56 καὶ ὅπου ἂν εἰσεπορεύετο
that he is(was). And wherever he entered

εἰς κώμας ἢ εἰς πόλεις ἢ εἰς ἀγρούς,
into villages or into cities or into country,

ἐν ταῖς ἀγοραῖς ἐτίθεσαν τοὺς ἀσθενοῦντας
in the marketplaces they put the ailing [ones],

καὶ παρεκάλουν αὐτὸν ἵνα κἂν τοῦ
and besought him that if even the

κρασπέδου τοῦ ἱματίου αὐτοῦ ἅψωνται·
fringe of the garment of him they might touch;

καὶ ὅσοι ἂν ἥψαντο αὐτοῦ ἐσώζοντο.
and as many as touched him were healed.

123

King James Version

7 Then came together unto him the Pharisees, and certain of the scribes, which came from Jerusalem. 2And when they saw some of his disciples eat bread with defiled, that is to say, with unwashen hands, they found fault. 3 For the Pharisees, and all the Jews, except they wash *their* hands oft, eat not, holding the tradition of the elders. 4And *when they come* from the market, except they wash, they eat not. And many other things there be, which they have received to hold, *as* the washing of cups, and pots, brazen vessels, and of tables. 5 Then the Pharisees and scribes asked him, Why walk not thy disciples according to the tradition of the elders, but eat bread with unwashen hands? 6 He answered and said unto them, Well hath Esaias prophesied of you hypocrites, as it is written, This people honoureth me with *their* lips, but their heart is far from me. 7 Howbeit in vain do they worship me, teaching *for* doctrines the commandments of men. 8 For laying aside the commandment of God, ye hold the tradition of men, *as* the washing of pots and cups: and many other such like things ye do. 9And he said unto them, Full well ye reject the commandment of God, that ye may keep your own tradition. 10 For Moses said, Honour thy father and thy mother; and, Whoso curseth father or mother, let him die the death: 11 But ye say, If a man shall say to his father or mother, *It is* Corban, that is to say, a gift, by whatsoever thou mightest be profited by me; *he shall be free.* 12And ye suffer him no more to do aught for his father or his mother; 13 Making the word of God of none effect through your tradition, which ye have delivered: and many such like things do ye. 14 And when he had called all the people *unto him,* he said unto them, Hearken unto me every one *of you,* and understand: 15 There is nothing from without a man, that entering into him can defile him: but the things which come out of him, those are they that defile the man. 16 If any man have ears to hear, let him hear. 17And when he was entered into the house from the people, his disciples asked him concerning the parable. 18And he saith unto them, Are ye so without understanding also? Do ye not perceive, that whatsoever thing from without entereth into the man, *it* cannot defile him; 19 Because it entereth not into his heart, but into the belly, and goeth out into the draught, purging all meats? 20And he said, That which cometh out of the man, that defileth the man. 21 For within, out of the heart of men, proceed evil thoughts, adulteries, fornications, murders, 22 Thefts, covetousness, wickedness, deceit, lasciviousness, an evil eye, blasphemy, pride, foolishness: 23All these evil things come from within, and defile the man.

24 And from thence he arose, and went into the borders of Tyre and Sidon, and entered into a house, and would have no man know *it:* but he could not be hid. 25 For a *certain* woman, whose young daughter had an unclean spirit,

New International Version

Clean and unclean

7 The Pharisees and some of the teachers of the law who had come from Jerusalem gathered around Jesus and 2 saw some of his disciples eating food with "unclean"—that is, ceremonially unwashed—hands. 3 (The Pharisees and all the Jews do not eat unless they give their hands a ceremonial washing, holding to the tradition of the elders. 4 When they come from the marketplace they do not eat unless they wash. And they observe many other traditions, such as the washing of cups, pitchers and kettles.[s])

5 So the Pharisees and teachers of the law asked Jesus, "Why don't your disciples live according to the tradition of the elders instead of eating their food with 'unclean' hands?"

6 He replied, "Isaiah was right when he prophesied about you hypocrites; as it is written:

'These people honor me with their lips,
but their hearts are far from me.

7 They worship me in vain;
their teachings are but rules made by men.'[t]

8 You have let go of the commands of God and are holding on to the traditions of men."

9 And he said to them: "You have a fine way of setting aside the commands of God in order to observe[u] your own traditions! 10 For Moses said, 'Honor your father and mother,'[v] and, 'Anyone who curses his father or mother must be put to death.'[w] 11 But you say that if a man says to his father or mother: 'Whatever help you might otherwise have received from me is Corban' (that is, a gift devoted to God), 12 then you no longer let him do anything for his father or mother. 13 Thus you nullify the word of God by your tradition that you have handed down. And you do many things like that."

14 Again Jesus called the crowd to him and said, "Listen to me, everyone, and understand this. 15 Nothing outside a man can make him 'unclean' by going into him. Rather, it is what comes out of a man that makes him 'unclean.' "[x]

17 After he had left the crowd and entered the house, his disciples asked him about this parable. 18 "Are you so dull?" he asked. "Don't you see that nothing that enters a man from the outside can make him 'unclean'? 19 For it doesn't go into his heart but into his stomach, and then out of his body." (In saying this, Jesus declared all foods "clean.")

20 He went on: "What comes out of a man is what makes him 'unclean.' 21 For from within, out of men's hearts, come evil thoughts, sexual immorality, theft, murder, adultery, 22 greed, malice, deceit, lewdness, envy, slander, arrogance and folly. 23All these evils come from inside and make a man 'unclean.' "

The faith of a Syrian Phoenician woman

24 Jesus left that place and went to the vicinity of Tyre.[y] He entered a house and did not want anyone to know it; yet he could not keep his presence secret. 25 In fact, as soon as she heard about him, a woman whose little daughter

---

[s] Some early MSS add *and dining couches.* [t] Isaiah 29:13. [u] Some MSS read *set up.* [v] Exodus 20:12; Deut; 5:16. [w] Exodus 21:17. [x] Some early MSS add verse 16: *If anyone has ears to hear, let him hear.* [y] Many early MSS add *and Sidon.*

Greek Interlinear

Chapter 7

Καὶ συνάγονται πρὸς αὐτὸν οἱ Φαρισαῖοι
And assemble to him the Pharisees

καὶ τινες τῶν γραμματέων ἐλθόντες ἀπὸ
and some of the scribes coming from

Ἱεροσολύμων. 2 καὶ ἰδόντες τινὰς τῶν
Jerusalem. And seeing some of the

μαθητῶν αὐτοῦ ὅτι κοιναῖς χερσίν, τοῦτ'
disciples of him that with unclean hands, this

ἔστιν ἀνίπτοις, ἐσθίουσιν τοὺς ἄρτους,
is unwashed, they eat bread,

3 — οἱ γὰρ Φαρισαῖοι καὶ πάντες οἱ
— for the Pharisees and all the

Ἰουδαῖοι ἐὰν μὴ πυγμῇ νίψωνται τὰς
Jews unless with [the] fist they wash the
= ? carefully

χεῖρας οὐκ ἐσθίουσιν, κρατοῦντες τὴν
hands eat not, holding the

παράδοσιν τῶν πρεσβυτέρων, 4 καὶ ἀπ'
tradition of the elders, and from

ἀγορᾶς ἐὰν μὴ ῥαντίσωνται οὐκ ἐσθίουσιν, καὶ
marketplaces unless they sprinkle they eat not, and

ἄλλα πολλά ἐστιν ἃ παρέλαβον κρατεῖν,
other things many there are which they received to hold,

βαπτισμοὺς ποτηρίων καὶ ξεστῶν καὶ
washings of cups and of utensils and

χαλκίων, — 5 καὶ ἐπερωτῶσιν αὐτὸν οἱ
of bronze vessels, — and questioned him the

Φαρισαῖοι καὶ οἱ γραμματεῖς· διὰ τί
Pharisees and the scribes: Why

οὐ περιπατοῦσιν οἱ μαθηταί σου κατὰ τὴν
walk not the disciples of thee according to the

παράδοσιν τῶν πρεσβυτέρων, ἀλλὰ κοιναῖς
tradition of the elders, but with unclean

χερσὶν ἐσθίουσιν τὸν ἄρτον; 6 ὁ δὲ εἶπεν
hands eat bread? And he said

αὐτοῖς· καλῶς ἐπροφήτευσεν Ἠσαΐας περὶ
to them: Well prophesied Esaias concerning

ὑμῶν τῶν ὑποκριτῶν, ὡς γέγραπται ὅτι
you the hypocrites, as it has been written[:] –

οὗτος ὁ λαὸς τοῖς χείλεσίν με τιμᾷ,
This – people with the lips me honours,

ἡ δὲ καρδία αὐτῶν πόρρω ἀπέχει ἀπ'
but the heart of them ²far ¹is ³away from

ἐμοῦ· 7 μάτην δὲ σέβονταί με, διδάσκοντες
me; and in vain they worship me, teaching

διδασκαλίας ἐντάλματα ἀνθρώπων. 8 ἀφέντες
teachings [which are] commands of men. Leaving

τὴν ἐντολὴν τοῦ θεοῦ κρατεῖτε τὴν
the commandment – of God ye hold the

παράδοσιν τῶν ἀνθρώπων. 9 καὶ ἔλεγεν
tradition of men. And he said

αὐτοῖς· καλῶς ἀθετεῖτε τὴν ἐντολὴν τοῦ
to them: Well ye set aside the commandment –

θεοῦ, ἵνα τὴν παράδοσιν ὑμῶν τηρήσητε.
of God, that the tradition of you ye may keep.

10 Μωϋσῆς γὰρ εἶπεν· τίμα τὸν πατέρα σου
For Moses said: Honour the father of thee

καὶ τὴν μητέρα σου, καί· ὁ κακολογῶν
and the mother of thee, and: The [one] speaking evil of

πατέρα ἢ μητέρα θανάτῳ τελευτάτω. 11 ὑμεῖς
father or mother by death let him end(die). ye

δὲ λέγετε· ἐὰν εἴπῃ ἄνθρωπος τῷ πατρὶ
But say: If says a man to the(his) father

ἢ τῇ μητρί· κορβᾶν, ὅ ἐστιν δῶρον,
or to the mother: Korban, which is a gift,

ὃ ἐὰν ἐξ ἐμοῦ ὠφεληθῇς, 12 οὐκέτι ἀφίετε
whatever by me thou mightest profit, no longer ye allow

αὐτὸν οὐδὲν ποιῆσαι τῷ πατρὶ ἢ τῇ
him no(any)thing to do for the father or the

μητρί, 13 ἀκυροῦντες τὸν λόγον τοῦ θεοῦ
mother, annulling the word – of God

τῇ παραδόσει ὑμῶν ᾗ παρεδώκατε· καὶ
by the tradition of you which ye received; and

παρόμοια τοιαῦτα πολλὰ ποιεῖτε. 14 καὶ
²similar things ³such ¹many ye do. And

προσκαλεσάμενος πάλιν τὸν ὄχλον ἔλεγεν
calling to [him] again the crowd he said

αὐτοῖς· ἀκούσατέ μου πάντες καὶ σύνετε.
to them: Hear ye me all and understand.

15 οὐδέν ἐστιν ἔξωθεν τοῦ ἀνθρώπου
Nothing there is from without – a man

εἰσπορευόμενον εἰς αὐτὸν ὃ δύναται κοινῶσαι
entering into him which can to defile

αὐτόν· ἀλλὰ τὰ ἐκ τοῦ ἀνθρώπου ἐκπο-
him; but the things out of – a man coming

ρευόμενά ἐστιν τὰ κοινοῦντα τὸν ἄνθρωπον. ‡
forth are the [ones] defiling – a man.

17 Καὶ ὅτε εἰσῆλθεν εἰς οἶκον ἀπὸ τοῦ
And when he entered into a house from the

ὄχλου, ἐπηρώτων αὐτὸν οἱ μαθηταὶ αὐτοῦ
crowd, questioned him the disciples of him

τὴν παραβολήν. 18 καὶ λέγει αὐτοῖς·
the parable. And he says to them:

οὕτως καὶ ὑμεῖς ἀσύνετοί ἐστε; οὐ
Thus also ye undiscerning are ? do ye not

νοεῖτε ὅτι πᾶν τὸ ἔξωθεν εἰσπορευόμενον
understand that everything from without entering

εἰς τὸν ἄνθρωπον οὐ δύναται αὐτὸν
into – a man cannot him

κοινῶσαι, 19 ὅτι οὐκ εἰσπορεύεται αὐτοῦ
to defile, because it enters not of him

εἰς τὴν καρδίαν ἀλλ' εἰς τὴν κοιλίαν,
into the heart but into the belly,

καὶ εἰς τὸν ἀφεδρῶνα ἐκπορεύεται, καθα-
and into the drain goes out, purg-

ρίζων πάντα τὰ βρώματα; 20 ἔλεγεν δὲ
ing all – foods ? And he said[,]

ὅτι τὸ ἐκ τοῦ ἀνθρώπου ἐκπορευόμενον,
– The thing out of – a man coming forth,

ἐκεῖνο κοινοῖ τὸν ἄνθρωπον. 21 ἔσωθεν
that defiles – a man. from within

γὰρ ἐκ τῆς καρδίας τῶν ἀνθρώπων
For out of the heart – of men

οἱ διαλογισμοὶ οἱ κακοὶ ἐκπορεύονται,
– thoughts – evil come forth,

πορνεῖαι, κλοπαί, φόνοι, 22 μοιχεῖαι,
fornications, thefts, murders, adulteries,

πλεονεξίαι, πονηρίαι, δόλος, ἀσέλγεια, ὀφθαλμὸς
greedinesses, iniquities, deceit, lewdness, eye

πονηρός, βλασφημία, ὑπερηφανία, ἀφροσύνη·
an evil, blasphemy, arrogance, foolishness;

23 πάντα ταῦτα τὰ πονηρὰ ἔσωθεν ἐκπορεύεται
all these – evil things from within comes forth

καὶ κοινοῖ τὸν ἄνθρωπον.
and defile – a man.

24 Ἐκεῖθεν δὲ ἀναστὰς ἀπῆλθεν εἰς τὰ ὅρια
And thence rising up he went away into the district

Τύρου. Καὶ εἰσελθὼν εἰς οἰκίαν οὐδένα ἤθελε
of Tyre. And entering into a house no one he wished

γνῶναι, καὶ οὐκ ἠδυνάσθη λαθεῖν· 25 ἀλλ'
to know, and could not to be hidden; but

εὐθὺς ἀκούσασα γυνὴ περὶ αὐτοῦ, ἧς
immediately ²hearing ¹a woman about him, of whom
= whose

‡ Verse 16 omitted by Nestle

125

King James Version

heard of him, and came and fell at his feet: 26 The woman was a Greek, a Syrophenician by nation; and she besought him that he would cast forth the devil out of her daughter. 27 But Jesus said unto her, Let the children first be filled: for it is not meet to take the children's bread, and to cast *it* unto the dogs. 28And she answered and said unto him, Yes, Lord: yet the dogs under the table eat of the children's crumbs. 29And he said unto her, For this saying go thy way; the devil is gone out of thy daughter. 30And when she was come to her house, she found the devil gone out, and her daughter laid upon the bed.

31 And again, departing from the coasts of Tyre and Sidon, he came unto the sea of Galilee, through the midst of the coasts of Decapolis. 32And they bring unto him one that was deaf, and had an impediment in his speech; and they beseech him to put his hand upon him. 33And he took him aside from the multitude, and put his fingers into his ears, and he spit, and touched his tongue; 34And looking up to heaven, he sighed, and saith unto him, Ephphatha, that is, Be opened. 35And straightway his ears were opened, and the string of his tongue was loosed, and he spake plain. 36And he charged them that they should tell no man: but the more he charged them, so much the more a great deal they published *it;* 37And were beyond measure astonished, saying, He hath done all things well: he maketh both the deaf to hear, and the dumb to speak.

8 In those days the multitude being very great and having nothing to eat, Jesus called his disciples *unto him,* and saith unto them, 2 I have compassion on the multitude, because they have now been with me three days, and have nothing to eat: 3And if I send them away fasting to their own houses, they will faint by the way: for divers of them came from far. 4And his disciples answered him, From whence can a man satisfy these *men* with bread here in the wilderness? 5And he asked them, How many loaves have ye? And they said, Seven. 6And he commanded the people to sit down on the ground; and he took the seven loaves, and gave thanks, and brake, and gave to his disciples to set before *them;* and they did set *them* before the people. 7And they had a few small fishes: and he blessed, and commanded to set them also before *them.* 8 So they did eat, and were filled: and they took up of the broken *meat* that was left seven baskets. 9And they that had eaten were about four thousand: and he sent them away.

10 And straightway he entered into a ship with his disciples, and came into the parts of Dalmanutha. 11And the Pharisees came forth, and began to question with him, seeking of him

New International Version

was possessed by an evil [z] spirit came and fell at his feet. 26 The woman was a Greek, born in Syrian Phoenicia. She begged Jesus to drive the demon out of her daughter.

27 "First let the children eat all they want," he told her, "for it is not right to take the children's bread and toss it to their dogs."

28 "Yes, Lord," she replied, "but even the dogs under the table eat the children's crumbs."

29 Then he told her, "For such a reply, you may go; the demon has left your daughter."

30 She went home and found her child lying on the bed, and the demon gone.

The healing of a deaf and dumb man

31 Then Jesus left the vicinity of Tyre and went through Sidon, down to the Sea of Galilee and into the region of the Decapolis.[a] 32 There some people brought a man to him who was deaf and could hardly talk, and they begged him to place his hand on the man.

33 After he took him aside, away from the crowd, Jesus put his fingers into the man's ears. Then he spit and touched the man's tongue. 34 He looked up to heaven and with a deep sigh said to him, *"Ephphatha!"* (which means, "Be opened!"). 35At this, the man's ears were opened, his tongue was loosened and he began to speak plainly.

36 Jesus commanded them not to tell anyone. But the more he did so, the more they kept talking about it. 37 People were overwhelmed with amazement. "He has done everything well," they said. "He even makes the deaf hear and the dumb speak."

Jesus feeds the four thousand

8 During those days another large crowd gathered. Since they had nothing to eat, Jesus called his disciples to him and said, 2 "I have compassion for these people; they have already been with me three days and have nothing to eat. 3 If I send them home hungry, they will collapse on the way, because some of them have come a long distance."

4 His disciples answered, "But where in this remote place can anyone get enough bread to feed them?"

5 "How many loaves do you have?" Jesus asked.

"Seven," they replied.

6 He told the crowd to sit down on the ground. When he had taken the seven loaves and given thanks, he broke them and gave them to his disciples to set before the people, and they did so. 7 They had a few small fish as well; he gave thanks for them also and told the disciples to distribute them. 8 The people ate and were satisfied. Afterward the disciples picked up seven basketfuls of broken pieces that were left over. 9About four thousand men were present. And having sent them away, 10 he got into the boat with his disciples and went to the region of Dalmanutha.

11 The Pharisees came and began to question Jesus. To test him, they asked him for a sign

[z] Greek *unclean.* [a] That is, *the Ten Cities.*

Greek Interlinear

εἶχεν τὸ θυγάτριον αὐτῆς πνεῦμα ἀκάθαρτον,
had the daughter of her spirit an unclean,
daughter had

ἐλθοῦσα προσέπεσεν πρὸς τοὺς πόδας αὐτοῦ·
coming fell at the feet of him;

26 ἡ δὲ γυνὴ ἦν Ἑλληνίς, Συροφοινίκισσα
and the woman was a Greek, a Syrophenician

τῷ γένει· καὶ ἠρώτα αὐτὸν ἵνα τὸ
- by race; and she asked him that the

δαιμόνιον ἐκβάλῃ ἐκ τῆς θυγατρὸς αὐτῆς.
demon he would expel out of the daughter of her.

27 καὶ ἔλεγεν αὐτῇ· ἄφες πρῶτον
And he said to her: Permit first

χορτασθῆναι τὰ τέκνα· οὐ γάρ ἐστιν καλὸν
to be satisfied the children; for it is not good

λαβεῖν τὸν ἄρτον τῶν τέκνων καὶ τοῖς
to take the bread of the children and to the

κυναρίοις βαλεῖν. 28 ἡ δὲ ἀπεκρίθη καὶ
dogs to throw [it]. And she answered and

λέγει αὐτῷ· ναί, κύριε· καὶ τὰ κυνάρια
says to him· Yes, Lord· and yet the dogs

ὑποκάτω τῆς τραπέζης ἐσθίουσιν ἀπὸ τῶν
under the table eat from the

ψιχίων τῶν παιδίων. 29 καὶ εἶπεν αὐτῇ·
crumbs of the children. And he said to her:

διὰ τοῦτον τὸν λόγον ὕπαγε, ἐξελήλυθεν
Because of this - word go, has gone forth

ἐκ τῆς θυγατρός σου τὸ δαιμόνιον. 30 καὶ
out of the daughter of thee the demon. And

ἀπελθοῦσα εἰς τὸν οἶκον αὐτῆς εὗρεν τὸ
going away to the house of her she found the

παιδίον βεβλημένον ἐπὶ τὴν κλίνην καὶ τὸ
child having been laid on the couch and the

δαιμόνιον ἐξεληλυθός. 31 Καὶ πάλιν ἐξελθὼν
demon having gone forth. And again going forth

ἐκ τῶν ὁρίων Τύρου ἦλθεν διὰ Σιδῶνος
out of the district of Tyre he came through Sidon

εἰς τὴν θάλασσαν τῆς Γαλιλαίας ἀνὰ
to the sea - of Galilee in the

μέσον τῶν ὁρίων Δεκαπόλεως. 32 Καὶ
midst of the district of Decapolis. And

φέρουσιν αὐτῷ κωφὸν καὶ μογιλάλον, καὶ
they bring to him a man deaf and speaking with difficulty, and

παρακαλοῦσιν αὐτὸν ἵνα ἐπιθῇ αὐτῷ τὴν
they beseech him that he would put on on him the(his)

χεῖρα. 33 καὶ ἀπολαβόμενος αὐτὸν ἀπὸ
hand. And taking away him from

τοῦ ὄχλου κατ᾽ ἰδίαν ἔβαλεν τοὺς δακτύλους
the crowd privately he put the fingers

αὐτοῦ εἰς τὰ ὦτα αὐτοῦ καὶ πτύσας
of him into the ears of him and spitting

ἥψατο τῆς γλώσσης αὐτοῦ, 34 καὶ
he touched the tongue of him, and

ἀναβλέψας εἰς τὸν οὐρανὸν ἐστέναξεν,
looking up to heaven he groaned,

καὶ λέγει αὐτῷ· ἐφφαθά, ὅ ἐστιν διανοίχθητι.
and says to him: Ephphatha, which is Be thou opened.

35 καὶ ἠνοίγησαν αὐτοῦ αἱ ἀκοαί, καὶ
And were opened of him the ears, and

εὐθὺς ἐλύθη ὁ δεσμὸς τῆς γλώσσης αὐτοῦ,
immediately was loosened the bond of the tongue of him,

καὶ ἐλάλει ὀρθῶς. 36 καὶ διεστείλατο
and he spoke correctly. And he ordered

αὐτοῖς ἵνα μηδενὶ λέγωσιν· ὅσον δὲ
them that no one they should tell; but as much as

αὐτοῖς διεστέλλετο, αὐτοὶ μᾶλλον περισσότερον
them he ordered, they more exceedingly

ἐκήρυσσον. 37 καὶ ὑπερπερισσῶς ἐξεπλήσσοντο
proclaimed. And most exceedingly they were astounded

λέγοντες· καλῶς πάντα πεποίηκεν, καὶ
saying: Well all things he has done, both

τοὺς κωφοὺς ποιεῖ ἀκούειν καὶ ἀλάλους
the deaf he makes to hear and dumb

λαλεῖν.
to speak.

Chapter 8

Ἐν ἐκείναις ταῖς ἡμέραις πάλιν πολλοῦ
In those - days again a much(great)
= there being

ὄχλου ὄντος καὶ μὴ ἐχόντων τί φάγωσιν,
crowd being* and not having* anything they might eat,
a great crowd

προσκαλεσάμενος τοὺς μαθητὰς λέγει αὐτοῖς·
calling to [him] the disciples he says to them:

2 σπλαγχνίζομαι ἐπὶ τὸν ὄχλον, ὅτι ἤδη
I have compassion on the crowd, because now

ἡμέραι τρεῖς προσμένουσίν μοι καὶ οὐκ
days three they remain with me and not

ἔχουσιν τί φάγωσιν· 3 καὶ ἐὰν ἀπολύσω
they have anything they may eat; and if I dismiss

αὐτοὺς νήστεις εἰς οἶκον αὐτῶν, ἐκλυθήσονται
them fasting to house of them, they will faint

ἐν τῇ ὁδῷ· καί τινες αὐτῶν ἀπὸ μακρόθεν
in the way; and some of them from afar

εἰσίν. 4 καὶ ἀπεκρίθησαν αὐτῷ οἱ μαθηταὶ
are. And answered him the disciples

αὐτοῦ ὅτι πόθεν τούτους δυνήσεταί τις
of him[,] that ¹Whence ⁴these people ⁴will ⁴be able ²anyone

ὧδε χορτάσαι ἄρτων ἐπ᾽ ἐρημίας; 5 καὶ
⁵here ⁴to satisfy ⁷of(with) loaves ⁶on(in) ³a desert? And

ἠρώτα αὐτούς· πόσους ἔχετε ἄρτους;
he asked them: How many have ye loaves?

οἱ δὲ εἶπαν· ἑπτά. 6 καὶ παραγγέλλει τῷ
And they said: Seven. And he commands the

ὄχλῳ ἀναπεσεῖν ἐπὶ τῆς γῆς· καὶ λαβὼν
crowd to recline on the ground; and taking

τοὺς ἑπτὰ ἄρτους εὐχαριστήσας ἔκλασεν
the seven loaves giving thanks he broke

καὶ ἐδίδου τοῖς μαθηταῖς αὐτοῦ ἵνα
and gave to the disciples of him that

παρατιθῶσιν, καὶ παρέθηκαν τῷ ὄχλῳ.
they might serve, and they served the crowd.

7 καὶ εἶχον ἰχθύδια ὀλίγα· καὶ εὐλογήσας
And they had fishes a few; and blessing

αὐτὰ εἶπεν καὶ ταῦτα παρατιθέναι. 8 καὶ
them he told also these to be served. And

ἔφαγον καὶ ἐχορτάσθησαν, καὶ ἦραν
they ate and were satisfied, and took

περισσεύματα κλασμάτων, ἑπτὰ σπυρίδας.
excesses of fragments, seven baskets.

9 ἦσαν δὲ ὡς τετρακισχίλιοι. καὶ ἀπέλυσεν
Now they were about four thousand. And he dismissed

αὐτούς. 10 Καὶ εὐθὺς ἐμβὰς εἰς τὸ
them. And immediately embarking in the

πλοῖον μετὰ τῶν μαθητῶν αὐτοῦ
ship with the disciples of him

ἦλθεν εἰς τὰ μέρη Δαλμανουθά.
he came into the region of Dalmanutha.

11 Καὶ ἐξῆλθον οἱ Φαρισαῖοι καὶ ἤρξαντο
And came forth the Pharisees and began

συζητεῖν αὐτῷ, ζητοῦντες παρ᾽ αὐτοῦ
to debate with him, seeking from him

King James Version

a sign from heaven, tempting him. 12And he sighed deeply in his spirit, and saith, Why doth this generation seek after a sign? verily I say unto you, There shall no sign be given unto this generation. 13And he left them, and entering into the ship again departed to the other side.

14 Now *the disciples* had forgotten to take bread, neither had they in the ship with them more than one loaf. 15And he charged them, saying, Take heed, beware of the leaven of the Pharisees, and *of* the leaven of Herod. 16And they reasoned among themselves, saying, It *is* because we have no bread. 17And when Jesus knew *it,* he saith unto them, Why reason ye, because ye have no bread? perceive ye not yet, neither understand? have ye your heart yet hardened? 18 Having eyes, see ye not? and having ears, hear ye not? and do ye not remember? 19When I brake the five loaves among five thousand, how many baskets full of fragments took ye up? They say unto him, Twelve. 20And when the seven among four thousand, how many baskets full of fragments took ye up? And they said, Seven. 21And he said unto them, How is it that ye do not understand?

22 And he cometh to Bethsaida; and they bring a blind man unto him, and besought him to touch him. 23And he took the blind man by the hand, and led him out of the town; and when he had spit on his eyes, and put his hands upon him, he asked him if he saw aught. 24And he looked up, and said, I see men as trees, walking. 25After that he put *his* hands again upon his eyes, and made him look up; and he was restored, and saw every man clearly. 26And he sent him away to his house, saying, Neither go into the town, nor tell *it* to any in the town.

27 And Jesus went out, and his disciples, into the towns of Cesarea Philippi: and by the way he asked his disciples, saying unto them, Whom do men say that I am? 28And they answered, John the Baptist: but some *say,* Elias; and others, One of the prophets. 29And he saith unto them, But whom say ye that I am? And Peter answereth and saith unto him, Thou art the Christ. 30And he charged them that they should tell no man of him. 31And he began to teach them, that the Son of man must suffer many things, and be rejected of the elders, and *of* the

New International Version

from heaven. 12 He sighed deeply and said, "Why does this generation ask for a miraculous sign? I tell you the truth, no sign will be given to it." 13 Then he left them, got back into the boat and crossed to the other side.

The yeast of the Pharisees and Herod

14 The disciples had forgotten to bring bread, except for one loaf they had with them in the boat. 15 "Be careful," Jesus warned them. "Watch out for the yeast of the Pharisees and that of Herod."

16 They discussed this with one another and said, "It is because we have no bread."

17 Aware of their discussion, Jesus asked them: "Why are you talking about having no bread? Do you still not see or understand? Are your hearts hardened? 18 Do you have eyes but fail to see, and ears but fail to hear? And don't you remember? 19 When I broke the five loaves for the five thousand, how many basketfuls of pieces did you pick up?"

"Twelve," they replied.

20 "And when I broke the seven loaves for the four thousand, how many basketfuls of pieces did you pick up?"

They answered, "Seven."

21 He said to them, "Do you still not understand?"

The healing of a blind man at Bethsaida

22 They came to Bethsaida, and some people brought a blind man and begged Jesus to touch him. 23 He took the blind man by the hand and led him outside the village. When he had spit on the man's eyes and put his hands on him, Jesus asked, "Do you see anything?"

24 He looked up and said, "I see people; they look like trees walking around."

25 Once more Jesus put his hands on the man's eyes. Then his eyes were opened, his sight was restored, and he saw everything clearly. 26 Jesus sent him home, saying, "Don't go into the village." [b]

Peter's confession of Christ

27 Jesus and his disciples went on to the villages around Caesarea Philippi. On the way he asked them, "Who do people say I am?"

28 They replied, "Some say John the Baptist; others say Elijah; and still others, one of the prophets."

29 "But what about you?" he asked. "Who do you say I am?"

Peter answered, "You are the Christ." [c]

30 Jesus warned them not to tell anyone about him.

Jesus predicts his death

31 He then began to teach them that the Son of Man must suffer many things and be rejected by the elders, chief priests and teachers of the

[b] Some MSS read *Don't go and tell anyone in the village.* [c] Or *Messiah.* "The Christ" (Greek) and "the Messiah" (Hebrew) both mean "the Anointed One."

Greek Interlinear

σημεῖον ἀπὸ τοῦ οὐρανοῦ, πειράζοντες
a sign   from   -   heaven,   tempting

αὐτόν. 12 καὶ ἀναστενάξας τῷ πνεύματι
him.   And   groaning   in the   spirit

αὐτοῦ λέγει· τί ἡ γενεὰ αὕτη ζητεῖ
of him he says: Why - ²generation ³this ¹does ⁴seek

σημεῖον; ἀμὴν λέγω ὑμῖν, εἰ δοθήσεται
a sign?   Truly I tell you, if will be given

τῇ γενεᾷ ταύτῃ σημεῖον. 13 καὶ ἀφεὶς
- generation to this   a sign.   And leaving

αὐτοὺς πάλιν ἐμβὰς ἀπῆλθεν εἰς τὸ
them   again embarking he went away to   the

πέραν. 14 Καὶ ἐπελάθοντο λαβεῖν ἄρτους,
other side. And they forgot   to take   loaves,

καὶ εἰ μὴ ἕνα ἄρτον οὐκ εἶχον μεθ'
and except one loaf   they had not with

ἑαυτῶν ἐν τῷ πλοίῳ. 15 καὶ διεστέλλετο
themselves in the ship.   And he charged

αὐτοῖς λέγων· ὁρᾶτε, βλέπετε ἀπὸ τῆς
them   saying : See,   look ye from the
                                      ═Beware of

ζύμης τῶν Φαρισαίων καὶ τῆς ζύμης
leaven of the Pharisees   and of the leaven

Ἡρώδου. 16 καὶ διελογίζοντο πρὸς ἀλλήλους
of Herod.   And they reasoned   with one another

ὅτι ἄρτους οὐκ ἔχουσιν. 17 καὶ γνοὺς
because loaves they have(had) not.   And knowing

λέγει αὐτοῖς· τί διαλογίζεσθε ὅτι ἄρτους
he says to them: Why reason ye   because loaves

οὐκ ἔχετε; οὔπω νοεῖτε οὐδὲ συνίετε;
ye have not? not yet understand ye nor realize?

πεπωρωμένην ἔχετε τὴν καρδίαν ὑμῶν,
having been hardened have ye the heart   of you?

18 ὀφθαλμοὺς ἔχοντες οὐ βλέπετε, καὶ
eyes   having   see ye not, and

ὦτα ἔχοντες οὐκ ἀκούετε; καὶ
ears having   hear ye not?   and

οὐ μνημονεύετε, 19 ὅτε τοὺς πέντε ἄρτους
do ye not remember,   when the five loaves

ἔκλασα εἰς τοὺς πεντακισχιλίους, πόσους
I broke to the   five thousand,   how many

κοφίνους κλασμάτων πλήρεις ἤρατε; λέγουσιν
baskets of fragments   full ye took? They say

αὐτῷ· δώδεκα. 20 ὅτε τοὺς ἑπτὰ εἰς
to him: Twelve.   When the seven to

τοὺς τετρακισχιλίους, πόσων σπυρίδων
the   four thousand, ⁵of how many baskets

πληρώματα κλασμάτων ἤρατε; καὶ λέγουσιν·
¹fullnesses ⁴of fragments ye took? And they say:

ἑπτά. 21 καὶ ἔλεγεν αὐτοῖς· οὔπω συνίετε;
Seven.   And he said to them: Not yet do ye realize?

22 Καὶ ἔρχονται εἰς Βηθσαϊδάν. Καὶ
And   they come to   Bethsaida.   And

φέρουσιν αὐτῷ τυφλόν, καὶ παρακαλοῦσιν
they bring to him a blind man, and beseech

αὐτὸν ἵνα αὐτοῦ ἅψηται. 23 καὶ ἐπιλαβόμενος
him   that him he would touch. And laying hold of

τῆς χειρὸς τοῦ τυφλοῦ ἐξήνεγκεν αὐτὸν
the hand   of the blind man he led forth   him

ἔξω τῆς κώμης, καὶ πτύσας εἰς τὰ
outside the village,   and spitting in the

ὄμματα αὐτοῦ, ἐπιθεὶς τὰς χεῖρας αὐτῷ,
eyes   of him, putting on the hands on him,

ἐπηρώτα αὐτόν· εἴ τι βλέπεις; 24 καὶ
questioned   him: If anything thou seest? And

ἀναβλέψας ἔλεγεν· βλέπω τοὺς ἀνθρώπους,
looking up   he said : I see   -   men,

ὅτι ὡς δένδρα ὁρῶ περιπατοῦντας.
that as trees I behold   walking.

25 εἶτα πάλιν ἐπέθηκεν τὰς χεῖρας ἐπὶ
Then   again he put on   the hands   on

τοὺς ὀφθαλμοὺς αὐτοῦ, καὶ διέβλεψεν καὶ
the   eyes   of him, and he looked steadily and

ἀπεκατέστη, καὶ ἐνέβλεπεν τηλαυγῶς ἅπαντα.
was restored, and saw   clearly   all things.

26 καὶ ἀπέστειλεν αὐτὸν εἰς οἶκον αὐτοῦ
And   he sent   him   to house of him

λέγων· μηδὲ εἰς τὴν κώμην εἰσέλθῃς.
saying: Not into the village thou mayest enter.

27 Καὶ ἐξῆλθεν ὁ Ἰησοῦς καὶ οἱ μαθηταὶ
And went forth - Jesus and the disciples

αὐτοῦ εἰς τὰς κώμας Καισαρείας τῆς
of him to the villages of Cæsarea   -

Φιλίππου· καὶ ἐν τῇ ὁδῷ ἐπηρώτα τοὺς
of Philip;   and in the way he questioned the

μαθητὰς αὐτοῦ λέγων αὐτοῖς· τίνα με
disciples of him saying to them: Whom me

λέγουσιν οἱ ἄνθρωποι εἶναι; 28 οἱ δὲ
say   -   men   to be?   And they

εἶπαν αὐτῷ λέγοντες ὅτι Ἰωάννην τὸν
told   him saying   that John   the

βαπτιστήν, καὶ ἄλλοι Ἡλίαν, ἄλλοι δὲ
Baptist,   and others Elias, but others[.]

ὅτι εἷς τῶν προφητῶν. 29 καὶ αὐτὸς
- one of the prophets.   And he

ἐπηρώτα αὐτούς· ὑμεῖς δὲ τίνα με λέγετε
questioned them: But ye   whom me say ye

εἶναι; ἀποκριθεὶς ὁ Πέτρος λέγει αὐτῷ·
to be? Answering - Peter   says to him:

σὺ εἶ ὁ χριστός. 30 καὶ ἐπετίμησεν
Thou art the Christ.   And   he warned

αὐτοῖς ἵνα μηδενὶ λέγωσιν περὶ αὐτοῦ.
them   that no one they might tell about him.

31 Καὶ ἤρξατο διδάσκειν αὐτοὺς ὅτι δεῖ
And he began to teach   them that it behoves

τὸν υἱὸν τοῦ ἀνθρώπου πολλὰ παθεῖν,
the Son   - of man   many things to suffer,

καὶ ἀποδοκιμασθῆναι ὑπὸ τῶν πρεσβυτέρων
and to be rejected   by the   elders

King James Version

chief priests, and scribes, and be killed, and after three days rise again. 32And he spake that saying openly. And Peter took him, and began to rebuke him. 33 But when he had turned about and looked on his disciples, he rebuked Peter, saying, Get thee behind me, Satan: for thou savourest not the things that be of God, but the things that be of men.

34 And when he had called the people *unto him* with his disciples also, he said unto them, Whosoever will come after me, let him deny himself, and take up his cross, and follow me. 35 For whosoever will save his life shall lose it; but whosoever shall lose his life for my sake and the gospel's, the same shall save it. 36 For what shall it profit a man, if he shall gain the whole world, and lose his own soul? 37 Or what shall a man give in exchange for his soul? 38 Whosoever therefore shall be ashamed of me and of my words, in this adulterous and sinful generation, of him also shall the Son of man be ashamed, when he cometh in the glory of his Father with the holy angels.

9 And he said unto them, Verily I say unto you, That there be some of them that stand here, which shall not taste of death, till they have seen the kingdom of God come with power.

2 And after six days Jesus taketh *with him* Peter, and James, and John, and leadeth them up into a high mountain apart by themselves: and he was transfigured before them. 3And his raiment became shining, exceeding white as snow; so as no fuller on earth can white them. 4And there appeared unto them Elias with Moses: and they were talking with Jesus. 5And Peter answered and said to Jesus, Master, it is good for us to be here: and let us make three tabernacles; one for thee, and one for Moses, and one for Elias. 6 For he wist not what to say; for they were sore afraid. 7And there was a cloud that overshadowed them: and a voice came out of the cloud, saying, This is my beloved Son: hear him. 8And suddenly, when they had looked round about, they saw no man any more, save Jesus only with themselves. 9And as they came down from the mountain, he charged them that they should tell no man what things they had seen, till the Son of man were risen from the dead. 10And they kept that saying with themselves, questioning one with another what the rising from the dead should mean.

11 And they asked him, saying, Why say the scribes that Elias must first come? 12And he answered and told them, Elias verily cometh first, and restoreth all things; and how it is written of the Son of man, that he must suffer many things, and be set at nought. 13 But I say unto you, That Elias is indeed come, and they have

New International Version

law, and that he must be killed and after three days rise again. 32 He spoke plainly about this, and Peter took him aside and began to rebuke him.

33 But when Jesus turned and looked at his disciples, he rebuked Peter. "Out of my sight, Satan!" he said. "You do not have in mind the things of God, but the things of men."

34 Then he called the crowd to him along with his disciples and said: "If anyone would come after me, he must deny himself and take up his cross and follow me. 35 For whoever wants to save his life[d] will lose it, but whoever loses his life for me and for the gospel will save it. 36 What good is it for a man to gain the whole world, yet forfeit his soul? [d] 37 Or what can a man give in exchange for his soul? 38 If anyone is ashamed of me and my words in this adulterous and sinful generation, the Son of Man will be ashamed of him when he comes in his Father's glory with the holy angels."

9 And he said to them, "I tell you the truth, some who are standing here will not taste death before they see the kingdom of God come with power."

The transfiguration

2 After six days Jesus took Peter, James and John with him and led them up a high mountain, where they were all alone. There he was transfigured before them. 3 His clothes became dazzling white, whiter than anyone in the world could bleach them. 4And there appeared before them Elijah and Moses, who were talking with Jesus.

5 Peter said to Jesus, "Rabbi, it is good for us to be here. Let us put up three shelters[e]—one for you, one for Moses and one for Elijah." 6 (He did not know what to say, they were so frightened.)

7 Then a cloud appeared and enveloped them, and a voice came from the cloud: "This is my Son, whom I love. Listen to him!"

8 Suddenly, when they looked around, they no longer saw anyone with them except Jesus.

9 As they were coming down the mountain, Jesus gave them orders not to tell anyone what they had seen until the Son of Man had risen from the dead. 10 They kept the matter to themselves, discussing what "rising from the dead" meant.

11 And they asked him, "Why do the teachers of the law say that Elijah must come first?"

12 Jesus replied, "To be sure, Elijah does come first, and restores all things. Why then is it written that the Son of Man must suffer much and be rejected? 13 But I tell you, Elijah has come,

[d] The Greek word means either *life* or *soul*. [e] Or *sanctuaries*.

Greek Interlinear

καὶ τῶν ἀρχιερέων καὶ τῶν γραμματέων
and the chief priests and the   scribes

καὶ ἀποκτανθῆναι καὶ μετὰ τρεῖς ἡμέρας
and to be killed   and after three days

ἀναστῆναι· 32 καὶ παρρησίᾳ τὸν λόγον
to rise again; and openly   the   word

ἐλάλει.   καὶ προσλαβόμενος ὁ Πέτρος
he spoke. And ²taking ⁴aside   - ¹Peter

αὐτὸν ἤρξατο ἐπιτιμᾶν αὐτῷ. 33 ὁ δὲ
³him   began to rebuke   him.   But he

ἐπιστραφεὶς καὶ ἰδὼν τοὺς μαθητὰς αὐτοῦ
turning round and seeing the disciples of him

ἐπετίμησεν Πέτρῳ καὶ λέγει· ὕπαγε ὀπίσω
rebuked   Peter   and says: Go   behind

μου, σατανᾶ, ὅτι οὐ φρονεῖς τὰ τοῦ
me, Satan, because thou mindest not the things -

θεοῦ ἀλλὰ τὰ τῶν ἀνθρώπων. 34 Καὶ
of God but the things - of men.   And

προσκαλεσάμενος τὸν ὄχλον σὺν τοῖς μαθηταῖς
calling to [him]   the crowd with the disciples

αὐτοῦ εἶπεν αὐτοῖς· εἴ τις θέλει ὀπίσω
of him he said to them: If anyone wishes after

μου ἐλθεῖν, ἀπαρνησάσθω ἑαυτὸν καὶ ἀράτω
me to come, let him deny   himself and take

τὸν σταυρὸν αὐτοῦ, καὶ ἀκολουθείτω μοι.
the cross   of him,   and let him follow   me.

35 ὃς γὰρ ἐὰν θέλῃ τὴν ψυχὴν αὐτοῦ σῶ-
For whoever wishes the life of him to

σαι, ἀπολέσει αὐτήν· ὃς δ' ἂν ἀπολέσει
save, will lose   it;   but whoever will lose

τὴν ψυχὴν αὐτοῦ ἕνεκεν ἐμοῦ καὶ τοῦ
the   life of him for the sake of me and the

εὐαγγελίου, σώσει αὐτήν. 36 τί γὰρ ὠφελεῖ
gospel,   will save it.   For what profits

ἄνθρωπον κερδῆσαι τὸν κόσμον ὅλον καὶ
a man   to gain   the world   whole and

ζημιωθῆναι τὴν ψυχὴν αὐτοῦ; 37 τί γὰρ
to be fined   the soul   of him?   For what

δοῖ ἄνθρωπος ἀντάλλαγμα τῆς ψυχῆς αὐτοῦ;
might give a man an exchange of the soul of him?

38 ὃς γὰρ ἐὰν ἐπαισχυνθῇ με καὶ
For whoever   is ashamed of me and

τοὺς ἐμοὺς λόγους ἐν τῇ γενεᾷ ταύτῃ
-   my   words in the generation this

τῇ μοιχαλίδι καὶ ἁμαρτωλῷ, καὶ ὁ
- adulterous and   sinful,   also the

υἱὸς τοῦ ἀνθρώπου ἐπαισχυνθήσεται αὐτόν,
Son   - of man   will be ashamed of   him,

ὅταν ἔλθῃ ἐν τῇ δόξῃ τοῦ πατρὸς
when he comes in the glory of the Father

αὐτοῦ μετὰ τῶν ἀγγέλων τῶν ἁγίων.
of him with the   angels   -   holy.

Chapter 9

καὶ ἔλεγεν αὐτοῖς· ἀμὴν λέγω ὑμῖν
And he said to them: Truly I tell you

ὅτι εἰσίν τινες ὧδε τῶν ἑστηκότων
that there are some here of the [ones] standing

οἵτινες οὐ μὴ γεύσωνται θανάτου ἕως ἂν
who by no means may taste of death until

ἴδωσιν τὴν βασιλείαν τοῦ θεοῦ ἐληλυθυῖαν
they see the kingdom - of God having come

ἐν δυνάμει.
in power.

2 Καὶ μετὰ ἡμέρας ἓξ παραλαμβάνει
And after days six takes

ὁ Ἰησοῦς τὸν Πέτρον καὶ τὸν Ἰάκωβον
- Jesus   the Peter   and - James

καὶ Ἰωάννην, καὶ ἀναφέρει αὐτοὺς εἰς
and John,   and leads up   them into

ὄρος ὑψηλὸν κατ' ἰδίαν μόνους. καὶ
mountain a high privately alone. And

μετεμορφώθη ἔμπροσθεν αὐτῶν, 3 καὶ τὰ
he was transfigured before them,   and the

ἱμάτια αὐτοῦ ἐγένετο στίλβοντα λευκὰ λίαν,
garments of him became gleaming white exceedingly,

οἷα γναφεὺς ἐπὶ τῆς γῆς οὐ δύναται
such as fuller on the earth cannot

οὕτως λευκᾶναι. 4 καὶ ὤφθη αὐτοῖς Ἡλίας
so to whiten.   And appeared to them Elias

σὺν Μωϋσεῖ, καὶ ἦσαν συλλαλοῦντες τῷ
with Moses,   and they were conversing with

Ἰησοῦ. 5 καὶ ἀποκριθεὶς ὁ Πέτρος λέγει
Jesus.   And answering   - Peter says

τῷ Ἰησοῦ· ῥαββί, καλόν ἐστιν ἡμᾶς ὧδε
- to Jesus: Rabbi, good it is us here

εἶναι, καὶ ποιήσωμεν τρεῖς σκηνάς, σοὶ
to be, and let us make three tents, for thee

μίαν καὶ Μωϋσεῖ μίαν καὶ Ἡλίᾳ μίαν.
one and for Moses one and for Elias one.

6 οὐ γὰρ ᾔδει τί ἀποκριθῇ· ἔκφοβοι γὰρ
For he knew not what he answered; for exceedingly afraid

ἐγένοντο. 7 καὶ ἐγένετο νεφέλη ἐπισκιάζουσα
they became. And there came a cloud overshadowing

αὐτοῖς, καὶ ἐγένετο φωνὴ ἐκ τῆς νεφέλης·
them,   and there came a voice out of the cloud:

οὗτός ἐστιν ὁ υἱός μου ὁ ἀγαπητός,
This is the Son of me the beloved,

ἀκούετε αὐτοῦ. 8 καὶ ἐξάπινα περιβλεψάμενοι
hear ye him.   And suddenly looking round

οὐκέτι οὐδένα εἶδον εἰ μὴ τὸν Ἰησοῦν
no longer no(any)one they saw except - Jesus

μόνον μεθ' ἑαυτῶν. 9 Καὶ καταβαινόντων
only with themselves. And coming down
                              = as they came down

αὐτῶν ἐκ τοῦ ὄρους διεστείλατο αὐτοῖς
them⁴ out of the mountain he ordered them

ἵνα μηδενὶ ἃ εἶδον διηγήσωνται,
that to no one [the] things which they saw they should relate,

εἰ μὴ ὅταν ὁ υἱὸς τοῦ ἀνθρώπου ἐκ νεκρῶν
except when the Son - of man out of [the] dead

ἀναστῇ. 10 καὶ τὸν λόγον ἐκράτησαν πρὸς
should rise. And the word they held to

ἑαυτοὺς συζητοῦντες τί ἐστιν τὸ ἐκ
themselves debating what is the "out of

νεκρῶν ἀναστῆναι. 11 Καὶ ἐπηρώτων αὐτὸν
[the] dead to rise."   And they questioned him

λέγοντες· ὅτι λέγουσιν οἱ γραμματεῖς ὅτι
saying: Why say   the scribes that

Ἡλίαν δεῖ ἐλθεῖν πρῶτον; 12 ὁ δὲ ἔφη
Elias it behoves to come first?   And he said

αὐτοῖς· Ἡλίας μὲν ἐλθὼν πρῶτον
to them: Elias indeed coming first

ἀποκαθιστάνει πάντα· καὶ πῶς γέγραπται
will restore all things; and how has it been written

ἐπὶ τὸν υἱὸν τοῦ ἀνθρώπου, ἵνα πολλὰ
on(concerning) the Son - of man, that many things

πάθῃ καὶ ἐξουδενηθῇ; 13 ἀλλὰ λέγω ὑμῖν
he should suffer and be set at naught? But I tell you

ὅτι καὶ Ἡλίας ἐλήλυθεν, καὶ ἐποίησαν
that indeed Elias has come,   and they did

131

King James Version

done unto him whatsoever they listed, as it is written of him.

14 And when he came to *his* disciples, he saw a great multitude about them, and the scribes questioning with them. 15And straightway all the people, when they beheld him, were greatly amazed, and running to *him* saluted him. 16And he asked the scribes, What question ye with them? 17And one of the multitude answered and said, Master, I have brought unto thee my son, which hath a dumb spirit; 18And wheresoever he taketh him, he teareth him; and he foameth, and gnasheth with his teeth, and pineth away: and I spake to thy disciples that they should cast him out; and they could not. 19 He answereth him, and saith, O faithless generation, how long shall I be with you? how long shall I suffer you? bring him unto me. 20And they brought him unto him: and when he saw him, straightway the spirit tare him; and he fell on the ground, and wallowed foaming. 21And he asked his father, How long is it ago since this came unto him? And he said, Of a child. 22And ofttimes it hath cast him into the fire, and into the waters, to destroy him: but if thou canst do any thing, have compassion on us, and help us. 23 Jesus said unto him, If thou canst believe, all things *are* possible to him that believeth. 24And straightway the father of the child cried out, and said with tears, Lord, I believe; help thou mine unbelief. 25 When Jesus saw that the people came running together, he rebuked the foul spirit, saying unto him, *Thou* dumb and deaf spirit, I charge thee, come out of him, and enter no more into him. 26And *the spirit* cried, and rent him sore, and came out of him: and he was as one dead; insomuch that many said, He is dead. 27 But Jesus took him by the hand, and lifted him up; and he arose. 28And when he was come into the house, his disciples asked him privately, Why could not we cast him out? 29And he said unto them, This kind can come forth by nothing, but by prayer and fasting.

30 And they departed thence, and passed through Galilee; and he would not that any man should know *it*. 31 For he taught his disciples, and said unto them, The Son of man is delivered into the hands of men, and they shall kill him; and after that he is killed, he shall rise the third day. 32 But they understood not that saying, and were afraid to ask him.

33 And he came to Capernaum: and being in the house he asked them, What was it that ye disputed among yourselves by the way? 34 But they held their peace: for by the way they had disputed among themselves, who *should be* the greatest. 35And he sat down, and called the twelve, and saith unto them, If any man desire to be first, *the same* shall be last of all, and servant of all. 36And he took a child, and set him in the midst of them: and when he had taken

New International Version

and they have done to him everything they wished, just as it is written about him."

The healing of a boy with an evil spirit

14 When they came to the other disciples, they saw a large crowd around them and the teachers of the law arguing with them. 15As soon as all the people saw Jesus, they were overwhelmed with wonder and ran to greet him.

16 "What are you arguing with them about?" he asked.

17 A man in the crowd answered, "Teacher, I brought you my son, who is possessed by a spirit that has robbed him of speech. 18 Whenever it seizes him, it throws him to the ground. He foams at the mouth, grinds his teeth and becomes rigid. I asked your disciples to drive out the spirit, but they could not."

19 "O unbelieving generation," Jesus replied, "how long shall I stay with you? How long shall I put up with you? Bring the boy to me."

20 So they brought him. When the spirit saw Jesus, it immediately threw the boy into a convulsion. He fell to the ground and rolled around, foaming at the mouth.

21 Jesus asked the boy's father, "How long has he been like this?"

"From childhood," he answered. 22 "It has often thrown him into fire or water to kill him. But if you can do anything, take pity on us and help us."

23 "What do you mean, 'If you can'?" said Jesus. "Everything is possible for him who believes."

24 Immediately the boy's father exclaimed, "I do believe; help me overcome my unbelief!"

25 When Jesus saw that a crowd was running to the scene, he rebuked the evil *f* spirit. "You deaf and dumb spirit," he said, "I command you, come out of him and never enter him again."

26 The spirit shrieked, convulsed him violently and came out. The boy looked so much like a corpse that many said, "He's dead." 27 But Jesus took him by the hand and lifted him to his feet, and he stood up.

28 After Jesus had gone indoors, his disciples asked him privately, "Why couldn't we drive it out?"

29 He replied, "This kind can come out only by prayer." *g*

30 They left that place and passed through Galilee. Jesus did not want anyone to know where they were, 31 because he was teaching his disciples. He said to them, "The Son of Man is going to be betrayed into the hands of men. They will kill him, and after three days he will rise." 32 But they did not understand what he meant and were afraid to ask him about it.

Who is the greatest?

33 They came to Capernaum. When he was in the house, he asked them, "What were you arguing about on the road?" 34 But they kept quiet because on the way they had argued about who was the greatest.

35 Sitting down, Jesus called the Twelve and said, "If anyone wants to be first, he must be the very last, and the servant of all."

36 He took a little child and had him stand among them. Taking him in his arms, he said

[f] Greek unclean. [g] Some MSS add and fasting.

Greek Interlinear

αὐτῷ   ὅσα   ἤθελον,   καθὼς   γέγραπται
to him   what   they wished,   as   it has been written
ἐπ᾽   αὐτόν.
on(concerning) him.

14 Καὶ   ἐλθόντες   πρὸς   τοὺς   μαθητὰς
   And   coming   to   the   disciples
εἶδον   ὄχλον   πολὺν   περὶ   αὐτοὺς   καὶ
they saw   crowd   a much(great) around   them   and
γραμματεῖς   συζητοῦντας   πρὸς   αὐτούς.
scribes   debating   with   them.

15 καὶ   εὐθὺς   πᾶς   ὁ   ὄχλος   ἰδόντες   αὐτὸν
   And   immediately all   the   crowd   seeing   him
ἐξεθαμβήθησαν,   καὶ   προστρέχοντες   ἠσπάζοντο
were greatly astonished, and   running up to   greeted
αὐτόν.   16 καὶ   ἐπηρώτησεν   αὐτούς·   τί
him.   And   he questioned   them: What
συζητεῖτε   πρὸς   αὐτούς;   17 καὶ   ἀπεκρίθη
are ye debating with   them?   And   answered
αὐτῷ   εἷς   ἐκ   τοῦ   ὄχλου·   διδάσκαλε,
him   one   of   the   crowd: Teacher,
ἤνεγκα   τὸν   υἱόν   μου   πρὸς   σέ,   ἔχοντα
I brought   the   son   of me   to   thee,   having
πνεῦμα   ἄλαλον·   18 καὶ   ὅπου   ἐὰν   αὐτὸν
spirit   a dumb;   and   wherever   him
καταλάβῃ,   ῥήσσει   αὐτόν,   καὶ   ἀφρίζει   καὶ
it seizes,   it tears   him,   and   he foams   and
τρίζει   τοὺς   ὀδόντας   καὶ   ξηραίνεται·   καὶ
grinds   the(his) teeth   and   he wastes away;   and
εἶπα   τοῖς   μαθηταῖς   σου   ἵνα   αὐτὸ
I told   the   disciples   of thee   that   it
ἐκβάλωσιν,   καὶ   οὐκ   ἴσχυσαν.   19 ὁ   δὲ
they might expel, and   they were not able.   And he
ἀποκριθεὶς   αὐτοῖς   λέγει·   ὦ   γενεὰ   ἄπιστος,
answering   them   says: O   generation unbelieving,
ἕως   πότε   πρὸς   ὑμᾶς   ἔσομαι;   ἕως   πότε
until   when   with   you   shall I be?   how long
= how long
ἀνέξομαι   ὑμῶν;   φέρετε   αὐτὸν   πρός   με.
shall I endure you?   bring   him   to   me.

20 καὶ   ἤνεγκαν   αὐτὸν   πρὸς   αὐτόν.   καὶ
   And   they brought   him   to   him.   And
ἰδὼν   αὐτὸν   τὸ   πνεῦμα   εὐθὺς   συνεσπάραξεν
seeing   him   the   spirit   immediately violently threw
αὐτόν,   καὶ   πεσὼν   ἐπὶ   τῆς   γῆς   ἐκυλίετο
him,   and   falling   on   the   earth   he wallowed
ἀφρίζων.   21 καὶ   ἐπηρώτησεν   τὸν   πατέρα
foaming.   And   he questioned   the   father
αὐτοῦ·   πόσος   χρόνος   ἐστὶν   ὡς   τοῦτο
of him: What   time   is it   while   this
γέγονεν   αὐτῷ;   ὁ   δὲ   εἶπεν·   ἐκ   παιδιόθεν·
has happened to him? And he said: From childhood;
22 καὶ   πολλάκις   καὶ   εἰς   πῦρ   αὐτὸν
   and   often   both   into   fire   him
ἔβαλεν   καὶ   εἰς   ὕδατα   ἵνα   ἀπολέσῃ   αὐτόν·   ἀλλ᾽
it threw   and   into   waters   that   it may destroy   him;   but
εἴ   τι   δύνῃ,   βοήθησον   ἡμῖν   σπλαγχνισθεὶς
if anything thou canst, help   us   having compassion
ἐφ᾽   ἡμᾶς.   23 ὁ   δὲ   Ἰησοῦς   εἶπεν   αὐτῷ·   τὸ   εἰ
on   us.   And Jesus   said   to him: The " if
δύνῃ,   πάντα   δυνατὰ   τῷ   πιστεύοντι.
thou canst," all things possible to the [one] believing.
24 εὐθὺς   κράξας   ὁ   πατὴρ   τοῦ   παιδίου
   Immediately crying out the   father   of the   child
ἔλεγεν·   πιστεύω·   βοήθει   μου   τῇ   ἀπιστίᾳ.
said: I believe;   help thou   of me   the   unbelief.
25 ἰδὼν   δὲ   ὁ   Ἰησοῦς   ὅτι   ἐπισυντρέχει
   And ²seeing -   ¹Jesus   that is(was) running together
ὄχλος,   ἐπετίμησεν   τῷ   πνεύματι   τῷ   ἀκαθάρτῳ
a crowd, rebuked   the   spirit   -   unclean

λέγων   αὐτῷ·   τὸ   ἄλαλον   καὶ   κωφὸν
saying   to it: -   Dumb   and   deaf
πνεῦμα,   ἐγὼ   ἐπιτάσσω   σοι,   ἔξελθε   ἐξ
spirit,   I   command   thee,   come forth out of
αὐτοῦ   καὶ   μηκέτι   εἰσέλθῃς   εἰς   αὐτόν.
him   and   no more mayest thou enter into   him.
26 καὶ   κράξας   καὶ   πολλὰ   σπαράξας
   And   crying out and   much convulsing [him]
ἐξῆλθεν·   καὶ   ἐγένετο   ὡσεὶ   νεκρός,   ὥστε
it came out; and   he was   as   dead,   so as
τοὺς   πολλοὺς   λέγειν   ὅτι   ἀπέθανεν.   27 ὁ
-   many   to sayᵇ   that   he died.   -
= many said
δὲ   Ἰησοῦς   κρατήσας   τῆς   χειρὸς   αὐτοῦ
But   Jesus   taking hold of the   hand   of him
ἤγειρεν   αὐτόν,   καὶ   ἀνέστη.   28 καὶ
raised   him,   and   he stood up.   And
εἰσελθόντος   αὐτοῦ   εἰς   οἶκον   οἱ   μαθηταὶ
entering   himᵃ   into   a house   the   disciples
= when he entered
αὐτοῦ   κατ᾽   ἰδίαν   ἐπηρώτων   αὐτόν·   ὅτι
of him   privately   questioned   him: Why
ἡμεῖς   οὐκ   ἠδυνήθημεν   ἐκβαλεῖν   αὐτό;
we   were not able   to expel   it?
29 καὶ   εἶπεν   αὐτοῖς·   τοῦτο   τὸ   γένος   ἐν
   And   he told   them: This   -   kind   by
οὐδενὶ   δύναται   ἐξελθεῖν   εἰ   μὴ   ἐν   προσευχῇ.
nothing   can   to come out except   by   prayer.
30 Κἀκεῖθεν   ἐξελθόντες   παρεπορεύοντο   διὰ
   And thence   going forth   they passed   through
τῆς   Γαλιλαίας,   καὶ   οὐκ   ἤθελεν   ἵνα
-   Galilee,   and   he wished not   that
τις   γνοῖ·   31 ἐδίδασκεν   γὰρ   τοὺς   μαθητὰς
anyone should know; for he was teaching the   disciples
αὐτοῦ,   καὶ   ἔλεγεν   αὐτοῖς   ὅτι   ὁ   υἱὸς   τοῦ
of him,   and   he said   to them   that[,]   -   The Son -
ἀνθρώπου   παραδίδοται   εἰς   χεῖρας   ἀνθρώπων,
of man   is betrayed   into [the] hands   of men,
καὶ   ἀποκτενοῦσιν   αὐτόν,   καὶ   ἀποκτανθεὶς
and   they will kill   him,   and   being killed
μετὰ   τρεῖς   ἡμέρας   ἀναστήσεται.   32 οἱ
after   three   days   he will rise up.   they
δὲ   ἠγνόουν   τὸ   ῥῆμα,   καὶ   ἐφοβοῦντο
But   did not know the   word,   and   feared
αὐτὸν   ἐπερωτῆσαι.
him   to question.
33 Καὶ   ἦλθον   εἰς   Καφαρναούμ.   Καὶ
   And   they came   to   Capernaum.   And
ἐν   τῇ   οἰκίᾳ   γενόμενος   ἐπηρώτα   αὐτούς·
in   the   house   being   he questioned   them:
τί   ἐν   τῇ   ὁδῷ   διελογίζεσθε;   34 οἱ   δὲ
What in   the   way   were ye debating?   And they
ἐσιώπων·   πρὸς   ἀλλήλους   γὰρ   διελέχθησαν
were silent; ᵇwith   ᶜone another   ᵃfor   they debated
ἐν   τῇ   ὁδῷ   τίς   μείζων.   35 καὶ   καθίσας
in   the   way   who [was] greater.   And   sitting
ἐφώνησεν   τοὺς   δώδεκα   καὶ   λέγει   αὐτοῖς·
he called   the   twelve   and   says   to them:
εἴ   τις   θέλει   πρῶτος   εἶναι,   ἔσται   πάντων
If anyone wishes   first   to be, he shall be   of all
ἔσχατος   καὶ   πάντων   διάκονος.   36 καὶ
last   and   of all   servant.   And
λαβὼν   παιδίον   ἔστησεν   αὐτὸ   ἐν   μέσῳ
taking   a child   he set   it(him)   in [the] midst
αὐτῶν,   καὶ   ἐναγκαλισάμενος   αὐτὸ   εἶπεν
of them,   and   folding in [his] arms   it   he said

King James Version

him in his arms, he said unto them, 37 Whosoever shall receive one of such children in my name, receiveth me; and whosoever shall receive me, receiveth not me, but him that sent me.

38 And John answered him, saying, Master, we saw one casting out devils in thy name, and he followeth not us; and we forbade him, because he followeth not us. 39 But Jesus said, Forbid him not: for there is no man which shall do a miracle in my name, that can lightly speak evil of me. 40 For he that is not against us is on our part. 41 For whosoever shall give you a cup of water to drink in my name, because ye belong to Christ, verily I say unto you, he shall not lose his reward. 42And whosoever shall offend one of *these* little ones that believe in me, it is better for him that a millstone were hanged about his neck, and he were cast into the sea. 43And if thy hand offend thee, cut it off: it is better for thee to enter into life maimed, than having two hands to go into hell, into the fire that never shall be quenched: 44 Where their worm dieth not, and the fire is not quenched. 45And if thy foot offend thee, cut it off: it is better for thee to enter halt into life, than having two feet to be cast into hell, into the fire that never shall be quenched: 46 Where their worm dieth not, and the fire is not quenched. 47And if thine eye offend thee, pluck it out: it is better for thee to enter into the kingdom of God with one eye, than having two eyes to be cast into hell fire: 48 Where their worm dieth not, and the fire is not quenched. 49 For every one shall be salted with fire, and every sacrifice shall be salted with salt. 50 Salt *is* good: but if the salt have lost his saltness, wherewith will ye season it? Have salt in yourselves, and have peace one with another.

10 And he arose from thence, and cometh into the coasts of Judea by the farther side of Jordan: and the people resort unto him again; and, as he was wont, he taught them again.

2 And the Pharisees came to him, and asked him, Is it lawful for a man to put away *his* wife? tempting him. 3And he answered and said unto them, What did Moses command you? 4And they said, Moses suffered to write a bill of divorcement, and to put *her* away. 5And Jesus answered and said unto them, For the hardness of your heart he wrote you this precept. 6 But from the beginning of the creation God made them male and female. 7 For this cause shall a man leave his father and mother, and cleave to his wife; 8And they twain shall be one flesh: so then they are no more twain, but one flesh. 9 What therefore God hath joined together, let not man put asunder. 10And in the house his disciples asked him again of the same *matter.* 11And he saith unto them, Whosoever shall put away his

New International Version

to them, 37 "Whoever welcomes one of these little children in my name welcomes me; and whoever welcomes me does not welcome me but the one who sent me."

Whoever is not against us is for us

38 "Teacher," said John, "we saw a man driving out demons in your name and we told him to stop, because he was not one of us."

39 "Do not stop him," Jesus said. "No one who does a miracle in my name can in the next moment say anything bad about me, 40 for whoever is not against us is for us. 41 I tell you the truth, anyone who gives you a cup of water in my name because you belong to Christ will certainly not lose his reward.

Causing to sin

42 "And if anyone causes one of these little ones who believe in me to sin, it would be better for him to be thrown into the sea with a large millstone tied around his neck. 43 If your hand causes you to sin, cut it off. It is better for you to enter life maimed than with two hands to go into hell, where the fire never goes out.[h] 45And if your foot causes you to sin, cut it off. It is better for you to enter life crippled, than to have two feet and be thrown into hell.[i] 47And if your eye causes you to sin, pluck it out. It is better for you to enter the kingdom of God with one eye, than to have two eyes and be thrown into hell, 48 where

'their worm does not die,
   and the fire is not put out.'[j]

49 Everyone will be salted with fire.

50 "Salt is good, but if it loses its saltiness, how can you make it salty again? Have salt in yourselves, and be at peace with each other."

Divorce

10 Jesus then left that place and went into the region of Judea and across the Jordan. Again crowds of people came to him, and as was his custom, he taught them.

2 Some Pharisees came and tested him by asking, "Is it lawful for a man to divorce his wife?"

3 "What did Moses command you?" he replied.

4 They said, "Moses permitted a man to write a certificate of divorce and send her away."

5 "It was because your hearts were hard that Moses wrote you this law," Jesus replied. 6 "But at the beginning of creation, God 'made them male and female.'[k] 7 'For this reason a man will leave his father and mother and be united to his wife,[l] 8 and the two will become one flesh.'[m] So they are no longer two, but one. 9 Therefore what God has joined together, let man not separate."

10 When they were in the house again, the disciples asked Jesus about this. 11 He answered, "Anyone who divorces his wife and marries

---

[h] Some MSS add verse 44, which reads the same as verse 48. [i] Some MSS add verse 46, which reads the same as verse 48. [j] Isaiah 66:24. [k] Gen. 1:27. [l] Some early MSS omit *and be united to his wife.* [m] Gen. 2:24.

Greek Interlinear

αὐτοῖς· 37 ὃς ἂν ἓν τῶν τοιούτων παιδίων
to them: Whoever one - of such   children

δέξηται ἐπὶ τῷ ὀνόματί μου, ἐμὲ δέχεται·
receives on(in) the name   of me, me receives;

καὶ ὃς ἂν ἐμὲ δέχηται, οὐχ ἐμὲ δέχεται
and whoever me   receives, not me   receives

ἀλλὰ τὸν ἀποστείλαντά με. 38 Ἔφη αὐτῷ
but the [one] having sent   me.   Said to him

ὁ Ἰωάννης· διδάσκαλε, εἴδομέν τινα ἐν
- John: Teacher,   we saw someone in

τῷ ὀνόματί σου ἐκβάλλοντα δαιμόνια, ὃς
the name   of thee expelling   demons,   who

οὐκ ἀκολουθεῖ ἡμῖν, καὶ ἐκωλύομεν αὐτόν,
does not follow us,   and we forbade   him,

ὅτι οὐκ ἠκολούθει ἡμῖν. 39 ὁ δὲ Ἰησοῦς
because he was not following us. - But Jesus

εἶπεν· μὴ κωλύετε αὐτόν· οὐδεὶς γὰρ
said: Do not forbid   him: for no one

ἔστιν ὃς ποιήσει δύναμιν ἐπὶ τῷ ὀνόματί
there is who shall do a mighty work on(in) the name

μου καὶ δυνήσεται ταχὺ κακολογῆσαί με·
of me and will be able quickly to speak evil of me;

40 ὃς γὰρ οὐκ ἔστιν καθ᾽ ἡμῶν, ὑπὲρ
for who is not against us,   for

ἡμῶν ἐστιν. 41 Ὃς γὰρ ἂν ποτίσῃ
us   is.   For whoever ¹gives ²drink

ὑμᾶς ποτήριον ὕδατος ἐν ὀνόματι, ὅτι
²you   a cup   of water in [the] name, because

Χριστοῦ ἐστε, ἀμὴν λέγω ὑμῖν ὅτι
of Christ ye are, truly I tell you   that

οὐ μὴ ἀπολέσῃ τὸν μισθὸν αὐτοῦ. 42 Καὶ
by no means he will lose the reward of him.   And

ὃς ἂν σκανδαλίσῃ ἕνα τῶν μικρῶν τούτων
whoever offends   one - ³little [ones] ¹of these

τῶν πιστευόντων, καλόν ἐστιν αὐτῷ μᾶλλον
-   ²believing,   good is it for him rather

εἰ περίκειται μύλος ὀνικὸς περὶ τὸν
if be laid round a [heavy] millstone round the

τράχηλον αὐτοῦ καὶ βέβληται εἰς τὴν
neck   of him and he be thrown into the

θάλασσαν. 43 Καὶ ἐὰν σκανδαλίσῃ σε ἡ
sea.   And if   offends   thee the

χείρ σου, ἀπόκοψον αὐτήν· καλόν ἐστίν
hand of thee, cut off   it;   good   is it

σε κυλλὸν εἰσελθεῖν εἰς τὴν ζωήν, ἢ τὰς
thee maimed to enter into - life, than the

δύο χεῖρας ἔχοντα ἀπελθεῖν εἰς τὴν
two hands having to go away into -

γέενναν, εἰς τὸ πῦρ τὸ ἄσβεστον.‡ 45 καὶ
gehenna, into the fire the unquenchable.   And

ἐὰν ὁ πούς σου σκανδαλίζῃ σε, ἀπόκοψον
if the foot of thee offends   thee,   cut off

αὐτόν· καλόν ἐστίν σε εἰσελθεῖν εἰς τὴν
it;   good is it thee to enter into -

ζωὴν χωλόν, ἢ τοὺς δύο πόδας ἔχοντα
life lame, than the two feet having

βληθῆναι εἰς τὴν γέενναν.✶ 47 καὶ ἐὰν ὁ
to be cast into - gehenna.   And if the

ὀφθαλμός σου σκανδαλίζῃ σε, ἔκβαλε αὐτόν·
eye   of thee offends   thee, cast out it;

καλόν σέ ἐστιν μονόφθαλμον εἰσελθεῖν εἰς
good thee is it   one-eyed   to enter into

τὴν βασιλείαν τοῦ θεοῦ, ἢ δύο ὀφθαλμοὺς
the kingdom   - of God, than two   eyes

ἔχοντα βληθῆναι εἰς τὴν γέενναν, 48 ὅπου
having to be cast into - gehenna,   where

ὁ σκώληξ αὐτῶν οὐ τελευτᾷ καὶ τὸ
the worm of them dies not and the

πῦρ οὐ σβέννυται. 49 Πᾶς γὰρ πυρὶ
fire is not quenched.   For everyone with fire

ἁλισθήσεται. 50 καλὸν τὸ ἅλας· ἐὰν δὲ
shall be salted.   Good [is] - salt;   but if

τὸ ἅλας ἄναλον γένηται, ἐν τίνι αὐτὸ
- salt saltless becomes, by what it

ἀρτύσετε; ἔχετε ἐν ἑαυτοῖς ἅλα καὶ
will ye season? Have in yourselves salt and

εἰρηνεύετε ἐν ἀλλήλοις.
be at peace among one another.

Chapter 10

Καὶ ἐκεῖθεν ἀναστὰς ἔρχεται εἰς τὰ
And thence rising up he comes into the

ὅρια τῆς Ἰουδαίας καὶ πέραν τοῦ
territory - of Judæa and beyond the

Ἰορδάνου, καὶ συμπορεύονται πάλιν ὄχλοι
Jordan,   and   ²go with   ¹again ²crowds

πρὸς αὐτόν, καὶ ὡς εἰώθει πάλιν ἐδίδασκεν
⁴with ³him, and as he was wont again he taught

αὐτούς. 2 Καὶ προσελθόντες Φαρισαῖοι
them.   And   ²approaching   ¹Pharisees

ἐπηρώτων αὐτὸν εἰ ἔξεστιν ἀνδρὶ γυναῖκα
questioned him if it is(was) lawful for a man a wife

ἀπολῦσαι, πειράζοντες αὐτόν. 3 ὁ δὲ
to dismiss,   testing   him.   And he

ἀποκριθεὶς εἶπεν αὐτοῖς· 4 τί ὑμῖν ἐνετείλατο
answering   said to them: What you   ordered

Μωϋσῆς; οἱ δὲ εἶπαν· ἐπέτρεψεν Μωϋσῆς
Moses? And they said: permitted   Moses

βιβλίον ἀποστασίου γράψαι καὶ ἀπολῦσαι.
a roll   of divorce to write and to dismiss.

5 ὁ δὲ Ἰησοῦς εἶπεν αὐτοῖς· πρὸς τὴν
- And Jesus   said to them: For the

σκληροκαρδίαν ὑμῶν ἔγραψεν ὑμῖν τὴν
hardheartedness of you he wrote to you -

ἐντολὴν ταύτην. 6 ἀπὸ δὲ ἀρχῆς κτίσεως
this commandment.   But from [the] beginning of creation

ἄρσεν καὶ θῆλυ ἐποίησεν αὐτούς· 7 ἕνεκεν
male and female he made   them; for the sake of

τούτου καταλείψει ἄνθρωπος τὸν πατέρα
this   shall leave   a man   the father

αὐτοῦ καὶ τὴν μητέρα, 8 καὶ ἔσονται
of him and the mother,   and shall be

οἱ δύο εἰς σάρκα μίαν· ὥστε οὐκέτι
the two - flesh   one; so as no longer

εἰσὶν δύο ἀλλὰ μία σάρξ. 9 ὃ οὖν ὁ
are they two but one flesh. What then -

θεὸς συνέζευξεν, ἄνθρωπος μὴ χωριζέτω.
God yoked together, ¹man   ²not ³let ⁴separate.

10 καὶ εἰς τὴν οἰκίαν πάλιν οἱ μαθηταὶ
And in   the house   again the disciples

περὶ τούτου ἐπηρώτων αὐτόν. 11 καὶ
about this   questioned   him.   And

λέγει αὐτοῖς· ὃς ἂν ἀπολύσῃ τὴν γυναῖκα
he says to them: Whoever dismisses the   wife

---

‡ Verse 44 omitted by Nestle
✶ Verse 46 omitted by Nestle

King James Version

wife, and marry another, committeth adultery against her. 12And if a woman shall put away her husband, and be married to another, she committeth adultery.

13 And they brought young children to him, that he should touch them; and *his* disciples rebuked those that brought *them*. 14 But when Jesus saw *it*, he was much displeased, and said unto them, Suffer the little children to come unto me, and forbid them not; for of such is the kingdom of God. 15 Verily I say unto you, Whosoever shall not receive the kingdom of God as a little child, he shall not enter therein. 16And he took them up in his arms, put *his* hands upon them, and blessed them.

17 And when he was gone forth into the way, there came one running, and kneeled to him, and asked him, Good Master, what shall I do that I may inherit eternal life? 18And Jesus said unto him, Why callest thou me good? *there is* none good but one, *that is*, God. 19 Thou knowest the commandments, Do not commit adultery, Do not kill, Do not steal, Do not bear false witness, Defraud not, Honour thy father and mother. 20And he answered and said unto him, Master, all these have I observed from my youth. 21 Then Jesus beholding him loved him, and said unto him, One thing thou lackest: go thy way, sell whatsoever thou hast, and give to the poor, and thou shalt have treasure in heaven: and come, take up the cross, and follow me. 22And he was sad at that saying, and went away grieved: for he had great possessions.

23 And Jesus looked round about, and saith unto his disciples, How hardly shall they that have riches enter into the kingdom of God! 24And the disciples were astonished at his words. But Jesus answereth again, and saith unto them, Children, how hard is it for them that trust in riches to enter into the kingdom of God! 25 It is easier for a camel to go through the eye of a needle, than for a rich man to enter into the kingdom of God. 26And they were astonished out of measure, saying among themselves, Who then can be saved? 27And Jesus looking upon them saith, With men *it is* impossible, but not with God: for with God all things are possible.

28 Then Peter began to say unto him, Lo, we have left all, and have followed thee. 29And Jesus answered and said, Verily I say unto you, There is no man that hath left house, or brethren, or sisters, or father, or mother, or wife, or children, or lands, for my sake, and the gospel's, 30 But he shall receive a hundredfold now in this time, houses, and brethren, and sisters, and mothers, and children, and lands, with persecutions; and in the world to come eternal life. 31 But many *that are* first shall be last; and the last first.

32 And they were in the way going up to Jerusalem; and Jesus went before them: and they were amazed; and as they followed, they were afraid. And he took again the twelve, and began to tell them what things should happen unto him, 33 *Saying*, Behold, we go up to Jerusalem;

New International Version

another woman commits adultery against her. 12And if she divorces her husband and marries another man, she commits adultery."

The little children and Jesus

13 People were bringing little children to Jesus to have him touch them, but the disciples rebuked them. 14 When Jesus saw this, he was indignant. He said to them, "Let the little children come to me, and do not hinder them, for the kingdom of God belongs to such as these. 15 I tell you the truth, anyone who will not receive the kingdom of God like a little child will never enter it." 16And he took the children in his arms, put his hands on them and blessed them.

The rich young man

17 As Jesus started on his way, a man ran up to him and fell on his knees before him. "Good teacher," he asked, "what must I do to inherit eternal life?"

18 "Why do you call me good?" Jesus answered. "No one is good—except God alone. 19 You know the commandments: 'Do not murder, do not commit adultery, do not steal, do not give false testimony, do not defraud, honor your father and mother.'[n]"

20 "Teacher," he declared, "all these I have kept since I was a boy."

21 Jesus looked at him and loved him. "One thing you lack," he said. "Go, sell everything you have and give to the poor, and you will have treasure in heaven. Then come, follow me."

22 At this the man's face fell. He went away sad, because he had great wealth.

23 Jesus looked around and said to his disciples, "How hard it is for the rich to enter the kingdom of God!"

24 The disciples were amazed at his words. But Jesus said again, "Children, how hard it is[o] to enter the kingdom of God! 25 It is easier for a camel to go through the eye of a needle than for a rich man to enter the kingdom of God."

26 The disciples were even more amazed, and said to each other, "Who then can be saved?"

27 Jesus looked at them and said, "With man this is impossible, but not with God; all things are possible with God."

28 Peter said to him, "We have left everything to follow you!"

29 "I tell you the truth," Jesus replied, "no one who has left home or brothers or sisters or mother or father or children or fields for me and the gospel 30 will fail to receive a hundred times as much in this present age (homes, brothers, sisters, mothers, children and fields—and with them, persecutions) and in the age to come, eternal life. 31 But many who are first will be last, and the last first."

Jesus again predicts his death

32 They were on their way up to Jerusalem, with Jesus leading the way, and the disciples were astonished, while those who followed were afraid. Again he took the Twelve aside and told them what was going to happen to him. 33 "We are going up to Jerusalem," he said, "and the

[n] Exodus 20:12-16; Deut. 5:16-20. [o] Some MSS add *for those who trust in riches.*

136

Greek Interlinear

αὐτοῦ καὶ γαμήσῃ ἄλλην, μοιχᾶται ἐπ'
of him and marries another, commits adultery with

αὐτήν· 12 καὶ ἐὰν αὐτὴ ἀπολύσασα τὸν
her; and if she having dismissed the

ἄνδρα αὐτῆς γαμήσῃ ἄλλον, μοιχᾶται.
husband of her marries another, she commits adultery.

13 Καὶ προσέφερον αὐτῷ παιδία ἵνα
And they brought to him children that

αὐτῶν ἅψηται· οἱ δὲ μαθηταὶ ἐπετίμησαν
them he might touch; but the disciples rebuked

αὐτοῖς. 14 ἰδὼν δὲ ὁ Ἰησοῦς ἠγανάκτησεν
them. But ²seeing - ¹Jesus was angry

καὶ εἶπεν αὐτοῖς· ἄφετε τὰ παιδία
and said to them: Allow the children

ἔρχεσθαι πρός με, μὴ κωλύετε αὐτά·
to come to me, do not prevent them;

τῶν γὰρ τοιούτων ἐστὶν ἡ βασιλεία τοῦ
- for of such is the kingdom -

θεοῦ. 15 ἀμὴν λέγω ὑμῖν, ὃς ἂν
of God. Truly I tell you, whoever

μὴ δέξηται τὴν βασιλείαν τοῦ θεοῦ ὡς
receives not the kingdom - of God as

παιδίον, οὐ μὴ εἰσέλθῃ εἰς αὐτήν. 16 καὶ
a child, by no means may enter into it. And

ἐναγκαλισάμενος αὐτὰ κατευλόγει τιθεὶς τὰς
folding in [his] arms them he blesses putting the(his)

χεῖρας ἐπ' αὐτά.
hands on them.

17 Καὶ ἐκπορευομένου αὐτοῦ εἰς ὁδὸν
And going forth him* into [the] way
= as he went forth

προσδραμὼν εἷς καὶ γονυπετήσας αὐτὸν
running to one and kneeling to him

ἐπηρώτα αὐτόν· διδάσκαλε ἀγαθέ, τί ποιήσω
questioned him: Teacher good, what may I do

ἵνα ζωὴν αἰώνιον κληρονομήσω; 18 ὁ δὲ
that life eternal I may inherit ? - And

Ἰησοῦς εἶπεν αὐτῷ· τί με λέγεις ἀγαθόν;
Jesus said to him: Why me callest thou good ?

οὐδεὶς ἀγαθὸς εἰ μὴ εἷς ὁ θεός. 19 τὰς ἐντολὰς
no one good except one - God. The commandments

οἶδας· μὴ φονεύσῃς, μὴ μοιχεύσῃς,
thou knowest: Do not kill, Do not commit adultery,

μὴ κλέψῃς, μὴ ψευδομαρτυρήσῃς, μὴ
Do not steal, Do not bear false witness, Do

ἀποστερήσῃς, τίμα τὸν πατέρα σου καὶ
not defraud, Honour the father of thee and

τὴν μητέρα. 20 ὁ δὲ ἔφη αὐτῷ· διδάσκαλε,
the mother. And he said to him: Teacher,

ταῦτα πάντα ἐφυλαξάμην ἐκ νεότητός μου.
all these things I observed from youth of me.

21 ὁ δὲ Ἰησοῦς ἐμβλέψας αὐτῷ ἠγάπησεν
- But Jesus looking at him loved

αὐτὸν καὶ εἶπεν αὐτῷ· ἕν σε ὑστερεῖ·
him and said to him: One thing thee is wanting:

ὕπαγε, ὅσα ἔχεις πώλησον καὶ δὸς [τοῖς]
go, what things thou hast sell and give to the

πτωχοῖς, καὶ ἕξεις θησαυρὸν ἐν οὐρανῷ,
poor, and thou wilt have treasure in heaven,

καὶ δεῦρο ἀκολούθει μοι. 22 ὁ δὲ στυγνάσας
and come follow me. But he being sad

ἐπὶ τῷ λόγῳ ἀπῆλθεν λυπούμενος, ἦν
at the word went away grieving, ²he was

γὰρ ἔχων κτήματα πολλά. 23 Καὶ
¹for having possessions many. And

περιβλεψάμενος ὁ Ἰησοῦς λέγει τοῖς
looking round - Jesus says to the

μαθηταῖς αὐτοῦ· πῶς δυσκόλως οἱ τὰ
disciples of him: How hardly the [ones] the

χρήματα ἔχοντες εἰς τὴν βασιλείαν τοῦ
riches having into the kingdom -

θεοῦ εἰσελεύσονται. 24 οἱ δὲ μαθηταὶ
of God shall enter. And the disciples

ἐθαμβοῦντο ἐπὶ τοῖς λόγοις αὐτοῦ. ὁ δὲ
were amazed at the words of him. - And

Ἰησοῦς πάλιν ἀποκριθεὶς λέγει αὐτοῖς·
Jesus again answering says to them:

τέκνα, πῶς δύσκολόν ἐστιν εἰς τὴν
Children, how hard it is into the

βασιλείαν τοῦ θεοῦ εἰσελθεῖν· 25 εὐκοπώτερόν
kingdom - of God to enter; easier

ἐστιν κάμηλον διὰ τῆς τρυμαλιᾶς τῆς
it is a camel through the eye

ῥαφίδος διελθεῖν ἢ πλούσιον εἰς τὴν
of a needle to go through than a rich man into the

βασιλείαν τοῦ θεοῦ εἰσελθεῖν. 26 οἱ δὲ
kingdom - of God to enter. But they

περισσῶς ἐξεπλήσσοντο λέγοντες πρὸς
exceedingly were astonished saying to

ἑαυτούς· καὶ τίς δύναται σωθῆναι;
themselves: And who can to be saved ?

27 ἐμβλέψας αὐτοῖς ὁ Ἰησοῦς λέγει· παρὰ
Looking at them - Jesus says: With

ἀνθρώποις ἀδύνατον, ἀλλ' οὐ παρὰ θεῷ·
men [it is] impossible, but not with God;

πάντα γὰρ δυνατὰ παρὰ τῷ θεῷ. 28 Ἤρξατο
for all things [are] possible with - God. Began

λέγειν ὁ Πέτρος αὐτῷ· ἰδοὺ ἡμεῖς ἀφήκαμεν
to say - Peter to him: Behold [,] we left

πάντα καὶ ἠκολουθήκαμέν σοι. 29 ἔφη ὁ
all things and have followed thee. Said -

Ἰησοῦς· ἀμὴν λέγω ὑμῖν, οὐδείς ἐστιν
Jesus: Truly I tell you, no one there is

ὃς ἀφῆκεν οἰκίαν ἢ ἀδελφοὺς ἢ ἀδελφὰς
who left house or brothers or sisters

ἢ μητέρα ἢ πατέρα ἢ τέκνα ἢ ἀγροὺς
or mother or father or children or fields

ἕνεκεν ἐμοῦ καὶ ἕνεκεν τοῦ εὐαγγελίου,
for the sake of me and for the sake of the gospel,

30 ἐὰν μὴ λάβῃ ἑκατονταπλασίονα νῦν
but he receives a hundredfold now

ἐν τῷ καιρῷ τούτῳ οἰκίας καὶ ἀδελφοὺς
in - time this houses and brothers

καὶ ἀδελφὰς καὶ μητέρας καὶ τέκνα καὶ
and sisters and mothers and children and

ἀγροὺς μετὰ διωγμῶν, καὶ ἐν τῷ αἰῶνι
fields with persecutions, and in the age

τῷ ἐρχομένῳ ζωὴν αἰώνιον. 31 πολλοὶ δὲ
- coming life eternal. And ¹many

ἔσονται πρῶτοι ἔσχατοι καὶ οἱ ἔσχατοι
²will be ³first ⁴last and the last

πρῶτοι.
first.

32 Ἦσαν δὲ ἐν τῇ ὁδῷ ἀναβαίνοντες
Now they were in the way going up

εἰς Ἱεροσόλυμα, καὶ ἦν προάγων αὐτοὺς
to Jerusalem, and was going before them

ὁ Ἰησοῦς, καὶ ἐθαμβοῦντο, οἱ δὲ
- Jesus, and they were astonished, and the

ἀκολουθοῦντες ἐφοβοῦντο. καὶ παραλαβὼν
[ones] following were afraid. And taking

πάλιν τοὺς δώδεκα ἤρξατο αὐτοῖς λέγειν
again the twelve he began them to tell

τὰ μέλλοντα αὐτῷ συμβαίνειν, 33 ὅτι ἰδοὺ
the things about to him to happen, - Behold

ἀναβαίνομεν εἰς Ἱεροσόλυμα, καὶ ὁ υἱὸς
we are going up to Jerusalem, and the Son

King James Version

and the Son of man shall be delivered unto the chief priests, and unto the scribes; and they shall condemn him to death, and shall deliver him to the Gentiles: 34And they shall mock him, and shall scourge him, and shall spit upon him, and shall kill him; and the third day he shall rise again.

35 And James and John, the sons of Zebedee, come unto him, saying, Master, we would that thou shouldest do for us whatsoever we shall desire. 36And he said unto them, What would ye that I should do for you? 37 They said unto him, Grant unto us that we may sit, one on thy right hand, and the other on thy left hand, in thy glory. 38 But Jesus said unto them, Ye know not what ye ask: can ye drink of the cup that I drink of? and be baptized with the baptism that I am baptized with? 39And they said unto him, We can. And Jesus said unto them, Ye shall indeed drink of the cup that I drink of; and with the baptism that I am baptized withal shall ye be baptized: 40 But to sit on my right hand and on my left hand is not mine to give; but *it shall be given to them* for whom it is prepared. 41And when the ten heard *it*, they began to be much displeased with James and John. 42 But Jesus called them *to him*, and saith unto them, Ye know that they which are accounted to rule over the Gentiles exercise lordship over them; and their great ones exercise authority upon them. 43 But so shall it not be among you: but whosoever will be great among you, shall be your minister: 44And whosoever of you will be the chiefest, shall be servant of all. 45 For even the Son of man came not to be ministered unto, but to minister, and to give his life a ransom for many.

46 And they came to Jericho: and as he went out of Jericho with his disciples and a great number of people, blind Bartimeus, the son of Timeus, sat by the highway side begging. 47And when he heard that it was Jesus of Nazareth, he began to cry out, and say, Jesus, *thou* Son of David, have mercy on me. 48And many charged him that he should hold his peace: but he cried the more a great deal, *Thou* Son of David, have mercy on me. 49And Jesus stood still, and commanded him to be called. And they call the blind man, saying unto him, Be of good comfort, rise; he calleth thee. 50And he, casting away his garment, rose, and came to Jesus. 51And Jesus answered and said unto him, What wilt thou that I should do unto thee? The blind man said unto him, Lord, that I might receive my sight. 52And Jesus said unto him, Go thy way; thy faith hath made thee whole. And immediately he received his sight, and followed Jesus in the way.

New International Version

Son of Man will be betrayed to the chief priests and teachers of the law. They will condemn him to death and will hand him over to the Gentiles, 34 who will mock him and spit on him, flog him and kill him. Three days later he will rise."

The request of James and John

35 Then James and John, the sons of Zebedee, came to him. "Teacher," they said, "we want you to do for us whatever we ask."

36 "What do you want me to do for you?" he asked.

37 They replied, "Let one of us sit at your right and the other at your left in your glory."

38 "You don't know what you are asking," Jesus said. "Can you drink the cup I drink or be baptized with the baptism I am baptized with?"

39 "We can," they answered.

Jesus said to them, "You will drink the cup I drink and be baptized with the baptism I am baptized with, 40 but to sit at my right or left is not for me to grant. These places belong to those for whom they have been prepared."

41 When the ten heard about this, they became indignant with James and John. 42 Jesus called them together and said, "You know that those who are regarded as rulers of the Gentiles lord it over them, and their high officials exercise authority over them. 43 Not so with you. Instead, whoever wants to become great among you must be your servant, 44 and whoever wants to be first must be slave of all. 45 For even the Son of Man did not come to be served, but to serve, and to give his life a ransom for many."

Blind Bartimaeus receives his sight

46 Then they came to Jericho. As Jesus and his disciples, together with a large crowd, were leaving the city, a blind man, Bartimaeus (that is, the Son of Timaeus), was sitting by the roadside begging. 47 When he heard that it was Jesus of Nazareth, he began to shout, "Jesus, Son of David, have mercy on me!"

48 Many rebuked him and told him to be quiet, but he shouted all the more, "Son of David, have mercy on me!"

49 Jesus stopped and said, "Call him."

So they called to the blind man, "Cheer up! On your feet! He's calling you." 50 Throwing his cloak aside, he jumped to his feet and came to Jesus.

51 "What do you want me to do for you?" Jesus asked him.

The blind man said, "Rabbi, I want to see."

52 "Go," said Jesus, "your faith has healed you." Immediately he received his sight and followed Jesus along the road.

The triumphal entry

11 And when they came nigh to Jerusalem, unto Bethphage and Bethany, at the mount of Olives, he sendeth forth two of his disciples, 2And saith unto them, Go your way into the

11 As they approached Jerusalem and came to Bethphage and Bethany at the Mount of Olives, Jesus sent two of his disciples, 2 saying to them, "Go to the village ahead of you,

Greek Interlinear

τοῦ ἀνθρώπου παραδοθήσεται τοῖς
\- of man will be betrayed to the

ἀρχιερεῦσιν καὶ τοῖς γραμματεῦσιν, καὶ
chief priests and to the scribes, and

κατακρινοῦσιν αὐτὸν θανάτῳ καὶ παραδώσουσιν
they will condemn him to death and will deliver

αὐτὸν τοῖς ἔθνεσιν 34 καὶ ἐμπαίξουσιν
him to the nations and they will mock

αὐτῷ καὶ ἐμπτύσουσιν αὐτῷ καὶ μαστι-
him and will spit at him and will

γώσουσιν αὐτὸν καὶ ἀποκτενοῦσιν, καὶ
scourge him and will kill, and

μετὰ τρεῖς ἡμέρας ἀναστήσεται.
after three days he will rise again.

35 Καὶ προσπορεύονται αὐτῷ Ἰάκωβος
And approach to him James

καὶ Ἰωάννης οἱ [δύο] υἱοὶ Ζεβεδαίου
and John the two sons of Zebedee

λέγοντες αὐτῷ· διδάσκαλε, θέλομεν ἵνα ὃ ἐὰν
saying to him: Teacher, we wish that whatever

αἰτήσωμέν σε ποιήσῃς ἡμῖν. 36 ὁ
we may ask thee thou mayest do for us. he

δὲ εἶπεν αὐτοῖς· τί θέλετέ με ποιήσω
And said to them: What wish ye me I may do

ὑμῖν; 37 οἱ δὲ εἶπαν αὐτῷ· δὸς ἡμῖν
for you? And they said to him: Give us

ἵνα εἷς σου ἐκ δεξιῶν καὶ εἷς ἐξ
that one of thee out of(on) [the] right and one on
= on thy right

ἀριστερῶν καθίσωμεν ἐν τῇ δόξῃ σου.
[thy] left we may sit in the glory of thee.

38 ὁ δὲ Ἰησοῦς εἶπεν αὐτοῖς· οὐκ οἴδατε
\- And Jesus said to them: Ye know not

τί αἰτεῖσθε. δύνασθε πιεῖν τὸ ποτήριον
what ye ask. Can ye to drink the cup

ὃ ἐγὼ πίνω, ἢ τὸ βάπτισμα ὃ ἐγὼ
which I drink, or the baptism which I

βαπτίζομαι βαπτισθῆναι; 39 οἱ δὲ εἶπαν
am baptized to be baptized [with]? And they said

αὐτῷ· δυνάμεθα. ὁ δὲ Ἰησοῦς εἶπεν
to him: We can. \- And Jesus said

αὐτοῖς· τὸ ποτήριον ὃ ἐγὼ πίνω πίεσθε,
to them: The cup which I drink shall ye drink,

καὶ τὸ βάπτισμα ὃ ἐγὼ βαπτίζομαι
and the baptism which I am baptized [with]

βαπτισθήσεσθε· 40 τὸ δὲ καθίσαι ἐκ δεξιῶν
ye shall be baptized; \- but to sit on right

μου ἢ ἐξ εὐωνύμων οὐκ ἔστιν ἐμὸν
of me or on [my] left is not mine

δοῦναι, ἀλλ' οἷς ἡτοίμασται. 41 Καὶ
to give, but for whom it has been prepared. And

ἀκούσαντες οἱ δέκα ἤρξαντο ἀγανακτεῖν
²hearing ¹the ³ten began to be incensed

περὶ Ἰακώβου καὶ Ἰωάννου. 42 Καὶ
about James and John. And

προσκαλεσάμενος αὐτοὺς ὁ Ἰησοῦς λέγει
²calling ¹to ³[him] ²them \- Jesus says

αὐτοῖς· οἴδατε ὅτι οἱ δοκοῦντες ἄρχειν
to them: Ye know that the [ones] thinking to rule

τῶν ἐθνῶν κατακυριεύουσιν αὐτῶν καὶ
the nations lord it over them and

οἱ μεγάλοι αὐτῶν κατεξουσιάζουσιν αὐτῶν.
the great [ones] of them exercise authority over them.

43 οὐχ οὕτως δέ ἐστιν ἐν ὑμῖν· ἀλλ'
²not ³so ¹But is it among you; but

ὃς ἂν θέλῃ μέγας γενέσθαι ἐν ὑμῖν,
whoever wishes great to become among you,

ἔσται ὑμῶν διάκονος, 44 καὶ ὃς ἂν
shall be of you servant, and whoever

θέλῃ ἐν ὑμῖν εἶναι πρῶτος, ἔσται πάντων
wishes among you to be first, shall be of all

δοῦλος· 45 καὶ γὰρ ὁ υἱὸς τοῦ ἀνθρώπου
slave; for even the Son \- of man

οὐκ ἦλθεν διακονηθῆναι ἀλλὰ διακονῆσαι
did not come to be served but to serve

καὶ δοῦναι τὴν ψυχὴν αὐτοῦ λύτρον ἀντὶ
and to give the life of him a ransom instead of

πολλῶν.
many.

46 Καὶ ἔρχονται εἰς Ἰεριχώ. Καὶ
And they come to Jericho. And

ἐκπορευομένου αὐτοῦ ἀπὸ Ἰεριχὼ καὶ τῶν
going out himᵃ from Jericho and the
= as he was going out

μαθητῶν αὐτοῦ καὶ ὄχλου ἱκανοῦ ὁ υἱὸς
disciplesᵃ of him and crowd a considerableᵃ the son

Τιμαίου Βαρτιμαῖος, τυφλὸς προσαίτης,
.of Timæus Bartimæus, a blind beggar,

ἐκάθητο παρὰ τὴν ὁδόν. 47 καὶ ἀκούσας
sat by the way. And hearing

ὅτι Ἰησοῦς ὁ Ναζαρηνός ἐστιν ἤρξατο
that Jesus the Nazarene it is(was) he began

κράζειν καὶ λέγειν· υἱὲ Δαυίδ Ἰησοῦ,
to cry out and to say: Son of David Jesus,

ἐλέησόν με. 48 καὶ ἐπετίμων αὐτῷ πολλοὶ
pity me. And rebuked him many

ἵνα σιωπήσῃ· ὁ δὲ πολλῷ μᾶλλον ἔκραζεν·
that he should be quiet. But he much more cried out:

υἱὲ Δαυίδ, ἐλέησόν με. 49 καὶ στὰς
Son of David, pity me. And standing

ὁ Ἰησοῦς εἶπεν· φωνήσατε αὐτόν. καὶ
\- Jesus said: Call him. And

φωνοῦσιν τὸν τυφλὸν λέγοντες αὐτῷ·
they call the blind man saying to him:

θάρσει, ἔγειρε, φωνεῖ σε. 50 ὁ δὲ
Be of good courage, rise, he calls thee. So he

ἀποβαλὼν τὸ ἱμάτιον αὐτοῦ ἀναπηδήσας ἦλθεν
throwing away the garment of him leaping up came

πρὸς τὸν Ἰησοῦν. 51 καὶ ἀποκριθεὶς αὐτῷ ὁ
to \- Jesus. And answering him \-

Ἰησοῦς εἶπεν· τί σοι θέλεις ποιήσω;
Jesus said: What for thee wishest thou I may do?

ὁ δὲ τυφλὸς εἶπεν αὐτῷ· ῥαββουνί, ἵνα
And the blind man said to him: Rabboni, that

ἀναβλέψω. 52 καὶ ὁ Ἰησοῦς εἶπεν αὐτῷ·
I may see again. And \- Jesus said to him:

ὕπαγε, ἡ πίστις σου σέσωκέν σε. καὶ
Go, the faith of thee has healed thee. And

εὐθὺς ἀνέβλεψεν, καὶ ἠκολούθει αὐτῷ ἐν
immediately he saw again, and followed him in

τῇ ὁδῷ.
the way.

Chapter 11

Καὶ ὅτε ἐγγίζουσιν εἰς Ἰεροσόλυμα
And when they draw near to Jerusalem

εἰς Βηθφαγὴ καὶ Βηθανίαν πρὸς τὸ
to Bethphage and Bethany at the

ὄρος τῶν ἐλαιῶν, ἀποστέλλει δύο τῶν
mount of the olives, he sends two of the

μαθητῶν αὐτοῦ 2 καὶ λέγει αὐτοῖς· ὑπάγετε
disciples of him and tells them: Go ye

King James Version

village over against you: and as soon as ye be
entered into it, ye shall find a colt tied, whereon
never man sat; loose him, and bring *him*. 3And
if any man say unto you, Why do ye this? say
ye that the Lord hath need of him; and straightway he will send him hither. 4And they went
their way, and found the colt tied by the door
without in a place where two ways met; and
they loose him. 5And certain of them that stood
there said unto them, What do ye, loosing the
colt? 6And they said unto them even as Jesus
had commanded: and they let them go. 7And
they brought the colt to Jesus, and cast their
garments on him; and he sat upon him. 8And
many spread their garments in the way; and
others cut down branches off the trees, and
strewed *them* in the way. 9And they that went
before, and they that followed, cried, saying,
Hosanna; Blessed *is* he that cometh in the name
of the Lord: 10 Blessed *be* the kingdom of our
father David, that cometh in the name of the
Lord: Hosanna in the highest. 11And Jesus entered into Jerusalem, and into the temple: and
when he had looked round about upon all things,
and now the eventide was come, he went out
unto Bethany with the twelve.
12 And on the morrow, when they were come
from Bethany; he was hungry: 13And seeing a
fig tree afar off having leaves, he came, if haply
he might find any thing thereon: and when he
came to it, he found nothing but leaves; for the
time of figs was not *yet*. 14And Jesus answered
and said unto it, No man eat fruit of thee hereafter for ever. And his disciples heard *it*.
15 And they come to Jerusalem: and Jesus
went into the temple, and began to cast out
them that sold and bought in the temple, and
overthrew the tables of the money changers, and
the seats of them that sold doves; 16And would
not suffer that any man should carry *any* vessel
through the temple. 17And he taught, saying unto
them, Is it not written, My house shall be called
of all nations the house of prayer? but ye have
made it a den of thieves. 18And the scribes and
chief priests heard *it*, and sought how they might
destroy him: for they feared him, because all
the people was astonished at his doctrine. 19And
when even was come, he went out of the city.
20 And in the morning, as they passed by,
they saw the fig tree dried up from the roots.
21And Peter calling to remembrance saith unto
him, Master, behold, the fig tree which thou
cursedst is withered away. 22And Jesus answering saith unto them, Have faith in God. 23 For
verily I say unto you, That whosoever shall say
unto this mountain, Be thou removed, and be
thou cast into the sea; and shall not doubt in
his heart, but shall believe that those things
which he saith shall come to pass; he shall have
whatsoever he saith. 24 Therefore I say unto you,
What things soever ye desire, when ye pray, believe that ye receive *them*, and ye shall have

New International Version

and just as you enter it, you will find a colt tied
there, which no one has ever ridden. Untie it
and bring it here. 3 If anyone asks you, 'Why
are you doing this?' tell him, 'The Lord needs it
and will send it back here shortly.' "
4 They went and found a colt outside in the
street, tied at a doorway. As they untied it,
5 some people standing there asked, "What are
you doing, untying that colt?" 6 They answered
as Jesus had told them to, and the people let
them go. 7 When they brought the colt to Jesus
and threw their cloaks over it, he sat on it.
8 Many people spread their cloaks on the road,
while others spread branches they had cut in the
fields. 9 Those who went ahead and those who
followed shouted,

"Hosanna! [p]
Blessed is he who comes in the name of the
Lord! [q]
10 Blessed is the coming kingdom of our father
David!
Hosanna[p] in the highest!"

11 Jesus entered Jerusalem and went to the
temple. He looked around at everything, but
since it was already late, he went out to Bethany
with the Twelve.

Jesus clears the temple

12 The next day as they were leaving Bethany, Jesus was hungry. 13 Seeing in the distance
a fig tree in leaf, he went to find out if it had
any fruit. When he reached it, however, he found
nothing but leaves, because it was not the season
for figs. 14 Then he said to the tree, "May no
one ever eat fruit from you again." And his
disciples heard him say it.
15 On reaching Jerusalem, Jesus entered the
temple area and began driving out those who
were buying and selling there. He overturned
the tables of the money-changers and the
benches of those selling doves, 16 and would
not allow anyone to carry merchandise through
the temple courts. 17And as he taught them, he
said, "Is it not written:

'My house will be called a house of prayer
for all nations' [r] ?

But you have made it 'a den of robbers.' [s] "
18 The chief priests and the teachers of the
law heard this and began looking for a way to
kill him, for they feared him, because the whole
crowd was amazed at his teaching.
19 When evening came, they[t] went out of the
city.

The withered fig tree

20 In the morning, as they went along, they
saw the fig tree withered from the roots. 21 Peter
remembered and said to Jesus, "Rabbi, look!
The fig tree you cursed has withered!"
22 "Have[u] faith in God," Jesus answered.
23 "I tell you the truth, if anyone says to this
mountain, 'Go, throw yourself into the sea,' and
does not doubt in his heart but believes that
what he says will happen, it will be done for
him. 24 Therefore I tell you, whatever you ask
for in prayer, believe that you will receive it, and

[*p*] A Hebrew expression meaning "Save!" which became an exclamation of praise. [*q*] Psalm 118:25, 26. [*r*] Isaiah 56:7. [*s*] Jer. 7:11. [*t*] Some early MSS read *he*. [*u*] Some early MSS read *If you have*.

Greek Interlinear

εἰς τὴν κώμην τὴν κατέναντι ὑμῶν, καὶ
into the village – opposite you, and

εὐθὺς εἰσπορευόμενοι εἰς αὐτὴν εὑρήσετε
immediately entering into it ye will find

πῶλον δεδεμένον ἐφ' ὃν οὐδεὶς οὔπω
a colt having been tied on which ¹no one ²not yet

ἀνθρώπων ἐκάθισεν· λύσατε αὐτὸν καὶ
¹of men ⁴sat; loosen it and

φέρετε. 3 καὶ ἐάν τις ὑμῖν εἴπῃ· τί
bring. And if anyone to you says: Why

ποιεῖτε τοῦτο; εἴπατε· ὁ κύριος αὐτοῦ
do ye this? say: The Lord of it

χρείαν ἔχει, καὶ εὐθὺς αὐτὸν ἀποστέλλει
need has, and immediately it he sends

πάλιν ὧδε. 4 καὶ ἀπῆλθον καὶ εὗρον
again here. And they went and found

πῶλον δεδεμένον πρὸς θύραν ἔξω ἐπὶ
a colt having been tied at a door outside on

τοῦ ἀμφόδου, καὶ λύουσιν αὐτόν. 5 καὶ
the open street, and they loosen it. And

τινες τῶν ἐκεῖ ἑστηκότων ἔλεγον αὐτοῖς·
some of the [ones] there standing said to them:

τί ποιεῖτε λύοντες τὸν πῶλον; 6 οἱ δὲ
What do ye loosening the colt? And they

εἶπαν αὐτοῖς καθὼς εἶπεν ὁ Ἰησοῦς·
said to them as said – Jesus;

καὶ ἀφῆκαν αὐτούς. 7 καὶ φέρουσιν τὸν
and they let go them. And they bring the

πῶλον πρὸς τὸν Ἰησοῦν, καὶ ἐπιβάλλουσιν
colt to – Jesus, and they throw on

αὐτῷ τὰ ἱμάτια αὐτῶν, καὶ ἐκάθισεν
it the garments of them, and he sat

ἐπ' αὐτόν. 8 καὶ πολλοὶ τὰ ἱμάτια αὐτῶν
on it. And many the garments of them

ἔστρωσαν εἰς τὴν ὁδόν, ἄλλοι δὲ στιβάδας,
strewed in the way, and others wisps of twigs,

κόψαντες ἐκ τῶν ἀγρῶν. 9 καὶ οἱ
cutting out of the fields. And the [ones]

προάγοντες καὶ οἱ ἀκολουθοῦντες ἔκραζον·
going before and the [ones] following cried out:

ὡσαννά· εὐλογημένος ὁ ἐρχόμενος ἐν
Hosanna; blessed the [one] coming in

ὀνόματι κυρίου· 10 εὐλογημένη ἡ ἐρχομένη
[the] name of [the] Lord; blessed the coming

βασιλεία τοῦ πατρὸς ἡμῶν Δαυίδ· ὡσαννὰ
kingdom of the father of us David; Hosanna

ἐν τοῖς ὑψίστοις]. 11 Καὶ εἰσῆλθεν εἰς
in the highest [places]. And he entered into

Ἱεροσόλυμα εἰς τὸ ἱερόν· καὶ περιβλεψάμενος
Jerusalem into the temple; and looking round at

πάντα, ὀψὲ ἤδη οὔσης τῆς ὥρας, ἐξῆλθεν
all things, ²late ¹now ²being ¹the ³hour,ᵃ he went forth

εἰς Βηθανίαν μετὰ τῶν δώδεκα.
to Bethany with the twelve.

12 Καὶ τῇ ἐπαύριον ἐξελθόντων αὐτῶν
And on the morrow going forth themᵃ
= as they went forth

ἀπὸ Βηθανίας ἐπείνασεν. 13 καὶ ἰδὼν
from Bethany he hungered. And seeing

συκῆν ἀπὸ μακρόθεν ἔχουσαν φύλλα ἦλθεν
a fig-tree from afar having leaves he came

εἰ ἄρα τι εὑρήσει ἐν αὐτῇ, καὶ ἐλθὼν
if perhaps something he will find in it, and coming

ἐπ' αὐτὴν οὐδὲν εὗρεν εἰ μὴ φύλλα·
upon it nothing he found except leaves;

ὁ γὰρ καιρὸς οὐκ ἦν σύκων. 14 καὶ
for the time was not of figs. And

ἀποκριθεὶς εἶπεν αὐτῇ· μηκέτι εἰς τὸν
answering he said to it: No more to the

αἰῶνα ἐκ σοῦ μηδεὶς καρπὸν φάγοι.
age of thee no one fruit may eat.
= May no one eat fruit of thee for ever.

καὶ ἤκουον οἱ μαθηταὶ αὐτοῦ. 15 Καὶ
And ⁴heard ¹the ²disciples ²of him. And

ἔρχονται εἰς Ἱεροσόλυμα. Καὶ εἰσελθὼν
they come to Jerusalem. And entering

εἰς τὸ ἱερὸν ἤρξατο ἐκβάλλειν τοὺς
into the temple he began to cast out the [ones]

πωλοῦντας καὶ τοὺς ἀγοράζοντας ἐν τῷ
selling and the [ones] buying in the

ἱερῷ, καὶ τὰς τραπέζας τῶν κολλυβιστῶν
temple, and the tables of the moneychangers

καὶ τὰς καθέδρας τῶν πωλούντων τὰς
and the seats of the [ones] selling the

περιστερὰς κατέστρεψεν, 16 καὶ οὐκ ἤφιεν
doves he overturned, and did not permit

ἵνα τις διενέγκῃ σκεῦος διὰ τοῦ
that anyone should carry through a vessel through the

ἱεροῦ, 17 καὶ ἐδίδασκεν καὶ ἔλεγεν αὐτοῖς· οὐ
temple, and taught and said to them: Not

γέγραπται ὅτι ὁ οἶκός μου οἶκος προσευχῆς
has it been written that the house of me a house of prayer

κληθήσεται πᾶσιν τοῖς ἔθνεσιν; ὑμεῖς δὲ
shall be called for all the nations? but ye

πεποιήκατε αὐτὸν σπήλαιον λῃστῶν. 18 καὶ
have made it a den of robbers. And

ἤκουσαν οἱ ἀρχιερεῖς καὶ οἱ γραμματεῖς,
²heard ¹the ²chief priests ²and ⁴the ⁵scribes,

καὶ ἐζήτουν πῶς αὐτὸν ἀπολέσωσιν·
and they sought how him they might destroy;

ἐφοβοῦντο γὰρ αὐτόν, πᾶς γὰρ ὁ ὄχλος
for they feared him, for all the crowd

ἐξεπλήσσετο ἐπὶ τῇ διδαχῇ αὐτοῦ. 19 Καὶ
was astounded at the teaching of him. And

ὅταν ὀψὲ ἐγένετο, ἐξεπορεύοντο ἔξω τῆς
when late it became, they went forth outside the

πόλεως. 20 Καὶ παραπορευόμενοι πρωὶ
city. And passing along early

εἶδον τὴν συκῆν ἐξηραμμένην ἐκ ῥιζῶν.
they saw the fig-tree having been withered from [the] roots.

21 καὶ ἀναμνησθεὶς ὁ Πέτρος λέγει αὐτῷ·
And ²remembering – ¹Peter says to him:

ῥαββί, ἴδε ἡ συκῆ ἣν κατηράσω
Rabbi, behold[,] the fig-tree which thou cursedst

ἐξήρανται. 22 καὶ ἀποκριθεὶς ὁ Ἰησοῦς λέγει
has been withered. And answering – Jesus says

αὐτοῖς· ἔχετε πίστιν θεοῦ. 23 ἀμὴν λέγω ὑμῖν
to them: Have [the] faith of God. Truly I tell you

ὅτι ὃς ἂν εἴπῃ τῷ ὄρει τούτῳ· ἄρθητι
that whoever says – mountain to this: Be thou taken

καὶ βλήθητι εἰς τὴν θάλασσαν, καὶ μὴ
and be thou cast into the sea, and not

διακριθῇ ἐν τῇ καρδίᾳ αὐτοῦ ἀλλὰ πιστεύῃ
doubts in the heart of him but believes

ὅτι ὃ λαλεῖ γίνεται, ἔσται αὐτῷ. 24 διὰ
that what he says happens, it will be to him.ᵉ There-
= he will have it.

τοῦτο λέγω ὑμῖν, πάντα ὅσα προσεύχεσθε
fore I tell you, all things which ye pray

καὶ αἰτεῖσθε, πιστεύετε ὅτι ἐλάβετε, καὶ
and ask, believe that ye received, and

King James Version

them. 25And when ye stand praying, forgive, if ye have aught against any; that your Father also which is in heaven may forgive you your trespasses. 26 But if ye do not forgive, neither will your Father which is in heaven forgive your trespasses.

27 And they come again to Jerusalem: and as he was walking in the temple, there come to him the chief priests, and the scribes, and the elders, 28And say unto him, By what authority doest thou these things? and who gave thee this authority to do these things? 29And Jesus answered and said unto them, I will also ask of you one question, and answer me, and I will tell you by what authority I do these things. 30 The baptism of John, was *it* from heaven, or of men? answer me. 31And they reasoned with themselves, saying, If we shall say, From heaven; he will say,. Why then did ye not believe him? 32 But if we shall say, Of men; they feared the people: for all *men* counted John, that he was a prophet indeed. 33And they answered and said unto Jesus, We cannot tell. And Jesus answering saith unto them, Neither do I tell you by what authority I do these things.

12 And he began to speak unto them by parables. A *certain* man planted a vineyard, and set a hedge about *it*, and digged *a place for* the winefat, and built a tower, and let it out to husbandmen, and went into a far country. 2And at the season he sent to the husbandmen a servant, that he might receive from the husbandmen of the fruit of the vineyard. 3And they caught *him*, and beat him, and sent *him* away empty. 4And again he sent unto them another servant; and at him they cast stones, and wounded *him* in the head, and sent *him* away shamefully handled. 5And again he sent another; and him they killed, and many others; beating some, and killing some. 6 Having yet therefore one son, his well beloved, he sent him also last unto them, saying, They will reverence my son. 7 But those husbandmen said among themselves, This is the heir; come, let us kill him, and the inheritance shall be ours. 8And they took him, and killed *him*, and cast *him* out of the vineyard. 9 What shall therefore the lord of the vineyard do? he will come and destroy the husbandmen, and will give the vineyard unto others. 10And have ye not read this Scripture; The stone which the builders rejected is become the head of the corner: 11 This was the Lord's doing, and it is marvellous in our eyes? 12And they sought to lay hold on him, but feared the people; for they knew that he had spoken the parable against them: and they left him, and went their way.

13 And they send unto him certain of the Pharisees and of the Herodians, to catch him in *his* words. 14And when they were come, they say unto him, Master, we know that thou art

New International Version

it will be yours. 25And when you stand praying, if you hold anything against anyone, forgive him, so that your Father in heaven may forgive you your sins." *v*

The authority of Jesus questioned

27 They arrived again in Jerusalem, and while Jesus was walking in the temple courts, the chief priests, the teachers of the law and the elders came to him. 28 "By what authority are you doing these things?" they asked. "And who gave you authority to do this?"

29 Jesus replied, "I will ask you one question. Answer me, and I will tell you by what authority I am doing these things. 30 John's baptism —was it from heaven, or from men? Tell me!"

31 They discussed it among themselves and said, "If we say, 'From heaven,' he will ask, 'Then why didn't you believe him?' 32 But if we say, 'From men'. . . ." (They feared the people, for everyone held that John really was a prophet.)

33 So they answered Jesus, "We don't know." Jesus said, "Neither will I tell you by what authority I am doing these things."

The parable of the tenants

12 He then began to speak to them in parables: "A man planted a vineyard. He put a wall around it, dug a pit for the winepress and built a tower. Then he rented the vineyard to some farmers and went away on a journey. 2At harvest time he sent a servant to the tenants to collect from them some of the fruit of the vineyard. 3 But they seized him, beat him and sent him away empty-handed. 4 Then he sent another servant to them; they struck this man on the head and treated him shamefully. 5 He sent still another, and that one they killed. He sent many others; some of them they beat, others they killed.

6 "He had one left to send, a son, whom he loved. He sent him last of all, saying, 'They will respect my son.'

7 "But the tenants said to one another, 'This is the heir. Come, let's kill him, and the inheritance will be ours.' 8 So they took him and killed him, and threw him out of the vineyard.

9 "What then will the owner of the vineyard do? He will come and kill those tenants and give the vineyard to others. 10 Haven't you read this scripture:

" 'The stone the builders rejected
   has become the capstone;
11 the Lord has done this,
   and it is marvelous in our eyes' *w* ?"

12 Then they looked for a way to arrest him because they knew he had spoken the parable against them. But they were afraid of the crowd; so they left him and went away.

Paying taxes to Caesar

13 Later they sent some of the Pharisees and Herodians to Jesus to catch him in his words. 14 They came to him and said, "Teacher, we know you are a man of integrity. You aren't

[v] Some MSS add verse 26: *But if you do not forgive, neither will your Father who is in heaven forgive your sins.* [w] Psalm 118:22,23.

142

Greek Interlinear

ἔσται ὑμῖν, **25** καὶ ὅταν στήκετε
it will be to you.[c] And when ye stand
= ye will have it.

προσευχόμενοι, ἀφίετε εἴ τι ἔχετε κατά
praying, forgive if anything ye have against

τινος, ἵνα καὶ ὁ πατὴρ ὑμῶν ὁ ἐν τοῖς
anyone, that also the Father of you – in the

οὐρανοῖς ἀφῇ ὑμῖν τὰ παραπτώματα ὑμῶν.‡
heavens may forgive you the trespasses of you.

27 Καὶ ἔρχονται πάλιν εἰς Ἱεροσόλυμα.
And they come again to Jerusalem.

καὶ ἐν τῷ ἱερῷ περιπατοῦντος αὐτοῦ
And in the temple walking him[a]
=as he walked

ἔρχονται πρὸς αὐτὸν οἱ ἀρχιερεῖς καὶ οἱ
come to him the chief priests and the

γραμματεῖς καὶ οἱ πρεσβύτεροι, **28** καὶ
scribes and the elders, and

ἔλεγον αὐτῷ· ἐν ποίᾳ ἐξουσίᾳ ταῦτα
said to him: By what authority these things

ποιεῖς; ἢ τίς σοι ἔδωκεν τὴν ἐξουσίαν
doest thou? or who thee gave – authority

ταύτην ἵνα ταῦτα ποιῇς; **29** ὁ δὲ Ἰησοῦς
this that these things thou mayest do? – And Jesus

εἶπεν αὐτοῖς· ἐπερωτήσω ὑμᾶς ἕνα λόγον,
said to them: I will question you one word,

καὶ ἀποκρίθητέ μοι, καὶ ἐρῶ ὑμῖν ἐν
and answer ye me, and I will tell you by

ποίᾳ ἐξουσίᾳ ταῦτα ποιῶ. **30** τὸ βάπτισμα
what authority these things I do. The baptism

τὸ Ἰωάννου ἐξ οὐρανοῦ ἦν ἢ ἐξ ἀνθρώπων;
– of John of heaven was it or of men?

ἀποκρίθητέ μοι. **31** καὶ διελογίζοντο πρὸς
answer ye me. And they debated with

ἑαυτοὺς λέγοντες· ἐὰν εἴπωμεν· ἐξ οὐρανοῦ,
themselves saying: If we say: Of heaven,

ἐρεῖ· διὰ τί οὖν οὐκ ἐπιστεύσατε αὐτῷ;
he will say: Why then did ye not believe him?

32 ἀλλὰ εἴπωμεν· ἐξ ἀνθρώπων;—ἐφοβοῦντο
But may we say: Of men? – they feared

τὸν ὄχλον· ἅπαντες γὰρ εἶχον τὸν Ἰωάννην
the crowd; for all men held – John

ὄντως ὅτι προφήτης ἦν. **33** καὶ
'really 'that a prophet 'he was. And

ἀποκριθέντες τῷ Ἰησοῦ λέγουσιν· οὐκ
answering – Jesus they say: not

οἴδαμεν. καὶ ὁ Ἰησοῦς λέγει αὐτοῖς·
We know. And – Jesus says to them:

οὐδὲ ἐγὼ λέγω ὑμῖν ἐν ποίᾳ ἐξουσίᾳ
Neither I tell you by what authority

Chapter 12

ταῦτα ποιῶ. **12** Καὶ ἤρξατο αὐτοῖς ἐν
these things I do. And he began to them in

παραβολαῖς λαλεῖν. ἀμπελῶνα ἄνθρωπος
parables to speak. ²a vineyard ¹A man

ἐφύτευσεν, καὶ περιέθηκεν φραγμὸν καὶ ὤρυξεν
²planted, and put round [it] a hedge and dug

ὑπολήνιον καὶ ᾠκοδόμησεν πύργον, καὶ
a winepress and built a tower, and

ἐξέδοτο αὐτὸν γεωργοῖς, καὶ ἀπεδήμησεν.
let out it to husbandmen, and went away.

2 καὶ ἀπέστειλεν πρὸς τοὺς γεωργοὺς τῷ
And he sent to the husbandmen at the

καιρῷ δοῦλον, ἵνα παρὰ τῶν γεωργῶν
time a slave, that from the husbandmen

λάβῃ ἀπὸ τῶν καρπῶν τοῦ ἀμπελῶνος·
he might receive from(of) the fruits of the vineyard;

3 καὶ λαβόντες αὐτὸν ἔδειραν καὶ ἀπέστειλαν
And taking him they beat and sent away

κενόν. **4** καὶ πάλιν ἀπέστειλεν πρὸς αὐτοὺς
empty. And again he sent to them

ἄλλον δοῦλον· κἀκεῖνον ἐκεφαλαίωσαν καὶ
another slave; and that one they wounded in the head and

ἠτίμασαν. **5** καὶ ἄλλον ἀπέστειλεν· κἀκεῖνον
insulted. And another he sent; and that one

ἀπέκτειναν, καὶ πολλοὺς ἄλλους, οὓς μὲν
they killed, and many others, ²some

δέροντες, οὓς δὲ ἀποκτέννοντες. **6** ἔτι ἕνα
¹beating, ²others ¹killing. Still one

εἶχεν, υἱὸν ἀγαπητόν· ἀπέστειλεν αὐτὸν
he had, a son beloved; he sent him

ἔσχατον πρὸς αὐτοὺς λέγων ὅτι ἐντραπήσονται
last to them saying[,] – They will reverence

τὸν υἱόν μου. **7** ἐκεῖνοι δὲ οἱ γεωργοὶ
the son of me. But those – husbandmen

πρὸς ἑαυτοὺς εἶπαν ὅτι οὗτός ἐστιν ὁ
to themselves said[,] – This is the

κληρονόμος· δεῦτε ἀποκτείνωμεν αὐτόν, καὶ
heir; come[,] let us kill him, and

ἡμῶν ἔσται ἡ κληρονομία. **8** καὶ λαβόντες
of us will be the inheritance. And taking

ἀπέκτειναν αὐτόν, καὶ ἐξέβαλον αὐτὸν
they killed him, and cast out him

ἔξω τοῦ ἀμπελῶνος. **9** τί ποιήσει ὁ
outside the vineyard. What will do the

κύριος τοῦ ἀμπελῶνος; ἐλεύσεται καὶ
lord of the vineyard? he will come and

ἀπολέσει τοὺς γεωργούς, καὶ δώσει τὸν
will destroy the husbandmen, and will give the

ἀμπελῶνα ἄλλοις. **10** οὐδὲ τὴν γραφὴν
vineyard to others. ²not – 'scripture

ταύτην ἀνέγνωτε· λίθον ὃν ἀπεδοκίμασαν
³this ¹Read ye: A stone which ⁴rejected

οἱ οἰκοδομοῦντες, οὗτος ἐγενήθη εἰς κεφαλὴν
¹the [ones] ²building, this became for head

γωνίας· **11** παρὰ κυρίου ἐγένετο αὕτη,
of corner; from [the] Lord was this,

καὶ ἔστιν θαυμαστὴ ἐν ὀφθαλμοῖς ἡμῶν;
and it is marvellous in eyes of us?

12 Καὶ ἐζήτουν αὐτὸν κρατῆσαι, καὶ
And they sought him to seize, and

ἐφοβήθησαν τὸν ὄχλον· ἔγνωσαν γὰρ
feared the crowd; for they knew

ὅτι πρὸς αὐτοὺς τὴν παραβολὴν
that to them the parable

εἶπεν. καὶ ἀφέντες αὐτὸν ἀπῆλθον.
he told. And leaving him they went away.

13 Καὶ ἀποστέλλουσιν πρὸς αὐτόν τινας τῶν
And they send to him some of the

Φαρισαίων καὶ τῶν Ἡρωδιανῶν ἵνα αὐτὸν
Pharisees and of the Herodians that him

ἀγρεύσωσιν λόγῳ. **14** καὶ ἐλθόντες
they might catch in a word. And coming

λέγουσιν αὐτῷ· διδάσκαλε, οἴδαμεν ὅτι
they say to him: Teacher, we know that

ἀληθὴς εἶ καὶ οὐ μέλει σοι περὶ
true thou art and it matters not to thee about

‡ Verse 26 omitted by Nestle

King James Version

true, and carest for no man; for thou regardest not the person of men, but teachest the way of God in truth: Is it lawful to give tribute to Cesar, or not? 15 Shall we give, or shall we not give? But he, knowing their hypocrisy, said unto them, Why tempt ye me? bring me a penny, that I may see it. 16And they brought it. And he saith unto them, Whose is this image and superscription? And they said unto him, Cesar's. 17And Jesus answering said unto them, Render to Cesar the things that are Cesar's, and to God the things that are God's. And they marvelled at him.

18 Then come unto him the Sadducees, which say there is no resurrection; and they asked him, saying, 19 Master, Moses wrote unto us, If a man's brother die, and leave his wife behind him, and leave no children, that his brother should take his wife, and raise up seed unto his brother. 20 Now there were seven brethren: and the first took a wife, and dying left no seed. 21And the second took her, and died, neither left he any seed: and the third likewise. 22And the seven had her, and left no seed: last of all the woman died also. 23 In the resurrection therefore, when they shall rise, whose wife shall she be of them? for the seven had her to wife. 24And Jesus answering said unto them, Do ye not therefore err, because ye know not the Scriptures, neither the power of God? 25 For when they shall rise from the dead, they neither marry, nor are given in marriage; but are as the angels which are in heaven. 26And as touching the dead, that they rise; have ye not read in the book of Moses, how in the bush God spake unto him, saying, I am the God of Abraham, and the God of Isaac, and the God of Jacob? 27 He is not the God of the dead, but the God of the living: ye therefore do greatly err.

28 And one of the scribes came, and having heard them reasoning together, and perceiving that he had answered them well, asked him, Which is the first commandment of all? 29And Jesus answered him, The first of all the commandments is, Hear, O Israel; The Lord our God is one Lord: 30And thou shalt love the Lord thy God with all thy heart, and with all thy soul, and with all thy mind, and with all thy strength: this is the first commandment. 31And the second is like, namely this, Thou shalt love thy neighbour as thyself. There is none other commandment greater than these. 32And the scribe said unto him, Well, Master, thou hast said the truth: for there is one God; and there is none other but he: 33And to love him with all the heart, and with all the understanding, and with all the soul, and with all the strength, and to love his neighbour as himself, is more than all whole burnt offerings and sacrifices. 34And when Jesus saw that he answered discreetly, he said unto him, Thou art not far from the kingdom of God. And no man after that durst ask him any question.

New International Version

swayed by men, because you pay no attention to who they are; but you teach the way of God in accordance with the truth. Is it right to pay taxes to Caesar or not? 15 Should we pay or shouldn't we?"

But Jesus knew their hypocrisy. "Why are you trying to trap me?" he asked. "Bring me a denarius and let me look at it." 16 They brought the coin, and he asked them, "Whose portrait is this? And whose inscription?"

"Caesar's," they replied.

17 Then Jesus said to them, "Give to Caesar what is Caesar's and to God what is God's."

And they were amazed at him.

Marriage at the resurrection

18 Then the Sadducees, who say there is no resurrection, came to him with a question. 19 "Teacher," they said, "Moses wrote for us that if a man's brother dies and leaves a wife but no children, the man must marry the widow and have children for his brother. 20 Now there were seven brothers. The first one married and died without leaving any children. 21 The second one married the widow, but he also died, leaving no child. It was the same with the third. 22 In fact, none of the seven left any children. Last of all, the woman died too. 23At the resurrection* whose wife will she be, since the seven were married to her?"

24 Jesus replied, "Are you not in error because you do not know the Scriptures or the power of God? 25 When the dead rise, they will neither marry nor be given in marriage; they will be like the angels in heaven. 26 Now about the dead rising—have you not read in the book of Moses, in the account of the bush, how God said to him, 'I am the God of Abraham, the God of Isaac, and the God of Jacob' ʸ ? 27 He is not the God of the dead, but of the living. You are badly mistaken!"

The greatest commandment

28 One of the teachers of the law came and heard them debating. Noticing that Jesus had given them a good answer, he asked him, "Of all the commandments, which is the most important?"

29 "The most important one," answered Jesus, "is this: 'Hear, O Israel, the Lord our God, the Lord is one;ᶻ 30 love the Lord your God with all your heart, with all your soul, with all your mind and with all your strength.' ᵃ 31 The second is this: 'Love your neighbor as yourself.' ᵇ There is no greater commandment than these."

32 "Well said, teacher," the man replied. "You are right in saying that God is one and there is no other but him. 33 To love him with all your heart, with all your understanding and with all your strength, and to love your neighbor as yourself is more important than all burnt offerings and sacrifices."

34 When Jesus saw that he had answered wisely, he said to him, "You are not far from the kingdom of God." And from then on no one dared ask him any more questions.

[x] Some MSS add when men rise from the dead. [y] Exodus 3:6. [z] Or the Lord our God is the one Lord. [a] Deut. 6:4, 5. [b] Lev. 19:18.

Greek Interlinear

οὐδενός· οὐ γὰρ βλέπεις εἰς πρόσωπον
no(any)one; for thou lookest not at [the] face

ἀνθρώπων, ἀλλ' ἐπ' ἀληθείας τὴν ὁδὸν
of men, but on(in) truth the way

τοῦ θεοῦ διδάσκεις· ἔξεστιν δοῦναι κῆνσον
– of God teachest; is it lawful to give tribute

Καίσαρι ἢ οὔ; δῶμεν ἢ μὴ δῶμεν;
to Cæsar or no? may we give or may we not give?

15 ὁ δὲ εἰδὼς αὐτῶν τὴν ὑπόκρισιν εἶπεν
But he knowing of them the hypocrisy said

αὐτοῖς· τί με πειράζετε; φέρετέ μοι
to them: Why me tempt ye? bring me

δηνάριον ἵνα ἴδω. 16 οἱ δὲ ἤνεγκαν. καὶ
a denarius that I may see. And they brought. And

λέγει αὐτοῖς· τίνος ἡ εἰκὼν αὕτη καὶ ἡ
he says to them: Of whom image this and the

ἐπιγραφή; οἱ δὲ εἶπαν αὐτῷ· Καίσαρος.
superscription? And they tell him: Of Cæsar.

17 ὁ δὲ Ἰησοῦς εἶπεν αὐτοῖς· τὰ Καίσαρος
– So Jesus said to them: The things of Cæsar

ἀπόδοτε Καίσαρι καὶ τὰ τοῦ θεοῦ τῷ
render to Cæsar and the things – of God

θεῷ. καὶ ἐξεθαύμαζον ἐπ' αὐτῷ.
to God. And they marvelled at him.

18 Καὶ ἔρχονται Σαδδουκαῖοι πρὸς αὐτόν,
And come Sadducees to him,

οἵτινες λέγουσιν ἀνάστασιν μὴ εἶναι, καὶ
who say resurrection not to be, and
= that there is no resurrection,

ἐπηρώτων αὐτὸν λέγοντες· 19 διδάσκαλε,
questioned him saying: Teacher,

Μωϋσῆς ἔγραψεν ἡμῖν ὅτι ἐάν τινος
Moses wrote to us that if of anyone

ἀδελφὸς ἀποθάνῃ καὶ καταλίπῃ γυναῖκα
a brother should die and leave behind a wife

καὶ μὴ ἀφῇ τέκνον, ἵνα λάβῃ ὁ ἀδελφὸς
and leave not a child, – ¹may take ¹the ²brother

αὐτοῦ τὴν γυναῖκα καὶ ἐξαναστήσῃ σπέρμα
³of him the wife and may raise up seed

τῷ ἀδελφῷ αὐτοῦ. 20 ἑπτὰ ἀδελφοὶ ἦσαν·
to the brother of him. Seven brothers there were;

καὶ ὁ πρῶτος ἔλαβεν γυναῖκα, καὶ
and the first took a wife, and

ἀποθνῄσκων οὐκ ἀφῆκεν σπέρμα· 21 καὶ
dying left not seed; and

ὁ δεύτερος ἔλαβεν αὐτήν, καὶ ἀπέθανεν μὴ
the second took her, and died not

καταλιπὼν σπέρμα· καὶ ὁ τρίτος ὡσαύτως·
leaving behind seed; and the third similarly;

22 καὶ οἱ ἑπτὰ οὐκ ἀφῆκαν σπέρμα.
and the seven left not seed.

ἔσχατον πάντων καὶ ἡ γυνὴ ἀπέθανεν.
Last of all also the wife died.

23 ἐν τῇ ἀναστάσει, ὅταν ἀναστῶσιν,
In the resurrection, when they rise again,

τίνος αὐτῶν ἔσται γυνή; οἱ γὰρ ἑπτὰ
of which of them will she be wife? for the seven

ἔσχον αὐτὴν γυναῖκα. 24 ἔφη αὐτοῖς ὁ
had her [as] wife. Said to them –

Ἰησοῦς· οὐ διὰ τοῦτο πλανᾶσθε μὴ
Jesus: ²not ⁴therefore ¹Do ³ye ⁵err not

εἰδότες τὰς γραφὰς μηδὲ τὴν δύναμιν
knowing the scriptures nor the power

τοῦ θεοῦ; 25 ὅταν γὰρ ἐκ νεκρῶν
– of God? for when out of [the] dead

ἀναστῶσιν, οὔτε γαμοῦσιν οὔτε γαμίζονται,
they rise again, they neither marry nor are given in marriage,

ἀλλ' εἰσὶν ὡς ἄγγελοι ἐν τοῖς οὐρανοῖς.
but are as angels in the heavens.

26 περὶ δὲ τῶν νεκρῶν ὅτι ἐγείρονται,
But concerning the dead that they are raised,

οὐκ ἀνέγνωτε ἐν τῇ βίβλῳ Μωϋσέως ἐπὶ
did ye not read in the roll of Moses at

τοῦ βάτου πῶς εἶπεν αὐτῷ ὁ θεὸς λέγων·
the bush how said to him – God saying:

ἐγὼ ὁ θεὸς Ἀβραὰμ καὶ θεὸς Ἰσαὰκ
I [am] the God of Abraham and God of Isaac

καὶ θεὸς Ἰακώβ; 27 οὐκ ἔστιν θεὸς
and God of Jacob? he is not God

νεκρῶν ἀλλὰ ζώντων. πολὺ πλανᾶσθε.
of dead [persons] but of living [ones]. Much ye err.

28 Καὶ προσελθὼν εἷς τῶν γραμματέων,
And ⁴approaching ¹one ²of the ³scribes,

ἀκούσας αὐτῶν συζητούντων, εἰδὼς ὅτι
hearing them debating, knowing that

καλῶς ἀπεκρίθη αὐτοῖς, ἐπηρώτησεν αὐτόν·
well he answered them, questioned him:

ποία ἐστὶν ἐντολὴ πρώτη πάντων;
What is [the] commandment first of all?

29 ἀπεκρίθη ὁ Ἰησοῦς ὅτι πρώτη ἐστίν·
Answered – Jesus[,] – [The] first is:

ἄκουε, Ἰσραήλ, κύριος ὁ θεὸς ἡμῶν κύριος
Hear, Israel, Lord the God of us Lord
= The Lord our God is one Lord,

εἷς ἐστιν, 30 καὶ ἀγαπήσεις κύριον τὸν
one is, and thou shalt love Lord the

θεόν σου ἐξ ὅλης τῆς καρδίας σου καὶ
God of thee from(with) all the heart of thee and

ἐξ ὅλης τῆς ψυχῆς σου καὶ ἐξ ὅλης
with all the soul of thee and with all

τῆς διανοίας σου καὶ ἐξ ὅλης τῆς ἰσχύος
the mind of thee and with all the strength

σου. 31 δευτέρα αὕτη· ἀγαπήσεις τὸν
of thee. [The] second [is] this: Thou shalt love the

πλησίον σου ὡς σεαυτόν. μείζων τούτων
neighbour of thee as thyself. Greater [than] these

ἄλλη ἐντολὴ οὐκ ἔστιν. 32 καὶ εἶπεν
other commandment there is not. And said

αὐτῷ ὁ γραμματεύς· καλῶς, διδάσκαλε, ἐπ'
to him the scribe: Well, teacher, on(in)

ἀληθείας εἶπες ὅτι εἷς ἐστιν καὶ οὐκ
truth thou sayest that one there is and not

ἔστιν ἄλλος πλὴν αὐτοῦ· 33 καὶ τὸ
there is another besides him; and –

ἀγαπᾶν αὐτὸν ἐξ ὅλης τῆς καρδίας καὶ ἐξ
to love him with all the heart and with

ὅλης τῆς συνέσεως καὶ ἐξ ὅλης τῆς
all the understanding and with all the

ἰσχύος, καὶ τὸ ἀγαπᾶν τὸν πλησίον ὡς
strength, and – to love the(one's) neighbour as

ἑαυτὸν περισσότερόν ἐστιν πάντων τῶν
himself more is [than] all the

ὁλοκαυτωμάτων καὶ θυσιῶν. 34 καὶ ὁ
burnt offerings and sacrifices. And –

Ἰησοῦς, ἰδὼν αὐτὸν ὅτι νουνεχῶς ἀπεκρίθη,
Jesus, seeing him that sensibly he answered,

εἶπεν αὐτῷ· οὐ μακρὰν εἶ ἀπὸ τῆς
said to him: Not far thou art from the

βασιλείας τοῦ θεοῦ. καὶ οὐδεὶς οὐκέτι
kingdom – of God. And no one no(any) more

ἐτόλμα αὐτὸν ἐπερωτῆσαι.
dared him to question.

35 And Jesus answered and said, while he taught in the temple, How say the scribes that Christ is the son of David? 36 For David himself said by the Holy Ghost, The Lord said to my Lord, Sit thou on my right hand, till I make thine enemies thy footstool. 37 David therefore himself calleth him Lord; and whence is he *then* his son? And the common people heard him gladly.

38 And he said unto them in his doctrine, Beware of the scribes, which love to go in long clothing, and *love* salutations in the marketplaces, 39 And the chief seats in the synagogues, and the uppermost rooms at feasts: 40 Which devour widows' houses, and for a pretence make long prayers: these shall receive greater damnation.

41 And Jesus sat over against the treasury, and beheld how the people cast money into the treasury: and many that were rich cast in much. 42 And there came a certain poor widow, and she threw in two mites, which make a farthing. 43 And he called *unto him* his disciples, and saith unto them, Verily I say unto you, That this poor widow hath cast more in, than all they which have cast into the treasury: 44 For all *they* did cast in of their abundance; but she of her want did cast in all that she had, *even* all her living.

13 And as he went out of the temple, one of his disciples saith unto him, Master, see what manner of stones and what buildings *are here!* 2 And Jesus answering said unto him, Seest thou these great buildings? there shall not be left one stone upon another, that shall not be thrown down. 3 And as he sat upon the mount of Olives, over against the temple, Peter and James and John and Andrew asked him privately, 4 Tell us, when shall these things be? and what *shall be* the sign when all these things shall be fulfilled? 5 And Jesus answering them began to say, Take heed lest any *man* deceive you: 6 For many shall come in my name, saying, I am *Christ;* and shall deceive many. 7 And when ye shall hear of wars and rumours of wars, be ye not troubled: for *such things* must needs be; but the end *shall* not *be* yet. 8 For nation shall rise against nation, and kingdom against kingdom: and there shall be earthquakes in divers places, and there shall be famines and troubles: these *are* the beginnings of sorrows.

9 But take heed to yourselves: for they shall deliver you up to councils; and in the synagogues ye shall be beaten: and ye shall be brought before rulers and kings for my sake, for a testimony against them. 10 And the gospel must first be published among all nations. 11 But when they shall lead *you,* and deliver you up, take no thought beforehand what ye shall speak, neither do ye premeditate: but whatsoever shall be given

Whose son is the Christ?

. 35 While Jesus was teaching in the temple courts, he asked, "How is it that the teachers of the law say that the Christ *c* is the son of David? 36 David himself, speaking by the Holy Spirit, declared:

'The Lord said to my Lord:
Sit at my right hand
until I put your enemies under your feet.' *d*
37 David himself calls him 'Lord.' How then can he be his son?"

The large crowd listened to him with delight.

38 As he taught, Jesus said, "Watch out for the teachers of the law. They like to walk around in flowing robes and be greeted in the marketplaces, 39 and have the most important seats in the synagogues and the places of honor at banquets. 40 They devour widows' houses and for a show make lengthy prayers. Such men will be punished most severely."

The widow's offering

41 Jesus sat down opposite the place where the offerings were put and watched the crowd putting their money into the temple treasury. Many rich people threw in large amounts. 42 But a poor widow came and put in two very small copper coins, worth only a fraction of a penny.

43 Calling his disciples to him, Jesus said, "I tell you the truth, this poor widow has put more into the treasury than all the others. 44 They all gave of their wealth; but she, out of her poverty, put in everything—all she had to live on."

Signs of the end of the age

13 As he was leaving the temple, one of his disciples said to him, "Look, Teacher! What massive stones! What magnificent buildings!"

2 "Do you see all these great buildings?" replied Jesus. "Not one stone here will be left on another; every one will be thrown down."

3 As Jesus was sitting on the Mount of Olives opposite the temple, Peter, James, John and Andrew asked him privately, 4 "Tell us, when will these things happen? And what will be the sign that they are all about to be fulfilled?"

5 Jesus said to them: "Watch out that no one deceives you. 6 Many will come in my name, claiming, 'I am he,' and will deceive many. 7 When you hear of wars and rumors of wars, do not be alarmed. Such things must happen, but the end is still to come. 8 Nation will rise against nation, and kingdom against kingdom. There will be earthquakes in various places, and famines. These are the beginning of birth pains.

9 "You must be on your guard. You will be handed over to the local councils and flogged in the synagogues. On account of me you will stand before governors and kings as witnesses to them. 10 And the gospel must first be preached to all nations. 11 Whenever you are arrested and brought to trial, do not worry beforehand about what to say. Just say whatever is given you at

[c] Or *Messiah.* [d] Psalm 110:1.

Greek Interlinear

35 Καὶ   ἀποκριθεὶς   ὁ   Ἰησοῦς   ἔλεγεν
And   answering   -   Jesus   said

διδάσκων   ἐν   τῷ   ἱερῷ·   πῶς   λέγουσιν   οἱ
teaching   in   the   temple: How   say   the

γραμματεῖς   ὅτι   ὁ   χριστὸς   υἱός   Δαυίδ
scribes   that   the   Christ   son   of David

ἐστιν;   **36** αὐτὸς   Δαυὶδ   εἶπεν   ἐν   τῷ   πνεύματι
is?   himself   David   said   by   the   Spirit

τῷ   ἁγίῳ·   εἶπεν   κύριος   τῷ   κυρίῳ   μου·
-   Holy: said [the] LORD   to the   Lord   of me:

κάθου   ἐκ   δεξιῶν   μου   ἕως   ἂν   θῶ   τοὺς
Sit   at [the]   right [hand]   of me   until   I put   the

ἐχθρούς   σου   ὑποκάτω   τῶν   ποδῶν   σου.
enemies   of thee   under   the   feet   of thee.

37 αὐτὸς   Δαυὶδ   λέγει   αὐτὸν   κύριον,   καὶ
himself   David   says(calls)   him   Lord,   and

πόθεν   αὐτοῦ   ἐστιν   υἱός;
whence   of him   is he   son?

Καὶ   ὁ   πολὺς   ὄχλος   ἤκουεν   αὐτοῦ
And   the   much   crowd   heard   him

ἡδέως.   **38** Καὶ   ἐν   τῇ   διδαχῇ   αὐτοῦ
gladly.   And   in   the   teaching   of him

ἔλεγεν·   βλέπετε   ἀπὸ   τῶν   γραμματέων
he said: Beware   from(of)   the   scribes

τῶν   θελόντων   ἐν   στολαῖς   περιπατεῖν   καὶ
the [ones] wishing   in   robes   to walk about   and

ἀσπασμοὺς   ἐν   ταῖς   ἀγοραῖς   **39** καὶ
greetings   in   the   marketplaces   and

πρωτοκαθεδρίας   ἐν   ταῖς   συναγωγαῖς   καὶ
chief seats   in   the   synagogues   and

πρωτοκλισίας   ἐν   τοῖς   δείπνοις·   **40**   οἱ
chief places   in   the   dinners;   the [ones]

κατέσθοντες   τὰς   οἰκίας   τῶν   χηρῶν   καὶ
devouring   the   houses   of the   widows   and

προφάσει   μακρὰ   προσευχόμενοι,   οὗτοι
under pretence   long   praying,   these

λήμψονται   περισσότερον   κρίμα.   **41** Καὶ
will receive   greater   condemnation.   And

καθίσας   κατέναντι   τοῦ   γαζοφυλακείου   ἐθεώρει
sitting   opposite   the   treasury   he beheld

πῶς   ὁ   ὄχλος   βάλλει   χαλκὸν   εἰς   τὸ
how   the   crowd   puts   copper money   into   the

γαζοφυλακεῖον·   καὶ   πολλοὶ   πλούσιοι   ἔβαλλον
treasury;   and   many   rich men   put

πολλά·   **42** καὶ   ἐλθοῦσα   μία   χήρα   πτωχὴ
much;   and   coming   one   widow   poor

ἔβαλεν   λεπτὰ   δύο,   ὅ   ἐστιν   κοδράντης.
put   lepta   two,   which   is   a quadrans.

43 καὶ   προσκαλεσάμενος   τοὺς   μαθητὰς   αὐτοῦ
And   calling to [him]   the   disciples   of him

εἶπεν   αὐτοῖς·   ἀμὴν   λέγω   ὑμῖν   ὅτι
he said to them: Truly   I tell   you   that

ἡ   χήρα   αὕτη   ἡ   πτωχὴ   πλεῖον   πάντων
- ¹widow   ²this   - ³poor   ⁵more [than]   ⁴all

ἔβαλεν   τῶν   βαλλόντων   εἰς   τὸ   γαζοφυλακεῖον·
⁶put   the [ones] putting   into   the   treasury;

44 πάντες   γὰρ   ἐκ   τοῦ   περισσεύοντος   αὐτοῖς
for all   out of   the   abounding   to them
= their abundance

ἔβαλον,   αὕτη   δὲ   ἐκ   τῆς   ὑστερήσεως   αὐτῆς
put,   but this woman   out of   the   want   of her

πάντα   ὅσα   εἶχεν   ἔβαλεν,   ὅλον   τὸν   βίον
¹all things   ³how many   ⁴she had   ²put,   all   the   living

αὐτῆς.
of her.

Chapter 13

Καὶ   ἐκπορευομένου   αὐτοῦ   ἐκ   τοῦ
And   going forth   him^a   out of   the
= as he went forth

ἱεροῦ   λέγει   αὐτῷ   εἷς   τῶν   μαθητῶν   αὐτοῦ·
temple   says   to him   one   of the   disciples   of him:

διδάσκαλε,   ἴδε   ποταποὶ   λίθοι   καὶ   ποταπαὶ
Teacher,   behold[,] what great stones   and   what great

οἰκοδομαί.   **2** καὶ   ὁ   Ἰησοῦς   εἶπεν   αὐτῷ·
buildings.   And   -   Jesus   said   to him:

βλέπεις   ταύτας   τὰς   μεγάλας   οἰκοδομάς;
Seest thou   these   -   great   buildings?

οὐ   μὴ   ἀφεθῇ   λίθος   ἐπὶ   λίθον   ὃς   οὐ
by no means be left   stone   on   stone   which by no
= there shall by no means be left stone on stone which will not

μὴ   καταλυθῇ.   **3** Καὶ   καθημένου   αὐτοῦ
means be overthrown.   And   sitting   him^a
be overthrown.   = as he sat

εἰς   τὸ   ὄρος   τῶν   ἐλαιῶν   κατέναντι   τοῦ
in(on)   the   mount   of the   olives   opposite   the

ἱεροῦ,   ἐπηρώτα   αὐτὸν   κατ'   ἰδίαν   Πέτρος
temple,   questioned   him   privately   Peter

καὶ   Ἰάκωβος   καὶ   Ἰωάννης   καὶ   Ἀνδρέας·
and   James   and   John   and   Andrew:

4 εἰπὸν   ἡμῖν,   πότε   ταῦτα   ἔσται,   καὶ   τί
Tell   us,   when   these things will be,   and   what

τὸ   σημεῖον   ὅταν   μέλλῃ   ταῦτα   συντελεῖσθαι
the   sign   when   ²are about   ¹these things   ⁴to be completed

πάντα;   **5** ὁ   δὲ   Ἰησοῦς   ἤρξατο   λέγειν
³all?   -   And   Jesus   began   to say

αὐτοῖς·   βλέπετε   μή   τις   ὑμᾶς   πλανήσῃ.
to them: See   lest anyone   you   lead astray.

6 πολλοὶ   ἐλεύσονται   ἐπὶ   τῷ   ὀνόματί   μου
Many   will come   on(in)   the   name   of me

λέγοντες   ὅτι   ἐγώ   εἰμι,   καὶ   πολλοὺς
saying[,]   -   I   am,   and   many

πλανήσουσιν.   **7** ὅταν   δὲ   ἀκούσητε   πολέμους
they will lead astray.   But when   ye hear   [of] wars

καὶ   ἀκοὰς   πολέμων,   μὴ   θροεῖσθε·   δεῖ
and   rumours   of wars,   be not disturbed;   it behoves

γενέσθαι,   ἀλλ'   οὔπω   τὸ   τέλος.   **8** ἐγερθήσεται
to happen,   but not yet   the   end.   will be raised

γὰρ   ἔθνος   ἐπ'   ἔθνος   καὶ   βασιλεία   ἐπὶ
For   nation   against   nation   and   kingdom   against

βασιλείαν.   ἔσονται   σεισμοὶ   κατὰ   τόπους,
kingdom.   There will be   earthquakes   in places,

ἔσονται   λιμοί·   ἀρχὴ   ὠδίνων   ταῦτα.
there will be famines;   beginning   of birth-pangs   these things [are].

9 Βλέπετε   δὲ   ὑμεῖς   ἑαυτούς·   παραδώσουσιν
But see   ye   yourselves;   they will deliver

ὑμᾶς   εἰς   συνέδρια   καὶ   εἰς   συναγωγὰς
you   to   councils   and   in   synagogues

δαρήσεσθε   καὶ   ἐπὶ   ἡγεμόνων   καὶ   βασιλέων
ye will be beaten   and   before   rulers   and   kings

σταθήσεσθε   ἕνεκεν   ἐμοῦ,   εἰς   μαρτύριον
ye will stand   for the sake   of me,   for   a testimony

αὐτοῖς.   **10** καὶ   εἰς   πάντα   τὰ   ἔθνη   πρῶτον
to them.   And   to   all   the   nations   first

δεῖ   κηρυχθῆναι   τὸ   εὐαγγέλιον.   **11** καὶ   ὅταν
it behoves to be proclaimed the   gospel.   And   when
= the gospel must be proclaimed.

ἄγωσιν   ὑμᾶς   παραδιδόντες,   μὴ   προμεριμνᾶτε
they lead   you   delivering,   be not anxious beforehand

τί   λαλήσητε,   ἀλλ'   ὃ   ἐὰν   δοθῇ   ὑμῖν   ἐν
what   ye speak,   but   whatever   is given   you   in

ἐκείνῃ   τῇ   ὥρᾳ,   τοῦτο   λαλεῖτε·   οὐ   γὰρ
that   -   hour.   this   speak ye;   for not

King James Version

you in that hour, that speak ye: for it is not ye that speak, but the Holy Ghost. 12 Now the brother shall betray his brother to death, and the father the son; and children shall rise up against *their* parents, and shall cause them to be put to death. 13And ye shall be hated of all *men* for my name's sake: but he that shall endure unto the end, the same shall be saved.

14 But when ye shall see the abomination of desolation, spoken of by Daniel the prophet, standing where it ought not, (let him that readeth understand,) then let them that be in Judea flee to the mountains: 15And let him that is on the housetop not go down into the house, neither enter *therein*, to take any thing out of his house: 16And let him that is in the field not turn back again for to take up his garment. 17 But woe to them that are with child, and to them that give suck in those days! 18And pray ye that your flight be not in the winter. 19 For *in* those days shall be affliction, such as was not from the beginning of the creation which God created unto this time, neither shall be. 20And except that the Lord had shortened those days, no flesh should be saved: but for the elect's sake, whom he hath chosen, he hath shortened the days. 21And then if any man shall say to you, Lo, here *is* Christ; or, lo, *he is* there; believe *him* not: 22 For false Christs and false prophets shall rise, and shall shew signs and wonders, to seduce, if *it were* possible, even the elect. 23 But take ye heed: behold, I have foretold you all things.

24 But in those days, after that tribulation, the sun shall be darkened, and the moon shall not give her light, 25And the stars of heaven shall fall, and the powers that are in heaven shall be shaken. 26And then shall they see the Son of man coming in the clouds with great power and glory. 27And then shall he send his angels, and shall gather together his elect from the four winds, from the uttermost part of the earth to the uttermost part of heaven. 28 Now learn a parable of the fig tree: When her branch is yet tender, and putteth forth leaves, ye know that summer is near: 29 So ye in like manner, when ye shall see these things come to pass, know that it is nigh, *even* at the doors. 30 Verily I say unto you, that this generation shall not pass, till all these things be done. 31 Heaven and earth shall pass away: but my words shall not pass away.

32 But of that day and *that* hour knoweth no man, no, not the angels which are in heaven, neither the Son, but the Father. 33 Take ye heed, watch and pray: for ye know not when the time is. 34 *For the Son of man* is as a man taking a far journey, who left his house, and gave authority to his servants, and to every man his work, and commanded the porter to watch. 35 Watch ye therefore: for ye know not when the master of the house cometh, at even, or at midnight, or at the cockcrowing, or in the morning: 36 Lest coming suddenly he find you sleeping. 37And what I say unto you I say unto all, Watch.

New International Version

the time, for it is not you speaking, but the Holy Spirit.

12 "Brother will betray brother to death, and a father his child. Children will rebel against their parents and have them put to death. 13All men will hate you because of me, but he who stands firm to the end will be saved.

14 "When you see 'the abomination that causes desolation' *e* standing where it does not belong—let the reader understand—then let those who are in Judea flee to the mountains. 15 Let no one on the roof of his house go down or enter the house to take anything out. 16 Let no one in the field go back to get his cloak. 17 How dreadful it will be in those days for pregnant women and nursing mothers! 18 Pray that this will not take place in winter, 19 because those will be days of distress unequaled from the beginning, when God created the world, until now—and never to be equaled again. 20 If the Lord had not cut short those days, no one would survive. But for the sake of the elect, whom he has chosen, he has shortened them. 21At that time if anyone says to you, 'Look, here is the Christ!' *f* or, 'Look, there he is!' do not believe it. 22 For false Christs and false prophets will appear and perform signs and miracles to deceive the elect—if that were possible. 23 So be on your guard; I have told you everything ahead of time.

24 "But in those days, following that distress,

'the sun will be darkened,
    and the moon will not give its light;
25 the stars will fall from the sky,
    and the heavenly bodies will be shaken.' *g*

26 "At that time men will see the Son of Man coming in clouds with great power and glory. 27And he will send his angels and gather his elect from the four winds, from the ends of the earth to the ends of the heavens.

28 "Now learn this lesson from the fig tree: As soon as its twigs get tender and its leaves come out, you know that summer is near. 29 Even so, when you see these things happening, you know that it *h* is near, right at the door. 30 I tell you the truth, this generation *i* will certainly not pass away until all these things have happened. 31 Heaven and earth will pass away, but my words will never pass away.

The day and hour unknown

32 "No one knows about that day or hour, not even the angels in heaven, nor the Son, but only the Father. 33 Be on guard! Be alert! *j* You do not know when that time will come. 34 It's like a man going away: He leaves his house in charge of his servants, each with his assigned task, and tells the one at the door to keep watch. 35 So you also must keep watch because you do not know when the owner of the house will come back—whether in the evening, or at midnight, or when the rooster crows, or at dawn. 36 If he comes suddenly, don't let him find you sleeping. 37 What I say to you, I say to everyone: 'Watch!' "

[e] Dan. 9:27; 11:31; 12:11. [f] Or *Messiah*. [g] Isaiah 13:10; 34:4. [h] Or *he*. [i] Or *race*. [j] Some MSS add *and pray*.

Greek Interlinear

ἐστε   ὑμεῖς   οἱ   λαλοῦντες   ἀλλὰ   τὸ   πνεῦμα
are   ye   the [ones] speaking   but   the   Spirit

τὸ   ἅγιον.   **12** καὶ   παραδώσει   ἀδελφὸς
-   Holy.   And   ²will deliver   ¹a brother

ἀδελφὸν   εἰς   θάνατον   καὶ   πατὴρ   τέκνον,   καὶ
a brother   to   death   and   a father   a child,   and

ἐπαναστήσονται   τέκνα   ἐπὶ   γονεῖς   καὶ
²will rise against   ¹children   against   parents   and

θανατώσουσιν   αὐτούς·   **13** καὶ   ἔσεσθε
will put to death   them;   and   ye will be

μισούμενοι   ὑπὸ   πάντων   διὰ   τὸ   ὄνομά
being hated   by   all men   on account of   the   name

μου·   ὁ   δὲ   ὑπομείνας   εἰς   τέλος,   οὗτος
of me;   but   the [one]   enduring   to [the] end,   . this

σωθήσεται.   **14** Ὅταν   δὲ   ἴδητε   τὸ   βδέλυγμα
will be saved.   But when   ye see   the   abomination

τῆς   ἐρημώσεως   ἑστηκότα   ὅπου   οὐ   δεῖ,   ὁ
-   of desolation   stand   where it behoves not, the

ἀναγινώσκων   νοείτω,   τότε   οἱ   ἐν   τῇ
[one] reading   let him understand,   then   the [ones]   in   the

Ἰουδαίᾳ   φευγέτωσαν   εἰς   τὰ   ὄρη,   **15** ὁ   ἐπὶ
Judea   let them flee   to   the   mountains,   the [one]   on

τοῦ   δώματος   μὴ   καταβάτω   μηδὲ   εἰσελθάτω
the   roof   let him not come down   nor   let him enter

τι   ἆραι   ἐκ   τῆς   οἰκίας   αὐτοῦ,   **16** καὶ   ὁ
anything to take out of   the   house   of him,   and the [one]

εἰς   τὸν   ἀγρὸν   μὴ   ἐπιστρεψάτω   εἰς   τὰ
in   the   field   let him not return   to the things

ὀπίσω   ἆραι   τὸ   ἱμάτιον   αὐτοῦ.   **17** οὐαὶ
behind   to take   the   garment   of him.   woe

δὲ   ταῖς   ἐν   γαστρὶ   ἐχούσαις   καὶ   ταῖς
But to the women   pregnant†   and   to the

θηλαζούσαις   ἐν   ἐκείναις   ταῖς   ἡμέραις.
[ones] giving suck   in   those   -   days.

18 προσεύχεσθε   δὲ   ἵνα   μὴ   γένηται   χειμῶνος·
But pray ye   that it may not happen   of(in) winter;

19 ἔσονται   γὰρ   αἱ   ἡμέραι   ἐκεῖναι   θλῖψις,   οἵα
for ²will be   -   ³days   ¹those   ⁴affliction, of such

οὐ   γέγονεν   τοιαύτη   ἀπ᾿   ἀρχῆς   κτίσεως
²has not happened   ¹as   from [the] beginning of [the] creation

ἣν   ἔκτισεν   ὁ   θεὸς   ἕως   τοῦ   νῦν   καὶ .   οὐ
which created   -   God   until   -   now   and   by

μὴ   γένηται.   **20** καὶ   εἰ   μὴ   ἐκολόβωσεν
no means   may be.   And   unless   ²shortened

κύριος   τὰς   ἡμέρας,   οὐκ   ἂν   ἐσώθη   πᾶσα
¹[the] Lord   the   days,   would not be saved   all

σάρξ·   ἀλλὰ   διὰ   τοὺς   ἐκλεκτοὺς   οὓς
= no flesh would be saved;

flesh;   but   on account of   the   chosen   whom

ἐξελέξατο   ἐκολόβωσεν   τὰς   ἡμέρας.   **21** καὶ
he chose   he shortened   the   days.   And

τότε   ἐάν   τις   ὑμῖν   εἴπῃ·   ἴδε   ὧδε   ὁ
then   if   anyone   ²you   ¹tells: Behold here [is]   the

χριστός,   ἴδε   ἐκεῖ,   μὴ   πιστεύετε·   **22** ἐγερθή-
Christ,   behold there,   believe ye not;   ¹will be

σονται   δὲ   ψευδόχριστοι   καὶ   ψευδοπροφῆται
raised   ¹and   ²false Christs   ³and   ⁴false prophets

καὶ   ποιήσουσιν   σημεῖα   καὶ   τέρατα   πρὸς
and   they will do   signs   and   wonders   for

τὸ   ἀποπλανᾶν,   εἰ   δυνατόν,   τοὺς   ἐκλεκτούς.
- to lead astray,   if   possible,   the   chosen.

23 ὑμεῖς   δὲ   βλέπετε·   προείρηκα   ὑμῖν   πάντα.
But ²ye   ¹see;   ¹I have told   ²before ³you   ⁴all things.

24 Ἀλλὰ   ἐν   ἐκείναις   ταῖς   ἡμέραις   μετὰ
But   in   those   -   days   after

τὴν   θλῖψιν   ἐκείνην   ὁ   ἥλιος   σκοτισθήσεται,
-   affliction   that   the   sun   will be darkened,

καὶ   ἡ   σελήνη   οὐ   δώσει   τὸ   φέγγος   αὐτῆς,
and   the   moon   will not give   the   light   of her,

25 καὶ   οἱ   ἀστέρες   ἔσονται   ἐκ   τοῦ   οὐρανοῦ
and   the   stars   ¹will be   ²out of   -   ⁴heaven

πίπτοντες,   καὶ   αἱ   δυνάμεις   αἱ   ἐν   τοῖς
³falling,   and   the   powers   -   in   the

οὐρανοῖς   σαλευθήσονται.   **26** καὶ   τότε   ὄψονται
heavens   will be shaken.   And then   they will see

τὸν   υἱὸν   τοῦ   ἀνθρώπου   ἐρχόμενον   ἐν
the   Son   - of man   coming   in

νεφέλαις   μετὰ   δυνάμεως   πολλῆς   καὶ   δόξης.
clouds   with   power   much   and   glory.

27 καὶ   τότε   ἀποστελεῖ   τοὺς   ἀγγέλους   καὶ
And   then   he will send   the   angels   and

ἐπισυνάξει   τοὺς   ἐκλεκτοὺς   [αὐτοῦ]   ἐκ   τῶν
they will assemble   the   chosen   of him   out of   the

τεσσάρων   ἀνέμων   ἀπ᾿   ἄκρου   γῆς   ἕως
four   winds   from [the] extremity of earth   to

ἄκρου   οὐρανοῦ.   **28** Ἀπὸ   δὲ   τῆς   συκῆς
[the] extremity of heaven.   Now from   -   the   fig-tree

μάθετε   τὴν   παραβολήν·   ὅταν   ἤδη   ὁ
learn   the   parable;   when   now   the

κλάδος   αὐτῆς   ἁπαλὸς   γένηται   καὶ   ἐκφύῃ
branch   of it   tender   becomes   and   puts forth

τὰ   φύλλα,   γινώσκετε   ὅτι   ἐγγὺς   τὸ   θέρος
the   leaves,   ye know   that   near   the   summer

ἐστίν·   **29** οὕτως   καὶ   ὑμεῖς,   ὅταν   ἴδητε
is;   so   also   ye,   when   ye see

ταῦτα   γινόμενα,   γινώσκετε   ὅτι   ἐγγύς   ἐστιν
these things happening,   know   that   near   he/it is

ἐπὶ   θύραις.   **30** ἀμὴν   λέγω   ὑμῖν   ὅτι   οὐ
at [the] doors.   Truly   I tell   you   that by no

μὴ   παρέλθῃ   ἡ   γενεὰ   αὕτη   μέχρις   οὗ
means   passes   -   generation   this   until

ταῦτα   πάντα   γένηται.   **31** ὁ   οὐρανὸς   καὶ
these things   all   happen.   The   heaven   and

ἡ   γῆ   παρελεύσονται,   οἱ   δὲ   λόγοι   μου
the   earth   will pass away,   but the   words   of me

οὐ   παρελεύσονται.   **32** Περὶ   δὲ   τῆς   ἡμέρας
will not pass away.   But concerning   -   day

ἐκείνης   ἢ   τῆς   ὥρας   οὐδεὶς   οἶδεν,   οὐδὲ
that   or   -   hour   no one   knows,   not

οἱ   ἄγγελοι   ἐν   οὐρανῷ   οὐδὲ   ὁ   υἱός,   εἰ
the   angels   in   heaven   neither   the   Son, ex-

μὴ   ὁ   πατήρ.   **33** Βλέπετε,   ἀγρυπνεῖτε·
cept   the   Father.   Look,   be wakeful;

οὐκ   οἴδατε   γὰρ   πότε   ὁ   καιρός   ἐστιν.
for ye know not   when   the   time   is.

34 ὡς   ἄνθρωπος   ἀπόδημος   ἀφεὶς   τὴν   οἰκίαν
As   a man   away from home   leaving   the   house

αὐτοῦ   καὶ   δοὺς   τοῖς   δούλοις   αὐτοῦ   τὴν
of him   and   giving   to the   slaves   of him   -

ἐξουσίαν,   ἑκάστῳ   τὸ   ἔργον   αὐτοῦ,   καὶ
authority,   to each   the   work   of him,   and

τῷ   θυρωρῷ   ἐνετείλατο   ἵνα   γρηγορῇ.
the   doorkeeper   he commanded   that   he should watch.

35 γρηγορεῖτε   οὖν·   οὐκ   οἴδατε   γὰρ   πότε
Watch ye therefore;   for ye know not   when

ὁ   κύριος   τῆς   οἰκίας   ἔρχεται,   ἢ   ὀψὲ   ἢ
the   lord   of the house   comes,   either   late   ot

μεσονύκτιον   ἢ   ἀλεκτοροφωνίας   ἢ   πρωΐ·
at midnight   or   at cock-crowing   or   early;

36 μὴ   ἐλθὼν   ἐξαίφνης   εὕρῃ   ὑμᾶς   καθεύδ-
lest   coming   suddenly   he find you   sleep-

οντας.   **37** ὃ   δὲ   ὑμῖν   λέγω,   πᾶσιν   λέγω,
ing.   And what to you   I say,   to all   I say,

γρηγορεῖτε.
watch ye.

King James Version

14 After two days was *the feast of* the passover, and of unleavened ˙bread: and the chief priests and the scribes sought how they might take him by craft, and put *him* to death. 2 But they said, Not on the feast *day,* lest there be an uproar of the people.

3 And being in Bethany, in the house of Simon the leper, as he sat at meat, there came a woman having an alabaster box of ointment of spikenard very precious; and she brake the box, and poured *it* on his head. 4And there were some that had indignation within themselves, and said, Why was this waste of the ointment made? 5 For it might have been sold for more than three hundred pence, and have been given to the poor. And they murmured against her. 6And Jesus said, Let her alone; why trouble ye her? she hath wrought a good work on me. 7 For ye have the poor with you always, and whensoever ye will ye may do them good: but me ye have not always. 8 She hath done what she could: she is come aforehand to anoint my body to the burying. 9 Verily I say unto you, Wheresoever this gospel shall be preached throughout the whole world, *this* also that she hath done shall be spoken of for a memorial of her.

10 And Judas Iscariot, one of the twelve, went unto the chief priests, to betray him unto them. 11And when they heard *it,* they were glad, and promised to give him money. And he sought how he might conveniently betray him.

12 And the first day of unleavened bread, when they killed the passover, his disciples said unto him, Where wilt thou that we go and prepare that thou mayest eat the passover? 13And he sendeth forth two of his disciples, and saith unto them, Go ye into the city, and there shall meet you a man bearing a pitcher of water: follow him. 14And wheresoever he shall go in, say ye to the goodman of the house, The Master saith, Where is the guestchamber, where I shall eat the passover with my disciples? 15And he will shew you a large upper room furnished *and* prepared: there make ready for us. 16And his disciples went forth, and came into the city, and found as he had said unto them: and they made ready the passover. 17And in the evening he cometh with the twelve. 18And as they sat and did eat, Jesus said, Verily I say unto you, One of you which eateth with me shall betray me. 19And they began to be sorrowful, and to say unto him one by one, *Is* it I? and another *said, Is* it I? 20And he answered and said unto them, *It is* one of the twelve, that dippeth with me in the dish. 21 The Son of man indeed goeth, as it is written of him: but woe to that man by whom the Son of man is betrayed! good were it for that man if he had never been born.

22 And as they did eat, Jesus took bread, and blessed, and brake *it,* and gave to them, and

New International Version

Jesus anointed at Bethany

14 Now the Passover and the Feast of Unleavened Bread were only two days away, and the chief priests and the teachers of the law were looking for some sly way to arrest Jesus and kill him. 2 "But not during the feast," they said, "or the people may riot."

3 While he was in Bethany, reclining at the table in the home of a man known as Simon the Leper, a woman came with an alabaster jar of very expensive perfume, made of pure nard. She broke the jar and poured the perfume on his head.

4 Some of those present were saying indignantly to one another, "Why this waste of perfume? 5 It could have been sold for more than a year's wages[k] and the money given to the poor." And they rebuked her harshly.

6 "Leave her alone," said Jesus. "Why are you bothering her? She has done a beautiful thing to me. 7 The poor you will always have with you, and you can help them any time you want. But you will not always have me. 8 She did what she could. She poured perfume on my body beforehand to prepare for my burial. 9 I tell you the truth, wherever the gospel is preached throughout the world, what she has done will also be told, in memory of her."

10 Then Judas Iscariot, one of the Twelve, went to the chief priests to betray Jesus to them. 11 They were delighted to hear this and promised to give him money. So he watched for an opportunity to hand him over.

The Lord's supper

12 On the first day of the Feast of Unleavened Bread, when it was customary to sacrifice the Passover lamb, Jesus' disciples asked him, "Where do you want us to go and make preparations for you to eat the Passover?"

13 So he sent two of his disciples, telling them, "Go into the city, and a man carrying a jar of water will meet you. Follow him. 14 Say to the owner of the house he enters, 'The Teacher asks: Where is my guest room, where I may eat the Passover with my disciples?' 15 He will show you a large upper room, furnished and ready. Make preparations for us there."

16 The disciples left, went into the city and found things just as Jesus had told them. So they prepared the Passover.

17 When evening came, Jesus arrived with the Twelve. 18 While they were reclining at the table eating, he said, "I tell you the truth, one of you will betray me—one who is eating with me."

19 They were saddened, and one by one they said to him, "Surely not I?"

20 "It is one of the Twelve," he replied, "one who dips bread into the bowl with me. 21 The Son of Man will go just as it is written about him. But woe to that man who betrays the Son of Man! It would be better for him if he had not been born."

22 While they were eating, Jesus took bread, gave thanks and broke it, and gave it to his disciples, saying, "Take it; this is my body."

[k] Greek *300 denarii.*

Greek Interlinear

Chapter 14

Ἦν δὲ τὸ πάσχα καὶ τὰ ἄζυμα
Now it was the Passover and [the feast of] the
unleavened bread†

μετὰ δύο ἡμέρας. καὶ ἐζήτουν οἱ ἀρχιερεῖς
after two days. And sought the chief priests

καὶ οἱ γραμματεῖς πῶς αὐτὸν ἐν δόλῳ
and the scribes how ²him ³by ⁴guile

κρατήσαντες ἀποκτείνωσιν. 2 ἔλεγον γάρ·
¹seizing they might kill. For they said:

μὴ ἐν τῇ ἑορτῇ, μήποτε ἔσται θόρυβος
Not at the feast, lest there will be a disturbance

τοῦ λαοῦ.
of the people.

3 Καὶ ὄντος αὐτοῦ ἐν Βηθανίᾳ ἐν τῇ
And being him² in Bethany in the
— when he was

οἰκίᾳ Σίμωνος τοῦ λεπροῦ, κατακειμένου
house of Simon the leper, reclining
— as he reclined

αὐτοῦ ἦλθεν γυνὴ ἔχουσα ἀλάβαστρον
him² came a woman having an alabaster phial

μύρου νάρδου πιστικῆς πολυτελοῦς·
of ointment ²nard ¹of pure ²costly;

συντρίψασα τὴν ἀλάβαστρον κατέχεεν αὐτοῦ
breaking the alabaster phial she poured over of him

τῆς κεφαλῆς. 4 ἦσαν δέ τινες ἀγανακτοῦντες
the head. Now there were some being angry

πρὸς ἑαυτούς· εἰς τί ἡ ἀπώλεια αὕτη
with themselves: Why — waste this

τοῦ μύρου γέγονεν; 5 ἠδύνατο γὰρ τοῦτο
of the ointment has occurred? for ²could ¹this

τὸ μύρον πραθῆναι ἐπάνω δηναρίων
— ²ointment to be sold [for] over denarii

τριακοσίων καὶ δοθῆναι τοῖς πτωχοῖς·
three hundred and to be given to the poor;

καὶ ἐνεβριμῶντο αὐτῇ. 6 ὁ δὲ Ἰησοῦς
and they were indignant with her. — But Jesus

εἶπεν· ἄφετε αὐτήν· τί αὐτῇ κόπους
said: Leave her; why ²to her ¹troubles

παρέχετε; καλὸν ἔργον ἠργάσατο ἐν ἐμοί.
¹cause ye? a good work she wrought in me.

7 πάντοτε γὰρ τοὺς πτωχοὺς ἔχετε μεθ'
For always the poor ye have with

ἑαυτῶν, καὶ ὅταν θέλητε δύνασθε αὐτοῖς
yourselves, and whenever ye wish ye can to them

εὖ ποιῆσαι, ἐμὲ δὲ οὐ πάντοτε ἔχετε.
well to do, but me not always ye have.

8 ὃ ἔσχεν ἐποίησεν· προέλαβεν μυρίσαι τὸ
What she had she did; she was beforehand to anoint the

σῶμά μου εἰς τὸν ἐνταφιασμόν. 9 ἀμὴν
body of me for the burial. truly

δὲ λέγω ὑμῖν, ὅπου ἐὰν κηρυχθῇ τὸ
And I tell you, wherever is proclaimed the

εὐαγγέλιον εἰς ὅλον τὸν κόσμον, καὶ ὃ
gospel in all the world, also what

ἐποίησεν αὕτη λαληθήσεται εἰς μνημόσυνον
did this woman will be spoken for a memorial

αὐτῆς. 10 Καὶ Ἰούδας Ἰσκαριώθ, ὁ εἷς
of her. And Judas Iscariot, the one

τῶν δώδεκα, ἀπῆλθεν πρὸς τοὺς ἀρχιερεῖς
of the twelve, went to the chief priests

ἵνα αὐτὸν παραδοῖ αὐτοῖς. 11 οἱ δὲ
that him he might betray to them. And they

ἀκούσαντες ἐχάρησαν καὶ ἐπηγγείλαντο αὐτῷ
hearing rejoiced and promised him

ἀργύριον δοῦναι. καὶ ἐζήτει πῶς αὐτὸν
silver to give. And he sought how him

εὐκαίρως παραδοῖ.
opportunely he might betray.

12 Καὶ τῇ πρώτῃ ἡμέρᾳ τῶν ἀζύμων,
And on the first day of unleavened bread,†

ὅτε τὸ πάσχα ἔθυον, λέγουσιν αὐτῷ οἱ
when the passover they sacrificed, say to him the

μαθηταὶ αὐτοῦ· ποῦ θέλεις ἀπελθόντες
disciples of him: Where wishest thou , going

ἑτοιμάσωμεν ἵνα φάγῃς τὸ πάσχα; 13 καὶ
we may prepare that thou eatest the passover? And

ἀποστέλλει δύο τῶν μαθητῶν αὐτοῦ καὶ
he sends two of the disciples of him and

λέγει αὐτοῖς· ὑπάγετε εἰς τὴν πόλιν, καὶ
tells them: Go ye into the city, and

ἀπαντήσει ὑμῖν ἄνθρωπος κεράμιον ὕδατος
will meet you a man a pitcher of water

βαστάζων· ἀκολουθήσατε αὐτῷ, 14 καὶ ὅπου
carrying; follow him, and wher-

ἐὰν εἰσέλθῃ εἴπατε τῷ οἰκοδεσπότῃ ὅτι ὁ
ever he enters tell the housemaster[,] — The

διδάσκαλος λέγει· ποῦ ἐστιν τὸ κατάλυμά
teacher says: Where is the guest room

μου, ὅπου τὸ πάσχα μετὰ τῶν μαθητῶν
of me, where the passover with the disciples

μου φάγω; 15 καὶ αὐτὸς ὑμῖν δείξει
of me I may eat? And he you will show

ἀνάγαιον μέγα ἐστρωμένον ἕτοιμον· καὶ
upper room a large having been spread ready; and

ἐκεῖ ἑτοιμάσατε ἡμῖν. 16 καὶ ἐξῆλθον οἱ
there prepare ye for us. And went forth the

μαθηταὶ καὶ ἦλθον εἰς τὴν πόλιν καὶ
disciples and came into the city and

εὗρον καθὼς εἶπεν αὐτοῖς, καὶ ἡτοίμασαν
found as he told them, and they prepared

τὸ πάσχα. 17 Καὶ ὀψίας γενομένης ἔρχεται
the passover. And evening coming² he comes
— when evening came

μετὰ τῶν δώδεκα. 18 καὶ ἀνακειμένων
with the twelve. And reclining
— as they reclined and ate

αὐτῶν καὶ ἐσθιόντων ὁ Ἰησοῦς εἶπεν·
them and eating² — Jesus said:

ἀμὴν λέγω ὑμῖν ὅτι εἷς ἐξ ὑμῶν παραδώσει
Truly I tell you that one of you will betray

με, ὁ ἐσθίων μετ' ἐμοῦ. 19 ἤρξαντο
me, the [one] eating with me. They began

λυπεῖσθαι καὶ λέγειν αὐτῷ εἷς ἐξ εἷς·
to grieve and to say to him one by one:

μήτι ἐγώ; 20 ὁ δὲ εἶπεν αὐτοῖς· εἷς τῶν
Not I? And he said to them: One of the

δώδεκα, ὁ ἐμβαπτόμενος μετ' ἐμοῦ εἰς
twelve, the [one] dipping with me in

τὸ [ἓν] τρύβλιον. 21 ὅτι ὁ μὲν υἱὸς τοῦ
the one dish. Because indeed the Son

ἀνθρώπου ὑπάγει καθὼς γέγραπται περὶ
of man is going as it has been written concerning

αὐτοῦ· οὐαὶ δὲ τῷ ἀνθρώπῳ ἐκείνῳ δι'
him; but woe — man to that through

οὗ ὁ υἱὸς τοῦ ἀνθρώπου παραδίδοται·
whom the Son of man is betrayed;

καλὸν αὐτῷ εἰ οὐκ ἐγεννήθη ὁ ἄνθρωπος
good for him if was not born — man

ἐκεῖνος. 22 Καὶ ἐσθιόντων αὐτῶν λαβὼν
that. And eating them² taking
— as they were eating

ἄρτον εὐλογήσας ἔκλασεν καὶ ἔδωκεν αὐτοῖς
a loaf blessing he broke and gave to them

καὶ εἶπεν· λάβετε· τοῦτό ἐστιν τὸ σῶμά
and said: Take ye; this is the body

King James Version

said, Take, eat; this is my body. 23And he took the cup, and when he had given thanks, he gave *it* to them: and they all drank of it. 24And he said unto them, This is my blood of the new testament, which is shed for many. 25 Verily I say unto you, I will drink no more of the fruit of the vine, until that day that I drink it new in the kingdom of God.

26 And when they had sung a hymn, they went out into the mount of Olives. 27And Jesus saith unto them, All ye shall be offended because of me this night: for it is written, I will smite the Shepherd, and the sheep shall be scattered. 28 But after that I am risen, I will go before you into Galilee. 29 But Peter said unto him, Although all shall be offended, yet *will* not I. 30And Jesus saith unto him, Verily I say unto thee, That this day, *even* in this night, before the cock crow twice, thou shalt deny me thrice. 31 But he spake the more vehemently, If I should die with thee, I will not deny thee in any wise. Likewise also said they all. 32And they came to a place which was named Gethsemane: and he saith to his disciples, Sit ye here, while I shall pray. 33And he taketh with him Peter and James and John, and began to be sore amazed, and to be very heavy; 34And saith unto them, My soul is exceeding sorrowful unto death: tarry ye here, and watch. 35And he went forward a little, and fell on the ground, and prayed that, if it were possible, the hour might pass from him. 36And he said, Abba, Father, all things *are* possible unto thee; take away this cup from me: nevertheless, not what I will, but what thou wilt. 37And he cometh, and findeth them sleeping, and saith unto Peter, Simon, sleepest thou? couldest not thou watch one hour? 38 Watch ye and pray, lest ye enter into temptation. The spirit truly *is* ready, but the flesh *is* weak. 39And again he went away, and prayed, and spake the same words. 40And when he returned, he found them asleep again, (for their eyes were heavy,) neither wist they what to answer him. 41And he cometh the third time, and saith unto them, Sleep on now, and take *your* rest: it is enough, the hour is come; behold, the Son of man is betrayed into the hands of sinners. 42 Rise up, let us go; lo, he that betrayeth me is at hand.

43 And immediately, while he yet spake, cometh Judas, one of the twelve, and with him a great multitude with swords and staves, from the chief priests and the scribes and the elders. 44And he that betrayed him had given them a token, saying, Whomsoever I shall kiss, that same is he; take him, and lead *him* away safely. 45And as soon as he was come, he goeth straightway to him, and saith, Master, Master; and kissed him.

46 And they laid their hands on him, and took him. 47And one of them that stood by drew a sword, and smote a servant of the high priest,

New International Version

23 Then he took the cup, gave thanks and offered it to them, and they all drank from it.

24 "This is my blood of the *l* covenant, which is poured out for many," he said. 25 "I tell you the truth, I will not drink again from the fruit of the vine until that day when I drink it anew in the kingdom of God."

26 When they had sung a hymn, they went out to the Mount of Olives.

Jesus predicts Peter's denial

27 "You will all fall away," Jesus told them, "for it is written:

'I will strike the shepherd,
  and the sheep will be scattered.' *m*

28 But after I have risen, I will go ahead of you into Galilee."

29 Peter declared, "Even if all fall away, I will not."

30 "I tell you the truth," Jesus answered, "today—yes, tonight—before the rooster crows twice*n* you yourself will disown me three times."

31 But Peter insisted emphatically, "Even if I have to die with you, I will never disown you." And all the others said the same.

Gethsemane

32 They went to a place called Gethsemane, and Jesus said to his disciples, "Sit here while I pray." 33 He took Peter, James and John along with him, and he began to be deeply distressed and troubled. 34 "My soul is overwhelmed with sorrow to point of death," he said to them. "Stay here and keep watch."

35 Going a little farther, he fell to the ground and prayed that if possible the hour might pass from him. 36 "*Abba,°* Father," he said, "everything is possible for you. Take this cup from me. Yet not what I will, but what you will."

37 Then he returned to his disciples and found them sleeping. "Simon," he said to Peter, "are you asleep? Could you not keep watch for one hour? 38 Watch and pray so that you will not fall into temptation. The spirit is willing, but the body is weak."

39 Once more he went away and prayed the same thing. 40 When he came back, he again found them sleeping, because their eyes were heavy. They did not know what to say to him.

41 Returning the third time, he said to them, "Are you still sleeping and resting? Enough! The hour has come. Look, the Son of Man is betrayed into the hands of sinners. 42 Rise! Let us go! Here comes my betrayer!"

Jesus arrested

43 Just as he was speaking, Judas, one of the Twelve, appeared. With him was a crowd armed with swords and clubs, sent from the chief priests, the teachers of the law, and the elders. 44 Now the betrayer had arranged a signal with them: "The one I kiss is the man; arrest him and lead him away under guard." 45 Going at once to Jesus, Judas said, "Rabbi!" and kissed him. 46 The men seized Jesus and arrested him. 47 Then one of those standing near drew his sword and struck the servant of the high priest, cutting off his ear.

[*l*] Some MSS add *new.* [*m*] Zech. 13:7. [*n*] Some early MSS omit *twice.* [*o*] Aramaic for *Father.*

Greek Interlinear

μου. 23 καὶ λαβὼν ποτήριον εὐχαριστήσας
of me.   And taking   a cup   giving thanks

ἔδωκεν αὐτοῖς, καὶ ἔπιον ἐξ αὐτοῦ πάντες.
he gave   to them,   and   drank   of   it   all.

24 καὶ εἶπεν αὐτοῖς· τοῦτό ἐστιν τὸ αἷμά
   And he said to them: This   is   the blood

μου τῆς διαθήκης τὸ ἐκχυννόμενον ὑπὲρ
of me of the covenant   -   being shed   for

πολλῶν. 25 ἀμὴν λέγω ὑμῖν ὅτι οὐκέτι
many.   Truly   I tell   you[,]   -   No more

οὐ μὴ πίω ἐκ τοῦ γενήματος τῆς ἀμπέλου
by no(any) will I drink of the   fruit   of the   vine
means

ἕως τῆς ἡμέρας ἐκείνης ὅταν αὐτὸ πίνω
until   -   day   that   when   it   I drink

καινὸν ἐν τῇ βασιλείᾳ τοῦ θεοῦ.
new   in   the   kingdom   -   of God.

26 Καὶ ὑμνήσαντες ἐξῆλθον εἰς τὸ
   And having sung a hymn they went forth   to   the

ὄρος τῶν ἐλαιῶν. 27 Καὶ λέγει αὐτοῖς ὁ
mount of the   olives.   And   says   to them   -

Ἰησοῦς ὅτι πάντες σκανδαλισθήσεσθε, ὅτι
Jesus[,]   -   'All   'ye 'will 'be offended, because

γέγραπται· πατάξω τὸν ποιμένα, καὶ τὸ
it has been written: I will strike   the   shepherd,   and   the

πρόβατα διασκορπισθήσονται. 28 ἀλλὰ μετὰ
sheep   will be scattered.   But   after

τὸ ἐγερθῆναί με προάξω ὑμᾶς εἰς τὴν
the to be raised me I will go before you   to   -
= I am raised

Γαλιλαίαν. 29 ὁ δὲ Πέτρος ἔφη αὐτῷ·
Galilee.   -   And Peter   said   to him·

εἰ καὶ πάντες σκανδαλισθήσονται, ἀλλ'
If   even   all men   shall be offended,   yet

οὐκ ἐγώ. 30 καὶ λέγει αὐτῷ ὁ Ἰησοῦς·
not   I.   And says   to him   the Jesus:

ἀμὴν λέγω σοι ὅτι σὺ σήμερον ταύτῃ τῇ
Truly   I tell   thee[,]   -   Thou to-day   in this   -

νυκτὶ πρὶν ἢ δὶς ἀλέκτορα φωνῆσαι τρίς
night   before twice a cock   to sound   thrice

με ἀπαρνήσῃ. 31 ὁ δὲ ἐκπερισσῶς ἐλάλει·
me thou wilt deny.   But he more exceedingly   said:

ἐὰν δέῃ με συναποθανεῖν σοι, οὐ μὴ
If it should behove me to die with thee,   by no means
= I must

σε ἀπαρνήσομαι. ὡσαύτως [δὲ] καὶ πάντες
thee will I deny.   And similarly   also   all

ἔλεγον.
said.

32 Καὶ ἔρχονται εἰς χωρίον οὗ τὸ
   And they come   to a piece of land of which the

ὄνομα Γεθσημανί, καὶ λέγει τοῖς μαθηταῖς
name [was] Gethsemani,   and   he says   to the   disciples

αὐτοῦ· καθίσατε ὧδε ἕως προσεύξωμαι.
of him: Sit ye   here   while   I pray.

33 καὶ παραλαμβάνει τὸν Πέτρον καὶ τὸν
   And he takes   -   Peter   and   -

Ἰάκωβον καὶ τὸν Ἰωάννην μετ' αὐτοῦ,
James   and   the   John   with   him,

καὶ ἤρξατο ἐκθαμβεῖσθαι καὶ ἀδημονεῖν,
and   began   to be greatly astonished and to be distressed,

34 καὶ λέγει αὐτοῖς· περίλυπός ἐστιν ἡ
   And says   to them: Deeply grieved   is   the

ψυχή μου ἕως θανάτου· μείνατε ὧδε καὶ
soul   of me unto   death;   remain ye   here   and

γρηγορεῖτε. 35 καὶ προελθὼν μικρὸν ἔπιπτεν
watch.   And going forward a little   he fell

ἐπὶ τῆς γῆς, καὶ προσηύχετο ἵνα εἰ
on   the ground, and   prayed   that   if

δυνατόν ἐστιν παρέλθῃ ἀπ' αὐτοῦ ἡ ὥρα,
possible   it is   might pass away from him   the hour,

36 καὶ ἔλεγεν· ἀββὰ ὁ πατήρ, πάντα
   and   said·   Abba   -   Father,   all things

δυνατά σοι· παρένεγκε τὸ ποτήριον τοῦτο
[are] possible to thee; remove   -   cup   this

ἀπ' ἐμοῦ· ἀλλ' οὐ τί ἐγὼ θέλω ἀλλὰ
from me;   but   not what   I   wish   but

τί σύ. 37 καὶ ἔρχεται καὶ εὑρίσκει
what thou.   And he comes   and   finds

αὐτοὺς καθεύδοντας, καὶ λέγει τῷ Πέτρῳ·
them   sleeping,   and   says   to Peter:

Σίμων, καθεύδεις; οὐκ ἴσχυσας μίαν ὥραν
Simon,   sleepest thou? couldest thou not one   hour

γρηγορῆσαι; 38 γρηγορεῖτε καὶ προσεύχεσθε,
to watch?   Watch ye   and   pray,

ἵνα μὴ ἔλθητε εἰς πειρασμόν· τὸ μὲν
lest   ye come into   temptation;   indeed the

πνεῦμα πρόθυμον, ἡ δὲ σὰρξ ἀσθενής.
spirit   [is] eager,   but the flesh   weak.

39 καὶ πάλιν ἀπελθὼν προσηύξατο τὸν
   And again   going away   he prayed   'the

αὐτὸν λόγον εἰπών. 40 καὶ πάλιν ἐλθὼν
'same   'word 'saying.   And   again   coming

εὗρεν αὐτοὺς καθεύδοντας, ἦσαν γὰρ αὐτῶν
he found them   sleeping,   for were   of them

οἱ ὀφθαλμοὶ καταβαρυνόμενοι, καὶ οὐκ
the   eyes   becoming heavy,   and   not

ᾔδεισαν τί ἀποκριθῶσιν αὐτῷ. 41 καὶ
they knew   what they might answer   him.   And

ἔρχεται τὸ τρίτον καὶ λέγει αὐτοῖς·
he comes   the third [time] and   says   to them:

καθεύδετε τὸ λοιπὸν καὶ ἀναπαύεσθε·
Sleep ye   the   now†   and   rest;

ἀπέχει· ἦλθεν ἡ ὥρα, ἰδοὺ παραδίδοται ὁ
it is enough; came the hour, behold is betrayed   the

υἱὸς τοῦ ἀνθρώπου εἰς τὰς χεῖρας τῶν
Son   -   man   into   the   hands   -

ἁμαρτωλῶν. 42 ἐγείρεσθε, ἄγωμεν· ἰδοὺ ὁ
of sinners.   Rise ye,   let us go;   behold the

παραδιδούς με ἤγγικεν. 43 Καὶ εὐθὺς ἔτι
[one] betraying me has drawn near.   And immediately yet

αὐτοῦ λαλοῦντος παραγίνεται [ὁ] Ἰούδας
him   speaking·   arrives   -   Judas
= while he was still speaking

εἷς τῶν δώδεκα, καὶ μετ' αὐτοῦ ὄχλος
one   of the   twelve,   and   with   him   a crowd

μετὰ μαχαιρῶν καὶ ξύλων παρὰ τῶν
with   swords   and   clubs   from   the

ἀρχιερέων καὶ τῶν γραμματέων καὶ τῶν
chief priests   and   the   scribes   and   the

πρεσβυτέρων. 44 δεδώκει δὲ ὁ παραδιδοὺς
elders.   'Now 'had given 'the [one] 'betraying

αὐτὸν σύσσημον αὐτοῖς λέγων· ὃν ἂν
'him   'a signal   'them   saying: Whomever

φιλήσω αὐτός ἐστιν· κρατήσατε αὐτὸν καὶ
I may kiss he   is;   seize ye   him   and

ἀπάγετε ἀσφαλῶς. 45 καὶ ἐλθὼν εὐθὺς
lead away securely.   And   coming immediately

προσελθὼν αὐτῷ λέγει· ῥαββί, καὶ
approaching to him he says: Rabbi,   and

κατεφίλησεν αὐτόν· 46 οἱ δὲ ἐπέβαλον τὰς
fervently kissed him;   and they 'laid 'on 'the(their)

χεῖρας αὐτῷ καὶ ἐκράτησαν αὐτόν. 47 εἷς
'hands   him and   seized   him.   'one

δὲ τις τῶν παρεστηκότων σπασάμενος
'But 'a certain of the [ones] standing by   drawing

τὴν μάχαιραν ἔπαισεν τὸν δοῦλον τοῦ ἀρχιερέως
the   sword   struck   the   slave   of the high priest

King James Version

and cut off his ear. 48And Jesus answered and said unto them, Are ye come out, as against a thief, with swords and *with* staves to take me? 49 I was daily with you in the temple teaching, and ye took me not: but the Scriptures must be fulfilled. 50And they all forsook him, and fled. 51And there followed him a certain young man, having a linen cloth cast about *his* naked *body;* and the young men laid hold on him: 52And he left the linen cloth, and fled from them naked.

53 And they led Jesus away to the high priest: and with him were assembled all the chief priests and the elders and the scribes. 54And Peter followed him afar off, even into the palace of the high priest: and he sat with the servants, and warmed himself at the fire. 55And the chief priests and all the council sought for witness against Jesus to put him to death; and found none. 56 For many bare false witness against him, but their witness agreed not together. 57And there arose certain, and bare false witness against him, saying, 58 We heard him say, I will destroy this temple that is made with hands, and within three days I will build another made without hands. 59 But neither so did their witness agree together. 60And the high priest stood up in the midst, and asked Jesus, saying, Answerest thou nothing? what *is it which* these witness against thee? 61 But he held his peace, and answered nothing. Again the high priest asked him, and said unto him, Art thou the Christ, the Son of the Blessed? 62And Jesus said, I am: and ye shall see the Son of man sitting on the right hand of power, and coming in the clouds of heaven. 63 Then the high priest rent his clothes, and saith, What need we any further witnesses? 64 Ye have heard the blasphemy: what think ye? And they all condemned him to be guilty of death. 65And some began to spit on him, and to cover his face, and to buffet him, and to say unto him, Prophesy: and the servants did strike him with the palms of their hands.

66 And as Peter was beneath in the palace, there cometh one of the maids of the high priest: 67And when she saw Peter warming himself, she looked upon him, and said, And thou also wast with Jesus of Nazareth. 68 But he denied, saying, I know not, neither understand I what thou sayest. And he went out into the porch; and the cock crew. 69And a maid saw him again, and began to say to them that stood by, This is *one* of them. 70And he denied it again. And a little after, they that stood by said again to Peter, Surely thou art *one* of them: for thou art a Galilean, and thy speech agreeth *thereto.* 71 But he began to curse and to swear, *saying,* I know not this man of whom ye speak. 72And the second time the cock crew. And Peter called to mind the word that Jesus said unto him, Before the cock crow twice, thou shalt deny me thrice. And when he thought thereon, he wept.

New International Version

48 "Am I leading a rebellion," said Jesus, "that you have come out with swords and clubs to capture me? 49 Every day I was with you, teaching in the temple courts, and you did not arrest me. But the Scriptures must be fulfilled." 50 Then everyone deserted him and fled.

51 A young man, wearing nothing but a linen garment, was following Jesus. When they seized him, 52 he fled naked, leaving his garment behind.

Before the Sanhedrin

53 They took Jesus to the high priest, and all the chief priests, elders and teachers of the law came together. 54 Peter followed him at a distance, right into the courtyard of the high priest. There he sat with the guards and warmed himself at the fire.

55 The chief priests and the whole Sanhedrin were looking for evidence against Jesus so that they could put him to death, but they did not find any. 56 Many testified falsely against him, but their statements did not agree.

57 Then some stood up and gave this false testimony against him: 58 "We heard him say, 'I will destroy this man-made temple and in three days will build another, not made by man.'" 59 Yet even then their testimony did not agree.

60 Then the high priest stood up before them and asked Jesus, "Are you not going to answer? What is this testimony that these men are bringing against you?" 61 But Jesus remained silent and gave no answer.

Again the high priest asked him, "Are you the Christ,[p] the Son of the Blessed One?"

62 "I am," said Jesus. "And you will see the Son of Man sitting at the right hand of the Mighty One and coming on the clouds of heaven."

63 The high priest tore his clothes. "Why do we need any more witnesses?" he asked. 64 "You have heard the blasphemy. What do you think?"

They all condemned him as worthy of death. 65 Then some began to spit at him; they blindfolded him, struck him with their fists, and said, "Prophesy!" And the guards took him and beat him.

Peter disowns Jesus

66 While Peter was below in the courtyard, one of the servant girls of the high priest came by. 67 When she saw Peter warming himself, she looked closely at him.

"You also were with that Nazarene, Jesus," she said.

68 But he denied it. "I don't know or understand what you're talking about," he said, and went out into the entryway.[q]

69 When the servant girl saw him there, she said again to those standing around, "This fellow is one of them." 70 Again he denied it.

After a little while, those standing near said to Peter, "Surely you are one of them, for you are a Galilean."

71 He began to call down curses on himself, and he swore to them, "I don't know this man you're talking about."

72 Immediately the rooster crowed the second time.[r] Then Peter remembered the word Jesus had spoken to him: "Before the rooster crows twice,[s] you will disown me three times." And he broke down and wept.

[p] Or *Messiah.* [q] Some early MSS add *and the rooster crowed.* [r] Some early MSS omit *the second time.* [s] Some early MSS omit *twice.*

154

Greek Interlinear

καὶ ἀφεῖλεν αὐτοῦ τὸ ὠτάριον. 48 καὶ
and cut off of him the ear. And

ἀποκριθεὶς ὁ Ἰησοῦς εἶπεν αὐτοῖς· ὡς
answering – Jesus said to them: As

ἐπὶ λῃστὴν ἐξήλθατε μετὰ μαχαιρῶν καὶ
against a robber came ye forth with swords and

ξύλων συλλαβεῖν με; 49 καθ᾽ ἡμέραν ἤμην
clubs to arrest me? Daily I was

πρὸς ὑμᾶς ἐν τῷ ἱερῷ διδάσκων, καὶ οὐκ
with you in the temple teaching, and not

ἐκρατήσατέ με· ἀλλ᾽ ἵνα πληρωθῶσιν αἱ
ye did seize me; but that may be fulfilled the

γραφαί. 50 καὶ ἀφέντες αὐτὸν ἔφυγον
scriptures. And leaving him they fled

πάντες. 51 Καὶ νεανίσκος τις συνηκολούθει
all. And a certain young man accompanied

αὐτῷ περιβεβλημένος σινδόνα ἐπὶ γυμνοῦ,
him having been clothed [in] a nightgown over [his] naked [body],

καὶ κρατοῦσιν αὐτόν· 52 ὁ δὲ καταλιπὼν
and they seize him; and he leaving

τὴν σινδόνα γυμνὸς ἔφυγεν.
the nightgown naked fled.

53 Καὶ ἀπήγαγον τὸν Ἰησοῦν πρὸς τὸν
And they led away – Jesus to the

ἀρχιερέα, καὶ συνέρχονται πάντες οἱ
high priest, and come together all the

ἀρχιερεῖς καὶ οἱ πρεσβύτεροι καὶ οἱ
chief priests and the elders and the

γραμματεῖς. 54 καὶ ὁ Πέτρος ἀπὸ μακρόθεν
scribes. And – Peter from afar

ἠκολούθησεν αὐτῷ ἕως ἔσω εἰς τὴν αὐλὴν
followed him until within in the court

τοῦ ἀρχιερέως, καὶ ἦν συγκαθήμενος μετὰ
of the high priest, and was sitting with with

τῶν ὑπηρετῶν καὶ θερμαινόμενος πρὸς τὸ
the attendants and warming himself by the

φῶς. 55 Οἱ δὲ ἀρχιερεῖς καὶ ὅλον τὸ
bright fire. Now the chief priests and all the

συνέδριον ἐζήτουν κατὰ τοῦ Ἰησοῦ
council sought against – Jesus

μαρτυρίαν εἰς τὸ θανατῶσαι αὐτόν, καὶ
witness for the to put to death him, and
= so as

οὐχ ηὕρισκον· 56 πολλοὶ γὰρ ἐψευδομαρτύρουν
found not; for many falsely witnessed

κατ᾽ αὐτοῦ, καὶ ἴσαι αἱ μαρτυρίαι οὐκ
against him, and ¹identical ¹the ⁴testimonies ⁴not

ἦσαν. 57 καί τινες ἀναστάντες ἐψευδομαρτύρουν
²were. And some standing up falsely witnessed

κατ᾽ αὐτοῦ λέγοντες 58 ὅτι ἡμεῖς ἠκούσαμεν
against him saying[,] – We heard

αὐτοῦ λέγοντος ὅτι ἐγὼ καταλύσω τὸν
him saying[,] – I will overthrow the

ναὸν τοῦτον τὸν χειροποίητον καὶ διὰ
²shrine ¹this – ³handmade and through(after)

τριῶν ἡμερῶν ἄλλον ἀχειροποίητον οἰκο-
three days another not handmade I will

δομήσω. 59 καὶ οὐδὲ οὕτως ἴση ἦν ἡ
build. And not so identical was the

μαρτυρία αὐτῶν. 60 καὶ ἀναστὰς ὁ
witness of them. And standing up the

ἀρχιερεὺς εἰς μέσον ἐπηρώτησεν τὸν Ἰησοῦν
high priest in [the] midst questioned – Jesus

λέγων· οὐκ ἀποκρίνῃ οὐδὲν τί οὗτοί σου
saying: Answerest thou not no(any)thing what these men ¹thee

καταμαρτυροῦσιν; 61 ὁ δὲ ἐσιώπα καὶ
¹testify against? But he was silent and

οὐκ ἀπεκρίνατο οὐδέν. πάλιν ὁ ἀρχιερεὺς
answered not no(any)thing. Again the high priest

ἐπηρώτα αὐτὸν καὶ λέγει αὐτῷ· σὺ εἶ ὁ
questioned him and says to him: Thou art the

χριστὸς ὁ υἱὸς τοῦ εὐλογητοῦ; 62 ὁ δὲ
Christ the Son of the Blessed [one]? – And

Ἰησοῦς εἶπεν· ἐγώ εἰμι, καὶ ὄψεσθε
Jesus said: I am, and ye will see

τὸν υἱὸν τοῦ ἀνθρώπου ἐκ δεξιῶν καθήμενον
the Son – of man ²at [the] right [hand] ¹sitting

τῆς δυνάμεως καὶ ἐρχόμενον μετὰ τῶν
of the Power and coming with the

νεφελῶν τοῦ οὐρανοῦ. 63 ὁ δὲ ἀρχιερεὺς
clouds – of heaven. And the high priest

διαρρήξας τοὺς χιτῶνας αὐτοῦ λέγει· τί
rending the tunics of him says: What

ἔτι χρείαν ἔχομεν μαρτύρων; 64 ἠκούσατε
more need have we of witnesses? ye heard

τῆς βλασφημίας· τί ὑμῖν φαίνεται; οἱ δὲ
the blasphemy; what to you appears it? And they

πάντες κατέκριναν αὐτὸν ἔνοχον εἶναι
all condemned him liable to be

θανάτου. 65 Καὶ ἤρξαντό τινες ἐμπτύειν
of(to) death. And began some to spit at

αὐτῷ καὶ περικαλύπτειν αὐτοῦ τὸ πρόσωπον
him and to cover of him the face

καὶ κολαφίζειν αὐτὸν καὶ λέγειν αὐτῷ·
and to maltreat him and to say to him:

προφήτευσον, καὶ οἱ ὑπηρέται ῥαπίσμασιν
Prophesy, and the attendants with slaps

αὐτὸν ἔλαβον. 66 Καὶ ὄντος τοῦ Πέτρου
²him ¹took. And being – Peter³
= as Peter was

κάτω ἐν τῇ αὐλῇ ἔρχεται μία τῶν
below in the court comes one of the

παιδισκῶν τοῦ ἀρχιερέως, 67 καὶ ἰδοῦσα
maidservants of the high priest, and seeing

τὸν Πέτρον θερμαινόμενον ἐμβλέψασα αὐτῷ
– Peter warming himself looking at him

λέγει· καὶ σὺ μετὰ τοῦ Ναζαρηνοῦ ἦσθα
says: And ¹thou ²with ⁴the ⁵Nazarene ³wast

τοῦ Ἰησοῦ. 68 ὁ δὲ ἠρνήσατο λέγων· ⁵οὔτε
– ⁶Jesus. But he denied saying: ⁵neither

οἶδα οὔτε ἐπίσταμαι σὺ τί λέγεις. καὶ
¹I ²know ⁴nor ³understand ⁷thou ⁸what ⁶sayest. And

ἐξῆλθεν ἔξω εἰς τὸ προαύλιον· 69 καὶ ἡ
he went forth outside into the forecourt; and the

παιδίσκη ἰδοῦσα αὐτὸν ἤρξατο πάλιν λέγειν
maidservant seeing him began again to say

τοῖς παρεστῶσιν ὅτι οὗτος ἐξ αὐτῶν ἐστιν.
to the [ones] standing by[.] – This man of them is.

70 ὁ δὲ πάλιν ἠρνεῖτο. καὶ μετὰ μικρὸν
But he again denied. And after a little

πάλιν οἱ παρεστῶτες ἔλεγον τῷ Πέτρῳ·
again the [ones] standing by said – to Peter:

ἀληθῶς ἐξ αὐτῶν εἶ· καὶ γὰρ Γαλιλαῖος
Truly of them thou art; ²indeed ¹for ⁴a Galilæan

εἶ. 71 ὁ δὲ ἤρξατο ἀναθεματίζειν καὶ
³thou art. And he began to curse and

ὀμνύναι ὅτι οὐκ οἶδα τὸν ἄνθρωπον
to swear[,] – I know not the man

τοῦτον ὃν λέγετε. 72 καὶ εὐθὺς ἐκ
this whom ye say. And immediately –

δευτέρου ἀλέκτωρ ἐφώνησεν. καὶ ἀνεμνήσθη
second time a cock crew. And remembered

ὁ Πέτρος τὸ ῥῆμα ὡς εἶπεν αὐτῷ ὁ
– Peter the word as said to him the

Ἰησοῦς ὅτι πρὶν ἀλέκτορα δὶς φωνῆσαι
Jesus[,] – Before a cock twice to crow⁰

τρίς με ἀπαρνήσῃ. καὶ ἐπιβαλὼν ἔκλαιεν.
thrice me thou wilt deny; and thinking thereon he wept.

King James Version

15 And straightway in the morning the chief priests held a consultation with the elders and scribes and the whole council, and bound Jesus, and carried *him* away, and delivered *him* to Pilate. 2And Pilate asked him, Art thou the King of the Jews? And he answering said unto him, Thou sayest *it.* 3And the chief priests accused him of many things; but he answered nothing. 4And Pilate asked him again, saying, Answerest thou nothing? behold how many things they witness against thee. 5 But Jesus yet answered nothing; so that Pilate marvelled. 6 Now at *that* feast he released unto them one prisoner, whomsoever they desired. 7And there was *one* named Barabbas, *which lay* bound with them that had made insurrection with him, who had committed murder in the insurrection. 8And the multitude crying aloud began to desire *him to do* as he had ever done unto them. 9 But Pilate answered them, saying, Will ye that I release unto you the King of the Jews? 10 For he knew that the chief priests had delivered him for envy. 11 But the chief priests moved the people, that he should rather release Barabbas unto them. 12And Pilate answered and said again unto them, What will ye then that I shall do *unto him* whom ye call the King of the Jews? 13And they cried out again, Crucify him. 14 Then Pilate said unto them, Why, what evil hath he done? And they cried out the more exceedingly, Crucify him.

15 And *so* Pilate, willing to content the people, released Barabbas unto them, and delivered Jesus, when he had scourged *him,* to be crucified. 16And the soldiers led him away into the hall, called Pretorium; and they call together the whole band. 17And they clothed him with purple, and platted a crown of thorns, and put it about his *head,* 18And began to salute him, Hail, King of the Jews! 19And they smote him on the head with a reed, and did spit upon him, and bowing *their* knees worshipped him. 20And when they had mocked him, they took off the purple from him, and put his own clothes on him, and led him out to crucify him. 21And they compel one Simon a Cyrenian, who passed by, coming out of the country, the father of Alexander and Rufus, to bear his cross. 22And they bring him unto the place Golgotha, which is, being interpreted, The place of a skull. 23And they gave him to drink wine mingled with myrrh: but he received *it* not. 24And when they had crucified him, they parted his garments, casting lots upon them, what every man should take. 25And it was the third hour, and they crucified him. 26And the superscription of his accusation was written over, THE KING OF THE JEWS. 27And with him they crucify two thieves; the one on his right hand, and the other on his left. 28And the Scripture was fulfilled, which saith, And he was numbered with the transgressors. 29And they that passed by railed on him, wagging

New International Version

Jesus before Pilate

15 Very early in the morning, the chief priests, with the elders, the teachers of the law and the whole Sanhedrin, reached a decision. They bound Jesus, led him away and handed him over to Pilate.

2 "Are you the king of the Jews?" asked Pilate.

"Yes, it is as you say," Jesus replied.

3 The chief priests accused him of many things. 4 So again Pilate asked him, "Aren't you going to answer? See how many things they are accusing you of."

5 But Jesus still made no reply, and Pilate was amazed.

6 Now it was the custom at the Feast to release a prisoner whom the people requested. 7A man called Barabbas was in prison with the insurrectionists who had committed murder in the uprising. 8 The crowd came up and asked Pilate to do for them what he usually did.

9 "Do you want me to release to you the king of the Jews?" asked Pilate, 10 knowing it was out of envy that the chief priests had handed Jesus over to him. 11 But the chief priests stirred up the crowd to have Pilate release Barabbas instead.

12 "What shall I do, then, with the one you call the king of the Jews?" Pilate asked them.

13 "Crucify him!" they shouted.

14 "Why? What crime has he committed?" asked Pilate.

But they shouted all the louder, "Crucify him!"

15 Wanting to satisfy the crowd, Pilate released Barabbas to them. He had Jesus flogged, and handed him over to be crucified.

The soldiers mock Jesus

16 The soldiers led Jesus away into the palace (that is, the Praetorium) and called together the whole company of soldiers. 17 They put a purple robe on him, then wove a crown of thorns and set it on him. 18And they began to call out to him, "Hail, King of the Jews!" 19Again and again they struck him on the head with a staff and spit on him. Falling on their knees, they worshiped him. 20And when they had mocked him, they took off the purple robe and put his own clothes on him. Then they led him out to crucify him.

The crucifixion

21 A certain man from Cyrene, Simon, the father of Alexander and Rufus, was passing by on his way in from the country, and they forced him to carry the cross. 22 They brought Jesus to the place called Golgotha (which means, The Place of the Skull). 23 Then they offered him wine mixed with myrrh, but he did not take it. 24And they crucified him. Dividing up his clothes, they cast lots to see what each would get.

25 It was the third hour when they crucified him. 26 The written notice of the charge against him read: THE KING OF THE JEWS. 27 They crucified two robbers with him, one on his right and one on his left.* 29 Those who passed by hurled

---

[*t*] Some MSS add verse 28: *and the scripture was fulfilled which says, "He was counted with the lawless ones."* (Isaiah 53:12).

Greek Interlinear

Chapter 15

Καὶ εὐθὺς πρωῒ συμβούλιον ἑτοιμάσαντες
And immediately early   ²a council   ¹preparing

οἱ ἀρχιερεῖς μετὰ τῶν πρεσβυτέρων καὶ
the chief priests with the elders and

γραμματέων καὶ ὅλον τὸ συνέδριον, δήσαντες
scribes and all the council, having bound

τὸν Ἰησοῦν ἀπήνεγκαν καὶ παρέδωκαν
- Jesus led [him] away and delivered [him]

Πιλάτῳ. 2 καὶ ἐπηρώτησεν αὐτὸν ὁ
to Pilate. And questioned him -

Πιλᾶτος· σὺ εἶ ὁ βασιλεὺς τῶν Ἰουδαίων;
Pilate: Thou art the king of the Jews?

ὁ δὲ ἀποκριθεὶς αὐτῷ λέγει· σὺ λέγεις.
And he answering him says: Thou sayest.

3 καὶ κατηγόρουν αὐτοῦ οἱ ἀρχιερεῖς πολλά.
And accused him the chief priests many things.

4 ὁ δὲ Πιλᾶτος πάλιν ἐπηρώτα αὐτὸν [λέγων]·
- But Pilate again questioned him saying:

οὐκ ἀποκρίνῃ οὐδέν; ἴδε πόσα
Answerest thou not no(any)thing? Behold how many things

σου κατηγοροῦσιν. 5 ὁ δὲ Ἰησοῦς οὐκ-
thee they accuse. - But Jesus no(any)

ἔτι οὐδὲν ἀπεκρίθη, ὥστε θαυμάζειν
more nothing answered, so as to marvel

τὸν Πιλᾶτον. 6 Κατὰ δὲ ἑορτὴν ἀπέλυεν
- Pilate[b]. Now at a feast he released

αὐτοῖς ἕνα δέσμιον ὃν παρῃτοῦντο. 7 ἦν δὲ
to them one prisoner whom they begged. Now there was

ὁ λεγόμενος Βαραββᾶς μετὰ τῶν
the [one] named Barabbas with the

στασιαστῶν δεδεμένος, οἵτινες ἐν τῇ στάσει
rebels having been bound, who* in the rebellion

φόνον πεποιήκεισαν. 8 καὶ ἀναβὰς ὁ ὄχλος
murder had done. And going up the crowd

ἤρξατο αἰτεῖσθαι καθὼς ἐποίει αὐτοῖς.
began to ask as he used to do for them.

9 ὁ δὲ Πιλᾶτος ἀπεκρίθη αὐτοῖς λέγων·
- But Pilate answered them saying:

θέλετε ἀπολύσω ὑμῖν τὸν βασιλέα τῶν
Do you wish I may release to you the king of the

Ἰουδαίων; 10 ἐγίνωσκεν γὰρ ὅτι διὰ φθόνον
Jews? For he knew that on account of envy

παραδεδώκεισαν αὐτὸν οἱ ἀρχιερεῖς. 11 οἱ
had delivered him the chief priests.

δὲ ἀρχιερεῖς ἀνέσεισαν τὸν ὄχλον ἵνα
But chief priests stirred up the crowd that

μᾶλλον τὸν Βαραββᾶν ἀπολύσῃ αὐτοῖς.
rather - Barabbas he should release to them.

12 ὁ δὲ Πιλᾶτος πάλιν ἀποκριθεὶς ἔλεγεν
- So Pilate again answering said

αὐτοῖς· τί οὖν ποιήσω [ὃν] λέγετε τὸν
to them: What then may I do [to him] whom ye call the

βασιλέα τῶν Ἰουδαίων; 13 οἱ δὲ πάλιν
king of the Jews? And they again

ἔκραξαν· σταύρωσον αὐτόν. 14 ὁ δὲ
cried out: Crucify him. - But

Πιλᾶτος ἔλεγεν αὐτοῖς· τί γὰρ ἐποίησεν
Pilate said to them: Indeed what ¹did he

κακόν; οἱ δὲ περισσῶς ἔκραξαν· σταύρωσον
¹evil? and they more cried out: Crucify

αὐτόν. 15 ὁ δὲ Πιλᾶτος βουλόμενος τῷ
him. - And Pilate resolving the

ὄχλῳ τὸ ἱκανὸν ποιῆσαι ἀπέλυσεν αὐτοῖς
crowd to satisfy† released to them

τὸν Βαραββᾶν, καὶ παρέδωκεν τὸν Ἰησοῦν
- Barabbas, and delivered - Jesus

φραγελλώσας ἵνα σταυρωθῇ.
having scourged [him] that he might be crucified.

16 Οἱ δὲ στρατιῶται ἀπήγαγον αὐτὸν
Then the soldiers led away him

ἔσω τῆς αὐλῆς, ὅ ἐστιν πραιτώριον, καὶ
inside the court, which is prætorium, and

συγκαλοῦσιν ὅλην τὴν σπεῖραν. 17 καὶ
they call together all the cohort. And

ἐνδιδύσκουσιν αὐτὸν πορφύραν καὶ περιτιθέασιν
they put on him a purple [robe] and place round

αὐτῷ πλέξαντες ἀκάνθινον στέφανον· 18 καὶ
him plaiting a thorny crown; and

ἤρξαντο ἀσπάζεσθαι αὐτόν· χαῖρε, βασιλεῦ
they began to salute him: Hail, king

τῶν Ἰουδαίων· 19 καὶ ἔτυπτον αὐτοῦ τὴν
of the Jews; and they struck of him the

κεφαλὴν καλάμῳ καὶ ἐνέπτυον αὐτῷ, καὶ
head with a reed and spat at him, and

τιθέντες τὰ γόνατα προσεκύνουν αὐτῷ.
placing(bending) the(their) knees worshipped him.

20 καὶ ὅτε ἐνέπαιξαν αὐτῷ, ἐξέδυσαν
And when they mocked him, they took off

αὐτὸν τὴν πορφύραν καὶ ἐνέδυσαν αὐτὸν
him the purple [robe] and put on him

τὰ ἱμάτια αὐτοῦ. Καὶ ἐξάγουσιν αὐτὸν
the garments of him. And they lead forth him

ἵνα σταυρώσωσιν αὐτόν. 21 καὶ ἀγγαρεύουσιν
that they might crucify him. And they impress

παράγοντά τινα Σίμωνα Κυρηναῖον ἐρχόμενον
passing by a certain Simon a Cyrenian coming

ἀπ' ἀγροῦ, τὸν πατέρα Ἀλεξάνδρου καὶ
from [the] country, the father of Alexander and

Ῥούφου, ἵνα ἄρῃ τὸν σταυρὸν αὐτοῦ.
of Rufus, that he might bear the cross of him.

22 καὶ φέρουσιν αὐτὸν ἐπὶ τὸν Γολγοθᾶν
And they bring him to the Golgotha

τόπον, ὅ ἐστιν μεθερμηνευόμενος κρανίου
place, which is being interpreted of a skull

τόπος. 23 καὶ ἐδίδουν αὐτῷ ἐσμυρνισμένον
place. And they gave him ¹having been spiced
with myrrh

οἶνον· ὃς δὲ οὐκ ἔλαβεν. 24 καὶ σταυροῦσιν
¹wine; but who(he) received not. And they crucify

αὐτόν, καὶ διαμερίζονται τὰ ἱμάτια αὐτοῦ,
him, and divide the garments of him,

βάλλοντες κλῆρον ἐπ' αὐτὰ τίς τί ἄρῃ.
casting a lot on them ²one ¹what might take.

25 ἦν δὲ ὥρα τρίτη καὶ ἐσταύρωσαν
Now it was hour third and they crucified

αὐτόν. 26 καὶ ἦν ἡ ἐπιγραφὴ τῆς αἰτίας
him. And was the superscription of the accusation

αὐτοῦ ἐπιγεγραμμένη· Ο ΒΑΣΙΛΕΥΣ ΤΩΝ
of him having been written over: THE KING OF THE

ΙΟΥΔΑΙΩΝ. 27 Καὶ σὺν αὐτῷ σταυροῦσιν
JEWS. And with him they crucify

δύο λῃστάς, ἕνα ἐκ δεξιῶν καὶ ἕνα ἐξ
two robbers, one on [the] right and one on

εὐωνύμων αὐτοῦ. ‡ 29 Καὶ οἱ παραπορευόμενοι
[the] left of him. And the [ones] passing by

---

* Note the plural.

‡ Verse 28 omitted by Nestle

King James Version

their heads, and saying, Ah, thou that destroyest the temple, and buildest *it* in three days, 30 Save thyself, and come down from the cross. 31 Likewise also the chief priests mocking said among themselves with the scribes, He saved others; himself he cannot save. 32 Let Christ the King of Israel descend now from the cross, that we may see and believe. And they that were crucified with him reviled him. 33And when the sixth hour was come, there was darkness over the whole land until the ninth hour. 34And at the ninth hour Jesus cried with a loud voice, saying, Eloi, Eloi, lama sabachthani? which is, being interpreted, My God, my God, why hast thou forsaken me? 35And some of them that stood by, when they heard *it*, said, Behold, he calleth Elias. 36And one ran and filled a sponge full of vinegar, and put *it* on a reed, and gave him to drink, saying, Let alone; let us see whether Elias will come to take him down. 37And Jesus cried with a loud voice, and gave up the ghost. 38And the vail of the temple was rent in twain from the top to the bottom.

39 And when the centurion, which stood over against him, saw that he so cried out, and gave up the ghost, he said, Truly this man was the Son of God. 40 There were also women looking on afar off: among whom was Mary Magdalene, and Mary the mother of James the less and of Joses, and Salome; 41 Who also, when he was in Galilee, followed him, and ministered unto him; and many other women which came up with him unto Jerusalem.

42 And now when the even was come, because it was the preparation, that is, the day before the sabbath, 43 Joseph of Arimathea, an honourable counsellor, which also waited for the kingdom of God, came, and went in boldly unto Pilate, and craved the body of Jesus. 44And Pilate marvelled if he were already dead: and calling *unto him* the centurion, he asked him whether he had been any while dead. 45And when he knew *it* of the centurion, he gave the body to Joseph. 46And he bought fine linen, and took him down, and wrapped him in the linen, and laid him in a sepulchre which was hewn out of a rock, and rolled a stone unto the door of the sepulchre. 47And Mary Magdalene and Mary *the mother* of Joses beheld where he was laid.

16 And when the sabbath was past, Mary Magdalene, and Mary the *mother* of James, and Salome, had bought sweet spices, that they might come and anoint him. 2And very early in the morning, the first *day* of the week, they came unto the sepulchre at the rising of the sun. 3And they said among themselves, Who shall roll us away the stone from the door of the

New International Version

insults at him, shaking their heads and saying, "So! You who are going to destroy the temple and build it in three days, 30 come down from the cross and save yourself!"

31 In the same way the chief priests and the teachers of the law mocked him among themselves. "He saved others," they said, "but he can't save himself! 32 Let this Christ,ᵘ this King of Israel, come down now from the cross, that we may see and believe." Those crucified with him also heaped insults on him.

The death of Jesus

33 At the sixth hour darkness came over the whole land until the ninth hour. 34And at the ninth hour Jesus cried out in a loud voice, *"Eloi, Eloi, lama sabachthani?"*—which means, "My God, my God, why have you forsaken me?" ᵛ

35 When some of those standing near heard this, they said, "Listen, he's calling Elijah."

36 One man ran, filled a sponge with wine vinegar, put it on a stick, and offered it to Jesus to drink. "Leave him alone now. Let's see if Elijah comes to take him down," he said.

37 With a loud cry, Jesus breathed his last.

38 The curtain of the temple was torn in two from top to bottom. 39And when the centurion, who stood there in front of Jesus, heard his cry and ʷ saw how he died, he said, "Surely this man was the Sonˣ of God!"

40 Some women were watching from a distance. Among them were Mary Magdalene, Mary the mother of James the younger and of Joses, and Salome. 41 In Galilee these women had followed him and cared for his needs. Many other women who had come up with him to Jerusalem were also there.

The burial of Jesus

42 It was Preparation Day (that is, the day before the Sabbath). So as evening approached, 43 Joseph of Arimathea, a prominent member of the Council, who was himself waiting for the kingdom of God, went boldly to Pilate and asked for Jesus' body. 44 Pilate was surprised to hear that he was already dead. Summoning the centurion, he asked him if Jesus had already died. 45 When he learned from the centurion that it was so, he gave the body to Joseph. 46 So Joseph bought some linen cloth, took down the body, wrapped it in the linen, and placed it in a tomb cut out of rock. Then he rolled a stone against the entrance of the tomb. 47 Mary Magdalene and Mary the mother of Joses saw where he was laid.

The resurrection

16 When the Sabbath was over, Mary Magdalene, Mary the mother of James, and Salome bought spices so that they might go to anoint Jesus' body. 2 Very early on the first day of the week, just after sunrise, they were on their way to the tomb 3 and they asked each other, "Who will roll the stone away from the entrance of the tomb?"

[u] Or *Messiah.* [v] Psalm 22:1. [w] Some MSS omit *heard his cry and.* [x] Or *a son.*

Greek Interlinear

ἐβλασφήμουν αὐτὸν κινοῦντες τὰς κεφαλὰς
blasphemed him wagging the heads

αὐτῶν καὶ λέγοντες· οὐὰ ὁ καταλύων
of them and saying· Ah the [one] overthrowing

τὸν ναὸν καὶ οἰκοδομῶν [ἐν] τρισὶν
the shrine and building in three

ἡμέραις, 30 σῶσον σεαυτὸν καταβὰς ἀπὸ
days, save thyself coming down from

τοῦ σταυροῦ. 31 ὁμοίως καὶ οἱ ἀρχιερεῖς
the cross. Likewise also the chief priests

ἐμπαίζοντες πρὸς ἀλλήλους μετὰ τῶν
mocking to one another with the

γραμματέων ἔλεγον· ἄλλους ἔσωσεν, ἑαυτὸν
scribes said· Others he saved, himself

οὐ δύναται σῶσαι· 32 ὁ χριστὸς ὁ βασιλεὺς
he cannot to save; the Christ the king

Ἰσραὴλ καταβάτω νῦν ἀπὸ τοῦ σταυροῦ,
of Israel let come down now from the cross,

ἵνα ἴδωμεν καὶ πιστεύσωμεν. καὶ οἱ
that we may see and believe. And the

συνεσταυρωμένοι σὺν αὐτῷ ὠνείδιζον αὐτόν.
[ones] crucified with with him reproached him.

33 Καὶ γενομένης ὥρας ἕκτης σκότος
And becoming hour sixth* darkness
= when it was the sixth hour

ἐγένετο ἐφ᾽ ὅλην τὴν γῆν ἕως ὥρας
came over all the land until [the] hour

ἐνάτης. 34 καὶ τῇ ἐνάτῃ ὥρᾳ ἐβόησεν ὁ
ninth. And at the ninth hour cried

Ἰησοῦς φωνῇ μεγάλῃ· ἐλωῒ ἐλωῒ λαμὰ
Jesus with a voice great(loud): Eloi[,] Eloi[,] lama

σαβαχθάνι; ὅ ἐστιν μεθερμηνευόμενον·
sabachthani? which is being interpreted: The

θεός μου ὁ θεός μου, εἰς τί ἐγκατέλιπές
God of me[,] the God of me, why didst thou forsake

με; 35 καί τινες τῶν παρεστηκότων
me ? And some of the [ones] standing by

ἀκούσαντες ἔλεγον· ἴδε Ἠλίαν φωνεῖ.
hearing said: Behold Elias he calls.

36 δραμὼν δέ τις γεμίσας σπόγγον ὄξους
And running one having filled a sponge of(with) vinegar

περιθεὶς καλάμῳ ἐπότιζεν αὐτόν, λέγων·
placing it round a reed ¹gave ²to drink ³him, saying:

ἄφετε ἴδωμεν εἰ ἔρχεται Ἠλίας καθελεῖν
Leave[,] let us see if comes Elias ¹to take ³down

αὐτόν. 37 ὁ δὲ Ἰησοῦς ἀφεὶς φωνὴν
²him. - But Jesus letting go voice

μεγάλην ἐξέπνευσεν. 38 Καὶ τὸ καταπέτασμα
a great(loud) expired. And the veil

τοῦ ναοῦ ἐσχίσθη εἰς δύο ἀπ᾽ ἄνωθεν
of the shrine was rent in two from top

ἕως κάτω. 39 Ἰδὼν δὲ ὁ κεντυρίων
to bottom. And ⁶seeing ¹the ²centurion -

παρεστηκὼς ἐξ ἐναντίας αὐτοῦ ὅτι οὕτως
³standing by ⁴opposite ⁵him that thus

ἐξέπνευσεν, εἶπεν· ἀληθῶς οὗτος ὁ ἄνθρωπος
he expired, said: Truly this - man

υἱὸς θεοῦ ἦν. 40 Ἦσαν δὲ καὶ γυναῖκες
son of God was. Now there were also women

ἀπὸ μακρόθεν θεωροῦσαι, ἐν αἷς καὶ
from afar beholding, among whom both

Μαρία ἡ Μαγδαληνὴ καὶ Μαρία ἡ
Mary the Magdalene and Mary ¹the

Ἰακώβου τοῦ μικροῦ καὶ Ἰωσῆτος μήτηρ
²of James ⁴the ⁵little ⁶and ⁷of Joses ³mother

καὶ Σαλώμη, 41 αἳ ὅτε ἦν ἐν τῇ Γαλιλαίᾳ
and Salome, who when he was in - Galilee

ἠκολούθουν αὐτῷ καὶ διηκόνουν αὐτῷ, καὶ
followed him and served him, and

ἄλλαι πολλαὶ αἱ συναναβᾶσαι αὐτῷ εἰς
others many - having come up with him to

Ἱεροσόλυμα.
Jerusalem.

42 Καὶ ἤδη ὀψίας γενομένης, ἐπεὶ ἦν
And now evening coming,* since it was
= when it was evening,

παρασκευή, ὅ ἐστιν προσάββατον, 43 ἐλθὼν
[the] preparation, which is the day before the sabbath, coming

Ἰωσὴφ ὁ ἀπὸ Ἀριμαθαίας, εὐσχήμων
Joseph the [one] from Arimathœa, an honourable

βουλευτής, ὃς καὶ αὐτὸς ἦν προσδεχόμενος
councillor, who also [him]self was expecting

τὴν βασιλείαν τοῦ θεοῦ, τολμήσας εἰσῆλθεν
the kingdom - of God, taking courage went in

πρὸς τὸν Πιλᾶτον καὶ ᾐτήσατο τὸ σῶμα
to - Pilate and asked the body

τοῦ Ἰησοῦ. 44 ὁ δὲ Πιλᾶτος ἐθαύμασεν
- of Jesus. - And Pilate marvelled

εἰ ἤδη τέθνηκεν, καὶ προσκαλεσάμενος τὸν
if already he has died, and calling to [him] the

κεντυρίωνα ἐπηρώτησεν αὐτὸν εἰ πάλαι
centurion questioned him f long ago

ἀπέθανεν· 45 καὶ γνοὺς ἀπὸ τοῦ κεντυρίωνος
he died; and knowing from the centurion

ἐδωρήσατο τὸ πτῶμα τῷ Ἰωσήφ. 46 καὶ
he granted the corpse - to Joseph. And

ἀγοράσας σινδόνα καθελὼν αὐτὸν ἐνείλησεν
having bought a piece of taking down him he wrapped
unused linen

τῇ σινδόνι καὶ κατέθηκεν αὐτὸν ἐν μνήματι
with the linen and deposited him in a tomb

ὃ ἦν λελατομημένον ἐκ πέτρας, καὶ
which was having been hewn out of rock, and

προσεκύλισεν λίθον ἐπὶ τὴν θύραν τοῦ
rolled a stone against the door of the

μνημείου. 47 ἡ δὲ Μαρία ἡ Μαγδαληνὴ
tomb. - And Mary the Magdalene

καὶ Μαρία ἡ Ἰωσῆτος ἐθεώρουν ποῦ
and Mary the [mother] of Joses beheld where

τέθειται.
he has been laid.

Chapter 16

Καὶ διαγενομένου τοῦ σαββάτου [ἡ]
And passing the sabbath* -
= when the sabbath was past

Μαρία ἡ Μαγδαληνὴ καὶ Μαρία ἡ [τοῦ]
Mary the Magdalene and Mary the [mother] -

Ἰακώβου καὶ Σαλώμη ἠγόρασαν ἀρώματα
of James and Salome bought spices

ἵνα ἐλθοῦσαι ἀλείψωσιν αὐτόν. 2 καὶ λίαν
that coming they might anoint him. And very

πρωῒ [τῇ] μιᾷ τῶν σαββάτων ἔρχονται
early on the first day of the week† they come

ἐπὶ τὸ μνῆμα, ἀνατείλαντος τοῦ ἡλίου.
upon the tomb, rising the sun.*
= as the sun rose.

3 καὶ ἔλεγον πρὸς ἑαυτάς· τίς ἀποκυλίσει
And they said to themselves: Who will roll away

ἡμῖν τὸν λίθον ἐκ τῆς θύρας τοῦ μνημείου;
for us the stone out of the door of the tomb ?

King James Version

sepulchre? 4And when they looked, they saw that the stone was rolled away: for it was very great. 5And entering into the sepulchre, they saw a young man sitting on the right side, clothed in a long white garment; and they were affrighted. 6And he saith unto them, Be not affrighted: ye seek Jesus of Nazareth, which was crucified: he is risen; he is not here: behold the place where they laid him. 7 But go your way, tell his disciples and Peter that he goeth before you into Galilee: there shall ye see him, as he said unto you. 8And they went out quickly, and fled from the sepulchre; for they trembled and were amazed: neither said they any thing to any *man;* for they were afraid.

9 Now when *Jesus* was risen early the first *day* of the week, he appeared first to Mary Magdalene, out of whom he had cast seven devils. 10*And* she went and told them that had been with him, as they mourned and wept. 11And they, when they had heard that he was alive, and had been seen of her, believed not.

12 After that he appeared in another form unto two of them, as they walked, and went into the country. 13And they went and told *it* unto the residue: neither believed they them.

14 Afterward he appeared unto the eleven as they sat at meat, and upbraided them with their unbelief and hardness of heart, because they believed not them which had seen him after he was risen. 15And he said unto them, Go ye into all the world, and preach the gospel to every creature. 16 He that believeth and is baptized shall be saved; but he that believeth not shall be damned. 17These signs shall follow them that believe; In my name shall they cast out devils; they shall speak with new tongues; 18 They shall take up serpents; and if they drink any deadly thing, it shall not hurt them; they shall lay hands on the sick, and they shall recover.

19 So then, after the Lord had spoken unto them, he was received up into heaven, and sat on the right hand of God. 20And they went forth, and preached every where, the Lord working with *them,* and confirming the word with signs following. Amen.

New International Version

4 But when they looked up, they saw that the stone, which was very large, had been rolled away. 5As they entered the tomb, they saw a young man dressed in a white robe sitting on the right side, and they were alarmed.

6 "Don't be alarmed," he said. "You are looking for Jesus the Nazarene, who was crucified. He has risen! He is not here. See the place where they laid him. 7 But go, tell his disciples and Peter, 'He is going ahead of you into Galilee. There you will see him, just as he told you.'"

8 Trembling and bewildered, the women went out and fled from the tomb. They said nothing to anyone, because they were afraid.

[The most reliable early manuscripts omit Mark 16:9–20.]

The appearances and ascension of Jesus

9 When Jesus rose early on the first day of the week, he appeared first to Mary Magdalene, out of whom he had driven seven demons. 10 She went and told those who had been with him and who were mourning and weeping. 11 When they heard that Jesus was alive and that she had seen him, they did not believe it.

12 Afterward Jesus appeared in a different form to two of them while they were walking in the country. 13 These returned and reported it to the rest; but they did not believe them either.

14 Later Jesus appeared to the Eleven as they were eating; he rebuked them for their lack of faith and their stubborn refusal to believe those who had seen him after he had risen.

15 He said to them, "Go into all the world and preach the good news to all creation. 16 Whoever believes and is baptized will be saved, but whoever does not believe will be condemned. 17And these signs will accompany those who believe: In my name they will drive out demons; they will speak in new tongues; 18they will pick up snakes with their hands; and when they drink deadly poison, it will not hurt them at all; they will place their hands on sick people, and they will get well."

19 After the Lord Jesus had spoken to them, he was taken up into heaven and he sat at the right hand of God. 20 Then the disciples went out and preached everywhere, and the Lord worked with them and confirmed his word by the signs that accompanied it.

Greek Interlinear

4 καὶ ἀναβλέψασαι θεωροῦσιν ὅτι ἀνακεκύλισται
And   looking up   they behold that has been rolled back
ὁ λίθος· ἦν γὰρ μέγας σφόδρα. **5** καὶ
the stone; for it was great exceedingly.   And
εἰσελθοῦσαι εἰς τὸ μνημεῖον εἶδον νεανίσκον
entering   into the tomb   they saw a young man
καθήμενον ἐν τοῖς δεξιοῖς περιβεβλημένον
sitting   on the right having been clothed
στολὴν λευκήν, καὶ ἐξεθαμβήθησαν. **6** ὁ δὲ
robe [in] a white, and they were greatly astonished. But he
λέγει αὐταῖς· μὴ ἐκθαμβεῖσθε· Ἰησοῦν
says to them: Be not greatly astonished; Jesus
ζητεῖτε τὸν Ναζαρηνὸν τὸν ἐσταυρωμένον·
ye seek the Nazarene the - having been crucified·
ἠγέρθη, οὐκ ἔστιν ὧδε· ἴδε ὁ τόπος
he was raised, he is not here; behold[,] the place
ὅπου ἔθηκαν αὐτόν. **7** ἀλλὰ ὑπάγετε εἴπατε
where they put him.   But go ye tell
τοῖς μαθηταῖς αὐτοῦ καὶ τῷ Πέτρῳ ὅτι
the disciples of him and - Peter that
προάγει ὑμᾶς εἰς τὴν Γαλιλαίαν· ἐκεῖ
he goes before you to - Galilee; there
αὐτὸν ὄψεσθε, καθὼς εἶπεν ὑμῖν. **8** καὶ
him ye will see, as he told you.   And
ἐξελθοῦσαι ἔφυγον ἀπὸ τοῦ μνημείου, εἶχεν
going forth they fled from the tomb,   'had
γὰρ αὐτὰς τρόμος καὶ ἔκστασις· καὶ
'for 'them 'trembling 'and 'bewilderment; and
οὐδενὶ οὐδὲν εἶπαν· ἐφοβοῦντο γάρ.
no one no(any)thing they told; for they were afraid.
9 Ἀναστὰς δὲ πρωὶ πρώτῃ σαββάτου
And rising early on the first day of the week†
ἐφάνη πρῶτον Μαρίᾳ τῇ Μαγδαληνῇ, παρ᾽
he appeared first to Mary the Magdalene, from
ἧς ἐκβεβλήκει ἑπτὰ δαιμόνια. **10** ἐκείνη
whom he had expelled seven demons.   That [one]
                                        = She
πορευθεῖσα ἀπήγγειλεν τοῖς μετ᾽ αὐτοῦ
going reported to the [ones] with him
                           = those who had been with him
γενομένοις πενθοῦσι καὶ κλαίουσιν· **11** κἀκεῖνοι
having been mourning and weeping; and those
ἀκούσαντες ὅτι ζῇ καὶ ἐθεάθη ὑπ᾽ αὐτῆς
hearing that he lives and was seen by her
ἠπίστησαν. **12** Μετὰ δὲ ταῦτα δυσὶν ἐξ
disbelieved.   And after these things to two of
αὐτῶν περιπατοῦσιν ἐφανερώθη ἐν ἑτέρᾳ
them walking he was manifested in a different
μορφῇ πορευομένοις εἰς ἀγρόν· **13** κἀκεῖνοι
form going into [the] country; and those

ἀπελθόντες ἀπήγγειλαν τοῖς λοιποῖς· οὐδὲ
going reported to the rest; neither
ἐκείνοις ἐπίστευσαν. **14** Ὕστερον [δὲ]
those they believed.   And later
ἀνακειμένοις αὐτοῖς τοῖς ἕνδεκα ἐφανερώθη,
to the reclining them the eleven he was manifested,
= to the eleven as they reclined
καὶ ὠνείδισεν τὴν ἀπιστίαν αὐτῶν καὶ
and reproached the disbelief of them and
σκληροκαρδίαν ὅτι τοῖς θεασαμένοις αὐτὸν
hardness of heart because the [ones] beholding him
ἐγηγερμένον οὐκ ἐπίστευσαν. **15** καὶ εἶπεν
having been raised they did not believe.   And he said
αὐτοῖς· πορευθέντες εἰς τὸν κόσμον ἅπαντα
to them: Going into 'the 'world 'all
κηρύξατε τὸ εὐαγγέλιον πάσῃ τῇ κτίσει.
proclaim ye the gospel to all the creation.
16 ὁ πιστεύσας καὶ βαπτισθεὶς σωθήσεται,
The [one] believing and being baptized will be saved,
ὁ δὲ ἀπιστήσας κατακριθήσεται. **17** σημεῖα
but the [one] disbelieving will be condemned.   'signs
δὲ τοῖς πιστεύσασιν ταῦτα παρακολουθήσει·
'And 'the [ones] 'believing 'these 'will follow:
ἐν τῷ ὀνόματί μου δαιμόνια ἐκβαλοῦσιν,
in the name of me demons they will expel,
γλώσσαις λαλήσουσιν καιναῖς, **18** ὄφεις
'tongues 'they will speak 'with new, serpents
ἀροῦσιν κἂν θανάσιμόν τι πίωσιν
they will take and if 'deadly 'anything 'they drink
οὐ μὴ αὐτοὺς βλάψῃ, ἐπὶ ἀρρώστους χεῖρας
by no means them it will hurt, on sick [ones] hands
ἐπιθήσουσιν καὶ καλῶς ἕξουσιν. **19** Ὁ μὲν
they will place on and well they will have. 'The 'there-
= they will recover.
οὖν κύριος [Ἰησοῦς] μετὰ τὸ λαλῆσαι
fore 'Lord 'Jesus after the to speak
                              = speaking
αὐτοῖς ἀνελήμφθη εἰς τὸν οὐρανὸν καὶ
to them was taken up into - heaven and
ἐκάθισεν ἐκ δεξιῶν τοῦ θεοῦ. **20** ἐκεῖνοι
sat at [the] right [hand] - of God. those
δὲ ἐξελθόντες ἐκήρυξαν πανταχοῦ, τοῦ
But going forth proclaimed everywhere, the
κυρίου συνεργοῦντος καὶ τὸν λόγον
Lord working with and the word
= while the Lord worked with [them] and confirmed the word
βεβαιοῦντος διὰ τῶν ἐπακολουθούντων
confirming· through the accompanying
σημείων.
signs.

King James Version

New International Version

THE
GOSPEL ACCORDING TO
SAINT LUKE

LUKE

Introduction

1 Forasmuch as many have taken in hand to set forth in order a declaration of those things which are most surely believed among us, 2 Even as they delivered them unto us, which from the beginning were eyewitnesses, and ministers of the word; 3 It seemed good to me also, having had perfect understanding of all things from the very first, to write unto thee in order, most excellent Theophilus, 4 That thou mightest know the certainty of those things, wherein thou hast been instructed.

5 There was in the days of Herod, the king of Judea, a certain priest named Zacharias, of the course of Abia: and his wife *was* of the daughters of Aaron, and her name *was* Elisabeth. 6And they were both righteous before God, walking in all the commandments and ordinances of the Lord blameless. 7And they had no child, because that Elisabeth was barren; and they both were *now* well stricken in years. 8And it came to pass, that, while he executed the priest's office before God in the order of his course, 9According to the custom of the priest's office, his lot was to burn incense when he went into the temple of the Lord. 10And the whole multitude of the people were praying without at the time of incense. 11And there appeared unto him an angel of the Lord standing on the right side of the altar of incense. 12And when Zacharias saw *him,* he was troubled, and fear fell upon him. 13 But the angel said unto him, Fear not, Zacharias: for thy prayer is heard; and thy wife Elisabeth shall bear thee a son, and thou shalt call his name John. 14And thou shalt have joy and gladness; and many shall rejoice at his birth. 15 For he shall be great in the sight of the Lord, and shall drink neither wine nor strong drink; and he shall be filled with the Holy Ghost, even from his mother's womb. 16And many of the children of Israel shall he turn to the Lord their God. 17And he shall go before him in the spirit and power of Elias, to turn the hearts of the fathers to the children, and the disobedient to the wisdom of the just; to make ready a people prepared for the Lord. 18And Zacharias said unto the angel, Whereby shall I know this? for I am an old man, and my wife well stricken in years. 19And the angel answering said unto him, I am Gabriel, that stand in the presence of God; and am sent to speak unto thee, and to shew thee these glad tidings. 20And, behold, thou shalt be dumb, and not able to speak, until the day that

1 Many have undertaken to draw up an account of the things that have been fulfilled [a] among us, 2 just as they were handed down to us by those who from the first were eyewitnesses and servants of the word. 3 Therefore, since I myself have carefully investigated everything from the beginning, it seemed good also to me to write an orderly account for you, most excellent Theophilus, 4 so that you may know the certainty of the things you have been taught.

The birth of John the Baptist foretold

5 In the time of Herod, king of Judea, there was a priest named Zechariah, who belonged to the priestly division of Abijah; his wife Elizabeth was also a descendant of Aaron. 6 Both of them were upright in the sight of God, observing all the Lord's commandments and regulations blamelessly. 7 But they had no children, because Elizabeth was barren; and they were both well along in years.

8 Once when Zechariah's division was on duty and he was serving as priest before God, 9 he was chosen by lot, according to the custom of the priesthood, to go into the temple of the Lord and burn incense. 10And when the time for the burning of incense came, all the assembled worshipers were praying outside.

11 Then an angel of the Lord appeared to him, standing at the right side of the altar of incense. 12 When Zechariah saw him, he was startled and was gripped with fear. 13 But the angel said to him: "Do not be afraid, Zechariah; your prayer has been heard. Your wife Elizabeth will bear you a son, and you are to give him the name John. 14 He will be a joy and delight to you, and many will rejoice because of his birth, 15 for he will be great in the sight of the Lord. He is never to take wine or other fermented drink, and he will be filled with the Holy Spirit even from birth.[b] 16 Many of the people of Israel will he bring back to the Lord their God. 17And he will go on before the Lord, in the spirit and power of Elijah, to turn the hearts of the fathers to their children and the disobedient to the wisdom of the righteous—to make ready a people prepared for the Lord."

18 Zechariah asked the angel, "How can I be sure of this? I am an old man and my wife is well along in years."

19 The angel answered, "I am Gabriel. I stand in the presence of God, and I have been sent to speak to you and to tell you this good news. 20And now you will be silent and not able to speak until the day this happens, because you

[a] Or *surely believed.* [b] Or *from his mother's womb.*

ΚΑΤΑ   ΛΟΥΚΑΝ

Chapter 1

'Επειδήπερ πολλοὶ ἐπεχείρησαν ἀνατάξασθαι
Since   many   took in hand   to draw up

διήγησιν   περὶ   τῶν   πεπληροφορημένων
a narrative concerning ¹the   ²having been fully carried out

ἐν ἡμῖν πραγμάτων, 2 καθὼς παρέδοσαν ἡμῖν
⁴among ⁵us   ²matters,   as   delivered   to us

οἱ   ἀπ'   ἀρχῆς   αὐτόπται καὶ ὑπηρέται
the [ones] from [the] beginning eyewitnesses and attendants

γενόμενοι   τοῦ   λόγου, 3 ἔδοξε   κἀμοὶ
becoming   of the   Word,   it seemed good to me also

παρηκολουθηκότι ἄνωθεν πᾶσιν   ἀκριβῶς
having investigated from their source all things   accurately

καθεξῆς   σοι   γράψαι, κράτιστε Θεόφιλε,
¹in order ²to thee ³to write, most excellent Theophilus,

4 ἵνα   ἐπιγνῷς   περὶ   ὧν
that   thou mightest know   ⁴concerning ¹which

κατηχήθης   λόγων   τὴν   ἀσφάλειαν.
¹thou wast instructed ²of [the] things ³the   ⁴reliability.

5 'Εγένετο   ἐν   ταῖς   ἡμέραις
There was   in   the   days

'Ηρώδου   βασιλέως   τῆς   'Ιουδαίας   ἱερεύς
of Herod   king   -   of Judæa   ⁴priest

τις   ὀνόματι Ζαχαρίας ἐξ ἐφημερίας 'Αβιά,
¹a certain by name Zacharias of [the] course of Abia,

καὶ γυνὴ αὐτῷ ἐκ τῶν θυγατέρων 'Ααρών,
and   wife to him⁶ of the daughters of Aaron,
= his wife

καὶ τὸ ὄνομα αὐτῆς 'Ελισάβετ. 6 ἦσαν δὲ
and the name of her Elisabeth.   And they were

δίκαιοι ἀμφότεροι ἐναντίον   τοῦ   θεοῦ,
righteous   both   before   -   God,

πορευόμενοι ἐν πάσαις ταῖς ἐντολαῖς καὶ
going   in all   the commandments and

δικαιώμασιν τοῦ κυρίου ἄμεμπτοι. 7 καὶ
ordinances   of the Lord blameless.   And

οὐκ ἦν αὐτοῖς τέκνον, καθότι   ἦν   ἡ
there was not to them a child,⁶ because ²was -
= they had no child,

'Ελισάβετ στεῖρα, καὶ ἀμφότεροι προβεβηκότες
¹Elisabeth barren, and   both   having advanced

ἐν ταῖς ἡμέραις αὐτῶν ἦσαν. 8 'Εγένετο
in the   days   of them were.   it came to pass

δὲ ἐν τῷ ἱερατεύειν αὐτὸν ἐν τῇ τάξει
Now in the to serve as priest himᵇᵉ in the order
= while he served as priest

τῆς ἐφημερίας αὐτοῦ ἔναντι τοῦ θεοῦ,
of the course   of him before   - God,

9 κατὰ τὸ ἔθος τῆς ἱερατείας ἔλαχε τοῦ
according to the custom of the priesthood his lot was -

θυμιᾶσαι εἰσελθὼν εἰς τὸν ναὸν τοῦ κυρίου,
to burn incenseᵈ entering into the shrine of the Lord,

10 καὶ πᾶν τὸ πλῆθος ἦν τοῦ λαοῦ
and   all ¹the "multitude "was ³of the ⁴people

προσευχόμενον ἔξω τῇ ὥρᾳ τοῦ θυμιάματος.
praying   outside at the hour - of incense.

11 ὤφθη δὲ αὐτῷ ἄγγελος κυρίου ἑστὼς
And there appeared to him an angel of [the] Lord standing

ἐκ δεξιῶν τοῦ θυσιαστηρίου τοῦ θυμιάματος.
on [the] right of the altar   - of incense.

12 καὶ ἐταράχθη Ζαχαρίας ἰδών, καὶ φόβος
And was troubled Zacharias seeing, and   fear

ἐπέπεσεν ἐπ' αὐτόν. 13 εἶπεν δὲ πρὸς
fell on   upon him.   But said to

αὐτὸν ὁ ἄγγελος· μὴ φοβοῦ, Ζαχαρία,
him the angel: Fear not,   Zacharias,

διότι εἰσηκούσθη ἡ δέησίς σου, καὶ ἡ
because was heard the request of thee, and the

γυνή σου 'Ελισάβετ γεννήσει υἱόν σοι,
wife of thee Elisabeth   will bear a son to thee,

καὶ καλέσεις τὸ ὄνομα αὐτοῦ 'Ιωάννην·
and thou shalt call the name of him   John;

14 καὶ ἔσται χαρά σοι καὶ ἀγαλλίασις,
and there shall be joy to thee and   gladness,⁶
= thou shalt have joy and gladness,

καὶ πολλοὶ ἐπὶ τῇ γενέσει αὐτοῦ χαρή-
and   many   over the birth   of him   will

σονται. 15 ἔσται γὰρ μέγας ἐνώπιον
rejoice.   For he will be great in the eyes of

κυρίου, καὶ οἶνον καὶ σίκερα οὐ μὴ
[the] Lord, and wine and strong drink by no means

πίῃ,   καὶ πνεύματος ἁγίου πλησθήσεται
may he drink, and of(with) Spirit [the] Holy he will be filled

ἔτι ἐκ κοιλίας μητρὸς αὐτοῦ, 16 καὶ
even from [the] womb of [the] mother of him,   and

πολλοὺς τῶν υἱῶν 'Ισραὴλ ἐπιστρέψει ἐπὶ κύριον
many of the sons of Israel he will turn to [the] Lord

τὸν θεὸν αὐτῶν· 17 καὶ αὐτὸς προελεύσεται
the God of them;   and   he   will go before

ἐνώπιον αὐτοῦ ἐν πνεύματι καὶ δυνάμει
before   him in [the] spirit and power

'Ηλίου, ἐπιστρέψαι καρδίας πατέρων ἐπὶ
of Elias,   to turn   [the] hearts of fathers to

τέκνα καὶ ἀπειθεῖς ἐν φρονήσει
children and disobedient [ones] to [the] understanding

δικαίων, ἑτοιμάσαι κυρίῳ λαὸν κατεσκευασ-
of [the] just, to prepare for [the] Lord a people having been

μένον. 18 καὶ εἶπεν Ζαχαρίας πρὸς τὸν ἄγγελον·
prepared. And said Zacharias   to   the   angel:

κατὰ τί γνώσομαι τοῦτο; ἐγὼ γάρ εἰμι
By what shall I know this ?   for I   am

πρεσβύτης καὶ ἡ γυνή μου προβεβηκυῖα
old   and the wife of me having advanced

ἐν ταῖς ἡμέραις αὐτῆς. 19 καὶ ἀποκριθεὶς
in the   days   of her.   And answering

ὁ ἄγγελος εἶπεν αὐτῷ· ἐγώ εἰμι Γαβριὴλ
the angel   said to him : I   am Gabriel

ὁ παρεστηκὼς ἐνώπιον τοῦ θεοῦ, καὶ
the [one] standing   before   - God,   and

ἀπεστάλην λαλῆσαι πρὸς σὲ καὶ εὐαγ-
I was sent to speak   to thee and to

γελίσασθαί σοι ταῦτα· 20 καὶ ἰδοὺ
announce   to thee these things;   and behold

ἔσῃ   σιωπῶν καὶ μὴ δυνάμενος λαλῆσαι
thou shalt be being silent and not being able   to speak

163

King James Version

these things shall be performed, because thou believest not my words, which shall be fulfilled in their season. 21And the people waited for Zacharias, and marvelled that he tarried so long in the temple. 22And when he came out, he could not speak unto them: and they perceived that he had seen a vision in the temple; for he beckoned unto them, and remained speechless. 23And it came to pass, that, as soon as the days of his ministration were accomplished, he departed to his own house. 24And after those days his wife Elisabeth conceived, and hid herself five months, saying, 25 Thus hath the Lord dealt with me in the days wherein he looked on *me*, to take away my reproach among men. 26And in the sixth month the angel Gabriel was sent from God unto a city of Galilee, named Nazareth, 27 To a virgin espoused to a man whose name was Joseph, of the house of David; and the virgin's name *was* Mary. 28And the angel came in unto her, and said, Hail, *thou that art* highly favoured, the Lord *is* with thee: blessed *art* thou among women. 29And when she saw *him*, she was troubled at his saying, and cast in her mind what manner of salutation this should be. 30And the angel said unto her, Fear not, Mary: for thou hast found favour· with God. 31And, behold, thou shalt conceive in thy womb, and bring forth a son, and shalt call his name JESUS. 32 He shall be great, and shall be called the Son of the Highest; and the Lord God shall give unto him the throne of his father David: 33And he shall reign over the house of Jacob for ever; and of his kingdom there shall be no end. 34 Then said Mary unto the angel, How shall this be, seeing I know not a man? 35And the angel answered and said unto her, The Holy Ghost shall come upon thee, and the power of the Highest shall overshadow thee: therefore also that holy thing which shall be born of thee shall be called the Son of God. 36And, behold, thy cousin Elisabeth, she hath also conceived a son in her old age; and this is the sixth month with her, who was called barren. 37 For with God nothing shall be impossible. 38And Mary said, Behold the handmaid of the Lord; be it unto me according to thy word. And the angel departed from her. 39And Mary arose in those days, and went into the hill country with haste, into a city of Juda; 40And entered into the house of Zacharias, and saluted Elisabeth. 41And it came to pass, that, when Elisabeth heard the salutation of Mary, the babe leaped in her womb; and Elisabeth was filled with the Holy Ghost: 42And she spake out with a loud voice, and said, Blessed *art* thou among women, and blessed *is* the fruit of thy womb. 43And whence *is* this to me, that the mother of my Lord should come to me? 44 For, lo, as soon as the voice of thy salutation sounded in mine ears, the babe leaped in my womb for joy. 45And blessed *is* she that believed: for there shall be a performance of those things which were told her from the

New International Version

did not believe my words, which will come true at their proper time."

21 Meanwhile, the people were waiting for Zechariah and wondering why he stayed so long in the temple. 22 When he came out, he could not speak to them. They realized he had seen a vision in the temple, for he kept making signs to them but remained unable to speak.

23 When his time of service was completed, he returned home. 24After this his wife Elizabeth became pregnant and for five months remained in seclusion. 25 "The Lord has done this for me," she said. "In these days he has shown his favor and taken away my disgrace among the people."

The birth of Jesus foretold

26 In the sixth month, God sent the angel Gabriel to Nazareth, a town in Galilee, 27 to a virgin pledged to be married to a man named Joseph, a descendant of David. The virgin's name was Mary. 28 The angel went to her and said, "Greetings, you who are highly favored! The Lord is with you."

29 Mary was greatly troubled at his words and wondered what kind of greeting this might be. 30 But the angel said to her, "Do not be afraid, Mary, you have found favor with God. 31 You will be with child and give birth to a son, and you are to give him the name Jesus. 32 He will be great and will be called the Son of the Most High. The Lord God will give him the throne of his father David, 33 and he will reign over the house of Jacob forever; his kingdom will never end."

34 "How can this be," Mary asked the angel, "since I am a virgin?"

35 The angel answered, "The Holy Spirit will come upon you, and the power of the Most High will overshadow you. So the holy one to be born will be called the Son of God. 36 Even Elizabeth your relative is going to have a child in her old age, and she who was said to be barren is in her sixth month. 37 For nothing is impossible with God."

38 "I am the Lord's servant," Mary answered. "May it be to me as you have said." Then the angel left her.

Mary visits Elizabeth

39 At that time Mary got ready and hurried to a town in the hill country of Judah, 40 where she entered Zechariah's home and greeted Elizabeth. 41 When Elizabeth heard Mary's greeting, the baby leaped in her womb, and Elizabeth was filled with the Holy Spirit. 42 In a loud voice she exclaimed: "Blessed are you among women, and blessed is the child you will bear! 43 But why am I so favored, that the mother of my Lord should come to me? 44As soon as the sound of your greeting reached my ears, the baby in my womb leaped for joy. 45 Blessed is she who has believed that what the Lord has said to her will be accomplished!"

ἄχρι ἧς ἡμέρας γένηται ταῦτα, ἀνθ' ὧν οὐκ
until which day happens these things, because not
= the day when these things happen,

ἐπίστευσας τοῖς λόγοις μου, οἵτινες πληρω-
thou believedst the words of me, which will be

θήσονται εἰς τὸν καιρὸν αὐτῶν. 21 καὶ ἦν
fulfilled in the time of them. And was

ὁ λαὸς προσδοκῶν τὸν Ζαχαρίαν, καὶ
the people expecting - Zacharias, and

ἐθαύμαζον ἐν τῷ χρονίζειν ἐν τῷ ναῷ
they marvelled in(at) the to delay in the shrine
= when he delayed in the shrine.

αὐτόν. 22 ἐξελθὼν δὲ οὐκ ἐδύνατο λαλῆσαι
him.be And going out he was not able to speak

αὐτοῖς καὶ ἐπέγνωσαν ὅτι ὀπτασίαν ἑώρακεν
to them, and they knew that a vision he has(had) seen

ἐν τῷ ναῷ· καὶ αὐτὸς ἦν διανεύων
in the shrine; and he was beckoning

αὐτοῖς, καὶ διέμενεν κωφός. 23 καὶ
to them, and remained dumb. And

ἐγένετο ὡς ἐπλήσθησαν αἱ ἡμέραι τῆς
it came to pass when were fulfilled the days of the

λειτουργίας αὐτοῦ, ἀπῆλθεν εἰς τὸν οἶκον
service of him, he went away to the house

αὐτοῦ. 24 Μετὰ δὲ ταύτας τὰς ἡμέρας
of him. And after these - days

συνέλαβεν Ἐλισάβετ ἡ γυνὴ αὐτοῦ, καὶ
conceived Elisabeth the wife of him, and

περιέκρυβεν ἑαυτὴν μῆνας πέντε, λέγουσα
hid herself months five, saying[.]

25 ὅτι οὕτως μοι πεποίηκεν κύριος ἐν
- Thus to me has done [the] Lord in

ἡμέραις αἷς ἐπεῖδεν ἀφελεῖν ὄνειδός
days in which he looked upon to take away reproach

μου ἐν ἀνθρώποις.
of me among men.

26 Ἐν δὲ τῷ μηνὶ τῷ ἕκτῳ ἀπεστάλη
Now in the month - sixth was sent

ὁ ἄγγελος Γαβριὴλ ἀπὸ τοῦ θεοῦ εἰς
the angel Gabriel from - God to

πόλιν τῆς Γαλιλαίας ᾗ ὄνομα Ναζαρέθ,
a city - of Galilee to which name· Nazareth,
= the name of which [was]

27 πρὸς παρθένον ἐμνηστευμένην ἀνδρὶ ᾧ ὄνομα
to a virgin having been betrothed to a man to whom name·

Ἰωσήφ, ἐξ οἴκου Δαυίδ, καὶ τὸ ὄνομα
Joseph, of [the] house of David, and the name

τῆς παρθένου Μαριάμ. 28 καὶ εἰσελθὼν
of the virgin [was] Mary. And entering

πρὸς αὐτὴν εἶπεν· χαῖρε, κεχαριτωμένη, ὁ
to her he said: Hail, having been favoured [one], the

κύριος μετὰ σοῦ. 29 ἡ δὲ ἐπὶ τῷ λόγῳ
Lord [is] with thee. And she at the saying

διεταράχθη, καὶ διελογίζετο ποταπὸς εἴη
was greatly disturbed, and considered of what sort ᵃmight be

ὁ ἀσπασμὸς οὗτος. 30 καὶ εἶπεν ὁ ἄγγελος
- ᵃgreeting ¹this.. And said the angel

αὐτῇ· μὴ φοβοῦ, Μαριάμ· εὗρες γὰρ
to her: Fear not, Mary· for thou didst find

χάριν παρὰ τῷ θεῷ. 31 καὶ ἰδοὺ συλλήμψῃ
favour with - God. And behold thou wilt conceive

ἐν γαστρὶ καὶ τέξῃ υἱόν, καὶ καλέσεις τὸ
in womb and bear a son, and thou shalt call the

ὄνομα αὐτοῦ Ἰησοῦν. 32 οὗτος ἔσται μέγας
name of him Jesus. This will be great

καὶ υἱὸς ὑψίστου κληθήσεται, καὶ δώσει
and Son of [the] Most High will be called, and will give

αὐτῷ κύριος ὁ θεὸς τὸν θρόνον Δαυὶδ
him [the] Lord - God the throne of David

τοῦ πατρὸς αὐτοῦ, 33 καὶ βασιλεύσει ἐπὶ
the father of him, and he will reign over

τὸν οἶκον Ἰακὼβ εἰς τοὺς αἰῶνας, καὶ
the house of Jacob unto the ages, and
= for ever,

τῆς βασιλείας αὐτοῦ οὐκ ἔσται τέλος.
of the kingdom of him there will not be an end.

34 εἶπεν δὲ Μαριὰμ πρὸς τὸν ἄγγελον·
And said Mary to the angel:

πῶς ἔσται τοῦτο, ἐπεὶ ἄνδρα οὐ γινώσκω;
How will be this, since a man I know not?

35 καὶ ἀποκριθεὶς ὁ ἄγγελος εἶπεν αὐτῇ·
And answering the angel said to her:

πνεῦμα ἅγιον ἐπελεύσεται ἐπὶ σέ, καὶ
¹[The] ²Spirit ¹Holy will come upon upon thee, and

δύναμις ὑψίστου ἐπισκιάσει σοι· διὸ
[the] power of [the] Most High will overshadow thee; wherefore

καὶ τὸ γεννώμενον ἅγιον κληθήσεται υἱὸς θεοῦ.
also the thing being born holy will be called[,] Son of God.

36 καὶ ἰδοὺ Ἐλισάβετ ἡ συγγενίς σου καὶ
And behold Elisabeth the relative of thee also

αὐτὴ συνείληφεν υἱὸν ἐν γήρει αὐτῆς, καὶ
she conceived a son in old age of her, and

οὗτος μὴν ἕκτος ἐστὶν αὐτῇ τῇ καλουμένῃ
this month sixth is with her the [one] being called

στείρᾳ· 37 ὅτι οὐκ ἀδυνατήσει παρὰ τοῦ
barren; because will not be impossible with -

θεοῦ πᾶν ῥῆμα. 38 εἶπεν δὲ Μαριάμ· ἰδοὺ ἡ
God every word. And said Mary: Behold[,] the

δούλη κυρίου· γένοιτό μοι κατὰ
handmaid of [the] Lord; may it be to me according to

τὸ ῥῆμά σου. καὶ ἀπῆλθεν ἀπ' αὐτῆς
the word of thee. And went away from her

ὁ ἄγγελος. 39 Ἀναστᾶσα δὲ Μαριὰμ ἐν
the angel. And rising up Mary in

ταῖς ἡμέραις ταύταις ἐπορεύθη εἰς τὴν
- days these she went to the

ὀρεινὴν μετὰ σπουδῆς εἰς πόλιν Ἰούδα,
mountain country with haste to a city of Juda,

40 καὶ εἰσῆλθεν εἰς τὸν οἶκον Ζαχαρίου
and entered into the house of Zacharias

καὶ ἠσπάσατο τὴν Ἐλισάβετ. 41 καὶ
and greeted - Elisabeth. And

ἐγένετο ὡς ἤκουσεν τὸν ἀσπασμὸν τῆς
it came to pass when ²heard ¹the ⁴greeting

Μαρίας ἡ Ἐλισάβετ, ἐσκίρτησεν τὸ βρέφος
³of Mary ¹Elisabeth, leaped the babe

ἐν τῇ κοιλίᾳ αὐτῆς, καὶ ἐπλήσθη πνεύματος
in the womb of her, and ²was filled ³of(with) ⁴Spirit

ἁγίου ἡ Ἐλισάβετ, 42 καὶ ἀνεφώνησεν
⁴[the] Holy - ¹Elisabeth, and she called out

κραυγῇ μεγάλῃ καὶ εἶπεν· εὐλογημένη
cry with a great and said: Blessed [art]

σὺ ἐν γυναιξίν, καὶ εὐλογημένος ὁ καρπὸς
thou among women, and blessed [is] the fruit

τῆς κοιλίας σου. 43 καὶ πόθεν μοι τοῦτο
of the womb of thee. And whence to me this

ἵνα ἔλθῃ ἡ μήτηρ τοῦ κυρίου μου πρὸς
that comes the mother of the Lord of me to

ἐμέ; 44 ἰδοὺ γὰρ ὡς ἐγένετο ἡ φωνὴ τοῦ
me? For behold when came the sound of the

ἀσπασμοῦ σου εἰς τὰ ὦτά μου, ἐσκίρτησεν
greeting of thee in the ears of me, leaped

ἐν ἀγαλλιάσει τὸ βρέφος ἐν τῇ κοιλίᾳ
in gladness the babe in the womb

μου. 45 καὶ μακαρία ἡ πιστεύσασα ὅτι
of me. And blessed the [one] believing because

ἔσται τελείωσις τοῖς λελαλημένοις αὐτῇ
there shall be a completion to the things having been to her
spoken

King James Version

Lord. 46And Mary said, My soul doth magnify the Lord, 47And my spirit hath rejoiced in God my Saviour. 48 For he hath regarded the low estate of his handmaiden: for, behold, from henceforth all generations shall call me blessed. 49 For he that is mighty hath done to me great things; and holy *is* his name. 50And his mercy *is* on them that fear him from generation to generation. 51 He hath shewed strength with his arm; he hath scattered the proud in the imagination of their hearts. 52 He hath put down the mighty from *their* seats, and exalted them of low degree. 53 He hath filled the hungry with good things; and the rich he hath sent empty away. 54 He hath holpen his servant Israel, in remembrance of *his* mercy; 55As he spake to our fathers, to Abraham, and to his seed for ever. 56And Mary abode with her about three months, and returned to her own house. 57 Now Elisabeth's full time came that she should be delivered; and she brought forth a son. 58And her neighbours and her cousins heard how the Lord had shewed great mercy upon her; and they rejoiced with her. 59And it came to pass, that on the eighth day they came to circumcise the child; and they called him Zacharias, after the name of his father. 60And his mother answered and said, Not so; but he _hall be called John. 61And they said unto her, There is none of thy kindred that is called by this name. 62And they made signs to his father, how he would have him called. 63And he asked for a writing table, and wrote, saying, His name is John. And they marvelled all. 64And his mouth was opened immediately, and his tongue *loosed,* and he spake, and praised God. 65And fear came on all that dwelt round about them: and all these sayings were noised abroad throughout all the hill country of Judea. 66And all they that heard *them* laid *them* up in their hearts, saying, What manner of child shall this be! And the hand of the Lord was with him. 67And his father Zacharias was filled with the Holy Ghost, and prophesied, saying, 68 Blessed *be* the Lord God of Israel; for he hath visited and redeemed his people, 69And hath raised up a horn of salvation for us in the house of his servant David; 70As he spake by the mouth of his holy prophets, which have been since the world began: 71 That we should be saved from our enemies, and from the hand of all that hate us; 72 To perform the mercy *promised* to our fathers, and to remember his holy covenant; 73 The oath which he sware to our father Abra-

New International Version

Mary's song

46 And Mary said:
"My soul praises the Lord
47 and my spirit rejoices in God my Savior,
48 for he has been mindful of the humble state of his servant.
From now on all generations will call me blessed,
49 for the Mighty One has done great things for me—
holy is his name.
50 His mercy extends to those who fear him, from generation to generation.
51 He has performed mighty deeds with his arm;
he has scattered those who are proud in their inmost thoughts.
52 He has brought down rulers from their thrones
but has lifted up the humble.
53 He has filled the hungry with good things but has sent the rich away empty.
54 He has helped his servant Israel, remembering to be merciful
55 to Abraham and his descendants forever, even as he said to our fathers."
56 Mary stayed with Elizabeth for about three months and then returned home.

The birth of John the Baptist

57 When it was time for Elizabeth to have her baby, she gave birth to a son. 58 Her neighbors and relatives heard that the Lord had shown her great mercy, and they shared her joy.
59 On the eighth day they came to circumcise the child, and they were going to name him after his father Zechariah, 60 but his mother spoke up and said, "No! He is to be called John."
61 They said to her, "There is no one among your relatives who has that name."
62 Then they made signs to his father, to find ou. what he would like to name the child. 63 He asked for a writing tablet, and to everyone's astonishment he wrote, "His name is John." 64 Immediately his mouth was opened and his tongue was loosed, and he began to speak, praising God. 65 The neighbors were all filled with awe, and throughout the hill country of Judea people were talking about all these things. 66 Everyone who heard this wondered about it, asking, "What then is this child going to be?" For the Lord's hand was with him.

Zechariah's song

67 His father Zechariah was filled with the Holy Spirit and prophesied:
68 "Praise the Lord, the God of Israel, because he has come and has redeemed his people.
69 He has raised up a horn[c] of salvation for us
in the house of his servant David
70 (as he said through his holy prophets of long ago),
71 salvation from our enemies
and from the hand of all who hate us—
72 to show mercy to our fathers
and to remember his holy covenant,
73 the oath he swore to our father Abraham:

166   [c] *Horn* in the Old Testament symbolizes strength.

Greek Interlinear

παρὰ κυρίου. **46** Καὶ εἶπεν Μαριάμ·
from [the] Lord. And said Mary :

Μεγαλύνει ἡ ψυχή μου τὸν κύριον, **47** καὶ
Magnifies the soul of me the Lord, and

ἠγαλλίασεν τὸ πνεῦμά μου ἐπὶ τῷ θεῷ
exulted the spirit of me in - God

τῷ σωτῆρί μου· **48** ὅτι ἐπέβλεψεν ἐπὶ τὴν
the saviour of me; because he looked on upon the

ταπείνωσιν τῆς δούλης αὐτοῦ. ἰδοὺ γὰρ
humiliation of the handmaid of him. For behold

ἀπὸ τοῦ νῦν μακαριοῦσίν με πᾶσαι αἱ
from - now ⁴will ⁵deem ⁶blessed ¹me ²all ³the

γενεαί· **49** ὅτι ἐποίησέν μοι μεγάλα ὁ
³generations; because did to me great things the

δυνατός. καὶ ἅγιον τὸ ὄνομα αὐτοῦ,
Mighty [one]. And holy the name of him,

50 καὶ τὸ ἔλεος αὐτοῦ εἰς γενεὰς καὶ
and the mercy of him to generations and

γενεὰς τοῖς φοβουμένοις αὐτόν. **51** Ἐποίησεν
generations to the [ones] fearing him. He did

κράτος ἐν βραχίονι αὐτοῦ, διεσκόρπισεν
might with [the] arm of him, he scattered

ὑπερηφάνους διανοίᾳ καρδίας αὐτῶν·
haughty [ones] in [the] understanding of [the] heart of them;

52 καθεῖλεν δυνάστας ἀπὸ θρόνων καὶ ὕψω-
he pulled down potentates from thrones and exalt-

σεν ταπεινούς, **53** πεινῶντας ἐνέπλησεν
ed humble [ones], hungering [ones] he filled

ἀγαθῶν καὶ πλουτοῦντας ἐξαπέστειλεν
of(with) good things and rich [ones] he sent away

κενούς. **54** ἀντελάβετο Ἰσραὴλ παιδὸς αὐτοῦ,
empty. He succoured Israel servant of him,

μνησθῆναι ἐλέους, **55** καθὼς ἐλάλησεν
to remember mercy, as he spoke

πρὸς τοὺς πατέρας ἡμῶν, τῷ Ἀβραὰμ
to the fathers of us, - to Abraham

καὶ τῷ σπέρματι αὐτοῦ εἰς τὸν αἰῶνα.
and to the seed of him unto the age.
=for ever.

56 Ἔμεινεν δὲ Μαριὰμ σὺν αὐτῇ ὡς
And remained Mary with her about

μῆνας τρεῖς, καὶ ὑπέστρεψεν εἰς τὸν
months three, and returned to the

οἶκον αὐτῆς.
house of her.

57 Τῇ δὲ Ἐλισάβετ ἐπλήσθη ὁ χρόνος
- Now ⁴to Elisabeth ²was fulfilled ¹the ³time

τοῦ τεκεῖν αὐτήν, καὶ ἐγέννησεν υἱόν.
- to bear her,ᵇᵈ and she brought forth a son.
=that she should bear,

58 καὶ ἤκουσαν οἱ περίοικοι καὶ οἱ
And heard the neighbours and the

συγγενεῖς αὐτῆς ὅτι ἐμεγάλυνεν κύριος τὸ
relatives of her that magnified [the] Lord the

ἔλεος αὐτοῦ μετ' αὐτῆς, καὶ συνέχαιρον
mercy of him with her, and they rejoiced with

αὐτῇ. **59** Καὶ ἐγένετο ἐν τῇ ἡμέρᾳ τῇ
her. And it came to pass on the day the

ὀγδόῃ ἦλθον περιτεμεῖν τὸ παιδίον, καὶ
eighth they came to circumcise the child, and

ἐκάλουν αὐτὸ ἐπὶ τῷ ὀνόματι τοῦ πατρὸς
were calling it(him) by the name of the father

αὐτοῦ Ζαχαρίαν. **60** καὶ ἀποκριθεῖσα ἡ
of him Zacharias. And answering the

μήτηρ αὐτοῦ εἶπεν· οὐχί, ἀλλὰ κληθήσεται
mother of him said : No, but he shall be called

Ἰωάνης. **61** καὶ εἶπαν πρὸς αὐτὴν ὅτι
John. And they said to her[.]

οὐδείς ἐστιν ἐκ τῆς συγγενείας σου ὃς
No one there is of the kindred of thee who

καλεῖται τῷ ὀνόματι τούτῳ. **62** ἐνένευον
is called - name by this. they nodded

δὲ τῷ πατρὶ αὐτοῦ τὸ τί ἂν θέλοι
And to the father of him - what he might wish

καλεῖσθαι αὐτό. **63** καὶ αἰτήσας πινακίδιον
²to be called ¹him. And asking for a tablet

ἔγραψεν λέγων· Ἰωάνης ἐστὶν ὄνομα
he wrote saying : John is name

αὐτοῦ. καὶ ἐθαύμασαν πάντες. **64** καὶ ἀνεῴχθη δὲ
of him. And they marvelled all. And was opened

τὸ στόμα αὐτοῦ παραχρῆμα καὶ ἡ
the mouth of him instantly and the

γλῶσσα αὐτοῦ, καὶ ἐλάλει εὐλογῶν τὸν
tongue of him, and he spoke blessing -

θεόν. **65** Καὶ ἐγένετο ἐπὶ πάντας φόβος
God. And ⁵came ⁶on ⁴all ¹fear

τοὺς περιοικοῦντας αὐτούς, καὶ ἐν ὅλῃ τῇ
the [ones] dwelling round them, and in all the

ὀρεινῇ τῆς Ἰουδαίας διελαλεῖτο πάντα
mountain country - of Judæa ⁴were talked over ¹all

τὰ ῥήματα ταῦτα, **66** καὶ ἔθεντο πάντες
²facts ³these, and ⁴put ¹all

οἱ ἀκούσαντες ἐν τῇ καρδίᾳ αὐτῶν,
²the [ones] ³hearing in the heart of them,

λέγοντες· τί ἄρα τὸ παιδίον τοῦτο ἔσται;
saying : What then - child this will be ?

καὶ γὰρ χεὶρ κυρίου ἦν μετ' αὐτοῦ.
for indeed [the] hand of [the] Lord was with him.

67 Καὶ Ζαχαρίας ὁ πατὴρ αὐτοῦ ἐπλήσθη
And Zacharias the father of him was filled

πνεύματος ἁγίου καὶ ἐπροφήτευσεν λέγων·
of(with) Spirit [the] Holy and prophesied saying :

68 Εὐλογητὸς κύριος ὁ θεὸς τοῦ Ἰσραήλ,
Blessed [be] [the] Lord the God - of Israel,

ὅτι ἐπεσκέψατο καὶ ἐποίησεν λύτρωσιν τῷ
because he visited and wrought redemption for the

λαῷ αὐτοῦ, **69** καὶ ἤγειρεν κέρας σωτηρίας
people of him, and raised a horn of salvation

ἡμῖν ἐν οἴκῳ Δαυὶδ παιδὸς αὐτοῦ, **70** καθὼς
for us in [the] house of David servant of him, as

ἐλάλησεν διὰ στόματος τῶν ἁγίων ἀπ'
he spoke through [the] mouth of the ³holy ⁴from

αἰῶνος προφητῶν αὐτοῦ, **71** σωτηρίαν ἐξ
⁵[the] age ²prophets ¹of him, salvation out of

ἐχθρῶν ἡμῶν καὶ ἐκ χειρὸς πάντων τῶν
[the] enemies of us and out of [the] hand of all the [ones]

μισούντων ἡμᾶς, **72** ποιῆσαι ἔλεος μετὰ
hating us, to perform mercy with

τῶν πατέρων ἡμῶν καὶ μνησθῆναι διαθήκης
the fathers of us and to remember [the] covenant

ἁγίας αὐτοῦ, **73** ὅρκον ὃν ὤμοσεν πρὸς Ἀβραὰμ
holy of him, [the] oath which he swore to Abraham

τὸν πατέρα ἡμῶν, τοῦ δοῦναι ἡμῖν
the father of us, - to giveᵈ us

King James Version

ham, 74 That he would grant unto us, that we, being delivered out of the hand of our enemies, might serve him without fear, 75 In holiness and righteousness before him, all the days of our life. 76And thou, child, shalt be called the prophet of the Highest: for thou shalt go before the face of the Lord to prepare his ways; 77 To give knowledge of salvation unto his people by the remission of their sins, 78 Through the tender mercy of our God; whereby the dayspring from on high hath visited us, 79 To give light to them that sit in darkness and *in* the shadow of death, to guide our feet into the way of peace. 80And the child grew, and waxed strong in spirit, and was in the deserts till the day of his shewing unto Israel.

2 And it came to pass in those days, that there went out a decree from Cesar Augustus, that all the world should be taxed. 2 (*And* this taxing was first made when Cyrenius was governor of Syria.) 3And all went to be taxed, every one into his own city. 4And Joseph also went up from Galilee, out of the city of Nazareth, into Judea, unto the city of David, which is called Bethlehem, (because he was of the house and lineage of David,) 5 To be taxed with Mary his espoused wife, being great with child. 6And so it was, that, while they were there, the days were accomplished that she should be delivered. 7And she brought forth her firstborn son, and wrapped him in swaddling clothes, and laid him in a manger; because there was no room for them in the inn. 8And there were in the same country shepherds abiding in the field, keeping watch over their flock by night. 9And, lo, the angel of the Lord came upon them, and the glory of the Lord shone round about them; and they were sore afraid. 10And the angel said unto them, Fear not: for, behold, I bring you good tidings of great joy, which shall be to all people. 11 For unto you is born this day in the city of David a Saviour, which is Christ the Lord. 12And this *shall be* a sign unto you; Ye shall find the babe wrapped in swaddling clothes, lying in a manger. 13And suddenly there was with the angel a multitude of the heavenly host praising God, and saying, 14 Glory to God in the highest, and on earth peace, good will toward men. 15And it came to pass, as the angels were gone away from them into heaven, the shepherds said one to another, Let us now go even unto Bethlehem, and see this thing which is come to pass, which the Lord hath made known unto us. 16And they came with haste, and found Mary and Joseph, and the babe lying in a manger. 17And when they had seen *it,* they made known abroad the saying which was told them concerning this child. 18And all they that heard

New International Version

74 to rescue us from the hand of our enemies,
and to enable us to serve him without fear
75 in holiness and righteousness before him all our days.
76 And you, my child, will be called a prophet of the Most High;
for you will go on before the Lord to prepare the way for him,
77 to give his people the knowledge of salvation
through the forgiveness of their sins,
78 because of the tender mercy of our God,
by which the rising sun will come to us from heaven
79 to shine on those living in darkness and in the shadow of death,
to guide our feet into the path of peace."
80 And the child grew and became strong in spirit; and he lived in the desert until he appeared publicly to Israel.

The birth of Jesus

2 In those days Caesar Augustus issued a decree that a census should be taken of the entire Roman world. 2 (This was the first census that took place while Quirinius was governor of Syria.) 3And everyone went to his own town to register.
4 So Joseph also went up from the town of Nazareth in Galilee to Judea, to Bethlehem the town of David, because he belonged to the house and line of David. 5 He went there to register with Mary, who was pledged to be married to him and was expecting a child. 6 While they were there, the time came for the baby to be born, 7 and she gave birth to her firstborn, a son. She wrapped him in strips of cloth and placed him in a manger, because there was no room for them in the inn.

The shepherds and the angels

8 And there were shepherds living out in the fields nearby, keeping watch over their flocks at night. 9An angel of the Lord appeared to them, and the glory of the Lord shone around them, and they were terrified. 10 But the angel said to them, "Do not be afraid. I bring you good news of great joy that will be for all the people. 11 Today in the town of David a Savior has been born to you; he is Christ[d] the Lord. 12 This will be a sign to you: You will find a baby wrapped in strips of cloth and lying in a manger."
13 Suddenly a great company of the heavenly host appeared with the angel, praising God and saying,
14 "Glory to God in the highest,
and on earth peace to men on whom his favor rests."
15 When the angels had left them and gone into heaven, the shepherds said to one another, "Let's go to Bethlehem and see this thing that has happened, which the Lord has told us about."
16 So they hurried off and found Mary and Joseph, and the baby, who was lying in the manger. 17 When they had seen him, they spread the word concerning what had been told them about this child, 18 and all who heard it

[d] Or *Messiah*. "The Christ" (Greek) and "the Messiah" (Hebrew) both mean "the Anointed One."

Greek Interlinear

74 ἀφόβως ἐκ χειρὸς ἐχθρῶν ῥυσθέντας
¹fearlessly ²out of ³[the] hand ⁴of[our] enemies ¹having been delivered

λατρεύειν αὐτῷ 75 ἐν ὁσιότητι καὶ δικαιοσύνῃ
⁵to serve him in holiness and righteousness

ἐνώπιον αὐτοῦ πάσαις ταῖς ἡμέραις ἡμῶν.
before him all the days⁸ of us.

76 Καὶ σὺ δέ, παιδίον, προφήτης ὑψίστου
And thou also, child, a prophet of [the] Most High

κληθήσῃ· προπορεύσῃ γὰρ ἐνώπιον κυρίου
wilt be called; for thou wilt go before before [the] Lord

ἑτοιμάσαι ὁδοὺς αὐτοῦ, 77 τοῦ δοῦναι
to prepare [the] ways of him, - to give⁴

γνῶσιν σωτηρίας τῷ λαῷ αὐτοῦ ἐν
a knowledge of salvation to the people of him by

ἀφέσει ἁμαρτιῶν αὐτῶν, 78 διὰ σπλάγχνα
forgiveness of sins of them, because of [the] bowels

ἐλέους θεοῦ ἡμῶν, ἐν οἷς ἐπισκέψεται
of mercy of God of us, whereby will visit

ἡμᾶς ἀνατολὴ ἐξ ὑψους, 79 ἐπιφᾶναι τοῖς
us a [sun]rising from [the] height, to appear ¹to the [ones]

ἐν σκότει καὶ σκιᾷ θανάτου καθημένοις,
²in ⁴darkness ³and ⁵in a shadow ⁶of death ¹sitting,

τοῦ κατευθῦναι τοὺς πόδας ἡμῶν εἰς ὁδὸν
- to guide⁴ the feet of us into a way

εἰρήνης.
of peace.

80 Τὸ δὲ παιδίον ηὔξανεν καὶ ἐκραταιοῦτο
And the child grew and became strong

πνεύματι, καὶ ἦν ἐν ταῖς ἐρήμοις ἕως
in spirit, and was in the deserts until

ἡμέρας ἀναδείξεως αὐτοῦ πρὸς τὸν Ἰσραήλ.
[the] days of showing of him to - Israel.

Chapter 2

Ἐγένετο δὲ ἐν ταῖς ἡμέραις ἐκείναις
Now it came to pass in - days those

ἐξῆλθεν δόγμα παρὰ Καίσαρος Αὐγούστου
went out a decree from Cæsar Augustus

ἀπογράφεσθαι πᾶσαν τὴν οἰκουμένην. 2 αὕτη
to be enrolled all the inhabited earth. This

ἀπογραφὴ πρώτη ἐγένετο ἡγεμονεύοντος τῆς
²enrolment ¹first was governing - = when Cyrenius governed Syria.

Συρίας Κυρηνίου. 3 καὶ ἐπορεύοντο πάντες
Syria Cyrenius.ˢ And went all

ἀπογράφεσθαι, ἕκαστος εἰς τὴν ἑαυτοῦ
to be enrolled, each man to the of himselꞏ

πόλιν. 4 Ἀνέβη δὲ καὶ Ἰωσὴφ ἀπὸ τῆς
city. So went up also Joseph from -

Γαλιλαίας ἐκ πόλεως Ναζαρὲθ εἰς τὴꞏ
Galilee out of a city Nazareth to -

Ἰουδαίαν εἰς πόλιꞏ Δαυὶδ ἥτις καλεῖται Βηθλέεμ,
Judæa to a city of David which is called Bethlehem,

διὰ τὸ εἶναι αὐτὸν ἐξ οἴκου καὶ
because of the to be himᵇ out of [the] house and
= because he was

πατριᾶς Δαυίδ, 5 ἀπογράψασθαι σὺν Μαριὰμ
family of David, to be enrolled with Mary

τῇ ἐμνηστευμένῃ αὐτῷ, οὔσῃ ἐγκύῳ.
the [one] having been betrothed to him, being pregnant.

6 Ἐγένετο δὲ ἐν τῷ εἶναι αὐτοὺς ἐκεῖ
And it came to pass in the to be themᵇᵉ there
= while they were

ἐπλήσθησαν αἱ ἡμέραι τοῦ τεκεῖν αὐτήν,
were fulfilled the days - to bear her,ᵇᵈ
= for her to bear,

7 καὶ ἔτεκεν τὸν υἱὸν αὐτῆς τὸν πρωτότοκον,
and she bore the son of her the firstborn,

καὶ ἐσπαργάνωσεν αὐτὸν καὶ ἀνέκλινεν
and she swathed him and laid

αὐτὸν ἐν φάτνῃ, διότι οὐκ ἦν αὐτοῖς
him in a manger, because there was not for them

τόπος ἐν τῷ καταλύματι. 8 Καὶ ποιμένες
place in the inn. And shepherds

ἦσαν ἐν τῇ χώρᾳ τῇ αὐτῇ ἀγραυλοῦντες
there were in the country - same living in the fields

καὶ φυλάσσοντες φυλακὰς τῆς νυκτὸς ἐπὶ
and keeping guard of(in) the night over

τὴν ποίμνην αὐτῶν. 9 καὶ ἄγγελος κυρίου
the flock of them. And an angel of [the] Lord

ἐπέστη αὐτοῖς καὶ δόξα κυρίου περιέλαμψεν
came upon them and [the] glory of [the]Lord shone around

αὐτούς, καὶ ἐφοβήθησαν φόβον μέγαν.
them, and they feared fear a great.
= exceedingly.

10 καὶ εἶπεν αὐτοῖς ὁ ἄγγελος· μὴ
And said to them the angel : noꞏ

φοβεῖσθε· ἰδοὺ γὰρ εὐαγγελίζομαι ὑμιꞏ
Fear ye; for behold I announce to you

χαρὰν μεγάλην, ἥτις ἔσται παντὶ τῷ λαῷ,
joy a great, which will be to all the people,

11 ὅτι ἐτέχθη ὑμῖν σήμερον σωτήρ, ὃς
because was born to you to-day a Saviour, who

ἐστιν χριστὸς κύριος, ἐν πόλει Δαυίδ
is Christ [the] Lord, in a city of David

12 καὶ τοῦτο ὑμῖν σημεῖον, εὑρήσετε βρέφος
And this to you a sign, ye will find a babe

ἐσπαργανωμένον καὶ κείμενον ἐν φάτνῃ.
having been swathed and lying in a manger.

13 καὶ ἐξαίφνης ἐγένετο σὺν τῷ ἀγγέλῳ
And suddenly there was with the angel

πλῆθος στρατιᾶς οὐρανίου αἰνούντων τὸν
a multitude army of a heavenly praising -

θεὸν καὶ λεγόντων· 14 δόξα ἐν ὑψίστοις
God and saying : Glory in highest [places]

θεῷ καὶ ἐπὶ γῆς εἰρήνη ἐν ἀνθρώποις
to God and on earth peace among men

εὐδοκίας. 15 Καὶ ἐγένετο ὡς ἀπῆλθον
of goodwill. And it came to pass when went away

ἀπ᾽ αὐτῶν εἰς τὸν οὐρανὸν οἱ ἄγγελοι,
from them to - heaven the angels,

οἱ ποιμένες ἐλάλουν πρὸς ἀλλήλους·
the shepherds said to one another :

διέλθωμεν δὴ ἕως Βηθλέεμ καὶ ἴδωμεν
Let us go then unto Bethlehem and let us see

τὸ ῥῆμα τοῦτο τὸ γεγονὸς ὃ ὁ κύριος
- thing this - having happened which the Lord

ἐγνώρισεν ἡμῖν. 16 καὶ ἦλθαν σπεύσαντες,
made known to us. And they came hastening,

καὶ ἀνεῦραν τήν τε Μαριὰμ καὶ τὸν
and found - both Mary and -

Ἰωσὴφ καὶ τὸ βρέφος κείμενον ἐν τῇ
Joseph and the babe lying in the

φάτνῃ· 17 ἰδόντες δὲ ἐγνώρισαν περὶ τοῦ
manger; and seeing they made known concerning the

ῥήματος τοῦ λαληθέντος αὐτοῖς περὶ τοῦ
word - spoken to them concerning -

παιδίου τούτου. 18 καὶ πάντες οἱ ἀκούσαντες
child this. And all the [ones] hearing

169

King James Version

it wondered at those things which were told them by the shepherds. 19 But Mary kept all these things, and pondered *them* in her heart. 20And the shepherds returned, glorifying and praising God for all the things that they had heard and seen, as it was told unto them. 21And when eight days were accomplished for the circumcising of the child, his name was called JESUS, which was so named of the angel before he was conceived in the womb. 22And when the days of her purification according to the law of Moses were accomplished, they brought him to Jerusalem, to present *him* to the Lord; 23 (As it is written in the law of the Lord, Every male that openeth the womb shall be called holy to the Lord;) 24And to offer a sacrifice according to that which is said in the law of the Lord, A pair of turtledoves, or two young pigeons. 25And, behold, there was a man in Jerusalem, whose name *was* Simeon; and the same man *was* just and devout, waiting for the consolation of Israel: and the Holy Ghost was upon him. 26And it was revealed unto him by the Holy Ghost, that he should not see death, before he had seen the Lord's Christ. 27And he came by the Spirit into the temple: and when the parents brought in the child Jesus, to do for him after the custom of the law, 28 Then took he him up in his arms, and blessed God, and said, 29 Lord, now lettest thou thy servant depart in peace, according to thy word: 30 For mine eyes have seen thy salvation, 31 Which thou hast prepared before the face of all people; 32A light to lighten the Gentiles, and the glory of thy people Israel. 33And Joseph and his mother marvelled at those things which were spoken of him. 34And Simeon blessed them, and said unto Mary his mother, Behold, this *child* is set for the fall and rising again of many in Israel; and for a sign which shall be spoken against; 35 (Yea, a sword shall pierce through thy own soul also;) that the thoughts of many hearts may be revealed. 36And there was one Anna, a prophetess, the daughter of Phanuel, of the tribe of Aser: she was of a great age, and had lived with a husband seven years from her virginity; 37And she *was* a widow of about fourscore and four years, which departed not from the temple, but served *God* with fastings and prayers night and day. 38And she coming in that instant gave thanks likewise unto the Lord, and spake of him to all them that looked for redemption in Jerusalem. 39And when they had performed all things according to the law of the Lord, they returned into Gal-

New International Version

were amazed at what the shepherds said to them. 19 But Mary treasured up all these things and pondered them in her mind. 20 The shepherds returned, glorifying and praising God for all the things they had heard and seen, which were just as they had been told.

Jesus presented in the temple

21 On the eighth day, when it was time to circumcise him, he was named Jesus, the name the angel had given him before he had been conceived.

22 When the time of their purification according to the Law of Moses had been completed, Joseph and Mary took him to Jerusalem to present him to the Lord "Every firstborn male is to be consecrated to the Lord" *e*), 24 and to offer a sacrifice in keeping with what is said in the Law of the Lord: "A pair of doves or two young pigeons." *f*

25 Now there was a man in Jerusalem called Simeon, who was righteous and devout. He was waiting for the consolation of Israel, and the Holy Spirit was upon him. 26 It had been revealed to him by the Holy Spirit that he would not die before he had seen the Lord's Christ.*g* 27 Moved by the Spirit, he went into the temple courts. When the parents brought in the child Jesus to do for him as the custom of the Law required, 28 Simeon took him in his arms and praised God, saying:

29 "Sovereign Lord, as you promised,
　　now dismiss your servant in peace,
30 For my eyes have seen your salvation,
31 　which you have prepared in the sight of
　　all people,
32 a light for revelation to the Gentiles
　　and for glory to your people Israel."

33 The child's father and mother marveled at what was said about him. 34 Then Simeon blessed them and said to Mary, his mother: "This child is destined to cause the falling and rising of many in Israel, and to be a sign that will be spoken against, 35 so that the thoughts of many hearts will be revealed. And a sword will pierce your own soul too."

36 There was also a prophetess, Anna, the daughter of Phanuel, of the tribe of Asher. She was very old; she had lived with her husband seven years after her marriage, 37 and then was a widow until she was eighty-four. She never left the temple but worshiped night and day, fasting and praying. 38 Coming up to them at that very moment, she gave thanks to God and spoke about the child to all who were looking forward to the redemption of Jerusalem.

39 When Joseph and Mary had done everything required by the Law of the Lord, they returned to Galilee to their own town of Nazareth.

[e] Exodus 13:2, 12, 15. [f] Lev. 12:8. [g] Or *Messiah*.

Greek Interlinear

ἐθαύμασαν περὶ τῶν λαληθέντων ὑπὸ τῶν
marvelled concerning the things spoken by the

ποιμένων πρὸς αὐτούς· 19 ἡ δὲ Μαρία
shepherds to them;   -   but Mary

πάντα συνετήρει τὰ ῥήματα ταῦτα συμβάλλουσα
²all ¹kept - ⁴things ³these pondering

ἐν τῇ καρδίᾳ αὐτῆς. 20 καὶ ὑπέστρεψαν
in the heart of her.   And returned

οἱ ποιμένες δοξάζοντες καὶ αἰνοῦντες τὸν
the shepherds glorifying and praising -

θεὸν ἐπὶ πᾶσιν οἷς ἤκουσαν καὶ εἶδον
God at all things which they heard and saw

καθὼς ἐλαλήθη πρὸς αὐτούς.
as was spoken to them.

21 Καὶ ὅτε ἐπλήσθησαν ἡμέραι ὀκτὼ
And when were completed days eight

τοῦ περιτεμεῖν αὐτόν, καὶ ἐκλήθη τὸ
- to circumcise himᵈ, and was called the

ὄνομα αὐτοῦ Ἰησοῦς, τὸ κληθὲν ὑπὸ τοῦ
name of him Jesus, the [name] called by the

ἀγγέλου πρὸ τοῦ συλλημφθῆναι αὐτὸν ἐν
angel before the to be conceived himᵇ in
= he was conceived

τῇ κοιλίᾳ.
the womb.

22 Καὶ ὅτε ἐπλήσθησαν αἱ ἡμέραι τοῦ
And when were completed the days of the

καθαρισμοῦ αὐτῶν κατὰ τὸν νόμον
cleansing of them according to the law

Μωϋσέως, ἀνήγαγον αὐτὸν εἰς Ἰεροσόλυμα
of Moses, they took up him to Jerusalem

παραστῆσαι τῷ κυρίῳ, 23 καθὼς γέγραπται
to present to the Lord, as it has been written

ἐν νόμῳ κυρίου ὅτι πᾶν ἄρσεν διανοῖγον
in [the] law of the Lordᵃ[,] - Every male opening

μήτραν ἅγιον τῷ κυρίῳ κληθήσεται, 24 καὶ
a womb holy to the Lord shall be called, and

τοῦ δοῦναι θυσίαν κατὰ τὸ εἰρημένον ἐν
- to giveᵈ a sacrifice according to the thing said in

τῷ νόμῳ κυρίου, ζεῦγος τρυγόνων ἢ δύο
the law of [the] Lord, a pair of turtledoves or two

νοσσοὺς περιστερῶν. 25 Καὶ ἰδοὺ ἄνθρωπος
nestlings of doves.   And behold[,] a man

ἦν ἐν Ἰερουσαλὴμ ᾧ ὄνομα Συμεών, καὶ
was in Jerusalem to whom nameᶜ Simeon, and
= whose name was

ὁ ἄνθρωπος οὗτος δίκαιος καὶ εὐλαβής,
- man this [was] just and devout,

προσδεχόμενος παράκλησιν τοῦ Ἰσραήλ, καὶ
expecting [the] consolation - of Israel, and

πνεῦμα ἦν ἅγιον ἐπ' αὐτ'ν· 26 καὶ ἦν
¹[the] ³Spirit ²was ¹Holy upon him; and it was

αὐτῷ κεχρηματισμένον ὑπὸ τοῦ πνεύματος
to him having been communicated by the Spirit

τοῦ ἁγίου μὴ ἰδεῖν θάνατον πρὶν ἢ ἂν
- Holy not to see death before

ἴδῃ τὸν χριστὸν κυρίου. 27 καὶ ἦλθεν
he should see the Christ of [the] Lord. And he came

ἐν τῷ πνεύματι εἰς τὸ ἱερόν· καὶ ἐν τῷ
by the Spirit into the temple; and in the
= as the(his) parents brought in

εἰσαγαγεῖν τοὺς γονεῖς τὸ παιδίον Ἰησοῦν
to bring in the parentsᵇᵉ the child Jesus

τοῦ ποιῆσαι αὐτοὺς κατὰ τὸ εἰθισμένον
- to do themᵇᵈ according to the custom
= for them to do

τοῦ νόμου περὶ αὐτοῦ, 28 καὶ αὐτὸς
of the law concerning him, and he

ἐδέξατο αὐτὸ εἰς τὰς ἀγκάλας καὶ
received him in the(his) arms and

εὐλόγησεν τὸν θεὸν καὶ εἶπεν· 29 νῦν
blessed - God and said: Now

ἀπολύεις τὸν δοῦλόν σου, δέσποτα, κατὰ
thou releasest the slave of thee, Master, according to

τὸ ῥῆμά σου ἐν εἰρήνῃ· 30 ὅτι εἶδον οἱ
the word of thee in peace; because saw the

ὀφθαλμοί μου τὸ σωτήριόν σου, 31 ὃ
eyes of me the salvation of thee, which

ἡτοίμασας κατὰ πρόσωπον πάντων τῶν
thou didst prepare before [the] face of all the

λαῶν, 32 φῶς εἰς ἀποκάλυψιν ἐθνῶν καὶ
peoples, a light for a revelation of [the] nations and

δόξαν λαοῦ σου Ἰσραήλ. 33 καὶ ἦν
a glory of [the] people of thee Israel. And ²was(were)

ὁ πατὴρ αὐτοῦ καὶ ἡ μήτηρ θαυμάζοντες
¹the ³father ²of him ⁴and ⁵the ⁶mother ⁸marvelling

ἐπὶ τοῖς λαλουμένοις περὶ αὐτοῦ. 34 καὶ
at the things being said concerning him. And

εὐλόγησεν αὐτοὺς Συμεὼν καὶ εἶπεν πρὸς
blessed them Simeon and said to

Μαριὰμ τὴν μητέρα αὐτοῦ· ἰδοὺ οὗτος
Mary the mother of him: Behold[,] this

κεῖται εἰς πτῶσιν καὶ ἀνάστασιν πολλῶν
is set for fall and rising again of many

ἐν τῷ Ἰσραὴλ καὶ εἰς σημεῖον ἀντιλεγ-
in - Israel and for a sign spoken

όμενον — 35 καὶ σοῦ δὲ αὐτῆς τὴν ψυχὴν
against — and ³of thee ²also ⁴[thy]self ⁵the ¹soul

διελεύσεται ῥομφαία—, ὅπως ἂν ἀποκαλυφθῶσιν
¹will go through ²a sword —, so as - may be revealed

ἐκ πολλῶν καρδιῶν διαλογισμοί. 36 Καὶ
of many hearts [the] thoughts.   And

ἦν Ἄννα προφῆτις, θυγάτηρ Φανουήλ, ἐκ
there was Anna a prophetess, a daughter of Phanuel, of

φυλῆς Ἀσήρ· αὕτη προβεβηκυῖα ἐν ἡμέραις
[the] tribe of Asher; this having advanced in days

πολλαῖς, ζήσασα μετὰ ἀνδρὸς ἔτη ἑπτὰ
many, having lived with a husband years seven

ἀπὸ τῆς παρθενίας αὐτῆς, 37 καὶ αὐτὴ
from the virginity of her, and she [was]

χήρα ἕως ἐτῶν ὀγδοήκοντα τεσσάρων, ἣ
a widow until years eighty-four, who

οὐκ ἀφίστατο τοῦ ἱεροῦ νηστείαις καὶ
withdrew not from the temple with fastings and

δεήσεσιν λατρεύουσα νύκτα καὶ ἡμέραν.
petitionings serving night and day.

38 καὶ αὐτῇ τῇ ὥρᾳ ἐπιστᾶσα ἀνθωμολογεῖτο
And at the very hourᵃ coming upon she gave thanks

τῷ θεῷ καὶ ἐλάλει περὶ αὐτοῦ πᾶσιν τοῖς
- to God and spoke about him to all the [ones]

προσδεχομένοις λύτρωσιν Ἰερουσαλήμ. 39 Καὶ
expecting redemption in Jerusalem.   And

ὡς ἐτέλεσαν πάντα τὰ κατὰ τὸν νόμον
when they finished all things - according to the law

κυρίου, ἐπέστρεψαν εἰς τὴν Γαλιλαίαν εἰς
of [the] Lord, they returned to - Galilee to

πόλιν ἑαυτῶν Ναζαρέθ.
a city of themselves Nazareth.

ᵃ Strictly, this construction should mean "the hour itself"; but the context demands "the same hour". See 10. 7, 21; 12. 12; 13. 1, 31; 20. 19; 23. 12; 24. 13. "Luke seems to be the only N.T. writer who affects the construction" (C. F. D. Moule). See also Acts 16. 18; 22. 13. Of course there is not a great difference between "the hour itself", "the very hour", and "the same hour".

King James Version

ilee, to their own city Nazareth. 40And the child grew, and waxed strong in spirit, filled with wisdom; and the grace of God was upon him. 41 Now his parents went to Jerusalem every year at the feast of the passover. 42And when he was twelve years old, they went up to Jerusalem after the custom of the feast. 43And when they had fulfilled the days, as they returned, the child Jesus tarried behind in Jerusalem; and Joseph and his mother knew not *of it.* 44 But they, supposing him to have been in the company, went a day's journey; and they sought him among *their* kinsfolk and acquaintance. 45And when they found him not, they turned back again to Jerusalem, seeking him. 46And it came to pass, that after three days they found him in the temple, sitting in the midst of the doctors, both hearing them, and asking them questions. 47And all that heard him were astonished at his understanding and answers. 48And when they saw him, they were amazed: and his mother said unto him, Son, why hast thou thus dealt with us? behold, thy father and I have sought thee sorrowing. 49And he said unto them, How is it that ye sought me? wist ye not that I must be about my Father's business? 50And they understood not the saying which he spake unto them. 51And he went down with them, and came to Nazareth, and was subject unto them: but his mother kept all these sayings in her heart. 52And Jesus increased in wisdom and stature, and in favour with God and man.

New International Version

40And the child grew and became strong; he was filled with wisdom, and the grace of God was upon him.

The boy Jesus at the temple

41 Every year his parents went to Jerusalem for the Feast of the Passover. 42 When he was twelve years old, they went up to the feast, according to the custom. 43After the feast was over, while his parents were returning home, the boy Jesus stayed behind in Jerusalem, but they were unaware of it. 44 Thinking he was in their company, they traveled on for a day. Then they began looking for him among their relatives and friends. 45 When they did not find him, they went back to Jerusalem to look for him. 46After three days they found him in the temple courts, sitting among the teachers, listening to them and asking them questions. 47 Everyone who heard him was amazed at his understanding and his answers. 48 When his parents saw him, they were astonished. His mother said to him, "Son, why have you treated us like this? Your father and I have been anxiously searching for you."

49 "Why were you searching for me?" he asked. "Didn't you know I had to be in my Father's house?" 50 But they did not understand what he meant.

51 Then he went down to Nazareth with them and was obedient to them. But his mother treasured all these things in her heart. 52And Jesus grew in wisdom and stature, and in favor with God and men.

John the Baptist prepares the way

3 Now in the fifteenth year of the reign of Tiberius Cesar, Pontius Pilate being governor of Judea, and Herod being tetrarch of Galilee, and his bother Philip tetrarch of Iturea and of the region of Trachonitis, and Lysanias the tetrarch of Abilene, 2Annas and Caiaphas being the high priests, the word of God came unto John the son of Zacharias in the wilderness. 3And he came into all the country about Jordan, preaching the baptism of repentance for the remission of sins; 4As it is written in the book of the words of Esaias the prophet, saying, The voice of one crying in the wilderness, Prepare ye the way of the Lord, make his paths straight. 5 Every valley shall be filled, and every mountain and hill shall be brought low; and the crooked shall be made straight, and the rough ways *shall be* made smooth; 6And all flesh shall see the salvation of God. 7 Then said he to the multitude that came forth to be baptized of him, O generation of vipers, who hath warned you to flee from the wrath to come? 8 Bring forth therefore fruits worthy of repentance, and begin not to say within yourselves, We have Abraham to

3 In the fifteenth year of the reign of Tiberius Caesar—when Pontius Pilate was governor of Judea, Herod tetrarch of Galilee, his brother Philip tetrarch of Iturea and Trachonitis, and Lysanias tetrarch of Abilene—2 and during the high-priesthood of Annas and Caiaphas, the word of God came to John son of Zechariah in the desert. 3 He went into all the country around the Jordan, preaching a baptism of repentance for the forgiveness of sins. 4As is written in the book of the words of Isaiah the prophet:

"A voice of one calling in the desert,
'Prepare the way for the Lord,
   make straight paths for him.
5 Every valley shall be filled in,
   and every mountain and hill leveled off.
The crooked roads shall become straight,
   and the rough ways smooth.
6 And all mankind shall see God's salvation.' [h] "

7 John said to the crowds coming out to be baptized by him, "You brood of vipers! Who warned you to flee from the coming wrath? 8 Produce fruit in keeping with repentance. And do not begin to say to yourselves, 'We have

[h] Isaiah 40:3-5.

Greek Interlinear

40 Τὸ δὲ παιδίον ηὔξανεν καὶ ἐκραταιοῦτο
And the child grew and became strong

πληρούμενον σοφίᾳ, καὶ χάρις θεοῦ ἦν ἐπ'
being filled with wisdom, and [the] grace of God was upon

αὐτό.
him.

41 Καὶ ἐπορεύοντο οἱ γονεῖς αὐτοῦ κατ'
And went the parents of him year

ἔτος εἰς Ἰερουσαλὴμ τῇ ἑορτῇ τοῦ πάσχα.
by year† to Jerusalem at the feast of the Passover.

42 Καὶ ὅτε ἐγένετο ἐτῶν δώδεκα, ἀναβαινόντων
And when he became of years twelve, going up
= as they went up

αὐτῶν κατὰ τὸ ἔθος τῆς ἑορτῆς, **43** καὶ
them according to the custom of the feast, and

τελειωσάντων τὰς ἡμέρας, ἐν τῷ ὑποστρέφειν
fulfilling* the days, in the to return
= when they returned

αὐτοὺς ὑπέμεινεν Ἰησοῦς ὁ παῖς ἐν
them** *remained *Jesus ¹the *boy in

Ἰερουσαλήμ, καὶ οὐκ ἔγνωσαν οἱ γονεῖς
Jerusalem, and knew not ¹the ²parents

αὐτοῦ. **44** νομίσαντες δὲ αὐτὸν εἶναι ἐν
²of him. But supposing him to be in

τῇ συνοδίᾳ ἦλθον ἡμέρας ὁδὸν καὶ ἀνεζήτουν
the company they went of a day a journey and sought

αὐτὸν ἐν τοῖς συγγενεῦσιν καὶ τοῖς
him among the(ir) relatives and the(ir)

γνωστοῖς, **45** καὶ μὴ εὑρόντες ὑπέστρεψαν
acquaintances, and not finding returned

εἰς Ἰερουσαλὴμ ἀναζητοῦντες αὐτόν. **46** καὶ
to Jerusalem seeking him. And

ἐγένετο μετὰ ἡμέρας τρεῖς εὗρον αὐτὸν
it came to pass after days three they found him

ἐν τῷ ἱερῷ καθεζόμενον ἐν μέσῳ τῶν
in the temple sitting in [the] midst of the

διδασκάλων καὶ ἀκούοντα αὐτῶν καὶ
teachers both hearing them and

ἐπερωτῶντα αὐτούς· **47** ἐξίσταντο δὲ πάντες
questioning them; and were astonished all

οἱ ἀκούοντες αὐτοῦ ἐπὶ τῇ συνέσει καὶ
the [ones] hearing him at the intelligence and

ταῖς ἀποκρίσεσιν αὐτοῦ. **48** καὶ ἰδόντες
the answers of him. And seeing

αὐτὸν ἐξεπλάγησαν, καὶ εἶπεν πρὸς αὐτὸν
him they were astounded, and said to him

ἡ μήτηρ αὐτοῦ· τέκνον, τί ἐποίησας ἡμῖν
the mother of him : Child, why didst thou to us

οὕτως; ἰδοὺ ὁ πατήρ σου κἀγὼ ὀδυνώμενοι
thus? behold[,] the father of thee and I greatly distressed

ζητοῦμέν σε. **49** καὶ εἶπεν πρὸς αὐτούς·
are seeking thee. And he said to them :

τί ὅτι ἐζητεῖτέ με; οὐκ ᾔδειτε ὅτι ἐν
Why [is it] that ye sought me? did ye not know that in
= I

τοῖς τοῦ πατρός μου δεῖ εἶναί με;
the [affairs] of the Father of me it behoves to be me?
must be about my Father's business?

50 καὶ αὐτοὶ οὐ συνῆκαν τὸ ῥῆμα ὃ
And they did not understand the word which

ἐλάλησεν αὐτοῖς. **51** καὶ κατέβη μετ'
he spoke to them. And he went down with

αὐτῶν καὶ ἦλθεν εἰς Ναζαρέθ, καὶ ἦν
them and came to Nazareth, and was

ὑποτασσόμενος αὐτοῖς. καὶ ἡ μήτηρ
being subject to them. And the mother

αὐτοῦ διετήρει πάντα τὰ ῥήματα ἐν τῇ
of him carefully kept all the matters in the

καρδίᾳ αὐτῆς. **52** Καὶ Ἰησοῦς προέκοπτεν
heart of her. And Jesus progressed

ἐν τῇ σοφίᾳ καὶ ἡλικίᾳ καὶ χάριτι παρὰ
in wisdom and age and favour before

θεῷ καὶ ἀνθρώποις.
God and men.

Chapter 3

Ἐν ἔτει δὲ πεντεκαιδεκάτῳ τῆς
Now in [the] year fifteenth of the

ἡγεμονίας Τιβερίου Καίσαρος, ἡγεμονεύοντος
government of Tiberius Cæsar, governing
= while Pontius Pilate

Ποντίου Πιλάτου τῆς Ἰουδαίας, καὶ
Pontius Pilate* - of Judæa, and
was governing

τετρααρχοῦντος τῆς Γαλιλαίας Ἡρώδου,
ruling as tetrarch of Galilee Herod,*
= while Herod was ruling as tetrarch of Galilee,

Φιλίππου δὲ τοῦ ἀδελφοῦ αὐτοῦ τετρα-
and Philip the brother of him ruling

αρχοῦντος τῆς Ἰτουραίας καὶ Τραχωνίτιδος
as tetrarch* ²of the *of Ituræa *and *of Trachonitis

χώρας, καὶ Λυσανίου τῆς Ἀβιληνῆς
¹country, and Lysanias of Abilene

τετρααρχοῦντος, **2** ἐπὶ ἀρχιερέως Ἄννα
ruling as tetrarch*, in the time of [the] high priest Anna

καὶ Καϊάφα, ἐγένετο ῥῆμα θεοῦ ἐπὶ Ἰωάννην
and Caiaphas, came a word of God to John

τὸν Ζαχαρίου υἱὸν ἐν τῇ ἐρήμῳ. **3** καὶ
the of Zacharias son in the desert. And

ἦλθεν εἰς πᾶσαν τὴν περίχωρον· τοῦ
he came into all the neighbourhood of the

Ἰορδάνου κηρύσσων βάπτισμα μετανοίας
Jordan proclaiming a baptism of repentance

εἰς ἄφεσιν ἁμαρτιῶν, **4** ὡς γέγραπται ἐν
for forgiveness of sins, as it has been written in

βίβλῳ λόγων Ἡσαΐου τοῦ προφήτου·
[the] roll of [the] words of Esaias the prophet :

φωνὴ βοῶντος ἐν τῇ ἐρήμῳ· ἑτοιμάσατε
Voice of [one] crying in the desert : Prepare ye

τὴν ὁδὸν κυρίου, εὐθείας ποιεῖτε τὰς
the way of [the] Lord, straight make the

τρίβους αὐτοῦ· **5** πᾶσα φάραγξ πληρωθήσεται
paths of him; every valley shall be filled up

καὶ πᾶν ὄρος καὶ βουνὸς ταπεινωθήσεται,
and every mountain and hill shall be laid low,

καὶ ἔσται τὰ σκολιὰ εἰς εὐθείας καὶ αἱ
and shall be the crooked [places] into straight [ones] and the

τραχεῖαι εἰς ὁδοὺς λείας· **6** καὶ ὄψεται
rough [places] into ways smooth; and *shall see

πᾶσα σὰρξ τὸ σωτήριον τοῦ θεοῦ.
¹all ²flesh the salvation - of God.

7 Ἔλεγεν οὖν τοῖς ἐκπορευομένοις ὄχλοις
He said therefore to the 'going out 'crowds

βαπτισθῆναι ὑπ' αὐτοῦ· γεννήματα ἐχιδνῶν,
to be baptized by him : Offspring of vipers,

τίς ὑπέδειξεν ὑμῖν φυγεῖν ἀπὸ τῆς
who warned you to flee from the

μελλούσης ὀργῆς; **8** ποιήσατε οὖν καρποὺς
coming wrath? Produce therefore fruits

ἀξίους τῆς μετανοίας· καὶ μὴ ἄρξησθε
worthy - of repentance; and do not begin

λέγειν ἐν ἑαυτοῖς· πατέρα ἔχομεν τὸν
to say among yourselves : Father we have -

173

King James Version

our father: for I say unto you, That God is able of these stones to raise up children unto Abraham. 9And now also the axe is laid unto the root of the trees: every tree therefore which bringeth not forth good fruit is hewn down, and cast into the fire. 10And the people asked him, saying, What shall we do then? 11 He answereth and saith unto them, He that hath two coats, let him impart to him that hath none; and he that hath meat, let him do likewise. 12 Then came also publicans to be baptized, and said unto him, Master, what shall we do? 13And he said unto them, Exact no more than that which is appointed you. 14And the soldiers likewise demanded of him, saying, And what shall we do? And he said unto them, Do violence to no man, neither accuse *any* falsely; and be content with your wages. 15And as the people were in expectation, and all men mused in their hearts of John, whether he were the Christ, or not; 16John answered, saying unto *them* all, I indeed baptize you with water; but one mightier than I cometh, the latchet of whose shoes I am not worthy to unloose: he shall baptize you with the Holy Ghost and with fire: 17 Whose fan *is* in his hand, and he will thoroughly purge his floor, and will gather the wheat into his garner; but the chaff he will burn with fire unquenchable. 18And many other things in his exhortation preached he unto the people. 19 But Herod the tetrarch, being reproved by him for Herodias his brother Philip's wife, and for all the evils which Herod had done, 20Added yet this above all, that he shut up John in prison. 21 Now when all the people were baptized, it came to pass, that Jesus also being baptized, and praying, the heaven was opened, 22And the Holy Ghost descended in a bodily shape like a dove upon him, and a voice came from heaven, which said, Thou art my beloved Son; in thee I am well pleased. 23And Jesus himself began to be about thirty years of age, being (as was supposed) the son of Joseph, which was *the son* of Heli, 24 Which was *the son* of Matthat, which was *the son* of Levi, which was *the son* of Melchi, which was *the son* of Janna, which was *the son* of Joseph, 25 Which was *the son* of Mattathias, which was *the son* of Amos, which was *the son* of Naum, which was *the son* of Esli, which was *the son* of Nagge, 26 Which was *the son* of Maath, which was *the son* of Mattathias, which was *the son* of Semei, which was *the son* of Joseph, which was *the son* of Juda, 27 Which was *the son* of Joanna, which was *the son* of Rhesa, which was *the son* of Zorobabel, which was *the son* of Salathiel, which was *the son* of Neri, 28 Which was *the son* of Melchi, which was *the son* of Addi, which was *the son* of Cosam, which was *the son* of Elmodam, which was *the son* of Er, 29 Which was *the son* of Jose, which was *the son* of Eliezer, which was *the son* of Jorim, which was *the son* of Matthat, which was *the son* of Levi, 30 Which was *the son* of Simeon, which was *the son* of Juda, which was *the son* of Joseph, which was *the son* of Jonan, which was *the son* of Eliakim, 31 Which was *the son* of Melea, which was *the son* of Menan, which was *the son* of Mattatha, which was *the son* of Nathan, which was *the son* of David, 32 Which was *the son* of Jesse, which was *the son* of Obed, which was *the son* of Booz, which was *the son* of Salmon, which was *the son* of Naasson, 33 Which was *the son* of Aminadab, which was *the son* of Aram, which was *the son* of Esrom, which was *the son*

New International Version

Abraham as our father.' For I tell you that out of these stones God can raise up children for Abraham. 9 The ax is already at the root of the trees, and every tree that does not produce good fruit will be cut down and thrown into the fire."
10 "What should we do then?" the crowd asked.
11 John answered, "The man with two tunics should share with him who has none, and the one who has food should do the same."
12 Tax collectors also came to be baptized. "Teacher," they asked, "what should we do?"
13 "Don't collect any more than you are required to," he told them.
14 Then some soldiers asked him, "And what should we do?"
He replied, "Don't extort money and don't accuse people falsely—be content with your pay."
15 The people were waiting expectantly and were all wondering in their hearts if John might possibly be the Christ.[i] 16 John answered them all, "I baptize you with[j] water. But one more powerful than I will come, the thongs of whose sandals I am not worthy to untie. He will baptize you with the Holy Spirit and fire. 17 His winnowing fork is in his hand to clear his threshing floor and to gather the wheat into his barn, but he will burn up the chaff with unquenchable fire." 18And with many other words John exhorted the people and preached the good news to them.
19 But when John rebuked Herod the tetrarch because of Herodias, his brother's wife, and all the other evil things he had done, 20 Herod added this to them all: He locked John up in prison.

The baptism and genealogy of Jesus

21 When all the people were being baptized, Jesus was baptized too. And as he was praying, heaven was opened 22 and the Holy Spirit descended on him in bodily form like a dove. And a voice came from heaven: "You are my Son, whom I love; with you I am well-pleased."
23 Now Jesus himself was about thirty years old when he began his ministry. He was the son, so it was thought, of Joseph,
    the son of Heli, 24 the son of Matthat,
    the son of Levi, the son of Melchi,
    the son of Jannai, the son of Joseph,
    25 the son of Mattathias, the son of Amos,
    the son of Nahum, the son of Esli,
    the son of Naggai, 26 the son of Maath,
    the son of Mattathias, the son of Semein,
    the son of Josech, the son of Joda,
    27 the son of Joanan, the son of Rhesa,
    the son of Zerubbabel, the son of Shealtiel,
    the son of Neri, 28 the son of Melchi,
    the son of Addi, the son of Cosam,
    the son of Elmadam, the son of Er,
    29 the son of Joshua, the son of Eliezer,
    the son of Jorim, the son of Matthat,
    the son of Levi, 30 the son of Simeon,
    the son of Judah, the son of Joseph,
    the son of Jonam, the son of Eliakim,
    31 the son of Melea, the son of Menna,
    the son of Mattatha, the son of Nathan,
    the son of David, 32 the son of Jesse,
    the son of Obed, the son of Boaz,
    the son of Salmon,[k] the son of Nahshon,
    33 the son of Amminadab, the son of Ram,[l]
    the son of Hezron, the son of Perez,

[i] Or *Messiah.* [j] Or *in.* [k] Some MSS read *Sala.* [l] Some MSS read *Amminadab, the son of Admin, the son of Arni;* other MSS vary widely.

Greek Interlinear

Ἀβραάμ· λέγω γὰρ ὑμῖν ὅτι δύναται ὁ
Abraham; for I tell you that 'can -

θεὸς ἐκ τῶν λίθων τούτων ἐγεῖραι τέκνα
¹God out of - stones these to raise children

τῷ Ἀβραάμ. 9 ἤδη δὲ καὶ ἡ ἀξίνη πρὸς
- to Abraham. And ²already ¹even the axe at

τὴν ῥίζαν τῶν δένδρων κεῖται· πᾶν οὖν
the root of the trees is laid; ²every ¹therefore

δένδρον μὴ ποιοῦν καρπὸν καλὸν
tree not producing fruit good

ἐκκόπτεται καὶ εἰς πῦρ βάλλεται. 10 Καὶ
is being cut down and into fire is being cast. And

ἐπηρώτων αὐτὸν οἱ ὄχλοι λέγοντες· τί
asked him the crowds saying : What

οὖν ποιήσωμεν; 11 ἀποκριθεὶς δὲ ἔλεγεν
then may we do? And answering he told

αὐτοῖς· ὁ ἔχων δύο χιτῶνας μεταδότω
them : The [one] having two tunics let him impart

τῷ μὴ ἔχοντι, καὶ ὁ ἔχων βρώματα
to the [one] not having, and the [one] having foods

ὁμοίως ποιείτω. 12 ἦλθον δὲ καὶ τελῶναι
likewise let him do. And there came also tax-collectors

βαπτισθῆναι καὶ εἶπαν πρὸς αὐτόν·
to be baptized and they said to him :

διδάσκαλε, τί ποιήσωμεν; 13 ὁ δὲ εἶπεν
Teacher, what may we do? And he said

πρὸς αὐτούς· μηδὲν πλέον παρὰ τὸ
to them : Nothing more besides the [thing]

διατεταγμένον ὑμῖν πράσσετε. 14 ἐπηρώτων δὲ
having been commanded you do ye. And asked

αὐτὸν καὶ στρατευόμενοι λέγοντες· τί
him also men serving in the army saying : What

ποιήσωμεν καὶ ἡμεῖς; καὶ εἶπεν αὐτοῖς·
may do also we? And he told them :

μηδένα διασείσητε μηδὲ συκοφαντήσητε,
No one intimidate nor accuse falsely,

καὶ ἀρκεῖσθε τοῖς ὀψωνίοις ὑμῶν.
and be satisfied with the pay of you.

15 Προσδοκῶντος δὲ τοῦ λαοῦ καὶ
Now expecting the people* and

= while the people were expecting and all were debating

διαλογιζομένων πάντων ἐν ταῖς καρδίαις
debating all* in the hearts

αὐτῶν περὶ τοῦ Ἰωάννου, μήποτε αὐτὸς
of them concerning - John, perhaps he

εἴη ὁ χριστός, 16 ἀπεκρίνατο λέγων πᾶσιν
might be the Christ, ²answered ³saying ⁴to all

ὁ Ἰωάννης· ἐγὼ μὲν ὕδατι βαπτίζω ὑμᾶς·
- 'John : I indeed with water baptize you;

ἔρχεται δὲ ὁ ἰσχυρότερός μου, οὗ οὐκ
but there comes the [one] stronger of me, of whom not
= than I,

εἰμὶ ἱκανὸς λῦσαι τὸν ἱμάντα τῶν ὑποδημά-
I am competent to loosen the thong of the san-

των αὐτοῦ· αὐτὸς ὑμᾶς βαπτίσει ἐν
dals of him; he you will baptize with

πνεύματι ἁγίῳ καὶ πυρί· 17 οὗ τὸ πτύον
Spirit [the] Holy and fire; of whom the fan [is]

ἐν τῇ χειρὶ αὐτοῦ διακαθᾶραι τὴν ἅλωνα
in the hand of him thoroughly to cleanse the threshing-floor

αὐτοῦ καὶ συναγαγεῖν τὸν σῖτον εἰς τὴν
of him and to gather the wheat into the

ἀποθήκην αὐτοῦ, τὸ δὲ ἄχυρον κατακαύσει
barn of him, but the chaff he will burn up

πυρὶ ἀσβέστῳ. 18 Πολλὰ μὲν οὖν καὶ
with fire unquenchable. Many things indeed therefore and

ἕτερα παρακαλῶν εὐηγγελίζετο τὸν λαόν·
different exhorting he evangelized the people;

19 ὁ δὲ Ἡρῴδης ὁ τετραάρχης, ἐλεγχόμενος
- but Herod the tetrarch, being reproved

ὑπ᾽ αὐτοῦ περὶ Ἡρῳδιάδος τῆς γυναικὸς
by him concerning Herodias the wife

τοῦ ἀδελφοῦ αὐτοῦ καὶ περὶ πάντων ὧν
of the brother of him and concerning ¹all ²things ⁴which

ἐποίησεν πονηρῶν ὁ Ἡρῴδης, 20 προσέθηκεν
³did ⁵evil - 'Herod, added

καὶ τοῦτο ἐπὶ πᾶσιν, κατέκλεισεν τὸν
also this above all, he shut up

Ἰωάννην ἐν φυλακῇ.
John in prison.

21 Ἐγένετο δὲ ἐν τῷ βαπτισθῆναι ἅπαντα
Now it came to pass in the to be baptized all
= when all the people were baptized

τὸν λαὸν καὶ Ἰησοῦ βαπτισθέντος καὶ
the people^be and Jesus being baptized and
= as Jesus had been baptized and was praying

προσευχομένου ἀνεῳχθῆναι τὸν οὐρανὸν 22 καὶ
praying* to be opened the heaven and
= the heaven was opened and the Holy Spirit came down

καταβῆναι τὸ πνεῦμα τὸ ἅγιον σωματικῷ
to come down the Spirit the Holy^b in a bodily

εἴδει ὡς περιστερὰν ἐπ᾽ αὐτόν, καὶ φωνὴν
form as a dove upon him, and a voice

ἐξ οὐρανοῦ γενέσθαι· σὺ εἶ ὁ υἱός μου
out of heaven to come^b : Thou art the Son of me

ὁ ἀγαπητός, ἐν σοὶ εὐδόκησα. 23 Καὶ
- beloved, in thee I was well pleased. And

αὐτὸς ἦν Ἰησοῦς ἀρχόμενος ὡσεὶ ἐτῶν
'himself ²was 'Jesus 'beginning about years

τριάκοντα, ὢν υἱός, ὡς ἐνομίζετο, Ἰωσήφ,
thirty, being son, as was supposed, of Joseph,

τοῦ Ἠλὶ 24 τοῦ Ματθὰτ τοῦ Λευὶ τοῦ
- of Eli - of Matthat - of Levi -

Μελχὶ τοῦ Ἰανναὶ τοῦ Ἰωσὴφ 25 τοῦ
of Melchi - of Jannai - of Joseph -

Ματταθίου τοῦ Ἀμὼς τοῦ Ναοὺμ τοῦ
of Mattathias - of Amos - of Naum -

Ἑσλὶ τοῦ Ναγγαὶ 26 τοῦ Μάαθ τοῦ
of Hesli - of Naggai - of Maath -

Ματταθίου τοῦ Σεμεῒν τοῦ Ἰωσὴχ τοῦ
of Mattathias - of Semein - of.Josech -

Ἰωδὰ 27 τοῦ Ἰωανὰν τοῦ Ῥησὰ τοῦ
of Jodah - of Joanan - of Rhesa -

Ζοροβαβὲλ τοῦ Σαλαθιὴλ τοῦ Νηρὶ 28 τοῦ
of Zorobabel - of Salathiel - of Neri -

Μελχὶ τοῦ Ἀδδὶ τοῦ Κωσὰμ τοῦ
of Melchi - of Addi - of Kosam -

Ἐλμαδὰμ τοῦ Ἢρ 29 τοῦ Ἰησοῦ τοῦ
of Elmadam - of Er - of Jesus -

Ἐλιέζερ τοῦ Ἰωρὶμ τοῦ Ματθὰτ τοῦ
of Eliezer - of Jorim - of Matthat -

Λευὶ 30 τοῦ Συμεὼν τοῦ Ἰούδα τοῦ
of Levi - of Simeon - of Juda -

Ἰωσὴφ τοῦ Ἰωνὰμ τοῦ Ἐλιακὶμ 31 τοῦ
of Joseph - of Jonam - of Eliakim -

Μελεὰ τοῦ Μεννὰ τοῦ Ματταθὰ τοῦ
of Melea - of Menna - of Mattatha -

Ναθὰμ τοῦ Δαυὶδ 32 τοῦ Ἰεσσαὶ τοῦ
of Natham - of David - of Jesse -

Ἰωβὴδ τοῦ Βόος τοῦ Σάλα τοῦ Ναασσὼν
of Jobed - of Boos - of Sala - of Naasson

33 τοῦ Ἀμιναδὰβ τοῦ Ἀδμὶν τοῦ Ἀρνὶ
- of Aminadab - of Admin - of Arni

τοῦ Ἑσρὼμ τοῦ Φάρες τοῦ Ἰούδα
- of Hesrom - of Phares - of Juda

King James Version

of Phares, which was *the son* of Juda, 34 Which was *the son* of Jacob, which was *the son* of Isaac, which was *the son* of Abraham, which was *the son* of Thara, which was *the son* of Nachor, 35 Which was *the son* of Saruch, which was *the son* of Ragau, which was *the son* of Phalec, which was *the son* of Heber, which was *the son* of Sala, 36 Which was *the son* of Cainan, which was *the son* of Arphaxad, which was *the son* of Sem, which was *the son* of Noe, which was *the son* of Lamech, 37 Which was *the son* of Mathusala, which was *the son* of Enoch, which was *the son* of Jared, which was *the son* of Maleleel, which was *the son* of Cainan, 38 Which was *the son* of Enos, which was *the son* of Seth, which was *the son* of Adam, which was *the son* of God.

4 And Jesus being full of the Holy Ghost returned from Jordan, and was led by the Spirit into the wilderness, 2 Being forty days tempted of the devil. And in those days he did eat nothing: and when they were ended, he afterward hungered. 3 And the devil said unto him, If thou be the Son of God, command this stone that it be made bread. 4 And Jesus answered him, saying, It is written, That man shall not live by bread alone, but by every word of God. 5 And the devil, taking him up into a high mountain, shewed unto him all the kingdoms of the world in a moment of time. 6 And the devil said unto him, All this power will I give thee, and the glory of them: for that is delivered unto me; and to whomsoever I will, I give it. 7 If thou therefore wilt worship me, all shall be thine. 8 And Jesus answered and said unto him, Get thee behind me, Satan: for it is written, Thou shalt worship the Lord thy God, and him only shalt thou serve. 9 And he brought him to Jerusalem, and set him on a pinnacle of the temple, and said unto him, If thou be the Son of God, cast thyself down from hence: 10 For it is written, He shall give his angels charge over thee, to keep thee: 11 And in *their* hands they shall bear thee up, lest at any time thou dash thy foot against a stone. 12 And Jesus answering said unto him, It is said, Thou shalt not tempt the Lord thy God. 13 And when the devil had ended all the temptation, he departed from him for a season.

14 And Jesus returned in the power of the Spirit into Galilee: and there went out a fame of him through all the region round about. 15 And he taught in their synagogues, being glorified of all.

16 And he came to Nazareth, where he had been brought up: and, as his custom was, he went into the synagogue on the sabbath day, and stood up for to read. 17 And there was delivered unto him the book of the prophet Esaias. And when he had opened the book, he found the place where it was written, 18 The Spirit of the Lord *is* upon me, because he hath anointed me to preach the gospel to the poor; he hath sent me to heal the brokenhearted, to preach deliverance to the captives, and recovering of sight to the blind, to set at liberty them that are bruised, 19 To preach the acceptable year of the

New International Version

the son of Judah, 34 the son of Jacob, the son of Isaac, the son of Abraham, the son of Terah, the son of Nahor, 35 the son of Serug, the son of Reu, the son of Peleg, the son of Eber, the son of Shelah, 36 the son of Cainan, the son of Arphaxad, the son of Shem, the son of Noah, the son of Lamech, 37 the son of Methuselah, the son of Enoch, the son of Jared, the son of Mahalaleel, the son of Cainan, 38 the son of Enos, the son of Seth, the son of Adam, the son of God.

The temptations of Jesus

4 Jesus, full of the Holy Spirit, returned from the Jordan and was led by the Spirit in the desert, 2 where for forty days he was tempted by the devil. He ate nothing during those days, and at the end of them he was hungry.

3 The devil said to him, "If you are the Son of God, tell this stone to become bread."

4 Jesus answered, "It is written: 'Man does not live on bread alone.' *m* "

5 The devil led him up to a high place and showed him in an instant all the kingdoms of the world. 6 And he said to him, "I will give you all their authority and splendor, for it has been given to me, and I can give it to anyone I want to. 7 So if you worship me, it will all be yours."

8 Jesus answered, "It is written: 'Worship the Lord your God and serve him only.' *n* "

9 The devil led him to Jerusalem and had him stand on the highest point of the temple. "If you are the Son of God," he said, "throw yourself down from here. 10 For it is written:

'He will command his angels concerning you
    to guard you carefully;
11 and they will lift you up in their hands,
    so that you will not strike your foot
        against a stone.' *o* "

12 Jesus answered, "It says: 'Do not put the Lord your God to the test.' *p* "

Jesus rejected at Nazareth

13 When the devil had finished all these temptations, he left him until an opportune time.

14 Jesus returned to Galilee in the power of the Spirit, and news about him spread through the whole countryside. 15 He taught in their synagogues, and everyone praised him.

16 He went to Nazareth, where he had been brought up, and on the Sabbath day he went into the synagogue, as was his custom. And he stood up to read. 17 The scroll of the prophet Isaiah was handed to him. Unrolling it, he found the place where it is written:
18 "The Spirit of the Lord is on me;
    therefore he has anointed me to preach
        good news to the poor.
He has sent me to proclaim freedom for
        the prisoners
    and recovery of sight for the blind,
to release the oppressed,
19   to proclaim the year of the Lord's
        favor." *q*

[m] Deut. 8:3. [n] Deut. 6:13. [o] Psalm 91:11, 12. [p] Deut. 6:16. [q] Isaiah 61:1, 2.

176

Greek Interlinear

34 τοῦ Ἰακὼβ τοῦ Ἰσαὰκ τοῦ Ἀβραάμ
\- of Jacob - of Isaac - of Abraham

τοῦ Θάρα τοῦ Ναχὼρ **35** τοῦ Σερούχ
\- of Thara - of Nachor - of Seruch

τοῦ Ῥαγαὺ τοῦ Φάλεκ τοῦ Ἔβερ τοῦ
\- of Rhagau - of Phalek - of Eber -

Σάλα **36** τοῦ Καϊνὰμ τοῦ Ἀρφαξὰδ τοῦ
of Sala - of Cainam - of Arphaxad -

Σὴμ τοῦ Νῶε τοῦ Λάμεχ **37** τοῦ Μαθουσάλα
of Sem - of Noe - of Lamech - of Mathusala

τοῦ Ἐνὼχ τοῦ Ἰάρετ τοῦ Μαλελεὴλ
\- of Henoch - of Jaret - of Maleleel

τοῦ Καϊνὰμ **38** τοῦ Ἐνὼς τοῦ Σὴθ τοῦ
\- of Cainam - of Enos - of Seth -

Ἀδὰμ τοῦ θεοῦ.
of Adam - of God.

Chapter 4

Ἰησοῦς δὲ πλήρης πνεύματος ἁγίου
And Jesus full of ¹[the] ²Spirit ³Holy

ὑπέστρεψεν ἀπὸ τοῦ Ἰορδάνου, καὶ ἤγετο
returned from the Jordan, and was led

ἐν τῷ πνεύματι ἐν τῇ ἐρήμῳ **2** ἡμέρας
by the Spirit in the desert days

τεσσεράκοντα πειραζόμενος ὑπὸ τοῦ διαβόλου.
forty being tempted by the devil.

Καὶ οὐκ ἔφαγεν οὐδὲν ἐν ταῖς ἡμέραις
And he ate not no(any)thing in - days

ἐκείναις, καὶ συντελεσθεισῶν αὐτῶν ἐπεί-
those, and being ended them* = when they were ended he

νασεν. **3** εἶπεν δὲ αὐτῷ ὁ διάβολος·
hungered. And said to him the devil :

εἰ υἱὸς εἶ τοῦ θεοῦ, εἰπὲ τῷ λίθῳ
If Son thou art - of God, tell - stone

τούτῳ ἵνα γένηται ἄρτος. **4** καὶ ἀπεκρίθη
this that it become a loaf. And made answer

πρὸς αὐτὸν ὁ Ἰησοῦς· γέγραπται ὅτι
to him - Jesus : It has been written[,] -

οὐκ ἐπ' ἄρτῳ μόνῳ ζήσεται ὁ ἄνθρωπος.
Not on bread only shall live - man.

5 Καὶ ἀναγαγὼν αὐτὸν ἔδειξεν αὐτῷ πάσας
And leading up him he showed him all

τὰς βασιλείας τῆς οἰκουμένης ἐν στιγμῇ
the kingdoms of the inhabited earth in a moment

χρόνου. **6** καὶ εἶπεν αὐτῷ ὁ διάβολος·
of time. And said to him the devil :

σοὶ δώσω τὴν ἐξουσίαν ταύτην ἅπασαν καὶ
To thee I will give - authority this all and

τὴν δόξαν αὐτῶν, ὅτι ἐμοὶ παραδέδοται
the glory of them, because to me it has been delivered

καὶ ᾧ ἐὰν θέλω δίδωμι αὐτήν· **7** σὺ οὖν
and to whomever I wish I give it; *thou ¹therefore

ἐὰν προσκυνήσῃς ἐνώπιον ἐμοῦ, ἔσται σοῦ
²if worship before me, will be of thee

πᾶσα. **8** καὶ ἀποκριθεὶς ὁ Ἰησοῦς εἶπεν
all. And answering Jesus said

αὐτῷ· γέγραπται· προσκυνήσεις κύριον τὸν
to him : It has been written : Thou shalt worship [the] Lord the

θεόν σου καὶ αὐτῷ μόνῳ λατρεύσεις.
God of thee and him only shalt thou serve.

9 Ἤγαγεν δὲ αὐτὸν εἰς Ἰερουσαλὴμ καὶ
And he led him to Jerusalem and

ἔστησεν ἐπὶ τὸ πτερύγιον τοῦ ἱεροῦ, καὶ
set on the gable of the temple, and

εἶπεν αὐτῷ· εἰ υἱὸς εἶ τοῦ θεοῦ, βάλε
said to him : If Son thou art - of God, throw

σεαυτὸν ἐντεῦθεν κάτω· **10** γέγραπται γὰρ ὅτι
thyself hence down; for it has been written[,] -

τοῖς ἀγγέλοις αὐτοῦ ἐντελεῖται περὶ
The angels of him he will command concerning

σοῦ τοῦ διαφυλάξαι σε, **11** καὶ ὅτι ἐπὶ
thee - to preserveᵈ thee, and - on

χειρῶν ἀροῦσίν σε, μήποτε προσκόψῃς
[their] hands they will bear thee, lest thou dash

πρὸς λίθον τὸν πόδα σου. **12** καὶ
against a stone the foot of thee. And

ἀποκριθεὶς εἶπεν αὐτῷ ὁ Ἰησοῦς ὅτι
answering said to him - Jesus[,]

εἴρηται· οὐκ ἐκπειράσεις κύριον τὸν
It has been said : Thou shalt not overtempt [the] Lord the

θεόν σου. **13** Καὶ συντελέσας πάντα πειρασμὸν
God of thee. And having finished every temptation

ὁ διάβολος ἀπέστη ἀπ' αὐτοῦ ἄχρι καιροῦ.
the devil went away from him until a season.

14 Καὶ ὑπέστρεψεν ὁ Ἰησοῦς ἐν τῇ
And returned - Jesus in the

δυνάμει τοῦ πνεύματος εἰς τὴν Γαλιλαίαν·
power of the Spirit to - Galilee;

καὶ φήμη ἐξῆλθεν καθ' ὅλης τῆς περιχώρου
and a rumour went forth throughout all the neighbourhood

περὶ αὐτοῦ. **15** καὶ αὐτὸς ἐδίδασκεν ἐν
concerning him. And he taught in

ταῖς συναγωγαῖς αὐτῶν, δοξαζόμενος ὑπὸ
the synagogues of them, being glorified by

πάντων.
all.

16 Καὶ ἦλθεν εἰς Ναζαρά, οὗ ἦν
And he came to Nazareth, where he was

τεθραμμένος, καὶ εἰσῆλθεν κατὰ τὸ εἰωθὸς
having been and entered accord- the custom
brought up, ing to =his custom

αὐτῷ ἐν τῇ ἡμέρᾳ τῶν σαββάτων εἰς τὴν
to himᵉ on the day of the sabbaths into the

συναγωγήν, καὶ ἀνέστη ἀναγνῶναι. **17** καὶ
synagogue, and stood up to read. And

ἐπεδόθη αὐτῷ βιβλίον τοῦ προφήτου
was handed to him a roll of the prophet

Ἠσαΐου, καὶ ἀνοίξας τὸ βιβλίον εὗρεν
Esaias, and having opened the roll he found

[τὸν] τόπον οὗ ἦν γεγραμμένον· **18** πνεῦμα
the place where it was having been written : [The] Spirit

κυρίου ἐπ' ἐμέ, οὗ εἵνεκεν ἔχρισέν με
of [the] Lord [is] upon me, wherefore he anointed me

εὐαγγελίσασθαι πτωχοῖς, ἀπέσταλκέν με
to evangelize [the] poor, he has sent me

κηρῦξαι αἰχμαλώτοις ἄφεσιν καὶ τυφλοῖς
to proclaim to captives release and to blind [ones]

ἀνάβλεψιν, ἀποστεῖλαι τεθραυσμένους ἐν
sight, to send away having been crushed [ones] in

ἀφέσει, **19** κηρῦξαι ἐνιαυτὸν κυρίου δεκτόν.
release, to proclaim a year of [the] Lord acceptable.

177

King James Version

Lord. 20And he closed the book, and he gave *it* again to the minister, and sat down. And the eyes of all them that were in the synagogue were fastened on him. 21And he began to say unto them, This day is this Scripture fulfilled in your ears. 22And all bare him witness, and wondered at the gracious words which proceeded out of his mouth. And they said, Is not this Joseph's son? 23And he said unto them, Ye will surely say unto me this proverb, Physician, heal thyself: whatsoever we have heard done in Capernaum, do also here in thy country. 24And he said, Verily I say unto you, No prophet is accepted in his own country. 25 But I tell you of a truth, many widows were in Israel in the days of Elias, when the heaven was shut up three years and six months, when great famine was throughout all the land; 26 But unto none of them was Elias sent, save unto Sarepta, *a city* of Sidon, unto a woman *that was* a widow. 27And many lepers were in Israel in the time of Eliseus the prophet; and none of them was cleansed, saving Naaman the Syrian. 28And all they in the synagogue, when they heard these things, were filled with wrath, 29And rose up, and thrust him out of the city, and led him unto the brow of the hill whereon their city was built, that they might cast him down headlong. 30 But he, passing through the midst of them, went his way, 31And came down to Capernaum, a city of Galilee, and taught them on the sabbath days. 32And they were astonished at his doctrine: for his word was with power.

33 And in the synagogue there was a man, which had a spirit of an unclean devil, and cried out with a loud voice, 34 Saying, Let *us* alone; what have we to do with thee, *thou* Jesus of Nazareth? art thou come to destroy us? I know thee who thou art; the Holy One of God. 35And Jesus rebuked him, saying, Hold thy peace, and come out of him. And when the devil had thrown him in the midst, he came out of him, and hurt him not. 36And they were all amazed, and spake among themselves, saying, What a word *is* this! for with authority and power he commandeth the unclean spirits, and they come out. 37And the fame of him went out into every place of the country round about.

38 And he arose out of the synagogue, and entered into Simon's house. And Simon's wife's mother was taken with a great fever; and they besought him for her. 39And he stood over her, and rebuked the fever; and it left her: and immediately she arose and ministered unto them.

40 Now when the sun was setting, all they that had any sick with divers diseases brought them unto him; and he laid his hands on every one of them, and healed them. 41And devils also came out of many, crying out, and saying, Thou art Christ the Son of God. And he rebuking *them* suffered them not to speak: for they knew

New International Version

20 Then he rolled up the scroll, gave it back to the attendant and sat down. The eyes of everyone in the synagogue were fastened on him, 21 and he said to them, "Today this scripture is fulfilled in your hearing."

22 All spoke well of him and were amazed at the gracious words that came from his lips. "Isn't this Joseph's son?" they asked.

23 Jesus said to them, "Surely you will quote this proverb to me: 'Physician, heal yourself! Do here in your home town what we have heard that you did in Capernaum.' "

24 "I tell you the truth," he continued, "no prophet is accepted in his home town. 25 I assure you that there were many widows in Israel in Elijah's time, when the sky was shut for three and a half years and there was a severe famine throughout the land. 26 Yet Elijah was not sent to any of them, but to a widow in Zarephath in the region of Sidon. 27And there were many in Israel with leprosy[r] in the time of Elisha the prophet, yet not one of them was cleansed except Naaman the Syrian."

28 All the people in the synagogue were furious when they heard this. 29 They got up, drove him out of the town, and took him to the brow of the hill on which the town was built, in order to throw him down the cliff. 30 But he walked right through the crowd and went on his way.

Jesus drives out an evil spirit

31 Then he went down to Capernaum, a town in Galilee, and on the Sabbath began to teach the people. 32 They were amazed at his teaching, because his message had authority.

33 In the synagogue there was a man possessed by a demon, an evil[s] spirit. He cried out at the top of his voice, 34 "Ha! What do you want with us, Jesus of Nazareth? Have you come to destroy us? I know who you are—the Holy One of God!"

35 "Be quiet!" Jesus said sternly. "Come out of him!" Then the demon threw the man down before them all and came out without injuring him.

36 All the people were amazed and said to each other, "What is this teaching? With authority and power he gives orders to evil[s] spirits and they come out!" 37And the news about him spread throughout the surrounding area.

Jesus heals many

38 Jesus left the synagogue and went to the home of Simon. Now Simon's mother-in-law was suffering from a high fever, and they asked Jesus to help her. 39 So he bent over her and rebuked the fever, and it left her. She got up at once and began to wait on them.

40 When the sun was setting, the people brought to Jesus all who had various kinds of sickness, and laying his hands on each one, he healed them. 41 Moreover, demons came out of many people, shouting, "You are the Son of God!" But he rebuked them and would not allow them to speak, because they knew he was the Christ.[u]

[r] The Greek word probably designated other related diseases also. [s] Greek *unclean.* [u] Or *Messiah.*

Greek Interlinear

20 καὶ πτύξας τὸ βιβλίον ἀποδοὺς τῷ
And having closed the roll returning [it] to the

ὑπηρέτῃ ἐκάθισεν· καὶ πάντων οἱ ὀφθαλμοὶ
attendant he sat; and of all the eyes

ἐν τῇ συναγωγῇ ἦσαν ἀτενίζοντες αὐτῷ.
in the synagogue were gazing at him.

21 ἤρξατο δὲ λέγειν πρὸς αὐτοὺς ὅτι
And he began to say to them[,] -

σήμερον πεπλήρωται ἡ γραφὴ αὕτη ἐν
To-day has been fulfilled - scripture this in

τοῖς ὠσὶν ὑμῶν. 22 καὶ πάντες ἐμαρτύρουν
the ears of you. And all bore witness

αὐτῷ καὶ ἐθαύμαζον ἐπὶ τοῖς λόγοις τῆς
to him and marvelled at the words -

χάριτος τοῖς ἐκπορευομένοις ἐκ τοῦ στόματος
of grace proceeding out of the mouth

αὐτοῦ, καὶ ἔλεγον· οὐχὶ υἱός ἐστιν Ἰωσὴφ
of him, and they said: ²not ⁴son ¹Is ³of Joseph

οὗτος; 23 καὶ εἶπεν πρὸς αὐτούς· πάντως
¹this man? And he said to them: To be sure

ἐρεῖτέ μοι τὴν παραβολὴν ταύτην· ἰατρέ,
ye will say to me - parable this; Physician,

θεράπευσον σεαυτόν· ὅσα ἠκούσαμεν γεν-
heal thyself; what things we heard hap-

όμενα εἰς τὴν Καφαρναούμ, ποίησον καὶ
pening in - Capernaum, do also

ὧδε ἐν τῇ πατρίδι σου. 24 εἶπεν δέ·
here in the native place of thee. And he said:

ἀμὴν λέγω ὑμῖν ὅτι οὐδεὶς προφήτης
Truly I tell you that no prophet

δεκτός ἐστιν ἐν τῇ πατρίδι αὐτοῦ. 25 ἐπ'
acceptable is in the native place of him. ⁵on(in)

ἀληθείας δὲ λέγω ὑμῖν, πολλαὶ χῆραι ἦσαν
³truth ¹But I tell you, many widows were

ἐν ταῖς ἡμέραις Ἠλίου ἐν τῷ Ἰσραήλ,
in the days of Elias in - Israel,

ὅτε ἐκλείσθη ὁ οὐρανὸς ἐπὶ ἔτη τρία καὶ
when was shut up the heaven over years three and

μῆνας ἕξ, ὡς ἐγένετο λιμὸς μέγας ἐπὶ
months six, when came famine a great over

πᾶσαν τὴν γῆν, 26 καὶ πρὸς οὐδεμίαν
all the land, and to not one

αὐτῶν ἐπέμφθη Ἠλίας εἰ μὴ εἰς Σάρεπτα
of them was sent Elias except to Sarepta

τῆς Σιδωνίας πρὸς γυναῖκα χήραν. 27 καὶ
- of Sidon to a woman a widow. And

πολλοὶ λεπροὶ ἦσαν ἐν τῷ Ἰσραὴλ ἐπὶ
many lepers were in - Israel during

Ἐλισαίου τοῦ προφήτου, καὶ οὐδεὶς αὐτῶν
Elisæus the prophet, and not one of them

ἐκαθαρίσθη εἰ μὴ Ναιμὰν ὁ Σύρος.
was cleansed except Naaman the Syrian.

28 καὶ ἐπλήσθησαν πάντες θυμοῦ ἐν τῇ
And ²were filled ¹all of(with) anger in the

συναγωγῇ ἀκούοντες ταῦτα, 29 καὶ ἀναστάντες
synagogue hearing these things, and rising up

ἐξέβαλον αὐτὸν ἔξω τῆς πόλεως, καὶ
they cast out him outside the city, and

ἤγαγον αὐτὸν ἕως ὀφρύος τοῦ ὄρους ἐφ'
led him to a brow of the hill on

οὗ ἡ πόλις ᾠκοδόμητο αὐτῶν, ὥστε
which the city was built of them, so as

κατακρημνίσαι αὐτόν· 30 αὐτὸς δὲ διελθὼν
to throw down him; but he passing through

διὰ μέσου αὐτῶν ἐπορεύετο.
through [the] midst of them went.

31 Καὶ κατῆλθεν εἰς Καφαρναοὺμ πόλιν
And he went down to Capernaum a city

τῆς Γαλιλαίας. καὶ ἦν διδάσκων αὐτοὺς
- of Galilee. And he was teaching them

ἐν τοῖς σάββασιν· 32 καὶ ἐξεπλήσσοντο
on the sabbaths; and they were astounded

ἐπὶ τῇ διδαχῇ αὐτοῦ, ὅτι ἐν ἐξουσίᾳ
at the teaching of him, because with authority

ἦν ὁ λόγος αὐτοῦ. 33 καὶ ἐν τῇ συναγωγῇ
was the word of him. And in the synagogue

ἦν ἄνθρωπος ἔχων πνεῦμα δαιμονίου
there was a man having a spirit ²demon

ἀκαθάρτου, καὶ ἀνέκραξεν φωνῇ μεγάλῃ·
¹of an unclean, and he shouted voice with a great:

34 ἔα, τί ἡμῖν καὶ σοί, Ἰησοῦ Ναζαρηνέ;
Ah, what to us and to thee, Jesus Nazarene?

ἦλθες ἀπολέσαι ἡμᾶς; οἶδά σε τίς εἶ,
Camest thou to destroy us? I know thee who thou art,

ὁ ἅγιος τοῦ θεοῦ. 35 καὶ ἐπετίμησεν αὐτῷ
the holy one - of God. And rebuked him

ὁ Ἰησοῦς λέγων· φιμώθητι καὶ ἔξελθε
- Jesus saying: Be muzzled and come out

ἀπ' αὐτοῦ. καὶ ῥῖψαν αὐτὸν τὸ δαιμόνιον
from him. And ³throwing ⁴him ¹the ²demon

εἰς τὸ μέσον ἐξῆλθεν ἀπ' αὐτοῦ μηδὲν
in the midst came out from him nothing

βλάψαν αὐτόν. 36 καὶ ἐγένετο θάμβος
injuring him. And came astonishment

ἐπὶ πάντας, καὶ συνελάλουν πρὸς ἀλλήλους
on all, and they spoke to one another

λέγοντες· τίς ὁ λόγος οὗτος, ὅτι ἐν
saying: What [is] - word this, because with

ἐξουσίᾳ καὶ δυνάμει ἐπιτάσσει τοῖς
authority and power he commands the

ἀκαθάρτοις πνεύμασιν καὶ ἐξέρχονται; 37 καὶ
unclean spirits and they come out? And

ἐξεπορεύετο ἦχος περὶ αὐτοῦ εἰς πάντα
went forth a rumour concerning him into every

τόπον τῆς περιχώρου. 38 Ἀναστὰς δὲ
place of the neighbourhood. And rising up

ἀπὸ τῆς συναγωγῆς εἰσῆλθεν εἰς τὴν
from the synagogue he entered into the

οἰκίαν Σίμωνος. πενθερὰ δὲ τοῦ Σίμωνος
house of Simon. And [the] mother-in-law - of Simon

ἦν συνεχομένη πυρετῷ μεγάλῳ, καὶ
was being seized fever with a great, and

ἠρώτησαν αὐτὸν περὶ αὐτῆς. 39 καὶ
they ask ₁him about her. And

ἐπιστὰς ἐπάνω αὐτῆς ἐπετίμησεν τῷ πυρετῷ,
standing over her he rebuked the fever,

καὶ ἀφῆκεν αὐτήν· παραχρῆμα δὲ ἀναστᾶσα
and it left her; and at once rising up

διηκόνει αὐτοῖς. 40 Δύνοντος δὲ τοῦ
she served them. And setting = as the sun was setting

ἡλίου ἅπαντες ὅσοι εἶχον ἀσθενοῦντας
sun² all as many as had ailing [ones]

νόσοις ποικίλαις ἤγαγον αὐτοὺς πρὸς αὐτόν·
diseases with various brought them to him;

ὁ δὲ ἑνὶ ἑκάστῳ αὐτῶν τὰς χεῖρας
and he ²one ³on each ¹of them ⁵the(his) ⁴hands

ἐπιτιθεὶς ἐθεράπευεν αὐτούς. 41 ἐξήρχετο
¹putting on healed them. came out

δὲ καὶ δαιμόνια ἀπὸ πολλῶν, κραυγάζοντα
And also demons from many, crying out

καὶ λέγοντα ὅτι σὺ εἶ ὁ υἱὸς τοῦ θεοῦ.
and saying[,] - Thou art the Son - of God.

καὶ ἐπιτιμῶν οὐκ εἴα αὐτὰ λαλεῖν, ὅτι
And rebuking he allowed not them to speak, because

179

King James Version

that he was Christ. 42And when it was day, he departed and went into a desert place: and the people sought him, and came unto him, and stayed him, that he should not depart from them. 43And he said unto them, I must preach the kingdom of God to other cities also: for therefore am I sent. 44And he preached in the synagogues of Galilee.

5 And it came to pass, that, as the people pressed upon him to hear the word of God, he stood by the lake of Gennesaret, 2And saw two ships standing by the lake: but the fishermen were gone out of them, and were washing *their* nets. 3And he entered into one of the ships, which was Simon's, and prayed him that he would thrust out a little from the land. And he sat down, and taught the people out of the ship. 4 Now when he had left speaking, he said unto Simon, Launch out into the deep, and let down your nets for a draught. 5And Simon answering said unto him, Master, we have toiled all the night, and have taken nothing: nevertheless at thy word I will let down the net. 6And when they had this done, they inclosed a great multitude of fishes: and their net brake. 7And they beckoned unto *their* partners, which were in the other ship, that they should come and help them. And they came, and filled both the ships, so that they began to sink. 8 When Simon Peter saw *it,* he fell down at Jesus' knees, saying, Depart from me; for I am a sinful man, O Lord. 9 For he was astonished, and all that were with him, at the draught of the fishes which they had taken: 10And so *was* also James, and John, the sons of Zebedee, which were partners with Simon. And Jesus said unto Simon, Fear not; from henceforth thou shalt catch men. 11And when they had brought their ships to land, they forsook all, and followed him.

12 And it came to pass, when he was in a certain city, behold a man full of leprosy: who seeing Jesus fell on *his* face, and besought him, saying, Lord, if thou wilt, thou canst make me clean. 13And he put forth *his* hand, and touched him, saying, I will: be thou clean. And immediately the leprosy departed from him. 14And he charged him to tell no man: but go, and shew thyself to the priest, and offer for thy cleansing, according as Moses commanded, for a testimony unto them. 15 But so much the more went there a fame abroad of him: and great multitudes came together to hear, and to be healed by him of their infirmities. 16 And he withdrew himself into the wilder-

New International Version

42 At daybreak Jesus went out to a solitary place. The people were looking for him and when they came to where he was, they tried to keep him from leaving them. 43 But he said, "I must preach the good news of the kingdom of God to the other towns also, because that is why I was sent." 44And he kept on preaching in the synagogues of Judea.[v]

The calling of the first disciples

5 One day as Jesus was standing by the Lake of Gennesaret,[w] with the people crowding around him and listening to the word of God, 2 he saw at the water's edge two boats, left there by the fishermen, who were washing their nets. 3 He got into one of the boats, the one belonging to Simon, and asked him to put out a little from shore. Then he sat down and taught the people from the boat.

4 When he had finished speaking, he said to Simon, "Put out into deep water, and let down the nets for a catch."

5 Simon answered, "Master, we've worked hard all night and haven't caught anything. But because you say so, I will let down the nets."

6 When they had done so, they caught such a large number of fish that their nets began to break. 7 So they signaled their partners in the other boat to come and help them, and they came and filled both boats so full that they began to sink.

8 When Simon Peter saw this, he fell at Jesus' knees and said, "Go away from me, Lord; I am a sinful man!" 9 For he and all his companions were astonished at the catch of fish they had taken, 10 and so were James and John, the sons of Zebedee, Simon's partners.

Then Jesus said to Simon, "Don't be afraid; from now on you will catch men." 11 So they pulled their boats up on shore, left everything and followed him.

The man with leprosy

12 While Jesus was in one of the towns, a man came along who was covered with leprosy.[x] When he saw Jesus, he fell with his face to the ground and begged him, "Lord, if you are willing, you can make me clean."

13 Jesus reached out his hand and touched the man. "I am willing," he said. "Be clean!" And immediately the leprosy left him.

14 Then Jesus ordered him, "Don't tell anyone, but go, show yourself to the priest and offer the sacrifices that Moses commanded for your cleansing, as a testimony to them."

15 Yet the news about him spread all the more, so that crowds of people came to hear him and to be healed of their sicknesses. 16 But Jesus often withdrew to lonely places and prayed.

[v] Or *the land of the Jews.* Some MSS read *Galilee.* [w] That is, the Sea of Galilee. [x] The Greek word probably designated other related diseases also.

Greek Interlinear

ἤδεισαν τὸν χριστὸν αὐτὸν εἶναι. 42 Γενομένης
they knew ³the ⁴Christ ¹him ²to be.   coming
                                                 = And when

δὲ ἡμέρας ἐξελθὼν ἐπορεύθη εἰς ἔρημον
And day³ going forth he went to a desert
day came

τόπον· καὶ οἱ ὄχλοι ἐπεζήτουν αὐτόν, καὶ
place; and the crowds sought him,   and

ἦλθον ἕως αὐτοῦ, καὶ κατεῖχον αὐτὸν
came up to him,   and detained him

τοῦ μὴ πορεύεσθαι ἀπ᾽ αὐτῶν. 43 ὁ δὲ
 - not to go⁴ from them.   And he
= so that he should not go

εἶπεν πρὸς αὐτοὺς ὅτι καὶ ταῖς ἑτέραις
said   to   them[,] - Also to the other

πόλεσιν εὐαγγελίσασθαί με δεῖ τὴν
cities ³to preach ²me ¹it behoves the

βασιλείαν τοῦ θεοῦ, ὅτι ἐπὶ τοῦτο ἀπεστάλην.
kingdom - of God, because on this I was sent.

44 καὶ ἦν κηρύσσων εἰς τὰς συναγωγὰς
And he was proclaiming in the synagogues

τῆς Ἰουδαίας.
 - of Judæa.

Chapter 5

Ἐγένετο δὲ ἐν τῷ τὸν ὄχλον ἐπικεῖσθαι
Now it came to pass in the the crowd to press upon
                     = as the crowd pressed upon him and heard

αὐτῷ καὶ ἀκούειν τὸν λόγον τοῦ θεοῦ,
him   and to hear⁵ᵉ the word - of God,

καὶ αὐτὸς ἦν ἑστὼς παρὰ τὴν λίμνην
and he was standing by the lake

Γεννησαρέτ, 2 καὶ εἶδεν δύο πλοιάρια
Gennesaret, and saw two boats

ἑστῶτα παρὰ τὴν λίμνην· οἱ δὲ ἁλεεῖς
standing by the lake; but the fishermen

ἀπ᾽ αὐτῶν ἀποβάντες ἔπλυνον τὰ δίκτυα.
from them having gone away were washing the nets.

3 ἐμβὰς δὲ εἰς ἓν τῶν πλοίων, ὃ ἦν
And embarking into one of the boats, which was

Σίμωνος, ἠρώτησεν αὐτὸν ἀπὸ τῆς γῆς
of Simon, he asked him from the land

ἐπαναγαγεῖν ὀλίγον· καθίσας δὲ ἐκ τοῦ
to put out a little; and sitting ⁴out of ¹the

πλοίου ἐδίδασκεν τοὺς ὄχλους. 4 ὡς δὲ
⁵boat ³he taught ²the ³crowds. And when

ἐπαύσατο λαλῶν, εἶπεν πρὸς τὸν Σίμωνα·
he ceased speaking, he said to - Simon :

ἐπανάγαγε εἰς τὸ βάθος, καὶ χαλάσατε
Put out into the deep, and let down

τὰ δίκτυα ὑμῶν εἰς ἄγραν. 5 καὶ
the nets of you for a draught. And

ἀποκριθεὶς Σίμων εἶπεν· ἐπιστάτα, δι᾽
answering Simon said : Master, through

ὅλης νυκτὸς κοπιάσαντες οὐδὲν ἐλάβομεν·
[the] whole night labouring nothing we took;

ἐπὶ δὲ τῷ ῥήματί σου χαλάσω τὰ δίκτυα.
but at the word of thee I will let down the nets.

6 καὶ τοῦτο ποιήσαντες συνέκλεισαν πλῆθος
And this doing they enclosed multitude

ἰχθύων πολύ· διερρήσσετο δὲ τὰ δίκτυα
of fishes a much; and were being torn the nets

αὐτῶν. 7 καὶ κατένευσαν τοῖς μετόχοις
of them. And they nodded to the(ir) partners

ἐν τῷ ἑτέρῳ πλοίῳ τοῦ ἐλθόντας
in the other boat - coming
                        = that they should come

συλλαβέσθαι αὐτοῖς· καὶ ἦλθαν, καὶ ἔπλησαν
to help⁴ them; and they came, and filled

ἀμφότερα τὰ πλοῖα ὥστε βυθίζεσθαι αὐτά.ᵇ
both the boats so as to be sinking them.ᵇ
                                          = so that they were sinking.

8 ἰδὼν δὲ Σίμων Πέτρος προσέπεσεν τοῖς
And seeing Simon Peter fell at the

γόνασιν Ἰησοῦ λέγων· ἔξελθε ἀπ᾽ ἐμοῦ,
knees of Jesus saying : Depart from me,

ὅτι ἀνὴρ ἁμαρτωλός εἰμι, κύριε. 9 θάμβος
because man a sinful I am, Lord. astonishment

γὰρ περιέσχεν αὐτὸν καὶ πάντας τοὺς
For seized him and all the [ones]

σὺν αὐτῷ ἐπὶ τῇ ἄγρᾳ τῶν ἰχθύων ᾗ
with him at the draught of the fishes which

συνέλαβον, 10 ὁμοίως δὲ καὶ Ἰάκωβον καὶ
they took, and likewise both James and

Ἰωάννην υἱοὺς Ζεβεδαίου, οἳ ἦσαν κοινωνοὶ
John sons of Zebedee, who were sharers

τῷ Σίμωνι. καὶ εἶπεν πρὸς τὸν Σίμωνα
 - with Simon. And said to - Simon

ὁ Ἰησοῦς· μὴ φοβοῦ· ἀπὸ τοῦ νῦν
 - Jesus: Fear thou not; from the now

ἀνθρώπους ἔσῃ ζωγρῶν. 11 καὶ καταγαγόντες
men thou wilt be taking alive. And bringing down

τὰ πλοῖα ἐπὶ τὴν γῆν, ἀφέντες πάντα
the boats onto the land, leaving all things

ἠκολούθησαν αὐτῷ.
they followed him.

12 Καὶ ἐγένετο ἐν τῷ εἶναι αὐτὸν ἐν
And it came to pass in the to be him⁵ᵉ in
                                = as he was

μιᾷ τῶν πόλεων καὶ ἰδοὺ ἀνὴρ πλήρης
one of the cities and behold[,] a man full

λέπρας· ἰδὼν δὲ τὸν Ἰησοῦν, πεσὼν ἐπὶ
of leprosy; and seeing - Jesus, falling on

πρόσωπον ἐδεήθη αὐτοῦ λέγων· κύριε,
[his] face he begged him saying : Lord,

ἐὰν θέλῃς, δύνασαί με καθαρίσαι. 13 καὶ
if thou willest, thou canst me to cleanse. And

ἐκτείνας τὴν χεῖρα ἥψατο αὐτοῦ λέγων·
stretching out the(his) hand he touched him saying :

θέλω, καθαρίσθητι· καὶ εὐθέως ἡ λέπρα
I am willing, be thou cleansed; and immediately the leprosy

ἀπῆλθεν ἀπ᾽ αὐτοῦ. 14 καὶ αὐτὸς παρήγγειλεν
departed from him. And he charged

αὐτῷ μηδενὶ εἰπεῖν, ἀλλὰ ἀπελθὼν δεῖξον
him no one to tell, but going away show

σεαυτὸν τῷ ἱερεῖ, καὶ προσένεγκε περὶ
thyself to the priest, and offer concerning

τοῦ καθαρισμοῦ σου καθὼς προσέταξεν
the cleansing of thee as commanded

Μωϋσῆς, εἰς μαρτύριον αὐτοῖς. 15 διήρχετο
Moses, for a testimony to them. went

δὲ μᾶλλον ὁ λόγος περὶ αὐτοῦ, καὶ
But rather the word concerning him. and

συνήρχοντο ὄχλοι πολλοὶ ἀκούειν καὶ
³accompanied ²crowds ¹many to hear and

θεραπεύεσθαι ἀπὸ τῶν ἀσθενειῶν αὐτῶν·
to be healed from the infirmities of them;

16 αὐτὸς δὲ ἦν ὑποχωρῶν ἐν ταῖς ἐρήμοις
but he was withdrawing in the deserts

καὶ προσευχόμενος.
and praying.

181

King James Version

ness, and prayed. 17And it came to pass on a certain day, as he was teaching, that there were Pharisees and doctors of the law sitting by, which were come out of every town of Galilee, and Judea, and Jerusalem: and the power of the Lord was *present* to heal them.

18 And, behold, men brought in a bed a man which was taken with a palsy: and they sought *means* to bring him in, and to lay *him* before him. 19And when they could not find by what *way* they might bring him in because of the multitude, they went upon the housetop, and let him down through the tiling with *his* couch into the midst before Jesus. 20And when he saw their faith, he said unto him, Man, thy sins are forgiven thee. 21And the scribes and the Pharisees began to reason, saying, Who is this which speaketh blasphemies? Who can forgive sins, but God alone? 22 But when Jesus perceived their thoughts, he answering said unto them, What reason ye in your hearts? 23 Whether is easier, to say, Thy sins be forgiven thee; or to say, Rise up and walk? 24 But that ye may know that the Son of man hath power upon earth to forgive sins, (he said unto the sick of the palsy,) I say unto thee, Arise, and take up thy couch, and go into thine house. 25And immediately he rose up before them, and took up that whereon he lay, and departed to his own house, glorifying God. 26 And they were all amazed, and they glorified God, and were filled with fear, saying, We have seen strange things to day.

27 And after these things he went forth, and saw a publican, named Levi, sitting at the receipt of custom: and he said unto him, Follow me. 28And he left all, rose up, and followed him. 29And Levi made him a great feast in his own house: and there was a great company of publicans and of others that sat down with them. 30 But their scribes and Pharisees murmured against his disciples, saying, Why do ye eat and drink with publicans and sinners? 31And Jesus answering said unto them, They that are whole need not a physician; but they that are sick. 32 I came not to call the righteous, but sinners to repentance.

33 And they said unto him, Why do the disciples of John fast often, and make prayers, and likewise *the disciples* of the Pharisees; but thine eat and drink? 34And he said unto them, Can ye make the children of the bridechamber fast, while the bridegroom is with them? 35 But the days will come, when the bridegroom shall be taken away from them, and then shall they fast in those days.

36 And he spake also a parable unto them; No man putteth a piece of a new garment upon an old; if otherwise, then both the new maketh a rent, and the piece that was *taken* out of the new agreeth not with the old. 37And no man putteth new wine into old bottles; else the new wine will burst the bottles, and be spilled, and

New International Version

Jesus heals a paralytic

17 One day as he was teaching, Pharisees and teachers of the law, who had come from every village of Galilee and from Judea and Jerusalem, were sitting there. And the power of the Lord was present for him to heal the sick. 18 Some men came carrying a paralytic on a mat and tried to take him into the house to lay him before Jesus. 19 When they could not find a way to do this because of the crowd, they went up on the roof and lowered him on his mat through the tiles into the middle of the crowd, right in front of Jesus.

20 When Jesus saw their faith, he said, "Friend, your sins are forgiven."

21 The Pharisees and the teachers of the law began thinking to themselves, "Who is this fellow who speaks blasphemy? Who can forgive sins but God alone?"

22 Jesus knew what they were thinking and asked, "Why are you thinking these things in your hearts? 23 Which is easier: to say, 'Your sins are forgiven,' or to say, 'Get up and walk'? 24 But that you may know that the Son of Man has authority on earth to forgive sins. . . ." He said to the paralyzed man, "I tell you, get up, take your mat and go home." 25 Immediately he stood up in front of them, took what he had been lying on and went home praising God. 26 Everyone was amazed and gave praise to God. They were filled with awe and said, "We have seen remarkable things today."

The calling of Levi

27 After this, Jesus went out and saw a tax collector by the name of Levi sitting at his tax booth. "Follow me," Jesus said to him, 28 and Levi got up, left everything and followed him.

29 Then Levi held a great banquet for Jesus at his house, and a large crowd of tax collectors and others were eating with them. 30 But the Pharisees and the teachers of the law who belonged to their sect complained to his disciples, "Why do you eat and drink with tax collectors and 'sinners'?"

31 Jesus answered them, "It is not the healthy who need a doctor, but the sick. 32 I have not come to call the righteous, but sinners to repentance."

Jesus questioned about fasting

33 They said to him, "John's disciples often fast and pray, and so do the disciples of the Pharisees, but yours go on eating and drinking."

34 Jesus answered, "Can you make the guests of the bridegroom fast while he is with them? 35 But the time will come when the bridegroom will be taken from them; in those days they will fast."

36 He told them this parable: "No one tears a patch from a new garment and sews it on an old one. If he does, he will have torn the new garment, and the patch from the new will not match the old. 37And no one pours new wine into old wineskins. If he does, the new wine will burst the skins, the wine will run out and the

Greek Interlinear

17 Καὶ ἐγένετο ἐν μιᾷ τῶν ἡμερῶν καὶ
And it came to pass on one of the days and

αὐτὸς ἦν διδάσκων, καὶ ἦσαν καθήμενοι
he was teaching, and were sitting

Φαρισαῖοι καὶ νομοδιδάσκαλοι οἳ ἦσαν
Pharisees and law-teachers who were

ἐληλυθότες ἐκ πάσης κώμης τῆς Γαλιλαίας
having come out of every village - of Galilee

καὶ Ἰουδαίας καὶ Ἰερουσαλήμ· καὶ δύναμις
and Judæa and Jerusalem; and [the] power

κυρίου ἦν εἰς τὸ ἰᾶσθαι αὐτόν. 18 καὶ
of [the] Lord was ¹in - ²to cure ³him. And

ἰδοὺ ἄνδρες φέροντες ἐπὶ κλίνης ἄνθρωπον
behold[,] men bearing on a couch a man

ὃς ἦν παραλελυμένος, καὶ ἐζήτουν αὐτὸν
who was having been paralysed, and they sought ²him

εἰσενεγκεῖν καὶ θεῖναι [αὐτὸν] ἐνώπιον
¹to carry in and to lay him before

αὐτοῦ. 19 καὶ μὴ εὑρόντες ποίας εἰσ-
him. And not finding how† they

ἐνέγκωσιν αὐτὸν διὰ τὸν ὄχλον, ἀναβάντες
might carry in him because of the crowd, going up

ἐπὶ τὸ δῶμα διὰ τῶν κεράμων καθῆκαν
onto the roof through the tiles they let down

αὐτὸν σὺν τῷ κλινιδίῳ εἰς τὸ μέσον
him with the couch into the midst

ἔμπροσθεν τοῦ Ἰησοῦ. 20 καὶ ἰδὼν τὴν
in front of - Jesus. And seeing the

πίστιν αὐτῶν εἶπεν· ἄνθρωπε, ἀφέωνταί
faith of them he said: Man, have been forgiven

σοι αἱ ἁμαρτίαι σου. 21 καὶ ἤρξαντο
thee the sins of thee. And began

διαλογίζεσθαι οἱ γραμματεῖς καὶ οἱ Φαρισαῖοι
to reason the scribes and the Pharisees

λέγοντες· τίς ἐστιν οὗτος ὃς λαλεῖ
saying: Who is this man who speaks

βλασφημίας; τίς δύναται ἁμαρτίας ἀφεῖναι
blasphemies? Who can sins to forgive

εἰ μὴ μόνος ὁ θεός; 22 ἐπιγνοὺς δὲ ὁ
except only - God? But knowing -

Ἰησοῦς τοὺς διαλογισμοὺς αὐτῶν, ἀποκριθεὶς
Jesus the reasonings of them, answering

εἶπεν πρὸς αὐτούς· τί διαλογίζεσθε ἐν
said to them: Why reason ye in

ταῖς καρδίαις ὑμῶν; 23 τί ἐστιν εὐκοπώτερον,
the hearts of you? What is easier,

εἰπεῖν· ἀφέωνταί σοι αἱ ἁμαρτίαι σου, ἢ
to say: Have been forgiven thee the sins of thee, or

εἰπεῖν· ἔγειρε καὶ περιπάτει; 24 ἵνα δὲ
to say: Rise and walk? but that

εἰδῆτε ὅτι ὁ υἱὸς τοῦ ἀνθρώπου ἐξουσίαν
ye may know that the Son - of man authority

ἔχει ἐπὶ τῆς γῆς ἀφιέναι ἁμαρτίας, —
has on the earth to forgive sins, —

εἶπεν τῷ παραλελυμένῳ· σοὶ λέγω, ἔγειρε
he said to the paralysed [one]: To thee I say, rise

καὶ ἄρας τὸ κλινίδιόν σου πορεύου εἰς
and taking the pallet of thee go to

τὸν οἶκόν σου. 25 καὶ παραχρῆμα ἀναστὰς
the house of thee. And at once rising up

ἐνώπιον αὐτῶν, ἄρας ἐφ' ὃ κατέκειτο,
before them, taking [that] on which he was lying,

ἀπῆλθεν εἰς τὸν οἶκον αὐτοῦ δοξάζων τὸν
he went away to the house of him glorifying -

θεόν. 26 καὶ ἔκστασις ἔλαβεν ἅπαντας, καὶ
God. And bewilderment took all, and

ἐδόξαζον τὸν θεόν, καὶ ἐπλήσθησαν φόβου
they glorified - God, and were filled of(with) fear

λέγοντες ὅτι εἴδομεν παράδοξα σήμερον.
saying[,] We saw wonderful things to-day.

27 Καὶ μετὰ ταῦτα ἐξῆλθεν, καὶ ἐθεάσατο
And after these things he went forth, and saw

τελώνην ὀνόματι Λευὶν καθήμενον ἐπὶ τὸ
a tax-collector by name Levi sitting on(in) the

τελώνιον, καὶ εἶπεν αὐτῷ· ἀκολούθει μοι.
custom house, and said to him: Follow me.

28 καὶ καταλιπὼν πάντα ἀναστὰς ἠκολούθει
And abandoning all things rising up he followed

αὐτῷ. 29 Καὶ ἐποίησεν δοχὴν μεγάλην
him. And ²made ¹feast ³a great

Λευὶς αὐτῷ ἐν τῇ οἰκίᾳ αὐτοῦ· καὶ ἦν
¹Levi for him in the house of him; and there was

ὄχλος πολὺς τελωνῶν καὶ ἄλλων οἳ ἦσαν
crowd a much of tax-collectors and of others who were

μετ' αὐτῶν κατακείμενοι. 30 καὶ ἐγόγγυζον
²with ³them ¹reclining. And grumbled

οἱ Φαρισαῖοι καὶ οἱ γραμματεῖς αὐτῶν
the Pharisees and the scribes of them

πρὸς τοὺς μαθητὰς αὐτοῦ λέγοντες· διὰ
at the disciples of him saying: Why

τί μετὰ τῶν τελωνῶν καὶ ἁμαρτωλῶν
with the tax-collectors and sinners

ἐσθίετε καὶ πίνετε; 31 καὶ ἀποκριθεὶς ὁ
eat ye and drink ye? And answering -

Ἰησοῦς εἶπεν πρὸς αὐτούς· οὐ χρείαν
Jesus said to them: not need

ἔχουσιν οἱ ὑγιαίνοντες ἰατροῦ ἀλλὰ οἱ
have the [ones] being healthy of a physician but the
= those who are ill;

κακῶς ἔχοντες· 32 οὐκ ἐλήλυθα καλέσαι
[ones] ill having; I have not come to call

δικαίους ἀλλὰ ἁμαρτωλοὺς εἰς μετάνοιαν.
righteous persons but sinners to repentance.

33 Οἱ δὲ εἶπαν πρὸς αὐτόν· οἱ μαθηταὶ
And they said to him: The disciples

Ἰωάννου νηστεύουσιν πυκνὰ καὶ δεήσεις
of John fast often and prayers

ποιοῦνται, ὁμοίως καὶ οἱ τῶν Φαρισαίων,
make, likewise also those of the Pharisees,

οἱ δὲ σοὶ ἐσθίουσιν καὶ πίνουσιν. 34 ὁ
but those to thee° eat and drink.
= but thine

δὲ Ἰησοῦς εἶπεν πρὸς αὐτούς· μὴ δύνασθε
And Jesus said to them: not ¹Can ye

τοὺς υἱοὺς τοῦ νυμφῶνος, ἐν ᾧ ὁ νυμφίος
²the ⁴sons ³of the ⁵bride-chamber, ⁶while °the ¹⁰bridegroom

μετ' αὐτῶν ἐστιν, ποιῆσαι νηστεῦσαι;
¹¹with ¹²them ¹¹is, ⁶to make ⁷to fast?

35 ἐλεύσονται δὲ ἡμέραι, καὶ ὅταν ἀπαρθῇ
but will come days, and when is taken away

ἀπ' αὐτῶν ὁ νυμφίος, τότε νηστεύσουσιν
from them the bridegroom, then they will fast

ἐν ἐκείναις ταῖς ἡμέραις. 36 Ἔλεγεν δὲ
in those days. And he told

καὶ παραβολὴν πρὸς αὐτοὺς ὅτι οὐδεὶς
also a parable to them[:] - No one

ἐπίβλημα ἀπὸ ἱματίου καινοῦ σχίσας
²a patch ³from ⁴garment ⁶a new ¹tearing

ἐπιβάλλει ἐπὶ ἱμάτιον παλαιόν· εἰ δὲ μή γε,
⁷puts [it] ⁸on ⁹a garment ⁸an old; otherwise,

καὶ τὸ καινὸν σχίσει καὶ τῷ παλαιῷ
both the new will tear and ⁷with the ⁶old

οὐ συμφωνήσει τὸ ἐπίβλημα τὸ ἀπὸ τοῦ
⁵will not agree ¹the ²patch - ³from ⁴the

καινοῦ. 37 καὶ οὐδεὶς βάλλει οἶνον νέον
⁵new. And no one puts wine new

εἰς ἀσκοὺς παλαιούς· εἰ δὲ μή γε, ῥήξει
into wineskins old; otherwise, ⁶will burst

ὁ οἶνος ὁ νέος τοὺς ἀσκούς, καὶ αὐτὸς
³the ¹wine ²new ⁴the ⁵wineskins, and it

ἐκχυθήσεται καὶ οἱ ἀσκοὶ ἀπολοῦνται.
will be poured out and the wineskins will perish.

King James Version

the bottles shall perish. 38 But new wine must be put into new bottles; and both are preserved. 39 No man also having drunk old *wine* straightway desireth new; for he saith, The old is better.

6 And it came to pass on the second sabbath after the first, that he went through the corn fields; and his disciples plucked the ears of corn, and did eat, rubbing *them* in *their* hands. 2And certain of the Pharisees said unto them, Why do ye that which is not lawful to do on the sabbath days? 3And Jesus answering them said, Have ye not read so much as this, what David did, when himself was a hungered, and they which were with him; 4 How he went into the house of God, and did take and eat the shewbread, and gave also to them that were with him; which it is not lawful to eat but for the priests alone? 5And he said unto them, That the Son of man is Lord also of the sabbath. 6And it came to pass also on another sabbath, that he entered into the synagogue and taught: and there was a man whose right hand was withered. 7And the scribes and Pharisees watched him, whether he would heal on the sabbath day; that they might find an accusation against him. 8 But he knew their thoughts, and said to the man which had the withered hand, Rise up, and stand forth in the midst. And he arose and stood forth. 9 Then said Jesus unto them, I will ask you one thing; Is it lawful on the sabbath days to do good, or to do evil? to save life, or to destroy *it?* 10And looking round about upon them all, he said unto the man, Stretch forth thy hand. And he did so: and his hand was restored whole as the other. 11And they were filled with madness; and communed one with another what they might do to Jesus. 12And it came to pass in those days, that he went out into a mountain to pray, and continued all night in prayer to God. 13 And when it was day, he called *unto him* his disciples: and of them he chose twelve, whom also he named apostles; 14 Simon, (whom he also named Peter,) and Andrew his brother, James and John, Philip and Bartholomew, 15 Matthew and Thomas, James the *son* of Alpheus, and Simon called Zelotes, 16And Judas *the brother* of James, and Judas Iscariot, which also was the traitor.

17 And he came down with them, and stood in the plain, and the company of his disciples, and a great multitude of people out of all Judea and Jerusalem, and from the sea coast of Tyre and Sidon, which came to hear him, and to be healed of their diseases; 18And they that were vexed with unclean spirits: and they were healed. 19And the whole multitude sought to touch him: for there went virtue out of him, and healed *them* all.

20 And he lifted up his eyes on his disciples, and said, Blessed *be ye* poor: for yours is the kingdom of God. 21 Blessed *are ye* that hunger

New International Version

wineskins will be ruined. 38 No, new wine must be poured into new wineskins. 39And no one after drinking old wine wants the new, for he says, 'The old is better.' "

Lord of the Sabbath

6 One Sabbath Jesus was going through the grainfields, and his disciples began to pick some heads of grain, rub them in their hands and eat the kernels. 2 Some of the Pharisees asked, "Why are you doing what is unlawful on the Sabbath?"

3 Jesus answered them, "Have you never read what David did when he and his companions were hungry? 4 He entered the house of God, and taking the consecrated bread, which is lawful only for priests to eat. And he also gave some to his companions." 5 Then Jesus said to them, "The Son of Man is Lord of the Sabbath."

6 On another Sabbath he went into the synagogue and was teaching, and a man was there whose right hand was shriveled. 7 The Pharisees and the teachers of the law were looking for a reason to accuse Jesus, so they watched him closely to see if he would heal on the Sabbath. 8 But Jesus knew what they were thinking and said to the man with the shriveled hand, "Get up and stand in front of everyone." So he got up and stood there.

9 Then Jesus said to them, "I ask you, which is lawful on the Sabbath: to do good or to do evil, to save life or to destroy it?"

10 He looked around at them all, and then said to the man, "Stretch out your hand." He did so, and his hand was completely restored. 11 But they were furious and began to discuss with one another what they might do to Jesus.

The twelve apostles

12 One of those days Jesus went out into the hills to pray, and spent the night praying to God. 13 When morning came, he called his disciples to him and chose twelve of them, whom he also designated apostles: 14 Simon (whom he named Peter), his brother Andrew, James, John, Philip, Bartholomew, 15 Matthew, Thomas, James son of Alphaeus, Simon who was called the Zealot, 16 Judas son of James, and Judas Iscariot, who became a traitor.

Blessings and woes

17 He went down with them and stood on a level place. A large crowd of his disciples was there and a great number of people from all over Judea, from Jerusalem, and from the seacoast of Tyre and Sidon, 18 who had come to hear him and to be healed of their diseases. Those troubled by evil *y* spirits were cured, 19 and the people all tried to touch him, because power was coming from him and healing them all.

20 Looking at his disciples, he said:
"Blessed are you who are poor,
    for yours is the kingdom of God.
21 Blessed are you who hunger now,

[y] Greek *unclean.*

184

Greek Interlinear

38 ἀλλὰ οἶνον νέον εἰς ἀσκοὺς καινοὺς
But wine new into wineskins new
βλητέον. 39 καὶ οὐδεὶς πιὼν παλαιὸν
one must put. And no one having drunk old

θέλει νέον· λέγει γάρ· ὁ παλαιὸς χρηστός
desires new; for he says: The old good
ἐστιν.
is.

Chapter 6

Ἐγένετο δὲ ἐν σαββάτῳ διαπορεύεσθαι
And it came to pass on a sabbath   to go through
= he went through
αὐτὸν διὰ σπορίμων, καὶ ἔτιλλον οἱ
him through cornfields, and 'plucked 'the
μαθηταὶ αὐτοῦ καὶ ἤσθιον τοὺς στάχυας
²disciples ³of him and ate the ears
ψώχοντες ταῖς χερσίν. 2 τινὲς δὲ τῶν
rubbing with the(ir) hands. And some of the
Φαρισαίων εἶπαν· τί ποιεῖτε ὃ οὐκ ἔξεστιν
Pharisees said: Why do ye what is not lawful
τοῖς σάββασιν; 3 καὶ ἀποκριθεὶς πρὸς
on the sabbaths?   And replying to
αὐτοὺς εἶπεν ὁ Ἰησοῦς· οὐδὲ τοῦτο ἀνέγνωτε
them said – Jesus: 'not ³this ¹read ye
ὃ ἐποίησεν Δαυίδ, ὁπότε ἐπείνασεν αὐτὸς
which did David, when hungered he
καὶ οἱ μετ' αὐτοῦ ὄντες; 4 ὡς εἰσῆλθεν
and the [ones] with him being? how he entered
εἰς τὸν οἶκον τοῦ θεοῦ καὶ τοὺς ἄρτους
into the house – of God and the loaves
τῆς προθέσεως λαβὼν ἔφαγεν καὶ ἔδωκεν
of the setting forth taking he ate and gave
τοῖς μετ' αὐτοῦ, οὓς οὐκ ἔξεστιν φαγεῖν
to the [ones] with him, which it is not lawful to eat
εἰ μὴ μόνους τοὺς ἱερεῖς; 5 καὶ ἔλεγεν
except only the priests? And he said
αὐτοῖς· κύριός ἐστιν τοῦ σαββάτου ὁ
to them: Lord is of the sabbath the
υἱὸς τοῦ ἀνθρώπου. 6 Ἐγένετο δὲ ἐν
Son – of man.   And it came to pass on
ἑτέρῳ σαββάτῳ εἰσελθεῖν αὐτὸν εἰς τὴν
another sabbath to enter him into the
= he entered into the synagogue and
συναγωγὴν καὶ διδάσκειν· καὶ ἦν ἄνθρωπος
synagogue and to teach; and there was a man
taught;
ἐκεῖ καὶ ἡ χεὶρ αὐτοῦ ἡ δεξιὰ ἦν ξηρά·
there and the ²hand ³of him – ¹right was withered;
7 παρετηροῦντο δὲ αὐτὸν οἱ γραμματεῖς
and carefully watched him the scribes
καὶ οἱ Φαρισαῖοι εἰ ἐν τῷ σαββάτῳ
and the Pharisees if on the sabbath
θεραπεύει, ἵνα εὕρωσιν κατηγορεῖν αὐτοῦ.
he heals, that they might find to accuse him.
8 αὐτὸς δὲ ᾔδει τοὺς διαλογισμοὺς αὐτῶν,
But he knew the reasonings of them,
εἶπεν δὲ τῷ ἀνδρὶ τῷ ξηρὰν ἔχοντι τὴν
and said to the man – ²withered ¹having 'the
χεῖρα· ἔγειρε καὶ στῆθι εἰς τὸ μέσον·
'hand: Rise and stand in the midst;
καὶ ἀναστὰς ἔστη. 9 εἶπεν δὲ ὁ Ἰησοῦς
and rising up he stood. And said – Jesus
πρὸς αὐτούς· ἐπερωτῶ ὑμᾶς εἰ ἔξεστιν
to them: I ask you if it is lawful
τῷ σαββάτῳ ἀγαθοποιῆσαι ἢ κακοποιῆσαι,
on the sabbath to do good or to do evil,
ψυχὴν σῶσαι ἢ ἀπολέσαι; 10 καὶ περι-
life to save or to destroy? And looking
βλεψάμενος πάντας αὐτοὺς εἶπεν αὐτῷ·
round at all them he said to him:
ἔκτεινον τὴν χεῖρά σου. ὁ δὲ ἐποίησεν,
Stretch out the hand of thee. And he did,

καὶ ἀπεκατεστάθη ἡ χεὶρ αὐτοῦ. 11 αὐτοὶ
and was restored the hand of him. they
δὲ ἐπλήσθησαν ἀνοίας, καὶ διελάλουν πρὸς
But were filled of(with) madness, and talked to
ἀλλήλους τί ἂν ποιήσαιεν τῷ Ἰησοῦ.
one another what they might do – to Jesus.
12 Ἐγένετο δὲ ἐν ταῖς ἡμέραις ταύταις
Now it came to pass in – days these
ἐξελθεῖν αὐτὸν εἰς τὸ ὄρος προσεύξασθαι,
to go forth him to the mountain to pray,
= he went forth
καὶ ἦν διανυκτερεύων ἐν τῇ προσευχῇ τοῦ
and was spending the whole in the prayer –
night
θεοῦ. 13 καὶ ὅτε ἐγένετο ἡμέρα, προσεφώνησεν
of God. And when it became day, he called to [him]
τοὺς μαθητὰς αὐτοῦ, καὶ ἐκλεξάμενος ἀπ'
the disciples of him, and choosing from
αὐτῶν δώδεκα, οὓς καὶ ἀποστόλους ὠνόμασεν,
them twelve, whom also apostles he named,
14 Σίμωνα, ὃν καὶ ὠνόμασεν Πέτρον, καὶ
Simon, whom also he named Peter, and
Ἀνδρέαν τὸν ἀδελφὸν αὐτοῦ, καὶ Ἰάκωβον
Andrew the brother of him, and James
καὶ Ἰωάννην, καὶ Φίλιππον καὶ Βαρθο-
and John, and Philip and Bartho-
λομαῖον, 15 καὶ Μαθθαῖον καὶ Θωμᾶν,
lomew, and Matthew and Thomas,
[καὶ] Ἰάκωβον Ἁλφαίου καὶ Σίμωνα τὸν
and James [son] of Alphæus and Simon the [one]
καλούμενον ζηλωτήν, καὶ Ἰούδαν Ἰακώβου,
being called a Zealot, and Judas of James,
16 καὶ Ἰούδαν Ἰσκαριώθ, ὃς ἐγένετο προδότης,
and Judas Iscariot, who became betrayer,
17 καὶ καταβὰς μετ' αὐτῶν ἔστη ἐπὶ
and coming down with them he stood on
τόπου πεδινοῦ, καὶ ὄχλος πολὺς μαθητῶν
place a level, and crowd a much of disciples
αὐτοῦ, καὶ πλῆθος πολὺ τοῦ λαοῦ ἀπὸ
of him, and multitude a much of the people from
πάσης τῆς Ἰουδαίας καὶ Ἰερουσαλὴμ καὶ
all – Judæa and Jerusalem and
τῆς παραλίου Τύρου καὶ Σιδῶνος, 18 οἳ
the coast country of Tyre and Sidon, who
ἦλθον ἀκοῦσαι αὐτοῦ καὶ ἰαθῆναι ἀπὸ
came to hear him and to be cured from
τῶν νόσων αὐτῶν, καὶ οἱ ἐνοχλούμενοι
the diseases of them, and the [ones] being tormented
ἀπὸ πνευμάτων ἀκαθάρτων ἐθεραπεύοντο.
from spirits unclean were healed.
19 καὶ πᾶς ὁ ὄχλος ἐζήτουν ἅπτεσθαι
And all the crowd sought to touch
αὐτοῦ, ὅτι δύναμις παρ' αὐτοῦ ἐξήρχετο
him, because power from him went forth
καὶ ἰᾶτο πάντας. 20 Καὶ αὐτὸς ἐπάρας
and cured all. And he lifting up
τοὺς ὀφθαλμοὺς αὐτοῦ εἰς τοὺς μαθητὰς
the eyes of him to the disciples
αὐτοῦ ἔλεγεν·
of him said:
Μακάριοι οἱ πτωχοί, ὅτι ὑμετέρα ἐστὶν
Blessed [are] the poor, because yours is
ἡ βασιλεία τοῦ θεοῦ. 21 μακάριοι οἱ
the kingdom – of God. Blessed [are] the [ones]

King James Version

now: for ye shall be filled. Blessed *are ye* that weep now: for ye shall laugh. 22 Blessed are ye, when men shall hate you, and when they shall separate you *from their company,* and shall reproach *you,* and cast out your name as evil, for the Son of man's sake. 23 Rejoice ye in that day, and leap for joy: for, behold, your reward *is* great in heaven: for in the like manner did their fathers unto the prophets. 24 But woe unto you that are rich! for ye have received your consolation. 25 Woe unto you that are full! for ye shall hunger. Woe unto you that laugh now! for ye shall mourn and weep. 26 Woe unto you, when all men shall speak well of you! for so did their fathers to the false prophets.

27 But I say unto you which hear, Love your enemies, do good to them which hate you, 28 Bless them that curse you, and pray for them which despitefully use you. 29And unto him that smiteth thee on the *one* cheek offer also the other; and him that taketh away thy cloak forbid not *to take thy* coat also. 30 Give to every man that asketh of thee; and of him that taketh away thy goods ask *them* not again. 31And as ye would that men should do to you, do ye also to them likewise. 32 For if ye love them which love you, what thank have ye? for sinners also love those that love them. 33And if ye do good to them which do good to you, what thank have ye? for sinners also do even the same. 34And if ye lend *to them* of whom ye hope to receive, what thank have ye? for sinners also lend to sinners, to receive as much again. 35 But love ye your enemies, and do good, and lend, hoping for nothing again; and your reward shall be great, and ye shall be the children of the Highest: for he is kind unto the unthankful and *to* the evil. 36 Be ye therefore merciful, as your Father also is merciful. 37 Judge not, and ye shall not be judged: condemn not, and ye shall not be condemned: forgive, and ye shall be forgiven: 38 Give, and it shall be given unto you; good measure, pressed down, and shaken together, and running over, shall men give into your bosom. For with the same measure that ye mete withal it shall be measured to you again.

39 And he spake a parable unto them; Can the blind lead the blind? shall they not both fall into the ditch? 40 The disciple is not above his master: but every one that is perfect shall be as his master. 41And why beholdest thou the mote that is in thy brother's eye, but perceivest not the beam that is in thine own eye? 42 Either how canst thou say to thy brother, Brother, let me pull out the mote that is in thine eye, when thou thyself beholdest not the beam that is in thine own eye? Thou hypocrite, cast out first the beam out of thine own eye, and then shalt thou see clearly to pull out the mote that is in thy

New International Version

for you will be satisfied.
Blessed are you who weep now,
    for you will laugh.
22 Blessed are you when men hate you,
    when they exclude you and insult you
    and reject your name as evil,
        because of the Son of Man.
23 "Rejoice in that day and leap for joy, because great is your reward in heaven. For that is how their fathers treated the prophets.
24 "But woe to you who are rich,
    for you have already received your comfort.
25 Woe to you who are well fed now,
    for you will go hungry.
Woe to you who laugh now,
    for you will mourn and weep.
26 Woe to you when all men speak well of you,
    for that is how their fathers treated the false prophets.

Love for enemies

27 "But I tell you who hear me: Love your enemies, do good to those who hate you, 28 bless those who curse you, pray for those who mistreat you. 29 If someone strikes you on one cheek, turn to him the other also. If someone takes your cloak, do not stop him from taking your tunic. 30 Give to everyone who asks you, and if anyone takes what belongs to you, do not demand it back. 31 Do to others as you would have them do to you.

32 "If you love those who love you, what credit is that to you? Even 'sinners' love those who love them. 33And if you do good to those who are good to you, what credit is that to you? Even 'sinners' do that. 34And if you lend to those from whom you expect repayment, what credit is that to you? Even 'sinners' lend to 'sinners,' expecting to be repaid in full. 35 But love your enemies, do good to them, and lend to them without expecting to get anything back. Then your reward will be great, and you will be sons of the Most High, because he is kind to the ungrateful and wicked. 36 Be merciful, just as your Father is merciful.

Judging others

37 "Do not judge, and you will not be judged. Do not condemn, and you will not be condemned. Forgive, and you will be forgiven. 38 Give, and it will be given to you. A good measure, pressed down, shaken together and running over, will be poured into your lap. For with the measure you use, it will be measured to you."

39 He also told them this parable: "Can a blind man lead a blind man? Will they not both fall into a pit? 40A student is not above his teacher, but everyone who is fully trained will be like his teacher.

41 "Why do you look at the speck of sawdust in your brother's eye and pay no attention to the plank in your own eye? 42 How can you say to your brother, 'Brother, let me take the speck out of your eye,' when you yourself fail to see the plank in your own eye? You hypocrite, first take the plank out of your eye, and then you will see clearly to remove the speck from your brother's eye.

Greek Interlinear

πεινῶντες νῦν, ὅτι χορτασθήσεσθε. μακάριοι
hungering now, because ye will be satisfied. Blessed [are]

οἱ κλαίοντες νῦν, ὅτι γελάσετε. 22 μακάριοί
the [ones] weeping now, because ye will laugh. Blessed

ἐστε ὅταν μισήσωσιν ὑμᾶς οἱ ἄνθρωποι,
are ye when ²hate ³you - ¹men,

καὶ ὅταν ἀφορίσωσιν ὑμᾶς καὶ ὀνειδίσωσιν
and when they separate you and reproach

καὶ ἐκβάλωσιν τὸ ὄνομα ὑμῶν ὡς πονηρὸν
and cast out the name of you as evil

ἕνεκα τοῦ υἱοῦ τοῦ ἀνθρώπου. 23 χάρητε
for the sake of the Son - of man.   Rejoice

ἐν ἐκείνῃ τῇ ἡμέρᾳ καὶ σκιρτήσατε·
in that the - day and leap for joy;

ἰδοὺ γὰρ ὁ μισθὸς ὑμῶν πολὺς ἐν τῷ
for behold[,] the reward of you much in -

οὐρανῷ· κατὰ τὰ αὐτὰ γὰρ ἐποίουν τοῖς
heaven; for according to the same things ⁴did ⁵to the
= in the same way

προφήταις οἱ πατέρες αὐτῶν.
⁶prophets ¹the ²fathers ³of them.

24 Πλὴν οὐαὶ ὑμῖν τοῖς πλουσίοις, ὅτι
But Woe to you the rich [ones], because

ἀπέχετε τὴν παράκλησιν ὑμῶν. οὐαὶ ὑμῖν,
ye have the consolation of you. Woe to you,

οἱ ἐμπεπλησμένοι νῦν, ὅτι πεινάσετε.
the [ones] having been filled up now, because ye will hunger.

25 οὐαί, οἱ γελῶντες νῦν, ὅτι πενθήσετε
Woe, the [ones] laughing now, because ye will mourn

καὶ κλαύσετε. 26 οὐαὶ ὅταν καλῶς ὑμᾶς
and lament. Woe when well [of] you

εἴπωσιν πάντες οἱ ἄνθρωποι· κατὰ τὰ
say all - men; for according to the
= in the same way

αὐτὰ γὰρ ἐποίουν τοῖς ψευδοπροφήταις οἱ
the same things did to the false prophets the

πατέρες αὐτῶν. 27 Ἀλλὰ ὑμῖν λέγω
fathers of them. But you I tell

τοῖς ἀκούουσιν· ἀγαπᾶτε τοὺς ἐχθροὺς
the [ones] hearing: Love ye the enemies

ὑμῶν, καλῶς ποιεῖτε τοῖς μισοῦσιν ὑμᾶς,
of you, ¹well ²do to the [ones] hating you,

28 εὐλογεῖτε τοὺς καταρωμένους ὑμᾶς,
bless the [ones] cursing you,

προσεύχεσθε περὶ τῶν ἐπηρεαζόντων ὑμᾶς.
pray about the [ones] insulting you.

29 τῷ τύπτοντί σε ἐπὶ τὴν σιαγόνα
To the [one] striking thee on the cheek

πάρεχε καὶ τὴν ἄλλην, καὶ ἀπὸ τοῦ
turn also the other, and from the [one]

αἴροντός σου τὸ ἱμάτιον καὶ τὸν χιτῶνα
taking of thee the garment also the tunic

μὴ κωλύσῃς. 30 παντὶ αἰτοῦντί σε δίδου,
do not prevent. To everyone asking thee give,

καὶ ἀπὸ τοῦ αἴροντος τὰ σὰ μὴ ἀπαίτει.
and from the [one] taking thy things do not ask back.

31 καὶ καθὼς θέλετε ἵνα ποιῶσιν ὑμῖν
And as ye wish that may do to you

οἱ ἄνθρωποι, ποιεῖτε αὐτοῖς ὁμοίως. 32 καὶ
- men, do ye to them likewise. And

εἰ ἀγαπᾶτε τοὺς ἀγαπῶντας ὑμᾶς, ποία
if ye love the [ones] loving you, what

ὑμῖν χάρις ἐστίν; καὶ γὰρ οἱ ἁμαρτωλοὶ
to you thanks is there?ᶜ for even - sinners
= thanks have ye?

τοὺς ἀγαπῶντας αὐτοὺς ἀγαπῶσιν. 33 καὶ
²the [ones] ²loving ⁴them ¹love. even

γὰρ ἐὰν ἀγαθοποιῆτε τοὺς ἀγαθοποιοῦντας
For if ye do good to the [ones] doing good to

ὑμᾶς, ποία ὑμῖν χάρις ἐστίν; καὶ οἱ
you, what to you thanks is there?ᶜ even -
= thanks have ye?

ἁμαρτωλοὶ τὸ αὐτὸ ποιοῦσιν. 34 καὶ ἐὰν
sinners the same thing do. And if

δανείσητε παρ' ὧν ἐλπίζετε λαβεῖν, ποία
ye lend from whom ye hope to receive, what

ὑμῖν χάρις [ἐστίν]; καὶ ἁμαρτωλοὶ
to you thanks is there?ᶜ even sinners
= thanks have ye?

ἁμαρτωλοῖς δανείζουσιν ἵνα ἀπολάβωσιν τὰ
to sinners lend that they may receive back the

ἴσα. 35 πλὴν ἀγαπᾶτε τοὺς ἐχθροὺς ὑμῶν
equal things. But love ye the enemies of you

καὶ ἀγαθοποιεῖτε καὶ δανείζετε μηδὲν
and do good and lend nothing

ἀπελπίζοντες· καὶ ἔσται ὁ μισθὸς ὑμῶν
despairing; and will be the reward of you
= despairing not at all;

πολύς, καὶ ἔσεσθε υἱοὶ ὑψίστου, ὅτι
much, and ye will be sons of [the] Most High, because

αὐτὸς χρηστός ἐστιν ἐπὶ τοὺς ἀχαρίστους
he kind is to the unthankful

καὶ πονηρούς. 36 Γίνεσθε οἰκτίρμονες,
and evil. Be ye compassionate,

καθὼς ὁ πατὴρ ὑμῶν οἰκτίρμων ἐστίν.
as the Father of you compassionate is.

37 καὶ μὴ κρίνετε, καὶ οὐ μὴ κριθῆτε· καὶ
And do not judge, and by no means ye may be and
judged;

μὴ καταδικάζετε, καὶ οὐ μὴ καταδικασθῆτε.
do not condemn, and by no means ye may be condemned.

ἀπολύετε, καὶ ἀπολυθήσεσθε· 38 δίδοτε, καὶ
Forgive, and ye will be forgiven; give, and

δοθήσεται ὑμῖν· μέτρον καλὸν πεπιεσμένον
it will be given to you; measure good having been pressed
down

σεσαλευμένον ὑπερεκχυννόμενον δώσουσιν εἰς
having been shaken running over they will give into

τὸν κόλπον ὑμῶν· ᾧ γὰρ μέτρῳ μετρεῖτε
the bosom of you; for in what measure ye measure

ἀντιμετρηθήσεται ὑμῖν. 39 Εἶπεν δὲ καὶ
it will be measured in return to you. And he told also

παραβολὴν αὐτοῖς· μήτι δύναται τυφλὸς
a parable to them: Not can a blind man

τυφλὸν ὁδηγεῖν; οὐχὶ ἀμφότεροι εἰς βόθυνον
²a blind man ¹guide? not both into a ditch

ἐμπεσοῦνται; 40 οὐκ ἔστιν μαθητὴς ὑπὲρ
will fall in? ²not ¹is ¹A disciple above

τὸν διδάσκαλον· κατηρτισμένος δὲ πᾶς
the teacher; ¹but ²having been perfected ³everyone

ἔσται ὡς ὁ διδάσκαλος αὐτοῦ. 41 Τί δὲ
²will be as the teacher of him. And why

βλέπεις τὸ κάρφος τὸ ἐν τῷ ὀφθαλμῷ
seest thou the mote - in the eye

τοῦ ἀδελφοῦ σου, τὴν δὲ δοκὸν τὴν ἐν
of the brother of thee, but the beam - in

τῷ ἰδίῳ ὀφθαλμῷ οὐ κατανοεῖς; 42 πῶς
thine own eye thou considerest not? how

δύνασαι λέγειν τῷ ἀδελφῷ σου· ἀδελφέ,
canst thou to say to the brother of thee: Brother,

ἄφες ἐκβάλω τὸ κάρφος τὸ ἐν τῷ
allow I may take out the mote - in the
= allow me to take out

ὀφθαλμῷ σου, αὐτὸς τὴν ἐν τῷ ὀφθαλμῷ
eye of thee, ¹[thy]self ²the ³in ⁴the ⁵eye

σου δοκὸν οὐ βλέπων; ὑποκριτά, ἔκβαλε
⁶of thee ⁷beam ⁸not ⁹seeing? hypocrite, take out

πρῶτον τὴν δοκὸν ἐκ τοῦ ὀφθαλμοῦ σου,
first the beam out of the eye of thee,

καὶ τότε διαβλέψεις τὸ κάρφος τὸ ἐν τῷ
and then thou wilt see clearly the mote - in the

King James Version

brother's eye. 43 For a good tree bringeth not forth corrupt fruit; neither doth a corrupt tree bring forth good fruit. 44 For every tree is known by his own fruit. For of thorns men do not gather figs, nor of a bramble bush gather they grapes. 45 A good man out of the good treasure of his heart bringeth forth that which is good; and an evil man out of the evil treasure of his heart bringeth forth that which is evil: for of the abundance of the heart his mouth speaketh.

46 And why call ye me, Lord, Lord, and do not the things which I say? 47 Whosoever cometh to me, and heareth my sayings, and doeth them, I will shew you to whom he is like: 48 He is like a man which built a house, and digged deep, and laid the foundation on a rock: and when the flood arose, the stream beat vehemently upon that house, and could not shake it; for it was founded upon a rock. 49 But he that heareth, and doeth not, is like a man that without a foundation built a house upon the earth; against which the stream did beat vehemently, and immediately it fell; and the ruin of that house was great.

7 Now when he had ended all his sayings in the audience of the people, he entered into Capernaum. 2 And a certain centurion's servant, who was dear unto him, was sick, and ready to die. 3 And when he heard of Jesus, he sent unto him the elders of the Jews, beseeching him that he would come and heal his servant. 4 And when they came to Jesus, they besought him instantly, saying, That he was worthy for whom he should do this: 5 For he loveth our nation, and he hath built us a synagogue. 6 Then Jesus went with them. And when he was now not far from the house, the centurion sent friends to him, saying unto him, Lord, trouble not thyself; for I am not worthy that thou shouldest enter under my roof: 7 Wherefore neither thought I myself worthy to come unto thee: but say in a word, and my servant shall be healed. 8 For I also am a man set under authority, having under me soldiers, and I say unto one, Go, and he goeth; and to another, Come, and he cometh; and to my servant, Do this, and he doeth it. 9 When Jesus heard these things, he marvelled at him, and turned him about, and said unto the people that followed him, I say unto you, I have not found so great faith, no, not in Israel. 10 And they that were sent, returning to the house, found the servant whole that had been sick.

11 And it came to pass the day after, that he went into a city called Nain; and many of his disciples went with him, and much people. 12 Now when he came nigh to the gate of the

New International Version

A tree and its fruit

43 "No good tree bears bad fruit, nor does a bad tree bear good fruit. 44 Each tree is recognized by its own fruit. People do not pick figs from thornbushes, or grapes from briars. 45 The good man brings good things out of the good stored up in his heart, and the evil man brings evil things out of the evil stored up in his heart. For out of the overflow of his heart his mouth speaks.

The wise and foolish builders

46 "Why do you call me, 'Lord, Lord,' and do not do what I say? 47 I will show you what he is like who comes to me and hears my words and puts them into practice. 48 He is like a man building a house, who dug down deep and laid the foundation on rock. When a flood came, the torrent struck that house but could not shake it, because it was well built. 49 But the one who hears my words and does not put them into practice is like a man who built a house on the ground without a foundation. The moment the torrent struck that house, it collapsed and its destruction was complete."

The faith of the centurion

7 When Jesus had finished saying all this in the hearing of the people, he entered Capernaum. 2 There a centurion's servant, whom his master valued highly, was sick and about to die. 3 The centurion heard of Jesus and sent some elders of the Jews to him, asking him to come and heal his servant. 4 When they came to Jesus, they pleaded earnestly with him, "This man deserves to have you do this, 5 because he loves our nation and has built our synagogue." 6 So Jesus went with them.

He was not far from the house when the centurion sent friends to say to him: "Lord, don't trouble yourself, for I do not deserve to have you come under my roof. 7 That is why I did not even consider myself worthy to come to you. But say the word, and my servant will be healed. 8 For I myself am a man under authority, with soldiers under me. I tell this one, 'Go,' and he goes; and that one, 'Come,' and he comes. I say to my servant, 'Do this,' and he does it."

9 When Jesus heard this, he was amazed at him, and turning to the crowd following him, he said, "I tell you, I have not found such great faith even in Israel." 10 Then the men who had been sent returned to the house and found the servant well.

Jesus raises a widow's son

11 Soon afterward, Jesus went to a town called Nain, and his disciples and a large crowd went along with him. 12 As he approached the

Greek Interlinear

ὀφθαλμῷ τοῦ ἀδελφοῦ σου ἐκβαλεῖν. 43 Οὐ
eye   of the   brother   of thee   to take out.   ²no

γάρ ἐστιν δένδρον καλὸν ποιοῦν καρπὸν
¹For   ³there is   ⁴tree   ⁶good   producing   fruit

σαπρόν, οὐδὲ πάλιν δένδρον σαπρὸν ποιοῦν
bad,   nor   again   tree   a bad   producing

καρπὸν. καλόν. 44 ἕκαστον γὰρ δένδρον
fruit   good.   For each   tree

ἐκ τοῦ ἰδίου καρποῦ γινώσκεται· οὐ γὰρ
by the(its)   own   fruit   is known;   for not

ἐξ ἀκανθῶν συλλέγουσιν σῦκα, οὐδὲ ἐκ
of   thorns   do they gather   figs,   nor   of

βάτου σταφυλὴν τρυγῶσιν. 45 ὁ ἀγαθὸς
a thorn bush   a grape   do they pick.   The   good

ἄνθρωπος ἐκ τοῦ ἀγαθοῦ θησαυροῦ τῆς
man   out of the   good   treasure   of the(his)

καρδίας προφέρει τὸ ἀγαθόν, καὶ ὁ
heart   brings forth   the   good,   and the
               =that which is good,

πονηρὸς ἐκ τοῦ πονηροῦ προφέρει τὸ
evil man   out of the   evil   brings forth   the

πονηρόν· ἐκ γὰρ περισσεύματος καρδίας
evil;   for out of   [the] abundance   of [his] heart
=that which is evil;

λαλεῖ τὸ στόμα αὐτοῦ. 46 Τί δέ με καλεῖτε·
speaks the mouth of him.   And why me call ye :

κύριε κύριε, καὶ οὐ ποιεῖτε ἃ
Lord[,]   Lord,   and   do not [the things] which

λέγω; 47 Πᾶς ὁ ἐρχόμενος πρός με καὶ
I say?   Everyone   coming   to   me   and

ἀκούων μου τῶν λόγων καὶ ποιῶν αὐτούς,
hearing   of me the   words   and   doing   them,

ὑποδείξω ὑμῖν τίνι ἐστὶν ὅμοιος. 48 ὅμοιός
I will show   you to whom he is   like.   Like

ἐστιν ἀνθρώπῳ οἰκοδομοῦντι οἰκίαν, ὃς
he is   to a man   building   a house, who

ἔσκαψεν καὶ ἐβάθυνεν καὶ ἔθηκεν θεμέλιον
dug   and   deepened   and   laid   a foundation

ἐπὶ τὴν πέτραν· πλημμύρης δὲ γενομένης
on   the   rock;   and a flood   occurring°
               =when a flood occurred

προσέρρηξεν ὁ ποταμὸς τῇ οἰκίᾳ ἐκείνῃ,
²dashed against ¹the ³river   house   that,

καὶ οὐκ ἴσχυσεν σαλεῦσαι αὐτὴν διὰ
and   was not able   to shake   it because of

τὸ καλῶς οἰκοδομῆσθαι αὐτήν. 49 ὁ δὲ
the   well   to be built   it.ᵇ   But the
=because it was well built.   [one]

ἀκούσας καὶ μὴ ποιήσας ὅμοιός ἐστιν
hearing   and not   doing   ²like   ¹is

ἀνθρώπῳ οἰκοδομήσαντι οἰκίαν ἐπὶ τὴν
a man   having built   a house   on   the

γῆν χωρὶς θεμελίου, ᾗ προσέρρηξεν ὁ
earth without   a foundation, ²which ¹dashed ³against ⁴the

ποταμός, καὶ εὐθὺς συνέπεσεν, καὶ ἐγένετο
⁵river,   and   immediately it collapsed,   and   ²was

τὸ ῥῆγμα τῆς οἰκίας ἐκείνης μέγα.
¹the   ⁴ruin   -   ⁵house   ⁶of that   ³great.

Chapter 7

Ἐπειδὴ ἐπλήρωσεν πάντα τὰ ῥήματα
When   he completed   all   the   words

αὐτοῦ εἰς τὰς ἀκοὰς τοῦ λαοῦ, εἰσῆλθεν
of him   in   the   ears   of the people,   he entered

εἰς Καφαρναούμ. 2 Ἑκατοντάρχου δέ
into   Capernaum.   Now ⁴of ¹a ⁵centurion

τινος δοῦλος κακῶς ἔχων ἤμελλεν τελευτᾶν,
²certain ¹a slave   ⁷ill   ⁶having(being) ¹²was about ¹³to die,

ὃς ἦν αὐτῷ ἔντιμος. 3 ἀκούσας δὲ περὶ
¹who ²was ¹¹to him ¹²dear.   And hearing   about

τοῦ Ἰησοῦ ἀπέστειλεν πρὸς αὐτὸν πρε-
-   Jesus   he sent   to   him   eld-

σβυτέρους τῶν Ἰουδαίων, ἐρωτῶν αὐτὸν
ers   of the   Jews,   asking   him

ὅπως ἐλθὼν διασώσῃ τὸν δοῦλον αὐτοῦ.
that   coming he might recover   the   slave   of him.

4 οἱ δὲ παραγενόμενοι πρὸς τὸν Ἰησοῦν
And they   coming   to   -   Jesus

παρεκάλουν αὐτὸν σπουδαίως, λέγοντες ὅτι ἄξιός
besought   him   earnestly,   saying[,] -   Worthy

ἐστιν ᾧ παρέξῃ τοῦτο· 5 ἀγαπᾷ γὰρ
he is for whom thou shouldest grant this;   for he loves

τὸ ἔθνος ἡμῶν καὶ τὴν συναγωγὴν
the   nation   of us   and   the   synagogue

αὐτὸς ᾠκοδόμησεν ἡμῖν. 6 ὁ δὲ Ἰησοῦς
he   built   for us.   - And Jesus

ἐπορεύετο σὺν αὐτοῖς. ἤδη δὲ αὐτοῦ οὐ
went   with   them.   And yet   him   not
               =while he was not

μακρὰν ἀπέχοντος ἀπὸ τῆς οἰκίας, ἔπεμψεν
far   being away°   from   the   house,   sent
not far away

φίλους ὁ ἑκατοντάρχης λέγων αὐτῷ· κύριε,
friends   the   centurion   saying   to him :   Lord,

μὴ σκύλλου· οὐ γὰρ ἱκανός εἰμι ἵνα ὑπὸ
do not trouble;   for not   worthy   am I that under

τὴν στέγην μου εἰσέλθῃς· 7 διὸ οὐδὲ
the   roof   of me thou shouldest enter;   wherefore   not

ἐμαυτὸν ἠξίωσα πρός σὲ ἐλθεῖν· ἀλλὰ εἰπὲ
myself I accounted worthy to thee to come; but say

λόγῳ, καὶ ἰαθήτω ὁ παῖς μου. 8 καὶ
in a word, and   let be cured the servant   of me.   ²also

γὰρ ἐγὼ ἄνθρωπός εἰμι ὑπὸ ἐξουσίαν
¹For   ³I   ⁶a man   ⁴am   ⁵under   ⁷authority

τασσόμενος, ἔχων ὑπ' ἐμαυτὸν στρατιώτας,
⁸being set,   having under   myself   soldiers,

καὶ λέγω τούτῳ· πορεύθητι, καὶ πορεύεται,
and   I tell   this one :   Go,   and   he goes,

καὶ ἄλλῳ· ἔρχου, καὶ ἔρχεται, καὶ τῷ
and another · Come,   and he comes,   and   the

δούλῳ μου· ποίησον τοῦτο, καὶ ποιεῖ.
slave   of me :   Do   this,   and   he does.

9 ἀκούσας δὲ ταῦτα ὁ Ἰησοῦς ἐθαύμασεν
And hearing   these [words] -   Jesus   marvelled at

αὐτόν, καὶ στραφεὶς τῷ ἀκολουθοῦντι αὐτῷ
him,   and   turning to the   following   ²him

ὄχλῳ εἶπεν· λέγω ὑμῖν, οὐδὲ ἐν τῷ
¹crowd   said :   I tell   you,   not   in   -

Ἰσραὴλ τοσαύτην πίστιν εὗρον. 10 καὶ
Israel   such   faith   I found.   And

ὑποστρέψαντες εἰς τὸν οἶκον οἱ πεμφθέντες
returning   to   the   house   the [ones] sent

εὗρον τὸν δοῦλον ὑγιαίνοντα. 11 Καὶ
found   the   slave   well.   And

ἐγένετο ἐν τῷ ἑξῆς ἐπορεύθη εἰς πόλιν
it came to pass on the   next day   he went   into   a city

καλουμένην Ναΐν, καὶ συνεπορεύοντο αὐτῷ
being called   Nain,   and   went with   him

οἱ μαθηταὶ αὐτοῦ καὶ ὄχλος πολύς.
the   disciples   of him   and   crowd   a much.

12 ὡς δὲ ἤγγισεν τῇ πύλῃ τῆς πόλεως, καὶ
And as he drew near to the gate   of the city,   and

King James Version

city, behold, there was a dead man carried out, the only son of his mother, and she was a widow: and much people of the city was with her. 13And when the Lord saw her, he had compassion on her, and said unto her, Weep not. 14And he came and touched the bier: and they that bare *him* stood still. And he said, Young man, I say unto thee, Arise. 15And he that was dead sat up, and began to speak. And he delivered him to his mother. 16And there came a fear on all: and they glorified God, saying, That a great prophet is risen up among us: and, That God hath visited his people. 17And this rumour of him went forth throughout all Judea, and throughout all the region round about. 18And the disciples of John shewed him of all these things.

19 And John calling *unto him* two of his dis-·· ciples sent *them* to Jesus, saying, Art thou he that should come? or look we for another? 20 When the men were come unto him, they said, John Baptist hath sent us unto thee, saying, Art thou he that should come? or look we for another? 21And in that same hour he cured many of *their* infirmities and plagues, and of evil spirits; and unto many *that were* blind he gave sight. 22 Then Jesus answering said unto them, Go your way, and tell John what things ye have seen and heard; how that the blind see, the lame walk, the lepers are cleansed, the deaf hear, the dead are raised, to the poor the gospel is preached. 23And blessed is *he,* whosoever shall not be offended in me.

24 And when the messengers of John were departed, he began to speak unto the people concerning John, What went ye out into the wilderness for to see? A reed shaken with the wind? 25 But what went ye out for to see? A man clothed in soft raiment? Behold, they which are gorgeously apparelled, and live delicately, are in kings' courts. 26 But what went ye out for to see? A prophet? Yea, I say unto you, and much more than a prophet. 27 This is *he,* of whom it is written, Behold, I send my messenger before thy face, which shall prepare thy way before thee. 28 For I say unto you, Among those that are born of women there is not a greater prophet than John the Baptist: but he that is least in the kingdom of God is greater than he. 29And all the people that heard *him,* and the publicans, justified God, being baptized with the baptism of John. 30 But the Pharisees and lawyers rejected the counsel of God against themselves, being not baptized of him.

31 And the Lord said, Whereunto then shall I liken the men of this generation? and to what are they like? 32 They are like unto children sitting in the marketplace, and calling one to another, and saying, We have piped unto you, and ye have not danced; we have mourned to you, and ye have not wept. 33 For John the Baptist came neither eating bread nor drinking wine; and ye say He hath a devil. 34 The Son of man is come eating and drinking; and ye say, Behold a gluttonous man, and a winebibber, a friend of publicans and sinners! 35 But wisdom is justified of all her children.

New International Version

town gate, a dead person was being carried out —the only son of his mother, and she was a widow. And a large crowd from the town was with her. 13 When the Lord saw her, his heart went out to her and he said, "Don't cry."

14 Then he went up and touched the coffin, and those carrying it stood still. He said, "Young man, I say to you, get up!" 15 The dead man sat up and began to talk, and Jesus gave him back to his mother.

16 They were all filled with awe and praised God. "A great prophet has appeared among us," they said. "God has come to help his people." 17 This news about Jesus spread throughout Judea[z] and the surrounding country.

Jesus and John the Baptist

18 John's disciples told him about all these things. Calling two of them, 19 he sent them to the Lord to ask, "Are you the one who was to come, or should we expect someone else?"

20 When the men came to Jesus, they said, "John the Baptist sent us to you to ask, 'Are you the one who was to come, or should we expect someone else?' "

21 At that very time Jesus cured many who had diseases, sicknesses and evil spirits, and gave sight to many who were blind. 22 So he replied to the messengers, "Go back and report to John what you have seen and heard: The blind receive sight, the lame walk, those who have leprosy[a] are cured, the deaf hear, the dead are raised, and the good news is preached to the poor. 23 Blessed is the man who does not fall away on account of me."

24 After John's messengers left, Jesus began to speak to the crowd about John: "What did you go out into the desert to see? A reed swayed by the wind? 25 If not, what did you go out to see? A man dressed in fine clothes? No, those who wear expensive clothes and indulge in luxury are in palaces. 26 But what did you go out to see? A prophet? Yes, I tell you, and more than a prophet. 27 This is the one about whom it is written:

'I will send my messenger ahead of you,
  who will prepare your way before you.' [b]
28 I tell you, among those born of women there is no one greater than John; yet the one who is least in the kingdom of God is greater than he."

29 (All the people, even the tax collectors, when they heard Jesus' words, acknowledged that God's way was right, because they had been baptized by John. 30 But the Pharisees and experts in the law rejected God's purpose for themselves, because they had not been baptized by John.)

31 "To what, then, can I compare the people of this generation? What are they like? 32 They are like children sitting in the marketplace and calling out to each other:

'We played the flute for you, and you did not
    dance;
  we sang a dirge, and you did not cry.'
33 For John the Baptist came neither eating bread nor drinking wine, and you say, 'He has a demon.' 34 The Son of Man came eating and drinking, and you say, 'Here is a glutton and a drunkard, a friend of tax collectors and "sinners." ' 35 But wisdom is proved right by all her children."

[z] Or *the land of the Jews.* [a] The Greek word probably designated other related diseases also. [b] Mal. 3:1.

Greek Interlinear

ἰδοὺ   ἐξεκομίζετο   τεθνηκὼς   μονογενὴς
behold was being carried out   having died   an only born
[for burial]

υἱὸς   τῇ   μητρὶ   αὐτοῦ,   καὶ   αὕτη   ἦν   χήρα,
son to the   mother   of him,   and   this   was   a widow,

καὶ   ὄχλος   τῆς   πόλεως   ἱκανὸς   ἦν   σὺν
and   a 'crowd   'of the   'city   'considerable   was   with

αὐτῇ.   13 καὶ   ἰδὼν   αὐτὴν   ὁ   κύριος
her.   And   seeing   her   the   Lord

ἐσπλαγχνίσθη   ἐπ'   αὐτῇ   καὶ   εἶπεν   αὐτῇ·
felt compassion   over   her   and   said   to her:

μὴ   κλαῖε.   14 καὶ   προσελθὼν   ἥψατο   τῆς
Do not weep.   And   approaching   he touched   the

σοροῦ,   οἱ   δὲ   βαστάζοντες   ἔστησαν,   καὶ
bier,   and the [ones]   bearing   stood,   and

εἶπεν·   νεανίσκε,   σοὶ   λέγω,   ἐγέρθητι.   15 καὶ
he said :   Young man,   to thee I say,   Arise.   And

ἀνεκάθισεν   ὁ   νεκρὸς   καὶ   ἤρξατο   λαλεῖν,
sat up   the   dead man   and   began   to speak,

καὶ   ἔδωκεν   αὐτὸν   τῇ   μητρὶ   αὐτοῦ.
and   he gave   him   to the   mother   of him.

16 ἔλαβεν   δὲ   φόβος   πάντας,   καὶ   ἐδόξαζον
And 'took   'fear   'all,   and   they glorified

τὸν   θεὸν   λέγοντες   ὅτι   προφήτης   μέγας
-    God   saying[,]   -   prophet   A great

ἠγέρθη   ἐν   ἡμῖν,   καὶ   ὅτι   ἐπεσκέψατο   ὁ
was raised   among us,   and[,]   -   'visited   -

θεὸς   τὸν   λαὸν   αὐτοῦ.   17 καὶ   ἐξῆλθεν   ὁ
'God   the   people   of him.   And   went forth   the

λόγος   οὗτος   ἐν   ὅλῃ   τῇ   Ἰουδαίᾳ   περὶ
word   this   in   all   -   Judæa   'concerning

αὐτοῦ   καὶ   πάσῃ   τῇ   περιχώρῳ.
'him   'and   'all   'the   'neighbourhood.

18 Καὶ   ἀπήγγειλαν   Ἰωάννῃ   οἱ   μαθηταὶ
And   reported   to John   the   disciples

αὐτοῦ   περὶ   πάντων   τούτων.   καὶ
of him   about   all   these things.   And

προσκαλεσάμενος   δύο   τινὰς   τῶν   μαθητῶν
calling to [him]   'two   'a certain   of the   disciples

αὐτοῦ   ὁ   Ἰωάννης   19 ἔπεμψεν   πρὸς   τὸν
of him   -   John   sent   to   the

κύριον   λέγων·   σὺ   εἶ   ὁ   ἐρχόμενος,   ἢ   ἄλλον
Lord   saying : Thou art   the   coming [one],   or   another

προσδοκῶμεν;   20 παραγενόμενοι   δὲ   πρὸς
may we expect?   And coming   to

αὐτὸν   οἱ   ἄνδρες   εἶπαν·   Ἰωάννης   ὁ   βαπτιστὴς
him   the   men   said :   John   the   Baptist

ἀπέστειλεν   ἡμᾶς   πρὸς   σὲ   λέγων·   σὺ   εἶ   ὁ
sent   us   to   thee   saying : Thou art   the

ἐρχόμενος,   ἢ   ἄλλον   προσδοκῶμεν;   21 ἐν
coming [one],   or   another   may we expect?   In

ἐκείνῃ   τῇ   ὥρᾳ   ἐθεράπευσεν   πολλοὺς   ἀπὸ
that   -   hour   he healed   many   from(of)

νόσων   καὶ   μαστίγων   καὶ   πνευμάτων   πονηρῶν,
diseases   and   plagues   and   spirits   evil,

καὶ   τυφλοῖς   πολλοῖς   ἐχαρίσατο   βλέπειν.
and   blind persons   to many   he gave   to see.

22 καὶ   ἀποκριθεὶς   εἶπεν   αὐτοῖς·   πορευθέντες
And   answering   he said   to them :   Going

ἀπαγγείλατε   Ἰωάννῃ   ἃ   εἴδετε   καὶ
report   to John   [the things] which   ye saw   and

ἠκούσατε·   τυφλοὶ   ἀναβλέπουσιν,   χωλοὶ
heard :   blind men   see again,   lame men

περιπατοῦσιν,   λεπροὶ   καθαρίζονται,   καὶ   κωφοὶ
walk,   lepers   are being cleansed,   and   deaf men

ἀκούουσιν,   νεκροὶ   ἐγείρονται,   πτωχοὶ
hear,   dead men   are raised,   poor people

εὐαγγελίζονται·   23 καὶ   μακάριός   ἐστιν   ὃς   ἐὰν
are evangelized;   and   blessed   is   whoever

μὴ   σκανδαλισθῇ   ἐν   ἐμοί.   24 Ἀπελθόντων   δὲ
is not offended   in   me.   And going away
= as the

τῶν   ἀγγέλων   Ἰωάννου   ἤρξατο   λέγειν   πρὸς
the   messengers   of John°   he began   to say   to
messengers of John went away

τοὺς   ὄχλους   περὶ   Ἰωάννου·   τί   ἐξήλθατε
the   crowds   concerning   John :   What   went ye forth

εἰς   τὴν   ἔρημον   θεάσασθαι;   κάλαμον   ὑπὸ
into   the   desert   to see?   a reed   by

ἀνέμου   σαλευόμενον;   25 ἀλλὰ   τί   ἐξήλθατε
wind   being shaken?   But   what   went ye forth

ἰδεῖν;   ἄνθρωπον   ἐν   μαλακοῖς   ἱματίοις
to see?   a man   in   soft   garments

ἠμφιεσμένον;   ἰδοὺ   οἱ   ἐν   ἱματισμῷ   ἐνδόξῳ
having been   behold[,]   the   'in   'raiment   'splendid
clothed?   [ones]

καὶ   τρυφῇ   ὑπάρχοντες   ἐν   τοῖς   βασιλείοις
'and   'in luxury   'being   'in   -   'royal palaces

εἰσίν.   26 ἀλλὰ   τί   ἐξήλθατε   ἰδεῖν;   προφήτην;
'are.   But   what   went ye forth to see?   a prophet?

ναὶ   λέγω   ὑμῖν,   καὶ   περισσότερον   προφήτου.
yes   I tell   you,   and   more [than]   a prophet.

27 οὗτός   ἐστιν   περὶ   οὗ   γέγραπται·   ἰδοὺ
This   is he concerning whom   it has been written : Behold

ἀποστέλλω   τὸν   ἄγγελόν   μου   πρὸ   προσώπου
I send   the   messenger   of me   before   [the] face

σου,   ὃς   κατασκευάσει   τὴν   ὁδόν   σου
of thee,   who   will prepare   the   way   of thee

ἔμπροσθέν   σου.   28 λέγω   ὑμῖν,   μείζων
before   thee.   I tell   you,   'greater

ἐν   γεννητοῖς   γυναικῶν   Ἰωάννου   οὐδεὶς
'among '[those] born 'of women ['than]   'John   'no one

ἐστιν·   ὁ   δὲ   μικρότερος   ἐν   τῇ   βασιλείᾳ   τοῦ
'is;   but   the   less   in   the   kingdom   -

θεοῦ   μείζων   αὐτοῦ   ἐστιν.   29 καὶ   πᾶς   ὁ
of God   greater [than] he   is.   And   all   the

λαὸς   ἀκούσας   καὶ   οἱ   τελῶναι   ἐδικαίωσαν
people   hearing   and   the   tax-collectors   justified

τὸν   θεόν,   βαπτισθέντες   τὸ   βάπτισμα
-    God,   being baptized [with] the   baptism

Ἰωάννου·   30 οἱ   δὲ   Φαρισαῖοι   καὶ   οἱ
of John;   but the   Pharisees   and   the

νομικοὶ   τὴν   βουλὴν   τοῦ   θεοῦ   ἠθέτησαν   εἰς
lawyers   'the   'counsel   -   'of God   'rejected   'for

ἑαυτούς,   μὴ   βαπτισθέντες   ὑπ'   αὐτοῦ.   31 Τίνι
'themselves,   not   being baptized   by   him.   To what

οὖν   ὁμοιώσω   τοὺς   ἀνθρώπους   τῆς   γενεᾶς
then   may I liken   the   men   -   generation

ταύτης,   καὶ   τίνι   εἰσὶν   ὅμοιοι;   32 ὅμοιοί   εἰσιν
of this,   and to what are they like?   Like   are they

παιδίοις   τοῖς   ἐν   ἀγορᾷ   καθημένοις   καὶ
to children   -   in   a marketplace   sitting   and

προσφωνοῦσιν   ἀλλήλοις   ἃ   λέγει·   ηὐλήσαμεν
calling   to one another who says :   We piped

ὑμῖν   καὶ   οὐκ   ὠρχήσασθε·   ἐθρηνήσαμεν   καὶ
to you and   ye did not dance;   we mourned   and

οὐκ   ἐκλαύσατε.   33 ἐλήλυθεν   γὰρ   Ἰωάννης
ye did not weep.   For has come   John

ὁ   βαπτιστὴς   μὴ   ἐσθίων   ἄρτον   μήτε   πίνων
the   Baptist   not   eating   bread   nor   drinking

οἶνον,   καὶ   λέγετε·   δαιμόνιον   ἔχει.
wine,   and   ye say :   A demon   he has.

34 ἐλήλυθεν   ὁ   υἱὸς   τοῦ   ἀνθρώπου   ἐσθίων
Has come   the   Son   -   of man   eating

καὶ   πίνων,   καὶ   λέγετε·   ἰδοὺ   ἄνθρωπος
and   drinking,   and   ye say :   Behold[,]   a man

φάγος   καὶ   οἰνοπότης,   φίλος   τελωνῶν   καὶ
a glutton   and   a winebibber,   a friend   of tax-collectors and

ἁμαρτωλῶν.   35 καὶ   ἐδικαιώθη   ἡ   σοφία
of sinners.   And   was(is) justified   the   wisdom

ἀπὸ   πάντων   τῶν   τέκνων   αὐτῆς.
from(by)   all   the   children   of her.

King James Version

36 And one of the Pharisees desired him that he would eat with him. And he went into the Pharisee's house, and sat down to meat. 37And, behold, a woman in the city, which was a sinner, when she knew that *Jesus* sat at meat in the Pharisee's house, brought an alabaster box of ointment, 38And stood at his feet behind *him* weeping, and began to wash his feet with tears, and did wipe *them* with the hairs of her head, and kissed his feet, and anointed *them* with the ointment. 39 Now when the Pharisee which had bidden him saw *it*, he spake within himself, saying, This man, if he were a prophet, would have known who and what manner of woman *this is* that toucheth him; for she is a sinner. 40And Jesus answering said unto him, Simon, I have somewhat to say unto thee. And he saith, Master, say on. 41 There was a certain creditor which had two debtors: the one owed five hundred pence, and the other fifty. 42 And when they had nothing to pay, he frankly forgave them both. Tell me therefore, which of them will love him most? 43 Simon answered and said, I suppose that *he*, to whom he forgave most. And he said unto him, Thou hast rightly judged. 44And he turned to the woman, and said unto Simon, Seest thou *this* woman? I entered into thine house, thou gavest me no water for my feet: but she hath washed my feet with tears, and wiped *them* with the hairs of her head. 45 Thou gavest me no kiss: but this woman, since the time I came in, hath not ceased to kiss my feet. 46 My head with oil thou didst not anoint: but this woman hath anointed my feet with ointment. 47 Wherefore I say unto thee, Her sins, which are many, are forgiven; for she loved much: but to whom little is forgiven, *the same* loveth little. 48And he said unto her, Thy sins are forgiven. 49And they that sat at meat with him began to say within themselves, Who is this that forgiveth sins also? 50And he said to the woman, Thy faith hath saved thee; go in peace.

New International Version

Jesus anointed by a sinful woman

36 Now one of the Pharisees invited Jesus to have dinner with him, so he went to the Pharisee's house and reclined at the table. 37 When a woman who lived a sinful life in that town learned that Jesus was eating at the Pharisee's house, she brought an alabaster jar of perfume, 38 and as she stood behind him at his feet weeping, she began to wet his feet with her tears. Then she wiped them with her hair, kissed them and poured perfume on them.

39 When the Pharisee who had invited him saw this, he said to himself, "If this man were a prophet, he would know who is touching him and what kind of woman she is—that she is a sinner."

40 Jesus answered him, "Simon, I have something to tell you."

"Tell me, teacher," he said.

41 "Two men owed money to a certain moneylender. One owed him five hundred denarii,*e* and the other fifty. 42 Neither of them had the money to pay him back, so he canceled the debts of both. Now which of them will love him more?"

43 Simon replied, "I suppose the one who had the bigger debt canceled."

"You have judged correctly," Jesus said.

44 Then he turned toward the woman and said to Simon, "Do you see this woman? I came into your house. You did not give me any water for my feet, but she wet my feet with her tears and wiped them with her hair. 45 You did not give me a kiss, but this woman, from the time I entered, has not stopped kissing my feet. 46 You did not anoint my head with oil, but she has anointed my feet with perfume. 47 Therefore, I tell you, her many sins have been forgiven—for she loved much. But he loves little who has been forgiven little."

48 Then Jesus said to her, "Your sins are forgiven."

49 The other guests began to say among themselves, "Who is this who even forgives sins?"

50 Jesus said to the woman, "Your faith has saved you; go in peace."

The parable of the sower

8 And it came to pass afterward, that he went throughout every city and village, preaching and shewing the glad tidings of the kingdom of God: and the twelve *were* with him, 2And certain women, which had been healed of evil spirits and infirmities, Mary called Magdalene, out of whom went seven devils, 3And Joanna the wife of Chuza Herod's steward, and Susanna, and many others, which ministered unto him of their substance.

4 And when much people were gathered together, and were come to him out of every city, he spake by a parable: 5A sower went out to sow his seed: and as he sowed, some fell by the way side; and it was trodden down, and the

8 After this, Jesus traveled about from one city and village to another, proclaiming the good news of the kingdom of God. The Twelve were with him, 2 and also some women who had been cured of evil spirits and diseases: Mary, called Magdalene, from whom seven demons had come out; 3 Joanna the wife of Chuza, the manager of Herod's household; Susanna; and many others. These women were helping to support them out of their own means.

4 While a large crowd was gathering and people were coming to Jesus from town after town, he told this parable: 5 "A farmer went out to sow his seed. As he was scattering the seed, some fell along the path; it was trampled

[c] A denarius was a coin worth about a day's wage.

192

Greek Interlinear

36 Ἠρώτα δέ τις αὐτὸν τῶν Φαρισαίων
And ᵃasked ¹a certain one ᵇhim ¹of the ²Pharisees

ἵνα φάγῃ μετ᾽ αὐτοῦ· καὶ εἰσελθὼν εἰς
that he would eat with him; and entering into

τὸν οἶκον τοῦ Φαρισαίου κατεκλίθη. **37** καὶ
the house of the Pharisee he reclined. And[,]

ἰδοὺ γυνὴ ἥτις ἦν ἐν τῇ πόλει ἁμαρτωλός,
behold[,] a woman who was in the city a sinner,

καὶ ἐπιγνοῦσα ὅτι κατάκειται ἐν τῇ
and knowing that he reclines in the

οἰκίᾳ τοῦ Φαρισαίου, κομίσασα ἀλάβαστρον
house of the Pharisee, bringing an alabaster box

μύρου **38** καὶ στᾶσα ὀπίσω παρὰ τοὺς
of ointment and standing behind at the

πόδας αὐτοῦ κλαίουσα, τοῖς δάκρυσιν
feet of him weeping, with the(her) tears

ἤρξατο βρέχειν τοὺς πόδας αὐτοῦ, καὶ
began to wet the feet of him, and

ταῖς θριξὶν τῆς κεφαλῆς αὐτῆς ἐξέμασσεν,
with the hairs of the head of her wiped off,

καὶ κατεφίλει τοὺς πόδας αὐτοῦ καὶ
and fervently kissed the feet of him and

ἤλειφεν τῷ μύρῳ. **39** ἰδὼν δὲ ὁ Φαρισαῖος
anointed with the ointment. But ²seeing ¹the ²Pharisee

ὁ καλέσας αὐτὸν εἶπεν ἐν ἑαυτῷ λέγων·
- ²having invited ᵇhim spoke within himself saying :

οὗτος εἰ ἦν [ὁ] προφήτης, ἐγίνωσκεν ἂν
This man if he was [the] prophet, would have known

τίς καὶ ποταπὴ ἡ γυνὴ ἥτις ἅπτεται
who and what sort the woman who is touching

αὐτοῦ, ὅτι ἁμαρτωλός ἐστιν. **40** καὶ
him, because a sinner she is. And

ἀποκριθεὶς ὁ Ἰησοῦς εἶπεν πρὸς αὐτόν·
answering - Jesus said to him :

Σίμων, ἔχω σοί τι εἰπεῖν. ὁ δέ· διδάσκαλε,
Simon, I have to thee something to say. And he : Teacher,

εἰπέ, φησίν. **41** δύο χρεοφειλέται ἦσαν
say, says. Two debtors were
= A certain creditor had two debtors;

δανειστῇ τινι· ὁ εἷς ὤφειλεν δηνάρια
creditor to a certain;ᶜ the one owed denarii

πεντακόσια, ὁ δὲ ἕτερος πεντήκοντα. **42** μὴ
five hundred, and the other fifty. Not
= As they had no[thing]

ἐχόντων αὐτῶν ἀποδοῦναι ἀμφοτέροις
having themᵃ to repay ᵇboth

ἐχαρίσατο. τίς οὖν αὐτῶν πλεῖον ἀγαπήσει
¹he freely forgave. Who then of them more will love

αὐτόν; **43** ἀποκριθεὶς Σίμων εἶπεν·
him? Answering Simon said :

ὑπολαμβάνω ὅτι ᾧ τὸ πλεῖον ἐχαρίσατο.
I suppose[.] - to whom the more he freely forgave.

ὁ δὲ εἶπεν αὐτῷ· ὀρθῶς ἔκρινας. **44** καὶ
And he said to him : Rightly thou didst judge. And

στραφεὶς πρὸς τὴν γυναῖκα τῷ Σίμωνι
turning to the woman - to Simon

ἔφη· βλέπεις ταύτην τὴν γυναῖκα; εἰσῆλθόν
he said : Seest thou this - woman? I entered

σου εἰς τὴν οἰκίαν, ὕδωρ μοι ἐπὶ πόδας
of thee into the house, water to me on(for) [my] feet

οὐκ ἔδωκας· αὕτη δὲ τοῖς δάκρυσιν
thou gavest not; but this woman with the(her) tears

ἔβρεξέν μου τοὺς πόδας καὶ ταῖς θριξὶν
wet of me the feet and with the hairs

αὐτῆς ἐξέμαξεν. **45** φίλημά μοι οὐκ ἔδωκας·
of her wiped off. A kiss to me thou gavest not;

αὕτη δὲ ἀφ᾽ ἧς εἰσῆλθον οὐ διέλειπεν
but this woman from [the time] I entered ceased not
which

καταφιλοῦσά μου τοὺς πόδας. **46** ἐλαίῳ
fervently kissing of me the feet. With oil

τὴν κεφαλήν μου οὐκ ἤλειψας· αὕτη δὲ
the head of me thou didst not anoint; but this woman

μύρῳ ἤλειψεν τοὺς πόδας μου. **47** οὗ
with ointment anointed the feet of me. Of which
= Wherefore

χάριν λέγω σοι, ἀφέωνται αἱ ἁμαρτίαι
for the sake of I tell thee, ²have been forgiven ¹the ²sins

αὐτῆς αἱ πολλαί, ὅτι ἠγάπησεν πολύ·
²of her - ¹many, because she loved much;

ᾧ δὲ ὀλίγον ἀφίεται, ὀλίγον ἀγαπᾷ.
but to whom little is forgiven, little he loves.

48 εἶπεν δὲ αὐτῇ· ἀφέωνταί σου αἱ
And he said to her : Have been forgiven of thee the

ἁμαρτίαι. **49** καὶ ἤρξαντο οἱ συνανακείμενοι
sins. And began the [ones] reclining with [him]

λέγειν ἐν ἑαυτοῖς· τίς οὗτός ἐστιν, ὃς καὶ
to say among themselves : Who this is, who even

ἁμαρτίας ἀφίησιν; **50** εἶπεν δὲ πρὸς τὴν
sins forgives? But he said to the

γυναῖκα· ἡ πίστις σου σέσωκέν σε·
woman : The faith of thee has saved thee;

πορεύου εἰς εἰρήνην.
go in peace.

Chapter 8

Καὶ ἐγένετο ἐν τῷ καθεξῆς καὶ αὐτὸς
And it came to pass afterwards and he

διώδευεν κατὰ πόλιν καὶ κώμην κηρύσσων
journeyed through everyᵗ city and village proclaiming

καὶ εὐαγγελιζόμενος τὴν βασιλείαν τοῦ
and preaching the kingdom -

θεοῦ, καὶ οἱ δώδεκα σὺν αὐτῷ, **2** καὶ
of God, and the twelve with him, and

γυναῖκές τινες αἳ ἦσαν τεθεραπευμέναι ἀπὸ
women certain who were having been healed from

πνευμάτων πονηρῶν καὶ ἀσθενειῶν, Μαρία
spirits evil and infirmities, Mary

ἡ καλουμένη Μαγδαληνή, ἀφ᾽ ἧς δαιμόνια
- being called Magdalene, from whom demons

ἑπτὰ ἐξεληλύθει, **3** καὶ Ἰωάννα γυνὴ Χουζᾶ
seven had gone out, and Joanna wife of Chuza

ἐπιτρόπου Ἡρῴδου καὶ Σουσάννα καὶ
steward of Herod and Susanna and

ἕτεραι πολλαί, αἵτινες διηκόνουν αὐτοῖς
others many, who ministered to them

ἐκ τῶν ὑπαρχόντων αὐταῖς.
out of the possessions to them.ᵉ

4 Συνιόντος δὲ ὄχλου πολλοῦ καὶ τῶν
And coming together crowd a much and the [ones]
= when a great crowd came together and people in each city

κατὰ πόλιν ἐπιπορευομένων πρὸς αὐτὸν
in each cityᵗ resortingᵃ to him
resorted

εἶπεν διὰ παραβολῆς· **5** ἐξῆλθεν ὁ σπείρων
he said by a parable : Went forth the [one] sowing

τοῦ σπεῖραι τὸν σπόρον αὐτοῦ. καὶ ἐν τῷ
- to sowᵈ the seed of him. And in the

σπείρειν αὐτὸν ὃ μὲν ἔπεσεν παρὰ τὴν
to sow himᵇᵉ this fell by the
= as he sowed

ὁδὸν καὶ κατεπατήθη, καὶ τὰ πετεινὰ τοῦ
way and was trodden down, and the birds of the

King James Version

fowls of the air devoured it. 6And some fell
upon a rock; and as soon as it was sprung up, it
withered away, because it lacked moisture. 7And
some fell among thorns; and the thorns sprang
up with it, and choked it. 8And other fell on
good ground, and sprang up, and bare fruit a
hundredfold. And when he had said these things,
he cried, He that hath ears to hear, let him
hear. 9And his disciples asked him, saying, What
might this parable be? 10And he said, Unto you
it is given to know the mysteries of the kingdom
of God: but to others in parables; that seeing
they might not see, and hearing they might not
understand. 11 Now the parable is this: The seed
is the word of God. 12 Those by the way side are
they that hear; then cometh the devil, and
taketh away the word out of their hearts, lest
they should believe and be saved. 13 They on the
rock *are they,* which, when they hear, receive
the word with joy; and these have no root, which
for a while believe, and in time of temptation fall
away. 14And that which fell among thorns are
they, which, when they have heard, go forth,
and are choked with cares and riches and pleasures of *this* life, and bring no fruit to perfection.
15 But that on the good ground are they, which
in an honest and good heart, having heard the
word, keep *it,* and bring forth fruit with patience.

16 No man, when he hath lighted a candle,
covereth it with a vessel, or putteth *it* under a
bed; but setteth *it* on a candlestick, that they
which enter in may see the light. 17 For nothing
is secret, that shall not be made manifest;
neither *any thing* hid, that shall not be known
and come abroad. 18 Take heed therefore how
ye hear: for whosoever hath, to him shall be
given; and whosoever hath not, from him shall
be taken even that which he seemeth to have.

19 Then came to him *his* mother and his
brethren, and could not come at him for the
press. 20And it was told him *by certain* which
said, Thy mother and thy brethren stand without, desiring to see thee. 21And he answered and
said unto them, My mother and my brethren
are these which hear the word of God, and do it.

22 Now it came to pass on a certain day, that
he went into a ship with his disciples: and he
said unto them, Let us go over unto the other
side of the lake. And they launched forth. 23 But
as they sailed, he fell asleep: and there came
down a storm of wind on the lake; and they
were filled *with water,* and were in jeopardy.
24And they came to him, and awoke him, saying,
Master, Master, we perish. Then he arose, and
rebuked the wind and the raging of the water:
and they ceased, and there was a calm. 25And
he said unto them, Where is your faith? And
they being afraid wondered, saying one to another, What manner of man is this! for he commandeth even the winds and water, and they
obey him.

New International Version

on, and the birds of the air ate it up. 6 Some
fell on rock, and when it came up, the plants
withered because they had no moisture. 7 Other
seed fell among thorns, which grew up with it
and choked the plants. 8 Still other seed fell on
good soil. It came up and yielded a crop, a
hundred times more than was sown."

When he said this, he called out, "He who
has ears to hear, let him hear."

9 His disciples asked him what this parable
meant. 10 He said, "The knowledge of the secrets of the kingdom of God has been given to
you, but to others I speak in parables, so that,

'though seeing, they may not see;
    though hearing, they may not understand.' [d]

11 "This is the meaning of the parable: The
seed is the word of God. 12 Those along the path
are the ones who hear, and then the devil comes
and takes away the word from their hearts, so
that they cannot believe and be saved. 13 Those
on the rock are the ones who receive the word
with joy when they hear it, but they have no
root. They believe for a while, but in the time of
testing they fall away. 14 The seed that fell among
thorns stands for those who hear, but as they
go on their way they are choked by life's worries, riches and pleasures, and they do not mature. 15 But the seed on good soil stands for
those with a noble and good heart, who hear the
word, retain it, and by persevering produce a
crop.

A lamp on a stand

16 "No one lights a lamp and hides it in a
jar or puts it under a bed. Instead, he puts it
on a stand, so that those who come in can see
the light. 17 For there is nothing hidden that
will not be disclosed, and nothing concealed
that will not be known or brought out into the
open. 18 Therefore consider carefully how you
listen. Whoever has will be given more; whoever
does not have, even what he thinks he has will
be taken from him."

Jesus' mother and brothers

19 Now Jesus' mother and brothers came to
see him, but they were not able to get near him
because of the crowd. 20 Someone told him,
"Your mother and brothers are standing outside,
wanting to see you."

21 He replied, "My mother and brothers are
those who hear God's word and put it into
practice."

Jesus calms the storm

22 One day Jesus said to his disciples, "Let's
go over to the other side of the lake." So they
got into a boat and set out. 23 As they sailed, he
fell asleep. A squall came down on the lake, so
that the boat was being swamped, and they were
in great danger.

24 The disciples went and woke him, saying,
"Master, Master, we're going to drown!"

He got up and rebuked the wind and the
raging waters; the storm subsided, and all was
calm. 25 "Where is your faith?" he asked his
disciples.

In fear and amazement they asked one another, "Who is this? He commands even the
winds and the water, and they obey him."

[d] Isaiah 6:9.

Greek Interlinear

οὐρανοῦ κατέφαγεν αὐτό.   6 καὶ ἔτερον
heaven(air) devoured it.   And other [seed]

κατέπεσεν ἐπὶ τὴν πέτραν, καὶ φυὲν
fell   on   the   rock,   and grown

ἐξηράνθη διὰ τὸ μὴ ἔχειν ἰκμάδα.
it was withered because of the not to have moisture.
= because it had no moisture.

7 καὶ ἔτερον ἔπεσεν ἐν μέσῳ τῶν ἀκανθῶν, καὶ
And other fell   in [the] of the thorns, and
                       midst

συμφυεῖσαι αἱ ἄκανθαι ἀπέπνιξαν αὐτό.
growing up with [it] the thorns choked   it.

8 καὶ ἔτερον ἔπεσεν εἰς τὴν γῆν τὴν
And other fell   in the soil –

ἀγαθὴν καὶ φυὲν ἐποίησεν καρπὸν
good   and grown it produced fruit

ἑκατονταπλασίονα. ταῦτα λέγων ἐφώνει·   ὁ
a hundredfold.   These things saying he called: The [one]

ἔχων ὦτα ἀκούειν ἀκουέτω.   9 Ἐπηρώτων δὲ
having ears to hear let him hear.   And questioned

αὐτὸν οἱ μαθηταὶ αὐτοῦ τίς εἴη ἡ
him the disciples of him what ¹this ²might be –

παραβολή. 10 ὁ δὲ εἶπεν· ὑμῖν δέδοται
²parable.   And he said : To you it has been given

γνῶναι τὰ μυστήρια τῆς βασιλείας τοῦ
to know the mysteries of the kingdom   –

θεοῦ, τοῖς δὲ λοιποῖς ἐν παραβολαῖς, ἵνα
of God, but to the rest   in parables,   that

βλέποντες μὴ βλέπωσιν καὶ ἀκούοντες μὴ
seeing   they may not see and hearing not

συνιῶσιν.   11 ἔστιν δὲ αὕτη ἡ παραβολή.
they may understand. ¹is ¹Now ²this – ³parable.

ὁ σπόρος ἐστὶν ὁ λόγος τοῦ θεοῦ.
The seed   is   the word – of God.

12 οἱ δὲ παρὰ τὴν ὁδόν εἰσιν οἱ ἀκούσαντες,
And the [ones] by the way are the [ones] hearing,

εἶτα ἔρχεται ὁ διάβολος καὶ αἴρει τὸν
then comes   the devil   and takes the

λόγον ἀπὸ τῆς καρδίας αὐτῶν, ἵνα μὴ
word from the   heart   of them, lest

πιστεύσαντες σωθῶσιν. 13 οἱ δὲ ἐπὶ τῆς
believing   they may be saved. And the [ones] on the

πέτρας οἳ ὅταν ἀκούσωσιν μετὰ χαρᾶς
rock   who when they hear   with   joy

δέχονται τὸν λόγον· καὶ οὗτοι ῥίζαν
receive   the word;   and these   root

οὐκ ἔχουσιν, οἳ πρὸς καιρὸν πιστεύουσιν
have not,   who for a time   believe

καὶ ἐν καιρῷ πειρασμοῦ ἀφίστανται. 14 τὸ
and in time of trial   withdraw. the [one]

δὲ εἰς τὰς ἀκάνθας πεσόν, οὗτοί εἰσιν
And in the thorns falling, these   are

οἱ ἀκούσαντες, καὶ ὑπὸ μεριμνῶν καὶ
the [ones] hearing, ¹and ⁴by ⁵cares ⁶and

πλούτου καὶ ἡδονῶν τοῦ βίου πορευόμενοι
⁷riches ⁸and ⁹pleasures – ¹⁰of life ²going

συμπνίγονται καὶ οὐ τελεσφοροῦσιν. 15 τὸ
²are choked and do not bear [fruit] to maturity. the [one]

δὲ ἐν τῇ καλῇ γῇ, οὗτοί εἰσιν οἵτινες ἐν
And in the good soil, these are [those] who in

καρδίᾳ καλῇ καὶ ἀγαθῇ ἀκούσαντες
heart a worthy and good   hearing the

λόγον κατέχουσιν καὶ καρποφοροῦσιν ἐν
word hold fast   and   bear fruit   in

ὑπομονῇ. 16 Οὐδεὶς δὲ λύχνον ἅψας
patience.   Now no one   a lamp having lit

καλύπτει αὐτὸν σκεύει ἢ ὑποκάτω κλίνης
hides   it   with a vessel or underneath a couch

τίθησιν, ἀλλ' ἐπὶ λυχνίας τίθησιν, ἵνα οἱ
puts,   but on a lampstand puts, that the

εἰσπορευόμενοι βλέπωσιν τὸ φῶς. 17 οὐ
[ones] coming in may see the light.   not

γάρ ἐστιν κρυπτὸν ὃ οὐ φανερὸν
For [anything] is hidden which ³not ⁴manifest

γενήσεται, οὐδὲ ἀπόκρυφον ὃ οὐ μὴ
¹will ²become, nor   secret which by no means

γνωσθῇ καὶ εἰς φανερὸν ἔλθῃ. 18 βλέπετε
will be known and to [be] manifest come.   See

οὖν πῶς ἀκούετε· ὃς ἂν γὰρ ἔχῃ,
therefore how ye hear;   for whoever   has,

δοθήσεται αὐτῷ· καὶ ὃς ἂν μὴ ἔχῃ,
it will be given to him; and whoever has not,

καὶ ὃ δοκεῖ ἔχειν ἀρθήσεται ἀπ' αὐτοῦ.
even what he seems to have will be taken from him.

19 Παρεγένετο δὲ πρὸς αὐτὸν ἡ μήτηρ
And came   to him the mother

καὶ οἱ ἀδελφοὶ αὐτοῦ, καὶ οὐκ ἠδύναντο
and the brothers of him, and were not able

συντυχεῖν αὐτῷ διὰ τὸν ὄχλον. 20 ἀπηγγέλη δὲ
to come up with him be- the crowd.   And it was reported
                                        cause of

αὐτῷ· ἡ μήτηρ σου καὶ οἱ ἀδελφοί σου
to him : The mother of thee and the brothers of thee

ἑστήκασιν ἔξω ἰδεῖν θέλοντές σε. 21 ὁ δὲ
are standing outside ²to see ¹wishing thee.   But he

ἀποκριθεὶς εἶπεν πρὸς αὐτούς· μήτηρ μου
answering   said to them : Mother of me

καὶ ἀδελφοί μου οὗτοί εἰσιν οἱ τὸν λόγον
and brothers of me ²these ¹are ³the [ones] ⁷the ⁸word

τοῦ θεοῦ ἀκούοντες καὶ ποιοῦντες.
– ⁵of God ⁴hearing   and ⁶doing.

22 Ἐγένετο δὲ ἐν μιᾷ τῶν ἡμερῶν καὶ
And it came to pass on one of the days   and

αὐτὸς ἐνέβη εἰς πλοῖον καὶ οἱ μαθηταὶ
he   embarked in a boat and the disciples

αὐτοῦ, καὶ εἶπεν πρὸς αὐτούς· διέλθωμεν
of him, and he said to   them; Let us go over

εἰς τὸ πέραν τῆς λίμνης· καὶ ἀνήχθησαν.
to the other side of the lake;   and they put to sea.

23 πλεόντων δὲ αὐτῶν ἀφύπνωσεν. καὶ
And sailing   them⁰ he fell asleep. And
= as they sailed

κατέβη λαῖλαψ ἀνέμου εἰς τὴν λίμνην, καὶ
came down a storm of wind to the   lake,   and

συνεπληροῦντο καὶ ἐκινδύνευον. 24 προσ-
they were filling up and were in danger.   ap-

ελθόντες δὲ διήγειραν αὐτὸν λέγοντες·
proaching And they awaken him   saying :

ἐπιστάτα ἐπιστάτα, ἀπολλύμεθα. ὁ δὲ
Master[,]   Master, we are perishing. But he

διεγερθεὶς ἐπετίμησεν τῷ ἀνέμῳ καὶ τῷ
being awakened rebuked the wind   and the

κλύδωνι τοῦ ὕδατος· καὶ ἐπαύσαντο, καὶ ἐγένετο
roughness of the water; and they ceased, and there was

γαλήνη. 25 εἶπεν δὲ αὐτοῖς· ποῦ ἡ πίστις ὑμῶν;
a calm.   Then he said to them: Where the faith of you?

φοβηθέντες δὲ ἐθαύμασαν, λέγοντες πρὸς
And fearing   they marvelled, saying   to

ἀλλήλους· τίς ἄρα οὗτός ἐστιν, ὅτι καὶ
one another : Who then ²this man ¹is,   that ²even

τοῖς ἀνέμοις ἐπιτάσσει καὶ τῷ ὕδατι, καὶ
³the ⁴winds ⁵he commands and the water,   and

195

King James Version

26 And they arrived at the country of the Gadarenes, which is over against Galilee. 27And when he went forth to land, there met him out of the city a certain man, which had devils long time, and ware no clothes, neither abode in *any* house, but in the tombs. 28 When he saw Jesus, he cried out, and fell down before him, and with a loud voice said, What have I to do with thee, Jesus, *thou* Son of God most high? I beseech thee, torment me not. 29 (For he had commanded the unclean spirit to come out of the man. For oftentimes it had caught him: and he was kept bound with chains and in fetters; and he brake the bands, and was driven of the devil into the wilderness.) 30And Jesus asked him, saying, What is thy name? And he said, Legion: because many devils were entered into him. 31And they besought him that he would not command them to go out into the deep. 32And there was there a herd of many swine feeding on the mountain: and they besought him that he would suffer them to enter into them. And he suffered them. 33 Then went the devils out of the man, and entered into the swine: and the herd ran violently down a steep place into the lake, and were choked. 34 When they that fed *them* saw what was done, they fled, and went and told *it* in the city and in the country. 35 Then they went out to see what was done; and came to Jesus, and found the man, out of whom the devils were departed, sitting at the feet of Jesus, clothed, and in his right mind: and they were afraid. 36 They also which saw *it* told them by what means he that was possessed of the devils was healed.

37 Then the whole multitude of the country of the Gadarenes round about besought him to depart from them; for they were taken with great fear: and he went up into the ship, and returned back again. 38 Now the man, out of whom the devils were departed, besought him that he might be with him: but Jesus sent him away, saying, 39 Return to thine own house, and shew how great things God hath done unto thee. And he went his way, and published throughout the whole city how great things Jesus had done unto him. 40And it came to pass, that, when Jesus was returned, the people *gladly* received him: for they were all waiting for him.

41 And, behold, there came a man named Jairus, and he was a ruler of the synagogue; and he fell down at Jesus' feet, and besought him that he would come into his house: 42 For he had one only daughter, about twelve years of age, and she lay a dying. But as he went the people thronged him.

43 And a woman having an issue of blood twelve years, which had spent all her living upon physicians, neither could be healed of any, 44 Came behind *him*, and touched the border of his garment: and immediately her issue of blood stanched. 45And Jesus said, Who touched me? When all denied, Peter and they that were with him said, Master, the multitude throng thee and press *thee*, and sayest thou, Who touched me?

New International Version

The healing of a demon-possessed man

26 They sailed to the region of the Gerasenes,[e] which is across the lake from Galilee. 27 When Jesus stepped ashore, he was met by a demon-possessed man from the town. For a long time this man had not worn clothes or lived in a house, but had lived in the tombs. 28 When he saw Jesus, he cried out and fell at his feet, shouting at the top of his voice, "What do you want with me, Jesus, Son of the Most High God? I beg you, don't torture me!" 29 For Jesus had commanded the evil [f] spirit to come out of the man. Many times it had seized him, and though he was chained hand and foot and kept under guard, he had broken his chains and had been driven by the demon into solitary places.

30 Jesus asked him, "What is your name?"

"Legion," he replied, because many demons had gone into him. 31And they begged him repeatedly not to order them to go into the Abyss.

32 A herd of many pigs was feeding there on the hillside. The demons begged Jesus to let them go into them, and he gave them permission. 33 When the demons came out of the man, they went into the pigs, and the herd rushed down the steep bank into the lake and was drowned.

34 When those tending the pigs saw what had happened, they ran off and reported this in the town and countryside, 35 and the people went out to see what had happened. When they came to Jesus, they found the man from whom the demons had gone out, sitting at Jesus' feet, dressed and in his right mind; and they were afraid. 36 Those who had seen it told the people how the demon-possessed man had been cured. 37 Then all the people of the region of the Gerasenes[e] asked Jesus to leave them, because they were overcome with fear. So he got into the boat and left.

38 The man from whom the demons had gone out begged to go with him, but Jesus sent him away, saying, 39 "Return home and tell how much God has done for you." So the man went away and told all over town how much Jesus had done for him.

A dead girl and a sick woman

40 Now when Jesus returned, a crowd welcomed him, for they were all expecting him. 41 Just then a man named Jairus, a ruler of the synagogue, came and fell at Jesus' feet, pleading with him to come to his house 42 because his only daughter, a girl of about twelve, was dying.

As Jesus was on his way, the crowds almost crushed him. 43And a woman was there who had been subject to bleeding for twelve years,[g] but no one could heal her. 44 She came up behind him and touched the edge of his cloak, and immediately her bleeding stopped.

45 "Who touched me?" Jesus asked.

When they all denied it, Peter said, "Master, the people are crowding and pressing against you."

---

[e] Some MSS read *Gadarenes;* others read *Gergesenes.* [f] Greek *unclean.* [g] Many MSS add *and she had spent all she had on doctors.*

Greek Interlinear

ὑπακούουσιν αὐτῷ; 26 Καὶ κατέπλευσαν εἰς
they obey him? And they sailed down to

τὴν χώραν τῶν Γερασηνῶν, ἥτις ἐστὶν
the country of the Gerasenes, which is

ἀντιπέρα τῆς Γαλιλαίας. 27 ἐξελθόντι δὲ
opposite - Galilee. And going out
= as he went out

αὐτῷ ἐπὶ τὴν γῆν ὑπήντησεν ἀνήρ τις
him* onto the land met [him] man a certain

ἐκ τῆς πόλεως ἔχων δαιμόνια, καὶ χρόνῳ
out of the city having demons, and 'time

ἱκανῷ οὐκ ἐνεδύσατο ἱμάτιον, καὶ ἐν οἰκίᾳ
'for a con- put not on a garment, and in a house
siderable

οὐκ ἔμενεν ἀλλ' ἐν τοῖς μνήμασιν. 28 ἰδὼν
remained not but among the tombs. seeing

δὲ τὸν Ἰησοῦν ἀνακράξας προσέπεσεν αὐτῷ
And - Jesus crying out he fell prostrate before him

καὶ φωνῇ μεγάλῃ εἶπεν· τί ἐμοὶ καὶ σοί,
and voice in a great(loud) said : What to me and to thee,

Ἰησοῦ υἱὲ τοῦ θεοῦ τοῦ ὑψίστου; δέομαί
Jesus Son - of God - most high? I beg

σου, μή με βασανίσῃς. 29 παρήγγελλεν
of thee, do not me torment. he charged

γὰρ τῷ πνεύματι τῷ ἀκαθάρτῳ ἐξελθεῖν
For the spirit - unclean to come out

ἀπὸ τοῦ ἀνθρώπου. πολλοῖς γὰρ χρόνοις
from the man. For many times

συνηρπάκει αὐτόν, καὶ ἐδεσμεύετο ἁλύσεσιν·
it had seized him, and he was bound with chains

καὶ πέδαις φυλασσόμενος, καὶ διαρήσσων
and fetters being guarded, and tearing asunder

τὰ δεσμὰ ἠλαύνετο ἀπὸ τοῦ δαιμονίου εἰς
the bonds he was driven from(by) the demon into

τὰς ἐρήμους. 30 ἐπηρώτησεν δὲ αὐτὸν ὁ
the deserts. And questioned him -

Ἰησοῦς· τί σοι ὄνομά ἐστιν; ὁ δὲ εἶπεν·
Jesus : What to thee name is?° And he said :

λεγιών, ὅτι εἰσῆλθεν δαιμόνια πολλὰ εἰς
Legion, because ²entered ¹demons ¹many into

αὐτόν. 31 καὶ παρεκάλουν αὐτὸν ἵνα μὴ
him. And they besought him that not

ἐπιτάξῃ αὐτοῖς εἰς τὴν ἄβυσσον ἀπελθεῖν.
he would order them into the abyss to go away.

32 ἦν δὲ ἐκεῖ ἀγέλη χοίρων ἱκανῶν
Now there was there a herd pigs of many

βοσκομένη ἐν τῷ ὄρει· καὶ παρεκάλεσαν
feeding in the mountain; and they besought

αὐτὸν ἵνα ἐπιτρέψῃ αὐτοῖς εἰς ἐκείνους
him that he would allow them into those

εἰσελθεῖν· καὶ ἐπέτρεψεν αὐτοῖς. 33 ἐξελθόντα
to enter; and he allowed them. ⁴coming out

δὲ τὰ δαιμόνια ἀπὸ τοῦ ἀνθρώπου εἰσῆλθον
¹So ³the ²demons from the man entered

εἰς τοὺς χοίρους, καὶ ὥρμησεν ἡ ἀγέλη
into the pigs, and rushed the herd

κατὰ τοῦ κρημνοῦ εἰς τὴν λίμνην καὶ
down the precipice into the lake and

ἀπεπνίγη. 34 ἰδόντες δὲ οἱ βόσκοντες
was choked. And ²seeing ¹the [ones] ³feeding

τὸ γεγονὸς ἔφυγον καὶ ἀπήγγειλαν εἰς
⁴the thing ⁵having fled and reported in
happened
= what had happened

τὴν πόλιν καὶ εἰς τοὺς ἀγρούς. 35 ἐξῆλθον
the city and in the farms. they went out

δὲ ἰδεῖν τὸ γεγονός, καὶ ἦλθον πρὸς τὸν
And to see the thing having and came to -
happened,
= what had happened,

Ἰησοῦν, καὶ εὗρον καθήμενον τὸν ἄνθρωπον
Jesus, and found sitting the man

ἀφ' οὗ τὰ δαιμόνια ἐξῆλθεν ἱματισμένον
from whom the demons went out having been clothed

καὶ σωφρονοῦντα παρὰ τοὺς πόδας τοῦ
and being in his senses by the feet -

Ἰησοῦ, καὶ ἐφοβήθησαν. 36 ἀπήγγειλαν δὲ
of Jesus, and they were afraid. And ²reported

αὐτοῖς οἱ ἰδόντες πῶς ἐσώθη ὁ δαιμο-
⁴to them ¹the [ones] ³seeing ⁴how ⁵was healed ⁶the ⁷demon-

νισθείς. 37 καὶ ἠρώτησεν αὐτὸν ἅπαν τὸ
possessed. And asked him all the

πλῆθος τῆς περιχώρου τῶν Γερασηνῶν
multitude of the neighbourhood of the Gerasenes

ἀπελθεῖν ἀπ' αὐτῶν, ὅτι φόβῳ μεγάλῳ
to go away from them, because fear with a great

συνείχοντο· αὐτὸς δὲ ἐμβὰς εἰς πλοῖον
they were seized; so he embarking in a boat

ὑπέστρεψεν. 38 ἐδεῖτο δὲ αὐτοῦ ὁ ἀνὴρ
returned. And begged of him the man

ἀφ' οὗ ἐξεληλύθει τὰ δαιμόνια εἶναι σὺν
from whom had gone out the demons to be with

αὐτῷ· ἀπέλυσεν δὲ αὐτὸν λέγων· 39 ὑπόστρεφε
him; but he dismissed him saying : Return

εἰς τὸν οἶκόν σου, καὶ διηγοῦ ὅσα σοι
to the house of thee, and relate what ²to thee
things

ἐποίησεν ὁ θεός. καὶ ἀπῆλθεν καθ' ὅλην
¹did - ¹God. And he went away throughout all

τὴν πόλιν κηρύσσων ὅσα ἐποίησεν αὐτῷ
the city proclaiming what things ¹did ²to him

ὁ Ἰησοῦς.
- ¹Jesus.

40 Ἐν δὲ τῷ ὑποστρέφειν τὸν Ἰησοῦν
Now in the to return - Jesus^{be}
= when Jesus returned

ἀπεδέξατο αὐτὸν ὁ ὄχλος· ἦσαν γὰρ
welcomed him the crowd; for they were

πάντες προσδοκῶντες αὐτόν. 41 καὶ ἰδοὺ
all expecting him. And behold

ἦλθεν ἀνὴρ ᾧ ὄνομα Ἰάϊρος, καὶ οὗτος
came a man to whom name Jairus,° and this man

ἄρχων τῆς συναγωγῆς ὑπῆρχεν· καὶ πεσὼν
a ruler of the synagogue was; and falling

παρὰ τοὺς πόδας Ἰησοῦ παρεκάλει αὐτὸν
at the feet of Jesus he besought him

εἰσελθεῖν εἰς τὸν οἶκον αὐτοῦ, 42 ὅτι
to enter into the house of him, because

θυγάτηρ μονογενὴς ἦν αὐτῷ ὡς ἐτῶν
daughter an only born was to him° about of years
= he had an only daughter

δώδεκα καὶ αὐτὴ ἀπέθνησκεν. Ἐν δὲ τῷ
twelve and this(she) was dying. Now in the
= as he went

ὑπάγειν αὐτὸν οἱ ὄχλοι συνέπνιγον αὐτόν.
to go him^{be} the crowds pressed upon him.

43 καὶ γυνὴ οὖσα ἐν ῥύσει αἵματος ἀπὸ
And a woman being in a flow of blood from
= having

ἐτῶν δώδεκα, ἥτις οὐκ ἴσχυσεν ἀπ'
years twelve, who was not able from

οὐδενὸς θεραπευθῆναι, 44 προσελθοῦσα ὄπισθεν
no(any)one to be healed, approaching behind

ἥψατο τοῦ κρασπέδου τοῦ ἱματίου αὐτοῦ,
touched the fringe of the garment of him,

καὶ παραχρῆμα ἔστη ἡ ῥύσις τοῦ αἵματος
and at once stood the flow of the blood

αὐτῆς. 45 καὶ εἶπεν ὁ Ἰησοῦς· τίς ὁ
of her. And said - Jesus : Who the

ἁψάμενός μου; ἀρνουμένων δὲ πάντων
[one] touching me? And denying all*
= when all denied

εἶπεν ὁ Πέτρος· ἐπιστάτα, οἱ ὄχλοι
said - Peter : Master, the crowds

King James Version

46And Jesus said, Somebody hath touched me: for I perceive that virtue is gone out of me. 47And when the woman saw that she was not hid, she came trembling, and falling down before him, she declared unto him before all the people for what cause she had touched him, and how she was healed immediately. 48And he said unto her, Daughter, be of good comfort: thy faith hath made thee whole; go in peace.

49 While he yet spake, there cometh one from the ruler of the synagogue's *house*, saying to him, Thy daughter is dead; trouble not the Master. 50 But when Jesus heard *it*, he answered him, saying, Fear not: believe only, and she shall be made whole. 51And when he came into the house, he suffered no man to go in, save Peter, and James, and John, and the father and the mother of the maiden. 52And all wept, and bewailed her: but he said, Weep not; she is not dead, but sleepeth. 53And they laughed him to scorn, knowing that she was dead. 54And he put them all out, and took her by the hand, and called, saying, Maid, arise. 55And her spirit came again, and she arose straightway: and he commanded to give her meat. 56And her parents were astonished: but he charged them that they should tell no man what was done.

9 Then he called his twelve disciples together, and gave them power and authority over all devils, and to cure diseases. 2And he sent them to preach the kingdom of God, and to heal the sick. 3And he said unto them, Take nothing for *your* journey, neither staves, nor scrip, neither bread, neither money; neither have two coats apiece. 4And whatsoever house ye enter into, there abide, and thence depart. 5And whosoever will not receive you, when ye go out of that city, shake off the very dust from your feet for a testimony against them. 6And they departed, and went through the towns, preaching the gospel, and healing every where.

7 Now Herod the tetrarch heard of all that was done by him: and he was perplexed, because that it was said of some, that John was risen from the dead; 8And of some, that Elias had appeared; and of others, that one of the old prophets was risen again. 9And Herod said, John have I beheaded; but who is this, of whom I hear such things? And he desired to see him.

10 And the apostles, when they were returned, told him all that they had done. And he took them, and went aside privately into a desert place belonging to the city called Bethsaida. 11And the people, when they knew *it*, followed him: and he received them, and spake unto them of the kingdom of God, and healed them that had need of healing. 12And when the day began to wear away, then came the twelve, and said unto him, Send the multitude away, that they

New International Version

46 But Jesus said, "Someone touched me; I know that power has gone out from me."

47 Then the woman, seeing that she could not go unnoticed, came trembling and fell at his feet. In the presence of all the people, she told why she had touched him and how she had been instantly healed. 48 Then he said to her, "Daughter, your faith has healed you. Go in peace."

49 While Jesus was still speaking, someone came from the house of Jairus, the synagogue ruler. "Your daughter is dead," he said. "Don't bother the teacher any more."

50 Hearing this, Jesus said to Jairus, "Don't be afraid; just believe, and she will be healed."

51 When he arrived at the house of Jairus, he did not let anyone go in with him except Peter, John and James, and the child's father and mother. 52 Meanwhile, all the people were wailing and mourning for her. "Stop wailing," Jesus said. "She is not dead but asleep."

53 They laughed at him, knowing that she was dead. 54 But he took her by the hand and said, "My child, get up!" 55 Her spirit returned, and at once she stood up. Then Jesus told them to give her something to eat. 56 Her parents were astonished, but he ordered them not to tell anyone what had happened.

Jesus sends out the Twelve

9 When Jesus had called the Twelve together, he gave them power and authority to drive out all demons and to cure diseases, 2 and he sent them out to preach the kingdom of God and to heal the sick. 3 He told them: "Take nothing for the journey—no staff, no bag, no bread, no money, no extra tunic. 4 Whatever house you enter, stay there until you leave that town. 5 If people do not welcome you, shake the dust off your feet when you leave their town, as a testimony against them." 6 So they set out and went from village to village, preaching the gospel and healing people everywhere.

7 Now Herod the tetrarch heard about all that was going on. And he was perplexed, because some were saying that John had been raised from the dead, 8 others that Elijah had appeared, and still others that one of the prophets of long ago had come back to life. 9 But Herod said, "I beheaded John. Who, then, is this I hear such things about?" And he tried to see him.

Jesus feeds the five thousand

10 When the apostles returned, they reported to Jesus what they had done. Then he took them with him and they withdrew by themselves to a town called Bethsaida, 11 but the crowds learned about it and followed him. He welcomed them and spoke to them about the kingdom of God, and healed those who needed healing.

12 Late in the afternoon the Twelve came to him and said, "Send the crowd away so they can go to the surrounding villages and country-

Greek Interlinear

συνέχουσίν σε καὶ ἀποθλίβουσιν. **46** ὁ δὲ
press upon thee and jostle.   - But

Ἰησοῦς εἶπεν· ἥψατό μού τις· ἐγὼ γὰρ
Jesus said: Touched me someone; for I

ἔγνων δύναμιν ἐξεληλυθυῖαν ἀπ' ἐμοῦ.
knew power having gone forth from me.

47 ἰδοῦσα δὲ ἡ γυνὴ ὅτι οὐκ ἔλαθεν,
And ³seeing ¹the ²woman that she was not hidden,

τρέμουσα ἦλθεν καὶ προσπεσοῦσα αὐτῷ δι'
trembling came and prostrating before him ⁸for

ἦν αἰτίαν ἥψατο αὐτοῦ ἀπήγγειλεν ἐνώπιον
⁷what ⁸cause ⁹she touched ¹⁰him ¹declared ²before

παντὸς τοῦ λαοῦ, καὶ ὡς ἰάθη παραχρῆμα.
³all ⁴the ⁵people, and how she was cured at once.

48 ὁ δὲ εἶπεν αὐτῇ· θυγάτηρ, ἡ πίστις
And he said to her: Daughter, the faith

σου σέσωκέν σε· πορεύου εἰς εἰρήνην.
of thee has healed thee; go in peace.

49 Ἔτι αὐτοῦ λαλοῦντος ἔρχεταί τις παρὰ
Yet him speaking² comes someone from
= While he was yet speaking

τοῦ ἀρχισυναγώγου λέγων ὅτι τέθνηκεν
the synagogue ruler saying[,] - Has died

ἡ θυγάτηρ σου· μηκέτι σκύλλε τὸν
the daughter of thee; no more trouble the

διδάσκαλον. **50** ὁ δὲ Ἰησοῦς ἀκούσας
teacher. - But Jesus hearing

ἀπεκρίθη αὐτῷ· μὴ φοβοῦ· μόνον πίστευσον,
answered him: Fear thou not; only believe,

καὶ σωθήσεται. **51** ἐλθὼν δὲ εἰς τὴν
and she will be healed. And coming into the

οἰκίαν οὐκ ἀφῆκεν εἰσελθεῖν τινα σὺν
house he allowed not to enter anyone with

αὐτῷ εἰ μὴ Πέτρον καὶ Ἰωάννην καὶ
him except Peter and John and

Ἰάκωβον καὶ τὸν πατέρα τῆς παιδὸς καὶ
James and the father of the maid and

τὴν μητέρα. **52** ἔκλαιον δὲ πάντες καὶ
the mother. And were weeping all and

ἐκόπτοντο αὐτήν. ὁ δὲ εἶπεν· μὴ κλαίετε·
bewailing her. But he said: Weep ye not;

οὐκ ἀπέθανεν ἀλλὰ καθεύδει. **53** καὶ
she did not die but sleeps. And

κατεγέλων αὐτοῦ, εἰδότες ὅτι ἀπέθανεν.
they ridiculed him, knowing that she died.

54 αὐτὸς δὲ κρατήσας τῆς χειρὸς αὐτῆς
But he holding the hand of her

ἐφώνησεν λέγων· ἡ παῖς, ἔγειρε. **55** καὶ
called saying: - Maid, arise. And

ἐπέστρεψεν τὸ πνεῦμα αὐτῆς, καὶ ἀνέστη
returned the spirit of her, and she rose up

παραχρῆμα, καὶ διέταξεν αὐτῇ δοθῆναι
at once, and he commanded ²to her ¹to be given

φαγεῖν. **56** καὶ ἐξέστησαν οἱ γονεῖς
to eat. And were amazed the parents

αὐτῆς· ὁ δὲ παρήγγειλεν αὐτοῖς μηδενὶ
of her; but he enjoined them ²no one

εἰπεῖν τὸ γεγονός.
¹to tell the thing having happened.
= what had happened.

Chapter 9

Συγκαλεσάμενος δὲ τοὺς δώδεκα ἔδωκεν
And having called together the twelve he gave

αὐτοῖς δύναμιν καὶ ἐξουσίαν ἐπὶ πάντα τὰ
them power and authority over all the

δαιμόνια καὶ νόσους θεραπεύειν· **2** καὶ
demons and diseases to heal; and

ἀπέστειλεν αὐτοὺς κηρύσσειν τὴν βασιλείαν
sent them to proclaim the kingdom

τοῦ θεοῦ καὶ ἰᾶσθαι, **3** καὶ εἶπεν πρὸς
- of God and to cure, and said to

αὐτούς· μηδὲν αἴρετε εἰς τὴν ὁδόν, μήτε
them: Nothing take ye for the way, neither

ῥάβδον μήτε πήραν μήτε ἄρτον μήτε
staff nor wallet nor bread nor

ἀργύριον μήτε ἀνὰ δύο χιτῶνας ἔχειν.
silver nor each two tunics to have.

4 καὶ εἰς ἣν ἂν οἰκίαν εἰσέλθητε, ἐκεῖ
And into whatever house ye may enter, there

μένετε καὶ ἐκεῖθεν ἐξέρχεσθε. **5** καὶ
remain and thence go forth. And

ὅσοι ἂν μὴ δέχωνται ὑμᾶς, ἐξερχόμενοι
as many as may not receive you, going forth

ἀπὸ τῆς πόλεως ἐκείνης τὸν κονιορτὸν
from - city that the dust

ἀπὸ τῶν ποδῶν ὑμῶν ἀποτινάσσετε εἰς
from the feet of you shake off for

μαρτύριον ἐπ' αὐτούς. **6** ἐξερχόμενοι δὲ
a testimony against them. And going forth

διήρχοντο κατὰ τὰς κώμας εὐαγγελιζόμενοι
they went throughout the villages evangelizing
through

καὶ θεραπεύοντες πανταχοῦ. **7** Ἤκουσεν
and healing everywhere. ⁴heard

δὲ Ἡρώδης ὁ τετραάρχης τὰ γινόμενα
¹And ²Herod ³the ⁴tetrarch the things happening

πάντα, καὶ διηπόρει διὰ τὸ λέγεσθαι
all, and was in perplexity because of the to be said
= because it was said

ὑπό τινων ὅτι Ἰωάννης ἠγέρθη ἐκ νεκρῶν,
by some that John was raised from [the] dead,

8 ὑπό τινων δὲ ὅτι Ἠλίας ἐφάνη, ἄλλων
and by some that Elias appeared, ²others

δὲ ὅτι προφήτης τις τῶν ἀρχαίων ἀνέστη.
¹but that prophet a certain of the ancients rose again.

9 εἶπεν δὲ [ὁ] Ἡρώδης· Ἰωάννην ἐγὼ
But said - Herod: John I

ἀπεκεφάλισα· τίς δέ ἐστιν οὗτος περὶ οὗ
beheaded; but who is this about whom

ἀκούω τοιαῦτα; καὶ ἐζήτει ἰδεῖν αὐτόν.
I hear such things? And he sought to see him.

10 Καὶ ὑποστρέψαντες οἱ ἀπόστολοι
And having returned the apostles

διηγήσαντο αὐτῷ ὅσα ἐποίησαν. Καὶ
narrated to him what things they did. And

παραλαβὼν αὐτοὺς ὑπεχώρησεν κατ' ἰδίαν
taking them he departed privately

εἰς πόλιν καλουμένην Βηθσαϊδά. **11** οἱ δὲ
to a city being called Bethsaida. But the

ὄχλοι γνόντες ἠκολούθησαν αὐτῷ· καὶ
crowds knowing followed him; and

ἀποδεξάμενος αὐτοὺς ἐλάλει αὐτοῖς περὶ
welcoming them he spoke to them about

τῆς βασιλείας τοῦ θεοῦ, καὶ τοὺς χρείαν
the kingdom - of God, and the [ones] ²need

ἔχοντας θεραπείας ἰᾶτο. **12** Ἡ δὲ ἡμέρα
¹having of healing he cured. But the day

ἤρξατο κλίνειν· προσελθόντες δὲ οἱ δώδεκα
began to decline; and approaching the twelve

εἶπαν αὐτῷ· ἀπόλυσον τὸν ὄχλον, ἵνα
said to him: Dismiss the crowd, that

King James Version

may go into the towns and country round about, and lodge, and get victuals: for we are here in a desert place. 13 But he said unto them, Give ye them to eat. And they said, We have no more but five loaves and two fishes; except we should go and buy meat for all this people. 14 For they were about five thousand men. And he said to his disciples, Make them sit down by fifties in a company. 15And they did so, and made them all sit down. 16 Then he took the five loaves and the two fishes, and looking up to heaven, he blessed them, and brake, and gave to the disciples to set before the multitude. 17And they did eat, and were all filled: and there was taken up of fragments that remained to them twelve baskets.

18 And it came to pass, as he was alone praying, his disciples were with him; and he asked them, saying, Whom say the people that I am? 19 They answering said, John the Baptist; but some say, Elias; and others say, that one of the old prophets is risen again. 20 He said unto them, But whom say ye that I am? Peter answering said, The Christ of God. 21And he straitly charged them, and commanded them to tell no man that thing; 22 Saying, The Son of man must suffer many things, and be rejected of the elders and chief priests and scribes, and be slain, and be raised the third day.

23 And he said to them all, If any man will come after me, let him deny himself, and take up his cross daily, and follow me. 24 For whosoever will save his life shall lose it: but whosoever will lose his life for my sake, the same shall save it. 25 For what is a man advantaged, if he gain the whole world, and lose himself, or be cast away? 26 For whosoever shall be ashamed of me and of my words, of him shall the Son of man be ashamed, when he shall come in his own glory, and in his Father's, and of the holy angels. 27 But I tell you of a truth, there be some standing here, which shall not taste of death, till they see the kingdom of God.

28 And it came to pass about an eight days after these sayings, he took Peter and John and James, and went into a mountain to pray. 29And as he prayed, the fashion of his countenance was altered, and his raiment was white and glistering. 30And, behold, there talked with him two men, which were Moses and Elias: 31 Who appeared in glory, and spake of his decease which he should accomplish at Jerusalem. 32 But Peter and they that were with him were heavy with sleep: and when they were awake, they saw his glory, and the two men that stood with him. 33And it came to pass, as they

New International Version

side and find food and lodging, because we are in a remote place here."

13 He replied, "You give them something to eat."

They answered, "We have only five loaves of bread and two fish—unless we go and buy food for all this crowd." 14 (About five thousand men were there.)

But he said to his disciples, "Have them sit down in groups of about fifty each." 15 The disciples did so, and everybody sat down. 16 Taking the five loaves and the two fish and looking up to heaven, he gave thanks and broke them. Then he gave them to the disciples to set before the people. 17 They all ate and were satisfied, and the disciples picked up twelve basketfuls of broken pieces that were left over.

Peter's confession of Christ

18 Once when Jesus was praying in private and his disciples were with him, he asked them, "Who do the crowds say I am?"

19 They replied, "Some say John the Baptist; others say Elijah; and still others, that one of the prophets of long ago has come back to life."

20 "But what about you?" he asked. "Who do you say I am?"

Peter answered, "The Christ[h] of God."

21 Jesus strictly warned them not to tell this to anyone. 22And he said, "The Son of Man must suffer many things and be rejected by the elders, chief priests and teachers of the law, and he must be killed and on the third day be raised to life."

23 Then he said to them all: "If anyone would come after me, he must deny himself and take up his cross daily and follow me. 24 For whoever wants to save his life will lose it, but whoever loses his life for me will save it. 25 What good is it for a man to gain the whole world, and yet lose or forfeit his very self? 26 If anyone is ashamed of me and my words, the Son of Man will be ashamed of him when he comes in his glory and in the glory of the Father and of the holy angels. 27 I tell you the truth, some who are standing here will not taste death before they see the kingdom of God."

The transfiguration

28 About eight days after Jesus said this, he took Peter, John and James with him and went up onto a mountain to pray. 29As he was praying, the appearance of his face changed, and his clothes became as bright as a flash of lightning. 30 Two men, Moses and Elijah, 31 appeared in glorious splendor, talking with Jesus. They spoke about his departure, which he was about to bring to fulfillment at Jerusalem. 32 Peter and his companions were very sleepy, but when they became fully awake, they saw his glory and the two men standing with him. 33As the men were

[h] Or Messiah.

Greek Interlinear

πορευθέντες εἰς τὰς κύκλω κώμας καὶ
going to ¹the ²around ³villages ²and

ἀγροὺς καταλύσωσιν καὶ εὕρωσιν ἐπισιτισμόν,
⁴farms they may lodge and may find provisions,

ὅτι ὧδε ἐν ἐρήμῳ τόπῳ ἐσμέν. 13 εἶπεν
because here in a desert place we are. he said

δὲ πρὸς αὐτούς· δότε αὐτοῖς φαγεῖν
And to them : ¹Give ²them ³to eat

ὑμεῖς. οἱ δὲ εἶπαν· οὐκ εἰσὶν ἡμῖν
⁴ye. But they said : There are not to us
=We have not

πλεῖον ἢ ἄρτοι πέντε καὶ ἰχθύες δύο, εἰ
more than loaves five and fishes two, un-

μήτι πορευθέντες ἡμεῖς ἀγοράσωμεν εἰς
less going we may buy for

πάντα τὸν λαὸν τοῦτον βρώματα. 14 ἦσαν
all - people this foods. there were

γὰρ ὡσεὶ ἄνδρες πεντακισχίλιοι. εἶπεν δὲ
For about men five thousand. And he said

πρὸς τοὺς μαθητὰς αὐτοῦ· κατακλίνατε
to the disciples of him : ¹Make ²to recline

αὐτοὺς κλισίας ὡσεὶ ἀνὰ πεντήκοντα.
³them [in] groups ¹about ²each ⁴fifty.

15 καὶ ἐποίησαν οὕτως καὶ κατέκλιναν
And they did so and made to recline

ἅπαντας. 16 λαβὼν δὲ τοὺς πέντε ἄρτους
all. And taking the five loaves

καὶ τοὺς δύο ἰχθύας, ἀναβλέψας εἰς τὸν
and the two fishes, looking up to -

οὐρανὸν εὐλόγησεν αὐτοὺς καὶ κατέκλασεν,
heaven he blessed them and broke,

καὶ ἐδίδου τοῖς μαθηταῖς παραθεῖναι τῷ
and gave to the disciples to set before the

ὄχλῳ. 17 καὶ ἔφαγον καὶ ἐχορτάσθησαν
crowd. And they ate and were satisfied

πάντες· καὶ ἤρθη τὸ περισσεῦσαν αὐτοῖς
all; and were taken the excess to them

κλασμάτων κόφινοι δώδεκα.
of fragments baskets twelve.

18 Καὶ ἐγένετο ἐν τῷ εἶναι αὐτὸν
And it came to pass in the to be him
= as he was

προσευχόμενον κατὰ μόνας συνῆσαν αὐτῷ
praying alone were with him

οἱ μαθηταί, καὶ ἐπηρώτησεν αὐτοὺς λέγων·
the disciples, and he questioned them saying :

τίνα με οἱ ὄχλοι λέγουσιν εἶναι; 19 οἱ δὲ
Whom me the crowds say to be? And they
= Whom do the crowds say that I am?

ἀποκριθέντες εἶπαν· Ἰωάννην τὸν βαπτιστήν,
answering said : John the Baptist,

ἄλλοι δὲ Ἠλίαν, ἄλλοι δὲ ὅτι προφήτης
but others Elias, and others that prophet

τις τῶν ἀρχαίων ἀνέστη. 20 εἶπεν δὲ
a certain of the ancients rose again. And he said

αὐτοῖς· ὑμεῖς δὲ τίνα με λέγετε εἶναι;
to them : But ye whom me say to be?
= whom say ye that I am?

Πέτρος δὲ ἀποκριθεὶς εἶπεν· τὸν χριστὸν
And Peter answering said : The Christ

τοῦ θεοῦ. 21 ὁ δὲ ἐπιτιμήσας αὐτοῖς
- of God. But he warning ³them

παρήγγειλεν μηδενὶ λέγειν τοῦτο, 22 εἰπὼν
¹charged ⁴no one ⁵to tell ⁶this, saying

ὅτι δεῖ τὸν υἱὸν τοῦ ἀνθρώπου πολλὰ
that it behoves the Son - of man many things

παθεῖν καὶ ἀποδοκιμασθῆναι ἀπὸ τῶν
to suffer and to be rejected from(by) the

πρεσβυτέρων καὶ ἀρχιερέων καὶ γραμματέων
elders and chief priests and scribes

καὶ ἀποκτανθῆναι καὶ τῇ τρίτῃ ἡμέρᾳ
and to be killed and on the third day

ἐγερθῆναι. 23 Ἔλεγεν δὲ πρὸς πάντας·
to be raised. And he said to all :

εἴ τις θέλει ὀπίσω μου ἔρχεσθαι, ἀρνησάσθω
If anyone wishes after me to come, let him deny

ἑαυτὸν καὶ ἀράτω τὸν σταυρὸν
himself and take the cross

αὐτοῦ καθ᾽ ἡμέραν, καὶ ἀκολουθείτω μοι.
of him daily, and let him follow me.

24 ὃς γὰρ ἐὰν θέλῃ τὴν ψυχὴν αὐτοῦ
For whoever wishes the life of him

σῶσαι, ἀπολέσει αὐτήν· ὃς δ᾽ ἂν ἀπολέσῃ
to save, he will lose it; but whoever loses

τὴν ψυχὴν αὐτοῦ ἕνεκεν ἐμοῦ, οὗτος
the life of him for the sake of me, this [one]

σώσει αὐτήν. 25 τί γὰρ ὠφελεῖται
will save it. For what is profited

ἄνθρωπος κερδήσας τὸν κόσμον ὅλον ἑαυτὸν
a man gaining the world whole ³himself

δὲ ἀπολέσας ἢ ζημιωθείς; 26 ὃς γὰρ ἂν
¹but ²losing or suffering loss? For whoever

ἐπαισχυνθῇ με καὶ τοὺς ἐμοὺς λόγους,
is ashamed of me and - my words,

τοῦτον ὁ υἱὸς τοῦ ἀνθρώπου ἐπαι-
this [one] the Son - of man will be

σχυνθήσεται, ὅταν ἔλθῃ ἐν τῇ δόξῃ
ashamed of, when he comes in the glory

αὐτοῦ καὶ τοῦ πατρὸς καὶ τῶν ἁγίων
of him and of the Father and of the holy

ἀγγέλων. 27 λέγω δὲ ὑμῖν ἀληθῶς,
angels. But I tell you truly,

εἰσίν τινες τῶν αὐτοῦ ἑστηκότων οἳ
there are some of the [ones] here standing who

οὐ μὴ γεύσωνται θανάτου ἕως ἂν ἴδωσιν
by no means may taste of death until they see

τὴν βασιλείαν τοῦ θεοῦ.
the kingdom - of God.

28 Ἐγένετο δὲ μετὰ τοὺς λόγους τούτους
And it came to pass ⁴after - ¹sayings ²these

ὡσεὶ ἡμέραι ὀκτώ, καὶ παραλαβὼν Πέτρον
¹about ³days ²eight, and taking Peter

καὶ Ἰωάννην καὶ Ἰάκωβον ἀνέβη εἰς τὸ
and John and James he went up into the

ὄρος προσεύξασθαι. 29 καὶ ἐγένετο ἐν τῷ
mountain to pray. And ³became in the
= as ¹he ²prayed

προσεύχεσθαι αὐτὸν τὸ εἶδος τοῦ προσώπου
to pray him ⁴the ⁵appearance ⁶of the ⁷face

αὐτοῦ ἕτερον καὶ ὁ ἱματισμὸς αὐτοῦ
⁸of him ¹⁰different and the raiment of him

λευκὸς ἐξαστράπτων. 30 καὶ ἰδοὺ ἄνδρες
⁹white ¹gleaming. And[,] behold[,] men

δύο συνελάλουν αὐτῷ, οἵτινες ἦσαν Μωϋσῆς
two conversed with him, who were Moses

καὶ Ἠλίας, 31 οἳ ὀφθέντες ἐν δόξῃ ἔλεγον
and Elias, who appearing in glory spoke of

τὴν ἔξοδον αὐτοῦ, ἣν ἤμελλεν πληροῦν
the exodus of him, which he was about to accomplish

ἐν Ἱερουσαλήμ. 32 ὁ δὲ Πέτρος καὶ οἱ
in Jerusalem. - But Peter and the [ones]

σὺν αὐτῷ ἦσαν βεβαρημένοι ὕπνῳ· δια-
with him were having been burdened with sleep; ¹wak-

γρηγορήσαντες δὲ εἶδαν τὴν δόξαν αὐτοῦ
ing thoroughly ²but they saw the glory of him

καὶ τοὺς δύο ἄνδρας τοὺς συνεστῶτας
and the two men the standing with

αὐτῷ. 33 καὶ ἐγένετο ἐν τῷ διαχωρίζεσθαι
him. And it came to pass in the to part
= when they parted

201

King James Version

departed from him, Peter said unto Jesus, Master, it is good for us to be here: and let us make three tabernacles; one for thee, and one for Moses, and one for Elias: not knowing what he said. 34 While he thus spake, there came a cloud, and overshadowed them: and they feared as they entered into the cloud. 35And there came a voice out of the cloud, saying, This is my beloved Son: hear him. 36And when the voice was past, Jesus was found alone. And they kept *it* close, and told no man in those days any of those things which they had seen.

37 And it came to pass, that on the next day, when they were come down from the hill, much people met him. 38And, behold, a man of the company cried out, saying, Master, I beseech thee, look upon my son; for he is mine only child. 39And, lo, a spirit taketh him, and he suddenly crieth out; and it teareth him that he foameth again, and bruising him, hardly departeth from him. 40And I besought thy disciples to cast him out; and they could not. 41And Jesus answering said, O faithless and perverse generation, how long shall I be with you, and suffer you? Bring thy son hither. 42And as he was yet a coming, the devil threw him down, and tare *him*. And Jesus rebuked the unclean spirit, and healed the child, and delivered him again to his father.

43 And they were all amazed at the mighty power of God. But while they wondered every one at all things which Jesus did, he said unto his disciples, 44 Let these sayings sink down into your ears: for the Son of man shall be delivered into the hands of men. 45 But they understood not this saying, and it was hid from them, that they perceived it not: and they feared to ask him of that saying.

46 Then there arose a reasoning among them, which of them should be greatest. 47And Jesus, perceiving the thought of their heart, took a child, and set him by him, 48And said unto them, Whosoever shall receive this child in my name receiveth me; and whosoever shall receive me, receiveth him that sent me: for he that is least among you all, the same shall be great.

49 And John answered and said, Master, we saw one casting out devils in thy name; and we forbade him, because he followeth not with us. 50And Jesus said unto him, Forbid *him* not: for he that is not against us is for us.

51 And it came to pass, when the time was come that he should be received up, he stedfastly set his face to go to Jerusalem, 52And sent messengers before his face: and they went, and entered into a village of the Samaritans, to make ready for him. 53And they did not receive him, because his face was as though he would go to

New International Version

leaving Jesus, Peter said to him, "Master, it is good for us to be here. Let us put up three shelters[i]—one for you, one for Moses and one for Elijah." (He did not know what he was saying.)

34 While he was speaking, a cloud appeared and enveloped them, and they were afraid as they entered the cloud. 35A voice came from the cloud, saying, "This is my Son whom I have chosen; listen to him." 36 When the voice had spoken, they found that Jesus was alone. The disciples kept this to themselves, and told no one at that time what they had seen.

The healing of a boy with an evil spirit

37 The next day, when they came down from the mountain, a large crowd met him. 38A man in the crowd called out, "Teacher, I beg you to look at my son, for he is my only child. 39A spirit seizes him and he suddenly screams; it throws him into convulsions so that he foams at the mouth. It scarcely ever leaves him and is destroying him. 40 I begged your disciples to drive it out, but they could not."

41 "O unbelieving and perverse generation," Jesus replied, "how long shall I stay with you and put up with you? Bring your son here."

42 Even while the boy was coming, the demon threw him to the ground in a convulsion. But Jesus rebuked the evil[j] spirit, healed the boy and gave him back to his father. 43And they were all amazed at the greatness of God.

While everyone was marveling at all that Jesus did, he said to his disciples, 44 "Listen carefully to what I am about to tell you: The Son of Man is going to be betrayed into the hands of men." 45 But they did not understand what this meant. It was hidden from them, so that they did not grasp it, and they were afraid to ask him about it.

Who will be the greatest?

46 An argument started among the disciples as to which of them would be the greatest. 47 Jesus, knowing their thoughts, took a little child and had him stand beside him. 48 Then he said to them, "Whoever welcomes this little child in my name welcomes me; and whoever welcomes me welcomes the one who sent me. For he who is least among you all—he is the greatest."

49 "Master," said John, "we saw a man driving out demons in your name and we tried to stop him, because he is not one of us."

50 "Do not stop him," Jesus said, "for whoever is not against you is for you."

Samaritan opposition

51 As the time approached for him to be taken up to heaven, Jesus resolutely set out for Jerusalem, 52 and he sent messengers on ahead. They went into a Samaritan village to get things ready for him, 53 but the people there did not welcome him, because he was heading for Jerusalem.

Greek Interlinear

αὐτοὺς ἀπ' αὐτοῦ εἶπεν ὁ Πέτρος πρὸς
them[be] from him said - Peter to

τὸν Ἰησοῦν· ἐπιστάτα, καλόν ἐστιν ἡμᾶς,
- Jesus : Master, good it is [for] us

ὧδε εἶναι, καὶ ποιήσωμεν σκηνὰς τρεῖς,
here to be, and let us make tents three,

μίαν σοὶ καὶ μίαν Μωϋσεῖ καὶ μίαν
one for thee and one for Moses and one

Ἠλίᾳ, μὴ εἰδὼς ὃ λέγει. 34 ταῦτα δὲ
for Elias, not knowing what he says. And these things

αὐτοῦ λέγοντος ἐγένετο νεφέλη καὶ
him saying[a] came a cloud and
= while he said these things

ἐπεσκίαζεν αὐτούς· ἐφοβήθησαν δὲ ἐν τῷ
overshadowed them; and they feared in the
= as they entered

εἰσελθεῖν αὐτοὺς εἰς τὴν νεφέλην. 35 καὶ
to enter them[be] into the cloud. And

φωνὴ ἐγένετο ἐκ τῆς νεφέλης λέγουσα·
a voice came out of the cloud saying :

οὗτός ἐστιν ὁ υἱός μου ὁ ἐκλελεγμένος,
This is the Son of me - having been chosen,

αὐτοῦ ἀκούετε, 36 καὶ ἐν τῷ γενέσθαι
him hear ye, and in the to become
= when the voice came

τὴν φωνὴν εὑρέθη Ἰησοῦς μόνος. καὶ
the voice[be] was found Jesus alone. And

αὐτοὶ ἐσίγησαν καὶ οὐδενὶ ἀπήγγειλαν ἐν ἐκείναις
they were silent and to no one reported in those

ταῖς ἡμέραις οὐδὲν ὧν ἑώρακαν.
- days no(any) of [the things] they have
thing which (had) seen.

37 Ἐγένετο δὲ τῇ ἑξῆς ἡμέρᾳ κατελ-
And it came to pass on the following day coming

θόντων αὐτῶν ἀπὸ τοῦ ὄρους συνήντησεν
down them[a] from the mountain met
= as they came down

αὐτῷ ὄχλος πολύς. 38 καὶ ἰδοὺ ἀνὴρ
him crowd a much. And[,] behold[,] a man

ἀπὸ τοῦ ὄχλου ἐβόησεν λέγων· διδάσκαλε,
from the crowd called aloud saying : Teacher,

δέομαί σου ἐπιβλέψαι ἐπὶ τὸν υἱόν μου,
I beg of thee to look at at the son of me,

ὅτι μονογενής μοί ἐστιν, 39 καὶ ἰδοὺ
because only born to me he is, and[,] behold[,]

πνεῦμα λαμβάνει αὐτόν, καὶ ἐξαίφνης
a spirit takes him, and suddenly

κράζει καὶ σπαράσσει αὐτὸν μετὰ ἀφροῦ,
cries out and throws him with foam,

καὶ μόλις ἀποχωρεῖ ἀπ' αὐτοῦ συντρῖβον
and scarcely departs from him bruising

αὐτόν· 40 καὶ ἐδεήθην τῶν μαθητῶν σου
him; and I begged of the disciples of thee

ἵνα ἐκβάλωσιν αὐτό, καὶ οὐκ ἠδυνήθησαν.
that they would expel it, and they were not able.

41 ἀποκριθεὶς δὲ ὁ Ἰησοῦς εἶπεν· ὦ
And answering - Jesus said : O

γενεὰ ἄπιστος καὶ διεστραμμένη, ἕως πότε
generation unbelieving and having been perverted, until when

ἔσομαι πρὸς ὑμᾶς καὶ ἀνέξομαι ὑμῶν;
shall I be with you and endure you?

προσάγαγε ὧδε τὸν υἱόν σου. 42 ἔτι
Bring here the son of thee. yet

δὲ προσερχομένου αὐτοῦ ἔρρηξεν αὐτὸν τὸ
But approaching him[a] tore him the
= But while he was yet approaching

δαιμόνιον καὶ συνεσπάραξεν· ἐπετίμησεν δὲ
demon and threw violently; but [e]rebuked

ὁ Ἰησοῦς τῷ πνεύματι τῷ ἀκαθάρτῳ, καὶ
- [1]Jesus [3]the [2]spirit - [4]unclean, and

ἰάσατο τὸν παῖδα καὶ ἀπέδωκεν αὐτὸν τῷ
cured the boy and restored him to the

πατρὶ αὐτοῦ. 43 ἐξεπλήσσοντο δὲ πάντες
father of him. And were astounded all

ἐπὶ τῇ μεγαλειότητι τοῦ θεοῦ.
at the majesty - of God.

Πάντων δὲ θαυμαζόντων ἐπὶ πᾶσιν οἷς
And all marvelling[a] at all things which
= while all marvelled

ἐποίει εἶπεν πρὸς τοὺς μαθητὰς αὐτοῦ·
he did he said to the disciples of him :

44 θέσθε ὑμεῖς εἰς τὰ ὦτα ὑμῶν τοὺς
Lay ye in the ears of you

λόγους τούτους· ὁ γὰρ υἱὸς τοῦ ἀνθρώπου
sayings these; for the Son - of man

μέλλει παραδίδοσθαι εἰς χεῖρας ἀνθρώπων.
is about to be betrayed into [the] hands of men.

45 οἱ δὲ ἠγνόουν τὸ ῥῆμα τοῦτο, καὶ ἦν
But they knew not - word this, and it was

παρακεκαλυμμένον ἀπ' αὐτῶν ἵνα μὴ
having been veiled from them lest

αἴσθωνται αὐτό, καὶ ἐφοβοῦντο ἐρωτῆσαι
they should perceive it, and they feared to ask

αὐτὸν περὶ τοῦ ῥήματος τούτου. 46 Εἰσῆλθεν
him about - word this. entered

δὲ διαλογισμὸς ἐν αὐτοῖς, τὸ τίς ἂν εἴη
And a debate among them, - who might be
= a debate arose

μείζων αὐτῶν. 47 ὁ δὲ Ἰησοῦς εἰδὼς τὸν
greater(est) of them. - And Jesus knowing the

διαλογισμὸν τῆς καρδίας αὐτῶν, ἐπιλαβόμενος
debate of the heart of them, taking

παιδίον ἔστησεν αὐτὸ παρ' ἑαυτῷ, 48 καὶ
a child stood it(him) beside himself, and

εἶπεν αὐτοῖς· ὃς ἐὰν δέξηται τοῦτο τὸ
said to them : Whoever receives this -

παιδίον ἐπὶ τῷ ὀνόματί μου, ἐμὲ δέχεται·
child on(in) the name of me, me receives;

καὶ ὃς ἂν ἐμὲ δέξηται, δέχεται τὸν
and whoever me receives, receives the [one]

ἀποστείλαντά με· ὁ γὰρ μικρότερος ἐν
having sent me; for [1]the [one] [3]lesser [4]among

πᾶσιν ὑμῖν ὑπάρχων, οὗτός ἐστιν μέγας.
[5]all [2]you being, this [one] is great.

49 Ἀποκριθεὶς δὲ ὁ Ἰωάννης εἶπεν· ἐπιστάτα,
And answering - John said : Master,

εἴδομέν τινα ἐν τῷ ὀνόματί σου ἐκβάλλοντα
we saw someone in the name of thee expelling

δαιμόνια, καὶ ἐκωλύομεν αὐτόν, ὅτι
demons, and we prevented him, because

οὐκ ἀκολουθεῖ μεθ' ἡμῶν. 50 εἶπεν δὲ πρὸς
he does not follow with us. And said to

αὐτὸν Ἰησοῦς· μὴ κωλύετε· ὃς γὰρ οὐκ
him Jesus: Do not prevent; for [he] who not

ἔστιν καθ' ὑμῶν, ὑπὲρ ὑμῶν ἐστιν.
is against you, for you is.

51 Ἐγένετο δὲ ἐν τῷ συμπληροῦσθαι
And it came to pass in the to be fulfilled

τὰς ἡμέρας τῆς ἀναλήμψεως αὐτοῦ καὶ
the days of the assumption of him[be] and
= as the days of his assumption were fulfilled

αὐτὸς τὸ πρόσωπον ἐστήρισεν τοῦ
he the(his) face set -

πορεύεσθαι εἰς Ἰερουσαλήμ, 52 καὶ ἀπέστειλεν
to go[d] to Jerusalem, and sent

ἀγγέλους πρὸ προσώπου αὐτοῦ. καὶ
messengers before face of him. And

πορευθέντες εἰσῆλθον εἰς κώμην Σαμαριτῶν,
going they entered into a village of Samaritans,

ὥστε ἑτοιμάσαι αὐτῷ· 53 καὶ οὐκ ἐδέξαντο
so as to prepare for him; and they did not receive

αὐτόν, ὅτι τὸ πρόσωπον αὐτοῦ ἦν
him, because the face of him was

King James Version

Jerusalem. 54And when his disciples James and John saw *this,* they said, Lord, wilt thou that we command fire to come down from heaven, and consume them, even as Elias did? 55 But he turned, and rebuked them, and said, Ye know not what manner of spirit ye are of. 56 For the Son of man is not come to destroy men's lives, but to save *them.* And they went to another village.

57 And it came to pass, that, as they went in the way, a certain *man* said unto him, Lord, I will follow thee whithersoever thou goest. 58And Jesus said unto him, Foxes have holes, and birds of the air *have* nests; but the Son of man hath not where to lay *his* head. 59And he said unto another, Follow me. But he said, Lord, suffer me first to go and bury my father. 60 Jesus said unto him, Let the dead bury their dead: but go thou and preach the kingdom of God. 61And another also said, Lord, I will follow thee; but let me first go bid them farewell, which are at home at my house. 62And Jesus said unto him, No man, having put his hand to the plough, and looking back, is fit for the kingdom of God.

10 After these things the Lord appointed other seventy also, and sent them two and two before his face into every city and place, whither he himself would come. 2 Therefore said he unto them, The harvest truly *is* great, but the labourers *are* few: pray ye therefore the Lord of the harvest, that he would send forth labourers into his harvest. 3 Go your ways: behold, I send you forth as lambs among wolves. 4 Carry neither purse, nor scrip, nor shoes: and salute no man by the way. 5And into whatsoever house ye enter, first say, Peace *be* to this house. 6And if the son of peace be there, your peace shall rest upon it: if not, it shall turn to you again. 7And in the same house remain, eating and drinking such things as they give: for the labourer is worthy of his hire. Go not from house to house. 8And into whatsoever city ye enter, and they receive you, eat such things as are set before you: 9And heal the sick that are therein, and say unto them, The kingdom of God is come nigh unto you. 10 But into whatsoever city ye enter, and they receive you not, go your ways out into the streets of the same, and say, 11 Even the very dust of your city, which cleaveth on us, we do wipe off against you: notwithstanding, be ye sure of this, that the kingdom of God is come nigh unto you. 12 But I say unto you, that it shall be more tolerable in that day for Sodom, than for that city. 13 Woe unto thee, Chorazin! woe unto thee, Bethsaida! for if the mighty works had been done in Tyre and Sidon, which have been done in you, they had a great

New International Version

54 When the disciples James and John saw this, they asked, "Lord, do you want us to call fire down from heaven to destroy them*k*?" 55 But Jesus turned and rebuked them,*l* 56 and they went to another village.

The cost of following Jesus

57 As they were walking along the road, a man said to him, "I will follow you wherever you go."

58 Jesus replied, "Foxes have holes and birds of the air have nests, but the Son of Man has no place to lay his head."

59 He said to another man, "Follow me."

But the man replied, "Lord, first let me go and bury my father."

60 Jesus said to him, "Let the dead bury their own dead, but you go and proclaim the kingdom of God."

61 Still another said, "I will follow you, Lord; but first let me go back and say good-by to my family."

62 Jesus replied, "No one who puts his hand to the plow and looks back is fit for service in the kingdom of God."

Jesus sends out the seventy-two

10 After this the Lord appointed seventy-two*m* others and sent them two by two ahead of him to every town and place where he was about to go. 2 He told them, "The harvest is plentiful, but the workers are few. Ask the Lord of the harvest, therefore, to send out workers into his harvest field. 3 Go! I am sending you out like lambs among wolves. 4 Do not take a purse or bag or sandals; and do not greet anyone on the road.

5 "When you enter a house, first say, 'Peace to this house.' 6 If a man of peace is there, your peace will rest on him; if not, it will return to you. 7 Stay in that house, eating and drinking whatever they give you, for the worker deserves his wages. Do not move around from house to house.

8 "When you enter a town and are welcomed, eat what is set before you. 9 Heal the sick who are there and tell them, 'The kingdom of God is near you.' 10 But when you enter a town and are not welcomed, go into its streets and say, 11 'Even the dust of your town that sticks to our feet we wipe off against you. Yet be sure of this: The kingdom of God is near.' 12 I tell you, it will be more bearable on that day for Sodom than for that town.

13 "Woe to you, Chorazin! Woe to you, Bethsaida! For if the miracles that were performed in you had been performed in Tyre and Sidon, they

---

[k] Some MSS add *even as Elijah did.* [l] Some MSS add *And he said, "You do not know what kind of spirit you are of, for the Son of Man did not come to destroy men's lives, but to save them."* [m] Some MSS read *seventy.*

πορευόμενον εἰς Ἱερουσαλήμ. 54 ἰδόντες
going to Jerusalem. ⁵seeing

δὲ οἱ μαθηταὶ Ἰάκωβος καὶ Ἰωάννης
And ¹the ²disciples ³James ⁴and ⁵John

εἶπαν· κύριε, θέλεις εἴπωμεν πῦρ κατα-
²said· Lord, wilt thou we may tell fire to come

βῆναι ἀπὸ τοῦ οὐρανοῦ καὶ ἀναλῶσαι
down from - heaven and to destroy

αὐτούς; 55 στραφεὶς δὲ ἐπετίμησεν αὐτοῖς.
them? But turning he rebuked them.

56 καὶ ἐπορεύθησαν εἰς ἑτέραν κώμην.
And they went to another village.

57 Καὶ πορευομένων αὐτῶν ἐν τῇ ὁδῷ
And going them² in the way
▬as they went

εἶπέν τις πρὸς αὐτόν· ἀκολουθήσω σοι
said one to him: I will follow thee

ὅπου ἐὰν ἀπέρχῃ. 58 καὶ εἶπεν αὐτῷ ὁ
wherever thou goest. And said to him -

Ἰησοῦς· αἱ ἀλώπεκες φωλεοὺς ἔχουσιν καὶ
Jesus· The foxes holes have and

τὰ πετεινὰ τοῦ οὐρανοῦ κατασκηνώσεις, ὁ
the birds of heaven nests, ²the

δὲ υἱὸς τοῦ ἀνθρώπου οὐκ ἔχει ποῦ τὴν
¹but Son - of man has not where the(his)

κεφαλὴν κλίνῃ. 59 Εἶπεν δὲ πρὸς ἕτερον·
head he may lay. And he said to another :

ἀκολούθει μοι. ὁ δὲ εἶπεν· ἐπίτρεψόν μοι
Follow me. But he said : Allow me

πρῶτον ἀπελθόντι θάψαι τὸν πατέρα μου.
first going to bury the father of me.

60 εἶπεν δὲ αὐτῷ· ἄφες τοὺς νεκροὺς
But he said to him : Leave the dead

θάψαι τοὺς ἑαυτῶν νεκρούς, σὺ δὲ ἀπελθὼν
to bury the of themselves dead, but thou going
=their own dead,

διάγγελλε τὴν βασιλείαν τοῦ θεοῦ. 61 Εἶπεν
announce the kingdom - of God. said

δὲ καὶ ἕτερος· ἀκολουθήσω σοι, κύριε·
And also another : I will follow thee, Lord ;

πρῶτον δὲ ἐπίτρεψόν μοι ἀποτάξασθαι τοῖς
but first allow me to say farewell to the [ones]

εἰς τὸν οἶκόν μου. 62 εἶπεν δὲ [πρὸς
in the house of me. But said to

αὐτὸν] ὁ Ἰησοῦς· οὐδεὶς ἐπιβαλὼν τὴν
him - Jesus : No one putting on the(his)

χεῖρα ἐπ᾽ ἄροτρον καὶ βλέπων εἰς τὰ
hand on a plough and looking at the things

ὀπίσω εὐθετός ἐστιν τῇ βασιλείᾳ τοῦ θεοῦ.
behind fit is for the kingdom - of God.

Chapter 10

Μετὰ δὲ ταῦτα ἀνέδειξεν ὁ κύριος
Now after these things appointed the Lord

ἑτέρους ἑβδομήκοντα [δύο], καὶ ἀπέστειλεν
others seventy-two, and sent

αὐτοὺς ἀνὰ δύο† πρὸ προσώπου αὐτοῦ εἰς
them two by two† before face of him into

πᾶσαν πόλιν καὶ τόπον οὗ ἤμελλεν αὐτὸς
every city and place where ²was about ¹he

ἔρχεσθαι. 2 ἔλεγεν δὲ πρὸς αὐτούς· ὁ
to come. And he said to them : the

μὲν θερισμὸς πολύς, οἱ δὲ ἐργάται ὀλίγοι·
Indeed harvest much, but the workmen few ;

δεήθητε οὖν τοῦ κυρίου τοῦ θερισμοῦ
beg ye therefore of the Lord of the harvest

ὅπως ἐργάτας ἐκβάλῃ εἰς τὸν θερισμὸν
that workmen he would thrust forth into the harvest

αὐτοῦ. 3 ὑπάγετε· ἰδοὺ ἀποστέλλω ὑμᾶς
of him. Go ye; behold I send you

ὡς ἄρνας ἐν μέσῳ λύκων. 4 μὴ βαστάζετε
as lambs in [the] midst of wolves. Do not carry

βαλλάντιον, μὴ πήραν, μὴ ὑποδήματα· καὶ
a purse, nor a wallet, nor sandals; and

μηδένα κατὰ τὴν ὁδὸν ἀσπάσησθε. 5 εἰς
no one by the way greet. ²into

ἣν δ᾽ ἂν εἰσέλθητε οἰκίαν, πρῶτον λέγετε·
¹And ²whatever ³ye enter ⁴house, first say :

εἰρήνη τῷ οἴκῳ τούτῳ. 6 καὶ ἐὰν ἐκεῖ
Peace - house to this. And if there

ᾖ υἱὸς εἰρήνης, ἐπαναπαήσεται ἐπ᾽ αὐτὸν
there is a son of peace, shall rest on it(?him)

ἡ εἰρήνη ὑμῶν· εἰ δὲ μή γε, ἐφ᾽ ὑμᾶς
the peace of you; otherwise, on you

ἀνακάμψει. 7 ἐν αὐτῇ δὲ τῇ οἰκίᾳ μένετε,
it shall return. ²in ⁴same ¹And ³the ⁴house* remain,

ἔσθοντες καὶ πίνοντες τὰ παρ᾽ αὐτῶν·
eating and drinking the things with them;

ἄξιος γὰρ ὁ ἐργάτης τοῦ μισθοῦ αὐτοῦ.
for worthy [is] the workman of the pay of him.

μὴ μεταβαίνετε ἐξ οἰκίας εἰς οἰκίαν.
Do not remove from house to house.

8 καὶ εἰς ἣν ἂν πόλιν εἰσέρχησθε καὶ
And into whatever city ye enter and

δέχωνται ὑμᾶς, ἐσθίετε τὰ παρατιθέμενα
they receive you, eat the things being set before

ὑμῖν, 9 καὶ θεραπεύετε τοὺς ἐν αὐτῇ
you, and heal the ²in ³it

ἀσθενεῖς, καὶ λέγετε αὐτοῖς· ἤγγικεν ἐφ᾽
¹sick, and tell them : Has drawn near on(to)

ὑμᾶς ἡ βασιλεία τοῦ θεοῦ. 10 καὶ εἰς ἣν δ᾽
you the kingdom - of God. And into what-

ἂν πόλιν εἰσέλθητε καὶ μὴ δέχωνται ὑμᾶς,
ever city ye enter and they do not receive you,

ἐξελθόντες εἰς τὰς πλατείας αὐτῆς εἴπατε·
going forth into the streets of it say :

11 καὶ τὸν κονιορτὸν τὸν κολληθέντα ἡμῖν
Even the dust - adhering to us
=the dust of your city adhering to us, on our feet,

ἐκ τῆς πόλεως ὑμῶν εἰς τοὺς πόδας
of the city of you on the(our) feet

ἀπομασσόμεθα ὑμῖν· πλὴν τοῦτο γινώσκετε,
we shake off to you; nevertheless this know ye,

ὅτι ἤγγικεν ἡ βασιλεία τοῦ θεοῦ. 12 λέγω
that has drawn near the kingdom - of God. I tell

ὑμῖν ὅτι Σοδόμοις ἐν τῇ ἡμέρᾳ ἐκείνῃ
you that for Sodom in - day that

ἀνεκτότερον ἔσται ἢ τῇ πόλει ἐκείνῃ.
more endurable it will be than - city for that.

13 Οὐαί σοι, Χοραζίν, οὐαί σοι, Βηθσαϊδά·
Woe to thee, Chorazin, woe to thee, Bethsaida ;

ὅτι εἰ ἐν Τύρῳ καὶ Σιδῶνι ἐγενήθησαν αἱ
because if in Tyre and Sidon happened the

δυνάμεις αἱ γενόμεναι ἐν ὑμῖν, πάλαι ἂν ἐν
powerful deeds - happening in you, long ago - in

---

* Luke here, and in 2. 38; 10. 21; 12. 12; 13. 31; 24. 13, as
well as in Acts 16. 18; 22. 13, ignores the strict idiomatic construction of αὐτός when in apposition. The words here should
mean " in the house itself " but obviously do mean " in the same
house ". So elsewhere. See note on Luke 2. 38.

King James Version

while ago repented, sitting in sackcloth and ashes. 14 But it shall be more tolerable for Tyre and Sidon at the judgment, than for you. 15And thou, Capernaum, which art exalted to heaven, shalt be thrust down to hell. 16 He that heareth you heareth me; and he that despiseth you despiseth me; and he that despiseth me despiseth him that sent me.

17 And the seventy returned again with joy, saying, Lord, even the devils are subject unto us through thy name. 18And he said unto them, I beheld Satan as lightning fall from heaven. 19 Behold, I give unto you power to tread on serpents and scorpions, and over all the power of the enemy; and nothing shall by any means hurt you. 20 Notwithstanding, in this rejoice not, that the spirits are subject unto you; but rather rejoice, because your names are written in heaven. 21 In that hour Jesus rejoiced in spirit, and said, I thank thee, O Father, Lord of heaven and earth, that thou hast hid these things from the wise and prudent, and hast revealed them unto babes: even so, Father; for so it seemed good in thy sight. 22All things are delivered to me of my Father: and no man knoweth who the Son is, but the Father; and who the Father is, but the Son, and *he* to whom the Son will reveal *him*.

23 And he turned him unto *his* disciples, and said privately, Blessed *are* the eyes which see the things that ye see: 24 For I tell you, that many prophets and kings have desired to see those things which ye see, and have not seen *them;* and to hear those things which ye hear, and have not heard *them.*

25 And, behold, a certain lawyer stood up, and tempted him, saying, Master, what shall I do to inherit eternal life? 26 He said unto him, What is written in the law? how readest thou? 27And he answering said, Thou shalt love the Lord thy God with all thy heart, and with all thy soul, and with all thy strength, and with all thy mind; and thy neighbour as thyself. 28And he said unto him, Thou hast answered right: this do, and thou shalt live. 29 But he, willing to justify himself, said unto Jesus, And who is my neighbour? 30And Jesus answering said, A certain *man* went down from Jerusalem to Jericho, and fell among thieves, which stripped him of his raiment, and wounded *him,* and departed, leaving *him* half dead. 31And by chance there came down a certain priest that way; and when he saw him, he passed by on the other side. 32And likewise a Levite, when he was at the place, came and looked *on him,* and passed by on the other side. 33 But a certain Samaritan, as he journeyed, came where he was; and when he saw him, he had compassion *on him,* 34And went to *him,* and bound up his wounds, pouring in oil and wine, and set him on his own beast, and brought him to an inn, and took care of him. 35And on the morrow when he departed, he took out two pence, and gave *them* to the host, and said unto him, Take care of him: and whatsoever thou spendest more, when I come

New International Version

would have repented long ago, sitting in sackcloth and ashes. 14 But it will be more bearable for Tyre and Sidon at the judgment than for you. 15And you, Capernaum, will you be lifted up to the skies? No, you will go down to the depths.[n]

16 "He who listens to you listens to me; he who rejects you rejects me; but he who rejects me rejects him who sent me."

17 The seventy-two[o] returned with joy and said, "Lord, even the demons submit to us in your name."

18 He replied, "I saw Satan fall like lightning from heaven. 19 I have given you authority to trample on snakes and scorpions, and to overcome all the power of the enemy; nothing will harm you. 20 However, do not rejoice that the spirits submit to you, but rejoice that your names are recorded in heaven."

21 At that time Jesus, full of joy through the Holy Spirit, said, "I praise you, Father, Lord of heaven and earth, because you have hidden these things from the wise and learned, and revealed them to little children. Yes, Father, for this was your good pleasure.

22 "All things have been committed to me by my Father. No one knows who the Son is except the Father, and no one knows who the Father is except the Son and those to whom the Son chooses to reveal him."

23 Then he turned to his disciples and said privately, "Blessed are the eyes that see what you see. 24 For I tell you that many prophets and kings wanted to see what you see but did not see it, and to hear what you hear but did not hear it."

The parable of the good Samaritan

25 On one occasion an expert in the law stood up to test Jesus. "Teacher," he asked, "what must I do to inherit eternal life?"

26 "What is written in the Law?" he replied. "How do you read it?"

27 He answered: " 'Love the Lord your God with all your heart, with all your soul, with all your strength and with all your mind'[p]; and, 'Love your neighbors as yourself.'[q] "

28 "You have answered correctly," Jesus replied. "Do this and you will live."

29 But he wanted to justify himself, so he asked Jesus, "And who is my neighbor?"

30 In reply Jesus said: "A man was going down from Jerusalem to Jericho, when he fell into the hands of robbers. They stripped him of his clothes, beat him and went away, leaving him half dead. 31A priest happened to be going down the same road, and when he saw the man, passed by on the other side. 32 So too, a Levite, when he came to the place and saw him, passed by on the other side. 33 But a Samaritan, as he traveled, came where the man was; and when he saw him, he took pity on him. 34 He went to him and bandaged his wounds, pouring on oil and wine. Then he put the man on his own donkey, took him to an inn and took care of him. 35 The next day he took out two silver coins[r] and gave them to the innkeeper. 'Look after him,' he said, 'and when I return, I will reimburse you for any extra expense you may have.'

[n] Greek *Hades.* [o] Some MSS read *seventy.* [p] Deut 6:5. [q] Lev. 19:18. [r] Greek *two denarii.*

Greek Interlinear

σάκκῳ καὶ σποδῷ καθήμενοι μετενόησαν.
sackcloth and ashes sitting they would have repented.

14 πλὴν Τύρῳ καὶ Σιδῶνι ἀνεκτότερον
Nevertheless for Tyre and Sidon more endurable

ἔσται ἐν τῇ κρίσει ἢ ὑμῖν. **15** καὶ σύ,
it will be in the judgment than for you. And thou,

Καφαρναούμ, μὴ ἕως οὐρανοῦ ὑψωθήσῃ;
Capernaum, not to heaven wast thou lifted?

ἕως τοῦ ᾅδου καταβήσῃ. **16** Ὁ ἀκούων
to - hades thou shalt come down. The [one] hearing

ὑμῶν ἐμοῦ ἀκούει, καὶ ὁ ἀθετῶν ὑμᾶς
you me hears, and the [one] rejecting you

ἐμὲ ἀθετεῖ· ὁ δὲ ἐμὲ ἀθετῶν ἀθετεῖ τὸν
me rejects; and the [one] me rejecting rejects the [one]

ἀποστείλαντά με. **17** Ὑπέστρεψαν δὲ οἱ
having sent me. And returned the

ἑβδομήκοντα [δύο] μετὰ χαρᾶς λέγοντες·
seventy-two with joy saying:

κύριε, καὶ τὰ δαιμόνια ὑποτάσσεται ἡμῖν
Lord, even the demons submits to us

ἐν τῷ ὀνόματί σου. **18** εἶπεν δὲ αὐτοῖς·
in the name of thee. And he said to them:

ἐθεώρουν τὸν σατανᾶν ὡς ἀστραπὴν ἐκ
I beheld - Satan as lightning out of

τοῦ οὐρανοῦ πεσόντα. **19** ἰδοὺ δέδωκα
- heaven fall. Behold I have given

ὑμῖν τὴν ἐξουσίαν τοῦ πατεῖν ἐπάνω
you the authority - to tread[d] on

ὄφεων καὶ σκορπίων, καὶ ἐπὶ πᾶσαν τὴν
serpents and scorpions, and on all the

δύναμιν τοῦ ἐχθροῦ, καὶ οὐδὲν ὑμᾶς οὐ μὴ
power of the enemy, and nothing you by no(any) means

ἀδικήσει. **20** πλὴν ἐν τούτῳ μὴ χαίρετε
shall hurt. Nevertheless in this rejoice not

ὅτι τὰ πνεύματα ὑμῖν ὑποτάσσεται, χαίρετε
that the spirits to you submits, ¹rejoice

δὲ ὅτι τὰ ὀνόματα ὑμῶν ἐγγέγραπται ἐν
¹but that the names of you have been enrolled in

τοῖς οὐρανοῖς. **21** Ἐν αὐτῇ τῇ ὥρᾳ
the heavens. In ²same ¹the hour

ἠγαλλιάσατο τῷ πνεύματι τῷ ἁγίῳ καὶ
he exulted in(?by) the Spirit - Holy and

εἶπεν· ἐξομολογοῦμαί σοι, πάτερ, κύριε
said: I praise thee, Father, Lord

τοῦ οὐρανοῦ καὶ τῆς γῆς, ὅτι ἀπέκρυψας
- of heaven and - of earth, because thou didst hide

ταῦτα ἀπὸ σοφῶν καὶ συνετῶν, καὶ
these things from wise and intelligent [ones], and

ἀπεκάλυψας αὐτὰ νηπίοις· ναί, ὁ πατήρ,
didst reveal them to infants; yes - Father,

ὅτι οὕτως εὐδοκία ἐγένετο ἔμπροσθέν σου.
because thus good pleasure it was before thee.

22 πάντα μοι παρεδόθη ὑπὸ τοῦ πατρός
All things to me were delivered by the Father

μου, καὶ οὐδεὶς γινώσκει τίς ἐστιν ὁ
of me, and no one knows who is the

υἱὸς εἰ μὴ ὁ πατήρ, καὶ τίς ἐστιν ὁ πατὴρ
Son except the Father, and who is the Father

εἰ μὴ ὁ υἱὸς καὶ ᾧ ἐὰν βούληται
except the Son and [he] to whomever wills

ὁ υἱὸς ἀποκαλύψαι. **23** Καὶ στραφεὶς
the Son to reveal [him]. And turning

πρὸς τοὺς μαθητὰς κατ᾽ ἰδίαν εἶπεν·
to the disciples privately he said:

μακάριοι οἱ ὀφθαλμοὶ οἱ βλέποντες ἃ
Blessed the eyes - seeing the things which

βλέπετε. **24** λέγω γὰρ ὑμῖν ὅτι πολλοὶ
ye see. For I tell you that many

προφῆται καὶ βασιλεῖς ἠθέλησαν ἰδεῖν ἃ
prophets and kings desired to see the things which

ὑμεῖς βλέπετε καὶ οὐκ εἶδαν, καὶ ἀκοῦσαι
ye see and did not see, and to hear

ἃ ἀκούετε καὶ οὐκ ἤκουσαν.
the things which ye hear and did not hear.

25 Καὶ ἰδοὺ νομικός τις ἀνέστη
And[,] behold[,] lawyer a certain stood up

ἐκπειράζων αὐτὸν λέγων· διδάσκαλε, τί
tempting him saying: Teacher, what

ποιήσας ζωὴν αἰώνιον κληρονομήσω; **26** ὁ
doing ³life ²eternal ¹I ¹may ²inherit? he

δὲ εἶπεν πρὸς αὐτόν· ἐν τῷ νόμῳ τί
And said to him: In the law what

γέγραπται; πῶς ἀναγινώσκεις; **27** ὁ δὲ
has been written? how readest thou? And he

ἀποκριθεὶς εἶπεν· ἀγαπήσεις κύριον τὸν
answering said: Thou shalt love [the] Lord the

θεόν σου ἐξ ὅλης τῆς καρδίας σου καὶ
God of thee from all the heart of thee and

ἐν ὅλῃ τῇ ψυχῇ σου καὶ ἐν ὅλῃ τῇ
with all the soul of thee and with all the

ἰσχύϊ σου καὶ ἐν ὅλῃ τῇ διανοίᾳ σου,
strength of thee and with all the mind of thee.

καὶ τὸν πλησίον σου ὡς σεαυτόν. **28** εἶπεν
and the neighbour of thee as thyself. he said

δὲ αὐτῷ· ὀρθῶς ἀπεκρίθης· τοῦτο ποίει
And to him: Rightly thou didst answer; this do

καὶ ζήσῃ. **29** ὁ δὲ θέλων δικαιῶσαι ἑαυτὸν
and thou shalt live. But he wishing to justify himself

εἶπεν πρὸς τὸν Ἰησοῦν· καὶ τίς ἐστίν
said to - Jesus: And who is

μου πλησίον; **30** ὑπολαβὼν ὁ Ἰησοῦς
of me neighbour? Taking [him] up - Jesus

εἶπεν· ἄνθρωπός τις κατέβαινεν ἀπὸ
said: A certain man was going down from

Ἰερουσαλὴμ εἰς Ἰεριχώ, καὶ λῃσταῖς
Jerusalem to Jericho, and ²robbers

περιέπεσεν, οἳ καὶ ἐκδύσαντες αὐτὸν καὶ
¹fell in with, who both stripping him and

πληγὰς ἐπιθέντες ἀπῆλθον ἀφέντες ἡμιθανῆ.
³blows ¹laying ²on ⁴[him] went away leaving [him] half dead.

31 κατὰ συγκυρίαν δὲ ἱερεύς τις κατέβαινεν
And by a coincidence a certain priest was going down

ἐν τῇ ὁδῷ ἐκείνῃ, καὶ ἰδὼν αὐτὸν
in - way that, and seeing him

ἀντιπαρῆλθεν. **32** ὁμοίως δὲ καὶ Λευίτης
passed by opposite. And likewise also a Levite

κατὰ τὸν τόπον ἐλθὼν καὶ ἰδὼν
upon the place coming and seeing

ἀντιπαρῆλθεν. **33** Σαμαρίτης δέ τις ὁδεύων
passed by opposite. And a certain Samaritan journeying

ἦλθεν κατ᾽ αὐτὸν καὶ ἰδὼν ἐσπλαγχνίσθη,
came upon him and seeing was filled with pity,

34 καὶ προσελθὼν κατέδησεν τὰ τραύματα
and approaching bound up the wounds

αὐτοῦ ἐπιχέων ἔλαιον καὶ οἶνον, ἐπιβιβάσας
of him pouring on oil and wine, ²placing

δὲ αὐτὸν ἐπὶ τὸ ἴδιον κτῆνος ἤγαγεν
¹and him on the(his) own beast brought

αὐτὸν εἰς πανδοχεῖον καὶ ἐπεμελήθη αὐτοῦ.
him to an inn and cared for him.

35 καὶ ἐπὶ τὴν αὔριον ἐκβαλὼν δύο
And on the morrow taking out two

δηνάρια ἔδωκεν τῷ πανδοχεῖ καὶ εἶπεν·
denarii he gave to the innkeeper and said:

ἐπιμελήθητι αὐτοῦ, καὶ ὅ τι ἂν προσδα-
Care thou for him, and whatever thou spendest

πανήσῃς ἐγὼ ἐν τῷ ἐπανέρχεσθαί με
in addition I in the to return me[be]
=when I return

King James Version

again, I will repay thee. 36 Which now of these three, thinkest thou, was neighbour unto him that fell among the thieves? 37And he said, He that shewed mercy on him. Then said Jesus unto him, Go, and do thou likewise.

38 Now it came to pass, as they went, that he entered into a certain village: and a certain woman named Martha received him into her house. 39And she had a sister called Mary, which also sat at Jesus' feet, and heard his word. 40 But Martha was cumbered about much serving, and came to him, and said, Lord, dost thou not care that my sister hath left me to serve alone? bid her therefore that she help me. 41And Jesus answered and said unto her, Martha, Martha, thou art careful and troubled about many things: 42 But one thing is needful; and Mary hath chosen that good part, which shall not be taken away from her.

11 And it came to pass, that, as he was praying in a certain place, when he ceased, one of his disciples said unto him, Lord, teach us to pray, as John also taught his disciples. 2And he said unto them, When ye pray, say, Our Father which art in heaven, Hallowed be thy name. Thy kingdom come. Thy will be done, as in heaven, so in earth. 3 Give us day by day our daily bread. 4And forgive us our sins; for we also forgive every one that is indebted to us. And lead us not into temptation; but deliver us from evil. 5And he said unto them, Which of you shall have a friend, and shall go unto him at midnight, and say unto him, Friend, lend me three loaves; 6 For a friend of mine in his journey is come to me, and I have nothing to set before him? 7And he from within shall answer and say, Trouble me not: the door is now shut, and my children are with me in bed; I cannot rise and give thee. 8 I say unto you, Though he will not rise and give him, because he is his friend, yet because of his importunity he will rise and give him as many as he needeth. 9And I say unto you, Ask, and it shall be given you; seek, and ye shall find; knock, and it shall be opened unto you. 10 For every one that asketh receiveth; and he that seeketh findeth; and to him that knocketh it shall be opened. 11 If a son shall ask bread of any of you that is a father, will he give him a stone? or if he ask a fish, will he for a fish give him a serpent? 12 Or if he shall ask an egg, will he offer him a scorpion? 13 If ye then, being evil, know how to give good gifts unto your children; how much more shall your heavenly Father give the Holy Spirit to them that ask him?

14 And he was casting out a devil, and it was dumb. And it came to pass, when the devil was

New International Version

36 "Which of these three do you think was a neighbor to the man who fell into the hands of robbers?"

37 The expert in the law replied, "The one who had mercy on him."

Jesus told him, "Go and do likewise."

At the home of Martha and Mary

38 As Jesus and his disciples were on their way, he came to a village where a woman named Martha opened her home to him. 39 She had a sister called Mary, who sat at the Lord's feet listening to what he said. 40 But Martha was distracted by all the preparations that had to be made. She came to him and asked, "Lord, don't you care that my sister has left me to do the work by myself? Tell her to help me!"

41 "Martha, Martha," the Lord answered, "you are worried and upset about many things, 42 but only one thing is needed.ˢ Mary has chosen what is better, and it will not be taken away from her."

Jesus' teaching on prayer

11 One day Jesus was praying in a certain place. When he finished, one of his disciples said to him, "Lord, teach us to pray, just as John taught his disciples."

2 He said to them, "When you pray, say:
'Father,ᵗ
hallowed be your name,
your kingdom come.ᵘ
3 Give us each day our daily bread.
4 Forgive us our sins,
for we also forgive everyone who sins against us.ᵛ
And lead us not into temptation.' ʷ "

5 Then he said to them, "Suppose one of you has a friend, and he goes to him at midnight and says, 'Friend, lend me three loaves of bread, 6 because a friend of mine on a journey has come to me, and I have nothing to set before him.'

7 "Then the one inside answers, 'Don't bother me. The door is already locked, and my children are with me in bed. I can't get up and give you anything.' 8 I tell you, though he will not get up and give him the bread because he is his friend, yet because of the man's persistence he will get up and give him as much as he needs.

9 "So I say to you: Ask and it will be given to you; seek and you will find; knock and the door will be opened to you. 10 For everyone who asks receives; he who seeks finds; and to him who knocks, the door will be opened.

11 "Which of you fathers, if your son asks for a fish, will give him a snake instead? 12 Or if he asks for an egg, will give him a scorpion? 13 If you then, though you are evil, know how to give good gifts to your children, how much more will your Father in heaven give the Holy Spirit to those who ask him!"

Jesus and Beelzebub

14 Jesus was driving out a demon that was mute. When the demon left, the man who had

[s] Or but few things are needed-or only one. [t] Some MSS read Our Father in heaven. [u] Some MSS add May your will be done on earth as it is in heaven. [v] Greek everyone who is indebted to us. [w] Some MSS add but deliver us from the evil one.

Greek Interlinear

ἀποδώσω σοι. 36 τίς τούτων τῶν τριῶν πλησίον
will repay thee.   Who of these — three ⁴neighbour

δοκεῖ σοι γεγονέναι τοῦ ἐμπεσόντος
¹seems it ²to thee ³to have become of the [one] falling into

εἰς τοὺς λῃστάς; 37 ὁ δὲ εἶπεν· ὁ ποιήσας
among the robbers?   And he said : The [one] doing

τὸ ἔλεος μετ᾽ αὐτοῦ. εἶπεν δὲ αὐτῷ ὁ
the mercy with him.   And said to him

'Ιησοῦς· πορεύου καὶ σὺ ποίει ὁμοίως.
Jesus :   Go and thou do likewise.

38 'Εν δὲ τῷ πορεύεσθαι αὐτοὺς αὐτὸς
And in the to go them^be he
      = as they went

εἰσῆλθεν εἰς κώμην τινά· γυνὴ δέ τις
entered into a certain village; and a certain woman

ὀνόματι Μάρθα ὑπεδέξατο αὐτὸν εἰς τὴν
by name Martha received him into the

οἰκίαν. 39 καὶ τῇδε ἦν ἀδελφὴ καλουμένη
house.   And to this was a sister° being called
                              = she had a sister

Μαριάμ, ἣ καὶ παρακαθεσθεῖσα πρὸς τοὺς
Mary, who also sitting beside at the

πόδας τοῦ κυρίου ἤκουεν τὸν λόγον αὐτοῦ.
feet of the Lord heard the word of him.

40 ἡ δὲ Μάρθα περιεσπᾶτο περὶ πολλὴν
— But Martha was distracted about much

διακονίαν· ἐπιστᾶσα δὲ εἶπεν· κύριε, οὐ
serving; and coming upon [him] she said : Lord, not

μέλει σοι ὅτι ἡ ἀδελφή μου μόνην με
matters it to thee that the sister of me ²alone ¹me

κατέλειπεν διακονεῖν; εἰπὸν οὖν αὐτῇ ἵνα
¹left to serve? tell therefore her that

μοι συναντιλάβηται. 41 ἀποκριθεὶς δὲ εἶπεν
²me ¹sne may help.   And answering said

αὐτῇ ὁ κύριος· Μάρθα Μάρθα, μεριμνᾷς
to her the Lord : Martha[.] Martha, thou art anxious

καὶ θορυβάζῃ περὶ πολλά, 42 ὀλίγων δέ
and disturbed about many things, but of few things

ἐστιν χρεία ἢ ἑνός· Μαριὰμ γὰρ τὴν
there is need or of one; for Mary the

ἀγαθὴν μερίδα ἐξελέξατο, ἥτις οὐκ
good part chose, which not

ἀφαιρεθήσεται αὐτῆς.
shall be taken from her.

Chapter 11

Καὶ ἐγένετο ἐν τῷ εἶναι αὐτὸν ἐν
And it came to pass in the to be him^be in
                          = when he was

τόπῳ τινὶ προσευχόμενον, ὡς ἐπαύσατο,
a certain place praying, as he ceased,

εἶπέν τις τῶν μαθητῶν αὐτοῦ πρὸς
said a certain one of the disciples of him to

αὐτόν· κύριε, δίδαξον ἡμᾶς προσεύχεσθαι,
him : Lord, teach us to pray,

καθὼς καὶ 'Ιωάννης ἐδίδαξεν τοὺς μαθητὰς
even as also John taught the disciples

αὐτοῦ. 2 εἶπεν δὲ αὐτοῖς· ὅταν
of him. And he said to them : When

προσεύχησθε, λέγετε· Πάτερ, ἁγιασθήτω τὸ
ye pray, say : Father, let be hallowed the

ὄνομά σου· ἐλθάτω ἡ βασιλεία σου·
name of thee; let come the kingdom of thee;

3 τὸν ἄρτον ἡμῶν τὸν ἐπιούσιον δίδου
the bread of us — belonging to the morrow give

ἡμῖν τὸ καθ᾽ ἡμέραν· 4 καὶ ἄφες ἡμῖν τὰς
us each day†; and forgive us the

ἁμαρτίας ἡμῶν, καὶ γὰρ αὐτοὶ ἀφίομεν
sins of us, for indeed [our]selves we forgive

παντὶ ὀφείλοντι ἡμῖν· καὶ μὴ εἰσενέγκῃς
everyone owing to us; and lead not

ἡμᾶς εἰς πειρασμόν. 5 Καὶ εἶπεν πρὸς
us into temptation. And he said to

αὐτούς· τίς ἐξ ὑμῶν ἕξει φίλον, καὶ
them : Who of you shall have a friend, and

πορεύσεται πρὸς αὐτὸν μεσονυκτίου καὶ
will come to him at midnight and

εἴπῃ αὐτῷ· φίλε, χρῆσόν μοι τρεῖς ἄρτους,
say to him : Friend, lend me three loaves,

6 ἐπειδὴ φίλος μου παρεγένετο ἐξ ὁδοῦ
since a friend of me arrived off a journey

πρός με καὶ οὐκ ἔχω ὃ παραθήσω αὐτῷ·
to me and I have not what I may set before him;

7 κἀκεῖνος ἔσωθεν ἀποκριθεὶς εἴπῃ· μή
and that one within answering may say : Not

μοι κόπους πάρεχε· ἤδη ἡ θύρα κέκλεισται,
me troubles cause; now the door has been shut,

καὶ τὰ παιδία μου μετ᾽ ἐμοῦ εἰς τὴν
and the children of me with me in the

κοίτην εἰσίν· οὐ δύναμαι ἀναστὰς δοῦναί
bed are; I cannot rising up to give

σοι. 8 λέγω ὑμῖν, εἰ καὶ οὐ δώσει
thee. I tell you, if even he will not give

αὐτῷ ἀναστὰς διὰ τὸ εἶναι φίλον αὐτοῦ,
him rising up on account of the to be friend of him,
                    = because he is his friend,

διά γε τὴν ἀναίδειαν αὐτοῦ ἐγερθεὶς
yet on account of the importunity of him rising

δώσει αὐτῷ ὅσων χρῄζει. 9 Κἀγὼ ὑμῖν
he will give him as many as he needs. And I ²you

λέγω, αἰτεῖτε, καὶ δοθήσεται ὑμῖν· ζητεῖτε,
¹tell, ask, and it will be given you; seek,

καὶ εὑρήσετε· κρούετε, καὶ ἀνοιγήσεται
and ye will find; knock, and it will be opened

ὑμῖν. 10 πᾶς γὰρ ὁ αἰτῶν λαμβάνει, καὶ
to you. For everyone asking receives, and

ὁ ζητῶν εὑρίσκει, καὶ τῷ κρούοντι
the [one] seeking finds, and to the [one] knocking

ἀνοιγήσεται. 11 τίνα δὲ ἐξ ὑμῶν τὸν
it will be opened. And ¹what ⁴of ²you —

πατέρα αἰτήσει ὁ υἱὸς ἰχθύν, μὴ
¹father ³[is there] ⁶[of whom] ⁷will ask ⁵the ⁸son ¹⁰a fish, not

ἀντὶ ἰχθύος ὄφιν αὐτῷ ἐπιδώσει; 12 ἢ
instead of a fish ²a serpent ¹to him ¹will hand? or

καὶ αἰτήσει ᾠόν, ἐπιδώσει αὐτῷ σκορπίον;
even he will ask an egg, will hand to him a scorpion?

13 εἰ οὖν ὑμεῖς πονηροὶ ὑπάρχοντες οἴδατε δόματα
If therefore ye ²evil ¹being know gifts

ἀγαθὰ διδόναι τοῖς τέκνοις ὑμῶν, πόσῳ
good to give to the children of you, how much

μᾶλλον ὁ πατὴρ ὁ ἐξ οὐρανοῦ δώσει
more the Father — of heaven will give

πνεῦμα ἅγιον τοῖς αἰτοῦσιν αὐτόν.
Spirit [the] Holy to the [ones] asking him.

14 Καὶ ἦν ἐκβάλλων δαιμόνιον, καὶ αὐτὸ
And he was expelling a demon, and it

ἦν κωφόν· ἐγένετο δὲ τοῦ δαιμονίου
was dumb; and it came to pass the demon
              = as the demon went out

King James Version

gone out, the dumb spake; and the people wondered. 15 But some of them said, He casteth out devils through Beelzebub the chief of the devils. 16 And others, tempting *him,* sought of him a sign from heaven. 17 But he, knowing their thoughts, said unto them, Every kingdom divided against itself is brought to desolation; and a house *divided* against a house falleth. 18 If Satan also be divided against himself, how shall his kingdom stand? because ye say that I cast out devils through Beelzebub. 19 And if I by Beelzebub cast out devils, by whom do your sons cast *them* out? therefore shall they be your judges. 20 But if I with the finger of God cast out devils, no doubt the kingdom of God is come upon you. 21 When a strong man armed keepeth his palace, his goods are in peace: 22 But when a stronger than he shall come upon him, and overcome him, he taketh from him all his armour wherein he trusted, and divideth his spoils. 23 He that is not with me is against me; and he that gathereth not with me scattereth. 24 When the unclean spirit is gone out of a man, he walketh through dry places, seeking rest; and finding none, he saith, I will return unto my house whence I came out. 25 And when he cometh, he findeth *it* swept and garnished. 26 Then goeth he, and taketh *to him* seven other spirits more wicked than himself; and they enter in, and dwell there: and the last *state* of that man is worse than the first.

27 And it came to pass, as he spake these things, a certain woman of the company lifted up her voice, and said unto him, Blessed *is* the womb that bare thee, and the paps which thou hast sucked. 28 But he said, Yea, rather, blessed *are* they that hear the word of God, and keep it.

29 And when the people were gathered thick together, he began to say, This is an evil generation: they seek a sign; and there shall no sign be given it, but the sign of Jonas the prophet. 30 For as Jonas was a sign unto the Ninevites, so shall also the Son of man be to this generation. 31 The queen of the south shall rise up in the judgment with the men of this generation, and condemn them: for she came from the utmost parts of the earth to hear the wisdom of Solomon; and, behold, a greater than Solomon *is* here. 32 The men of Nineveh shall rise up in the judgment with this generation, and shall condemn it: for they repented at the preaching of Jonas; and, behold, a greater than Jonas *is* here. 33 No man, when he hath lighted a candle, putteth *it* in a secret place, neither under a bushel, but on a candlestick, that they which come in may see the light. 34 The light of the body is the eye: therefore when thine eye is single, thy whole body also is full of light; but when *thine eye* is evil, thy body also *is* full of darkness. 35 Take heed therefore, that the light which is in thee be not darkness. 36 If thy whole body therefore *be* full of light, having no part dark, the whole shall be full of light, as when the bright shining of a candle doth give thee light.

New International Version

been dumb spoke, and the crowd was amazed. 15 But some of them said, "By Beelzebub,[x] the prince of demons, he is driving out demons." 16 Others tested him by asking for a sign from heaven.

17 Jesus knew their thoughts and said to them: "Any kingdom divided against itself will be ruined, and a house divided against itself will fall. 18 If Satan is divided against himself, how can his kingdom stand? I say this because you claim that I drive out demons by Beelzebub.[x] 19 Now if I drive out demons by Beelzebub,[x] by whom do your followers drive them out? So then, they will be your judges. 20 But if I drive out demons by the finger of God, then the kingdom of God has come to you.

21 "When a strong man, fully armed, guards his own house, his possessions are safe. 22 But when someone stronger attacks and overpowers him, he takes away the armor in which the man trusted and divides up the spoils.

23 "He who is not with me is against me, and he who does not gather with me, scatters.

24 "When an evil[y] spirit comes out of a man, it goes through arid places seeking rest and does not find it. Then it says, 'I will return to the house I left.' 25 When it arrives, it finds the house swept clean and put in order. 26 Then it goes and takes seven other spirits more wicked than itself, and they go in and live there. And the final condition of that man is worse than the first."

27 As Jesus was saying these things, a woman in the crowd called out, "Blessed is the mother who gave you birth and nursed you."

28 He replied, "Blessed rather are those who hear the word of God and obey it."

The sign of Jonah

29 As the crowds increased, Jesus said, "This is a wicked generation. It asks for a miraculous sign, but none will be given it except the sign of Jonah. 30 For as Jonah was a sign to the Ninevites, so also will the Son of Man be to this generation. 31 The Queen of the South will rise at the judgment with the men of this generation and condemn them, for she came from the ends of the earth to listen to Solomon's wisdom, and now one greater than Solomon is here. 32 The men of Nineveh will stand up at the judgment with this generation and condemn it, for they repented at the preaching of Jonah, and now one greater than Jonah is here.

The lamp of the body

33 "No one lights a lamp and puts it in a place where it will be hidden, or under a bowl. Instead he puts it on its stand, so that those who come in may see the light. 34 Your eye is the lamp of your body. When your eyes are good, your whole body also is full of light. But when they are bad, your body also is full of darkness. 35 See to it, then, that the light within you is not darkness. 36 Therefore, if your whole body is full of light, and no part of it dark, it will be completely lighted, as when the light of a lamp shines on you."

[x] Greek MSS *Beelzeboul* or *Beezeboul.* [y] Greek *unclean.*

ἐξελθόντος ἐλάλησεν ὁ κωφός· καὶ
going out* spoke the dumb man; and

ἐθαύμασαν οἱ ὄχλοι· 15 τινὲς δὲ ἐξ
marvelled the crowds; but some of

αὐτῶν εἶπαν· ἐν Βεελζεβοὺλ τῷ ἄρχοντι
them said : By Beelzebub the chief

τῶν δαιμονίων ἐκβάλλει τὰ δαιμόνια·
of the demons he expels the demons;

16 ἕτεροι δὲ πειράζοντες σημεῖον ἐξ οὐρανοῦ
and others tempting a sign out of heaven

ἐζήτουν παρ' αὐτοῦ. 17 αὐτὸς δὲ εἰδὼς
sought from him. But he knowing

αὐτῶν τὰ διανοήματα εἶπεν αὐτοῖς· πᾶσα
of them the thoughts said to them : Every

βασιλεία ἐφ' ἑαυτὴν διαμερισθεῖσα ἐρημοῦται,
kingdom against itself divided is made desolate,

καὶ οἶκος ἐπὶ οἶκον πίπτει. 18 εἰ δὲ
and a house against a house falls. And if

καὶ ὁ σατανᾶς ἐφ' ἑαυτὸν διεμερίσθη,
also - Satan against himself was divided,

πῶς σταθήσεται ἡ βασιλεία αὐτοῦ; ὅτι
how will stand the kingdom of him? because

λέγετε ἐν Βεελζεβοὺλ ἐκβάλλειν με τὰ
ye say by Beelzebub to expel me[b] the
=[that] by Beelzebub I expel

δαιμόνια. 19 εἰ δὲ ἐγὼ ἐν Βεελζεβοὺλ
demons. But if I by Beelzebub

ἐκβάλλω τὰ δαιμόνια, οἱ υἱοὶ ὑμῶν ἐν
expel the demons, the sons of you by

τίνι ἐκβάλλουσιν; διὰ τοῦτο αὐτοὶ ὑμῶν
what do they expel? therefore they of you

κριταὶ ἔσονται. 20 εἰ δὲ ἐν δακτύλῳ
judges shall be. But if by [the] finger

θεοῦ [ἐγὼ] ἐκβάλλω τὰ δαιμόνια, ἄρα
of God I expel the demons, then

ἔφθασεν ἐφ' ὑμᾶς ἡ βασιλεία τοῦ θεοῦ.
came upon you the kingdom - of God.

21 ὅταν ὁ ἰσχυρὸς καθωπλισμένος φυλάσσῃ
When the strong man having been well armed guards

τὴν ἑαυτοῦ αὐλήν, ἐν εἰρήνῃ ἐστὶν τὰ
the of himself palace, in peace is(are) the

ὑπάρχοντα αὐτοῦ· 22 ἐπὰν δὲ ἰσχυρότερος
goods of him; but when a stronger

αὐτοῦ ἐπελθὼν νικήσῃ αὐτόν, τὴν πανοπλίαν
[than] him coming upon overcomes him, the armour

αὐτοῦ αἴρει, ἐφ' ᾗ ἐπεποίθει, καὶ τὰ
of him he takes, on which he had relied, and the

σκῦλα αὐτοῦ διαδίδωσιν. 23 Ὁ μὴ ὢν
arms of him distributes. The [one] not being

μετ' ἐμοῦ κατ' ἐμοῦ ἐστιν, καὶ ὁ μὴ
with me against me is, and the [one] not

συνάγων μετ' ἐμοῦ σκορπίζει. 24 Ὅταν
gathering with me scatters. When

τὸ ἀκάθαρτον πνεῦμα ἐξέλθῃ ἀπὸ τοῦ
the unclean spirit goes out from the

ἀνθρώπου, διέρχεται δι' ἀνύδρων τόπων
man, he goes through through dry places

ζητοῦν ἀνάπαυσιν, καὶ μὴ εὑρίσκον λέγει·
seeking rest, and not finding says :

ὑποστρέψω εἰς τὸν οἶκόν μου ὅθεν ἐξῆλθον·
I will return to the house of me whence I came out;

25 καὶ ἐλθὸν εὑρίσκει σεσαρωμένον καὶ
and coming he finds [it] having been swept and

κεκοσμημένον. 26 τότε πορεύεται καὶ
having been furnished. Then he goes and

παραλαμβάνει ἕτερα πνεύματα πονηρότερα
takes other spirits more wicked

ἑαυτοῦ ἑπτά, καὶ εἰσελθόντα κατοικεῖ
[than] himself seven, and entering he dwells

ἐκεῖ· καὶ γίνεται τὰ ἔσχατα τοῦ ἀνθρώπου
there; and becomes the last things - man

ἐκείνου χείρονα τῶν πρώτων. 27 Ἐγένετο
of that worse [than] the first. it came to pass

δὲ ἐν τῷ λέγειν αὐτὸν ταῦτα ἐπάρασά τις
And in the to say him[be] these things [e]lifting up [a] certain
= as he said

φωνὴν γυνὴ ἐκ τοῦ ὄχλου εἶπεν αὐτῷ·
[her] [e]voice [e]woman [e]of [e]the [e]crowd said to him :

μακαρία ἡ κοιλία ἡ βαστάσασά σε καὶ
Blessed the womb - having borne thee and

μαστοὶ οὓς ἐθήλασας. 28 αὐτὸς δὲ εἶπεν·
[the] breasts which thou didst suck. But he said :

μενοῦν μακάριοι οἱ ἀκούοντες τὸν λόγον
Nay rather blessed the [ones] hearing the word

τοῦ θεοῦ καὶ φυλάσσοντες.
- of God and keeping.

29 Τῶν δὲ ὄχλων ἐπαθροιζομένων ἤρξατο
And the crowds pressing upon* he began
= as the crowds pressed upon [him]

λέγειν· ἡ γενεὰ αὕτη γενεὰ πονηρά ἐστιν·
to say : - [e]generation [1]This [e]generation [e]an evil [e]is;

σημεῖον ζητεῖ, καὶ σημεῖον οὐ δοθήσεται
a sign it seeks, and a sign will not be given

αὐτῇ εἰ μὴ τὸ σημεῖον Ἰωνᾶ. 30 καθὼς
to it except the sign of Jonas. even as

γὰρ ἐγένετο [ὁ] Ἰωνᾶς τοῖς Νινευίταις
For [e]became - [1]Jonas [e]to the [e]Ninevites

σημεῖον, οὕτως ἔσται καὶ ὁ υἱὸς τοῦ
[e]a sign, so will be also the Son -

ἀνθρώπου τῇ γενεᾷ ταύτῃ. 31 βασίλισσα
of man - generation to this. [The] queen

νότου ἐγερθήσεται ἐν τῇ κρίσει μετὰ τῶν
of [the] south will be raised in the judgment with the

ἀνδρῶν τῆς γενεᾶς ταύτης καὶ κατακρινεῖ
men - generation of this and will condemn

αὐτούς· ὅτι ἦλθεν ἐκ τῶν περάτων τῆς
them; because she came from the extremities of the

γῆς ἀκοῦσαι τὴν σοφίαν Σολομῶνος, καὶ
earth to hear the wisdom of Solomon, and

ἰδοὺ πλεῖον Σολομῶνος ὧδε. 32 ἄνδρες
behold a greater [than] Solomon [is] here. Men

Νινευῖται ἀναστήσονται ἐν τῇ κρίσει μετὰ
Ninevites will rise up in the judgment with

τῆς γενεᾶς ταύτης καὶ κατακρινοῦσιν αὐτήν·
- generation this and will condemn it;

ὅτι μετενόησαν εἰς τὸ κήρυγμα Ἰωνᾶ, καὶ
because they repented at the proclamation of Jonas, and

ἰδοὺ πλεῖον Ἰωνᾶ ὧδε. 33 Οὐδεὶς λύχνον
behold a greater [than] Jonas [is] here. No one [a] a lamp

ἅψας εἰς κρύπτην τίθησιν οὐδὲ ὑπὸ τὸν
[1]having lit [a]in [e]secret [e]places [it] nor under the

μόδιον, ἀλλ' ἐπὶ τὴν λυχνίαν, ἵνα οἱ
bushel, but on the lampstand, that the

εἰσπορευόμενοι τὸ φέγγος βλέπωσιν. 34 ὁ
ones] entering the light may see. The

λύχνος τοῦ σώματός ἐστιν ὁ ὀφθαλμός σου.
lamp of the body is the eye of thee.

ὅταν ὁ ὀφθαλμός σου ἁπλοῦς ᾖ, καὶ
When the eye of thee single is, also

ὅλον τὸ σῶμά σου φωτεινόν ἐστιν· ἐπὰν
all the body of thee bright is; [a]when

δὲ πονηρὸς ᾖ, καὶ τὸ σῶμά σου σκοτεινόν.
[1]but evil it is, also the body of thee [is] dark.

35 σκόπει οὖν μὴ τὸ φῶς τὸ ἐν σοὶ
Watch therefore lest the light - in thee

σκότος ἐστίν. 36 εἰ οὖν τὸ σῶμά σου
darkness is. If therefore [e]the [e]body [e]of thee

ὅλον φωτεινόν, μὴ ἔχον μέρος τι σκοτεινόν,
[1]whole [is] bright, not having [a]part [1]any dark,

ἔσται φωτεινὸν ὅλον ὡς ὅταν ὁ λύχνος
[1]will be [e]bright [1]all as when the lamp

τῇ ἀστραπῇ φωτίζῃ σε.
with the(its) shining enlightens thee.

King James Version

37 And as he spake, a certain Pharisee besought him to dine with him: and he went in, and sat down to meat. 38And when the Pharisee saw *it*, he marvelled that he had not first washed before dinner. 39And the Lord said unto him, Now do ye Pharisees make clean the outside of the cup and the platter; but your inward part is full of ravening and wickedness. 40 *Ye* fools, did not he, that made that which is without, make that which is within also? 41 But rather give alms of such things as ye have; and, behold, all things are clean unto you. 42 But woe unto you, Pharisees! for ye tithe mint and rue and all manner of herbs, and pass over judgment and the love of God: these ought ye to have done, and not to leave the other undone. 43 Woe unto you, Pharisees! for ye love the uppermost seats in the synagogues, and greetings in the markets. 44 Woe unto you, scribes and Pharisees, hypocrites! for ye are as graves which appear not, and the men that walk over *them* are not aware *of them*.

45 Then answered one of the lawyers, and said unto him, Master, thus saying thou reproachest us also. 46And he said, Woe unto you also, *ye* lawyers! for ye lade men with burdens grievous to be borne, and ye yourselves touch not the burdens with one of your fingers. 47 Woe unto you! for ye build the sepulchres of the prophets, and your fathers killed them. 48 Truly ye bear witness that ye allow the deeds of your fathers: for they indeed killed them, and ye build their sepulchres. 49 Therefore also said the wisdom of God, I will send them prophets and apostles, and *some* of them they shall slay and persecute: 50 That the blood of all the prophets, which was shed from the foundation of the world, may be required of this generation; 51 From the blood of Abel unto the blood of Zacharias, which perished between the altar and the temple: verily I say unto you, It shall be required of this generation. 52 Woe unto you, lawyers! for ye have taken away the key of knowledge: ye entered not in yourselves, and them that were entering in ye hindered. 53And as he said these things unto them, the scribes and the Pharisees began to urge *him* vehemently, and to provoke him to speak of many things: 54 Laying wait for him, and seeking to catch something out of his mouth, that they might accuse him.

12 In the mean time, when there were gathered together an innumerable multitude of people, insomuch that they trode one upon another, he began to say unto his disciples first of all, Beware ye of the leaven of the Pharisees, which is hypocrisy. 2 For there is nothing covered, that shall not be revealed; neither hid, that shall not be known. 3 Therefore, whatsoever ye have spoken in darkness shall be heard in the light; and that which ye have spoken in the ear in closets shall be proclaimed upon the house-

New International Version

Six woes

37 When Jesus had finished speaking, a Pharisee invited him to eat with him; so he went in and reclined at the table. 38 But the Pharisee, noticing that Jesus did not first wash before the meal, was surprised.

39 Then the Lord said to him, "Now then, you Pharisees clean the outside of the cup and dish, but inside you are full of greed and wickedness. 40 You foolish people! Did not the one who made the outside make the inside also? 41 But give what is inside to the poor, and everything will be clean for you.

42 "Woe to you Pharisees, because you give God a tenth of your mint, rue and all other kinds of garden herbs, but you neglect justice and the love of God. You should have practiced the latter without leaving the former undone.

43 "Woe to you Pharisees, because you love the most important seats in the synagogues and greetings in the marketplaces.

44 "Woe to you, because you are like unmarked graves, which men walk over without knowing it."

45 One of the experts in the law answered him, "Teacher, when you say these things, you insult us also."

46 Jesus replied, "And you experts in the law, woe to you, because you load people down with burdens they can hardly carry, and you yourselves will not lift one finger to help them.

47 "Woe to you, because you build tombs for the prophets, and it was your forefathers who killed them. 48 So you testify that you approve of what your forefathers did; they killed the prophets, and you build their tombs. 49 Because of this, God in his wisdom said, 'I will send them prophets and apostles, some of whom they will kill and others they will persecute.' 50 Therefore this generation will be held responsible for the blood of all the prophets that has been shed since the beginning of the world, 51 from the blood of Abel to the blood of Zechariah, who was killed between the altar and the sanctuary. Yes, I tell you, this generation will be held responsible for it all.

52 "Woe to you experts in the law, because you have taken away the key to knowledge. You yourselves have not entered, and you have hindered those who were entering."

53 When Jesus left there, the Pharisees and the teachers of the law began to oppose him fiercely and to besiege him with questions, 54 waiting to catch him in something he might say.

Warnings and encouragements

12 Meanwhile, when a crowd of many thousands had gathered, so that they were trampling on one another, Jesus began to speak first to his disciples, saying: "Be on your guard against the yeast of the Pharisees, which is hypocrisy. 2 There is nothing concealed that will not be disclosed, or hidden that will not be made known. 3 What you have said in the dark will be heard in the daylight, and what you have whispered in the ear behind closed doors will be proclaimed from the housetops.

Greek Interlinear

37 Ἐν δὲ τῷ λαλῆσαι ἐρωτᾷ αὐτὸν
Now in the to speak* asks him
= as [he] spoke

Φαρισαῖος ὅπως ἀριστήσῃ παρ' αὐτῷ·
a Pharisee that he would dine with him;
εἰσελθὼν δὲ ἀνέπεσεν. 38 ὁ δὲ Φαρισαῖος
and entering he reclined. But the Pharisee
ἰδὼν ἐθαύμασεν ὅτι οὐ πρῶτον ἐβαπτίσθη
seeing marvelled that not first he washed
πρὸ τοῦ ἀρίστου. 39 εἶπεν δὲ ὁ κύριος
before the dinner. But said the Lord
πρὸς αὐτόν· νῦν ὑμεῖς οἱ Φαρισαῖοι τὸ
to him: Now ye - Pharisees the
ἔξωθεν τοῦ ποτηρίου καὶ τοῦ πίνακος
outside of the cup and of the dish
καθαρίζετε, τὸ δὲ ἔσωθεν ὑμῶν γέμει
cleanse, but the inside of you is full
ἁρπαγῆς καὶ πονηρίας. 40 ἄφρονες, οὐχ
of robbery and wickedness. Foolish men, not
ὁ ποιήσας τὸ ἔξωθεν καὶ τὸ ἔσωθεν
the [one] making the outside also the inside
ἐποίησεν; 41 πλὴν τὰ ἐνόντα δότε
made? Nevertheless the things being within give
ἐλεημοσύνην, καὶ ἰδοὺ πάντα καθαρὰ ὑμῖν
alms, and behold all things clean to you
ἐστιν. 42 ἀλλὰ οὐαὶ ὑμῖν τοῖς Φαρισαίοις,
is(are). But woe to you - Pharisees,
ὅτι ἀποδεκατοῦτε τὸ ἡδύοσμον καὶ τὸ
because ye tithe the mint and the
πήγανον καὶ πᾶν λάχανον, καὶ παρέρχεσθε
rue and every herb, and pass by
τὴν κρίσιν καὶ τὴν ἀγάπην τοῦ θεοῦ·
the judgment and the love - of God;
ταῦτα δὲ ἔδει ποιῆσαι κἀκεῖνα μὴ
but these things it behoved to do and those not
παρεῖναι. 43 οὐαὶ ὑμῖν τοῖς Φαρισαίοις,
to pass by. Woe to you - Pharisees,
ὅτι ἀγαπᾶτε τὴν πρωτοκαθεδρίαν ἐν ταῖς
because ye love the chief seat in the
συναγωγαῖς καὶ τοὺς ἀσπασμοὺς ἐν ταῖς
synagogues and the greetings in the
ἀγοραῖς. 44 οὐαὶ ὑμῖν, ὅτι ἐστὲ ὡς τὰ
marketplaces. Woe to you, because ye are as the
μνημεῖα τὰ ἄδηλα, καὶ οἱ ἄνθρωποι οἱ
tombs - unseen, and the men -
περιπατοῦντες ἐπάνω οὐκ οἴδασιν.
walking over do not know.

45 Ἀποκριθεὶς δέ τις τῶν νομικῶν λέγει
And answering one of the lawyers says
αὐτῷ· διδάσκαλε, ταῦτα λέγων καὶ ἡμᾶς
to him: Teacher, these things saying also us
ὑβρίζεις. 46 ὁ δὲ εἶπεν· καὶ ὑμῖν τοῖς
thou insultest. And he said: Also to you -
νομικοῖς οὐαί, ὅτι φορτίζετε τοὺς ἀνθρώπους
lawyers woe, because ye burden - men

φορτία δυσβάστακτα, καὶ αὐτοὶ ἑνὶ τῶν
[with] burdens difficult to carry, and [your]selves with one of the
δακτύλων ὑμῶν οὐ προσψαύετε τοῖς φορτίοις.
fingers of you ye do not touch the burdens.
47 οὐαὶ ὑμῖν, ὅτι οἰκοδομεῖτε τὰ μνημεῖα
Woe to you, because ye build the tombs
τῶν προφητῶν, οἱ δὲ πατέρες ὑμῶν
of the prophets, and the fathers of you
ἀπέκτειναν αὐτούς. 48 ἄρα μάρτυρές ἐστε
killed them. Therefore witnesses ye are
καὶ συνευδοκεῖτε τοῖς ἔργοις τῶν πατέρων
and ye entirely approve the works of the fathers
ὑμῶν, ὅτι αὐτοὶ μὲν ἀπέκτειναν αὐτούς,
of you, because they on one hand killed them,
ὑμεῖς δὲ οἰκοδομεῖτε. 49 διὰ τοῦτο καὶ
ye on the other hand build. Therefore also
ἡ σοφία τοῦ θεοῦ εἶπεν· ἀποστελῶ εἰς
the Wisdom - of God said: I will send to
αὐτοὺς προφήτας καὶ ἀποστόλους, καὶ ἐξ
them prophets and apostles, and of
αὐτῶν ἀποκτενοῦσιν καὶ διώξουσιν, 50 ἵνα
them they will kill and persecute, that
ἐκζητηθῇ τὸ αἷμα πάντων τῶν προφητῶν
[11]may be required [the] [3]blood [2]of all [4]the [5]prophets
τὸ ἐκκεχυμένον ἀπὸ καταβολῆς κόσμου
- [6]having been shed [7]from [8][the] [9]foundation [10]of [the] world
ἀπὸ τῆς γενεᾶς ταύτης, 51 ἀπὸ αἵματος
[12]from - generation this, from [the] blood
Ἄβελ ἕως αἵματος Ζαχαρίου τοῦ
of Abel to [the] blood of Zacharias -
ἀπολομένου μεταξὺ τοῦ θυσιαστηρίου καὶ
destroyed between the altar and
τοῦ οἴκου· ναὶ λέγω ὑμῖν, ἐκζητηθήσεται
the house; yes I tell you, it will be required
ἀπὸ τῆς γενεᾶς ταύτης. 52 οὐαὶ ὑμῖν τοῖς
from - generation this. Woe to you -
νομικοῖς, ὅτι ἤρατε τὴν κλεῖδα τῆς
lawyers, because ye took the key of the
γνώσεως· αὐτοὶ οὐκ εἰσήλθατε καὶ τοὺς
of knowledge; [your]selves ye did not enter and the
εἰσερχομένους ἐκωλύσατε. 53 Κἀκεῖθεν ἐξελ-
[ones] entering ye prevented. And thence going
θόντος αὐτοῦ ἤρξαντο οἱ γραμματεῖς καὶ
= as he went forth thence
forth him began the scribes and
οἱ Φαρισαῖοι δεινῶς ἐνέχειν καὶ ἀποστοματίζειν
the Pharisees [2]terribly [1]to be [3]angry and to [1]draw [3]out
αὐτὸν περὶ πλειόνων, 54 ἐνεδρεύοντες
[1]him concerning a great number of things, lying in wait for
αὐτὸν θηρεῦσαί τι ἐκ τοῦ στόματος αὐτοῦ.
him to catch something out of the mouth of him.

Chapter 12

Ἐν οἷς ἐπισυναχθεισῶν τῶν μυριάδων
In which things being assembled the thousands
= Meanwhile as the thousands of the crowd were assembled,
τοῦ ὄχλου, ὥστε καταπατεῖν ἀλλήλους,
of the crowd, so as to tread on one another,
ἤρξατο λέγειν πρὸς τοὺς μαθητὰς αὐτοῦ
he began to say to the disciples of him
πρῶτον· προσέχετε ἑαυτοῖς ἀπὸ τῆς ζύμης,
first: Take heed to yourselves from the leaven,
ἥτις ἐστὶν ὑπόκρισις, τῶν Φαρισαίων.
which is hypocrisy, of the Pharisees.

2 οὐδὲν δὲ συγκεκαλυμμένον ἐστὶν ὃ οὐκ
And [2]nothing [3]having been [1]there is which not
completely covered
ἀποκαλυφθήσεται, καὶ κρυπτὸν ὃ οὐ γνωσθήσεται.
will be uncovered, and hidden which will not be known.
3 ἀνθ' ὧν ὅσα ἐν τῇ σκοτίᾳ εἴπατε ἐν
Therefore what things in the darkness ye said in
τῷ φωτὶ ἀκουσθήσεται, καὶ ὃ πρὸς τὸ
the light will be heard, and what to the
οὖς ἐλαλήσατε ἐν τοῖς ταμείοις κηρυχθήσεται
ear ye spoke in the private rooms will be proclaimed

213

King James Version

tops. 4And I say unto you my friends, Be not afraid of them that kill the body, and after that have no more that they can do. 5 But I will forewarn you whom ye shall fear: Fear him, which after he hath killed hath power to cast into hell; yea, I say unto you, Fear him. 6Are not five sparrows sold for two farthings, and not one of them is forgotten before God? 7 But even the very hairs of your head are all numbered. Fear not therefore: ye are of more value than many sparrows. 8Also I say unto you, Whosoever shall confess me before men, him shall the Son of man also confess before the angels of God: 9 But he that denieth me before men shall be denied before the angels of God. 10And whosoever shall speak a word against the Son of man, it shall be forgiven him: but unto him that blasphemeth against the Holy Ghost it shall not be forgiven. 11And when they bring you unto the synagogues, and *unto* magistrates, and powers, take ye no thought how or what thing ye shall answer, or what ye shall say: 12 For the Holy Ghost shall teach you in the same hour what ye ought to say.

13 And one of the company said unto him, Master, speak to my brother, that he divide the inheritance with me. 14And he said unto him, Man, who made me a judge or a divider over you? 15And he said unto them, Take heed, and beware of covetousness: for a man's life consisteth not in the abundance of the things which he possesseth. 16And he spake a parable unto them, saying, The ground of a certain rich man brought forth plentifully: 17And he thought within himself, saying, What shall I do, because I have no room where to bestow my fruits? 18And he said, This will I do: I will pull down my barns, and build greater; and there will I bestow all my fruits and my goods. 19And I will say to my soul, Soul, thou hast much goods laid up for many years; take thine ease, eat, drink, *and* be merry. 20 But God said unto him, *Thou* fool, this night thy soul shall be required of thee: then whose shall those things be, which thou hast provided? 21 So *is* he that layeth up treasure for himself, and is not rich toward God.

22 And he said unto his disciples, Therefore I say unto you, Take no thought for your life, what ye shall eat; neither for the body, what ye shall put on. 23 The life is more than meat, and the body *is more* than raiment. 24 Consider the ravens: for they neither sow nor reap; which neither have storehouse nor barn; and God feedeth them: how much more are ye better than the fowls? 25And which of you with taking thought can add to his stature one cubit? 26 If ye then be not able to do that thing which is least, why take ye thought for the rest? 27 Consider the lilies how they grow: they toil not, they spin not; and yet I say unto you, that Solomon in all his glory was not arrayed like one of these. 28 If then God so clothe the grass, which is to day in the field, and to morrow is cast into the oven; how much more *will he clothe* you,

New International Version

4 "I tell you, my friends, do not be afraid of those who kill the body and after that can do no more. 5 But I will show you whom you should fear: Fear him who, after the killing of the body, has power to throw you into hell. Yes, I tell you, fear him. 6Are not five sparrows sold for two pennies? Yet not one of them is forgotten by God. 7 Indeed, the very hairs of your head are all numbered. Don't be afraid; you are worth more than many sparrows.

8 "I tell you, whoever acknowledges me before men, the Son of Man will also acknowledge him before the angels of God. 9 But he who disowns me before men will be disowned before the angels of God. 10And everyone who speaks a word against the Son of Man will be forgiven, but anyone who blasphemes against the Holy Spirit will not be forgiven.

11 "When you are brought before synagogues, rulers and authorities, do not worry about how you will defend yourselves or what you will say, 12 for the Holy Spirit will teach you at that time what you should say."

The parable of the rich fool

13 Someone in the crowd said to him, "Teacher, tell my brother to divide the inheritance with me."

14 Jesus replied, "Man, who appointed me a judge or an arbiter between you?" 15 Then he said to them, "Watch out! Be on your guard against all kinds of greed; a man's life does not consist in the abundance of his possessions."

16 And he told them this parable: "The ground of a certain rich man produced a good crop. 17 He thought to himself, 'What shall I do? I have no place to store my crops.'

18 "Then he said, 'This is what I'll do. I will tear down my barns and build bigger ones, and there I will store all my grain and my goods. 19And I'll say to myself, "You have plenty of good things laid up for many years. Take life easy; eat, drink and be merry." '

20 "But God said to him, 'You fool! This very night your life will be demanded from you. Then who will get what you have prepared for yourself?'

21 "This is how it will be with anyone who stores things up for himself but is not rich toward God."

Do not worry

22 Then Jesus said to his disciples: "Therefore I tell you, do not worry about your life, what you will eat; or about your body, what you will wear. 23 Life is more than food, and the body more than clothes. 24 Consider the ravens: They do not sow or reap, they have no storeroom or barn; yet God feeds them. And how much more valuable you are than birds! 25 Who of you by worrying can add a single hour to his life? *z* 26 Since you cannot do this very little thing, why do you worry about the rest?

27 "Consider how the lilies grow. They do not labor or spin. Yet I tell you, not even Solomon in all his splendor was dressed like one of these. 28 If that is how God clothes the grass of the field, which is here today and tomorrow is thrown into the fire, how much more will he

[z] Or *single cubit to his height?*

Greek Interlinear

ἐπὶ τῶν δωμάτων. 4 Λέγω δὲ ὑμῖν τοῖς
on the roofs. And I say to you the

φίλοις μου, μὴ φοβηθῆτε ἀπὸ τῶν
friends of me, do not be afraid from(of) the [ones]

ἀποκτεννόντων τὸ σῶμα καὶ μετὰ ταῦτα
killing the body and after these things

μὴ ἐχόντων περισσότερόν τι ποιῆσαι.
not having anything more to do.

5 ὑποδείξω δὲ ὑμῖν τίνα φοβηθῆτε·
But I will warn you whom ye may fear:

φοβήθητε τὸν μετὰ τὸ ἀποκτεῖναι ἔχοντα
¹fear ²the [one] ⁴after the ³to kill(killing) ³having

ἐξουσίαν ἐμβαλεῖν εἰς τὴν γέενναν. ναὶ
⁴authority ⁵to cast in into gehenna. Yes[,]

λέγω ὑμῖν, τοῦτον φοβήθητε. 6 οὐχὶ
I say to you, this one fear ye. Not

πέντε στρουθία πωλοῦνται ἀσσαρίων δύο;
five sparrows are sold of(for) farthings two?

καὶ ἐν αὐτῶν οὐκ ἔστιν ἐπιλελησμένον
and one of them is not having been forgotten

ἐνώπιον τοῦ θεοῦ. 7 ἀλλὰ καὶ αἱ τρίχες
before God. But even the hairs

τῆς κεφαλῆς ὑμῶν πᾶσαι ἠρίθμηνται.
of the head of you all have been numbered.

μὴ φοβεῖσθε· πολλῶν στρουθίων διαφέρετε.
Fear ye not; from many sparrows ye differ.

8 λέγω δὲ ὑμῖν, πᾶς ὃς ἂν ὁμολογήσῃ
But I tell you, everyone whoever confesses

ἐν ἐμοὶ ἔμπροσθεν τῶν ἀνθρώπων, καὶ ὁ
- me before - men, also the

υἱὸς τοῦ ἀνθρώπου ὁμολογήσει ἐν αὐτῷ
Son - of man will confess - him

ἔμπροσθεν τῶν ἀγγέλων τοῦ θεοῦ· 9 ὁ δὲ
before the angels - of God; and the

ἀρνησάμενός με ἐνώπιον τῶν ἀνθρώπων
[one] denying me before - men

ἀπαρνηθήσεται ἐνώπιον τῶν ἀγγέλων τοῦ
will be denied before the angels -

θεοῦ. 10 καὶ πᾶς ὃς ἐρεῖ λόγον εἰς τὸν
of God. And everyone who shall say a word against the

υἱὸν τοῦ ἀνθρώπου, ἀφεθήσεται αὐτῷ· τῷ
Son - of man, it will be forgiven him; ²the [one]

δὲ εἰς τὸ ἅγιον πνεῦμα βλασφημήσαντι
¹but against the Holy Spirit blaspheming

οὐκ ἀφεθήσεται. 11 ὅταν δὲ εἰσφέρωσιν
will not be forgiven. And when they bring in

ὑμᾶς ἐπὶ τὰς συναγωγὰς καὶ τὰς ἀρχὰς
you before - synagogues and - rulers

καὶ τὰς ἐξουσίας, μὴ μεριμνήσητε πῶς ἢ
and - authorities, do not be anxious how or

τί ἀπολογήσησθε ἢ τί εἴπητε· 12 τὸ γὰρ
what ye may answer or what ye may say; for the

ἅγιον πνεῦμα διδάξει ὑμᾶς ἐν αὐτῇ τῇ
Holy Spirit will teach you in ¹same ¹the

ὥρᾳ ἃ δεῖ εἰπεῖν. 13 Εἶπεν δέ τις
hour what things it behoves [you] to say. And said someone

ἐκ τοῦ ὄχλου αὐτῷ· διδάσκαλε, εἰπὲ τῷ
out of the crowd to him : Teacher, tell the

ἀδελφῷ μου μερίσασθαι μετ' ἐμοῦ τὴν
brother of me to divide with me the

κληρονομίαν. 14 ὁ δὲ εἶπεν αὐτῷ· ἄνθρωπε,
inheritance But he said to him: Man,

τίς με κατέστησεν κριτὴν ἢ μεριστὴν ἐφ'
who me appointed a judge or a divider over

ὑμᾶς; 15 εἶπεν δὲ πρὸς αὐτούς· ὁρᾶτε
you? And he said to them : Beware

καὶ φυλάσσεσθε ἀπὸ πάσης πλεονεξίας,
and guard from(against) all covetousness,

ὅτι οὐκ ἐν τῷ περισσεύειν τινὶ ἡ ζωὴ
because ⁵not ¹in ²the ³to abound ⁴to anyone ¹the ²life

αὐτοῦ ἐστιν ἐκ τῶν ὑπαρχόντων αὐτῷ.
²of him ⁴is ¹⁰of the things existing to him.ᵉ
=¹¹his ¹²possessions.

16 Εἶπεν δὲ παραβολὴν πρὸς αὐτοὺς λέγων·
And he told a parable to them saying:

ἀνθρώπου τινὸς πλουσίου εὐφόρησεν ἡ
²of a certain ³man ¹rich ⁸bore well ¹The

χώρα. 17 καὶ διελογίζετο ἐν ἑαυτῷ λέγων·
²land. And he reasoned in himself saying :

τί ποιήσω, ὅτι οὐκ ἔχω ποῦ συνάξω τοὺς
What may I do, because I have not where I may gather the

καρπούς μου; 18 καὶ εἶπεν· τοῦτο ποιήσω·
fruits of me? And he said : This will I do :

καθελῶ μου τὰς ἀποθήκας καὶ μείζονας
I will pull down of me the barns and larger ones

οἰκοδομήσω, καὶ συνάξω ἐκεῖ πάντα τὸν
I will build, and I will gather there all the

σῖτον καὶ τὰ ἀγαθά μου, 19 καὶ ἐρῶ τῇ
wheat and the goods of me, and I will say to the

ψυχῇ μου· ψυχή, ἔχεις πολλὰ ἀγαθὰ
soul of me : Soul, thou hast many goods

κείμενα εἰς ἔτη πολλά· ἀναπαύου, φάγε,
laid [up] for years many; take rest, eat,

πίε, εὐφραίνου. 20 εἶπεν δὲ αὐτῷ ὁ
drink, be glad. But said to him -

θεός· ἄφρων, ταύτῃ τῇ νυκτὶ τὴν ψυχήν
God : Foolish man, in this - night the soul

σου ἀπαιτοῦσιν ἀπὸ σοῦ· ἃ δὲ
of thee they demand from thee; then [the] things which

ἡτοίμασας, τίνι ἔσται; 21 οὕτως ὁ
thou preparedst, to whom will they be?ᵉ So the [one]

=whose will they be?

θησαυρίζων αὑτῷ καὶ μὴ εἰς θεὸν πλουτῶν.
treasuring to himself and not toward God being rich.

22 Εἶπεν δὲ πρὸς τοὺς μαθητὰς [αὐτοῦ]· διὰ τοῦτο
And he said to the disciples of him : Therefore

λέγω ὑμῖν· μὴ μεριμνᾶτε τῇ ψυχῇ τί
I tell you : Do not be anxious for the life what

φάγητε, μηδὲ τῷ σώματι [ὑμῶν] τί
ye may eat, nor for the body of you what

ἐνδύσησθε. 23 ἡ γὰρ ψυχὴ πλεῖόν ἐστιν
ye may put on. For the life more is

τῆς τροφῆς καὶ τὸ σῶμα τοῦ ἐνδύματος.
[than] the food and the body [than] the clothing.

24 κατανοήσατε τοὺς κόρακας, ὅτι οὔτε
Consider ye the ravens, that neither

σπείρουσιν οὔτε θερίζουσιν, οἷς οὐκ ἔστινᵉ
they sow nor reap, to which is not
=which have not

ταμιεῖον οὐδὲ ἀποθήκη, καὶ ὁ θεὸς τρέφει
storehouse nor barn, and - God feeds

αὐτούς· πόσῳ μᾶλλον ὑμεῖς διαφέρετε τῶν
them; by how much rather ye differ from the

πετεινῶν. 25 τίς δὲ ἐξ ὑμῶν μεριμνῶν
birds. And who of you being anxious

δύναται ἐπὶ τὴν ἡλικίαν αὐτοῦ προσθεῖναι
can on the stature of him to add

πῆχυν; 26 εἰ οὖν οὐδὲ ἐλάχιστον δύνασθε,
a cubit? If therefore not [the] least ye can,

τί περὶ τῶν λοιπῶν μεριμνᾶτε; 27 κατα-
why concerning the other things are ye anxious? Con-

νοήσατε τὰ κρίνα, πῶς οὔτε νήθει οὔτε
sider ye the lilies, how neither they spin nor

ὑφαίνει· λέγω δὲ ὑμῖν, οὐδὲ Σολομὼν ἐν
weave; but I tell you, not Solomon in

πάσῃ τῇ δόξῃ αὐτοῦ περιεβάλετο ὡς ἓν
all the glory of him was arrayed as one

τούτων. 28 εἰ δὲ ἐν ἀγρῷ τὸν χόρτον
of these. ¹And ²if ³in ¹⁰a field ⁴the ⁷grass

ὄντα σήμερον καὶ αὔριον εἰς κλίβανον
⁶being ¹¹to-day ¹²and ¹³tomorrow ¹²into ¹⁶an oven

βαλλόμενον ὁ θεὸς οὕτως ἀμφιάζει, πόσῳ
¹⁴being thrown - ⁸God ⁴so ⁵clothes, by how much

King James Version

O ye of little faith? 29And seek not ye what ye shall eat, or what ye shall drink, neither be ye of doubtful mind. 30 For all these things do the nations of the world seek after: and your Father knoweth that ye have need of these things.

31 But rather seek ye the kingdom of God; and all these things shall be added unto you. 32 Fear not, little flock; for it is your Father's good pleasure to give you the kingdom. 33 Sell that ye have, and give alms; provide yourselves bags which wax not old, a treasure in the heavens that faileth not, where no thief approacheth, neither moth corrupteth. 34 For where your treasure is, there will your heart be also. 35 Let your loins be girded about, and *your* lights burning; 36And ye yourselves like unto men that wait for their lord, when he will return from the wedding; that, when he cometh and knocketh, they may open unto him immediately. 37 Blessed *are* those servants, whom the lord when he cometh shall find watching: verily I say unto you, that he shall gird himself, and make them to sit down to meat, and will come forth and serve them. 38And if he shall come in the second watch, or come in the third watch, and find *them* so, blessed are those servants. 39And this know, that if the goodman of the house had known what hour the thief would come, he would have watched, and not have suffered his house to be broken through. 40 Be ye therefore ready also: for the Son of man cometh at an hour when ye think not.

41 Then Peter said unto him, Lord, speakest thou this parable unto us, or even to all? 42And the Lord said, Who then is that faithful and wise steward, whom *his* lord shall make ruler over his household, to give *them their* portion of meat in due season? 43 Blessed *is* that servant, whom his lord when he cometh shall find so doing. 44 Of a truth I say unto you, that he will make him ruler over all that he hath. 45 But and if that servant say in his heart, My lord delayeth his coming; and shall begin to beat the menservants and maidens, and to eat and drink, and to be drunken; 46 The lord of that servant will come in a day when he looketh not for *him*, and at an hour when he is not aware, and will cut him in sunder, and will appoint him his portion with the unbelievers. 47And that servant, which knew his lord's will, and prepared not *himself*, neither did according to his will, shall be beaten with many *stripes*. 48 But he that knew not, and did commit things worthy of stripes, shall be beaten with few *stripes*. For unto whomsoever much is given, of him shall be much required; and to whom men have committed much, of him they will ask the more.

49 I am come to send fire on the earth: and what will I, if it be already kindled? 50 But I have a baptism to be baptized with; and how am I straitened till it be accomplished! 51 Suppose ye that I am come to give peace on earth? I tell you, Nay; but rather division: 52 For from henceforth there shall be five in one house divided, three against two, and two against three. 53 The father shall be divided against the son, and the son against the father; the mother against the daughter, and the daughter against the mother;

New International Version

clothe you, O you of little faith! 29And do not set your heart on what you will eat or drink; do not worry about it. 30 For the pagan world runs after all such things, and your Father knows that you need them. 31 But seek his kingdom, and these things will be given to you as well.

32 "Do not be afraid, little flock, for your Father has been pleased to give you the kingdom. 33 Sell your possessions and give to the poor. Provide purses for yourselves that will not wear out, a treasure in heaven that will not be exhausted, where no thief comes near and no moth destroys. 34 For where your treasure is, there your heart will be also.

Watchfulness

35 "Be dressed ready for service and keep your lamps burning, 36 like men waiting for their master to return from a wedding banquet, so that when he comes and knocks they can immediately open the door for him. 37 It will be good for those servants whose master finds them watching when he comes. I tell you the truth, he will dress himself to serve, will have them recline at the table and will come and wait on them. 38 It will be good for those servants whose master finds them ready, even if he comes in the second or third watch of the night. 39 But understand this: If the owner of the house had known at what hour the thief was coming, he would not have let his house be broken into. 40 You also must be ready, because the Son of Man will come at an hour when you do not expect him."

41 Peter asked, "Lord, are you telling this parable to us, or to everyone?"

42 The Lord answered, "Who then is the faithful and wise manager, whom the master puts in charge of his servants to give them their food allowance at the proper time? 43 It will be good for that servant whom the master finds doing so when he returns. 44 I tell you the truth, he will put him in charge of all his possessions. 45 But suppose the servant says to himself, 'My master is taking a long time in coming,' and he then begins to beat the men and women servants and to eat and drink and get drunk. 46 The master of that servant will come on a day when he does not expect him and at an hour he is not aware of. He will cut him to pieces and assign him a place with the unbelievers.

47 "That servant who knows his master's will and does not get ready or does not do what his master wants will be beaten with many blows. 48 But the one who does not know and does things deserving punishment will be beaten with few blows. From everyone who has been given much, much will be demanded; and from the one who has been entrusted with much, much more will be asked.

Not peace but division

49 "I have come to bring fire on the earth, and how I wish it were already kindled! 50 But I have a baptism to undergo, and how distressed I am until it is completed! 51 Do you think I came to bring peace on earth? No, I tell you, but division. 52 From now on there will be five in one family divided against each other, three against two and two against three. 53 They will be divided, father against son and son against father, mother against daughter and daughter

Greek Interlinear

μᾶλλον ὑμᾶς, ὀλιγόπιστοι. 29 καὶ ὑμεῖς
rather you, little-faiths. And ye

μὴ ζητεῖτε τί φάγητε καὶ τί πίητε, καὶ
do not seek what ye may eat and what ye may drink, and

μὴ μετεωρίζεσθε· 30 ταῦτα γὰρ πάντα τὰ
do not be in suspense; for these things all the

ἔθνη τοῦ κόσμου ἐπιζητοῦσιν· ὑμῶν δὲ
nations of the world seek after; but of you

ὁ πατὴρ οἶδεν ὅτι χρῄζετε τούτων·
the Father knows that ye have need of them;

31 πλὴν ζητεῖτε τὴν βασιλείαν αὐτοῦ, καὶ
but seek ye the kingdom of him, and

ταῦτα προστεθήσεται ὑμῖν. 32 Μὴ φοβοῦ,
these things will be added to you. Fear not,

τὸ μικρὸν ποίμνιον· ὅτι εὐδόκησεν ὁ
- little flock; because was well pleased the

πατὴρ ὑμῶν δοῦναι ὑμῖν τὴν βασιλείαν.
Father of you to give you the kingdom.

33 Πωλήσατε τὰ ὑπάρχοντα ὑμῶν καὶ
Sell the possessions of you and

δότε ἐλεημοσύνην· ποιήσατε ἑαυτοῖς βαλ-
give alms; make for yourselves

λάντια μὴ παλαιούμενα, θησαυρὸν ἀνέκλειπτον
purses not becoming old, a treasure unfailing

ἐν τοῖς οὐρανοῖς, ὅπου κλέπτης οὐκ
in the heavens, where a thief not

ἐγγίζει οὐδὲ σὴς διαφθείρει· 34 ὅπου γάρ
comes near nor moth corrupts; for where

ἐστιν ὁ θησαυρὸς ὑμῶν, ἐκεῖ καὶ ἡ
is the treasure of you, there also the

καρδία ὑμῶν ἔσται. 35 Ἔστωσαν ὑμῶν αἱ
heart of you will be. Let be of you the

ὀσφύες περιεζωσμέναι καὶ οἱ λύχνοι
loins *having been* girded and the lamps

καιόμενοι· 36 καὶ ὑμεῖς ὅμοιοι ἀνθρώποις
burning; and ye like men

προσδεχομένοις τὸν κύριον ἑαυτῶν, πότε
awaiting the lord of them*selves*, when

ἀναλύσῃ ἐκ τῶν γάμων, ἵνα ἐλθόντος
he returns from the wedding festivities, that coming[a]

καὶ κρούσαντος εὐθέως ἀνοίξωσιν αὐτῷ.
and knocking[a] immediately they may open to him.

37 μακάριοι οἱ δοῦλοι ἐκεῖνοι, οὓς ἐλθὼν
Blessed - slaves those, whom coming

ὁ κύριος εὑρήσει γρηγοροῦντας· ἀμὴν λέγω
the lord will find watching; truly I tell

ὑμῖν ὅτι περιζώσεται καὶ ἀνακλινεῖ αὐτοὺς
you that he will gird himself and [1]make [2]to recline [1]them

καὶ παρελθὼν διακονήσει αὐτοῖς. 38 κἂν
and coming up to will serve them. And if

ἐν τῇ δευτέρᾳ κἂν ἐν τῇ τρίτῃ φυλακῇ
in the second and if in the third watch

ἔλθῃ καὶ εὕρῃ οὕτως, μακάριοί εἰσιν
he comes and finds so, blessed are

ἐκεῖνοι. 39 τοῦτο δὲ γινώσκετε, ὅτι εἰ
those [slaves]. But this know ye, that if

ᾔδει ὁ οἰκοδεσπότης ποίᾳ ὥρᾳ ὁ κλέπτης
knew the house-master in what hour the thief

ἔρχεται, οὐκ ἂν ἀφῆκεν διορυχθῆναι τὸν
comes, he would not have allowed to be dug through the

οἶκον αὐτοῦ. 40 καὶ ὑμεῖς γίνεσθε ἕτοιμοι,
house of him. And [1]ye [1]be prepared,

ὅτι ᾗ ὥρᾳ οὐ δοκεῖτε ὁ υἱὸς τοῦ
because in what hour ye think not the Son -

ἀνθρώπου ἔρχεται. 41 Εἶπεν δὲ ὁ Πέτρος·
of man comes. And said - Peter:

κύριε, πρὸς ἡμᾶς τὴν παραβολὴν ταύτην
Lord, to us - parable this

λέγεις ἢ καὶ πρὸς πάντας; 42 καὶ εἶπεν
sayest thou or also to all? And said

ὁ κύριος· τίς ἄρα ἐστὶν ὁ πιστὸς
the Lord: Who then is the faithful

οἰκονόμος ὁ φρόνιμος, ὃν καταστήσει ὁ
steward the prudent, whom will appoint the

κύριος ἐπὶ τῆς θεραπείας αὐτοῦ τοῦ
lord over the household attendants of him -

διδόναι ἐν καιρῷ [τὸ]d σιτομέτριον;
to give[d] in season the portion of food?

43 μακάριος ὁ δοῦλος ἐκεῖνος, ὃν ἐλθὼν
Blessed - slave that, whom coming

ὁ κύριος αὐτοῦ εὑρήσει ποιοῦντα οὕτως.
the lord of him will find doing so.

44 ἀληθῶς λέγω ὑμῖν ὅτι ἐπὶ πᾶσιν τοῖς
Truly I tell you that over all the

ὑπάρχουσιν αὐτοῦ καταστήσει αὐτόν. 45 ἐὰν
possessions of him he will appoint him. if

δὲ εἴπῃ ὁ δοῦλος ἐκεῖνος ἐν τῇ καρδίᾳ
But says - slave that in the heart

αὐτοῦ· χρονίζει ὁ κύριός μου ἔρχεσθαι,
of him: Delays the lord of me to come,

καὶ ἄρξηται τύπτειν τοὺς παῖδας καὶ τὰς
and begins to strike the menservants and the

παιδίσκας, ἐσθίειν τε καὶ πίνειν καὶ
maidservants, [2]to eat [1]both and to drink and

μεθύσκεσθαι, 46 ἥξει ὁ κύριος τοῦ δούλου
to become drunk, will come the lord - slave

ἐκείνου ἐν ἡμέρᾳ ᾗ οὐ προσδοκᾷ καὶ ἐν
of that in a day in which he does not expect and in

ὥρᾳ ᾗ οὐ γινώσκει, καὶ διχοτομήσει
an hour *in* which he knows not, and will cut asunder

αὐτόν, καὶ τὸ μέρος αὐτοῦ μετὰ τῶν
him, and the portion of him with the

ἀπίστων θήσει. 47 ἐκεῖνος δὲ ὁ δοῦλος
unbelievers will place. But that - slave

ὁ γνοὺς τὸ θέλημα τοῦ κυρίου αὐτοῦ
- having known the will of the lord of him

καὶ μὴ ἑτοιμάσας ἢ ποιήσας πρὸς τὸ θέλημα
and not having prepared or done according to the will

αὐτοῦ δαρήσεται πολλάς· 48 ὁ δὲ
of him will be beaten [with] many [stripes]; but the [one]

μὴ γνούς, ποιήσας δὲ ἄξια πληγῶν,
not having known, but having done things worthy of stripes,

δαρήσεται ὀλίγας. παντὶ δὲ ᾧ
will be beaten [with] few [stripes]. But to everyone to whom

ἐδόθη πολύ, πολὺ ζητηθήσεται παρ' αὐτοῦ, καὶ
was given much, much will be demanded from him, and

ᾧ παρέθεντο πολύ, περισσότερον αἰτήσουσιν
with whom was deposited much, more exceedingly they will ask

αὐτόν. 49 Πῦρ ἦλθον βαλεῖν ἐπὶ τὴν γῆν,
him. Fire I came to cast on the earth,

καὶ τί θέλω εἰ ἤδη ἀνήφθη. 50 βάπτισμα
and what will I if already it was kindled. [a]a baptism

δὲ ἔχω βαπτισθῆναι, καὶ πῶς συνέχομαι
[1]And[1]I have to be baptized [with], and how am I pressed

ἕως ὅτου τελεσθῇ. 51 δοκεῖτε ὅτι εἰρήνην
until it is accomplished. Think ye that peace

παρεγενόμην δοῦναι ἐν τῇ γῇ; οὐχί, λέγω
I came to give in the earth? No, I tell

ὑμῖν, ἀλλ' ἢ διαμερισμόν. 52 ἔσονται γὰρ
you, but rather division. For there will be

ἀπὸ τοῦ νῦν πέντε ἐν ἑνὶ οἴκῳ διαμεμε-
from - now five in one house *having been*

ρισμένοι, τρεῖς ἐπὶ δυσὶν καὶ δύο ἐπὶ
divided, three against two and two against

τρισὶν 53 διαμερισθήσονται, πατὴρ ἐπὶ υἱῷ
three will be divided, father against son

καὶ υἱὸς ἐπὶ πατρί, μήτηρ ἐπὶ θυγατέρα
and son against father, mother against daughter

217

King James Version

the mother in law against her daughter in law, and the daughter in law against her mother in law.

54 And he said also to the people, When ye see a cloud rise out of the west, straightway ye say, There cometh a shower; and so it is. 55And when *ye see* the south wind blow, ye say, There will be heat; and it cometh to pass. 56 *Ye* hypocrites, ye can discern the face of the sky and of the earth; but how is it that ye do not discern this time? 57 Yea, and why even of yourselves judge ye not what is right?

58 When thou goest with thine adversary to the magistrate, *as thou art* in the way, give diligence that thou mayest be delivered from him; lest he hale thee to the judge, and the judge deliver thee to the officer, and the officer cast thee into prison. 59 I tell thee, thou shalt not depart thence, till thou hast paid the very last mite.

13 There were present at that season some that told him of the Galileans, whose blood Pilate had mingled with their sacrifices. 2And Jesus answering said unto them, Suppose ye that these Galileans were sinners above all the Galileans, because they suffered such things? 3 I tell you, Nay: but, except ye repent, ye shall all likewise perish. 4 Or those eighteen, upon whom the tower in Siloam fell, and slew them, think ye that they were sinners above all men that dwelt in Jerusalem? 5 I tell you, Nay: but, except ye repent, ye shall all likewise perish.

6 He spake also this parable; A certain *man* had a fig tree planted in his vineyard; and he came and sought fruit thereon, and found none. 7 Then said he unto the dresser of his vineyard, Behold, these three years I come seeking fruit on this fig tree, and find none: cut it down; why cumbereth it the ground? 8And he answering said unto him, Lord, let it alone this year also, till I shall dig about it, and dung *it:* 9And if it bear fruit, *well:* and if not, *then* after that thou shalt cut it down.

10 And he was teaching in one of the synagogues on the sabbath. 11And, behold, there was a woman which had a spirit of infirmity eighteen years, and was bowed together, and could in no wise lift up *herself.* 12And when Jesus saw her, he called *her to him,* and said unto her, Woman, thou art loosed from thine infirmity. 13And he laid *his* hands on her: and immediately she was made straight, and glorified God. 14And the ruler of the synagogue answered with indignation, because that Jesus had healed on the sabbath day, and said unto the people, There are six days in which men ought to work: in them therefore come and be healed, and not on the sabbath day. 15 The Lord then answered him, and said, *Thou* hypocrite, doth not each

New International Version

against mother, mother-in-law against daughter-in-law and daughter-in-law against mother-in-law."

Interpreting the times

54 He said to the crowd: "When you see a cloud rising in the west, immediately you say, 'It's going to rain,' and it does. 55And when the south wind blows, you say, 'It's going to be hot,' and it is. 56 Hypocrites! You know how to interpret the appearance of the earth and the sky. How is it that you don't know how to interpret this present time?

57 "Why don't you judge for yourselves what is right? 58As you are going with your adversary to the magistrate, try hard to be reconciled to him on the way, or he may drag you off to the judge, and the judge turn you over to the officer, and the officer throw you into prison. 59 I tell you, you will not get out until you have paid the last penny."

Repent or perish

13 Now there were some present at that time who told Jesus about the Galileans whose blood Pilate had mixed with their sacrifices. 2 Jesus answered, "Do you think that these Galileans were worse sinners than all the other Galileans because they suffered this way? 3 I tell you, no! But unless you repent, you too will all perish. 4 Or those eighteen who died when the tower in Siloam fell on them—do you think they were more guilty than all the others living in Jerusalem? 5 I tell you, no! But unless you repent, you too will all perish."

6 Then he told this parable: "A man had a fig tree, planted in his vineyard, and he went to look for fruit on it, but did not find any. 7 So he said to the man who took care of the vineyard, 'For three years now I've been coming to look for fruit on this fig tree and haven't found any. Cut it down! Why should it use up the soil?'

8 "'Sir,' the man replied, 'leave it alone for one more year, and I'll dig around it and fertilize it. 9 If it bears fruit next year, fine! If not, then cut it down.'"

A crippled woman healed on the Sabbath

10 On a Sabbath Jesus was teaching in one of the synagogues, 11 and a woman was there who had been crippled by a spirit for eighteen years. She was bent over and could not straighten up at all. 12 When Jesus saw her, he called her forward and said to her, "Woman, you are set free from your infirmity." 13 Then he put his hands on her, and immediately she straightened up and praised God.

14 Indignant because Jesus had healed on the Sabbath, the synagogue ruler said to the people, "There are six days for work. So come and be healed on those days, not on the Sabbath."

15 The Lord answered him, "You hypocrites!

Greek Interlinear

καὶ θυγάτηρ ἐπὶ τὴν μητέρα, πενθερὰ
and daughter against the mother, mother-in-law

ἐπὶ τὴν νύμφην αὐτῆς καὶ νύμφη ἐπὶ
against the daughter-in-law of her and daughter-in-law against

τὴν πενθεράν. 54 Ἔλεγεν δὲ καὶ τοῖς
the mother-in-law. And he said also to the

ὄχλοις· ὅταν ἴδητε νεφέλην ἀνατέλλουσαν
crowds : When ye see a cloud rising

ἐπὶ δυσμῶν, εὐθέως λέγετε ὅτι ὄμβρος
over [the] west, immediately ye say that a storm

ἔρχεται, καὶ γίνεται οὕτως· 55 καὶ ὅταν
is coming, and it becomes so; and when

νότον πνέοντα, λέγετε ὅτι καύσων ἔσται,
a south wind blowing, ye say that heat there will be,

καὶ γίνεται. 56 ὑποκριταί, τὸ πρόσωπον
and it becomes. Hypocrites, the face

τῆς γῆς καὶ τοῦ οὐρανοῦ οἴδατε δοκιμάζειν,
of the earth and of the heaven ye know* to discern,

τὸν καιρὸν δὲ τοῦτον πῶς οὐ δοκιμάζετε;
- ²time ¹but ³this how do ye not discern?

57 Τί δὲ καὶ ἀφ' ἑαυτῶν οὐ κρίνετε
And why even from yourselves do ye not judge

τὸ δίκαιον; 58 ὡς γὰρ ὑπάγεις μετὰ τοῦ
the righteous thing? For as thou goest with the

ἀντιδίκου σου ἐπ' ἄρχοντα, ἐν τῇ ὁδῷ
adversary of thee to a ruler, in the way

δὸς ἐργασίαν ἀπηλλάχθαι ἀπ' αὐτοῦ, μήποτε
give(take) pains to be rid from(of) him, lest

κατασύρῃ σε πρὸς τὸν κριτήν, καὶ ὁ
he drag thee to the judge, and the

κριτής σε παραδώσει τῷ πράκτορι, καὶ ὁ
judge thee will deliver to the usher, and the

πράκτωρ σε βαλεῖ εἰς φυλακήν. 59 λέγω
usher thee will cast into prison. I tell

σοι, οὐ μὴ ἐξέλθῃς ἐκεῖθεν ἕως
thee, by no means mayest thou come out thence until

καὶ τὸ ἔσχατον λεπτὸν ἀποδῷς.
even the last lepton thou payest.

Chapter 13

Παρῆσαν δέ τινες ἐν αὐτῷ τῷ
And there were present some at ⁴same ¹the

καιρῷ ἀπαγγέλλοντες αὐτῷ περὶ τῶν
time reporting to him about the

Γαλιλαίων ὧν τὸ αἷμα Πιλᾶτος ἔμιξεν
Galilæans of whom the blood Pilate mixed

μετὰ τῶν θυσιῶν αὐτῶν. 2 καὶ ἀποκριθεὶς
with the sacrifices of them. And answering

εἶπεν αὐτοῖς· δοκεῖτε ὅτι οἱ Γαλιλαῖοι
he said to them : Think ye that - Galilæans

οὗτοι ἁμαρτωλοὶ παρὰ πάντας τοὺς Γαλι-
these sinners above all ¹he Gali-

λαίους ἐγένοντο, ὅτι ταῦτα πεπόνθασιν;
læans were, because these things they have suffered?

3 οὐχί, λέγω ὑμῖν, ἀλλ' ἐὰν μὴ μετανοῆτε,
No, I tell you, but unless ye repent,

πάντες ὁμοίως ἀπολεῖσθε. 4 ἢ ἐκεῖνοι οἱ
all likewise ye will perish. Or those -

δεκαοκτὼ ἐφ' οὓς ἔπεσεν ὁ πύργος ἐν
eighteen on whom fell the tower in

τῷ Σιλωὰμ καὶ ἀπέκτεινεν αὐτούς, δοκεῖτε
- Siloam and killed them, think ye

ὅτι αὐτοὶ ὀφειλέται ἐγένοντο παρὰ πάντας
that they debtors were above all

τοὺς ἀνθρώπους τοὺς κατοικοῦντας Ἰερου-
the men - dwelling in Jeru-

σαλήμ; 5 οὐχί, λέγω ὑμῖν, ἀλλ' ἐὰν μὴ
salem? No, I tell you, but unless

μετανοήσητε, πάντες ὡσαύτως ἀπολεῖσθε.
ye repent, all similarly ye will perish.

6 Ἔλεγεν δὲ ταύτην τὴν παραβολήν. συκῆν
And he told this - parable. ³A fig-tree

εἶχέν τις πεφυτευμένην ἐν τῷ ἀμπελῶνι
¹had ¹a certain man *having been* planted in the vineyard

αὐτοῦ, καὶ ἦλθεν ζητῶν καρπὸν ἐν αὐτῇ
of him, and came seeking fruit in it

καὶ οὐχ εὗρεν. 7 εἶπεν δὲ πρὸς τὸν
and found not. And he said to the

ἀμπελουργόν· ἰδοὺ τρία ἔτη ἀφ' οὗ
vinedresser : Behold[,] three years [it is] since

ἔρχομαι ζητῶν καρπὸν ἐν τῇ συκῇ ταύτῃ
I come seeking fruit in - fig-tree this

καὶ οὐχ εὑρίσκω· ἔκκοψον αὐτήν· ἱνατί
and find not; cut down it; why

καὶ τὴν γῆν καταργεῖ; 8 ὁ δὲ ἀποκριθεὶς
even the ground it spoils? But he answering

λέγει αὐτῷ· κύριε, ἄφες αὐτὴν καὶ τοῦτο
says to him : Lord, leave it also this

τὸ ἔτος, ἕως ὅτου σκάψω περὶ αὐτὴν καὶ
- year, until I may dig round it and

βάλω κόπρια, 9 κἂν μὲν ποιήσῃ καρπὸν
may throw dung, and if indeed it makes fruit

εἰς τὸ μέλλον· εἰ δὲ μή γε, ἐκκόψεις
in the future; otherwise, thou shalt cut down

αὐτήν.
it.

10 Ἦν δὲ διδάσκων ἐν μιᾷ τῶν συναγωγῶν
And he was teaching in one of the synagogues

ἐν τοῖς σάββασιν. 11 καὶ ἰδοὺ γυνὴ
on the sabbaths. And[,] behold[,] a woman

πνεῦμα ἔχουσα ἀσθενείας ἔτη δεκαοκτώ,
²a spirit ¹having of infirmity years eighteen,

καὶ ἦν συγκύπτουσα καὶ μὴ δυναμένη
and was bending double and not being able

ἀνακύψαι εἰς τὸ παντελές. 12 ἰδὼν δὲ
to become erect entirely.† And seeing

αὐτὴν ὁ Ἰησοῦς προσεφώνησεν καὶ εἶπεν
her - Jesus called to [him] and said

αὐτῇ· γύναι, ἀπολέλυσαι τῆς ἀσθενείας
to her : Woman, thou hast been loosed from the infirmity

σου, 13 καὶ ἐπέθηκεν αὐτῇ τὰς χεῖρας·
of thee, and he put on her the(his) hands;

καὶ παραχρῆμα ἀνωρθώθη, καὶ ἐδόξαζεν
and at once she was straightened, and glorified

τὸν θεόν. 14 ἀποκριθεὶς δὲ ὁ ἀρχι-
- God. But answering the syn-

συνάγωγος, ἀγανακτῶν ὅτι τῷ σαββάτῳ
agogue ruler, being angry that ²on the ⁴sabbath

ἐθεράπευσεν ὁ Ἰησοῦς, ἔλεγεν τῷ ὄχλῳ
³healed - ¹Jesus, said to the crowd[,]

ὅτι ἓξ ἡμέραι εἰσὶν ἐν αἷς δεῖ ἐργάζεσθαι·
six days there are on which it behoves to work;

ἐν αὐταῖς οὖν ἐρχόμενοι θεραπεύεσθε καὶ
on them therefore coming be ye healed and

μὴ τῇ ἡμέρᾳ τοῦ σαββάτου. 15 ἀπεκρίθη δὲ
not on the day of the sabbath. But answered

αὐτῷ ὁ κύριος καὶ εἶπεν· ὑποκριταί,
him the Lord and said : Hypocrites,

* can, as Mat. 16. 3. See note on page xxxviii

King James Version

one of you on the sabbath loose his ox or *his* ass from the stall, and lead *him* away to watering? 16And ought not this woman, being a daughter of Abraham, whom Satan hath bound, lo, these eighteen years, be loosed from this bond on the sabbath day? 17And when he had said these things, all his adversaries were ashamed: and all the people rejoiced for all the glorious things that were done by him.

18 Then said he, Unto what is the kingdom of God like? and whereunto shall I resemble it? 19 It is like a grain of mustard seed, which a man took, and cast into his garden; and it grew, and waxed a great tree; and the fowls of the air lodged in the branches of it. 20And again he said, Whereunto shall I liken the kingdom of God? 21 It is like leaven, which a woman took and hid in three measures of meal, till the whole was leavened. 22And he went through the cities and villages, teaching, and journeying toward Jerusalem. 23 Then said one unto him, Lord, are there few that be saved? And he said unto them,

24 Strive to enter in at the strait gate: for many, I say unto you, will seek to enter in, and shall not be able. 25 When once the master of the house is risen up, and hath shut to the door, and ye begin to stand without, and to knock at the door, saying, Lord, Lord, open unto us; and he shall answer and say unto you, I know you not whence ye are: 26 Then shall ye begin to say, We have eaten and drunk in thy presence, and thou hast taught in our streets. 27 But he shall say, I tell you, I know you not whence ye are; depart from me, all *ye* workers of iniquity. 28 There shall be weeping and gnashing of teeth, when ye shall see Abraham, and Isaac, and Jacob, and all the prophets, in the kingdom of God, and you *yourselves* thrust out. 29And they shall come from the east, and *from* the west, and from the north, and *from* the south, and shall sit down in the kingdom of God. 30And, behold, there are last which shall be first; and there are first which shall be last.

31 The same day there came certain of the Pharisees, saying unto him, Get thee out, and depart hence; for Herod will kill thee. 32And he said unto them, Go ye, and tell that fox, Behold, I cast out devils, and I do cures to day and to morrow, and the third *day* I shall be perfected. 33 Nevertheless I must walk to day, and to morrow, and the *day* following: for it cannot be that a prophet perish out of Jerusalem. 34 O Jerusalem, Jerusalem, which killest the prophets, and stonest them that are sent unto thee; how often would I have gathered thy children together, as a hen *doth gather* her brood under *her* wings, and ye would not! 35 Behold, your house is left unto you desolate: and verily I say unto you, Ye shall not see me, until *the time* come when ye shall say, Blessed *is* he that cometh in the name of the Lord.

New International Version

Doesn't each of you on the Sabbath untie his ox or donkey from the stall and lead it out to give it water? 16 Then should not this woman, a daughter of Abraham, whom Satan has kept bound for eighteen long years, be set free on the Sabbath day from what bound her?"

17 When he said this, all his opponents were humiliated, but the people were delighted with all the wonderful things he was doing.

The parables of the mustard seed and yeast

18 Then Jesus asked, "What is the kingdom of God like? What shall I compare it to? 19 It is like a mustard seed, which a man took and planted in his garden. It grew, became a tree, and the birds of the air perched in its branches."

20 Again he asked, "What shall I compare the kingdom of God to? 21 It is like yeast that a woman took and mixed into a large amount*a* of flour until it worked all through the dough."

The narrow door

22 Then Jesus went through the cities and villages, teaching as he made his way to Jerusalem. 23 Someone asked him, "Lord, are only a few people going to be saved?"

He said to them, 24 "Make every effort to enter through the narrow door, because many, I tell you, will try to enter and will not be able to. 25 Once the owner of the house gets up and closes the door, you will stand outside knocking and pleading, 'Sir, open the door for us.'

"But he will answer, 'I don't know you or where you come from.'

26 "Then you will say, 'We ate and drank with you, and you taught in our streets.'

27 "But he will reply, 'I don't know you or where you come from. Away from me, all you evildoers!'

28 "There will be weeping and grinding of teeth when you see Abraham, Isaac and Jacob and all the prophets in the kingdom of God, but you yourselves thrown out. 29 People will come from east and west and north and south, and will take their places at the feast in the kingdom of God. 30 Indeed there are those who are last who will be first, and first who will be last."

Jesus' sorrow for Jerusalem

31 At that time some Pharisees came to Jesus and said to him, "Leave this place and go somewhere else. Herod wants to kill you."

32 He replied, "Go tell that fox, 'I will drive out demons and heal people today and tomorrow, and on the third day I will reach my goal.' 33 In any case, I must keep going today and tomorrow and the next day—for surely no prophet can die outside Jerusalem!

34 "O Jerusalem, Jerusalem, you who kill the prophets and stone those sent to you, how often I have longed to gather your children together, as a hen gathers her chicks under her wings, but you were not willing! 35 Look, your house is left to you desolate. I tell you, you will not see me again until you say, 'Blessed is he who comes in the name of the Lord.' *b* "

[a] Greek *three satas* (about a bushel). [b] Psalm 118:26.

Greek Interlinear

ἕκαστος ὑμῶν τῷ σαββάτῳ οὐ λύει τὸν
each one   of you on the sabbath does he not loosen the

βοῦν αὐτοῦ ἢ τὸν ὄνον ἀπὸ τῆς φάτνης
ox   of him or the ass   from the   manger

καὶ ἀπαγαγὼν ποτίζει; 16 ταύτην δὲ
and leading [it] away give drink? And this woman

θυγατέρα Ἀβραὰμ οὖσαν, ἣν ἔδησεν ὁ
a daughter of Abraham being, whom bound   -

σατανᾶς ἰδοὺ δέκα καὶ ὀκτὼ ἔτη, οὐκ ἔδει
Satan behold ten and eight years, behoved it not

λυθῆναι ἀπὸ τοῦ δεσμοῦ τούτου τῇ
to be loosened from - bond   this on the

ἡμέρᾳ τοῦ σαββάτου; 17 καὶ ταῦτα λέγοντος
day   of the sabbath?   And these things saying
                                    = when he said these things

αὐτοῦ κατῃσχύνοντο πάντες οἱ ἀντικείμενοι
him[a] were put to shame all the [ones] opposing

αὐτῷ, καὶ πᾶς ὁ ὄχλος ἔχαιρεν ἐπὶ
him, and all the crowd rejoiced over

πᾶσι τοῖς ἐνδόξοις τοῖς γινομένοις ὑπ'
all the glorious things the happening by

αὐτοῦ. 18 Ἔλεγεν οὖν· τίνι ὁμοία ἐστὶν ἡ
him.   He said therefore: To what like is the

βασιλεία τοῦ θεοῦ, καὶ τίνι ὁμοιώσω
kingdom   - of God, and to what may I liken

αὐτήν; 19 ὁμοία ἐστὶν κόκκῳ σινάπεως, ὃν
it?   Like it is to a grain of mustard, which

λαβὼν ἄνθρωπος ἔβαλεν εἰς κῆπον ἑαυτοῦ,
[a]taking [a] a man cast into a garden of himself,

καὶ ηὔξησεν καὶ ἐγένετο εἰς δένδρον, καὶ
and it grew and became into a tree, and

τὰ πετεινὰ τοῦ οὐρανοῦ κατεσκήνωσεν
the birds   of the heaven(air) lodged

ἐν τοῖς κλάδοις αὐτοῦ. 20 Καὶ πάλιν
in the branches of it.   And again

εἶπεν· τίνι ὁμοιώσω τὴν βασιλείαν τοῦ
he said : To what may I liken the kingdom -

θεοῦ; 21 ὁμοία ἐστὶν ζύμῃ, ἣν λαβοῦσα
of God? Like it is to leaven, which [a]taking

γυνὴ ἔκρυψεν εἰς ἀλεύρου σάτα τρία,
[a] a woman hid in of meal measures three,

ἕως οὗ ἐζυμώθη ὅλον.
until was leavened all.

22 Καὶ διεπορεύετο κατὰ πόλεις καὶ
And he journeyed through throughout cities and

κώμας διδάσκων καὶ πορείαν ποιούμενος
villages teaching and journey making

εἰς Ἱεροσόλυμα. 23 Εἶπεν δέ τις αὐτῷ·
to Jerusalem.   And said someone to him :

κύριε, εἰ ὀλίγοι οἱ σωζόμενοι; ὁ δὲ εἶπεν
Lord, if few the [ones] being saved? And he said

πρὸς αὐτούς· 24 ἀγωνίζεσθε εἰσελθεῖν διὰ
to   them :   Struggle   to enter through

τῆς στενῆς θύρας, ὅτι πολλοί, λέγω ὑμῖν,
the strait door, because many, I tell you,

ζητήσουσιν εἰσελθεῖν καὶ οὐκ ἰσχύσουσιν.
will seek to enter and will not be able.

25 ἀφ' οὗ ἂν ἐγερθῇ ὁ οἰκοδεσπότης καὶ
From [the time] when is risen the house-master and

ἀποκλείσῃ τὴν θύραν, καὶ ἄρξησθε ἔξω
he shuts the door, and ye begin outside

ἑστάναι καὶ κρούειν τὴν θύραν λέγοντες·
to stand and to knock the door saying :

κύριε, ἄνοιξον ἡμῖν, καὶ ἀποκριθεὶς ἐρεῖ
Lord, open to us, and answering he will say

ὑμῖν· οὐκ οἶδα ὑμᾶς πόθεν ἐστέ. 26 τότε
to you : I know not you whence ye are.   Then

ἄρξεσθε λέγειν· ἐφάγομεν ἐνώπιόν σου καὶ
ye will begin to say : We ate before thee and

ἐπίομεν, καὶ ἐν ταῖς πλατείαις ἡμῶν
drank, and in the streets of us

ἐδίδαξας· 27 καὶ ἐρεῖ λέγων ὑμῖν· οὐκ
thou didst teach; and he will say telling you : not

οἶδα πόθεν ἐστέ· ἀπόστητε ἀπ' ἐμοῦ
I know whence ye are; stand away from me

πάντες ἐργάται ἀδικίας. 28 ἐκεῖ ἔσται ὁ
all workers of unrighteousness. There will be the

κλαυθμὸς καὶ ὁ βρυγμὸς τῶν ὀδόντων,
weeping and the gnashing of the teeth,

ὅταν ὄψησθε Ἀβραὰμ καὶ Ἰσαὰκ καὶ
when ye see Abraham and Isaac and

Ἰακὼβ καὶ πάντας τοὺς προφήτας ἐν τῇ
Jacob and all the prophets in the

βασιλείᾳ τοῦ θεοῦ, ὑμᾶς δὲ ἐκβαλλομένους
kingdom   - of God, but you being thrust out

ἔξω. 29 καὶ ἥξουσιν ἀπὸ ἀνατολῶν καὶ
outside.   And they will come from east and

δυσμῶν καὶ ἀπὸ βορρᾶ καὶ νότου, καὶ
west and from north and south, and

ἀνακλιθήσονται ἐν τῇ βασιλείᾳ τοῦ θεοῦ.
will recline in the kingdom - of God.

30 καὶ ἰδοὺ εἰσὶν ἔσχατοι οἳ ἔσονται
And behold there are last [ones] who will be

πρῶτοι, καὶ εἰσὶν πρῶτοι οἳ ἔσονται
first, and there are first [ones] who will be

ἔσχατοι. 31 Ἐν αὐτῇ τῇ ὥρᾳ προσῆλθάν
last.   In [2]same [1]the hour approached

τινες Φαρισαῖοι λέγοντες αὐτῷ· ἔξελθε καὶ
some Pharisees saying to him : Depart and

πορεύου ἐντεῦθεν, ὅτι Ἡρῴδης θέλει σε
go hence, because Herod wishes thee

ἀποκτεῖναι. 32 καὶ εἶπεν αὐτοῖς· πορευθέντες
to kill.   And he said to them : Going

εἴπατε τῇ ἀλώπεκι ταύτῃ· ἰδοὺ ἐκβάλλω
tell - fox this : Behold I expel

δαιμόνια καὶ ἰάσεις ἀποτελῶ σήμερον καὶ
demons and [2]cures [1]accomplish to-day and .

αὔριον, καὶ τῇ τρίτῃ τελειοῦμαι. 33 πλὴν
to-morrow, and on the third [day] I am perfected. Nevertheless

δεῖ με σήμερον καὶ αὔριον καὶ τῇ ἐχομένῃ
it be- me to-day and to- and on the following
hoves   morrow   [day]

πορεύεσθαι, ὅτι οὐκ ἐνδέχεται προφήτην
to journey, because it is not possible a prophet

ἀπολέσθαι ἔξω Ἱερουσαλήμ. 34 Ἱερουσαλὴμ
to perish outside Jerusalem.   Jerusalem[.]

Ἱερουσαλήμ, ἡ ἀποκτείνουσα τοὺς προφήτας
Jerusalem, the [one] killing the prophets

καὶ λιθοβολοῦσα τοὺς ἀπεσταλμένους πρὸς
and stoning the [ones] having been sent to

αὐτήν, ποσάκις ἠθέλησα ἐπισυνάξαι τὰ
her, how often I wished to gather the

τέκνα σου ὃν τρόπον ὄρνις τὴν ἑαυτῆς
children of thee as † a bird the of herself

νοσσιὰν ὑπὸ τὰς πτέρυγας, καὶ οὐκ
brood under the(her) wings, and not

ἠθελήσατε. 35 ἰδοὺ ἀφίεται ὑμῖν ὁ οἶκος
ye wished.   Behold is left to you the house

ὑμῶν. λέγω [δὲ] ὑμῖν, οὐ μὴ ἴδητέ με
of you. And I tell you, by no means ye may see me

ἕως ἥξει ὅτε εἴπητε· εὐλογημένος ὁ
until shall come [the ye say : Blessed the
      time] when

ἐρχόμενος ἐν ὀνόματι κυρίου.
[one] coming in [the] name of [the] Lord.

King James Version

14 And it came to pass, as he went into the house of one of the chief Pharisees to eat bread on the sabbath day, that they watched him. 2And, behold, there was a certain man before him which had the dropsy. 3And Jesus answering spake unto the lawyers and Pharisees, saying, Is it lawful to heal on the sabbath day? 4And they held their peace. And he took *him*, and healed him, and let him go; 5And answered them, saying, Which of you shall have an ass or an ox fallen into a pit, and will not straightway pull him out on the sabbath day? 6And they could not answer him again to these things.

7 And he put forth a parable to those which were bidden, when he marked how they chose out the chief rooms; saying unto them, 8 When thou art bidden of any *man* to a wedding, sit not down in the highest room; lest a more honourable man than thou be bidden of him; 9And he that bade thee and him come and say to thee, Give this man place; and thou begin with shame to take the lowest room. 10 But when thou art bidden, go and sit down in the lowest room; that when he that bade thee cometh, he may say unto thee, Friend, go up higher: then shalt thou have worship in the presence of them that sit at meat with thee. 11 For whosoever exalteth himself shall be abased; and he that humbleth himself shall be exalted.

12 Then said he also to him that bade him, When thou makest a dinner or a supper, call not thy friends, nor thy brethren, neither thy kinsmen, nor *thy* rich neighbours; lest they also bid thee again, and a recompense be made thee. 13 But when thou makest a feast, call the poor, the maimed, the lame, the blind: 14And thou shalt be blessed; for they cannot recompense thee: for thou shalt be recompensed at the resurrection of the just.

15 And when one of them that sat at meat with him heard these things, he said unto him, Blessed *is* he that shall eat bread in the kingdom of God. 16 Then said he unto him, A certain man made a great supper, and bade many: 17And sent his servant at supper time to say to them that were bidden, Come; for all things are now ready. 18And they all with one *consent* began to make excuse. The first said unto him, I have bought a piece of ground, and I must needs go and see it: I pray thee have me excused. 19And another said, I have bought five yoke of oxen, and I go to prove them: I pray thee have me excused. 20And another said, I have married a wife, and therefore I cannot come. 21 So that servant came, and shewed his lord these things. Then the master of the house being angry said to his servant, Go out quickly into the streets and lanes of the city, and bring in hither the poor, and the maimed, and the halt, and the blind. 22And the servant said, Lord, it is done as thou hast commanded, and yet there is room. 23And the lord said unto the servant, Go out into the highways and hedges, and compel *them*

New International Version

Jesus at a Pharisee's house

14 One Sabbath, when Jesus went to eat in the house of a prominent Pharisee, he was being carefully watched. 2 There in front of him was a man suffering from dropsy. 3 Jesus asked the Pharisees and experts in the law, "Is it lawful to heal on the Sabbath or not?" 4 But they remained silent. So taking hold of the man, he healed him and sent him away.

5 Then he asked them, "If one of you has a son[c] or an ox that falls into a well on the Sabbath day, will you not immediately pull him out?" 6And they had nothing to say.

7 When he noticed how the guests picked the places of honor at the table, he told them this parable: 8 "When someone invites you to a wedding feast, do not take the place of honor, for a person more distinguished than you may have been invited. 9 If so, the host who invited both of you will come and say to you, 'Give this man your seat.' Then, humiliated, you will have to take the least important place. 10 But when you are invited, take the lowest place, so that when your host comes, he will say to you, 'Friend, move up to a better place.' Then you will be honored in the presence of all your fellow guests. 11 For everyone who exalts himself will be humbled, and he who humbles himself will be exalted."

12 Then Jesus said to his host, "When you give a luncheon or dinner, do not invite your friends, your brothers or relatives, or your rich neighbors; if you do, they may invite you back and so you will be repaid. 13 But when you give a banquet, invite the poor, the crippled, the lame, the blind, 14 and you will be blessed. Although they cannot repay you, you will be repaid at the resurrection of the righteous."

The parable of the great banquet

15 When one of those at the table with him heard this, he said to Jesus, "Blessed is the man who will eat at the feast in the kingdom of God."

16 Jesus replied: "A certain man was preparing a great banquet and invited many guests. 17At the time of the banquet he sent his servant to tell those who had been invited, 'Come, for everything is now ready.'

18 "But they all alike began to make excuses. The first said, 'I have just bought a field, and I must go and see it. Please excuse me.'

19 "Another said, 'I have just bought five yoke of oxen, and I'm on my way to try them out. Please excuse me.'

20 "Still another said, 'I just got married, so I can't come.'

21 "The servant came back and reported this to his master. Then the owner of the house became angry and ordered his servant, 'Go out quickly into the streets and alleys of the town and bring in the poor, the crippled, the blind and the lame.'

22 " 'Sir,' the servant said, 'what you ordered has been done, but there is still room.'

23 "Then the master told his servant, 'Go out to the roads and country lanes and make them

Greek Interlinear

Chapter 14

Καὶ ἐγένετο ἐν τῷ ἐλθεῖν αὐτὸν εἰς
And it came to pass in the to go him[be] into
=as he went

οἶκόν τινος τῶν ἀρχόντων τῶν Φαρισαίων
a house of one of the leaders of the Pharisees

σαββάτῳ φαγεῖν ἄρτον, καὶ αὐτοὶ ἦσαν
on a sabbath to eat bread, and they were

παρατηρούμενοι αὐτόν. 2 καὶ ἰδοὺ ἄνθρωπός
carefully watching him. And[,] behold[,] man

τις ἦν ὑδρωπικὸς ἔμπροσθεν αὐτοῦ. 3 καὶ
a certain was dropsical before him. And

ἀποκριθεὶς ὁ Ἰησοῦς εἶπεν πρὸς τοὺς
answering - Jesus spoke to the

νομικοὺς καὶ Φαρισαίους λέγων: ἔξεστιν
lawyers and Pharisees saying: Is it lawful

τῷ σαββάτῳ θεραπεῦσαι ἢ οὔ; 4 οἱ δὲ
on the sabbath to heal or not? And they

ἡσύχασαν. καὶ ἐπιλαβόμενος ἰάσατο αὐτὸν
were silent. And taking he cured him

καὶ ἀπέλυσεν. 5 καὶ πρὸς αὐτοὺς εἶπεν·
and dismissed. And to them he said:

τίνος ὑμῶν υἱὸς ἢ βοῦς εἰς φρέαρ πεσεῖται,
Of whom of you a son or an ox into a pit shall fall,

καὶ οὐκ εὐθέως ἀνασπάσει αὐτὸν ἐν
and not immediately he will pull up it on

ἡμέρᾳ τοῦ σαββάτου; 6 καὶ οὐκ ἴσχυσαν
a day of the sabbath? And they were not able

ἀνταποκριθῆναι πρὸς ταῦτα. 7 Ἔλεγεν δὲ
to reply against these things. And he said

πρὸς τοὺς κεκλημένους παραβολήν, ἐπέχων
to the [ones] having invited a parable, noting

πῶς τὰς πρωτοκλισίας ἐξελέγοντο, λέγων
how ¹the ²chief seats ¹they were choosing, saying

πρὸς αὐτούς· 8 ὅταν κληθῇς ὑπό τινος εἰς
to them: When thou art invited by anyone to

γάμους, μὴ κατακλιθῇς εἰς τὴν πρωτοκλισίαν,
wedding festivities, do not recline in the chief seat,

μήποτε ἐντιμότερός σου ᾖ κεκλημένος ὑπ'
lest a more honour- thou be having been invited by
able [than]

αὐτοῦ, 9 καὶ ἐλθὼν ὁ σὲ καὶ αὐτὸν καλέσας
him, and coming ¹the[one] ²thee ³and ⁴him ¹inviting

ἐρεῖ σοι· δὸς τούτῳ τόπον, καὶ τότε
will say to thee: Give this man place, and then

ἄρξῃ μετὰ αἰσχύνης τὸν ἔσχατον τόπον
thou wilt begin with shame the last place

κατέχειν. 10 ἀλλ' ὅταν κληθῇς, πορευθεὶς
to take. But when thou art invited, going

ἀνάπεσε εἰς τὸν ἔσχατον τόπον, ἵνα ὅταν ἔλθῃ
recline in the last place, that when ⁴comes

ὁ κεκληκώς σε ἐρεῖ σοι· φίλε,
¹the [one] ²having invited ³thee he will say to thee: Friend,

προσανάβηθι ἀνώτερον· τότε ἔσται σοι δόξα
go up higher; then there will be to thee[e] glory

ἐνώπιον πάντων τῶν συνανακειμένων σοι.
before all the [ones] reclining with thee.

11 ὅτι πᾶς ὁ ὑψῶν ἑαυτὸν ταπεινωθήσεται,
Because everyone exalting himself will be humbled,

καὶ ὁ ταπεινῶν ἑαυτὸν ὑψωθήσεται.
and the [one] humbling himself will be exalted.

12 Ἔλεγεν δὲ καὶ τῷ κεκληκότι αὐτόν·
And he said also to the [one] having invited him:

ὅταν ποιῇς ἄριστον ἢ δεῖπνον, μὴ φώνει
When thou makest a dinner or a supper, do not call

τοὺς φίλους σου μηδὲ τοὺς ἀδελφούς
the friends of thee nor the brothers

σου μηδὲ τοὺς συγγενεῖς σου μηδὲ
of thee nor the relatives of thee nor

γείτονας πλουσίους, μήποτε καὶ αὐτοὶ
neighbours rich, lest also they

ἀντικαλέσωσίν σε καὶ γένηται ἀνταπόδομά
¹invite ²in ³return ¹thee and it becomes a recompence

σοι. 13 ἀλλ' ὅταν δοχὴν ποιῇς, κάλει
to thee. But when a party thou makest, invite

πτωχούς, ἀναπήρους, χωλούς, τυφλούς·
poor [persons], maimed, lame, blind;

14 καὶ μακάριος ἔσῃ, ὅτι οὐκ ἔχουσιν
and blessed thou shalt be, because they have not

ἀνταποδοῦναί σοι· ἀνταποδοθήσεται γάρ σοι
to recompense thee; for it will be recompensed to thee

ἐν τῇ ἀναστάσει τῶν δικαίων. 15 Ἀκούσας
in the resurrection of the just. ¹hearing

δέ τις τῶν συνανακειμένων ταῦτα εἶπεν
¹And ⁴one ²of the [ones] ⁵reclining with ⁶these things said

αὐτῷ· μακάριος ὅστις φάγεται ἄρτον ἐν
to him: Blessed [is he] who eats bread in

τῇ βασιλείᾳ τοῦ θεοῦ. 16 ὁ δὲ εἶπεν
the kingdom - of God. And he said

αὐτῷ· ἄνθρωπός τις ἐποίει δεῖπνον μέγα,
to him: A certain man made supper a great,

καὶ ἐκάλεσεν πολλούς, 17 καὶ ἀπέστειλεν
and invited many, and sent

τὸν δοῦλον αὐτοῦ τῇ ὥρᾳ τοῦ δείπνου
the slave of him at the hour of the supper

εἰπεῖν τοῖς κεκλημένοις· ἔρχεσθε, ὅτι ἤδη
to say to the [ones] having been invited: Come, because ²now

ἕτοιμά ἐστιν. 18 καὶ ἤρξαντο ἀπὸ μιᾶς
²prepared ¹it is. And they began from one [mind]

πάντες παραιτεῖσθαι. ὁ πρῶτος εἶπεν
all to beg off. The first said

αὐτῷ· ἀγρὸν ἠγόρασα, καὶ ἔχω ἀνάγκην
to him: ²A farm ¹I bought, and I am obliged†

ἐξελθὼν ἰδεῖν αὐτόν· ἐρωτῶ σε, ἔχε με
going out to see it; I ask thee, have me

παρῃτημένον. 19 καὶ ἕτερος εἶπεν· ζεύγη
begged off. And another said: ²Yoke

βοῶν ἠγόρασα πέντε, καὶ πορεύομαι
¹of oxen ¹I bought ³five, and I am going

δοκιμάσαι αὐτά· ἐρωτῶ σε, ἔχε με
to prove them; I ask thee, have me

παρῃτημένον. 20 καὶ ἕτερος εἶπεν· γυναῖκα
begged off. And another said: ¹A wife

ἔγημα, καὶ διὰ τοῦτο οὐ δύναμαι ἐλθεῖν.
¹I married, and therefore I cannot to come.

21 καὶ παραγενόμενος ὁ δοῦλος ἀπήγγειλεν
And coming up the slave reported

τῷ κυρίῳ αὐτοῦ ταῦτα. τότε ὀργισθεὶς ὁ
to the lord of him these things. Then being angry the

οἰκοδεσπότης εἶπεν τῷ δούλῳ αὐτοῦ· ἔξελθε
house-master told the slave of him: Go out

ταχέως εἰς τὰς πλατείας καὶ ῥύμας τῆς
quickly into the streets and lanes of the

πόλεως, καὶ τοὺς πτωχοὺς καὶ ἀναπήρους
city, and the poor and maimed

καὶ τυφλοὺς καὶ χωλοὺς εἰσάγαγε ὧδε.
and blind and lame bring in here.

22 καὶ εἶπεν ὁ δοῦλος· κύριε, γέγονεν ὃ
And said the slave: Lord, has happened what

ἐπέταξας, καὶ ἔτι τόπος ἐστίν. 23 καὶ
thou didst command, and yet room there is. And

εἶπεν ὁ κύριος πρὸς τὸν δοῦλον· ἔξελθε εἰς
said the lord to the slave: Go out into

τὰς ὁδοὺς καὶ φραγμοὺς καὶ ἀνάγκασον
the ways and hedges and compel

εἰσελθεῖν, ἵνα γεμισθῇ μου ὁ οἶκος·
to come in, that may be filled of me the house;

King James Version

to come in, that my house may be filled. 24 For I say unto you, That none of those men which were bidden shall taste of my supper.

25 And there went great multitudes with him: and he turned, and said unto them, 26 If any *man* come to me, and hate not his father, and mother, and wife, and children, and brethren, and sisters, yea, and his own life also, he cannot be my disciple. 27And whosoever doth not bear his cross, and come after me, cannot be my disciple. 28 For which of you, intending to build a tower, sitteth not down first, and counteth the cost, whether he have *sufficient* to finish *it?* 29 Lest haply, after he hath laid the foundation, and is not able to finish *it,* all that behold *it* begin to mock him, 30 Saying, This man began to build, and was not able to finish. 31 Or what king, going to make war against another king, sitteth not down first, and consulteth whether he be able with ten thousand to meet him that cometh against him with twenty thousand? 32 Or else, while the other is yet a great way off, he sendeth an ambassage, and desireth conditions of peace. 33 So likewise, whosoever he be of you that forsaketh not all that he hath, he cannot be my disciple.

34 Salt *is* good: but if the salt have lost his savour, wherewith shall it be seasoned? 35 It is neither fit for the land, nor yet for the dunghill; *but* men cast it out. He that hath ears to hear, let him hear.

New International Version

come in, so that my house will be full. 24 I tell you, not one of those men who were invited will get a taste of my banquet.' "

The cost of being a disciple

25 Large crowds were traveling with Jesus, and turning to them he said: 26 "If anyone comes to me and does not hate his father and mother, his wife and children, his brothers and sisters—yes, even his own life—he cannot be my disciple. 27And anyone who does not carry his cross and follow me cannot be my disciple.

28 "Suppose one of you wants to build a tower. Will he not first sit down and estimate the cost to see if he has enough money to complete it? 29 For if he lays the foundation and is not able to finish it, everyone who sees it will ridicule him, 30 saying, 'This fellow began to build and was not able to finish.'

31 "Or suppose a king is about to go to war against another king. Will he not first sit down and consider whether he is able with ten thousand men to oppose the one coming against him with twenty thousand? 32 If he is not able, he will send a delegation while the other is still a long way off and will ask for terms of peace. 33 In the same way, any of you who does not give up everything he has cannot be my disciple.

34 "Salt is good, but if it loses its saltiness, how can it be made salty again? 35 It is fit neither for the soil nor for the manure pile; it is thrown out.

"He who has ears to hear, let him hear."

The parable of the lost sheep

15 Then drew near unto him all the publicans and sinners for to hear him. 2And the Pharisees and scribes murmured, saying, This man receiveth sinners, and eateth with them.

3 And he spake this parable unto them, saying, 4 What man of you, having a hundred sheep, if he lose one of them, doth not leave the ninety and nine in the wilderness, and go after that which is lost, until he find it? 5And when he hath found *it,* he layeth *it* on his shoulders, rejoicing. 6And when he cometh home, he calleth together *his* friends and neighbours, saying unto them, Rejoice with me; for I have found my sheep which was lost. 7 I say unto you, that likewise joy shall be in heaven over one sinner that repenteth, more than over ninety and nine just persons, which need no repentance.

8 Either what woman having ten pieces of silver, if she lose one piece, doth not light a candle, and sweep the house, and seek diligently till she find *it?* 9And when she hath found *it,* she calleth *her* friends and *her* neighbours together, saying, Rejoice with me; for I have found the piece which I had lost. 10 Likewise, I say unto you, there is joy in the presence of the angels of God over one sinner that repenteth.

15 Now the tax collectors and "sinners" were all gathering around to hear him. 2 But the Pharisees and the teachers of the law muttered, "This man welcomes sinners and eats with them."

3 Then Jesus told them this parable: 4 "Suppose one of you has a hundred sheep and loses one of them. Does he not leave the ninety-nine in the open country and go after the lost sheep until he finds it? 5And when he finds it, he joyfully puts it on his shoulders 6 and goes home. Then he calls his friends and neighbors together and says, 'Rejoice with me; I have found my lost sheep.' 7 I tell you that in the same way there is more rejoicing in heaven over one sinner who repents than over ninety-nine righteous persons who do not need to repent.

The parable of the lost coin

8 "Or suppose a woman has ten silver coins[d] and loses one. Does she not light a lamp, sweep the house and search carefully until she finds it? 9And when she finds it, she calls her friends and neighbors together and says, 'Rejoice with me; I have found my lost coin.' 10 In the same way, I tell you, there is rejoicing in the presence of the angels of God over one sinner who repents."

[d] Greek *drachmas,* each worth about a day's wage.

Greek Interlinear

24 λέγω γὰρ ὑμῖν ὅτι οὐδεὶς τῶν ἀνδρῶν
for I tell　you　that　not one　－　men

ἐκείνων τῶν κεκλημένων γεύσεταί μου
of those　－　having been invited　shall taste　of me

τοῦ δείπνου.
the　supper.

25 Συνεπορεύοντο δὲ αὐτῷ ὄχλοι πολλοί,
And came together　to him　crowds　many,

καὶ στραφεὶς εἶπεν πρὸς αὐτούς· **26** εἴ τις
and　turning　he said　to　them :　If anyone

ἔρχεται πρός με καὶ οὐ μισεῖ τὸν πατέρα
comes　to me　and　hates not　the　father

αὐτοῦ καὶ τὴν μητέρα καὶ τὴν γυναῖκα
of him　and　the　mother　and　the　wife

καὶ τὰ τέκνα καὶ τοὺς ἀδελφοὺς καὶ τὰς
and the children　and　the　brothers　and the

ἀδελφάς, ἔτι τε καὶ τὴν ψυχὴν ἑαυτοῦ,
sisters,　and besides also　the　life　of himself,

οὐ δύναται εἶναί μου μαθητής. **27** ὅστις
he cannot　to be　of me　a disciple.　Who

οὐ βαστάζει τὸν σταυρὸν ἑαυτοῦ καὶ
bears not　the　cross　of himself　and

ἔρχεται ὀπίσω μου, οὐ δύναται εἶναί μου
comes　after me,　he cannot　to be　of me

μαθητής. **28** Τίς γὰρ ἐξ ὑμῶν θέλων
a disciple.　For who　of　you　wishing

πύργον οἰκοδομῆσαι οὐχὶ πρῶτον καθίσας
a tower　to build　not　first　sitting

ψηφίζει τὴν δαπάνην, εἰ ἔχει εἰς ἀπαρ-
counts　the　cost,　if　he has for　com-

τισμόν; **29** ἵνα μή ποτε θέντος αὐτοῦ
pletion?　Lest　when　laying　him*
　　　　　　　　　　　　　　= he has laid

θεμέλιον καὶ μὴ ἰσχύοντος ἐκτελέσαι πάντες
a foundation and not　being able*　to finish　all

οἱ θεωροῦντες ἄρξωνται αὐτῷ ἐμπαίζειν
the [ones]　seeing　begin　him　to mock

30 λέγοντες ὅτι οὗτος ὁ ἄνθρωπος ἤρξατο
saying[,]　－　This　－　man　began

οἰκοδομεῖν καὶ οὐκ ἴσχυσεν ἐκτελέσαι.
to build　and　was not able　to finish.

31 Ἢ τίς βασιλεὺς πορευόμενος ἑτέρῳ βασιλεῖ
Or what　king　¹going　²another　⁴king

συμβαλεῖν εἰς πόλεμον οὐχὶ καθίσας πρῶτον
¹to attack　³in　⁴war　not　sitting　first

βουλεύσεται εἰ δυνατός ἐστιν ἐν δέκα
will deliberate　if　able　he is　with　ten

χιλιάσιν ὑπαντῆσαι τῷ μετὰ εἴκοσι χιλιάδων
thousands　to meet　¹the [one] ⁴with ⁵twenty ²thousands

ἐρχομένῳ ἐπ᾽ αὐτόν; **32** εἰ δὲ μή γε, ἔτι
²coming　³upon　⁴him?　Otherwise,　yet
　　　　　　　　　　　　　　　　　　　= while

αὐτοῦ πόρρω ὄντος πρεσβείαν ἀποστείλας
him　afar　being*　a delegation　sending

he is yet at a distance

ἐρωτᾷ τὰ πρὸς εἰρήνην. **33** οὕτως οὖν
he asks　the things for　peace.　So therefore

πᾶς ἐξ ὑμῶν ὃς οὐκ ἀποτάσσεται πᾶσιν
everyone of　you　who　does not say farewell　to all

τοῖς ἑαυτοῦ ὑπάρχουσιν οὐ δύναται εἶναί
¹the ²of himself ³possessions　cannot　to be

μου μαθητής. **34** Καλὸν οὖν τὸ ἅλας·
of me　a disciple.　Good therefore the　salt;

ἐὰν δὲ καὶ τὸ ἅλας μωρανθῇ, ἐν τίνι
but if　even　the　salt　becomes useless, with　what

ἀρτυθήσεται; **35** οὔτε εἰς γῆν οὔτε εἰς
will it be seasoned?　neither　for　soil　nor　for

κοπρίαν εὔθετόν ἐστιν· ἔξω βάλλουσιν
manure　suitable　is it;　outside　they cast

αὐτό. ὁ ἔχων ὦτα ἀκούειν ἀκουέτω.
it　The [one] having　ears　to hear　let him hear.

Chapter 15

Ἦσαν δὲ αὐτῷ ἐγγίζοντες πάντες
Now there were　to him　drawing near　all

οἱ τελῶναι καὶ οἱ ἁμαρτωλοὶ ἀκούειν
the tax-collectors and　the　sinners　to hear

αὐτόν. **2** καὶ διεγόγγυζον οἵ τε Φαρισαῖοι
him.　And greatly murmured both the　Pharisees

καὶ οἱ γραμματεῖς λέγοντες ὅτι οὗτος
and　the　scribes　saying[,]　－ This man

ἁμαρτωλοὺς προσδέχεται καὶ συνεσθίει αὐ-
sinners　receives　and　eats with　them.

τοῖς. **3** εἶπεν δὲ πρὸς αὐτοὺς τὴν παρα-
And he spoke　to　them　－　para-

βολὴν ταύτην λέγων· **4** τίς ἄνθρωπος ἐξ
ble　this　saying :　What　man　of

ὑμῶν ἔχων ἑκατὸν πρόβατα καὶ ἀπολέσας
you　having　a hundred　sheep　and　losing

ἐξ αὐτῶν ἓν οὐ καταλείπει τὰ ἐνενήκοντα
of them　one　does not leave　the　ninety-

ἐννέα ἐν τῇ ἐρήμῳ καὶ πορεύεται ἐπὶ
nine　in　the　desert　and　goes　after

τὸ ἀπολωλὸς ἕως εὕρῃ αὐτό; **5** καὶ
the [one] having been lost until　he finds　it?　and

εὑρὼν ἐπιτίθησιν ἐπὶ τοὺς ὤμους αὐτοῦ
finding　places on [it]　on　the　shoulders of him

χαίρων, **6** καὶ ἐλθὼν εἰς τὸν οἶκον
rejoicing,　and　coming　into　the　house

συγκαλεῖ τοὺς φίλους καὶ τοὺς γείτονας,
he calls together　the　friends　and the　neighbours,

λέγων αὐτοῖς· συγχάρητέ μοι, ὅτι εὗρον
saying　to them :　Rejoice with　me, because I found

τὸ πρόβατόν μου τὸ ἀπολωλός. **7** λέγω
the　sheep　of me － having been lost.　I tell

ὑμῖν ὅτι οὕτως χαρὰ ἐν τῷ οὐρανῷ
you　that　thus　joy　in　－　heaven

ἔσται ἐπὶ ἑνὶ ἁμαρτωλῷ μετανοοῦντι ἢ
will be　over　one　sinner　repenting　than

ἐπὶ ἐνενήκοντα ἐννέα δικαίοις οἵτινες οὐ
over　ninety-nine　just men　who　no

χρείαν ἔχουσιν μετανοίας. **8** Ἢ τίς γυνὴ
need　have　of repentance.　Or what woman

δραχμὰς ἔχουσα δέκα, ἐὰν ἀπολέσῃ
²drachmae　¹having　³ten,　if　she loses

δραχμὴν μίαν, οὐχὶ ἅπτει λύχνον καὶ
drachma　one,　does not light　a lamp　and

σαροῖ τὴν οἰκίαν καὶ ζητεῖ ἐπιμελῶς
sweep　the　house　and　seek　carefully

ἕως οὗ εὕρῃ; **9** καὶ εὑροῦσα συγκαλεῖ
until　she finds?　and　finding　she calls together

τὰς φίλας καὶ γείτονας λέγουσα· συγχάρητέ
the　friends and neighbours　saying :　Rejoice with

μοι, ὅτι εὗρον τὴν δραχμὴν ἣν ἀπώλεσα.
me, because I found　the　drachma　which　I lost.

10 οὕτως, λέγω ὑμῖν, γίνεται χαρὰ ἐνώπιον
So,　I tell　you,　there is　joy　before

τῶν ἀγγέλων τοῦ θεοῦ ἐπὶ ἑνὶ ἁμαρτωλῷ
the　angels　－ of God　over　one　sinner

King James Version

11 And he said, A certain man had two sons: 12And the younger of them said to *his* father, Father, give me the portion of goods that falleth *to me*. And he divided unto them *his* living. 13And not many days after the younger son gathered all together, and took his journey into a far country, and there wasted his substance with riotous living. 14And when he had spent all, there arose a mighty famine in that land; and he began to be in want. 15And he went and joined himself to a citizen of that country; and he sent him into his fields to feed swine. 16And he would fain have filled his belly with the husks that the swine did eat: and no man gave unto him. 17And when he came to himself, he said, How many hired servants of my father's have bread enough and to spare, and I perish with hunger! 18 I will arise and go to my father, and will say unto him, Father, I have sinned against heaven, and before thee, 19And am no more worthy to be called thy son: make me as one of thy hired servants. 20And he arose, and came to his father. But when he was yet a great way off, his father saw him, and had compassion, and ran, and fell on his neck, and kissed him. 21And the son said unto him, Father, I have sinned against heaven, and in thy sight, and am no more worthy to be called thy son. 22 But the father said to his servants, Bring forth the best robe, and put *it* on him; and put a ring on his hand, and shoes on *his* feet: 23And bring hither the fatted calf, and kill *it;* and let us eat, and be merry: 24 For this my son was dead, and is alive again; he was lost, and is found. And they began to be merry. 25 Now his elder son was in the field: and as he came and drew nigh to the house, he heard music and dancing. 26And he called one of the servants, and asked what these things meant. 27And he said unto him, Thy brother is come; and thy father hath killed the fatted calf, because he hath received him safe and sound. 28And he was angry, and would not go in: therefore came his father out, and entreated him. 29And he answering said to *his* father, Lo, these many years do I serve thee, neither transgressed I at any time thy commandment; and yet thou never gavest me a kid, that I might make merry with my friends: 30 But as soon as this thy son was come, which hath devoured thy living with harlots, thou hast killed for him the fatted calf. 31And he said unto him, Son, thou art ever with me, and all that I have is thine. 32 It was meet that we should make merry, and be glad: for this thy brother was dead, and is alive again; and was lost, and is found.

New International Version

The parable of the lost son

11 Jesus continued: "There was a man who had two sons. 12 The younger one said to his father, 'Father, give me my share of the estate.' So he divided his property between them.

13 "Not long after that, the younger son got together all he had, set off for a distant country and there squandered his wealth in wild living. 14After he had spent everything, there was a severe famine in that whole country, and he began to be in need. 15 So he went and hired himself out to a citizen of that country, who sent him to his fields to feed pigs. 16 He longed to fill his stomach with the pods that the pigs were eating, but no one gave him anything.

17 "When he came to his senses, he said, 'How many of my father's hired men have food to spare, and here I am starving to death! 18 I will set out and go back to my father and say to him: Father, I have sinned against heaven and against you. 19 I am no longer worthy to be called your son; make me like one of your hired men.' 20 So he got up and went to his father.

"But while he was still a long way off, his father saw him and was filled with compassion for him. He ran to his son, threw his arms around him and kissed him.

21 "The son said to him, 'Father, I have sinned against heaven and against you. I am no longer worthy to be called your son.' *[e]*

22 "But the father said to his servants, 'Quick! Bring the best robe and put it on him. Put a ring on his finger and sandals on his feet. 23 Bring the fattened calf and kill it. Let's have a feast and celebrate. 24 For this son of mine was dead and is alive again; he was lost and is found.' So they began to celebrate.

25 "Meanwhile, the older son was in the field. When he came near the house, he heard music and dancing. 26 So he called one of the servants and asked him what was going on. 27 'Your brother has come,' he replied, 'and your father has killed the fattened calf because he has him back safe and sound.'

28 "The older brother became angry and refused to go in. So his father went out and pleaded with him. 29 But he answered his father, 'Look! All these years I've been slaving for you and never disobeyed your orders. Yet you never gave me even a young goat so I could celebrate with my friends. 30 But when this son of yours who has squandered your property with prostitutes comes home, you kill the fattened calf for him!'

31 " 'My son,' the father said, 'you are always with me, and everything I have is yours. 32 But we had to celebrate and be glad, because this brother of yours was dead and is alive again; he was lost and is found.' "

[e] Some early MSS add *Make me like on of your hired men.*

μετανοοῦντι. **11** Εἶπεν δέ· ἄνθρωπός τις
repenting.   And he said: A certain man

εἶχεν δύο υἱούς. **12** καὶ εἶπεν ὁ νεώτερος
had   two sons.   And said the younger

αὐτῶν τῷ πατρί· πάτερ, δός μοι τὸ
of them to the father: Father, give me the

ἐπιβάλλον μέρος τῆς οὐσίας. ὁ δὲ διεῖλες
falling upon share of the property. And he divided
= share of the property falling to [me].

αὐτοῖς τὸν βίον. **13** καὶ μετ᾽ οὐ πολλὰς
to them the living.   And after not many

ἡμέρας συναγαγὼν πάντα ὁ νεώτερος υἱὸς
days   having gathered all things the younger son

ἀπεδήμησεν εἰς χώραν μακράν, καὶ ἐκεῖ
departed   to country a far,   and there

διεσκόρπισεν τὴν οὐσίαν αὐτοῦ ζῶν ἀσώτως.
scattered   the property of him living prodigally.

14 δαπανήσαντος δὲ αὐτοῦ πάντα ἐγένετο
But having spent   him⁴ all things there came
= when he had spent

λιμὸς ἰσχυρὰ κατὰ τὴν χώραν ἐκείνην,
famine a severe throughout - country   that,

καὶ αὐτὸς ἤρξατο ὑστερεῖσθαι. **15** καὶ
and he   began   to be in want.   And

πορευθεὶς ἐκολλήθη ἑνὶ τῶν πολιτῶν τῆς
going   he was joined to one of the citizens -

χώρας ἐκείνης, καὶ ἔπεμψεν αὐτὸν εἰς
country of that, and he sent   him   into

τοὺς ἀγροὺς αὐτοῦ βόσκειν χοίρους· **16** καὶ
the fields of him to feed pigs;   and

ἐπεθύμει γεμίσαι τὴν κοιλίαν αὐτοῦ ἐκ
he longed to fill the stomach of him out of (with)

τῶν κερατίων ὧν ἤσθιον οἱ χοῖροι, καὶ
the husks   which ²ate ¹the ³pigs,   and

οὐδεὶς ἐδίδου αὐτῷ. **17** εἰς ἑαυτὸν δὲ
no one gave   to him.   ²to ⁴himself ¹But

ἐλθὼν ἔφη· πόσοι μίσθιοι τοῦ πατρός μου
³coming he said: How many hired servants of the father of me

περισσεύονται ἄρτων, ἐγὼ δὲ λιμῷ ὧδε
abound   of loaves, but I with famine here
= have abundance of bread,

ἀπόλλυμαι. **18** ἀναστὰς πορεύσομαι πρὸς
am perishing.   Rising up I will go   to

τὸν πατέρα μου καὶ ἐρῶ αὐτῷ· πάτερ,
the father   of me and I will say to him : Father,

ἥμαρτον εἰς τὸν οὐρανὸν καὶ ἐνώπιόν σου,
I sinned against - heaven   and before   thee,

19 οὐκέτι εἰμὶ ἄξιος κληθῆναι υἱός σου·
no longer am I worthy to be called a son of thee;

ποίησόν με ὡς ἕνα τῶν μισθίων σου.
make   me as one of the hired servants of thee.

20 καὶ ἀναστὰς ἦλθεν πρὸς τὸν πατέρα
And rising up he came to the father

ἑαυτοῦ. ἔτι δὲ αὐτοῦ μακρὰν ἀπέχοντος
of himself. But yet him   afar   being away⁸
= while he was yet far away

εἶδεν αὐτὸν ὁ πατὴρ αὐτοῦ καὶ ἐσπλαγχνίσθη,
saw   him the father of him and was moved with pity,

καὶ δραμὼν ἐπέπεσεν ἐπὶ τὸν τράχηλον
and running fell on   on the neck

αὐτοῦ καὶ κατεφίλησεν αὐτόν. **21** εἶπεν δὲ
of him and fervently kissed   him.   And said

ὁ υἱὸς αὐτῷ· πάτερ, ἥμαρτον εἰς τὸν
the son to him: Father, I sinned against -

οὐρανὸν καὶ ἐνώπιόν σου, οὐκέτι εἰμὶ
heaven   and before   thee, no longer am I

ἄξιος κληθῆναι υἱός σου. **22** εἶπεν δὲ
worthy to be called a son of thee.   But said

ὁ πατὴρ πρὸς τοὺς δούλους αὐτοῦ· ταχὺ
the father to the slaves   of him : Quickly

ἐξενέγκατε στολὴν τὴν πρώτην καὶ ἐνδύσατε
bring ye out a robe the first and clothe

αὐτόν, καὶ δότε δακτύλιον εἰς τὴν χεῖρα
him,   and give(put) a ring   to the hand

αὐτοῦ καὶ ὑποδήματα εἰς τοὺς πόδας,
of him and sandals   to the feet,

23 καὶ φέρετε τὸν μόσχον τὸν σιτευτόν,
and bring the calf   -   fattened,

θύσατε, καὶ φαγόντες εὐφρανθῶμεν, **24** ὅτι
kill,   and eating   let us be merry,   because

οὗτος ὁ υἱός μου νεκρὸς ἦν καὶ ἀνέζησεν,
this - son of me dead   was and lived again,

ἦν ἀπολωλὼς καὶ εὑρέθη. καὶ ἤρξαντο
was having been lost and was found. And they began

εὐφραίνεσθαι. **25** ἦν δὲ ὁ υἱὸς αὐτοῦ
to be merry.   But was the son of him

ὁ πρεσβύτερος ἐν ἀγρῷ· καὶ ὡς ἐρχόμενος
- older   in a field; and as coming

ἤγγισεν τῇ οἰκίᾳ, ἤκουσεν συμφωνίας καὶ
he drew near to the house, he heard music   and

χορῶν, **26** καὶ προσκαλεσάμενος ἕνα τῶν
dances,   and calling to [him]   one of the

παίδων ἐπυνθάνετο τί ἂν εἴη ταῦτα.
lads   he inquired what might be these things.

27 ὁ δὲ εἶπεν αὐτῷ ὅτι ὁ ἀδελφός σου
And he said to him[,] - The brother of thee

ἥκει, καὶ ἔθυσεν ὁ πατήρ σου τὸν μόσχον τὸν
has come, and ⁴killed ¹the ²father ³of thee ⁵the ⁷calf -

σιτευτόν, ὅτι ὑγιαίνοντα αὐτὸν ἀπέλαβεν.
⁶fattened, because ⁸being in health ³him ¹he ²received ⁴back.

28 ὠργίσθη δὲ καὶ οὐκ ἤθελεν εἰσελθεῖν·
But he was angry and did not wish to enter:

ὁ δὲ πατὴρ αὐτοῦ ἐξελθὼν παρεκάλει
so the father of him coming out besought

αὐτόν. **29** ὁ δὲ ἀποκριθεὶς εἶπεν τῷ
him.   But he answering   said to the

πατρί· ἰδοὺ τοσαῦτα ἔτη δουλεύω σοι καὶ
father : Behold[,] so many years I serve thee and

οὐδέποτε ἐντολήν σου παρῆλθον, καὶ ἐμοὶ
never   a command of thee I transgressed, and - to me

οὐδέποτε ἔδωκας ἔριφον ἵνα μετὰ τῶν
never   thou gavest a goat that with the

φίλων μου εὐφρανθῶ· **30** ὅτε δὲ ὁ υἱός
friends of me I might be merry; but when - ³son

σου οὗτος ὁ καταφαγών σου τὸν βίον
²of thee ¹this - having devoured of thee the living

μετὰ πορνῶν ἦλθεν, ἔθυσας αὐτῷ τὸν
with harlots came, thou killedst for him the

σιτευτὸν μόσχον. **31** ὁ δὲ εἶπεν αὐτῷ·
fattened calf.   And he said to him:

τέκνον, σὺ πάντοτε μετ᾽ ἐμοῦ εἶ, καὶ
Child,   thou always with me art,   and

πάντα τὰ ἐμὰ σά ἐστιν· **32** εὐφρανθῆναι
¹all ³things - ²my ⁴thine ⁵is(are).   ²to be merry

δὲ καὶ χαρῆναι ἔδει, ὅτι ὁ ἀδελφός
¹And ⁴and ³to rejoice ²it be- because - ²brother
                          hoved [us],

σου οὗτος νεκρὸς ἦν καὶ ἔζησεν, καὶ ἀπο-
³of thee ¹this ⁴dead ⁶was and came to life, and having

λωλὼς καὶ εὑρέθη:
been lost also was found.

King James Version

16 And he said also unto his disciples, There was a certain rich man, which had a steward; and the same was accused unto him that he had wasted his goods. 2And he called him, and said unto him, How is it that I hear this of thee? give an account of thy stewardship; for thou mayest be no longer steward. 3 Then the steward said within himself, What shall I do? for my lord taketh away from me the stewardship: I cannot dig; to beg I am ashamed. 4 I am resolved what to do, that, when I am put out of the stewardship, they may receive me into their houses. 5 So he called every one of his lord's debtors *unto him*, and said unto the first, How much owest thou unto my lord? 6And he said, A hundred measures of oil. And he said unto him, Take thy bill, and sit down quickly, and write fifty. 7 Then said he to another, And how much owest thou? And he said, A hundred measures of wheat. And he said unto him, Take thy bill, and write fourscore. 8And the lord commended the unjust steward, because he had done wisely: for the children of this world are in their generation wiser than the children of light. 9And I say unto you, Make to yourselves friends of the mammon of unrighteousness; that, when ye fail, they may receive you into everlasting habitations. 10 He that is faithful in that which is least is faithful also in much: and he that is unjust in the least is unjust also in much. 11 If therefore ye have not been faithful in the unrighteous mammon, who will commit to your trust the true *riches?* 12And if ye have not been faithful in that which is another man's, who shall give you that which is your own?

13 No servant can serve two masters: for either he will hate the one, and love the other; or else he will hold to the one, and despise the other. Ye cannot serve God and mammon. 14And the Pharisees also, who were covetous, heard all these things: and they derided him. 15And he said unto them, Ye are they which justify yourselves before men; but God knoweth your hearts: for that which is highly esteemed among men is abomination in the sight of God. 16 The law and the prophets *were* until John: since that time the kingdom of God is preached, and every man presseth into it. 17And it is easier for heaven and earth to pass, than one tittle of the law to fail. 18 Whosoever putteth away his wife, and marrieth another, committeth adultery: and whosoever marrieth her that is put away from *her* husband committeth adultery.

19 There was a certain rich man, which was clothed in purple and fine linen, and fared sumptuously every day: 20And there was a certain beggar named Lazarus, which was laid at his gate, full of sores, 21And desiring to be fed with the crumbs which fell from the rich man's table: moreover the dogs came and licked his sores. 22And it came to pass, that the beggar died, and was carried by the angels into Abraham's bosom:

New International Version

The parable of the shrewd manager

16 Jesus told his disciples: "There was a rich man whose manager was accused of wasting his possessions. 2 So he called him in and asked him, 'What is this I hear about you? Give an account of your management, because you cannot be manager any longer.'

3 "The manager said to himself, 'What shall I do now? My master is taking away my job. I'm not strong enough to dig, and I'm ashamed to beg—4 I know what I'll do so that, when I lose my job here, people will welcome me into their houses.'

5 "So he called in each one of his master's debtors. He asked the first, 'How much do you owe my master?'

6 " 'Eight hundred gallons of olive oil,' he replied.

"The manager told him, 'Take your bill, sit down quickly, and make it four hundred.'

7 "Then he asked the second, 'And how much do you owe?'

" 'A thousand bushels of wheat,' he replied.

"He told him, 'Take your bill and make it eight hundred.'

8 "The master commended the dishonest manager because he had acted shrewdly. For the people of this world are more shrewd in dealing with their own kind than are the people of the light. 9 I tell you, use worldly wealth to gain friends for yourselves, so that when it is gone, you will be welcomed into eternal dwellings.

10 "Whoever can be trusted with very little can also be trusted with much, and whoever is dishonest with very little will also be dishonest with much. 11 So if you have not been trustworthy in handling worldly wealth, who will trust you with true riches? 12And if you have not been truthworthy with someone else's property, who will give you property of your own?

13 "No servant can serve two masters. Either he will hate the one and love the other, or he will be devoted to the one and despise the other. You cannot serve both God and Money."

14 The Pharisees, who loved money, heard all this and were sneering at Jesus. 15 He said to them, "You are the ones who justify yourselves in the eyes of men, but God knows your hearts. What is highly valued among men is detestable in God's sight.

16 "The Law and the Prophets were proclaimed until John. Since that time, the good news of the kingdom of God is being preached, and everyone is forcing his way into it. 17 It is easier for heaven and earth to disappear than for the least stroke of a pen to drop out of the Law.

18 "Anyone who divorces his wife and marries another woman commits adultery, and the man who marries a divorced woman commits adultery.

The rich man and Lazarus

19 "There was a rich man who was dressed in purple and fine linen and lived in luxury every day. 20At his gate was laid a beggar named Lazarus, covered with sores 21 and longing to eat what fell from the rich man's table. Even the dogs came and licked his sores. 22 "The time came when the beggar died and the angels carried him to Abraham's side. The

Greek Interlinear

Chapter 16

Ἔλεγεν δὲ καὶ πρὸς τοὺς μαθητάς·
And he said also to the disciples :

ἄνθρωπός τις ἦν πλούσιος ὃς εἶχεν
[A] certain [man] [there was] [rich] who had

οἰκονόμον, καὶ οὗτος διεβλήθη αὐτῷ ὡς
a steward, and this was complained of to him as

διασκορπίζων τὰ ὑπάρχοντα αὐτοῦ. 2 καὶ
wasting the possessions of him. And

φωνήσας αὐτὸν εἶπεν αὐτῷ· τί τοῦτο
calling him he said to him : What [is] this

ἀκούω περὶ σοῦ; ἀπόδος τὸν λόγον τῆς
I hear about thee? render the account of the

οἰκονομίας σου· οὐ γὰρ δύνῃ ἔτι οἰκονομεῖν.
stewardship of thee; for thou canst not longer to be steward.

3 εἶπεν δὲ ἐν ἑαυτῷ ὁ οἰκονόμος· τί
And said in himself the steward : What

ποιήσω, ὅτι ὁ κύριός μου ἀφαιρεῖται τὴν
may I do, because the lord of me takes away the

οἰκονομίαν ἀπ᾽ ἐμοῦ; σκάπτειν οὐκ ἰσχύω,
stewardship from me? to dig I am not able,

ἐπαιτεῖν αἰσχύνομαι. 4 ἔγνων τί ποιήσω,
to beg I am ashamed. I knew(know) what I may do,

ἵνα ὅταν μετασταθῶ ἐκ τῆς οἰκονομίας
that when I am removed out of the stewardship

δέξωνταί με εἰς τοὺς οἴκους ἑαυτῶν.
they may receive me into the houses of themselves.

5 καὶ προσκαλεσάμενος ἕνα ἕκαστον τῶν
And calling to [him] 'one 'each of the

χρεοφειλετῶν τοῦ κυρίου ἑαυτοῦ ἔλεγεν τῷ
debtors of the lord of himself he said to the

πρώτῳ· πόσον ὀφείλεις τῷ κυρίῳ μου;
first : How much owest thou to the lord of me?

6 ὁ δὲ εἶπεν· ἑκατὸν βάτους ἐλαίου. ὁ δὲ
And he said : A hundred baths of oil. And he

εἶπεν αὐτῷ· δέξαι σου τὰ γράμματα καὶ
told him : Take of thee the letters(bill) and

καθίσας ταχέως γράψον πεντήκοντα. 7 ἔπειτα
sitting quickly write fifty. Then

ἑτέρῳ εἶπεν· σὺ δὲ πόσον ὀφείλεις; ὁ δὲ
to another he said : 'thou 'And 'how much 'owest? And he

εἶπεν· ἑκατὸν κόρους σίτου. λέγει αὐτῷ·
said : A hundred cors of wheat. He tells him :

δέξαι σου τὰ γράμματα καὶ γράψον
Take of thee the bill and write

ὀγδοήκοντα. 8 καὶ ἐπῄνεσεν ὁ κύριος τὸν
eighty. And 'praised 'the 'lord the

οἰκονόμον τῆς ἀδικίας ὅτι φρονίμως
steward – of unrighteousness because prudently

ἐποίησεν· ὅτι οἱ υἱοὶ τοῦ αἰῶνος τούτου
he acted; because the sons – age of this

φρονιμώτεροι ὑπὲρ τοὺς υἱοὺς τοῦ φωτὸς
more prudent than the sons of the light

εἰς τὴν γενεὰν τὴν ἑαυτῶν εἰσιν. 9 Καὶ
in the generation – of themselves are. And

ἐγὼ ὑμῖν λέγω, ἑαυτοῖς ποιήσατε φίλους
I 'you 'tell, To yourselves make friends

ἐκ τοῦ μαμωνᾶ τῆς ἀδικίας, ἵνα ὅταν
by the mammon – of unrighteousness, that when

ἐκλίπῃ δέξωνται ὑμᾶς εἰς τὰς αἰωνίους
it fails they may receive you into the eternal

σκηνάς. 10 ὁ πιστὸς ἐν ἐλαχίστῳ καὶ ἐν
tabernacles. The man faithful in least also in

πολλῷ πιστός ἐστιν, καὶ ὁ ἐν ἐλαχίστῳ
much faithful is, and the man in least

ἄδικος καὶ ἐν πολλῷ ἄδικός ἐστιν. 11 εἰ
unrighteous also in much unrighteous is. If

οὖν ἐν τῷ ἀδίκῳ μαμωνᾷ πιστοὶ οὐκ
therefore in the unrighteous mammon faithful not

ἐγένεσθε, τὸ ἀληθινὸν τίς ὑμῖν πιστεύσει;
ye were, the true who to you will entrust ?

12 καὶ εἰ ἐν τῷ ἀλλοτρίῳ πιστοὶ οὐκ
And if in the thing belonging to another faithful no[t]

ἐγένεσθε, τὸ ἡμέτερον τίς δώσει ὑμῖν;
ye were, the ours who will give you?
=that which is ours

13 Οὐδεὶς οἰκέτης δύναται δυσὶ κυρίοις
No household slave can two lords

δουλεύειν· ἢ γὰρ τὸν ἕνα μισήσει καὶ τὸν
to serve; for either the one he will hate and the

ἕτερον ἀγαπήσει, ἢ ἑνὸς ἀνθέξεται καὶ
other he will love, or one he will hold fast to and

τοῦ ἑτέρου καταφρονήσει. οὐ δύνασθε
the the other he will despise. Ye cannot

θεῷ δουλεύειν καὶ μαμωνᾷ. 14 Ἤκουον
God to serve and mammon. 'heard

δὲ ταῦτα πάντα οἱ Φαρισαῖοι φιλάργυροι
'Now 'these things 'all 'the 'Pharisees 'moneylovers

ὑπάρχοντες, καὶ ἐξεμυκτήριζον αὐτόν. 15 καὶ
'being, and they scoffed at him. And

εἶπεν αὐτοῖς· ὑμεῖς ἐστε οἱ δικαιοῦντες
he said to them : Ye are the [ones] justifying

ἑαυτοὺς ἐνώπιον τῶν ἀνθρώπων, ὁ δὲ
yourselves before – men, – but

θεὸς γινώσκει τὰς καρδίας ὑμῶν· ὅτι τὸ
God knows the hearts of you; because the thing

ἐν ἀνθρώποις ὑψηλὸν βδέλυγμα ἐνώπιον
'among 'men 'lofty [is] an abomination before

τοῦ θεοῦ. 16 Ὁ νόμος καὶ οἱ προφῆται
– God. The law and the prophets

μέχρι Ἰωάννου· ἀπὸ τότε ἡ βασιλεία τοῦ
[were] until John; from then the kingdom –

θεοῦ εὐαγγελίζεται καὶ πᾶς εἰς αὐτὴν
of God is being preached and everyone into it

βιάζεται. 17 εὐκοπώτερον δέ ἐστιν τὸν οὐρανὸν
is pressing. But easier it is the heaven

καὶ τὴν γῆν παρελθεῖν ἢ τοῦ νόμου μίαν
and the earth to pass away than of the law one

κεραίαν πεσεῖν. 18 Πᾶς ὁ ἀπολύων τὴν
little horn* to fall. Everyone dismissing the

γυναῖκα αὐτοῦ καὶ γαμῶν ἑτέραν μοιχεύει,
wife of him and marrying another commits adultery,

καὶ ὁ ἀπολελυμένην ἀπὸ
and 'the [one] 'a woman having been dismissed 'from

ἀνδρὸς γαμῶν μοιχεύει. 19 Ἄνθρωπος δέ
'a husband 'marrying 'commits adultery. Now a certain

τις ἦν πλούσιος, καὶ ἐνεδιδύσκετο πορφύραν
man was rich, and used to put on a purple robe

καὶ βύσσον εὐφραινόμενος καθ᾽ ἡμέραν
and fine linen being merry every day†

λαμπρῶς. 20 πτωχὸς δέ τις ὀνόματι
splendidly. And a certain poor man by name

Λάζαρος ἐβέβλητο πρὸς τὸν πυλῶνα αὐτοῦ
Lazarus had been placed at the gate of him

εἱλκωμένος 21 καὶ ἐπιθυμῶν χορτασθῆναι
being covered with sores and desiring to be satisfied

ἀπὸ τῶν πιπτόντων ἀπὸ τῆς τραπέζης
from the things falling from the table

τοῦ πλουσίου· ἀλλὰ καὶ οἱ κύνες ἐρχόμενοι
of the rich man; but even the dogs coming

ἐπέλειχον τὰ ἕλκη αὐτοῦ. 22 ἐγένετο δὲ
licked the sores of him. And it came to pass

ἀποθανεῖν τὸν πτωχὸν καὶ ἀπενεχθῆναι
to die the poor man and to be carried away
=that the poor man died and he was carried away

αὐτὸν[b] ὑπὸ τῶν ἀγγέλων εἰς τὸν κόλπον
him[b] by the angels into the bosom

* The little projection which distinguishes some Hebrew letters
from those otherwise similar.

King James Version

the rich man also died, and was buried; 23And in hell he lifted up his eyes, being in torments, and seeth Abraham afar off, and Lazarus in his bosom. 24And he cried and said, Father Abraham, have mercy on me, and send Lazarus, that he may dip the tip of his finger in water, and cool my tongue; for I am tormented in this flame. 25 But Abraham said, Son, remember that thou in thy lifetime receivedst thy good things, and likewise Lazarus evil things: but now he is comforted, and thou art tormented. 26And beside all this, between us and you there is a great gulf fixed: so that they which would pass from hence to you cannot; neither can they pass to us, that *would come* from thence. 27 Then he said, I pray thee therefore, father, that thou wouldest send him to my father's house: 28 For I have five brethren; that he may testify unto them, lest they also come into this place of torment. 29Abraham saith unto them, They have Moses and the prophets; let them hear them. 30And he said, Nay, father Abraham: but if one went unto them from the dead, they will repent. 31And he said unto him, If they hear not Moses and the prophets, neither will they be persuaded, though one rose from the dead.

17 Then said he unto the disciples, It is impossible but that offences will come: but woe *unto him*, through whom they come! 2 It were better for him that a millstone were hanged about his neck, and he cast into the sea, than that he should offend one of these little ones. 3 Take heed to yourselves: If thy brother trespass against thee, rebuke him; and if he repent, forgive him. 4And if he trespass against thee seven times in a day, and seven times in a day turn again to thee, saying, I repent; thou shalt forgive him. 5And the apostles said unto the Lord, Increase our faith. 6And the Lord said, If ye had faith as a grain of mustard seed, ye might say unto this sycamine tree, Be thou plucked up by the root, and be thou planted in the sea; and it should obey you. 7 But which of you, having a servant ploughing or feeding cattle, will say unto him by and by, when he is come from the field, Go and sit down to meat? 8And will not rather say unto him, Make ready wherewith I may sup, and gird thyself, and serve me, till I have eaten and drunken; and afterward thou shalt eat and drink? 9 Doth he thank that servant because he did the things that were commanded him? I trow not. 10 So likewise ye, when ye shall have done all those things which are commanded you, say, We are unprofitable servants: we have done that which was our duty to do.

11 And it came to pass, as he went to Jerusalem, that he passed through the midst of Samaria and Galilee. 12And as he entered into a certain village, there met him ten men that were

New International Version

rich man also died and was buried. 23 In hell,*f* where he was in torment, he looked up and saw Abraham far away, with Lazarus by his side. 24 So he called to him, 'Father Abraham, have pity on me and send Lazarus to dip the tip of his finger in water and cool my tongue, because I am in agony in this fire.' 25 "But Abraham replied, 'Son, remember that in your lifetime you received your good things, while Lazarus received bad things, but now he is comforted here and you are in agony. 26And besides all this, between us and you a great chasm has been fixed, so that those who want to go from here to you cannot, nor can anyone cross over from there to us.' 27 "He answered, 'Then I beg you, father, send Lazarus to my father's house, 28 for I have five brothers. Let him warn them, so that they will not also come to this place of torment.' 29 "Abraham replied, 'They have Moses and the Prophets; let them listen to them.' 30 " 'No, father Abraham,' he said, 'but if someone from the dead goes to them, they will repent.' 31 "He said to him, 'If they do not listen to Moses and the Prophets, they will not be convinced even if someone rises from the dead.' "

Sin, faith, duty

17 Jesus said to his disciples: "Things that cause people to sin are bound to come, but woe to that person through whom they come. 2 It would be better for him to be thrown into the sea with a millstone tied around his neck than for him to cause one of these little ones to sin. 3 So watch yourselves.
"If your brother sins, rebuke him, and if he repents, forgive him. 4 If he sins against you seven times in a day, and seven times comes back to you and says, 'I repent,' forgive him."
5 The apostles said to the Lord, "Increase our faith!"
6 He replied, "If you have faith as small as a mustard seed, you can say to this mulberry tree, 'Be uprooted and planted in the sea,' and it will obey you.
7 "Suppose one of you had a servant plowing or looking after the sheep. Would he say to the servant when he comes in from the field, 'Come along now and sit down to eat'? 8 Would he not rather say, 'Prepare my supper, get yourself ready and wait on me while I eat and drink; after that you may eat and drink'? 9 Would he thank the servant because he did what he was told to do? 10 So you also, when you have done everything you were told to do, should say, 'We are unworthy servants; we have only done our duty.' "

Ten healed of leprosy

11 Now on his way to Jerusalem, Jesus traveled along the border between Samaria and Galilee. 12As he was going into a village, ten men who had leprosy*g* met him. They stood at

[f] Greek *Hades*. [g] The Greek word probably designated other related diseases also.

Greek Interlinear

Ἀβραάμ· ἀπέθανεν δὲ καὶ ὁ πλούσιος καὶ
of Abraham;   and died   · also the   rich man   and

ἐτάφη. 23 καὶ ἐν τῷ ᾅδη ἐπάρας τοὺς
was buried.   And in   -   hades lifting up the

ὀφθαλμοὺς αὐτοῦ, ὑπάρχων ἐν βασάνοις,
eyes   of him,   being   in   torments,

ὁρᾷ Ἀβραάμ ἀπὸ μακρόθεν καὶ Λάζαρον
he sees Abraham from   afar   and   Lazarus

ἐν τοῖς κόλποις αὐτοῦ. 24 καὶ αὐτὸς
in the   bosoms   of him.   And   he

φωνήσας εἶπεν· πάτερ Ἀβραάμ, ἐλέησόν
calling   said :   Father   Abraham,   pity

με καὶ πέμψον Λάζαρον ἵνα βάψῃ τὸ
me and   send   Lazarus   that he may dip the

ἄκρον τοῦ δακτύλου αὐτοῦ ὕδατος καὶ
tip   of the   finger   of him   of(in) water and

καταψύξῃ τὴν γλῶσσάν μου, ὅτι ὀδυνῶμαι
may cool the   tongue   of me, because I am suffering

ἐν τῇ φλογὶ ταύτῃ. 25 εἶπεν δὲ Ἀβραάμ·
in - flame   this.   But said   Abraham :

τέκνον, μνήσθητι ὅτι ἀπέλαβες τὰ ἀγαθά
Child,   remember   that thou didst receive the good things

σου ἐν τῇ ζωῇ σου, καὶ Λάζαρος ὁμοίως
of thee in · the   life   of thee, and   Lazarus   likewise

τὰ κακά· νῦν δὲ ὧδε παρακαλεῖται, σὺ δὲ
the bad;   but now here   he is comforted,   but thou

ὀδυνᾶσαι. 26 καὶ ἐν πᾶσι τούτοις μεταξὺ
art suffering.   And among   all   these things between

ἡμῶν καὶ ὑμῶν χάσμα μέγα ἐστήρικται,
us   and   you   chasm   a great has been firmly fixed,

ὅπως οἱ θέλοντες διαβῆναι ἔνθεν πρὸς
so that the [ones] wishing   to pass   hence   to

ὑμᾶς μὴ δύνωνται, μηδὲ ἐκεῖθεν πρὸς
you   cannot,   neither   thence   to

ἡμᾶς διαπερῶσιν. 27 εἶπεν δέ· ἐρωτῶ
us   may they cross over.   And he said :   I ask

σε οὖν, πάτερ, ἵνα πέμψῃς αὐτὸν εἰς
thee therefore, father,   that thou mayest send him   in

τὸν οἶκον τοῦ πατρός μου· 28 ἔχω γὰρ
the   house of the father of me;   for I have

πέντε ἀδελφούς· ὅπως διαμαρτύρηται αὐτοῖς,
five   brothers·   so that   he may witness   to them,

ἵνα μὴ καὶ αὐτοὶ ἔλθωσιν εἰς τὸν τόπον
lest   also   they   come   to -   place

τοῦτον τῆς βασάνου. 29 λέγει δὲ Ἀβραάμ·
this   - of torment.   But says   Abraham :

ἔχουσι Μωϋσέα καὶ τοὺς προφήτας·
They have   Moses   and   the   prophets;

ἀκουσάτωσαν αὐτῶν. 30 ὁ δὲ εἶπεν·
let them hear   them.   But he   said :

οὐχί, πάτερ Ἀβραάμ, ἀλλ᾽ ἐάν τις ἀπὸ
No,   father   Abraham,   but   if someone from

νεκρῶν πορευθῇ πρὸς αὐτούς, μετανοήσουσιν.
[the] dead should go   to   them,   they will repent.

31 εἶπεν δὲ αὐτῷ· εἰ Μωϋσέως καὶ τῶν
But he said to him : If   Moses   and the

προφητῶν οὐκ ἀκούουσιν, οὐδὲ ἐάν τις
prophets   they do not hear,   neither   if someone

ἐκ νεκρῶν ἀναστῇ πεισθήσονται.
out of [the] dead should rise again will they be persuaded.

Chapter 17

Εἶπεν δὲ πρὸς τοὺς μαθητὰς αὐτοῦ·
And he said   to   the   disciples   of him :

ἀνένδεκτόν ἐστιν τοῦ τὰ σκάνδαλα μὴ ἐλθεῖν,d
Impossible   it is   - the   offences   not to come,d

οὐαὶ δὲ δι᾽ οὗ ἔρχεται· 2 λυσιτελεῖ
but woe [to him] through whom they come;   it profits

αὐτῷ εἰ λίθος μυλικὸς περίκειται περὶ
him   if   a millstone   is put round   round

τὸν τράχηλον αὐτοῦ καὶ ἔρριπται εἰς τὴν
the   neck   of him   and he has been thrown into the

θάλασσαν, ἢ ἵνα σκανδαλίσῃ τῶν μικρῶν
sea,   than that he should offend - little ones

τούτων ἕνα. 3 προσέχετε ἑαυτοῖς. ἐὰν
²of these   ¹one.   Take heed   to yourselves.   If

ἁμάρτῃ ὁ ἀδελφός σου, ἐπιτίμησον αὐτῷ,
sins   the brother of thee,   rebuke   him,

καὶ ἐὰν μετανοήσῃ, ἄφες αὐτῷ. 4 καὶ
and   if   he repents,   forgive   him.   And

ἐὰν ἑπτάκις τῆς ἡμέρας ἁμαρτήσῃ εἰς σὲ
if   seven times of(in) the day   he sins against thee

καὶ ἑπτάκις ἐπιστρέψῃ πρὸς σὲ λέγων·
and   seven times   turns   to   thee   saying :

μετανοῶ, ἀφήσεις αὐτῷ. 5 Καὶ εἶπαν οἱ
I repent, thou shalt forgive him.   And   said   the

ἀπόστολοι τῷ κυρίῳ· πρόσθες ἡμῖν πίστιν.
apostles   to the Lord :   Add   to us   faith.

6 εἶπεν δὲ ὁ κύριος· εἰ ἔχετε πίστιν ὡς
And said the Lord :   If ye have   faith   as

κόκκον σινάπεως, ἐλέγετε ἂν τῇ συκαμίνῳ
a grain   of mustard, ye would have said - sycamine-tree

ταύτῃ· ἐκριζώθητι καὶ φυτεύθητι ἐν τῇ
to this :   Be thou uprooted and be thou planted in the

θαλάσσῃ· καὶ ὑπήκουσεν ἂν ὑμῖν. 7 Τίς
sea;   and   it would have obeyed   you.   who

δὲ ἐξ ὑμῶν δοῦλον ἔχων ἀροτριῶντα ἢ
But of you   ²a slave   ¹having   ploughing   or

ποιμαίνοντα, ὃς εἰσελθόντι ἐκ τοῦ ἀγροῦ
herding,   who on [his] coming ine out of the   farm

ἐρεῖ αὐτῷ· εὐθέως παρελθὼν ἀνάπεσε,
will say to him :   Immediately   coming up   recline,

8 ἀλλ᾽ οὐχὶ ἐρεῖ αὐτῷ· ἑτοίμασον τί
but   will not say   to him :   Prepare something

δειπνήσω, καὶ περιζωσάμενος διακόνει μοι
I may dine,   and   having girded thyself   serve   me

ἕως φάγω καὶ πίω, καὶ μετὰ ταῦτα
until   I eat   and   drink,   and   after these things

φάγεσαι καὶ πίεσαι σύ; 9 μὴ ἔχει χάριν
eat   and   drink thou? Not he has thanks

τῷ δούλῳ ὅτι ἐποίησεν τὰ διαταχθέντα;
to the slave because he did the things commanded?

10 οὕτως καὶ ὑμεῖς, ὅταν ποιήσητε πάντα
So   also   ye,   when   ye do   all

τὰ διαταχθέντα ὑμῖν, λέγετε ὅτι δοῦλοι
the things commanded   you,   say[,]   - Slaves

ἀχρεῖοί ἐσμεν, ὃ ὠφείλομεν ποιῆσαι
unprofitable   we are,   what   we ought   to do

πεποιήκαμεν.
we have done.

11 Καὶ ἐγένετο ἐν τῷ πορεύεσθαι εἰς
And it came to pass in   the   to goe   to
=as [he] went

Ἰερουσαλήμ, καὶ αὐτὸς διήρχετο διὰ μέσον
Jerusalem,   and   he   passed through [the]
through   midst

Σαμαρείας καὶ Γαλιλαίας. 12 καὶ εἰσερχομένου
of Samaria   and   Galilee.   And   entering
=as he entered

αὐτοῦ εἴς τινα κώμην ἀπήντησαν δέκα
hima   into   a certain   village   met [him]   ten

231

King James Version

lepers, which stood afar off: 13And they lifted up *their* voices, and said, Jesus, Master, have mercy on us. 14And when he saw *them,* he said unto them, Go shew yourselves unto the priests. And it came to pass, that, as they went, they were cleansed. 15And one of them, when he saw that he was healed, turned back, and with a loud voice glorified God, 16And fell down on *his* face at his feet, giving him thanks: and he was a Samaritan. 17And Jesus answering said, Were there not ten cleansed? but where *are* the nine? 18 There are not found that returned to give glory to God, save this stranger. 19And he said unto him, Arise, go thy way: thy faith hath made thee whole.

20 And when he was demanded of the Pharisees, when the kingdom of God should come, he answered them and said, The kingdom of God cometh not with observation: 21 Neither shall they say, Lo here! or, lo there! for, behold, the kingdom of God is within you. 22And he said unto the disciples, The days will come, when ye shall desire to see one of the days of the Son of man, and ye shall not see *it.* 23And they shall say to you, See here; or, see there: go not after *them,* nor follow *them.* 24 For as the lightning, that lighteneth out of the one *part* under heaven, shineth unto the other *part* under heaven; so shall also the Son of man be in his day. 25 But first must he suffer many things, and be rejected of this generation. 26And as it was in the days of Noe, so shall it be also in the days of the Son of man. 27 They did eat, they drank, they married wives, they were given in marriage, until the day that Noe entered into the ark, and the flood came, and destroyed them all. 28 Likewise also as it was in the days of Lot; they did eat, they drank, they bought, they sold, they planted, they builded; 29 But the same day that Lot went out of Sodom it rained fire and brimstone from heaven, and destroyed *them* all. 30 Even thus shall it be in the day when the Son of man is revealed. 31 In that day, he which shall be upon the housetop, and his stuff in the house, let him not come down to take it away: and he that is in the field, let him likewise not return back. 32 Remember Lot's wife. 33 Whosoever shall seek to save his life shall lose it; and whosoever shall lose his life shall preserve it. 34 I tell you, in that night there shall be two *men* in one bed; the one shall be taken, and the other shall be left. 35 Two *women* shall be grinding together; the one shall be taken, and the other left. 36 Two *men* shall be in the field; the one shall be taken, and the other left. 37And they answered and said unto him, Where, Lord? And he said unto them, Wheresoever the body *is,* thither will the eagles be gathered together.

New International Version

a distance 13 and called out in a loud voice, "Jesus, Master, have pity on us!"

14 When he saw them, he said, "Go, show yourselves to the priests." And as they went, they were cleansed.

15 One of them, when he saw he was healed, came back, praising God in a loud voice. 16 He threw himself at Jesus' feet and thanked him— and he was a Samaritan.

17 Jesus asked, "Were not all ten cleansed? Where are the other nine? 18 Was no one found to return and give praise to God except this foreigner?" 19 Then he said to him, "Rise and go; your faith has made you well."

The coming of the kingdom of God

20 Once, having been asked by the Pharisees when the kingdom of God would come, Jesus replied, "The kingdom of God does not come visibly, 21 nor will people say, 'Here it is,' or 'There it is,' because the kingdom of God is within you.*h* "

22 Then he said to his disciples, "The time is coming when you will long to see one of the days of the Son of Man, but you will not see it. 23 Men will tell you, 'There he is!' or 'Here he is!' Do not go running off after them. 24 For the Son of Man in his day*i* will be like the lightning, which flashes and lights up the sky from one end to the other. 25 But first he must suffer many things and be rejected by this generation.

26 "Just as it was in the days of Noah, so also will it be in the days of the Son of Man. 27 People were eating, drinking, marrying and being given in marriage up to the day Noah entered the ark. Then the flood came and destroyed them all.

28 "It was the same in the days of Lot. People were eating, drinking, buying, selling, planting and building. 29 But the day Lot left Sodom, fire and sulfur rained down from heaven and destroyed them all.

30 "It will be just like this on the day the Son of Man is revealed. 31 On that day no one who is on the roof of his house, with his goods inside, should go down to get them. Likewise, no one in the field should go back for anything. 32 Remember Lot's wife! 33 Whoever tries to keep his life will lose it, and whoever loses his life will preserve it. 34 I tell you, on that night two people will be in one bed; one will be taken and the other left. 35 Two women will be grinding grain together; one will be taken and the other left." *j*

37 "Where, Lord?" they asked.

He replied, "Where there is a dead body, there the vultures will gather."

[*h*] Or *is among you.* [*i*] Some MSS omit *in his day.* [*j*] Some MSS add verse 36: *Two men will be in the field; one will be taken and the other left.*

Greek Interlinear

λεπροὶ ἄνδρες, οἳ ἔστησαν πόρρωθεν, 13 καὶ
leprous men, who stood afar off, and

αὐτοὶ ἦραν φωνὴν λέγοντες· Ἰησοῦ
they lifted voice saying : Jesus

ἐπιστάτα, ἐλέησον ἡμᾶς. 14 καὶ ἰδὼν εἶπεν
Master, pity us. And seeing he said

αὐτοῖς· πορευθέντες ἐπιδείξατε ἑαυτοὺς τοῖς
to them : Going show yourselves to the

ἱερεῦσιν. καὶ ἐγένετο ἐν τῷ ὑπάγειν
priests. And it came to pass in the to go
= as they went

αὐτοὺς ἐκαθαρίσθησαν. 15 εἷς δὲ ἐξ
them[be] they were cleansed. But one of

αὐτῶν, ἰδὼν ὅτι ἰάθη, ὑπέστρεψεν μετὰ
them, seeing that he was cured, returned with

φωνῆς μεγάλης δοξάζων τὸν θεόν, 16 καὶ
voice a great glorifying - God, and

ἔπεσεν ἐπὶ πρόσωπον παρὰ τοὺς πόδας
fell on [his] face at the feet

αὐτοῦ εὐχαριστῶν αὐτῷ· καὶ αὐτὸς ἦν
of him thanking him; and he was

Σαμαρίτης. 17 ἀποκριθεὶς δὲ ὁ Ἰησοῦς
a Samaritan. And answering - Jesus

εἶπεν· οὐχ οἱ δέκα ἐκαθαρίσθησαν; οἱ [δὲ]
said : Not the ten were cleansed? but the

ἐννέα ποῦ; 18 οὐχ εὑρέθησαν ὑποστρέψαντες
nine where? were there not found returning

δοῦναι δόξαν τῷ θεῷ εἰ μὴ ὁ ἀλλογενὴς
to give glory - to God only - stranger

οὗτος; 19 καὶ εἶπεν αὐτῷ· ἀναστὰς πορεύου·
this ? And he said to him : Rising up go;

ἡ πίστις σου σέσωκέν σε.
the faith of thee has healed thee.

20 Ἐπερωτηθεὶς δὲ ὑπὸ τῶν Φαρισαίων
And being questioned by the Pharisees

πότε ἔρχεται ἡ βασιλεία τοῦ θεοῦ,
when comes the kingdom - of God,

ἀπεκρίθη αὐτοῖς καὶ εἶπεν· οὐκ ἔρχεται
he answered them and said : Comes not

ἡ βασιλεία τοῦ θεοῦ μετὰ παρατηρήσεως,
the kingdom - of God with observation,

21 οὐδὲ ἐροῦσιν· ἰδοὺ ὧδε ἤ· ἐκεῖ· ἰδοὺ
nor will they say : Behold[,] here or: there; [b]behold

γὰρ ἡ βασιλεία τοῦ θεοῦ ἐντὸς ὑμῶν
[1]for the kingdom - of God within you

ἐστιν. 22 Εἶπεν δὲ πρὸς τοὺς μαθητάς·
is. And he said to the disciples :

ἐλεύσονται ἡμέραι ὅτε ἐπιθυμήσετε μίαν
Will come days when ye will long one

τῶν ἡμερῶν τοῦ υἱοῦ τοῦ ἀνθρώπου ἰδεῖν
of the days of the Son - of man to see

καὶ οὐκ ὄψεσθε. 23 καὶ ἐροῦσιν ὑμῖν·
and will not see. And they will say to you :

ἰδοὺ ἐκεῖ, ἰδοὺ ὧδε· μὴ ἀπέλθητε μηδὲ
Behold there, behold here; do not go away nor

διώξητε. 24 ὥσπερ γὰρ ἡ ἀστραπὴ
follow. For as the lightning

ἀστράπτουσα ἐκ τῆς ὑπὸ τὸν οὐρανὸν
flashing out of the [one part] under - heaven

εἰς τὴν ὑπ᾽ οὐρανὸν λάμπει, οὕτως ἔσται
to the [other part] under heaven shines, so will be

ὁ υἱὸς τοῦ ἀνθρώπου ἐν τῇ ἡμέρᾳ αὐτοῦ.
the Son - of man in the day of him.

25 πρῶτον δὲ δεῖ αὐτὸν πολλὰ παθεῖν καὶ
But first it behoves him many things to suffer and

ἀποδοκιμασθῆναι ἀπὸ τῆς γενεᾶς ταύτης.
to be rejected from - generation this.

26 καὶ καθὼς ἐγένετο ἐν ταῖς ἡμέραις
And as it was in the days

Νῶε, οὕτως ἔσται καὶ ἐν ταῖς ἡμέραις
of Noah, so it will be also in the days

τοῦ υἱοῦ τοῦ ἀνθρώπου· 27 ἤσθιον, ἔπινον,
of the Son - of man; they were eating, drinking,

ἐγάμουν, ἐγαμίζοντο, ἄχρι ἧς ἡμέρας
marrying, giving in marriage, until which day
= the day when

εἰσῆλθεν Νῶε εἰς τὴν κιβωτόν, καὶ
entered Noah into the ark, and

ἦλθεν ὁ κατακλυσμὸς καὶ ἀπώλεσεν πάντας.
came the flood and destroyed all.

28 ὁμοίως καθὼς ἐγένετο ἐν ταῖς ἡμέραις
Likewise as it was in the days

Λώτ· ἤσθιον, ἔπινον, ἠγόραζον, ἐπώλουν,
of Lot; they were eating, drinking, buying, selling,

ἐφύτευον, ᾠκοδόμουν· 29 ᾗ δὲ ἡμέρᾳ ἐξῆλθεν
planting, building; but on which day went forth

Λὼτ ἀπὸ Σοδόμων, ἔβρεξεν πῦρ καὶ
Lot from Sodom, it rained fire and

θεῖον ἀπ᾽ οὐρανοῦ καὶ ἀπώλεσεν πάντας.
brimstone from heaven and destroyed all.

30 κατὰ τὰ αὐτὰ ἔσται ᾗ ἡμέρᾳ ὁ υἱὸς
According to the same things it will be on which day the Son
= In the same way   = on the day when

τοῦ ἀνθρώπου ἀποκαλύπτεται. 31 ἐν ἐκείνῃ
- of man is revealed. In that

τῇ ἡμέρᾳ ὃς ἔσται ἐπὶ τοῦ δώματος καὶ
- day who will be on the roof and

τὰ σκεύη αὐτοῦ ἐν τῇ οἰκίᾳ, μὴ καταβάτω
the goods of him in the house, let him not come down

ἆραι αὐτά, καὶ ὁ ἐν ἀγρῷ ὁμοίως μὴ
to take them, and the [one] in a field likewise not

ἐπιστρεψάτω εἰς τὰ ὀπίσω. 32 μνημονεύετε
let him turn back to the things behind. Remember

τῆς γυναικὸς Λώτ. 33 ὃς ἐὰν ζητήσῃ
the wife of Lot. Whoever seeks

τὴν ψυχὴν αὐτοῦ περιποιήσασθαι, ἀπολέσει
the life of him to preserve, he will lose

αὐτήν, καὶ ὃς ἂν ἀπολέσει, ζῳογονήσει
it, and whoever will lose, will preserve

αὐτήν. 34 λέγω ὑμῖν, ταύτῃ τῇ νυκτὶ
it. I tell you, in this - night

ἔσονται δύο ἐπὶ κλίνης μιᾶς, ὁ εἷς
there will be two men on couch one, the one

παραλημφθήσεται καὶ ὁ ἕτερος ἀφεθήσεται·
will be taken and the other will be left;

35 ἔσονται δύο ἀλήθουσαι ἐπὶ τὸ αὐτό, ἡ
there will be two women grinding together,† the

μία παραλημφθήσεται ἡ δὲ ἑτέρα ἀφεθήσεται.‡
one will be taken but the other will be left.

37 καὶ ἀποκριθέντες λέγουσιν αὐτῷ· ποῦ,
And answering they say to him : Where,

κύριε; ὁ δὲ εἶπεν αὐτοῖς· ὅπου τὸ σῶμα,
Lord? And he said to them : Where the body,

ἐκεῖ καὶ οἱ ἀετοὶ ἐπισυναχθήσονται.
there also the eagles will be gathered together.

---

‡ Verse 36 omitted by Nestle

King James Version

18 And he spake a parable unto them *to this end,* that men ought always to pray, and not to faint; 2 Saying, There was in a city a judge, which feared not God, neither regarded man: 3And there was a widow in that city; and she came unto him, saying, Avenge me of mine adversary. 4And he would not for a while: but afterward he said within himself, Though I fear not God, nor regard man; 5 Yet because this widow troubleth me, I will avenge her, lest by her continual coming she weary me. 6And the Lord said, Hear what the unjust judge saith. 7And shall not God avenge his own elect, which cry day and night unto him, though he bear long with them? 8 I tell you that he will avenge them speedily. Nevertheless, when the Son of man cometh, shall he find faith on the earth? 9And he spake this parable unto certain which trusted in themselves that they were righteous, and despised others: 10 Two men went up into the temple to pray; the one a Pharisee, and the other a publican. 11 The Pharisee stood and prayed thus with himself, God, I thank thee, that I am not as other men *are,* extortioners, unjust, adulterers, or even as this publican. 12 I fast twice in the week, I give tithes of all that I possess. 13And the publican, standing afar off, would not lift up so much as *his* eyes unto heaven, but smote upon his breast, saying, God be merciful to me a sinner. 14 I tell you, this man went down to his house justified *rather* than the other: for every one that exalteth himself shall be abased; and he that humbleth himself shall be exalted. 15And they brought unto him also infants, that he would touch them: but when *his* disciples saw *it,* they rebuked them. 16 But Jesus called them *unto him,* and said, Suffer little children to come unto me, and forbid them not: for of such is the kingdom of God. 17 Verily I say unto you, Whosoever shall not receive the kingdom of God as a little child shall in no wise enter therein. 18And a certain ruler asked him, saying, Good Master, what shall I do to inherit eternal life? 19And Jesus said unto him, Why callest thou me good? none *is* good, save one, *that is,* God. 20 Thou knowest the commandments, Do not commit adultery, Do not kill, Do not steal, Do not bear false witness, Honour thy father and thy mother. 21And he said, All these have I kept from my youth up. 22 Now when Jesus heard these things, he said unto him, Yet lackest thou one thing: sell all

New International Version

The parable of the persistent widow

18 Then Jesus told his disciples a parable to show them that they should always pray and not give up. 2 He said: "In a certain town there was a judge who neither feared God nor cared about men. 3And there was a widow in that town who kept coming to him with the plea, 'Grant me justice against my adversary.'

4 "For some time he refused. But finally he said to himself, 'Even though I don't fear God or care about men, 5 yet because this widow keeps bothering me, I will see that she gets justice, so that she won't eventually wear me out with her coming!' "

6 And the Lord said, "Listen to what the unjust judge says. 7And will not God bring about justice for his chosen ones, who cry out to him day and night? Will he keep putting them off? 8 I tell you, he will see that they get justice, and quickly. However, when the Son of Man comes, will he find faith on the earth?"

The parable of the Pharisee and the tax collector

9 To some who were confident of their own righteousness and looked down on everybody else, Jesus told this parable: 10 "Two men went up to the temple to pray, one a Pharisee and the other a tax collector. 11 The Pharisee stood up and prayed about himself: 'God, I thank you that I am not like all other men—robbers, evildoers, adulterers—or even like this tax collector. 12 I fast twice a week and give a tenth of all my income.'

13 "But the tax collector stood at a distance. He would not even look up to heaven, but beat his breast and said, 'God, have mercy on me, a sinner.'

14 "I tell you that this man, rather than the other, went home justified before God. For everyone who exalts himself will be humbled, and he who humbles himself will be exalted."

The little children and Jesus

15 People were also bringing babies to Jesus to have him touch them. When the disciples saw this, they rebuked them. 16 But Jesus called the children to him and said, "Let the little children come to me, and do not hinder them, for the kingdom of God belongs to such as these. 17 I tell you the truth, anyone who will not receive the kingdom of God like a little child will never enter it."

The rich ruler

18 A certain ruler asked him, "Good teacher, what must I do to inherit eternal life?"

19 "Why do you call me good?" Jesus answered. "No one is good—except God alone. 20 You know the commandments: 'Do not commit adultery, do not murder, do not steal, do not give false testimony, honor your father and mother.' *k* "

21 "All these I have kept since I was a boy," he said.

22 When Jesus heard this, he said to him, "You still lack one thing. Sell everything you

[k] Exodus 20:12-16; Deut. 5:16-20.

Greek Interlinear

Chapter 18

Ἔλεγεν δὲ παραβολὴν αὐτοῖς πρὸς
And he told ³a parable ¹them to
=that

τὸ δεῖν πάντοτε προσεύχεσθαι αὐτοὺς καὶ
the ¹to behove ²always ⁴to pray ³them and
they must always pray and not faint,

μὴ ἐγκακεῖν, 2 λέγων· κριτής τις ἦν ἔν
not to faint, saying : ²judge ¹a certain ¹There ⁴in
was

τινι πόλει τὸν θεὸν μὴ φοβούμενος καὶ
²a certain ⁶city - ³God ¹not ⁵fearing and

ἄνθρωπον μὴ ἐντρεπόμενος. 3 χήρα δὲ ἦν
³man ¹not ²regarding. And ²a widow ¹there was

ἐν τῇ πόλει ἐκείνῃ, καὶ ἤρχετο πρὸς
in - city that, and she came to

αὐτὸν λέγουσα· ἐκδίκησόν με ἀπὸ τοῦ
him saying : Vindicate me from the

ἀντιδίκου μου. 4 καὶ οὐκ ἤθελεν ἐπὶ
opponent of me. And he would not for

χρόνον· μετὰ ταῦτα δὲ εἶπεν ἐν ἑαυτῷ·
a time; but after these things he said in himself :

εἰ καὶ τὸν θεὸν οὐ φοβοῦμαι οὐδὲ ἄνθρωπον
If indeed - God I fear not nor man

ἐντρέπομαι, 5 διά γε τὸ παρέχειν
regard, at least because of - to cause
=because this widow causes me trouble

μοι κόπον τὴν χήραν ταύτην ἐκδικήσω αὐτήν,
me trouble - widow this⁵ I will vindicate her,

ἵνα μὴ εἰς τέλος ἐρχομένη ὑπωπιάζῃ με.
lest in [the] end coming she exhausts me.

6 Εἶπεν δὲ ὁ κύριος· ἀκούσατε τί ὁ κριτὴς
And said the Lord : Hear ye what the judge

τῆς ἀδικίας λέγει· 7 ὁ δὲ θεὸς οὐ μὴ
- of unrighteousness says; - and God by no means

ποιήσῃ τὴν ἐκδίκησιν τῶν ἐκλεκτῶν
will he make the vindication of the chosen [ones]

αὐτοῦ τῶν βοώντων αὐτῷ ἡμέρας καὶ
of him - crying to him day and

νυκτός, καὶ μακροθυμεῖ ἐπ' αὐτοῖς; 8 λέγω
night, and be patient over them? I tell

ὑμῖν ὅτι ποιήσει τὴν ἐκδίκησιν αὐτῶν
you that he will make the vindication of them

ἐν τάχει. πλὴν ὁ υἱὸς τοῦ ἀνθρώπου ἐλθὼν
quickly. Nevertheless the Son - of man coming

ἆρα εὑρήσει τὴν πίστιν ἐπὶ τῆς γῆς;
then will he find the faith on the earth?

9 Εἶπεν δὲ καὶ πρός τινας τοὺς
And he said also to some the [ones]

πεποιθότας ἐφ' ἑαυτοῖς ὅτι εἰσὶν
relying on themselves that they are

δίκαιοι καὶ ἐξουθενοῦντας τοὺς λοιποὺς
righteous and despising the rest

τὴν παραβολὴν ταύτην. 10 Ἄνθρωποι δύο
- parable this. Men two

ἀνέβησαν εἰς τὸ ἱερὸν προσεύξασθαι, ὁ εἷς
went up to the temple to pray, the one

Φαρισαῖος καὶ ὁ ἕτερος τελώνης. 11 ὁ
a Pharisee and the other a tax-collector. The

Φαρισαῖος σταθεὶς ταῦτα πρὸς ἑαυτὸν
Pharisee standing these things to himself

προσηύχετο· ὁ θεός, εὐχαριστῶ σοι ὅτι
prayed : - God, I thank thee that

οὐκ εἰμὶ ὥσπερ οἱ λοιποὶ τῶν ἀνθρώπων,
I am not as the rest - of men,

ἅρπαγες, ἄδικοι, μοιχοί, ἢ καὶ ὡς οὗτος
rapacious, unjust, adulterers, or even as this

ὁ τελώνης· 12 νηστεύω δὶς τοῦ σαββάτου,
- tax-collector; I fast twice of(in) the week,

ἀποδεκατεύω πάντα ὅσα κτῶμαι. 13 ὁ δὲ
I tithe all things how many I get. But the

τελώνης μακρόθεν ἑστὼς οὐκ ἤθελεν οὐδὲ
tax-collector far off standing would not not even

τοὺς ὀφθαλμοὺς ἐπᾶραι εἰς τὸν οὐρανόν,
the(his) eyes to lift up to - heaven,

ἀλλ' ἔτυπτεν τὸ στῆθος αὐτοῦ λέγων· ὁ
but smote the breast of him saying : -

θεός, ἱλάσθητί μοι τῷ ἁμαρτωλῷ. 14 λέγω
God, be propitious to me the sinner. I tell

ὑμῖν, κατέβη οὗτος δεδικαιωμένος εἰς τὸν
you, went down this man having been justified to the

οἶκον αὐτοῦ παρ' ἐκεῖνον· ὅτι πᾶς ὁ
house of him [rather] than that one; because everyone

ὑψῶν ἑαυτὸν ταπεινωθήσεται, ὁ δὲ ταπεινῶν
exalting himself will be humbled, and the [one] humbling

ἑαυτὸν ὑψωθήσεται.
himself will be exalted.

15 Προσέφερον δὲ αὐτῷ καὶ τὰ βρέφη
And they brought to him also the babes

ἵνα αὐτῶν ἅπτηται· ἰδόντες δὲ οἱ μαθηταὶ
that them he might touch; but ²seeing ¹the ³disciples

ἐπετίμων αὐτοῖς. 16 ὁ δὲ Ἰησοῦς
rebuked them. - But Jesus

προσεκαλέσατο αὐτὰ λέγων· ἄφετε τὰ
called to [him] them* saying : Allow the

παιδία ἔρχεσθαι πρός με καὶ μὴ κωλύετε
children to come to me and do not prevent

αὐτά· τῶν γὰρ τοιούτων ἐστὶν ἡ βασιλεία
them; - for of such is the kingdom

τοῦ θεοῦ. 17 ἀμὴν λέγω ὑμῖν, ὃς ἂν
- of God. Truly I tell you, whoever

μὴ δέξηται τὴν βασιλείαν τοῦ θεοῦ ὡς
does not receive the kingdom - of God as

παιδίον, οὐ μὴ εἰσέλθῃ εἰς αὐτήν.
a child, by no means enters into it.

18 Καὶ ἐπηρώτησέν τις αὐτὸν ἄρχων
And ²questioned ¹a certain ⁴him ³ruler

λέγων· διδάσκαλε ἀγαθέ, τί ποιήσας ζωὴν
saying : Teacher good, what doing life

αἰώνιον κληρονομήσω; 19 εἶπεν δὲ αὐτῷ
eternal may I inherit? And said to him

ὁ Ἰησοῦς· τί με λέγεις ἀγαθόν; οὐδεὶς
- Jesus : Why me sayest thou good? no one

ἀγαθὸς εἰ μὴ εἷς [ὁ] θεός. 20 τὰς ἐντολὰς
[is] good except one[,] - God. The commandments

οἶδας· μὴ μοιχεύσῃς, μὴ φονεύσῃς,
thou knowest : Do not commit adultery, Do not kill,

μὴ κλέψῃς, μὴ ψευδομαρτυρήσῃς, τίμα
Do not steal, Do not bear false witness, Honour

τὸν πατέρα σου καὶ τὴν μητέρα. 21 ὁ δὲ
the father of thee and the mother. And he

εἶπεν· ταῦτα πάντα ἐφύλαξα ἐκ νεότητος.
said : All these things I kept from youth.

22 ἀκούσας δὲ ὁ Ἰησοῦς εἶπεν αὐτῷ· ἔτι
But hearing - Jesus said to him : Yet

ἕν σοι λείπει· πάντα ὅσα ἔχεις
one thing to thee is lacking; all things how many thou hast

That is, "the babes" (τὰ βρέφη in ver. 15).

King James Version

that thou hast, and distribute unto the poor, and thou shalt have treasure in heaven: and come, follow me. 23And when he heard this, he was very sorrowful: for he was very rich. 24And when Jesus saw that he was very sorrowful, he said, How hardly shall they that have riches enter into the kingdom of God! 25 For it is easier for a camel to go through a needle's eye, than for a rich man to enter into the kingdom of God. 26And they that heard it said, Who then can be saved? 27And he said, The things which are impossible with men are possible with God. 28 Then Peter said, Lo, we have left all, and followed thee. 29And he said unto them, Verily I say unto you, There is no man that hath left house, or parents, or brethren, or wife, or children, for the kingdom of God's sake, 30 Who shall not receive manifold more in this present time, and in the world to come life everlasting.

31 Then he took unto him the twelve, and said unto them, Behold, we go up to Jerusalem, and all things that are written by the prophets concerning the Son of man shall be accomplished. 32 For he shall be delivered unto the Gentiles, and shall be mocked, and spitefully entreated, and spitted on: 33And they shall scourge him, and put him to death; and the third day he shall rise again. 34And they understood none of these things: and this saying was hid from them, neither knew they the things which were spoken.

35 And it came to pass, that as he was come nigh unto Jericho, a certain blind man sat by the way side begging: 36And hearing the multitude pass by, he asked what it meant. 37And they told him, that Jesus of Nazareth passeth by. 38And he cried, saying, Jesus, thou Son of David, have mercy on me. 39And they which went before rebuked him, that he should hold his peace: but he cried so much the more, Thou Son of David, have mercy on me. 40And Jesus stood, and commanded him to be brought unto him: and when he was come near, he asked him, 41 Saying, What wilt thou that I shall do unto thee? And he said, Lord, that I may receive my sight. 42And Jesus said unto him, Receive thy sight: thy faith hath saved thee. 43And immediately he received his sight, and followed him, glorifying God: and all the people, when they saw it, gave praise unto God.

New International Version

have and give to the poor, and you will have treasure in heaven. Then come, follow me."

23 When he heard this, he became very sad, because he was a man of great wealth. 24 Jesus looked at him and said, "How hard it is for the rich to enter the kingdom of God! 25 Indeed, it is easier for a camel to go through the eye of a needle than for a rich man to enter the kingdom of God."

26 Those who heard this asked, "Who then can be saved?"

27 Jesus replied, "What is impossible with men is possible with God."

28 Peter said to him, "We have left all we had to follow you!"

29 "I tell you the truth," Jesus said to them, "no one who has left home or wife or brothers or parents or children for the sake of the kingdom of God 30 will fail to receive many times as much in this age and, in the age to come, eternal life."

Jesus again predicts his death

31 Jesus took the Twelve aside and told them, "We are going up to Jerusalem, and everything that is written by the prophets about the Son of Man will be fulfilled. 32 He will be handed over to the Gentiles. They will mock him, insult him, spit on him, flog him and kill him. 33 On the third day he will rise again."

34 The disciples did not understand any of this. Its meaning was hidden from them, and they did not know what he was talking about.

A blind beggar receives his sight

35 As Jesus approached Jericho, a blind man was sitting by the roadside begging. 36 When he heard the crowd going by, he asked what was happening. 37 They told him, "Jesus of Nazareth is passing by."

38 He called out, "Jesus, Son of David, have mercy on me!"

39 Those who led the way rebuked him and told him to be quiet, but he shouted all the more, "Son of David, have mercy on me!"

40 Jesus stopped and ordered the man to be brought to him. When he came near, Jesus asked him, 41 "What do you want me to do for you?"

"Lord, I want to see," he replied.

42 Jesus said to him, "Receive your sight; your faith has healed you." 43 Immediately he received his sight and followed Jesus, praising God. When all the people saw it, they also praised God.

Zacchaeus the tax collector

19 And Jesus entered and passed through Jericho. 2And, behold, there was a man named Zaccheus, which was the chief among the publicans, and he was rich. 3And he sought to see Jesus who he was; and could not for the press, because he was little of stature. 4And he ran before, and climbed up into a sycamore tree to see him; for he was to pass that way. 5And when Jesus came to the place, he looked up,

19 Jesus entered Jericho and was passing through. 2A man was there by the name of Zacchaeus; he was a chief tax collector and was wealthy. 3 He wanted to see who Jesus was, but being a short man he could not, because of the crowd. 4 So he ran ahead and climbed a sycamore-fig tree to see him, since Jesus was coming that way.

5 When Jesus reached the spot, he looked up

Greek Interlinear

πώλησον καὶ διάδος πτωχοῖς, καὶ ἕξεις
sell   and distribute to poor people, and thou wilt have

θησαυρὸν ἐν . [τοῖς] οὐρανοῖς, καὶ δεῦρο
treasure in   [-]   heavens,   and   come

ἀκολούθει μοι.   23 ὁ δὲ ἀκούσας ταῦτα
follow   me.   But he hearing these things

περίλυπος ἐγενήθη, ἦν γὰρ πλούσιος σφόδρα.
very grieved became, for he was rich   exceedingly.

24 ἰδὼν δὲ αὐτὸν ὁ Ἰησοῦς εἶπεν· πῶς
And seeing him   -   Jesus   said : How

δυσκόλως οἱ τὰ χρήματα ἔχοντες εἰς τὴν
hardly ¹the [ones] - ²property ³having into the

βασιλείαν τοῦ θεοῦ εἰσπορεύονται· 25 εὐκο-
kingdom   - of God go in;   ²easi-

πώτερον γάρ ἐστιν κάμηλον διὰ τρήματος
er   ¹for it is [for] a camel through [the] eye

βελόνης εἰσελθεῖν ἢ πλούσιον εἰς τὴν
of a needle to enter than a rich man into the

βασιλείαν τοῦ θεοῦ εἰσελθεῖν. 26 εἶπαν
kingdom   - of God to enter.   said

δὲ οἱ ἀκούσαντες· καὶ τίς δύναται
And the [ones] hearing :   And who can

σωθῆναι; 27 ὁ δὲ εἶπεν· τὰ ἀδύνατα παρὰ
to be saved? And he said : The things impossible with

ἀνθρώποις δυνατὰ παρὰ τῷ θεῷ ἐστιν.
men   possible with   - God is(are).

28 Εἶπεν δὲ ὁ Πέτρος· ἰδοὺ ἡμεῖς ἀφέντες
And said   -   Peter : Behold[,] we leaving

τὰ ἴδια ἠκολουθήσαμέν σοι. 29 ὁ δὲ
our own things followed   thee.   And he

εἶπεν αὐτοῖς· ἀμὴν λέγω ὑμῖν ὅτι οὐδείς
said   to them : Truly I tell you that no one

ἐστιν ὃς ἀφῆκεν οἰκίαν ἢ γυναῖκα ἢ
there is who left   house or   wife   or

ἀδελφοὺς ἢ γονεῖς ἢ τέκνα εἵνεκεν τῆς
brothers   or parents or children for the sake of the

βασιλείας τοῦ θεοῦ, 30 ὃς οὐχὶ μὴ λάβῃ
kingdom   - of God,   who by no means receives

πολλαπλασίονα ἐν τῷ καιρῷ τούτῳ καὶ ἐν
many times over in - time   this   and in

τῷ αἰῶνι τῷ ἐρχομένῳ ζωὴν αἰώνιον.
the age -   coming   life eternal.

31 Παραλαβὼν δὲ τοὺς δώδεκα εἶπεν πρὸς
And taking   the twelve he said to

αὐτούς· ἰδοὺ ἀναβαίνομεν εἰς Ἰερουσαλήμ,
them·   Behold we are going up to Jerusalem,

καὶ τελεσθήσεται πάντα τὰ γεγραμ-
and will be accomplished all things - having been

μένα διὰ τῶν προφητῶν τῷ υἱῷ τοῦ
written through the prophets to the Son -

ἀνθρώπου· 32 παραδοθήσεται γὰρ τοῖς ἔθνεσιν
of man·   for he will be delivered to the nations

καὶ ἐμπαιχθήσεται καὶ ὑβρισθήσεται καὶ
and will be mocked   and   will be insulted and

ἐμπτυσθήσεται, 33 καὶ μαστιγώσαντες
will be spit at,   and   having scourged

ἀποκτενοῦσιν αὐτόν, καὶ τῇ ἡμέρᾳ τῇ
they will kill   him,   and on the day   -

τρίτῃ ἀναστήσεται. 34 καὶ αὐτοὶ οὐδὲν
third he will rise again.   And they   none

τούτων συνῆκαν, καὶ ἦν τὸ ῥῆμα τοῦτο
of these things understood, and ²was - ³utterance ¹this

κεκρυμμένον ἀπ' αὐτῶν, καὶ οὐκ ἐγίνωσκον
⁴having been hidden from them, and   they knew not

τὰ λεγόμενα.
the things being said.

35 Ἐγένετο δὲ ἐν τῷ ἐγγίζειν αὐτὸν εἰς
And it came to pass in the to draw near himᵇᵉ to
= as he drew near

Ἰεριχὼ τυφλός τις ἐκάθητο παρὰ τὴν ὁδὸν
Jericho a certain blind man sat by   the   way

ἐπαιτῶν. 36 ἀκούσας δὲ ὄχλου διαπορευομένου
begging.   And hearing a crowd passing through

ἐπυνθάνετο τί εἴη τοῦτο. 37 ἀπήγγειλαν
he inquired what ²might be ¹this.   And they re-

δὲ αὐτῷ ὅτι Ἰησοῦς ὁ Ναζωραῖος
ported to him[,] -   Jesus the   Nazarene

παρέρχεται. 38 καὶ ἐβόησεν λέγων· Ἰησοῦ
is passing by.   And he cried saying :   Jesus

υἱὲ Δαυίδ, ἐλέησόν με. 39 καὶ οἱ
son of David, pity   me.   And the [ones]

προάγοντες ἐπετίμων αὐτῷ ἵνα σιγήσῃ·
going before rebuked   him that he should be quiet;

αὐτὸς δὲ πολλῷ μᾶλλον ἔκραζεν· υἱὲ
but he   by much   more   cried out : Son

Δαυίδ, ἐλέησόν με. 40 σταθεὶς δὲ ὁ
of David, pity   me.   And standing   -

Ἰησοῦς ἐκέλευσεν αὐτὸν ἀχθῆναι πρὸς
Jesus   commanded   him to be brought to

αὐτόν. ἐγγίσαντος δὲ αὐτοῦ ἐπηρώτησεν
him.   And drawing near   himᵃ   he questioned
= as he drew near

αὐτόν· 41 τί σοι θέλεις ποιήσω; ὁ δὲ
him :   What for thee wishest thou I may do? And he

εἶπεν· κύριε, ἵνα ἀναβλέψω. 42 καὶ ὁ Ἰησοῦς
said : Lord, that I may see again.   And - Jesus

εἶπεν αὐτῷ· ἀνάβλεψον· ἡ πίστις σου
said to him : See again; the faith of thee

σέσωκέν σε. 43 καὶ παραχρῆμα ἀνέβλεψεν,
has healed thee.   And at once   he saw again,

καὶ ἠκολούθει αὐτῷ δοξάζων τὸν θεόν.
and followed   him glorifying - God.

καὶ πᾶς ὁ λαὸς ἰδὼν ἔδωκεν αἶνον τῷ
And all the people seeing gave praise -

θεῷ.
to God.

Chapter 19

Καὶ εἰσελθὼν διήρχετο τὴν Ἰεριχώ.
And having entered he passed through - Jericho.

2 Καὶ ἰδοὺ ἀνὴρ ὀνόματι καλούμενος
And behold[,] a man by name   being called

Ζακχαῖος, καὶ αὐτὸς ἦν ἀρχιτελώνης, καὶ
Zacchæus,   and   he was a chief tax-collector, and

αὐτὸς πλούσιος· 3 καὶ ἐζήτει ἰδεῖν τὸν
he [was] rich·   and he sought to see   -

Ἰησοῦν τίς ἐστιν, καὶ οὐκ ἠδύνατο ἀπὸ
Jesus   who he is(was), and was not able from

τοῦ ὄχλου, ὅτι τῇ ἡλικίᾳ μικρὸς ἦν.
the crowd, because - ²in stature ³little ¹he was.

4 καὶ προδραμὼν εἰς τὸ ἔμπροσθεν ἀνέβη
And having run forward to the   front   he went up

ἐπὶ συκομορέαν, ἵνα ἴδῃ αὐτόν, ὅτι
onto a sycamore-tree, that he might see him, because

ἐκείνης ἤμελλεν διέρχεσθαι. 5 καὶ ὡς
²that [way] ¹he was about ²to pass along.   And as

ἦλθεν ἐπὶ τὸν τόπον, ἀναβλέψας ὁ Ἰησοῦς
he came upon the place,   looking up   -   Jesus

King James Version

and saw him, and said unto him, Zaccheus, make haste, and come down; for to day I must abide at thy house. 6And he made haste, and came down, and received him joyfully. 7And when they saw *it*, they all murmured, saying, That he was gone to be guest with a man that is a sinner. 8And Zaccheus stood, and said unto the Lord; Behold, Lord, the half of my goods I give to the poor; and if I have taken any thing from any man by false accusation, I restore *him* fourfold. 9And Jesus said unto him, This day is salvation come to this house, forasmuch as he also is a son of Abraham. 10 For the Son of man is come to seek and to save that which was lost. 11And as they heard these things, he added and spake a parable, because he was nigh to Jerusalem, and because they thought that the kingdom of God should immediately appear. 12 He said therefore, A certain nobleman went into a far country to receive for himself a kingdom, and to return. 13And he called his ten servants, and delivered them ten pounds, and said unto them, Occupy till I come. 14 But his citizens hated him, and sent a message after him, saying, We will not have this *man* to reign over us. 15And it came to pass, that when he was returned, having received the kingdom, then he commanded these servants to be called unto him, to whom he had given the money, that he might know how much every man had gained by trading. 16 Then came the first, saying, Lord, thy pound hath gained ten pounds. 17And he said unto him, Well, thou good servant: because thou hast been faithful in a very little, have thou authority over ten cities. 18And the second came, saying, Lord, thy pound hath gained five pounds. 19And he said likewise to him, Be thou also over five cities. 20And another came, saying, Lord, behold, *here is* thy pound, which I have kept laid up in a napkin: 21 For I feared thee, because thou art an austere man: thou takest up that thou layedst not down, and reapest that thou didst not sow. 22And he saith unto him, Out of thine own mouth will I judge thee, *thou* wicked servant. Thou knewest that I was an austere man, taking up that I laid not down, and reaping that I did not sow: 23 Wherefore then gavest not thou my money into the bank, that at my coming I might have required mine own with usury? 24And he said unto them that stood by, Take from him the pound, and give *it* to him that hath ten pounds. 25 (And they said unto him, Lord, he hath ten pounds.) 26 For I say unto you, That unto every one which hath shall be given; and from him that hath not, even that he hath shall be taken away from him. 27 But those mine enemies, which would not that I should reign over them, bring hither, and slay *them* before me.

28 And when he had thus spoken, he went before, ascending up to Jerusalem. 29And it came to pass, when he was come nigh to Bethphage and Bethany, at the mount called *the mount* of

New International Version

and said to him, "Zacchaeus, come down immediately. I must stay at your house today." 6 So he came down at once and welcomed him gladly.

7 All the people saw this and began to mutter, "He has gone to be the guest of a sinner."

8 But Zacchaeus stood up and said to the Lord, "Look, Lord! Here and now I give half of my possessions to the poor, and if I have cheated anybody out of anything, I will pay back four times the amount."

9 Jesus said to him, "Today salvation has come to this house, because this man, too, is a son of Abraham. 10 For the Son of Man came to seek and to save what was lost."

The parable of the ten minas

11 While they were listening to this, he went on to tell them a parable, because he was near Jerusalem and the people thought that the kingdom of God was going to appear at once. 12 He said: "A man of noble birth went to a distant country to have himself appointed king and then to return. 13 So he called ten of his servants and gave them ten minas.[l] 'Put this money to work,' he said, 'until I come back.'

14 "But his subjects hated him and sent a delegation after him to say, 'We don't want this man to be our king.'

15 "He was made king, however, and returned home. Then he sent for the servants to whom he had given the money, in order to find out what they had gained with it.

16 "The first one came and said, 'Sir, your mina has earned ten more.'

17 " 'Well done, my good servant!' his master replied. 'Because you have been trustworthy in a very small matter, take charge of ten cities.'

18 "The second came and said, 'Sir, your mina has earned five more.'

19 "His master answered, 'You take charge of five cities.'

20 "Then another servant came and said, 'Sir, here is your mina; I have kept it laid away in a piece of cloth. 21 I was afraid of you, because you are a hard man. You take out what you did not put in and reap what you did not sow.'

22 "His master replied, 'I will judge you by your own words, you wicked servant! You knew, did you, that I am a hard man, taking out what I did not put in, and reaping what I did not sow? 23 Why then didn't you put my money on deposit, so that when I came back, I could have collected it with interest?

24 "Then he said to those standing by, 'Take his mina away from him and give it to the one who has ten minas.'

25 " 'Sir,' they said, 'he already has ten!'

26 "He replied, 'I tell you that to everyone who has, more will be given, but as for the one who has nothing, even what he has will be taken away. 27 But those enemies of mine who did not want me to be king over them—bring them here and kill them in front of me.' "

The triumphal entry

28 After Jesus had said this, he went on ahead, going up to Jerusalem. 29As he approached Bethphage and Bethany at the hill called the Mount of Olives, he sent two of his disciples,

[l] A mina was about three months' wages.

Greek Interlinear

εἶπεν πρὸς αὐτόν· Ζακχαῖε, σπεύσας
said   to   him : Zacchæus, making haste

κατάβηθι· σήμερον γὰρ ἐν τῷ οἴκῳ σου
come down; for to-day in the house of thee

δεῖ με μεῖναι. 6 καὶ σπεύσας κατέβη,
it behoves me to remain.   And making haste he came down,

καὶ ὑπεδέξατο αὐτὸν χαίρων. 7 καὶ
and   welcomed   him   rejoicing.   And

ἰδόντες πάντες διεγόγγυζον λέγοντες ὅτι
seeing   all   murmured   saying[,] –

παρὰ ἁμαρτωλῷ ἀνδρὶ εἰσῆλθεν καταλῦσαι.
With a sinful   man he entered to lodge.

8 σταθεὶς δὲ Ζακχαῖος εἶπεν πρὸς τὸν
  And standing Zacchæus said to   the

κύριον· ἰδοὺ τὰ ἡμίση μου τῶν ὑπαρχόντων,
Lord : Behold[,] the half of me of the possessions,

κύριε, τοῖς πτωχοῖς δίδωμι, καὶ εἴ τινός
Lord, to the poor   I give, and if anyone

τι ἐσυκοφάντησα, ἀποδίδωμι τετραπλοῦν.
anything I accused falsely, I restore fourfold.

9 εἶπεν δὲ πρὸς αὐτὸν ὁ Ἰησοῦς ὅτι
  And said to   him   – Jesus[,] –

σήμερον σωτηρία τῷ οἴκῳ τούτῳ ἐγένετο,
To-day salvation – house to this came,

καθότι καὶ αὐτὸς υἱὸς Ἀβραάμ [ἐστιν]·
because even he a son of Abraham   is;

10 ἦλθεν γὰρ ὁ υἱὸς τοῦ ἀνθρώπου ζητῆσαι
   for came the Son   – of man   to seek

καὶ σῶσαι τὸ ἀπολωλός.
and to save the having been lost.

11 Ἀκουόντων δὲ αὐτῶν ταῦτα προσθεὶς
   And hearing   them* these things adding
                = as they heard

εἶπεν παραβολήν, διὰ τὸ ἐγγὺς εἶναι
he told a parable, because of the near to be
                   = because he was near to Jerusalem and they thought

Ἰερουσαλὴμ αὐτὸν καὶ δοκεῖν αὐτοὺς ὅτι
Jerusalem   him and to think themᵇ that

παραχρῆμα μέλλει ἡ βασιλεία τοῦ θεοῦ
at once is(was) about the kingdom – of God

ἀναφαίνεσθαι· 12 εἶπεν οὖν· ἄνθρωπός τις
to appear;   he said therefore : A certain man

εὐγενὴς ἐπορεύθη εἰς χώραν μακρὰν λαβεῖν
well born went to country a far to receive

ἑαυτῷ βασιλείαν καὶ ὑποστρέψαι. 13 καλέσας
for himself a kingdom and to return.   having called

δὲ δέκα δούλους ἑαυτοῦ ἔδωκεν αὐτοῖς
And ten slaves of himself he gave them

δέκα μνᾶς, καὶ εἶπεν πρὸς αὐτούς·
ten   minas, and said to   them :

πραγματεύσασθε ἐν ᾧ ἔρχομαι. 14 οἱ δὲ
Trade ye   while I am coming.*   But the

πολῖται αὐτοῦ ἐμίσουν αὐτόν, καὶ ἀπέστειλαν
citizens of him hated   him, and sent

πρεσβείαν ὀπίσω αὐτοῦ λέγοντες· οὐ θέλομεν
a delegation after him saying : We do not wish

τοῦτον βασιλεῦσαι ἐφ' ἡμᾶς. 15 καὶ
this man to reign   over us.   And

ἐγένετο ἐν τῷ ἐπανελθεῖν αὐτὸν λαβόντα
it came to pass in the to return   himᵇᵉ having received
                = when he returned

τὴν βασιλείαν καὶ εἶπεν φωνηθῆναι αὐτῷ
the kingdom   and he said to be called to him

τοὺς δούλους τούτους οἷς δεδώκει τὸ
–   slaves   these to whom he had given the

ἀργύριον, ἵνα γνοῖ τίς τί
money,   that he might know ⁱanyone ¹what

διεπραγματεύσατο. 16 παρεγένετο δὲ ὁ πρῶτος
gained by trading.   And came the first

λέγων· κύριε, ἡ μνᾶ σου δέκα προσηργάσατο
saying : Lord, the mina of thee ¹ten   ¹gained

μνᾶς. 17 καὶ εἶπεν αὐτῷ· εὖ γε, ἀγαθὲ δοῦλε,
ᵃminas.   And he said to him : Well, good slave,

ὅτι ἐν ἐλαχίστῳ πιστὸς ἐγένου, ἴσθι
because in a least thing faithful thou wast, be thou

ἐξουσίαν ἔχων ἐπάνω δέκα πόλεων. 18 καὶ
ᵃauthority ¹having over   ten cities.   And

ἦλθεν ὁ δεύτερος λέγων· ἡ μνᾶ σου,
came   the second   saying: The mina of thee,

κύριε, ἐποίησεν πέντε μνᾶς. 19 εἶπεν δὲ
lord, made   five minas.   And he said

καὶ τούτῳ· καὶ σὺ ἐπάνω γίνου πέντε
also to this one : And ²thou ²over   ¹be   five

πόλεων. 20 καὶ ὁ ἕτερος ἦλθεν λέγων·
cities.   And the other came   saying :

κύριε, ἰδοὺ ἡ μνᾶ σου, ἣν εἶχον
Lord, behold[,] the mina of thee, which I had

ἀποκειμένην ἐν σουδαρίῳ· 21 ἐφοβούμην γάρ
being put away in a napkin;   for I feared

σε, ὅτι ἄνθρωπος αὐστηρὸς εἶ, αἴρεις ὃ
thee, because man an exacting thou art, thou takest what

οὐκ ἔθηκας, καὶ θερίζεις ὃ οὐκ ἔσπειρας.
thou didst not lay, and thou reapest what thou didst not sow.

22 λέγει αὐτῷ· ἐκ τοῦ στόματός σου
He says to him : Out of the mouth of thee

κρινῶ σε, πονηρὲ δοῦλε. ᾔδεις ὅτι ἐγὼ
I will judge thee, wicked slave. Knewest thou that   I

ἄνθρωπος αὐστηρός εἰμι, αἴρων ὃ οὐκ
man   an exacting am, taking what not

ἔθηκα, καὶ θερίζων ὃ οὐκ ἔσπειρα; 23 καὶ
I laid, and reaping what I sowed not ?   And

διὰ τί οὐκ ἔδωκάς μου τὸ ἀργύριον ἐπὶ
why didst thou not give of me the money on

τράπεζαν; κἀγὼ ἐλθὼν σὺν τόκῳ ἂν
a table?★ And I coming with interest

αὐτὸ ἔπραξα. 24 καὶ τοῖς παρεστῶσιν
it would have exacted. And to the [ones] standing by

εἶπεν· ἄρατε ἀπ' αὐτοῦ τὴν μνᾶν καὶ
he said : Take from him   the mina and

δότε τῷ τὰς δέκα μνᾶς ἔχοντι. 25 καὶ
give ¹to the [one] ³the ⁴ten ²minas ¹having.   And

εἶπαν αὐτῷ· κύριε, ἔχει δέκα μνᾶς.
they said to him : Lord, he has ten minas.

26 λέγω ὑμῖν ὅτι παντὶ τῷ ἔχοντι
   I tell you that to everyone having

δοθήσεται, ἀπὸ δὲ τοῦ μὴ ἔχοντος καὶ
it will be given, and from the [one] not having even

ὃ ἔχει ἀρθήσεται. 27 πλὴν τοὺς ἐχθρούς
what he has will be taken. Nevertheless – enemies

μου τούτους τοὺς μὴ θελήσαντάς με
of me these the [ones] not   wishing   me

βασιλεῦσαι ἐπ' αὐτοὺς ἀγάγετε ὧδε καὶ
to reign   over them   bring ye here and

κατασφάξατε αὐτοὺς ἔμπροσθέν μου.
slay   them   before   me.

28 Καὶ εἰπὼν ταῦτα ἐπορεύετο ἔμπροσθεν
   And having said these things he went   in front

ἀναβαίνων εἰς Ἰεροσόλυμα. 29 Καὶ ἐγένετο
going up   to Jerusalem.   And it came to pass

ὡς ἤγγισεν εἰς Βηθφαγὴ καὶ Βηθανίαν
as he drew near to Bethphage and Bethany

πρὸς τὸ ὄρος τὸ καλούμενον ἐλαιῶν,
toward the mount – being called of olives,

ἀπέστειλεν δύο τῶν μαθητῶν λέγων·
he sent   two of the disciples saying :

* That is, " again." The present of this verb often has a
futurist significance; cf. John 14. 3.
★ That is, a moneychanger's or banker's table.

King James Version

Olives, he sent two of his disciples, 30 Saying, Go ye into the village over against *you;* in the which at your entering ye shall find a colt tied, whereon yet never man sat: loose him, and bring *him hither.* 31And if any man ask you, Why do ye loose *him?* thus shall ye say unto him, Because the Lord hath need of him. 32And they that were sent went their way, and found even as he had said unto them. 33And as they were loosing the colt, the owners thereof said unto them, Why loose ye the colt? 34And they said, The Lord hath need of him. 35And they brought him to Jesus: and they cast their garments upon the colt, and they set Jesus thereon. 36And as he went, they spread their clothes in the way. 37And when he was come nigh, even now at the descent of the mount of Olives, the whole multitude of the disciples began to rejoice and praise God with a loud voice for all the mighty works that they had seen; 38 Saying, Blessed *be* the King that cometh in the name of the Lord: peace in heaven, and glory in the highest. 39And some of the Pharisees from among the multitude said unto him, Master, rebuke thy disciples. 40And he answered and said unto them, I tell you that, if these should hold their peace, the stones would immediately cry out.

41 And when he was come near, he beheld the city, and wept over it, 42 Saying, If thou hadst known, even thou, at least in this thy day, the things *which belong* unto thy peace! but now they are hid from thine eyes. 43 For the days shall come upon thee, that thine enemies shall cast a trench about thee, and compass thee round, and keep thee in on every side, 44And shall lay thee even with the ground, and thy children within thee; and they shall not leave in thee one stone upon another; because thou knewest not the time of thy visitation. 45And he went into the temple, and began to cast out them that sold therein, and them that bought; 46 Saying unto them, It is written, My house is the house of prayer; but ye have made it a den of thieves. 47And he taught daily in the temple. But the chief priests and the scribes and the chief of the people sought to destroy him, 48And could not find what they might do: for all the people were very attentive to hear him.

20 And it came to pass, *that* on one of those days, as he taught the people in the temple, and preached the gospel, the chief priests and the scribes came upon *him* with the elders, 2And spake unto him, saying, Tell us, by what authority doest thou these things? or who is he that gave thee this authority? 3And he answered and said unto them, I will also ask you one thing; and answer me: 4 The baptism of John, was it from heaven, or of men? 5And they reasoned with themselves, saying, If we shall say, From heaven; he will say, Why then believed ye him not? 6 But and if ye say, Of men; all the people will stone us: for they be persuaded that

New International Version

saying to them: 30 "Go to the village ahead of you, and as you enter it, you will find a colt tied there, which no one has ever ridden. Untie it and bring it here. 31 If anyone asks you, 'Why are you untying it?' tell him, 'The Lord needs it.' "

32 Those who were sent went and found it just as he had told them. 33As they were untying the colt, its owners asked them, "Why are you untying the colt?"

34 They replied, "The Lord needs it."

35 They brought it to Jesus, threw their cloaks on the colt and put Jesus on it. 36As he went along, people spread their cloaks on the road.

37 When he came near the place where the road goes down the Mount of Olives, the whole crowd of disciples began joyfully to praise God in loud voices for all the miracles they had seen:

38 "Blessed is the king who comes in the name of the Lord! [m]

Peace in heaven and glory in the highest!"

39 Some of the Pharisees in the crowd said to Jesus, "Teacher, rebuke your disciples!"

40 "I tell you," he replied, "if they keep quiet, the stones will cry out."

41 As he approached Jerusalem and saw the city, he wept over it 42 and said, "If you, even you, had only known on this day what would bring you peace—but now it is hidden from your eyes. 43 The days will come upon you when your enemies will build an embankment against you and encircle you and hem you in on every side. 44 They will dash you to the ground, you and the children within your walls. They will not leave one stone on another, because you did not recognize the time of God's coming to you."

Jesus at the temple

45 Then he entered the temple area and began driving out those who were selling. 46 "It is written," he said to them, " 'My house will be a house of prayer' [n]; but you have made it 'a den of robbers.' [o]"

47 Every day he was teaching at the temple. But the chief priests, the teachers of the law and the leaders among the people were trying to kill him. 48 Yet they could not find any way to do it, because all the people hung on his words.

The authority of Jesus questioned

20 One day as he was teaching the people in the temple courts and preaching the gospel, the chief priests and the teachers of the law, together with the elders, came up to him. 2 "Tell us by what authority you are doing these things," they said. "Who gave you this authority?"

3 He replied, "I will also ask you a question. Tell me, 4 John's baptism—was it from heaven, or from men?"

5 They discussed it among themselves and said, "If we say, 'From heaven,' he will ask, 'Why didn't you believe him?' 6 But if we say, 'From men,' all the people will stone us, because they are persuaded that John was a prophet."

[m] Psalm 118:26. [n] Isaiah 56:7. [o] Jer. 7:11.

Greek Interlinear

30 ὑπάγετε εἰς τὴν κατέναντι κώμην, ἐν ᾗ
Go ye into the opposite village, in which

εἰσπορευόμενοι εὑρήσετε πῶλον δεδεμένον,
entering ye will find a colt having been tied,

ἐφ᾽ ὃν οὐδεὶς πώποτε ἀνθρώπων ἐκάθισεν,
on which no one ever yet of men sat,

καὶ λύσαντες αὐτὸν ἀγάγετε. **31** καὶ ἐάν
and loosening it bring. And if

τις ὑμᾶς ἐρωτᾷ· διὰ τί λύετε; οὕτως
anyone you asks: Why loosen ye? thus

ἐρεῖτε ὅτι ὁ κύριος αὐτοῦ χρείαν ἔχει.
shall ye say: Because the Lord of it need has.

32 ἀπελθόντες δὲ οἱ ἀπεσταλμένοι εὗρον
And going the [ones] having been sent found

καθὼς εἶπεν αὐτοῖς. **33** λυόντων δὲ
as he told them. And loosening
=as they were

αὐτῶν τὸν πῶλον εἶπαν οἱ κύριοι αὐτοῦ
them⁺ the colt said the owners of it
loosening

πρὸς αὐτούς· τί λύετε τὸν πῶλον; **34** οἱ
to them· Why loosen ye the colt? ²they

δὲ εἶπαν· ὅτι ὁ κύριος αὐτοῦ χρείαν ἔχει.
¹And said: Because the Lord of it need has.

35 καὶ ἤγαγον αὐτὸν πρὸς τὸν Ἰησοῦν,
And they led it to Jesus,

καὶ ἐπιρίψαντες αὐτῶν τὰ ἱμάτια ἐπὶ τὸν
and throwing on of them the garments on the

πῶλον ἐπεβίβασαν τὸν Ἰησοῦν. **36** πορευ-
colt they put on [it] Jesus. And

ομένου δὲ αὐτοῦ ὑπεστρώννυον τὰ ἱμάτια
going him⁺ they strewed the garments
=as he went

ἑαυτῶν ἐν τῇ ὁδῷ. **37** ἐγγίζοντος δὲ
of themselves in the way. And drawing near
=as he drew near

αὐτοῦ ἤδη πρὸς τῇ καταβάσει τοῦ ὄρους
him⁺ now to the descent of the mount

τῶν ἐλαιῶν ἤρξαντο ἅπαν τὸ πλῆθος τῶν
of the olives began all the multitude of the

μαθητῶν χαίροντες αἰνεῖν τὸν θεὸν φωνῇ
disciples rejoicing to praise - God voice

μεγάλῃ περὶ πασῶν ὧν εἶδον δυνάμεων,
with a about ¹all ²which ⁴they saw ³[the] powerful
great deeds,

38 λέγοντες· εὐλογημένος ὁ ἐρχόμενος, ὁ
saying: Blessed the coming [one], the

βασιλεὺς ἐν ὀνόματι κυρίου· ἐν οὐρανῷ
king in [the] name of [the] Lord; in heaven

εἰρήνη καὶ δόξα ἐν ὑψίστοις. **39** καὶ
peace and glory in highest places. And

τινες τῶν Φαρισαίων ἀπὸ τοῦ ὄχλου
some of the Pharisees from the crowd

εἶπαν πρὸς αὐτόν· διδάσκαλε, ἐπιτίμησον
said to him: Teacher, rebuke

τοῖς μαθηταῖς σου. **40** καὶ ἀποκριθεὶς
the disciples of thee. And answering

εἶπεν· λέγω ὑμῖν, ἐὰν οὗτοι σιωπήσουσιν,
he said: I tell you, if these shall(should) be silent,

οἱ λίθοι κράξουσιν. **41** Καὶ ὡς ἤγγισεν,
the stones will cry out. And as he drew near,

ἰδὼν τὴν πόλιν ἔκλαυσεν ἐπ᾽ αὐτήν,
seeing the city he wept over it,

42 λέγων ὅτι εἰ ἔγνως ἐν τῇ ἡμέρᾳ
saying[,] - If thou knewest in - day

ταύτῃ καὶ σὺ τὰ πρὸς εἰρήνην· νῦν δὲ
this even thou the things for peace; but now

ἐκρύβη ἀπὸ ὀφθαλμῶν σου. **43** ὅτι ἥξουσιν
they were hidden from eyes of thee. Because will come

ἡμέραι ἐπὶ σὲ καὶ παρεμβαλοῦσιν οἱ
days upon thee and ²will raise up ¹the

ἐχθροί σου χάρακά σοι καὶ περικυκλώσουσίν
²enemies ³of thee ³a rampart to thee and will surround

σε καὶ συνέξουσίν σε πάντοθεν, **44** καὶ
thee and will press thee on all sides, and

ἐδαφιοῦσίν σε καὶ τὰ τέκνα σου ἐν σοί,
dash to the ground thee and the children of thee in thee,

καὶ οὐκ ἀφήσουσιν λίθον ἐπὶ λίθον ἐν σοί,
and will not leave stone upon stone in thee,

ἀνθ᾽ ὧν οὐκ ἔγνως τὸν καιρὸν τῆς
because† thou knewest not the time of the

ἐπισκοπῆς σου. **45** Καὶ εἰσελθὼν εἰς τὸ
visitation of thee. And entering into the

ἱερὸν ἤρξατο ἐκβάλλειν τοὺς πωλοῦντας,
temple he began to expel the [ones] selling,

46 λέγων αὐτοῖς· γέγραπται καὶ ἔσται ὁ
telling them: It has been written: And shall be the

οἶκός μου οἶκος προσευχῆς· ὑμεῖς δὲ
house of me a house of prayer; but ye

αὐτὸν ἐποιήσατε σπήλαιον λῃστῶν.
it made a den of robbers.

47 Καὶ ἦν διδάσκων τὸ καθ᾽ ἡμέραν ἐν
And he was teaching - daily† in

τῷ ἱερῷ· οἱ δὲ ἀρχιερεῖς καὶ οἱ
the temple; but the chief priests and the

γραμματεῖς ἐζήτουν αὐτὸν ἀπολέσαι καὶ οἱ
scribes ²sought ³him ¹to destroy ¹and ⁴the

πρῶτοι τοῦ λαοῦ, **48** καὶ οὐχ εὕρισκον
²chief men ³of the ⁵people, and did not find

τὸ τί ποιήσωσιν· ὁ λαὸς γὰρ ἅπας
- what they might do; ²the ³people ¹for ²all

ἐξεκρέματο αὐτοῦ ἀκούων.
hung upon him hearing.

Chapter 20

Καὶ ἐγένετο ἐν μιᾷ τῶν ἡμερῶν
And it came to pass on one of the days

διδάσκοντος αὐτοῦ τὸν λαὸν ἐν τῷ ἱερῷ
teaching him⁺ the people in the temple
=as he was teaching

καὶ εὐαγγελιζομένου ἐπέστησαν οἱ ἀρχιερεῖς
and preaching good news⁺ came upon [him] the chief priests

καὶ οἱ γραμματεῖς σὺν τοῖς πρεσβυτέροις,
and the scribes with the elders,

2 καὶ εἶπαν λέγοντες πρὸς αὐτόν· εἰπὸν
and spoke saying to him: Tell

ἡμῖν ἐν ποίᾳ ἐξουσίᾳ ταῦτα ποιεῖς, ἢ τίς
us by what authority these things thou doest, or who

ἐστιν ὁ δούς σοι τὴν ἐξουσίαν ταύτην;
is the [one] having given thee - authority this?

3 ἀποκριθεὶς δὲ εἶπεν πρὸς αὐτούς·
And answering he said to them:

ἐρωτήσω ὑμᾶς κἀγὼ λόγον, καὶ εἴπατέ
Will ask you I also a word, and tell ye

μοι· **4** τὸ βάπτισμα Ἰωάννου ἐξ οὐρανοῦ
me: The baptism of John from heaven

ἦν ἢ ἐξ ἀνθρώπων; **5** οἱ δὲ συνελογίσαντο
was it or from men? And they debated

πρὸς ἑαυτοὺς λέγοντες ὅτι ἐὰν εἴπωμεν·
with themselves saying[,] - If we say:

ἐξ οὐρανοῦ, ἐρεῖ· διὰ τί οὐκ ἐπιστεύσατε
From heaven, he will say: Why did ye not believe

αὐτῷ; **6** ἐὰν δὲ εἴπωμεν· ἐξ ἀνθρώπων, ὁ
him? And if we say: From men, the

λαὸς ἅπας καταλιθάσει ἡμᾶς· πεπεισμένος
people all will stone us; for having been per-

241

King James Version

John was a prophet. 7And they answered, that they could not tell whence *it was.* 8And Jesus said unto them, Neither tell I you by what authority I do these things. 9 Then began he to speak to the people this parable; A certain man planted a vineyard, and let it forth to husbandmen, and went into a far country for a long time. 10And at the season he sent a servant to the husbandmen, that they should give him of the fruit of the vineyard: but the husbandmen beat him, and sent *him* away empty. 11And again he sent another servant: and they beat him also, and entreated *him* shamefully, and sent *him* away empty. 12And again he sent a third: and they wounded *him* also, and cast *him* out. 13 Then said the lord of the vineyard, What shall I do? I will send my beloved son: it may be they will reverence *him* when they see him. 14 But when the husbandmen saw him, they reasoned among themselves, saying, This is the heir: come, let us kill him, that the inheritance may be ours. 15 So they cast him out of the vineyard, and killed *him.* What therefore shall the lord of the vineyard do unto them? 16 He shall come and destroy these husbandmen, and shall give the vineyard to others. And when they heard *it,* they said, God forbid. 17And he beheld them, and said, What is this then that is written, The stone which the builders rejected, the same is become the head of the corner? 18 Whosoever shall fall upon that stone shall be broken; but on whomsoever it shall fall, it will grind him to powder.

19 And the chief priests and the scribes the same hour sought to lay hands on him; and they feared the people: for they perceived that he had spoken this parable against them. 20And they watched *him,* and sent forth spies, which should feign themselves just men, that they might take hold of his words, that so they might deliver him unto the power and authority of the governor. 21And they asked him, saying, Master, we know that thou sayest and teachest rightly, neither acceptest thou the person *of any,* but teachest the way of God truly: 22 Is it lawful for us to give tribute unto Cesar, or no? 23 But he perceived their craftiness, and said unto them, Why tempt ye me? 24 Shew me a penny. Whose image and superscription hath it? They answered and said, Cesar's. 25And he said unto them, Render therefore unto Cesar the things which be Cesar's, and unto God the things which be God's. 26And they could not take hold of his words before the people: and they marvelled at his answer, and held their peace.

27 Then came to *him* certain of the Sadducees, which deny that there is any resurrection; and they asked him, 28 Saying, Master,

New International Version

7 So they answered, "We don't know where it was from."

8 Jesus said, "Neither will I tell you by what authority I am doing these things."

The parable of the tenants

9 He went on to tell the people this parable: "A man planted a vineyard, rented it to some farmers and went away for a long time. 10At harvest time he sent a servant to the tenants so they would give him some of the fruit of the vineyard. But the tenants beat him and sent him away empty-handed. 11 He sent another servant, but that one also they beat and treated shamefully and sent away empty-handed. 12 He sent still a third, and they wounded him and threw him out.

13 "Then the owner of the vineyard said, 'What shall I do? I will send my son, whom I love; perhaps they will respect him.'

14 "But when the tenants saw him, they talked the matter over. 'This is the heir,' they said. 'Let's kill him, and the inheritance will be ours.' 15 So they threw him out of the vineyard and killed him.

"What then will the owner of the vineyard do to them? 16 He will come and kill those tenants and give the vineyard to others."

When the people heard this, they said, "May this never be!"

17 Jesus looked directly at them and asked, "Then what is the meaning of that which is written:

'The stone the builders rejected
　　has become the capstone' *p* ?

18 Everyone who falls on that stone will be broken to pieces, but he on whom it falls will be crushed."

19 The teachers of the law and the chief priests looked for a way to arrest him immediately, because they knew he had spoken this parable against them. But they were afraid of the people.

Paying taxes to Caesar

20 Keeping a close watch on him, they sent spies, who pretended to be honest. They hoped to catch Jesus in something he said so that they might hand him over to the power and authority of the governor. 21 So the spies questioned him: "Teacher, we know that you speak and teach what is right, and that you do not show partiality but teach the way of God in accordance with the truth. 22 Is it right for us to pay taxes to Caesar or not?"

23 He saw through their duplicity and said to them, 24 "Show me a denarius. Whose portrait and inscription are on it?"

25 "Caesar's," they replied.

He said to them, "Then give to Caesar what is Caesar's, and to God what is God's."

26 They were unable to trap him in what he had said there in public. And astonished by his answer, they became silent.

The resurrection and marriage

27 Some of the Sadducees, who say there is no resurrection, came to Jesus with a question. 28 "Teacher," they said, "Moses wrote for us

[p] Psalm 118:22.

Greek Interlinear

γάρ ἐστιν Ἰωάννην προφήτην εἶναι. 7 καὶ
suaded it is* John a prophet to be. And

ἀπεκρίθησαν μὴ εἰδέναι πόθεν. 8 καὶ ὁ
they answered not to know whence. And

Ἰησοῦς εἶπεν αὐτοῖς· οὐδὲ ἐγὼ λέγω
Jesus said to them : Neither I tell

ὑμῖν ἐν ποίᾳ ἐξουσίᾳ ταῦτα ποιῶ. 9 Ἤρξατο
you by what authority these things I do. he began

δὲ πρὸς τὸν λαὸν λέγειν τὴν παραβολὴν
And to the people to tell - parable

ταύτην. ἄνθρωπος ἐφύτευσεν ἀμπελῶνα,
this. A man planted a vineyard,

καὶ ἐξέδοτο αὐτὸν γεωργοῖς, καὶ ἀπεδή-
and let out it to husbandmen, and went

μησεν χρόνους ἱκανούς. 10 καὶ καιρῷ
away periods for considerable. And in time
=a long time.

ἀπέστειλεν πρὸς τοὺς γεωργοὺς δοῦλον,
he sent to the husbandmen a slave,

ἵνα ἀπὸ τοῦ καρποῦ τοῦ ἀμπελῶνος
that from the fruit of the vineyard

δώσουσιν αὐτῷ· οἱ δὲ γεωργοὶ ἐξαπέστειλαν
they will give him; but the husbandmen ²sent ⁴away out

αὐτὸν δείραντες κενόν. 11 καὶ προσέθετο
³him ¹beating ²empty. And he added

ἕτερον πέμψαι δοῦλον· οἱ δὲ κἀκεῖνον
²another ¹to send slave; but they that one also
= he sent another slave in addition;

δείραντες καὶ ἀτιμάσαντες ἐξαπέστειλαν
beating and insulting sent away out

κενόν. 12 καὶ προσέθετο τρίτον πέμψαι·
empty. And he added a third to send;

οἱ δὲ καὶ τοῦτον τραυματίσαντες ἐξέβαλον.
but they also this one wounding threw out.

13 εἶπεν δὲ ὁ κύριος τοῦ ἀμπελῶνος· τί
And said the owner of the vineyard : What

ποιήσω; πέμψω τὸν υἱόν μου τὸν ἀγαπητόν·
may I do? I will send the son of me - beloved;

ἴσως τοῦτον ἐντραπήσονται. 14 ἰδόντες δὲ
perhaps this one they will regard. But seeing

αὐτὸν οἱ γεωργοὶ διελογίζοντο πρὸς
him the husbandmen debated with

ἀλλήλους λέγοντες· οὗτός ἐστιν ὁ κληρονόμος·
one another saying : This is the heir;

ἀποκτείνωμεν αὐτόν, ἵνα ἡμῶν γένηται
let us kill him, that of us may become

ἡ κληρονομία. 15 καὶ ἐκβαλόντες αὐτὸν
the inheritance. And throwing out him

ἔξω τοῦ ἀμπελῶνος ἀπέκτειναν. τί οὖν
outside the vineyard they killed. What therefore

ποιήσει αὐτοῖς ὁ κύριος τοῦ ἀμπελῶνος;
will do to them the owner of the vineyard?

16 ἐλεύσεται καὶ ἀπολέσει τοὺς γεωργοὺς
he will come and will destroy - husbandmen

τούτους, καὶ δώσει τὸν ἀμπελῶνα ἄλλοις.
these, and will give the vineyard to others.

ἀκούσαντες δὲ εἶπαν· μὴ γένοιτο. 17 ὁ δὲ
And hearing they said : May it not be. And he

ἐμβλέψας αὐτοῖς εἶπεν· τί οὖν ἐστιν τὸ
looking at them said : What therefore is -

γεγραμμένον τοῦτο· λίθον ὃν ἀπεδοκίμασαν
having been written this : [The] stone which ²rejected

οἱ οἰκοδομοῦντες, οὗτος ἐγενήθη εἰς κεφαλὴν
¹the [ones] ²building, this came to be for [the] head

γωνίας; 18 πᾶς ὁ πεσὼν ἐπ’ ἐκεῖνον τὸν
of [the] corner? Everyone falling on that -

λίθον συνθλασθήσεται· ἐφ’ ὃν δ’ ἂν πέσῃ,
stone will be broken in pieces; but on whomever it falls,

λικμήσει αὐτόν. 19 Καὶ ἐζήτησαν οἱ
it will crush to powder him. And sought the

γραμματεῖς καὶ οἱ ἀρχιερεῖς ἐπιβαλεῖν ἐπ’
scribes and the chief priests to lay on on

αὐτὸν τὰς χεῖρας ἐν αὐτῇ τῇ ὥρᾳ, καὶ
him the(ir) hands in ²same ¹the hour, and

ἐφοβήθησαν τὸν λαόν· ἔγνωσαν γὰρ ὅτι
feared the people; for they knew that

πρὸς αὐτοὺς εἶπεν τὴν παραβολὴν ταύτην.
at them he told - parable this.

20 Καὶ παρατηρήσαντες ἀπέστειλαν ἐγκαθέτους
And watching carefully they sent spies

ὑποκρινομένους ἑαυτοὺς δικαίους εἶναι, ἵνα
pretending themselves righteous to be, that

ἐπιλάβωνται αὐτοῦ λόγου, ὥστε παραδοῦναι
they might seize of him a word, so as to deliver

αὐτὸν τῇ ἀρχῇ καὶ τῇ ἐξουσίᾳ τοῦ
him to the rule and to the authority of the

ἡγεμόνος. 21 καὶ ἐπηρώτησαν αὐτὸν
governor. And they questioned him

λέγοντες· διδάσκαλε, οἴδαμεν ὅτι ὀρθῶς
saying : Teacher, we know that ²rightly

λέγεις καὶ διδάσκεις καὶ οὐ λαμβάνεις
¹thou speakest ²and ³teachest and receivest not
=regarded not persons,

πρόσωπον, ἀλλ’ ἐπ’ ἀληθείας τὴν ὁδὸν τοῦ
a face, but on [the basis of] truth the way -

θεοῦ διδάσκεις· 22 ἔξεστιν ἡμᾶς Καίσαρι
of God teachest; is it lawful for us to Cæsar

φόρον δοῦναι ἢ οὔ; 23 κατανοήσας δὲ
tribute to give or not? And perceiving

αὐτῶν τὴν πανουργίαν εἶπεν πρὸς αὐτούς·
of them the cleverness he said to them :

24 δείξατέ μοι δηνάριον· τίνος ἔχει εἰκόνα
Show me a denarius; of whom has it an image

καὶ ἐπιγραφήν; οἱ δὲ εἶπαν· Καίσαρος.
and superscription? And they said : Of Cæsar.

25 ὁ δὲ εἶπεν πρὸς αὐτούς· τοίνυν ἀπόδοτε
And he said to them : So render

τὰ Καίσαρος Καίσαρι καὶ τὰ τοῦ θεοῦ
the things of Cæsar to Cæsar and the things - of God

τῷ θεῷ. 26 καὶ οὐκ ἴσχυσαν ἐπιλαβέσθαι
- to God. And they were not able to seize

αὐτοῦ ῥήματος ἐναντίον τοῦ λαοῦ, καὶ
of him a word in the presence of the people, and

θαυμάσαντες ἐπὶ τῇ ἀποκρίσει αὐτοῦ
marvelling at the answer of him

ἐσίγησαν.
they were silent.

27 Προσελθόντες δέ τινες τῶν Σαδ-
And ⁴approaching ¹some ²of the ³Sad-

δουκαίων, οἱ ἀντιλέγοντες ★ ἀνάστασιν μὴ
ducees, the [ones] saying in opposition a resurrection not

εἶναι, ἐπηρώτησαν αὐτὸν 28 λέγοντες·
to be, they questioned him saying :

---

* That is, the people (a collective singular) have been (=are)
persuaded.
★ That is, to the Pharisees and to the generally held opinion.

King James Version

Moses wrote unto us, If any man's brother die, having a wife, and he die without children, that his brother should take his wife, and raise up seed unto his brother. 29 There were therefore seven brethren: and the first took a wife, and died without children. 30And the second took her to wife, and he died childless. 31And the third took her; and in like manner the seven also: and they left no children, and died. 32 Last of all the woman died also. 33 Therefore in the resurrection whose wife of them is she? for seven had her to wife. 34And Jesus answering said unto them, The children of this world marry, and are given in marriage: 35 But they which shall be accounted worthy to obtain that world, and the resurrection from the dead, neither marry, nor are given in marriage: 36 Neither can they die any more: for they are equal unto the angels; and are the children of God, being the children of the resurrection. 37 Now that the dead are raised, even Moses shewed at the bush, when he calleth the Lord the God of Abraham, and the God of Isaac, and the God of Jacob. 38 For he is not a God of the dead, but of the living: for all live unto him.

39 Then certain of the scribes answering said, Master, thou hast well said. 40And after that they durst not ask him any *question at all.* 41And he said unto them, How say they that Christ is David's son? 42And David himself saith in the book of Psalms, The Lord said unto my Lord, Sit thou on my right hand, 43 Till I make thine enemies thy footstool. 44 David therefore calleth him Lord, how is he then his son?

45 Then in the audience of all the people he said unto his disciples, 46 Beware of the scribes, which desire to walk in long robes, and love greetings in the markets, and the highest seats in the synagogues, and the chief rooms at feasts; 47 Which devour widows' houses, and for a shew make long prayers: the same shall receive greater damnation.

21 And he looked up, and saw the rich men casting their gifts into the treasury. 2And he saw also a certain poor widow casting in thither two mites. 3And he said, Of a truth I say unto you, that this poor widow hath cast in more than they all: 4 For all these have of their abundance cast in unto the offerings of God: but she of her penury hath cast in all the living that she had.

5 And as some spake of the temple, how it was adorned with goodly stones and gifts, he said, 6*As for* these things which ye behold, the days will come, in the which there shall not be left one stone upon another, that shall not be

New International Version

that if a man's brother dies and leaves a wife but no children, the man must marry the widow and have children for his brother. 29 Now there were seven brothers. The first one married a woman and died childless. 30 The second 31 and then the third married her, and in the same way the seven died, leaving no children. 32 Finally, the woman died too. 33 Now then, at the resurrection whose wife will she be, since the seven were married to her?"

34 Jesus replied, "The people of this age marry and are given in marriage. 35 But those who are considered worthy of taking part in that age and in the resurrection from the dead will neither marry nor be given in marriage, 36 and they can no longer die; for they are like the angels. They are God's children, since they are children of the resurrection. 37 But in the account of the bush, even Moses showed that the dead rise, for he calls the Lord 'the God of Abraham, and the God of Isaac, and the God of Jacob.' *q* 38 He is not the God of the dead, but of the living, for to him all are alive."

39 Some of the teachers of the law responded, "Well said, teacher!" 40And no one dared to ask him any *q* more questions.

Whose son is the Christ?

41 Then Jesus said to them, "How is it that they say the Christ*r* is the Son of David? 42 David himself declares in the Book of Psalms:

'The Lord said to my Lord:
  Sit at my right hand,
43   until I make your enemies your footstool.' *s*

44 David calls him 'Lord.' How then can he be his son?"

45 While all the people were listening, Jesus said to his disciples, 46 "Beware of the teachers of the law. They like to walk around in flowing robes and love to be greeted in the marketplaces and have the most important seats in the synagogues and the places of honor at banquets. 47 They devour widows' houses and for a show make lengthy prayers. Such men will be punished most severely."

The widow's offering

21 As he looked up, Jesus saw the rich putting their gifts into the temple treasury. 2 He also saw a poor widow put in two very small copper coins. 3 "I tell you the truth," he said, "this poor widow has put in more than all the others. 4All these people gave their gifts out of their wealth; but she out of her poverty put in all she had to live on."

Signs of the end of the age

5 Some of his disciples were remarking about how the temple was adorned with beautiful stones and with gifts dedicated to God. But Jesus said, 6 "As for what you see here, the time will come when not one stone will be left on another; every one of them will be thrown down."

[q] Exodus 3:6. [r] Or *Messiah.* [s] Psalm 110:1.

Greek Interlinear

διδάσκαλε, Μωϋσῆς ἔγραψεν ἡμῖν, ἐάν
Teacher,   Moses   wrote   to us,   If

τινος ἀδελφὸς ἀποθάνῃ ἔχων γυναῖκα, καὶ
of anyone a brother dies   having a wife, and

οὗτος ἄτεκνος ᾖ, ἵνα λάβῃ ὁ ἀδελφὸς
this man childless is, that ²should take ¹the ³brother

αὐτοῦ τὴν γυναῖκα καὶ ἐξαναστήσῃ σπέρμα
⁴of him ¹the ⁵wife   and   raise up   seed

τῷ ἀδελφῷ αὐτοῦ. 29 ἑπτὰ οὖν ἀδελφοὶ
to the brother of him.   Seven therefore brothers

ἦσαν· καὶ ὁ πρῶτος λαβὼν γυναῖκα
there were; and the first   having taken a wife

ἀπέθανεν ἄτεκνος· 30 καὶ ὁ δεύτερος 31 καὶ
died   childless;   and the second   and

ὁ τρίτος ἔλαβεν αὐτήν, ὡσαύτως δὲ καὶ
the third took   her,   and similarly also

οἱ ἑπτὰ οὐ κατέλιπον τέκνα καὶ ἀπέθανον.
the seven did not leave children and   died.

32 ὕστερον καὶ ἡ γυνὴ ἀπέθανεν. 33 ἡ
Lastly   also the woman died.   The

γυνὴ οὖν ἐν τῇ ἀναστάσει τίνος αὐτῶν
woman therefore in the resurrection of which of them

γίνεται γυνή; οἱ γὰρ ἑπτὰ ἔσχον αὐτὴν
becomes she wife? for the seven   had   her

γυναῖκα. 34 καὶ εἶπεν αὐτοῖς ὁ Ἰησοῦς·
[as] wife.   And   said   to them - Jesus:

οἱ υἱοὶ τοῦ αἰῶνος τούτου γαμοῦσιν καὶ
The sons -   age   of this   marry   and

γαμίσκονται, 35 οἱ δὲ καταξιωθέντες τοῦ
are given in marriage, but the [ones] counted worthy   -

αἰῶνος ἐκείνου τυχεῖν καὶ τῆς ἀναστάσεως
²age ³of that ¹to obtain and of the resurrection

τῆς ἐκ νεκρῶν οὔτε γαμοῦσιν οὔτε
the out of [the] dead neither marry   nor

γαμίζονται· 36 οὐδὲ γὰρ ἀποθανεῖν ἔτι
are given in marriage; for not even to die   more

δύνανται, ἰσάγγελοι γάρ εἰσιν, καὶ υἱοί
can they,   for equal to angels they are, and ²sons

εἰσιν θεοῦ τῆς ἀναστάσεως υἱοὶ ὄντες.
¹they are ³of God ⁴of the ⁷resurrection ⁵sons ⁶being.

37 ὅτι δὲ ἐγείρονται οἱ νεκροί, καὶ
But that - are raised the dead,   even

Μωϋσῆς ἐμήνυσεν ἐπὶ τῆς βάτου, ὡς
Moses   pointed out at the bush,   as

λέγει κύριον τὸν θεὸν Ἀβραὰμ καὶ θεὸν
he calls [the] Lord the God of Abraham and God

Ἰσαὰκ καὶ θεὸν Ἰακώβ· 38 θεὸς δὲ οὐκ
of Isaac and God of Jacob;   but God not

ἔστιν νεκρῶν ἀλλὰ ζώντων· πάντες γὰρ
he is of dead persons but of living;   for all

αὐτῷ ζῶσιν. 39 ἀποκριθέντες δέ τινες
to him live.   And answering   some

τῶν γραμματέων εἶπαν· διδάσκαλε, κελῶς
of the scribes   said : Teacher,   well

εἶπας. 40 οὐκέτι γὰρ ἐτόλμων ἐπερωτᾶν
thou sayest. For no more dared they to question

αὐτὸν οὐδέν.
him   no(any)thing.

41 Εἶπεν δὲ πρὸς αὐτούς· πῶς λέγουσιν
And he said to   them : How say they

τὸν χριστὸν εἶναι Δαυὶδ υἱόν; 42 αὐτὸς
the Christ   to be of David son?   himself

γὰρ Δαυὶδ λέγει ἐν βίβλῳ ψαλμῶν·
For David says in [the] roll of psalms :

εἶπεν κύριος τῷ κυρίῳ μου· κάθου ἐκ
Said [the] LORD to the Lord of me : Sit thou at

δεξιῶν μου 43 ἕως ἂν θῶ τοὺς ἐχθρούς σου
[the] right of me until I put the   enemies of thee

ὑποπόδιον τῶν ποδῶν σου. 44 Δαυὶδ
a footstool of the feet   of thee.   David

οὖν αὐτὸν κύριον καλεῖ, καὶ πῶς αὐτοῦ
therefore him Lord   calls, and how of him

υἱός ἐστιν;
son is he?

45 Ἀκούοντος δὲ παντὸς τοῦ λαοῦ εἶπεν
And hearing   all   the people⁶ he said
= as all the people heard

τοῖς μαθηταῖς· 46 προσέχετε ἀπὸ τῶν
to the disciples : Beware   from(of) the

γραμματέων τῶν θελόντων περιπατεῖν ἐν
scribes   -   wishing   to walk about in

στολαῖς καὶ φιλούντων ἀσπασμοὺς ἐν ταῖς
robes   and liking   greetings   in the

ἀγοραῖς καὶ πρωτοκαθεδρίας ἐν ταῖς
marketplaces and chief seats   in the

συναγωγαῖς καὶ πρωτοκλισίας ἐν τοῖς
synagogues and chief couches   in the

δείπνοις, 47 οἳ κατεσθίουσιν τὰς οἰκίας
suppers,   who devour   the houses

τῶν χηρῶν καὶ προφάσει μακρὰ προσεύχονται·
of the widows and under pretence long pray;

οὗτοι λήμψονται περισσότερον κρίμα.
these will receive severer   judgment.

Chapter 21

Ἀναβλέψας δὲ εἶδεν τοὺς βάλλοντας
And looking up he saw ¹the   ²putting

εἰς τὸ γαζοφυλακεῖον τὰ δῶρα αὐτῶν
⁵into ⁶the ⁷treasury   ³the ⁸gifts ⁴of them

πλουσίους. 2 εἶδεν δέ τινα χήραν πενιχρὰν
⁹rich [ones]. And he saw a certain widow poor

βάλλουσαν ἐκεῖ λεπτὰ δύο, 3 καὶ εἶπεν·
putting   there lepta two,   and he said :

ἀληθῶς λέγω ὑμῖν ὅτι ἡ χήρα αὕτη ἡ
Truly   I tell you that the ²widow ¹this -

πτωχὴ πλεῖον πάντων ἔβαλεν· 4 πάντες
³poor more [than] all   put;   ⁵all

γὰρ οὗτοι ἐκ τοῦ περισσεύοντος αὐτοῖς
⁴for these out of the abounding   to them⁶
= their abundance

ἔβαλον εἰς τὰ δῶρα, αὕτη δὲ ἐκ τοῦ
put   into the gifts, but this woman out of the

ὑστερήματος αὐτῆς πάντα τὸν βίον ὃν
want   of her ²all   ³the ⁴living ⁵which

εἶχεν ἔβαλεν.
¹she had ³put.

5 Καί τινων λεγόντων περὶ τοῦ ἱεροῦ, ὅτι
And some speaking³ about the temple, that
= as some spoke

λίθοις καλοῖς καὶ ἀναθήμασιν κεκόσμηται,
stones with beautiful and gifts   it has(had)
been adorned,

εἶπεν· 6 ταῦτα ἃ θεωρεῖτε, ἐλεύσονται
he said : These things which ye behold, will come

ἡμέραι ἐν αἷς οὐκ ἀφεθήσεται λίθος ἐπὶ
days   in which there will not be left stone on

245

King James Version

thrown down. 7And they asked him, saying, Master, but when shall these things be? and what sign *will there be* when these things shall come to pass? 8And he said, Take heed that ye be not deceived: for many shall come in my name, saying, I am *Christ;* and the time draweth near: go ye not therefore after them. 9 But when ye shall hear of wars and commotions, be not terrified: for these things must first come to pass; but the end *is* not by and by. 10 Then said he unto them, Nation shall rise against nation, and kingdom against kingdom: 11And great earthquakes shall be in divers places, and famines, and pestilences; and fearful sights and great signs shall there be from heaven. 12 But before all these, they shall lay their hands on you, and persecute *you,* delivering *you* up to the synagogues, and into prisons, being brought before kings and rulers for my name's sake. 13And it shall turn to you for a testimony. 14 Settle *it* therefore in your hearts, not to meditate before what ye shall answer: 15 For I will give you a mouth and wisdom, which all your adversaries shall not be able to gainsay nor resist. 16And ye shall be betrayed both by parents, and brethren, and kinsfolks, and friends; and *some* of you shall they cause to be put to death. 17And ye shall be hated of all *men* for my name's sake. 18 But there shall not a hair of your head perish. 19 In your patience possess ye your souls. 20And when ye shall see Jerusalem compassed with armies, then know that the desolation thereof is nigh. 21 Then let them which are in Judea flee to the mountains; and let them which are in the midst of it depart out; and let not them that are in the countries enter thereinto. 22 For these be the days of vengeance, that all things which are written may be fulfilled. 23 But woe unto them that are with child, and to them that give suck, in those days! for there shall be great distress in the land, and wrath upon this people. 24And they shall fall by the edge of the sword, and shall be led away captive into all nations: and Jerusalem shall be trodden down of the Gentiles, until the times of the Gentiles be fulfilled.

25 And there shall be signs in the sun, and in the moon, and in the stars; and upon the earth distress of nations, with perplexity; the sea and the waves roaring; 26 Men's hearts failing them for fear, and for looking after those things which are coming on the earth: for the powers of heaven shall be shaken. 27And then shall they see the Son of man coming in a cloud with power and great glory. 28And when these things begin to come to pass, then look up, and lift up your heads; for your redemption draweth nigh. 29And he spake to them a parable; Behold the fig tree, and all the trees; 30 When they now shoot forth, ye see and know of your own selves that summer is now nigh at hand. 31 So likewise ye, when ye see these things come to pass, know ye that the kingdom of God is nigh at hand. 32 Verily I say unto you, This generation shall not pass away, till all be fulfilled. 33 Heaven and earth shall pass away; but my words shall not pass away.

New International Version

7 "Teacher," they asked, "when will these things happen? And what will be the sign that they are about to take place?"

8 He replied: "Watch out that you are not deceived. For many will come in my name, claiming, 'I am he,' and, 'The time is near.' Do not follow them. 9 When you hear of wars and revolutions, do not be frightened. These things must happen first, but the end will not come right away."

10 Then he said to them: "Nation will rise against nation, and kingdom against kingdom. 11 There will be great earthquakes, famines and pestilences in various places, and fearful events and great signs from heaven.

12 "But before all this, they will lay hands on you and persecute you. They will deliver you to synagogues and prisons, and you will be brought before kings and governors, and all on account of my name. 13 This will result in your being witnesses to them. 14 But make up your mind not to worry beforehand how you will defend yourselves. 15 For I will give you words and wisdom that none of your adversaries will be able to resist or contradict. 16 You will be betrayed by parents, brothers, relatives and friends, and they will put some of you to death. 17 All men will hate you because of me. 18 But not a hair of your head will perish. 19 By standing firm you will save yourselves.

20 "When you see Jerusalem surrounded by armies, you will know that its desolation is near. 21 Then let those who are in Judea flee to the mountains, let those in the city get out, and let those in the country not enter the city. 22 For this is the time of punishment in fulfillment of all that has been written. 23 How dreadful it will be in those days for pregnant women and nursing mothers! There will be great distress in the land and wrath against this people. 24 They will fall by the sword and will be taken as prisoners to all the nations. Jerusalem will be trampled on by the Gentiles until the times of the Gentiles are fulfilled.

25 "There will be signs in the sun, moon and stars. On the earth, nations will be in anguish and perplexity at the roaring and tossing of the sea. 26 Men will faint from terror, apprehensive of what is coming on the world, for the heavenly bodies will be shaken. 27 At that time they will see the Son of Man coming in a cloud with power and great glory. 28 When these things begin to take place, stand up and lift up your heads, because your redemption is drawing near."

29 He told them this parable: "Look at the fig tree and all the trees. 30 When they sprout leaves, you can see for yourselves and know that summer is near. 31 Even so, when you see these things happening, you know that the kingdom of God is near.

32 "I tell you the truth, this generation[t] will certainly not pass away until all these things have happened. 33 Heaven and earth will pass away, but my words will never pass away.

[t] Or *race.*

Greek Interlinear

λίθῳ ὃς οὐ καταλυθήσεται. 7 ἐπηρώτησαν δὲ
stone which will not be overthrown.   And they questioned

αὐτὸν λέγοντες· διδάσκαλε, πότε οὖν
him   saying :   Teacher,   when therefore

ταῦτα ἔσται; καὶ τί τὸ σημεῖον ὅταν
these things will be? And what [will be] the sign   when

μέλλῃ ταῦτα γίνεσθαι; 8 ὁ δὲ εἶπεν·
ᵃare about ¹these things ²to happen   And he   said :

βλέπετε μὴ πλανηθῆτε· πολλοὶ γὰρ
Beware   lest ye be led astray;   for many

ἐλεύσονται ἐπὶ τῷ ὀνόματί μου λέγοντες·
will come   on(in) the name   of me   saying :

ἐγώ εἰμι, καί· ὁ καιρὸς ἤγγικεν· μὴ
I   am, and : The time has drawn near; not

πορευθῆτε ὀπίσω αὐτῶν. 9 ὅταν δὲ
go ye   after them.   And when

ἀκούσητε πολέμους καὶ ἀκαταστασίας, μὴ
ye hear [of] wars   and commotions,   not

πτοηθῆτε· δεῖ γὰρ ταῦτα γενέσθαι
be ye scared; for it behoves these things to happen

πρῶτον, ἀλλ' οὐκ εὐθέως τὸ τέλος. 10 Τότε
first,   but not immediately the end.   Then

ἔλεγεν αὐτοῖς· ἐγερθήσεται ἔθνος ἐπ' ἔθνος
he said to them· Will be raised nation against nation

καὶ βασιλεία ἐπὶ βασιλείαν, 11 σεισμοί τε
and kingdom against kingdom,   and earthquakes

μεγάλοι καὶ κατὰ τόπους λοιμοὶ καὶ λιμοὶ
great   and from place to place† pestilences and famines

ἔσονται, φόβητρά τε καὶ ἀπ' οὐρανοῦ
there will be, and terrors and ²from ⁴heaven

σημεῖα μεγάλα ἔσται. 12 πρὸ δὲ τούτων
²signs ¹great there will be.   But before these things

πάντων ἐπιβαλοῦσιν ἐφ' ὑμᾶς τὰς χεῖρας
all   they will lay on on you   the hands

αὐτῶν καὶ διώξουσιν, παραδιδόντες εἰς τὰς
of them and will persecute, delivering   to the

συναγωγὰς καὶ φυλακάς, ἀπαγομένους ἐπὶ
synagogues and prisons,   being led away on(before)

βασιλεῖς καὶ ἡγεμόνας ἕνεκεν τοῦ ὀνόματός
kings   and governors for the sake of the name

μου· 13 ἀποβήσεται ὑμῖν εἰς μαρτύριον.
of me;   it will turn out to you for a testimony.

14 θέτε οὖν ἐν ταῖς καρδίαις ὑμῶν μὴ
Put therefore in the hearts   of you not

προμελετᾶν ἀπολογηθῆναι· 15 ἐγὼ γὰρ
to practise beforehand to defend [yourselves];   for I

δώσω ὑμῖν στόμα καὶ σοφίαν, ᾗ οὐ
will give you a mouth and wisdom, which not

δυνήσονται ἀντιστῆναι ἢ ἀντειπεῖν ἅπαντες οἱ
will be able to withstand or to contradict all the

ἀντικείμενοι ὑμῖν. 16 παραδοθήσεσθε δὲ καὶ
[ones] opposing you.   ye will be betrayed also

ὑπὸ γονέων καὶ ἀδελφῶν καὶ συγγενῶν
by parents and brothers and relatives

καὶ φίλων, καὶ θανατώσουσιν ἐξ ὑμῶν,
and friends, and they will put to death [some] of you,

17 καὶ ἔσεσθε μισούμενοι ὑπὸ πάντων διὰ
and ye will be being hated by all men because of

τὸ ὄνομά μου. 18 καὶ θρὶξ ἐκ τῆς
the name of me.   And a hair of the

κεφαλῆς ὑμῶν οὐ μὴ ἀπόληται· 19 ἐν τῇ
head   of you by no means will perish;   in the

ὑπομονῇ ὑμῶν κτήσεσθε τὰς ψυχὰς ὑμῶν.
endurance of you ye will gain the souls of you.

20 Ὅταν δὲ ἴδητε κυκλουμένην ὑπὸ
But when ye see   being surrounded ²by

στρατοπέδων Ἰερουσαλήμ, τότε γνῶτε ὅτι
¹camps   Jerusalem, then know ye that

ἤγγικεν ἡ ἐρήμωσις αὐτῆς. 21 τότε οἱ ἐν
has drawn near the desolation of it. Then the [ones] in

τῇ Ἰουδαίᾳ φευγέτωσαν εἰς τὰ ὄρη, καὶ
- Judæa let them flee to the mountains, and

οἱ ἐν μέσῳ αὐτῆς ἐκχωρείτωσαν, καὶ
the [ones] in [the] midst of it let them depart out, and

οἱ ἐν ταῖς χώραις μὴ εἰσερχέσθωσαν εἰς
the [ones] in the districts let them not enter into

αὐτήν, 22 ὅτι ἡμέραι ἐκδικήσεως αὗταί
it,   because days of vengeance these

εἰσιν τοῦ πλησθῆναι πάντα τὰ γεγραμμένα.
are - to be fulfilledᵈ all the things having been written.

23 οὐαὶ ταῖς ἐν γαστρὶ ἐχούσαις καὶ ταῖς
Woe to the pregnant women† and to the

θηλαζούσαις ἐν ἐκείναις ταῖς ἡμέραις·
[ones] giving suck in those   - days;

ἔσται γὰρ ἀνάγκη μεγάλη ἐπὶ τῆς γῆς
for there will be distress great on the land

καὶ ὀργὴ τῷ λαῷ τούτῳ, 24 καὶ πεσοῦνται
and wrath - people to this,   and they will fall

στόματι μαχαίρης καὶ αἰχμαλωτισθή-
by [the] mouth(edge) of [the] sword and   will be led

σονται εἰς τὰ ἔθνη πάντα, καὶ Ἰερουσαλὴμ
captive to the nations all, and Jerusalem

ἔσται πατουμένη ὑπὸ ἐθνῶν, ἄχρι οὗ
will be being trodden down by nations,   until

πληρωθῶσιν καιροὶ ἐθνῶν. 25 Καὶ ἔσονται
are accomplished [the] times of [the] nations. And there will be

σημεῖα ἐν ἡλίῳ καὶ σελήνῃ καὶ ἄστροις,
signs in sun and moon and stars,

καὶ ἐπὶ τῆς γῆς συνοχὴ ἐθνῶν ἐν ἀπορίᾳ
and on the earth anxiety of nations in perplexity

ἤχους θαλάσσης καὶ σάλου, 26 ἀποψυχόντων
of [the] sound of [the] sea and surf, fainting
                                    =while men faint

ἀνθρώπων ἀπὸ φόβου καὶ προσδοκίας τῶν
menᵃ   from fear and expectation of the

ἐπερχομένων τῇ οἰκουμένῃ· αἱ γὰρ δυνάμεις
things coming on the inhabited earth; for the powers

τῶν οὐρανῶν σαλευθήσονται. 27 καὶ τότε
of the heavens will be shaken.   And then

ὄψονται τὸν υἱὸν τοῦ ἀνθρώπου ἐρχόμενον
they will see the Son   - of man   coming

ἐν νεφέλῃ μετὰ δυνάμεως καὶ δόξης
in a cloud with power   and glory

πολλῆς. 28 ἀρχομένων δὲ τούτων γίνεσθαι
much(great). And beginning these things to happen
                                    =when these things begin

ἀνακύψατε καὶ ἐπάρατε τὰς κεφαλὰς ὑμῶν,
stand erect and lift up the heads of you,

διότι ἐγγίζει ἡ ἀπολύτρωσις ὑμῶν. 29 Καὶ
because draws near the redemption of you.   And

εἶπεν παραβολὴν αὐτοῖς· ἴδετε τὴν συκῆν
he told ²a parable ¹them : Ye see the fig-tree

καὶ πάντα τὰ δένδρα· 30 ὅταν προβάλωσιν
and all the trees;   when they burst into leaf

ἤδη, βλέποντες ἀφ' ἑαυτῶν γινώσκετε ὅτι
now, seeing from(of) yourselves ye know that

ἤδη ἐγγὺς τὸ θέρος ἐστίν· 31 οὕτως καὶ
now near the summer is;   so also

ὑμεῖς, ὅταν ἴδητε ταῦτα γινόμενα,
ye,   when ye see these things happening,

γινώσκετε ὅτι ἐγγύς ἐστιν ἡ βασιλεία
know   that near is the kingdom

τοῦ θεοῦ. 32 ἀμὴν λέγω ὑμῖν ὅτι οὐ μὴ
- of God.   Truly I tell you that by no means

παρέλθῃ ἡ γενεὰ αὕτη ἕως ἂν πάντα
will pass away - generation this until all things

γένηται. 33 ὁ οὐρανὸς καὶ ἡ γῆ παρ-
happens.   The heaven and the earth will

ελεύσονται, οἱ δὲ λόγοι μου οὐ μὴ παρελεύ-
pass away, but the words of me by no means will pass

King James Version

34 And take heed to yourselves, lest at any time your hearts be overcharged with surfeiting, and drunkenness, and cares of this life, and so that day come upon you unawares. 35 For as a snare shall it come on all them that dwell on the face of the whole earth. 36 Watch ye therefore, and pray always, that ye may be accounted worthy to escape all these things that shall come to pass, and to stand before the Son of man. 37And in the daytime he was teaching in the temple; and at night he went out, and abode in the mount that is called *the mount* of Olives. 38And all the people came early in the morning to him in the temple, for to hear him.

22 Now the feast of unleavened bread drew nigh, which is called the passover. 2And the chief priests and scribes sought how they might kill him; for they feared the people. 3 Then entered Satan into Judas surnamed Iscariot, being of the number of the twelve. 4And he went his way, and communed with the chief priests and captains, how he might betray him unto them. 5And they were glad, and covenanted to give him money. 6And he promised, and sought opportunity to betray him unto them in the absence of the multitude. 7 Then came the day of unleavened bread, when the passover must be killed. 8And he sent Peter and John, saying, Go and prepare us the passover, that we may eat. 9And they said unto him, Where wilt thou that we prepare? 10And he said unto them, Behold, when ye are entered into the city, there shall a man meet you, bearing a pitcher of water; follow him into the house where he entereth in. 11And ye shall say unto the goodman of the house, The Master saith unto thee, Where is the guestchamber, where I shall eat the passover with my disciples? 12And he shall shew you a large upper room furnished: there make ready. 13And they went, and found as he had said unto them: and they made ready the passover. 14And when the hour was come, he sat down, and the twelve apostles with him. 15And he said unto them, With desire I have desired to eat this passover with you before I suffer: 16 For I say unto you, I will not any more eat thereof, until it be fulfilled in the kingdom of God. 17And he took the cup, and gave thanks, and said, Take this, and divide *it* among yourselves: 18 For I say unto you, I will not drink of the fruit of the vine, until the kingdom of God shall come. 19 And he took bread, and gave thanks, and brake *it*, and gave unto them, saying, This is my body which is given for you: this do in remembrance of me. 20 Likewise also the cup after supper, saying, This cup *is* the new testament in my blood, which is shed for you.

New International Version

34 "Be careful, or your hearts will be weighed down with dissipation, drunkenness and the anxieties of life, and that day will close on you unexpectedly like a trap. 35 For it will come upon all those who live on the face of the whole earth. 36 Be always on the watch, and pray that you may be able to escape all that is about to happen, and that you may be able to stand before the Son of Man."

37 Each day Jesus was teaching at the temple, and each evening he went out to spend the night on the hill called the Mount of Olives, 38 and all the people came early in the morning to hear him at the temple.

Judas agrees to betray Jesus

22 Now the Feast of Unleavened Bread, called the Passover, was approaching, 2 and the chief priests and the teachers of the law were looking for some way to get rid of Jesus, for they were afraid of the people. 3 Then Satan entered Judas, called Iscariot, one of the Twelve. 4And Judas went to the chief priests and the officers of the temple guard and discussed with them how he might betray Jesus. 5 They were delighted and agreed to give him money. 6 He consented, and watched for an opportunity to hand Jesus over to them when no crowd was present.

The Last Supper

7 Then came the day of Unleavened Bread on which the Passover lamb had to be sacrificed. 8 Jesus sent Peter and John, saying, "Go and make preparations for us to eat the Passover."

9 "Where do you want us to prepare for it?" they asked.

10 He replied, "As you enter the city, a man carrying a jar of water will meet you. Follow him to the house that he enters, 11 and say to the owner of the house, 'The Teacher asks: Where is the guest room, where I may eat the Passover with my disciples?' 12 He will show you a large upper room, all furnished. Make preparations there."

13 They left and found things just as Jesus had told them. So they prepared the Passover.

14 When the hour came, Jesus and his apostles reclined at the table. 15And he said to them, "I have eagerly desired to eat this Passover with you before I suffer. 16 For I tell you, I will not eat it again until it finds fulfillment in the kingdom of God."

17 After taking the cup, he gave thanks and said, "Take this and divide it among you. 18 For I tell you I will not drink again from the fruit of the vine until the kingdom of God comes."

19 And he took some bread, gave thanks and broke it, and gave it to them, saying, "This is my body given for you; do this in remembrance of me."

20 In the same way, after the supper he took the cup, saying, "This cup is the new covenant

Greek Interlinear

σονται. **34** Προσέχετε δὲ ἑαυτοῖς μήποτε
away. And take heed to yourselves lest

βαρηθῶσιν ὑμῶν αἱ καρδίαι ἐν κραιπάλῃ
become burdened of you the hearts with surfeiting

καὶ μέθῃ καὶ μερίμναις βιωτικαῖς, καὶ
and deep drinking and anxieties of life,† and

ἐπιστῇ ἐφ' ὑμᾶς αἰφνίδιος ἡ ἡμέρα ἐκείνη
come on on you suddenly - day that

35 ὡς παγίς· ἐπεισελεύσεται γὰρ ἐπὶ πάντας
as a snare; for it will come in on all

τοὺς καθημένους ἐπὶ πρόσωπον πάσης τῆς
the [ones] sitting on [the] face of all the

γῆς. **36** ἀγρυπνεῖτε δὲ ἐν παντὶ καιρῷ
earth. But be ye watchful at every time

δεόμενοι ἵνα κατισχύσητε ἐκφυγεῖν ταῦτα
begging that ye may be able to escape these things

πάντα τὰ μέλλοντα γίνεσθαι, καὶ σταθῆναι
all - being about to happen, and to stand

ἔμπροσθεν τοῦ υἱοῦ τοῦ ἀνθρώπου.
before the Son - of man.

37 Ἦν δὲ τὰς ἡμέρας ἐν τῷ ἱερῷ
Now he was [in] the days in the temple

διδάσκων, τὰς δὲ νύκτας ἐξερχόμενος
teaching, and [in] the nights going forth

ηὐλίζετο εἰς τὸ ὄρος τὸ καλούμενον
he lodged in the mountain - being called

ἐλαιών. **38** καὶ πᾶς ὁ λαὸς ὤρθριζεν
of olives. And all the people came in the morning

πρὸς αὐτὸν ἐν τῷ ἱερῷ ἀκούειν αὐτοῦ.
to him in the temple to hear him.

Chapter 22

Ἤγγιζεν δὲ ἡ ἑορτὴ τῶν ἀζύμων ἡ
Now drew near the feast of unleavened bread -

λεγομένη πάσχα. **2** καὶ ἐζήτουν οἱ ἀρχιερεῖς
being called Passover. And ¹sought ¹the ²chief priests

καὶ οἱ γραμματεῖς τὸ πῶς ἀνέλωσιν
²and ⁴the ⁵scribes - how they might destroy

αὐτόν· ἐφοβοῦντο γὰρ τὸν λαόν. **3** Εἰσῆλθεν δὲ
him; for they feared the people. And entered

σατανᾶς εἰς Ἰούδαν τὸν καλούμενον
Satan into Judas - being called

Ἰσκαριώτην, ὄντα ἐκ τοῦ ἀριθμοῦ τῶν
Iscariot, being of the number of the

δώδεκα· **4** καὶ ἀπελθὼν συνελάλησεν τοῖς
twelve; and going he conversed with the

ἀρχιερεῦσιν καὶ στρατηγοῖς τὸ πῶς αὐτοῖς
chief priests and captains - how to them

παραδῷ αὐτόν. **5** καὶ ἐχάρησαν, καὶ
he might betray him. And they rejoiced, and

συνέθεντο αὐτῷ ἀργύριον δοῦναι. **6** καὶ
they agreed ³him ²money ¹to give. And

ἐξωμολόγησεν, καὶ ἐζήτει εὐκαιρίαν τοῦ
he fully consented, and sought opportunity

παραδοῦναι αὐτὸν ἄτερ ὄχλου αὐτοῖς.
to betray[d] him apart from a crowd to them.

7 Ἦλθεν δὲ ἡ ἡμέρα τῶν ἀζύμων, ᾗ
And came the day of unleavened bread, on which

ἔδει θύεσθαι τὸ πάσχα· **8** καὶ ἀπέστειλεν
it behoved to kill the passover [lamb]; and he sent

Πέτρον καὶ Ἰωάννην εἰπών· πορευθέντες
Peter and John saying: Going

ἑτοιμάσατε ἡμῖν τὸ πάσχα, ἵνα φάγωμεν. **9** οἱ
prepare ye for us the passover, that we may eat. they

δὲ εἶπαν αὐτῷ· ποῦ θέλεις ἑτοιμάσωμεν;
And said to him: Where wishest thou [that] we may prepare?

10 ὁ δὲ εἶπεν αὐτοῖς· ἰδοὺ εἰσελθόντων
And he told them: Behold[,] entering
=as ye enter

ὑμῶν εἰς τὴν πόλιν συναντήσει ὑμῖν
you[a] into the city will meet you

ἄνθρωπος κεράμιον ὕδατος βαστάζων·
a man a pitcher of water bearing;

ἀκολουθήσατε αὐτῷ εἰς τὴν οἰκίαν εἰς ἣν
follow him into the house into which

εἰσπορεύεται· **11** καὶ ἐρεῖτε τῷ οἰκοδεσπότῃ
he enters; and ye will say to the house-master

τῆς οἰκίας· λέγει σοι ὁ διδάσκαλος·
of the house: Says to thee the teacher:

ποῦ ἐστιν τὸ κατάλυμα ὅπου τὸ πάσχα
Where is the guest room where the passover

μετὰ τῶν μαθητῶν μου φάγω; **12** κἀκεῖνος
with the disciples of me I may eat? And that man

ὑμῖν δείξει ἀνάγαιον μέγα ἐστρωμένον·
you will show upper room a large having been spread;[a]

ἐκεῖ ἑτοιμάσατε. **13** ἀπελθόντες δὲ εὗρον
there prepare ye. And going they found

καθὼς εἰρήκει αὐτοῖς, καὶ ἡτοίμασαν τὸ
as he had told them, and they prepared the

πάσχα. **14** Καὶ ὅτε ἐγένετο ἡ ὥρα,
passover. And when came the hour,

ἀνέπεσεν, καὶ οἱ ἀπόστολοι σὺν αὐτῷ.
he reclined, and the apostles with him.

15 καὶ εἶπεν πρὸς αὐτούς· ἐπιθυμίᾳ
And he said to them: With desire

ἐπεθύμησα τοῦτο τὸ πάσχα φαγεῖν μεθ'
I desired this - passover to eat with

ὑμῶν πρὸ τοῦ με παθεῖν·[b] **16** λέγω γὰρ
you before the me to suffer; for I tell
=I suffer;

ὑμῖν ὅτι οὐκέτι οὐ μὴ φάγω αὐτὸ
you that no more by no(any) means I eat it

ἕως ὅτου πληρωθῇ ἐν τῇ βασιλείᾳ τοῦ θεοῦ.
until it is fulfilled in the kingdom - of God.

17 καὶ δεξάμενος ποτήριον εὐχαριστήσας
And taking a cup having given thanks

εἶπεν· λάβετε τοῦτο καὶ διαμερίσατε εἰς
he said: Take this and divide among

ἑαυτούς· **18** λέγω γὰρ ὑμῖν, οὐ μὴ πίω
yourselves; for I tell you, by no means I drink

ἀπὸ τοῦ νῦν ἀπὸ τοῦ γενήματος τῆς
from - now [on] from the produce of the

ἀμπέλου ἕως οὗ ἡ βασιλεία τοῦ θεοῦ
vine until the kingdom - of God

ἔλθῃ. **19** καὶ λαβὼν ἄρτον εὐχαριστήσας
comes. And taking a loaf having given thanks

ἔκλασεν καὶ ἔδωκεν αὐτοῖς λέγων· τοῦτο
he broke and gave to them saying: This

ἐστιν τὸ σῶμά μου [τὸ ὑπὲρ ὑμῶν
is the body of me [- for you

διδόμενον· τοῦτο ποιεῖτε εἰς τὴν ἐμὴν
being given; this do ye into - my

ἀνάμνησιν. **20** καὶ τὸ ποτήριον ὡσαύτως
memorial. And the cup similarly

μετὰ τὸ δειπνῆσαι, λέγων· τοῦτο τὸ
after the to sup, saying: This -

ποτήριον ἡ καινὴ διαθήκη ἐν τῷ αἵματι
cup [is] the new covenant in the blood

---

[a] That is, with carpets, and the dining couches supplied with cushions.

King James Version

21 But, behold, the hand of him that betrayeth me *is* with me on the table. 22And truly the Son of man goeth, as it was determined: but woe unto that man by whom he is betrayed! 23And they began to inquire among themselves, which of them it was that should do this thing.

24 And there was also a strife among them, which of them should be accounted the greatest. 25And he said unto them, The kings of the Gentiles exercise lordship over them; and they that exercise authority upon them are called benefactors. 26 But ye *shall* not *be* so: but he that is greatest among you, let him be as the younger; and he that is chief, as he that doth serve. 27 For whether *is* greater, he that sitteth at meat, or he that serveth? *is* not he that sitteth at meat? but I am among you as he that serveth. 28 Ye are they which have continued with me in my temptations. 29And I appoint unto you a kingdom, as my Father hath appointed unto me; 30 That ye may eat and drink at my table in my kingdom, and sit on thrones judging the twelve tribes of Israel.

31 And the Lord said, Simon, Simon, behold, Satan hath desired *to have* you, that he may sift *you* as wheat: 32 But I have prayed for thee, that thy faith fail not: and when thou art converted, strengthen thy brethren. 33And he said unto him, Lord, I am ready to go with thee, both into prison, and to death. 34And he said, I tell thee, Peter, the cock shall not crow this day, before that thou shalt thrice deny that thou knowest me. 35And he said unto them, When I sent you without purse, and scrip, and shoes, lacked ye any thing? And they said, Nothing. 36 Then said he unto them, But now, he that hath a purse, let him take *it*, and likewise *his* scrip: and he that hath no sword, let him sell his garment, and buy one. 37 For I say unto you, that this that is written must yet be accomplished in me, And he was reckoned among the transgressors: for the things concerning me have an end. 38And they said, Lord, behold, here *are* two swords. And he said unto them, It is enough.

39 And he came out, and went, as he was wont, to the mount of Olives; and his disciples also followed him. 40And when he was at the place, he said unto them, Pray that ye enter not into temptation. 41And he was withdrawn from them about a stone's cast, and kneeled down, and prayed, 42 Saying, Father, if thou be willing, remove this cup from me: nevertheless, not my will, but thine, be done. 43And there appeared an angel unto him from heaven, strengthening him. 44And being in an agony he prayed more earnestly: and his sweat was as it were great drops of blood falling down to the ground. 45And when he rose up from prayer, and was come to his disciples, he found them sleeping for sorrow, 46And said unto them, Why sleep ye? rise and pray, lest ye enter into temptation.

47 And while he yet spake, behold a multitude, and he that was called Judas, one of the

New International Version

in my blood, which is poured out for you. 21 But the hand of him who is going to betray me is with mine on the table. 22 The Son of Man will go as it has been decreed, but woe to that man who betrays him." 23 They began to question among themselves which of them it might be who would do this.

24 Also a dispute arose among them as to which of them was considered to be greatest. 25 Jesus said to them, "The kings of the Gentiles lord it over them; and those who exercise authority over them are given the title Benefactor. 26 But you are not to be like that. Instead, the greatest among you should be like the youngest, and the one who rules like the one who serves. 27 For who is greater, the one who is at the table or the one who serves? Is it not the one who is at the table? But I am among you as one who serves. 28 You are those who have stood by me in my trials. 29And I confer on you a kingdom, just as my Father conferred one on me, 30 so that you may eat and drink at my table in my kingdom and sit on thrones, judging the twelve tribes of Israel.

31 "Simon, Simon, Satan has asked to sift you all as wheat. 32 But I have prayed for you, Simon, that your faith may not fail. And when you have returned to me, strengthen your brothers."

33 But he replied, "Lord, I am ready to go with you to prison and to death."

34 Jesus answered, "I tell you, Peter, before the rooster crows today, you will deny three times that you know me."

35 Then Jesus asked them, "When I sent you without purse, bag or sandals, did you lack anything?"

"Nothing," they answered.

36 He said to them, "But now if you have a purse, take it, and also a bag; and if you don't have a sword, sell your cloak and buy one. 37 It is written: 'And he was numbered with the transgressors' *u*; and I tell you that this must be fulfilled in me. Yes, what is written about me is reaching its fulfillment."

38 The disciples said, "See, Lord, here are two swords."

"That is enough," he replied.

Jesus prays on the Mount of Olives

39 Jesus went out as usual to the Mount of Olives, and his disciples followed him. 40 On reaching the place, he said to them, "Pray so that you will not fall into temptation." 41 He withdrew about a stone's throw beyond them, knelt down and prayed, 42 "Father, if you are willing, take this cup from me; yet not my will, but yours, be done." 43An angel from heaven appeared to him and strengthened him. 44And being in anguish, he prayed more earnestly, and his sweat was like drops of blood falling to the ground.*v*

45 When he rose from prayer and went back to the disciples, he found them asleep, exhausted from sorrow. 46 "Why are you sleeping?" he asked them. "Get up and pray so that you will not fall into temptation."

Jesus arrested

47 While he was still speaking a crowd came up, and the man who was called Judas, one of

[*u*] Isaiah 53:12. [*v*] Some early MSS omit verses 43 and 44.

250

Greek Interlinear

μου, τὸ ὑπὲρ ὑμῶν ἐκχυννόμενον.] 21 πλὴν
of me, - for you being shed. However

ἰδοὺ ἡ χεὶρ τοῦ παραδιδόντος με μετ'
behold[,] the hand of the [one] betraying me with

ἐμοῦ ἐπὶ τῆς τραπέζης. 22 ὅτι ὁ υἱὸς μὲν
me on the table. Because ᵇthe ᵃSon ¹indeed

τοῦ ἀνθρώπου κατὰ τὸ ὡρισμένον
- of man according to the [thing] having been determined

πορεύεται, πλὴν οὐαὶ τῷ ἀνθρώπῳ ἐκείνῳ
goes, nevertheless woe - man to that

δι' οὗ παραδίδοται. 23 καὶ αὐτοὶ ἤρξαντο
through whom he is betrayed. And they began

συζητεῖν πρὸς ἑαυτοὺς τὸ τίς ἄρα εἴη
to debate with themselves - who then it might be

ἐξ αὐτῶν ὁ τοῦτο μέλλων πράσσειν.
of them the [one] ᵇthis ¹being about ²to do.

24 Ἐγένετο δὲ καὶ φιλονεικία ἐν αὐτοῖς,
And there was also a rivalry among them,

τὸ τίς αὐτῶν δοκεῖ εἶναι μείζων. 25 ὁ δὲ
- who of them seems to be greater. So he

εἶπεν αὐτοῖς· οἱ βασιλεῖς τῶν ἐθνῶν
said to them: The kings of the nations

κυριεύουσιν αὐτῶν, καὶ οἱ ἐξουσιάζοντες
lord it over them, and the [ones] having authority over

αὐτῶν εὐεργέται καλοῦνται. 26 ὑμεῖς δὲ
them benefactors are called. But ye

οὐχ οὕτως, ἀλλ' ὁ μείζων ἐν ὑμῖν
not so, but the greater among you

γινέσθω ὡς ὁ νεώτερος, καὶ ὁ ἡγούμενος
let him become as the younger, and the [one] governing

ὡς ὁ διακονῶν. 27 τίς γὰρ μείζων, ὁ
as the [one] serving. For who [is] greater, the

ἀνακείμενος ἢ ὁ διακονῶν; οὐχὶ ὁ
[one] reclining or the [one] serving? not the

ἀνακείμενος; ἐγὼ δὲ ἐν μέσῳ ὑμῶν εἰμι
[one] reclining? But I in [the] midst of you am

ὡς ὁ διακονῶν. 28 ὑμεῖς δέ ἐστε οἱ
as the [one] serving. But ye are the [ones]

διαμεμενηκότες μετ' ἐμοῦ ἐν τοῖς πειρα-
having remained throughout with me in the tempta-

σμοῖς μου· 29 κἀγὼ διατίθεμαι ὑμῖν καθὼς
tions of me; and I appoint to you as

διέθετό μοι ὁ πατήρ μου βασιλείαν,
appointed to me the Father of me a kingdom,

30 ἵνα ἔσθητε καὶ πίνητε ἐπὶ τῆς -ραπέζης
that ye may eat and drink at the table

μου ἐν τῇ βασιλείᾳ μου, καὶ καθήσεσθε
of me in the kingdom of me, and ye will sit

ἐπὶ θρόνων τὰς δώδεκα φυλὰς κρίνοντες
on thrones ᵇthe ¹twelve ²tribes ³judging

τοῦ Ἰσραήλ. 31 Σίμων Σίμων, ἰδοὺ ὁ
- of Israel. Simon[,] Simon, behold[,] -

σατανᾶς ἐξητήσατο ὑμᾶς τοῦ σινιάσαι ὡς
Satan begged earnestly for you - to sift ᵈ as

τὸν σῖτον· 32 ἐγὼ δὲ ἐδεήθην περὶ σοῦ
the wheat; but I requested concerning thee

ἵνα μὴ ἐκλίπῃ ἡ πίστις σου· καὶ σύ
that might not fail the faith of thee; and thou

ποτε ἐπιστρέψας στήριξον τοὺς ἀδελφούς
when having turned support the brothers

σου. 33 ὁ δὲ εἶπεν αὐτῷ· κύριε, μετὰ
of thee. And he said to him: Lord, with

σοῦ ἑτοιμός εἰμι καὶ εἰς φυλακὴν καὶ εἰς
thee prepared I am both to prison and to

θάνατον πορεύεσθαι. 34 ὁ δὲ εἶπεν· λέγω
death to go. But he said: I tell

σοι, Πέτρε, οὐ φωνήσει σήμερον ἀλέκτωρ
thee, Peter, will not sound to-day a cock

ἕως τρίς με ἀπαρνήσῃ μὴ εἰδέναι. 35 Καὶ
until thrice me thou wilt deny not to know. And

εἶπεν αὐτοῖς· ὅτε ἀπέστειλα ὑμᾶς ἄτερ
he said to them: When I sent you without

βαλλαντίου καὶ πήρας καὶ ὑποδημάτων, μὴ
a purse and a wallet and sandals, not

τινος ὑστερήσατε; οἱ δὲ εἶπαν· οὐθενός.
of anything were ye short? And they said: Of nothing.

36 εἶπεν δὲ αὐτοῖς· ἀλλὰ νῦν ὁ ἔχων
And he said to them: But now the [one] having

βαλλάντιον ἀράτω, ὁμοίως καὶ πήραν, καὶ
a purse let him take [it], likewise also a wallet, and

ὁ μὴ ἔχων πωλησάτω τὸ ἱμάτιον αὐτοῦ
the [one] not having let him sell the garment of him

καὶ ἀγορασάτω μάχαιραν. 37 λέγω γὰρ
and let him buy a sword. For I tell

ὑμῖν ὅτι τοῦτο τὸ γεγραμμένον δεῖ
you that this - having been written it behoves

τελεσθῆναι ἐν ἐμοί, τό· καὶ μετὰ ἀνόμων
to be finished in me, - And with lawless men

ἐλογίσθη· καὶ γὰρ τὸ περὶ ἐμοῦ τέλος
he was reckoned; for indeed the thing concerning me an end

ἔχει. 38 οἱ δὲ εἶπαν· κύριε, ἰδοὺ μάχαιραι
has. And they said: Lord, behold[,] swords

ὧδε δύο. ὁ δὲ εἶπεν αὐτοῖς· ἱκανόν ἐστιν.
here two. And he said to them: Enough it is.

39 Καὶ ἐξελθὼν ἐπορεύθη κατὰ τὸ ἔθος
And going forth he went according to the(his) habit

εἰς τὸ ὄρος τῶν ἐλαιῶν· ἠκολούθησαν δὲ
to the mountain of the olives; and ⁴followed

αὐτῷ καὶ οἱ μαθηταί. 40 γενόμενος δὲ
²him ³also ¹the ¹disciples. And coming

ἐπὶ τοῦ τόπου εἶπεν αὐτοῖς· προσεύχεσθε
upon the place he said to them: Pray ye

μὴ εἰσελθεῖν εἰς πειρασμόν. 41 καὶ αὐτὸς
not to enter into temptation. And he

ἀπεσπάσθη ἀπ' αὐτῶν ὡσεὶ λίθου βολήν,
was withdrawn from them about of a stone a throw,

καὶ θεὶς τὰ γόνατα προσηύχετο 42 λέγων·
and placing the knees he prayed saying:

πάτερ, εἰ βούλει παρένεγκε τοῦτο τὸ
Father, if thou wilt take away this -

ποτήριον ἀπ' ἐμοῦ· πλὴν μὴ τὸ θέλημά
cup from me; nevertheless not the will

μου ἀλλὰ τὸ σὸν γινέσθω. 43 [ὤφθη δὲ
of me but the thine let be. And appeared

αὐτῷ ἄγγελος ἀπ' οὐρανοῦ ἐνισχύων αὐτόν.
to him an angel from heaven strengthening him.

44 καὶ γενόμενος ἐν ἀγωνίᾳ ἐκτενέστερον
And becoming in an agony more earnestly

προσηύχετο· καὶ ἐγένετο ὁ ἱδρὼς αὐτοῦ
he prayed; and became the sweat of him

ὡσεὶ θρόμβοι αἵματος καταβαίνοντες ἐπὶ
as drops of blood falling down onto

τὴν γῆν.] 45 καὶ ἀναστὰς ἀπὸ τῆς
the earth. And rising up from the

προσευχῆς, ἐλθὼν πρὸς τοὺς μαθητὰς
prayer, coming to the disciples

εὗρεν κοιμωμένους αὐτοὺς ἀπὸ τῆς λύπης,
he found ¹sleeping ²them from the grief,

46 καὶ εἶπεν αὐτοῖς· τί καθεύδετε;
and said to them: Why sleep ye?

ἀναστάντες προσεύχεσθε, ἵνα μὴ εἰσέλθητε
rising up pray ye, lest ye enter

εἰς πειρασμόν. 47 Ἔτι αὐτοῦ λαλοῦντος
into temptation. Yet him speaking²
= While he was yet speaking

ἰδοὺ ὄχλος, καὶ ὁ λεγόμενος Ἰούδας εἷς
behold[,] a crowd, and the [one] being named Judas one

251

King James Version

twelve, went before them, and drew near unto Jesus to kiss him. 48 But Jesus said unto him, Judas, betrayest thou the Son of man with a kiss? 49 When they which were about him saw what would follow, they said unto him, Lord, shall we smite with the sword?

50 And one of them smote the servant of the high priest, and cut off his right ear. 51 And Jesus answered and said, Suffer ye thus far. And he touched his ear, and healed him. 52 Then Jesus said unto the chief priests, and captains of the temple, and the elders, which were come to him, Be ye come out, as against a thief, with swords and staves? 53 When I was daily with you in the temple, ye stretched forth no hands against me: but this is your hour, and the power of darkness.

54 Then took they him, and led *him,* and brought him into the high priest's house. And Peter followed afar off. 55 And when they had kindled a fire in the midst of the hall, and were set down together, Peter sat down among them. 56 But a certain maid beheld him as he sat by the fire, and earnestly looked upon him, and said, This man was also with him. 57 And he denied him, saying, Woman, I know him not. 58 And after a little while another saw him, and said, Thou art also of them. And Peter said, Man, I am not. 59 And about the space of one hour after another confidently affirmed, saying, Of a truth this *fellow* also was with him; for he is a Galilean. 60 And Peter said, Man, I know not what thou sayest. And immediately, while he yet spake, the cock crew. 61 And the Lord turned, and looked upon Peter. And Peter remembered the word of the Lord, how he had said unto him, Before the cock crow, thou shalt deny me thrice. 62 And Peter went out, and wept bitterly.

63 And the men that held Jesus mocked him, and smote *him.* 64 And when they had blindfolded him, they struck him on the face, and asked him, saying, Prophesy, who is it that smote thee? 65 And many other things blasphemously spake they against him.

66 And as soon as it was day, the elders of the people and the chief priests and the scribes came together, and led him into their council, saying, 67 Art thou the Christ? tell us. And he said unto them, If I tell you, ye will not believe: 68 And if I also ask *you,* ye will not answer me, nor let *me* go. 69 Hereafter shall the Son of man sit on the right hand of the power of God. 70 Then said they all, Art thou then the Son of God? And he said unto them, Ye say that I am. 71 And they said, What need we any further witness? for we ourselves have heard of his own mouth.

New International Version

the Twelve, was leading them. He approached Jesus to kiss him, 48 but Jesus asked him, "Judas, are you betraying the Son of Man with a kiss?" 49 When Jesus' followers saw what was going to happen, they said, "Lord, should we strike with our swords?" 50 And one of them struck the servant of the high priest, cutting off his right ear.

51 But Jesus answered, "No more of this!" And he touched the man's ear and healed him.

52 Then Jesus said to the chief priests, the officers of the temple guard, and the elders, who had come for him, "Am I leading a rebellion, that you have come with swords and clubs? 53 Every day I was with you in the temple courts, and you did not lay a hand on me. But this is your hour—when darkness reigns."

Peter disowns Jesus

54 Then seizing him, they led him away and took him into the house of the high priest. Peter followed at a distance. 55 But when they had kindled a fire in the midde of the courtyard and had sat down together, Peter sat down with them. 56 A servant girl saw him seated there in the firelight. She looked closely at him and said, "This man was with him."

57 But he denied it. "Girl, I don't know him," he said.

58 A little later someone else saw him and said, "You also are one of them."

"Man, I am not!" Peter replied.

59 About an hour later another asserted, "Certainly this fellow was with him, for he is a Galilean."

60 Peter replied, "Man, I don't know what you're talking about!" Just as he was speaking, the rooster crowed. 61 The Lord turned and looked straight at Peter. Then Peter remembered the word the Lord had spoken to him: "Before the rooster crows today, you will disown me three times." 62 And he went outside and wept bitterly.

The soldiers mock Jesus

63 The men who were guarding Jesus began mocking and beating him. 64 They blindfolded him and demanded, "Prophesy! Who hit you?" 65 And they said many other insulting things to him.

Jesus before Pilate and Herod

66 At daybreak the council of the elders of the people, both the chief priests and teachers of the law, met together, and Jesus was led before them. 67 "If you are the Christ,*w* " they said, "tell us."

Jesus answered, "If I tell you, you will not believe me, 68 and if I asked you, you would not answer. 69 But from now on, the Son of Man will be seated at the right hand of the mighty God."

70 They all asked, "Are you then the Son of God?"

He replied, "You are right in saying I am." 71 Then they said, "Why do we need any more testimony? We have heard it from his own lips."

[w] Or *Messiah.*

252

Greek Interlinear

τῶν δώδεκα προήρχετο αὐτούς, καὶ ἤγγισεν
of the   twelve came before them,   and drew near

τῷ Ἰησοῦ φιλῆσαι αὐτόν. **48** Ἰησοῦς δὲ
- to Jesus to kiss   him.   But Jesus

εἶπεν αὐτῷ· Ἰούδα, φιλήματι τὸν υἱὸν
said   to him : Judas, with a kiss the   Son

τοῦ ἀνθρώπου παραδίδως; **49** ἰδόντες δὲ
-    of man   betrayest thou?   And ⁵seeing

οἱ περὶ αὐτὸν τὸ ἐσόμενον εἶπαν· κύριε,
¹the [ones] ²round ³him the thing going to be said : Lord,

εἰ πατάξομεν ἐν μαχαίρῃ; **50** καὶ ἐπάταξεν
if we shall strike with a sword?   And ⁶struck

εἷς τις ἐξ αὐτῶν τοῦ ἀρχιερέως τὸν
¹a certain one ³of ⁴them ⁵of the ⁶high priest ⁷the

δοῦλον καὶ ἀφεῖλεν τὸ οὖς αὐτοῦ τὸ .
⁸slave and cut off ¹the ²ear ³of him

δεξιόν. **51** ἀποκριθεὶς δὲ ὁ Ἰησοῦς εἶπεν·
⁴right.   And answering   -   Jesus   said :

ἐᾶτε ἕως τούτου· καὶ ἁψάμενος τοῦ
Permit ye until this;   and touching the

ὠτίου ἰάσατο αὐτόν. **52** Εἶπεν δὲ Ἰησοῦς
ear   he cured him.   And said Jesus

πρὸς τοὺς παραγενομένους ἐπ’ αὐτὸν
³to   ¹the   ²coming   ¹⁰upon ¹¹him

ἀρχιερεῖς καὶ στρατηγοὺς τοῦ ἱεροῦ καὶ
⁴chief priests ⁵and ⁶captains ⁷of the ⁸temple ⁹and

πρεσβυτέρους· ὡς ἐπὶ λῃστὴν ἐξήλθατε·
⁴elders :   As against a robber came ye out

μετὰ μαχαιρῶν καὶ ξύλων; **53** καθ’ ἡμέραν
with   swords   and clubs?   daily

ὄντος μου μεθ’ ὑμῶν ἐν τῷ ἱερῷ οὐκ
being me² with you in the temple not
=while I was

ἐξετείνατε τὰς χεῖρας ἐπ’ ἐμέ· ἀλλ’ αὕτη
ye stretched out the(your) hands against me; but this

ἐστὶν ὑμῶν ἡ ὥρα καὶ ἡ ἐξουσία τοῦ
is   of you the hour and the authority of the

σκότους.
darkness.

54 Συλλαβόντες δὲ αὐτὸν ἤγαγον καὶ
And having arrested   him   they led and

εἰσήγαγον εἰς τὴν οἰκίαν τοῦ ἀρχιερέως·
brought in   into the house of the high priest;

ὁ δὲ Πέτρος ἠκολούθει μακρόθεν. **55** περι-
- and Peter   followed   afar off.   light-

αἱψάντων δὲ πῦρ ἐν μέσῳ τῆς αὐλῆς καὶ
ing   And a fire in [the] centre of the court and
=when they had lit a fire . . . and had sat down together

συγκαθισάντων ἐκάθητο ὁ Πέτρος μέσος
sitting down together² sat   - Peter   among

αὐτῶν. **56** ἰδοῦσα δὲ αὐτὸν παιδίσκη τις
them.   And ²seeing   ³him ¹a certain maidservant

καθήμενον πρὸς τὸ φῶς καὶ ἀτενίσασα
sitting   near the light and gazing at

αὐτῷ εἶπεν· καὶ οὗτος σὺν αὐτῷ ἦν. **57** ὁ
him   said : And this man with him was.   he

δὲ ἠρνήσατο λέγων· οὐκ οἶδα αὐτόν,
But denied   saying : I know not him,

γύναι. **58** καὶ μετὰ βραχὺ ἕτερος ἰδὼν
woman.   And after a short while another seeing

αὐτὸν ἔφη· καὶ σὺ ἐξ αὐτῶν εἶ. ὁ
him   said : And thou of them art.   the

δὲ Πέτρος ἔφη· ἄνθρωπε, οὐκ εἰμί.
But Peter   said : Man,   I am not.

59 καὶ διαστάσης ὡσεὶ ὥρας μιᾶς ἄλλος
And intervening about hour one² ²other man
=when about an hour had intervened

τις διϊσχυρίζετο λέγων· ἐπ’ ἀληθείας καὶ
¹a cer- emphatically saying : Of a truth   also
tain   asserted

οὗτος μετ’ αὐτοῦ ἦν, καὶ γὰρ Γαλιλαῖός
this man with him was, for indeed a Galilean

ἐστιν. **60** εἶπεν δὲ ὁ Πέτρος· ἄνθρωπε,
he is.   But said - Peter :   Man,

οὐκ οἶδα ὃ λέγεις. καὶ παραχρῆμα ἔτι
I know not what thou sayest. And at once yet

λαλοῦντος αὐτοῦ ἐφώνησεν ἀλέκτωρ. **61** καὶ
speaking   him² sounded   a cock.   And
=while he was yet speaking

στραφεὶς ὁ κύριος ἐνέβλεψεν τῷ Πέτρῳ,
turning   the Lord looked at   - Peter,

καὶ ὑπεμνήσθη ὁ Πέτρος τοῦ λόγου τοῦ
and remembered - Peter the word of the

κυρίου, ὡς εἶπεν αὐτῷ ὅτι πρὶν ἀλέκτορα
Lord, as he told him that before a cock

φωνῆσαι σήμερον ἀπαρνήσῃ με τρίς. **62** καὶ
to sound⁵ to-day thou wilt deny me thrice.   And

ἐξελθὼν ἔξω ἔκλαυσεν πικρῶς. **63** Καὶ οἱ
going out outside he wept   bitterly.   And the

ἄνδρες οἱ συνέχοντες αὐτὸν ἐνέπαιζον αὐτῷ
men   - having in charge him² mocked   him

δέροντες, **64** καὶ περικαλύψαντες αὐτὸν
beating,   and covering over   him

ἐπηρώτων λέγοντες· προφήτευσον, τίς ἐστιν
questioned saying :   Prophesy,   who is

ὁ παίσας σε; **65** καὶ ἕτερα πολλὰ
the [one] playing thee?   And other things many

βλασφημοῦντες ἔλεγον εἰς αὐτόν.
blaspheming   they said against him.

66 Καὶ ὡς ἐγένετο ἡμέρα, συνήχθη τὸ
And when came   day,   was assembled the

πρεσβυτέριον τοῦ λαοῦ, ἀρχιερεῖς τε καὶ
body of elders of the people, both chief priests and

γραμματεῖς, καὶ ἀπήγαγον αὐτὸν εἰς τὸ
scribes,   and led away   him   to the

συνέδριον αὐτῶν, **67** λέγοντες· εἰ σὺ εἶ ὁ
council   of them,   saying : If thou art the

χριστός, εἰπὸν ἡμῖν. εἶπεν δὲ αὐτοῖς·
Christ, tell us.   And he said to them :

ἐὰν ὑμῖν εἴπω, οὐ μὴ πιστεύσητε· **68** ἐὰν
If you I tell, by no means will ye believe;   ²if

δὲ ἐρωτήσω, οὐ μὴ ἀποκριθῆτε. **69** ἀπὸ
¹and I question, by no means will ye answer.   ³from

τοῦ νῦν δὲ ἔσται ὁ υἱὸς τοῦ ἀνθρώπου
- ²now ¹But ⁴will be ³the ⁵Son - ⁶of man

καθήμενος ἐκ δεξιῶν τῆς δυνάμεως τοῦ
⁷sitting   at [the] right of the power -

θεοῦ. **70** εἶπαν δὲ πάντες· σὺ οὖν εἶ ὁ
of God.   And they said all : Thou therefore art the

υἱὸς τοῦ θεοῦ; ὁ δὲ πρὸς αὐτοὺς ἔφη·
Son   - of God? And he to them   said :

ὑμεῖς λέγετε ὅτι ἐγώ εἰμι. **71** οἱ δὲ
Ye say   that I am.   And they

εἶπαν· τί ἔτι ἔχομεν μαρτυρίας χρείαν;
said : Why yet have we of witness   need ?

αὐτοὶ γὰρ ἠκούσαμεν ἀπὸ τοῦ στόματος
for [our]selves we heard from the mouth

αὐτοῦ.
of him.

---

* That is, Jesus (as some texts have it).

King James Version

23 And the whole multitude of them arose, and led him unto Pilate. 2And they began to accuse him, saying, We found this *fellow* perverting the nation, and forbidding to give tribute to Cesar, saying that he himself is Christ a king. 3And Pilate asked him, saying, Art thou the King of the Jews? And he answered him and said, Thou sayest *it*. 4 Then said Pilate to the chief priests and *to* the people, I find no fault in this man. 5And they were the more fierce, saying, He stirreth up the people, teaching throughout all Jewry, beginning from Galilee to this place. 6 When Pilate heard of Galilee, he asked whether the man were a Galilean. 7And as soon as he knew that he belonged unto Herod's jurisdiction, he sent him to Herod, who himself also was at Jerusalem at that time.

8 And when Herod saw Jesus, he was exceeding glad: for he was desirous to see him of a long *season*, because he had heard many things of him; and he hoped to have seen some miracle done by him. 9 Then he questioned with him in many words; but he answered him nothing. 10And the chief priests and scribes stood and vehemently accused him. 11And Herod with his men of war set him at nought, and mocked *him*, and arrayed him in a gorgeous robe, and sent him again to Pilate.

12 And the same day Pilate and Herod were made friends together; for before they were at enmity between themselves.

13 And Pilate, when he had called together the chief priests and the rulers and the people, 14 Said unto them, Ye have brought this man unto me, as one that perverteth the people; and, behold, I, having examined *him* before you, have found no fault in this man touching those things whereof ye accuse him: 15 No, nor yet Herod: for I sent you to him; and, lo, nothing worthy of death is done unto him. 16 I will therefore chastise him, and release *him*. 17 (For of necessity he must release one unto them at the feast.) 18And they cried out all at once, saying, Away with this *man*, and release unto us Barabbas: 19 (Who for a certain sedition made in the city, and for murder, was cast into prison.) 20 Pilate therefore, willing to release Jesus, spake again to them. 21 But they cried, saying, Crucify *him*, crucify him. 22And he said unto them the third time, Why, what evil hath he done? I have found no cause of death in him: I will therefore chastise him, and let *him* go. 23And they were instant with loud voices, requiring that he might be crucified: and the voices of them and of the chief priests prevailed. 24And Pilate gave sentence that it should be as they required. 25And he released unto them him that for sedition and murder was cast into prison, whom they had desired; but he delivered Jesus to their will. 26And as they led him away, they laid hold upon one Simon, a Cyrenian, coming out of the country, and on him they laid the cross, that he might bear *it* after Jesus.

New International Version

23 Then the whole assembly rose and led him off to Pilate. 2And they began to accuse him, saying, "We have found this man subverting our nation. He opposes payment of taxes to Caesar and claims to be Christ,[w] a king."

3 So Pilate asked Jesus, "Are you the king of the Jews?"

"Yes, it is as you say," Jesus replied.

4 Then Pilate announced to the chief priests and the crowd, "I find no basis for a charge against this man."

5 But they insisted, "He stirs up the people all over Judea[x] by his teaching. He started in Galilee and has come all the way here."

6 On hearing this, Pilate asked if the man was a Galilean. 7 When he learned that Jesus was under Herod's jurisdiction, he sent him to Herod, who was also in Jerusalem at that time.

8 When Herod saw Jesus, he was greatly pleased, because for a long time he had been wanting to see him. From what he had heard about him, he hoped to see him perform some miracle. 9 He plied him with many questions, but Jesus gave him no answer. 10 The chief priests and the teachers of the law were standing there, vehemently accusing him. 11 Then Herod and his soldiers ridiculed and mocked him. Dressing him in an elegant robe, they sent him back to Pilate. 12 That day Herod and Pilate became friends—before this they had been enemies.

13 Pilate called together the chief priests, the rulers and the people, 14 and said to them, "You brought me this man as one who was inciting the people to rebellion. I have examined him in your presence and have found no basis for your charges against him. 15 Neither has Herod, for he sent him back to us; as you can see, he has done nothing to deserve death. 16 Therefore, I will punish him and then release him." [y]

18 With one voice they cried out, "Away with this man! Release Barabbas to us!" 19 (Barabbas had been thrown into prison for an insurrection in the city, and for murder.)

20 Wanting to release Jesus, Pilate appealed to them again. 21 But they kept shouting, "Crucify him! Crucify him!"

22 For the third time he spoke to them: "Why? What crime has this man committed? I have found in him no grounds for the death penalty. Therefore, I will have him punished and then release him."

23 But with loud shouts they insistently demanded that he be crucified, and their shouts prevailed. 24 So Pilate decided to grant their demand. 25 He released the man who had been thrown into prison for insurrection and murder, the one they asked for, and surrendered Jesus to their will.

The crucifixion

26 As they led him away, they seized Simon from Cyrene, who was on his way in from the country, and put the cross on him and made

---

[w] Or *Messiah*. [x] Or *the land of the Jews*. [y] Some MSS add verse 17: *Now he was obliged to release one man to them at the feast.*

Greek Interlinear

Chapter 23

Καὶ ἀναστὰν ἅπαν τὸ πλῆθος αὐτῶν
And rising up all the multitude of them

ἤγαγον αὐτὸν ἐπὶ τὸν Πιλᾶτον. 2 ἤρξαντο
led him before - Pilate. they began

δὲ κατηγορεῖν αὐτοῦ λέγοντες· τοῦτον
And to accuse him saying : This man

εὕραμεν διαστρέφοντα τὸ ἔθνος ἡμῶν καὶ
we found perverting the nation of us and

κωλύοντα φόρους Καίσαρι διδόναι, καὶ
forbidding tribute to Cæsar to give, and

λέγοντα ἑαυτὸν χριστὸν βασιλέα εἶναι.
saying himself Christ a king to be.

3 ὁ δὲ Πιλᾶτος ἠρώτησεν αὐτὸν λέγων·
- And Pilate questioned him saying :

σὺ εἶ ὁ βασιλεὺς τῶν Ἰουδαίων; ὁ δὲ
Thou art the king of the Jews? And he

ἀποκριθεὶς αὐτῷ ἔφη· σὺ λέγεις. 4 ὁ δὲ
answering him said : Thou sayest. - And

Πιλᾶτος εἶπεν πρὸς τοὺς ἀρχιερεῖς καὶ
Pilate said to the chief priests and

τοὺς ὄχλους· οὐδὲν εὑρίσκω αἴτιον ἐν
the crowds : ¹No ¹I find ¹crime in

τῷ ἀνθρώπῳ τούτῳ. 5 οἱ δὲ ἐπίσχυον λέγοντες
- man this. But they insisted saying[.]

ὅτι ἀνασείει τὸν λαόν, διδάσκων καθ᾽
- He excites the people, teaching throughout

ὅλης τῆς Ἰουδαίας, καὶ ἀρξάμενος ἀπὸ
all the Judæa, even beginning from

τῆς Γαλιλαίας ἕως ὧδε. 6 Πιλᾶτος δὲ
- Galilee to here. And Pilate

ἀκούσας ἐπηρώτησεν εἰ ὁ ἄνθρωπος
hearing questioned if the man

Γαλιλαῖός ἐστιν, 7 καὶ ἐπιγνοὺς ὅτι ἐκ
a Galilæan is(was), and perceiving that of

τῆς ἐξουσίας Ἡρώδου ἐστίν, ἀνέπεμψεν
the authority of Herod he is(was), he sent up

αὐτὸν πρὸς Ἡρώδην, ὄντα καὶ αὐτὸν ἐν
him to Herod, being also him(he) in

Ἱεροσολύμοις ἐν ταύταις ταῖς ἡμέραις.
Jerusalem in these the days.

8 ὁ δὲ Ἡρώδης ἰδὼν τὸν Ἰησοῦν ἐχάρη
- And Herod seeing - Jesus rejoiced

λίαν· ἦν γὰρ ἐξ ἱκανῶν χρόνων θέλων
greatly; for he was of a long times wishing

ἰδεῖν αὐτὸν διὰ τὸ ἀκούειν περὶ αὐτοῦ,
to see him because of the to hear[b] about him,
                            =because he had heard

καὶ ἤλπιζέν τι σημεῖον ἰδεῖν ὑπ᾽ αὐτοῦ
and he hoped some sign to see by him

γινόμενον. 9 ἐπηρώτα δὲ αὐτὸν ἐν λόγοις
brought about. And he questioned him in words

ἱκανοῖς· αὐτὸς δὲ οὐδὲν ἀπεκρίνατο αὐτῷ.
many; but he nothing answered him.

10 εἱστήκεισαν δὲ οἱ ἀρχιερεῖς καὶ οἱ
And stood the chief priests and the

γραμματεῖς εὐτόνως κατηγοροῦντες αὐτοῦ.
scribes vehemently accusing him.

11 ἐξουθενήσας δὲ αὐτὸν ὁ Ἡρώδης σὺν
And despising him - Herod with

τοῖς στρατεύμασιν αὐτοῦ καὶ ἐμπαίξας,
the soldiery of him and mocking,

περιβαλὼν ἐσθῆτα λαμπρὰν ἀνέπεμψεν αὐτὸν
throwing round clothing splendid sent back him

τῷ Πιλάτῳ. 12 ἐγένοντο δὲ φίλοι ὅ τε
- to Pilate. And became friends - both

Ἡρώδης καὶ ὁ Πιλᾶτος ἐν αὐτῇ τῇ
Herod and - Pilate on ⁵same ⁶the

ἡμέρᾳ μετ᾽ ἀλλήλων· προϋπῆρχον γὰρ ἐν
day with⁴ each other; for they were previously in

ἔχθρᾳ ὄντες πρὸς αὐτούς. 13 Πιλᾶτος δὲ
enmity being with themselves. And Pilate

συγκαλεσάμενος τοὺς ἀρχιερεῖς καὶ τοὺς
calling together the chief priests and the

ἄρχοντας καὶ τὸν λαὸν 14 εἶπεν πρὸς
leaders and the people said to

αὐτούς· προσηνέγκατέ μοι τὸν ἄνθρωπον
them : Ye brought to me - man

τοῦτον ὡς ἀποστρέφοντα τὸν λαόν, καὶ
this as perverting the people, and

ἰδοὺ ἐγὼ ἐνώπιον ὑμῶν ἀνακρίνας οὐθὲν
behold I ²before ³you ¹examining ⁴nothing

εὗρον ἐν τῷ ἀνθρώπῳ τούτῳ αἴτιον ὧν
⁵found ⁷in ⁸man ⁸this ⁶crime of the
                                        [things]
                                        which

κατηγορεῖτε κατ᾽ αὐτοῦ. 15 ἀλλ᾽ οὐδὲ
ye bring accusation against him. And neither

Ἡρώδης· ἀνέπεμψεν γὰρ αὐτὸν πρὸς ἡμᾶς·
Herod; for he sent back him to us;

καὶ ἰδοὺ οὐδὲν ἄξιον θανάτου ἐστὶν
and behold nothing worthy of death is

πεπραγμένον αὐτῷ. 16 παιδεύσας οὖν αὐτὸν
having been done by him; chastising therefore him

ἀπολύσω. ‡ 18 ἀνέκραγον δὲ παμπληθεὶ
I will release. But they shouted with the whole
                                        multitude

λέγοντες· αἶρε τοῦτον, ἀπόλυσον δὲ ἡμῖν
saying : Take this man, and release to us

τὸν Βαραββᾶν· 19 ὅστις ἦν διὰ στάσιν
- Barabbas; who was because ²insurrec-
                                      of   tion

τινὰ γενομένην ἐν τῇ πόλει καὶ φόνον
¹some happening in the city and murder

βληθεὶς ἐν τῇ φυλακῇ. 20 πάλιν δὲ
thrown in the prison. But again

ὁ Πιλᾶτος προσεφώνησεν αὐτοῖς, θέλων
- Pilate called to them, wishing

ἀπολύσαι τὸν Ἰησοῦν. 21 οἱ δὲ ἐπεφώνουν
to release - Jesus. But they shouted

λέγοντες· σταύρου σταύρου αὐτόν. 22 ὁ δὲ
saying : Crucify[.] crucify thou him. But he

τρίτον εἶπεν πρὸς αὐτούς· τί γὰρ κακὸν
a third time said to them : But what evil

ἐποίησεν οὗτος; οὐδὲν αἴτιον θανάτου
did this man? nothing cause of death

εὗρον ἐν αὐτῷ· παιδεύσας οὖν αὐτὸν
I found in him; chastising therefore ○ him

ἀπολύσω. 23 οἱ δὲ ἐπέκειντο φωναῖς
I will release. But they insisted voices

μεγάλαις αἰτούμενοι αὐτὸν σταυρωθῆναι,
with great asking him to be crucified,

καὶ κατίσχυον αἱ φωναὶ αὐτῶν. 24 καὶ
and prevailed the voices of them. And

Πιλᾶτος ἐπέκρινεν γενέσθαι τὸ αἴτημα
Pilate decided to be [carried out] the request

αὐτῶν· 25 ἀπέλυσεν δὲ τὸν διὰ στάσιν
of them; and he released the [one] because of insurrection

καὶ φόνον βεβλημένον εἰς φυλακήν, ὃν
and murder having been thrown into prison, whom

ᾐτοῦντο, τὸν Ἰησοῦν παρέδωκεν τῷ
they asked, - but Jesus he delivered to the

θελήματι αὐτῶν.
will of them.

26 Καὶ ὡς ἀπήγαγον αὐτόν, ἐπιλαβόμενοι
And as they led away him, seizing

Σίμωνά τινα Κυρηναῖον ἐρχόμενον ἀπ᾽
Simon a certain Cyrenian coming from

ἀγροῦ ἐπέθηκαν αὐτῷ τὸν σταυρὸν φέρειν
[the] country they placed on him the cross to carry

‡ Ver. 17 omitted by Nestle

King James Version

27 And there followed him a great company of people, and of women, which also bewailed and lamented him. 28 But Jesus turning unto them said, Daughters of Jerusalem, weep not for me, but weep for yourselves, and for your children. 29 For, behold, the days are coming, in the which they shall say, Blessed *are* the barren, and the wombs that never bare, and the paps which never gave suck. 30 Then shall they begin to say to the mountains, Fall on us; and to the hills, Cover us. 31 For if they do these things in a green tree, what shall be done in the dry? 32And there were also two others, malefactors, led with him to be put to death. 33And when they were come to the place, which is called Calvary, there they crucified him, and the malefactors, one on the right hand, and the other on the left.

34 Then said Jesus, Father, forgive them; for they know not what they do. And they parted his raiment, and cast lots. 35And the people stood beholding. And the rulers also with them derided *him*, saying, He saved others; let him save himself, if he be Christ, the chosen of God. 36And the soldiers also mocked him, coming to him, and offering him vinegar, 37And saying, If thou be the King of the Jews, save thyself. 38And a superscription also was written over him in letters of Greek, and Latin, and Hebrew, THIS IS THE KING OF THE JEWS.

39 And one of the malefactors which were hanged railed on him, saying, If thou be Christ, save thyself and us. 40 But the other answering rebuked him, saying, Dost not thou fear God, seeing thou art in the same condemnation? 41And we indeed justly; for we receive the due reward of our deeds: but this man hath done nothing amiss. 42And he said unto Jesus, Lord, remember me when thou comest into thy kingdom. 43And Jesus said unto him, Verily I say unto thee, To day shalt thou be with me in paradise. 44And it was about the sixth hour, and there was a darkness over all the earth until the ninth hour. 45And the sun was darkened, and the vail of the temple was rent in the midst.

46 And when Jesus had cried with a loud voice, he said, Father, into thy hands I commend my spirit: and having said thus, he gave up the ghost. 47 Now when the centurion saw what was done, he glorified God, saying, Certainly this was a righteous man. 48And all the people that came together to that sight, beholding the things which were done, smote their breasts, and returned. 49And all his acquaintance, and the women that followed him from Galilee, stood afar off, beholding these things.

50 And, behold, *there was* a man named Joseph, a counsellor; *and he was* a good man, and a just: 51 (The same had not consented to the counsel and deed of them:) *he was* of Arimathea, a city of the Jews; who also himself

New International Version

him carry it behind Jesus. 27A large number of people followed him, including women who mourned and wailed for him. 28 Jesus turned and said to them, "Daughters of Jerusalem, do not weep for me; weep for yourselves and for your children. 29 For the time will come when you will say, 'Blessed are the barren women, the wombs that never bore and the breasts that never nursed!' 30 Then,

'they will say to the mountains: Fall on us;
    and to the hills: Cover us.' [z]

31 For if men do these things when the tree is green, what will happen when it is dry?"

32 Two other men, both criminals, were also led out with him to be executed. 33 When they came to the place called The Skull, there they crucified him, along with the criminals—one on his right, the other on his left. 34 Jesus said, "Father, forgive them, for they do not know what they are doing." [a] And they divided up his clothes by casting lots.

35 The people stood watching, and the rulers even sneered at him. They said, "He saved others; let him save himself if he is the Christ[b] of God, the Chosen One."

36 The soldiers also came up and mocked him. They offered him wine vinegar 37 and said, "If you are the king of the Jews, save yourself."

38 There was a written notice above him, which read: THIS IS THE KING OF THE JEWS.

39 One of the criminals who hung there hurled insults at him: "Aren't you the Christ[b]? Save yourself and us!"

40 But the other criminal rebuked him. "Don't you fear God," he said, "since you are under the same sentence? 41 We are punished justly, for we are getting what our deeds deserve. But this man has done nothing wrong."

42 Then he said, "Jesus, remember me when you come into your kingdom."

43 Jesus answered him, "I tell you the truth, today you will be with me in paradise."

Jesus' death

44 It was now about the sixth hour, and darkness came over the whole land until the ninth hour, 45 for the sun stopped shining. And the curtain of the temple was torn in two. 46 Jesus called out with a loud voice, "Father, into your hands I commit my spirit." When he had said this, he breathed his last.

47 The centurion, seeing what had happened, praised God and said, "Surely this was a righteous man." 48 When all the people who had gathered to witness this sight saw what took place, they beat their breasts and went away. 49 But all those who knew him, including the women who had followed him from Galilee, stood at a distance, watching these things.

Jesus' burial

50 Now there was a man named Joseph, a member of the Council, a good and upright man, 51 who had not consented to their decision and action. He came from the Judean town of Arimathea and he was waiting for the king-

[z] Hosea 10:8. [a] Some early MSS omit verse 34a. [b] Or *Messiah*.

Greek Interlinear

ὄπισθεν τοῦ Ἰησοῦ. 27 Ἠκολούθει δὲ
behind — Jesus. And followed

αὐτῷ πολὺ πλῆθος τοῦ λαοῦ καὶ γυναικῶν
him a much multitude of the people and of women

αἳ ἐκόπτοντο καὶ ἐθρήνουν αὐτόν. 28 στρα-
who mourned and lamented him. turn

φεὶς δὲ πρὸς αὐτὰς Ἰησοῦς εἶπεν·
ing And to them Jesus said :

θυγατέρες Ἰερουσαλήμ, μὴ κλαίετε ἐπ'
Daughters of Jerusalem, do not weep over

ἐμέ· πλὴν ἐφ' ἑαυτὰς κλαίετε καὶ ἐπὶ
me; but over yourselves weep and over

τὰ τέκνα ὑμῶν, 29 ὅτι ἰδοὺ ἔρχονται
the children of you, because behold come

ἡμέραι ἐν αἷς ἐροῦσιν· μακάριαι αἱ
days in which they will say : Blessed the

στεῖραι, καὶ αἱ κοιλίαι αἳ οὐκ ἐγέννησαν,
barren, and the wombs which bare not,

καὶ μαστοὶ οἳ οὐκ ἔθρεψαν. 30 τότε
and breasts which gave not suck. Then

ἄρξονται λέγειν τοῖς ὄρεσιν· πέσατε ἐφ'
they will begin to say to the mountains : Fall on

ἡμᾶς, καὶ τοῖς βουνοῖς· καλύψατε ἡμᾶς·
us, and to the hills : Cover us;

31 ὅτι εἰ ἐν ὑγρῷ ξύλῳ ταῦτα ποιοῦσιν,
because if in ¹full of sap ¹a tree these things they do,

ἐν τῷ ξηρῷ τί γένηται; 32 Ἤγοντο δὲ
in the dry what may happen? And were led

καὶ ἕτεροι κακοῦργοι δύο σὺν αὐτῷ
also others* criminals two with him

ἀναιρεθῆναι. 33 Καὶ ὅτε ἦλθον ἐπὶ τὸν
to be killed. And when they came upon the

τόπον τὸν καλούμενον Κρανίον, ἐκεῖ ἐσταύ-
place — being called Skull, there they

ρωσαν αὐτὸν καὶ τοὺς κακούργους, ὃν μὲν
crucified him and the criminals, one†

ἐκ δεξιῶν ὃν δὲ ἐξ ἀριστερῶν. 34 [ὁ δὲ
on [the] right and one† on [the] left. — And

Ἰησοῦς ἔλεγεν· πάτερ, ἄφες αὐτοῖς· οὐ
Jesus said : Father, forgive them; ²not

γὰρ οἴδασιν τί ποιοῦσιν.] διαμεριζόμενοι
¹for ²they know what they are doing.] dividing

δὲ τὰ ἱμάτια αὐτοῦ ἔβαλον κλήρους.
And the garments of him they cast lots.

35 καὶ εἱστήκει, ὁ λαὸς θεωρῶν. ἐξεμυκ-
And stood the people beholding. scoff-

τήριζον δὲ καὶ οἱ ἄρχοντες λέγοντες·
ed And also the rulers saying :

ἄλλους ἔσωσεν, σωσάτω ἑαυτόν, εἰ οὗτός
Others he saved, let him save himself, if this man

ἐστιν ὁ χριστὸς τοῦ θεοῦ ὁ ἐκλεκτός.
is the Christ — of God the chosen [one].

36 ἐνέπαιξαν δὲ αὐτῷ καὶ οἱ στρατιῶται
And mocked him also the soldiers

προσερχόμενοι, ὄξος προσφέροντες αὐτῷ
approaching, vinegar offering to him

37 καὶ λέγοντες· εἰ σὺ εἶ ὁ βασιλεὺς
and saying : If thou art the king

τῶν Ἰουδαίων, σῶσον σεαυτόν. 38 ἦν δὲ
of the Jews, save thyself. And there was

καὶ ἐπιγραφὴ ἐπ' αὐτῷ· Ο ΒΑΣΙΛΕΥΣ
also a superscription over him : THE KING

ΤΩΝ ΙΟΥΔΑΙΩΝ ΟΥΤΟΣ. 39 Εἷς δὲ
OF THE JEWS THIS. And one

τῶν κρεμασθέντων κακούργων ἐβλασφήμει
of the hanged criminals blasphemed

αὐτόν· οὐχὶ σὺ εἶ ὁ χριστός; σῶσον
him : Not thou art the Christ? save

σεαυτὸν καὶ ἡμᾶς. 40 ἀποκριθεὶς δὲ ὁ
thyself and us. But answering the

ἕτερος ἐπιτιμῶν αὐτῷ ἔφη· οὐδὲ φοβῇ σὺ
other rebuking him said : Not fearest thou

τὸν θεόν, ὅτι ἐν τῷ αὐτῷ κρίματι εἶ;
— God, because in the same judgment thou art?

41 καὶ ἡμεῖς μὲν δικαίως, ἄξια γὰρ ὧν
And we indeed justly, for things worthy of what

ἐπράξαμεν ἀπολαμβάνομεν· οὗτος δὲ οὐδὲν
we did we receive back; but this man nothing

ἄτοπον ἔπραξεν. 42 καὶ ἔλεγεν Ἰησοῦ,
amiss did. And he said : Jesus,

μνήσθητί μου ὅταν ἔλθῃς εἰς τὴν βασιλείαν
remember me when thou comest into the kingdom

σου. 43 καὶ εἶπεν αὐτῷ· ἀμήν σοι λέγω,
of thee. And he said to him : Truly thee I tell,

σήμερον μετ' ἐμοῦ ἔσῃ ἐν τῷ παραδείσῳ.
to-day with me thou wilt be in the paradise.

44 Καὶ ἦν ἤδη ὡσεὶ ὥρα ἕκτη καὶ
And it was now about hour sixth and

σκότος ἐγένετο ἐφ' ὅλην τὴν γῆν ἕως
darkness came over all the land until

ὥρας ἐνάτης 45 τοῦ ἡλίου ἐκλιπόντος·
hour ninth the sun failing;*
=as the sun failed;

ἐσχίσθη δὲ τὸ καταπέτασμα τοῦ ναοῦ
and was torn the veil of the shrine

μέσον. 46 καὶ φωνήσας φωνῇ μεγάλῃ ὁ
in the middle. And crying voice with a great —

Ἰησοῦς εἶπεν· πάτερ, εἰς χεῖράς σου
Jesus said : Father, into hands of thee

παρατίθεμαι τὸ πνεῦμά μου. τοῦτο δὲ
I commit the spirit of me. And this

εἰπὼν ἐξέπνευσεν. 47 ἰδὼν δὲ ὁ ἑκατον-
saying he expired. And ¹seeing ¹the ²cen-

τάρχης τὸ γενόμενον ἐδόξαζεν τὸν θεὸν
turion the thing happening glorified — God

λέγων· ὄντως ὁ ἄνθρωπος οὗτος δίκαιος
saying : Really — man this righteous

ἦν. 48 καὶ πάντες οἱ συμπαραγενόμενοι
was. And all ¹the ²arriving together

ὄχλοι ἐπὶ τὴν θεωρίαν ταύτην, θεωρήσαντες τὰ
²crowds at — sight this, beholding the things

γενόμενα, τύπτοντες τὰ στήθη ὑπέστρεφον.
happening, smiting the(ir) breasts returned.

49 εἱστήκεισαν δὲ πάντες οἱ γνωστοὶ αὐτῷ
And ¹stood ¹all ²the [ones] ²known ⁴to him

ἀπὸ μακρόθεν, καὶ γυναῖκες αἱ συνακο-
³afar off, and women the [ones] accom-

λουθοῦσαι αὐτῷ ἀπὸ τῆς Γαλιλαίας, ὁρῶσαι
panying him from — Galilee, seeing

ταῦτα.
these things.

50 Καὶ ἰδοὺ ἀνὴρ ὀνόματι Ἰωσὴφ
And behold[,] a man by name Joseph

βουλευτὴς ὑπάρχων, ἀνὴρ ἀγαθὸς καὶ
a councillor being, a man good and

δίκαιος, — 51 οὗτος οὐκ ἦν συγκατατεθειμένος
righteous, — this man was not agreeing with

τῇ βουλῇ καὶ τῇ πράξει αὐτῶν, — ἀπὸ
the counsel and the action of them, — from

Ἀριμαθαίας πόλεως τῶν Ἰουδαίων, ὃς
Arimathæa a city of the Jews, who

προσεδέχετο τὴν βασιλείαν τοῦ θεοῦ,
was awaiting the kingdom — of God,

* Luke uses ἕτεροι here with strict accuracy = "different."
Jesus was not himself a criminal. Note punctuation of A.V. Cf.
Acts 28. 1.

King James Version

waited for the kingdom of God. 52 This *man* went unto Pilate, and begged the body of Jesus. 53And he took it down, and wrapped it in linen, and laid it in a sepulchre that was hewn in stone, wherein never man before was laid. 54And that day was the preparation, and the sabbath drew on. 55And the women also, which came with him from Galilee, followed after, and beheld the sepulchre, and how his body was laid. 56And they returned, and prepared spices and ointments; and rested the sabbath day according to the commandment.

24 Now upon the first *day* of the week, very early in the morning, they came unto the sepulchre, bringing the spices which they had prepared, and certain *others* with them. 2And they found the stone rolled away from the sepulchre. 3And they entered in, and found not the body of the Lord Jesus. 4And it came to pass, as they were much perplexed thereabout, behold, two men stood by them in shining garments: 5And as they were afraid, and bowed down *their* faces to the earth, they said unto them, Why seek ye the living among the dead? 6 He is not here, but is risen: remember how he spake unto you when he was yet in Galilee, 7 Saying, The Son of man must be delivered into the hands of sinful men, and be crucified, and the third day rise again. 8And they remembered his words, 9And returned from the sepulchre, and told all these things unto the eleven, and to all the rest. 10 It was Mary Magdalene, and Joanna, and Mary *the mother* of James, and other *women that were* with them, which told these things unto the apostles. 11And their words seemed to them as idle tales, and they believed them not. 12 Then arose Peter, and ran unto the sepulchre; and stooping down, he beheld the linen clothes laid by themselves, and departed, wondering in himself at that which was come to pass.

13 And, behold, two of them went that same day to a village called Emmaus, which was from Jerusalem *about* threescore furlongs. 14And they talked together of all these things which had happened. 15And it came to pass, that, while they communed *together* and reasoned, Jesus himself drew near, and went with them. 16 But their eyes were holden that they should not know him. 17And he said unto them, What manner of communications *are* these that ye have one to another, as ye walk, and are sad? 18And the one of them, whose name was Cleopas, answering said unto him, Art thou only a stranger in Jerusalem, and hast not known the things which are come to pass there in these days? 19And he said unto them, What things? And they said unto him, Concerning Jesus of Nazareth, which was a prophet mighty in deed and word before God and all the people: 20And how the chief priests and our rulers delivered him to be condemned to death, and have crucified him.

New International Version

dom of God. 52 Going to Pilate, he asked for Jesus' body. 53 Then he took it down, wrapped it in linen cloth and placed it in a tomb cut in the rock, one in which no one had yet been laid. 54 It was Preparation Day, and the Sabbath was about to begin.

55 The women who had come with Jesus from Galilee followed Joseph and saw the tomb and how his body was laid in it. 56 Then they went home and prepared spices and perfumes. But they rested on the Sabbath in obedience to the commandment.

The resurrection

24 On the first day of the week, very early in the morning, the women took the spices they had prepared and went to the tomb. 2 They found the stone rolled away from the tomb, 3 but when they entered, they did not find the body of the Lord Jesus. 4 While they were wondering about this, suddenly two men in clothes that gleamed like lightning stood beside them. 5 In their fright the women bowed down with their faces to the ground, but the men said to them, "Why do you look for the living among the dead? 6 He is not here; he has risen! Remember how he told you, while he was still with you in Galilee: 7 'The Son of Man must be delivered into the hands of sinful men, be crucified and on the third day be raised again.' " 8 Then they remembered his words.

9 When they came back from the tomb, they told all these things to the Eleven and to all the others. 10 It was Mary Magdalene, Joanna, Mary the mother of James, and the others with them who told this to the apostles. 11 But they did not believe the women, because their words seemed to them like nonsense. 12 Peter, however, got up and ran to the tomb. Stooping down, he saw the strips of linen lying by themselves, and he went away, wondering to himself what had happened.

On the road to Emmaus

13 Now that same day two of them were going to a village called Emmaus, about seven miles from Jerusalem. 14 They were talking with each other about everything that had happened. 15As they talked and discussed these things with each other, Jesus himself came up and walked along with them; 16 but they were kept from recognizing him.

17 He asked them, "What are you discussing together as you walk along?"

They stood still, their faces downcast. 18 One of them, named Cleopas, asked him, "Are you the only one living in Jerusalem who doesn't know what things have happened there in these days?"

19 "What things?" he asked.

"About Jesus of Nazareth," they replied. "He was a prophet, powerful in word and deed before God and all the people. 20 The chief priests and our rulers handed him over to be sentenced

Greek Interlinear

52 οὗτος προσελθὼν τῷ Πιλάτῳ ἠτήσατο
this man approaching - to Pilate asked

τὸ σῶμα τοῦ Ἰησοῦ, **53** καὶ καθελὼν
the body of Jesus, and taking down

ἐνετύλιξεν αὐτὸ σινδόνι, καὶ ἔθηκεν αὐτὸν
wrapped it in linen, and placed him

ἐν μνήματι λαξευτῷ, οὗ οὐκ ἦν οὐδεὶς
in tomb a hewn, where was not no(any)one

οὔπω κείμενος. **54** καὶ ἡμέρα ἦν παρασκευῆς,
not yet laid. And day it was of preparation,

καὶ σάββατον ἐπέφωσκεν. **55** Κατακολουθήσασαι
and a sabbath was coming on. ⁶following after

δὲ αἱ γυναῖκες, αἵτινες ἦσαν συνεληλυθυῖαι
¹And ²the ³women, who were ⁴having come with

ἐκ τῆς Γαλιλαίας αὐτῷ, ἐθεάσαντο τὸ
⁵out of - ⁶Galilee ⁷with him, beheld the

μνημεῖον καὶ ὡς ἐτέθη τὸ σῶμα αὐτοῦ,
tomb and how was placed the body of him,

56 ὑποστρέψασαι δὲ ἡτοίμασαν ἀρώματα καὶ
and returning prepared spices and

μύρα.
ointment.

Καὶ τὸ μὲν σάββατον ἡσύχασαν κατὰ
And [on] the ²indeed ¹sabbath they rested according to

Chapter 24

τὴν ἐντολήν. **24** τῇ δὲ μιᾷ τῶν σαββάτων
the commandment. But on the one of the week

ὄρθρου βαθέως ἐπὶ τὸ μνῆμα ἦλθον φέρουσαι
while still very early† upon the tomb they came carrying

ἃ ἡτοίμασαν ἀρώματα. **2** εὗρον δὲ τὸν
²which ¹they prepared ³spices. And they found the

λίθον ἀποκεκυλισμένον ἀπὸ τοῦ μνημείου,
stone having been rolled away from the tomb,

3 εἰσελθοῦσαι δὲ οὐχ εὗρον τὸ σῶμα
and entering they found not the body

τοῦ κυρίου Ἰησοῦ. **4** καὶ ἐγένετο ἐν τῷ
of the Lord Jesus. And it was in the
= as they were perplexed

ἀπορεῖσθαι αὐτὰς περὶ τούτου καὶ ἰδοὺ
to be perplexed them⁶ᵉ about this and behold[.]

ἄνδρες δύο ἐπέστησαν αὐταῖς ἐν ἐσθῆτι
men two stood by them in clothing

ἀστραπτούσῃ· **5** ἐμφόβων δὲ γενομένων
shining; and terrified becoming
= as they became terrified and bent their faces

αὐτῶν καὶ κλινουσῶν τὰ πρόσωπα εἰς τὴν
them and bending the(ir) faces⁶ to the

γῆν, εἶπαν πρὸς αὐτάς· τί ζητεῖτε τὸν
earth, they said to them : Why seek ye the

ζῶντα μετὰ τῶν νεκρῶν; **6** [οὐκ ἔστιν
living [one] with the dead [ones]? He is not

ὧδε, ἀλλὰ ἠγέρθη.] μνήσθητε ὡς ἐλάλησεν
here, but was raised.] Remember how he spoke

ὑμῖν ἔτι ὢν ἐν τῇ Γαλιλαίᾳ, **7** λέγων
to you yet being in - Galilee, saying[,]

τὸν υἱὸν τοῦ ἀνθρώπου ὅτι δεῖ παραδο-
The Son - of man - it behoves to be de-

θῆναι εἰς χεῖρας ἀνθρώπων ἁμαρτωλῶν καὶ
livered into hands men of sinful and

σταυρωθῆναι καὶ τῇ τρίτῃ ἡμέρᾳ ἀναστῆναι.
to be crucified and on the third day to rise again.

8 καὶ ἐμνήσθησαν τῶν ῥημάτων αὐτοῦ,
And they remembered the words of him,

9 καὶ ὑποστρέψασαι ἀπὸ τοῦ μνημείου
and returning from the tomb

ἀπήγγειλαν ταῦτα πάντα τοῖς ἔνδεκα καὶ
reported these things all to the eleven and

πᾶσιν τοῖς λοιποῖς. **10** ἦσαν δὲ ἡ
to all the rest. Now they were the

Μαγδαληνὴ Μαρία καὶ Ἰωάννα καὶ Μαρία
Magdalene Mary and Joanna and Mary

ἡ Ἰακώβου· καὶ αἱ λοιπαὶ* σὺν αὐταῖς*
the [mother] of James; and the rest with them

ἔλεγον πρὸς τοὺς ἀποστόλους ταῦτα. **11** καὶ
told to the apostles these things. And

ἐφάνησαν ἐνώπιον αὐτῶν ὡσεὶ λῆρος
seemed before them as folly

τὰ ῥήματα ταῦτα, καὶ ἠπίστουν αὐταῖς.* ‡
- words these, and they disbelieved them.

13 Καὶ ἰδοὺ δύο ἐξ αὐτῶν ἐν αὐτῇ τῇ
And behold[,] two of them on same the

ἡμέρᾳ ἦσαν πορευόμενοι εἰς κώμην ἀπέχουσαν
day were journeying to a village being distant

σταδίους ἑξήκοντα ἀπὸ Ἰερουσαλήμ, ᾗ
furlongs sixty from Jerusalem, to which

ὄνομα Ἐμμαοῦς, **14** καὶ αὐτοὶ ὡμίλουν
name Emmaus, and they talked

πρὸς ἀλλήλους περὶ πάντων τῶν συμβεβηκότων
to each other about all - ²having occurred

τούτων. **15** καὶ ἐγένετο ἐν τῷ ὁμιλεῖν
¹these things. And it came to pass in the to talk

αὐτοὺς καὶ συζητεῖν, καὶ αὐτὸς Ἰησοῦς
them and to discuss⁶ᵉ, and [him]self Jesus
= as they talked and discussed,

ἐγγίσας συνεπορεύετο αὐτοῖς· **16** οἱ δὲ
drawing near journeyed with them; but the⁴

ὀφθαλμοὶ αὐτῶν ἐκρατοῦντο τοῦ μὴ
eyes of them were held - not

ἐπιγνῶναι αὐτόν. **17** εἶπεν δὲ πρὸς αὐτούς·
to recognize⁴ him. And he said to them :

τίνες οἱ λόγοι οὗτοι οὓς ἀντιβάλλετε
What - words these which ye exchange

πρὸς ἀλλήλους περιπατοῦντες; καὶ ἐστάθησαν
with each other walking? And they stood

σκυθρωποί. **18** ἀποκριθεὶς δὲ εἷς ὀνόματι
sad-faced. And answering one by name

Κλεοπᾶς εἶπεν πρὸς αὐτόν· σὺ μόνος
Cleopas said to him : Thou only

παροικεῖς Ἰερουσαλὴμ καὶ οὐκ ἔγνως τὰ
a stranger in Jerusalem and knewest not the things

γενόμενα ἐν αὐτῇ ἐν ταῖς ἡμέραις ταύταις;
happening in it in - days these ?

19 καὶ εἶπεν αὐτοῖς· ποῖα; οἱ δὲ εἶπαν
And he said to them : What things? And they said

αὐτῷ· τὰ περὶ Ἰησοῦ τοῦ Ναζαρηνοῦ, ὃς
to him : The things about Jesus the Nazarene, who

ἐγένετο ἀνὴρ προφήτης δυνατὸς ἐν ἔργῳ
was a man prophet powerful in work

καὶ λόγῳ ἐναντίον τοῦ θεοῦ καὶ παντὸς
and word before - God and all

τοῦ λαοῦ, **20** ὅπως τε παρέδωκαν αὐτὸν οἱ
the people, how both ¹delivered ²him ¹the

ἀρχιερεῖς καὶ οἱ ἄρχοντες ἡμῶν εἰς
²chief priests ³and ⁴the ⁵rulers ⁶of us to

κρίμα θανάτου καὶ ἐσταύρωσαν αὐτόν.
[the] judgment of death and crucified him.

---

* Note the feminines.
‡ Verse 12 omitted by Nestle

King James Version

21 But we trusted that it had been he which should have redeemed Israel: and beside all this, to day is the third day since these things were done. 22 Yea, and certain women also of our company made us astonished, which were early at the sepulchre; 23 And when they found not his body, they came, saying, that they had also seen a vision of angels, which said that he was alive. 24 And certain of them which were with us went to the sepulchre, and found it even so as the women had said: but him they saw not. 25 Then he said unto them, O fools, and slow of heart to believe all that the prophets have spoken: 26 Ought not Christ to have suffered these things, and to enter into his glory? 27 And beginning at Moses and all the prophets, he expounded unto them in all the Scriptures the things concerning himself. 28 And they drew nigh unto the village, whither they went: and he made as though he would have gone further. 29 But they constrained him, saying, Abide with us; for it is toward evening, and the day is far spent. And he went in to tarry with them. 30 And it came to pass, as he sat at meat with them, he took bread, and blessed it, and brake, and gave to them. 31 And their eyes were opened, and they knew him; and he vanished out of their sight. 32 And they said one to another, Did not our heart burn within us, while he talked with us by the way, and while he opened to us the Scriptures? 33 And they rose up the same hour, and returned to Jerusalem, and found the eleven gathered together, and them that were with them, 34 Saying, The Lord is risen indeed, and hath appeared to Simon. 35 And they told what things were done in the way, and how he was known of them in breaking of bread.

36 And as they thus spake, Jesus himself stood in the midst of them, and saith unto them, Peace be unto you. 37 But they were terrified and affrighted, and supposed that they had seen a spirit. 38 And he said unto them, Why are ye troubled? and why do thoughts arise in your hearts? 39 Behold my hands and my feet, that it is I myself: handle me, and see; for a spirit hath not flesh and bones, as ye see me have. 40 And when he had thus spoken, he shewed them his hands and his feet. 41 And while they yet believed not for joy, and wondered, he said unto them, Have ye here any meat? 42 And they gave him a piece of a broiled fish, and of a honeycomb. 43 And he took it, and did eat before them. 44 And he said unto them, These are the words which I spake unto you, while I was yet with you, that all things must be fulfilled, which were written in the law of Moses, and in the prophets, and in the psalms, concerning me. 45 Then opened he their understanding, that they might understand the Scriptures, 46 And said unto them, Thus it is written, and thus it behoved Christ to suffer, and to rise from the dead the third day: 47 And

New International Version

to death, and they crucified him; 21 but we had hoped that he was the one who was going to redeem Israel. And what is more, it is the third day since all this took place. 22 In addition, some of our women amazed us. They went to the tomb early this morning 23 but didn't find his body. They came and told us that they had seen a vision of angels, who said he was alive. 24 Then some of our companions went to the tomb and found it just as the women had said, but him they did not see.

25 He said to them, "How foolish you are, and how slow of heart that you do not believe all that the prophets have spoken! 26 Did not the Christ[d] have to suffer these things and then enter his glory?" 27 And beginning with Moses and all the Prophets, he explained to them what was said in all the Scriptures concerning himself.

28 As they approached the village to which they were going, Jesus acted as if he were going farther. 29 But they urged him strongly, "Stay with us, for it is nearly evening; the day is almost over." So he went in to stay with them.

30 When he was at the table with them, he took bread, gave thanks, broke it and began to give it to them. 31 Then their eyes were opened and they recognized him, and he disappeared from their sight. 32 They asked each other, "Were not our hearts burning within us while he talked with us on the road and opened the Scriptures to us?"

33 They got up and returned at once to Jerusalem. There they found the Eleven and those with them, assembled together 34 and saying, "It is true! The Lord has risen and has appeared to Simon." 35 Then the two told what had happened on the way, and how Jesus was recognized by them when he broke the bread.

Jesus appears to the disciples

36 While they were still talking about this, Jesus himself stood among them and said to them, "Peace be with you."

37 They were startled and frightened, thinking they saw a ghost. 38 He said to them, "Why are you troubled, and why do doubts rise in your minds? 39 Look at my hands and my feet. It is I myself! Touch me and see; a ghost does not have flesh and bones, as you see I have."

40 When he had said this, he showed them his hands and feet. 41 And while they still did not believe it because of joy and amazement, he asked them, "Do you have anything here to eat?" 42 They gave him a piece of broiled fish, 43 and he took it and ate it in their presence.

44 He said to them, "This is what I told you while I was still with you: Everything must be fulfilled that is written about me in the Law of Moses, the Prophets and the Psalms."

45 Then he opened their minds so they could understand the Scriptures. 46 He told them, "This is what is written: The Christ[e] will suffer and rise from the dead on the third day, 47 and re-

[d] Or Messiah.

260

Greek Interlinear

21 ἡμεῖς δὲ ἠλπίζομεν ὅτι αὐτός ἐστιν
But we were hoping that he it is(was)
ὁ μέλλων λυτροῦσθαι τὸν Ἰσραήλ· ἀλλά
the [one] being about to redeem - Israel; but
γε καὶ σὺν πᾶσιν τούτοις τρίτην ταύτην
- also with all these things third this
= this is the third day
ἡμέραν ἄγει ἀφ' οὗ ταῦτα ἐγένετο.
day it leads since these things happened.
22 ἀλλὰ καὶ γυναῖκές τινες ἐξ ἡμῶν
But also ²women ¹some of us
ἐξέστησαν ἡμᾶς, γενόμεναι ὀρθριναὶ ἐπὶ τὸ
astonished us, being early at the
μνημεῖον, **23** καὶ μὴ εὑροῦσαι τὸ σῶμα
tomb, and not finding the body
αὐτοῦ ἦλθον λέγουσαι καὶ ὀπτασίαν ἀγγέλων
of him came saying also a vision of angels
ἑωρακέναι, οἳ λέγουσιν αὐτὸν ζῆν. **24** καὶ
to have seen, who say him to live. And
= that he lives.
ἀπῆλθόν τινες τῶν σὺν ἡμῖν ἐπὶ τὸ
²went ¹some ²of the [ones] ³with ⁴us to the
μνημεῖον, καὶ εὗρον οὕτως καθὼς καὶ αἱ
tomb, and found so as indeed the
γυναῖκες εἶπον, αὐτὸν δὲ οὐκ εἶδον.
women said, but him they saw not.
25 καὶ αὐτὸς εἶπεν πρὸς αὐτούς· ὦ
And he said to them : O
ἀνόητοι καὶ βραδεῖς τῇ καρδίᾳ τοῦ πιστεύειν
foolish [ones] and slow in heart - to believe
ἐπὶ πᾶσιν οἷς ἐλάλησαν οἱ προφῆται·
on(in) all things which spoke the prophets.
26 οὐχὶ ταῦτα ἔδει παθεῖν τὸν χριστὸν καὶ
²not ⁴these things ¹behoved it ³to suffer ⁵the ⁶Christ and
εἰσελθεῖν εἰς τὴν δόξαν αὐτοῦ; **27** καὶ
to enter into the glory of him? And
ἀρξάμενος ἀπὸ Μωϋσέως καὶ ἀπὸ πάντων
beginning from Moses and from all
τῶν προφητῶν διηρμήνευσεν αὐτοῖς ἐν
the prophets he explained to them in
πάσαις ταῖς γραφαῖς τὰ περὶ ἑαυτοῦ.
all the scriptures the things concerning himself.
28 Καὶ ἤγγισαν εἰς τὴν κώμην οὗ
And they drew near to the village whither
ἐπορεύοντο, καὶ αὐτὸς προσεποιήσατο
they were journeying, and he pretended
πορρώτερον πορεύεσθαι. **29** καὶ παρε-
farther to journey. And they
βιάσαντο αὐτὸν λέγοντες· μεῖνον μεθ'
urged him saying : Remain with
ἡμῶν, ὅτι πρὸς ἑσπέραν ἐστὶν καὶ κέκλικεν
us, because toward evening it is and has declined
ἤδη ἡ ἡμέρα. καὶ εἰσῆλθεν τοῦ μεῖναι
now the day. And he went in - to remain
σὺν αὐτοῖς. **30** καὶ ἐγένετο ἐν τῷ
with them. And it came to pass in the
= as he reclined
κατακλιθῆναι αὐτὸν μετ' αὐτῶν λαβὼν τὸν
to recline him with them taking the
ἄρτον εὐλόγησεν καὶ κλάσας ἐπεδίδου
loaf he blessed and having broken he handed
αὐτοῖς· **31** αὐτῶν δὲ διηνοίχθησαν οἱ
to them; and of them were opened up the
ὀφθαλμοί, καὶ ἐπέγνωσαν αὐτόν· καὶ αὐτὸς
eyes, and they recognized him; and he
ἄφαντος ἐγένετο ἀπ' αὐτῶν. **32** καὶ
invisible became from them. And
εἶπαν πρὸς ἀλλήλους· οὐχὶ ἡ καρδία
they said to each other : Not the heart

ἡμῶν καιομένη ἦν ἐν ἡμῖν, ὡς ἐλάλει
of us burning was in us, as he spoke
ἡμῖν ἐν τῇ ὁδῷ, ὡς διήνοιγεν ἡμῖν τὰς
to us in the way, as he opened up to us the
γραφάς; **33** Καὶ ἀναστάντες αὐτῇ τῇ ὥρᾳ
scriptures? And rising up ²same ¹in the hour
ὑπέστρεψαν εἰς Ἰερουσαλήμ, καὶ εὗρον
they returned to Jerusalem, and found
ἠθροισμένους τοὺς ἕνδεκα καὶ τοὺς σὺν
having been collected the eleven and the [ones] with
αὐτοῖς, **34** λέγοντας ὅτι ὄντως ἠγέρθη ὁ
them, saying[,] - Really was raised the
κύριος καὶ ὤφθη Σίμωνι. **35** καὶ αὐτοὶ ἐξηγοῦντο
Lord and appeared to Simon. And they related
τὰ ἐν τῇ ὁδῷ καὶ ὡς ἐγνώσθη
the things in the way and how he was known
αὐτοῖς ἐν τῇ κλάσει τοῦ ἄρτου. **36** Ταῦτα
by them in the breaking of the loaf. these things
δὲ αὐτῶν λαλούντων αὐτὸς ἔστη ἐν
And them saying⁸ he stood in
= as they said these things
μέσῳ αὐτῶν. **37** πτοηθέντες δὲ καὶ
[the] midst of them. But scared and
ἔμφοβοι γενόμενοι ἐδόκουν πνεῦμα θεωρεῖν.
terrified becoming they thought a spirit to behold.
38 καὶ εἶπεν αὐτοῖς· τί τεταραγμένοι ἐστέ,
And he said to them : Why having been troubled are ye,
καὶ διὰ τί διαλογισμοὶ ἀναβαίνουσιν ἐν
and why thoughts come up in
τῇ καρδίᾳ ὑμῶν; **39** ἴδετε τὰς χεῖράς
the heart of you? See the hands
μου καὶ τοὺς πόδας μου, ὅτι ἐγώ εἰμι
of me and the feet of me, that I am
αὐτός· ψηλαφήσατέ με καὶ ἴδετε, ὅτι
[my]self; feel me and see, because
πνεῦμα σάρκα καὶ ὀστέα οὐκ ἔχει καθὼς
a spirit flesh and bones has not as
ἐμὲ θεωρεῖτε ἔχοντα. ‡ **41** ἔτι δὲ ἀπιστούντων
me ye behold having. And yet disbelieving
= while they yet disbelieved
αὐτῶν ἀπὸ τῆς χαρᾶς καὶ θαυμαζόντων,
them⁸ from the joy and marvelling⁸,
εἶπεν αὐτοῖς· ἔχετέ τι βρώσιμον ἐνθάδε;
he said to them : Have ye any food here?
42 οἱ δὲ ἐπέδωκαν αὐτῷ ἰχθύος ὀπτοῦ
And they handed to him ²fish ¹of a broiled
μέρος· **43** καὶ λαβὼν ἐνώπιον αὐτῶν ἔφαγεν.
¹part; and taking before them he ate.
44 Εἶπεν δὲ πρὸς αὐτούς· οὗτοι οἱ λόγοι
And he said to them : These - words
μου οὓς ἐλάλησα πρὸς ὑμᾶς ἔτι ὢν σὺν
of me which I spoke to you yet being with
ὑμῖν, ὅτι δεῖ πληρωθῆναι πάντα τὰ
you, that it behoves to be fulfilled all the things
γεγραμμένα ἐν τῷ νόμῳ Μωϋσέως καὶ
having been written in the law of Moses and
τοῖς προφήταις καὶ ψαλμοῖς περὶ ἐμοῦ.
the prophets and psalms concerning me.
45 τότε διήνοιξεν αὐτῶν τὸν νοῦν τοῦ
Then he opened up of them the mind -
συνιέναι τὰς γραφάς· **46** καὶ εἶπεν αὐτοῖς
to understand the scriptures; and said to them[,]
ὅτι οὕτως γέγραπται παθεῖν τὸν χριστὸν
- Thus it has been written ²to suffer ¹the ⁴Christ
καὶ ἀναστῆναι ἐκ νεκρῶν τῇ τρίτῃ ἡμέρᾳ,
and to rise again out of [the] dead on the third day,
47 καὶ κηρυχθῆναι ἐπὶ τῷ ὀνόματι αὐτοῦ
and ⁴ to be proclaimed on(in) the name of him

‡ Verse 40 omitted by Nestle

King James Version

that repentance and remission of sins should be preached in his name among all nations, beginning at Jerusalem. 48And ye are witnesses of these things.

49 And, behold, I send the promise of my Father upon you: but tarry ye in the city of Jerusalem, until ye be endued with power from on high.

50 And he led them out as far as to Bethany, and he lifted up his hands, and blessed them. 51And it came to pass, while he blessed them, he was parted from them, and carried up into heaven. 52And they worshipped him, and returned to Jerusalem with great joy: 53And were continually in the temple, praising and blessing God. Amen.

New International Version

pentance and forgiveness of sins will be preached in his name to all nations, beginning at Jerusalem. 48 You are witnesses of these things. 49 I am going to send you what my Father has promised; but stay in the city until you have been clothed with power from on high."

The ascension

50 When he had led them out to the vicinity of Bethany, he lifted up his hands and blessed them. 51 While he was blessing them, he left them and was taken up into heaven. 52 Then they worshiped him and returned to Jerusalem with great joy. 53And they stayed continually at the temple, praising God.

Greek Interlinear

μετάνοιαν εἰς ἄφεσιν ἁμαρτιῶν εἰς πάντα
repentance unto forgiveness of sins to all

τὰ ἔθνη, — ἀρξάμενοι ἀπὸ Ἰερουσαλήμ.
the nations, — beginning from Jerusalem.

48 ὑμεῖς μάρτυρες τούτων. **49** καὶ ἰδοὺ
Ye [are] witnesses of these things. And behold

ἐγὼ ἐξαποστέλλω τὴν ἐπαγγελίαν τοῦ
I send forth the promise of the

πατρός μου ἐφ' ὑμᾶς· ὑμεῖς δὲ καθίσατε
Father of me on you; but ye sit

ἐν τῇ πόλει ἕως οὗ ἐνδύσησθε ἐξ ὕψους
in the city until ¹ye are clothed[with]²out of ³height

δύναμιν.
²power.

50 Ἐξήγαγεν δὲ αὐτοὺς ἕως πρὸς
And he led out them until toward

Βηθανίαν, καὶ ἐπάρας τὰς χεῖρας αὐτοῦ
Bethany, and lifting up the hands of him

εὐλόγησεν αὐτούς. **51** καὶ ἐγένετο ἐν τῷ
he blessed them. And it came to pass in the

εὐλογεῖν αὐτὸν αὐτοὺς διέστη ἀπ' αὐτῶν.
to bless him^be them he withdrew from them.
= while he blessed

52 καὶ αὐτοὶ ὑπέστρεψαν εἰς Ἰερουσαλὴμ
And they returned to Jerusalem

μετὰ χαρᾶς μεγάλης, **53** καὶ ἦσαν διὰ παντὸς
with joy great, and were continually

ἐν τῷ ἱερῷ εὐλογοῦντες τὸν θεόν.
in the temple blessing - God.

King James Version
THE GOSPEL
ACCORDING TO
SAINT JOHN

New International Version
JOHN

The Word became flesh

1 In the beginning was the Word, and the Word was with God, and the Word was God. 2 The same was in the beginning with God. 3 All things were made by him; and without him was not any thing made that was made. 4 In him was life; and the life was the light of men. 5 And the light shineth in darkness; and the darkness comprehended it not.

6 There was a man sent from God, whose name *was* John. 7 The same came for a witness, to bear witness of the Light, that all *men* through him might believe. 8 He was not that Light, but *was sent* to bear witness of that Light. 9 *That* was the true Light, which lighteth every man that cometh into the world. 10 He was in the world, and the world was made by him, and the world knew him not. 11 He came unto his own, and his own received him not. 12 But as many as received him, to them gave he power to become the sons of God, *even* to them that believe on his name: 13 Which were born, not of blood, nor of the will of the flesh, nor of the will of man, but of God. 14 And the Word was made flesh, and dwelt among us, (and we beheld his glory, the glory as of the only begotten of the Father,) full of grace and truth.

15 John bare witness of him, and cried, saying, This was he of whom I spake, He that cometh after me is preferred before me; for he was before me. 16 And of his fulness have all we received, and grace for grace. 17 For the law was given by Moses, *but* grace and truth came by Jesus Christ. 18 No man hath seen God at any time; the only begotten Son, which is in the bosom of the Father, he hath declared *him*.

19 And this is the record of John, when the Jews sent priests and Levites from Jerusalem to ask him, Who art thou? 20 And he confessed, and denied not; but confessed, I am not the Christ. 21 And they asked him, What then? Art thou Elias? And he saith, I am not. Art thou that Prophet? And he answered, No. 22 Then said they unto him, Who art thou? that we may give an answer to them that sent us. What sayest

1 In the beginning was the Word, and the Word was with God, and the Word was God. 2 He was with God in the beginning. 3 Through him all things were made; without him nothing was made that has been made. 4 In him was life, and that life was the light of men. 5 The light shines in the darkness, but the darkness has not understood *a* it.

6 There came a man who was sent from God; his name was John. 7 He came as a witness to testify concerning that light, so that through him all men might believe. 8 He himself was not the light; he came only as a witness to the light. 9 The true light that gives light to every man was coming into the world. *b*

10 He was in the world, and though the world was made through him, the world did not recognize him. 11 He came to that which was his own, but his own did not receive him. 12 Yet to all who received him, to those who believed in his name, he gave the right to become children of God— 13 children born not of natural descent, *c* nor of human decision or a husband's will, but born of God. 14 The Word became flesh and lived for a while among us. We have seen his glory, the glory of the one and only [Son] *d*, who came from the Father, full of grace and truth.

15 John testifies concerning him. He cries out, saying, "This was he of whom I said, 'He who comes after me has surpassed me because he was before me.'" 16 From the fullness of his grace we have all received one blessing after another. 17 For the law was given through Moses; grace and truth came through Jesus Christ. 18 No man has ever seen God, but God the only *e* [Son], *f* who is at the Father's side, has made him known.

John the Baptist denies being the Christ

19 Now this was John's testimony when the Jews of Jerusalem sent priests and Levites to ask him who he was. 20 He did not fail to confess, but confessed freely, "I am not the Christ. *g* "

21 They asked him, "Then who are you? Are you Elijah?"
He said, "I am not."
"Are you the Prophet?"
He answered, "No."

22 Finally they said, "Who are you? Give us an answer to take back to those who sent us. What do you say about yourself?"

[a] Or *overpowered.* [b] Or *This was the true light that gives light to every man who comes into the world.* [c] Greek *of bloods.* [d] Or the *Only Begotten.* [e] Or *but God the only Begotten.* [f] Some MSS read *but the only Son* (or *but the only begotten Son*). [g] Or *Messiah.* "The Christ" (Greek) and "the Messiah" (Hebrew) both mean "the Anointed One."

ΚΑΤΑ   ΙΩΑΝΝΗΝ

Chapter 1

'Εν ἀρχῇ ἦν ὁ λόγος, καὶ ὁ λόγος
In [the] beginning was the Word, and the Word
ἦν πρὸς τὸν θεόν, καὶ θεὸς ἦν ὁ λόγος.
was with - God, and God was the Word.*
2 οὗτος ἦν ἐν ἀρχῇ πρὸς τὸν θεόν.
This one was in [the] beginning with - God.
3 πάντα δι' αὐτοῦ ἐγένετο, καὶ χωρὶς
All things through him became, and without
αὐτοῦ ἐγένετο οὐδὲ ἕν ὃ γέγονεν. 4 ἐν
him became not one thing which has become. In
αὐτῷ ζωὴ ἦν, καὶ ἡ ζωὴ ἦν τὸ φῶς
him life was, and the life was the light
τῶν ἀνθρώπων· 5 καὶ τὸ φῶς ἐν τῇ
- of men; and the light in the
σκοτίᾳ φαίνει, καὶ ἡ σκοτία αὐτὸ οὐ
darkness shines, and the darkness it not
κατέλαβεν. 6 'Εγένετο ἄνθρωπος, ἀπεσταλμένος
overtook. There was a man, having been sent
παρὰ θεοῦ, ὄνομα αὐτῷ 'Ιωάννης· 7 οὗτος
from God, name to him⁰ John; this man
ἦλθεν εἰς μαρτυρίαν, ἵνα μαρτυρήσῃ περὶ
came for witness, that he might witness concerning
τοῦ φωτός, ἵνα πάντες πιστεύσωσιν δι'
the light, that all men might believe through
αὐτοῦ. 8 οὐκ ἦν ἐκεῖνος τὸ φῶς, ἀλλ' ἵνα
him. He was not that - light, but that
μαρτυρήσῃ περὶ τοῦ φωτός. 9 Ἦν τὸ φῶς
he might witness concerning the light. It was the light
τὸ ἀληθινόν, ὃ φωτίζει πάντα ἄνθρωπον,
- true, which enlightens every man,
ἐρχόμενον εἰς τὸν κόσμον. 10 ἐν τῷ
coming into the world. In the
κόσμῳ ἦν, καὶ ὁ κόσμος δι' αὐτοῦ
world he was, and the world through him
ἐγένετο, καὶ ὁ κόσμος αὐτὸν οὐκ ἔγνω.
became, and the world him knew not.
11 εἰς τὰ ἴδια ἦλθεν, καὶ οἱ ἴδιοι αὐτὸν
To his own things he came, and his own people him
οὐ παρέλαβον. 12 ὅσοι δὲ ἔλαβον αὐτόν,
received not. But as many as received him,
ἔδωκεν αὐτοῖς ἐξουσίαν τέκνα θεοῦ γεν-
he gave to them right children of God to be-
έσθαι, τοῖς πιστεύουσιν εἰς τὸ ὄνομα αὐτοῦ,
come, to the [ones] believing in the name of him,
13 οἳ οὐκ ἐξ αἱμάτων οὐδὲ ἐκ θελήματος
who not of bloods nor of [the] will
σαρκὸς οὐδὲ ἐκ θελήματος ἀνδρὸς ἀλλ'
of [the] flesh nor of [the] will of a man but
ἐκ θεοῦ ἐγεννήθησαν. 14 Καὶ ὁ λόγος
of God were born. And the Word

σὰρξ ἐγένετο καὶ ἐσκήνωσεν ἐν ἡμῖν,
flesh became and tabernacled among us,
καὶ ἐθεασάμεθα τὴν δόξαν αὐτοῦ, δόξαν
and we beheld the glory of him, glory
ὡς μονογενοῦς παρὰ πατρός, πλήρης χάριτος
as of an only begotten from a father, full of grace
καὶ ἀληθείας. 15 'Ιωάννης μαρτυρεῖ περὶ
and of truth. John witnesses concerning
αὐτοῦ καὶ κέκραγεν λέγων· οὗτος ἦν ὃν
him and has cried out saying : This man was he whom
εἶπον· ὁ ὀπίσω μου ἐρχόμενος ἔμπροσθέν
I said : The [one] after me coming before
μου γέγονεν, ὅτι πρῶτός μου ἦν. 16 ὅτι
me has become, because first of me he was. Because
ἐκ τοῦ πληρώματος αὐτοῦ ἡμεῖς πάντες
of the fulness of him we all
ἐλάβομεν, καὶ χάριν ἀντὶ χάριτος· 17 ὅτι
received, and grace instead of grace; because
ὁ νόμος διὰ Μωϋσέως ἐδόθη, ἡ χάρις καὶ
the law through Moses was given, the grace and
ἡ ἀλήθεια διὰ 'Ιησοῦ Χριστοῦ ἐγένετο.
the truth through Jesus Christ became.
18 Θεὸν οὐδεὶς ἑώρακεν πώποτε· μονογενὴς
God no man has seen never; [the] only begotten
θεὸς ὁ ὢν εἰς τὸν κόλπον τοῦ πατρός,
God the [one] being in the bosom of the Father,
ἐκεῖνος ἐξηγήσατο.
that one declared [?him].

19 Καὶ αὕτη ἐστὶν ἡ μαρτυρία τοῦ
And this is the witness of the
'Ιωάννου, ὅτε ἀπέστειλαν πρὸς αὐτὸν οἱ
of John, when ³sent ⁴to ⁵him ¹the
'Ιουδαῖοι ἐξ 'Ιεροσολύμων ἱερεῖς καὶ Λευίτας
²Jews ⁶from ¹⁰Jerusalem ⁷priests ⁸'Levites
ἵνα ἐρωτήσωσιν αὐτόν· σὺ τίς εἶ; 20 καὶ
that they might ask him : Thou who art? And
ὡμολόγησεν καὶ οὐκ ἠρνήσατο, καὶ
he confessed and denied not, and
ὡμολόγησεν ὅτι ἐγὼ οὐκ εἰμὶ ὁ χριστός.
he confessed[,] - I am not the Christ.
21 καὶ ἠρώτησαν αὐτόν· τί οὖν; 'Ηλίας εἶ
And they asked him: What then? Elias art
σύ; καὶ λέγει· οὐκ εἰμί. ὁ προφήτης εἶ σύ;
thou? And he says : I am not. The prophet art thou?
καὶ ἀπεκρίθη· οὔ. 22 εἶπαν οὖν αὐτῷ·
And he answered : No. They said therefore to him :
τίς εἶ; ἵνα ἀπόκρισιν δῶμεν τοῖς
Who art thou? that an answer we may give to the [ones]
πέμψασιν ἡμᾶς· τί λέγεις περὶ σεαυτοῦ;
having sent us; What sayest thou concerning thyself?

---

* But note that the subject has the article and the predicate
has it not; hence translate—" the Word was God ."

265

King James Version

thou of thyself? 23 He said, I *am* the voice of one crying in the wilderness, Make straight the way of the Lord, as said the prophet Esaias. 24And they which were sent were of the Pharisees. 25And they asked him, and said unto him, Why baptizest thou then, if thou be not that Christ, nor Elias, neither that Prophet? 26 John answered them, saying, I baptize with water: but there standeth one among you, whom ye know not; 27 He it is, who coming after me is preferred before me, whose shoe's latchet I am not worthy to unloose. 28 These things were done in Bethabara beyond Jordan, where John was baptizing.

29 The next day John seeth Jesus coming unto him, and saith, Behold the Lamb of God, which taketh away the sin of the world! 30 This is he of whom I said, After me cometh a man which is preferred before me; for he was before me. 31And I knew him not: but that he should be made manifest to Israel, therefore am I come baptizing with water. 32And John bare record, saying, I saw the Spirit descending from heaven like a dove, and it abode upon him. 33And I knew him not: but he that sent me to baptize with water, the same said unto me, Upon whom thou shalt see the Spirit descending, and remaining on him, the same is he which baptizeth with the Holy Ghost. 34And I saw, and bare record that this is the Son of God.

35 Again the next day after, John stood, and two of his disciples; 36And looking upon Jesus as he walked, he saith, Behold the Lamb of God! 37And the two disciples heard him speak, and they followed Jesus. 38 Then Jesus turned, and saw them following, and saith unto them, What seek ye? They said unto him, Rabbi, (which is to say, being interpreted, Master,) where dwellest thou? 39 He saith unto them, Come and see. They came and saw where he dwelt, and abode with him that day: for it was about the tenth hour. 40 One of the two which heard John *speak,* and followed him, was Andrew, Simon Peter's brother. 41 He first findeth his own brother Simon, and saith unto him, We have found the Messias, which is, being interpreted, the Christ. 42And he brought him to Jesus. And when Jesus beheld him, he said, Thou art Simon the son of Jona: thou shalt be called Cephas, which is by interpretation, A stone.

43 The day following Jesus would go forth into Galilee, and findeth Philip, and saith unto him, Follow me. 44 Now Philip was of Bethsaida, the city of Andrew and Peter. 45 Philip findeth Nathanael, and saith unto him, We have found him, of whom Moses in the law, and the proph-

New International Version

23 John replied in the words of Isaiah the prophet, "I am the voice of one calling in the desert, 'Make straight the way for the Lord.' " [h]

24 Now some Pharisees who had been sent 25 questioned him, "Why then do you baptize if you are not the Christ,[g] nor Elijah, nor the Prophet?"

26 "I baptize with[i] water," John replied, "but among you stands one you do not know. 27 He is the one who comes after me, the thongs of whose sandals I am not worthy to untie."

28 This all happened at Bethany on the other side of the Jordan, where John was baptizing.

Jesus the Lamb of God

29 The next day John saw Jesus coming toward him and said, "Look, the Lamb of God, who takes away the sin of the world! 30 This is the one I meant when I said, 'A man who comes after me has surpassed me because he was before me.' 31 I myself did not know him, but the reason I came baptizing with[i] water was that he might be revealed to Israel."

32 Then John gave this testimony: "I saw the Spirit come down from heaven as a dove and remain on him. 33 I would not have known him, except that the one who sent me to baptize with[i] water told me, 'The man on whom you see the Spirit come down and remain is he who will baptize with the Holy Spirit.' 34 I have seen and I testify that this is the Son of God."

Jesus' first disciples

35 The next day John was there again with two of his disciples. 36 When he saw Jesus passing by, he said, "Look, the Lamb of God!"

37 When the two disciples heard him say this, they followed Jesus. 38 Turning around, Jesus saw them following and asked, "What do you want?"

They said, "Rabbi" (which means, Teacher), "where are you staying?"

39 "Come," he replied, "and you will see."

So they went and saw where he was staying, and spent that day with him. It was about the tenth hour.

40 Andrew, Simon Peter's brother, was one of the two who heard what John had said and who had followed Jesus. 41 The first thing Andrew did was to find his brother Simon and tell him, "We have found the Messiah" (that is, the Christ).

42 Then he brought Simon to Jesus, who looked at him and said, "You are Simon, the son of John. You will be called Cephas" (which, when translated, is Peter[k]).

Jesus calls Philip and Nathanael

43 The next day Jesus decided to leave for Galilee. Finding Philip, he said to him, "Follow me."

44 Philip, like Andrew and Peter, was from the town of Bethsaida. 45 Philip found Nathanael and told him, "We have found the one Moses wrote about in the Law, and about

---

[h] Isaiah 40:3. [g] Or *Messiah.* "The Christ" (Greek) and "the Messiah" (Hebrew) both men "the Anointed One." [i] Or *in.* [k] Both Cephas (Aramaic) and Peter (Greek) mean *rock.*

Greek Interlinear

23 ἔφη· ἐγὼ φωνὴ βοῶντος ἐν τῇ ἐρήμῳ·
He said : I [am] a voice of [one] crying in the desert :

εὐθύνατε τὴν ὁδὸν κυρίου, καθὼς εἶπεν
Make straight the way of [the] Lord, as said

Ἡσαΐας ὁ προφήτης. **24** Καὶ ἀπεσταλμένοι
Esaias the prophet. And [the ones] *having been* sent

ἦσαν ἐκ τῶν Φαρισαίων. **25** καὶ ἠρώτησαν
were of the Pharisees. And they asked

αὐτὸν καὶ εἶπαν αὐτῷ· τι οὖν βαπτίζεις
him and said to him: Why then baptizest thou

εἰ σὺ οὐκ εἶ ὁ χριστὸς οὐδὲ Ἠλίας
if thou art not the Christ nor Elias

οὐδὲ ὁ προφήτης; **26** ἀπεκρίθη αὐτοῖς ὁ
nor the prophet? Answered them -

Ἰωάννης λέγων· ἐγὼ βαπτίζω ἐν ὕδατι·
John saying : I baptize in water;

μέσος ὑμῶν στήκει ὃν ὑμεῖς οὐκ οἴδατε,
among you stands [one] whom ye know not,

27 ὁ ὀπίσω μου ἐρχόμενος, οὗ οὐκ εἰμὶ
the [one] after me coming, of whom am not

ἐγὼ ἄξιος ἵνα λύσω αὐτοῦ τὸν ἱμάντα
I worthy that I should loosen of him the thong

τοῦ ὑποδήματος. **28** Ταῦτα ἐν Βηθανίᾳ
of the sandal. These things in Bethany

ἐγένετο πέραν τοῦ Ἰορδάνου, ὅπου ἦν ὁ
happened beyond the Jordan, where was -

Ἰωάννης βαπτίζων. **29** Τῇ ἐπαύριον βλέπει
John baptizing. On the morrow he sees

τὸν Ἰησοῦν ἐρχόμενον πρὸς αὐτόν, καὶ
- Jesus coming toward him, and

λέγει· ἴδε ὁ ἀμνὸς τοῦ θεοῦ ὁ αἴρων
says : Behold[,] the Lamb - of God - taking

τὴν ἁμαρτίαν τοῦ κόσμου. **30** οὗτός ἐστιν
the sin of the world. This is he

ὑπὲρ οὗ ἐγὼ εἶπον· ὀπίσω μου ἔρχεται
as to whom I said : After me comes

ἀνὴρ ὃς ἔμπροσθέν μου γέγονεν, ὅτι
a man who before me has become, because

πρῶτός μου ἦν. **31** κἀγὼ οὐκ ᾔδειν
first of me he was. And I knew not

αὐτόν, ἀλλ᾽ ἵνα φανερωθῇ τῷ Ἰσραήλ,
him, but that he might be manifested - to Israel,

διὰ τοῦτο ἦλθον ἐγὼ ἐν ὕδατι βαπτίζων.
therefore came I in water baptizing.

32 Καὶ ἐμαρτύρησεν Ἰωάννης λέγων ὅτι
And witnessed John saying[,] -

τεθέαμαι τὸ πνεῦμα καταβαῖνον ὡς
I have beheld the Spirit coming down as

περιστερὰν ἐξ οὐρανοῦ, καὶ ἔμεινεν ἐπ᾽
a dove out of heaven, and he remained on

αὐτόν. **33** κἀγὼ οὐκ ᾔδειν αὐτόν, ἀλλ᾽
him. And I knew not him, but

ὁ πέμψας με βαπτίζειν ἐν ὕδατι, ἐκεῖνός
the [one] having sent me to baptize in water, that [one]

μοι εἶπεν· ἐφ᾽ ὃν ἂν ἴδῃς τὸ πνεῦμα
to me said : On whomever thou seest the Spirit

καταβαῖνον καὶ μένον ἐπ᾽ αὐτόν, οὗτός
coming down and remaining on him, this

ἐστιν ὁ βαπτίζων ἐν πνεύματι ἁγίῳ.
is the [one] baptizing in Spirit Holy.

34 κἀγὼ ἑώρακα, καὶ μεμαρτύρηκα ὅτι
And I have seen, and have witnessed that

οὗτός ἐστιν ὁ υἱὸς τοῦ θεοῦ.
this [one] is the Son - of God.

35 Τῇ ἐπαύριον πάλιν εἱστήκει ὁ Ἰωάννης
On the morrow again stood - John

καὶ ἐκ τῶν μαθητῶν αὐτοῦ δύο, **36** καὶ
and of the disciples of him two, and

ἐμβλέψας τῷ Ἰησοῦ περιπατοῦντι λέγει·
looking at - Jesus walking he says :

ἴδε ὁ ἀμνὸς τοῦ θεοῦ. **37** καὶ ἤκουσαν
Behold[,] the Lamb - of God. And ⁴heard

οἱ δύο μαθηταὶ αὐτοῦ λαλοῦντος καὶ
¹the ²two ³disciples ⁴him ⁵speaking and

ἠκολούθησαν τῷ Ἰησοῦ. **38** στραφεὶς δὲ
they followed - Jesus. And ³turning

ὁ Ἰησοῦς καὶ θεασάμενος αὐτοὺς ἀκολουθοῦντας
- ¹Jesus and beholding them following

λέγει αὐτοῖς· τί ζητεῖτε; οἱ δὲ εἶπαν
says to them : What seek ye? And they said

αὐτῷ· ῥαββὶ (ὃ λέγεται μεθερμηνευόμενον
to him : Rabbi (which is called being translated

διδάσκαλε), ποῦ μένεις; **39** λέγει αὐτοῖς·
Teacher), where remainest thou? He says to them :

ἔρχεσθε καὶ ὄψεσθε. ἦλθαν οὖν καὶ εἶδαν
Come and ye will see. They went therefore and saw

ποῦ μένει, καὶ παρ᾽ αὐτῷ ἔμειναν τὴν
where he remains(ed), and with him remained -

ἡμέραν ἐκείνην· ὥρα ἦν ὡς δεκάτη.
day that; hour was about tenth.

40 Ἦν Ἀνδρέας ὁ ἀδελφὸς Σίμωνος Πέτρου
It was Andrew the brother of Simon Peter

εἷς ἐκ τῶν δύο τῶν ἀκουσάντων παρὰ
one of the two - hearing from

Ἰωάννου καὶ ἀκολουθησάντων αὐτῷ·
John and following him;

41 εὑρίσκει οὗτος πρῶτον τὸν ἀδελφὸν τὸν
²finds ¹this one ³first ⁴the(his) ⁵brother -

ἴδιον Σίμωνα καὶ λέγει αὐτῷ· εὑρήκαμεν
⁶own Simon and tells him : We have found

τὸν Μεσσίαν (ὅ ἐστιν μεθερμηνευόμενον
the Messiah (which is being translated

χριστός). **42** ἤγαγεν αὐτὸν πρὸς τὸν
Christ). He led him to -

Ἰησοῦν. ἐμβλέψας αὐτῷ ὁ Ἰησοῦς εἶπεν·
Jesus. Looking at him - Jesus said :

σὺ εἶ Σίμων ὁ υἱὸς Ἰωάννου, σὺ κληθήσῃ
Thou art Simon the son of John, thou shalt be called

Κηφᾶς (ὃ ἑρμηνεύεται Πέτρος). **43** Τῇ
Cephas (which is translated Peter). On the

ἐπαύριον ἠθέλησεν ἐξελθεῖν εἰς τὴν Γαλιλαίαν,
morrow he wished to go forth into - Galilee,

καὶ εὑρίσκει Φίλιππον. καὶ λέγει αὐτῷ ὁ
and finds Philip. And says to him -

Ἰησοῦς· ἀκολούθει μοι. **44** ἦν δὲ ὁ
Jesus : Follow me. Now was -

Φίλιππος ἀπὸ Βηθσαϊδά, ἐκ τῆς πόλεως
Philip from Bethsaida, of the city

Ἀνδρέου καὶ Πέτρου. **45** εὑρίσκει Φίλιππος
of Andrew and of Peter. ²Finds ¹Philip

τὸν Ναθαναὴλ καὶ λέγει αὐτῷ· ὃν ἔγραψεν
- ²Nathanael and tells him : [He] whom wrote

Μωϋσῆς ἐν τῷ νόμῳ καὶ οἱ προφῆται
Moses in the law and the prophets

King James Version

ets, did write, Jesus of Nazareth, the son of Joseph. 46And Nathanael said unto him, Can there any good thing come out of Nazareth? Philip saith unto him, Come and see. 47 Jesus saw Nathanael coming to him, and saith of him, Behold an Israelite indeed, in whom is no guile! 48 Nathanael saith unto him, Whence knowest thou me? Jesus answered and said unto him, Before that Philip called thee, when thou wast under the fig tree, I saw thee. 49 Nathanael answered and saith unto him, Rabbi, thou art the Son of God; thou art the King of Israel. 50 Jesus answered and said unto him, Because I said unto thee, I saw thee under the fig tree, believest thou? thou shalt see greater things than these. 51And he saith unto him, Verily, verily, I say unto you, Hereafter ye shall see heaven open, and the angels of God ascending and descending upon the Son of man.

2 And the third day there was a marriage in Cana of Galilee; and the mother of Jesus was there: 2And both Jesus was called, and his disciples, to the marriage. 3And when they wanted wine, the mother of Jesus saith unto him, They have no wine. 4 Jesus saith unto her, Woman, what have I to do with thee? mine hour is not yet come. 5 His mother saith unto the servants, Whatsoever he saith unto you, do it. 6And there were set there six waterpots of stone, after the manner of the purifying of the Jews, containing two or three firkins apiece. 7 Jesus saith unto them, Fill the waterpots with water. And they filled them up to the brim. 8And he saith unto them, Draw out now, and bear unto the governor of the feast. And they bare it. 9 When the ruler of the feast had tasted the water that was made wine, and knew not whence it was, (but the servants which drew the water knew,) the governor of the feast called the bridegroom, 10And saith unto him, Every man at the beginning doth set forth good wine; and when men have well drunk, then that which is worse: but thou hast kept the good wine until now. 11 This beginning of miracles did Jesus in Cana of Galilee, and manifested forth his glory; and his disciples believed on him.

12 After this he went down to Capernaum, he, and his mother, and his brethren, and his disciples; and they continued there not many days.

13 And the Jews' passover was at hand, and Jesus went up to Jerusalem, 14And found in the temple those that sold oxen and sheep and doves, and the changers of money sitting: 15And when he had made a scourge of small cords, he drove them all out of the temple, and the sheep, and the oxen; and poured out the changers' money, and overthrew the tables; 16And said unto them that sold doves, Take these things hence; make not my Father's house a house of

New International Version

whom the prophets also wrote—Jesus of Nazareth, the son of Joseph."

46 "Nazareth! Can anything good come from there?" Nathanael asked.

"Come and see," said Philip.

47 When Jesus saw Nathanael approaching, he said of him, "Here is a true Israelite, in whom there is nothing false."

48 "How do you know me?" Nathanael asked.

Jesus answered, "I saw you while you were still under the fig tree before Philip called you."

49 Then Nathanael declared, "Rabbi, you are the Son of God; you are the King of Israel."

50 Jesus said, "You believe[l] because I told you I saw you under the fig tree. You shall see greater things than that." 51 He then added, "I tell you the truth, you shall all see heaven open, and the angels of God ascending and descending on the Son of Man."

Jesus changes water to wine

2 On the third day a wedding took place at Cana in Galilee. Jesus' mother was there, 2 and Jesus and his disciples had also been invited to the wedding. 3 When the wine was gone, Jesus' mother said to him, "They have no more wine."

4 "Why do you involve me[m]?" Jesus replied, "My time has not yet come."

5 His mother said to the servants, "Do whatever he tells you."

6 Nearby stood six stone water jars, the kind used by the Jews for ceremonial washing, each holding from twenty to thirty gallons.

7 Jesus said to the servants, "Fill the jars with water"; so they filled them to the brim.

8 Then he told them, "Now draw some out and take it to the master of the banquet."

They did so, 9 and the master of the banquet tasted the water that had been turned into wine. He did not realize where it had come from, though the servants who had drawn the water knew. Then he called the bridegroom aside 10 and said, "Everyone brings out the choice wine first and then the cheaper wine after the guests have had too much to drink; but you have saved the best till now."

11 This, the first of his miraculous signs, Jesus performed in Cana of Galilee. He thus revealed his glory, and his disciples put their faith in him.

Jesus clears the temple

12 After this he went down to Capernaum with his mother and brothers and his disciples. Here they stayed for a few days.

13 When it was almost time for the Jewish Passover, Jesus went up to Jerusalem. 14 In the temple court he found men selling cattle, sheep and doves, and others sitting at tables exchanging money. 15 So he made a whip out of cords, and drove all from the temple area, both sheep and cattle; he scattered the coins of the moneychangers and overturned their tables. 16 To those who sold doves, he said, "Get these out of here! How dare you turn my Father's house into a market!"

[l] Or Do you believe. . . ? [m] Greek involve me, woman (a polite form of address).

Greek Interlinear

εὑρήκαμεν, Ἰησοῦν υἱὸν τοῦ Ἰωσὴφ τὸν
we have found, Jesus   son   - of Joseph -

ἀπὸ Ναζαρέθ. 46 καὶ εἶπεν αὐτῷ
from Nazareth.   And said to him

Ναθαναήλ· ἐκ Ναζαρὲθ δύναταί τι ἀγαθὸν
Nathanael : Out of Nazareth can anything good

εἶναι; λέγει αὐτῷ ὁ Φίλιππος· ἔρχου καὶ
to be? Says to him - Philip : Come and

ἴδε. 47 εἶδεν Ἰησοῦς τὸν Ναθαναὴλ
see.   ᵇSaw ᶦJesus   - ²Nathanael

ἐρχόμενον πρὸς αὐτὸν καὶ λέγει περὶ
coming   toward him   and says concerning

αὐτοῦ· ἴδε ἀληθῶς Ἰσραηλίτης, ἐν ᾧ
him :   Behold truly an Israelite, in whom

δόλος οὐκ ἔστιν. 48 λέγει αὐτῷ Ναθαναήλ·
guile   is not.   Says to him Nathanael :

πόθεν με γινώσκεις; ἀπεκρίθη Ἰησοῦς καὶ
Whence me knowest thou? Answered Jesus and

εἶπεν αὐτῷ· πρὸ τοῦ σε Φίλιππον φωνῆσαι
said to him : Before the thee Philip   to callᵇ
                                        = Philip called thee

ὄντα ὑπὸ τὴν συκῆν εἶδόν σε. 49 ἀπεκρίθη
being under the fig-tree I saw thee.   Answered

αὐτῷ Ναθαναήλ· ῥαββί, σὺ εἶ ὁ υἱὸς τοῦ
him Nathanael : Rabbi, thou art the Son -

θεοῦ, σὺ βασιλεὺς εἶ τοῦ Ἰσραήλ.
of God, thou king art - of Israel.

50 ἀπεκρίθη Ἰησοῦς καὶ εἶπεν αὐτῷ·
   Answered Jesus and said to him :

ὅτι εἶπόν σοι ὅτι εἶδόν σε ὑποκάτω τῆς
Because I told thee that I saw thee underneath the

συκῆς, πιστεύεις; μείζω τούτων ὄψῃ.
fig-tree, believest thou? greater [than] these things thou shalt see.

51 καὶ λέγει αὐτῷ· ἀμὴν ἀμὴν λέγω
   And he says to him : Truly truly I tell

ὑμῖν, ὄψεσθε τὸν οὐρανὸν ἀνεῳγότα καὶ
you, ye shall see the heaven having been opened and

τοὺς ἀγγέλους τοῦ θεοῦ ἀναβαίνοντας καὶ
the   angels   - of God going up   and

καταβαίνοντας ἐπὶ τὸν υἱὸν τοῦ ἀνθρώπου.
coming down   on the Son - of man.

Chapter 2

Καὶ τῇ ἡμέρᾳ τῇ τρίτῃ γάμος ἐγένετο
And on the day the third a wedding there was

ἐν Κανὰ τῆς Γαλιλαίας, καὶ ἦν ἡ μήτηρ
in Cana - of Galilee, and was the mother

τοῦ Ἰησοῦ ἐκεῖ· 2 ἐκλήθη δὲ καὶ ὁ
- of Jesus there;   and was invited both -

Ἰησοῦς καὶ οἱ μαθηταὶ αὐτοῦ εἰς τὸν
Jesus and the disciples of him to the

γάμον. 3 καὶ ὑστερήσαντος οἴνου λέγει ἡ
wedding. And lacking   wineᵇ says the
                          = when wine was lacking

μήτηρ τοῦ Ἰησοῦ πρὸς αὐτόν· οἶνον
mother - of Jesus to   him :   Wine

οὐκ ἔχουσιν. 4 καὶ λέγει αὐτῇ ὁ Ἰησοῦς·
they have not.   And says to her - Jesus :

τί ἐμοὶ καὶ σοί, γύναι; οὔπω ἥκει ἡ
What to me and to thee, woman? not yet is come the

ὥρα μου. 5 λέγει ἡ μήτηρ αὐτοῦ τοῖς
hour of me.   Says the mother of him to the

διακόνοις· ὅ τι ἂν λέγῃ ὑμῖν, ποιήσατε.
servants : Whatever he tells you, do ye.

6 ἦσαν δὲ ἐκεῖ λίθιναι ὑδρίαι ἓξ κατὰ
Now there were there stone water-pots six according to

τὸν καθαρισμὸν τῶν Ἰουδαίων κείμεναι,
the purifying of the Jews   lying,

χωροῦσαι ἀνὰ μετρητὰς δύο ἢ τρεῖς.
containing each† measures two or three.

7 λέγει αὐτοῖς ὁ Ἰησοῦς· γεμίσατε τὰς
Tells them   - Jesus : Fill ye the

ὑδρίας ὕδατος. καὶ ἐγέμισαν αὐτὰς ἕως
water-pots of(with) water. And they filled them up to

ἄνω. 8 καὶ λέγει αὐτοῖς· ἀντλήσατε νῦν
[the] top. And he tells them : Draw   now

καὶ φέρετε τῷ ἀρχιτρικλίνῳ. οἱ δὲ
and carry to the master of the feast. And they

ἤνεγκαν. 9 ὡς δὲ ἐγεύσατο ὁ ἀρχιτρίκλινος
carried.   But when tasted the master of the feast

τὸ ὕδωρ οἶνον γεγενημένον, καὶ οὐκ ᾔδει
the water ¹wine ²having become, and did not know

πόθεν ἐστίν, οἱ δὲ διάκονοι ᾔδεισαν οἱ
whence it is(was), but the servants knew the [ones]

ἠντληκότες τὸ ὕδωρ, φωνεῖ τὸν νυμφίον
having drawn the water, ᵇcalls ᵃthe ᵇbridegroom

ὁ ἀρχιτρίκλινος 10 καὶ λέγει αὐτῷ· πᾶς
¹the ²master of the feast   and says to him : Every

ἄνθρωπος πρῶτον τὸν καλὸν οἶνον τίθησιν,
man   first   the good wine sets forth,

καὶ ὅταν μεθυσθῶσιν τὸν ἐλάσσω· σὺ
and when they become drunk the worse; thou

τετήρηκας τὸν καλὸν οἶνον ἕως ἄρτι.
hast kept the good wine until now.

11 Ταύτην ἐποίησεν ἀρχὴν τῶν σημείων ὁ
   ¹This ⁴did ²beginning ³of the ⁵signs -

Ἰησοῦς ἐν Κανὰ τῆς Γαλιλαίας καὶ
Jesus in Cana - of Galilee and

ἐφανέρωσεν τὴν δόξαν αὐτοῦ, καὶ ἐπίστευσαν
manifested the glory of him, and believed

εἰς αὐτὸν οἱ μαθηταὶ αὐτοῦ.
in him   the disciples of him.

12 Μετὰ τοῦτο κατέβη εἰς Καφαρναοὺμ
   After this went down to Capernaum

αὐτὸς καὶ ἡ μήτηρ αὐτοῦ καὶ
he   and the mother of him and

οἱ ἀδελφοὶ καὶ οἱ μαθηταὶ αὐτοῦ, καὶ
the brothers and the disciples of him, and

ἐκεῖ ἔμειναν οὐ πολλὰς ἡμέρας.
there remained not many days.

13 Καὶ ἐγγὺς ἦν τὸ πάσχα τῶν Ἰουδαίων,
   And near was the Passover of the Jews,

καὶ ἀνέβη εἰς Ἱεροσόλυμα ὁ Ἰησοῦς.
and went up to Jerusalem - Jesus.

14 καὶ εὗρεν ἐν τῷ ἱερῷ τοὺς πωλοῦντας
   And he found in the temple the [ones] selling

βόας καὶ πρόβατα καὶ περιστερὰς καὶ τοὺς
oxen and sheep and doves   and the

κερματιστὰς καθημένους, 15 καὶ ποιήσας
coindealers sitting,   and having made

φραγέλλιον ἐκ σχοινίων πάντας ἐξέβαλεν
a lash   out of ropes ²all ¹he expelled

ἐκ τοῦ ἱεροῦ, τά τε πρόβατα καὶ τοὺς
out of the temple, both the sheep and the

βόας, καὶ τῶν κολλυβιστῶν ἐξέχεεν τὰ
oxen, and ⁴of the ⁵moneychangers ¹poured out ²the

κέρματα καὶ τὰς τραπέζας ἀνέτρεψεν,
³coins and ⁶the ⁷tables ¹overturned,

16 καὶ τοῖς τὰς περιστερὰς πωλοῦσιν
   and ²to the [ones] ⁴the ⁵doves ³selling

εἶπεν· ἄρατε ταῦτα ἐντεῦθεν, μὴ ποιεῖτε
¹said : Take these things hence, do not make

τὸν οἶκον τοῦ πατρός μου οἶκον ἐμπορίου.
the house of the Father of me a house of merchandise.

269

King James Version

merchandise. 17And his disciples remembered that it was written, The zeal of thine house hath eaten me up.

18 Then answered the Jews and said unto him, What sign shewest thou unto us, seeing that thou doest these things? 19 Jesus answered and said unto them, Destroy this temple, and in three days I will raise it up. 20 Then said the Jews, Forty and six years was this temple in building, and wilt thou rear it up in three days? 21 But he spake of the temple of his body. 22 When therefore he was risen from the dead, his disciples remembered that he had said this unto them; and they believed the Scripture, and the word which Jesus had said.

23 Now when he was in Jerusalem at the passover, in the feast *day,* many believed in his name, when they saw the miracles which he did. 24 But Jesus did not commit himself unto them, because he knew all *men,* 25And needed not that any should testify of man: for he knew what was in man.

3 There was a man of the Pharisees, named Nicodemus, a ruler of the Jews: 2 The same came to Jesus by night, and said unto him, Rabbi, we know that thou art a teacher come from God: for no man can do these miracles that thou doest, except God be with him. 3 Jesus answered and said unto him, Verily, verily, I say unto thee, Except a man be born again, he cannot see the kingdom of God. 4 Nicodemus saith unto him, How can a man be born when he is old? can he enter the second time into his mother's womb, and be born? 5 Jesus answered, Verily, verily, I say unto thee, Except a man be born of water and *of* the Spirit, he cannot enter into the kingdom of God. 6 That which is born of the flesh is flesh; and that which is born of the Spirit is spirit. 7 Marvel not that I said unto thee, Ye must be born again. 8 The wind bloweth where it listeth, and thou hearest the sound thereof, but canst not tell whence it cometh, and whither it goeth: so is every one that is born of the Spirit. 9 Nicodemus answered and said unto him, How can these things be? 10 Jesus answered and said unto him, Art thou a master of Israel, and knowest not these things? 11 Verily, verily, I say unto thee, We speak that we do know, and testify that we have seen; and ye receive not our witness. 12 If I have told you earthly things, and ye believe not, how shall ye believe, if I tell you *of* heavenly things? 13And no man hath ascended up to heaven, but he that came down from heaven, *even* the Son of man which is in heaven.

14 And as Moses lifted up the serpent in the wilderness, even so must the Son of man be

New International Version

17 His disciples remembered that it is written: "Zeal for your house will consume me." *n*

18 Then the Jews demanded of him, "What miraculous sign can you show us to prove your authority to do all this?"

19 Jesus answered them, "Destroy this temple, and I will raise it again in three days."

20 The Jews replied, "It has taken forty-six years to build this temple, and you are going to raise it in three days?" 21 But the temple he had spoken of was his body. 22After he was raised from the dead, his disciples recalled what he had said. Then they believed the Scripture and the words that Jesus had spoken.

23 Now while he was in Jerusalem at the Passover Feast, many people saw the miraculous signs he was doing and trusted in his name.*o* 24 But Jesus would not trust himself to them, for he knew all men. 25 He did not need man's testimony about man, for he knew what was in a man.

Jesus teaches Nicodemus

3 Now there was a man of the Pharisees named Nicodemus, a member of the Jewish ruling council. 2 He came to Jesus at night and said, "Rabbi, we know you are a teacher who has come from God. For no one could perform the miraculous signs you are doing if God were not with him."

3 In reply Jesus declared, "I tell you the truth, unless a man is born again,*p* he cannot see the kingdom of God."

4 "But," said Nicodemus, "how can a man be born when he is old? Surely he cannot enter a second time into his mother's womb to be born!"

5 Jesus answered, "I tell you the truth, unless a man is born of water and the Spirit, he cannot enter the kingdom of God. 6 Flesh gives birth to flesh, but the Spirit*q* gives birth to spirit. 7 You should not be surprised at my saying, 'You*r* must be born again.'*p* 8 The wind blows wherever it pleases. You may hear its sound, but you cannot tell where it comes from or where it is going. So it is with everyone born of the Spirit."

9 "How can this be?" Nicodemus asked.

10 "You are a teacher of Israel," said Jesus, "and do you not understand these things? 11 I tell you the truth, we speak of what we know, and we testify to what we have seen, but still you people do not accept our testimony. 12 I have spoken to you of earthly things and you do not believe; how then will you believe if I speak of heavenly things? 13 No one has ever gone into heaven except the one who came from heaven—the Son of Man. 14 Just as Moses lifted up the snake in the desert, so the Son of Man

[n] Psalm 69:9. [o] Or *and put their trust in him.* [p] Or *born from above.* [q] Or *but spirit.* [r] The Greek is plural.

Greek Interlinear

17 ἐμνήσθησαν οἱ μαθηταὶ αὐτοῦ ὅτι
Remembered the disciples of him that
γεγραμμένον ἐστίν· ὁ ζῆλος τοῦ οἴκου
having been written it is : The zeal of the house
σου καταφάγεταί με. **18** ἀπεκρίθησαν οὖν
of thee will consume me. Answered therefore
οἱ Ἰουδαῖοι καὶ εἶπαν αὐτῷ· τί σημεῖον
the Jews and said to him: What sign
δεικνύεις ἡμῖν, ὅτι ταῦτα ποιεῖς;
showest thou to us, because these things thou doest?
19 ἀπεκρίθη Ἰησοῦς καὶ εἶπεν αὐτοῖς· λύσατε τὸν
Answered Jesus and said to them: Destroy -
ναὸν τοῦτον, καὶ ἐν τρισὶν ἡμέραις ἐγερῶ αὐτόν.
shrine this, and in three days I will raise it.
20 εἶπαν οὖν οἱ Ἰουδαῖοι· τεσσεράκοντα
Said therefore the Jews : In forty
καὶ ἓξ ἔτεσιν οἰκοδομήθη ὁ ναὸς οὗτος,
and six years was built - shrine this,
καὶ σὺ ἐν τρισὶν ἡμέραις ἐγερεῖς αὐτόν;
and thou in three days wilt raise it?
21 ἐκεῖνος δὲ ἔλεγεν περὶ τοῦ ναοῦ τοῦ
But that [one]* spoke about the shrine of the
σώματος αὐτοῦ. **22** ὅτε οὖν ἠγέρθη ἐκ
body of him. When therefore he was raised from

νεκρῶν, ἐμνήσθησαν οἱ μαθηταὶ αὐτοῦ
[the] dead, remembered the disciples of him
ὅτι τοῦτο ἔλεγεν, καὶ ἐπίστευσαν τῇ
that this he said, and they believed the
γραφῇ καὶ τῷ λόγῳ ὃν εἶπεν ὁ Ἰησοῦς.
scripture and the word which said - Jesus.
23 Ὡς δὲ ἦν ἐν τοῖς Ἱεροσολύμοις ἐν
And when he was in - Jerusalem at
τῷ πάσχα ἐν τῇ ἑορτῇ, πολλοὶ ἐπίστευσαν
the Passover at the feast, many believed
εἰς τὸ ὄνομα αὐτοῦ, θεωροῦντες αὐτοῦ τὰ
in the name of him, beholding of him the
σημεῖα ἃ ἐποίει· **24** αὐτὸς δὲ Ἰησοῦς
signs which he was doing; ¹but ²[him]self, ¹Jesus
οὐκ ἐπίστευεν αὐτὸν αὐτοῖς διὰ τὸ αὐτὸν
did not commit himself to them because of the him
                                   =because he knew
γινώσκειν πάντας, **25** καὶ ὅτι οὐ χρείαν εἶχεν
to know[b] all men, and because no need he had
ἵνα τις μαρτυρήσῃ περὶ τοῦ ἀνθρώπου·
that anyone should witness concerning - man;
αὐτὸς γὰρ ἐγίνωσκεν τί ἦν ἐν τῷ ἀνθρώπῳ.
for he knew what was in - man.

Chapter 3

Ἦν δὲ ἄνθρωπος ἐκ τῶν Φαρισαίων,
Now there was a man of the Pharisees,
Νικόδημος ὄνομα αὐτῷ, ἄρχων τῶν
Nicodemus name to him[e], a ruler of the
                       =his name,
Ἰουδαίων· **2** οὗτος ἦλθεν πρὸς αὐτὸν νυκτὸς
Jews; this man came to him of(by) night
καὶ εἶπεν αὐτῷ· ῥαββί, οἴδαμεν ὅτι ἀπὸ
and said to him : Rabbi, we know that from
θεοῦ ἐλήλυθας διδάσκαλος· οὐδεὶς γὰρ
God thou hast come a teacher; for no one
δύναται ταῦτα τὰ σημεῖα ποιεῖν ἃ σὺ
can these - signs to do which thou
ποιεῖς, ἐὰν μὴ ᾖ ὁ θεὸς μετ' αὐτοῦ.
doest, except ³is - ¹God with him.
3 ἀπεκρίθη Ἰησοῦς καὶ εἶπεν αὐτῷ· ἀμὴν
Answered Jesus and said to him : Truly
ἀμὴν λέγω σοι, ἐὰν μή τις γεννηθῇ
truly I tell thee, except anyone is born
ἄνωθεν, οὐ δύναται ἰδεῖν τὴν βασιλείαν
from above, he cannot to see the kingdom
τοῦ θεοῦ. **4** λέγει πρὸς αὐτὸν ὁ Νικόδημος·
- of God. Says to him - Nicodemus :
πῶς δύναται ἄνθρωπος γεννηθῆναι γέρων ὤν;
How can a man to be born old being?
μὴ δύναται εἰς τὴν κοιλίαν τῆς μητρὸς
not can he into the womb of the mother
αὐτοῦ δεύτερον εἰσελθεῖν καὶ γεννηθῆναι;
of him secondly to enter and to be born?
5 ἀπεκρίθη Ἰησοῦς· ἀμὴν ἀμὴν λέγω σοι,
Answered Jesus : Truly truly I tell thee,
ἐὰν μή τις γεννηθῇ ἐξ ὕδατος καὶ
except anyone is born of water and
πνεύματος, οὐ δύναται εἰσελθεῖν εἰς τὴν
spirit, he cannot to enter into the
βασιλείαν τοῦ θεοῦ. **6** τὸ γεγεννημένον ἐκ
kingdom - of God. The thing having been born of
τῆς σαρκὸς σάρξ ἐστιν, καὶ τὸ γεγεννημένον
the flesh flesh is, and the thing having been born
ἐκ τοῦ πνεύματος πνεῦμά ἐστιν. **7** μὴ
of the Spirit spirit is. not

θαυμάσῃς ὅτι εἶπόν σοι· δεῖ ὑμᾶς
Marvel because I told thee : It behoves you
γεννηθῆναι ἄνωθεν. **8** τὸ πνεῦμα ὅπου θέλει
to be born from above. The spirit(?wind) where it wishes
πνεῖ, καὶ τὴν φωνὴν αὐτοῦ ἀκούεις, ἀλλ'
blows, and the sound of it thou hearest, but
οὐκ οἶδας πόθεν ἔρχεται καὶ ποῦ ὑπάγει·
thou knowest not whence it comes and whither it goes;
οὕτως ἐστὶν πᾶς ὁ γεγεννημένος ἐκ τοῦ
so is everyone having been born of the
πνεύματος. **9** ἀπεκρίθη Νικόδημος καὶ
Spirit. Answered Nicodemus and
εἶπεν αὐτῷ· πῶς δύναται ταῦτα γενέσθαι;
said to him : How can these things to come about?
10 ἀπεκρίθη Ἰησοῦς καὶ εἶπεν αὐτῷ· σὺ
Answered Jesus and said to him : Thou
εἶ ὁ διδάσκαλος τοῦ Ἰσραὴλ καὶ ταῦτα
art the teacher - of Israel and these things
οὐ γινώσκεις; **11** ἀμὴν ἀμὴν λέγω σοι ὅτι
knowest not? Truly truly I tell thee[,]
ὃ οἴδαμεν λαλοῦμεν καὶ ὃ ἑωράκαμεν
What we know we speak and what we have seen
μαρτυροῦμεν, καὶ τὴν μαρτυρίαν ἡμῶν
we witness, and the witness of us
οὐ λαμβάνετε. **12** εἰ τὰ ἐπίγεια εἶπον
ye receive not. If the earthly things I told
ὑμῖν καὶ οὐ πιστεύετε, πῶς ἐὰν εἴπω
you and ye believe not, how if I tell
ὑμῖν τὰ ἐπουράνια πιστεύσετε; **13** καὶ
you the heavenly things will ye believe? And
οὐδεὶς ἀναβέβηκεν εἰς τὸν οὐρανὸν εἰ μὴ
no man has gone up into - heaven except
ὁ ἐκ τοῦ οὐρανοῦ καταβάς, ὁ υἱὸς
the[one] out of - heaven having come down, the Son
τοῦ ἀνθρώπου. **14** Καὶ καθὼς Μωϋσῆς ὕψωσεν
- of man. And as Moses lifted up
τὸν ὄφιν ἐν τῇ ἐρήμῳ, οὕτως ὑψωθῆναι
the serpent in the desert, so to be lifted up

---

* John repeatedly uses the demonstrative adjective ἐκεῖνος in
the sense of " he," referring to Christ.

King James Version

lifted up: 15 That whosoever believeth in him should not perish, but have eternal life.

16 For God so loved the world, that he gave his only begotten Son, that whosoever believeth in him should not perish, but have everlasting life. 17 For God sent not his Son into the world to condemn the world; but that the world through him might be saved.

18 He that believeth on him is not condemned: but he that believeth not is condemned already, because he hath not believed in the name of the only begotten Son of God. 19And this is the condemnation, that light is come into the world, and men loved darkness rather than light, because their deeds were evil. 20 For every one that doeth evil hateth the light, neither cometh to the light, lest his deeds should be reproved. 21 But he that doeth truth cometh to the light, that his deeds may be made manifest, that they are wrought in God.

22 After these things came Jesus and his disciples into the land of Judea; and there he tarried with them, and baptized.

23 And John also was baptizing in Enon near to Salim, because there was much water there: and they came, and were baptized. 24 For John was not yet cast into prison.

25 Then there arose a question between *some* of John's disciples and the Jews about purifying. 26And they came unto John, and said unto him, Rabbi, he that was with thee beyond Jordan, to whom thou barest witness, behold, the same baptizeth, and all *men* come to him. 27 John answered and said, A man can receive nothing, except it be given him from heaven. 28 Ye yourselves bear me witness, that I said, I am not the Christ, but that I am sent before him. 29 He that hath the bride is the bridegroom: but the friend of the bridegroom, which standeth and heareth him, rejoiceth greatly because of the bridegroom's voice: this my joy therefore is fulfilled. 30 He must increase, but I *must* decrease. 31 He that cometh from above is above all: he that is of the earth is earthly, and speaketh of the earth: he that cometh from heaven is above all. 32And what he hath seen and heard, that he testifieth; and no man receiveth his testimony. 33 He that hath received his testimony hath set to his seal that God is true. 34 For he whom God hath sent speaketh the words of God: for God giveth not the Spirit by measure *unto him.* 35 The Father loveth the Son, and hath given all things into his hand. 36 He that believeth on the son hath everlasting life: and he that believeth not the Son shall not see life; but the wrath of God abideth on him.

New International Version

must be lifted up, 15 that everyone who believes in him may have eternal life.[s]

16 "For God so loved the world that he gave his one and only Son,[t] that whoever believes in him shall not perish but have everlasting life. 17 For God did not send his Son into the world to condemn the world, but to save the world through him. 18 Whoever believes in him is not condemned, but whoever does not believe stands condemned already because he has not believed in the name of God's one and only Son.[u] 19 This is the verdict: Light has come into the world, but men loved darkness instead of light because their deeds were evil. 20 Everyone who does evil hates the light, and will not come into the light for fear that his deeds will be exposed. 21 But whoever lives by the truth comes into the light, so that it may be seen plainly that what he has done has been done through God." [v]

John the Baptist's testimony about Jesus

22 After this, Jesus and his disciples went out into the Judean countryside, where he spent some time with them, and baptized. 23 Now John also was baptizing at Aenon near Salim, because there was plenty of water, and people were constantly coming to be baptized. 24 (This was before John was put in prison.) 25An argument developed between some of John's disciples and a certain Jew over the matter of ceremonial washing. 26 They came to John and said to him, "Rabbi, that man who was with you on the other side of the Jordan—the one about whom you testified—well, he is baptizing, and everyone is going to him."

27 To this John replied, "A man can receive only what is given him from heaven. 28 You yourselves can testify that I said, 'I am not the Christ[w] but am sent ahead of him.' 29 The bride belongs to the bridegroom. The friend who attends the bridegroom waits and listens for him, and is full of joy when he hears the bridegroom's voice. That joy is mine, and it is now complete. 30 He must become greater; I must become less important.

31 "The one who comes from above is above all; the one who is from the earth belongs to the earth, and speaks as one from the earth. The one who comes from heaven is above all. 32 He testifies to what he has seen and heard, but no one accepts his testimony. 33 The man who has accepted it has certified that God is truthful. 34 For the one whom God has sent speaks the words of God; to him God gives the Spirit without limit. 35 The Father loves the Son and has placed everything in his hands. 36 Whoever puts his faith in the Son has eternal life, but whoever rejects the Son will not see that life, for God's wrath remains on him."

[s] Or *believes may have eternal life in him.* [t] Or *his only begotten Son.* [u] Or *God's only begotten Son.* [v] Some interpreters end the quotation after verse 15. [w] Or *Messiah.*

Greek Interlinear

δεῖ   τὸν   υἱὸν   τοῦ   ἀνθρώπου, 15 ἵνα πᾶς ὁ
it behoves the Son   -   of man,   that everyone

πιστεύων ἐν   αὐτῷ   ἔχῃ   ζωὴν   αἰώνιον.
believing in   him   may have life   eternal.

16 οὕτως γὰρ   ἠγάπησεν   ὁ θεὸς   τὸν
     For thus   ²loved   - ¹God the

κόσμον, ὥστε   τὸν υἱὸν τὸν μονογενῆ
world,   so as   the Son   the only begotten

ἔδωκεν, ἵνα πᾶς ὁ πιστεύων εἰς αὐτὸν
he gave,   that everyone believing in him

μὴ ἀπόληται ἀλλ' ἔχῃ ζωὴν αἰώνιον.
may not perish but may have life eternal.

17 οὐ γὰρ ἀπέστειλεν ὁ θεὸς τὸν υἱὸν
     For ²not ²sent   - ¹God the Son

εἰς τὸν κόσμον ἵνα κρίνῃ τὸν κόσμον,
into the   world that he might judge the world,

ἀλλ' ἵνα   σωθῇ   ὁ κόσμος δι' αὐτοῦ.
but   that ²might be saved ¹the ²world through him.

18 ὁ   πιστεύων εἰς αὐτὸν οὐ κρίνεται·
The [one] believing in   him   is not judged;

ὁ μὴ πιστεύων ἤδη κέκριται, ὅτι
the[one]not believing already has been judged, because

μὴ πεπίστευκεν εἰς τὸ ὄνομα τοῦ μονογενοῦς
he has not believed in the name of the only begotten

υἱοῦ τοῦ θεοῦ. **19** αὕτη δέ ἐστιν ἡ
Son   -   of God.   And this is   the

κρίσις, ὅτι τὸ φῶς ἐλήλυθεν εἰς τὸν
judgment, that the light has come into the

κόσμον καὶ ἠγάπησαν οἱ ἄνθρωποι μᾶλλον
world and ²loved   ¹men   ²rather

τὸ σκότος ἢ τὸ φῶς· ἦν γὰρ αὐτῶν
³the ³darkness ⁴than the light; for was(were) of them

πονηρὰ τὰ ἔργα. **20** πᾶς γὰρ ὁ φαῦλα
evil   the works.   For everyone evil things

πράσσων μισεῖ τὸ φῶς καὶ οὐκ ἔρχεται
doing   hates the light and does not come

πρὸς τὸ φῶς, ἵνα μὴ ἐλεγχθῇ τὰ ἔργα
to the light, lest is(are) reproved the works

αὐτοῦ· **21** ὁ δὲ ποιῶν τὴν ἀλήθειαν ἔρχεται
of him;   but the [one] doing the truth comes

πρὸς τὸ φῶς, ἵνα φανερωθῇ αὐτοῦ τὰ
to the light, that may be manifested of him the

ἔργα ὅτι ἐν θεῷ ἐστιν εἰργασμένα.
works that in God they are having been wrought.

22 Μετὰ ταῦτα ἦλθεν ὁ Ἰησοῦς καὶ οἱ
     After these things came - Jesus and the

μαθηταὶ αὐτοῦ εἰς τὴν Ἰουδαίαν γῆν, καὶ
disciples of him into the Judæan land, and

ἐκεῖ διέτριβεν μετ' αὐτῶν καὶ ἐβάπτιζεν.
there continued with them and baptized.

23 ἦν δὲ καὶ Ἰωάννης βαπτίζων ἐν
     And was also John baptizing in

Αἰνὼν ἐγγὺς τοῦ Σαλίμ, ὅτι ὕδατα
Ainon near   - Salim, because waters

πολλὰ ἦν ἐκεῖ, καὶ παρεγίνοντο καὶ
many was(were) there, and they came and

ἐβαπτίζοντο· **24** οὔπω γὰρ ἦν βεβλημένος
were baptized;   for ²not yet ²was ³having been cast

εἰς τὴν φυλακὴν Ἰωάννης. **25** Ἐγένετο
⁴into ⁵the ⁵prison ¹John.   There was

οὖν ζήτησις ἐκ τῶν μαθητῶν Ἰωάννου
therefore a questioning of the disciples of John

μετὰ Ἰουδαίου περὶ καθαρισμοῦ. **26** καὶ
with a Jew about purifying.   And

ἦλθον πρὸς τὸν Ἰωάννην καὶ εἶπαν αὐτῷ·
they came to   -   John and said to him :

ῥαββί, ὃς ἦν μετὰ σοῦ πέραν τοῦ
Rabbi, [he] who was with thee beyond the

Ἰορδάνου, ᾧ σὺ μεμαρτύρηκας, ἴδε
Jordan, to whom thou hast borne witness, behold[,]

οὗτος βαπτίζει καὶ πάντες ἔρχονται πρὸς
this man baptizes and all men are coming to

αὐτόν. **27** ἀπεκρίθη Ἰωάννης καὶ εἶπεν·
him.   Answered John and said :

οὐ δύναται ἄνθρωπος λαμβάνειν οὐδὲν ἐὰν μὴ
Cannot   a man   to receive no(any)thing unless

ᾖ δεδομένον αὐτῷ ἐκ τοῦ οὐρανοῦ.
it is having been given to him out of - heaven.

28 αὐτοὶ ὑμεῖς μοι μαρτυρεῖτε ὅτι εἶπον·
     [Your]selves ye to me bear witness that I said :

οὐκ εἰμὶ ἐγὼ ὁ χριστός, ἀλλ' ὅτι
²not ²am ¹I the Christ, but that

ἀπεσταλμένος εἰμὶ ἔμπροσθεν ἐκείνου. **29** ὁ
having been sent I am before that one.*   The [one]

ἔχων τὴν νύμφην νυμφίος ἐστίν· ὁ δὲ
having the bride a bridegroom is; but the

φίλος τοῦ νυμφίου, ὁ ἑστηκὼς καὶ ἀκούων
friend of the bridegroom, - standing and hearing

αὐτοῦ, χαρᾷ χαίρει διὰ τὴν φωνὴν τοῦ
him,   with joy rejoices because of the voice of the

νυμφίου. αὕτη οὖν ἡ χαρὰ ἡ ἐμὴ
bridegroom. ²This ²therefore ²joy - ¹my

πεπλήρωται. **30** ἐκεῖνον δεῖ αὐξάνειν, ἐμὲ
has been fulfilled.   That one it behoves to increase, ²me

δὲ ἐλαττοῦσθαι. **31** Ὁ ἄνωθεν ἐρχόμενος
¹but to decrease.   The [one] from above coming

ἐπάνω πάντων ἐστίν· ὁ ὢν ἐκ τῆς γῆς
over   all   is; the [one] being of the earth

ἐκ τῆς γῆς ἐστιν καὶ ἐκ τῆς γῆς λαλεῖ.
of the earth is and of the earth speaks.

ὁ ἐκ τοῦ οὐρανοῦ ἐρχόμενος ἐπάνω
The [one] of   -   heaven coming over

πάντων ἐστίν· **32** ὃ ἑώρακεν καὶ ἤκουσεν,
all   is;   what he has seen and heard,

τοῦτο μαρτυρεῖ, καὶ τὴν μαρτυρίαν αὐτοῦ
this he witnesses [to], and the witness of him

οὐδεὶς λαμβάνει. **33** ὁ λαβὼν αὐτοῦ τὴν
no man receives.   The [one] receiving of him the

μαρτυρίαν ἐσφράγισεν ὅτι ὁ θεὸς ἀληθής
witness sealed that - God true

ἐστιν. **34** ὃν γὰρ ἀπέστειλεν ὁ θεὸς τὰ
is.   For [he] whom ²sent   -   ¹God the

ῥήματα τοῦ θεοῦ λαλεῖ· οὐ γὰρ ἐκ
words   of God speaks; for not by

μέτρου δίδωσιν τὸ πνεῦμα. **35** ὁ πατὴρ
measure he gives the Spirit.   The Father

ἀγαπᾷ τὸν υἱόν, καὶ πάντα δέδωκεν ἐν
loves the Son, and all things has given in[to]

τῇ χειρὶ αὐτοῦ. **36** ὁ πιστεύων εἰς τὸν
the hand of him.   The [one] believing in the

υἱὸν ἔχει ζωὴν αἰώνιον· ὁ δὲ ἀπειθῶν
Son has life eternal; but the [one] disobeying

τῷ υἱῷ οὐκ ὄψεται ζωήν, ἀλλ' ἡ ὀργὴ
the Son will not see life, but the wrath

τοῦ θεοῦ μένει ἐπ' αὐτόν.
-   of God remains on him.

* See note to 2. 21.

King James Version

4 When therefore the Lord knew how the Pharisees had heard that Jesus made and baptized more disciples than John, 2 (Though Jesus himself baptized not, but his disciples,) 3 He left Judea, and departed again into Galilee. 4 And he must needs go through Samaria. 5 Then cometh he to a city of Samaria, which is called Sychar, near to the parcel of ground that Jacob gave to his son Joseph. 6 Now Jacob's well was there. Jesus therefore, being wearied with *his* journey, sat thus on the well: *and* it was about the sixth hour. 7 There cometh a woman of Samaria to draw water: Jesus saith unto her, Give me to drink. 8 (For his disciples were gone away unto the city to buy meat.) 9 Then saith the woman of Samaria unto him, How is it that thou, being a Jew, askest drink of me, which am a woman of Samaria? for the Jews have no dealings with the Samaritans. 10 Jesus answered and said unto her, If thou knewest the gift of God, and who it is that saith to thee, Give me to drink; thou wouldest have asked of him, and he would have given thee living water. 11 The woman saith unto him, Sir, thou hast nothing to draw with, and the well is deep: from whence then hast thou that living water? 12 Art thou greater than our father Jacob, which gave us the well, and drank thereof himself, and his children, and his cattle? 13 Jesus answered and said unto her, Whosoever drinketh of this water shall thirst again: 14 But whosoever drinketh of the water that I shall give him shall never thirst; but the water that I shall give him shall be in him a well of water springing up into everlasting life. 15 The woman saith unto him, Sir, give me this water, that I thirst not, neither come hither to draw. 16 Jesus saith unto her, Go, call thy husband, and come hither. 17 The woman answered and said, I have no husband. Jesus said unto her, Thou hast well said, I have no husband: 18 For thou hast had five husbands; and he whom thou now hast is not thy husband: in that saidst thou truly. 19 The woman saith unto him, Sir, I perceive that thou art a prophet. 20 Our fathers worshipped in this mountain; and ye say, that in Jerusalem is the place where men ought to worship. 21 Jesus saith unto her, Woman, believe me, the hour cometh, when ye shall neither in this mountain, nor yet at Jerusalem, worship the Father. 22 Ye worship ye know not what: we know what we worship; for salvation is of the Jews. 23 But the hour cometh, and now is, when the true worshippers shall worship the Father in spirit and in truth: for the Father seeketh such to worship him. 24 God *is* a Spirit: and they that worship him

New International Version

Jesus talks with a Samaritan woman

4 The Pharisees heard that Jesus was gaining and baptizing more disciples than John, 2 although in fact it was not Jesus who baptized, but his disciples. 3 When the Lord learned of this, he left Judea and went back once more to Galilee.

4 Now he had to go through Samaria. 5 So he came to a town in Samaria called Sychar, near the plot of ground Jacob had given to his son Joseph. 6 Jacob's well was there, and Jesus, tired as he was from the journey, sat down by the well. It was about the sixth hour.

7 When a Samaritan woman came to draw water, Jesus said to her, "Will you give me a drink?" 8 (His disciples had gone into the town to buy food.)

9 The Samaritan woman said to him, "You are a Jew and I am a Samaritan woman. How can you ask me for a drink?" (For Jews do not associate with Samaritans.*)

10 Jesus answered her, "If you knew the gift of God and who it is that asks you for a drink, you would have asked him and he would have given you living water."

11 "Sir," the woman said, "you have nothing to draw with and the well is deep. Where can you get this living water? 12 Are you greater than our father Jacob, who gave us the well and drank from it himself, as did also his sons and his flocks and herds?"

13 Jesus answered, "Everyone who drinks this water will be thirsty again, 14 but whoever drinks the water I give him will never thirst. Indeed, the water I give him will become in him a spring of water welling up to everlasting life."

15 The woman said to him, "Sir, give me this water so that I won't get thirsty and have to keep coming here to draw water."

16 He told her, "Go, call your husband and come back."

17 "I have no husband," she replied.

Jesus said to her, "You are right when you say you have no husband. 18 The fact is, you have had five husbands, and the man you now have is not your husband. What you have just said is quite true."

19 "Sir," the woman said, "I can see that you are a prophet. 20 Our fathers worshiped on this mountain, but you Jews claim that the place where we must worship is in Jerusalem." 21 Jesus declared, "Believe me, woman, a time is coming when you will worship the Father neither on this mountain nor in Jerusalem. 22 You Samaritans worship what you do not know; we worship what we do know, for salvation is from the Jews. 23 Yet a time is coming and has now come when the true worshipers will worship the Father in spirit and truth, for they are the kind of worshipers the Father seeks. 24 God is spirit, and his worshipers must worship in spirit and in truth."

Greek Interlinear

Chapter 4

Ὡς οὖν ἔγνω ὁ κύριος ὅτι ἤκουσαν
²When ¹therefore ³knew ²the ⁴Lord ⁵that ⁶heard

οἱ Φαρισαῖοι ὅτι Ἰησοῦς πλείονας μαθητὰς
⁷the ⁸Pharisees that Jesus more disciples

ποιεῖ καὶ βαπτίζει ἢ Ἰωάννης, — 2 καίτοι γε
makes and baptizes than John, — though

Ἰησοῦς αὐτὸς οὐκ ἐβάπτιζεν ἀλλ' οἱ
Jesus [him]self baptized not but the

μαθηταὶ αὐτοῦ, — 3 ἀφῆκεν τὴν Ἰουδαίαν
disciples of him, — he left Judæa

καὶ ἀπῆλθεν πάλιν εἰς τὴν Γαλιλαίαν.
and went away again into — Galilee.

4 Ἔδει δὲ αὐτὸν διέρχεσθαι διὰ τῆς
And it behoved him to pass through *through* —

Σαμαρείας. 5 ἔρχεται οὖν εἰς πόλιν τῆς
Samaria. He comes therefore to a city of the

Σαμαρείας λεγομένη Σύχαρ, πλησίον τοῦ
of Samaria *being* called Sychar, near the

χωρίου ὃ ἔδωκεν Ἰακὼβ [τῷ] Ἰωσὴφ
piece of land which ⁸gave ⁹Jacob — to Joseph

τῷ υἱῷ αὐτοῦ· 6 ἦν δὲ ἐκεῖ πηγὴ τοῦ
the son of him; and was there a fountain —

Ἰακώβ. ὁ οὖν Ἰησοῦς κεκοπιακὼς ἐκ
of Jacob. — Therefore Jesus having become wearied from

τῆς ὁδοιπορίας ἐκαθέζετο οὕτως ἐπὶ τῇ
the journey sat thus at the

πηγῇ· ὥρα ἦν ὡς ἕκτη. 7 ἔρχεται γυνὴ
fountain; [the] hour was about sixth. Comes a woman

ἐκ τῆς Σαμαρείας ἀντλῆσαι ὕδωρ. λέγει
of — Samaria to draw water. Says

αὐτῇ ὁ Ἰησοῦς· δός μοι πεῖν. 8 οἱ γὰρ
to her — Jesus· Give me to drink. For the

μαθηταὶ αὐτοῦ ἀπεληλύθεισαν εἰς τὴν
disciples of him had gone away into the

πόλιν, ἵνα τροφὰς ἀγοράσωσιν. 9 λέγει
city, that foods they might buy. Says

οὖν αὐτῷ ἡ γυνὴ ἡ Σαμαρῖτις· πῶς
therefore to him the woman — Samaritan· How

σὺ Ἰουδαῖος ὢν παρ' ἐμοῦ πεῖν
thou ²a Jew ¹being ³from ⁴me ⁶to drink

αἰτεῖς γυναικὸς Σαμαρίτιδος οὔσης;
⁵askest ⁸woman ⁷a Samaritan ⁹being?

[οὐ γὰρ συγχρῶνται Ἰουδαῖοι Σαμαρίταις.]
¹For ²not ³associate ⁴Jews ⁶with Samaritans.]

10 ἀπεκρίθη Ἰησοῦς καὶ εἶπεν αὐτῇ· εἰ ᾔδεις
Answered Jesus and said to her: If thou knewest

τὴν δωρεὰν τοῦ θεοῦ, καὶ τίς ἐστιν ὁ
the gift — of God, and who is the [one]

λέγων σοι· δός μοι πεῖν, σὺ ἂν ᾔτησας
saying to thee· Give me to drink, thou wouldest have asked

αὐτὸν καὶ ἔδωκεν ἄν σοι ὕδωρ ζῶν.
him and he would have given thee water living.

11 λέγει αὐτῷ· κύριε, οὔτε ἄντλημα ἔχεις
She says to him: Sir, no pail thou hast

καὶ τὸ φρέαρ ἐστὶν βαθύ· πόθεν οὖν
and the well is deep; whence then

ἔχεις τὸ ὕδωρ τὸ ζῶν; 12 μὴ σὺ μείζων
hast thou the water — living? *not* thou greater

εἶ τοῦ πατρὸς ἡμῶν Ἰακώβ, ὃς ἔδωκεν
art [than] the father of us Jacob, who gave

ἡμῖν τὸ φρέαρ, καὶ αὐτὸς ἐξ αὐτοῦ
us the well, and [him]self of it

ἔπιεν καὶ οἱ υἱοὶ αὐτοῦ καὶ τὰ θρέμματα
drank and the sons of him and the cattle

αὐτοῦ; 13 ἀπεκρίθη Ἰησοῦς καὶ εἶπεν αὐτῇ·
of him; Answered Jesus and said to her:

πᾶς ὁ πίνων ἐκ τοῦ ὕδατος τούτου
Everyone drinking of — water this

διψήσει πάλιν· 14 ὃς δ' ἂν πίῃ ἐκ τοῦ
will thirst again; but whoever drinks of the

ὕδατος οὗ ἐγὼ δώσω αὐτῷ, οὐ μὴ
water which I will give him, by no means

διψήσει εἰς τὸν αἰῶνα, ἀλλὰ τὸ ὕδωρ ὃ
will thirst unto the age, but the water which

δώσω αὐτῷ γενήσεται ἐν αὐτῷ πηγὴ
I will give him will become in him a fountain

ὕδατος ἁλλομένου εἰς ζωὴν αἰώνιον. 15 λέγει
of water springing to life eternal. Says

πρὸς αὐτὸν ἡ γυνή· κύριε, δός μοι
to him the woman· Sir, give me

τοῦτο τὸ ὕδωρ, ἵνα μὴ διψῶ μηδὲ
this — water, that I thirst not nor

διέρχωμαι ἐνθάδε ἀντλεῖν. 16 λέγει αὐτῇ·
come through hither to draw. He says to her·

ὕπαγε φώνησον τὸν ἄνδρα σου καὶ ἐλθὲ
Go call the husband of thee and come

ἐνθάδε. 17 ἀπεκρίθη ἡ γυνὴ καὶ εἶπεν·
hither. Answered the woman and said:

οὐκ ἔχω ἄνδρα. λέγει αὐτῇ ὁ Ἰησοῦς·
I have not a husband. Says to her — Jesus:

καλῶς εἶπες ὅτι ἄνδρα οὐκ ἔχω· 18 πέντε
Well sayest thou[.] — A husband I have not; ⁵five

γὰρ ἄνδρας ἔσχες, καὶ νῦν ὃν ἔχεις
¹for husbands thou hadst, and now [he] whom thou hast

οὐκ ἔστιν σου ἀνήρ· τοῦτο ἀληθὲς εἴρηκας.
is not of thee husband; this truly thou hast said.

19 λέγει αὐτῷ ἡ γυνή· κύριε, θεωρῶ
Says to him the woman: Sir, I perceive

ὅτι προφήτης εἶ σύ. 20 οἱ πατέρες
that a prophet art thou. The fathers

ἡμῶν ἐν τῷ ὄρει τούτῳ προσεκύνησαν·
of us in — mountain this worshipped;

καὶ ὑμεῖς λέγετε ὅτι ἐν Ἰεροσολύμοις
and ye say that in Jerusalem

ἐστὶν ὁ τόπος ὅπου προσκυνεῖν δεῖ.
is the place where to worship it behoves.

21 λέγει αὐτῇ ὁ Ἰησοῦς· πίστευέ μοι,
Says to her — Jesus· Believe me,

γύναι, ὅτι ἔρχεται ὥρα ὅτε οὔτε ἐν
woman, that is coming an hour when neither in

τῷ ὄρει τούτῳ οὔτε ἐν Ἰεροσολύμοις
— mountain this nor in Jerusalem

προσκυνήσετε τῷ πατρί. 22 ὑμεῖς προσκυ-
will ye worship the Father. Ye wor-

νεῖτε ὃ οὐκ οἴδατε, ἡμεῖς προσκυνοῦμεν
ship what ye know not, we worship what

οἴδαμεν, ὅτι ἡ σωτηρία ἐκ τῶν Ἰουδαίων
we know, because — salvation of the Jews

ἐστίν· 23 ἀλλὰ ἔρχεται ὥρα καὶ νῦν
is; but is coming an hour and now

ἐστιν, ὅτε οἱ ἀληθινοὶ προσκυνηταὶ προσκυνή-
is, when the true worshippers will

σουσιν τῷ πατρὶ ἐν πνεύματι καὶ ἀληθείᾳ·
worship the Father in spirit and truth;

καὶ γὰρ ὁ πατὴρ τοιούτους ζητεῖ τοὺς
for indeed the Father ⁵such ⁶seeks the [ones]

προσκυνοῦντας αὐτόν. 24 πνεῦμα ὁ θεός,
worshipping him; God [is] spirit,*

καὶ τοὺς προσκυνοῦντας ἐν πνεύματι καὶ
and ⁸the [ones] ⁹worshipping ⁴in ⁵spirit ⁶and

---

* See note on 1. 1.

King James Version

must worship *him* in spirit and in truth. 25 The woman saith unto him, I know that Messias cometh, which is called Christ: when he is come, he will tell us all things. 26 Jesus saith unto her, I that speak unto thee am *he.*

27 And upon this came his disciples, and marvelled that he talked with the woman: yet no man said, What seekest thou? or, Why talkest thou with her? 28 The woman then left her waterpot, and went her way into the city, and saith to the men, 29 Come, see a man, which told me all things that ever I did: is not this the Christ? 30 Then they went out of the city, and came unto him.

31 In the mean while his disciples prayed him, saying, Master, eat. 32 But he said unto them, I have meat to eat that ye know not of. 33 Therefore said the disciples one to another, Hath any man brought him *aught* to eat? 34 Jesus saith unto them, My meat is to do the will of him that sent me, and to finish his work. 35 Say not ye, There are yet four months, and *then* cometh harvest? behold, I say unto you, Lift up your eyes, and look on the fields; for they are white already to harvest. 36 And he that reapeth receiveth wages, and gathereth fruit unto life eternal: that both he that soweth and he that reapeth may rejoice together. 37 And herein is that saying true, One soweth, and another reapeth. 38 I sent you to reap that whereon ye bestowed no labour: other men laboured, and ye are entered into their labours.

39 And many of the Samaritans of that city believed on him for the saying of the woman, which testified, He told me all that ever I did. 40 So when the Samaritans were come unto him, they besought him that he would tarry with them: and he abode there two days. 41 And many more believed because of his own word; 42 And said unto the woman, Now we believe, not because of thy saying: for we have heard *him* ourselves, and know that this is indeed the Christ, the Saviour of the world.

43 Now after two days he departed thence, and went into Galilee. 44 For Jesus himself testified, that a prophet hath no honour in his own country. 45 Then when he was come into Galilee, the Galileans received him, having seen all the things that he did at Jerusalem at the feast: for they also went unto the feast. 46 So Jesus came again into Cana of Galilee, where he made the water wine. And there was a certain nobleman, whose son was sick at Capernaum. 47 When he heard that Jesus was come out of Judea into Galilee, he went unto him, and besought him that he would come down, and heal his son: for he was at the point of death. 48 Then said Jesus unto him, Except ye see signs and wonders, ye will not believe. 49 The nobleman saith unto him,

New International Version

25 The woman said, "I know that Messiah" (called Christ) "is coming. When he comes, he will explain everything to us."

26 Then Jesus declared, "I who speak to you am he."

The disciples rejoin Jesus

27 Just then his disciples returned and were surprised to find him talking with a woman. But no one asked, "What do you want?" or "Why are you talking with her?"

28 Then, leaving her water jar, the woman went back to the town and said to the people, 29 "Come, see a man who told me everything I ever did. Could this be the Christ[y]?" 30 They came out of the town and made their way toward him.

31 Meanwhile his disciples urged him, "Rabbi, eat something."

32 But he said to them, "I have food to eat that you know nothing about."

33 Then his disciples said to each other, "Could someone have brought him food?"

34 "My food," said Jesus, "is to do the will of him who sent me and to finish his work. 35 Do you not say, 'Four months more and then the harvest'? I tell you, open your eyes and look at the fields! They are ripe for harvest. 36 Even now the reaper draws his wages, even now he harvests the crop for eternal life, so that the sower and the reaper may be glad together. 37 Thus the saying 'One sows and another reaps' is true. 38 I sent you to reap what you have not worked for. Others have done the hard work, and you have reaped the benefits of their labor."

Many Samaritans believe

39 Many of the Samaritans from that town believed in him because of the woman's testimony, "He told me everything I ever did." 40 So when the Samaritans came to him, they urged him to stay with them, and he stayed two days. 41 And because of his words many more became believers.

42 They said to the woman, "We no longer believe just because of what you said; now we have heard for ourselves, and we know that this man really is the Savior of the world."

Jesus heals the official's son

43 After the two days he left for Galilee. 44 (Now Jesus himself had pointed out that a prophet has no honor in his own country.) 45 When he arrived in Galilee, the Galileans welcomed him. They had seen all that he had done in Jerusalem at the Passover Feast, for they also had been there.

46 Once more he visited Cana in Galilee, where he had turned the water into wine. And there was a certain royal official whose son lay sick at Capernaum. 47 When this man heard that Jesus had arrived in Galilee from Judea, he went to him and begged him to come and heal his son, who was close to death.

48 "Unless you people see miraculous signs and wonders," Jesus told him, "you will never believe."

49 The royal official said, "Sir, come down before my child dies."

[y] Or *Messiah.*

Greek Interlinear

ἀληθείᾳ δεῖ προσκυνεῖν. 25 λέγει αὐτῷ
'truth ²it behoves 'to worship.   Says   to him

ἡ γυνή· οἶδα ὅτι Μεσσίας ἔρχεται, ὁ
the woman : I know that Messiah is coming, the [one]

λεγόμενος χριστός· ὅταν ἔλθῃ ἐκεῖνος,
being called   Christ;   when comes that one,

ἀναγγελεῖ ἡμῖν ἅπαντα. 26 λέγει αὐτῇ
he will announce to us all things.   Says   to her

ὁ Ἰησοῦς· ἐγώ εἰμι, ὁ λαλῶν σοι.
- Jesus :   I am, the [one] speaking to thee.

27 Καὶ ἐπὶ τούτῳ ἦλθαν οἱ μαθηταὶ
And on this came   the disciples

αὐτοῦ, καὶ ἐθαύμαζον ὅτι μετὰ γυναικὸς
of him, and marvelled that with a woman

ἐλάλει· οὐδεὶς μέντοι εἶπεν· τί ζητεῖς
he was speaking; no one however said : What seekest thou

ἢ τί λαλεῖς μετ' αὐτῆς; 28 ἀφῆκεν οὖν
or why speakest thou with her?   'Left ²therefore

τὴν ὑδρίαν αὐτῆς ἡ γυνὴ καὶ ἀπῆλθεν
'the 'waterpot 'of her 'the 'woman and went away

εἰς τὴν πόλιν, καὶ λέγει τοῖς ἀνθρώποις·
into the city, and says to the men :

29 δεῦτε ἴδετε ἄνθρωπον ὃς εἶπέν μοι
Come see   a man   who told me

πάντα ἃ ἐποίησα· μήτι οὗτός ἐστιν ὁ
all things which I did; not this is the

χριστός; 30 ἐξῆλθον ἐκ τῆς πόλεως καὶ
Christ?   They went forth out of the city and

ἤρχοντο πρὸς αὐτόν. 31 Ἐν τῷ μεταξὺ
came   to him.   In the meantime

ἠρώτων αὐτὸν οἱ μαθηταὶ λέγοντες· ῥαββί,
asked   him the disciples saying : Rabbi,

φάγε. 32 ὁ δὲ εἶπεν αὐτοῖς· ἐγὼ βρῶσιν
eat.   But he said to them : I   food

ἔχω φαγεῖν ἣν ὑμεῖς οὐκ οἴδατε. 33 ἔλεγον
have to eat which ye   do not know.   Said

οὖν οἱ μαθηταὶ πρὸς ἀλλήλους· μή τις
therefore the disciples to one another : Not anyone

ἤνεγκεν αὐτῷ φαγεῖν; 34 λέγει αὐτοῖς ὁ
brought   him to eat?   Says to them -

Ἰησοῦς· ἐμὸν βρῶμά ἐστιν ἵνα ποιῶ τὸ
Jesus : My   food is that I may do the

θέλημα τοῦ πέμψαντός με καὶ τελειώσω
will of the [one] having sent me and may finish

αὐτοῦ τὸ ἔργον. 35 οὐχ ὑμεῖς λέγετε ὅτι
of him the work.   'Not ²ye 'say that

ἔτι τετράμηνός ἐστιν καὶ ὁ θερισμὸς
yet four months it is and the harvest

ἔρχεται; ἰδοὺ λέγω ὑμῖν, ἐπάρατε τοὺς
comes?   Behold I tell you, lift up the

ὀφθαλμοὺς ὑμῶν καὶ θεάσασθε τὰς χώρας,
eyes   of you and behold the fields.

ὅτι λευκαί εἰσιν πρὸς θερισμόν. ἤδη
because white they are to harvest.   Already

36 ὁ θερίζων μισθὸν λαμβάνει καὶ συνάγει
the [one] reaping wages receives and gathers

καρπὸν εἰς ζωὴν αἰώνιον, ἵνα ὁ σπείρων
fruit to life eternal, that 'the [one] ²sowing

ὁμοῦ χαίρῃ καὶ ὁ θερίζων. 37 ἐν γὰρ
'together ²may rejoice ²and 'the [one] ²reaping.   For in

τούτῳ ὁ λόγος ἐστὶν ἀληθινὸς ὅτι ἄλλος
this the word is   true that another(one)

ἐστὶν ὁ σπείρων καὶ ἄλλος ὁ θερίζων.
is the [one] sowing and another the [one] reaping.

38 ἐγὼ ἀπέστειλα ὑμᾶς θερίζειν ὃ οὐχ
I   sent   you   to reap what not

ὑμεῖς κεκοπιάκατε· ἄλλοι κεκοπιάκασιν, καὶ
ye   have laboured; others have laboured, and

ὑμεῖς εἰς τὸν κόπον αὐτῶν εἰσεληλύθατε.
ye   into the labour of them have entered.

39 Ἐκ δὲ τῆς πόλεως ἐκείνης πολλοὶ
And out of - city that   many

ἐπίστευσαν εἰς αὐτὸν τῶν Σαμαριτῶν διὰ
believed in him of the Samaritans because of

τὸν λόγον τῆς γυναικὸς μαρτυρούσης ὅτι
the word of the woman witnessing[,] -

εἶπέν μοι πάντα ἃ ἐποίησα. 40 ὡς
He told me all things which I did.   When

οὖν ἦλθον πρὸς αὐτὸν οἱ Σαμαρῖται,
therefore came to him the Samaritans,

ἠρώτων αὐτὸν μεῖναι παρ' αὐτοῖς· καὶ
they asked him to remain with them; and

ἔμεινεν ἐκεῖ δύο ἡμέρας. 41 καὶ πολλῷ
he remained there two days.   And 'more

πλείους ἐπίστευσαν διὰ τὸν λόγον αὐτοῦ,
'many believed because of the word of him,

42 τῇ τε γυναικὶ ἔλεγον ὅτι οὐκέτι διὰ
and to the woman they said[.] - No longer because of

τὴν σὴν λαλιὰν πιστεύομεν· αὐτοὶ γὰρ
- thy talk we believe; for [our]selves

ἀκηκόαμεν, καὶ οἴδαμεν ὅτι οὗτός ἐστιν
we have heard, and we know that this man is

ἀληθῶς ὁ σωτὴρ τοῦ κόσμου.
truly the Saviour of the world.

43 Μετὰ δὲ τὰς δύο ἡμέρας ἐξῆλθεν
And after - the two days he went forth

ἐκεῖθεν εἰς τὴν Γαλιλαίαν. 44 αὐτὸς γὰρ
thence into - Galilee.   For ²[him]self

Ἰησοῦς ἐμαρτύρησεν ὅτι προφήτης ἐν
'Jesus witnessed that a prophet in

τῇ ἰδίᾳ πατρίδι τιμὴν οὐκ ἔχει. 45 ὅτε
the(his) own native place honour has not.   When

οὖν ἦλθεν εἰς τὴν Γαλιλαίαν, ἐδέξαντο
therefore he came into - Galilee, received

αὐτὸν οἱ Γαλιλαῖοι, πάντα ἑωρακότες
him the Galileans, all things having seen

ὅσα ἐποίησεν ἐν Ἱεροσολύμοις ἐν τῇ
which he did in Jerusalem at the

ἑορτῇ· καὶ αὐτοὶ γὰρ ἦλθον εἰς τὴν
feast; ²also ³they 'for went to the

ἑορτήν. 46 Ἦλθεν οὖν πάλιν εἰς τὴν
feast.   He came therefore again to -

Κανὰ τῆς Γαλιλαίας, ὅπου ἐποίησεν τὸ
Cana - of Galilee, where he made the

ὕδωρ οἶνον. καὶ ἦν τις βασιλικὸς
water wine. And there was a certain courtier

οὗ ὁ υἱὸς ἠσθένει ἐν Καφαρναούμ· 47 οὗτος
of whom the son ailed in Capernaum.   this man

ἀκούσας ὅτι Ἰησοῦς ἥκει ἐκ τῆς Ἰουδαίας
hearing that Jesus comes(came) out of - Judæa

εἰς τὴν Γαλιλαίαν, ἀπῆλθεν πρὸς αὐτὸν καὶ
into - Galilee, went to him and

ἠρώτα ἵνα καταβῇ καὶ ἰάσηται αὐτοῦ
asked that he would come down and would cure of him

τὸν υἱόν· ἤμελλεν γὰρ ἀποθνήσκειν. 48 εἶπεν
the son; for he was about to die.   Said

οὖν ὁ Ἰησοῦς πρὸς αὐτόν· ἐὰν μὴ σημεῖα
therefore - Jesus to him : Except signs

καὶ τέρατα ἴδητε, οὐ μὴ πιστεύσητε.
and prodigies ye see, by no means ye believe.

49 λέγει πρὸς αὐτὸν ὁ βασιλικός· κύριε,
Says to him the courtier : Sir,

κατάβηθι πρὶν ἀποθανεῖν τὸ παιδίον μου.
come down before to die the child of me.

King James Version

Sir, come down ere my child die. 50 Jesus saith unto him, Go thy way; thy son liveth. And the man believed the word that Jesus had spoken unto him, and he went his way. 51And as he was now going down, his servants met him, and told *him*, saying, Thy son liveth. 52 Then inquired he of them the hour when he began to amend. And they said unto him, Yesterday at the seventh hour the fever left him. 53 So the father knew that *it was* at the same hour, in the which Jesus said unto him, Thy son liveth: and himself believed, and his whole house. 54 This *is* again the second miracle *that* Jesus did, when he was come out of Judea into Galilee.

5 After this there was a feast of the Jews; and Jesus went up to Jerusalem. 2 Now there is at Jerusalem by the sheep *market* a pool, which is called in the Hebrew tongue Bethesda, having five porches. 3 In these lay a great multitude of impotent folk, of blind, halt, withered, waiting for the moving of the water. 4 For an angel went down at a certain season into the pool, and troubled the water: whosoever then first after the troubling of the water stepped in was made whole of whatsoever disease he had. 5And a certain man was there, which had an infirmity thirty and eight years. 6 When Jesus saw him lie, and knew that he had been now a long time *in that case*, he saith unto him, Wilt thou be made whole? 7 The impotent man answered him, Sir, I have no man, when the water is troubled, to put me into the pool: but while I am coming, another steppeth down before me. 8 Jesus saith unto him, Rise, take up thy bed, and walk. 9And immediately the man was made whole, and took up his bed, and walked: and on the same day was the sabbath.

10 The Jews therefore said unto him that was cured, It is the sabbath day: it is not lawful for thee to carry *thy* bed. 11 He answered them, He that made me whole, the same said unto me, Take up thy bed, and walk. 12 Then asked they him, What man is that which said unto thee, Take up thy bed, and walk? 13And he that was healed wist not who it was: for Jesus had conveyed himself away, a multitude being in *that* place. 14Afterward Jesus findeth him in the temple, and said unto him, Behold, thou art made whole: sin no more, lest a worse thing come unto thee. 15 The man departed, and told the Jews that it was Jesus, which had made him whole. 16And therefore did the Jews persecute Jesus, and sought to slay him, because he had done these things on the sabbath day.

17 But Jesus answered them, My Father worketh hitherto, and I work. 18 Therefore the Jews sought the more to kill him, because he not only had broken the sabbath, but said also that God was his Father, making himself equal with God. 19 Then answered Jesus and said unto them, Verily, verily, I say unto you, The Son can do

New International Version

50 Jesus replied, "You may go. Your son will live."

The man took Jesus at his word and departed. 51 While he was still on the way, his servants met him with the news that his boy was living. 52 When he inquired as to the time when his son had gotten better, they said to him, "The fever left him yesterday at the seventh hour."

53 Then the father realized that this was the exact time at which Jesus had said to him, "Your son will live." So he and all his household believed.

54 This was the second miraculous sign that Jesus performed, having come from Judea to Galilee.

The healing at the pool

5 Some time later, Jesus went up to Jerusalem for a feast of the Jews. 2 Now there is in Jerusalem near the Sheep Gate a pool, which in Aramaic is called Bethesda*z* and which is surrounded by five covered colonnades. 3 Here a great number of disabled people used to lie —the blind, the lame, the paralyzed.*a* 5 One who was there had been an invalid for thirty-eight years. 6 When Jesus saw him lying there and learned that he had been in this condition for a long time, he asked him, "Do you want to get well?"

7 "Sir," the invalid replied, "I have no one to help me into the pool when the water is stirred. While I am trying to get in, someone else goes down ahead of me."

8 Then Jesus said to him, "Get up! Pick up your mat and walk." 9At once the man was cured; he picked up his mat and walked.

The day on which this took place was a Sabbath, 10 and so the Jews said to the man who had been healed, "It is the Sabbath; the law forbids you to carry your mat."

11 But he replied, "The man who made me well said to me, 'Pick up your mat and walk.'"

12 So they asked him, "Who is this fellow who told you to pick it up and walk?"

13 The man who was healed had no idea who it was, for Jesus had slipped away in the crowd.

14 Later Jesus found him at the temple and said to him, "See, you are well again. Stop sinning or something worse may happen to you."

15 The man went away and told the Jews that it was Jesus who had made him well.

Life through the Son

16 So, because Jesus was doing these things on the Sabbath, the Jews persecuted him. 17 Jesus said to them, "My Father is always at his work to this very day, and I, too, am working." 18 For this reason the Jews tried all the harder to kill him; not only was he breaking the Sabbath, but he was even calling God his own Father, making himself equal with God. 19 Jesus gave them this answer: "I tell you the truth, the Son can do nothing by himself; he can do

[z] Some early MSS read *Bethzatha;* others *Bethsaida.* [a] Some MSS add-*and they waited for the moving of the waters.* Some less important MSS also add verse 4: *From time to time an angel of the Lord would come down and stir up the waters. The first one into the pool after each such disturbance would be cured of whatever disease he had.*

Greek Interlinear

50 λέγει αὐτῷ ὁ Ἰησοῦς· πορεύου, ὁ
Tells him - Jesus : Go, the

υἱός σου ζῇ. ἐπίστευσεν ὁ ἄνθρωπος τῷ
son of thee lives. ²Believed ¹the ¹man ⁴the

λόγῳ ὃν εἶπεν αὐτῷ ὁ Ἰησοῦς, καὶ
¹word ²which ³said ⁴to him - ⁵Jesus, and

ἐπορεύετο. **51** ἤδη δὲ αὐτοῦ καταβαίνοντος
went. And already him going down²
=while he was going down

οἱ δοῦλοι ὑπήντησαν αὐτῷ λέγοντες ὅτι
the slaves met him saying that

ὁ παῖς αὐτοῦ ζῇ. **52** ἐπύθετο οὖν τὴν
the boy of him lives. He inquired therefore the

ὥραν παρ' αὐτῶν ἐν ᾗ κομψότερον ἔσχεν·
hour from them in which better he had;
=he got better;

εἶπαν οὖν αὐτῷ ὅτι ἐχθὲς ὥραν ἑβδόμην
they said therefore to him[,] - Yesterday [at] hour seventh

ἀφῆκεν αὐτὸν ὁ πυρετός. **53** ἔγνω οὖν
left him the fever. Knew therefore

ὁ πατὴρ ὅτι ἐκείνῃ τῇ ὥρᾳ ἐν ᾗ εἶπεν
the father that in that - hour in which told

αὐτῷ ὁ Ἰησοῦς· ὁ υἱός σου ζῇ· καὶ
him - Jesus : The son of thee lives; and

ἐπίστευσεν αὐτὸς καὶ ἡ οἰκία αὐτοῦ ὅλη.
believed he and the household of him whole.

54 Τοῦτο [δὲ] πάλιν δεύτερον σημεῖον
And this again a second sign

ἐποίησεν ὁ Ἰησοῦς ἐλθὼν ἐκ τῆς Ἰουδαίας
did - Jesus having come out of - Judæa

εἰς τὴν Γαλιλαίαν.
into - Galilee.

Chapter 5

Μετὰ ταῦτα ἦν ἑορτὴ τῶν Ἰουδαίων,
After these things there was a feast of the Jews,

καὶ ἀνέβη Ἰησοῦς εἰς Ἱεροσόλυμα. **2** ἔστιν
and went up Jesus to Jerusalem. there is

δὲ ἐν τοῖς Ἱεροσολύμοις ἐπὶ τῇ προβατικῇ
Now in - Jerusalem at the sheepgate

κολυμβήθρα, ἡ ἐπιλεγομένη Ἑβραϊστὶ
a pool, the [one] being called in Hebrew

Βηθζαθά, πέντε στοὰς ἔχουσα. **3** ἐν
Bethzatha, five porches having. In

ταύταις κατέκειτο πλῆθος τῶν ἀσθενούντων,
these lay a multitude of the ailing [ones],

τυφλῶν, χωλῶν, ξηρῶν. ‡ **5** ἦν δὲ τις
blind, lame, withered. And there was¹ a

ἄνθρωπος ἐκεῖ τριάκοντα καὶ ὀκτὼ ἔτη
certain man there thirty-eight years

ἔχων ἐν τῇ ἀσθενείᾳ αὐτοῦ· **6** τοῦτον
having in the ailment of him; ²this man

ἰδὼν ὁ Ἰησοῦς κατακείμενον, καὶ γνοὺς
²seeing - ¹Jesus ⁴lying, and knowing

ὅτι πολὺν ἤδη χρόνον ἔχει, λέγει αὐτῷ·
that ²much ¹already ³time ¹he has, says to him :

θέλεις ὑγιὴς γενέσθαι; **7** ἀπεκρίθη αὐτῷ
Wishest thou whole to become? Answered him

ὁ ἀσθενῶν· κύριε, ἄνθρωπον οὐκ ἔχω,
the ailing [one] : Sir, a man I have not,

ἵνα ὅταν ταραχθῇ τὸ ὕδωρ βάλῃ με εἰς
that when is troubled the water he may put me into

τὴν κολυμβήθραν· ἐν ᾧ δὲ ἔρχομαι ἐγώ,
the pool; but while am coming I,

ἄλλος πρὸ ἐμοῦ καταβαίνει. **8** λέγει αὐτῷ
another before me goes down. Says to him

ὁ Ἰησοῦς· ἔγειρε ἆρον τὸν κράβατόν
- Jesus : Rise[,] take the mattress

σου καὶ περιπάτει. **9** καὶ εὐθέως ἐγένετο
of thee and walk. And immediately became

ὑγιὴς ὁ ἄνθρωπος, καὶ ἦρεν τὸν κράβατον
whole the man, and took the mattress

αὐτοῦ καὶ περιεπάτει. ⁷Ην δὲ σάββατον
of him and walked. And it was a sabbath

ἐν ἐκείνῃ τῇ ἡμέρα. **10** ἔλεγον οὖν οἱ
on that - day. Said therefore the

Ἰουδαῖοι τῷ τεθεραπευμένῳ· σάββατόν ἐστιν,
Jews to the [one] having been healed : A sabbath it is,

καὶ οὐκ ἔξεστίν σοι ἆραι τὸν κράβατον.
and it is not lawful for thee to take the mattress.

11 ὃς δὲ ἀπεκρίθη αὐτοῖς· ὁ ποιήσας
But who(he) answered them : The [one] making

με ὑγιῆ, ἐκεῖνός μοι εἶπεν· ἆρον τὸν
me whole, that one me told : Take the

κράβατόν σου καὶ περιπάτει. **12** ἠρώτησαν
mattress of thee and walk. They asked

αὐτόν· τίς ἐστιν ὁ ἄνθρωπος ὁ εἰπών·
him : Who is the man the telling

σοι· ἆρον καὶ περιπάτει; **13** ὁ δὲ ἰαθεὶς
thee : Take and walk? But the [one] cured

οὐκ ᾔδει τίς ἐστιν· ὁ γὰρ Ἰησοῦς
did not know who it is(was); - for Jesus

ἐξένευσεν ὄχλου ὄντος ἐν τῷ τόπῳ.
withdrew a crowd being² in the place.
=as there was a crowd

14 μετὰ ταῦτα εὑρίσκει αὐτὸν ὁ Ἰησοῦς
After these things finds him - Jesus

ἐν τῷ ἱερῷ καὶ εἶπεν αὐτῷ· ἴδε ὑγιὴς
in the temple and said to him : Behold[,] whole

γέγονας· μηκέτι ἁμάρτανε, ἵνα μὴ χεῖρόν
thou hast become; no longer sin, lest ³worse

σοί τι γένηται. **15** ἀπῆλθεν ὁ ἄνθρωπος
⁴to thee ¹something ²happens. Went away the man

καὶ εἶπεν τοῖς Ἰουδαίοις ὅτι Ἰησοῦς
and told the Jews that Jesus

ἐστιν ὁ ποιήσας αὐτὸν ὑγιῆ. **16** καὶ διὰ
it is(was) the [one] having made him whole. And there-

τοῦτο ἐδίωκον οἱ Ἰουδαῖοι τὸν Ἰησοῦν,
fore ²persecuted ¹the ³Jews - ¹Jesus,

ὅτι ταῦτα ἐποίει ἐν σαββάτῳ. **17** ὁ δὲ
because these things he did on a sabbath. But he

ἀπεκρίνατο αὐτοῖς· ὁ πατήρ μου ἕως
answered them : The Father of me until

ἄρτι ἐργάζεται, κἀγὼ ἐργάζομαι· **18** διὰ
now works, and I work; because of

τοῦτο οὖν μᾶλλον ἐζήτουν αὐτὸν οἱ
this therefore ⁴the more ¹sought ³him ⁵the

Ἰουδαῖοι ἀποκτεῖναι, ὅτι οὐ μόνον ἔλυεν
²Jews ⁶to kill, because not only he broke

τὸ σάββατον, ἀλλὰ καὶ πατέρα ἴδιον
the sabbath, but also Father [his] own

ἔλεγεν τὸν θεόν, ἴσον ἑαυτὸν ποιῶν
said - God [to be], equal himself making -

θεῷ. **19** Ἀπεκρίνατο οὖν ὁ Ἰησοῦς καὶ
to God. Answered therefore - Jesus and

ἔλεγεν αὐτοῖς· ἀμὴν ἀμὴν λέγω ὑμῖν,
said to them : Truly truly I say to you,

οὐ δύναται ὁ υἱὸς ποιεῖν ἀφ' ἑαυτοῦ
cannot the Son to do from himself

‡ End of ver. 3 and ver. 4 omitted by Nestle

King James Version

nothing of himself, but what he seeth the Father do: for what things soever he doeth, these also doeth the Son likewise. 20 For the Father loveth the Son, and sheweth him all things that himself doeth: and he will shew him greater works than these, that ye may marvel. 21 For as the Father raiseth up the dead, and quickeneth *them;* even so the Son quickeneth whom he will. 22 For the Father judgeth no man, but hath committed all judgment unto the Son: 23 That all *men* should honour the Son, even as they honour the Father. He that honoureth not the Son honoureth not the Father which hath sent him. 24 Verily, verily, I say unto you, He that heareth my word, and believeth on him that sent me, hath everlasting life, and shall not come into condemnation; but is passed from death unto life. 25 Verily, verily, I say unto you, The hour is coming, and now is, when the dead shall·hear the voice of the Son of God: and they that hear shall live. 26 For as the Father hath life in himself; so hath he given to the Son to have life in himself; 27And hath given him authority to execute judgment also, because he is the Son of man. 28 Marvel not at this: for the hour is coming, in the which all that are in the graves shall hear his voice, 29And shall come forth; they that have done good, unto the resurrection of life; and they that have done evil, unto the resurrection of damnation. 30 I can of mine own self do nothing: as I hear, I judge: and my judgment is just; because I seek not mine own will, but the will of the Father which hath sent me. 31 If I bear witness of myself, my witness is not true.

32 There is another that beareth witness of me; and I know that the witness which he witnesseth of me is true. 33 Ye sent unto John, and he bare witness unto the truth. 34 But I receive not testimony from man: but these things I say, that ye might be saved. 35 He was a burning and a shining light; and ye were willing for a season to rejoice in his light.

36 But I have greater witness than *that* of John: for the works which the Father hath given me to finish, the same works that I do, bear witness of me, that the Father hath sent me. 37And the Father himself, which hath sent me, hath borne witness of me. Ye have neither heard his voice at any time, nor seen his shape. 38And ye have not his word abiding in you: for whom he hath sent, him ye believe not.

39 Search the Scriptures; for in them ye think ye have eternal life: and they are they which testify of me. 40And ye will not come to me, that ye might have life. 41 I receive not honour from men. 42 But I know you, that ye have not the love of God in you. 43 I am come in my Father's name, and ye receive me not: if another shall come in his own name, him ye will receive. 44 How can ye believe, which receive honour one

New International Version

only what he sees his Father doing, because whatever the Father does the Son also does. 20 For the Father loves the Son and shows him all he does. Yes, to your amazement he will show him even greater things than these. 21 For just as the Father raises the dead and gives them life, even so the Son gives life to whom he is pleased to give it. 22 Moreover, the Father judges no one, but has entrusted all judgment to the Son, 23 that all may honor the Son just as they honor the Father. He who does not honor the Son does not honor the Father who sent him.

24 "I tell you the truth, whoever hears my word and believes him who sent me has eternal life and will not be condemned; he has crossed over from death to life. 25 I tell you the truth, a time is coming and has now come when the dead will hear the voice of the Son of God and those who hear will live. 26 For as the Father has life in himself, so he has granted the Son to have life in himself. 27And he has given him authority to judge because he is the Son of Man.

28 "Do not be amazed at this, for a time is coming when all who are in their graves will hear his voice 29 and come out—those who have done good will rise to live, and those who have done evil will rise to be condemned. 30 By myself I can do nothing; I judge only as I hear, and my judgment is just, for I seek not to please myself but him who sent me.

Testimonies about Jesus

31 "If I testify about myself, my testimony is not valid. 32 There is another who testifies in my favor, and I know that his testimony about me is valid.

33 "You have sent to John and he has testified to the truth. 34 Not that I accept human testimony; but I mention it that you may be saved. 35 John was a lamp that burned and gave light, and you chose for a time to enjoy his light.

36 "I have testimony weightier than that of John. For the very work that the Father has given me to finish, and which I am doing, testifies that the Father has sent me. 37And the Father who sent me has himself testified concerning me. You have never heard his voice nor seen his form, 38 nor does his word dwell in you, for you do not believe the one he sent. 39 You diligently study[b] the Scriptures because you think that by them you possess eternal life. These are the Scriptures that testify about me, 40 yet you refuse to come to me to have life.

41 "I do not accept praise from men, 42 but I know you. I know that you do not have God's love in your hearts. 43 I have come in my Father's name, and you do not accept me; but if someone else comes in his own name, you will accept him. 44 How can you believe if you ac-

[b] Or *Study diligently* (the imperative).

Greek Interlinear

οὐδέν, ἂν μή τι βλέπῃ τὸν πατέρα
no(any)thing, except what he sees the Father

ποιοῦντα· ἃ γὰρ ἂν ἐκεῖνος ποιῇ, ταῦτα
doing; for whatever things that one does, these

καὶ ὁ υἱὸς ὁμοίως ποιεῖ. 20 ὁ γὰρ
also the Son likewise does. For the

πατὴρ φιλεῖ τὸν υἱὸν καὶ πάντα δείκνυσιν
Father loves the Son and all things shows

αὐτῷ ἃ αὐτὸς ποιεῖ, καὶ μείζονα τούτων
him which he does, and ¹greater ²[than] ³these

δείξει αὐτῷ ἔργα, ἵνα ὑμεῖς θαυμάζητε.
¹he will show ³him ²works, that ye may marvel.

21 ὥσπερ γὰρ ὁ πατὴρ ἐγείρει τοὺς
For as the Father raises the

νεκροὺς καὶ ζωοποιεῖ, οὕτως καὶ ὁ υἱὸς
dead and quickens, so also the Son

οὓς θέλει ζωοποιεῖ. 22 οὐδὲ γὰρ ὁ
whom he wills quickens. For not the

πατὴρ κρίνει οὐδένα, ἀλλὰ τὴν κρίσιν
Father judges no(any) one, but – judgment

πᾶσαν δέδωκεν τῷ υἱῷ, 23 ἵνα πάντες
all he has given to the Son, that all men

τιμῶσι τὸν υἱὸν καθὼς τιμῶσι τὸν πατέρα.
may honour the Son as they honour the Father.

ὁ μὴ τιμῶν τὸν υἱὸν οὐ τιμᾷ τὸν πατέρα
The [one] not honouring the Son honours not the Father

τὸν πέμψαντα αὐτόν. 24 Ἀμὴν ἀμὴν
– having sent him. Truly truly

λέγω ὑμῖν ὅτι ὁ τὸν λόγον μου ἀκούων
I say to you[,] – The [one] the word of me hearing

καὶ πιστεύων τῷ πέμψαντί με ἔχει
and believing the [one] having sent me has

ζωὴν αἰώνιον, καὶ εἰς κρίσιν οὐκ ἔρχεται
life eternal, and into judgment comes not

ἀλλὰ μεταβέβηκεν ἐκ τοῦ θανάτου εἰς
but has passed over out of – death into

τὴν ζωήν. 25 ἀμὴν ἀμὴν λέγω ὑμῖν ὅτι
life. Truly truly I say to you[,] –

ἔρχεται ὥρα καὶ νῦν ἐστιν ὅτε οἱ νεκροὶ
Comes an hour and now is when the dead

ἀκούσουσιν τῆς φωνῆς τοῦ υἱοῦ τοῦ
will hear the voice of the Son of

θεοῦ καὶ οἱ ἀκούσαντες ζήσουσιν. 26 ὥσπερ
of God and the[ones] hearing will live. as

γὰρ ὁ πατὴρ ἔχει ζωὴν ἐν ἑαυτῷ, οὕτως
For the Father has life in himself, so

καὶ τῷ υἱῷ ἔδωκεν ζωὴν ἔχειν ἐν ἑαυτῷ.
also to the Son he gave life to have in himself.

27 καὶ ἐξουσίαν ἔδωκεν αὐτῷ κρίσιν ποιεῖν,
And authority he gave him judgment to do,

ὅτι υἱὸς ἀνθρώπου ἐστίν. 28 μὴ θαυμάζετε
because son of man* he is. Marvel not [at]

τοῦτο, ὅτι ἔρχεται ὥρα ἐν ᾗ πάντες οἱ
this, because comes an hour in which all the [ones]

ἐν τοῖς μνημείοις ἀκούσουσιν τῆς φωνῆς
in the tombs will hear the voice

αὐτοῦ 29 καὶ ἐκπορεύσονται οἱ τὰ ἀγαθὰ
of him and will come forth the [ones] the good things

ποιήσαντες εἰς ἀνάστασιν ζωῆς, οἱ τὰ
having done to a resurrection of life, the [ones] the

φαῦλα πράξαντες εἰς ἀνάστασιν κρίσεως.
evil things having done to a resurrection of judgment.

30 Οὐ δύναμαι ἐγὼ ποιεῖν ἀπ' ἐμαυτοῦ
Cannot I to do from myself

οὐδέν· καθὼς ἀκούω κρίνω, καὶ ἡ κρίσις
no(any)thing; as I hear I judge, and – judgment

ἡ ἐμὴ δικαία ἐστίν, ὅτι οὐ ζητῶ τὸ
– my just is, because I seek not –

θέλημα τὸ ἐμὸν ἀλλὰ τὸ θέλημα τοῦ
will – my but the will of the [one]

πέμψαντός με. 31 Ἐὰν ἐγὼ μαρτυρῶ
having sent me. If I witness

περὶ ἐμαυτοῦ, ἡ μαρτυρία μου οὐκ ἔστιν
concerning myself, the witness of me is not

ἀληθής· 32 ἄλλος ἐστὶν ὁ μαρτυρῶν περὶ
true; another there is the [one] witnessing concerning

ἐμοῦ, καὶ οἶδα ὅτι ἀληθής ἐστιν ἡ
me, and I know that true is the

μαρτυρία ἣν μαρτυρεῖ περὶ ἐμοῦ. 33 ὑμεῖς
witness which he witnesses concerning me. Ye

ἀπεστάλκατε πρὸς Ἰωάννην, καὶ μεμαρ-
have sent to John, and he has

τύρηκεν τῇ ἀληθείᾳ· 34 ἐγὼ δὲ οὐ παρὰ
witnessed to the truth; but I not from

ἀνθρώπου τὴν μαρτυρίαν λαμβάνω, ἀλλὰ
man the witness receive, but

ταῦτα λέγω ἵνα ὑμεῖς σωθῆτε. 35 ἐκεῖνος
these things I say that ye may be saved. That man

ἦν ὁ λύχνος ὁ καιόμενος καὶ φαίνων,
was the lamp – burning and shining,

ὑμεῖς δὲ ἠθελήσατε ἀγαλλιαθῆναι πρὸς
and ye were willing to exult for

ὥραν ἐν τῷ φωτὶ αὐτοῦ. 36 Ἐγὼ δὲ
an hour in the light¹ of him. But I

ἔχω τὴν μαρτυρίαν μείζω τοῦ Ἰωάννου·
have the witness greater [than] – of John;

τὰ γὰρ ἔργα ἃ δέδωκέν μοι ὁ πατὴρ ἵνα
for the works which has given me the Father that

τελειώσω αὐτά, αὐτὰ τὰ ἔργα ἃ ποιῶ,
I may finish them, ²[them]selves ¹the ³works which I do,

μαρτυρεῖ περὶ ἐμοῦ ὅτι ὁ πατήρ με
witnesses concerning me that the Father me

ἀπέσταλκεν. 37 καὶ ὁ πέμψας με πατήρ,
has sent. And ¹the ²having sent ⁴me ³Father,

ἐκεῖνος μεμαρτύρηκεν περὶ ἐμοῦ. οὔτε
that [one] has witnessed concerning me. Neither

φωνὴν αὐτοῦ πώποτε ἀκηκόατε οὔτε εἶδος
voice of him never ye have heard nor form

αὐτοῦ ἑωράκατε, 38 καὶ τὸν λόγον αὐτοῦ
of him ye have seen, and the word of him

οὐκ ἔχετε ἐν ὑμῖν μένοντα, ὅτι ὃν
ye have not in you remaining, because [he] whom

ἀπέστειλεν ἐκεῖνος, τούτῳ ὑμεῖς οὐ πιστεύετε.
¹sent ²that [one], this [one] ye do not believe.

39 ἐρευνᾶτε τὰς γραφάς, ὅτι ὑμεῖς δοκεῖτε
Ye search the scriptures, because ye think

ἐν αὐταῖς ζωὴν αἰώνιον ἔχειν· καὶ ἐκεῖναί
in them life eternal to have; and those

εἰσιν αἱ μαρτυροῦσαι περὶ ἐμοῦ· 40 καὶ
are the [ones] witnessing concerning me; and

οὐ θέλετε ἐλθεῖν πρός με ἵνα ζωὴν
ye wish not to come to me that life

ἔχητε. 41 Δόξαν παρὰ ἀνθρώπων οὐ
ye may have. Glory from men not

λαμβάνω, 42 ἀλλὰ ἔγνωκα ὑμᾶς ὅτι τὴν
I receive, but I have known you that the

ἀγάπην τοῦ θεοῦ οὐκ ἔχετε ἐν ἑαυτοῖς.
love – of God ye have not in yourselves.

43 ἐγὼ ἐλήλυθα ἐν τῷ ὀνόματι τοῦ πατρός
I have come in the name of the Father

μου, καὶ οὐ λαμβάνετέ με· ἐὰν ἄλλος
of me, and ye receive not me; if another

ἔλθῃ ἐν τῷ ὀνόματι τῷ ἰδίῳ, ἐκεῖνον
comes in name the(his) own, that [one]

λήμψεσθε. 44 πῶς δύνασθε ὑμεῖς πιστεῦσαι,
ye will receive. How can ye to believe,

---

* Note the absence of the definite article here. See also Rev.
1. 13 and 14. 14.

King James Version

of another, and seek not the honour that *cometh* from God only? 45 Do not think that I will accuse you to the Father: there is *one* that accuseth you, *even* Moses, in whom ye trust. 46 For had ye believed Moses, ye would have believed me: for he wrote of me. 47 But if ye believe not his writings, how shall ye believe my words?

6 After these things Jesus went over the sea of Galilee, which is *the sea* of Tiberias. 2And a great multitude followed him, because they saw his miracles which he did on them that were diseased. 3And Jesus went up into a mountain, and there he sat with his disciples. 4And the passover, a feast of the Jews, was nigh.

5 When Jesus then lifted up *his* eyes, and saw a great company come unto him, he saith unto Philip, Whence shall we buy bread, that these may eat? 6And this he said to prove him: for he himself knew what he would do. 7 Philip answered him, Two hundred pennyworth of bread is not sufficient for them, that every one of them may take a little. 8 One of his disciples, Andrew, Simon Peter's brother, saith unto him, 9 There is a lad here, which hath five barley loaves, and two small fishes: but what are they among so many? 10And Jesus said, Make the men sit down. Now there was much grass in the place. So the men sat down, in number about five thousand. 11And Jesus took the loaves; and when he had given thanks, he distributed to the disciples, and the disciples to them that were set down; and likewise of the fishes as much as they would. 12 When they were filled, he said unto his disciples, Gather up the fragments that remain, that nothing be lost. 13 Therefore they gathered *them* together, and filled twelve baskets with the fragments of the five barley loaves, which remained over and above unto them that had eaten. 14 Then those men, when they had seen the miracle that Jesus did, said, This is of a truth that Prophet that should come into the world.

15 When Jesus therefore perceived that they would come and take him by force, to make him a king, he departed again into a mountain himself alone. 16And when even was *now* come, his disciples went down unto the sea, 17And entered into a ship, and went over the sea toward Capernaum. And it was now dark, and Jesus was not come to them. 18And the sea arose by reason of a great wind that blew. 19 So when they had rowed about five and twenty or thirty furlongs, they see Jesus walking on the sea, and drawing nigh unto the ship: and they were afraid. 20 But he saith unto them, It is I; be not afraid. 21 Then

New International Version

cept praise from one another, yet make no effort to obtain the praise that comes from the only God? [c]

45 "But do not think I will accuse you before the Father. Your accuser is Moses, on whom your hopes are set. 46 If you believed Moses, you would believe me, for he wrote about me. 47 But since you do not believe what he wrote, how are you going to believe what I say?"

Jesus feeds the five thousand

6 Some time after this, Jesus crossed to the far shore of the Sea of Galilee (that is, the Sea of Tiberias), 2 and a great crowd of people followed him because they saw the miraculous signs he had performed on the sick. 3 Then Jesus went up on the hillside and sat down with his disciples. 4 The Jewish Passover Feast was near.

5 When Jesus looked up and saw a great crowd coming toward him, he said to Philip, "Where shall we buy bread for these people to eat?" 6 He asked this only to test him, for he already had in mind what he was going to do.

7 Philip answered him, "Eight months' wages[d] would not buy enough bread for each one to have a bite!"

8 Another of his disciples, Andrew, Simon Peter's brother, spoke up, 9 "Here is a boy with five small barley loaves and two small fish, but how far will they go among so many?"

10 Jesus said, "Have the people sit down." There was plenty of grass in that place, and the men sat down, above five thousand of them. 11 Jesus then took the loaves, gave thanks, and distributed to those who were seated as much as they wanted. He did the same with the fish.

12 When they had all had enough to eat, he said to his disciples, "Gather the pieces that are left over. Let nothing be wasted." 13 So they gathered them and filled twelve baskets with the pieces of the five barley loaves left over by those who had eaten.

14 After the people saw the miraculous sign that Jesus did, they began to say, "Surely this is the Prophet who is to come into the world." 15 Jesus, knowing that they intended to come and make him king by force, withdrew again into the hills by himself.

Jesus walks on the water

16 When evening came, his disciples went down to the lake, 17 where they got into a boat and set off across the lake for Capernaum. By now it was dark, and Jesus had not yet joined them. 18 A strong wind was blowing and the waters grew rough. 19 When they had rowed three or four miles, they saw Jesus approaching the boat, walking on the water; and they were terrified. 20 But he said to them, "It is I; don't be afraid." 21 Then they were willing to take

[c] Some early MSS read *the Only One.* [d] Greek *200 denarii.*

Greek Interlinear

δόξαν παρὰ ἀλλήλων λαμβάνοντες, καὶ
glory from one another receiving, and

τὴν δόξαν τὴν παρὰ τοῦ μόνου θεοῦ
the glory - from the only God

οὐ ζητεῖτε; 45 μὴ δοκεῖτε ὅτι ἐγὼ κατηγορήσω
ye seek not? Do not think that I will accuse

ὑμῶν πρὸς τὸν πατέρα· ἐστιν ὁ κατηγορῶν
you to the Father; there is the [one] accusing

ὑμῶν Μωϋσῆς, εἰς ὃν ὑμεῖς ἠλπίκατε. 46 εἰ
you[,] Moses, in whom ye have hoped. if

γὰρ ἐπιστεύετε Μωϋσεῖ, ἐπιστεύετε ἂν
For ye believed Moses, ye would have believed

ἐμοί· περὶ γὰρ ἐμοῦ ἐκεῖνος ἔγραψεν.
me; for concerning me that [one] wrote.

47 εἰ δὲ τοῖς ἐκείνου γράμμασιν οὐ
But ¹if ³the ²of that [one] letters ²not

πιστεύετε, πῶς τοῖς ἐμοῖς ῥήμασιν
¹ye believe, how - my words

πιστεύσετε;
will ye believe?

Chapter 6

Μετὰ ταῦτα ἀπῆλθεν ὁ Ἰησοῦς πέραν
After these things went away - Jesus across

τῆς θαλάσσης τῆς Γαλιλαίας τῆς Τιβεριάδος.
the sea - of Galilee[,] - of Tiberias.

2 ἠκολούθει δὲ αὐτῷ ὄχλος πολύς, ὅτι
And followed him crowd a much, because

ἑώρων τὰ σημεῖα ἃ ἐποίει ἐπὶ τῶν
they saw the signs which he did on the

ἀσθενούντων. 3 ἀνῆλθεν δὲ εἰς τὸ ὄρος
ailing [ones]. And went up to the mountain

Ἰησοῦς, καὶ ἐκεῖ ἐκάθητο μετὰ τῶν
Jesus, and there sat with the

μαθητῶν αὐτοῦ. 4 ἦν δὲ ἐγγὺς τὸ πάσχα,
disciples of him. And was near the Passover,

ἡ ἑορτὴ τῶν Ἰουδαίων. 5 ἐπάρας οὖν
the feast of the Jews. Lifting up therefore

τοὺς ὀφθαλμοὺς ὁ Ἰησοῦς καὶ θεασάμενος
the(his) eyes - Jesus and beholding

ὅτι πολὺς ὄχλος ἔρχεται πρὸς αὐτόν,
that a much crowd is(was) coming toward him,

λέγει πρὸς Φίλιππον· πόθεν ἀγοράσωμεν
he says to Philip : Whence may we buy

ἄρτους ἵνα φάγωσιν οὗτοι; 6 τοῦτο δὲ
loaves that may eat these? And this

ἔλεγεν πειράζων αὐτόν· αὐτὸς γὰρ ᾔδει
he said testing him; for he knew

τί ἔμελλεν ποιεῖν. 7 ἀπεκρίθη αὐτῷ ὁ
what he was about to do. Answered him -

Φίλιππος· διακοσίων δηναρίων ἄρτοι οὐκ
Philip : ²Of two hundred ³denarii ¹loaves not

ἀρκοῦσιν αὐτοῖς, ἵνα ἕκαστος βραχύ τι
are enough for them, that each a little

λάβῃ. 8 λέγει αὐτῷ εἷς ἐκ τῶν μαθητῶν
may take. Says to him one of the disciples

αὐτοῦ, Ἀνδρέας ὁ ἀδελφὸς Σίμωνος
of him, Andrew the brother of Simon

Πέτρου· 9 ἔστιν παιδάριον ὧδε ὃς ἔχει
Peter : There is a lad here who has

πέντε ἄρτους κριθίνους καὶ δύο ὀψάρια·
five loaves barley and two fishes;

ἀλλὰ ταῦτα τί ἐστιν εἰς τοσούτους;
but ²these ¹what ³is(are) among so many?

10 εἶπεν ὁ Ἰησοῦς· ποιήσατε τοὺς ἀνθρώπους
Said - Jesus : Make the men*

ἀναπεσεῖν. ἦν δὲ χόρτος πολὺς ἐν τῷ
to recline. Now there was grass much in the

τόπῳ. ἀνέπεσαν οὖν οἱ ἄνδρες τὸν ἀριθμὸν
place. reclined therefore the men the number

ὡς πεντακισχίλιοι. 11 ἔλαβεν οὖν τοὺς
about five thousand. Took therefore the

ἄρτους ὁ Ἰησοῦς καὶ εὐχαριστήσας
loaves - Jesus and having given thanks

διέδωκεν τοῖς ἀνακειμένοις, ὁμοίως καὶ
distributed to the [ones] lying down, likewise also

ἐκ τῶν ὀψαρίων ὅσον ἤθελον. 12 ὡς δὲ
of the fishes as much as they wished. Now when

ἐνεπλήσθησαν, λέγει τοῖς μαθηταῖς αὐτοῦ·
they were filled, he tells the disciples of him:

συναγάγετε τὰ περισσεύσαντα κλάσματα, ἵνα
Gather ye the left over fragments, that

μή τι ἀπόληται. 13 συνήγαγον οὖν, καὶ
not anything is lost. They gathered therefore, and

ἐγέμισαν δώδεκα κοφίνους κλασμάτων ἐκ
filled twelve baskets of fragments of

τῶν πέντε ἄρτων τῶν κριθίνων ἃ ἐπερίσσευσαν
the five loaves - barley which were left over

τοῖς βεβρωκόσιν. 14 Οἱ οὖν ἄνθρωποι
to the [ones] having eaten. Therefore the men*

ἰδόντες ὃ ἐποίησεν σημεῖον ἔλεγον ὅτι
seeing ¹what ³he did ²sign said[,] -

οὗτός ἐστιν ἀληθῶς ὁ προφήτης ὁ
This is truly the prophet -

ἐρχόμενος εἰς τὸν κόσμον. 15 Ἰησοῦς
coming into the world. Jesus

οὖν γνοὺς ὅτι μέλλουσιν ἔρχεσθαι καὶ
therefore knowing that they are(were) about to come and

ἁρπάζειν αὐτὸν ἵνα ποιήσωσιν βασιλέα,
seize him that they might make a king,

ἀνεχώρησεν πάλιν εἰς τὸ ὄρος αὐτὸς
departed again to the mountain [him]self

μόνος. 16 Ὡς δὲ ὀψία ἐγένετο, κατέβησαν
alone. And when evening came, went down

οἱ μαθηταὶ αὐτοῦ ἐπὶ τὴν θάλασσαν,
the disciples of him to the sea,

17 καὶ ἐμβάντες εἰς πλοῖον ἤρχοντο πέραν
and embarking in a boat came across

τῆς θαλάσσης εἰς Καφαρναούμ. καὶ
the sea to Capernaum. And

σκοτία ἤδη ἐγεγόνει καὶ οὔπω ἐληλύθει
darkness now had come and not yet had come

πρὸς αὐτοὺς ὁ Ἰησοῦς, 18 ἥ τε θάλασσα
to them - Jesus, and the sea

ἀνέμου μεγάλου πνέοντος διηγείρετο.
wind a great blowing* was roused.
= as a great wind blew

19 ἐληλακότες οὖν ὡς σταδίους εἴκοσι
Having rowed therefore about furlongs twenty-

πέντε ἢ τριάκοντα θεωροῦσιν τὸν Ἰησοῦν
five or thirty they behold - Jesus

περιπατοῦντα ἐπὶ τῆς θαλάσσης καὶ ἐγγὺς
walking on the sea and near

τοῦ πλοίου γινόμενον, καὶ ἐφοβήθησαν.
the boat becoming, and they feared.

20 ὁ δὲ λέγει αὐτοῖς· ἐγώ εἰμι· μὴ
But he says to them : I am; not

φοβεῖσθε. 21 ἤθελον οὖν λαβεῖν αὐτὸν εἰς
fear ye. They wished therefore to take him into

---

* That is, people. Compare ἄνδρες in ver. 10.

King James Version

they willingly received him into the ship: and immediately the ship was at the land whither they went. 22 The day following, when the people, which stood on the other side of the sea, saw that there was none other boat there, save that one whereinto his disciples were entered, and that Jesus went not with his disciples into the boat, but *that* his disciples were gone away alone; 23 Howbeit there came other boats from Tiberias nigh unto the place where they did eat bread, after that the Lord had given thanks: 24 When the people therefore saw that Jesus was not there, neither his disciples, they also took shipping, and came to Capernaum, seeking for Jesus. 25And when they had found him on the other side of the sea, they said unto him, Rabbi, when camest thou hither? 26 Jesus answered them and said, Verily, verily, I say unto you, Ye seek me, not because ye saw the miracles, but because ye did eat of the loaves, and were filled. 27 Labour not for the meat which perisheth, but for that meat which endureth unto everlasting life, which the Son of man shall give unto you: for him hath God the Father sealed. 28 Then said they unto him, What shall we do, that we might work the works of God? 29 Jesus answered and said unto them, This is the work of God, that ye believe on him whom he hath sent. 30 They said therefore unto him, What sign shewest thou then, that we may see, and believe thee? what dost thou work? 31 Our fathers did eat manna in the desert; as it is written, He gave them bread from heaven to eat. 32 Then Jesus said unto them, Verily, verily, I say unto you, Moses gave you not that bread from heaven; but my Father giveth you the true bread from heaven. 33 For the bread of God is he which cometh down from heaven, and giveth life unto the world. 34 Then said they unto him, Lord, evermore give us this bread. 35And Jesus said unto them, I am the bread of life: he that cometh to me shall never hunger; and he that believeth on me shall never thirst. 36 But I said unto you, That ye also have seen me, and believe not. 37All that the Father giveth me shall come to me; and him that cometh to me I will in no wise cast out. 38 For I came down from heaven, not to do mine own will, but the will of him that sent me. 39And this is the Father's will which hath sent me, that of all which he hath given me I should lose nothing, but should raise it up again at the last day. 40And this is the will of him that sent me, that every one which seeth the Son, and believeth on him, may have everlasting life: and I will raise him up at the last day. 41 The Jews then murmured at him, because he said, I am the bread which came down from heaven. 42And they said, Is not this Jesus, the son of Joseph, whose father and mother we know? how is it then that he saith, I came down from heaven? 43 Jesus therefore answered and said unto them, Murmur not

New International Version

him into the boat, and immediately the boat reached the shore where they were heading. 22 The next day the crowd that had stayed on the opposite shore of the lake realized that only one boat had been there, and that Jesus had not entered it with his disciples, but that they had gone away alone. 23 Then some boats from Tiberias landed near the place where the people had eaten the bread after the Lord had given thanks. 24 Once the crowd realized that neither Jesus nor his disciples were there, they got into the boats and went to Capernaum in search of Jesus.

Jesus the bread of life

25 When they found him on the other side of the lake, they asked him, "Rabbi, when did you get here?"

26 Jesus answered, "I tell you the truth, you are looking for me, not because you saw miraculous signs but because you ate the loaves and had your fill. 27 Do not work for food that spoils, but for food that endures to eternal life, which the Son of Man will give you. On him God the Father has placed his seal of approval."

28 Then they asked him, "What must we do to do the work of God?"

29 Jesus answered, "The work of God is this: to believe in the one whom he has sent."

30 So they asked him, "What miraculous sign then will you give that we may see it and believe you? What will you do? 31 Our forefathers ate the manna in the desert; as it is written: 'He gave them bread from heaven to eat.' *e* "

32 Jesus said to them, "I tell you the truth, it is not Moses who has given you the bread from heaven, but it is my Father who gives you the true bread from heaven. 33 For the bread of God is he who comes down from heaven and gives life to the world."

34 "Sir," they said, "from now on give us this bread."

35 Then Jesus declared, "I am the bread of life. He who comes to me will never go hungry, and he who believes in me will never be thirsty. 36 But as I told you, you have seen me and still you do not believe. 37All that the Father gives me will come to me, and whoever comes to me I will never drive away. 38 For I have come down from heaven not to do my will but to do the will of him who sent me. 39And this is the will of him who sent me, that I shall lose none of all that he has given me, but raise them up at the last day. 40 For my Father's will is that everyone who looks to the Son and believes in him shall have eternal life, and I will raise him up at the last day."

41 At this the Jews began to murmur against him because he said, "I am the bread that came down from heaven." 42 They said, "Is this not Jesus, the son of Joseph, whose father and mother we know? How can he now say, 'I came down from heaven'?"

43 "Stop murmuring among yourselves," Je-

[e] Exodus 16:4; Psalm 78:24

Greek Interlinear

τὸ πλοῖον, καὶ εὐθέως ἐγένετο τὸ πλοῖον
the boat, and immediately was the boat

ἐπὶ τῆς γῆς εἰς ἣν ὑπῆγον.
at the land to which they were going.

22 Τῇ ἐπαύριον ὁ ὄχλος ὁ ἑστηκὼς
On the morrow the crowd – standing

πέραν τῆς θαλάσσης εἶδον ὅτι πλοιάριον
across the sea saw that boat

ἄλλο οὐκ ἦν ἐκεῖ εἰ μὴ ἓν, καὶ ὅτι
other was not there except one, and that

οὐ συνεισῆλθεν τοῖς μαθηταῖς αὐτοῦ ὁ
²did not come in with ³the ⁴disciples ⁵of him –

'Ιησοῦς εἰς τὸ πλοῖον ἀλλὰ μόνοι οἱ
¹Jesus in the boat but alone the

μαθηταὶ αὐτοῦ ἀπῆλθον· **23** ἄλλα ἦλθεν
disciples of him went away; ¹other ²came

πλοιάρια ἐκ Τιβεριάδος ἐγγὺς τοῦ τόπου
²boats from Tiberias near the place

ὅπου ἔφαγον τὸν ἄρτον εὐχαριστήσαντος
where they ate the bread having given thanks

τοῦ κυρίου. **24** ὅτε οὖν εἶδεν ὁ ὄχλος
the Lord.* When therefore saw the crowd
=when the Lord had given thanks.

ὅτι 'Ιησοῦς οὐκ ἔστιν ἐκεῖ οὐδὲ οἱ
that Jesus is(was) not there nor the

μαθηταὶ αὐτοῦ, ἐνέβησαν αὐτοὶ εἰς τὰ
disciples of him, embarked they in the

πλοιάρια καὶ ἦλθον εἰς Καφαρναοὺμ
boats and came to Capernaum

ζητοῦντες τὸν 'Ιησοῦν. **25** καὶ εὑρόντες
seeking – Jesus. And finding

αὐτὸν πέραν τῆς θαλάσσης εἶπον αὐτῷ·
him across the sea they said to him:

ῥαββί, πότε ὧδε γέγονας; **26** ἀπεκρίθη
Rabbi, when here hast thou come? Answered

αὐτοῖς ὁ 'Ιησοῦς καὶ εἶπεν· ἀμὴν ἀμὴν
them – Jesus and said: Truly truly

λέγω ὑμῖν, ζητεῖτέ με οὐχ ὅτι εἴδετε
I say to you, ye seek me not because ye saw

σημεῖα, ἀλλ' ὅτι ἐφάγετε ἐκ τῶν ἄρτων
signs, but because ye ate of the loaves

καὶ ἐχορτάσθητε. **27** ἐργάζεσθε μὴ τὴν
and were satisfied. Work not [for] the

βρῶσιν τὴν ἀπολλυμένην, ἀλλὰ τὴν βρῶσιν
food – perishing, but [for] the food

τὴν μένουσαν εἰς ζωὴν αἰώνιον, ἣν ὁ
– remaining to life eternal, which the

υἱὸς τοῦ ἀνθρώπου ὑμῖν δώσει· τοῦτον γὰρ
Son – of man you will give; for this [one]

ὁ πατὴρ ἐσφράγισεν ὁ θεός. **28** εἶπον
¹the ³Father ⁴sealed – ²God. They said

οὖν πρὸς αὐτόν· τί ποιῶμεν ἵνα ἐργαζ-
therefore to him: What may we do that we may

ώμεθα τὰ ἔργα τοῦ θεοῦ; **29** ἀπεκρίθη
work the works of God? Answered

'Ιησοῦς καὶ εἶπεν αὐτοῖς· τοῦτό ἐστιν τὸ
Jesus and said to them: This is the

ἔργον τοῦ θεοῦ, ἵνα πιστεύητε εἰς ὃν
work of God, that ye believe in [him] whom

ἀπέστειλεν ἐκεῖνος. **30** εἶπον οὖν αὐτῷ·
sent that [one]. They said therefore to him:

τί οὖν ποιεῖς σὺ σημεῖον, ἵνα ἴδωμεν
¹What ²then ⁴doest ³thou ⁵sign, that we may see

καὶ πιστεύσωμέν σοι; τί ἐργάζῃ; **31** οἱ
and believe thee? what workest thou? The

πατέρες ἡμῶν τὸ μάννα ἔφαγον ἐν τῇ
fathers of us the manna ate in the

ἐρήμῳ, καθώς ἐστιν γεγραμμένον· ἄρτον
desert, as it is having been written: Bread

ἐκ τοῦ οὐρανοῦ ἔδωκεν αὐτοῖς φαγεῖν.
out of – heaven he gave them to eat.

32 Εἶπεν οὖν αὐτοῖς ὁ 'Ιησοῦς· ἀμὴν
Said therefore to them – Jesus: Truly

ἀμὴν λέγω ὑμῖν, οὐ Μωϋσῆς δέδωκεν
truly I say to you, not Moses has given

ὑμῖν τὸν ἄρτον ἐκ τοῦ οὐρανοῦ, ἀλλ' ὁ
you the bread out of – heaven, but the

πατήρ μου δίδωσιν ὑμῖν τὸν ἄρτον ἐκ
Father of me gives you ¹the ²bread ⁴out of

τοῦ οὐρανοῦ τὸν ἀληθινόν· **33** ὁ γὰρ ἄρτος
– ³heaven the ²true; for the bread

τοῦ θεοῦ ἐστιν ὁ καταβαίνων ἐκ τοῦ
– of God is the [one] coming down out of –

οὐρανοῦ καὶ ζωὴν διδοὺς τῷ κόσμῳ.
heaven and life giving to the world.

34 εἶπον οὖν πρὸς αὐτόν· κύριε, πάντοτε
They said therefore to him: Lord, always

δὸς ἡμῖν τὸν ἄρτον τοῦτον. **35** εἶπεν
give us – bread this. Said

αὐτοῖς ὁ 'Ιησοῦς· ἐγώ εἰμι ὁ ἄρτος τῆς
to them – Jesus: I am the bread

ζωῆς· ὁ ἐρχόμενος πρὸς ἐμὲ οὐ μὴ
of life; the [one] coming to me by no means

πεινάσῃ, καὶ ὁ πιστεύων εἰς ἐμὲ οὐ μὴ
hungers, and the [one] believing in me by no means

διψήσει πώποτε. **36** Ἀλλ' εἶπον ὑμῖν ὅτι
will thirst never. But I told you that

καὶ ἑωράκατέ [με] καὶ οὐ πιστεύετε.
both ye have seen me and do not believe.

37 πᾶν ὃ δίδωσίν μοι ὁ πατὴρ πρὸς
All which gives to me the Father to

ἐμὲ ἥξει, καὶ τὸν ἐρχόμενον πρός με
me will come, and the [one] coming to me

οὐ μὴ ἐκβάλω ἔξω, **38** ὅτι καταβέβηκα
by no means I will cast out outside, because I have come down

ἀπὸ τοῦ οὐρανοῦ οὐχ ἵνα ποιῶ τὸ θέλημα
from – heaven not that I may do the ¹will

τὸ ἐμὸν ἀλλὰ τὸ θέλημα τοῦ πέμψαντός
– ¹my but the will of the [one] having sent

με. **39** τοῦτο δέ ἐστιν τὸ θέλημα τοῦ
me. And this is the will of the [one]

πέμψαντός με, ἵνα πᾶν ὃ δέδωκέν μοι
having sent me, that all which he has given me

μὴ ἀπολέσω ἐξ αὐτοῦ, ἀλλὰ ἀναστήσω
I shall not lose of it, but shall raise up

αὐτὸ ἐν τῇ ἐσχάτῃ ἡμέρᾳ. **40** τοῦτο
it in the last day. this

γάρ ἐστιν τὸ θέλημα τοῦ πατρός μου,
For is the will of the Father of me,

ἵνα πᾶς ὁ θεωρῶν τὸν υἱὸν καὶ πιστεύων
that everyone beholding the Son and believing

εἰς αὐτὸν ἔχῃ ζωὴν αἰώνιον, καὶ ἀναστήσω
in him may have life eternal, and will raise up

αὐτὸν ἐγὼ ἐν τῇ ἐσχάτῃ ἡμέρᾳ. **41** Ἐγόγ-
him I in the last day. Mur-

γυζον οὖν οἱ 'Ιουδαῖοι περὶ αὐτοῦ ὅτι
mured therefore the Jews about him because

εἶπεν· ἐγώ εἰμι ὁ ἄρτος ὁ καταβὰς ἐκ
he said: I am the bread – having come down out

τοῦ οὐρανοῦ, **42** καὶ ἔλεγον· οὐχ οὗτός
– of heaven, and they said: Not this man

ἐστιν 'Ιησοῦς ὁ υἱὸς 'Ιωσήφ, οὗ ἡμεῖς
is Jesus the son of Joseph, of whom we

οἴδαμεν τὸν πατέρα καὶ τὴν μητέρα;
know the father and the mother?

πῶς νῦν λέγει ὅτι ἐκ τοῦ οὐρανοῦ
how now says he[,] that Out of – heaven

καταβέβηκα; **43** ἀπεκρίθη 'Ιησοῦς καὶ εἶπεν
I have come down? Answered Jesus and said

αὐτοῖς· μὴ γογγύζετε μετ' ἀλλήλων.
to them: Do not murmur with one another.

King James Version

among yourselves. 44 No man can come to me, except the Father which hath sent me draw him: and I will raise him up at the last day. 45 It is written in the prophets, And they shall be all taught of God. Every man therefore that hath heard, and hath learned of the Father, cometh unto me. 46 Not that any man hath seen the Father, save he which is of God, he hath seen the Father. 47 Verily, verily, I say unto you, He that believeth on me hath everlasting life. 48 I am that bread of life. 49 Your fathers did eat manna in the wilderness, and are dead. 50 This is the bread which cometh down from heaven, that a man may eat thereof, and not die. 51 I am the living bread which came down from heaven: if any man eat of this bread, he shall live for ever: and the bread that I will give is my flesh, which I will give for the life of the world. 52 The Jews therefore strove among themselves, saying, How can this man give us *his* flesh to eat? 53 Then Jesus said unto them, Verily, verily, I say unto you, Except ye eat the flesh of the Son of man, and drink his blood, ye have no life in you. 54 Whoso eateth my flesh, and drinketh my blood, hath eternal life; and I will raise him up at the last day. 55 For my flesh is meat indeed, and my blood is drink indeed. 56 He that eateth my flesh, and drinketh my blood, dwelleth in me, and I in him. 57 As the living Father hath sent me, and I live by the Father; so he that eateth me, even he shall live by me. 58 This is that bread which came down from heaven: not as your fathers did eat manna, and are dead: he that eateth of this bread shall live for ever. 59 These things said he in the synagogue, as he taught in Capernaum. 60 Many therefore of his disciples, when they had heard *this*, said, This is a hard saying; who can hear it? 61 When Jesus knew in himself that his disciples murmured at it, he said unto them, Doth this offend you? 62 *What* and if ye shall see the Son of man ascend up where he was before? 63 It is the Spirit that quickeneth; the flesh profiteth nothing: the words that I speak unto you, *they* are spirit, and *they* are life. 64 But there are some of you that believe not. For Jesus knew from the beginning who they were that believed not, and who should betray him. 65 And he said, Therefore said I unto you, that no man can come unto me, except it were given unto him of my Father.

66 From that *time* many of his disciples went back, and walked no more with him. 67 Then said Jesus unto the twelve, Will ye also go away? 68 Then Simon Peter answered him, Lord, to whom shall we go? thou hast the words of eternal life. 69 And we believe and are sure that thou

New International Version

sus answered. 44 "No one can come to me unless the Father who sent me draws him, and I will raise him up at the last day. 45 It is written in the Prophets: 'They will all be taught by God.' *f* Everyone who listens to the Father and learns from him comes to me. 46 No one has seen the Father except the one who is from God; only he has seen the Father. 47 I tell you the truth, he who believes has everlasting life. 48 I am the bread of life. 49 Your forefathers ate the manna in the desert, yet they died. 50 But here is the bread that comes down from heaven, which a man may eat and not die. 51 I am the living bread that came down from heaven. If a man eats of this bread, he will live forever. This bread is my flesh, which I will give for the life of the world."

52 Then the Jews began to argue sharply among themselves, "How can this man give us his flesh to eat?"

53 Jesus said to them, "I tell you the truth, unless you eat the flesh of the Son of Man and drink his blood, you have no life in you. 54 Whoever eats my flesh and drinks my blood has eternal life, and I will raise him up at the last day. 55 For my flesh is real food and my blood is real drink. 56 Whoever eats my flesh and drinks my blood remains in me, and I in him. 57 Just as the living Father sent me and I live because of the Father, so the one who feeds on me will live because of me. 58 This is the bread that came down from heaven. Our forefathers ate [manna] and died, but he who feeds on this bread will live forever." 59 He said this while teaching in the synagogue in Capernaum.

Many disciples desert Jesus

60 On hearing it, many of his disciples said, "This is a hard teaching. Who can accept it?"

61 Aware that his disciples were grumbling about this, Jesus said to them, "Does this offend you? 62 What if you see the Son of Man ascend to where he was before! 63 The Spirit gives life; the flesh counts for nothing. The words I have spoken to you are spirit *g* and they are life. 64 Yet there are some of you who do not believe." For Jesus had known from the beginning which of them did not believe and who would betray him. 65 He went on to say, "This is why I told you that no one can come to me unless the Father has enabled him."

66 From this time many of his disciples turned back and no longer followed him.

67 "Do you want to leave too?" Jesus asked the Twelve.

68 Simon Peter answered him, "Lord, to whom shall we go? You have the words of eternal life. 69 We believe and know that you are the Holy One of God."

[*f*] Isaiah 54:13. [*g*] Or *Spirit*.

Greek Interlinear

44 Οὐδεὶς δύναται ἐλθεῖν πρός με ἐὰν μὴ
No one can to come to me unless

ὁ πατὴρ ὁ πέμψας με ἑλκύσῃ αὐτόν,
the Father the [one] having sent me should draw him,

κἀγὼ ἀναστήσω αὐτὸν ἐν τῇ ἐσχάτῃ
and I will raise up him in the last

ἡμέρᾳ. 45 ἔστιν γεγραμμένον ἐν τοῖς
day. It is *having been* written in the

προφήταις· καὶ ἔσονται πάντες διδακτοὶ
prophets: And they shall be all taught

θεοῦ· πᾶς ὁ ἀκούσας παρὰ τοῦ πατρὸς
of God; everyone hearing from the Father

καὶ μαθὼν ἔρχεται πρὸς ἐμέ. 46 οὐχ
and learning comes to me. Not

ὅτι τὸν πατέρα ἑώρακέν τις, εἰ μὴ ὁ
that the Father has seen anyone, except the [one]

ὢν παρὰ τοῦ θεοῦ, οὗτος ἑώρακεν τὸν
being with - God, this [one] has seen the

πατέρα. 47 ἀμὴν ἀμὴν λέγω ὑμῖν, ὁ
Father. Truly truly I say to you, the

πιστεύων ἔχει ζωὴν αἰώνιον. 48 Ἐγώ
[one] believing has life eternal. I

εἰμι ὁ ἄρτος τῆς ζωῆς. 49 οἱ πατέρες
am the bread - of life. The fathers

ὑμῶν ἔφαγον ἐν τῇ ἐρήμῳ τὸ μάννα καὶ
of you ate in the desert the manna and

ἀπέθανον· 50 οὗτός ἐστιν ὁ ἄρτος ὁ ἐκ
died; this is the bread - out of

τοῦ οὐρανοῦ καταβαίνων, ἵνα τις ἐξ
- heaven coming down, that anyone of

αὐτοῦ φάγῃ καὶ μὴ ἀποθάνῃ. 51 ἐγώ
it may eat and may not die. I

εἰμι ὁ ἄρτος ὁ ζῶν ὁ ἐκ τοῦ οὐρανοῦ
am the bread - living the [one] out of - heaven

καταβάς· ἐάν τις φάγῃ ἐκ τούτου τοῦ
having come down; if anyone eats of this -

ἄρτου, ζήσει εἰς τὸν αἰῶνα· καὶ ὁ ἄρτος
bread, he will live to the age; indeed the bread

δὲ ὃν ἐγὼ δώσω ἡ σάρξ μού ἐστιν
and which I will give the flesh of me is

ὑπὲρ τῆς τοῦ κόσμου ζωῆς. 52 Ἐμάχοντο
for the of the world life. Fought

οὖν πρὸς ἀλλήλους οἱ Ἰουδαῖοι λέγοντες·
therefore with one another the Jews saying:

πῶς δύναται οὗτος ἡμῖν δοῦναι τὴν
How can this man us to give the(his)

σάρκα φαγεῖν; 53 εἶπεν οὖν αὐτοῖς ὁ
flesh to eat? Said therefore to them -

Ἰησοῦς· ἀμὴν ἀμὴν λέγω ὑμῖν, ἐὰν μὴ
Jesus: Truly truly I say to you, unless

φάγητε τὴν σάρκα τοῦ υἱοῦ τοῦ ἀνθρώπου
ye eat the flesh of the Son - of man

καὶ πίητε αὐτοῦ τὸ αἷμα, οὐκ ἔχετε
and drink of him the blood, ye have not

ζωὴν ἐν ἑαυτοῖς. 54 ὁ τρώγων μου τὴν
life in yourselves. The [one] eating of me the

σάρκα καὶ πίνων μου τὸ αἷμα ἔχει ζωὴν
flesh and drinking of me the blood has life

αἰώνιον, κἀγὼ ἀναστήσω αὐτὸν τῇ ἐσχάτῃ
eternal, and I will raise up him in the last

ἡμέρᾳ. 55 ἡ γὰρ σάρξ μου ἀληθής
day. For the flesh of me true

ἐστιν βρῶσις, καὶ τὸ αἷμά μου ἀληθής
is food, and the blood of me true

ἐστιν πόσις. 56 ὁ τρώγων μου τὴν
is drink. The [one] eating of me the

σάρκα καὶ πίνων μου τὸ αἷμα ἐν ἐμοὶ
flesh and drinking of me the blood in me

μένει κἀγὼ ἐν αὐτῷ. 57 καθὼς ἀπέστειλέν
remains and I in him. As sent

με ὁ ζῶν πατὴρ κἀγὼ ζῶ διὰ τὸν
me the living Father and I live because of the

πατέρα, καὶ ὁ τρώγων με κἀκεῖνος
Father, also the [one] eating me even that one

ζήσει δι' ἐμέ. 58 οὗτός ἐστιν ὁ ἄρτος ὁ
will live because of me. This is the bread -

ἐξ οὐρανοῦ καταβάς, οὐ καθὼς ἔφαγον
out of heaven having come down, not as ate

οἱ πατέρες καὶ ἀπέθανον· ὁ τρώγων
the fathers and died; the [one] eating

τοῦτον τὸν ἄρτον ζήσει εἰς τὸν αἰῶνα.
this - bread will live unto the age.

59 Ταῦτα εἶπεν ἐν συναγωγῇ διδάσκων ἐν
These things he said in a synagogue teaching in

Καφαρναούμ. 60 Πολλοὶ οὖν ἀκούσαντες
Capernaum. Many therefore hearing

ἐκ τῶν μαθητῶν αὐτοῦ εἶπαν· σκληρός
of the disciples of him said: Hard

ἐστιν ὁ λόγος οὗτος· τίς δύναται αὐτοῦ
is - word this; who can it

ἀκούειν; 61 εἰδὼς δὲ ὁ Ἰησοῦς ἐν ἑαυτῷ
to hear? But knowing - Jesus in himself

ὅτι γογγύζουσιν περὶ τούτου οἱ μαθηταὶ
that are murmuring about this the disciples

αὐτοῦ, εἶπεν αὐτοῖς· τοῦτο ὑμᾶς σκανδαλίζει;
of him, said to them: This you offends?

62 ἐὰν οὖν θεωρῆτε τὸν υἱὸν τοῦ ἀνθρώπου
If then ye behold the Son - of man

ἀναβαίνοντα ὅπου ἦν τὸ πρότερον; 63 τὸ
ascending where he was at first? † The

πνεῦμά ἐστιν τὸ ζωοποιοῦν, ἡ σὰρξ οὐκ
spirit is the [thing] quickening, the flesh not

ὠφελεῖ οὐδέν· τὰ ῥήματα ἃ ἐγὼ λελάληκα
profits no(any)thing; the words which I have spoken

ὑμῖν πνεῦμά ἐστιν καὶ ζωή ἐστιν. 64 ἀλλ'
to you spirit is(are) and life is(are). But

εἰσὶν ἐξ ὑμῶν τινες οἳ οὐ πιστεύουσιν. ᾔδει
there are of you some who do not believe. knew

γὰρ ἐξ ἀρχῆς ὁ Ἰησοῦς τίνες εἰσὶν
For from [the] beginning - Jesus who are(were)

οἱ μὴ πιστεύοντες καὶ τίς ἐστιν ὁ
the [ones] not believing and who is(was) the

παραδώσων αὐτόν. 65 καὶ ἔλεγεν·
[one] betraying him. And he said:

διὰ τοῦτο εἴρηκα ὑμῖν ὅτι οὐδεὶς δύναται
Therefore I have told you that no one can

ἐλθεῖν πρός με ἐὰν μὴ ᾖ δεδομένον
to come to me unless it is *having been* given

αὐτῷ ἐκ τοῦ πατρός.
to him of the Father.

66 Ἐκ τούτου πολλοὶ τῶν μαθητῶν
From this many of the disciples

αὐτοῦ ἀπῆλθον εἰς τὰ ὀπίσω καὶ οὐκέτι
of him went away back† and no longer

μετ' αὐτοῦ περιεπάτουν. 67 εἶπεν οὖν ὁ
with him walked. Said therefore -

Ἰησοῦς τοῖς δώδεκα· μὴ καὶ ὑμεῖς
Jesus to the twelve: Not also ye

θέλετε ὑπάγειν; 68 ἀπεκρίθη αὐτῷ Σίμων
wish to go? Answered him Simon

Πέτρος· κύριε, πρὸς τίνα ἀπελευσόμεθα;
Peter: Lord, to whom shall we go away?

ῥήματα ζωῆς αἰωνίου ἔχεις· 69 καὶ ἡμεῖς
words of life eternal thou hast; and we

πεπιστεύκαμεν καὶ ἐγνώκαμεν ὅτι σὺ εἶ
have believed and have known that thou art

King James Version

art that Christ, the Son of the living God. 70 Jesus answered them, Have not I chosen you twelve, and one of you is a devil? 71 He spake of Judas Iscariot *the son* of Simon: for he it was that should betray him, being one of the twelve.

7 After these things Jesus walked in Galilee: for he would not walk in Jewry, because the Jews sought to kill him. 2 Now the Jews' feast of tabernacles was at hand. 3 His brethren therefore said unto him, Depart hence, and go into Judea, that thy disciples also may see the works that thou doest. 4 For *there is* no man *that* doeth any thing in secret, and he himself seeketh to be known openly. If thou do these things, shew thyself to the world. 5 For neither did his brethren believe in him. 6 Then Jesus said unto them, My time is not yet come: but your time is always ready. 7 The world cannot hate you; but me it hateth, because I testify of it, that the works thereof are evil. 8 Go ye up unto this feast: I go not up yet unto this feast; for my time is not yet full come. 9 When he had said these words unto them, he abode *still* in Galilee.

10 But when his brethren were gone up, then went he also up unto the feast, not openly, but as it were in secret. 11 Then the Jews sought him at the feast, and said, Where is he? 12 And there was much murmuring among the people concerning him: for some said, He is a good man: others said, Nay; but he deceiveth the people. 13 Howbeit no man spake openly of him for fear of the Jews.

14 Now about the midst of the feast Jesus went up into the temple, and taught. 15 And the Jews marvelled, saying, How knoweth this man letters, having never learned? 16 Jesus answered them, and said, My doctrine is not mine, but his that sent me. 17 If any man will do his will, he shall know of the doctrine, whether it be of God, or *whether* I speak of myself. 18 He that speaketh of himself seeketh his own glory: but he that seeketh his glory that sent him, the same is true, and no unrighteousness is in him. 19 Did not Moses give you the law, and *yet* none of you keepeth the law? Why go ye about to kill me? 20 The people answered and said, Thou hast a devil: who goeth about to kill thee? 21 Jesus answered and said unto them, I have done one work, and ye all marvel. 22 Moses therefore gave unto you circumcision; (not because it is of Moses, but of the fathers;) and ye on the sabbath day circumcise a man. 23 If a man on the sabbath day receive circumcision, that the law of

New International Version

70 Then Jesus replied, "Have I not chosen you, the Twelve? Yet one of you is a devil!" 71 (He meant Judas, the son of Simon Iscariot, who, though one of the Twelve, was later to betray him.)

Jesus goes to the Feast of Tabernacles

7 After this, Jesus went around in Galilee, purposely staying away from Judea because the Jews there were waiting to take his life. 2 But when the Jewish Feast of Tabernacles was near, 3 Jesus' brothers said to him, "You ought to leave here and go to Judea, so that your disciples may see the miracles you do. 4 No one who wants to become a public figure acts in secret. Since you are doing these things, show yourself to the world." 5 For even his own brothers did not believe in him.

6 Therefore Jesus told them, "The right time for me has not yet come; for you any time is right. 7 The world cannot hate you, but it hates me because I testify that what it does is evil. 8 You go to the Feast. I am not yet[h] going up to this Feast, because for me the right time has not yet come." 9 Having said this, he stayed in Galilee.

10 However, after his brothers had left for the Feast, he went also, but not publicly, in secret. 11 Now at the Feast the Jews were watching for him and asking, "Where is that man?"

12 Among the crowds there was widespread whispering about him. Some said, "He is a good man."

Others replied, "No, he deceives the people." 13 But no one would say anything publicly about him for fear of the Jews.

Jesus teaches at the Feast

14 Not until halfway through the Feast did Jesus go up to the temple court and begin to teach. 15 The Jews were amazed and asked, "How did this man get such learning without having studied?"

16 Jesus answered, "My teaching is not my own. It comes from him who sent me. 17 If a man chooses to do God's will, he will find out whether my teaching comes from God or whether I speak on my own. 18 He who speaks on his own does so to gain honor for himself, but he who works for the honor of the one who sent him is a man of truth; there is nothing false about him. 19 Has not Moses given you the law? Yet not one of you keeps the law. Why are you trying to kill me?"

20 "You are demon-possessed," the crowd answered. "Who is trying to kill you?"

21 Jesus said to them, "I did one miracle, and you are all astonished. 22 Yet, because Moses gave you circumcision (though actually it did not come from Moses, but from the patriarchs), you circumcise a child on the Sabbath. 23 Now if a child can be circumcised on the Sabbath so

Greek Interlinear

ὁ ἅγιος τοῦ θεοῦ. **70** ἀπεκρίθη αὐτοῖς ὁ
the holy one – of God.   Answered them –

'Ιησοῦς· οὐκ ἐγὼ ὑμᾶς τοὺς δώδεκα
Jesus : ²Not ¹I ⁴you ³the ⁵twelve

ἐξελεξάμην; καὶ ἐξ ὑμῶν εἷς διάβολός
¹chose? and of you one a devil

ἐστιν. **71** ἔλεγεν δὲ τὸν 'Ιούδαν Σίμωνος
is.   Now he spoke [of] – Judas [son] of Simon

'Ισκαριώτου· οὗτος γὰρ ἔμελλεν παραδιδόναι
Iscariot;   for this one was about to betray

αὐτόν, εἷς ἐκ τῶν δώδεκα.
him, one of the twelve.

Chapter 7

Καὶ μετὰ ταῦτα περιεπάτει ὁ 'Ιησοῦς
And after these things walked – Jesus

ἐν τῇ Γαλιλαίᾳ· οὐ γὰρ ἤθελεν ἐν τῇ
in – Galilee; for he did not wish in –

'Ιουδαίᾳ περιπατεῖν, ὅτι ἐζήτουν αὐτὸν οἱ
Judæa to walk, because ²were seeking ³him ¹the

'Ιουδαῖοι ἀποκτεῖναι. **2** ἦν δὲ ἐγγὺς ἡ
²Jews ⁴to kill.   Now was near the

ἑορτὴ τῶν 'Ιουδαίων ἡ σκηνοπηγία. **3** εἶπον
feast of the Jews the Tabernacles. Said

οὖν πρὸς αὐτὸν οἱ ἀδελφοὶ αὐτοῦ·
therefore to him the brothers of him :

μετάβηθι ἐντεῦθεν καὶ ὕπαγε εἰς τὴν 'Ιουδαίαν,
Depart hence and go into – Judæa,

ἵνα καὶ οἱ μαθηταί σου θεωρήσουσιν τὰ
that also the disciples of thee will behold the

ἔργα σου ἃ ποιεῖς· **4** οὐδεὶς γάρ τι ἐν
works of thee which thou doest; for no one anything in

κρυπτῷ ποιεῖ καὶ ζητεῖ αὐτὸς ἐν παρρησίᾳ
secret does and seeks [him]self in [the] open

εἶναι. εἰ ταῦτα ποιεῖς, φανέρωσον σεαυτὸν
to be. If these things thou doest, manifest thyself

τῷ κόσμῳ. **5** οὐδὲ γὰρ οἱ ἀδελφοὶ
to the world. For not the brothers

αὐτοῦ ἐπίστευον εἰς αὐτόν. **6** λέγει οὖν
of him believed in him. Says therefore

αὐτοῖς ὁ 'Ιησοῦς· The ²time – ¹my
to them – Jesus: The ²time – ¹my

οὔπω πάρεστιν, ὁ δὲ καιρὸς ὁ ὑμέτερος
not yet is arrived, but the ²time – ¹your

πάντοτέ ἐστιν ἕτοιμος. **7** οὐ δύναται ὁ
always is ready.   Cannot the

κόσμος μισεῖν ὑμᾶς, ἐμὲ δὲ μισεῖ, ὅτι
world to hate you, but me it hates, because

ἐγὼ μαρτυρῶ περὶ αὐτοῦ ὅτι τὰ ἔργα
I witness about it that the works

αὐτοῦ πονηρά ἐστιν. **8** ὑμεῖς ἀνάβητε εἰς
of it evil is(are). ²Ye ¹go ²up to

τὴν ἑορτήν· ἐγὼ οὐκ ἀναβαίνω εἰς τὴν
the feast; I am not going up to –

ἑορτὴν ταύτην, ὅτι ὁ ἐμὸς καιρὸς οὔπω
feast this, because the my time not yet

πεπλήρωται. **9** ταῦτα δὲ εἰπὼν αὐτοῖς
has been fulfilled. And these things saying to them

ἔμεινεν ἐν τῇ Γαλιλαίᾳ. **10** Ὡς δὲ
he remained in – Galilee.   But when

ἀνέβησαν οἱ ἀδελφοὶ αὐτοῦ εἰς τὴν ἑορτήν,
went up the brothers of him to the feast,

τότε καὶ αὐτὸς ἀνέβη, οὐ φανερῶς ἀλλὰ
then also he went up, not manifestly but

ὡς ἐν κρυπτῷ. **11** οἱ οὖν 'Ιουδαῖοι
as in secret.   Therefore the Jews

ἐζήτουν αὐτὸν ἐν τῇ ἑορτῇ καὶ ἔλεγον·
sought him at the feast and said :

ποῦ ἐστιν ἐκεῖνος; **12** καὶ γογγυσμὸς περὶ
Where is that man? And ²murmuring ⁴about

αὐτοῦ ἦν πολὺς ἐν τοῖς ὄχλοις· οἱ μὲν
³him ¹there was ²much in the crowds; some

ἔλεγον ὅτι ἀγαθός ἐστιν· ἄλλοι [δὲ]
said[.] – A good man he is; but others

ἔλεγον· οὔ, ἀλλὰ πλανᾷ τὸν ὄχλον.
said : No, but he deceives the crowd.

13 οὐδεὶς μέντοι παρρησίᾳ ἐλάλει περὶ
No one however openly spoke about

αὐτοῦ διὰ τὸν φόβον τῶν 'Ιουδαίων.
him because of the fear of the Jews.

14 Ἤδη δὲ τῆς ἑορτῆς μεσούσης ἀνέβη
But now the feast being in [its] middle² went up
                      = in the middle of the feast

'Ιησοῦς εἰς τὸ ἱερὸν καὶ ἐδίδασκεν.
Jesus to the temple and taught.

15 ἐθαύμαζον οὖν οἱ 'Ιουδαῖοι λέγοντες·
Marvelled therefore the Jews saying :

πῶς οὗτος γράμματα οἶδεν μὴ μεμαθηκώς;
How this man letters knows not having learned?

16 ἀπεκρίθη οὖν αὐτοῖς 'Ιησοῦς καὶ εἶπεν·
Answered therefore them Jesus and said :

ἡ ἐμὴ διδαχὴ οὐκ ἔστιν ἐμὴ ἀλλὰ τοῦ
The my teaching is not mine but of the

πέμψαντός με· **17** ἐάν τις θέλῃ τὸ θέλημα
[one] having sent me; if anyone wishes the will

αὐτοῦ ποιεῖν, γνώσεται περὶ τῆς διδαχῆς,
of him to do, he will know concerning the teaching,

πότερον ἐκ τοῦ θεοῦ ἐστιν ἢ ἐγὼ ἀπ'
whether of – God it is or I from

ἐμαυτοῦ λαλῶ. **18** ὁ ἀφ' ἑαυτοῦ λαλῶν
myself speak. The [one] from himself speaking

τὴν δόξαν τὴν ἰδίαν ζητεῖ· ὁ δὲ ζητῶν
his own glory seeks; but the [one] seeking

τὴν δόξαν τοῦ πέμψαντος αὐτόν, οὗτος
the glory of the [one] having sent him, this man

ἀληθής ἐστιν καὶ ἀδικία ἐν αὐτῷ οὐκ
true is and unrighteousness in him not

ἔστιν. **19** οὐ Μωϋσῆς ἔδωκεν ὑμῖν τὸν
is.   Not Moses gave you the

νόμον; καὶ οὐδεὶς ἐξ ὑμῶν ποιεῖ τὸν
law? and no one of you does the

νόμον. τί με ζητεῖτε ἀποκτεῖναι;
law. Why me seek ye to kill?

20 ἀπεκρίθη ὁ ὄχλος· δαιμόνιον ἔχεις·
Answered the crowd : A demon thou hast;

τίς σε ζητεῖ ἀποκτεῖναι; **21** ἀπεκρίθη
who thee seeks to kill?   Answered

'Ιησοῦς καὶ εἶπεν αὐτοῖς· ἐν ἔργον ἐποίησα
Jesus and said to them : One work I did

καὶ πάντες θαυμάζετε. **22** διὰ τοῦτο
and all ye marvel.   Because of this

Μωϋσῆς δέδωκεν ὑμῖν τὴν περιτομήν, —
Moses has given you – circumcision, –

οὐχ ὅτι ἐκ τοῦ Μωϋσέως ἐστιν ἀλλ' ἐκ
not that of – Moses it is but of

τῶν πατέρων, — καὶ ἐν σαββάτῳ
the fathers, – and on a sabbath

περιτέμνετε ἄνθρωπον. **23** εἰ περιτομὴν
ye circumcise a man.   If circumcision

λαμβάνει [ὁ] ἄνθρωπος ἐν σαββάτῳ ἵνα
²receives   ¹a man on a sabbath that

King James Version

Moses should not be broken; are ye angry at me, because I have made a man every whit whole on the sabbath day? 24 Judge not according to the appearance, but judge righteous judgment. 25 Then said some of them of Jerusalem, Is not this he, whom they seek to kill? 26 But, lo, he speaketh boldly, and they say nothing unto him. Do the rulers know indeed that this is the very Christ? 27 Howbeit we know this man whence he is: but when Christ cometh, no man knoweth whence he is. 28 Then cried Jesus in the temple as he taught, saying, Ye both know me, and ye know whence I am: and I am not come of myself, but he that sent me is true, whom ye know not. 29 But I know him; for I am from him, and he hath sent me. 30 Then they sought to take him: but no man laid hands on him, because his hour was not yet come. 31 And many of the people believed on him, and said, When Christ cometh, will he do more miracles than these which this *man* hath done?

32 The Pharisees heard that the people murmured such things concerning him; and the Pharisees and the chief priests sent officers to take him. 33 Then said Jesus unto them, Yet a little while am I with you, and *then* I go unto him that sent me. 34 Ye shall seek me, and shall not find *me:* and where I am, *thither* ye cannot come. 35 Then said the Jews among themselves, Whither will he go, that we shall not find him? will he go unto the dispersed among the Gentiles, and teach the Gentiles? 36 What *manner of* saying is this that he said, Ye shall seek me, and shall not find *me:* and where I am, *thither* ye cannot come? 37 In the last day, that great *day* of the feast, Jesus stood and cried, saying, If any man thirst, let him come unto me, and drink. 38 He that believeth on me, as the Scripture hath said, out of his belly shall flow rivers of living water. 39 (But this spake he of the Spirit, which they that believe on him should receive: for the Holy Ghost was not yet *given;* because that Jesus was not yet glorified.)

40 Many of the people therefore, when they heard this saying, said, Of a truth this is the Prophet. 41 Others said, This is the Christ. But some said, Shall Christ come out of Galilee? 42 Hath not the Scripture said, That Christ cometh of the seed of David, and out of the town of Bethlehem, where David was? 43 So there was a division among the people because of him. 44 And some of them would have taken him; but no man laid hands on him.

45 Then came the officers to the chief priests and Pharisees; and they said unto them, Why have ye not brought him? 46 The officers answered, Never man spake like this man. 47 Then answered them the Pharisees, Are ye also de-

New International Version

that the law of Moses may not be broken, why are you angry with me for healing the whole man on the Sabbath? 24 Stop judging by mere appearances, and make a right judgment."

Is Jesus the Christ?

25 At that point some of the people of Jerusalem began to ask, "Isn't this the man they are trying to kill? 26 Here he is, speaking publicly, and they are not saying a word to him. Have the authorities really concluded that he is the Christ*? 27 But we know where this man is from; when the Christ* comes, no one will know where he is from."

28 Then Jesus, still teaching in the temple court, cried out, "Yes, you know me, and you know where I am from. I am not here on my own, but he who sent me is true. You do not know him, 29 but I know him because I am from him and he sent me."

30 At this they tried to seize him, but no one laid a hand on him, because his time had not yet come. 31 Still, many in the crowd put their faith in him. They said, "When the Christ* comes, will he do more miraculous signs than this man?"

32 The Pharisees heard the crowd whispering such things about him. Then the chief priests and the Pharisees sent temple guards to arrest him.

33 Jesus said, "I am with you for only a short time, and then I go to the one who sent me. 34 You will look for me, but you will not find me; and where I am, you cannot come."

35 The Jews said to one another, "Where does this man intend to go that we cannot find him? Will he go where our people live scattered among the Greeks, and teach the Greeks? 36 What did he mean when he said, 'You will look for me, but you will not find me,' and 'Where I am, you cannot come'?"

37 On the last and greatest day of the Feast, Jesus stood and said in a loud voice, "If a man is thirsty, let him come to me and drink. 38 Whoever believes in me, as the Scripture has said, streams of living water will flow from within him." 39 By this he meant the Spirit, whom those who believed in him were later to receive. Up to that time the Spirit had not been given, since Jesus had not yet been glorified.

40 On hearing his words, some of the people said, "Surely this man is the Prophet."

41 Others said, "He is the Christ.*"

Still others asked, "How can the Christ* come from Galilee? 42 Does not the Scripture say that the Christ* will come from David's family* and from Bethlehem, the town where David lived?" 43 Thus the people were divided because of Jesus. 44 Some wanted to seize him, but no one laid a hand on him.

Unbelief of the Jewish leaders

45 Finally the temple guards went back to the chief priests and Pharisees, who asked them, "Why didn't you bring him in?"

46 "No one ever spoke the way this man does," the guards declared.

47 "You mean he has deceived you also?" the

[i] Or *Messiah.* [j] Or *If a man is thirsty, let him come to me. And let him drink, who believes in me.* [l] Greek *seed.*

Greek Interlinear

μὴ λυθῇ ὁ νόμος Μωϋσέως, ἐμοὶ χολᾶτε
is not broken the law of Moses, with me are ye angry

ὅτι ὅλον ἄνθρωπον ὑγιῆ ἐποίησα ἐν
because a whole man healthy I made on

σαββάτῳ; 24 μὴ κρίνετε κατ' ὄψιν, ἀλλὰ
a sabbath? Judge not according to face, but

τὴν δικαίαν κρίσιν κρίνατε. 25 Ἔλεγον
- righteous judgment judge. Said

οὖν τινες ἐκ τῶν Ἱεροσολυμιτῶν· οὐχ
therefore some of the Jerusalemites : ¹Not

οὗτός ἐστιν ὃν ζητοῦσιν ἀποκτεῖναι; 26 καὶ
²this man ¹is it whom they are seeking to kill? and

ἴδε παρρησίᾳ λαλεῖ, καὶ οὐδὲν αὐτῷ
behold openly he speaks, and nothing to him

λέγουσιν. μήποτε ἀληθῶς ἔγνωσαν οἱ
they say. Perhaps indeed knew the

ἄρχοντες ὅτι οὗτός ἐστιν ὁ χριστός; *
rulers that this is the Christ?

27 ἀλλὰ τοῦτον οἴδαμεν πόθεν ἐστίν· ὁ δὲ
But this man we know whence he is; but ²the

χριστὸς ὅταν ἔρχηται, οὐδεὶς γινώσκει
²Christ ¹when comes, no one knows

πόθεν ἐστίν. 28 ἔκραξεν οὖν ἐν τῷ ἱερῷ
whence he is. ¹Cried out therefore ²in ³the ⁴temple

διδάσκων ὁ Ἰησοῦς καὶ λέγων· κἀμὲ
³teaching - ¹Jesus ²and ⁴saying : Both me

οἴδατε καὶ οἴδατε πόθεν εἰμί· καὶ ἀπ'
ye know and ye know whence I am; and from

ἐμαυτοῦ οὐκ ἐλήλυθα, ἀλλ' ἔστιν ἀληθινὸς
myself I have not come, but he is true

ὁ πέμψας με, ὃν ὑμεῖς οὐκ οἴδατε·
the [one] having sent me, whom ye know not;

29 ἐγὼ οἶδα αὐτόν, ὅτι παρ' αὐτοῦ εἰμι
I know him, because ²from ³him ¹I am

κἀκεῖνός με ἀπέστειλεν. 30 Ἐζήτουν οὖν
²and that one ¹me ³sent. They sought therefore

αὐτὸν πιάσαι, καὶ οὐδεὶς ἐπέβαλεν ἐπ'
him to arrest, and no one laid on on

αὐτὸν τὴν χεῖρα, ὅτι οὔπω ἐληλύθει ἡ
him the hand, because not yet had come the

ὥρα αὐτοῦ. 31 Ἐκ τοῦ ὄχλου δὲ πολλοὶ
hour of him. ²of ³the ⁴crowd ¹But ⁵many

ἐπίστευσαν εἰς αὐτόν, καὶ ἔλεγον· ὁ
believed in him, and said : ²The

χριστὸς ὅταν ἔλθῃ, μὴ πλείονα σημεῖα
²Christ ¹when ³comes, not more signs

ποιήσει ὧν οὗτος ἐποίησεν; 32 ἤκουσαν
will he do [than] which this man did? ¹Heard

οἱ Φαρισαῖοι τοῦ ὄχλου γογγύζοντος περὶ
²the ³Pharisees ⁴the ⁵crowd ⁶murmuring ⁷about

αὐτοῦ ταῦτα, καὶ ἀπέστειλαν οἱ ἀρχιερεῖς
⁸him ⁹these things, and ²sent ¹the ³chief priests

καὶ οἱ Φαρισαῖοι ὑπηρέτας ἵνα πιάσωσιν
²and ⁴the ⁵Pharisees ⁶attendants that they might arrest

αὐτόν. 33 εἶπεν οὖν ὁ Ἰησοῦς· ἔτι
him. Said therefore - Jesus : Yet

χρόνον μικρὸν μεθ' ὑμῶν εἰμι καὶ ὑπάγω
time a little with you I am and I go

πρὸς τὸν πέμψαντά με. 34 ζητήσετέ με
to the [one] having sent me. Ye will seek me

καὶ οὐχ εὑρήσετε, καὶ ὅπου εἰμὶ ἐγὼ
and will not find, and where am I

ὑμεῖς οὐ δύνασθε ἐλθεῖν. 35 εἶπον οὖν
ye cannot to come. Said therefore

οἱ Ἰουδαῖοι πρὸς ἑαυτούς· ποῦ οὗτος
the Jews to themselves : Where this man

μέλλει πορεύεσθαι, ὅτι ἡμεῖς οὐχ εὑρήσομεν
is about to go, that we will not find

αὐτόν; μὴ εἰς τὴν διασπορὰν τῶν Ἑλλήνων
him? not to the dispersion of the Greeks

μέλλει πορεύεσθαι καὶ διδάσκειν τοὺς
is he about to go and to teach the

Ἕλληνας; 36 τίς ἐστιν ὁ λόγος οὗτος
Greeks? What is - word this

ὃν εἶπεν· ζητήσετέ με καὶ οὐχ εὑρήσετε,
which he said : Ye will seek me and will not find,

καὶ ὅπου εἰμὶ ἐγὼ ὑμεῖς οὐ δύνασθε
and where am I ye cannot

ἐλθεῖν;
to come?

37 Ἐν δὲ τῇ ἐσχάτῃ ἡμέρᾳ τῇ μεγάλῃ
Now in the last day the great [day]

τῆς ἑορτῆς εἱστήκει ὁ Ἰησοῦς καὶ ἔκραξεν
of the feast stood - Jesus and cried out

λέγων· ἐάν τις διψᾷ, ἐρχέσθω πρός με
saying : If anyone thirsts, let him come to me

καὶ πινέτω. 38 ὁ πιστεύων εἰς ἐμέ,
and drink. The [one] believing in me,

καθὼς εἶπεν ἡ γραφή, ποταμοὶ ἐκ τῆς
as said the scripture, ²rivers ¹out of ³the

κοιλίας αὐτοῦ ῥεύσουσιν ὕδατος ζῶντος.
⁴belly ⁵of him ⁶will flow ⁷water ⁸of living.

39 τοῦτο δὲ εἶπεν περὶ τοῦ πνεύματος
But this he said concerning the Spirit

οὗ ἔμελλον λαμβάνειν οἱ πιστεύσαντες
whom were about to receive the [ones] believing

εἰς αὐτόν· οὔπω γὰρ ἦν πνεῦμα, ὅτι
in him; for not yet was [?the] Spirit, because

Ἰησοῦς οὐδέπω ἐδοξάσθη. 40 Ἐκ τοῦ
Jesus not yet was glorified. [Some] of the

ὄχλου οὖν ἀκούσαντες τῶν λόγων τούτων
crowd therefore hearing - words these

ἔλεγον [ὅτι]· οὗτός ἐστιν ἀληθῶς ὁ
said : This man is truly the

προφήτης· 41 ἄλλοι ἔλεγον· οὗτός ἐστιν ὁ
prophet; Others said : This man is the

χριστός· οἱ δὲ ἔλεγον· μὴ γὰρ ἐκ τῆς
Christ; But others† said : Not then out of -

Γαλιλαίας ὁ χριστὸς ἔρχεται; 42 οὐχ ἡ
Galilee the Christ comes? not the

γραφὴ εἶπεν ὅτι ἐκ τοῦ σπέρματος Δαυίδ,
scripture said that of the seed of David,

καὶ ἀπὸ Βηθλέεμ τῆς κώμης ὅπου ἦν
and from Bethlehem the village where was

Δαυίδ, ἔρχεται ὁ χριστός; 43 σχίσμα
David, comes the Christ? A division

οὖν ἐγένετο ἐν τῷ ὄχλῳ δι' αὐτόν·
therefore became in the crowd because of him;

44 τινὲς δὲ ἤθελον ἐξ αὐτῶν πιάσαι αὐτόν,
and ²some ¹wished ³of ⁴them to arrest him,

ἀλλ' οὐδεὶς ἐπέβαλεν ἐπ' αὐτὸν τὰς χεῖρας.
but no one laid on on him the(his) hands.

45 Ἦλθον οὖν οἱ ὑπηρέται πρὸς τοὺς
Came therefore the attendants to the

ἀρχιερεῖς καὶ Φαρισαίους, καὶ εἶπον αὐτοῖς
chief priests and Pharisees, and ²said ¹to them

ἐκεῖνοι· διὰ τί οὐκ ἠγάγετε αὐτόν;
¹those: Why did ye not bring him?

46 ἀπεκρίθησαν οἱ ὑπηρέται· οὐδέποτε
Answered the attendants : Never

ἐλάλησεν οὕτως ἄνθρωπος, ὡς οὗτος λαλεῖ
spoke so a man, as ¹this ²speaks

ὁ ἄνθρωπος. 47 ἀπεκρίθησαν οὖν αὐτοῖς
³man. Answered therefore them

οἱ Φαρισαῖοι· μὴ καὶ ὑμεῖς πεπλάνησθε;
the Pharisees : Not also ye have been deceived?

---

* As this question is introduced by μήποτε , a negative answer is expected; see page xxxiii, and note ver. 31 below.

King James Version

ceived? 48 Have any of the rulers or of the Pharisees believed on him? 49 But this people who knoweth not the law are cursed. 50 Nicodemus saith unto them, (he that came to Jesus by night, being one of them,) 51 Doth our law judge *any* man, before it hear him, and know what he doeth? 52 They answered and said unto him, Art thou also of Galilee? Search, and look: for out of Galilee ariseth no prophet.

53 And every man went unto his own house.

8 Jesus went unto the mount of Olives. 2 And early in the morning he came again into the temple, and all the people came unto him; and he sat down, and taught them. 3 And the scribes and Pharisees brought unto him a woman taken in adultery; and when they had set her in the midst, 4 They say unto him, Master, this woman was taken in adultery, in the very act. 5 Now Moses in the law commanded us, that such should be stoned: but what sayest thou? 6 This they said, tempting him, that they might have to accuse him. But Jesus stooped down, and with *his* finger wrote on the ground, *as though he heard them not.* 7 So when they continued asking him, he lifted up himself, and said unto them, He that is without sin among you, let him first cast a stone at her. 8 And again he stooped down, and wrote on the ground. 9 And they which heard *it,* being convicted by *their own* conscience, went out one by one, beginning at the eldest, *even* unto the last: and Jesus was left alone, and the woman standing in the midst. 10 When Jesus had lifted up himself, and saw none but the woman, he said unto her, Woman, where are those thine accusers? hath no man condemned thee? 11 She said, No man, Lord. And Jesus said unto her, Neither do I condemn thee: go, and sin no more.

12 Then spake Jesus again unto them, saying, I am the light of the world: he that followeth me shall not walk in darkness, but shall have the light of life. 13 The Pharisees therefore said unto him, Thou bearest record of thyself; thy record is not true. 14 Jesus answered and said unto them, Though I bear record of myself, *yet* my record is true: for I know whence I came, and whither I go; but ye cannot tell whence I come, and whither I go. 15 Ye judge after the flesh; I judge no man. 16 And yet if I judge, my judgment is true: for I am not alone, but I and the Father that sent me. 17 It is also written in your law, that the testimony of two men is true. 18 I am one that bear witness of myself, and the Father that sent me beareth witness of me. 19 Then said they unto him, Where is thy Father?

New International Version

Pharisees retorted. 48 "Has any of the rulers or of the Pharisees put his trust in him? 49 No! But this mob that knows nothing of the law—there is a curse on them."

50 Nicodemus, who had gone to Jesus earlier and who was one of their own number, asked, 51 "Does our law condemn a man without first hearing him to find out what he is doing?"

52 They replied, "Are you from Galilee, too? Look into it, and you will find that a prophet[m] does not come out of Galilee."

[The most reliable early manuscripts omit John 7:53–8:11.]

53 Then they all left, each to his own home.

The woman caught in adultery

8 But Jesus went to the Mount of Olives. 2 At dawn he appeared again in the temple court, where all the people gathered around him, and he sat down to teach them. 3 The teachers of the law and the Pharisees brought in a woman caught in adultery. They made her stand before the group and 4 said to Jesus, "Teacher, this woman was caught in the act of adultery. 5 In the Law Moses commanded us to stone such women. Now what do you say?" 6 They were using this question as a trap, in order to have a basis for accusing him.

But Jesus bent down and started to write on the ground with his finger. 7 When they kept on questioning him, he straightened up and said to them, "If any one of you is without sin, let him begin stoning her." 8 Again he stooped down and wrote on the ground.

9 At this, those who heard began to go away one at a time, the older ones first, until only Jesus was left, with the woman still standing there. 10 Jesus straightened up and asked her, "Woman, where are they? Has no one condemned you?"

11 "No one, sir," she said.

"Then neither do I condemn you," Jesus declared. "Go now and leave your life of sin."

The validity of Jesus' testimony

12 When Jesus spoke again to the people, he said, "I am the light of the world. Whoever follows me will never walk in darkness, but will have the light of life."

13 The Pharisees challenged him, "Here you are, appearing as your own witness; your testimony is not valid."

14 Jesus answered, "Even if I testify on my own behalf, my testimony is valid, for I know where I came from and where I am going. But you have no idea where I come from or where I am going. 15 You judge by human standards; I pass judgment on no one. 16 But if I do judge, my decisions are right, because I am not alone. I stand with the Father who sent me. 17 In your own Law it is written that the testimony of two men is valid. 18 I am one who testifies for myself; my other witness is the one who sent me—the Father."

19 Then they asked him, "Where is your father?"

[m] Or *the Prophet.*

Greek Interlinear

48 μή τις ἐκ τῶν ἀρχόντων ἐπίστευσεν
not anyone of the rulers believed

εἰς αὐτόν ἢ ἐκ τῶν Φαρισαίων; **49** ἀλλὰ
in him or of the Pharisees? But

ὁ ὄχλος οὗτος ὁ μὴ γινώσκων τὸν
- crowd this - not knowing the

νόμον ἐπάρατοί εἰσιν. **50** λέγει Νικόδημος
law cursed are. Says Nicodemus

πρὸς αὐτούς, ὁ ἐλθὼν πρὸς αὐτὸν πρότερον,
to them, the [one] having come to him firstly,

εἷς ὢν ἐξ αὐτῶν· **51** μὴ ὁ νόμος ἡμῶν
²one ¹being of them· Not the law of us

κρίνει τὸν ἄνθρωπον ἐὰν μὴ ἀκούσῃ
judges the man unless it hears

πρῶτον παρ' αὐτοῦ καὶ γνῷ τί ποιεῖ;
first from him and knows what he does?

52 ἀπεκρίθησαν καὶ εἶπαν αὐτῷ· μὴ καὶ
They answered and said to him : Not also

σὺ ἐκ τῆς Γαλιλαίας εἶ; ἐρεύνησον καὶ
thou of - Galilee art? search and

ἴδε ὅτι ἐκ τῆς Γαλιλαίας προφήτης οὐκ
see that out of - Galilee a prophet not

ἐγείρεται.
is raised.

53 Καὶ ἐπορεύθησαν ἕκαστος εἰς τὸν οἶκον
And they went each one to the house

Chapter 8

αὐτοῦ, **8** Ἰησοῦς δὲ ἐπορεύθη εἰς τὸ
of him, but Jesus went to the

Ὄρος τῶν Ἐλαιῶν. **2** Ὄρθρου δὲ πάλιν
Mount of the Olives. And at dawn again

παρεγένετο εἰς τὸ ἱερόν [, καὶ πᾶς ὁ
he arrived in the temple, and all the

λαὸς ἤρχετο πρὸς αὐτόν, καὶ καθίσας
people came to him, and sitting

ἐδίδασκεν αὐτούς]. **3** Ἄγουσιν δὲ οἱ
he taught them. And lead the

γραμματεῖς καὶ οἱ Φαρισαῖοι γυναῖκα ἐπὶ
scribes and the Pharisees a woman in

μοιχείᾳ κατειλημμένην, καὶ στήσαντες αὐτὴν
adultery having been caught, and standing her

ἐν μέσῳ **4** λέγουσιν αὐτῷ Διδάσκαλε,
in [the] midst they say to him[,] Teacher,

αὕτη ἡ γυνὴ κατείληπται ἐπ' αὐτοφώρῳ
this - woman has been caught in the act

μοιχευομένη· **5** ἐν δὲ τῷ νόμῳ [ἡμῖν]
committing adultery; now in the law [to us]

Μωυσῆς ἐνετείλατο τὰς τοιαύτας λιθάζειν·
Moses enjoined - ²such ¹to stone;

σὺ οὖν τί λέγεις; **6** [τοῦτο δὲ ἔλεγον
thou therefore what sayest thou? But this they said

πειράζοντες αὐτόν, ἵνα ἔχωσιν κατηγορεῖν
tempting him, that they might have to accuse

αὐτοῦ.] ὁ δὲ Ἰησοῦς κάτω κύψας τῷ
him. - But Jesus down stooping with the

δακτύλῳ κατέγραφεν εἰς τὴν γῆν. **7** ὡς δὲ
finger wrote in the earth. But as

ἐπέμενον ἐρωτῶντες [αὐτόν], ἀνέκυψεν καὶ
they remained questioning him, he stood erect and

εἶπεν [αὐτοῖς,] Ὁ ἀναμάρτητος ὑμῶν
said to them[,] The [one] sinless of you

πρῶτος ἐπ' αὐτὴν βαλέτω λίθον. **8** καὶ
first on her let him cast a stone. And

πάλιν κατακύψας ἔγραφεν εἰς τὴν γῆν.
again stooping down he wrote in the earth.

9 οἱ δὲ ἀκούσαντες ἐξήρχοντο εἰς καθ'
And they hearing went out one by

εἷς ἀρξάμενοι ἀπὸ τῶν πρεσβυτέρων, καὶ
one beginning from the older ones, and

κατελείφθη μόνος, καὶ ἡ γυνὴ ἐν μέσῳ
he was left alone, and the woman in [the] midst

οὖσα. **10** ἀνακύψας δὲ ὁ Ἰησοῦς εἶπεν
being. And standing erect - Jesus said

αὐτῇ Γύναι, ποῦ εἰσιν; οὐδείς σε κατέκρινεν;
to her[,] Woman, where are they? no one thee condemned?

11 ἡ δὲ εἶπεν Οὐδείς, κύριε. εἶπεν δὲ
And she said[,] No one, sir. So said

ὁ Ἰησοῦς Οὐδὲ ἐγώ σε κατακρίνω·
- Jesus[,] Neither I thee condemn;

πορεύου, ἀπὸ τοῦ νῦν μηκέτι ἁμάρτανε.
go, from - now no longer sin.

12 Πάλιν οὖν αὐτοῖς ἐλάλησεν ὁ Ἰησοῦς
Again therefore to them spoke - Jesus

λέγων· ἐγώ εἰμι τὸ φῶς τοῦ κόσμου·
saying: I am the light of the world;

ὁ ἀκολουθῶν μοι οὐ μὴ περιπατήσῃ ἐν
the [one] following me by no means will walk in

τῇ σκοτίᾳ, ἀλλ' ἕξει τὸ φῶς τῆς ζωῆς.
the darkness, but will have the light - of life.

13 εἶπον οὖν αὐτῷ οἱ Φαρισαῖοι· σὺ περὶ
Said therefore to him the Pharisees; Thou concerning

σεαυτοῦ μαρτυρεῖς· ἡ μαρτυρία σου οὐκ
thyself witnessest; the witness of thee not

ἔστιν ἀληθής. **14** ἀπεκρίθη Ἰησοῦς καὶ
is true. Answered Jesus and

εἶπεν αὐτοῖς· κἂν ἐγὼ μαρτυρῶ περὶ
said to them : Even if I witness concerning

ἐμαυτοῦ, ἀληθής ἐστιν ἡ μαρτυρία μου,
myself, true is the witness of me,

ὅτι οἶδα πόθεν ἦλθον καὶ ποῦ ὑπάγω·
because I know whence I came and where I go;

ὑμεῖς δὲ οὐκ οἴδατε πόθεν ἔρχομαι ἢ
but ye know not whence I come or

ποῦ ὑπάγω. **15** ὑμεῖς κατὰ τὴν σάρκα
where I go. Ye according to the flesh

κρίνετε, ἐγὼ οὐ κρίνω οὐδένα. **16** ²καὶ
judge, I judge not no(any)one. ²even

ἐὰν κρίνω δὲ ἐγώ, ἡ κρίσις ἡ ἐμὴ
¹if ³judge ¹But ⁴I, the ¹judgment - ¹my

ἀληθινή ἐστιν, ὅτι μόνος οὐκ εἰμί, ἀλλ'
true is, because alone I am not, but

ἐγὼ καὶ ὁ πέμψας με. **17** καὶ ἐν τῷ
I and the [one] having sent me. ²even ³in the

νόμῳ δὲ τῷ ὑμετέρῳ γέγραπται ὅτι δύο
¹law ¹And - ⁴your it has been written that of two

ἀνθρώπων ἡ μαρτυρία ἀληθής ἐστιν.
men the witness true is.

18 ἐγώ εἰμι ὁ μαρτυρῶν περὶ ἐμαυτοῦ,
I am the [one] witnessing concerning myself,

καὶ μαρτυρεῖ περὶ ἐμοῦ ὁ πέμψας με
and witnesses concerning me ¹the ²having sent ⁴me

πατήρ. **19** ἔλεγον οὖν αὐτῷ· ποῦ ἐστιν ὁ
³Father. They said therefore to him : Where is the

King James Version

Jesus answered, Ye neither know me, nor my Father: if ye had known me, ye should have known my Father also. 20 These words spake Jesus in the treasury, as he taught in the temple: and no man laid hands on him; for his hour was not yet come. 21 Then said Jesus again unto them, I go my way, and ye shall seek me, and shall die in your sins: whither I go, ye cannot come. 22 Then said the Jews, Will he kill himself? because he saith, Whither I go, ye cannot come. 23And he said unto them, Ye are from beneath; I am from above: ye are of this world; I am not of this world. 24 I said therefore unto you, that ye shall die in your sins: for if ye believe not that I am *he*, ye shall die in your sins. 25 Then said they unto him, Who art thou? And Jesus saith unto them, Even *the same* that I said unto you from the beginning. 26 I have many things to say and to judge of you: but he that sent me is true; and I speak to the world those things which I have heard of him. 27 They understood not that he spake to them of the Father. 28 Then said Jesus unto them, When ye have lifted up the Son of man, then shall ye know that I am *he*, and *that* I do nothing of myself; but as my Father hath taught me, I speak these things. 29And he that sent me is with me: the Father hath not left me alone; for I do always those things that please him. 30As he spake these words, many believed on him. 31 Then said Jesus to those Jews which believed on him, If ye continue in my word, *then* are ye my disciples indeed; 32And ye shall know the truth, and the truth shall make you free.

33 They answered him, We be Abraham's seed, and were never in bondage to any man: how sayest thou, Ye shall be made free? 34 Jesus answered them, Verily, verily, I say unto you, Whosoever committeth sin is the servant of sin. 35And the servant abideth not in the house for ever: *but* the Son abideth ever. 36 If the Son therefore shall make you free, ye shall be free indeed. 37 I know that ye are Abraham's seed; but ye seek to kill me, because my word hath no place in you. 38 I speak that which I have seen with my Father: and ye do that which ye have seen with your father. 39 They answered and said unto him, Abraham is our father. Jesus saith unto them, If ye were Abraham's children, ye would do the works of Abraham. 40 But now ye seek to kill me, a man that hath told you the truth, which I have heard of God: this did not Abraham. 41 Ye do the deeds of your father. Then said they to him, We be not born of fornication; we have one Father, *even* God. 42 Jesus said unto them, If God were your Father, ye would love me: for I proceeded forth and came from God;

New International Version

"You do not know me or my Father," Jesus replied. "If you knew me, you would know my Father also." 20 He spoke these words while teaching in the temple area near the place where the offerings were put. Yet no one seized him, because his time had not yet come.

21 Once more Jesus said to them, "I am going away, and you will look for me, and you will die in your sin. Where I go, you cannot come."

22 This made the Jews ask, "Will he kill himself? Is that why he says, 'Where I go, you cannot come'?"

23 But he continued, "You are from below; I am from above. You are of this world; I am not of this world. 24 I told you that you would die in your sins; if you do not believe that I am [the one I claim to be],[n] you will indeed die in your sins."

25 "Who are you, anyway?" they asked.

"Just what I have been claiming all along," Jesus replied. 26 "I have much to say in judgment of you. But he who sent me is reliable, and what I have heard from him I tell the world."

27 They did not understand that he was telling them about his Father. 28 So Jesus said, "When you have lifted up the Son of Man, then you will know who I am[o] and that I do nothing on my own but speak just what the Father has taught me. 29 The one who sent me is with me; he has not left me alone, for I always do what pleases him." 30 Even as he spoke, many put their faith in him.

The children of Abraham

31 To the Jews who had believed him, Jesus said, "If you hold to my teaching, you are really my disciples. 32 Then you will know the truth, and the truth will set you free."

33 They answered him, "We are Abraham's descendants[p] and have never been slaves of anyone. How can you say that we shall be set free?"

34 Jesus replied, "I tell you the truth, everyone who sins is a slave to sin. 35 Now a slave has no permanent place in the family, but a son belongs to it forever. 36 So if the Son sets you free, you will be free indeed. 37 I know you are Abraham's descendants. Yet you are ready to kill me, because you have no room for my word. 38 I am telling you what I have seen in the Father's presence, and you do what you have heard from your father." [q]

39 "Abraham is our father," they answered.

"If you were Abraham's children," said Jesus, "then you would do the things Abraham did.[r] 40As it is, you are determined to kill me, a man who has told you the truth that I heard from God. Abraham did not do such things. 41 You are doing the things your own father does."

"We are not illegitimate children," they protested. "The only Father we have is God himself."

The children of the devil

42 Jesus said to them, "If God were your Father, you would love me, for I came from God and now am here. I have not come on my own;

---

[n] Or *I am he.* [o] Or *know that I am he.* [p] Greek *seed.* [q] Or *presence. Therefore do what you have heard from the Father.* [r] Some early MSS read *then do the things Abraham did.*

Greek Interlinear

πατήρ σου; ἀπεκρίθη Ἰησοῦς· οὔτε ἐμὲ
Father of thee? Answered Jesus : Neither me

οἴδατε οὔτε τὸν πατέρα μου· εἰ ἐμὲ
ye know nor the Father of me; if me

ᾔδειτε, καὶ τὸν πατέρα μου ἂν ᾔδειτε.
ye knew, also the Father of me ye would have known.

20 Ταῦτα τὰ ῥήματα ἐλάλησεν ἐν τῷ
These - words he spoke in the

γαζοφυλακείῳ διδάσκων ἐν τῷ ἱερῷ· καὶ
treasury teaching in the temple; and

οὐδεὶς ἐπίασεν αὐτόν, ὅτι οὔπω ἐληλύθει
no one seized him, because not yet had come

ἡ ὥρα αὐτοῦ.
the hour of him.

21 Εἶπεν οὖν πάλιν αὐτοῖς· ἐγὼ ὑπάγω
He said therefore again to them : I go

καὶ ζητήσετέ με, καὶ ἐν τῇ ἁμαρτίᾳ
and ye will seek me, and in the sin

ὑμῶν ἀποθανεῖσθε· ὅπου ἐγὼ ὑπάγω ὑμεῖς
of you ye will die; where I go ye

οὐ δύνασθε ἐλθεῖν. **22** ἔλεγον οὖν οἱ
cannot to come. Said therefore the

Ἰουδαῖοι· μήτι ἀποκτενεῖ ἑαυτόν, ὅτι
Jews : Not will he kill himself, because

λέγει· ὅπου ἐγὼ ὑπάγω ὑμεῖς οὐ δύνασθε
he says : Where I go ye cannot

ἐλθεῖν; **23** καὶ ἔλεγεν αὐτοῖς· ὑμεῖς ἐκ
to come? And he said to them : Ye of

τῶν κάτω ἐστέ, ἐγὼ ἐκ τῶν ἄνω εἰμί·
the things below are, I of the things above am;

ὑμεῖς ἐκ τούτου τοῦ κόσμου ἐστέ, ἐγὼ
ye of this - world are, I

οὐκ εἰμὶ ἐκ τοῦ κόσμου τούτου. **24** εἶπον
am not of - world this. I said

οὖν ὑμῖν ὅτι ἀποθανεῖσθε ἐν ταῖς ἁμαρτίαις
therefore to you that ye will die in the sins

ὑμῶν· ἐὰν γὰρ μὴ πιστεύσητε ὅτι ἐγώ
of you ; for if ye believe not that I

εἰμι, ἀποθανεῖσθε ἐν ταῖς ἁμαρτίαις ὑμῶν.
am, ye will die in the sins of you.

25 ἔλεγον οὖν αὐτῷ· σὺ τίς εἶ; εἶπεν
They said therefore to him : ²Thou ¹who ³art? Said

αὐτοῖς ὁ Ἰησοῦς· τὴν ἀρχὴν ὅ τι καὶ
to them - Jesus : ²at all † ¹Why ³indeed

λαλῶ ὑμῖν; **26** πολλὰ ἔχω περὶ ὑμῶν
³speak I ⁴to you? Many things I have about you

λαλεῖν καὶ κρίνειν· ἀλλ' ὁ πέμψας με
to speak and to judge; but the [one] having sent me

ἀληθής ἐστιν, κἀγὼ ἃ ἤκουσα παρ'
true is, and I what I heard from

αὐτοῦ, ταῦτα λαλῶ εἰς τὸν κόσμον.
him, these things I speak in the world.

27 οὐκ ἔγνωσαν ὅτι τὸν πατέρα αὐτοῖς
They did not know that ²the ³Father ⁴to them

ἔλεγεν. **28** εἶπεν οὖν ὁ Ἰησοῦς· ὅταν
¹he spoke [of]. Said therefore - Jesus : When

ὑψώσητε τὸν υἱὸν τοῦ ἀνθρώπου, τότε
ye lift up the Son - of man, then

γνώσεσθε ὅτι ἐγώ εἰμι, καὶ ἀπ' ἐμαυτοῦ
ye will know that I am, and from myself

ποιῶ οὐδέν, ἀλλὰ καθὼς ἐδίδαξέν με ὁ
I do nothing, but as taught me the

πατήρ, ταῦτα λαλῶ. **29** καὶ ὁ πέμψας
Father, these things I speak. And the [one] having sent

με μετ' ἐμοῦ ἐστιν· οὐκ ἀφῆκέν με
me with me is; he did not leave me

μόνον, ὅτι ἐγὼ τὰ ἀρεστὰ αὐτῷ ποιῶ
alone, because I the things pleasing to him do

πάντοτε.
always.

30 Ταῦτα αὐτοῦ λαλοῦντος πολλοὶ ἐπίσ-
These things him saying⁸ many be-
= As he said these things

τευσαν εἰς αὐτόν. **31** ἔλεγεν οὖν ὁ Ἰησοῦς
lieved in him. Said therefore - Jesus

πρὸς τοὺς πεπιστευκότας αὐτῷ Ἰουδαίους·
to ¹the ²having believed ⁴him ³Jews :

ἐὰν ὑμεῖς μείνητε ἐν τῷ λόγῳ τῷ ἐμῷ,
If ye continue in *the* ²word - ¹my,

ἀληθῶς μαθηταί μού ἐστε, **32** καὶ γνώσεσθε
truly disciples of me ye are, and ye will know

τὴν ἀλήθειαν, καὶ ἡ ἀλήθεια ἐλευθερώσει
the truth, and the truth will free

ὑμᾶς. **33** ἀπεκρίθησαν πρὸς αὐτόν· σπέρμα
you. They answered to him : Seed

Ἀβραάμ ἐσμεν, καὶ οὐδενὶ δεδουλεύκαμεν
of Abraham we are, and to no one have we been enslaved

πώποτε· πῶς σὺ λέγεις ὅτι ἐλεύθεροι
never; how thou sayest that free

γενήσεσθε; **34** ἀπεκρίθη αὐτοῖς ὁ Ἰησοῦς·
ye will become? Answered them - Jesus :

ἀμὴν ἀμὴν λέγω ὑμῖν ὅτι πᾶς ὁ ποιῶν
Truly truly I tell you that everyone doing

τὴν ἁμαρτίαν δοῦλός ἐστιν τῆς ἁμαρτίας.
- sin a slave is - of sin.

35 ὁ δὲ δοῦλος οὐ μένει ἐν τῇ οἰκίᾳ
But the slave does not remain in the house

εἰς τὸν αἰῶνα· ὁ υἱὸς μένει εἰς τὸν
unto the age; the son remains unto the

αἰῶνα. **36** ἐὰν οὖν ὁ υἱὸς ὑμᾶς ἐλευθερώσῃ,
age. If therefore the Son you frees,

ὄντως ἐλεύθεροι ἔσεσθε. **37** Οἶδα ὅτι
really free ye will be. I know that

σπέρμα Ἀβραάμ ἐστε· ἀλλὰ ζητεῖτέ με
seed of Abraham ye are; but ye seek me

ἀποκτεῖναι, ὅτι ὁ λόγος ὁ ἐμὸς οὐ χωρεῖ
to kill, because the *word - ¹my finds no room

ἐν ὑμῖν. **38** ἃ ἐγὼ ἑώρακα παρὰ τῷ
in you. What I have seen with the

πατρὶ λαλῶ· καὶ ὑμεῖς οὖν ἃ ἠκού-
Father I speak; and ye therefore what ye

σατε παρὰ τοῦ πατρὸς ποιεῖτε. **39** ἀπεκρί-
heard from the father ye do. They

θησαν καὶ εἶπαν αὐτῷ· ὁ πατὴρ ἡμῶν Ἀβραάμ
answered and said to him: The father of us Abraham

ἐστιν. λέγει αὐτοῖς ὁ Ἰησοῦς· εἰ τέκνα
is. Says to them - Jesus : If children

τοῦ Ἀβραάμ ἐστε, τὰ ἔργα τοῦ Ἀβραὰμ
- of Abraham ye are, the works - of Abraham

ποιεῖτε· **40** νῦν δὲ ζητεῖτέ με ἀποκτεῖναι,
ye do; but now ye seek me to kill,

ἄνθρωπον ὃς τὴν ἀλήθειαν ὑμῖν λελάληκα,
a man who the truth to you has spoken,

ἣν ἤκουσα παρὰ τοῦ θεοῦ· τοῦτο Ἀβραὰμ
which I heard from - God; this Abraham

οὐκ ἐποίησεν. **41** ὑμεῖς ποιεῖτε τὰ ἔργα
did not. Ye do the works

τοῦ πατρὸς ὑμῶν. εἶπαν αὐτῷ· ἡμεῖς ἐκ
of the father of you. They said to him : We of

πορνείας οὐκ ἐγεννήθημεν, ἕνα πατέρα
fornication were not born, one father

ἔχομεν τὸν θεόν. **42** εἶπεν αὐτοῖς ὁ
we have[.] - God. Said to them -

Ἰησοῦς· εἰ ὁ θεὸς πατὴρ ὑμῶν ἦν,
Jesus : If - God father of you was,

ἠγαπᾶτε ἂν ἐμέ· ἐγὼ γὰρ ἐκ τοῦ θεοῦ
ye would have loved me; for I of - God

ἐξῆλθον καὶ ἥκω· οὐδὲ γὰρ ἀπ' ἐμαυτοῦ
came forth and have come; for not from myself

King James Version

neither came I of myself, but he sent me. 43 Why do ye not understand my speech? *even* because ye cannot hear my word. 44 Ye are of *your* father the devil, and the lusts of your father ye will do: he was a murderer from the beginning, and abode not in the truth, because there is no truth in him. When he speaketh a lie, he speaketh of his own: for he is a liar, and the father of it. 45And because I tell *you* the truth, ye believe me not. 46 Which of you convinceth me of sin? And if I say the truth, why do ye not believe me? 47 He that is of God heareth God's words: ye therefore hear *them* not, because ye are not of God. 48 Then answered the Jews, and said unto him, Say we not well that thou art a Samaritan, and hast a devil? 49 Jesus answered, I have not a devil; but I honour my Father, and ye do dishonour me. 50And I seek not mine own glory: there is one that seeketh and judgeth. 51 Verily, verily, I say unto you, If a man keep my saying, he shall never see death. 52 Then said the Jews unto him, Now we know that thou hast a devil. Abraham is dead, and the prophets; and thou sayest, If a man keep my saying, he shall never taste of death. 53Art thou greater than our father Abraham, which is dead? and the prophets are dead: whom makest thou thyself? 54 Jesus answered, If I honour myself, my honour is nothing: it is my Father that honoureth me; of whom ye say, that he is your God: 55 Yet ye have not known him; but I know him: and if I should say, I know him not, I shall be a liar like unto you: but I know him, and keep his saying. 56 Your father Abraham rejoiced to see my day: and he saw *it,* and was glad. 57 Then said the Jews unto him, Thou art not yet fifty years old, and hast thou seen Abraham? 58 Jesus said unto them, Verily, verily, I say unto you, Before Abraham was, I am. 59 Then took they up stones to cast at him: but Jesus hid himself, and went out of the temple, going through the midst of them, and so passed by.

New International Version

but he sent me. 43 Why is my language not clear to you? Because you are unable to hear what I say. 44 You belong to your father, the devil, and you want to carry out your father's desire. He was a murderer from the beginning, not holding to the truth, for there is no truth in him. When he lies, he speaks his native language, for he is a liar and the father of lies. 45 Yet because I tell the truth, you do not believe me! 46 Can any of you prove me guilty of sin? If I am telling the truth, why don't you believe me? 47 He who belongs to God hears what God says. The reason you do not hear is that you do not belong to God."

The claims of Jesus about himself

48 The Jews answered him, "Aren't we right in saying that you are a Samaritan and demon-possessed?"

49 "I am not possessed by a demon," said Jesus, "but I honor my Father and you dishonor me. 50 I am not seeking glory for myself; but there is one who seeks it, and he is the judge. 51 I tell you the truth, if a man keeps my word, he will never see death."

52 At this the Jews exclaimed, "Now we know that you are demon-possessed! Abraham died and so did the prophets, yet you say that if a man keeps your word, he will never taste death. 53Are you greater than our father Abraham? He died, and so did the prophets. Who do you think you are?"

54 Jesus replied, "If I glorify myself, my glory means nothing. My Father, whom you claim as your God, is the one who glorifies me. 55 Though you do not know him, I know him. If I said I did not, I would be a liar like you, but I do know him and keep his word. 56 Your father Abraham rejoiced at the thought of seeing my day; he saw it and was glad."

57 "You are not yet fifty years old," the Jews said to him, "and you have seen Abraham!"

58 "I tell you the truth," Jesus answered, "before Abraham was born, I am!" 59At this, they picked up stones to stone him, but Jesus hid himself, slipping away from the temple grounds.

Jesus heals a man born blind

9 And as *Jesus* passed by, he saw a man which was blind from *his* birth. 2And his disciples asked him, saying, Master, who did sin, this man, or his parents, that he was born blind? 3 Jesus answered, Neither hath this man sinned, nor his parents: but that the works of God should be made manifest in him. 4 I must work the works of him that sent me, while it is day: the night cometh, when no man can work. 5As long as I am in the world, I am the light of the world. 6 When he had thus spoken, he spat on the ground, and made clay of the spittle, and he anointed the eyes of the blind man with the

9 As he went along, he saw a man blind from birth. 2 His disciples asked him, "Rabbi, who sinned, this man or his parents, that he was born blind?"

3 "Neither this man nor his parents sinned," said Jesus, "but this happened so that the work of God might be displayed in his life. 4As long as it is day, we must do the work of him who sent me. Night is coming, when no one can work. 5 While I am in the world, I am the light of the world."

6 Having said this, he spit on the ground, made some mud with the saliva, and put it on

Greek Interlinear

ἐλήλυθα, ἀλλ' ἐκεῖνός με ἀπέστειλεν. **43** διὰ τί
I have come, but that one me sent. Why

τὴν λαλιὰν τὴν ἐμὴν οὐ γινώσκετε;
the ²speech - ¹my know ye not?

ὅτι οὐ δύνασθε ἀκούειν τὸν λόγον τὸν
because ye cannot to hear the ²word -

ἐμόν. **44** ὑμεῖς ἐκ τοῦ πατρὸς τοῦ
¹my. Ye of the father of the

διαβόλου ἐστὲ καὶ τὰς ἐπιθυμίας τοῦ
devil are and the desires of the

πατρὸς ὑμῶν θέλετε ποιεῖν. ἐκεῖνος
father of you ye wish to do. That one

ἀνθρωποκτόνος ἦν ἀπ' ἀρχῆς, καὶ ἐν
a murderer was from [the] beginning, and in

τῇ ἀληθείᾳ οὐκ ἔστηκεν, ὅτι οὐκ ἔστιν
the truth stood not, because not is

ἀλήθεια ἐν αὐτῷ. ὅταν λαλῇ τὸ ψεῦδος,
truth in him. When he speaks the lie,

ἐκ τῶν ἰδίων λαλεῖ, ὅτι ψεύστης ἐστὶν
out of his own things he speaks, because a liar he is

καὶ ὁ πατὴρ αὐτοῦ. **45** ἐγὼ δὲ ὅτι τὴν
and the father of it. But ³I ¹because ⁴the

ἀλήθειαν λέγω, οὐ πιστεύετέ μοι. **46** τίς
²truth ³say, ye do not believe me. Who

ἐξ ὑμῶν ἐλέγχει με περὶ ἁμαρτίας; εἰ
of you reproves me concerning sin? If

ἀλήθειαν λέγω, διὰ τί ὑμεῖς οὐ πιστεύετέ
truth I say, why ⁴ye ¹do not believe

μοι; **47** ὁ ὢν ἐκ τοῦ θεοῦ τὰ ῥήματα
me? The [one] being of - God the words

τοῦ θεοῦ ἀκούει· διὰ τοῦτο ὑμεῖς οὐκ
- of God hears; therefore ye not

ἀκούετε, ὅτι ἐκ τοῦ θεοῦ οὐκ ἐστέ.
hear, because of - God ye are not.

48 Ἀπεκρίθησαν οἱ Ἰουδαῖοι καὶ εἶπαν
Answered the Jews and said

αὐτῷ· οὐ καλῶς λέγομεν ἡμεῖς ὅτι
to him : ²Not ⁴well ¹say ³we ⁵that

Σαμαρίτης εἶ σὺ καὶ δαιμόνιον ἔχεις;
⁶a Samaritan ⁸art ⁷thou ⁹and ¹¹a demon ¹⁰hast?

49 ἀπεκρίθη Ἰησοῦς· ἐγὼ δαιμόνιον οὐκ
Answered Jesus : I a demon not

ἔχω, ἀλλὰ τιμῶ τὸν πατέρα μου, καὶ
have, but I honour the Father of me, and

ὑμεῖς ἀτιμάζετέ με. **50** ἐγὼ δὲ οὐ ζητῶ
ye dishonour me. But I seek not

τὴν δόξαν μου· ἔστιν ὁ ζητῶν καὶ
the glory of me; there is the [one] seeking and

κρίνων. **51** ἀμὴν ἀμὴν λέγω ὑμῖν, ἐάν
judging. Truly truly I tell you, if

τις τὸν ἐμὸν λόγον τηρήσῃ, θάνατον
anyone - my word keeps, death

οὐ μὴ θεωρήσῃ εἰς τὸν αἰῶνα. **52** εἶπαν
by no means will he behold unto the age. Said

αὐτῷ οἱ Ἰουδαῖοι· νῦν ἐγνώκαμεν ὅτι
to him the Jews : Now we have known that

δαιμόνιον ἔχεις. Ἀβραὰμ ἀπέθανεν καὶ οἱ
a demon thou hast. Abraham died and the

προφῆται, καὶ σὺ λέγεις· ἐάν τις τὸν
prophets, and thou sayest : If anyone the

λόγον μου τηρήσῃ, οὐ μὴ γεύσηται
word of me keeps, by no means will he taste

θανάτου εἰς τὸν αἰῶνα. **53** μὴ σὺ μείζων
of death unto the age. Not thou greater

εἶ τοῦ πατρὸς ἡμῶν Ἀβραάμ, ὅστις
art [than] the father of us Abraham, who

ἀπέθανεν; καὶ οἱ προφῆται ἀπέθανον· τίνα
died? and the prophets died; . whom

σεαυτὸν ποιεῖς; **54** ἀπεκρίθη Ἰησοῦς· ἐὰν
thyself makest thou? Answered Jesus : If

ἐγὼ δοξάσω ἐμαυτόν, ἡ δόξα μου οὐδέν
I glorify myself, the glory of me nothing

ἐστιν· ἔστιν ὁ πατήρ μου ὁ δοξάζων με,
is; ⁴is ¹the ²Father ³of me the [one] glorifying me,

ὃν ὑμεῖς λέγετε ὅτι θεὸς ἡμῶν ἐστιν,
whom ye say[.] - God of us he is,

55 καὶ οὐκ ἐγνώκατε αὐτόν, ἐγὼ δὲ
and ye have not known him, but I

οἶδα αὐτόν. κἂν εἴπω ὅτι οὐκ οἶδα
know him. Even if I say that I know not

αὐτόν, ἔσομαι ὅμοιος ὑμῖν ψεύστης· ἀλλὰ
him, I shall be like you a liar; but

οἶδα αὐτὸν καὶ τὸν λόγον αὐτοῦ τηρῶ.
I know him and the word of him I keep.

56 Ἀβραὰμ ὁ πατὴρ ὑμῶν ἠγαλλιάσατο
Abraham the father of you was glad

ἵνα ἴδῃ τὴν ἡμέραν τὴν ἐμήν, καὶ εἶδεν
that he should see the ²day - ¹my, and he saw

καὶ ἐχάρη. **57** εἶπαν οὖν οἱ Ἰουδαῖοι
and rejoiced. Said therefore the Jews

πρὸς αὐτόν· πεντήκοντα ἔτη οὔπω ἔχεις
to him : Fifty years not yet thou hast

καὶ Ἀβραὰμ ἑώρακας; **58** εἶπεν αὐτοῖς
and Abraham hast thou seen? Said to them

Ἰησοῦς· ἀμὴν ἀμὴν λέγω ὑμῖν, πρὶν
Jesus : Truly truly I tell you, before

Ἀβραὰμ γενέσθαι ἐγὼ εἰμί. **59** ἦραν
Abraham to become[b] I am. They took
=became

οὖν λίθους ἵνα βάλωσιν ἐπ' αὐτόν·
therefore stones that they might cast on him;

Ἰησοῦς δὲ ἐκρύβη καὶ ἐξῆλθεν ἐκ τοῦ
but Jesus was hidden and went forth out of the

ἱεροῦ.
temple.

Chapter 9

Καὶ παράγων εἶδεν ἄνθρωπον τυφλὸν
And passing along he saw a man blind

ἐκ γενετῆς. **2** καὶ ἠρώτησαν αὐτὸν οἱ
from birth. And asked him the

μαθηταὶ αὐτοῦ λέγοντες· ῥαββί, τίς ἥμαρτεν,
disciples of him saying : Rabbi, who sinned,

οὗτος ἢ οἱ γονεῖς αὐτοῦ, ἵνα τυφλὸς
this man or the parents of him, that blind

γεννηθῇ; **3** ἀπεκρίθη Ἰησοῦς· οὔτε οὗτος
he was born? Answered Jesus : Neither this man

ἥμαρτεν οὔτε οἱ γονεῖς αὐτοῦ, ἀλλ' ἵνα
sinned nor the parents of him, but that

φανερωθῇ τὰ ἔργα τοῦ θεοῦ ἐν αὐτῷ.
might be manifested the works - of God in him.

4 ἡμᾶς δεῖ ἐργάζεσθαι τὰ ἔργα τοῦ
Us it behoves to work the works of the

πέμψαντός με ἕως ἡμέρα ἐστίν· ἔρχεται
[one] having sent me while day it is; comes

νὺξ ὅτε οὐδεὶς δύναται ἐργάζεσθαι. **5** ὅταν
night when no one can to work. When

ἐν τῷ κόσμῳ ᾦ, φῶς εἰμι τοῦ κόσμου.
in the world I am, light I am of the world.

6 ταῦτα εἰπὼν ἔπτυσεν χαμαὶ καὶ ἐποίησεν
These things having said he spat on the ground and made

πηλὸν ἐκ τοῦ πτύσματος, καὶ ἐπέθηκεν
clay out of the spittle, and ¹put on

αὐτοῦ τὸν πηλὸν ἐπὶ τοὺς ὀφθαλμούς,
²of him ⁴the ³clay ⁵on ⁶the ⁷eyes,

King James Version

clay, 7And said unto him, Go, wash in the pool of Siloam, (which is by interpretation, Sent.) He went his way therefore, and washed, and came seeing.

8 The neighbours therefore, and they which before had seen him that he was blind, said, Is not this he that sat and begged? 9 Some said, This is he: others *said*, He is like him: *but* he said, I am *he.* 10 Therefore said they unto him, How were thine eyes opened? 11 He answered and said, A man that is called Jesus made clay, and anointed mine eyes, and said unto me, Go to the pool of Siloam, and wash: and I went and washed, and I received sight. 12 Then said they unto him, Where is he? He said, I know not.

13 They brought to the Pharisees him that aforetime was blind. 14And it was the sabbath day when Jesus made the clay, and opened his eyes. 15 Then again the Pharisees also asked him how he had received his sight. He said unto them, He put clay upon mine eyes, and I washed, and do see. 16 Therefore said some of the Pharisees, This man is not of God, because he keepeth not the sabbath day. Others said, How can a man that is a sinner do such miracles? And there was a division among them. 17 They say unto the blind man again, What sayest thou of him, that he hath opened thine eyes? He said, He is a prophet. 18 But the Jews did not believe concerning him, that he had been blind, and received his sight, until they called the parents of him that had received his sight. 19And they asked them, saying, Is this your son, who ye say was born blind? how then doth he now see? 20 His parents answered them and said, We know that this is our son, and that he was born blind: 21 But by what means he now seeth, we know not; or who hath opened his eyes, we know not: he is of age; ask him: he shall speak for himself. 22 These *words* spake his parents, because they feared the Jews: for the Jews had agreed already, that if any man did confess that he was Christ, he should be put out of the synagogue. 23 Therefore said his parents, He is of age; ask him. 24 Then again called they the man that was blind, and said unto him, Give God the praise: we know that this man is a sinner. 25 He answered and said, Whether he be a sinner *or no,* I know not: one thing I know, that, whereas I was blind, now I see. 26 Then said they to him again, What did he to thee? how opened he thine eyes? 27 He answered them, I have told you already, and ye did not hear: wherefore would ye hear *it* again? will ye also be his disciples? 28 Then they reviled him, and said, Thou art his disciple; but we are Moses' disciples. 29 We know that God spake unto Moses: *as for* this *fellow*, we know not from whence he is. 30 The man answered and said unto them, Why

New International Version

the man's eyes. 7 "Go," he told him, "wash in the pool of Siloam" (this word means Sent). So the man went and washed, and came home seeing.

8 His neighbors and those who had formerly seen him begging asked, "Isn't this the same man who used to sit and beg?" 9 Some claimed that he was.

Others said, "No, he only looks like him."

But he himself insisted, "I am the man."

10 "How then were your eyes opened?" they demanded.

11 He replied, "The man they call Jesus made some mud and put it on my eyes. He told me to go to Siloam and wash. So I went and washed, and then I could see."

12 "Where is this man?" they asked him.

"I don't know," he said.

The Pharisees investigate the healing

13 They brought to the Pharisees the man who had been blind. 14 Now the day on which Jesus had made the mud and opened the man's eyes was a Sabbath. 15 Therefore the Pharisees also asked him how he had received his sight. "He put mud on my eyes," the man replied, "and I washed, and now I see."

16 Some of the Pharisees said, "This man is not from God, for he does not keep the Sabbath."

But others asked, "How can a sinner do such miraculous signs?" So they were divided.

17 Finally they turned again to the blind man, "What have you to say about him? It was your eyes he opened."

The man replied, "He is a prophet."

18 The Jews still did not believe that he had been blind and had received his sight until they sent for the man's parents. 19 "Is this your son?" they asked. "Is this the one you say was born blind? How is it that now he can see?"

20 "We know he is our son," the parents answered, "and we know he was born blind. 21 But how he can see now, or who opened his eyes, we don't know. Ask him. He is of age; he will speak for himself." 22 His parents said this because they were afraid of the Jews, for already the Jews had decided that anyone who acknowledged that Jesus was the Christ*s* would be put out of the synagogue. 23 That was why his parents said, "He is of age; ask him."

24 A second time they summoned the man who had been blind. "Give glory to God," *t* they said. "We know this man is a sinner."

25 He replied, "Whether he is a sinner or not, I don't know. One thing I do know. I was blind but now I see!"

26 Then they asked him, "What did he do to you? How did he open your eyes?"

27 He answered, "I have told you already and you did not listen. Why do you want to hear it again? Do you want to become his disciples, too?"

28 Then they hurled insults at him and said, "You are this fellow's disciple! We are disciples of Moses! 29 We know that God spoke to Moses, but as for this fellow, we don't even know where he comes from."

30 The man answered, "Now that is remarka-

---

[s] Or *Messiah.* [t] A solemn charge to tell the truth (see Joshua 7:19).

Greek Interlinear

7 καὶ εἶπεν αὐτῷ· ὕπαγε νίψαι εἰς τὴν
and said to him: Go wash in the

κολυμβήθραν τοῦ Σιλωάμ (ὃ ἑρμηνεύεται
pool of Siloam (which is translated

ἀπεσταλμένος). ἀπῆλθεν οὖν καὶ ἐνίψατο,
having been sent). He went therefore and washed,

καὶ ἦλθεν βλέπων. 8 Οἱ οὖν γείτονες
and came seeing. Therefore the neighbours

καὶ οἱ θεωροῦντες αὐτὸν τὸ πρότερον,
and the [ones] beholding him formerly, †

ὅτι προσαίτης ἦν, ἔλεγον· οὐχ οὗτός
that a beggar he was, said: ²Not ³this man

ἐστιν ὁ καθήμενος καὶ προσαιτῶν; 9 ἄλλοι
¹is the [one] sitting and begging? Some

ἔλεγον ὅτι οὗτός ἐστιν· ἄλλοι ἔλεγον·
said[,] – This is he; others said:

οὐχί, ἀλλὰ ὅμοιος αὐτῷ ἐστιν. ἐκεῖνος
No, but like to him he is. That [one]

ἔλεγεν ὅτι ἐγώ εἰμι. 10 ἔλεγον οὖν
said[,] – I am. They said therefore

αὐτῷ· πῶς [οὖν] ἠνεῴχθησάν σου οἱ
to him: How then were opened of thee the

ὀφθαλμοί; 11 ἀπεκρίθη ἐκεῖνος· ὁ ἄνθρωπος
eyes? Answered that [one]: The man

ὁ λεγόμενος Ἰησοῦς πηλὸν ἐποίησεν καὶ
– being named Jesus clay made and

ἐπέχρισέν μου τοὺς ὀφθαλμοὺς καὶ εἶπέν
anointed of me the eyes and told

μοι ὅτι ὕπαγε εἰς τὸν Σιλωὰμ καὶ
me[,] – Go to – Siloam and

νίψαι· ἀπελθὼν οὖν καὶ νιψάμενος ἀνέβλεψα.
wash; going therefore and washing I saw.

12 καὶ εἶπαν αὐτῷ· ποῦ ἐστιν ἐκεῖνος;
And they said to him: Where is that [one]?

λέγει· οὐκ οἶδα. 13 Ἄγουσιν αὐτὸν
He says: I do not know. They lead him

πρὸς τοὺς Φαρισαίους, τόν ποτε τυφλόν.
to the Pharisees, the at one time blind.

14 ἦν δὲ σάββατον ἐν ᾗ ἡμέρᾳ τὸν
Now it was a sabbath on which day ²the

πηλὸν ἐποίησεν ὁ Ἰησοῦς καὶ ἀνέῳξεν
⁴clay ³made – ¹Jesus and opened

αὐτοῦ τοὺς ὀφθαλμούς. 15 πάλιν οὖν
of him the eyes. Again therefore

ἠρώτων αὐτὸν καὶ οἱ Φαρισαῖοι πῶς
⁴asked ³him ²also ¹the ⁵Pharisees how

ἀνέβλεψεν. ὁ δὲ εἶπεν αὐτοῖς· πηλὸν
he saw. And he said to them: Clay

ἐπέθηκέν μου ἐπὶ τοὺς ὀφθαλμούς, καὶ
he put on ⁴of me ¹on ²the ³eyes, and

ἐνιψάμην, καὶ βλέπω. 16 ἔλεγον οὖν ἐκ
I washed, and I see. Said therefore of

τῶν Φαρισαίων τινές· οὐκ ἔστιν οὗτος
the Pharisees some: ⁴not ³is ¹This

παρὰ θεοῦ ὁ ἄνθρωπος, ὅτι τὸ σάββατον
²from ³God – man, because the sabbath

οὐ τηρεῖ. ἄλλοι [δὲ] ἔλεγον· πῶς δύναται
he keeps not. But others said: How can

ἄνθρωπος ἁμαρτωλὸς τοιαῦτα σημεῖα ποιεῖν;
man a sinful such signs to do?

καὶ σχίσμα ἦν ἐν αὐτοῖς. 17 λέγουσιν
And a division there was among them. They say

οὖν τῷ τυφλῷ πάλιν· τί σὺ λέγεις
therefore to the blind man again: What thou sayest

περὶ αὐτοῦ, ὅτι ἠνέῳξέν σου τοὺς
about him, because he opened of thee the

ὀφθαλμούς; ὁ δὲ εἶπεν ὅτι προφήτης ἐστίν.
eyes? And he said[,] – A prophet he is.

18 οὐκ ἐπίστευσαν οὖν οἱ Ἰουδαῖοι περὶ
Did not believe therefore the Jews about

αὐτοῦ ὅτι ἦν τυφλὸς καὶ ἀνέβλεψεν,
him that he was blind and saw,

ἕως ὅτου ἐφώνησαν τοὺς γονεῖς αὐτοῦ
until they called the parents of him

τοῦ ἀναβλέψαντος 19 καὶ ἠρώτησαν αὐτοὺς
of the [one] having seen and asked them

λέγοντες· οὗτός ἐστιν ὁ υἱὸς ὑμῶν, ὃν
saying: This is the son of you, whom

ὑμεῖς λέγετε ὅτι τυφλὸς ἐγεννήθη; πῶς
ye say that blind he was born? how

οὖν βλέπει ἄρτι; 20 ἀπεκρίθησαν οὖν οἱ
then sees he now? Answered therefore the

γονεῖς αὐτοῦ καὶ εἶπαν· οἴδαμεν ὅτι
parents of him and said: We know that

οὗτός ἐστιν ὁ υἱὸς ἡμῶν καὶ ὅτι τυφλὸς
this is the son of us and that blind

ἐγεννήθη· 21 πῶς δὲ νῦν βλέπει οὐκ
he was born; but how now he sees not

οἴδαμεν, ἢ τίς ἤνοιξεν αὐτοῦ τοὺς ὀφθαλμοὺς
we know, or who opened of him the eyes

ἡμεῖς οὐκ οἴδαμεν· αὐτὸν ἐρωτήσατε,
we know not; him ask ye,

ἡλικίαν ἔχει, αὐτὸς περὶ ἑαυτοῦ λαλήσει.
age he has, he about himself will speak.

22 ταῦτα εἶπαν οἱ γονεῖς αὐτοῦ ὅτι ἐφο-
These things said the parents of him because they

βοῦντο τοὺς Ἰουδαίους· ἤδη γὰρ συνετέθειντο
feared the Jews; for already had agreed

οἱ Ἰουδαῖοι ἵνα ἐάν τις αὐτὸν ὁμολογήσῃ
the Jews that if anyone him should acknowledge

χριστόν, ἀποσυνάγωγος γένηται.
[to be] Christ, put away from [the] synagogue he would be.

23 διὰ τοῦτο οἱ γονεῖς αὐτοῦ εἶπαν ὅτι
Therefore the parents of him said[,] –

ἡλικίαν ἔχει, αὐτὸν ἐπερωτήσατε. 24 Ἐφώνησαν
Age he has, him question ye. They called

οὖν τὸν ἄνθρωπον ἐκ δευτέρου ὃς ἦν
therefore the man a second time who was

τυφλός, καὶ εἶπαν αὐτῷ· δὸς δόξαν τῷ
blind, and said to him: Give glory –

θεῷ· ἡμεῖς οἴδαμεν ὅτι οὗτος ὁ ἄνθρωπος
to God; we know that this man

ἁμαρτωλός ἐστιν. 25 ἀπεκρίθη οὖν ἐκεῖνος·
sinful is. Answered therefore that [one]:

εἰ ἁμαρτωλός ἐστιν οὐκ οἶδα· ἓν οἶδα,
If sinful he is I know not; one thing I know,

ὅτι τυφλὸς ὢν ἄρτι βλέπω. 26 εἶπαν
that blind being now I see. They said

οὖν αὐτῷ· τί ἐποίησέν σοι; πῶς ἤνοιξέν
therefore to him: What did he to thee? how opened he

σου τοὺς ὀφθαλμούς; 27 ἀπεκρίθη αὐτοῖς·
of thee the eyes? He answered them:

εἶπον ὑμῖν ἤδη καὶ οὐκ ἠκούσατε· τί
I told you already and ye heard not; why

πάλιν θέλετε ἀκούειν; μὴ καὶ ὑμεῖς
again wish ye to hear? not also ye

θέλετε αὐτοῦ μαθηταὶ γενέσθαι; 28 καὶ
wish of him disciples to become? And

ἐλοιδόρησαν αὐτὸν καὶ εἶπαν· σὺ μαθητὴς
they reviled him and said: Thou a disciple

εἶ ἐκείνου, ἡμεῖς δὲ τοῦ Μωϋσέως ἐσμὲν
art of that man, but we – of Moses are

μαθηταί· 29 ἡμεῖς οἴδαμεν ὅτι Μωϋσεῖ
disciples; we know that by Moses

λελάληκεν ὁ θεός, τοῦτον δὲ οὐκ οἴδαμεν
has spoken – God, but this man we know not

πόθεν ἐστίν. 30 ἀπεκρίθη ὁ ἄνθρωπος
whence he is. Answered the man

καὶ εἶπεν αὐτοῖς· ἐν τούτῳ γὰρ τὸ
and said to them: In this then the

King James Version

herein is a marvellous thing, that ye know not from whence he is, and *yet* he hath opened mine eyes. 31 Now we know that God heareth not sinners: but if any man be a worshipper of God, and doeth his will, him he heareth. 32 Since the world began was it not heard that any man opened the eyes of one that was born blind. 33 If this man were not of God, he could do nothing. 34 They answered and said unto him, Thou wast altogether born in sins, and dost thou teach us? And they cast him out. 35 Jesus heard that they had cast him out; and when he had found him, he said unto him, Dost thou believe on the Son of God? 36 He answered and said, Who is he, Lord, that I might believe on him? 37 And Jesus said unto him, Thou hast both seen him, and it is he that talketh with thee. 38 And he said, Lord, I believe. And he worshipped him.

39 And Jesus said, For judgment I am come into this world, that they which see not might see; and that they which see might be made blind. 40 And *some* of the Pharisees which were with him heard these words, and said unto him, Are we blind also? 41 Jesus said unto them, If ye were blind, ye should have no sin: but now ye say, We see; therefore your sin remaineth.

10 Verily, verily, I say unto you, He that entereth not by the door into the sheepfold, but climbeth up some other way, the same is a thief and a robber. 2 But he that entereth in by the door is the shepherd of the sheep. 3 To him the porter openeth; and the sheep hear his voice: and he calleth his own sheep by name, and leadeth them out. 4 And when he putteth forth his own sheep, he goeth before them, and the sheep follow him: for they know his voice. 5 And a stranger will they not follow, but will flee from him; for they know not the voice of strangers. 6 This parable spake Jesus unto them: but they understood not what things they were which he spake unto them. 7 Then said Jesus unto them again, Verily, verily, I say unto you, I am the door of the sheep. 8 All that ever came before me are thieves and robbers: but the sheep did not hear them. 9 I am the door: by me if any man enter in, he shall be saved, and shall go in and out, and find pasture. 10 The thief cometh not, but for to steal, and to kill, and to destroy: I am come that they might have life, and that they might have *it* more abundantly. 11 I am the good shepherd: the good shepherd giveth his life for the sheep. 12 But he that is a hireling, and not the shepherd, whose own the sheep are not, seeth the wolf coming, and leaveth the sheep, and fleeth; and the wolf catcheth them, and scattereth the sheep. 13 The hireling fleeth, because he is a hireling, and careth not

New International Version

ble! You don't know where he comes from, yet he opened my eyes. 31 We know that God does not listen to sinners. He listens to the godly man who does his will. 32 Nobody has ever heard of opening the eyes of a man born blind. 33 If this man were not from God, he could do nothing."

34 To this they replied, "You were steeped in sin at birth; how dare you lecture us!" And they threw him out.

Spiritual blindness

35 Jesus heard that they had thrown him out, and when he found him, he said, "Do you believe in the Son of Man?"

36 "Who is he, sir?" the man asked. "Tell me so that I may believe in him."

37 Jesus said, "You have now seen him; in fact, he is the one speaking with you."

38 Then the man said, "Lord, I believe," and he worshiped him.

39 Jesus said, "For judgment I have come into this world, so that the blind will see and those who see will turn out to be blind."

40 Some Pharisees who were with him heard him say this and asked, "What? Are we blind too?"

41 Jesus said, "If you were blind, you would not be guilty of sin; but now that you claim you can see, your guilt remains.

The shepherd and his flock

10 "I tell you the truth, the man who does not enter the sheep pen by the gate, but climbs in by some other way, is a thief and a robber. 2 The man who enters by the gate is the shepherd of his sheep. 3 The watchman opens the gate for him, and the sheep listen to his voice. He calls his own sheep by name and leads them out. 4 When he has brought out all his own, he goes on ahead of them, and his sheep follow him because they know his voice. 5 But they will never follow a stranger; in fact, they will run away from him because they do not recognize a stranger's voice." 6 Jesus used this figure of speech, but they did not understand what he was telling them.

7 Therefore Jesus said again, "I tell you the truth, I am the gate for the sheep. 8 All who ever came before me were thieves and robbers, but the sheep did not listen to them. 9 I am the gate; whoever enters through me will be saved." He will come in and go out, and find pasture. 10 The thief comes only to steal and kill and destroy; I have come that they may have life, and have it to the full.

11 "I am the good shepherd. The good shepherd lays down his life for the sheep. 12 The hired hand is not the shepherd who owns the sheep. So when he sees the wolf coming, he abandons the sheep and runs away. Then the wolf attacks the flock and scatters it. 13 The man runs away because he is a hired hand and cares nothing for the sheep.

[u] Or *kept safe.*

Greek Interlinear

θαυμαστὸν ἐστιν, ὅτι ὑμεῖς οὐκ οἴδατε
marvellous thing is, that ye do not know

πόθεν ἐστίν, καὶ ἤνοιξέν μου τοὺς
whence he is, and he opened of me the

ὀφθαλμούς. 31 οἴδαμεν ὅτι ὁ θεὸς
eyes. We know that - God

ἁμαρτωλῶν οὐκ ἀκούει, ἀλλ' ἐάν τις
sinful men does not hear, ͑ but if anyone

θεοσεβὴς ᾖ καὶ τὸ θέλημα αὐτοῦ ποιῇ,
godfearing is and the will of him does,

τούτου ἀκούει. 32 ἐκ τοῦ αἰῶνος οὐκ
this man he hears. From the age not

ἠκούσθη ὅτι ἠνέῳξέν τις ὀφθαλμοὺς τυφλοῦ
it was heard that ¹opened ²anyone eyes of a blind man

γεγεννημένου· 33 εἰ μὴ ἦν οὗτος παρὰ
having been born· if ¹not ²was ³this man ⁴from

θεοῦ, οὐκ ἠδύνατο ποιεῖν οὐδέν. 34 ἀπεκρίθησαν
God, he could not to do no(any)thing. They answered

καὶ εἶπαν αὐτῷ· ἐν ἁμαρτίαις σὺ ἐγεννήθης
and said to him: In sins thou wast born

ὅλος, καὶ σὺ διδάσκεις ἡμᾶς; καὶ ἐξέβαλον
wholly, and thou teachest us? and they cast out

αὐτὸν ἔξω. 35 Ἤκουσεν Ἰησοῦς ὅτι
him outside. Heard Jesus that

ἐξέβαλον αὐτὸν ἔξω, καὶ εὑρὼν αὐτὸν
they cast out him outside, and finding him

εἶπεν· Σὺ πιστεύεις εἰς τὸν υἱὸν τοῦ
said: Thou believest in the Son of the

ἀνθρώπου; 36 ἀπεκρίθη ἐκεῖνος καὶ εἶπεν·
of man? Answered that [one] and said:

καὶ τίς ἐστιν, κύριε, ἵνα πιστεύσω εἰς
And who is he, sir, that I may believe in

αὐτόν; 37 εἶπεν αὐτῷ ὁ Ἰησοῦς· καὶ
him? Said to him - Jesus: Both

ἑώρακας αὐτὸν καὶ ὁ λαλῶν μετὰ σοῦ
thou hast seen him and the [one] speaking with thee

ἐκεῖνός ἐστιν. 38 ὁ δὲ ἔφη· πιστεύω, κύριε·
that [one] is. And he said: I believe, sir;

καὶ προσεκύνησεν αὐτῷ. 39 καὶ εἶπεν ὁ
and he worshipped him. And said -

Ἰησοῦς· εἰς κρίμα ἐγὼ εἰς τὸν κόσμον
Jesus: For judgment I into - world

τοῦτον ἦλθον, ἵνα οἱ μὴ βλέποντες
this came, that the [ones] not seeing

βλέπωσιν καὶ οἱ βλέποντες τυφλοὶ γένωνται.
may see and the [ones] seeing blind may become.

40 Ἤκουσαν ἐκ τῶν Φαρισαίων ταῦτα
¹heard ¹[Some] ²of ³the ⁴Pharisees ⁵these things

οἱ μετ' αὐτοῦ ὄντες, καὶ εἶπαν αὐτῷ·
- ⁴with ⁵him ⁵being, and they said to him:

μὴ καὶ ἡμεῖς τυφλοί ἐσμεν; 41 εἶπεν
Not also we blind are? Said

αὐτοῖς ὁ Ἰησοῦς· εἰ τυφλοὶ ἦτε, οὐκ
to them - Jesus: If blind ye were, not

ἂν εἴχετε ἁμαρτίαν· νῦν δὲ λέγετε ὅτι
ye would have had sin; but now ye say[,] -

βλέπομεν· ἡ ἁμαρτία ὑμῶν μένει.
We see; the sin of you remains.

Chapter 10

Ἀμὴν ἀμὴν λέγω ὑμῖν, ὁ μὴ
Truly truly I say to you, the [one] not

εἰσερχόμενος διὰ τῆς θύρας εἰς τὴν
entering through the door into the

αὐλὴν τῶν προβάτων ἀλλὰ ἀναβαίνων
fold of the sheep but going up

ἀλλαχόθεν, ἐκεῖνος κλέπτης ἐστὶν καὶ
by another way, that [one] a thief is and

λῃστής· 2 ὁ δὲ εἰσερχόμενος διὰ τῆς
a robber; but the [one] entering through the

θύρας ποιμήν ἐστιν τῶν προβάτων. 3 τούτῳ
door shepherd is of the sheep. To this [one]

ὁ θυρωρὸς ἀνοίγει, καὶ τὰ πρόβατα τῆς
the doorkeeper opens, and the sheep the

φωνῆς αὐτοῦ ἀκούει, καὶ τὰ ἴδια πρόβατα
voice of him hears, and the(his) own sheep

φωνεῖ κατ' ὄνομα καὶ ἐξάγει αὐτά.
he calls by name and leads out them.

4 ὅταν τὰ ἴδια πάντα ἐκβάλῃ, ἔμπροσθεν
When the(his) own all he puts forth, in front of

αὐτῶν πορεύεται, καὶ τὰ πρόβατα αὐτῷ
them he goes, and the sheep him

ἀκολουθεῖ, ὅτι οἴδασιν τὴν φωνὴν αὐτοῦ·
follows, because they know the voice of him:

5 ἀλλοτρίῳ δὲ οὐ μὴ ἀκολουθήσουσιν,
but a stranger by no means will they follow,

ἀλλὰ φεύξονται ἀπ' αὐτοῦ, ὅτι οὐκ
but will flee from him, because not

οἴδασιν τῶν ἀλλοτρίων τὴν φωνήν.
they know of the strangers the voice.

6 Ταύτην τὴν παροιμίαν εἶπεν αὐτοῖς ὁ
This - allegory told them -

Ἰησοῦς· ἐκεῖνοι δὲ οὐκ ἔγνωσαν τίνα
Jesus; but those men knew not what things

ἦν ἃ ἐλάλει αὐτοῖς. 7 Εἶπεν οὖν πάλιν
they were which he spoke to them. Said therefore again

ὁ Ἰησοῦς· ἀμὴν ἀμὴν λέγω ὑμῖν ὅτι
- Jesus: Truly truly I say to you that

ἐγώ εἰμι ἡ θύρα τῶν προβάτων. 8 πάντες
I am the door of the sheep. All

ὅσοι ἦλθον πρὸ ἐμοῦ κλέπται εἰσὶν καὶ
who came before me thieves are and

λῃσταί· ἀλλ' οὐκ ἤκουσαν αὐτῶν τὰ
robbers; but did not hear them the

πρόβατα. 9 ἐγώ εἰμι ἡ θύρα· δι' ἐμοῦ
sheep. I am the door; through me

ἐάν τις εἰσέλθῃ, σωθήσεται, καὶ εἰσελεύ-
if anyone enters, he will be saved, and will go

σεται καὶ ἐξελεύσεται καὶ νομὴν εὑρήσει.
in and will go out and pasture will find.

10 ὁ κλέπτης οὐκ ἔρχεται εἰ μὴ ἵνα
The thief comes not except that

κλέψῃ καὶ θύσῃ καὶ ἀπολέσῃ· ἐγὼ ἦλθον
he may steal and kill and destroy; I came

ἵνα ζωὴν ἔχωσιν καὶ περισσὸν ἔχωσιν.
that life they may have and abundantly they may have.

11 Ἐγώ εἰμι ὁ ποιμὴν ὁ καλός. ὁ
I am the shepherd - good. The

ποιμὴν ὁ καλὸς τὴν ψυχὴν αὐτοῦ τίθησιν
shepherd - good the life of him lays down

ὑπὲρ τῶν προβάτων· 12 ὁ μισθωτὸς καὶ
for the sheep; the hireling and

οὐκ ὢν ποιμήν, οὗ οὐκ ἔστιν τὰ πρόβατα
not being a shepherd, of whom is(are) not the sheep

ἴδια, θεωρεῖ τὸν λύκον ἐρχόμενον καὶ
[his] own, beholds the wolf coming and

ἀφίησιν τὰ πρόβατα καὶ φεύγει, — καὶ
leaves the sheep and flees, — and

ὁ λύκος ἁρπάζει αὐτὰ καὶ σκορπίζει·
the wolf seizes them and scatters;

13 ὅτι μισθωτός ἐστιν καὶ οὐ μέλει
because a hireling he is and it matters not

King James Version

for the sheep. 14 I am the good shepherd, and know my *sheep*, and am known of mine. 15As the Father knoweth me, even so know I the Father: and I lay down my life for the sheep. 16And other sheep I have, which are not of this fold: them also I must bring, and they shall hear my voice; and there shall be one fold, *and* one shepherd. 17 Therefore doth my Father love me, because I lay down my life, that I might take it again. 18 No man taketh it from me, but I lay it down of myself. I have power to lay it down, and I have power to take it again. This commandment have I received of my Father.

19 There was a division therefore again among the Jews for these sayings. 20And many of them said, He hath a devil, and is mad; why hear ye him? 21 Others said, These are not the words of him that hath a devil. Can a devil open the eyes of the blind?

22 And it was at Jerusalem the feast of the dedication, and it was winter. 23And Jesus walked in the temple in Solomon's porch. 24 Then came the Jews round about him, and said unto him, How long dost thou make us to doubt? If thou be the Christ, tell us plainly. 25 Jesus answered them, I told you, and ye believed not: the works that I do in my Father's name, they bear witness of me. 26But ye believe not, because ye are not of my sheep, as I said unto you. 27 My sheep hear my voice, and I know them, and they follow me: 28And I give unto them eternal life; and they shall never perish, neither shall any *man* pluck them out of my hand. 29 My Father, which gave *them* me, is greater than all; and no *man* is able to pluck *them* out of my Father's hand. 30 I and *my* Father are one. 31 Then the Jews took up stones again to stone him. 32 Jesus answered them, Many good works have I shewed you from my Father; for which of those works do ye stone me? 33 The Jews answered him, saying, For a good work we stone thee not; but for blasphemy; and because that thou, being a man, makest thyself God. 34 Jesus answered them, Is it not written in your law, I said, Ye are gods? 35 If he called them gods, unto whom the word of God came, and the Scripture cannot be broken; 36 Say ye of him, whom the Father hath sanctified, and sent into the world, Thou blasphemest; because I said, I am the Son of God? 37 If I do not the works of my Father, believe me not. 38 But if I do, though ye believe not me, believe the works; that ye may know, and believe, that the Father *is* in me, and I in him. 39 Therefore they sought again to take him; but he escaped out of their

New International Version

14 "I am the good shepherd; I know my sheep and my sheep know me—15 just as the Father knows me and I know the Father—and I lay down my life for the sheep. 16 I have other sheep that are not of this flock. I must bring them also. They too will listen to my voice, and there shall be one flock and one shepherd. 17 The reason my Father loves me is that I lay down my life —only to take it up again. 18 No one takes it from me, but I lay it down of my own accord. I have authority to lay it down and authority to take it up again. This command I received from my Father."

19 At these words the Jews were again divided. 20 Many of them said, "He is demon-possessed and raving mad. Why listen to him?"

21 But others said, "These are not the sayings of a man possessed by a demon. How can a demon open the eyes of the blind?"

The unbelief of the Jews

22 Then came the Feast of Dedication[v] at Jerusalem. It was winter, 23 and Jesus was in the temple area walking in Solomon's Colonnade. 24 The Jews gathered around him, saying, "How long will you keep us in suspense? If you are the Christ,[w] tell us plainly."

25 Jesus answered, "I did tell you, but you do not believe. The miracles I do in my Father's name speak for me, 26 but you do not believe because you do not belong to my flock. 27 My sheep listen to my voice; I know them, and they follow me. 28 I give them eternal life, and they shall never perish; no one can snatch them out of my hand. 29 My Father, who has given them to me, is greater than all[x]; no one can snatch them out of my Father's hand. 30 I and the Father are one."

31 Again the Jews picked up stones to stone him, 32 but Jesus said to them, "I have shown you many great miracles from the Father. For which of these do you stone me?"

33 "We are not stoning you for any of these," replied the Jews, "but for blasphemy, because you, a mere man, claim to be God."

34 Jesus answered them, "Is it not written in your Law, 'I have said you are gods'[y]? 35 If he called them 'gods,' to whom the word of God came—and the Scripture cannot be broken— 36 what about the one whom the Father set apart as his very own and sent into the world? Why then do you accuse me of blasphemy because I said, 'I am God's Son'? 37 Do not believe me unless I do what my Father does. 38 But if I do it, even though you do not believe me, believe the evidence of the miracles, that you may learn and understand that the Father is in me, and I in the Father." 39Again they tried to seize him, but he escaped their grasp.

[v] That is, Hanukkah. [w] Or *Messiah*. [x] Many early MSS read *What my Father has given me greater than all*. [y] Psalm 82:6.

Greek Interlinear

αὐτῷ περὶ τῶν προβάτων. 14 ἐγώ εἰμι
to him about the sheep. I am

ὁ ποιμὴν ὁ καλός, καὶ γινώσκω τὰ
the shepherd - good, and I know

ἐμὰ καὶ γινώσκουσί με τὰ ἐμά, 15 καθὼς
mine and 'know 'me - 'mine, as

γινώσκει με ὁ πατὴρ κἀγώ γινώσκω τὸν
'knows 'me 'the 'Father and I know the

πατέρα, καὶ τὴν ψυχήν μου τίθημι ὑπὲρ
Father, and the life of me I lay down for

τῶν προβάτων. 16 καὶ ἄλλα πρόβατα
the sheep. And other sheep

ἔχω ἃ οὐκ ἔστιν ἐκ τῆς αὐλῆς ταύτης·
I have which is(are) not of - fold this;

κἀκεῖνα δεῖ με ἀγαγεῖν, καὶ τῆς φωνῆς
those also it behoves me to bring, and the voice

μου ἀκούσουσιν, καὶ γενήσεται μία ποίμνη,
of me they will hear, and there will become one flock,

εἰς ποιμήν. 17 διὰ τοῦτό με ὁ πατὴρ
one shepherd. Therefore me the Father

ἀγαπᾷ ὅτι ἐγώ τίθημι τὴν ψυχήν μου,
loves because I lay down the life of me,

ἵνα πάλιν λάβω αὐτήν. 18 οὐδεὶς ἦρεν
that again I may take it. No one took

αὐτὴν ἀπ' ἐμοῦ, ἀλλ' ἐγώ τίθημι αὐτὴν
it from me, but I lay down it

ἀπ' ἐμαυτοῦ. ἐξουσίαν ἔχω θεῖναι αὐτήν,
from myself. Authority I have to lay down it,

καὶ ἐξουσίαν ἔχω πάλιν λαβεῖν αὐτήν·
and authority I have again to take it;

ταύτην τὴν ἐντολὴν ἔλαβον παρὰ τοῦ
this - commandment I received from the

πατρός μου. 19 Σχίσμα πάλιν ἐγένετο ἐν
Father of me. A division again there was among

τοῖς Ἰουδαίοις διὰ τοὺς λόγους τούτους.
the Jews because of - words these.

20 ἔλεγον δὲ πολλοὶ ἐξ αὐτῶν· δαιμόνιον
And said many of them: A demon

ἔχει καὶ μαίνεται· τί αὐτοῦ ἀκούετε;
he has and raves; why him hear ye?

21 ἄλλοι ἔλεγον· ταῦτα τὰ ῥήματα οὐκ
Others said: These - words not

ἔστιν δαιμονιζομένου· μὴ δαιμόνιον δύναται
is(are) of one demon-possessed; not a demon can

τυφλῶν ὀφθαλμοὺς ἀνοῖξαι;
of blind men eyes to open?

22 Ἐγένετο τότε τὰ ἐγκαίνια ἐν τοῖς
There was then the Dedication in -

Ἰεροσολύμοις· χειμὼν ἦν· 23 καὶ περιεπάτει
Jerusalem: winter it was; and walked

ὁ Ἰησοῦς ἐν τῷ ἱερῷ ἐν τῇ στοᾷ τοῦ
- Jesus in the temple in the porch -

Σολομῶνος. 24 ἐκύκλωσαν οὖν αὐτὸν οἱ
of Solomon. Surrounded therefore him the

Ἰουδαῖοι καὶ ἔλεγον αὐτῷ· ἕως πότε
Jews and said to him: Until when

τὴν ψυχὴν ἡμῶν αἴρεις; εἰ σὺ εἶ
the life(soul) of us holdest thou * ? if thou art

ὁ χριστός, εἰπὸν ἡμῖν παρρησίᾳ. 25 ἀπεκρίθη
the Christ, tell us plainly. Answered

αὐτοῖς ὁ Ἰησοῦς· εἶπον ὑμῖν, καὶ
them - Jesus: I told you, and

οὐ πιστεύετε· τὰ ἔργα ἃ ἐγώ ποιῶ ἐν τῷ
ye do not believe; the works which I do in the

ὀνόματι τοῦ πατρός μου, ταῦτα μαρτυρεῖ
name of the Father of me, these witnesses

περὶ ἐμοῦ· ἀλλὰ ὑμεῖς οὐ πιστεύετε,
concerning me; but ye do not believe,

26 ὅτι οὐκ ἐστὲ ἐκ τῶν προβάτων τῶν
because ye are not of the 'sheep -

ἐμῶν. 27 τὰ πρόβατα τὰ ἐμὰ τῆς φωνῆς
'my. the sheep - My the voice

μου ἀκούουσιν, κἀγώ γινώσκω αὐτά, καὶ
of me hear, and I know them, and

ἀκολουθοῦσίν μοι, 28 κἀγώ δίδωμι αὐτοῖς
they follow me, and I give to them

ζωὴν αἰώνιον, καὶ οὐ μὴ ἀπόλωνται εἰς
life eternal, and by no means they perish unto

τὸν αἰῶνα, καὶ οὐχ ἁρπάσει τις αὐτὰ
the age, and 'shall not seize 'anyone them

ἐκ τῆς χειρός μου. 29 ὁ πατὴρ μου ὃ
out of the hand of me. The Father of me who

δέδωκέν μοι πάντων μεῖζόν ἐστιν, καὶ
has given to me [than] all greater is, and

οὐδεὶς δύναται ἁρπάζειν ἐκ τῆς χειρὸς
no one can to seize out of the hand

τοῦ πατρός. 30 ἐγώ καὶ ὁ πατὴρ ἕν
of the Father. I and the Father one

ἐσμεν. 31 Ἐβάστασαν πάλιν λίθους οἱ
we are. Lifted again stones the

Ἰουδαῖοι ἵνα λιθάσωσιν αὐτόν. 32 ἀπ-
Jews that they might stone him. An-

εκρίθη αὐτοῖς ὁ Ἰησοῦς· πολλὰ ἔργα
swered them - Jesus: Many 'works

ἔδειξα ὑμῖν καλὰ ἐκ τοῦ πατρός· διὰ
'I showed 'you 'good of the Father; because of

ποῖον αὐτῶν ἔργον ἐμὲ λιθάζετε;
which of them 'work 'me 'stone ye?

33 ἀπεκρίθησαν αὐτῷ οἱ Ἰουδαῖοι· περὶ
Answered him the Jews: Concerning

καλοῦ ἔργου οὐ λιθάζομέν σε ἀλλὰ περὶ
a good work we do not stone thee but concerning

βλασφημίας, καὶ ὅτι σὺ ἄνθρωπος ὢν
blasphemy, and because thou a man being

ποιεῖς σεαυτὸν θεόν. 34 ἀπεκρίθη αὐτοῖς
makest thyself God. Answered them

ὁ Ἰησοῦς· οὐκ ἔστιν γεγραμμένον ἐν τῷ
- Jesus: Is it not having been written in the

νόμῳ ὑμῶν ὅτι ἐγώ εἶπα· θεοί ἐστε;
law of you[,] - I said: Gods ye are?

35 εἰ ἐκείνους εἶπεν θεοὺς πρὸς οὓς ὁ
'if 'those 'he called 'gods with whom the

λόγος τοῦ θεοῦ ἐγένετο, καὶ οὐ δύναται
word - of God was, and cannot

λυθῆναι ἡ γραφή, 36 ὃν ὁ πατὴρ
to be broken the scripture, '[him] whom 'the 'Father

ἡγίασεν καὶ ἀπέστειλεν εἰς τὸν κόσμον
'sanctified 'and 'sent 'into 'the "world

ὑμεῖς λέγετε ὅτι βλασφημεῖς, ὅτι εἶπον·
'ye 'tell[,] - Thou blasphemest, because I said:

υἱὸς τοῦ θεοῦ εἰμι; 37 εἰ οὐ ποιῶ τὰ ἔργα
Son - of God I am? If I do not the works

τοῦ πατρός μου, μὴ πιστεύετέ μοι· 38 εἰ δὲ
of the Father of me, do not believe me; but if

ποιῶ, κἂν ἐμοὶ μὴ πιστεύητε, τοῖς ἔργοις
I do, even if me ye do not believe, the works

πιστεύετε, ἵνα γνῶτε καὶ γινώσκητε★
believe, that ye may know★ and continue to know★

ὅτι ἐν ἐμοὶ ὁ πατὴρ κἀγώ ἐν τῷ πατρί.
that in me the Father [is] and I in the Father.

39 Ἐζήτουν οὖν αὐτὸν πάλιν πιάσαι· καὶ
They sought therefore him again to arrest; and

ἐξῆλθεν ἐκ τῆς χειρὸς αὐτῶν.
he went forth out of the hand of them.

---

* That is, in suspense.

★ Different tenses (aorist and present) of the same verb.

King James Version

hand, 40And went away again beyond Jordan into the place where John at first baptized; and there he abode. 41And many resorted unto him, and said, John did no miracle: but all things that John spake of this man were true. 42And many believed on him there.

11 Now a certain *man* was sick, *named* Lazarus, of Bethany, the town of Mary and her sister Martha. 2 (It was *that* Mary which anointed the Lord with ointment, and wiped his feet with her hair, whose brother Lazarus was sick.) 3 Therefore his sisters sent unto him, saying, Lord, behold, he whom thou lovest is sick. 4 When Jesus heard *that,* he said, This sickness is not unto death, but for the glory of God, that the Son of God might be glorified thereby. 5 Now Jesus loved Martha, and her sister, and Lazarus. 6 When he had heard therefore that he was sick, he abode two days still in the same place where he was. 7 Then after that saith he to *his* disciples, Let us go into Judea again. 8 *His* disciples say unto him, Master, the Jews of late sought to stone thee; and goest thou thither again? 9 Jesus answered, Are there not twelve hours in the day? If any man walk in the day, he stumbleth not, because he seeth the light of this world. 10 But if a man walk in the night, he stumbleth, because there is no light in him. 11 These things said he: and after that he saith unto them, Our friend Lazarus sleepeth; but I go, that I may awake him out of sleep. 12 Then said his disciples, Lord, if he sleep, he shall do well. 13 Howbeit Jesus spake of his death: but they thought that he had spoken of taking of rest in sleep. 14 Then said Jesus unto them plainly, Lazarus is dead. 15And I am glad for your sakes that I was not there, to the intent ye may believe; nevertheless let us go unto him. 16 Then said Thomas, which is called Didymus, unto his fellow disciples, Let us also go, that we may die with him. 17 Then when Jesus came, he found that he had *lain* in the grave four days already. 18 Now Bethany was nigh unto Jerusalem, about fifteen furlongs off: 19And many of the Jews came to Martha and Mary, to comfort them concerning their brother. 20 Then Martha, as soon as she heard that Jesus was coming, went and met him: but Mary sat *still* in the house. 21 Then said Martha unto Jesus, Lord, if thou hadst been here, my brother had not died. 22 But I know, that even now, whatsoever thou wilt ask of God, God will give *it* thee. 23 Jesus saith unto her, Thy brother shall rise again. 24 Martha saith unto him, I know that he shall rise again in the

New International Version

40 Then Jesus went back across the Jordan to the place where John had been baptizing in the early days. Here he stayed 41 and many people came to him. They said, "Though John never performed a miraculous sign, all that John said about this man was true." 42And in that place many believed in Jesus.

The death of Lazarus

11 Now a man named Lazarus was sick. He was from Bethany, the village of Mary and her sister Martha. 2 This Mary, whose brother Lazarus now lay sick, was the same one who poured perfume on the Lord and wiped his feet with her hair. 3 So the sisters sent word to Jesus, "Lord, the one you love is sick." 4 When he heard this, Jesus said, "This sickness will not end in death. No, it is for God's glory so that God's Son may be glorified through it." 5 Jesus loved Martha and her sister and Lazarus. 6 Yet when he heard that Lazarus was sick, he stayed where he was two more days. 7 Then he said to his disciples, "Let us go back to Judea." 8 "But Rabbi," they said, "a short while ago the Jews tried to stone you, and yet you are going back there?" 9 Jesus answered, "Are there not twelve hours of daylight? A man who walks by day will not stumble, for he sees by this world's light. 10 It is when he walks by night that he stumbles, for he has no light." 11 After he had said this, he went on to tell them, "Our friend Lazarus has fallen asleep; but I am going there to wake him up." 12 His disciples replied, "Lord, if he sleeps, he will get better." 13 Jesus had been speaking of his death, but his disciples thought he meant natural sleep. 14 So then he told them plainly, "Lazarus is dead, 15 yet for your sake so that you may believe, I am glad I was not there. But let us go to him." 16 Then Thomas, called Didymus, said to the rest of the disciples, "Let us also go, that we may die with him."

Jesus comforts the sisters

17 On his arrival, Jesus found that Lazarus had already been in the tomb for four days. 18 Bethany was less than two miles from Jerusalem, 19 and many Jews had come to Martha and Mary to comfort them in the loss of their brother. 20 When Martha heard that Jesus was coming, she went out to meet him, but Mary stayed at home. 21 "Lord," Martha said to Jesus, "if you had been here, my brother would not have died. 22 But I know that even now God will give you whatever you ask." 23 Jesus said to her, "Your brother will rise again." 24 Martha answered, "I know he will rise again in the resurrection at the last day."

Greek Interlinear

40 Καὶ ἀπῆλθεν πάλιν πέραν τοῦ
And he went away again across the
'Ιορδάνου εἰς τὸν τόπον ὅπου ἦν 'Ιωάννης
Jordan to the place where was John
τὸ πρῶτον βαπτίζων, καὶ ἔμενεν ἐκεῖ.
at first baptizing, and remained there.
41 καὶ πολλοὶ ἦλθον πρὸς αὐτὸν καὶ
And many came to him and

ἔλεγον ὅτι 'Ιωάννης μὲν σημεῖον ἐποίησεν
said[,] - John indeed sign did
οὐδέν, πάντα δὲ ὅσα εἶπεν 'Ιωάννης περὶ
none, but all things how many said John about
τούτου ἀληθῆ ἦν. **42** καὶ πολλοὶ ἐπίστευσαν
this man true was(were). And many believed
εἰς αὐτὸν ἐκεῖ.
in him there.

Chapter 11

'Ην δέ τις ἀσθενῶν, Λάζαρος ἀπὸ
Now there was a certain [man] ailing, Lazarus from
Βηθανίας, ἐκ τῆς κώμης Μαρίας καὶ
Bethany, of the village of Mary and
Μάρθας τῆς ἀδελφῆς αὐτῆς. **2** ἦν δὲ
Martha the sister of her. And it was
Μαριὰμ ἡ ἀλείψασα τὸν κύριον μύρῳ
Mary the [one] anointing the Lord with ointment
καὶ ἐκμάξασα τοὺς πόδας αὐτοῦ ταῖς
and wiping off the feet of him with the
θριξὶν αὐτῆς, ἧς ὁ ἀδελφὸς Λάζαρος
hairs of her, of whom the brother Lazarus
ἠσθένει. **3** ἀπέστειλαν οὖν αἱ ἀδελφαὶ
ailed. Sent therefore the sisters
πρὸς αὐτὸν λέγουσαι· κύριε, ἴδε ὃν
to him saying : Lord, behold[,] [he] whom
φιλεῖς ἀσθενεῖ. **4** ἀκούσας δὲ ὁ 'Ιησοῦς
thou lovest ails. And hearing - Jesus
εἶπεν· αὕτη ἡ ἀσθένεια οὐκ ἔστιν πρὸς
said: This - ailment is not to
θάνατον ἀλλ' ὑπὲρ τῆς δόξης τοῦ θεοῦ,
death but for the glory - of God,
ἵνα δοξασθῇ ὁ υἱὸς τοῦ θεοῦ δι' αὐτῆς.
that may be glorified the Son - of God through it.
5 ἠγάπα δὲ ὁ 'Ιησοῦς τὴν Μάρθαν καὶ
Now ¹loved - ¹Jesus - Martha and
τὴν ἀδελφὴν αὐτῆς καὶ τὸν Λάζαρον.
the sister of her and - Lazarus.
6 ὡς οὖν ἤκουσεν ὅτι ἀσθενεῖ, τότε μὲν
When therefore he heard that he ails(ed), then -
ἔμεινεν ἐν ᾧ ἦν τόπῳ δύο ἡμέρας·
he remained ¹in ²which ⁴he was ³place two days;
7 ἔπειτα μετὰ τοῦτο λέγει τοῖς μαθηταῖς·
then after this he says to the disciples :
ἄγωμεν εἰς τὴν 'Ιουδαίαν πάλιν. **8** λέγουσιν
Let us go into - Judæa again. Say
αὐτῷ οἱ μαθηταί· ῥαββί, νῦν ἐζήτουν
to him the disciples : Rabbi, ⁴now ²were ³seeking
σε λιθάσαι οἱ 'Ιουδαῖοι, καὶ πάλιν ὑπάγεις
⁷thee ⁶to stone ¹the ⁵Jews, and again goest thou
ἐκεῖ; **9** ἀπεκρίθη 'Ιησοῦς· οὐχὶ δώδεκα
there? Answered Jesus : Not twelve
ὥραί εἰσιν τῆς ἡμέρας; ἐάν τις περιπατῇ
hours are there of the day? If anyone walks
ἐν τῇ ἡμέρᾳ, οὐ προσκόπτει, ὅτι τὸ φῶς
in the day, he does not stumble, because the light
τοῦ κόσμου τούτου βλέπει· **10** ἐὰν δέ
- world of this he sees; but if
τις περιπατῇ ἐν τῇ νυκτί, προσκόπτει,
anyone walks in the night, he stumbles,
ὅτι τὸ φῶς οὐκ ἔστιν ἐν αὐτῷ. **11** ταῦτα
because the light is not in him. These things
εἶπεν, καὶ μετὰ τοῦτο λέγει αὐτοῖς·
he said, and after this he says to them :
Λάζαρος ὁ φίλος ἡμῶν κεκοίμηται· ἀλλὰ
Lazarus the friend of us has fallen asleep; but

πορεύομαι ἵνα ἐξυπνίσω αὐτόν. **12** εἶπαν
I am going that I may awaken him. Said
οὖν οἱ μαθηταὶ αὐτῷ· κύριε, εἰ κεκοίμηται,
there- the disciples to him: Lord, if he has fallen asleep,
fore
σωθήσεται. **13** εἰρήκει δὲ ὁ 'Ιησοῦς περὶ
he will be healed. Now had spoken - Jesus concerning
τοῦ θανάτου αὐτοῦ· ἐκεῖνοι δὲ ἔδοξαν ὅτι
the death of him; but those men thought that
περὶ τῆς κοιμήσεως τοῦ ὕπνου λέγει.
concerning the sleep - of slumber he says.
14 τότε οὖν εἶπεν αὐτοῖς ὁ 'Ιησοῦς
Then therefore told them - Jesus
παρρησίᾳ· Λάζαρος ἀπέθανεν, **15** καὶ χαίρω
plainly : Lazarus died, and I rejoice
δι' ὑμᾶς, ἵνα πιστεύσητε, ὅτι οὐκ ἤμην
because of you, that ye may believe, that I was not
ἐκεῖ· ἀλλὰ ἄγωμεν πρὸς αὐτόν. **16** εἶπεν
there; but let us go to him. Said
οὖν Θωμᾶς ὁ λεγόμενος Δίδυμος τοῖς
therefore Thomas - being called Twin to the(his)
συμμαθηταῖς· ἄγωμεν καὶ ἡμεῖς ἵνα
fellow-disciples : Let go also we(us) that
ἀποθάνωμεν μετ' αὐτοῦ. **17** 'Ελθὼν οὖν
we may die with him. Coming therefore
ὁ 'Ιησοῦς εὗρεν αὐτὸν τέσσαρας ἤδη
- Jesus found him ²four ¹already
ἡμέρας ἔχοντα ἐν τῷ μνημείῳ. **18** ἦν δὲ
³days having(being) in the tomb. Now was
Βηθανία ἐγγὺς τῶν 'Ιεροσολύμων ὡς ἀπὸ
Bethany near - Jerusalem about ²away
σταδίων δεκαπέντε. **19** πολλοὶ δὲ ἐκ τῶν
¹furlongs ¹fifteen. And many of the
'Ιουδαίων ἐληλύθεισαν πρὸς τὴν Μάρθαν
Jews had come to - Martha
καὶ Μαριάμ, ἵνα παραμυθήσωνται αὐτὰς
and Mary, that they might console them
περὶ τοῦ ἀδελφοῦ. **20** ἡ οὖν Μάρθα ὡς
concerning the(ir) brother. - Therefore Martha when
ἤκουσεν ὅτι 'Ιησοῦς ἔρχεται, ὑπήντησεν
she heard that Jesus is(was) coming, met
αὐτῷ· Μαριὰμ δὲ ἐν τῷ οἴκῳ ἐκαθέζετο.
him; but Mary in the house sat.
21 εἶπεν οὖν ἡ Μάρθα πρὸς 'Ιησοῦν·
Said therefore - Martha to Jesus :
κύριε, εἰ ἦς ὧδε, οὐκ ἂν ἀπέθανεν
Lord, if thou wast here, would not have died the
ὁ ἀδελφός μου. **22** καὶ νῦν οἶδα ὅτι ὅσα ἂν
brother of me. And now I know that whatever things
αἰτήσῃ τὸν θεὸν δώσει σοι ὁ θεός.
thou askest - God ²will give ³thee - ¹God.
23 λέγει αὐτῇ ὁ 'Ιησοῦς· ἀναστήσεται ὁ
Says to her - Jesus : Will rise again the
ἀδελφός σου. **24** λέγει αὐτῷ ἡ Μάρθα·
brother of thee. Says to him - Martha :
οἶδα ὅτι ἀναστήσεται ἐν τῇ ἀναστάσει
I know that he will rise again in the resurrection

305

King James Version

resurrection at the last day. 25 Jesus said unto her, I am the resurrection, and the life: he that believeth in me, though he were dead, yet shall he live: 26And whosoever liveth and believeth in me shall never die. Believest thou this? 27 She saith unto him, Yea, Lord: I believe that thou art the Christ, the Son of God, which should come into the world. 28And when she had so said, she went her way, and called Mary her sister secretly, saying, The Master is come, and calleth for thee. 29As soon as she heard *that,* she arose quickly, and came unto him. 30 Now Jesus was not yet come into the town, but was in that place where Martha met him. 31 The Jews then which were with her in the house, and comforted her, when they saw Jesus, that she rose up hastily and went out, followed her, saying, She goeth unto the grave to weep there. 32 Then when Mary was come where Jesus was, and saw him, she fell down at his feet, saying unto him, Lord, if thou hadst been here, my brother had not died. 33 When Jesus therefore saw her weeping, and the Jews also weeping which came with her, he groaned in the spirit, and was troubled, 34And said, Where have ye laid him? They say unto him, Lord, come and see. 35 Jesus wept. 36 Then said the Jews, Behold how he loved him! 37And some of them said, Could not this man, which opened the eyes of the blind, have caused that even this man should not have died? 38 Jesus therefore again groaning in himself cometh to the grave. It was a cave, and a stone lay upon it. 39 Jesus said, Take ye away the stone. Martha, the sister of him that was dead, saith unto him, Lord, by this time he stinketh: for he hath been *dead* four days. 40 Jesus saith unto her, Said I not unto thee, that, if thou wouldest believe, thou shouldest see the glory of God? 41 Then they took away the stone *from the place* where the dead was laid. And Jesus lifted up *his* eyes, and said, Father, I thank thee that thou hast heard me. 42And I knew that thou hearest me always: but because of the people which stand by I said *it,* that they may believe that thou hast sent me. 43And when he thus had spoken, he cried with a loud voice, Lazarus, come forth. 44And he that was dead came forth, bound hand and foot with graveclothes; and his face wa s bound about with a napkin. Jesus saith unto them, Loose him, and let him go. 45 Then many of the Jews which came to Mary, and had seen the things which Jesus did, believed on him. 46 But some of them went their ways to the Pharisees, and told them what things Jesus had done.

47 Then gathered the chief priests and the Pharisees a council, and said, What do we? for this man doeth many miracles. 48 If we let him thus alone, all *men* will believe on him; and the Romans shall come and take away both our

New International Version

25 Jesus said to her, "I am the resurrection and the life. He who believes in me will live, even though he dies; 26 and whoever lives and believes in me will never die. Do you believe this?"

27 "Yes, Lord," she told him, "I believe that you are the Christ,[z] the Son of God, who was to come into the world."

28 And after she had said this, she went back and called her sister Mary aside. "The Teacher is here," she said, "and is asking for you." 29 When Mary heard this, she got up quickly and went to him. 30 Now Jesus had not yet entered the village, but was still at the place where Martha had met him. 31 When the Jews who had been with Mary in the house, comforting her, noticed how quickly she got up and went out, they followed her, supposing she was going to the tomb to mourn there.

32 When Mary reached the place where Jesus was and saw him, she fell at his feet and said, "Lord, if you had been here, my brother would not have died."

33 When Jesus saw her weeping, and the Jews who had come along with her also weeping, he was deeply moved and troubled. 34 Where have you laid him?" he asked.

"Come and see, Lord," they replied.

35 Jesus wept.

36 Then the Jews said, "See how he loved him!"

37 But some of them said, "Could not he who opened the eyes of the blind man have kept this man from dying?"

Jesus raises Lazarus from the dead

38 Jesus, once more deeply moved, came to the tomb. It was a cave with a stone laid across the entrance. 39 "Take away the stone," he said.

"But, Lord," said Martha, the sister of the dead man, "by this time there is a bad odor, for he has been there four days."

40 Then Jesus said, "Did I not tell you that if you believed, you would see the glory of God?"

41 So they took away the stone. Then Jesus looked up and said, "Father, I thank you that you have heard me. 42 I knew that you always hear me, but I said this for the benefit of the people standing here, that they may believe that you sent me."

43 When he had said this, Jesus called in a loud voice, "Lazarus, come out!" 44 The dead man came out, his hands and feet wrapped with strips of linen, and a cloth around his face.

Jesus said to them, "Take off the grave clothes and let him go."

The plot to kill Jesus

45 Therefore many of the Jews who had come to visit Mary, and had seen what Jesus did, put their faith in him. 46 But some of them went to the Pharisees and told them what Jesus had done. 47 Then the chief priests and the Pharisees called a meeting of the Sanhedrin.

"What are we accomplishing?" they asked. "Here is this man performing many miraculous signs. 48 If we let him go on like this, everyone will put his trust in him, and then the Romans will come and take away both our place[a] and our nation."

[z] Or *Messiah.* [a] Or *temple.*

Greek Interlinear

ἐν τῇ ἐσχάτῃ ἡμέρᾳ. **25** εἶπεν αὐτῇ ὁ
in the last day. Said to her -

'Ιησοῦς· ἐγώ εἰμι ἡ ἀνάστασις καὶ ἡ
Jesus: I am the resurrection and the

ζωή· ὁ πιστεύων εἰς ἐμὲ κἂν ἀποθάνῃ
life; the [one] believing in me even if he should die

ζήσεται, **26** καὶ πᾶς ὁ ζῶν καὶ πιστεύων
will live, and everyone living and believing

εἰς ἐμὲ οὐ μὴ ἀποθάνῃ εἰς τὸν αἰῶνα·
in me by no means dies unto the age:

πιστεύεις τοῦτο; **27** λέγει αὐτῷ· ναί, κύριε·
believest thou this? She says to him: Yes, Lord;

ἐγὼ πεπίστευκα ὅτι σὺ εἶ ὁ χριστὸς ὁ
I have believed that thou art the Christ the

υἱὸς τοῦ θεοῦ ὁ εἰς τὸν κόσμον ἐρχόμενος.
Son - of God ¹the ²into ⁴the ³world ⁵[one] coming.

28 καὶ τοῦτο εἰποῦσα ἀπῆλθεν καὶ ἐφώνησεν
And this saying she went away and called

Μαριὰμ τὴν ἀδελφὴν αὐτῆς λάθρα εἰποῦσα·
Mary the sister of her secretly saying:

ὁ διδάσκαλος πάρεστιν καὶ φωνεῖ σε.
The Teacher is here and calls thee.

29 ἐκείνη δὲ ὡς ἤκουσεν, ἐγείρεται ταχὺ
And that [one] when she heard, rose quickly

καὶ ἤρχετο πρὸς αὐτόν· **30** οὔπω δὲ
and came to him; now not yet

ἐληλύθει ὁ 'Ιησοῦς εἰς τὴν κώμην, ἀλλ'
had come - Jesus into the village, but

ἦν ἔτι ἐν τῷ τόπῳ ὅπου ὑπήντησεν
was still in the place where met

αὐτῷ ἡ Μάρθα. **31** οἱ οὖν 'Ιουδαῖοι
him - Martha. Therefore the Jews

οἱ ὄντες μετ' αὐτῆς ἐν τῇ οἰκίᾳ καὶ
the [ones] being with her in the house and

παραμυθούμενοι αὐτήν, ἰδόντες τὴν Μαριὰμ
consoling her, seeing - Mary

ὅτι ταχέως ἀνέστη καὶ ἐξῆλθεν,
that quickly she rose up and went out,

ἠκολούθησαν αὐτῇ, δόξαντες ὅτι ὑπάγει
followed her, thinking[,] - She is going

εἰς τὸ μνημεῖον ἵνα κλαύσῃ ἐκεῖ. **32** ἡ
to the tomb that she may weep there. -

οὖν Μαριὰμ ὡς ἦλθεν ὅπου ἦν 'Ιησοῦς,
Therefore Mary when she came where was Jesus,

ἰδοῦσα αὐτὸν ἔπεσεν αὐτοῦ πρὸς τοὺς
seeing him fell of him at the

πόδας, λέγουσα αὐτῷ· κύριε, εἰ ἦς ὧδε,
feet, saying to him: Lord, if thou wast here,

οὐκ ἄν μου ἀπέθανεν ὁ ἀδελφός.
⁴would not ³of me ²have died ¹the ⁵brother.

33 'Ιησοῦς οὖν ὡς εἶδεν αὐτὴν κλαίουσαν
Jesus therefore when he saw her weeping

καὶ τοὺς συνελθόντας αὐτῇ 'Ιουδαίους
and ¹the ²coming with ⁴her ³Jews

κλαίοντας, ἐνεβριμήσατο τῷ πνεύματι καὶ
weeping, groaned in the(his) spirit and

ἐτάραξεν ἑαυτόν, **34** καὶ εἶπεν· ποῦ
troubled himself, and said: Where

τεθείκατε αὐτόν; λέγουσιν αὐτῷ· κύριε,
have ye put him? They say to him: Lord,

ἔρχου καὶ ἴδε. **35** ἐδάκρυσεν ὁ 'Ιησοῦς.
come and see. Shed tears - Jesus.

36 ἔλεγον οὖν οἱ 'Ιουδαῖοι· ἴδε πῶς
Said therefore the Jews: See how

ἐφίλει αὐτόν. **37** τινὲς δὲ ἐξ αὐτῶν
he loved him. But some of them

εἶπαν· οὐκ ἐδύνατο οὗτος ὁ ἀνοίξας
said: Could not this man the [one] opening

τοὺς ὀφθαλμοὺς τοῦ τυφλοῦ ποιῆσαι ἵνα
the eyes of the blind man to cause that

καὶ οὗτος μὴ ἀποθάνῃ; **38** 'Ιησοῦς οὖν
even this man should not die? Jesus therefore

πάλιν ἐμβριμώμενος ἐν ἑαυτῷ ἔρχεται
again groaning in himself comes

εἰς τὸ μνημεῖον· ἦν δὲ σπήλαιον, καὶ
to the tomb; now it was a cave, and

λίθος ἐπέκειτο ἐπ' αὐτῷ. **39** λέγει ὁ
a stone was lying on on it. Says -

'Ιησοῦς· ἄρατε τὸν λίθον. λέγει αὐτῷ
Jesus: Lift ye the stone. Says to him

ἡ ἀδελφὴ τοῦ τετελευτηκότος Μάρθα·
the sister of the [one] having died Martha:

κύριε, ἤδη ὄζει· τεταρταῖος γάρ ἐστιν.
Lord, now he smells; for fourth [day] it is.

40 λέγει αὐτῇ ὁ 'Ιησοῦς· οὐκ εἶπόν
Says to her - Jesus: Not I told

σοι ὅτι ἐὰν πιστεύσῃς ὄψῃ τὴν δόξαν
thee that if thou believest thou wilt see the glory

τοῦ θεοῦ; **41** ἦραν οὖν τὸν λίθον. ὁ
- of God? They lifted therefore the stone. -

δὲ 'Ιησοῦς ἦρεν τοὺς ὀφθαλμοὺς ἄνω
And Jesus lifted the(his) eyes up

καὶ εἶπεν· πάτερ, εὐχαριστῶ σοι ὅτι
and said: Father, I thank thee that

ἤκουσάς μου. **42** ἐγὼ δὲ ᾔδειν ὅτι
thou didst hear me. And I knew that

πάντοτέ μου ἀκούεις· ἀλλὰ διὰ τὸν
always me thou hearest; but because of the

ὄχλον τὸν περιεστῶτα εἶπον, ἵνα
crowd - standing round I said, that

πιστεύσωσιν ὅτι σύ με ἀπέστειλας.
they may believe that thou me didst send.

43 καὶ ταῦτα εἰπὼν φωνῇ μεγάλῃ
And these things saying voice with a great

ἐκραύγασεν· Λάζαρε, δεῦρο ἔξω. **44** ἐξῆλθεν
he cried out: Lazarus, come out. Came out

ὁ τεθνηκὼς δεδεμένος τοὺς πόδας καὶ
the [one] having died having been bound the feet and

τὰς χεῖρας κειρίαις, καὶ ἡ ὄψις αὐτοῦ
the hands with bandages, and the face of him

σουδαρίῳ περιεδέδετο. λέγει αὐτοῖς ὁ
with a napkin had been bound round. Says to them -

'Ιησοῦς· λύσατε αὐτὸν καὶ ἄφετε αὐτὸν ὑπάγειν.
Jesus: Loosen him and let him to go.

45 Πολλοὶ οὖν ἐκ τῶν 'Ιουδαίων, οἱ
Many therefore of the Jews, the [ones]

ἐλθόντες πρὸς τὴν Μαριὰμ καὶ θεασάμενοι
having come to - Mary and having beheld

ὃ ἐποίησεν, ἐπίστευσαν εἰς αὐτόν· **46** τινὲς δὲ
what he did, believed in him; but some

ἐξ αὐτῶν ἀπῆλθον πρὸς τοὺς Φαρισαίους
of them went away to the Pharisees

καὶ εἶπαν αὐτοῖς ἃ ἐποίησεν 'Ιησοῦς.
and told them what things did Jesus.

47 συνήγαγον οὖν οἱ ἀρχιερεῖς καὶ οἱ
Assembled therefore the chief priests and the

Φαρισαῖοι συνέδριον, καὶ ἔλεγον· τί
Pharisees a council, and said: What

ποιοῦμεν, ὅτι οὗτος ὁ ἄνθρωπος πολλὰ
are we doing, because this - man ¹many

ποιεῖ σημεῖα; **48** ἐὰν ἀφῶμεν αὐτὸν οὕτως,
²does ³signs? If we leave him thus,

πάντες πιστεύσουσιν εἰς αὐτόν, καὶ
all men will believe in him, and

ἐλεύσονται οἱ 'Ρωμαῖοι καὶ ἀροῦσιν ἡμῶν
will come the Romans and will take of us

King James Version

place and nation. 49And one of them, *named* Caiaphas, being the high priest that same year, said unto them, Ye know nothing at all, 50 Nor consider that it is expedient for us, that one man should die for the people, and that the whole nation perish not. 51And this spake he not of himself: but being high priest that year, he prophesied that Jesus should die for that nation; 52And not for that nation only, but that also he should gather together in one the children of God that were scattered abroad. 53 Then from that day forth they took counsel together for to put him to death. 54 Jesus therefore walked no more openly among the Jews; but went thence unto a country near to the wilderness, into a city called Ephraim, and there continued with his disciples.

55 And the Jews' passover was nigh at hand: and many went out of the country up to Jerusalem before the passover, to purify themselves. 56 Then sought they for Jesus, and spake among themselves, as they stood in the temple, What think ye, that he will not come to the feast? 57 Now both the chief priests and the Pharisees had given a commandment, that, if any man knew where he were, he should shew *it,* that they might take him.

12 Then Jesus six days before the passover came to Bethany, where Lazarus was which had been dead, whom he raised from the dead. 2 There they made him a supper; and Martha served: but Lazarus was one of them that sat at the table with him. 3 Then took Mary a pound of ointment of spikenard, very costly, and anointed the feet of Jesus, and wiped his feet with her hair: and the house was filled with the odour of the ointment. 4 Then saith one of his disciples, Judas Iscariot, Simon's *son,* which should betray him, 5 Why was not this ointment sold for three hundred pence, and given to the poor? 6 This he said, not that he cared for the poor; but because he was a thief, and had the bag, and bare what was put therein. 7 Then said Jesus, Let her alone: against the day of my burying hath she kept this. 8 For the poor always ye have with you; but me ye have not always. 9 Much people of the Jews therefore knew that he was there: and they came not for Jesus' sake only, but that they might see Lazarus also, whom he had raised from the dead.

10 But the chief priests consulted that they might put Lazarus also to death; 11 Because that by reason of him many of the Jews went away, and believed on Jesus.

12 On the next day much people that were come to the feast, when they heard that Jesus

New International Version

49 Then one of them, named Caiaphas, who was high priest that year, spoke up, "You know nothing at all! 50 You do not realize that it is better for you that one man die for the people than that the whole nation perish."

51 He did not say this on his own, but as high priest that year he prophesied that Jesus would die for the Jewish nation, 52 and not only for that nation but also for the scattered children of God, to bring them together and make them one. 53 So from that day on they plotted to take his life.

54 Therefore Jesus no longer moved about publicly among the Jews. Instead he withdrew to a region near the desert, to a village called Ephraim, where he stayed with his disciples.

55 When it was almost time for the Jewish Passover, many went up from the country to Jerusalem for their ceremonial cleansing before the Passover. 56 They kept looking for Jesus, and as they stood in the temple area they asked one another, "What do you think? Isn't he coming to the Feast at all?" 57 But the chief priests and Pharisees had given orders that if anyone found out where Jesus was, he should report it so that they might arrest him.

Jesus anointed at Bethany

12 Six days before the Passover, Jesus arrived at Bethany, where Lazarus lived, whom Jesus had raised from the dead. 2 Here a dinner was given in Jesus' honor. Martha served, while Lazarus was among those reclining at the table with him. 3 Then Mary took about a pint of pure nard, an expensive perfume; she poured it on Jesus' feet and wiped his feet with her hair. And the house was filled with the fragrance of the perfume.

4 But one of his disciples, Judas Iscariot, who was later to betray him, objected, 5 "Why wasn't this perfume sold and the money given to the poor? It was worth a year's wages.*b*" 6 He did not say this because he cared about the poor but because he was a thief; as keeper of the money bag, he used to help himself to what was put into it.

7 "Leave her alone," Jesus replied. "It was meant that she should save this perfume for the day of my burial. 8 You will always have the poor among you, but you will not always have me."

9 Meanwhile a large crowd of Jews found out that Jesus was there and came, not only because of him but also to see Lazarus, whom he had raised from the dead. 10 So the chief priests made plans to kill Lazarus as well, 11 for on account of him many of the Jews were going over to Jesus and putting their faith in him.

The triumphal entry

12 The next day the great crowd that had come for the Feast heard that Jesus was on his

[b] Greek *300 denarii*

Greek Interlinear

καὶ τὸν τόπον καὶ τὸ ἔθνος. 49 εἰς
both the place and the nation. *one

δέ τις ἐξ αὐτῶν Καϊάφας, ἀρχιερεὺς
¹But ²a certain of them[,] Caiaphas, high priest

ὢν τοῦ ἐνιαυτοῦ ἐκείνου, εἶπεν αὐτοῖς·
being – year of that, said to them :

ὑμεῖς οὐκ οἴδατε οὐδέν, 50 οὐδὲ λογίζεσθε
Ye know not no(any)thing, nor reckon

ὅτι συμφέρει ὑμῖν ἵνα εἷς ἄνθρωπος
that it is expedient for us that one man

ἀποθάνῃ ὑπὲρ τοῦ λαοῦ καὶ μὴ ὅλον
should die for the people and not all

τὸ ἔθνος ἀπόληται. 51 τοῦτο δὲ ἀφ'
the nation perish. But this from

ἑαυτοῦ οὐκ εἶπεν, ἀλλὰ ἀρχιερεὺς ὢν
himself he said not, but high priest being

τοῦ ἐνιαυτοῦ ἐκείνου ἐπροφήτευσεν ὅτι
– year of that he prophesied that

ἔμελλεν Ἰησοῦς ἀποθνήσκειν ὑπὲρ τοῦ
was about Jesus to die for the

ἔθνους, 52 καὶ οὐχ ὑπὲρ τοῦ ἔθνους
nation, and not for the nation

μόνον, ἀλλ' ἵνα καὶ τὰ τέκνα τοῦ θεοῦ
only, but that also the children – of God

τὰ διεσκορπισμένα συναγάγῃ εἰς ἕν.
– having been scattered he might gather into one.

53 ἀπ' ἐκείνης οὖν τῆς ἡμέρας ἐβουλεύσαντο
From ¹that ²therefore – ³day ³they took counsel

ἵνα ἀποκτείνωσιν αὐτόν. 54 Ὁ οὖν
that they might kill him. – Therefore

Ἰησοῦς οὐκέτι παρρησίᾳ περιεπάτει ἐν
Jesus no longer openly walked among

τοῖς Ἰουδαίοις, ἀλλὰ ἀπῆλθεν ἐκεῖθεν εἰς
the Jews, but went away thence into

τὴν χώραν ἐγγὺς τῆς ἐρήμου, εἰς Ἐφραὶμ
the country near the desert, to ¹Ephraim

λεγομένην πόλιν, κἀκεῖ ἔμεινεν μετὰ τῶν
²being called ¹a city, and there remained with the

μαθητῶν.
disciples.

55 Ἦν δὲ ἐγγὺς τὸ πάσχα τῶν
Now was near the Passover of the

Ἰουδαίων, καὶ ἀνέβησαν πολλοὶ εἰς
Jews, and went up many to

Ἱεροσόλυμα ἐκ τῆς χώρας πρὸ τοῦ
Jerusalem out of the country before the

πάσχα, ἵνα ἁγνίσωσιν ἑαυτούς.
Passover, that they might purify themselves.

56 ἐζήτουν οὖν τὸν Ἰησοῦν καὶ ἔλεγον
They sought therefore – Jesus and said

μετ' ἀλλήλων ἐν τῷ ἱερῷ ἑστηκότες·
with one another in the temple standing :

τί δοκεῖ ὑμῖν; ὅτι οὐ μὴ ἔλθῃ εἰς
What seems it to you? that by no means he comes to

τὴν ἑορτήν; 57 δεδώκεισαν δὲ οἱ ἀρχιερεῖς
the feast? Now had given the chief priests

καὶ οἱ Φαρισαῖοι ἐντολὰς ἵνα ἐάν τις
and the Pharisees commands that if anyone

γνῷ ποῦ ἐστιν μηνύσῃ, ὅπως πιάσωσιν
knew where he is (was) he should inform, so as they might

αὐτόν.
arrest

Chapter 12

αὐτόν. 12 Ὁ οὖν Ἰησοῦς πρὸ ἓξ ἡμερῶν
him. – Therefore Jesus ²before ³six ¹days

τοῦ πάσχα ἦλθεν εἰς Βηθανίαν, ὅπου
the Passover came to Bethany, where

ἦν Λάζαρος, ὃν ἤγειρεν ἐκ νεκρῶν
was Lazarus, whom ¹raised ²out of [the] ²dead

Ἰησοῦς. 2 ἐποίησαν οὖν αὐτῷ δεῖπνον ἐκεῖ,
¹Jesus. They made therefore for him a supper there,

καὶ ἡ Μάρθα διηκόνει, ὁ δὲ Λάζαρος εἷς
and – Martha served, – but Lazarus one

ἦν ἐκ τῶν ἀνακειμένων σὺν αὐτῷ· 3 ἡ
was of the [ones] reclining with him; –

οὖν Μαριὰμ λαβοῦσα λίτραν μύρου
therefore Mary taking a pound ²ointment

νάρδου πιστικῆς πολυτίμου ἤλειψεν τοὺς
⁴of spikenard ³of pure ⁵costly anointed the

πόδας τοῦ Ἰησοῦ καὶ ἐξέμαξεν ταῖς
feet – of Jesus and wiped off with the

θριξὶν αὐτῆς τοὺς πόδας αὐτοῦ· ἡ δὲ
hairs of her the feet of him; and the

οἰκία ἐπληρώθη ἐκ τῆς ὀσμῆς τοῦ
house was filled of(with) the odour of the

μύρου. 4 λέγει δὲ Ἰούδας ὁ Ἰσκαριώτης
ointment. And says Judas the Iscariot

εἷς τῶν μαθητῶν αὐτοῦ, ὁ μέλλων
one of the disciples of him, the [one] being about

αὐτὸν παραδιδόναι· 5 διὰ τί τοῦτο τὸ
him to betray : Why this –

μύρον οὐκ ἐπράθη τριακοσίων δηναρίων
ointment not was sold of(for) three hundred denarii

καὶ ἐδόθη πτωχοῖς; 6 εἶπεν δὲ τοῦτο
and given to [the] poor? But he said this

οὐχ ὅτι περὶ τῶν πτωχῶν ἔμελεν αὐτῷ,
not because about the poor it mattered to him,

ἀλλ' ὅτι κλέπτης ἦν καὶ τὸ γλωσσόκομον
but because a thief he was and ²the ²bag

ἔχων τὰ βαλλόμενα ἐβάσταζεν.
¹having ³the things ⁶being put [in] ⁷carried. *

7 εἶπεν οὖν ὁ Ἰησοῦς· ἄφες αὐτήν,
Said therefore – Jesus : Leave her,

ἵνα εἰς τὴν ἡμέραν τοῦ ἐνταφιασμοῦ
that to the day of the burial

μου τηρήσῃ αὐτό· 8 τοὺς πτωχοὺς γὰρ
of me she may keep it; ²the ²poor ¹for

πάντοτε ἔχετε μεθ' ἑαυτῶν, ἐμὲ δὲ
always ye have with yourselves, but me

οὐ πάντοτε ἔχετε. 9 Ἔγνω οὖν ὁ ὄχλος
not always ye have. Knew therefore the crowd

πολὺς ἐκ τῶν Ἰουδαίων ὅτι ἐκεῖ ἐστιν,
great of the Jews that there he is(was),

καὶ ἦλθον οὐ διὰ τὸν Ἰησοῦν μόνον,
and they came not because of – Jesus only,

ἀλλ' ἵνα καὶ τὸν Λάζαρον ἴδωσιν ὃν
but that also – Lazarus they might see whom

ἤγειρεν ἐκ νεκρῶν. 10 ἐβουλεύσαντο δὲ
he raised out of [the] dead. But took counsel

οἱ ἀρχιερεῖς ἵνα καὶ τὸν Λάζαρον
the chief priests that also – Lazarus

ἀποκτείνωσιν, 11 ὅτι πολλοὶ δι' αὐτὸν
they might kill, because ¹many ⁴because of ²him

ὑπῆγον τῶν Ἰουδαίων καὶ ἐπίστευον εἰς
³went ⁵of the ⁶Jews and believed in

τὸν Ἰησοῦν.
– Jesus.

12 Τῇ ἐπαύριον ὁ ὄχλος πολὺς ὁ
On the morrow the crowd much the

ἐλθὼν εἰς τὴν ἑορτήν, ἀκούσαντες ὅτι
coming to the feast, hearing that

* This may mean " stole "; cf. our euphemism for " steal "—to " lift " a thing.

309

King James Version

was coming to Jerusalem, 13 Took branches of palm trees, and went forth to meet him, and cried, Hosanna: blessed *is* the King of Israel that cometh in the name of the Lord. 14And Jesus, when he had found a young ass, sat thereon; as it is written, 15 Fear not, daughter of Sion: behold, thy King cometh, sitting on an ass's colt. 16 These things understood not his disciples at the first: but when Jesus was glorified, then remembered they that these things were written of him, and *that* they had done these things unto him. 17 The people therefore that was with him when he called Lazarus out of his grave, and raised him from the dead, bare record. 18 For this cause the people also met him, for that they heard that he had done this miracle. 19 The Pharisees therefore said among themselves, Perceive ye how ye prevail nothing? behold, the world is gone after him.

20 And there were certain Greeks among them that came up to worship at the feast: 21 The same came therefore to Philip, which was of Bethsaida of Galilee, and desired him, saying, Sir, we would see Jesus. 22 Philip cometh and telleth Andrew: and again Andrew and Philip tell Jesus.

23 And Jesus answered them, saying, The hour is come, that the Son of man should be glorified. 24 Verily, verily, I say unto you, Except a corn of wheat fall into the ground and die, it abideth alone: but if it die, it bringeth forth much fruit. 25 He that loveth his life shall lose it; and he that hateth his life in this world shall keep it unto life eternal. 26 If any man serve me, let him follow me; and where I am, there shall also my servant be: if any man serve me, him will *my* Father honour. 27 Now is my soul troubled; and what shall I say? Father, save me from this hour: but for this cause came I unto this hour. 28 Father, glorify thy name. Then came there a voice from heaven, *saying,* I have both glorified *it,* and will glorify *it* again. 29 The people therefore that stood by, and heard *it,* said that it thundered: others said, An angel spake to him. 30 Jesus answered and said, This voice came not because of me, but for your sakes. 31 Now is the judgment of this world: now shall the prince of this world be cast out. 32And I, if I be lifted up from the earth, will draw all *men* unto me. 33 This he said, signifying what death he should die. 34 The people answered him, We have heard out of the law that Christ abideth for ever: and how sayest thou, The Son of man must be lifted up? who is this Son of man? 35 Then Jesus said unto them, Yet a little while is the light with you. Walk while ye have the light, lest darkness come upon you: for he that walketh in darkness knoweth not

New International Version

way to Jerusalem. 13 They took palm branches and went out to meet him, shouting,
    "Hosanna! *c*
    Blessed is he who comes in the name of the Lord! *d*
    Blessed is the King of Israel!"
14 Jesus found a young donkey and sat upon it, as Scripture says,
    15 "Do not be afraid, O Zion;
    see, your king is coming,
    seated on a donkey's colt." *e*
16 At first his disciples did not understand all this. Only after Jesus was glorified did they realize that these things had been written about him and that they had done these things to him.

17 Now the crowd that was with him had continued to spread the word that he had called Lazarus from the tomb, raising him from the dead.*f* 18 Many people, because they had heard that he had given this miraculous sign, went out to meet him. 19 So the Pharisees said to one another, "See, this is getting us nowhere. Look how the whole world has gone after him!"

Jesus predicts his death

20 Now there were some Greeks among those who went up to worship at the Feast. 21 They came to Philip, who was from Bethsaida in Galilee, with a request. "Sir," they said, "we would like to see Jesus." 22 Philip went to tell Andrew; Andrew and Philip in turn told Jesus.

23 Jesus replied, "The hour has come for the Son of Man to be glorified. 24 I tell you the truth, unless a kernel of wheat falls to the ground and dies, it remains only a single seed. But if it dies, it produces many seeds. 25 The man who loves his life will lose it, while the man who hates his life in this world will keep it for eternal life. 26 Whoever serves me must follow me; and where I am, my servant also will be. My Father will honor the one who serves me.

27 "Now my heart is troubled, and what shall I say? 'Father, save me from this hour'? No, it was for this very reason I came to this hour. 28 Father, glorify your name!"

Then a voice came from heaven, "I have glorified it, and will glorify it again." 29 The crowd that was there and heard it said it had thundered; others said an angel had spoken to him.

30 Jesus said, "This voice was for your benefit, not mine. 31 Now is the time for judgment on this world; now the prince of this world will be driven out. 32 But I, when I am lifted up from the earth, will draw all men to myself." 33 He said this to show the kind of death he was going to die.

34 The crowd spoke up, "We have heard from the Law that the Christ*g* will remain forever, so how can you say, 'The Son of Man must be lifted up?' Who is this 'Son of Man'?"

35 Then Jesus told them, "You are going to have the light just a little while longer. Walk while you have the light, before darkness overtakes you. The man who walks in the dark does

[c] A Hebrew expression meaning "Save!" which became an exclamation of praise. [d] Psalm 118:25,26. [e] Zech. 9:9. [f] Or *Now the crowd that had been with him when he called Lazarus from the tomb and raised him from the dead were telling everyone.* [g] Or *Messiah.*

Greek Interlinear

ἔρχεται ᾽Ιησοῦς εἰς ᾽Ιεροσόλυμα, 13 ἔλαβον
is(was) coming Jesus to Jerusalem, took

τὰ βαΐα τῶν φοινίκων καὶ ἐξῆλθον εἰς
the branches of the palm-trees and went out to

ὑπάντησιν αὐτῷ, καὶ ἐκραύγαζον· ὡσαννά,
a meeting with him, and cried out : Hosanna,

εὐλογημένος ὁ ἐρχόμενος ἐν ὀνόματι
being blessed the [one] coming in [the] name

κυρίου, καὶ ὁ βασιλεὺς τοῦ ᾽Ισραήλ.
of [the] Lord, even the king – of Israel.

14 εὑρὼν δὲ ὁ ᾽Ιησοῦς ὀνάριον ἐκάθισεν
And ²having found – ¹Jesus a young ass sat

ἐπ᾽ αὐτό, καθώς ἐστιν γεγραμμένον·
on it, as it is having been written :

15 μὴ φοβοῦ, θυγάτηρ Σιών· ἰδοὺ ὁ
Fear not, daughter of Sion : behold[,] the

βασιλεύς σου ἔρχεται, καθήμενος ἐπὶ
king of thee comes, sitting on

πῶλον ὄνου. 16 ταῦτα οὐκ ἔγνωσαν
a foal of an ass. These things knew not

αὐτοῦ οἱ μαθηταὶ τὸ πρῶτον, ἀλλ᾽ ὅτε
of him the disciples at first, but when

ἐδοξάσθη ᾽Ιησοῦς, τότε ἐμνήσθησαν ὅτι
was glorified Jesus, then they remembered that

ταῦτα ἦν ἐπ᾽ αὐτῷ γεγραμμένα καὶ
these things were on him having been written and

ταῦτα ἐποίησαν αὐτῷ. 17 ἐμαρτύρει οὖν
these things they did to him. Witnessed therefore

ὁ ὄχλος ὁ ὢν μετ᾽ αὐτοῦ ὅτε τὸν
the crowd – being with him when –

Λάζαρον ἐφώνησεν ἐκ τοῦ μνημείου καὶ
Lazarus he called out of the tomb and

ἤγειρεν αὐτὸν ἐκ νεκρῶν. 18 διὰ τοῦτο
raised him out of [the] dead. Therefore

καὶ ὑπήντησεν αὐτῷ ὁ ὄχλος, ὅτι
also met him the crowd, because

ἤκουσαν τοῦτο αὐτὸν πεποιηκέναι τὸ
¹they heard ⁴this ²him ³to have done⁵ –

σημεῖον. 19 οἱ οὖν Φαρισαῖοι εἶπαν
sign. Therefore the Pharisees said

πρὸς ἑαυτούς· θεωρεῖτε ὅτι οὐκ ὠφελεῖτε
to themselves : Behold ye that ye profit not

οὐδέν· ἴδε ὁ κόσμος ὀπίσω αὐτοῦ ἀπῆλθεν.
no(any)thing; see[,] the world after him went(is gone).

20 ῏Ησαν δὲ ῞Ελληνές τινες ἐκ τῶν
Now there were ²Greeks ¹some of the

ἀναβαινόντων ἵνα προσκυνήσωσιν ἐν τῇ
[ones] going up that they might worship at the

ἑορτῇ· 21 οὗτοι οὖν προσῆλθον Φιλίππῳ
feast; these therefore approached to Philip

τῷ ἀπὸ Βηθσαϊδὰ τῆς Γαλιλαίας. καὶ
the [one] from Bethsaida – of Galilee, and

ἠρώτων αὐτὸν λέγοντες· κύριε, θέλομεν
asked him saying : Sir, we wish

τὸν ᾽Ιησοῦν ἰδεῖν. 22 ἔρχεται ὁ Φίλιππος
– Jesus to see. Comes – Philip

καὶ λέγει τῷ ᾽Ανδρέᾳ· ἔρχεται ᾽Ανδρέας
and tells – Andrew; comes Andrew

καὶ Φίλιππος καὶ λέγουσιν τῷ ᾽Ιησοῦ.
and Philip and tell – Jesus.

23 ὁ δὲ ᾽Ιησοῦς ἀποκρίνεται αὐτοῖς λέγων·
– And Jesus answers them saying :

ἐλήλυθεν ἡ ὥρα ἵνα δοξασθῇ ὁ υἱὸς τοῦ
Has come the hour that is glorified the Son –

ἀνθρώπου. 24 ἀμὴν ἀμὴν λέγω ὑμῖν,
of man. Truly truly I say to you,

ἐὰν μὴ ὁ κόκκος τοῦ σίτου πεσὼν εἰς
unless the grain – of wheat falling into

τὴν γῆν ἀποθάνῃ, αὐτὸς μόνος μένει·
the ground dies, it alone remains;

ἐὰν δὲ ἀποθάνῃ, πολὺν καρπὸν φέρει.
but if it dies, much fruit it bears.

25 ὁ φιλῶν τὴν ψυχὴν αὐτοῦ ἀπολλύει
The [one] loving the life of him loses

αὐτήν, καὶ ὁ μισῶν τὴν ψυχὴν αὐτοῦ
it, and the [one] hating the life of him

ἐν τῷ κόσμῳ τούτῳ εἰς ζωὴν αἰώνιον
in – world this unto life eternal

φυλάξει αὐτήν. 26 ἐὰν ἐμοί τις διακονῇ,
will keep it. If me anyone serves,

ἐμοὶ ἀκολουθείτω, καὶ ὅπου εἰμὶ ἐγώ,
me let him follow, and where am I,

ἐκεῖ καὶ ὁ διάκονος ὁ ἐμὸς ἔσται·
there also the ²servant – ¹my will be;

ἐάν τις ἐμοὶ διακονῇ, τιμήσει αὐτὸν
if anyone me serves, will honour him

ὁ πατήρ. 27 νῦν ἡ ψυχή μου τετάρακται,
the Father. Now the soul of me has been troubled,

καὶ τί εἴπω; πάτερ, σῶσόν με ἐκ
and what may I say? Father, save me out of

τῆς ὥρας ταύτης. ἀλλὰ διὰ τοῦτο ἦλθον
– hour this. But therefore I came

εἰς τὴν ὥραν ταύτην. 28 πάτερ, δόξασόν
to – hour this. Father, glorify

σου τὸ ὄνομα. ἦλθεν οὖν φωνὴ ἐκ
of thee the name. Came therefore a voice out of

τοῦ οὐρανοῦ· καὶ ἐδόξασα καὶ πάλιν
– heaven : Both I glorified and again

δοξάσω. 29 ὁ οὖν ὄχλος ὁ ἑστὼς καὶ
I will glorify. Therefore the crowd – standing and

ἀκούσας ἔλεγεν βροντὴν γεγονέναι· ἄλλοι
hearing said thunder to have happened; others

ἔλεγον· ἄγγελος αὐτῷ λελάληκεν.
said : An angel to him has spoken.

30 ἀπεκρίθη ᾽Ιησοῦς καὶ εἶπεν· οὐ δι᾽ ἐμὲ
Answered Jesus and said : Not because of me

ἡ φωνὴ αὕτη γέγονεν ἀλλὰ δι᾽ ὑμᾶς.
– voice this has happened but because of you.

31 νῦν κρίσις ἐστὶν τοῦ κόσμου τούτου·
Now judgment is – world of this ;

νῦν ὁ ἄρχων τοῦ κόσμου τούτου
now the ruler – world of this

ἐκβληθήσεται ἔξω· 32 κἀγὼ ἐὰν ὑψωθῶ
shall be cast out outside; and I if I am lifted up

ἐκ τῆς γῆς, πάντας ἑλκύσω πρὸς
out of the earth, all men will draw to

ἐμαυτόν. 33 τοῦτο δὲ ἔλεγεν σημαίνων
myself. And this he said signifying

ποίῳ θανάτῳ ἤμελλεν ἀποθνήσκειν.
by what kind of death he was about to die.

34 ἀπεκρίθη οὖν αὐτῷ ὁ ὄχλος· ἡμεῖς
Answered therefore him the crowd : We

ἠκούσαμεν ἐκ τοῦ νόμου ὅτι ὁ χριστὸς
heard out of the law that the Christ

μένει εἰς τὸν αἰῶνα, καὶ πῶς λέγεις
remains unto the age, and how sayest

σὺ ὅτι δεῖ ὑψωθῆναι τὸν υἱὸν τοῦ
thou that it behoves to be lifted up the Son –

ἀνθρώπου; τίς ἐστιν οὗτος ὁ υἱὸς τοῦ
of man? who is this – Son –

ἀνθρώπου; 35 εἶπεν οὖν αὐτοῖς ὁ ᾽Ιησοῦς·
of man? Said therefore to them – Jesus :

ἔτι μικρὸν χρόνον τὸ φῶς ἐν ὑμῖν
Yet a little time the light among you

ἐστιν. περιπατεῖτε ὡς τὸ φῶς ἔχετε,
is. Walk while the light ye have,

ἵνα μὴ σκοτία ὑμᾶς καταλάβῃ· καὶ
lest darkness you overtakes; and

ὁ περιπατῶν ἐν τῇ σκοτίᾳ οὐκ οἶδεν
the [one] walking in the darkness knows not

311

King James Version

whither he goeth. 36 While ye have light, believe in the light, that ye may be the children of light. These things spake Jesus, and departed, and did hide himself from them.

37 But though he had done so many miracles before them, yet they believed not on him: 38 That the saying of Esaias the prophet might be fulfilled, which he spake, Lord, who hath believed our report? and to whom hath the arm of the Lord been revealed? 39 Therefore they could not believe, because that Esaias said again, 40 He hath blinded their eyes, and hardened their heart; that they should not see with *their* eyes, nor understand with *their* heart, and be converted, and I should heal them. 41 These things said Esaias, when he saw his glory, and spake of him.

42 Nevertheless among the chief rulers also many believed on him; but because of the Pharisees they did not confess *him,* lest they should be put out of the synagogue: 43 For they loved the praise of men more than the praise of God. 44 Jesus cried and said, He that believeth on me, believeth not on me, but on him that sent me. 45 And he that seeth me seeth him that sent me. 46 I am come a light into the world, that whosoever believeth on me should not abide in darkness. 47 And if any man hear my words, and believe not, I judge him not: for I came not to judge the world, but to save the world. 48 He that rejecteth me, and receiveth not my words, hath one that judgeth him: the word that I have spoken, the same shall judge him in the last day. 49 For I have not spoken of myself; but the Father which sent me, he gave me a commandment, what I should say, and what I should speak. 50 And I know that his commandment is life everlasting: whatsoever I speak therefore, even as the Father said unto me, so I speak.

13 Now before the feast of the passover, when Jesus knew that his hour was come that he should depart out of this world unto the Father, having loved his own which were in the world, he loved them unto the end. 2 And supper being ended, the devil having now put into the heart of Judas Iscariot, Simon's *son,* to betray him; 3 Jesus knowing that the Father had given all things into his hands, and that he was come from God, and went to God; 4 He riseth from supper, and laid aside his garments; and took a towel, and girded himself. 5 After that he poureth water into a basin, and began to wash the disciples' feet, and to wipe *them* with the towel

New International Version

not know where he is going. 36 Put your trust in the light while you have it, so that you may become sons of light." When he had finished speaking, Jesus left and hid himself from them.

The Jews continue in their unbelief

37 Even after Jesus had done all these miraculous signs in their presence, they still would not believe in him. 38 This was to fulfill the word of Isaiah the prophet:

"Lord, who has believed our message,
  and to whom has the arm of the Lord been
    revealed?" [h]

39 For this reason they could not believe, because, as Isaiah says elsewhere:

40 "He has blinded their eyes
  and deadened their hearts,
so they can neither see with their eyes,
  nor understand with their hearts,
    nor turn—and I would heal them." [i]

41 Isaiah said this because he saw Jesus' glory, and spoke about him.

42 Yet at the same time many even among the leaders believed in him. But because of the Pharisees they would not confess their faith for fear they would be put out of the synagogue; 43 for they loved praise from men more than praise from God.

44 Then Jesus cried out, "When a man believes in me, he does not believe in me only, but in the one who sent me. 45 When he looks at me, he sees the one who sent me. 46 I have come into the world as a light, so that no one who believes in me should stay in darkness.

47 "As for the person who hears my words but does not keep them, I do not judge him. For I did not come to judge the world, but to save it. 48 There is a judge for the one who rejects me and does not accept my words; that very word which I spoke will condemn him at the last day. 49 For I did not speak of my own accord, but the Father who sent me commanded me what to say and how to say it. 50 I know that his command leads to eternal life. So whatever I say is just what the Father has told me to say."

Jesus washes his disciples' feet

13 It was just before the Passover Feast. Jesus knew that the time had come for him to leave this world and go to the Father. Having loved his own who were in the world, he now showed them the full extent of his love.

2 The evening meal was being served, and the devil had already prompted Judas Iscariot, son of Simon, to betray Jesus. 3 Jesus knew that the Father had put all things under his power, and that he had come from God and was returning to God, 4 so he got up from the meal, took off his outer clothing, and wrapped a towel around his waist. 5 After that, he poured water into a basin and began to wash his disciples' feet, drying them with the towel that was wrapped around him.

[h] Isaiah 53:1. [i] Isaiah 6:10.

312

Greek Interlinear

ποῦ ὑπάγει. **36** ὡς τὸ φῶς ἔχετε,
where he is going. While the light ye have,

πιστεύετε εἰς τὸ φῶς, ἵνα υἱοὶ φωτὸς
believe in the light, that sons of light

γένησθε.
ye may become.

Ταῦτα ἐλάλησεν Ἰησοῦς, καὶ ἀπελθὼν
These things spoke Jesus, and going away

ἐκρύβη ἀπ' αὐτῶν. **37** Τοσαῦτα δὲ αὐτοῦ
was hidden from them. But so many him

σημεῖα πεποιηκότος ἔμπροσθεν αὐτῶν οὐκ
signs having done* before them not
= But while he did so many signs

ἐπίστευον εἰς αὐτόν, **38** ἵνα ὁ λόγος
they believed in him, that the word

Ἡσαΐου τοῦ προφήτου πληρωθῇ ὃν
of Esaias the prophet might be fulfilled which

εἶπεν· κύριε, τίς ἐπίστευσεν τῇ ἀκοῇ
he said: Lord, who believed the report

ἡμῶν; καὶ ὁ βραχίων κυρίου τίνι
of us? and the arm of [the] Lord to whom

ἀπεκαλύφθη; **39** διὰ τοῦτο οὐκ ἠδύναντο
was it revealed? Therefore they could not

πιστεύειν, ὅτι πάλιν εἶπεν Ἡσαΐας·
to believe, because again said Esaias:

40 τετύφλωκεν αὐτῶν τοὺς ὀφθαλμοὺς καὶ
He has blinded of them the eyes and

ἐπώρωσεν αὐτῶν τὴν καρδίαν, ἵνα
hardened of them the heart, that

μὴ ἴδωσιν τοῖς ὀφθαλμοῖς καὶ νοήσωσιν
they might not see with the eyes and understand

τῇ καρδίᾳ καὶ στραφῶσιν, καὶ ἰάσομαι
with the heart and might turn, and I will cure

αὐτούς. **41** ταῦτα εἶπεν Ἡσαΐας ὅτι
them. These things said Esaias because

εἶδεν τὴν δόξαν αὐτοῦ, καὶ ἐλάλησεν
he saw the glory of him, and spoke

περὶ αὐτοῦ. **42** ὅμως μέντοι καὶ ἐκ
about him. Nevertheless however even of

τῶν ἀρχόντων πολλοὶ ἐπίστευσαν εἰς αὐτόν,
the rulers many believed in him,

ἀλλὰ διὰ τοὺς Φαρισαίους οὐχ ὡμολόγουν,
but because of the Pharisees did not confess,

ἵνα μὴ ἀποσυνάγωγοι γένωνται·
lest put out of [the] synagogue they should become;

43 ἠγάπησαν γὰρ τὴν δόξαν τῶν ἀνθρώπων
for they loved the glory - of men

μᾶλλον ἤπερ τὴν δόξαν τοῦ θεοῦ.
more than the ' glory - of God.

44 Ἰησοῦς δὲ ἔκραξεν καὶ εἶπεν· ὁ
But Jesus cried out and said : The

πιστεύων εἰς ἐμὲ οὐ πιστεύει εἰς ἐμὲ
[one] believing in me believes not in me

ἀλλὰ εἰς τὸν πέμψαντά με, **45** καὶ ὁ
but in the [one] having sent me, and the

θεωρῶν ἐμὲ θεωρεῖ τὸν πέμψαντά με.
[one] beholding me beholds the [one] having sent me.

46 ἐγὼ φῶς εἰς τὸν κόσμον ἐλήλυθα,
I a light into the world have come,

ἵνα πᾶς ὁ πιστεύων εἰς ἐμὲ ἐν τῇ
that everyone believing in me in the

σκοτίᾳ μὴ μείνῃ. **47** καὶ ἐάν τίς μου
darkness may not remain. And if anyone of me

ἀκούσῃ τῶν ῥημάτων καὶ μὴ φυλάξῃ,
hears the words and keeps not,

ἐγὼ οὐ κρίνω αὐτόν· οὐ γὰρ ἦλθον
I do not judge him; for I came not

ἵνα κρίνω τὸν κόσμον, ἀλλ' ἵνα σώσω
that I might judge the world, but that I might save

τὸν κόσμον. **48** ὁ ἀθετῶν ἐμὲ καὶ μὴ
the world. The [one] rejecting me and not

λαμβάνων τὰ ῥήματά μου ἔχει τὸν
receiving the words of me has the

κρίνοντα αὐτόν· ὁ λόγος ὃν ἐλάλησα,
[one] judging him; the word which I spoke,

ἐκεῖνος κρινεῖ αὐτὸν ἐν τῇ ἐσχάτῃ ἡμέρᾳ.
that will judge him in the last day.

49 ὅτι ἐγὼ ἐξ ἐμαυτοῦ οὐκ ἐλάλησα,
Because I of myself did not speak,

ἀλλ' ὁ πέμψας με πατὴρ αὐτός μοι
but 'the 'having sent 'me 'Father 'he 'me

ἐντολὴν δέδωκεν τί εἴπω καὶ τί
'commandment 'has given what I may say and what

λαλήσω. **50** καὶ οἶδα ὅτι ἡ ἐντολὴ
I may speak. And I know that the commandment

αὐτοῦ ζωὴ αἰώνιός ἐστιν. ἃ οὖν ἐγὼ
of him life eternal is. What things therefore I

λαλῶ, καθὼς εἴρηκέν μοι ὁ πατήρ,
speak, as has said to me the Father,

οὕτως λαλῶ.
so I speak.

Chapter 13

Πρὸ δὲ τῆς ἑορτῆς τοῦ πάσχα
Now before the feast of the Passover

εἰδὼς ὁ Ἰησοῦς ὅτι ἦλθεν αὐτοῦ ἡ
'knowing - 'Jesus that came of him the

ὥρα ἵνα μεταβῇ ἐκ τοῦ κόσμου τούτου
hour that he should remove out of - world this

πρὸς τὸν πατέρα, ἀγαπήσας τοὺς ἰδίους
to the Father, loving the(his) own

τοὺς ἐν τῷ κόσμῳ, εἰς τέλος ἠγάπησεν
- in the world, to [the] end he loved

αὐτούς. **2** καὶ δείπνου γινομένου, τοῦ
them. And supper taking place,* the
= during supper,

διαβόλου ἤδη βεβληκότος εἰς τὴν καρδίαν
devil now having put* into the heart
= as the devil had now put

ἵνα παραδοῖ αὐτὸν Ἰούδας Σίμωνος
that 'should betray 'him 'Judas '[son] of Simon

Ἰσκαριώτης, **3** εἰδὼς ὅτι πάντα ἔδωκεν
'Iscariot, knowing* that all things gave

αὐτῷ ὁ πατὴρ εἰς τὰς χεῖρας, καὶ
him the Father into the(his) hands, and

ὅτι ἀπὸ θεοῦ ἐξῆλθεν καὶ πρὸς τὸν
that from God he came forth and to -

θεὸν ὑπάγει, **4** ἐγείρεται ἐκ τοῦ δείπνου
God goes, he rises out of(from) the supper

καὶ τίθησιν τὰ ἱμάτια, καὶ λαβὼν
and places [aside] the(his) garments, and taking

λέντιον διέζωσεν ἑαυτόν· **5** εἶτα βάλλει
a towel he girded himself; then he puts

ὕδωρ εἰς τὸν νιπτῆρα, καὶ ἤρξατο νίπτειν
water into the basin, and began to wash

τοὺς πόδας τῶν μαθητῶν καὶ ἐκμάσσειν
the feet of the disciples and to wipe off

τῷ λεντίῳ ᾧ ἦν διεζωσμένος.
with the towel with which he was *having been* girded.

* Repeated from ver. 1; the subject is therefore again "Jesus".

313

King James Version

wherewith he was girded. 6 Then cometh he to Simon Peter: and Peter saith unto him, Lord, dost thou wash my feet? 7 Jesus answered and said unto him, What I do thou knowest not now; but thou shalt know hereafter. 8 Peter saith unto him, Thou shalt never wash my feet. Jesus answered him, If I wash thee not, thou hast no part with me. 9 Simon Peter saith unto him, Lord, not my feet only, but also *my* hands and *my* head. 10 Jesus saith to him, He that is washed needeth not save to wash *his* feet, but is clean every whit: and ye are clean, but not all. 11 For he knew who should betray him; therefore said he, Ye are not all clean. 12 So after he had washed their feet, and had taken his garments, and was set down again, he said unto them, Know ye what I have done to you? 13 Ye call me Master and Lord: and ye say well; for *so* I am. 14 If I then, *your* Lord and Master, have washed your feet; ye also ought to wash one another's feet. 15 For I have given you an example, that ye should do as I have done to you. 16 Verily, verily, I say unto you, The servant is not greater than his lord; neither he that is sent greater than he that sent him. 17 If ye know these things, happy are ye if ye do them.

18 I speak not of you all: I know whom I have chosen: but that the Scripture may be fulfilled, He that eateth bread with me hath lifted up his heel against me. 19 Now I tell you before it come, that, when it is come to pass, ye may believe that I am *he.* 20 Verily, verily, I say unto you, He that receiveth whomsoever I send receiveth me; and he that receiveth me receiveth him that sent me. 21 When Jesus had thus said, he was troubled in spirit, and testified, and said, Verily, verily, I say unto you, that one of you shall betray me. 22 Then the disciples looked one on another, doubting of whom he spake. 23 Now there was leaning on Jesus' bosom one of his disciples, whom Jesus loved. 24 Simon Peter therefore beckoned to him, that he should ask who it should be of whom he spake. 25 He then lying on Jesus' breast saith unto him, Lord, who is it? 26 Jesus answered, He it is, to whom I shall give a sop, when I have dipped *it.* And when he had dipped the sop, he gave *it* to Judas Iscariot, *the son* of Simon. 27 And after the sop Satan entered into him. Then said Jesus unto him, That thou doest, do quickly. 28 Now no man at the table knew for what intent he spake this unto him. 29 For some *of them* thought, because Judas had the bag, that Jesus had said unto him, Buy *those things* that we have need of against the feast; or, that he should give something to the poor. 30 He then, having received the sop, went immediately out: and it was night.

New International Version

6 He came to Simon Peter, who said to him, "Lord, are you going to wash my feet?"

7 Jesus replied, "You do not realize now what I am doing, but later you will understand."

8 "No," said Peter, "you shall never wash my feet."

Jesus answered, "Unless I wash you, you have no part with me."

9 "Then, Lord," Simon Peter replied, "not just my feet but my hands and my head as well!"

10 Jesus answered, "A person who has had a bath needs only to wash his feet; his whole body is clean. And you are clean, though not every one of you." 11 For he knew who was going to betray him, and that was why he said not every one was clean.

12 When he had finished washing their feet, he put on his clothes and returned to his place. "Do you understand what I have done for you?" he asked them. 13 "You call me 'Teacher' and 'Lord,' and rightly so, for that is what I am. 14 Now that I, your Lord and Teacher, have washed your feet, you also should wash one another's feet. 15 I have set you an example that you should do as I have done for you. 16 I tell you the truth, no servant is greater than his master, nor is a messenger greater than the one who sent him. 17 Once you know these things, you will be blessed if you do them.

Jesus predicts his betrayal

18 "I am not referring to all of you; I know those I have chosen. But this is to fulfill the scripture: 'He who shares my bread has lifted up his heel against me.' [j]

19 "I am telling you now before it happens, so that when it does happen you will believe that I am He. 20 I tell you the truth, whoever accepts anyone I send accepts me; and whoever accepts me accepts the one who sent me."

21 After he had said this, Jesus was deeply troubled and testified, "I tell you the truth, one of you is going to betray me."

22 His disciples stared at one another, at a loss to know which of them he meant. 23 One of them, the disciple whom Jesus loved, was reclining next to him. 24 Simon Peter motioned to this disciple and said, "Ask him which one he means."

25 Leaning back against Jesus, he asked him, "Lord, who is it?"

26 Jesus answered, "It is the one to whom I will give this piece of bread when I have dipped it in the dish." Then, dipping the piece of bread, he gave it to Judas Iscariot, son of Simon. 27 As soon as Judas took the bread, Satan entered into him.

"What you are about to do, do quickly," Jesus told him, 28 but no one at the meal understood why Jesus said this to him. 29 Since Judas had charge of the money, some thought Jesus was telling him to buy what was needed for the Feast, or to give something to the poor. 30 As soon as Judas had taken the bread, he went out. And it was night.

[j] Psalm 41:9.

Greek Interlinear

6 ἔρχεται οὖν πρὸς Σίμωνα Πέτρον·
He comes therefore to Simon Peter;
λέγει αὐτῷ· κύριε, σύ μου νίπτεις τοὺς
he says to him : Lord, thou of me washest the
πόδας; 7 ἀπεκρίθη Ἰησοῦς καὶ εἶπεν αὐτῷ·
feet? Answered Jesus and said to him :
ὃ ἐγὼ ποιῶ σὺ οὐκ οἶδας ἄρτι,
What I am doing thou knowest not yet,
γνώσῃ δὲ μετὰ ταῦτα. 8 λέγει αὐτῷ
but thou wilt know after these things. Says to him
Πέτρος· οὐ μὴ νίψῃς μου τοὺς πόδας
Peter : By no means shalt thou wash of me the feet
εἰς τὸν αἰῶνα. ἀπεκρίθη Ἰησοῦς αὐτῷ·
unto the age. ²Answered ¹Jesus ʰim :
ἐὰν μὴ νίψω σε, οὐκ ἔχεις μέρος μετ᾽
Unless I wash thee, thou hast no part with
ἐμοῦ. 9 λέγει αὐτῷ Σίμων Πέτρος :
me. Says to him Simon Peter :
κύριε, μὴ τοὺς πόδας μου μόνον ἀλλὰ
Lord, not the feet of me only but
καὶ τὰς χεῖρας καὶ τὴν κεφαλήν. 10 λέγει
also the hands and the head. Says
αὐτῷ Ἰησοῦς· ὁ λελουμένος οὐκ ἔχει
to him Jesus : The [one] having been bathed has not
χρείαν [εἰ μὴ τοὺς πόδας] νίψασθαι,
need except the feet to wash,
ἀλλ᾽ ἔστιν καθαρὸς ὅλος· καὶ ὑμεῖς
but is clean wholly; and ye
καθαροί ἐστε, ἀλλ᾽ οὐχὶ πάντες. 11 ᾔδει
clean are, but not all. he knew
γὰρ τὸν παραδιδόντα αὐτόν· διὰ τοῦτο
For the [one] betraying him; therefore
εἶπεν ὅτι οὐχὶ πάντες καθαροί ἐστε.
he said[,] – Not all clean ye are.
12 Ὅτε οὖν ἔνιψεν τοὺς πόδας αὐτῶν
When therefore he washed the feet of them
καὶ ἔλαβεν τὰ ἱμάτια αὐτοῦ καὶ ἀνέπεσεν
and took the garments of him and reclined
πάλιν, εἶπεν αὐτοῖς· γινώσκετε τί πε-
again, he said to them : Do ye know what I
ποίηκα ὑμῖν, 13 ὑμεῖς φωνεῖτέ με· ὁ
have done to you? Ye call me : The
διδάσκαλος καὶ ὁ κύριος, καὶ καλῶς
Teacher and the Lord, and well
λέγετε· εἰμὶ γάρ. 14 εἰ οὖν ἐγὼ ἔνιψα
ye say; for I am. If therefore I washed
ὑμῶν τοὺς πόδας ὁ κύριος καὶ ὁ
of you the feet the Lord and the
διδάσκαλος, καὶ ὑμεῖς ὀφείλετε ἀλλήλων
Teacher, also ye ought of one another
νίπτειν τοὺς πόδας· 15 ὑπόδειγμα γὰρ
to wash the feet; for an example
ἔδωκα ὑμῖν ἵνα καθὼς ἐγὼ ἐποίησα
I gave you that as I did
ὑμῖν καὶ ὑμεῖς ποιῆτε. 16 ἀμὴν ἀμὴν
to you also ye may do. Truly truly
λέγω ὑμῖν, οὐκ ἔστιν δοῦλος μείζων
I tell you, is not a slave greater [than]
τοῦ κυρίου αὐτοῦ, οὐδὲ ἀπόστολος μείζων
the lord of him, nor a sent one greater [than]
τοῦ πέμψαντος αὐτόν. 17 εἰ ταῦτα
the [one] sending him. If these things
οἴδατε, μακάριοί ἐστε ἐὰν ποιῆτε αὐτά.
ye know, blessed are ye if ye do them.
18 Οὐ περὶ πάντων ὑμῶν λέγω· ἐγὼ
Not concerning ²all ¹you I speak; I
οἶδα τίνας ἐξελεξάμην· ἀλλ᾽ ἵνα ἡ
know whom I chose; but that the
γραφὴ πληρωθῇ· ὁ τρώγων μου τὸν
scripture may be fulfilled : The [one] eating of me the

ἄρτον ἐπῆρεν ἐπ᾽ ἐμὲ τὴν πτέρναν αὐτοῦ.
bread lifted up against me the heel of him.
19 ἀπ᾽ ἄρτι λέγω ὑμῖν πρὸ τοῦ γενέσθαι,
From now I tell you before the to happen,
= it happens,
ἵνα πιστεύητε ὅταν γένηται ὅτι ἐγώ
that ye may believe when it happens that I
εἰμι. 20 ἀμὴν ἀμὴν λέγω ὑμῖν, ὁ
am. Truly truly I say to you, the
λαμβάνων ἄν τινα πέμψω ἐμὲ λαμβάνει,
[one] receiving whomever I may send me receives,
ὁ δὲ ἐμὲ λαμβάνων λαμβάνει τὸν
and the [one] me receiving receives the [one]
πέμψαντά με. 21 ταῦτα εἰπὼν Ἰησοῦς
having sent me. These things saying Jesus
ἐταράχθη τῷ πνεύματι καὶ ἐμαρτύρησεν
was troubled in the(his) spirit and witnessed
καὶ εἶπεν· ἀμὴν ἀμὴν λέγω ὑμῖν ὅτι
and said : Truly truly I tell you that
εἷς ἐξ ὑμῶν παραδώσει με. 22 ἔβλεπον
one of you will betray me. Looked
εἰς ἀλλήλους οἱ μαθηταὶ ἀπορούμενοι περὶ
at one another the disciples being perplexed about
τίνος λέγει. 23 ἦν ἀνακείμενος εἷς ἐκ
whom he speaks. Was reclining one of
τῶν μαθητῶν αὐτοῦ ἐν τῷ κόλπῳ τοῦ
the disciples of him in the bosom –
Ἰησοῦ, ὃν ἠγάπα ὁ Ἰησοῦς· 24 νεύει
of Jesus, whom ²loved – ¹Jesus; nods
οὖν τούτῳ Σίμων Πέτρος καὶ λέγει
therefore to this one Simon Peter and says
αὐτῷ· εἰπὲ τίς ἐστιν περὶ οὗ λέγει.
to him : Say who it is about whom he speaks.
25 ἀναπεσὼν ἐκεῖνος οὕτως ἐπὶ τὸ
Falling back that one thus on the
στῆθος τοῦ Ἰησοῦ λέγει αὐτῷ· κύριε,
breast – of Jesus he says to him : Lord,
τίς ἐστιν; 26 ἀποκρίνεται οὖν ὁ Ἰησοῦς·
who is it? Answers therefore – Jesus :
ἐκεῖνός ἐστιν ᾧ ἐγὼ βάψω τὸ ψωμίον
That one it is to whom I shall dip the morsel
καὶ δώσω αὐτῷ. βάψας οὖν [τὸ]
and shall give him. Dipping therefore the
ψωμίον λαμβάνει καὶ δίδωσιν Ἰούδᾳ
morsel he takes and gives to Judas
Σίμωνος Ἰσκαριώτου. 27 καὶ μετὰ τὸ
[son] of Simon Iscariot. And after the
ψωμίον τότε εἰσῆλθεν εἰς ἐκεῖνον ὁ
morsel then entered into that one –
σατανᾶς. λέγει οὖν αὐτῷ Ἰησοῦς· ὃ
Satan. Says therefore to him Jesus : What
ποιεῖς ποίησον τάχιον. 28 τοῦτο [δὲ]
thou doest do quickly. But this
οὐδεὶς ἔγνω τῶν ἀνακειμένων πρὸς τί
no one knew of the [ones] reclining for what
εἶπεν αὐτῷ· 29 τινὲς γὰρ ἐδόκουν, ἐπεὶ
he told him; for some thought, since
τὸ γλωσσόκομον εἶχεν Ἰούδας, ὅτι λέγει
²the ⁴bag ³had ¹Judas, that tells
αὐτῷ Ἰησοῦς· ἀγόρασον ὧν χρείαν
him Jesus : Buy [the] things of which need
ἔχομεν εἰς τὴν ἑορτήν, ἢ τοῖς πτωχοῖς
we have for the feast, or to the poor
ἵνα τι δῷ. 30 λαβὼν οὖν τὸ
that something he should give. Having taken therefore the
ψωμίον ἐκεῖνος ἐξῆλθεν εὐθύς· ἦν δὲ
morsel that one went out immediately; and it was
νύξ.
night.

King James Version

31 Therefore, when he was gone out, Jesus said, Now is the Son of man glorified, and God is glorified in him. 32 If God be glorified in him, God shall also glorify him in himself, and shall straightway glorify him. 33 Little children, yet a little while I am with you. Ye shall seek me; and as I said unto the Jews, Whither I go, ye cannot come; so now I say to you. 34 A new commandment I give unto you, That ye love one another; as I have loved you, that ye also love one another. 35 By this shall all *men* know that ye are my disciples, if ye have love one to another.

36 Simon Peter said unto him, Lord, whither goest thou? Jesus answered him, Whither I go, thou canst not follow me now; but thou shalt follow me afterwards. 37 Peter said unto him, Lord, why cannot I follow thee now? I will lay down my life for thy sake. 38 Jesus answered him, Wilt thou lay down thy life for my sake? Verily, verily, I say unto thee, The cock shall not crow, till thou hast denied me thrice.

14 Let not your heart be troubled: ye believe in God, believe also in me. 2 In my Father's house are many mansions: if *it were* not *so,* I would have told you. I go to prepare a place for you. 3 And if I go and prepare a place for you, I will come again, and receive you unto myself; that where I am, *there* ye may be also. 4 And whither I go ye know, and the way ye know. 5 Thomas saith unto him, Lord, we know not whither thou goest; and how can we know the way? 6 Jesus saith unto him, I am the way, the truth, and the life: no man cometh unto the Father, but by me. 7 If ye had known me, ye should have known my Father also: and from henceforth ye know him, and have seen him. 8 Philip saith unto him, Lord, shew us the Father, and it sufficeth us. 9 Jesus saith unto him, Have I been so long time with you, and yet hast thou not known me, Philip? he that hath seen me hath seen the Father; and how sayest thou *then,* Shew us the Father? 10 Believest thou not that I am in the Father, and the Father in me? the words that I speak unto you I speak not of myself: but the Father that dwelleth in me, he doeth the works. 11 Believe me that I *am* in the Father, and the Father in me: or else believe me for the very works' sake. 12 Verily, verily, I say unto you, He that believeth on me, the works that I do shall he do also; and greater *works* than these shall he do; because I go unto my Father. 13 And whatsoever ye shall ask in my name, that will I do, that the Father may be glorified in the Son. 14 If ye shall ask any thing in my name, I will do *it.*
15 If ye love me, keep my commandments.

New International Version

Jesus predicts Peter's denial

31 When he was gone, Jesus said, "Now is the Son of Man glorified and God is glorified in him. 32 If God is glorified in him,[k] then God will glorify the Son in himself, and will glorify him at once.
33 "My children, I will be with you only a little longer. You will look for me, and just as I told the Jews, so I tell you now: Where I am going, you cannot come.
34 "A new commandment I give you: Love one another. As I have loved you, so you must love one another. 35 All men will know that you are my disciples if you love one another."
36 Simon Peter asked him, "Lord, where are you going?"
Jesus replied, "Where I am going, you cannot follow now, but you will follow later."
37 Peter asked, "Lord, why can't I follow you now? I will lay down my life for you."
38 Then Jesus answered, "Will you really lay down your life for me? I tell you the truth, before the rooster crows, you will disown me three times!

Jesus comforts his disciples

14 "Do not let your hearts be troubled. Trust in God[l]; trust also in me. 2 There are many rooms in my Father's house; otherwise, I would have told you. I am going there to prepare a place for you. 3 And if I go and prepare a place for you, I will come back and take you to be with me that you also may be where I am. 4 You know the way to the place where I am going."

Jesus the way to the Father

5 Thomas said to him, "Lord, we don't know where you are going, so how can we know the way?"
6 Jesus answered, "I am the way—and the truth and the life. No one comes to the Father except through me. 7 If you really knew me, you would know[m] my Father as well. From now on, you do know him and have seen him."
8 Philip said, "Lord, show us the Father and that will be enough for us."
9 Jesus answered, "Don't you know me, Philip, even after I have been among you such a long time? Anyone who has seen me has seen the Father. How can you say, 'Show us the Father'? 10 Don't you believe that I am in the Father, and that the Father is in me? The words I say to you are not just my own. Rather, it is the Father, living in me, who is doing his work. 11 Believe me when I say that I am in the Father and the Father is in me; or at least believe on the evidence of the miracles themselves. 12 I tell you the truth, anyone who has faith in me will do what I have been doing. He will do even greater things than these, because I am going to the Father. 13 And I will do whatever you ask in my name, so that the Son may bring glory to the Father. 14 You may ask me for anything in my name, and I will do it. 15 If you love me, you will do what I command.

---

[k] Many early MSS omit *If God is glorified in him.* [l] Or *You trust in God.* [m] Some early MSS read *If you really have known me, you will know.*

Greek Interlinear

31 Ὅτε   οὖν   ἐξῆλθεν,   λέγει   Ἰησοῦς·
When therefore he went out,   says   Jesus :

νῦν   ἐδοξάσθη   ὁ   υἱὸς   τοῦ   ἀνθρώπου,
Now was(is) glorified the   Son   -   of man,

καὶ   ὁ   θεὸς   ἐδοξάσθη   ἐν   αὐτῷ·   32 εἰ
and   -   God was(is) glorified in   him;   if

ὁ   θεὸς   ἐδοξάσθη   ἐν   αὐτῷ,   καὶ   ὁ   θεὸς
- God was(is) glorified in   him,   both - God

δοξάσει   αὐτὸν   ἐν   αὐτῷ,   καὶ   εὐθὺς
will glorify   him   in   him,   and immediately

δοξάσει   αὐτόν.   33 τεκνία,   ἔτι   μικρὸν
will glorify   him.   Children,   yet a little while

μεθ'   ὑμῶν   εἰμι·   ζητήσετέ   με,   καὶ   καθὼς
with   you   I am; ye will seek me,   and   as

εἶπον   τοῖς   Ἰουδαίοις   ὅτι   ὅπου   ἐγὼ
I said   to the   Jews   that   where   I

ὑπάγω   ὑμεῖς   οὐ   δύνασθε   ἐλθεῖν,   καὶ
go   ye   cannot   to come,   also

ὑμῖν   λέγω   ἄρτι.   34 Ἐντολὴν   καινὴν
to you   I say   now.   commandment A new

δίδωμι   ὑμῖν,   ἵνα   ἀγαπᾶτε   ἀλλήλους,
I give   you,   that   ye love   one another,

καθὼς   ἠγάπησα   ὑμᾶς   ἵνα   καὶ   ὑμεῖς
as   I loved   you   that   also   ye

ἀγαπᾶτε   ἀλλήλους.   35 ἐν   τούτῳ   γνώσονται
love   one another.   By   this   will know

πάντες   ὅτι   ἐμοὶ   μαθηταί   ἐστε,   ἐὰν
all men   that   to me°   disciples   ye are,   if

ἀγάπην   ἔχητε   ἐν   ἀλλήλοις.   36 Λέγει
love   ye have   among   one another.   Says

αὐτῷ   Σίμων   Πέτρος·   κύριε,   ποῦ   ὑπάγεις;
to him   Simon   Peter :   Lord,   where   goest thou?

ἀπεκρίθη   Ἰησοῦς·   ὅπου   ὑπάγω   οὐ   δύνασαί
Answered   Jesus :   Where   I go   thou canst not

μοι   νῦν   ἀκολουθῆσαι,   ἀκολουθήσεις   δὲ
me   now   to follow,   but thou wilt follow

ὕστερον.   37 λέγει   αὐτῷ   [ὁ]   Πέτρος·
later.   Says   to him   -   Peter :

κύριε,   διὰ   τί   οὐ   δύναμαί   σοι   ἀκολουθῆσαι
Lord,   why   can I not   thee   to follow

ἄρτι;   τὴν   ψυχήν   μου   ὑπὲρ   σοῦ   θήσω.
yet?   the   life   of me   for   thee I will lay down.

38 ἀποκρίνεται   Ἰησοῦς·   τὴν   ψυχήν   σου
Answers   Jesus :   The   life   of thee

ὑπὲρ   ἐμοῦ   θήσεις;   ἀμὴν   ἀμὴν   λέγω
for   me   wilt thou lay down?   truly   truly   I tell

σοι,   οὐ   μὴ   ἀλέκτωρ   φωνήσῃ   ἕως   οὗ
thee,   by no means   a cock   crows   until

Chapter 14

ἀρνήσῃ   με   τρίς.   14 Μὴ   ταρασσέσθω
thou deniest   me   thrice.   Let not be troubled

ὑμῶν   ἡ   καρδία·   πιστεύετε   εἰς   τὸν   θεόν,   καὶ
of you the   heart;   believe   in -   the God,   also

εἰς   ἐμὲ   πιστεύετε.   2 ἐν   τῇ   οἰκίᾳ   τοῦ
in   me   believe.   In   the   house of the

πατρός   μου   μοναὶ   πολλαί   εἰσιν·   εἰ   δὲ   μή,
Father of me   abodes   many   there are;   otherwise,

εἶπον   ἂν   ὑμῖν·   ὅτι   πορεύομαι   ἑτοιμάσαι
I would have told you;   because   I go   to prepare

τόπον   ὑμῖν·   3 καὶ   ἐὰν   πορευθῶ   καὶ
a place   for you;   and   if   I go   and

ἑτοιμάσω   τόπον   ὑμῖν,   πάλιν   ἔρχομαι   καὶ
prepare   a place   for you,   again   I come   and

παραλήμψομαι   ὑμᾶς   πρὸς   ἐμαυτόν,   ἵνα
will receive   you   to   myself,   that

ὅπου   εἰμὶ   ἐγὼ   καὶ   ὑμεῖς   ἦτε.   4 Καὶ
where   am   I   also   ye   may be.   And

ὅπου   ἐγὼ   ὑπάγω   οἴδατε   τὴν   ὁδόν.
where   I   go   ye know   the   way.

5 λέγει   αὐτῷ   Θωμᾶς·   κύριε,   οὐκ   οἴδαμεν
Says   to him   Thomas :   Lord,   we know not

ποῦ   ὑπάγεις·   πῶς   οἴδαμεν   τὴν   ὁδόν;
where   thou goest;   how   do we know   the   way?

6 λέγει   αὐτῷ   Ἰησοῦς·   ἐγώ   εἰμι   ἡ   ὁδὸς
Says   to him   Jesus :   I   am   the   way

καὶ   ἡ   ἀλήθεια   καὶ   ἡ   ζωή·   οὐδεὶς   ἔρχεται
and   the   truth   and   the life;   no one   comes

πρὸς   τὸν   πατέρα   εἰ   μὴ   δι'   ἐμοῦ.   7 εἰ
to   the   Father   except through me.   If

ἐγνώκειτέ   με,   καὶ   τὸν   πατέρα   μου
ye had known   me,   also   the   Father   of me

ἂν   ᾔδειτε.   ἀπ'   ἄρτι   γινώσκετε   αὐτὸν
ye would have known. From now   ye know   him

καὶ   ἑωράκατε.   8 Λέγει   αὐτῷ   Φίλιππος·
and   have seen.   Says   to him   Philip:

κύριε,   δεῖξον   ἡμῖν   τὸν   πατέρα,   καὶ
Lord,   show   us   the   Father,   and

ἀρκεῖ   ἡμῖν.   9 λέγει   αὐτῷ   ὁ   Ἰησοῦς·
it suffices   for us.   Says   to him   -   Jesus:

τοσοῦτον   χρόνον   μεθ'   ὑμῶν   εἰμι   καὶ
So long   time   with   you   I am   and

οὐκ   ἔγνωκάς   με,   Φίλιππε;   ὁ   ἑωρακὼς
thou hast not known me,   Philip?   The [one] having seen

ἐμὲ   ἑώρακεν   τὸν   πατέρα·   πῶς   σὺ   λέγεις·
me   has seen   the   Father;   how thou sayest:

δεῖξον   ἡμῖν   τὸν   πατέρα;   10 οὐ   πιστεύεις
Show   us   the   Father?   believest thou not

ὅτι   ἐγὼ   ἐν   τῷ   πατρὶ   καὶ   ὁ   πατὴρ
that   I   in   the   Father   and   the   Father

ἐν   ἐμοί   ἐστιν;   τὰ   ῥήματα   ἃ   ἐγὼ   λέγω
in   me   is?   the   words   which I   say

ὑμῖν   ἀπ'   ἐμαυτοῦ   οὐ   λαλῶ·   ὁ   δὲ   πατὴρ
to you from   myself   I speak not;   but the Father

ἐν   ἐμοὶ   μένων   ποιεῖ   τὰ   ἔργα   αὐτοῦ.
in   me   remaining   does   the   works   of him.

11 πιστεύετέ   μοι   ὅτι   ἐγὼ   ἐν   τῷ   πατρὶ
Believe ye   me   that   I   in   the   Father

καὶ   ὁ   πατὴρ   ἐν   ἐμοί·   εἰ   δὲ   μή,   διὰ
and   the   Father   in   me;   otherwise,   because of

τὰ   ἔργα   αὐτὰ   πιστεύετε.   12 ἀμὴν   ἀμὴν
the   works [them]selves believe ye.   Truly   truly

λέγω   ὑμῖν,   ὁ   πιστεύων   εἰς   ἐμὲ   τὰ
I tell   you, the [one]   believing   in   me   the

ἔργα   ἃ   ἐγὼ   ποιῶ   κἀκεῖνος   ποιήσει,
works   which   I   do   that one also   will do,

καὶ   μείζονα   τούτων   ποιήσει,   ὅτι   ἐγὼ
and   greater [than]   these   he will do,   because   I

πρὸς   τὸν   πατέρα   πορεύομαι·   13 καὶ   ὅ   τι
to   the   Father   am going;   and   what-

ἂν   αἰτήσητε   ἐν   τῷ   ὀνόματί   μου,   τοῦτο
ever   ye ask   in   the   name   of me,   this

ποιήσω,   ἵνα   δοξασθῇ   ὁ   πατὴρ   ἐν   τῷ
I will do,   that may be glorified the   Father   in   the

υἱῷ.   14 ἐάν   τι   αἰτήσητέ   με   ἐν   τῷ
Son.   If   anything   ye ask   me   in   the

ὀνόματί   μου,   ἐγὼ   ποιήσω.   15 Ἐὰν
name   of me,   I   will do.   If

ἀγαπᾶτέ   με,   τὰς   ἐντολὰς   τὰς   ἐμὰς
ye love   me,   the   ¹commandments   -   ¹my

317

King James Version

16And I will pray the Father, and he shall give you another Comforter, that he may abide with you for ever; 17 *Even* the Spirit of truth; whom the world cannot receive, because it seeth him not, neither knoweth him: but ye know him; for he dwelleth with you, and shall be in you. 18 I will not leave you comfortless: I will come to you. 19 Yet a little while, and the world seeth me no more; but ye see me: because I live, ye shall live also. 20 At that day ye shall know that I *am* in my Father, and ye in me, and I in you. 21 He that hath my commandments, and keepeth them, he it is that loveth me: and he that loveth me shall be loved of my Father, and I will love him, and will manifest myself to him. 22 Judas saith unto him, not Iscariot, Lord, how is it that thou wilt manifest thyself unto us, and not unto the world? 23 Jesus answered and said unto him, If a man love me, he will keep my words: and my Father will love him, and we will come unto him, and make our abode with him. 24 He that loveth me not keepeth not my sayings: and the word which ye hear is not mine, but the Father's which sent me. 25 These things have I spoken unto you, being *yet* present with you. 26 But the Comforter, *which is* the Holy Ghost, whom the Father will send in my name, he shall teach you all things, and bring all things to your remembrance, whatsoever I have said unto you. 27 Peace I leave with you, my peace I give unto you: not as the world giveth, give I unto you. Let not your heart be troubled, neither let it be afraid. 28 Ye have heard how I said unto you, I go away, and come *again* unto you. If ye loved me, ye would rejoice, because I said, I go unto the Father: for my Father is greater than I. 29And now I have told you before it come to pass, that, when it is come to pass, ye might believe. 30 Hereafter I will not talk much with you: for the prince of this world cometh, and hath nothing in me. 31 But that the world may know that I love the Father; and as the Father gave me commandment, even so I do. Arise, let us go hence.

New International Version

Jesus promises the Holy Spirit

16 "I will ask the Father, and he will give you another Counselor, 17 the Spirit of truth, to be with you forever. The world cannot accept this Counselor, because it neither sees him nor knows him. But you know him, for he lives with you and will be in you. 18 I will not leave you as orphans; I will come to you. 19 Before long, the world will not see me any more, but you will see me. Because I live, you also will live. 20 On that day you will realize that I am in my Father, and you are in me, and I am in you. 21 Whoever has my commands and obeys them, he is the one who loves me. He who loves me will be loved by my Father, and I too will love him and show myself to him."

22 Then Judas (not Judas Iscariot) said, "But, Lord, why do you intend to show yourself to us and not to the world?"

23 Jesus replied, "If anyone loves me, he will obey my teaching. My Father will love him, and we will come to him and make our home with him. 24 He who does not love me will not obey my teaching. These words you hear are not my own; they belong to the Father who sent me.

25 "All this I have spoken while still with you. 26 But the Counselor, the Holy Spirit, whom the Father will send in my name, will teach you all things and will remind you of everything I have said to you. 27 Peace I leave with you; my peace I give you. I do not give to you as the world gives. Do not let your hearts be troubled and do not be afraid.

28 "You heard me say, 'I am going away and I am coming back to you.' If you loved me, you would be glad that I am going to the Father, for the Father is greater than I. 29 I have told you now before it happens, so that when it does happen you will believe. 30 I will not speak with you much longer, for the prince of this world is coming. He has no effect on me, 31 but the world must learn that I love the Father and that I do exactly what my Father has commanded me. Come now; let us leave.

The vine and the branches

15 I am the true vine, and my Father is the husbandman. 2 Every branch in me that beareth not fruit he taketh away: and every *branch* that beareth fruit, he purgeth it, that it may bring forth more fruit. 3 Now ye are clean through the word which I have spoken unto you. 4 Abide in me, and I in you. As the branch cannot bear fruit of itself, except it abide in the vine; no more can ye, except ye abide in me.

15 "I am the true vine and my Father is the gardener. 2 He cuts off every branch in me that bears no fruit, while every branch that does bear fruit he trims clean so that it will be even more fruitful. 3 You are already clean because of the word I have spoken to you. 4 Remain in me, and I will remain in you. No branch can bear fruit by itself; it must remain in the vine. Neither can you bear fruit unless you remain in me.

Greek Interlinear

τηρήσετε. **16** κἀγὼ ἐρωτήσω τὸν πατέρα
ye will keep.　And I　will request　the　Father

καὶ ἄλλον παράκλητον δώσει ὑμῖν, ἵνα
and another Comforter he will give you, that

ᾖ μεθ᾽ ὑμῶν εἰς τὸν αἰῶνα, **17** τὸ
he may be with you unto the age, the

πνεῦμα τῆς ἀληθείας, ὃ ὁ κόσμος
Spirit - of truth, which* the world

οὐ δύναται λαβεῖν, ὅτι οὐ θεωρεῖ αὐτὸ
cannot to receive, because it beholds not it*

οὐδὲ γινώσκει· ὑμεῖς γινώσκετε αὐτό,
nor knows· ye know it,*

ὅτι παρ᾽ ὑμῖν μένει καὶ ἐν ὑμῖν ἔσται.
because with you he remains and in you will be.

18 Οὐκ ἀφήσω ὑμᾶς ὀρφανούς, ἔρχομαι
I will not leave you orphans, I am coming

πρὸς ὑμᾶς. **19** ἔτι μικρὸν καὶ ὁ κόσμος
to you. Yet a little and the world

με οὐκέτι θεωρεῖ, ὑμεῖς δὲ θεωρεῖτέ
me no longer beholds, but ye behold

με, ὅτι ἐγὼ ζῶ καὶ ὑμεῖς ζήσετε.
me, because I live also ye will live.

20 ἐν ἐκείνῃ τῇ ἡμέρᾳ γνώσεσθε ὑμεῖς
In that - day will know ye

ὅτι ἐγὼ ἐν τῷ πατρί μου καὶ ὑμεῖς
that I in the Father of me and ye

ἐν ἐμοὶ κἀγὼ ἐν ὑμῖν. **21** Ὁ ἔχων
in me and I in you. The [one] having

τὰς ἐντολάς μου καὶ τηρῶν αὐτάς,
the commandments of me and keeping them,

ἐκεῖνός ἐστιν ὁ ἀγαπῶν με· ὁ δὲ ἀγαπῶν
that is the [one] loving me; and the [one] loving

με ἀγαπηθήσεται ὑπὸ τοῦ πατρός μου,
me will be loved by the Father of me,

κἀγὼ ἀγαπήσω αὐτὸν καὶ ἐμφανίσω αὐτῷ
and I will love him and will manifest to him

ἐμαυτόν. **22** λέγει αὐτῷ Ἰούδας, οὐχ
myself. Says to him Judas, not

ὁ Ἰσκαριώτης· κύριε, καὶ τί γέγονεν
the Iscariot: Lord, and what has happened

ὅτι ἡμῖν μέλλεις ἐμφανίζειν σεαυτὸν καὶ
that to us thou art about to manifest thyself and

οὐχὶ τῷ κόσμῳ; **23** ἀπεκρίθη Ἰησοῦς
not to the world? Answered Jesus

καὶ εἶπεν αὐτῷ· ἐάν τις ἀγαπᾷ με,
and said to him: If anyone loves me,

τὸν λόγον μου τηρήσει, καὶ ὁ πατὴρ
the word of me he will keep, and the Father

μου ἀγαπήσει αὐτόν, καὶ πρὸς αὐτὸν
of me will love him, and to him

ἐλευσόμεθα καὶ μονὴν παρ᾽ αὐτῷ
we will come and abode with him

ποιησόμεθα. **24** ὁ μὴ ἀγαπῶν με τοὺς
we will make. The [one] not loving me the

λόγους μου οὐ τηρεῖ· καὶ ὁ λόγος ὃν
words of me keeps not; and the word which

ἀκούετε οὐκ ἔστιν ἐμὸς ἀλλὰ τοῦ
ye hear is not mine but ¹of the

πέμψαντός με πατρός. **25** Ταῦτα λελάληκα
³having sent ¹me ²Father. These things I have spoken

ὑμῖν παρ᾽ ὑμῖν μένων· **26** ὁ δὲ παρά-
to you with you remaining; but the Com-

κλητος, τὸ πνεῦμα τὸ ἅγιον ὃ πέμψει ὁ
forter, the Spirit - Holy which will send the

πατὴρ ἐν τῷ ὀνόματί μου, ἐκεῖνος ὑμᾶς
Father in the name of me, that one you

διδάξει πάντα καὶ ὑπομνήσει ὑμᾶς πάντα
will teach all things and remind you [of] all things

ἃ εἶπον ὑμῖν ἐγώ. **27** Εἰρήνην ἀφίημι
which ²told ³you ¹I. Peace I leave

ὑμῖν, εἰρήνην τὴν ἐμὴν δίδωμι ὑμῖν·
to you, ²peace ¹my I give you;

οὐ καθὼς ὁ κόσμος δίδωσιν ἐγὼ δίδωμι
not as the world gives I give

ὑμῖν. μὴ ταρασσέσθω ὑμῶν ἡ καρδία
you. Let not be troubled of you the heart

μηδὲ δειλιάτω. **28** ἠκούσατε ὅτι ἐγὼ
nor let it be fearful. Ye heard that I

εἶπον ὑμῖν· ὑπάγω καὶ ἔρχομαι πρὸς
told you: I go and come to

ὑμᾶς. εἰ ἠγαπᾶτέ με, ἐχάρητε ἂν ὅτι
you. If ye loved me, ye would have rejoiced that

πορεύομαι πρὸς τὸν πατέρα, ὅτι ὁ πατὴρ
I am going to the Father, because the Father

μείζων μού ἐστιν. **29** καὶ νῦν εἴρηκα
greater [than] me(I) is. And now I have told

ὑμῖν πρὶν γενέσθαι, ἵνα ὅταν γένηται
you before to happen, that when it happens
=it happens,

πιστεύσητε. **30** οὐκέτι πολλὰ λαλήσω μεθ᾽
ye may believe. No longer many things I will speak with

ὑμῶν, ἔρχεται γὰρ ὁ τοῦ κόσμου ἄρχων·
you, for ²is coming ¹the ³the ⁴of the ⁵world ⁶ruler;

καὶ ἐν ἐμοὶ οὐκ ἔχει οὐδέν, **31** ἀλλ᾽
and in me he has not no(any)thing, but

ἵνα γνῷ ὁ κόσμος ὅτι ἀγαπῶ τὸν
that may know the world that I love the

πατέρα, καὶ καθὼς ἐνετείλατό μοι ὁ
Father, and as commanded me the

πατήρ, οὕτως ποιῶ. Ἐγείρεσθε, ἄγωμεν
Father, so I do. Rise, let us go

ἐντεῦθεν.
hence.

Chapter 15

1 Ἐγώ εἰμι ἡ ἄμπελος ἡ ἀληθινή,
I am the vine - true,

καὶ ὁ πατήρ μου ὁ γεωργός ἐστιν.
and the Father of me the husbandman is.

2 πᾶν κλῆμα ἐν ἐμοὶ μὴ φέρον καρπόν,
Every branch in me not bearing fruit,

αἴρει αὐτό, καὶ πᾶν τὸ καρπὸν φέρον,
he takes it, and every [branch] the fruit bearing,

καθαίρει αὐτὸ ἵνα καρπὸν πλείονα φέρῃ.
he prunes it that fruit more it may bear.

3 ἤδη ὑμεῖς καθαροί ἐστε διὰ τὸν λόγον
Now ye clean are because of the word

ὃν λελάληκα ὑμῖν· μείνατε ἐν ἐμοί,
which I have spoken to you; remain in me,

κἀγὼ ἐν ὑμῖν. **4** καθὼς τὸ κλῆμα
and I in you. As the branch

οὐ δύναται καρπὸν φέρειν ἀφ᾽ ἑαυτοῦ ἐὰν μὴ
cannot fruit to bear from itself unless

μένῃ ἐν τῇ ἀμπέλῳ, οὕτως οὐδὲ ὑμεῖς
it remains in the vine, so not ye

---

* The gender of these pronouns agrees, of course, with the antecedent πνεῦμα (neuter); and this has been kept though the personal
Spirit of God is meant. Elsewhere, masculine pronouns are in
fact used.

King James Version

5 I am the vine, ye *are* the branches. He that abideth in me, and I in him, the same bringeth forth much fruit; for without me ye can do nothing. 6 If a man abide not in me, he is cast forth as a branch, and is withered; and men gather them, and cast *them* into the fire, and they are burned. 7 If ye abide in me, and my words abide in you, ye shall ask what ye will, and it shall be done unto you. 8 Herein is my Father glorified, that ye bear much fruit; so shall ye be my disciples. 9 As the Father hath loved me, so have I loved you: continue ye in my love. 10 If ye keep my commandments, ye shall abide in my love; even as I have kept my Father's commandments, and abide in his love. 11 These things have I spoken unto you, that my joy might remain in you, and *that* your joy might be full. 12 This is my commandment, That ye love one another, as I have loved you. 13 Greater love hath no man than this, that a man lay down his life for his friends. 14 Ye are my friends, if ye do whatsoever I command you. 15 Henceforth I call you not servants; for the servant knoweth not what his lord doeth: but I have called you friends; for all things that I have heard of my Father I have made known unto you. 16 Ye have not chosen me, but I have chosen you, and ordained you, that ye should go and bring forth fruit, and *that* your fruit should remain; that whatsoever ye shall ask of the Father in my name, he may give it you. 17 These things I command you, that ye love one another. 18 If the world hate you, ye know that it hated me before *it hated* you. 19 If ye were of the world, the world would love his own; but because ye are not of the world, but I have chosen you out of the world, therefore the world hateth you. 20 Remember the word that I said unto you, The servant is not greater than his lord. If they have persecuted me, they will also persecute you; if they have kept my saying, they will keep yours also. 21 But all these things will they do unto you for my name's sake, because they know not him that sent me. 22 If I had not come and spoken unto them, they had not had sin: but now they have no cloak for their sin. 23 He that hateth me hateth my Father also. 24 If I had not done among them the works which none other man did, they had not had sin: but now have they both seen and hated both me and my Father. 25 But *this cometh to pass,* that the word might be fulfilled that is written in their law, They hated me without a cause. 26 But when the Comforter is come, whom I will send unto you from the Father, *even* the Spirit of truth, which proceedeth from the Father, he shall testify of me: 27 And ye also shall bear witness, because ye have been with me from the beginning.

New International Version

5 "I am the vine; you are the branches. If a man remains in me and I in him, he will bear much fruit; apart from me you can do nothing. 6 If anyone does not remain in me, he is like a branch that is thrown away and withers; such branches are picked up, thrown into the fire and burned. 7 If you remain in me and my words remain in you, ask whatever you wish, and it will be given you. 8 This is to my Father's glory, that you bear much fruit, showing yourselves to be my disciples.

9 "As the Father has loved me, so have I loved you. Now remain in my love. 10 If you obey my commands, you will remain in my love, just as I have obeyed my Father's commands and remain in his love. 11 I have told you this so that my joy may be in you and that your joy may be complete. 12 My command is this: Love each other as I have loved you. 13 No one has greater love than the one who lays down his life for his friends. 14 You are my friends if you do what I command. 15 I no longer call you servants, because a servant does not know his master's business. Instead, I have called you friends, for everything that I learned from my Father I have made known to you. 16 You did not choose me, but I chose you to go and bear fruit—fruit that will last. Then the Father will give you whatever you ask in my name. 17 This is my command: Love each other.

The world hates the disciples

18 "If the world hates you, keep in mind that it hated me first. 19 If you belonged to the world, it would love you as its own. As it is, you do not belong to the world, but I have chosen you out of the world. That is why the world hates you. 20 Remember the words I spoke to you: 'No servant is greater than his master.' [n] If they persecuted me, they will persecute you also. If they obeyed my teaching, they will obey yours also. 21 They will treat you this way because of my name, for they do not know the one who sent me. 22 If I had not come and spoken to them, they would not be guilty of sin. Now, however, they have no excuse for their sin. 23 He who hates me hates my Father as well. 24 If I had not done among them what no one else did, they would not be guilty of sin. But now they have seen these miracles, and yet they have hated both me and my Father. 25 But this is to fulfill what is written in their Law: 'They hated me without reason.' [o]

26 "When the Counselor comes, whom I will send to you from the Father, the Spirit of truth who goes out from the Father, he will testify about me; 27 but you also must testify, for you have been with me from the beginning.

Greek Interlinear

ἐὰν μὴ ἐν ἐμοὶ μένητε. **5** ἐγώ εἰμι
unless   in   me   ye remain.   I   am

ἡ ἄμπελος, ὑμεῖς τὰ κλήματα. ὁ μένων
the vine,   ye   the branches. The [one] remaining

ἐν ἐμοὶ κἀγὼ ἐν αὐτῷ, οὗτος φέρει
in me   and I   in   him,   this one   bears

καρπὸν πολύν, ὅτι χωρὶς ἐμοῦ οὐ δύνασθε
fruit   much,   because apart from me   ye cannot

ποιεῖν οὐδέν. **6** ἐὰν μή τις μένῃ ἐν
to do no(any)thing.   Unless   anyone remains in

ἐμοί, ἐβλήθη ἔξω ὡς τὸ κλῆμα καὶ
me,   he was(is) cast outside as   the branch   and

ἐξηράνθη, καὶ συνάγουσιν αὐτὰ καὶ εἰς
was(is) dried,   and   they gather   them   and   into

τὸ πῦρ βάλλουσιν, καὶ καίεται. **7** ἐὰν
the fire   they cast,   and they are burned.   If

μείνητε ἐν ἐμοὶ καὶ τὰ ῥήματά μου
ye remain in   me   and   the   words   of me

ἐν ὑμῖν μείνῃ, ὃ ἐὰν θέλητε αἰτήσασθε,
in you   remain, whatever   ye wish   ask,

καὶ γενήσεται ὑμῖν. **8** ἐν τούτῳ ἐδοξάσθη
and it shall happen to you.   By   this   was glorified

ὁ πατήρ μου, ἵνα καρπὸν πολὺν φέρητε
the Father of me,   that   fruit   much   ye bear

καὶ γενήσεσθε ἐμοὶ μαθηταί. **9** καθὼς
and   ye will be   to me°   disciples.   As

ἠγάπησέν με ὁ πατήρ, κἀγὼ ὑμᾶς
loved   me   the Father,   I also   you

ἠγάπησα· μείνατε ἐν τῇ ἀγάπῃ τῇ ἐμῇ·
loved;   remain ye in   the ²love   - ¹my.

10 ἐὰν τὰς ἐντολάς μου τηρήσητε, μενεῖτε
If the commandments of me ye keep, ye will remain

ἐν τῇ ἀγάπῃ μου, καθὼς ἐγὼ τοῦ πατρός
in the love   of me,   as   I   of the Father

μου τὰς ἐντολὰς τετήρηκα καὶ μένω
of me   the commandments   have kept   and   remain

αὐτοῦ ἐν τῇ ἀγάπῃ. **11** Ταῦτα λελάληκα
of him   in   the   love.   These things I have spoken

ὑμῖν ἵνα ἡ χαρὰ ἡ ἐμὴ ἐν ὑμῖν ᾖ
to you that the ²joy   - ¹my   in   you may be

καὶ ἡ χαρὰ ὑμῶν πληρωθῇ. **12** αὕτη
and the   joy   of you   may be filled.   This

ἐστὶν ἡ ἐντολὴ ἡ ἐμή, ἵνα ἀγαπᾶτε
is   the ²commandment - ¹my,   that   ye love

ἀλλήλους καθὼς ἠγάπησα ὑμᾶς. **13** μείζονα
one another   as   I loved   you.   ¹Greater

ταύτης ἀγάπην οὐδεὶς ἔχει, ἵνα τις
[²than] ⁴this   ³love   no one   has,   that anyone

τὴν ψυχὴν αὐτοῦ θῇ ὑπὲρ τῶν φίλων
the   life of him should lay down for   the   friends

αὐτοῦ. **14** ὑμεῖς φίλοι μού ἐστε, ἐὰν
of him.   Ye   friends   of me   are,   if

ποιῆτε ὃ ἐγὼ ἐντέλλομαι ὑμῖν. **15** οὐκέτι
ye do what   I   command   you.   No longer

λέγω ὑμᾶς δούλους, ὅτι ὁ δοῦλος οὐκ οἶδεν
I call   you   slaves, because the slave   knows not

τί ποιεῖ αὐτοῦ ὁ κύριος· ὑμᾶς δὲ
what does   of him   the   lord;   but you

εἴρηκα φίλους, ὅτι πάντα ἃ ἤκουσα
I have called 'friends, because all things which   I heard

παρὰ τοῦ πατρός μου ἐγνώρισα ὑμῖν.
from   the   Father   of me I made known to you.

16 οὐχ ὑμεῖς με ἐξελέξασθε, ἀλλ' ἐγὼ
Not   ye   me   chose,   but   I

ἐξελεξάμην ὑμᾶς, καὶ ἔθηκα ὑμᾶς ἵνα
chose   you,   and appointed   you   that

ὑμεῖς ὑπάγητε καὶ καρπὸν φέρητε καὶ
ye   should go   and   fruit   should bear and

ὁ καρπὸς ὑμῶν μένῃ, ἵνα ὅ τι ἂν
the fruit of you should remain, that   whatever

αἰτήσητε τὸν πατέρα ἐν τῷ ὀνόματί
ye may ask   the   Father   in   the   name

μου δῷ ὑμῖν. **17** ταῦτα ἐντέλλομαι ὑμῖν,
of me he may give you.   These things I command   you,

ἵνα ἀγαπᾶτε ἀλλήλους. **18** Εἰ ὁ κόσμος
that   ye love   one another.   If the   world

ὑμᾶς μισεῖ, γινώσκετε ὅτι ἐμὲ πρῶτον
you   hates,   ye know   that   me   before

ὑμῶν μεμίσηκεν. **19** εἰ ἐκ τοῦ κόσμου ἦτε,
you   it has hated.   If of   the   world ye were,

ὁ κόσμος ἂν τὸ ἴδιον ἐφίλει· ὅτι δὲ
the   world   ¹would ²the(its) ⁴own   ³have loved; but because

ἐκ τοῦ κόσμου οὐκ ἐστέ, ἀλλ' ἐγὼ
of   the   world   ye are not,   but   I

ἐξελεξάμην ὑμᾶς ἐκ τοῦ κόσμου, διὰ τοῦτο
chose   you out of the   world,   therefore

μισεῖ ὑμᾶς ὁ κόσμος. **20** μνημονεύετε
hates   you   the world.   Remember ye

τοῦ λόγου οὗ ἐγὼ εἶπον ὑμῖν· οὐκ
the   word   which I   said   to you : Not

ἔστιν δοῦλος μείζων τοῦ κυρίου αὐτοῦ.
is   a slave   greater [than] the   lord   of him.

εἰ ἐμὲ ἐδίωξαν, καὶ ὑμᾶς διώξουσιν·
If me   they persecuted,   also   you they will persecute;

εἰ τὸν λόγον μου ἐτήρησαν, καὶ τὸν
if   the   word   of me they kept,   also   -

ὑμέτερον τηρήσουσιν. **21** ἀλλὰ ταῦτα πάντα
yours   they will keep.   But these things   all

ποιήσουσιν εἰς ὑμᾶς διὰ τὸ ὄνομά μου,
they will do   to   you because of the   name   of me,

ὅτι οὐκ οἴδασιν τὸν πέμψαντα με.
because   they know not   the [one] having sent   me.

22 εἰ μὴ ἦλθον καὶ ἐλάλησα αὐτοῖς, ἁμαρτίαν
Unless I came and   spoke   to them,   sin

οὐκ εἴχοσαν· νῦν δὲ πρόφασιν οὐκ ἔχουσιν
they had not had; but now   cloak   they have not

περὶ τῆς ἁμαρτίας αὐτῶν. **23** ὁ ἐμὲ
concerning the   sin   of them.   The [one] me

μισῶν καὶ τὸν πατέρα μου μισεῖ. **24** εἰ
hating also   the   Father   of me hates.   If

τὰ ἔργα μὴ ἐποίησα ἐν αὐτοῖς ἃ οὐδεὶς
the   works   I did not   among them which no man

ἄλλος ἐποίησεν, ἁμαρτίαν οὐκ εἴχοσαν
other   did,   sin   they had not had;

νῦν δὲ καὶ ἑωράκασιν καὶ μεμισήκασιν
but now   both   they have seen   and   have hated

καὶ ἐμὲ καὶ τὸν πατέρα μου. **25** ἀλλ'
both   me   and   the   Father   of me.   But

ἵνα πληρωθῇ ὁ λόγος ὁ ἐν τῷ νόμῳ
that may be fulfilled the   word   - in   the   law

αὐτῶν γεγραμμένος ὅτι ἐμίσησάν με
of them having been written[,]   -   They hated   me

δωρεάν. **26** Ὅταν ἔλθῃ ὁ παράκλητος
freely.   When   comes   the   Comforter

ὃν ἐγὼ πέμψω ὑμῖν παρὰ τοῦ πατρός,
whom I   will send to you from   the   Father,

τὸ πνεῦμα τῆς ἀληθείας ὃ παρὰ τοῦ
the   Spirit   -   of truth   which from   the

πατρὸς ἐκπορεύεται, ἐκεῖνος μαρτυρήσει
Father   proceeds,   that one   will witness

περὶ ἐμοῦ· **27** καὶ ὑμεῖς δὲ μαρτυρεῖτε,
concerning me;   ²also   ³ye   ¹and   witness,

ὅτι ἀπ' ἀρχῆς μετ' ἐμοῦ ἐστε.
because from [the] beginning with   me   ye are.

16 These things have I spoken unto you, that ye should not be offended. 2 They shall put you out of the synagogues: yea, the time cometh, that whosoever killeth you will think that he doeth God service. 3And these things will they do unto you, because they have not known the Father, nor me. 4 But these things have I told you, that when the time shall come, ye may remember that I told you of them. And these things I said not unto you at the beginning, because I was with you. 5 But now I go my way to him that sent me; and none of you asketh me, Whither goest thou? 6 But because I have said these things unto you, sorrow hath filled your heart. 7 Nevertheless I tell you the truth; It is expedient for you that I go away: for if I go not away, the Comforter will not come unto you; but if I depart, I will send him unto you. 8And when he is come, he will reprove the world of sin, and of righteousness, and of judgment: 9 Of sin, because they believe not on me; 10 Of righteousness, because I go to my Father, and ye see me no more; 11 Of judgment, because the prince of this world is judged. 12 I have yet many things to say unto you, but ye cannot bear them now. 13 Howbeit when he, the Spirit of truth, is come, he will guide you into all truth: for he shall not speak of himself; but whatsoever he shall hear, *that* shall he speak: and he will shew you things to come. 14 He shall glorify me: for he shall receive of mine, and shall shew *it* unto you. 15All things that the Father hath are mine: therefore said I, that he shall take of mine, and shall shew *it* unto you. 16A little while, and ye shall not see me: and again, a little while, and ye shall see me, because I go to the Father. 17 Then said *some* of his disciples among themselves, What is this that he saith unto us, A little while, and ye shall not see me: and again, a little while, and ye shall see me: and, Because I go to the Father? 18 They said therefore, What is this that he saith, A little while? we cannot tell what he saith. 19 Now Jesus knew that they were desirous to ask him, and said unto them, Do ye inquire among yourselves of that I said, A little while, and ye shall not see me: and again, a little while, and ye shall see me? 20 Verily, verily, I say unto you, That ye shall weep and lament, but the world shall rejoice: and ye shall be sorrowful, but your sorrow shall be turned into joy. 21 A woman when she is in travail hath sorrow, because her hour is come: but as soon as she is delivered of the child, she remembereth no more the anguish, for joy that a man is born into the world. 22And when ye therefore have sorrow: but I will see you again, and your heart shall rejoice, and your joy no man taketh from you. 23And in that day ye shall ask me nothing. Verily, verily, I say unto you, Whatsoever ye shall ask the Father in my name, he will give *it* you. 24 Hitherto have ye asked nothing in my name: ask, and ye shall receive, that your joy may be full. 25 These things have I

16 "All this I have told you so that you will not go astray. 2 They will put you out of the synagogue; in fact, a time is coming when anyone who kills you will think he is offering a service to God. 3 They will do such things because they have not known the Father or me. 4 I have told you this, so that when the time comes you will remember that I warned you. I did not tell you this at first because I was with you.

The work of the Holy Spirit

5 "Now I am going to him who sent me, yet none of you even asks me, 'Where are you going?' 6 Because I have said these things, you are filled with grief. 7 But I tell you the truth: It is for your good that I am going away. Unless I go away, the Counselor will not come to you; but if I go, I will send him to you. 8 When he comes, he will prove the world wrong about sin and righteousness and judgment: 9 about sin, because men do not believe in me; 10 about righteousness, because I am going to the Father, where you can see me no longer; 11 and about judgment, because the prince of this world now stands condemned.

12 "I have much more to say to you, more than you can now bear. 13 But when he, the Spirit of truth, comes, he will guide you into all truth. He will not speak on his own; he will speak only what he hears, and he will tell you what is yet to come. 14 He will bring glory to me by taking from what is mine and making it known to you. 15All that belongs to the Father is mine. That is why I said the Spirit will take from what is mine and make it known to you.

16 "In a little while you will see me no more, and then after a little while you will see me."

The disciples' grief will turn to joy

17 Some of his disciples said to one another, "What does he mean by saying, 'In a little while you will see me no more,' and 'Then after a little while you will see me,' and 'Because I am going to the Father'?" 18 They kept asking, "What does he mean by 'a little while'? We don't understand what he is saying."

19 Jesus saw that they wanted to ask him about this, so he said to them, "Are you asking one another what I meant when I said, 'In a little while you will see me no more,' and 'Then after a little while you will see me'? 20 I tell you the truth, you will weep and mourn while the world rejoices. You will grieve, but your grief will turn to joy. 21A woman giving birth to a child has pain because her time has come; but when her baby is born she forgets the anguish because of her joy that a child is born into the world. 22 So with you: Now is your time of grief, but I will see you again and you will rejoice, and no one will take away your joy. 23 In that day you will no longer ask me anything. I tell you the truth, my Father will give you whatever you ask in my name. 24 Until now you have not asked for anything in my name. Ask and you will receive, and your joy will be complete.

25 "Though I have been speaking figuratively,

Greek Interlinear

Chapter 16

Ταῦτα λελάληκα ὑμῖν ἵνα μὴ
These things I have spoken to you that not
σκανδαλισθῆτε. 2 ἀποσυναγώγους ποιή-
ye be offended. Put away from [the] synagogue they
σουσιν ὑμᾶς· ἀλλ' ἔρχεται ὥρα ἵνα πᾶς ὁ
will make you; but comes an hour that everyone
ἀποκτείνας ὑμᾶς δόξῃ λατρείαν προσφέρειν
killing you thinks service to offer
τῷ θεῷ. 3 καὶ ταῦτα ποιήσουσιν ὅτι
- to God. And these things they will do because
οὐκ ἔγνωσαν τὸν πατέρα οὐδὲ ἐμέ.
they knew not the Father nor me.
4 ἀλλὰ ταῦτα λελάληκα ὑμῖν ἵνα ὅταν
But these things I have spoken to you that when
ἔλθῃ ἡ ὥρα αὐτῶν μνημονεύητε αὐτῶν,
comes the hour of them ye may remember them,
ὅτι ἐγὼ εἶπον ὑμῖν. Ταῦτα δὲ ὑμῖν
that I told you. And these things to you
ἐξ ἀρχῆς οὐκ εἶπον, ὅτι μεθ' ὑμῶν
from [the] beginning I said not, because with you
ἤμην. 5 νῦν δὲ ὑπάγω πρὸς τὸν πέμψαντά
I was. But now I am going to the [one] having sent
με, καὶ οὐδεὶς ἐξ ὑμῶν ἐρωτᾷ με·
me, and not one of you asks me:
ποῦ ὑπάγεις; 6 ἀλλ' ὅτι ταῦτα λελάληκα
Where goest thou? but because these things I have spoken
ὑμῖν, ἡ λύπη πεπλήρωκεν ὑμῶν τὴν
to you, - grief has filled of you the
καρδίαν. 7 ἀλλ' ἐγὼ τὴν ἀλήθειαν λέγω
heart. But I the truth tell
ὑμῖν, συμφέρει ὑμῖν ἵνα ἐγὼ ἀπέλθω.
you, it is expedient for you that I should go away.
ἐὰν γὰρ μὴ ἀπέλθω, ὁ παράκλητος
For if I go not away, the Comforter
οὐ μὴ ἔλθῃ πρὸς ὑμᾶς· ἐὰν δὲ πορευθῶ,
by no means comes to you; but if I go,
πέμψω αὐτὸν πρὸς ὑμᾶς. 8 καὶ ἐλθὼν
I will send him to you. And coming
ἐκεῖνος ἐλέγξει τὸν κόσμον περὶ ἁμαρτίας
that one will reprove the world concerning sin
καὶ περὶ δικαιοσύνης καὶ περὶ κρίσεως·
and concerning righteousness and concerning judgment;
9 περὶ ἁμαρτίας μέν, ὅτι οὐ πιστεύουσιν
concerning sin, - because they believe not
εἰς ἐμέ· 10 περὶ δικαιοσύνης δέ, ὅτι
in me; concerning righteousness - because
πρὸς τὸν πατέρα ὑπάγω καὶ οὐκέτι
to the Father I am going and no longer
θεωρεῖτέ με· 11 περὶ δὲ κρίσεως, ὅτι
ye behold me; concerning - judgment, because
ὁ ἄρχων τοῦ κόσμου τούτου κέκριται.
the ruler - world of this has been judged.
12 Ἔτι πολλὰ ἔχω ὑμῖν λέγειν, ἀλλ'
Yet many things I have you to tell, but
οὐ δύνασθε βαστάζειν ἄρτι· 13 ὅταν δὲ
ye cannot to bear now; but when
ἔλθῃ ἐκεῖνος, τὸ πνεῦμα τῆς ἀληθείας,
comes that one, the Spirit - of truth,
ὁδηγήσει ὑμᾶς εἰς τὴν ἀλήθειαν πᾶσαν·
he will guide you into the truth all;
οὐ γὰρ λαλήσει ἀφ' ἑαυτοῦ, ἀλλ' ὅσα
for not will he speak from himself, but what things
ἀκούει λαλήσει, καὶ τὰ ἐρχόμενα
he hears he will speak, and the coming things
ἀναγγελεῖ ὑμῖν. 14 ἐκεῖνος ἐμὲ δοξάσει,
he will announce to you. That one me will glorify,
ὅτι ἐκ τοῦ ἐμοῦ λήμψεται καὶ ἀναγγελεῖ
because of the of me * he will receive and will announce
ὑμῖν. 15 πάντα ὅσα ἔχει ὁ πατὴρ ἐμά
to you. All things which has the Father mine

ἐστιν· διὰ τοῦτο εἶπον ὅτι ἐκ τοῦ ἐμοῦ
is(are); therefore I said that of the of me *
λαμβάνει καὶ ἀναγγελεῖ ὑμῖν. 16 Μικρὸν
he receives and will announce to you. A little while
καὶ οὐκέτι θεωρεῖτέ με, καὶ πάλιν
and no longer ye behold me, and again
μικρὸν καὶ ὄψεσθέ με. 17 εἶπαν οὖν
a little while and ye will see me. Said therefore
ἐκ τῶν μαθητῶν αὐτοῦ πρὸς ἀλλήλους·
[some] of the disciples of him to one another :
τί ἐστιν τοῦτο ὃ λέγει ἡμῖν· μικρὸν
What is this which he tells us : A little while
καὶ οὐ θεωρεῖτέ με, καὶ πάλιν μικρὸν
and ye behold not me, and again a little while
καὶ ὄψεσθέ με; καί· ὅτι ὑπάγω
and ye will see me? and : Because I am going
πρὸς τὸν πατέρα; 18 ἔλεγον οὖν· τοῦτο
to the Father? They said therefore : *This
τί ἐστιν ὃ λέγει τὸ μικρόν; οὐκ οἴδαμεν
¹what ²is which he says[,] the "little while"? We do not know
τί λαλεῖ. 19 ἔγνω Ἰησοῦς ὅτι ἤθελον
what he speaks. Knew Jesus that they wished
αὐτὸν ἐρωτᾶν, καὶ εἶπεν αὐτοῖς· περὶ
him to question, and said to them : Concerning
τούτου ζητεῖτε μετ' ἀλλήλων ὅτι εἶπον·
this seek ye with one another because I said :
μικρὸν καὶ οὐ θεωρεῖτέ με, καὶ πάλιν
A little while and ye behold not me, and again
μικρὸν καὶ ὄψεσθέ με; 20 ἀμὴν ἀμὴν
a little while and ye will see me? Truly truly
λέγω ὑμῖν ὅτι κλαύσετε καὶ θρηνήσετε
I tell you that will weep and will lament
ὑμεῖς, ὁ δὲ κόσμος χαρήσεται· ὑμεῖς
ye, and the world will rejoice; ye
λυπηθήσεσθε, ἀλλ' ἡ λύπη ὑμῶν εἰς
will be grieved, but the grief of you into
χαρὰν γενήσεται. 21 ἡ γυνὴ ὅταν τίκτῃ
joy will become. The woman when she gives birth
λύπην ἔχει, ὅτι ἦλθεν ἡ ὥρα αὐτῆς·
grief has, because came the hour of her;
ὅταν δὲ γεννήσῃ τὸ παιδίον, οὐκέτι
but when she brings forth the child, no longer
μνημονεύει τῆς θλίψεως διὰ τὴν χαρὰν
she remembers the distress because of the joy
ὅτι ἐγεννήθη ἄνθρωπος εἰς τὸν κόσμον.
that was born a man into the world.
22 καὶ ὑμεῖς οὖν νῦν μὲν λύπην ἔχετε·
And ye therefore now indeed grief have;
πάλιν δὲ ὄψομαι ὑμᾶς, καὶ χαρήσεται
but again I will see you, and *will rejoice
ὑμῶν ἡ καρδία, καὶ τὴν χαρὰν ὑμῶν
*of you ¹the ²heart, and the joy of you
οὐδεὶς αἴρει ἀφ' ὑμῶν. 23 καὶ ἐν ἐκείνῃ τῇ
no one takes from you. And in that -
ἡμέρᾳ ἐμὲ οὐκ ἐρωτήσετε οὐδέν.
day me ye will not question no(any)thing.
ἀμὴν ἀμὴν λέγω ὑμῖν, ἄν τι αἰτήσητε
Truly truly I tell you, whatever ye ask
τὸν πατέρα δώσει ὑμῖν ἐν τῷ ὀνόματί
the Father he will give you in the name
μου. 24 ἕως ἄρτι οὐκ ᾐτήσατε οὐδὲν
of me. Until now ye asked not no(any)thing
ἐν τῷ ὀνόματί μου· αἰτεῖτε, καὶ λήμψεσθε,
in the name of me; ask, and ye will receive,
ἵνα ἡ χαρὰ ὑμῶν ᾖ πεπληρωμένη.
that the joy of you may be *having been filled.
25 Ταῦτα ἐν παροιμίαις λελάληκα ὑμῖν·
These things in allegories I have spoken to you;

* Understand "that which is mine".

King James Version

spoken unto you in proverbs: but the time cometh, when I shall no more speak unto you in proverbs, but I shall shew you plainly of the Father. 26At that day ye shall ask in my name: and I say not unto you, that I will pray the Father for you: 27 For the Father himself loveth you, because ye have loved me, and have believed that I came out from God. 28 I came forth from the Father, and am come into the world: again, I leave the world, and go to the Father. 29 His disciples said unto him, Lo, now speakest thou plainly, and speakest no proverb. 30 Now are we sure that thou knowest all things, and needest not that any man should ask thee: by this we believe that thou camest forth from God. 31 Jesus answered them, Do ye now believe? 32 Behold, the hour cometh, yea, is now come, that ye shall be scattered, every man to his own, and shall leave me alone: and yet I am not alone, because the Father is with me. 33 These things I have spoken unto you, that in me ye might have peace. In the world ye shall have tribulation: but be of good cheer; I have overcome the world.

17 These words spake Jesus, and lifted up his eyes to heaven, and said, Father, the hour is come; glorify thy Son, that thy Son also may glorify thee: 2As thou hast given him power over all flesh, that he should give eternal life to as many as thou hast given him. 3And this is life eternal, that they might know thee the only true God, and Jesus Christ, whom thou hast sent. 4 I have glorified thee on the earth: I have finished the work which thou gavest me to do. 5And now, O Father, glorify thou me with thine own self with the glory which I had with thee before the world was. 6 I have manifested thy name unto the men which thou gavest me out of the world: thine they were, and thou gavest them me; and they have kept thy word. 7 Now they have known that all things whatsoever thou hast given me are of thee. 8 For I have given unto them the words which thou gavest me; and they have received them, and have known surely that I came out from thee, and they have believed that thou didst send me. 9 I pray for them: I pray not for the world, but for them which thou hast given me; for they are thine. 10And all mine are thine, and thine are mine; and I am glorified in them. 11And now I am no more in the world, but these are in the world, and I come to thee. Holy Father, keep through thine own name those whom thou hast given me, that they may be one, as we are. 12 While I was with them in the world, I kept them in thy name: those that thou gavest me I have kept, and none of them is lost, but the son of perdition; that the Scripture might be fulfilled. 13And now come I to thee; and these things I speak in the world, that they

New International Version

a time is coming when I will no longer use this kind of language but will tell you plainly about my Father. 26 In that day you will ask in my name. I am not saying that I will ask the Father on your behalf. 27 No, the Father himself loves you because you have loved me and have believed that I came from God. 28 I came from the Father and entered the world; now I am leaving the world and going back to the Father."

29 Then Jesus' disciples said, "Now you are speaking clearly and without figures of speech. 30 Now we can see that you know all things and that you do not even need to have anyone ask you questions. This makes us believe that you came from God."

31 "You believe at last!" [p] Jesus answered. 32 "But a time is coming, and has come, when you will be scattered, each to his own home. You will leave me all alone. Yet I am not alone, for my Father is with me.

33 "I have told you these things, so that in me you may have peace. In this world you will have trouble. But take heart! I have overcome the world."

Jesus prays for himself

17 After Jesus said this, he looked toward heaven and prayed: "Father, the time has come. Glorify your Son, that your Son may glorify you. 2 For you granted him authority over all men that he might give eternal life to all those you have given to him. 3 Now this is eternal life: that they may know you, the only true God, and Jesus Christ, whom you have sent. 4 I have brought you glory on earth by completing the work you gave me to do. 5And now, Father, glorify me in your presence with the glory I had with you before the world began.

Jesus prays for his disciples

6 "I have revealed you to those whom you gave me out of the world. They were yours; you gave them to me and they have obeyed your word. 7 Now they know that everything you have given me comes from you. 8 For I gave them the words you gave me and they accepted them. They knew with certainty that I came from you, and they believed that you sent me. 9 I pray for them. I am not praying for the world, but for those you have given me, for they are yours. 10All I have is yours, and all you have is mine. And glory has come to me through them. 11 I will remain in the world no longer, but they are still in the world, and I am coming to you. Holy Father, protect them by the power of your name —the name you gave me—so that they may be one as we are one. 12 While I was with them, I protected them and kept them safe by that name you gave me. None has been lost except the child of hell so that Scripture would be fulfilled.

13 "I am coming to you now, but I say these things while I am still in the world, so that they may have the full measure of my joy within

[p] Or "Do you now believe?"

Greek Interlinear

ἔρχεται ὥρα ὅτε οὐκέτι ἐν παροιμίαις
comes   an hour when no longer in allegories

λαλήσω ὑμῖν, ἀλλὰ παρρησίᾳ περὶ τοῦ
I will speak to you, but plainly concerning the

πατρὸς ἀπαγγελῶ ὑμῖν. 26 ἐν ἐκείνῃ τῇ
Father will declare to you. In that -

ἡμέρᾳ ἐν τῷ ὀνόματί μου αἰτήσεσθε,
day in the name of me ye will ask,

καὶ οὐ λέγω ὑμῖν ὅτι ἐγὼ ἐρωτήσω
and I tell not you that I will request

τὸν πατέρα περὶ ὑμῶν· 27 αὐτὸς γὰρ
the Father concerning you; for [him]self

ὁ πατὴρ φιλεῖ ὑμᾶς, ὅτι ὑμεῖς ἐμὲ
the Father loves you, because ye me

πεφιλήκατε καὶ πεπιστεύκατε ὅτι ἐγὼ
have loved and have believed that I

παρὰ τοῦ θεοῦ ἐξῆλθον. 28 ἐξῆλθον
from - God came forth. I came forth

ἐκ τοῦ πατρὸς καὶ ἐλήλυθα εἰς τὸν
out of the Father and have come into the

κόσμον· πάλιν ἀφίημι τὸν κόσμον καὶ
world; again I leave the world and

πορεύομαι πρὸς τὸν πατέρα. 29 Λέγουσιν
go to the Father. Say

οἱ μαθηταὶ αὐτοῦ· ἴδε νῦν ἐν παρρησίᾳ
the disciples of him : Behold[,] now in plainness

λαλεῖς, καὶ παροιμίαν οὐδεμίαν λέγεις.
thou speakest, and ªallegory ¹no thou sayest.

30 νῦν οἴδαμεν ὅτι οἶδας πάντα καὶ
Now we know that thou knowest all things and

οὐ χρείαν ἔχεις ἵνα τίς σε ἐρωτᾷ· ἐν
no need hast that anyone thee should question; by

τούτῳ πιστεύομεν ὅτι ἀπὸ θεοῦ ἐξῆλθες.
this we believe that from God thou camest forth.

31 ἀπεκρίθη αὐτοῖς Ἰησοῦς· ἄρτι πιστεύετε;
Answered them Jesus : Now believe ye?

32 ἰδοὺ ἔρχεται ὥρα καὶ ἐλήλυθεν ἵνα
behold[,] comes an hour and has come that

σκορπισθῆτε ἕκαστος εἰς τὰ ἴδια κἀμὲ
ye are scattered each one to the(his) own and me

μόνον ἀφῆτε· καὶ οὐκ εἰμὶ μόνος, ὅτι
alone ye leave; and I am not alone, because

ὁ πατὴρ μετ' ἐμοῦ ἐστιν. 33 ταῦτα
the Father with me is. These things

λελάληκα ὑμῖν ἵνα ἐν ἐμοὶ εἰρήνην
I have spoken to you that in me peace

ἔχητε. ἐν τῷ κόσμῳ θλῖψιν ἔχετε·
ye may have. In the world distress ye have;

ἀλλὰ θαρσεῖτε, ἐγὼ νενίκηκα τὸν κόσμον.
but cheer ye up, I have overcome the world.

Chapter 17

Ταῦτα ἐλάλησεν Ἰησοῦς, καὶ ἐπάρας
These things spoke Jesus, and lifting up

τοὺς ὀφθαλμοὺς αὐτοῦ εἰς τὸν οὐρανὸν
the eyes of him to the heaven

εἶπεν· πάτερ, ἐλήλυθεν ἡ ὥρα· δόξασόν
said : Father, has come the hour; glorify

σου τὸν υἱόν, ἵνα ὁ υἱὸς δοξάσῃ σέ,
of thee the Son, that the Son may glorify thee,

2 καθὼς ἔδωκας αὐτῷ ἐξουσίαν πάσης
as thou gavest him authority of(over) all

σαρκός, ἵνα πᾶν ὃ δέδωκας αὐτῷ δώσῃ
flesh, that all which thou hast given him he may give

αὐτοῖς ζωὴν αἰώνιον. 3 αὕτη δέ ἐστιν
to them life eternal. And this is

ἡ αἰώνιος ζωή, ἵνα γινώσκωσιν σὲ τὸν
- eternal life, that they may know thee the

μόνον ἀληθινὸν θεὸν καὶ ὃν ἀπέστειλας
only true God and [he] whom thou didst send

Ἰησοῦν Χριστόν. 4 ἐγώ σε ἐδόξασα
Jesus Christ. I thee glorified

ἐπὶ τῆς γῆς, τὸ ἔργον τελειώσας ὃ
on the earth, the work finishing which

δέδωκάς μοι ἵνα ποιήσω· 5 καὶ νῦν
thou hast given to me that I should do; and now

δόξασόν με σύ, πάτερ, παρὰ σεαυτῷ
glorify me thou, Father, . with thyself

τῇ δόξῃ ᾗ εἶχον πρὸ τοῦ τὸν κόσμον
with the glory which I had before the the world
= before the world was

εἶναι παρὰ σοί. 6 Ἐφανέρωσά σου τὸ
to beᵇ with thee. I manifested of thee the

ὄνομα τοῖς ἀνθρώποις οὓς ἔδωκάς μοι
name to the men whom thou gavest to me

ἐκ τοῦ κόσμου. σοὶ ἦσαν κἀμοὶ αὐτοὺς
out of the world. To theeᶜ they were and to me them
= Thine

ἔδωκας, καὶ τὸν λόγον σου τετήρηκαν.
thou gavest, and the word of thee they have kept.

7 νῦν ἔγνωκαν ὅτι πάντα ὅσα δέδωκάς
Now they have known that all things as many as thou hast given

μοι παρὰ σοῦ εἰσιν· 8 ὅτι τὰ ῥήματα
to me from thee are; because the words

ἃ ἔδωκάς μοι δέδωκα αὐτοῖς, καὶ αὐτοὶ
which thou gavest to me I have given to them, and they

ἔλαβον, καὶ ἔγνωσαν ἀληθῶς ὅτι παρὰ
received, and knew truly that from

σοῦ ἐξῆλθον, καὶ ἐπίστευσαν ὅτι σύ
thee I came forth, and they believed that thou

με ἀπέστειλας. 9 ἐγὼ περὶ αὐτῶν ἐρωτῶ·
me didst send. I concerning them make request;

οὐ περὶ τοῦ κόσμου ἐρωτῶ, ἀλλὰ περὶ
not concerning the world do I make request, but concerning

ὧν δέδωκάς μοι, ὅτι σοί εἰσιν,
[those] whom thou hast given to me, because to theeᵉ they are,
= thine

10 καὶ τὰ ἐμὰ πάντα σά ἐστιν καὶ
and ⁸the ¹my things ¹all ⁴thine ⁴is(are) and

τὰ σὰ ἐμά, καὶ δεδόξασμαι ἐν αὐτοῖς.
the thy things mine, and I have been glorified in them.

11 καὶ οὐκέτι εἰμὶ ἐν τῷ κόσμῳ, καὶ
And no longer am I in the world, and

αὐτοὶ ἐν τῷ κόσμῳ εἰσίν, κἀγὼ πρὸς
they in the world are, and I to

σὲ ἔρχομαι. πάτερ ἅγιε, τήρησον αὐτοὺς
thee come. Father holy, keep them

ἐν τῷ ὀνόματί σου ᾧ δέδωκάς μοι,
in the name of thee which thou hast given to me,

ἵνα ὦσιν ἓν καθὼς ἡμεῖς. 12 ὅτε ἤμην
that they may be one as we. When I was

μετ' αὐτῶν, ἐγὼ ἐτήρουν αὐτοὺς ἐν
with them, I kept them in

τῷ ὀνόματί σου ᾧ δέδωκάς μοι, καὶ
the name of thee which thou hast given to me, and

ἐφύλαξα, καὶ οὐδεὶς ἐξ αὐτῶν ἀπώλετο
I guarded, and not one of them perished

εἰ μὴ ὁ υἱὸς τῆς ἀπωλείας, ἵνα ἡ
except the son - perdition, that the

γραφὴ πληρωθῇ. 13 νῦν δὲ πρὸς σὲ
scripture might be fulfilled. But now to thee

ἔρχομαι, καὶ ταῦτα λαλῶ ἐν τῷ κόσμῳ
I come, and these things I speak in the world

ἵνα ἔχωσιν τὴν χαρὰν τὴν ἐμὴν
that they may have the ¹joy - ¹my

325

King James Version

might have my joy fulfilled in themselves. 14 I have given them thy word; and the world hath hated them, because they are not of the world, even as I am not of the world. 15 I pray not that thou shouldest take them out of the world, but that thou shouldest keep them from the evil. 16 They are not of the world, even as I am not of the world. 17 Sanctify them through thy truth: thy word is truth. 18As thou hast sent me into the world, even so have I also sent them into the world. 19And for their sakes I sanctify myself, that they also might be sanctified through the truth. 20 Neither pray I for these alone, but for them also which shall believe on me through their word; 21 That they all may be one; as thou, Father, *art* in me, and I in thee, that they also may be one in us: that the world may believe that thou hast sent me. 22And the glory which thou gavest me I have given them; that they may be one, even as we are one: 23 I in them, and thou in me, that they may be made perfect in one; and that the world may know that thou hast sent me, and hast loved them, as thou hast loved me. 24 Father, I will that they also, whom thou hast given me, be with me where I am; that they may behold my glory, which thou hast given me: for thou lovedst me before the foundation of the world. 25 O righteous Father, the world hath not known thee: but I have known thee, and these have known that thou hast sent me. 26And I have declared unto them thy name, and will declare *it;* that the love wherewith thou hast loved me may be in them, and I in them.

New International Version

them. 14 I have given them your word and the world has hated them, for they are not of the world any more than I am of the world. 15 My prayer is not that you take them out of the world but that you protect them from the evil one. 16 They are not of the world, even as I am not of it. 17 Sanctify[q] them by the truth; your word is truth. 18As you sent me into the world, I have sent them into the world. 19 For them I sanctify[q] myself, that they too may be truly sanctified.[q]

Jesus prays for all believers

20 "My prayer is not for them alone. I pray also for those who will believe in me through their message, 21 that all of them may be one, Father, just as you are in me and I am in you. May they also be in us so that the world may believe that you have sent me. 22 I have given them the glory that you gave me, that they may be one as we are one: 23 I in them and you in me. May they be brought to complete unity to let the world know that you sent me and have loved them even as you have loved me.

24 "Father, I want those you have given me to be with me where I am, and to see my glory, the glory you have given me because you loved me before the creation of the world.

25 "Righteous Father, though the world does not know you, I know you, and they know that you have sent me. 26 I have revealed you[r] to them, and will continue to make you known in order that the love you have for me may be theirs and that I myself may be in them."

Jesus arrested

18 When Jesus had spoken these words, he went forth with his disciples over the brook Cedron, where was a garden, into the which he entered, and his disciples. 2And Judas also, which betrayed him, knew the place: for Jesus ofttimes resorted thither with his disciples. 3 Judas then, having received a band *of men* and officers from the chief priests and Pharisees, cometh thither with lanterns and torches and weapons. 4 Jesus therefore, knowing all things that should come upon him, went forth, and said unto them, Whom seek ye? 5 They answered him, Jesus of Nazareth. Jesus saith unto them, I am *he.* And Judas also, which betrayed him, stood with them. 6As soon then as he had said unto them, I am *he,* they went backward, and fell to the ground. 7 Then asked he them again, Whom seek ye? And they said, Jesus of Nazareth. 8 Jesus answered, I have told you that I am *he:* if therefore ye seek me, let these go their way: 9 That the saying might be fulfilled, which he spake, Of them which thou gavest me have I lost none. 10 Then Simon Peter having a sword drew it, and smote the high priest's serv-

18 When he had finished praying, Jesus left with his disciples and crossed the Kidron Valley. On the other side there was an olive grove, and he and his disciples went into it.

2 Now Judas, who betrayed him, knew the place, because Jesus had often met there with his disciples. 3 So Judas came to the grove, guiding a detachment of soldiers and some officials from the chief priests and Pharisees. They were carrying torches, lanterns and weapons.

4 Jesus, knowing all that was going to happen to him, went out and asked them, "Who is it you want?"

5 "Jesus of Nazareth," they replied.

"I am he," Jesus said. (And Judas the traitor was standing there with them.) 6 When Jesus said, "I am he," they drew back and fell to the ground.

7 Again he asked them, "Who is it you want?" And they said, "Jesus of Nazareth."

8 "I told you that I am he," Jesus answered. "If you are looking for me, then let these men go." 9 This happened so that the words he had spoken would be fulfilled: "I have not lost one of those you gave me."[s]

10 Then Simon Peter, who had a sword, drew it and struck the high priest's servant, cutting off

---

[q] Greek *hagiazo* (*set apart for sacred use or make holy*). [r] Or *have made your name known.* [s] John 6:39.

Greek Interlinear

πεπληρωμένην ἐν ἑαυτοῖς. **14** ἐγὼ δέδωκα
having been fulfilled in themselves.   I   have given

αὐτοῖς τὸν λόγον σου, καὶ ὁ κόσμος
to them the word of thee, and the world

ἐμίσησεν αὐτούς, ὅτι οὐκ εἰσὶν ἐκ τοῦ
hated   them, because they are not- of the

κόσμου καθὼς ἐγὼ οὐκ εἰμὶ ἐκ τοῦ
world   as   I   am not of the

κόσμου. **15** οὐκ ἐρωτῶ ἵνα ἄρῃς αὐτούς
world.   I do not request that thou shouldest take them

ἐκ τοῦ κόσμου, ἀλλ᾽ ἵνα τηρήσῃς αὐτοὺς
out of the world, but that thou shouldest keep them

ἐκ τοῦ πονηροῦ. **16** ἐκ τοῦ κόσμου
out of the evil [?one].   Of the world

οὐκ εἰσὶν καθὼς ἐγὼ οὐκ εἰμὶ ἐκ τοῦ
they are not as   I   am not of the

κόσμου. **17** ἁγίασον αὐτοὺς ἐν τῇ
world.   Sanctify   them in(?by) the

ἀληθείᾳ· ὁ λόγος ὁ σὸς ἀλήθειά ἐστιν.
truth;   the 'word the 'thy truth is.

18 καθὼς ἐμὲ ἀπέστειλας εἰς τὸν κόσμον,
As   me thou didst send into the world,

κἀγὼ ἀπέστειλα αὐτοὺς εἰς τὸν κόσμον·
I also   sent   them into the world;

19 καὶ ὑπὲρ αὐτῶν [ἐγὼ] ἁγιάζω ἐμαυτόν,
and on behalf of them   I sanctify myself,

ἵνα ὦσιν καὶ αὐτοὶ ἡγιασμένοι ἐν ἀληθείᾳ.
that 'may be 'also 'they having been sanctified in truth.

20 Οὐ περὶ τούτων δὲ ἐρωτῶ μόνον,
'Not 'concerning 'these 'but I make request only,

ἀλλὰ καὶ περὶ τῶν πιστευόντων διὰ
but also concerning the [ones] believing through

τοῦ λόγου αὐτῶν εἰς ἐμέ, **21** ἵνα πάντες
the word of them in me,   that all

ἓν ὦσιν, καθὼς σύ, πάτηρ, ἐν ἐμοὶ
one may be, as thou, Father, in me

κἀγὼ ἐν σοί, ἵνα καὶ αὐτοὶ ἐν ἡμῖν
and I in thee, that also they in us

ὦσιν, ἵνα ὁ κόσμος πιστεύῃ ὅτι σύ
may be, that the world may believe that thou

με ἀπέστειλας. **22** κἀγὼ τὴν δόξαν ἣν
me didst send.   And I the glory which

δέδωκάς μοι δέδωκα αὐτοῖς, ἵνα ὦσιν
thou hast given to me have given to them, that they may be

ἓν καθὼς ἡμεῖς ἕν· **23** ἐγὼ ἐν αὐτοῖς
one as we [are] one;   I in them

καὶ σὺ ἐν ἐμοί, ἵνα ὦσιν τετελειωμένοι
and thou in me, that they may be having been perfected

εἰς ἕν, ἵνα γινώσκῃ ὁ κόσμος ὅτι σύ
in one, that may know the world that thou

με ἀπέστειλας καὶ ἠγάπησας αὐτοὺς
me didst send and didst love them

καθὼς ἐμὲ ἠγάπησας. **24** Πάτηρ, ὃ
as   me thou didst love.   Father, what

δέδωκάς μοι, θέλω ἵνα ὅπου εἰμὶ ἐγὼ
thou hast given to me, I wish that where am I

κἀκεῖνοι ὦσιν μετ᾽ ἐμοῦ, ἵνα θεωρῶσιν
those also may be with me, that they may behold

τὴν δόξαν τὴν ἐμήν, ἣν δέδωκάς μοι
the 'glory – 'my, which thou hast given to me

ὅτι ἠγάπησάς με πρὸ καταβολῆς κόσμου.
because thou didst love me before [the] foundation of [the] world.

25 πάτηρ δίκαιε, καὶ ὁ κόσμος σε
Father righteous, indeed the world thee

οὐκ ἔγνω, ἐγὼ δέ σε ἔγνων, καὶ οὗτοι
knew not, but I thee knew, and these

ἔγνωσαν ὅτι σύ με ἀπέστειλας· **26** καὶ
knew   that thou me didst send;   and

ἐγνώρισα αὐτοῖς τὸ ὄνομά σου καὶ
I made known to them the name of thee and

γνωρίσω, ἵνα ἡ ἀγάπη ἣν ἠγάπησάς
will make known, that the love [with] which thou lovedst

με ἐν αὐτοῖς ᾖ κἀγὼ ἐν αὐτοῖς.
me in them may be and I in them.

Chapter 18

Ταῦτα εἰπὼν Ἰησοῦς ἐξῆλθεν σὺν
These things having said Jesus went forth with

τοῖς μαθηταῖς αὐτοῦ πέραν τοῦ χειμάρρου
the disciples of him across the torrent

τοῦ Κεδρών, ὅπου ἦν κῆπος, εἰς ὃν
– Kedron, where there was a garden, into which

εἰσῆλθεν αὐτὸς καὶ οἱ μαθηταὶ αὐτοῦ.
entered   he and the disciples of him.

2 ᾔδει δὲ καὶ Ἰούδας ὁ παραδιδοὺς
'Now 'knew 'also 'Judas 'the [one] 'betraying

αὐτὸν τὸν τόπον, ὅτι πολλάκις συνήχθη
'him 'the 'place, because often assembled

Ἰησοῦς ἐκεῖ μετὰ τῶν μαθητῶν αὐτου.
Jesus there with the disciples of him.

3 ὁ οὖν Ἰούδας λαβὼν τὴν σπεῖραν
– Therefore Judas taking the band

καὶ ἐκ τῶν ἀρχιερέων καὶ [ἐκ] τῶν
and 'from 'the 'chief priests 'and 'from 'the

Φαρισαίων ὑπηρέτας ἔρχεται ἐκεῖ μετὰ
'Pharisees 'attendants comes there with

φανῶν καὶ λαμπάδων καὶ ὅπλων. **4** Ἰησοῦς
lanterns and lamps and weapons. Jesus

οὖν εἰδὼς πάντα τὰ ἐρχόμενα ἐπ᾽ αὐτὸν
therefore knowing all the things coming on him

ἐξῆλθεν καὶ λέγει αὐτοῖς· τίνα ζητεῖτε;
went forth and says to them : Whom seek ye?

5 ἀπεκρίθησαν αὐτῷ· Ἰησοῦν τὸν
They answered   him :   Jesus the

Ναζωραῖον. λέγει αὐτοῖς· ἐγώ εἰμι.
Nazarene. He tells them : I am.

εἱστήκει δὲ καὶ Ἰούδας ὁ παραδιδοὺς
Now stood also Judas the [one] betraying

αὐτὸν μετ᾽ αὐτῶν. **6** ὡς οὖν εἶπεν
him with them.   When therefore he told

αὐτοῖς· ἐγώ εἰμι, ἀπῆλθαν εἰς τὰ ὀπίσω
them :   I am, they went away back †

καὶ ἔπεσαν χαμαί. **7** πάλιν οὖν
and fell on the ground. Again therefore

ἐπηρώτησεν αὐτούς· τίνα ζητεῖτε; οἱ δὲ
he questioned them : Whom seek ye? And they

εἶπαν· Ἰησοῦν τὸν Ναζωραῖον. **8** ἀπεκρίθη
said : Jesus the Nazarene.   Answered

Ἰησοῦς· εἶπον ὑμῖν ὅτι ἐγώ εἰμι· εἰ
Jesus : I told you that I am; if

οὖν ἐμὲ ζητεῖτε, ἄφετε τούτους ὑπάγειν·
therefore me ye seek, allow these to go;

9 ἵνα πληρωθῇ ὁ λόγος ὃν εἶπεν, ὅτι
that might be fulfilled the word which he said,

οὓς δέδωκάς μοι, οὐκ ἀπώλεσα ἐξ
[Those] whom thou hast given to me, I lost not of

αὐτῶν οὐδένα. **10** Σίμων οὖν Πέτρος
them no(any)one.   'Simon 'therefore 'Peter

ἔχων μάχαιραν εἵλκυσεν αὐτὴν καὶ ἔπαισεν
having a sword drew it and smote

τὸν τοῦ ἀρχιερέως δοῦλον καὶ ἀπέκοψεν
'the 'of the 'high priest 'slave and cut off

King James Version

ant, and cut off his right ear. The servant's name was Malchus. 11 Then said Jesus unto Peter, Put up thy sword into the sheath: the cup which my Father hath given me, shall I not drink it? 12 Then the band and the captain and officers of the Jews took Jesus, and bound him, 13And led him away to Annas first; for he was father in law to Caiaphas, which was the high priest that same year. 14 Now Caiaphas was he, which gave counsel to the Jews, that it was expedient that one man should die for the people.

15 And Simon Peter followed Jesus, and *so did* another disciple: that disciple was known unto the high priest, and went in with Jesus into the palace of the high priest. 16 But Peter stood at the door without. Then went out that other disciple, which was known unto the high priest, and spake unto her that kept the door, and brought in Peter. 17 Then saith the damsel that kept the door unto Peter, Art not thou also *one* of this man's disciples? He saith, I am not. 18And the servants and officers stood there, who had made a fire of coals, for it was cold; and they warmed themselves: and Peter stood with them, and warmed himself.

19 The high priest then asked Jesus of his disciples, and of his doctrine. 20 Jesus answered him, I spake openly to the world; I ever taught in the synagogue, and in the temple, whither the Jews always resort; and in secret have I said nothing. 21 Why askest thou me? ask them which heard me, what I have said unto them: behold, they know what I said. 22And when he had thus spoken, one of the officers which stood by struck Jesus with the palm of his hand, saying, Answerest thou the high priest so? 23 Jesus answered him, If I have spoken evil, bear witness of the evil: but if well, why smitest thou me? 24 Now Annas had sent him bound unto Caiaphas the high priest. 25And Simon Peter stood and warmed himself. They said therefore unto him, Art not thou also *one* of his disciples? He denied *it,* and said, I am not. 26 One of the servants of the high priest, being *his* kinsman whose ear Peter cut off, saith, Did not I see thee in the garden with him? 27 Peter then denied again; and immediately the cock crew.

28 Then led they Jesus from Caiaphas unto the hall of judgment: and it was early; and they

New International Version

his right ear. (The servant's name was Malchus.)

11 Jesus commanded Peter, "Put your sword away! Shall I not drink the cup the Father has given me?"

Jesus taken to Annas

12 Then the detachment of soldiers with its commander and the Jewish officials arrested Jesus. They bound him 13 and brought him first to Annas, who was the father-in-law of Caiaphas, the high priest that year. 14 Caiaphas was the one who had advised the Jews that it would be good if one man died for the people.

Peter's first denial

15 Simon Peter and another disciple were following Jesus. Because this disciple was known to the high priest, he went with Jesus into the high priest's courtyard, 16 but Peter had to wait outside at the door. The other disciple, who was known to the high priest, came back, spoke to the girl on duty there, and brought Peter in.

17 "Surely you are not another of this man's disciples?" the girl at the door asked Peter.

He replied, "I am not."

18 It was cold, and the servants and officials stood around a fire they had made to keep warm. Peter also was standing with them, warming himself.

The high priest questions Jesus

19 Meanwhile, the high priest questioned Jesus about his disciples and his teaching.

20 "I have spoken openly to the world," Jesus replied. "I always taught in synagogues or at the temple, where all the Jews come together. I said nothing in secret. 21 Why question me? Ask those who heard me. Surely they know what I said."

22 When Jesus had said this, one of the officials nearby struck him in the face. "Is that any way to answer the high priest?" he demanded.

23 "If I said something wrong," Jesus replied, "speak up about it. But if I spoke the truth, why did you hit me?" 24 Then Annas sent him, still bound, to Caiaphas the high priest.*

Peter's second and third denials

25 As Simon Peter stood warming himself, he was asked, "Surely you are not another of his disciples?"

He denied it, saying, "I am not."

26 One of the high priest's servants, a relative of the man whose ear Peter had cut off, challenged him, "Didn't I see you with him in the olive grove?" 27Again Peter denied it, and at that moment a rooster began to crow.

Jesus before Pilate

28 Then the Jews led Jesus from Caiaphas to the palace of the Roman governor. By now it

[t] Or (*Now Annas had sent him, still bound to Caiaphas the high priest.*)

Greek Interlinear

αὐτοῦ τὸ ὠτάριον τὸ δεξιόν· ἦν δὲ
of him the 'ear - 'right; and was

ὄνομα τῷ δούλῳ Μάλχος. 11 εἶπεν οὖν
name to the slave⁰ Malchus. Said therefore

ὁ Ἰησοῦς τῷ Πέτρῳ· βάλε τὴν μάχαιραν
- Jesus - to Peter : Put the sword

εἰς τὴν θήκην· τὸ ποτήριον ὃ δέδωκέν
into the sheath; the cup which has given

μοι ὁ πατήρ, οὐ μὴ πίω αὐτό;
to me the Father, by no means shall I drink it?

12 Ἡ οὖν σπεῖρα καὶ ὁ χιλίαρχος
Therefore the band and the chiliarch

καὶ οἱ ὑπηρέται τῶν Ἰουδαίων συνέλαβον
and the attendants of the Jews took

τὸν Ἰησοῦν · καὶ ἔδησαν αὐτόν, 13 καὶ
- Jesus and bound him, and

ἤγαγον πρὸς Ἄνναν πρῶτον· ἦν γὰρ
led to Annas first; for he was

πενθερὸς τοῦ Καϊάφα, ὃς ἦν ἀρχιερεὺς
father-in-law of Caiaphas, who was high priest

τοῦ ἐνιαυτοῦ ἐκείνου· 14 ἦν δὲ Καϊάφας
- year of that; now it was Caiaphas

ὁ συμβουλεύσας τοῖς Ἰουδαίοις ὅτι
the [one] having advised the Jews that

συμφέρει ἕνα ἄνθρωπον ἀποθανεῖν ὑπὲρ
it is(was) expedient one man to die on behalf of

τοῦ λαοῦ. 15 Ἠκολούθει δὲ τῷ Ἰησοῦ
the people. And followed - Jesus

Σίμων Πέτρος καὶ ἄλλος μαθητής. ὁ δὲ
Simon Peter and another disciple. - And

μαθητὴς ἐκεῖνος ἦν γνωστὸς τῷ ἀρχιερεῖ,
disciple that was known to the high priest,

καὶ συνεισῆλθεν τῷ Ἰησοῦ εἰς τὴν αὐλὴν
and entered with - Jesus into the court

τοῦ ἀρχιερέως, 16 ὁ δὲ Πέτρος εἱστήκει
of the high priest, - but Peter stood

πρὸς τῇ θύρᾳ ἔξω. ἐξῆλθεν οὖν ὁ
at the door outside. Went out therefore the

μαθητὴς ὁ ἄλλος ὁ γνωστὸς τοῦ ἀρχιερέως
¹disciple - 'other - known of(to) the high priest

καὶ εἶπεν τῇ θυρωρῷ, καὶ εἰσήγαγεν
and told the portress, and brought in

τὸν Πέτρον. 17 λέγει οὖν τῷ Πέτρῳ ἡ
- Peter. Says therefore - to Peter the

παιδίσκη ἡ θυρωρός· μὴ καὶ σὺ ἐκ
maidservant the portress: Not also thou of

τῶν μαθητῶν εἶ τοῦ ἀνθρώπου τούτου;
the disciples art - man of this?

λέγει ἐκεῖνος· οὐκ εἰμί. 18 εἱστήκεισαν δὲ
Says that one : I am not. And stood

οἱ δοῦλοι καὶ οἱ ὑπηρέται ἀνθρακιὰν
the slaves and the attendants a fire

πεποιηκότες, ὅτι ψῦχος ἦν, καὶ
having made, because cold it was, and

ἐθερμαίνοντο· ἦν δὲ καὶ ὁ Πέτρος μετ'
were warming themselves; and was also - Peter with

αὐτῶν ἑστὼς καὶ θερμαινόμενος. 19 Ὁ
them standing and warming himself. - ¹The

οὖν ἀρχιερεὺς ἠρώτησεν τὸν Ἰησοῦν
⁰therefore ⁴high priest questioned - Jesus

περὶ τῶν μαθητῶν αὐτοῦ καὶ περὶ τῆς
about the disciples of him and about the

διδαχῆς αὐτοῦ. 20 ἀπεκρίθη αὐτῷ Ἰησοῦς·
teaching of him. Answered him Jesus :

ἐγὼ παρρησίᾳ λελάληκα τῷ κόσμῳ· ἐγὼ
I with plainness have spoken to the world; I

πάντοτε ἐδίδαξα ἐν συναγωγῇ καὶ ἐν
always taught in a synagogue and in

τῷ ἱερῷ, ὅπου πάντες οἱ Ἰουδαῖοι
the temple, where all the Jews

συνέρχονται, καὶ ἐν κρυπτῷ ἐλάλησα
come together, and in secret I spoke

οὐδέν. 21 τί με ἐρωτᾷς; ἐρώτησον
nothing. Why me questionest thou? question

τοὺς ἀκηκοότας τί ἐλάλησα αὐτοῖς· ἴδε
the [ones] having heard what I spoke to them; behold[,]

οὗτοι οἴδασιν ἃ εἶπον ἐγώ. 22 ταῦτα
these know what things said I. These things

δὲ αὐτοῦ εἰπόντος εἷς παρεστηκὼς τῶν
and him saying⁰ one standing by of the
= And as he said this

ὑπηρετῶν ἔδωκεν ῥάπισμα τῷ Ἰησοῦ
attendants gave a blow - to Jesus

εἰπών· οὕτως ἀποκρίνῃ τῷ ἀρχιερεῖ;
saying: Thus answerest thou the high priest?

23 ἀπεκρίθη αὐτῷ Ἰησοῦς· εἰ κακῶς
Answered him Jesus: If ill

ἐλάλησα, μαρτύρησον περὶ τοῦ κακοῦ·
I spoke, witness concerning the evil;

εἰ δὲ καλῶς, τί με δέρεις; 24 ἀπέστειλεν
but if well, why me beatest thou? ¹Sent

οὖν αὐτὸν ὁ Ἄννας δεδεμένον πρὸς
⁰therefore ⁴him ¹ 'Annas having been bound to

Καϊάφαν τὸν ἀρχιερέα. 25 Ἦν δὲ Σίμων
Caiaphas the high priest. Now was Simon

Πέτρος ἑστὼς καὶ θερμαινόμενος. εἶπον
Peter standing and warming himself. They said

οὖν αὐτῷ· μὴ καὶ σὺ ἐκ τῶν μαθητῶν
therefore to him: Not also thou of the disciples

αὐτοῦ εἶ; ἠρνήσατο ἐκεῖνος καὶ εἶπεν·
of him art? Denied that one and said :

οὐκ εἰμί. 26 λέγει εἷς ἐκ τῶν δούλων τοῦ
I am not. Says one of the slaves of the

ἀρχιερέως, συγγενὴς ὢν οὗ ἀπέκοψεν
high priest, ¹a relative 'being ³[of him] of whom ²cut off

Πέτρος τὸ ὠτίον· οὐκ ἐγώ σε εἶδον
⁴Peter ⁵the ⁶ear : ²Not ⁸I ⁴thee ¹saw

ἐν τῷ κήπῳ μετ' αὐτοῦ; 27 πάλιν οὖν
in the garden with him? Again therefore

ἠρνήσατο Πέτρος, καὶ εὐθέως ἀλέκτωρ
denied Peter, and immediately a cock

ἐφώνησεν.
sounded(crew).

28 Ἄγουσιν οὖν τὸν Ἰησοῦν ἀπὸ τοῦ
They lead therefore - Jesus from -

Καϊάφα εἰς τὸ πραιτώριον· ἦν δὲ πρωΐ·
Caiaphas .to the prætorium; and it was early;

King James Version

themselves went not into the judgment hall, lest they should be defiled; but that they might eat the passover. 29 Pilate then went out unto them, and said, What accusation bring ye against this man? 30 They answered and said unto him, If he were not a malefactor, we would not have delivered him up unto thee. 31 Then said Pilate unto them, Take ye him, and judge him according to your law. The Jews therefore said unto him, It is not lawful for us to put any man to death: 32 That the saying of Jesus might be fulfilled, which he spake, signifying what death he should die. 33 Then Pilate entered into the judgment hall again, and called Jesus, and said unto him, Art thou the King of the Jews? 34 Jesus answered him, Sayest thou this thing of thyself, or did others tell it thee of me? 35 Pilate answered, Am I a Jew? Thine own nation and the chief priests have delivered thee unto me: what hast thou done? 36 Jesus answered, My kingdom is not of this world: if my kingdom were of this world, then would my servants fight, that I should not be delivered to the Jews: but now is my kingdom not from hence. 37 Pilate therefore said unto him, Art thou a king then? Jesus answered, Thou sayest that I am a king. To this end was I born, and for this cause came I into the world, that I should bear witness unto the truth. Every one that is of the truth heareth my voice. 38 Pilate saith unto him, What is truth? And when he had said this, he went out again unto the Jews, and saith unto them, I find in him no fault *at all*. 39 But ye have a custom, that I should release unto you one at the passover: will ye therefore that I release unto you the King of the Jews? 40 Then cried they all again, saying, Not this man, but Barabbas. Now Barabbas was a robber.

New International Version

was early morning, and to avoid ceremonial uncleanness the Jews did not enter the palace; they wanted to be able to eat the Passover. 29 So Pilate came out to them and asked, "What charges are you bringing against this man?"

30 "If he were not a criminal," they replied, "we would not have handed him over to you."

31 Pilate said, "Take him yourselves and judge him by your own law."

"But we have no right to execute anyone," the Jews objected. 32 This happened so that the words Jesus had spoken indicating the kind of death he was going to die would be fulfilled.

33 Pilate then went back inside the palace, summoned Jesus, and asked him, "Are you the king of the Jews?"

34 "Is that your own idea," Jesus asked, "or did others talk to you about me?"

35 "Do you think I am a Jew?" Pilate replied. "It was your people and your chief priests who handed you over to me. What is it you have done?"

36 Jesus said, "My kingdom is not of this world. If it were, my servants would fight to prevent my arrest by the Jews. But now my kingdom is from another place."

37 "You are a king, then!" said Pilate.

Jesus answered, "You are right in saying I am a king. In fact, for this reason I was born, and for this I came into the world, to testify to the truth. Everyone on the side of truth listens to me."

38 "What is truth?" Pilate asked. With this he went out again to the Jews and said, "I find no basis for a charge against him. 39 But it is your custom for me to release to you one prisoner at the time of the Passover. Do you want me to release 'the king of the Jews'?"

40 They shouted back, "No, not him! Give us Barabbas!" Now Barabbas had taken part in a rebellion.

Jesus sentenced to be crucified

19 Then Pilate therefore took Jesus, and scourged *him*. 2 And the soldiers platted a crown of thorns, and put *it* on his head, and they put on him a purple robe, 3 And said, Hail, King of the Jews! and they smote him with their hands. 4 Pilate therefore went forth again, and saith unto them, Behold, I bring him forth to you, that ye may know that I find no fault in him. 5 Then came Jesus forth, wearing the crown of thorns, and the purple robe. And *Pilate* saith unto them, Behold the man! 6 When the chief priests therefore and officers saw him, they cried out, saying, Crucify *him*, crucify *him*. Pilate saith unto them, Take ye him, and crucify *him*: for I find no fault in him. 7 The Jews answered him, We have a law, and by our law he ought to die, because he made himself the Son of God.

19 Then Pilate took Jesus and had him flogged. 2 The soldiers twisted together a crown of thorns and put it on his head. They clothed him in a purple robe 3 and went up to him again and again, saying, "Hail, O king of the Jews!" And they struck him in the face.

4 Once more Pilate came out and said to the Jews, "Look, I am bringing him out to you to let you know that I find no basis for a charge against him." 5 When Jesus came out wearing the crown of thorns and the purple robe, Pilate said to them, "Here is the man!"

6 As soon as the chief priests and their officials saw him, they shouted, "Crucify! Crucify!"

But Pilate answered, "You take him and crucify him. As for me, I find no basis for a charge against him."

7 The Jews insisted, "We have a law, and according to that law he must die, because he claimed to be the Son of God."

Greek Interlinear

καὶ αὐτοὶ οὐκ εἰσῆλθον εἰς τὸ πραιτώριον,
and they entered not into the prætorium,

ἵνα μὴ μιανθῶσιν ἀλλὰ φάγωσιν τὸ
lest they should be defiled but might eat the

πάσχα. **29** ἐξῆλθεν οὖν ὁ Πιλᾶτος ἔξω
passover. Went forth therefore – Pilate outside

πρὸς αὐτοὺς καὶ φησίν· τίνα κατηγορίαν
to them and says: What accusation

φέρετε τοῦ ἀνθρώπου τούτου; **30** ἀπεκρίθησαν
bring ye – man of this? They answered

καὶ εἶπαν αὐτῷ· εἰ μὴ ἦν
and said to him: Unless was

οὗτος κακὸν ποιῶν, οὐκ ἄν σοι
this man evil doing, ¹would ²not ³to thee

παρεδώκαμεν αὐτόν. **31** εἶπεν οὖν αὐτοῖς
¹we ⁴have ⁵delivered ⁶him. Said therefore to them

ὁ Πιλᾶτος· λάβετε αὐτὸν ὑμεῖς, καὶ
– Pilate: Take him ye, and

κατὰ τὸν νόμον ὑμῶν κρίνατε αὐτόν.
according to the law of you judge ye him.

εἶπον αὐτῷ οἱ Ἰουδαῖοι· ἡμῖν οὐκ ἔξεστιν
Said to him the Jews: For us it is not lawful

ἀποκτεῖναι οὐδένα· **32** ἵνα ὁ λόγος τοῦ
to kill no(any)one; that the word –

Ἰησοῦ πληρωθῇ ὃν εἶπεν σημαίνων ποίῳ
of Jesus might be fulfilled which he said signifying by what

θανάτῳ ἤμελλεν ἀποθνήσκειν. **33** Εἰσῆλθεν
death he was about to die. Entered

οὖν πάλιν εἰς τὸ πραιτώριον ὁ Πιλᾶτος
therefore again into the prætorium – Pilate

καὶ ἐφώνησεν τὸν Ἰησοῦν καὶ εἶπεν
and called – Jesus and said

αὐτῷ· σὺ εἶ ὁ βασιλεὺς τῶν Ἰουδαίων;
to him: Thou art the king of the Jews?

34 ἀπεκρίθη Ἰησοῦς· ἀφ᾽ ἑαυτοῦ σὺ τοῦτο
Answered Jesus: From [thy]self ¹thou ²this

λέγεις, ἢ ἄλλοι εἶπόν σοι περὶ ἐμοῦ;
¹sayest, or others told thee about me?

35 ἀπεκρίθη ὁ Πιλᾶτος· μήτι ἐγὼ
Answered – Pilate: not I

Ἰουδαῖός εἰμι; τὸ ἔθνος τὸ σὸν καὶ
a Jew am? the ²nation – ¹thy and

οἱ ἀρχιερεῖς παρέδωκάν σε ἐμοί· τί
the chief priests delivered thee to me; what

ἐποίησας; **36** ἀπεκρίθη Ἰησοῦς· ἡ βασιλεία
didst thou? Answered Jesus: The ¹kingdom

ἡ ἐμὴ οὐκ ἔστιν ἐκ τοῦ κόσμου τούτου·
– ¹my is not of – world this;

εἰ ἐκ τοῦ κόσμου τούτου ἦν ἡ βασιλεία
if of – world this was the ¹kingdom

ἡ ἐμή, οἱ ὑπηρέται ἂν οἱ ἐμοὶ ἠγωνίζοντο,
– ¹my, the ²attendants ¹would – ¹my ⁴have struggled,

ἵνα μὴ παραδοθῶ τοῖς Ἰουδαίοις· νῦν
that I should not be delivered to the Jews; ¹now

δὲ ἡ βασιλεία ἡ ἐμὴ οὐκ ἔστιν ἐντεῦθεν.
¹but the ¹kingdom – ¹my is not hence.

37 εἶπεν οὖν αὐτῷ ὁ Πιλᾶτος· οὐκοῦν
Said therefore to him – Pilate: Not really

βασιλεὺς εἶ σύ; ἀπεκρίθη [ὁ] Ἰησοῦς·
a king art thou? Answered Jesus:

σὺ λέγεις ὅτι βασιλεύς εἰμι. ἐγὼ εἰς
Thou sayest that a king I am. I for

τοῦτο γεγέννημαι καὶ εἰς τοῦτο ἐλήλυθα
this have been born and for this I have come

εἰς τὸν κόσμον, ἵνα μαρτυρήσω τῇ
into the world, that I might witness to the

ἀληθείᾳ· πᾶς ὁ ὢν ἐκ τῆς ἀληθείας
truth; everyone being of the truth

ἀκούει μου τῆς φωνῆς. **38** λέγει αὐτῷ
hears of me the voice. Says to him

ὁ Πιλᾶτος· τί ἐστιν ἀλήθεια; Καὶ
– Pilate: What is truth? And

τοῦτο εἰπὼν πάλιν ἐξῆλθεν πρὸς τοὺς
this having said again he went forth to the

Ἰουδαίους, καὶ λέγει αὐτοῖς· ἐγὼ οὐδεμίαν
Jews, and tells them: ¹I ²no

εὑρίσκω ἐν αὐτῷ αἰτίαν. **39** ἔστιν δὲ
³find ⁴in ⁵him ⁴crime. But there is

συνήθεια ὑμῖν ἵνα ἕνα ἀπολύσω ὑμῖν
a custom to you⁴ that one I should release to you

ἐν τῷ πάσχα· βούλεσθε οὖν ἀπολύσω
at the Passover; will ye therefore [that] I release

ὑμῖν τὸν βασιλέα τῶν Ἰουδαίων; **40** ἐκραύ-
to you the king of the Jews? They cried

γασαν οὖν πάλιν λέγοντες· μὴ τοῦτον,
out therefore again saying: Not this man,

ἀλλὰ τὸν Βαραββᾶν. ἦν δὲ ὁ Βαραββᾶς
but – Barabbas. ¹But ²was – ²Barabbas

Chapter 19

λῃστής. **19** Τότε οὖν ἔλαβεν ὁ Πιλᾶτος
²a robber. Then therefore ²took – ¹Pilate

τὸν Ἰησοῦν καὶ ἐμαστίγωσεν. **2** καὶ οἱ
– ²Jesus and scourged [him]. And the

στρατιῶται πλέξαντες στέφανον ἐξ ἀκανθῶν
soldiers having plaited a wreath out of thorns

ἐπέθηκαν αὐτοῦ τῇ κεφαλῇ, καὶ ἱμάτιον
put [it] on of him the head, and ²garment

πορφυροῦν περιέβαλον αὐτόν, **3** καὶ ἤρχοντο
²a purple ¹threw round ²him, and came

πρὸς αὐτὸν καὶ ἔλεγον· χαῖρε ὁ βασιλεὺς
to him and said: Hail[,] king

τῶν Ἰουδαίων· καὶ ἐδίδοσαν αὐτῷ
of the Jews; and they gave him

ῥαπίσματα. **4** Καὶ ἐξῆλθεν πάλιν ἔξω
blows. And went forth again outside

ὁ Πιλᾶτος καὶ λέγει αὐτοῖς· ἴδε ἄγω
– Pilate and says to them: Behold ¹I bring

ὑμῖν αὐτὸν ἔξω, ἵνα γνῶτε ὅτι οὐδεμίαν
²to you ³him ⁴out, that ye may know that no

αἰτίαν εὑρίσκω ἐν αὐτῷ. **5** ἐξῆλθεν
crime I find in him. Came forth

οὖν ὁ Ἰησοῦς ἔξω, φορῶν τὸν ἀκάνθινον
therefore – Jesus outside, wearing the thorny

στέφανον καὶ τὸ πορφυροῦν ἱμάτιον. καὶ
wreath and the purple garment. And

λέγει αὐτοῖς· ἰδοὺ ὁ ἄνθρωπος. **6** ὅτε
he says to them: Behold[,] the man. When

οὖν εἶδον αὐτὸν οἱ ἀρχιερεῖς καὶ οἱ
therefore saw him the chief priests and the

ὑπηρέται, ἐκραύγασαν λέγοντες· σταύρωσον
attendants, they shouted saying: Crucify[,]

σταύρωσον. λέγει αὐτοῖς ὁ Πιλᾶτος·
crucify. Says to them – Pilate:

λάβετε αὐτὸν ὑμεῖς καὶ σταυρώσατε·
¹Take ²him ³ye and crucify;

ἐγὼ γὰρ οὐχ εὑρίσκω ἐν αὐτῷ αἰτίαν.
for I find not in him crime.

7 ἀπεκρίθησαν αὐτῷ οἱ Ἰουδαῖοι· ἡμεῖς
Answered him the Jews: We

νόμον ἔχομεν, καὶ κατὰ τὸν νόμον
a law have, and according to the law

ὀφείλει ἀποθανεῖν, ὅτι υἱὸν θεοῦ ἑαυτὸν
he ought to die, because Son of God himself

King James Version

8 When Pilate therefore heard that saying, he was the more afraid; 9And went again into the judgment hall, and saith unto Jesus, Whence art thou? But Jesus gave him no answer. 10 Then saith Pilate unto him, Speakest thou not unto me? knowest thou not that I have power to crucify thee, and have power to release thee? 11 Jesus answered, Thou couldest have no power *at all* against me, except it were given thee from above: therefore he that delivered me unto thee hath the greater sin. 12And from thenceforth Pilate sought to release him: but the Jews cried out, saying, If thou let this man go, thou art not Cesar's friend: whosoever maketh himself a king speaketh against Cesar.

13 When Pilate therefore heard that saying, he brought Jesus forth, and sat down in the judgment seat in a place that is called the Pavement, but in the Hebrew, Gabbatha. 14And it was the preparation of the passover, and about the sixth hour: and he saith unto the Jews, Behold your King! 15 But they cried out, Away with *him*, away with *him*, crucify him. Pilate saith unto them, Shall I crucify your King? The chief priests answered, We have no king but Cesar. 16 Then delivered he him therefore unto them to be crucified. And they took Jesus, and led *him* away. 17And he bearing his cross went forth into a place called *the place* of a skull, which is called in the Hebrew Golgotha: 18 Where they crucified him, and two others with him, on either side one, and Jesus in the midst.

19 And Pilate wrote a title, and put *it* on the cross. And the writing was, JESUS OF NAZARETH THE KING OF THE JEWS. 20 This title then read many of the Jews; for the place where Jesus was crucified was nigh to the city: and it was written in Hebrew, *and* Greek, *and* Latin. 21 Then said the chief priests of the Jews to Pilate, Write not, The King of the Jews; but that he said, I am King of the Jews. 22 Pilate answered, What I have written I have written.

23 Then the soldiers, when they had crucified Jesus, took his garments, and made four parts, to every soldier a part; and also *his* coat: now the coat was without seam, woven from the top throughout. 24 They said therefore among themselves, Let us not rend it, but cast lots for it, whose it shall be: that the Scripture might be fulfilled, which saith, They parted my raiment among them, and for my vesture they did cast lots. These things therefore the soldiers did.

25 Now there stood by the cross of Jesus his mother, and his mother's sister, Mary the *wife* of Cleophas, and Mary Magdalene. 26 When Jesus therefore saw his mother, and the disciple standing by, whom he loved, he saith unto his mother, Woman, behold thy son! 27 Then saith he to the disciple, Behold thy mother! And from that hour that disciple took her unto his own *home*.

New International Version

8 When Pilate heard this, he was even more afraid, 9 and he went back inside the palace. "Where do you come from?" he asked Jesus, but Jesus gave him no answer. 10 "Do you refuse to speak to me?" Pilate said. "Don't you realize I have power either to free you or to crucify you?"

11 Jesus answered, "You have no power over me that was not given to you from above. Therefore the one who handed me over to you is guilty of a greater sin."

12 From then on, Pilate tried to set Jesus free, but the Jews kept shouting, "If you let this man go, you are no friend of Caesar. Anyone who claims to be a king opposes Caesar."

13 When Pilate heard this, he brought Jesus out and sat down on the judge's seat at a place known as The Stone Pavement (which in Aramaic is Gabbatha). 14 It was the day of Preparation of Passover Week, about the sixth hour.

"Here is your king," Pilate said to the Jews.

15 But they shouted, "Take him away! Take him away! Crucify him!"

"Shall I crucify your king?" Pilate asked.

"We have no king but Caesar," the chief priests answered.

16 Finally Pilate handed him over to them to be crucified.

The crucifixion

So the soldiers took charge of Jesus. 17 Carrying his own cross, he went out to The Place of the Skull (which in Aramaic is called Golgotha). 18 Here they crucified him, with him two others—one on either side and Jesus in the middle.

19 Pilate had a notice prepared and fastened to the cross. It read, JESUS OF NAZARETH, THE KING OF THE JEWS. 20 Many of the Jews read this sign, for the place where Jesus was crucified was near the city, and the sign was written in Aramaic, Latin and Greek. 21 The chief priests of the Jews protested to Pilate, "Do not write 'The King of the Jews,' but that this man claimed to be king of the Jews."

22 Pilate answered, "What I have written, I have written."

23 When the soldiers crucified Jesus, they took his clothes, dividing them into four shares, one for each of them, with the undergarment remaining. This garment was seamless, woven in one piece from top to bottom.

24 "Let's not tear it," they said to one another. "Let's decide by lot who will get it."

This happened that the scripture might be fulfilled which said,

"They divided my garments among themselves
    and cast lots for my clothing." [u]
So this is what the soldiers did.

25 Near the cross of Jesus stood his mother, his mother's sister, Mary the wife of Clopas, and Mary of Magdala. 26 When Jesus saw his mother there, and the disciple whom he loved standing nearby, he said to his mother, "Here is[v] your son," 27 and to the disciple, "Here is your mother." From that time on, this disciple took her into his home.

[u] Psalm 22:18. [v] Greek *"Woman, here is . . ."* (a polite form of address).

332

Greek Interlinear

ἐποίησεν. 8 Ὅτε οὖν ἤκουσεν ὁ Πιλᾶτος
he made. When therefore heard – Pilate

τοῦτον τὸν λόγον, μᾶλλον ἐφοβήθη, 9 καὶ
this – word, more he was afraid, and

εἰσῆλθεν εἰς τὸ πραιτώριον πάλιν καὶ
entered into the prætorium again and

λέγει τῷ Ἰησοῦ· πόθεν εἶ σύ; ὁ δὲ
says – to Jesus: Whence art thou? – But

Ἰησοῦς ἀπόκρισιν οὐκ ἔδωκεν αὐτῷ.
Jesus answer did not give him.

10 λέγει οὖν αὐτῷ ὁ Πιλᾶτος· ἐμοὶ
Says therefore to him – Pilate· To me

οὐ λαλεῖς; οὐκ οἶδας ὅτι ἐξουσίαν ἔχω
speakest thou not? knowest thou not that authority I have

ἀπολῦσαί σε καὶ ἐξουσίαν ἔχω σταυρῶσαί
to release thee and authority I have to crucify

σε; 11 ἀπεκρίθη Ἰησοῦς· οὐκ εἶχες
thee? Answered Jesus: Thou hadst not

ἐξουσίαν κατ᾽ ἐμοῦ οὐδεμίαν εἰ μὴ ἦν
authority ¹against ²me ¹no(any) unless it was

δεδομένον σοι ἄνωθεν· διὰ τοῦτο ὁ
having been given thee from above; therefore the [one]

παραδούς μέ σοι μείζονα ἁμαρτίαν ἔχει.
having delivered me to thee a greater sin has.

12 ἐκ τούτου ὁ Πιλᾶτος ἐζήτει ἀπολῦσαι
From this – Pilate sought to release

αὐτόν· οἱ δὲ Ἰουδαῖοι ἐκραύγασαν λέγοντες·
him; but the Jews shouted saying:

ἐὰν τοῦτον ἀπολύσῃς, οὐκ εἶ φίλος τοῦ
If this man thou releasest, thou art not a friend –

Καίσαρος· πᾶς ὁ βασιλέα ἑαυτὸν ποιῶν
of Cæsar; everyone a king himself making

ἀντιλέγει τῷ Καίσαρι. 13 Ὁ οὖν Πιλᾶτος
speaks against – Cæsar. – Therefore Pilate

ἀκούσας τῶν λόγων τούτων ἤγαγεν ἔξω
hearing – words these brought outside

τὸν Ἰησοῦν, καὶ ἐκάθισεν ἐπὶ βήματος
– Jesus, and sat on a tribunal

εἰς τόπον λεγόμενον Λιθόστρωτον, Ἑβραϊστὶ δὲ
in a place being called Pavement, but in Hebrew

Γαββαθά. 14 ἦν δὲ παρασκευὴ τοῦ
Gabbatha. Now it was preparation of the

πάσχα, ὥρα ἦν ὡς ἕκτη· καὶ λέγει
Passover, hour it was about sixth; and he says

τοῖς Ἰουδαίοις· ἴδε ὁ βασιλεὺς ὑμῶν.
to the Jews: Behold[,] the king of you.

15 ἐκραύγασαν οὖν ἐκεῖνοι· ἆρον ἆρον,
Shouted therefore those: Take[,] take,

σταύρωσον αὐτόν. λέγει αὐτοῖς ὁ Πιλᾶτος·
crucify him. Says to them – Pilate·

τὸν βασιλέα ὑμῶν σταυρώσω; ἀπεκρίθησαν
The king of you shall I crucify? Answered

οἱ ἀρχιερεῖς· οὐκ ἔχομεν βασιλέα εἰ
the chief priests· We have not a king ex-

μὴ Καίσαρα. 16 τότε οὖν παρέδωκεν
cept Cæsar. Then therefore he delivered

αὐτὸν αὐτοῖς ἵνα σταυρωθῇ.
him to them that he should be crucified.

Παρέλαβον οὖν τὸν Ἰησοῦν· 17 καὶ
They took therefore – Jesus; and

βαστάζων ἑαυτῷ τὸν σταυρὸν ἐξῆλθεν
carrying ⁶to himself ¹the ²cross he went forth

εἰς τὸν λεγόμενον κρανίου τόπον, ὃ
to ¹the ⁴being called ²of a skull ³place, which

λέγεται Ἑβραϊστὶ Γολγοθά, 18 ὅπου αὐτὸν
is called in Hebrew Golgotha, where him

ἐσταύρωσαν, καὶ μετ᾽ αὐτοῦ ἄλλους δύο
they crucified, and with him others two

ἐντεῦθεν καὶ ἐντεῦθεν, μέσον δὲ τὸν
on this side and on that, † and in the middle –

Ἰησοῦν. 19 ἔγραψεν δὲ καὶ τίτλον ὁ
Jesus. And wrote also a title –

Πιλᾶτος καὶ ἔθηκεν ἐπὶ τοῦ σταυροῦ·
Pilate and put [it] on the cross;

ἦν δὲ γεγραμμένον· ΙΗΣΟΥΣ Ο
and it was having been written: JESUS THE

ΝΑΖΩΡΑΙΟΣ Ο ΒΑΣΙΛΕΥΣ ΤΩΝ
NAZARENE THE KING OF THE

ΙΟΥΔΑΙΩΝ. 20 τοῦτον οὖν τὸν τίτλον
JEWS. ¹This ²therefore – ⁵title

πολλοὶ ἀνέγνωσαν τῶν Ἰουδαίων, ὅτι
¹many ³read ⁴of the ³Jews, because

ἐγγὺς ἦν ὁ τόπος τῆς πόλεως ὅπου
¹near ²was ¹the ³place ⁴the ⁵city ⁶where

ἐσταυρώθη ὁ Ἰησοῦς· καὶ ἦν γεγραμμένον
⁷was crucified – ²Jesus; and it was having been written

Ἑβραϊστί, Ῥωμαϊστί, Ἑλληνιστί. 21 ἔλεγον
in Hebrew, in Latin, in Greek. Said

οὖν τῷ Πιλάτῳ οἱ ἀρχιερεῖς τῶν Ἰουδαίων·
therefore – to Pilate the chief priests of the Jews:

μὴ γράφε· ὁ βασιλεὺς τῶν Ἰουδαίων,
Write not: The king of the Jews,

ἀλλ᾽ ὅτι ἐκεῖνος εἶπεν· βασιλεύς εἰμι
but that that man said: King I am

τῶν Ἰουδαίων. 22 ἀπεκρίθη ὁ Πιλᾶτος·
of the Jews. Answered – Pilate:

ὃ γέγραφα, γέγραφα. 23 Οἱ οὖν
What I have written, I have written. Therefore the

στρατιῶται, ὅτε ἐσταύρωσαν τὸν Ἰησοῦν,
soldiers, when they crucified – Jesus,

ἔλαβον τὰ ἱμάτια αὐτοῦ καὶ ἐποίησαν
took the garments of him and made

τέσσερα μέρη, ἑκάστῳ στρατιώτῃ μέρος,
four parts, to each soldier a part,

καὶ τὸν χιτῶνα. ἦν δὲ ὁ χιτὼν ἄρραφος,
and the tunic. Now was the tunic seamless,

ἐκ τῶν ἄνωθεν ὑφαντὸς δι᾽ ὅλου. 24 εἶπαν
from the top woven throughout. They said

οὖν πρὸς ἀλλήλους· μὴ σχίσωμεν αὐτόν,
therefore to one another: Let us not tear it,

ἀλλὰ λάχωμεν περὶ αὐτοῦ τίνος ἔσται·
but let us cast lots about it of whom it shall be;

ἵνα ἡ γραφὴ πληρωθῇ· διεμερίσαντο τὰ
that the scripture might be fulfilled: They parted the

ἱμάτιά μου ἑαυτοῖς καὶ ἐπὶ τὸν ἱματισμόν
garments of me to themselves and over the raiment

μου ἔβαλον κλῆρον. Οἱ μὲν οὖν στρατιῶται
of me they cast a lot. ²The –⁴ therefore ⁴soldiers

ταῦτα ἐποίησαν. 25 εἱστήκεισαν δὲ παρὰ
¹these things did. ¹there stood ²But by

τῷ σταυρῷ τοῦ Ἰησοῦ ἡ μήτηρ αὐτοῦ
the cross – of Jesus the mother of him

καὶ ἡ ἀδελφὴ τῆς μητρὸς αὐτοῦ, Μαρία
and the sister of the mother of him, Mary

ἡ τοῦ Κλωπᾶ καὶ Μαρία ἡ Μαγδαληνή.
the [?wife] – of Clopas and Mary the Magdalene.

26 Ἰησοῦς οὖν ἰδὼν τὴν μητέρα καὶ
Jesus therefore seeing the(his) mother and

τὸν μαθητὴν παρεστῶτα ὃν ἠγάπα, λέγει
the disciple standing by whom he loved, says

τῇ μητρί· γύναι, ἴδε ὁ υἱός σου.
to the(his) mother: Woman, behold[,] the son of thee.

27 εἶτα λέγει τῷ μαθητῇ· ἴδε ἡ μήτηρ
Then he says to the disciple: Behold[,] the mother

σου. καὶ ἀπ᾽ ἐκείνης τῆς ὥρας ἔλαβεν
of thee. And from that – hour took

---

* μέν is scarcely translatable. But note the δέ in ver. 25 : John
contrasts two groups—the soldiers and the women.

King James Version

28 After this, Jesus knowing that all things were now accomplished, that the Scripture might be fulfilled, saith, I thirst. 29 Now there was set a vessel full of vinegar: and they filled a sponge with vinegar, and put *it* upon hyssop, and put *it* to his mouth. 30 When Jesus therefore had received the vinegar, he said, It is finished: and he bowed his head, and gave up the ghost. 31 The Jews therefore, because it was the preparation, that the bodies should not remain upon the cross on the sabbath day, (for that sabbath day was a high day,) besought Pilate that their legs might be broken, and *that* they might be taken away. 32 Then came the soldiers, and brake the legs of the first, and of the other which was crucified with him. 33 But when they came to Jesus, and saw that he was dead already, they brake not his legs: 34 But one of the soldiers with a spear pierced his side, and forthwith came there out blood and water. 35 And he that saw *it* bare record, and his record is true: and he knoweth that he saith true, that ye might believe. 36 For these things were done, that the Scripture should be fulfilled, A bone of him shall not be broken. 37 And again another Scripture saith, They shall look on him whom they pierced.

38 And after this Joseph of Arimathea, being a disciple of Jesus, but secretly for fear of the Jews, besought Pilate that he might take away the body of Jesus: and Pilate gave *him* leave. He came therefore, and took the body of Jesus. 39 And there came also Nicodemus, (which at the first came to Jesus by night,) and brought a mixture of myrrh and aloes, about a hundred pound *weight*. 40 Then took they the body of Jesus, and wound it in linen clothes with the spices, as the manner of the Jews is to bury. 41 Now in the place where he was crucified there was a garden; and in the garden a new sepulchre, wherein was never man yet laid. 42 There laid they Jesus therefore because of the Jews' preparation *day;* for the sepulchre was nigh at hand.

20 The first *day* of the week cometh Mary Magdalene early, when it was yet dark, unto the sepulchre, and seeth the stone taken away from the sepulchre. 2 Then she runneth, and cometh to Simon Peter, and to the other disciple, whom Jesus loved, and saith unto them, They have taken away the Lord out of the sepulchre, and we know not where they have laid him. 3 Peter therefore went forth, and that other disciple, and came to the sepulchre. 4 So they ran both together: and the other disciple

New International Version

The death of Jesus

28 Later, knowing that all was now completed, and so that the scripture would be fulfilled, Jesus said, "I am thirsty." 29 A jar of wine vinegar was there, so they soaked a sponge in it, put the sponge on a stalk of the hyssop plant, and lifted it to Jesus' lips. 30 When he had received the drink, Jesus said, "It is finished." With that, he bowed his head and gave up his life.

31 Now it was the day of Preparation, and the next day was to be a special Sabbath. Because the Jews did not want the bodies left on the crosses during the Sabbath, they asked Pilate to have the legs broken and the bodies taken down. 32 The soldiers therefore came and broke the legs of the first man who had been crucified with Jesus, and then those of the other. 33 But when they came to Jesus and found that he was already dead, they did not break his legs. 34 Instead, one of the soldiers pierced Jesus' side with a spear, bringing a sudden flow of blood and water. 35 The man who saw it has given testimony, and his testimony is true. He knows that he tells the truth, and he testifies so that you also may have faith. 36 These things happened so that the scripture would be fulfilled: "Not one of his bones will be broken," [w] 37 and, as another scripture says, "They will look on the one they have pierced." [x]

The burial of Jesus

38 Later, Joseph of Arimathea asked Pilate for the body of Jesus. Now Joseph was a disciple of Jesus, but secretly because he feared the Jews. With Pilate's permission, he came and took the body. 39 He was accompanied by Nicodemus, the man who earlier had visited Jesus at night. Nicodemus brought a mixture of myrrh and aloes, about seventy-five pounds. 40 Taking Jesus' body, the two of them wrapped it, with the spices, in strips of linen. This was in accordance with Jewish burial customs. 41 At the place where Jesus was crucified, there was a garden, and in the garden a new tomb, in which no one had ever been laid. 42 Because it was the Jewish day of Preparation and since the tomb was nearby, they laid Jesus there.

The empty tomb

20 Early on the first day of the week, while it was still dark, Mary of Magdala went to the tomb and saw that the stone had been removed from the entrance. 2 So she came running to Simon Peter and the other disciple, the one Jesus loved, and said, "They have taken the Lord out of the tomb, and we don't know where they have put him!"

3 So Peter and the other disciple started for the tomb. 4 Both were running, but the other

[w] Exodus 12:46; Num. 9:12; Psalm 34:20. [x] Zech. 12:10.

334

Greek Interlinear

ὁ μαθητὴς αὐτὴν εἰς τὰ ἴδια. **28** Μετὰ
the disciple her to his own [home].† After

τοῦτο εἰδὼς ὁ Ἰησοῦς ὅτι ἤδη πάντα
this knowing - Jesus that now all things

τετέλεσται, ἵνα τελειωθῇ ἡ γραφή, λέγει·
have been finished, that might be fulfilled the scripture, says:

διψῶ. **29** σκεῦος ἔκειτο ὄξους μεστόν·
I thirst. A vessel was set of vinegar full;

σπόγγον οὖν μεστὸν τοῦ ὄξους ὑσσώπῳ
ᵃa sponge therefore ⁴full ¹of the ᵛvinegar ³a hyssop §

περιθέντες προσήνεγκαν αὐτοῦ τῷ στόματι.
²putting ³round they brought [it] to of him the mouth.

30 ὅτε οὖν ἔλαβεν τὸ ὄξος [ὁ] Ἰησοῦς
When therefore he took the vinegar - Jesus

εἶπεν· τετέλεσται, καὶ κλίνας τὴν κεφαλὴν
he said: It has been finished, and inclining the(his) head

παρέδωκεν τὸ πνεῦμα.
delivered up the(his) spirit.

31 Οἱ οὖν Ἰουδαῖοι, ἐπεὶ παρασκευὴ
The ²therefore ¹Jews, since preparation

ἦν, ἵνα μὴ μείνῃ ἐπὶ τοῦ σταυροῦ τὰ
it was, that might not remain on the cross the

σώματα ἐν τῷ σαββάτῳ, ἦν γὰρ μεγάλη
bodies on the sabbath, for was great

ἡ ἡμέρα ἐκείνου τοῦ σαββάτου, ἠρώτησαν
the day of that - sabbath, they asked

τὸν Πιλᾶτον ἵνα κατεαγῶσιν αὐτῶν τὰ
- Pilate that might be broken of them the

σκέλη καὶ ἀρθῶσιν. **32** ἦλθον οὖν οἱ
legs and they might be taken. Came therefore the

στρατιῶται, καὶ τοῦ μὲν πρώτου κατέαξαν
soldiers, and of the -ᵃ first broke

τὰ σκέλη καὶ τοῦ ἄλλου τοῦ
the legs and of the other the

συσταυρωθέντος αὐτῷ· **33** ἐπὶ δὲ τὸν
crucified with him; ²on ¹but -

Ἰησοῦν ἐλθόντες, ὡς εἶδον αὐτὸν
³Jesus ¹coming, when they saw already him

τεθνηκότα, οὐ κατέαξαν αὐτοῦ τὰ σκέλη,
to have died, they did not break of him the legs,

34 ἀλλ᾽ εἷς τῶν στρατιωτῶν λόγχῃ αὐτοῦ
but one of the soldiers with a lance of him

τὴν πλευρὰν ἔνυξεν, καὶ ἐξῆλθεν εὐθὺς αἷμα
the side pricked, and there came imme-diately blood
out

καὶ ὕδωρ. **35** καὶ ὁ ἑωρακὼς μεμαρτύρηκεν,
and water. And the [one] having seen has witnessed,

καὶ ἀληθινὴ αὐτοῦ ἐστιν ἡ μαρτυρία,
and true of him is the witness,

καὶ ἐκεῖνος οἶδεν ὅτι ἀληθῆ λέγει, ἵνα
and that one knows that truly he says, that

καὶ ὑμεῖς πιστεύητε. **36** ἐγένετο γὰρ
also ye may believe. For happened

ταῦτα ἵνα ἡ γραφὴ πληρωθῇ· ὀστοῦν
these things that the scripture might be fulfilled: A bone

οὐ συντριβήσεται αὐτοῦ. **37** καὶ πάλιν
shall not be broken of him. And again

ἑτέρα γραφὴ λέγει· ὄψονται εἰς ὃν
another scripture says: They shall look at [him] whom

ἐξεκέντησαν. **38** Μετὰ δὲ ταῦτα ἠρώτησεν
they pierced. Now after these things ¹⁴asked

τὸν Πιλᾶτον Ἰωσὴφ ἀπὸ Ἀριμαθαίας,
- ¹¹Pilate ¹Joseph ²from ³Arimathæa,

ὢν μαθητὴς [τοῦ] Ἰησοῦ κεκρυμμένος
⁴being ⁵a disciple - ⁶of Jesus ⁵having been hidden

δὲ διὰ τὸν φόβον τῶν Ἰουδαίων, ἵνα
⁷but ⁸because ¹⁰the ¹¹fear ¹²of the ¹³Jews, that
of

ἄρῃ τὸ σῶμα τοῦ Ἰησοῦ· καὶ
he might take the body - of Jesus; and

ἐπέτρεψεν ὁ Πιλᾶτος. ἦλθεν οὖν καὶ ἦρεν
allowed - Pilate. He came there- and took
fore

τὸ σῶμα αὐτοῦ. **39** ἦλθεν δὲ καὶ Νικόδημος,
the body of him. And came also Nicodemus,

ὁ ἐλθὼν πρὸς αὐτὸν νυκτὸς τὸ πρῶτον,
the [one] having come to him of(by) night at first,†

φέρων μίγμα σμύρνης καὶ ἀλόης ὡς
bearing a mixture of myrrh and aloes about

λίτρας ἑκατόν. **40** ἔλαβον οὖν τὸ σῶμα
pounds a hundred. They took there- the body
fore

τοῦ Ἰησοῦ καὶ ἔδησαν αὐτὸ ὀθονίοις
- of Jesus and bound it in sheets

μετὰ τῶν ἀρωμάτων, καθὼς ἔθος ἐστὶν
with the spices, as custom is

τοῖς Ἰουδαίοις ἐνταφιάζειν. **41** ἦν δὲ
with the Jews to bury. Now there was

ἐν τῷ τόπῳ ὅπου ἐσταυρώθη κῆπος,
in the place where he was crucified a garden,

καὶ ἐν τῷ κήπῳ μνημεῖον καινόν, ἐν
and in the garden tomb a new, in

ᾧ οὐδέπω οὐδεὶς ἦν τεθειμένος· **42** ἐκεῖ
which never yet no(any) was *having been* put; there
one

οὖν διὰ τὴν παρασκευὴν τῶν Ἰουδαίων,
therefore because of the preparation of the Jews,

ὅτι ἐγγὺς ἦν τὸ μνημεῖον, ἔθηκαν τὸν
because near was the tomb, they put -

Ἰησοῦν.
Jesus.

Chapter 20

Τῇ δὲ μιᾷ τῶν σαββάτων Μαρία
Now on the one(first) [day] of the week Mary

ἡ Μαγδαληνὴ ἔρχεται πρωῒ σκοτίας ἔτι
the Magdalene comes early darkness yet
= while it was yet dark

οὔσης εἰς τὸ μνημεῖον, καὶ βλέπει τὸν
being² to the tomb, and sees the

λίθον ἠρμένον ἐκ τοῦ μνημείου.
stone having been taken out of the tomb.

2 τρέχει οὖν καὶ ἔρχεται πρὸς Σίμωνα
She runs therefore and comes to Simon

Πέτρον καὶ πρὸς τὸν ἄλλον μαθητὴν ὃν
Peter and to the other disciple whom

ἐφίλει ὁ Ἰησοῦς, καὶ λέγει αὐτοῖς· ἦραν
²loved — ¹Jesus, and says to them: They
took

τὸν κύριον ἐκ τοῦ μνημείου, καὶ οὐκ οἴδαμεν
the Lord out of the tomb, and we do not know

ποῦ ἔθηκαν αὐτόν. **3** Ἐξῆλθεν οὖν ὁ
where they put him. Went forth therefore -

Πέτρος καὶ ὁ ἄλλος μαθητής, καὶ ἤρχοντο
Peter and the other disciple, and came

εἰς τὸ μνημεῖον. **4** ἔτρεχον δὲ οἱ δύο
to the tomb. And ran the two

ὁμοῦ· καὶ ὁ ἄλλος μαθητὴς προέδραμεν
together; and the other disciple ran before

---

§ It has been suggested that ὑσσώπῳ is a graphic error for ὑσσῷ
(*pilum*), pike; but *cf.* Mat. 27. 48.
ᵃ See note on 19. 24. Here see ver. 33—two actions contrasted.

King James Version

did outrun Peter, and came first to the sepulchre. 5And he stooping down, *and looking in,* saw the linen clothes lying; yet went he not in. 6 Then cometh Simon Peter following him, and went into the sepulchre, and seeth the linen clothes lie, 7And the napkin, that was about his head, not lying with the linen clothes, but wrapped together in a place by itself. 8 Then went in also that other disciple, which came first to the sepulchre, and he saw, and believed. 9 For as yet they knew not the Scripture, that he must rise again from the dead. 10 Then the disciples went away again unto their own home.

11 But Mary stood without at the sepulchre weeping: and as she wept, she stooped down, *and looked* into the sepulchre, 12And seeth two angels in white sitting, the one at the head, and the other at the feet, where the body of Jesus had lain. 13And they say unto her, Woman, why weepest thou? She saith unto them, Because they have taken away my Lord, and I know not where they have laid him. 14And when she had thus said, she turned herself back, and saw Jesus standing, and knew not that it was Jesus. 15 Jesus saith unto her, Woman, why weepest thou? whom seekest thou? She, supposing him to be the gardener, saith unto him, Sir, if thou have borne him hence, tell me where thou hast laid him, and I will take him away. 16 Jesus saith unto her, Mary. She turned herself, and saith unto him, Rabboni; which is to say, Master. 17 Jesus saith unto her, Touch me not; for I am not yet ascended to my Father: but go to my brethren, and say unto them, I ascend unto my Father, and your Father; and *to* my God, and your God. 18 Mary Magdalene came and told the disciples that she had seen the Lord, and *that* he had spoken these things unto her.

19 Then the same day at evening, being the first *day* of the week, when the doors were shut where the disciples were assembled for fear of the Jews, came Jesus and stood in the midst, and saith unto them, Peace *be* unto you. 20And when he had so said, he shewed unto them *his* hands and his side. Then were the disciples glad, when they saw the Lord. 21 Then said Jesus to them again, Peace *be* unto you: as *my* Father hath sent me, even so send I you. 22And when he had said this, he breathed on *them,* and saith unto them, Receive ye the Holy Ghost: 23 Whosesoever sins ye remit, they are remitted unto them; *and* whosesoever *sins* ye retain, they are retained.

24 But Thomas, one of the twelve, called Didymus, was not with them when Jesus came. 25 The other disciples therefore said unto him, We have seen the Lord. But he said unto them, Except I shall see in his hands the print of the nails, and put my finger into the print of the nails, and thrust my hand into his side, I will not believe.

26 And after eight days again his disciples

New International Version

disciple outran Peter, and reached the tomb first. 5 He bent over and looked in at the strips of linen lying there but did not go in. 6 Then Simon Peter, who was behind him, arrived and went into the tomb. He saw the strips of linen lying there, 7 as well as the burial cloth that had been around Jesus' head. The cloth was folded up by itself, separate from the linen. 8 Finally the other disciple, who had reached the tomb first, also went inside. He saw and believed. 9 (They still did not understand from Scripture that Jesus had to rise from the dead.)

Jesus appears to Mary of Magdala

10 Then the disciples went back to their homes, 11 but Mary stood outside the tomb crying. As she wept, she bent over to look into the tomb 12 and saw two angels in white, seated where Jesus' body had been, one at the head and the other at the foot.

13 They asked her, "Woman, why are you crying?"

"They have taken my Lord away," she said, "and I don't know where they have put him." 14At this, she turned around and saw Jesus standing there, but she did not realize that it was Jesus.

15 "Woman," he said, "why are you crying? Who is it you are looking for?"

Thinking he was the gardener, she said, "Sir, if you have carried him away, tell me where you have put him, and I will get him."

16 Jesus said to her, "Mary."

She turned toward him and cried out in Aramaic, "Rabboni!" (which means Teacher).

17 Jesus said, "Do not hold on to me, for I have not yet returned to the Father. Go instead to my brothers and tell them, 'I am returning to my Father and your Father, to my God and your God.'" 18 Mary of Magdala went to the disciples with the news that she had seen the Lord and that he had told her this.

Jesus appears to his disciples

19 On the evening of that first day of the week, when the disciples were together, with the doors locked for fear of the Jews, Jesus came and stood among them and said, "Peace be with you!" 20After he said this, he showed them his hands and side. The disciples were overjoyed when they saw the Lord.

21 Again Jesus said, "Peace be with you! As the Father has sent me, I am sending you." 22And with that he breathed on them and said, "Receive the Holy Spirit. 23 If you forgive anyone his sins, they are forgiven; if you do not forgive them, they are not forgiven."

Jesus appears to Thomas

24 Now Thomas (called Didymus), one of the Twelve, was not with the disciples when Jesus came. 25 When the other disciples told him that they had seen the Lord, he declared, "Unless I see the nail marks in his hands and put my finger where the nails were, and put my hand into his side, I will not believe it."

26 A week later his disciples were in the

Greek Interlinear

τάχιον τοῦ Πέτρου καὶ ἦλθεν πρῶτος
more quickly [than] - Peter and came first
εἰς τὸ μνημεῖον, 5 καὶ παρακύψας βλέπει
to the tomb, and stooping sees
κείμενα τὰ ὀθόνια, οὐ μέντοι εἰσῆλθεν.
lying the sheets, not however he entered.
6 ἔρχεται οὖν καὶ Σίμων Πέτρος ἀκο-
Comes therefore also Simon Peter follow-
λουθῶν αὐτῷ, καὶ εἰσῆλθεν εἰς τὸ
ing him, and entered into the
μνημεῖον· καὶ θεωρεῖ τὰ ὀθόνια κείμενα,
tomb; and he beholds the sheets lying,
7 καὶ τὸ σουδάριον, ὃ ἦν ἐπὶ τῆς
and the kerchief, which was on the
κεφαλῆς αὐτοῦ, οὐ μετὰ τῶν ὀθονίων
head of him, not with the sheets
κείμενον ἀλλὰ χωρὶς ἐντετυλιγμένον εἰς
lying but apart having been wrapped up in
ἕνα τόπον. 8 τότε οὖν εἰσῆλθεν καὶ
one place. Then therefore entered also
ὁ ἄλλος μαθητὴς ὁ ἐλθὼν πρῶτος εἰς
the other disciple - having come first to
τὸ μνημεῖον, καὶ εἶδεν καὶ ἐπίστευσεν·
the tomb, and he saw and believed;
9 οὐδέπω γὰρ ᾔδεισαν τὴν γραφήν, ὅτι
for not yet they knew the scripture, that
δεῖ αὐτὸν ἐκ νεκρῶν ἀναστῆναι.
it behoves him from [the] dead to rise again.
10 ἀπῆλθον οὖν πάλιν πρὸς αὐτοὺς οἱ
Went away therefore again to themselves* the
μαθηταί. 11 Μαρία δὲ εἱστήκει πρὸς
disciples. But Mary stood at
τῷ μνημείῳ ἔξω κλαίουσα. ὡς οὖν
the tomb outside weeping. As therefore
ἔκλαιεν, παρέκυψεν εἰς τὸ μνημεῖον,
she was weeping, she stooped into the tomb,
12 καὶ θεωρεῖ δύο ἀγγέλους ἐν λευκοῖς
and beholds two angels in white
καθεζομένους, ἕνα πρὸς τῇ κεφαλῇ καὶ
sitting, one at the head and
ἕνα πρὸς τοῖς ποσίν, ὅπου ἔκειτο τὸ
one at the feet, where lay the
σῶμα τοῦ Ἰησοῦ. 13 καὶ λέγουσιν αὐτῇ
body of Jesus. And say to her
ἐκεῖνοι· γύναι, τί κλαίεις; λέγει αὐτοῖς[,]
those : Woman, why weepest thou? She says to them[,]
ὅτι ἦραν τὸν κύριόν μου, καὶ οὐκ οἶδα
- They took the Lord of me, and I know not
ποῦ ἔθηκαν αὐτόν. 14 ταῦτα εἰποῦσα
where they put him. These things saying
ἐστράφη εἰς τὰ ὀπίσω, καὶ θεωρεῖ τὸν
she turned back,† and beholds -
Ἰησοῦν ἑστῶτα, καὶ οὐκ ᾔδει ὅτι Ἰησοῦς
Jesus standing, and knew not that Jesus
ἐστιν. 15 λέγει αὐτῇ Ἰησοῦς· γύναι,
it is(was). Says to her Jesus : Woman,
τί κλαίεις; τίνα ζητεῖς; ἐκείνη δοκοῦσα
why weepest thou? whom seekest thou? That one thinking
ὅτι ὁ κηπουρός ἐστιν, λέγει αὐτῷ· κύριε,
that the gardener it is(was), says to him : Sir,
εἰ σὺ ἐβάστασας αὐτόν, εἰπέ μοι ποῦ
if thou didst carry him, tell me where
ἔθηκας αὐτόν, κἀγὼ αὐτὸν ἀρῶ. 16 λέγει
thou didst put him, and I him will take. Says
αὐτῇ Ἰησοῦς· Μαριάμ. στραφεῖσα ἐκείνη
to her Jesus : Mary. Turning that one
λέγει αὐτῷ Ἑβραϊστί· ῥαββουνί (ὃ λέγεται
says to him in Hebrew : Rabboni (which is said
διδάσκαλε). 17 λέγει αὐτῇ Ἰησοῦς· μή
Teacher). Says to her Jesus : Not

μου ἅπτου, οὔπω γὰρ ἀναβέβηκα πρὸς
me touch, for not yet have I ascended to
τὸν πατέρα· πορεύου δὲ πρὸς τοὺς
the Father; but go thou to the
ἀδελφούς μου καὶ εἰπὲ αὐτοῖς· ἀναβαίνω
brothers of me and tell them : I ascend
πρὸς τὸν πατέρα μου καὶ πατέρα ὑμῶν
to the Father of me and Father of you
καὶ θεόν μου καὶ θεὸν ὑμῶν. 18 ἔρχεται
and God of me and God of you. Comes
Μαριὰμ ἡ Μαγδαληνὴ ἀγγέλλουσα τοῖς
Mary the Magdalene announcing to the
μαθηταῖς ὅτι ἑώρακα τὸν κύριον, καὶ
disciples[,] - I have seen the Lord, and
ταῦτα εἶπεν αὐτῇ.
these things he said to her.
19 Οὔσης οὖν ὀψίας τῇ ἡμέρᾳ ἐκείνῃ
Being therefore early evening* - day on that
=Therefore when it was early evening
τῇ μιᾷ σαββάτων, καὶ τῶν θυρῶν
the one(first) of the week, and the doors
κεκλεισμένων ὅπου ἦσαν οἱ μαθηταὶ διὰ
having been shut* where were the disciples because of
τὸν φόβον τῶν Ἰουδαίων, ἦλθεν ὁ Ἰησοῦς
the fear of the Jews, came - Jesus
καὶ ἔστη εἰς τὸ μέσον, καὶ λέγει αὐτοῖς·
and stood in the midst, and says to them :
εἰρήνη ὑμῖν. 20 καὶ τοῦτο εἰπὼν ἔδειξεν
Peace to you. And this saying he showed
καὶ τὰς χεῖρας καὶ τὴν πλευρὰν αὐτοῖς.
both the(his) hands and the(his) side to them.
ἐχάρησαν οὖν οἱ μαθηταὶ ἰδόντες τὸν
Rejoiced therefore the disciples seeing the
κύριον. 21 εἶπεν οὖν αὐτοῖς [ὁ Ἰησοῦς]
Lord. Said therefore to them - Jesus
πάλιν· εἰρήνη ὑμῖν· καθὼς ἀπέσταλκέν
again : Peace to you; as has sent
με ὁ πατήρ, κἀγὼ πέμπω ὑμᾶς. 22 καὶ
me the Father, I also send you. And
τοῦτο εἰπὼν ἐνεφύσησεν καὶ λέγει αὐτοῖς·
this saying he breathed in and says to them :
λάβετε πνεῦμα ἅγιον. 23 ἄν τινων
Receive ye Spirit Holy. Of whomever
ἀφῆτε τὰς ἁμαρτίας, ἀφέωνται αὐτοῖς·
ye forgive the sins, they have been to them;
forgiven
ἄν τινων κρατῆτε, κεκράτηνται.
of whomever ye hold, they have been held.
24 Θωμᾶς δὲ εἷς ἐκ τῶν δώδεκα,
But Thomas one of the twelve,
ὁ λεγόμενος Δίδυμος, οὐκ ἦν μετ' αὐτῶν
- being called Twin, was not with them
ὅτε ἦλθεν Ἰησοῦς. 25 ἔλεγον οὖν αὐτῷ
when came Jesus. Said therefore to him
οἱ ἄλλοι μαθηταί· ἑωράκαμεν τὸν κύριον.
the other disciples : We have seen the Lord.
ὁ δὲ εἶπεν αὐτοῖς· ἐὰν μὴ ἴδω ἐν
But he said to them : Unless I see in
ταῖς χερσὶν αὐτοῦ τὸν τύπον τῶν ἥλων
the hands of him the mark of the nails
καὶ βάλω τὸν δάκτυλόν μου εἰς τὸν
and put the finger of me into the
τόπον τῶν ἥλων καὶ βάλω μου τὴν
place of the nails and put of me the
χεῖρα εἰς τὴν πλευρὰν αὐτοῦ, οὐ μὴ
hand into the side of him, by no means
πιστεύσω. 26 Καὶ μεθ' ἡμέρας ὀκτὼ
will I believe. And after days eight
πάλιν ἦσαν ἔσω οἱ μαθηταὶ αὐτοῦ, καὶ
again were within the disciples of him, and

* That is, to their own home; cf. 19. 27.
337

King James Version

were within, and Thomas with them: *then* came Jesus, the doors being shut, and stood in the midst, and said, Peace *be* unto you. 27 Then saith he to Thomas, Reach hither thy finger, and behold my hands; and reach hither thy hand, and thrust *it* into my side; and be not faithless, but believing. 28 And Thomas answered and said unto him, My Lord and my God. 29 Jesus saith unto him, Thomas, because thou hast seen me, thou hast believed: blessed *are* they that have not seen, and *yet* have believed.

30 And many other signs truly did Jesus in the presence of his disciples, which are not written in this book: 31 But these are written, that ye might believe that Jesus is the Christ, the Son of God; and that believing ye might have life through his name.

21 After these things Jesus shewed himself again to the disciples at the sea of Tiberias; and on this wise shewed he *himself*. 2 There were together Simon Peter, and Thomas called Didymus, and Nathanael of Cana in Galilee, and the *sons* of Zebedee, and two other of his disciples. 3 Simon Peter saith unto them, I go a fishing. They say unto him, We also go with thee. They went forth, and entered into a ship immediately; and that night they caught nothing. 4 But when the morning was now come, Jesus stood on the shore; but the disciples knew not that it was Jesus. 5 Then Jesus saith unto them, Children, have ye any meat? They answered him, No. 6 And he said unto them, Cast the net on the right side of the ship, and ye shall find. They cast therefore, and now they were not able to draw it for the multitude of fishes. 7 Therefore that disciple whom Jesus loved saith unto Peter, It is the Lord. Now when Simon Peter heard that it was the Lord, he girt *his* fisher's coat *unto him,* (for he was naked,) and did cast himself into the sea. 8 And the other disciples came in a little ship, (for they were not far from land, but as it were two hundred cubits,) dragging the net with fishes. 9 As soon then as they were come to land, they saw a fire of coals there, and fish laid thereon, and bread. 10 Jesus saith unto them, Bring of the fish which ye have now caught. 11 Simon Peter went up, and drew the net to land full of great fishes, a hundred and fifty and three: and for all there were so many, yet was not the net broken. 12 Jesus saith unto them, Come *and* dine. And none of the disciples durst ask him, Who art thou? knowing that it was the Lord. 13 Jesus then cometh, and taketh bread, and giveth them, and fish likewise. 14 This is now the third time that Jesus shewed himself to his disciples, after that he was risen from the dead.

New International Version

house again, and Thomas was with them. Though the doors were locked, Jesus came and stood among them, and said, "Peace be with you!" 27 Then he said to Thomas, "Put your finger here; see my hands. Reach out your hand and put it into my side. Stop doubting and believe."

28 Thomas said to him, "My Lord and my God!"

29 Then Jesus told him, "Because you have seen me, you have believed; blessed are those who have not seen and yet have believed."

30 Jesus did many other miraculous signs in the presence of his disciples, which are not recorded in this book. 31 But these are written that you may believe[y] that Jesus is the Christ, the Son of God, and that by believing you may have life in his name.

Jesus and the miraculous catch of fish

21 Afterward Jesus appeared again to his disciples by the Sea of Tiberias. It happened this way: 2 Simon Peter, Thomas (called Didymus), Nathanael from Cana in Galilee, the sons of Zebedee, and two other disciples were together. 3 "I'm going out to fish," Simon Peter told them, and they said, "We'll go with you." So they went out and got into the boat, but that night they caught nothing.

4 Early in the morning, Jesus stood on the shore, but the disciples did not realize that it was Jesus.

5 He called out to them, "Friends, haven't you caught any fish?"

"No," they answered.

6 He said, "Throw your net on the right side of the boat and you will find some." When they did, they were unable to haul the net in because of the large number of fish.

7 Then the disciple whom Jesus loved said to Peter, "It is the Lord!" As soon as Simon Peter heard him say, "It is the Lord," he wrapped his outer garment around him (for he had taken it off) and jumped into the water. 8 The other disciples followed in the boat, towing the net full of fish, for they were not far from shore, about a hundred yards. 9 When they landed, they saw a fire of burning coals there with fish on it, and some bread.

10 Jesus said to them, "Bring some of the fish you have just caught."

11 Simon Peter climbed aboard and dragged the net ashore. It was full of large fish, 153, but even with so many the net was not torn. 12 Jesus said to them, "Come and have breakfast." None of the disciples dared ask him, "Who are you?" They knew it was the Lord. 13 Jesus came, took the bread and gave it to them, and did the same with the fish. 14 This was now the third time Jesus appeared to his disciples after he was raised from the dead.

Greek Interlinear

Θωμᾶς μετ' αὐτῶν. ἔρχεται ὁ Ἰησοῦς
Thomas with them. Comes - Jesus

τῶν θυρῶν κεκλεισμένων, καὶ ἔστη εἰς
the doors having been shut[a], and stood in

τὸ μέσον καὶ εἶπεν· εἰρήνη ὑμῖν. 27 εἶτα
the midst and said: Peace to you. Then

λέγει τῷ Θωμᾷ· φέρε τὸν δάκτυλόν
he says - to Thomas: Bring the finger

σου ὧδε καὶ ἴδε τὰς χεῖράς μου, καὶ
of thee here and see the hands of me, and

φέρε τὴν χεῖρά σου καὶ βάλε εἰς τὴν
bring the hand of thee and put into the

πλευράν μου, καὶ μὴ γίνου ἄπιστος
side of me, and be not faithless

ἀλλὰ πιστός. 28 ἀπεκρίθη Θωμᾶς καὶ
but faithful. Answered Thomas and

εἶπεν αὐτῷ· ὁ κύριός μου καὶ ὁ θεός
said to him: The Lord of me and the God

μου. 29 λέγει αὐτῷ ὁ Ἰησοῦς· ὅτι
of me. Says to him - Jesus: Because

ἑώρακάς με, πεπίστευκας; μακάριοι οἱ
thou hast seen me, hast thou believed? blessed the [ones]

μὴ ἰδόντες καὶ πιστεύσαντες.
not seeing and§ believing.

30 Πολλὰ μὲν οὖν καὶ ἄλλα σημεῖα
Many -* therefore and other signs

ἐποίησεν ὁ Ἰησοῦς ἐνώπιον τῶν μαθητῶν,
did - Jesus before the disciples,

ἃ οὐκ ἔστιν γεγραμμένα ἐν τῷ βιβλίῳ
which is(are) not having been written in - roll

τούτῳ· 31 ταῦτα δὲ γέγραπται ἵνα
this; but these* has(ve) been written that

πιστεύητε ὅτι Ἰησοῦς ἐστιν ὁ χριστὸς ὁ
ye may believe that Jesus is the Christ the

υἱὸς τοῦ θεοῦ, καὶ ἵνα πιστεύοντες ζωὴν
Son - of God, and that believing life

ἔχητε ἐν τῷ ὀνόματι αὐτοῦ.
ye may have in the name of him.

Chapter 21

Μετὰ ταῦτα ἐφανέρωσεν ἑαυτὸν πάλιν
After these things manifested himself again

Ἰησοῦς τοῖς μαθηταῖς ἐπὶ τῆς θαλάσσης
Jesus to the disciples on the sea

τῆς Τιβεριάδος· ἐφανέρωσεν δὲ οὕτως.
- of Tiberias; and he manifested [himself] thus.

2 ἦσαν ὁμοῦ Σίμων Πέτρος καὶ Θωμᾶς
There were together Simon Peter and Thomas

ὁ λεγόμενος Δίδυμος καὶ Ναθαναὴλ ὁ
- being called Twin and Nathanael -

ἀπὸ Κανὰ τῆς Γαλιλαίας καὶ οἱ τοῦ
from Cana - of Galilee and the [sons] -

Ζεβεδαίου καὶ ἄλλοι ἐκ τῶν μαθητῶν
of Zebedee and others of the disciples

αὐτοῦ δύο. 3 λέγει αὐτοῖς Σίμων Πέτρος·
of him two. Says to them Simon Peter:

ὑπάγω ἁλιεύειν. λέγουσιν αὐτῷ· ἐρχόμεθα
I am going to fish. They say to him: Are coming

καὶ ἡμεῖς σὺν σοί. ἐξῆλθον καὶ ἐνέβησαν
also we with thee. They went forth and embarked

εἰς τὸ πλοῖον, καὶ ἐν ἐκείνῃ τῇ νυκτὶ
in the boat, and in that - night

ἐπίασαν οὐδέν. 4 πρωΐας δὲ ἤδη γινομένης
they caught nothing. Early morning but now becoming*
- But when it became early morning

ἔστη Ἰησοῦς εἰς τὸν αἰγιαλόν· οὐ μέντοι
stood Jesus in(on) the shore; not however

ᾔδεισαν οἱ μαθηταὶ ὅτι Ἰησοῦς ἐστιν.
knew the disciples that Jesus it is(was).

5 λέγει οὖν αὐτοῖς Ἰησοῦς· παιδία, μή
Says therefore to them Jesus: Children, not

τι προσφάγιον ἔχετε; ἀπεκρίθησαν αὐτῷ·
any fish have ye? They answered him:

οὔ. 6 ὁ δὲ εἶπεν αὐτοῖς· βάλετε εἰς τὰ
No. So he said to them: Cast in the

δεξιὰ μέρη τοῦ πλοίου τὸ δίκτυον, καὶ
right parts of the boat the net, and

εὑρήσετε. ἔβαλον οὖν, καὶ οὐκέτι αὐτὸ
ye will find. They cast therefore, and ¹no longer ⁴it

ἑλκύσαι ἴσχυον ἀπὸ τοῦ πλήθους τῶν
²to drag ³were they able from the multitude of the

ἰχθύων. 7 λέγει οὖν ὁ μαθητὴς ἐκεῖνος
fishes. Says therefore - disciple that

ὃν ἠγάπα Ἰησοῦς τῷ Πέτρῳ· ὁ κύριός
whom ²loved - ¹Jesus - to Peter: The Lord

ἐστιν. Σίμων οὖν Πέτρος, ἀκούσας ὅτι
it is. ³Simon ¹therefore ²Peter, hearing that

ὁ κύριός ἐστιν, τὸν ἐπενδύτην διεζώσατο,
the Lord it is(was), ⁸[with]the ²coat ¹girded himself,

ἦν γὰρ γυμνός, καὶ ἔβαλεν ἑαυτὸν εἰς
for he was naked, and threw himself into

τὴν θάλασσαν. 8 οἱ δὲ ἄλλοι μαθηταὶ
the sea; but the other disciples

τῷ πλοιαρίῳ ἦλθον, οὐ γὰρ ἦσαν μακρὰν
in the little boat came, for not they were far

ἀπὸ τῆς γῆς ἀλλὰ ὡς ἀπὸ πηχῶν
from the land but about from cubits

διακοσίων, σύροντες τὸ δίκτυον τῶν ἰχθύων.
two hundred, dragging the net of the fishes.

9 ὡς οὖν ἀπέβησαν εἰς τὴν γῆν, βλέπουσιν
When therefore they disembarked onto the land, they see

ἀνθρακιὰν κειμένην καὶ ὀψάριον ἐπικείμενον
a coal fire lying and a fish lying on

καὶ ἄρτον. 10 λέγει αὐτοῖς ὁ Ἰησοῦς·
and bread. Says to them - Jesus:

ἐνέγκατε ἀπὸ τῶν ὀψαρίων ὧν ἐπιάσατε
Bring from the fishes which ye caught

νῦν. 11 ἀνέβη Σίμων Πέτρος καὶ εἵλκυσεν
now. Went up Simon Peter and dragged

τὸ δίκτυον εἰς τὴν γῆν μεστὸν ἰχθύων
the net to the land full fishes

μεγάλων ἑκατὸν πεντήκοντα τριῶν· καὶ
of great a hundred fifty three; and

τοσούτων ὄντων οὐκ ἐσχίσθη τὸ δίκτυον.
so many being* was not torn the net.

12 λέγει αὐτοῖς ὁ Ἰησοῦς· δεῦτε ἀριστήσατε.
Says to them - Jesus: Come breakfast ye.

οὐδεὶς ἐτόλμα τῶν μαθητῶν ἐξετάσαι
No one dared of the disciples to question

αὐτόν· σὺ τίς εἶ; εἰδότες ὅτι ὁ κύριός
him: Thou who art? knowing that the Lord

ἐστιν. 13 ἔρχεται Ἰησοῦς καὶ λαμβάνει
it is(was). Comes Jesus and takes

τὸν ἄρτον καὶ δίδωσιν αὐτοῖς, καὶ τὸ
the bread and gives to them, and the

ὀψάριον ὁμοίως. 14 τοῦτο ἤδη τρίτον
fish likewise. This [was] now [the] third [time]
[that]

ἐφανερώθη Ἰησοῦς τοῖς μαθηταῖς ἐγερθεὶς
⁵was manifested ¹Jesus to the disciples raised

ἐκ νεκρῶν.
from [the] dead.

* See note on 19. 24 and 32.

§ καί sometimes = and yet; see 5. 40; 8. 55; 9. 30; 16. 32; 17. 11.

King James Version

15 So when they had dined, Jesus saith to Simon Peter, Simon, *son* of Jonas, lovest thou me more than these? He saith unto him, Yea, Lord; thou knowest that I love thee. He saith unto him, Feed my lambs. 16 He saith to him again the second time, Simon, *son* of Jonas, lovest thou me? He saith unto him, Yea, Lord; thou knowest that I love thee. He saith unto him, Feed my sheep. 17 He saith unto him the third time, Simon, *son* of Jonas, lovest thou me? Peter was grieved because he said unto him the third time, Lovest thou me? And he said unto him, Lord, thou knowest all things; thou knowest that I love thee. Jesus saith unto him, Feed my sheep. 18 Verily, verily, I say unto thee, When thou wast young, thou girdedst thyself, and walkedst whither thou wouldest: but when thou shalt be old, thou shalt stretch forth thy hands, and another shall gird thee, and carry *thee* whither thou wouldest not. 19 This spake he, signifying by what death he should glorify God. And when he had spoken this, he saith unto him, Follow me. 20 Then Peter, turning about, seeth the disciple whom Jesus loved following; which also leaned on his breast at supper, and said, Lord, which is he that betrayeth thee? 21 Peter seeing him saith to Jesus, Lord, and what *shall* this man *do?* 22 Jesus saith unto him, If I will that he tarry till I come, what *is that* to thee? follow thou me. 23 Then went this saying abroad among the brethren, that that disciple should not die: yet Jesus said not unto him, He shall not die; but, If I will that he tarry till I come, what *is that* to thee? 24 This is the disciple which testifieth of these things, and wrote these things: and we know that his testimony is true. 25And there are also many other things which Jesus did, the which, if they should be written every one, I suppose that even the world itself could not contain the books that should be written. Amen.

New International Version

Jesus reinstates Peter

15 When they had finished eating, Jesus said to Simon Peter, "Simon son of John, do you truly love me more than these?"

"Yes, Lord," he said, "you know that I love you."

Jesus said, "Feed my lambs."

16 Again Jesus said, "Simon son of John, do you truly love me?"

He answered, "Yes, Lord, you know that I love you."

Jesus said, "Take care of my sheep."

17 The third time he said to him, "Simon son of John, do you love me?"

Peter was hurt because Jesus asked him the third time, "Do you love me?" He said, "Lord, you know all things; you know that I love you."

Jesus said, "Feed my sheep. 18 I tell you the truth, when you were younger you dressed yourself and went where you wanted; but when you are old you will stretch out your hands, and someone else will dress you and lead you where you do not want to go." 19 Jesus said this to indicate the kind of death by which Peter would glorify God. Then he said to him, "Follow me!"

20 Peter turned and saw that the disciple whom Jesus loved was following them. (This was the one who had leaned back against Jesus at the supper and had said, "Lord, who is going to betray you?") 21 When Peter saw him, he asked, "Lord, what about him?"

22 Jesus answered, "If I want him to remain alive until I return, what is that to you? You must follow me." 23 Because of this, the rumor spread among the brothers that this disciple would not die. But Jesus did not say that he would not die; he only said, "If I want him to remain alive until I return, what is that to you?"

24 This is the disciple who testifies to these things and who wrote them down. We know that his testimony is true.

25 Jesus did many other things as well. If every one of them were written down, I suppose that even the whole world would not have room for the books that would be written.

Greek Interlinear

15 Ὅτε οὖν ἠρίστησαν, λέγει τῷ
When therefore they breakfasted, says -

Σίμωνι Πέτρῳ ὁ Ἰησοῦς· Σίμων Ἰωάννου,
to Simon Peter - Jesus: Simon [son] of John,

ἀγαπᾷς με πλέον τούτων; λέγει αὐτῷ·
lovest thou me more [than] these? He says to him:

ναί, κύριε, σὺ οἶδας ὅτι φιλῶ σε. λέγει
Yes, Lord, thou knowest that I love thee. He says

αὐτῷ· βόσκε τὰ ἀρνία μου. **16** λέγει
to him: Feed the lambs of me. He says

αὐτῷ πάλιν δεύτερον· Σίμων [son] Ἰωάννου,
to him again secondly: Simon [son] of John,

ἀγαπᾷς με; λέγει αὐτῷ· ναί, κύριε,
lovest thou me? He says to him: Yes, Lord,

σὺ οἶδας ὅτι φιλῶ σε. λέγει αὐτῷ·
thou knowest that I love thee. He says to him:

ποίμαινε τὰ προβάτιά μου. **17** λέγει
Shepherd the little sheep of me. He says

αὐτῷ τὸ τρίτον· Σίμων Ἰωάννου, φιλεῖς
to him the third [time]: Simon [son] of John, lovest thou

με; ἐλυπήθη ὁ Πέτρος ὅτι εἶπεν αὐτῷ
me? Was grieved - Peter that he said to him

τὸ τρίτον· φιλεῖς με; καὶ εἶπεν αὐτῷ·
the third [time]: Lovest thou me? and said to him:

κύριε, πάντα σὺ οἶδας, σὺ γινώσκεις
Lord, all things thou knowest, thou knowest

ὅτι φιλῶ σε· λέγει αὐτῷ Ἰησοῦς· βόσκε
that I love thee; says to him Jesus: Feed

τὰ προβάτιά μου. **18** ἀμὴν ἀμὴν λέγω
the little sheep of me. Truly truly I tell

σοι, ὅτε ἦς νεώτερος, ἐζώννυες σεαυτὸν
thee, when thou wast younger, thou girdedst thyself

καὶ περιεπάτεις ὅπου ἤθελες· ὅταν δὲ
and walkedst where thou wishedst; but when

γηράσῃς, ἐκτενεῖς τὰς χεῖράς σου, καὶ
thou growest old, thou wilt stretch out the hands of thee, and

ἄλλος ζώσει σε καὶ οἴσει ὅπου οὐ θέλεις.
another will gird thee and will carry where thou wishest not.

19 τοῦτο δὲ εἶπεν σημαίνων ποίῳ θανάτῳ
And this he said signifying by what death

δοξάσει τὸν θεόν. καὶ τοῦτο εἰπὼν λέγει
he will glorify - God. And this saying he tells

αὐτῷ· ἀκολούθει μοι. **20** ἐπιστραφεὶς ὁ
him: Follow me. Turning -

Πέτρος βλέπει τὸν μαθητὴν ὃν ἠγάπα ὁ
Peter sees the disciple whom ²loved -

Ἰησοῦς ἀκολουθοῦντα, ὃς καὶ ἀνέπεσεν
¹Jesus following, who also leaned

ἐν τῷ δείπνῳ ἐπὶ τὸ στῆθος αὐτοῦ καὶ
at the supper on the breast of him and

εἶπεν· κύριε, τίς ἐστιν ὁ παραδιδούς σε;
said: Lord, who is the[one] betraying thee?

21 τοῦτον οὖν ἰδὼν ὁ Πέτρος λέγει τῷ
⁴This one ³therefore ²seeing - ¹Peter says

Ἰησοῦ· κύριε, οὗτος δὲ τί; **22** λέγει
to Jesus: Lord, and this one what? Says

αὐτῷ ὁ Ἰησοῦς· ἐὰν αὐτὸν θέλω μένειν
to him - Jesus: If him I wish to remain

ἕως ἔρχομαι, τί πρὸς σέ; σύ μοι
until I come, what to thee? ²thou ³me

ἀκολούθει. **23** ἐξῆλθεν οὖν οὗτος ὁ λόγος
¹follow. Went forth therefore this - word

εἰς τοὺς ἀδελφοὺς ὅτι ὁ μαθητὴς ἐκεῖνος
to the brothers that - disciple that

οὐκ ἀποθνῄσκει· οὐκ εἶπεν δὲ αὐτῷ ὁ
does not die; but said not to him -

Ἰησοῦς ὅτι οὐκ ἀποθνῄσκει, ἀλλ'· ἐὰν
Jesus that he does not die, but: If

αὐτὸν θέλω μένειν ἕως ἔρχομαι, τί πρὸς
him I wish to remain until I come, what to

σέ;
thee?

24 Οὗτός ἐστιν ὁ μαθητὴς ὁ μαρτυρῶν
This is the disciple - witnessing

περὶ τούτων καὶ ὁ γράψας ταῦτα,
concerning these and - having these
things written things,

καὶ οἴδαμεν ὅτι ἀληθὴς αὐτοῦ ἡ μαρτυρία
and we know that true of him the witness

ἐστίν. **25** Ἔστιν δὲ καὶ ἄλλα πολλὰ ἃ
is. And there are also other many which
things

ἐποίησεν ὁ Ἰησοῦς, ἅτινα ἐὰν γράφηται
did - Jesus, which if they were written

καθ' ἕν, οὐδ' αὐτὸν οἶμαι τὸν κόσμον
singly,† ²not ⁴[it]self ¹I think ³the ⁴world

χωρήσειν τὰ γραφόμενα βιβλία.
⁵to contain ⁷the ⁸being written ⁶rolls.

King James Version

New International Version

THE ACTS OF THE

APOSTLES

ACTS

Jesus taken up into heaven

1 The former treatise have I made, O Theophilus, of all that Jesus began both to do and teach, 2 Until the day in which he was taken up, after that he through the Holy Ghost had given commandments unto the apostles whom he had chosen: 3 To whom also he shewed himself alive after his passion by many infallible proofs, being seen of them forty days, and speaking of the things pertaining to the kingdom of God: 4And, being assembled together with *them,* commanded them that they should not depart from Jerusalem, but wait for the promise of the Father, which, *saith he,* ye have heard of me. 5 For John truly baptized with water; but ye shall be baptized with the Holy Ghost not many days hence. 6 When they therefore were come together, they asked of him, saying, Lord, wilt thou at this time restore again the kingdom to Israel? 7And he said unto them, It is not for you to know the times or the seasons, which the Father hath put in his own power. 8 But ye shall receive power, after that the Holy Ghost is come upon you: and ye shall be witnesses unto me both in Jerusalem, and in all Judea, and in Samaria, and unto the uttermost part of the earth. 9And when he had spoken these things, while they beheld, he was taken up; and a cloud received him out of their sight. 10And while they looked steadfastly toward heaven as he went up, behold, two men stood by them in white apparel; 11 Which also said, Ye men of Galilee, why stand ye gazing up into heaven? this same Jesus, which is taken up from you into heaven, shall so come in like manner as ye have seen him go into heaven. 12 Then returned they unto Jerusalem from the mount called Olivet, which is from Jerusalem a sabbath day's journey. 13And when they were come in, they went up into an upper room, where abode both Peter and James, and John, and Andrew, Philip, and Thomas, Bartholomew, and Matthew, James *the son* of Alpheus, and Simon Zelotes, and Judas *the brother* of James. 14 These all continued with one accord in prayer and supplication, with the women, and Mary the mother of Jesus, and with his brethren.

15 And in those days Peter stood up in the midst of the disciples, and said, (the number of names together were about a hundred and twenty,) 16 Men *and* brethren, this Scripture must needs have been fulfilled, which the Holy Ghost by the mouth of David spake before concerning Judas, which was guide to them that

1 In my former book, Theophilus, I wrote about all that Jesus began to do and to teach 2 until the day he was taken up to heaven, after giving instructions through the Holy Spirit to the apostles he had chosen. 3After his suffering, he showed himself to these men and gave many convincing proofs that he was alive. He appeared to them over a period of forty days and spoke about the kingdom of God. 4 On one occasion, while he was eating with them, he gave them this command: "Do not leave Jerusalem, but wait for the gift my Father promised, which you have heard me speak about. 5 For John baptized with water, but in a few days you will be baptized with the Holy Spirit."

6 So when they met together, they asked him, "Lord, are you at this time going to restore the kingdom to Israel?"

7 He said to them: "It is not for you to know the times or dates the Father has set by his own authority. 8 But you will receive power when the Holy Spirit comes on you; and you will be my witnesses in Jerusalem, and in all Judea and Samaria, and to the ends of the earth."

9 After he said this, he was taken up before their very eyes, and a cloud hid him from their sight.

10 They were looking intently up into the sky as he was going, when suddenly two men dressed in white stood beside them. 11 "Men of Galilee," they said, "why do you stand here looking into the sky? This same Jesus, who has been taken from you into heaven, will come back in the same way you have seen him go into heaven."

Matthias chosen to replace Judas

12 Then they returned to Jerusalem from the hill called the Mount of Olives, a Sabbath day's walk[a] from the city. 13 When they arrived, they went upstairs to the room where they were staying. Those present were Peter, John, James and Andrew; Philip and Thomas, Bartholomew and Matthew; James son of Alphaeus and Simon the Zealot, and Judas son of James. 14 They all joined together constantly in prayer, along with the women and Mary the mother of Jesus, and his brothers.

15 In those days Peter stood up among the believers (a group numbering about one hundred and twenty) 16 and said, "Brothers, the Scripture had to be fulfilled which the Holy Spirit spoke long ago through the mouth of David concerning Judas, who served as guide

[a] That is, about half a mile.

ΠΡΑΞΕΙΣ   ΑΠΟΣΤΟΛΩΝ

Chapter 1

Τὸν μὲν πρῶτον λόγον ἐποιησάμην
The -   first   account   I made

περὶ πάντων, ὦ Θεόφιλε, ὧν ἤρξατο
concerning all things, O Theophilus, which began

ὁ Ἰησοῦς ποιεῖν τε καὶ διδάσκειν,
- Jesus both to do and to teach,

2 ἄχρι ἧς ἡμέρας ἐντειλάμενος τοῖς
until which day 'having given injunctions 'to the
=the day on which

ἀποστόλοις διὰ πνεύματος ἁγίου οὓς
'apostles 'through 'Spirit 'Holy 'whom

ἐξελέξατο ἀνελήμφθη· 3 οἷς καὶ παρέστησεν
'he chose 'he was taken up; to whom also he presented

ἑαυτὸν ζῶντα μετὰ τὸ παθεῖν αὐτὸν ἐν
himself living after the to suffer him' by
=he suffered

πολλοῖς τεκμηρίοις, δι' ἡμερῶν τεσσεράκοντα
many infallible proofs, through days forty

ὀπτανόμενος αὐτοῖς καὶ λέγων τὰ περὶ
being seen by them and speaking the things concerning

τῆς βασιλείας τοῦ θεοῦ· 4 καὶ συναλιζόμενος
the kingdom - of God; and meeting with [them]

παρήγγειλεν αὐτοῖς ἀπὸ Ἱεροσολύμων μὴ
he charged them from Jerusalem not

χωρίζεσθαι, ἀλλὰ περιμένειν τὴν ἐπαγγελίαν
to depart, but to await the promise

τοῦ πατρὸς ἣν ἠκούσατέ μου· 5 ὅτι
of the Father which ye heard of me : because

Ἰωάννης μὲν ἐβάπτισεν ὕδατι, ὑμεῖς δὲ
John indeed baptized in water, but ye

ἐν πνεύματι βαπτισθήσεσθε ἁγίῳ οὐ μετὰ
in 'Spirit 'will be baptized 'Holy not after

πολλὰς ταύτας ἡμέρας. 6 Οἱ μὲν οὖν
many these days. 'the [ones] 'So then

συνελθόντες ἠρώτων αὐτὸν λέγοντες· κύριε,
'coming together questioned him saying : Lord,

εἰ ἐν τῷ χρόνῳ τούτῳ ἀποκαθιστάνεις
if at the this time restorest thou

τὴν βασιλείαν τῷ Ἰσραήλ; 7 εἶπεν πρὸς
the kingdom - to Israel? He said to

αὐτούς· οὐχ ὑμῶν ἐστιν γνῶναι χρόνους
them : Not of you it is to know times

ἢ καιροὺς οὓς ὁ πατὴρ ἔθετο ἐν τῇ
or seasons which the Father placed in the(his)

ἰδίᾳ ἐξουσίᾳ, 8 ἀλλὰ λήμψεσθε δύναμιν
own authority, but ye will receive power

ἐπελθόντος τοῦ ἁγίου πνεύματος ἐφ' ὑμᾶς,
coming upon the Holy Spirit' upon you,
=when the Holy Spirit comes

καὶ ἔσεσθέ μου μάρτυρες ἔν τε Ἱερουσαλὴμ
and ye will be of me witnesses both in Jerusalem

καὶ ἐν πάσῃ τῇ Ἰουδαίᾳ καὶ Σαμαρείᾳ
and in all - Judæa and Samaria

καὶ ἕως ἐσχάτου τῆς γῆς. 9 καὶ ταῦτα
and unto [the] extremity of the earth. And these things

εἰπὼν βλεπόντων αὐτῶν ἐπήρθη, καὶ
saying looking them' he was taken up, and
=as they looked

νεφέλη ὑπέλαβεν αὐτὸν ἀπὸ τῶν ὀφθαλμῶν
a cloud received him from the eyes

αὐτῶν. 10 καὶ ὡς ἀτενίζοντες ἦσαν εἰς
of them. And as gazing they were to

τὸν οὐρανὸν πορευομένου αὐτοῦ, καὶ ἰδοὺ
- heaven going him,' - behold[,]
=as he went,

ἄνδρες δύο παρειστήκεισαν αὐτοῖς ἐν ἐσθήσεσι
men two stood by them in garments

λευκαῖς, 11 οἳ καὶ εἶπαν· ἄνδρες Γαλιλαῖοι,
white, who also said : Men Galilæans;

τί ἑστήκατε βλέποντες εἰς τὸν οὐρανόν;
why stand ye looking to - heaven ?

οὗτος ὁ Ἰησοῦς ὁ ἀναλημφθεὶς
This - Jesus the [one] having been taken up

ἀφ' ὑμῶν εἰς τὸν οὐρανὸν οὕτως ἐλεύσεται
from you to - heaven thus will come

ὃν τρόπον ἐθεάσασθε αὐτὸν πορευόμενον
in the way† ye beheld him going

εἰς τὸν οὐρανόν. 12 Τότε ὑπέστρεψαν
to - heaven. Then they returned

εἰς Ἱερουσαλὴμ ἀπὸ ὄρους τοῦ καλου-
to Jerusalem from [the] mount the [one] being

μένου ἐλαιῶνος, ὅ ἐστιν ἐγγὺς Ἱερουσαλὴμ
called of [the] olive grove, which is near Jerusalem

σαββάτου ἔχον ὁδόν. 13 καὶ ὅτε εἰσῆλθον,
of a sabbath having a way. And when they entered,
=a sabbath's journey off.

εἰς τὸ ὑπερῷον ἀνέβησαν οὗ ἦσαν
into the upper room they went up where they were

καταμένοντες, ὅ τε Πέτρος καὶ Ἰωάννης
waiting, - both Peter and John

καὶ Ἰάκωβος καὶ Ἀνδρέας, Φίλιππος καὶ
and James and Andrew, Philip and

Θωμᾶς, Βαρθολομαῖος καὶ Μαθθαῖος,
Thomas, Bartholomew and Matthew,

Ἰάκωβος Ἀλφαίου καὶ Σίμων ὁ ζηλωτὴς
James [son] of Alphæus and Simon the zealot

καὶ Ἰούδας Ἰακώβου. 14 οὗτοι πάντες
and Judas [brother] of James. These all

ἦσαν προσκαρτεροῦντες ὁμοθυμαδὸν τῇ
were continuing steadfastly with one mind -

προσευχῇ σὺν γυναιξὶν καὶ Μαριὰμ τῇ
in prayer with [the] women and Mary the

μητρὶ [τοῦ] Ἰησοῦ καὶ σὺν τοῖς ἀδελφοῖς
mother of Jesus and with the brothers

αὐτοῦ.
of him.

15 Καὶ ἐν ταῖς ἡμέραις ταύταις ἀναστὰς
And in these days standing up

Πέτρος ἐν μέσῳ τῶν ἀδελφῶν εἶπεν·
Peter in [the] midst of the brothers said :

ἦν τε ὄχλος ὀνομάτων ἐπὶ τὸ αὐτὸ
'was 'and '[the] 'crowd of names 'together

ὡσεὶ ἑκατὸν εἴκοσι· 16 ἄνδρες ἀδελφοί,
about a hundred twenty : Men brothers,

ἔδει πληρωθῆναι τὴν γραφὴν ἣν
it behoved to be fulfilled the scripture which

προεῖπεν τὸ πνεῦμα τὸ ἅγιον διὰ στόματος
spoke before the Spirit - Holy through [the] mouth

Δαυὶδ περὶ Ἰούδα τοῦ γενομένου ὁδηγοῦ
of David concerning Judas the [one] having become guide

King James Version

took Jesus. 17 For he was numbered with us, and had obtained part of this ministry. 18 Now this man purchased a field with the reward of iniquity; and falling headlong, he burst asunder in the midst, and all his bowels gushed out. 19And it was known unto all the dwellers at Jerusalem; insomuch as that field is called, in their proper tongue, Aceldama, that is to say, The field of blood. 20 For it is written in the book of Psalms, Let his habitation be desolate, and let no man dwell therein: and, His bishoprick let another take. 21 Wherefore of these men which have companied with us all the time that the Lord Jesus went in and out among us, 22 Beginning from the baptism of John, unto that same day that he was taken up from us, must one be ordained to be a witness with us of his resurrection. 23 And they appointed two, Joseph called Barsabas, who was surnamed Justus, and Matthias. 24And they prayed, and said, Thou, Lord, which knowest the hearts of all *men*, shew whether of these two thou hast chosen, 25 That he may take part of this ministry and apostleship, from which Judas by transgression fell, that he might go to his own place. 26And they gave forth their lots; and the lot fell upon Matthias; and he was numbered with the eleven apostles.

2 And when the day of Pentecost was fully come, they were all with one accord in one place. 2And suddenly there came a sound from heaven as of a rushing mighty wind, and it filled all the house where they were sitting. 3And there appeared unto them cloven tongues like as of fire, and it sat upon each of them. 4And they were all filled with the Holy Ghost, and began to speak with other tongues, as the Spirit gave them utterance. 5And there were dwelling at Jerusalem Jews, devout men, out of every nation under heaven. 6 Now when this was noised abroad, the multitude came together, and were confounded, because that every man heard them speak in his own language. 7And they were all amazed and marvelled, saying one to another, Behold, are not all these which speak Galileans? 8And how hear we every man in our own tongue, wherein we were born? 9 Parthians, and Medes, and Elamites, and the dwellers in Mesopotamia, and in Judea, and Cappadocia, in Pontus, and Asia, 10 Phrygia, and Pamphylia, in Egypt, and in the parts of Libya about Cyrene, and strangers of Rome, Jews and proselytes, 11 Cretes and Arabians, we do hear them speak in our tongues

New International Version

for those who arrested Jesus—17 he was one of our number and shared in this ministry."

18 (With the reward he got for his wickedness, Judas bought a field; there he fell headlong, his body burst open and all his intestines spilled out. 19 Everyone in Jerusalem heard about this, so they called that field in their language Akeldama, that is, Field of Blood.)

20 "For," said Peter, "it is written in the book of Psalms,

'May his place be deserted;
    let there be no one to dwell in it,' *b*
and,
'May another take his place of leadership.' *c*

21 Therefore it is necessary to choose one of the men who have been with us the whole time the Lord Jesus went in and out among us, 22 beginning from John's baptism to the time when Jesus was taken up from us. For one of these must become a witness with us of his resurrection."

23 So they proposed two men: Joseph called Barsabbas (also known as Justus) and Matthias. 24 Then they prayed, "Lord, you know everyone's. heart. Show us which of these two you have chosen 25 to take over this apostolic ministry, which Judas left to go where he belongs." 26 Then they drew lots, and the lot fell to Matthias; so he was added to the eleven apostles.

The Holy Spirit comes at Pentecost

2 When the day of Pentecost came, they were all together in one place. 2 Suddenly a sound like the blowing of a violent wind came from heaven and filled the whole house where they were sitting. 3 They saw what seemed to be tongues of fire that separated and came to rest on each of them. 4All of them were filled with the Holy Spirit and began to speak in other tongues*d* as the Spirit enabled them.

5 Now there were staying in Jerusalem Godfearing Jews from every nation of the world. 6 When they heard this sound, a crowd came together in bewilderment, because each one heard them speaking in his own language. 7 Utterly amazed, they asked: "Are not all these men who are speaking Galileans? 8 Then how is it that each of us hears them in his own native language? 9 Parthians, Medes and Elamites; residents of Mesopotamia, Judea and Cappadocia, Pontus and Asia, 10 Phrygia and Pamphylia, Egypt and the parts of Libya near Cyrene; visitors from Rome 11 (both Jews and converts to Judaism); Cretans and Arabs—we hear them declaring the wonders of God in our own

[b] Psalm 69:25. [c] Psalm 109:8. [d] Or *languages*.

Greek Interlinear

τοῖς συλλαβοῦσιν Ἰησοῦν, 17 ὅτι κατ-
to the [ones] taking Jesus, because having

ηριθμημένος ἦν ἐν ἡμῖν καὶ ἔλαχεν τὸν
been numbered he was among us and obtained the

κλῆρον τῆς διακονίας ταύτης. 18 οὗτος μὲν οὖν
portion of this ministry. This one therefore

ἐκτήσατο χωρίον ἐκ μισθοῦ τῆς
bought a field out of [the] reward -

ἀδικίας, καὶ πρηνὴς γενόμενος ἐλάκησεν
of unrighteousness, and swollen up having become he burst asunder

μέσος, καὶ ἐξεχύθη πάντα τὰ σπλάγχνα
in the middle, and were poured out all the bowels

αὐτοῦ· 19 καὶ γνωστὸν ἐγένετο πᾶσι τοῖς
of him; and known it became to all the

κατοικοῦσιν Ἰερουσαλήμ, ὥστε κληθῆναι
[ones] inhabiting Jerusalem, so as to be called

τὸ χωρίον ἐκεῖνο τῇ ἰδίᾳ διαλέκτῳ αὐτῶν
that field in their own language

Ἀκελδαμάχ, τοῦτ' ἔστιν χωρίον
Aceldamach, this is Field

αἵματος. 20 γέγραπται γὰρ ἐν βίβλῳ
of blood. For it has been written in [the] roll

ψαλμῶν· γενηθήτω ἡ ἔπαυλις αὐτοῦ ἔρημος
of Psalms : Let become the estate of him deserted

καὶ μὴ ἔστω ὁ κατοικῶν ἐν αὐτῇ, καὶ·
and let not be the [one] dwelling in it, and :

τὴν ἐπισκοπὴν αὐτοῦ λαβέτω ἕτερος.
The office of him let take another.

21 δεῖ οὖν τῶν συνελθόντων ἡμῖν ἀνδρῶν
It behoves* therefore ²of the ³accompanying ⁴us ¹men

ἐν παντὶ χρόνῳ ᾧ εἰσῆλθεν καὶ
in all [the] time in which went in and

ἐξῆλθεν ἐφ' ἡμᾶς ὁ κύριος Ἰησοῦς,
went out among us the Lord Jesus,

22 ἀρξάμενος ἀπὸ τοῦ βαπτίσματος
beginning from the baptism

Ἰωάννου ἕως τῆς ἡμέρας ἧς ἀνελήμφθη
of John until the day when he was taken up

ἀφ' ἡμῶν, μάρτυρα τῆς ἀναστάσεως
from us, ⁴a witness* ²of the ³resurrection

αὐτοῦ σὺν ἡμῖν γενέσθαι ἕνα τούτων.
¹of him ²with ³us ¹to become ¹one* ¹of these.

23 Καὶ ἔστησαν δύο, Ἰωσὴφ τὸν καλού-
And they set two, Joseph the [one] being

μενον Βαρσαββᾶν, ὃς ἐπεκλήθη Ἰοῦστος,
called Barsabbas, who was surnamed Justus,

καὶ Μαθθίαν. 24 καὶ προσευξάμενοι εἶπαν·
and Matthias. And praying they said :

σὺ κύριε καρδιογνῶστα πάντων, ἀνάδειξον
Thou Lord Heart-knower of all men, show

ὃν ἐξελέξω ἐκ τούτων τῶν δύο ἕνα
whom thou didst choose of these - two one

25 λαβεῖν τὸν τόπον τῆς διακονίας ταύτης
to take the place of this ministry

καὶ ἀποστολῆς, ἀφ' ἧς παρέβη Ἰούδας
and apostleship, from which fell Judas

πορευθῆναι εἰς τὸν τόπον τὸν ἴδιον.
to go to the(his) place - own.

26 καὶ ἔδωκαν κλήρους αὐτοῖς, καὶ ἔπεσεν
And they gave lots for them, and fell

ὁ κλῆρος ἐπὶ Μαθθίαν, καὶ συγκατεψηφίσθη
the lot on Matthias, and he was reckoned along with

μετὰ τῶν ἕνδεκα ἀποστόλων.
with the eleven apostles.

Chapter 2

Καὶ ἐν τῷ συμπληροῦσθαι τὴν ἡμέραν
And in the to be completed the day
= when the day of Pentecost was completed

τῆς πεντηκοστῆς ἦσαν πάντες ὁμοῦ ἐπὶ
- of Pentecost* they were all together to-

τὸ αὐτό· 2 καὶ ἐγένετο ἄφνω ἐκ τοῦ
gether;† and there was suddenly out of

οὐρανοῦ ἦχος ὥσπερ φερομένης πνοῆς
heaven a sound as ¹being borne ¹of²a ⁴wind

βιαίας καὶ ἐπλήρωσεν ὅλον τὸν οἶκον
²violent and it filled all the house

οὗ ἦσαν καθήμενοι, 3 καὶ ὤφθησαν αὐτοῖς
where they were sitting, and there appeared to them

διαμεριζόμεναι γλῶσσαι ὡσεὶ πυρός, καὶ
being distributed tongues as of fire, and

ἐκάθισεν ἐφ' ἕνα ἕκαστον αὐτῶν, 4 καὶ
it sat on ²one ¹each of them, and

ἐπλήσθησαν πάντες πνεύματος ἁγίου, καὶ
they were filled all of(with) Spirit Holy, and

ἤρξαντο λαλεῖν ἑτέραις γλώσσαις καθὼς
began to speak in other tongues as

τὸ πνεῦμα ἐδίδου ἀποφθέγγεσθαι αὐτοῖς.
the Spirit gave ¹to speak out ¹them.

5 Ἦσαν δὲ εἰς Ἰερουσαλὴμ κατοικοῦντες
Now there were in Jerusalem dwelling

Ἰουδαῖοι, ἄνδρες εὐλαβεῖς ἀπὸ παντὸς ἔθνους
Jews, men devout from every nation

τῶν ὑπὸ τὸν οὐρανόν· 6 γενομένης
of the [ones] under - heaven; happening

δὲ τῆς φωνῆς ταύτης συνῆλθεν τὸ πλῆθος
and this sound* came together the multitude
= when this sound happened

καὶ συνεχύθη, ὅτι ἤκουον εἷς ἕκαστος
and were confounded, because they heard ⁴one ²each

τῇ ἰδίᾳ διαλέκτῳ λαλούντων αὐτῶν.
¹in his own language ²speaking ¹them.

7 ἐξίσταντο δὲ καὶ ἐθαύμαζον λέγοντες·
And they were amazed and marvelled saying :

οὐχὶ ἰδοὺ πάντες οὗτοί εἰσιν οἱ λαλοῦντες
²not ¹behold ⁴all ⁵these ²are *the [ones] ³speaking

Γαλιλαῖοι; 8 καὶ πῶς ἡμεῖς ἀκούομεν
⁵Galilæans? and how ¹we ¹hear

ἕκαστος τῇ ἰδίᾳ διαλέκτῳ ἡμῶν ἐν ᾗ
²each ¹in his own language ¹of us in which

ἐγεννήθημεν, 9 Πάρθοι καὶ Μῆδοι καὶ
we were born, Parthians and Medes and

Ἐλαμῖται, καὶ οἱ κατοικοῦντες τὴν
Elamites, and the [ones] inhabiting -

Μεσοποταμίαν, Ἰουδαίαν τε καὶ Καππα-
Mesopotamia, both Judæa and Cappa-

δοκίαν, Πόντον καὶ τὴν Ἀσίαν, 10 Φρυγίαν
docia, Pontus and - Asia, Phrygia

τε καὶ Παμφυλίαν, Αἴγυπτον καὶ τὰ
both and Pamphylia, Egypt and the

μέρη τῆς Λιβύης τῆς κατὰ Κυρήνην,
regions - of Libya - over against Cyrene,

καὶ οἱ ἐπιδημοῦντες Ῥωμαῖοι, 11 Ἰουδαῖοί
and the temporarily residing Romans, ¹Jews

τε καὶ προσήλυτοι, Κρῆτες καὶ Ἄραβες,
¹both and proselytes, Cretans and Arabians,

ἀκούομεν λαλούντων αὐτῶν ταῖς ἡμετέραις
we hear ²speaking ¹them in the our

γλώσσαις τὰ μεγαλεῖα τοῦ θεοῦ;
tongues the great deeds - of God?

* The object (according to the Greek construction) of the verb
δεῖ is ἕνα, with μάρτυρα as its complement after γενέσθαι.

345

King James Version

the wonderful works of God. 12And they were all amazed, and were in doubt, saying one to another, What meaneth this? 13 Others mocking said, These men are full of new wine.

14 But Peter, standing up with the eleven, lifted up his voice, and said unto them, Ye men of Judea, and all *ye* that dwell at Jerusalem, be this known unto you, and hearken to my words: 15 For these are not drunken, as ye suppose, seeing it is *but* the third hour of the day. 16 But this is that which was spoken by the prophet Joel; 17And it shall come to pass in the last days, saith God, I will pour out of my Spirit upon all flesh: and your sons and your daughters shall prophesy, and your young men shall see visions, and your old men shall dream dreams: 18And on my servants and on my handmaidens I will pour out in those days of my Spirit; and they shall prophesy: 19And I will shew wonders in heaven above, and signs in the earth beneath; blood, and fire, and vapour of smoke: 20 The sun shall be turned into darkness, and the moon into blood, before that great and notable day of the Lord come: 21And it shall come to pass, *that* whosoever shall call on the name of the Lord shall be saved. 22 Ye men of Israel, hear these words; Jesus of Nazareth, a man approved of God among you by miracles and wonders and signs, which God did by him in the midst of you, as ye yourselves also know: 23 Him, being delivered by the determinate counsel and foreknowledge of God, ye have taken, and by wicked hands have crucified and slain: 24 Whom God hath raised up, having loosed the pains of death: because it was not possible that he should be holden of it. 25 For David speaketh concerning him, I foresaw the Lord always before my face; for he is on my right hand, that I should not be moved: 26 Therefore did my heart rejoice, and my tongue was glad; moreover also my flesh shall rest in hope: 27 Because thou wilt not leave my soul in hell, neither wilt thou suffer thine Holy One to see corruption. 28 Thou hast made known to me the ways of life; thou shalt make me full of joy with thy countenance. 29 Men *and* brethren, let me freely speak unto you of the patriarch David, that he is both dead and buried, and his sepulchre is with us unto this day. 30 Therefore being a prophet, and knowing that God had sworn with an oath to him, that of the fruit of his loins, according to the flesh, he would raise up Christ to sit on his throne; 31 He, seeing this before, spake of the resurrection of Christ, that his soul was not left in hell, neither his flesh did see corruption. 32 This Jesus hath God raised up, whereof we all are witnesses. 33 Therefore being by the right hand of God exalted, and having received of the Father the promise of the Holy Ghost, he hath shed forth

New International Version

tongues[d]!" 12Amazed and perplexed, they asked one another, "What does this mean?"
13 Some, however, made fun of them and said, "They have had too much wine.[e]"

Peter addresses the crowd

14 Then Peter stood up with the Eleven, raised his voice and addressed the crowd: "Fellow Jews and all of you who are in Jerusalem, let me explain this to you; listen carefully to what I say. 15 These men are not drunk, as you suppose. It's only nine in the morning! 16 No, this is what was spoken by the prophet Joel:
17 'In the last days, God says,
   I will pour out my Spirit on all people.
   Your sons and daughters will prophesy,
      your young men will see visions,
      and your old men will dream dreams.
18 Even on my servants, both men and women,
   I will pour out my Spirit in those days,
      and they will prophesy.
19 And I will show wonders in the heaven above
   and signs on the earth below,
      blood and fire and billows of smoke.
20 The sun will be turned to darkness
   and the moon become as blood
      before the coming of the great and glorious day of the Lord.
21 And everyone who calls on the name of the Lord will be saved.'[f]
22 "Men of Israel, listen to this: Jesus of Nazareth was a man accredited by God to you by miracles, wonders and signs, which God did among you through him, as you yourselves know. 23 This man was handed over to you by God's set purpose and foreknowledge; and you, with the help of wicked men, put him to death by nailing him to the cross. 24 But God raised him from the dead, freeing him from the agony of death, because it was impossible for death to keep its hold on him. 25 David said about him:
'I saw the Lord always before me.
   Because he is at my right hand, I will not be shaken.
26 Therefore my heart is glad and my tongue rejoices;
   my body also will live in hope,
27 because you will not abandon me to the grave,
   nor will you let your Holy One undergo decay.
28 You have made known to me the paths of life;
   you will fill me with joy in your presence.'[g]
29 "Brothers, I can tell you confidently that the patriarch David died and was buried, and his tomb is here to this day. 30 But he was a prophet and knew that God had promised with an oath that he would place one of his descendants on his throne. 31 Seeing what was ahead, he spoke of the resurrection of the Christ,[h] that he was not abandoned to the grave, nor did his body undergo decay. 32 God has raised this Jesus to life, and we are all witnesses of the fact. 33 Exalted to the right hand of God, he has received from the Father the promised Holy Spirit, and has poured out what you now see

[d] Or *languages.* [e] Or *sweet wine.* [f] Joel 2:28-32. [g] Psalm 16:8-11. [h] Or *Messiah.* "The Christ" (Greek) and "the Messiah" (Hebrew) both mean "the Anointed One."

Greek Interlinear

12 ἐξίσταντο δὲ πάντες καὶ διηποροῦντο,
And were amazed all and were troubled,

ἄλλος πρὸς ἄλλον λέγοντες· τί θέλει
other to other saying : What wishes

τοῦτο εἶναι; 13 ἕτεροι δὲ διαχλευάζοντες
this to be? But others mocking

ἔλεγον ὅτι γλεύκους μεμεστωμένοι εἰσίν.
said[.] - Of(with) sweet wine having been filled they are.

14 Σταθεὶς δὲ ὁ Πέτρος σὺν τοῖς ἕνδεκα
But standing - Peter with the eleven

ἐπῆρεν τὴν φωνὴν αὐτοῦ καὶ ἀπεφθέγξατο
lifted up the voice of him and spoke out

αὐτοῖς·
to them :

Ἄνδρες Ἰουδαῖοι καὶ οἱ κατοικοῦντες
Men Jews and the [ones] inhabiting

Ἰερουσαλὴμ πάντες, τοῦτο ὑμῖν γνωστὸν
Jerusalem all, this to you known

ἔστω, καὶ ἐνωτίσασθε τὰ ῥήματά μου.
let be, and give ear to the words of me.

15 οὐ γὰρ ὡς ὑμεῖς ὑπολαμβάνετε οὗτοι
For not as ye imagine these men

μεθύουσιν, ἔστιν γὰρ ὥρα τρίτη τῆς
are drunk, for it is hour third of the

ἡμέρας, 16 ἀλλὰ τοῦτό ἐστιν τὸ εἰρημένον
day, but this is the thing having been spoken

διὰ τοῦ προφήτου Ἰωήλ· 17 καὶ ἔσται
through the prophet Joel : And it shall be

ἐν ταῖς ἐσχάταις ἡμέραις, λέγει ὁ θεός,
in the last days, says - God,

ἐκχεῶ ἀπὸ τοῦ πνεύματός μου ἐπὶ
I will pour out from the Spirit of me on

πᾶσαν σάρκα, καὶ προφητεύσουσιν οἱ υἱοὶ
all flesh, and will prophesy the sons

ὑμῶν καὶ αἱ θυγατέρες ὑμῶν, καὶ οἱ
of you and the daughters of you, and the

νεανίσκοι ὑμῶν ὁράσεις ὄψονται, καὶ οἱ
young men of you visions will see, and the

πρεσβύτεροι ὑμῶν ἐνυπνίοις ἐνυπνιασθήσονται·
old men of you dreams will dream;

18 καὶ γε ἐπὶ τοὺς δούλους μου καὶ ἐπὶ
and - on the male slaves of me and on

τὰς δούλας μου ἐν ταῖς ἡμέραις ἐκείναις
the female slaves of me in those days

ἐκχεῶ ἀπὸ τοῦ πνεύματός μου, καὶ
I will pour out from the Spirit of me, and

προφητεύσουσιν. 19 καὶ δώσω τέρατα ἐν
they will prophesy. And I will give wonders in

τῷ οὐρανῷ ἄνω καὶ σημεῖα ἐπὶ τῆς
the heaven above and signs on the

γῆς κάτω, αἷμα καὶ πῦρ καὶ ἀτμίδα
earth below, blood and fire and vapour

καπνοῦ. 20 ὁ ἥλιος μεταστραφήσεται εἰς
of smoke. The sun will be turned into

σκότος καὶ ἡ σελήνη εἰς αἷμα, πρὶν
darkness and the moon into blood, before

ἐλθεῖν ἡμέραν κυρίου τὴν μεγάλην καὶ
¹to come(comes) ²day ⁶of [the] Lord ¹the ⁴great ³and

ἐπιφανῆ. 21 καὶ ἔσται πᾶς ὃς ἐὰν
⁴notable.[b] And it will be everyone whoever

ἐπικαλέσηται τὸ ὄνομα κυρίου σωθήσεται.
invokes the name of [the] Lord will be saved.

22 Ἄνδρες Ἰσραηλῖται, ἀκούσατε τοὺς
Men Israelites, hear ye -

λόγους τούτους· Ἰησοῦν τὸν Ναζωραῖον,
words these: Jesus the Nazarene,

ἄνδρα ἀποδεδειγμένον ἀπὸ τοῦ θεοῦ εἰς
a man having been approved from - God among

ὑμᾶς δυνάμεσι καὶ τέρασι καὶ σημείοις,
you by powerful deeds and wonders and signs,

οἷς ἐποίησεν δι᾽ αὐτοῦ ὁ θεὸς ἐν μέσῳ
which did through him - God in [the] midst

ὑμῶν, καθὼς αὐτοὶ οἴδατε, 23 τοῦτον
of you, as [your]selves ye know, this man

τῇ ὡρισμένῃ βουλῇ καὶ προγνώσει τοῦ
¹by the ³having been fixed ⁴counsel ¹and ⁶foreknowledge -

θεοῦ ἔκδοτον διὰ χειρὸς ἀνόμων
⁷of God ¹given up ⁸through ¹⁰[the] hand ¹¹of lawless men

προσπήξαντες ἀνείλατε, 24 ὃν ὁ θεὸς
⁹fastening⁹ ¹²ye killed, whom - God

ἀνέστησεν λύσας τὰς ὠδῖνας τοῦ θανάτου,
raised up loosening the pangs - of death,

καθότι οὐκ ἦν δυνατὸν κρατεῖσθαι αὐτὸν
because it was not possible ¹to be held ¹him

ὑπ᾽ αὐτοῦ. 25 Δαυὶδ γὰρ λέγει εἰς
by it. For David says [as] to

αὐτόν· προορώμην τὸν κύριον ἐνώπιόν
him : I foresaw the Lord before

μου διὰ παντός, ὅτι ἐκ δεξιῶν μού
me always, because on right of me

ἐστιν, ἵνα μὴ σαλευθῶ. 26 διὰ τοῦτο
he is, lest I be moved. Therefore

ηὐφράνθη μου ἡ καρδία καὶ ἠγαλλιάσατο
was glad of me the heart and exulted

ἡ γλῶσσά μου, ἔτι δὲ καὶ ἡ σάρξ
the tongue of me, and now also the flesh

μου κατασκηνώσει ἐπ᾽ ἐλπίδι, 27 ὅτι οὐκ
of me will dwell on(in) hope, because not

ἐγκαταλείψεις τὴν ψυχήν μου εἰς ᾅδην
thou wilt abandon the soul of me in hades

οὐδὲ δώσεις τὸν ὅσιόν σου ἰδεῖν
nᵒ⁻ wilt thou give the holy one of thee to see

διαφθοράν. 28 ἐγνώρισάς μοι ὁδοὺς ζωῆς,
corruption. Thou madest known to me the ways of life,

πληρώσεις με εὐφροσύνης μετὰ τοῦ προσώ-
thou wilt fill me of(with) gladness with the pres-

που σου. 29 Ἄνδρες ἀδελφοί, ἐξὸν εἰπεῖν
ence of thee. Men brothers, it is permitted to speak

μετὰ παρρησίας πρὸς ὑμᾶς περὶ τοῦ
with plainness to you concerning the

πατριάρχου Δαυίδ, ὅτι καὶ ἐτελεύτησεν
patriarch David, that both he died

καὶ ἐτάφη, καὶ τὸ μνῆμα αὐτοῦ ἔστιν
and was buried, and the tomb of him is

ἐν ἡμῖν ἄχρι τῆς ἡμέρας ταύτης.
among us until this day.

30 προφήτης οὖν ὑπάρχων καὶ εἰδὼς ὅτι
A prophet therefore being and knowing that

ὅρκῳ ὤμοσεν αὐτῷ ὁ θεὸς ἐκ καρποῦ
with an oath swore to him - God of [the] fruit

τῆς ὀσφύος αὐτοῦ καθίσαι ἐπὶ τὸν θρόνον
of the ¹oin[s] of him to sit on the throne

αὐτοῦ, 31 προϊδὼν ἐλάλησεν περὶ τῆς
of him, foreseeing he spoke concerning the

ἀναστάσεως τοῦ Χριστοῦ, ὅτι οὔτε
resurrection of the Christ, that neither

ἐγκατελείφθη εἰς ᾅδην οὔτε ἡ σὰρξ
he was abandoned in hades nor the flesh

αὐτοῦ εἶδεν διαφθοράν. 32 τοῦτον τὸν
of him saw corruption. This -

Ἰησοῦν ἀνέστησεν ὁ θεός, οὗ πάντες
Jesus ¹raised up - ¹God, of which all

ἡμεῖς ἐσμεν μάρτυρες· 33 τῇ δεξιᾷ οὖν
we are witnesses; to the right [hand] therefore

τοῦ θεοῦ ὑψωθεὶς τήν τε ἐπαγγελίαν
- of God having been exalted ²the ¹and ²promise

τοῦ πνεύματος τοῦ ἁγίου λαβὼν παρὰ
¹of the ¹⁰Spirit - ⁹Holy ⁶receiving ⁸from

τοῦ πατρὸς ἐξέχεεν τοῦτο ὃ ὑμεῖς καὶ
⁴the ⁵Father he poured out this which ye both

* That is, to a tree; see ch. 5. 30.

King James Version

this, which ye now see and hear. 34 For David is not ascended into the heavens: but he saith himself, The LORD said unto my Lord, Sit thou on my right hand, 35 Until I make thy foes thy footstool. 36 Therefore let all the house of Israel know assuredly, that God hath made that same Jesus, whom ye have crucified, both Lord and Christ.

37 Now when they heard *this,* they were pricked in their heart, and said unto Peter and to the rest of the apostles, Men *and* brethren, what shall we do? 38 Then Peter said unto them, Repent, and be baptized every one of you in the name of Jesus Christ for the remission of sins, and ye shall receive the gift of the Holy Ghost. 39 For the promise is unto you, and to your children, and to all that are afar off, *even* as many as the Lord our God shall call. 40And with many other words did he testify and exhort, saying, Save yourselves from this untoward generation.

41 Then they that gladly received his word were baptized: and the same day there were added *unto them* about three thousand souls. 42And they continued steadfastly in the apostles' doctrine and fellowship, and in breaking of bread, and in prayers. 43And fear came upon every soul: and many wonders and signs were done by the apostles. 44And all that believed were together, and had all things common; 45And sold their possessions and goods, and parted them to all *men,* as every man had need. 46And they, continuing daily with one accord in the temple, and breaking bread from house to house, did eat their meat with gladness and singleness of heart, 47 Praising God, and having favour with all the people. And the Lord added to the church daily such as should be saved.

3 Now Peter and John went up together into the temple at the hour of prayer, *being* the ninth *hour.* 2And a certain man lame from his mother's womb was carried, whom they laid daily at the gate of the temple which is called Beautiful, to ask alms of them that entered into the temple; 3 Who, seeing Peter and John about to go into the temple, asked an alms. 4And Peter, fastening his eyes upon him with John, said, Look on us. 5And he gave heed unto them, expecting to receive something of them. 6 Then Peter said, Silver and gold have I none; but such as I have give I thee: In the name of Jesus Christ of Nazareth rise up and walk. 7And he took him by the right hand, and lifted *him* up: and immediately his feet and ankle bones received strength. 8And he leaping up stood, and walked,

New International Version

and hear. 34 For David did not ascend to heaven, and yet he said,

'The Lord said to my Lord:
　　Sit at my right hand
35　until I make your enemies your footstool.' [i]

36 "Therefore, let all Israel be assured of this: God has made this Jesus whom you crucified both Lord and Christ.[h] "

37 When the people heard this, they were cut to the heart and said to Peter and the other apostles, "Brothers, what shall we do?"

38 Peter replied: "Repent and be baptized, every one of you, in the name of Jesus Christ so that your sins may be forgiven. And you will receive the gift of the Holy Spirit. 39 The promise is for you and your children and for all who are far off—for all whom the Lord our God will call."

40 With many other words he warned them; and he pleaded with them, "Save yourselves from this corrupt generation." 41 Those who accepted his message were baptized, and about three thousand were added to their number that day.

The fellowship of the believers

42 They devoted themselves to the apostles' teaching and to the fellowship, to the breaking of bread and to prayer. 43 Everyone was filled with awe, and many wonders and miracles were done by the apostles. 44All the believers were together and had everything in common. 45 Selling their possessions and goods, they gave to anyone as he had need. 46 Every day they continued to meet together in the temple courts. They broke bread in their homes and ate together with glad and sincere hearts, 47 praising God and enjoying the favor of all the people. And the Lord added to their number daily those who were being saved.

Peter heals the crippled beggar

3 One day Peter and John were going up to the temple at the time of prayer—at three in the afternoon. 2 Now a man crippled from birth was being carried to the temple gate called Beautiful, where he was put every day to beg from those going into the temple courts. 3 When he saw Peter and John about to enter, he asked them for money. 4 Peter looked straight at him, as did John. Then Peter said, "Look at us!" 5 So the man gave them his attention, expecting to get something from them.

6 Then Peter said, "I have no silver or gold, but what I have I give you. In the name of Jesus Christ of Nazareth, walk." 7 Taking him by the right hand, he helped him up, and instantly the man's feet and ankles became strong. 8 He

[i] Psalm 110:1. [h] Or *Messiah.* "The Christ" (Greek) and "the Messiah" (Hebrew) both mean "the Anointed One."

Greek Interlinear

βλέπετε καὶ ἀκούετε. **34** οὐ γὰρ Δαυὶδ
see and hear. For not David

ἀνέβη εἰς τοὺς οὐρανούς, λέγει δὲ αὐτός·
ascended to the heavens, but says he:

εἶπεν κύριος τῷ κυρίῳ μου· κάθου ἐκ
Said [the] LORD to the Lord of me: Sit at

δεξιῶν μου, **35** ἕως ἂν θῶ τοὺς ἐχθρούς
right of me, until I put the enemies

σου ὑποπόδιον τῶν ποδῶν σου. **36** ἀσφαλῶς
of thee a footstool of the feet of thee. Assuredly

οὖν γινωσκέτω πᾶς οἶκος Ἰσραὴλ ὅτι
therefore ¹let ²know ³all! ²[the] ⁴house ⁵of Israel that

καὶ κύριον αὐτὸν καὶ χριστὸν ἐποίησεν
⁶both ⁹Lord ⁷him ⁸and ⁷Christ ¹made

ὁ θεος, τοῦτον τὸν Ἰησοῦν ὃν ὑμεῖς
- ¹God, this - Jesus whom ye

ἐσταυρώσατε. **37** Ἀκούσαντες δὲ κατενύγ-
crucified. And hearing they were

ησαν τὴν καρδίαν, εἶπόν τε πρὸς τὸν
stung [in] the heart, and said to the

Πέτρον καὶ τοὺς λοιποὺς ἀποστόλους·
Peter and the remaining apostles:

τί ποιήσωμεν, ἄνδρες ἀδελφοί; **38** Πέτρος
What may we do, men brothers? Peter

δὲ πρὸς αὐτούς· μετανοήσατε, καὶ
And to them: Repent ye, and

βαπτισθήτω ἕκαστος ὑμῶν ἐπὶ τῷ ὀνόματι
let be baptized each of you on the name

Ἰησοῦ Χριστοῦ εἰς ἄφεσιν τῶν
of Jesus Christ [with a view to] forgiveness of the

ἁμαρτιῶν ὑμῶν, καὶ λήμψεσθε τὴν δωρεὰν
sins of you, and ye will receive the gift

τοῦ ἁγίου πνεύματος. **39** ὑμῖν γάρ ἐστιν
of the Holy Spirit. For to you is

ἡ ἐπαγγελία καὶ τοῖς τέκνοις ὑμῶν καὶ
the promise and to the children of you and

πᾶσιν τοῖς εἰς μακράν, ὅσους ἂν
to all the [ones] far away, as many as

προσκαλέσηται κύριος ὁ θεὸς ἡμῶν.
may call to [him] [the] Lord the God of us.

40 ἑτέροις τε λόγοις πλείοσιν διεμαρτύρατο,
And with other words many he solemnly witnessed,

καὶ παρεκάλει αὐτοὺς λέγων· σώθητε
and exhorted them saying: Be ye saved

ἀπὸ τῆς γενεᾶς τῆς σκολιᾶς ταύτης. **41** οἱ
from - ²generation ¹perverse ¹this. The [ones]

μὲν οὖν ἀποδεξάμενοι τὸν λόγον αὐτοῦ
- therefore welcoming the word of him

ἐβαπτίσθησαν, καὶ προσετέθησαν ἐν
were baptized, and there were added in

τῇ ἡμέρᾳ ἐκείνῃ ψυχαὶ ὡσεὶ τρισχίλιαι·
that day souls about three thousand;

42 ἦσαν δὲ προσκαρτεροῦντες τῇ διδαχῇ
and they were continuing steadfastly in the teaching

τῶν ἀποστόλων καὶ τῇ κοινωνίᾳ, τῇ
of the apostles and in the fellowship, in the

κλάσει τοῦ ἄρτου καὶ ταῖς προσευχαῖς.
breaking of the loaf and in the prayers.

43 Ἐγίνετο δὲ πάσῃ ψυχῇ φόβος· πολλὰ δὲ
And came to every soul fear; and many

τέρατα καὶ σημεῖα διὰ τῶν ἀποστόλων
wonders and signs through the apostles

ἐγίνετο. **44** πάντες δὲ οἱ πιστεύσαντες
happened. And all the believing [ones]

ἐπὶ τὸ αὐτὸ εἶχον ἅπαντα κοινά, **45** καὶ
together had all things common, and

τὰ κτήματα καὶ τὰς ὑπάρξεις ἐπίπρασκον
the properties and the possessions they sold

καὶ διεμέριζον αὐτὰ πᾶσιν, καθότι ἄν
and distributed them to all, according as

τις χρείαν εἶχεν. **46** καθ᾽ ἡμέραν τε
anyone need had. And from day to day†

προσκαρτεροῦντες ὁμοθυμαδὸν ἐν τῷ ἱερῷ,
continuing steadfastly with one mind in the temple,

κλῶντές τε κατ᾽ οἶκον ἄρτον, μετε-
and ¹breaking ²from house to house† ³bread, they

λάμβανον τροφῆς ἐν ἀγαλλιάσει καὶ
shared food in gladness and

ἀφελότητι καρδίας, **47** αἰνοῦντες τὸν θεὸν
simplicity of heart, praising - God

καὶ ἔχοντες χάριν πρὸς ὅλον τὸν λαόν.
and having favour with all the people.

ὁ δὲ κύριος προσετίθει τοὺς σωζομένους
And the Lord added the [ones] being saved

καθ᾽ ἡμέραν ἐπὶ τὸ αὐτό.
from day to day† together.†

Chapter 3

Πέτρος δὲ καὶ Ἰωάννης ἀνέβαινον
Now Peter and John were going up

εἰς τὸ ἱερὸν ἐπὶ τὴν ὥραν τῆς προσευχῆς
to the temple at the hour of the prayer

τὴν ἐνάτην. **2** καί τις ἀνὴρ χωλὸς ἐκ
the ninth. And a certain man ²lame ¹from

κοιλίας μητρὸς αὐτοῦ ὑπάρχων ἐβαστάζετο,
⁴[the] ³of [the] ⁵of him ¹being was being carried, womb mother

ὃν ἐτίθουν καθ᾽ ἡμέραν πρὸς τὴν θύραν
whom they used from day to day† at the door

τοῦ ἱεροῦ τὴν λεγομένην ὡραίαν τοῦ
of the temple - being called Beautiful -

αἰτεῖν ἐλεημοσύνην παρὰ τῶν εἰσπορευομέ-
to ask alms from the [ones] enter-

νων εἰς τὸ ἱερόν· **3** ὃς ἰδὼν Πέτρον καὶ
ing into the temple; who seeing Peter and

Ἰωάννην μέλλοντας εἰσιέναι εἰς τὸ ἱερὸν
John being about to go in into the temple

ἠρώτα ἐλεημοσύνην λαβεῖν. **4** ἀτενίσας δὲ
asked alms to receive. And ⁵gazing

Πέτρος εἰς αὐτὸν σὺν τῷ Ἰωάννῃ εἶπεν·
¹Peter at him with - John said:

βλέψον εἰς ἡμᾶς. **5** ὁ δὲ ἐπεῖχεν αὐτοῖς
Look at us. And he paid heed to them

προσδοκῶν τι παρ᾽ αὐτῶν λαβεῖν. **6** εἶπεν
expecting something from them to receive. said

δὲ Πέτρος· ἀργύριον καὶ χρυσίον οὐχ
And Peter: Silver and gold not

ὑπάρχει μοι· ὃ δὲ ἔχω, τοῦτό σοι δίδωμι·
is to me°; but what I have, this to thee I give;
=I have not;

ἐν τῷ ὀνόματι Ἰησοῦ Χριστοῦ τοῦ
in the name of Jesus Christ the

Ναζωραίου περιπάτει. **7** καὶ πιάσας αὐτὸν τῆς
Nazarene walk. And seizing him of (by) the

δεξιᾶς χειρὸς ἤγειρεν αὐτόν· παραχρῆμα
the right hand he raised him; ²at once

δὲ ἐστερεώθησαν αἱ βάσεις αὐτοῦ καὶ τὰ
¹and were made firm the feet of him and the

σφυδρά, **8** καὶ ἐξαλλόμενος ἔστη, καὶ
ankle-bones, and leaping up he stood, and

King James Version

and entered with them into the temple, walking and leaping, and praising God. 9And all the people saw him walking and praising God: 10And they knew that it was he which sat for alms at the Beautiful gate of the temple: and they were filled with wonder and amazement at that which had happened unto him. 11And as the lame man which was healed held Peter and John, all the people ran together unto them in the porch that is called Solomon's, greatly wondering.

12 And when Peter saw it, he answered unto the people, Ye men of Israel, why marvel ye at this? or why look ye so earnestly on us, as though by our own power or holiness we had made this man to walk? 13 The God of Abraham, and of Isaac, and of Jacob, the God of our fathers, hath glorified his Son Jesus; whom ye delivered up, and denied him in the presence of Pilate, when he was determined to let him go. 14 But ye denied the Holy One and the Just, and desired a murderer to be granted unto you; 15And killed the Prince of life, whom God hath raised from the dead; whereof we are witnesses. 16And his name, through faith in his name, hath made this man strong, whom ye see and know: yea, the faith which is by him hath given him this perfect soundness in the presence of you all. 17And now, brethren, I wot that through ignorance ye did it, as did also your rulers. 18 But those things, which God before had shewed by the mouth of all his prophets, that Christ should suffer, he hath so fulfilled.

19 Repent ye therefore, and be converted, that your sins may be blotted out, when the times of refreshing shall come from the presence of the Lord; 20And he shall send Jesus Christ, which before was preached unto you: 21 Whom the heaven must receive until the times of restitution of all things, which God hath spoken by the mouth of all his holy prophets since the world began. 22 For Moses truly said unto the fathers, A Prophet shall the Lord your God raise up unto you of your brethren, like unto me; him shall ye hear in all things whatsoever he shall say unto you. 23And it shall come to pass, that every soul, which will not hear that Prophet, shall be destroyed from among the people. 24 Yea, and all the prophets from Samuel and those that follow after, as many as have spoken, have likewise foretold of these days. 25 Ye are the children of the prophets, and of the covenant which God made with our fathers, saying unto Abraham, And in thy seed shall all the kindreds of the earth be blessed. 26 Unto you first God, having raised up his Son Jesus, sent him to bless you, in turning away every one of you from his iniquities.

New International Version

jumped to his feet and began to walk. Then he went with them into the temple courts, walking and jumping, and praising God. 9 When all the people saw him walking and praising God, 10 they recognized him as the same man who used to sit begging at the temple gate called Beautiful, and they were filled with wonder and amazement at what had happened to him.

Peter speaks to the onlookers

11 While the beggar held on to Peter and John, all the people were astonished and came running to them in the place called Solomon's Colonnade. 12 When Peter saw this, he said to them: "Men of Israel, why does this surprise you? Why do you stare at us as if by our own power or godliness we had made this man walk? 13 The God of Abraham, Isaac and Jacob, the God of our fathers, has glorified his servant Jesus. You handed him over to be killed, and you disowned him before Pilate, though he had decided to let him go. 14 You disowned the Holy and Righteous One and asked that a murderer be released to you. 15 You killed the author of life, but God raised him from the dead. We are witnesses of this. 16 By faith in the name of Jesus, this man whom you see and know was made strong. It is Jesus' name and the faith that comes through him that has given this complete healing to him, as you can all see.

17 "Now, brothers, I know that you acted in ignorance, as did your leaders. 18 But this is how God fulfilled what he had foretold through all the prophets, saying that his Christ[j] would suffer. 19 Repent, then, and turn to God, so that your sins may be wiped out, 20 that times of refreshing may come from the Lord, and that he may send the Christ,[j] who has been appointed for you—even Jesus. 21 He must remain in heaven until the time comes for God to restore everything, as he promised long ago through his holy prophets. 22 For Moses said, 'The Lord your God will raise up for you a prophet like me from among your own people; you must listen to everything he tells you. 23Anyone who does not listen to him will be completely cut off from among his people.'[k]

24 "Indeed, all the prophets from Samuel on, as many as have spoken, have foretold these days. 25And you are heirs of the prophets and of the covenant God made with your fathers. He said to Abraham, 'Through your offspring all peoples on earth will be blessed.'[l] 26 When God raised up his servant, he sent him first to you to bless you by turning each of you from his wicked ways."

[j] Or Messiah. [k] Deut. 18:15, 18, 19. [l] Gen. 22:18, 26:4.

Greek Interlinear

περιεπάτει, καὶ εἰσῆλθεν σὺν αὐτοῖς εἰς
walked, and entered with them into

τὸ ἱερὸν περιπατῶν καὶ ἁλλόμενος καὶ
the temple walking and leaping and

αἰνῶν τὸν θεόν. 9 καὶ εἶδεν πᾶς ὁ
praising - God. And ⁴saw ¹all ²the

λαὸς αὐτὸν περιπατοῦντα καὶ αἰνοῦντα
²people him walking and praising

τὸν θεόν· 10 ἐπεγίνωσκον δὲ αὐτόν, ὅτι
- God; and they recognized him, that

οὗτος ἦν ὁ πρὸς τὴν ἐλεημοσύνην
this was the [one] for - alms

καθήμενος ἐπὶ τῇ ὡραίᾳ πύλῃ τοῦ ἱεροῦ,
sitting at the Beautiful gate of the temple,

καὶ ἐπλήσθησαν θάμβους καὶ ἐκστάσεως
and they were filled of(with) and bewilderment
amazement

ἐπὶ τῷ συμβεβηκότι αὐτῷ. 11 Κρατοῦντος δὲ
at the thing having happened to him. And holding
= as he held

αὐτοῦ τὸν Πέτρον καὶ τὸν Ἰωάννην
him· - Peter and - John

συνέδραμεν πᾶς ὁ λαὸς πρὸς αὐτοὺς
ran together all the people to them

ἐπὶ τῇ στοᾷ τῇ καλουμένῃ Σολομῶντος
at the porch - being called of Solomon

ἔκθαμβοι. 12 Ἰδὼν δὲ ὁ Πέτρος ἀπεκρίνατο
greatly amazed. And ²seeing - ¹Peter answered

πρὸς τὸν λαόν· ἄνδρες Ἰσραηλῖται, τί
to the people: Men Israelites, why

θαυμάζετε ἐπὶ τούτῳ, ἢ ἡμῖν τί ἀτενίζετε
marvel ye at this man, or at us why gaze ye

ὡς ἰδίᾳ δυνάμει ἢ εὐσεβείᾳ πεποιηκόσιν
as by [our] own power or piety having made

τοῦ περιπατεῖν αὐτόν; 13 ὁ θεὸς Ἀβραὰμ
- to walk⁴ him? The God of Abraham

καὶ Ἰσαὰκ καὶ Ἰακώβ, ὁ θεὸς τῶν
and Isaac and Jacob, the God of the

πατέρων ἡμῶν, ἐδόξασεν τὸν παῖδα αὐτοῦ
fathers of us, glorified the servant of him

Ἰησοῦν, ὃν ὑμεῖς μὲν παρεδώκατε καὶ
Jesus, whom ye - delivered and

ἠρνήσασθε κατὰ πρόσωπον Πιλάτου,
denied in [the] presence of Pilate,

κρίναντος ἐκείνου ἀπολύειν· 14 ὑμεῖς δὲ
having decided that oneᵃ to release [him]; but ye
= when he had decided

τὸν ἅγιον καὶ δίκαιον ἠρνήσασθε, καὶ
the holy and just one denied, and

ᾐτήσασθε ἄνδρα φονέα χαρισθῆναι ὑμῖν,
asked a man a murderer to be granted you,

15 τὸν δὲ ἀρχηγὸν τῆς ζωῆς ἀπεκτείνατε,
and the Author - of life ye killed,

ὃν ὁ θεὸς ἤγειρεν ἐκ νεκρῶν, οὗ ἡμεῖς
whom - God raised from [the] dead, of which we

μάρτυρές ἐσμεν. 16 καὶ ἐπὶ τῇ πίστει
witnesses are. And on the faith

τοῦ ὀνόματος αὐτοῦ τοῦτον, ὃν θεωρεῖτε
of(in) name* of him ³this man, ⁴whom ²ye behold
the

καὶ οἴδατε, ἐστερέωσεν τὸ ὄνομα αὐτοῦ,
¹and ¹know, ⁴made firm ¹the ²name ³of him,

καὶ ἡ πίστις ἡ δι' αὐτοῦ ἔδωκεν αὐτῷ
and the faith - through him gave him

τὴν ὁλοκληρίαν ταύτην ἀπέναντι πάντων
this soundness before all

ὑμῶν. 17 καὶ νῦν, ἀδελφοί, οἶδα ὅτι
you. And now, brothers, I know that

κατὰ ἄγνοιαν ἐπράξατε, ὥσπερ καὶ οἱ
by way of ignorance ye acted, as also the

ἄρχοντες ὑμῶν· 18 ὁ δὲ θεὸς ἃ
rulers of you; - but God the things which

προκατήγγειλεν διὰ στόματος πάντων
he foreannounced through [the] mouth of all

τῶν προφητῶν, παθεῖν τὸν χριστὸν αὐτοῦ,
the prophets, to suffer the Christ of himᵇ,
= that his Christ was to suffer,

ἐπλήρωσεν οὕτως. 19 μετανοήσατε οὖν
fulfilled thus. Repent ye therefore

καὶ ἐπιστρέψατε πρὸς τὸ ἐξαλειφθῆναι
and turn for the to be wiped away
= that your sins may be wiped away,

ὑμῶν τὰς ἁμαρτίας, 20 ὅπως ἂν ἔλθωσιν
of you the sins, so as may come

καιροὶ ἀναψύξεως ἀπὸ προσώπου τοῦ
times of refreshing from [the] presence of the

κυρίου καὶ ἀποστείλῃ τὸν προκεχειρισμένον
Lord and he may send the ¹the ²having been foreappointed

ὑμῖν χριστὸν Ἰησοῦν, 21 ὃν δεῖ οὐρανὸν
²for you ³Christ ³Jesus, whom it behoves heaven

μὲν δέξασθαι ἄχρι χρόνων ἀποκαταστάσεως
- to receive until [the] times of restitution

πάντων ὧν ἐλάλησεν ὁ θεὸς διὰ στόματος
of all things which ²spoke - ¹God ³through ⁴[the] mouth

τῶν ἁγίων ἀπ' αἰῶνος αὐτοῦ προφητῶν.
⁵of the ⁶holy ⁹from ⁷[the] age ⁸of him ⁹prophets.

22 Μωϋσῆς μὲν εἶπεν ὅτι προφήτην ὑμῖν
Moses indeed said[,] - ⁴A prophet ⁵for you

ἀναστήσει κύριος ὁ θεὸς ἐκ τῶν ἀδελφῶν
²will raise up ¹(the) Lord - ¹God of the brothers

ὑμῶν ὡς ἐμέ· αὐτοῦ ἀκούσεσθε κατὰ
of you as me; him shall ye hear according to

πάντα ὅσα ἂν λαλήσῃ πρὸς ὑμᾶς.
all things whatever he may speak to you.

23 ἔσται δὲ πᾶσα ψυχὴ ἥτις ἐὰν μὴ ἀκούσῃ
And it shall be every soul whoever hears not

τοῦ προφήτου ἐκείνου ἐξολεθρευθήσεται
that prophet will be utterly destroyed

ἐκ τοῦ λαοῦ. 24 καὶ πάντες δὲ οἱ
out of the people. ²also ¹all ¹And the

προφῆται ἀπὸ Σαμουὴλ καὶ τῶν καθεξῆς
prophets from Samuel and the [ones] in order

ὅσοι ἐλάλησαν καὶ κατήγγειλαν τὰς ἡμέρας
as many as spoke also announced - days

ταύτας. 25 ὑμεῖς ἐστε οἱ υἱοὶ τῶν
these. Ye are the sons of the

προφητῶν καὶ τῆς διαθήκης ἧς ὁ θεὸς
prophets and of the covenant which - God

διέθετο πρὸς τοὺς πατέρας ὑμῶν, λέγων
made with the fathers of us, saying

πρὸς Ἀβραάμ· καὶ ἐν τῷ σπέρματί
to Abraham: And in the seed

σου ἐνευλογηθήσονται πᾶσαι αἱ πατριαὶ
of thee shall be blessed all the families

τῆς γῆς. 26 ὑμῖν πρῶτον ἀναστήσας ὁ
of the earth. To you first ²having raised up -

θεὸς τὸν παῖδα αὐτοῦ ἀπέστειλεν αὐτὸν
¹God the servant of him sent him

εὐλογοῦντα ὑμᾶς ἐν τῷ ἀποστρέφειν
blessing you in the to turn away
= in turning away

ἕκαστον ἀπὸ τῶν πονηριῶν ὑμῶν.
each one from the iniquities of you.

---

* Objective genitive; cf. "the fear of God" = the fear which has God for its object; and see Gal. 2. 20, etc.

King James Version

4 And as they spake unto the people, the priests, and the captain of the temple, and the Sadducees, came upon them, 2 Being grieved that they taught the people, and preached through Jesus the resurrection from the dead. 3And they laid hands on them, and put *them* in hold unto the next day: for it was now eventide. 4 Howbeit many of them which heard the word believed; and the number of the men was about five thousand.

5 And it came to pass on the morrow that their rulers, and elders, and scribes, 6And Annas the high priest, and Caiaphas, and John, and Alexander, and as many as were of the kindred of the high priest, were gathered together at Jerusalem. 7And when they had set them in the midst, they asked, By what power, or by what name, have ye done this? 8 Then Peter, filled with the Holy Ghost, said unto them, Ye rulers of the people, and elders of Israel, 9 If we this day be examined of the good deed done to the impotent man, by what means he is made whole; 10 Be it known unto you all, and to all the people of Israel, that by the name of Jesus Christ of Nazareth, whom ye crucified, whom God raised from the dead, *even* by him doth this man stand here before you whole. 11 This is the stone which was set at nought of you builders, which is become the head of the corner. 12 Neither is there salvation in any other: for there is none other name under heaven given among men, whereby we must be saved.

13 Now when they saw the boldness of Peter and John, and perceived that they were unlearned and ignorant men, they marvelled; and they took knowledge of them, that they had been with Jesus. 14And beholding the man which was healed standing with them, they could say nothing against it. 15 But when they had commanded them to go aside out of the council, they conferred among themselves, 16 Saying, What shall we do to these men? for that indeed a notable miracle hath been done by them *is* manifest to all them that dwell in Jerusalem; and we cannot deny *it.* 17 But that it spread no further among the people, let us straitly threaten them, that they speak henceforth to no man in this name. 18And they called them, and commanded them not to speak at all nor teach in the name of Jesus. 19 But Peter and John answered and said unto them, Whether it be right in the sight of God to hearken unto you more than unto God, judge ye. 20 For we cannot but speak the things which we have seen and heard. 21 So when they had further threatened them, they let them go, finding nothing how they might punish them, because of the people: for all *men* glorified God

New International Version

Peter and John before the Sanhedrin

4 The priests and the captain of the temple guard and the Sadducees came up to Peter and John while they were speaking to the people. 2 They were greatly disturbed because the apostles were teaching the people and proclaiming in Jesus the resurrection of the dead. 3 They seized Peter and John, and because it was evening, they put them in jail until the next day. 4 But many who heard the message believed, and the number of men grew to about five thousand.

5 The next day the rulers, elders and teachers of the law met in Jerusalem. 6Annas the high priest was there, and so were Caiaphas, John, Alexander and the other men of the high priest's family. 7 They had Peter and John brought before them and began to question them: "By what power or what name did you do this?"

8 Then Peter, filled with the Holy Spirit, said to them: "Rulers and elders of the people! 9 If we are being called to account today for an act of kindness shown to a cripple and are asked how he was healed, 10 then know this, you and everyone else in Israel: It is by the name of Jesus Christ of Nazareth, whom you crucified but whom God raised from the dead, that this man stands before you completely healed. 11 He is

'the stone you builders rejected,
  which has become the capstone.' *m*
12 Salvation is found in no one else; for there is no other name under heaven given to men by which we must be saved."

13 When they saw the courage of Peter and John and realized that they were unschooled, ordinary men, they were astonished and they took note that these men had been with Jesus. 14 But since they could see the man who had been healed standing there with them, there was nothing they could say. 15 So they ordered them to withdraw from the Sanhedrin and then conferred together. 16 "What are we going to do with these men?" they asked. "Everybody living in Jerusalem knows they have done an outstanding miracle, and we cannot deny it. 17 But to stop this thing from spreading any further among the people, we must warn these men to speak no longer to anyone in this name."

18 Then they called them in again and commanded them not to speak or teach at all in the name of Jesus. 19 But Peter and John replied, "Judge for yourselves whether it is right in God's sight to obey you rather than God. 20 For we cannot help speaking about what we have seen and heard."

21 After further threats they let them go. They could not decide how to punish them, because all the people were praising God for what

[*m*] Psalm 118:22.

Greek Interlinear

Chapter 4

Λαλούντων δὲ αὐτῶν πρὸς τὸν λαόν,
And speaking   them*   to   the   people,
=while they were speaking

ἐπέστησαν αὐτοῖς οἱ ἱερεῖς καὶ ὁ στρατηγὸς
came upon   them   the priests and the commandant

τοῦ ἱεροῦ καὶ οἱ Σαδδουκαῖοι, 2 διαπονούμενοι
of the . temple and the Sadducees,   being greatly troubled

διὰ   τὸ διδάσκειν αὐτοὺς τὸν λαὸν καὶ
because of the to teach   themᵇ   the   people and
=because they taught ... announced

καταγγέλλειν ἐν τῷ Ἰησοῦ τὴν ἀνάστασιν
to announceᵇ   by -   Jesus   the   resurrection

τὴν ἐκ νεκρῶν, 3 καὶ ἐπέβαλον αὐτοῖς
-    from [the] dead, and   laid on   them

τὰς χεῖρας καὶ ἔθεντο εἰς τήρησιν εἰς
the(ir) hands and   put   in   guard   till

τὴν αὔριον· ἦν γὰρ ἑσπέρα ἤδη. 4 πολλοὶ
the   morrow;   for it was evening   now.   many

δὲ τῶν ἀκουσάντων τὸν λόγον ἐπίστευσαν,
But of the [ones] hearing   the   word   believed,

καὶ ἐγενήθη ἀριθμὸς τῶν ἀνδρῶν ὡς
and became [the] number of the   men   about

χιλιάδες πέντε.
thousands   five.

5 Ἐγένετο δὲ ἐπὶ τὴν αὔριον
Now it came to pass on   the   morrow

συναχθῆναι αὐτῶν τοὺς ἄρχοντας καὶ τοὺς
to be assembled of them the   rulers   and the

πρεσβυτέρους καὶ τοὺς γραμματεῖς ἐν
elders   and the   scribes   in

Ἰερουσαλήμ, 6 καὶ Ἄννας ὁ ἀρχιερεὺς
Jerusalem,   and Annas*   the high priest

καὶ Καϊάφας καὶ Ἰωάννης καὶ Ἀλέξανδρος
and Caiaphas and   John   and   Alexander

καὶ ὅσοι ἦσαν ἐκ γένους ἀρχιερατικοῦ,
and as many as were of [the] race   high-priestly,

7 καὶ στήσαντες αὐτοὺς ἐν τῷ μέσῳ
and   having stood   them   in the   midst

ἐπυνθάνοντο· ἐν ποίᾳ δυνάμει ἢ ἐν ποίῳ
inquired :   By what   power   or in   what

ὀνόματι ἐποιήσατε τοῦτο ὑμεῖς; 8 τότε
name   did   this   ye?   Then

Πέτρος πλησθεὶς πνεύματος ἁγίου εἶπεν
Peter   filled   of(with) [the] Spirit Holy   said

πρὸς αὐτούς· ἄρχοντες τοῦ λαοῦ καὶ
to   them :   Rulers   of the people and

πρεσβύτεροι, 9 εἰ ἡμεῖς σήμερον ἀνα-
elders,   if   we   to-day   are be-

κρινόμεθα ἐπὶ εὐεργεσίᾳ ἀνθρώπου ἀσθενοῦς,
ing examined on a good deed   man   of an infirm,
=[done to] an infirm man,

ἐν τίνι οὗτος σέσωσται, 10 γνωστὸν ἔστω
by what this man has been healed,   known   let it be

πᾶσιν ὑμῖν καὶ παντὶ τῷ λαῷ Ἰσραήλ,
to all   you and to all the people of Israel,

ὅτι ἐν τῷ ὀνόματι Ἰησοῦ Χριστοῦ τοῦ
that in the   name   of Jesus Christ   the

Ναζωραίου, ὃν ὑμεῖς ἐσταυρώσατε, ὃν ὁ
Nazarene,   whom ye   crucified,   whom -

θεὸς ἤγειρεν ἐκ νεκρῶν, ἐν τούτῳ οὗτος
God raised from [the] dead, in this [name] this man

παρέστηκεν ἐνώπιον ὑμῶν ὑγιής. 11 οὗτός
stands   before   you   whole.   This

ἐστιν ὁ λίθος ὁ ἐξουθενηθεὶς ὑφ' ὑμῶν
is   the stone   -   despised   by   you

τῶν οἰκοδόμων, ὁ γενόμενος εἰς κεφαλὴν
the [ones] building, the [one] become to   head

γωνίας. 12 καὶ οὐκ ἔστιν ἐν ἄλλῳ οὐδενὶ
of [the] corner.   And there is not ¹in ²other ³no(any)

ἡ σωτηρία· οὐδὲ γὰρ ὄνομά ἐστιν ἕτερον
the salvation: for neither ¹name ²is there ²other

ὑπὸ τὸν οὐρανὸν τὸ δεδομένον ἐν
under   -   heaven   - having been given among

ἀνθρώποις ἐν ᾧ δεῖ σωθῆναι ἡμᾶς.
men   by which it behoves ⁴to be saved ¹us.

13 Θεωροῦντες δὲ τὴν τοῦ Πέτρου
And beholding   the   -   of Peter

παρρησίαν καὶ Ἰωάννου, καὶ καταλαβόμενοι
boldness   and of John,   and   perceiving

ὅτι ἄνθρωποι ἀγράμματοί εἰσιν καὶ
that   men   unlettered   they are(were) and

ἰδιῶται, ἐθαύμαζον, ἐπεγίνωσκόν τε αὐτοὺς
laymen, they marvelled, and recognized   them

ὅτι σὺν τῷ Ἰησοῦ ἦσαν, 14 τόν τε
that with   -   Jesus they were(had been), ³the ¹and

ἄνθρωπον βλέποντες σὺν αὐτοῖς ἑστῶτα τὸν
⁴man   ²seeing   ⁵with ⁶them   ³standing   -

τεθεραπευμένον, οὐδὲν εἶχον ἀντειπεῖν.
⁷having been healed,   nothing they had to say against.

15 κελεύσαντες δὲ αὐτοὺς ἔξω τοῦ συνεδρίου
So having commanded   them   outside the   council

ἀπελθεῖν, συνέβαλλον πρὸς ἀλλήλους
to go,   they discussed with   with   one another

16 λέγοντες· τί ποιήσωμεν τοῖς ἀνθρώποις
saying :   What may we do   -   men

τούτοις; ὅτι μὲν γὰρ γνωστὸν σημεῖον
to these?   for that indeed   a notable   sign

γέγονεν δι' αὐτῶν, πᾶσιν τοῖς κατοικοῦσιν
has happened through t...m, to all the [ones] inhabiting

Ἰερουσαλὴμ φανερόν, καὶ οὐ δυνάμεθα
Jerusalem [is]   manifest,   and -   we cannot

ἀρνεῖσθαι· 17 ἀλλ' ἵνα μὴ ἐπὶ πλεῖον
to deny [it];   but   ¹lest   ²more†

διανεμηθῇ εἰς τὸν λαόν, ἀπειλησώμεθα
⁴it is spread abroad ⁴to   the   people,   let us threaten

αὐτοῖς μηκέτι λαλεῖν ἐπὶ τῷ ὀνόματι
them   no longer to speak on   -   name

τούτῳ μηδενὶ ἀνθρώπων. 18 καὶ καλέσαντες
this   to no(any)one of men.   And   calling

αὐτοὺς παρήγγειλαν καθόλου μὴ φθέγγεσθαι
them   they charged   at all   not   to utter

μηδὲ διδάσκειν ἐπὶ τῷ ὀνόματι τοῦ
nor   to teach   on   -   name   -

Ἰησοῦ. 19 ὁ δὲ Πέτρος καὶ Ἰωάννης
of Jesus.   -   But Peter   and   John

ἀποκριθέντες εἶπον πρὸς αὐτούς· εἰ
answering   said   to   them :   If

δίκαιόν ἐστιν ἐνώπιον τοῦ θεοῦ, ὑμῶν
right   it is   before   -   God,   you

ἀκούειν μᾶλλον ἢ τοῦ θεοῦ, κρίνατε·
to hear   rather than -   God,   decide ye;

20 οὐ δυνάμεθα γὰρ ἡμεῖς ἃ εἴδαμεν
for cannot   we   [the] things which we saw

καὶ ἠκούσαμεν μὴ λαλεῖν. 21 οἱ δὲ
and   heard   not   to speak.   And they

προσαπειλησάμενοι ἀπέλυσαν αὐτούς, μηδὲν
having added threats   released   them,   nothing

εὑρίσκοντες τὸ πῶς κολάσωνται αὐτούς,
finding   -   how   they might punish   them,

διὰ τὸν λαόν, ὅτι πάντες ἐδόξαζον τὸν
because of the people, because all men   glorified   -

* The rough breathing in the Greek is ignored in the trans-
literation of some familiar proper names.

353

King James Version

for that which was done. 22 For the man was above forty years old, on whom this miracle of healing was shewed.

23 And being let go, they went to their own company, and reported all that the chief priests and elders had said unto them. 24And when they heard that, they lifted up their voice to God with one accord, and said, Lord, thou *art* God, which hast made heaven, and earth, and the sea, and all that in them is; 25 Who by the mouth of thy servant David hast said, Why did the heathen rage, and the people imagine vain things? 26 The kings of the earth stood up, and the rulers were gathered together against the Lord, and against his Christ. 27 For of a truth against thy holy child Jesus, whom thou hast anointed, both Herod, and Pontius Pilate, with the Gentiles, and the people of Israel, were gathered together, 28 For to do whatsoever thy hand and thy counsel determined before to be done. 29And now, Lord, behold their threatenings: and grant unto thy servants, that with all boldness they may speak thy word, 30 By stretching forth thine hand to heal; and that signs and wonders may be done by the name of thy holy child Jesus.

31 And when they had prayed, the place was shaken where they were assembled together; and they were all filled with the Holy Ghost, and they spake the word of God with boldness. 32And the multitude of them that believed were of one heart and of one soul: neither said any *of them* that aught of the things which he possessed was his own; but they had all things common. 33And with great power gave the apostles witness of the resurrection of the Lord Jesus: and great grace was upon them all. 34 Neither was there any among them that lacked: for as many as were possessors of lands or houses sold them, and brought the prices of the things that were sold, 35And laid *them* down at the apostles' feet: and distribution was made unto every man according as he had need. 36And Joses, who by the apostles was surnamed Barnabas, (which is, being interpreted, The son of consolation,) a Levite, *and* of the country of Cyprus, 37 Having land, sold *it*, and brought the money, and laid *it* at the apostles' feet.

5 But a certain man named Ananias, with Sapphira his wife, sold a possession, 2And kept back *part* of the price, his wife also being privy *to it*, and brought a certain part, and laid *it* at the apostles' feet. 3 But Peter said, Ananias, why hath Satan filled thine heart to lie to the Holy

New International Version

had happened. 22 For the man who was miraculously healed was over forty years old.

The believers' prayer

23 On their release, Peter and John went back to their own people and reported all that the chief priests and elders had said to them. 24 When they heard this, they raised their voices together in prayer to God. "Sovereign Lord," they said, "you made the heaven and the earth and the sea, and everything in them. 25 You spoke by the Holy Spirit through the mouth of your servant, our father David:

'Why do the nations rage,
    and the people plot in vain?
26 The kings of the earth take their stand,
    and the rulers gather together
against the Lord
    and against his Anointed One." ' [o]

27 Indeed Herod and Pontius Pilate met together with the Gentiles and the people of Israel in this city to conspire against your holy servant Jesus, whom you anointed. 28 They did what your power and will had decided beforehand should happen. 29 Now, Lord, consider their threats and enable your servants to speak your word with great boldness. 30 Stretch out your hand to heal and perform miraculous signs and wonders through the name of your holy servant Jesus."

31 After they prayed, the place where they were meeting was shaken. And they were all filled with the Holy Spirit and spoke the word of God boldly.

The believers share their possessions

32 All the believers were one in heart and mind. No one claimed that any of his possessions was his own, but they shared everything they had. 33 With great power the apostles continued to testify to the resurrection of the Lord Jesus, and much grace was with them all. 34 There were no needy persons among them. For from time to time those who owned lands or houses sold them, brought the money from the sales 35 and put it at the apostles' feet, and it was distributed to anyone as he had need.

36 Joseph, a Levite from Cyprus, whom the apostles called Barnabas (which means, Son of Encouragement), 37 sold a field he owned and brought the money and put it at the apostles' feet.

Ananias and Sapphira

5 Now a man named Ananias, together with his wife Sapphira, also sold a piece of property. 2 With his wife's full knowledge he kept back part of the money for himself, but brought the rest and put it at the apostles' feet.

3 Then Peter said, "Ananias, how is it that Satan has so filled your heart that you have lied to the Holy Spirit and have kept for yourself

[n] That is, Christ of Messiah. [o] Psalm 2:1,2.

Greek Interlinear

θεὸν ἐπὶ τῷ γεγονότι· **22** ἐτῶν γὰρ
God   on   the thing having happened;   for of years

ἦν πλειόνων τεσσεράκοντα ὁ ἄνθρωπος
was   more [than]   forty   the   man

ἐφ' ὃν γεγόνει τὸ σημεῖον τοῦτο τῆς
on whom had happened this   sign   -

ἰάσεως. **23** Ἀπολυθέντες δὲ ἦλθον πρὸς
of cure.   And being released   they went to

τοὺς ἰδίους καὶ ἀπήγγειλαν ὅσα πρὸς
the(ir) own [people] and   reported   what things to

αὐτοὺς οἱ ἀρχιερεῖς καὶ οἱ πρεσβύτεροι
them   the chief priests and the   elders

εἶπαν. **24** οἱ δὲ ἀκούσαντες ὁμοθυμαδὸν
said.   And they having heard   with one mind

ἦραν φωνὴν πρὸς τὸν θεὸν καὶ εἶπαν·
lifted voice   to   -   God   and said :

δέσποτα, σὺ ὁ ποιήσας τὸν οὐρανὸν καὶ
Master,   thou the [one] having made the heaven and

τὴν γῆν καὶ τὴν θάλασσαν καὶ πάντα
the earth and the   sea   and   all things

τὰ ἐν αὐτοῖς, **25** ὁ τοῦ πατρὸς ἡμῶν
-   in them,   ¹the ⁴the ²father ¹⁰of us
                              [one]

διὰ πνεύματος ἁγίου στόματος Δαυὶδ
²through ⁵[the] Spirit ⁴Holy ⁷[by] mouth ⁹of David

παιδός σου εἰπών· ἱνατί ἐφρύαξαν ἔθνη
¹¹servant ¹²of thee ⁸saying :⁸ Why   raged   nations

καὶ λαοὶ ἐμελέτησαν κενά; **26** παρέστησαν
and peoples devised   vain things?   came

οἱ βασιλεῖς τῆς γῆς καὶ οἱ ἄρχοντες
the kings   of the earth and the rulers

συνήχθησαν ἐπὶ τὸ αὐτὸ κατὰ τοῦ κυρίου
assembled   together   against the Lord

καὶ κατὰ τοῦ χριστοῦ αὐτοῦ.
and against the   Christ   of him.

27 συνήχθησαν γὰρ ἐπ' ἀληθείας ἐν τῇ
     For assembled   in   truth   in

πόλει ταύτῃ ἐπὶ τὸν ἅγιον παῖδά σου
city   this against the holy servant of thee

Ἰησοῦν, ὃν ἔχρισας, Ἡρῴδης τε καὶ
Jesus, whom thou didst anoint, both Herod and

Πόντιος Πιλᾶτος σὺν ἔθνεσιν καὶ λαοῖς
Pontius   Pilate with nations   and peoples

Ἰσραήλ, **28** ποιῆσαι ὅσα ἡ χείρ σου καὶ
of Israel,   to do   what the hand of thee and
                                            things

ἡ βουλὴ προώρισεν γενέσθαι. **29** καὶ τὰ
the counsel foreordained to happen.   And -

νῦν, κύριε, ἔπιδε ἐπὶ τὰς ἀπειλὰς αὐτῶν,
now, Lord, look on on the threatenings of them,

καὶ δὸς τοῖς δούλοις σου μετὰ παρρησίας
and give to the slaves of thee with ᵇboldness

πάσης λαλεῖν τὸν λόγον σου, **30** ἐν τῷ
¹all   to speak the word of thee,   by the

τὴν χεῖρα ἐκτείνειν σε εἰς ἴασιν καὶ
the hand to stretch forth thee for cure   and
= by stretching forth thy hand

σημεῖα καὶ τέρατα γίνεσθαι διὰ τοῦ
signs   and wonders to happen through the

ὀνόματος τοῦ ἁγίου παιδός σου Ἰησοῦ.
name   of the holy servant of thee Jesus.

31 καὶ δεηθέντων αὐτῶν ἐσαλεύθη ὁ τόπος
     And requesting them⁵ was shaken the place
                      = as they were making request

ἐν ᾧ ἦσαν συνηγμένοι, καὶ ἐπλήσθησαν
in which they were having been   and they were filled
                    assembled,

ἅπαντες τοῦ ἁγίου πνεύματος, καὶ ἐλάλουν
all   of(with) the Holy   Spirit,   and   spoke

τὸν λόγον τοῦ θεοῦ μετὰ παρρησίας.
the word   - of God with boldness.

32 Τοῦ δὲ πλήθους τῶν πιστευσάντων
¹Now ⁶of ⁴the ⁵multitude ⁸of the [ones] ¹⁰having believed

ἦν καρδία καὶ ψυχὴ μία, καὶ οὐδὲ
¹¹was ³[the] ²heart ³and ⁴soul ¹one, and ¹not

εἰς τι τῶν ὑπαρχόντων αὐτῷ ἔλεγεν
²one ²any- ⁴of the ⁵possessions [belonging] ²said
        thing   ⁶to him

ἴδιον εἶναι, ἀλλ' ἦν αὐτοῖς πάντα κοινά.
²[his] own ¹to be, but were to them² all things common.

33 καὶ δυνάμει μεγάλῃ ἀπεδίδουν τὸ
    And ¹with ²power ⁴great   ³gave   ⁵the

μαρτύριον οἱ ἀπόστολοι τοῦ κυρίου Ἰησοῦ
⁶testimony ⁸the ⁷apostles ¹⁰of the ¹¹Lord ¹²Jesus

τῆς ἀναστάσεως, χάρις τε μεγάλη ἦν
⁹of the ¹³resurrection, and ²grace ¹great was

ἐπὶ πάντας αὐτούς. **34** οὐδὲ γὰρ ἐνδεής
upon all   them.   ¹For ²neither ³needy

τις ἦν ἐν αὐτοῖς· ὅσοι γὰρ κτήτορες
⁴anyone ⁵was among them; for as many as owners

χωρίων ἢ οἰκιῶν ὑπῆρχον, πωλοῦντες
of lands or of houses were,   selling

ἔφερον τὰς τιμὰς τῶν πιπρασκομένων
brought the prices of the things   being sold

35 καὶ ἐτίθουν παρὰ τοὺς πόδας τῶν
    and   placed   at   the feet   of the

ἀποστόλων· διεδίδοτο δὲ ἑκάστῳ καθότι ἄν
apostles;   and it was distributed to each   according as

τις χρείαν εἶχεν. **36** Ἰωσὴφ δὲ ὁ
anyone need   had.   And Joseph the [one]

ἐπικληθεὶς Βαρναβᾶς ἀπὸ τῶν ἀποστόλων,
surnamed   Barnabas from(by) the apostles,

ὃ ἐστιν μεθερμηνευόμενον υἱὸς παρακλήσεως,
which is   being translated   Son of consolation,

Λευίτης, Κύπριος τῷ γένει, **37** ὑπάρχοντος
a Levite, a Cypriote -   by race,   being

αὐτῷ ἀγροῦ, πωλήσας ἤνεγκεν τὸ χρῆμα
to him⁸ a field,⁸ having sold [it] brought the proceeds
= as he had a field,

καὶ ἔθηκεν πρὸς τοὺς πόδας τῶν ἀποστόλων.
and placed   at   the feet   of the apostles.

Chapter 5

Ἀνὴρ δέ τις Ἀνανίας ὀνόματι σὺν
And a certain man Ananias★ by name with

Σαπφίρῃ τῇ γυναικὶ αὐτοῦ ἐπώλησεν
Sapphira the wife   of him   sold

κτῆμα, **2** καὶ ἐνοσφίσατο ἀπὸ τῆς τιμῆς,
a property, and appropriated from the   price,

συνειδυίης καὶ τῆς γυναικός, καὶ ἐνέγκας
aware of [it] also the(his) wife,⁸   and bringing
= his wife also being aware of it,

μέρος τι παρὰ τοὺς πόδας τῶν ἀποστόλων
a certain part at   the   feet   of the   apostles

ἔθηκεν. **3** εἶπεν δὲ ὁ Πέτρος· Ἀνανία,
placed [it].   But said   -   Peter :   Ananias,

διὰ τί ἐπλήρωσεν ὁ σατανᾶς τὴν καρδίαν
why   filled   -   Satan   the   heart

σου, ψεύσασθαί σε τὸ πνεῦμα τὸ ἅγιον
of thee, to deceive theeᵇ the Spirit   -   Holy
= that thou shouldest deceive

* It is recognized that there is a primitive error in the text in the
first half of ver. 25; it is impossible to construe it as it stands.
See ch. 1. 16.

★ See note to 4. 6.

355

King James Version

Ghost, and to keep back *part* of the price of the
land? 4 While it remained, was it not thine own?
and after it was sold, was it not in thine own
power? why hast thou conceived this thing in
thine heart? thou hast not lied unto men, but
unto God. 5And Ananias hearing these words
fell down, and gave up the ghost: and great fear
came on all them that heard these things. 6And
the young men arose, wound him up, and carried
him out, and buried *him*. 7And it was about the
space of three hours after, when his wife, not
knowing what was done, came in. 8And Peter
answered unto her, Tell me whether ye sold the
land for so much? And she said, Yea, for so
much. 9 Then Peter said unto her, How is it that
ye have agreed together to tempt the Spirit of
the Lord? behold, the feet of them which have
buried thy husband *are* at the door, and shall
carry thee out. 10 Then fell she down straightway
at his feet, and yielded up the ghost: and the
young men came in, and found her dead, and,
carrying *her* forth, buried *her* by her husband.
11And great fear came upon all the church, and
upon as many as heard these things.

12 And by the hands of the apostles were
many signs and wonders wrought among the people; (and they were all with one accord in Solomon's porch. 13And of the rest durst no man
join himself to them: but the people magnified
them. 14And believers were the more added to
the Lord, multitudes both of men and women;)
15 Insomuch that they brought forth the sick into
the streets, and laid *them* on beds and couches,
that at the least the shadow of Peter passing by
might overshadow some of them. 16 There came
also a multitude *out* of the cities round about
unto Jerusalem, bringing sick folks, and them
which were vexed with unclean spirits: and they
were healed every one.

17 Then the high priest rose up, and all they
that were with him, (which is the sect of the
Sadducees,) and were filled with indignation,
18And laid their hands on the apostles, and put
them in the common prison. 19 But the angel of
the Lord by night opened the prison doors, and
brought them forth, and said, 20 Go, stand and
speak in the temple to the people all the words
of this life. 21And when they heard *that*, they
entered into the temple early in the morning,
and taught. But the high priest came, and they
that were with him, and called the council together, and all the senate of the children of
Israel, and sent to the prison to have them
brought. 22 But when the officers came, and
found them not in the prison, they returned, and
told, 23 Saying, The prison truly found we shut
with all safety, and the keepers standing without
before the doors: but when we had opened, we
found no man within. 24 Now when the high
priest and the captain of the temple and the
chief priests heard these things, they doubted

New International Version

some of the money you received for the land?
4 Didn't it belong to you before it was sold? And
after it was sold, wasn't the money at your disposal? What made you think of doing such a
thing? You have not lied to man but to God."
5 When Ananias heard this, he fell down and
died. And great fear seized all who heard what
had happened. 6 Then the young men came forward, wrapped up his body, and carried him out
and buried him.
7 About three hours later his wife came in,
not knowing what had happened. 8 Peter asked
her, "Tell me, is this the price you and Ananias
got for the land?"
"Yes," she said, "that is the price."
9 Peter said to her, "How could you agree to
test the Spirit of the Lord? Look! The feet of
the men who buried your husband are at the
door, and they will carry you out also."
10 At that moment she fell down at his feet
and died. Then the young men came in and, finding her dead, carried her out and buried her beside her husband. 11 Great fear seized the whole
church and all who heard about these events.

The apostles heal many

12 The apostles performed many miraculous
signs and wonders among the people. And all
the believers used to meet together in Solomon's
Colonnade. 13 No one else dared join them, even
though they were highly regarded by the people.
14 Nevertheless, more and more men and women
believed in the Lord and were added to their
number. 15As a result, people brought the sick
into the streets and laid them on beds and mats
so that at least Peter's shadow might fall on
some of them as he passed by. 16 Crowds gathered also from the towns around Jerusalem,
bringing their sick and those tormented by evil *p*
spirits, and all of them were healed.

The apostles persecuted

17 Then the high priest and all his associates,
who were members of the party of the Sadducees, were filled with jealousy. 18 They arrested
the apostles and put them in the public jail.
19 But during the night an angel of the Lord
opened the doors of the jail and brought them
out. 20 "Go, stand in the temple courts," he said,
"and tell the people the full message of this
new life."
21 At daybreak they entered the temple
courts, as they had been told, and began to teach
the people.
When the high priest and his associates arrived, they called together the Sanhedrin—the
full assembly of the elders of Israel—and sent
to the jail for the apostles. 22 But on arriving
at the jail, the officers did not find them there.
So they went back and reported, 23 "We found
the jail securely locked, with the guards standing at the doors; but when we opened them, we
found no one inside." 24 On hearing this report,
the captain of the temple guard and the chief
priests were puzzled, wondering what would
come of this.

[p] Greek *unclean.*

356

Greek Interlinear

καὶ νοσφίσασθαι ἀπὸ τῆς τιμῆς τοῦ
and to appropriate from the price of the

χωρίου; **4** οὐχὶ μένον σοὶ ἔμενεν καὶ
land? Not remaining to thee it remained and

πραθὲν ἐν τῇ σῇ ἐξουσίᾳ ὑπῆρχεν; τί ὅτι
sold in - thy authority it was? Why

ἔθου ἐν τῇ καρδίᾳ σου τὸ πρᾶγμα
was put in the heart of thee - action

τοῦτο; οὐκ ἐψεύσω ἀνθρώποις ἀλλὰ
this? thou didst not lie to men but

τῷ θεῷ. **5** ἀκούων δὲ ὁ Ἁνανίας
- to God. And hearing - Ananias

τοὺς λόγους τούτους πεσὼν ἐξέψυξεν· καὶ
these words falling expired; and

ἐγένετο φόβος μέγας ἐπὶ πάντας τοὺς
came fear great on all the [ones]

ἀκούοντας. **6** ἀναστάντες δὲ οἱ νεώτεροι
hearing. And rising up the young men

συνέστειλαν αὐτὸν καὶ ἐξενέγκαντες ἔθαψαν.
wrapped him and carrying out buried [him].

7 Ἐγένετο δὲ ὡς ὡρῶν τριῶν διάστημα
¹And there was ³of about ⁵hours ⁴three ²an interval

καὶ ἡ γυνὴ αὐτοῦ μὴ εἰδυῖα τὸ γεγονὸς
and the wife of him not knowing the thing having
happened

εἰσῆλθεν. **8** ἀπεκρίθη δὲ πρὸς αὐτὴν
entered. And answered to her

Πέτρος· εἰπέ μοι, εἰ τοσούτου τὸ χωρίον
Peter: Tell me, if of so much the land

ἀπέδοσθε; ἡ δὲ εἶπεν· ναί, τοσούτου.
ye sold? And she said : Yes, of(for) so much.

9 ὁ δὲ Πέτρος πρὸς αὐτήν· τί ὅτι
- And Peter to her: Why

συνεφωνήθη ὑμῖν πειράσαι τὸ πνεῦμα
was it agreed with you to tempt the Spirit

κυρίου; ἰδοὺ οἱ πόδες τῶν θαψάντων τὸν
of the Lord? behold[,] the feet of the [ones] having
buried

ἄνδρα σου ἐπὶ τῇ θύρᾳ καὶ ἐξοίσουσίν
husband of thee at the door and they will
carry out

σε. **10** ἔπεσεν δὲ παραχρῆμα πρὸς τοὺς
thee. And she fell at once at the

πόδας αὐτοῦ καὶ ἐξέψυξεν· εἰσελθόντες δὲ
feet of him and expired; and entering

οἱ νεανίσκοι εὗρον αὐτὴν νεκράν, καὶ
the young men found her dead, and

ἐξενέγκαντες ἔθαψαν πρὸς τὸν ἄνδρα
carrying out buried [her] beside the husband

αὐτῆς. **11** Καὶ ἐγένετο φόβος μέγας
of her. And came fear great

ἐφ᾽ ὅλην τὴν ἐκκλησίαν καὶ ἐπὶ πάντας
on all the church and on all

τοὺς ἀκούοντας ταῦτα.
the [ones] hearing these things.

12 Διὰ δὲ τῶν χειρῶν τῶν ἀποστόλων
And through the hands of the apostles

ἐγίνετο σημεῖα καὶ τέρατα πολλὰ ἐν
¹happened ²signs ³and ⁴wonders ⁵many among

τῷ λαῷ· καὶ ἦσαν ὁμοθυμαδὸν πάντες
the people; and were with one mind all

ἐν τῇ στοᾷ Σολομῶντος· **13** τῶν δὲ
in the porch of Solomon: and of the

λοιπῶν οὐδεὶς ἐτόλμα κολλᾶσθαι αὐτοῖς,
rest no one dared to be joined to them,

ἀλλ᾽ ἐμεγάλυνεν αὐτοὺς ὁ λαός· **14** μᾶλλον
but magnified them the people; ²more

δὲ προσετίθεντο πιστεύοντες τῷ κυρίῳ,
¹and were added believing [ones] to the Lord,

πλήθη ἀνδρῶν τε καὶ γυναικῶν· **15** ὥστε
multitudes both of men and of women; so as

καὶ εἰς τὰς πλατείας ἐκφέρειν τοὺς
even into the streets to bring out the
=they brought out

ἀσθενεῖς καὶ τιθέναι ἐπὶ κλιναρίων καὶ
ailing and to place on pallets and

κραβάτων, ἵνα ἐρχομένου Πέτρου κἂν ἡ σκιὰ
mattresses, that ⁶coming ⁷of Peter ¹if even ²the ³shadow

ἐπισκιάσῃ τινὶ αὐτῶν. **16** συνήρχετο δὲ
might overshadow some one of them. And came together

καὶ τὸ πλῆθος τῶν πέριξ πόλεων
also the multitude of the ³round about ¹cities

Ἰερουσαλήμ, φέροντες ἀσθενεῖς καὶ
Jerusalem, carrying ailing [ones] and

ὀχλουμένους ὑπὸ πνευμάτων ἀκαθάρτων,
being tormented by spirits unclean,

οἵτινες ἐθεραπεύοντο ἅπαντες.
who were healed all.

17 Ἀναστὰς δὲ ὁ ἀρχιερεὺς καὶ πάντες
And rising up the high priest and all

οἱ σὺν αὐτῷ, ἡ οὖσα αἵρεσις τῶν
the [ones] with him, the existing sect of the

Σαδδουκαίων, ἐπλήσθησαν ζήλου **18** καὶ
Sadducees, were filled of(with) jealousy and

ἐπέβαλον τὰς χεῖρας ἐπὶ τοὺς ἀποστόλους
laid on the(ir) hands on the apostles

καὶ ἔθεντο αὐτοὺς ἐν τηρήσει δημοσίᾳ.
and put them in custody publicly.

19 Ἄγγελος δὲ κυρίου διὰ νυκτὸς
But an angel of [the] Lord through(during) [the] night

ἤνοιξε τὰς θύρας τῆς φυλακῆς ἐξαγαγών τε
opened the doors of the prison and leading out

αὐτοὺς εἶπεν· **20** πορεύεσθε καὶ σταθέντες
them said : Go ye and standing

λαλεῖτε ἐν τῷ ἱερῷ τῷ λαῷ πάντα
speak in the temple to the people all

τὰ ῥήματα τῆς ζωῆς ταύτης.
the words of this life.

21 ἀκούσαντες δὲ εἰσῆλθον ὑπὸ τὸν ὄρθρον
And having heard they entered about the dawn

εἰς τὸ ἱερὸν καὶ ἐδίδασκον. Παραγενόμενος δὲ
into the temple and taught. And having come

ὁ ἀρχιερεὺς καὶ οἱ σὺν αὐτῷ
the high priest and the [ones] with him

συνεκάλεσαν τὸ συνέδριον καὶ πᾶσαν τὴν
called together the council and all the

γερουσίαν τῶν υἱῶν Ἰσραήλ, καὶ ἀπέστειλαν
senate of the sons of Israel, and sent

εἰς τὸ δεσμωτήριον ἀχθῆναι αὐτούς.
to the jail to be brought them.

22 οἱ δὲ παραγενόμενοι ὑπηρέται οὐχ εὗρον
¹But ²the ⁴having come ³attendants found not

αὐτοὺς ἐν τῇ φυλακῇ· ἀναστρέψαντες δὲ
them in the prison; and having returned

ἀπήγγειλαν **23** λέγοντες ὅτι τὸ δεσμωτήριον
they reported saying[,] - The jail

εὕρομεν κεκλεισμένον ἐν πάσῃ ἀσφαλείᾳ
we found having been shut in all security

καὶ τοὺς φύλακας ἑστῶτας ἐπὶ τῶν
and the guards standing at the

θυρῶν, ἀνοίξαντες δὲ ἔσω οὐδένα εὕρομεν.
doors, but having opened ³inside ²no one ¹we found.

24 ὡς δὲ ἤκουσαν τοὺς λόγους τούτους
And as ¹heard ¹⁰these ¹¹words

ὅ τε στρατηγὸς τοῦ ἱεροῦ καὶ οἱ ἀρχιερεῖς,
²the ³both ⁵commandant ⁴of the ⁶temple ⁸and ⁷the ⁹chief priests,

διηπόρουν περὶ αὐτῶν τί ἂν γένοιτο
they were in doubt about them what ²might become

357

King James Version

of them whereunto this would grow. 25 Then came one and told them, saying, Behold, the men whom ye put in prison are standing in the temple, and teaching the people. 26 Then went the captain with the officers, and brought them without violence: for they feared the people, lest they should have been stoned. 27And when they had brought them, they set *them* before the council: and the high priest asked them, 28 Saying, Did not we straitly command you that ye should not teach in this name? and, behold, ye have filled Jerusalem with your doctrine, and intend to bring this man's blood upon us.

29 Then Peter and the *other* apostles answered and said, We ought to obey God rather than men. 30 The God of our fathers raised up Jesus, whom ye slew and hanged on a tree. 31 Him hath God exalted with his right hand *to be* a Prince and a Saviour, for to give repentance to Israel, and forgiveness of sins. 32And we are his witnesses of these things; and *so is* also the Holy Ghost, whom God hath given to them that obey him.

33 When they heard *that,* they were cut *to the heart,* and took counsel to slay them. 34 Then stood there up one in the council, a Pharisee, named Gamaliel, a doctor of the law, had in reputation among all the people, and commanded to put the apostles forth a little space; 35And said unto them, Ye men of Israel, take heed to yourselves what ye intend to do as touching these men. 36 For before these days rose up Theudas, boasting himself to be somebody; to whom a number of men, about four hundred, joined themselves: who was slain; and all, as many as obeyed him, were scattered, and brought to nought. 37After this man rose up Judas of Galilee in the days of the taxing, and drew away much people after him: he also perished; and all, *even* as many as obeyed him, were dispersed. 38And now I say unto you, Refrain from these men, and let them alone: for if this counsel or this work be of men, it will come to nought: 39 But if it be of God, ye cannot overthrow it; lest haply ye be found even to fight against God. 40And to him they agreed: and when they had called the apostles, and beaten *them,* they commanded that they should not speak in the name of Jesus, and let them go.

41 And they departed from the presence of the council, rejoicing that they were counted worthy to suffer shame for his name. 42And daily in the temple, and in every house, they ceased not to teach and preach Jesus Christ.

New International Version

25 Then someone came and said, "Look! The men you put in jail are standing in the temple courts teaching the people." 26At that, the captain went with his officers and brought the apostles. They did not use force, because they feared that the people would stone them.

27 Having brought the apostles, they made them appear before the Sanhedrin to be questioned by the high priest. 28 "We gave you strict orders not to teach in this name," he said. "Yet you have filled Jerusalem with your teaching and are determined to make us guilty of this man's blood."

29 Peter and the other apostles replied: "We must obey God rather than men! 30 The God of our fathers raised Jesus from the dead—whom you had killed by hanging him on a tree. 31 God exalted him to his own right hand as Prince and Savior that he might give repentance and forgiveness of sins to Israel. 32 We are witnesses of these things, and so is the Holy Spirit, whom God has given to those who obey him."

33 When they heard this, they were furious and wanted to put them to death. 34 But a Pharisee named Gamaliel, a teacher of the law, who was honored by all the people, stood up in the Sanhedrin and ordered that the men be put outside for a little while. 35 Then he addressed them: "Men of Israel, consider carefully what you intend to do to these men. 36 Some time ago Theudas appeared, claiming to be somebody, and about four hundred men rallied to him. He was killed, all his followers were dispersed, and it all came to nothing. 37After him, Judas the Galilean appeared in the days of the census and led a band of people in revolt. He too was killed, and all his followers were scattered. 38 Therefore, in the present case I advise you: Leave these men alone! Let them go! For if their purpose or activity is of human origin, it will fail. 39 But if it is from God, you will not be able to stop these men; you will only find yourselves fighting against God."

40 His speech persuaded them. They called the apostles in and had them flogged. Then they ordered them not to speak in the name of Jesus, and let them go.

41 The apostles left the Sanhedrin, rejoicing because they had been counted worthy of suffering disgrace for the Name. 42 Day after day, in the temple courts and from house to house, they never stopped teaching and proclaiming the good news that Jesus is the Christ.[q]

[q] Or *Messiah.*

Greek Interlinear

τοῦτο. **25** παραγενόμενος δέ τις ἀπήγγειλεν
¹this thing.   And having come   someone   reported

αὐτοῖς ὅτι ἰδοὺ οἱ ἄνδρες, οὓς
to them[,] – Behold[,] the men, whom

ἔθεσθε ἐν τῇ φυλακῇ, εἰσὶν ἐν τῷ ἱερῷ
ye put in the prison, are in the temple

ἑστῶτες καὶ διδάσκοντες τὸν λαόν.
standing and teaching the people.

26 Τότε ἀπελθὼν ὁ στρατηγὸς σὺν τοῖς
Then going the commandant with the

ὑπηρέταις ἦγεν αὐτούς, οὐ μετὰ βίας,
attendants brought them, not with force,

ἐφοβοῦντο γὰρ τὸν λαόν, μὴ λιθασθῶσιν·
for they feared the people, lest they should be stoned;

27 ἀγαγόντες δὲ αὐτοὺς ἔστησαν ἐν τῷ
and bringing them they stood in the

συνεδρίῳ. καὶ ἐπηρώτησεν αὐτοὺς ὁ
council. And questioned them the

ἀρχιερεὺς **28** λέγων· παραγγελίᾳ παρηγ-
high priest saying : With charge we
= We strictly

γείλαμεν ὑμῖν μὴ διδάσκειν ἐπὶ
charged you not to teach on(in)

τῷ ὀνόματι τούτῳ, καὶ ἰδοὺ πεπληρώκατε
this name, and behold ye have filled

τὴν Ἰερουσαλὴμ τῆς διδαχῆς ὑμῶν, καὶ
– Jerusalem of(with) the teaching of you, and

βούλεσθε ἐπαγαγεῖν ἐφ' ἡμᾶς τὸ αἷμα
intend to bring on on us the blood

τοῦ ἀνθρώπου τούτου. **29** ἀποκριθεὶς δὲ
of this man. And answering

Πέτρος καὶ οἱ ἀπόστολοι εἶπαν· πειθαρχεῖν
Peter and the apostles said : ¹to obey

δεῖ θεῷ μᾶλλον ἢ ἀνθρώποις. **30** ὁ
¹It behoves God rather than men. The

θεὸς τῶν πατέρων ἡμῶν ἤγειρεν Ἰησοῦν,
God of the fathers of us raised Jesus,

ὃν ὑμεῖς διεχειρίσασθε κρεμάσαντες ἐπὶ
whom ye killed hanging on

ξύλου· **31** τοῦτον ὁ θεὸς ἀρχηγὸν καὶ
a tree; this man – God a Ruler and

σωτῆρα ὕψωσεν τῇ δεξιᾷ αὐτοῦ τοῦ
a Saviour exalted to the right [hand] of him –

δοῦναι μετάνοιαν τῷ Ἰσραὴλ καὶ ἄφεσιν
to give⁴ repentance – to Israel and forgiveness

ἁμαρτιῶν. **32** καὶ ἡμεῖς ἐσμεν μάρτυρες
of sins. And we · are witnesses

τῶν ῥημάτων τούτων, καὶ τὸ πνεῦμα
of these words(things), and the Spirit

τὸ ἅγιον ὃ ἔδωκεν ὁ θεὸς τοῖς
– Holy which ²gave – ¹God to the

πειθαρχοῦσιν αὐτῷ. **33** οἱ δὲ ἀκούσαντες
[ones] obeying him. And the [ones] hearing

διεπρίοντο καὶ ἐβούλοντο ἀνελεῖν αὐτούς.
were cut⁸ and intended to kill them.

34 Ἀναστὰς δέ τις ἐν τῷ συνεδρίῳ
¹But ⁴standing up ²a certain ³in ⁵the ⁷council

Φαρισαῖος ὀνόματι Γαμαλιήλ, νομοδιδάσκαλος
⁸Pharisee by name Gamaliel, a teacher of the law

τίμιος παντὶ τῷ λαῷ, ἐκέλευσεν ἔξω
honoured by all the people, commanded ⁴outside

βραχὺ τοὺς ἀνθρώπους ποιῆσαι, **35** εἶπέν
⁵a little ³the ⁶men ¹to make(put), ⁸said

τε πρὸς αὐτούς· ἄνδρες Ἰσραηλῖται,
¹and to them : Men Israelites,

προσέχετε ἑαυτοῖς ἐπὶ τοῖς ἀνθρώποις τούτοις
take heed to yourselves ⁶on(to) ⁸these ⁶men

τί μέλλετε πράσσειν. **36** πρὸ γὰρ
¹what ²ye intend ³to do. For before

τούτων τῶν ἡμερῶν ἀνέστη Θευδᾶς, λέγων
these – days stood up Theudas, saying

εἶναί τινα ἑαυτόν, ᾧ προσεκλίθη ἀνδρῶν
to be someone himself, ¹to whom ⁶were attached ²of men

ἀριθμὸς ὡς τετρακοσίων· ὃς ἀνῃρέθη, καὶ
²a number ⁴about ⁵four hundreds; who was killed, and

πάντες ὅσοι ἐπείθοντο αὐτῷ διελύθησαν
all as many as obeyed him were dispersed

καὶ ἐγένοντο εἰς οὐδέν. **37** μετὰ τοῦτον
and came to nothing. After this

ἀνέστη Ἰούδας ὁ Γαλιλαῖος ἐν ταῖς
stood up Judas the Galilæan in the

ἡμέραις τῆς ἀπογραφῆς καὶ ἀπέστησεν
days of the enrolment and drew away

λαὸν ὀπίσω αὐτοῦ· κἀκεῖνος ἀπώλετο,
people after him; and that man perished,

καὶ πάντες ὅσοι ἐπείθοντο αὐτῷ
and all as many as obeyed him

διεσκορπίσθησαν. **38** καὶ τὰ νῦν λέγω
were scattered. And – now I say

ὑμῖν, ἀπόστητε ἀπὸ τῶν ἀνθρώπων τούτων
to you, stand away from these men

καὶ ἄφετε αὐτούς· ὅτι ἐὰν ᾖ ἐξ ἀνθρώπων
and leave them; because if be of men

ἡ βουλὴ αὕτη ἢ τὸ ἔργον τοῦτο,
this counsel or this work,

καταλυθήσεται· **39** εἰ δὲ ἐκ θεοῦ ἐστιν,
it will be destroyed; but if of God it is,

οὐ δυνήσεσθε καταλῦσαι αὐτούς, μήποτε
ye will not be able to destroy them, lest

καὶ θεομάχοι εὑρεθῆτε. ἐπείσθησαν δὲ
even fighters against God ye be found. And they obeyed

αὐτῷ, **40** καὶ προσκαλεσάμενοι τοὺς
him, and having called to [them] the

ἀποστόλους δείραντες παρήγγειλαν μὴ
apostles beating charged not

λαλεῖν ἐπὶ τῷ ὀνόματι τοῦ Ἰησοῦ καὶ
to speak on(in) the name – of Jesus and

ἀπέλυσαν. **41** Οἱ μὲν οὖν ἐπορεύοντο
released [them]. They – therefore went

χαίροντες ἀπὸ προσώπου τοῦ συνεδρίου,
rejoicing from [the] presence of the council,

ὅτι κατηξιώθησαν ὑπὲρ τοῦ ὀνόματος
because they were deemed worthy on behalf of the name

ἀτιμασθῆναι· **42** πᾶσάν τε ἡμέραν ἐν τῷ
to be dishonoured; and every day in the

ἱερῷ καὶ κατ' οἶκον οὐκ ἐπαύοντο
temple and from house to house† they ceased not

διδάσκοντες καὶ εὐαγγελιζόμενοι τὸν χριστὸν
teaching and preaching the Christ

Ἰησοῦν.
Jesus.

---

* That is, to the heart; cf. 7. 54.

King James Version

6 And in those days, when the number of the disciples was multiplied, there arose a murmuring of the Grecians against the Hebrews, because their widows were neglected in the daily ministration. 2 Then the twelve called the multitude of the disciples *unto them,* and said, It is not reason that we should leave the word of God, and serve tables. 3 Wherefore, brethren, look ye out among you seven men of honest report, full of the Holy Ghost and wisdom, whom we may appoint over this business. 4 But we will give ourselves continually to prayer, and to the ministry of the word.

5 And the saying pleased the whole multitude: and they chose Stephen, a man full of faith and of the Holy Ghost, and Philip, and Prochorus, and Nicanor, and Timon, and Parmenas, and Nicolas a proselyte of Antioch; 6 Whom they set before the apostles: and when they had prayed, they laid *their* hands on them. 7 And the word of God increased; and the number of the disciples multiplied in Jerusalem greatly; and a great company of the priests were obedient to the faith. 8 And Stephen, full of faith and power, did great wonders and miracles among the people.

9 Then there arose certain of the synagogue, which is called *the synagogue* of the Libertines, and Cyrenians, and Alexandrians, and of them of Cilicia and of Asia, disputing with Stephen. 10 And they were not able to resist the wisdom and the spirit by which he spake. 11 Then they suborned men, which said, We have heard him speak blasphemous words against Moses, and *against* God. 12 And they stirred up the people, and the elders, and the scribes, and came upon *him,* and caught him, and brought *him* to the council, 13 And set up false witnesses, which said, This man ceaseth not to speak blasphemous words against this holy place, and the law: 14 For we have heard him say, that this Jesus of Nazareth shall destroy this place, and shall change the customs which Moses delivered us. 15 And all that sat in the council, looking stedfastly on him, saw his face as it had been the face of an. angel.

7 Then said the high priest, Are these things so? 2 And he said, Men, brethren, and fathers, hearken; The God of glory appeared unto our father Abraham, when he was in Mesopotamia, before he dwelt in Charran, 3 And said unto him, Get thee out of thy country, and from thy kindred, and come into the land which I shall shew thee. 4 Then came he out of the land of the Chaldeans, and dwelt in Charran: and from 'hence, when his father was dead, he removed

New International Version

The choosing of the seven

6 In those days when the number of disciples was increasing, the Grecian Jews among them complained against those of the Aramaic-speaking community because their widows were being overlooked in the daily distribution of food. 2 So the Twelve gathered all the disciples together and said: "It would not be right for us to neglect the ministry of the word of God in order to wait on tables. 3 Brothers, choose seven men from among you who are known to be full of the Spirit and wisdom. We will turn this responsibility over to them 4 and will give our attention to prayer and the ministry of the word."

5 This proposal pleased the whole group. They chose Stephen, a man full of faith and of the Holy Spirit; also Philip, Prochorus, Nicanor, Timon, Parmenas, and Nicolas from Antioch, a convert to Judaism. 6 They presented these men to the apostles, who prayed and laid their hands on them.

7 So the word of God spread. The number of disciples in Jerusalem increased rapidly, and a large number of priests became obedient to the faith.

Stephen seized

8 Now Stephen, a man full of God's grace and power, did great wonders and miraculous signs among the people. 9 Opposition arose, however, from members of the Synagogue of the Freedmen (as it was called)—Jews of Cyrene and Alexandria as well as the provinces of Cilicia and Asia. These men began to argue with Stephen, 10 but they could not stand up against his wisdom or the Spirit by which he spoke.

11 Then they secretly persuaded some men to say, "We have heard Stephen speak words of blasphemy against Moses and against God."

12 So they stirred up the people and the elders and the teachers of the law. They seized Stephen and brought him before the Sanhedrin. 13 They produced false witnesses, who testified, "This fellow never stops speaking against the holy place and against the law. 14 For we have heard him say that this Jesus of Nazareth will destroy this place and change the customs Moses handed down to us."

15 All who were sitting in the Sanhedrin looked intently at Stephen, and they saw that his face was like the face of an angel.

Stephen's speech to the Sanhedrin

7 Then the high priest asked him, "Are these charges true?"

2 To this he replied: "Brothers and fathers, listen to me! The God of glory appeared to our father Abraham while he was still in Mesopotamia, before he lived in Haran. 3 'Leave your country and your people,' God said, 'and go to the land I will show you.' *r*

4 "So he left Chaldea and settled in Haran. After the death of his father, God sent him to

Greek Interlinear

Chapter 6

Ἐν δὲ ταῖς ἡμέραις ταύταις
Now in these days

πληθυνόντων τῶν μαθητῶν ἐγένετο
being multiplied the disciples* there was
=as the disciples were multiplied

γογγυσμὸς τῶν Ἑλληνιστῶν πρὸς τοὺς
a murmuring of the Hellenists against the

Ἑβραίους, ὅτι παρεθεωροῦντο ἐν τῇ
Hebrews, because ⁴were overlooked ⁵in ¹the

διακονίᾳ τῇ καθημερινῇ αἱ χῆραι αὐτῶν.
²service - ³daily ¹the ⁴widows ⁵of them.

2 προσκαλεσάμενοι δὲ οἱ δώδεκα τὸ
²having called to [them] ¹And ³the ⁴twelve the

πλῆθος τῶν μαθητῶν εἶπαν· οὐκ ἀρεστόν
multitude of the disciples said : not pleasing

ἐστιν ἡμᾶς καταλείψαντας τὸν λόγον τοῦ
It is us leaving the word of

θεοῦ διακονεῖν τραπέζαις. 3 ἐπισκέψασθε
of God to serve tables. look ye out

δέ, ἀδελφοί, ἄνδρας ἐξ ὑμῶν μαρτυρουμένους
But, brothers, ²men ⁴of ⁵you ¹being witnessed to

ἑπτὰ πλήρεις πνεύματος καὶ σοφίας, οὓς
³seven [as] full of Spirit and of wisdom, whom

καταστήσομεν ἐπὶ τῆς χρείας ταύτης·
we will appoint over this office;

4 ἡμεῖς δὲ τῇ προσευχῇ καὶ τῇ διακονίᾳ
but we to the prayer and to the service

τοῦ λόγου προσκαρτερήσομεν. 5 καὶ ἤρεσεν
of the word will keep. And ²pleased

ὁ λόγος ἐνώπιον παντὸς τοῦ πλήθους,
¹the ²word before all the multitude,

καὶ ἐξελέξαντο Στέφανον, ἄνδρα πλήρη
and they chose Stephen, a man full

πίστεως καὶ πνεύματος ἁγίου, καὶ Φίλιππον
of faith and Spirit of Holy, and Philip

καὶ Πρόχορον καὶ Νικάνορα καὶ Τίμωνα
and Prochorus and Nicanor and Timon

καὶ Παρμενᾶν καὶ Νικόλαον προσήλυτον
and Parmenas and Nicolaus a proselyte

Ἀντιοχέα, 6 οὓς ἔστησαν ἐνώπιον τῶν
of Antioch, whom they set before the

ἀποστόλων, καὶ προσευξάμενοι ἐπέθηκαν
apostles, and having prayed they placed on

αὐτοῖς τὰς χεῖρας.
them the(ir) hands.

7 Καὶ ὁ λόγος τοῦ θεοῦ ηὔξανεν, καὶ
And the word - of God grew, and

ἐπληθύνετο ὁ ἀριθμὸς τῶν μαθητῶν ἐν
was multiplied the number of the disciples in

Ἰερουσαλὴμ σφόδρα, πολύς τε ὄχλος τῶν
Jerusalem greatly, and a much(great) crowd of the

ἱερέων ὑπήκουον τῇ πίστει.
priests obeyed the faith.

8 Στέφανος δὲ πλήρης χάριτος καὶ
And Stephen full of grace and

δυνάμεως ἐποίει τέρατα καὶ σημεῖα μεγάλα
of power did wonders and signs great

ἐν τῷ λαῷ. 9 ἀνέστησαν δέ τινες τῶν
among the people. But rose up some of the [ones]

ἐκ τῆς συναγωγῆς τῆς λεγομένης
of the synagcgue - being called

Λιβερτίνων καὶ Κυρηναίων καὶ Ἀλεξ-
of Freedmen and of Cyrenians and of

ανδρέων καὶ τῶν ἀπὸ Κιλικίας καὶ
Alexandrians and of the [ones] from Cilicia and

Ἀσίας συζητοῦντες τῷ Στεφάνῳ, 10 καὶ
Asia discussing - with Stephen, and

οὐκ ἴσχυον ἀντιστῆναι τῇ σοφίᾳ καὶ
were not able to withstand the wisdom and

τῷ πνεύματι ᾧ ἐλάλει. 11 τότε ὑπέβαλον
the spirit with which he spoke. Then they suborned

ἄνδρας λέγοντας ὅτι ἀκηκόαμεν αὐτοῦ
men saying[.] - We have heard him

λαλοῦντος ῥήματα βλάσφημα εἰς Μωϋσῆν
speaking words blasphemous against Moses

καὶ τὸν θεόν· 12 συνεκίνησάν τε τὸν
and - God; and they stirred up the

λαὸν καὶ τοὺς πρεσβυτέρους καὶ τοὺς
people and the elders and the

γραμματεῖς, καὶ ἐπιστάντες συνήρπασαν
scribes, and coming on they seized

αὐτὸν καὶ ἤγαγον εἰς τὸ συνέδριον,
him and led to the council,

13 ἔστησάν τε μάρτυρας ψευδεῖς λέγοντας·
and stood witnesses false saying :

ὁ ἄνθρωπος οὗτος οὐ παύεται λαλῶν
This man ceases not speaking

ῥήματα κατὰ τοῦ τόπου τοῦ ἁγίου [τούτου]
words against - ²place - ³holy ¹this

καὶ τοῦ νόμου· 14 ἀκηκόαμεν γὰρ αὐτοῦ
and the law; for we have heard him

λέγοντος ὅτι Ἰησοῦς ὁ Ναζωραῖος οὗτος
saying that ²Jesus ³the ⁴Nazarene ¹this

καταλύσει τὸν τόπον τοῦτον καὶ ἀλλάξει
will destroy the place this and will change

τὰ ἔθη ἃ παρέδωκεν ἡμῖν Μωϋσῆς.
the customs which delivered to us Moses.

15 καὶ ἀτενίσαντες εἰς αὐτὸν πάντες οἱ
And gazing at him all the

καθεζόμενοι ἐν τῷ συνεδρίῳ εἶδον τὸ
[ones] sitting in the council saw the

πρόσωπον αὐτοῦ ὡσεὶ πρόσωπον ἀγγέλου.
face of him as a face of an angel.

Chapter 7

Εἶπεν δὲ ὁ ἀρχιερεύς· εἰ ταῦτα
And said the high priest : If these things

οὕτως ἔχει; 2 ὁ δὲ ἔφη·
thus have(are)? And he said:

Ἄνδρες ἀδελφοὶ καὶ πατέρες, ἀκούσατε.
Men brothers and fathers, hear ye.

Ὁ θεὸς τῆς δόξης ὤφθη τῷ πατρὶ
The God - of glory appeared to the father

ἡμῶν Ἀβραὰμ ὄντι ἐν τῇ Μεσοποταμίᾳ
of us Abraham being in - Mesopotamia

πρὶν ἢ κατοικῆσαι αὐτὸν ἐν Χαρράν,
before to dwell himᵇ in Charran,
=he dwelt

3 καὶ εἶπεν πρὸς αὐτόν· ἔξελθε ἐκ τῆς
and said to him : Go forth out of the

γῆς σου καὶ τῆς συγγενείας σου, καὶ
land of thee and the kindred of thee, and

δεῦρο εἰς τὴν γῆν ἣν ἄν σοι δείξω.
come into the land whichever to thee I may show.

4 τότε ἐξελθὼν ἐκ γῆς Χαλδαίων
Then going forth out of [the] land of [the] Chaldæans

κατῴκησεν ἐν Χαρράν. κἀκεῖθεν μετὰ
he dwelt in Charran. And thence after

τὸ ἀποθανεῖν τὸν πατέρα αὐτοῦ μετῴκισεν
the to die the father of himᵇ [God] removed
=his father died

King James Version

him into this land, wherein ye now dwell. 5And he gave him none inheritance in it, no, not *so much as* to set his foot on: yet he promised that he would give it to him for a possession, and to his seed after him, when *as yet* he had no child. 6And God spake on this wise, That his seed should sojourn in a strange land; and that they should bring them into bondage, and entreat *them* evil four hundred years. 7And the nation to whom they shall be in bondage will I judge, said God: and after that shall they come forth, and serve me in this place. 8And he gave him the covenant of circumcision: and so *Abraham* begat Isaac, and circumcised him the eighth day; and Isaac *begat* Jacob; and Jacob *begat* the twelve patriarchs. 9And the patriarchs, moved with envy, sold Joseph into Egypt: but God was with him, 10And delivered him out of all his afflictions, and gave him favour and wisdom in the sight of Pharaoh king of Egypt; and he made him governor over Egypt and all his house. 11 Now there came a dearth over all the land of Egypt and Chanaan, and great affliction: and our fathers found no sustenance. 12 But when Jacob heard that there was corn in Egypt, he sent out our fathers first. 13And at the second *time* Joseph was made known to his brethren; and Joseph's kindred was made known unto Pharaoh. 14 Then sent Joseph, and called his father Jacob to *him*, and all his kindred, threescore and fifteen souls. 15 So Jacob went down into Egypt, and died, he, and our fathers, 16And were carried over into Sychem, and laid in the sepulchre that Abraham bought for a sum of money of the sons of Emmor, *the father* of Sychem. 17 But when the time of the promise drew nigh, which God had sworn to Abraham, the people grew and multiplied in Egypt, 18 Till another king arose, which knew not Joseph. 19 The same dealt subtilely with our kindred, and evil entreated our fathers, so that they cast out their young children, to the end they might not live. 20 In which time Moses was born, and was exceeding fair, and nourished up in his father's house three months: 21And when he was cast out, Pharaoh's daughter took him up, and nourished him for her own son. 22And Moses was learned in all the wisdom of the Egyptians, and was mighty in words and in deeds. 23And when he was full forty years old, it came into his heart to visit his brethren the children of Israel. 24And seeing one *of them* suffer wrong, he defended *him*, and avenged him that was oppressed, and smote the Egyptian: 25 For he supposed his brethren would have understood how that God by his hand would deliver them; but they understood not. 26And the next day he

New International Version

this land where you are now living. 5 He gave him no inheritance here, not even a foot of ground. But God promised him that he and his descendants after him would possess the land, even though at that time Abraham had no child. 6 God spoke to him in this way: 'Your descendants will be strangers in a foreign country, and they will be enslaved and mistreated four hundred years. 7 I will punish the nation that makes them slaves,' God said, 'and afterward they will come out of that country and worship me in this place.' [s] 8 Then he gave Abraham the covenant of circumcision. And Abraham became the father of Isaac and circumcised him eight days after his birth. Later Isaac became the father of Jacob, and Jacob became the father of the twelve patriarchs.

9 "Because the patriarchs were jealous of Joseph, they sold him as a slave into Egypt. But God was with him 10 and rescued him from all his troubles. He gave Joseph wisdom and enabled him to gain the good will of Pharaoh, king of Egypt; so he made him ruler over Egypt and all his palace.

11 "Then a famine struck all Egypt and Canaan, bringing great suffering, and our fathers could not find food. 12 When Jacob heard that there was grain in Egypt, he sent our fathers on their first visit. 13 On their second visit, Joseph told his brothers who he was, and Pharaoh learned about Joseph's family. 14After this, Joseph sent for his father Jacob and his whole family, seventy-five in all. 15 Then Jacob went down to Egypt, where he and our fathers died. 16 Their bodies were brought back to Shechem and placed in the tomb that Abraham had bought from the sons of Hamor at Shechem for a certain sum of money.

17 "As the time drew near for God to fulfill his promise to Abraham, the number of our people in Egypt greatly increased. 18 Then another king, who knew nothing about Joseph, became ruler of Egypt. 19 He dealt treacherously with our people and oppressed our ancestors by forcing them to throw out their newborn babies so that they would die.

20 "At that time Moses was born, and he was no ordinary child.[t] For three months he was cared for in his father's house. 21 When he was placed outside, Pharaoh's daughter took him and brought him up as her own son. 22 Moses was educated in all the wisdom of the Egyptians and was powerful in speech and action.

23 "When Moses was forty years old, he decided to visit his fellow Israelites. 24 He saw one of them being mistreated by an Egyptian, so he went to his defense and avenged him by killing the Egyptian. 25 Moses thought that his own people would realize that God was using him to rescue them, but they did not. 26 The next day

[s] Gen. 15:13,14. [t] Or *was fair in the sight of God.*

Greek Interlinear

αὐτὸν εἰς τὴν γῆν ταύτην εἰς ἣν ὑμεῖς
him into this land in which ye

νῦν κατοικεῖτε, **5** καὶ οὐκ ἔδωκεν αὐτῷ
now dwell, and gave not to him

κληρονομίαν ἐν αὐτῇ οὐδὲ βῆμα ποδός,
an inheritance in it nor a foot's space,

καὶ ἐπηγγείλατο δοῦναι αὐτῷ εἰς
and promised to give him for

κατάσχεσιν αὐτὴν καὶ τῷ σπέρματι αὐτοῦ
a possession it and to the seed of him

μετ' αὐτόν, οὐκ ὄντος αὐτῷ τέκνου.
after him, not being to him a child.
=while he had no child.

6 ἐλάλησεν δὲ οὕτως ὁ θεός, ὅτι ἔσται
And spoke thus - God, that will be

τὸ σπέρμα αὐτοῦ πάροικον ἐν γῇ ἀλλοτρίᾳ,
the seed of him a sojourner in a land belonging to others,

καὶ δουλώσουσιν αὐτὸ καὶ κακώσουσιν
and they will enslave it and will ill-treat

ἔτη τετρακόσια· **7** καὶ τὸ ἔθνος ᾧ ἐὰν
years four hundred; and the nation whichever

δουλεύσουσιν κρινῶ ἐγώ, ὁ θεὸς εἶπεν,
they will serve will judge I, - God said,

καὶ μετὰ ταῦτα ἐξελεύσονται καὶ
and after these things they will come forth and

λατρεύσουσίν μοι ἐν τῷ τόπῳ τούτῳ.
will worship me in this place.

8 καὶ ἔδωκεν αὐτῷ διαθήκην περιτομῆς·
And he gave him a covenant of circumcision;

καὶ οὕτως ἐγέννησεν τὸν Ἰσαὰκ καὶ
and thus he begat - Isaac and

περιέτεμεν αὐτὸν τῇ ἡμέρᾳ τῇ ὀγδόῃ,
circumcised him on the day - eighth,

καὶ Ἰσαὰκ τὸν Ἰακώβ, καὶ Ἰακὼβ
and Isaac [begat] - Jacob, and Jacob [begat]

τοὺς δώδεκα πατριάρχας. **9** Καὶ οἱ
the twelve patriarchs. And the

πατριάρχαι ζηλώσαντες τὸν Ἰωσὴφ
patriarchs becoming jealous - Joseph

ἀπέδοντο εἰς Αἴγυπτον· καὶ ἦν ὁ θεὸς
sold into Egypt; and was - God

μετ' αὐτοῦ, **10** καὶ ἐξείλατο αὐτὸν ἐκ
with him, and rescued him out of

πασῶν τῶν θλίψεων αὐτοῦ, καὶ ἔδωκεν
all the afflictions of him, and gave

αὐτῷ χάριν καὶ σοφίαν ἐναντίον Φαραὼ
him favour and wisdom before Pharaoh

βασιλέως Αἰγύπτου, καὶ κατέστησεν αὐτὸν
king of Egypt, and he appointed him

ἡγούμενον ἐπ' Αἴγυπτον καὶ ὅλον τὸν
governor over Egypt and all the

οἶκον αὐτοῦ. **11** ἦλθεν δὲ λιμὸς ἐφ'
household of him. But came a famine over

ὅλην τὴν Αἴγυπτον καὶ Χανάαν καὶ
all - Egypt and Canaan and

θλῖψις μεγάλη, καὶ οὐχ ηὕρισκον
affliction great, and found not

χορτάσματα οἱ πατέρες ἡμῶν. **12** ἀκούσας
sustenance the fathers of us. having heard

δὲ Ἰακὼβ ὄντα σιτία εἰς Αἴγυπτον
But Jacob being corn in Egypt

ἐξαπέστειλεν τοὺς πατέρας ἡμῶν πρῶτον·
sent forth the fathers of us first;

13 καὶ ἐν τῷ δευτέρῳ ἐγνωρίσθη Ἰωσὴφ
and at the second [time] was made known Joseph

τοῖς ἀδελφοῖς αὐτοῦ, καὶ φανερὸν ἐγένετο τῷ
to the brothers of him, and manifest became -

Φαραὼ τὸ γένος Ἰωσήφ. **14** ἀποστείλας δὲ
to Pharaoh the race of Joseph. And sending

Ἰωσὴφ μετεκαλέσατο Ἰακὼβ τὸν πατέρα
Joseph called Jacob the father

αὐτοῦ καὶ πᾶσαν τὴν συγγένειαν ἐν
of him and all the(his) kindred in

ψυχαῖς ἑβδομήκοντα πέντε. **15** καὶ κατέβη
souls seventy-five. And went down

Ἰακὼβ εἰς Αἴγυπτον, καὶ ἐτελεύτησεν
Jacob to Egypt, and died

αὐτὸς καὶ οἱ πατέρες ἡμῶν, **16** καὶ
he and the fathers of us, and

μετετέθησαν εἰς Συχὲμ καὶ ἐτέθησαν ἐν
were transferred to Sychem and were put in

τῷ μνήματι ᾧ ὠνήσατο Ἀβραὰμ τιμῆς
the tomb which bought Abraham of(for) a price

ἀργυρίου παρὰ τῶν υἱῶν Ἐμμὼρ ἐν
of silver from the sons of Emmor in

Συχέμ. **17** Καθὼς δὲ ἤγγιζεν ὁ χρόνος
Sychem. And as drew near the time

τῆς ἐπαγγελίας ἧς ὡμολόγησεν ὁ θεὸς
of the promise which declared - God

τῷ Ἀβραάμ, ηὔξησεν ὁ λαὸς καὶ
to Abraham, grew the people and

ἐπληθύνθη ἐν Αἰγύπτῳ, **18** ἄχρι οὗ ἀνέστη
were multiplied in Egypt, until rose up

βασιλεὺς ἕτερος ἐπ' Αἴγυπτον, ὃς οὐκ ᾔδει
king another over Egypt, who did not know

τὸν Ἰωσήφ. **19** οὗτος κατασοφισάμενος
- Joseph. This man dealing craftily with

τὸ γένος ἡμῶν ἐκάκωσεν τοὺς πατέρας
the race of us ill-treated the fathers

τοῦ ποιεῖν τὰ βρέφη ἔκθετα αὐτῶν
- to make the babes exposed of them

εἰς τὸ μὴ ζωογονεῖσθαι. **20** Ἐν ᾧ
to the not to be preserved alive. At which
=so that they should not be . . .

καιρῷ ἐγεννήθη Μωϋσῆς, καὶ ἦν ἀστεῖος
time was born Moses, and was fair

τῷ θεῷ· ὃς ἀνετράφη μῆνας τρεῖς ἐν
- to God; who was reared months three in

τῷ οἴκῳ τοῦ πατρός· **21** ἐκτεθέντος δὲ
the house of the(his) father; and when he was exposed

αὐτοῦ ἀνείλατο αὐτὸν ἡ θυγάτηρ Φαραὼ
him took up him the daughter of Pharaoh

καὶ ἀνεθρέψατο αὐτὸν ἑαυτῇ εἰς υἱόν.
and reared him to herself for a son.
=as her own son.

22 καὶ ἐπαιδεύθη Μωϋσῆς πάσῃ σοφίᾳ
And was trained Moses in all [the] wisdom

Αἰγυπτίων, ἦν δὲ δυνατὸς ἐν λόγοις
of [the] Egyptians, and was powerful in words

καὶ ἔργοις αὐτοῦ. **23** Ὡς δὲ ἐπληροῦτο
and works of him. But when was fulfilled

αὐτῷ τεσσερακονταετὴς χρόνος, ἀνέβη ἐπὶ
to him of forty years a time, it came up upon

τὴν καρδίαν αὐτοῦ ἐπισκέψασθαι τοὺς
the heart of him to visit the

ἀδελφοὺς αὐτοῦ τοὺς υἱοὺς Ἰσραήλ. **24** καὶ
brothers of him the sons of Israel. And

ἰδών τινα ἀδικούμενον ἠμύνατο, καὶ
seeing one being injured he defended [him], and

ἐποίησεν ἐκδίκησιν τῷ καταπονουμένῳ
he wrought vengeance for the [one] getting the worse

πατάξας τὸν Αἰγύπτιον. **25** ἐνόμιζεν δὲ
striking the Egyptian. Now he supposed

συνιέναι τοὺς ἀδελφοὺς ὅτι ὁ θεὸς διὰ
to understand the(his) brothers that - God through
=that his brothers would understand

χειρὸς αὐτοῦ δίδωσιν σωτηρίαν αὐτοῖς·
hand of him would give salvation to them;

οἱ δὲ οὐ συνῆκαν. **26** τῇ τε ἐπιούσῃ
but they understood not. And on the coming

King James Version

shewed himself unto them as they strove, and
would have set them at one again, saying, Sirs,
ye are brethren; why do ye wrong one to another? 27 But he that did his neighbour wrong
thrust him away, saying, Who made thee a ruler
and a judge over us? ·28 Wilt thou kill me, as
thou didst the Egyptian yesterday? 29 Then fled
Moses at this saying, and was a stranger in the
land of Madian, where he begat two sons. 30And
when forty years were expired, there appeared
to him in the wilderness of mount Sina an angel
of the Lord in a flame of fire in a bush. 31 When
Moses saw *it*, he wondered at the sight: and as
he drew near to behold *it*, the voice of the Lord
came unto him, 32 *Saying*, I *am* the God of thy
fathers, the God of Abraham, and the God of
Isaac, and the God of Jacob. Then Moses trembled, and durst not behold. 33 Then said the
Lord to him, Put off thy shoes from thy feet:
for the place where thou standest is holy ground.
34 I have seen, I have seen the affliction of my
people which is in Egypt, and I have heard their
groaning, and am come down to deliver them.
And now come, I will send thee into Egypt.
35 This Moses whom they refused, saying, Who
made thee a ruler and a judge? the same did
God send *to be* a ruler and a deliverer by the
hand of the angel which appeared to him in the
bush. 36 He brought them out, after that he had
shewed wonders and signs in the land of Egypt,
and in the Red sea, and in the wilderness forty
years.

37 This is that Moses, which said unto the
children of Israel, A Prophet shall the Lord your
God raise up unto you of your brethren, like
unto me; him shall ye hear. 38 This is he, that
was in the church in the wilderness with the
angel which spake to him in the mount Sina,
and *with* our fathers: who received the lively
oracles to give unto us: 39 To whom our fathers
would not obey, but thrust *him* from them, and
in their hearts turned back again into Egypt,
40 Saying unto Aaron, Make us gods to go before us: for *as for* this Moses, which brought
us out of the land of Egypt, we wot not what
is become of him. 41And they made a calf in
those days, and offered sacrifice unto the idol,
and rejoiced in the works of their own hands.
42 Then God turned, and gave them up to worship the host of heaven; as it is written in the
book of the prophets, O ye house of Israel, have
ye offered to me slain beasts and sacrifices *by the
space of* forty years in the wilderness? 43 Yea,
ye took up the tabernacle of Moloch, and the
star of your god Remphan, figures which ye
made to worship them: and I will carry you
away beyond Babylon. 44 Our fathers had the
tabernacle of witness in the wilderness, as he had
appointed, speaking unto Moses, that he should
make it according to the fashion that he had
seen. 45 Which also our fathers that came after
brought in with Jesus into the possession of the
Gentiles, whom God drave out before the face

New International Version

Moses came upon two Israelites who were fighting. He tried to reconcile them by saying, 'Men,
you are brothers; why do you want to hurt each
other?'

27 "But the man who was mistreating the
other pushed Moses aside and said, 'Who made
you ruler and judge over us? 28 Do you want to
kill me as you killed the Egyptian yesterday?' *u*
29 When Moses heard this, he fled to Midian,
where he settled as a foreigner and had two sons.

30 "After forty years had passed, an angel
appeared to Moses in the flames of a burning
bush in the desert near Mount Sinai. 31 When
he saw this, he was amazed at the sight. As he
went over to look more closely, he heard the
Lord's voice: 32 'I am the God of your fathers,
the God of Abraham, Isaac and Jacob.' *v* Moses
trembled with fear and did not dare to look.

33 "Then the Lord said to him, 'Take off your
sandals; the place where you are standing is holy
ground. 34 I have indeed seen the oppression of
my people in Egypt. I have heard their groaning
and have come down to set them free. Now
come, I will send you back to Egypt.' *w*

35 "This is the same Moses whom they had
rejected with the words, 'Who made you ruler
and judge?' He was sent to be their ruler and
deliverer by God himself, through the angel who
appeared to him in the bush. 36 He led them
out of Egypt and did wonders and miraculous
signs in Egypt, at the Red Sea*x* and for forty
years in the desert. 37 This is that Moses who
told the Israelites, 'God will send you a prophet
like me from your own people.' *y* 38 He was in
the congregation in the desert, with our fathers
and with the angel who spoke to him on Mount
Sinai; and he received living words to pass on
to us.

39 "But our fathers refused to obey him. Instead, they rejected him and in their hearts
turned back to Egypt. 40 They told Aaron,
'Make some gods who will lead the way for us.
As for this fellow Moses who led us out of
Egypt—we don't know what has happened to
him!' *z* 41 That was the time they made an idol
in the form of a calf. They brought sacrifices to
it and held a celebration in honor of what their
hands had made. 42 But God turned away and
gave them over to the worship of the heavenly
bodies. This agrees with what is written in the
book of the prophets:

'Did you bring me sacrifices and offerings
   forty years in the desert, O Israel?
43 No, you have lifted up the shrine of Moloch
   and the star of your god Rephan,
   the idols you made to worship.
Therefore, I will send you into exile' *a* beyond Babylon.

44 "Our ancestors had the tabernacle of testimony with them in the desert. It had been made
as God directed Moses, according to the pattern
he had seen. 45 Having received the tabernacle,
our fathers under Joshua brought it with them
when they took the land from the nations God

[*u*] Exodus 2:14. [*v*] Exodus 3:6. [*w*] Exodus 3:5,7,8,10. [*x*] That is,
Sea of Reeds. [*y*] Deut. 18:15. [*z*] Exodus 32:1. [*a*] Amos 5:25-27.

Greek Interlinear

ἡμέρᾳ ὤφθη αὐτοῖς μαχομένοις, καὶ
day he appeared to them fighting, and

συνήλλασσεν αὐτοὺς εἰς εἰρήνην εἰπών·
attempted to reconcile them in peace saying :

ἄνδρες, ἀδελφοί ἐστε· ἱνατί ἀδικεῖτε
Men, brothers ye are; why injure ye

ἀλλήλους; 27 ὁ δὲ ἀδικῶν τὸν πλησίον
each other? But the [one] injuring the(his) neighbour

ἀπώσατο αὐτόν εἰπών· τίς σε κατέστησεν
thrust away him saying : Who thee appointed

ἄρχοντα καὶ δικαστὴν ἐφ' ἡμῶν; 28 μὴ
a ruler and a judge over us? not

ἀνελεῖν με σὺ θέλεις ὃν τρόπον ἀνεῖλες
to kill me thou wishest in the same way ast thou killedst

ἐχθὲς τὸν Αἰγύπτιον; 29 ἔφυγεν δὲ
yesterday the Egyptian? So fled

Μωϋσῆς ἐν τῷ λόγῳ τούτῳ, καὶ ἐγένετο
Moses at this word, and became

πάροικος ἐν γῇ Μαδιάμ, οὗ ἐγέννησεν
a sojourner in [the] land Midian, where he begat

υἱοὺς δύο. 30 Καὶ πληρωθέντων ἐτῶν
sons two. And being fulfilled years
= when forty years were fulfilled

τεσσεράκοντα ὤφθη αὐτῷ ἐν τῇ ἐρήμῳ
forty* appeared to him in the desert

τοῦ ὄρους Σινὰ ἄγγελος ἐν φλογὶ πυρὸς
of the mount Sinai an angel in a flame of fire

βάτου. 31 ὁ δὲ Μωϋσῆς ἰδὼν ἐθαύμαζεν
of a thorn bush. - And Moses seeing marvelled at

τὸ ὅραμα· προσερχομένου δὲ αὐτοῦ κατα-
the vision; and approaching him⁸ to take
= as he approached

νοῆσαι ἐγένετο φωνὴ κυρίου· 32 ἐγὼ ὁ
notice there was a voice of [the] Lord : I the

θεὸς τῶν πατέρων σου, ὁ θεὸς Ἀβραὰμ
God of the fathers of thee, the God of Abraham

καὶ Ἰσαὰκ καὶ Ἰακώβ. ἔντρομος δὲ
and of Isaac and of Jacob. But trembling

γενόμενος Μωϋσῆς οὐκ ἐτόλμα κατανοῆσαι.
becoming Moses dared not to take notice.

33 εἶπεν δὲ αὐτῷ ὁ κύριος· λῦσον τὸ
And said to him the Lord : Loosen the

ὑπόδημα τῶν ποδῶν σου· ὁ γὰρ τόπος
sandal of the feet of thee; for the place

ἐφ' ᾧ ἕστηκας γῆ ἁγία ἐστίν. 34 ἰδὼν
on which thou standest ground holy is. Seeing

εἶδον τὴν κάκωσιν τοῦ λαοῦ μου τοῦ
I saw the ill-treatment of the people of me -

ἐν Αἰγύπτῳ, καὶ τοῦ στεναγμοῦ αὐτοῦ
in Egypt, and the groan of it

ἤκουσα, καὶ κατέβην ἐξελέσθαι αὐτούς·
I heard, and I came down to rescue them;

καὶ νῦν δεῦρο ἀποστείλω σε εἰς Αἴγυπτον.
and now come I will send thee to Egypt.

35 Τοῦτον τὸν Μωϋσῆν, ὃν ἠρνήσαντο
This - Moses, whom they denied

εἰπόντες· τίς σε κατέστησεν ἄρχοντα καὶ
saying : Who thee appointed a ruler and

δικαστήν; τοῦτον ὁ θεὸς καὶ ἄρχοντα
a judge? this man - God both a ruler

καὶ λυτρωτὴν ἀπέσταλκεν σὺν χειρὶ
and a redeemer has sent with [the] hand

ἀγγέλου τοῦ ὀφθέντος αὐτῷ ἐν τῇ βάτῳ.
of [the] angel - appearing to him in the bush.

36 οὗτος ἐξήγαγεν αὐτοὺς ποιήσας τέρατα
This man led forth them doing wonders

καὶ σημεῖα ἐν γῇ Αἰγύπτῳ καὶ ἐν
and signs in [the] land Egypt and in

ἐρυθρᾷ θαλάσσῃ καὶ ἐν τῇ ἐρήμῳ ἔτη
[the] Red Sea and in the desert years

τεσσεράκοντα. 37 οὗτός ἐστιν ὁ Μωϋσῆς
forty. This is the Moses

ὁ εἴπας τοῖς υἱοῖς Ἰσραήλ· προφήτην
- saying to the sons of Israel : A prophet

ὑμῖν ἀναστήσει ὁ θεὸς ἐκ τῶν ἀδελφῶν
for you will raise up - God of the brothers

ὑμῶν ὡς ἐμέ. 38 οὗτός ἐστιν ὁ γενόμενος
of you as me. This is the [one] having been

ἐν τῇ ἐκκλησίᾳ ἐν τῇ ἐρήμῳ μετὰ τοῦ
in the church in the desert with the

ἀγγέλου τοῦ λαλοῦντος αὐτῷ ἐν τῷ
angel - speaking to him in the

ὄρει Σινὰ καὶ τῶν πατέρων ἡμῶν, ὃς
mount Sinai and [with] the fathers of us, who

ἐδέξατο λόγια ζῶντα δοῦναι ὑμῖν, 39 ᾧ
received oracles living to give to you, ¹to whom

οὐκ ἠθέλησαν ὑπήκοοι γενέσθαι οἱ πατέρες
*wished ²not *obedient ⁷to become ³the ⁴fathers

ἡμῶν, ἀλλὰ ἀπώσαντο καὶ ἐστράφησαν
⁵of us, but thrust away and turned

ἐν ταῖς καρδίαις αὐτῶν εἰς Αἴγυπτον,
in the hearts of them to Egypt,

40 εἰπόντες τῷ Ἀαρών· ποίησον ἡμῖν
saying - to Aaron : Make for us

θεοὺς οἳ προπορεύσονται ἡμῶν· ὁ γὰρ
gods which will go before us; - for

Μωϋσῆς οὗτος, ὃς ἐξήγαγεν ἡμᾶς ἐκ
this Moses, who led forth us out of

γῆς Αἰγύπτου, οὐκ οἴδαμεν τί ἐγένετο
[the] land Egypt, we know not what happened

αὐτῷ. 41 καὶ ἐμοσχοποίησαν ἐν
to him. And they made [a model of] a calf in

ταῖς ἡμέραις ἐκείναις καὶ ἀνήγαγον θυσίαν τῷ
those days and brought up a sacrifice to the

εἰδώλῳ, καὶ εὐφραίνοντο ἐν τοῖς ἔργοις
idol, and made merry in the works

τῶν χειρῶν αὐτῶν. 42 ἔστρεψεν δὲ ὁ
of the hands of them. And ³turned -

θεὸς καὶ παρέδωκεν αὐτοὺς λατρεύειν
¹God and delivered them to worship

τῇ στρατιᾷ τοῦ οὐρανοῦ, καθὼς γέγραπται
the host - of heaven, as it has been written

ἐν βίβλῳ τῶν προφητῶν· μὴ σφάγια
in [the] roll of the prophets : Not victims

καὶ θυσίας προσηνέγκατέ μοι ἔτη
and sacrifices ye offered to me years

τεσσεράκοντα ἐν τῇ ἐρήμῳ, οἶκος Ἰσραήλ,
forty in the desert, [O] house of Israel,

43 καὶ ἀνελάβετε τὴν σκηνὴν τοῦ Μόλοχ
and ye took up the tent - of Moloch

καὶ τὸ ἄστρον τοῦ θεοῦ Ῥομφά, τοὺς
and the star of the god Rompha, the

τύπους οὓς ἐποιήσατε προσκυνεῖν αὐτοῖς·
models which ye made to worship them?

καὶ μετοικιῶ ὑμᾶς ἐπέκεινα Βαβυλῶνος.
and I will deport you beyond Babylon.

44 Ἡ σκηνὴ τοῦ μαρτυρίου ἦν τοῖς
The tent - of witness was to the
= Our fathers had the tent of witness

πατράσιν ἡμῶν ἐν τῇ ἐρήμῳ, καθὼς
fathers of us⁹ in the desert, as

διετάξατο ὁ λαλῶν τῷ Μωϋσῆ ποιῆσαι
commanded the [one] speaking - to Moses to make

αὐτὴν κατὰ τὸν τύπον ὃν ἑωράκει·
it according to the model which he had seen;

45 ἣν καὶ εἰσήγαγον διαδεξάμενοι οἱ
which also ³brought in ²having received ¹the

πατέρες ἡμῶν μετὰ Ἰησοῦ ἐν τῇ κατα-
²fathers ³of us with Jesus in the pos-

σχέσει τῶν ἐθνῶν, ὧν ἐξῶσεν ὁ θεὸς
session of the nations, whom put out - God

King James Version

of our fathers, unto the days of David; 46 Who found favour before God, and desired to find a tabernacle for the God of Jacob. 47 But Solomon built him a house. 48 Howbeit the Most High dwelleth not in temples made with hands; as saith the prophet, 49 Heaven *is* my throne, and earth *is* my footstool: what house will ye build me? saith the Lord: or what *is* the place of my rest? 50 Hath not my hand made all these things?

51 Ye stiffnecked and uncircumcised in heart and ears, ye do always resist the Holy Ghost: as your fathers *did*, so *do* ye. 52 Which of the prophets have not your fathers persecuted? and they have slain them which shewed before of the coming of the Just One; of whom ye have been now the betrayers and murderers: 53 Who have received the law by the disposition of angels, and have not kept *it*.

54 When they heard these things, they were cut to the heart, and they gnashed on him with *their* teeth. 55 But he, being full of the Holy Ghost, looked up steadfastly into heaven, and saw the glory of God, and Jesus standing on the right hand of God, 56 And said, Behold, I see the heavens opened, and the Son of man standing on the right hand of God. 57 Then they cried out with a loud voice, and stopped their ears, and ran upon him with one accord, 58 And cast *him* out of the city, and stoned *him:* and the witnesses laid down their clothes at a young man's feet, whose name was Saul. 59 And they stoned Stephen, calling upon *God,* and saying, Lord Jesus, receive my spirit. 60 And he kneeled down, and cried with a loud voice, Lord, lay not this sin to their charge. And when he had said **this,** he fell asleep.

8 And Saul was consenting unto his death. And at that time there was a great persecution against the church which was at Jerusalem; and they were all scattered abroad throughout the regions of Judea and Samaria, except the apostles. 2 And devout men carried Stephen *to his burial,* and made great lamentation over him. 3 As for Saul, he made havoc of the church, entering into every house, and haling men and women committed *them* to prison. 4 Therefore they that were scattered abroad went every where preaching the word. 5 Then Philip went down to the city of Samaria, and preached Christ unto them. 6 And the people with one accord gave heed unto those things which Philip spake, hear-

New International Version

drove out before them. It remained in the land until the time of David, 46 who enjoyed God's favor and asked that he might provide a dwelling place for the God of Jacob.[b] 47 But it was Solomon who built the house for him.

48 "However, the Most High does not live in houses made by men. As the prophet says:

49 'Heaven is my throne,
  and the earth is my footstool.
What kind of house will you make for me?
                              says the Lord.
Or where will my resting place be?
50 Has not my hand made all these things?'[c]

51 "You stubborn people, with uncircumcised hearts and ears! You are just like your fathers: You always resist the Holy Spirit! 52 Was there ever a prophet your fathers did not persecute? They even killed those who predicted the coming of the Righteous One. And now you have betrayed and murdered him—53 you who have received the law that was put into effect through angels but have not obeyed it."

The stoning of Stephen

54 When they heard this, they were furious and ground their teeth at him. 55 But Stephen, filled with the Holy Spirit, looked up to heaven and saw the glory of God, and Jesus standing at the right hand of God. 56 "Look," he said, "I see heaven open and the Son of Man standing at the right hand of God."

57 At this they covered their ears and, yelling at the top of their voices, they all rushed at him, 58 dragged him out of the city and began to stone him. Meanwhile, the witnesses laid their clothes at the feet of a young man named Saul.

59 While they were stoning him, Stephen prayed, "Lord Jesus, receive my spirit." 60 Then he fell on his knees and cried out, "Lord, do not hold this sin against them." When he had said this, he fell asleep.

8 And Saul was there, giving approval to his death.

The church persecuted and scattered

On that day a great persecution broke out against the church at Jerusalem, and all except the apostles were scattered throughout Judea and Samaria. 2 Godly men buried Stephen and mourned deeply for him. 3 But Saul began to destroy the church. Going from house to house, he dragged off men and women and put them in prison.

Philip in Samaria

4 Those who had been scattered preached the word wherever they went. 5 Philip went down to a city in Samaria and proclaimed the Christ[d] there. 6 When the crowds heard Philip and saw the miraculous signs he did, they all paid close

[b] Some early MSS read *house of Jacob.* [c] Isaiah 66:1,2. [d] Or *Messiah.*

Greek Interlinear

ἀπὸ προσώπου τῶν πατέρων ἡμῶν, ἕως
from [the] face of the fathers of us, until

τῶν ἡμερῶν Δαυίδ· 46 ὃς εὗρεν χάριν
the days of David; who found favour

ἐνώπιον τοῦ θεοῦ καὶ ᾐτήσατο εὑρεῖν
before – God and asked to find

σκήνωμα τῷ οἴκῳ Ἰακώβ. 47 Σολομὼν δὲ
a tent for the house of Jacob. But Solomon

οἰκοδόμησεν αὐτῷ οἶκον. 48 ἀλλ'
built for him a house. But

οὐχ ὁ ὕψιστος ἐν χειροποιήτοις κατοικεῖ·
⁴not ¹the ²Most High ³in ⁵[places] made by hand ⁶dwells;

καθὼς ὁ προφήτης λέγει· 49 ὁ οὐρανός
as the prophet says: The heaven

μοι θρόνος, ἡ δὲ γῆ ὑποπόδιον τῶν
to me a throne, and the earth a footstool of the

ποδῶν μου· ποῖον οἶκον οἰκοδομήσετέ μοι,
feet of me; what house will ye build for me,

λέγει κύριος, ἢ τίς τόπος τῆς καταπαύσεώς
says [the] Lord, or what place of the rest

μου; 50 οὐχὶ ἡ χείρ μου ἐποίησεν ταῦτα
of me? not the hand of me made these things

πάντα; 51 Σκληροτράχηλοι καὶ ἀπερίτμητοι
all? Hard-necked and uncircumcised

καρδίαις καὶ τοῖς ὠσίν, ὑμεῖς ἀεὶ τῷ
in hearts and the ears, ye always the

πνεύματι τῷ ἁγίῳ ἀντιπίπτετε, ὡς οἱ
Spirit – Holy oppose, as the

πατέρες ὑμῶν καὶ ὑμεῖς. 52 τίνα τῶν
fathers of you also ye. Which of the

προφητῶν οὐκ ἐδίωξαν οἱ πατέρες ὑμῶν;
prophets persecuted not the fathers of you?

καὶ ἀπέκτειναν τοὺς προκαταγγείλαντας
and they killed the [ones] announcing beforehand

περὶ τῆς ἐλεύσεως τοῦ δικαίου, οὗ
concerning the coming of the righteous one, of whom

νῦν ὑμεῖς προδόται καὶ φονεῖς ἐγένεσθε,
now ye. betrayers and murderers became,

53 οἵτινες ἐλάβετε τὸν νόμον εἰς διαταγὰς
who received the law in(by) dispositions

ἀγγέλων, καὶ οὐκ ἐφυλάξατε.
of angels, and did not keep [it].

54 Ἀκούοντες δὲ ταῦτα διεπρίοντο ταῖς
And hearing these things they were cut to the

καρδίαις αὐτῶν καὶ ἔβρυχον τοὺς ὀδόντας
hearts of them and gnashed the teeth

ἐπ' αὐτόν. 55 ὑπάρχων δὲ πλήρης
at him. But being full

πνεύματος ἁγίου ἀτενίσας εἰς τὸν οὐρανὸν
of [the] Spirit Holy gazing into – heaven

εἶδεν δόξαν θεοῦ καὶ Ἰησοῦν ἑστῶτα ἐκ
he saw [the] glory of God and Jesus standing at

δεξιῶν τοῦ θεοῦ, 56 καὶ εἶπεν· ἰδοὺ
[the] right [hand] – of God, and said: Behold

θεωρῶ τοὺς οὐρανοὺς διηνοιγμένους καὶ
I see the heavens having been opened up and

τὸν υἱὸν τοῦ ἀνθρώπου ἐκ δεξιῶν ἑστῶτα
the Son – of man at [the] right [hand] standing

τοῦ θεοῦ. 57 κράξαντες δὲ φωνῇ μεγάλῃ
– of God. And crying out voice with a great

συνέσχον τὰ ὦτα αὐτῶν, καὶ ὥρμησαν
they closed the ears of them, and rushed

ὁμοθυμαδὸν ἐπ' αὐτόν, 58 καὶ ἐκβαλόντες
with one mind on him, and casting out

ἔξω τῆς πόλεως ἐλιθοβόλουν. καὶ οἱ
outside the city they stoned [him]. And the

μάρτυρες ἀπέθεντο τὰ ἱμάτια αὐτῶν παρὰ
witnesses put off the garments of them at

τοὺς πόδας νεανίου καλουμένου Σαύλου.
the feet of a young man being called Saul.

59 καὶ ἐλιθοβόλουν τὸν Στέφανον, ἐπικαλ-
And they stoned – Stephen, invok-

ούμενον καὶ λέγοντα· κύριε Ἰησοῦ, δέξαι
ing [God] and saying: Lord Jesus, receive

τὸ πνεῦμά μου. 60 θεὶς δὲ τὰ γόνατα
the spirit of me. And placing the knees
=kneeling down

ἔκραξεν φωνῇ μεγάλῃ· κύριε, μὴ στήσῃς
he cried voice with a great: Lord, place not

αὐτοῖς ταύτην τὴν ἁμαρτίαν. καὶ τοῦτο
to them this – sin. And ¹this

Chapter 8

εἰπὼν ἐκοιμήθη. 8 Σαῦλος δὲ ἦν συνευδοκῶν
¹saying he fell asleep. And Saul was consenting

τῇ ἀναιρέσει αὐτοῦ.
to the killing of him.

Ἐγένετο δὲ ἐν ἐκείνῃ τῇ ἡμέρᾳ
And there was in that – day

διωγμὸς μέγας ἐπὶ τὴν ἐκκλησίαν τὴν
persecution a great on(against) the church

ἐν Ἱεροσολύμοις· πάντες [δὲ] διεσπάρησαν
in Jerusalem; and all were scattered

κατὰ τὰς χώρας τῆς Ἰουδαίας καὶ
throughout the countries – of Judea and

Σαμαρείας πλὴν τῶν ἀποστόλων.
Samaria except . the apostles.

2 συνεκόμισαν δὲ τὸν Στέφανον ἄνδρες
And ²recovered – ⁴Stephen ³men

εὐλαβεῖς καὶ ἐποίησαν κοπετὸν μέγαν
¹devout and made lamentation great

ἐπ' αὐτῷ. 3 Σαῦλος δὲ ἐλυμαίνετο τὴν
over him. But Saul ravaged the

ἐκκλησίαν κατὰ τοὺς οἴκους εἰσπορευόμενος,
church house by house† entering,

σύρων τε ἄνδρας καὶ γυναῖκας παρεδίδου
dragging both men and women delivered

εἰς φυλακήν.
to prison.

4 Οἱ μὲν οὖν διασπαρέντες διῆλθον
The [ones] –* therefore being scattered passed through

εὐαγγελιζόμενοι τὸν λόγον. 5 Φίλιππος
preaching the word. But Philip

κατελθὼν εἰς τὴν πόλιν τῆς
going down to the city

Σαμαρείας ἐκήρυσσεν αὐτοῖς τὸν Χριστόν.
of Samaria proclaimed to them the Christ.

6 προσεῖχον δὲ οἱ ὄχλοι τοῖς
And gave heed the crowds to the things

λεγομένοις ὑπὸ τοῦ Φιλίππου ὁμοθυμαδὸν
being said by – Philip with one mind

ἐν τῷ ἀκούειν αὐτοὺς καὶ βλέπειν τὰ
in the to hear them and to see*ᵇᵉ the
=as they heard and saw

* See note on John 19. 24.

King James Version

ing and seeing the miracles which he did. 7 For unclean spirits, crying with loud voice, came out of many that were possessed *with them:* and many taken with palsies, and that were lame, were healed. 8And there was great joy in that city. 9 But there was a certain man, called Simon, which beforetime in the same city used sorcery, and bewitched the people of Samaria, giving out that himself was some great one: 10 To whom they all gave heed, from the least to the greatest, saying, This man is the great power of God. 11And to him they had regard, because that of long time he had bewitched them.with sorceries. 12 But when they believed Philip preaching the things concerning the kingdom of God, and the name of Jesus Christ, they were baptized, both men and women. 13 Then Simon himself believed also: and when he was baptized, he continued with Philip, and wondered, beholding the miracles and signs which were done. 14 Now when the apostles which were at Jerusalem heard that Samaria had received the word of God, they sent unto them Peter and John: 15 Who, when they were come down, prayed for them, that they might receive the Holy Ghost: 16 (For as yet he was fallen upon none of them: only they were baptized in the name of the Lord Jesus.) 17 Then laid they *their* hands on them, and they received the Holy Ghost. 18And when Simon saw that through laying on of the apostles' hands the Holy Ghost was given, he offered them money, 19 Saying, Give me also this power, that on whomsoever I lay hands, he may receive the Holy Ghost. 20 But Peter said unto him, Thy money perish with thee, because thou hast thought that the gift of God may be purchased with money. 21 Thou hast neither part nor lot in this matter: for thy heart is not right in the sight of God. 22 Repent therefore of this thy wickedness, and pray God, if perhaps the thought of thine heart may be forgiven thee. 23 For I perceive that thou art in the gall of bitterness, and *in* the bond of iniquity. 24 Then answered Simon, and said, Pray ye to the Lord for me, that none of these things which ye have spoken come upon me. 25And they, when they had testified and preached ·the word of the Lord, returned to Jerusalem, and preached the gospel in many villages of the Samaritans. 26And the angel of the Lord spake unto Philip, saying, Arise, and go toward the south, unto the way that goeth down from Jerusalem unto Gaza, which is desert. 27And he arose and went: and, behold, a man of Ethiopia, a eunuch of great authority under Candace queen of the Ethiopians, who had the charge of all her treasure, and had come to Jerusalem for to worship, 28 Was returning, and sitting in his chariot read Esaias the prophet. 29 Then the Spirit said unto Philip, Go near, and

New International Version

attention to what he said. 7 With shrieks, evil [e] spirits came out of many, and many paralytics and cripples were healed. 8 So there was great joy in that city.

Simon the sorcerer

9 Now for some time a man named Simon had practiced sorcery in the city and amazed all the people of Samaria. He boasted that he was someone great, 10 and all the people, both high and low, gave him their attention and exclaimed, "This man is the divine power known as the Great Power." 11 They followed him because he had amazed them for a long time with his magic. 12 But when they believed Philip as he preached the good news of the kingdom of God and the name of Jesus Christ, they were baptized, both men and women. 13 Simon himself believed and was baptized. And he followed Philip everywhere, astonished by the great signs and miracles he saw.

14 When the apostles in Jerusalem heard that Samaria had accepted the word of God, they sent Peter and John to them. 15 When they arrived, they prayed for them that they might receive the Holy Spirit, 16 because the Holy Spirit had not yet come upon any of them; they had simply been baptized into[f] the name of the Lord Jesus. 17 Then Peter and John placed their hands on them, and they received the Holy Spirit.

18 When Simon saw that the Spirit was given at the laying on of the apostles' hands, he offered them money and said, 19 "Give me also this ability so that everyone on whom I lay my hands may receive the Holy Spirit."

20 Peter answered: "May your money perish with you, because you thought you could buy the gift of God with money! 21 You have no part or share in this ministry, because your heart is not right before God. 22 Repent of this wickedness and pray to the Lord. Perhaps he will forgive you for having such a thought in your heart. 23 For I see that you are full of bitterness and captive to sin."

24 Then Simon answered, "Pray to the Lord for me so that nothing you have said may happen to me."

25 When they had testified and proclaimed the word of the Lord, Peter and John returned to Jerusalem, preaching the gospel in many Samaritan villages.

Philip and the Ethiopian

26 Now an angel of the Lord said to Philip, "Go south to the road—the desert road—that goes down from Jerusalem to Gaza." 27 So he started out, and on his way he met an Ethiopian eunuch, an important official in charge of all the treasury of Candace, queen of the Ethiopians. This man had gone to Jerusalem to worship, 28 and on his way home was sitting in his chariot reading the book of Isaiah the prophet. 29 The Spirit told Philip, "Go to that chariot and stay near it."

[e] Greek *unclean.* [f] Or *in.*

Greek Interlinear

σημεῖα ἃ ἐποίει. 7 πολλοὶ γὰρ τῶν
signs   which he was doing. For many   of the

ἐχόντων πνεύματα ἀκάθαρτα βοῶντα φωνῇ
[ones] having spirits   unclean   crying ²voice

μεγάλῃ ἐξήρχοντο· πολλοὶ δὲ παραλελυμένοι
¹with a great came out; and many having been paralysed

καὶ χωλοὶ ἐθεραπεύθησαν· 8 ἐγένετο δὲ
and lame were healed;   and there was

πολλὴ χαρὰ ἐν τῇ πόλει ἐκείνῃ. 9 Ἀνὴρ δέ τις
much joy in the city that city. And a certain man

ὀνόματι Σίμων προϋπῆρχεν ἐν τῇ
by name Simon· was previously in the

πόλει μαγεύων καὶ ἐξιστάνων τὸ
city practising sorcery and astonishing the

ἔθνος τῆς Σαμαρείας, λέγων εἶναί τινα
nation of Samaria, saying ¹to be ²someone

ἑαυτὸν μέγαν, 10 ᾧ προσεῖχον πάντες
¹himself ²great, to whom gave heed all

ἀπὸ μικροῦ ἕως μεγάλου λέγοντες· οὗτός
from small to great   saying : This man

ἐστιν ἡ δύναμις τοῦ θεοῦ ἡ καλουμένη
is the power   of God being called

μεγάλη. 11 προσεῖχον δὲ αὐτῷ διὰ τὸ
great. And they gave heed to him because of the

ἱκανῷ χρόνῳ ταῖς μαγείαις ἐξεστακέναι
for a considerable time by the sorceries to have astonished
=because for a considerable time he had astonished them by his sorceries

αὐτούς. 12 ὅτε δὲ ἐπίστευσαν τῷ Φιλίππῳ
them. But when they believed - Philip

εὐαγγελιζομένῳ περὶ τῆς βασιλείας τοῦ
preaching about the kingdom

θεοῦ καὶ τοῦ ὀνόματος Ἰησοῦ Χριστοῦ,
of God and the name of Jesus Christ,

ἐβαπτίζοντο ἄνδρες τε καὶ γυναῖκες.
they were baptized both men and women.

13 ὁ δὲ Σίμων καὶ αὐτὸς ἐπίστευσεν,
- And Simon also [him]self believed,

καὶ βαπτισθεὶς ἦν προσκαρτερῶν τῷ
and having been baptized was attaching himself

Φιλίππῳ, θεωρῶν τε σημεῖα καὶ δυνάμεις
to Philip, and beholding signs and powerful deeds

μεγάλας γινομένας ἐξίστατο. 14 Ἀκούσαντες
great happening he was amazed. ²hearing

δὲ οἱ ἐν Ἱεροσολύμοις ἀπόστολοι ὅτι
¹And ²the ³in Jerusalem apostles that

δέδεκται ἡ Σαμάρεια τὸν λόγον τοῦ
²has received - ¹Samaria the word

θεοῦ, ἀπέστειλαν πρὸς αὐτοὺς Πέτρον
of God, they sent to them Peter

καὶ Ἰωάννην, 15 οἵτινες καταβάντες
and John, who going down

προσηύξαντο περὶ αὐτῶν ὅπως λάβωσιν
prayed concerning them so as they might receive

πνεῦμα ἅγιον· 16 οὐδέπω γὰρ ἦν ἐπ'
Spirit Holy· for ¹not yet ¹he was ²on

οὐδενὶ αὐτῶν ἐπιπεπτωκός, μόνον δὲ
¹no(any)one ²of them ³having fallen on, but only

βεβαπτισμένοι ὑπῆρχον εἰς τὸ ὄνομα τοῦ
having been baptized they were in the name

κυρίου Ἰησοῦ. 17 τότε ἐπετίθεσαν τὰς
Lord Jesus. Then they laid on the(ir)

χεῖρας ἐπ' αὐτούς, καὶ ἐλάμβανον πνεῦμα
hands on them, and they received ²Spirit

ἅγιον. 18 ἰδὼν δὲ ὁ Σίμων ὅτι διὰ
¹Holy. And ²seeing - ¹Simon that through

τῆς ἐπιθέσεως τῶν χειρῶν τῶν ἀποστόλων
the laying on of the hands of the apostles

δίδοται τὸ πνεῦμα, προσήνεγκεν αὐτοῖς
is(was) given the Spirit, he offered them

χρήματα λέγων· 19 δότε κἀμοὶ τὴν
money saying : Give me also -

ἐξουσίαν ταύτην ἵνα ᾧ ἐὰν ἐπιθῶ τὰς
authority this that whomever I lay on the(my)

χεῖρας λαμβάνῃ πνεῦμα ἅγιον. 20 Πέτρος δὲ
hands he may receive Spirit Holy. But Peter

εἶπεν πρὸς αὐτόν· τὸ ἀργύριόν σου
said to him : The silver of thee

σὺν σοὶ εἴη εἰς ἀπώλειαν, ὅτι τὴν δωρεὰν
with thee may it be into perdition, because the gift

τοῦ θεοῦ ἐνόμισας διὰ χρημάτων κτᾶσθαι.
- of God thou didst suppose through money to get.

21 οὐκ ἔστιν σοι μερὶς οὐδὲ κλῆρος
There is not to thee² part nor lot
=Thou hast no

ἐν τῷ λόγῳ τούτῳ· ἡ γὰρ καρδία σου
in this matter ; for the heart of thee

οὐκ ἔστιν εὐθεῖα ἔναντι τοῦ θεοῦ.
is not right before - God.

22 μετανόησον οὖν ἀπὸ τῆς κακίας σου
Repent thou therefore from - ²wickedness ²of thee

ταύτης, καὶ δεήθητι τοῦ κυρίου εἰ ἄρα
¹this, and petition the Lord if perhaps

ἀφεθήσεταί σοι ἡ ἐπίνοια τῆς καρδίας
will be forgiven thee the thought of the heart

σου· 23 εἰς γὰρ χολὴν πικρίας καὶ
of thee; for in gall of bitterness and

σύνδεσμον ἀδικίας ὁρῶ σε ὄντα.
bond of unrighteousness I see thee being.

24 ἀποκριθεὶς δὲ ὁ Σίμων εἶπεν· δεήθητε
And answering - Simon said : Petition

ὑμεῖς ὑπὲρ ἐμοῦ πρὸς τὸν κύριον, ὅπως
ye for me to the Lord, so as

μηδὲν ἐπέλθῃ ἐπ' ἐμὲ ὧν εἰρήκατε.
¹not one ³may come on ²on ⁴me ⁵of the ⁶things which ⁷ye have ⁸spoken.

25 Οἱ μὲν οὖν διαμαρτυράμενοι καὶ λαλή-
They - therefore having solemnly witnessed and

σαντες τὸν λόγον τοῦ κυρίου ὑπέστρεφον
spoken the word of the Lord returned

εἰς Ἱεροσόλυμα, πολλάς τε κώμας τῶν
to Jerusalem, and ²many ³villages ⁴of the

Σαμαριτῶν εὐηγγελίζοντο.
⁵Samaritans ¹evangelized.

26 Ἄγγελος δὲ κυρίου ἐλάλησεν πρὸς
But an angel of [the] Lord spoke to

Φίλιππον λέγων· ἀνάστηθι καὶ πορεύου
Philip saying : Rise up and go

κατὰ μεσημβρίαν ἐπὶ τὴν ὁδὸν τὴν
along south on the way -

καταβαίνουσαν ἀπὸ Ἱερουσαλὴμ εἰς Γάζαν·
going down from Jerusalem to Gaza;

αὕτη ἐστὶν ἔρημος. 27 καὶ ἀναστὰς
this is desert. And rising up

ἐπορεύθη. καὶ ἰδοὺ ἀνὴρ Αἰθίοψ εὐνοῦχος
he went. And behold[,] a man Ethiopian a eunuch

δυνάστης Κανδάκης βασιλίσσης Αἰθιόπων,
a courtier of Candace queen of [the] Ethiopians,

ὃς ἦν ἐπὶ πάσης τῆς γάζης αὐτῆς,
who was over all the treasure of her,

[ὃς] ἐληλύθει προσκυνήσων εἰς Ἱερουσαλήμ,
who had come worshipping in Jerusalem,

28 ἦν δὲ ὑποστρέφων καὶ καθήμενος ἐπὶ
and was returning and sitting on

τοῦ ἅρματος αὐτοῦ καὶ ἀνεγίνωσκεν τὸν
the chariot of him and was reading the

προφήτην Ἡσαΐαν. 29 εἶπεν δὲ τὸ πνεῦμα
prophet Esaias. And said the Spirit

τῷ Φιλίππῳ· πρόσελθε καὶ κολλήθητι
- to Philip : Approach and keep company with

369

King James Version

join thyself to this chariot. 30And Philip ran thither to *him,* and heard him read the prophet Esaias, and said, Understandest thou what thou readest? 31And he said, How can I, except some man should guide me? And he desired Philip that he would come up and sit with him. 32 The place of the Scripture which he read was this, He was led as a sheep to the slaughter; and like a lamb dumb before his shearer, so opened he not his mouth: 33 In his humiliation his judgment was taken away: and who shall declare his generation? for his life is taken from the earth. 34And the eunuch answered Philip, and said, I pray thee, of whom speaketh the prophet this? of himself, or of some other man? 35 Then Philip opened his mouth, and began at the same Scripture, and preached unto him Jesus. 36And as they went on *their* way, they came unto a certain water: and the eunuch said, See, *here is* water; what doth hinder me to be baptized? 37And Philip said, If thou believest with all thine heart, thou mayest. And he answered and said, I believe that Jesus Christ is the Son of God. 38And he commanded the chariot to stand still: and they went down both into the water, both Philip and the eunuch; and he baptized him. 39And when they were come up out of the water, the Spirit of the Lord caught away Philip, that the eunuch saw him no more: and he went on his way rejoicing. 40 But Philip was found at Azotus: and passing through he preached in all the cities, till he came to Cesarea.

9 And Saul, yet breathing out threatenings and slaughter against the disciples of the Lord, went unto the high priest, 2And desired of him letters to Damascus to the synagogues, that if he found any of this way, whether they were men or women, he might bring them bound unto Jerusalem. 3And as he journeyed, he came near Damascus: and suddenly there shined round about him a light from heaven: 4And he fell to the earth, and heard a voice saying unto him, Saul, Saul, why persecutest thou me? 5And he said, Who art thou, Lord? And the Lord said, I am Jesus whom thou persecutest: *it is* hard for thee to kick against the pricks. 6And he trembling and astonished said, Lord, what wilt thou have me to do? And the Lord *said* unto him, Arise, and go into the city, and it shall be told thee what thou must do. 7And the men which journeyed with him stood speechless, hearing a voice, but seeing no man. 8And Saul arose from the earth; and when his eyes were opened, he saw no man: but they led him by the hand, and brought *him* into Damascus. 9And he was three days without sight, and neither did eat nor drink.

10 And there was a certain disciple at Damascus, named Ananias; and to him said the Lord in a vision, Ananias. And he said, Behold,

New International Version

30 Then Philip ran up to the chariot and heard the man reading Isaiah the prophet. "Do you understand what you are reading?" Philip asked.

31 "How can I," he said, "unless someone explains it to me?" So he invited Philip to come up and sit with him.

32 The eunuch was reading this passage of Scripture:

"He was led like a sheep to the slaughter,
and as a lamb before the shearer is silent,
so he did not open his mouth.
33 In his humiliation he was deprived of justice.
Who can speak of his descendants?
For his life was taken from the earth." *g*

34 The eunuch asked Philip, "Tell me, please, who is the prophet talking about, himself or someone else?" 35 Then Philip began with that very passage of Scripture and told him the good news about Jesus.

36 As they traveled along the road, they came to some water and the eunuch said, "Look, here is water. Why shouldn't I be baptized?" *h* 38And he ordered the chariot to stop. Then both Philip and the eunuch went down into the water and Philip baptized him. 39 When they came up out of the water, the Spirit of the Lord suddenly took Philip away, and the eunuch did not see him again, but went on his way rejoicing. 40 Philip, however, appeared at Azotus and traveled about, preaching the gospel in all the towns until he reached Caesarea.

Saul's conversion

9 Meanwhile, Saul was still breathing out murderous threats against the Lord's disciples. He went to the high priest 2 and asked him for letters to the synagogues in Damascus, so that if he found any there who belonged to the Way, whether men or women, he might take them as prisoners to Jerusalem. 3As he neared Damascus on his journey, suddenly a light from heaven flashed around him. 4 He fell to the ground and heard a voice say to him, "Saul, Saul, why do you persecute me?"

5 "Who are you, Lord?" Saul asked.

"I am Jesus whom you are persecuting," he replied. 6 "Now get up and go into the city, and you will be told what you must do."

7 The men traveling with Saul stood there speechless; they heard the sound but did not see anyone. 8 Saul got up from the ground, but when he opened his eyes he could see nothing. So they led him by the hand into Damascus. 9 For three days he was blind, and did not eat or drink anything.

10 In Damascus there was a disciple named Ananias. The Lord called to him in a vision, "Ananias!"

"Yes, Lord," he answered.

[g] Isaiah 53:7,8. [h] Some MSS add verse 37: *Philip said, "If you believe with all your heart, you may." The official answered, "I believe that Jesus Christ is the Son of God."*

370

Greek Interlinear

τῷ ἅρματι τούτῳ. 30 προσδραμὼν δὲ
this chariot. And running up

ὁ Φίλιππος ἤκουσεν αὐτοῦ ἀναγινώσκοντος
- Philip heard him reading

'Ησαΐαν τὸν προφήτην, καὶ εἶπεν· ἆρά γε
Esaias the prophet, and said: Then

γινώσκεις ἃ ἀναγινώσκεις; 31 ὁ δὲ
knowest thou what things thou art reading? And he

εἶπεν· πῶς γὰρ ἂν δυναίμην ἐὰν μή
said: How indeed should I be able unless

τις ὁδηγήσει με; παρεκάλεσέν τε τὸν
someone shall guide me? And he besought

Φίλιππον ἀναβάντα καθίσαι σὺν αὐτῷ.
Philip coming up to sit with him.

32 ἡ δὲ περιοχὴ τῆς γραφῆς ἣν ἀνεγίνω-
Now the passage of the scripture which he was

σκεν ἦν αὕτη· ὡς πρόβατον ἐπὶ σφαγὴν
reading was this: As a sheep to slaughter

ἤχθη, καὶ ὡς ἀμνὸς ἐναντίον τοῦ κείροντος
he was led, and as a lamb before the [one] shearing

αὐτὸν ἄφωνος, οὕτως οὐκ ἀνοίγει τὸ
it [is] dumb, so he opens not the

στόμα αὐτοῦ. 33 'Εν τῇ ταπεινώσει
mouth of him. In the humiliation

ἡ κρίσις αὐτοῦ ἤρθη· τὴν γενεὰν αὐτοῦ
the judgment of him was taken away; the generation of him

τίς διηγήσεται; ὅτι αἴρεται ἀπὸ τῆς
who will relate? because is taken from the

γῆς ἡ ζωὴ αὐτοῦ. 34 ἀποκριθεὶς δὲ ὁ
earth the life of him. And answering the

εὐνοῦχος τῷ Φιλίππῳ εἶπεν· δέομαί σου,
eunuch to Philip said: I ask thee,

περὶ τίνος ὁ προφήτης λέγει τοῦτο;
about whom the prophet says this?

περὶ ἑαυτοῦ ἢ περὶ ἑτέρου τινός;
about himself or about other someone?

35 ἀνοίξας δὲ ὁ Φίλιππος τὸ στόμα
And opening - Philip the mouth

αὐτοῦ καὶ ἀρξάμενος ἀπὸ τῆς γραφῆς ταύτης
of him and beginning from this scripture

εὐηγγελίσατο αὐτῷ τὸν 'Ιησοῦν.
preached to him the - Jesus.

36 ὡς δὲ ἐπορεύοντο κατὰ τὴν ὁδόν,
And as they were going along the way,

ἦλθον ἐπί τι ὕδωρ, καί φησιν ὁ εὐνοῦχος·
they came upon certain water, and says the eunuch:

ἰδοὺ ὕδωρ· τί κωλύει με βαπτισθῆναι;‡
Behold[.] water; what prevents me to be baptized?

38 καὶ ἐκέλευσεν στῆναι τὸ ἅρμα, καὶ
And he commanded to stand the chariot, and

κατέβησαν ἀμφότεροι εἰς τὸ ὕδωρ, ὅ
went down both into the water, -

τε Φίλιππος καὶ ὁ εὐνοῦχος, καὶ ἐβάπτισεν
both Philip and the eunuch, and he baptized

αὐτόν. 39 ὅτε δὲ ἀνέβησαν ἐκ τοῦ ὕδατος,
him. And when they came up out of the water,

πνεῦμα κυρίου ἥρπασεν τὸν Φίλιππον,
[the] Spirit of [the] Lord seized - Philip,

καὶ οὐκ εἶδεν αὐτὸν οὐκέτι ὁ εὐνοῦχος,
and saw not him no(any) more the eunuch,

ἐπορεύετο γὰρ τὴν ὁδὸν αὐτοῦ χαίρων.
for he went the way of him rejoicing.

40 Φίλιππος δὲ εὑρέθη εἰς "Αζωτον, καὶ
But Philip was found in Azotus, and

διερχόμενος εὐηγγελίζετο τὰς πόλεις πάσας
passing through he evangelized the cities all

ἕως τοῦ ἐλθεῖν αὐτὸν εἰς Καισάρειαν.
until the to come him[b] to Cæsarea.
=he came

Chapter 9

'Ο δὲ Σαῦλος ἔτι ἐμπνέων ἀπειλῆς
- But Saul still breathing threatening

καὶ φόνου εἰς τοὺς μαθητὰς τοῦ κυρίου,
and murder against the disciples of the Lord,

προσελθὼν τῷ ἀρχιερεῖ 2 ᾐτήσατο παρ'
approaching to the high priest asked from

αὐτοῦ ἐπιστολὰς εἰς Δαμασκὸν πρὸς τὰς
him letters to Damascus for the

συναγωγάς, ὅπως ἐάν τινας εὕρῃ τῆς
synagogues, so as if any [he found b]of the

ὁδοῦ ὄντας, ἄνδρας τε καὶ γυναῖκας, δεδεμένους
[way b]being, both men and women, [having been bound b]

ἀγάγῃ εἰς 'Ιερουσαλήμ. 3 'Εν
[he might bring [them] to b] Jerusalem. in

δὲ τῷ πορεύεσθαι ἐγένετο αὐτὸν ἐγγίζειν
Now the to go[b] it came to pass him to draw near[b]
=as he went =he drew near

τῇ Δαμασκῷ, ἐξαίφνης τε αὐτὸν περιήστ-
- to Damascus, and suddenly [him b] [shone-

ραψεν φῶς ἐκ τοῦ οὐρανοῦ, 4 καὶ πεσὼν
round b]a light [out of b] - [heaven, b] and falling

ἐπὶ τὴν γῆν ἤκουσεν φωνὴν λέγουσαν
on the earth he heard a voice saying

αὐτῷ· Σαοὺλ Σαούλ, τί με διώκεις;
to him: Saul[,] Saul, why me persecutest thou?

5 εἶπεν δέ· τίς εἶ, κύριε; ὁ δέ· ἐγώ
And he said: Who art thou, Lord? And he [said]: I

εἰμι 'Ιησοῦς ὃν σὺ διώκεις· 6 ἀλλὰ
am Jesus whom thou persecutest· but

ἀνάστηθι καὶ εἴσελθε εἰς τὴν πόλιν,
rise thou up, and enter into the city,

καὶ λαληθήσεταί σοι ὅ τί σε δεῖ ποιεῖν.
and it shall be told thee what thee it behoves to do.

7 οἱ δὲ ἄνδρες οἱ συνοδεύοντες αὐτῷ
Now the men - journeying with him

εἱστήκεισαν ἐνεοί, ἀκούοντες μὲν τῆς
stood speechless, hearing indeed the

φωνῆς, μηδένα δὲ θεωροῦντες. 8 ἠγέρθη δὲ
sound, but no man beholding. And was raised

Σαῦλος ἀπὸ τῆς γῆς, ἀνεῳγμένων δὲ
Saul from the ground, and having been opened
=when his eyes were opened

τῶν ὀφθαλμῶν αὐτοῦ οὐδὲν ἔβλεπεν·
the eyes of him[a] nothing he saw;

χειραγωγοῦντες δὲ αὐτὸν εἰσήγαγον εἰς
and leading by the hand him they brought in into

Δαμασκόν. 9 καὶ ἦν ἡμέρας τρεῖς μὴ
Damascus. and he was days three not

βλέπων, καὶ οὐκ ἔφαγεν οὐδὲ ἔπιεν.
seeing, and ate not nor drank.

10 'Ην δέ τις μαθητὴς ἐν Δαμασκῷ
Now there was a certain disciple in Damascus

ὀνόματι 'Ανανίας, καὶ εἶπεν πρὸς αὐτὸν
by name Ananias, and said to him

ἐν ὁράματι ὁ κύριος· 'Ανανία. ὁ δὲ
in a vision the Lord: Ananias. And he

‡ Verse 37 omitted by Nestle

King James Version

I *am here*, Lord. 11And the Lord *said* unto him, Arise, and go into the street which is called Straight, and inquire in the house of Judas for *one* called Saul, of Tarsus: for, behold, he prayeth, 12And hath seen in a vision a man named Ananias coming in, and putting *his* hand on him, that he might receive his sight. 13 Then Ananias answered, Lord, I have heard by many of this man, how much evil he hath done to thy saints at Jerusalem: 14And here he hath authority from the chief priests to bind all that call on thy name. 15 But the Lord said unto him, Go thy way: for he is a chosen vessel unto me, to bear my name before the Gentiles, and kings, and the children of Israel: 16 For I will shew him how great things he must suffer for my name's sake. 17And Ananias went his way, and entered into the house; and putting his hands on him said, Brother Saul, the Lord, *even* Jesus, that appeared unto thee in the way as thou camest, hath sent me, that thou mightest receive thy sight, and be filled with the Holy Ghost. 18And immediately there fell from his eyes as it had been scales: and he received sight forthwith, and arose, and was baptized. 19And when he had received meat, he was strengthened. Then was Saul certain days with the disciples which were at Damascus. 20And straightway he preached Christ in the synagogues, that he is the Son of God. 21 But all that heard *him* were amazed, and said; Is not this he that destroyed them which called on this name in Jerusalem, and came hither for that intent, that he might bring them bound unto the chief priests? 22 But Saul increased the more in strength, and confounded the Jews which dwelt at Damascus, proving that this is very Christ.

23 And after that many days were fulfilled, the Jews took counsel to kill him: 24 But their laying wait was known of Saul. And they watched the gates day and night to kill him. 25 Then the disciples took him by night, and let *him* down by the wall in a basket. 26And when Saul was come to Jerusalem he assayed to join himself to the disciples: but they were all afraid of him, and believed not that he was a disciple. 27 But Barnabas took him, and brought *him* to the apostles, and declared unto them how he had seen the Lord in the way, and that he had spoken to him, and how he had preached boldly at Damascus in the name of Jesus. 28And he was with them coming in and going out at Jerusalem. 29And he spake boldly in the name of the Lord Jesus, and disputed against the Grecians: but they went about to slay him. 30 *Which* when the brethren knew, they brought him down to Cesarea, and sent him forth to Tarsus. 31 Then had the churches rest throughout all Judea and Galilee and Samaria, and were edified; and walking in the fear of the Lord, and in the comfort of the Holy Ghost, were multiplied.

New International Version

11 The Lord told him, "Go to the house of Judas on Straight Street and ask for a man from Tarsus named Saul, for he is praying. 12 In a vision he has seen a man named Ananias come and place his hands on him to restore his sight."

13 "Lord," Ananias answered, "I have heard many reports about this man and all the harm he has done to your saints in Jerusalem. 14And he has come here with authority from the chief priests to arrest all who call on your name."

15 But the Lord said to Ananias, "Go! This man is my chosen instrument to carry my name before the Gentiles and their kings and before the people of Israel. 16 I will show him how much he must suffer for my name."

17 Then Ananias went to the house and entered it. Placing his hands on Saul, he said, "Brother Saul, the Lord—Jesus, who appeared to you on the road as you were coming here—has sent me so that you may see again and be filled with the Holy Spirit." 18 Immediately, something like scales fell from Saul's eyes, and he could see again. He got up and was baptized, 19 and after taking some food, he regained his strength.

Saul in Damascus and Jerusalem

Saul spent several days with the disciples in Damascus. 20At once he began to preach in the synagogues that Jesus is the Son of God. 21All those who heard him were astonished and asked, "Isn't he the man who raised havoc in Jerusalem among those who call on this name? And hasn't he come here to take them as prisoners to the chief priests?" 22 Yet Saul grew more and more powerful and baffled the Jews living in Damascus by proving that Jesus is the Christ.[i]

23 After many days had gone by, the Jews conspired to kill him, 24 but Saul learned of their plan. Day and night they kept close watch on the city gates in order to kill him. 25 But his followers took him by night and lowered him in a basket through an opening in the wall.

26 When he came to Jerusalem, he tried to join the disciples, but they were all afraid of him, not believing that he really was a disciple. 27 But Barnabas took him and brought him to the apostles. He told them how Saul on his journey had seen the Lord and that the Lord had spoken to him, and how in Damascus he had preached fearlessly in the name of Jesus. 28 So Saul stayed with them and moved about freely in Jerusalem, speaking boldly in the name of the Lord. 29 He talked and debated with the Grecian Jews, but they tried to kill him. 30 When the brothers learned of this, they took him down to Caesarea and sent him off to Tarsus.

31 Then the church throughout Judea, Galilee and Samaria enjoyed a time of peace. It was strengthened; and encouraged by the Holy Spirit, it grew in numbers, living in the fear of the Lord.

[i] Or *Messiah*.

Greek Interlinear

εἶπεν· ἰδοὺ ἐγώ, κύριε. 11 ὁ δὲ κύριος
said : Behold[,] I, Lord.   And the Lord

πρὸς αὐτόν· ἀναστὰς πορεύθητι ἐπὶ τὴν
[said] to him : Rising up go thou to the

ῥύμην τὴν καλουμένην εὐθεῖαν καὶ ζήτησον
street - being called Straight and seek

ἐν οἰκίᾳ Ἰούδα Σαῦλον ὀνόματι Ταρσέα·
in [the] house of Judas ³Saul ²by name ¹a Tarsian;

ἰδοὺ γὰρ προσεύχεται, 12 καὶ εἶδεν ἄνδρα
for behold he is praying, and saw ²a man

[ἐν ὁράματι] Ἀνανίαν ὀνόματι εἰσελθόντα
¹in ²a vision Ananias by name coming in

καὶ ἐπιθέντα αὐτῷ χεῖρας, ὅπως ἀναβλέψῃ.
and putting on him hands, so as he may see again.

13 ἀπεκρίθη δὲ Ἀνανίας· κύριε, ἤκουσα
And answered Ananias : Lord, I heard

ἀπὸ πολλῶν περὶ τοῦ ἀνδρὸς τούτου,
from many about the man this,

ὅσα κακὰ τοῖς ἁγίοις σου ἐποίησεν
how many evil things to the saints of thee he did

ἐν Ἰερουσαλήμ· 14 καὶ ὧδε ἔχει ἐξουσίαν
in Jerusalem; and here he has authority

παρὰ τῶν ἀρχιερέων δῆσαι πάντας τοὺς
from the chief priests to bind all the

ἐπικαλουμένους τὸ ὄνομά σου. 15 εἶπεν
[ones] invoking the name of thee. said

δὲ πρὸς αὐτὸν ὁ κύριος· πορεύου, ὅτι
But to him the Lord : Go thou, because

σκεῦος ἐκλογῆς ἐστίν μοι οὗτος τοῦ
²a vessel ¹of choice ³is ⁴to me this man of

βαστάσαι τὸ ὄνομά μου ἐνώπιον [τῶν]
to bearᵈ the name of me ³before ¹the

ἐθνῶν τε καὶ βασιλέων υἱῶν τε Ἰσραήλ·
²nations ³both ⁴and ⁵kings ⁶sons ⁷and ⁸of Israel;

16 ἐγὼ γὰρ ὑποδείξω αὐτῷ ὅσα δεῖ
for I will show him how many things it behoves

αὐτὸν ὑπὲρ τοῦ ὀνόματός μου παθεῖν.
him on behalf of the name of me to suffer.

17 Ἀπῆλθεν δὲ Ἀνανίας καὶ εἰσῆλθεν
And went away Ananias and entered

εἰς τὴν οἰκίαν, καὶ ἐπιθεὶς ἐπ' αὐτὸν
into the house, and putting on on him

τὰς χεῖρας εἶπεν· Σαοὺλ ἀδελφέ, ὁ
the(his) hands said : Saul brother, the

κύριος ἀπέσταλκέν με, Ἰησοῦς ὁ ὀφθείς σοι
Lord has sent me, Jesus the [one] appear- to thee
ing

ἐν τῇ ὁδῷ ᾗ ἤρχου, ὅπως ἀναβλέψῃς
in the way which thou camest, so as thou mayest see again

καὶ πλησθῇς πνεύματος ἁγίου. 18 καὶ
and be filled of(with) Spirit Holy. And

εὐθέως ἀπέπεσαν αὐτοῦ ἀπὸ τῶν ὀφθαλμῶν
immediately fell away of him from the eyes

ὡς λεπίδες, ἀνέβλεψέν τε, καὶ ἀναστὰς
as scales, and he saw again, and rising up

ἐβαπτίσθη, 19 καὶ λαβὼν τροφὴν ἐνίσχυσεν.
was baptized, and taking food was strengthened.

Ἐγένετο δὲ μετὰ τῶν ἐν Δαμασκῷ
Now he was with the in Damascus

μαθητῶν ἡμέρας τινάς, 20 καὶ εὐθέως
disciples days some, and immediately

ἐν ταῖς συναγωγαῖς ἐκήρυσσεν τὸν Ἰησοῦν,
in the synagogues he proclaimed - Jesus,

ὅτι οὗτός ἐστιν ὁ υἱὸς τοῦ θεοῦ.
that this one is the Son - of God.

21 ἐξίσταντο δὲ πάντες οἱ ἀκούοντες καὶ
And were amazed all the [ones] hearing and

ἔλεγον· οὐχ οὗτός ἐστιν ὁ πορθήσας
said : Not this man is the [one] having destroyed

εἰς Ἰερουσαλὴμ τοὺς ἐπικαλουμένους
in Jerusalem the [ones] invoking

τὸ ὄνομα τοῦτο, καὶ ὧδε εἰς τοῦτο ἐληλύθει,
this name, and here for this he had come,

ἵνα δεδεμένους αὐτοὺς ἀγάγῃ ἐπὶ τοὺς
that having been bound them he might bring before the

ἀρχιερεῖς; 22 Σαῦλος δὲ μᾶλλον ἐνε-
chief priests? But Saul more was filled

δυναμοῦτο καὶ συνέχυννεν Ἰουδαίους τοὺς κατ-
with power and confounded · Jews the [ones]

οικοῦντας ἐν Δαμασκῷ, συμβιβάζων ὅτι οὗτός
dwelling in Damascus, proving that this one

ἐστιν ὁ χριστός. 23 Ὡς δὲ ἐπληροῦντο
is the Christ. And when were fulfilled

ἡμέραι ἱκαναί, 24 συνεβουλεύσαντο
days considerable(many), consulted together

οἱ Ἰουδαῖοι ἀνελεῖν αὐτόν· ἐγνώσθη δὲ
the Jews to kill him; but was known

τῷ Σαύλῳ ἡ ἐπιβουλὴ αὐτῶν. παρετη-
- to Saul the plot of them. And they

ροῦντο δὲ καὶ τὰς πύλας ἡμέρας τε καὶ
carefully watched also the gates both by day and

νυκτὸς ὅπως αὐτὸν ἀνέλωσιν· 25 λαβόντες δὲ
by night so as him they might but ⁴taking
destroy;

οἱ μαθηταὶ αὐτοῦ νυκτὸς διὰ τοῦ
¹the ²disciples ³of him by night through the

τείχους καθῆκαν αὐτὸν χαλάσαντες ἐν
wall let down him lowering in

σπυρίδι. 26 Παραγενόμενος δὲ εἰς
a basket. And arriving at

Ἰερουσαλὴμ ἐπείραζεν κολλᾶσθαι τοῖς
Jerusalem he tried to be joined to the

μαθηταῖς· καὶ πάντες ἐφοβοῦντο αὐτόν,
disciples; and all feared him,

μὴ πιστεύοντες ὅτι ἐστὶν μαθητής.
not believing that he is(was) a disciple.

27 Βαρνάβας δὲ ἐπιλαβόμενος αὐτὸν ἤγαγεν
But Barnabas taking hold of him led

πρὸς τοὺς ἀποστόλους, καὶ διηγήσατο
to the apostles, and narrated

αὐτοῖς πῶς ἐν τῇ ὁδῷ εἶδεν τὸν κύριον
to them how in the way he saw the Lord

καὶ ὅτι ἐλάλησεν αὐτῷ, καὶ πῶς ἐν
and that he spoke to him, and how in

Δαμασκῷ ἐπαρρησιάσατο ἐν τῷ ὀνόματι
Damascus he spoke boldly in the name

Ἰησοῦ. 28 καὶ ἦν μετ' αὐτῶν εἰσπορευόμενος
of Jesus. And he was with them going in

καὶ ἐκπορευόμενος εἰς Ἰερουσαλήμ,
and going out in Jerusalem,

παρρησιαζόμενος ἐν τῷ ὀνόματι τοῦ
speaking boldly in the name of the

κυρίου, 29 ἐλάλει τε καὶ συνεζήτει πρὸς
Lord, ²spoke ¹both ²and ⁴discussed with

τοὺς Ἑλληνιστάς· οἱ δὲ ἐπεχείρουν ἀνελεῖν
the Hellenists; and they attempted to kill

αὐτόν. 30 ἐπιγνόντες δὲ οἱ ἀδελφοὶ
him. But ²knowing ¹the ³brothers

κατήγαγον αὐτὸν εἰς Καισάρειαν καὶ
brought down him to Cæsarea and

ἐξαπέστειλαν αὐτὸν εἰς Ταρσόν.
sent forth him to Tarsus.

31 Ἡ μὲν οὖν ἐκκλησία καθ' ὅλης
²The - ¹therefore ³church throughout all

τῆς Ἰουδαίας καὶ Γαλιλαίας καὶ Σαμαρείας
- Judæa and Galilee and Samaria

εἶχεν εἰρήνην οἰκοδομουμένη καὶ πορευομένη
had peace being built and going

τῷ φόβῳ τοῦ κυρίου, καὶ τῇ παρακλήσει
in the fear of the Lord, and in the comfort

τοῦ ἁγίου πνεύματος ἐπληθύνετο.
of the Holy Spirit was multiplied.

King James Version

32 And it came to pass, as Peter passed throughout all *quarters*, he came down also to the saints which dwelt at Lydda. 33And there he found a certain man named Eneas, which had kept his bed eight years, and was sick of the palsy. 34And Peter said unto him, Eneas, Jesus Christ maketh thee whole: arise, and make thy bed. And he arose immediately. 35And all that dwelt at Lydda and Saron saw him, and turned to the Lord.

36 Now there was at Joppa a certain disciple named Tabitha, which by interpretation is called Dorcas: this woman was full of good works and almsdeeds which she did. 37And it came to pass in those days, that she was sick, and died: whom when they had washed, they laid *her* in an upper chamber. 38And forasmuch as Lydda was nigh to Joppa, and the disciples had heard that Peter was there, they sent unto him two men, desiring *him* that he would not delay to come to them. 39 Then Peter arose and went with them. When he was come, they brought him into the upper chamber: and all the widows stood by him weeping, and shewing the coats and garments which Dorcas made, while she was with them. 40 But Peter put them all forth, and kneeled down, and prayed; and turning *him* to the body said, Tabitha, arise. And she opened her eyes: and when she saw Peter, she sat up. 41And he gave her *his* hand, and lifted her up; and when he had called the saints and widows, he presented her alive. 42And it was known throughout all Joppa; and many believed in the Lord. 43And it came to pass, that he tarried many days in Joppa with one Simon a tanner.

10 There was a certain man in Cesarea called Cornelius, a centurion of the band called the Italian *band,* 2*A* devout *man,* and one that feared God with all his house, which gave much alms to the people, and prayed to God always. 3 He saw in a vision evidently, about the ninth hour of the day, an angel of God coming in to him, and saying unto him, Cornelius. 4And when he looked on him, he was afraid, and said, What is it, Lord? And he said unto him, Thy prayers and thine alms are come up for a memorial before God. 5And now send men to Joppa, and call for *one* Simon, whose surname is Peter: 6 He lodgeth with one Simon a tanner, whose house is by the sea side: he shall tell thee what thou oughtest to do. 7And when the angel which spake unto Cornelius was departed, he called two of his household servants, and a devout soldier of them that waited on him continually; 8And when he had declared all *these* things unto them, he sent them to Joppa.

9 On the morrow, as they went on their journey, and drew nigh unto the city, Peter went up

New International Version

Aeneas and Dorcas

32 As Peter traveled about the country, he went to visit the saints in Lydda. 33 There he found a man named Aeneas, a paralytic who had been bedridden for eight years. 34 "Aeneas," Peter said to him, "Jesus Christ heals you. Get up and arrange your things." Immediately Aeneas got up. 35All those who lived in Lydda and Sharon saw him and turned to the Lord.

36 In Joppa there was a disciple named Tabitha (which, when translated, is Dorcas*J*), who was always doing good and helping the poor. 37About that time she became sick and died, and her body was washed and placed in an upstairs room. 38 Lydda was near Joppa; so when the disciples heard that Peter was in Lydda, they sent two men to him and urged him, "Please come at once!"

39 Peter went with them, and when he arrived he was taken upstairs to the room. All the widows stood around him, crying and showing him the robes and other clothing that Dorcas had made while she was still with them.

40 Peter sent them all out of the room; then he got down on his knees and prayed. Turning toward the dead woman, he said, "Tabitha, get up." She opened her eyes, and seeing Peter she sat up. 41 He took her by the hand and helped her to her feet. Then he called the believers and the widows and presented her to them alive. 42 This became known all over Joppa, and many people believed in the Lord. 43 Peter stayed in Joppa for some time with a tanner named Simon.

Cornelius calls for Peter

10 At Caesarea there was a man named Cornelius, a centurion in what was known as the Italian Regiment. 2 He and all his family were devout and God-fearing; he gave generously to those in need and prayed to God regularly. 3 One day at about three in the afternoon he had a vision. He distinctly saw an angel of God, who came to him and said, "Cornelius!"

4 Cornelius stared at him in fear. "What is it, Lord?" he asked.

The angel answered, "Your prayers and gifts to the poor have come up as a remembrance before God. 5 Now send men to Joppa to bring back a man named Simon who is called Peter. 6 He is staying with Simon the tanner, whose house is by the sea."

7 When the angel who spoke to him had gone, Cornelius called two of his servants and one of his military aides who was a devout man. 8 He told them everything that had happened and sent them to Joppa.

Peter's vision

9 About noon the following day as they were approaching the city, Peter went up on the roof

[*j*] Both *Tabitha* (Aramaic) and *Dorcas* (Greek) mean *gazelle.*

Greek Interlinear

32 Ἐγένετο δὲ Πέτρον διερχόμενον· διὰ
Now it came to pass Peter passing *through* through

πάντων κατελθεῖν καὶ πρὸς τοὺς ἁγίους
all [quarters] to come down[b] also to the saints

τοὺς κατοικοῦντας Λύδδα. **33** εὗρεν δὲ
- inhabiting Lydda. And he found

ἐκεῖ ἄνθρωπόν τινα ὀνόματι Αἰνέαν ἐξ
there a certain man by name Aeneas of

ἐτῶν ὀκτὼ κατακείμενον ἐπὶ κραβάτου,
years eight lying on a mattress,

ὃς ἦν παραλελυμένος. **34** καὶ εἶπεν αὐτῷ
who was *having been* paralysed. And said to him

ὁ Πέτρος· Αἰνέα, ἰᾶταί σε Ἰησοῦς Χριστός·
- Peter: Aeneas, cures thee Jesus Christ;

ἀνάστηθι καὶ στρῶσον σεαυτῷ. καὶ
rise up and gird thyself. And

εὐθέως ἀνέστη. **35** καὶ εἶδαν αὐτὸν
immediately he rose up. And saw him

πάντες οἱ κατοικοῦντες Λύδδα καὶ τὸν
all the [ones] inhabiting Lydda and -

Σαρῶνα, οἵτινες ἐπέστρεψαν ἐπὶ τὸν κύριον.
Saron, who turned to the Lord.

Ἐν Ἰόππῃ δέ τις ἦν μαθήτρια ὀνόματι
[b]in Joppa [1]Now [a]a certain [4]was [5]disciple by name

Ταβιθά, **36** ἣ διερμηνευομένη λέγεται
Tabitha, who being translated is called

Δορκάς· αὕτη ἦν πλήρης ἔργων ἀγαθῶν
Dorcas; this woman was full works of good

καὶ ἐλεημοσυνῶν ὧν ἐποίει. **37** ἐγένετο δὲ
and of alms which she did. And it happened

ἐν ταῖς ἡμέραις ἐκείναις ἀσθενήσασαν
in . those days ailing

αὐτὴν ἀποθανεῖν· λούσαντες δὲ ἔθηκαν
she to die[b]; and having washed they put [her]
= being ill she died;

ἐν ὑπερῴῳ. **38** ἐγγὺς δὲ οὔσης Λύδδας
in an upper room. Now [a]near [b]being [1]Lydda[a]

τῇ Ἰόππῃ οἱ μαθηταὶ ἀκούσαντες ὅτι
- to Joppa the disciples having heard that

Πέτρος ἐστὶν ἐν αὐτῇ ἀπέστειλαν δύο
Peter is(was) in it sent two

ἄνδρας πρὸς αὐτὸν παρακαλοῦντες· μὴ
men to him beseeching: [a]not

ὀκνήσῃς διελθεῖν ἕως ἡμῶν. **39** ἀναστὰς δὲ
[1]hesitate to come to us. And rising up

Πέτρος συνῆλθεν αὐτοῖς· ὃν παραγενόμενον
Peter went with them; whom arriving

ἀνήγαγον εἰς τὸ ὑπερῷον, καὶ παρέστησαν
they led up into the upper room, and stood by

αὐτῷ πᾶσαι αἱ χῆραι κλαίουσαι καὶ
him all the widows weeping and

ἐπιδεικνύμεναι χιτῶνας καὶ ἱμάτια, ὅσα
showing tunics and garments, which

ἐποίει μετ᾽ αὐτῶν οὖσα ἡ Δορκάς.
[1]made [4]with [5]them [3]being - [1]Dorcas.

40 ἐκβαλὼν δὲ ἔξω πάντας ὁ Πέτρος
And [2]putting out [4]outside [3]all - [1]Peter

καὶ θεὶς τὰ γόνατα προσηύξατο, καὶ
and placing the knees he prayed, and
= kneeling down

ἐπιστρέψας πρὸς τὸ σῶμα εἶπεν· Ταβιθά,
turning to the body said : Tabitha,

ἀνάστηθι. ἡ δὲ ἤνοιξεν τοὺς ὀφθαλμοὺς
rise up. And she opened the eyes

αὐτῆς, καὶ ἰδοῦσα τὸν Πέτρον ἀνεκάθισεν.
of her, and seeing - Peter sat up.

41 δοὺς δὲ αὐτῇ χεῖρα ἀνέστησεν αὐτήν·
And giving her a hand he raised up her;

φωνήσας δὲ τοὺς ἁγίους καὶ τὰς χήρας
and calling the saints and the widows

παρέστησεν αὐτὴν ζῶσαν. **42** γνωστὸν δὲ
he presented her living. And known

ἐγένετο καθ᾽ ὅλης τῆς Ἰόππης, καὶ
it became throughout all - Joppa, and

ἐπίστευσαν πολλοὶ ἐπὶ τὸν κύριον.
believed many on the Lord.

43 Ἐγένετο δὲ ἡμέρας ἱκανὰς μεῖναι ἐν
And it came to pass days several to remain in
= he remained many days

Ἰόππῃ παρά τινι Σίμωνι βυρσεῖ.
Joppa with one Simon a tanner.

Chapter 10

Ἀνὴρ δέ τις ἐν Καισαρείᾳ ὀνόματι
Now a certain man in Cæsarea by name

Κορνήλιος, ἑκατοντάρχης ἐκ σπείρης· τῆς
Cornelius, a centurion of a cohort [the]

καλουμένης Ἰταλικῆς, **2** εὐσεβὴς καὶ
being called Italian, devout and

φοβούμενος τὸν θεὸν σὺν παντὶ τῷ οἴκῳ
fearing - God with all the household

αὐτοῦ, ποιῶν ἐλεημοσύνας πολλὰς τῷ
of him, doing alms many to the

λαῷ καὶ δεόμενος τοῦ θεοῦ διὰ παντός,
people and petitioning - God continually,

3 εἶδεν ἐν ὁράματι φανερῶς, ὡσεὶ περὶ
saw in a vision clearly, as it were around

ὥραν ἐνάτην τῆς ἡμέρας, ἄγγελον τοῦ
hour ninth of the day, an angel -

θεοῦ εἰσελθόντα πρὸς αὐτὸν καὶ εἰπόντα
of God entering to him and saying

αὐτῷ· Κορνήλιε. **4** ὁ δὲ ἀτενίσας αὐτῷ
to him: Cornelius. And he gazing at him

καὶ ἔμφοβος γενόμενος εἶπεν· τί ἐστιν,
and terrified becoming said : What is it,

κύριε; εἶπεν δὲ αὐτῷ· αἱ προσευχαί
lord? And he said to him : The prayers

σου καὶ αἱ ἐλεημοσύναι σου ἀνέβησαν
of thee and the alms of thee went up

εἰς μνημόσυνον ἔμπροσθεν τοῦ θεοῦ. **5** καὶ
for a memorial before - God. And

νῦν πέμψον ἄνδρας εἰς Ἰόππην καὶ
now send men to Joppa and

μετάπεμψαι Σίμωνά τινα ὃς ἐπικαλεῖται
[summon] [2]Simon [1]one who is surnamed

Πέτρος· **6** οὗτος ξενίζεται παρά τινι
Peter: this man is lodged with one

Σίμωνι βυρσεῖ, ᾧ ἐστιν οἰκία παρὰ
Simon a tanner, to whom is a house[e] by
= who has a house

θάλασσαν. **7** ὡς δὲ ἀπῆλθεν ὁ ἄγγελος ὁ
[the] sea. And as went away the angel -

λαλῶν αὐτῷ, φωνήσας δύο τῶν οἰκετῶν
speaking to him, calling two of the household
slaves

καὶ στρατιώτην εὐσεβῆ τῶν προσκαρτερούν-
and soldier a devout of the [ones] waiting

των αὐτῷ, **8** καὶ ἐξηγησάμενος ἅπαντα
on him, and explaining all things

αὐτοῖς ἀπέστειλεν αὐτοὺς εἰς τὴν Ἰόππην.
to them sent them to - Joppa.

9 Τῇ δὲ ἐπαύριον ὁδοιπορούντων ἐκείνων
And on the morrow journeying those

καὶ τῇ πόλει ἐγγιζόντων[a] ἀνέβη Πέτρος
and to the city drawing near[a] went up Peter
= as they journeyed and drew near to the city

King James Version

upon the housetop to pray about the sixth hour:
10And he became very hungry, and would have
eaten: but while they made ready, he fell into a
trance, 11And saw heaven opened, and a certain
vessel descending unto him, as it had been a
great sheet knit at the four corners, and let down
to the earth: 12 Wherein were all manner of
fourfooted beasts of the earth, and wild beasts,
and creeping things, and fowls of the air. 13And
there came a voice to him, Rise, Peter; kill, and
eat. 14 But Peter said, Not so, Lord; for I have
never eaten any thing that is common or unclean. 15And the voice spake unto him again the
second time, What God hath cleansed, *that* call
not thou common. 16 This was done thrice: and
the vessel was received up again into heaven.
17 Now while Peter doubted in himself what this
vision which he had seen should mean, behold,
the men which were sent from Cornelius had
made inquiry for Simon's house, and stood before the gate, 18And called, and asked whether
Simon, which was surnamed Peter, were lodged
there.

19 While Peter thought on the vision, the
Spirit said unto him, Behold, three men seek
thee. 20Arise therefore, and get thee down, and
go with them, doubting nothing: for I have sent
them. 21 Then Peter went down to the men
which were sent unto him from Cornelius; and
said, Behold, I am he whom ye seek: what *is*
the cause wherefore ye are come? 22And they
said, Cornelius the centurion, a just man, and
one that feareth God, and of good report among
all the nation of the Jews, was warned from God
by a holy angel to send for thee into his house,
and to hear words of thee. 23 Then called he
them in, and lodged *them.* And on the morrow
Peter went away with them, and certain brethren
from Joppa accompanied him. 24And the morrow after they entered into Cesarea. And Cornelius waited for them, and had called together his
kinsmen and near friends. 25And as Peter was
coming in, Cornelius met him, and fell down at
his feet, and worshipped *him.* 26 But Peter took
him up, saying, Stand up; I myself also am a
man. 27And as he talked with him, he went in,
and found·many there were come together. 28And
he said unto them, Ye know how that it is an
unlawful thing for a man that is a Jew to keep
company, or come unto one of another nation;
but God hath shewed me that I should not call
any man common or unclean. 29 Therefore came
I *unto you* without gainsaying, as soon as I was
sent for: I ask therefore for what intent ye have
sent for me? 30And Cornelius said, Four days
ago I was fasting until this hour; and at the
ninth hour I prayed in my house, and, behold, a
man stood before me in bright clothing, 31And
said, Cornelius, thy prayer is heard, and thine
alms are had in remembrance in the sight of
God. 32 Send therefore to Joppa, and call hither
Simon, whose surname is Peter; he is lodged in
the house of *one* Simon a tanner by the sea side:
who, when he cometh, shall speak unto thee.
33 Immediately therefore I sent to thee; and

New International Version

to pray. 10 He became hungry and wanted
something to eat, and while the meal was being
prepared, he fell into a trance. 11 He saw heaven
opened and something like a large sheet being
let down to earth by its four corners. 12 It contained all kinds of four-footed animals, as well
as reptiles of the earth and birds of the air.
13 Then a voice told him, "Get up, Peter. Kill
and eat."

14 "Surely not, Lord!" Peter replied. "I have
never eaten anything impure or unclean."

15 The voice spoke to him a second time, "Do
not call anything impure that God has made
clean."

16 This happened three times, and immediately the sheet was taken back to heaven.

17 While Peter was wondering about the
meaning of the vision, the men sent by Cornelius
found out where Simon's house was and stopped
at the gate. 18 They called out asking if Simon
who was known as Peter was staying there.

19 While Peter was still thinking about the
vision, the Spirit said to him, "Simon, three[k]
men are looking for you. 20 So get up and go
downstairs. Do not hesitate to go with them, for
I have sent them."

21 Peter went down and said to the men, "I'm
the one you're looking for. Why have you
come?"

22 The men replied, "We have come from
Cornelius the centurion. He is a righteous and
God-fearing man, who is respected by all the
Jewish people. A holy angel told him to have
you come to his house so that he could hear
what you have to say." 23 Then Peter invited the
men into the house to be his guests.

Peter at Cornelius' house

The next day Peter started out with them, and
some of the brothers from Joppa went along.
24 The following day he arrived in Caesarea.
Cornelius was expecting them and had called
together his relatives and close friends. 25As
Peter entered the house, Cornelius met him and
fell at his feet in reverence. 26 But Peter made
him get up. "Stand up," he said, "I am only a
man myself."

27 Talking with him, Peter went inside and
found a large gathering of people. 28 He said to
them: "You are well aware that it is against our
law for a Jew to associate with a Gentile or visit
him. But God has shown me that I should not
call any man impure or unclean. 29 So when I
was sent for, I came without raising any objec-
tion. May I ask why you sent for me?"

30 Cornelius answered: "Four days ago I was
in my house praying at this hour, at three in the
afternoon. Suddenly a man in shining clothes
stood before me 31 and said, 'Cornelius, God has
heard your prayer and remembered your gifts to
the poor. 32 Send to Joppa for Simon who is
called Peter. He is a guest in the home of Simon
the tanner, who lives by the sea.' 33 So I sent for

---

[k] One early MSS reads *two;* other MSS omit the number.

Greek Interlinear

ἐπὶ τὸ δῶμα προσεύξασθαι περὶ ὥραν
onto the roof to pray about hour

ἕκτην. 10 ἐγένετο δὲ πρόσπεινος καὶ
sixth. And he became hungry and

ἤθελεν γεύσασθαι· παρασκευαζόντων δὲ
wished to taste(eat); and preparing
= while they prepared

αὐτῶν ἐγένετο ἐπ' αὐτὸν ἔκστασις, 11 καὶ
them⁴ there came on him an ecstasy, and

θεωρεῖ τὸν οὐρανὸν ἀνεῳγμένον καὶ
he beholds the heaven having been opened and

καταβαῖνον σκεῦός τι ὡς ὀθόνην μεγάλην,
coming down a certain vessel like sheet a great,

τέσσαρσιν ἀρχαῖς καθιέμενον ἐπὶ τῆς γῆς,
by four corners being let down onto the earth,

12 ἐν ᾧ ὑπῆρχεν πάντα τὰ τετράποδα
in which were all the quadrupeds

καὶ ἑρπετὰ τῆς γῆς καὶ πετεινὰ τοῦ
and reptiles of the earth and birds of the

οὐρανοῦ. 13 καὶ ἐγένετο φωνὴ πρὸς
heaven(air). And there came a voice to

αὐτόν· ἀναστάς, Πέτρε, θῦσον καὶ φάγε.
him : Rise up, Peter, slay and eat.

14 ὁ δὲ Πέτρος εἶπεν· μηδαμῶς, κύριε,
- But Peter said : Not at all, Lord,

ὅτι οὐδέποτε ἔφαγον πᾶν κοινὸν καὶ
because never did I eat every(any)thing common and

ἀκάθαρτον. 15 καὶ φωνὴ πάλιν ἐκ δευτέρου
unclean. And a voice again a second [time]

πρὸς αὐτόν· ἃ ὁ θεὸς ἐκαθάρισεν σὺ
[came] to him : What things - God cleansed ²thou

μὴ κοίνου. 16 τοῦτο δὲ ἐγένετο
¹not ¹treat ⁴as ²unclean. And this occurred on

τρίς, καὶ εὐθὺς ἀνελήμφθη τὸ σκεῦος
three [occasions], and immediately was taken up the vessel

εἰς τὸν οὐρανόν. 17 Ὡς δὲ ἐν ἑαυτῷ
into - heaven. Now as in himself

διηπόρει ὁ Πέτρος τί ἂν εἴη τὸ ὅραμα
was doubting - Peter what might be the vision

ὃ εἶδεν, ἰδοὺ οἱ ἄνδρες οἱ ἀπεσταλμένοι
which he saw, behold[,] the men - having been sent

ὑπὸ τοῦ Κορνηλίου διερωτήσαντες τὴν
by - Cornelius asking for the

οἰκίαν τοῦ Σίμωνος ἐπέστησαν ἐπὶ τὸν
house of Simon stood at at the

πυλῶνα, 18 καὶ · φωνήσαντες ἐπυνθάνοντο
porch, and calling inquired

εἰ Σίμων ὁ ἐπικαλούμενος Πέτρος ἐνθάδε
if Simon - being surnamed Peter here

ξενίζεται. 19 Τοῦ δὲ Πέτρου διενθυμουμένου
is lodged. - And Peter pondering⁴
= while Peter pondered

περὶ τοῦ ὁράματος εἶπεν τὸ πνεῦμα·
about the vision ¹said ¹the ²Spirit :

ἰδοὺ ἄνδρες δύο ζητοῦντές σε· 20 ἀλλὰ
Behold[,] men two seeking thee; but

ἀναστὰς κατάβηθι, καὶ πορεύου σὺν αὐτοῖς
rising up go down, and go with them

μηδὲν διακρινόμενος, ὅτι ἐγὼ ἀπέσταλκα
nothing doubting, because I have sent

αὐτούς. 21 καταβὰς δὲ Πέτρος πρὸς
them. And going down Peter to

τοὺς ἄνδρας εἶπεν· ἰδοὺ ἐγώ εἰμι ὃν
the men said : Behold[,] I am [he] whom

ζητεῖτε· τίς ἡ αἰτία δι' ἣν πάρεστε;
ye seek ; what [is] the cause for which ye are here?

22 οἱ δὲ εἶπαν· Κορνήλιος ἑκατοντάρχης,
And they said : Cornelius a centurion,

ἀνὴρ δίκαιος καὶ φοβούμενος τὸν θεόν,
a man just and fearing - God,

μαρτυρούμενός τε ὑπὸ ὅλου τοῦ ἔθνους
and being witnessed to by all the nation

τῶν Ἰουδαίων, ἐχρηματίσθη ὑπὸ ἀγγέλου
of the Jews, was warned by angel

ἁγίου μεταπέμψασθαί σε εἰς τὸν οἶκον
a holy to summon thee to the house

αὐτοῦ καὶ ἀκοῦσαι ῥήματα παρὰ σοῦ.
of him and to hear words from thee.

23 εἰσκαλεσάμενος οὖν αὐτοὺς ἐξένισεν.
Calling in therefore them he lodged.

Τῇ δὲ ἐπαύριον ἀναστὰς ἐξῆλθεν σὺν
And on the morrow rising up he went forth with

αὐτοῖς, καί τινες τῶν ἀδελφῶν τῶν
them, and some of the brothers the

ἀπὸ Ἰόππης συνῆλθον αὐτῷ. 24 τῇ δὲ
from Joppa accompanied him. And on the

ἐπαύριον εἰσῆλθεν εἰς τὴν Καισάρειαν·
morrow he entered into - Cæsarea ;

ὁ δὲ Κορνήλιος ἦν προσδοκῶν αὐτούς,
- and Cornelius was awaiting them,

συγκαλεσάμενος τοὺς συγγενεῖς αὐτοῦ καὶ
having called together the relatives of him and

τοὺς ἀναγκαίους φίλους. 25 Ὡς δὲ
the intimate friends. Now when

ἐγένετο τοῦ εἰσελθεῖν τὸν Πέτρον,
it came to pass the to enter - Peter,ᵇ
= Now it came to pass when Peter entered,

συναντήσας αὐτῷ ὁ Κορνήλιος πεσὼν
²meeting ³him - ¹Cornelius falling

ἐπὶ τοὺς πόδας προσεκύνησεν. 26 ὁ δὲ
at the(his) feet worshipped. - But

Πέτρος ἤγειρεν αὐτὸν λέγων· ἀνάστηθι·
Peter raised him saying: Stand up ;

καὶ ἐγὼ αὐτὸς ἄνθρωπός εἰμι. 27 καὶ
also I [my]self a man am. And

συνομιλῶν αὐτῷ εἰσῆλθεν, καὶ εὑρίσκει
talking with him he entered, and finds

συνεληλυθότας πολλούς, 28 ἔφη τε πρὸς
having come together many, and said to

αὐτούς· ὑμεῖς ἐπίστασθε ὡς ἀθέμιτόν ἐστιν
them: Ye understand how unlawful it is

ἀνδρὶ Ἰουδαίῳ κολλᾶσθαι ἢ προσέρχεσθαι
for a man a Jew to adhere or to approach

ἀλλοφύλῳ· κἀμοὶ ὁ θεὸς ἔδειξεν μηδένα
a foreigner ; and to me - God showed ²not any

κοινὸν ἢ ἀκάθαρτον λέγειν ἄνθρωπον·
⁴common ²or ⁵unclean ¹to call ³man ;

29 διὸ καὶ ἀναντιρρήτως ἦλθον μετα-
wherefore indeed ³unquestionably ²I came ¹being

πεμφθείς. πυνθάνομαι οὖν, τίνι λόγῳ
summoned. I inquire therefore, for what reason

μετεπέμψασθέ με; 30 καὶ ὁ Κορνήλιος
ye summoned me? And - Cornelius

ἔφη· ἀπὸ τετάρτης ἡμέρας μέχρι ταύτης τῆς
said : From fourth day until this -
= Four days ago

ὥρας ἤμην τὴν ἐνάτην προσευχόμενος
hour I was [at] the ninth praying

ἐν τῷ οἴκῳ μου, καὶ ἰδοὺ ἀνὴρ ἔστη
in the house of me, and behold[,] a man stood

ἐνώπιόν μου ἐν ἐσθῆτι λαμπρᾷ, 31 καὶ
before me in clothing bright, and

φησίν· Κορνήλιε, εἰσηκούσθη σου ἡ
says: Cornelius, was heard of thee the

προσευχὴ καὶ αἱ ἐλεημοσύναι σου ἐμνήσθησαν
prayer and the alms of thee were remembered

ἐνώπιον τοῦ θεοῦ. 32 πέμψον οὖν εἰς
before - God. Send thou therefore to

Ἰόππην καὶ μετακάλεσαι Σίμωνα ὃς ἐπι-
Joppa and send for Simon who is

καλεῖται Πέτρος· οὗτος ξενίζεται ἐν οἰκίᾳ
surnamed Peter ; this man is lodged in [the] house

Σίμωνος βυρσέως παρὰ θάλασσαν. 33 ἐξαυτῆς
of Simon a tanner by [the] sea. At once

King James Version

thou hast well done that thou art come. Now therefore are we all here present before God, to hear all things that are commanded thee of God.

34 Then Peter opened *his* mouth, and said, Of a truth I perceive that God is no respecter of persons: 35 But in every nation he that feareth him, and worketh righteousness, is accepted with him. 36 The word which *God* sent unto the children of Israel, preaching peace by Jesus Christ: (he is Lord of all:) 37 That word, *I say,* ye know, which was published throughout all Judea, and began from Galilee, after the baptism which John preached; 38 How God anointed Jesus of Nazareth with the Holy Ghost and with power: who went about doing good, and healing all that were oppressed of the devil; for God was with him. 39And we are witnesses of all things which he did both in the land of the Jews, and in Jerusalem; whom they slew and hanged on a tree: 40 Him God raised up the third day, and shewed him openly; 41 Not to all the people, but unto witnesses chosen before of God, *even* to us, who did eat and drink with him after he rose from the dead. 42And he commanded us to preach unto the people, and to testify that it is he which was ordained of God *to be* the Judge of quick and dead. 43 To him give all the prophets witness, that through his name whosoever believeth in him shall receive remission of sins.

44 While Peter yet spake these words, the Holy Ghost fell on all them which heard the word. 45And they of the circumcision which believed were astonished, as many as came with Peter, because that on the Gentiles also was poured out the gift of the Holy Ghost. 46 For they heard them speak with tongues, and magnify God. Then answered Peter, 47 Can any man forbid water, that these should not be baptized, which have received the Holy Ghost as well as we? 48And he commanded them to be baptized in the name of the Lord. Then prayed they him to tarry certain days.

11 And the apostles and brethren that were in Judea heard that the Gentiles had also received the word of God. 2And when Peter was come up to Jerusalem, they that were of the circumcision contended with him, 3 Saying, Thou wentest in to men uncircumcised, and didst eat with them. 4 But Peter rehearsed *the matter* from the beginning, and expounded *it* by order unto them, saying, 5 I was in the city of Joppa praying: and in a trance I saw a vision, A certain vessel descend, as it had been a great sheet, let down from heaven by four corners; and it came even to me: 6 Upon the which when I had

New International Version

you immediately, and it was good of you to come. Now we are all here in the presence of God to listen to everything the Lord has commanded you to tell us."

34 Then Peter began to speak: "I now realize how true it is that God does not show favoritism 35 but accepts men from every nation who fear him and do what is right. 36 This is the message God sent to the people of Israel, telling the good news of peace through Jesus Christ, who is Lord of all. 37 You know what has happened throughout Judea, beginning in Galilee after the baptism that John preached— 38 how God anointed Jesus of Nazareth with the Holy Spirit and power, and how he went around doing good and healing all who were under the power of the devil, because God was with him.

39 "We are witnesses of everything he did in the country of the Jews and in Jerusalem. They killed him by hanging him on a tree, 40 but God raised him from the dead on the third day and caused him to be seen. 41 He was not seen by all the people, but by witnesses whom God had already chosen—by us who ate and drank with him after he rose from the dead. 42 He commanded us to preach to the people and to testify that he is the one whom God appointed as judge of the living and the dead. 43All the prophets testify about him that everyone who believes in him receives forgiveness of sins through his name."

44 While Peter was still speaking these words, the Holy Spirit came on all who heard the message. 45 The circumcised believers who had come with Peter were astonished that the gift of the Holy Spirit had been poured out even on the Gentiles. 46 For they heard them speaking in tongues[1] and praising God.

Then Peter said, 47 "Can anyone keep these people from being baptized with water? They have received the Holy Spirit just as we have." 48 So he ordered that they be baptized in the name of Jesus Christ. Then they asked Peter to stay with them for a few days.

Peter explains his actions

11 The apostles and the brothers throughout Judea heard that the Gentiles also had received the word of God. 2 So when Peter went up to Jerusalem, the circumcised believers criticized him 3 and said, "You went into the house of uncircumcised men and ate with them."

4 Peter began and explained everything to them precisely as it had happened: 5 "I was in the city of Joppa praying, and in a trance I saw a vision. I saw something like a large sheet being let down from heaven by its four corners, and it came down to where I was. 6 I looked into it

[*l*] Or *other languages.*

Greek Interlinear

οὖν ἔπεμψα πρὸς σέ, σύ τε καλῶς
therefore I sent to thee, and thou well

ἐποίησας παραγενόμενος. νῦν οὖν πάντες
didst arriving. Now therefore all

ἡμεῖς ἐνώπιον τοῦ θεοῦ πάρεσμεν ἀκοῦσαι
we before - God are present to hear

πάντα τὰ προστεταγμένα σοι ὑπὸ τοῦ
all the things having been commanded thee by the

κυρίου. 34 Ἀνοίξας δὲ Πέτρος τὸ στόμα
Lord. And opening Peter the(his) mouth

εἶπεν· ἐπ' ἀληθείας καταλαμβάνομαι ὅτι
said: On(in) truth I perceive that

οὐκ ἔστιν προσωπολήμπτης ὁ θεός, 35 ἀλλ'
¹not ²is ⁴a respecter of persons - ¹God, but

ἐν παντὶ ἔθνει ὁ φοβούμενος αὐτὸν καὶ
in every nation the [one] fearing him and

ἐργαζόμενος δικαιοσύνην δεκτὸς αὐτῷ ἐστιν·
working righteousness acceptable to him is;

36 τὸν λόγον ὃν ἀπέστειλεν τοῖς υἱοῖς
the word which he sent to the sons

Ἰσραὴλ εὐαγγελιζόμενος εἰρήνην διὰ Ἰησοῦ
of Israel preaching peace through Jesus

Χριστοῦ· οὗτός ἐστιν πάντων κύριος.
Christ: this one is of all Lord.

37 ὑμεῖς οἴδατε τὸ γενόμενον ῥῆμα καθ'
Ye know the having become thing throughout
= that which took place

ὅλης τῆς Ἰουδαίας, ἀρξάμενος ἀπὸ τῆς
all - Judæa, beginning from -

Γαλιλαίας μετὰ τὸ βάπτισμα ὃ ἐκήρυξεν
Galilee after the baptism which ²proclaimed

Ἰωάννης, 38 Ἰησοῦν τὸν ἀπὸ Ναζαρέθ,
¹John, Jesus the one from Nazareth,

ὡς ἔχρισεν αὐτὸν ὁ θεὸς πνεύματι ἁγίῳ
how anointed him - God with Spirit Holy

καὶ δυνάμει, ὃς διῆλθεν εὐεργετῶν καὶ
and power, who went about doing good and

ἰώμενος πάντας τοὺς καταδυναστευομένους
curing all the [ones] being oppressed

ὑπὸ τοῦ διαβόλου, ὅτι ὁ θεὸς ἦν μετ'
by the devil, because - God was with

αὐτοῦ· 39 καὶ ἡμεῖς μάρτυρες πάντων
him; and we [are] witnesses of all things

ὧν ἐποίησεν ἔν τε τῇ χώρᾳ τῶν Ἰουδαίων
which he did both in the country of the Jews

καὶ Ἰερουσαλήμ· ὃν καὶ ἀνεῖλαν
and Jerusalem; whom indeed they killed

κρεμάσαντες ἐπὶ ξύλου. 40 τοῦτον ὁ
hanging on a tree. This one -

θεὸς ἤγειρεν ἐν τῇ τρίτῃ ἡμέρᾳ καὶ
God raised on the third day and

ἔδωκεν αὐτὸν ἐμφανῆ γενέσθαι, 41 οὐ
gave him visible to become, not

παντὶ τῷ λαῷ, ἀλλὰ μάρτυσιν τοῖς
to all the people, but to witnesses -

προκεχειροτονημένοις ὑπὸ τοῦ θεοῦ, ἡμῖν,
having been previously appointed by - God, to us,

οἵτινες συνεφάγομεν καὶ συνεπίομεν αὐτῷ
who ate with and drank with him

μετὰ τὸ ἀναστῆναι αὐτὸν ἐκ νεκρῶν·
after the to rise again himᵇ out of [the] dead;
= he rose again

42 καὶ παρήγγειλεν ἡμῖν κηρῦξαι τῷ λαῷ
and he commanded us to proclaim to the people

καὶ διαμαρτύρασθαι ὅτι οὗτός ἐστιν ὁ
and solemnly to witness that this man is the [one]

ὡρισμένος ὑπὸ τοῦ θεοῦ κριτὴς ζώντων
having been by - God judge of living
designated

καὶ νεκρῶν. 43 τούτῳ πάντες οἱ προφῆται
and of dead. To this man all the prophets

μαρτυροῦσιν, ἄφεσιν ἁμαρτιῶν λαβεῖν διὰ
witness, ⁸forgiveness ⁷of sins ⁶to receive ⁵through

τοῦ ὀνόματος αὐτοῦ πάντα τὸν πιστεύοντα
⁹the ¹⁰name ¹¹of him ¹everyone ²believing

εἰς αὐτόν. 44 Ἔτι λαλοῦντος τοῦ Πέτρου
³in ⁴him. Yet speaking - Peterᵃ
= While Peter was still speaking

τὰ ῥήματα ταῦτα ἐπέπεσεν τὸ πνεῦμα
these words ⁴fell on ¹the ³Spirit

τὸ ἅγιον ἐπὶ πάντας τοὺς ἀκούοντας
- ²Holy on all the [ones] hearing

τὸν λόγον. 45 καὶ ἐξέστησαν οἱ ἐκ
the discourse. And ⁴were amazed ¹the ²of [the]

περιτομῆς πιστοὶ ὅσοι συνῆλθαν τῷ Πέτρῳ,
³circumcision ⁵faithful as many as accompanied - Peter,

ὅτι καὶ ἐπὶ τὰ ἔθνη ἡ δωρεὰ τοῦ ἁγίου
because also on the nations the gift of the Holy

πνεύματος ἐκκέχυται· 46 ἤκουον γὰρ
Spirit has been poured out; for they heard

αὐτῶν λαλούντων γλώσσαις καὶ μεγαλυνόν-
them speaking in tongues and magnify-

των τὸν θεόν. τότε ἀπεκρίθη Πέτρος·
ing - God. Then answered Peter:

47 μήτι τὸ ὕδωρ δύναται κωλῦσαί τις
Not ⁴the ⁵water ¹can ⁶to forbid ²anyone

τοῦ μὴ βαπτισθῆναι τούτους, οἵτινες τὸ
- ³not ⁷to be baptized ⁸these, ⁹who the

πνεῦμα τὸ ἅγιον ἔλαβον ὡς καὶ ἡμεῖς;
Spirit - Holy received as also we?

48 προσέταξεν δὲ αὐτοὺς ἐν τῷ ὀνόματι
And he commanded them in the name

Ἰησοῦ Χριστοῦ βαπτισθῆναι. τότε ἠρώτησαν
of Jesus Christ to be baptized. Then they asked

αὐτὸν ἐπιμεῖναι ἡμέρας τινάς.
him to remain days some.

Chapter 11

Ἤκουσαν δὲ οἱ ἀπόστολοι καὶ οἱ
Now heard the apostles and the

ἀδελφοὶ οἱ ὄντες κατὰ τὴν Ἰουδαίαν
brothers - being throughout - Judæa

ὅτι καὶ τὰ ἔθνη ἐδέξαντο τὸν λόγον
that also the nations received the word

τοῦ θεοῦ. 2 Ὅτε δὲ ἀνέβη Πέτρος εἰς
- of God. And when went up Peter to

Ἰερουσαλήμ, διεκρίνοντο πρὸς αὐτὸν οἱ
Jerusalem, disputed with him the [ones]

ἐκ περιτομῆς 3 λέγοντες ὅτι εἰσῆλθες
of [the] circumcision saying[.] - Thou enteredst

πρὸς ἄνδρας ἀκροβυστίαν ἔχοντας καὶ
to men uncircumcision having and

συνέφαγες αὐτοῖς. 4 ἀρξάμενος δὲ Πέτρος
didst eat with them. And beginning Peter

ἐξετίθετο αὐτοῖς καθεξῆς λέγων· 5 ἐγὼ
explained to them in order saying: I

ἤμην ἐν πόλει Ἰόππῃ προσευχόμενος, καὶ
was in [the] city Joppa praying, and

εἶδον ἐν ἐκστάσει ὅραμα, καταβαῖνον
I saw in an ecstasy a vision, coming down

σκεῦός τι ὡς ὀθόνην μεγάλην τέσσαρσιν
a certain vessel as sheet a great by four

ἀρχαῖς καθιεμένην ἐκ τοῦ οὐρανοῦ, καὶ
corners having been let down out of - heaven, and

ἦλθεν ἄχρι ἐμοῦ· 6 εἰς ἣν ἀτενίσας
it came up to me; into which gazing

379

King James Version

fastened mine eyes, I considered, and saw four-footed beasts of the earth, and wild beasts, and creeping things, and fowls of the air. 7And I heard a voice saying unto me, Arise, Peter; slay and eat. 8 But I said, Not so, Lord: for nothing common or unclean hath at any time entered into my mouth. 9 But the voice answered me again from heaven, What God hath cleansed, *that* call not thou common. 10And this was done three times: and all were drawn up again into heaven. 11And, behold, immediately there were three men already come unto the house where I was, sent from Cesarea unto me. 12And the Spirit bade me go with them, nothing doubting. Moreover these six brethren accompanied me, and we entered into the man's house: 13And he shewed us how he had seen an angel in his house, which stood and said unto him, Send men to Joppa, and call for Simon, whose surname is Peter; 14 Who shall tell thee words, whereby thou and all thy house shall be saved. 15And as I began to speak, the Holy Ghost fell on them, as on us at the beginning. 16 Then remembered I the word of the Lord, how that he said, John indeed baptized with water; but ye shall be baptized with the Holy Ghost. 17 Forasmuch then as God gave them the like gift as *he did* unto us, who believed on the Lord Jesus Christ, what was I, that I could withstand God? 18 When they heard these things, they held their peace, and glorified God, saying, Then hath God also to the Gentiles granted repentance unto life.

19 Now they which were scattered abroad upon the persecution that arose about Stephen travelled as far as Phenice, and Cyprus, and Antioch, preaching the word to none but unto the Jews only. 20And some of them were men of Cyprus and Cyrene, which, when they were come to Antioch, spake unto the Grecians, preaching the Lord Jesus. 21And the hand of the Lord was with them: and a great number believed, and turned unto the Lord.

22 Then tidings of these things came unto the ears of the church which was in Jerusalem: and they sent forth Barnabas, that he should go as far as Antioch. 23 Who, when he came, and had seen the grace of God, was glad, and exhorted them all, that with purpose of heart they would cleave unto the Lord. 24 For he was a good man, and full of the Holy Ghost and of faith: and much people was added unto the Lord. 25 Then departed Barnabas to Tarsus, for to seek Saul: 26And when he had found him, he brought him unto Antioch. And it came to pass, that a whole year they assembled themselves with the church, and taught much people. And the disciples were called Christians first in Antioch.

27 And in these days came prophets from Jerusalem unto Antioch. 28And there stood up one of them named Agabus, and signified by the Spirit that there should be great dearth throughout all the world: which came to pass

New International Version

and saw four-footed animals of the earth, wild beasts, reptiles, and birds of the air. 7 Then I heard a voice telling me, 'Get up, Peter. Kill and eat.'

8 "I replied, 'Surely not, Lord! Nothing impure or unclean has ever entered my mouth.'

9 "The voice spoke from heaven a second time, 'Do not call anything impure that God has made clean.' 10 This happened three times, and then it was all pulled up to heaven again.

11 "Right then three men who had been sent to me from Caesarea stopped at the house where I was staying. 12 The Spirit told me to have no hesitation about going with them. These six brothers also went with me, and we entered the man's house. 13 He told us how he had seen an angel appear in his house and say, 'Send to Joppa for Simon who is called Peter. 14 He will bring you a message through which you and all your household will be saved.'

15 "Just as I was starting to speak, the Holy Spirit came on them as he had come on us at the beginning. 16 Then I remembered what the Lord had said, 'John baptized with water, but you will be baptized with the Holy Spirit.' 17 So if God gave them the same gift as he gave us when we believed in the Lord Jesus Christ, who was I to think that I could oppose God!"

18 When they heard this, they had no further objections and praised God, saying, "So then, God has even granted the Gentiles repentance unto life."

The church in Antioch

19 Now those who had been scattered by the persecution in connection with Stephen traveled as far as Phoenicia, Cyprus and Antioch, telling the message only to Jews. 20 Some of them, however, men from Cyprus and Cyrene, went to Antioch and began to speak to Greeks also, telling them the good news about the Lord Jesus. 21 The Lord's hand was with them, and a great number of people believed and turned to the Lord.

22 News of this reached the ears of the church at Jerusalem, and they sent Barnabas to Antioch. 23 When he arrived and saw the evidence of the grace of God, he was glad and encouraged them all to remain true to the Lord with all their hearts. 24 He was a good man, full of the Holy Spirit and faith, and a great number of people were brought to the Lord.

25 Then Barnabas went to Tarsus to look for Saul, 26 and when he found him, he brought him to Antioch. So for a whole year Barnabas and Saul met with the church and taught great numbers of people. The disciples were first called Christians at Antioch.

27 During this time some prophets came down from Jerusalem to Antioch. 28 One of them, named Agabus, stood up and through the Spirit predicted that a severe famine would spread over the entire Roman world. (This happened

Greek Interlinear

κατενόουν, καὶ εἶδον τὰ τετράποδα τῆς
I perceived, and I saw the quadrupeds of the

γῆς καὶ τὰ θηρία καὶ τὰ ἑρπετὰ καὶ τὰ
earth and the wild beasts and the reptiles and the

πετεινὰ τοῦ οὐρανοῦ. 7 ἤκουσα δὲ καὶ
birds of the heaven(air). And I heard also

φωνῆς λεγούσης μοι· ἀναστάς, Πέτρε,
a voice saying to me: Rise up, Peter,

θῦσον καὶ φάγε. 8 εἶπον δέ· μηδαμῶς,
slay and eat. And I said: Not at all,

κύριε, ὅτι κοινὸν ἢ ἀκάθαρτον οὐδέποτε
Lord, because a common or unclean thing never

εἰσῆλθεν εἰς τὸ στόμα μου. 9 ἀπεκρίθη δὲ
entered into the mouth of me. And answered

ἐκ δευτέρου φωνὴ ἐκ τοῦ οὐρανοῦ·
a second [time] a voice out of - heaven:

ἃ ὁ θεὸς ἐκαθάρισεν σὺ μὴ κοίνου.
What things God cleansed thou regard not common.

10 τοῦτο δὲ ἐγένετο ἐπὶ τρίς, καὶ
And this happened on three [occasions], and

ἀνεσπάσθη πάλιν ἅπαντα εἰς τὸν οὐρανόν.
was pulled up again all things to - heaven.

11 καὶ ἰδοὺ ἐξαυτῆς τρεῖς ἄνδρες ἐπέστησαν
And behold at once three men stood at

ἐπὶ τὴν οἰκίαν ἐν ᾗ ἦμεν, ἀπεσταλμένοι
at the house in which I was, having been sent

ἀπὸ Καισαρείας πρός με. 12 εἶπεν δὲ
from Cæsarea to me. And told

τὸ πνεῦμά μοι συνελθεῖν αὐτοῖς μηδὲν
the Spirit me to go with them nothing

διακρίναντα. ἦλθον δὲ σὺν ἐμοὶ καὶ
doubting. And came with me also

οἱ ἓξ ἀδελφοὶ οὗτοι, καὶ εἰσήλθομεν εἰς
- six brothers these, and we entered into

τὸν οἶκον τοῦ ἀνδρός. 13 ἀπήγγειλεν δὲ
the house of the man. And he reported

ἡμῖν πῶς εἶδεν τὸν ἄγγελον ἐν τῷ
to us how he saw the angel in the

οἴκῳ αὐτοῦ σταθέντα καὶ εἰπόντα·
house of him standing and saying:

ἀπόστειλον εἰς Ἰόππην καὶ μετάπεμψαι
Send to Joppa and summon

Σίμωνα τὸν ἐπικαλούμενον Πέτρον, 14 ὃς
Simon being surnamed Peter, who

λαλήσει ῥήματα πρὸς σὲ ἐν οἷς σωθήσῃ
will speak words to thee by which mayest be saved

σὺ καὶ πᾶς ὁ οἶκός σου. 15 ἐν δὲ
thou and all the household of thee. And in

τῷ ἄρξασθαί με λαλεῖν ἐπέπεσεν τὸ
the to begin me to speak fell on the
= as I began

πνεῦμα τὸ ἅγιον ἐπ' αὐτοὺς ὥσπερ καὶ
Spirit - Holy on them as also

ἐφ' ἡμᾶς ἐν ἀρχῇ. 16 ἐμνήσθην δὲ τοῦ
on us at [the] beginning. And I remembered the

ῥήματος τοῦ κυρίου, ὡς ἔλεγεν· Ἰωάννης
word of the Lord, how he said: John

μὲν ἐβάπτισεν ὕδατι, ὑμεῖς δὲ βαπτισθήσεσθε
indeed baptized with water, but ye will be baptized

ἐν πνεύματι ἁγίῳ. 17 εἰ οὖν τὴν ἴσην
in Spirit Holy. If therefore the equal

δωρεὰν ἔδωκεν αὐτοῖς ὁ θεὸς ὡς καὶ
gift gave them - God as also

ἡμῖν, πιστεύσασιν ἐπὶ τὸν κύριον Ἰησοῦν
to us, having believed on the Lord Jesus

Χριστόν, ἐγὼ τίς ἤμην δυνατὸς κωλῦσαι
Christ, I who was [to be] able to hinder

τὸν θεόν; 18 ἀκούσαντες δὲ ταῦτα ἡσύχασαν,
- God? And hearing these things they kept silence

καὶ ἐδόξασαν τὸν θεὸν λέγοντες· ἄρα καὶ
and glorified - God saying: Then also

τοῖς ἔθνεσιν ὁ θεὸς τὴν μετάνοιαν εἰς
to the nations - God - repentance to

ζωὴν ἔδωκεν.
life gave.

19 Οἱ μὲν οὖν διασπαρέντες ἀπὸ τῆς
The [ones] - therefore being scattered from the

θλίψεως τῆς γενομένης ἐπὶ Στεφάνῳ
affliction the occurring over Stephen

διῆλθον ἕως Φοινίκης καὶ Κύπρου καὶ
passed through to Phœnicia and Cyprus and

Ἀντιοχείας, μηδενὶ λαλοῦντες τὸν λόγον
Antioch, to no one speaking the word

εἰ μὴ μόνον Ἰουδαίοις. 20 Ἦσαν δὲ
except only to Jews. But were

τινες ἐξ αὐτῶν ἄνδρες Κύπριοι καὶ
some of them men Cypriotes and

Κυρηναῖοι, οἵτινες ἐλθόντες εἰς Ἀντιόχειαν
Cyrenians, who coming to Antioch

ἐλάλουν καὶ πρὸς τοὺς Ἕλληνας,
spoke also to the Greeks,

εὐαγγελιζόμενοι τὸν κύριον Ἰησοῦν. 21 καὶ ἦν
preaching the Lord Jesus. And was

χεὶρ κυρίου μετ' αὐτῶν, πολύς τε
[the] hand of [the] Lord with them, and a much(great)

ἀριθμὸς ὁ πιστεύσας ἐπέστρεψεν ἐπὶ τὸν
number - believing turned to the

κύριον. 22 Ἠκούσθη δὲ ὁ λόγος εἰς
Lord. And was heard the account in

τὰ ὦτα τῆς ἐκκλησίας τῆς οὔσης ἐν
the ears of the church - being in

Ἰερουσαλὴμ περὶ αὐτῶν, καὶ ἐξαπέστειλαν
Jerusalem about them, and they sent out

Βαρναβᾶν ἕως Ἀντιοχείας· 23 ὃς παραγεν-
Barnabas to Antioch; who arriv-

όμενος καὶ ἰδὼν τὴν χάριν τὴν τοῦ
ing and seeing the grace the

θεοῦ ἐχάρη, καὶ παρεκάλει πάντας τῇ
of God rejoiced, and exhorted all

προθέσει τῆς καρδίας προσμένειν τῷ
with purpose - of heart to remain with the

κυρίῳ, 24 ὅτι ἦν ἀνὴρ ἀγαθὸς καὶ
Lord, because he was man a good and

πλήρης πνεύματος ἁγίου καὶ πίστεως.
full of [the] Spirit Holy and of faith.

καὶ προσετέθη ὄχλος ἱκανὸς τῷ κυρίῳ.
And was added a crowd considerable to the Lord.

25 ἐξῆλθεν δὲ εἰς Ταρσὸν ἀναζητῆσαι
And he went forth to Tarsus to seek

Σαῦλον, 26 καὶ εὑρὼν ἤγαγεν εἰς Ἀντιόχειαν.
Saul, and finding brought to Antioch.

ἐγένετο δὲ αὐτοῖς καὶ ἐνιαυτὸν ὅλον
And it happened to them also year a whole

συναχθῆναι ἐν τῇ ἐκκλησίᾳ καὶ διδάξαι
to be assembled in the church and to teach

ὄχλον ἱκανόν, χρηματίσαι τε πρώτως ἐν
a crowd considerable, and to call firstly in

Ἀντιοχείᾳ τοὺς μαθητὰς Χριστιανούς.
Antioch the disciples Christians.

27 Ἐν ταύταις δὲ ταῖς ἡμέραις κατῆλθον
And in these - days came down

ἀπὸ Ἰεροσολύμων προφῆται εἰς Ἀντιόχειαν·
from Jerusalem prophets to Antioch;

28 ἀναστὰς δὲ εἷς ἐξ αὐτῶν ὀνόματι
and rising up one of them by name

Ἄγαβος ἐσήμαινεν διὰ τοῦ πνεύματος
Agabus signified through the Spirit

λιμὸν μεγάλην μέλλειν ἔσεσθαι ἐφ' ὅλην τὴν
famine a great to be about to be over all the

οἰκουμένην· ἥτις ἐγένετο ἐπὶ Κλαυδίου.
inhabited earth; which happened in the time of Claudius.

King James Version

in the days of Claudius Cesar. 29 Then the disciples, every man according to his ability, determined to send relief unto the brethren which
dwelt in Judea: 30 Which also they did, and
sent it to the elders by the hands of Barnabas
and Saul.

12 Now about that time Herod the king
stretched forth *his* hands to vex certain of
the church. 2And he killed James the brother of
John with the sword. 3And because he saw it
pleased the Jews, he proceeded further to take
Peter also. (Then were the days of unleavened
bread.) 4And when he had apprehended him, he
put *him* in prison, and delivered *him* to four
quaternions of soldiers to keep him; intending
after Easter to bring him forth to the people.
5 Peter therefore was kept in prison: but prayer
was made without ceasing of the church unto
God for him. 6And when Herod would have
brought him forth, the same night Peter was
sleeping between two soldiers, bound with two
chains: and the keepers before the door kept the
prison. 7And, behold, the angel of the Lord
came upon *him*, and a light shined in the prison:
and he smote Peter on the side, and raised him
up, saying, Arise up quickly. And his chains fell
off from *his* hands. 8And the angel said unto
him, Gird thyself, and bind on thy sandals: and
so he did. And he saith unto him, Cast thy
garment about thee, and follow me. 9And he
went out, and followed him; and wist not that it
was true which was done by the angel; but
thought he saw a vision. 10 When they were past
the first and the second ward, they came unto
the iron gate that leadeth unto the city; which
opened to them of his own accord: and they
went out, and passed on through one street; and
forthwith the angel departed from him. 11And
when Peter was come to himself, he said, Now I
know of a surety, that the Lord hath sent his
angel, and hath delivered me out of the hand
of Herod, and *from* all the expectation of the
people of the Jews. 12And when he had considered *the thing*, he came to the house of Mary
the mother of John, whose surname was Mark;
where many were gathered together praying.
13And as Peter knocked at the door of the gate,
a damsel came to hearken, named Rhoda. 14And
when she knew Peter's voice, she opened not the
gate for gladness, but ran in, and told how Peter
stood before the gate. 15And they said unto her,
Thou art mad. But she constantly affirmed that
it was even so. Then said they, It is his angel.
16 But Peter continued knocking: and when they
had opened *the door*, and saw him, they were
astonished. 17 But he, beckoning unto them with
the hand to hold their peace, declared unto them
how the Lord had brought him out of the prison.

New International Version

during the reign of Claudius.) 29 The disciples,
each according to his ability, decided to provide
help for the brothers living in Judea. 30 This
they did, sending their gift to the elders by
Barnabas and Saul.

Peter's miraculous escape from prison

12 It was about this time that King Herod
arrested some who belonged to the church,
intending to persecute them. 2 He had James, the
brother of John, put to death with the sword.
3 When he saw that this pleased the Jews, he
proceeded to seize Peter also. This happened during the Feast of Unleavened Bread. 4After arresting him, he put him in prison, handing him
over to be guarded by four squads of four soldiers each. Herod intended to bring him out for
public trial after the Passover.
5 So Peter was kept in prison, but the church
was earnestly praying to God for him.
6 The night before Herod was to bring him to
trial, Peter was sleeping between two soldiers,
bound with two chains, and sentries stood
guard at the entrance. 7 Suddenly an angel of
the Lord appeared and a light shone in the cell.
He struck Peter on the side and woke him up.
"Quick, get up!" he said, and the chains fell off
Peter's wrists.
8 Then the angel said to him, "Put on your
clothes and sandals." And Peter did so. "Wrap
your cloak around you and follow me," the angel
told him. 9 Peter followed him out of the prison,
but he had no idea that what the angel was
doing was really happening; he thought he was
seeing a vision. 10 They passed the first and second guards and came to the iron gate leading to
the city. It opened for them by itself, and they
went through it. When they had walked the
length of one street, suddenly the angel left him.
11 Then Peter came to himself and said,
"Now I know without a doubt that the Lord
sent his angel and rescued me from Herod's
clutches and from everything the Jewish people
were anticipating."
12 When this had dawned on him, he went to
the house of Mary the mother of John, also
called Mark, where many people had gathered
and were praying. 13 Peter knocked at the outer
entrance, and a servant girl named Rhoda came
to answer the door. 14 When she recognized
Peter's voice, she was so overjoyed she ran back
without opening it and exclaimed, "Peter is at
the door!"
15 "You're out of your mind," they told her.
When she kept insisting that it was so, they said,
"It must be his angel."
16 But Peter kept on knocking, and when they
opened the door and saw him, they were astonished. 17 Peter motioned for them to be quiet
and described how the Lord had brought him

Greek Interlinear

29 τῶν δὲ μαθητῶν καθὼς εὐπορεῖτό
So ²of the ⁴disciples ¹as ²was prosperous

τις, ὥρισαν ἕκαστος αὐτῶν εἰς διακονίαν
¹anyone, they determined each of them for ministration

πέμψαι τοῖς κατοικοῦσιν ἐν τῇ Ἰουδαίᾳ
to send ¹to the ²dwelling ⁴in - ³Judæa

ἀδελφοῖς· **30** ὃ καὶ ἐποίησαν ἀποστείλαντες
³brothers; which indeed they did sending

πρὸς τοὺς πρεσβυτέρους διὰ χειρὸς
to the elders through [the] hand

Βαρναβᾶ καὶ Σαύλου.
of Barnabas and of Saul.

Chapter 12

Κατ' ἐκεῖνον δὲ τὸν καιρὸν ἐπέβαλεν
Now at that - time laid on

Ἡρώδης ὁ βασιλεὺς τὰς χεῖρας κακῶσαί
Herod the king the(his) hands to ill-treat

τινας τῶν ἀπὸ τῆς ἐκκλησίας. **2** ἀνεῖλεν δὲ
some of the [ones] from the church. And he killed

Ἰάκωβον τὸν ἀδελφὸν Ἰωάννου μαχαίρῃ.
James the brother of John with a sword.

3 ἰδὼν δὲ ὅτι ἀρεστόν ἐστιν τοῖς Ἰουδαίοις
And seeing that pleasing it is(was) to the Jews

προσέθετο συλλαβεῖν καὶ Πέτρον, ἦσαν δὲ
he added to arrest also Peter, and they were

ἡμέραι τῶν ἀζύμων, **4** ὃν καὶ πιάσας
days - of unleavened bread, whom also seizing

ἔθετο εἰς φυλακήν, παραδοὺς τέσσαρσιν
he put in prison, delivering to four

τετραδίοις στρατιωτῶν φυλάσσειν αὐτόν,
quaternions of soldiers to guard him,

βουλόμενος μετὰ τὸ πάσχα ἀναγαγεῖν
intending after the Passover to bring up

αὐτὸν τῷ λαῷ. **5** ὁ μὲν οὖν Πέτρος
him to the people. -ᵃ therefore Peter

ἐτηρεῖτο ἐν τῇ φυλακῇ· προσευχὴ δὲ ἦν
was kept in the prison; but prayer was

ἐκτενῶς γινομένη ὑπὸ τῆς ἐκκλησίας πρὸς
earnestly being made by the church to

τὸν θεὸν περὶ αὐτοῦ. **6** Ὅτε δὲ ἤμελλεν
- God concerning him. And when ²was about

προαγαγεῖν αὐτὸν ὁ Ἡρώδης, τῇ νυκτὶ
²to bring forward ⁴him ¹Herod, - ³night

ἐκείνῃ ἦν ὁ Πέτρος κοιμώμενος μεταξὺ
¹in that was - Peter sleeping between

δύο στρατιωτῶν δεδεμένος ἁλύσεσιν δυσίν,
two soldiers having been bound with chains two,

φύλακές τε πρὸ τῆς θύρας ἐτήρουν τὴν
and guards before the door were keeping the

φυλακήν. **7** καὶ ἰδοὺ ἄγγελος κυρίου
prison. And behold[,] an angel of [the] Lord

ἐπέστη, καὶ φῶς ἔλαμψεν ἐν τῷ οἰκήματι·
came upon, and a light shone in the building;

πατάξας δὲ τὴν πλευρὰν τοῦ Πέτρου
and striking the side - of Peter

ἤγειρεν αὐτὸν λέγων· ἀνάστα ἐν τάχει.
he raised him saying: Rise up in haste.

καὶ ἐξέπεσαν αὐτοῦ αἱ ἁλύσεις ἐκ τῶν
And fell off of him the chains off the(his)

χειρῶν. **8** εἶπεν δὲ ὁ ἄγγελος πρὸς
hands. And said the angel to

αὐτόν· ζῶσαι καὶ ὑπόδησαι τὰ σανδάλιά
him: Gird thyself and put on the sandals

σου. ἐποίησεν δὲ οὕτως. καὶ λέγει
of thee. And he did so. And he tells

αὐτῷ· περιβαλοῦ τὸ ἱμάτιόν σου καὶ
him: Cast round the garment of thee and

ἀκολούθει μοι. **9** καὶ ἐξελθὼν ἠκολούθει,
follow me. And going forth he followed,

καὶ οὐκ ᾔδει ὅτι ἀληθές ἐστιν τὸ
and knew not that ²true ³is(was) ¹the thing

γινόμενον διὰ τοῦ ἀγγέλου, ἐδόκει δὲ
happening through the angel, but he thought

ὅραμα βλέπειν. **10** διελθόντες δὲ πρώτην
a vision to see. And going through [the] first

φυλακὴν καὶ δευτέραν ἦλθαν ἐπὶ τὴν
prison and [the] second they came on the

πύλην τὴν σιδηρᾶν τὴν φέρουσαν εἰς τὴν
gate - iron - leading to the

πόλιν, ἥτις αὐτομάτη ἠνοίγη αὐτοῖς, καὶ
city, which of itself was opened to them, and

ἐξελθόντες προῆλθον ῥύμην μίαν, καὶ
going out they went forward street one, and

εὐθέως ἀπέστη ὁ ἄγγελος ἀπ' αὐτοῦ.
immediately departed the angel from him.

11 καὶ ὁ Πέτρος ἐν ἑαυτῷ γενόμενος
And - Peter in himself having become

εἶπεν· νῦν οἶδα ἀληθῶς ὅτι ἐξαπέστειλεν
said: Now I know truly that sent forth

ὁ κύριος τὸν ἄγγελον αὐτοῦ καὶ ἐξείλατό
the Lord the angel of him and delivered

με ἐκ χειρὸς Ἡρώδου καὶ πάσης τῆς
me out of [the] hand of Herod and of all the

προσδοκίας τοῦ λαοῦ τῶν Ἰουδαίων.
expectation of the people of the Jews.

12 συνιδών τε ἦλθεν ἐπὶ τὴν οἰκίαν τῆς
And realizing he came on the house -

Μαρίας τῆς μητρὸς Ἰωάννου τοῦ
of Mary the mother of John -

ἐπικαλουμένου Μάρκου, οὗ ἦσαν ἱκανοὶ
being surnamed Mark, where were many

συνηθροισμένοι καὶ προσευχόμενοι. **13** κρού-
having been assembled and praying. And

σαντος δὲ αὐτοῦ τὴν θύραν τοῦ πυλῶνος
knocking himᵃ the door of the porch
= as he knocked

προσῆλθεν παιδίσκη ὑπακοῦσαι ὀνόματι
approached a maidservant to listen by name

Ῥόδη, **14** καὶ ἐπιγνοῦσα τὴν φωνὴν τοῦ
Rhoda, and recognizing the voice -

Πέτρου ἀπὸ τῆς χαρᾶς οὐκ ἤνοιξεν τὸν
of Peter from - joy she did not open the

πυλῶνα, εἰσδραμοῦσα δὲ ἀπήγγειλεν ἑστάναι
porch, but running in announced ²to stand

τὸν Πέτρον πρὸ τοῦ πυλῶνος. **15** οἱ δὲ
¹Peter before the porch. But they

πρὸς αὐτὴν εἶπαν· μαίνῃ. ἡ δὲ διϊσχυρίζετο
to her said: Thou ravest. But she emphatically asserted

οὕτως ἔχειν. οἱ δὲ ἔλεγον· ὁ ἄγγελός
so to have(be). So they said: The angel

ἐστιν αὐτοῦ. **16** ὁ δὲ Πέτρος ἐπέμενεν
it is of him. - But Peter continued

κρούων· ἀνοίξαντες δὲ εἶδαν αὐτὸν καὶ
knocking; and having opened they saw him and

ἐξέστησαν. **17** κατασείσας δὲ αὐτοῖς τῇ
were amazed. And beckoning to them with the

χειρὶ σιγᾶν διηγήσατο αὐτοῖς πῶς ὁ
hand to be quiet he related to them how the

κύριος αὐτὸν ἐξήγαγεν ἐκ τῆς φυλακῆς,
Lord him led out out of the prison,

ᵃ μέν and δέ are in contrast : " on one hand..."—" on the other..."

383

King James Version

And he said, Go shew these things unto James, and to the brethren. And he departed, and went into another place. 18 Now as soon as it was day, there was no small stir among the soldiers, what was become of Peter. 19And when Herod had sought for him, and found him not, he examined the keepers, and commanded that *they* should be put to death. And he went down from Judea to Cesarea, and *there* abode.

20 And Herod was highly displeased with them of Tyre and Sidon: but they came with one accord to him, and, having made Blastus the king's chamberlain their friend, desired peace; because their country was nourished by the king's *country.* 21And upon a set day Herod, arrayed in royal apparel, sat upon his throne, and made an oration unto them. 22And the people gave a shout, *saying, It is* the voice of a god, and not of a man. 23And immediately the angel of the Lord smote him, because he gave not God the glory: and he was eaten of worms, and gave up the ghost.

24 But the word of God grew and multiplied. 25And Barnabas and Saul returned from Jerusalem, when they had fulfilled *their* ministry, and took with them John, whose surname was Mark.

13 Now there were in the church that was at Antioch certain prophets and teachers; as Barnabas, and Simeon that was called Niger, and Lucius of Cyrene, and Manaen, which had been brought up with Herod the tetrarch, and Saul. 2As they ministered to the Lord, and fasted, the Holy Ghost said, Separate me Barnabas and Saul for the work whereunto I have called them. 3And when they had fasted and prayed, and laid *their* hands on them, they sent *them* away.

4 So they, being sent forth by the Holy Ghost, departed unto Seleucia; and from thence they sailed to Cyprus. 5And when they were at Salamis, they preached the word of God in the synagogues of the Jews: and they had also John to *their* minister. 6And when they had gone through the isle unto Paphos, they found a certain sorcerer, a false prophet, a Jew, whose name *was* Bar-jesus: 7 Which was with the deputy of the country, Sergius Paulus, a prudent man; who called for Barnabas and Saul, and desired to hear the word of God. 8 But Elymas the sorcerer (for so is his name by interpretation) withstood them, seeking to turn away the deputy from the faith. 9 Then Saul, (who also *is called* Paul,) filled with the Holy Ghost, set his eyes on him, 10And said, O full of all subtilty and all mischief, *thou* child of the devil, *thou* enemy of all righteousness, wilt thou not cease to pervert the right ways of the Lord? 11And now, behold,

New International Version

out of prison. "Tell James and the brothers about this," he said, and then he left for another place.

18 In the morning, there was a great commotion among the soldiers. "What could have happened to Peter?" they asked. 19After Herod had a thorough search made for him and did not find him, he cross-examined the guards and ordered that they be executed.

Herod's death

Then Herod went from Judea to Caesarea and stayed there a while. 20 He had been quarreling with the people of Tyre and Sidon; they now joined together and sought an audience with him. Having secured the support of Blastus, a trusted personal servant of the king, they asked for peace, because they depended on the king's country for their food supply.

21 On the appointed day Herod, wearing his royal robes, sat on his throne and delivered a public address to the people. 22 They shouted, "This is the voice of a god, not of a man." 23 Immediately, because Herod did not give praise to God, an angel of the Lord struck him down, and he was eaten by worms and died.

24 But the word of God continued to increase and spread.

25 When Barnabas and Saul had finished their mission, they returned from Jerusalem,*m* taking with them John, also called Mark.

Barnabas and Saul sent off

13 In the church at Antioch there were prophets and teachers: Barnabas, Simeon called Niger, Lucius of Cyrene, Manaen (who had been brought up with Herod the tetrarch) and Saul. 2 While they were worshiping the Lord and fasting, the Holy Spirit said, "Set apart for me Barnabas and Saul for the work to which I have called them." 3 So after they had fasted and prayed, they placed their hands on them and sent them off.

On Cyprus

4 The two of them, sent on their way by the Holy Spirit, went down to Seleucia and sailed from there to Cyprus. 5 When they arrived at Salamis, they proclaimed the word of God in the Jewish synagogues. John was with them as their helper.

6 They traveled through the whole island until they came to Paphos. There they met a Jewish sorcerer and false prophet named Bar-Jesus, 7 who was an attendant of the proconsul, Sergius Paulus. The proconsul, an intelligent man, sent for Barnabas and Saul because he wanted to hear the word of God. 8 But Elymas the sorcerer (for that is what his name means) opposed them and tried to turn the proconsul from the faith. 9 Then Saul, who was also called Paul, filled with the Holy Spirit, looked straight at Elymas and said, 10 "You are a child of the devil and an enemy of everything that is right! You are full of all kinds of deceit and trickery. Will you never stop perverting the right ways of the Lord? 11 Now the hand of the Lord is against you. You

[m] Some MSS read *to Jerusalem.*

Greek Interlinear

εἰπέν τε· ἀπαγγείλατε Ἰακώβω καὶ τοῖς
and said: Report to James and to the

ἀδελφοῖς ταῦτα. καὶ ἐξελθὼν ἐπορεύθη εἰς
brothers these things. And going out he went to

ἕτερον τόπον. 18 Γενομένης δὲ ἡμέρας ἦν
another place. And becoming day* there was
= when it became day

τάραχος οὐκ ὀλίγος ἐν τοῖς στρατιώταις,
disturbance not a little among the soldiers,

τί ἄρα ὁ Πέτρος ἐγένετο. 19 Ἡρῴδης δὲ
what then - [of] Peter became. And Herod

ἐπιζητήσας αὐτὸν καὶ μὴ εὑρών,
searching for him and not finding,

ἀνακρίνας τοὺς φύλακας ἐκέλευσεν ἀπ-
examining the guards commanded to

αχθῆναι,* καὶ κατελθὼν ἀπὸ τῆς Ἰουδαίας
be led away,* and going down from - Judæa

εἰς Καισάρειαν διέτριβεν. 20 Ἦν δὲ
to Cæsarea stayed. Now he was

θυμομαχῶν Τυρίοις καὶ Σιδωνίοις·
being furiously angry with Tyrians and Sidonians;

ὁμοθυμαδὸν δὲ παρῆσαν πρὸς αὐτόν, καὶ
and with one mind they came to him, and

πείσαντες Βλάστον τὸν ἐπὶ τοῦ κοιτῶνος
having persuaded Blastus the one over the bedchamber

τοῦ βασιλέως ἠτοῦντο εἰρήνην, διὰ τὸ
of the king they asked peace, because the

τρέφεσθαι αὐτῶν τὴν χώραν ᾽ ἀπὸ τῆς
to be fed of them the country from the
= their country was fed

βασιλικῆς. 21 τακτῇ δὲ ἡμέρᾳ ὁ Ἡρῴδης
royal. And on an appointed day - Herod

ἐνδυσάμενος ἐσθῆτα βασιλικὴν καθίσας ἐπὶ
having been arrayed with clothing regal sitting on

τοῦ βήματος ἐδημηγόρει πρὸς αὐτούς·
the tribunal made a public speech to them;

22 ὁ δὲ δῆμος ἐπεφώνει· θεοῦ φωνὴ
and the mob cried out : Of a god a voice

καὶ οὐκ ἀνθρώπου. 23 παραχρῆμα δὲ
and not of a man. And at once

ἐπάταξεν αὐτὸν ἄγγελος κυρίου ἀνθ' ὧν
smote him an angel of [the] Lord because

οὐκ ἔδωκεν τὴν δόξαν τῷ θεῷ, καὶ
he gave not the glory - to God, and

γενόμενος σκωληκόβρωτος ἐξέψυξεν.
becoming eaten by worms he expired.

24 Ὁ δὲ λόγος τοῦ κυρίου ηὔξανεν
But the word of the Lord grew

καὶ ἐπληθύνετο. 25 Βαρναβᾶς δὲ καὶ
and increased. And Barnabas and

Σαῦλος ὑπέστρεψαν ἐξ Ἰερουσαλήμ,
Saul returned out of Jerusalem,

πληρώσαντες τὴν διακονίαν, συμπαρα-
having completed the ministration, taking

λαβόντες Ἰωάννην τὸν ἐπικληθέντα Μᾶρκον.
with [them] John - surnamed Mark.

Chapter 13

Ἦσαν δὲ ἐν Ἀντιοχείᾳ κατὰ τὴν
Now there were in Antioch among the

οὖσαν ἐκκλησίαν προφῆται καὶ διδάσκαλοι
existing church prophets and teachers

ὅ τε Βαρναβᾶς καὶ Συμεὼν ὁ καλούμενος
- both Barnabas and Simeon - being called

Νίγερ, καὶ Λούκιος ὁ Κυρηναῖος, Μαναήν τε
Niger, and Lucius the Cyrenian, and Manaen

Ἡρῴδου τοῦ τετραάρχου σύντροφος
of Herod the tetrarch foster brother

καὶ Σαῦλος. 2 Λειτουργούντων δὲ αὐτῶν
and Saul. And ministering them*
= as they ministered

τῷ κυρίῳ καὶ νηστευόντων εἶπεν τὸ
to the Lord and fasting* said the

πνεῦμα τὸ ἅγιον· ἀφορίσατε δή μοι
Spirit - Holy: ¹Separate ye ²so then ³to me

τὸν Βαρναβᾶν καὶ Σαῦλον εἰς τὸ ἔργον
- Barnabas and Saul for the work

ὃ προσκέκλημαι αὐτούς· 3 τότε νηστεύ-
[to] which I have called them; then having

σαντες καὶ προσευξάμενοι καὶ ἐπιθέντες
fasted and having prayed and ¹laying ⁴on

τὰς χεῖρας αὐτοῖς ἀπέλυσαν.
²the(ir) ³hands them they dismissed [them].

4 Αὐτοὶ μὲν οὖν ἐκπεμφθέντες ὑπὸ τοῦ
They - therefore sent out by the

ἁγίου πνεύματος κατῆλθον εἰς Σελεύκειαν,
Holy Spirit went down to Seleucia,

ἐκεῖθέν τε ἀπέπλευσαν εἰς Κύπρον, 5 καὶ
and thence sailed away to Cyprus, and

γενόμενοι ἐν Σαλαμῖνι κατήγγελλον τὸν
being in Salamis they announced the

λόγον τοῦ θεοῦ ἐν ταῖς συναγωγαῖς τῶν
word - of God in the synagogues of the

Ἰουδαίων· εἶχον δὲ καὶ Ἰωάννην ὑπηρέτην.
Jews; and they had also John [as] attendant.

6 Διελθόντες δὲ ὅλην τὴν νῆσον ἄχρι
And passing through all the island unto

Πάφου εὗρον ἄνδρα τινὰ μάγον ψευδο-
Paphos they found a certain man a sorcerer a ²false

προφήτην Ἰουδαῖον, ᾧ ὄνομα Βαριησοῦς,
¹prophet ¹Jewish, to whom name* Barjesus,
= whose name was

7 ὃς ἦν σὺν τῷ ἀνθυπάτῳ Σεργίῳ
who was with the proconsul Sergius

Παύλῳ, ἀνδρὶ συνετῷ. οὗτος προσ-
Paulus, man an intelligent. This man calling

καλεσάμενος Βαρναβᾶν καὶ Σαῦλον ἐπεζήτησεν
to [him] Barnabas and Saul sought

ἀκοῦσαι τὸν λόγον τοῦ θεοῦ· 8 ἀνθίστατο δὲ
to hear the word - of God; but opposed

αὐτοῖς Ἐλύμας ὁ μάγος, οὕτως γὰρ
them Elymas the sorcerer, for so

μεθερμηνεύεται τὸ ὄνομα αὐτοῦ, ζητῶν
is translated the name of him, seeking

διαστρέψαι τὸν ἀνθύπατον ἀπὸ τῆς
to divert the proconsul from the

πίστεως. 9 Σαῦλος δέ, ὁ καὶ Παῦλος,
faith. But Saul, the [one] also Paul,

πλησθεὶς πνεύματος ἁγίου ἀτενίσας εἰς
filled of(with) Spirit Holy gazing on

αὐτὸν εἶπεν· 10 ὦ πλήρης παντὸς δόλου
him said: O full of all deceit

καὶ πάσης ῥᾳδιουργίας, υἱὲ διαβόλου,
and of all fraud, son of [the] devil,

ἐχθρὲ πάσης δικαιοσύνης, οὐ παύσῃ
enemy of all righteousness, wilt thou not cease

διαστρέφων τὰς ὁδοὺς τοῦ κυρίου τὰς
perverting the ways of the Lord -

εὐθείας; 11 καὶ νῦν ἰδοὺ χεὶρ κυρίου
right? And now behold[,] [the] hand of [the] Lord

---

* That is, to execution.

King James Version

the hand of the Lord *is* upon thee, and thou shalt be blind, not seeing the sun for a season. And immediately there fell on him a mist and a darkness; and he went about seeking some to lead him by the hand. 12 Then the deputy, when he saw what was done, believed, being astonished at the doctrine of the Lord. 13 Now when Paul and his company loosed from Paphos, they came to Perga in Pamphylia: and John departing from them returned to Jerusalem.

14 But when they departed from Perga, they came to Antioch in Pisidia, and went into the synagogue on the sabbath day, and sat down. 15And after the reading of the law and the prophets, the rulers of the synagogue sent unto them, saying, *Ye* men *and* brethren, if ye have any word of exhortation for the people, say on. 16 Then Paul stood up, and beckoning with *his* hand said, Men of Israel, and ye that fear God, give audience. 17 The God of this people of Israel chose our fathers, and exalted the people when they dwelt as strangers in the land of Egypt, and with a high arm brought he them out of it. 18And about the time of forty years suffered he their manners in the wilderness. 19And when he had destroyed seven nations in the land of Chanaan, he divided their land to them by lot. 20And after that he gave *unto them* judges about the space of four hundred and fifty years, until Samuel the prophet. 21And afterward they desired a king: and God gave unto them Saul the son of Cis, a man of the tribe of Benjamin, by the space of forty years. 22And when he had removed him, he raised up unto them David to be their king; to whom also he gave testimony, and said, I have found David the *son* of Jesse, a man after mine own heart, which shall fulfil all my will. 23 Of this man's seed hath God, according to *his* promise, raised unto Israel a Saviour, Jesus: 24 When John had first preached before his coming the baptism of repentance to all the people of Israel. 25And as John fulfilled his course, he said, Whom think ye that I am? I am not *he.* But, behold, there cometh one after me, whose shoes of *his* feet I am not worthy to loose. 26 Men *and* brethren, children of the stock of Abraham, and whosoever among you feareth God, to you is the word of this salvation sent. 27 For they that dwell at Jerusalem, and their rulers, because they knew him not, nor yet the voices of the prophets which are read every sabbath day, they have fulfilled *them* in condemning *him.* 28And though they found no cause of death *in him,* yet desired they Pilate that he should be slain. 29And when they had fulfilled all that was written of him, they took *him* down from the tree, and laid *him* in a sepulchre. 30 But God raised him from the dead: 31And he was seen many days of them which came up with him from Galilee to Jerusalem, who are his witnesses unto the people. 32And we declare unto you glad tidings, how that the promise

New International Version

are going to be blind, and for a time you will be unable to see the light of the sun."

Immediately mist and darkness came over him, and he groped about, seeking someone to lead him by the hand. 12 When the proconsul saw what had happened, he believed, for he was amazed at the teaching about the Lord.

In Pisidian Antioch

13 From Paphos, Paul and his companions sailed to Perga in Pamphylia, where John left them to return to Jerusalem. 14 From Perga they went on to Pisidian Antioch. On the Sabbath they entered the synagogue and sat down. 15After the reading from the Law and the Prophets, the synagogue rulers sent word to them, saying, "Brothers, if you have a message of encouragement for the people, please speak."

16 Standing up, Paul motioned with his hand and said: "Men of Israel and you Gentiles who worship God, listen to me! 17 The God of the people of Israel chose our fathers and made the people prosper during their stay in Egypt. With mighty power he led them out of that country 18 and endured their conduct[n] forty years in the desert. 19 He overthrew seven nations in Canaan and gave their land to his people as their inheritance. 20All this took about 450 years.

"After this, God gave them judges until the time of Samuel the prophet. 21 Then the people asked for a king, and he gave them Saul son of Kish, of the tribe of Benjamin, who ruled forty years. 22After removing Saul, he made David their king. He testified concerning him: 'I have found David son of Jesse, a man after my own heart; he will do everything I want him to do.' 23 From this man's descendants God has brought to Israel the Savior Jesus, as he promised. 24 Before the coming of Jesus, John preached repentance and baptism to all the people of Israel. 25As John was completing his work, he said: 'Who do you think I am? I am not that one. No, but he is coming after me, whose sandals I am not worthy to untie.'

26 "Brothers, children of Abraham, and you God-fearing Gentiles, it is to us that this message of salvation has been sent. 27 The people of Jerusalem and their rulers did not recognize Jesus, yet in condemning him they fulfilled the words of the prophets that are read every Sabbath. 28 Though they found no proper ground for a death sentence, they asked Pilate to have him executed. 29 When they had carried out all that was written about him, they took him down from the tree and laid him in a tomb. 30 But God raised him from the dead, 31 and for many days he was seen by those who had traveled with him from Galilee to Jerusalem. They are now his witnesses to our people.

32 "We tell you the good news: What God

[n] Some MSS read *and cared for them.*

386

Greek Interlinear

ἐπὶ σέ, καὶ ἔσῃ τυφλὸς μὴ βλέπων
[is] on thee, and thou wilt be blind not seeing

τὸν ἥλιον ἄχρι καιροῦ. παραχρῆμα δὲ
the sun until [such] a time. And at once

ἔπεσεν ἐπ᾽ αὐτὸν ἀχλὺς καὶ σκότος, καὶ
fell on him a mist and darkness, and

περιάγων ἐζήτει χειραγωγούς. 12 τότε
going about he sought leaders by the hand. Then

ἰδὼν ὁ ἀνθύπατος τὸ γεγονὸς
²seeing ¹the ²proconsul the thing having occurred

ἐπίστευσεν, ἐκπλησσόμενος ἐπὶ τῇ διδαχῇ
believed, being astounded at the teaching

τοῦ κυρίου.
of the Lord.

13 Ἀναχθέντες δὲ ἀπὸ τῆς Πάφου οἱ
And setting sail from - Paphos the ones

περὶ Παῦλον ἦλθον εἰς Πέργην τῆς
around(with) Paul came to Perga

Παμφυλίας· Ἰωάννης δὲ ἀποχωρήσας ἀπ᾽
of Pamphylia; and John departing from

αὐτῶν ὑπέστρεψεν εἰς Ἱεροσόλυμα.
them returned to Jerusalem.

14 Αὐτοὶ δὲ διελθόντες ἀπὸ τῆς Πέργης
And they going through from - Perga

παρεγένοντο εἰς Ἀντιόχειαν τὴν Πισιδίαν,
arrived in Antioch the Pisidian,

καὶ ἐλθόντες εἰς τὴν συναγωγὴν τῇ
and going into the synagogue on the

ἡμέρᾳ τῶν σαββάτων ἐκάθισαν. 15 μετὰ δὲ
day of the sabbaths sat down. And after

τὴν ἀνάγνωσιν τοῦ νόμου καὶ τῶν
the reading of the law and of the

προφητῶν ἀπέστειλαν οἱ ἀρχισυνάγωγοι
prophets sent the synagogue rulers

πρὸς αὐτοὺς λέγοντες· ἄνδρες ἀδελφοί,
to them saying: Men brothers,

εἴ τίς ἐστιν ἐν ὑμῖν λόγος παρακλήσεως
¹if ²any ³there is ⁴among ⁵you ⁶word of exhortation

πρὸς τὸν λαόν, λέγετε. 16 ἀναστὰς δὲ
to the people, say ye. And ¹rising up

Παῦλος καὶ κατασείσας τῇ χειρὶ εἶπεν·
⁶Paul ⁵and ²beckoning ⁴with the(his) ³hand said:

ἄνδρες Ἰσραηλῖται καὶ οἱ φοβούμενοι τὸν
Men Israelites and the [ones] fearing

θεόν, ἀκούσατε. 17 ὁ θεὸς τοῦ λαοῦ
God, hear ye. The God of the people

τούτου Ἰσραὴλ ἐξελέξατο τοὺς πατέρας
of this Israel chose the fathers

ἡμῶν, καὶ τὸν λαὸν ὕψωσεν ἐν τῇ
of us, and ²the ³people ¹exalted in the

παροικίᾳ ἐν γῇ Αἰγύπτου, καὶ μετὰ
sojourn in [the] land of Egypt, and with

βραχίονος ὑψηλοῦ ἐξήγαγεν αὐτοὺς ἐξ
arm a high he led forth them out of

αὐτῆς, 18 καὶ ὡς τεσσερακονταετῆ χρόνον
it, and about forty years time

ἐτροποφόρησεν αὐτοὺς ἐν τῇ ἐρήμῳ, 19 καὶ
endured them in the desert, and

καθελὼν ἔθνη ἑπτὰ ἐν γῇ Χανάαν
having destroyed nations seven in [the] land Canaan

κατεκληρονόμησεν τὴν γῆν αὐτῶν 20 ὡς
gave as an inheritance the land of them about

ἔτεσιν τετρακοσίοις καὶ πεντήκοντα. καὶ
years four hundreds and fifty. And

μετὰ ταῦτα ἔδωκεν κριτὰς ἕως Σαμουὴλ
after these things he gave judges until Samuel

προφήτου. 21 κἀκεῖθεν ᾐτήσαντο βασιλέα,
a prophet. And thence they asked a king,

καὶ ἔδωκεν αὐτοῖς ὁ θεὸς τὸν Σαοὺλ
and gave them - God - Saul

υἱὸν Κίς, ἄνδρα ἐκ φυλῆς Βενιαμίν,
son of Cis, a man of [the] tribe of Benjamin,

ἔτη τεσσεράκοντα· 22 καὶ μεταστήσας
years forty; and removing

αὐτὸν ἤγειρεν τὸν Δαυὶδ αὐτοῖς εἰς
him he raised - David to them for

βασιλέα, ᾧ καὶ εἶπεν μαρτυρήσας·
a king, to whom also he said giving witness:

εὗρον Δαυὶδ τὸν τοῦ Ἰεσσαί, ἄνδρα
I found David the [son] - of Jesse, a man

κατὰ τὴν καρδίαν μου, ὃς ποιήσει πάντα
according to the heart of me, who will do all

τὰ θελήματά μου. 23 τούτου ὁ θεὸς
the wishes of me. ¹Of this man ²God

ἀπὸ τοῦ σπέρματος κατ᾽ ἐπαγγελίαν
¹from ²the ³seed according to promise

ἤγαγεν τῷ Ἰσραὴλ σωτῆρα Ἰησοῦν,
brought - to Israel a Saviour Jesus,

24 προκηρύξαντος Ἰωάννου πρὸ προσώπου
previously proclaiming John[a] before face
= when John had previously proclaimed

τῆς εἰσόδου αὐτοῦ βάπτισμα μετανοίας
of the entrance of him a baptism of repentance

παντὶ τῷ λαῷ Ἰσραήλ. 25 ὡς δὲ
to all the people of Israel. Now as

ἐπλήρου Ἰωάννης τὸν δρόμον, ἔλεγεν·
completed John the (his) course, he said:

τί ἐμὲ ὑπονοεῖτε εἶναι; οὐκ εἰμὶ ἐγώ·
What me suppose ye to be? ²Not ¹am ¹I;

ἀλλ᾽ ἰδοὺ ἔρχεται μετ᾽ ἐμὲ οὗ οὐκ εἰμὶ
but behold he comes after me of whom I am not

ἄξιος τὸ ὑπόδημα τῶν ποδῶ λῦσαι.
worthy the sandal of the feet to loosen.

26 Ἄνδρες ἀδελφοί, υἱοὶ γένους Ἀβραὰμ
Men brothers, sons of [the] race of Abraham

καὶ οἱ ἐν ὑμῖν φοβούμενοι τὸν θεόν,
and the [ones] among you fearing - God,

ἡμῖν ὁ λόγος τῆς σωτηρίας ταύτης
to us the word of this salvation

ἐξαπεστάλη. 27 οἱ γὰρ κατοικοῦντες ἐν
was sent forth. For the [ones] dwelling in

Ἱερουσαλὴμ καὶ οἱ ἄρχοντες αὐτῶν τοῦτον
Jerusalem and the rulers of them ²this man

ἀγνοήσαντες καὶ τὰς φωνὰς τῶν προφητῶν τὰς
¹not knowing and the voices of the prophets -

κατὰ πᾶν σάββατον ἀναγινωσκομένας
²throughout(on) ¹every ²sabbath ¹being read

κρίναντες ἐπλήρωσαν, 28 καὶ μηδεμίαν
judging they fulfilled, and no

αἰτίαν θανάτου εὑρόντες ᾐτήσαντο Πιλᾶτον
cause of death finding they asked Pilate

ἀναιρεθῆναι αὐτόν· 29 ὡς δὲ ἐτέλεσαν πάντα
to be destroyed him; and when they finished all

τὰ περὶ αὐτοῦ γεγραμμένα, καθελόντες
the things concerning him having been written, taking down

ἀπὸ τοῦ ξύλου ἔθηκαν εἰς μνημεῖον.
from the tree they laid in a tomb.

30 ὁ δὲ θεὸς ἤγειρεν αὐτὸν ἐκ νεκρῶν·
- But God raised him out of [the] dead;

31 ὃς ὤφθη ἐπὶ ἡμέρας πλείους
who appeared over days many to the [ones]

συναναβᾶσιν αὐτῷ ἀπὸ τῆς Γαλιλαίας εἰς
having come up with him from - Galilee to

Ἱερουσαλήμ, οἵτινες {νῦν} εἰσιν μάρτυρες
Jerusalem, who now are witnesses

αὐτοῦ πρὸς τὸν λαόν. 32 καὶ ἡμεῖς
of him to the people. And we

ὑμᾶς εὐαγγελιζόμεθα τὴν πρὸς τοὺς
[to] you preach ²the ¹to ²the

King James Version

which was made unto the fathers, 33 God hath fulfilled the same unto us their children, in that he hath raised up Jesus again; as it is also written in the second psalm, Thou art my Son, this day have I begotten thee. 34And as concerning that he raised him up from the dead, *now* no more to return to corruption, he said on this wise, I will give you the sure mercies of David. 35 Wherefore he saith also in another *psalm*, Thou shalt not suffer thine Holy One to see corruption. 36 For David, after he had served his own generation by the will of God, fell on sleep, and was laid unto his fathers, and saw corruption: 37 But he, whom God raised again, saw no corruption.

38 Be it known unto you therefore, men *and* brethren, that through this man is preached unto you the forgiveness of sins: 39And by him all that believe are justified from all things, from which ye could not be justified by the law of Moses. 40 Beware therefore, lest that come upon you, which is spoken of in the prophets; 41 Behold, ye despisers, and wonder, and perish: for I work a work in your days, a work which ye shall in no wise believe, though a man declare it unto you. 42And when the Jews were gone out of the synagogue, the Gentiles besought that these words might be preached to them the next sabbath. 43 Now when the congregation was broken up, many of the Jews and religious proselytes followed Paul and Barnabas; who, speaking to them, persuaded them to continue in the grace of God.

44 And the next sabbath day came almost the whole city together to hear the word of God. 45 But when the Jews saw the multitudes, they were filled with envy, and spake against those things which were spoken by Paul, contradicting and blaspheming. 46 Then Paul and Barnabas waxed bold, and said, It was necessary that the word of God should first have been spoken to you: but seeing ye put it from you, and judge yourselves unworthy of everlasting life, lo, we turn to the Gentiles. 47 For so hath the Lord commanded us, *saying*, I have set thee to be a light of the Gentiles, that thou shouldest be for salvation unto the ends of the earth. 48And when the Gentiles heard this, they were glad, and glorified the word of the Lord: and as many as were ordained to eternal life believed. 49And the word of the Lord was published throughout all the region. 50 But the Jews stirred up the devout and honourable women, and the chief men of the city, and raised persecution against Paul and Barnabas, and expelled them out of their coasts. 51 But they shook off the dust of their feet against them, and came unto Iconium. 52And the disciples were filled with joy, and with the Holy Ghost.

New International Version

promised our fathers 33 he has fulfilled for us, their children, by raising Jesus from the dead. As it is written in the second Psalm:

'You are my Son;
    today I have become your Father.'[o] '[p]

34 The fact that God raised him from the dead, never to decay, is stated in these words:

'I will give you the holy and sure blessings
    promised to David.' [q]

35 So it is stated elsewhere:

'You will not let your Holy One undergo decay.' [r]

36 "For when David had served God's purpose in his own generation, he fell asleep; he was buried with his ancestors and his body decayed. 37 But the one whom God raised from the dead did not undergo decay. 38, 39 Therefore, my brothers, I want you to know that through Jesus the forgiveness of sins is proclaimed to you. Through him everyone who believes is justified from everything from which you could not be justified by the law of Moses. 40 Take care that what the prophets have said does not happen to you:

41 'Look, you scoffers,
    wonder and perish,
    because I am going to do something in
        your days
    that you would never believe,
    even if someone told you.' [s] "

42 As Paul and Barnabas were leaving the synagogue, the people invited them to speak further about these things on the next Sabbath. 43 When the congregation was dismissed, many of the Jews and devout converts to Judaism followed Paul and Barnabas, who talked with them and urged them to continue in the grace of God.

44 On the next Sabbath almost the whole city gathered to hear the word of the Lord. 45 When the Jews saw the crowds, they were filled with jealousy and talked abusively against what Paul was saying.

46 Then Paul and Barnabas answered them boldly: "We had to speak the word of God to you first. Since you reject it and do not consider yourselves worthy of eternal life, we now turn to the Gentiles. 47 For this is what the Lord has commanded us:

'I have made you a light for the Gentiles,
    that you may bring salvation to the ends of
        the earth.' [t] "

48 When the Gentiles heard this, they were glad and honored the word of the Lord; and all who were appointed for eternal life believed.

49 The word of the Lord spread through the whole region. 50 But the Jews incited the God-fearing women of high standing and the leading men of the city. They stirred up persecution against Paul and Barnabas, and expelled them from their region. 51 So they shook the dust from their feet in protest against them and went to Iconium. 52And the disciples were filled with joy and with the Holy Spirit.

In Iconium

14 And it came to pass in Iconium, that they went both together into the synagogue of the Jews, and so spake, that a great multitude both of the Jews and also of the Greeks be-

14 At Iconium Paul and Barnabas went as usual into the Jewish synagogue. There they spoke so effectively that a great number of

[o] Or *have begotten you.* [p] Psalm 2:7. [q] Isaiah 55:3. [r] Psalm 16:10. [s] Hab. 1:5. [t] Isaiah 49:6.

Greek Interlinear

πατέρας ἐπαγγελίαν γενομένην, 33 ὅτι
fathers *promise* *having come,* that

ταύτην ὁ θεὸς ἐκπεπλήρωκεν τοῖς τέκνοις
this [promise] - God has fulfilled *to the *children

ἡμῖν ἀναστήσας Ἰησοῦν, ὡς καὶ ἐν τῷ
*to us raising up Jesus, as also in the

ψαλμῷ γέγραπται τῷ δευτέρῳ· υἱός μου
*psalm *it has been written - *second : Son of me

εἶ σύ, ἐγὼ σήμερον γεγέννηκά σε. 34 ὅτι δὲ
art thou, I to-day have begotten thee. And that

ἀνέστησεν αὐτὸν ἐκ νεκρῶν μηκέτι
he raised up him out of [the] dead no more

μέλλοντα ὑποστρέφειν εἰς διαφθοράν, οὕτως
being about to return to corruption, thus

εἴρηκεν ὅτι δώσω ὑμῖν τὰ ὅσια Δαυὶδ τὰ
he has said[,] - I will give you the *holy things *of David the

πιστά. 35 διότι καὶ ἐν ἑτέρῳ λέγει·
*faithful. Wherefore also in another [psalm] he says:

οὐ δώσεις τὸν ὅσιόν σου ἰδεῖν διαφθοράν.
Thou wilt not give the holy one of thee to see corruption.

36 Δαυὶδ μὲν γὰρ ἰδίᾳ γενεᾷ ὑπηρετήσας
For David indeed [his] own generation having served

τῇ τοῦ θεοῦ βουλῇ ἐκοιμήθη καὶ προσετέθη
by the - of God counsel fell asleep and was added

πρὸς τοὺς πατέρας αὐτοῦ καὶ εἶδεν
to the fathers of him and saw

διαφθοράν· 37 ὃν δὲ ὁ θεὸς ἤγειρεν,
corruption; but [he] whom - God raised,

οὐκ εἶδεν διαφθοράν. 38 γνωστὸν οὖν
did not see corruption. Known therefore

ἔστω ὑμῖν, ἄνδρες ἀδελφοί, ὅτι διὰ
let it be to you, *men* brothers, that through

τούτου ὑμῖν ἄφεσις ἁμαρτιῶν καταγγέλ-
this man to you forgiveness of sins is an-

λεται, καὶ ἀπὸ πάντων ὧν οὐκ ἠδυνήθητε
nounced, and from all things from which ye could not

ἐν νόμῳ Μωϋσέως δικαιωθῆναι, 39 ἐν
by [the] law of Moses *to be* justified, by

τούτῳ πᾶς ὁ πιστεύων δικαιοῦται. 40 βλέπετε
this man everyone believing is justified. Look ye

οὖν μὴ ἐπέλθῃ τὸ εἰρημένον
therefore lest come on [you] the thing having been said

ἐν τοῖς προφήταις· 41 ἴδετε, οἱ κατα-
in the prophets: See, the the des-

φρονηταί, καὶ θαυμάσατε καὶ ἀφανίσθητε,
pisers, and marvel ye and perish,

ὅτι ἔργον ἐργάζομαι ἐγὼ ἐν ταῖς ἡμέραις
because a work work I in the days

ὑμῶν, ἔργον ὃ οὐ μὴ πιστεύσητε ἐάν
of you, a work which by no means ye believe if

τις ἐκδιηγῆται ὑμῖν. 42 Ἐξιόντων δὲ
anyone declares to you. And going out

αὐτῶν παρεκάλουν εἰς τὸ μεταξὺ σάββατον
them* they besought in the intervening sabbath(week)

λαληθῆναι αὐτοῖς τὰ ῥήματα ταῦτα.
to be spoken to them these words.

43 λυθείσης δὲ τῆς συναγωγῆς ἠκολούθησαν
And being broken up the assembly* *followed
= when the assembly was broken up

πολλοὶ τῶν Ἰουδαίων καὶ τῶν σεβομένων
*many *of the *Jews *and *of the *worshipping

προσηλύτων τῷ Παύλῳ καὶ τῷ Βαρναβᾷ,
*proselytes *Paul and - Barnabas,

οἵτινες προσλαλοῦντες αὐτοῖς ἔπειθον αὐτοὺς
who speaking to them persuaded them

προσμένειν τῇ χάριτι τοῦ θεοῦ. 44 Τῷ δὲ
to continue in the grace - of God. And on the

ἐρχομένῳ σαββάτῳ σχεδὸν πᾶσα ἡ
coming sabbath almost all the

πόλις συνήχθη ἀκοῦσαι τὸν λόγον τοῦ
city was assembled to hear the word -

θεοῦ. 45 ἰδόντες δὲ οἱ Ἰουδαῖοι τοὺς
of God. But *seeing *the *Jews the

ὄχλους ἐπλήσθησαν ζήλου, καὶ ἀντέλεγον
crowds were filled of(with) jealousy, and contradicted

τοῖς ὑπὸ Παύλου λαλουμένοις βλασφημοῦντες.
the things by Paul being spoken blaspheming.

46 παρρησιασάμενοί τε ὁ Παῦλος καὶ ὁ
And speaking boldly - Paul and -

Βαρναβᾶς εἶπαν· ὑμῖν ἦν ἀναγκαῖον πρῶτον
Barnabas said: To you it was necessary firstly

λαληθῆναι τὸν λόγον τοῦ θεοῦ· ἐπειδὴ
to be spoken the word - of God; since

ἀπωθεῖσθε αὐτὸν καὶ οὐκ ἀξίους κρίνετε
ye put away it and not worthy judge

ἑαυτοὺς τῆς αἰωνίου ζωῆς, ἰδοὺ στρεφόμεθα
yourselves of the eternal life, behold we turn

εἰς τὰ ἔθνη. 47 οὕτως γὰρ ἐντέταλται
to the nations. For thus has commanded

ἡμῖν ὁ κύριος· τέθεικά σε εἰς φῶς
us the Lord: I have set thee for a light

ἐθνῶν τοῦ εἶναί σε εἰς σωτηρίαν ἕως
of nations - to be thee^b for salvation to

ἐσχάτου τῆς γῆς. 48 ἀκούοντα δὲ τὰ ἔθνη
[the] end of the earth. And *hearing *the *nations

ἔχαιρον καὶ ἐδόξαζον τὸν λόγον τοῦ κυρίου, καὶ
rejoiced and glorified the word of the Lord, and

ἐπίστευσαν ὅσοι ἦσαν τεταγμένοι εἰς
*believed *as many as *were *having been disposed *to

ζωὴν αἰώνιον· 49 διεφέρετο δὲ ὁ λόγος τοῦ
*life *eternal; and was carried *through* the word of the

κυρίου δι' ὅλης τῆς χώρας. 50 οἱ δὲ
Lord through all the country. But the

Ἰουδαῖοι παρώτρυναν τὰς σεβομένας γυναῖκας
Jews urged on the *worshipping *women

τὰς εὐσχήμονας καὶ τοὺς πρώτους τῆς
- *honourable and the chief men of the

πόλεως, καὶ ἐπήγειραν διωγμὸν ἐπὶ τὸν
city, and raised up persecution against -

Παῦλον καὶ Βαρναβᾶν, καὶ ἐξέβαλον αὐτοὺς
Paul and Barnabas, and expelled them

ἀπὸ τῶν ὁρίων αὐτῶν. 51 οἱ δὲ ἐκτιναξάμενοι
from the borders of them. But they shaking off

τὸν κονιορτὸν τῶν ποδῶν ἐπ' αὐτοὺς ἦλθον
the dust of the(ir) feet on them came

εἰς Ἰκόνιον, 52 οἱ τε μαθηταὶ ἐπλη-
to Iconium, and the disciples were

ροῦντο χαρᾶς καὶ πνεύματος ἁγίου.
filled of(with) joy and of(with) Spirit Holy.

Chapter 14

Ἐγένετο δὲ ἐν Ἰκονίῳ κατὰ τὸ αὐτὸ
Now it happened in Iconium *together†

εἰσελθεῖν αὐτοὺς εἰς τὴν συναγωγὴν
*to enter them^b into the synagogue
= they entered

τῶν Ἰουδαίων καὶ λαλῆσαι οὕτως ὥστε
of the Jews and to speak^b so as

πιστεῦσαι Ἰουδαίων τε καὶ Ἑλλήνων
to believe both of Jews and of Greeks

King James Version

lieved. 2 But the unbelieving Jews stirred up the Gentiles, and made their minds evil affected against the brethren. 3 Long time therefore abode they speaking boldly in the Lord, which gave testimony unto the word of his grace, and granted signs and wonders to be done by their hands. 4 But the multitude of the city was divided: and part held with the Jews, and part with the apostles. 5And when there was an assault made both of the Gentiles, and also of the Jews with their rulers, to use *them* despitefully, and to stone them, 6 They were ware of *it,* and fled unto Lystra and Derbe, cities of Lycaonia, and unto the region that lieth round about: 7And there they preached the gospel.

8 And there sat a certain man at Lystra, impotent in his feet, being a cripple from his mother's womb, who never had walked: 9 The same heard Paul speak: who steadfastly beholding him, and perceiving that he had faith to be healed, 10 Said with a loud voice, Stand upright on thy feet. And he leaped and walked. 11And when the people saw what Paul had done, they lifted up their voices, saying in the speech of Lycaonia, The gods are come down to us in the likeness of men. 12And they called Barnabas, Jupiter; and Paul, Mercurius, because he was the chief speaker. 13 Then the priest of Jupiter, which was before their city, brought oxen and garlands unto the gates, and would have done sacrifice with the people. 14 *Which* when the apostles, Barnabas and Paul, heard *of,* they rent their clothes, and ran in among the people, crying out, 15And saying, Sirs, why do ye these things? We also are men of like passions with you, and preach unto you that ye should turn from these vanities unto the living God, which made heaven, and earth, and the sea, and all things that are therein: 16 Who in times past suffered all nations to walk in their own ways. 17 Nevertheless he left not himself without witness, in that he did good, and gave us rain from heaven, and fruitful seasons, filling our hearts with food and gladness. 18And with these sayings scarce restrained they the people, that they had not done sacrifice unto them.

19 And there came thither *certain* Jews from Antioch and Iconium, who persuaded the people, and, having stoned Paul, drew *him* out of the city, supposing he had been dead. 20 Howbeit, as the disciples stood round about him, he rose up, and came into the city: and the next day he departed with Barnabas to Derbe. 21And when they had preached the gospel to that city, and had taught many, they returned again to Lystra, and *to* Iconium, and Antioch, 22 Confirming the souls of the disciples, *and* exhorting them to continue in the faith, and that we must through much tribulation enter into the kingdom of God. 23And when they had ordained them elders in every church, and had prayed with fasting, they commended them to the Lord,

New International Version

Jews and Gentiles believed. 2 But the Jews who refused to believe stirred up the Gentiles and poisoned their minds against the brothers. 3 Paul and Barnabas spent considerable time there, speaking boldly for the Lord, who confirmed the message of his grace by enabling them to do miraculous signs and wonders. 4 The people of the city were divided; some sided with the Jews, others with the apostles. 5 There was a plot afoot among the Gentiles and Jews, together with their leaders, to mistreat them and stone them. 6 But they found out about it and fled to the Lycaonian cities of Lystra and Derbe and to the surrounding country, 7 where they continued to preach the good news.

In Lystra and Derbe

8 In Lystra there sat a man crippled in his feet, who was lame from birth and had never walked. 9 He listened to Paul as he was speaking. Paul looked directly at him, saw that he had faith to be healed 10 and called out, "Stand up on your feet!" At that, the man jumped up and began to walk.

11 When the crowd saw what Paul had done, they shouted in the Lycaonian language, "The gods have come down to us in human form!" 12 Barnabas they called Zeus, and Paul they called Hermes because he was the chief speaker. 13 The priest of Zeus, whose temple was just outside the city, brought bulls and wreaths to the city gates because he and the crowd wanted to offer sacrifices to them.

14 But when the apostles Barnabas and Paul heard of this, they tore their clothes and rushed into the crowd, shouting: 15 "Men, why are you doing this? We too are only men, human like you. We are bringing you good news, telling you to turn from these worthless things to the living God, who made heaven and earth and sea and everything in them. 16 In the past, he let all nations go their own way. 17 Yet he has not left himself without testimony: He has shown kindness by giving you rain from heaven and crops in their seasons; he provides you with plenty of food and fills your hearts with joy." 18 Even with these words, they had difficulty keeping the crowd from sacrificing to them.

19 Then some Jews came from Antioch and Iconium and won the crowd over. They stoned Paul and dragged him outside the city, thinking he was dead. 20 But after the disciples had gathered around him, he got up and went back into the city. The next day he and Barnabas left for Derbe.

The return to Antioch in Syria

21 They preached the good news in that city and won a large number of disciples. Then they returned to Lystra, Iconium and Antioch, 22 strengthening the disciples and encouraging them to remain true to the faith. "We must go through many hardships to enter the kingdom of God," they said. 23 Paul and Barnabas appointed elders[u] for them in each church and, with prayer and fasting, committed them to the

[u] Or Barnabas *ordained elders;* or *Barnabas had elders elected.*

Greek Interlinear

πολὺ　πλῆθος.　2 οἱ　δὲ　ἀπειθήσαντες
a much(great) multitude.　But the　　disobeying

'Ιουδαῖοι　ἐπήγειραν　καὶ　ἐκάκωσαν　τὰς
Jews　　　excited　　and　embittered　the

ψυχὰς　τῶν　ἐθνῶν　κατὰ　τῶν　ἀδελφῶν.
minds　of the　nations　against　the　brothers.

3 ἱκανὸν　μὲν　οὖν　χρόνον　διέτριψαν
A considerable　²therefore　¹time　　they continued

παρρησιαζόμενοι　ἐπὶ　τῷ　κυρίῳ　τῷ　μαρ-
speaking boldly　on　the　Lord　-　wit-

τυροῦντι　ἐπὶ　τῷ　λόγῳ　τῆς　χάριτος　αὐτοῦ,
nessing　to　the　word　of the　grace　of him,

διδόντι　σημεῖα　καὶ　τέρατα　γίνεσθαι　διὰ
giving　signs　and　wonders　to happen　through

τῶν　χειρῶν　αὐτῶν.　4 ἐσχίσθη　δὲ　τὸ
the　hands　of them.　But was divided　-　the

πλῆθος　τῆς　πόλεως,　καὶ　οἱ　μὲν　ἦσαν
multitude of the　city,　and　some　were

σὺν　τοῖς　'Ιουδαίοις,　οἱ　δὲ　σὺν　τοῖς
with　the　Jews,　but others　with　the

ἀποστόλοις.　5 ὡς　δὲ　ἐγένετο　ὁρμὴ　τῶν
apostles.　And when　there was　a rush　²of the

ἐθνῶν　τε　καὶ　'Ιουδαίων　σὺν　τοῖς　ἄρχουσιν
¹nations ¹both ⁴and　of Jews　with　the　rulers

αὐτῶν　ὑβρίσαι　καὶ　λιθοβολῆσαι　αὐτούς,
of them　to insult　and　to stone　them,

6 συνιδόντες　κατέφυγον　εἰς　τὰς　πόλεις
perceiving　they escaped　to　the　cities

τῆς　Λυκαονίας　Λύστραν　καὶ　Δέρβην　καὶ
-　of Lycaonia　Lystra　and　Derbe　and

τὴν　περίχωρον·　7 κἀκεῖ　εὐαγγελιζόμενοι
the　neighbourhood;　and there　evangelizing

ἦσαν.　8 Καί　τις　ἀνὴρ　ἀδύνατος　ἐν
they were.　And a certain man　impotent　in

Λύστροις　τοῖς　ποσὶν　ἐκάθητο,　χωλὸς　ἐκ
Lystra　in the　feet　sat,　lame　from

κοιλίας　μητρὸς　αὐτοῦ,　ὃς　οὐδέποτε
[the] womb　of [the] mother　of him　who　never

περιεπάτησεν.　9 οὗτος　ἤκουεν　τοῦ　Παύλου
walked.　This man　heard　-　Paul

λαλοῦντος·　ὃς　ἀτενίσας　αὐτῷ　καὶ　ἰδὼν
speaking;　who　gazing　at him　and　seeing

ὅτι　ἔχει　πίστιν　τοῦ　σωθῆναι,　10 εἶπεν
that he has(had)　faith　-　to be healed,ᵈ　said

μεγάλῃ　φωνῇ·　ἀνάστηθι　ἐπὶ　τοὺς　πόδας
with a　voice:　Stand up　on　the　feet
great(loud)

σου　ὀρθός.　καὶ　ἥλατο　καὶ　περιεπάτει.
of thee　erect.　And　he leaped up and　walked.

11 οἱ　τε　ὄχλοι　ἰδόντες　ὃ　ἐποίησεν　Παῦλος
And the　crowds　seeing　what　did　Paul

ἐπῆραν　τὴν　φωνὴν　αὐτῶν　Λυκαονιστὶ
lifted up　the　voice　of them　in Lycaonian

λέγοντες·　οἱ　θεοὶ　ὁμοιωθέντες　ἀνθρώποις
saying:　The gods　made like　men

κατέβησαν　πρὸς　ἡμᾶς,　12 ἐκάλουν　τε　τὸν
came down　to　us,　and they called

Βαρναβᾶν　Δία,　τὸν　δὲ　Παῦλον　'Ερμῆν,
Barnabas　Zeus,　-　and　Paul　Hermes,

ἐπειδὴ　αὐτὸς　ἦν　ὁ　ἡγούμενος　τοῦ　λόγου.
since　he　was　the　leader　of the discourse.

13 ὅ　τε　ἱερεὺς　τοῦ　Διὸς　τοῦ　ὄντος　πρὸ
And the　priest　-　of Zeus　-　being　before

τῆς　πόλεως,　ταύρους　καὶ　στέμματα　ἐπὶ
the　city,　bulls　and　garlands　on

τοὺς　πυλῶνας　ἐνέγκας,　σὺν　τοῖς　ὄχλοις
the　gates　bringing,　with　the　crowds

ἤθελεν　θύειν.　14 ἀκούσαντες　δὲ　οἱ
wished　to sacrifice.　But ²hearing　¹the

ἀπόστολοι　Βαρναβᾶς　καὶ　Παῦλος,　διαρ-
¹apostles　²Barnabas　⁴and　⁵Paul,　rend-

ρήξαντες　τὰ　ἱμάτια　ἑαυτῶν　ἐξεπήδησαν　εἰς
ing　the　garments of themselves　rushed out　into

τὸν　ὄχλον,　κράζοντες　15 καὶ　λέγοντες·
the　crowd,　crying out　and　saying:

ἄνδρες,　τί　ταῦτα　ποιεῖτε;　καὶ　ἡμεῖς
Men,　why　these things　do ye?　²also　¹we

ὁμοιοπαθεῖς　ἐσμεν　ὑμῖν　ἄνθρωποι,　εὐαγ-
³of like nature　¹are　⁴to you　²men,　preach-

γελιζόμενοι　ὑμᾶς　ἀπὸ　τούτων　τῶν　ματαίων
ing [to]　you　from　these　-　vanities

ἐπιστρέφειν　ἐπὶ　θεὸν　ζῶντα,　ὃς　ἐποίησεν
to turn　to　God　a living,　who　made

τὸν　οὐρανὸν　καὶ　τὴν　γῆν　καὶ　τὴν
the　heaven　and　the　earth　and　the

θάλασσαν　καὶ　πάντα　τὰ　ἐν　αὐτοῖς·　16 ὃς
sea　and　all　the things　in　them;　who

ἐν　ταῖς　παρῳχημέναις　γενεαῖς　εἴασεν　πάντα
in　the　having passed　generations　allowed　all

τὰ　ἔθνη　πορεύεσθαι　ταῖς　ὁδοῖς　αὐτῶν·
the　nations　to go　in the　ways　of them;

17 καίτοι　οὐκ　ἀμάρτυρον　αὐτὸν　ἀφῆκεν
and yet　²not　³unwitnessed　¹himself　¹left

ἀγαθουργῶν,　οὐρανόθεν　ὑμῖν　ὑετοὺς　διδοὺς
doing good,　⁴from heaven　²us　⁴rain　¹giving

καὶ　καιροὺς　καρποφόρους,　ἐμπιπλῶν　τροφῆς
and　times　fruit-bearing,　filling　of(with) food

καὶ　εὐφροσύνης　τὰς　καρδίας　ὑμῶν.　18 καὶ
and　of(with) gladness　the　hearts　of us.　And

ταῦτα　λέγοντες　μόλις　κατέπαυσαν　τοὺς
these things　saying　scarcely　they restrained　the

ὄχλους　τοῦ　μὴ　θύειν　αὐτοῖς.　19 'Επῆλθαν
crowds　-　not to sacrificeᵈ　to them.　¹came upon
[the scene]

δὲ　ἀπὸ　'Αντιοχείας　καὶ　'Ικονίου　'Ιουδαῖοι,
And ²from　³Antioch　⁴and　⁵Iconium　¹Jews,

καὶ　πείσαντες　τοὺς　ὄχλους　καὶ　λιθάσαντες
and　persuading　the　crowds　and　stoning

τὸν　Παῦλον　ἔσυρον　ἔξω　τῆς　πόλεως,
-　Paul　dragged　outside　the　city,

νομίζοντες　αὐτὸν　τεθνηκέναι.　20 κυκλω-
supposing　him　to have died.　But sur-

σάντων　δὲ　τῶν　μαθητῶν　αὐτὸν　ἀναστὰς
rounding　-　the　disciplesᵃ　him　rising up
= as the disciples surrounded

εἰσῆλθεν　εἰς　τὴν　πόλιν.　Καὶ　τῇ　ἐπαύριον
he entered　into　the　city.　And on the　morrow

ἐξῆλθεν　σὺν　τῷ　Βαρναβᾷ　εἰς　Δέρβην.
he went forth with　-　Barnabas　to　Derbe.

21 εὐαγγελισάμενοί　τε　τὴν　πόλιν　ἐκείνην
And evangelizing　that　city

καὶ　μαθητεύσαντες　ἱκανοὺς　ὑπέστρεψαν　εἰς
and　having made disciples　many　they returned　to

τὴν　Λύστραν　καὶ　εἰς　'Ικόνιον　καὶ　[εἰς]
-　Lystra　and　to　Iconium　and　to

'Αντιόχειαν,　22 ἐπιστηρίζοντες　τὰς　ψυχὰς
Antioch,　confirming　the　minds

τῶν　μαθητῶν,　παρακαλοῦντες　ἐμμένειν　τῇ
of the　disciples,　exhorting　to continue in the

πίστει,　καὶ　ὅτι　διὰ　πολλῶν　θλίψεων
faith,　and　that　through　many　afflictions

δεῖ　ἡμᾶς　εἰσελθεῖν　εἰς　τὴν　βασιλείαν　τοῦ
it behoves　us　to enter　into　the　kingdom　-

θεοῦ.　23 χειροτονήσαντες　δὲ　αὐτοῖς　κατ'
of God.　And having appointed　for them　in

ἐκκλησίαν　πρεσβυτέρους,　προσευξάμενοι
every church　elders,　praying

μετὰ　νηστειῶν　παρέθεντο　αὐτοὺς　τῷ　κυρίῳ
with　fastings　they committed　them　to the Lord

King James Version

on whom they believed. 24And after they had passed throughout Pisidia, they came to Pamphylia. 25And when they had preached the word in Perga, they went down into Attalia: 26And thence sailed to Antioch, from whence they had been recommended to the grace of God for the work which they fulfilled. 27And when they were come, and had gathered the church together, they rehearsed all that God had done with them, and how he had opened the door of faith unto the Gentiles. 28And there they abode long time with the disciples.

15 And certain men which came down from Judea taught the brethren, *and said,* Except ye be circumcised after the manner of Moses, ye cannot be saved. 2 When therefore Paul and Barnabas had no small dissension and disputation with them, they determined that Paul and Barnabas, and certain other of them, should go up to Jerusalem unto the apostles and elders about this question. 3And being brought on their way by the church, they passed through Phenice and Samaria, declaring the conversion of the Gentiles: and they caused great joy unto all the brethren. 4And when they were come to Jerusalem, they were received of the church, and *of* the apostles and elders, and they declared all things that God had done with them. 5 But there rose up certain of the sect of the Pharisees which believed, saying, That it was needful to circumcise them, and to command *them* to keep the law of Moses.

6 And the apostles and elders came together for to consider of this matter. 7And when there had been much disputing, Peter rose up, and said unto them, Men *and* brethren, ye know how that a good while ago God made choice among us, that the Gentiles by my mouth should hear the word of the gospel, and believe. 8And God, which knoweth the hearts, bare them witness, giving them the Holy Ghost, even as *he did* unto us; 9And put no difference between us and them, purifying their hearts by faith. 10 Now therefore why tempt ye God, to put a yoke upon the neck of the disciples, which neither our fathers nor we were able to bear? 11 But we believe that through the grace of the Lord Jesus Christ we shall be saved, even as they.

12 Then all the multitude kept silence, and gave audience to Barnabas and Paul, declaring what miracles and wonders God had wrought among the Gentiles by them.

13 And after they had held their peace, James answered, saying, Men *and* brethren, hearken unto me: 14 Simeon hath declared how God at the first did visit the Gentiles, to take out of them a people for his name. 15And to this agree

New International Version

Lord in whom they had put their trust. 24After going through Pisidia, they came into Pamphylia, 25 and when they had preached the word in Perga, they went down to Attalia.

26 From Attalia they sailed back to Antioch, where they had been committed to the grace of God for the work they had now completed. 27 On arriving there, they gathered the church together and reported all that God had done through them and how he had opened the door of faith to the Gentiles. 28And they stayed there a long time with the disciples.

The council at Jerusalem

15 Some men came down from Judea to Antioch and were teaching the brothers: "Unless you are circumcised according to the custom taught by Moses, you cannot be saved." 2 This brought Paul and Barnabas into sharp dispute and debate with them. So Paul and Barnabas were appointed, along with some other believers, to go up to Jerusalem to see the apostles and elders about this question. 3 The church sent them on their way, and as they traveled through Phoenicia and Samaria, they told how the Gentiles had been converted. This news made all the brothers very glad. 4 When they came to Jerusalem, they were welcomed by the church and the apostles and elders, to whom they reported everything God had done through them.

5 Then some of the believers who belonged to the party of the Pharisees stood up and said, "The Gentiles must be circumcised and required to obey the law of Moses."

6 The apostles and elders met to consider this question. 7After much discussion, Peter got up and addressed them: "Brothers, you know that some time ago God made a choice among you that the Gentiles might hear from my lips the message of the gospel and believe. 8 God, who knows the heart, showed that he accepted them by giving the Holy Spirit to them, just as he did to us. 9 He made no distinction between us and them, for he purified their hearts by faith. 10 Now then, why do you try to test God by putting on the necks of the disciples a yoke that neither we nor our fathers have been able to bear? 11 No! We believe it is through the grace of our Lord Jesus that we are saved, just as they are."

12 The whole assembly became silent as they listened to Barnabas and Paul telling about the miraculous signs and wonders God had done among the Gentiles through them. 13 When they finished, James spoke up: "Brothers, listen to me. 14 Simon[v] has described to us how God at first showed his concern by taking from the Gentiles a people for himself. 15 The words of

Greek Interlinear

εἰς   ὃν   πεπιστεύκεισαν.   **24** καὶ   διελθόντες
in whom they had believed.   And passing through

τὴν   Πισιδίαν   ἦλθον   εἰς   τὴν   Παμφυλίαν,
 -    Pisidia   they came to   -   Pamphylia,

25 καὶ   λαλήσαντες   εἰς   τὴν   Πέργην   τὸν
     and   speaking   in   -   Perga   the

λόγον   κατέβησαν   εἰς   'Αττάλειαν,   κἀκεῖθεν
word   they came down to   Attalia,   and thence

ἀπέπλευσαν   εἰς   'Αντιόχειαν,   **26** ὅθεν   ἦσαν
sailed away   to   Antioch,   whence they were

παραδεδομένοι   τῇ   χάριτι   τοῦ   θεοῦ   εἰς
having been commended to the grace   -   of God   for

τὸ   ἔργον   ὃ   ἐπλήρωσαν.   **27** Παραγεν-
the work which they accomplished.   And having

όμενοι   δὲ   καὶ   συναγαγόντες   τὴν   ἐκκλησίαν,
arrived   and   and   assembling   the   church,

ἀνήγγελλον   ὅσα   ἐποίησεν   ὁ   θεὸς   μετ'
they reported what things did   -   God   with

αὐτῶν,   καὶ   ὅτι   ἤνοιξεν   τοῖς   ἔθνεσιν
them,   and   that   he opened to the nations

θύραν   πίστεως.   **28** διέτριβον   δὲ   χρόνον
a door of faith.   And they continued   time

οὐκ   ὀλίγον   σὺν   τοῖς   μαθηταῖς.
not   a little   with   the   disciples.

Chapter 15

Καὶ   τινες   κατελθόντες   ἀπὸ   τῆς
And   some   going down   from   the

'Ιουδαίας   ἐδίδασκον   τοὺς   ἀδελφοὺς   ὅτι
Judæa   taught   the   brothers[,]   -

ἐὰν   μὴ   περιτμηθῆτε   τῷ   ἔθει   τῷ   Μωϋσέως,
Unless ye are circumcised by the custom   -   of Moses,

οὐ   δύνασθε   σωθῆναι.   **2** γενομένης   δὲ
ye cannot   to be saved.   And taking place

στάσεως   καὶ   ζητήσεως   οὐκ   ὀλίγης   τῷ
discord   and   questioning   not   a little*

=when there took place not a little . . .

Παύλῳ   καὶ   τῷ   Βαρναβᾷ   πρὸς   αὐτούς,
by Paul   and   -   Barnabas   with   them,

ἔταξαν   ἀναβαίνειν   Παῦλον   καὶ   Βαρναβᾶν
they assigned to go up   Paul   and   Barnabas

καὶ   τινας   ἄλλους   ἐξ   αὐτῶν   πρὸς   τοὺς
and   some   others   of them   to   the

ἀποστόλους   καὶ   πρεσβυτέρους   εἰς   'Ιερουσαλὴμ
apostles   and   elders   in   Jerusalem

περὶ   τοῦ   ζητήματος   τούτου.   **3** Οἱ   μὲν
about   the   question   this.   They   -

οὖν   προπεμφθέντες   ὑπὸ   τῆς   ἐκκλησίας
therefore being set forward   by   the   church

διήρχοντο   τήν   τε   Φοινίκην   καὶ   Σαμάρειαν
passed through   -   both   Phœnicia   and   Samaria

ἐκδιηγούμενοι   τὴν   ἐπιστροφὴν   τῶν   ἐθνῶν,
telling in detail   the   conversion   of the   nations,

καὶ   ἐποίουν   χαρὰν   μεγάλην   πᾶσιν   τοῖς
and   caused   joy   great   to all   the

ἀδελφοῖς.   **4** παραγενόμενοι   δὲ   εἰς   'Ιεροσόλυμα
brothers.   And having arrived   in   Jerusalem

παρεδέχθησαν   ἀπὸ   τῆς   ἐκκλησίας   καὶ   τῶν
they were welcomed from   the   church   and   the

ἀποστόλων   καὶ   τῶν   πρεσβυτερων,   ἀνήγ-
apostles   and   the   elders,   and

γειλάν   τε   ὅσα   ὁ   θεὸς   ἐποίησεν   μετ'
reported   -   what things   -   God   did   with

αὐτῶν.   **5** 'Εξανέστησαν   δέ   τινες   τῶν
them.   But stood forth   some of the [ones]

ἀπὸ   τῆς   αἱρέσεως   τῶν   Φαρισαίων
from   the   sect   of the   Pharisees

πεπιστευκότες,   λέγοντες   ὅτι   δεῖ   περιτέμνειν
having believed,   saying[.]   -   It be- to circumcise
                                      hoves

αὐτοὺς   παραγγέλλειν   τε   τηρεῖν   τὸν   νόμον
them   and to charge   -   to keep   the   law

Μωϋσέως.
of Moses.

6 Συνήχθησάν   τε   οἱ   ἀπόστολοι   καὶ   οἱ
    And were assembled   -   the   apostles   and   the

πρεσβύτεροι   ἰδεῖν   περὶ   τοῦ   λόγου   τούτου.
elders   to see   about   the   this matter.

7 Πολλῆς   δὲ   ζητήσεως   γενομένης   ἀναστὰς
    And much   questioning having taken place* rising up
=When much questioning had . . .

Πέτρος   εἶπεν   πρὸς   αὐτούς·   ἄνδρες   ἀδελφοί,
Peter   said   to   them: Men   brothers,

ὑμεῖς   ἐπίστασθε   ὅτι   ἀφ'   ἡμερῶν   ἀρχαίων
ye   understand   that   from   days   olden

ἐν   ὑμῖν   ἐξελέξατο   ὁ   θεὸς   διὰ   τοῦ   στόματός
²among ²you   ¹chose   -   ¹God through   the   mouth

μου   ἀκοῦσαι   τὰ   ἔθνη   τὸν   λόγον   τοῦ
of me   ²to hear   ¹the ²nations the   word   of the

εὐαγγελίου   καὶ   πιστεῦσαι.   **8** καὶ   ὁ
gospel   and   to believe.   And   ²the

καρδιογνώστης   θεὸς   ἐμαρτύρησεν   αὐτοῖς
³Heart-knower   ¹God   witnessed   to them

δοὺς   τὸ   πνεῦμα   τὸ   ἅγιον   καθὼς   καὶ
giving the   Spirit   -   Holy   as   also

ἡμῖν,   **9** καὶ   οὐθὲν   διέκρινεν   μεταξὺ   ἡμῶν
to us,   and   nothing distinguished between   ²us

τε   καὶ   αὐτῶν,   τῇ   πίστει   καθαρίσας   τὰς
¹both   and   them,   -   by faith   cleansing   the

καρδίας   αὐτῶν.   **10** νῦν   οὖν   τί   πειράζετε
hearts   of them.   Now therefore why   test ye

τὸν   θεόν,   ἐπιθεῖναι   ζυγὸν   ἐπὶ   τὸν
 -    God,   to put on   a yoke   on   the

τράχηλον   τῶν   μαθητῶν,   ὃν   οὔτε   οἱ
neck   of the disciples,   which neither the

πατέρες   ἡμῶν   οὔτε   ἡμεῖς   ἰσχύσαμεν
fathers   of us   nor   we   were able

βαστάσαι;   **11** ἀλλὰ   διὰ   τῆς   χάριτος   τοῦ
to bear?   but   through   the   grace   of the

κυρίου   'Ιησοῦ   πιστεύομεν   σωθῆναι   καθ'
Lord   Jesus   we believe   to be saved   in

ὃν   τρόπον   κἀκεῖνοι.   **12** 'Εσίγησεν   δὲ
the same way as† those also.   And was silent

πᾶν   τὸ   πλῆθος,   καὶ   ἤκουον   Βαρναβᾶ
all   the   multitude,   and   heard   Barnabas

καὶ   Παύλου   ἐξηγουμένων   ὅσα   ἐποίησεν
and   Paul   relating   ¹what   ¹did

ὁ   θεὸς   σημεῖα   καὶ   τέρατα   ἐν   τοῖς
 -   ¹God   ²signs   ²and   ⁴wonders among   the

ἔθνεσιν   δι'   αὐτῶν.   **13** Μετὰ   δὲ   τὸ   σιγῆσαι
nations   through them.   And after the to keep silence
                                           =they kept silence

αὐτοὺς   ἀπεκρίθη   'Ιάκωβος   λέγων·   **14** ἄνδρες
them‡   answered   James   saying: Men

ἀδελφοί,   ἀκούσατέ   μου.   Συμεὼν   ἐξηγήσατο
brothers,   hear ye   me.   Simeon   declared

καθὼς   πρῶτον   ὁ   θεὸς   ἐπεσκέψατο   λαβεῖν   ἐξ
even as   firstly   -   God   visited   to take out of

ἐθνῶν   λαὸν   τῷ   ὀνόματι   αὐτοῦ.   **15** καὶ
[the] nations a people for the   name   of him.   And

King James Version

the words of the prophets; as it is written,
16After this I will return, and will build again
the tabernacle of David, which is fallen down;
and I will build again the ruins thereof, and I
will set it up: 17 That the residue of men might
seek after the Lord, and all the Gentiles, upon
whom my name is called, saith the Lord, who
doeth all these things. 18 Known unto God are
all his works from the beginning of the world.
19 Wherefore my sentence is, that we trouble
not them, which from among the Gentiles are
turned to God: 20 But that we write unto them,
that they abstain from pollutions of idols, and
from fornication, and *from* things strangled,
and *from* blood. 21 For Moses of old time hath
in every city them that preach him, being read
in the synagogues every sabbath day. 22 Then
pleased it the apostles and elders, with the whole
church, to send chosen men of their own company to Antioch with Paul and Barnabas;
namely, Judas surnamed Barsabas, and Silas,
chief men among the brethren: 23And they
wrote *letters* by them after this manner; The
apostles and elders and brethren *send* greeting
unto the brethren which are of the Gentiles in
Antioch and Syria and Cilicia: 24 Forasmuch as
we have heard, that certain which went out
from us have troubled you with words, subverting your souls, saying, *Ye must* be circumcised, and keep the law; to whom we gave no
such commandment: 25 It seemed good unto us,
being assembled with one accord, to send chosen
men unto you with our beloved Barnabas and
Paul, 26 Men that have hazarded their lives for
the name of our Lord Jesus Christ. 27 We have
sent therefore Judas and Silas, who shall also
tell *you* the same things by mouth. 28 For it
seemed good to the Holy Ghost, and to us, to
lay upon you no greater burden than these necessary things; 29 That ye abstain from meats offered to idols, and from blood, and from things
strangled, and from fornication: from which if
ye keep yourselves, ye shall do well. Fare ye
well. 30 So when they were dismissed, they came
to Antioch: and when they had gathered the
multitude together, they delivered the epistle:
31 *Which* when they had read, they rejoiced for
the consolation. 32And Judas and Silas, being
prophets also themselves, exhorted the brethren
with many words, and confirmed *them.* 33And
after they had tarried *there* a space, they were
let go in peace from the brethren unto the
apostles. 34 Notwithstanding it pleased Silas to
abide there still. 35 Paul also and Barnabas continued in Antioch, teaching and preaching the
word of the Lord, with many others also.

New International Version

the prophets are in agreement with this, as it is
written:
16 'After this I will return
    and rebuild the fallen house of David.
  Its ruins I will rebuild,
    and I will restore it,
17 that the rest of mankind may seek the
    Lord,
  and all the Gentiles who bear my name,
  says the Lord, who does these things' *w*
18   that have been known for ages.*x*
19 "It is my judgment, therefore, that we
should not make it difficult for the Gentiles who
are turning to God. 20 Instead we should write
to them, telling them to abstain from food polluted by idols, from sexual immorality, from
the meat of strangled animals and from blood.
21 For Moses has been preached in every city
from the earliest times and is read in the synagogues on every Sabbath."

The council's letter to Gentile believers

22 Then the apostles and elders, with the
whole church, decided to choose some of their
own men and send them to Antioch with Paul
and Barnabas. They chose Judas, called Barsabbas, and Silas, two men who were leaders among
the brothers. 23 With them they sent the following letter:

The apostles and elders, your brothers,

To the Gentile believers in Antioch, Syria
and Cilicia:

Greetings.

24 We have heard that some went out from
us without our authorization and disturbed
you, troubling your minds by what they said.
25 So we all agreed to choose some men and
send them to you with our dear friends
Barnabas and Paul—26 men who have risked
their lives for the name of our Lord Jesus
Christ. 27 Therefore we are sending Judas
and Silas to confirm by word of mouth what
we are writing. 28 It seemed good to the Holy
Spirit and to us not to burden you with anything beyond the following requirements:
29 You are to abstain from food offered to
idols, from blood, from the meat of strangled
animals and from sexual immorality. You will
do well to avoid these things.

Farewell.

30 The men were sent off and went down to
Antioch, where they gathered the church together and delivered the letter. 31 The people
read it and were glad for its encouraging message. 32 Judas and Silas, who themselves
were prophets, said much to encourage and strengthen
the brothers. 33After spending some time there,
they were sent off by the brothers with the blessing of peace to return to those who had sent
them.*y* 35 But Paul and Barnabas remained in
Antioch, where they and many others taught and
preached the word of the Lord.

[w] Amos 9:11, 12. [x] Some MSS read *things'* - 18*known to the
Lord for ages in his work.* [y] Some MSS add verse 34: *but Silas
decided to remain there.*

Greek Interlinear

τούτῳ συμφωνοῦσιν οἱ λόγοι τῶν προφητῶν,
to this　agree　the words　of the　prophets,

καθὼς γέγραπται· 16 μετὰ ταῦτα
even as　it has been written:　After　these things

ἀναστρέψω καὶ ἀνοικοδομήσω τὴν σκηνὴν
I will return　and　I will rebuild　the　tent

Δαυὶδ τὴν πεπτωκυῖαν, καὶ τὰ κατεστραμ-
of David　-　having fallen,　and　the　having been
　　　　　　　　　　　　　　　　　things

μένα αὐτῆς ἀνοικοδομήσω καὶ ἀνορθώσω
overturned　of it　I will rebuild　and　I will rear again
= its ruins

αὐτήν, 17 ὅπως ἂν ἐκζητήσωσιν οἱ
it,　　so as　-　⁴may seek　¹the

κατάλοιποι τῶν ἀνθρώπων τὸν κύριον,
²rest　-　³of men　⁵the　⁶Lord,

καὶ πάντα τὰ ἔθνη ἐφ᾽ οὓς ἐπικέκληται
even　all　the　nations　on　whom has been invoked

τὸ ὄνομά μου ἐπ᾽ αὐτούς, λέγει κύριος
the　name　of me　on　them,　says　[the] Lord

ποιῶν ταῦτα 18 γνωστὰ ἀπ᾽ αἰῶνος.
doing these things　known　from　[the] age.

19 διὸ ἐγὼ κρίνω μὴ παρενοχλεῖν τοῖς
Wherefore I　decide　not　to trouble　the [ones]

ἀπὸ τῶν ἐθνῶν ἐπιστρέφουσιν ἐπὶ τὸν
from　the　nations　turning　to　-

θεόν, 20 ἀλλὰ ἐπιστεῖλαι αὐτοῖς τοῦ
God,　but　to write word　to them

ἀπέχεσθαι τῶν ἀλισγημάτων τῶν εἰδώλων
to abstain from⁴ the　pollutions　-　of idols

καὶ τῆς πορνείας καὶ πνικτοῦ καὶ τοῦ
and　-　fornication　and　a thing strangled and -

αἵματος. 21 Μωϋσῆς γὰρ ἐκ γενεῶν
blood.　For ¹Moses　³from ⁴generations

ἀρχαίων κατὰ πόλιν τοὺς κηρύσσοντας
²ancient　⁶in every city　⁷the [ones]　⁸proclaiming

αὐτὸν ἔχει ἐν ταῖς συναγωγαῖς κατὰ
⁵him　⁹has　¹¹in　¹²the　¹³synagogues　¹⁴on

πᾶν σάββατον ἀναγινωσκόμενος. 22 Τότε
¹⁵every ¹⁶sabbath　¹⁰being read.　Then

ἔδοξε τοῖς ἀποστόλοις καὶ τοῖς πρεσ-
it seemed [good] to the　apostles　and　to the　el-

βυτέροις σὺν ὅλῃ τῇ ἐκκλησίᾳ ἐκλεξαμένους
ders　with　all　the　church　chosen

ἄνδρας ἐξ αὐτῶν πέμψαι εἰς Ἀντιόχειαν
men　of them　to send　to　Antioch

σὺν τῷ Παύλῳ καὶ Βαρναβᾷ, Ἰούδαν
with　-　Paul　and　Barnabas,　Judas

τὸν καλούμενον Βαρσαββᾶν καὶ Σιλᾶν,
-　being called　Barsabbas　and　Silas,

ἄνδρας ἡγουμένους ἐν τοῖς ἀδελφοῖς,
men　leading　among　the　brothers,

23 γράψαντες διὰ χειρὸς αὐτῶν· Οἱ
writing　through　[the] hand　of them:　The

ἀπόστολοι καὶ οἱ πρεσβύτεροι ἀδελφοὶ
apostles　and　the　elder　brothers

τοῖς κατὰ τὴν Ἀντιόχειαν καὶ Συρίαν
¹to the　⁴throughout -　²Antioch　³and　⁵Syria

καὶ Κιλικίαν ἀδελφοῖς τοῖς ἐξ ἐθνῶν
⁶and　¹⁰Cilicia　⁷brothers　-　⁸of [the] ⁹nations

χαίρειν. 24 Ἐπειδὴ ἠκούσαμεν ὅτι τινὲς
¹¹greeting.　Since　we heard　that　some

ἐξ ἡμῶν ἐτάραξαν ὑμᾶς λόγοις ἀνασκευάζ-
of　us　troubled　you　with words　unsettl-

οντες τὰς ψυχὰς ὑμῶν, οἷς οὐ διεστειλάμεθα,
ing　the　minds　of you,　to　we did not give
　　　　　　　　　　　whom　commission,

25 ἔδοξεν ἡμῖν γενομένοις ὁμοθυμαδόν,
it seemed [good]　to us　becoming　of one mind,

ἐκλεξαμένους ἄνδρας πέμψαι πρὸς ὑμᾶς
chosen　men　to send　to　you

σὺν τοῖς ἀγαπητοῖς ἡμῶν Βαρναβᾷ καὶ
with　the　beloved　of us　Barnabas　and

Παύλῳ, 26 ἀνθρώποις παραδεδωκόσι τὰς
Paul,　men　having given up　the

ψυχὰς αὐτῶν ὑπὲρ τοῦ ὀνόματος τοῦ
lives　of them　on behalf of the　name　of the

κυρίου ἡμῶν Ἰησοῦ Χριστοῦ. 27 ἀπεστάλ-
Lord　of us　Jesus　Christ.　We have

καμεν οὖν Ἰούδαν καὶ Σιλᾶν, καὶ αὐτοὺς
sent　therefore Judas　and　Silas,　and　they

διὰ λόγου ἀπαγγέλλοντας τὰ αὐτά.
through　speech　announcing　the　same
(by)　　　　　　　　　　　　things.

28 ἔδοξεν γὰρ τῷ πνεύματι τῷ ἁγίῳ
For it seemed [good]　to the　Spirit　-　Holy

καὶ ἡμῖν μηδὲν πλέον ἐπιτίθεσθαι ὑμῖν
and　to us　¹nothing　²more　¹to be put on　³you

βάρος πλὴν τούτων τῶν ἐπάναγκες,
⁴burden　than　these　-　, necessary things,

29 ἀπέχεσθαι εἰδωλοθύτων καὶ αἵματος καὶ
to abstain from　idol sacrifices　and　blood　and

πνικτῶν καὶ πορνείας· ἐξ ὧν διατηροῦντες
things　and　fornication;　from　which　keeping
strangled

ἑαυτοὺς εὖ πράξετε. Ἔρρωσθε.
yourselves　well　ye will do.　Farewell.

30 Οἱ μὲν οὖν ἀπολυθέντες κατῆλθον εἰς
They　- therefore being dismissed　went down　to

Ἀντιόχειαν, καὶ συναγαγόντες τὸ πλῆθος
Antioch,　and　assembling　the　multitude

ἐπέδωκαν τὴν ἐπιστολήν. 31 ἀναγνόντες δὲ
handed in the　letter.　And having read

ἐχάρησαν ἐπὶ τῇ παρακλήσει. 32 Ἰούδας τε
they rejoiced　at　the　exhortation.　And Judas

καὶ Σιλᾶς, καὶ αὐτοὶ προφῆται ὄντες,
and　Silas,　also　[them]selves　prophets　being,

διὰ λόγου πολλοῦ παρεκάλεσαν τοὺς
through　speech　much　exhorted　the
(by)

ἀδελφοὺς καὶ ἐπεστήριξαν· 33 ποιήσαντες δὲ
brothers　and　confirmed;　and having continued

χρόνον ἀπελύθησαν μετ᾽ εἰρήνης ἀπὸ
a time　they were dismissed　with　peace　from

τῶν ἀδελφῶν πρὸς τοὺς ἀποστείλαντας
the　brothers　to　the [ones]　having sent

αὐτούς. ‡ 35 Παῦλος δὲ καὶ Βαρναβᾶς
them.　But Paul　and　Barnabas

διέτριβον ἐν Ἀντιοχείᾳ, διδάσκοντες καὶ
stayed　in　Antioch,　teaching　and

εὐαγγελιζόμενοι μετὰ καὶ ἑτέρων πολλῶν
preaching　¹with　⁴also　³others　²many

τὸν λόγον τοῦ κυρίου.
the　word　of the　Lord.

---

‡ Verse 34 omitted by Nestle

King James Version

36 And some days after, Paul said unto Barnabas, Let us go again and visit our brethren in every city where we have preached the word of the Lord, *and see* how they do. 37And Barnabas determined to take with them John, whose surname was Mark. 38 But Paul thought not good to take him with them, who departed from them from Pamphylia, and went not with them to the work. 39And the contention was so sharp between them, that they departed asunder one from the other: and so Barnabas took Mark, and sailed unto Cyprus; 40And Paul chose Silas, and departed, being recommended by the brethren unto the grace of God. 41And he went through Syria and Cilicia, confirming the churches.

16 Then came he to Derbe and Lystra: and, behold, a certain disciple was there, named Timotheus, the son of a certain woman, which was a Jewess, and believed; but his father *was* a Greek. 2 Which was well reported of by the brethren that were at Lystra and Iconium. 3 Him would Paul have to go forth with him; and took and circumcised him because of the Jews which were in those quarters: for they knew all that his father was a Greek. 4And as they went through the cities, they delivered them the decrees for to keep, that were ordained of the apostles and elders which were at Jerusalem. 5And so were the churches established in the faith, and increased in number daily. 6 Now when they had gone throughout Phrygia and the region of Galatia, and were forbidden of the Holy Ghost to preach the word in Asia, 7After they were come to Mysia, they assayed to go into Bithynia: but the Spirit suffered them not. 8And they passing by Mysia came down to Troas. 9And a vision appeared to Paul in the night; There stood a man of Macedonia, and prayed him, saying, Come over into Macedonia, and help us. 10And after he had seen the vision, immediately we endeavoured to go into Macedonia, assuredly gathering that the Lord had called us for to preach the gospel unto them. 11 Therefore loosing from Troas, we came with a straight course to Samothracia, and the next *day* to Neapolis; 12And from thence to Philippi, which is the chief city of that part of Macedonia, *and* a colony: and we were in that city abiding certain days. 13And on the sabbath we went out of the city by a river side, where prayer was wont to be made; and we sat down, and spake unto the women which resorted *thither*. 14 And a certain woman named Lydia, a seller of purple, of the city of Thyatira, which worshipped God, heard *us:* whose heart the Lord opened, that she attended unto the things

New International Version

Disagreement between Paul and Barnabas

36 Some time later Paul said to Barnabas, "Let us go back and visit the brothers in all the towns where we preached the word of the Lord and see how they are doing." 37 Barnabas wanted to take John, also called Mark, with them, 38 but Paul did not think it wise to take him, because he had deserted them in Pamphylia and had not continued with them in the work. 39 They had such a sharp disagreement that they parted company. Barnabas took Mark and sailed for Cyprus, 40 but Paul chose Silas and left, commended by the brothers to the grace of the Lord. 41 He went through Syria and Cilicia, strengthening the churches.

Timothy joins Paul and Silas

16 He came to Derbe and then to Lystra, where a disciple named Timothy lived, whose mother was a Jewess and a believer, but whose father was a Greek. 2 The brothers at Lystra and Iconium spoke well of him. 3 Paul wanted to take him along on the journey, so he circumcised him because of the Jews who lived in that area, for they all knew that his father was a Greek. 4As they traveled from town to town, they delivered the decisions reached by the apostles and elders in Jerusalem for the people to obey. 5 So the churches were strengthened in the faith and grew daily in numbers.

Paul's vision of the Macedonian

6 Paul and his companions traveled throughout the region of Phrygia and Galatia, having been kept by the Holy Spirit from preaching the word in the province of Asia. 7 When they came to the border of Mysia, they tried to enter Bithynia, but the Spirit of Jesus would not allow them to. 8 So they passed by Mysia and went down to Troas. 9 During the night Paul had a vision of a man of Macedonia standing and begging him, "Come over to Macedonia and help us." 10After Paul had seen the vision, we got ready at once to leave for Macedonia, concluding that God had called us to preach the gospel to them.

Lydia's conversion in Philippi

11 From Troas we put out to sea and sailed straight for Samothrace, and the next day on to Neapolis. 12 From there we traveled to Philippi, a Roman colony and the leading city of that district of Macedonia. And we stayed there several days.

13 On the Sabbath we went outside the city gate to the river, where we expected to find a place of prayer. We sat down and began to speak to the women who had gathered there. 14 One of those listening was a woman named Lydia, a dealer in purple cloth from the city of Thyatira, who was a worshiper of God. The Lord opened her heart to respond to Paul's

Greek Interlinear

36 Μετὰ δέ τινας ἡμέρας εἶπεν πρὸς
Now after some days ¹said ²to

Βαρναβᾶν Παῦλος· ἐπιστρέψαντες δὴ
⁴Barnabas ¹Paul: Returning then

ἐπισκεψώμεθα τοὺς ἀδελφοὺς κατὰ πόλιν
let us visit the brothers throughout ¹city

πᾶσαν ἐν αἷς κατηγγείλαμεν τὸν λόγον
¹every in which we announced the word

τοῦ κυρίου, πῶς ἔχουσιν. **37** Βαρναβᾶς
of the Lord, how they have(are). Barnabas

δὲ ἐβούλετο συμπαραλαβεῖν καὶ τὸν
And wished to take with [them] also –

᾿Ιωάννην τὸν καλούμενον Μᾶρκον· **38** Παῦλος
John – being called Mark; ¹Paul

δὲ ἠξίου, τὸν ἀποστάντα ἀπ᾿ αὐτῶν
¹but ²thought fit, – ⁷withdrawing ⁶from ⁷them

ἀπὸ Παμφυλίας καὶ μὴ συνελθόντα αὐτοῖς
¹⁰from ¹¹Pamphylia ¹²and ¹³not ¹⁴going with ¹⁵them

39 ἐγένετο δὲ παροξυσμός, ὥστε ἀποχωρισ-
And there was sharp feeling, so as to separ-

θῆναι αὐτοὺς ἀπ᾿ ἀλλήλων, τόν τε
ate them from each other, – and

Βαρναβᾶν παραλαβόντα τὸν Μᾶρκον
Barnabas taking the Mark

ἐκπλεῦσαι εἰς Κύπρον. **40** Παῦλος δὲ
to sail away to Cyprus. But Paul

ἐπιλεξάμενος Σιλᾶν ἐξῆλθεν, παραδοθεὶς
having chosen Silas went forth, being commended

τῇ χάριτι τοῦ κυρίου ὑπὸ τῶν
to the grace of the Lord by the

ἀδελφῶν· **41** διήρχετο δὲ τὴν Συρίαν
brothers; and he went through – Syria

καὶ Κιλικίαν ἐπιστηρίζων τὰς ἐκκλησίας.
and Cilicia confirming the churches.

Chapter 16

Κατήντησεν δὲ καὶ εἰς Δέρβην καὶ
And he came down also to Derbe and

εἰς Λύστραν. καὶ ἰδοὺ μαθητής τις ἦν
to Lystra. And behold[,] a certain disciple was

ἐκεῖ ὀνόματι Τιμόθεος, υἱὸς γυναικὸς
there by name Timothy, son ¹woman

᾿Ιουδαίας πιστῆς πατρὸς δὲ ῞Ελληνος,
¹Jewish ²of a faithful ¹but ²father ¹of a Greek,

2 ὃς ἐμαρτυρεῖτο ὑπὸ τῶν ἐν Λύστροις
who was witnessed to by ¹the ²in ¹Lystra

καὶ ᾿Ικονίῳ ἀδελφῶν. **3** τοῦτον ἠθέλησεν
²and ³Iconium ¹brothers. ¹This one ²wished

ὁ Παῦλος σὺν αὐτῷ ἐξελθεῖν, καὶ λαβὼν
– ¹Paul with him to go forth, and taking

περιέτεμεν αὐτὸν διὰ τοὺς ᾿Ιουδαίους τοὺς
circumcised him on account the Jews –
        of

ὄντας ἐν τοῖς τόποις ἐκείνοις· ᾔδεισαν
being in those places; ¹they knew

γὰρ ἅπαντες ὅτι ῞Ελλην ὁ πατὴρ αὐτοῦ
¹for all that a Greek the father of him

ὑπῆρχεν. **4** ῾Ως δὲ διεπορεύοντο τὰς
was. Now as they went through the

πόλεις, παρεδίδοσαν αὐτοῖς φυλάσσειν τὰ
cities, they delivered to them* to keep the

δόγματα τὰ κεκριμένα ὑπὸ τῶν ἀποστόλων
decrees – having been by the apostles
    decided [on]

καὶ πρεσβυτέρων τῶν ἐν ᾿Ιεροσολύμοις.
and elders – in Jerusalem.

5 Αἱ μὲν οὖν ἐκκλησίαι ἐστερεοῦντο
¹The ¹therefore ³churches were strengthened

τῇ πίστει καὶ ἐπερίσσευον τῷ ἀριθμῷ
in the faith and increased – in number

καθ᾿ ἡμέραν.
daily.

6 Διῆλθον δὲ τὴν Φρυγίαν καὶ Γαλατικὴν
And they went through the Phrygian and Galatian

χώραν, κωλυθέντες ὑπὸ τοῦ ἁγίου
country, being prevented by the Holy

πνεύματος λαλῆσαι τὸν λόγον ἐν τῇ
Spirit to speak the word in –
   =from speaking

᾿Ασίᾳ· **7** ἐλθόντες δὲ κατὰ τὴν Μυσίαν
Asia; but coming against – Mysia

ἐπείραζον εἰς τὴν Βιθυνίαν πορευθῆναι,
they attempted into – Bithynia to go,

καὶ οὐκ εἴασεν αὐτοὺς τὸ πνεῦμα ᾿Ιησοῦ·
and ²not ¹allowed ⁴them ¹the ⁵Spirit ¹of Jesus;

8 παρελθόντες δὲ τὴν Μυσίαν κατέβησαν
so passing by – Mysia they came down

εἰς Τρωάδα. **9** καὶ ὅραμα διὰ νυκτὸς
to Troas. And a vision through [the]
      (during) night

τῷ Παύλῳ ὤφθη, ἀνὴρ Μακεδών τις
– to Paul appeared, a man Macedonian certain

ἦν ἑστὼς καὶ παρακαλῶν αὐτὸν καὶ
was standing and beseeching him and

λέγων· διαβὰς εἰς Μακεδονίαν βοήθησον
saying: Crossing into Macedonia help

ἡμῖν. **10** ὡς δὲ τὸ ὅραμα εἶδεν, εὐθέως
us. So when the vision he saw, immediately

ἐζητήσαμεν ἐξελθεῖν εἰς Μακεδονίαν,
we sought to go forth to Macedonia,

συμβιβάζοντες ὅτι προσκέκληται ἡμᾶς ὁ
concluding that ²has(had) called ¹us ¹the

θεὸς εὐαγγελίσασθαι αὐτούς.
¹God to evangelize them.

11 ᾿Αναχθέντες δὲ ἀπὸ Τρωάδος εὐθυδρο-
And setting sail from Troas we ran a

μήσαμεν εἰς Σαμοθρᾴκην, τῇ δὲ ἐπιούσῃ
straight course to Samothracia, and on the next day

εἰς Νέαν πόλιν, **12** κἀκεῖθεν εἰς Φιλίππους,
to Neapolis, and thence to Philippi,

ἥτις ἐστὶν πρώτη τῆς μερίδος Μακεδονίας
which is [the] ¹first ¹of the ¹part ²of Macedonia

πόλις, κολωνία. ῏Ημεν δὲ ἐν ταύτῃ τῇ
²city, a colony. And we were in this –

πόλει διατρίβοντες ἡμέρας τινάς. **13** τῇ τε
city staying days some. And on the

ἡμέρᾳ τῶν σαββάτων ἐξήλθομεν ἔξω τῆς
day of the sabbaths we went forth outside the

πύλης παρὰ ποταμὸν οὗ ἐνομίζομεν
gate by a river where we supposed

προσευχὴν εἶναι, καὶ καθίσαντες ἐλαλοῦμεν
a place of prayer to be, and sitting we spoke

ταῖς συνελθούσαις γυναιξίν. **14** καί τις
to the ¹coming together ¹women. And a certain

γυνὴ ὀνόματι Λυδία, πορφυρόπωλις
woman by name Lydia, a dealer in purple-
     dyed [garments]

πόλεως Θυατίρων, σεβομένη τὸν θεόν,
of [the] city of Thyatira, worshipping – God,

ἤκουεν, ἧς ὁ κύριος διήνοιξεν τὴν καρδίαν
heard, of whom the Lord opened up the heart

προσέχειν τοῖς λαλουμένοις ὑπὸ Παύλου.
to take heed to the things being spoken by Paul.

* Note the gender: πόλις is feminine.

King James Version

which were spoken of Paul. 15And when she was baptized, and her household, she besought *us*, saying, If ye have judged me to be faithful to the Lord, come into my house, and abide *there*. And she constrained us.

16 And it came to pass, as we went to prayer, a certain damsel possessed with a spirit of divination met us, which brought her masters much gain by soothsaying: 17 The same followed Paul and us, and cried, saying, These men are the servants of the most high God, which shew unto us the way of salvation. 18 And this did she many days. But Paul, being grieved, turned and said to the spirit, I command thee in the name of Jesus Christ to come out of her. And he came out the same hour.

19 And when her masters saw that the hope of their gains was gone, they caught Paul and Silas, and drew *them* into the marketplace unto the rulers, 20And brought them to the magistrates, saying, These men, being Jews, do exceedingly trouble our city, 21And teach customs, which are not lawful for us to receive, neither to observe, being Romans. 22And the multitude rose up together against them; and the magistrates rent off their clothes, and commanded to beat *them*. 23And when they had laid many stripes upon them, they cast *them* into prison, charging the jailer to keep them safely: 24 Who, having received such a charge, thrust them into the inner prison, and made their feet fast in the stocks.

25 And at midnight Paul and Silas prayed, and sang praises unto God: and the prisoners heard them. 26And suddenly there was a great earthquake, so that the foundations of the prison were shaken: and immediately all the doors were opened, and every one's hands were loosed. 27And the keeper of the prison awaking out of his sleep, and seeing the prison doors open, he drew out his sword, and would have killed himself, supposing that the prisoners had been fled. 28 But Paul cried with a loud voice, saying, Do thyself no harm: for we are all here. 29 Then he called for a light, and sprang in, and came trembling, and fell down before Paul and Silas, 30And brought them out, and said, Sirs, what must I do to be saved? 31And they said, Believe on the Lord Jesus Christ, and thou shalt be saved, and thy house. 32And they spake unto him the word of the Lord, and to all that were in his house. 33And he took them the same hour of the night, and washed *their* stripes; and was baptized, he and all his, straightway. 34And when he had brought them into his house, he set meat before them, and rejoiced, believing in God with all his house. 35And when it was day, the magistrates sent the serjeants, saying, Let those men go. 36And the

New International Version

message. 15 When she and the members of her household were baptized, she invited us to her home. "If you consider me a believer in the Lord," she said, "come and stay at my house." And she persuaded us.

Paul and Silas in prison

16 Once when we were going to the place of prayer, we were met by a slave girl who had a spirit by which she predicted the future. She earned a lot of money for her owners by fortune-telling. 17 This girl followed Paul and the rest of us, shouting, "These men are servants of the Most High God, who are telling you the way to be saved." 18 She kept this up for many days. Finally Paul became so troubled that he turned around and said to the spirit, "In the name of Jesus Christ I command you to come out of her!" At that moment the spirit left her.

19 When the owners of the slave girl realized that their hope of making money was gone, they seized Paul and Silas and dragged them into the marketplace to face the authorities. 20 They brought them before the magistrates and said, "These men are Jews, and are throwing our city into an uproar 21 by advocating customs unlawful for us Romans to accept or practice."

22 The crowd joined in the attack against Paul and Silas, and the magistrates ordered them to be stripped and beaten. 23After they had been severely flogged, they were thrown into prison, and the jailer was commanded to guard them carefully. 24 Upon receiving such orders, he put them in the inner cell and fastened their feet in the stocks.

25 About midnight Paul and Silas were praying and singing hymns to God, and the other prisoners were listening to them. 26 Suddenly there was such a violent earthquake that the foundations of the prison were shaken. At once all the prison doors flew open, and everybody's chains came loose. 27 The jailer woke up, and when he saw the prison doors open, he drew his sword and was about to kill himself because he thought the prisoners had escaped. 28 But Paul shouted, "Don't harm yourself! We are all here!"

29 The jailer called for lights, rushed in and fell trembling before Paul and Silas. 30 He then brought them out and asked, "Men, what must I do to be saved?"

31 They replied, "Believe in the Lord Jesus, and you will be saved—you and your household." 32 Then they spoke the word of the Lord to him and to all the others in his house. 33At that hour of the night the jailer took them and washed their wounds; then immediately he and all his family were baptized. 34 The jailer brought them into his house and set a meal before them, and the whole family was filled with joy, because they had come to believe in God.

35 When it was daylight, the magistrates sent their officers to the jailer with the order: "Release those men." 36 The jailer told Paul, "The

Greek Interlinear

15 ὡς δὲ ἐβαπτίσθη καὶ ὁ οἶκος αὐτῆς,
And when she was baptized and the household of her,

παρεκάλεσεν λέγουσα· εἰ κεκρίκατέ με
she besought saying: If ye have decided me

πιστὴν τῷ κυρίῳ εἶναι, εἰσελθόντες εἰς
faithful to the Lord to be, entering into

τὸν οἶκόν μου μένετε· καὶ παρεβιάσατο
the house of me remain; and she urged

ἡμᾶς. **16** Ἐγένετο δὲ πορευομένων ἡμῶν
us. And it happened going us*
= as we went

εἰς τὴν προσευχήν, παιδίσκην τινὰ ἔχουσαν
to the place of prayer, a certain maid having

πνεῦμα πύθωνα ὑπαντῆσαι ἡμῖν, ἥτις
a spirit of a python to meet us, who

ἐργασίαν πολλὴν παρεῖχεν τοῖς κυρίοις
²gain ¹much ¹brought to the masters

αὐτῆς μαντευομένη. **17** αὕτη κατακολουθοῦσα
of her practising soothsaying. This one following after

τῷ Παύλῳ καὶ ἡμῖν ἔκραζεν λέγουσα·
- Paul and us cried out saying:

οὗτοι οἱ ἄνθρωποι δοῦλοι τοῦ θεοῦ τοῦ
These - men slaves of the God of the

ὑψίστου εἰσίν, οἵτινες καταγγέλλουσιν ὑμῖν
most high are, who announce to you

ὁδὸν σωτηρίας. **18** τοῦτο δὲ ἐποίει ἐπὶ
a way of salvation. And this she did over

πολλὰς ἡμέρας. διαπονηθεὶς δὲ Παῦλος
many days. But becoming greatly troubled Paul

καὶ ἐπιστρέψας τῷ πνεύματι εἶπεν· παραγ-
and turning ¹to the ²spirit ¹he said: I

γέλλω σοι ἐν ὀνόματι Ἰησοῦ Χριστοῦ
charge thee in [the] name of Jesus Christ

ἐξελθεῖν ἀπ' αὐτῆς· καὶ ἐξῆλθεν αὐτῇ
to come out from her; and it came out in the

τῇ ὥρα. **19** Ἰδόντες δὲ οἱ κύριοι αὐτῆς
same hour.* And ²seeing ¹the ¹masters ²of her

ὅτι ἐξῆλθεν ἡ ἐλπὶς τῆς ἐργασίας αὐτῶν,
²that ¹went out ¹the ¹hope of the ¹gain ²of them,

ἐπιλαβόμενοι τὸν Παῦλον καὶ τὸν Σιλᾶν
having seized - Paul and - Silas

εἵλκυσαν εἰς τὴν ἀγορὰν ἐπὶ τοὺς ἄρχοντας,
dragged to the marketplace before the rulers,

20 καὶ προσαγαγόντες αὐτοὺς τοῖς στρατηγοῖς
and ¹bringing ²to ²them the prætors

εἶπαν· οὗτοι οἱ ἄνθρωποι ἐκταράσσουσιν
said: These - men are greatly troubling

ἡμῶν τὴν πόλιν, Ἰουδαῖοι ὑπάρχοντες,
of us the city, ¹Jews ¹being,

21 καὶ καταγγέλλουσιν ἔθη ἃ οὐκ ἔξεστιν
and they announce customs which it is not lawful

ἡμῖν παραδέχεσθαι οὐδὲ ποιεῖν Ῥωμαίοις
for us to receive nor to do ¹Romans

οὖσιν. **22** καὶ συνεπέστη ὁ ὄχλος κατ'
¹being. And rose up together the crowd against

αὐτῶν, καὶ οἱ στρατηγοὶ περιρήξαντες
them, and the prætors tearing off

αὐτῶν τὰ ἱμάτια ἐκέλευον ῥαβδίζειν,
of them the garments commanded to flog,

23 πολλὰς δὲ ἐπιθέντες αὐτοῖς πληγὰς
and ¹many ¹laying on ²them ²stripes

ἔβαλον εἰς φυλακήν, παραγγείλαντες τῷ
threw into prison, charging the

δεσμοφύλακι ἀσφαλῶς τηρεῖν αὐτούς· **24** ὃς
jailer securely to keep them; who

παραγγελίαν τοιαύτην λαβὼν ἔβαλεν αὐτοὺς
²a charge ¹such ²having received threw them

εἰς τὴν ἐσωτέραν φυλακὴν καὶ τοὺς
into the inner prison and ²the

πόδας ἠσφαλίσατο αὐτῶν εἰς τὸ ξύλον.
¹feet ¹secured ²of them in the stocks.

25 Κατὰ δὲ τὸ μεσονύκτιον Παῦλος καὶ
And about - midnight Paul and

Σιλᾶς προσευχόμενοι ὕμνουν τὸν θεόν,
Silas praying ¹praised ²in a hymn - ²God,

ἐπηκροῶντο δὲ αὐτῶν οἱ δέσμιοι· **26** ἄφνω δὲ
and ²listened to ⁴them ¹the ²prisoners; and suddenly

σεισμὸς ἐγένετο μέγας, ὥστε σαλευ-
²earthquake ¹there was ²a great, so as to be

θῆναι τὰ θεμέλια τοῦ δεσμωτηρίου·
shaken the foundations of the jail;

ἠνεώχθησαν δὲ παραχρῆμα αἱ θύραι πᾶσαι,
and ³were opened ¹at once ²the ³doors ⁴all,

καὶ πάντων τὰ δεσμὰ ἀνέθη. **27** ἔξυπνος δὲ
and ²of all ¹the ²bonds were And ²awake
loosened.

γενόμενος ὁ δεσμοφύλαξ καὶ ἰδὼν
¹having become ²the ¹jailer and seeing

ἀνεῳγμένας τὰς θύρας τῆς φυλακῆς,
having been opened the doors of the prison,

σπασάμενος τὴν μάχαιραν ἤμελλεν ἑαυτὸν
having drawn the sword was about himself

ἀναιρεῖν, νομίζων ἐκπεφευγέναι τοὺς
to kill, supposing to have escaped the

δεσμίους. **28** ἐφώνησεν δὲ Παῦλος μεγάλῃ
prisoners. But called Paul with a
great(loud)

φωνῇ λέγων· μηδὲν πράξῃς σεαυτῷ κακόν,
voice saying: ¹Nothing ²do ⁴thyself ³harm,

ἅπαντες γάρ ἐσμεν ἐνθάδε. **29** αἰτήσας
for ¹all ¹we are ¹here. asking

δὲ φῶτα εἰσεπήδησεν, καὶ ἔντρομος
And lights he rushed in, and trembling

γενόμενος προσέπεσεν τῷ Παύλῳ καὶ
becoming he fell before - Paul and

Σιλᾷ, **30** καὶ προαγαγὼν αὐτοὺς ἔξω ἔφη·
Silas, and ¹leading ²forward ³them outside said:

κύριοι, τί με δεῖ ποιεῖν ἵνα σωθῶ;
Sirs, what ¹me ¹behoves it to do that I may
be saved?

31 οἱ δὲ εἶπαν· πίστευσον ἐπὶ τὸν κύριον
And they said: Believe on the Lord

Ἰησοῦν, καὶ σωθήσῃ σὺ καὶ ὁ οἶκός
Jesus, and shalt be saved thou and the household

σου. **32** καὶ ἐλάλησαν αὐτῷ τὸν λόγον
of thee. And they spoke to him the word

τοῦ θεοῦ σὺν πᾶσιν τοῖς ἐν τῇ οἰκίᾳ
- of God with all the [ones] in the house

αὐτοῦ. **33** καὶ παραλαβὼν αὐτοὺς ἐν
of him. And taking them in

ἐκείνῃ τῇ ὥρᾳ τῆς νυκτὸς ἔλουσεν ἀπὸ
that - hour of the night he washed from

τῶν πληγῶν, καὶ ἐβαπτίσθη αὐτὸς καὶ
the stripes, and was baptized he and

οἱ αὐτοῦ ἅπαντες παραχρῆμα, **34** ἀναγαγών
the of him all at once, ¹bringing up
= all his

τε αὐτοὺς εἰς τὸν οἶκον παρέθηκεν
¹and them to the house he set
before [them]

τράπεζαν, καὶ ἠγαλλιάσατο πανοικεὶ πεπι-
a table, and exulted with all the having
household

στευκὼς τῷ θεῷ. **35** Ἡμέρας δὲ γενομένης
believed - God. And day coming
= when day came

ἀπέστειλαν οἱ στρατηγοὶ τοὺς ῥαβδούχους
¹sent the ²prætors the tipstaffs

λέγοντες· ἀπόλυσον τοὺς ἀνθρώπους
saying: Release - men

ἐκείνους. **36** ἀπήγγειλεν δὲ ὁ δεσμοφύλαξ
those. And announced the jailer

* See Luke 2. 38.

399

King James Version

keeper of the prison told this saying to Paul, The magistrates have sent to let you go: now therefore depart, and go in peace. 37 But Paul said unto them, They have beaten us openly uncondemned, being Romans, and have cast *us* into prison; and now do they thrust us out privily? nay verily; but let them come themselves and fetch us out. 38And the serjeants told these words unto the magistrates: and they feared, when they heard that they were Romans. 39And they came and besought them, and brought *them* out, and desired *them* to depart out of the city. 40And they went out of the prison, and entered into *the house of* Lydia: and when they had seen the brethren, they comforted them, and departed.

17 Now when they had passed through Amphipolis and Apollonia, they came to Thessalonica, where was a synagogue of the Jews: 2And Paul, as his manner was, went in unto them, and three sabbath days reasoned with them out of the Scriptures, 3 Opening and alleging, that Christ must needs have suffered, and risen again from the dead; and that this Jesus, whom I preach unto you, is Christ. 4And some of them believed, and consorted with Paul and Silas; and of the devout Greeks a great multitude, and of the chief women not a few.
5 But the Jews which believed not, moved with envy, took unto them certain lewd fellows of the baser sort, and gathered a company, and set all the city on an uproar, and assaulted the house of Jason, and sought to bring them out to the people. 6And when they found them not, they drew Jason and certain brethren unto the rulers of the city, crying, These that have turned the world upside down are come hither also; 7 Whom Jason hath received: and these all do contrary to the decrees of Cesar, saying that there is another king, *one* Jesus. 8And they troubled the people and the rulers of the city, when they heard these things. 9And when they had taken security of Jason, and of the others, they let them go.
10 And the brethren immediately sent away Paul and Silas by night unto Berea: who coming *thither* went into the synagogue of the Jews. 11 These were more noble than those in Thessalonica, in that they received the word with all readiness of mind, and searched the Scriptures daily, whether those things were so. 12 Therefore many of them believed; also of honourable women which were Greeks, and of men, not a few. 13 But when the Jews of Thessalonica had knowledge that the word of God was preached of Paul at Berea, they came thither also, and

New International Version

magistrates have ordered that you and Silas be released. Now you can leave. Go in peace."
37 But Paul said to the officers: "They beat us publicly without a trial, even though we are Roman citizens, and threw us into prison. And now do they want to get rid of us quietly? No! Let them come themselves and escort us out."
38 The officers reported this to the magistrates, and when they heard that Paul and Silas were Roman citizens, they were alarmed. 39 They came to appease them and escorted them from the prison, requesting them to leave the city. 40After Paul and Silas came out of the prison, they went to Lydia's house, where they met with the brothers and encouraged them. Then they left.

In Thessalonica

17 When they had passed through Amphipolis and Apollonia, they came to Thessalonica, where there was a Jewish synagogue. 2As his custom was, Paul went into the synagogue, and on three Sabbath days he reasoned with them from the Scriptures, 3 explaining and proving that the Christ[z] had to suffer and rise from the dead. "This Jesus I am proclaiming to you is the Christ,[z]" he said. 4 Some of the Jews were persuaded and joined Paul and Silas, as did a large number of God-fearing Greeks and not a few prominent women.
5 But the Jews were jealous; so they rounded up some bad characters from the marketplace, formed a mob and started a riot in the city. They rushed to Jason's house in search of Paul and Silas in order to bring them out to the crowd.[a] 6 But when they did not find them, they dragged Jason and some other brothers before the city officials, shouting: "These men who have caused trouble all over the world have now come here, 7 and Jason has welcomed them into his house. They are all defying Caesar's decrees, saying that there is another king, one called Jesus." 8 When they heard this, the crowd and the city officials were thrown into turmoil. 9 Then they made Jason and the others post bond and let them go.

In Berea

10 As soon as it was night, the brothers sent Paul and Silas away to Berea. On arriving there, they went to the Jewish synagogue. 11 Now the Bereans were of more noble character than the Thessalonians, for they received the message with great eagerness and examined the Scriptures every day to see if what Paul said was true. 12 Many of the Jews believed, as did also a number of prominent Greek women and many Greek men. 13 When the Jews in Thessalonica learned that Paul was preaching the word of God at Berea, they went there too, agitating the crowds and

[z] Or *Messiah*. [a] Or *assembly of the people.*

Greek Interlinear

τοὺς λόγους τούτους πρὸς τὸν Παῦλον,
these words   to   –   Paul,

ὅτι ἀπέσταλκαν οἱ στρατηγοὶ ἵνα ἀπολυθῆτε.
– ²have sent ¹The ³prætors   that   ye may be released.

νῦν οὖν ἐξελθόντες πορεύεσθε ἐν εἰρήνῃ.
Now therefore going forth   proceed   in   peace.

37 ὁ δὲ Παῦλος ἔφη πρὸς αὐτούς·
– But   Paul   said   to   them:

δείραντες ἡμᾶς δημοσίᾳ ἀκατακρίτους,
Having beaten   us   publicly   uncondemned,

ἀνθρώπους Ῥωμαίους ὑπάρχοντας, ἔβαλαν
men   ¹Romans   ¹being,   they threw [us]

εἰς φυλακήν· καὶ νῦν λάθρα ἡμᾶς ἐκβάλ-
into   prison;   and now   secretly   us   they

λουσιν; οὐ γάρ, ἀλλὰ ἐλθόντες αὐτοὶ
expel?   No   indeed,   but   coming   [them]selves

ἡμᾶς ἐξαγαγέτωσαν. 38 ἀπήγγειλαν δὲ τοῖς
us   let them bring out.   And ²reported   ⁴to the

στρατηγοῖς οἱ ῥαβδοῦχοι τὰ ῥήματα ταῦτα.
²prætors ¹the ³tipstaffs   these words.

ἐφοβήθησαν δὲ ἀκούσαντες ὅτι Ῥωμαῖοί
And they were afraid   hearing   that   Romans

εἰσιν, 39 καὶ ἐλθόντες παρεκάλεσαν
they are(were),   and   coming   besought

αὐτούς, καὶ ἐξαγαγόντες ἠρώτων ἀπελθεῖν
them,   and   bringing out   asked   to go away

ἀπὸ τῆς πόλεως. 40 ἐξελθόντες δὲ ἀπὸ
from   the   city.   And going out   from

τῆς φυλακῆς εἰσῆλθον πρὸς τὴν Λυδίαν,
the   prison   they entered   to [the]   –   Lydia,
        house of]

καὶ ἰδόντες παρεκάλεσαν τοὺς ἀδελφοὺς
and   seeing   they exhorted   the   brothers

καὶ ἐξῆλθαν.
and   went forth.

Chapter 17

Διοδεύσαντες δὲ τὴν Ἀμφίπολιν καὶ
And travelling through   –   Amphipolis   and

τὴν Ἀπολλωνίαν ἦλθον εἰς Θεσσαλονίκην,
–   Apollonia   they came to   Thessalonica,

ὅπου ἦν συναγωγὴ τῶν Ἰουδαίων. 2 κατὰ
where was a synagogue of the   Jews.   according to

δὲ τὸ εἰωθὸς τῷ Παύλῳ εἰσῆλθεν πρὸς
And the   custom   – with Paul⁹   he entered   to

αὐτούς, καὶ ἐπὶ σάββατα τρία διελέξατο
them,   and   on   sabbaths   three   lectured

αὐτοῖς ἀπὸ τῶν γραφῶν, 3 διανοίγων
to them   from   the   scriptures,   opening up

καὶ παρατιθέμενος ὅτι τὸν χριστὸν ἔδει
and setting before [them]   that   ¹the   ¹it behoved

παθεῖν καὶ ἀναστῆναι ἐκ νεκρῶν, καὶ
to suffer   and   to rise again   out of [the] dead,   and

ὅτι οὗτός ἐστιν ὁ χριστός, ὁ Ἰησοῦς,
that   this   is(was)   the   Christ,   –   Jesus,

ὃν ἐγὼ καταγγέλλω ὑμῖν. 4 καί τινες
whom   I   announce   to you.   And   some

ἐξ αὐτῶν ἐπείσθησαν καὶ προσεκληρώθησαν
of   them   were persuaded   and   threw in their lot

τῷ Παύλῳ καὶ τῷ Σιλᾷ, τῶν τε
–   with Paul   and   –   Silas,   both of the

σεβομένων Ἑλλήνων πλῆθος πολύ, γυναικῶν τε
worshipping   Greeks   ²multitude ¹a   much   and of ²women (great),

τῶν πρώτων οὐκ ὀλίγαι. 5 Ζηλώσαντες δὲ
¹the   ²chief   not   a few.   But becoming jealous

οἱ Ἰουδαῖοι καὶ προσλαβόμενοι τῶν
the   Jews   and   taking aside   of the

ἀγοραίων ἄνδρας τινὰς πονηροὺς καὶ
loungers in the   men   some   wicked   and
marketplace

ὀχλοποιήσαντες ἐθορύβουν τὴν πόλιν, καὶ
having gathered a   disturbed   the   city,   and
crowd

ἐπιστάντες τῇ οἰκίᾳ Ἰάσονος ἐζήτουν
coming on   the   house   of Jason   sought

αὐτοὺς προαγαγεῖν εἰς τὸν δῆμον· 6 μὴ
them   to bring forward   to   the   mob;   ¹not

εὑρόντες δὲ αὐτοὺς ἔσυρον Ἰάσονα καί
¹finding   ²but   them   they dragged   Jason   and

τινας ἀδελφοὺς ἐπὶ τοὺς πολιτάρχας,
some   brothers   to   the   politarchs,

βοῶντες ὅτι οἱ τὴν οἰκουμένην ἀναστατώ-
crying[,]   –   ²the   ⁴the   ³inhabited   ⁵having turned
     [ones]   earth

σαντες οὗτοι καὶ ἐνθάδε πάρεισιν, 7 οὓς
upside   ¹these   also   here   have arrived,   whom
down   men

ὑποδέδεκται Ἰάσων· καὶ οὗτοι πάντες
²has received   ¹Jason;   and   these   all

ἀπέναντι τῶν δογμάτων Καίσαρος
²contrary to   ¹the   ³decrees   ⁴of Cæsar

πράσσουσιν, βασιλέα ἕτερον λέγοντες εἶναι
¹act,   ⁴king   ³another   ¹saying   ²to be

Ἰησοῦν. 8 ἐτάραξαν δὲ τὸν ὄχλον καὶ
²Jesus.   And they troubled   the   crowd   and

τοὺς πολιτάρχας ἀκούοντας ταῦτα, 9 καὶ
the   politarchs   hearing   these things,   and

λαβόντες τὸ ἱκανὸν παρὰ τοῦ Ἰάσονος
taking   the   surety   from   –   Jason

καὶ τῶν λοιπῶν ἀπέλυσαν αὐτούς. 10 Οἱ δὲ
and   the   rest   released   them.   And the

ἀδελφοὶ εὐθέως διὰ νυκτὸς ἐξεπεμψαν
brothers   immediately   through [the] night   sent forth
        (during)

τόν τε Παῦλον καὶ τὸν Σιλᾶν εἰς Βέροιαν,
– both   Paul   and   –   Silas   to   Berœa,

οἵτινες παραγενόμενοι εἰς τὴν συναγωγὴν
who   having arrived   ²into   ¹the   synagogue

τῶν Ἰουδαίων ἀπῄεσαν· 11 οὗτοι δὲ ἦσαν
⁴of the   ⁵Jews   ¹went;   and these   were

εὐγενέστεροι τῶν ἐν Θεσσαλονίκῃ, οἵτινες
more noble [than] the [ones] in   Thessalonica,   who

ἐδέξαντο τὸν λόγον μετὰ πάσης προθυμίας,
received   the   word   with   all   eagerness,

[τὸ] καθ' ἡμέραν ἀνακρίνοντες τὰς γραφὰς
–   daily   examining   the   scriptures

εἰ ἔχοι ταῦτα οὕτως. 12 πολλοὶ μὲν
if   ²have(are) ¹these things   ³so.   Many   –

οὖν ἐξ αὐτῶν ἐπίστευσαν, καὶ τῶν
therefore   of   them   believed,   and   of the

Ἑλληνίδων γυναικῶν τῶν εὐσχημόνων καὶ
²Greek   ¹women   –   ³honourable   and

ἀνδρῶν οὐκ ὀλίγοι. 13 Ὡς δὲ ἔγνωσαν
of men   not   a few.   But when   ¹knew

οἱ ἀπὸ τῆς Θεσσαλονίκης Ἰουδαῖοι ὅτι
¹the   ²from   –   ⁴Thessalonica   ³Jews   that

καὶ ἐν τῇ Βεροίᾳ κατηγγέλη ὑπὸ τοῦ
also   in   –   Berœa   was announced   by   –

Παύλου ὁ λόγος τοῦ θεοῦ, ἦλθον κάκεῖ
Paul   the   word   – of God,   they came there also

σαλεύοντες καὶ ταράσσοντες τοὺς ὄχλους.
shaking   and   troubling   the   crowds.

King James Version

stirred up the people. 14And then immediately the brethren sent away Paul to go as it were to the sea: but Silas and Timotheus abode there still. 15And they that conducted Paul brought him unto Athens: and receiving a commandment unto Silas and Timotheus for to come to him with all speed, they departed.

16 Now while Paul waited for them at Athens, his spirit was stirred in him, when he saw the city wholly given to idolatry. 17 Therefore disputed he in the synagogue with the Jews, and with the devout persons, and in the market daily with them that met with him. 18 Then certain philosophers of the Epicureans, and of the Stoics, encountered him. And some said, What will this babbler say? other some, He seemeth to be a setter forth of strange gods: because he preached unto them Jesus, and the resurrection. 19And they took him, and brought him unto Areopagus, saying, May we know what this new doctrine, whereof thou speakest, is? 20 For thou bringest certain strange things to our ears: we would know therefore what these things mean. 21 (For all the Athenians, and strangers which were there, spent their time in nothing else, but either to tell or to hear some new thing.)

22 Then Paul stood in the midst of Mars' hill, and said, Ye men of Athens, I perceive that in all things ye are too superstitious. 23 For as I passed by, and beheld your devotions, I found an altar with this inscription, TO THE UNKNOWN GOD. Whom therefore ye ignorantly worship, him declare I unto you. 24 God that made the world and all things therein, seeing that he is Lord of heaven and earth, dwelleth not in temples made with hands; 25 Neither is worshipped with men's hands, as though he needed any thing, seeing he giveth to all life, and breath, and all things; 26And hath made of one blood all nations of men for to dwell on all the face of the earth, and hath determined the times before appointed, and the bounds of their habitation; 27 That they should seek the Lord, if haply they might feel after him, and find him, though he be not far from every one of us: 28 For in him we live, and move, and have our being; as certain also of your own poets have said, For we are also his offspring. 29 Forasmuch then as we are the offspring of God, we ought not to think that the Godhead is like unto gold, or silver, or stone, graven by art and man's device. 30And the times of this ignorance God winked at; but now commandeth all men every where to repent: 31 Because he hath appointed a day, in the which he will judge the world in righteousness by that man whom he hath ordained; whereof he hath given assurance unto all men, in that he hath raised him from the dead.

32 And when they heard of the resurrection of the dead, some mocked: and others said, We

New International Version

stirring them up. 14 The brothers immediately sent Paul to the coast, but Silas and Timothy stayed at Berea. 15 The men who accompanied Paul brought him to Athens and then left with instructions for Silas and Timothy to join him as soon as possible.

In Athens

16 While Paul was waiting for them in Athens, he was greatly distressed to see that the city was full of idols. 17 So he reasoned in the synagogue with the Jews and the God-fearing Greeks, as well as in the marketplace day by day with those who happened to be there. 18A group of Epicurean and Stoic philosophers began to dispute with him. Some of them asked, "What is this babbler trying to say?" Others remarked, "He seems to be advocating foreign gods." They said this because Paul was preaching about Jesus and the resurrection. 19 Then they took him and brought him to a meeting of the Areopagus, where they said to him, "May we know what this new teaching is that you are presenting? 20 You are bringing some strange ideas to our ears, and we want to know what they mean." 21 (All the Athenians and the foreigners who lived there spent their time doing nothing but talking about and listening to the latest ideas.)

22 Paul then stood up in the meeting of the Areopagus and said: "Men of Athens! I see that in every way you are very religious. 23 For as I walked around and observed your objects of worship, I even found an altar with this inscription: TO AN UNKNOWN GOD. Now what you worship as something unknown I am going to proclaim to you.

24 "The God who made the world and everything in it is the Lord of heaven and earth and does not live in temples built by hands. 25And he is not served by human hands, as if he needed anything, because he himself gives all men life and breath and everything else. 26 From one man he made every nation of men, that they should inhabit the whole earth; and he determined the times set for them and the exact places where they should live. 27 God did this so that men would seek him and perhaps reach out for him and find him, though he is not far from each one of us. 28 'For in him we live and move and have our being.' As some of your own poets have said, 'We are his children.'

29 "Therefore since we are God's children, we should not think that the divine being is like gold or silver or stone—an image made by man's design and skill. 30 In the past God overlooked such ignorance, but now he commands all people everywhere to repent. 31 For he has set a day when he will judge the world with justice by the man he has appointed. He has given proof of this to all men by raising him from the dead."

32 When they heard about the resurrection of the dead, some of them sneered, but others said, "We want to hear you again on this sub-

14 εὐθέως δὲ τότε τὸν Παῦλον ἐξαπέστειλαν
So immediately then – ²Paul ¹sent away

οἱ ἀδελφοὶ πορεύεσθαι ἕως ἐπὶ τὴν
¹the ²brothers to go as far as to the

θάλασσαν· ὑπέμεινάν τε ὅ τε Σιλᾶς καὶ
sea; ¹but ²remained – ²both ³Silas ⁴and

ὁ Τιμόθεος ἐκεῖ. **15** οἱ δὲ καθιστάνοντες
– ²Timothy ⁷there. And the [ones] conducting

τὸν Παῦλον ἤγαγον ἕως ᾿Αθηνῶν, καὶ
– Paul brought [him] as far as Athens, and

λαβόντες ἐντολὴν πρὸς τὸν Σιλᾶν καὶ τὸν
receiving a command to – Silas and –

Τιμόθεον ἵνα ὡς τάχιστα ἔλθωσιν πρὸς
Timothy that as quickly they should to
[as possible] come

αὐτὸν ἐξῄεσαν.
him they departed.

16 ᾿Εν δὲ ταῖς ᾿Αθήναις ἐκδεχομένου
And in – Athens awaiting
=while Paul awaited them,

αὐτοὺς τοῦ Παύλου, παρωξύνετο τὸ πνεῦμα
them – Paul,* ⁴was provoked ¹the ²spirit

αὐτοῦ ἐν αὐτῷ θεωροῦντος κατείδωλον
³of him in him beholding ⁴full of images

οὖσαν τὴν πόλιν. **17** διελέγετο μὲν οὖν
²being ¹the ²city. He addressed –* therefore

ἐν τῇ συναγωγῇ τοῖς ᾿Ιουδαίοις καὶ
in the synagogue the Jews and

τοῖς σεβομένοις καὶ ἐν τῇ ἀγορᾷ κατὰ
the [ones] worshipping and in the marketplace –

πᾶσαν ἡμέραν πρὸς τοὺς παρατυγχάνοντας.
every day to the [ones] chancing to be [there].

18 τινὲς δὲ καὶ τῶν ᾿Επικουρείων καὶ
But some also of the Epicurean and

Στωικῶν φιλοσόφων συνέβαλλον αὐτῷ, καὶ
Stoic philosophers fell in with him, and

τινες ἔλεγον· τί ἂν θέλοι ὁ σπερμολόγος
some said: What may wish – ²ignorant plagiarist

οὗτος λέγειν; οἱ δέ· ξένων δαιμονίων
¹this to say? And others [said]: Of foreign demons

δοκεῖ καταγγελεὺς εἶναι· ὅτι τὸν ᾿Ιησοῦν
he seems an announcer to be; because – Jesus

καὶ τὴν ἀνάστασιν εὐηγγελίζετο. **19** ἐπιλα-
and the resurrection he preached. taking

βόμενοι δὲ αὐτοῦ ἐπὶ τὸν ῎Αρειον πάγον
hold And of him to the Areopagus

ἤγαγον, λέγοντες· δυνάμεθα γνῶναι τίς
they led [him], saying: Can we to know what

ἡ καινὴ αὕτη ἡ ὑπὸ σοῦ λαλουμένη
¹this ⁴new – ⁴by ⁴thee ⁴being spoken

διδαχή; **20** ξενίζοντα γάρ τινα εἰσφέρεις
⁴teaching [is]? for ⁴startling things ⁴some thou bringest in

εἰς τὰς ἀκοὰς ἡμῶν· βουλόμεθα θεροφερε
to the ears of us; we are minded therefore

γνῶναι τίνα θέλει ταῦτα εἶναι. **21** ᾿Αθηναῖοι
to know what wishes these things to be. ²Athenians

δὲ πάντες καὶ οἱ ἐπιδημοῦντες ξένοι εἰς
Now ¹all ²and ⁴the ⁴dwelling ⁴strangers ⁸for

οὐδὲν ἕτερον ηὐκαίρουν ἢ λέγειν τι ἢ
²nothing ¹different ⁷have leisure either ⁸to say something or

ἀκούειν τι καινότερον. **22** Σταθεὶς δὲ
to hear something newer. And standing

Παῦλος ἐν μέσῳ τοῦ ᾿Αρείου πάγου
¹Paul ¹in ²[the] midst ²of the ⁴Areopagus

ἔφη· ἄνδρες ᾿Αθηναῖοι, κατὰ πάντα ὡς
said: Men Athenians, in everything how

δεισιδαιμονεστέρους ὑμᾶς θεωρῶ. **23** διερχόμενος
very religious ²you ¹I behold. passing along

γὰρ καὶ ἀναθεωρῶν τὰ σεβάσματα ὑμῶν
For and looking up at the objects of worship of you

εὗρον καὶ βωμὸν ἐν ᾧ ἐπεγέγραπτο·
I found also an altar in which had been inscribed:

ΑΓΝΩΣΤΩ ΘΕΩ. ὃ οὖν ἀγνοοῦντες
TO AN UNKNOWN GOD. What therefore being ignorant

εὐσεβεῖτε, τοῦτο ἐγὼ καταγγέλλω ὑμῖν.
ye reverence, this I announce to you.

24 ὁ θεὸς ὁ ποιήσας τὸν κόσμον καὶ
The God the [one] having made the world and

πάντα τὰ ἐν αὐτῷ, οὗτος οὐρανοῦ καὶ
all the things in it, this one ⁴of heaven ⁴and

γῆς ὑπάρχων κύριος οὐκ ἐν χειροποιήτοις
³of earth ¹being ²lord ³not ⁴in ⁴hand-made

ναοῖς κατοικεῖ, **25** οὐδὲ ὑπὸ χειρῶν
⁴shrines ¹dwells, nor ⁸by ⁸hands

ἀνθρωπίνων θεραπεύεται προσδεόμενός
³human ¹is served having need

τινος, αὐτὸς διδοὺς πᾶσι ζωὴν καὶ πνοὴν
of anything, he giving to all life and breath

καὶ τὰ πάντα· **26** ἐποίησέν τε ἐξ ἑνὸς
and – all things; and he made of one

πᾶν ἔθνος ἀνθρώπων κατοικεῖν ἐπὶ παντὸς
every nation of men to dwell on all

προσώπου τῆς γῆς, ὁρίσας προστεταγμένους
[the] face of the earth, fixing having been appointed

καιροὺς καὶ τὰς ὁροθεσίας τῆς κατοικίας
seasons and the boundaries of the dwelling

αὐτῶν, **27** ζητεῖν τὸν θεόν, εἰ ἄρα γε
of them, to seek – God, if perchance

ψηλαφήσειαν αὐτὸν καὶ εὕροιεν, καί γε
they might feel after him and might find, though

οὐ μακρὰν ἀπὸ ἑνὸς ἑκάστου ἡμῶν
²not ³far ⁴from ⁵one ⁵each ⁷of us

ὑπάρχοντα. **28** ἐν αὐτῷ γὰρ ζῶμεν καὶ
¹being. ³in ⁴him ¹For ²we live and

κινούμεθα καὶ ἐσμέν, ὡς καὶ τινες τῶν
move and are, as indeed some of the

καθ᾿ ὑμᾶς ποιητῶν εἰρήκασιν· τοῦ γὰρ
⁴among ⁴you ¹poets have said: ⁴of him ¹For

καὶ γένος ἐσμέν. **29** γένος οὖν ὑπάρχοντες
²also ⁴offspring ⁴we are. Offspring therefore being

τοῦ θεοῦ οὐκ ὀφείλομεν νομίζειν, χρυσῷ
– of God we ought not to suppose, ¹to gold

ἢ ἀργύρῳ ἢ λίθῳ, χαράγματι τέχνης
⁸or ⁷to silver ⁸or ⁸to stone, ¹⁰to an ¹¹of art
engraved work

καὶ ἐνθυμήσεως ἀνθρώπου, τὸ θεῖον εἶναι
¹²and ¹³of meditation ¹⁴of man, ¹the ²divine ⁴to be
nature

ὅμοιον. **30** τοὺς μὲν οὖν χρόνους τῆς
¹like. ²The ⁴so ⁴then ³times –

ἀγνοίας ὑπεριδὼν ὁ θεὸς τὰ νῦν
¹of ignorance ²having – ²God – now
overlooked

ἀπαγγέλλει τοῖς ἀνθρώποις πάντας πανταχοῦ
declares – to men all men everywhere

μετανοεῖν, **31** καθότι ἔστησεν ἡμέραν ἐν
to repent, because he set a day in

ᾗ μέλλει κρίνειν τὴν οἰκουμένην ἐν
which he is about to judge the inhabited earth in

δικαιοσύνῃ, ἐν ἀνδρὶ ᾧ ὥρισεν, πίστιν
righteousness, by a man whom he desig- ²a
nated, . guarantee

παρασχὼν πᾶσιν ἀναστήσας αὐτὸν ἐκ
¹offering to all having raised up him out of

νεκρῶν. **32** ἀκούσαντες δὲ ἀνάστασιν
[the] dead. And hearing [of] a resurrection

νεκρῶν, οἱ μὲν ἐχλεύαζον, οἱ δὲ εἶπαν·
of dead some scoffed, others said:
persons,

ἀκουσόμεθά σου περὶ τούτου καὶ πάλιν.
We will hear thee concerning this also again.

* See note on ch. 12. 5.

King James Version

will hear thee again of this *matter* 33 So Paul departed from among them. 34 Howbeit certain men clave unto him, and believed: among the which *was* Dionysius the Areopagite, and a woman named Damaris, and others with them.

18 After these things Paul departed from Athens, and came to Corinth; 2And found a certain Jew named Aquila, born in Pontus, lately come from Italy, with his wife Priscilla, (because that Claudius had commanded all Jews to depart from Rome,) and came unto them. 3And because he was of the same craft, he abode with them, and wrought: (for by their occupation they were tentmakers.) 4And he reasoned in the synagogue every sabbath, and persuaded the Jews and the Greeks. 5And when Silas and Timotheus were come from Macedonia, Paul was pressed in the spirit, and testified to the Jews *that* Jesus *was* Christ. 6And when they opposed themselves, and blasphemed, he shook *his* raiment, and said unto them, Your blood *be* upon your own heads; I *am* clean: from henceforth I will go unto the Gentiles.

7 And he departed thence, and entered into a certain *man's* house, named Justus, *one* that worshipped God, whose house joined hard to the synagogue. 8And Crispus, the chief ruler of the synagogue, believed on the Lord with all his house; and many of the Corinthians hearing believed, and were baptized. 9 Then spake the Lord to Paul in the night by a vision, Be not afraid, but speak, and hold not thy peace: 10 For I am with thee, and no man shall set on thee to hurt thee: for I have much people in this city. 11And he continued *there* a year and six months, teaching the word of God among them.

12 And when Gallio was the deputy of Achaia, the Jews made insurrection with one accord against Paul, and brought him to the judgment seat, 13 Saying, This *fellow* persuadeth men to worship God contrary to the law. 14And when Paul was now about to open *his* mouth, Gallio said unto the Jews, If it were a matter of wrong or wicked lewdness, O *ye* Jews, reason would that I should bear with you: 15 But if it be a question of words and names, and *of* your law, look ye *to it;* for I will be no judge of such *matters.* 16And he drave them from the judgment seat. 17 Then all the Greeks took Sosthenes, the chief ruler of the synagogue, and beat *him* before the judgment seat. And Gallio cared for none of those things.

18 And Paul *after this* tarried *there* yet a good while, and then took his leave of the brethren, and sailed thence into Syria, and with

New International Version

ject." 33At that, Paul left the Council. 34A few men became followers of Paul and believed. Among them was Dionysius, a member of the Areopagus, also a woman named Damaris, and a number of others.

In Corinth

18 After this, Paul left Athens and went to Corinth. 2 There he met a Jew named Aquila, a native of Pontus, who had recently come from Italy with his wife Priscilla, because Claudius had ordered all the Jews to leave Rome. Paul went to see them, 3 and because he was a tentmaker as they were, he stayed and worked with them. 4 Every Sabbath he reasoned in the synagogue, trying to persuade Jews and Greeks.

5 When Silas and Timothy came from Macedonia, Paul devoted himself exclusively to preaching, testifying to the Jews that Jesus was the Christ.[b] 6 But when the Jews opposed Paul and became abusive, he shook out his clothes in protest and said to them, "Your blood be on your own heads! I am clear of my responsibility. From now on I will go to the Gentiles."

7 Then Paul left the synagogue and went next door to the house of Titius Justus, a worshiper of God. 8 Crispus, the synagogue ruler, and his entire household believed in the Lord; and many of the Corinthians who heard him believed and were baptized.

9 One night the Lord spoke to Paul in a vision: "Do not be afraid; keep on speaking, do not be silent. 10 For I am with you, and no one is going to attack and harm you, because I have many people in this city." 11 So Paul stayed for a year and a half, teaching them the word of God.

12 While Gallio was proconsul of Achaia, the Jews made a united attack on Paul and brought him into court. 13 "This man," they charged, "is persuading the people to worship God in ways contrary to the law."

14 Just as Paul was about to speak, Gallio said to the Jews, "If you Jews were making a complaint about some misdemeanor or serious crime, it would be reasonable for me to listen to you. 15 But since it involves questions about words and names and your own law—settle the matter yourselves. I will not be a judge of such things." 16 So he had them ejected from the court. 17 Then they all turned on Sosthenes, the synagogue ruler, and beat him in front of the court. But Gallio showed no concern whatever.

Priscilla, Aquila and Apollos

18 Paul stayed on in Corinth for some time. Then he left the brothers and sailed for Syria,

Greek Interlinear

33 οὕτως   ὁ   Παῦλος   ἐξῆλθεν   ἐκ   μέσου
Thus   -   Paul   went forth from [the] midst
αὐτῶν.   34 τινὲς   δὲ   ἄνδρες   κολληθέντες
of them.   But some   men   adhering
αὐτῷ   ἐπίστευσαν,   ἐν   οἷς   καὶ   Διονύσιος
to him   believed,   among whom both   Dionysius

ὁ   ’Αρεοπαγίτης   καὶ   γυνὴ   ὀνόματι   Δαμαρὶς
the   Areopagite   and a woman by name   Damaris
καὶ   ἕτεροι   σὺν   αὐτοῖς.
and   others   with   them.

Chapter 18

Μετὰ   ταῦτα   χωρισθεὶς   ἐκ   τῶν
After   these things   departing   out of   -
’Αθηνῶν   ἦλθεν   εἰς   Κόρινθον.   2 καὶ
Athens   he came   to   Corinth.   And
εὑρών   τινα   ’Ιουδαῖον   ὀνόματι   ’Ακύλαν,
finding a certain   Jew   by name   Aquila,
Ποντικὸν   τῷ   γένει,   προσφάτως   ἐληλυθότα
belonging to   -   by race,   recently   having come
Pontus
ἀπὸ   τῆς   ’Ιταλίας,   καὶ   Πρίσκιλλαν   γυναῖκα
from   -   Italy,   and   Priscilla   wife
αὐτοῦ,   διὰ   τὸ   διατεταχέναι   Κλαύδιον
of him, because of the to have commanded Claudius[b]
=because Claudius had commanded
χωρίζεσθαι   πάντας   τοὺς   ’Ιουδαίους   ἀπὸ
to depart   all   the   Jews   from
τῆς   ’Ρώμης,   προσῆλθεν   αὐτοῖς,   3 καὶ
-   Rome,   he came to   them,   and
διὰ   τὸ   ὁμότεχνον   εἶναι   ἔμενεν   παρ’
because of the of the same trade to be[b] he remained with
=because [he] was of the same trade
αὐτοῖς,   καὶ   ἠργάζοντο·   ἦσαν   γὰρ   σκηνοποιοὶ
them,   and they wrought; for they were   tentmakers
τῇ   τέχνῃ.   4 διελέγετο   δὲ   ἐν   τῇ   συναγωγῇ
- by trade.   And he lectured in the   synagogue
κατὰ   πᾶν   σάββατον,   ἔπειθέν   τε   ’Ιουδαίους
on   every   sabbath,   he persuaded both   Jews
καὶ   ῞Ελληνας.   5 ῾Ως   δὲ   κατῆλθον   ἀπὸ
and   Greeks.   And when came down from
τῆς   Μακεδονίας   ὅ   τε   Σιλᾶς   καὶ   ὁ
-   Macedonia   -   both   Silas   and   -
Τιμόθεος,   συνείχετο   τῷ   λόγῳ   ὁ   Παῦλος,
Timothy,   was pressed   by the word   -   Paul,
διαμαρτυρόμενος   τοῖς   ’Ιουδαίοις   εἶναι   τὸν
solemnly witnessing to the   Jews   to be   the
=that Jesus was the Christ.
χριστὸν   ’Ιησοῦν.   6 ἀντιτασσομένων   δὲ   αὐτῶν
Christ   Jesus.   But resisting   them
=when they resisted and blasphemed
καὶ   βλασφημούντων   ἐκτιναξάμενος   τὰ   ἱμάτια
and   blaspheming[a] shaking off   the(his) garments
εἶπεν   πρὸς   αὐτούς·   τὸ   αἷμα   ὑμῶν   ἐπὶ
he said   to   them: The blood of you   on
τὴν   κεφαλὴν   ὑμῶν·   καθαρὸς   ἐγὼ   ἀπὸ
the   head   of you;   clean   I   from
τοῦ   νῦν   εἰς   τὰ   ἔθνη   πορεύσομαι.   7 καὶ
-   now   to   the nations will go.   And
μεταβὰς   ἐκεῖθεν   ἦλθεν   εἰς   οἰκίαν   τινὸς
removing   thence   he went into [the] house of one
ὀνόματι   Τιτίου   ’Ιούστου   σεβομένου   τὸν
by name   Titius   Justus   worshipping   -
θεόν,   οὗ   ἡ   οἰκία   ἦν   συνομοροῦσα   τῇ
God, of whom the house was being next door to the
συναγωγῇ.   8 Κρίσπος   δὲ   ὁ   ἀρχισυνάγωγος
synagogue.   Now Crispus the   synagogue ruler
ἐπίστευσεν   τῷ   κυρίῳ   σὺν   ὅλῳ   τῷ   οἴκῳ
believed   the Lord with all the household
αὐτοῦ,   καὶ   πολλοὶ   τῶν   Κορινθίων   ἀκούοντες
of him,   and   many of the   Corinthians   hearing
ἐπίστευον   καὶ   ἐβαπτίζοντο.   9 Εἶπεν   δὲ
believed   and   were baptized.   And said

ὁ   κύριος   ἐν   νυκτὶ   δι’   ὁράματος   τῷ
the Lord   in [the] night through a vision   -
Παύλῳ·   μὴ   φοβοῦ,   ἀλλὰ   λάλει   καὶ
to Paul: Do not fear,   but   speak   and
μὴ   σιωπήσῃς,   10 διότι   ἐγώ   εἰμι   μετὰ   σοῦ
keep not silence,   because   I   am   with   thee
καὶ   οὐδεὶς   ἐπιθήσεταί   σοι   τοῦ   κακῶσαί
and   no one   shall set on   thee   -   to illtreat[d]
σε,   διότι   λαός   ἐστί   μοι   πολὺς   ἐν
thee,   because   people   is   to me   much[a]   in
=I have a great people
τῇ   πόλει   ταύτῃ.   11 ’Εκάθισεν   δὲ   ἐνιαυτὸν
this city.   And he sat   a year
καὶ   μῆνας   ἓξ   διδάσκων   ἐν   αὐτοῖς   τὸν
and   months   six   teaching   among them   the
λόγον   τοῦ   θεοῦ.   12 Γαλλίωνος   δὲ
word   -   of God.   And Gallio
=when Gallio
ἀνθυπάτου   ὄντος   τῆς   ’Αχαΐας   κατεπέστησαν
proconsul   being[a]   - of Achaia   [a]set on
was proconsul
ὁμοθυμαδὸν   οἱ   ’Ιουδαῖοι   τῷ   Παύλῳ   καὶ
[a]with one mind [1]the [2]Jews   -   Paul   and
ἤγαγον   αὐτὸν   ἐπὶ   τὸ   βῆμα,   13 λέγοντες
brought   him   to   the   tribunal,   saying[,]
ὅτι   παρὰ]   τὸν   νόμον   ἀναπείθει   οὗτος
- [differently] from [1]the [2]law   [1]urges [3]This man
τοὺς   ἀνθρώπους   σέβεσθαι   τὸν   θεόν.
-   [2]men   [4]to worship   -   [3]God.
14 μέλλοντος   δὲ   τοῦ   Παύλου   ἀνοίγειν   τὸ
And being about   -   Paul[a]   to open the(his)
=when Paul was about
στόμα   εἶπεν   ὁ   Γαλλίων   πρὸς   τοὺς
mouth   said   -   Gallio   to   the
’Ιουδαίους·   εἰ   μὲν   ἦν   ἀδίκημά   τι
Jews: If indeed it was crime   some
ἢ   ῥᾳδιούργημα   πονηρόν,   ὦ   ’Ιουδαῖοι,
or   villainy   evil,   O   Jews,
κατὰ   λόγον   ἂν   ἀνεσχόμην   ὑμῶν·   15 εἰ   δὲ   ζητή-
rightly   I would endure you;   but if ques-
ματά   ἐστιν   περὶ   λόγου   καὶ   ὀνομάτων   καὶ
tions it is concerning a word and   names   and
νόμου   τοῦ   καθ’   ὑμᾶς,   ὄψεσθε   αὐτοί·
law the according to you, ye will see [your]selves;
=your law,
κριτὴς   ἐγὼ   τούτων   οὐ   βούλομαι   εἶναι.
a judge [1]I [2]of these things [3]do not intend [4]to be.
16 καὶ   ἀπήλασεν   αὐτοὺς   ἀπὸ   τοῦ   βήματος.
And he drove away   them from the   tribunal.
17 ἐπιλαβόμενοι   δὲ   πάντες   Σωσθένην   τὸν
But [2]seizing   [1]all   Sosthenes   the
ἀρχισυνάγωγον   ἔτυπτον   ἔμπροσθεν   τοῦ
synagogue ruler they struck [him] in front of the
βήματος·   καὶ   οὐδὲν   τούτων   τῷ   Γαλλίωνι
tribunal;   and not one of these things - [2]to Gallio
ἔμελεν.   18 ῾Ο   δὲ   Παῦλος   ἔτι   προσμείνας
[1]mattered.   But   Paul yet having remained
ἡμέρας   ἱκανάς,   τοῖς   ἀδελφοῖς   ἀποταξάμενος
days   many,   to the   brothers   bidding farewell
ἐξέπλει   εἰς   τὴν   Συρίαν,   καὶ   σὺν   αὐτῷ
he sailed away to   -   Syria,   and   with   him

405

King James Version

him Priscilla and Aquila; having shorn *his* head in Cenchrea: for he had a vow. 19And he came to Ephesus, and left them there: but he himself entered into the synagogue, and reasoned with the Jews. 20 When they desired *him* to tarry longer time with them, he consented not; 21 But bade them farewell, saying, I must by all means keep this feast that cometh in Jerusalem: but I will return again unto you, if God will. And he sailed from Ephesus. 22And when he had landed at Cesarea, and gone up, and saluted the church, he went down to Antioch. 23And after he had spent some time *there,* he departed, and went over *all* the country of Galatia and Phrygia in order, strengthening all the disciples.

24 And a certain Jew named Apollos, born at Alexandria, an eloquent man, *and* mighty in the Scriptures, came to Ephesus. 25 This man was instructed in the way of the Lord; and being fervent in the spirit, he spake and taught diligently the things of the Lord, knowing only the baptism of John. 26And he began to speak boldly in the synagogue: whom when Aquila and Priscilla had heard, they took him unto *them,* and expounded unto him the way of God more perfectly. 27And when he was disposed to pass into Achaia, the brethren wrote, exhorting the disciples to receive him: who, when he was come, helped them much which had believed through grace: 28 For he mightily convinced the Jews, *and that* publicly, shewing by the Scriptures that Jesus was Christ.

19 And it came to pass, that, while Apollos was at Corinth, Paul having passed through the upper coasts came to Ephesus; and finding certain disciples, 2 He said unto them, Have ye received the Holy Ghost since ye believed? And they said unto him, We have not so much as heard whether there be any Holy Ghost. 3And he said unto them, Unto what then were ye baptized? And they said, Unto John's baptism. 4 Then said Paul, John verily baptized with the baptism of repentance, saying unto the people, that they should believe on him which should come after him, that is, on Christ Jesus. 5 When they heard *this,* they were baptized in the name of the Lord Jesus. 6And when Paul had laid *his* hands upon them, the Holy Ghost came on them; and they spake with tongues, and prophesied. 7And all the men were about twelve. 8And he went into the synagogue, and spake boldly for the space of three months, disputing and persuading the things concerning the kingdom of God. 9 But when divers were hardened, and believed not, but spake evil of that way before the multitude, he departed from them, and separated the disciples, disputing daily in the school of one Tyrannus. 10And this continued by the space of two years; so that all they which dwelt

New International Version

accompanied by Priscilla and Aquila. Before he sailed, he had his hair cut off at Cenchrea because of a vow he had taken. 19 They arrived at Ephesus, where Paul left Priscilla and Aquila. He himself went into the synagogue and reasoned with the Jews. 20 When they asked him to spend more time with them, he declined. 21 But as he left, he promised, "I will come back if it is God's will." Then he set sail from Ephesus.

22 When he landed at Caesarea, he went up and greeted the church and then went down to Antioch. 23After spending some time in Antioch, Paul set out from there and traveled from place to place throughout the region of Galatia and Phrygia, strengthening all the disciples.

24 Meanwhile a Jew named Apollos, a native of Alexandria, came to Ephesus. He was a learned man, with a thorough knowledge of the Scriptures. 25 He had been instructed in the way of the Lord, and he spoke with great fervor and taught about Jesus accurately, knowing only the baptism of John. 26 He began to speak boldly in the synagogue. When Priscilla and Aquila heard him, they invited him to their home and explained to him the way of God more adequately.

27 When Apollos wanted to go to Achaia, the brothers encouraged him and wrote to the disciples there to welcome him. On arriving, he was a great help to those who by grace had believed. 28 For he vigorously refuted the Jews in public debate, proving from the Scriptures that Jesus was the Christ.[c]

Paul in Ephesus

19 While Apollos was at Corinth, Paul took the road through the interior and arrived at Ephesus. There he found some disciples 2 and asked them, "Did you receive the Holy Spirit when you believed?"

They answered, "No, we have not even heard that there is a Holy Spirit."

3 So Paul asked, "Then what baptism did you receive?"

"John's baptism," they replied.

4 Paul said, "John's baptism was a baptism of repentance. He told the people to believe in the one coming after him, that is, in Jesus." 5 On hearing this, they were baptized into[d] the name of the Lord Jesus. 6 When Paul placed his hands on them, the Holy Spirit came on them, and they spoke in tongues[e] and prophesied. 7 There were about twelve men in all.

8 Paul entered the synagogue and spoke boldly there for three months, arguing persuasively about the kingdom of God. 9 But some of them became obstinate; they refused to believe and publicly maligned the Way. So Paul left them. He took the disciples with him and had discussions daily in the lecture hall of Tyrannus. 10 This went on for two years, so that all the

[c] Or *Messiah.* [d] Or *in.* [e] Or *other languages.*

Greek Interlinear

Πρίσκιλλα καὶ 'Ακύλας, κειράμενος ἐν
Priscilla and Aquila, having shorn in

Κεγχρεαῖς τὴν κεφαλήν· εἶχεν γὰρ εὐχήν.
Cenchrea the(his) head; for he had a vow.

19 κατήντησαν δὲ εἰς "Εφεσον, κἀκείνους
And they came down to Ephesus, and those

κατέλιπεν αὐτοῦ, αὐτὸς δὲ εἰσελθὼν εἰς
he left there, but he entering into

τὴν συναγωγὴν διελέξατο τοῖς 'Ιουδαίοις.
the synagogue lectured to the Jews.

20 ἐρωτώντων δὲ αὐτῶν ἐπὶ πλείονα
And asking them⁰ over a more(longer)
=as they asked

χρόνον μεῖναι οὐκ ἐπένευσεν, **21** ἀλλὰ
time to remain he consented not, but

ἀποταξάμενος καὶ εἰπών· πάλιν ἀνακάμψω
bidding farewell and saying: Again I will return

πρὸς ὑμᾶς τοῦ θεοῦ θέλοντος, ἀνήχθη
to you - God willing,⁰ he set sail
=if God wills,

ἀπὸ τῆς 'Εφέσου, **22** καὶ κατελθὼν εἰς
from - Ephesus, and coming down to

Καισάρειαν, ἀναβὰς καὶ ἀσπασάμενος τὴν
Cæsarea, going up and greeting the

ἐκκλησίαν, κατέβη εἰς 'Αντιόχειαν, **23** καὶ
church, he went down to Antioch, and

ποιήσας χρόνον τινὰ ἐξῆλθεν, διερχόμενος
having spent time some he went forth, passing through

καθεξῆς τὴν Γαλατικὴν χώραν καὶ Φρυγίαν,
in order the Galatian country and Phrygia,

στηρίζων πάντας τοὺς μαθητάς.
confirming all the disciples.

24 'Ιουδαῖος δέ τις 'Απολλῶς ὀνόματι,
And a certain Jew Apollos by name,

'Αλεξανδρεὺς τῷ γένει, ἀνὴρ λόγιος,
an Alexandrian - by race, a man eloquent,

κατήντησεν εἰς "Εφεσον, δυνατὸς ὢν ἐν
came to Ephesus, powerful being in

ταῖς γραφαῖς. **25** οὗτος ἦν κατηχημένος
the scriptures. This man was orally instructed [in]

τὴν ὁδὸν τοῦ κυρίου, καὶ ζέων τῷ
the way of the Lord, and burning -

πνεύματι ἐλάλει καὶ ἐδίδασκεν ἀκριβῶς
in spirit he spoke and taught accurately

τὰ περὶ τοῦ 'Ιησοῦ, ἐπιστάμενος
the things concerning - Jesus, understanding

μόνον τὸ βάπτισμα 'Ιωάννου· **26** οὗτός τε
only the baptism of John; and this man

ἤρξατο παρρησιάζεσθαι ἐν τῇ συναγωγῇ.
began to speak boldly in the synagogue.

ἀκούσαντες δὲ αὐτοῦ Πρίσκιλλα καὶ
And hearing him Priscilla and

'Ακύλας προσελάβοντο αὐτὸν καὶ ἀκριβέστε-
Aquila took him and more accurate-

ρον αὐτῷ ἐξέθεντο τὴν ὁδὸν τοῦ θεοῦ.
ly to him explained the way - of God.

27 βουλομένου δὲ αὐτοῦ διελθεῖν εἰς τὴν
And intending him⁰ to go through into -
=when he intended

'Αχαΐαν, προτρεψάμενοι οἱ ἀδελφοὶ ἔγραψαν
Achaia, being encouraged the brothers wrote

τοῖς μαθηταῖς ἀποδέξασθαι αὐτόν· ὃς
to the disciples to welcome him; who

παραγενόμενος συνεβάλετο πολὺ τοῖς
arriving contributed much to the [ones]

πεπιστευκόσιν διὰ τῆς χάριτος· **28** εὐτόνως
having believed through - grace; ⁰vehemently

γὰρ τοῖς 'Ιουδαίοις διακατηλέγχετο δημοσίᾳ
¹for ⁴the ³Jews ²he confuted publicly

ἐπιδεικνὺς διὰ τῶν γραφῶν εἶναι τὸν
proving through the scriptures ¹to be ²the

χριστὸν 'Ιησοῦν.
⁴Christ ³Jesus.

Chapter 19

'Εγένετο δὲ ἐν τῷ τὸν 'Απολλῶ
Now it came to pass in the the Apollos was
=while Apollos was

εἶναι ἐν Κορίνθῳ Παῦλον διελθόντα τὰ
to be⁰⁰ in Corinth Paul having passed through the

ἀνωτερικὰ μέρη ἐλθεῖν εἰς "Εφεσον καὶ
higher parts to come⁰ to Ephesus and

εὑρεῖν τινας μαθητάς, **2** εἶπέν τε πρὸς
to find⁰ some disciples, and said to

αὐτούς· εἰ πνεῦμα ἅγιον ἐλάβετε πιστεύσαν-
them: If Spirit Holy ye received believ-

τες; οἱ δὲ πρὸς αὐτόν· ἀλλ' οὐδ' εἰ
ing? And they [said] to him: But ²not ¹if

πνεῦμα ἅγιον ἔστιν ἠκούσαμεν. **3** εἶπέν τε·
⁴Spirit ³Holy ⁵there is ¹we heard. And he said:

εἰς τί οὖν ἐβαπτίσθητε; οἱ δὲ εἶπαν·
To what therefore were ye baptized? And they said:

εἰς τὸ 'Ιωάννου βάπτισμα. **4** εἶπεν δὲ
To the of John baptism. And said

Παῦλος· 'Ιωάννης ἐβάπτισεν βάπτισμα μετα-
Paul: John baptized [with] a baptism of repent-

νοίας, τῷ λαῷ λέγων εἰς τὸν ἐρχόμενον
ance, to the ⁵people ¹saying ²in ³the [one] ⁴coming

μετ' αὐτὸν ἵνα πιστεύσωσιν, τοῦτ' ἔστιν
⁶after ¹⁰him ⁷that ⁸they should believe, this is

εἰς τὸν 'Ιησοῦν. **5** ἀκούσαντες δὲ ἐβαπτίσ-
in - Jesus. And hearing they were

θησαν εἰς τὸ ὄνομα τοῦ κυρίου 'Ιησοῦ.
baptized in the name of the Lord Jesus.

6 καὶ ἐπιθέντος αὐτοῖς τοῦ Παύλου χεῖρας
And laying on them - Paul hands⁰
=as Paul laid [his] hands on them

ἦλθε τὸ πνεῦμα τὸ ἅγιον ἐπ' αὐτούς,
came the Spirit the Holy on them,

ἐλάλουν τε γλώσσαις καὶ ἐπροφήτευον.
and they spoke in tongues and prophesied.

7 ἦσαν δὲ οἱ πάντες ἄνδρες ὡσεὶ δώδεκα.
And ⁴were ³the ¹all ²men about twelve.

8 Εἰσελθὼν δὲ εἰς τὴν συναγωγὴν
And entering into the synagogue

ἐπαρρησιάζετο ἐπὶ μῆνας τρεῖς διαλεγόμενος
he spoke boldly over months three lecturing

καὶ πείθων περὶ τῆς βασιλείας τοῦ θεοῦ.
and persuading concerning the· kingdom - of God.

9 ὡς δέ τινες ἐσκληρύνοντο καὶ ἠπείθουν
But as some were hardened and disobeyed

κακολογοῦντες τὴν ὁδὸν ἐνώπιον τοῦ
speaking ill [of] the way before the

πλήθους, ἀποστὰς ἀπ' αὐτῶν ἀφώρισεν
multitude, withdrawing from them he separated

τοὺς μαθητάς, καθ' ἡμέραν διαλεγόμενος
the disciples, daily lecturing

ἐν τῇ σχολῇ Τυράννου. **10** τοῦτο δὲ
in the school of Tyrannus. And this

ἐγένετο ἐπὶ ἔτη δύο, ὥστε πάντας τοὺς
happened over years two, so as all the
=so that all who inhabited

King James Version

in Asia heard the word of the Lord Jesus, both Jews and Greeks. 11And God wrought special miracles by the hands of Paul: 12 So that from his body were brought unto the sick handkerchiefs or aprons, and the diseases departed from them, and the evil spirits went out of them.

13 Then certain of the vagabond Jews, exorcists, took upon them to call over them which had evil spirits the name of the Lord Jesus, saying, We adjure you by Jesus whom Paul preacheth. 14And there were seven sons of one Sceva, a Jew, and chief of the priests, which did so. 15And the evil spirit answered and said, Jesus I know, and Paul I know; but who are ye? 16And the man in whom the evil spirit was leaped on them, and overcame them, and prevailed against them, so that they fled out of that house naked and wounded. 17And this was known to all the Jews and Greeks also dwelling at Ephesus; and fear fell on them all, and the name of the Lord Jesus was magnified. 18And many that believed came, and confessed, and shewed their deeds. 19 Many of them also which used curious arts brought their books together, and burned them before all men: and they counted the price of them, and found it fifty thousand pieces of silver. 20 So mightily grew the word of God and prevailed.

21 After these things were ended, Paul purposed in the spirit, when he had passed through Macedonia and Achaia, to go to Jerusalem, saying, After I have been there, I must also see Rome. 22 So he sent into Macedonia two of them that ministered unto him, Timotheus and Erastus; but he himself stayed in Asia for a season. 23And the same time there arose no small stir about that way. 24 For a certain man named Demetrius, a silversmith, which made silver shrines for Diana, brought no small gain unto the craftsmen; 25 Whom he called together with the workmen of like occupation, and said, Sirs, ye know that by this craft we have our wealth. 26 Moreover ye see and hear, that not alone at Ephesus, but almost throughout all Asia, this Paul hath persuaded and turned away much people, saying that they be no gods, which are made with hands: 27 So that not only this our craft is in danger to be set at nought; but also that the temple of the great goddess Diana should be despised, and her magnificence should be destroyed, whom all Asia and the world worshippeth. 28And when they heard these sayings, they were full of wrath, and cried out, saying,

New International Version

Jews and Greeks who lived in the province of Asia heard the word of the Lord.

11 God did extraordinary miracles through Paul. 12 Handkerchiefs and aprons that had touched him were taken to the sick, and their illnesses were cured and the evil spirits left them.

13 Some Jews who went around driving out evil spirits tried to invoke the name of the Lord Jesus over those who were demon-possessed. They would say, "In the name of Jesus whom Paul preaches, I command you to come out." 14 Seven sons of Sceva, a Jewish chief priest, were doing this. 15 The evil spirit answered them, "Jesus I know and Paul I know, but who are you?" 16 Then the man who had the evil spirit jumped on them and overpowered them all. He gave them such a beating that they ran out of the house naked and bleeding.

17 When this became known to the Jews and Greeks living in Ephesus, they were all seized with fear, and the name of the Lord Jesus was held in high honor. 18 Many of those who believed now came and openly confessed their evil deeds. 19A number who had practiced sorcery brought their scrolls together and burned them publicly. When they calculated the value of the scrolls, the total came to fifty thousand drachmas.[f] 20 In this way the word of the Lord spread widely and grew in power.

21 After all this had happened, Paul decided to go to Jerusalem, passing through Macedonia and Achaia. "After I have been there," he said, "I must visit Rome also." 22 He sent two of his helpers, Timothy and Erastus, to Macedonia, while he stayed in the province of Asia a little longer.

The riot in Ephesus

23 About that time there arose a great disturbance about the Way. 24A silversmith named Demetrius, who made silver shrines of Artemis, brought in no little business for the craftsmen. 25 He called them together, along with the workmen in related trades, and said: "Men, you know we receive a good income from this business. 26And you see and hear how this fellow Paul has convinced and led astray large numbers of people here in Ephesus and in practically the whole province of Asia. He says that man-made gods are no gods at all. 27 There is danger not only that 'our trade will lose its good name, but also that the temple of the great goddess Artemis will be discredited, and the goddess herself, who is worshiped throughout the province of Asia and the world, will be robbed of her divine majesty."

28 When they heard this, they were furious and began shouting: "Great is Artemis of the

[f] A drachma was about a day's wage.

Greek Interlinear

κατοικοῦντας τὴν Ἀσίαν ἀκοῦσαι τὸν
[ones] inhabiting – Asia to hear[b] the
Asia heard

λόγον τοῦ κυρίου, Ἰουδαίους τε καὶ
word of the Lord, ²Jews ¹both and

Ἕλληνας. 11 Δυνάμεις τε οὐ τὰς τυχούσας
Greeks. And powerful deeds not the ordinary

ὁ θεὸς ἐποίει διὰ τῶν χειρῶν Παύλου,
– God did through the hands of Paul,

12 ὥστε καὶ ἐπὶ τοὺς ἀσθενοῦντας
so as even onto the [ones] ailing
=so that there were even brought away from his skin hand-

ἀποφέρεσθαι ἀπὸ τοῦ χρωτὸς αὐτοῦ
to be brought away from the skin of him
kerchiefs or aprons onto those who ailed and the diseases were rid

σουδάρια ἢ σιμικίνθια καὶ ἀπαλλάσσεσθαι
handkerchiefs or aprons and to be rid
from them, and the evil spirits went out.

ἀπ' αὐτῶν τὰς νόσους, τά τε πνεύματα
from them the diseases, and the spirits

τὰ πονηρὰ ἐκπορεύεσθαι. 13 Ἐπεχείρησαν δέ
evil to go out. But ²attempted

τινες καὶ τῶν περιερχομένων Ἰουδαίων
¹some ²also ³of the ⁴strolling ⁵Jews

ἐξορκιστῶν ὀνομάζειν ἐπὶ τοὺς ἔχοντας
⁶exorcists to name over the [ones] having

τὰ πνεύματα τὰ πονηρὰ τὸ ὄνομα τοῦ
the spirits – evil the name of the

κυρίου Ἰησοῦ λέγοντες· ὁρκίζω ὑμᾶς τὸν
Lord Jesus saying: · I exorcise you [by] –

Ἰησοῦν ὃν Παῦλος κηρύσσει. 14 ἦσαν δέ
Jesus whom Paul proclaims. And there were

τινος Σκευᾶ Ἰουδαίου ἀρχιερέως ἑπτὰ
²of one ¹Sceva ³a Jewish ⁴chief priest ⁵seven

υἱοὶ τοῦτο ποιοῦντες. 15 ἀποκριθὲν δὲ
⁶sons ⁷this ⁷doing. And answering

τὸ πνεῦμα τὸ πονηρὸν εἶπεν αὐτοῖς·
the spirit – evil said to them:

τὸν [μὲν] Ἰησοῦν γινώσκω καὶ τὸν
– ²indeed ¹Jesus I know and the

Παῦλον ἐπίσταμαι· ὑμεῖς δὲ τίνες ἐστέ;
Paul I understand; but ye who are?

16 καὶ ἐφαλόμενος ὁ ἄνθρωπος ἐπ' αὐτούς,
And ²leaping on ¹the ¹man ¹⁰on ¹¹them,

ἐν ᾧ ἦν τὸ πνεῦμα τὸ πονηρόν,
²in ¹whom ²was ³the ⁴spirit – ⁴evil,

κατακυριεύσας ἀμφοτέρων ἴσχυσεν κατ'
overmastering both was strong against

αὐτῶν, ὥστε γυμνοὺς καὶ τετραυματισμένους
them, so as naked and having been wounded
=so that they escaped out of that house naked and

ἐκφυγεῖν ἐκ τοῦ οἴκου ἐκείνου. 17 τοῦτο
to escape out of that house. this
wounded.

δὲ ἐγένετο γνωστὸν πᾶσιν Ἰουδαίοις τε
And became known to all ³Jews ¹both

καὶ Ἕλλησιν τοῖς κατοικοῦσιν τὴν Ἐφεσον,
and Greeks – inhabiting – Ephesus,

καὶ ἐπέπεσεν φόβος ἐπὶ πάντας αὐτούς,
and ²fell on ¹fear ³on ⁴all ⁵them,

καὶ ἐμεγαλύνετο τὸ ὄνομα τοῦ κυρίου
and was magnified the name of the Lord

Ἰησοῦ· 18 πολλοί τε τῶν πεπιστευκότων
Jesus; and many of the [ones] having believed

ἤρχοντο ἐξομολογούμενοι καὶ ἀναγγέλλοντες
came confessing and telling

τὰς πράξεις αὐτῶν. 19 ἱκανοὶ δὲ τῶν τὰ
the doings of them. And a consider- of the the
able number [ones]

περίεργα πραξάντων συνενέγκαντες τὰς βίβλους
curious things doing bringing together the rolls

κατέκαιον ἐνώπιον πάντων· καὶ συνεψήφισαν
burnt before all; and they reckoned up

τὰς τιμὰς αὐτῶν καὶ εὗρον ἀργυρίου μυριάδας
the prices of them and found [pieces] ¹thousand
²of silver

πέντε. 20 Οὕτως κατὰ κράτος τοῦ κυρίου
¹five. Thus by might ²of the ⁴Lord

ὁ λόγος ηὔξανεν καὶ ἴσχυεν.
¹the ³word increased and was strong.

21 Ὡς δὲ ἐπληρώθη ταῦτα, ἔθετο ὁ
And when were fulfilled these things, purposed –

Παῦλος ἐν τῷ πνεύματι διελθὼν τὴν
Paul in the(his) spirit passing through –

Μακεδονίαν καὶ Ἀχαΐαν πορεύεσθαι εἰς
Macedonia and Achaia to go to

Ἱεροσόλυμα, εἰπὼν ὅτι μετὰ τὸ γενέσθαι
Jerusalem, saying[,] – After the to become
= After I am

με ἐκεῖ δεῖ με καὶ Ῥώμην ἰδεῖν.
me[b] there it behoves me ²also ¹Rome ¹to see.

22 ἀποστείλας δὲ εἰς Μακεδονίαν δύο
And sending into Macedonia two

τῶν διακονούντων αὐτῷ, Τιμόθεον καὶ
of the [ones] ministering to him, Timothy and

Ἔραστον, αὐτὸς ἐπέσχεν χρόνον εἰς τὴν
Erastus, he delayed a time in –

Ἀσίαν. 23 Ἐγένετο δὲ κατὰ τὸν καιρὸν
Asia. Now there was about – time

ἐκεῖνον τάραχος οὐκ ὀλίγος περὶ τῆς
that ²trouble ¹no ²little concerning the

ὁδοῦ. 24 Δημήτριος γάρ τις ὀνόματι,
way. For ²Demetrius ¹one by name,

ἀργυροκόπος, ποιῶν ναοὺς ἀργυροῦς
a silversmith, making shrines silver

Ἀρτέμιδος παρείχετο τοῖς τεχνίταις οὐκ
of Artemis provided the artisans no

ὀλίγην ἐργασίαν, 25 οὓς συναθροίσας καὶ
little trade, ¹whom ²assembling also

τοὺς περὶ τὰ τοιαῦτα ἐργάτας εἶπεν·
¹the ²about(in) – ⁴such things ³workmen said:

ἄνδρες, ἐπίστασθε ὅτι ἐκ ταύτης τῆς
Men, ye understand that from this –

ἐργασίας ἡ εὐπορία ἡμῖν ἐστιν, 26 καὶ
trade the gain to us is,⁹ and
=we have [our] gain,

θεωρεῖτε καὶ ἀκούετε ὅτι οὐ μόνον
ye behold and hear that ²not ¹only

Ἐφέσου ἀλλὰ σχεδὸν πάσης τῆς Ἀσίας
²of Ephesus ¹⁰but ¹¹almost ¹²of all – ¹³Asia

ὁ Παῦλος οὗτος πείσας μετέστησεν ἱκανὸν
– ²Paul ¹this ³having ⁵perverted ⁶a considerable
persuaded

ὄχλον, λέγων ὅτι οὐκ εἰσὶν θεοὶ οἱ διὰ
⁶crowd, saying that they are not gods ¹the ²through
[ones]

χειρῶν γινόμενοι. 27 οὐ μόνον δὲ τοῦτο
³hands ⁴coming into being. ²not ¹only ³Now ⁴this

κινδυνεύει ἡμῖν τὸ μέρος εἰς ἀπελεγμὸν
²is in danger to us the share⁶ ²into ³disrepute
=our share

ἐλθεῖν, ἀλλὰ καὶ τὸ τῆς μεγάλης θεᾶς
¹to come, but also ¹the ²of the ³great ⁴goddess

Ἀρτέμιδος ἱερὸν εἰς οὐθὲν λογισθῆναι,
⁵Artemis ⁶temple ⁷for(as) ⁸nothing ¹to be reckoned,

μέλλειν τε καὶ καθαιρεῖσθαι τῆς μεγα-
¹to be about ²and ²also ⁴to be diminished the great-

λειότητος αὐτῆς, ἣν ὅλη ἡ Ἀσία καὶ
ness of her, whom all – Asia and

ἡ οἰκουμένη σέβεται. 28 ἀκούσαντες δὲ
the inhabited earth worships. And hearing

καὶ γενόμενοι πλήρεις θυμοῦ ἔκραζον
and becoming full of anger they cried out

λέγοντες· μεγάλη ἡ Ἀρτεμις Ἐφεσίων.
saying: Great [is] Artemis of [the] Ephesians.

King James Version

Great *is* Diana of the Ephesians. 29And the whole city was filled with confusion: and having caught Gaius and Aristarchus, men of Macedonia, Paul's companions in travel, they rushed with one accord into the theatre. 30And when Paul would have entered in unto the people, the disciples suffered him not. 31And certain of the chief of Asia, which were his friends, sent unto him, desiring *him* that he would not adventure himself into the theatre. 32 Some therefore cried one thing, and some another: for the assembly was confused; and the more part knew not wherefore they were come together. 33And they drew Alexander out of the multitude, the Jews putting him forward. And Alexander beckoned with the hand, and would have made his defence unto the people. 34 But when they knew that he was a Jew, all with one voice about the space of two hours cried out, Great *is* Diana of the Ephesians. 35And when the townclerk had appeased the people, he said, *Ye* men of Ephesus, what man is there that knoweth not how that the city of the Ephesians is a worshipper of the great goddess Diana, and of the *image* which fell down from Jupiter? 36 Seeing then that these things cannot be spoken against, ye ought to be quiet, and to do nothing rashly. 37 For ye have brought hither these men, which are neither robbers of churches, nor yet blasphemers of your goddess. 38 Wherefore if Demetrius, and the craftsmen which are with him, have a matter against any man, the law is open, and there are deputies: let them implead one another. 39 But if ye inquire any thing concerning other matters, it shall be determined in a lawful assembly. 40 For we are in danger to be called in question for this day's uproar, there being no cause whereby we may give an account of this concourse. 41And when he had thus spoken, he dismissed the assembly.

20 And after the uproar was ceased, Paul called unto *him* the disciples, and embraced *them*, and departed for to go into Macedonia. 2And when he had gone over those parts, and had given them much exhortation, he came into Greece, 3And *there* abode three months. And when the Jews laid wait for him, as he was about to sail into Syria, he purposed to return through Macedonia. 4And there accompanied him into Asia Sopater of Berea; and of the Thessalonians, Aristarchus and Secundus; and Gaius of Derbe, and Timotheus; and of Asia, Tychicus and Trophimus. 5These going before tarried for us at Troas. 6And we sailed away from Philippi after the days of unleavened bread, and came unto them to Troas in five days; where we abode

New International Version

Ephesians!" 29 Soon the whole city was in an uproar. The people seized Gaius and Aristarchus, Paul's traveling companions from Macedonia, and rushed as one man into the theater. 30 Paul wanted to appear before the crowd, but the disciples would not let him. 31 Even some of the officials of the province, friends of Paul, sent him a message begging him not to venture into the theater. 32 The assembly was in confusion: Some were shouting one thing, some another. Most of the people did not even know why they were there. 33 The Jews pushed Alexander to the front, and some of the crowd shouted instructions to him. He motioned for silence in order to make a defense before the people. 34 But when they realized he was a Jew, they all shouted in unison for about two hours: "Great is Artemis of the Ephesians!"

35 The city clerk quieted the crowd and said: "Men of Ephesus, doesn't all the world know that the city of Ephesus is the guardian of the temple of the great Artemis and of her image, which fell from heaven? 36 Therefore, since these facts are undeniable, you ought to be quiet and not do anything rash. 37 You have brought these men here, though they have neither robbed temples nor blasphemed our goddess. 38 If, then, Demetrius and his fellow craftsmen have a grievance against anybody, the courts are open and there are proconsuls. They can press charges. 39 If there is anything further you want to bring up, it must be settled in a legal assembly. 40As it is, we are in danger of being charged with rioting because of today's events. In that case we would not be able to account for this commotion, since there is no reason for it." 41After he had said this, he dismissed the assembly.

Through Macedonia and Greece

20 When the uproar had ended, Paul sent for the disciples and, after encouraging them, said good-by and set out for Macedonia. 2 He traveled through that area, speaking many words of encouragement to the people, and finally arrived in Greece, 3 where he stayed three months. Because the Jews made a plot against him just as he was about to sail for Syria, he decided to go back through Macedonia. 4 He was accompanied by Sopater son of Pyrrhus from Berea, Aristarchus and Secundus from Thessalonica, Gaius from Derbe, Timothy also, and from the province of Asia Tychicus and Trophimus. 5 These men went on ahead and waited for us at Troas. 6 But we sailed from Philippi after the Feast of Unleavened Bread, and five days later joined the others at Troas, where we stayed seven days.

Greek Interlinear

29 καὶ ἐπλήσθη ἡ πόλις τῆς συγχύσεως,
And was filled the city of(with) the confusion,

ὥρμησάν τε ὁμοθυμαδὸν εἰς τὸ θέατρον,
and they rushed with one mind into the theatre,

συναρπάσαντες Γάϊον καὶ ᾿Αρίσταρχον
keeping a firm grip on Gaius and Aristarchus[,]

Μακεδόνας, συνεκδήμους Παύλου. 30 Παύλου
Macedonians, travelling companions of Paul. Paul

δὲ βουλομένου εἰσελθεῖν εἰς τὸν δῆμον
And intending* to enter into the mob
= as Paul intended

οὐκ εἴων αὐτὸν οἱ μαθηταί· 31 τινὲς
*not *allowed *him ¹the *disciples; some

δὲ καὶ τῶν ᾿Ασιαρχῶν, ὄντες αὐτῷ
and also of the Asiarchs, being to him

φίλοι, πέμψαντες πρὸς αὐτὸν παρεκάλουν
friends, sending to him besought

μὴ δοῦναι ἑαυτὸν εἰς τὸ θέατρον. 32 ἄλλοι
not to give himself in the theatre. Others

μὲν οὖν ἄλλο τι ἔκραζον· ἦν γὰρ
indeed therefore *different ¹something cried out; for ²was

ἡ ἐκκλησία συγκεχυμένη, καὶ οἱ πλείους
¹the *assembly *having been* confounded, and the majority

οὐκ ᾔδεισαν τίνος ἕνεκα συνεληλύθεισαν.
knew not *of what ¹on account they had come together.

33 ἐκ δὲ τοῦ ὄχλου συνεβίβασαν ᾿Αλέξανδρον,
But [some] of the crowd instructed Alexander,

προβαλόντων αὐτὸν τῶν ᾿Ιουδαίων· ὁ δὲ
putting forward him the Jews*; - and
= as the Jews put him forward;

᾿Αλέξανδρος κατασείσας τὴν χεῖρα ἤθελεν
Alexander waving the(his) hand wished

ἀπολογεῖσθαι τῷ δήμῳ. 34 ἐπιγνόντες δὲ
to defend himself to the mob. But knowing

ὅτι ᾿Ιουδαῖός ἐστιν, φωνὴ ἐγένετο μία
that a Jew he is(was), *voice ¹there was ¹one

ἐκ πάντων, ὡς ἐπὶ ὥρας δύο κράζοντες·
from all, about over hours two crying out:

μεγάλη ἡ ῎Αρτεμις ᾿Εφεσίων. 35 κατα-
Great [is] - Artemis of [the] Ephesians. *having

στείλας δὲ ὁ γραμματεὺς τὸν ὄχλον
quietened ¹And *the *town clerk the crowd

φησίν· ἄνδρες ᾿Εφέσιοι, τίς γὰρ ἐστιν
says: Men Ephesians, who indeed is there

ἀνθρώπων ὃς οὐ γινώσκει τὴν ᾿Εφεσίων
of men who does not know ¹the *of [the] Ephesians

πόλιν νεωκόρον οὖσαν τῆς μεγάλης
*city *temple warden *being of the great

᾿Αρτέμιδος καὶ τοῦ διοπετοῦς; 36 ἀναντιρ-
Artemis and of the fallen from undeni-
[image] the sky?

ρήτων οὖν ὄντων τούτων δέον ἐστὶν
able therefore being these things* necessary it is
= as these things are undeniable

ὑμᾶς κατεσταλμένους ὑπάρχειν καὶ μηδὲν
you *having been quietened ¹to be and *nothing

προπετὲς πράσσειν. 37 ἠγάγετε γὰρ τοὺς
¹rash ¹to do. For ye brought -

ἄνδρας τούτους οὔτε ἱεροσύλους οὔτε
men these neither temple robbers nor

βλασφημοῦντας τὴν θεὰν ἡμῶν. 38 εἰ
blaspheming the goddess of you. If

μὲν οὖν Δημήτριος καὶ οἱ σὺν αὐτῷ
indeed therefore Demetrius and ¹the *with *him

τεχνῖται ἔχουσι πρός τινα λόγον, ἀγοραῖοι
*artisans have against anyone an account, assizes

ἄγονται καὶ ἀνθύπατοί εἰσιν, ἐγκαλείτωσαν
are and proconsuls there are, let them bring a
being(held) charge against

ἀλλήλοις. 39 εἰ δέ τι περαιτέρω ἐπιζητεῖτε,
one another. But if *anything *further ¹ye seek,

ἐν τῇ ἐννόμῳ ἐκκλησίᾳ ἐπιλυθήσεται.
in the lawful assembly it will be settled.

40 καὶ γὰρ κινδυνεύομεν ἐγκαλεῖσθαι
For indeed we are in danger to be charged with

στάσεως περὶ τῆς σήμερον, μηδενὸς
insurrection concerning to-day, nothing

αἰτίου ὑπάρχοντος, περὶ οὗ οὐ δυνησόμεθα
cause being*, concerning which we shall not be able
= there being no cause,

ἀποδοῦναι λόγον περὶ τῆς συστροφῆς
to give account concerning - *crowding together

ταύτης. 41 καὶ ταῦτα εἰπὼν ἀπέλυσεν τὴν
¹this. And these things saying he dismissed the

ἐκκλησίαν.
assembly.

Chapter 20

Μετὰ δὲ τὸ παύσασθαι τὸν θόρυβον
And after the to cease the uproar[b]
= after the uproar ceased

μεταπεμψάμενος ὁ Παῦλος τοὺς μαθητὰς
*summoning - ¹Paul *the *disciples

καὶ παρακαλέσας, ἀσπασάμενος ἐξῆλθεν
*and *exhorting, taking leave he went forth

πορεύεσθαι εἰς Μακεδονίαν. 2 διελθὼν δὲ
to go to Macedonia. And having gone through

τὰ μέρη ἐκεῖνα καὶ παρακαλέσας αὐτοὺς
those parts and having exhorted them

λόγῳ πολλῷ ἦλθεν εἰς τὴν ῾Ελλάδα,
¹with *speech *much he came into - Greece,

3 ποιήσας τε μῆνας τρεῖς, γενομένης
and spending months three, there being

ἐπιβουλῆς αὐτῷ ὑπὸ τῶν ᾿Ιουδαίων
a plot* against] him by the Jews

μέλλοντι ἀνάγεσθαι εἰς τὴν Συρίαν, ἐγένετο
being about to set sail to(for) - Syria, he was
= as he was about

γνώμης τοῦ ὑποστρέφειν διὰ Μακεδονίας.
of a mind - to return[d] through Macedonia.

4 συνείπετο δὲ αὐτῷ Σώπατρος Πύρρου
And there accompanied him Sopater [son] of Pyrrhus

Βεροιαῖος, Θεσσαλονικέων δὲ ᾿Αρίσταρχος
a Berœan, and of Thessalonians Aristarchus

καὶ Σέκουνδος, καὶ Γάϊος Δερβαῖος καὶ
and Secundus, and Gaius a Derbæan and

Τιμόθεος, ᾿Ασιανοὶ δὲ Τύχικος καὶ
Timothy, and Asians Tychicus and

Τρόφιμος. 5 οὗτοι δὲ προελθόντες ἔμενον
Trophimus. And these men going forward awaited

ἡμᾶς ἐν Τρῳάδι· 6 ἡμεῖς δὲ ἐξεπλεύσαμεν
us in Troas; and we sailed away

μετὰ τὰς ἡμέρας τῶν ἀζύμων ἀπὸ
after the days - of unleavened bread from

Φιλίππων, καὶ ἤλθομεν πρὸς αὐτοὺς εἰς
Philippi, and came to them in

τὴν Τρῳάδα ἄχρι ἡμερῶν πέντε, ὅπου
- Troas until days five, where

411

King James Version

seven days. 7And upon the first *day* of the week, when the disciples came together to break bread, Paul preached unto them, ready to depart on the morrow; and continued his speech until midnight. 8And there were many lights in the upper chamber, where they were gathered together. 9And there sat in a window a certain young man named Eutychus, being fallen into a deep sleep: and as Paul was long preaching, he sunk down with sleep, and fell down from the third loft, and was taken up dead. 10And Paul went down, and fell on him, and embracing *him* said, Trouble not yourselves; for his life is in him. 11 When he therefore was come up again, and had broken bread, and eaten, and talked a long while, even till break of day, so he departed. 12And they brought the young man alive, and were not a little comforted.

13 And we went before to ship, and sailed unto Assos, there intending to take in Paul: for so had he appointed, minding himself to go afoot. 14And when he met with us at Assos, we took him in, and came to Mitylene. 15And we sailed thence, and came the next *day* over against Chios; and the next *day* we arrived at Samos, and tarried at Trogyllium; and the next *day* we came to Miletus. 16 For Paul had determined to sail by Ephesus, because he would not spend the time in Asia: for he hasted, if it were possible for him, to be at Jerusalem the day of Pentecost.

17 And from Miletus he sent to Ephesus, and called the elders of the church. 18And when they were come to him, he said unto them, Ye know, from the first day that I came into Asia, after what manner I have been with you at all seasons, 19 Serving the Lord with all humility of mind, and with many tears, and temptations, which befell me by the lying in wait of the Jews: 20And how I kept back nothing that was profitable *unto you,* but have shewed you, and have taught you publicly, and from house to house, 21 Testifying both to the Jews, and also to the Greeks, repentance toward God, and faith toward our Lord Jesus Christ. 22And now, behold, I go bound in the spirit unto Jerusalem, not knowing the things that shall befall me there: 23 Save that the Holy Ghost witnesseth in every city, saying that bonds and afflictions abide me. 24 But none of these things move me, neither count I my life dear unto myself, so that I might finish my course with joy, and the ministry, which I have received of the Lord Jesus, to testify the gospel of the grace of God. 25And now, behold, I know that ye all among whom I have gone preaching the kingdom of God, shall see my face no more. 26 Wherefore I take you

New International Version

Eutychus raised from the dead at Troas

7 On the first day of the week we came together to break bread. Paul preached to the people and, because he intended to leave the next day, kept on talking until midnight. 8 There were many lamps in the upstairs room where we were meeting. 9 Seated in a window was a young man named Eutychus, who was sinking into a deep sleep as Paul talked on and on. When he was sound asleep, he fell to the ground from the third story and was picked up dead. 10 Paul went down, threw himself on the young man and put his arms around him. "Don't be alarmed," he said. "He's alive!" 11 Then he went upstairs again and broke bread and ate. After talking until daylight, he left. 12 The people took the young man home alive and were greatly comforted.

Paul's farewell to the Ephesian elders

13 We went on ahead to the ship and sailed for Assos, where we were going to take Paul aboard. He had made this arrangement because he was going there on foot. 14 When he met us at Assos, we took him aboard and went on to Mitylene. 15 The next day we set sail from there and arrived off Chios. The day after that we crossed over to Samos, and on the following day arrived at Miletus. 16 Paul had decided to sail past Ephesus to avoid spending time in the province of Asia, for he was in a hurry to reach Jerusalem, if possible, by the day of Pentecost.

17 From Miletus, Paul sent to Ephesus for the elders of the church. 18 When they arrived, he said to them: "You know how I lived the whole time I was with you, from the first day I came into the province of Asia. 19 I served the Lord with great humility and with tears, although I was severely tested by the plots of the Jews. 20 You know that I have not hesitated to preach anything that would be helpful to you but have taught you publicly and from house to house. 21 I have declared to both Jews and Greeks that they must turn to God in repentance and have faith in our Lord Jesus.

22 "And now, compelled by the Spirit, I am going to Jerusalem, not knowing what will happen to me there. 23 I only know that in every city the Holy Spirit warns me that prison and hardships are facing me. 24 However, I consider my life worth nothing to me, if only I may finish the race and complete the task the Lord Jesus has given me—the task of testifying to the gospel of God's grace.

25 "Now I know that none of you among whom I have gone about preaching the kingdom will ever see me again. 26 Therefore, I declare

Greek Interlinear

διετρίψαμεν ἡμέρας ἑπτά. 7 Ἐν δὲ τῇ
we stayed   days   seven.   And on   the

μιᾷ   τῶν   σαββάτων   συνηγμένων   ἡμῶν
one(first) of the sabbaths(week) having been   us*
[day]   assembled
=as we were assembled

κλάσαι   ἄρτον   ὁ Παῦλος διελέγετο αὐτοῖς,
to break bread   - Paul   lectured   to them,

μέλλων   ἐξιέναι   τῇ ἐπαύριον, παρέτεινέν τε
being about to depart on the morrow,   and continued

τὸν λόγον   μέχρι   μεσονυκτίου. 8 ἦσαν   δὲ
the speech   until   midnight.   Now there were

λαμπάδες ἱκαναὶ   ἐν   τῷ ὑπερῴῳ   οὗ
lamps   a considerable in the upper room where
          number of

ἦμεν   συνηγμένοι. 9 καθεζόμενος δέ τις
we were having been assembled. And sitting a certain

νεανίας ὀνόματι Εὔτυχος ἐπὶ τῆς θυρίδος,
young man by name Eutychus on   the window sill,

καταφερόμενος ὕπνῳ βαθεῖ,   διαλεγομένου
being overborne sleep by a deep, lecturing

τοῦ Παύλου ἐπὶ πλεῖον,   κατενεχθεὶς ἀπὸ
-    Paul*   for a longer time, having been   from
=while Paul lectured   overborne

τοῦ ὕπνου ἔπεσεν ἀπὸ τοῦ τριστέγου
the sleep   he fell   from the third floor*

κάτω καὶ ἤρθη   νεκρός. 10 καταβὰς δὲ
down and was taken up dead.   But going down

ὁ Παῦλος ἐπέπεσεν αὐτῷ καὶ συμπεριλαβὼν
- Paul   fell on   him   and closely embracing
                                     [him]

εἶπεν· μὴ θορυβεῖσθε·   ἡ γὰρ ψυχὴ αὐτοῦ
said: Be ye not terrified; for the life of him

ἐν αὐτῷ ἐστιν. 11 ἀναβὰς   δὲ καὶ κλάσας
in him   is.   And going up and breaking

τὸν ἄρτον καὶ γευσάμενος, ἐφ᾽ ἱκανόν τε
the bread   and tasting,   and over a considerable
                                 [time]

ὁμιλήσας   ἄχρι   αὐγῆς,   οὕτως ἐξῆλθεν.
conversing   until light [of day], thus   he went forth.

12 ἤγαγον δὲ τὸν παῖδα ζῶντα,   καὶ
And they brought the lad   living,   and

παρεκλήθησαν οὐ μετρίως. 13 Ἡμεῖς δὲ
were comforted   not moderately.   And we

προελθόντες   ἐπὶ τὸ πλοῖον ἀνήχθημεν
going before   onto the ship   set sail

ἐπὶ τὴν Ἄσσον, ἐκεῖθεν μέλλοντες ἀνα-
to(for) - Assos,   thence   intending   to

λαμβάνειν τὸν Παῦλον· οὕτως γὰρ
take up   -   Paul;   for thus

διατεταγμένος ἦν, μέλλων αὐτὸς πεζεύειν.
having been arranged it was, *intending *he to go afoot.

14 ὡς δὲ συνέβαλλεν ἡμῖν εἰς τὴν Ἄσσον,
Now when he met with   us   in   -   Assos,

ἀναλαβόντες αὐτὸν ἤλθομεν   εἰς Μιτυλήνην·
taking up   him   we came   to   Mitylene;

15 κἀκεῖθεν   ἀποπλεύσαντες τῇ ἐπιούσῃ
and thence   sailing away   on the next [day]

κατηντήσαμεν ἄντικρυς Χίου, τῇ δὲ ἑτέρᾳ
we arrived   off   Chios, and the other(next)

παρεβάλομεν   εἰς Σάμον, τῇ δὲ ἐχομένῃ
we crossed over to   Samos,   and on the next

ἤλθομεν εἰς Μίλητον. 16 κεκρίκει γὰρ ὁ
we came   to   Miletus.   For had decided -

Παῦλος παραπλεῦσαι τὴν Ἔφεσον, ὅπως
Paul   to sail past   -   Ephesus,   so as

μὴ γένηται αὐτῷ χρονοτριβῆσαι ἐν τῇ
not be   to him to spend time   in   -
=so that he should not . . .

Ἀσίᾳ· ἔσπευδεν γάρ, εἰ δυνατὸν εἴη
Asia;   for he hasted,   if   possible it might be

αὐτῷ, τὴν ἡμέραν τῆς πεντηκοστῆς
to him, the day   -   of Pentecost

γενέσθαι εἰς Ἱεροσόλυμα.
to be   in   Jerusalem.

17 Ἀπὸ δὲ τῆς Μιλήτου πέμψας εἰς
And from -   Miletus   sending   to

Ἔφεσον μετεκαλέσατο τοὺς πρεσβυτέρους
Ephesus   he summoned   the   elders

τῆς ἐκκλησίας. 18 ὡς δὲ παρεγένοντο
of the church.   And when   they came

πρὸς αὐτόν, εἶπεν αὐτοῖς· ὑμεῖς ἐπίστασθε,
to   him,   he said to them: Ye   understand,

ἀπὸ πρώτης   ἡμέρας ἀφ᾽ ἧς ἐπέβην εἰς
from [the] first day   from which I set foot on in

τὴν Ἀσίαν, πῶς μεθ᾽ ὑμῶν τὸν πάντα
-    Asia,   how with   you   the   whole

χρόνον ἐγενόμην, 19 δουλεύων τῷ κυρίῳ
time   I was,   serving   the Lord

μετὰ πάσης ταπεινοφροσύνης καὶ δακρύων
with   all   humility   and   tears

καὶ πειρασμῶν τῶν συμβάντων μοι ἐν
and   trials   -   happening   to me by

ταῖς ἐπιβουλαῖς τῶν Ἰουδαίων, 20 ὡς
the   plots   of the Jews,   as

οὐδὲν ὑπεστειλάμην τῶν συμφερόντων τοῦ
*nothing *I kept back   of the things   beneficial -

μὴ ἀναγγεῖλαι ὑμῖν καὶ διδάξαι ὑμᾶς
not to declare*   to you and to teach*   you

δημοσίᾳ καὶ κατ᾽ οἴκους, 21 διαμαρτυρόμενος
publicly and from house to house,† solemnly witnessing

Ἰουδαίοις τε καὶ Ἕλλησιν τὴν εἰς θεὸν
*to Jews   *both and to Greeks   -   toward God

μετάνοιαν καὶ πίστιν εἰς τὸν κύριον
repentance and faith   toward(?in) the Lord

ἡμῶν Ἰησοῦν. 22 καὶ νῦν ἰδοὺ δεδεμένος
of us   Jesus.   And now behold having been
                                       bound

ἐγὼ τῷ πνεύματι πορεύομαι εἰς Ἱερου-
I   by the Spirit   am going   to   Jeru-

σαλήμ, τὰ ἐν αὐτῇ συναντήσοντα ἐμοὶ
salem,   *the things *in   *it   *going to meet   *me

μὴ εἰδώς, 23 πλὴν ὅτι τὸ πνεῦμα τὸ
*not *knowing,   except that the Spirit   -

ἅγιον κατὰ πόλιν διαμαρτύρεται μοι λέγον
Holy   in every city† solemnly witnesses to me saying

ὅτι δεσμὰ καὶ θλίψεις με μένουσιν.
that bonds   and afflictions me await.

24 ἀλλ᾽ οὐδενὸς λόγου ποιοῦμαι τὴν ψυχὴν
But *of nothing *account   *I make   *the(my) *life

τιμίαν ἐμαυτῷ ὡς τελειώσω τὸν δρόμον
precious to myself so as I may finish the   course

μου καὶ τὴν διακονίαν ἣν ἔλαβον παρὰ
of me and the ministry   which I received from

τοῦ κυρίου Ἰησοῦ, διαμαρτύρασθαι τὸ
the Lord   Jesus,   to witness solemnly the

εὐαγγέλιον τῆς χάριτος τοῦ θεοῦ. 25 καὶ
gospel   of the grace   -   of God.   And

νῦν ἰδοὺ ἐγὼ οἶδα ὅτι οὐκέτι ὄψεσθε
now behold I   know that *no more *will see

τὸ πρόσωπόν μου ὑμεῖς πάντες ἐν οἷς
*the *face   *of me *ye   *all   among whom

διῆλθον κηρύσσων τὴν βασιλείαν. 26 διότι
I went about proclaiming the kingdom.   Wherefore

* Souter remarks that it is uncertain whether the ground floor was counted or not in the enunciation; " if so, we should have to translate ' the second floor '."

413

King James Version

to record this day, that I *am* pure from the blood of all *men*. 27 For I have not shunned to declare unto you all the counsel of God.

28 Take heed therefore unto yourselves, and to all the flock, over the which the Holy Ghost hath made you overseers, to feed the church of God, which he hath purchased with his own blood. 29 For I know this, that after my departing shall grievous wolves enter in among you, not sparing the flock. 30 Also of your own selves shall men arise, speaking perverse things, to draw away disciples after them. 31 Therefore watch, and remember, that by the space of three years I ceased not to warn every one night and day with tears. 32 And now, brethren, I commend you to God, and to the word of his grace, which is able to build you up, and to give you an inheritance among all them which are sanctified. 33 I have coveted no man's silver, or gold, or apparel. 34 Yea, ye yourselves know, that these hands have ministered unto my necessities, and to them that were with me. 35 I have shewed you all things, how that so labouring ye ought to support the weak, and to remember the words of the Lord Jesus, how he said, It is more blessed to give than to receive.

36 And when he had thus spoken, he kneeled down, and prayed with them all. 37 And they all wept sore, and fell on Paul's neck, and kissed him, 38 Sorrowing most of all for the words which he spake, that they should see his face no more. And they accompanied him unto the ship.

21 And it came to pass, that after we were gotten from them, and had launched, we came with a straight course unto Coos, and the day following unto Rhodes, and from thence unto Patara: 2 And finding a ship sailing over unto Phenicia, we went aboard, and set forth. 3 Now when we had discovered Cyprus, we left it on the left hand, and sailed into Syria, and landed at Tyre: for there the ship was to unlade her burden. 4 And finding disciples, we tarried there seven days: who said to Paul through the Spirit, that he should not go up to Jerusalem. 5 And when we had accomplished those days, we departed and went our way; and they all brought us on our way, with wives and children, till *we were* out of the city: and we kneeled down on the shore, and prayed. 6 And when we had taken our leave one of another, we took ship; and they returned home again. 7 And when we had finished *our* course from Tyre, we came to Ptolemais, and saluted the brethren, and abode

New International Version

to you today that I am innocent of the blood of all men. 27 For I have not hesitated to proclaim to you the whole will of God. 28 Guard yourselves and all the flock of which the Holy Spirit has made you overseers.[g] Be shepherds of the church of God,[h] which he bought with his own blood. 29 I know that after I leave, savage wolves will come in among you and will not spare the flock. 30 Even from your own number men will arise and distort the truth in order to draw away disciples after them. 31 So be on your guard! Remember that for three years I never stopped warning each of you night and day with tears.

32 "Now I commit you to God and to the word of his grace, which can build you up and give you an inheritance among all those who are sanctified. 33 I have not coveted anyone's silver or gold or clothing. 34 You yourselves know that these hands of mine have supplied my own needs and the needs of my companions. 35 In everything I did, I showed you that by this kind of hard work we must help the weak, remembering the words of the Lord Jesus: 'It is more blessed to give than to receive.'"

36 When he had said this, he knelt down with all of them and prayed. 37 They all wept as they embraced him and kissed him. 38 What grieved them most was his statement that they would never see his face again. Then they accompanied him to the ship.

On to Jerusalem

21 After we had torn ourselves away from them, we put out to sea and sailed straight to Cos. The next day we went to Rhodes and from there to Patara. 2 We found a ship crossing over to Phoenicia, went on board and set sail. 3 After sighting Cyprus and passing to the south of it, we sailed on to Syria. We landed at Tyre, where our ship was to unload its cargo. 4 Finding the disciples there, we stayed with them seven days. Through the Spirit they urged Paul not to go on to Jerusalem. 5 But when our time was up, we left and continued on our way. All the disciples and their wives and children accompanied us out of the city, and there on the beach we knelt to pray. 6 After saying good-by to each other, we went aboard the ship, and they returned home.

7 We continued our voyage from Tyre and landed at Ptolemais, where we greeted the broth-

[g] Or *bishops.* [h] Some MSS read *of the Lord.*

414

Greek Interlinear

μαρτύρομαι ὑμῖν ἐν τῇ σήμερον ἡμέρᾳ
I witness to you on this day

ὅτι καθαρός εἰμι ἀπὸ τοῦ αἵματος πάντων·
that clean I am from the blood of all men;

27 οὐ γὰρ ὑπεστειλάμην τοῦ μὴ ἀναγγεῖλαι
for I kept not back — not to declare[d]

πᾶσαν τὴν βουλὴν τοῦ θεοῦ ὑμῖν.
all the counsel — of God to you.

28 προσέχετε ἑαυτοῖς καὶ παντὶ τῷ
Take heed to yourselves and to all the

ποιμνίῳ, ἐν ᾧ ὑμᾶς τὸ πνεῦμα τὸ
flock, in which ²you ¹the ³Spirit the

ἅγιον ἔθετο ἐπισκόπους, ποιμαίνειν τὴν
³Holy ⁴placed overseers, to shepherd the

ἐκκλησίαν τοῦ θεοῦ, ἣν περιεποιήσατο
church — of God, which he acquired

διὰ τοῦ αἵματος τοῦ ἰδίου. 29 ἐγὼ
through the blood of the(his) own.* I

οἶδα ὅτι εἰσελεύσονται μετὰ τὴν ἄφιξίν
know that ²will come in ¹after ¹the ²departure

μου λύκοι βαρεῖς εἰς ὑμᾶς μὴ φειδόμενοι
⁴of me ³wolves ⁵grievous ⁶into you not sparing

τοῦ ποιμνίου, 30 καὶ ἐξ ὑμῶν αὐτῶν
the flock, and of you [your]selves

ἀναστήσονται ἄνδρες λαλοῦντες διεστραμμένα
will rise up men speaking *having been perverted things*

τοῦ ἀποσπᾶν τοὺς μαθητὰς ὀπίσω ἑαυτῶν.
— to drag away[d] the disciples after themselves.

31 διὸ γρηγορεῖτε, μνημονεύοντες ὅτι
Wherefore watch ye, remembering that

τριετίαν νύκτα καὶ ἡμέραν οὐκ ἐπαυσάμην
for three years night and day I ceased not

μετὰ δακρύων νουθετῶν ἕνα ἕκαστον.
with tears admonishing ²one ¹each.

32 καὶ τὰ νῦν παρατίθεμαι ὑμᾶς τῷ
And — now I commend you to the

κυρίῳ καὶ τῷ λόγῳ τῆς χάριτος αὐτοῦ
Lord and to the word of the grace of him

τῷ δυναμένῳ οἰκοδομῆσαι καὶ δοῦναι τὴν
— being able to build and to give the

κληρονομίαν ἐν τοῖς ἡγιασμένοις πᾶσιν.
inheritance among ²the [ones] ¹having been ¹all.
sanctified

33 ἀργυρίου ἢ χρυσίου ἢ ἱματισμοῦ οὐδενὸς
Silver or gold or raiment of no one

ἐπεθύμησα· 34 αὐτοὶ γινώσκετε ὅτι ταῖς
I coveted; [your]selves ye know that ⁴to the

χρείαις μου καὶ τοῖς οὖσιν μετ’ ἐμοῦ
⁵needs ⁶of me ⁷and ⁸to the [ones] ⁹being ¹⁰with ¹¹me

ὑπηρέτησαν αἱ χεῖρες αὗται. 35 πάντα
¹ministered ²these ³hands. All things

ὑπέδειξα ὑμῖν, ὅτι οὕτως κοπιῶντας δεῖ
I showed you, that thus labouring it behoves

ἀντιλαμβάνεσθαι τῶν ἀσθενούντων, μνημονεύειν
to succour the ailing [ones], ²to remember

τε τῶν λόγων τοῦ κυρίου Ἰησοῦ, ὅτι
¹and the words of the Lord Jesus, that

αὐτὸς εἶπεν· μακάριόν ἐστιν μᾶλλον, διδόναι
he said: Blessed it is rather to give

ἢ λαμβάνειν. 36 καὶ ταῦτα εἰπών,
than to receive. And ²these things ¹having said,

θεὶς τὰ γόνατα αὐτοῦ σὺν πᾶσιν αὐτοῖς
placing the knees of him with ²all ¹them
= kneeling down

προσηύξατο. 37 ἱκανὸς δὲ κλαυθμὸς ἐγένετο
he prayed. And ¹considerable ³weeping ¹there was

πάντων, καὶ ἐπιπεσόντες ἐπὶ τὸν τράχηλον
of all, and falling on on the neck

τοῦ Παύλου κατεφίλουν αὐτόν, 38 ὀδυνώ-
— of Paul they kissed fervently him, suffer-

μενοι μάλιστα ἐπὶ τῷ λόγῳ ᾧ εἰρήκει,
ing most over the word which he had said,

ὅτι οὐκέτι μέλλουσιν τὸ πρόσωπον αὐτοῦ
that no more they are(were) the face of him

θεωρεῖν. προέπεμπον δὲ αὐτὸν εἰς τὸ
to behold. And they escorted him to the

πλοῖον.
ship.

Chapter 21

Ὡς δὲ ἐγένετο ἀναχθῆναι ἡμᾶς
Now when it came to pass to set sail we

ἀποσπασθέντας ἀπ’ αὐτῶν, εὐθυδρομήσαντες
having been withdrawn from them, taking a straight course

ἤλθομεν εἰς τὴν Κῶ, τῇ δὲ ἑξῆς εἰς
we came to — Cos, and on the next [day] to

τὴν Ῥόδον κἀκεῖθεν εἰς Πάταρα· 2 καὶ
— Rhodes and thence to Patara; and

εὑρόντες πλοῖον διαπερῶν εἰς Φοινίκην,
having found a ship crossing over to Phœnice,

ἐπιβάντες ἀνήχθημεν. 3 ἀναφάναντες δὲ
embarking we set sail. And sighting

τὴν Κύπρον καὶ καταλιπόντες αὐτὴν
the Cyprus and leaving it

εὐώνυμον ἐπλέομεν εἰς Συρίαν, καὶ κατήλ-
on the left we sailed to Syria, and came

θομεν εἰς Τύρον· ἐκεῖσε γὰρ τὸ πλοῖον
down to Tyre; for there the ship

ἦν ἀποφορτιζόμενον τὸν γόμον. 4 ἀνευρ-
was unloading the cargo. find-

όντες δὲ τοὺς μαθητὰς ἐπεμείναμεν αὐτοῦ
ing And the disciples we remained there

ἡμέρας ἑπτά· οἵτινες τῷ Παύλῳ ἔλεγον
days seven; who — ¹Paul ¹told

διὰ τοῦ πνεύματος μὴ ἐπιβαίνειν εἰς
through the Spirit not to go up to

Ἰεροσόλυμα. 5 ὅτε δὲ ἐγένετο ἐξαρτίσαι
Jerusalem. But when it came to pass to accomplish
= we accomplished

ἡμᾶς τὰς ἡμέρας, ἐξελθόντες ἐπορευόμεθα
us[b] the days, going forth we journeyed

προπεμπόντων ἡμᾶς πάντων σὺν γυναιξὶ
¹escorting ²us ¹all³ with women

καὶ τέκνοις ἕως ἔξω τῆς πόλεως, καὶ
and children as far as outside the city, and

θέντες τὰ γόνατα ἐπὶ τὸν αἰγιαλὸν
placing the knees on the shore
= kneeling

προσευξάμενοι 6 ἀπησπασάμεθα ἀλλήλους,
praying we gave parting greetings to one another,

καὶ ἐνέβημεν εἰς τὸ πλοῖον, ἐκεῖνοι δὲ
and embarked in the ship, and those

ὑπέστρεψαν εἰς τὰ ἴδια. 7 Ἡμεῖς δὲ
returned to ¹the(ir) ²things ²own. But we
= home.

τὸν πλοῦν διανύσαντες ἀπὸ Τύρου κατηντή-
²the ¹voyage finishing from Tyre ar-

σαμεν εἰς Πτολεμαΐδα, καὶ ἀσπασάμενοι
rived at Ptolemais, and greeting

* This = his own blood or the blood of his own [?Son].

415

King James Version

with them one day. 8And the next *day* we that were of Paul's company departed, and came unto Cesarea; and we entered into the house of Philip the evangelist, which was *one* of the seven; and abode with him. 9And the same man had four daughters, virgins, which did prophesy. 10And as we tarried *there* many days, there came down from Judea a certain prophet, named Agabus. 11And when he was come unto us, he took Paul's girdle, and bound his own hands and feet, and said, Thus saith the Holy Ghost, So shall the Jews at Jerusalem bind the man that owneth this girdle, and shall deliver *him* into the hands of the Gentiles. 12And when we heard these things, both we, and they of that place, besought him not to go up to Jerusalem. 13 Then Paul answered, What mean ye to weep and to break mine heart? for I am ready not to be bound only, but also to die at Jerusalem for the name of the Lord Jesus. 14And when he would not be persuaded, we ceased, saying, The will of the Lord be done. 15And after those days we took up our carriages, and went up to Jerusalem. 16 There went with us also *certain* of the disciples of Cesarea, and brought with them one Mnason of Cyprus, an old disciple, with whom we should lodge. 17And when we were come to Jerusalem, the brethren received us gladly. 18And the *day* following Paul went in with us unto James; and all the elders were present. 19And when he had saluted them, he declared particularly what things God had wrought among the Gentiles by his ministry. 20And when they heard *it*, they glorified the Lord, and said unto him, Thou seest, brother, how many thousands of Jews there are which believe; and they are all zealous of the law: 21And they are informed of thee, that thou teachest all the Jews which are among the Gentiles to forsake Moses, saying that they ought not to circumcise *their* children, neither to walk after the customs. 22 What is it therefore? the multitude must needs come together: for they will hear that thou art come. 23 Do therefore this that we say to thee: We have four men which have a vow on them; 24 Them take, and purify thyself with them, and be at charges with them, that they may shave *their* heads: and all may know that those things, whereof they were informed concerning thee, are nothing; but *that* thou thyself also walkest orderly, and keepest the law. 25As touching the Gentiles which believe, we have written *and* concluded that they observe no such thing, save only that they keep themselves from *things* offered to idols, and from blood, and from strangled, and from fornication. 26 Then Paul took the men, and the next day purifying himself with them entered into the temple, to signify the accomplishment of the days of purification, until that an offering should be offered for every one of them. 27And when the seven days were almost ended, the Jews which were of Asia,

New International Version

ers and stayed with them for a day. 8 Leaving the next day, we reached Caesarea and stayed at the house of Philip the evangelist, one of the Seven. 9 He had four unmarried daughters who had the gift of prophecy.

10 After we had been there a number of days, a prophet named Agabus came down from Judea. 11 Coming over to us, he took Paul's belt, tied his own hands and feet with it and said, "The Holy Spirit says, 'In this way the Jews of Jerusalem will bind the owner of this belt and will hand him over to the Gentiles.' "

12 When we heard this, we and the people there pleaded with Paul not to go up to Jerusalem. 13 Then Paul answered, "Why are you weeping and breaking my heart? I am ready not only to be bound, but also to die in Jerusalem for the name of the Lord Jesus." 14 When he would not be dissuaded, we gave up and said, "The Lord's will be done."

15 After this, we got ready and went up to Jerusalem. 16 Some of the disciples from Caesarea accompanied us and brought us to the home of Mnason, where we were to stay. He was a man from Cyprus and one of the early disciples.

Paul's arrival at Jerusalem

17 When we arrived at Jerusalem, the brothers received us warmly. 18 The next day Paul and the rest of us went to see James, and all the elders were present. 19 Paul greeted them and reported in detail what God had done among the Gentiles through his ministry.

20 When they heard this, they praised God. Then they said to Paul: "You see, brother, how many thousands of Jews have believed, and all of them are zealous for the law. 21 They have been informed that you teach all the Jews who live among the Gentiles to turn away from Moses, telling them not to circumcise their children or live according to our customs. 22 What shall we do? They will certainly hear that you have come, 23 so do what we tell you. There are four men with us who have made a vow. 24 Take these men, join in their purification rites and pay their expenses, so that they can have their heads shaved. Then everybody will know there is no truth in these reports about you, but that you yourself are living in obedience to the law. 25As for the Gentile believers, we have written to them our decision that they should abstain from food offered to idols, from blood, from the meat of strangled animals and from sexual immorality."

26 The next day Paul took the men and purified himself along with them. Then he went to the temple to give notice of the date when the days of purification would end and the offering would be made for each of them.

Paul arrested

27 When the seven days were nearly over, some Jews from the province of Asia saw Paul

Greek Interlinear

τοὺς ἀδελφοὺς ἐμείναμεν ἡμέραν μίαν
the brothers we remained day one

παρ’ αὐτοῖς. 8 τῇ δὲ ἐπαύριον ἐξελθόντες
with them. And on the morrow going forth

ἤλθομεν εἰς Καισάρειαν, καὶ εἰσελθόντες
we came to Cæsarea, and entering

εἰς τὸν οἶκον Φιλίππου τοῦ εὐαγγελιστοῦ
into the house of Philip the evangelist

ὄντος ἐκ τῶν ἑπτά, ἐμείναμεν παρ’
being of the seven, we remained with

αὐτῷ. 9 τούτῳ δὲ ἦσαν θυγατέρες
him. Now to this man were daughters
=this man had four daughters

τέσσαρες παρθένοι προφητεύουσαι. 10 Ἐπιμεν-
four° virgins prophesying. remain-

όντων δὲ ἡμέρας πλείους κατῆλθέν τις
ing° And days more(many) ²came down ¹a certain

ἀπὸ τῆς Ἰουδαίας προφήτης ὀνόματι
°from – ⁷Judæa ¹prophet ²by name

Ἄγαβος, 11 καὶ ἐλθὼν πρὸς ἡμᾶς καὶ
⁴Agabus, and coming to us and

ἄρας τὴν ζώνην τοῦ Παύλου, δήσας
taking the girdle – of Paul, having bound

ἑαυτοῦ τοὺς πόδας καὶ τὰς χεῖρας εἶπεν·
of himself the feet and the hands said:

τάδε λέγει τὸ πνεῦμα τὸ ἅγιον· τὸν
These things says the Spirit – Holy: ⁷The

ἄνδρα οὗ ἐστιν ἡ ζώνη αὕτη οὕτως
⁸man of whom ¹⁰is the ¹¹girdle ¹thus

δήσουσιν ἐν Ἰερουσαλὴμ οἱ Ἰουδαῖοι καὶ
⁴will bind ⁵in ⁶Jerusalem ¹the ²Jews and

παραδώσουσιν εἰς χεῖρας ἐθνῶν. 12 ὡς
will deliver into [the] hands of [the] nations. when

δὲ ἠκούσαμεν ταῦτα, παρεκαλοῦμεν ἡμεῖς
And we heard these things, ⁴besought ¹we

τε καὶ οἱ ἐντόπιοι τοῦ μὴ ἀναβαίνειν
²both ³and ⁴the ⁵residents – ¹not ²to go up

αὐτὸν εἰς Ἰερουσαλήμ. 13 τότε ἀπεκρίθη
⁷him to Jerusalem. Then answered

ὁ Παῦλος τί ποιεῖτε κλαίοντες καὶ
– Paul: What are ye doing weeping and

συνθρύπτοντές μου τὴν καρδίαν; ἐγὼ γὰρ
weakening of me the heart? For I

οὐ μόνον δεθῆναι ἀλλὰ καὶ ἀποθανεῖν
not only to be bound but also to die

εἰς Ἰερουσαλὴμ ἑτοίμως ἔχω ὑπὲρ τοῦ
in Jerusalem readily have on behalf of the
= am ready

ὀνόματος τοῦ κυρίου Ἰησοῦ. 14 μὴ
name of the Lord Jesus. Not

πειθομένου δὲ αὐτοῦ ἡσυχάσαμεν εἰπόντες·
being persuaded and him we kept silence having said:
= And when he was not persuaded

τοῦ κυρίου τὸ θέλημα γινέσθω.
⁴Of the ¹Lord ²the ³will ⁵let ⁶be [done].

15 Μετὰ δὲ τὰς ἡμέρας ταύτας
And after these days

ἐπισκευασάμενοι ἀνεβαίνομεν εἰς Ἰεροσόλυμα·
having made ready we went up to Jerusalem;

16 συνῆλθον δὲ καὶ τῶν μαθητῶν ἀπὸ
and went with also [some] of the disciples from

Καισαρείας σὺν ἡμῖν, ἄγοντες παρ’ ᾧ
Cæsarea with us, bringing [one] with whom

ξενισθῶμεν Μνάσωνί τινι Κυπρίῳ,
we might be lodged Mnason a certain Cypriote,

ἀρχαίῳ μαθητῇ. 17 Γενομένων δὲ ἡμῶν εἰς
an ancient disciple. And being us² in
(early) = when we were

Ἰεροσόλυμα ἀσμένως ἀπεδέξαντο ἡμᾶς οἱ
Jerusalem ²joyfully ¹received ³us ⁴the

ἀδελφοί. 18 τῇ δὲ ἐπιούσῃ εἰσῄει ὁ
⁵brothers. And on the next day went in –

Παῦλος σὺν ἡμῖν πρὸς Ἰάκωβον, πάντες
Paul with us to James, ²all

τε παρεγένοντο οἱ πρεσβύτεροι. 19 καὶ
¹and ⁴came ³the ⁵elders. And

ἀσπασάμενος αὐτοὺς ἐξηγεῖτο καθ’ ἓν
having greeted them he related according to one
= singly

ἕκαστον ὧν ἐποίησεν ὁ θεὸς ἐν τοῖς
each of [the did – God among the
things] which

ἔθνεσιν διὰ τῆς διακονίας αὐτοῦ. 20 οἱ
nations through the ministry of him. they

δὲ ἀκούσαντες ἐδόξαζον τὸν θεόν, εἶπάν τε
And hearing glorified – God, and said

αὐτῷ· θεωρεῖς, ἀδελφέ, πόσαι μυριάδες
to him: Thou beholdest, brother, how many ten thousands

εἰσὶν ἐν τοῖς Ἰουδαίοις τῶν πεπιστευκότων,
there are among the Jews – having believed,

καὶ πάντες ζηλωταὶ τοῦ νόμου ὑπάρχουσιν·
and all zealots of the law are;

21 κατηχήθησαν δὲ περὶ σοῦ ὅτι ἀποστα-
and they were informed about thee that ²apo-

σίαν διδάσκεις ἀπὸ Μωϋσέως τοὺς κατὰ
stasy ¹thou teachest °from ¹⁰Moses ¹the ²throughout

τὰ ἔθνη πάντας Ἰουδαίους, λέγων μὴ
³the ⁴nations ⁵all ⁶Jews, ⁷telling ⁸not

περιτέμνειν αὐτοὺς τὰ τέκνα μηδὲ τοῖς
⁹to circumcise ¹⁰them the children nor in the

ἔθεσιν περιπατεῖν. 22 τί οὖν ἐστιν;
customs to walk. What therefore is it?

πάντως ἀκούσονται ὅτι ἐλήλυθας. 23 τοῦτο
At all events they will hear that thou hast come. This

οὖν ποίησον ὅ σοι λέγομεν· εἰσὶν ἡμῖν
therefore do thou which thee we tell: There are to us²
= We have

ἄνδρες τέσσαρες εὐχὴν ἔχοντες ἐφ’ ἑαυτῶν·
men four a vow having on themselves;

24 τούτους παραλαβὼν ἁγνίσθητι σὺν αὐτοῖς,
these taking be thou purified with them,

καὶ δαπάνησον ἐπ’ αὐτοῖς ἵνα ξυρήσονται
and spend on them that they will shave

τὴν κεφαλήν, καὶ γνώσονται πάντες ὅτι
the head, and will know all men that

ὧν κατήχηνται περὶ σοῦ οὐδέν
²[of the things] ³they have been ⁴about ⁵thee ¹nothing
of which informed

ἐστιν, ἀλλὰ στοιχεῖς καὶ αὐτὸς φυλάσσων τὸν
¹there is, but thou walkest also [thy]self keeping the

νόμον. 25 περὶ δὲ τῶν πεπιστευκότων
law. And concerning ¹the ²having believed

ἐθνῶν ἡμεῖς ἐπεστείλαμεν κρίναντες φυλάσ-
³nations we joined in writing ¹judging ²to keep

σεσθαι αὐτοὺς τό τε εἰδωλόθυτον καὶ
themselves ⁴them ⁵[from] ⁶the ⁷both idol sacrifice and

αἷμα καὶ πνικτὸν καὶ πορνείαν. 26 τότε
blood and a thing strangled and fornication. Then

ὁ Παῦλος παραλαβὼν τοὺς ἄνδρας τῇ
– Paul taking the men on the

ἐχομένῃ ἡμέρᾳ σὺν αὐτοῖς ἁγνισθεὶς εἰσῄει
next day with them having been purified went in

εἰς τὸ ἱερόν, διαγγέλλων τὴν ἐκπλήρωσιν
to the temple, announcing the completion

τῶν ἡμερῶν τοῦ ἁγνισμοῦ, ἕως οὗ
of the days of the purification, until

προσηνέχθη ὑπὲρ ἑνὸς ἑκάστου αὐτῶν ἡ
should be offered on behalf of ¹one ²each of them the

προσφορά.
offering.

27 Ὡς δὲ ἔμελλον αἱ ἑπτὰ ἡμέραι
Now when were about the seven days

συντελεῖσθαι, οἱ ἀπὸ τῆς Ἀσίας Ἰουδαῖοι
to be fulfilled, ¹the ²from – ⁴Asia ³Jews

King James Version

when they saw him in the temple, stirred up all the people, and laid hands on him, 28 Crying out, Men of Israel, help: This is the man, that teacheth all *men* every where against the people, and the law, and this place: and further brought Greeks also into the temple, and hath polluted this holy place. 29 (For they had seen before with him in the city Trophimus an Ephesian, whom they supposed that Paul had brought into the temple.) 30And all the city was moved, and the people ran together: and they took Paul, and drew him out of the temple: and forthwith the doors were shut. 31And as they went about to kill him, tidings came unto the chief captain of the band, that all Jerusalem was in an uproar: 32 Who immediately took soldiers and centurions, and ran down unto them: and when they saw the chief captain and the soldiers, they left beating of Paul. 33 Then the chief captain came near, and took him, and commanded *him* to be bound with two chains; and demanded who he was, and what he had done. 34And some cried one thing, some another, among the multitude: and when he could not know the certainty for the tumult, he commanded him to be carried into the castle. 35And when he came upon the stairs, so it was, that he was borne of the soldiers for the violence of the people. 36 For the multitude of the people followed after, crying, Away with him. 37And as Paul was to be led into the castle, he said unto the chief captain, May I speak unto thee? Who said, Canst thou speak Greek? 38Art not thou that Egyptian, which before these days madest an uproar, and leddest out into the wilderness four thousand men that were murderers? 39 But Paul said, I am a man *which am* a Jew of Tarsus, *a city* in Cilicia, a citizen of no mean city: and, I beseech thee, suffer me to speak unto the people. 40And when he had given him license, Paul stood on the stairs, and beckoned with the hand unto the people. And when there was made a great silence, he spake unto *them* in the Hebrew tongue, saying,

22 Men, brethren, and fathers, hear ye my defence *which I make* now unto you. 2 (And when they heard that he spake in the Hebrew tongue to them, they kept the more silence: and he saith,) 3 I am verily a man *which am* a Jew, born in Tarsus, *a city* in Cilicia, yet brought up in this city at the feet of Gamaliel, *and* taught according to the perfect manner of the law of the fathers, and was zealous toward God, as ye all are this day. 4And I persecuted this way unto the death, binding

New International Version

at the temple. They stirred up the whole crowd and seized him, 28 shouting, "Men of Israel, help us! This is the man who teaches all men everywhere against our people and our law and this place. And besides, he has brought Greeks into the temple area and defiled this holy place." 29 (They had previously seen Trophimus the Ephesian in the city with Paul and assumed that Paul had brought him into the temple area.) 30 The whole city was aroused, and the people came running from all directions. Seizing Paul, they dragged him from the temple, and immediately the gates were shut. 31 While they were trying to kill him, news reached the commander of the Roman troops that the whole city of Jerusalem was in an uproar. 32 He at once took some officers and soldiers and ran down to the crowd. When the rioters saw the commander and his soldiers, they stopped beating Paul.

33 The commander came up and arrested him and ordered him to be bound with two chains. Then he asked who he was and what he had done. 34 Some in the crowd shouted one thing and some another, and since the commander could not get at the truth because of the uproar, he ordered that Paul be taken into the barracks. 35 When Paul reached the steps, the violence of the mob was so great he had to be carried by the soldiers. 36 The crowd that followed kept shouting, "Away with him!"

Paul speaks to the crowd

37 As the soldiers were about to take Paul into the barracks, he asked the commander, "May I say something to you?"

"Do you speak Greek?" he replied. 38 "Aren't you the Egyptian who started a revolt and led four thousand terrorists out into the desert some time ago?"

39 Paul answered, "I am a Jew, from Tarsus in Cilicia, a citizen of no ordinary city. Please let me speak to the people."

40 Having received the commander's permission, Paul stood on the steps and motioned to the crowd. When they were all silent, he said to

22 them in Aramaic: 1 "Brothers and fathers, listen now to my defense."

2 When they heard him speak to them in Aramaic, they became very quiet.

Then Paul said: 3 "I am a Jew, born in Tarsus of Cilicia, but brought up in this city. Under Gamaliel I was thoroughly trained in the law of our fathers and was just as zealous for God as any of you are today. 4 I persecuted the followers of this Way to their death, arresting both

Greek Interlinear

θεασάμενοι   αὐτὸν   ἐν   τῷ   ἱερῷ   συνέχεον
seeing   him   in   the   temple stirred up

πάντα   τὸν   ὄχλον,   καὶ   ἐπέβαλαν   ἐπ'
all   the   crowd,   and   laid on   on

αὐτὸν   τὰς   χεῖρας,   28 κράζοντες·   ἄνδρες
him   the(ir) hands,   crying out: Men

'Ισραηλῖται,   βοηθεῖτε·   οὗτός   ἐστιν   ὁ
Israelites,   help: this   is   the

ἄνθρωπος   ὁ   κατὰ   τοῦ   λαοῦ   καὶ   τοῦ
man   ¹the [one] ²against ⁴the   ⁷people ⁸and   ⁹the

νόμου   καὶ   τοῦ   τόπου   τούτου   πάντας
¹⁰law   ¹¹and   ¹²the ¹⁴this ¹³place   ³all men

πανταχῇ   διδάσκων,   ἔτι   τε   καὶ   Ἕλληνας
⁴everywhere ⁵teaching,   and even also   Greeks

εἰσήγαγεν   εἰς   τὸ   ἱερὸν   καὶ   κεκοίνωκεν
brought in   into   the   temple   and   has profaned

τὸν   ἅγιον   τόπον   τοῦτον.   29 ἦσαν   γὰρ
-      ²holy   ¹place   ¹this.   For they were

προεωρακότες   Τρόφιμον   τὸν   Ἐφέσιον   ἐν
having previously seen Trophimus the   Ephesian   in

τῇ   πόλει   σὺν   αὐτῷ,   ὃν   ἐνόμιζον   ὅτι
the   city   with   him,   whom they supposed that

εἰς   τὸ   ἱερὸν   εἰσήγαγεν   ὁ   Παῦλος.   30 ἐκινήθη
²into ⁴the ⁵temple ³brought in -   ¹Paul.   ⁴was moved

τε   ἡ   πόλις   ὅλη   καὶ   ἐγένετο   συνδρομὴ
¹And ³the ²city   ³whole and   there was a running together

τοῦ   λαοῦ,   καὶ   ἐπιλαβόμενοι   τοῦ   Παύλου
of the people,   and   laying hold   -   of Paul

εἷλκον   αὐτὸν   ἔξω   τοῦ   ἱεροῦ,   καὶ   εὐθέως
they dragged him   outside the   temple,   and   immediately

ἐκλείσθησαν   αἱ   θύραι.   31 Ζητούντων   τε
were shut   the   doors.   And [while they were] seeking⁸

αὐτὸν   ἀποκτεῖναι   ἀνέβη   φάσις   τῷ
⁹him   ¹to kill   ²came up ³information to the

χιλιάρχῳ   τῆς   σπείρης   ὅτι   ὅλη   συγχύν-
chiliarch   of the cohort   that   all   ⁸is(was) in

νεται   Ἰερουσαλήμ·   32 ὃς   ἐξαυτῆς   παρα-
confusion ⁷Jerusalem;   who   at once   tak-

λαβὼν   στρατιώτας   καὶ   ἑκατοντάρχας
ing   soldiers   and   centurions

κατέδραμεν   ἐπ'   αὐτούς·   οἱ   δὲ   ἰδόντες
ran down   on   them;   and they   seeing

τὸν   χιλίαρχον   καὶ   τοὺς   στρατιώτας
the   chiliarch   and   the   soldiers

ἐπαύσαντο   τύπτοντες   τὸν   Παῦλον.   33 τότε
ceased   beating   -   Paul.   Then

ἐγγίσας   ὁ   χιλίαρχος   ἐπελάβετο   αὐτοῦ
drawing near the chiliarch   laid hold   of him

καὶ   ἐκέλευσεν   δεθῆναι   ἁλύσεσι   δυσί,   καὶ
and   commanded   to be bound chains   with two, and

ἐπυνθάνετο   τίς   εἴη   καὶ   τί   ἐστιν   πεποιηκώς.
inquired   who   he   and   what he is   having done.
              might be

34 ἄλλοι   δὲ   ἄλλο   τι   ἐπεφώνουν   ἐν   τῷ
And ¹others ⁷different ⁶some- ⁵called out ⁴among ³the
                        thing

ὄχλῳ·   μὴ   δυναμένου   δὲ   αὐτοῦ   γνῶναι
⁴crowd; and not being able   him*   to know
                         = as he was not able

τὸ   ἀσφαλὲς   διὰ   τὸν   θόρυβον,   ἐκέλευσεν
the   certain thing because of the   uproar,   he commanded

ἄγεσθαι   αὐτὸν   εἰς   τὴν   παρεμβολήν.   35 ὅτε
to be brought him   into   the   fort.   when

δὲ   ἐγένετο   ἐπὶ   τοὺς   ἀναβαθμούς,   συνέβη
And   he was   on   the   steps,   it happened

βαστάζεσθαι   αὐτὸν   ὑπὸ   τῶν   στρατιωτῶν
to be carried himᵇ   by   he   soldiers
= he was carried

διὰ   τὴν   βίαν   τοῦ   ὄχλου·   36 ἠκολούθει
because of the violence of the crowd;   ⁶followed

γὰρ   τὸ   πλῆθος   τοῦ   λαοῦ   κράζοντες·
¹for   ⁵the ²multitude ³of the ⁴people crying out:

αἶρε   αὐτόν.   37 Μέλλων   τε   εἰσάγεσθαι
Take away him.   And being about to be brought in

εἰς   τὴν   παρεμβολὴν   ὁ   Παῦλος   λέγει   τῷ
into   the   fort   -   Paul   says   to the

χιλιάρχῳ·   εἰ   ἔξεστίν   μοι   εἰπεῖν   τι   πρὸς
chiliarch·   If   it is lawful for me to say   something to

σέ;   ὁ   δὲ   ἔφη·   Ἑλληνιστὶ   γινώσκεις;
thee? And he   said: in Greek   Knowest thou
                                       [to speak]?*

38 οὐκ   ἄρα   σὺ   εἶ   ὁ   Αἰγύπτιος   ὁ   πρὸ
¹Not   ²then ³thou ⁴art the   Egyptian   the [one] before

τούτων   τῶν   ἡμερῶν   ἀναστατώσας   καὶ
these   -   days   unsettling   and

ἐξαγαγὼν   εἰς   τὴν   ἔρημον   τοὺς   τετρα-
leading out into the   desert   the   four

κισχιλίους   ἄνδρας   τῶν   σικαρίων;   39 εἶπεν
thousand   men   of the Sicarii?   said

δὲ   ὁ   Παῦλος·   ἐγὼ   ἄνθρωπος   μέν   εἰμι
And   -   Paul·   I   a man   indeed am

Ἰουδαῖος,   Ταρσεύς,   τῆς   Κιλικίας   οὐκ
a Jew,   a Tarsian,   -   of Cilicia not

ἀσήμου   πόλεως   πολίτης·   δέομαι   δέ   σου,
of a mean city   a citizen; and I beg   of thee,

ἐπίτρεψόν   μοι   λαλῆσαι   πρὸς   τὸν   λαόν.
permit   me   to speak   to   the   people.

40 ἐπιτρέψαντος   δὲ   αὐτοῦ   ὁ   Παῦλος   ἑστὼς
And permitting   him*   -   Paul   standing
= when he gave permission

ἐπὶ   τῶν   ἀναβαθμῶν   κατέσεισεν   τῇ   χειρὶ
on   the   steps   beckoned   with the(his) hand

τῷ   λαῷ·   πολλῆς   δὲ   σιγῆς   γενομένης*
to the people; and much   silence   becoming*
= when there was great silence

προσεφώνησεν   τῇ   Ἑβραΐδι   διαλέκτῳ   λέγων·
he addressed   in the Hebrew   language   saying:

Chapter 22

Ἄνδρες   ἀδελφοὶ   καὶ   πατέρες,   ἀκούσατέ
Men   brothers   and   fathers,   hear ye

μου   τῆς   πρὸς   ὑμᾶς   νυνὶ   ἀπολογίας.
²of me ¹the   ⁴to   ⁵you   ⁶now   ³defence.

— 2 ἀκούσαντες   δὲ   ὅτι   τῇ   Ἑβραΐδι
(And hearing   that   in the Hebrew

διαλέκτῳ   προσεφώνει   αὐτοῖς   μᾶλλον
language   he addressed   them   more

παρέσχον   ἡσυχίαν.   καὶ   φησίν·   — 3 ἐγώ   εἰμι
they showed quietness.   And   he says:)   I   am

ἀνὴρ   Ἰουδαῖος,   γεγεννημένος   ἐν   Ταρσῷ
a man   a Jew,   having been born in   Tarsus

τῆς   Κιλικίας,   ἀνατεθραμμένος   δὲ   ἐν   τῇ
-      of Cilicia, and having been brought up in   the

πόλει   ταύτῃ,   παρὰ   τοὺς   πόδας   Γαμαλιὴλ
city   this,   at   the   feet   of Gamaliel

πεπαιδευμένος   κατὰ   ἀκρίβειαν   τοῦ   πατρῴου
having been trained according exactness of the ancestral
                                      to [the]

νόμου,   ζηλωτὴς   ὑπάρχων   τοῦ   θεοῦ   καθὼς
law   a zealot   being   -   of God even as

πάντες   ὑμεῖς   ἐστε   σήμερον·   4 ὃς   ταύτην
all   ye   are   to-day;   who   this

τὴν   ὁδὸν   ἐδίωξα   ἄχρι   θανάτου,   δεσμεύων
-      way   persecuted as far as to death,   binding

* See note on page xxxviii.

King James Version

and delivering into prisons both men and women. 5As also the high priest doth bear me witness, and all the estate of the elders: from whom also I received letters unto the brethren, and went to Damascus, to bring them which were there bound unto Jerusalem, for to be punished. 6And it came to pass, that, as I made my journey, and was come nigh unto Damascus about noon, suddenly there shone from heaven a great light round about me. 7And I fell unto the ground, and heard a voice saying unto me, Saul, Saul, why persecutest thou me? 8And I answered, Who art thou, Lord? And he said unto me, I am Jesus of Nazareth, whom thou persecutest. 9And they that were with me saw indeed the light, and were afraid; but they heard not the voice of him that spake to me. 10And I said, What shall I do, Lord? And the Lord said unto me, Arise, and go into Damascus; and there it shall be told thee of all things which are appointed for thee to do. 11And when I could not see for the glory of that light, being led by the hand of them that were with me, I came into Damascus. 12And one Ananias, a devout man according to the law, having a good report of all the Jews which dwelt *there,* 13 Came unto me, and stood, and said unto me, Brother Saul, receive thy sight. And the same hour I looked up upon him. 14And he said, The God of our fathers hath chosen thee, that thou shouldest know his will, and see that Just One, and shouldest hear the voice of his mouth. 15 For thou shalt be his witness unto all men of what thou hast seen and heard. 16And now why tarriest thou? arise, and be baptized, and wash away thy sins, calling on the name of the Lord. 17And it came to pass, that, when I was come again to Jerusalem, even while I prayed in the temple, I was in a trance; 18And saw him saying unto me, Make haste, and get thee quickly out of Jerusalem: for they will not receive thy testimony concerning me. 19And I said, Lord, they know that I imprisoned and beat in every synagogue them that believed on thee: 20And when the blood of thy martyr Stephen was shed, I also was standing by, and consenting unto his death, and kept the raiment of them that slew him. 21And he said unto me, Depart: for I will send thee far hence unto the Gentiles. 22And they gave him audience unto this word, and *then* lifted up their voices, and said, Away with such a *fellow* from the earth: for it is not fit that he should live. 23And as they cried out, and cast off *their* clothes, and threw dust into the air, 24 The chief captain commanded him to be brought into the castle, and bade that he should be examined by scourging; that he might know wherefore they cried so against him. 25And as they bound him with thongs, Paul said unto the centurion that stood by, Is it lawful for you to scourge a man that is a Roman, and uncondemned? 26 When the centurion heard *that,* he went and told the chief captain, saying, Take

New International Version

men and women and throwing them into prison, 5 as also the high priest and all the council can testify. I even obtained letters from them to their brothers in Damascus, and went there to bring these people as prisoners to Jerusalem to be punished.

6 "About noon as I came near Damascus, suddenly a bright light from heaven flashed around me. 7 I fell to the ground and heard a voice say to me, 'Saul! Saul! Why do you persecute me?'

8 " 'Who are you, Lord?' I asked.

" 'I am Jesus of Nazareth, whom you are persecuting,' he replied. 9 My companions saw the light, but they did not understand the voice of him who was speaking to me.

10 " 'What shall I do, Lord?' I asked.

" 'Get up,' the Lord said, 'and go into Damascus. There you will be told all that you have been assigned to do.' 11 My companions led me by the hand into Damascus, because the brilliance of the light had blinded me.

12 "A man named Ananias came to see me. He was a devout observer of the law and highly respected by all the Jews living there. 13 He stood beside me and said, 'Brother Saul, receive your sight!' And at that very moment I was able to see him.

14 "Then he said: 'The God of our fathers has chosen you to know his will and to see the Righteous One and to hear words from his mouth. 15 You will be his witness to all men of what you have seen and heard. 16 And now what are you waiting for? Get up, be baptized and wash your sins away, calling on his name.'

17 "When I returned to Jerusalem and was praying at the temple, I fell into a trance 18 and saw the Lord speaking. 'Quick!' he said to me. 'Leave Jerusalem immediately, because they will not accept your testimony about me.'

19 " 'Lord,' I replied, 'these men know that I went from one synagogue to another to imprison and beat those who believe in you. 20 And when the blood of your martyr Stephen was shed, I stood there giving my approval and guarding the clothes of those who were killing him.'

21 "Then the Lord said to me, 'Go; I will send you far away to the Gentiles.' "

Paul the Roman citizen

22 The crowd listened to Paul until he said this. Then they raised their voices and shouted, "Rid the earth of him! He's not fit to live!"

23 As they were shouting and throwing off their cloaks and flinging dust into the air, 24 the commander ordered Paul to be taken into the barracks. He directed that he be flogged and questioned in order to find out why the people were shouting at him like this. 25 As they stretched him out to flog him, Paul said to the centurion standing there, "Is it legal for you to flog a Roman citizen who hasn't even been found guilty?"

26 When the centurion heard this, he went to the commander and reported it. "What are you

Greek Interlinear

καὶ παραδιδοὺς εἰς φυλακὰς ἄνδρας τε
and delivering to prisons both men
καὶ γυναῖκας. 5 ὡς καὶ ὁ ἀρχιερεὺς
and women. As even the high priest
μαρτυρεῖ μοι καὶ πᾶν τὸ πρεσβυτέριον·
witnesses to me and all the senate;
παρ᾽ ὧν καὶ ἐπιστολὰς δεξάμενος πρὸς
from whom also letters having received to
τοὺς ἀδελφοὺς εἰς Δαμασκὸν ἐπορευόμην,
the brothers in Damascus I journeyed,
ἄξων καὶ τοὺς ἐκεῖσε ὄντας δεδεμένους
leading also the [ones] ¹there ²being having been bound
εἰς Ἰερουσαλὴμ ἵνα τιμωρηθῶσιν.
to Jerusalem that they might be punished.
6 Ἐγένετο δέ μοι πορευομένῳ καὶ ἐγγίζοντι
Now it happened to me journeying and drawing near
τῇ Δαμασκῷ περὶ μεσημβρίαν ἐξαίφνης ἐκ
to Damascus about midday suddenly out of
τοῦ οὐρανοῦ περιαστράψαι φῶς ἱκανὸν
– heaven to shine round ¹a ³light ²considerable
περὶ ἐμέ, 7 ἔπεσά τε εἰς τὸ ἔδαφος
round me, and I fell to the ground
καὶ ἤκουσα φωνῆς λεγούσης μοι· Σαοὺλ
and heard a voice saying to me: Saul[,]
Σαούλ, τί με διώκεις; 8 ἐγὼ δὲ ἀπεκρίθην·
Saul, why me persecutest thou? And I answered:
τίς εἶ, κύριε; εἶπέν τε πρὸς ἐμέ· ἐγώ
Who art thou, Lord? And he said to me: I
εἰμι Ἰησοῦς ὁ Ναζωραῖος, ὃν σὺ διώκεις.
am Jesus the Nazarene, whom thou persecutest.
9 οἱ δὲ σὺν ἐμοὶ ὄντες τὸ μὲν φῶς
Now ¹the [ones] ³with ⁴me ²being ⁷the ⁶indeed ⁸light
ἐθεάσαντο, τὴν δὲ φωνὴν οὐκ ἤκουσαν
⁵beheld, but the voice they heard not
τοῦ λαλοῦντός μοι. 10 εἶπον δέ· τί
of the [one] speaking to me. And I said: What
ποιήσω, κύριε; ὁ δὲ κύριος εἶπεν πρός
may I do, Lord? And the Lord said to
με· ἀναστὰς πορεύου εἰς Δαμασκόν, κἀκεῖ σοι
me: Rising up go into Damascus, and there to thee
λαληθήσεται περὶ πάντων ὧν τέτακταί
it will be told concerning all things which has(ve) been
arranged
σοι ποιῆσαι. 11 ὡς δὲ οὐκ ἐνέβλεπον
for thee to do. And as I saw not
ἀπὸ τῆς δόξης τοῦ φωτὸς ἐκείνου,
from the glory of the light of that light,
χειραγωγούμενος ὑπὸ τῶν συνόντων μοι
being led by the hand by the [ones] being with me
ἦλθον εἰς Δαμασκόν. 12 Ἀνανίας δέ τις,
I went into Damascus. And a certain Ananias,
ἀνὴρ εὐλαβὴς κατὰ τὸν νόμον, μαρτυρού-
a man devout according to the law, being attest-
μενος ὑπὸ πάντων τῶν κατοικούντων
[to] by all ¹the ²dwelling ³[there]
Ἰουδαίων, 13 ἐλθὼν πρὸς ἐμὲ καὶ ἐπιστὰς
³Jews, coming to me and standing by
εἶπέν μοι· Σαοὺλ ἀδελφέ, ἀνάβλεψον.
said to me: Saul brother, look up.
κἀγὼ αὐτῇ τῇ ὥρᾳ ἀνέβλεψα εἰς αὐτόν.
And I in that hour⁴ looked up at him.
14 ὁ δὲ εἶπεν· ὁ θεὸς τῶν πατέρων
And he said: The God of the fathers
ἡμῶν προεχειρίσατό σε γνῶναι τὸ θέλημα
of us previously appointed thee to know the will
αὐτοῦ καὶ ἰδεῖν τὸν δίκαιον καὶ ἀκοῦσαι
of him and to see the Just One and to hear
φωνὴν ἐκ τοῦ στόματος αὐτοῦ, 15 ὅτι
a voice out of the mouth of him, because
ἔσῃ μάρτυς αὐτῷ πρὸς πάντας ἀνθρώπους
thou wilt be a witness to him⁴ to all men

ὧν ἑώρακας καὶ ἤκουσας. 16 καὶ νῦν
of things which thou hast seen and didst hear. And now
τί μέλλεις; ἀναστὰς βάπτισαι καὶ ἀπόλου-
what intendest thou? Rising up be baptized and wash
σαι τὰς ἁμαρτίας σου, ἐπικαλεσάμενος τὸ
away the sins of thee, invoking the
ὄνομα αὐτοῦ. 17 Ἐγένετο δέ μοι ὑποστρέ-
name of him. And it happened to me having
ψαντι εἰς Ἰερουσαλὴμ καὶ προσευχομένου
returned to Jerusalem and praying
μου ἐν τῷ ἱερῷ γενέσθαι με ἐν ἐκστάσει,
me⁴ in the temple to become me⁵ in an ecstasy,
=as I was praying
=I became
18 καὶ ἰδεῖν αὐτὸν λέγοντά μοι· σπεῦσον
and to see⁵ him saying to me; Haste
=I saw
καὶ ἔξελθε ἐν τάχει ἐξ Ἰερουσαλήμ,
and go forth quickly out of Jerusalem,
διότι οὐ παραδέξονταί σου μαρτυρίαν
because they will not receive of thee witness
περὶ ἐμοῦ. 19 κἀγὼ εἶπον· κύριε, αὐτοὶ
concerning me. And I said: Lord, they
ἐπίστανται ὅτι ἐγὼ ἤμην φυλακίζων καὶ
understand that I was imprisoning and
δέρων κατὰ τὰς συναγωγὰς τοὺς πιστεύον-
beating throughout the synagogues the [ones] believ-
τας ἐπὶ σέ· 20 καὶ ὅτε ἐξεχύννετο τὸ αἷμα
ing on thee; and when was being shed the blood
Στεφάνου τοῦ μάρτυρός σου, καὶ αὐτὸς
of Stephen the witness of thee, even [my]self
ἤμην ἐφεστὼς καὶ συνευδοκῶν καὶ
I was standing by and consenting and
φυλάσσων τὰ ἱμάτια τῶν ἀναιρούντων
keeping the garments of the [ones] killing
αὐτόν. 21 καὶ εἶπεν πρός με· πορεύου,
him. And he said to me: Go,
ὅτι ἐγὼ εἰς ἔθνη μακρὰν ἐξαποστελῶ σε.
because I to nations afar will send forth thee.
22 Ἤκουον δὲ αὐτοῦ ἄχρι τούτου τοῦ
And they heard him as far as to this –
λόγου, καὶ ἐπῆραν τὴν φωνὴν αὐτῶν
word, and lifted up the voice of them
λέγοντες· αἶρε ἀπὸ τῆς γῆς τὸν τοιοῦτον·
saying: Take from the earth such a man;
οὐ γὰρ καθῆκεν αὐτὸν ζῆν. 23 κραυγαζόν-
for not it is fitting him to live. And shout-
των τε αὐτῶν καὶ ῥιπτούντων τὰ ἱμάτια
ing them and tearing* the(ir) garments
=as they shouted and tore . . .
καὶ κονιορτὸν βαλλόντων εἰς τὸν ἀέρα,
and ²dust ¹throwing* in the air,
=threw dust
24 ἐκέλευσεν ὁ χιλίαρχος εἰσάγεσθαι αὐτὸν
commanded the chiliarch to be brought in him
εἰς τὴν παρεμβολήν, εἴπας ¹with scourges
into the fort, bidding
ἀνετάζεσθαι αὐτόν, ἵνα ἐπιγνῷ δι᾽ ἣν
²to be examined ¹him, that he might fully know for what
αἰτίαν οὕτως ἐπεφώνουν αὐτῷ. 25 ὡς δὲ
crime thus they were calling against him. But as
προέτειναν αὐτὸν τοῖς ἱμᾶσιν, εἶπεν πρὸς
they stretched him with the thongs, ²said ¹to
forward
τὸν ἑστῶτα ἑκατόνταρχον ὁ Παῦλος· εἰ
⁴the ⁵standing [by] ⁶centurion – ¹Paul: ³If
ἄνθρωπον Ῥωμαῖον καὶ ἀκατάκριτον ἔξεστιν
a man ²a Roman ³and ¹uncondemned ²it is lawful
ὑμῖν μαστίζειν; 26 ἀκούσας δὲ ὁ ἑκατόν-
³for you ⁴to scourge? And ³hearing ¹the ²cen-
τάρχης προσελθὼν τῷ χιλιάρχῳ ἀπήγγειλεν
turion approaching to the chiliarch reported

* See Luke 2. 38.

King James Version

heed what thou doest; for this man is a Roman.
27 Then the chief captain came, and said unto
him, Tell me, art thou a Roman? He said, Yea.
28And the chief captain answered, With a great
sum obtained I this freedom. And Paul said,
But I was *free* born. 29 Then straightway they
departed from him which should have examined
him: and the chief captain also was afraid, after
he knew that he was a Roman, and because
he had bound him. 30 On the morrow, because he
would have known the certainty wherefore he
was accused of the Jews, he loosed him from
his bands, and commanded the chief priests and
all their council to appear, and brought Paul
down, and set him before them.

23 And Paul, earnestly beholding the council, said, Men *and* brethren, I have lived in
all good conscience before God until this day.
2And the high priest Ananias commanded them
that stood by him to smite him on the mouth.
3 Then said Paul unto him, God shall smite thee,
thou whited wall: for sittest thou to judge me
after the law, and commandest me to be smitten
contrary to the law? 4And they that stood by
said, Revilest thou God's high priest? 5 Then
said Paul, I wist not, brethren, that he was the
high priest: for it is written, Thou shalt not
speak evil of the ruler of thy people. 6 But when
Paul perceived that the one part were Sadducees, and the other Pharisees, he cried out in
the council, Men *and* brethren, I am a Pharisee,
the son of a Pharisee: of the hope and resurrection of the dead I am called in question.
7And when he had so said, there arose a dissension between the Pharisees and the Sadducees: and the multitude was divided. 8 For the
Sadducees say that there is no resurrection, neither angel, nor spirit: but the Pharisees confess
both. 9And there arose a great cry: and the
scribes *that were* of the Pharisees' part arose,
and strove, saying, We find no evil in this man:
but if a spirit or an angel hath spoken to him,
let us not fight against God. 10And when there
arose a great dissension, the chief captain, fearing lest Paul should have been pulled in pieces
of them, commanded the soldiers to go down,
and to take him by force from among them, and
to bring *him* into the castle. 11And the night
following the Lord stood by him, and said, Be
of good cheer, Paul: for as thou hast testified
of me in Jerusalem, so must thou bear witness
also at Rome. 12And when it was day, certain
of the Jews banded together, and bound themselves under a curse, saying that they would
neither eat nor drink till they had killed Paul.
13And they were more than forty which had

New International Version

going to do?" he asked. "This man is a Roman
citizen."
27 The commander went to Paul and asked,
"Tell me, are you a Roman citizen?"
"Yes, I am," he answered.
28 Then the commander said, "I had to pay
a big price for my citizenship."
"But I was born a citizen," Paul replied.
29 Those who were about to question him
withdrew immediately. The commander himself
was alarmed when he realized that he had put
Paul, a Roman citizen, in chains.

Before the Sanhedrin

30 The next day, since the commander wanted
to find out exactly why Paul was being accused
by the Jews, he released him and ordered the
chief priests and all the Sanhedrin to assemble.
Then he brought Paul and had him stand before
them.

23 Paul looked straight at the Sanhedrin and
said, "My brothers, I have fulfilled my
duty to God in all good conscience to this day."
2At this the high priest Ananias ordered those
standing near Paul to strike him on the mouth.
3 Then Paul said to him, "God will strike you,
you white-washed wall! You sit there to judge
me according to the law, yet you yourself violate
the law by commanding that I be struck!"
4 Those who were standing near Paul said,
"You dare to insult God's high priest?"
5 Paul replied, "Brothers, I did not realize
that he was the high priest; for it is written: 'Do
not speak evil about the ruler of your people.' [i] "
6 Then Paul, knowing that some of them were
Sadducees and the others Pharisees, called out
in the Sanhedrin, "My brothers, I am a Pharisee,
the son of a Pharisee. I stand on trial because
of my hope in the resurrection of the dead."
7 When he said this, a dispute broke out between the Pharisees and the Sadducees, and the
assembly was divided. 8 (The Sadducees say that
there is no resurrection, and that there are
neither angels nor spirits, but the Pharisees acknowledge them all.)
9 There was a great uproar, and some of the
teachers of the law who were Pharisees stood up
and argued vigorously. "We find nothing wrong
with this man," they said. "What if a spirit or
an angel has spoken to him?" 10 The dispute
became so violent that the commander was afraid
Paul would be torn to pieces by them. He ordered the troops to go down and take him away
from them by force and bring him into the
barracks.
11 The following night the Lord stood near
Paul and said, "Take courage! As you have
testified about me in Jerusalem, so you must
also testify in Rome."

The plot to kill Paul

12 The next morning the Jews formed a conspiracy and bound themselves with an oath not
to eat or drink until they had killed Paul.
13 More than forty men were involved in this

[i] Exodus 22:28.

Greek Interlinear

λέγων· τί μέλλεις ποιεῖν; ὁ γὰρ ἄνθρωπος
saying: What art thou about to do?   -   for   ¹man

οὗτος 'Ρωμαῖός ἐστιν. 27 προσελθὼν δὲ
¹this   ⁴a Roman   ²is.   And approaching

ὁ χιλίαρχος εἶπεν αὐτῷ· λέγε μοι, σὺ
the chiliarch said to him: Tell me, thou

'Ρωμαῖος εἶ; ὁ δὲ ἔφη· ναί. 28 ἀπεκρίθη
a Roman art? And he said: Yes.   answered

δὲ ὁ χιλίαρχος· ἐγὼ πολλοῦ κεφαλαίου
And the chiliarch: ¹I   ⁴of(for) ⁵sum [of money] much(great)

τὴν πολιτείαν ταύτην ἐκτησάμην. ὁ δὲ
²this ⁶citizenship   ³acquired.   -   So

Παῦλος ἔφη· ἐγὼ δὲ καὶ γεγέννημαι.
Paul said: But I indeed have been born.

29 εὐθέως οὖν ἀπέστησαν ἀπ' αὐτοῦ οἱ
Immediately therefore ⁵stood away ⁶from ⁷him ¹the [ones]

μέλλοντες αὐτὸν ἀνετάζειν· καὶ ὁ χιλίαρχος
³being about ⁴him ²to examine; ⁴also ³the ⁵chiliarch

δὲ ἐφοβήθη ἐπιγνοὺς ὅτι 'Ρωμαῖός ἐστιν
¹and feared fully knowing that a Roman he is(was)

καὶ ὅτι αὐτὸν ἦν δεδεκώς.
and that ¹him ¹he was ²having bound.

30 Τῇ δὲ ἐπαύριον βουλόμενος γνῶναι τὸ
And on the morrow being minded to know the

ἀσφαλές, τὸ τί κατηγορεῖται ὑπὸ τῶν
certain thing, - why he was accused by the

'Ιουδαίων, ἔλυσεν αὐτόν, καὶ ἐκέλευσεν
Jews, he released him, and commanded

συνελθεῖν τοὺς ἀρχιερεῖς καὶ πᾶν τὸ
to come together the chief priests and all the

συνέδριον, καὶ καταγαγὼν τὸν Παῦλον
council, and having brought down - Paul

Chapter 23

ἔστησεν εἰς αὐτούς. 23 ἀτενίσας δὲ
set [him] among them. And ²gazing

ὁ Παῦλος τῷ συνεδρίῳ εἶπεν· ἄνδρες
- ¹Paul at the council said: Men

ἀδελφοί, ἐγὼ πάσῃ συνειδήσει ἀγαθῇ
brothers, I in all conscience good

πεπολίτευμαι τῷ θεῷ ἄχρι ταύτης τῆς
have lived - to God until this -

ἡμέρας. 2 ὁ δὲ ἀρχιερεὺς 'Ανανίας
day. And the high priest Ananias

ἐπέταξεν τοῖς παρεστῶσιν αὐτῷ τύπτειν
gave order to the [ones] standing by him to strike

αὐτοῦ τὸ στόμα. 3 τότε ὁ Παῦλος πρὸς
of him the mouth. Then - Paul to

αὐτὸν εἶπεν· τύπτειν σε μέλλει ὁ θεός,
him said:- ²To strike ⁴thee ³is about - ¹God,

τοῖχε κεκονιαμένε· καὶ σὺ κάθῃ κρίνων
wall having been whitened; and thou sittest judging

με κατὰ τὸν νόμον, καὶ παρανομῶν
me according to the law, and contravening law

κελεύεις με τύπτεσθαι; 4 οἱ δὲ παρεστῶτες
commandest me to be struck? And the [ones] standing by

εἶπαν· τὸν ἀρχιερέα τοῦ θεοῦ λοιδορεῖς;
said: The high priest - of God revilest thou?

5 ἔφη τε ὁ Παῦλος· οὐκ ᾔδειν, ἀδελφοί,
And said - Paul: I did not know, brothers,

ὅτι ἐστὶν ἀρχιερεύς· γέγραπται γὰρ ὅτι
that is high priest; for it has been written[,]

ἄρχοντα τοῦ λαοῦ σου οὐκ ἐρεῖς κακῶς.
A ruler of the people of thee thou shalt not speak evilly.

6 γνοὺς δὲ ὁ Παῦλος ὅτι τὸ ἓν μέρος
And knowing - Paul that the one part

ἐστὶν Σαδδουκαίων τὸ δὲ ἕτερον Φαρισαίων
is(was) of Sadducees but the other of Pharisees

ἔκραζεν ἐν τῷ συνεδρίῳ· ἄνδρες ἀδελφοί,
cried out in the council: Men brothers,

ἐγὼ Φαρισαῖός εἰμι, υἱὸς Φαρισαίων· περὶ
I a Pharisee am, a son of Pharisees; concerning

ἐλπίδος καὶ ἀναστάσεως νεκρῶν κρίνομαι.
hope and resurrection of dead ones I am being judged.

7 τοῦτο δὲ αὐτοῦ λαλοῦντος ἐγένετο
And this him saying⁸ there was = as he said this

στάσις τῶν Φαρισαίων καὶ Σαδδουκαίων,
a discord of the Pharisees and Sadducees.

καὶ ἐσχίσθη τὸ πλῆθος. 8 Σαδδουκαῖοι
and was divided the multitude. Sadducees

γὰρ λέγουσιν μὴ εἶναι ἀνάστασιν μήτε
For say not to be a resurrection nor

ἄγγελον μήτε πνεῦμα, Φαρισαῖοι δὲ
angel nor spirit, but Pharisees

ὁμολογοῦσιν τὰ ἀμφότερα. 9 ἐγένετο δὲ
confess - both. And there was

κραυγὴ μεγάλη, καὶ ἀναστάντες τινὲς
cry a great, and rising up some

τῶν γραμματέων τοῦ μέρους τῶν Φαρισαίων
of the scribes of the part of the Pharisees

διεμάχοντο λέγοντες· οὐδὲν κακὸν εὑρίσκομεν
strove saying: Nothing evil we find

ἐν τῷ ἀνθρώπῳ τούτῳ· εἰ δὲ πνεῦμα
in this man; and if ¹a spirit

ἐλάλησεν αὐτῷ ἢ ἄγγελος —. 10 Πολλῆς δὲ
²spoke ³to him ²or ³an angel —. And much

γινομένης στάσεως φοβηθεὶς ὁ χιλίαρχος
arising discord³ ²fearing ¹the ⁵chiliarch = when much' discord arose

μὴ διασπασθῇ ὁ Παῦλος ὑπ' αὐτῶν,
⁴lest ⁶should be - ³Paul by them,
torn asunder

ἐκέλευσεν τὸ στράτευμα καταβὰν ἁρπάσαι
commanded the soldiery coming down to seize

αὐτὸν ἐκ μέσου αὐτῶν ἄγειν τε εἰς
him out of [the] midst of them and to bring [him] into

τὴν παρεμβολήν. 11 Τῇ δὲ ἐπιούσῃ
the fort. And in the following

νυκτὶ ἐπιστὰς αὐτῷ ὁ κύριος εἶπεν·
night ²coming on ⁴to him ¹the ³Lord said:

θάρσει· ὡς γὰρ διεμαρτύρω τὰ περὶ
Be of good for as thou didst the concerning courage; solemnly witness things

ἐμοῦ εἰς 'Ιερουσαλήμ, οὕτω σε δεῖ καὶ
me in Jerusalem, so thee it behoves also

εἰς 'Ρώμην μαρτυρῆσαι. 12 Γενομένης δὲ
in Rome to witness. And becoming

ἡμέρας ποιήσαντες συστροφὴν οἱ 'Ιουδαῖοι
day⁸ ²making ⁴a conspiracy ¹the ³Jews = when it became day

ἀνεθεμάτισαν ἑαυτούς, λέγοντες μήτε φαγεῖν
cursed themselves, saying neither to eat

μήτε πεῖν ἕως οὗ ἀποκτείνωσιν τὸν
nor to drink until they should kill -

Παῦλον. 13 ἦσαν δὲ πλείους τεσσεράκοντα
Paul. And there were more [than] forty

King James Version

made this conspiracy. 14And they came to the chief priests and elders, and said, We have bound ourselves under a great curse, that we will eat nothing until we have slain Paul. 15 Now therefore ye with the council signify to the chief captain that he bring him down unto you to morrow, as though ye would inquire something more perfectly concerning him: and we, or ever he come near, are ready to kill him. 16And when Paul's sister's son heard of their lying in wait, he went and entered into the castle, and told Paul. 17 Then Paul called one of the centurions unto him, and said, Bring this young man unto the chief captain: for he hath a certain thing to tell him. 18 So he took him, and brought him to the chief captain, and said, Paul the prisoner called me unto him, and prayed me to bring this young man unto thee, who hath something to say unto thee. 19 Then the chief captain took him by the hand, and went with him aside privately, and asked him, What is that thou hast to tell me? 20And he said, The Jews have agreed to desire thee that thou wouldest bring down Paul to morrow into the council, as though they would inquire somewhat of him more perfectly. 21 But do not thou yield unto them: for there lie in wait for him of them more than forty men, which have bound themselves with an oath, that they will neither eat nor drink till they have killed him: and now are they ready, looking for a promise from thee. 22 So the chief captain then let the young man depart, and charged him, See thou tell no man that thou hast shewed these things to me. 23And he called unto him two centurions, saying, Make ready two hundred soldiers to go to Cesarea, and horsemen threescore and ten, and spearmen two hundred, at the third hour of the night; 24And provide them beasts, that they may set Paul on, and bring him safe unto Felix the governor. 25And he wrote a letter after this manner: 26 Claudius Lysias unto the most excellent governor Felix sendeth greeting. 27 This man was taken of the Jews, and should have been killed of them: then came I with an army, and rescued him, having understood that he was a Roman. 28And when I would have known the cause wherefore they accused him, I brought him forth into their council: 29 Whom I perceived to be accused of questions of their law, but to have nothing laid to his charge worthy of death or of bonds. 30And when it was told me how that the Jews laid wait for the man, I sent straightway to thee, and gave commandment to his accusers also to say before thee what they had against him. Farewell. 31 Then the soldiers, as it was commanded them, took Paul, and brought him by night to Antipatris. 32 On the morrow they left the horsemen to go with him, and returned to the castle: 33 Who, when they came to Cesarea, and delivered the epistle to the governor, presented

New International Version

plot. 14 They went to the chief priests and elders and said, "We have taken a solemn oath not to eat anything until we have killed Paul. 15 Now then, you and the Sanhedrin petition the commander to bring him before you on the pretext of wanting more accurate information about his case. We are ready to kill him before he gets here."

16 But when the son of Paul's sister heard of this plot, he went into the barracks and told Paul.

17 Then Paul called one of the centurions and said, "Take this young man to the commander; he has something to tell him." 18 So he took him to the commander.

The centurion said, "The prisoner Paul sent for me and asked me to bring this young man to you because he has something to tell you."

19 The commander took the young man by the hand, drew him aside and asked, "What is it you want to tell me?"

20 He said: "The Jews have agreed to ask you to bring Paul before the Sanhedrin tomorrow on the pretext of wanting more accurate information about him. 21 Don't give in to them, because more than forty of them are waiting in ambush for him. They have taken an oath not to eat or drink until they have killed him. They are ready now, waiting for your consent to their request."

22 The commander dismissed the young man and cautioned him, "Don't tell anyone that you have reported this to me."

Paul transferred to Caesarea

23 Then he called two of his centurions and ordered them, "Get ready a detachment of two hundred soldiers, seventy horsemen and two hundred spearmen to go to Caesarea tonight at the third hour.[j] 24 Provide mounts for Paul so that he may be taken safely to Governor Felix."

25 He wrote a letter as follows:

26 Claudius Lysias,

To His Excellency, Governor Felix:

Greetings.

27 This man was seized by the Jews and they were about to kill him, but I came with my troops and rescued him, for I had learned that he is a Roman citizen. 28 I wanted to know why they were accusing him, so I brought him to their Sanhedrin. 29 I found that the accusation had to do with questions about their law, but there was no charge against him that deserved death or imprisonment. 30 When I was informed of a plot to be carried out against the man, I sent him to you at once. I also ordered his accusers to present to you their case against him.

31 So the soldiers, carrying out their orders, took Paul with them during the night and brought him as far as Antipatris. 32 The next day they let the cavalry go on with him, while they returned to the barracks. 33 When the cavalry arrived in Caesarea, they delivered the letter to the governor and handed Paul over to him.

[j] That is, about 9:00 P.M.

Greek Interlinear

οἱ   ταύτην   τὴν   συνωμοσίαν   ποιησάμενοι·
the [ones] this   –   plot   making;

14 οἵτινες   προσελθόντες   τοῖς   ἀρχιερεῦσιν
who   approaching   to the chief priests

καὶ   τοῖς   πρεσβυτέροις   εἶπαν·   ἀναθέματι
and   to the   elders   said·   With a curse

ἀνεθεματίσαμεν   ἑαυτοὺς   μηδενὸς   γεύσασθαι
we cursed   ourselves of nothing   to taste

ἕως   οὗ   ἀποκτείνωμεν   τὸν   Παῦλον.   **15** νῦν
until   we may kill   –   Paul.   Now

οὖν   ὑμεῖς   ἐμφανίσατε   τῷ   χιλιάρχῳ   σὺν
therefore ye   inform   the chiliarch   with

τῷ   συνεδρίῳ   ὅπως   καταγάγῃ   αὐτὸι   εἰς
the council   so as   he may bring down him   to

ὑμᾶς   ὡς   μέλλοντας   διαγινώσκειν   ἀκριβέστε-
you   as   intending   to ascertain exactly more accurate-

ρον   τὰ   περὶ   αὐτοῦ·   ἡμεῖς   δὲ   πρὸ   τοῦ
ly the things concerning him; and we   before   –

ἐγγίσαι   αὐτὸν   ἕτοιμοί   ἐσμεν   τοῦ   ἀνελεῖν
to draw near him   ready   are   –   to kill

αὐτόν.   **16** Ἀκούσας   δὲ   ὁ   υἱὸς   τῆς   ἀδελφῆς
him.   And hearing   the son   of the   sister

Παύλου   τὴν   ἐνέδραν,   παραγενόμενος   καὶ
of Paul   the   treachery,   coming   and

εἰσελθὼν   εἰς   τὴν   παρεμβολὴν   ἀπήγγειλεν
entering   into the   fort   reported

τῷ   Παύλῳ.   **17** προσκαλεσάμενος   δὲ   ὁ
–   to Paul.   And calling to [him]   –

Παῦλος   ἕνα   τῶν   ἑκατοντάρχων   ἔφη·   τὸν
Paul   one   of the centurions   said·

νεανίαν   τοῦτον   ἄπαγε   πρὸς   τὸν   χιλίαρχον,
youth   this   Bring up   to   the   chiliarch,

ἔχει   γὰρ   ἀπαγγεῖλαί   τι   αὐτῷ.   **18** ὁ
for he has   to report   something to him.   He

μὲν   οὖν   παραλαβὼν   αὐτὸν   ἤγαγεν   πρὸς
–   therefore taking   him   brought   to

τὸν   χιλίαρχον   καὶ   φησίν·   ὁ   δέσμιος
the   chiliarch   and   says: The prisoner

Παῦλος   προσκαλεσάμενός   με   ἠρώτησεν
Paul   calling to [him]   me   asked

τοῦτον   τὸν   νεανίσκον   ἀγαγεῖν   πρὸς   σέ,
this   –   young man   to bring   to   thee,

ἔχοντά   τι   λαλῆσαί   σοι.   **19** ἐπιλαβόμενος
having   something to tell   thee.   laying hold

δὲ   τῆς   χειρὸς   αὐτοῦ   ὁ   χιλίαρχος   καὶ
And of the hand   of him the chiliarch   and

ἀναχωρήσας   κατ’   ἰδίαν   ἐπυνθάνετο·   τί
retiring   privately   inquired: What

ἐστιν   ὃ   ἔχεις   ἀπαγγεῖλαί   μοι;   **20** εἶπεν
is it   which thou hast to report   to me?   he said[,]

δὲ   ὅτι   οἱ   Ἰουδαῖοι   συνέθεντο   τοῦ   ἐρωτῆσαί
And – The Jews   agreed   –   to ask

σε   ὅπως   αὔριον   τὸν   Παῦλον   καταγάγῃς
thee so as   to-morrow   –   Paul   thou shouldest bring down

εἰς   τὸ   συνέδριον   ὡς   μέλλον   τι   ἀκριβέστερον
to the council   as   intending some- more accurately
                                                    thing

πυνθάνεσθαι   περὶ   αὐτοῦ.   **21** σὺ   οὖν   μὴ
to inquire   concerning him.   Thou therefore not

πεισθῇς   αὐτοῖς·   ἐνεδρεύουσιν   γὰρ   αὐτὸν
be persuaded by them;   for there lie in wait for   him

ἐξ   αὐτῶν   ἄνδρες   πλείους   τεσσεράκοντα,
of   them   men   more [than]   forty,

οἵτινες   ἀνεθεμάτισαν   ἑαυτοὺς   μήτε   φαγεῖν
who   cursed   themselves neither to eat

μήτε   πεῖν   ἕως   οὗ   ἀνέλωσιν   αὐτόν,   καὶ   νῦν
nor   to drink until   they kill   him,   and now

εἰσιν   ἕτοιμοι   προσδεχόμενοι   τὴν   ἀπὸ   σοῦ
they are ready   awaiting   the   from   thee

ἐπαγγελίαν.   **22** ὁ   μὲν   οὖν   χιλίαρχος
promise.   the   –   Therefore chiliarch

ἀπέλυσε   τὸν   νεανίσκον,   παραγγείλας   μηδενὶ
dismissed   the   young man,   charging [him]   to no one

ἐκλαλῆσαι   ὅτι   ταῦτα   ἐνεφάνισας   πρὸς   ἐμέ.
to divulge   that these things thou reportedst to   me.

23 Καὶ   προσκαλεσάμενός   τινας   δύο   τῶν
And   calling to [him]   a certain two of the

ἑκατονταρχῶν   εἶπεν·   ἑτοιμάσατε   στρατιώτας
centurions   he said: Prepare ye   soldiers

διακοσίους   ὅπως   πορευθῶσιν   ἕως   Καισαρείας,
two hundred   so as   they may go as far as Caesarea,

καὶ   ἱππεῖς   ἑβδομήκοντα   καὶ   δεξιολάβους
and horsemen   seventy   and   spearmen

διακοσίους,   ἀπὸ   τρίτης   ὥρας   τῆς   νυκτός,
two hundred,   from   third   hour   of the   night,

24 κτήνη   τε   παραστῆσαι,   ἵνα   ἐπιβιβάσαντες
and beasts   to stand by,   that   putting on

τὸν   Παῦλον   διασώσωσι   πρὸς   Φήλικα   τὸν
–   Paul   they may bring   to   Felix   the
                                                  [him] safely

ἡγεμόνα,   **25** γράψας   ἐπιστολὴν   ἔχουσαν
governor,   writing   a letter   having

τὸν   τύπον   τοῦτον·   **26** Κλαύδιος   Λυσίας   τῷ
this pattern: Claudius   Lysias   to the

κρατίστῳ   ἡγεμόνι   Φήλικι   χαίρειν.   **27** Τὸν
most excellent governor   Felix   greeting.   –

ἄνδρα   τοῦτον   συλλημφθέντα   ὑπὸ   τῶν
man   This   having been arrested by   the

Ἰουδαίων   καὶ   μέλλοντα   ἀναιρεῖσθαι   ὑπ’
Jews   and   being about   to be killed   by

αὐτῶν   ἐπιστὰς   σὺν   τῷ   στρατεύματι
them   coming on   with the   soldiery
         [the scene]

ἐξειλάμην,   μαθὼν   ὅτι   Ῥωμαῖός   ἐστιν·
I rescued,   having learned that   a Roman   he is;

28 βουλόμενός   τε   ἐπιγνῶναι   τὴν   αἰτίαν
and being minded   to know fully   the   cause

δι’   ἣν   ἐνεκάλουν   αὐτῷ,   κατήγαγον   εἰς
on ac- which they were   him,   I brought   to
count of   accusing   [him] down

τὸ   συνέδριον   αὐτῶν·   **29** ὃν   εὗρον   ἐγκαλούμενον
the   council   of them;   whom I found   being accused

περὶ   ζητημάτων   τοῦ   νόμου   αὐτῶν,   μηδὲν
about questions   of the   law   of them,   nothing

δὲ   ἄξιον   θανάτου   ἢ   δεσμῶν   ἔχοντα
and worthy   of death   or   of bonds   having

ἔγκλημα.   **30** μηνυθείσης   δὲ   μοι   ἐπιβουλῆς
charge.   And being revealed   to me   a plot
                 = when it was revealed to me that there was a plot

εἰς   τὸν   ἄνδρα   ἔσεσθαι,   ἐξαυτῆς   ἔπεμψα
against the   man   to be,   at once   I sent

πρὸς   σέ,   παραγγείλας   καὶ   τοῖς   κατηγόροις
to   thee,   commanding   also   the   accusers

λέγειν   πρὸς   αὐτὸν   ἐπὶ   σοῦ.   **31** Οἱ   μὲν
to say   to   him   before thee.   the   –

οὖν   στρατιῶται   κατὰ   τὸ   διατεταγμένον
Therefore soldiers   according to the having been
             appointed

αὐτοῖς   ἀναλαβόντες   τὸν   Παῦλον   ἤγαγον
them   taking up   the   Paul   brought

διὰ   νυκτὸς   εἰς   τὴν   Ἀντιπατρίδα·   **32** τῇ   δὲ
through [the] night to   –   Antipatris;   and on the
(during)

ἐπαύριον   ἐάσαντες   τοὺς   ἱππεῖς   ἀπέρχεσθαι
morrow   allowing   the   horsemen   to depart

σὺν   αὐτῷ,   ὑπέστρεψαν   εἰς   τὴν   παρεμβολήν·
with him,   they returned   to   the   fort;

33 οἵτινες   εἰσελθόντες   εἰς   τὴν   Καισάρειαν
who   entering   into   –   Caesarea

καὶ   ἀναδόντες   τὴν   ἐπιστολὴν   τῷ   ἡγεμόνι,
and   handing over   the   letter   to the governor,

παρέστησαν   καὶ   τὸν   Παῦλον   αὐτῷ.
presented   also   –   Paul   to him.

King James Version

Paul also before him. 34And when the governor had read *the letter,* he asked of what province he was. And when he understood that *he was* of Cilicia; 35 I will hear thee, said he, when thine accusers are also come. And he commanded him to be kept in Herod's judgment hall.

24 And after five days Ananias the high priest descended with the elders, and *with* a certain orator *named* Tertullus, who informed the governor against Paul. 2And when he was called forth, Tertullus began to accuse *him,* saying, Seeing that by thee we enjoy great quietness, and that very worthy deeds are done unto this nation by thy providence, 3 We accept *it* always, and in all places, most noble Felix, with all thankfulness. 4 Notwithstanding, that I be not further tedious unto thee, I pray thee that thou wouldest hear us of thy clemency a few words. 5 For we have found this man *a* pestilent *fellow,* and a mover of sedition among all the Jews throughout the world, and a ringleader of the sect of the Nazarenes: 6 Who also hath gone about to profane the temple: whom we took, and would have judged according to our law. 7 But the chief captain Lysias came *upon us,* and with great violence took *him* away out of our hands, 8 Commanding his accusers to come unto thee: by examining of whom thyself mayest take knowledge of all these things, whereof we accuse him. 9And the Jews also assented, saying that these things were so. 10 Then Paul, after that the governor had beckoned unto him to speak, answered, Forasmuch as I know that thou hast been of many years a judge unto this nation, I do the more cheerfully answer for myself: 11 Because that thou mayest understand, that there are yet but twelve days since I went up to Jerusalem for to worship. 12And they neither found me in the temple disputing with any man, neither raising up the people, neither in the synagogues, nor in the city: 13 Neither can they prove the things whereof they now accuse me. 14 But this I confess unto thee, that after the way which they call heresy, so worship I the God of my fathers, believing all things which are written in the law and in the prophets: 15And have hope toward God, which they themselves also allow, that there shall be a resurrection of the dead, both of the just and unjust. 16And herein do I exercise myself, to have always a conscience void of offence toward God, and *toward* men. 17 Now after many years I came to bring alms to my nation, and offerings. 18 Whereupon certain Jews from Asia found me purified in the temple, neither with multitude, nor with tumult. 19 Who ought to have been here before thee, and object, if they had aught against me. 20 Or else let these same *here* say, if they have found any evil doing in me, while I stood before the council, 21 Except it be for this one voice, that I cried standing among

New International Version

34 The governor read the letter and asked what province he was from. Learning that he was from Cilicia, 35 he said, "I will hear your case when your accusers get here." Then he ordered that Paul be kept under guard in Herod's palace.

The trial before Felix

24 Five days later the high priest Ananias went down to Caesarea with some of the elders and a lawyer named Tertullus, and they brought their charges against Paul before the governor. 2 When Paul was called in, Tertullus presented his case before Felix: "We have enjoyed a long period of peace under you, and your foresight has brought about reforms in this nation. 3 Everywhere and in every way, most excellent Felix, we acknowledge this with profound gratitude. 4 But in order not to weary you further, I would request that you be kind enough to hear us briefly.

5 "We have found this man to be a troublemaker, stirring up riots among the Jews all over the world. He is a ringleader of the Nazarene sect 6 and even tried to desecrate the temple; so we seized him.[k] 8 By examining him yourself you will be able to learn the truth about all these charges we are bringing against him."

9 The Jews joined in the accusation, asserting that these things were true.

10 When the governor motioned for him to speak, Paul replied: "I know that for a number of years you have been a judge over this nation; so I gladly make my defense. 11 You can easily verify that no more than twelve days ago I went up to Jerusalem to worship. 12 My accusers did not find me arguing with anyone at the temple, or stirring up a crowd in the synagogues or anywhere else in the city. 13And they cannot prove to you the charges they are now making against me. 14 However, I admit that I worship the God of our fathers, as a follower of the Way, which they call a sect. I believe everything that agrees with the Law and that is written in the Prophets, 15 and I have the same hope in God as these men, that there will be a resurrection of both the righteous and the wicked. 16 So I strive always to keep my conscience clear before God and man.

17 "After an absence of several years, I came to Jerusalem to bring my people gifts for the poor and to present offerings. 18 I was ceremonially clean when they found me in the temple courts doing this. There was no crowd with me, nor was I involved in any disturbance. 19 But there are some Jews from the province of Asia, who ought to be here before you and bring charges if they have anything against me. 20 Or these who are here should state what crime they found in me, when I stood before the Sanhedrin —21 unless it was this one thing I shouted as I stood in their presence: 'It is concerning the

[k] Some MSS add *and wanted to judge him according to our law.* 7*But the commander, Lysias, came and with the use of much force snatched him from our hands* 8*and ordered his accusers to come before you.*

Greek Interlinear

34 ἀναγνοὺς   δὲ   καὶ   ἐπερωτήσας   ἐκ   ποίας
And having read   and   asking   of   what

ἐπαρχείας   ἐστίν,   καὶ   πυθόμενος   ὅτι   ἀπὸ
province   he is(was),   and   learning[,]   –   From

Κιλικίας,   **35** διακούσομαί   σου,   ἔφη,   ὅταν
Cilicia,   I will hear   thee,   he said,   when

καὶ   οἱ   κατήγοροί   σου   παραγένωνται·
also   the   accusers   of thee   arrive;

κελεύσας   ἐν   τῷ   πραιτωρίῳ   τοῦ   Ἡρῴδου
commanding   in   the   prætorium   –   of Herod
= that he be kept in Herod's prætorium.

φυλάσσεσθαι   αὐτόν.
to be kept   him.

Chapter 24

Μετὰ   δὲ   πέντε   ἡμέρας   κατέβη   ὁ
And after   five   days   came down   the

ἀρχιερεὺς   Ἀνανίας   μετὰ   πρεσβυτέρων   τινῶν
high priest   Ananias   with   elders   some

καὶ   ῥήτορος   Τερτύλλου   τινός,   οἵτινες
and   an orator   Tertullus   one,   who

ἐνεφάνισαν   τῷ   ἡγεμόνι   κατὰ   τοῦ   Παύλου.
informed   the   governor   against   –   Paul.

2 κληθέντος   δὲ   [αὐτοῦ]   ἤρξατο   κατηγορεῖν
And being called   him]   ¹began   ⁵to accuse
= when he was called

ὁ   Τέρτυλλος   λέγων·   πολλῆς   εἰρήνης
–   ¹Tertullus   saying: Much   peace

τυγχάνοντες   διὰ   σοῦ   καὶ   διορθωμάτων
obtaining   through   thee   and   reforms

γινομένων   τῷ   ἔθνει   τούτῳ   διὰ   τῆς   σῆς
coming   to this nation   through   –   thy

προνοίας,   **3** πάντῃ   τε   καὶ   πανταχοῦ
forethought,   both in everything   and   everywhere

ἀποδεχόμεθα,   κράτιστε   Φῆλιξ,   μετὰ   πάσης
we welcome,   most excellent   Felix,   with   all

εὐχαριστίας.   **4** ἵνα   δὲ   μὴ   ἐπὶ   πλεῖόν
thankfulness.   But that   ¹not   ⁴more

σε   ἐγκόπτω,   παρακαλῶ   ἀκοῦσαί   σε   ἡμῶν
²thee   ¹I hinder,   I beseech   ⁴to hear   ¹thee   us

συντόμως   τῇ   σῇ   ἐπιεικείᾳ.   **5** εὑρόντες   γὰρ
briefly   –   in thy   forbearance.   For having found

τὸν   ἄνδρα   τοῦτον   λοιμὸν   καὶ   κινοῦντα
this man   pestilent   and   moving

στάσεις   πᾶσιν   τοῖς   Ἰουδαίοις   τοῖς   κατὰ
seditions [among] all   the   Jews   – throughout

τὴν   οἰκουμένην   πρωτοστάτην   τε   τῆς   τῶν
the   inhabited [earth]   and a ringleader   of the ¹of the

Ναζωραίων   αἱρέσεως,   **6** ὃς   καὶ   τὸ   ἱερὸν
²Nazarenes   ¹sect,   who   also   ²the   ⁴temple

ἐπείρασεν   βεβηλῶσαι,   ὃν   καὶ   ἐκρατήσαμεν,
¹attempted   ²to profane,   whom   also   we laid hold of,‡

8 παρ᾽   οὗ   δυνήσῃ   αὐτὸς   ἀνακρίνας
from whom   thou wilt be able   [thy]self   ¹having examined

περὶ   πάντων   τούτων   ἐπιγνῶναι   ὧν   ἡμεῖς
²concerning   ⁴all   ⁵these things   ¹to know fully of which   we

κατηγοροῦμεν   αὐτοῦ.   **9** συνεπέθεντο   δὲ
accuse   him.   And ¹joined in

καὶ   οἱ   Ἰουδαῖοι·   φάσκοντες   ταῦτα   οὕτως
²also   ¹the   ³Jews   alleging   these things   thus

ἔχειν.   **10** Ἀπεκρίθη   τε   ὁ   Παῦλος,
to have(be).   And answered   –   Paul.

νεύσαντος   αὐτῷ   τοῦ   ἡγεμόνος   λέγειν·   ἐκ
³having   ⁴to him   ¹the   ²governor   to speak·   ⁵of
beckoned   (for)

πολλῶν   ἐτῶν   ὄντα   σε   κριτὴν   τῷ   ἔθνει   τούτῳ
⁴many   ⁵years   ²being   ³thee   ¹a judge   ⁶to ¹⁰this ¹¹nation
(to be)

ἐπιστάμενος   εὐθύμως   τὰ   περὶ
¹²understanding   ¹³cheerfully ¹⁵[as to]   ¹⁴the things ¹⁵concerning

ἐμαυτοῦ   ἀπολογοῦμαι,   **11** δυναμένου   σου
¹⁶myself   ¹¹I defend myself,   being able   thee⁴
= as thou art able

ἐπιγνῶναι   ὅτι   οὐ   πλείους   εἰσίν   μοι   ἡμέραι
to know fully   that   ²not   ⁴more   ⁵there   ¹to ⁷[than] ⁶days
are   me

δώδεκα   ἀφ᾽   ἧς   ἀνέβην   προσκυνήσων   εἰς
²twelve   from   which   I went up   worshipping   in
= since

Ἰερουσαλήμ.   **12** καὶ   οὔτε   ἐν   τῷ   ἱερῷ
Jerusalem.   And   neither   in   the   temple

εὑρόν   με   πρός   τινα   διαλεγόμενον   ἢ
they found me   ²with   ²anyone   ¹discoursing   or

ἐπίστασιν   ποιοῦντα   ὄχλου,   οὔτε   ἐν   ταῖς
¹collection   ¹making   of a crowd,   neither   in   the

συναγωγαῖς   οὔτε   κατὰ   τὴν   πόλιν,   **13** οὐδὲ
synagogues   nor   throughout   the   city,   nor

παραστῆσαι   δύνανταί   σοι   περὶ   ὧν   νυνὶ
²to prove   ¹are they able   to thee   con-   [the] things now
cerning of which

κατηγοροῦσίν   μου.   **14** ὁμολογῶ   δὲ   τοῦτό
they accuse   me.   But I confess   this

σοι,   ὅτι   κατὰ   τὴν   ὁδὸν   ἣν   λέγουσιν
to thee,   that   according to the   way   which they say(call)

αἵρεσιν   οὕτως   λατρεύω   τῷ   πατρῴῳ   θεῷ,
a sect   thus   I worship   the   ancestral   God,

πιστεύων   πᾶσι   τοῖς   κατὰ   τὸν   νόμον   καὶ
believing   all   the   according   the   law   and
things to

τοῖς   ἐν   τοῖς   προφήταις   γεγραμμένοις,
the things in   the   prophets   having been written,

15 ἐλπίδα   ἔχων   εἰς   τὸν   θεόν,   ἣν   καὶ
hope   having   toward   –   God, which   ²also

αὐτοὶ   οὗτοι   προσδέχονται,   ἀνάστασιν   μέλ-
²[them]selves   ¹these   expect,   a resurrection   to be

λειν   ἔσεσθαι   δικαίων   τε   καὶ   ἀδίκων.
about   to be   both of just   and   of unjust.

16 ἐν   τούτῳ   καὶ   αὐτὸς   ἀσκῶ   ἀπρόσκοπον
By   this   also   ²[my]self   ¹I exercise   ²a blameless

συνείδησιν   ἔχειν   πρὸς   τὸν   θεὸν   καὶ   τοὺς
¹conscience   ³to have   toward   –   God   and   –

ἀνθρώπους   διὰ   παντός.   **17** δι᾽   ἐτῶν   δὲ
men   always.   And after years

πλειόνων   ἐλεημοσύνας   ποιήσων   εἰς   τὸ
many   ²alms   ¹making(bringing)   ³to   ⁴the

ἔθνος   μου   παρεγενόμην   καὶ   προσφοράς,
²nation   ¹of me   ³I arrived   and   ⁴offerings,

18 ἐν   αἷς   εὗρόν   με   ἡγνισμένον   ἐν   τῷ
among   which   they found me   having been   purified   in   the

ἱερῷ,   οὐ   μετὰ   ὄχλου   οὐδὲ   μετὰ   θορύβου,
temple,   not   with   a crowd   nor   with   uproar.

19 τινὲς   δὲ   ἀπὸ   τῆς   Ἀσίας   Ἰουδαῖοι,
but some   ¹from   –   Asia   ¹Jews,

οὓς   ἔδει   ἐπὶ   σοῦ   παρεῖναι   καὶ   κατηγορεῖν
whom   it be-   before   thee   to be present   and   to accuse
hoved

εἴ   τι   ἔχοιεν   πρὸς   ἐμέ.   **20** ἢ   αὐτοὶ
if   anything they have   against   me.   Or ²[them]selves

οὗτοι   εἰπάτωσαν   τί   εὗρον   ἀδίκημα   στάντος
²these   ¹let ³say   ¹what ²they found   misdeed   standing

μου   ἐπὶ   τοῦ   συνεδρίου,   **21** ἢ   περὶ   μιᾶς
me⁴   before   the   council,   unless concerning ¹one
= while I stood

ταύτης   φωνῆς   ἧς   ἐκέκραξα   ἐν   αὐτοῖς
¹this   voice   which I have cried out   ²among   ³them

‡ Verse 7 omitted by Nestle

427

King James Version

them, Touching the resurrection of the dead I am called in question by you this day. 22And when Felix heard these things, having more perfect knowledge of *that* way, he deferred them, and said, When Lysias the chief captain shall come down, I will know the uttermost of your matter. 23And he commanded a centurion to keep Paul, and to let *him* have liberty, and that he should forbid none of his acquaintance to minister or come unto him. 24And after certain days, when Felix came with his wife Drusilla, which was a Jewess, he sent for Paul, and heard him concerning the faith in Christ. 25And as he reasoned of righteousness, temperance, and judgment to come, Felix trembled, and answered, Go thy way for this time; when I have a convenient season, I will call for thee. 26 He hoped also that money should have been given him of Paul, that he might loose him: wherefore he sent for him the oftener, and communed with him. 27 But after two years Porcius Festus came into Felix' room: and Felix, willing to shew the Jews a pleasure, left Paul bound.

25 Now when Festus was come into the province, after three days he ascended from Cesarea to Jerusalem. 2 Then the high priest and the chief of the Jews informed him against Paul, and besought him, 3And desired favour against him, that he would send for him to Jerusalem, laying wait in the way to kill him. 4 But Festus answered, that Paul should be kept at Cesarea, and that he himself would depart shortly *thither.* 5 Let them therefore, said he, which among you are able, go down with *me,* and accuse this man, if there be any wickedness in him. 6And when he had tarried among them more than ten days, he went down unto Cesarea; and the next day sitting on the judgment seat commanded Paul to be brought. 7And when he was come, the Jews which came down from Jerusalem stood round about, and laid many and grievous complaints against Paul, which they could not prove. 8 While he answered for himself, Neither against the law of the Jews, neither against the temple, nor yet against Cesar, have I offended any thing at all. 9 But Festus, willing to do the Jews a pleasure, answered Paul, and said, Wilt thou go up to Jerusalem, and there be judged of these things before me? 10 Then said Paul, I stand at Cesar's judgment seat, where I ought to be judged: to the Jews have I done no wrong, as thou very well knowest. 11 For if I be an offender, or have committed any thing worthy of death, I refuse not to die: but if there be none of these things whereof these accuse me, no man

New International Version

resurrection of the dead that I am on trial before you today.' "

22 Then Felix, who was well acquainted with the Way, adjourned the proceedings. "When Lysias the commander comes," he said, "I will decide your case." 23 He ordered the centurion to keep Paul under guard but to give him some freedom and permit his friends to take care of his needs.

24 Several days later Felix arrived with his wife Drusilla, who was a Jewess. He sent for Paul and listened to him as he spoke about faith in Christ Jesus. 25As Paul discoursed on righteousness, self-control and the judgment to come, Felix was afraid and said, "That's enough for now! You may leave. When I find it convenient, I will send for you." 26At the same time he was hoping that Paul would offer him a bribe, so he sent for him frequently and talked with him.

27 When two years had passed, Felix was succeeded by Porcius Festus, but because Felix wanted to grant a favor to the Jews, he left Paul in prison.

The trial before Festus

25 Three days after arriving in the province, Festus went up from Caesarea to Jerusalem, 2 where the chief priests and Jewish leaders appeared before him and presented the charges against Paul. 3 They urgently requested Festus, as a favor to them, to have Paul transferred to Jerusalem, for they were preparing an ambush to kill him along the way. 4 Festus answered, "Paul is being held at Caesarea, and I myself am going there soon. 5 Let some of your leaders come with me and press charges against the man there, if he has done anything wrong."

6 After spending eight or ten days with them, he went down to Caesarea, and the next day he convened the court and ordered that Paul be brought before him. 7 When Paul appeared, the Jews who had come down from Jerusalem stood around him, bringing many serious charges against him, which they could not prove.

8 Then Paul made his defense: "I have done nothing wrong against the law of the Jews or against the temple or against Caesar."

9 Festus, wishing to do the Jews a favor, said to Paul, "Are you willing to go up to Jerusalem and stand trial before me there on these charges?"

10 Paul answered: "I am now standing before Caesar's court, where I ought to be tried. I have not done any wrong to the Jews, as you yourself know very well. 11 If, however, I am guilty of doing anything deserving death, I do not refuse to die. But if the charges brought against me by these Jews are not true, no one has the right

ἐστὼς ὅτι περὶ ἀναστάσεως νεκρῶν ἐγὼ
¹standing[.] – Concerning a resurrection of dead persons I

κρίνομαι σήμερον ἐφ' ὑμῶν. 22 Ἀνεβάλετο
am being judged to-day before you.   ⁵postponed

δὲ αὐτοὺς ὁ Φῆλιξ, ἀκριβέστερον εἰδὼς
And ²them – ¹Felix,   more exactly   knowing

τὰ περὶ τῆς ὁδοῦ, εἴπας· ὅταν Λυσίας ὁ
the con-   the way,   saying: When Lysias the
things cerning

χιλίαρχος καταβῇ, διαγνώσομαι τὰ καθ'
chiliarch comes down, I will determine the things as to

ὑμᾶς· 23 διαταξάμενος τῷ ἑκατοντάρχῃ
you;   commanding   the   centurion

τηρεῖσθαι αὐτὸν ἔχειν τε ἄνεσιν καὶ
to keep   him   and to have indulgence and

μηδένα κωλύειν τῶν ἰδίων αὐτοῦ ὑπηρετεῖν
²no one ¹to forbid of his own [people]   to attend

αὐτῷ. 24 Μετὰ δὲ ἡμέρας τινὰς παραγενό-
him.   And after   days   some   ²arriv-

μενος ὁ Φῆλιξ σὺν Δρουσίλλῃ τῇ ἰδίᾳ
ing   – ¹Felix with Drusilla   the(his) own

γυναικὶ οὔσῃ Ἰουδαίᾳ μετεπέμψατο τὸν
wife   being a Jewess   he sent for   –

Παῦλον, καὶ ἤκουσεν αὐτοῦ περὶ τῆς
Paul,   and   heard   him   about ¹the(?his)

εἰς Χριστὸν Ἰησοῦν πίστεως. 25 διαλεγομέ-
²in ⁴Christ ⁵Jesus ³faith.   discours-
                                        = And as he discoursed

νου δὲ αὐτοῦ περὶ δικαιοσύνης καὶ
ing And him⁵ concerning righteousness and

ἐγκρατείας καὶ τοῦ κρίματος τοῦ μέλλοντος
self-control and the ³judgment   –   ⁴coming

ἔμφοβος γενόμενος ὁ Φῆλιξ ἀπεκρίθη·
afraid   becoming – Felix   answered:

τὸ νῦν ἔχον πορεύου, καιρὸν δὲ μεταλαβὼν
For the present† go thou,   but ²time ¹taking ⁴later

μετακαλέσομαί σε· 26 ἅμα καὶ ἐλπίζων
I will send for thee;   at the also   hoping
                       same time

ὅτι χρήματα δοθήσεται αὐτῷ ὑπὸ τοῦ
that money   will be given him   by   –

Παύλου· διὸ καὶ πυκνότερον αὐτὸν
Paul: wherefore also more frequently him

μεταπεμπόμενος ὡμίλει αὐτῷ. 27 Διετίας δὲ
sending for   he conversed him.   And two years

πληρωθείσης ἔλαβεν διάδοχον ὁ Φῆλιξ
being completed⁵ ²received ¹a successor – ¹Felix

Πόρκιον Φῆστον· θέλων τε χάριτα κατα-
Porcius Festus;   and wishing a favour ³to

θέσθαι τοῖς Ἰουδαίοις ὁ Φῆλιξ κατέλιπε
show   to the Jews   – ¹Felix   left

τὸν Παῦλον δεδεμένον.
–   Paul   having been bound.

Chapter 25

Φῆστος οὖν ἐπιβὰς τῇ ἐπαρχείῳ
Festus therefore having entered the province

μετὰ τρεῖς ἡμέρας ἀνέβη εἰς Ἰεροσόλυμα
after three   days   went up to   Jerusalem

ἀπὸ Καισαρείας, 2 ἐνεφάνισάν τε αὐτῷ
from Cæsarea,   and ²informed   ³him

οἱ ἀρχιερεῖς καὶ οἱ πρῶτοι τῶν Ἰουδαίων
¹the ⁴chief priests ²and ³the ⁴chiefs ⁵of the ⁶Jews

κατὰ τοῦ Παύλου, καὶ παρεκάλουν αὐτὸν
against –   Paul,   and   they besought him

3 αἰτούμενοι χάριν κατ' αὐτοῦ, ὅπως μετα-
asking   a favour against him, so as he might

πέμψηται αὐτὸν εἰς Ἰερουσαλήμ, ἐνέδραν
summon   him   to   Jerusalem,   a plot

ποιοῦντες ἀνελεῖν αὐτὸν κατὰ τὴν ὁδόν.
making   to kill   him   by   the way.

4 ὁ μὲν οὖν Φῆστος ἀπεκρίθη τηρεῖσθαι
– – Therefore Festus answered ²to be kept

τὸν Παῦλον εἰς Καισάρειαν, ἑαυτὸν δὲ
– ¹Paul in Cæsarea,   and ³himself

μέλλειν ἐν τάχει ἐκπορεύεσθαι· 5 οἱ οὖν
¹to intend in shortly to go forth; ⁴the ¹therefore

ἐν ὑμῖν, φησίν, δυνατοὶ συγκαταβάντες,
⁴among ⁵you, ²he says, ⁶able men going down with [me],

εἴ τί ἐστιν ἐν τῷ ἀνδρὶ ἄτοπον,
if anything there is in the   man   amiss,

κατηγορείτωσαν αὐτοῦ. 6 Διατρίψας δὲ ἐν
let them accuse   him.   And having stayed among

αὐτοῖς ἡμέρας οὐ πλείους ὀκτὼ ἢ δέκα,
them   days   not more [than] eight or ten,

καταβὰς εἰς Καισάρειαν, τῇ ἐπαύριον
going down to Cæsarea,   on the morrow

καθίσας ἐπὶ τοῦ βήματος ἐκέλευσεν τὸν
sitting on the tribunal   he commanded –

Παῦλον ἀχθῆναι. 7 παραγενομένου δὲ
Paul   to be brought.   And arriving
                           = when he arrived

αὐτοῦ περιέστησαν αὐτὸν οἱ ἀπὸ Ἰεροσο-
him⁵   ²stood round ⁷him ¹the ⁴from   ⁵Jeru-

λύμων καταβεβηκότες Ἰουδαῖοι, πολλὰ καὶ
salem ³having come down ⁶Jews,   many   and

βαρέα αἰτιώματα καταφέροντες, ἃ οὐκ
heavy   charges   bringing against [him], which not

ἴσχυον ἀποδεῖξαι, 8 τοῦ Παύλου ἀπολογου-
they were able to prove, – Paul   defending him-

μένου ὅτι οὔτε εἰς τὸν νόμον τῶν
self[.]² ¹Neither against the   law   of the
= while Paul defended himself,

Ἰουδαίων οὔτε εἰς τὸ ἱερὸν οὔτε εἰς
Jews   nor against the temple nor against

Καίσαρά τι ἥμαρτον. 9 ὁ Φῆστος δὲ,
Cæsar anything I sinned. – But Festus,

θέλων τοῖς Ἰουδαίοις χάριν καταθέσθαι,
wishing the Jews   a favour to show,

ἀποκριθεὶς τῷ Παύλῳ εἶπεν· θέλεις εἰς
answering   – Paul   said: Dost thou wish ²to

Ἰεροσόλυμα ἀναβὰς ἐκεῖ περὶ τούτων
³Jerusalem ¹going up ⁴there ⁵concerning ⁶these things

κριθῆναι ἐπ' ἐμοῦ; 10 εἶπεν δὲ ὁ Παῦλος·
⁷to be judged ⁸before ⁹me? And said – Paul:

ἐστὼς ἐπὶ τοῦ βήματος Καίσαρός εἰμι,
Standing before the tribunal   of Cæsar   I am,

οὗ με δεῖ κρίνεσθαι. Ἰουδαίους οὐδὲν
where me it behoves to be judged. Jews   nothing

ἠδίκηκα, ὡς καὶ σὺ κάλλιον ἐπιγινώσκεις.
I have wronged, as indeed thou very well knowest.

11 εἰ μὲν οὖν ἀδικῶ καὶ ἄξιον θανάτου
If – therefore I do wrong and worthy of death

πέπραχά τι, οὐ παραιτοῦμαι τὸ ἀποθανεῖν·
I have done anything, I do not refuse the to die;

εἰ δὲ οὐδέν ἐστιν ὧν οὗτοι κατηγοροῦσίν
but if not one there is of [the these accuse
                            things] which

429

King James Version

may deliver me unto them. I appeal unto Cesar. 12 Then Festus, when he had conferred with the council, answered, Hast thou appealed unto Cesar? unto Cesar shalt thou go. 13 And after certain days king Agrippa and Bernice came unto Cesarea to salute Festus. 14And when they had been there many days, Festus declared Paul's cause unto the king, saying, There is a certain man left in bonds by Felix: 15About whom, when I was at Jerusalem, the chief priests and the elders of the Jews informed *me*, desiring *to have* judgment against him. 16 To whom I answered, It is not the manner of the Romans to deliver any man to die, before that he which is accused have the accusers face to face, and have license to answer for himself concerning the crime laid against him. 17 Therefore, when they were come hither, without any delay on the morrow I sat on the judgment seat, and commanded the man to be brought forth. 18Against whom when the accusers stood up, they brought none accusation of such things as I supposed: 19 But had certain questions against him of their own superstition, and of one Jesus, which was dead, whom Paul affirmed to be alive. 20And because I doubted of such manner of questions, I asked *him* whether he would go to Jerusalem, and there be judged of these matters. 21 But when Paul had appealed to be reserved unto the hearing of Augustus, I commanded him to be kept till I might send him to Cesar. 22 Then Agrippa said unto Festus, I would also hear the man myself. To morrow, said he, thou shalt hear him. 23And on the morrow, when Agrippa was come, and Bernice, with great pomp, and was entered into the place of hearing, with the chief captains, and principal men of the city, at Festus' commandment Paul was brought forth. 24And Festus said, King Agrippa, and all men which are here present with us, ye see this man, about whom all the multitude of the Jews have dealt with me, both at Jerusalem, and *also* here, crying that he ought not to live any longer. 25 But when I found that he had committed nothing worthy of death, and that he himself hath appealed to Augustus, I have determined to send him. 26 Of whom I have no certain thing to write unto my lord. Wherefore I have brought him forth before you, and specially before thee, O king Agrippa, that, after examination had, I might have somewhat to write. 27 For it seemeth to me unreasonable to send a prisoner, and not withal to signify the crimes *laid* against him.

26 Then Agrippa said unto Paul, Thou art permitted to speak for thyself. Then Paul stretched forth the hand, and answered for himself: 2 I think myself happy, king Agrippa, be-

New International Version

to hand me over to them. I appeal to Caesar!" 12 After Festus had conferred with his council, he declared: "You have appealed to Caesar. To Caesar you will go!"

Festus consults King Agrippa

13 A few days later King Agrippa and Bernice arrived at Caesarea to pay their respects to Festus. 14 Since they were spending many days there, Festus discussed Paul's case with the king. He said: "There is a man here whom Felix left as a prisoner. 15 When I went to Jerusalem, the chief priests and elders of the Jews brought charges against him and asked that he be condemned.

16 "I told them that it is not the Roman custom to hand over any man before he has faced his accusers and has had an opportunity to defend himself against their charges. 17 When they came here with me, I did not delay the case, but convened the court the next day and ordered the man to be brought in. 18 When his accusers got up to speak, they did not charge him with any of the crimes I had expected. 19 Instead, they had some points of dispute with him about their own religion and about a dead man named Jesus who Paul claimed was alive. 20 I was at a loss how to investigate such matters; so I asked if he would be willing to go to Jerusalem and stand trial there on these charges. 21 When Paul made his appeal to be held over for the Emperor's decision, I ordered him held until I could send him to Caesar."

22 Then Agrippa said to Festus, "I would like to hear this man myself."

He replied, "Tomorrow you will hear him."

Paul before Agrippa

23 The next day Agrippa and Bernice came with great pomp and entered the audience room with the high ranking officers and the leading men of the city. At the command of Festus, Paul was brought in. 24 Festus said: "King Agrippa, and all who are present with us, you see this man! The whole Jewish community has petitioned me about him in Jerusalem and here in Caesarea, shouting that he ought not to live any longer. 25 I found he had done nothing deserving of death, but because he made his appeal to the Emperor I decided to send him to Rome. 26 But I have nothing definite to write to His Majesty about him. Therefore I have brought him before all of you, and especially before you, King Agrippa, so that as a result of this investigation I may have something to write. 27 For I think it is unreasonable to send on a prisoner without specifying the charges against him."

26 Then Agrippa said to Paul, "You have permission to speak for yourself."

So Paul motioned with his hand and began his defense: 2 "King Agrippa, I consider myself

Greek Interlinear

μου, οὐδείς με δύναται αὐτοῖς χαρίσασθαι·
me, no one me ¹can ⁴to them ⁵to grant;

Καίσαρα ἐπικαλοῦμαι.   12 τότε ὁ Φῆστος
¹Cæsar ¹I appeal to.   Then - Festus

συλλαλήσας μετὰ τοῦ συμβουλίου ἀπεκρίθη·
having talked with with the council answered:

Καίσαρα ἐπικέκλησαι, ἐπὶ Καίσαρα πορεύσῃ.
²Cæsar ¹thou hast appealed to, before Cæsar thou shalt go.

13 Ἡμερῶν δὲ διαγενομένων τινῶν
And days passing some*
= when some days had passed

Ἀγρίππας ὁ βασιλεὺς καὶ Βερνίκη
Agrippa the king and Bernice

κατήντησαν εἰς Καισάρειαν ἀσπασάμενοι
arrived at Cæsarea greeting

τὸν Φῆστον.   14 ὡς δὲ πλείους ἡμέρας
- Festus.   And as more days

διέτριβον ἐκεῖ, ὁ Φῆστος τῷ βασιλεῖ
they stayed there, - Festus ²to the ¹king

ἀνέθετο τὰ κατὰ τὸν Παῦλον λέγων·
¹set forth the matters regarding - Paul saying:

ἀνήρ τίς ἐστιν καταλελειμμένος ὑπὸ
A certain man there is having been left behind by

Φήλικος δέσμιος, 15 περὶ οὗ γενομένου
Felix prisoner, about whom being
= when I was

μου εἰς Ἰεροσόλυμα ἐνεφάνισαν οἱ ἀρχιερεῖς
me* in Jerusalem ²informed ¹the ²chief priests

καὶ οἱ πρεσβύτεροι τῶν Ἰουδαίων,
²and ²the ²elders ²of the ²Jews,

αἰτούμενοι κατ᾽ αὐτοῦ καταδίκην· 16 πρὸς
asking against him sentence; to

οὓς ἀπεκρίθην ὅτι οὐκ ἔστιν ἔθος Ῥωμαίοις
whom I answered that it is not a custom with Romans

χαρίζεσθαί τινα ἄνθρωπον πρὶν ἢ ὁ
to grant any man before the

κατηγορούμενος κατὰ πρόσωπον ἔχοι τοὺς
[one] being accused face to face† should have the

κατηγόρους τόπον τε ἀπολογίας λάβοι
accusers ²place* ¹and ⁴of defence ⁴receive

περὶ τοῦ ἐγκλήματος. 17 συνελθόντων
concerning the charge. Coming together*

οὖν ἐνθάδε ἀναβολὴν μηδεμίαν ποιησάμενος
therefore thither ²delay ²no ¹making

τῇ ἑξῆς καθίσας ἐπὶ τοῦ βήματος ἐκέλευσα
on the next [day] sitting on the tribunal I commanded

ἀχθῆναι τὸν ἄνδρα· 18 περὶ οὗ σταθέντες
to be brought the man; concerning whom standing

οἱ κατήγοροι οὐδεμίαν αἰτίαν ἔφερον ὧν
the accusers ²no ²charge ¹brought ⁴of ⁵things
                                                ²which

ἐγὼ ὑπενόουν πονηρῶν, 19 ζητήματα δέ
²I ¹suspected ⁵evil, but ²questions

τινα περὶ τῆς ἰδίας δεισιδαιμονίας εἶχον
¹certain ²about ⁴the(ir) own ⁶religion ¹they had

πρὸς αὐτὸν καὶ περί τινος Ἰησοῦ
with him and about one Jesus

τεθνηκότος, ὃν ἔφασκεν ὁ Παῦλος ζῆν.
having died, whom ²asserted - ¹Paul to live.

20 ἀπορούμενος δὲ ἐγὼ τὴν περὶ τούτων
And ²being perplexed at ¹I ⁴the ⁵about ⁴these things

ζήτησιν ἔλεγον εἰ βούλοιτο πορεύεσθαι εἰς
⁴debate said if he wished to go to

Ἰεροσόλυμα κἀκεῖ κρίνεσθαι περὶ τούτων.
Jerusalem and there to be judged about these things.

21 τοῦ δὲ Παύλου ἐπικαλεσαμένου τηρηθῆναι
- But Paul having appealed* to be kept
= when Paul appealed

αὐτὸν εἰς τὴν τοῦ Σεβαστοῦ διάγνωσιν,
him to the - ²of Augustus ¹decision,

ἐκέλευσα τηρεῖσθαι αὐτὸν ἕως οὗ ἀναπέμψω
I commanded to be kept him until I may send up

αὐτὸν πρὸς Καίσαρα. 22 Ἀγρίππας δὲ
him to Cæsar. And Agrippa

πρὸς τὸν Φῆστον· ἐβουλόμην καὶ αὐτὸς
[said] to - Festus: I was minded also [my]self

τοῦ ἀνθρώπου ἀκοῦσαι. αὔριον, φησίν, καὶ
the man to hear. Tomorrow, he says,

ἀκούσῃ αὐτοῦ. 23 Τῇ οὖν ἐπαύριον
thou shalt hear him. ²On the ¹therefore ²morrow

ἐλθόντος τοῦ Ἀγρίππα καὶ τῆς Βερνίκης
coming - Agrippa and - Bernice*
= when Agrippa and Bernice came

μετὰ πολλῆς φαντασίας καὶ εἰσελθόντων
with much display and entering*

εἰς τὸ ἀκροατήριον σύν τε χιλιάρχοις
into the place of audience with both chiliarchs

καὶ ἀνδράσιν τοῖς κατ᾽ ἐξοχὴν τῆς πόλεως,
and ²men ¹the ²chief † of the city,

καὶ κελεύσαντος τοῦ Φήστου ἤχθη ὁ
and having commanded - Festus* ²was brought -

Παῦλος. 24 καί φησιν ὁ Φῆστος· Ἀγρίππα
¹Paul. And says - Festus: Agrippa

βασιλεῦ καὶ πάντες οἱ συμπαρόντες ἡμῖν
king and all the ²present together with ²us

ἄνδρες, θεωρεῖτε τοῦτον περὶ οὗ ἅπαν τὸ
¹men, ye behold this man about whom all the

πλῆθος τῶν Ἰουδαίων ἐνέτυχόν μοι ἔν τε
multitude of the Jews petitioned me ²in ¹both

Ἰεροσολύμοις καὶ ἐνθάδε, βοῶντες μὴ
Jerusalem and here, crying not

δεῖν αὐτὸν ζῆν μηκέτι. 25 ἐγὼ δὲ κατε-
ought him to live no longer. But I dis-
= that he ought not to live any longer.

λαβόμην μηδὲν ἄξιον αὐτὸν θανάτου
covered ²nothing ⁴worthy ¹him ⁵of death

πεπραχέναι, αὐτοῦ δὲ τούτου ἐπικαλεσαμένου
³to have done, but [him]self this man appealing to*
= when he himself appealed to

τὸν Σεβαστὸν ἔκρινα πέμπειν. 26 περὶ
- Augustus I decided to send. Concerning

οὗ ἀσφαλές τι γράψαι τῷ κυρίῳ οὐκ
whom ²certain ¹anything ⁴to write ⁴to the ¹lord ²not

ἔχω· διὸ προήγαγον αὐτὸν ἐφ᾽ ὑμῶν καὶ
¹I have; where- I brought him before you and
   fore forth

μάλιστα ἐπὶ σοῦ, βασιλεῦ Ἀγρίππα, ὅπως
most of all before thee, king Agrippa, so as
= when

τῆς ἀνακρίσεως γενομένης σχῶ τί γράψω·
the examination being* I may what I may
there has been an examination have write;

27 ἄλογον γάρ μοι δοκεῖ πέμποντα δέσμιον
for ²unreasonable ²to me ¹it seems sending a prisoner

μὴ καὶ τὰς κατ᾽ αὐτοῦ αἰτίας σημάναι.
not also ²the ⁴against ⁴him ⁴charges ¹to signify.

Chapter 26

Ἀγρίππας δὲ πρὸς τὸν Παῦλον ἔφη·
And Agrippa to - Paul said:

ἐπιτρέπεταί σοι ὑπὲρ σεαυτοῦ λέγειν.
It is permitted to thee on behalf of thyself to speak.

τότε ὁ Παῦλος ἐκτείνας τὴν χεῖρα
Then - Paul stretching out the(his) hand

ἀπελογεῖτο· 2 Περὶ πάντων ὧν ἐγκαλοῦμαι
defended himself: Concerning all things of which I am being
                                                   accused

* That is, opportunity.

431

King James Version

cause I shall answer for myself this day before thee touching all the things whereof I am accused of the Jews: 3 Especially *because I know* thee to be expert in all customs and questions which are among the Jews: wherefore I beseech thee to hear me patiently. 4 My manner of life from my youth, which was at the first among mine own nation at Jerusalem, know all the Jews; 5 Which knew me from the beginning, if they would testify, that after the most straitest sect of our religion I lived a Pharisee. 6And now I stand and am judged for the hope of the promise made of God unto our fathers: 7 Unto which *promise* our twelve tribes, instantly serving *God* day and night, hope to come. For which hope's sake, king Agrippa, I am accused of the Jews. 8 Why should it be thought a thing incredible with you, that God should raise the dead? 9 I verily thought with myself, that I ought to do many things contrary to the name of Jesus of Nazareth. 10 Which thing I also did in Jerusalem: and many of the saints did I shut up in prison, having received authority from the chief priests; and when they were put to death, I gave my voice against *them*. 11And I punished them oft in every synagogue, and compelled *them* to blaspheme; and being exceedingly mad against them, I persecuted *them* even unto strange cities. 12 Whereupon as I went to Damascus with authority and commission from the chief priests, 13At midday, O king, I saw in the way a light from heaven, above the brightness of the sun, shining round about me and them which journeyed with me. 14And when we were all fallen to the earth, I heard a voice speaking unto me, and saying in the Hebrew tongue, Saul, Saul, why persecutest thou me? *it is* hard for thee to kick against the pricks. 15And I said, Who art thou, Lord? And he said, I am Jesus whom thou persecutest. 16 But rise, and stand upon thy feet: for I have appeared unto thee for this purpose, to make thee a minister and a witness both of these things which thou hast seen, and of those things in the which I will appear unto thee; 17 Delivering thee from the people, and *from* the Gentiles, unto whom now I send thee, 18.To open their eyes, *and* to turn *them* from darkness to light, and *from* the power of Satan unto God, that they may receive forgiveness of sins, and inheritance among them which are sanctified by faith that is in me. 19 Whereupon, O king Agrippa, I was not disobedient unto the heavenly vision: 20 But shewed first unto them of Damascus, and at Jerusalem, and throughout all the coasts of Judea, and *then* to the Gentiles, that they should repent and turn to God, and do works meet for repentance. 21 For these causes the Jews caught me in the temple, and went about to kill *me*. 22 Having therefore obtained help of God, I continue unto this day, witnessing both to small and great, saying none other things than those which the prophets and

New International Version

fortunate to stand before you today as I make my defense against all the accusations of the Jews, 3 and especially so because you are well acquainted with all the Jewish customs and controversies. Therefore, I beg you to listen to me patiently. 4 "The Jews all know the way I have lived ever since I was a child, from the beginning of my life in my own country, and also in Jerusalem. 5 They have known me for a long time and can testify, if they are willing, that according to the strictest sect of our religion, I lived as a Pharisee. 6And now it is because of my hope in what God has promised our fathers that I am on trial today. 7 This is the promise our twelve tribes are hoping to see fulfilled as they earnestly serve God day and night. Your Majesty, it is because of this hope that the Jews are accusing me. 8 Why should any of you consider it incredible that God raises the dead? 9 "I too was convinced that I ought to do all that was possible to oppose the name of Jesus of Nazareth. 10And that is just what I did in Jerusalem. On the authority of the chief priests I put many of the saints in prison, and when they were put to death, I cast my vote against them. 11 Many a time I went from one synagogue to another to have them punished, and I tried to force them to blaspheme. In my obsession against them, I even went to foreign cities to persecute them. 12 "On one of these journeys I was going to Damascus with the authority and commission of the chief priests. 13About noon, Your Majesty, as I was on the road, I saw a light from heaven, brighter than the sun, blazing around me and my companions. 14 We all fell to the ground, and I heard a voice saying to me in Aramaic,[1] 'Saul, Saul, why do you persecute me? It is hard for you to kick against the goads.' 15 "Then I asked, 'Who are you, Lord?' " 'I am Jesus, whom you are persecuting,' the Lord replied. 16 'Now get up and stand on your feet. I have appeared to you to appoint you as a servant and as a witness of what you have seen of me and what I will show you. 17 I will rescue you from your own people and from the Gentiles. I am sending you 18 to open their eyes and turn them from darkness to light, and from the power of Satan to God, so that they may receive forgiveness of sins and a place among those who are sanctified by faith in me.' 19 "So then, King Agrippa, I was not disobedient to the vision from heaven. 20 First to those in Damascus, then to those in Jerusalem and in all Judea, and to the Gentiles also, I preached that they should repent and turn to God and prove their repentance by their deeds. 21 That is why the Jews seized me in the temple courts and tried to kill me. 22 But I have had God's help to this very day, and so I stand here and testify to small and great alike. I am saying nothing beyond what the prophets and Moses

[1] Or *Hebrew.*

432

Greek Interlinear

ὑπὸ Ἰουδαίων, βασιλεῦ Ἀγρίππα, ἥγημαι
by Jews, king Agrippa, I consider

ἐμαυτὸν μακάριον ἐπὶ σοῦ μέλλων σήμερον
myself happy ²before ⁴thee ³being about ⁵to-day

ἀπολογεῖσθαι, 3 μάλιστα γνώστην ὄντα σε
¹to defend myself, most of all ²an expert ¹being ³thee

πάντων τῶν κατὰ Ἰουδαίους ἐθῶν τε
²of all ⁴the ⁵among ⁶Jews ⁷customs ⁸both

καὶ ζητημάτων· διὸ δέομαι μακροθύμως
¹⁰and ¹¹questions; wherefore I beg patiently

ἀκοῦσαί μου. 4 Τὴν μὲν οὖν βίωσίν
to hear me. ²the ¹So ²then ⁴manner of life

μου ἐκ νεότητος τὴν ἀπ᾽ ἀρχῆς γενομένην
of me from youth - ³from ⁴beginning ¹having been ²[the]

ἐν τῷ ἔθνει μου ἔν τε Ἱεροσολύμοις
in the nation of me ⁵in ¹and Jerusalem

ἴσασι πάντες Ἰουδαῖοι, 5 προγινώσκοντές
know all Jews, previously knowing

με ἄνωθεν, ἐὰν θέλωσι μαρτυρεῖν, ὅτι
me from the first, if they are willing to testify, that

κατὰ τὴν ἀκριβεστάτην αἵρεσιν τῆς
according to the most exact sect -

ἡμετέρας θρησκείας ἔζησα Φαρισαῖος. 6 καὶ
of our religion I lived a Pharisee. And

νῦν ἐπ᾽ ἐλπίδι τῆς εἰς τοὺς πατέρας
now on(in) hope of the ⁴to ¹the ²fathers

ἡμῶν ἐπαγγελίας γενομένης ὑπὸ τοῦ θεοῦ
²of us ¹promise ³having been [made] ²by - ⁴God

ἕστηκα κρινόμενος, 7 εἰς ἣν τὸ δωδεκά-
I stand being judged, to which the twelve-

φυλον ἡμῶν ἐν ἐκτενείᾳ νύκτα καὶ
tribes of us with earnestness night and

ἡμέραν λατρεῦον ἐλπίζει καταντῆσαι· περὶ
day worshipping hopes to arrive; concerning

ἧς ἐλπίδος ἐγκαλοῦμαι ὑπὸ Ἰουδαίων,
which hope I am accused by Jews,

βασιλεῦ. 8 τί ἄπιστον κρίνεται παρ᾽
[O] king. Why incredible is it judged by

ὑμῖν εἰ ὁ θεὸς νεκροὺς ἐγείρει; 9 ἐγὼ
you if - God ²dead persons ¹raises? ²I

μὲν οὖν ἔδοξα ἐμαυτῷ πρὸς τὸ ὄνομα
¹indeed ²then ¹thought ²to myself ⁴to ⁵the ¹⁴name

Ἰησοῦ τοῦ Ναζωραίου δεῖν πολλὰ ἐναντία
¹²of Jesus ¹⁴the ¹⁵Nazarene ⁶ought ⁷many ¹contrary
things

πρᾶξαι· 10 ὃ καὶ ἐποίησα ἐν Ἱεροσολύμοις,
⁷to do; which indeed I did in Jerusalem,

καὶ πολλούς τε τῶν ἁγίων ἐγὼ ἐν
and many ²- of the saints ³I ⁵in

φυλακαῖς κατέκλεισα τὴν παρὰ τῶν
⁶prisons ³shut up ⁴the ⁵from ³the

ἀρχιερέων ἐξουσίαν λαβών, ἀναιρουμένων τε
¹⁰chief priests ²authority ⁶having received, being killed and
= and when they were killed

αὐτῶν κατήνεγκα ψῆφον, 11 καὶ κατὰ
them² I cast a vote, and throughout

πάσας τὰς συναγωγὰς πολλάκις τιμωρῶν
all the synagogues often punishing

αὐτοὺς ἠνάγκαζον βλασφημεῖν, περισσῶς τε
them I compelled [them] to blaspheme, and excessively

ἐμμαινόμενος αὐτοῖς ἐδίωκον ἕως καὶ εἰς
raging against them I persecuted as far as even to

τὰς ἔξω πόλεις. 12 Ἐν οἷς πορευόμενος
the outside cities. In which journeying

εἰς τὴν Δαμασκὸν μετ᾽ ἐξουσίας καὶ
to - Damascus with authority and

ἐπιτροπῆς τῆς τῶν ἀρχιερέων, 13 ἡμέρας
power to decide - of the chief priests, at ⁴day

μέσης κατὰ τὴν ὁδόν, εἶδον, βασιλεῦ,
¹mid along the way, I saw, [O] king,

οὐρανόθεν ὑπὲρ τὴν λαμπρότητα τοῦ ἡλίου
²from heaven ³above ⁴the ⁵brightness ⁶of the ⁷sun

περιλάμψαν με φῶς καὶ τοὺς σὺν ἐμοὶ
⁸shining round ⁹me ¹a light ¹⁰and ¹¹the [ones] with

πορευομένους· 14 πάντων τε καταπεσόντων
¹¹journeying; and all having fallen down
= when we had all fallen

ἡμῶν εἰς τὴν γῆν ἤκουσα φωνὴν λέγουσαν
us² to the earth I heard a voice saying

πρός με τῇ Ἑβραΐδι διαλέκτῳ· Σαοὺλ
to me in the Hebrew language: Saul[,]

Σαούλ, τί με διώκεις; σκληρόν σοι
Saul, why me persecutest thou? hard for thee

πρὸς κέντρα λακτίζειν. 15 ἐγὼ δὲ εἶπα·
against goads to kick. And I said:

τίς εἶ, κύριε; ὁ δὲ κύριος εἶπεν· ἐγώ
Who art thou, Lord? And the Lord said: I

εἰμι Ἰησοῦς ὃν σὺ διώκεις. 16 ἀλλὰ
am Jesus whom thou persecutest. But

ἀνάστηθι καὶ στῆθι ἐπὶ τοὺς πόδας σου·
rise thou up and stand on the feet of thee;

εἰς τοῦτο γὰρ ὤφθην σοι, προχειρίσασθαί
²for ³this [purpose] ¹for I appeared to thee, to appoint

σε ὑπηρέτην καὶ μάρτυρα ὧν τε
thee an attendant and a witness ²of the things ¹both
which

εἰδές με ὧν τε ὀφθήσομαί σοι,
³thou sawest ⁴me ⁵of the things ⁵and I will appear to thee,
which

17 ἐξαιρούμενός σε ἐκ τοῦ λαοῦ καὶ ἐκ
delivering thee from the people and from

τῶν ἐθνῶν, εἰς οὓς ἐγὼ ἀποστέλλω σε,
the nations, to whom I send thee,

18 ἀνοῖξαι ὀφθαλμοὺς αὐτῶν, τοῦ ἐπιστρέψαι
to open eyes of them, - to turnᵇ

ἀπὸ σκότους εἰς φῶς καὶ τῆς ἐξουσίας
from darkness to light and [from] the authority

τοῦ σατανᾶ ἐπὶ τὸν θεόν, τοῦ λαβεῖν
- of Satan to - God, - to receive
= that they may receive

αὐτοὺς ἄφεσιν ἁμαρτιῶν καὶ κλῆρον ἐν
themᵇᵈ forgiveness of sins and a lot among

τοῖς ἡγιασμένοις πίστει τῇ εἰς ἐμέ.
the [ones] having been sanctified by faith - in me.

19 Ὅθεν, βασιλεῦ Ἀγρίππα, οὐκ ἐγενόμην
Whence, king Agrippa, I was not

ἀπειθὴς τῇ οὐρανίῳ ὀπτασίᾳ, 20 ἀλλὰ
disobedient to the heavenly vision, but

τοῖς ἐν Δαμασκῷ πρῶτόν τε καὶ
to the [ones] in Damascus firstly and also

Ἱεροσολύμοις, πᾶσάν τε τὴν χώραν τῆς
[in] Jerusalem, and all the country -

Ἰουδαίας καὶ τοῖς ἔθνεσιν ἀπήγγελλον
of Judæa and to the nations I announced

μετανοεῖν καὶ ἐπιστρέφειν ἐπὶ τὸν θεόν,
to repent and to turn to - God,

ἄξια τῆς μετανοίας ἔργα πράσσοντας.
⁴worthy ⁵of the ⁶repentance ³works ¹doing.

21 ἕνεκα τούτων με Ἰουδαῖοι συλλαβόμενοι
On these things ²me ¹Jews ³having seized
account of

ἐν τῷ ἱερῷ ἐπειρῶντο διαχειρίσασθαι.
in the temple tried to kill [me].

22 ἐπικουρίας οὖν τυχὼν τῆς ἀπὸ τοῦ
Succour therefore having - from -
obtained

θεοῦ ἄχρι τῆς ἡμέρας ταύτης ἕστηκα
God until this day I stand

μαρτυρόμενος μικρῷ τε καὶ μεγάλῳ, οὐδὲν
witnessing ²to small ¹both and to great, ²nothing

ἐκτὸς λέγων ὧν τε οἱ προφῆται
¹apart ³saying ⁴the things ⁵both ⁴the ⁵prophets
from which

King James Version

Moses did say should come: 23 That Christ should suffer, *and* that he should be the first that should rise from the dead, and should shew light unto the people, and to the Gentiles. 24And as he thus spake for himself, Festus said with a loud voice, Paul, thou art beside thyself; much learning doth make thee mad. 25 But he said, I am not mad, most noble Festus; but speak forth the words of truth and soberness. 26 For the king knoweth of these things, before whom also I speak freely: for I am persuaded that none of these things are hidden from him; for this thing was not done in a corner. 27 King Agrippa, believest thou the prophets? I know that thou believest. 28 Then Agrippa said unto Paul, Almost thou persuadest me to be a Christian. 29And Paul said, I would to God, that not only thou, but also all that hear me this day, were both almost, and altogether such as I am, except these bonds. 30And when he had thus spoken, the king rose up, and the governor, and Bernice, and they that sat with them: 31And when they were gone aside, they talked between themselves, saying, This man doeth nothing worthy of death or of bonds. 32 Then said Agrippa unto Festus, This man might have been set at liberty, if he had not appealed unto Cesar.

New International Version

said would happen—23 that the Christ[m] would suffer and, as the first to rise from the dead, would proclaim light to his own people and to the Gentiles."

24 At this point Festus interrupted Paul's defense. "You are out of your mind, Paul!" he shouted. "Your great learning is driving you insane."

25 "I am not insane, most excellent Festus," Paul replied. "What I am saying is true and reasonable. 26 The king is familiar with these things, and I can speak freely to him. I am convinced that none of this has escaped his notice, because it was not done in a corner. 27 King Agrippa, do you believe the prophets? I know you do."

28 Then Agrippa said to Paul, "Do you think that in such a short time you can persuade me to be a Christian?"

29 Paul replied, "Short time or long—I pray God that not only you but all who are listening to me today may become what I am, except for these chains."

30 The king rose, and with him the governor and Bernice and those sitting with them. 31 They left the room, and while talking with one another, they said, "This man is not doing anything that deserves death or imprisonment."

32 Agrippa said to Festus, "This man could have been set free, if he had not appealed to Caesar."

Paul sails for Rome

27 And when it was determined that we should sail into Italy, they delivered Paul and certain other prisoners unto *one* named Julius, a centurion of Augustus' band. 2And entering into a ship of Adramyttium, we launched, meaning to sail by the coasts of Asia; *one* Aristarchus, a Macedonian of Thessalonica, being with us. 3And the next *day* we touched at Sidon. And Julius courteously entreated Paul, and gave *him* liberty to go unto his friends to refresh himself. 4And when we had launched from thence, we sailed under Cyprus, because the winds were contrary. 5And when we had sailed over the sea of Cilicia and Pamphylia, we came to Myra, *a city* of Lycia. 6And there the centurion found a ship of Alexandria sailing into Italy; and he put us therein. 7And when we had sailed slowly many days, and scarce were come over against Cnidus, the wind not suffering us, we sailed under Crete, over against Salmone; 8And, hardly passing it, came unto a place which is called the Fair Havens; nigh whereunto was the city *of* Lasea. 9 Now when much time was spent, and when sailing was now dangerous, because the fast was now already past, Paul admonished *them*, 10And said unto them, Sirs, I perceive

27 When it was decided that we would sail for Italy, Paul and some other prisoners were handed over to a centurion named Julius, who belonged to the Imperial Regiment. 2 We boarded a ship from Adramyttium about to sail for ports along the coast of the province of Asia, and we put out to sea. Aristarchus, a Macedonian from Thessalonica, was with us.

3 The next day we landed at Sidon; and Julius, in kindness to Paul, allowed him to go to his friends so they might provide for his needs. 4 From there we put out to sea again and passed to the lee of Cyprus because the winds were against us. 5 When we had sailed across the open sea off the coast of Cilicia and Pamphylia, we landed at Myra in Lycia. 6 There the centurion found an Alexandrian ship sailing for Italy and put us on board. 7 We made slow headway for many days and had difficulty arriving off Cnidus. When the wind did not allow us to hold our course, we sailed to the lee of Crete, opposite Salmone. 8 We moved along the coast with difficulty and came to a place called Fair Havens, near the town of Lasea.

9 Much time had been lost, and sailing had already become dangerous because by now it was after the Fast.[n] So Paul warned them, 10 "Men, I can see that our voyage is going to

[m] Or *Messiah*. [n] That is, the Day of Atonement (Yom Kippur).

Greek Interlinear

ἐλάλησαν μελλόντων γίνεσθαι καὶ Μωϋσῆς,
¹⁴said ¹¹being about ¹²to happen ⁸and ⁹Moses,

23 εἰ παθητὸς ὁ χριστός, εἰ πρῶτος
if subject to suffering the Christ, if first

ἐξ ἀναστάσεως νεκρῶν φῶς μέλλει
by a resurrection of dead ⁸a light ¹he is
persons about

καταγγέλλειν τῷ τε λαῷ καὶ τοῖς ἔθνεσιν.
²to announce ⁴to the ⁶both people and to the nations.

24 Ταῦτα δὲ αὐτοῦ ἀπολογουμένου ὁ Φῆστος
And these things him defending himself⁸ - Festus
= as he defended himself with these things

μεγάλῃ τῇ φωνῇ φησιν· μαίνῃ, Παῦλε·
⁸great ¹with the(his) ²voice says: Thou ravest, Paul:

τὰ πολλά σε γράμματα εἰς μανίαν
¹the ⁵many ⁴thee ³letters ²to ⁷madness

περιτρέπει. 25 ὁ δὲ Παῦλος· οὐ μαίνομαι,
⁶turn[s]. - But · Paul: I do not rave,

φησίν, κράτιστε Φῆστε, ἀλλὰ ἀληθείας
he says, most excellent Festus, but ²of truth

καὶ σωφροσύνης ῥήματα ἀποφθέγγομαι.
⁴and ⁸of good sense ¹words ¹speak forth.

26 ἐπίσταται γὰρ περὶ τούτων ὁ βασιλεύς,
For ²understands ⁴about ³these things ¹the ⁵king,

πρὸς ὃν καὶ παρρησιαζόμενος λαλῶ·
to whom indeed being bold of speech I speak;

λανθάνειν γὰρ αὐτὸν τούτων οὐ πείθομαι
for ⁶to be hidden [from] ⁴him ⁵of these things not ¹I am persuaded

οὐθέν· οὐ γάρ ἐστιν ἐν γωνίᾳ πεπραγμένον
¹nothing; for ²not ³is ¹in ⁴a corner ⁵having been done

τοῦτο. 27 πιστεύεις, βασιλεῦ Ἀγρίππα,
¹this. Believest thou, king Agrippa,

τοῖς προφήταις; οἶδα ὅτι πιστεύεις. 28 ὁ
the prophets? I know that thou believest. -

δὲ Ἀγρίππας πρὸς τὸν Παῦλον· ἐν
And Agrippa [said] to - Paul: In

ὀλίγῳ με πείθεις Χριστιανὸν ποιῆσαι.
a little ¹me ¹thou persuadest ²a Christian ³to make(act).

29 ὁ δὲ Παῦλος· εὐξαίμην ἂν τῷ θεῷ
- And Paul [said]: I would pray - God

καὶ ἐν ὀλίγῳ καὶ ἐν μεγάλῳ οὐ μόνον
both in a little and in great not only

σὲ ἀλλὰ καὶ πάντας τοὺς ἀκούοντάς
thee but also all the [ones] hearing

μου σήμερον γενέσθαι τοιούτους ὁποῖος
me to-day ²to become ¹such of what kind

καὶ ἐγώ εἰμι, παρεκτὸς τῶν δεσμῶν
indeed I am, except - bonds

τούτων. 30 Ἀνέστη τε ὁ βασιλεὺς καὶ
these. Rose up both the king and

ὁ ἡγεμὼν ἥ τε Βερνίκη καὶ οἱ συγ-
the governor - and Bernice and the [ones] sit-

καθήμενοι αὐτοῖς, 31 καὶ ἀναχωρήσαντες
ting with them, and having left

ἐλάλουν πρὸς ἀλλήλους λέγοντες ὅτι οὐδὲν
spoke to one another saying [.] - ⁴nothing

θανάτου ἢ δεσμῶν ἄξιον πράσσει ὁ
⁶of death ⁷or ⁸of bonds ⁶worthy ²does -

ἄνθρωπος οὗτος. 32 Ἀγρίππας δὲ τῷ
⁸man ¹This. And Agrippa -

Φήστῳ ἔφη· ἀπολελύσθαι ἐδύνατο
to Festus said: ²to have been released ¹was able(could)

ὁ ἄνθρωπος οὗτος εἰ μὴ ἐπεκέκλητο Καίσαρα.
¹This man if he had not appealed to Cæsar.

Chapter 27

Ὡς δὲ ἐκρίθη τοῦ ἀποπλεῖν ἡμᾶς
And when it was decided - to sail us⁸ᵈ
= that we should sail

εἰς τὴν Ἰταλίαν, παρεδίδουν τόν τε
to - Italy, they delivered - both

Παῦλον καί τινας ἑτέρους δεσμώτας
Paul and some other prisoners

ἑκατοντάρχῃ ὀνόματι Ἰουλίῳ σπείρης
to a centurion by name Julius of a cohort

Σεβαστῆς. 2 ἐπιβάντες δὲ πλοίῳ Ἀδρα-
Augustan. And embarking in a ship belonging to

μυττηνῷ μέλλοντι πλεῖν εἰς τοὺς κατὰ
Adramyttium being about to sail ¹for ⁸the ⁴along [the
coast of]

τὴν Ἀσίαν τόπους ἀνήχθημεν, ὄντος σὺν
- ⁶Asia ⁸places we set sail, being with

ἡμῖν Ἀριστάρχου Μακεδόνος Θεσσαλονικέως·
us Aristarchus a Macedonian of Thessalonica;

3 τῇ τε ἑτέρᾳ κατήχθημεν εἰς Σιδῶνα,
and on the next [day] we were brought at Sidon,
to land

φιλανθρώπως τε ὁ Ἰούλιος τῷ Παύλῳ
and ²kindly - ¹Julius - ²Paul

χρησάμενος ἐπέτρεψεν πρὸς τοὺς φίλους
¹treating [him] allowed ³to ⁴the ⁵friends

πορευθέντι ἐπιμελείας τυχεῖν. 4 κἀκεῖθεν
⁶going ¹¹attention ¹²to obtain. And thence

ἀναχθέντες ὑπεπλεύσαμεν τὴν Κύπρον διὰ
putting to sea we sailed close to - Cyprus because
of

τὸ τοὺς ἀνέμους εἶναι ἐναντίους, 5 τό τε
- the winds to be(being) contrary, and ⁸the

πέλαγος τὸ κατὰ τὴν Κιλικίαν καὶ
³sea - ⁴against - ⁵Cilicia ⁶and

Παμφυλίαν διαπλεύσαντες κατήλθαμεν εἰς
⁷Pamphylia ¹sailing over we came down to

Μύρα τῆς Λυκίας. 6 Κἀκεῖ εὑρὼν ὁ
Myra - of Lycia. And there ⁸having found ¹the

ἑκατοντάρχης πλοῖον Ἀλεξανδρῖνον πλέον
²centurion ship an Alexandrian sailing

εἰς τὴν Ἰταλίαν ἐνεβίβασεν ἡμᾶς εἰς
to - Italy he embarked us in

αὐτό. 7 ἐν ἱκαναῖς δὲ ἡμέραις βραδυπλο-
it. And in a number of days sailing

οῦντες καὶ μόλις γενόμενοι κατὰ τὴν
slowly and hardly coming against -

Κνίδον, μὴ προσεῶντος ἡμᾶς τοῦ ἀνέμου,
Cnidus, not allowing us the wind,⁸
= as the wind did not allow us,

ὑπεπλεύσαμεν τὴν Κρήτην κατὰ Σαλμώνην,
we sailed close to - Crete against Salmone,

8 μόλις τε παραλεγόμενοι αὐτὴν ἤλθομεν
and hardly sailing along it we came

εἰς τόπον τινὰ καλούμενον Καλοὺς λιμένας,
to place a certain being called Fair Havens,

ᾧ ἐγγὺς ἦν πόλις Λασαία. 9 Ἱκανοῦ δὲ
⁸to which ¹near was a city Lasæa. And much
= when

χρόνου διαγενομένου καὶ ὄντος ἤδη
time having passed⁸ and being now
much time had passed = as the voyage

ἐπισφαλοῦς τοῦ πλοὸς διὰ τὸ καὶ τὴν
dangerous the voyage⁸ on account of - also the
was now dangerous = because also the fast had now

νηστείαν ἤδη παρεληλυθέναι, παρῄνει ὁ
fast now to have gone by, ²advised -
gone by,

Παῦλος 10 λέγων αὐτοῖς· ἄνδρες, θεωρῶ
¹Paul saying to them: Men, I see

435

King James Version

that this voyage will be with hurt and much damage, not only of the lading and ship, but also of our lives. 11 Nevertheless the centurion believed the master and the owner of the ship, more than those things which were spoken by Paul. 12And because the haven was not commodious to winter in, the more part advised to depart thence also, if by any means they might attain to Phenice, *and there* to winter; *which is* a haven of Crete, and lieth toward the southwest and northwest. 13And when the south wind blew softly, supposing that they had obtained *their* purpose, loosing *thence,* they sailed close by Crete. 14 But not long after there arose against it a tempestuous wind, called Euroclydon. 15And when the ship was caught, and could not bear up into the wind, we let *her* drive. 16And running under a certain island which is called Clauda, we had much work to come by the boat: 17 Which when they had taken up, they used helps, undergirding the ship; and, fearing lest they should fall into the quicksands, strake sail, and so were driven. 18And we being exceedingly tossed with a tempest, the next *day* they lightened the ship; 19And the third *day* we cast out with our own hands the tackling of the ship. 20And when neither sun nor stars in many days appeared, and no small tempest lay on *us,* all hope that we should be saved was then taken away. 21 But after long abstinence, Paul stood forth in the midst of them, and said, Sirs, ye should have hearkened unto me, and not have loosed from Crete, and to have gained this harm and loss. 22And now I exhort you to be of good cheer: for there shall be no loss of *any man's* life among you, but of the ship. 23 For there stood by me this night the angel of God, whose I am, and whom I serve, 24 Saying, Fear not, Paul; thou must be brought before Cesar: and, lo, God hath given thee all them that sail with thee. 25 Wherefore, sirs, be of good cheer: for I believe God, that it shall be even as it was told me. 26 Howbeit we must be cast upon a certain island. 27 But when the fourteenth night was come, as we were driven up and down in Adria, about midnight the shipmen deemed that they drew near to some country; 28And sounded, and found *it* twenty fathoms: and when they had gone a little further, they sounded again, and found *it* fifteen fathoms. 29 Then fearing lest we should have fallen upon rocks, they cast four anchors out of the stern, and wished for the day. 30And as the shipmen were about to flee out of the ship, when they had let down the boat into the sea, under colour as though they would have cast anchors out of the fore-

New International Version

be disastrous and bring great loss to ship and cargo, and to our own lives also." 11 But the centurion, instead of listening to what Paul said, followed the advice of the pilot and of the owner of the ship. 12 Since the harbor was unsuitable to winter in, the majority decided that we should sail on, hoping to reach Phoenix and winter there. This was a harbor in Crete, facing both southwest and northwest.

The storm

13 When a gentle south wind began to blow, they thought they had obtained what they wanted; so they weighed anchor and sailed along the shore of Crete. 14 Before very long, a wind of hurricane force, called the "Northeaster," swept down from the island. 15 The ship was caught by the storm and could not head into the wind; so we gave way to it and were driven along. 16 As we passed to the lee of a small island called Cauda, we were hardly able to make the lifeboat secure. 17 When the men had hoisted it aboard, they tied ropes around the ship itself to hold it together. Fearing that they would run aground on the sandbars of Syrtis, they lowered the sea anchor and let the ship be driven along. 18 We took such a violent battering from the storm that the next day they began to throw the cargo overboard. 19 On the third day, they threw the ship's tackle overboard with their own hands. 20 When neither sun nor stars appeared for many days and the storm continued raging, we finally gave up all hope of being saved.

21 After the men had gone a long time without food, Paul stood up before them and said: "Men, you should have taken my advice not to sail from Crete; then you would have spared yourselves this damage and loss. 22 But now I urge you to keep up your courage, because not one of you will be lost; only the ship will be destroyed. 23 Last night an angel of the God whose I am and whom I serve stood beside me 24 and said, 'Do not be afraid, Paul. You must stand trial before Caesar; and God has graciously given you the lives of all who sail with you.' 25 So keep up your courage, men, for I have faith in God that it will happen just as he told me. 26 Nevertheless, we must run aground on some island."

The shipwreck

27 On the fourteenth night we were still being driven across the Adriatic Sea, when about midnight the sailors sensed they were approaching land. 28 They took soundings and found that the water was one hundred and twenty feet deep. A short time later they took soundings again and found it was ninety feet deep. 29 Fearing that we would be dashed against the rocks, they dropped four anchors from the stern and prayed for daylight. 30 In an attempt to escape from the ship, the sailors let the lifeboat down into the sea, pretending they were going to lower

Greek Interlinear

ὅτι μετὰ ὕβρεως καὶ πολλῆς ζημίας οὐ
that with injury and much loss not

μόνον τοῦ φορτίου καὶ τοῦ πλοίου ἀλλὰ
only of the cargo and of the ship but

καὶ τῶν ψυχῶν ἡμῶν μέλλειν ἔσεσθαι
also of the lives of us ³to be about ⁴to be
= will be

τὸν πλοῦν. 11 ὁ δὲ ἑκατοντάρχης τῷ
¹the ²voyage. But the centurion ²the

κυβερνήτῃ καὶ τῷ ναυκλήρῳ μᾶλλον
¹steersman ⁴and ⁵the ⁶shipmaster ⁷rather

ἐπείθετο ἢ τοῖς ὑπὸ Παύλου λεγομένοις.
¹was persuaded by ⁸than ⁹the ¹¹by ¹²Paul ¹⁰things said.

12 ἀνευθέτου δὲ τοῦ λιμένος ὑπάρχοντος
But unsuitable the port being⁸
= as the port was unsuitable

πρὸς παραχειμασίαν οἱ πλείονες ἔθεντο
for wintering the majority placed
= decided

βουλὴν ἀναχθῆναι ἐκεῖθεν, εἴ πως δύναιντο
counsel to set sail thence, if some- they might
how be able

καταντήσαντες εἰς Φοίνικα παραχειμάσαι,
having arrived at Phœnix to pass the winter,

λιμένα τῆς Κρήτης βλέποντα κατὰ λίβα
a port - of Crete looking toward south-

καὶ κατὰ χῶρον. 13 Ὑποπνεύσαντος δὲ
and toward north-west. And blowing gently
= when a south wind

νότου δόξαντες τῆς προθέσεως κεκρατηκέναι,
a south wind⁸ thinking ²the(ir) ³purpose ¹to have obtained,
blew gently

ἄραντες ἆσσον παρελέγοντο τὴν Κρήτην.
raising ²close in- ¹they coasted by - ²Crete.
[anchor] shore

14 μετ᾽ οὐ πολὺ δὲ ἔβαλεν κατ᾽ αὐτῆς
And after not much there beat down it

ἄνεμος τυφωνικὸς ὁ καλούμενος εὐρακύλων·
wind tempestuous - being called Euraquilo·

15 συναρπασθέντος δὲ τοῦ πλοίου καὶ μὴ
and ²being seized ¹the ³ship⁸ and not

δυναμένου ἀντοφθαλμεῖν τῷ ἀνέμῳ ἐπιδόντες
being able⁸ to beat up against the wind giving way

ἐφερόμεθα. 16 νησίον δέ τι ὑποδραμόντες
we were borne. And ²islet ¹a certain ¹running under
the lee of

καλούμενον Κλαῦδα ἰσχύσαμεν μόλις
being called Clauda we were able hardly

περικρατεῖς γενέσθαι τῆς σκάφης, 17 ἣν
control to get of the boat, which

ἄραντες βοηθείαις ἐχρῶντο, ὑποζωννύντες
taking ⁹helps ¹they used, undergirding

τὸ πλοῖον· φοβούμενοί τε μὴ εἰς τὴν
the ship; and fearing lest into -

Σύρτιν ἐκπέσωσιν, χαλάσαντες τὸ σκεῦος,
Syrtis they might fall off,⁸ lowering the tackle,

οὕτως ἐφέροντο. 18 σφοδρῶς δὲ χειμαζ-
thus they were borne. But exceedingly being in . . .
= as we were exceedingly in . . .

ομένων ἡμῶν τῇ ἑξῆς ἐκβολὴν ἐποιοῦντο,
the grip us⁸ on the next a jettisoning they made,
of a storm [day]

19 καὶ τῇ τρίτῃ αὐτόχειρες τὴν σκευὴν
and on the third with their the tackle
[day] own hands

τοῦ πλοίου ἔρριψαν. 20 μήτε δὲ ἡλίου
of the ship they threw [out]. And neither sun
= when neither . . .

μήτε ἄστρων ἐπιφαινόντων ἐπὶ πλείονας
nor stars appearing⁸ over many
appeared

ἡμέρας, χειμῶνός τε οὐκ ὀλίγου ἐπικειμένου,
days, and stormy weather no little pressing hard,⁸

λοιπὸν περιῃρεῖτο ἐλπὶς πᾶσα τοῦ σῴζεσθαι
now was taken away ³hope ¹all - to be saved
= that we might

ἡμᾶς. 21 Πολλῆς τε ἀσιτίας ὑπαρχούσης
us.ᵇᵈ And much abstinence being⁸
be saved. = when there was long abstinence

τότε σταθεὶς ὁ Παῦλος ἐν μέσῳ αὐτῶν εἶπεν·
then ¹standing - ¹Paul in [the] midst of them said:

ἔδει μέν, ὦ ἄνδρες, πειθαρχήσαντάς
It behoved - O men, obeying
[you],

μοι μὴ ἀνάγεσθαι ἀπὸ τῆς Κρήτης
me not to set sail from - Crete

κερδῆσαί τε τὴν ὕβριν ταύτην καὶ τὴν
and to come by - injury this and -

ζημίαν. 22 καὶ τὰ νῦν παραινῶ ὑμᾶς
loss. And - now I advise you

εὐθυμεῖν· ἀποβολὴ γὰρ ψυχῆς οὐδεμία
to be of good for ³throwing away ⁴of life ²no
cheer;

ἔσται ἐξ ὑμῶν πλὴν τοῦ πλοίου.
¹there will be of you but of the ship.

23 παρέστη γάρ μοι ταύτῃ τῇ νυκτὶ
For there stood by me in this - night

τοῦ θεοῦ οὗ εἰμι, ᾧ καὶ λατρεύω,
- ²of God ¹of whom ⁴I am, ³whom ⁵also ⁶I serve,

ἄγγελος 24 λέγων· μὴ φοβοῦ, Παῦλε·
¹an angel saying· Fear not, Paul;

Καίσαρί σε δεῖ παραστῆναι, καὶ ἰδοὺ
⁴Cæsar ³thee ¹it behoves ²to stand before, and behold

κεχάρισταί σοι ὁ θεὸς πάντας τοὺς
¹has given ²thee - ³God all the [ones]

πλέοντας μετὰ σοῦ. 25 διὸ εὐθυμεῖτε,
sailing with thee. Wherefore be ye of
good cheer,

ἄνδρες· πιστεύω γὰρ τῷ θεῷ ὅτι οὕτως
men; for I believe - God that thus

ἔσται καθ᾽ ὃν τρόπον λελάληταί μοι.
it will be in the way in which† it has been spoken to me.

26 εἰς νῆσον δέ τινα δεῖ ἡμᾶς ἐκπεσεῖν.
⁵Onto ²island ¹but ⁴a ³it ²us ⁴to fall off.
certain behoves

27 Ὡς δὲ τεσσαρεσκαιδεκάτη νὺξ ἐγένετο
Now when [the] fourteenth night came

διαφερομένων ἡμῶν ἐν τῷ Ἀδρίᾳ, κατ᾽
being carried about us⁸ in the Adria, abou
= while we were being carried about

μέσον τῆς νυκτὸς ὑπενόουν οἱ ναῦται
[the] middle of the night ³supposed ¹the ²sailors

προσάγειν τινὰ αὐτοῖς χώραν. 28 καὶ
⁴to approach ⁵some ⁶to them ⁷country. And

βολίσαντες εὗρον ὀργυιὰς εἴκοσι, βραχὺ
sounding they found fathoms twenty, and ²a little

διαστήσαντες καὶ πάλιν βολίσαντες εὗρον
¹having moved and also sounding they found

ὀργυιὰς δεκαπέντε· 29 φοβούμενοί τε μή
fathoms fifteen; and fearing lest

που κατὰ τραχεῖς τόπους ἐκπέσωμεν,
⁸somewhere ⁹against ⁴rough ⁵places ¹we might fall off,

ἐκ πρύμνης ῥίψαντες ἀγκύρας τέσσαρας
out of [the] stern throwing anchors four

ηὔχοντο ἡμέραν γενέσθαι. 30 Τῶν δὲ
they prayed day to become. And the

ναυτῶν ζητούντων φυγεῖν ἐκ τοῦ πλοίου
sailors seeking to flee out of the ship
= when the sailors sought

καὶ χαλασάντων τὴν σκάφην εἰς τὴν
and lowering⁸ the boat into the
= lowered

θάλασσαν προφάσει ὡς ἐκ πρώρης ἀγκύρας
sea under pretence as ²out of ³[the] prow ¹anchors

* This is the classical Greek word for a ship being driven out of her course on to shoals, rocks, etc. (Page). See also vers 26 and 29.

437

King James Version

ship, 31 Paul said to the centurion and to the soldiers, Except these abide in the ship, ye cannot be saved. 32 Then the soldiers cut off the ropes of the boat, and let her fall off. 33And while the day was coming on, Paul besought *them* all to take meat, saying, This day is the fourteenth day that ye have tarried and continued fasting, having taken nothing. 34 Wherefore I pray you to take *some* meat; for this is for your health: for there shall not a hair fall from the head of any of you. 35And when he had thus spoken, he took bread, and gave thanks to God in presence of them all; and when he had broken *it*, he began to eat. 36 Then were they all of good cheer, and they also took *some* meat. 37And we were in all in the ship two hundred threescore and sixteen souls. 38And when they had eaten enough, they lightened the ship, and cast out the wheat into the sea. 39And when it was day, they knew not the land: but they discovered a certain creek with a shore, into the which they were minded, if it were possible, to thrust in the ship. 40And when they had taken up the anchors, they committed *themselves* unto the sea, and loosed the rudder bands, and hoised up the mainsail to the wind, and made toward shore. 41And falling into a place where two seas met, they ran the ship aground; and the forepart stuck fast, and remained unmoveable, but the hinder part was broken with the violence of the waves. 42And the soldiers' counsel was to kill the prisoners, lest any of them should swim out, and escape. 43 But the centurion, willing to save Paul, kept them from *their* purpose; and commanded that they which could swim should cast *themselves* first *into the sea*, and get to land: 44And the rest, some on boards, and some on *broken pieces* of the ship. And so it came to pass, that they escaped all safe to land.

New International Version

some anchors from the bow. 31 Then Paul said to the centurion and the soldiers, "Unless these men stay with the ship, you cannot be saved." 32 So the soldiers cut the ropes that held the lifeboat and let it fall away.

33 Just before dawn Paul urged them all to eat. "For the last fourteen days," he said, "you have been in constant suspense and have gone without food—you haven't eaten anything. 34 Now I urge you to take some food. You need it to survive. Not one of you will lose a single hair from his head." 35After he said this, he took some bread and gave thanks to God in front of them all. Then he broke it and began to eat. 36 They were all encouraged and ate some food themselves. 37Altogether there were 276 of us on board. 38 When they had eaten as much as they wanted, they lightened the ship by throwing the grain into the sea.

39 When daylight came, they did not recognize the land, but they saw a bay with a sandy beach, where they decided to run the ship aground if they could. 40 Cutting loose the anchors, they left them in the sea and at the same time untied the ropes that held the rudders. Then they hoisted the foresail to the wind and made for the beach. 41 But the ship struck a sandbar and ran aground. The bow stuck fast and would not move, and the stern was broken to pieces by the pounding of the surf. 42 The soldiers planned to kill the prisoners to prevent any of them from swimming away and escaping. 43 But the centurion wanted to spare Paul's life and kept them from carrying out their plan. He ordered those who could swim to jump overboard first and get to land. 44 The rest were to get there on planks or on pieces of the ship. In this way everyone reached land in safety.

Ashore on Malta

28 And when they were escaped, then they knew that the island was called Melita. 2And the barbarous people shewed us no little kindness: for they kindled a fire, and received us every one, because of the present rain, and because of the cold. 3And when Paul had gathered a bundle of sticks, and laid *them* on the fire, there came a viper out of the heat, and fastened on his hand. 4And when the barbarians saw the *venomous* beast hang on his hand, they said among themselves, No doubt this man is a murderer, whom, though he hath escaped the sea, yet vengeance suffereth not to live. 5And he shook off the beast into the fire, and felt no harm. 6Howbeit they looked when he should have swollen, or fallen down dead suddenly:

28 Once safely on shore, we found out that the island was called Malta. 2 The islanders showed us unusual kindness. They built a fire and welcomed us all because it was raining and cold. 3 Paul gathered a pile of brushwood and, as he put it on the fire, a viper, driven out by the heat, fastened itself on his hand. 4 When the islanders saw the snake hanging from his hand, they said to each other, "This man must be a murderer; for though he escaped from the sea, Justice has not allowed him to live." 5 But Paul shook the snake off into the fire and suffered no ill effects. 6 The people expected him to swell up or suddenly fall over dead, but after

Greek Interlinear

μελλόντων ἐκτείνειν, **31** εἶπεν ὁ Παῦλος
¹intending ²to cast out, said - Paul

τῷ ἑκατοντάρχῃ καὶ τοῖς στρατιώταις·
to the centurion and to the soldiers:

ἐὰν μὴ οὗτοι μείνωσιν ἐν τῷ πλοίῳ,
Unless these remain in the ship,

ὑμεῖς σωθῆναι οὐ δύνασθε. **32** τότε
ye ²to be saved ¹cannot. Then

ἀπέκοψαν οἱ στρατιῶται τὰ σχοινία τῆς
cut away the soldiers the ropes of the

σκάφης καὶ εἴασαν αὐτὴν ἐκπεσεῖν.
boat and let it to fall off.

33 Ἄχρι δὲ οὗ ἡμέρα ἤμελλεν γίνεσθαι,
And until day was about to come,

παρεκάλει ὁ Παῦλος ἅπαντας μεταλαβεῖν
besought - Paul all to partake

τροφῆς λέγων· τεσσαρεσκαιδεκάτην σήμερον
of food saying: ¹[the] fourteenth ¹To-day [is]

ἡμέραν προσδοκῶντες ἄσιτοι διατελεῖτε,
²day ³waiting ⁴without food ⁵ye continued,

μηθὲν προσλαβόμενοι. **34** διὸ παρακαλῶ
nothing taking. Wherefore I beseech

ὑμᾶς μεταλαβεῖν τροφῆς· τοῦτο γὰρ πρὸς
you to partake of food; for this to

τῆς ὑμετέρας σωτηρίας ὑπάρχει· οὐδενὸς
- your salvation is; ²of no one

γὰρ ὑμῶν θρὶξ ἀπὸ τῆς κεφαλῆς ἀπολεῖται.
¹for of you a hair from the head shall perish.

35 εἴπας δὲ ταῦτα καὶ λαβὼν ἄρτον
And saying these things and taking bread

εὐχαρίστησεν τῷ θεῷ ἐνώπιον πάντων
he gave thanks - to God before all

καὶ κλάσας ἤρξατο ἐσθίειν. **36** εὔθυμοι δὲ
and breaking began to eat. And ⁴in good spirits

γενόμενοι πάντες καὶ αὐτοὶ προσελάβοντο
²becoming ¹all ³also they took

τροφῆς. **37** ἤμεθα δὲ αἱ πᾶσαι ψυχαὶ
food. Now we were ³the ¹all souls

ἐν τῷ πλοίῳ διακόσιαι ἑβδομήκοντα ἕξ.
in the ship two hundreds [and] seventy six.

38 κορεσθέντες δὲ τροφῆς ἐκούφιζον τὸ
And having been satisfied of(with) food they lightened the

πλοῖον ἐκβαλλόμενοι τὸν σῖτον εἰς τὴν
ship ¹throwing out the wheat into the

θάλασσαν. **39** Ὅτε δὲ ἡμέρα ἐγένετο,
sea. And when day came,

τὴν γῆν οὐκ ἐπεγίνωσκον, κόλπον δὲ
²the ³land ¹they did not recognize, but ²bay

τινα κατενόουν ἔχοντα αἰγιαλόν, εἰς ὃν
²a certain ¹they noticed having a shore, into which

ἐβουλεύοντο εἰ δύναιντο ἐξῶσαι τὸ πλοῖον.
they were minded if they were able to drive the ship.

40 καὶ τὰς ἀγκύρας περιελόντες εἴων
And ²the ³anchors ¹having cast off they left [them]

εἰς τὴν θάλασσαν, ἅμα ἀνέντες τὰς
in the sea, at the same time loosening the

ζευκτηρίας τῶν πηδαλίων, καὶ ἐπάραντες
fastenings of the rudders, and raising

τὸν ἀρτέμωνα τῇ πνεούσῃ κατεῖχον εἰς
the foresail to the breeze they held [the ship] to

τὸν αἰγιαλόν. **41** περιπεσόντες δὲ εἰς
the shore. And coming upon to

τόπον διθάλασσον ἐπέκειλαν τὴν ναῦν,
a place between two seas they drove the vessel,

καὶ ἡ μὲν πρῷρα ἐρείσασα ἔμεινεν
and ²the ¹while prow having run aground remained

ἀσάλευτος, ἡ δὲ πρύμνα ἐλύετο ὑπὸ
immovable, ²the ¹yet stern was broken by

τῆς βίας.* **42** Τῶν δὲ στρατιωτῶν βουλὴ
the force.* Now ²of the ¹soldiers ¹[the] mind

ἐγένετο ἵνα τοὺς δεσμώτας ἀποκτείνωσιν,
was that ²the ³prisoners ¹they should kill,

μή τις ἐκκολυμβήσας διαφύγῃ· **43** ὁ δὲ
lest anyone swimming out should escape; but the

ἑκατοντάρχης βουλόμενος διασῶσαι τὸν
centurion being minded to save

Παῦλον ἐκώλυσεν αὐτοὺς τοῦ βουλήματος,
Paul forbade them the(ir) intention,

ἐκέλευσέν τε τοὺς δυναμένους κολυμβᾶν
and commanded the [ones] being able to swim

ἀπορίψαντας πρώτους ἐπὶ τὴν γῆν
casting [themselves] first onto the land
overboard

ἐξιέναι, **44** καὶ τοὺς λοιποὺς οὓς μὲν ἐπὶ
to go out, and the rest some on

σανίσιν, οὓς δὲ ἐπί τινων τῶν ἀπὸ τοῦ
planks, others on some of the things from the

πλοίου. καὶ οὕτως ἐγένετο πάντας
ship. And thus it came to pass all

διασωθῆναι ἐπὶ τὴν γῆν.
to be saved on the land.

Chapter 28

Καὶ διασωθέντες τότε ἐπέγνωμεν ὅτι
And having been saved then we found out that

Μελίτη ἡ νῆσος καλεῖται. **2** οἵ τε
Melita the island is(was) called. And the

βάρβαροι παρεῖχον οὐ τὴν τυχοῦσαν
foreigners ¹showed ²not ⁴the ³ordinary

φιλανθρωπίαν ἡμῖν· ἅψαντες γὰρ πυρὰν
⁵kindness ⁶us; for having lit a fire

προσελάβοντο πάντας ἡμᾶς διὰ τὸν ὑετὸν
they welcomed ²all ¹us because of the rain

τὸν ἐφεστῶτα καὶ διὰ τὸ ψῦχος. **3** συστρέ-
- coming on and because of the cold. col-

ψαντος δὲ τοῦ Παύλου φρυγάνων τι
lecting And - Paul ²of sticks ¹a
= when Paul collected

πλῆθος καὶ ἐπιθέντος ἐπὶ τὴν πυράν,
³quantity and putting on⁴ on the fire,
= put them

ἔχιδνα ἀπὸ τῆς θέρμης ἐξελθοῦσα καθῆψεν
a snake from the heat coming out fastened on

τῆς χειρὸς αὐτοῦ. **4** ὡς δὲ εἶδον οἱ
the hand of him. And when ²saw ¹the

βάρβαροι κρεμάμενον τὸ θηρίον ἐκ τῆς
²foreigners ⁴hanging ⁴the ⁵beast from the

χειρὸς αὐτοῦ, πρὸς ἀλλήλους ἔλεγον·
hand of him, to one another they said:

πάντως φονεύς ἐστιν ὁ ἄνθρωπος οὗτος,
To be sure ²a murderer ³is ¹this man,

ὃν διασωθέντα ἐκ τῆς θαλάσσης ἡ δίκη
whom having been out of the sea - justice
saved

ζῆν οὐκ εἴασεν. **5** ὁ μὲν οὖν ἀποτινάξας
²to live ¹did not allow. He - then shaking off

τὸ θηρίον εἰς τὸ πῦρ ἔπαθεν οὐδὲν
the beast into the fire suffered no

κακόν· **6** οἱ δὲ προσεδόκων αὐτὸν μέλλειν
harm; but they expected him to be about

πίμπρασθαι ἢ καταπίπτειν ἄφνω νεκρόν.
to swell or to fall down suddenly dead.

---

* That is, of the waves, as indeed some MSS have.

King James Version

but after they had looked a great while, and saw no harm come to him, they changed their minds, and said that he was a god. 7 In the same quarters were possessions of the chief man of the island, whose name was Publius; who received us, and lodged us three days courteously. 8And it came to pass, that the father of Publius lay sick of a fever and of a bloody flux: to whom Paul entered in, and prayed, and laid his hands on him, and healed him. 9 So when this was done, others also, which had diseases in the island, came, and were healed: 10 Who also honoured us with many honours; and when we departed, they laded *us* with such things as were necessary. 11And after three months we departed in a ship of Alexandria, which had wintered in the isle, whose sign was Castor and Pollux. 12And landing at Syracuse, we tarried *there* three days. 13And from thence we fetched a compass, and came to Rhegium: and after one day the south wind blew, and we came the next day to Puteoli: 14 Where we found brethren, and were desired to tarry with them seven days: and so we went toward Rome. 15And from thence, when the brethren heard of us, they came to meet us as far as Appii Forum, and the Three Taverns; whom when Paul saw, he thanked God, and took courage. 16And when we came to Rome, the centurion delivered the prisoners to the captain of the guard: but Paul was suffered to dwell by himself with a soldier that kept him. 17And it came to pass, that after three days Paul called the chief of the Jews together: and when they were come together, he said unto them, Men *and* brethren, though I have committed nothing against the people, or customs of our fathers, yet was I delivered prisoner from Jerusalem into the hands of the Romans: 18 Who, when they had examined me, would have let *me* go, because there was no cause of death in me. 19 But when the Jews spake against *it,* I was constrained to appeal unto Cesar; not that I had aught to accuse my nation of. 20 For this cause therefore have I called for you, to see *you,* and to speak with *you:* because that for the hope of Israel I am bound with this chain. 21And they said unto him, We neither received letters out of Judea concerning thee, neither any of the brethren that came shewed or spake any harm of thee. 22 But we desire to hear of thee what thou thinkest: for as concerning this sect, we know that every where it is spoken against. 23And when they had appointed him a day, there came many to him into *his* lodging; to whom he expounded and testified the kingdom of God, persuading them concerning Jesus, both out of the law of Moses, and *out of* the prophets, from morning till evening. 24And some believed the things which

New International Version

waiting a long time and seeing nothing unusual happen to him, they changed their minds and said he was a god.

7 There was an estate nearby that belonged to Publius, the chief official of the island. He welcomed us to his home and for three days entertained us hospitably. 8 His father was sick in bed, suffering from fever and dysentery. Paul went in to see him and, after prayer, placed his hands on him and healed him. 9 When this had happened, the rest of the sick on the island came and were cured. 10 They honored us in many ways and when we were ready to sail, they furnished us with the supplies we needed.

Arrival at Rome

11 After three months we put out to sea in a ship that had wintered in the island. It was an Alexandrian ship with the figurehead of the twin gods Castor and Pollux. 12 We put in at Syracuse and stayed there three days. 13 From there we set sail and arrived at Rhegium. The next day the south wind came up, and on the following day we reached Puteoli. 14 There we found some brothers who invited us to spend a week with them. And so we went to Rome. 15 The brothers there had heard that we were coming, and they traveled as far as the Forum of Appius and the Three Taverns to meet us. At the sight of these men Paul thanked God and was encouraged. 16 When we got to Rome, Paul was allowed to live by himself, with a soldier to guard him.

Paul preaches at Rome under guard

17 Three days later he called together the leaders of the Jews. When they had assembled, Paul said to them: "My brothers, although I have done nothing against our people or against the customs of our ancestors, I was arrested in Jerusalem and handed over to the Romans. 18 They examined me and wanted to release me, because I was not guilty of any crime deserving death. 19 But when the Jews objected, I was compelled to appeal to Caesar—not that I had any charge to bring against my own people. 20 For this reason I have asked to see you and talk with you. It is because of the hope of Israel that I am bound with this chain."

21 They replied, "We have not received any letters from Judea concerning you, and none of the brothers who had come from there has reported or said anything bad about you. 22 But we want to hear what your views are, for we know that people everywhere are talking against this sect."

23 They arranged to meet Paul on a certain day, and came in even larger numbers to the place where he was staying. From morning till evening he explained and declared to them the kingdom of God and tried to convince them about Jesus from the Law of Moses and from the Prophets. 24 Some were convinced by what

Greek Interlinear

ἐπὶ πολὺ δὲ αὐτῶν προσδοκώντων καὶ
But over much [time] they expecting and
= while they expected and beheld

θεωρούντων μηδὲν ἄτοπον εἰς αὐτὸν
beholding⁸ nothing amiss ²to ⁸him

γινόμενον, μεταβαλόμενοι ἔλεγον αὐτὸν εἶναι
¹happening, changing their minds they said him to be

θεόν. 7 Ἐν δὲ τοῖς περὶ τὸν τόπον
a god. Now in the [parts] about – place

ἐκεῖνον ὑπῆρχεν χωρία τῷ πρώτῳ τῆς
that were lands to the chief manᶜ of the
= the chief man . . . had lands

νήσου ὀνόματι Ποπλίῳ, ὃς ἀναδεξάμενος
island by name Publius, who welcoming

ἡμᾶς ἡμέρας τρεῖς φιλοφρόνως ἐξένισεν.
us ⁴days ³three ²friendlily ¹lodged [us].

8 ἐγένετο δὲ τὸν πατέρα τοῦ Ποπλίου
Now it happened the father – of Publius

πυρετοῖς καὶ δυσεντερίῳ συνεχόμενον
²feverish attacks ⁴and ³dysentery ¹suffering from

κατακεῖσθαι, πρὸς ὃν ὁ Παῦλος εἰσελθὼν
¹to be lying down, to whom – Paul entering

καὶ προσευξάμενος, ἐπιθεὶς τὰς χεῖρας
and praying, ¹putting ⁴on ²the(his) ³hands

αὐτῷ ἰάσατο αὐτόν. 9 τούτου δὲ γενομένου
⁵him cured him. And this happening⁸
= when this happened

καὶ οἱ λοιποὶ οἱ ἐν τῇ νήσῳ ἔχοντες
²also ¹the ²rest – in the island having

ἀσθενείας προσήρχοντο · καὶ ἐθεραπεύοντο,
ailments came up and were healed,

10 οἳ καὶ πολλαῖς τιμαῖς ἐτίμησαν ἡμᾶς
who also with many honours honoured us

καὶ ἀναγομένοις ἐπέθεντο τὰ πρὸς τὰς
and on our putting to sea placed on [us] the things for the(our)

χρείας.
needs.

11 Μετὰ δὲ τρεῖς μῆνας ἀνήχθημεν ἐν
And after three months we embarked in

πλοίῳ παρακεχειμακότι ἐν τῇ νήσῳ,
a ship having passed the winter in the island,

Ἀλεξανδρίνῳ, παρασήμῳ Διοσκούροις. 12 καὶ
an Alexandrian, with a sign Dioscuri. And

καταχθέντες εἰς Συρακούσας ἐπεμείναμεν
being brought to land to(at) Syracuse we remained

ἡμέρας τρεῖς, 13 ὅθεν περιελθόντες κατην-
days three, whence tacking we ar-

τήσαμεν εἰς Ῥήγιον. καὶ μετὰ μίαν
rived at Rhegium. And after one

ἡμέραν ἐπιγενομένου νότου δευτεραῖοι
day coming on a south wind⁸ on the
= as a south wind came on second day

ἤλθομεν εἰς Ποτιόλους, 14 οὗ εὑρόντες
we came to Puteoli, where having found

ἀδελφοὺς παρεκλήθημεν παρ' αὐτοῖς ἐπιμεῖναι
brothers we were besought with them to remain

ἡμέρας ἑπτά· καὶ οὕτως εἰς τὴν Ῥώμην
days seven; and thus to – Rome

ἤλθαμεν. 15 κἀκεῖθεν οἱ ἀδελφοὶ ἀκούσαντες
we went. And thence the brothers having heard

τὰ περὶ ἡμῶν ἦλθαν εἰς ἀπάντησιν ἡμῖν
the con- us came to a meeting with us
things cerning

ἄχρι Ἀππίου φόρου καὶ Τριῶν ταβερνῶν,
as far as Appii Forum and Three Taverns,

οὓς ἰδὼν ὁ Παῦλος εὐχαριστήσας τῷ
whom seeing – Paul thanking –

θεῷ ἔλαβε θάρσος. 16 Ὅτε δὲ εἰσήλθομεν
God he took courage. And when we entered

εἰς Ῥώμην, ἐπετράπη τῷ Παύλῳ μένειν
into Rome, he⁸ permitted – Paul to remain

καθ' ἑαυτὸν σὺν τῷ φυλάσσοντι αὐτὸν
by himself with ¹the ²guarding ⁴him

στρατιώτῃ.
¹soldier.

17 Ἐγένετο δὲ μετὰ ἡμέρας τρεῖς
And it came to pass after days three

συγκαλέσασθαι αὐτὸν τοὺς ὄντας τῶν
to call together himᵇ the [ones] being of the
= he called together

Ἰουδαίων πρώτους· συνελθόντων δὲ αὐτῶν
Jews first(chief); and coming together them⁸
= and when they came together

ἔλεγεν πρὸς αὐτούς· ἐγώ, ἄνδρες ἀδελφοί,
he said to them: I, men brothers,

οὐδὲν ἐναντίον ποιήσας τῷ λαῷ ἢ τοῖς
¹nothing ²contrary ¹having done to the people or to the

ἔθεσι τοῖς πατρῴοις, δέσμιος ἐξ Ἱεροσο-
customs – ancestral, a prisoner from Jeru-

λύμων παρεδόθην εἰς τὰς χεῖρας τῶν
salem I was delivered into the hands of the

Ῥωμαίων, 18 οἵτινες ἀνακρίναντές με ἐβούλοντο
Romans, who having examined me were minded

ἀπολῦσαι διὰ τὸ μηδεμίαν αἰτίαν θανάτου
to release on account – no cause of death
of

ὑπάρχειν ἐν ἐμοί· 19 ἀντιλεγόντων δὲ
to be in me; but speaking against [this]
= when the Jews spoke

τῶν Ἰουδαίων ἠναγκάσθην ἐπικαλέσασθαι
the Jews⁸ I was compelled to appeal to
against this

Καίσαρα, οὐχ ὡς τοῦ ἔθνους μου ἔχων
Cæsar, not as ⁴the ⁵nation ⁶of me ¹having

τι κατηγορεῖν. 20 διὰ ταύτην οὖν τὴν
²anything ³to accuse. ²On account of ⁴this ¹therefore –

αἰτίαν παρεκάλεσα ὑμᾶς ἰδεῖν καὶ προσ-
³cause I called you to see and to

λαλῆσαι· εἵνεκεν γὰρ τῆς ἐλπίδος τοῦ
speak to; for for the sake of the hope –

Ἰσραὴλ τὴν ἅλυσιν ταύτην περίκειμαι.
of Israel ⁴the ²chain ¹I have round [me].

21 οἱ δὲ πρὸς αὐτὸν εἶπαν· ἡμεῖς οὔτε
And they to him said: We neither

γράμματα περὶ σοῦ ἐδεξάμεθα ἀπὸ τῆς
²letters ³about ⁴thee ¹received from –

Ἰουδαίας, οὔτε παραγενόμενός τις τῶν
Judæa, nor arriving anyone of the

ἀδελφῶν ἀπήγγειλεν ἢ ἐλάλησέν τι περὶ
brothers told or spoke anything ¹about

σοῦ πονηρόν. 22 ἀξιοῦμεν δὲ παρὰ σοῦ
²thee ¹evil. But we think fit from thee

ἀκοῦσαι ἃ φρονεῖς· περὶ μὲν γὰρ τῆς
to hear what thou ²concerning ³indeed ¹for –
things thinkest;

αἱρέσεως ταύτης γνωστὸν ἡμῖν ἐστιν ὅτι
²sect ¹this ²known ¹to us ¹it is that

πανταχοῦ ἀντιλέγεται. 23 Ταξάμενοι δὲ
everywhere it is spoken against. And arranging

αὐτῷ ἡμέραν ἦλθον πρὸς αὐτὸν εἰς τὴν
with him a day ²came ³to ⁴him ⁵in ⁶the(his)

ξενίαν πλείονες, οἷς ἐξετίθετο διαμαρτυρ-
⁷lodging ¹more, to whom he set forth solemnly

ὅμενος τὴν βασιλείαν τοῦ θεοῦ, πείθων
witnessing the kingdom – of God, ¹persuading

τε αὐτοὺς περὶ τοῦ Ἰησοῦ ἀπό τε τοῦ
²and them concerning – Jesus from both the

νόμου Μωϋσέως καὶ τῶν προφητῶν, ἀπὸ
law of Moses and the prophets, from

πρωῒ ἕως ἑσπέρας. 24 καὶ οἱ μὲν
morning until evening. And some

---

* That is, the officer to whom Paul was handed over by the centurion Julius.

441

King James Version

New International Version

were spoken, and some believed not. 25And when they agreed not among themselves, they departed, after that Paul had spoken one word, Well spake the Holy Ghost by Esaias the prophet unto our fathers, 26 Saying, Go unto this people, and say, Hearing ye shall hear, and shall not understand; and seeing ye shall see, and not perceive: 27 For the heart of this people is waxed gross, and their ears are dull of hearing, and their eyes have they closed; lest they should see with *their* eyes, and hear with *their* ears, and understand with *their* heart, and should be converted, and I should heal them. 28 Be it known therefore unto you, that the salvation of God is sent unto the Gentiles, and *that* they will hear it. 29And when he had said these words, the Jews departed, and had great reasoning among themselves. 30And Paul dwelt two whole years in his own hired house, and received all that came in unto him, 31 Preaching the kingdom of God, and teaching those things which concern the Lord Jesus Christ, with all confidence, no man forbidding him.

he said, but others would not believe. 25 They disagreed among themselves and began to leave, after Paul had made this final statement: "The Holy Spirit spoke the truth to your ancestors when he said through Isaiah the prophet:
26 'Go to this people and say,
    You will be ever hearing but never under-
        standing;
    you will be ever seeing but never per-
        ceiving.
27 For this people's heart has become cal-
        loused;
    they hardly hear with their ears,
    and they have closed their eyes.
Otherwise they might see with their eyes,
    hear with their ears,
    understand with their hearts
    and turn and I would heal them.' *o*
28 "Therefore I want you to know that God's salvation has been sent to the Gentiles, and they will listen!" *p*
30 For two whole years Paul stayed there in his own rented house and welcomed all who came to see him. 31 Boldly and without hindrance he preached the kingdom of God and taught about the Lord Jesus Christ.

[o] Isaiah 6:9, 10. [p] Some MSS add verse 29: *After he said this, the Jews left, arguing vigorously among themselves.*

Greek Interlinear

ἐπείθοντο   τοῖς   λεγομένοις,   25 οἱ   δὲ
were persuaded by the things being said,   others

ἠπίστουν·   ἀσύμφωνοι   δὲ   ὄντες   πρὸς   ἀλλή-
disbelieved;   and ²disagreed   ¹being   with   one an-

λους ·   ἀπελύοντο,   εἰπόντος   τοῦ   Παύλου
other   they were dismissed, having said -   Paul²
                                           =after Paul had said

ῥῆμα   ἕν,   ὅτι   καλῶς   τὸ   πνεῦμα   τὸ   ἅγιον
word   one,   -   Well   the   Spirit   -   Holy

ἐλάλησεν   διὰ   Ἡσαΐου   τοῦ   προφήτου   πρὸς
spoke   through Esaias   the   prophet   to

τοὺς   πατέρας   ὑμῶν   26 λέγων·   πορεύθητι
the   fathers   of you   saying: Go thou

πρὸς   τὸν   λαὸν   τοῦτον   καὶ   εἰπόν·   ἀκοῇ
to   the   people this   and   say: In hearing

ἀκούσετε   καὶ   οὐ   μὴ   συνῆτε,   καὶ   βλέποντες
ye will hear and   by no means understand, and   looking

βλέψετε   καὶ   οὐ   μὴ   ἴδητε·   27 ἐπαχύνθη
ye will look and   by no means see;   ²was thickened

γὰρ   ἡ   καρδία   τοῦ   λαοῦ   τούτου,   καὶ
¹for   the   heart   of the   people of this people,   and

τοῖς   ὠσὶν   βαρέως   ἤκουσαν,   καὶ   τοὺς
with the(ir) ears heavily   they heard,   and   the

ὀφθαλμοὺς   αὐτῶν   ἐκάμμυσαν·   μήποτε   ἴδωσιν
eyes   of them   they closed;   lest at any time they see

τοῖς   ὀφθαλμοῖς   καὶ   τοῖς   ὠσὶν   ἀκούσωσιν
with the   eyes   and   with the   ears   hear

καὶ   τῇ   καρδίᾳ   συνῶσιν   καὶ   ἐπιστρέψωσιν,
and   with the heart   understand   and   turn,

καὶ   ἰάσομαι   αὐτούς.   28 γνωστὸν   οὖν
and   I shall cure them.   Known   therefore

ἔστω   ὑμῖν   ὅτι   τοῖς   ἔθνεσιν   ἀπεστάλη
let it be to you   that   to the   nations   was sent

τοῦτο   τὸ   σωτήριον   τοῦ   θεοῦ·   αὐτοὶ   καὶ
this   -   salvation   -   of God;   and they

ἀκούσονται.‡
will hear.

30 Ἐνέμεινεν   δὲ   διετίαν   ὅλην   ἐν   ἰδίῳ
And he remained   a whole two years   in [his] own

μισθώματι,   καὶ   ἀπεδέχετο   πάντας   τοὺς
hired apartment,   and   welcomed   all   the

εἰσπορευομένους   πρὸς   αὐτόν,   31 κηρύσσων
[ones] coming in   to   him,   proclaiming

τὴν   βασιλείαν   τοῦ   θεοῦ   καὶ   διδάσκων
the   kingdom   -   of God   and   teaching

τὰ   περὶ   τοῦ   κυρίου   Ἰησοῦ   Χριστοῦ
the things concerning the   Lord   Jesus   Christ

μετὰ   πάσης   παρρησίας   ἀκωλύτως.
with   all   boldness   unhinderedly.

‡ Verse 29 omitted by Nestle

King James Version

New International Version

THE EPISTLE OF
PAUL THE APOSTLE
TO THE

ROMANS

ROMANS

1 Paul, a servant of Jesus Christ, called *to be* an apostle, separated unto the gospel of God, 2 (Which he had promised afore by his prophets in the holy Scriptures,) 3 Concerning his Son Jesus Christ our Lord, which was made of the seed of David according to the flesh; 4 And declared *to be* the Son of God with power, according to the Spirit of holiness, by the resurrection from the dead: 5 By whom we have received grace and apostleship, for obedience to the faith among all nations, for his name: 6 Among whom are ye also the called of Jesus Christ: 7 To all that be in Rome, beloved of God, called *to be* saints: Grace to you, and peace, from God our Father and the Lord Jesus Christ. 8 First, I thank my God through Jesus Christ for you all, that your faith is spoken of throughout the whole world. 9 For God is my witness, whom I serve with my spirit in the gospel of his Son, that without ceasing I make mention of you always in my prayers; 10 Making request, if by any means now at length I might have a prosperous journey by the will of God to come unto you. 11 For I long to see you, that I may impart unto you some spiritual gift, to the end ye may be established; 12 That is, that I may be comforted together with you by the mutual faith both of you and me. 13 Now I would not have you ignorant, brethren, that oftentimes I purposed to come unto you, (but was let hitherto,) that I might have some fruit among you also, even as among other Gentiles. 14 I am debtor both to the Greeks, and to the Barbarians; both to the wise, and to the unwise. 15 So, as much as in me is, I am ready to preach the gospel to you that are at Rome also. 16 For I am not ashamed of the gospel of Christ: for it is the power of God unto salvation to every one that believeth; to the Jew first, and also to the Greek. 17 For therein is the righteousness of God revealed from faith to faith: as it is written, The just shall live by faith. 18 For the wrath of God is revealed from heaven against all ungodliness and unrighteousness of men, who hold the truth in unrighteousness; 19 Because that which may be known of God is manifest in them; for God hath shewed *it* unto them. 20 For the invisible things of him from the creation of the world are clearly seen, being understood by the things

1 Paul, a servant of Christ Jesus, called to be an apostle and set apart for the gospel of God —2 the gospel he promised beforehand through his prophets in the Holy Scriptures. 3 regarding his Son, who as to his human nature was a descendant of David, 4 and who through the Spirit of holiness[a] was declared with power to be the Son of God by his resurrection from the dead: Jesus Christ our Lord. 5 Through him and for his name's sake, we received grace and apostleship to call people from among all the Gentiles to the obedience that comes from faith. 6 And you also are among those who are called to belong to Jesus Christ.

7 To all in Rome who are loved by God and called to be saints:

Grace and peace to you from God our Father and from the Lord Jesus Christ.

Paul's longing to visit Rome

8 First, I thank my God through Jesus Christ for all of you, because your faith is being reported all over the world. 9 God, whom I serve with my whole heart in preaching the gospel of his Son, is my witness how constantly I remember you 10 in my prayers at all times; and I pray that now at last by God's will the way may be opened for me to come to you.

11 I long to see you so that I may impart to you some spiritual gift to make you strong— 12 that is, that you and I may be mutually encouraged by each other's faith. 13 I do not want you to be unaware, brothers, that I planned many times to come to you (but have been prevented from doing so until now) in order that I might have a harvest among you, just as I have had among the other Gentiles.

14 I am obligated both to Greeks and non-Greeks, both to the wise and the foolish. 15 That is why I am so eager to preach the gospel also to you who are at Rome.

16 I am not ashamed of the gospel, because it is the power of God for the salvation of everyone who believes: first for the Jew, then for the Gentile. 17 For in the gospel a righteousness from God is revealed, a righteousness that is by faith from first to last, just as it is written: "The righteous will live by faith." [b]

God's wrath against mankind

18 The wrath of God is being revealed from heaven against all the godlessness and wickedness of men who suppress the truth by their wickedness, 19 since what may be known about God is plain to them, because God has made it plain to them. 20 For since the creation of the world God's invisible qualities—his eternal power and divine nature—have been clearly seen, being

444

[a] Or *and who as to his spirit of holiness.* [b] Hab. 2:4.

(handwritten annotations: "Check at", "εν τω πνευματι μου", "II Cor 13:4", "N.nom/acc/s οντος", "Λ.3¹", "passive")

ΠΡΟΣ ΡΩΜΑΙΟΙΣ

Chapter 1

Παῦλος δοῦλος Χριστοῦ Ἰησοῦ, κλητὸς
Paul a slave of Christ Jesus, called

ἀπόστολος ἀφωρισμένος εἰς εὐαγγέλιον
an apostle having been separated to [the] gospel

θεοῦ, 2 ὃ προεπηγγείλατο διὰ τῶν
of God, which he promised beforehand through the

προφητῶν αὐτοῦ ἐν γραφαῖς ἁγίαις 3 περὶ
prophets of him in writings holy concerning

τοῦ υἱοῦ αὐτοῦ τοῦ γενομένου ἐκ
the Son of him come of

σπέρματος Δαυὶδ κατὰ σάρκα, 4 τοῦ
[the] seed of David according to [the] flesh,

ὁρισθέντος υἱοῦ θεοῦ ἐν δυνάμει
designated Son of God in power

κατὰ πνεῦμα ἁγιωσύνης ἐξ ἀναστάσεως
according to [the] Spirit of holiness by a resurrection

νεκρῶν, Ἰησοῦ Χριστοῦ τοῦ κυρίου ἡμῶν,
of dead persons, Jesus Christ the Lord of us,

5 δι᾿ οὗ ἐλάβομεν χάριν καὶ ἀποστολὴν
through whom we received grace and apostleship

εἰς ὑπακοὴν πίστεως ἐν πᾶσιν τοῖς
for obedience of faith among all the

ἔθνεσιν ὑπὲρ τοῦ ὀνόματος αὐτοῦ, 6 ἐν
nations on behalf of the name of him, among

οἷς ἐστε καὶ ὑμεῖς κλητοὶ Ἰησοῦ Χριστοῦ,
whom are also ye called of Jesus Christ,

7 πᾶσιν τοῖς οὖσιν ἐν Ῥώμῃ ἀγαπητοῖς
to all the [ones] being in Rome beloved

θεοῦ, κλητοῖς ἁγίοις· χάρις ὑμῖν καὶ
of God, called holy: Grace to you and

εἰρήνη ἀπὸ θεοῦ πατρὸς ἡμῶν καὶ κυρίου
peace from God [the] Father of us and Lord

Ἰησοῦ Χριστοῦ.
Jesus Christ.

8 Πρῶτον μὲν εὐχαριστῶ τῷ θεῷ μου
Firstly - I thank the God of me

διὰ Ἰησοῦ Χριστοῦ περὶ πάντων ὑμῶν,
through Jesus Christ concerning all you.

ὅτι ἡ πίστις ὑμῶν καταγγέλλεται ἐν
because the faith of you is being announced in

ὅλῳ τῷ κόσμῳ. 9 μάρτυς γάρ μού
all the world. For witness of me

ἐστιν ὁ θεός, ᾧ λατρεύω ἐν τῷ πνεύματί
is - God, whom I serve in the spirit

μου ἐν τῷ εὐαγγελίῳ τοῦ υἱοῦ αὐτοῦ,
of me in the gospel of the Son of him,

ὡς ἀδιαλείπτως μνείαν ὑμῶν ποιοῦμαι
how unceasingly mention of you I make

10 πάντοτε ἐπὶ τῶν προσευχῶν μου,
always on(in) the prayers of me,

δεόμενος εἴ πως ἤδη ποτὲ εὐοδω-
requesting if somehow now at some time I shall have

θήσομαι ἐν τῷ θελήματι τοῦ θεοῦ ἐλθεῖν
a happy journey in the will - of God to come

πρὸς ὑμᾶς. 11 ἐπιποθῶ γὰρ ἰδεῖν ὑμᾶς,
unto you. For I long to see you,

ἵνα τι μεταδῶ χάρισμα ὑμῖν πνευματικὸν
that some I may impart gift to you spiritual

εἰς τὸ στηριχθῆναι ὑμᾶς, 12 τοῦτο δέ
for the to be established you, and this
=that ye may be established,

ἐστιν συμπαρακληθῆναι ἐν ὑμῖν διὰ τῆς
is to be encouraged with among you through the

ἐν ἀλλήλοις πίστεως ὑμῶν τε καὶ ἐμοῦ.
in one another faith of you both and of me.

13 οὐ θέλω δὲ ὑμᾶς ἀγνοεῖν, ἀδελφοί,
not I wish But you to be ignorant, brothers,

ὅτι πολλάκις προεθέμην ἐλθεῖν πρὸς ὑμᾶς,
that often I purposed to come unto you,

καὶ ἐκωλύθην ἄχρι τοῦ δεῦρο, ἵνα τινὰ
and was hindered until the present, that some

καρπὸν σχῶ καὶ ἐν ὑμῖν καθὼς καὶ
fruit I may have also among you as indeed

ἐν τοῖς λοιποῖς ἔθνεσιν. 14 Ἕλλησίν
among the remaining nations, to Greeks

τε καὶ βαρβάροις, σοφοῖς τε καὶ ἀνοήτοις
Both and to foreigners, to wise men both and to foolish

ὀφειλέτης εἰμί· 15 οὕτως τὸ κατ᾿ ἐμὲ
a debtor I am; so as far as in me lies†

πρόθυμον καὶ ὑμῖν τοῖς ἐν Ῥώμῃ
[I am] eager also to you the [ones] in Rome

εὐαγγελίσασθαι. 16 οὐ γὰρ ἐπαισχύνομαι
to preach. For I am not ashamed of

τὸ εὐαγγέλιον· δύναμις γὰρ θεοῦ ἐστιν
the gospel; power for of God it is

εἰς σωτηρίαν παντὶ τῷ πιστεύοντι, Ἰουδαίῳ
to salvation to everyone believing, to Jew

τε πρῶτον καὶ Ἕλληνι. 17 δικαιοσύνη
both firstly and to Greek. a righteousness

γὰρ θεοῦ ἐν αὐτῷ ἀποκαλύπτεται ἐκ
For of God in it is revealed from

πίστεως εἰς πίστιν, καθὼς γέγραπται·
faith to faith, as it has been written:

ὁ δὲ δίκαιος ἐκ πίστεως ζήσεται.
Now the just man by faith will live.

18 Ἀποκαλύπτεται γὰρ ὀργὴ θεοῦ ἀπ᾿
For is revealed [the] wrath of God from

οὐρανοῦ ἐπὶ πᾶσαν ἀσέβειαν καὶ ἀδικίαν
heaven against all impiety and unrighteousness

ἀνθρώπων τῶν τὴν ἀλήθειαν ἐν ἀδικίᾳ
of men - the truth in unrighteousness

κατεχόντων, 19 διότι τὸ γνωστὸν τοῦ θεοῦ
holding fast, because the thing known - of God

φανερόν ἐστιν ἐν αὐτοῖς· ὁ θεὸς γὰρ αὐτοῖς
manifest is among them; - for God to them

ἐφανέρωσεν. 20 τὰ γὰρ ἀόρατα αὐτοῦ
manifested [it]. For the invisible things of him

ἀπὸ κτίσεως κόσμου τοῖς ποιήμασιν
from [the] creation of [the] world by the things made

νοούμενα καθορᾶται, ἥ τε
being understood is(are) clearly seen, the both

King James Version

that are made, *even* his eternal power and Godhead; so that they are without excuse: 21 Because that, when they knew God, they glorified *him* not as God, neither were thankful; but became vain in their imaginations, and their foolish heart was darkened. 22 Professing themselves to be wise, they became fools, 23 And changed the glory of the uncorruptible God into an image made like to corruptible man, and to birds, and fourfooted beasts, and creeping things. 24 Wherefore God also gave them up to uncleanness, through the lusts of their own hearts, to dishonour their own bodies between themselves: 25 Who changed the truth of God into a lie, and worshipped and served the creature more than the Creator, who is blessed for ever. Amen. 26 For this cause God gave them up unto vile affections: for even their women did change the natural use into that which is against nature: 27 And likewise also the men, leaving the natural use of the woman, burned in their lust one toward another; men with men working that which is unseemly, and receiving in themselves that recompense of their error which was meet. 28 And even as they did not like to retain God in *their* knowledge, God gave them over to a reprobate mind, to do those things which are not convenient; 29 Being filled with all unrighteousness, fornication, wickedness, covetousness, maliciousness; full of envy, murder, debate, deceit, malignity; whisperers, 30 Backbiters, haters of God, despiteful, proud, boasters, inventors of evil things, disobedient to parents, 31 Without understanding, covenant-breakers, without natural affection, implacable, unmerciful: 32 Who, knowing the judgment of God, that they which commit such things are worthy of death, not only do the same, but have pleasure in them that do them.

New International Version

understood from what has been made, so that men are without excuse.

21 For although they knew God, they neither glorified him as God nor gave thanks to him, but their thinking became futile and their foolish hearts were darkened. 22 Although they claimed to be wise, they became fools 23 and exchanged the glory of the immortal God for images made to look like mortal man and birds and animals and reptiles.

24 Therefore God gave them over in the sinful desires of their hearts to sexual impurity for the degrading of their bodies with one another. 25 They exchanged the truth of God for a lie, and worshiped and served created things rather than the Creator—who is forever praised. Amen.

26 Because of this, God gave them over to shameful lusts. Even their women exchanged natural relations for unnatural ones. 27 In the same way the men also abandoned natural relations with women and were inflamed with lust for one another. Men committed indecent acts with other men, and received in themselves the due penalty for their perversion.

28 Furthermore, since they did not think it worthwhile to retain the knowledge of God, he gave them over to a depraved mind, to do what ought not to be done. 29 They have become filled with every kind of wickedness, evil, greed and depravity. They are full of envy, murder, strife, deceit and malice. They are gossips, 30 slanderers, God-haters, insolent, arrogant and boastful; they invent ways of doing evil; they disobey their parents; 31 they are senseless, faithless, heartless, ruthless. 32 Although they know God's righteous decree that those who do such things deserve death, they not only continue to do these very things, but also approve of those who practice them.

God's righteous judgment

2 Therefore thou art inexcusable, O man, whosoever thou art that judgest: for wherein thou judgest another, thou condemnest thyself; for thou that judgest doest the same things. 2 But we are sure that the judgment of God is according to truth against them which commit such things. 3 And thinkest thou this, O man, that judgest them which do such things, and doest the same, that thou shalt escape the judgment of God? 4 Or despisest thou the riches of his goodness and forbearance and long suffering; not knowing that the goodness of God leadeth thee to repentance? 5 But, after thy hardness and impenitent heart, treasurest up unto thyself wrath against the day of wrath and revelation of the righteous judgment of God; 6 Who will render to every man according to his deeds: 7 To them who by patient continuance

2 You, therefore, have no excuse, you who pass judgment on someone else, for at whatever point you judge the other, you are condemning yourself, because you who pass judgment do the same things. 2 Now we know that God's judgment against those who do such things is based on truth. 3 So when you, a mere man, pass judgment on them and yet do the same things, do you think you will escape God's judgment? 4 Or do you show contempt for the riches of his kindness, tolerance and patience, not realizing that God's kindness should lead you to repentance?

5 But because of your stubbornness and your unrepentant heart, you are storing up wrath against yourself for the day of God's wrath, when his righteous judgment will be revealed. 6 God "will give to each person according to what he has done." *c* 7 To those who by persist-

[c] Psalm 62:12; Prov. 24:12.

Greek Interlinear

ἀΐδιος αὐτοῦ δύναμις καὶ θειότης, εἰς
[11]everlasting [15]of him [13]power [12]and [14]divinity, for

τὸ εἶναι αὐτοὺς ἀναπολογήτους, 21 διότι
the to be them[b] without excuse, because
=so that they are

γνόντες τὸν θεὸν οὐχ ὡς θεὸν ἐδόξασαν
knowing – God [3]not [2]as [3]God [1]they glorified [him]

ἢ ηὐχαρίστησαν, ἀλλὰ ἐματαιώθησαν ἐν
[1]or [3]thanked [him], but became vain in

τοῖς διαλογισμοῖς αὐτῶν, καὶ ἐσκοτίσθη
the reasonings of them, and [3]was darkened

ἡ ἀσύνετος αὐτῶν καρδία. 22 φάσκοντες
[1]the [2]undiscerning [4]of them [5]heart. Asserting

εἶναι σοφοὶ ἐμωράνθησαν, 23 καὶ ἤλλαξαν
to be wise they became foolish, and changed

τὴν δόξαν τοῦ ἀφθάρτου θεοῦ ἐν ὁμοιώματι
the glory of the incorruptible God in[to] a likeness

εἰκόνος φθαρτοῦ ἀνθρώπου καὶ πετεινῶν
of an image of corruptible man and birds

καὶ τετραπόδων καὶ ἑρπετῶν· 24 διὸ
and quadrupeds and reptiles; wherefore

παρέδωκεν αὐτοὺς ὁ θεὸς ἐν ταῖς
[2]gave up [3]them – [1]God in the

ἐπιθυμίαις τῶν καρδιῶν αὐτῶν εἰς ἀκαθαρ-
desires of the hearts of them to unclean-

σίαν τοῦ ἀτιμάζεσθαι τὰ σώματα αὐτῶν
ness – to be dishonoured[d] the bodies of them

ἐν αὐτοῖς. 25 Οἵτινες μετήλλαξαν τὴν
among them[selves]. Who changed the

ἀλήθειαν τοῦ θεοῦ ἐν τῷ ψεύδει, καὶ
truth – of God in[to] the lie, and

ἐσεβάσθησαν καὶ ἐλάτρευσαν τῇ κτίσει
worshipped and served the creature

παρὰ τὸν κτίσαντα, ὅς ἐστιν εὐλογητὸς
rather the [one] having created, who is blessed
than

εἰς τοὺς αἰῶνας· ἀμήν. 26 διὰ τοῦτο
unto the ages: Amen. Therefore

παρέδωκεν αὐτοὺς ὁ θεὸς εἰς πάθη
[2]gave up [3]them – [1]God to passions

ἀτιμίας· αἵ τε γὰρ θήλειαι αὐτῶν
of dishonour; [3]the [2]even [1]for females of them

μετήλλαξαν τὴν φυσικὴν χρῆσιν εἰς τὴν
changed the natural use to the [use]

παρὰ φύσιν, 27 ὁμοίως τε καὶ οἱ ἄρσενες
against nature, [3]likewise [1]and also the males

ἀφέντες τὴν φυσικὴν χρῆσιν τῆς θηλείας
leaving the natural use of the female

ἐξεκαύθησαν ἐν τῇ ὀρέξει αὐτῶν εἰς
burned in the desire of them toward

ἀλλήλους, ἄρσενες ἐν ἄρσεσιν τὴν
one another, males among males [3]the

ἀσχημοσύνην κατεργαζόμενοι καὶ τὴν
[2]unseemliness [1]working and [4]the

ἀντιμισθίαν ἣν ἔδει τῆς πλάνης αὐτῶν
[3]requital [4]which [10]behoved [5]of the [7]error [6]of them

ἐν ἑαυτοῖς ἀπολαμβάνοντες. 28 Καὶ
[8]in [9]themselves [1]receiving back. And

καθὼς οὐκ ἐδοκίμασαν τὸν θεὸν ἔχειν
as they thought not fit – God to have

ἐν ἐπιγνώσει, παρέδωκεν αὐτοὺς ὁ θεὸς
in knowledge, [2]gave up [3]them – [1]God

εἰς ἀδόκιμον νοῦν, ποιεῖν τὰ μὴ καθήκοντα
to a reprobate mind, to do the not being proper,
things

29 πεπληρωμένους πάσῃ ἀδικίᾳ πονηρίᾳ
having been filled with all unrighteousness wickedness

πλεονεξίᾳ κακίᾳ, μεστοὺς φθόνου φόνου
covetousness evil, full of envy of murder

ἔριδος δόλου κακοηθείας, ψιθυριστάς,*
of strife of guile of malignity, whisperers,*

30 καταλάλους, θεοστυγεῖς, ὑβριστάς, ὑπερ-
railers, God-haters, insolent, arro-

ηφάνους, ἀλαζόνας, ἐφευρετὰς κακῶν,
gant, boasters, inventors of evil things,

γονεῦσιν ἀπειθεῖς, 31 ἀσυνέτους, ἀσυνθέτους,
to parents disobedient, undiscerning, faithless,

ἀστόργους, ἀνελεήμονας· 32 οἵτινες τὸ
without unmerciful; who [3]the
natural affection,

δικαίωμα τοῦ θεοῦ ἐπιγνόντες, ὅτι οἱ
[2]ordinance – [4]of God [1]knowing, that the

τὰ τοιαῦτα πράσσοντες ἄξιοι θανάτου
the [5]such things [4][ones] practising worthy of death

εἰσίν, οὐ μόνον αὐτὰ ποιοῦσιν, ἀλλὰ
are, not only them do, but

καὶ συνευδοκοῦσιν τοῖς πράσσουσιν.
also consent to the [ones] practising.

Chapter 2

Διὸ ἀναπολόγητος εἶ, ὦ ἄνθρωπε
Wherefore inexcusable thou art, O man

πᾶς ὁ κρίνων· ἐν ᾧ γὰρ κρίνεις τὸν
everyone judging; [2]in [3]what [1]for thou judgest the

ἕτερον, σεαυτὸν κατακρίνεις· τὰ γὰρ αὐτὰ
other, thyself thou condemnest; for the same
things

πράσσεις ὁ κρίνων. 2 οἴδαμεν δὲ ὅτι τὸ
thou the judging. But we know that the
practisest [one]

κρίμα τοῦ θεοῦ ἐστιν κατὰ ἀλήθειαν ἐπὶ
judg- – of is accord- truth on
ment God ing to

τοὺς τὰ τοιαῦτα πράσσοντας. 3 λογίζῃ
the the [2]such things [1][ones] practising. reckonest thou

δὲ τοῦτο, ὦ ἄνθρωπε ὁ κρίνων τοὺς
And this, O man the judging the
[one] [ones]

τὰ τοιαῦτα πράσσοντας καὶ ποιῶν αὐτά,
the such things practising and doing them,

ὅτι σὺ ἐκφεύξῃ τὸ κρίμα τοῦ θεοῦ;
that thou wilt escape the judgment – of God?

4 ἢ τοῦ πλούτου τῆς χρηστότητος αὐτοῦ
or the riches of the kindness of him

καὶ τῆς ἀνοχῆς καὶ τῆς μακροθυμίας
and the forbearance and the longsuffering

καταφρονεῖς, ἀγνοῶν ὅτι τὸ χρηστὸν τοῦ
despisest thou, not knowing that the kindness –

θεοῦ εἰς μετάνοιάν σε ἄγει; 5 κατὰ δὲ
of God to repentance thee leads? but according to

τὴν σκληρότητά σου καὶ ἀμετανόητον
the hardness of thee and impenitent

καρδίαν θησαυρίζεις σεαυτῷ ὀργὴν ἐν
heart treasurest for thyself wrath in

ἡμέρᾳ ὀργῆς καὶ ἀποκαλύψεως δικαιοκρισίας
a day of wrath and of revelation of a righteous
judgment

τοῦ θεοῦ, 6 ὃς ἀποδώσει ἑκάστῳ κατὰ τὰ
– of God, who will requite to each man accord- the
ing to

ἔργα αὐτοῦ· 7 τοῖς μὲν καθ’ ὑπομονὴν
works of him : to the on [2]by [1]endurance
[ones] one hand

* " In a bad sense " (Abbott-Smith).

447

King James Version

in well doing seek for glory and honour and immortality, eternal life: 8 But unto them that are contentious, and do not obey the truth, but obey unrighteousness, indignation and wrath, 9 Tribulation and anguish, upon every soul of man that doeth evil; of the Jew first, and also of the Gentile; 10 But glory, honour, and peace, to every man that worketh good; to the Jew first, and also to the Gentile: 11 For there is no respect of persons with God. 12 For as many as have sinned without law shall also perish without law; and as many as have sinned in the law shall be judged by the law; 13 (For not the hearers of the law *are* just before God, but the doers of the law shall be justified. 14 For when the Gentiles, which have not the law, do by nature the things contained in the law, these, having not the law, are a law unto themselves: 15 Which shew the work of the law written in their hearts, their conscience also bearing witness, and *their* thoughts the mean while accusing or else excusing one another;) 16 In the day when God shall judge the secrets of men by Jesus Christ according to my gospel. 17 Behold, thou art called a Jew, and restest in the law, and makest thy boast of God, 18And knowest *his* will, and approvest the things that are more excellent, being instructed out of the law; 19And art confident that thou thyself art a guide of the blind, a light of them which are in darkness, 20An instructor of the foolish, a teacher of babes, which hast the form of knowledge and of the truth in the law. 21 Thou therefore which teachest another, teachest thou not thyself? thou that preachest a man should not steal, dost thou steal? 22 Thou that sayest a man should not commit adultery, dost thou commit adultery? thou that abhorrest idols, dost thou commit sacrilege? 23 Thou that makest thy boast of the law, through breaking the law dishonourest thou God? 24 For the name of God is blasphemed among the Gentiles through you, as it is written. 25 For circumcision verily profiteth, if thou keep the law: but if thou be a breaker of the law, thy circumcision is made uncircumcision. 26 Therefore, if the uncircumcision keep the righteousness of the law, shall not his uncircumcision be counted for circumcision? 27And shall not uncircumcision which is by nature, if it fulfil the law, judge thee, who by the letter and circumcision dost transgress the law? 28 For he is not a Jew, which is one outwardly; neither *is that* circumcision, which is outward in the flesh: 29 But he *is* a Jew, which is one inwardly; and circumcision *is that* of the heart, in the spirit, *and* not in the letter; whose praise *is* not of men, but of God.

New International Version

ence in doing good seek glory, honor and immortality, he will give eternal life. 8 But for those who are self-seeking and who reject the truth and follow evil, there will be wrath and anger. 9 There will be trouble and distress for every human being who does evil: first for the Jew, then for the Gentile; 10 but glory, honor and peace for everyone who does good: first for the Jew, then for the Gentile. 11 For God does not show favoritism.

12 All who sin apart from the law will also perish apart from the law, and all who sin under the law will be judged by the law. 13 For it is not those who hear the law who are righteous in God's sight, but it is those who obey the law who will be declared righteous. 14 (Indeed, when Gentiles, who do not have the law, do by nature things required by the law, they are a law for themselves, even though they do not have the law, 15 since they show that the requirements of the law are written on their hearts, their consciences also bearing witness, and their thoughts now accusing, now even defending them.) 16 This will take place on the day when God will judge men's secrets through Jesus Christ, as my gospel declares.

The Jews and the law

17 Now you, if you call yourself a Jew; if you rely on the law and brag about your relationship to God; 18 if you know his will and approve of what is superior because you are instructed by the law; 19 if you are convinced that you are a guide for the blind, a light for those who are in the dark, 20 an instructor of the foolish, a teacher of infants, because you have in the law the embodiment of knowledge and truth —21 you, then, who teach others, do you not teach yourself? You who preach against stealing, do you steal? 22 You who say that people should not commit adultery, do you commit adultery? You who abhor idols, do you rob temples? 23 You who brag about the law, do you dishonor God by breaking the law? 24As it is written: "God's name is blasphemed among the Gentiles because of you." [d]

25 Circumcision has value if you observe the law, but if you break the law, you have become as though you had not been circumcised. 26 If those who are not circumcised keep the law's requirements, will they not be regarded as though they were circumcised? 27 The one who is not circumcised physically and yet obeys the law will condemn you who, even though you have the[e] written code and circumcision, are a lawbreaker. 28 A man is not a Jew if he is only one outwardly, nor is circumcision merely outward and physical. 29 No, a man is a Jew if he is one inwardly; and circumcision is circumcision of the heart, by the Spirit, not by the written code. Such a man's praise is not from men, but from God.

God's faithfulness

3 What advantage then hath the Jew? or what profit *is there* of circumcision? 2 Much every way: chiefly, because that unto them were com-

3 What advantage, then, is there in being a Jew, or what value is there in circumcision? 2 Much in every way! First of all, they have been entrusted with the very words of God.

[d] Isaiah 52:5; Ezek. 36:22. [e] Or *who by means of a.*

Greek Interlinear

ἔργου ἀγαθοῦ δόξαν καὶ τιμὴν καὶ
⁹work ⁴of(in) good ⁸glory ⁷and ⁶honour ⁵and
ἀφθαρσίαν ζητοῦσιν ζωὴν αἰώνιον·
¹⁰incorruption ³seeking ¹²life ¹¹eternal;
8 τοῖς δὲ ἐξ ἐριθείας καὶ ἀπειθοῦσι τῇ
to the [ones] of self-seeking and disobeying the
on the other

ἀληθείᾳ πειθομένοις δὲ τῇ ἀδικίᾳ, ὀργὴ
truth ²obeying ¹but - unrighteousness, wrath
καὶ θυμός. 9 θλῖψις καὶ στενοχωρία ἐπὶ
and anger. Affliction and anguish on
πᾶσαν ψυχὴν ἀνθρώπου τοῦ κατεργαζομένου
every soul of man - working
τὸ κακόν, Ἰουδαίου τε πρῶτον καὶ
the evil, both of Jew firstly and
Ἕλληνος· 10 δόξα δὲ καὶ τιμὴ καὶ
of Greek; but glory and honour and
εἰρήνη παντὶ τῷ ἐργαζομένῳ τὸ ἀγαθόν,
peace to everyone working the good,
Ἰουδαίῳ τε πρῶτον καὶ Ἕλληνι. 11 οὐ
both to Jew firstly and to Greek. not
γάρ ἐστιν προσωπολημψία παρὰ τῷ θεῷ.
For is respect of persons with - God.
12 Ὅσοι γὰρ ἀνόμως ἥμαρτον, ἀνόμως
For as many as without law sinned, without law
καὶ ἀπολοῦνται· καὶ ὅσοι ἐν νόμῳ
also will perish; and as in law
many as (under)
ἥμαρτον, διὰ νόμου κριθήσονται· 13 οὐ
sinned, through law will be judged; ²not
γὰρ οἱ ἀκροαταὶ νόμου δίκαιοι παρὰ
¹for the hearers of law [are] just with
[τῷ] θεῷ, ἀλλ' οἱ ποιηταὶ νόμου
- God, but the doers of law
δικαιωθήσονται. 14 ὅταν γὰρ ἔθνη τὰ
will be justified. For whenever nations -
μὴ νόμον ἔχοντα φύσει τὰ τοῦ νόμου
¹not ²law ³having by nature the things of the law
ποιῶσιν, οὗτοι νόμον μὴ ἔχοντες ἑαυτοῖς
do, these ²law ¹not ³having to themselves
εἰσιν νόμος· 15 οἵτινες ἐνδείκνυνται τὸ
are a law; who show, the
ἔργον τοῦ νόμου γραπτὸν ἐν ταῖς καρδίαις
work of the law written in the hearts
αὐτῶν, συμμαρτυρούσης αὐτῶν τῆς συνει-
of them, witnessing with of them the con-
=while their conscience witnesses with and their
δήσεως καὶ μεταξὺ ἀλλήλων τῶν λογισμῶν
science and between one another the thoughts
thoughts among themselves accuse or even excuse,
κατηγορούντων ἢ καὶ ἀπολογουμένων, 16 ἐν
accusing or even excusing,⁸ in
ᾗ ἡμέρα κρίνει ὁ θεὸς τὰ κρυπτὰ τῶν
what day judges - God the hidden things
ἀνθρώπων κατὰ τὸ εὐαγγέλιόν μου διὰ
of men according to the gospel of me through
Χριστοῦ Ἰησοῦ. 17 Εἰ δὲ σὺ Ἰουδαῖος
Christ Jesus. But if thou ²a Jew
ἐπονομάζῃ καὶ ἐπαναπαύῃ νόμῳ καὶ
¹art named and restest on law and
καυχᾶσαι ἐν θεῷ 18 καὶ γινώσκεις τὸ
boastest in God and knowest the
θέλημα καὶ δοκιμάζεις τὰ διαφέροντα
will and approvest the things excelling

κατηχούμενος ἐκ τοῦ νόμου, 19 πέποιθάς τε
being instructed out of the law, and having persuaded
σεαυτὸν ὁδηγὸν εἶναι τυφλῶν, φῶς
thyself a guide to be of blind a light
[persons],
τῶν ἐν σκότει, 20 παιδευτὴν ἀφρόνων,
of the in darkness, an instructor of foolish
[ones] [persons],
διδάσκαλον νηπίων, ἔχοντα τὴν μόρφωσιν
a teacher of infants, having the form
τῆς γνώσεως καὶ τῆς ἀληθείας ἐν τῷ
- of knowledge and of the truth in the
νόμῳ· 21 ὁ οὖν διδάσκων ἕτερον ςεαυτὸν
law: the there- teaching another thyself
[one] fore
οὐ διδάσκεις; ὁ κηρύσσων μὴ κλέπτειν
teachest thou not? the [one] proclaiming not to steal
κλέπτεις; 22 ὁ λέγων μὴ μοιχεύειν
stealest thou? the [one] saying not to commit adultery
μοιχεύεις; ὁ βδελυσσόμενος τὰ εἴδωλα
dost thou com- the detesting the idols
mit adultery? [one]
ἱεροσυλεῖς; 23 ὃς ἐν νόμῳ καυχᾶσαι, διὰ
dost thou rob who in law boastest, through
temples?
τῆς παραβάσεως τοῦ νόμου τὸν θεὸν
- transgression of the law - ²God
ἀτιμάζεις; 24 τὸ γὰρ ὄνομα τοῦ θεοῦ
¹dishonourest thou? for the name - of God
δι' ὑμᾶς βλασφημεῖται ἐν τοῖς ἔθνεσιν,
because you is blasphemed among the nations,
of
καθὼς γέγραπται. 25 περιτομὴ μὲν γὰρ
as it has been written. circumcision indeed For
ὠφελεῖ ἐὰν νόμον πράσσῃς· ἐὰν δὲ
profits if law thou practisest; but if
παραβάτης νόμου ᾖς, ἡ περιτομή σου
a transgressor of law thou art, the circumcision of thee
ἀκροβυστία γέγονεν. 26 ἐὰν οὖν ἡ ἀκρο-
uncircumcision has become. If therefore the uncir-
βυστία τὰ δικαιώματα τοῦ νόμου φυλάσσῃ,
cumcision the ordinances of the law keeps,
οὐχ ἡ ἀκροβυστία αὐτοῦ εἰς περιτομὴν
not the uncircumcision of him for circumcision
λογισθήσεται; 27 καὶ κρινεῖ ἡ ἐκ φύσεως
will be reckoned? and ²will judge the ³by ²nature
ἀκροβυστία τὸν νόμον τελοῦσα σὲ τὸν
³uncircumcision ⁴the ⁷law ⁵keeping ⁸thee ¹⁰the
διὰ γράμματος καὶ περιτομῆς παραβάτην
¹¹through ¹²letter ¹³and ¹⁴circumcision ¹⁵transgressor
νόμου. 28 οὐ γὰρ ἐν τῷ φανερῷ
¹²of law. For ¹not ³the ⁴in ⁵the ⁶open
Ἰουδαῖός ἐστιν, οὐδὲ ἡ ἐν τῷ φανερῷ
²Jew ¹he is, nor ³the ⁴in ⁵the ⁶open
ἐν σαρκὶ περιτομή· 29 ἀλλ' ὁ ἐν τῷ
⁸in ⁷flesh ⁹circumcision; but ¹the ⁴in ⁵the
κρυπτῷ Ἰουδαῖος, καὶ περιτομὴ καρδίας
²secret ³Jew [is], and circumcision [is] of heart
ἐν πνεύματι οὐ γράμματι, οὗ ὁ ἔπαινος
in spirit not letter, of the praise [is]
whom
οὐκ ἐξ ἀνθρώπων ἀλλ' ἐκ τοῦ θεοῦ.
not from men but from - God.

Chapter 3

Τί οὖν τὸ περισσὸν τοῦ Ἰουδαίου,
What therefore the advantage of the Jew,
ἢ τίς ἡ ὠφέλεια τῆς περιτομῆς; 2 πολὺ
or what the profit - of circumcision? Much

κατὰ πάντα τρόπον. πρῶτον μὲν [γὰρ]
by every way. ²Firstly ²indeed ¹For
ὅτι ἐπιστεύθησαν τὰ λόγια τοῦ θεοῦ.
because they were the oracles - of God.
entrusted [with]

King James Version

mitted the oracles of God. 3 For what if some did not believe? shall their unbelief make the faith of God without effect? 4 God forbid: yea, let God be true, but every man a liar; as it is written, That thou mightest be justified in thy sayings, and mightest overcome when thou art judged. 5 But if our unrighteousness commend the righteousness of God, what shall we say? *Is* God unrighteous who taketh vengeance? (I speak as a man) 6 God forbid: for then how shall God judge the world? 7 For if the truth of God hath more abounded through my lie unto his glory; why yet am I also judged as a sinner? 8 And not *rather,* (as we be slanderously reported, and as some affirm that we say,) Let us do evil, that good may come? whose damnation is just. 9 What then? are we better *than they?* No, in no wise: for we have before proved both Jews and Gentiles, that they are all under sin; 10 As it is written, There is none righteous, no, not one: 11 There is none that understandeth, there is none that seeketh after God. 12 They are all gone out of the way, they are together become unprofitable; there is none that doeth good, no, not one. 13 Their throat *is* an open sepulchre; with their tongues they have used deceit; the poison of asps *is* under their lips: 14 Whose mouth *is* full of cursing and bitterness: 15 Their feet *are* swift to shed blood: 16 Destruction and misery *are* in their ways: 17 And the way of peace have they not known: 18 There is no fear of God before their eyes. 19 Now we know that what things soever the law saith, it saith to them who are under the law: that every mouth may be stopped, and all the world may become guilty before God. 20 Therefore by the deeds of the law there shall no flesh be justified in his sight: for by the law *is* the knowledge of sin. 21 But now the righteousness of God without the law is manifested, being witnessed by the law and the prophets; 22 Even the righteousness of God *which is* by faith of Jesus Christ unto all and upon all them that believe; for there is no difference: 23 For all have sinned, and come short of the glory of God; 24 Being justified freely by his grace through the redemption that is in Christ Jesus: 25 Whom God hath set forth *to be* a propitiation through faith in his blood, to declare his righteousness for the remission of sins that are past, through the forbearance of God; 26 To declare, *I say,* at this time his righteousness: that he might be just, and the justifier of him which believeth in Jesus. 27 Where *is* boasting then? It is excluded. By what law? of works? Nay; but by the law of faith. 28 Therefore we conclude that a man is

New International Version

3 What if some did not have faith? Will their lack of faith nullify God's faithfulness? 4 Not at all! Let God be true, and every man a liar. As it is written:

"So that you may be proved right in your words
  and prevail in your judging." *f*

5 But if our unrighteousness brings out God's righteousness more clearly, what shall we say? That God is unjust in bringing his wrath on us? (I am using a human argument.) 6 Certainly not! If that were so, how could God judge the world? 7 Someone might argue, "If my falsehood enhances God's truthfulness and so increases his glory, why am I still condemned as a sinner?" 8 Why not say—as we are being slanderously reported and as some claim that we say—"Let us do evil that good may result"? Their condemnation is deserved.

No one is righteous

9 What shall we conclude then? Are we any better *g*? Not at all! We have already made the charge that Jews and Gentiles alike are all under sin. 10 As it is written:

"There is no one righteous, not even one;
11   there is no one who understands,
      no one who searches for God.
12 All have turned away
      and together become worthless.
  There is no one who does good,
      not even one." *h*

13 "Their throats are open graves;
      their tongues practice deceit." *i*
  "The poison of vipers is on their lips." *j*
14   "Their mouths are full of cursing and
      bitterness." *k*
15 "Their feet are swift to shed blood;
16   ruin and misery mark their paths,
17 and the way of peace they do not know." *l*
18   "There is no fear of God before their
      eyes." *m*

19 Now we know that whatever the law says, it says to those who are under the law, so that every mouth may be silenced and the whole world held accountable to God. 20 Therefore no one will be declared righteous in his sight by observing the law; rather, through the law we become conscious of sin.

Righteousness through faith

21 But now a righteousness from God, apart from law, has been made known, to which the Law and the Prophets testify. 22 This righteousness from God comes through faith in Jesus Christ to all who believe. There is no difference, 23 for all have sinned and fall short of the glory of God, 24 and are justified freely by his grace through the redemption that came by Christ Jesus. 25 God presented him as a sacrifice of atonement, through faith in his blood. He did this to demonstrate his justice, because in his forbearance he had left the sins committed beforehand unpunished—26 he did it to demonstrate his justice at the present time, so as to be just and the one who justifies the man who has faith in Jesus.

27 Where, then, is boasting? It is excluded. On what principle? On that of observing the law? No, but on that of faith. 28 For we main-

[*f*] Psalm 51:4. [*g*] Or *worse.* [*h*] Psalm 14:1-3; 53:1-3; Eccles. 7:20.
[*i*] Psalm 5:9. [*j*] Psalm 140:3. [*k*] Psalm 10:7. [*l*] Isaiah 59:7,8. [*m*]
Psalm 36:1.

Greek Interlinear

3 τί γάρ; εἰ ἠπίστησάν τινες, μὴ ἡ
For what? If ²disbelieved ¹some, not the

ἀπιστία αὐτῶν τὴν πίστιν τοῦ θεοῦ
unbelief of them the faith - of God

καταργήσει; **4** μὴ γένοιτο· γινέσθω δὲ
will destroy? May it not be; but let be

ὁ θεὸς ἀληθής, πᾶς δὲ ἄνθρωπος ψεύστης,
- God true, and every man a liar,

καθάπερ γέγραπται· ὅπως ἂν δικαιωθῇς
as it has been So as - thou mayest
written: be justified

ἐν τοῖς λόγοις σου καὶ νικήσεις ἐν
in the sayings of thee and wilt overcome in

τῷ κρίνεσθαί σε. **5** εἰ δὲ ἡ ἀδικία
the to be judged thee. Now if the unright-
=when thou art judged. eousness

ἡμῶν θεοῦ δικαιοσύνην συνίστησιν, τί
of us ⁴of God ¹a righteousness ²commends, what

ἐροῦμεν; μὴ ἄδικος ὁ θεὸς ὁ ἐπιφέρων
shall we say? not unrighteous - God the [one] inflicting

τὴν ὀργήν; κατὰ ἄνθρωπον λέγω. **6** μὴ
- wrath? according to man I say. not

γένοιτο· ἐπεὶ πῶς κρινεῖ ὁ θεὸς τὸν
May it be; otherwise how will judge - God the

κόσμον; **7** εἰ δὲ ἡ ἀλήθεια τοῦ θεοῦ
world? But if the truth - of God

ἐν τῷ ἐμῷ ψεύσματι ἐπερίσσευσεν εἰς
by - my lie abounded to

τὴν δόξαν αὐτοῦ, τί ἔτι κἀγὼ ὡς
the glory of him, why still I also as

ἁμαρτωλὸς κρίνομαι; **8** καὶ μὴ καθὼς
a sinner am judged? and not as

βλασφημούμεθα καὶ καθώς φασίν τινες
we are blasphemed and as ²say ¹some

ἡμᾶς λέγειν ὅτι ποιήσωμεν τὰ κακὰ
us to say[,] - Let us do - evil things
=that we say,

ἵνα ἔλθῃ τὰ ἀγαθά; ὧν τὸ κρίμα
that may come - good things? of whom the judgment

ἔνδικόν ἐστιν. **9** Τί οὖν; προεχόμεθα;
just is. What therefore? Do we excel?

οὐ πάντως· προῃτιασάμεθα γὰρ Ἰουδαίους
not at all; for we previously accused ²Jews

τε καὶ Ἕλληνας πάντας ὑφ' ἁμαρτίαν
¹both and Greeks all under sin

εἶναι, **10** καθὼς γέγραπται ὅτι οὐκ ἔστιν
to be, as it has been written[,] - There is not

δίκαιος οὐδὲ εἷς, οὐκ ἔστιν ὁ
a righteous man not one, there is not the [one]

συνίων, **11** οὐκ ἔστιν ὁ ἐκζητῶν τὸν θεόν·
under- there is not the seeking - God;
standing, [one]

12 πάντες ἐξέκλιναν, ἅμα ἠχρεώθησαν·
all turned away, together became unprofitable:

οὐκ ἔστιν ὁ ποιῶν χρηστότητα, οὐκ
there is not the [one] doing kindness, not

ἔστιν ἕως ἑνός. **13** τάφος ἀνεῳγμένος
there is so much as one. A grave having been opened

ὁ λάρυγξ αὐτῶν, ταῖς γλώσσαις αὐτῶν
the throat of them, with the tongues of them

ἐδολιοῦσαν, ἰὸς ἀσπίδων ὑπὸ τὰ χείλη
they acted poison of asps under the lips
deceitfully,

αὐτῶν· **14** ὧν τὸ στόμα ἀρᾶς καὶ πικρίας
of them; of whom the mouth ²of cursing ³and ⁴bitterness

γέμει· **15** ὀξεῖς οἱ πόδες αὐτῶν ἐκχέαι
¹is full; swift the feet of them to shed

αἷμα, **16** σύντριμμα καὶ ταλαιπωρία ἐν
blood, ruin and misery in

ταῖς ὁδοῖς αὐτῶν, **17** καὶ ὁδὸν εἰρήνης
the ways of them, and a way of peace

οὐκ ἔγνωσαν. **18** οὐκ ἔστιν φόβος θεοῦ
they knew not. There is not fear of God

ἀπέναντι τῶν ὀφθαλμῶν αὐτῶν. **19** οἴδαμεν
before the eyes of them. We know

δὲ ὅτι ὅσα ὁ νόμος λέγει τοῖς ἐν τῷ
But that whatever the law says to the in the
things [ones]

νόμῳ λαλεῖ, ἵνα πᾶν στόμα φραγῇ καὶ
law it speaks, in order that every mouth may be stopped and

ὑπόδικος γένηται πᾶς ὁ κόσμος τῷ
⁵under ⁴may become ¹all ²the ³world -
judgment

θεῷ· **20** διότι ἐξ ἔργων νόμου οὐ
to God; because by works of law not

δικαιωθήσεται πᾶσα σὰρξ ἐνώπιον αὐτοῦ·
will be justified all flesh* before him;

διὰ γὰρ νόμου ἐπίγνωσις ἁμαρτίας.
for through law [is] full knowledge of sin.

21 Νυνὶ δὲ χωρὶς νόμου δικαιοσύνη
But now without law a righteousness

θεοῦ πεφανέρωται, μαρτυρουμένη ὑπὸ τοῦ
of God has been manifested, being witnessed by the

νόμου καὶ τῶν προφητῶν, **22** δικαιοσύνη
law and the prophets, ²a righteousness

δὲ θεοῦ διὰ πίστεως [Ἰησοῦ] Χριστοῦ,
¹and of God through faith of(in) Jesus Christ,

εἰς πάντας τοὺς πιστεύοντας· οὐ γάρ
to all the [ones] believing; for not

ἐστιν διαστολή· **23** πάντες γὰρ ἥμαρτον
there is difference; for all sinned

καὶ ὑστεροῦνται τῆς δόξης τοῦ θεοῦ,
and come short of the glory - of God,

24 δικαιούμενοι δωρεὰν τῇ αὐτοῦ χάριτι
being justified freely by the of him grace

διὰ τῆς ἀπολυτρώσεως τῆς ἐν Χριστῷ
through the redemption - in Christ

Ἰησοῦ· **25** ὃν προέθετο ὁ θεὸς ἱλαστήριον
Jesus; whom set forth - God a propitiation

διὰ πίστεως ἐν τῷ αὐτοῦ αἵματι, εἰς
through faith by the of him blood, for

ἔνδειξιν τῆς δικαιοσύνης αὐτοῦ διὰ τὴν
a showing of the righteousness of him because of the
forth

πάρεσιν τῶν προγεγονότων ἁμαρτημάτων
passing by of the ²having previously ¹sins
occurred

26 ἐν τῇ ἀνοχῇ τοῦ θεοῦ, πρὸς τὴν
in the forbearance - of God, for the

ἔνδειξιν τῆς δικαιοσύνης αὐτοῦ ἐν τῷ
showing of the righteousness of him in the
forth

νῦν καιρῷ, εἰς τὸ εἶναι αὐτὸν δίκαιον
present time, for the to be himᵇ just
=that he should be

καὶ δικαιοῦντα τὸν ἐκ πίστεως Ἰησοῦ.
and justifying the [one] of faith of(in) Jesus.

27 Ποῦ οὖν ἡ καύχησις; ἐξεκλείσθη. διὰ
Where there- the boasting? It was shut out. Through
fore

ποίου νόμου; τῶν ἔργων; οὐχί, ἀλλὰ
what law? of works? no, but

διὰ νόμου πίστεως. **28** λογιζόμεθα γὰρ
through a law of faith. For we reckon

---

* That is, no flesh will be justified . . .

King James Version

justified by faith without the deeds of the law. 29 *Is he* the God of the Jews only? *is he* not also of the Gentiles? Yes, of the Gentiles also: 30 Seeing *it is* one God, which shall justify the circumcision by faith, and uncircumcision through faith. 31 Do we then make void the law through faith? God forbid: yea, we establish the law.

4 What shall we say then that Abraham our father, as pertaining to the flesh, hath found? 2 For if Abraham were justified by works, he hath *whereof* to glory; but not before God. 3 For what saith the Scripture? Abraham believed God, and it was counted unto him for righteousness. 4 Now to him that worketh is the reward not reckoned of grace, but of debt. 5 But to him that worketh not, but believeth on him that justifieth the ungodly, his faith is counted for righteousness. 6 Even as David also describeth the blessedness of the man, unto whom God imputeth righteousness without works, 7 *Saying*, Blessed *are* they whose iniquities are forgiven, and whose sins are covered. 8 Blessed *is* the man to whom the Lord will not impute sin. 9 *Cometh* this blessedness then upon the circumcision *only*, or upon the uncircumcision also? for we say that faith was reckoned to Abraham for righteousness. 10 How was it then reckoned? when he was in circumcision, or in uncircumcision? Not in circumcision, but in uncircumcision. 11And he received the sign of circumcision, a seal of the righteousness of the faith which *he had yet* being uncircumcised: that he might be the father of all them that believe, though they be not circumcised; that righteousness might be imputed unto them also: 12And the father of circumcision to them who are not of the circumcision only, but who also walk in the steps of that faith of our father Abraham, which *he had* being *yet* uncircumcised. 13 For the promise, that he should be the heir of the world, *was* not to Abraham, or to his seed, through the law, but through the righteousness of faith. 14 For if they which are of the law *be* heirs, faith is made void, and the promise made of none effect: 15 Because the law worketh wrath: for where no law is, *there is* no transgression. 16 Therefore *it is* of faith, that *it might be* by grace; to the end the promise might be sure to all the seed; not to that only which is of the law, but to that also which is of the faith of Abraham; who is the father of us all, 17 (As it is written, I have made thee a father of many nations,) before him whom he believed, *even* God, who quickeneth the dead, and calleth those things which be not as though they were: 18 Who against hope believed in hope, that he might become the father of many nations, according to that which was spoken, So shall thy

New International Version

tain that a man is justified by faith apart from observing the law. 29 Is God the God of Jews only? Is he not the God of Gentiles too? Yes, of Gentiles too, 30 since there is only one God, who will justify the circumcised by faith and the uncircumcised through that same faith. 31 Do we, then, nullify the law by this faith? Not at all! Rather, we uphold the law.

Abraham justified by faith

4 What then shall we say that Abraham, our forefather, discovered in this matter? 2 If, in fact, Abraham was justified by works, he had something to boast about—but not before God. 3 What does the Scripture say? "Abraham believed God, and it was credited to him as righteousness." [n]

4 Now when a man works, his wages are not credited to him as a gift, but as an obligation. 5 However, to the man who does not work but trusts God who justifies the wicked, his faith is credited as righteousness. 6 David says the same thing when he speaks of the blessedness of the man to whom God credits righteousness apart from works:

7 "Blessed are they whose offenses have been forgiven
and whose sins have been covered.
8 Blessed is the man whose sin the Lord will never count against him." [o]

9 Is this blessedness only for the circumcised, or also for the uncircumcised? We have been saying that Abraham's faith was credited to him as righteousness. 10 Under what circumstances was it credited? Was it after he was circumcised, or before? It was not after, but before! 11And he received circumcision as a sign and seal of the righteousness that he had by faith while he was still uncircumcised. So then, he is the father of all who believe but have not been circumcised, in order that righteousness might be credited to them. 12And he is also the father of the circumcised who not only are circumcised but who also walk in the footsteps of the faith that our father Abraham had before he was circumcised.

13 It was not through law that Abraham and his offspring received the promise that he would be heir of the world, but through the righteousness that comes by faith. 14 For if those who live by law are heirs, faith has no value and the promise is worthless, 15 because law brings wrath. And where there is no law there is no transgression.

16 Therefore, the promise comes by faith, so that it may be by grace and may be guaranteed to all Abraham's offspring—not only to those who are of the law but also to those who are of the faith of Abraham. He is the father of us all. 17 As it is written: "I have made you a father of many nations." [p] He is our father in the sight of God, in whom he believed—the God who gives life to the dead and calls things that are not as though they were.

18 Against all hope, Abraham in hope believed and so became the father of many nations, just as it had been said to him, "So shall your

Greek Interlinear

δικαιοῦσθαι   πίστει   ἄνθρωπον   χωρὶς   ἔργων
¹to be justified   ³by faith   ¹a man   without   works

νόμου.   29 ἢ   'Ιουδαίων   ὁ θεὸς   μόνον;
of law.   Or   of Jews [is he]   the   God   only?

οὐχὶ   καὶ   ἐθνῶν;   ναὶ   καὶ   ἐθνῶν,   30 εἴπερ
not   also   of nations?   Yes[,]   also   of nations,   since [there is]

εἷς   ὁ   θεὸς   ὃς   δικαιώσει   περιτομὴν   ἐκ
one   -   God   who   will justify   circumcision   by

πίστεως   καὶ   ἀκροβυστίαν   διὰ   τῆς   πίστεως.
faith   and   uncircumcision   through the   faith.

31 νόμον   οὖν   καταργοῦμεν   διὰ   τῆς
¹Law   ²therefore   ¹do we destroy   through   the

πίστεως;   μὴ   γένοιτο,   ἀλλὰ   νόμον   ἱστάνομεν.
faith?   May it not be,   but   ²law   ¹we establish.

Chapter 4

Τί   οὖν   ἐροῦμεν   εὑρηκέναι   'Αβραὰμ
What   therefore   shall we say   to have found   Abraham

τὸν   προπάτορα   ἡμῶν   κατὰ   σάρκα;   2 εἰ
the   forefather   of us   according to   flesh?   if

γὰρ   'Αβραὰμ   ἐξ   ἔργων   ἐδικαιώθη,   ἔχει
For   Abraham   by   works   was justified,   he has

καύχημα·   ἀλλ'   οὐ   πρὸς   θεόν.   3 τί   γὰρ
a boast;   but   not   with   God.   For what

ἡ γραφὴ   λέγει;   ἐπίστευσεν   δὲ   'Αβραὰμ
the scripture   says?   And ²believed   ¹Abraham

τῷ   θεῷ,   καὶ   ἐλογίσθη   αὐτῷ   εἰς
-   God,   and   it was reckoned   to him   for

δικαιοσύνην.   4 τῷ   δὲ   ἐργαζομένῳ   ὁ
righteousness.   Now to the [one]   working   the

μισθὸς   οὐ   λογίζεται   κατὰ   χάριν   ἀλλὰ
reward   is not reckoned   according to   grace   but

κατὰ   ὀφείλημα·   τῷ   δὲ   μὴ   ἐργαζομένῳ,
according to   debt;   but to the [one] not   working,

5 πιστεύοντι   δὲ   ἐπὶ   τὸν   δικαιοῦντα   τὸν
but believing   on   the [one] justifying   the

ἀσεβῆ,   λογίζεται   ἡ   πίστις   αὐτοῦ   εἰς
impious man,   is reckoned   the   faith   of him   for

δικαιοσύνην,   6 καθάπερ   καὶ   Δαυὶδ   λέγει
righteousness,   even as   also   David   says

τὸν   μακαρισμὸν   τοῦ   ἀνθρώπου   ᾧ   ὁ
the   blessedness   of the   man   to whom   -

θεὸς   λογίζεται   δικαιοσύνην   χωρὶς   ἔργων·
God   reckons   righteousness   without   works :

7 μακάριοι   ὧν   ἀφέθησαν   αἱ   ἀνομίαι
Blessed [are they]   of whom   were forgiven   the   lawlessnesses

καὶ   ὧν   ἐπεκαλύφθησαν   αἱ   ἁμαρτίαι·
and   of whom   were covered over   the   sins;

8 μακάριος   ἀνὴρ   οὗ   οὐ   μὴ   λογίσηται
blessed   [is] a man   of whom   by no means   ⁴may reckon

κύριος   ἁμαρτίαν   9 ὁ   μακαρισμὸς   οὖν
¹[the] Lord   sin.   -   ²blessedness   ¹then

οὗτος   ἐπὶ   τὴν   περιτομὴν   ἢ   καὶ   ἐπὶ
¹This   on   the   circumcision   or   also   on

τὴν   ἀκροβυστίαν;   λέγομεν   γάρ·   ἐλογίσθη
the   uncircumcision?   for we say :   ¹was reckoned

τῷ   'Αβραὰμ   ἡ   πίστις   εἰς   δικαιοσύνην.
-   ⁴to Abraham   ¹The(his)   ³faith   for   righteousness.

10 πῶς   οὖν   ἐλογίσθη;   ἐν   περιτομῇ   ὄντι
How   then   was it reckoned?   in   circumcision   being

ἢ   ἐν   ἀκροβυστίᾳ;   οὐκ   ἐν   περιτομῇ   ἀλλ'
or   in   uncircumcision?   not   in   circumcision   but

ἐν   ἀκροβυστίᾳ·   11 καὶ   σημεῖον   ἔλαβεν
in   uncircumcision·   and   ²a sign   ¹he received

περιτομῆς   σφραγῖδα   τῆς   δικαιοσύνης   τῆς
of circumcision   a seal   of the   righteousness   of the

πίστεως   τῆς   ἐν   τῇ   ἀκροβυστίᾳ,   εἰς
faith   -   [while] in   -   uncircumcision,   for
=so

τὸ   εἶναι   αὐτὸν   πατέρα   πάντων   τῶν
the   to be   him[b]   a father   of all   the
that he should be

πιστευόντων   δι'   ἀκροβυστίας,   εἰς   τὸ
[ones] believing   through   uncircumcision,   for   the
=that right-

λογισθῆναι   αὐτοῖς   [τὴν]   δικαιοσύνην,   12 καὶ
to be reckoned   to them   -   righteousness,[b]   and
eousness should be reckoned to them,

πατέρα   περιτομῆς   τοῖς   οὐκ   ἐκ   περιτομῆς
a father   of circumcision   to the   not   of   circumcision
[ones]

μόνον   ἀλλὰ   καὶ   τοῖς   στοιχοῦσιν   τοῖς
only   but   also   to the [ones] walking   in the

ἴχνεσιν   τῆς   ἐν   ἀκροβυστίᾳ   πίστεως   τοῦ
steps   ¹of the   ⁵in   ⁴uncircumcision   ²faith   ³of the

πατρὸς   ἡμῶν   'Αβραάμ.   13 Οὐ   γὰρ   διὰ
⁴father   of us   ⁶Abraham.   For not   through

νόμου   ἡ   ἐπαγγελία   τῷ   'Αβραὰμ   ἢ   τῷ
law   the   promise   -   to Abraham   or   to the

σπέρματι   αὐτοῦ,   τὸ   κληρονόμον   αὐτὸν
seed   of him,   the   heir   him
=that he should be heir

εἶναι   κόσμου,   ἀλλὰ   διὰ   δικαιοσύνης   πίστεως.
to be[b]   of [the] world,   but   through   a righteousness   of faith.

14 εἰ   γὰρ   οἱ   ἐκ   νόμου   κληρονόμοι,
For if   ¹the   ³[are] ⁴of   ²law   ⁵heirs,

κεκένωται   ἡ   πίστις   καὶ   κατήργηται
¹has been emptied   -   ²faith   and   ³has been destroyed

ἡ   ἐπαγγελία·   15 ὁ   γὰρ   νόμος   ὀργὴν
¹the   ²promise;   for the   law   ²wrath

κατεργάζεται·   οὗ   δὲ   οὐκ   ἔστιν   νόμος,
¹works;   and where   there is not   law,

οὐδὲ   παράβασις.   16 Διὰ   τοῦτο   ἐκ   πίστεως,
neither   [is there]   Therefore   [it is]   of   faith,
transgression.

ἵνα   κατὰ   χάριν,   εἰς   τὸ   εἶναι   βεβαίαν
in   [it may be]   grace,   for   the   to be   firm
order according   =so that the promise shall be firm
that to

τὴν   ἐπαγγελίαν   παντὶ   τῷ   σπέρματι,   οὐ
the   promise[b]   to all   the   seed,   not

τῷ   ἐκ   τοῦ   νόμου   μόνον   ἀλλὰ   καὶ   τῷ
to the   of   the   law   only   but   also to the
[seed]   [seed]

ἐκ   πίστεως   'Αβραάμ,   ὃς   ἐστιν   πατὴρ
of   [the] faith   of Abraham,   who   is   father

πάντων   ἡμῶν,   17 καθὼς   γέγραπται   ὅτι
of all   us,   as   it has been written[,]

πατέρα   πολλῶν   ἐθνῶν   τέθεικά   σε,
A father   of many   of many   nations   I have appointed   thee,

κατέναντι   οὗ   ἐπίστευσεν   θεοῦ   τοῦ   ζωο-
before   ²whom   ³he believed   ¹God   the [one] quick-

ποιοῦντος   τοὺς   νεκροὺς   καὶ   καλοῦντος
ening   the   dead [ones]   and   calling

τὰ   μὴ   ὄντα   ὡς   ὄντα·   18 ὃς   παρ'   ἐλπίδα
the   not being   as   being·   who beyond   hope
things

ἐπ'   ἐλπίδι   ἐπίστευσεν,   εἰς   τὸ   γενέσθαι
on   hope   believed,   for   the   to become
=so that he should become

αὐτὸν   πατέρα   πολλῶν   ἐθνῶν   κατὰ   τὸ
him[b]   a father   of many   nations   accord-   the
ing to   thing

εἰρημένον·   οὕτως   ἔσται   τὸ   σπέρμα   σου·
having been said :   So   shall be   the   seed   of thee;

King James Version

seed be. 19And being not weak in faith, he considered not his own body now dead, when he was about a hundred years old, neither yet the deadness of Sarah's womb: 20 He staggered not at the promise of God through unbelief; but was strong in faith, giving glory to God; 21And being fully persuaded, that what he had promised, he was able also to perform. 22And therefore it was imputed to him for righteousness. 23 Now it was not written for his sake alone, that it was imputed to him; 24 But for us also, to whom it shall be imputed, if we believe on him that raised up Jesus our Lord from the dead; 25 Who was delivered for our offences, and was raised again for our justification.

5 Therefore being justified by faith, we have peace with God through our Lord Jesus Christ: 2 By whom also we have access by faith into this grace wherein we stand, and rejoice in hope of the glory of God. 3And not only so, but we glory in tribulations also; knowing that tribulation worketh patience; 4And patience, experience; and experience, hope: 5And hope maketh not ashamed; because the love of God is shed abroad in our hearts by the Holy Ghost which is given unto us. 6 For when we were yet without strength, in due time Christ died for the ungodly. 7 For scarcely for a righteous man will one die: yet peradventure for a good man some would even dare to die. 8 But God commendeth his love toward us, in that, while we were yet sinners, Christ died for us. 9 Much more then, being now justified by his blood, we shall be saved from wrath through him. 10 For if, when we were enemies, we were reconciled to God by the death of his Son; much more, being reconciled, we shall be saved by his life. 11And not only so, but we also joy in God through our Lord Jesus Christ, by whom we have now received the atonement. 12 Wherefore, as by one man sin entered into the world, and death by sin; and so death passed upon all men, for that all have sinned: 13 (For until the law sin was in the world: but sin is not imputed when there is no law. 14 Nevertheless death reigned from Adam to Moses, even over them that had not sinned after the similitude of Adam's transgression, who is the figure of him that was to come. 15 But not as the offence, so also is the free gift: for if through the offence of one many be

New International Version

offspring be." q 19 Without weakening in his faith, he faced the fact that his body was as good as dead—since he was about a hundred years old —and that Sarah's womb was also dead. 20 Yet he did not waver through unbelief regarding the promise of God, but was strengthened in his faith and gave glory to God, 21 being fully persuaded that God had power to do what he had promised. 22 This is why "it was credited to him as righteousness." r 23 The words "it was credited to him" were written not for him alone, 24 but also for us, to whom God will credit righteousness— for us who believe in him who raised Jesus our Lord from the dead. 25 He was delivered over to death for our sins and was raised to life for our justification.

Peace and joy

5 Therefore, since we have been justified through faith, we s have peace with God through our Lord Jesus Christ, 2 through whom we have gained access by faith into this grace in which we now stand. And we rejoice in the hope of the glory of God. 3 Not only so, but we s also rejoice in our sufferings, because we know that suffering produces perseverance; 4 perseverance, character; and character, hope. 5And hope does not disappoint us, because God has poured out his love into our hearts by the Holy Spirit, whom he has given us.

6 You see, at just the right time, when we were still powerless, Christ died for the ungodly. 7 Very rarely will anyone die for a righteous man, though for a good man someone might possibly dare to die. 8 But God demonstrates his own love for us in this: While we were still sinners, Christ died for us.

9 Since we have now been justified by his blood, how much more shall we be saved from God's wrath through him! 10 For if, when we were God's enemies, we were reconciled to him through the death of his Son, how much more, having been reconciled, shall we be saved through his life! 11 Not only is this so, but we also rejoice in God through our Lord Jesus Christ, through whom we have now received reconciliation.

Death through Adam, life through Christ

12 Therefore, just as sin entered the world through one man, and death through sin, and in this way death came to all men, because all sinned—13 for before the law was given, sin was in the world. But sin is not taken into account when there is no law. 14 Nevertheless, death reigned from the time of Adam to the time of Moses, even over those who did not sin by breaking a command, as did Adam, who was a pattern of the one to come.

15 But the gift is not like the trespass. For if the many died by the trespass of the one man,

[q] Gen. 15:5. [r] Gen. 15:6. [s] Or let us.

Greek Interlinear

19 καὶ μὴ ἀσθενήσας τῇ πίστει κατενόησεν
and not weakening – in faith he considered
τὸ ἑαυτοῦ σῶμα νενεκρωμένον, ἑκατονταέτης
¹the ²of himself ¹body to have died, a hundred years
που ὑπάρχων, καὶ τὴν νέκρωσιν τῆς
about being, and the death of the
μήτρας Σάρρας· **20** εἰς δὲ τὴν ἐπαγγελίαν
womb of Sarah; but ²against ³the ⁴promise
τοῦ θεοῦ οὐ διεκρίθη τῇ ἀπιστίᾳ, ἀλλὰ
– ⁵of God ¹he did not decide – ⁶by unbelief, but
ἐνεδυναμώθη τῇ πίστει, δοὺς δόξαν τῷ
was empowered – by faith, giving glory –
θεῷ **21** καὶ πληροφορηθεὶς ὅτι ὃ ἐπήγγελται
to God and being fully that what he has
                        persuaded   promised
δυνατός ἐστιν καὶ ποιῆσαι. **22** διὸ [καὶ]
able he is also to do. Wherefore also
ἐλογίσθη αὐτῷ εἰς δικαιοσύνην. **23** Οὐκ
it was to him for righteousness. not
reckoned

ἐγράφη δὲ δι’ αὐτὸν μόνον ὅτι ἐλογίσθη
it was Now because him only that it was
written of   reckoned
αὐτῷ, **24** ἀλλὰ καὶ δι’ ἡμᾶς, οἷς μέλλει
to him, but also because us, to whom it is
                        of   about
λογίζεσθαι, τοῖς πιστεύουσιν ἐπὶ τὸν
to be reckoned, to the [ones] believing on the [one]
ἐγείραντα Ἰησοῦν τὸν κύριον ἡμῶν ἐκ
having raised Jesus the Lord of us out of
νεκρῶν, **25** ὃς παρεδόθη διὰ τὰ παραπ-
[the] dead, who was delivered because of the of-
τώματα ἡμῶν καὶ ἠγέρθη διὰ τὴν
fences of us and was raised because of the
δικαίωσιν ἡμῶν.
justification of us.

Chapter 5

Δικαιωθέντες οὖν ἐκ πίστεως εἰρήνην
Having been justified therefore by faith peace
ἔχομεν πρὸς τὸν θεὸν διὰ τοῦ κυρίου
we have with – God through the Lord
ἡμῶν Ἰησοῦ Χριστοῦ, **2** δι’ οὗ καὶ τὴν
of us Jesus Christ, through whom also the
προσαγωγὴν ἐσχήκαμεν [τῇ πίστει] εἰς
access we have had – by faith into
τὴν χάριν ταύτην ἐν ᾗ ἑστήκαμεν, καὶ
this grace in which we stand, and
καυχώμεθα ἐπ’ ἐλπίδι τῆς δόξης τοῦ
boast on hope of the glory –
θεοῦ. **3** οὐ μόνον δέ, ἀλλὰ καὶ καυχώμεθα
of God. And not only [so], but also we boast
ἐν ταῖς θλίψεσιν, εἰδότες ὅτι ἡ θλῖψις
in afflictions, knowing that the affliction
ὑπομονὴν κατεργάζεται, **4** ἡ δὲ ὑπομονὴ
patience works, – and patience
δοκιμήν, ἡ δὲ δοκιμὴ ἐλπίδα· **5** ἡ δὲ
proof, – and proof hope; – and
ἐλπὶς οὐ καταισχύνει, ὅτι ἡ ἀγάπη
hope does not put to shame, because the love
τοῦ θεοῦ ἐκκέχυται ἐν ταῖς καρδίαις
– of God has been poured out in the hearts
ἡμῶν διὰ πνεύματος ἁγίου τοῦ δοθέντος
of us through Spirit Holy – given
ἡμῖν· **6** εἴ γε Χριστὸς ὄντων ἡμῶν
to us; indeed ⁷Christ ⁸being ¹us
ἀσθενῶν ἔτι κατὰ καιρὸν ὑπὲρ ἀσεβῶν
⁶weak² ³yet ⁴accord- ⁵time ⁶on ¹⁰impious
                    ing to   behalf of ones
ἀπέθανεν. **7** μόλις γὰρ ὑπὲρ δικαίου
⁹died. For hardly on behalf of a just man
τις ἀποθανεῖται· ὑπὲρ γὰρ τοῦ ἀγαθοῦ
anyone will die; for on behalf of the good man
τάχα τις καὶ τολμᾷ ἀποθανεῖν· **8** συνίστησιν
perhaps some- even dares to die; ³commends
one
δὲ τὴν ἑαυτοῦ ἀγάπην εἰς ἡμᾶς ὁ θεὸς
but ²the ⁴of himself ⁵love ⁶to ¹us – ¹God
ὅτι ἔτι ἁμαρτωλῶν ὄντων ἡμῶν Χριστὸς
that yet sinners being us⁶ Christ
= while we were yet sinners
ὑπὲρ ἡμῶν ἀπέθανεν. **9** πολλῷ οὖν μᾶλλον
on be- us died. By much there- rather
half of   fore

δικαιωθέντες νῦν ἐν τῷ αἵματι αὐτοῦ
having been justified now by the blood of him
σωθησόμεθα δι’ αὐτοῦ ἀπὸ τῆς ὀργῆς.
we shall be saved through him from the wrath.
10 εἰ γὰρ ἐχθροὶ ὄντες κατηλλάγημεν
For if enemies being we were reconciled
τῷ θεῷ διὰ τοῦ θανάτου τοῦ υἱοῦ αὐτοῦ,
– to God through the death of the Son of him,
πολλῷ μᾶλλον καταλλαγέντες σωθησόμεθα
by much rather having been reconciled we shall be saved
ἐν τῇ ζωῇ αὐτοῦ· **11** οὐ μόνον δέ, ἀλλὰ
by the life of him; and not only [so], but
καὶ καυχώμενοι ἐν τῷ θεῷ διὰ τοῦ
also boasting in – God through the
κυρίου ἡμῶν Ἰησοῦ [Χριστοῦ], δι’ οὗ
Lord of us Jesus Christ, through whom
νῦν τὴν καταλλαγὴν ἐλάβομεν.
now the reconciliation we received.
12 Διὰ τοῦτο ὥσπερ δι’ ἑνὸς ἀνθρώπου
Therefore as through one man
ἡ ἁμαρτία εἰς τὸν κόσμον εἰσῆλθεν,
– sin into the world entered,
καὶ διὰ τῆς ἁμαρτίας ὁ θάνατος, καὶ
and through – sin – death, ²also
οὕτως εἰς πάντας ἀνθρώπους ὁ θάνατος
¹so to all men – death
διῆλθεν, ἐφ’ ᾧ πάντες ἥμαρτον· **13** ἄχρι
passed, inasmuch as all sinned· until
γὰρ νόμου ἁμαρτία ἦν ἐν κόσμῳ, ἁμαρτία
for law sin was in [the] world, sin
δὲ οὐκ ἐλλογεῖται μὴ ὄντος νόμου·
but is not reckoned not being law²;
= when there is no law;
14 ἀλλὰ ἐβασίλευσεν ὁ θάνατος ἀπὸ Ἀδὰμ
but ²reigned – ¹death from Adam
μέχρι Μωϋσέως καὶ ἐπὶ τοὺς μὴ
until Moses even over the [ones] not
ἁμαρτήσαντας ἐπὶ τῷ ὁμοιώματι τῆς
sinning on the likeness of the
παραβάσεως Ἀδάμ, ὅς ἐστιν τύπος τοῦ
transgression of Adam, who is a type of the
μέλλοντος. **15** Ἀλλ’ οὐχ ὡς τὸ παράπτωμα
[one] coming. But not as the offence,
οὕτως [καὶ] τὸ χάρισμα· εἰ γὰρ τῷ
so also the free gift; for if ¹by the
τοῦ ἑνὸς παραπτώματι οἱ πολλοὶ
²of the ⁴one [man] ³offence the many

455

King James Version

dead, much more the grace of God, and the gift by grace, *which is* by one man, Jesus Christ, hath abounded unto many. 16And not as *it was* by one that sinned, *so is* the gift: for the judgment *was* by one to condemnation, but the free gift *is* of many offences unto justification. 17 For if by one man's offence death reigned by one; much more they which receive abundance of grace and of the gift of righteousness shall reign in life by one, Jesus Christ.) 18 Therefore, as by the offence of one *judgment came* upon all men to condemnation; even so by the righteousness of one *the free gift came* upon all men unto justification of life. 19 For as by one man's disobedience many were made sinners, so by the obedience of one shall many be made righteous. 20 Moreover the law entered, that the offence might abound. But where sin abounded, grace did much more abound: 21 That as sin hath reigned unto death, even so might grace reign through righteousness unto eternal life by Jesus Christ our Lord.

6 What shall we say then? Shall we continue in sin, that grace may abound? 2 God forbid. How shall we, that are dead to sin, live any longer therein? 3 Know ye not, that so many of us as were baptized into Jesus Christ were baptized into his death? 4 Therefore we are buried with him by baptism into death: that like as Christ was raised up from the dead by the glory of the Father, even so we also should walk in newness of life. 5 For if we have been planted together in the likeness of his death, we shall be also *in the likeness* of *his* resurrection: 6 Knowing this, that our old man is crucified with *him,* that the body of sin might be destroyed, that henceforth we should not serve sin. 7 For he that is dead is freed from sin. 8 Now if we be dead with Christ, we believe that we shall also live with him: 9 Knowing that Christ being raised from the dead dieth no more; death hath no more dominion over him. 10 For in that he died, he died unto sin once: but in that he liveth, he liveth unto God. 11 Likewise reckon ye also yourselves to be dead indeed unto sin, but alive unto God through Jesus Christ our Lord. 12 Let not sin therefore reign in your mortal body, that ye should obey it in the lusts thereof. 13 Neither yield ye your members *as* instruments of unrighteousness unto sin: but yield yourselves unto God, as those that are alive from the dead, and your members *as* instruments of

New International Version

how much more did God's grace and the gift that came by the grace of the one man, Jesus Christ, overflow to the many! 16Again, the gift of God is not like the result of the one man's sin: The judgment followed one sin and brought condemnation, but the gift followed many trespasses and brought justification. 17 For if, by the trespass of the one man, death reigned through that one man, how much more will those who receive God's abundant provision of grace and of the gift of righteousness reign in life through the one man, Jesus Christ.

18 Consequently, just as the result of one trespass was condemnation for all men, so also the result of one act of righteousness was justification that brings life for all men. 19 For just as through the disobedience of the one man the many were made sinners, so also through the obedience of the one man the many will be made righteous.

20 The law was added so that the trespass might increase. But where sin increased, grace increased all the more, 21 so that, just as sin reigned in death, so also grace might reign through righteousness to bring eternal life through Jesus Christ our Lord.

Dead to sin, alive in Christ

6 What shall we say, then? Shall we go on sinning so that grace may increase? 2 By no means! We died to sin; how can we live in it any longer? 3 Or don't you know that all of us who were baptized into Christ Jesus were baptized into his death? 4 We were therefore buried with him through baptism into death in order that, just as Christ was raised from the dead through the glory of the Father, we too may live a new life.

5 If we have been united with him in his death, we will certainly also be united with him in his resurrection. 6 For we know that our old self was crucified with him so that the body of sin might be rendered powerless, that we should no longer be slaves to sin—7 because anyone who has died has been freed from sin.

8 Now if we died with Christ, we believe that we will also live with him. 9 For we know that since Christ was raised from the dead, he cannot die again; death no longer has mastery over him. 10 The death he died, he died to sin once for all; but the life he lives, he lives to God.

11 In the same way, count yourselves dead to sin but alive to God in Christ Jesus. 12 Therefore, do not let sin reign in your mortal body so that you obey its evil desires. 13 Do not offer the parts of your body to sin, as instruments of wickedness, but rather offer yourselves to God, as those who have returned from death to life; and offer the parts of your body to him as in-

Greek Interlinear

ἀπέθανον, πολλῷ μᾶλλον ἡ χάρις τοῦ θεοῦ
died,   by much   rather   the   grace   -   of God

καὶ ἡ δωρεὰ ἐν χάριτι τῇ τοῦ ἑνὸς
and the   gift   in   grace   -   of the   one

ἀνθρώπου Ἰησοῦ Χριστοῦ εἰς τοὺς πολλοὺς
man   Jesus   Christ   to   the   many

ἐπερίσσευσεν. 16 καὶ οὐχ ὡς δι' ἑνὸς
abounded.   And   not   as   through   one
    [man]

ἁμαρτήσαντος τὸ δώρημα· τὸ μὲν γὰρ
sinning   the   gift;   ²the ¹on one hand ¹for

κρίμα ἐξ ἑνὸς εἰς κατάκριμα, τὸ δὲ
judgment [is] of   one   to   condemna-   on the other
   [offence]   tion,   the

χάρισμα ἐκ πολλῶν παραπτωμάτων εἰς
free gift [is]   of   many   offences   to

δικαίωμα. 17 εἰ γὰρ τῷ τοῦ ἑνὸς
justification.   For if   ¹by   the ²of the ⁴one [man]

παραπτώματι ὁ θάνατος ἐβασίλευσεν διὰ
⁴offence   -   death   reigned   through

τοῦ ἑνός, πολλῷ μᾶλλον οἱ τὴν περισσείαν
the   one   by much   rather   ¹the ²the ⁴abundance
[man],   [ones]

τῆς χάριτος καὶ τῆς δωρεᾶς τῆς
⁵of the   ⁶grace   ⁷and   ⁸of the   ⁹gift   -

δικαιοσύνης λαμβάνοντες ἐν ζωῇ βασιλεύ-
¹⁰of righteousness   ²receiving   ¹³in   ¹³life   ¹¹will

σουσιν διὰ τοῦ ἑνὸς Ἰησοῦ Χριστοῦ.
reign   through   the one [man]   Jesus   Christ.

18 Ἄρα οὖν ὡς δι' ἑνὸς παραπτώματος
So   therefore   as   through one   offence

εἰς πάντας ἀνθρώπους εἰς κατάκριμα,
to   all   men   to   condemnation,

οὕτως καὶ δι' ἑνὸς δικαιώματος εἰς
so   also   through   one   righteous act   to

πάντας ἀνθρώπους εἰς δικαίωσιν ζωῆς·
all   men   to   justification   of life·

19 ὥσπερ γὰρ διὰ τῆς παρακοῆς τοῦ
for as   through   the   disobedience   of the

ἑνὸς ἀνθρώπου ἁμαρτωλοὶ κατεστάθησαν
one   man   ⁴sinners   ³were constituted

οἱ πολλοί, οὕτως καὶ διὰ τῆς ὑπακοῆς
¹the ²many,   so   also   through   the   obedience

τοῦ ἑνὸς δίκαιοι κατασταθήσονται οἱ
of the one [man]   ²righteous   ³will be constituted   ¹the

πολλοί. 20 νόμος δὲ παρεισῆλθεν ἵνα
²many.   But law   entered   in order
    that

πλεονάσῃ τὸ παράπτωμα· οὗ δὲ ἐπλεόνασεν
might abound the   offence;   but where   abounded

ἡ ἁμαρτία, ὑπερεπερίσσευσεν ἡ χάρις,
-   sin,   more abounded   -   grace,

21 ἵνα ὥσπερ ἐβασίλευσεν ἡ ἁμαρτία ἐν
in order that   as   reigned   -   sin   by

τῷ θανάτῳ, οὕτως καὶ ἡ χάρις βασιλεύσῃ
-   death,   so   also -   grace   might reign

διὰ δικαιοσύνης εἰς ζωὴν αἰώνιον διὰ
through righteousness   to   life   eternal   through

Ἰησοῦ Χριστοῦ τοῦ κυρίου ἡμῶν.
Jesus   Christ   the   Lord   of us.

Chapter 6

Τί οὖν ἐροῦμεν; ἐπιμένωμεν τῇ
What therefore shall we say? May we continue   -

ἁμαρτίᾳ, ἵνα ἡ χάρις πλεονάσῃ; 2 μὴ
in sin,   in order that   -   grace   may abound?   not

γένοιτο. οἵτινες ἀπεθάνομεν τῇ ἁμαρτίᾳ,
May it be.   Who   we died   -   to sin,

πῶς ἔτι ζήσομεν ἐν αὐτῇ; 3 ἢ ἀγνοεῖτε
how   yet shall we live   in   it?   or are ye ignorant

ὅτι ὅσοι ἐβαπτίσθημεν εἰς Χριστὸν
that   as many as   we were baptized   into   Christ

Ἰησοῦν, εἰς τὸν θάνατον αὐτοῦ ἐβαπτίσ-
Jesus,   into   the   death   of him   we were

θημεν; 4 συνετάφημεν οὖν αὐτῷ διὰ τοῦ
baptized?   ²We were   ¹there   him   through   -
   buried with   fore

βαπτίσματος εἰς τὸν θάνατον, ἵνα ὥσπερ
baptism   into   -   death,   in order   as
    that

ἠγέρθη Χριστὸς ἐκ νεκρῶν διὰ τῆς
was raised   Christ   from   [the] dead   through   the

δόξης τοῦ πατρός, οὕτως καὶ ἡμεῖς ἐν
glory   of the   Father,   so   also   we   in

καινότητι ζωῆς περιπατήσωμεν. 5 εἰ γὰρ
newness   of life   might walk.   For if

σύμφυτοι γεγόναμεν τῷ ὁμοιώματι τοῦ
united with   we have become   in the   likeness   of the

θανάτου αὐτοῦ, ἀλλὰ καὶ τῆς ἀναστάσεως
death   of him,   but(so)   also of the(his) resurrection

ἐσόμεθα· 6 τοῦτο γινώσκοντες, ὅτι ὁ
we shall be;   this   knowing,   that   the

παλαιὸς ἡμῶν ἄνθρωπος συνεσταυρώθη, ἵνα
¹old   ²of us   ³man   was crucified   in or-
    with [him],   der that

καταργηθῇ τὸ σῶμα τῆς ἁμαρτίας, τοῦ
might be   the   body   -   of sin,   -
destroyed

μηκέτι δουλεύειν ἡμᾶς τῇ ἁμαρτίᾳ· 7 ὁ
no longer   to serve   us^bd   -   sin;   ²the
= that we should no longer serve   (one)

γὰρ ἀποθανὼν δεδικαίωται ἀπὸ τῆς
¹for   having died   has been justified   from   -

ἁμαρτίας. 8 εἰ δὲ ἀπεθάνομεν σὺν Χριστῷ,
sin.   But if   we died   with   Christ

πιστεύομεν ὅτι καὶ συζήσομεν αὐτῷ,
we believe   that   also   we shall live with   him,

9 εἰδότες ὅτι Χριστὸς ἐγερθεὶς ἐκ νεκρῶν
knowing   that   Christ   having   from [the] dead
    been raised

οὐκέτι ἀποθνήσκει, θάνατος αὐτοῦ οὐκέτι
no more   dies,   death   ²of him   ¹no more

κυριεύει. 10 ὃ γὰρ ἀπέθανεν, τῇ ἁμαρτίᾳ
²lords it over.   For in that†   he died,   -   to sin

ἀπέθανεν ἐφάπαξ· ὃ δὲ ζῇ, ζῇ τῷ θεῷ.
he died   once;   but in that†   he   he   -   to
    lives,   lives   God.

11 οὕτως καὶ ὑμεῖς λογίζεσθε ἑαυτοὺς
So   also   ²ye   ¹reckon   yourselves

εἶναι νεκροὺς μὲν τῇ ἁμαρτίᾳ ζῶντας
to be   dead   indeed   -   to sin   ²living

δὲ τῷ θεῷ ἐν Χριστῷ Ἰησοῦ. 12 μὴ
¹but   -   to God   in   Christ   Jesus.   ³not

οὖν βασιλευέτω ἡ ἁμαρτία ἐν τῷ θνητῷ
¹There-   ²let ³reign   -   ⁴sin   ⁵in ⁶the   ⁸mortal
fore

ὑμῶν σώματι εἰς τὸ ὑπακούειν ταῖς
¹⁰of you   ⁹body   for   the   to obey   the
    = to obey its lusts,

ἐπιθυμίαις αὐτοῦ, 13 μηδὲ παριστάνετε τὰ
lusts   of it,   neither   present ye   the

μέλη ὑμῶν ὅπλα ἀδικίας τῇ ἁμαρτίᾳ,
members of you   weapons   of unright-   -   to sin,
    eousness

ἀλλὰ παραστήσατε ἑαυτοὺς τῷ θεῷ ὡσεὶ
but   present ye   yourselves   -   to God   as

ἐκ νεκρῶν ζῶντας καὶ τὰ μέλη ὑμῶν
from [the] dead   living   and   the   members   of you

King James Version

righteousness unto God. 14 For sin shall not have dominion over you: for ye are not under the law, but under grace. 15 What then? shall we sin, because we are not under the law, but under grace? God forbid. 16 Know ye not, that to whom ye yield yourselves servants to obey, his servants ye are to whom ye obey; whether of sin unto death, or of obedience unto righteousness? 17 But God be thanked, that ye were the servants of sin, but ye have obeyed from the heart that form of doctrine which was delivered you. 18 Being then made free from sin, ye became the servants of righteousness. 19 I speak after the manner of men because of the infirmity of your flesh: for as ye have yielded your members servants to uncleanness and to iniquity unto iniquity; even so now yield your members servants to righteousness unto holiness. 20 For when ye were the servants of sin, ye were free from righteousness. 21 What fruit had ye then in those things whereof ye are now ashamed? for the end of those things *is* death. 22 But now being made free from sin, and become servants to God, ye have your fruit unto holiness, and the end everlasting life. 23 For the wages of sin *is* death; but the gift of God *is* eternal life through Jesus Christ our Lord.

7 Know ye not, brethren, (for I speak to them that know the law,) how that the law hath dominion over a man as long as he liveth? 2 For the woman which hath a husband is bound by the law to *her* husband so long as he liveth; but if the husband be dead, she is loosed from the law of *her* husband. 3 So then if, while *her* husband liveth, she be married to another man, she shall be called an adulteress: but if her husband be dead, she is free from that law; so that she is no adulteress, though she be married to another man. 4 Wherefore, my brethren, ye also are become dead to the law by the body of Christ; that ye should be married to another, *even* to him who is raised from the dead, that we should bring forth fruit unto God. 5 For when we were in the flesh, the motions of sins, which were by the law, did work in our members to bring forth fruit unto death. 6 But now we are delivered from the law, that being dead wherein we were held; that we should serve in newness of spirit, and not *in* the oldness of the letter. 7 What shall we say then? *Is* the law sin? God forbid. Nay, I had not known sin, but by the law: for I had not known lust, except the law had said, Thou shalt not covet. 8 But sin, taking occasion by the commandment, wrought in me all manner of concupiscence. For without the law sin *was* dead. 9 For I was alive without the law once: but when the commandment

New International Version

struments of righteousness. 14 For sin shall not be your master, because you are not under law, but under grace.

Slaves to righteousness

15 What then? Shall we sin because we are not under law but under grace? By no means! 16 Don't you know that when you offer yourselves to someone to obey him as slaves, you are slaves to the one whom you obey—whether you are slaves to sin, which leads to death, or to obedience, which leads to righteousness? 17 But thanks be to God that, though you used to be slaves to sin, you wholeheartedly obeyed the form of teaching to which you were committed. 18 You have been set free from sin and have become slaves to righteousness.

19 I put this in human terms because you are weak in your natural selves. Just as you used to offer the parts of your body in slavery to impurity and to ever-increasing wickedness, so now offer them in slavery to righteousness and holiness. 20 When you were slaves to sin, you were free from the control of righteousness. 21 What benefit did you reap at that time from the things you are now ashamed of? Those things result in death! 22 But now that you have been set free from sin and have become slaves to God, the benefit you reap leads to holiness, and the result is eternal life. 23 For the wages of sin is death, but the gift of God is eternal life through Christ Jesus our Lord.

An illustration from marriage

7 Do you not know, brothers—for I am speaking to men who know the law—that the law has authority over a man only as long as he lives? 2 For example, by law a married woman is bound to her husband as long as he is alive, but if her husband dies, she is released from the law of marriage. 3 So then, if she marries another man while her husband is still alive, she is called an adulteress. But if her husband dies, she is released from that law and is not an adulteress, even though she marries another man.

4 So, my brothers, you also died to the law through the body of Christ, that you might belong to another, to him who was raised from the dead, in order that we might bear fruit to God. 5 For when we were controlled by our sinful nature, the sinful passions aroused by the law were at work in our bodies, so that we bore fruit for death. 6 But now, by dying to what once bound us, we have been released from the law so that we serve in the new way of the Spirit, and not in the old way of the written code.

Struggling with sin

7 What shall we say, then? Is the law sin? Far from it! Indeed I would not have known what sin was except through the law. For I would not have known what it was to covet if the law had not said, "Do not covet." [t] 8 But sin, seizing the opportunity afforded by the commandment, produced in me every kind of covetous desire. For apart from law, sin is dead. 9 Once I was alive apart from law; but when the command-

[t] Exodus 20:17; Deut. 5:21.

Greek Interlinear

ὅπλα δικαιοσύνης τῷ θεῷ, **14** ἁμαρτία
weapons of righteousness - to God, ¹sin

γὰρ ὑμῶν οὐ κυριεύσει· οὐ γάρ ἐστε
¹for ªof you ²shall not lord it over; for ye are not

ὑπὸ νόμον ἀλλὰ ὑπὸ χάριν. **15** Τί οὖν;
under law but under grace. What therefore?

ἁμαρτήσωμεν, ὅτι οὐκ ἐσμὲν ὑπὸ νόμον
may we sin, because we are not under law

ἀλλὰ ὑπὸ χάριν; μὴ γένοιτο. **16** οὐκ
but under grace? May it not be. not

οἴδατε ὅτι ᾧ παριστάνετε ἑαυτοὺς δούλους
Know ye that to ye present yourselves slaves
     whom

εἰς ὑπακοήν, δοῦλοί ἐστε ᾧ ὑπακούετε,
for obedience,   slaves   ye are whom ye obey,

ἤτοι ἁμαρτίας εἰς θάνατον ἢ ὑπακοῆς
whether of sin to death or of obedience

εἰς δικαιοσύνην, **17** χάρις δὲ τῷ θεῷ
to righteousness? But thanks - to God

ὅτι ἦτε δοῦλοι τῆς ἁμαρτίας, ὑπηκούσατε
that ye were slaves of sin, ªye obeyed

δὲ ἐκ καρδίας εἰς ὃν παρεδόθητε τύπον
¹but out of [the] heart ²to ³which ⁵ye were delivered ⁴a form

διδαχῆς, **18** ἐλευθερωθέντες δὲ ἀπὸ τῆς
¹of teaching, and having been freed from -

ἁμαρτίας ἐδουλώθητε τῇ δικαιοσύνῃ.
sin ye were enslaved - to righteousness.

19 ἀνθρώπινον λέγω διὰ τὴν ἀσθένειαν
Humanly I say because of the weakness

τῆς σαρκὸς ὑμῶν. ὥσπερ γὰρ παρεστήσατε
of the flesh of you. For as ye presented

τὰ μέλη ὑμῶν δοῦλα τῇ ἀκαθαρσίᾳ καὶ
the members of you slaves - to uncleanness and

τῇ ἀνομίᾳ εἰς τὴν ἀνομίαν, οὕτως νῦν
- to iniquity unto - iniquity, so now

παραστήσατε τὰ μέλη ὑμῶν δοῦλα τῇ
present ye the members of you slaves -

δικαιοσύνῃ εἰς ἁγιασμόν. **20** ὅτε γὰρ
to righteousness unto sanctification. For when

δοῦλοι ἦτε τῆς ἁμαρτίας, ἐλεύθεροι ἦτε
slaves ye were - of sin, free ye were

τῇ δικαιοσύνῃ. **21** τίνα οὖν καρπὸν εἴχετε
- to righteousness. What ²therefore ¹fruit had ye

τότε; ἐφ' οἷς νῦν ἐπαισχύνεσθε· τὸ γὰρ
then? Over which now ye are ashamed; for the
     things

τέλος ἐκείνων θάνατος. **22** νυνὶ δὲ ἐλευ-
end of those things [is] death. But now having

θερωθέντες ἀπὸ τῆς ἁμαρτίας δουλωθέντες
been freed from - sin ªhaving been enslaved

δὲ τῷ θεῷ, ἔχετε τὸν καρπὸν ὑμῶν εἰς
¹and - to God, ye have the fruit of you to

ἁγιασμόν, τὸ δὲ τέλος ζωὴν αἰώνιον.
sanctification, and the end life eternal.

23 τὰ γὰρ ὀψώνια τῆς ἁμαρτίας θάνατος,
For the wages - of sin [is] death,

τὸ δὲ χάρισμα τοῦ θεοῦ ζωὴ αἰώνιος
but the free gift of God life eternal

ἐν Χριστῷ Ἰησοῦ τῷ κυρίῳ ἡμῶν.
in Christ Jesus the Lord of us.

Chapter 7

Ἢ ἀγνοεῖτε, ἀδελφοί, γινώσκουσιν γὰρ
Or are ye ignorant, brothers, for to [ones] knowing

νόμον λαλῶ, ὅτι ὁ νόμος κυριεύει τοῦ
law I speak, that the law lords it over the

ἀνθρώπου ἐφ' ὅσον χρόνον ζῇ; **2** ἡ γὰρ
man over such time [as] he lives? For the

ὕπανδρος γυνὴ τῷ ζῶντι ἀνδρὶ δέδεται
ªmarried ¹woman to the living husband has
     been bound

νόμῳ· ἐὰν δὲ ἀποθάνῃ ὁ ἀνήρ, κατήργηται
by law; but if dies the husband, she has been
     discharged

ἀπὸ τοῦ νόμου τοῦ ἀνδρός. **3** ἄρα οὖν
from the law of the husband. Therefore

ζῶντος τοῦ ἀνδρὸς μοιχαλὶς χρηματίσει
living the husbandª an adulteress she will be called
= while the husband lives

ἐὰν γένηται ἀνδρὶ ἑτέρῳ· ἐὰν δὲ ἀποθάνῃ
if she ²husband ¹to a but if dies
     becomes   different;

ὁ ἀνήρ, ἐλευθέρα ἐστὶν ἀπὸ τοῦ νόμου,
the husband, free she is from the law,

τοῦ μὴ εἶναι αὐτὴν μοιχαλίδα γενομένην
- not to be herᵈ an adulteress having become
= so that she is not

ἀνδρὶ ἑτέρῳ. **4** ὥστε, ἀδελφοί μου, καὶ
ªhusband ¹to a So, brothers of me, also
different.

ὑμεῖς ἐθανατώθητε τῷ νόμῳ διὰ τοῦ
ye were put to death to the law through the

σώματος τοῦ Χριστοῦ, εἰς τὸ γενέσθαι
body - of Christ, for the to become
= that ye might belong

ὑμᾶς ἑτέρῳ, τῷ ἐκ νεκρῶν ἐγερθέντι,
youᵇ to a to the from dead having been
different, [one] [the] raised,

ἵνα καρποφορήσωμεν τῷ θεῷ. **5** ὅτε
in order we may bear fruit - to God. when
that

γὰρ ἦμεν ἐν τῇ σαρκί, τὰ παθήματα
For we were in the flesh, the passions

τῶν ἁμαρτιῶν τὰ διὰ τοῦ νόμου ἐνηργεῖτο
- of sins - through the law operated

ἐν τοῖς μέλεσιν ἡμῶν εἰς τὸ καρποφορῆσαι
in the members of us for the to bear fruit

τῷ θανάτῳ· **6** νυνὶ δὲ κατηργήθημεν ἀπὸ
- to death; but now we were discharged from

τοῦ νόμου, ἀποθανόντες ἐν ᾧ κατειχόμεθα,
the law, having died [to that] in which we were held fast,

ὥστε δουλεύειν [ἡμᾶς] ἐν καινότητι
so as to serve usᵇ in newness

πνεύματος καὶ οὐ παλαιότητι γράμματος.
of spirit and not [in] oldness of letter.

7 Τί οὖν ἐροῦμεν; ὁ νόμος ἁμαρτία;
What therefore shall we say? the law sin?

μὴ γένοιτο· ἀλλὰ τὴν ἁμαρτίαν οὐκ
May it not be; yet - sin not

ἔγνων εἰ μὴ διὰ νόμου· τήν τε γὰρ
I knew except through law; ªalso ¹for

ἐπιθυμίαν οὐκ ᾔδειν εἰ μὴ ὁ νόμος
lust I knew not except the law

ἔλεγεν· οὐκ ἐπιθυμήσεις· **8** ἀφορμὴν δὲ
said : Thou shalt not lust; but ¹occasion

λαβοῦσα ἡ ἁμαρτία διὰ τῆς ἐντολῆς
²taking - ¹sin through the commandment

κατειργάσατο ἐν ἐμοὶ πᾶσαν ἐπιθυμίαν·
wrought in me every lust;

χωρὶς γὰρ νόμου ἁμαρτία νεκρά. **9** ἐγὼ
for without law sin [is] dead. I

δὲ ἔζων χωρὶς νόμου ποτέ· ἐλθούσης δὲ
And was living without law then; but coming
= when the

King James Version

came, sin revived, and I died. 10And the commandment, which *was ordained* to life, I found *to be* unto death. 11 For sin, taking occasion by the commandment, deceived me, and by it slew *me*. 12 Wherefore the law *is* holy, and the commandment holy, and just, and good. 13 Was then that which is good made death unto me? God forbid. But sin, that it might appear sin, working death in me by that which is good; that sin by the commandment might become exceeding sinful. 14 For we know that the law is spiritual: but I am carnal, sold under sin. 15 For that which I do, I allow not: for what I would, that do I not; but what I hate, that do I. 16 If then I do that which I would not, I consent unto the law that *it is* good. 17 Now then it is no more I that do it, but sin that dwelleth in me. 18 For I know that in me (that is, in my flesh,) dwelleth no good thing: for to will is present with me; but *how* to perform that which is good I find not. 19 For the good that I would, I do not: but the evil which I would not, that I do. 20 Now if I do that I would not, it is no more I that do it, but sin that dwelleth in me. 21 I find then a law, that, when I would do good, evil is present with me. 22 For I delight in the law of God after the inward man: 23 But I see another law in my members, warring against the law of my mind, and bringing me into captivity to the law of sin which is in my members. 24 O wretched man that I am! who shall deliver me from the body of this death? 25 I thank God through Jesus Christ our Lord. So then with the mind I myself serve the law of God; but with the flesh the law of sin.

8 *There is* therefore now no condemnation to them which are in Christ Jesus, who walk not after the flesh, but after the Spirit. 2 For the law of the Spirit of life in Christ Jesus hath made me free from the law of sin and death. 3 For what the law could not do, in that it was weak through the flesh, God sending his own Son in the likeness of sinful flesh, and for sin, condemned sin in the flesh: 4 That the righteousness of the law might be fulfilled in us, who walk not after the flesh, but after the Spirit. 5 For they that are after the flesh do mind the things of the flesh; but they that are after the Spirit, the things of the Spirit. 6 For to be carnally minded *is* death; but to be spiritually minded *is* life and peace. 7 Because the carnal

New International Version

ment came, sin sprang to life 10 and I died. I found that the very commandment that was intended to bring life actually brought death. 11 For sin, seizing the opportunity afforded by the commandment, deceived me, and through the commandment put me to death. 12 So then, the law is holy, and the commandment is holy, righteous and good.

13 Did that which is good, then, become death to me? By no means! But in order that sin might be recognized as sin, it produced death in me through what was good, so that through the commandment sin might become utterly sinful.

14 We know that the law is spiritual; but I am unspiritual, sold as a slave to sin. 15 I do not know what I am doing. For what I want to do I do not do, but what I hate I do. 16And if I do what I do not want to do, I agree that the law is good. 17As it is, it is no longer I myself who do it, but it is sin living in me. 18 I know that nothing good lives in me, that is, in my sinful nature. For I have the desire to do what is good, but I cannot carry it out. 19 For what I do is not the good I want to do; no, the evil I do not want to do—this I keep on doing. 20 Now if I do what I do not want to do, it is no longer I who do it, but it is sin living in me that does it.

21 So I find this law at work: When I want to do good, evil is right there with me. 22 For in my inner being I delight in God's law; 23 but I see another law at work in the members of my body, waging war against the law of my mind and making me a prisoner of the law of sin at work within my members. 24 What a wretched man I am! Who will rescue me from this body of death? 25 Thanks be to God—through Jesus Christ our Lord!

So then, I myself in my mind am a slave to God's law, but in my sinful nature a slave to the law of sin.

Life through the Spirit

8 Therefore, there is now no condemnation for those who are in Christ Jesus,ᵘ 2 because through Christ Jesus the law of the Spirit of life set me free from the law of sin and death. 3 For what the law was powerless to do in that it was weakened by our sinful nature, God did by sending his own Son in the likeness of sinful man to be a sin offering.ᵛ And so he condemned sin in sinful man, 4 in order that the righteous requirements of the law might be fully met in us, who do not live according to our sinful nature but according to the Spirit.

5 Those who live according to their sinful nature have their minds set on what that nature desires; but those who live in accordance with the Spirit have their minds set on what the Spirit desires. 6 The mind of sinful man is death, but the mind controlled by the Spirit is life and peace, 7 because the sinful mind is hostile to

[u] Some later MSS add *who do not live according to their sinful nature but according to the Spirit.* [v] Or *man, for sin.*

460

Greek Interlinear

τῆς ἐντολῆς ἡ ἁμαρτία ἀνέζησεν, 10 ἐγὼ
the commandment° - sin revived, ¹I
commandment came

δὲ ἀπέθανον, καὶ εὑρέθη μοι ἡ ἐντολὴ
¹and died, and ²was ³to me ¹the ¹command-
found ment

ἡ εἰς ζωήν, αὕτη εἰς θάνατον· 11 ἡ γὰρ
- ¹for ²life, ³this to death; - for

ἁμαρτία ἀφορμὴν λαβοῦσα διὰ τῆς
sin ²occasion ¹taking through the

ἐντολῆς ἐξηπάτησέν με καὶ δι᾽ αὐτῆς
commandment deceived me and through it

ἀπέκτεινεν. 12 ὥστε ὁ μὲν νόμος ἅγιος,
killed [me]. So the - law [is] holy,

καὶ ἡ ἐντολὴ ἁγία καὶ δικαία καὶ ἀγαθή.
and the command- holy and just and good.
ment

13 Τὸ οὖν ἀγαθὸν ἐμοὶ ἐγένετο θάνατος;
¹The ¹therefore good to me became death?

μὴ γένοιτο· ἀλλὰ ἡ ἁμαρτία, ἵνα φανῇ
May it not be; yet - sin, in or- it might
der that appear

ἁμαρτία, διὰ τοῦ ἀγαθοῦ μοι κατεργα-
sin, through the good ²to me ¹work-

ζομένη θάνατον, ἵνα γένηται καθ᾽ ὑπερβολὴν
ing ²death, in or- ¹might ⁴excessively†
der that become

ἁμαρτωλὸς ἡ ἁμαρτία διὰ τῆς ἐντολῆς.
²sinful - ¹sin ³through ⁴the ⁵command-
ment.

14 οἴδαμεν γὰρ ὅτι ὁ νόμος πνευματικός
For we know that the law spiritual

ἐστιν· ἐγὼ δὲ σάρκινός εἰμι, πεπραμένος
is; but I fleshy am, having been sold

ὑπὸ τὴν ἁμαρτίαν. 15 ὃ γὰρ κατεργάζομαι
under - sin. For what I work

οὐ γινώσκω· οὐ γὰρ ὃ θέλω τοῦτο
I know not; for not what I wish this

πράσσω, ἀλλ᾽ ὃ μισῶ τοῦτο ποιῶ. 16 εἰ
I practise, but what I hate this I do. if

δὲ ὃ οὐ θέλω τοῦτο ποιῶ, σύμφημι
But what I wish not this I do, I agree with

τῷ νόμῳ ὅτι καλός. 17 νυνὶ δὲ οὐκέτι
the law that [it is] good. But now no longer

ἐγὼ κατεργάζομαι αὐτὸ ἀλλὰ ἡ ἐνοικοῦσα
I work it but the ²indwelling

ἐν ἐμοὶ ἁμαρτία. 18 οἶδα γὰρ ὅτι οὐκ
⁴in ⁵me ¹sin. For I know that not

οἰκεῖ ἐν ἐμοί, τοῦτ᾽ ἔστιν ἐν τῇ σαρκί
dwells in me, this is in the flesh

μου, ἀγαθόν· τὸ γὰρ θέλειν παράκειταί
of me, [that which is] - for to wish is present
good;

μοι, τὸ δὲ κατεργάζεσθαι τὸ καλὸν
to me, ²the - but ²to work ²the ⁴good

οὔ· 19 οὐ γὰρ ὃ θέλω ποιῶ ἀγαθόν,
¹not; for not what ²I wish ¹I do ²good,

ἀλλὰ ὃ οὐ θέλω κακὸν τοῦτο πράσσω.
but what ¹I wish not ²evil this I practise.

20 εἰ δὲ ὃ οὐ θέλω ἐγὼ τοῦτο ποιῶ,
But if what ²wish not ¹I this I do,

οὐκέτι ἐγὼ κατεργάζομαι αὐτὸ ἀλλὰ ἡ
no longer I work it but ¹the

οἰκοῦσα ἐν ἐμοὶ ἁμαρτία. 21 εὑρίσκω
²dwelling ⁴in ⁵me ³sin. I find

ἄρα τὸν νόμον τῷ θέλοντι ἐμοὶ ποιεῖν
then the law ²the [one] ¹wishing ³to me to do

τὸ καλόν, 22 ὅτι ἐμοὶ τὸ κακὸν παράκειται·
the good, that to me the evil is present;

συνήδομαι γὰρ τῷ νόμῳ τοῦ θεοῦ κατὰ
for I delight in the law - of God according to

τὸν ἔσω ἄνθρωπον, 23 βλέπω δὲ ἕτερον
the inner man, but I see a different

νόμον ἐν τοῖς μέλεσίν μου ἀντιστρατευόμενον
law in the members of me warring against

τῷ νόμῳ τοῦ νοός μου καὶ αἰχμαλωτίζοντά
the law of the mind of me and taking captive

με ἐν τῷ νόμῳ τῆς ἁμαρτίας τῷ ὄντι
me by the law - of sin the [one] being

ἐν τοῖς μέλεσίν μου. 24 Ταλαίπωρος
in the members of me. ¹Wretched

ἐγὼ ἄνθρωπος· τίς με ῥύσεται ἐκ τοῦ
²I ³man; who me will deliver from the

σώματος τοῦ θανάτου τούτου; 25 χάρις
body of this death? Thanks

τῷ θεῷ διὰ Ἰησοῦ Χριστοῦ τοῦ κυρίου
- to God through Jesus Christ the Lord

ἡμῶν. Ἄρα οὖν αὐτὸς ἐγὼ τῷ μὲν
of us. So then ²[my]self ¹I ²with ⁴on one
the hand

νοῒ δουλεύω νόμῳ θεοῦ, τῇ δὲ σαρκὶ
⁵mind serve [the] law of God, on the other flesh
with the

Chapter 8

νόμῳ ἁμαρτίας. 8 οὐδὲν ἄρα νῦν κατάκριμα
[the] law of sin. ⁴No ¹then ²now ⁵condemnation
³[there is]

τοῖς ἐν Χριστῷ Ἰησοῦ. 2 ὁ γὰρ νόμος τοῦ
to the in Christ Jesus. For the law of the
[ones]

πνεύματος τῆς ζωῆς ἐν Χριστῷ Ἰησοῦ
spirit - of life in Christ Jesus

ἠλευθέρωσέν σε ἀπὸ τοῦ νόμου τῆς
freed thee from the law -

ἁμαρτίας καὶ τοῦ θανάτου. 3 τὸ γὰρ
of sin and - of death. For the

ἀδύνατον τοῦ νόμου, ἐν ᾧ ἠσθένει διὰ
impossible of the law, in which it was through
thing weak

τῆς σαρκός, ὁ θεὸς τὸν ἑαυτοῦ υἱὸν
the flesh, - ¹God ²the ⁴of himself ⁵Son

πέμψας ἐν ὁμοιώματι σαρκὸς ἁμαρτίας
³sending in likeness of flesh of sin

καὶ περὶ ἁμαρτίας κατέκρινεν τὴν ἁμαρτίαν
and concerning sin condemned - sin

ἐν τῇ σαρκί, 4 ἵνα τὸ δικαίωμα τοῦ
in the flesh, in order the ordinance of the
that

νόμου πληρωθῇ ἐν ἡμῖν τοῖς μὴ κατὰ
law may be in us the not accord-
fulfilled [ones] ing to

σάρκα περιπατοῦσιν ἀλλὰ κατὰ πνεῦμα.
flesh walking but according to spirit.

5 οἱ γὰρ κατὰ σάρκα ὄντες τὰ τῆς
For the [ones] accord- flesh being the of the
ing to things

σαρκὸς φρονοῦσιν, οἱ δὲ κατὰ πνεῦμα
flesh mind, but the accord- spirit
[ones] ing to

τὰ τοῦ πνεύματος. 6 τὸ γὰρ φρόνημα
the of the Spirit. For the mind
things

τῆς σαρκὸς θάνατος, τὸ δὲ φρόνημα
of the flesh [is] death, but the mind

τοῦ πνεύματος ζωὴ καὶ εἰρήνη. 7 διότι
of the Spirit life and peace. Wherefore

461

King James Version

mind *is* enmity against God: for it is not subject to the law of God, neither indeed can be. 8 So then they that are in the flesh cannot please God. 9 But ye are not in the flesh, but in the Spirit, if so be that the Spirit of God dwell in you. Now if any man have not the Spirit of Christ, he is none of his. 10And if Christ *be* in you, the body *is* dead because of sin; but the Spirit *is* life because of righteousness. 11 But if the Spirit of him that raised up Jesus from the dead dwell in you, he that raised up Christ from the dead shall also quicken your mortal bodies by his Spirit that dwelleth in you. 12 Therefore, brethren, we are debtors, not to the flesh, to live after the flesh. 13 For if ye live after the flesh, ye shall die: but if ye through the Spirit do mortify the deeds of the body, ye shall live. 14 For as many as are led by the Spirit of God, they are the sons of God. 15 For ye have not received the spirit of bondage again to fear; but ye have received the Spirit of adoption, whereby we cry, Abba, Father. 16 The Spirit itself beareth witness with our spirit, that we are the children of God: 17And if children, then heirs; heirs of God, and joint heirs with Christ; if so be that we suffer with *him*, that we may be also glorified together. 18 For I reckon that the sufferings of this present time *are* not worthy *to be compared* with the glory which shall be revealed in us. 19 For the earnest expectation of the creature waiteth for the manifestation of the sons of God. 20 For the creature was made subject to vanity, not willingly, but by reason of him who hath subjected *the same* in hope; 21 Because the creature itself also shall be delivered from the bondage of corruption into the glorious liberty of the children of God. 22 For we know that the whole creation groaneth and travaileth in pain together until now. 23And not only *they,* but ourselves also, which have the firstfruits of the Spirit, even we ourselves groan within ourselves, waiting for the adoption, *to wit,* the redemption of our body. 24 For we are saved by hope: but hope that is seen is not hope: for what a man seeth, why doth he yet hope for? 25 But if we hope for that we see not, *then* do we with patience wait for *it.* 26 Likewise the Spirit also helpeth our infirmities: for we know not what we should pray for as we ought: but the Spirit itself maketh intercession for us with groanings which cannot be uttered. 27And he that searcheth the hearts knoweth what *is* the mind of the Spirit, because he maketh intercession for the saints according to *the will of* God. 28And we know that all things work together for good to them that love God, to them who are the called according to *his* purpose. 29 For whom he did foreknow, he also did predestinate *to be* conformed to the image of his Son, that he might be the firstborn among many brethren. 30 More-

New International Version

God. It does not submit to God's law, nor can it do so. 8 Those controlled by their sinful nature cannot please God.

9 You, however, are controlled not by your sinful nature but by the Spirit, if the Spirit of God lives in you. And if anyone does not have the Spirit of Christ, he does not belong to Christ. 10 But if Christ is in you, your body is dead because of sin, yet your spirit is alive because of righteousness. 11And if the Spirit of him who raised Jesus from the dead is living in you, he who raised Christ from the dead will also give life to your mortal bodies through his Spirit, who lives in you.

12 Therefore, brothers, we have an obligation —but it is not to our sinful nature, to live according to it. 13 For if you live according to the sinful nature, you will die; but if by the Spirit you put to death the misdeeds of the body, you will live.

14 Those who are led by the Spirit of God are sons of God. 15 For you did not receive a spirit that makes you a slave again to fear, but you received the Spirit who makes you sons. And by him we cry, *"Abba,*[w] Father." 16 The Spirit himself testifies with our spirit that we are God's children. 17 Now if we are children, then we are heirs—heirs of God and co-heirs with Christ, if indeed we share in his sufferings in order that we may also share in his glory.

Future glory

18 I consider that our present sufferings are not worth comparing with the glory that will be revealed in us. 19 The creation waits in eager expectation for the sons of God to be revealed. 20 For the creation was subjected to frustration, not by its own choice, but by the will of the one who subjected it, in hope 21 that the creation itself will be liberated from its bondage to decay and brought into the glorious freedom of the children of God.

22 We know that the whole creation has been groaning as in the pains of childbirth right up to the present time. 23 Not only so, but we ourselves, who have the firstfruits of the Spirit, groan inwardly as we wait eagerly for our adoption as sons, the redemption of our bodies. 24 For in this hope we were saved. But hope that is seen is no hope at all. Who hopes for what he already has? 25 But if we hope for what we do not yet have, we wait for it patiently.

26 In the same way, the Spirit helps us in our weakness. We do not know how we ought to pray, but the Spirit himself intercedes for us with groans that words cannot express. 27And he who searches our hearts knows the mind of the Spirit, because the Spirit intercedes for the saints in accordance with God's will.

More than conquerors

28 And we know that in all things God works for the good of those who love him,[x] who have been called according to his purpose. 29 For those God foreknew he also predestined to be conformed to the likeness of his Son, that he might be the firstborn among many brothers. 30And those he predestined, he also called; those

[w] Aramaic for *Father.* [x] Some MSS read *And we know that all things work together for good to those who love God.*

Greek Interlinear

τὸ φρόνημα τῆς σαρκὸς ἔχθρα εἰς θεόν·
the mind of the flesh [is] enmity against God;

τῷ γὰρ νόμῳ τοῦ θεοῦ οὐχ ὑποτάσσεται,
for to the law – of God it is not subject,

οὐδὲ γὰρ δύναται· 8 οἱ δὲ ἐν σαρκὶ
neither indeed can it; and the [ones] ²in ¹flesh

ὄντες θεῷ ἀρέσαι οὐ δύνανται. 9 ὑμεῖς
¹being ⁴God ²to please ³cannot. ye

δὲ οὐκ ἐστὲ ἐν σαρκὶ ἀλλὰ ἐν πνεύματι,
But are not in flesh but in Spirit,

εἴπερ πνεῦμα θεοῦ οἰκεῖ ἐν ὑμῖν. εἰ
since [the] Spirit of God dwells in you. if

δέ τις πνεῦμα Χριστοῦ οὐκ ἔχει, οὗτος
But anyone [the] Spirit of Christ has not, this one

οὐκ ἔστιν αὐτοῦ. 10 εἰ δὲ Χριστὸς
is not of him. But if Christ

ἐν ὑμῖν, τὸ μὲν σῶμα νεκρὸν διὰ
[is] in you, ²the ¹on one ²body [is] dead because of
hand

ἁμαρτίαν, τὸ δὲ πνεῦμα ζωὴ διὰ
sin, ²the ¹on the ²spirit [is] because
other life of

δικαιοσύνην. 11 εἰ δὲ τὸ πνεῦμα τοῦ
righteousness. But if the Spirit of the [one]

ἐγείραντος τὸν Ἰησοῦν ἐκ νεκρῶν οἰκεῖ ἐν
having raised – Jesus from [the] dead dwells in

ὑμῖν, ὁ ἐγείρας ἐκ νεκρῶν Χριστὸν
you, the having from [the] dead Christ
[one] raised

Ἰησοῦν ζωοποιήσει καὶ τὰ θνητὰ σώματα
Jesus will quicken also the mortal bodies

ὑμῶν διὰ τοῦ ἐνοικοῦντος αὐτοῦ πνεύματος
of you through the ²indwelling ³of him ¹Spirit

ἐν ὑμῖν.
²in ¹you.

12 Ἄρα οὖν, ἀδελφοί, ὀφειλέται ἐσμέν,
So then, brothers, debtors we are,

οὐ τῇ σαρκὶ τοῦ κατὰ σάρκα ζῆν. 13 εἰ
not to the flesh – accord- flesh to liveᵈ. if
ing to

γὰρ κατὰ σάρκα ζῆτε, μέλλετε ἀποθνῄσκειν·
For accord- flesh ye live, ye are to die:
ing to about

εἰ δὲ πνεύματι τὰς πράξεις τοῦ σώματος
but if by [the] Spirit the practices of the body

θανατοῦτε, ζήσεσθε. 14 ὅσοι γὰρ πνεύματι
ye put to death; ye will live. For as many as by [the] Spirit

θεοῦ ἄγονται, οὗτοι υἱοί εἰσιν θεοῦ.
of God are led, these sons are of God.

15 οὐ γὰρ ἐλάβετε πνεῦμα δουλείας πάλιν
For ye received not a spirit of slavery again

εἰς φόβον, ἀλλὰ ἐλάβετε πνεῦμα υἱοθεσίας,
for fear, but ye received a spirit of adoption,

ἐν ᾧ κράζομεν· ἀββὰ ὁ πατήρ. 16 αὐτὸ
by which we cry: Abba – Father. ²it(him)self

τὸ πνεῦμα συμμαρτυρεῖ τῷ πνεύματι ἡμῶν
¹The ²Spirit witnesses with the spirit of us

ὅτι ἐσμὲν τέκνα θεοῦ. 17 εἰ δὲ τέκνα,
that we are children of God. And if children,

καὶ κληρονόμοι· κληρονόμοι μὲν θεοῦ,
also heirs; heirs on one hand of God,

συγκληρονόμοι δὲ Χριστοῦ, εἴπερ συμπάσ-
joint heirs on the of Christ, since we suffer
other

χομεν ἵνα καὶ συνδοξασθῶμεν. 18 Λογίζομαι
with[him] in or- also we may be glorified I reckon
der that with [him].

γὰρ ὅτι οὐκ ἄξια τὰ παθήματα τοῦ
For that ⁶[are] ¹not ⁵worthy ¹the ²sufferings ³of the

νῦν καιροῦ πρὸς τὴν μέλλουσαν δόξαν
⁴now ⁵time [to with the coming glory
(present) be compared]

ἀποκαλυφθῆναι εἰς ἡμᾶς. 19 ἡ γὰρ
to be revealed to us. For the

ἀποκαραδοκία τῆς κτίσεως τὴν ἀποκάλυψιν
anxious watching of the creation ²the ¹revelation

τῶν υἱῶν τοῦ θεοῦ ἀπεκδέχεται. 20 τῇ
³of the ⁴sons – ⁵of God ¹is eagerly expecting.

γὰρ ματαιότητι ἡ κτίσις ὑπετάγη, οὐχ
For to vanity the creation was subjected, not

ἑκοῦσα, ἀλλὰ διὰ τὸν ὑποτάξαντα, ἐφ'
willing[ly], but because of the [one] subjecting, in

ἐλπίδι 21 διότι καὶ αὐτὴ ἡ κτίσις
hope because even itself the creation

ἐλευθερωθήσεται ἀπὸ τῆς δουλείας τῆς
will be freed from the slavery

φθορᾶς εἰς τὴν ἐλευθερίαν τῆς δόξης
of corruption to the freedom of the glory

τῶν τέκνων τοῦ θεοῦ. 22 οἴδαμεν γὰρ
of the children – of God. For we know

ὅτι πᾶσα ἡ κτίσις συστενάζει καὶ
that all the creation groans together and

συνωδίνει ἄχρι τοῦ νῦν· 23 οὐ μόνον δέ,
travails together until – now; and not only [so],

ἀλλὰ καὶ αὐτοὶ τὴν ἀπαρχὴν τοῦ πνεύματος
but also [our]selves ²the ²firstfruit ³of the ¹Spirit

ἔχοντες [ἡμεῖς] καὶ αὐτοὶ ἐν ἑαυτοῖς
¹having we also [our]selves in ourselves

στενάζομεν υἱοθεσίαν ἀπεκδεχόμενοι, τὴν
groan adoption eagerly expecting, the

ἀπολύτρωσιν τοῦ σώματος ἡμῶν. 24 τῇ
redemption of the body of us. –

γὰρ ἐλπίδι ἐσώθημεν· ἐλπὶς δὲ βλεπομένη
For by hope we were saved; but hope being seen

οὐκ ἔστιν ἐλπίς· ὃ γὰρ βλέπει τις,
is not hope; for what sees anyone,

τί καὶ ἐλπίζει; 25 εἰ δὲ ὃ οὐ βλέπομεν
why also he hopes? but if what we do not see

ἐλπίζομεν, δι' ὑπομονῆς ἀπεκδεχόμεθα.
we hope [for], through patience we eagerly expect.

26 ὡσαύτως δὲ καὶ τὸ πνεῦμα συναντιλαμ-
And similarly also the Spirit takes

βάνεται τῇ ἀσθενείᾳ ἡμῶν· τὸ γὰρ τί
share in the weakness of us; – for what

προσευξώμεθα καθὸ δεῖ οὐκ οἴδαμεν, ἀλλὰ
we may pray as it behoves we know not, but

αὐτὸ τὸ πνεῦμα ὑπερεντυγχάνει στεναγμοῖς
it(him)self the Spirit supplicates on [our] behalf with groanings

ἀλαλήτοις· 27 ὁ δὲ ἐρευνῶν τὰς καρδίας
unutterable; and the [one] searching the hearts

οἶδεν τί τὸ φρόνημα τοῦ πνεύματος,
knows what [is] the mind of the Spirit,

ὅτι κατὰ θεὸν ἐντυγχάνει ὑπὲρ ἁγίων.
be- according God he supplicates on behalf saints.
cause to of

28 οἴδαμεν δὲ ὅτι τοῖς ἀγαπῶσιν τὸν
And we know that to the [ones] loving –

θεὸν πάντα συνεργεῖ [ὁ θεὸς] εἰς ἀγαθόν,
God ²all things ³works together – ¹God for good.

τοῖς κατὰ πρόθεσιν κλητοῖς οὖσιν. 29 ὅτι
to the ²accord- ³purpose ²called ¹being. Because
[ones] ing to

οὓς προέγνω, καὶ προώρισεν συμμόρφους
whom he foreknew, also he foreordained conformed to

τῆς εἰκόνος τοῦ υἱοῦ αὐτοῦ, εἰς τὸ
of the image of the Son of him, for the
= that he should be

εἶναι αὐτὸν πρωτότοκον ἐν πολλοῖς
to be himᵇ firstborn among many

ἀδελφοῖς· 30 οὓς δὲ προώρισεν, τούτους
brothers; but whom he foreordained, these

King James Version

over, whom he did predestinate, them he also called: and whom he called, them he also justified: and whom he justified, them he also glorified. 31 What shall we then say to these things? If God *be* for us, who *can be* against us? 32 He that spared not his own Son, but delivered him up for us all, how shall he not with him also freely give us all things? 33 Who shall lay any thing to the charge of God's elect? *It is* God that justifieth. 34 Who *is* he that condemneth? *It is* Christ that died, yea rather, that is risen again, who is even at the right hand of God, who also maketh intercession for us. 35 Who shall separate us from the love of Christ? *shall* tribulation, or distress, or persecution, or famine, or nakedness, or peril, or sword? 36As it is written, For thy sake we are killed all the day long; we are accounted as sheep for the slaughter. 37 Nay, in all these things we are more than conquerors through him that loved us. 38 For I am persuaded, that neither death, nor life, nor angels, nor principalities, nor powers, nor things present, nor things to come, 39 Nor height, nor depth, nor any other creature, shall be able to separate us from the love of God, which is in Christ Jesus our Lord.

9 I say the truth in Christ, I lie not, my conscience also bearing me witness in the Holy Ghost, 2 That I have great heaviness and continual sorrow in my heart. 3 For I could wish that myself were accursed from Christ for my brethren, my kinsmen according to the flesh: 4 Who are Israelites; to whom *pertaineth* the adoption, and the glory, and the covenants, and the giving of the law, and the service *of God,* and the promises; 5 Whose *are* the fathers, and of whom as concerning the flesh Christ *came,* who is over all, God blessed for ever. Amen. 6 Not as though the word of God hath taken none effect. For they *are* not all Israel, which are of Israel: 7 Neither, because they are the seed of Abraham, *are they* all children: but, In Isaac shall thy seed be called. 8 That is, They which are the children of the flesh, these *are* not the children of God: but the children of the promise are counted for the seed. 9 For this *is* the word of promise, At this time will I come, and Sarah shall have a son. 10And not only *this;* but when Rebecca also had conceived by one, *even* by our father Isaac, 11 (For *the children* being not yet born, neither having done any good or evil, that the purpose of God according to election might stand, not of works, but of him that calleth;) 12 It was said unto her, The elder shall serve the younger. 13 As it is written, Jacob have I loved, but Esau have I hated. 14 What shall we say then? *Is there* unrighteousness with God? God forbid. 15 For he

New International Version

he called, he also justified; those he justified, he also glorified.
31 What, then, shall we say in response to this? If God is for us, who can be against us? 32 He who did not spare his own Son, but gave him up for us all—how will he not also, along with him, graciously give us all things? 33 Who will bring any charge against those whom God has chosen? It is God who justifies. 34 Who is he that condemns? Christ Jesus, who died—more than that, who was raised to life—is at the right hand of God and is also interceding for us. 35 Who shall separate us from the love of Christ? Shall trouble or hardship or persecution or famine or nakedness or danger or sword? 36As it is written:

"For your sake we face death all the day long;
    we are considered as sheep to be slaughtered." [y]

37 No, in all these things we are more than conquerors through him who loved us. 38 For I am convinced that neither death nor life, neither angels nor demons, neither the present nor the future, nor any powers, 39 neither height nor depth, nor anything else in all creation, will be able to separate us from the love of God that is in Christ Jesus our Lord.

God's sovereign choice

9 I speak the truth in Christ—I am not lying, my conscience confirms it in the Holy Spirit —2 I have great sorrow and unceasing anguish in my heart. 3 For I could wish that I myself were cursed and cut off from Christ for the sake of my brothers, those of my own race, 4 the people of Israel. Theirs is the adoption as sons; theirs the divine glory, the covenants, the receiving of the law, the temple worship and the promises. 5 Theirs are the patriarchs, and from them is traced the human ancestry of Christ, who is God over all, forever praised! [z] Amen.
6 It is not as though God's word had failed. For not all who are descended from Israel are Israel. 7 Nor because they are his descendants are they all Abraham's children. On the contrary, "Through Isaac shall your offspring come." [a] 8 In other words, it is not the natural children who are God's children, but it is the children of the promise who are regarded as Abraham's offspring. 9 For this was how the promise was stated: "At the appointed time I will return, and Sarah shall have a son." [b]
10 Not only that, but Rebecca's children had one and the same father, our ancestor Isaac. 11 Yet, before the twins were born or had done anything good or bad—in order that God's purpose in election might stand: 12 not by works but by him who calls—she was told, "The older will serve the younger." [c] 13 Just as it is written: "Jacob I loved, but Esau I hated." [d]
14 What then shall we say? Is God unjust? Not at all! 15 For he says to Moses,

[y] Psalm 44:22. [z] Or *Christ, who is over all. God forever be praised!* Or *Christ. God who is over all be forever praised!.* [a] Gen. 21:12. [b] Gen. 18:10,14. [c] Gen. 25:23. [d] Mal. 1:2,3.

Greek Interlinear

καὶ ἐκάλεσεν· καὶ οὓς ἐκάλεσεν, τούτους
also he called; and whom he called, these

καὶ ἐδικαίωσεν· οὓς δὲ ἐδικαίωσεν, τούτους
also he justified; but whom he justified, these

καὶ ἐδόξασεν. 31 Τί οὖν ἐροῦμεν πρὸς
also he glorified. What therefore shall we say to

ταῦτα; εἰ ὁ θεὸς ὑπὲρ ἡμῶν, τίς καθ'
these things? If - God on behalf of us, who against

ἡμῶν; ὅς γε τοῦ ἰδίου υἱοῦ οὐκ ἐφείσατο,
us? Who indeed the(his) own Son spared not,

32 ἀλλὰ ὑπὲρ ἡμῶν πάντων παρέδωκεν
but on behalf of us all delivered

αὐτόν, πῶς οὐχὶ καὶ σὺν αὐτῷ τὰ πάντα
him, how not also with him - all things

ἡμῖν χαρίσεται; 33 τίς ἐγκαλέσει κατὰ
to us will he Who will bring a against
freely give? charge against

ἐκλεκτῶν θεοῦ; θεὸς ὁ δικαιῶν· 34 τίς
chosen ones of God? God [is] the [one] justifying; who

ὁ κατακρινῶν; Χριστὸς Ἰησοῦς ὁ ἀποθανών,
the condemning? Christ Jesus [is] the having died,
[one] [one]

μᾶλλον δὲ ἐγερθείς, ὅς ἐστιν ἐν δεξιᾷ
but rather having who is at [the] right
been raised, [hand]

τοῦ θεοῦ, ὃς καὶ ἐντυγχάνει ὑπὲρ ἡμῶν.
- of God, who also supplicates on behalf of us.

35 τίς ἡμᾶς χωρίσει ἀπὸ τῆς ἀγάπης
Who us will separate from the love

τοῦ Χριστοῦ; θλῖψις ἢ στενοχωρία ἢ
- of Christ? affliction or distress or

διωγμὸς ἢ λιμὸς ἢ γυμνότης ἢ κίνδυνος
persecution or famine or nakedness or peril

ἢ μάχαιρα; 36 καθὼς γέγραπται ὅτι ἕνεκεν
or sword? As it has been - For the
written[,] sake

σοῦ θανατούμεθα ὅλην τὴν ἡμέραν,
of thee we are being put to death all the day,

ἐλογίσθημεν ὡς πρόβατα σφαγῆς. 37 ἀλλ'
we were reckoned as sheep of(for) slaughter. But

ἐν τούτοις πᾶσιν ὑπερνικῶμεν διὰ τοῦ
in these things all we overconquer through the

ἀγαπήσαντος ἡμᾶς. 38 πέπεισμαι γὰρ
[one] having loved us. For I have been persuaded

ὅτι οὔτε θάνατος οὔτε ζωὴ οὔτε ἄγγελοι
that not death nor life nor angels

οὔτε ἀρχαὶ οὔτε ἐνεστῶτα οὔτε μέλλοντα
nor rulers nor things present nor things coming

οὔτε δυνάμεις 39 οὔτε ὕψωμα οὔτε βάθος
nor powers nor height nor depth

οὔτε τις κτίσις ἑτέρα δυνήσεται ἡμᾶς
nor any creature other will be able us

χωρίσαι ἀπὸ τῆς ἀγάπης τοῦ θεοῦ τῆς
to separate from the love - of God the

ἐν Χριστῷ Ἰησοῦ τῷ κυρίῳ ἡμῶν.
in Christ Jesus the Lord of us.

Chapter 9

Ἀλήθειαν λέγω ἐν Χριστῷ, οὐ
Truth I say in Christ, not

ψεύδομαι, συμμαρτυρούσης μοι τῆς
I lie, witnessing with me the

συνειδήσεώς μου ἐν πνεύματι ἁγίῳ, 2 ὅτι
conscience of me in [the] Spirit Holy, that

λύπη μοί ἐστιν μεγάλη καὶ ἀδιάλειπτος
grief to me is great and incessant
=I have great grief and . . .

ὀδύνη τῇ καρδίᾳ μου. 3 ηὐχόμην γὰρ
pain in the heart of me. For I was praying

ἀνάθεμα εἶναι αὐτὸς ἐγὼ ἀπὸ τοῦ Χριστοῦ
a curse to be [my]self I from - Christ

ὑπὲρ τῶν ἀδελφῶν μου τῶν συγγενῶν
on behalf of the brothers of me the kinsmen

μου κατὰ σάρκα, 4 οἵτινές εἰσιν Ἰσραη-
of me according to flesh, who are Israel-

λῖται, ὧν ἡ υἱοθεσία καὶ ἡ δόξα καὶ
ites, of whom the adoption and the glory and

αἱ διαθῆκαι καὶ ἡ νομοθεσία καὶ ἡ
the covenants and the giving of [the] law and the

λατρεία καὶ αἱ ἐπαγγελίαι, 5 ὧν οἱ
service and the promises, of whom the

πατέρες, καὶ ἐξ ὧν ὁ Χριστὸς τὸ κατὰ
fathers, and from whom the Christ - according to

σάρκα· ὁ ὢν ἐπὶ πάντων θεὸς εὐλογητὸς
flesh; the [one] being over all God blessed

εἰς τοὺς αἰῶνας, ἀμήν. 6 Οὐχ οἷον δὲ
unto the ages, amen. Not of course

ὅτι ἐκπέπτωκεν ὁ λόγος τοῦ θεοῦ. οὐ
that has failed the word - of God. not

γὰρ πάντες οἱ ἐξ Ἰσραήλ, οὗτοι Ἰσραήλ·
For all the [ones] of Israel, these [are of] Israel;

7 οὐδ' ὅτι εἰσὶν σπέρμα Ἀβραάμ, πάντες
neither because they are seed of [are they] all
Abraham,

τέκνα, ἀλλ'· ἐν Ἰσαὰκ κληθήσεταί σοι
children, but: In Isaac will be called to thee

σπέρμα. 8 τοῦτ' ἔστιν, οὐ τὰ τέκνα τῆς
seed. This is, not the children of the
=thy seed.

σαρκὸς ταῦτα τέκνα τοῦ θεοῦ, ἀλλὰ
flesh these children of God, but

τὰ τέκνα τῆς ἐπαγγελίας λογίζεται εἰς
the children of the promise is(are) reckoned for

σπέρμα. 9 ἐπαγγελίας γὰρ ὁ λόγος οὗτος·
a seed. For of promise the word this [is]:

κατὰ τὸν καιρὸν τοῦτον ἐλεύσομαι καὶ
According to this time I will come and

ἔσται τῇ Σάρρᾳ υἱός. 10 οὐ μόνον δέ,
will be to Sara a son. And not only [so],
=Sarah will have a son.

ἀλλὰ καὶ Ῥεβέκκα ἐξ ἑνὸς κοίτην ἔχουσα,
but also Rebecca from one conceiving,†

Ἰσαὰκ τοῦ πατρὸς ἡμῶν· 11 μήπω γὰρ
Isaac the father of us; for not yet

γεννηθέντων μηδὲ πραξάντων τι ἀγαθὸν
being born nor practising anything good

ἢ φαῦλον, ἵνα ἡ κατ' ἐκλογὴν πρόθεσις
or bad, in order the accord- choice purpose
that ing to

τοῦ θεοῦ μένῃ, 12 οὐκ ἐξ ἔργων ἀλλ'
- of God might not of works but
remain,

ἐκ τοῦ καλοῦντος, ἐρρέθη αὐτῇ ὅτι ὁ
of the [one] calling, it was said to her[,] - The

μείζων δουλεύσει τῷ ἐλάσσονι· 13 καθάπερ
greater will serve the lesser; even as

γέγραπται· τὸν Ἰακὼβ ἠγάπησα, τὸν δὲ
it has been - Jacob I loved, but
written:

Ἠσαῦ ἐμίσησα.
Esau I hated.

14 Τί οὖν ἐροῦμεν; μὴ ἀδικία παρὰ
What therefore shall we say? not unrighteousness with

τῷ θεῷ; μὴ γένοιτο. 15 τῷ Μωϋσεῖ
- God? May it not be. - to Moses

King James Version

saith to Moses, I will have mercy on whom I will have mercy, and I will have compassion on whom I will have compassion. 16 So then *it is* not of him that willeth, nor of him that runneth, but of God that sheweth mercy. 17 For the Scripture saith unto Pharaoh, Even for this same purpose have I raised thee up, that I might shew my power in thee, and that my name might be declared throughout all the earth. 18 Therefore hath he mercy on whom he will *have mercy,* and whom he will he hardeneth. 19 Thou wilt say then unto me, Why doth he yet find fault? For who hath resisted his will? 20 Nay but, O man, who art thou that repliest against God? Shall the thing formed say to him that formed *it,* Why hast thou made me thus? 21 Hath not the potter power over the clay, of the same lump to make one vessel unto honour, and another unto dishonour? 22 *What* if God, willing to shew *his* wrath, and to make his power known, endured with much longsuffering the vessels of wrath fitted to destruction: 23 And that he might make known the riches of his glory on the vessels of mercy, which he had afore prepared unto glory, 24 Even us, whom he hath called, not of the Jews only, but also of the Gentiles? 25 As he saith also in Osee, I will call them my people, which were not my people; and her beloved, which was not beloved. 26 And it shall come to pass, *that* in the place where it was said unto them, Ye *are* not my people; there shall they be called the children of the living God. 27 Esaias also crieth concerning Israel, Though the number of the children of Israel be as the sand of the sea, a remnant shall be saved: 28 For he will finish the work, and cut *it* short in righteousness: because a short work will the Lord make upon the earth. 29 And as Esaias said before, Except the Lord of Sabaoth had left us a seed, we had been as Sodoma, and been made like unto Gomorrha. 30 What shall we say then? That the Gentiles, which followed not after righteousness, have attained to righteousness, even the righteousness which is of faith. 31 But Israel, which followed after the law of righteousness, hath not attained to the law of righteousness. 32 Wherefore? Because *they sought it* not by faith, but as it were by the works of the law. For they stumbled at that stumblingstone; 33 As it is written, Behold, I lay in Sion a stumblingstone and rock of offence: and whosoever believeth on him shall not be ashamed.

10 Brethren, my heart's desire and prayer to God for Israel is, that they might be saved. 2 For I bear them record that they have a zeal of God, but not according to knowledge. 3 For they, being ignorant of God's righteousness, and going about to establish their own righteousness, have not submitted themselves unto the righteousness of God. 4 For Christ *is* the end of

New International Version

"I will have mercy on whom I have mercy,
    and I will have compassion on whom I
    have compassion." [e]
16 It does not, therefore, depend on man's desire or effort, but on God's mercy. 17 For the Scripture says to Pharaoh: "I raised you up for this very purpose, that I might display my power in you and that my name might be proclaimed in all the earth." [f] 18 Therefore God has mercy on whom he wants to have mercy, and he hardens whom he wants to harden.

19 One of you will say to me: "Then why does God still blame us? For who resists his will?" 20 But who are you, O man, to talk back to God? "Shall what is formed say to him who formed it, 'Why did you make me like this?'" [g] 21 Does not the potter have the right to make out of the same lump of clay some pottery for noble purposes and some for common use?

22 What if God, choosing to show his wrath and make his power known, bore with great patience the objects of his wrath—prepared for destruction? 23 What if he did this to make the riches of his glory known to the objects of his mercy, whom he prepared in advance for glory—24 even us, whom he also called, not only from the Jews but also from the Gentiles? 25 As he says in Hosea:
"I will call them 'my people' who are not my
    people;
and I will call her 'my loved one' who is
    not my loved one," [h]
26 and,
"It will happen that in the very place where it
    was said to them,
    'You are not my people,'
they will be called 'sons of the living God.'" [i]
27 Isaiah cries out concerning Israel: "Though the number of the Israelites should be like the sand by the sea, only the remnant will be saved. 28 For the Lord will carry out his sentence on earth with speed and finality." [j] 29 It is just as Isaiah said previously:
"Unless the Lord All-powerful had left us
    descendants,
we would have become like Sodom,
    and we would have been like Gomorrah." [k]

Israel's unbelief

30 What then shall we say? That the Gentiles, who did not pursue righteousness, have obtained it, a righteousness that is by faith; 31 but Israel, who pursued a law of righteousness, has not attained it. 32 Why not? Because they pursued it not by faith but as if it were by works. They stumbled over the "stumbling stone." 33 As it is written:
"See, I lay in Zion a stone that causes men to
    stumble
and a rock that makes them fall,
    and the one who trusts in him will never be
    put to shame." [l]

10 Brothers, my heart's desire and prayer to God for the Israelites is that they may be saved. 2 For I can testify about them that they are zealous for God, but their zeal is not based on knowledge. 3 Since they disregarded the righteousness that comes from God and sought to establish their own, they did not submit to God's righteousness. 4 Christ is the end

[e] Exodus 33:19. [f] Exodus 9:16. [g] Isaiah 29:16; 45:9. [h] Hosea 2:23. [i] Hosea 1:10. [j] Isaiah 10:22,23. [k] Isaiah 1:9. [l] Isaiah 8:14; 28:16.

Greek Interlinear

γὰρ λέγει· ἐλεήσω ὃν ἂν ἐλεῶ, καὶ
[1]For   he says: I will   whomever I have   and
                            have mercy on
οἰκτιρήσω ὃν ἂν οἰκτίρω.   16 ἄρα οὖν
I will pity whomever I pity.   So therefore
                                    [it is]
οὐ τοῦ θέλοντος οὐδὲ τοῦ τρέχοντος,
not of the [one] wishing nor of the [one] running,
ἀλλὰ τοῦ ἐλεῶντος θεοῦ.   17 λέγει γὰρ
but of the [one] having mercy God.   For says
ἡ γραφὴ τῷ Φαραὼ ὅτι εἰς αὐτὸ τοῦτο
the scripture - to Pharaoh[,] - For this very thing
ἐξήγειρά σε, ὅπως ἐνδείξωμαι ἐν σοὶ
I raised up thee, so as I may show forth in thee
τὴν δύναμίν μου, καὶ ὅπως διαγγελῇ τὸ
the power of me, and so as might be pub- the
                                    lished abroad
ὄνομά μου ἐν πάσῃ τῇ γῇ.   18 ἄρα οὖν
name of me in all the earth.   So therefore
ὃν θέλει ἐλεεῖ, ὃν δὲ θέλει σκληρύνει.
whom he he has but whom he wishes he hardens.
        wishes mercy,
19 Ἐρεῖς μοι οὖν· τί ἔτι μέμφεται;
Thou wilt say to me therefore: Why still finds he fault?
τῷ γὰρ βουλήματι αὐτοῦ τίς ἀνθέστηκεν;
for [2]the [3]counsel [2]of him [1]who [4]resisted?
20 ὦ ἄνθρωπε, μενοῦν γε σὺ τίς εἶ ὁ
O man, nay rather [2]thou [1]who [3]art the
ἀνταποκρινόμενος τῷ θεῷ; μὴ ἐρεῖ τὸ
[one] replying against - God? not [1]Will say [2]the
πλάσμα τῷ πλάσαντι· τί με ἐποίησας
[3]thing to the having formed: Why [5]me [4]madest
formed [one]   thou
οὕτως; 21 ἢ οὐκ ἔχει ἐξουσίαν ὁ κεραμεὺς
thus? or has not [2]authority [1]the [2]potter
τοῦ πηλοῦ ἐκ τοῦ αὐτοῦ φυράματος
of the clay out of the same lump
ποιῆσαι ὃ μὲν εἰς τιμὴν σκεῦος, ὃ δὲ
to make [1]this [2]to [4]honour [3]vessel, that
εἰς ἀτιμίαν; 22 εἰ δὲ θέλων ὁ θεὸς
to dishonour? But if wishing - God
ἐνδείξασθαι τὴν ὀργὴν καὶ γνωρίσαι τὸ
to show forth the(his) wrath and to make known the
δυνατὸν αὐτοῦ ἤνεγκεν ἐν πολλῇ μακρο-
ability of him bore in much long-
θυμίᾳ σκεύη ὀργῆς κατηρτισμένα εἰς
suffering vessels of wrath having been fitted for
ἀπώλειαν, 23 καὶ ἵνα γνωρίσῃ τὸν πλοῦτον
destruction, and in or- he might the riches
                    der that make known
τῆς δόξης αὐτοῦ ἐπὶ σκεύη ἐλέους, ἃ
of the glory of him on vessels of mercy, which
προητοίμασεν εἰς δόξαν, 24 οὓς καὶ
he previously prepared for glory,   whom also
ἐκάλεσεν ἡμᾶς οὐ μόνον ἐξ Ἰουδαίων
he called[,] us not only of Jews

ἀλλὰ καὶ ἐξ ἐθνῶν; 25 ὡς καὶ ἐν τῷ
but also of nations?   As also in -
Ὡσηὲ λέγει· καλέσω τὸν οὐ λαόν μου
Osee he says: I will call the [2]not [3]people of me
λαόν μου καὶ τὴν οὐκ ἠγαπημένην
a people of me and the not having been loved
ἠγαπημένην· 26 καὶ ἔσται ἐν τῷ τόπῳ
having been loved; and it shall be in the place
οὗ ἐρρέθη [αὐτοῖς]· οὐ λαός μου ὑμεῖς,
where it was said to them: not a people of me ye [are],
ἐκεῖ κληθήσονται υἱοὶ θεοῦ ζῶντος.
there they will be called sons [2]God [1]of a living.
27 Ἡσαΐας δὲ κράζει ὑπὲρ τοῦ Ἰσραήλ·
But Esaias cries on behalf of - Israel:
ἐὰν ᾖ ὁ ἀριθμὸς τῶν υἱῶν Ἰσραὴλ
If be the number of the sons of Israel
ὡς ἡ ἄμμος τῆς θαλάσσης, τὸ ὑπόλειμμα
as the sand of the sea, the remnant
σωθήσεται· 28 λόγον γὰρ συντελῶν καὶ
will be saved; for [2]an account [1]cutting short [3]and
συντέμνων ποιήσει κύριος ἐπὶ τῆς γῆς.
[2]cutting short [5]will make [4][the] Lord on the earth.
29 καὶ καθὼς προείρηκεν Ἡσαΐας· εἰ μὴ
And as [2]has previously said [1]Esaias: Except
κύριος σαβαὼθ ἐγκατέλιπεν ἡμῖν σπέρμα,
[the] Lord of hosts left to us a seed,
ὡς Σόδομα ἂν ἐγενήθημεν καὶ ὡς Γόμορρα
as Sodom we would have become and as Gomorra
ἂν ὡμοιώθημεν.
we would have been likened.
30 Τί οὖν ἐροῦμεν; ὅτι ἔθνη τὰ μὴ
What therefore shall we say? that nations - not
διώκοντα δικαιοσύνην κατέλαβεν δικαιοσύνην,
pursuing righteousness apprehended righteousness,
δικαιοσύνην δὲ τὴν ἐκ πίστεως· 31 Ἰσραὴλ
but a righteousness - of faith; [1]Israel
δὲ διώκων νόμον δικαιοσύνης εἰς νόμον
[1]but pursuing a law of righteousness [2]to(at) [3]a law
οὐκ ἔφθασεν. 32 διὰ τί; ὅτι οὐκ ἐκ
[1]did not arrive. Why? Because not of
πίστεως ἀλλ᾽ ὡς ἐξ ἔργων· προσέκοψαν
faith but as of works; they stumbled
τῷ λίθῳ τοῦ προσκόμματος, 33 καθὼς
at the stone - of stumbling, as
γέγραπται· ἰδοὺ τίθημι ἐν Σιὼν λίθον
it has been Behold I place in Sion a stone
written:
προσκόμματος καὶ πέτραν σκανδάλου, καὶ
of stumbling and a rock of offence, and
ὁ πιστεύων ἐπ᾽ αὐτῷ οὐ καταισχυνθήσεται.
the [one] believing on him will not be put to shame.

Chapter 10

Ἀδελφοί, ἡ μὲν εὐδοκία τῆς ἐμῆς
Brothers, the - good pleasure - of my
καρδίας καὶ ἡ δέησις πρὸς τὸν θεὸν
heart and the request to - God
ὑπὲρ αὐτῶν εἰς σωτηρίαν. 2 μαρτυρῶ
on behalf of them [is] for salvation.   I witness
γὰρ αὐτοῖς ὅτι ζῆλον θεοῦ ἔχουσιν, ἀλλ᾽
For to them that a zeal of God they have, but

οὐ κατ᾽ ἐπίγνωσιν· 3 ἀγνοοῦντες γὰρ τὴν
not according to knowledge; for not knowing the
τοῦ θεοῦ δικαιοσύνην, καὶ τὴν ἰδίαν
- [2]of God [1]righteousness, and the(ir) own
ζητοῦντες στῆσαι, τῇ δικαιοσύνῃ τοῦ θεοῦ
seeking to establish, to the righteousness - of God
οὐχ ὑπετάγησαν. 4 τέλος γὰρ νόμου
they did not submit.   For end of law

King James Version

the law for righteousness to every one that believeth. 5 For Moses describeth the righteousness which is of the law, That the man which doeth those things shall live by them. 6 But the righteousness which is of faith speaketh on this wise, Say not in thine heart, Who shall ascend into heaven? (that is, to bring Christ down *from above:*) 7 Or, Who shall descend into the deep? (that is, to bring up Christ again from the dead.) 8 But what saith it? The word is nigh thee, *even* in thy mouth, and in thy heart: that is, the word of faith, which we preach; 9 That if thou shalt confess with thy mouth the Lord Jesus, and shalt believe in thine heart that God hath raised him from the dead, thou shalt be saved. 10 For with the heart man believeth unto righteousness; and with the mouth confession is made unto salvation. 11 For the Scripture saith, Whosoever believeth on him shall not be ashamed. 12 For there is no difference between the Jew and the Greek: for the same Lord over all is rich unto all that call upon him. 13 For whosoever shall call upon the name of the Lord shall be saved. 14 How then shall they call on him in whom they have not believed? and how shall they believe in him of whom they have not heard? and how shall they hear without a preacher? 15 And how shall they preach, except they be sent? as it is written, How beautiful are the feet of them that preach the gospel of peace, and bring glad tidings of good things! 16 But they have not all obeyed the gospel. For Esaias saith, Lord, who hath believed our report? 17 So then faith *cometh* by hearing, and hearing by the word of God. 18 But I say, Have they not heard? Yes verily, their sound went into all the earth, and their words unto the ends of the world. 19 But I say, Did not Israel know? First Moses saith, I will provoke you to jealousy by *them that are* no people, *and* by a foolish nation I will anger you. 20 But Esaias is very bold, and saith, I was found of them that sought me not; I was made manifest unto them that asked not after me. 21 But to Israel he saith, All day long I have stretched forth my hands unto a disobedient and gainsaying people.

11 I say then, Hath God cast away his people? God forbid. For I also am an Israelite, of the seed of Abraham, *of* the tribe of Benjamin. 2 God hath not cast away his people which he foreknew. Wot ye not what the Scripture saith of Elias? how he maketh intercession to God against Israel, saying, 3 Lord, they have killed thy prophets, and digged down thine altars; and I am left alone, and they seek my life. 4 But what saith the answer of God unto him? I have reserved to myself seven thousand

New International Version

of the law so that there may be righteousness for everyone who believes.

5 Moses describes in this way the righteousness that is by the law: "The man who does these things will live by them." [m] 6 But the righteousness that is by faith says: "Do not say in your heart, 'Who will ascend into heaven?' [n]" (that is, to bring Christ down), 7 or "'Who will descend into the deep?' [o]" (that is, to bring Christ up from the dead? 8 But what does it say?

"The word is near you;
    it is in your mouth and in your heart" [p];

that is, the word of faith we are proclaiming: 9 That if you confess with your mouth, "Jesus is Lord," and believe in your heart that God raised him from the dead, you will be saved. 10 For it is with your heart that you believe and are justified, and it is with your mouth that you confess and are saved. 11 As the Scripture says, "He who believes in him will not be put to shame." [q] 12 For there is no difference between Jew and Gentile—the same Lord is Lord of all and richly blesses all who call on him, 13 for, "Everyone who calls on the name of the Lord will be saved." [r]

14 How, then, can they call on the one they have not believed in? And how can they believe in the one of whom they have not heard? And how can they hear without someone preaching to them? 15 And how can they preach unless they are sent? As it is written, "How beautiful are the feet of those who bring good news!" [s]

16 But not all the Israelites responded to the good news. For Isaiah says, "Lord, who has believed our message?" [t] 17 Consequently, faith comes from hearing the message, and the message is heard through the word of Christ. 18 But I ask, did they not hear? Of course they did:

"Their voice has gone out into all the earth,
    their words to the ends of the world." [u]

19 Again I ask, did Israel not understand? First, Moses says,

"I will make you envious by means of those
    who are not a nation;
I will make you angry by a nation that has
    no understanding." [v]

20 Then Isaiah boldly says,

"I was found by those who did not seek me;
    I revealed myself to those who did not ask
    for me." [w]

21 But concerning Israel he says, "All day long I have held out my hands to a disobedient and obstinate people." [x]

The remnant of Israel

11 I ask then, Did God reject his people? By no means! I am an Israelite myself, a descendant of Abraham, from the tribe of Benjamin. 2 God did not reject his people, whom he foreknew. Don't you know what the Scripture says in the passage about Elijah—how he appealed to God against Israel: 3 "Lord, they have killed your prophets and torn down your altars; I am the only one left, and they are trying to kill me" [y]? 4 And what was God's answer to him? "I have reserved for myself seven thou-

---

[m] Lev. 18:5. [n] Deut. 30:12. [o] Deut. 30:13. [p] Deut. 30:14. [q] Isaiah 28:16. [r] Joel 2:32. [s] Isaiah 52:7. [t] Isaiah 53:1. [u] Psalm 19:4. [v] Deut. 32:21l. [w] Isaiah 65:1. [x] Isaiah 65:2. [y] I Kings 19:10,14.

468

Greek Interlinear

Χριστὸς   εἰς   δικαιοσύνην   παντὶ   τῷ
Christ [is]   for   righteousness   to everyone

πιστεύοντι.   5 Μωϋσῆς γὰρ γράφει ὅτι
believing.   For Moses   writes[.]   -

τὴν δικαιοσύνην τὴν ἐκ νόμου ὁ ποιήσας
⁴the   ⁵righteousness   -   ⁶of   ⁷law   ¹The   ²doing

ἄνθρωπος ζήσεται ἐν αὐτῇ.   6 ἡ δὲ
³man   will live   by   it.   But the

ἐκ πίστεως δικαιοσύνη οὕτως λέγει·   μὴ
²of   ³faith   ¹righteousness   thus   says: not

εἴπῃς ἐν τῇ καρδίᾳ σου· τίς ἀναβήσεται
Say   in   the   heart   of thee: Who   will ascend

εἰς τὸν οὐρανόν; τοῦτ' ἔστιν Χριστὸν
into   -   heaven?   this   is   Christ

καταγαγεῖν· 7 ἤ· τίς καταβήσεται εἰς
to bring down;   or: Who   will descend   into

τὴν ἄβυσσον; τοῦτ' ἔστιν Χριστὸν ἐκ
the   abyss?   this   is   Christ   from

νεκρῶν ἀναγαγεῖν.   8 ἀλλὰ τί λέγει;
[the] dead   to bring up.   But   what   says it?

ἐγγύς σου τὸ ῥῆμά ἐστιν, ἐν τῷ στόματί
Near   thee   the   word   is,   in   the   mouth

σου καὶ ἐν τῇ καρδίᾳ σου· τοῦτ' ἔστιν
of thee   and   in   the   heart   of thee;   this   is

τὸ ῥῆμα τῆς πίστεως ὃ κηρύσσομεν.
the   word   -   of faith   which   we proclaim.

9 ὅτι ἐὰν ὁμολογήσῃς ἐν τῷ στόματί
Because   if   thou confessest   with   the   mouth

σου κύριον Ἰησοῦν, καὶ πιστεύσῃς ἐν
of thee   Lord   Jesus,   and   believest   in

τῇ καρδίᾳ σου ὅτι ὁ θεὸς αὐτὸν ἤγειρεν
the   heart   of thee   that   -   God   him   raised

ἐκ νεκρῶν, σωθήσῃ.   10 καρδίᾳ γὰρ
from   [the] dead,   thou wilt be saved;   for with heart

πιστεύεται εἰς δικαιοσύνην, στόματι δὲ
[one] believes   to   righteousness,   and with mouth

ὁμολογεῖται εἰς σωτηρίαν.   11 λέγει γὰρ
[one] confesses   to   salvation.   For says

ἡ γραφή· πᾶς ὁ πιστεύων ἐπ' αὐτῷ
the   scripture: Everyone   believing   on   him

οὐ καταισχυνθήσεται.   12 οὐ γάρ ἐστιν
will not be put to shame.   For there is no

διαστολὴ Ἰουδαίου τε καὶ Ἕλληνος. ὁ
difference   ²of Jew   ¹both   ³and   ⁴of Greek.*   the

γὰρ αὐτὸς κύριος πάντων, πλουτῶν εἰς
For   same   Lord   of all,   is rich   to

πάντας τοὺς ἐπικαλουμένους αὐτόν· 13 πᾶς
all   the [ones]   calling on   him;   ²everyone

γὰρ ὃς ἂν ἐπικαλέσηται τὸ ὄνομα κυρίου
¹for   whoever   calls on   the   name   of [the]
Lord

σωθήσεται.   14 Πῶς οὖν ἐπικαλέσωνται εἰς
will be saved.   How therefore   may they call on   in
[one]

ὃν οὐκ ἐπίστευσαν; πῶς δὲ πιστεύσωσιν
whom they believed not?   And how   may they believe

οὗ οὐκ ἤκουσαν; πῶς δὲ ἀκούσωσιν
of whom they heard not?   And how   may they hear

χωρὶς κηρύσσοντος; 15 πῶς δὲ κηρύξωσιν
without   [one] heralding?   And how   may they herald

ἐὰν μὴ ἀποσταλῶσιν; καθάπερ γέγραπται·
if   they are not sent?   As   it has been written:

ὡς ὡραῖοι οἱ πόδες τῶν εὐαγγελιζομένων
How beautiful   the   feet   of the [ones] announcing good

ἀγαθά. 16 ἀλλ' οὐ πάντες ὑπήκουσαν τῷ
good things.   But not   all   obeyed   the

εὐαγγελίῳ. Ἡσαΐας γὰρ λέγει· κύριε,
gospel.   For Esaias   says: Lord,

τίς ἐπίστευσεν τῇ ἀκοῇ ἡμῶν; 17 ἄρα
who   believed   the   hearing   of us?   Then

ἡ πίστις ἐξ ἀκοῆς, ἡ δὲ ἀκοὴ διὰ
-    faith [is] from   hearing,   and the   hearing through

ῥήματος Χριστοῦ. 18 ἀλλὰ λέγω, μὴ
a word   of Christ.   But   I say,   not

οὐκ ἤκουσαν; μενοῦν γε· εἰς πᾶσαν
did they not hear?   Nay   rather: To   all

τὴν γῆν ἐξῆλθεν ὁ φθόγγος αὐτῶν,
the   earth   went out   the   utterance   of them,

καὶ εἰς τὰ πέρατα τῆς οἰκουμένης τὰ
and   to   the   ends   of the inhabited earth the

ῥήματα αὐτῶν. 19 ἀλλὰ λέγω, μὴ Ἰσραὴλ
words   of them.   But   I say,   not   Israel

οὐκ ἔγνω; πρῶτος Μωϋσῆς λέγει· ἐγὼ
did not know?   First   Moses   says :   I

παραζηλώσω ὑμᾶς ἐπ' οὐκ ἔθνει, ἐπ'
will provoke to   you   on(by)   not   a nation, on(by)
jealousy

ἔθνει ἀσυνέτῳ παροργιῶ ὑμᾶς. 20 Ἡσαΐας
a nation unintelligent   I will anger   you.   Esaias

δὲ ἀποτολμᾷ καὶ λέγει· εὑρέθην τοῖς
But   is quite bold   and   says :   I was found   by the
[ones]

ἐμὲ μὴ ζητοῦσιν, ἐμφανὴς ἐγενόμην τοῖς
²me   ¹not   ³seeking,   manifest   I became   to the
[ones]

ἐμὲ μὴ ἐπερωτῶσιν. 21 πρὸς δὲ τὸν
²me   ¹not   ³inquiring [for].   But to   -

Ἰσραὴλ λέγει· ὅλην τὴν ἡμέραν ἐξεπέτασα
Israel   he says: All   the   day   I stretched out

τὰς χεῖράς μου πρὸς λαὸν ἀπειθοῦντα
the   hands   of me   to   a people   disobeying

καὶ ἀντιλέγοντα.
and   contradicting.

Chapter 11

Λέγω οὖν, μὴ ἀπώσατο ὁ θεὸς
I say   therefore,   ²did not put away   -   ¹God

τὸν λαὸν αὐτοῦ; μὴ γένοιτο· καὶ γὰρ
the   people   of him?   May it not be;   for even

ἐγὼ Ἰσραηλίτης εἰμί, ἐκ σπέρματος
I   an Israelite   am,   of   [the] seed

Ἀβραάμ, φυλῆς Βενιαμίν. 2 οὐκ ἀπώσατο
of Abraham,   of [the]   tribe   of Benjamin.   did not put away
tribe

ὁ θεὸς τὸν λαὸν αὐτοῦ ὃν προέγνω.
-    God   the   people   of him   whom he foreknew.

ἢ οὐκ οἴδατε ἐν Ἠλίᾳ τί λέγει ἡ
Or   know ye not   in   Elias   what   says   the

γραφή, ὡς ἐντυγχάνει τῷ θεῷ κατὰ τοῦ
scripture,   how   he supplicates   -   God   against   -

Ἰσραήλ; 3 κύριε, τοὺς προφήτας σου
Israel?   Lord,   the   prophets   of thee

ἀπέκτειναν, τὰ θυσιαστήριά σου κατέσκαψαν,
they killed,   the   altars   of thee   they dug down,

κἀγὼ ὑπελείφθην μόνος καὶ ζητοῦσιν τὴν
and I   was left behind   alone   and   they seek   the

ψυχήν μου. 4 ἀλλὰ τί λέγει αὐτῷ ὁ
life   of me.   But   what   says   to him   the

χρηματισμός; κατέλιπον ἐμαυτῷ ἑπτακισ-
[divine] response?   I reserved   to myself   seven

* That is, between these two classes.

469

King James Version

men, who have not bowed the knee to *the image of* Baal. 5 Even so then at this present time also there is a remnant according to the election of grace. 6And if by grace, then *is it* no more of works: otherwise grace is no more grace. But if *it be* of works, then is it no more grace: otherwise work is no more work. 7 What then? Israel hath not obtained that which he seeketh for; but the election hath obtained it, and the rest were blinded 8 (According as it is written, God hath given them the spirit of slumber, eyes that they should not see, and ears that they should not hear;) unto this day. 9And David saith, Let their table be made a snare, and a trap, and a stumblingblock, and a recompense unto them: 10 Let their eyes be darkened, that they may not see, and bow down their back alway. 11 I say then, Have they stumbled that they should fall? God forbid: but *rather* through their fall salvation *is come* unto the Gentiles, for to provoke them to jealousy. 12 Now if the fall of them *be* the riches of the world, and the diminishing of them the riches of the Gentiles; how much more their fulness? 13 For I speak to you Gentiles, inasmuch as I am the apostle of the Gentiles, I magnify mine office: 14 If by any means I may provoke to emulation *them which are* my flesh, and might save some of them. 15 For if the casting away of them *be* the reconciling of the world, what *shall* the receiving *of them be*, but life from the dead? 16 For if the firstfruit *be* holy, the lump *is* also *holy:* and if the root *be* holy, so *are* the branches. 17 And if some of the branches be broken off, and thou, being a wild olive tree, wert graffed in among them, and with them partakest of the root and fatness of the olive tree; 18 Boast not against the branches. But if thou boast, thou bearest not the root, but the root thee. 19 Thou wilt say then, The branches were broken off, that I might be graffed in. 20 Well; because of unbelief they were broken off, and thou standest by faith. Be not highminded, but fear: 21 For if God spared not the natural branches, *take heed* lest he also spare not thee. 22 Behold therefore the goodness and severity of God: on them which fell, severity; but toward thee, goodness, if thou continue in *his* goodness: otherwise thou also shalt be cut off. 23And they also, if they abide not still in unbelief, shall be graffed in: for God is able to graff them in again. 24 For if thou wert cut out of the olive tree which is wild by nature, and wert graffed contrary to nature into a good olive tree; how much more shall these, which be the natural *branches,* be graffed into their own olive tree? 25 For I would not, brethren, that ye should be ignorant of this mystery, lest ye should be wise in your own conceits, that blindness in part is happened to Israel, until the fulness of the Gentiles be come in. 26And so all Israel shall be saved: as it is written,

New International Version

sand who have not bowed the knee to Baal." [z] 5 So too, at the present time there is a remnant chosen by grace. 6And if by grace, then it is no longer by works; if it were, grace would no longer be grace.[a] 7 What then? What Israel sought so earnestly it did not obtain, but the elect did. The others became hardened, 8 as it is written:

> "God gave them a spirit of stupor,
>   eyes so that they could not see
>   and ears so that they could not hear,
>   to this very day." [b]

9And David says:

> "May their table become a snare and a trap,
>   a stumbling block and a retribution for
>   them.
> 10 "May their eyes be darkened so that they
>   cannot see,
>   and their backs be bent forever." [c]

Ingrafted branches

11 Again I ask, Did they stumble so as to fall beyond recovery? Not at all! Rather, because of their transgression, salvation has come to the Gentiles to make Israel envious. 12 But if their transgression means riches for the world, and their loss means riches for the Gentiles, how much greater riches will their fullness bring!

13 I am talking to you Gentiles. Inasmuch as I am the apostle to the Gentiles, I make much of my ministry 14 in the hope that I may somehow arouse my own people to envy and save some of them. 15 For if their rejection is the reconciliation of the world, what will their acceptance be, but life from the dead? 16 If the part of the dough offered as firstfruits is holy, then the whole batch is holy; if the root is holy, so are the branches.

17 If some of the branches have been broken off, and you, though a wild olive shoot, have been grafted in among the others and now share in the nourishing sap from the olive root, 18 do not boast over those branches. If you do, consider this: You do not support the root, but the root supports you. 19 You will say then, "Branches were broken off so that I could be grafted in." 20 Granted. But they were broken off because of unbelief, and you stand by faith. Do not be arrogant, but be afraid. 21 For if God did not spare the natural branches, he will not spare you either.

22 Consider therefore the kindness and sternness of God: sternness to those who fell, but kindness to you, provided that you continue in his kindness. Otherwise, you also will be cut off. 23And if they do not persist in unbelief, they will be grafted in, for God is able to graft them in again. 24After all, if you were cut out of an olive tree that is wild by nature, and contrary to nature were grafted into a cultivated olive tree, how much more readily will these, the natural branches, be grafted into their own olive tree?

All Israel will be saved

25 I do not want you to be ignorant of this mystery, brothers, so that you may not be conceited: Israel has experienced a hardening in part until the full number of the Gentiles has come in. 26And so all Israel will be saved, as it is written:

[z] I Kings 19:18 [a] Some MSS add *But if by works, then it is no longer grace; if it were, work would no longer be work.* [b] Deut. 29:4; Isaiah 29:10 [c] Psalm 69:22,23.

Greek Interlinear

χιλίους ἄνδρας, οἵτινες οὐκ ἔκαμψαν γόνυ
thousands men, who bowed not knee

τῇ Βάαλ. 5 οὕτως οὖν καὶ ἐν τῷ νῦν
- to Baal. So therefore also in the present

καιρῷ λεῖμμα κατ᾽ ἐκλογὴν χάριτος
time a remnant according to a choice of grace

γέγονεν· 6 εἰ δὲ χάριτι, οὐκέτι ἐξ ἔργων,
has become; and if by grace, no more of works,

ἐπεὶ ἡ χάρις οὐκέτι γίνεται χάρις. 7 Τί
since - grace no more becomes grace. What

οὖν; ὃ ἐπιζητεῖ Ἰσραήλ, τοῦτο οὐκ
there- What ²seeks after ¹Israel, this not
fore?

ἐπέτυχεν, ἡ δὲ ἐκλογὴ ἐπέτυχεν· οἱ δὲ
he obtained, the choice obtained [it]; and the

λοιποὶ ἐπωρώθησαν, 8 καθάπερ γέγραπται·
rest were hardened, as it has been written·

ἔδωκεν αὐτοῖς ὁ θεὸς πνεῦμα κατανύξεως,
Gave to them - God a spirit of torpor,

ὀφθαλμοὺς τοῦ μὴ βλέπειν καὶ ὦτα
eyes - not to see[d] and ears

τοῦ μὴ ἀκούειν, ἕως τῆς σήμερον ἡμέρας
- not to hear,[d] until the present† day.

9 καὶ Δαυὶδ λέγει· γενηθήτω ἡ τράπεζα
And David says: Let become the table

αὐτῶν εἰς παγίδα καὶ εἰς θήραν καὶ
of them for a snare and for a net and

εἰς σκάνδαλον καὶ εἰς ἀνταπόδομα αὐτοῖς,
for an offence and for a recompence to them,

10 σκοτισθήτωσαν οἱ ὀφθαλμοὶ αὐτῶν τοῦ
let be darkened the eyes of them -

μὴ βλέπειν, καὶ τὸν νῶτον αὐτῶν διὰ
not to see[d] and the back of them al-

παντὸς σύγκαμψον.
ways bending.

11 Λέγω οὖν, μὴ ἔπταισαν ἵνα πέσωσιν;
I say therefore, did they not in order they might
stumble that fall?

μὴ γένοιτο· ἀλλὰ τῷ αὐτῶν παραπτώματι
May it not be; but by the ²of them ¹trespass

ἡ σωτηρία τοῖς ἔθνεσιν, εἰς τὸ παραζηλῶσαι
- salvation to the nations, for the to provoke to
[came] jealousy

αὐτούς. 12 εἰ δὲ τὸ παράπτωμα αὐτῶν
them. But if the trespass of them

πλοῦτος κόσμου καὶ τὸ ἥττημα αὐτῶν
[is] [the] of [the] and the defect of them
riches world

πλοῦτος ἐθνῶν, πόσῳ μᾶλλον τὸ πλήρωμα
[is] [the] of [the] by how more the fulness
riches nations, much

αὐτῶν. 13 Ὑμῖν δὲ λέγω τοῖς ἔθνεσιν.
of them. But to you ¹I say[,] ¹the ²nations.

ἐφ᾽ ὅσον μὲν οὖν εἰμι ἐγὼ ἐθνῶν ἀπόστο-
Forasmuch in- there- ²am ¹I ⁴of ²an apos-
as deed fore nations

λος, τὴν διακονίαν μου δοξάζω, 14 εἴ πως
tle, the ministry of me I glorify, if somehow

παραζηλώσω μου τὴν σάρκα καὶ σώσω
I may provoke to of me the flesh and may save
jealousy

τινὰς ἐξ αὐτῶν. 15 εἰ γὰρ ἡ ἀποβολὴ
some of them. For if the casting away

αὐτῶν καταλλαγὴ κόσμου, τίς ἡ πρόσλημψις
of them [is] [the] of [the] what the reception
reconciliation world,

εἰ μὴ ζωὴ ἐκ νεκρῶν; 16 εἰ δὲ ἡ
if not life from [the] dead? And if the

ἀπαρχὴ ἁγία, καὶ τὸ φύραμα· καὶ εἰ
firstfruit [is] holy, also the lump; and if

ἡ ῥίζα ἁγία, καὶ οἱ κλάδοι. 17 Εἰ δὲ
the root [is] holy, also the branches. But if

τινες τῶν κλάδων ἐξεκλάσθησαν, σὺ δὲ
some of the branches were broken off, and thou

ἀγριέλαιος ὢν ἐνεκεντρίσθης ἐν αὐτοῖς
¹a wild olive ¹being wast grafted in among them

καὶ συγκοινωνὸς τῆς ῥίζης τῆς πιότητος
and ²a partaker ¹of the ⁴root* ³of the ⁵fatness

τῆς ἐλαίας ἐγένου, 18 μὴ κατακαυχῶ
⁷of the ⁸olive-tree ¹didst become, boast not against

τῶν κλάδων· εἰ δὲ κατακαυχᾶσαι, οὐ
of the branches; but if thou boastest, not

σὺ τὴν ῥίζαν βαστάζεις ἀλλὰ ἡ ῥίζα σέ.
thou the root bearest but the root thee.

19 ἐρεῖς οὖν· ἐξεκλάσθησαν κλάδοι ἵνα
Thou wilt therefore· ²Were broken off ¹branches in order
say that

ἐγὼ ἐγκεντρισθῶ. 20 καλῶς· τῇ ἀπιστίᾳ
I might be grafted in. Well: - for unbelief

ἐξεκλάσθησαν, σὺ δὲ τῇ πίστει ἕστηκας.
they were broken off, and thou - by faith standest.

μὴ ὑψηλὰ φρόνει, ἀλλὰ φοβοῦ· 21 εἰ
²Not ³high things ¹mind, but fear; ¹if

γὰρ ὁ θεὸς τῶν κατὰ φύσιν κλάδων
¹for ²God ³the ⁷according to ⁴nature ⁶branches

οὐκ ἐφείσατο, οὐδὲ σοῦ φείσεται. 22 ἴδε
⁵spared not, neither thee he will spare. See

οὖν χρηστότητα καὶ ἀποτομίαν θεοῦ· ἐπὶ
therefore [the] kindness and [the] severity of God: ³on

μὲν τοὺς πεσόντας ἀποτομία, ἐπὶ δὲ
¹on one, the having fallen severity, ²on ¹on the
hand [ones] other

σὲ χρηστότης θεοῦ, ἐὰν ἐπιμένῃς τῇ
thee [the] kindness of God, if thou continuest in the
(his)

χρηστότητι, ἐπεὶ καὶ σὺ ἐκκοπήσῃ.
kindness, since also thou wilt be cut off.

23 κἀκεῖνοι δέ, ἐὰν μὴ ἐπιμένωσιν τῇ
And those also, if they continue not -

ἀπιστίᾳ, ἐγκεντρισθήσονται· δυνατὸς γὰρ
in unbelief, will be grafted in; for ²able

ἐστιν ὁ θεὸς πάλιν ἐγκεντρίσαι αὐτούς.
²is - ¹God ³again ⁴to graft ⁵in ⁶them.

24 εἰ γὰρ σὺ ἐκ τῆς κατὰ φύσιν ἐξεκόπης
For if thou ²out ³the ⁵according ⁴nature ¹wast cut
of to out

ἀγριελαίου καὶ παρὰ φύσιν ἐνεκεντρίσθης
⁶wild olive and against nature wast grafted in

εἰς καλλιέλαιον, πόσῳ μᾶλλον οὗτοι οἱ
into a cultivated by how more these the
olive, much [ones]

κατὰ φύσιν ἐγκεντρισθήσονται τῇ ἰδίᾳ
according to nature will be grafted in the(ir) own

ἐλαίᾳ. 25 Οὐ γὰρ θέλω ὑμᾶς ἀγνοεῖν,
olive-tree. For I wish not you to be ignorant,

ἀδελφοί, τὸ μυστήριον τοῦτο, ἵνα μὴ
brothers, [of] this mystery, lest

ἦτε ἐν ἑαυτοῖς φρόνιμοι, ὅτι πώρωσις
ye be in yourselves wise, that hardness

ἀπὸ μέρους τῷ Ἰσραὴλ γέγονεν ἄχρι οὗ
from(in) part - to Israel has happened until

τὸ πλήρωμα τῶν ἐθνῶν εἰσέλθῃ, 26 καὶ
the fulness of the nations comes in, and

οὕτως πᾶς Ἰσραὴλ σωθήσεται, καθὼς
so all Israel will be saved, as

---

* Some MSS insert καί (and) here; as it is, the two nouns in the
genitive must be in apposition; cf. Col. 1. 18, 2. 2; John 8. 44.

King James Version

There shall come out of Sion the Deliverer, and shall turn away ungodliness from Jacob: 27 For this *is* my covenant unto them, when I shall take away their sins. 28As concerning the gospel, *they are* enemies for your sakes: but as touching the election, *they are* beloved for the fathers' sakes. 29 For the gifts and calling of God *are* without repentance. 30 For as ye in times past have not believed God, yet have now obtained mercy through their unbelief: 31 Even so have these also now not believed, that through your mercy they also may obtain mercy. 32 For God hath concluded them all in unbelief, that he might have mercy upon all. 33 O the depth of the riches both of the wisdom and knowledge of God! how unsearchable *are* his judgments, and his ways past finding out! 34 For who hath known the mind of the Lord? or who hath been his counsellor? 35 Or who hath first given to him, and it shall be recompensed unto him again? 36 For of him, and through him, and to him, *are* all things: to whom *be* glory for ever. Amen.

12 I beseech you therefore, brethren, by the mercies of God, that ye present your bodies a living sacrifice, holy, acceptable unto God, *which is* your reasonable service. 2And be not conformed to this world: but be ye transformed by the renewing of your mind, that ye may prove what *is* that good, and acceptable, and perfect will of God. 3 For I say, through the grace given unto me, to every man that is among you, not to think *of himself* more highly than he ought to think; but to think soberly, according as God hath dealt to every man the measure of faith. 4 For as we have many members in one body, and all members have not the same office: 5 So we, *being* many, are one body in Christ, and every one members one of another. 6 Having then gifts differing according to the grace that is given to us, whether prophecy, *let us prophesy* according to the proportion of faith; 7 Or ministry, *let us wait* on *our* ministering; or he that teacheth, on teaching; 8 Or he that exhorteth, on exhortation: he that giveth, *let him do it* with simplicity; he that ruleth, with diligence; he that sheweth mercy, with cheerfulness. 9 *Let* love be without dissimulation. Abhor that which is evil; cleave to that which is good. 10 *Be* kindly affectioned one to another with brotherly love; in honour preferring one another; 11 Not slothful in business; fervent in spirit; serving the Lord; 12 Rejoicing in hope; patient in tribulation; con-

New International Version

"The deliverer will come from Zion;
　he will turn godlessness away from Jacob.
27And this is*d* my covenant with them
　when I take away their sins." *e*
28 As far as the gospel is concerned, they are enemies on your account; but as far as election is concerned, they are loved on account of the patriarchs, 29 for God's gifts and his call are irrevocable. 30 Just as you who were at one time disobedient to God have now received mercy as a result of their disobedience, 31 so they too, as a result of God's mercy to you, have now become disobedient in order that they too may now receive mercy. 32 For God has bound all men over to disobedience so that he may have mercy on them all.

Doxology

33 Oh the depth of the riches, the wisdom
　and the knowledge of God!
How unsearchable his judgments,
　and his paths beyond tracing out!
34 "Who has known the mind of the Lord?
　Or who has been his adviser?" *f*
35 "Who has ever given to God,
　that God should repay him?" *g*
36 For from him and through him and to him
　are all things.
To him be the glory forever! Amen.

Living sacrifices

12 Therefore, I urge you, brothers, in view of God's mercy, to offer yourselves as living sacrifices, holy and pleasing to God—which is your spiritual worship. 2 Do not conform any longer to the pattern of this world, but be transformed by the renewing of your mind. Then you will be able to test and approve what God's will is—his good, pleasing and perfect will.

3 For by the grace given to me I say to every one of you: Do not think of yourself more highly than you ought, but rather think of yourself with sober judgment, in accordance with the measure of faith God has given you. 4 Just as each of us has one body with many members, and these members do not all have the same function, 5 so in Christ we who are many form one body, and each member belongs to all the others. 6 We have different gifts, according to the grace given us. If a man's gift is prophesying, let him use it in proportion to his faith. 7 If it is serving, let him serve; if it is teaching, let him teach; 8 if it is encouraging, let him encourage; if it is contributing to the needs of others, let him give generously; if it is leadership, let him govern diligently; if it is showing mercy, let him do it cheerfully.

Love

9 Love must be sincere. Hate what is evil; cling to what is good. 10 Be devoted to one another in brotherly love. Honor one another above yourselves. 11 Never be lacking in zeal, but keep your spiritual fervor, serving the Lord. 12 Be joyful in hope, patient in affliction, faithful in

[*d*] Or *will be.* [*e*] Isaiah 59:20,21; 27:9. [*f*] Isaiah 40:13; Jer. 23:18. [*g*] Job 41:11.

Greek Interlinear

γέγραπται· ἥξει ἐκ Σιὼν ὁ ῥυόμενος,
it has been ²will ⁴out ⁵Sion ¹The ³delivering,
written: come of [one]

ἀποστρέψει ἀσεβείας ἀπὸ Ἰακώβ. 27 καὶ
he will turn away impiety from Jacob. And

αὕτη αὐτοῖς ἡ παρ' ἐμοῦ διαθήκη, ὅταν
this [is] ⁵with them ¹the ³from ⁴me ²covenant, when

ἀφέλωμαι τὰς ἁμαρτίας αὐτῶν. 28 κατὰ
I take away the sins of them. ⁸According to

μὲν τὸ εὐαγγέλιον ἐχθροὶ δι' ὑμᾶς,
¹on one the gospel enemies because you,
hand of

κατὰ δὲ τὴν ἐκλογὴν ἀγαπητοὶ διὰ
²accord- ¹on the the choice beloved because
ing to other of

τοὺς πατέρας· 29 ἀμεταμέλητα γὰρ τὰ
the fathers; for unrepented the

χαρίσματα καὶ ἡ κλῆσις τοῦ θεοῦ.
free gifts and the calling - of God.

30 ὥσπερ γὰρ ὑμεῖς ποτε ἠπειθήσατε
For as ye then disobeyed

τῷ θεῷ, νῦν δὲ ἠλεήθητε τῇ τούτων
- God, but now ye obtained mercy ¹by the ²of these

ἀπειθείᾳ, 31 οὕτως καὶ οὗτοι νῦν ἠπείθησαν
³disobedience, so also these now disobeyed

τῷ ὑμετέρῳ ἐλέει ἵνα καὶ αὐτοὶ νῦν
- ²by your ³mercy ¹in order also they now
that

ἐλεηθῶσιν. 32 συνέκλεισεν γὰρ ὁ θεὸς
may obtain mercy. For ²shut up - ¹God

τοὺς πάντας εἰς ἀπείθειαν ἵνα τοὺς
- all in disobedience in order that -

πάντας ἐλεήσῃ.
to all he may show mercy.

33 Ὦ βάθος πλούτου καὶ σοφίας καὶ
O [the] depth of [the] riches and of [the] wisdom and

γνώσεως θεοῦ· ὡς ἀνεξερεύνητα τὰ κρίματα
of [the] of God; how inscrutable the judgments
knowledge

αὐτοῦ καὶ ἀνεξιχνίαστοι αἱ ὁδοὶ αὐτοῦ.
of him and unsearchable the ways of him.

34 τίς γὰρ ἔγνω νοῦν κυρίου; ἢ τίς
For who knew [the] mind of [the] Lord? or who

σύμβουλος αὐτοῦ ἐγένετο; 35 ἢ τίς
counsellor of him became? or who

προέδωκεν αὐτῷ, καὶ ἀνταποδοθήσεται
previously gave to him, and it will be repaid

αὐτῷ; 36 ὅτι ἐξ αὐτοῦ καὶ δι' αὐτοῦ
to him? Because of him and through him

καὶ εἰς αὐτὸν τὰ πάντα· αὐτῷ ἡ δόξα
and to him - all things; to him the glory

εἰς τοὺς αἰῶνας· ἀμήν.
unto the ages: Amen.

Chapter 12

Παρακαλῶ οὖν ὑμᾶς, ἀδελφοί, διὰ
I beseech therefore you, brothers, through

τῶν οἰκτιρμῶν τοῦ θεοῦ, παραστῆσαι τὰ
the compassions - of God, to present the

σώματα ὑμῶν θυσίαν ζῶσαν ἁγίαν τῷ
bodies of you sacrifice a living holy -

θεῷ εὐάρεστον, τὴν λογικὴν λατρείαν
to God well-pleasing, the reasonable service

ὑμῶν· 2 καὶ μὴ συσχηματίζεσθε τῷ αἰῶνι
of you; and be ye not conformed - age

τούτῳ, ἀλλὰ μεταμορφοῦσθε τῇ ἀνακαινώσει
to this, but be ye transformed by the renewing

τοῦ νοός, εἰς τὸ δοκιμάζειν ὑμᾶς τί τὸ
of the mind, for the to prove you what the
=so that ye may prove

θέλημα τοῦ θεοῦ, τὸ ἀγαθὸν καὶ εὐάρεστον
will - of God, the good and well-pleasing

καὶ τέλειον.
and perfect.

3 Λέγω γὰρ διὰ τῆς χάριτος τῆς
For I say through the grace -

δοθείσης μοι παντὶ τῷ ὄντι ἐν ὑμῖν,
given to me to everyone being among you,

μὴ ὑπερφρονεῖν παρ' ὃ δεῖ φρονεῖν,
not to have high beyond what it to think,
thoughts behoves

ἀλλὰ φρονεῖν εἰς τὸ σωφρονεῖν, ἑκάστῳ
but to think to the to be sober-minded, ⁴to each

ὡς ὁ θεὸς ἐμέρισεν μέτρον πίστεως.
¹as - ²God ³divided a measure of faith.

4 καθάπερ γὰρ ἐν ἑνὶ σώματι πολλὰ
For as in one body many

μέλη ἔχομεν, τὰ δὲ μέλη πάντα οὐ τὴν
members we have, but ²the ³members ¹all ⁴not ⁵the

αὐτὴν ἔχει πρᾶξιν, 5 οὕτως οἱ πολλοὶ
⁶same ⁷has(ve) ⁸action, so the many

ἓν σῶμά ἐσμεν ἐν Χριστῷ, τὸ δὲ καθ'
one body we are in Christ, - and each

εἰς ἀλλήλων μέλη. 6 ἔχοντες δὲ χαρίσματα
one ²of one ¹members. And having gifts
another

κατὰ τὴν χάριν τὴν δοθεῖσαν ἡμῖν διάφορα,
²accord- ³the ⁴grace - ⁵given ⁶to us ¹differing,
ing to

εἴτε προφητείαν, κατὰ τὴν ἀναλογίαν τῆς
whether prophecy, according to the proportion of the

πίστεως· 7 εἴτε διακονίαν, ἐν τῇ διακονίᾳ·
faith; or ministry, in the ministry;

εἴτε ὁ διδάσκων, ἐν τῇ διδασκαλίᾳ·
or the [one] teaching, in the teaching;

8 εἴτε ὁ παρακαλῶν, ἐν τῇ παρακλήσει·
or the [one] exhorting, in the exhortation;

ὁ μεταδιδοὺς ἐν ἁπλότητι, ὁ προϊστάμενος
the [one] sharing in simplicity, the [one] taking the lead

ἐν σπουδῇ, ὁ ἐλεῶν ἐν ἱλαρότητι. 9 ἡ
in diligence, the showing in cheerfulness. -
[one] mercy

ἀγάπη ἀνυπόκριτος. ἀποστυγοῦντες τὸ
[Let] love [be] unassumed. Shrinking from the

πονηρόν, κολλώμενοι τῷ ἀγαθῷ· 10 τῇ
evil, cleaving to the good; -

φιλαδελφίᾳ εἰς ἀλλήλους φιλόστοργοι, τῇ
in brotherly love to one another loving warmly, -

τιμῇ ἀλλήλους προηγούμενοι, 11 τῇ σπουδῇ
in one another preferring, - in zeal
honour

μὴ ὀκνηροί, τῷ πνεύματι ζέοντες, τῷ
not slothful, - in spirit burning, the

κυρίῳ δουλεύοντες, 12 τῇ ἐλπίδι χαίροντες,
Lord serving, - in hope rejoicing,

τῇ θλίψει ὑπομένοντες, τῇ προσευχῇ
- in affliction showing endurance, - in prayer

473

King James Version

tinuing instant in prayer; 13 Distributing to the necessity of saints; given to hospitality. 14 Bless them which persecute you: bless, and curse not. 15 Rejoice with them that do rejoice, and weep with them that weep. 16 *Be* of the same mind one toward another. Mind not high things, but condescend to men of low estate. Be not wise in your own conceits. 17 Recompense to no man evil for evil. Provide things honest in the sight of all men. 18 If it be possible, as much as lieth in you, live peaceably with all men. 19 Dearly beloved, avenge not yourselves, but *rather* give place unto wrath: for it is written, Vengeance *is* mine; I will repay, saith the Lord. 20 Therefore if thine enemy hunger, feed him; if he thirst, give him drink: for in so doing thou shalt heap coals of fire on his head. 21 Be not overcome of evil, but overcome evil with good.

13 Let every soul be subject unto the higher powers. For there is no power but of God: the powers that be are ordained of God. 2 Whosoever therefore resisteth the power, resisteth the ordinance of God: and they that resist shall receive to themselves damnation. 3 For rulers are not a terror to good works, but to the evil. Wilt thou then not be afraid of the power? do that which is good, and thou shalt have praise of the same: 4 For he is the minister of God to thee for good. But if thou do that which is evil, be afraid; for he beareth not the sword in vain: for he is the minister of God, a revenger to *execute* wrath upon him that doeth evil. 5 Wherefore *ye* must needs be subject, not only for wrath, but also for conscience' sake. 6 For, for this cause pay ye tribute also: for they are God's ministers, attending continually upon this very thing. 7 Render therefore to all their dues: tribute to whom tribute *is due;* custom to whom custom; fear to whom fear; honour to whom honour. 8 Owe no man any thing, but to love one another: for he that loveth another hath fulfilled the law. 9 For this, Thou shalt not commit adultery, Thou shalt not kill, Thou shalt not steal, Thou shalt not bear false witness, Thou shalt not covet; and if *there be* any other commandment, it is briefly comprehended in this saying, namely, Thou shalt love thy neighbour as thyself. 10 Love worketh no ill to his neighbour: therefore love *is* the fulfilling of the law. 11 And that, knowing the time, that now *it is* high time to awake out of sleep: for now *is* our salvation nearer than when we believed. 12 The night is far spent, the day is at hand: let us therefore cast off the works of darkness,

New International Version

prayer. 13 Share with God's people who are in need. Practice hospitality.

14 Bless those who persecute you; bless and do not curse. 15 Rejoice with those who rejoice; mourn with those who mourn. 16 Live in harmony with one another. Don't be proud, but be willing to associate with people of low position.[h] Don't be conceited.

17 Do not repay anyone evil for evil. Be careful to do what is right in the sight of everybody. 18 If it is possible, as far as it depends on you, live at peace with everyone. 19 Do not take revenge, my friends, but leave room for God's wrath, for it is written: "It is mine to avenge, I will repay,"[i] says the Lord. 20 On the contrary: "If your enemy is hungry, feed him; if he is thirsty, give him something to drink. In doing this, you will heap burning coals on his head."[j] 21 Do not be overcome by evil, but overcome evil with good.

Submission to the authorities

13 Everyone must submit himself to the governing authorities, for there is no authority except that which God has established. The authorities that exist have been established by God. 2 Consequently, he who rebels against the authority is rebelling against what God has instituted, and those who do so will bring judgment on themselves. 3 For rulers hold no terror for those who do right, but for those who do wrong. Do you want to be free from fear of the one in authority? Then do what is right and he will commend you. 4 For he is God's servant to do you good. But if you do wrong, be afraid, for he does not bear the sword for nothing. He is God's servant, an agent of justice to bring punishment on the wrongdoer. 5 Therefore, it is necessary to submit to the authorities, not only because of possible punishment but also because of conscience.

6 This is also why you pay taxes, for the authorities are God's servants, who give their full time to governing. 7 Give everyone what you owe him: If you owe taxes, pay taxes; if revenue, then revenue; if respect, then respect; if honor, then honor.

Love, for the day is near

8 Let no debt remain outstanding, except the continuing debt to love one another, for he who loves his fellow man has fulfilled the law. 9 The commandments, "Do not commit adultery," "Do not murder," "Do not steal," "Do not covet,"[k] and whatever other commandment there may be, are summed up in this one rule: "Love your neighbor as yourself."[l] 10 Love does no harm to its neighbor. Therefore love is the fulfillment of the law.

11 And do this, understanding the present time. The hour has come for you to wake up from your slumber, because our salvation is nearer now than when we first believed. 12 The night is nearly over; the day is almost here. So let us put aside the deeds of darkness and put

[h] Or *willing to do menial work.* [i] Deut. 32:35. [j] Prov. 25:21,22. [k] Exodus 20:13-15,17; Deut. 5:17-19,21. [l] Lev. 19:18.

Greek Interlinear

προσκαρτεροῦντες, **13** ταῖς χρείαις τῶν
steadfastly continuing,   to the   needs   of the

ἁγίων κοινωνοῦντες, τὴν φιλοξενίαν
saints   imparting,   -   hospitality

διώκοντες. **14** εὐλογεῖτε τοὺς διώκοντας,
pursuing.   Bless ye   the [ones] persecuting,

εὐλογεῖτε καὶ μὴ καταρᾶσθε. **15** χαίρειν
bless   and   do not curse.   To rejoice

μετὰ χαιρόντων, κλαίειν μετὰ κλαιόντων.
with rejoicing [ones], to weep with weeping [ones].

16 τὸ αὐτὸ εἰς ἀλλήλους φρονοῦντες· μὴ
The same thing toward one another minding;   not

τὰ ὑψηλὰ φρονοῦντες ἀλλὰ τοῖς ταπεινοῖς
the high things minding   but to the   humble

συναπαγόμενοι. μὴ γίνεσθε φρόνιμοι παρ'
condescending. Become not   wise   with

ἑαυτοῖς. **17** μηδενὶ κακὸν ἀντὶ κακοῦ
yourselves. To no one   evil instead of evil

ἀποδιδόντες· προνοούμενοι καλὰ ἐνώπιον
returning;   ;roviding for good things before

πάντων ἀνθρώπων· **18** εἰ δυνατόν, τὸ ἐξ
all   men;   if possible, as far as it

ὑμῶν, μετὰ πάντων ἀνθρώπων εἰρηνεύοντες·
rests with with all   men   seeking peace;
you,†

19 μὴ ἑαυτοὺς ἐκδικοῦντες, ἀγαπητοί, ἀλλὰ
not yourselves avenging, beloved, but

δότε τόπον τῇ ὀργῇ· γέγραπται γάρ·
give place - to wrath; for it has been written:

ἐμοὶ ἐκδίκησις, ἐγὼ ἀνταποδώσω, λέγει
To me vengeance,ᵉ   I   will repay,   says
= Vengeance is mine,

κύριος. **20** ἀλλὰ ἐὰν πεινᾷ ὁ ἐχθρός
[the] Lord.   But if hungers the enemy

σου, ψώμιζε αὐτόν· ἐὰν διψᾷ, πότιζε
of thee, feed him;   if he thirsts, give drink

αὐτόν· τοῦτο γὰρ ποιῶν ἄνθρακας πυρὸς
him;   for this doing   coals   of fire

σωρεύσεις ἐπὶ τὴν κεφαλὴν αὐτοῦ. **21** μὴ
thou wilt heap on the   head   of him.   not

νικῶ ὑπὸ τοῦ κακοῦ, ἀλλὰ νίκα
Be conquered by the   evil,   but   conquer

Chapter 13

ἐν τῷ ἀγαθῷ τὸ κακόν. **13** Πᾶσα
by the good   the evil.   Every

ψυχὴ ἐξουσίαις ὑπερεχούσαις ὑποτασσέσθω.
soul authorities to superior let be subject.

οὐ γὰρ ἔστιν ἐξουσία εἰ μὴ
For there is no authority   except

ὑπὸ θεοῦ, αἱ δὲ οὖσαι ὑπὸ θεοῦ
by God, and the existing [ones] by God

τεταγμέναι εἰσίν. **2** ὥστε ὁ ἀντιτασσόμενος
having been are.   So the [one] resisting
ordained

τῇ ἐξουσίᾳ τῇ τοῦ θεοῦ διαταγῇ ἀνθέστη-
the authority the - of God ordinance has op-

κεν· οἱ δὲ ἀνθεστηκότες ἑαυτοῖς κρίμα
posed; and the [ones] having opposed to themselves judgment

λήμψονται. **3** οἱ γὰρ ἄρχοντες οὐκ εἰσὶν
will receive.   For the rulers are not

φόβος τῷ ἀγαθῷ ἔργῳ ἀλλὰ τῷ κακῷ.
a fear to the good   work   but to the evil.

θέλεις δὲ μὴ φοβεῖσθαι τὴν ἐξουσίαν;
And wishest thou not to fear the authority?

τὸ ἀγαθὸν ποίει, καὶ ἕξεις ἔπαινον ἐξ
the good   do,   and thou wilt praise from
have

αὐτῆς· **4** θεοῦ γὰρ διάκονός ἐστιν σοί
it;   for of God a minister he is to thee

εἰς τὸ ἀγαθόν. ἐὰν δὲ τὸ κακὸν ποιῇς,
for the good.   But if the evil thou doest,

φοβοῦ· οὐ γὰρ εἰκῇ τὴν μάχαιραν φορεῖ·
fear;   for not in vain the sword he bears;

θεοῦ γὰρ διάκονός ἐστιν ἔκδικος εἰς
for of God a minister he is an avenger for

ὀργὴν τῷ τὸ κακὸν πράσσοντι. **5** διὸ
wrath to the [one] the evil practising.   Wherefore

ἀνάγκη ὑποτάσσεσθαι, οὐ μόνον διὰ τὴν
it is necessary to be subject, not only because of -

ὀργὴν ἀλλὰ καὶ διὰ τὴν συνείδησιν.
wrath but also because of - conscience.

6 διὰ τοῦτο γὰρ καὶ φόρους τελεῖτε·
For therefore   also   taxes   pay ye;

λειτουργοὶ γὰρ θεοῦ εἰσιν εἰς αὐτὸ τοῦτο
for ministers of God they are for this very thing

προσκαρτεροῦντες. **7** ἀπόδοτε πᾶσιν τὰς
attending constantly.   Render to all men the

ὀφειλάς, τῷ τὸν φόρον τὸν φόρον,
dues,   to the [one] the tax   the tax,

τῷ τὸ τέλος τὸ τέλος, τῷ τὸν φόβον
to the the tribute the tribute, to the [one] the fear
[one]

τὸν φόβον, τῷ τὴν τιμὴν τὴν τιμήν.
the fear, to the [one] the honour the honour.

8 Μηδενὶ μηδὲν ὀφείλετε, εἰ μὴ τὸ
To no one no(any)thing owe ye, except the

ἀλλήλους ἀγαπᾶν· ὁ γὰρ ἀγαπῶν τὸν
one another to love; for the [one] loving the

ἕτερον νόμον πεπλήρωκεν. **9** τὸ γὰρ
other law has fulfilled.   For

οὐ μοιχεύσεις, οὐ φονεύσεις, οὐ κλέψεις,
Thou shalt not Thou shalt not kill, Thou shalt not
commit adultery,   steal,

οὐκ ἐπιθυμήσεις, καὶ εἴ τις ἑτέρα ἐντολή,
Thou shalt not covet, and if any other command-
[there is]   ment,

ἐν τῷ λόγῳ τούτῳ ἀνακεφαλαιοῦται, [ἐν
in this word   it is summned up, in

τῷ]· ἀγαπήσεις τὸν πλησίον σου ὡς
- : Thou shalt love the neighbour of thee as

σεαυτόν. **10** ἡ ἀγάπη τῷ πλησίον κακὸν
thyself.   - Love to the neighbour evil
(one's)

οὐκ ἐργάζεται· πλήρωμα οὖν νόμου ἡ
works not;   [is] fulfilment therefore of law -

ἀγάπη. **11** Καὶ τοῦτο εἰδότες τὸν καιρόν,
love.   And this[,] knowing the time,

ὅτι ὥρα ἤδη ὑμᾶς ἐξ ὕπνου ἐγερθῆναι·
that hour now you out of sleep to be raised;ᵇ
= it is now an hour for you to be raised out of sleep;

νῦν γὰρ ἐγγύτερον ἡμῶν ἡ σωτηρία
for now nearer   [is] of us the salvation

ἢ ὅτε ἐπιστεύσαμεν. **12** ἡ νὺξ προέκοψεν,
than when we believed.   The night advanced,

ἡ δὲ ἡμέρα ἤγγικεν. ἀποθώμεθα οὖν
and the day has drawn near. Let us cast off therefore

τὰ ἔργα τοῦ σκότους, ἐνδυσώμεθα δὲ
the works of the darkness, and let us put on

---

* The phrase between the commas is elliptical; understand—
to the [one demanding] the tax [render] the tax. So of the
following phrases.

King James Version

and let us put on the armour of light. 13 Let us walk honestly, as in the day; not in rioting and drunkenness, not in chambering and wantonness, not in strife and envying: 14 But put ye on the Lord Jesus Christ, and make not provision for the flesh, to *fulfil* the lusts *thereof.*

14 Him that is weak in the faith receive ye, *but* not to doubtful disputations. 2 For one believeth that he may eat all things: another, who is weak, eateth herbs. 3 Let not him that eateth despise him that eateth not; and let not him which eateth not judge him that eateth: for God hath received him. 4 Who art thou that judgest another man's servant? to his own master he standeth or falleth; yea, he shall be holden up: for God is able to make him stand. 5 One man esteemeth one day above another: another esteemeth every day *alike.* Let every man be fully persuaded in his own mind. 6 He that regardeth the day, regardeth *it* unto the Lord; and he that regardeth not the day, to the Lord he doth not regard *it.* He that eateth, eateth to the Lord, for he giveth God thanks; and he that eateth not, to the Lord he eateth not, and giveth God thanks. 7 For none of us liveth to himself, and no man dieth to himself. 8 For whether we live, we live unto the Lord; and whether we die, we die unto the Lord: whether we live therefore, or die, we are the Lord's. 9 For to this end Christ both died, and rose, and revived, that he might be Lord both of the dead and living. 10 But why dost thou judge thy brother? or why dost thou set at nought thy brother? for we shall all stand before the judgment seat of Christ. 11 For it is written, *As* I live, saith the Lord, every knee shall bow to me, and every tongue shall confess to God. 12 So then every one of us shall give account of himself to God. 13 Let us not therefore judge one another any more: but judge this rather, that no man put a stumblingblock or an occasion to fall in *his* brother's way. 14 I know, and am persuaded by the Lord Jesus, that *there is* nothing unclean of itself: but to him that esteemeth any thing to be unclean, to him *it is* unclean. 15 But if thy brother be grieved with *thy* meat, now walkest thou not charitably. Destroy not him with thy meat, for whom Christ died. 16 Let not then your good be evil spoken of: 17 For the kingdom of God is not meat and drink; but righteousness, and peace, and joy in the Holy Ghost. 18 For he that in these things serveth Christ *is* acceptable to God, and approved of men. 19 Let us therefore follow after the things which make for peace, and things wherewith one may edify another. 20 For meat destroy not the work of God. All things indeed *are* pure; but *it is* evil for that man who eateth with offence. 21 *It is* good neither to eat flesh, nor to drink wine, nor *any thing* whereby thy

New International Version

on the armor of light. 13 Let us behave decently, as in the daytime, not in orgies and drunkenness, not in sexual immorality and debauchery, not in dissension and jealousy. 14 Rather, clothe yourselves with the Lord Jesus Christ, and do not think about how to gratify the desires of your sinful nature.

The weak and the strong

14 Accept him whose faith is weak, without passing judgment on disputable matters. 2 One man's faith allows him to eat everything, but another man, whose faith is weak, eats only vegetables. 3 The man who eats everything must not look down on him who does not, and the man who does not eat everything must not condemn the man who does, for God has accepted him. 4 Who are you to judge someone else's servant? To his own master he stands or falls. And he will stand, for the Lord is able to make him stand. 5 One man considers one day more sacred than another; another man considers every day alike. Each one should be fully convinced in his own mind. 6 He who regards one day as special, does so to the Lord. He who eats meat, eats to the Lord, for he gives thanks to God; and he who abstains, does so to the Lord, and gives thanks to God. 7 For none of us lives to himself alone and none of us dies to himself alone. 8 If we live, we live to the Lord; and if we die, we die to the Lord. So, whether we live or die, we belong to the Lord. 9 For this very reason, Christ died and returned to life so that he might be the Lord of both the dead and the living. 10 You, then, why do you judge your brother? Or why do you look down on your brother? For we will all stand before God's judgment seat. 11 It is written:

" 'As I live,' says the Lord,
   'Every knee will bow before me;
      every tongue will confess to God.' " [m]
12 So then, each of us will give an account of himself to God.

13 Therefore, let us stop passing judgment on one another. Instead, make up your mind not to put any stumbling block or obstacle in your brother's way. 14 As one who is in the Lord Jesus, I am fully convinced that no food is unclean in itself. But if anyone regards something as unclean, then for him it is unclean. 15 If your brother is distressed because of what you eat, you are no longer acting in love. Do not by your eating destroy your brother for whom Christ died. 16 Do not allow what you consider good to be spoken of as evil. 17 For the kingdom of God is not a matter of eating and drinking, but of righteousness, peace and joy in the Holy Spirit, 18 because anyone who serves Christ in this way is pleasing to God and approved by men.

19 Let us therefore make every effort to do what leads to peace and to mutual edification. 20 Do not destroy the work of God for the sake of food. All food is clean, but it is wrong for a man to eat anything that causes someone else to stumble. 21 It is better not to eat meat or drink

[m] Isaiah 49:18; 45:23.

Greek Interlinear

τὰ ὅπλα τοῦ φωτός. **13** ὡς ἐν ἡμέρᾳ
the weapons of the light. As in [the] day

εὐσχημόνως περιπατήσωμεν, μὴ κώμοις καὶ
becomingly let us walk, not in revellings and

μέθαις, μὴ κοίταις καὶ ἀσελγείαις, μὴ
in drunken not in beds* and excesses, not
bouts,

ἔριδι καὶ ζήλῳ· **14** ἀλλὰ ἐνδύσασθε τὸν
in strife and in jealousy; but put ye on the

κύριον Ἰησοῦν Χριστόν, καὶ τῆς σαρκὸς
Lord Jesus Christ, and of the flesh

πρόνοιαν μὴ ποιεῖσθε εἰς ἐπιθυμίας.
forethought make not for [its] lusts.

Chapter 14

Τὸν δὲ ἀσθενοῦντα τῇ πίστει
Now the [one] being weak in the faith

προσλαμβάνεσθε, μὴ εἰς διακρίσεις διαλογισ-
receive ye, not to judgments of

μῶν. **2** ὃς μὲν πιστεύει φαγεῖν πάντα,
thoughts. One indeed believes to eat all things,
man†

ὁ δὲ ἀσθενῶν λάχανα ἐσθίει. **3** ὁ ἐσθίων
but the being weak herbs eats. ³The ⁴eating
[one] [one]

τὸν μὴ ἐσθίοντα μὴ ἐξουθενείτω, ὁ δὲ
⁵the ³not ⁴eating ²not ¹let ⁶despise, and ³the
[one] [one]

μὴ ἐσθίων τὸν ἐσθίοντα μὴ κρινέτω,
⁴not ⁶eating ³the [one] ⁵eating ²not ¹let ⁷judge,

ὁ θεὸς γὰρ αὐτὸν προσελάβετο. **4** σὺ
- for God him received. ²Thou

τίς εἶ ὁ κρίνων ἀλλότριον οἰκέτην; τῷ
¹who ²art ³the ⁴judging ⁷belonging to ⁶a household to
[one] another servant? the(his)

ἰδίῳ κυρίῳ στήκει ἢ πίπτει· σταθήσεται
own lord he stands or falls; ²he will stand

δέ, δυνατεῖ γὰρ ὁ κύριος στῆσαι αὐτόν.
¹but, for is able the Lord to stand him.

5 ὃς μὲν [γὰρ] κρίνει ἡμέραν παρ'
one man† indeed judges a day above

ἡμέραν, ὃς δὲ κρίνει πᾶσαν ἡμέραν·
a day, another† judges every day;

ἕκαστος ἐν τῷ ἰδίῳ νοΐ πληροφορείσθω.
each man in the(his) own mind let him be fully
persuaded.

6 ὁ φρονῶν τὴν ἡμέραν κυρίῳ φρονεῖ.
The minding the day to [the] he minds
[one] Lord [it].

καὶ ὁ ἐσθίων κυρίῳ ἐσθίει, εὐχαριστεῖ γὰρ
And the eating to [the] he eats, for he gives thanks
[one] Lord

τῷ θεῷ· καὶ ὁ μὴ ἐσθίων κυρίῳ
- to God; and the [one] not eating to [the] Lord

οὐκ ἐσθίει, καὶ εὐχαριστεῖ τῷ θεῷ.
he eats not, and gives thanks - to God.

7 οὐδεὶς γὰρ ἡμῶν ἑαυτῷ ζῇ, καὶ οὐδεὶς
For no one of us to himself lives, and no one

ἑαυτῷ ἀποθνῄσκει· **8** ἐάν τε γὰρ ζῶμεν,
to himself dies; for whether we live,

τῷ κυρίῳ ζῶμεν, ἐάν τε ἀποθνῄσκωμεν,
to the Lord we live, or if we die,

τῷ κυρίῳ ἀποθνῄσκομεν. ἐάν τε οὖν
to the Lord we die. Whether therefore

ζῶμεν ἐάν τε ἀποθνῄσκωμεν, τοῦ κυρίου
we live or if we die, of the Lord

ἐσμέν. **9** εἰς τοῦτο γὰρ Χριστὸς ἀπέθανεν
we are. for this For Christ died

καὶ ἔζησεν, ἵνα καὶ νεκρῶν καὶ ζώντων
and lived [again], in order both of dead and of living
that [ones]

κυριεύσῃ. **10** σὺ δὲ τί κρίνεις τὸν ἀδελφόν
he might be Lord. ²thou And ¹why ³judgest the brother

σου; ἢ καὶ σὺ τί ἐξουθενεῖς τὸν ἀδελφόν
of thee? or ²indeed ⁴thou ¹why ³despisest the brother

σου; πάντες γὰρ παραστησόμεθα τῷ
of thee? for all we shall stand before the

βήματι τοῦ θεοῦ. **11** γέγραπται γάρ·
tribunal - of God. For it has been written:

ζῶ ἐγώ, λέγει κύριος, ὅτι ἐμοὶ κάμψει
Live I, says [the] Lord, that to me will bend

πᾶν γόνυ, καὶ πᾶσα γλῶσσα ἐξομολογήσεται
every knee, and every tongue will confess

τῷ θεῷ. **12** ἄρα [οὖν] ἕκαστος ἡμῶν
- to God. So therefore each one of us

περὶ ἑαυτοῦ λόγον δώσει [τῷ θεῷ].
concerning himself account will give - to God.

13 Μηκέτι οὖν ἀλλήλους κρίνωμεν· ἀλλὰ
No longer therefore one another let us judge; but

τοῦτο κρίνατε μᾶλλον, τὸ μὴ τιθέναι
this judge ye rather, - not to put

πρόσκομμα τῷ ἀδελφῷ ἢ σκάνδαλον.
a stumbling-block to the brother or an offence.

14 οἶδα καὶ πέπεισμαι ἐν κυρίῳ Ἰησοῦ
I know and have been by [the] Lord Jesus
persuaded

ὅτι οὐδὲν κοινὸν δι' ἑαυτοῦ· εἰ μὴ
that nothing [is] common through itself; except

τῷ λογιζομένῳ τι κοινὸν εἶναι, ἐκείνῳ
to the reckoning anything common to be, to that man
[one] [it is]

κοινόν. **15** εἰ γὰρ διὰ βρῶμα ὁ ἀδελφός
common. For if because food the brother
of

σου λυπεῖται, οὐκέτι κατὰ ἀγάπην
of thee is grieved, no longer according to love

περιπατεῖς. μὴ τῷ βρώματί σου ἐκεῖνον
thou walkest. ²Not ³by the ⁴food ⁵of thee ¹that man

ἀπόλλυε, ὑπὲρ οὗ Χριστὸς ἀπέθανεν.
¹destroy, on behalf of whom Christ died.

16 μὴ βλασφημείσθω οὖν ὑμῶν τὸ ἀγαθόν.
Let not be blasphemed therefore of you the good.

17 οὐ γάρ ἐστιν ἡ βασιλεία τοῦ θεοῦ
For not is the kingdom - of God

βρῶσις καὶ πόσις, ἀλλὰ δικαιοσύνη καὶ
eating and drinking, but righteousness and

εἰρήνη καὶ χαρὰ ἐν πνεύματι ἁγίῳ·
peace and joy in [the] Spirit Holy;

18 ὁ γὰρ ἐν τούτῳ δουλεύων τῷ Χριστῷ
for the [one] in this serving - Christ

εὐάρεστος τῷ θεῷ καὶ δόκιμος τοῖς
[is] well-pleasing - to God and approved -

ἀνθρώποις. **19** ἄρα οὖν τὰ τῆς εἰρήνης
by men. So there- the - of peace
fore things

διώκωμεν καὶ τὰ τῆς οἰκοδομῆς τῆς
let us pursue and the things - of building [up] -

εἰς ἀλλήλους. **20** μὴ ἕνεκεν βρώματος
for one another. Not for the sake of food

κατάλυε τὸ ἔργον τοῦ θεοῦ. πάντα
undo thou the work - of God. All things

μὲν καθαρά, ἀλλὰ κακὸν τῷ ἀνθρώπῳ
indeed [are] clean, but evil to the man

τῷ διὰ προσκόμματος ἐσθίοντι. **21** καλὸν
- ¹through ²a stumbling-block ¹eating. Good [it is]

τὸ μὴ φαγεῖν κρέα μηδὲ πιεῖν οἶνον
- not to eat flesh nor to drink wine

---

* That is, illicit sexual intercourse.

King James Version

brother stumbleth, or is offended, or is made weak. 22 Hast thou faith? have *it* to thyself before God. Happy *is* he that condemneth not himself in that thing which he alloweth. 23And he that doubteth is damned if he eat, because *he eateth* not of faith: for whatsoever *is* not of faith is sin.

15 We then that are strong ought to bear the infirmities of the weak, and not to please ourselves. 2 Let every one of us please *his* neighbour for *his* good to edification. 3 For even Christ pleased not himself; but, as it is written, The reproaches of them that reproached thee fell on me. 4 For whatsoever things were written aforetime were written for our learning, that we through patience and comfort of the Scriptures might have hope. 5 Now the God of patience and consolation grant you to be likeminded one toward another according to Christ Jesus: 6 That ye may with one mind *and* one mouth glorify God, even the Father of our Lord Jesus Christ. 7 Wherefore receive ye one another, as Christ also received us, to the glory of God. 8 Now I say that Jesus Christ was a minister of the circumcision for the truth of God, to confirm the promises *made* unto the fathers: 9And that the Gentiles might glorify God for *his* mercy; as it is written, For this cause I will confess to thee among the Gentiles, and sing unto thy name. 10And again he saith, Rejoice, ye Gentiles, with his people. 11And again, Praise the Lord, all ye Gentiles; and laud him, all ye people. 12 And again, Esaias saith, There shall be a root of Jesse, and he that shall rise to reign over the Gentiles; in him shall the Gentiles trust. 13 Now the God of hope fill you with all joy and peace in believing, that ye may abound in hope, through the power of the Holy Ghost. 14And I myself also am persuaded of you, my brethren, that ye also are full of goodness, filled with all knowledge, able also to admonish one another. 15 Nevertheless, brethren, I have written the more boldly unto you in some sort, as putting you in mind, because of the grace that is given to me of God, 16 That I should be the minister of Jesus Christ to the Gentiles, ministering the gospel of God, that the offering up of the Gentiles might be acceptable, being sanctified by the Holy Ghost. 17 I have therefore whereof I may glory through Jesus Christ in those things which pertain to God. 18 For I will not dare to speak of any of

New International Version

wine or to do anything else that will cause your brother to fall.

22 So whatever you believe about these things keep between yourself and God. Blessed is the man who does not condemn himself by what he approves. 23 But the man who has doubts is condemned if he eats, because his eating is not from faith; and everything that does not come from faith is sin.

15 We who are strong ought to bear with the failings of the weak, and not to please ourselves. 2 Each of us should please his neighbor for his good, to build him up. 3 For even Christ did not please himself but, as it is written: "The insults of those who insult you have fallen on me." [n] 4 For everything that was written in the past was written to teach us, so that through endurance and the encouragement of the Scriptures we might have hope.

5 May the God who gives endurance and encouragement give you a spirit of unity among yourselves as you follow Christ Jesus, 6 so that with one heart and mouth you may glorify the God and Father of our Lord Jesus Christ.

7 Accept one another, then, just as Christ accepted you, in order to bring praise to God. 8 For I tell you that Christ has become a servant of the Jews[o] on behalf of God's truth, to confirm the promises made to the patriarchs 9 so that the Gentiles may glorify God for his mercy, as it is written:

"For this reason I will praise you among the
　Gentiles;
　I will sing hymns to your name." [p]
10Again, it says,
　"Rejoice,[q] Gentiles, with his people."
11And again,
　"Praise the Lord, all you Gentiles,
　and sing praises to him, all you peoples." [r]
12And again, Isaiah says,
　"The root of Jesse will spring up,
　one who will arise to rule over the nations;
　the Gentiles will hope in him." [s]
13 May the God of hope fill you with great joy and peace as you trust in him, so that you may overflow with hope by the power of the Holy Spirit.

Paul the minister to the Gentiles

14 I myself am convinced, my brothers, that you yourselves are full of goodness, complete in knowledge and competent to instruct one another. 15 I have written you quite boldly on some points, as if to remind you of them again, because of the grace God gave me 16 to be a minister of Christ Jesus to the Gentiles with the priestly duty of proclaiming the gospel of God, so that the Gentiles might become an offering acceptable to God, sanctified by the Holy Spirit.

17 Therefore, I glory in Christ Jesus in my service to God. 18 I will not venture to speak of

[n] Psalm 69:9. [o] Greek *circumcision*. [p] Psalm 18:49. [q] Deut. 32:43. [r] Psalm 117:1. [s] Isaiah 11:10.

Greek Interlinear

μηδὲ ἐν ᾧ ὁ ἀδελφός σου προσκόπτει.
nor   by which the brother of thee stumbles.
[anything]

22 σὺ   πίστιν   ἣν   ἔχεις   κατὰ   σεαυτὸν
³Thou ¹faith ²which ⁴hast ⁵by   ⁶thyself

ἔχε   ἐνώπιον   τοῦ   θεοῦ.   μακάριος   ὁ
²have before   -   God.   Blessed   the
                                          [one]

μὴ   κρίνων   ἑαυτὸν   ἐν   ᾧ   δοκιμάζει·
not judging himself   in what he approves;

23 ὁ   δὲ   διακρινόμενος   ἐὰν   φάγῃ   κατα-
   but the [one] doubting   if   he eats has been

κέκριται,   ὅτι   οὐκ   ἐκ   πίστεως·   πᾶν
condemned, because not of   faith;   ⁸all

δὲ   ὃ   οὐκ   ἐκ   πίστεως   ἁμαρτία   ἐστίν.
¹and which [is] not of   faith   sin   is.

Chapter 15

Ὀφείλομεν   δὲ   ἡμεῖς   οἱ   δυνατοὶ   τὰ
⁵Ought   ¹so   ²we   ³the ⁴strong   ⁶the

ἀσθενήματα   τῶν   ἀδυνάτων   βαστάζειν,   καὶ
⁷weaknesses ⁸of the ¹⁰not strong ⁹to bear,   and

μὴ   ἑαυτοῖς   ἀρέσκειν.   2 ἕκαστος   ἡμῶν
not [our]selves to please.   Each one   of us

τῷ   πλησίον   ἀρεσκέτω   εἰς   τὸ   ἀγαθὸν
the(his) neighbour let him please for   -   good

πρὸς   οἰκοδομήν·   3 καὶ   γὰρ   ὁ   Χριστὸς
to   building [up];   for even   -   Christ

οὐχ   ἑαυτῷ   ἤρεσεν·   ἀλλὰ   καθὼς   γέ-
²not   ¹himself ²pleased;   but   as   it has

γραπται·   οἱ   ὀνειδισμοὶ   τῶν   ὀνειδιζόντων
been written: The reproaches of the [ones] reproaching

σε   ἐπέπεσαν   ἐπ᾽   ἐμέ.   4 ὅσα   γὰρ
thee   fell on   on   me. For whatever things

προεγράφη,   εἰς   τὴν   ἡμετέραν   διδασκαλίαν
were previously for   -   our   teaching
written,

ἐγράφη,   ἵνα   διὰ   τῆς   ὑπομονῆς   καὶ
were   in order through   -   patience   and
written,   that

διὰ   τῆς   παρακλήσεως   τῶν   γραφῶν   τὴν
through the   comfort   of the writings

ἐλπίδα   ἔχωμεν.   5 ὁ   δὲ   θεὸς   τῆς   ὑπομονῆς
hope   we may have. And the God   -   of patience

καὶ   τῆς   παρακλήσεως   δῴη   ὑμῖν   τὸ
and   -   of comfort   give to you   ³the

αὐτὸ   φρονεῖν   ἐν   ἀλλήλοις   κατὰ   Χριστὸν
²same   ¹to mind among one another according to Christ
thing

Ἰησοῦν,   6 ἵνα   ὁμοθυμαδὸν   ἐν   ἑνὶ   στόματι
Jesus,   in order with one accord with one   mouth
                  that

δοξάζητε   τὸν   θεὸν   καὶ   πατέρα   τοῦ
ye may glorify the   God   and   Father   of the

κυρίου   ἡμῶν   Ἰησοῦ   Χριστοῦ.
Lord   of us   Jesus   Christ.

7 Διὸ   προσλαμβάνεσθε   ἀλλήλους,   καθὼς
Wherefore   receive ye   one another,   as

καὶ   ὁ   Χριστὸς   προσελάβετο   ἡμᾶς   εἰς
also   -   Christ   received   us   to

δόξαν   τοῦ   θεοῦ.   8 λέγω   γὰρ   Χριστὸν
[the] glory   -   of God.   For I say   Christ

διάκονον   γεγενῆσθαι   περιτομῆς   ὑπὲρ
a minister   to have become   of [the]   on be-
                            circumcision   half of

ἀληθείας   θεοῦ,   εἰς   τὸ   βεβαιῶσαι   τὰς
[the] truth   of God.   -   to confirm   the

ἐπαγγελίας   τῶν   πατέρων,   9 τὰ   δὲ   ἔθνη
promises   of the fathers,   and ¹the ²nations

ὑπὲρ   ἐλέους   δοξάσαι   τὸν   θεόν,   καθὼς
³on be- ⁴mercy   ⁵to glorify   -   ⁶God,   as
half of

γέγραπται·   διὰ   τοῦτο   ἐξομολογήσομαί   σοι
it has been written: Therefore   I will confess   to thee

ἐν   ἔθνεσιν   καὶ   τῷ   ὀνόματί   σου   ψαλῶ.
among nations   and to the   name   of thee I will sing
                                                 praise.

10 καὶ   πάλιν   λέγει·   εὐφράνθητε,   ἔθνη,
And   again   he says: Be glad,   nations,

μετὰ   τοῦ   λαοῦ   αὐτοῦ.   11 καὶ   πάλιν·
with   the   people   of him.   And   again:

αἰνεῖτε,   πάντα   τὰ   ἔθνη,   τὸν   κύριον,
Praise,   all   the nations, the   Lord,

καὶ   ἐπαινεσάτωσαν   αὐτὸν   πάντες   οἱ   λαοί.
and   let praise   him   all   the peoples.

12 καὶ   πάλιν   Ἠσαΐας   λέγει·   ἔσται
And   again   Esaias   says: There
                                     shall be

ἡ   ῥίζα   τοῦ   Ἰεσσαί,   καὶ   ὁ   ἀνιστάμενος
the root   -   of Jesse,   and the [one] rising up

ἄρχειν   ἐθνῶν·   ἐπ᾽   αὐτῷ   ἔθνη   ἐλπιοῦσιν.
to rule   nations;   on   him   nations will hope.

13 Ὁ   δὲ   θεὸς   τῆς   ἐλπίδος   πληρώσαι
Now the   God   -   of hope   fill

ὑμᾶς   πάσης   χαρᾶς   καὶ   εἰρήνης   ἐν   τῷ
you   of(with) all   joy   and   peace   in   -

πιστεύειν,   εἰς   τὸ   περισσεύειν   ὑμᾶς   [in]
to believe   for   -   to abound   you[b]   in
(believing),

τῇ   ἐλπίδι   ἐν   δυνάμει   πνεύματος   ἁγίου.
-    hope   by   [the] power of [the] Spirit   Holy.

14 Πέπεισμαι   δέ,   ἀδελφοί   μου,   καὶ
But I have been persuaded, brothers   of me,   even

αὐτὸς   ἐγὼ   περὶ   ὑμῶν,   ὅτι   καὶ   αὐτοὶ
²[my]self ¹I concerning you,   that also [your]-
                                               selves

μεστοί   ἐστε   ἀγαθωσύνης,   πεπληρωμένοι
full   ye are   of goodness,   having been filled

πάσης   τῆς   γνώσεως,   δυνάμενοι   καὶ
of(with) all   -   knowledge,   being able   also

ἀλλήλους   νουθετεῖν.   15 τολμηρότερως   δὲ
one another   to admonish.   And more daringly

ἔγραψα   ὑμῖν   ἀπὸ   μέρους,   ὡς   ἐπαναμιμνή-
I wrote   to you   in   part,   as   remind-

σκων   ὑμᾶς   διὰ   τὴν   χάριν   τὴν   δοθεῖσάν
ing   you   by   the   grace   the   given

μοι   ἀπὸ   τοῦ   θεοῦ   16 εἰς   τὸ   εἶναί   με
to me from   -   God   for   the   to be   me[b]
                                  =that I should be

λειτουργὸν   Χριστοῦ   Ἰησοῦ   εἰς   τὰ   ἔθνη,
a minister   of Christ   Jesus   to   the nations,

ἱερουργοῦντα   τὸ   εὐαγγέλιον   τοῦ   θεοῦ,
sacrificing   the   gospel   -   of God,

ἵνα   γένηται   ἡ   προσφορὰ   τῶν   ἐθνῶν
in order ⁵may be ¹the ²offering   ³of the ⁴nations
that

εὐπρόσδεκτος,   ἡγιασμένη   ἐν   πνεύματι
acceptable,   having been sanctified by [the] Spirit

ἁγίῳ.   17 ἔχω   οὖν   τὴν   καύχησιν   ἐν
Holy.   I have therefore the   boasting   in

Χριστῷ   Ἰησοῦ   τὰ   πρὸς   τὸν   θεόν·   18 οὐ
Christ   Jesus the things with*   -   God;   ⁴not

---

* That is, the things that have to do with . . .

King James Version

those things which Christ hath not wrought by me, to make the Gentiles obedient, by word and deed, 19 Through mighty signs and wonders, by the power of the Spirit of God; so that from Jerusalem, and round about unto Illyricum, I have fully preached the gospel of Christ. 20 Yea, so have I strived to preach the gospel, not where Christ was named, lest I should build upon another man's foundation: 21 But as it is written, To whom he was not spoken of, they shall see: and they that have not heard shall understand. 22 For which cause also I have been much hindered from coming to you. 23 But now having no more place in these parts, and having a great desire these many years to come unto you; 24 Whensoever I take my journey into Spain, I will come to you: for I trust to see you in my journey, and to be brought on my way thitherward by you, if first I be somewhat filled with your *company*. 25 But now I go unto Jerusalem to minister unto the saints. 26 For it hath pleased them of Macedonia and Achaia to make a certain contribution for the poor saints which are at Jerusalem. 27 It hath pleased them verily; and their debtors they are. For if the Gentiles have been made partakers of their spiritual things, their duty is also to minister unto them in carnal things. 28 When therefore I have performed this, and have sealed to them this fruit, I will come by you into Spain. 29And I am sure that, when I come unto you, I shall come in the fullness of the blessing of the gospel of Christ. 30 Now I beseech you, brethren, for the Lord Jesus Christ's sake, and for the love of the Spirit, that ye strive together with me in *your* prayers to God for me; 31 That I may be delivered from them that do not believe in Judea; and that my service which *I have* for Jerusalem may be accepted of the saints; 32 That I may come unto you with joy by the will of God, and may with you be refreshed. 33 Now the God of peace *be* with you all Amẹn.

New International Version

anything except what Christ has accomplished through me in leading the Gentiles to obey God by what I have said and done—19 by the power of signs and miracles, through the power of the Spirit. So from Jerusalem all the way around to Illyricum, I have fully proclaimed the gospel of Christ. 20 It has always been my ambition to preach the gospel where Christ was not known, so that I would not be building on someone else's foundation. 21 Rather, as it is written:
> "Those who were not told about him will see,
> and those who have not heard will understand." [t]

22 This is why I have often been hindered from coming to you.

Paul's plan to visit Rome

23 But now that there is no more place for me to work in these regions, and since I have been longing for many years to see you, 24 I plan to do so when I go to Spain. I hope to visit you while passing through and to have you assist me on my journey there, after I have enjoyed your company for a while. 25 Now, however, I am on my way to Jerusalem in the service of the saints there. 26 For Macedonia and Achaia were pleased to make a contribution for the poor among the saints in Jerusalem. 27 They were pleased to do it, and indeed they owe it to them. For if the Gentiles have shared in the Jews' spiritual blessings, they owe it to the Jews to share with them their material blessings. 28 So after I have completed this task and have made sure that they have received this fruit, I will go to Spain and visit you on the way. 29 I know that when I come to you, I will come in the full measure of the blessing of Christ.

30 I urge you, brothers, by our Lord Jesus Christ and by the love of the Spirit, to join me in my struggle by praying to God for me. 31 Pray that I may be rescued from the unbelievers in Judea and that my service in Jerusalem may be acceptable to the saints there. 32 Then by God's will I can come to you with joy and together with you be refreshed. 33 The God of peace be with all. Amen.

Personal greetings

16 I commend unto you Phebe our sister, which is a servant of the church which is at Cenchrea: 2 That ye receive her in the Lord, as becometh saints, and that ye assist her in whatsoever business she hath need of you: for she hath been a succourer of many, and of myself also. 3 Greet Priscilla and Aquila, my helpers in Christ Jesus: 4 Who have for my life laid down their own necks: unto whom not only I give thanks, but also all the churches of the Gentiles. 5 Likewise *greet* the church that is in their house. Salute my well beloved Epenetus,

16 I commend to you our sister Phoebe, a servant[u] of the church in Cenchreae. 2 I ask you to receive her in the Lord in a way worthy of the saints and to give her any help she may need from you, for she has been a great help to many people, including me.
3 Greet Priscilla[v] and Aquila, my fellow workers in Christ Jesus. 4 They risked their lives for me. Not only I but all the churches of the Gentiles are grateful to them.
5 Greet also the church that meets at their house. Greet my dear friend Epaenetus, who was the

γὰρ   τολμήσω   τι   λαλεῖν   ὧν   οὐ
¹for   ⁸I ¹will ⁶dare ⁷any- ⁵to speak of [the] ⁴not
                       thing   things which

κατειργάσατο   Χριστὸς   δι' ἐμοῦ   εἰς ὑπακοὴν
¹did ⁴work ⁵out   ¹Christ   through me   for   obedience

ἐθνῶν,   λόγῳ   καὶ   ἔργῳ,   19 ἐν   δυνάμει
of [the] in word and   work,   by   power
nations,

σημείων   καὶ   τεράτων,   ἐν   δυνάμει   πνεύματος·
of signs   and   wonders,   by   power   of [the] Spirit;

ὥστε   με   ἀπὸ   Ἰερουσαλὴμ   καὶ   κύκλῳ
so as   me   from   Jerusalem   and   around
=I should fulfil the gospel . . . from . . . Illyricum.

μέχρι   τοῦ   Ἰλλυρικοῦ   πεπληρωκέναι   τὸ
unto   the   Illyricum   to have fulfilled[b] the

εὐαγγέλιον   τοῦ   Χριστοῦ.   20 οὕτως   δὲ
gospel   -   of Christ.   And so

φιλοτιμούμενον   εὐαγγελίζεσθαι   οὐχ   ὅπου
eagerly striving   to evangelize   not   where

ὠνομάσθη   Χριστός,   ἵνα   μὴ   ἐπ'   ἀλλότριον
²was named   ¹Christ,   in order not   on   ³belonging to
                         that   another

θεμέλιον   οἰκοδομῶ,   21 ἀλλὰ   καθὼς
¹a foundation I should build,   but   as

γέγραπται·   ὄψονται   οἷς   οὐκ   ἀνηγγέλη
it has been   They shall see to whom it was not announced
written:

περὶ   αὐτοῦ,   καὶ   οἳ   οὐκ   ἀκηκόασιν
concerning him,   and [those] who   have not heard

συνήσουσιν.   22 διὸ   καὶ   ἐνεκοπτόμην   τὰ
will understand.   Wherefore also   I was hindered   -

πολλὰ   τοῦ   ἐλθεῖν   πρὸς   ὑμᾶς·   23 νυνὶ
many(much) -   to come[d] to   you;   ¹now

δὲ   μηκέτι   τόπον   ἔχων   ἐν   τοῖς   κλίμασι
¹but   no longer   ⁴place ¹having in   -   ³regions

τούτοις,   ἐπιποθίαν   δὲ   ἔχων   τοῦ   ἐλθεῖν
¹these,   and ²a desire   ¹having   -   to come[d]

πρὸς   ὑμᾶς   ἀπὸ   ἱκανῶν   ἐτῶν,   24 ὡς   ἂν
to   you   from   several   years,   whenever

πορεύωμαι   εἰς   τὴν   Σπανίαν·   ἐλπίζω   γὰρ
I journey   to   -   Spain;   for I hope

διαπορευόμενος   θεάσασθαι   ὑμᾶς   καὶ   ὑφ'
journeying through   to behold   you   and   by

ὑμῶν   προπεμφθῆναι   ἐκεῖ,   ἐὰν   ὑμῶν   πρῶτον
you   to be set forward   there,   if   of(with) you   firstly

ἀπὸ   μέρους   ἐμπλησθῶ,   25 —   νυνὶ   δὲ
in   part   I may be filled,   —   but now

πορεύομαι   εἰς   Ἰερουσαλὴμ   διακονῶν   τοῖς
I am going   to   Jerusalem   ministering   to the

ἁγίοις.   26 ηὐδόκησαν   γὰρ   Μακεδονία   καὶ
saints.   For thought it good   Macedonia   and

Ἀχαΐα   κοινωνίαν   τινὰ   ποιήσασθαι   εἰς
Achaia   ²contribution   ³some   ¹to make   for

τοὺς   πτωχοὺς   τῶν   ἁγίων   τῶν   ἐν   Ἰερου-
the   poor   of the   saints   -   in   Jeru-

σαλήμ.   27 ηὐδόκησαν   γάρ,   καὶ   ὀφειλέται
salem.   For they thought it good,   and   debtors

εἰσὶν   αὐτῶν·   εἰ   γὰρ   τοῖς   πνευματικοῖς
they are   of them;   for if   in the   spiritual things

αὐτῶν   ἐκοινώνησαν   τὰ   ἔθνη,   ὀφείλουσιν
of them   ³shared   ¹the   ²nations,   they ought

καὶ   ἐν   τοῖς   σαρκικοῖς   λειτουργῆσαι   αὐτοῖς.
also   in   the   fleshly things   to minister   to them.

28 τοῦτο   οὖν   ἐπιτελέσας,   καὶ   σφραγισάμενος
This therefore   having   and   having sealed
                 completed,

αὐτοῖς   τὸν   καρπὸν   τοῦτον,   29 ἀπελεύσομαι
to them   this fruit,   I will go away

δι'   ὑμῶν   εἰς   Σπανίαν·   οἶδα   δὲ   ὅτι
through you   to   Spain;   and I know   that

ἐρχόμενος   πρὸς   ὑμᾶς   ἐν   πληρώματι
coming   to   you   in [the]   fulness

εὐλογίας   Χριστοῦ   ἐλεύσομαι.   30 Παρακαλῶ
of [the]   of Christ   I will come.   I beseech
blessing

δὲ   ὑμᾶς,   [ἀδελφοί],   διὰ   τοῦ   κυρίου
Now   you,   brothers,   through   the   Lord

ἡμῶν   Ἰησοῦ   Χριστοῦ   καὶ   διὰ   τῆς   ἀγάπης
of us   Jesus   Christ   and through   the   love

τοῦ   πνεύματος,   συναγωνίσασθαί   μοι   ἐν
of the   Spirit,   to strive with   me   in

ταῖς   προσευχαῖς   ὑπὲρ   ἐμοῦ   πρὸς   τὸν
the   prayers   on behalf of   me   to   -

θεόν,   31 ἵνα   ῥυσθῶ   ἀπὸ   τῶν   ἀπειθούντων
God,   in order I may be   from   the   disobeying
        that   delivered   [ones]

ἐν   τῇ   Ἰουδαίᾳ   καὶ   ἡ   διακονία   μου
in   the   Judæa   and   the   ministry   of me

ἡ   εἰς   Ἰερουσαλὴμ   εὐπρόσδεκτος   τοῖς
-    to   Jerusalem   ²acceptable   ³to the

ἁγίοις   γένηται,   32 ἵνα   ἐν   χαρᾷ   ἐλθὼν
⁴saints   ¹may be,   in order that in   joy   coming

πρὸς   ὑμᾶς   διὰ   θελήματος   θεοῦ   συνανα-
to   you   through   [the] will   of God   I may

παύσωμαι   ὑμῖν.   33 ὁ   δὲ   θεὸς   τῆς
rest with   you.   And the   God   -

εἰρήνης   μετὰ   πάντων   ὑμῶν·   ἀμήν.
of peace   [be] with   all   you: Amen.

Chapter 16

Συνίστημι   δὲ   ὑμῖν   Φοίβην   τὴν
Now I commend   to you   Phœbe   the

ἀδελφὴν   ἡμῶν,   οὖσαν   [καὶ]   διάκονον   τῆς
sister   of us,   being   also   a minister   of the

ἐκκλησίας   τῆς   ἐν   Κεγχρεαῖς,   2 ἵνα
church   -   in   Cenchrea,   in order that

αὐτὴν   προσδέξησθε   ἐν   κυρίῳ   ἀξίως   τῶν
²her   ¹ye may receive   in [the] Lord   worthily   of the

ἁγίων,   καὶ   παραστῆτε   αὐτῇ   ἐν   ᾧ   ἂν
saints,   and   may stand by   her   in   ¹whatever

ὑμῶν   χρῄζῃ   πράγματι·   καὶ   γὰρ   αὐτὴ
²of you   ³she may ⁴thing;   for indeed   she
        have need

προστάτις   πολλῶν   ἐγενήθη   καὶ   ἐμοῦ   αὐτοῦ.
a protectress   of many   became   and   of myself.

3 Ἀσπάσασθε   Πρίσκαν   καὶ   Ἀκύλαν   τοὺς
Greet ye   Prisca   and   Aquila   the

συνεργούς   μου   ἐν   Χριστῷ   Ἰησοῦ,   4 οἵτινες
fellow-workers   of me   in   Christ   Jesus,   who

ὑπὲρ   τῆς   ψυχῆς   μου   τὸν   ἑαυτῶν   τράχηλον
on be-   the   life   of me   ²the   ³of   ⁴neck
half of   themselves

ὑπέθηκαν,   οἷς   οὐκ   ἐγὼ   μόνος   εὐχαριστῶ
¹risked,   to whom not   I   only   give thanks

ἀλλὰ   καὶ   πᾶσαι   αἱ   ἐκκλησίαι   τῶν   ἐθνῶν,
but   also   all   the   churches   of the   nations,

5 καὶ   τὴν   κατ'   οἶκον   αὐτῶν   ἐκκλησίαν.
and   ¹the   ²in   ⁴house   ³of them   ⁵church.

ἀσπάσασθε   Ἐπαίνετον   τὸν   ἀγαπητόν   μου,
Greet   Epænetus   the   beloved   of me,

481

King James Version

who is the firstfruits of Achaia unto Christ.
6 Greet Mary, who bestowed much labour on us.
7 Salute Andronicus and Junia, my kinsmen,
and my fellow prisoners, who are of note among
the apostles, who also were in Christ before me.
8 Greet Amplias, my beloved in the Lord. 9 Salute Urbane, our helper in Christ, and Stachys
my beloved. 10 Salute Apelles approved in
Christ. Salute them which are of Aristobulus'
household. 11 Salute Herodion my kinsman.
Greet them that be of the *household* of Narcissus, which are in the Lord. 12 Salute Tryphena
and Tryphosa, who labour in the Lord. Salute
the beloved Persis, which laboured much in the
Lord. 13 Salute Rufus chosen in the Lord, and
his mother and mine. 14 Salute Asyncritus,
Phlegon, Hermas, Patrobas, Hermes, and the
brethren which are with them. 15 Salute Philologus, and Julia, Nereus, and his sister, and
Olympas, and all the saints which are with
them. 16 Salute one another with a holy kiss. The
churches of Christ salute you. 17 Now I beseech you, brethren, mark them which cause
divisions and offences contrary to the doctrine
which ye have learned; and avoid them. 18 For
they that are such serve not our Lord Jesus
Christ, but their own belly; and by good words
and fair speeches deceive the hearts of the simple. 19 For your obedience is come abroad unto
all *men.* I am glad therefore on your behalf: but
yet I would have you wise unto that which is
good, and simple concerning evil. 20 And the
God of peace shall bruise Satan under your feet
shortly. The grace of our Lord Jesus Christ *be*
with you. Amen. 21 Timotheus my workfellow,
and Lucius, and Jason, and Sosipater, my kinsmen, salute you. 22 I Tertius, who wrote *this*
epistle, salute you in the Lord. 23 Gaius mine
host, and of the whole church, saluteth you.
Erastus the chamberlain of the city saluteth you,
and Quartus a brother. 24 The grace of our Lord
Jesus Christ *be* with you all. Amen. 25 Now to
him that is of power to stablish you according
to my gospel, and the preaching of Jesus Christ,
according to the revelation of the mystery, which
was kept secret since the world began, 26 But
now is made manifest, and by the Scriptures of
the prophets, according to the commandment of
the everlasting God, made known to all nations for the obedience of faith: 27 To God only
wise, *be* glory through Jesus Christ for ever.
Amen.

Written to the Romans from Corinthus, *and
sent* by Phebe servant of the church at Cenchrea.

New International Version

first convert to Christ in the province of
Asia.
6 Greet Mary, who worked very hard for you.
7 Greet Andronicus and Junias, my relatives who
have been in prison with me. They are outstanding among the apostles, and they were
in Christ before I was.
8 Greet Ampliatus, whom I love in the Lord.
9 Greet Urbanus, our fellow worker in Christ,
and my dear friend Stachys.
10 Greet Apelles, tested and approved in Christ.
Greet those who belong to the household of
Aristobulus.
11 Greet Herodion, my relative.
Greet those in the household of Narcissus who
are in the Lord.
12 Greet Tryphaena and Tryphosa, those women
who work hard in the Lord.
Greet my dear friend Persis, another woman
who has worked very hard in the Lord.
13 Greet Rufus, chosen in the Lord, and his
mother, who has been a mother to me, too.
14 Greet Asyncritus, Phlegon, Hermes, Patrobas,
Hermas and the brothers with them.
15 Greet Philologus, Julia, Nereus and his sister,
and Olympas and all the saints with them.
16 Greet one another with a holy kiss.
All the churches of Christ send greetings.
17 I urge you, brothers, to watch out for those
who cause divisions and put obstacles in your
way, contrary to the teaching you have learned.
Keep away from them. 18 For such people are
not serving our Lord Christ, but their own ap-
petites. By smooth talk and flattery they deceive
the minds of naive people. 19 Everyone has heard
about your obedience, so I am full of joy over
you; but I want you to be wise about what is
good, and innocent about what is evil.
20 The God of peace will soon crush Satan
under your feet.
The grace of our Lord Jesus be with you.
21 Timothy, my fellow worker, sends his
greetings to you, as do Lucius, Jason and Sosipater, my relatives.
22 I, Tertius, who wrote down this letter, greet
you in the Lord.
23 Gaius, whose hospitality I and the whole
church here enjoy, sends you his greetings.
Erastus, who is the city's director of public
works, and our brother Quartus send you their
greetings.[w]
25 Now to him who is able to establish you by
my gospel and the proclamation of Jesus Christ,
according to the revelation of the mystery hidden for long ages past, 26 but now revealed and
made known through the prophetic writings by
the command of the eternal God, so that all na- .
tions might believe and obey him—27 to the only
wise God be glory forever through Jesus Christ!
Amen.

[w] Some MSS add verse 24: *May the grace of our Lord Jesus
Christ be with all of you. Amen.*

ὅς ἐστιν ἀπαρχὴ τῆς Ἀσίας εἰς Χριστόν.
who is firstfruit – of Asia for Christ.

6 ἀσπάσασθε Μαρίαν, ἥτις πολλὰ ἐκοπίασεν
Greet Mary, who many things laboured
(much)

εἰς ὑμᾶς. 7 ἀσπάσασθε Ἀνδρόνικον καὶ
for you. Greet Andronicus and

Ἰουνιᾶν τοὺς συγγενεῖς μου καὶ συναιχμα-
Junius the kinsmen of me and fellow-

λώτους μου, οἵτινές εἰσιν ἐπίσημοι ἐν
captives of me, who are notable among

τοῖς ἀποστόλοις, οἳ καὶ πρὸ ἐμοῦ γέγοναν
the apostles, who indeed before me have been

ἐν Χριστῷ. 8 ἀσπάσασθε Ἀμπλιᾶτον τὸν
in Christ. Greet Ampliatus the

ἀγαπητόν μου ἐν κυρίῳ. 9 ἀσπάσασθε
beloved of me in [the] Lord. Greet

Οὐρβανὸν τὸν συνεργὸν ἡμῶν ἐν Χριστῷ
Urbanus the fellow-worker of us in Christ

καὶ Στάχυν τὸν ἀγαπητόν μου. 10 ἀσπάσ-
and Stachys the beloved of me. Greet

ασθε Ἀπελλῆν τὸν δόκιμον ἐν Χριστῷ.
Apelles the approved in Christ.

ἀσπάσασθε τοὺς ἐκ τῶν Ἀριστοβούλου.
Greet the [ones] of the [family] of Aristobulus.

11 ἀσπάσασθε Ἡρῳδίωνα τὸν συγγενῆ μου.
Greet Herodion the kinsman of me.

ἀσπάσασθε τοὺς ἐκ τῶν Ναρκίσσου τοὺς
Greet the [ones] of the [family] of Narcissus –

ὄντας ἐν κυρίῳ. 12 ἀσπάσασθε Τρύφαιναν
being in [the] Lord. Greet Tryphæna

καὶ Τρύφωσαν τὰς κοπιώσας ἐν κυρίῳ.
and Tryphosa the [ones] labouring in [the] Lord.

ἀσπάσασθε Περσίδα τὴν ἀγαπητήν, ἥτις
Greet Persis the beloved, who

πολλὰ ἐκοπίασεν ἐν κυρίῳ. 13 ἀσπάσασθε
many things laboured in [the] Lord. Greet
(much)

Ῥοῦφον τὸν ἐκλεκτὸν ἐν κυρίῳ καὶ
Rufus the chosen in [the] Lord and

τὴν μητέρα αὐτοῦ καὶ ἐμοῦ. 14 ἀσπάσασθε
the mother of him and of me. Greet

Ἀσύγκριτον, Φλέγοντα, Ἑρμῆν, Πατροβᾶν,
Asyncritus, Phlegon, Hermes, Patrobas,

Ἑρμᾶν, καὶ τοὺς σὺν αὐτοῖς ἀδελφούς.
Hermas, and the ¹with ²them ¹brothers.

15 ἀσπάσασθε Φιλόλογον καὶ Ἰουλίαν,
Greet Philologus and Julia,

Νηρέα καὶ τὴν ἀδελφὴν αὐτοῦ, καὶ
Nereus and the sister of him, and

Ὀλυμπᾶν, καὶ τοὺς σὺν αὐτοῖς πάντας
Olympas, and ¹the ⁴with ²them ³all

ἁγίους. 16 ἀσπάσασθε ἀλλήλους ἐν φιλήματι
²saints. Greet one another with kiss

ἁγίῳ. ἀσπάζονται ὑμᾶς αἱ ἐκκλησίαι
a holy. ⁵greet ⁴you ²the ³churches

πᾶσαι τοῦ Χριστοῦ.
¹All – ⁴of Christ.

17 Παρακαλῶ δὲ ὑμᾶς, ἀδελφοί, σκοπεῖν
Now I beseech you, brothers, to watch

τοὺς τὰς διχοστασίας καὶ τὰ σκάνδαλα
¹the ²the ³divisions ⁴and ⁵the ⁶offences
[ones]

παρὰ τὴν διδαχὴν ἣν ὑμεῖς ἐμάθετε
⁹beside ¹⁰the ¹³teaching ¹¹which ¹²ye ¹³learned

ποιοῦντας, καὶ ἐκκλίνετε ἀπ' αὐτῶν· 18 οἱ
¹making, and turn away from them; –

γὰρ τοιοῦτοι τῷ κυρίῳ ἡμῶν Χριστῷ
for such men ²the ³Lord ¹of us ¹Christ

οὐ δουλεύουσιν ἀλλὰ τῇ ἑαυτῶν κοιλίᾳ,
¹serve not but the of themselves belly,

καὶ διὰ τῆς χρηστολογίας καὶ εὐλογίας
and through – fair speech and flattering
speech

ἐξαπατῶσιν τὰς καρδίας τῶν ἀκάκων.
deceive the hearts of the guileless.

19 ἡ γὰρ ὑμῶν ὑπακοὴ εἰς πάντας
²the ¹For ⁴of you ³obedience ⁵to ⁶all men

ἀφίκετο· ἐφ' ὑμῖν οὖν χαίρω, θέλω
¹came; over you therefore I rejoice, ¹I wish

δὲ ὑμᾶς σοφοὺς εἶναι εἰς τὸ ἀγαθόν,
²and you wise to be to the good,

ἀκεραίους δὲ εἰς τὸ κακόν. 20 ὁ δὲ
but simple to the evil. And the

θεὸς τῆς εἰρήνης συντρίψει τὸν σατανᾶν
God – of peace will crush – Satan

ὑπὸ τοὺς πόδας ὑμῶν ἐν τάχει.
under the feet ⁵of you soon.

Ἡ χάρις τοῦ κυρίου ἡμῶν Ἰησοῦ
The grace of the Lord of us Jesus [be]

μεθ' ὑμῶν.
with you.

21 Ἀσπάζεται ὑμᾶς Τιμόθεος ὁ συνεργός
²greets ⁴you ¹Timothy ¹the ³fellow-worker

μου, καὶ Λούκιος καὶ Ἰάσων καὶ
⁴of me, and Lucius and Jason and

Σωσίπατρος οἱ συγγενεῖς μου. 22 ἀσπάζ-
Sosipater the kinsmen of me. ²greet

ομαι ὑμᾶς ἐγὼ Τέρτιος ὁ γράψας τὴν
¹you ²I ¹Tertius ³the [one] ⁴writing ⁵the

ἐπιστολὴν ἐν κυρίῳ. 23 ἀσπάζεται ὑμᾶς
⁶epistle in [the] Lord. ¹greets ¹⁰you

Γάιος ὁ ξένος μου καὶ ὅλης τῆς
¹Gaius ³the ⁴host ²of me ⁵and ⁶of all ⁷the

ἐκκλησίας. ἀσπάζεται ὑμᾶς Ἔραστος ὁ
⁸church. ²greets ³you ¹Erastus ²the

οἰκονόμος τῆς πόλεως καὶ Κούαρτος ὁ
³treasurer ⁴of the ⁵city and Quartus the

ἀδελφός.‡
brother. (?his)

25 Τῷ δὲ δυναμένῳ ὑμᾶς στηρίξαι κατὰ
Now to the being able ¹you ¹to establish accord-
[one] ing to

τὸ εὐαγγέλιόν μου καὶ τὸ κήρυγμα
the gospel of me and the proclamation

Ἰησοῦ Χριστοῦ, κατὰ ἀποκάλυψιν μυστηρίου
of Jesus Christ, according [the] revelation of [the]
to mystery

χρόνοις αἰωνίοις σεσιγημένου, 26 φανερω-
²in times ¹eternal ³having been kept silent, ¹mani-

θέντος δὲ νῦν διά τε γραφῶν προφητικῶν
fested ¹but now and through writings prophetic

κατ' ἐπιταγὴν τοῦ αἰωνίου θεοῦ εἰς
accord- [the] of the eternal God ²for
ing to command

ὑπακοὴν πίστεως εἰς πάντα τὰ ἔθνη
¹obedience ³of faith ¹to ⁴all ¹the ²nations

γνωρισθέντος, 27 μόνῳ σοφῷ θεῷ, διὰ
¹made known, ²only ³wise ¹to God, through

Ἰησοῦ Χριστοῦ, ᾧ ἡ δόξα εἰς τοὺς
Jesus Christ, to whom of the glory unto the
(him)ᶜ

αἰῶνας τῶν αἰώνων· ἀμήν.
ages of the ages: Amen.

King James Version

the wisdom of the wise, and will bring to nothing the understanding of the prudent. 20 Where *is* the wise? where *is* the scribe? where *is* the disputer of this world? hath not God made foolish the wisdom of this world? 21 For after that in the wisdom of God the world by wisdom knew not God, it pleased God by the foolishness of preaching to save them that believe. 22 For the Jews require a sign, and the Greeks seek after wisdom: 23 But we preach Christ crucified, unto the Jews a stumblingblock, and unto the Greeks foolishness; 24 But unto them which are called, both Jews and Greeks, Christ the power of God, and the wisdom of God. 25 Because the foolishness of God is wiser than men; and the weakness of God is stronger than men. 26 For ye see your calling, brethren, how that not many wise men after the flesh, not many mighty, not many noble, *are called:* 27 But God hath chosen the foolish things of the world to confound the wise; and God hath chosen the weak things of the world to confound the things which are mighty; 28And base things of the world, and things which are despised, hath God chosen, *yea,* and things which are not, to bring to nought things that are: 29 That no flesh should glory in his presence. 30 But of him are ye in Christ Jesus, who of God is made unto us wisdom, and righteousness, and sanctification, and redemption: 31 That, according as it is written, He that glorieth, let him glory in the Lord.

2 And I, brethren, when I came to you, came not with excellency of speech or of wisdom, declaring unto you the testimony of God. 2 For I determined not to know any thing among you, save Jesus Christ, and him crucified. 3And I was with you in weakness, and in fear, and in much trembling. 4And my speech and my preaching *was* not with enticing words of man's wisdom, but in demonstration of the Spirit and of power: 5 That your faith should not stand in the wisdom of men, but in the power of God. 6 Howbeit we speak wisdom among them that are perfect: yet not the wisdom of this world, nor of the princes of this world, that come to nought: 7 But we speak the wisdom of God in a mystery, *even* the hidden *wisdom,* which God ordained before the world unto our glory: 8 Which none of the princes of this world knew: for had they known *it,* they would not have crucified the Lord of glory. 9 But as it is written, Eye hath not seen, nor ear heard, neither have entered into the heart of man, the things which God hath pre-

New International Version

"I will destroy the wisdom of the wise;
  the intelligence of the intelligent I will
  frustrate." *c*
20 Where is the wise man? Where is the scholar? Where is the philosopher of this age? Has not God made foolish the wisdom of the world? 21 For since in the wisdom of God the world through its wisdom did not know him, God was pleased through the foolishness of what was preached to save those who believe. 22 Jews demand miraculous signs and Greeks look for wisdom, 23 but we preach Christ crucified: a stumbling block to Jews and foolishness to Gentiles, 24 but to those whom God has called, both Jews and Greeks, Christ the power of God and the wisdom of God. 25 For the foolishness of God is wiser than man's wisdom, and the weakness of God is stronger than man's strength.

26 Brothers, think of what you were when you were called. Not many of you were wise by human standards; not many were influential; not many were of noble birth. 27 But God chose the foolish things of the world to shame the wise; God chose the weak things of the world to shame the strong. 28 He chose the lowly things of this world and the despised things—and the things that are not—to nullify the things that are, 29 so that no man may boast before him. 30 It is because of him that you are in Christ Jesus, who has become for us wisdom from God—that is, our righteousness, holiness and redemption. 31 Therefore, as it is written: "Let him who boasts boast in the Lord." *d*

2 When I came to you, brothers, I did not come with eloquence or superior wisdom as I proclaimed to you the testimony about God.*e* 2 For I resolved to know nothing while I was with you except Jesus Christ and him crucified. 3 I came to you in weakness and fear, and with much trembling. 4 My message and my preaching were not with wise and persuasive words, but with a demonstration of the Spirit's power, 5 so that your faith might not rest on men's wisdom, but on God's power.

Wisdom from the Spirit

6 We do, however, speak a message of wisdom among the mature, but not the wisdom of this age or of the rulers of this age, who are coming to nothing. 7 No, we speak of God's secret wisdom, a wisdom that has been hidden and that God destined for our glory before time began. 8 None of the rulers of this age understood it, for if they had, they would not have crucified the Lord of glory. 9 However, as it is written:
"No eye has seen,
  no ear has heard,
  no mind has conceived
    what God has prepared for those who love
    him" *f*—

[c] Isaiah 29:14. [d] Jer. 9:24. [e] Some MSS read *proclaimed to you God's mystery.* [f] Isaiah 64:4.

Greek Interlinear

τῶν σοφῶν, καὶ τὴν σύνεσιν τῶν συνετῶν
of the wise ones, and the understanding of the prudent

ἀθετήσω. 20 ποῦ σοφός; ποῦ γραμματεύς;
I will set Where [is the] where [is the] scribe?
aside.   wise man?

ποῦ συζητητὴς τοῦ αἰῶνος τούτου; οὐχὶ
where disputant   of this age?   ¹Not
[is the]

ἐμώρανεν ὁ θεὸς τὴν σοφίαν τοῦ κόσμου;
¹made ²foolish - ³God ⁴the ⁴wisdom ⁵of the ⁵world?

21 ἐπειδὴ γὰρ ἐν τῇ σοφίᾳ τοῦ θεοῦ
for since   in the wisdom - of God

οὐκ ἔγνω ὁ κόσμος διὰ τῆς σοφίας
⁴knew ¹not ¹the ²world ³through ³the(its) ⁴wisdom

τὸν θεόν, εὐδόκησεν ὁ θεὸς διὰ τῆς
- ²God, ²thought well - ¹God through the

μωρίας τοῦ κηρύγματος σῶσαι τοὺς
folly of the proclamation to save the

πιστεύοντας. 22 ἐπειδὴ καὶ Ἰουδαῖοι σημεῖα
[ones] believing. Seeing that both Jews ²signs

αἰτοῦσιν καὶ Ἕλληνες σοφίαν ζητοῦσιν,
¹ask and Greeks ¹wisdom ²seek,

23 ἡμεῖς δὲ κηρύσσομεν Χριστὸν ἐσταυρωμένον,
²we ¹yet proclaim Christ having been crucified,

Ἰουδαίοις μὲν σκάνδαλον, ἔθνεσιν δὲ
to Jews on one hand an offence, to nations on the
                                              other

μωρίαν, 24 αὐτοῖς δὲ τοῖς κλητοῖς,
folly, but to them the called ones,

Ἰουδαίοις τε καὶ Ἕλλησιν, Χριστὸν θεοῦ
²to Jews ¹both and to Greeks, Christ of God

δύναμιν καὶ θεοῦ σοφίαν. 25 ὅτι τὸ
power and of God wisdom. Because the

μωρὸν τοῦ θεοῦ σοφώτερον τῶν ἀνθρώπων
foolish - of God wiser [than] - men
thing

ἐστίν, καὶ τὸ ἀσθενὲς τοῦ θεοῦ ἰσχυρότερον
is, and the weak thing - of God stronger [than]

τῶν ἀνθρώπων. 26 Βλέπετε γὰρ τὴν
- men. For ye see the

κλῆσιν ὑμῶν, ἀδελφοί, ὅτι οὐ πολλοὶ
calling of you, brothers, that not many

σοφοὶ κατὰ σάρκα, οὐ πολλοὶ δυνατοί,
wise men according flesh, not many powerful,
to

οὐ πολλοὶ εὐγενεῖς· 27 ἀλλὰ τὰ μωρὰ
not many well born; but the foolish
                                              things

τοῦ κόσμου ἐξελέξατο ὁ θεὸς ἵνα καται-
of the world ²chose - ¹God in order he might
                                              that

σχύνῃ τοὺς σοφούς, καὶ τὰ ἀσθενῆ τοῦ
shame the wise men, and the weak things of the

κόσμου ἐξελέξατο ὁ θεὸς ἵνα καταισχύνῃ
world ²chose - ¹God in order he might shame
                                              that

τὰ ἰσχυρά, 28 καὶ τὰ ἀγενῆ τοῦ κόσμου
the strong things, and the base things of the world

καὶ τὰ ἐξουθενημένα ἐξελέξατο ὁ θεός,
and the things being despised ²chose - ¹God,

τὰ μὴ ὄντα, ἵνα τὰ ὄντα καταργήσῃ,
the not being, in order ²the ²being ²he might
things   that things abolish,

29 ὅπως μὴ καυχήσηται πᾶσα σὰρξ
so as not might boast all flesh*

ἐνώπιον τοῦ θεοῦ. 30 ἐξ αὐτοῦ δὲ ὑμεῖς
before - God. And of him ²ye

ἐστε ἐν Χριστῷ Ἰησοῦ, ὃς ἐγενήθη
are in Christ Jesus, who became

σοφία ἡμῖν ἀπὸ θεοῦ, δικαιοσύνη τε
wisdom to us from God, ²righteousness ¹both

καὶ ἁγιασμὸς καὶ ἀπολύτρωσις, 31 ἵνα καθὼς
and sanctification and redemption, in order that as

γέγραπται· ὁ καυχώμενος ἐν κυρίῳ καυχάσθω.
it has been The [one] boasting ²in ¹[the] ¹let him boast.
written: Lord

Chapter 2

Κἀγὼ ἐλθὼν πρὸς ὑμᾶς, ἀδελφοί,
And I coming to you, brothers,

ἦλθον οὐ καθ' ὑπεροχὴν λόγου ἢ σοφίας
came not accord- excellence of speech or of wisdom
           ing to

καταγγέλλων ὑμῖν τὸ μαρτύριον τοῦ θεοῦ.
announcing to you the testimony - of God.

2 οὐ γὰρ ἔκρινά τι εἰδέναι ἐν ὑμῖν
For I decided not anything to know among you

εἰ μὴ Ἰησοῦν Χριστὸν καὶ τοῦτον
except Jesus Christ and this one

ἐσταυρωμένον. 3 κἀγὼ ἐν ἀσθενείᾳ καὶ
having been crucified. And I in weakness and

ἐν φόβῳ καὶ ἐν τρόμῳ πολλῷ ἐγενόμην
in fear and in trembling much was

πρὸς ὑμᾶς, 4 καὶ ὁ λόγος μου καὶ τὸ
with you, and the speech of me and the

κήρυγμά μου οὐκ ἐν πειθοῖς σοφίας
proclamation of me not in ¹persuasive ²of wisdom

λόγοις, ἀλλ' ἐν ἀποδείξει πνεύματος καὶ
¹words, but in demonstration of spirit and

δυνάμεως, 5 ἵνα ἡ πίστις ὑμῶν μὴ ᾖ
of power, in order that the faith of you may not be

ἐν σοφίᾳ ἀνθρώπων ἀλλ' ἐν δυνάμει
in [the] wisdom of men but in [the] power

θεοῦ.
of God.

6 Σοφίαν δὲ λαλοῦμεν ἐν τοῖς τελείοις,
But ²wisdom ¹we speak among the perfect ones,

σοφίαν δὲ οὐ τοῦ αἰῶνος τούτου οὐδὲ
yet wisdom not of this age neither

τῶν ἀρχόντων τοῦ αἰῶνος τούτου τῶν
of the leaders of this age of the
                                              [ones]

καταργουμένων· 7 ἀλλὰ λαλοῦμεν θεοῦ
being brought to naught; but we speak ¹of God

σοφίαν ἐν μυστηρίῳ, τὴν ἀποκεκρυμμένην,
²a wisdom in mystery, - having been hidden,

ἣν προώρισεν ὁ θεὸς πρὸ τῶν αἰώνων
which ²foreordained - ¹God before the ages

εἰς δόξαν ἡμῶν· 8 ἣν οὐδεὶς τῶν ἀρχόντων
for glory of us; which not one of the leaders

τοῦ αἰῶνος τούτου ἔγνωκεν· εἰ γὰρ
of this age has known; for if

ἔγνωσαν, οὐκ ἂν τὸν κύριον τῆς δόξης
they knew, not - the Lord - of glory

ἐσταύρωσαν· 9 ἀλλὰ καθὼς γέγραπται· ἃ
they would have but as it has been written: Things
crucified;★   which

ὀφθαλμὸς οὐκ εἶδεν καὶ οὖς οὐκ ἤκουσεν
eye saw not and ear heard not

καὶ ἐπὶ καρδίαν ἀνθρώπου οὐκ ἀνέβη,
and on heart of man came not up,

ὅσα ἡτοίμασεν ὁ θεὸς τοῖς ἀγαπῶσιν
how many ¹prepared - ¹God for the [ones] loving

* That is, so that no flesh might boast. Cf. Mat. 24. 22.
★ This rendering is demanded by the preceding ἄν.

King James Version

pared for them that love him. 10 But God hath revealed *them* unto us by his Spirit: for the Spirit searcheth all things, yea, the deep things of God. 11 For what man knoweth the things of a man, save the spirit of man which is in him? even so the things of God knoweth no man, but the Spirit of God. 12 Now we have received, not the spirit of the world, but the Spirit which is of God; that we might know the things that are freely given to us of God. 13 Which things also we speak, not in the words which man's wisdom teacheth, but which the Holy Ghost teacheth; comparing spiritual things with spiritual. 14 But the natural man receiveth not the things of the Spirit of God: for they are foolishness unto him: neither can he know *them,* because they are spiritually discerned. 15 But he that is spiritual judgeth all things, yet he himself is judged of no man. 16 For who hath known the mind of the Lord, that he may instruct him? But we have the mind of Christ.

3 And I, brethren, could not speak unto you as unto spiritual, but as unto carnal, *even* as unto babes in Christ. 2 I have fed you with milk, and not with meat: for hitherto ye were not able *to bear it,* neither yet now are ye able. 3 For ye are yet carnal: for whereas *there is* among you envying, and strife, and divisions, are ye not carnal, and walk as men? 4 For while one saith, I am of Paul; and another, I *am* of Apollos; are ye not carnal? 5 Who then is Paul, and who *is* Apollos, but ministers by whom ye believed, even as the Lord gave to every man? 6 I have planted, Apollos watered; but God gave the increase. 7 So then neither is he that planteth any thing, neither he that watereth; but God that giveth the increase. 8 Now he that planteth and he that watereth are one: and every man shall receive his own reward according to his own labour. 9 For we are labourers together with God: ye are God's husbandry, *ye are* God's building. 10 According to the grace of God which is given unto me, as a wise masterbuilder, I have laid the foundation, and another buildeth thereon. But let every man take heed how he buildeth thereupon. 11 For other foundation can no man lay than that is laid, which is Jesus Christ. 12 Now if any man build upon this foundation gold, silver, precious stones, wood, hay, stubble; 13 Every man's work shall be made manifest: for the day shall declare it, because it shall be revealed by fire; and the fire shall try every man's work of what sort it is. 14 If any man's work abide which he hath built thereupon, he shall receive a reward. 15 If any man's work shall be burned, he shall suffer loss: but he himself shall be saved; yet so as by fire. 16 Know ye not that ye are the temple of God,

New International Version

10 but God has revealed it to us by his Spirit.

The Spirit searches all things, even the deep things of God. 11 For who among men knows the thoughts of a man except the man's spirit within him? In the same way no one knows the thoughts of God except the Spirit of God. 12 We have not received the spirit of the world but the Spirit who is from God, that we may understand what God has freely given us. 13 This is what we speak, not in words taught us by human wisdom but in words taught by the Spirit, expressing spiritual truths in spiritual words.*g* 14 The man without the Spirit does not accept the things that come from the Spirit of God, for they are foolishness to him, and he cannot understand them, because they are spiritually discerned. 15 The spiritual man makes judgments about all things, but he himself is not subject to any man's judgment:

16 "For who has known the mind of the Lord
　　that he may instruct him?" *h*

But we have the mind of Christ.

On divisions in the church

3 Brothers, I could not address you as spiritual but as worldly—mere infants in Christ. 2 I gave you milk, not solid food, for you were not yet ready for it. Indeed, you are still not ready. 3 You are still worldly. For since there is jealousy and quarreling among you, are you not worldly? Are you not acting like mere men? 4 For when one says, "I follow Paul," and another, "I follow Apollos," are you not mere men?

5 What, after all, is Apollos? And what is Paul? Only servants, through whom you came to believe—as the Lord has assigned to each his task. 6 I planted the seed, Apollos watered it, but God made it grow. 7 So neither he who plants nor he who waters is anything, but only God, who makes things grow. 8 The man who plants and the man who waters have one purpose, and each will be rewarded according to his own labor. 9 For we are God's fellow workers; you are God's field, God's building.

10 By the grace God has given me, I laid a foundation as an expert builder, and others are building on it. But each one should be careful how he builds. 11 For no one can lay any foundation other than the one already laid, which is Jesus Christ. 12 If any man builds on this foundation using gold, silver, costly stones, wood, hay or straw, 13 his work will be shown for what it is, because the Day will bring it to light. It will be revealed with fire, and the fire will test the quality of each man's work. 14 If what he has built survives, he will receive his reward. 15 If it is burned up, he will suffer loss; he himself will be saved, but only as one escaping through the flames.

16 Don't you know that you yourselves are God's temple and that God's Spirit lives in you?

[g] Or *Spirit, interpreting spiritual truths to spiritual men.* [h] Isaiah 40:13.

Greek Interlinear

αὐτόν.   10 ἡμῖν   γὰρ   ἀπεκάλυψεν ὁ θεός
him.   ¹For ²to us   ²revealed   - ³God

διὰ   τοῦ   πνεύματος· τὸ γὰρ πνεῦμα πάντα
through the   Spirit;   for the Spirit all things

ἐρευνᾷ,   καὶ τὰ βάθη τοῦ θεοῦ. 11 τίς
searches, even the deep things - of God.   ⁵who

γὰρ οἶδεν ἀνθρώπων τὰ τοῦ ἀνθρώπου
¹For ⁴knows   ²of men the things - of a man

εἰ μὴ τὸ πνεῦμα τοῦ ἀνθρώπου τὸ
except the spirit   - of a man   -

ἐν αὐτῷ; οὕτως καὶ τὰ τοῦ θεοῦ οὐδεὶς
in him?   so   also the things - of God no one

ἔγνωκεν εἰ μὴ τὸ πνεῦμα τοῦ θεοῦ.
has known except the Spirit   - of God.

12 ἡμεῖς δὲ οὐ τὸ πνεῦμα τοῦ κόσμου
And we   not the spirit of the world

ἐλάβομεν ἀλλὰ τὸ πνεῦμα τὸ ἐκ τοῦ θεοῦ,
received   but the Spirit   - from - God,

ἵνα εἰδῶμεν τὰ ὑπὸ τοῦ θεοῦ
in order we may the things by   - God
that   know

χαρισθέντα ἡμῖν· 13 ἃ καὶ λαλοῦμεν οὐκ
freely given to us; which things also we speak not

ἐν διδακτοῖς ἀνθρωπίνης σοφίας λόγοις,
in   ⁵taught   ⁶of human   ⁴wisdom ¹words,

ἀλλ’ ἐν διδακτοῖς πνεύματος, πνευματικοῖς
but   in [words] taught of [the] Spirit, ⁸with spiritual things

πνευματικὰ συγκρίνοντες. 14 ψυχικὸς δὲ
⁵spiritual things ⁷comparing.   But a natural

ἄνθρωπος οὐ δέχεται τὰ τοῦ πνεύματος
man   receives not the things of the Spirit

τοῦ θεοῦ· μωρία γὰρ αὐτῷ ἐστιν, καὶ
- of God; for folly to him they are, and

οὐ δύναται γνῶναι, ὅτι πνευματικῶς
he cannot to know, because ⁵spiritually

ἀνακρίνεται. 15 ὁ δὲ πνευματικὸς ἀνακρίνει
¹they are ⁴discerned. But the spiritual man ³discerns

μὲν πάντα, αὐτὸς δὲ ὑπ’ οὐδενὸς
¹on one all things, ⁴he ¹on the ⁴by ⁵no one
hand   other

ἀνακρίνεται. 16 τίς γὰρ ἔγνω νοῦν
⁴is discerned.   For who knew [the] mind

κυρίου, ὃς συμβιβάσει αὐτόν; ἡμεῖς δὲ
of [the] who will instruct him?   But we
Lord,

νοῦν Χριστοῦ ἔχομεν.
[the] mind of Christ have.

Chapter 3

Κἀγώ, ἀδελφοί, οὐκ ἠδυνήθην λαλῆσαι
And I,   brothers,   was not able   to speak

ὑμῖν ὡς πνευματικοῖς ἀλλ’ ὡς σαρκίνοις,
to you as   to spiritual men but as to fleshy,

ὡς νηπίοις ἐν Χριστῷ. 2 γάλα ὑμᾶς
as to infants in Christ.   ²Milk ³you

ἐπότισα, οὐ βρῶμα· οὔπω γὰρ ἐδύνασθε.
¹I gave not food;   for ye were not then able.
²to drink,

ἀλλ’ οὐδὲ [ἔτι] νῦν δύνασθε, 3 ἔτι γὰρ
But neither yet   now are ye able, for still

σαρκικοί ἐστε. ὅπου γὰρ ἐν ὑμῖν ζῆλος
fleshly ye are. For whereas among you [there is]
jealousy

καὶ ἔρις, οὐχὶ σαρκικοί ἐστε καὶ κατὰ
and   strife, ²not ³fleshly ¹are ye ⁴and ⁵according to

ἄνθρωπον περιπατεῖτε; 4 ὅταν γὰρ λέγῃ
³man   ¹walk?   For whenever says

τις· ἐγὼ μέν εἰμι Παύλου, ἕτερος δέ·
anyone: I   -   am of Paul, and another:

ἐγὼ Ἀπολλῶ, οὐκ ἄνθρωποί ἐστε; 5 Τί
I   of Apollos, ²not ³men   ¹are ye? What

οὖν ἐστιν Ἀπολλῶς; τί δέ ἐστιν Παῦλος;
there- is Apollos? and what is Paul?
fore

διάκονοι δι’ ὧν ἐπιστεύσατε, καὶ ἑκάστῳ
Ministers through whom ye believed, even ²to each one

ὡς ὁ κύριος ἔδωκεν. 6 ἐγὼ ἐφύτευσα,
¹as the Lord gave.   I   planted,

Ἀπολλῶς ἐπότισεν, ἀλλὰ ὁ θεὸς ηὔξανεν·
Apollos watered, but - God made to
grow;

7 ὥστε οὔτε ὁ φυτεύων ἐστίν τι οὔτε
so as neither the [one] planting is anything nor

ὁ ποτίζων, ἀλλ’ ὁ αὐξάνων θεός. 8 ὁ
the watering, but ¹the ²making to ¹God. ¹The
[one]   [one] grow   [one]

φυτεύων δὲ καὶ ὁ ποτίζων ἓν εἰσιν,
²planting ¹so and the [one] watering one* are,

ἕκαστος δὲ τὸν ἴδιον μισθὸν λήμψεται
and each one the(his) own reward will receive

κατὰ τὸν ἴδιον κόπον. 9 θεοῦ γὰρ ἐσμεν
accord- his   own labour. For of God we are
ing to

συνεργοί· θεοῦ γεώργιον, θεοῦ οἰκοδομή
fellow-workers; ¹of God ²a tillage, ¹of God ²a building

ἐστε. 10 Κατὰ τὴν χάριν τοῦ θεοῦ τὴν
¹ye are. According to the grace - of God -

δοθεῖσάν μοι ὡς σοφὸς ἀρχιτέκτων
given   to me as a wise master builder

θεμέλιον ἔθηκα· ἄλλος δὲ ἐποικοδομεῖ.
a foundation I laid, but another builds on [it].

ἕκαστος δὲ βλεπέτω πῶς ἐποικοδομεῖ.
But each one let him look how he builds on [it].

11 θεμέλιον γὰρ ἄλλον οὐδεὶς δύναται θεῖναι
For foundation other no one is able to lay

παρὰ τὸν κείμενον, ὅς ἐστιν Ἰησοῦς
beside the [one] being laid, who is Jesus

Χριστός. 12 εἰ δέ τις ἐποικοδομεῖ ἐπὶ
Christ.   Now if anyone builds on   on

τὸν θεμέλιον χρυσίον, ἀργύριον, λίθους
the foundation gold,   silver,   stones

τιμίους, ξύλα, χόρτον, καλάμην, 13 ἑκάστου
precious, woods, hay,   stubble,   of each one

τὸ ἔργον φανερὸν γενήσεται· ἡ γὰρ ἡμέρα
the work manifest will become; for the day

δηλώσει, ὅτι ἐν πυρὶ ἀποκαλύπτεται,
will declare because by fire it is revealed,
[it],

καὶ ἑκάστου τὸ ἔργον ὁποῖόν ἐστιν
and ⁵of each one ¹the ²work ⁴of what sort ³it is

τὸ πῦρ αὐτὸ δοκιμάσει. 14 εἴ τινος
⁴the ⁵fire ⁶it   ⁸will prove.   If of anyone

τὸ ἔργον μενεῖ ὃ ἐποικοδόμησεν, μισθὸν
the work remains which he built on, a reward

λήμψεται· 15 εἴ τινος τὸ ἔργον κατακαή-
he will receive; if of anyone the work will be con-

εται, ζημιωθήσεται, αὐτὸς δὲ σωθήσεται,
sumed, he will suffer loss, but he will be saved,

οὕτως δὲ ὡς διὰ πυρός. 16 Οὐκ οἴδατε
yet so   as through fire.   Know ye not

ὅτι ναὸς θεοῦ ἐστε καὶ τὸ πνεῦμα τοῦ
that a shrine of God ye are and the Spirit   -

* Notice the neuter gender, though " thing " cannot very well be
expressed; cf. John 10. 30.

King James Version

and *that* the Spirit of God dwelleth in you? 17 If any man defile the temple of God, him shall God destroy; for the temple of God is holy, which *temple* ye are. 18 Let no man deceive himself. If any man among you seemeth to be wise in this world, let him become a fool, that he may be wise. 19 For the wisdom of this world is foolishness with God: for it is written, He taketh the wise in their own craftiness. 20And again, The Lord knoweth the thoughts of the wise, that they are vain. 21 Therefore let no man glory in men: for all things are yours; 22 Whether Paul, or Apollos, or Cephas, or the world, or life, or death, or things present, or things to come; all are yours; 23And ye are Christ's; and Christ *is* God's.

New International Version

17 If anyone destroys God's temple, God will destroy him; for God's temple is sacred, and you are that temple.
18 Do not deceive yourselves. If any one of you thinks he is wise by the standards of this age, he should become a "fool" so that he may become wise. 19 For the wisdom of this world is foolishness in God's sight. As it is written: "He catches the wise in their craftiness" [i]; 20 and again, "The Lord knows that the thoughts of the wise are futile." [j] 21 So then, no more boasting about men! All things are yours, 22 whether Paul or Apollos or Cephas [k] or the world or life or death or the present or the future—all are yours, 23 and you are of Christ, and Christ is of God.

Apostles of Christ

4 Let a man so account of us, as of the ministers of Christ, and stewards of the mysteries of God. 2 Moreover it is required in stewards, that a man be found faithful. 3 But with me it is a very small thing that I should be judged of you, or of man's judgment: yea, I judge not mine own self. 4 For I know nothing by myself; yet am I not hereby justified: but he that judgeth me is the Lord. 5 Therefore judge nothing before the time, until the Lord come, who both will bring to light the hidden things of darkness, and will make manifest the counsels of the hearts: and then shall every man have praise of God. 6And these things, brethren, I have in a figure transferred to myself and *to* Apollos for your sakes; that ye might learn in us not to think *of men* above that which is written, that no one of you be puffed up for one against another. 7 For who maketh thee to differ *from another?* and what hast thou that thou didst not receive? now if thou didst receive *it,* why dost thou glory, as if thou hadst not received *it?* 8 Now ye are full, now ye are rich, ye have reigned as kings without us: and I would to God ye did reign, that we also might reign with you. 9 For I think that God hath set forth us the apostles last, as it were appointed to death: for we are made a spectacle unto the world, and to angels, and to men. 10 We *are* fools for Christ's sake, but ye *are* wise in Christ; we *are* weak, but ye *are* strong; ye *are* honourable, but we *are* despised. 11 Even unto this present hour we both hunger, and thirst, and are naked, and are buffeted, and have no certain dwellingplace; 12And labour, working with our own hands: being reviled, we bless; being persecuted, we suffer it: 13 Being defamed, we entreat: we are made as the filth of the world, *and are* the offscouring of all things unto this day. 14 I write not these things to shame you, but as my beloved sons I warn *you.* 15 For though ye have ten thousand instructors in Christ, yet *have ye* not many fathers: for in

4 So then, men ought to regard us as servants of Christ and as those entrusted with the secret things of God. 2 Now it is required that those who have been given a trust must prove faithful. 3 I care very little if I am judged by you or by any human court; indeed, I do not even judge myself. 4 My conscience is clear, but that does not make me innocent. It is the Lord who judges me. 5 Therefore, judge nothing before the appointed time; wait till the Lord comes. He will bring to light what is hidden in darkness and will expose the motives of men's hearts. At that time each will receive his praise from God.
6 Now, brothers, I have applied these things to myself and Apollos for your benefit, so that you may learn from us the meaning of the saying, "Do not go beyond what is written." Then you will not take pride in one man over against another. 7 For who makes you different from anyone else? What do you have that you did not receive? And if you did receive it, why do you boast as though you did not?
8 Already you have all you want! Already you have become rich! You have become kings—and that without us! How I wish that you really had become kings so that we might be kings with you! 9 For it seems to me that God has put us apostles on display at the end of the procession, like men condemned to die in the arena. We have been made a spectacle to the whole universe, to angels as well as to men. 10 We are fools for Christ, but you are so wise in Christ! We are weak, but you are strong! You are honored, we are dishonored! 11 To this very hour we go hungry and thirsty, we are in rags, we are brutally treated, we are homeless. 12 We work hard with our own hands. When we are cursed, we bless; when we are persecuted, we endure it; 13 when we are slandered, we answer kindly. Up to this moment we have become the scum of the earth, the refuse of the world.
14 I am not writing this to shame you, but to warn you, as my dear children. 15 Even though you have ten thousand guardians in Christ, you

---

[i] Job 5:13. [j] Psalm 94:11. [k] That is, Peter.

Greek Interlinear

θεοῦ ἐν ὑμῖν οἰκεῖ; 17 εἴ τις τὸν ναὸν
of God in you dwells? If anyone the shrine

τοῦ θεοῦ φθείρει, φθερεῖ τοῦτον ὁ θεός·
- of God defiles, ²will defile ³this man - ¹God;

ὁ γὰρ ναὸς τοῦ θεοῦ ἅγιός ἐστιν, οἵτινές
for the shrine - of God holy is, who(which)

ἐστε ὑμεῖς.
are ye.

18 Μηδεὶς ἑαυτὸν ἐξαπατάτω· εἴ τις
No one himself let deceive; if anyone

δοκεῖ σοφὸς εἶναι ἐν ὑμῖν ἐν τῷ αἰῶνι
thinks wise to be among you in - age

τούτῳ, μωρὸς γενέσθω, ἵνα γένηται
this, foolish let him become, in order that he may become

σοφός. 19 ἡ γὰρ σοφία τοῦ κόσμοι
wise. For the wisdom - world

τούτου μωρία παρὰ τῷ θεῷ ἐστιν.
of this folly with - God is.

γέγραπται γάρ· ὁ δρασσόμενος τοὺς σοφοὺς
For it has been written: The [one] grasping the wise

ἐν τῇ πανουργίᾳ αὐτῶν· 20 καὶ πάλιν·
in the craftiness of them; and again :

κύριος γινώσκει τοὺς διαλογισμοὺς τῶν
[The] Lord knows the reasonings of the

σοφῶν, ὅτι εἰσὶν μάταιοι. 21 ὥστε μηδεὶς
wise, that they are vain. So as no one

καυχάσθω ἐν ἀνθρώποις· πάντα γὰρ ὑμῶν
let boast in men; for all things of you

ἐστιν, 22 εἴτε Παῦλος εἴτε Ἀπολλῶς
is(are), whether Paul or Apollos

εἴτε Κηφᾶς, εἴτε κόσμος εἴτε ζωὴ εἴτε
or Cephas, or [the] world or life or

θάνατος, εἴτε ἐνεστῶτα εἴτε μέλλοντα,
death, or things present or things coming,

πάντα ὑμῶν, 23 ὑμεῖς δὲ Χριστοῦ, Χριστὸς δὲ
all things of you, and ye of Christ, and Christ

Chapter 4

θεοῦ. 4 Οὕτως ἡμᾶς λογιζέσθω ἄνθρωπος ὡς
of God. So ⁴us ¹let ²reckon ³a man as

ὑπηρέτας Χριστοῦ καὶ οἰκονόμους μυστηρίων
attendants of Christ and stewards of mysteries

θεοῦ. 2 ὧδε λοιπὸν ζητεῖται ἐν τοῖς
of God. Here for the rest it is sought among -

οἰκονόμοις ἵνα πιστός τις εὑρεθῇ. 3 ἐμοὶ
stewards in order that ²faithful ¹anyone ³be found. to me

δὲ εἰς ἐλάχιστόν ἐστιν ἵνα ὑφ᾽ ὑμῶν
And for a very little thing it is in order that by you

ἀνακριθῶ ἢ ὑπὸ ἀνθρωπίνης ἡμέρας· ἀλλ᾽
I am judged or by a human day;* but

οὐδὲ ἐμαυτὸν ἀνακρίνω· 4 οὐδὲν γὰρ
not myself I judge; for nothing

ἐμαυτῷ σύνοιδα, ἀλλ᾽ οὐκ ἐν τούτῳ
against myself I know, but not by this

δεδικαίωμαι· ὁ δὲ ἀνακρίνων με κύριός
have I been but the [one] judging me [the] Lord
justified;

ἐστιν. 5 ὥστε μὴ πρὸ καιροῦ τι κρίνετε,
is. So as not before time anything judge ye,

ἕως ἂν ἔλθῃ ὁ κύριος, ὃς καὶ φωτίσει
until comes the Lord, who both will shed light on

τὰ κρυπτὰ τοῦ σκότους καὶ φανερώσει
the hidden things of the darkness and will manifest

τὰς βουλὰς τῶν καρδιῶν· καὶ τότε ὁ
the counsels of the hearts; and then the

ἔπαινος γενήσεται ἑκάστῳ ἀπὸ τοῦ θεοῦ.
praise will be to each one⁰ from - God.

6 Ταῦτα δέ, ἀδελφοί, μετεσχημάτισα εἰς
Now these things, brothers, I adapted to

ἐμαυτὸν καὶ Ἀπολλῶν δι᾽ ὑμᾶς, ἵνα
myself and Apollos because of you, in order that

ἐν ἡμῖν μάθητε τὸ μὴ ὑπὲρ ἃ
among us ye may learn - not [to think] above what things

γέγραπται, ἵνα μὴ εἷς ὑπὲρ τοῦ ἑνὸς
has(ve) been written, lest ²one ³on behalf of ⁴the ¹one

φυσιοῦσθε κατὰ τοῦ ἑτέρου. 7 τίς γάρ σε
²ye are puffed up against the other. For who thee

διακρίνει; τί δὲ ἔχεις ὃ οὐκ ἔλαβες;
distinguishes? and what hast thou which thou didst not receive?

εἰ δὲ καὶ ἔλαβες, τί καυχᾶσαι ὡς μὴ
and if indeed thou didst why boastest thou as not
receive,

λαβών; 8 ἤδη κεκορεσμένοι ἐστέ· ἤδη
receiving? Now having been glutted ye are; now

ἐπλουτήσατε· χωρὶς ἡμῶν ἐβασιλεύσατε· καὶ
ye became rich; without us ye reigned; and

ὄφελόν γε ἐβασιλεύσατε, ἵνα
²an advantage ¹really ³[it is] [that] ye reigned, in order that

καὶ ἡμεῖς ὑμῖν συμβασιλεύσωμεν. 9 δοκῶ
also we ²you ¹might reign with. I think

γάρ, ὁ θεὸς ἡμᾶς τοὺς ἀποστόλους
For, - God us the apostles

ἐσχάτους ἀπέδειξεν ὡς ἐπιθανατίους, ὅτι
last showed forth as doomed to death, because

θέατρον ἐγενήθημεν τῷ κόσμῳ καὶ ἀγγέλοις
a spectacle we became to the world both to angels

καὶ ἀνθρώποις. 10 ἡμεῖς μωροὶ διὰ
and to men. We [are] fools because of

Χριστόν, ὑμεῖς δὲ φρόνιμοι ἐν Χριστῷ·
Christ, but ye [are] prudent in Christ;

ἡμεῖς ἀσθενεῖς, ὑμεῖς δὲ ἰσχυροί· ὑμεῖς
we [are] weak, but ye [are] strong; ye [are]

ἔνδοξοι, ἡμεῖς δὲ ἄτιμοι. 11 ἄχρι τῆς
held in honour, but we [are] unhonoured. Until the

ἄρτι ὥρας καὶ πεινῶμεν καὶ διψῶμεν
present hour ²both ¹we ²hunger and thirst

καὶ γυμνιτεύομεν καὶ κολαφιζόμεθα καὶ
and are naked and are buffeted and

ἀστατοῦμεν 12 καὶ κοπιῶμεν ἐργαζόμενοι
are unsettled and labour working

ταῖς ἰδίαις χερσίν· λοιδορούμενοι εὐλο-
with the(our) own hands; being reviled we

γοῦμεν, διωκόμενοι ἀνεχόμεθα, 13 δυσφημού-
bless, being persecuted we endure, being de-

μενοι παρακαλοῦμεν· ὡς περικαθάρματα τοῦ
famed we beseech; as refuse of the

κόσμου ἐγενήθημεν, πάντων περίψημα ἕως
world we became, ²of all things ¹offscouring until

ἄρτι.
now.

14 Οὐκ ἐντρέπων ὑμᾶς γράφω ταῦτα,
Not shaming you I write these things,

ἀλλ᾽ ὡς τέκνα μου ἀγαπητὰ νουθετῶν.
but as children of me beloved admonishing.

15 ἐὰν γὰρ μυρίους παιδαγωγοὺς ἔχητε
For if ten thousand trainers ye have

ἐν Χριστῷ, ἀλλ᾽ οὐ πολλοὺς πατέρας·
in Christ, yet not many fathers;

* ? of judgment.

King James Version

Christ Jesus I have begotten you through the gospel. 16 Wherefore I beseech you, be ye followers of me. 17 For this cause have I sent unto you Timotheus, who is my beloved son, and faithful in the Lord, who shall bring you into remembrance of my ways which be in Christ, as I teach every where in every church. 18 Now some are puffed up, as though I would not come to you. 19 But I will come to you shortly, if the Lord will, and will know, not the speech of them which are puffed up, but the power. 20 For the kingdom of God *is* not in word, but in power. 21 What will ye? shall I come unto you with a rod, or in love, and *in* the spirit of meekness?

5 It is reported commonly *that there is* fornication among you, and such fornication as is not so much as named among the Gentiles, that one should have his father's wife. 2 And ye are puffed up, and have not rather mourned, that he that hath done this deed might be taken away from among you. 3 For I verily, as absent in body, but present in spirit, have judged already, as though I were present, *concerning* him that hath so done this deed, 4 In the name of our Lord Jesus Christ, when ye are gathered together, and my spirit, with the power of our Lord Jesus Christ, 5 To deliver such a one unto Satan for the destruction of the flesh, that the spirit may be saved in the day of the Lord Jesus. 6 Your glorying *is* not good. Know ye not that a little leaven leaveneth the whole lump? 7 Purge out therefore the old leaven, that ye may be a new lump, as ye are unleavened. For even Christ our passover is sacrificed for us: 8 Therefore let us keep the feast, not with old leaven, neither with the leaven of malice and wickedness; but with the unleavened *bread* of sincerity and truth. 9 I wrote unto you in an epistle not to company with fornicators: 10 Yet not altogether with the fornicators of this world, or with the covetous, or extortioners, or with idolaters; for then must ye needs go out of the world. 11 But now I have written unto you not to keep company, if any man that is called a brother be a fornicator, or covetous, or an idolater, or a railer, or a drunkard, or an extortioner; with such a one no not to eat. 12 For what have I to do to judge them also that are without? do not ye judge them that are within? 13 But them that are without God judgeth. Therefore put away from among yourselves that wicked person.

6 Dare any of you, having a matter against another, go to law before the unjust, and not before the saints? 2 Do ye not know that the

New International Version

do not have many fathers, for in Christ Jesus I became your father through the gospel. 16 Therefore I urge you to imitate me. 17 For this reason I am sending to you Timothy, my son whom I love, who is faithful in the Lord. He will remind you of my way of life in Christ Jesus, which agrees with what I teach everywhere in every church.

18 Some of you have become arrogant, as if I were not coming to you. 19 But I will come to you very soon, if the Lord is willing, and then I will find out not only how these arrogant people are talking, but what power they have. 20 For the kingdom of God is not a matter of talk but of power. 21 What do you prefer? Shall I come to you with punishment, or in love and with a gentle spirit?

Expel the immoral brother!

5 It is actually reported that there is sexual immorality among you, and of a kind that does not occur even among pagans: A man has his father's wife. 2 And you are proud! Shouldn't you rather have been filled with grief and have put out of your fellowship the man who did this? 3 Even though I am not physically present, I am with you in spirit. And I have already passed judgment on the one who did this, just as if I were present. 4 When you are assembled in the name of our Lord Jesus and I am with you in spirit, and the power of our Lord Jesus is present, 5 hand this man over to Satan, so that his sinful nature[l] may be destroyed and his spirit saved on the day of the Lord.

6 Your boasting is not good. Don't you know that a little yeast works through the whole batch of dough? 7 Get rid of the old yeast that you may be a new batch without yeast—as you really are. For Christ, our Passover lamb, has been sacrificed. 8 Therefore, let us keep the Festival, not with the old yeast, the yeast of malice and wickedness, but with bread without yeast, the bread of sincerity and truth.

9 I have written you in my letter not to associate with sexually immoral people—10 not at all meaning the people of this world who are immoral, or the greedy and swindlers, or idolaters. In that case you would have to leave this world. 11 But now I am writing you that you must not associate with anyone who calls himself a brother but is sexually immoral or greedy, an idolater or a slanderer, a drunkard or a swindler. With such a man do not even eat.

12 What business is it of mine to judge those outside the church? Are you not to judge those inside? 13 God will judge those outside. "Expel the wicked man from your number." *m*

Lawsuits among believers

6 If any of you has a dispute with another, dare he take it before the ungodly for judgment instead of before the saints? 2 Do you not

[*l*] Or *his body.* [*m*] Deut. 17:7, 19:19; 22:21,24; 24:7.

Greek Interlinear

ἐν γὰρ Χριστῷ Ἰησοῦ διὰ τοῦ εὐαγγελίου
for in   Christ   Jesus   through the   gospel

ἐγὼ ὑμᾶς ἐγέννησα. 16 παρακαλῶ οὖν
I   ²you   ¹begat.   I beseech   therefore

ὑμᾶς, μιμηταί μου γίνεσθε. 17 Διὰ τοῦτο
you,   imitators   of me   become ye.   Because of this

αὐτὸ ἔπεμψα ὑμῖν Τιμόθεον, ὅς ἐστίν
very thing I sent   to you   Timothy,   who   is

μου τέκνον ἀγαπητὸν καὶ πιστὸν ἐν
of me   a child   beloved   and   faithful   in

κυρίῳ, ὃς ὑμᾶς ἀναμνήσει τὰς ὁδούς
[the] Lord, who   ¹you   ¹will remind [of] the   ways

μου τὰς ἐν Χριστῷ [Ἰησοῦ], καθὼς
of me   -   in   Christ   Jesus,   as

πανταχοῦ ἐν πάσῃ ἐκκλησίᾳ διδάσκω.
everywhere   in   every   church   I teach.

18 ὡς μὴ ἐρχομένου δέ μου πρὸς ὑμᾶς
When not   coming   now   me⁸   to   you
= Now when I did not come

ἐφυσιώθησάν τινες· 19 ἐλεύσομαι δὲ ταχέως
⁸were puffed up ¹some;   but I will come   shortly

πρὸς ὑμᾶς, ἐὰν ὁ κύριος θελήσῃ, καὶ
to you,   if   the   Lord   wills,   and

γνώσομαι οὐ τὸν λόγον τῶν πεφυσιωμένων
I will know   not   the   speech   of the   having been
[ones]   puffed up

ἀλλὰ τὴν δύναμιν· 20 οὐ γὰρ ἐν λόγῳ
but   the   power;   for ³[is] ¹not ⁴in ⁵speech

ἡ βασιλεία τοῦ θεοῦ, ἀλλ᾽ ἐν δυνάμει.
¹the   ²kingdom   -   ⁶of God,   but   in   power.

21 τί θέλετε; ἐν ῥάβδῳ ἔλθω πρὸς ὑμᾶς,
What will ye?   with   a rod   I come   to   you,

ἢ ἐν ἀγάπῃ πνεύματί τε πραΰτητος;
or   in   love   and a spirit   of meekness?

Chapter 5

Ὅλως ἀκούεται ἐν ὑμῖν πορνεία,
Actually   is heard   among   you   fornication,

καὶ τοιαύτη πορνεία ἥτις οὐδὲ ἐν τοῖς
and   such   fornication which [is] not   among   the

ἔθνεσιν, ὥστε γυναῖκά τινα τοῦ πατρὸς
nations,   so as   ²wife   ¹one ⁴of the ³father

ἔχειν. 2 καὶ ὑμεῖς πεφυσιωμένοι ἐστέ,
⁵to have.ᵇ   And   ye   *having been* puffed up   are,

καὶ οὐχὶ μᾶλλον ἐπενθήσατε, ἵνα ἀρθῇ
and   not   rather   mourned,   *in order* ⁵might be
       that   removed

ἐκ μέσου ὑμῶν ὁ τὸ ἔργον τοῦτο πράξας;
¹from ²midst ³of you ⁶the   ⁸this ⁹deed   ⁷having done?
[the]   [one]

3 ἐγὼ μὲν γάρ, ἀπὼν τῷ σώματι,
For I indeed,   being absent in the   body,

παρὼν δὲ τῷ πνεύματι, ἤδη κέκρικα
but being present in the   spirit,   already   have judged

ὡς παρὼν τὸν οὕτως τοῦτο. κατεργα-
as   being present ¹the [one]   ³thus ²this thing   ⁴having

σάμενον 4 ἐν τῷ ὀνόματι τοῦ κυρίου
wrought   in   the   name   of the   Lord

Ἰησοῦ συναχθέντων ὑμῶν καὶ τοῦ ἐμοῦ
Jesus   being assembled   you   and   -   my
= when you are assembled ...

πνεύματος σὺν τῇ δυνάμει τοῦ κυρίου
spirit   with   the   power   of the   Lord

ἡμῶν Ἰησοῦ 5 παραδοῦναι τὸν τοιοῦτον
of us   Jesus   to deliver   such a person

τῷ σατανᾷ εἰς ὄλεθρον τῆς σαρκός,
-   to Satan   for   destruction   of the   flesh,

ἵνα τὸ πνεῦμα σωθῇ ἐν τῇ ἡμέρᾳ τοῦ
in order the   spirit   may be   in   the   day   of the
that   saved

κυρίου. 6 Οὐ καλὸν τὸ καύχημα ὑμῶν.
Lord.   Not   good [is] .the   boast   of you.

οὐκ οἴδατε ὅτι μικρὰ ζύμη ὅλον τὸ
Know ye not   that   a little   leaven   all   the

φύραμα ζυμοῖ; 7 ἐκκαθάρατε τὴν παλαιὰν
lump   leavens?   Purge out   the   old

ζύμην, ἵνα ἦτε νέον φύραμα, καθὼς
leaven,   in order ye   a new   lump,   as
     that   may be

ἐστε ἄζυμοι. καὶ γὰρ τὸ πάσχα ἡμῶν
ye are unleavened.   For indeed   the   passover   of us

ἐτύθη Χριστός. 8 ὥστε ἑορτάζωμεν μὴ
was   Christ.   So as   let us keep feast   not
sacrificed[,]

ἐν ζύμῃ παλαιᾷ μηδὲ ἐν ζύμῃ κακίας
with   leaven   old   nor   with   leaven   of malice

καὶ πονηρίας, ἀλλ᾽ ἐν ἀζύμοις εἰλικρινείας
and   of evil,   but   with   unleavened   of sincerity
       [loaves]

καὶ ἀληθείας. 9 Ἔγραψα ὑμῖν ἐν τῇ
and   of truth.   I wrote   to you   in   the

ἐπιστολῇ μὴ συναναμίγνυσθαι πόρνοις,
epistle   not   to associate   with
       intimately *with*   fornicators,

10 οὐ πάντως τοῖς πόρνοις τοῦ κόσμου
not   altogether   with the fornicators   -   world

τούτου ἢ τοῖς πλεονέκταις καὶ ἅρπαξιν
of this   or   with the   covetous   and   rapacious

ἢ εἰδωλολάτραις, ἐπεὶ ὠφείλετε ἄρα ἐκ
or   idolaters,   since   ye ought   then out of

τοῦ κόσμου ἐξελθεῖν. 11 νῦν δὲ ἔγραψα
the   world   to go *out*.   But now   I wrote

ὑμῖν μὴ συναναμίγνυσθαι ἐάν τις ἀδελφὸς
to you not to associate intimately with if   anyone   a brother

ὀνομαζόμενος ἢ πόρνος ἢ πλεονέκτης ἢ
being named   is a fornicator   or   a covetous man   or

εἰδωλολάτρης ἢ λοίδορος ἢ μέθυσος ἢ
an idolater   or   a railer   or   a drunkard   or

ἅρπαξ, τῷ τοιούτῳ μηδὲ συνεσθίειν. 12 τί
a rapa-   with such a man   not   to eat *with*.   what
cious man,

γάρ μοι τοὺς ἔξω κρίνειν; οὐχὶ τοὺς
For [is it] to me ²the ones ¹without ¹to judge?   ²Not ⁴the ones

ἔσω ὑμεῖς κρίνετε; 13 τοὺς δὲ ἔξω
³within   ¹ye   ³judge?   But the ones   without

ὁ θεὸς κρινεῖ. ἐξάρατε τὸν πονηρὸν ἐξ
-   God   will judge.   Remove   the   evil man out of

ὑμῶν αὐτῶν.
yourselves.

Chapter 6

Τολμᾷ τις ὑμῶν πρᾶγμα ἔχων πρὸς
Dares   anyone   of you   ²a matter   ¹having   against

τὸν ἕτερον κρίνεσθαι ἐπὶ τῶν ἀδίκων,
the(an)   other   to be judged   before   the   unjust,

καὶ οὐχὶ ἐπὶ τῶν ἁγίων; 2 ἢ οὐκ οἴδατε
and   not   before   the   saints?   or   know ye not

King James Version

saints shall judge the world? and if the world shall be judged by you, are ye unworthy to judge the smallest matters? 3 Know ye not that we shall judge angels? how much more things that pertain to this life? 4 If then ye have judgments of things pertaining to this life, set them to judge who are least esteemed in the church. 5 I speak to your shame. Is it so, that there is not a wise man among you? no, not one that shall be able to judge between his brethren? 6 But brother goeth to law with brother, and that before the unbelievers. 7 Now therefore there is utterly a fault among you, because ye go to law one with another. Why do ye not rather take wrong? Why do ye not rather *suffer yourselves to* be defrauded? 8 Nay, ye do wrong, and defraud, and that *your* brethren. 9 Know ye not that the unrighteous shall not inherit the kingdom of God? Be not deceived: neither fornicators, nor idolaters, nor adulterers, nor effeminate, nor abusers of themselves with mankind, 10 Nor thieves, nor covetous, nor drunkards, nor revilers, nor extortioners, shall inherit the kingdom of God. 11 And such were some of you: but ye are washed, but ye are sanctified, but ye are justified in the name of the Lord Jesus, and by the Spirit of our God. 12 All things are lawful unto me, but all things are not expedient: all things are lawful for me, but I will not be brought under the power of any. 13 Meats for the belly, and the belly for meats: but God shall destroy both it and them. Now the body *is* not for fornication, but for the Lord; and the Lord for the body. 14 And God hath both raised up the Lord, and will also raise up us by his own power. 15 Know ye not that your bodies are the members of Christ? shall I then take the members of Christ, and make *them* the members of a harlot? God forbid. 16 What! know ye not that he which is joined to a harlot is one body? for two, saith he, shall be one flesh. 17 But he that is joined unto the Lord is one spirit. 18 Flee fornication. Every sin that a man doeth is without the body; but he that committeth fornication sinneth against his own body. 19 What! know ye not that your body is the temple of the Holy Ghost *which is* in you, which ye have of God, and ye are not your own? 20 For ye are bought with a price: therefore glorify God in your body, and in your spirit, which are God's.

7 Now concerning the things whereof ye wrote unto me: *It is* good for a man not to touch a woman. 2 Nevertheless, *to avoid* fornication, let every man have his own wife, and let every woman have her own husband. 3 Let the husband render unto the wife due benevolence: and

New International Version

know that God's people will judge the world? And if you are to judge the world, are you not competent to judge trivial cases? 3 Do you not know that we will judge angels? How much more the things of this life! 4 Therefore, if you have disputes about such matters, appoint as judges even men of little account in the church![n] 5 I say this to shame you. Is it possible that there is nobody among you wise enough to judge a dispute between believers? 6 But instead, one brother goes to law against another—and this in front of unbelievers!

7 The very fact that you have lawsuits among you means you have been completely defeated already. Why not rather be wronged? Why not rather be cheated? 8 Instead, you yourselves cheat and do wrong, and you do this to your brothers.

9 Don't you know that the wicked will not inherit the kingdom of God? Do not be deceived: Neither the sexually immoral nor idolaters nor adulterers nor male prostitutes nor homosexual offenders 10 nor thieves nor the greedy nor drunkards nor slanderers nor swindlers will inherit the kingdom of God. 11 And that is what some of you were. But you were washed, you were sanctified, you were justified in the name of the Lord Jesus Christ and by the Spirit of our God.

Sexual immorality

12 "Everything is permissible for me"—but not everything is beneficial. "Everything is permissible for me"—but I will not be mastered by anything. 13 "Food for the stomach and the stomach for food"—but God will destroy them both. The body is not meant for sexual immorality, but for the Lord, and the Lord for the body. 14 By his power God raised the Lord from the dead, and he will raise us also. 15 Do you not know that your bodies are members of Christ himself? Shall I then take the members of Christ and unite them with a prostitute? Never! 16 Do you not know that he who unites himself with a prostitute is one with her in body? For it is said, "The two will become one flesh."[o] 17 But he who unites himself with the Lord is one with him in spirit.

18 Flee from sexual immorality. All other sins a man commits are outside his body, but he who sins sexually sins against his own body. 19 Do you not know that your body is a temple of the Holy Spirit, who is in you, whom you have received from God? You are not your own; 20 you were bought at a price. Therefore honor God with your body.

Marriage

7 Now for the matters you wrote about: It is good for a man not to marry. 2 But since there is so much immorality, each man should have his own wife, and each woman her own husband. 3 The husband should fulfill his marital duty to his wife, and likewise the wife to her

[n] Or *matters, do you appoint as judges men of little account in the Church?* [o] Gen. 2:24.

494

Greek Interlinear

ὅτι οἱ ἅγιοι τὸν κόσμον κρινοῦσιν; καὶ
that the saints the world will judge? and

εἰ ἐν ὑμῖν κρίνεται ὁ κόσμος, ἀνάξιοί
if ⁴by ²you ³is judged ¹the ⁵world, ⁶unworthy

ἐστε κριτηρίων ἐλαχίστων; 3 οὐκ οἴδατε
¹are ye ⁴judgments? ²of very little? Know ye not

ὅτι ἀγγέλους κρινοῦμεν, μήτι γε βιωτικά;
that angels we will judge, not to speak of things
of this life?

4 βιωτικὰ μὲν οὖν κριτήρια ἐὰν ἔχητε,
⁴Of this life ²indeed ³therefore ⁵judgments ¹if ⁶ye have,

τοὺς ἐξουθενημένους ἐν τῇ ἐκκλησίᾳ,
the ones being despised in the church,

τούτους καθίζετε; 5 πρὸς ἐντροπὴν ὑμῖν
these sit ye? For shame to you

λέγω. οὕτως οὐκ ἔνι ἐν ὑμῖν οὐδεὶς
I say. Thus there is no room among you [for] no one

σοφός, ὃς δυνήσεται διακρῖναι ἀνὰ μέσον
wise man, who will be able to discern in your midst

τοῦ ἀδελφοῦ αὐτοῦ; 6 ἀλλὰ ἀδελφὸς μετὰ
the brother of him? But brother with

ἀδελφοῦ κρίνεται, καὶ τοῦτο ἐπὶ ἀπίστων;
brother is judged, and this before unbelievers?

7 ἤδη μὲν οὖν ὅλως ἥττημα ὑμῖν ἐστιν
Now indeed there- ²altogether ¹a failure ⁴with ³there is
fore you

ὅτι κρίματα ἔχετε μεθ᾽ ἑαυτῶν. διὰ τί
²that ¹lawsuits ³ye have with yourselves. Why

οὐχὶ μᾶλλον ἀδικεῖσθε; διὰ τί οὐχὶ
not rather be wronged? Why not

μᾶλλον ἀποστερεῖσθε; 8 ἀλλὰ ὑμεῖς ἀδικεῖτε
rather be deprived? But ye do wrong

καὶ ἀποστερεῖτε, καὶ τοῦτο ἀδελφούς.
and deprive, and this brothers.

9 ἢ οὐκ οἴδατε ὅτι ἄδικοι θεοῦ βασιλείαν
Or know ye not that unrighteous ²of God ¹[the]
men kingdom

οὐ κληρονομήσουσιν; μὴ πλανᾶσθε· οὔτε
¹will not inherit? Be not led astray; not

πόρνοι οὔτε εἰδωλολάτραι οὔτε μοιχοὶ
fornicators nor idolaters nor adulterers

οὔτε μαλακοὶ οὔτε ἀρσενοκοῖται 10 οὔτε
nor voluptuous nor sodomites nor
persons

κλέπται οὔτε πλεονέκται, οὐ μέθυσοι,
thieves nor covetous persons, not drunkards,

οὐ λοίδοροι, οὐχ ἅρπαγες βασιλείαν θεοῦ
not revilers, not rapacious ²[the] kingdom ³of
persons God

κληρονομήσουσιν. 11 καὶ ταῦτά τινες ἦτε·
¹will inherit. And these ²some ¹ye
things [of you] were;

ἀλλὰ ἀπελούσασθε, ἀλλὰ ἡγιάσθητε, ἀλλὰ
but ye were washed, but were sanctified, but

ἐδικαιώθητε ἐν τῷ ὀνόματι τοῦ κυρίου
ye were justified in the name of the Lord

Ἰησοῦ Χριστοῦ καὶ ἐν τῷ πνεύματι
Jesus Christ and by the Spirit

τοῦ θεοῦ ἡμῶν.
of the God of us.

12 Πάντα μοι ἔξεστιν, ἀλλ᾽ οὐ πάντα
All things to me [are] lawful, but not all things

συμφέρει. πάντα μοι ἔξεστιν, ἀλλ᾽ οὐκ
expedient. All things to me [are] lawful, but not

ἐγὼ ἐξουσιασθήσομαι ὑπό τινος. 13 τὰ
I will be ruled by anyone. -

βρώματα τῇ κοιλίᾳ, καὶ ἡ κοιλία τοῖς
Foods for the belly, and the belly -

βρώμασιν· ὁ δὲ θεὸς καὶ ταύτην καὶ
for foods; - but God both this and

ταῦτα καταργήσει. τὸ δὲ σῶμα οὐ τῇ
these will destroy. But the body [is] not -

πορνείᾳ ἀλλὰ τῷ κυρίῳ, καὶ ὁ κύριος
for fornication but for the Lord, and the Lord

τῷ σώματι· 14 ὁ δὲ θεὸς καὶ τὸν κύριον
for the body; - and God both the Lord

ἤγειρεν καὶ ἡμᾶς ἐξεγερεῖ διὰ τῆς
raised and us will raise up through the

δυνάμεως αὐτοῦ. 15 οὐκ οἴδατε ὅτι τὰ
power of him. Know ye not that the

σώματα ὑμῶν μέλη Χριστοῦ ἐστιν; ἄρας
bodies of you members of Christ (is)are? Taking

οὖν τὰ μέλη τοῦ Χριστοῦ ποιήσω πόρνης
there- the members - of Christ shall I make ²of a
fore [them] harlot

μέλη; μὴ γένοιτο. 16 ἢ οὐκ οἴδατε ὅτι
¹members? May it not be. Or know ye not that

ὁ κολλώμενος τῇ πόρνῃ ἓν σῶμά ἐστιν;
the being joined - to a harlot one body is?
[one]

ἔσονται γάρ, φησίν, οἱ δύο εἰς σάρκα
For ⁴will be, ²he says, ¹the ³two ⁵into ⁶flesh

μίαν. 17 ὁ δὲ κολλώμενος τῷ κυρίῳ
⁷one. But the [one] being joined to the Lord

ἓν πνεῦμά ἐστιν. 18 φεύγετε τὴν πορνείαν.
one spirit is. Flee ye - fornication.

πᾶν ἁμάρτημα ὃ ἐὰν ποιήσῃ ἄνθρωπος
Every sin whichever ²may do ¹a man

ἐκτὸς τοῦ σώματός ἐστιν· ὁ δὲ πορνεύων
outside the body is; but the committing
[one] fornication

εἰς τὸ ἴδιον σῶμα ἁμαρτάνει. 19
against the(his) own body sins. Or

οὐκ οἴδατε ὅτι τὸ σῶμα ὑμῶν ναός
know ye not that the body of you ²a shrine

τοῦ ἐν ὑμῖν ἁγίου πνεύματός ἐστιν,
³of the ⁴in ⁷you ⁵Holy ⁶Spirit ¹is,

οὗ ἔχετε ἀπὸ θεοῦ, καὶ οὐκ ἐστὲ ἑαυτῶν;
which ye from God, and ye are not of
have yourselves?

20 ἠγοράσθητε γὰρ τιμῆς· δοξάσατε δὴ
For ye were bought of(with) a price; glorify ye then

τὸν θεὸν ἐν τῷ σώματι ὑμῶν.
- God in the body of you.

Chapter 7

Περὶ δὲ ὧν ἐγράψατε, καλὸν ἀνθρώπῳ
Now about things ye wrote, [it is] good for a man
of which

γυναικὸς μὴ ἅπτεσθαι· 2 διὰ δὲ τὰς
²a woman* ¹not ³to touch; but because of the

πορνείας ἕκαστος τὴν ἑαυτοῦ γυναῖκα
fornications each man ²the ¹of himself ³wife

ἐχέτω, καὶ ἑκάστη τὸν ἴδιον ἄνδρα
¹let him have, and each woman the(her) own husband

ἐχέτω. 3 τῇ γυναικὶ ὁ ἀνὴρ τὴν ὀφειλὴν
let her have. To the wife ²the ¹husband ⁴the ³debt

ἀποδιδότω, ὁμοίως δὲ καὶ ἡ γυνὴ τῷ
¹let him pay, and likewise also the wife to the

* As the same Greek word γυνή means "wife" or " (?married)
woman" it is not always easy to differentiate in translating. So
also the one Greek word ἀνήρ means "man" or "husband"

495

King James Version

likewise also the wife unto the husband. 4 The wife hath not power of her own body, but the husband: and likewise also the husband hath not power of his own body, but the wife. 5 Defraud ye not one the other, except *it be* with consent for a time, that ye may give yourselves to fasting and prayer; and come together again, that Satan tempt you not for your incontinency. 6 But I speak this by permission, *and* not of commandment. 7 For I would that all men were even as I myself. But every man hath his proper gift of God, one after this manner, and another after that. 8 I say therefore to the unmarried and widows, It is good for them if they abide even as I. 9 But if they cannot contain, let them marry: for it is better to marry than to burn. 10And unto the married I command, *yet* not I, but the Lord, Let not the wife depart from *her* husband: 11 But and if she depart, let her remain unmarried, or be reconciled to *her* husband: and let not the husband put away *his* wife. 12 But to the rest speak I, not the Lord: If any brother hath a wife that believeth not, and she be pleased to dwell with him, let him not put her away. 13And the woman which hath a husband that believeth not, and if he be pleased to dwell with her, let her not leave him. 14 For the unbelieving husband is sanctified by the wife, and the unbelieving wife is sanctified by the husband: else were your children unclean; but now are they holy. 15 But if the unbelieving depart, let him depart. A brother or a sister is not under bondage in such *cases:* but God hath called us to peace. 16 For what knowest thou, O wife, whether thou shalt save *thy* husband? or how knowest thou, O man, whether thou shalt save *thy* wife? 17 But as God hath distributed to every man, as the Lord hath called every one, so let him walk. And so ordain I in all churches. 18 Is any man called being circumcised? let him not become uncircumcised. Is any called in uncircumcision? let him not be circumcised. 19 Circumcision is nothing, and uncircumcision is nothing, but the keeping of the commandments of God. 20 Let every man abide in the same calling wherein he was called. 21Art thou called *being* a servant? care not for it: but if thou mayest be made free, use *it* rather. 22 For he that is called in the Lord, *being* a servant, is the Lord's freeman: likewise also he that is called, *being* free, is Christ's servant. 23 Ye are bought with a price; be not ye the servants of men. 24 Brethren, let every man, wherein he is called, therein abide with God. 25 Now concerning virgins I have no commandment of the Lord: yet I give my judgment, as one that hath obtained mercy of the Lord to be faithful. 26 I suppose therefore that this is good for the present distress, *I say,* that *it is* good for a man so to be. 27Art thou bound unto a wife? seek not to be loosed. Art thou loosed from a wife? seek not a wife. 28 But and if thou marry, thou hast

New International Version

husband. 4 The wife's body does not belong to her alone but also to her husband. In the same way, the husband's body does not belong to him alone but also to his wife. 5 Do not deprive each other except by mutual consent and for a time, so that you may devote yourselves to prayer. Then come together again so that Satan will not tempt you because of your lack of self-control. 6 I say this as a concession, not as a command. 7 I wish that all men were as I am. But each man has his own gift from God; one has this gift, another has that.

8 Now to the unmarried and the widows I say: It is good for them to stay unmarried, as I am. 9 But if they cannot control themselves, they should marry, for it is better to marry than to burn with passion.

10 To the married I give this command (not I, but the Lord): A wife must not separate from her husband. 11 But if she does, she must remain unmarried or else be reconciled to her husband. And a husband must not divorce his wife.

12 To the rest I say this (I, not the Lord): If any brother has a wife who is not a believer and she is willing to live with him, he must not divorce her. 13And if a woman has a husband who is not a believer and he is willing to live with her, she must not divorce him. 14 For the unbelieving husband has been sanctified through his wife, and the unbelieving wife has been sanctified through her believing husband. Otherwise your children would be "unclean," but as it is, they are holy.

15 But if the unbeliever leaves, let him do so. A believing man or woman is not bound in such circumstances; God has called us to live in peace. 16 How do you know, wife, whether you will save your husband? Or, how do you know, husband, whether you will save your wife?

17 Nevertheless, each one should retain the place in life that the Lord assigned to him and to which God has called him. This is the rule I lay down in all the churches. 18 Was a man already circumcised when he was called? He should not become uncircumcised. Was a man uncircumcised when he was called? He should not be circumcised. 19 Circumcision is nothing and uncircumcision is nothing. Keeping God's commands is what counts. 20 Each one should remain in the situation which he was in when God called him. 21 Were you a slave when you were called? Don't let it trouble you—although if you can gain your freedom, do so. 22 For he who was a slave when he was called by the Lord is the Lord's freedman; similarly, he who was a free man when he was called is Christ's slave. 23 You were bought at a price; do not become slaves of men. 24 Brothers, each man, as responsible to God, should remain in the situation God called him to.

25 Now about virgins: I have no command from the Lord, but I give a judgment as one who by the Lord's mercy is trustworthy. 26 Because of the present crisis, I think that it is good for you to remain as you are. 27Are you married? Do not seek a divorce. Are you unmarried? Do not look for a wife. 28 But if you do marry,

ἀνδρί. **4** ἡ γυνὴ τοῦ ἰδίου σώματος
husband. The wife of the(her) own body

οὐκ ἐξουσιάζει ἀλλὰ ὁ ἀνήρ· ὁμοίως
has not authority but the husband; ²likewise

δὲ καὶ ὁ ἀνὴρ τοῦ ἰδίου σώματος οὐκ
¹and also the husband of the(his) own body not

ἐξουσιάζει ἀλλὰ ἡ γυνή. **5** μὴ ἀποστερεῖτε
has authority but the wife. Deprive not ye

ἀλλήλους, εἰ μήτι ἂν ἐκ συμφώνου πρὸς
each other, unless by agreement for

καιρὸν ἵνα σχολάσητε τῇ προσευχῇ καὶ
a time in order ye may have - for prayer and
that leisure

πάλιν ἐπὶ τὸ αὐτὸ ἦτε, ἵνα μὴ πειράζῃ
²again ¹together ¹ye may be, lest ²tempt

ὑμᾶς ὁ σατανᾶς διὰ τὴν ἀκρασίαν [ὑμῶν].
³you - ¹Satan because the want of of you.
of self-control

6 τοῦτο δὲ λέγω κατὰ συγγνώμην, οὐ
Now this I say by allowance, not

κατ' ἐπιταγήν. **7** θέλω δὲ πάντας
by command. And I wish all

ἀνθρώπους εἶναι ὡς καὶ ἐμαυτόν· ἀλλὰ
men to be as even myself· but

ἕκαστος ἴδιον ἔχει χάρισμα ἐκ θεοῦ,
each man ²[his] own ¹has gift of God,

ὁ μὲν οὕτως, ὁ δὲ οὕτως.
one thus, another thus.

8 Λέγω δὲ τοῖς ἀγάμοις καὶ ταῖς χήραις,
Now I say to the unmarried men and to the widows,

καλὸν αὐτοῖς ἐὰν μείνωσιν ὡς κἀγώ· **9** εἰ δὲ
[it is] good for them if they remain as I also; but if

οὐκ ἐγκρατεύονται, γαμησάτωσαν· κρεῖττον
they do not exercise self-control, let them marry· better

γάρ ἐστιν γαμεῖν ἢ πυροῦσθαι. **10** τοῖς
for it is to marry than to burn. to the [ones]

δὲ γεγαμηκόσιν παραγγέλλω, οὐκ ἐγὼ
But having married I enjoin, not I

ἀλλὰ ὁ κύριος, γυναῖκα ἀπὸ ἀνδρὸς μὴ
but the Lord, a woman from [her] husband not

χωρισθῆναι, **11** — ἐὰν δὲ καὶ χωρισθῇ,
to be separated,ᵇ but if indeed she is separated,

μενέτω ἄγαμος ἢ τῷ ἀνδρὶ καταλλαγήτω,
let her unmarried or to husband be reconciled,
remain the(her)

— καὶ ἄνδρα γυναῖκα μὴ ἀφιέναι. **12** Τοῖς
and a husband [his] wife not to leave.ᵇ to the

δὲ λοιποῖς λέγω ἐγώ, οὐχ ὁ κύριος·
And rest say I, not the Lord:

εἴ τις ἀδελφὸς γυναῖκα ἔχει ἄπιστον, καὶ
If any brother ²a wife ¹has unbelieving, and

αὕτη συνευδοκεῖ οἰκεῖν μετ' αὐτοῦ, μὴ
this one consents to dwell with him, not

ἀφιέτω αὐτήν· **13** καὶ γυνὴ ἥτις ἔχει
let him leave her; and a woman who has

ἄνδρα ἄπιστον, καὶ οὗτος συνευδοκεῖ οἰκεῖν
a husband unbelieving, and this one consents to dwell

μετ' αὐτῆς, μὴ ἀφιέτω τὸν ἄνδρα.
with her, not let her not leave the(her) husband.

14 ἡγίασται γὰρ ὁ ἀνὴρ ὁ ἄπιστος ἐν
For ⁴has been sanctified ¹the ²husband - ³unbelieving by

τῇ γυναικί, καὶ ἡγίασται ἡ γυνὴ ἡ
the wife, and ⁴has been ¹the ²wife -
sanctified

ἄπιστος ἐν τῷ ἀδελφῷ· ἐπεὶ ἄρα τὰ
³unbelieving by the brother; since then the

τέκνα ὑμῶν ἀκάθαρτά ἐστιν, νῦν δὲ
children of you ⁴unclean ³is(are), but now

ἅγιά ἐστιν. **15** εἰ δὲ ὁ ἄπιστος χωρίζ-
²holy ¹they are. But if the unbelieving separates
one

εται, χωριζέσθω· οὐ δεδούλωται ὁ
him/herself, let him/her be ²has not been enslaved ¹the
separated;

ἀδελφὸς ἢ ἡ ἀδελφὴ ἐν τοῖς τοιούτοις·
³brother ²or ⁴the ⁵sister in such matters;

ἐν δὲ εἰρήνῃ κέκληκεν ὑμᾶς ὁ θεός.
but ⁴in ²peace ³has called ¹you - ¹God.

16 τί γὰρ οἶδας, γύναι, εἰ τὸν ἄνδρα
For what know'st thou, wife, if the(thy) husband

σώσεις; ἢ τί οἶδας, ἄνερ, εἰ τὴν
thou wilt or what knowest husband, if the(thy)
save?

γυναῖκα σώσεις; **17** Εἰ μὴ ἑκάστῳ ὡς
wife thou wilt save? Only ²to each , ¹as

μεμέρικεν ὁ κύριος, ἕκαστον ὡς κέκληκεν
⁴has divided ⁵the ⁶Lord, ¹each ²as ³has called

ὁ θεός, οὕτως περιπατείτω. καὶ οὕτως
- ⁷God, so let him walk. And so

ἐν ταῖς ἐκκλησίαις πάσαις διατάσσομαι.
²in ³the ⁴churches ¹all ¹I command.

18 περιτετμημένος τις ἐκλήθη; μὴ
⁴Having been circumcised ²anyone ¹was ³called? not

ἐπισπάσθω· ἐν ἀκροβυστίᾳ κέκληταί τις;
let him be un- in uncircumcision has been anyone?
circumcised; called

μὴ περιτεμνέσθω. **19** ἡ περιτομὴ οὐδέν
let him not be circumcised. - Circumcision nothing

ἐστιν, καὶ ἡ ἀκροβυστία οὐδέν ἐστιν,
is, and - uncircumcision nothing is,

ἀλλὰ τήρησις ἐντολῶν θεοῦ. **20** ἕκαστος
but [the] keeping of command- of God. Each one
ments

ἐν τῇ κλήσει ᾗ ἐκλήθη, ἐν ταύτῃ
²in ³the ⁴calling in which he was called, in this

μενέτω. **21** δοῦλος ἐκλήθης; μή σοι
let him remain. A slave wast thou called? not to thee

μελέτω· ἀλλ' εἰ καὶ δύνασαι ἐλεύθερος
let it matter; but if indeed thou art able ¹free

γενέσθαι, μᾶλλον χρῆσαι. **22** ὁ γὰρ ἐν
¹to become, ²rather ³use [it]. For ¹the [one] ⁴in

κυρίῳ κληθεὶς δοῦλος ἀπελεύθερος κυρίου
²[the'] ³called ⁵a slave ⁷a freed man ⁶of [the]
Lord Lord

ἐστίν· ὁμοίως ὁ ἐλεύθερος κληθεὶς δοῦλός
⁸is; likewise ¹the ²a free man ³called ⁴a slave
[one]

ἐστιν Χριστοῦ. **23** τιμῆς ἠγοράσθητε· μὴ
⁵is ⁶of Christ. Of(with) a price ye were bought; not

γίνεσθε δοῦλοι ἀνθρώπων. **24** ἕκαστος ἐν
become ye slaves of men. Each one in

ᾧ ἐκλήθη, ἀδελφοί, ἐν τούτῳ μενέτω
what he was brothers, in this let him
[state] called, remain

παρὰ θεῷ.
with God.

25 Περὶ δὲ τῶν παρθένων ἐπιταγὴν
Now about the virgins a command

κυρίου οὐκ ἔχω, γνώμην δὲ δίδωμι ὡς
of [the] Lord I have not, but an opinion I give as

ἠλεημένος ὑπὸ κυρίου πιστὸς εἶναι.
having had mercy by [the] Lord faithful to be.

26 Νομίζω οὖν τοῦτο καλὸν ὑπάρχειν
I suppose therefore this good to be

διὰ τὴν ἐνεστῶσαν ἀνάγκην, ὅτι καλὸν
because the present necessity, that [it is] good
of

ἀνθρώπῳ τὸ οὕτως εἶναι. **27** δέδεσαι
for a man - so to be. Hast thou
been bound

γυναικί; μὴ ζήτει λύσιν· λέλυσαι ἀπὸ
to a woman? do not seek release; hast thou been from
released

γυναικός; μὴ ζήτει γυναῖκα. **28** ἐὰν
a woman? do not seek a woman. if

497

King James Version

not sinned; and if a virgin marry, she hath not sinned. Nevertheless such shall have trouble in the flesh: but I spare you. 29 But this I say, brethren, the time *is* short: it remaineth, that both they that have wives be as though they had none; 30And they that weep, as though they wept not; and they that rejoice, as though they rejoiced not; and they that buy, as though they possessed not; 31And they that use this world, as not abusing *it:* for the fashion of this world passeth away. 32 But I would have you without carefulness. He that is unmarried careth for the things that belong to the Lord, how he may please the Lord: 33 But he that is married careth for the things that are of the world, how he may please *his* wife. 34 There is difference *also* between a wife and a virgin. The unmarried woman careth for the things of the Lord, that she may be holy both in body and in spirit: but she that is married careth for the things of the world, how she may please *her* husband. 35And this I speak for your own profit; not that I may cast a snare upon you, but for that which is comely, and that ye may attend upon the Lord without distraction. 36 But if any man think that he behaveth himself uncomely toward his virgin, if she pass the flower of *her* age, and need so require, let him do what he will, he sinneth not: let them marry. 37 Nevertheless he that standeth steadfast in his heart, having no necessity, but hath power over his own will, and hath so decreed in his heart that he will keep his virgin, doeth well. 38 So then he that giveth *her* in marriage doeth well; but he that giveth *her* not in marriage doeth better. 39 The wife is bound by the law as long as her husband liveth; but if her husband be dead, she is at liberty to be married to whom she will; only in the Lord. 40 But she is happier if she so abide, after my judgment: and I think also that I have the Spirit of God.

New International Version

you have not sinned; and if a virgin marries, she has not sinned. But those who marry will face many troubles in this life, and I want to spare you this. 29 What I mean, brothers, is that the time is short. From now on those who have wives should live as if they had none; 30 those who mourn, as if they did not; those who are happy, as if they were not; those who buy something, as if it were not theirs to keep; 31 those who use the things of the world, as if not engrossed in them. For this world in its present form is passing away.

32 I would like you to be free from concern. An unmarried man is concerned about the Lord's affairs—how he can please the Lord. 33 But a married man is concerned about the affairs of this world—how he can please his wife—34 and his interests are divided. An unmarried woman or virgin is concerned about the Lord's affairs: Her aim is to be devoted to the Lord in both body and spirit. But a married woman is concerned about the affairs of this world—how she can please her husband. 35 I am saying this for your own good, not to restrict you. I want you to live in a right way in undivided devotion to the Lord.

36 If anyone thinks he is acting improperly toward the virgin he is engaged to, and if she is getting along in years and he feels he ought to marry, he should do as he wants. He is not sinning. They should get married. 37 But the man who has settled the matter in his own mind, who is under no compulsion but has control over his own will, and who has made up his mind not to marry the virgin—this man also does the right thing. 38 So then, he who marries the virgin does right, but he who does not marry her does even better.*p*

39 A woman is bound to her husband as long as he lives. But if her husband dies, she is free to marry anyone she wishes, but he must belong to the Lord. 40 In my judgment, she is happier if she stays as she is—and I think that I have the Spirit of God.

Meat sacrificed to idols

8 Now as touching things offered unto idols, we know that we all have knowledge. Knowledge puffeth up, but charity edifieth. 2And if any man think that he knoweth any thing, he knoweth nothing yet as he ought to know. 3 But if any man love God, the same is known of him. 4As concerning therefore the eating of those things that are offered in sacrifice unto idols, we know that an idol *is* nothing in the world,

8 Now about meat sacrificed to idols: We know that we all possess knowledge.*q* Knowledge puffs up, but love builds up. 2 The man who thinks he knows something does not yet know as he ought to know. 3 But the man who loves God is known by God.

4 So then, about eating meat sacrificed to idols: We know that an idol is nothing at all in the world, and that there is no God but one.

[p] Or ³⁶*If anyone thinks he is not treating his daughter properly, and if she is getting along in years, and he feels she ought to marry, he should do as he wants. He is not sinning. They should get married.* ³⁷*But the man who has settled the matter in his own mind, who is under no compulsion but has control over his own will, and who has made up his mind to keep the virgin unmarried-this man also does the right thing.* ³⁸*So then, he who gives his virgin in marriage does right, but he who does not give her in marriage does even better.* [q] Or *"We all possess knowledge,"* as you say.

Greek Interlinear

δὲ καὶ γαμήσῃς, οὐχ ἥμαρτες, καὶ ἐὰν
But indeed thou marriest, thou sinnedst not, and if

γήμῃ ἡ παρθένος, οὐχ ἥμαρτεν· θλῖψιν
¹marries ¹the ²virgin, she sinned not; ²affliction

δὲ τῇ σαρκὶ ἕξουσιν οἱ τοιοῦτοι, ἐγὼ
but ⁴in the ⁵flesh ¹will have - ¹such, ³I

δὲ ὑμῶν φείδομαι. 29 Τοῦτο δέ φημι,
¹and ⁴you ²am sparing. But this I say,

ἀδελφοί, ὁ καιρὸς συνεσταλμένος ἐστίν·
brothers, the time having been shortened is;

τὸ λοιπὸν ἵνα καὶ οἱ ἔχοντες γυναῖκας
for the rest in order both the [ones] having wives
that

ὡς μὴ ἔχοντες ὦσιν, 30 καὶ οἱ κλαίοντες
as not having may be, and the [ones] weeping

ὡς μὴ κλαίοντες, καὶ οἱ χαίροντες ὡς
as not weeping, and the [ones] rejoicing as

μὴ χαίροντες, καὶ οἱ ἀγοράζοντες ὡς
not rejoicing, and the [ones] buying as

μὴ κατέχοντες, 31 καὶ οἱ χρώμενοι τὸν
not holding, and the [ones] using the

κόσμον ὡς μὴ καταχρώμενοι· παράγει
world as not abusing [it]; ⁴is passing
away

γὰρ τὸ σχῆμα τοῦ κόσμου τούτου.
for ¹the ²fashion ²of this world.

32 Θέλω δὲ ὑμᾶς ἀμερίμνους εἶναι. ὁ
But I wish you without care to be. The

ἄγαμος μεριμνᾷ τὰ τοῦ κυρίου, 33 πῶς
unmarried cares for the of the Lord, how
man things

ἀρέσῃ τῷ κυρίῳ· ὁ δὲ γαμήσας μεριμνᾷ
he may the Lord; but the having married cares for
please [one]

τὰ τοῦ κόσμου, πῶς ἀρέσῃ τῇ γυναικί,
the of the world, how he may the(his) wife,
things please

34 καὶ μεμέρισται. καὶ ἡ γυνὴ ἡ ἄγαμος
and has been divided. And the ²woman - ¹unmarried

καὶ ἡ παρθένος μεριμνᾷ τὰ τοῦ κυρίου,
and the virgin cares for the things of the Lord,

ἵνα ᾖ ἁγία καὶ τῷ σώματι καὶ τῷ
in she holy both in the body and in
order may the
that be

πνεύματι· ἡ δὲ γαμήσασα μεριμνᾷ τὰ
spirit; but the [one] having married cares for the
things

τοῦ κόσμου, πῶς ἀρέσῃ τῷ ἀνδρί.
of the world, how she may please the(her) husband.

35 τοῦτο δὲ πρὸς τὸ ὑμῶν αὐτῶν σύμφορον
And ²this ²for ⁴the ⁶of yourselves ⁵advantage

λέγω, οὐχ ἵνα βρόχον ὑμῖν ἐπιβάλω,
¹I say, not in order ²a restraint ⁵you ¹I may put on,
that

ἀλλὰ πρὸς τὸ εὔσχημον καὶ εὐπάρεδρον
but for the thing comely and waiting on

τῷ κυρίῳ ἀπερισπάστως. 36 Εἰ δέ τις
the Lord undistractedly. But if anyone

ἀσχημονεῖν ἐπὶ τὴν παρθένον αὐτοῦ
²to behave ²toward ⁴the ⁵virgin ⁶of him
dishonourably

νομίζει, ἐὰν ᾖ ὑπέρακμος, καὶ οὕτως
¹thinks, if he/she is past the bloom and - so
of youth,

ὀφείλει γίνεσθαι, ὃ θέλει ποιείτω· οὐχ
ought to be, what he wishes let him do; not

ἁμαρτάνει· γαμείτωσαν. 37 ὃς δὲ ἕστηκεν
he sins; let them marry. But [he] who stands

ἐν τῇ καρδίᾳ αὐτοῦ ἑδραῖος, μὴ
in the heart of him firm, not

ἔχων ἀνάγκην, ἐξουσίαν δὲ ἔχει περὶ
having necessity, but authority has concerning

τοῦ ἰδίου θελήματος, καὶ τοῦτο κέκρικεν
the(his) own will, and this has decided

ἐν τῇ ἰδίᾳ καρδίᾳ, τηρεῖν τὴν ἑαυτοῦ
in the(his) own heart, to keep the of himself

παρθένον, καλῶς ποιήσει. 38 ὥστε καὶ
virgin, ²well ¹he will do. So as both

ὁ γαμίζων τὴν ἑαυτοῦ παρθένον καλῶς
the marrying the of himself virgin ²well
[one]

ποιεῖ, καὶ ὁ μὴ γαμίζων κρεῖσσον ποιήσει.
¹does, and the not marrying ²better ¹will do.
[one]

39 Γυνὴ δέδεται ἐφ' ὅσον χρόνον ζῇ
A wife has been bound for so long a time as lives

ὁ ἀνὴρ αὐτῆς· ἐὰν δὲ κοιμηθῇ ὁ ἀνήρ,
the husband of her; but if sleeps the husband,

ἐλευθέρα ἐστὶν ᾧ θέλει γαμηθῆναι, μόνον
²free ¹she is ²to ⁴she ³to be married, only
whom wishes

ἐν κυρίῳ. 40 μακαριωτέρα δέ ἐστιν
in [the] Lord. But happier she is

ἐὰν οὕτως μείνῃ, κατὰ τὴν ἐμὴν γνώμην·
if so she according - my opinion;
remains, to

δοκῶ δὲ κἀγὼ πνεῦμα θεοῦ ἔχειν.
and I think I also [the] Spirit of God to have.

Chapter 8

Περὶ δὲ τῶν εἰδωλοθύτων, οἴδαμεν
Now about the idolatrous sacrifices, we know

ὅτι πάντες γνῶσιν ἔχομεν. ἡ γνῶσις
that ²all ⁴knowledge ¹we ³have. - Knowledge

φυσιοῖ, ἡ δὲ ἀγάπη οἰκοδομεῖ· εἴ τις
puffs up, - but love builds up; if anyone

δοκεῖ ἐγνωκέναι τι, 2 οὔπω ἔγνω καθὼς
thinks to have known anything, not yet he knew as

δεῖ γνῶναι· 3 εἰ δέ τις ἀγαπᾷ τὸν
it be- to know; but if anyone loves -
hoves [him]

θεόν, οὗτος ἔγνωσται ὑπ' αὐτοῦ. 4 Περὶ
God, this one has been known by him. About

τῆς βρώσεως οὖν τῶν εἰδωλοθύτων
the eating therefore - of idolatrous sacrifices

οἴδαμεν ὅτι οὐδὲν εἴδωλον ἐν κόσμῳ,
we know that [there is] no idol in [the] world,

King James Version

and that *there is* none other God but one. 5 For though there be that are called gods, whether in heaven or in earth, (as there be gods many, and lords many,) 6 But to us *there is but* one God, the Father, of whom *are* all things, and we in him; and one Lord Jesus Christ, by whom *are* all things, and we by him. 7 Howbeit *there is* not in every man that knowledge: for some with conscience of the idol unto this hour eat *it* as a thing offered unto an idol; and their conscience being weak is defiled. 8 But meat commendeth us not to God: for neither, if we eat, are we the better; neither, if we eat not, are we the worse. 9 But take heed lest by any means this liberty of yours become a stumblingblock to them that are weak. 10 For if any man see thee which hast knowledge sit at meat in the idol's temple, shall not the conscience of him which is weak be emboldened to eat those things which are offered to idols; 11 And through thy knowledge shall the weak brother perish, for whom Christ died? 12 But when ye sin so against the brethren, and wound their weak conscience, ye sin against Christ. 13 Wherefore, if meat make my brother to offend, I will eat no flesh while the world standeth, lest I make my brother to offend.

New International Version

5 For even if there are so-called gods, whether in heaven or on earth (as indeed there are many "gods" and many "lords"), 6 yet for us there is but one God, the Father, from whom all things came and for whom we live; and there is but one Lord, Jesus Christ, through whom all things came and through whom we live.

7 But not everyone knows this. Some people are still so accustomed to idols that when they eat such meat, they think of it as having been sacrificed to an idol, and since their conscience is weak, it is defiled. 8 But food does not bring us near to God; we are no worse if we do not eat, and no better if we do.

9 Be careful, however, that the exercise of your freedom does not become a stumbling block to the weak. 10 For if anyone with a weak conscience sees you who have this knowledge eating in an idol's temple, won't he be emboldened to eat what has been sacrificed to idols? 11 So this weak brother, for whom Christ died, is destroyed by your knowledge. 12 When you sin against your brothers in this way and wound their weak conscience, you sin against Christ. 13 Therefore, if what I eat causes my brother to fall into sin, I will never eat meat again, so that I will not cause him to fall.

The rights of an apostle

9 Am I not an apostle? am I not free? have I not seen Jesus Christ our Lord? are not ye my work in the Lord? 2 If I be not an apostle unto others, yet doubtless I am to you: for the seal of mine apostleship are ye in the Lord. 3 Mine answer to them that do examine me is this: 4 Have we not power to eat and to drink? 5 Have we not power to lead about a sister, a wife, as well as other apostles, and *as* the brethren of the Lord, and Cephas? 6 Or I only and Barnabas, have not we power to forbear working? 7 Who goeth a warfare any time at his own charges? who planteth a vineyard, and eateth not of the fruit thereof? or who feedeth a flock, and eateth not of the milk of the flock? 8 Say I these things as a man? or saith not the law the same also? 9 For it is written in the law of Moses, Thou shalt not muzzle the mouth of the ox that treadeth out the corn. Doth God take care for oxen? 10 Or saith he *it* altogether for our sakes? For our sakes, no doubt, *this* is written: that he that plougheth should plough in hope; and that he that thresheth in hope should be partaker of his hope. 11 If we have sown unto you spiritual things, *is it* a great thing if we shall reap your carnal things? 12 If others be partakers of *this* power over you, *are* not we rather? Nevertheless we have not used this power; but suffer all things, lest we should hinder the gospel of Christ. 13 Do ye not know that they which minister about holy things live *of*

9 Am I not free? Am I not an apostle? Have I not seen Jesus our Lord? Are you not the result of my work in the Lord? 2 Even though I may not be an apostle to others, surely I am to you! For you are the seal of my apostleship in the Lord.

3 This is my defense to those who sit in judgment on me. 4 Don't we have the right to food and drink? 5 Don't we have the right to take a believing wife along with us, as do the other apostles and the Lord's brothers and Cephas? [r] 6 Or is it only I and Barnabas who must work for a living?

7 Who serves as a soldier at his own expense? Who plants a vineyard and does not eat of its grapes? Who tends a flock and does not drink of the milk? 8 Do I say this merely from a human point of view? Doesn't the Law say the same thing? 9 For it is written in the Law of Moses: "Do not muzzle an ox when it is treading out the grain." [s] Is it about oxen that God is concerned? 10 Surely he says this for us, doesn't he? Yes, this was written for us, because when the plowman plows and the thresher threshes, they ought to do so in the hope of sharing in the harvest. 11 If we have sown spiritual seed among you, is it too much if we reap a material harvest from you? 12 If others have this right of support from you, shouldn't we have it all the more?

But we did not use this right. On the contrary, we put up with anything rather than hinder the gospel of Christ. 13 Don't you know that those who work in the temple get their food from

---

[r] That is, Peter. [s] Deut. 25:4.

Greek Interlinear

καὶ ὅτι οὐδεὶς θεὸς εἰ μὴ εἶς. 5 καὶ
and that [there is] no God except one. even

γὰρ εἴπερ εἰσὶν λεγόμενοι θεοὶ εἴτε ἐν
For if there are being called gods either in

οὐρανῷ εἴτε ἐπὶ γῆς, ὥσπερ εἰσὶν θεοὶ
heaven or on earth, even as there are gods

πολλοὶ καὶ κύριοι πολλοί, 6 ἀλλ᾽ ἡμῖν
many and lords many, yet to us

εἶς θεὸς ὁ πατήρ, ἐξ οὗ τὰ πάντα καὶ
[there God the Father, of whom – [are] all and
is] one things

ἡμεῖς εἰς αὐτόν, καὶ εἷς κύριος Ἰησοῦς
we in him, and one Lord Jesus

Χριστός, δι᾽ οὗ τὰ πάντα καὶ ἡμεῖς
Christ, through whom – [are] all and we
things

δι᾽ αὐτοῦ. 7 Ἀλλ᾽ οὐκ ἐν πᾶσιν ἡ
through him. But [there is] not in all men the
(this)

γνῶσις· τινὲς δὲ τῇ συνηθείᾳ ἕως ἄρτι
knowledge; and some by the habit until now

τοῦ εἰδώλου ὡς εἰδωλόθυτον ἐσθίουσιν,
¹of the ²idol ⁴as ³an idolatrous sacrifice ¹eat,

καὶ ἡ συνείδησις αὐτῶν ἀσθενὴς οὖσα
and the conscience of them ¹weak ²being

μολύνεται. 8 βρῶμα δὲ ἡμᾶς οὐ παραστήσει
is defiled. But food ²us ¹will not commend

τῷ θεῷ· οὔτε ἐὰν μὴ φάγωμεν ὑστερούμεθα,
– to God; neither if we eat not are we behind,

οὔτε ἐὰν φάγωμεν περισσεύομεν. 9 βλέπετε
nor if we eat do we excel. look ye

δὲ μή πως ἡ ἐξουσία ὑμῶν αὕτη
But lest somehow the ²authority ³of you ¹this

πρόσκομμα γένηται τοῖς ἀσθενέσιν. 10 ἐὰν
a stumbling-block becomes to the weak ones. if

γάρ τις ἴδῃ σὲ τὸν ἔχοντα γνῶσιν ²in
For anyone sees thee the [one] having knowledge ²in

εἰδωλείῳ κατακείμενον, οὐχὶ ἡ συνείδησις
²an idol's temple ¹sitting, ¹not ²the ⁴conscience

αὐτοῦ ἀσθενοῦς ὄντος οἰκοδομηθήσεται εἰς
⁵of him ⁷weak ⁶[he]being ¹will ⁸be emboldened to

τὸ τὰ εἰδωλόθυτα ἐσθίειν; 11 ἀπόλλυται
– ¹⁰the ¹¹idolatrous sacrifices ⁹to eat? ²is destroyed

γὰρ ὁ ἀσθενῶν ἐν τῇ σῇ γνώσει, ὁ
For ¹the [one] ²being weak in thy knowledge, the

ἀδελφὸς δι᾽ ὃν Χριστὸς ἀπέθανεν. 12 οὕτως
brother because whom Christ died. so

δὲ ἁμαρτάνοντες εἰς τοὺς ἀδελφοὺς καὶ
And sinning against the brothers and

τύπτοντες αὐτῶν τὴν συνείδησιν ἀσθενοῦσαν
wounding of them the conscience being weak

εἰς Χριστὸν ἁμαρτάνετε. 13 διόπερ εἰ
²against ³Christ ¹ye sin. Wherefore if

βρῶμα σκανδαλίζει τὸν ἀδελφόν μου, οὐ
food offends the brother of me, by no

μὴ φάγω κρέα εἰς τὸν αἰῶνα, ἵνα μὴ
means I eat flesh unto the age, lest

τὸν ἀδελφόν μου σκανδαλίσω.
²the ³brother ⁴of me ¹I offend.

Chapter 9

Οὐκ εἰμὶ ἐλεύθερος; οὐκ εἰμὶ ἀπόστολος;
Am I not free? am I not an apostle?

οὐχὶ Ἰησοῦν τὸν κύριον ἡμῶν ἑόρακα;
not Jesus the Lord of us I have seen?

οὐ τὸ ἔργον μου ὑμεῖς ἐστε ἐν κυρίῳ;
not the work of me ye are in [the] Lord?

2 εἰ ἄλλοις οὐκ εἰμὶ ἀπόστολος, ἀλλά
If to others I am not an apostle, yet

γε ὑμῖν εἰμι· ἡ γὰρ σφραγίς μου τῆς
indeed to you I am; for the seal ¹of me ¹of the

ἀποστολῆς ὑμεῖς ἐστε ἐν κυρίῳ. 3 Ἡ
²apostleship ye are in [the] Lord.

ἐμὴ ἀπολογία τοῖς ἐμὲ ἀνακρίνουσίν ἐστιν
My defence to the ²me ¹examining is
[ones]

αὕτη. 4 μὴ οὐκ ἔχομεν ἐξουσίαν φαγεῖν
this. not Have we not authority to eat

καὶ πεῖν; 5 μὴ οὐκ ἔχομεν ἐξουσίαν
and to drink? not have we not authority

ἀδελφὴν γυναῖκα περιάγειν, ὡς καὶ οἱ
a sister a wife to lead about, as also the

λοιποὶ ἀπόστολοι καὶ οἱ ἀδελφοὶ τοῦ
remaining apostles and the brothers of the

κυρίου καὶ Κηφᾶς; 6 ἢ μόνος ἐγὼ καὶ
Lord and Cephas? or only I and

Βαρνάβας οὐκ ἔχομεν ἐξουσίαν μὴ
Barnabas have we not authority not

ἐργάζεσθαι; 7 Τίς στρατεύεται ἰδίοις
to work? Who soldiers at [his] own

ὀψωνίοις ποτέ; τίς φυτεύει ἀμπελῶνα καὶ
wages at any time? who plants a vineyard and

τὸν καρπὸν αὐτοῦ οὐκ ἐσθίει; ἢ τίς
the fruit of it eats not? or who

ποιμαίνει ποίμνην καὶ ἐκ τοῦ γάλακτος
shepherds a flock and of the milk

τῆς ποίμνης οὐκ ἐσθίει; 8 μὴ κατὰ
of the flock eats not? Not according to

ἄνθρωπον ταῦτα λαλῶ, ἢ καὶ ὁ νόμος
man these things I speak, or also the law

ταῦτα οὐ λέγει; 9 ἐν γὰρ τῷ Μωϋσέως
these things says not? for in the of Moses

νόμῳ γέγραπται· οὐ κημώσεις βοῦν
law it has been written: Thou shalt not muzzle an ox

ἀλοῶντα. μὴ τῶν βοῶν μέλει τῷ θεῷ;
threshing. not – of oxen matters it – to God?

10 ἢ δι᾽ ἡμᾶς πάντως λέγει; δι᾽ ἡμᾶς
or because of us altogether he says? because of us

γὰρ ἐγράφη, ὅτι ὀφείλει ἐπ᾽ ἐλπίδι
for it was written, because ²ought ⁶on(in) ⁷hope

ὁ ἀροτριῶν ἀροτριᾶν, καὶ ὁ ἀλοῶν ἐπ᾽
¹the ³ploughing ⁴to plough, and the threshing on(in)
[one] [one]

ἐλπίδι τοῦ μετέχειν. 11 εἰ ἡμεῖς ὑμῖν
hope to partake. If we to you
=of partaking.

τὰ πνευματικὰ ἐσπείραμεν, μέγα εἰ ἡμεῖς
– spiritual things ¹sowed, [is it] a great thing if we

ὑμῶν τὰ σαρκικὰ θερίσομεν; 12 εἰ ἄλλοι
of you – fleshly things shall reap? If others

τῆς ὑμῶν ἐξουσίας μετέχουσιν, οὐ
²of the ¹of you authority ¹have a share of, not

μᾶλλον ἡμεῖς; ἀλλ᾽ οὐκ ἐχρησάμεθα
rather we? But we did not use

τῇ ἐξουσίᾳ ταύτῃ, ἀλλὰ πάντα στέγομεν
this authority, but ¹all things ¹we put up with

ἵνα μή τινα ἐγκοπὴν δῶμεν τῷ εὐαγγελίῳ
lest ²anyone ³an obstacle ¹we should to the gospel
give

τοῦ Χριστοῦ. 13 Οὐκ οἴδατε ὅτι οἱ
– of Christ. Know ye not that the
[ones]

τὰ ἱερὰ ἐργαζόμενοι τὰ ἐκ τοῦ ἱεροῦ
– ²sacred things ¹working [at] ⁴the things ³of ⁶the ⁷temple

King James Version

the things of the temple? and they which wait at the altar are partakers with the altar? 14 Even so hath the Lord ordained that they which preach the gospel should live of the gospel. 15 But I have used none of these things: neither have I written these things, that it should be so done unto me: for *it were* better for me to die, than that any man should make my glorying void. 16 For though I preach the gospel, I have nothing to glory of: for necessity is laid upon me; yea, woe is unto me, if I preach not the gospel! 17 For if I do this thing willingly, I have a reward: but if against my will, a dispensation *of the gospel* is committed unto me. 18 What is my reward then? *Verily* that, when I preach the gospel, I may make the gospel of Christ without charge, that I abuse not my power in the gospel. 19 For though I be free from all *men,* yet have I made myself servant unto all, that I might gain the more. 20 And unto the Jews I became as a Jew, that I might gain the Jews; to them that are under the law, as under the law, that I might gain them that are under the law; 21 To them that are without law, as without law, (being not without law to God, but under the law to Christ,) that I might gain them that are without law. 22 To the weak became I as weak, that I might gain the weak: I am made all things to all *men,* that I might by all means save some. 23 And this I do for the gospel's sake, that I might be partaker thereof with *you.* 24 Know ye not that they which run in a race run all, but one receiveth the prize? So run, that ye may obtain. 25 And every man that striveth for the mastery is temperate in all things. Now they *do it* to obtain a corruptible crown; but we an incorruptible. 26 I therefore so run, not as uncertainly; so fight I, not as one that beateth the air: 27 But I keep under my body, and bring *it* into subjection: lest that by any means, when I have preached to others, I myself should be a castaway.

New International Version

the temple, and those who serve at the altar share in what is offered on the altar? 14 In the same way, the Lord has commanded that those who preach the gospel should receive their living from the gospel.

15 But I have not used any of these rights. And I am not writing this in the hope that you will do such things for me. I would rather die than have anyone deprive me of this boast. 16 Yet when I preach the gospel, I cannot boast, for I am compelled to preach. Woe to me if I do not preach the gospel! 17 If I preach voluntarily, I have a reward; if not voluntarily, I am simply discharging the trust committed to me. 18 What then is my reward? Just this: that in preaching the gospel I may offer it free of charge, and so not make use of my rights in preaching it.

19 Though I am free and belong to no man, I make myself a slave to everyone, to win as many as possible. 20 To the Jews I became like a Jew, to win the Jews. To those under the law I became like one under the law (though I myself am not under the law), so as to win those under the law. 21 To those not having the law I became like one not having the law (though I am not free from God's law but am under Christ's law), so as to win those not having the law. 22 To the weak I became weak, to win the weak. I have become all things to all men so that by all possible means I might save some. 23 I do all this for the sake of the gospel, that I may share in its blessings.

24 Do you not know that in a race all the runners run, but only one gets the prize? Run in such a way as to get the prize. 25 Everyone who competes in the games goes into strict training. They do it to get a crown of laurel that will not last; but we do it to get a crown that will last forever. 26 Therefore I do not run like a man running aimlessly; I do not fight like a man shadow boxing. 27 No, I beat my body and make it my slave so that after I have preached to others, I myself will not be disqualified for the prize.

Warnings from Israel's history

10 Moreover, brethren, I would not that ye should be ignorant, how that all our fathers were under the cloud, and all passed through the sea; 2 And were all baptized unto Moses in the cloud and in the sea; 3 And did all eat the same spiritual meat; 4 And did all drink the same spiritual drink: for they drank of that spiritual Rock that followed them: and that Rock was Christ. 5 But with many of them God was not well pleased: for they were overthrown in the wilderness. 6 Now these things were our examples, to the intent we should not lust after evil things, as they also lusted. 7 Neither be ye idolaters, as *were* some of them; as it is written, The people sat down to eat and drink, and rose up to play. 8 Neither let us commit fornication, as some of them committed, and fell in one day

10 For I do not want you to be ignorant of the fact, brothers, that our forefathers were all under the cloud and that they all passed through the sea. 2 They were all baptized into Moses in the cloud and in the sea. 3 They all ate the same spiritual food 4 and drank the same spiritual drink; for they drank from the spiritual rock that accompanied them, and that rock was Christ. 5 Nevertheless, God was not pleased with most of them, so their bodies were scattered over the desert.

6 Now these things occurred as examples,[t] to keep us from setting our hearts on evil things as they did. 7 Do not be idolaters, as some of them were; as it is written: "The people sat down to eat and drink and got up to indulge in pagan revelry."[u] 8 We should not commit sexual immorality, as some of them did—and in one day

[t] Or *types.* [u] Exodus 32:6.

Greek Interlinear

ἐσθίουσιν, οἱ τῷ θυσιαστηρίῳ παρεδρεύοντες
eat, the ²the ¹altar ¹attending [on]
[ones]

τῷ θυσιαστηρίῳ συμμερίζονται; 14 οὕτως
¹the ²altar ⁴partake with? So

καὶ ὁ κύριος διέταξεν τοῖς τὸ εὐαγγέλιον
also the Lord ordained the [ones] ¹the ²gospel

καταγγέλλουσιν ἐκ τοῦ εὐαγγελίου ζῆν.
¹announcing ²of ⁴the ³gospel ⁵to live.

15 ἐγὼ δὲ οὐ κέχρημαι οὐδενὶ τούτων.
But I have not used *not* one of these
things.

Οὐκ ἔγραψα δὲ ταῦτα ἵνα οὕτως γένηται
And I did not write these in order so it might be
things that

ἐν ἐμοί· καλὸν γάρ μοι μᾶλλον ἀποθανεῖν
in me; for good [it is] to me rather to die

ἢ — τὸ καύχημά μου οὐδεὶς κενώσει.
than — the boast of me no man shall empty.

16 ἐὰν γὰρ εὐαγγελίζωμαι, οὐκ ἔστιν
For if I preach good news, there is not
= I have no boast;

μοι καύχημα· ἀνάγκη γάρ μοι ἐπίκειται·
to me boast;ᶜ for necessity ¹me ²is laid on;

οὐαὶ γάρ μοί ἐστιν ἐὰν μὴ εὐαγγελίσωμαι.
for woe ²to me ¹is if I do not preach good tidings.

17 εἰ γὰρ ἑκὼν τοῦτο πράσσω, μισθὸν
For if willingly ¹this ²I do, ³a reward

ἔχω· εἰ δὲ ἄκων, οἰκονομίαν πεπίστευμαι.
¹I have; but if unwillingly, ²a stewardship ¹I have been
entrusted [with].

18 τίς οὖν μού ἐστιν ὁ μισθός; ἵνα
What therefore ⁴of me ¹is ²the ³reward? *in order
that*

εὐαγγελιζόμενος ἀδάπανον θήσω τὸ
preaching good tidings ⁴without charge ¹I may place ²the

εὐαγγέλιον, εἰς τὸ μὴ καταχρήσασθαι
³good tidings, so as† not to use to the full

τῇ ἐξουσίᾳ μου ἐν τῷ εὐαγγελίῳ.
the authority of me in the good tidings.

19 Ἐλεύθερος γὰρ ὢν ἐκ πάντων πᾶσιν
For ²free ¹being of all men ³to all men

ἐμαυτὸν ἐδούλωσα, ἵνα τοὺς πλείονας
²myself ¹I enslaved, in order that the more

κερδήσω· 20 καὶ ἐγενόμην τοῖς Ἰουδαίοις
I might gain; and I became to the Jews

ὡς Ἰουδαῖος, ἵνα Ἰουδαίους κερδήσω·
as a Jew, in order that Jews I might gain;

τοῖς ὑπὸ νόμον ὡς ὑπὸ νόμον, μὴ ὢν
to the under law as under law, not being
ones

αὐτὸς ὑπὸ νόμον, ἵνα τοὺς ὑπὸ νόμον
[my]self under law, in order the under law
that ones

κερδήσω· 21 τοῖς ἀνόμοις ὡς ἄνομος,
I might gain; to the ones without law as without law,

μὴ ὢν ἄνομος θεοῦ ἀλλ' ἔννομος Χριστοῦ,
not being without of God but under of Christ,
[the] law [the] law

ἵνα κερδάνω τοὺς ἀνόμους· 22 ἐγενόμην
in order I may gain the ones without law; I became
that

τοῖς ἀσθενέσιν ἀσθενής, ἵνα τοὺς ἀσθενεῖς
²to the ³weak ¹weak, in order the weak
that

κερδήσω· τοῖς πᾶσιν γέγονα πάντα, ἵνα
I might gain; – to all men I have become all in order
things, that

πάντως τινὰς σώσω. 23 πάντα δὲ ποιῶ
in any case ²some ¹I might save. But all things I do

διὰ τὸ εὐαγγέλιον, ἵνα συγκοινωνὸς αὐτοῦ
because the good tidings, in order ²a joint partaker ³of it
of that

γένωμαι. 24 Οὐκ οἴδατε ὅτι οἱ ἐν
¹I may become. Know ye not that the [ones] ³in

σταδίῳ τρέχοντες πάντες μὲν τρέχουσιν,
²a racecourse ¹running all indeed run,

εἷς δὲ λαμβάνει τὸ βραβεῖον; οὕτως
but one receives the prize? So

τρέχετε ἵνα καταλάβητε. 25 πᾶς δὲ ὁ
run in order that ye may obtain. And everyone

ἀγωνιζόμενος πάντα ἐγκρατεύεται, ἐκεῖνοι
struggling [in] all things exercises self-control, those

μὲν οὖν ἵνα φθαρτὸν στέφανον λάβωσιν,
indeed there- in order ²a corruptible ³crown ¹they may
fore that receive,

ἡμεῖς δὲ ἄφθαρτον. 26 ἐγὼ τοίνυν οὕτως
but we an incorruptible. I accordingly so

τρέχω ὡς οὐκ ἀδήλως, οὕτως πυκτεύω
run as not unclearly, so I box

ὡς οὐκ ἀέρα δέρων· 27 ἀλλὰ ὑπωπιάζω
as not ²air ¹beating; but I treat severely

μου τὸ σῶμα καὶ δουλαγωγῶ, μή πως
of me the body and lead [it] as a slave, lest

ἄλλοις κηρύξας αὐτὸς ἀδόκιμος γένωμαι.
to others having pro- ²[my]self ³disapproved ¹I ⁴may
claimed become.

Chapter 10

Οὐ θέλω γὰρ ὑμᾶς ἀγνοεῖν, ἀδελφοί,
For I wish not you to be ignorant, brothers,

ὅτι οἱ πατέρες ἡμῶν πάντες ὑπὸ τὴν
that the fathers of us all under the

νεφέλην ἦσαν καὶ πάντες διὰ τῆς θαλάσσης
cloud were and all through the sea

διῆλθον, 2 καὶ πάντες εἰς τὸν Μωϋσῆν
passed *through*, and all ²to – ¹Moses

ἐβαπτίσαντο ἐν τῇ νεφέλῃ καὶ ἐν τῇ
¹were baptized in the cloud and in the

θαλάσσῃ, 3 καὶ πάντες τὸ αὐτὸ πνευματικὸν
sea, and all ²the ³same ¹spiritual

βρῶμα ἔφαγον, 4 καὶ πάντες τὸ αὐτὸ
⁴food ⁵ate, and all ²the ³same

πνευματικὸν ἔπιον πόμα· ἔπινον γὰρ ἐκ
⁴spiritual ¹drank ⁵drink; for they drank of

πνευματικῆς ἀκολουθούσης πέτρας, ἡ πέτρα
a spiritual ²following ¹rock, ³the ⁴rock

δὲ ἦν ὁ Χριστός. 5 Ἀλλ' οὐκ ἐν τοῖς
⁵and was *the* Christ. But ²not ¹in(with) ⁴the

πλείοσιν αὐτῶν εὐδόκησεν ὁ θεός·
⁵majority ⁶of them ³was ⁷well ⁸pleased – ¹God;

κατεστρώθησαν γὰρ ἐν τῇ ἐρήμῳ.
for they were scattered in the desert.

6 ταῦτα δὲ τύποι ἡμῶν ἐγενήθησαν, εἰς
Now these things types of us were, for

τὸ μὴ εἶναι ἡμᾶς ἐπιθυμητὰς κακῶν,
the not to be usᵇ longers after evil things,
= so that we should not be . . .

καθὼς κάκεῖνοι ἐπεθύμησαν. 7 μηδὲ
as those indeed longed. Neither

εἰδωλολάτραι γίνεσθε, καθὼς τινες αὐτῶν·
idolaters be ye, as some of them;

ὥσπερ γέγραπται· ἐκάθισεν ὁ λαὸς φαγεῖν
as it has been written: Sat the people to eat

καὶ πεῖν, καὶ ἀνέστησαν παίζειν. 8 μηδὲ
and to drink, and stood up to play. Neither

πορνεύωμεν, καθὼς τινες αὐτῶν ἐπόρνευσαν
let us commit as some of them committed
fornication, fornication

King James Version

three and twenty thousand. 9 Neither let us tempt Christ, as some of them also tempted, and were destroyed of serpents. 10 Neither murmur ye, as some of them also murmured, and were destroyed of the destroyer. 11 Now all these things happened unto them for ensamples: and they are written for our admonition, upon whom the ends of the world are come. 12 Wherefore let him that thinketh he standeth take heed lest he fall. 13 There hath no temptation taken you but such as is common to man: but God *is* faithful, who will not suffer you to be tempted above that ye are able; but will with the temptation also make a way to escape, that ye may be able to bear *it*. 14 Wherefore, my dearly beloved, flee from idolatry. 15 I speak as to wise men; judge ye what I say. 16 The cup of blessing which we bless, is it not the communion of the blood of Christ? The bread which we break, is it not the communion of the body of Christ? 17 For we *being* many are one bread, *and* one body: for we are all partakers of that one bread. 18 Behold Israel after the flesh: are not they which eat of the sacrifices partakers of the altar? 19 What say I then? that the idol is any thing, or that which is offered in sacrifice to idols is any thing? 20 But *I say*, that the things which the Gentiles sacrifice, they sacrifice to devils, and not to God: and I would not that ye should have fellowship with devils. 21 Ye cannot drink the cup of the Lord, and the cup of devils: ye cannot be partakers of the Lord's table, and of the table of devils. 22 Do we provoke the Lord to jealousy? are we stronger than he? 23 All things are lawful for me, but all things are not expedient: all things are lawful for me, but all things edify not. 24 Let no man seek his own, but every man another's *wealth*. 25 Whatsoever is sold in the shambles, *that* eat, asking no question for conscience' sake: 26 For the earth *is* the Lord's, and the fulness thereof. 27 If any of them that believe not bid you *to a feast*, and ye be disposed to go; whatsoever is set before you, eat, asking no question for conscience' sake. 28 But if any man say unto you, This is offered in sacrifice unto idols, eat not for his sake that shewed it, and for conscience' sake: for the earth *is* the Lord's, and the fulness thereof: 29 Conscience, I say, not thine own, but of the other: for why is my liberty judged of another *man's* conscience? 30 For if I by grace be a partaker, why am I evil spoken of for that for which I give thanks? 31 Whether therefore ye eat, or drink, or whatsoever ye do, do all to the glory of God. 32 Give none offence, neither to the Jews, nor to the Gentiles, nor to the church of God: 33 Even as I please all *men* in all *things,* not seeking mine own profit, but the *profit* of many, that they may be saved.

New International Version

twenty-three thousand of them died. 9 We should not test the Lord, as some of them did— and were killed by snakes. 10 And do not grumble, as some of them did—and were killed by the destroying angel.

11 These things happened to them as examples[t] and were written down as warnings for us, on whom the fulfillment of the ages has come. 12 So, if you think you are standing firm, be careful that you don't fall! 13 No temptation has seized you except what is common to man. And God is faithful; he will not let you be tempted beyond what you can bear. But when you are tempted, he will also provide a way out so that you can stand up under it.

Idol feasts and the Lord's supper

14 Therefore, my dear friends, flee from idolatry. 15 I speak to sensible people; judge for yourselves what I say. 16 Is not the cup of thanksgiving for which we give thanks a participation in the blood of Christ? And is not the bread that we break a participation in the body of Christ? 17 Because there is one loaf, we, who are many, are one body, for we all partake of the one loaf.

18 Consider the people of Israel: Do not those who eat the sacrifices participate in the altar? 19 Do I mean then that a sacrifice offered to an idol is anything, or that an idol is anything? 20 No, but the sacrifices of pagans are offered to demons, not to God, and I do not want you to be participants with demons. 21 You cannot drink the cup of the Lord and the cup of demons too; you cannot have a part in both the Lord's table and the table of demons. 22 Are we trying to arouse the Lord's jealousy? Are we stronger than he?

The believer's freedom

23 "Everything is permissible"—but not everything is beneficial. "Everything is permissible" —but not everything is constructive. 24 Nobody should seek his own good, but the good of others.

25 Eat anything sold in the meat market without raising questions of conscience, 26 for, "The earth is the Lord's, and everything in it."[v]

27 If some unbeliever invites you to a meal and you want to go, eat whatever is put before you without raising questions of conscience. 28 But if anyone says to you, "This has been offered in sacrifice," then do not eat it, both for the sake of the man who told you and for conscience' sake[w]—29 the other man's conscience, I mean, not yours. For why should my freedom be judged by another's conscience? 30 If I take part in the meal with thankfulness, why am I denounced because of something I thank God for?

31 So whether you eat or drink or whatever you do, do it all for the glory of God. 32 Do not cause anyone to stumble, whether Jews, Greeks or the church of God—33 even as I try to please everybody in every way. For I am not seeking my own good but the good of many, so that they may be saved.

[v] Psalm 24:1. [w] Some MSS add *for "the earth is the Lord's and everything in it."*

Greek Interlinear

καὶ   ἔπεσαν   μιᾷ   ἡμέρᾳ   εἴκοσι   τρεῖς
and   fell   in one   day   twenty-three
χιλιάδες.   9 μηδὲ   ἐκπειράζωμεν   τὸν   κύριον,
thousands.   Neither   let us overtempt   the   Lord,
καθώς   τινες   αὐτῶν   ἐπείρασαν   καὶ   ὑπὸ
as   some   of them   tempted   and   by
τῶν   ὄφεων   ἀπώλλυντο.   10 μηδὲ   γογγύζετε,
the   serpents   were destroyed.   Neither   murmur ye,
καθάπερ   τινὲς   αὐτῶν   ἐγόγγυσαν,   καὶ
even as   some   of them   murmured,   and
ἀπώλοντο   ὑπὸ   τοῦ   ὀλεθρευτοῦ.   11 ταῦτα   δὲ
were destroyed   by   the   destroyer.   Now these things
τυπικῶς   συνέβαινεν   ἐκείνοις,   ἐγράφη   δὲ
²typically   ¹happened   ²to those men,   and was(were)
                                                written
πρὸς   νουθεσίαν   ἡμῶν,   εἰς   οὓς   τὰ
for   admonition   of us,   to   whom   the
τέλη   τῶν   αἰώνων   κατήντηκεν.   12 Ὥστε
ends   of the   ages   has(ve) arrived.   So as
ὁ   δοκῶν   ἑστάναι   βλεπέτω   μὴ   πέσῃ.
the   thinking   to stand   let him look   lest   he falls.
[one]
13 πειρασμὸς   ὑμᾶς   οὐκ   εἴληφεν   εἰ   μὴ
Temptation   you   has not taken   except
ἀνθρώπινος·   πιστὸς   δὲ   ὁ   θεός,   ὃς   οὐκ
[what is] human;   but faithful [is]   -   God,   who   not
ἐάσει   ὑμᾶς   πειρασθῆναι   ὑπὲρ   ὃ   δύνασθε,
will allow you   to be tempted   beyond   what you are able
                                                [to bear],
ἀλλὰ   ποιήσει   σὺν   τῷ   πειρασμῷ   καὶ   τὴν
but   will make   with   the   temptation   also   the
ἔκβασιν   τοῦ   δύνασθαι   ὑπενεγκεῖν.
way out   -   to be able   to endure.⁴
                                    — so that ye may be able . . .
14 Διόπερ,   ἀγαπητοί   μου,   φεύγετε   ἀπὸ
Wherefore,   beloved   of me,   flee ye   from
τῆς   εἰδωλολατρίας.   15 ὡς   φρονίμοις   λέγω·
-    idolatry.   ¹As   ²to prudent men   ¹I say;
κρίνατε   ὑμεῖς   ὃ   φημι.   16 Τὸ   ποτήριον
judge   ye   what   I say.   The   cup
τῆς   (εὐλογίας)   ὃ   εὐλογοῦμεν,   οὐχὶ   κοινωνία
-    of blessing   which   we bless,   ²not   ²a communion
ἐστὶν   τοῦ   αἵματος   τοῦ   Χριστοῦ;   τὸν
¹is it   of the   blood   -   of Christ?   the
ἄρτον   ὃν   κλῶμεν,   οὐχὶ   κοινωνία   τοῦ
bread   which   we break,   ²not   ²a communion   ²of the
σώματος   τοῦ   Χριστοῦ   ἐστιν;   17 ὅτι   εἷς
¹body   -   ²of Christ   ¹is it?   Because   ⁴one
ἄρτος,   ἓν   σῶμα   οἱ   πολλοί   ἐσμεν·   οἱ   γὰρ
¹bread,   ⁵one   ³body   ²the   ³many   ¹we are;   -   for
πάντες   ἐκ   τοῦ   ἑνὸς   ἄρτου   μετέχομεν.
all   of   the   one   bread   we partake.
18 βλέπετε   τὸν   Ἰσραὴλ   κατὰ   σάρκα·
See ye   -   Israel   according to [the] flesh;
οὐχ   οἱ   ἐσθίοντες   τὰς   θυσίας   κοινωνοὶ
²not   ²the [ones]   ⁴eating   ⁵the   ⁶sacrifices   ¹sharers
τοῦ   θυσιαστηρίου   εἰσὶν;   19 τί   οὖν   φημι;
³of the   altar   ¹are?   What there-   do I say?
                                    fore
ὅτι   εἰδωλόθυτόν   τί   ἐστιν;   ἢ   ὅτι   εἴδωλόν
that   an idolatrous   ²anything   ¹is?   or   that   an idol
                sacrifice
τί   ἐστιν;   20 ἀλλ'   ὅτι   ἃ   θύουσιν,
²anything   ¹is?   but   that   [the] things   they
                                    which   sacrifice,
δαιμονίοις   καὶ   οὐ   θεῷ   θύουσιν·   οὐ   θέλω
to demons   and   not   to God they sacrifice;   ²not   ¹I wish

δὲ   ὑμᾶς   κοινωνοὺς   τῶν   δαιμονίων   γίνεσθαι.
¹and   you   sharers   of the   demons   to become.
21 οὐ   δύνασθε   ποτήριον   κυρίου   πίνειν
Ye cannot   ²a cup   ⁸of [the] Lord   ¹to drink
καὶ   ποτήριον   δαιμονίων·   οὐ   δύνασθε
and   a cup   of demons;   ye cannot
τραπέζης   κυρίου   μετέχειν   καὶ   τραπέζης
²of a table   ⁸of [the] Lord   ¹to partake   and   of a table
δαιμονίων.   22 ἢ   παραζηλοῦμεν   τὸν   κύριον;
of demons.   Or   do we make jealous   the   Lord?
μὴ   ἰσχυρότεροι   αὐτοῦ   ἐσμεν;
Not   ²stronger [than]   ²he   ¹are we?
23 Πάντα   ἔξεστιν,   ἀλλ'   οὐ   πάντα
All things   [are] lawful,   but   not   all things
συμφέρει·   πάντα   ἔξεστιν,   ἀλλ'   οὐ   πάντα
¯are] expedient;   all things   lawful,   but   not   all things
                                                [are]
οἰκοδομεῖ.   24 μηδεὶς   τὸ   ἑαυτοῦ   ζητείτω
edifies(fy).   No one   the thing   of himself   let him seek
ἀλλὰ   τὸ   τοῦ   ἑτέρου.   25 Πᾶν   τὸ   ἐν
but   the thing   of the   other.   Everything   ¹in
μακέλλῳ   πωλούμενον   ἐσθίετε   μηδὲν
²a meat market   ¹being sold   eat ye   ²nothing
ἀνακρίνοντες   διὰ   τὴν   συνείδησιν·   26 τοῦ
¹examining   because of -   conscience;   ²of the
κυρίου   γὰρ   ἡ   γῆ   καὶ   τὸ   πλήρωμα
⁸Lord   ¹for   the   earth   and   the   fulness
αὐτῆς.   27 εἴ   τις   καλεῖ   ὑμᾶς   τῶν   ἀπίστων
of it.   If   anyone invites   you   of the unbelievers
καὶ   θέλετε   πορεύεσθαι,   πᾶν   τὸ   παρατι-
and   ye wish   to go,   ²everything   ³being set
θέμενον   ὑμῖν   ἐσθίετε   μηδὲν   ἀνακρίνοντες
before   ⁴you   ¹eat   ²nothing   ³examining
διὰ   τὴν   συνείδησιν.   28 ἐὰν   δέ   τις   ὑμῖν
because   -   conscience.   But if   anyone   ²to you
of
εἴπῃ·   τοῦτο   ἱερόθυτόν   ἐστιν,   μὴ   ἐσθίετε
¹says: This   ²slain in sacrifice   ¹is,   do not eat
δι'   ἐκεῖνον   τὸν   μηνύσαντα   καὶ   τὴν
because   that   the   pointing out   and   -
of   man   [one]
συνείδησιν·   29 συνείδησιν   δὲ   λέγω   οὐχὶ
conscience: ²conscience   ¹but   I say   not
τὴν   ἑαυτοῦ   ἀλλὰ   τὴν   τοῦ   ἑτέρου.   ἱνατί
the one of himself   but   the one   of the   other.*   why
γὰρ   ἡ   ἐλευθερία   μου   κρίνεται   ὑπὸ   ἄλλης
For   the   freedom   of me   is judged   by   ²of another
συνειδήσεως;   30 εἰ   ἐγὼ   χάριτι   μετέχω,
¹conscience?   If   I   by grace   partake,
τί   βλασφημοῦμαι   ὑπὲρ   οὗ   ἐγὼ   εὐχαριστῶ;
why   am I evil   because what   I   give thanks
spoken of   of   [for]?
31 Εἴτε   οὖν   ἐσθίετε   εἴτε   πίνετε   εἴτε
Whether therefore   ye eat   or   ye drink   or
τι   ποιεῖτε,   πάντα   εἰς   δόξαν   θεοῦ   ποιεῖτε.
what   ye do,   all things   to   [the] glory   of God   do ye.
[ever]
32 ἀπρόσκοποι   καὶ   Ἰουδαίοις   γίνεσθε   καὶ
²Without offence   ⁴both   ⁴to Jews   ¹be ye   ⁵and
Ἕλλησιν   καὶ   τῇ   ἐκκλησίᾳ   τοῦ   θεοῦ,
⁶to Greeks   and   ⁷to the   .church   -   of God,
33 καθὼς   κἀγὼ   πάντα   πᾶσιν   ἀρέσκω,
as   I also   [in] all things   all men   please,
μὴ   ζητῶν   τὸ   ἐμαυτοῦ   σύμφορον   ἀλλὰ
not   seeking   the   of myself   advantage   but

* That is, not the conscience of the person invited, to whom the
apostle's words are addressed, but the conscience of the person
" pointing out."

King James Version　　　　　New International Version

11 Be ye followers of me, even as I also *am* of Christ. 2 Now I praise you, brethren, that ye remember me in all things, and keep the ordinances, as I delivered *them* to you. 3 But I would have you know, that the head of every man is Christ; and the head of the woman *is* the man; and the head of Christ *is* God. 4 Every man praying or prophesying, having *his* head covered, dishonoureth his head. 5 But every woman that prayeth or prophesieth with *her* head uncovered dishonoureth her head: for that is even all one as if she were shaven. 6 For if the woman be not covered, let her also be shorn: but if it be a shame for a woman to be shorn or shaven, let her be covered. 7 For a man indeed ought not to cover *his* head, forasmuch as he is the image and glory of God: but the woman is the glory of the man. 8 For the man is not of the woman; but the woman of the man. 9 Neither was the man created for the woman; but the woman for the man. 10 For this cause ought the woman to have power on *her* head because of the angels. 11 Nevertheless neither is the man without the woman, neither the woman without the man, in the Lord. 12 For as the woman *is* of the man, even so *is* the man also by the woman; but all things of God. 13 Judge in yourselves: is it comely that a woman pray unto God uncovered? 14 Doth not even nature itself teach you, that, if a man have long hair, it is a shame unto him? 15 But if a woman have long hair, it is a glory to her: for *her* hair is given her for a covering. 16 But if any man seem to be contentious, we have no such custom, neither the churches of God. 17 Now in this that I declare *unto you* I praise *you* not, that ye come together not for the better, but for the worse. 18 For first of all, when ye come together in the church, I hear that there be divisions among you; and I partly believe it. 19 For there must be also heresies among you, that they which are approved may be made manifest among you. 20 When ye come together therefore into one place, *this* is not to eat the Lord's supper. 21 For in eating every one taketh before *other* his own supper: and one is hungry, and another is drunken. 22 What! have ye not houses to eat and to drink in? or despise ye the church of God, and shame them that have not? What shall I say to you? shall I praise you in this? I praise *you* not. 23 For I have received of the Lord that which also I delivered unto you, That the Lord Jesus, the *same* night in which he was betrayed, took bread: 24 And when he had given thanks, he brake *it*, and said, Take, eat; this is my body, which is broken for you: this do in remembrance of me. 25 After the same manner also *he*

11 Follow my example, as I follow the example of Christ.

Propriety in worship

2 I praise you for remembering me in everything and for holding to the teachings,[x] just as I passed them on to you. 3 Now I want you to realize that the head of every man is Christ, and the head of the woman is man, and the head of Christ is God. 4 Every man who prays or prophesies with his head covered dishonors his head. 5 And every woman who prays or prophesies with her head uncovered dishonors her head—it is just as though her head were shaved. 6 If a woman does not cover her head, she should have her hair cut off; and if it is a disgrace for a woman to have her hair cut or shaved off, she should cover her head. 7 A man ought not to cover his head,[y] since he is the image and glory of God; but the woman is the glory of man. 8 For man did not come from woman, but woman from man; 9 neither was man created for woman, but woman for man. 10 For this reason, and because of the angels, the woman ought to have a sign of authority on her head.

11 In the Lord, however, woman is not independent of man, nor is man independent of woman. 12 For as woman came from man, so also man is born of woman. But everything comes from God. 13 Judge for yourselves: Is it proper for a woman to pray to God with her head uncovered? 14 Does not the very nature of things teach you that if a man has long hair, it is a disgrace to him, 15 but that if a woman has long hair, it is her glory? For long hair is given to her as a covering. 16 If anyone wants to be contentious about this, we have no other practice—nor do the churches of God.

The Lord's Supper

17 In the following directives I have no praise for you, for your meetings do more harm than good. 18 In the first place, I hear that when you come together as a church, there are divisions among you, and to some extent I believe it. 19 No doubt there have to be differences among you to show which of you have God's approval. 20 When you come together, it is not the Lord's Supper you eat, 21 for as you eat, each of you goes ahead without waiting for anybody else. One remains hungry, another gets drunk. 22 Don't you have homes to eat and drink in? Or do you despise the church of God and humiliate those who have nothing? What shall I say to you? Shall I praise you for this? Certainly not!

23 For I received from the Lord what I also passed on to you: The Lord Jesus, on the night he was betrayed, took bread, 24 and when he had given thanks, he broke it and said, "This is my body, which is for you; do this in remembrance of me." 25 In the same way, after supper he took

---

[x] Or *traditions.* [y] Or *⁴Every man who prays or prophesies with long hair dishonors his head. ⁵And every woman who prays or prophesies with no covering (of hair) on her head dishonors her head-she is just like one of the "shorn women." ⁶If a woman has no covering, let her be for now with short hair, but since it is a disgrace for a woman to have her hair shorn or shaved, she should grow it again. ⁷A man ought not to have long hair.*

Greek Interlinear

τὸ τῶν πολλῶν, ἵνα σωθῶσιν. **11** μιμηταί
the of the many, in order they may Imitators
(that) that be saved.

μου γίνεσθε, καθὼς κἀγὼ Χριστοῦ.
of me be ye, as I also [am] of Christ.

2 Ἐπαινῶ δὲ ὑμᾶς ὅτι πάντα μου
But I praise you because ²all things ³of me

μέμνησθε καὶ καθὼς παρέδωκα ὑμῖν τὰς
¹ye have and ⁴as ⁵I delivered ⁶to you ⁷the
remembered

παραδόσεις κατέχετε. **3** Θέλω δὲ ὑμᾶς
¹traditions ¹ye hold fast. But I wish you

εἰδέναι ὅτι παντὸς ἀνδρὸς ἡ κεφαλὴ ὁ
to know that ⁴of every ²man ³the ⁴head –

Χριστός ἐστιν, κεφαλὴ δὲ γυναικὸς ὁ
¹Christ ¹is, and [the] head of a woman the

ἀνήρ, κεφαλὴ δὲ τοῦ Χριστοῦ ὁ θεός.
man, and [the] head – of Christ – God.

4 πᾶς ἀνὴρ προσευχόμενος ἢ προφητεύων
Every man praying or prophesying

κατὰ κεφαλῆς ἔχων καταισχύνει τὴν
³down over ⁴[his] head ²having shames the
¹[anything]

κεφαλὴν αὐτοῦ. **5** πᾶσα δὲ γυνὴ προσ-
head of him. But every woman pray-

ευχομένη ἢ προφητεύουσα ἀκατακαλύπτῳ
ing or prophesying ³unveiled

τῇ κεφαλῇ καταισχύνει τὴν κεφαλὴν αὐτῆς·
¹with ²head shames the head of her;
the(her)

ἐν γάρ ἐστιν καὶ τὸ αὐτὸ τῇ ἐξυρημένῃ.
for ²one ¹it is and the same with the having been
thing woman shaved.

6 εἰ γὰρ οὐ κατακαλύπτεται γυνή, καὶ
For if ²is not veiled ¹a woman, also

κειράσθω· εἰ δὲ αἰσχρὸν γυναικὶ τὸ
let her be shorn; but if shameful for a woman –

κείρασθαι ἢ ξυρᾶσθαι, κατακαλυπτέσθω.
to be shorn or to be shaved, let her be veiled.

7 ἀνὴρ μὲν γὰρ οὐκ ὀφείλει κατα-
For a man indeed ought not to be

καλύπτεσθαι τὴν κεφαλήν, εἰκὼν καὶ δόξα
veiled the head,b ¹[the] image ²and ³glory

θεοῦ ὑπάρχων· ἡ γυνὴ δὲ δόξα ἀνδρός
⁴of God ¹being; but the woman ¹[the] glory ²of a man

ἐστιν. **8** οὐ γάρ ἐστιν ἀνὴρ ἐκ γυναικός,
²is. For ²not ¹is ¹man ² of woman,

ἀλλὰ γυνὴ ἐξ ἀνδρός· **9** καὶ γὰρ οὐκ
but woman of man; for indeed ²not

ἐκτίσθη ἀνὴρ διὰ τὴν γυναῖκα, ἀλλὰ
¹was ⁴created ¹man because of the woman, but

γυνὴ διὰ τὸν ἄνδρα. **10** διὰ τοῦτο
woman because of the man. Therefore

ὀφείλει ἡ γυνὴ ἐξουσίαν ἔχειν ἐπὶ τῆς
ought the woman authority to have on the

κεφαλῆς διὰ τοὺς ἀγγέλους. **11** πλὴν
head because of the angels. Nevertheless

οὔτε γυνὴ χωρὶς ἀνδρὸς οὔτε ἀνὴρ χωρὶς
neither woman without man nor man without

γυναικὸς ἐν κυρίῳ· **12** ὥσπερ γὰρ ἡ
woman in [the] Lord; for as the

γυνὴ ἐκ τοῦ ἀνδρός, οὕτως καὶ ὁ ἀνὴρ
woman of the man, so also the man

διὰ τῆς γυναικός· τὰ δὲ πάντα ἐκ τοῦ
through the woman; – but all things of –

θεοῦ. **13** Ἐν ὑμῖν αὐτοῖς κρίνατε· πρέπον
God. Among you [your]selves judge: ²fitting

ἐστὶν γυναῖκα ἀκατακάλυπτον τῷ θεῷ
¹is it ³[for] ⁴a woman ⁵unveiled ⁶to God

προσεύχεσθαι; **14** οὐδὲ ἡ φύσις αὐτὴ
⁷to pray? Not – nature [her]self

διδάσκει ὑμᾶς ὅτι ἀνὴρ μὲν ἐὰν κομᾷ,
teaches you that a man indeed if he wears his
hair long,

ἀτιμία αὐτῷ ἐστιν, **15** γυνὴ δὲ ἐὰν
²a dishonour ³to him ¹it is, but a woman if

κομᾷ, δόξα αὐτῇ ἐστιν· ὅτι ἡ κόμη
she wears ¹a glory ²to her ³it is? because the long hair
her hair long,

ἀντὶ περιβολαίου δέδοται αὐτῇ. **16** Εἰ
instead of a veil has been given to her. if

δέ τις δοκεῖ φιλόνεικος εἶναι, ἡμεῖς
But anyone thinks ²contentious ¹to be, we

τοιαύτην συνήθειαν οὐκ ἔχομεν, οὐδὲ αἱ
²such ³a custom ¹have not, neither the

ἐκκλησίαι τοῦ θεοῦ.
churches – of God.

17 Τοῦτο δὲ παραγγέλλων οὐκ ἐπαινῶ
But this charging I do not praise

ὅτι οὐκ εἰς τὸ κρεῖσσον ἀλλὰ εἰς τὸ
because not for the better but for the

ἧσσον συνέρχεσθε. **18** πρῶτον μὲν γὰρ
worse ye come together. For firstly indeed

συνερχομένων ὑμῶν ἐν ἐκκλησίᾳ ἀκούω
coming together you² in church I hear
=when ye come together

σχίσματα ἐν ὑμῖν ὑπάρχειν, καὶ μέρος
divisions among you to be, and ²part

τι πιστεύω. **19** δεῖ γὰρ καὶ αἱρέσεις
¹some I believe. For it behoves indeed sects

ἐν ὑμῖν εἶναι, ἵνα [καὶ] οἱ δόκιμοι
among you to be, in order also the approved
that ones

φανεροὶ γένωνται ἐν ὑμῖν. **20** Συν-
manifest may become among you. Coming

ερχομένων οὖν ὑμῶν ἐπὶ τὸ αὐτὸ οὐκ
together therefore you² together not
=When therefore ye come

ἔστιν κυριακὸν δεῖπνον φαγεῖν· **21** ἕκαστος
it is of the Lord* a supper to eat; ²each one

γὰρ τὸ ἴδιον δεῖπνον προλαμβάνει ἐν
¹for the(his) own supper takes before in

τῷ φαγεῖν, καὶ ὃς μὲν πεινᾷ, ὃς δὲ
– to eat(eating), and one† hungers, another†

μεθύει. **22** μὴ γὰρ οἰκίας οὐκ ἔχετε
is drunken. Not indeed ¹houses ¹have ye not

εἰς τὸ ἐσθίειν καὶ πίνειν; ἢ τῆς ἐκκλησίας
– to eat and to drink? or the church

τοῦ θεοῦ καταφρονεῖτε, καὶ καταισχύνετε
– of God despise ye, and shame

τοὺς μὴ ἔχοντας; τί εἴπω ὑμῖν; ἐπαινέσω
the not having? What may I say to you? shall I praise
[ones]

ὑμᾶς; ἐν τούτῳ οὐκ ἐπαινῶ. **23** Ἐγὼ
you? In this I praise not. I

γὰρ παρέλαβον ἀπὸ τοῦ κυρίου, ὃ καὶ
For received from the Lord, what also

παρέδωκα ὑμῖν, ὅτι ὁ κύριος Ἰησοῦς
I delivered to you, that the Lord Jesus

ἐν τῇ νυκτὶ ᾗ παρεδίδοτο ἔλαβεν ἄρτον
in the night in which he was took bread
betrayed

24 καὶ εὐχαριστήσας ἔκλασεν καὶ εἶπεν·
and having given thanks broke and said:

τοῦτό μού ἐστιν τὸ σῶμα τὸ ὑπὲρ
This of me is the body – on behalf of

ὑμῶν· τοῦτο ποιεῖτε εἰς τὴν ἐμὴν
you; this do ye for the my

ἀνάμνησιν. **25** ὡσαύτως καὶ τὸ ποτήριον
remembrance. Similarly also the cup

* Note that κυριακός is an adjective, for which no exact English equivalent is available. Only other occurrence in N.T., Rev. 1. 10.

King James Version

took the cup, when he had supped, saying, This cup is the new testament in my blood: this do ye, as oft as ye drink *it*, in remembrance of me. 26 For as often as ye eat this bread, and drink this cup, ye do shew the Lord's death till he come. 27 Wherefore whosoever shall eat this bread, and drink *this* cup of the Lord, unworthily, shall be guilty of the body and blood of the Lord. 28 But let a man examine himself, and so let him eat of *that* bread, and drink of *that* cup. 29 For he that eateth and drinketh unworthily, eateth and drinketh damnation to himself, not discerning the Lord's body. 30 For this cause many *are* weak and sickly among you, and many sleep. 31 For if we would judge ourselves, we should not be judged. 32 But when we are judged, we are chastened of the Lord, that we should not be condemned with the world. 33 Wherefore, my brethren, when ye come together to eat, tarry one for another. 34And if any man hunger, let him eat at home; that ye come not together unto condemnation. And the rest will I set in order when I come.

12 Now concerning spiritual *gifts*, brethren, I would not have you ignorant. 2 Ye know that ye were Gentiles, carried away unto these dumb idols, even as ye were led. 3 Wherefore I give you to understand, that no man speaking by the Spirit of God calleth Jesus accursed: and *that* no man can say that Jesus is the Lord, but by the Holy Ghost. 4 Now there are diversities of gifts, but the same Spirit. 5And there are differences of administrations, but the same Lord. 6And there are diversities of operations, but it is the same God which worketh all in all. 7 But the manifestation of the Spirit is given to every man to profit withal. 8 For to one is given by the Spirit the word of wisdom; to another the word of knowledge by the same Spirit; 9 To another faith by the same Spirit; to another gifts of healing by the same Spirit; 10 To another the working of miracles; to another prophecy; to another discerning of spirits; to another *divers* kinds of tongues; to another the interpretation of tongues: 11 But all these worketh that one and the selfsame Spirit, dividing to every man severally as he will. 12 For as the body is one, and hath many members, and all the members of that one body, being many, are one body: so also *is* Christ. 13 For by one Spirit are we all baptized into one body, whether *we be* Jews or Gentiles, whether *we be* bond or free: and have been all made to drink into one Spirit. 14 For the body is not one member, but many. 15 If the foot shall say, Because I am not the hand, I am not of the body; is it therefore not

New International Version

the cup, saying, "This cup is the new covenant in my blood; do this, whenever you drink it, in remembrance of me." 26 For whenever you eat this bread and drink this cup, you proclaim the Lord's death until he comes. 27 Therefore, whoever eats the bread or drinks the cup of the Lord in an unworthy manner will be guilty of sinning against the body and blood of the Lord. 28A man ought to examine himself before he eats of the bread and drinks of the cup. 29 For anyone who eats and drinks without recognizing the body of the Lord eats and drinks judgment on himself. 30 That is why many among you are weak and sick, and a number of you have fallen asleep. 31 But if we judged ourselves, we would not come under judgment. 32 When we are judged by the Lord, we are being disciplined so that we will not be condemned with the world. 33 So then, my brothers, when you come together to eat, wait for each other. 34 If anyone is hungry, he should eat at home, so that when you meet together it may not result in judgment.

And when I come I will give further directions.

Spiritual gifts

12 Now about spiritual gifts, brothers, I do not want you to be ignorant. 2 You know that when you were pagans, somehow or other you were influenced and led astray to dumb idols. 3 Therefore I tell you that no one who is speaking by the Spirit of God says, "Jesus be cursed," and no one can say, "Jesus is Lord," except by the Holy Spirit.

4 There are different kinds of spiritual gifts, but the same Spirit. 5 There are different kinds of service, but the same Lord. 6 There are different kinds of working, but the same God works all of them in all men.

7 Now to each man the manifestation of the Spirit is given for the common good. 8 To one there is given through the Spirit the ability to speak with wisdom, to another the ability to speak with knowledge by means of the same Spirit, 9 to another faith by the same Spirit, to another gifts of healing by that one Spirit, 10 to another miraculous powers, to another prophecy, to another the ability to distinguish between spirits, to another the ability to speak in different kinds of tongues,*z* and to still another the interpretation of tongues.*z* 11All these are the work of one and the same Spirit, and he gives them to each man, just as he determines.

One body, many parts

12 The body is a unit, though it is made up of many parts; and though all its parts are many, they form one body. So it is with Christ. 13 For we were all baptized by one Spirit into one body—whether Jews or Greeks, slave or free—and we were all given the one Spirit to drink. 14 Now the body is not made up of one part but of many. 15 If the foot should say, "Because I am not a hand, I do not belong to the body," it would not for that reason cease to be part of

[z] Or *languages*.

Greek Interlinear

μετὰ   τὸ   δειπνῆσαι,   λέγων·   τοῦτο   τὸ
after   the   to sup,   saying: This   -

ποτήριον   ἡ   καινὴ   διαθήκη   ἐστὶν   ἐν   τῷ
cup   ²the   ³new   ⁴covenant   ¹is   in   -

ἐμῷ   αἵματι·   τοῦτο   ποιεῖτε,   ὁσάκις   ἐὰν
my   blood;   this   do ye,   as often as

πίνητε,   εἰς   τὴν   ἐμὴν   ἀνάμνησιν.   26 ὁσάκις
ye drink,   for   -   my   remembrance.   as often

γὰρ   ἐὰν   ἐσθίητε   τὸν   ἄρτον   τοῦτον   καὶ
For   as   ye eat   the   bread   this   and

τὸ   ποτήριον   πίνητε,   τὸν   θάνατον   τοῦ
²the   ³cup   ¹drink,   the   death   of the

κυρίου   καταγγέλλετε,   ἄχρι   οὗ   ἔλθῃ.
Lord   ye declare,   until   he comes.

27 Ὥστε   ὃς   ἂν   ἐσθίῃ   τὸν   ἄρτον   ἢ
So as   whoever   eats   the   bread   or

πίνῃ   τὸ   ποτήριον   τοῦ   κυρίου   ἀναξίως,
drinks   the   cup   of the   Lord   unworthily,

ἔνοχος   ἔσται   τοῦ   σώματος   καὶ   τοῦ
guilty   will be   of the   body   and   of the

αἵματος   τοῦ   κυρίου.   28 δοκιμαζέτω   δὲ
blood   of the   Lord.   But ¹let ²prove

ἄνθρωπος   ἑαυτόν,   καὶ   οὕτως   ἐκ   τοῦ
²a man   ⁴himself,   and   so   of   the

ἄρτου   ἐσθιέτω   καὶ   ἐκ   τοῦ   ποτηρίου
bread   let him eat   and   of   the   cup

πινέτω·   29 ὁ   γὰρ   ἐσθίων   καὶ   πίνων
let him drink;   for the [one]   eating   and   drinking

κρίμα   ἑαυτῷ   ἐσθίει   καὶ   πίνει   μὴ   διακρίνων
²judgment   ³to   ¹eats   ²and   ³drinks   not   discerning
himself

τὸ   σῶμα.   30 διὰ   τοῦτο   ἐν   ὑμῖν   πολλοὶ
the   body.   Therefore   among   you   many

ἀσθενεῖς   καὶ   ἄρρωστοι   καὶ   κοιμῶνται
[are] weak   and   feeble   and   ²sleep

ἱκανοί.   31 εἰ   δὲ   ἑαυτοὺς   διεκρίνομεν,
¹a number.   But if   ourselves   we discerned,

οὐκ   ἂν   ἐκρινόμεθα·   32 κρινόμενοι   δὲ   ὑπὸ
we should not be judged;   but being judged   by

τοῦ   κυρίου   παιδευόμεθα,   ἵνα   μὴ   σὺν
the   Lord   we are chastened,   lest   with

τῷ   κόσμῳ   κατακριθῶμεν.   33 Ὥστε,
the   world   we are condemned.   So as,

ἀδελφοί   μου,   συνερχόμενοι   εἰς   τὸ   φαγεῖν
brothers   of me,   coming together   for   the   to eat

ἀλλήλους   ἐκδέχεσθε.   34 εἰ   τις   πεινᾷ,
one another   await ye.   If   anyone   hungers,

ἐν   οἴκῳ   ἐσθιέτω,   ἵνα   μὴ   εἰς   κρίμα
at home   let him eat,   lest   to   judgment

συνέρχησθε.   τὰ   δὲ   λοιπὰ   ὡς   ἂν   ἔλθω
ye come together.   And the remaining matters whenever   I come

διατάξομαι.
I will arrange.

Chapter 12

Περὶ   δὲ   τῶν   πνευματικῶν,   ἀδελφοί,
Now about   the   spiritual matters,   brothers,

οὐ   θέλω   ὑμᾶς   ἀγνοεῖν.   2 Οἴδατε   ὅτι
I do not wish   you   to be ignorant.   Ye know   that

ὅτε   ἔθνη   ἦτε   πρὸς   τὰ   εἴδωλα   τὰ   ἄφωνα
when ¹nations ²ye were ³to   ⁴the   ⁷idols   -   ⁶voiceless

ὡς   ἂν   ἤγεσθε   ἀπαγόμενοι.   3 διὸ   γνωρίζω
⁸however   ⁹ye were led   ¹⁰[ye were]   Where-   I make
¹⁰being led away.⁹   fore   known

ὑμῖν   ὅτι   οὐδεὶς   ἐν   πνεύματι   θεοῦ   λαλῶν
to you   that   no one   ²by   ³[the] Spirit   ⁴of God   ¹speaking

λέγει·   ΑΝΑΘΕΜΑ   ΙΗΣΟΥΣ,   καὶ   οὐδεὶς
says: A CURSE [IS]   JESUS,   and   no one

δύναται   εἰπεῖν·   ΚΥΡΙΟΣ   ΙΗΣΟΥΣ,   εἰ   μὴ
can   to say: LORD   JESUS,   except

ἐν   πνεύματι   ἁγίῳ.
by   [the] ²Spirit   ¹Holy.

4 Διαιρέσεις   δὲ   χαρισμάτων   εἰσίν,   τὸ   δὲ   αὐτὸ
Now differences   of gifts   there are, but   the same

πνεῦμα·   5 καὶ   διαιρέσεις   διακονιῶν   εἰσιν,   καὶ
Spirit;   and   differences   of ministries   there are,   and

ὁ   αὐτὸς   κύριος·   6 καὶ   διαιρέσεις   ἐνεργημάτων
the same   Lord;   and   differences   of operations

εἰσίν,   ὁ   δὲ   αὐτὸς   θεὸς   ὁ   ἐνεργῶν   τὰ
there are,   but the   same   God   -   operating   -

πάντα   ἐν   πᾶσιν.   7 ἑκάστῳ   δὲ   δίδοται
all things   in   all.   But to each one   is given

ἡ   φανέρωσις   τοῦ   πνεύματος   πρὸς   τὸ
the   manifestation   of the   Spirit   to   the

συμφέρον.   8 ᾧ   μὲν   γὰρ   διὰ   τοῦ   πνεύματος
profiting.   For to one   through   the   Spirit

δίδοται   λόγος   σοφίας,   ἄλλῳ   δὲ   λόγος
is given   a word   of wisdom,   and to another   a word

γνώσεως   κατὰ   τὸ   αὐτὸ   πνεῦμα,   9 ἑτέρῳ
of   accord-   the   same   Spirit,   to
knowledge   ing to   another

πίστις   ἐν   τῷ   αὐτῷ   πνεύματι,   ἄλλῳ   δὲ
faith   by   the   same   Spirit,   and to another

χαρίσματα   ἰαμάτων   ἐν   τῷ   ἑνὶ   πνεύματι,
gifts   of cures   by   the   one   Spirit,

10 ἄλλῳ   δὲ   ἐνεργήματα   δυνάμεων,   ἄλλῳ
and to another   operations   of powers,   to another

[δὲ]   προφητεία,   ἄλλῳ   δὲ   διακρίσεις   πνευ-
and   prophecy,   and to another   discernings   of

μάτων,   ἑτέρῳ   γένη   γλωσσῶν,   ἄλλῳ   δὲ
spirits,   to another   kinds   of tongues,   and to another

ἑρμηνεία   γλωσσῶν·   11 πάντα   δὲ   ταῦτα
interpretation   of tongues: and ²all   ¹these things

ἐνεργεῖ   τὸ   ἓν   καὶ   τὸ   αὐτὸ   πνεῦμα,
²operates   ¹the   ²one   ²and   ⁴the   ⁵same   ⁶Spirit,

διαιροῦν   ἰδίᾳ   ἑκάστῳ   καθὼς   βούλεται.
distributing ²separately†   ¹to each one   as   he purposes.

12 Καθάπερ   γὰρ   τὸ   σῶμα   ἓν   ἐστιν
For as   the   body   ²one   ¹is

καὶ   μέλη   πολλὰ   ἔχει,   πάντα   δὲ   τὰ
and   ²members   ¹many   ¹has,   but all   the

μέλη   τοῦ   σώματος   πολλὰ   ὄντα   ἓν   ἐστιν
members   of the   body   ²many   ¹being   ²one   ²is(are)

σῶμα,   οὕτως   καὶ   ὁ   Χριστός·   13 καὶ   γὰρ
body,   so   also   the   Christ;   for indeed

ἐν   ἑνὶ   πνεύματι   ἡμεῖς   πάντες   εἰς   ἓν
⁴by   ⁵one   ⁶Spirit   ¹we   ²all   ⁷into   ⁸one

σῶμα   ἐβαπτίσθημεν,   εἴτε   Ἰουδαῖοι   εἴτε
⁹body   ³were baptized,   whether   Jews   or

Ἕλληνες,   εἴτε   δοῦλοι   εἴτε   ἐλεύθεροι,   καὶ
Greeks,   whether   slaves   or   free,   and

πάντες   ἐν   πνεῦμα   ἐποτίσθημεν.   14 καὶ
all   one   Spirit   we were given to drink.   indeed

γὰρ   τὸ   σῶμα   οὐκ   ἔστιν   ἓν   μέλος   ἀλλὰ
For   the   body   is not   one   member   but

πολλά.   15 ἐὰν   εἴπῃ   ὁ   πούς·   ὅτι   οὐκ
many.   If   ²says   ¹the   ²foot: Because   not

εἰμὶ   χείρ,   οὐκ   εἰμὶ   ἐκ   τοῦ   σώματος,
I am   a hand,   I am not   of   the   body,

οὐ   παρὰ   τοῦτο   οὐκ   ἔστιν   ἐκ   τοῦ   σώματος.
not   for   this   it is not   of   the   body.

---

* It is thought that there is a scribal error in this verse; see
commentaries on the Greek text. We have been guided by
G. G. Findlay, *The Expositor's Greek Testament*.

of the body? 16And if the ear shall say, Because I am not the eye, I am not of the body; is it therefore not of the body? 17 If the whole body were an eye, where were the hearing? If the whole were hearing, where were the smelling? 18 But now hath God set the members every one of them in the body, as it hath pleased him. 19And if they were all one member, where were the body? 20 But now are they many members, yet but one body. 21And the eye cannot say unto the hand, I have no need of thee: nor again the head to the feet, I have no need of you. 22 Nay, much more those members of the body, which seem to be more feeble, are necessary: 23And those members of the body, which we think to be less honourable, upon these we bestow more abundant honour; and our uncomely parts have more abundant comeliness. 24 For our comely parts have no need: but God hath tempered the body together, having given more abundant honour to that part which lacked: 25 That there should be no schism in the body; but that the members should have the same care one for another. 26And whether one member suffer, all the members suffer with it; or one member be honoured, all the members rejoice with it. 27 Now ye are the body of Christ, and members in particular. 28And God hath set some in the church, first apostles, secondarily prophets, thirdly teachers, after that miracles, then gifts of healings, helps, governments, diversities of tongues. 29Are all apostles? are all prophets? are all teachers? are all workers of miracles? 30 Have all the gifts of healing? do all speak with tongues? do all interpret? 31 But covet earnestly the best gifts: and yet shew I unto you a more excellent way.

the body. 16And if the ear should say, "Because I am not an eye, I do not belong to the body," it would not for that reason cease to be part of the body. 17 If the whole body were an eye, where would the sense of hearing be? If the whole body were an ear, where would the sense of smell be? 18 But in fact God has arranged the parts in the body, every one of them, just as he wanted them to be. 19 If they were all one part, where would the body be? 20As it is, there are many parts, but one body.

21 The eye cannot say to the hand, "I don't need you!" And the head cannot say to the feet, "I don't need you!" 22 On the contrary, those parts of the body that seem to be weaker are indispensable, 23 and the parts that we think are less honorable we treat with special honor. And the parts that are unpresentable are treated with special modesty, 24 while our presentable parts need no special treatment. But God has combined the members of the body and has given greater honor to the parts that lacked it, 25 so that there should be no division in the body, but that its parts should have equal concern for each other. 26 If one part suffers, every part suffers with it; if one part is honored, every part rejoices with it.

27 Now you are the body of Christ, and each one of you is a part of it. 28And in the church God has appointed first of all apostles, second prophets, third teachers, then workers of miracles, also those having gifts of healing, those able to help others, those with gifts of administration, and finally those speaking in different kinds of tongues.[a] 29Are all apostles? Are all prophets? Are all teachers? Do all work miracles? 30 Do all have gifts of healing? Do all speak in tongues?[b] Do all interpret? 31 But eagerly desire the greater gifts.

Love

And now I will show you the most excellent way.

13 Though I speak with the tongues of men and of angels, and have not charity, I am become as sounding brass, or a tinkling cymbal. 2And though I have the gift of prophecy, and understand all mysteries, and all knowledge; and though I have all faith, so that I could remove mountains, and have not charity, I am nothing. 3And though I bestow all my goods to feed the poor, and though I give my body to be burned, and have not charity, it profiteth me nothing. 4 Charity suffereth long, and is kind; charity envieth not; charity vaunteth not itself, is not puffed up, 5 Doth not behave itself unseemly, seeketh not her own, is not easily provoked, thinketh no evil; 6 Rejoiceth not in iniquity, but rejoiceth in the truth; 7 Beareth all things, believeth all things, hopeth all things, endureth all things. 8 Charity never faileth: but whether there be prophecies, they shall fail; whether there be tongues, they shall cease; whether there be knowledge, it shall vanish away. 9 For we know in part, and we prophesy in part. 10 But when that which is perfect is come, then that which

13 If I speak in the tongues[a] of men and of angels, but have not love, I am only a resounding gong or a clanging cymbal. 2 If I have the gift of prophecy, and can fathom all mysteries and all knowledge, and if I have a faith that can move mountains, but have not love, I am nothing. 3 If I give all I possess to the poor and surrender my body to the flames,[d] but have not love, I gain nothing.

4 Love is patient, love is kind. It does not envy, it does not boast, it is not proud. 5 It is not rude, it is not self-seeking, it is not easily angered, it keeps no record of wrongs. 6 Love does not delight in evil but rejoices in the truth. 7 It always protects, always trusts, always hopes, always perseveres.

8 Love never fails. But where there are prophecies, they will cease; where there are tongues, they will be stilled; where there is knowledge, it will pass away. 9 For we know in part and we prophesy in part, 10 but when perfection

[a] Or languages. [b] Or other languages. [d] Some early MSS read body that I may boast.

Greek Interlinear

16 καὶ ἐὰν εἴπῃ τὸ οὖς· ὅτι οὐκ εἰμὶ
And if says the ear: Because I am not

ὀφθαλμός, οὐκ εἰμὶ ἐκ τοῦ σώματος,
an eye, I am not of the body,

οὐ παρὰ τοῦτο οὐκ ἔστιν ἐκ τοῦ σώματος.
not for this it is not of the body.

17 εἰ ὅλον τὸ σῶμα ὀφθαλμός, ποῦ
If all the body [was] an eye, where

ἡ ἀκοή; εἰ ὅλον ἀκοή, ποῦ ἡ ὄσφρησις;
[would be] if all hearing, where the smelling?
the hearing?

18 νῦν δὲ ὁ θεὸς ἔθετο τὰ μέλη, ἐν
But now - God set the members, ¹one

ἕκαστον αὐτῶν ἐν τῷ σώματι καθὼς
¹each of them in the body as

ἠθέλησεν. 19 εἰ δὲ ἦν τὰ πάντα ἐν
he wished. And if ¹was - ¹all one

μέλος, ποῦ τὸ σῶμα; 20 νῦν δὲ πολλὰ
member, where the body? But now many

μὲν μέλη, ἓν δὲ σῶμα. 21 οὐ δύναται
¹indeed ¹members, but one body. ¹cannot

δὲ ὁ ὀφθαλμὸς εἰπεῖν τῇ χειρί· χρείαν
And ¹the ²eye to say to the hand: Need

σου οὐκ ἔχω, ἢ πάλιν ἡ κεφαλὴ τοῖς
of thee I have not, or again the head to the

ποσίν· χρείαν ὑμῶν οὐκ ἔχω· 22 ἀλλὰ
feet: Need of you I have not; but

πολλῷ μᾶλλον τὰ δοκοῦντα μέλη τοῦ
by much more ¹the ²seeming members ³of the

σώματος ἀσθενέστερα ὑπάρχειν ἀναγκαῖά ἐστιν,
⁴body ⁷weaker ⁵to be ⁶necessary ⁸is(are),

23 καὶ ἃ δοκοῦμεν ἀτιμότερα εἶναι
and ¹[members] ²we think ³less honourable ⁴to be

τοῦ σώματος, τούτοις τιμὴν περισσοτέραν
⁵of the ⁶body, to these honour more abundant

περιτίθεμεν, καὶ τὰ ἀσχήμονα ἡμῶν
we put round, and the uncomely [members] of us

εὐσχημοσύνην περισσοτέραν ἔχει, 24 τὰ δὲ
comeliness ¹more abundant ²has(ve), but th⌐

εὐσχήμονα ἡμῶν οὐ χρείαν ἔχει. ἀλλὰ
comely [members] of us ²no ¹need ²has(ve). But -

θεὸς συνεκέρασεν τὸ σῶμα, τῷ ὑστερουμένῳ
God blended together the body, ⁴to the [member] ¹lacking

περισσοτέραν δοὺς τιμήν, 25 ἵνα μὴ ᾖ
²more abundant ³giving ²honour, lest there
be

σχίσμα ἐν τῷ σώματι, ἀλλὰ τὸ αὐτὸ
division in the body, but ⁴the ⁵same

ὑπὲρ ἀλλήλων μεριμνῶσιν τὰ μέλη.
²on be- ⁷one ³should care ¹the ²members.
half of another

26 καὶ εἴτε πάσχει ἓν μέλος, συμπάσχει
And whether ²suffers ¹one ²member, ³suffers with [it]

πάντα τὰ μέλη· εἴτε δοξάζεται μέλος,
⁴all ⁵the ⁶members; or ¹is glorified ¹a member,

συγχαίρει πάντα τὰ μέλη. 27 ὑμεῖς
¹rejoices with [it] ²all ³the ²members. ye

δέ ἐστε σῶμα Χριστοῦ καὶ μέλη ἐκ
And are a body of Christ and members in

μέρους. 28 Καὶ οὓς μὲν ἔθετο ὁ θεὸς
part. And ¹some† ²placed - ¹God

ἐν τῇ ἐκκλησίᾳ πρῶτον ἀποστόλους, δεύτε-
in the church firstly apostles, second-

ρον προφήτας, τρίτον διδασκάλους, ἔπειτα
ly prophets, thirdly teachers, then

δυνάμεις, ἔπειτα χαρίσματα ἰαμάτων,
powers, then gifts of cures,

ἀντιλήμψεις, κυβερνήσεις, γένη γλωσσῶν.
helps, governings, kinds of tongues.

29 μὴ πάντες ἀπόστολοι; μὴ πάντες
Not all [are] apostles? not all

προφῆται; μὴ πάντες διδάσκαλοι; μὴ
prophets; not all teachers? not

πάντες δυνάμεις; 30 μὴ πάντες χαρίσματα
all powers? not all ¹gifts

ἔχουσιν ἰαμάτων; μὴ πάντες γλώσσαις
¹have of cures? not all ²with tongues

λαλοῦσιν; μὴ πάντες διερμηνεύουσιν;
¹speak? not all interpret?

31 ζηλοῦτε δὲ τὰ χαρίσματα τὰ μείζονα.
but desire ye eagerly the ²gifts - ¹greater.

Καὶ ἔτι καθ' ὑπερβολὴν ὁδὸν ὑμῖν
And yet ⁴according to ⁵excellence ²a way ¹to you

Chapter 13

δείκνυμι. 13 Ἐὰν ταῖς γλώσσαις τῶν ἀνθρώπων
¹I show. If in the tongues - of men

λαλῶ καὶ τῶν ἀγγέλων, ἀγάπην δὲ
I speak and - of angels, but love

μὴ ἔχω, γέγονα χαλκὸς ἠχῶν ἢ
I have not, I have become brass ¹sounding or

κύμβαλον ἀλαλάζον. 2 καὶ ἐὰν ἔχω
cymbal a tinkling. And if I have

προφητείαν καὶ εἰδῶ τὰ μυστήρια πάντα
prophecy and know ¹the ²mysteries ²all

καὶ πᾶσαν τὴν γνῶσιν, κἂν ἔχω πᾶσαν
and all - knowledge, and if I have all

τὴν πίστιν ὥστε ὄρη μεθιστάναι, ἀγάπην
- faith so as mountains to remove, ²love

δὲ μὴ ἔχω, οὐθέν εἰμι. 3 κἂν ψωμίσω
¹but I have not, nothing I am. And if I dole out

πάντα τὰ ὑπάρχοντά μου, καὶ ἐὰν παραδῶ
all the goods of me, and if I deliver

τὸ σῶμά μου ἵνα καυθήσομαι, ἀγάπην
the body of me in order I shall be ²love
that burned,

δὲ μὴ ἔχω, οὐδὲν ὠφελοῦμαι. 4 Ἡ
¹but I have not, nothing I am profited. -

ἀγάπη μακροθυμεῖ, χρηστεύεται ἡ ἀγάπη,
Love suffers long, is kind - love,

οὐ ζηλοῖ, ἡ ἀγάπη οὐ περπερεύεται,
is not jealous, - love does not vaunt itself,

οὐ φυσιοῦται, 5 οὐκ ἀσχημονεῖ, οὐ ζητεῖ
is not puffed up, does not act unbecomingly, does not seek

τὰ ἑαυτῆς, οὐ παροξύνεται, οὐ λογίζεται
the of is not provoked, does not reckon
things her(it)self,

τὸ κακόν, 6 οὐ χαίρει ἐπὶ τῇ ἀδικίᾳ,
the evil, rejoices not over the wrong,

συγχαίρει δὲ τῇ ἀληθείᾳ· 7 πάντα στέγει,
but rejoices with the truth: all things covers,

πάντα πιστεύει, πάντα ἐλπίζει, πάντα
all things believes, all things hopes, all things

ὑπομένει. 8 Ἡ ἀγάπη οὐδέποτε πίπτει·
endures. - Love never falls:

εἴτε δὲ προφητεῖαι, καταργηθήσονται· εἴτε
but whether prophecies, they will be abolished; or

γλῶσσαι, παύσονται· εἴτε γνῶσις, κατ-
tongues, they will cease: or knowledge, it will

αργηθήσεται. 9 ἐκ μέρους γὰρ γινώσκομεν
be abolished. For in part we know

καὶ ἐκ μέρους προφητεύομεν· 10 ὅταν
and in part we prophesy; ¹when

δὲ ἔλθῃ τὸ τέλειον, τὸ ἐκ μέρους
¹but ²comes ³the ⁴perfect thing, the thing in part

511

King James Version

is in part shall be done away. 11 When I was a child, I spake as a child, I understood as a child, I thought as a child: but when I became a man, I put away childish things. 12 For now we see through a glass, darkly; but then face to face: now I know in part; but then shall I know even as also I am known. 13And now abideth faith, hope, charity, these three; but the greatest of these is charity.

14 Follow after charity, and desire spiritual gifts, but rather that ye may prophesy. 2 For he that speaketh in an *unknown* tongue speaketh not unto men, but unto God: for no man understandeth *him;* howbeit in the spirit he speaketh mysteries. 3 But he that prophesieth speaketh unto men *to* edification, and exhortation, and comfort. 4 He that speaketh in an *unknown* tongue edifieth himself; but he that prophesieth edifieth the church. 5 I would that ye all spake with tongues, but rather that ye prophesied: for greater *is* he that prophesieth than he that speaketh with tongues, except he interpret, that the church may receive edifying. 6 Now, brethren, if I come unto you speaking with tongues, what shall I profit you, except I shall speak to you either by revelation, or by knowledge, or by prophesying, or by doctrine? 7And even things without life giving sound, whether pipe or harp, except they give a distinction in the sounds, how shall it be known what is piped or harped? 8 For if the trumpet give an uncertain sound, who shall prepare himself to the battle? 9 So likewise ye, except ye utter by the tongue words easy to be understood, how shall it be known what is spoken? for ye shall speak into the air. 10 There are, it may be, so many kinds of voices in the world, and none of them *is* without signification. 11 Therefore if I know not the meaning of the voice, I shall be unto him that speaketh a barbarian, and he that speaketh *shall be* a barbarian unto me. 12 Even so ye, forasmuch as ye are zealous of spiritual *gifts,* seek that ye may excel to the edifying of the church. 13 Wherefore let him that speaketh in an *unknown* tongue pray that he may interpret. 14 For if I pray in an *unknown* tongue, my spirit prayeth, but my understanding is unfruitful. 15 What is it then? I will pray with the spirit, and I will pray with the understanding also: I will sing with the spirit, and I will sing with the understanding also. 16 Else, when thou shalt bless with the spirit, how shall he that occupieth the room of the unlearned say Amen at thy giving of thanks, seeing he understandeth not what thou sayest? 17 For thou verily givest thanks well, but the other is not edified. 18 I thank my God, I speak with tongues more than ye all: 19 Yet in the church I had rather speak five words with my understanding, that *by my voice* I might teach others also, than ten thou-

New International Version

comes, the imperfect disappears. 11 When I was a child, I talked like a child, I thought like a child, I reasoned like a child. When I became a man, I put childish ways behind me. 12 Now we see but a poor reflection; then we shall see face to face. Now I know in part; then I shall know fully, even as I am fully known.

13 And now these three remain: faith, hope and love. But the greatest of these is love.

Gifts of prophecy and tongues

14 Follow the way of love and eagerly desire spiritual gifts, especially the gift of prophecy. 2 For anyone who speaks in a tongue[e] does not speak to men but to God. Indeed, no one understands him; he utters mysteries with his spirit.[f] 3 But everyone who prophesies speaks to men for their strengthening, encouragement and comfort. 4 He who speaks in a tongue edifies himself, but he who prophesies edifies the church. 5 I would like every one of you to speak in tongues,[g] but I would rather have you prophesy. He who prophesies is greater than one who speaks in tongues,[g] unless he interprets, so that the church may be edified.

6 Now, brothers, if I come to you and speak in tongues, what good will I be to you, unless I bring you some revelation or knowledge or prophecy or teaching? 7 Even in the case of lifeless things that make sounds, such as the flute or harp, how will anyone know what tune is being played unless there is a distinction in the notes? 8Again, if the trumpet does not sound a clear call, who will get ready for battle? 9 So it is with you. Unless you speak intelligible words with your tongue, how will anyone know what you are saying? You will just be speaking into the air. 10 Undoubtedly there are all sorts of languages in the world, yet none of them is without meaning. 11 If then I do not grasp the meaning of what someone is saying, I am a foreigner to the speaker, and he is a foreigner to me. 12 So it is with you. Since you are eager to have spiritual gifts, try to excel in gifts that build up the church.

13 For this reason the man who speaks in a tongue should pray that he may interpret what he says. 14 For if I pray in a tongue, my spirit prays, but my mind is unfruitful. 15 So what shall I do? I will pray with my spirit, but I will also pray with my mind; I will sing with my spirit, but I will also sing with my mind. 16 If you are praising God with your spirit, how can one who finds himself among those who do not understand[h] say "Amen" to your thanksgiving, since he does not know what you are saying? 17 You may be giving thanks well enough, but the other man is not edified.

18 I thank God that I speak in tongues more than all of you. 19 But in the church I would rather speak five intelligible words to instruct others than ten thousand words in a tongue.

[e] Or *another language.* Also in verses 4, 13, 14, 19, 26 and 27. [f] Or *by the Spirit.* [g] Or *other languages.* Also verses 6, 18, 22, 23 and 39. [h] Or *among the inquirers.*

Greek Interlinear

καταργηθήσεται. **11** ὅτε ἤμην νήπιος,
will be abolished.　　When　I was　an infant,

ἐλάλουν ὡς νήπιος, ἐφρόνουν ὡς νήπιος,
I spoke　as　an infant,　I thought　as　an infant,

ἐλογιζόμην ὡς νήπιος· ὅτε γέγονα ἀνήρ,
I reckoned　as　an infant;　when I have become a man,

κατήργηκα τὰ τοῦ νηπίου. **12** βλέπομεν
I have　　the　of the　infant.　　we see
abolished　things

γὰρ ἄρτι δι᾽ ἐσόπτρου ἐν αἰνίγματι,
For　yet　through　a mirror　in　a riddle,

τότε δὲ πρόσωπον πρὸς πρόσωπον· ἄρτι
but then　　face　　to　　face;　　yet

γινώσκω ἐκ μέρους, τότε δὲ ἐπιγνώσομαι
I know　in　part,　but then　I shall fully know

καθὼς καὶ ἐπεγνώσθην. **13** νυνὶ δὲ μένει
as　also　I was fully known.　　But now　remains

πίστις, ἐλπίς, ἀγάπη, τὰ τρία ταῦτα·
faith,　hope,　love,　these three;

μείζων δὲ τούτων ἡ ἀγάπη.
and [the] greater　of these [is] –　love.

Chapter 14

Διώκετε τὴν ἀγάπην, ζηλοῦτε δὲ
Pursue ye　　–　love,　but desire eagerly

τὰ πνευματικά, μᾶλλον δὲ ἵνα προφητεύητε.
the　spiritual [gifts],　and rather　in order　ye may prophesy.
　　　　　　　　　　　　　　　　that

2 ὁ γὰρ λαλῶν γλώσσῃ οὐκ ἀνθρώποις
For the [one]　speaking　in a tongue　¹not　　²to men

λαλεῖ ἀλλὰ θεῷ· οὐδεὶς γὰρ ἀκούει,
¹speaks　but　to God;　for no one　hears,

πνεύματι δὲ λαλεῖ μυστήρια· **3** ὁ δὲ
but in spirit　he speaks　mysteries;　but the [one]

προφητεύων ἀνθρώποις λαλεῖ οἰκοδομὴν καὶ
prophesying　to men　speaks　edification　and

παράκλησιν καὶ παραμυθίαν. **4** ὁ λαλῶν
encouragement　and　consolation.　The [one] speaking

γλώσσῃ ἑαυτὸν οἰκοδομεῖ· ὁ δὲ προφητεύων
in a tongue　himself　edifies;　but the [one] prophesying

ἐκκλησίαν οἰκοδομεῖ. **5** θέλω δὲ πάντας
a church　edifies.　　Now I wish　all

ὑμᾶς λαλεῖν γλώσσαις, μᾶλλον δὲ ἵνα
you　to speak　in tongues,　but rather　*in order*
　　　　　　　　　　　　　　　　　　that

προφητεύητε· μείζων δὲ ὁ προφητεύων ἢ
ye may prophesy;　and greater　the [one] prophesying　than

ὁ λαλῶν γλώσσαις, ἐκτὸς εἰ μὴ διερμηνεύῃ,
the speaking　in tongues,　except　unless　he interprets,
[one]

ἵνα ἡ ἐκκλησία οἰκοδομὴν λάβῃ. **6** νῦν δέ,
in or- the　church　edification may receive.　But now,
der that

ἀδελφοί, ἐὰν ἔλθω πρὸς ὑμᾶς γλώσσαις
brothers,　if　I come　to　you　in tongues

λαλῶν, τί ὑμᾶς ὠφελήσω, ἐὰν μὴ ὑμῖν
speaking,　what　you　¹shall I profit,　except　²to you

λαλήσω ἢ ἐν ἀποκαλύψει ἢ ἐν γνώσει
¹I speak　either in　a revelation　or　in knowledge

ἢ ἐν προφητείᾳ ἢ διδαχῇ; **7** ὅμως τὰ
or in　prophecy　or in teaching?　Yet　　–

ἄψυχα φωνὴν διδόντα, εἴτε αὐλὸς εἴτε
lifeless things　²a sound　¹giving,　whether　pipe　or

κιθάρα, ἐὰν διαστολὴν τοῖς φθόγγοις μὴ
harp,　if　²a distinction　³in the　⁴sounds　¹not

δῷ, πῶς γνωσθήσεται τὸ αὐλούμενον ἢ
³they　how　will it be known　the　being piped　or
give,　　　　　　　　　　　　thing

τὸ κιθαριζόμενον; **8** καὶ γὰρ ἐὰν ἄδηλον
the　being harped;　For indeed　if　²an
thing　　　　　　　　　　　　　uncertain

σάλπιγξ φωνὴν δῷ, τίς παρασκευάσεται
¹a trumpet　⁴sound　³gives, who　will prepare himself

εἰς πόλεμον; **9** οὕτως καὶ ὑμεῖς διὰ
for　war?　　so　also　²ye　²through

τῆς γλώσσης ἐὰν μὴ εὔσημον λόγον·
¹the　²tongue　unless　²a clear　²word

δῶτε, πῶς γνωσθήσεται τὸ λαλούμενον;
²give,　how　will it be known　the thing　being said?

ἔσεσθε γὰρ εἰς ἀέρα λαλοῦντες. **10** τοσαῦτα
for ¹ye will be　²into　⁴air　²speaking.　⁴So many

εἰ τύχοι γένη φωνῶν εἰσιν ἐν κόσμῳ,
²it may be†　⁴kinds　³of sounds ¹there are in ²the world,

καὶ οὐδὲν ἄφωνον· **11** ἐὰν οὖν μὴ εἰδῶ
and not one [is] voiceless;　if　therefore　I know not

τὴν δύναμιν τῆς φωνῆς, ἔσομαι τῷ
the　power　of the　sound,　I shall be　to the

λαλοῦντι βάρβαρος καὶ ὁ λαλῶν ἐν ἐμοὶ
[one] speaking　a foreigner　and　the speaking　in(to)　me
　　　　　　　　　　　　　　　[one]

βάρβαρος. **12** οὕτως καὶ ὑμεῖς. ἐπεὶ
a foreigner.　　So　also　ye,　since

ζηλωταί ἐστε πνευμάτων, πρὸς τὴν
zealots　ye are　of spirit[ual thing]s,　²to　¹the

οἰκοδομὴν τῆς ἐκκλησίας ζητεῖτε ἵνα περισ-
⁴edification　³of the　⁵church　¹seek ye in order ye may
　　　　　　　　　　　　　　　　　　　that

σεύητε. **13** Διὸ ὁ λαλῶν γλώσσῃ προσευχ-
abound.　Wherefore the speaking　in a tongue　let him
　　　　　　　　　[one]

έσθω ἵνα διερμηνεύῃ. **14** ἐὰν γὰρ προσεύχωμαι
pray *in order*　he may　For if　I pray
　　that　interpret.

γλώσσῃ, τὸ πνεῦμά μου προσεύχεται,
in a tongue,　the　spirit　of me　prays,

ὁ δὲ νοῦς μου ἄκαρπός ἐστιν. **15** τί
but the　mind　of me　unfruitful　is.　　What

οὖν ἐστιν; προσεύξομαι τῷ πνεύματι,
therefore　is it?　²I will pray　with the　spirit,

προσεύξομαι δὲ καὶ τῷ νοΐ· ψαλῶ τῷ
¹I will pray　²and　²also　with　mind;　I will　with
　　　　　　　　　　　　　　　the　sing　the

πνεύματι, ψαλῶ δὲ καὶ τῷ νοΐ. **16** ἐπεὶ
spirit,　²I will sing ¹and　²also with the mind.　Otherwise

ἐὰν εὐλογῇς [ἐν] πνεύματι, ὁ ἀναπληρῶν
if　thou blessest in　spirit,　the [one] occupying

τὸν τόπον τοῦ ἰδιώτου πῶς ἐρεῖ τὸ
the　place　of the　uninstructed　how　will he say　the

ἀμὴν ἐπὶ τῇ σῇ εὐχαριστίᾳ; ἐπειδὴ τί
"amen"　at　–　thy　giving thanks?　Since what

λέγεις οὐκ οἶδεν· **17** σὺ μὲν γὰρ καλῶς
thou sayest he knows not;　²thou ²indeed ¹for　⁴well

εὐχαριστεῖς, ἀλλ᾽ ὁ ἕτερος οὐκ οἰκοδομεῖται.
⁴givest thanks,　but　the other　is not edified.

18 εὐχαριστῶ τῷ θεῷ, πάντων ὑμῶν μᾶλ-
I give thanks　–　to God,　²all　¹you　²more

λον γλώσσαις λαλῶ· **19** ἀλλὰ ἐν ἐκκλησίᾳ
than　²in tongues　¹I speak;　but　in　a church

θέλω πέντε λόγους τῷ νοΐ μου λαλῆσαι,
²I wish　²five　²words ²with the ²mind ²of me ²to speak,

ἵνα καὶ ἄλλους κατηχήσω, ἢ μυρίους
in or-　also　others　I may instruct,　than　ten
der that　　　　　　　　　　　　　thousands

King James Version

sand words in an *unknown* tongue. 20 Brethren, be not children in understanding: howbeit in malice be ye children, but in understanding be men. 21 In the law it is written, With *men of* other tongues and other lips will I speak unto this people; and yet for all that will they not hear me, saith the Lord. 22 Wherefore tongues are for a sign, not to them that believe, but to them that believe not: but prophesying *serveth* not for them that believe not, but for them which believe. 23 If therefore the whole church be come together into one place, and all speak with tongues, and there come in *those that are* unlearned, or unbelievers, will they not say that ye are mad? 24 But if all prophesy, and there come in one that believeth not, or *one* unlearned, he is convinced of all, he is judged of all: 25 And thus are the secrets of his heart made manifest; and so falling down on *his* face he will worship God, and report that God is in you of a truth. 26 How is it then, brethren? when ye come together, every one of you hath a psalm, hath a doctrine, hath a tongue, hath a revelation, hath an interpretation. Let all things be done unto edifying. 27 If any man speak in an *unknown* tongue, *let it be* by two, or at the most *by* three, and *that* by course; and let one interpret. 28 But if there be no interpreter, let him keep silence in the church; and let him speak to himself, and to God. 29 Let the prophets speak two or three, and let the other judge. 30 If *any thing* be revealed to another that sitteth by, let the first hold his peace. 31 For ye may all prophesy one by one, that all may learn, and all may be comforted. 32 And the spirits of the prophets are subject to the prophets. 33 For God is not *the author* of confusion, but of peace, as in all churches of the saints. 34 Let your women keep silence in the churches: for it is not permitted unto them to speak; but *they are* commanded to be under obedience, as also saith the law. 35 And if they will learn any thing, let them ask their husbands at home: for it is a shame for women to speak in the church. 36 What! came the word of God out from you? or came it unto you only? 37 If any man think himself to be a prophet, or spiritual, let him acknowledge that the things that I write unto you are the commandments of the Lord. 38 But if any man be ignorant, let him be ignorant. 39 Wherefore, brethren, covet to prophesy, and forbid not to speak with tongues. 40 Let all things be done decently and in order.

15 Moreover, brethren, I declare unto you the gospel which I preached unto you, which also ye have received, and wherein ye stand; 2 By which also ye are saved, if ye keep in memory what I preached unto you, unless ye have believed in vain. 3 For I delivered unto you first of all that which I also received, how that Christ died for our sins according to the

New International Version

20 Brothers, stop thinking like children. In regard to evil be infants, but in your thinking be adults. 21 In the Law it is written:

"Through men of strange tongues
　　and through the lips of foreigners
I will speak to this people,
　　but even then they will not listen to me," *
says the Lord.
22 Tongues, then, are a sign, not for believers but for unbelievers; prophecy, however, is for believers, not for unbelievers. 23 So if the whole church comes together and everyone speaks in tongues, and some who do not understand *ʲ* or some unbelievers come in, will they not say that you are out of your mind? 24 But if an unbeliever or someone who does not understand *ᵏ* comes in while everybody is prophesying, he will be convinced by all that he is a sinner and will be judged by all, 25 and the secrets of his heart will be laid bare. So he will fall down and worship God, exclaiming, "God is really among you!"

Orderly worship

26 What then shall we say, brothers? When you come together, everyone has a hymn, or a word of instruction, a revelation, a tongue, or an interpretation. All of these must be done for the strengthening of the church. 27 If anyone speaks in a tongue, two—or at the most three—should speak, one at a time, and someone must interpret. 28 If there is no interpreter, the speaker should keep quiet in the church and speak to himself and God.

29 Two or three prophets should speak, and the others should weigh carefully what is said. 30 And if a revelation comes to someone who is sitting down, the first speaker should stop. 31 For you can all prophesy in turn so that everyone may be instructed and encouraged. 32 The spirits of prophets are subject to the control of prophets. 33 For God is not a God of disorder but of peace.

As in all the congregations of the saints, 34 women should remain silent in the churches. They are not allowed to speak, but must be in submission, as the Law says. 35 If they want to inquire about something, they should ask their own husbands at home; for it is disgraceful for a woman to speak in the church. 36 Did the word of God originate with you? Or are you the only people it has reached?

37 If anybody thinks he is a prophet or spiritually gifted, let him acknowledge that what I am writing to you is the Lord's command. 38 If he ignores this, he himself will be ignored. *ˡ*

39 Therefore, my brothers, be eager to prophesy, and do not forbid speaking in tongues. 40 But everything should be done in a fitting and orderly way.

The resurrection of Christ

15 Now, brothers, I want to remind you of the gospel I preached to you, which you received and on which you have taken your stand. 2 By this gospel you are saved, if you hold firmly to the word I preached to you. Otherwise, you have believed in vain.

3 For what I received I passed on to you as of first importance *ᵐ*: that Christ died for our sins

[i] Isaiah 28:11,12; Deut. 28:49. [j] Or *some inquirers*. [k] or *some inquirer.* [l] Some MSS read *If he ignores this, let him ignore this.* [m] Or *you at the first.*

Greek Interlinear

λόγους ἐν γλώσσῃ. 20 ’Αδελφοί, μὴ
words in a tongue. Brothers, ²not

παιδία γίνεσθε ταῖς φρεσίν, ἀλλὰ τῇ
²children ¹be ye in the(your) minds, but -

κακίᾳ νηπιάζετε, ταῖς δὲ φρεσὶν τέλειοι
in malice be ye infantlike, and in the(your) minds mature

γίνεσθε. 21 ἐν τῷ νόμῳ γέγραπται ὅτι
be ye. In the law it has been written that

ἐν ἑτερογλώσσοις καὶ ἐν χείλεσιν ἑτέρων
in other tongues and in lips of others

λαλήσω τῷ λαῷ τούτῳ, καὶ οὐδ’ οὕτως
I will speak to this people, and not so

εἰσακούσονταί μου, λέγει κύριος. 22 ὥστε
will they hear me, says [the] Lord. So as

αἱ γλῶσσαι εἰς σημεῖόν εἰσιν οὐ τοῖς
the tongues ²for ¹a sign ¹are not to the

πιστεύουσιν ἀλλὰ τοῖς ἀπίστοις, ἡ δὲ
[ones] believing but to the unbelievers, and the

προφητεία οὐ τοῖς ἀπίστοις ἀλλὰ τοῖς
prophecy [is] not to the unbelievers but to the

πιστεύουσιν. 23 ’Εὰν οὖν συνέλθῃ ἡ
[ones] believing. If therefore ²comes ¹the
together

ἐκκλησία ὅλη ἐπὶ τὸ αὐτὸ καὶ πάντες
²church ²whole together and all

λαλῶσιν γλώσσαις, εἰσέλθωσιν δὲ ἰδιῶται
speak in tongues, and ⁴enter ¹uninstructed

ἢ ἄπιστοι, οὐκ ἐροῦσιν ὅτι μαίνεσθε;
²or ¹unbelievers, will they not say that ye rave?

24 ἐὰν δὲ πάντες προφητεύωσιν, εἰσέλθῃ δέ
but if all prophesy, and ²enters

τις ἄπιστος ἢ ἰδιώτης, ἐλέγχεται ὑπὸ
¹some ¹unbeliever ²or ¹uninstructed, he is convicted by

πάντων, ἀνακρίνεται ὑπὸ πάντων, 25 τὰ
all, he is judged by all, the

κρυπτὰ τῆς καρδίας αὐτοῦ φανερὰ γίνεται,
hidden of the heart of him ¹manifest ¹becomes,
things

καὶ οὕτως πεσὼν ἐπὶ πρόσωπον προσκυνή-
and so falling on [his] face he will wor-

σει τῷ θεῷ, ἀπαγγέλλων ὅτι ὄντως
ship - God, declaring that really

ὁ θεὸς ἐν ὑμῖν ἐστιν. 26 Τί οὖν ἐστιν,
- God ²among ¹you ¹is. What therefore is it,

ἀδελφοί; ὅταν συνέρχησθε, ἕκαστος ψαλμὸν
brothers? whenever ye come together, each one a psalm

ἔχει, διδαχὴν ἔχει, ἀποκάλυψιν ἔχει, γλῶσ-
has, a teaching he has, a revelation he has, a

σαν ἔχει, ἑρμηνείαν ἔχει· πάντα πρὸς
tongue he has, an interpretation he has; ¹all things ²for

οἰκοδομὴν ¹let ²be. 27 εἴτε γλώσσῃ τις
²edification ¹let ²be. If in a tongue anyone

λαλεῖ, κατὰ δύο ἢ τὸ πλεῖστον τρεῖς,
speaks, by two or the most three,

καὶ ἀνὰ μέρος, 28 καὶ εἷς διερμηνευέτω·
and in turn,† and ²one ¹let ²interpret:

ἐὰν δὲ μὴ ᾖ διερμηνευτής, σιγάτω ἐν
but if there is not an interpreter, let him be silent in

ἐκκλησίᾳ, ἑαυτῷ δὲ λαλείτω καὶ τῷ
church, and to himself let him speak and -

θεῷ. 29 προφῆται δὲ δύο ἢ τρεῖς λαλεί-
to God. And prophets two or three let them

τωσαν, 30 καὶ οἱ ἄλλοι διακρινέτωσαν·
speak, and the others let discern;

ἐὰν δὲ ἄλλῳ ἀποκαλυφθῇ καθημένῳ, ὁ
but if ¹to another ²[something] ²sitting, the
¹is revealed

πρῶτος σιγάτω. 31 δύνασθε γὰρ καθ’
first let be silent. For ye can ²sin-

ἕνα πάντες προφητεύειν, ἵνα πάντες
gly† ¹all ²to prophesy, in order that all

μανθάνωσιν καὶ πάντες παρακαλῶνται.
may learn and all may be encouraged.

32 καὶ πνεύματα προφητῶν προφήταις
And [the] spirits of prophets to prophets

ὑποτάσσεται· 33 οὐ γάρ ἐστιν ἀκαταστασίας
is(are) subject; for ²not ¹is ⁴of tumult

ὁ θεὸς ἀλλὰ εἰρήνης. ‘Ως ἐν πάσαις
- ¹God but of peace. As in all

ταῖς ἐκκλησίαις τῶν ἁγίων, 34 αἱ γυναῖκες
the churches of the saints, ²the ²women

ἐν ταῖς ἐκκλησίαις σιγάτωσαν· οὐ γὰρ
²in ¹the ⁷churches ¹let ²be silent; ²not ¹for

ἐπιτρέπεται αὐταῖς λαλεῖν, ἀλλὰ ὑποτασ-
²it is ⁶permitted to them to speak, but let them

σέσθωσαν, καθὼς καὶ ὁ νόμος λέγει.
be subject, as also the law says.

35 εἰ δέ τι μαθεῖν θέλουσιν, ἐν οἴκῳ
But if ²anything ²to learn ¹they wish, ²at home

τοὺς ἰδίους ἄνδρας ἐπερωτάτωσαν· αἰσχρὸν
²the(ir) ²own ²husbands ¹let them question; ²a shame

γάρ ἐστιν γυναικὶ λαλεῖν ἐν ἐκκλησίᾳ.
¹for ¹it is for a woman to speak in a church.

36 ἢ ἀφ’ ὑμῶν ὁ λόγος τοῦ θεοῦ ἐξῆλθεν,
Or from you ²the ²word - ⁴of God ¹went forth,

ἢ εἰς ὑμᾶς μόνους κατήντησεν; 37 Εἴ
or to you only did it reach? If

τις δοκεῖ προφήτης εἶναι ἢ πνευματικός,
any- thinks ²a prophet ¹to be or a spiritual man,
one

ἐπιγινωσκέτω ἃ γράφω ὑμῖν ὅτι
let him clearly [the] things I write to you that
know which

κυρίου ἐστὶν ἐντολή· 38 εἰ δέ τις
of [the] Lord they are a commandment; but if anyone

ἀγνοεῖ, ἀγνοεῖται. 39 Ὥστε, ἀδελφοί
is ignorant, let him be ignorant. So as, brothers

μου, ζηλοῦτε τὸ προφητεύειν, καὶ τὸ
of me, be ye eager - to prophesy, and -

λαλεῖν μὴ κωλύετε γλώσσαις· 40 πάντα
²to speak ¹forbid not in tongues; ²all things

δὲ εὐσχημόνως καὶ κατὰ τάξιν γινέσθω.
and ⁴becomingly ²and ²according to ¹order ¹let ²be done.

Chapter 15

Γνωρίζω δὲ ὑμῖν, ἀδελφοί, τὸ
Now I make known to you, brothers, the

εὐαγγέλιον ὃ εὐηγγελισάμην ὑμῖν, ὃ καὶ
good tidings which I preached to you, which also

παρελάβετε, ἐν ᾧ καὶ ἑστήκατε, 2 δι’
ye received, in which also ye stand, through

οὗ καὶ σῴζεσθε, τίνι λόγῳ εὐηγγελισάμην
which also ye are saved, ²to what ⁴word ¹I preached

ὑμῖν εἰ κατέχετε, ἐκτὸς εἰ μὴ εἰκῇ
²to you ¹if ²ye hold fast, except unless in vain

ἐπιστεύσατε. 3 παρέδωκα γὰρ ὑμῖν ἐν
ye believed. For I delivered to you among

πρώτοις, ὃ καὶ παρέλαβον, ὅτι Χριστὸς
[the] first what also I received, that Christ
things,

ἀπέθανεν ὑπὲρ τῶν ἁμαρτιῶν ἡμῶν κατὰ
died on be- the sins of us accord-
half of ing to

515

King James Version

Scriptures; 4And that he was buried, and that he rose again the third day according to the Scriptures: 5And that he was seen of Cephas, then of the twelve: 6After that, he was seen of above five hundred brethren at once; of whom the greater part remain unto this present, but some are fallen asleep. 7After that, he was seen of James; then of all the apostles. 8And last of all he was seen of me also, as of one born out of due time. 9 For I am the least of the apostles, that am not meet to be called an apostle, because I persecuted the church of God. 10 But by the grace of God I am what I am: and his grace which was bestowed upon me was not in vain; but I laboured more abundantly than they all: yet not I, but the grace of God which was with me. 11 Therefore whether it were I or they, so we preach, and so ye believed. 12 Now if Christ be preached that he rose from the dead, how say some among you that there is no resurrection of the dead? 13 But if there be no resurrection of the dead, then is Christ not risen: 14And if Christ be not risen, then is our preaching vain, and your faith is also vain. 15 Yea, and we are found false witnesses of God; because we have testified of God that he raised up Christ: whom he raised not up, if so be that the dead rise not. 16 For if the dead rise not, then is not Christ raised: 17And if Christ be not raised, your faith is vain; ye are yet in your sins. 18 Then they also which are fallen asleep in Christ are perished. 19·If in this life only we have hope in Christ, we are of all men most miserable. 20 But now is Christ risen from the dead, and become the firstfruits of them that slept. 21 For since by man came death, by man came also the resurrection of the dead. 22 For as in Adam all die, even so in Christ shall all be made alive. 23 But every man in his own order: Christ the firstfruits; afterward they that are Christ's at his coming. 24 Then cometh the end, when he shall have delivered up the kingdom to God, even the Father; when he shall have put down all rule, and all authority and power. 25 For he must reign, till he hath put all enemies under his feet. 26 The last enemy that shall be destroyed is death. 27 For he hath put all things under his feet. But when he saith, All things are put under him, it is manifest that he is excepted, which did put all things under him. 28And when all things shall be subdued unto him, then shall the Son also himself be subject unto him that put all things under him, that God may be all in all. 29 Else what shall they do which are baptized for the dead, if the dead rise not at all? why are they then baptized for the dead? 30 And why stand we in jeopardy every hour? 31 I protest by your rejoicing which I have in Christ Jesus our Lord, I die daily. 32 If after the manner of men I have fought with beasts

New International Version

according to the Scriptures, 4 that he was buried, that he was raised on the third day according to the Scriptures, 5 and that he appeared to Peter,[n] and then to the Twelve. 6After that, he appeared to more than five hundred of the brothers at the same time, most of whom are still living, though some have fallen asleep. 7 Then he appeared to James, then to all the apostles, 8 and last of all he appeared to me also, as to one abnormally born.

9 For I am the least of the apostles and do not even deserve to be called an apostle, because I persecuted the church of God. 10 But by the grace of God I am what I am, and his grace to me was not without effect. No, I worked harder than all of them—yet not I, but the grace of God that was with me. 11 Whether, then, it was I or they, this is what we preach, and this is what you believed.

The resurrection of the dead

12 But if it is preached that Christ has been raised from the dead, how can some of you say that there is no resurrection of the dead? 13 If there is no resurrection of the dead, then not even Christ has been raised. 14And if Christ has not been raised, our preaching is useless and so is your faith. 15 More than that, we are then found to be false witnesses about God, for we have testified about God that he raised Christ from the dead. But he did not raise him if in fact the dead are not raised. 16 For if the dead are not raised, then Christ has not been raised either. 17And if Christ has not been raised, your faith is futile; you are still in your sins. 18 Then those also who have fallen asleep in Christ are lost. 19 If only for this life we have hope in Christ, we are to be pitied more than all men.

20 But Christ has indeed been raised from the dead, the firstfruits of those who have fallen asleep. 21 For since death came through a man, the resurrection of the dead comes also through a man. 22 For as in Adam all die, so in Christ all will be made alive. 23 But each in his own turn: Christ, the firstfruits; then, when he comes, those who belong to him. 24 Then the end will come, when he hands over the kingdom to God the Father after he has destroyed all dominion, authority and power. 25 For he must reign until God has put all his enemies under his feet. 26 The last enemy to be destroyed is death. 27 For God "has put everything under his feet." o Now when it says that "everything" has been put under him, it is clear that this does not include God himself, who put everything under Christ. 28 When he has done this, then the Son himself will be made subject to him who put everything under him, so that God may be all in all.

29 Now if there is no resurrection, what will those do who are baptized for the dead? If the dead are not raised at all, why are people baptized for them? 30And as for us, why do we endanger ourselves every hour? 31 I die every day —I mean that, brothers—just as surely as I glory over you in Christ Jesus our Lord. 32 If I fought wild beasts in Ephesus for merely human reasons,

(n) Greek Cephas. [o] Psalm 8:6.

τὰς γραφάς, 4 καὶ ὅτι ἐτάφη, καὶ ὅτι
the scriptures,   and   that he was buried, and   that

ἐγήγερται τῇ ἡμέρᾳ τῇ τρίτῃ κατὰ
he has   on the   *day   -   ¹third   accord-
been raised   ing to

τὰς γραφάς, 5 καὶ ὅτι ὤφθη Κηφᾷ,
the scriptures,   and   that he was seen by Cephas,

εἶτα τοῖς δώδεκα· 6 ἔπειτα ὤφθη ἐπάνω
then by the   twelve;   afterward he was seen ⁵over

πεντακοσίοις ἀδελφοῖς ἐφάπαξ, ἐξ ὧν οἱ
¹by ⁵five hundreds brothers   at one time, of whom the

πλείονες μένουσιν ἕως ἄρτι, τινὲς δὲ
majority   remain   until   now, though some

ἐκοιμήθησαν· 7 ἔπειτα ὤφθη Ἰακώβῳ, εἶτα
fell asleep;   afterward he was seen by James,   then

τοῖς ἀποστόλοις πᾶσιν· 8 ἔσχατον δὲ
by the   apostles   all;   and lastly

πάντων ὡσπερεὶ τῷ ἐκτρώματι ὤφθη
of all   even as if to the(an) abortion he was seen

κἀμοί. 9 Ἐγὼ γάρ εἰμι ὁ ἐλάχιστος
by me also.   For I   am the   least

τῶν ἀποστόλων, ὃς οὐκ εἰμὶ ἱκανὸς
of the apostles,   who am not   sufficient

καλεῖσθαι ἀπόστολος, διότι ἐδίωξα τὴν
to be called   an apostle,   because I persecuted the

ἐκκλησίαν τοῦ θεοῦ· 10 χάριτι δὲ θεοῦ
church   - of God;   but by [the] grace of God

εἰμι ὃ εἰμι, καὶ ἡ χάρις αὐτοῦ ἡ εἰς
I am what I am, and the grace of him –   to

ἐμὲ οὐ κενὴ ἐγενήθη, ἀλλὰ περισσότερον
me not empty   was,   but   ²more abundantly
                                    [than]

αὐτῶν πάντων ἐκοπίασα, οὐκ ἐγὼ δὲ
²them   ⁴all   ¹I laboured, ⁵not ³I ¹yet

ἀλλὰ ἡ χάρις τοῦ θεοῦ σὺν ἐμοί. 11 εἴτε
but the grace - of God with me.   Whether

οὖν ἐγὼ εἴτε ἐκεῖνοι, οὕτως κηρύσσομεν
therefore I or those,   so   we proclaim

καὶ οὕτως ἐπιστεύσατε.
and so   ye believed.

12 Εἰ δὲ Χριστὸς κηρύσσεται ὅτι ἐκ
But if   Christ   is proclaimed that from

νεκρῶν ἐγήγερται, πῶς λέγουσιν ἐν ὑμῖν
[the] dead he has been raised, how   say   ²among ¹you

τινες ὅτι ἀνάστασις νεκρῶν οὐκ ἔστιν;
¹some that a resurrection of dead persons there is not?

13 εἰ δὲ ἀνάστασις νεκρῶν οὐκ ἔστιν,
Now if a resurrection of dead persons there is not,

οὐδὲ Χριστὸς ἐγήγερται· 14 εἰ δὲ Χριστὸς
neither Christ has been raised;   and if   Christ

οὐκ ἐγήγερται, κενὸν ἄρα τὸ κήρυγμα
has not been raised, empty   then the   proclamation

ἡμῶν, κενὴ καὶ ἡ πίστις ὑμῶν· 15 εὑρισκ-
of us, empty also the faith of you;   ²we are

όμεθα δὲ καὶ ψευδομάρτυρες τοῦ θεοῦ,
found ¹and also   false witnesses   - of God,

ὅτι ἐμαρτυρήσαμεν κατὰ τοῦ θεοῦ ὅτι
because we witnessed as to -   God that

ἤγειρεν τὸν Χριστόν, ὃν οὐκ ἤγειρεν
he raised -   Christ, whom he raised not

εἴπερ ἄρα νεκροὶ οὐκ ἐγείρονται. 16 εἰ
if   then dead persons are not raised.

γὰρ νεκροὶ οὐκ ἐγείρονται, οὐδὲ Χριστὸς
For dead persons are not raised,   neither Christ

ἐγήγερται· 17 εἰ δὲ Χριστὸς οὐκ ἐγήγερται,
has been raised;   and if Christ has not been raised,

ματαία ἡ πίστις ὑμῶν [ἐστιν], ἔτι ἐστὲ
³useless ¹the ²faith ⁴of you ⁵is,   ⁶still ¹ye are

ἐν ταῖς ἁμαρτίαις ὑμῶν. 18 ἄρα καὶ οἱ
in the   sins   of you.   Then also the [ones]

κοιμηθέντες ἐν Χριστῷ ἀπώλοντο. 19 εἰ
having fallen asleep in Christ   perished.   If

ἐν τῇ ζωῇ ταύτῃ ἐν Χριστῷ ἠλπικότες
in this life   *in ⁴Christ ²having hoped

ἐσμὲν μόνον, ἐλεεινότεροι πάντων ἀνθρώπων
¹we are ⁵only, more pitiful [than]   all   men

ἐσμέν. 20 Νυνὶ δὲ Χριστὸς ἐγήγερται
we are.   But now   Christ   has been raised

ἐκ νεκρῶν, ἀπαρχὴ τῶν κεκοιμημένων.
from [the] dead, firstfruit of the [ones] having fallen asleep.

21 ἐπειδὴ γὰρ δι' ἀνθρώπου θάνατος, καὶ
For since   through a man   death [came], also

δι' ἀνθρώπου ἀνάστασις νεκρῶν. 22 ὥσπερ
through a man a resurrection of dead persons as
                                            [came].

γὰρ ἐν τῷ Ἀδὰμ πάντες ἀποθνῄσκουσιν,
For in -   Adam all   die,

οὕτως καὶ ἐν τῷ Χριστῷ πάντες ζῳοποιη-
so   also in -   Christ   all   will be

θήσονται. 23 Ἕκαστος δὲ ἐν τῷ ἰδίῳ
made alive.   But each one in the(his) own

τάγματι· ἀπαρχὴ Χριστός, ἔπειτα οἱ τοῦ
order: [the]   Christ,   afterward the -
          firstfruit   [ones]

Χριστοῦ ἐν τῇ παρουσίᾳ αὐτοῦ, 24 εἶτα
of Christ in the   presence   of him,   then

τὸ τέλος, ὅταν παραδιδοῖ τὴν βασιλείαν
the end, whenever he delivers the   kingdom

τῷ θεῷ καὶ πατρί, ὅταν καταργήσῃ
- to God even [the] Father, whenever he abolishes

πᾶσαν ἀρχὴν καὶ πᾶσαν ἐξουσίαν καὶ
all   rule   and   all   authority   and

δύναμιν. 25 δεῖ γὰρ αὐτὸν βασιλεύειν
power.   For it behoves   him   to reign

ἄχρι οὗ θῇ πάντας τοὺς ἐχθροὺς ὑπὸ
until   he puts all the(his)   enemies   under

τοὺς πόδας αὐτοῦ. 26 ἔσχατος ἐχθρὸς
the   feet of him.   [The] last   enemy

καταργεῖται ὁ θάνατος· πάντα γὰρ ὑπέταξεν
is abolished - death; for all things he subjected

ὑπὸ τοὺς πόδας αὐτοῦ. 27 ὅταν δὲ
under the   feet of him.   But whenever

εἴπῃ ὅτι πάντα ὑποτέτακται, δῆλον ὅτι
he says that all things have been subjected, [it is] clear that

ἐκτὸς τοῦ ὑποτάξαντος αὐτῷ τὰ πάντα.
[it is]   the having   to him - all
apart from [one] subjected   things.

28 ὅταν δὲ ὑποταγῇ αὐτῷ τὰ πάντα,
But whenever is(are) subjected to him - all things,

τότε καὶ αὐτὸς ὁ υἱὸς ὑποταγήσεται
then also ²[him]self ¹the ³Son   will be subjected

τῷ ὑποτάξαντι αὐτῷ τὰ πάντα, ἵνα
to the having   to him - all in order
[one]   subjected   things,   that

ᾖ ὁ θεὸς πάντα ἐν πᾶσιν. 29 Ἐπεὶ
¹may – ¹God all in all.   Other-
be   things   wise

τί ποιήσουσιν οἱ βαπτιζόμενοι ὑπὲρ τῶν
what will they do the [ones] being baptized on behalf of the

νεκρῶν; εἰ ὅλως νεκροὶ οὐκ ἐγείρονται,
dead?   if actually dead persons are not raised,

τί καὶ βαπτίζονται ὑπὲρ αὐτῶν; 30 τί
why indeed are they baptized on behalf of them?   why

καὶ ἡμεῖς κινδυνεύομεν πᾶσαν ὥραν;
also ²we   ¹are ²in danger   every   hour?

31 καθ' ἡμέραν ἀποθνῄσκω, νὴ τὴν
Daily   I die,   by   -

ὑμετέραν καύχησιν, ἀδελφοί, ἣν ἔχω ἐν
your   boasting,   brothers, which I have in

Χριστῷ Ἰησοῦ τῷ κυρίῳ ἡμῶν. 32 εἰ
Christ   Jesus the Lord   of us.   If

κατὰ ἄνθρωπον ἐθηριομάχησα ἐν Ἐφέσῳ,
according man   I fought with wild in   Ephesus,
                beasts

King James Version

at Ephesus, what advantageth it me, if the dead rise not? let us eat and drink; for to morrow we die. 33 Be not deceived: evil communications corrupt good manners. 34Awake to righteousness, and sin not; for some have not the knowledge of God: I speak *this* to your shame. 35 But some *man* will say, How are the dead raised up? and with what body do they come? 36 *Thou* fool, that which thou sowest is not quickened, except it die: 37And that which thou sowest, thou sowest not that body that shall be, but bare grain, it may chance of wheat, or of some other grain: 38 But God giveth it a body as it hath pleased him, and to every seed his own body. 39All flesh *is* not the same flesh: but *there is* one *kind of* flesh of men, another flesh of beasts, another of fishes, *and* another of birds. 40 *There are* also celestial bodies, and bodies terrestrial: but the glory of the celestial *is* one, and the *glory* of the terrestrial *is* another. 41 *There is* one glory of the sun, and another glory of the moon, and another glory of the stars; for *one* star differeth from *another* star in glory. 42 So also *is* the resurrection of the dead. It is sown in corruption; it is raised in incorruption: 43 It is sown in dishonour, it is raised in glory: it is sown in weakness, it is raised in power: 44 It is sown a natural body, it is raised a spiritual body. There is a natural body, and there is a spiritual body. 45And so it is written, The first man Adam was made a living soul; the last Adam *was made* a quickening spirit. 46 Howbeit that *was* not first which is spiritual, but that which is natural; and afterward that which is spiritual. 47 The first man *is* of the earth, earthy: the second man *is* the Lord from heaven. 48As *is* the earthy, such *are* they also that are earthy: and as *is* the heavenly, such *are* they also that are heavenly. 49And as we have borne the image of the earthy, we shall also bear the image of the heavenly. 50 Now this I say, brethren, that flesh and blood cannot inherit the kingdom of God; neither doth corruption inherit incorruption. 51 Behold, I shew you a mystery; We shall not all sleep, but we shall all be changed, 52 In a moment, in the twinkling of an eye, at the last trump: for the trumpet shall sound, and the dead shall be raised incorruptible, and we shall be changed. 53 For this corruptible must put on incorruption, and this mortal *must* put on immortality. 54 So when this corruptible shall have put on incorruption, and this mortal shall have put on immortality, then shall be brought to pass the saying that is written, Death is swallowed up in victory. 55 O death, where *is* thy sting? O grave, where *is* thy victory? 56 The sting of death *is* sin; and the strength of sin *is* the law. 57 But thanks *be* to God, which giveth us the victory through our Lord Jesus Christ. 58 Therefore, my beloved brethren, be ye steadfast, unmoveable, always abounding in the work of the Lord, forasmuch as ye know that your labour is not in vain in the Lord.

New International Version

what have I gained? If the dead are not raised,
"Let us eat and drink,
　for tomorrow we die." *p*
33 Do not be misled: "Bad company corrupts good character." 34 Come back to your senses as you ought, and stop sinning; for there are some who are ignorant of God—I say this to your shame.

The resurrection body

35 But someone may ask, "How are the dead raised? With what kind of body will they come?" 36 How foolish! What you sow does not come to life unless it dies. 37 When you sow, you do not plant the body that will be, but just a seed, perhaps of wheat or of something else. 38 But God gives it a body as he has determined, and to each kind of seed he gives its own body. 39All flesh is not the same: Men have one kind of flesh, animals have another, birds another and fish another. 40 There are also heavenly bodies and there are earthly bodies; but the splendor of the heavenly bodies is one kind, and the splendor of the earthly bodies is another. 41 The sun has one kind of splendor, the moon another and the stars another; and star differs from star in splendor.
42 So it will be with the resurrection of the dead. The body that is sown is perishable, it is raised imperishable; 43 it is sown in dishonor, it is raised in glory; it is sown in weakness, it is raised in power; 44 it is sown a natural body, it is raised a spiritual body.
If there is a natural body, there is also a spiritual body. 45 So it is written: "The first man Adam became a living being" *q*; the last Adam, a life-giving spirit. 46 The spiritual did not come first, but the natural, and after that the spiritual. 47 The first man was of the dust of the earth, the second man from heaven. 48As was the earthly man, so are those who are of the earth; and as is the man from heaven, so also are those who are of heaven. 49And just as we have borne the likeness of the earthly man, so we shall bear *r* the likeness of the man from heaven.
50 I declare to you, brothers, that flesh and blood cannot inherit the kingdom of God, nor does the perishable inherit the imperishable. 51 Listen, I tell you a mystery: We shall not all sleep, but we shall all be changed—52 in a flash, in the twinkling of an eye, at the last trumpet. For the trumpet will sound, the dead will be raised imperishable, and we shall be changed. 53 For the perishable must clothe itself with the imperishable, and the mortal with immortality. 54 When the perishable has been clothed with the imperishable, and the mortal with immortality, then the saying that is written will come true: "Death has been swallowed up in victory." *s*
55 "Where, O death, is your victory?
　Where, O death, is your sting?" *t*
56 The sting of death is sin, and the power of sin is the law. 57 But thanks be to God! He gives us the victory through our Lord Jesus Christ.
58 Therefore, my dear brothers, stand firm. Let nothing move you. Always give yourselves fully to the work of the Lord, because you know that your labor in the Lord is not in vain.

[p] Isaiah 22:13. [q] Gen. 2:7. [r] Some early MSS read *so let us bear*. [s] Isaiah 25:8. [t] Hosea 13:14.

τί μοι τὸ ὄφελος; εἰ νεκροὶ οὐκ ἐγείρονται,
what to me the profit?ᶜ If dead persons are not raised,
=what profit have I?

φάγωμεν καὶ πίωμεν, αὔριον γὰρ ἀποθνή-
let us eat and let us drink, for to-morrow we

σκομεν. 33 μὴ πλανᾶσθε· φθείρουσιν ἤθη
die. Be ye not led astray: ¹Corrupt ⁵customs

χρηστὰ ὁμιλίαι κακαί. 34 ἐκνήψατε δικαίως
⁴good ³associations ²bad. Become ye sober righteously

καὶ μὴ ἁμαρτάνετε· ἀγνωσίαν γὰρ θεοῦ
and do not sin; for ²ignorance ⁴of God

τινες ἔχουσιν· πρὸς ἐντροπὴν ὑμῖν λαλῶ.
¹some ³have: ⁴for ⁵shame ⁶to you ¹I speak.

35 Ἀλλὰ ἐρεῖ τις· πῶς ἐγείρονται οἱ
But ²will say ¹someone: How are raised the

νεκροί; ποίῳ δὲ σώματι ἔρχονται; 36 ἄφρων,
dead? and with what ⁹ body do they come? Foolish man,

σὺ ὃ σπείρεις, οὐ ζωοποιεῖται ἐὰν μὴ
¹thou ¹what sowest, is not made alive unless

ἀποθάνῃ·37 καὶ ὃ σπείρεις, οὐ τὸ σῶμα
it dies; and what thou sowest, not the body

τὸ γενησόμενον σπείρεις, ἀλλὰ γυμνὸν
- going to become thou sowest, but a naked

κόκκον εἰ τύχοι σίτου ἤ τινος τῶν
grain it may bet of wheat or some one of the

λοιπῶν· 38 ὁ δὲ θεὸς δίδωσιν αὐτῷ
rest; - but God gives to it

σῶμα καθὼς ἠθέλησεν, καὶ ἑκάστῳ τῶν
a body as he wished, and to each of the

σπερμάτων ἴδιον σῶμα. 39 οὐ πᾶσα
seeds [its] own body. ²[is] not ¹All

σὰρξ ἡ αὐτὴ σάρξ, ἀλλὰ ἄλλη μὲν
¹flesh the same flesh, but other(one) indeed

ἀνθρώπων, ἄλλη δὲ σὰρξ κτηνῶν, ἄλλη δὲ
of men, and another flesh of animals, and another

σὰρξ πτηνῶν, ἄλλη δὲ ἰχθύων. 40 καὶ
flesh of birds, and another of fishes. And [there

σώματα ἐπουράνια, καὶ σώματα ἐπίγεια·
are] bodies heavenly, and bodies earthly;

ἀλλὰ ἑτέρα μὲν ἡ τῶν ἐπουρανίων δόξα,
but ⁷other ⁵[is] ¹the ²of the ⁶heavenly ³glory,
(one) ⁴indeed [bodies]

ἑτέρα δὲ ἡ τῶν ἐπιγείων. 41 ἄλλη
and other the [glory] of the earthly [bodies]. Other(one)

δόξα ἡλίου, καὶ ἄλλη δόξα σελήνης,
glory of [the] sun, and another glory of [the] moon,

καὶ ἄλλη δόξα ἀστέρων· ἀστὴρ γὰρ
and another glory of [the] stars· for star

ἀστέρος διαφέρει ἐν δόξῃ. 42 οὕτως καὶ
from star differs in glory. So also

ἡ ἀνάστασις τῶν νεκρῶν. σπείρεται ἐν
the resurrection of the dead. It is sown in

φθορᾷ, ἐγείρεται ἐν ἀφθαρσίᾳ· 43 σπείρεται
corruption, it is raised in incorruption; it is sown

ἐν ἀτιμίᾳ, ἐγείρεται ἐν δόξῃ· σπείρεται
in dishonour, it is raised in glory; it is sown

ἐν ἀσθενείᾳ, ἐγείρεται ἐν δυνάμει· 44 σπείρ-
in weakness, it is raised in power; it is

εται σῶμα ψυχικόν, ἐγείρεται σῶμα
sown body a natural, it is raised body

πνευματικόν Εἰ ἔστιν σῶμα ψυχικόν,
a spiritual. If there is body a natural,

ἔστιν καὶ πνευματικόν. 45 οὕτως καὶ
there is also a spiritual [body]. So also

γέγραπται· ἐγένετο ὁ πρῶτος ἄνθρωπος
it has been written: ⁵became ¹The ²first ³man

Ἀδὰμ εἰς ψυχὴν ζῶσαν· ὁ ἔσχατος
⁴Adam – soul a living; the last

Ἀδὰμ εἰς πνεῦμα ζωοποιοῦν. 46 ἀλλ'
Adam – spirit a life-giving. But

οὐ πρῶτον τὸ πνευματικὸν ἀλλὰ τὸ
not firstly the spiritual [body] but the

ψυχικόν, ἔπειτα τὸ πνευματικόν. 47 ὁ
natural, afterward the spiritual. The

πρῶτος ἄνθρωπος ἐκ γῆς χοϊκός, ὁ
first man [was] out of earth earthy, the

δεύτερος ἄνθρωπος ἐξ οὐρανοῦ. 48 οἷος ὁ
second man [is] out of heaven. Such the

χοϊκός, τοιοῦτοι καὶ οἱ χοϊκοί, καὶ οἷος
earthy man, such also the earthy ones, and such

ὁ ἐπουράνιος, τοιοῦτοι καὶ οἱ ἐπουράνιοι·
the heavenly man, such also the heavenly ones;

49 καὶ καθὼς ἐφορέσαμεν τὴν εἰκόνα τοῦ
and as we bore the image of the

χοϊκοῦ, φορέσομεν καὶ τὴν εἰκόνα τοῦ
earthy man, we shall bear also the image of the

ἐπουρανίου. 50 Τοῦτο δέ φημι, ἀδελφοί,
heavenly man. And this I say, brothers,

ὅτι σὰρξ καὶ αἷμα βασιλείαν θεοῦ κληρο-
that flesh and blood ²[the] kingdom ⁴of God ¹to

νομῆσαι οὐ δύναται, οὐδὲ ἡ φθορὰ τὴν
inherit ¹cannot, neither the ⁵corruption –

ἀφθαρσίαν κληρονομεῖ. 51 ἰδοὺ μυστήριον
³incorruption ²inherits. Behold[,] a mystery

ὑμῖν λέγω· πάντες οὐ κοιμηθησόμεθα,
to you I tell: all We shall not fall asleep,

πάντες δὲ ἀλλαγησόμεθα, 52 ἐν ἀτόμῳ,
but all we shall be changed, in a moment,

ἐν ῥιπῇ ὀφθαλμοῦ, ἐν τῇ ἐσχάτῃ σάλπιγγι·
in a glance of an eye, at the last trumpet;

σαλπίσει γάρ, καὶ οἱ νεκροὶ ἐγερθήσονται
for a trumpet will and the dead will be raised
sound,

ἄφθαρτοι, καὶ ἡμεῖς ἀλλαγησόμεθα. 53 Δεῖ
incorruptible, and we shall be changed. It behoves

γὰρ τὸ φθαρτὸν τοῦτο ἐνδύσασθαι
For – corruptible this to put on

ἀφθαρσίαν καὶ τὸ θνητὸν τοῦτο ἐνδύσασθαι
incorruption and – mortal this to put on

ἀθανασίαν. 54 ὅταν δὲ τὸ φθαρτὸν τοῦτο
immortality. And whenever this [that is] corruptible

ἐνδύσηται ἀφθαρσίαν καὶ τὸ θνητὸν τοῦτο
shall put on incorruption and this [that is] mortal

ἐνδύσηται ἀθανασίαν, τότε γενήσεται ὁ
shall put on immortality, then will be the

λόγος ὁ γεγραμμένος· κατεπόθη ὁ θάνατος
word – having been ²was – ¹Death
written: swallowed up

εἰς νῖκος. 55 ποῦ σου, θάνατε, τὸ νῖκος;
in victory. Where of thee, [O] death, the victory?

ποῦ σου, θάνατε, τὸ κέντρον; 56 τὸ δὲ
where of thee, [O] death, the sting? Now the

κέντρον τοῦ θανάτου ἡ ἁμαρτία, ἡ δὲ
sting – of death [is] sin, and the

δύναμις τῆς ἁμαρτίας ὁ νόμος· 57 τῷ
power – of sin [is] the law; –

δὲ θεῷ χάρις τῷ διδόντι ἡμῖν τὸ νῖκος
but to God thanks the [one] giving to us the victory

διὰ τοῦ κυρίου ἡμῶν Ἰησοῦ Χριστοῦ.
through the Lord of us Jesus Christ.

58 Ὥστε, ἀδελφοί μου ἀγαπητοί, ἑδραῖοι
So as, brothers of me beloved, firm

γίνεσθε, ἀμετακίνητοι, περισσεύοντες ἐν τῷ
be ye, unmovable, abounding in the

ἔργῳ τοῦ κυρίου πάντοτε, εἰδότες ὅτι
work of the Lord always, knowing that

ὁ κόπος ὑμῶν οὐκ ἔστιν κενὸς ἐν κυρίῳ.
the labour of you is not empty in [the] Lord.

King James Version

16 Now concerning the collection for the saints, as I have given order to the churches of Galatia, even so do ye. 2 Upon the first *day* of the week let every one of you lay by him in store, as *God* hath prospered him, that there be no gatherings when I come. 3And when I come, whomsoever ye shall approve by *your* letters, them will I send to bring your liberality unto Jerusalem. 4And if it be meet that I go also, they shall go with me. 5 Now I will come unto you, when I shall pass through Macedonia: for I do pass through Macedonia. 6And it may be that I will abide, yea, and winter with you, that ye may bring me on my journey whithersoever I go. 7 For I will not come by the way; but I trust to tarry a while with you, if the Lord permit. 8 But I will tarry at Ephesus until Pentecost. 9 For a great door and effectual is opened unto me, and *there are* many adversaries. 10 Now if Timotheus come, see that he may be with you without fear: for he worketh the work of the Lord, as I also *do*. 11 Let no man therefore despise him: but conduct him forth in peace, that he may come unto me: for I look for him with the brethren. 12As touching *our* brother Apollos, I greatly desired him to come unto you with the brethren: but his will was not at all to come at this time; but he will come when he shall have convenient time. 13 Watch ye, stand fast in the faith, quit you like men, be strong. 14 Let all your things be done with charity. 15 I beseech you, brethren, (ye know the house of Stephanas, that it is the firstfruits of Achaia, and *that* they have addicted themselves to the ministry of the saints,) 16 That ye submit yourselves unto such, and to every one that helpeth with *us*, and laboureth. 17 I am glad of the coming of Stephanas and Fortunatus and Achaicus: for that which was lacking on your part they have supplied. 18 For they have refreshed my spirit and yours: therefore acknowledge ye them that are such. 19 The churches of Asia salute you. Aquila and Priscilla salute you much in the Lord, with the church that is in their house. 20All the brethren greet you. Greet ye one another with a holy kiss. 21 The salutation of *me* Paul with mine own hand. 22 If any man love not the Lord Jesus Christ, let him be Anathema, Maran atha. 23 The grace of our Lord Jesus Christ *be* with you. 24 My love *be* with you all in Christ Jesus. Amen.

The first *epistle* to the Corinthians was written from Philippi by Stephanas, and Fortunatus, and Achaicus, and Timotheus.

New International Version

The collection for God's people

16 Now about the collection for God's people: Do what I told the Galatian churches to do. 2 On the first day of every week, each one of you should set aside a sum of money in keeping with his income, saving it up, so that when I come no collections will have to be made. 3 Then, when I arrive, I will give letters of introduction to the men you approve and send them with your gift to Jerusalem. 4 If it seems advisable for me to go also, they will accompany me.

Personal requests

5 After I go through Macedonia, I will come to you—for I will be going through Macedonia. 6 Perhaps I will stay with you awhile, or even spend the winter, so that you can help me on my journey, wherever I go. 7 I do not want to see you now and make only a passing visit; I hope to spend some time with you, if the Lord permits. 8 But I will stay on at Ephesus until Pentecost, 9 because a great door for effective work has opened to me, and there are many who oppose me.

10 If Timothy comes, see to it that he has nothing to fear while he is with you, for he is carrying on the work of the Lord, just as I am. 11 No one, then, should refuse to accept him. Send him on his way in peace so that he may return to me. I am expecting him along with the brothers.

12 Now about our brother Apollos: I strongly urged him to go to you with the brothers. He was quite unwilling to go now, but he will go when he has the opportunity.

13 Be on your guard; stand firm in the faith; be men of courage; be strong. 14 Do everything in love.

15 You know that the household of Stephanas were the first converts in Achaia, and they have devoted themselves to the service of the saints. I urge you, brothers, 16 to submit to such as these and to everyone who joins in the work and labors at it. 17 I was glad when Stephanas, Fortunatus and Achaicus arrived, because they have supplied what was lacking from you. 18 For they refreshed my spirit and yours also. Such men deserve recognition.

Final greetings

19 The churches in the province of Asia send you greetings. Aquila and Priscilla[u] greet you warmly in the Lord, and so does the church that meets at their house. 20All the brothers here send you greetings. Greet one another with a holy kiss.

21 I, Paul, write this greeting in my own hand.

22 If anyone does not love the Lord—a curse be on him. Come, O Lord![v]

23 The grace of the Lord Jesus be with you.

24 My love to all of you in Christ Jesus.

[u] Greek *Prisca*. [v] The expression *Come, O Lord!* is in Aramaic *Maranatha!*

Greek Interlinear

Chapter 16

Περὶ δὲ τῆς λογείας τῆς εἰς τοὺς
Now about the collection – for the

ἁγίους, ὥσπερ διέταξα ταῖς ἐκκλησίαις
saints, as I charged the churches

τῆς Γαλατίας, οὕτως καὶ ὑμεῖς ποιήσατε.
– of Galatia, so also ²ye ¹do.

2 κατὰ μίαν σαββάτου ἕκαστος ὑμῶν
Every one of a week each of you
=On the first day of every week

παρ' ἑαυτῷ τιθέτω θησαυρίζων ὅ τι ἐὰν
by himself let him put storing up whatever

εὐοδῶται, ἵνα μὴ ὅταν ἔλθω τότε λογεῖαι
he is prospered, lest whenever I come then ²collections

γίνωνται. 3 ὅταν δὲ παραγένωμαι, οὓς
¹there are. And whenever I arrive, whom-

ἐὰν δοκιμάσητε, δι' ἐπιστολῶν τούτους
ever ye approve, through epistles these

πέμψω ἀπενεγκεῖν τὴν χάριν ὑμῶν εἰς
I will send to carry the grace(gift) of you to

Ἰερουσαλήμ· 4 ἐὰν δὲ ἄξιον ᾖ τοῦ κἀμὲ
Jerusalem; and if ²fitting ¹it is – me also

πορεύεσθαι, σὺν ἐμοὶ πορεύσονται.
to go,ᵈ with me they shall go.

5 Ἐλεύσομαι δὲ πρὸς ὑμᾶς ὅταν Μακε-
And I will come – to you whenever ²Mace-

δονίαν διέλθω· Μακεδονίαν γὰρ διέρχομαι,
donia ¹I pass for ²Macedonia ¹I am passing
through; through,*

6 πρὸς ὑμᾶς δὲ τυχὸν καταμενῶ ἢ
²with ³you ¹and ⁴possibly ⁵I will remain ⁶or

καὶ παραχειμάσω, ἵνα ὑμεῖς με προπέμ-
⁴even ⁵spend the winter, in order ³ye ¹me may set
that

ψητε οὗ ἐὰν πορεύωμαι. 7 οὐ θέλω γὰρ
forward wherever I may go. For I do not wish

ὑμᾶς ἄρτι ἐν παρόδῳ ἰδεῖν· ἐλπίζω γὰρ
²you ¹yet ⁴in ³passage ¹to see; for I am hoping

χρόνον τινὰ ἐπιμεῖναι πρὸς ὑμᾶς, ἐὰν
²time ¹some ³to remain with you, if

ὁ κύριος ἐπιτρέψῃ. 8 ἐπιμενῶ δὲ ἐν
the Lord permits. But I will remain in

Ἐφέσῳ ἕως τῆς πεντηκοστῆς· 9 θύρα
Ephesus until – Pentecost; ²door

γάρ μοι ἀνέῳγεν μεγάλη καὶ ἐνεργής,
¹for ²to me ⁴opened ³a great ⁵and ⁶effective,

καὶ ἀντικείμενοι πολλοί. 10 Ἐὰν δὲ
and ²opposing ¹many. Now if

ἔλθῃ Τιμόθεος, βλέπετε ἵνα ἀφόβως
²comes ¹Timothy, see in order that fearlessly

γένηται πρὸς ὑμᾶς· τὸ γὰρ ἔργον κυρίου
he is with you; for the work of [the] Lord

ἐργάζεται ὡς κἀγώ· 11 μή τις οὖν αὐτὸν
he works as I also; ²not ³any- ⁴there- ¹him
one fore

ἐξουθενήσῃ. προπέμψατε δὲ αὐτὸν ἐν
¹despise. But set ye forward him in

εἰρήνῃ, ἵνα ἔλθῃ πρός με· ἐκδέχομαι γὰρ
peace, in order he may to me; for I am awaiting
that come

αὐτὸν μετὰ τῶν ἀδελφῶν. 12 Περὶ δὲ
him with the brothers. Now about

Ἀπολλῶ τοῦ ἀδελφοῦ, πολλὰ παρεκάλεσα
¹Apollos the ²brother, ²much ¹I besought

αὐτὸν ἵνα ἔλθῃ πρὸς ὑμᾶς μετὰ τῶν
¹him in order he would to you with the
that come

ἀδελφῶν· καὶ πάντως οὐκ ἦν θέλημα
brothers; and altogether it was not [his] will

ἵνα νῦν ἔλθῃ, ἐλεύσεται δὲ ὅταν εὐκαιρήσῃ.
in ²now ¹he but he will come whenever he has
order should opportunity.
that come,

13 Γρηγορεῖτε, στήκετε ἐν τῇ πίστει,
Watch ye, stand in the faith,

ἀνδρίζεσθε, κραταιοῦσθε. 14 πάντα ὑμῶν
play the man, be strong. ¹All things ²of you

ἐν ἀγάπῃ γινέσθω.
²in ¹love ¹let be.

15 Παρακαλῶ δὲ ὑμᾶς, ἀδελφοί· οἴδατε
Now I beseech you, brothers: Know ye

τὴν οἰκίαν Στεφανᾶ, ὅτι ἐστὶν ἀπαρχὴ
the household of Stephanas, that it is firstfruit

τῆς Ἀχαΐας καὶ εἰς διακονίαν τοῖς
– of Achaia and to ministry to the

ἁγίοις ἔταξαν ἑαυτούς· 16 ἵνα καὶ ὑμεῖς
saints they themselves; in order also ye
appointed that

ὑποτάσσησθε τοῖς τοιούτοις καὶ παντὶ τῷ
may submit – to such ones and to everyone

συνεργοῦντι καὶ κοπιῶντι. 17 χαίρω δὲ
working with [?me] and labouring. Now I rejoice

ἐπὶ τῇ παρουσίᾳ Στεφανᾶ καὶ Φορτουνάτου
at the presence of Stephanas and of Fortunatus

καὶ Ἀχαϊκοῦ, ὅτι τὸ ὑμέτερον ὑστέρημα
and of Achaicus, that – ²your ³lack

οὗτοι ἀνεπλήρωσαν· 18 ἀνέπαυσαν γὰρ τὸ
¹these ⁴supplied; for they refreshed –

ἐμὸν πνεῦμα καὶ τὸ ὑμῶν. ἐπιγινώσκετε
my spirit and – of you(yours). Recognize ye

οὖν τοὺς τοιούτους.
therefore – such ones.

19 Ἀσπάζονται ὑμᾶς αἱ ἐκκλησίαι τῆς
⁴Greet ⁵you ¹the ²churches –

Ἀσίας. ἀσπάζεται ὑμᾶς ἐν κυρίῳ πολλὰ
³of Asia. ⁴Greets ⁵you ¹in ²[the] Lord ³much

Ἀκύλας καὶ Πρίσκα σὺν τῇ κατ' οἶκον
¹Aquila ²and ³Prisca ⁶with ¹³the ¹⁴in [the] house

αὐτῶν ἐκκλησίᾳ. 20 ἀσπάζονται ὑμᾶς οἱ
¹²of them ⁸church. ⁴Greet ⁵you ¹the

ἀδελφοὶ πάντες. Ἀσπάσασθε ἀλλήλους ἐν
²brothers ³all. Greet ye one another with

φιλήματι ἁγίῳ. 21 Ὁ ἀσπασμὸς τῇ
kiss a holy. ¹The ²greeting –

ἐμῇ χειρὶ Παύλου. 22 εἴ τις οὐ φιλεῖ
⁵with my ⁴hand ³of Paul. If anyone loves not

τὸν κύριον, ἤτω ἀνάθεμα. μαράνα θά.
the Lord, let him be a curse. Marana tha.

23 ἡ χάρις τοῦ κυρίου Ἰησοῦ μεθ' ὑμῶν.
The grace of the Lord Jesus [be] with you.

24 ἡ ἀγάπη μου μετὰ πάντων ὑμῶν ἐν
The love of me [be] with ¹all ²you in

Χριστῷ Ἰησοῦ.
Christ Jesus.

---

* " Futuristic present "; *cf.* John 14. 3 and ch. 15. 32.

King James Version   New International Version

THE SECOND EPISTLE OF
PAUL THE APOSTLE
TO THE

CORINTHIANS

2 CORINTHIANS

1 Paul, an apostle of Jesus Christ by the will of God, and Timothy *our* brother, unto the church of God which is at Corinth, with all the saints which are in all Achaia: 2 Grace *be* to you, and peace, from God our Father, and *from* the Lord Jesus Christ. 3 Blessed *be* God, even the Father of our Lord Jesus Christ, the Father of mercies, and the God of all comfort; 4 Who comforteth us in all our tribulation, that we may be able to comfort them which are in any trouble, by the comfort wherewith we ourselves are comforted of God. 5 For as the sufferings of Christ abound in us, so our consolation also aboundeth by Christ. 6And whether we be afflicted, *it is* for your consolation and salvation, which is effectual in the enduring of the same sufferings which we also suffer: or whether we be comforted, *it is* for your consolation and salvation. 7And our hope of you *is* steadfast, knowing, that as ye are partakers of the sufferings, so *shall ye be* also of the consolation. 8 For we would not, brethren, have you ignorant of our trouble which came to us in Asia, that we were pressed out of measure, above strength, insomuch that we despaired even of life: 9 But we had the sentence of death in ourselves, that we should not trust in ourselves, but in God which raiseth the dead: 10 Who delivered us from so great a death, and doth deliver: in whom we trust that he will yet deliver *us;* 11 Ye also helping together by prayer for us, that for the gift *bestowed* upon us by the means of many persons thanks may be given by many on our behalf. 12 For our rejoicing is this, the testimony of our conscience, that in simplicity and godly sincerity, not with fleshly wisdom, but by the grace of God, we have had our conversation in the world, and more abundantly to youward. 13 For we write none other things unto you, than what ye read or acknowledge; and I trust ye shall acknowledge even to the end; 14 As also ye have acknowledged us in part, that we are your rejoicing, even as ye also *are* ours

1 Paul, an apostle of Christ Jesus by the will of God, and Timothy our brother,
To the church of God in Corinth, together with all the saints throughout Achaia:
2 Grace and peace to you from God our Father and the Lord Jesus Christ.

The God of all comfort

3 Praise be to the God and Father of our Lord Jesus Christ, the Father of compassion and the God of all comfort, 4 who comforts us in all our troubles, so that we can comfort those in any trouble with the comfort we ourselves have received from God. 5 For just as the sufferings of Christ flow over into our lives, so also through Christ our comfort overflows. 6 If we are distressed, it is for your comfort and salvation; if we are comforted, it is for your comfort, which produces in you patient endurance of the same sufferings we suffer. 7And our hope for you is firm, because we know that just as you share in our sufferings, so also you share in our comfort.
8 We do not want you to be uninformed, brothers, about the hardships we suffered in the province of Asia. We were under great pressure, far beyond our ability to endure, so that we despaired even of life. 9 Indeed, in our hearts we felt the sentence of death. But this happened that we might not rely on ourselves but on God, who raises the dead. 10 He has delivered us from such a deadly peril, and he will deliver us. On him we have set our hope that he will continue to deliver us, 11 as you help us by your prayers. Then many will give thanks on our[a] behalf for the gracious favor granted us in answer to the prayers of many.

Paul's change of plans

12 Now this is our boast: Our conscience testifies that we have conducted ourselves in the world, and especially in our relations with you, in the holiness and sincerity that are from God. We have done so not according to worldly wisdom but according to God's grace. 13 For we do not write you anything you cannot read or understand. And I hope that, 14 as you have understood us in part, you will come to understand fully that you can boast of us just as we will boast of you in the day of the Lord Jesus.

[a] Many MSS read *your.*

522

ΠΡΟΣ   ΚΟΡΙΝΘΙΟΥΣ Β

Chapter 1

Παῦλος ἀπόστολος Χριστοῦ Ἰησοῦ
Paul   an apostle   of Christ Jesus

διὰ θελήματος θεοῦ καὶ Τιμόθεος ὁ
through [the] will of God and Timothy the

ἀδελφὸς τῇ ἐκκλησίᾳ τοῦ θεοῦ τῇ οὔσῃ
brother to the church - of God - being

ἐν Κορίνθῳ σὺν τοῖς ἁγίοις πᾶσιν τοῖς
in Corinth with ⁸the ⁵saints ¹all

οὖσιν ἐν ὅλῃ τῇ Ἀχαΐᾳ· 2 χάρις ὑμῖν καὶ
being in all - Achaia: Grace to you and

εἰρήνη ἀπὸ θεοῦ πατρὸς ἡμῶν καὶ κυρίου
peace from God [the] Father of us and [the] Lord

Ἰησοῦ Χριστοῦ.
Jesus Christ.

3 Εὐλογητὸς ὁ θεὸς καὶ πατὴρ τοῦ
Blessed [be] the God and Father of the

κυρίου ἡμῶν Ἰησοῦ Χριστοῦ, ὁ πατὴρ
Lord of us Jesus Christ, the Father

τῶν οἰκτιρμῶν καὶ θεὸς πάσης παρακλή-
- of compassions and God of all com-

εως, 4 ὁ παρακαλῶν ἡμᾶς ἐπὶ πάσῃ
fort, the [one] comforting us on(in) all

τῇ θλίψει ἡμῶν, εἰς τὸ δύνασθαι ἡμᾶς
the affliction of us, [with a - to be able us⁵
view] to =our being able

παρακαλεῖν τοὺς ἐν πάσῃ θλίψει διὰ
to comfort the ones in every affliction through

τῆς παρακλήσεως ἧς παρακαλούμεθα αὐτοὶ
the comfort of(with) we are comforted [our-]
which selves

ὑπὸ τοῦ θεοῦ. 5 ὅτι καθὼς περισσεύει τὰ
by - God. Because as abounds the

παθήματα τοῦ Χριστοῦ εἰς ἡμᾶς, οὕτως
sufferings - of Christ in us, so

διὰ τοῦ Χριστοῦ περισσεύει καὶ ἡ παρά-
through - Christ abounds also the com-

κλησις ἡμῶν. 6 εἴτε δὲ θλιβόμεθα, ὑπὲρ
fort of us. Now whether we are on be-
afflicted, half of

τῆς ὑμῶν παρακλήσεως καὶ σωτηρίας· εἴτε
the ⁴of you ¹comfort ⁸and ⁸salvation; or

παρακαλούμεθα, ὑπὲρ τῆς ὑμῶν παρακλή-
we are comforted, on behalf of the ⁸of you ¹com-

σεως τῆς ἐνεργουμένης ἐν ὑπομονῇ τῶν
fort - operating in endurance of the

αὐτῶν παθημάτων ὧν καὶ ἡμεῖς πάσχομεν,
same sufferings which also we suffer,

7 καὶ ἡ ἐλπὶς ἡμῶν βεβαία ὑπὲρ ὑμῶν·
and the hope of us [is] firm on behalf of you

εἰδότες ὅτι ὡς κοινωνοί ἐστε τῶν παθημά-
knowing that as partakers ye are of the suffer-

των, οὕτως καὶ τῆς παρακλήσεως. 8 Οὐ
ings, so also of the comfort. not

γὰρ θέλομεν ὑμᾶς ἀγνοεῖν, ἀδελφοί, ὑπὲρ
For we wish you to be ignorant, brothers, as to

τῆς θλίψεως ἡμῶν τῆς γενομένης ἐν
the affliction of us - having been in

τῇ Ἀσίᾳ, ὅτι καθ' ὑπερβολὴν ὑπὲρ
- Asia, that excessively† beyond

δύναμιν ἐβαρήθημεν, ὥστε ἐξαπορηθῆναι
power we were burdened, so as to despair
=so that we despaired even

ἡμᾶς καὶ τοῦ ζῆν· 9 ἀλλὰ αὐτοὶ ἐν
us⁵ even - to live; but [our]selves in
of life;

ἑαυτοῖς τὸ ἀπόκριμα τοῦ θανάτου ἐσχήκα-
ourselves the sentence - of death we have

μεν, ἵνα μὴ πεποιθότες ὦμεν ἐφ' ἑαυτοῖς
had, in order ⁸not ⁸having ¹we on ourselves
that trusted might be

ἀλλ' ἐπὶ τῷ θεῷ τῷ ἐγείροντι τοὺς
but on - God the [one] raising the

νεκρούς· 10 ὃς ἐκ τηλικούτου θανάτου
dead; who out of so great a death

ἐρρύσατο ἡμᾶς καὶ ῥύσεται, εἰς ὃν
delivered us and will deliver, in whom

ἠλπίκαμεν [ὅτι] καὶ ἔτι ῥύσεται, 11 συν-
we have hoped that indeed yet he will deliver, co-

υπουργούντων καὶ ὑμῶν ὑπὲρ ἡμῶν τῇ
operating also you⁸ on behalf of us -
=while ye also coöperate

δεήσει, ἵνα ἐκ πολλῶν προσώπων τὸ
in petition, in order ⁸by ⁸many ⁸persons ⁷[for]
that ⁶the

εἰς ἡμᾶς χάρισμα διὰ πολλῶν εὐχαριστηθῇ
¹⁰to ¹¹us ¹²gift ¹³through ¹³many ¹thanks may
be given

ὑπὲρ ἡμῶν.
⁹on behalf of ⁹us.

12 Ἡ γὰρ καύχησις ἡμῶν αὕτη ἐστίν,
For the boasting of us ⁸this ¹is,

τὸ μαρτύριον τῆς συνειδήσεως ἡμῶν, ὅτι
the testimony of the conscience of us, because

ἐν ἁγιότητι καὶ εἰλικρινείᾳ τοῦ θεοῦ,
in sanctity and sincerity - of God,

οὐκ ἐν σοφίᾳ σαρκικῇ ἀλλ' ἐν [τῇ] χάριτι
not in wisdom fleshly but in [the] grace

θεοῦ, ἀνεστράφημεν ἐν τῷ κόσμῳ, περισ-
of God, we behaved in the world, ⁵more

σοτέρως δὲ πρὸς ὑμᾶς. 13 οὐ γὰρ ἄλλα
⁸especially ¹and with you. ⁸Not ¹for ⁴other
things

γράφομεν ὑμῖν ἀλλ' ἢ ἃ ἀναγινώσκετε
⁵we write to you other than what ye read

ἢ καὶ ἐπιγινώσκετε, ἐλπίζω δὲ ὅτι
or even perceive, and I hope that

ἕως τέλους ἐπιγνώσεσθε, 14 καθὼς καὶ
to [the] end ye will perceive, as also

ἐπέγνωτε ἡμᾶς ἀπὸ μέρους, ὅτι καύχημα
ye perceived us from(in) part, because ⁸boast

ὑμῶν ἐσμεν καθάπερ καὶ ὑμεῖς ἡμῶν
⁹of you ¹we are even as also ye of us

ἐν τῇ ἡμέρᾳ τοῦ κυρίου ἡμῶν Ἰησοῦ.
in the day of the Lord of us Jesus.

King James Version

in the day of the Lord Jesus. 15And in this confidence I was minded to come unto you before, that ye might have a second benefit; 16And to pass by you into Macedonia, and to come again out of Macedonia unto you, and of you to be brought on my way toward Judea. 17 When I therefore was thus minded, did I use lightness? or the things that I purpose, do I purpose according to the flesh, that with me there should be yea, yea, and nay, nay? 18 But as God is true, our word toward you was not yea and nay. 19 For the Son of God, Jesus Christ, who was preached among you by us, even by me and Silvanus and Timotheus, was not yea and nay, but in him was yea. 20 For all the promises of God in him are yea, and in him Amen, unto the glory of God by us. 21 Now he which stablisheth us with you in Christ, and hath anointed us, is God; 22 Who hath also sealed us, and given the earnest of the Spirit in our hearts. 23 Moreover I call God for a record upon my soul, that to spare you I came not as yet unto Corinth. 24 Not for that we have dominion over your faith, but are helpers of your joy: for by faith ye stand.

2 But I determined this with myself, that I would not come again to you in heaviness. 2 For if I make you sorry, who is he then that maketh me glad, but the same which is made sorry by me? 3And I wrote this same unto you, lest, when I came, I should have sorrow from them of whom I ought to rejoice; having confidence in you all, that my joy is the joy of you all. 4 For out of much affliction and anguish of heart I wrote unto you with many tears; not that ye should be grieved, but that ye might know the love which I have more abundantly unto you. 5 But if any have caused grief, he hath not grieved me, but in part: that I may not overcharge you all. 6 Sufficient to such a man is this punishment, which was inflicted of many. 7 So that contrariwise ye ought rather to forgive him, and comfort him, lest perhaps such a one should be swallowed up with overmuch sorrow. 8 Wherefore I beseech you that ye would confirm your love toward him. 9 For to this end also did I write, that I might know the proof of you, whether ye be obedient in all things. 10 To whom ye forgive any thing, I forgive also: for if I forgave any thing, to whom I forgave it, for your sakes forgave I it in the person of Christ; 11 Lest Satan should get an advantage of us: for we are not ignorant of his devices. 12 Furthermore, when I came to Troas to preach Christ's gospel, and a door was opened unto me

New International Version

15 Because I was confident of this, I planned to visit you first so that you might benefit twice. 16 I planned to visit you on my way to Macedonia and to come back to you from Macedonia, and then to have you send me on my way to Judea. 17 When I planned this, did I do it lightly? Or do I make my plans in a worldly manner so that in the same breath I say, "Yes, yes" and "No, no"?

18 But as surely as God is faithful, our message to you is not "Yes" and "No." 19 For the Son of God, Jesus Christ, who was preached among you by me and Silas[b] and Timothy, was not "Yes" and "No," but in him it has always been "Yes." 20 For no matter how many promises God has made, they are "Yes" in Christ. And so through him the "Amen" is spoken by us to the glory of God. 21 Now it is God who makes both us and you stand firm in Christ. He anointed us, 22 set his seal of ownership on us, and put his Spirit in our hearts as a deposit, guaranteeing what is to come.

23 I call God as my witness that it was in order to spare you that I did not return to Corinth. 24 Not that we lord it over your faith, but we work with you for your joy, because it is

2 by faith you stand firm. 1 So I made up my mind that I would not make another painful visit to you. 2 For if I grieve you, who is left to make me glad but you whom I have grieved? 3 I wrote as I did so that when I came I should not be distressed by those who ought to make me rejoice. I had confidence in all of you, that you would all share my joy. 4 For I wrote you out of great distress and anguish of heart and with many tears, not to grieve you but to let you know the depth of my love for you.

Forgiveness for the sinner

5 If anyone has caused grief, he has not so much grieved me as he has grieved all of you, to some extent—not to put it too severely. 6 The punishment inflicted on him by the majority is sufficient for him. 7 Now instead, you ought to forgive and comfort him, so that he will not be overwhelmed by excessive sorrow. 8 I urge you, therefore, to reaffirm your love for him. 9 The reason I wrote you was to see if you would stand the test and be obedient in everything. 10 If you forgive anyone, I also forgive him. And what I have forgiven—if there was anything to forgive —I have forgiven in the sight of Christ for your sake, 11 in order that Satan might not outwit us. For we are not unaware of his schemes.

Ministers of the new covenant

12 Now when I went to Troas to preach the gospel of Christ and found that the Lord had

[b] Greek Silvanus.

Greek Interlinear

15 Καὶ ταύτῃ τῇ πεποιθήσει ἐβουλόμην
And in this – persuasion I determined

πρότερον πρὸς ὑμᾶς ἐλθεῖν ἵνα δευτέραν
formerly to you to come in order a second
that

χάριν σχῆτε, 16 καὶ δι' ὑμῶν διελθεῖν
grace ye might have, and through you to pass through

εἰς Μακεδονίαν, καὶ πάλιν ἀπὸ Μακεδονίας
into Macedonia, and again from Macedonia

ἐλθεῖν πρὸς ὑμᾶς καὶ ὑφ' ὑμῶν
to come to you and by you

προπεμφθῆναι εἰς τὴν Ἰουδαίαν. 17 τοῦτο
to be set forward to – Judæa. This

οὖν βουλόμενος μήτι ἄρα τῇ ἐλαφρίᾳ
therefore determining not ²then ¹fickleness

ἐχρησάμην; ἢ ἃ βουλεύομαι κατὰ σάρκα
¹did I use? or [the] I determine according [the]
things which to flesh

βουλεύομαι, ἵνα ᾖ παρ' ἐμοὶ τὸ ναὶ
do I determine, in order there with me the Yes
that may be

ναὶ καὶ τὸ οὒ οὔ; 18 πιστὸς δὲ ὁ
yes and the No no? But faithful [is] –

θεὸς ὅτι ὁ λόγος ἡμῶν ὁ πρὸς ὑμᾶς
God that the word of us – to you

οὐκ ἔστιν ναὶ καὶ οὔ. 19 ὁ τοῦ θεοῦ
is not yes and no. ²the – ⁴of God

γὰρ υἱὸς Χριστὸς Ἰησοῦς ὁ ἐν ὑμῖν
¹For ³Son Christ Jesus ¹the ²among ⁴you
[one]

δι' ἡμῶν κηρυχθείς, δι' ἐμοῦ καὶ Σιλουανοῦ
⁵through ⁶us ⁷proclaimed, through me and Silvanus

καὶ Τιμοθέου, οὐκ ἐγένετο ναὶ καὶ οὔ,
and Timothy, was not yes and no,

ἀλλὰ ναὶ ἐν αὐτῷ γέγονεν. 20 ὅσαι γὰρ
but ²Yes ³in ⁴him ¹has been. For as many

ἐπαγγελίαι θεοῦ, ἐν αὐτῷ τὸ ναί· διὸ
[as are] of God, in him [is] the Yes; where-
promises fore

καὶ δι' αὐτοῦ τὸ ἀμὴν τῷ θεῷ πρὸς
also through him the Amen – ¹to God ²unto

δόξαν δι' ἡμῶν. 21 ὁ δὲ βεβαιῶν ἡμᾶς
²glory through us. But the [one] making firm us

σὺν ὑμῖν εἰς Χριστὸν καὶ χρίσας ἡμᾶς
with you in Christ and having anointed us [is]

θεός, 22 ὁ καὶ σφραγισάμενος ἡμᾶς καὶ
God, the [one] both having sealed us and

δοὺς τὸν ἀρραβῶνα τοῦ πνεύματος ἐν
having the earnest of the Spirit in
given

ταῖς καρδίαις ἡμῶν.
the hearts of us.

23 Ἐγὼ δὲ μάρτυρα τὸν θεὸν ἐπικαλοῦμαι
Now ⁴I ¹[as] witness ²God ³invoke

ἐπὶ τὴν ἐμὴν ψυχήν, ὅτι φειδόμενος
¹on – ²my ³life, that sparing

ὑμῶν οὐκέτι ἦλθον εἰς Κόρινθον. 24 οὐχ ὅτι
you no more ¹I came to Corinth. Not that

κυριεύομεν ὑμῶν τῆς πίστεως, ἀλλὰ συνεργοὶ
we rule over ²of you ¹the ²faith, but ²fellow-
workers

ἐσμεν τῆς χαρᾶς ὑμῶν· τῇ γὰρ πίστει
¹we are of the joy of you; – for by faith

Chapter 2

ἑστήκατε. 2 ἔκρινα δὲ ἐμαυτῷ τοῦτο, τὸ μὴ
ye stand. But I decided in myself this, – not

πάλιν ἐν λύπῃ πρὸς ὑμᾶς ἐλθεῖν. 2 εἰ
again ⁴in ³grief ²to ¹you ²to come. if

γὰρ ἐγὼ λυπῶ ὑμᾶς, καὶ τίς ὁ εὐφραίνων
For I grieve you, then who the making glad
[one]

με εἰ μὴ ὁ λυπούμενος ἐξ ἐμοῦ; 3 καὶ
me except the [one] being grieved by me? And

ἔγραψα τοῦτο αὐτὸ ἵνα μὴ ἐλθὼν λύπην
I wrote this very thing lest coming grief

σχῶ ἀφ' ὧν ἔδει με χαίρειν, πεποιθὼς
I should from [those] it me to rejoice, having
have whom behoved confidence

ἐπὶ πάντας ὑμᾶς ὅτι ἡ ἐμὴ χαρὰ πάντων
in ²all ¹you that – my joy ²all

ὑμῶν ἐστιν. 4 ἐκ γὰρ πολλῆς θλίψεως
³of you ¹is. For out of much affliction

καὶ συνοχῆς καρδίας ἔγραψα ὑμῖν διὰ
and anxiety of heart I wrote to you through

πολλῶν δακρύων, οὐχ ἵνα λυπηθῆτε, ἀλλὰ
many tears, not in order ye should be but
that grieved,

τὴν ἀγάπην ἵνα γνῶτε ἣν ἔχω περισ-
²the ⁴love ¹in order ³ye should ⁵which I have more
that know

σοτέρως εἰς ὑμᾶς. 5 Εἰ δέ τις λελύπηκεν,
abundantly to you. But if anyone has grieved,

οὐκ ἐμὲ λελύπηκεν, ἀλλὰ ἀπὸ μέρους,
not me he has grieved, but from(in) part,

ἵνα μὴ ἐπιβαρῶ, πάντας ὑμᾶς. 6 ἱκανὸν
lest I am burdensome, ²all ¹you. Enough

τῷ τοιούτῳ ἡ ἐπιτιμία αὕτη ἡ ὑπὸ
for such a one this punishment – by

τῶν πλειόνων, 7 ὥστε τοὐναντίον μᾶλλον
the majority, so as on the contrary rather

ὑμᾶς χαρίσασθαι καὶ παρακαλέσαι, μή πως
you to forgive and to comfort,ᵇ lest
=ye should rather forgive and comfort,

τῇ περισσοτέρᾳ λύπῃ καταποθῇ ὁ τοιοῦτος.
²by ⁴more abundant ³grief ¹should be ²such a one.
the swallowed up

8 διὸ παρακαλῶ ὑμᾶς κυρῶσαι εἰς αὐτὸν
Wherefore I beseech you to confirm to him

ἀγάπην· 9 εἰς τοῦτο γὰρ καὶ ἔγραψα,
[your] love; ²to ²this [end] ¹for indeed I wrote,

ἵνα γνῶ τὴν δοκιμὴν ὑμῶν, εἰ εἰς πάντα
in or- I might the proof of you, if in all things
der that know

ὑπήκοοί ἐστε. 10 ᾧ δέ τι χαρίζεσθε,
obedient ye are. Now to whom anything ye forgive,

κἀγώ· καὶ γὰρ ἐγὼ ὃ κεχάρισμαι, εἴ
I also; for indeed ¹I ¹what ²have forgiven, if

τι κεχάρισμαι, δι' ὑμᾶς ἐν προσώπῳ
²any- ¹I have [it is] on you in [the] person
thing forgiven, account of

Χριστοῦ, 11 ἵνα μὴ πλεονεκτηθῶμεν ὑπὸ
of Christ, lest we are taken advantage of by

τοῦ σατανᾶ· οὐ γὰρ αὐτοῦ τὰ νοήματα
– Satan; for ²not ¹of him ¹the ²designs

ἀγνοοῦμεν. 12 Ἐλθὼν δὲ εἰς τὴν Τρωάδα εἰς
¹we ²are ²ignorant [of]. But coming to – Troas in

τὸ εὐαγγέλιον τοῦ Χριστοῦ, καὶ θύρας
the gospel – of Christ, and a door

King James Version

of the Lord, 13 I had no rest in my spirit, because I found not Titus my brother; but taking my leave of them, I went from thence into Macedonia. 14 Now thanks *be* unto God, which always causeth us to triumph in Christ, and maketh manifest the savour of his knowledge by us in every place. 15 For we are unto God a sweet savour of Christ, in them that are saved, and in them that perish: 16 To the one *we are* the savour of death unto death; and to the other the savour of life unto life. And who *is* sufficient for these things? 17 For we are not as many, which corrupt the word of God: but as of sincerity, but as of God, in the sight of God speak we in Christ.

New International Version

opened a door for me, 13 I still had no peace of mind, because I did not find my brother Titus there. So I said good-by and went on to Macedonia.

14 But thanks be to God, who always leads us in triumphal procession in Christ and through us spreads everywhere the fragrance of the knowledge of him. 15 For we are to God the aroma of Christ among those who are being saved and those who are perishing. 16 To the one we are the stench of death; to the other, the fragrance of life. And who is equal to such a task? 17 Unlike so many, we do not peddle the word of God for profit. On the contrary, in Christ we speak before God with sincerity, like men sent from God.

3 Do we begin again to commend ourselves? or need we, as some *others,* epistles of commendation to you, or *letters* of commendation from you? 2 Ye are our epistle written in our hearts, known and read of all men: 3 *Forasmuch as ye are* manifestly declared to be the epistle of Christ ministered by us, written not with ink, but with the Spirit of the living God; not in tables of stone, but in fleshly tables of the heart. 4And such trust have we through Christ to God-ward: 5 Not that we are sufficient of ourselves to think any thing as of ourselves; but our sufficiency *is* of God; 6 Who also hath made us able ministers of the new testament; not of the letter, but of the spirit: for the letter killeth, but the spirit giveth life. 7 But if the ministration of death, written *and* engraven in stones, was glorious, so that the children of Israel could not steadfastly behold the face of Moses for the glory of his countenance; which *glory* was to be done away; 8 How shall not the ministration of the spirit be rather glorious? 9 For if the ministration of condemnation *be* glory, much more doth the ministration of righteousness exceed in glory. 10 For even that which was made glorious had no glory in this respect, by reason of the glory that excelleth. 11 For if that which is done away *was* glorious, much more that which remaineth *is* glorious. 12 Seeing then that we have such hope, we use great plainness of speech: 13And not as Moses, *which* put a vail over his face, that the children of Israel could not steadfastly look to the end of that which is abolished: 14 But their minds were blinded: for until this day remaineth the same vail untaken away in the reading of the old testament; which *vail* is done away in Christ. 15 But even unto this day, when Moses is read, the vail is upon their heart. 16 Nevertheless, when it shall turn to the Lord,

3 Are we beginning to commend ourselves again? Or do we need, like some people, letters of recommendation to you or from you? 2 You yourselves are our letter, written on our hearts, known and read by everybody. 3 You show that you are a letter from Christ, the result of our ministry, written not with ink but with the Spirit of the living God, not on tablets of stone but on tablets of human hearts.

4 Such confidence as this is ours through Christ before God. 5 Not that we are competent to judge anything we do, but our competence comes from God. 6 He has enabled us to be ministers of a new covenant—not of the letter but of the Spirit; for the letter kills, but the Spirit gives life.

The glory of the new covenant

7 Now if the ministry that brought death, which was engraved in letters on stone, came with glory, so that the Israelites could not look steadily at the face of Moses because of its glory, fading though it was, 8 will not the ministry of the Spirit be even more glorious? 9 If the ministry that condemns men is glorious, how much more glorious is the ministry that brings righteousness! 10 For what was glorious has no glory now in comparison with the surpassing glory. 11And if what was fading away came with glory, how much greater is the glory of that which lasts!

12 Therefore, since we have such a hope, we are very bold. 13 We are not like Moses, who veiled his face to keep the Israelites from gazing at it while the radiance was fading away. 14 But their minds were made dull, for to this day the same veil remains when the old covenant is read. It has not been removed, because only in Christ is it taken away. 15 Even to this day when Moses is read, a veil covers their hearts. 16 But whenever anyone turns to the Lord, "the veil is taken

Greek Interlinear

μοι ἀνεῳγμένης ἐν κυρίῳ, 13 οὐκ ἔσχηκα
to me having been by [the] Lord, I *have* had no
opened*

ἄνεσιν τῷ πνεύματί μου τῷ μὴ εὑρεῖν
rest to the spirit of me in the not to find
= when I did not find ...

με Τίτον τὸν ἀδελφόν μου, ἀλλὰ ἀποτα-
me^{be} Titus the brother of me, but saying

ξάμενος αὐτοῖς ἐξῆλθον εἰς Μακεδονίαν.
farewell to them I went forth into Macedonia.

14 Τῷ δὲ θεῷ χάρις τῷ πάντοτε
- But ^ato God ^athanks the [one] always

θριαμβεύοντι ἡμᾶς ἐν τῷ Χριστῷ καὶ
leading in triumph us in - Christ and

τὴν ὀσμὴν τῆς γνώσεως αὐτοῦ φανεροῦντι
⁴the ⁶odour ⁴of the ⁵knowledge of him ⁵manifesting

δι' ἡμῶν ἐν παντὶ τόπῳ· 15 ὅτι Χριστοῦ
^athrough ^aus in every place; because of Christ

εὐωδία ἐσμὲν τῷ θεῷ ἐν τοῖς σῳζομένοις
a sweet we are - to God in the [ones] being saved
smell

καὶ ἐν τοῖς ἀπολλυμένοις, 16 οἷς μὲν
and in the [ones] perishing, to the [latter]†

ὀσμὴ ἐκ θανάτου εἰς θάνατον, οἷς δὲ
an odour out of death unto death, to the [former]†

ὀσμὴ ἐκ ζωῆς εἰς ζωήν. καὶ πρὸς
an odour out of life unto life. And for

ταῦτα τίς ἱκανός; 17 οὐ γάρ ἐσμεν
these things who [is] competent? For we are not

ὡς οἱ πολλοὶ καπηλεύοντες τὸν λόγον
as the many hawking the word

τοῦ θεοῦ, ἀλλ' ὡς ἐξ εἰλικρινείας, ἀλλ'
- of God, but as of sincerity, but

ὡς ἐκ θεοῦ κατέναντι θεοῦ ἐν Χριστῷ
as of God before God in Christ

λαλοῦμεν.
we speak.

Chapter 3

Ἀρχόμεθα πάλιν ἑαυτοὺς συνιστάνειν;
Do we begin again ourselves to commend?

ἢ μὴ χρῄζομεν ὥς τινες συστατικῶν
or not need we as some commendatory

ἐπιστολῶν πρὸς ὑμᾶς ἢ ἐξ ὑμῶν; 2 ἡ
epistles to you or from you? The

ἐπιστολὴ ἡμῶν ὑμεῖς ἐστε, ἐγγεγραμμένη
epistle of us ye are, *having been* inscribed

ἐν ταῖς καρδίαις ἡμῶν, γινωσκομένη καὶ
in the hearts of us, *being* known and

ἀναγινωσκομένη ὑπὸ πάντων ἀνθρώπων,
being read by all men,

3 φανερούμενοι ὅτι ἐστὲ ἐπιστολὴ Χριστοῦ
being manifested that ye are an epistle of Christ

διακονηθεῖσα ὑφ' ἡμῶν, ἐγγεγραμμένη οὐ
ministered by us, *having been* inscribed not

μέλανι ἀλλὰ πνεύματι θεοῦ ζῶντος, οὐκ
by ink but by [the] Spirit of ^aGod ^aa living, not

ἐν πλαξὶν λιθίναις ἀλλ' ἐν πλαξὶν καρδίαις
in ^atablets ^astony but in tablets [which are]

σαρκίναις.
^afleshy. ^ahearts

4 Πεποίθησιν δὲ τοιαύτην ἔχομεν διὰ
^aconfidence ¹And ²such we have through

τοῦ Χριστοῦ πρὸς τὸν θεόν. 5 οὐχ
- Christ toward - God. Not

ὅτι ἀφ' ἑαυτῶν ἱκανοί ἐσμεν λογίσασθαί
that ¹from ²ourselves ⁴competent ³we are to reckon

τι ὡς ἐξ ἑαυτῶν, ἀλλ' ἡ ἱκανότης
any- as of ourselves, but the competence
thing

ἡμῶν ἐκ τοῦ θεοῦ, 6 ὃς καὶ ἱκάνωσεν
of us [is] of - God, who also made competent

ἡμᾶς διακόνους καινῆς διαθήκης, οὐ
us [as] ministers of a new covenant, not

γράμματος ἀλλὰ πνεύματος· τὸ γὰρ γράμμα
of letter but of spirit; for the letter

ἀποκτείνει, τὸ δὲ πνεῦμα ζωοποιεῖ. 7 Εἰ
kills, but the spirit makes alive. if

δὲ ἡ διακονία τοῦ θανάτου ἐν γράμμασιν
Now the ministry - of death in letters

ἐντετυπωμένη λίθοις ἐγενήθη ἐν δόξῃ,
having been engraved in stones came to be in glory,

ὥστε μὴ δύνασθαι ἀτενίσαι τοὺς υἱοὺς
so as not to be able to gaze the sons
= so that the sons of Israel were not able to gaze

Ἰσραὴλ εἰς τὸ πρόσωπον Μωϋσέως διὰ
of Israel^b at the face of Moses on account of

τὴν δόξαν τοῦ προσώπου αὐτοῦ τὴν
the glory of the face of him -

καταργουμένην, 8 πῶς οὐχὶ μᾶλλον ἡ
being done away, how ^anot ¹rather ⁴the

διακονία τοῦ πνεύματος ἔσται ἐν δόξῃ;
²ministry ⁵of the ⁶Spirit ¹will ^abe in glory?

9 εἰ γὰρ ἡ διακονία τῆς κατακρίσεως
For if the ministry - of condemnation

δόξα, πολλῷ μᾶλλον περισσεύει ἡ διακονία
[was] by much rather ^aabounds ¹the ^aministry
glory,

τῆς δικαιοσύνης δόξῃ. 10 καὶ γὰρ οὐ
- ^aof righteousness in glory. For indeed ^anot

δεδόξασται τὸ δεδοξασμένον ἐν τούτῳ
¹has been the ³having been in this
glorified [thing] glorified

τῷ μέρει εἵνεκεν τῆς ὑπερβαλλούσης δόξης.
- respect for the the excelling glory.
sake of

11 εἰ γὰρ τὸ καταργούμενον διὰ δόξης,
For if the being done away [was] glory,
[thing] through

πολλῷ μᾶλλον τὸ μένον ἐν δόξῃ.
by much more the [thing] remaining [is] in glory.

12 Ἔχοντες οὖν τοιαύτην ἐλπίδα πολλῇ
Having therefore such hope ^amuch

παρρησίᾳ χρώμεθα, 13 καὶ οὐ καθάπερ
^aboldness ¹we use, and not as

Μωϋσῆς ἐτίθει κάλυμμα ἐπὶ τὸ πρόσωπον
Moses put a veil on the face

αὐτοῦ, πρὸς τὸ μὴ ἀτενίσαι τοὺς υἱοὺς
of him, for the ^anot ¹to gaze ¹the ^asons

Ἰσραὴλ εἰς τὸ τέλος τοῦ καταργουμένου.
^aof Israel^b at the end of the [thing] being done away.

14 ἀλλὰ ἐπωρώθη τὰ νοήματα αὐτῶν.
But were hardened the thoughts of them.

ἄχρι γὰρ τῆς σήμερον ἡμέρας τὸ αὐτὸ
For until the present day the same

κάλυμμα ἐπὶ τῇ ἀναγνώσει τῆς παλαιᾶς
veil ^aon(at) ^athe ¹reading ^aof the ^aold

διαθήκης μένει, μὴ ἀνακαλυπτόμενον ὅτι
^acovenant ¹remains, not being unveiled that

ἐν Χριστῷ καταργεῖται. 15 ἀλλ' ἕως
in Christ it is being done away. But until

σήμερον ἡνίκα ἂν ἀναγινώσκηται Μωϋσῆς
to-day whenever ¹is being read ^aMoses

κάλυμμα ἐπὶ τὴν καρδίαν αὐτῶν κεῖται·
a veil ^aon ^athe ¹heart ^aof them ¹lies;

16 ἡνίκα δὲ ἐὰν ἐπιστρέψῃ πρὸς κύριον,
but whenever it § turns to [the] Lord,

---

* That is, revealed (Conybeare and Howson). § ? their heart.

King James Version

the vail shall be taken away. 17 Now the Lord is that Spirit: and where the Spirit of the Lord *is,* there *is* liberty. 18 But we all, with open face beholding as in a glass the glory of the Lord, are changed into the same image from glory to glory, *even* as by the Spirit of the Lord.

4 Therefore, seeing we have this ministry, as we have received mercy, we faint not; 2 But have renounced the hidden things of dishonesty, not walking in craftiness, nor handling the word of God deceitfully; but, by manifestation of the truth, commending ourselves to every man's conscience in the sight of God. 3 But if our gospel be hid, it is hid to them that are lost: 4 In whom the god of this world hath blinded the minds of them which believe not, lest the light of the glorious gospel of Christ, who is the image of God, should shine unto them. 5 For we preach not ourselves, but Christ Jesus the Lord; and ourselves your servants for Jesus' sake. 6 For God, who commanded the light to shine out of darkness, hath shined in our hearts, to *give* the light of the knowledge of the glory of God in the face of Jesus Christ. 7 But we have this treasure in earthen vessels, that the excellency of the power may be of God, and not of us. 8 *We are* troubled on every side, yet not distressed; *we are* perplexed, but not in despair; 9 Persecuted, but not forsaken; cast down, but not destroyed; 10Always bearing about in the body the dying of the Lord Jesus, that the life also of Jesus might be made manifest in our body. 11 For we which live are alway delivered unto death for Jesus' sake, that the life also of Jesus might be made manifest in our mortal flesh. 12 So then death worketh in us, but life in you. 13 We having the same spirit of faith, according as it is written, I believed, and therefore have I spoken; we also believe, and therefore speak; 14 Knowing that he which raised up the Lord Jesus shall raise up us also by Jesus, and shall present *us* with you. 15 For all things *are* for your sakes, that the abundant grace might through the thanksgiving of many redound to the glory of God. 16 For which cause we faint not; but though our outward man perish, yet the inward *man* is renewed day by day. 17 For our light affliction, which is but for a moment, worketh for us a far more exceeding *and* eternal weight of glory;

New International Version

away." *c* 17 Now the Lord is the Spirit, and where the Spirit of the Lord is, there is freedom. 18And we, who with unveiled faces all reflect*d* the Lord's glory, are being transformed into his likeness with ever-increasing glory, which comes from the Lord, who is the Spirit.

Treasures in jars of clay

4 Therefore, since through God's mercy we have this ministry, we do not lose heart. 2 Rather, we have renounced secret and shameful ways; we do not use deception, nor do we distort the word of God. On the contrary, setting forth the truth plainly we commend ourselves to every man's conscience in the sight of God. 3And even if our gospel is veiled, it is veiled to those who are perishing. 4 The god of this age has blinded the minds of unbelievers, so that they cannot see the light of the gospel of the glory of Christ, who is the image of God. 5 For we do not preach ourselves, but Jesus Christ as Lord, and ourselves as your servants for Jesus' sake. 6 For God who said, "Let light shine out of darkness," *e* made his light shine in our hearts to give us the light of the knowledge of the glory of God in the face of Christ.

7 But we have this treasure in jars of clay to show that this all-surpassing power is from God and not from us. 8 We are hard pressed on every side, but not crushed; perplexed, but not in despair; 9 persecuted, but not abandoned; struck down, but not destroyed. 10 We always carry around in our body the death of Jesus, so that the life of Jesus may also be revealed in our body. 11 For we who are alive are always being given over to death for Jesus' sake, so that his life may be revealed in our mortal body. 12 So then, death is at work in us, but life is at work in you.

13 It is written: "I believed; therefore I have spoken." *f* With that same spirit of faith we also believe and therefore speak, 14 because we know that the one who raised the Lord Jesus from the dead will also raise us with Jesus and present us with you in his presence. 15All this is for your benefit, so that the grace that is reaching more and more people may cause thanksgiving to overflow to the glory of God.

16 Therefore we do not lose heart. Though outwardly we are wasting away, yet inwardly we are being renewed day by day. 17 For our light and momentary troubles are achieving for us an eternal glory that far outweighs them all.

[c] Exodus 34:34. [d] Or *Contemplate.* [e] Gen. 1:3. [f] Psalm 116:10.

Greek Interlinear

περιαιρεῖται τὸ κάλυμμα. **17** ὁ δὲ κύριος
²is taken away ¹the ⁸veil.   Now the   Lord
τὸ πνεῦμά ἐστιν· οὗ δὲ τὸ πνεῦμα
¹the ³Spirit ¹is;   and where the   Spirit
κυρίου, ἐλευθερία. **18** ἡμεῖς δὲ πάντες
of [the] [there is] freedom.   But we   all
Lord [is],
ἀνακεκαλυμμένῳ προσώπῳ τὴν δόξαν
¹having been unveiled ¹with face ²the ³glory

κυρίου κατοπτριζόμενοι τὴν αὐτὴν εἰκόνα
⁴of [the] ¹beholding in   ⁵the ⁷same ⁸image
Lord   a mirror
μεταμορφούμεθα ἀπὸ δόξης εἰς δόξαν,
⁴are being changed [into] from glory to   glory,
καθάπερ ἀπὸ κυρίου πνεύματος.
even as   from [the] Lord   Spirit.

Chapter 4

Διὰ τοῦτο, ἔχοντες τὴν διακονίαν
Therefore, having   -   ministry
ταύτην, καθὼς ἠλεήθημεν, οὐκ ἐγκακοῦμεν,
this,   as   we obtained mercy, we faint not,
2 ἀλλὰ ἀπειπάμεθα τὰ κρυπτὰ τῆς αἰσχύνης,
but we have renounced the hidden things - of shame,
μὴ περιπατοῦντες ἐν πανουργίᾳ μηδὲ
not walking   in   craftiness   nor
δολοῦντες τὸν λόγον τοῦ θεοῦ, ἀλλὰ
adulterating the   word   -   of God, but
τῇ φανερώσει τῆς ἀληθείας συνιστάνοντες
by the manifestation of the truth   commending
ἑαυτοὺς πρὸς πᾶσαν συνείδησιν ἀνθρώπων
ourselves to   every   conscience   of men
ἐνώπιον τοῦ θεοῦ. **3** εἰ δὲ καὶ ἔστιν
before   -   God.   But if indeed ⁴is
κεκαλυμμένον τὸ εὐαγγέλιον ἡμῶν, ἐν
¹having been hidden ¹the ⁵gospel   ⁶of us,   in
τοῖς ἀπολλυμένοις ἐστὶν κεκαλυμμένον, **4** ἐν
the [ones] perishing   it is having been hidden, in
οἷς ὁ θεὸς τοῦ αἰῶνος τούτου ἐτύφλωσεν
whom the god   of this age   blinded
τὰ νοήματα τῶν ἀπίστων εἰς τὸ μὴ
the thoughts   of the unbelieving [with a the not
                        [ones]   view] to
➡so that the enlightenment . . . should not shine forth,
αὐγάσαι τὸν φωτισμὸν τοῦ εὐαγγελίου
to shine forth the enlightenment of the   gospel
τῆς δόξης τοῦ Χριστοῦ, ὅς ἐστιν εἰκὼν
of the glory   - of Christ, who is [the] image
τοῦ θεοῦ. **5** οὐ γὰρ ἑαυτοὺς κηρύσσομεν
- of God. For ²not   ³ourselves ¹we proclaim
ἀλλὰ Χριστὸν Ἰησοῦν κύριον, ἑαυτοὺς δὲ
but   Christ   Jesus [as] Lord,   and ourselves
δούλους ὑμῶν διὰ Ἰησοῦν. **6** ὅτι ὁ
slaves   of you on account of Jesus.   Because -
θεὸς ὁ εἰπών· ἐκ σκότους φῶς λάμψει,
God the [one] saying: Out of darkness light shall shine,
ὃς ἔλαμψεν ἐν ταῖς καρδίαις ἡμῶν πρὸς
[is] [he] shone in   the   hearts   of us   for
who
φωτισμὸν τῆς γνώσεως τῆς δόξης τοῦ
enlightenment of the knowledge of the glory   -
θεοῦ ἐν προσώπῳ Χριστοῦ.
of God in [the] face   of Christ.
7 Ἔχομεν δὲ τὸν θησαυρὸν τοῦτον ἐν
And we have   -   the   this treasure   in
ὀστρακίνοις σκεύεσιν, ἵνα ἡ ὑπερβολὴ
earthenware   vessels, in order that the excellence
τῆς δυνάμεως ᾖ τοῦ θεοῦ καὶ μὴ ἐξ
of the power   may be - of God and not of
ἡμῶν· **8** ἐν παντὶ θλιβόμενοι ἀλλ' οὐ
us;   in every [way] afflicted   but not
στενοχωρούμενοι, ἀπορούμενοι ἀλλ' οὐκ
being restrained,   being in difficulties but not
ἐξαπορούμενοι, **9** διωκόμενοι ἀλλ' οὐκ
despairing,   being persecuted but not

ἐγκαταλειπόμενοι, καταβαλλόμενοι ἀλλ' οὐκ
being deserted,   being cast down   but not
ἀπολλύμενοι, **10** πάντοτε τὴν νέκρωσιν τοῦ
perishing,   always ²the ³dying
Ἰησοῦ ἐν τῷ σώματι περιφέροντες, ἵνα
¹of Jesus ⁴in ⁵the ⁶body   ¹bearing about, in order
                                        that
καὶ ἡ ζωὴ τοῦ Ἰησοῦ ἐν τῷ σώματι
also the life   - of Jesus in the body
ἡμῶν φανερωθῇ. **11** ἀεὶ γὰρ ἡμεῖς οἱ
of us might be manifested.   For always   we   the
ζῶντες εἰς θάνατον παραδιδόμεθα διὰ
[ones] living to death   are being   on ac-
                              delivered count of
Ἰησοῦν, ἵνα καὶ ἡ ζωὴ τοῦ Ἰησοῦ
Jesus, in order that also the life   - of Jesus
φανερωθῇ ἐν τῇ θνητῇ σαρκὶ ἡμῶν.
might be   in the mortal flesh of us.
manifested
12 ὥστε ὁ θάνατος ἐν ἡμῖν ἐνεργεῖται,
So as   -   death   in us   operates,
ἡ δὲ ζωὴ ἐν ὑμῖν. **13** ἔχοντες δὲ τὸ
- but life in you.   And having   the
αὐτὸ πνεῦμα τῆς πίστεως, κατὰ τὸ
same   spirit   of faith, according to the
                                        thing
γεγραμμένον· ἐπίστευσα, διὸ ἐλάλησα, καὶ
having been written: I believed, therefore I spoke, both
ἡμεῖς πιστεύομεν, διὸ καὶ λαλοῦμεν, **14** εἰδότες
we   believe, and therefore we speak,   knowing
ὅτι ὁ ἐγείρας τὸν κύριον Ἰησοῦν καὶ
that the having   the   Lord   Jesus   ²also
[one] raised
ἡμᾶς σὺν Ἰησοῦ ἐγερεῖ καὶ παραστήσει
¹us ⁴with ⁵Jesus ¹will raise and will present [us]
σὺν ὑμῖν. **15** τὰ γὰρ πάντα δι' ὑμᾶς,
with you.   -   For all things [are] on ac- you,
                                        count of
ἵνα ἡ χάρις πλεονάσασα διὰ τῶν πλειόνων
in or- grace increased   through the majority
der that
τὴν εὐχαριστίαν περισσεύσῃ εἰς τὴν δόξαν
¹the ²thanksgiving ¹may cause to abound to the   glory
τοῦ θεοῦ. **16** Διὸ οὐκ ἐγκακοῦμεν, ἀλλ'
- of God. Wherefore we faint not,   but
εἰ καὶ ὁ ἔξω ἡμῶν ἄνθρωπος διαφθείρεται,
if indeed the outward ⁵of us ¹man   is being disabled,
ἀλλ' ὁ ἔσω ἡμῶν ἀνακαινοῦται ἡμέρα
yet the inward [man] of us   is being renewed   day
καὶ ἡμέρα. **17** τὸ γὰρ παραυτίκα ἐλαφρὸν
and(by) day.   For the present   lightness
τῆς θλίψεως καθ' ὑπερβολὴν εἰς ὑπερβολὴν
of the affliction   ²excessively   ⁴to   ⁵excess
αἰώνιον βάρος δόξης κατεργάζεται ἡμῖν,
²an eternal ¹weight ³of glory ¹works   ²for us,

529

King James Version

18 While we look not at the things which are seen, but at the things which are not seen: for the things which are seen *are* temporal; but the things which are not seen *are* eternal.

5 For we know that, if our earthly house of *this* tabernacle were dissolved, we have a building of God, a house not made with hands, eternal in the heavens. 2 For in this we groan, earnestly desiring to be clothed upon with our house which is from heaven: 3 If so be that being clothed we shall not be found naked. 4 For we that are in *this* tabernacle do groan, being burdened: not for that we would be unclothed, but clothed upon, that mortality might be swallowed up of life. 5 Now he that hath wrought us for the selfsame thing *is* God, who also hath given unto us the earnest of the Spirit. 6 Therefore *we are* always confident, knowing that, whilst we are at home in the body, we are absent from the Lord: 7 (For we walk by faith, not by sight:) 8 We are confident, *I say,* and willing rather to be absent from the body, and to be present with the Lord. 9 Wherefore we labour, that, whether present or absent, we may be accepted of him. 10 For we must all appear before the judgment seat of Christ; that every one may receive the things *done* in his *body,* according to that he hath done, whether *it be* good or bad. 11 Knowing therefore the terror of the Lord, we persuade men; but we are made manifest unto God; and I trust also are made manifest in your consciences. 12 For we commend not ourselves again unto you, but give you occasion to glory on our behalf, that ye may have somewhat to *answer* them which glory in appearance, and not in heart. 13 For whether we be beside ourselves, *it is* to God: or whether we be sober, *it is* for your cause. 14 For the love of Christ constraineth us; because we thus judge, that if one died for all, then were all dead: 15And *that* he died for all, that they which live should not henceforth live unto themselves, but unto him which died for them, and rose again. 16 Wherefore henceforth know we no man after the flesh: yea, though we have known Christ after the flesh, yet now henceforth know we *him* no more. 17 Therefore if any man *be* in Christ, *he is* a new creature: old things are passed away; behold, all things are become new. 18And all things *are* of God, who hath reconciled us to himself by Jesus Christ, and hath given to us the ministry of reconciliation; 19 To wit, that God was in Christ, reconciling the world unto himself, not imputing their trespasses unto them;

New International Version

18 So we fix our eyes not on what is seen, but on what is unseen. For what is seen is temporary, but what is unseen is eternal.

Our heavenly dwelling

5 Now we know that if the earthly tent we live in is destroyed, we have a building from God, an eternal house in heaven, not built by human hands. 2 Meanwhile we groan, longing to be clothed with our heavenly dwelling, 3 since when we are clothed, we will not be found naked. 4 For while we are in this tent, we groan and are burdened, because we do not wish to be unclothed but to be clothed with our heavenly dwelling, so that what is mortal may be swallowed up by life. 5 Now it is God who has made us for this very purpose and has given us the Spirit as a deposit, guaranteeing what is to come.

6 Therefore we are always confident and know that as long as we are at home in the body we are away from the Lord. 7 We live by faith, not by sight. 8 We are confident, I say, and would prefer to be away from the body and at home with the Lord. 9 So we make it our goal to please him, whether we are at home in the body or away from it. 10 For we must all appear before the judgment seat of Christ, that each one may receive what is due him for the things done while in the body, whether good or bad.

The ministry of reconciliation

11 Since, then, we know what it is to fear the Lord, we try to persuade men. What we are is plain to God, and I hope it is also plain to your conscience. 12 We are not trying to commend ourselves to you again, but are giving you an opportunity to take pride in us, so that you can answer those who take pride in what is seen rather than in what is in the heart. 13 If we are out of our mind, it is for the sake of God; if we are in our right mind, it is for you. 14 For Christ's love compels us, because we are convinced that one died for all, and therefore all died. 15And he died for all that those who live should no longer live for themselves, but for him who died for them and was raised again.

16 So from now on we regard no one from a worldly point of view. Though we once regarded Christ in this way, we do so no longer. 17 Therefore, if anyone is in Christ, he is a new creation; the old has gone, the new has come! 18All this is from God, who reconciled us to himself through Christ and gave us the ministry of reconciliation: 19 that God was reconciling the world to himself in Christ, not counting men's sins against them. And he has committed

Greek Interlinear

18 μὴ σκοπούντων ἡμῶν τὰ βλεπόμενα
not considering usᵃ the things being seen
=while we do not consider

ἀλλὰ τὰ μὴ βλεπόμενα· τὰ γὰρ βλεπόμενα
but the not being seen; for the things being seen
things

πρόσκαιρα, τὰ δὲ μὴ βλεπόμενα αἰώνια.
[are] temporary, but the things not being seen [are] eternal.

Chapter 5

Οἴδαμεν γὰρ ὅτι ἐὰν ἡ ἐπίγειος
For we know that if the earthly

ἡμῶν οἰκία τοῦ σκήνους καταλυθῇ,
ᵇof us ¹house ²of the ²tabernacle is destroyed,

οἰκοδομὴν ἐκ θεοῦ ἔχομεν, οἰκίαν ἀχειρο-
a building of God we have, a house not made

ποίητον αἰώνιον ἐν τοῖς οὐρανοῖς. 2 καὶ
by hands eternal in the heavens. indeed

γὰρ ἐν τούτῳ στενάζομεν, τὸ οἰκητήριον
For in this² we groan, ²the ³dwelling-place

ἡμῶν τὸ ἐξ οὐρανοῦ ἐπενδύσασθαι ἐπιπο-
ᵇof us - ⁵out of ⁷heaven ⁴to put on ¹greatly

θοῦντες, 3 εἴ γε καὶ ἐνδυσάμενοι οὐ
desiring, if indeed being clothed not

γυμνοὶ εὑρεθησόμεθα. 4 καὶ γὰρ οἱ
naked we shall be found. For indeed ²the
[ones]

ὄντες ἐν τῷ σκήνει στενάζομεν βαρούμενοι,
¹being ⁴in ⁵the ⁶tabernacle ¹we groan being burdened,

ἐφ' ᾧ οὐ θέλομεν ἐκδύσασθαι ἀλλ'
inasmuch as we do not wish to put off but

ἐπενδύσασθαι, ἵνα καταποθῇ τὸ θνητὸν
to put on, in order ²may be ¹the ²mortal
that swallowed up

ὑπὸ τῆς ζωῆς. 5 ὁ δὲ κατεργασάμενος
by the life. Now the [one] having wrought

ἡμᾶς εἰς αὐτὸ τοῦτο θεός, ὁ δοὺς
us for this very thing [is] God, [one] the having

ἡμῖν τὸν ἀρραβῶνα τοῦ πνεύματος. 6 Θαρ-
to us the earnest of the Spirit. Being

ροῦντες οὖν πάντοτε καὶ εἰδότες ὅτι
of good therefore always and knowing that
cheer

ἐνδημοῦντες ἐν τῷ σώματι ἐκδημοῦμεν
being at home in the body we are away
from home

ἀπὸ τοῦ κυρίου· 7 διὰ πίστεως γὰρ
from the Lord; ¹through ²faith ¹for

περιπατοῦμεν, οὐ διὰ εἴδους· 8 θαρροῦμεν
we walk, not through appearance; we are of
good cheer

δὲ καὶ εὐδοκοῦμεν μᾶλλον ἐκδημῆσαι ἐκ
then and think it good rather to go away out
from home of

τοῦ σώματος καὶ ἐνδημῆσαι πρὸς τὸν
the body and to come home to the

κύριον. 9 διὸ καὶ φιλοτιμούμεθα, εἴτε
Lord. Wherefore also we are ambitious, whether

ἐνδημοῦντες εἴτε ἐκδημοῦντες, εὐάρεστοι
being at home or being away from home, wellpleasing

αὐτῷ εἶναι. 10 τοὺς γὰρ πάντας ἡμᾶς
to him to be. - For ²all ¹us

φανερωθῆναι δεῖ ἔμπροσθεν τοῦ βήματος
⁴to be manifested ¹it behoves before the tribunal

τοῦ Χριστοῦ, ἵνα κομίσηται ἕκαστος τὰ
- of Christ, in order ⁴may receive ¹each one the
that things

διὰ τοῦ σώματος πρὸς ἃ ἔπραξεν, εἴτε
through the body accord- what he either
ing to things practised,

ἀγαθὸν εἴτε φαῦλον.
good or worthless.

11 Εἰδότες οὖν τὸν φόβον τοῦ κυρίου
Knowing therefore the fear of the Lord

ἀνθρώπους πείθομεν, θεῷ δὲ πεφανερώμεθα·
²men ¹we persuade, and to God we have been made
manifest;

ἐλπίζω δὲ καὶ ἐν ταῖς συνειδήσεσιν
and I hope also in the consciences

ὑμῶν πεφανερῶσθαι. 12 οὐ πάλιν ἑαυτοὺς
of you to have been made Not again ²ourselves
manifest.

συνιστάνομεν ὑμῖν, ἀλλὰ ἀφορμὴν διδόντες
¹we commend to you, but ²an occasion ¹giving

ὑμῖν καυχήματος ὑπὲρ ἡμῶν, ἵνα ἔχητε
²to you of a boast on be- us, in order ye may
half of that have [it]

πρὸς τοὺς ἐν προσώπῳ καυχωμένους καὶ
in refer- the ³in ²face ¹boasting and
ence to [ones]

μὴ ἐν καρδίᾳ. 13 εἴτε γὰρ ἐξέστημεν,
not in heart. For whether we are mad,

θεῷ· εἴτε σωφρονοῦμεν. ὑμῖν. 14 ἡ γὰρ
[it is] or we are in our senses, [it is] For the
to God; for you.

ἀγάπη τοῦ Χριστοῦ συνέχει ἡμᾶς, κρίναντας
love - of Christ constrains us, judging

τοῦτο, ὅτι εἰς ὑπὲρ πάντων ἀπέθανεν·
this, that one on behalf of all men died;

ἄρα οἱ πάντες ἀπέθανον· 15 καὶ ὑπὲρ
then the all died; and ²on behalf of

πάντων ἀπέθανεν ἵνα οἱ ζῶντες μηκέτι
²all ¹he died in order the living no more
that [ones]

ἑαυτοῖς ζῶσιν ἀλλὰ τῷ ὑπὲρ αὐτῶν
to themselves may live but to the on behalf them
[one] of

ἀποθανόντι καὶ ἐγερθέντι. 16 Ὥστε ἡμεῖς
having died and having been raised. So as ²we

ἀπὸ τοῦ νῦν οὐδένα οἴδαμεν κατὰ σάρκα·
¹from - ²now ⁴no man ¹know according to flesh;

εἰ καὶ ἐγνώκαμεν κατὰ σάρκα Χριστόν,
if indeed ¹we have known ²according to ³flesh ⁴Christ,

ἀλλὰ νῦν οὐκέτι γινώσκομεν. 17 ὥστε
yet now no more we know [him]. So as

εἴ τις ἐν Χριστῷ, καινὴ κτίσις· τὰ
if anyone [is] in Christ, [he is] a new creation; the

ἀρχαῖα παρῆλθεν, ἰδοὺ γέγονεν καινά.
old things passed away, behold they have become new.

18 τὰ δὲ πάντα ἐκ τοῦ θεοῦ τοῦ καταλ-
- And all things [are] of - God the [one] having

λάξαντος ἡμᾶς ἑαυτῷ διὰ Χριστοῦ καὶ
reconciled us to himself through Christ and

δόντος ἡμῖν τὴν διακονίαν τῆς καταλλαγῆς,
having given to us the ministry - of reconciliation,

19 ὡς ὅτι θεὸς ἦν ἐν Χριστῷ κόσμον
as that God was in Christ ¹[the] world

καταλλάσσων ἑαυτῷ, μὴ λογιζόμενος αὐτοῖς
¹reconciling to himself, not reckoning to them

τὰ παραπτώματα αὐτῶν, καὶ θέμενος
the trespasses of them, and placing

---

* Neuter, going back to σκῆνος in the preceding verse.

and hath committed unto us the word of reconciliation. 20 Now then we are ambassadors for Christ, as though God did beseech *you* by us: we pray *you* in Christ's stead, be ye reconciled to God. 21 For he hath made him *to be* sin for us, who knew no sin; that we might be made the righteousness of God in him.

6 We then, *as* workers together *with him*, beseech *you* also that ye receive not the grace of God in vain. 2 (For he saith, I have heard thee in a time accepted, and in the day of salvation have I succoured thee: behold, now *is* the accepted time; behold, now *is* the day of salvation.) 3 Giving no offence in any thing, that the ministry be not blamed: 4 But in all *things* approving ourselves as the ministers of God, in much patience, in afflictions, in necessities, in distresses, 5 In stripes, in imprisonments, in tumults, in labours, in watchings, in fastings; 6 By pureness, by knowledge, by longsuffering, by kindness, by the Holy Ghost, by love unfeigned, 7 By the word of truth, by the power of God, by the armour of righteousness on the right hand and on the left, 8 By honour and dishonour, by evil report and good report: as deceivers, and *yet* true; 9 As unknown, and *yet* well known; as dying, and, behold, we live; as chastened, and not killed; 10 As sorrowful, yet alway rejoicing; as poor, yet making many rich; as having nothing, and *yet* possessing all things. 11 O *ye* Corinthians, our mouth is open unto you, our heart is enlarged. 12 Ye are not straitened in us, but ye are straitened in your own bowels. 13 Now for a recompense in the same, (I speak as unto *my* children,) be ye also enlarged. 14 Be ye not unequally yoked together with unbelievers: for what fellowship hath righteousness with unrighteousness? and what communion hath light with darkness? 15 And what concord hath Christ with Belial? or what part hath he that believeth with an infidel? 16 And what agreement hath the temple of God with idols? for ye are the temple of the living God; as God hath said, I will dwell in them, and walk in *them;* and I will be their God, and they shall be my people. 17 Wherefore come out from among them, and be ye separate, saith the Lord, and touch not the unclean *thing;* and I will receive you, 18 And will be a Father unto you, and ye shall be my sons and daughters, saith the Lord Almighty.

to us the message of reconciliation. 20 We are therefore Christ's ambassadors, as though God were making his appeal through us. We implore you on Christ's behalf: Be reconciled to God. 21 God made him who had no sin to be sin[g] for us, so that in him we might become the righteousness of God.

6 As God's fellow workers we urge you not to receive God's grace in vain. 2 For he says,

"At the time of my favor I heard you,
 and on the day of salvation I helped you."[h]

I tell you, now is the time of God's favor, now is the day of salvation.

Paul's hardships

3 We put no stumbling block in anyone's path, so that our ministry will not be discredited. 4 Rather, in every way we show ourselves to be servants of God: in great endurance; in troubles, hardships and distresses; 5 in beatings, imprisonments and riots; in hard work, sleepless nights and hunger; 6 in purity, understanding, patience and kindness; in the Holy Spirit and in sincere love; 7 in truthful speech and in the power of God; with weapons of righteousness in the right hand and in the left; 8 through glory and dishonor, praise and blame; genuine, yet regarded as impostors; 9 known, yet regarded as unknown; dying, and yet we live on; beaten, and yet not killed; 10 sorrowful, yet always rejoicing; poor, yet making many rich; having nothing, and yet possessing everything.

11 We have spoken freely to you, Corinthians, and opened wide our hearts to you. 12 We are not withholding our affection from you, but you are withholding yours from us. 13 As a fair exchange—I speak as to my children—open wide your hearts also.

Do not be yoked with unbelievers

14 Do not be yoked together with unbelievers. For what do righteousness and wickedness have in common? Or what fellowship can light have with darkness? 15 What harmony is there between Christ and Belial?[i] What does a believer have in common with an unbeliever? 16 What agreement is there between the temple of God and idols? For we are the temple of the living God. As God has said:

"I will live with them and walk among them,
 and I will be their God,
 and they will be my people."[j]

17 "Therefore come out from them
 and be separate,
                          says the Lord.
Touch no unclean thing,
 and I will receive you."[k]

18 "I will be a Father to you,
 and you will be my sons and daughters,
                          says the Lord Almighty."[l]

[g] Or *a sin offering.* [h] Isaiah 49:8. [i] Greek *Belair.* [j] Lev. 26:12; Jer. 32:38; Ezek. 37:27. [k] Isaiah 52:11; Ezek. 20:34,41. [l] II Samuel 7:14; 7:8.

Greek Interlinear

ἐν ἡμῖν τὸν λόγον τῆς καταλλαγῆς.
in us the word - of reconciliation.

20 'Υπὲρ Χριστοῦ οὖν πρεσβεύομεν ὡς
On behalf of Christ therefore we are ambassadors as

τοῦ θεοῦ παρακαλοῦντος δι' ἡμῶν· δεόμεθα
- God beseeching* through us; we beg

ὑπὲρ Χριστοῦ, καταλλάγητε τῷ θεῷ.
on behalf of Christ, Be ye reconciled - to God.

21 τὸν μὴ γνόντα ἁμαρτίαν ὑπὲρ ἡμῶν
*The [one] ¹not ⁴knowing ⁵sin ⁷on behalf of ⁶us

ἁμαρτίαν ἐποίησεν, ἵνα ἡμεῖς γενώμεθα
⁵sin ¹he made, in order that we might become

δικαιοσύνη θεοῦ ἐν αὐτῷ.
[the] righteousness of God in him.

Chapter 6

Συνεργοῦντες δὲ καὶ παρακαλοῦμεν μὴ
And working together also we beseech ²not

εἰς κενὸν τὴν χάριν τοῦ θεοῦ δέξασθαι
¹to no purpose ⁴the ³grace - ⁵of God ¹to receive

ὑμᾶς· 2 λέγει γάρ· καιρῷ δεκτῷ ἐπήκουσά
¹you; for he says: In a time acceptable I heard

σου καὶ ἐν ἡμέρᾳ σωτηρίας ἐβοήθησά
thee and in a day of salvation I helped

σοι· ἰδοὺ νῦν καιρὸς εὐπρόσδεκτος, ἰδοὺ
thee; behold now a time acceptable, behold

νῦν ἡμέρα σωτηρίας· 3 — μηδεμίαν ἐν
now a day of salvation; ²no ⁴in

μηδενὶ διδόντες προσκοπήν, ἵνα μὴ
¹no(any)thing ³giving ⁵cause of stumbling, lest

μωμηθῇ ἡ διακονία, 4 ἀλλ' ἐν παντὶ
²be blamed ¹the ³ministry, but in everything

συνιστάνοντες ἑαυτοὺς ὡς θεοῦ διάκονοι,
commending ourselves as ²of God ¹ministers,

ἐν ὑπομονῇ πολλῇ, ἐν θλίψεσιν, ἐν
in ²endurance ¹much, in afflictions, in

ἀνάγκαις, ἐν στενοχωρίαις, ἐν πληγαῖς,
necessities, in straits, in stripes,

5 ἐν φυλακαῖς, ἐν ἀκαταστασίαις, ἐν κόποις,
in prisons, in commotions, in labours,

ἐν ἀγρυπνίαις, ἐν νηστείαις, 6 ἐν ἁγνότητι,
in watchings, in fastings, in purity,

ἐν γνώσει, ἐν μακροθυμίᾳ, ἐν χρηστότητι,
in knowledge, in long-suffering, in kindness,

ἐν πνεύματι ἁγίῳ, ἐν ἀγάπῃ ἀνυποκρίτῳ,
in spirit a holy, in love unfeigned,

7 ἐν λόγῳ ἀληθείας, ἐν δυνάμει θεοῦ·
in a word of truth, in power of God;

διὰ τῶν ὅπλων τῆς δικαιοσύνης τῶν
through the weapons - of righteousness of the

δεξιῶν καὶ ἀριστερῶν, 8 διὰ δόξης καὶ
right [hand] and of left, through glory and

ἀτιμίας, διὰ δυσφημίας καὶ εὐφημίας·
dishonour, through ill report and good report;

ὡς πλάνοι καὶ ἀληθεῖς, 9 ὡς ἀγνοούμενοι
as deceivers and* true men, as being unknown

καὶ ἐπιγινωσκόμενοι, ὡς ἀποθνήσκοντες καὶ
and* being well known, as dying and

ἰδοὺ ζῶμεν, ὡς παιδευόμενοι καὶ μὴ
behold we live, as being chastened and not

θανατούμενοι, 10 ὡς λυπούμενοι ἀεὶ δὲ
being put to death, as being grieved *always ¹but

χαίροντες, ὡς πτωχοὶ πολλοὺς δὲ πλουτίζ-
rejoicing, as poor ²many ¹but ²en-

οντες, ὡς μηδὲν ἔχοντες καὶ πάντα
riching, as ²nothing ¹having ²and* ¹all things

κατέχοντες.
⁴possessing.

11 Τὸ στόμα ἡμῶν ἀνέῳγεν πρὸς ὑμᾶς,
The mouth of us has opened to you,

Κορίνθιοι, ἡ καρδία ἡμῶν πεπλάτυνται·
Corinthians, the heart of us has been enlarged;

12 οὐ στενοχωρεῖσθε ἐν ἡμῖν, στενοχωρεῖσθε
ye are not restrained in us, ²ye are restrained

δὲ ἐν τοῖς σπλάγχνοις ὑμῶν· 13 τὴν δὲ
¹but in the bowels of you; but [for] the

αὐτὴν ἀντιμισθίαν, ὡς τέκνοις λέγω,
same recompence, as to children I say,

πλατύνθητε καὶ ὑμεῖς.
be enlarged also ye.

14 Μὴ γίνεσθε ἑτεροζυγοῦντες ἀπίστοις·
Do not ye become unequally yoked [with] unbelievers;

τίς γὰρ μετοχὴ δικαιοσύνῃ καὶ ἀνομίᾳ,
for what share righteousnessᶜ and lawlessness,ᵉ
=have righteousness and lawlessness,

ἢ τίς κοινωνία φωτὶ πρὸς σκότος; 15 τίς
or what fellowship lightᶜ with darkness? what
=has light

δὲ συμφώνησις Χριστοῦ πρὸς Βελιάρ,
and agreement of Christ with Beliar,

ἢ τίς μερὶς πιστῷ μετὰ ἀπίστου; 16 τίς
or what part a believerᶜ with an unbeliever? what
=has a believer

δὲ συγκατάθεσις ναῷ θεοῦ μετὰ εἰδώλων;
and union a shrineᶜ of God with idols?
=has a shrine

ἡμεῖς γὰρ ναὸς θεοῦ ἐσμεν ζῶντος·
For ¹we ²a shrine ⁴God ³are ⁴of a living;

καθὼς εἶπεν ὁ θεὸς ὅτι ἐνοικήσω ἐν
as said - God[.] - I will dwell among

αὐτοῖς καὶ ἐμπεριπατήσω, καὶ ἔσομαι
them and I will walk among [them], and I will be

αὐτῶν θεός, καὶ αὐτοὶ ἔσονταί μου λαός.
of them God, and they shall be of me a people.

17 διὸ ἐξέλθατε ἐκ μέσου αὐτῶν καὶ
Wherefore come ye out from [the] midst of them and

ἀφορίσθητε, λέγει κύριος, καὶ ἀκαθάρτου
be ye separated, says [the] Lord, and an unclean thing

μὴ ἅπτεσθε· 18 κἀγὼ εἰσδέξομαι ὑμᾶς, καὶ
do not touch; and I will welcome in you, and

ἔσομαι ὑμῖν εἰς πατέρα, καὶ ὑμεῖς ἔσεσθέ
I will be to you for a father, and ye shall be

μοι εἰς υἱοὺς καὶ θυγατέρας, λέγει κύριος
to me for sons and daughters, says [the] Lord

---

* Evidently = and yet, as in some other places; cf. John 20. 29.

King James Version

7 Having therefore these promises, dearly beloved, let us cleanse ourselves from all filthiness of the flesh and spirit, perfecting holiness in the fear of God. 2 Receive us; we have wronged no man, we have corrupted no man, we have defrauded no man. 3 I speak not *this* to condemn *you:* for I have said before, that ye are in our hearts to die and live with *you.* 4 Great *is* my boldness of speech toward you, great *is* my glorying of you: I am filled with comfort, I am exceeding joyful in all our tribulation. 5 For, when we were come into Macedonia, our flesh had no rest, but we were troubled on every side; without *were* fightings, within *were* fears. 6 Nevertheless God, that comforteth those that are cast down, comforted us by the coming of Titus; 7And not by his coming only, but by the consolation wherewith he was comforted in you, when he told us your earnest desire, your mourning, your fervent mind toward me; so that I rejoiced the more. 8 For though I made you sorry with a letter, I do not repent, though I did repent: for I perceive that the same epistle hath made you sorry, though *it were* but for a season. 9 Now I rejoice, not that ye were made sorry, but that ye sorrowed to repentance: for ye were made sorry after a godly manner, that ye might receive damage by us in nothing. 10 For godly sorrow worketh repentance to salvation not to be repented of: but the sorrow of the world worketh death. 11 For behold this selfsame thing, that ye sorrowed after a godly sort, what carefulness it wrought in you, yea, *what* clearing of yourselves, yea, *what* indignation, yea, *what* fear, yea, *what* vehement desire, yea, *what* zeal, yea, *what* revenge! In all *things* ye have approved yourselves to be clear in this matter. 12 Wherefore, though I wrote unto you, *I did it* not for his cause that had done the wrong, nor for his cause that suffered wrong, but that our care for you in the sight of God might appear unto you. 13 Therefore we were comforted in your comfort: yea, and exceedingly the more joyed we for the joy of Titus, because his spirit was refreshed by you all. 14 For if I have boasted any thing to him of you, I am not ashamed; but as we spake all things to you in truth, even so our boasting, which *I made* before Titus, is found a truth. 15And his inward affection is more abundant toward you, whilst he remembereth the obedience of you all, how with fear and trembling ye received him. 16 I rejoice therefore that I have confidence in you in all *things.*

8 Moreover, brethren, we do you to wit of the grace of God bestowed on the churches of Macedonia; 2 How that in a great trial of affliction, the abundance of their joy and their deep poverty abounded unto the riches of their

New International Version

7 Since we have these promises, dear friends, let us purify ourselves from everything that contaminates body and spirit, and let us strive for perfection out of reverence for God.

Paul's joy

2 Make room for us in your hearts. We have wronged no one, we have corrupted no one, we have exploited no one. 3 I do not say this to condemn you; I have said before that you have such a place in our hearts that we would live or die with you. 4 I have great confidence in you; I take great pride in you. I am greatly encouraged; in all our troubles my joy knows no bounds.

5 For when we came into Macedonia, this body of ours had no rest, but we were harassed at every turn—conflicts on the outside, fears within. 6 But God, who comforts the downcast, comforted us by the coming of Titus, 7 and not only by his coming but also by the comfort you had given him. He told us about your affection, your deep sorrow, your ardent concern for me, so that my joy was greater than ever.

8 Even if I caused you sorrow by my letter, I do not regret it. Though I did regret it—I see that my letter hurt you, but only for a little while—9 yet now I am happy, not because you were made sorry, but because your sorrow led you to repentance. For you became sorrowful as God intended and so were not harmed in any way by us. 10 Godly sorrow brings repentance that leads to salvation and leaves no regret, but worldly sorrow brings death. 11 See what this godly sorrow has produced in you: what earnestness, what eagerness to clear yourselves, what indignation, what alarm, what affection, what concern, what readiness to see justice done. At every point you have proved yourselves to be innocent in this matter. 12 So even though I wrote to you, it was not on account of the one who did the wrong or of the injured party, but rather that before God you could see for yourselves how devoted to us you are. 13 By all this we are encouraged.

In addition to our own encouragement, we were especially delighted to see how happy Titus was, because all of you helped put his mind at ease. 14 I had boasted to him about you, and you have not embarrassed me. But just as everything we said to you was true, so our boasting about you to Titus has proved to be true as well. 15And his affection for you is all the greater when he remembers that you were all obedient, receiving him with fear and trembling. 16 I am glad I can have complete confidence in you.

Generosity encouraged

8 And now, brothers, we want you to know about the grace that God has given the Macedonian churches. 2 Out of the most severe trial, their overflowing joy and their extreme

Chapter 7

παντοκράτωρ. 7 ταύτας οὖν ἔχοντες τὰς ἐπ-
[the] Almighty.   These   therefore   having   -   pro-

αγγελίας, ἀγαπητοί, καθαρίσωμεν ἑαυτοὺς ἀπὸ
mises,   beloved,   let us cleanse   ourselves   from

παντὸς μολυσμοῦ σαρκὸς καὶ πνεύματος,
all   pollution   of flesh   and   of spirit,

ἐπιτελοῦντες ἁγιωσύνην ἐν φόβῳ θεοῦ.
perfecting   holiness   in [the] fear   of God.

2 Χωρήσατε ἡμᾶς· οὐδένα ἠδικήσαμεν,
Make room for   us;   no one   we wronged,

οὐδένα ἐφθείραμεν, οὐδένα ἐπλεονεκτήσαμεν.
no one   we injured,   no one   we defrauded.

3 πρὸς κατάκρισιν οὐ λέγω· προείρηκα
For   condemnation   I say not;   I have
previously said

γὰρ ὅτι ἐν ταῖς καρδίαις ἡμῶν ἐστε
for   that   in   the   hearts   of us   ye are

εἰς τὸ συναποθανεῖν καὶ συζῆν. 4 πολλή
for   -   to die with [you]   and to live with [you].   Much

μοι παρρησία πρὸς ὑμᾶς, πολλή μοι
to me   boldness   toward   you,   much   to me
= I have much   = I have much

καύχησις ὑπὲρ ὑμῶν· πεπλήρωμαι τῇ
boasting   on behalf of   you;   I have been filled   -

παρακλήσει, ὑπερπερισσεύομαι τῇ χαρᾷ ἐπὶ
with comfort,   I overflow   - with joy on(in)

πάσῃ τῇ θλίψει ἡμῶν. 5 Καὶ γὰρ
all   the   affliction   of us.   For indeed

ἐλθόντων ἡμῶν εἰς Μακεδονίαν οὐδεμίαν
coming   us   into   Macedonia   no
= when we came

ἔσχηκεν ἄνεσιν ἡ σὰρξ ἡμῶν, ἀλλ' ἐν
has had   rest   the   flesh   of us,   but   in

παντὶ θλιβόμενοι· ἔξωθεν μάχαι, ἔσωθεν
every way   being afflicted;   without [were] fightings,   within

φόβοι. 6 ἀλλ' ὁ παρακαλῶν τοὺς ταπεινοὺς
[were] fears.   But [the one] comforting   the   humble

παρεκάλεσεν ἡμᾶς ὁ θεὸς ἐν τῇ παρουσίᾳ
comforted   us   -   God   by   the   presence

Τίτου· 7 οὐ μόνον δὲ ἐν τῇ παρουσίᾳ
of Titus;   and not only   by   the   presence

αὐτοῦ, ἀλλὰ καὶ ἐν τῇ παρακλήσει ᾗ
of him,   but   also   by   the   comfort   with
which

παρεκλήθη ἐφ' ὑμῖν, ἀναγγέλλων ἡμῖν
he was comforted   over   you,   reporting   to us

τὴν ὑμῶν ἐπιπόθησιν, τὸν ὑμῶν ὀδυρμόν,
the   of you   eager longing,   the   of you   mourning,

τὸν ὑμῶν ζῆλον ὑπὲρ ἐμοῦ, ὥστε με
the   of you   zeal   on behalf of   me,   so as   me

μᾶλλον χαρῆναι. 8 Ὅτι εἰ καὶ ἐλύπησα
more   to rejoice.   Because if   indeed   I grieved
= so that I rejoiced more.

ὑμᾶς ἐν τῇ ἐπιστολῇ, οὐ μεταμέλομαι·
you   by   the   epistle,   I do not regret;

εἰ καὶ μετεμελόμην, βλέπω ὅτι ἡ ἐπιστολὴ
if indeed   I regretted,   I see   that   the   -   epistle

ἐκείνη εἰ καὶ πρὸς ὥραν ἐλύπησεν ὑμᾶς,
that   if indeed   for   an hour   it grieved   you,

9 νῦν χαίρω, οὐχ ὅτι ἐλυπήθητε, ἀλλ'
now   I rejoice,   not   that   ye were grieved,   but

ὅτι ἐλυπήθητε εἰς μετάνοιαν· ἐλυπήθητε
that   ye were grieved   to   repentance;   ye were grieved

γὰρ κατὰ θεόν, ἵνα ἐν μηδενὶ ζημιωθῆτε
for   according God,   in order in   nothing   ye might suffer
to   that   loss

ἐξ ἡμῶν. 10 ἡ γὰρ κατὰ θεὸν λύπη
by   us.   For the   according to God   grief

μετάνοιαν εἰς σωτηρίαν ἀμεταμέλητον
repentance   to   salvation   unregrettable

ἐργάζεται· ἡ δὲ τοῦ κόσμου λύπη θάνατον
works;   but the   of the   world   grief   death

κατεργάζεται. 11 ἰδοὺ γὰρ αὐτὸ τοῦτο
works out.   For behold   this very thing[,]

τὸ κατὰ θεὸν λυπηθῆναι πόσην κατειργά-
- according to God   to be grieved[,]   what   it worked

σατο ὑμῖν σπουδήν, ἀλλὰ ἀπολογίαν, ἀλλὰ
out   in you   earnestness,   but [what] defence,   but

ἀγανάκτησιν, ἀλλὰ φόβον, ἀλλὰ ἐπιπόθησιν,
vexation,   but   fear,   but   eager desire,

ἀλλὰ ζῆλον, ἀλλὰ ἐκδίκησιν. ἐν παντὶ
but   zeal,   but   vengeance.   In everything

συνεστήσατε ἑαυτοὺς ἁγνοὺς εἶναι τῷ
ye commended   yourselves   pure   to be   in the

πράγματι. 12 ἄρα εἰ καὶ ἔγραψα ὑμῖν,
affair.   Then   if   indeed   I wrote   to you,

οὐχ ἕνεκεν τοῦ ἀδικήσαντος οὐδὲ ἕνεκεν
not   for the   [one] having done   nor   for the
sake of   wrong   sake of

τοῦ ἀδικηθέντος, ἀλλ' ἕνεκεν τοῦ φανερω-
the   having been   but   for the   - to be mani-
[one]   wronged,   sake of

θῆναι τὴν σπουδὴν ὑμῶν τὴν ὑπὲρ ἡμῶν
fested   the   earnestness   of you   - on behalf of   us

πρὸς ὑμᾶς ἐνώπιον τοῦ θεοῦ. 13 διὰ
toward   you   before   -   God.   There-

τοῦτο παρακεκλήμεθα. Ἐπὶ δὲ τῇ
fore   we have been comforted.   But as to   the

παρακλήσει ἡμῶν περισσοτέρως μᾶλλον
comfort   of us   abundantly   more

ἐχάρημεν ἐπὶ τῇ χαρᾷ Τίτου, ὅτι ἀναπέ-
we rejoiced   over   the   joy   of Titus, because has been

παυται τὸ πνεῦμα αὐτοῦ ἀπὸ πάντων
rested   the   spirit   of him   from(by)   all

ὑμῶν· 14 ὅτι εἴ τι αὐτῷ ὑπὲρ ὑμῶν
you;   because if   anything   to him   on behalf of   you

κεκαύχημαι, οὐ κατῃσχύνθην, ἀλλ' ὡς
I have boasted,   I was not shamed,   but   as

πάντα ἐν ἀληθείᾳ ἐλαλήσαμεν ὑμῖν, οὕτως
all things   in   truth   we spoke   to you,   so

καὶ ἡ καύχησις ἡμῶν ἐπὶ Τίτου ἀλήθεια
also   the   boasting   of us   over   Titus   truth

ἐγενήθη. 15 καὶ τὰ σπλάγχνα αὐτοῦ
became.   And   the   bowels   of him

περισσοτέρως εἰς ὑμᾶς ἐστιν ἀναμιμνησκομέ-
abundantly   toward   you   is(are)   [he] remember-

νου τὴν πάντων ὑμῶν ὑπακοήν, ὡς μετὰ
ing   the   of all   you   obedience,   as   with

φόβου καὶ τρόμου ἐδέξασθε αὐτόν.
fear   and   trembling   ye received   him.

16 χαίρω ὅτι ἐν παντὶ θαρρῶ ἐν ὑμῖν.
I rejoice   that   in everything   I am confident in   you.

Chapter 8

Γνωρίζομεν δὲ ὑμῖν, ἀδελφοί, τὴν
Now we make known   to you,   brothers,   the

χάριν τοῦ θεοῦ τὴν δεδομένην ἐν ταῖς
grace   -   of God   - having been given among the

ἐκκλησίαις τῆς Μακεδονίας, 2 ὅτι ἐν πολλῇ
churches   - of Macedonia,   that in   much

δοκιμῇ θλίψεως ἡ περισσεία τῆς χαρᾶς
proving   of affliction   the   abundance   of the   joy

αὐτῶν καὶ ἡ κατὰ βάθους πτωχεία
of them   and   the   according to   depth   poverty
= their extreme poverty

αὐτῶν ἐπερίσσευσεν εἰς τὸ πλοῦτος τῆς
of them   abounded   to   the   riches   of the

535

King James Version

liberality. 3 For to *their* power, I bear record, yea, and beyond *their* power *they were* willing of themselves; 4 Praying us with much entreaty that we would receive the gift, and *take upon us* the fellowship of the ministering to the saints. 5And *this they did*, not as we hoped, but first gave their own selves to the Lord, and unto us by the will of God. 6 Insomuch that we desired Titus, that as he had begun, so he would also finish in you the same grace also. 7 Therefore, as ye abound in every *thing, in* faith, and utterance, and knowledge, and *in* all diligence, and *in* your love to us, *see* that ye abound in this grace also. 8 I speak not by commandment, but by occasion of the forwardness of others, and to prove the sincerity of your love. 9 For ye know the grace of our Lord Jesus Christ, that, though he was rich, yet for your sakes he became poor, that ye through his poverty might be rich. 10And herein I give *my* advice: for this is expedient for you, who have begun before, not only to do, but also to be forward a year ago. 11 Now therefore perform the doing *of it;* that as *there was* a readiness to will, so *there may be* a performance also out of that which ye have. 12 For if there be first a willing mind, *it is* accepted according to that a man hath, *and* not according to that he hath· not. 13 For *I mean* not that other men be eased, and ye burdened: 14 But by an equality, *that* now at this time your abundance *may be a supply* for their want, that their abundance also may be *a supply* for your want; that there may be equality: 15As it is written, He that *had gathered* much had nothing over; and he that *had gathered* little had no lack. 16 But thanks *be* to God, which put the same earnest care into the heart of Titus for you. 17 For indeed he accepted the exhortation; but being more forward, of his own accord he went unto you. 18And we have sent with him the brother, whose praise *is* in the gospel throughout all the churches; 19And not *that* only, but who was also chosen of the churches to travel with us with this grace, which is administered by us to the glory of the same Lord, and *declaration of* your ready mind: 20Avoiding this, that no man should blame us in this abundance which is administered by us: 21 Providing for honest things, not only in the sight of the Lord, but also in the sight of men. 22And we have sent with them our brother, whom we have oftentimes proved diligent in many things, but now much more diligent, upon the great confidence which *I have* in you. 23 Whether *any do inquire* of Titus, *he is* my partner and fellow helper concerning you: or our brethren *be inquired of, they are* the messengers of the churches, *and* the glory of Christ. 24 Wherefore shew ye to them, and before the churches, the proof of your love, and of our boasting on your behalf.

New International Version

poverty welled up in rich generosity. 3 For I testify that they gave as much as they were able, and even beyond their ability. Entirely on their own, 4 they urgently pleaded with us for the privilege of sharing in this service to the saints. 5And they did not do as we expected, but they gave themselves first to the Lord and then to us in keeping with God's will. 6 So we urged Titus, since he had earlier made a beginning, to bring also to completion this act of grace on your part. 7 But just as you excel in everything —in faith, in speech, in knowledge, in complete earnestness and in your love for us[m]—see that you also excel in this grace of giving.

8 I am not commanding you, but I want to test the sincerity of your love by comparing it with the earnestness of others. 9 For you know the grace of our Lord Jesus Christ, that though he was rich, yet for your sakes he became poor, so that you through his poverty might become rich.

10 And here is my advice about what is best for you in this matter: Last year you were the first not only to give but also to have the desire to do so. 11 Now finish the work, so that your eager willingness to do it may be matched by your completion of it, according to your means. 12 For if the willingness is there, the gift is acceptable according to what one has, not according to what he does not have.

13 Our desire is not that others might be relieved while you are hard pressed, but that there might be equality. 14At the present time your plenty will supply what they need, so that in turn their plenty will supply what you need. Then there will be equality, 15 as it is written:

"He that gathered much did not have too much, and he that gathered little did not have too little." [n]

Titus sent to Corinth

16 I thank God, who put into the heart of Titus the same concern I have for you. 17 For Titus not only welcomed our appeal, but he is coming to you with much enthusiasm and on his own initiative. 18And we are sending along with him the brother who is praised by all the churches for his service to the gospel. 19 What is more, he was chosen by the churches to accompany us as we carry the offering, which we administer in order to honor the Lord himself and to show our eagerness to help. 20 We want to avoid any criticism of the way we administer this liberal gift. 21 For we are taking pains to do what is right, not only in the eyes of the Lord but also in the eyes of men.

22 In addition, we are sending with them our brother who has often proved to us in many ways that he is zealous, and now even more so because of his great confidence in you. 23As for Titus, he is my partner and fellow worker among you; as for our brothers, they are representatives of the churches and an honor to Christ. 24 Therefore, show these men the proof of your love and the reason for our pride in you, so that all the churches can see it.

[m] Many MSS read *our love for you.* [n] Exodus 16:18.

Greek Interlinear

ἁπλότητος αὐτῶν· **3** ὅτι κατὰ δύναμιν,
liberality of them; that according [their]
to power,

μαρτυρῶ, καὶ παρὰ δύναμιν, αὐθαίρετοι
I witness, and beyond [their] power, of their own
accord

4 μετὰ πολλῆς παρακλήσεως δεόμενοι ἡμῶν
with much beseeching requesting of us

τὴν χάριν καὶ τὴν κοινωνίαν τῆς διακονίας
the grace and the fellowship of the ministry

τῆς εἰς τοὺς ἁγίους, **5** καὶ οὐ καθὼς
- to the saints, and not as

ἠλπίσαμεν, ἀλλὰ ἑαυτοὺς ἔδωκαν πρῶτον
we hoped, but themselves gave firstly

τῷ κυρίῳ καὶ ἡμῖν διὰ θελήματος θεοῦ,
to the Lord and to us through [the] will of God,

6 εἰς τὸ παρακαλέσαι ἡμᾶς Τίτον, ἵνα
for to beseech us[b] Titus, in order
=that we should beseech that

καθὼς προενήρξατο οὕτως καὶ ἐπιτελέσῃ
as previously he began so also he should
complete

εἰς ὑμᾶς καὶ τὴν χάριν ταύτην. **7** ἀλλ'
in you also this grace. But

ὥσπερ ἐν παντὶ περισσεύετε, πίστει καὶ
as in everything ye abound, in faith and

λόγῳ καὶ γνώσει καὶ πάσῃ σπουδῇ
in word and in knowledge and in all diligence

κι͘ τῇ ἐξ ἡμῶν ἐν ὑμῖν ἀγάπῃ, ἵνα
and - from us in(to) you in love, [see] that

καὶ ἐν ταύτῃ τῇ χάριτι περισσεύητε.
also in this - grace ye may abound.

8 Οὐ κατ' ἐπιταγὴν λέγω, ἀλλὰ διὰ
Not by way of command I say,* but through

τῆς ἑτέρων σπουδῆς καὶ τὸ τῆς ὑμετέρας
the of others diligence also the - of your

ἀγάπης γνήσιον δοκιμάζων· **9** γινώσκετε
love reality proving; ye know

γὰρ τὴν χάριν τοῦ κυρίου ἡμῶν Ἰησοῦ
for the grace of the Lord of us Jesus

[Χριστοῦ], ὅτι δι' ὑμᾶς ἐπτώχευσεν
Christ, that on account you he impoverished
of [himself]

πλούσιος ὤν, ἵνα ὑμεῖς τῇ ἐκείνου πτωχείᾳ
rich being, in or- ye by of that poverty
der that the one

πλουτήσητε. **10** καὶ γνώμην ἐν τούτῳ
might become rich. And an opinion in this

δίδωμι· τοῦτο γὰρ ὑμῖν συμφέρει, οἵτινες
I give; for this for you is expedient, who

οὐ μόνον τὸ ποιῆσαι ἀλλὰ καὶ τὸ θέλειν
not only the to do but also the to will

προενήρξασθε ἀπὸ πέρυσι· **11** νυνὶ δὲ καὶ
previously ye began from last year; but now also
=a year ago;

τὸ ποιῆσαι ἐπιτελέσατε, ὅπως καθάπερ ἡ
the to do complete ye, so as as the

προθυμία τοῦ θέλειν, οὕτως καὶ τὸ
eagerness of the to will, so also the

ἐπιτελέσαι ἐκ τοῦ ἔχειν. **12** εἰ γὰρ ἡ
to complete out of the to have. For if the
=what ye have.

προθυμία πρόκειται, καθὸ ἐὰν ἔχῃ
eagerness is already there, according to whatever one has

εὐπρόσδεκτος, οὐ καθὸ οὐκ ἔχει. **13** οὐ
it is acceptable, not according [what] one not
to has not.

γὰρ ἵνα ἄλλοις ἄνεσις, ὑμῖν θλῖψις,
For in order to others relief, to you distress,
that [there may be]

ἀλλ' ἐξ ἰσότητος **14** ἐν τῷ νῦν καιρῷ
but by equality at the present time

τὸ ὑμῶν περίσσευμα εἰς τὸ ἐκείνων
the of you abundance [may be] for the of those

ὑστέρημα, ἵνα καὶ τὸ ἐκείνων περίσσευμα
lack, in order also the of those abundance
that

γένηται εἰς τὸ ὑμῶν ὑστέρημα, ὅπως
may be for the of you lack, so as

γένηται ἰσότης, **15** καθὼς γέγραπται· ὁ
there may be equality, as it has been He
written:

τὸ πολὺ οὐκ ἐπλεόνασεν, καὶ ὁ τὸ
the much did not abound, and he the

ὀλίγον οὐκ ἠλαττόνησεν. **16** Χάρις δὲ
little had not less. But thanks [be]

τῷ θεῷ τῷ διδόντι τὴν αὐτὴν σπουδὴν
- to God - giving the same diligence

ὑπὲρ ὑμῶν ἐν τῇ καρδίᾳ Τίτου, **17** ὅτι
on be- you in the heart of Titus, because
half of

τὴν μὲν παράκλησιν ἐδέξατο, σπουδαιότερος
the indeed beseeching he received, more diligent

δὲ ὑπάρχων αὐθαίρετος ἐξῆλθεν πρὸς ὑμᾶς.
and being of his own he went to you.
accord forth

18 συνεπέμψαμεν δὲ μετ' αὐτοῦ τὸν
And we sent with with him the

ἀδελφὸν οὗ ὁ ἔπαινος ἐν τῷ εὐαγγελίῳ
brother of whom the praise in the gospel

διὰ πασῶν τῶν ἐκκλησιῶν, **19** οὐ μόνον δὲ
[is] all the churches, and not only [this]
through[out]

ἀλλὰ καὶ χειροτονηθεὶς ὑπὸ τῶν ἐκκλησιῶν
but also having been elected by the churches

συνέκδημος ἡμῶν ἐν τῇ χάριτι ταύτῃ
a travelling of us in this grace
companion

τῇ διακονουμένῃ ὑφ' ἡμῶν πρὸς τὴν
- being ministered by us to the

αὐτοῦ τοῦ κυρίου δόξαν καὶ προθυμίαν
[him]self of the Lord glory and eagerness

ἡμῶν, **20** στελλόμενοι τοῦτο, μή τις ἡμᾶς
of us, avoiding this, lest anyone us

μωμήσηται ἐν τῇ ἁδρότητι ταύτῃ τῇ
should blame in this bounty the

διακονουμένῃ ὑφ' ἡμῶν· **21** προνοοῦμεν γὰρ
being ministered by us; for we provide

καλὰ οὐ μόνον ἐνώπιον κυρίου ἀλλὰ καὶ
good not only before [the] Lord but also
things

ἐνώπιον ἀνθρώπων. **22** συνεπέμψαμεν δὲ
before men. And we sent with

αὐτοῖς τὸν ἀδελφὸν ἡμῶν, ὃν ἐδοκιμάσαμεν
them the brother of us, whom we proved

ἐν πολλοῖς πολλάκις σπουδαῖον ὄντα, νυνὶ
in many things many times diligent being, now

δὲ πολὺ σπουδαιότερον πεποιθήσει πολλῇ
and much more diligent in confidence much

τῇ εἰς ὑμᾶς. **23** εἴτε ὑπὲρ Τίτου, κοινωνὸς
- toward you. Whether as to Titus, partner

ἐμὸς καὶ εἰς ὑμᾶς συνεργός· εἴτε ἀδελφοὶ
my and for you fellow-worker; or brothers

ἡμῶν, ἀπόστολοι ἐκκλησιῶν, δόξα Χριστοῦ.
of us, apostles of churches, [the] of Christ.
glory

24 τὴν οὖν ἔνδειξιν τῆς ἀγάπης ὑμῶν
The therefore demon- of the love of you
stration

καὶ ἡμῶν καυχήσεως ὑπὲρ ὑμῶν εἰς
and of us boasting on behalf of you to

αὐτοὺς ἐνδεικνύμενοι εἰς πρόσωπον τῶν
them showing forth in [the] presence of the

ἐκκλησιῶν.
churches.

---

* That is, Paul is not issuing a command. Cf. I. Cor. 7. 6.

9 For as touching the ministering to the saints, it is superfluous for me to write to you: 2 For I know the forwardness of your mind, for which I boast of you to them of Macedonia, that Achaia was ready a year ago; and your zeal hath provoked very many. 3 Yet have I sent the brethren, lest our boasting of you should be in vain in this behalf; that, as I said, ye may be ready: 4 Lest haply if they of Macedonia come with me, and find you unprepared, we (that we say not, ye) should be ashamed in this same confident boasting. 5 Therefore I thought it necessary to exhort the brethren, that they would go before unto you, and make up beforehand your bounty, whereof ye had notice before, that the same might be ready, as *a matter of* bounty, and not as *of* covetousness. 6 But this *I say,* He which soweth sparingly shall reap also sparingly; and he which soweth bountifully shall reap also bountifully. 7 Every man according as he purposeth in his heart, *so let him give;* not grudgingly, or of necessity: for God loveth a cheerful giver. 8 And God *is* able to make all grace abound toward you; that ye, always having all sufficiency in all *things,* may abound to every good work: 9 (As it is written, He hath dispersed abroad; he hath given to the poor: his righteousness remaineth for ever. 10 Now he that ministereth seed to the sower both minister bread for *your* food, and multiply your seed sown, and increase the fruits of your righteousness:) 11 Being enriched in every thing to all bountifulness, which causeth through us thanksgiving to God. 12 For the administration of this service not only supplieth the want of the saints, but is abundant also by many thanksgivings unto God; 13 While by the experiment of this ministration they glorify God for your professed subjection unto the gospel of Christ, and for *your* liberal distribution unto them, and unto all *men;* 14 And by their prayer for you, which long after you for the exceeding grace of God in you. 15 Thanks *be* unto God for his unspeakable gift.

9 There is no need for me to write to you about this service to the saints. 2 For I know your eagerness to help, and I have been boasting about it to the Macedonians, telling them that since last year you in Achaia were ready to give; and your enthusiasm has stirred most of them to action. 3 But I am sending the brothers in order that our boasting about you in this matter should not prove hollow, but that you may be ready, as I said you would be. 4 For if any Macedonians come with me and find you unprepared, we—not to say anything about you— would be ashamed of having been so confident. 5 So I thought it necessary to urge the brothers to visit you in advance and finish the arrangements for the generous gift you had promised. Then it will be ready as a generous gift, not as one grudgingly given.

Sowing generously

6 Remember this: Whoever sows sparingly will also reap sparingly, and whoever sows generously will also reap generously. 7 Each man should give what he has decided in his heart to give, not reluctantly or under compulsion, for God loves a cheerful giver. 8 And God is able to make all grace abound to you, so that in all things at all times, having all that you need, you will abound in every good work. 9 As it is written:
"He has scattered abroad his gifts to the poor;
his righteousness endures for ever." *°*
10 Now he who supplies seed to the sower and bread for food will also supply and increase your store of seed and will enlarge the harvest of your righteousness. 11 You will be made rich in every way so that you can be generous on every occasion, and through us your generosity will result in thanksgiving to God.
12 This service that you perform is not only supplying the needs of God's people but is also overflowing in many expressions of thanks to God. 13 Because of the service by which you have proved yourselves, men will praise God for the obedience that accompanies your confession of the gospel of Christ, and for your generosity in sharing with them and with everyone else. 14 And in their prayers for you their hearts will go out to you, because of the surpassing grace God has given you. 15 Thanks be to God for his indescribable gift!

Paul's defense of his ministry

10 Now I Paul myself beseech you by the meekness and gentleness of Christ, who in presence *am* base among you, but being absent am bold toward you: 2 But I beseech *you,* that I may not be bold when I am present with that confidence, wherewith I think to be bold against some, which think of us as if we walked according to the flesh. 3 For though we walk in the flesh, we do not war after the flesh: 4 (For the weapons of our warfare *are* not carnal, but mighty through God to the pulling down of strong holds;) 5 Casting down imaginations, and every high thing that exalteth itself against the

10 By the meekness and gentleness of Christ, I appeal to you—I, Paul, who am "timid" when face to face with you, but "bold" when away! 2 I beg you that when I come I may not have to be as bold as I expect to be toward some people who think that we live by the standards of this world. 3 For though we live in the world, we do not wage war as the world does. 4 The weapons we fight with are not the weapons of the world. On the contrary, they have divine power to tear down strongholds. 5 We demolish arguments and every pretension that sets itself up against the knowledge of God,

[*o*] Psalm 112:9.

538

Greek Interlinear

Chapter 9

9 Περὶ μὲν γὰρ τῆς διακονίας τῆς
'Concerning 'indeed 'for the ministry -

εἰς τοὺς ἁγίους περισσόν μοί ἐστιν τὸ
to the saints 'superfluous 'for me 'it is -

γράφειν ὑμῖν· 2 οἶδα γὰρ τὴν προθυμίαν
to write to you; for I know the eagerness

ὑμῶν ἣν ὑπὲρ ὑμῶν καυχῶμαι Μακε-
of you which on behalf of you I boast to Mace-

δόσιν ὅτι Ἀχαΐα παρεσκεύασται ἀπὸ
donians that Achaia has made preparations from

πέρυσι, καὶ τὸ ὑμῶν ζῆλος ἠρέθισεν
last year, and the 'of you 'zeal stirred up
=a year ago,

τοὺς πλείονας. 3 ἔπεμψα δὲ τοὺς ἀδελφούς,
the greater number. And I sent the brothers,

ἵνα μὴ τὸ καύχημα ἡμῶν τὸ ὑπὲρ
lest the boast of us - on behalf

ὑμῶν κενωθῇ ἐν τῷ μέρει τούτῳ, ἵνα
of you should be in this respect, in order
emptied that

καθὼς ἔλεγον παρεσκευασμένοι ἦτε, 4 μή
as I said having been prepared ye were,

πως ἐὰν ἔλθωσιν σὺν ἐμοὶ Μακεδόνες
lest if 'come 'with 'me 'Macedonians

καὶ εὕρωσιν ὑμᾶς ἀπαρασκευάστους
and find you unprepared

καταισχυνθῶμεν ἡμεῖς, ἵνα μὴ λέγωμεν
'should be shamed 'we, in order we say not
that

ὑμεῖς, ἐν τῇ ὑποστάσει ταύτῃ. 5 ἀναγκαῖον
ye, in this confidence. 'Necessary

οὖν ἡγησάμην παρακαλέσαι τοὺς ἀδελφοὺς
'there- 'I thought [it] to beseech the brothers
fore

ἵνα προέλθωσιν εἰς ὑμᾶς καὶ προκαταρτί-
in order they go to you and arrange before-
that forward

σωσιν τὴν προεπηγγελμένην εὐλογίαν ὑμῶν,
hand 'the 'having been promised 'blessing 'of you,

ταύτην ἑτοίμην εἶναι οὕτως ὡς εὐλογίαν
this ready to be thus as a blessing

καὶ μὴ ὡς πλεονεξίαν. 6 Τοῦτο δέ,
and not as greediness. And this,

ὁ σπείρων φειδομένως φειδομένως καὶ
the [one] sowing sparingly 'sparingly 'also

θερίσει, καὶ ὁ σπείρων ἐπ' εὐλογίαις ἐπ'
'will reap, and the [one] sowing on(for) blessings 'on(for)

εὐλογίαις καὶ θερίσει. 7 ἕκαστος καθὼς
'blessings 'also 'will reap. Each one as

προῄρηται τῇ καρδίᾳ, μὴ ἐκ λύπης ἢ
he chose in the(his) heart, not of grief or

ἐξ ἀνάγκης· ἱλαρὸν γὰρ δότην ἀγαπᾷ ὁ
of necessity; for 'a cheerful 'giver 'loves -

θεός. 8 δυνατεῖ δὲ ὁ θεὸς πᾶσαν χάριν
'God. And 'is able - 'God 'all 'grace

περισσεῦσαι εἰς ὑμᾶς, ἵνα ἐν παντὶ
'to cause to abound toward you, in order that 'in 'everything

πάντοτε πᾶσαν αὐτάρκειαν ἔχοντες περισ-
'always 'all 'self-sufficiency 'having ye may

σεύητε εἰς πᾶν ἔργον ἀγαθόν, 9 καθὼς
abound to every work good, as

γέγραπται· ἐσκόρπισεν, ἔδωκεν τοῖς πένησιν,
it has been written: He scattered, he gave to the poor,

ἡ δικαιοσύνη αὐτοῦ μένει εἰς τὸν αἰῶνα.
the righteousness of him remains unto the age.

10 ὁ δὲ ἐπιχορηγῶν σπέρμα τῷ σπείροντι
Now the [one] providing seed for the [one] sowing

καὶ ἄρτον εἰς βρῶσιν χορηγήσει καὶ
'both 'bread 'for 'food 'will supply and

πληθυνεῖ τὸν σπόρον ὑμῶν καὶ αὐξήσει
will multiply the seed of you and will increase

τὰ γενήματα τῆς δικαιοσύνης ὑμῶν· 11 ἐν
the fruits of the righteousness of you; in

παντὶ πλουτιζόμενοι εἰς πᾶσαν ἁπλότητα,
everything being enriched to all liberality,

ἥτις κατεργάζεται δι' ἡμῶν εὐχαριστίαν
which works out through us thanksgiving

τῷ θεῷ· 12 ὅτι ἡ διακονία τῆς λειτουργίας
- to God; because the ministry - service

ταύτης οὐ μόνον ἐστὶν προσαναπληροῦσα
of this not only is making up

τὰ ὑστερήματα τῶν ἁγίων, ἀλλὰ καὶ
the things lacking of the saints, but [is] also

περισσεύουσα διὰ πολλῶν εὐχαριστιῶν τῷ
abounding through many thanksgivings -

θεῷ· 13 διὰ τῆς δοκιμῆς τῆς διακονίας
to God; through the proof - ministry

ταύτης δοξάζοντες τὸν θεὸν ἐπὶ τῇ
of this glorifying - God on the

ὑποταγῇ τῆς ὁμολογίας ὑμῶν εἰς τὸ
submission of the confession of you to the

εὐαγγέλιον τοῦ Χριστοῦ καὶ ἁπλότητι
gospel - of Christ and [on the] liberality

τῆς κοινωνίας εἰς αὐτοὺς καὶ εἰς πάντας,
of the fellowship toward them and toward all men,

14 καὶ αὐτῶν δεήσει ὑπὲρ ὑμῶν ἐπιποθούν-
and 'them 'with 'on be- 'you 'longing
request half of

των ὑμᾶς διὰ τὴν ὑπερβάλλουσαν χάριν
after' 'you on account the excelling grace
of

τοῦ θεοῦ ἐφ' ὑμῖν. 15 Χάρις τῷ θεῷ
- of God upon you. Thanks - to God

ἐπὶ τῇ ἀνεκδιηγήτῳ αὐτοῦ δωρεᾷ.
for the indescribable of him gift.

Chapter 10

Αὐτὸς δὲ ἐγὼ Παῦλος παρακαλῶ
[my]self Now I Paul beseech

ὑμᾶς διὰ τῆς πραΰτητος καὶ ἐπιεικείας
you through the meekness and forbearance

τοῦ Χριστοῦ, ὃς κατὰ πρόσωπον μὲν
- of Christ, who according to face indeed

ταπεινὸς ἐν ὑμῖν, ἀπὼν δὲ θαρρῶ εἰς
[am] humble among you, but being absent am bold toward

ὑμᾶς· 2 δέομαι δὲ τὸ μὴ παρὼν θαρρῆσαι
you: now I request - not being present to be bold

τῇ πεποιθήσει ᾗ λογίζομαι τολμῆσαι ἐπί
in the confidence which I reckon to be daring toward

τινας τοὺς λογιζομένους ἡμᾶς ὡς κατὰ
some the [ones] reckoning us as 'according to

σάρκα περιπατοῦντας. 3 Ἐν σαρκὶ γὰρ
'flesh 'walking. in flesh For

περιπατοῦντες οὐ κατὰ σάρκα στρατευόμεθα,
walking not accord- flesh we war,
ing to

4 τὰ γὰρ ὅπλα τῆς στρατείας ἡμῶν
for the weapons of the warfare of us [are]

οὐ σαρκικὰ ἀλλὰ δυνατὰ τῷ θεῷ πρὸς
not fleshly but powerful - to God to

καθαίρεσιν ὀχυρωμάτων, λογισμοὺς καθαιροῦν-
overthrow of strongholds, 'reasonings 'overthrow-

τες 5 καὶ πᾶν ὕψωμα ἐπαιρόμενον κατὰ
ing and every high thing rising up against

τῆς γνώσεως τοῦ θεοῦ, καὶ αἰχμαλωτίζοντες
the knowledge - of God, and taking captive

knowledge of God, and bringing into captivity every thought to the obedience of Christ; 6 And having in a readiness to revenge all disobedience, when your obedience is fulfilled. 7 Do ye look on things after the outward appearance? If any man trust to himself that he is Christ's, let him of himself think this again, that, as he *is* Christ's, even so *are* we Christ's. 8 For though I should boast somewhat more of our authority, which the Lord hath given us for edification, and not for your destruction, I should not be ashamed: 9 That I may not seem as if I would terrify you by letters. 10 For *his* letters, say they, *are* weighty and powerful; but *his* bodily presence *is* weak, and *his* speech contemptible. 11 Let such a one think this, that, such as we are in word by letters when we are absent, such *will we* be also in deed when we are present. 12 For we dare not make ourselves of the number, or compare ourselves with some that commend themselves: but they, measuring themselves by themselves, and comparing themselves among themselves, are not wise. 13 But we will not boast of things without *our* measure, but according to the measure of the rule which God hath distributed to us, a measure to reach even unto you. 14 For we stretch not ourselves beyond *our* measure, as though we reached not unto you; for we are come as far as to you also in *preaching* the gospel of Christ: 15 Not boasting of things without *our* measure, *that is,* of other men's labours; but having hope, when your faith is increased, that we shall be enlarged by you according to our rule abundantly, 16 To preach the gospel in the *regions* beyond you, *and* not to boast in another man's line of things made ready to our hand. 17 But he that glorieth, let him glory in the Lord. 18 For not he that commendeth himself is approved, but whom the Lord commendeth.

11 Would to God ye could bear with me a little in *my* folly: and indeed bear with me. 2 For I am jealous over you with godly jealousy: for I have espoused you to one husband, that I may present *you as* a chaste virgin to Christ. 3 But I fear, lest by any means, as the serpent beguiled Eve through his subtilty, so your minds should be corrupted from the simplicity that is in Christ. 4 For if he that cometh preacheth another Jesus, whom we have not preached, or *if* ye receive another spirit, which ye have not received, or another gospel, which ye have not accepted, ye might well bear with *him.* 5 For I suppose I was not a whit behind the very chiefest apostles. 6 But though *I be* rude in speech, yet not in knowledge; but we have been thoroughly

and we take captive every thought to make it obedient to Christ. 6 And we will be ready to punish every act of disobedience, once your obedience is complete.

7 You are looking only on the surface of things.[p] If anyone is confident that he belongs to Christ, he should consider again that we belong to Christ just as much as he. 8 For even if I boast somewhat freely about the authority the Lord gave us for building you up rather than pulling you down, I will not be ashamed of it. 9 I do not want to seem to be trying to frighten you with my letters. 10 For some say, "His letters are weighty and forceful, but in person he is unimpressive and his speaking amounts to nothing." 11 Such people should realize that what we are in our letters when we are absent, we will be in our actions when we are present. 12 We do not dare to classify or compare ourselves with some who commend themselves. When they measure themselves by themselves and compare themselves with themselves, they are not wise. 13 We, however, will not boast beyond proper limits, but will confine our boasting to the field God has assigned to us, a field that reaches even to you. 14 We are not going too far in our boasting, as would be the case if we had not come to you, for we did get as far as you with the gospel of Christ. 15 Neither do we go beyond our limits by boasting of work done by others.[q] Our hope is that, as your faith continues to grow, our area of activity among you will greatly expand, 16 so that we can preach the gospel in the regions beyond you. For we do not want to boast about work already done in another man's territory. 17 But, "Let him who boasts, boast in the Lord."[r] 18 For it is not the man who commends himself who is approved, but the man whom the Lord commends.

Paul and the false apostles

11 I hope you will put up with a little of my foolishness; but you are already doing that. 2 I am jealous for you with a godly jealousy. I promised you to one husband, to Christ, so that I might present you as a pure virgin to him. 3 But I am afraid that just as Eve was deceived by the serpent's cunning, your minds may somehow be led astray from your sincere and pure devotion to Christ. 4 For if someone comes to you and preaches a Jesus other than the Jesus we preached, or if you receive a different spirit from the one you received, or a different gospel from the one you accepted, you put up with it easily enough. 5 But I do not think I am in the least inferior to those "super-apostles." 6 I may not be a trained speaker, but I do have knowledge. We have made this perfectly clear to you in every way.

[p] Or *Look at the obvious facts.* [q] Or 13 *We, however, will not boast about things that cannot be measured, but we will boast according to the standard of measurement that the God of measure has assigned us-a measurement that relates even to you.* 14 . . . . 15 *Neither do we boast about things that cannot be measured in regard to the work done by others.* [r] Jer. 9:24.

Greek Interlinear

πᾶν νόημα εἰς τὴν ὑπακοὴν τοῦ Χριστοῦ,
every design to the obedience - of Christ,

6 καὶ ἐν ἑτοίμῳ ἔχοντες ἐκδικῆσαι πᾶσαν
and in readiness having to avenge all
= being ready

παρακοήν, ὅταν πληρωθῇ ὑμῶν ἡ ὑπακοή.
disobedience, whenever ⁴is fulfilled ²of you ¹the ³obedience.

7 Τὰ κατὰ πρόσωπον βλέπετε. εἴ τις
¹The ²according ⁴face ³ye look [at]. If any-
things to (appearance) one

πέποιθεν ἑαυτῷ Χριστοῦ εἶναι, τοῦτο
has persuaded himself ²of Christ ¹to be, this

λογιζέσθω πάλιν ἐφ' ἑαυτοῦ, ὅτι καθὼς
let him reckon again as to himself, that as

αὐτὸς Χριστοῦ, οὕτως καὶ ἡμεῖς. 8 ἐάν
he [is] of Christ, so also [are] we. ²if

τε γὰρ περισσότερόν τι καυχήσωμαι περὶ
³even ¹For ²more abundantly ⁵some- ⁴I should boast concern-
what ing

τῆς ἐξουσίας ἡμῶν, ἧς ἔδωκεν ὁ κύριος
the authority of us, which ²gave ¹the ²Lord

εἰς οἰκοδομὴν καὶ οὐκ εἰς καθαίρεσιν
for edification and not for overthrow

ὑμῶν, οὐκ αἰσχυνθήσομαι, 9 ἵνα μὴ δόξω
of you, I shall not be shamed, in order that I may not seem

ὡσὰν ἐκφοβεῖν ὑμᾶς διὰ τῶν ἐπιστολῶν.
as though to frighten you through the epistles.

10 ὅτι αἱ ἐπιστολαὶ μέν, φησίν, βαρεῖαι
Because the(his) epistles indeed, he says, [are] weighty

καὶ ἰσχυραί, ἡ δὲ παρουσία τοῦ σώματος
and strong, but the presence of the(his) body [is]

ἀσθενὴς καὶ ὁ λόγος ἐξουθενημένος.
weak and the(his) speech *being* despised.

11 τοῦτο λογιζέσθω ὁ τοιοῦτος, ὅτι οἷοί
This let reckon such a one, that such as

ἐσμεν τῷ λόγῳ δι' ἐπιστολῶν ἀπόντες,
we are in word through epistles being absent,

τοιοῦτοι καὶ παρόντες τῷ ἔργῳ. 12 Οὐ
such also being present - in work. ²not

γὰρ τολμῶμεν ἐγκρῖναι ἢ συγκρῖναι
¹For ³we dare to class with or to compare

ἑαυτούς τισιν τῶν ἑαυτοὺς συνιστανόντων·
ourselves with some of the ²themselves ¹commending;
[ones]

ἀλλὰ αὐτοὶ ἐν ἑαυτοῖς ἑαυτοὺς μετροῦντες
but they ²among ⁴them- ³them- ¹measuring
selves selves

καὶ συγκρίνοντες ἑαυτοὺς ἑαυτοῖς οὐ
and comparing themselves with themselves not

συνιᾶσιν. 13 ἡμεῖς δὲ οὐκ εἰς τὰ ἄμετρα
do understand. But we ²not ¹immeasurably†

καυχησόμεθα, ἀλλὰ κατὰ τὸ μέτρον τοῦ
¹will ³boast, but according to the measure of the

κανόνος οὗ ἐμέρισεν ἡμῖν ὁ θεὸς μέτρου,
rule which ³divided ²to us - ¹God of(in) measure,

ἐφικέσθαι ἄχρι καὶ ὑμῶν. 14 οὐ γὰρ
to reach as far as even you. For not

ὡς μὴ ἐφικνούμενοι εἰς ὑμᾶς ὑπερεκτείνομεν
as not reaching to you do we overstretch

ἑαυτούς, ἄχρι γὰρ καὶ ὑμῶν ἐφθάσαμεν
ourselves, for as far as even you we came

ἐν τῷ εὐαγγελίῳ τοῦ Χριστοῦ, 15 οὐκ
in the gospel - of Christ, not

εἰς τὰ ἄμετρα καυχώμενοι ἐν ἀλλοτρίοις
immeasurably† boasting in others']

κόποις, ἐλπίδα δὲ ἔχοντες αὐξανομένης
labours, but ²hope ¹having growing
= as your faith grows

τῆς πίστεως ὑμῶν ἐν ὑμῖν μεγαλυνθῆναι
the faith of youˢ ²among ³you ¹to be magnified

κατὰ τὸν κανόνα ἡμῶν· εἰς περισσείαν,
according the rule of us in abundance,
to

16 εἰς τὰ ὑπερέκεινα ὑμῶν εὐαγγελίσασθαι,
in the [parts] beyond you to preach good tidings,

οὐκ ἐν ἀλλοτρίῳ κανόνι εἰς τὰ ἕτοιμα
not ²in ³another's† ⁴rule ⁵in - ⁶things ready

καυχήσασθαι. 17 Ὁ δὲ καυχώμενος ἐν
¹to boast. But the [one] boasting ²in

κυρίῳ καυχάσθω· 18 οὐ γὰρ ὁ ἑαυτὸν
²[the] Lord ¹let him boast. for not the [one] himself

συνιστάνων, ἐκεῖνός ἐστιν δόκιμος, ἀλλὰ
commending, that one is approved, but

ὃν ὁ κύριος συνίστησιν.
whom the Lord commends.

Chapter 11

Ὄφελον ἀνείχεσθέ μου μικρόν τι
I would that ye endured me a little [bit]

ἀφροσύνης· ἀλλὰ καὶ ἀνέχεσθέ μου.
of foolishness; but indeed ye do endure me.

2 ζηλῶ γὰρ ὑμᾶς θεοῦ ζήλῳ, ἡρμοσάμην
For I am jealous [of] you ²of God ¹with a ¹I betrothed
jealousy,

γὰρ ὑμᾶς ἑνὶ ἀνδρὶ παρθένον ἁγνὴν
²for you to one husband ²virgin ¹a pure

παραστῆσαι τῷ Χριστῷ· 3 φοβοῦμαι δὲ
¹to present - to Christ; and I fear

μή πως, ὡς ὁ ὄφις ἐξηπάτησεν Εὔαν
lest somehow, as the serpent deceived Eve

ἐν τῇ πανουργίᾳ αὐτοῦ, φθαρῇ τὰ νοήματα
by the cleverness of him, ⁴should ¹the ³thoughts
be seduced

ὑμῶν ἀπὸ τῆς ἁπλότητος [καὶ τῆς
²of you from the simplicity [and the

ἁγνότητος] τῆς εἰς Χριστόν. 4 εἰ μὲν
purity] - in Christ. ²if ³indeed

γὰρ ὁ ἐρχόμενος ἄλλον Ἰησοῦν κηρύσσει
¹For the [one] coming ²another ³Jesus ¹proclaims

ὃν οὐκ ἐκηρύξαμεν, ἢ πνεῦμα ἕτερον
whom we did not proclaim, or ²spirit ¹a different

λαμβάνετε ὃ οὐκ ἐλάβετε, ἢ εὐαγγέλιον
¹ye receive which ye did not receive, or ¹gospel

ἕτερον ὃ οὐκ ἐδέξασθε, καλῶς ἀνέχεσθε.
¹a different which ye did not receive, ²[him] ¹well ye endure.

5 λογίζομαι γὰρ μηδὲν ὑστερηκέναι τῶν
For I reckon nothing to have come behind of the

ὑπερλίαν ἀποστόλων. 6 εἰ δὲ καὶ ἰδιώτης
super- apostles. But if indeed unskilled
[I am]

τῷ λόγῳ, ἀλλ' οὐ τῇ γνώσει, ἀλλ' ἐν
- in speech, yet not - in knowledge, but in

παντὶ φανερώσαντες ἐν πᾶσιν εἰς ὑμᾶς.
every having manifested in all things to you.
[way] [ourselves]

King James Version

made manifest among you in all things. 7 Have I committed an offence in abasing myself that ye might be exalted, because I have preached to you the gospel of God freely? 8 I robbed other churches, taking wages *of them*, to do you service. 9And when I was present with you, and wanted, I was chargeable to no man: for that which was lacking to me the brethren which came from Macedonia supplied: and in all *things* I have kept myself from being burdensome unto you, and *so* will I keep *myself*. 10As the truth of Christ is in me, no man shall stop me of this boasting in the regions of Achaia. 11 Wherefore? because I love you not? God knoweth. 12 But what I do, that I will do, that I may cut off occasion from them which desire occasion; that wherein they glory, they may be found even as we. 13 For such *are* false apostles, deceitful workers, transforming themselves into the apostles of Christ. 14And no marvel; for Satan himself is transformed into an angel of light. 15 Therefore *it is* no great thing if his ministers also be transformed as the ministers of righteousness; whose end shall be according to their works. 16 I say again, Let no man think me a fool; if otherwise, yet as a fool receive me, that I may boast myself a little. 17 That which I speak, I speak *it* not after the Lord, but as it were foolishly, in this confidence of boasting. 18 Seeing that many glory after the flesh, I will glory also. 19 For ye suffer fools gladly, seeing ye *yourselves* are wise. 20 For ye suffer, if a man bring you into bondage, if a man devour *you*, if a man take *of you*, if a man exalt himself, if a man smite you on the face. 21 I speak as concerning reproach, as though we had been weak. Howbeit, whereinsoever any is bold, (I speak foolishly,) I am bold also. 22Are they Hebrews? so *am* I. Are they Israelites? so *am* I. Are they the seed of Abraham? so *am* I. 23Are they ministers of Christ? (I speak as a fool,) I *am* more; in labours more abundant, in stripes above measure, in prisons more frequent, in deaths oft. 24 Of the Jews five times received I forty *stripes* save one. 25 Thrice was I beaten with rods, once was I stoned, thrice I suffered shipwreck, a night and a day I have been in the deep; 26 In journeyings often, *in* perils of waters, *in* perils of robbers, *in* perils by *mine own* countrymen, *in* perils by the heathen, *in* perils in the city, *in* perils in the wilderness, *in* perils in the sea, *in* perils among false brethren; 27 In weariness and painfulness, in watchings often, in hunger and thirst, in fastings often, in cold and nakedness. 28 Beside those things that are without, that which cometh upon me daily, the care of all the churches. 29 Who is weak, and I am not weak? who is offended, and I burn not? 30 If I must needs glory, I will glory of the things which concern mine infirmities. 31 The God and Father of our Lord Jesus Christ, which is blessed for evermore, knoweth that I lie not. 32 In Damascus

New International Version

7 Was it a sin for me to lower myself in order to elevate you by preaching the gospel of God to you free of charge? 8 I robbed other churches by receiving support from them so as to serve you. 9And when I was with you and needed something, I was not a burden to anyone, for the brothers who came from Macedonia supplied what I needed. I have kept myself from being a burden to you in any way, and will continue to do so. 10As surely as the truth of Christ is in me, nobody in the regions of Achaia will stop this boasting of mine. 11 Why? Because I do not love you? God knows I do! 12And I will keep on doing what I am doing in order to cut the ground from under those who want an opportunity to be considered equal with us in the things they boast about.

13 For such men are false apostles, deceitful workmen, masquerading as apostles of Christ. 14And no wonder, for Satan himself masquerades as an angel of light. 15 It is not surprising, then, if his servants masquerade as servants of righteousness. Their end will be what their actions deserve.

Paul boasts about his sufferings

16 I repeat: Let no one take me for a fool. But if you do, then receive me just as you would a fool, so that I may do a little boasting. 17 In this self-confident boasting I am not talking as the Lord would, but as a fool. 18 Since many are boasting in the way the world does, I too will boast. 19 You gladly put up with fools since you are so wise! 20 In fact, you even put up with anyone who enslaves you or exploits you or takes advantage of you or pushes himself forward or slaps you in the face. 21 To my shame I admit that we were too weak for that!

What anyone else dares to boast about—I am speaking as a fool—I also dare to boast about. 22Are they Hebrews? So am I. Are they Israelites? So am I. Are they Abraham's descendants? So am I. 23Are they servants of Christ? (I am out of my mind to talk like this.) I am more. I have worked much harder, been in prison more frequently, been flogged more severely, and been exposed to death again and again. 24 Five times I received from the Jews the forty lashes minus one. 25 Three times I was beaten with rods, once I was stoned, three times I was shipwrecked, I spent a night and a day in the open sea, 26 I have been constantly on the move. I have been in danger from rivers, in danger from bandits, in danger from my own countrymen, in danger from Gentiles; in danger in the city, in danger in the country, in danger at sea; and in danger from false brothers. 27 I have labored and toiled and have often gone without sleep; I have known hunger and thirst and have often gone without food; I have been cold and naked. 28 Besides everything else, I face daily the pressure of my concern for all the churches. 29 Who is weak, and I do not feel weak? Who is led into sin, and I do not inwardly burn?

30 If I must boast, I will boast of the things that show my weakness. 31 The God and Father of the Lord Jesus, who is to be praised forever, knows that I am not lying. 32 In Damascus

Greek Interlinear

7 Ἢ ἁμαρτίαν ἐποίησα ἐμαυτὸν ταπεινῶν
Or ²sin ¹did I commit ⁴myself ³humbling

ἵνα ὑμεῖς ὑψωθῆτε, ὅτι δωρεὰν τὸ τοῦ
in order ye might be because ⁵freely ³the –
that exalted,

θεοῦ εὐαγγέλιον εὐηγγελισάμην ὑμῖν;
⁴of God ⁵gospel ¹I preached *good tidings* to you?

8 ἄλλας ἐκκλησίας ἐσύλησα λαβὼν ὀψώνιον
Other churches I robbed taking wages

πρὸς τὴν ὑμῶν διακονίαν, 9 καὶ παρὼν
for ¹the ³of you ²ministry, and being present

πρὸς ὑμᾶς καὶ ὑστερηθεὶς οὐ κατενάρκησα
with you and lacking I was *not* an encumbrance

οὐθενός· τὸ γὰρ ὑστέρημά μου προσανε-
of no man; for the lack of me ²made

πλήρωσαν οἱ ἀδελφοὶ ἐλθόντες ἀπὸ Μακε-
up ¹the ³brothers ⁴coming ⁵from ⁶Mace-

δονίας· καὶ ἐν παντὶ ἀβαρῆ ἐμαυτὸν
donia; and in every [way] ²unburdensome ¹myself

ὑμῖν ἐτήρησα καὶ τηρήσω. 10 ἔστιν
⁴to you ¹I kept and I will keep. ²is

ἀλήθεια Χριστοῦ ἐν ἐμοί, ὅτι ἡ καύχησις
¹[The] truth ²of Christ in me, that the boasting

αὕτη οὐ φραγήσεται εἰς ἐμὲ ἐν τοῖς
this shall not be stopped in me in the

κλίμασιν τῆς Ἀχαΐας. 11 διὰ τί; ὅτι
regions – of Achaia. Why? because

οὐκ ἀγαπῶ ὑμᾶς; ὁ θεὸς οἶδεν. 12 Ὃ
I love not you? – God knows. what

δὲ ποιῶ, καὶ ποιήσω, ἵνα ἐκκόψω τὴν
But I do, also I will do, in order I may cut the
that off

ἀφορμὴν τῶν θελόντων ἀφορμήν, ἵνα ἐν
occasion of the desiring an occasion, in or- where-
[ones] der that

ᾧ καυχῶνται εὑρεθῶσιν καθὼς καὶ ἡμεῖς.
in they boast they may be found as also we.

13 οἱ γὰρ τοιοῦτοι ψευδαπόστολοι, ἐργάται
– For such [are] false apostles, ²workmen

δόλιοι, μετασχηματιζόμενοι εἰς ἀποστόλους
¹deceitful, transforming themselves into apostles

Χριστοῦ. 14 καὶ οὐ θαῦμα· αὐτὸς γὰρ
of Christ. And no wonder; ²[him]self ¹for

ὁ σατανᾶς μετασχηματίζεται εἰς ἄγγελον
– ²Satan transforms himself into an angel

φωτός. 15 οὐ μέγα οὖν εἰ καὶ οἱ
of light. No great thing therefore if also the

διάκονοι αὐτοῦ μετασχηματίζονται ὡς
ministers of him transform themselves as

διάκονοι δικαιοσύνης· ὧν τὸ τέλος ἔσται
ministers of righteousness; of whom the end will be

κατὰ τὰ ἔργα αὐτῶν.
according to the works of them.

16 Πάλιν λέγω, μή τίς με δόξῃ ἄφρονα
Again I say, ³not ¹anyone ⁴me ²think ⁵foolish

εἶναι· εἰ δὲ μή γε, κἂν ὡς ἄφρονα
⁶to be; otherwise, even if as foolish

δέξασθέ με, ἵνα κἀγὼ μικρόν τι καυχήσω-
receive ye me, in order I also a little [bit] may
that

μαι. 17 ὃ λαλῶ, οὐ κατὰ κύριον λαλῶ,
boast. What I speak, not according to [the] Lord I speak,
to

ἀλλ’ ὡς ἐν ἀφροσύνῃ, ἐν ταύτῃ τῇ
but as in folly, in this the

ὑποστάσει τῆς καυχήσεως. 18 ἐπεὶ πολλοὶ
confidence – of boasting. Since many

καυχῶνται κατὰ [τὴν] σάρκα, κἀγὼ
boast according to the flesh, I also

καυχήσομαι. 19 ἡδέως γὰρ ἀνέχεσθε τῶν
will boast. For gladly ye endure –

ἀφρόνων φρόνιμοι ὄντες· 20 ἀνέχεσθε γὰρ
fools ¹prudent ²being; for ye endure

εἴ τις ὑμᾶς καταδουλοῖ, εἴ τις κατεσθίει,
if anyone ²you ¹enslaves, if anyone devours [you],

εἴ τις λαμβάνει, εἴ τις ἐπαίρεται, εἴ
if anyone receives [you],* if anyone lifts himself up, if

τις εἰς πρόσωπον ὑμᾶς δέρει. 21 κατὰ
anyone ²in ³[the] face ⁴you ¹beats(hits). According to

ἀτιμίαν λέγω, ὡς ὅτι ἡμεῖς ἠσθενήκαμεν·
dishonour I say, as that we have been weak;

ἐν ᾧ δ’ ἄν τις τολμᾷ, ἐν ἀφροσύνῃ
but in whatever [respect] anyone dares, in folly

λέγω, τολμῶ κἀγώ. 22 Ἑβραῖοί εἰσιν;
I say, ²dare ¹I ³also. Hebrews are they?

κἀγώ. Ἰσραηλῖταί εἰσιν; κἀγώ. σπέρμα
I also. Israelites are they? I also. Seed

Ἀβραάμ εἰσιν; κἀγώ. 23 διάκονοι Χριστοῦ
of Abraham are they? I also. Ministers of Christ

εἰσιν; παραφρονῶν λαλῶ, ὑπὲρ ἐγώ· ἐν
are they? being out of I speak, ²beyond ¹I: in
my mind (more)

κόποις περισσοτέρως, ἐν φυλακαῖς περισ-
labours more abundantly, in prisons more

σοτέρως, ἐν πληγαῖς ὑπερβαλλόντως, ἐν
abundantly, in stripes excessively, in

θανάτοις πολλάκις. 24 ὑπὸ Ἰουδαίων
deaths many times. By Jews

πεντάκις τεσσεράκοντα παρὰ μίαν ἔλαβον,
five times forty [stripes] less one I received,

25 τρὶς ἐρραβδίσθην, ἅπαξ ἐλιθάσθην, τρὶς
thrice I was beaten with rods, once I was stoned, thrice

ἐναυάγησα, 26 νυχθήμερον ἐν τῷ βυθῷ
I was shipwrecked, a night and a day in the deep

πεποίηκα· ὁδοιπορίαις πολλάκις, κινδύνοις
I have done(been); in travels many times, in perils

ποταμῶν, κινδύνοις λῃστῶν, κινδύνοις ἐκ
of rivers, in perils of robbers, in perils of

γένους, κινδύνοις ἐξ ἐθνῶν, κινδύνοις ἐν
[my] kind, in perils of nations, in perils in

πόλει, κινδύνοις ἐν ἐρημίᾳ, κινδύνοις ἐν(at)
a city, in perils in a desert, in perils in(at)

θαλάσσῃ, κινδύνοις ἐν ψευδαδέλφοις, 27 κόπῳ
sea, in perils among false brothers, in labour

καὶ μόχθῳ, ἐν ἀγρυπνίαις πολλάκις, ἐν
and hardship, in watchings many times, in

λιμῷ καὶ δίψει, ἐν νηστείαις πολλάκις,
famine and thirst, in fastings many times,

ἐν ψύχει καὶ γυμνότητι· 28 χωρὶς τῶν
in cold and nakedness; apart from the things

παρεκτὸς ἡ ἐπίστασίς μοι ἡ καθ’ ἡμέραν,
without[.] the conspiring me – daily,
against

ἡ μέριμνα πασῶν τῶν ἐκκλησιῶν. 29 τίς
the care of all the churches. Who

ἀσθενεῖ, καὶ οὐκ ἀσθενῶ; τίς σκανδαλίζεται,
is weak, and I am not weak? who is offended,

καὶ οὐκ ἐγὼ πυροῦμαι; 30 εἰ καυχᾶσθαι
and ²not ¹I ³burn? If to boast

δεῖ, τὰ τῆς ἀσθενείας μου καυχήσομαι.
it be- the of the weakness of me I will boast.
hoves things
[me],

31 ὁ θεὸς καὶ πατὴρ τοῦ κυρίου Ἰησοῦ
The God and Father of the Lord Jesus

οἶδεν, ὁ ὢν εὐλογητὸς εἰς τοὺς αἰῶνας,
knows, the being blessed unto the ages,
[one]

ὅτι οὐ ψεύδομαι. 32 ἐν Δαμασκῷ ὁ
that I am not lying. In Damascus the

* ? takes [you in].

543

King James Version

the governor under Aretas the king kept the city of the Damascenes with a garrison, desirous to apprehend me: 33And through a window in a basket was I let down by the wall, and escaped his hands.

12 It is not expedient for me doubtless to glory. I will come to visions and revelations of the Lord. 2 I knew a man in Christ above fourteen years ago, (whether in the body, I cannot tell; or whether out of the body, I cannot tell: God knoweth;) such a one caught up to the third heaven. 3And I knew such a man, (whether in the body, or out of the body, I cannot tell: God knoweth;) 4 How that he was caught up into paradise, and heard unspeakable words, which it is not lawful for a man to utter. 5 Of such a one will I glory: yet of myself I will not glory, but in mine infirmities. 6 For though I would desire to glory, I shall not be a fool; for I will say the truth: but now I forbear, lest any man should think of me above that which he seeth me to be, or that he heareth of me. 7And lest I should be exalted above measure through the abundance of the revelations, there was given to me a thorn in the flesh, the messenger of Satan to buffet me, lest I should be exalted above measure. 8 For this thing I besought the Lord thrice, that it might depart from me. 9And he said unto me, My grace is sufficient for thee: for my strength is made perfect in weakness. Most gladly therefore will I rather glory in my infirmities, that the power of Christ may rest upon me. 10 Therefore I take pleasure in infirmities, in reproaches, in necessities, in persecutions, in distresses for Christ's sake: for when I am weak, then am I strong. 11 I am become a fool in glorying; ye have compelled me: for I ought to have been commended of you: for in nothing am I behind the very chiefest apostles, though I be nothing. 12 Truly the signs of an apostle were wrought among you in all patience, in signs, and wonders, and mighty deeds. 13 For what is it wherein ye were inferior to other churches, except it be that I myself was not burdensome to you? forgive me this wrong. 14 Behold, the third time I am ready to come to you; and I will not be burdensome to you: for I seek not yours, but you: for the children ought not to lay up for the parents, but the parents for the children. 15And I will very gladly spend and be spent for you; though the more abundantly I love you, the less I be loved. 16 But be it so, I did not burden you: nevertheless, being crafty, I caught you with guile. 17 Did I make a gain of you by any of them whom I sent unto you? 18 I desired Titus, and with him I sent a brother. Did Titus make a gain of you? walked we not in the same spirit? walked we not in the same

New International Version

the governor under King Aretas had the city of the Damascenes guarded in order to arrest me. 33 But I was lowered in a basket from a window in the wall and slipped through his hands.

Paul's vision and his thorn

12 I must go on boasting. Although there is nothing to be gained, I will go on to visions and revelations from the Lord. 2 I know a man in Christ who fourteen years ago was caught up to the third heaven. Whether it was in the body or out of the body I do not know—God knows. 3And I know that this man—whether in the body or apart from the body I do not know, but God knows—4 was caught up to Paradise. He heard inexpressible things, things that man is not permitted to tell. 5 I will boast about a man like that, but I will not boast about myself, except about my weaknesses. 6 Even if I should choose to boast, I would not be a fool, because I would be speaking the truth. But I refrain, so no one will think more of me than is warranted by what I do or say.

7 To keep me from becoming conceited because of these surpassingly great revelations, there was given me a thorn in my flesh, a messenger of Satan, to torment me. 8 Three times I pleaded with the Lord to take it away from me. 9 But he said to me, "My grace is sufficient for you, for my power is made perfect in weakness." Therefore, I will boast all the more gladly about my weaknesses, so that Christ's power may rest on me. 10 That is why, for Christ's sake, I delight in weaknesses, in insults, in hardships, in persecutions, in difficulties. For when I am weak, then I am strong.

Paul's concern for the Corinthians

11 I have made a fool of myself, but you drove me to it. I ought to have been commended by you, for I am not in the least inferior to the "super-apostles," even though I am nothing. 12 The things that mark an apostle—signs, wonders and miracles—were done among you with great perseverance. 13 How were you inferior to the other churches, except that I was never a burden to you? Forgive me this wrong! 14 Now I am ready to visit you for the third time, and I will not be a burden to you, because what I want is not your possessions but you. After all, children should not have to save up for their parents, but parents for their children. 15 So I will very gladly spend for you everything I have and expend myself as well. If I love you more, will you love me less? 16 Be that as it may, I have not been a burden to you. Yet, crafty fellow that I am, I caught you by trickery! 17 Did I exploit you through any of the men I sent you? 18 I urged Titus to go to you and I sent our brother with him. Titus did not exploit you, did he? Did we not act in the same spirit and follow the same course?

Greek Interlinear

ἐθνάρχης	Ἀρέτα	τοῦ	βασιλέως	ἐφρούρει
ethnarch	of Aretas	of the	king	guarded

τὴν	πόλιν	Δαμασκηνῶν	πιάσαι	με,	33 καὶ
the	city	of [the] Damascenes	to seize	me,	and

διὰ	θυρίδος	ἐν	σαργάνῃ	ἐχαλάσθην	διὰ
through a window	in	a basket	I was lowered through

τοῦ	τείχους	καὶ	ἐξέφυγον	τὰς	χεῖρας	αὐτοῦ.
the	wall	and	escaped	the	hands	of him.

Chapter 12

Καυχᾶσθαι δεῖ, οὐ συμφέρον μέν,
To boast it behoves not expedient indeed,
[me],

ἐλεύσομαι δὲ εἰς ὀπτασίας καὶ ἀποκαλύψεις
so I will come to visions and revelations

κυρίου. 2 οἶδα ἄνθρωπον ἐν Χριστῷ
of [the] Lord. I know a man in Christ

πρὸ ἐτῶν δεκατεσσάρων, — εἴτε ἐν
before years fourteen, (whether in

σώματι οὐκ οἶδα, εἴτε ἐκτὸς τοῦ σώματος
[the] body I know not, or outside the body

οὐκ οἶδα, ὁ θεὸς οἶδεν, — ἁρπαγέντα
I know not, - God knows,) - ¹caught

τὸν τοιοῦτον ἕως τρίτου οὐρανοῦ. 3 καὶ
- ¹such a one to [the] third heaven. And

οἶδα τὸν τοιοῦτον ἄνθρωπον — εἴτε
I know such a man (whether

ἐν σώματι εἴτε χωρὶς τοῦ σώματος
in [the] body or apart from the body

[οὐκ οἶδα], ὁ θεὸς οἶδεν, — 4 ὅτι
I know not, - God knows,) that

ἡρπάγη ε᾿ς τὸν παράδεισον καὶ ἤκουσεν
he was caught into the paradise and heard

ἄρρητα ῥήματα, ἃ οὐκ ἐξὸν ἀνθρώπῳ
unspeakable words, which it is not for a man
permissible

λαλῆσαι. 5 ὑπὲρ τοῦ τοιούτου καυχήσομαι,
to speak. On behalf of - such a one I will boast,

ὑπὲρ δὲ ἐμαυτοῦ οὐ καυχήσομαι εἰ
but on behalf of myself I will not boast ex-

μὴ ἐν ταῖς ἀσθενείαις. 6 ἐὰν γὰρ θελήσω
cept in the(my) weaknesses. For if I shall wish

καυχήσασθαι, οὐκ ἔσομαι ἄφρων, ἀλήθειαν
to boast, I shall not be foolish, ⁴truth

γὰρ ἐρῶ. φείδομαι δέ, μή τις εἰς ἐμὲ
¹for ²I will speak; but I spare, lest anyone to me

λογίσεται ὑπὲρ ὃ βλέπει με ἢ ἀκούει
reckons beyond what he sees me or hears

ἐξ ἐμοῦ 7 καὶ τῇ ὑπερβολῇ τῶν ἀποκα-
of me and by the excess of the revela-

λύψεων. διὸ ἵνα μὴ ὑπεραίρωμαι, ἐδόθη
tions. Where- lest I should be there was
fore exceedingly uplifted, given

μοι σκόλοψ τῇ σαρκί, ἄγγελος σατανᾶ,
to me a thorn in the flesh, a messenger of Satan,

ἵνα με κολαφίζῃ, ἵνα μὴ ὑπεραίρωμαι.
in order ²me ¹he might buffet, lest I should be
that exceedingly uplifted.

8 ὑπὲρ τούτου τρὶς τὸν κύριον παρεκάλεσα,
As to this thrice the Lord I besought,

ἵνα ἀποστῇ ἀπ᾿ ἐμοῦ. 9 καὶ εἴρηκέν
in or- it might from me. And he has said
der that depart

μοι· ἀρκεῖ σοι ἡ χάρις μου· ἡ γὰρ
to me· ⁴Suffices ⁵thee ¹the ²grace ³of me; for the(my)

δύναμις ἐν ἀσθενείᾳ τελεῖται. Ἥδιστα
power in weakness is perfected. Most gladly

οὖν μᾶλλον καυχήσομαι ἐν ταῖς ἀσθενείαις,
therefore rather I will boast in the(my) weaknesses,

ἵνα ἐπισκηνώσῃ ἐπ᾿ ἐμὲ ἡ δύναμις τοῦ
in order ²might over ⁴me ¹the ³power -
that overshadow

Χριστοῦ. 10 διὸ εὐδοκῶ ἐν ἀσθενείαις,
⁴of Christ. Wherefore I am well in weaknesses,
pleased

ἐν ὕβρεσιν, ἐν ἀνάγκαις, ἐν διωγμοῖς
in insults, in necessities, in persecutions

καὶ στενοχωρίαις, ὑπὲρ Χριστοῦ· ὅταν
and difficulties, on behalf of Christ; ¹whenever

γὰρ ἀσθενῶ, τότε δυνατός εἰμι.
¹for I am weak, then ²powerful ¹I am.

11 Γέγονα ἄφρων· ὑμεῖς με ἠναγκάσατε.
I have become foolish; ye me compelled.

ἐγὼ γὰρ ὤφειλον ὑφ᾿ ὑμῶν συνίστασθαι.
For I ought by you to be commended.

οὐδὲν γὰρ ὑστέρησα τῶν ὑπερλίαν
For nothing I lacked of the super-

ἀποστόλων, εἰ καὶ οὐδέν εἰμι. 12 τὰ
apostles, ³if ²even ¹nothing ²I am. ²The

μὲν σημεῖα τοῦ ἀποστόλου κατειργάσθη
¹indeed signs of the apostle were wrought

ἐν ὑμῖν ἐν πάσῃ ὑπομονῇ, σημείοις τε
among you in all endurance, ²by signs ¹both

καὶ τέρασιν καὶ δυνάμεσιν. 13 τί γὰρ
and by wonders and by powerful deeds. For what

ἐστιν ὃ ἡσσώθητε ὑπὲρ τὰς λοιπὰς
is it which ye were less than the remaining

ἐκκλησίας, εἰ μὴ ὅτι αὐτὸς ἐγὼ οὐ
churches, except that ²[my]self ¹I ¹not

κατενάρκησα ὑμῶν; χαρίσασθέ μοι τὴν
²encumbered ³of you? Forgive ye me -

ἀδικίαν ταύτην. 14 Ἰδοὺ τρίτον τοῦτο
wrong this. Behold ²[the] ¹this
third [time] [is]

ἑτοίμως ἔχω ἐλθεῖν πρὸς ὑμᾶς, καὶ
I am ready to come to you, and

οὐ καταναρκήσω· οὐ γὰρ ζητῶ τὰ ὑμῶν
I will not encumber [you]; ²not ¹for ²I seek the of
things you

ἀλλὰ ὑμᾶς. οὐ γὰρ ὀφείλει τὰ τέκνα
but you. For ²not ³ought ¹the ⁴children

τοῖς γονεῦσιν θησαυρίζειν, ἀλλὰ οἱ γονεῖς
for the parents to lay up treasure, but the parents

τοῖς τέκνοις. 15 ἐγὼ δὲ ἥδιστα δαπανήσω
for the children. But I most gladly will spend

καὶ ἐκδαπανηθήσομαι ὑπὲρ τῶν ψυχῶν
and will be spent out on behalf of the souls

ὑμῶν. εἰ περισσοτέρως ὑμᾶς ἀγαπῶ,
of you. If more abundantly ²you ¹I love,

ἧσσον ἀγαπῶμαι; 16 Ἔστω δέ, ἐγὼ οὐ
[the] less am I loved? But let it be, I not

κατεβάρησα ὑμᾶς· ἀλλὰ ὑπάρχων πανοῦργος
burdened you; but being crafty

δόλῳ ὑμᾶς ἔλαβον. 17 μή τινα ὧν
²with guile ³you ¹I took. Not anyone of
whom

ἀπέσταλκα πρὸς ὑμᾶς, 18 δι᾿ αὐτοῦ
I have sent to you, through him

ἐπλεονέκτησα ὑμᾶς; παρεκάλεσα Τίτον καὶ
did I defraud you? I besought Titus and

συναπέστειλα τὸν ἀδελφόν· μήτι ἐπλεο-
sent with [him] the brother; not ²de-

νέκτησεν ὑμᾶς Τίτος; οὐ τῷ αὐτῷ
frauded ³you ¹Titus? ¹not ²by the ⁴same

πνεύματι περιεπατήσαμεν; οὐ τοῖς αὐτοῖς
³spirit ¹walked we? not in the same

ἴχνεσιν;
steps?

545

King James Version

steps? 19Again, think ye that we excuse ourselves unto you? we speak before God in Christ: but *we do* all things, dearly beloved, for your edifying. 20 For I fear, lest, when I come, I shall not find you such as I would, and *that* I shall be found unto you such as ye would not: lest *there be* debates, envyings, wraths, strifes, backbitings, whisperings, swellings, tumults: 21*And* lest, when I come again, my God will humble me among you, and *that* I shall bewail many which have sinned already, and have not repented of the uncleanness and fornication and lasciviousness which they have committed.

13 This *is* the third *time* I am coming to you. In the mouth of two or three witnesses shall every word be established. 2 I told you before, and foretell you, as if I were present, the second time; and being absent now I write to them which heretofore have sinned, and to all other, that, if I come again, I will not spare: 3 Since ye seek a proof of Christ speaking in me, which to you-ward is not weak, but is mighty in you. 4 For though he was crucified through weakness, yet he liveth by the power of God. For we also are weak in him, but we shall live with him by the power of God toward you. 5 Examine yourselves, whether ye be in the faith; prove your own selves. Know ye not your own selves, how that Jesus Christ is in you, except ye be reprobates? 6 But I trust that ye shall know that we are not reprobates. 7 Now I pray to God that ye do no evil; not that we should appear approved, but that ye should do that which is honest, though we be as reprobates. 8 For we can do nothing against the truth, but for the truth. 9 For we are glad, when we are weak, and ye are strong: and this also we wish, *even* your perfection. 10 Therefore I write these things being absent, lest being present I should use sharpness, according to the power which the Lord hath given me to edification, and not to destruction. 11 Finally, brethren, farewell. Be perfect, be of good comfort, be of one mind, live in peace; and the God of love and peace shall be with you. 12 Greet one another with a holy kiss. 13All the saints salute you. 14 The grace of the Lord Jesus Christ, and the love of God, and the communion of the Holy Ghost, *be* with you all. Amen.

The second *epistle* to the Corinthians was written from Philippi, *a city* of Macedonia, by Titus and Lucas.

New International Version

19 Have you been thinking all along that we have been defending ourselves to you? We have been speaking in the sight of God as those in Christ; and everything we do, dear friends, is for your strengthening. 20 For I am afraid that when I come I may not find you as I want you to be, and you may not find me as you want me to be. I fear that there may be quarreling, jealousy, outbursts of anger, factions, slander, gossip, arrogance and disorder. 21 I am afraid that when I come again my God will humble me before you, and I will be grieved over many who have sinned earlier and have not repented of the impurity, sexual sin and debauchery in which they have indulged.

Final warnings

13 This will be my third visit to you. "Every matter must be established by the testimony of two or three witnesses." [a] 2 I already gave you a warning when I was with you the second time. I now repeat it while absent: On my return I will not spare those who sinned earlier or any of the others, 3 since you are demanding proof that Christ is speaking through me. He is not weak in dealing with you, but is powerful among you. 4 For to be sure, he was crucified in weakness, yet he lives by God's power. Likewise, we are weak in him, yet by God's power we will live with him to serve you.

5 Examine yourselves to see whether you are in the faith; test yourselves. Do you not realize that Christ Jesus is in you—unless, of course, you fail the test? 6 And I trust that you will discover that we have not failed the test. 7 Now we pray to God that you will not do anything wrong. Not that people will see that we have stood the test but that you will do what is right even though we may seem to have failed. 8 For we cannot do anything against the truth, but only for the truth. 9 We are glad whenever we are weak but you are strong; and our prayer is for your perfection. 10 This is why I write these things when I am absent, that when I come I may not have to be harsh in my use of authority—the authority the Lord gave me for building you up, not for tearing you down.

Final greetings

11 Finally, brothers, good-by. Aim for perfection, listen to my appeal, be of one mind, live in peace. And the God of love and peace will be with you. 12 Greet one another with a holy kiss. 13All the saints send their greetings.

14 May the grace of the Lord Jesus Christ, and the love of God, and the fellowship of the Holy Spirit be with you all.

[a] Deut. 19:15.

546

Greek Interlinear

19 Πάλαι δοκεῖτε ὅτι ὑμῖν ἀπολογούμεθα.
Already ye think that to you we are making a
defence.

κατέναντι θεοῦ ἐν Χριστῷ λαλοῦμεν· τὰ
Before God in Christ we speak; –

δὲ πάντα, ἀγαπητοί, ὑπὲρ τῆς ὑμῶν
but all things, beloved, [are] on behalf of ¹the ²of you

οἰκοδομῆς. 20 φοβοῦμαι γὰρ μή πως ἐλθὼν
²edification. For I fear lest coming

οὐχ οἵους θέλω εὕρω ὑμᾶς, κἀγὼ εὑρεθῶ
¹not ⁴such as ³I wish ²I may find ⁵you, and I am found

ὑμῖν οἷον οὐ θέλετε, μή πως ἔρις,
by you such as ye wish not, lest strife,

ζῆλος, θυμοί, ἐριθεῖαι, καταλαλιαί, ψιθυρισ-
jealousy, angers, rivalries, detractions, whisper-

μοί, φυσιώσεις, ἀκαταστασίαι· 21 μή πάλιν
ings, puffings up, disturbances; lest again

ἐλθόντος μου ταπεινώσῃ με ὁ θεός μου
coming me² ⁴may humble ²me ¹the ³God ⁵of me
–when I come

πρὸς ὑμᾶς, καὶ πενθήσω πολλοὺς τῶν
with you, and I shall mourn many of the
[ones]

προημαρτηκότων καὶ μὴ μετανοησάντων
having previously sinned and not repenting

ἐπὶ τῇ ἀκαθαρσίᾳ καὶ πορνείᾳ καὶ
over the uncleanness and fornication and

Chapter 13

ἀσελγείᾳ ᾗ ἔπραξαν. 13 Τρίτον τοῦτο
lewdness which they practised. ²[The] third ¹this
[time] [is]

ἔρχομαι πρὸς ὑμᾶς· ἐπὶ στόματος
I am coming to you; at [the] mouth

δύο μαρτύρων καὶ τριῶν σταθήσεται
of two witnesses and of three shall be established

πᾶν ῥῆμα. 2 προείρηκα καὶ προλέγω,
every word. I have previously and I say
said beforehand,

ὡς παρὼν τὸ δεύτερον καὶ ἀπὼν
as being present the second [time] and being absent

νῦν, τοῖς προημαρτηκόσιν καὶ τοῖς
now, to the [ones] having previously sinned and ¹to ²the

λοιποῖς πᾶσιν, ὅτι ἐὰν ἔλθω εἰς τὸ
⁴remaining ³all, that if I come in the
[ones]

πάλιν οὐ φείσομαι, 3 ἐπεὶ δοκιμὴν ζητεῖτε
again I will not spare, since ²a proof ¹ye seek

τοῦ ἐν ἐμοὶ λαλοῦντος Χριστοῦ, ὃς εἰς
– ¹in ²me ⁴speaking ³of Christ, who toward

ὑμᾶς οὐκ ἀσθενεῖ ἀλλὰ δυνατεῖ ἐν ὑμῖν.
you is not weak but is powerful in you.

4 καὶ γὰρ ἐσταυρώθη ἐξ ἀσθενείας, ἀλλὰ
For indeed he was crucified out of weakness, but

ζῆ ἐκ δυνάμεως θεοῦ. καὶ γὰρ ἡμεῖς
he lives by [the] power of God. For indeed we

ἀσθενοῦμεν ἐν αὐτῷ, ἀλλὰ ζήσομεν σὺν
are weak in him, but we shall live with

αὐτῷ ἐκ δυνάμεως θεοῦ εἰς ὑμᾶς.
him by [the] power of God toward you.

5 Ἑαυτοὺς πειράζετε εἰ ἐστὲ ἐν τῇ
¹Yourselves ²test if ye are in the

πίστει, ἑαυτοὺς δοκιμάζετε· ἢ οὐκ
faith, ²yourselves ¹prove; or not

ἐπιγινώσκετε ἑαυτοὺς ὅτι Ἰησοῦς Χριστὸς
perceive ye yourselves that Jesus Christ [is]

ἐν ὑμῖν, εἰ μήτι ἀδόκιμοί ἐστε. 6 ἐλπίζω
in you, unless ²counterfeits ¹ye are. I hope

δὲ ὅτι γνώσεσθε ὅτι ἡμεῖς οὐκ ἐσμὲν
But that ye will know that we are not

ἀδόκιμοι. 7 εὐχόμεθα δὲ πρὸς τὸν θεὸν
counterfeits. Now we pray to – God

μὴ ποιῆσαι ὑμᾶς κακὸν μηδέν, οὐχ
not to do you evil none, not
=that ye do no . . .

ἵνα ἡμεῖς δόκιμοι φανῶμεν, ἀλλ' ἵνα
in order we ²approved ¹may appear, but in order
that that

ὑμεῖς τὸ καλὸν ποιῆτε, ἡμεῖς δὲ ὡς
ye ²the ¹good ¹may do, and we ²as

ἀδόκιμοι ὦμεν. 8 οὐ γὰρ δυνάμεθά
²counterfeits ¹may be. For we cannot [do]

τι κατὰ τῆς ἀληθείας, ἀλλὰ ὑπὲρ τῆς
any- against the truth, but on behalf of the
thing

ἀληθείας. 9 χαίρομεν γὰρ ὅταν ἡμεῖς
truth. For we rejoice whenever we

ἀσθενῶμεν, ὑμεῖς δὲ δυνατοὶ ἦτε· τοῦτο
are weak, and ye powerful are; this

καὶ εὐχόμεθα, τὴν ὑμῶν κατάρτισιν. 10 Διὰ
also we pray, the ²of you ¹restoration. There-

τοῦτο ταῦτα ἀπὼν γράφω, ἵνα παρὼν
fore ³these things ²being ¹I write, in order being
absent that present

μὴ ἀποτόμως χρήσωμαι κατὰ τὴν ἐξουσίαν
²not ³sharply ¹I may deal according to the authority

ἣν ὁ κύριος ἔδωκέν μοι εἰς οἰκοδομὴν
which the Lord gave me for edification

καὶ οὐκ εἰς καθαίρεσιν.
and not for overthrow.

11 Λοιπόν, ἀδελφοί, χαίρετε, καταρτίζεσθε,
For the rest,† brothers, rejoice, restore yourselves,

παρακαλεῖσθε, τὸ αὐτὸ φρονεῖτε, εἰρηνεύετε,
admonish yourselves, the same thing think, be at peace,

καὶ ὁ θεὸς τῆς ἀγάπης καὶ εἰρήνης
and the God – of love and of peace

ἔσται μεθ' ὑμῶν. 12 Ἀσπάσασθε ἀλλήλους
will be with you. Greet ye one another

ἐν ἁγίῳ φιλήματι. Ἀσπάζονται ὑμᾶς οἱ
with a holy kiss. ⁴greet ²you ³the

ἅγιοι πάντες.
²saints ¹All.

13 Ἡ χάρις τοῦ κυρίου Ἰησοῦ Χριστοῦ
The grace of the Lord Jesus Christ

καὶ ἡ ἀγάπη τοῦ θεοῦ καὶ ἡ κοινωνία
and the love – of God and the fellowship

τοῦ ἁγίου πνεύματος μετὰ πάντων ὑμῶν.
of the Holy Spirit [be] with ²all ¹you.

547

King James Version

THE EPISTLE OF
PAUL THE APOSTLE
TO THE
GALATIANS

1 Paul, an apostle, (not of men, neither by man, but by Jesus Christ, and God the Father, who raised him from the dead;) 2And all the brethren which are with me, unto the churches of Galatia: 3 Grace *be* to you, and peace,'from God the Father, and *from* our Lord Jesus Christ, 4 Who gave himself for our sins, that he might deliver us from this present evil world, according to the will of God and our Father: 5 To whom *be* glory for ever and ever. Amen. 6 I marvel that ye are so soon removed from him that called you into the grace of Christ unto another gospel: 7 Which is not another; but there be some that trouble you, and would pervert the gospel of Christ. 8 But though we, or an angel from heaven, preach any other gospel unto you than that which we have preached unto you, let him be accursed. 9As we said before, so say I now again, If any *man* preach any other gospel unto you than that which ye have received, let him be accursed. 10 For do I now persuade men, or God? or do I seek to please men? for if I yet pleased men, I should not be the servant of Christ. 11 But I certify you, brethren, that the gospel which was preached of me is not after man. 12 For I neither received it of man, neither was I taught *it,* but by the revelation of Jesus Christ. 13 For ye have heard of my conversation in time past in the Jews' religion, how that beyond measure I persecuted the church of God, and wasted it: 14And profited in the Jews' religion above many my equals in mine own nation, being more exceedingly zealous of the traditions of my fathers. 15 But when it pleased God, who separated me from my mother's womb, and called *me* by his grace, 16 To reveal his Son in me, that I might preach him among the heathen; immediately I conferred not with flesh and blood: 17 Neither went I up to Jerusalem to them which were apostles before me; but I went into Arabia, and returned again unto Damascus. 18 Then after three years I went up to Jerusalem to see Peter, and abode with him fifteen days. 19 But other of the apostles saw I none, save James the Lord's brother. 20 Now the things which I write unto you, be-

New International Version

GALATIANS

1 Paul, an apostle—sent not from men nor by man, but by Jesus Christ and God the Father, who raised him from the dead—2 and all the brothers with me,
To the churches in Galatia:
3 Grace and peace to you from God our Father and the Lord Jesus Christ, 4 who gave himself for our sins to rescue us from the present evil age, according to the will of our God and Father, 5 to whom be glory for ever and ever. Amen.

No other gospel

6 I am astonished that you are so quickly deserting the one who called you by the grace of Christ and are turning to a different gospel— 7 which is really no gospel at all. Evidently some people are throwing you into confusion and trying to pervert the gospel of Christ. 8 But even if we or an angel from heaven should preach a gospel other than the one we preached to you, let him be eternally condemned! 9As we have already said, so now I say again: If anybody is preaching to you a gospel other than what you accepted, let him be eternally condemned!
10 Am I now trying to win the approval of men, or of God? Or am I trying to please men? If I were still trying to please men, I would not be a servant of Christ.

Paul called by God

11 I want you to know, brothers, that the gospel I preached is not something that man made up. 12 I did not receive it from any man, nor was I taught it; rather, I received it by revelation from Jesus Christ.
13 For you have heard of my previous way of life in Judaism, how I violently persecuted the church of God and tried to destroy it. 14 I was advancing in Judaism beyond many Jews of my own age and was extremely zealous for the traditions of my ancestors. 15 But when God, who set me apart from birth[a] and called me by his grace, was pleased 16 to reveal his Son in me so that I might preach him among the Gentiles, I did not consult any man. 17 I did not go up to Jerusalem to see those who were apostles before I was. Instead, I went immediately into Arabia and later returned to Damascus.
18 Then after three years, I went up to Jerusalem to get acquainted with Peter[b] and stayed with him fifteen days. 19 I saw none of the other apostles—only James, the Lord's brother. 20 I assure you before God that what I am writing

[a] Or *from my mother's womb.* [b] Greek *Cephas.*

ΠΡΟΣ ΓΑΛΑΤΑΣ

Chapter 1

Παῦλος ἀπόστολος, οὐκ ἀπ᾽ ἀνθρώπων
Paul   an apostle,   not from   men

οὐδὲ δι᾽ ἀνθρώπου ἀλλὰ διὰ Ἰησοῦ
nor through man   but through Jesus

Χριστοῦ καὶ θεοῦ πατρὸς τοῦ ἐγείραντος
Christ   and God [the] Father the [one] having raised

αὐτὸν ἐκ νεκρῶν, 2 καὶ οἱ σὺν ἐμοὶ
him   out of [the] dead, and ᵗthe ᵇwith ᵐe

πάντες ἀδελφοί, ταῖς ἐκκλησίαις τῆς
ᵃall   ᵇbrothers, to the churches   -

Γαλατίας· 3 χάρις ὑμῖν καὶ εἰρήνη ἀπὸ
of Galatia: Grace to you and   peace   from

θεοῦ πατρὸς ἡμῶν καὶ κυρίου Ἰησοῦ
God Father of us   and   Lord   Jesus

Χριστοῦ, 4 τοῦ δόντος ἑαυτὸν ὑπὲρ τῶν
Christ,   the [one] having given himself on behalf of the

ἁμαρτιῶν ἡμῶν, ὅπως ἐξέληται ἡμᾶς ἐκ
sins   of us.   so as he might deliver us   out of

τοῦ αἰῶνος τοῦ ἐνεστῶτος πονηροῦ κατὰ
the ²age   -   ¹present   ²evil   according to

τὸ θέλημα τοῦ θεοῦ καὶ πατρὸς ἡμῶν,
the will   of the God and Father of us,

5 ᾧ ἡ δόξα εἰς τοὺς αἰῶνας τῶν
to whom the glory unto   the   ages   of the
[be]

αἰώνων· ἀμήν.
ages·   Amen.

6 Θαυμάζω ὅτι οὕτως ταχέως μετατίθεσθε
I wonder   that thus   quickly ye are removing

ἀπὸ τοῦ καλέσαντος ὑμᾶς ἐν χάριτι
from the [one] having called you   by [the] grace

Χριστοῦ εἰς ἕτερον εὐαγγέλιον, 7 ὃ οὐκ
of Christ to another   gospel,   which not

ἔστιν ἄλλο· εἰ μή τινές εἰσιν οἱ ταράσ-
is another;   only ᵃsome ¹there are -   troubl-

σοντες ὑμᾶς καὶ θέλοντες μεταστρέψαι
ing   you   and   wishing   to pervert

τὸ εὐαγγέλιον τοῦ Χριστοῦ. 8 ἀλλὰ
the   gospel   of Christ.   But

καὶ ἐὰν ἡμεῖς ἢ ἄγγελος ἐξ οὐρανοῦ
even if we   or an angel out of heaven

εὐαγγελίσηται [ὑμῖν] παρ᾽ ὃ εὐηγγελισάμεθα
should preach to you beside what   we preached
a gospel

ὑμῖν, ἀνάθεμα ἔστω. 9 ὡς προειρήκαμεν,
to you, ᵃa curse ¹let him be. As we have previously said,

καὶ ἄρτι πάλιν λέγω, εἴ τις ὑμᾶς εὐαγγε-
also now   again I say, if anyone ²you ¹preaches

γελίζεται παρ᾽ ὃ παρελάβετε, ἀνάθεμα
ᵃa gospel beside what ye received,   ᵃa curse

ἔστω.
¹let him be.

10 Ἄρτι γὰρ ἀνθρώπους πείθω ἢ τὸν
For now   men   do I persuade or   -

θεόν; ἢ ζητῶ ἀνθρώποις ἀρέσκειν; εἰ
God? or do I seek men   to please? If

ἔτι ἀνθρώποις ἤρεσκον, Χριστοῦ δοῦλος
still men   I pleased,   ²of Christ ᵃa slave

οὐκ ἂν ἤμην. 11 γνωρίζω γὰρ ὑμῖν,
¹I would not have been.   For I make known   to you,

ἀδελφοί, τὸ εὐαγγέλιον τὸ εὐαγγελισθὲν
brothers,   the gospel   -   preached

ὑπ᾽ ἐμοῦ ὅτι οὐκ ἔστιν κατὰ ἄνθρωπον
by   me   that it is not according to man;

12 οὐδὲ γὰρ ἐγὼ παρὰ ἀνθρώπου παρέλαβον
for ¹not   ²I ¹from ⁴man   ³received

αὐτὸ οὔτε ἐδιδάχθην, ἀλλὰ δι᾽ ἀποκαλύψεως
²it   nor was I taught   but through a revelation
[by man],

Ἰησοῦ Χριστοῦ. 13 Ἠκούσατε γὰρ τὴν
of Jesus Christ.   For ye heard   -

ἐμὴν ἀναστροφήν ποτε ἐν τῷ Ἰουδαϊσμῷ,
my   conduct   then in -   Judaism,

ὅτι καθ᾽ ὑπερβολὴν ἐδίωκον τὴν ἐκκλησίαν
that   excessively†   I persecuted the   church

τοῦ θεοῦ καὶ ἐπόρθουν αὐτήν, 14 καὶ
-   of God and wasted   it,   and

προέκοπτον ἐν τῷ Ἰουδαϊσμῷ ὑπὲρ πολλοὺς
progressed   in -   Judaism   beyond many

συνηλικιώτας ἐν τῷ γένει μου, περισ-
contemporaries in the race of me,   ¹abun-

σοτέρως ζηλωτὴς ὑπάρχων τῶν πατρικῶν
dantly   ²a zealot   ¹being   ⁴of the ²ancestral

μου παραδόσεων. 15 Ὅτε δὲ εὐδόκησεν
³of me ¹traditions.   But when it was pleased

ὁ ἀφορίσας με ἐκ κοιλίας μητρός μου
¹the ²having   ³me ⁴from ⁵[the] womb ⁶of mother ⁷of me
[one] separated

καὶ καλέσας διὰ τῆς χάριτος αὐτοῦ
⁸and ⁹having called ¹⁰through ¹¹the   ¹²grace   ¹³of him

16 ἀποκαλύψαι τὸν υἱὸν αὐτοῦ ἐν ἐμοί,
to reveal   the Son of him   in   me,

ἵνα εὐαγγελίζωμαι αὐτὸν ἐν τοῖς ἔθνεσιν,
in order I might preach him among the nations,
that

εὐθέως οὐ προσανεθέμην σαρκὶ καὶ αἵματι,
immediately I conferred not   with flesh and blood,

17 οὐδὲ ἀνῆλθον εἰς Ἱεροσόλυμα πρὸς
neither did I go up to Jerusalem   to

τοὺς πρὸ ἐμοῦ ἀποστόλους, ἀλλὰ ἀπῆλθον
¹the ³before ⁴me   ²apostles,   but   I went away

εἰς Ἀραβίαν, καὶ πάλιν ὑπέστρεψα εἰς
into Arabia,   and again   returned   to

Δαμασκόν. 18 Ἔπειτα μετὰ τρία ἔτη
Damascus.   Then   after three years

ἀνῆλθον εἰς Ἱεροσόλυμα ἱστορῆσαι Κηφᾶν,
I went up to Jerusalem   to visit   Cephas,

καὶ ἐπέμεινα πρὸς αὐτὸν ἡμέρας δεκαπέντε·
and remained   with him   days   fifteen;

19 ἕτερον δὲ τῶν ἀποστόλων οὐκ εἶδον,
but other   of the apostles   I saw not,

εἰ μὴ Ἰάκωβον τὸν ἀδελφὸν τοῦ κυρίου.
except   James   the brother   of the Lord.

20 ἃ δὲ γράφω ὑμῖν, ἰδοὺ ἐνώπιον τοῦ
Now what I write to you, behold before   -
things

King James Version

New International Version

hold, before God, I lie not. 21Afterwards I came into the regions of Syria and Cilicia; 22And was unknown by face unto the churches of Judea which were in Christ: 23 But they had heard only, That he which persecuted us in times past now preacheth the faith which once he destroyed. 24And they glorified God in me.

you is no lie. 21 Later I went to Syria and Cilicia. 22 I was personally unknown to the churches of Judea that are in Christ. 23 They only heard the report: "The man who formerly persecuted us is now preaching the faith he once tried to destroy." 24And they praised God because of me.

Paul accepted by the apostles

2 Then fourteen years after I went up again to Jerusalem with Barnabas, and took Titus with *me* also. 2And I went up by revelation, and communicated unto them that gospel which I preach among the Gentiles, but privately to them which were of reputation, lest by any means I should run, or had run, in vain. 3 But neither Titus, who was with me, being a Greek, was compelled to be circumcised: 4And that because of false brethren unawares brought in, who came in privily to spy out our liberty which we have in Christ Jesus, that they might bring us into bondage: 5 To whom we gave place by subjection, no, not for an hour; that the truth of the gospel might continue with you. 6 But of those who seemed to be somewhat, whatsoever they were, it maketh no matter to me: God accepteth no man's person: for they who seemed *to be somewhat* in conference added nothing to me: 7 But contrariwise, when they saw that the gospel of the uncircumcision was committed unto me, as *the gospel* of the circumcision *was* unto Peter; 8 (For he that wrought effectually in Peter to the apostleship of the circumcision, the same was mighty in me toward the Gentiles;) 9And when James, Cephas, and John, who seemed to be pillars, perceived the grace that was given unto me, they gave to me and Barnabas the right hands of fellowship; that we *should go* unto the heathen, and they unto the circumcision. 10 Only *they would* that we should remember the poor; the same which I also was forward to do. 11 But when Peter was come to Antioch, I withstood him to the face, because he was to be blamed. 12 For before that certain came from James, he did eat with the Gentiles: but when they were come, he withdrew and separated himself, fearing them which were of the circumcision. 13And the other Jews dissembled likewise with him; insomuch that Barnabas also was carried away with their dissimulation. 14 But when I saw that they walked not uprightly according to the truth of the gospel, I said unto Peter before *them* all, If thou, being a Jew, livest after the manner of Gentiles, and not as do the Jews, why compellest thou the Gentiles to live as do the Jews? 15 We *who are* Jews by nature, and not sinners of the Gentiles, 16 Knowing that a man is not justified by the works of the law, but by the faith of Jesus Christ, even we have believed in Jesus Christ, that we might be justified by the faith of Christ, and not by the works of the law: for by the works of the

2 Fourteen years later I went up again to Jerusalem, this time with Barnabas. I took Titus along also. 2 I went in response to a revelation and set before them the gospel that I preach among the Gentiles. But I did this privately to those who seemed to be leaders, for fear that I was running or had run my race in vain. 3 Yet not even Titus, who was with me, was compelled to be circumcised, even though he was a Greek. 4 [This matter arose] because some false brothers had infiltrated our ranks to spy on the freedom we have in Christ Jesus and to make us slaves. 5 We did not give in to them for a moment, so that the truth of the gospel might remain with you.

6 As for those who seemed to be important—whatever they were makes no difference to me; God does not judge by external appearance—those men added nothing to my message. 7 On the contrary, they saw that I had been given the task of preaching the gospel to the Gentiles,[c] just as Peter had been given the task of preaching the gospel to the Jews.[d] 8 For God, who was at work in the ministry of Peter as an apostle to the Jews,[d] was also at work in my ministry as an apostle to the Gentiles. 9 James, Peter[e] and John, those reputed to be pillars, gave me and Barnabas the right hand of fellowship when they recognized the grace given to me. They agreed that we should go to the Gentiles, and they to the Jews.[d] 10All they asked was that we should continue to remember the poor, the very thing I was eager to do.

Paul opposes Peter

11 When Peter[e] came to Antioch, I opposed him to his face, because he was in the wrong. 12 Before certain men came from James, he used to eat with the Gentiles. But when they arrived, he began to draw back and separate himself from the Gentiles because he was afraid of those who belonged to the circumcision group. 13 The other Jews joined him in his hypocrisy, so that by their hypocrisy even Barnabas was led astray.

14 When I saw that they were not acting in line with the truth of the gospel, I said to Peter[e] in front of them all, "You are a Jew, yet you live like a Gentile and not like a Jew. How is it, then, that you force Gentiles to follow Jewish customs?

15 "We who are Jews by birth and not 'Gentile sinners' 16 know that a man is not justified by observing the law, but by faith in Jesus Christ. So we, too, have put our faith in Christ Jesus that we may be justified by faith in Christ and not by observing the law, because by observing the law no one will be justified.

Greek Interlinear

θεοῦ ὅτι οὐ ψεύδομαι. **21** ἔπειτα ἦλθον
God - I lie not. Then I went

εἰς τὰ κλίματα τῆς Συρίας καὶ τῆς
into the regions - of Syria and -

Κιλικίας. **22** ἤμην δὲ ἀγνοούμενος τῷ
of Cilicia. And I was being unknown -

προσώπῳ ταῖς ἐκκλησίαις τῆς Ἰουδαίας
by face to the churches - of Judæa

ταῖς ἐν Χριστῷ. **23** μόνον δὲ ἀκούοντες
- in Christ. But only hearing

ἦσαν ὅτι ὁ διώκων ἡμᾶς ποτε νῦν
they were that the [one] ²persecuting ¹us ¹then now

εὐαγγελίζεται τὴν πίστιν ἣν ποτε ἐπόρθει,
preaches the faith which then he was destroying,

24 καὶ ἐδόξαζον ἐν ἐμοὶ τὸν θεόν.
and they glorified ²in ³me - ¹God.

Chapter 2

Ἔπειτα διὰ δεκατεσσάρων ἐτῶν πάλιν
Then through fourteen years again

ἀνέβην εἰς Ἰεροσόλυμα μετὰ Βαρναβᾶ,
I went up to Jerusalem with Barnabas,

συμπαραλαβὼν καὶ Τίτον· **2** ἀνέβην δὲ
taking with [me] also Titus; and I went up

κατὰ ἀποκάλυψιν· καὶ ἀνεθέμην αὐτοῖς
according to a revelation; and I put before them

τὸ εὐαγγέλιον ὃ κηρύσσω ἐν τοῖς ἔθνεσιν,
the gospel which I proclaim among the nations,

κατ᾽ ἰδίαν δὲ τοῖς δοκοῦσιν, μή πως
²privately ¹but to the [ones] seeming,* lest

εἰς κενὸν τρέχω ἢ ἔδραμον. **3** ἀλλ᾽
in vain I run or I ran. But

οὐδὲ Τίτος ὁ σὺν ἐμοί, Ἕλλην ὤν,
not Titus the [one] with me, a Greek being,

ἠναγκάσθη περιτμηθῆναι· **4** διὰ δὲ τοὺς
was compelled to be circumcised; but on account of ¹the

παρεισάκτους ψευδαδέλφους, οἵτινες παρεισ-
²brought in secretly ¹false brothers, who stole

ἦλθον κατασκοπῆσαι τὴν ἐλευθερίαν ἡμῶν
in to spy on the freedom of us

ἣν ἔχομεν ἐν Χριστῷ Ἰησοῦ, ἵνα ἡμᾶς
which we have in Christ Jesus, in order that ¹us

καταδουλώσουσιν· **5** οἷς οὐδὲ πρὸς ὥραν
¹they will(might) enslave; to whom not for an hour

εἴξαμεν τῇ ὑποταγῇ, ἵνα ἡ ἀλήθεια
yielded we in subjection, in order that the truth

τοῦ εὐαγγελίου διαμείνῃ πρὸς ὑμᾶς. **6** ἀπὸ
of the gospel might continue with you. from

δὲ τῶν δοκούντων εἶναί τι, — ὁποῖοί
But the [ones] seeming to be something, (of what kind

ποτε ἦσαν οὐδέν μοι διαφέρει· πρόσωπον
¹then ¹they were ²nothing ⁴to me ³matters: ²[the] face

[ὁ] θεὸς ἀνθρώπου οὐ λαμβάνει — ἐμοὶ
- ¹God ³of a man ²receives not,) ⁴to me

γὰρ οἱ δοκοῦντες* οὐδὲν προσανέθεντο,
¹for the [ones] seeming* nothing added,

7 ἀλλὰ τοὐναντίον ἰδόντες ὅτι πεπίστευμαι
but on the contrary seeing that I have been entrusted [with]

τὸ εὐαγγέλιον τῆς ἀκροβυστίας καθὼς
the gospel of the uncircumcision as

Πέτρος τῆς περιτομῆς, **8** ὁ γὰρ ἐνεργήσας
Peter [that] of the circumcision, for the [one] operating

Πέτρῳ εἰς ἀποστολὴν τῆς περιτομῆς
in Peter to an apostleship of the circumcision

ἐνήργησεν καὶ ἐμοὶ εἰς τὰ ἔθνη, **9** καὶ
operated also in me to the nations, and

γνόντες τὴν χάριν τὴν δοθεῖσάν μοι,
knowing the grace - given to me,

Ἰάκωβος καὶ Κηφᾶς καὶ Ἰωάννης, οἱ
James and Cephas and John, the

δοκοῦντες στῦλοι εἶναι, δεξιὰς ἔδωκαν
[ones] seeming ¹pillars ¹to be, ¹right [hands] ¹gave

ἐμοὶ καὶ Βαρναβᾷ κοινωνίας, ἵνα ἡμεῖς
²to me ²and ⁴to Barnabas ⁵of fellowship, in order we
that [should

εἰς τὰ ἔθνη, αὐτοὶ δὲ εἰς τὴν περιτομήν·
go]to the nations, but they to the circumcision;

10 μόνον τῶν πτωχῶν ἵνα μνημονεύωμεν,
only ²the ⁴poor in order ¹that ³we might remember,

ὃ καὶ ἐσπούδασα αὐτὸ τοῦτο ποιῆσαι.
which indeed ²I was eager ¹this very thing to do.

11 Ὅτε δὲ ἦλθεν Κηφᾶς εἰς Ἀντιόχειαν,
But when ²came ¹Cephas to Antioch,

κατὰ πρόσωπον αὐτῷ ἀντέστην, ὅτι
against [his] face to him I opposed, because

κατεγνωσμένος ἦν. **12** πρὸ τοῦ γὰρ
²having been condemned ¹he was. Before the for
= For before some came . . .

ἐλθεῖν τινας ἀπὸ Ἰακώβου μετὰ τῶν
to come someᵇ from James ²with ¹the

ἐθνῶν συνήσθιεν· ὅτε δὲ ἦλθον, ὑπέστελλεν
²nations ¹he ate with; but when they came, he withdrew

καὶ ἀφώριζεν ἑαυτόν, φοβούμενος τοὺς
and separated himself, fearing the [ones]

ἐκ περιτομῆς· **13** καὶ συνυπεκρίθησαν αὐτῷ
of [the] circumcision; and dissembled along with him

[καὶ] οἱ λοιποὶ Ἰουδαῖοι, ὥστε καὶ
also the remaining Jews, so as even

Βαρναβᾶς συναπήχθη αὐτῶν τῇ ὑποκρίσει.
Barnabas was led away with ²of them ¹the ³dissembling.

14 ἀλλ᾽ ὅτε εἶδον ὅτι οὐκ ὀρθοποδοῦσιν
But when I saw that they walk[ed] not straight

πρὸς τὴν ἀλήθειαν τοῦ εὐαγγελίου, εἶπον
with the truth of the gospel, I said

τῷ Κηφᾷ ἔμπροσθεν πάντων· εἰ σὺ
- to Cephas in front of all: If thou

Ἰουδαῖος ὑπάρχων ἐθνικῶς καὶ οὐκ
²a Jew ¹being as a Gentile and not

Ἰουδαϊκῶς ζῆς, πῶς τὰ ἔθνη ἀναγκάζεις
as a Jew livest, how ²the ³nations ¹compellest thou

ἰουδαΐζειν; **15** Ἡμεῖς φύσει Ἰουδαῖοι καὶ
to judaize? We by nature Jews and

οὐκ ἐξ ἐθνῶν ἁμαρτωλοί, **16** εἰδότες δὲ
not ¹of ²nations ³sinners, and knowing

ὅτι οὐ δικαιοῦται ἄνθρωπος ἐξ ἔργων
that ²is not justified ¹a man by works

νόμου ἐὰν μὴ διὰ πίστεως Χριστοῦ
of law except(but) through faith of(in) Christ

Ἰησοῦ, καὶ ἡμεῖς εἰς Χριστὸν Ἰησοῦν
Jesus, ★ even we ²in ³Christ ⁴Jesus

ἐπιστεύσαμεν, ἵνα δικαιωθῶμεν ἐκ πίστεως
¹believed, in order that we might be by faith
justified

Χριστοῦ καὶ οὐκ ἐξ ἔργων νόμου, ὅτι
of(in) Christ* and not by works of law, because

ἐξ ἔργων νόμου οὐ δικαιωθήσεται πᾶσα
by works of law not will be justified all
=no flesh will be justified.

* Cf. the full expressions in vers. 6 (earlier) and 9.
★ Objective genitive, as is shown by the intervening sentence
see also 3. 22, 26). Cf. " fear of God".

551

King James Version

law shall no flesh be justified. 17 But if, while we seek to be justified by Christ, we ourselves also are found sinners, *is* therefore Christ the minister of sin? God forbid. 18 For if I build again the things which I destroyed, I make myself a transgressor. 19 For I through the law am dead to the law, that I might live unto God. 20 I am crucified with Christ: nevertheless I live; yet not I, but Christ liveth in me: and the life which I now live in the flesh I live by the faith of the Son of God, who loved me, and gave himself for me. 21 I do not frustrate the grace of God: for if righteousness *come* by the law, then Christ is dead in vain.

3 O foolish Galatians, who hath bewitched you, that ye should not obey the truth, before whose eyes Jesus Christ hath been evidently set forth, crucified among you? 2 This only would I learn of you, Received ye the Spirit by the works of the law, or by the hearing of faith? 3 Are ye so foolish? having begun in the Spirit, are ye now made perfect by the flesh? 4 Have ye suffered so many things in vain? if *it be* yet in vain. 5 He therefore that ministereth to you the Spirit, and worketh miracles among you, *doeth he it* by the works of the law, or by the hearing of faith? 6 Even as Abraham believed God, and it was accounted to him for righteousness. 7 Know ye therefore that they which are of faith, the same are the children of Abraham. 8 And the Scripture, foreseeing that God would justify the heathen through faith, preached before the gospel unto Abraham, *saying,* In thee shall all nations be blessed. 9 So then they which be of faith are blessed with faithful Abraham. 10 For as many as are of the works of the law are under the curse: for it is written, Cursed *is* every one that continueth not in all things which are written in the book of the law to do them. 11 But that no man is justified by the law in the sight of God, *it is* evident: for, The just shall live by faith. 12 And the law is not of faith: but, The man that doeth them shall live in them. 13 Christ hath redeemed us from the curse of the law, being made a curse for us: for it is written, Cursed *is* every one that hangeth on a tree: 14 That the blessing of Abraham might come on the Gentiles through Jesus Christ; that we might receive the promise of the Spirit through faith. 15 Brethren, I speak after the manner of men; Though *it be* but a man's covenant, yet *if it be* confirmed, no man disannulleth, or addeth thereto. 16 Now to Abraham and his seed were the promises made. He saith not, And to seeds, as of many; but as of one, And to thy seed, which is Christ. 17 And this I say, *that* the covenant, that was confirmed before of God in Christ, the law, which was four hundred and thirty years after, cannot disannul, that it should make the promise of none effect. 18 For if the inheritance *be* of the law, *it is* no more of prom-

New International Version

17 "If, while we seek to be justified in Christ, it becomes evident that we ourselves are sinners, does that mean that Christ promotes sin? Absolutely not! 18 If I rebuild what I destroyed, I prove that I am a lawbreaker. 19 For through the law I died to the law so that I might live for God. 20 I have been crucified with Christ and I no longer live, but Christ lives in me. The life I live in the body, I live by faith in the Son of God, who loved me and gave himself for me. 21 I do not set aside the grace of God, for if righteousness could be gained through the law, Christ died for nothing!" *f*

Faith or observance of the law

3 You foolish Galatians! Who has bewitched you? Before your very eyes Jesus Christ was clearly portrayed as crucified. 2 I would like to learn just one thing from you: Did you receive the Spirit by observing the law, or by believing what you heard? 3 Are you so foolish? After beginning with the Spirit, are you now trying to attain perfection by human effort? 4 Have you suffered so much for nothing—if it really was for nothing? 5 Does God give you his Spirit and work miracles among you because you observe the law, or because you believe what you heard? 6 Consider Abraham: "He believed God, and it was credited to him as righteousness." *g* 7 Understand, then, that those who believe are children of Abraham. 8 The Scripture foresaw that God would justify the Gentiles by faith, and announced the gospel in advance to Abraham: "All nations will be blessed in you." *h* 9 So those who have faith are blessed along with Abraham, the man of faith.

10 All who rely on observing the law are under a curse, for it is written: "Cursed is everyone who does not continue to do everything written in the book of the Law." *i* 11 Clearly no one is justified before God by the law, because, "The righteous will live by faith." *j* 12 The law is not based on faith; on the contrary, "The man who does these things will live by them." *k* 13 Christ redeemed us from the curse of the law by becoming a curse for us, for it is written: "Cursed is everyone who is hanged on a tree." *l* 14 He redeemed us in order that the blessing given to Abraham might come to the Gentiles through Christ Jesus, so that by faith we might receive the promise of the Spirit.

The law and the promise

15 Brothers, let me take an example from everyday life. Just as no one can set aside or add to a human covenant that has been duly established, so it is in this case. 16 The promises were spoken to Abraham and to his seed. The Scripture does not say "and to seeds," meaning many people, but "and to your seed," *m* meaning one person, who is Christ. 17 What I mean is this: The law, introduced 430 years later, does not set aside the covenant previously established by God and thus do away with the promise. 18 For if the inheritance depends on the law,

[*f*] Some interpreters end the quotation after verse 14. [*g*] Gen. 15:6. [*h*] Gen. 12:3; 18:18; 22:18. [*i*] Deut. 27:26. [*j*] Hab. 2:4. [*k*] Lev. 18:5. [*l*] Deut. 21:23. [*m*] Gen. 13:15; 24:7.

Greek Interlinear

σάρξ.   17 εἰ δὲ ζητοῦντες δικαιωθῆναι
flesh.   But if   seeking   to be justified

ἐν Χριστῷ εὑρέθημεν καὶ αὐτοὶ ἁμαρτωλοί,
in Christ we were found also [our]selves sinners,

ἆρα Χριστὸς ἁμαρτίας διάκονος; μὴ
then [is] Christ ²of sin   ¹a minister? not

γένοιτο. 18 εἰ γὰρ ἃ κατέλυσα ταῦτα
May it be.   For if what things I destroyed these things

πάλιν οἰκοδομῶ, παραβάτην ἐμαυτὸν συνισ-
again I build,   ²a transgressor ³myself   ¹I con-

τάνω.   19 ἐγὼ γὰρ διὰ νόμου νόμῳ
stitute.   For I   through law ²to law

ἀπέθανον ἵνα θεῷ ζήσω. Χριστῷ συνεσ-
¹died   in order to God I might live. With Christ I have
          that

ταύρωμαι· 20 ζῶ δὲ οὐκέτι ἐγώ, ζῇ δὲ
been co-crucified; ²live ¹no more ¹I,   but ³lives

ἐν ἐμοὶ Χριστός· ὃ δὲ νῦν ζῶ ἐν σαρκί,
²in ⁴me ¹Christ; and what now I live in [the] flesh,

ἐν πίστει ζῶ τῇ τοῦ υἱοῦ τοῦ θεοῦ
⁵by ²faith ¹I live - of(in) the Son - of God

τοῦ ἀγαπήσαντός με καὶ παραδόντος ἑαυτὸν
-    loving   me and giving up   himself

ὑπὲρ ἐμοῦ. 21 Οὐκ ἀθετῶ τὴν χάριν
on behalf of me.   I do not set aside the   grace

τοῦ θεοῦ· εἰ γὰρ διὰ νόμου δικαιοσύνη,
- of God; for if through law   righteousness,
                                   [comes],

ἄρα Χριστὸς δωρεὰν ἀπέθανεν.
then Christ without cause died.

Chapter 3

Ὦ ἀνόητοι Γαλάται, τίς ὑμᾶς
O foolish Galatians, who you

ἐβάσκανεν, οἷς κατ' ὀφθαλμοὺς Ἰησοῦς
bewitched, to before   eyes   Jesus

Χριστὸς προεγράφη ἐσταυρωμένος; 2 τοῦτο
Christ was portrayed having been crucified? This

μόνον θέλω μαθεῖν ἀφ' ὑμῶν, ἐξ ἔργων
only   I wish to learn from you, by works

νόμου τὸ πνεῦμα ἐλάβετε ἢ ἐξ ἀκοῆς
of law the Spirit received ye or by hearing

πίστεως; 3 οὕτως ἀνόητοί ἐστε; ἐναρξάμενοι
of faith?   thus   so foolish are ye? having begun

πνεύματι νῦν σαρκὶ ἐπιτελεῖσθε; 4 τοσαῦτα
in [the] Spirit now in [the] flesh are ye being so many things
                                perfected?

ἐπάθετε εἰκῇ; 5 εἴ γε καὶ εἰκῇ. ὁ
suffered ye in vain? if indeed in vain. The [one]

οὖν ἐπιχορηγῶν ὑμῖν τὸ πνεῦμα καὶ
therefore supplying to you the Spirit and

ἐνεργῶν δυνάμεις ἐν ὑμῖν ἐξ ἔργων
working powerful deeds among you [is it] by works

νόμου ἢ ἐξ ἀκοῆς πίστεως; 6 Καθὼς
of law or by hearing of faith?   As

Ἀβραὰμ ἐπίστευσεν τῷ θεῷ, καὶ ἐλογίσθη
Abraham believed   - God, and it was reckoned

αὐτῷ εἰς δικαιοσύνην. 7 γινώσκετε ἄρα
to him for righteousness.   Know ye   then

ὅτι οἱ ἐκ πίστεως, οὗτοι υἱοί εἰσιν
that the [ones] of faith, ¹these ²sons ¹are

Ἀβραάμ. 8 προϊδοῦσα δὲ ἡ γραφὴ ὅτι
⁴of Abraham. And ²foreseeing ¹the ³scripture ⁴that

ἐκ πίστεως δικαιοῖ τὰ ἔθνη ὁ θεός,
⁵by ¹⁰faith ⁹would justify ⁶the ⁷nations - ⁸God,

προευηγγελίσατο τῷ Ἀβραὰμ ὅτι ἐνευλογη-
preached good tidings - to Abraham that   ⁴will be
before

θήσονται ἐν σοὶ πάντα τὰ ἔθνη. 9 ὥστε
blessed ¹in ²thee ³all ⁴the ⁵nations. So as

οἱ ἐκ πίστεως εὐλογοῦνται σὺν τῷ πιστῷ
the[ones]of faith are blessed with the believing

Ἀβραάμ. 10 Ὅσοι γὰρ ἐξ ἔργων νόμου
Abraham.   For as many as ²of ³works ⁴of law

εἰσίν, ὑπὸ κατάραν εἰσίν· γέγραπται γὰρ
¹are, ⁵under ⁶a curse ⁴are; for it has been written[,]

ὅτι ἐπικατάρατος πᾶς ὃς οὐκ ἐμμένει
-     Accursed   everyone who continues not

πᾶσιν τοῖς γεγραμμένοις ἐν τῷ βιβλίῳ
in all the things having been written in the roll

τοῦ νόμου τοῦ ποιῆσαι αὐτά. 11 ὅτι
of the law   -   to doᵈ them.   that

δὲ ἐν νόμῳ οὐδεὶς δικαιοῦται παρὰ τῷ
Now by law no man is justified before -

θεῷ δῆλον, ὅτι ὁ δίκαιος ἐκ πίστεως
God [is] clear, because the just man by faith

ζήσεται· 12 ὁ δὲ νόμος οὐκ ἔστιν ἐκ
will live;   and the law   is not   of

πίστεως, ἀλλ' ὁ ποιήσας αὐτὰ ζήσεται
faith,   but the [one] doing them will live

ἐν αὐτοῖς. 13 Χριστὸς ἡμᾶς ἐξηγόρασεν
by them.   Christ   ¹us   ²redeemed

ἐκ τῆς κατάρας τοῦ νόμου γενόμενος
out of the curse of the law becoming

ὑπὲρ ἡμῶν κατάρα, ὅτι γέγραπται·
²on behalf of ¹us ¹a curse, because it has been
                               written:

ἐπικατάρατος πᾶς ὁ κρεμάμενος ἐπὶ
Accursed   everyone hanging   on

ξύλου, 14 ἵνα εἰς τὰ ἔθνη ἡ εὐλογία
a tree,   that to the ²nations ¹the ³blessing

τοῦ Ἀβραὰμ γένηται ἐν Ἰησοῦ Χριστῷ,
- ²of Abraham ⁴might be in Jesus Christ,

ἵνα τὴν ἐπαγγελίαν τοῦ πνεύματος λάβωμεν
in order ²the ³promise ⁴of the ⁵Spirit ¹we might
that   receive

διὰ τῆς πίστεως. 15 Ἀδελφοί, κατὰ
through the faith.   Brothers, according to

ἄνθρωπον λέγω. ὅμως ἀνθρώπου κεκυρω-
man   I say. Nevertheless ⁴of man ³having been

μένην διαθήκην οὐδεὶς ἀθετεῖ ἢ ἐπιδια-
ratified ²a covenant ¹no one ⁵sets aside ⁶or ⁷makes

τάσσεται. 16 τῷ δὲ Ἀβραὰμ ἐρρέθησαν
additions [to].   Now to Abraham were said

αἱ ἐπαγγελίαι καὶ τῷ σπέρματι αὐτοῦ.
the promises and to the seed   of him.

οὐ λέγει· καὶ τοῖς σπέρμασιν, ὡς ἐπὶ
It says not: And to the seeds,   as concerning

πολλῶν, ἀλλ' ὡς ἐφ' ἑνός· καὶ τῷ
many,   but as concerning one: And to the

σπέρματί σου, ὅς ἐστιν Χριστός. 17 τοῦτο δὲ
seed   of thee, who is   Christ.   And this

λέγω· διαθήκην προκεκυρωμένην ὑπὸ
I say: ¹⁰A covenant ¹¹having been previously ratified ¹⁵by

τοῦ θεοῦ ὁ μετὰ τετρακόσια καὶ τριάκοντα
- ¹²God ¹the ⁴after ²four hundred ³and ⁵thirty

ἔτη γεγονὼς νόμος οὐκ ἀκυροῖ, εἰς τὸ
⁷years ⁶having come ⁸law ⁹does not annul, so asᵗ
                                          into being

καταργῆσαι τὴν ἐπαγγελίαν. 18 εἰ γὰρ
to abolish   the   promise.   For if

ἐκ νόμου ἡ κληρονομία, οὐκέτι ἐξ
⁴of ⁵law ¹the ²inheritance ³[is], no more [is it] of

King James Version

ise: but God gave *it* to Abraham by promise. 19 Wherefore then *serveth* the law? It was added because of transgressions, till the seed should come to whom the promise was made; *and it was* ordained by angels in the hand of a mediator. 20 Now a mediator is not *a mediator* of one, but God is one. 21 *Is* the law then against the promises of God? God forbid: for if there had been a law given which could have given life, verily righteousness should have been by the law. 22 But the Scripture hath concluded all under sin, that the promise by faith of Jesus Christ might be given to them that believe. 23 But before faith came, we were kept under the law, shut up unto the faith which should afterwards be revealed. 24 Wherefore the law was our schoolmaster *to bring us* unto Christ, that we might be justified by faith. 25 But after that faith is come, we are no longer under a schoolmaster. 26 For ye are all the children of God by faith in Christ Jesus. 27 For as many of you as have been baptized into Christ have put on Christ. 28 There is neither Jew nor Greek, there is neither bond nor free, there is neither male nor female: for ye are all one in Christ Jesus. 29 And if ye *be* Christ's, then are ye Abraham's seed, and heirs according to the promise.

4 Now I say, *That* the heir, as long as he is a child, differeth nothing from a servant, though he be lord of all; 2 But is under tutors and governors until the time appointed of the father. 3 Even so we, when we were children, were in bondage under the elements of the world: 4 But when the fulness of the time was come, God sent forth his Son, made of a woman, made under the law, 5 To redeem them that were under the law, that we might receive the adoption of sons. 6 And because ye are sons, God hath sent forth the Spirit of his Son into your hearts, crying, Abba, Father. 7 Wherefore thou art no more a servant, but a son; and if a son, then an heir of God through Christ. 8 Howbeit then, when ye knew not God, ye did service unto them which by nature are no gods. 9 But now, after that ye have known God, or rather are known of God, how turn ye again to the weak and beggarly elements, whereunto ye desire again to be in bondage? 10 Ye observe days, and months, and times, and years. 11 I am afraid of you, lest I have bestowed upon you labour in vain. 12 Brethren, I beseech you, be as I *am;* for I *am* as ye *are:* ye have not injured me at all. 13 Ye know how through infirmity of the flesh I preached the gospel unto you at the first. 14 And my temptation which was in my flesh ye despised not, nor rejected; but received me as an angel of God, *even* as Christ Jesus. 15 Where is then the blessedness ye spake of? for I bear you record, that, if *it had been* possible, ye

New International Version

then it no longer depends on a promise; but God in his grace gave it to Abraham through a promise.

19 What, then, was the purpose of the law? It was added because of transgressions until the Seed to whom the promise referred had come. The law was put into effect through angels by a mediator. 20 A mediator, however, does not represent just one party; but God is one.

21 Is the law, therefore, opposed to the promises of God? Absolutely not! For if a law had been given that could impart life, then righteousness would certainly have come by the law. 22 But the Scripture declares that the whole world is a prisoner of sin, so that what was promised, being given through faith in Jesus Christ, might be given to those who believe. 23 Before this faith came, we were held prisoners by the law, locked up until faith should be revealed. 24 So the law was put in charge to lead us to Christ that we might be justified by faith. 25 Now that faith has come, we are no longer under the supervision of the law.

Sons of God

26 You are all sons of God through faith in Christ Jesus, 27 for all of you who were united with Christ in baptism have been clothed with Christ. 28 There is neither Jew nor Greek, slave nor free, male nor female, for you are all one in Christ Jesus. 29 If you belong to Christ, then you are Abraham's seed, and heirs according to the promise.

4 What I am saying is that as long as the heir is a child, he is no different from a slave, although he owns the whole estate. 2 He is subject to guardians and trustees until the time set by his father. 3 So also, when we were children, we were enslaved by the basic principles of the world. 4 But when the time had fully come, God sent his Son, born of a woman, born under law, 5 to redeem those under law, that we might receive the full rights of sons. 6 Because you are sons, God sent the Spirit of his Son into our hearts, the Spirit who calls out, "*Abba,*" Father." 7 So you are no longer a slave, but a son; and since you are a son, God has made you also an heir.

Paul's concern for the Galatians

8 Formerly, when you did not know God, you were slaves to those who by nature are not gods. 9 But now that you know God—or rather are known by God—how is it that you are turning back to those weak and miserable principles? Do you wish to be enslaved by them all over again? 10 You are observing special days and months and seasons and years! 11 I fear for you, that somehow I have wasted my efforts on you.

12 I plead with you, brothers, become like me, for I became like you. You have done me no wrong. 13 As you know, it was because of an illness that I first preached the gospel to you. 14 Even though my illness was a trial to you, you did not treat me with contempt or scorn. Instead, you welcomed me as if I were an angel of God, as if I were Christ Jesus himself. 15 What has happened to all your joy? I can testify that,

[n] Aramaic for *Father.*

Greek Interlinear

ἐπαγγελίας· τῷ δὲ Ἀβραὰμ δι' ἐπαγγελίας
promise; - but ⁴to Abraham ¹through ⁴promise

κεχάρισται ὁ θεός. 19 Τί οὖν ὁ νόμος;
¹has given ²[it] - ¹God.   Why therefore the law?

τῶν παραβάσεων χάριν προσετέθη, ἄχρις
²the ⁴transgressions ³by reason of ¹it was added,   until

ἂν ἔλθῃ τὸ σπέρμα ᾧ ἐπήγγελται,
²should come ¹the ²seed to whom it has been
                                    promised,

διαταγεὶς δι' ἀγγέλων, ἐν χειρὶ μεσίτου.
being ordained through angels, by [the] hand of a mediator.

20 ὁ δὲ μεσίτης ἑνὸς οὐκ ἔστιν, ὁ
   Now the mediator ²of one ¹is not, -

δὲ θεὸς εἷς ἐστιν. 21 ὁ οὖν νόμος κατὰ
but God ²is.   [Is] the ²therefore ¹law against

τῶν ἐπαγγελιῶν [τοῦ θεοῦ]; μὴ γένοιτο.
the promises [- of God? May it not be.

εἰ γὰρ ἐδόθη νόμος ὁ δυνάμενος ζῳοποι-
For if ²was given ¹a law - being able to make

ῆσαι, ὄντως ἐκ νόμου ἂν ἦν ἡ δικαιοσύνη·
alive, really ³by ⁴law ²would - ¹righteousness·
                have been

22 ἀλλὰ συνέκλεισεν ἡ γραφὴ τὰ πάντα
but ²shut up ¹the ³scripture all mankind†

ὑπὸ ἁμαρτίαν ἵνα ἡ ἐπαγγελία ἐκ πίστεως
under sin in or- that the promise by faith

Ἰησοῦ Χριστοῦ δοθῇ τοῖς πιστεύουσιν.
of(in) Jesus Christ might be given to the [ones] believing.

23 Πρὸ τοῦ δὲ ἐλθεῖν τὴν πίστιν ὑπὸ
before the But to come the faithᵇ under
= But before faith came

νόμον ἐφρουρούμεθα συγκλειόμενοι εἰς τὴν
law we were guarded being shut up to the

μέλλουσαν πίστιν ἀποκαλυφθῆναι. 24 ὥστε
²being about ¹faith to be revealed.   So as

ὁ νόμος παιδαγωγὸς ἡμῶν γέγονεν εἰς
the law ²a trainer ³of us ¹has become [up] to

Χριστόν, ἵνα ἐκ πίστεως δικαιωθῶμεν·
Christ, in order that by faith we might be justified·

25 ἐλθούσης δὲ τῆς πίστεως οὐκέτι ὑπὸ
   but ²having come ¹the ³faithᵃ ²no more ⁴under

παιδαγωγόν ἐσμεν. 26 Πάντες γὰρ υἱοὶ
¹a trainer ⁵we are.   For all sons

θεοῦ ἐστε διὰ τῆς πίστεως ἐν Χριστῷ
of God ye are through the faith in Christ

Ἰησοῦ· 27 ὅσοι γὰρ εἰς Χριστὸν ἐβαπτίσ-
Jesus; as many as ¹into ⁴Christ ²were

θητε, Χριστὸν ἐνεδύσασθε. 28 οὐκ ἔνι
baptized, ⁴Christ ³ye put on.   There cannot be

Ἰουδαῖος οὐδὲ Ἕλλην, οὐκ ἔνι δοῦλος
Jew nor Greek, there cannot be slave

οὐδὲ ἐλεύθερος, οὐκ ἔνι ἄρσεν καὶ θῆλυ·
nor freeman, there cannot be male and female·

πάντες γὰρ ὑμεῖς εἷς ἐστε ἐν Χριστῷ
for ²all ¹ye ³one ⁵are in Christ

Ἰησοῦ. 29 εἰ δὲ ὑμεῖς Χριστοῦ, ἄρα
Jesus.   But if ye [are] of Christ, then

τοῦ Ἀβραὰμ σπέρμα ἐστέ, κατ' ἐπαγγελίαν
- ²of Abraham ³a seed ¹are ye, according to promise

Chapter 4

κληρονόμοι. 4 Λέγω δέ, ἐφ' ὅσον χρόνον ὁ
heirs.   But I say, over so long a time as the

κληρονόμος νήπιός ἐστιν, οὐδὲν διαφέρει
heir ²an infant ¹is, ²nothing ¹he differs
                                    ³[from]

δούλου κύριος πάντων ὤν, 2 ἀλλὰ ὑπὸ
⁴a slave ¹lord ²of all ³being, but ¹under

ἐπιτρόπους ἐστὶν καὶ οἰκονόμους ἄχρι τῆς
²guardians ¹is and stewards until the

προθεσμίας τοῦ πατρός. 3 οὕτως καὶ
term previously of the father.   So also
appointed

ἡμεῖς, ὅτε ἦμεν νήπιοι, ὑπὸ τὰ στοιχεῖα
we, when we were infants, under the elements

τοῦ κόσμου ἤμεθα δεδουλωμένοι· 4 ὅτε
of the world we were having been enslaved;   when

δὲ ἦλθεν τὸ πλήρωμα τοῦ χρόνου,
but came the fulness of the time,

ἐξαπέστειλεν ὁ θεὸς τὸν υἱὸν αὐτοῦ,
sent forth - God the Son of him,

γενόμενον ἐκ γυναικός, γενόμενον ὑπὸ
becoming of a woman, becoming under

νόμον, 5 ἵνα τοὺς ὑπὸ νόμον ἐξαγοράσῃ,
law, in order that ²the ones ³under ⁴law ¹he might redeem,

ἵνα τὴν υἱοθεσίαν ἀπολάβωμεν. 6 Ὅτι δέ
in order ¹the ²adoption of sons ¹we might receive.   And because
that

ἐστε υἱοί, ἐξαπέστειλεν ὁ θεὸς τὸ
ye are sons, ²sent forth - ¹God the

πνεῦμα τοῦ υἱοῦ αὐτοῦ εἰς τὰς καρδίας
Spirit of the Son of him into the hearts

ἡμῶν, κρᾶζον· ἀββὰ ὁ πατήρ. 7 ὥστε
of us, crying· Abba - Father.   So as

οὐκέτι εἶ δοῦλος ἀλλὰ υἱός· εἰ δὲ υἱός,
no more art thou a slave but a son· and if a son,

καὶ κληρονόμος διὰ θεοῦ.
also an heir through God.

8 Ἀλλὰ τότε μὲν οὐκ εἰδότες θεὸν
But then indeed not knowing God

ἐδουλεύσατε τοῖς φύσει μὴ οὖσιν θεοῖς·
ye served as slaves ¹the ²by nature ⁴not ³being ⁴gods;

9 νῦν δὲ γνόντες θεόν, μᾶλλον δὲ
but now knowing God, but rather

γνωσθέντες ὑπὸ θεοῦ, πῶς ἐπιστρέφετε
being known by God, how turn ye

πάλιν ἐπὶ τὰ ἀσθενῆ καὶ πτωχὰ στοιχεῖα,
again to the weak and poor elements,

οἷς πάλιν ἄνωθεν δουλεῦσαι θέλετε;
to which again anew ²to serve ¹ye wish?

10 ἡμέρας παρατηρεῖσθε καὶ μῆνας καὶ
²days ¹Ye observe and months and

καιροὺς καὶ ἐνιαυτούς. 11 φοβοῦμαι ὑμᾶς
seasons and years.   I fear [for] you

μή πως εἰκῇ κεκοπίακα εἰς ὑμᾶς.
lest in vain I have laboured among you.

12 Γίνεσθε ὡς ἐγώ, ὅτι κἀγὼ ὡς
Be ye as I [am], because I also [am] as

ὑμεῖς, ἀδελφοί, δέομαι ὑμῶν. οὐδέν με
ye [are], brothers, I beg of you. Nothing me

ἠδικήσατε· 13 οἴδατε δὲ ὅτι δι' ἀσθένειαν
ye wronged· and ye know that on account of weakness

τῆς σαρκὸς εὐηγγελισάμην ὑμῖν τὸ
of the flesh I preached good tidings to you -

πρότερον, 14 καὶ τὸν πειρασμὸν ὑμῶν
formerly, and the trial of you

ἐν τῇ σαρκί μου οὐκ ἐξουθενήσατε οὐδὲ
in the flesh of me ye despised not nor

ἐξεπτύσατε, ἀλλὰ ὡς ἄγγελον θεοῦ ἐδέξασθέ
disdained ye, but as a messenger of God ye received

με, ὡς Χριστὸν Ἰησοῦν. 15 ποῦ οὖν
me, as Christ Jesus.   Where therefore

ὁ μακαρισμὸς ὑμῶν; μαρτυρῶ γὰρ ὑμῖν
the felicitation of you?* for I witness to you

* That is, "your felicitation [of me]".

King James Version

would have plucked out your own eyes, and have given them to me. 16Am I therefore become your enemy, because I tell you the truth? 17 They zealously affect you, *but* not well; yea, they would exclude you, that ye might affect them. 18 But *it is* good to be zealously affected always in *a* good *thing,* and not only when I am present with you. 19 My little children, of whom I travail in birth again until Christ be formed in you, 20 I desire to be present with you now, and to change my voice; for I stand in doubt of you. 21 Tell me, ye that desire to be under the law, do ye not hear the law? 22 For it is written, that Abraham had two sons, the one by a bondmaid, the other by a free woman. 23 But he *who was* of the bondwoman was born after the flesh; but he of the free woman *was* by promise. 24 Which things are an allegory: for these are the two covenants; the one from the mount Sinai, which gendereth to bondage, which is Agar. 25 For this Agar is mount Sinai in Arabia, and answereth to Jerusalem which now is, and is in bondage with her children. 26 But Jerusalem which is above is free, which is the mother of us all. 27 For it is written, Rejoice, thou barren that bearest not; break forth and cry, thou that travailest not: for the desolate hath many more children than she which hath a husband. 28 Now we, brethren, as Isaac was, are the children of promise. 29 But as then he that was born after the flesh persecuted him *that was born* after the Spirit, even so *it is* now. 30 Nevertheless what saith the Scripture? Cast out the bondwoman and her son: for the son of the bondwoman shall not be heir with the son of the free woman. 31 So then, brethren, we are not children of the bondwoman, but of the free.

5 Stand fast therefore in the liberty wherewith Christ hath made us free, and be not entangled again with the yoke of bondage. 2 Behold, I Paul say unto you, that if ye be circumcised, Christ shall profit you nothing. 3 For I testify again to every man that is circumcised, that he is a debtor to do the whole law. 4 Christ is become of no effect unto you, whosoever of you are justified by the law; ye are fallen from grace. 5 For we through the Spirit wait for the hope of righteousness by faith. 6 For in Jesus Christ neither circumcision availeth any thing, nor uncircumcision; but faith which worketh by love. 7 Ye did run well; who did hinder you that ye should not obey the truth? 8 This persuasion *cometh* not of him that calleth you. 9A little leaven leaveneth the whole lump. 10 I have confidence in you through the Lord, that ye will be none otherwise minded: but he that troubleth you shall bear his judgment, whosoever he be.

New International Version

if you could have done so, you would have torn out your eyes and given them to me. 16 Have I now become your enemy by telling you the truth? 17 Those people are zealous to win you over, but for no good. What they want is to alienate you [from us], so that you may be zealous for them. 18 It is fine to be zealous, provided the purpose is good, and to be so always and not just when I am with you. 19 My dear children, for whom I am again in the pains of childbirth until Christ is formed in you, 20 how I wish I could be with you now and change my tone, because I am perplexed about you!

Hagar and Sarah

21 Tell me, you who want to be under the law, are you not aware of what the law says? 22 For it is written that Abraham had two sons, one by the slave woman and the other by the free woman. 23 His son by the slave woman was born in the ordinary way; but his son by the free woman was born as the result of a promise.

24 These things may be taken figuratively, for the women represent two covenants. One covenant is from Mount Sinai and bears children who are to be slaves: This is Hagar. 25 Now Hagar stands for Mount Sinai in Arabia and corresponds to the present city of Jerusalem, because she is in slavery with her children. 26 But the Jerusalem that is above is free, and she is our mother. 27 For it is written:

"Be glad, O barren woman,
    who bears no children;
break forth and cry aloud,
    you who have no labor pains;
because more are the children of the desolate woman
    than of her who has a husband." [o]

28 Now you, brothers, like Isaac, are children of promise. 29At that time the son born in the ordinary way persecuted the son born by the power of the Spirit. It is the same now. 30 But what does the Scripture say? "Get rid of the slave woman and her son, for the slave woman's son will never share in the inheritance with the free woman's son." [p] 31 Therefore, brothers, we are not children of the slave woman, but of the free woman.

Freedom in Christ

5 It is for freedom that Christ has set us free. Stand firm, then, and do not let yourselves be burdened again by a yoke of slavery.

2 Mark my words! I, Paul, tell you that if you let yourselves be circumcised, Christ will be of no value to you at all. 3Again I declare to every man who lets himself be circumcised that he is obligated to obey the whole law. 4 You who are trying to be justified by law have been alienated from Christ; you have fallen away from grace. 5 But by faith we eagerly await through the Spirit the righteousness for which we hope. 6 For in Christ Jesus neither circumcision nor uncircumcision has any value. The only thing that counts is faith expressing itself through love.

7 You were running a good race. Who cut in on you and kept you from obeying the truth? 8 That kind of persuasion does not come from the one who calls you. 9 "A little yeast works through the whole batch of dough." 10 I am confident in the Lord that you will take no other view. The one who is throwing you into confusion will pay the penalty, whoever he may be.

Greek Interlinear

ὅτι εἰ δυνατὸν τοὺς ὀφθαλμοὺς ὑμῶν
that if possible ²the ¹eyes ⁴of you
ἐξορύξαντες ἐδώκατέ μοι. 16 ὥστε ἐχθρὸς
¹gouging out ye gave [them] to me. So that ²an enemy
ὑμῶν γέγονα ἀληθεύων ὑμῖν; 17 ζηλοῦσιν
³of you ¹have I become speaking truth to you? They are zealous of
ὑμᾶς οὐ καλῶς, ἀλλὰ ἐκκλεῖσαι ὑμᾶς
you not well, but ²to exclude ³you
θέλουσιν, 18 ἵνα αὐτοὺς ζηλοῦτε. καλὸν δὲ
¹wish, in order them ye may be But [it is] good
that zealous of.
ζηλοῦσθαι ἐν καλῷ πάντοτε, καὶ μὴ
to be zealous in a good thing always, and not
μόνον ἐν τῷ παρεῖναί με πρὸς ὑμᾶς,
only in the to be present meᵇᵉ with you,
—when I am present
19 τέκνα μου, οὓς πάλιν ὠδίνω μέχρις οὗ
children of me,[for] whom again I travail until
in birth
μορφωθῇ Χριστὸς ἐν ὑμῖν· 20 ἤθελον δὲ
²is formed ¹Christ in you; and I wished
παρεῖναι πρὸς ὑμᾶς ἄρτι καὶ ἀλλάξαι
to be present with you just now and to change
τὴν φωνήν μου, ὅτι ἀπορούμαι ἐν ὑμῖν.
the voice of me, because I am perplexed in(about) you.
21 Λέγετέ μοι, οἱ ὑπὸ νόμον θέλοντες
Tell me, the [ones] ²under ¹law ¹wishing
εἶναι, τὸν νόμον οὐκ ἀκούετε; 22 γέγραπται
²to be, ²the ¹law ¹hear ye not? ²it has been written
γὰρ ὅτι Ἀβραὰμ δύο υἱοὺς ἔσχεν, ἕνα
¹for that Abraham two sons had, one
ἐκ τῆς παιδίσκης καὶ ἕνα ἐκ τῆς ἐλευ-
of the maidservant and one of the free
θέρας. 23 ἀλλ' ὁ [μὲν] ἐκ τῆς παιδίσκης
woman. But the [one] indeed of the maidservant
κατὰ σάρκα γεγέννηται, ὁ δὲ ἐκ τῆς
according to flesh has been born, but the [one] of the
ἐλευθέρας διὰ τῆς ἐπαγγελίας. 24 ἅτινά
free woman through the promise. Which things
ἐστιν ἀλληγορούμενα· αὗται γάρ εἰσιν
is(are) being allegorized; for these are
δύο διαθῆκαι, μία μὲν ἀπὸ ὄρους Σινά,
two covenants, one indeed from mount Sina,

εἰς δουλείαν γεννῶσα, ἥτις ἐστὶν Ἀγάρ.
to slavery bringing forth, which is Hagar.
25 τὸ δὲ Ἀγὰρ Σινὰ ὄρος ἐστὶν ἐν
⁴The ²now ⁵Hagar ⁶Sina ⁷mount ³is in
τῇ Ἀραβίᾳ· συστοιχεῖ δὲ τῇ νῦν
- Arabia; and corresponds to the now
Ἰερουσαλήμ, δουλεύει γὰρ μετὰ τῶν
Jerusalem, for she serves as a slave with the
τέκνων αὐτῆς. 26 ἡ δὲ ἄνω Ἰερουσαλὴμ
children of her. But the above Jerusalem
ἐλευθέρα ἐστίν, ἥτις ἐστὶν μήτηρ ἡμῶν·
free is, who is mother of us;
27 γέγραπται γάρ· εὐφράνθητι, στεῖρα ἡ
for it has been written: Be thou glad, barren[,] the
[one]
οὐ τίκτουσα, ῥῆξον καὶ βόησον, ἡ οὐκ
not bearing, break forth and shout, the [one] not
ὠδίνουσα· ὅτι πολλὰ τὰ τέκνα τῆς ἐρήμου
travailing; because many [are] the children of the desolate
μᾶλλον ἢ τῆς ἐχούσης τὸν ἄνδρα. 28 ὑμεῖς
rather than of the having the husband. ye
δέ, ἀδελφοί, κατὰ Ἰσαὰκ ἐπαγγελίας τέκνα
But, brothers, ²according to ³Isaac ⁴of promise ⁵children
ἐστέ. 29 ἀλλ' ὥσπερ τότε ὁ κατὰ σάρκα
¹are. But even as then the [one] according to flesh
γεννηθεὶς ἐδίωκεν τὸν κατὰ πνεῦμα, οὕτως
born persecuted the [one] according spirit, so
[born] to
καὶ νῦν. 30 ἀλλὰ τί λέγει ἡ γραφή;
also now. But what says the scripture?
ἔκβαλε τὴν παιδίσκην καὶ τὸν υἱὸν αὐτῆς·
Cast out the maidservant and the son of her;
οὐ γὰρ μὴ κληρονομήσει ὁ υἱὸς τῆς
for by no means ²shall inherit ¹the ²son ²of the
παιδίσκης μετὰ τοῦ υἱοῦ τῆς ἐλευθέρας.
⁴maidservant with the son of the free woman.
31 διό, ἀδελφοί, οὐκ ἐσμὲν παιδίσκης
Wherefore, brothers, we are not ²of a maidservant
τέκνα ἀλλὰ τῆς ἐλευθέρας.
¹children but of the free woman.

Chapter 5

Τῇ ἐλευθερίᾳ ἡμᾶς Χριστὸς ἠλευθέρωσεν·
For the freedom ²us ¹Christ ²freed;
στήκετε οὖν καὶ μὴ πάλιν ζυγῷ δουλείας
stand firm therefore and not again with a yoke of slavery
ἐνέχεσθε.
be entangled.
2 Ἴδε ἐγὼ Παῦλος λέγω ὑμῖν ὅτι
Behold[,] I Paul te¹¹ you that
ἐὰν περιτέμνησθε Χριστὸς ὑμᾶς οὐδὲν
if ye are circumcised Christ ²you ¹nothing
ὠφελήσει. 3 μαρτύρομαι δὲ πάλιν παντὶ
¹will profit. And I testify again to every
ἀνθρώπῳ περιτεμνομένῳ ὅτι ὀφειλέτης ἐστὶν
man being circumcised that ²a debtor ¹he is
ὅλον τὸν νόμον ποιῆσαι. 4 κατηργήθητε
⁴all ¹the ⁴law ²to do. Ye were discharged
ἀπὸ Χριστοῦ οἵτινες ἐν νόμῳ δικαιοῦσθε,
from Christ who by law are justified,
τῆς χάριτος ἐξεπέσατε. 5 ἡμεῖς γὰρ
the ²grace ¹ye fell from. For we
πνεύματι ἐκ πίστεως ἐλπίδα δικαιοσύνης
in spirit by faith [the] hope of righteousness

ἀπεκδεχόμεθα. 6 ἐν γὰρ Χριστῷ Ἰησοῦ
eagerly expect. For in Christ Jesus
οὔτε περιτομή τι ἰσχύει οὔτε ἀκροβυστία,
neither circumcision ²anything ¹avails nor uncircumcision,
ἀλλὰ πίστις δι' ἀγάπης ἐνεργουμένη.
but faith ²through ²love ¹operating.
7 Ἐτρέχετε καλῶς· τίς ὑμᾶς ἐνέκοψεν
Ye were running well; who ²you ¹hindered
ἀληθείᾳ μὴ πείθεσθαι; 8 ἡ πεισμονὴ οὐκ
²by truth ¹not ²to be persuaded? the(this) persuasion not
ἐκ τοῦ καλοῦντος ὑμᾶς. 9 μικρὰ ζύμη
of the [one] calling you. A little leaven
ὅλον τὸ φύραμα ζυμοῖ. 10 ἐγὼ πέποιθα
all the lump leavens. I trust
εἰς ὑμᾶς ἐν κυρίῳ ὅτι οὐδὲν ἄλλο φρο-
as to² you in [the] Lord that ²nothing ¹other ²ye
νήσετε· ὁ δὲ ταράσσων ὑμᾶς βαστάσει
will think; but the [one] troubling you shall bear

King James Version

11And I, brethren, if I yet preach circumcision, why do I yet suffer persecution? then is the offence of the cross ceased. 12 I would they were even cut off which trouble you. 13 For, brethren, ye have been called unto liberty; only *use* not liberty for an occasion to the flesh, but by love serve one another. 14 For all the law is fulfilled in one word, *even* in this; Thou shalt love thy neighbour as thyself. 15 But if ye bite and devour one another, take heed that ye be not consumed one of another. 16 *This* I say then, Walk in the Spirit, and ye shall not fulfil the lust of the flesh. 17 For the flesh lusteth against the Spirit, and the Spirit against the flesh: and these are contrary the one to the other; so that ye cannot do the things that ye would. 18 But if ye be led of the Spirit, ye are not under the law. 19 Now the works of the flesh are manifest, which are *these*, Adultery, fornication, uncleanness, lasciviousness, 20 Idolatry, witchcraft, hatred, variance, emulations, wrath, strife, seditions, heresies, 21 Envyings, murders, drunkenness, revellings, and such like: of the which I tell you before, as I have also told *you* in time past, that they which do such things shall not inherit the kingdom of God. 22 But the fruit of the Spirit is love, joy, peace, longsuffering, gentleness, goodness, faith, 23 Meekness, temperance: against such there is no law. 24And they that are Christ's have crucified the flesh with the affections and lusts. 25 If we live in the Spirit, let us also walk in the Spirit. 26 Let us not be desirous of vainglory, provoking one another, envying one another.

6 Brethren, if a man be overtaken in a fault, ye which are spiritual, restore such a one in the spirit of meekness; considering thyself, lest thou also be tempted. 2 Bear ye one another's burdens, and so fulfil the law of Christ. 3 For if a man think himself to be something, when he is nothing, he deceiveth himself. 4 But let every man prove his own work, and then shall he have rejoicing in himself alone, and not in another. 5 For every man shall bear his own burden. 6 Let him that is taught in the word communicate unto him that teacheth in all good things. 7 Be not deceived; God is not mocked: for whatsoever a man soweth, that shall he also reap. 8 For he that soweth to his flesh shall of the flesh reap corruption; but he that soweth to the Spirit shall of the Spirit reap life everlasting. 9And let us not be weary in well doing: for in due season we shall reap, if we faint not. 10As we have therefore opportunity, let us do good unto all *men*, especially unto them who are of

New International Version

11 Brothers, if I am still preaching circumcision, why am I still being persecuted? In that case the offense of the cross has been abolished. 12As for those agitators, I wish they would go the whole way and emasculate themselves!

Life by the Spirit

13 You, my brothers, were called to be free. But do not use your freedom to indulge your sinful nature; rather, serve one another in love. 14 The entire law is summed up in a single command: "Love your neighbor as yourself." *q* 15 If you keep on biting and devouring each other, watch out or you will be destroyed by each other. 16 So I say, live by the Spirit, and you will not gratify the desires of your sinful nature. 17 For the sinful nature desires what is contrary to the Spirit, and the Spirit what is contrary to the sinful nature. They are in conflict with each other, so that you do not do what you want. 18 But if you are led by the Spirit, you are not under law.

19 The acts of the sinful nature are obvious: sexual immorality, impurity and debauchery; 20 idolatry and witchcraft; hatred, discord, jealousy, fits of rage, selfish ambition, dissensions, factions 21 and envy; drunkenness, orgies, and the like. I warn you, as I did before, that those who live like this will not inherit the kingdom of God.

22 But the fruit of the Spirit is love, joy, peace, patience, kindness, goodness, faithfulness, 23 gentleness and self-control. Against such things there is no law. 24 Those who belong to Christ Jesus have crucified their sinful nature with its passions and desires. 25 Since we live by the Spirit, let us keep in step with the Spirit. 26 Let us not become conceited, provoking and envying each other.

Doing good to all

6 Brothers, if a man is trapped in some sin, you who are spiritual should restore him gently. But watch yourself; you also may be tempted. 2 Carry each other's burdens, and in this way you will fulfill the law of Christ. 3 If anyone thinks he is something when he is nothing, he deceives himself. 4 Each man should test his own actions. Then he can take pride in himself, without comparing himself to somebody else, 5 for each man should carry his own load.

6 Anyone who receives instruction in the word must share all good things with his instructor.

7 Do not be deceived: God cannot be mocked. A man reaps what he sows. 8 The one who sows to please his sinful nature, from that nature will reap destruction; the one who sows to please the Spirit, from the Spirit will reap eternal life. 9 Let us not become weary in doing good, for at the proper time we will reap a harvest if we do not give up. 10 Therefore, as we have opportunity, let us do good to all people, especially to those who belong to the family of believers.

[q] Lev. 19:18.

Greek Interlinear

τὸ κρίμα, ὅστις ἐὰν ᾖ. 11 Ἐγὼ δέ,
the judgment, whoever he may be. ¹But ⁴I,

ἀδελφοί, εἰ περιτομὴν ἔτι κηρύσσω, τί
²brothers, ³if ⁷circumcision ⁵still ⁶proclaim, why

ἔτι διώκομαι; ἄρα κατήργηται τὸ
still am I being persecuted? then has been annulled the

σκάνδαλον τοῦ σταυροῦ. 12 Ὄφελον καὶ
offence of the cross. I would that indeed

ἀποκόψονται οἱ ἀναστατοῦντες ὑμᾶς.
⁴will(might) cut ¹the [ones] ²unsettling ³you.
themselves off

13 Ὑμεῖς γὰρ ἐπ' ἐλευθερίᾳ ἐκλήθητε,
For ye for freedom were called,

ἀδελφοί· μόνον μὴ τὴν ἐλευθερίαν εἰς
brothers; only [use] not the freedom for

ἀφορμὴν τῇ σαρκί, ἀλλὰ διὰ τῆς ἀγάπης
advantage to the flesh, but through – love

δουλεύετε ἀλλήλοις. 14 ὁ γὰρ πᾶς νόμος
serve ye as slaves one another. For the whole law

ἐν ἑνὶ λόγῳ πεπλήρωται, ἐν τῷ· ἀγα-
in one word has been summed up, in the [word]: Thou

πήσεις τὸν πλησίον σου ὡς σεαυτόν.
shalt love the neighbour of thee as thyself.

15 εἰ δὲ ἀλλήλους δάκνετε καὶ κατεσθίετε,
But if ⁴one another ¹ye bite ²and ³ye devour,

βλέπετε μὴ ὑπ' ἀλλήλων ἀναλωθῆτε.
see lest by one another ye are destroyed.

16 Λέγω δέ, πνεύματι περιπατεῖτε καὶ
Now I say, in spirit walk ye and

ἐπιθυμίαν σαρκὸς οὐ μὴ τελέσητε. 17 ἡ
[the] lust of [the] flesh by no means ye will perform. the

γὰρ σὰρξ ἐπιθυμεῖ κατὰ τοῦ πνεύματος,
For flesh lusts against the spirit,

τὸ δὲ πνεῦμα κατὰ τῆς σαρκός, ταῦτα
and the spirit against the flesh, ³these

γὰρ ἀλλήλοις ἀντίκειται, ἵνα μὴ ἃ ἐὰν
¹for ⁴each other ²opposes, lest whatever things

θέλητε ταῦτα ποιῆτε. 18 εἰ δὲ πνεύματι
ye wish these ye do. But if by [the] Spirit

ἄγεσθε, οὐκ ἐστὲ ὑπὸ νόμον. 19 φανερὰ δέ
ye are led, ye are not under law. Now ²manifest

ἐστιν τὰ ἔργα τῆς σαρκός, ἅτινά ἐστιν
¹is(are) ¹the ²works ³of the ⁴flesh, which is(are)

πορνεία, ἀκαθαρσία, ἀσέλγεια, 20 εἰδωλο-
fornication, uncleanness, lewdness, idola-

λατρία, φαρμακεία, ἔχθραι, ἔρις, ζῆλος,
try, sorcery, enmities, strife, jealousy,

θυμοί, ἐριθεῖαι, διχοστασίαι, αἱρέσεις,
angers, rivalries, divisions, sects,

21 φθόνοι, μέθαι, κῶμοι, καὶ τὰ ὅμοια
envyings, drunken- revellings, and – like
nesses, things

τούτοις, ἃ προλέγω ὑμῖν καθὼς προεῖπον,
to these, which I tell ²beforehand ¹you as I previously
said,

ὅτι οἱ τὰ τοιαῦτα πράσσοντες βασιλείαν
that the [ones] – ²such things ¹practising ⁴[the] kingdom

θεοῦ οὐ κληρονομήσουσιν. 22 ὁ δὲ καρπὸς
³of God ⁵will not inherit. But the fruit

τοῦ πνεύματός ἐστιν ἀγάπη, χαρά, εἰρήνη,
of the Spirit is love, joy, peace,

μακροθυμία, χρηστότης, ἀγαθωσύνη, πίστις,
longsuffering, kindness, goodness, faithfulness,

23 πραΰτης, ἐγκράτεια· κατὰ τῶν τοιούτων
meekness, self-control; against – such things

οὐκ ἔστιν νόμος. 24 οἱ δὲ τοῦ Χριστοῦ
there is no law. Now the ones – of Christ

Ἰησοῦ τὴν σάρκα ἐσταύρωσαν σὺν τοῖς
Jesus ²the ²flesh ¹crucified with the(its)

παθήμασιν καὶ ταῖς ἐπιθυμίαις. 25 Εἰ
passions and the(its) lusts. If

ζῶμεν πνεύματι, πνεύματι καὶ στοιχῶμεν.
we live in [the] Spirit, in [the] Spirit also let us walk.

26 μὴ γινώμεθα κενόδοξοι, ἀλλήλους
Let us not become vainglorious, one another

προκαλούμενοι, ἀλλήλοις φθονοῦντες.
provoking, one another envying.

Chapter 6

Ἀδελφοί, ἐὰν καὶ προλημφθῇ ἄνθρω-
Brothers, if indeed ²is overtaken ¹a

πος ἔν τινι παραπτώματι, ὑμεῖς οἱ
man in some trespass, ye the

πνευματικοὶ καταρτίζετε τὸν τοιοῦτον ἐν
spiritual [ones] restore – such a one in

πνεύματι πραΰτητος, σκοπῶν σεαυτόν, μὴ
a spirit of meekness, considering thyself, lest

καὶ σὺ πειρασθῇς. 2 Ἀλλήλων τὰ βάρη
also thou art tempted. Of one another the loads

βαστάζετε, καὶ οὕτως ἀναπληρώσετε τὸν
bear ye, and so ye will fulfil the

νόμον τοῦ Χριστοῦ. 3 εἰ γὰρ δοκεῖ
law – of Christ. For if ²thinks

τις εἶναί τι μηδὲν ὤν, φρεναπατᾷ ἑαυτόν.
¹anyone ²to be ³some- ⁶no- ⁵being, he deceives himself.
thing thing

4 τὸ δὲ ἔργον ἑαυτοῦ δοκιμαζέτω ἕκαστος,
But the work of himself ¹let ²prove ³each man,

καὶ τότε εἰς ἑαυτὸν μόνον τὸ καύχημα
and then in himself alone the boast

ἕξει καὶ οὐκ εἰς τὸν ἕτερον· 5 ἕκαστος
he will and not in the other man; ²each man
have

γὰρ τὸ ἴδιον φορτίον βαστάσει. 6 Κοινωνείτω δὲ
¹for the(his) own burden will bear. And ²let him share

ὁ κατηχούμενος τὸν λόγον τῷ κατη-
¹the ⁵being instructed [in] ³the ⁴word ⁶with the [one] in-
[one]

χοῦντι ἐν πᾶσιν ἀγαθοῖς. 7 Μὴ πλανᾶσθε,
structing in all good things. Be ye not led astray,

θεὸς οὐ μυκτηρίζεται. ὃ γὰρ ἐὰν σπείρῃ
God is not mocked. For whatever ²may sow

ἄνθρωπος, τοῦτο καὶ θερίσει· 8 ὅτι ὁ
¹a man, this also he will reap; because the

σπείρων εἰς τὴν σάρκα ἑαυτοῦ ἐκ τῆς
[one] sowing to the flesh of himself of the

σαρκὸς θερίσει φθοράν, ὁ δὲ σπείρων
flesh will reap corruption, but the [one] sowing

εἰς τὸ πνεῦμα ἐκ τοῦ πνεύματος θερίσει
to the spirit of the Spirit will reap

ζωὴν αἰώνιον. 9 τὸ δὲ καλὸν ποιοῦντες
life eternal. And ²the ²good ¹doing

μὴ ἐγκακῶμεν· καιρῷ γὰρ ἰδίῳ
let us not lose heart; for in its own time

θερίσομεν μὴ ἐκλυόμενοι. 10 Ἄρα οὖν
we shall reap not failing. Then therefore

ὡς καιρὸν ἔχομεν, ἐργαζώμεθα τὸ ἀγαθὸν
as ²time ¹we have, let us do the good

πρὸς πάντας, μάλιστα δὲ πρὸς τοὺς
to all men, and most of all to the

οἰκείους τῆς πίστεως.
members of of the faith.
the family

King James Version

the household of faith. 11Ye see how large a letter I have written unto you with mine own hand. 12As many as desire to make a fair shew in the flesh, they constrain you to be circumcised; only lest they should suffer persecution for the cross of Christ. 13 For neither they themselves who are circumcised keep the law; but desire to have you circumcised, that they may glory in your flesh. 14 But God forbid that I should glory, save in the cross of our Lord Jesus Christ, by whom the world is crucified unto me, and I unto the world. 15 For in Christ Jesus neither circumcision availeth any thing, nor uncircumcision, but a new creature. 16And as many as walk according to this rule, peace *be* on them, and mercy, and upon the Israel of God. 17 From henceforth let no man trouble me: for I bear in my body the marks of the Lord Jesus. 18 Brethren, the grace of our Lord Jesus Christ *be* with your spirit. Amen.

Unto the Galatians written from Rome.

New International Version

Not circumcision but a new creation

11 See what large letters I use as I write to you with my own hand!
12 Those who want to make a good impression outwardly are trying to compel you to be circumcised. The only reason they do this is to avoid being persecuted for the cross of Christ. 13 Not even those who are circumcised obey the law, yet they want you to be circumcised that they may boast about your flesh. 14 May I never boast except in the cross of our Lord Jesus Christ, through which the world has been crucified to me, and I to the world. 15 Neither circumcision nor uncircumcision means anything; what counts is a new creation. 16 Peace and mercy to all who follow this rule, even to the Israel of God.
17 Finally, let no one cause me trouble, for I bear on my body the marks of Jesus.
18 The grace of our Lord Jesus Christ be with your spirit, brothers. Amen.

11 Ἴδετε   πηλίκοις   ὑμῖν   γράμμασιν
Ye see   in how large   ⁸to you   ¹letters

ἔγραψα   τῇ   ἐμῇ   χειρί.   12 Ὅσοι   θέλουσιν
¹I wrote   -   with my   hand.   As many as   wish

εὐπροσωπῆσαι   ἐν   σαρκί,   οὗτοι   ἀναγκάζουσιν
to look well   in   [the] flesh,   these   compel

ὑμᾶς   περιτέμνεσθαι,   μόνον   ἵνα   τῷ
you   to be circumcised,   only   in order that   ⁸for the

σταυρῷ   τοῦ   Χριστοῦ   [Ἰησοῦ]   μὴ
⁴cross   -   ⁶of Christ   ⁵Jesus   ¹not

διώκωνται.   13 οὐδὲ   γὰρ   οἱ   περιτεμνόμενοι
²they are persecuted.   For ²not   ¹the [ones]   ⁸being circumcised

αὐτοὶ   νόμον   φυλάσσουσιν,   ἀλλὰ   θέλουσιν
³themselves   ⁵law   ⁴keep,   but   they wish

ὑμᾶς   περιτέμνεσθαι   ἵνα   ἐν   τῇ   ὑμετέρᾳ
you   to be circumcised in order that   ²in   -   ⁴your

σαρκὶ   καυχήσωνται.   14 ἐμοὶ   δὲ   μὴ   γένοιτο
⁴flesh   ¹they may boast.   But to me   may it not be

καυχᾶσθαι   εἰ   μὴ   ἐν   τῷ   σταυρῷ   τοῦ
to boast   except   in   the   cross   of the

κυρίου   ἡμῶν   Ἰησοῦ   Χριστοῦ,   δι’   οὗ
Lord   of us   Jesus   Christ,   through whom

ἐμοὶ   κόσμος   ἐσταύρωται   κἀγὼ   κόσμῳ.
to me   [the] world   has been crucified   and I to [the] world.

15 οὔτε   γὰρ   περιτομή   τί   ἐστιν   οὔτε
For neither   circumcision   ⁸anything   ¹is   nor

ἀκροβυστία,   ἀλλὰ   καινὴ   κτίσις.   16 καὶ
uncircumcision,   but   a new   creation.   And

ὅσοι   τῷ   κανόνι   τούτῳ   στοιχήσουσιν,
as many as   by this rule   will walk,

εἰρήνη   ἐπ’   αὐτοὺς   καὶ   ἔλεος,   καὶ   ἐπὶ   τὸν
peace   on   them   and   mercy,   and   on   the

Ἰσραὴλ   τοῦ   θεοῦ.
Israel   -   of God.

17 Τοῦ   λοιποῦ   κόπους   μοι   μηδεὶς
For the rest   ⁴troubles   ⁴me   ⁸no one

παρεχέτω·   ἐγὼ   γὰρ   τὰ   στίγματα   τοῦ
¹let ⁵cause;   for ¹I   ⁸the   ⁶brands   -

Ἰησοῦ   ἐν   τῷ   σώματί   μου   βαστάζω.
⁷of Jesus   ⁴in   ⁸the   ⁶body   ⁴of me   ²bear.

18 Ἡ   χάρις   τοῦ   κυρίου   ἡμῶν   Ἰησοῦ
The   grace   of the   Lord   of us   Jesus

Χριστοῦ   μετὰ   τοῦ   πνεύματος   ὑμῶν,
Christ   with   the   spirit   of you,

ἀδελφοί·   ἀμήν.
brothers :   Amen.

King James Version   New International Version

THE EPISTLE OF

PAUL THE APOSTLE

TO THE

EPHESIANS

EPHESIANS

1 Paul, an apostle of Jesus Christ by the will of God, to the saints which are at Ephesus, and to the faithful in Christ Jesus: 2 Grace *be* to you, and peace, from God our Father, and *from* the Lord Jesus Christ. 3 Blessed *be* the God and Father of our Lord Jesus Christ, who hath blessed us with all spiritual blessings in heavenly *places* in Christ: 4According as he hath chosen us in him before the foundation of the world, that we should be holy and without blame before him in love: 5 Having predestinated us unto the adoption of children by Jesus Christ to himself, according to the good pleasure of his will,. 6 To the praise of the glory of his grace, wherein he hath made us accepted in the beloved: 7 In whom we have redemption through his blood, the forgiveness of sins, according to the riches of his grace; 8 Wherein he hath abounded toward us in all wisdom and prudence; 9 Having made known unto us the mystery of his will, according to his good pleasure which he hath purposed in himself: 10 That in the dispensation of the fulness of times he might gather together in one all things in Christ, both which are in heaven, and which are on earth; *even* in him: 11 In whom also we have obtained an inheritance, being predestinated according to the purpose of him who worketh all things after the counsel of his own will: 12 That we should be to the praise of his glory, who first trusted in Christ. 13 In whom ye also *trusted,* after that ye heard the word of truth, the gospel of your salvation: in whom also, after that ye believed, ye were sealed with that Holy Spirit of promise, 14 Which is the earnest of our inheritance until the redemption of the purchased possession, unto the praise of his glory. 15 Wherefore I also, after I heard of your faith in the Lord Jesus, and love unto all the saints, 16 Cease not to give thanks for you, making mention of you in my prayers; 17 That the God of our Lord Jesus Christ, the Father of glory, may give unto you the spirit of wisdom and revelation in the knowledge of him: 18 The eyes of your understanding being enlightened; that ye may know what is the hope of his calling, and what the riches of the glory of his inheritance in the saints, 19And what *is* the exceeding greatness of his power to

1 Paul, an apostle of Christ Jesus by the will of God,
To the saints in Ephesus,*a* the faithful in Christ Jesus:
2 Grace and peace to you from God our Father and the Lord Jesus Christ.

Spiritual blessings in Christ

3 Praise be to the God and Father of our Lord Jesus Christ, who has blessed us in the heavenly realms with every spiritual blessing in Christ. 4 For he chose us in him before the creation of the world to be holy and blameless in his sight. In love 5 he*b* predestined us to be adopted as sons through Jesus Christ, in accordance with his pleasure and will—6 to the praise of his glorious grace, which he has freely given us in the One he loves. 7 In him we have redemption through his blood, the forgiveness of sins, in accordance with the riches of God's grace 8 that he lavished on us with all wisdom and understanding. 9And he*c* made known to us the mystery of his will according to his good pleasure, which he purposed in Christ, 10 to be put into effect when the times will have reached their fulfillment—to bring all things in heaven and on earth together under one head, even Christ.

11 In him we were also chosen, having been predestined according to the plan of him who works out everything in conformity with the purpose of his will, 12 in order that we, who were the first to hope in Christ, might be for the praise of his glory. 13And you also were included in Christ when you heard the word of truth, the gospel of your salvation. In him, when you believed, you were marked with a seal, the promised Holy Spirit, 14 who is a deposit guaranteeing our inheritance until the redemption of those who are God's possession—to the praise of his glory.

Thanksgiving and prayer

15 For this reason, I, since I heard about your faith in the Lord Jesus and your love for all the saints, 16 have never stopped giving thanks for you, remembering you in my prayers. 17 I keep asking that the God of our Lord Jesus Christ, the glorious Father, may give you the Spirit*d* of wisdom and revelation, so that you may know him better. 18 I pray also that the eyes of your heart may be enlightened in order that you may know the hope to which he has called you, the riches of his glorious inheritance in the saints, 19 and his incomparably great power for us who

[a] Some early MSS omit *in Ephesus.* [b] Or *sight in love.* *⁵He.* [c] Or *us. With all wisdom and understanding,* *⁹he.* [d] Or *a spirit.*

ΠΡΟΣ   ΕΦΕΣΙΟΥΣ

Chapter 1

Παῦλος ἀπόστολος Χριστοῦ Ἰησοῦ διὰ
Paul   an apostle of Christ Jesus through

θελήματος θεοῦ τοῖς ἁγίοις τοῖς οὖσιν
[the] will of God to the saints – being

[ἐν Ἐφέσῳ] καὶ πιστοῖς ἐν Χριστῷ
in Ephesus and faithful in Christ

Ἰησοῦ· 2 χάρις ὑμῖν καὶ εἰρήνη ἀπὸ
Jesus: Grace to you and peace from

θεοῦ πατρὸς ἡμῶν καὶ κυρίου Ἰησοῦ
God Father of us and Lord Jesus

Χριστοῦ.
Christ.

3 Εὐλογητὸς ὁ θεὸς καὶ πατὴρ τοῦ
Blessed   the God and Father of the

κυρίου ἡμῶν Ἰησοῦ Χριστοῦ, ὁ εὐλογήσας
Lord   of us Jesus Christ, the having
                                   [one] blessed

ἡμᾶς ἐν πάσῃ εὐλογίᾳ πνευματικῇ ἐν
us   with every blessing spiritual in

τοῖς ἐπουρανίοις ἐν Χριστῷ, 4 καθὼς
the heavenlies in Christ,   as

ἐξελέξατο ἡμᾶς ἐν αὐτῷ πρὸ καταβολῆς
he chose us in him before [the] foundation

κόσμου, εἶναι ἡμᾶς ἁγίους καὶ ἀμώμους
of [the] world, to be us holy and unblemished
                         –that we should be ...

κατενώπιον αὐτοῦ, ἐν ἀγάπῃ 5 προορίσας
before   him, in love   predestinating

ἡμᾶς εἰς υἱοθεσίαν διὰ Ἰησοῦ Χριστοῦ
us   to adoption of sons through Jesus Christ

εἰς αὐτόν, κατὰ τὴν εὐδοκίαν τοῦ
to him[self], according to the good pleasure of the

θελήματος αὐτοῦ, 6 εἰς ἔπαινον δόξης
will   of him,   to [the] praise of [the] glory

τῆς χάριτος αὐτοῦ, ἧς ἐχαρίτωσεν ἡμᾶς
of the grace of him, of(with) he favoured us
                              which

ἐν τῷ ἠγαπημένῳ, 7 ἐν ᾧ ἔχομεν τὴν
in the [one] having been loved, in whom we have the

ἀπολύτρωσιν διὰ τοῦ αἵματος αὐτοῦ, τὴν
redemption through the blood of him, the

ἄφεσιν τῶν παραπτωμάτων, κατὰ τὸ
forgiveness – of trespasses, according to the

πλοῦτος τῆς χάριτος αὐτοῦ, 8 ἧς ἐπερίσ-
riches of the grace of him, which he made to

σευσεν εἰς ἡμᾶς ἐν πάσῃ σοφίᾳ καὶ
abound to us in all wisdom and

φρονήσει 9 γνωρίσας ἡμῖν τὸ μυστήριον
intelligence making known to us the mystery

τοῦ θελήματος αὐτοῦ, κατὰ τὴν εὐδοκίαν
of the will of him, according to the good pleasure

αὐτοῦ, ἣν προέθετο ἐν αὐτῷ 10 εἰς
of him, which he purposed in him[self] for

οἰκονομίαν τοῦ πληρώματος τῶν καιρῶν,
a stewardship of the fulness of the times,

ἀνακεφαλαιώσασθαι τὰ πάντα ἐν τῷ
to head up – all things in –

Χριστῷ, τὰ ἐπὶ τοῖς οὐρανοῖς καὶ τὰ
Christ, the things on(in) the heavens and the
                                      things

ἐπὶ τῆς γῆς· ἐν αὐτῷ, 11 ἐν ᾧ καὶ
on the earth; in him, in whom also

ἐκληρώθημεν προορισθέντες κατὰ πρόθεσιν
we were chosen as being predestinated according to [the] purpose
[his] inheritance

τοῦ τὰ πάντα ἐνεργοῦντος κατὰ τὴν
of the – all things operating according to the
[one]

βουλὴν τοῦ θελήματος αὐτοῦ, 12 εἰς τὸ
counsel of the will of him,   for the

εἶναι ἡμᾶς εἰς ἔπαινον δόξης αὐτοῦ
to be us to [the] praise of [the] glory of him
–that we should be

τοὺς προηλπικότας ἐν τῷ Χριστῷ· 13 ἐν
the having previously in – Christ; in
[ones] hoped

ᾧ καὶ ὑμεῖς, ἀκούσαντες τὸν λόγον
whom also ye, hearing   the word

τῆς ἀληθείας, τὸ εὐαγγέλιον τῆς σωτηρίας
– of truth, the gospel   of the salvation

ὑμῶν, ἐν ᾧ καὶ πιστεύσαντες ἐσφραγίσθητε
of you, in whom also believing ye were sealed

τῷ πνεύματι τῆς ἐπαγγελίας τῷ ἁγίῳ,
with the Spirit of the of promise the holy,

14 ὅς ἐστιν ἀρραβὼν τῆς κληρονομίας
who is an earnest of the inheritance

ἡμῶν, εἰς ἀπολύτρωσιν τῆς περιποιήσεως,
of us, till [the] redemption of the possession.

εἰς ἔπαινον τῆς δόξης αὐτοῦ.
to [the] praise of the glory of him.

15 Διὰ τοῦτο κἀγώ, ἀκούσας τὴν καθ'
Therefore I also, hearing the among

ὑμᾶς πίστιν ἐν τῷ κυρίῳ Ἰησοῦ καὶ
you faith in the Lord Jesus and

τὴν ἀγάπην τὴν εἰς πάντας τοὺς ἁγίους,
the love – to all the saints,

16 οὐ παύομαι εὐχαριστῶν ὑπὲρ ὑμῶν
do not cease giving thanks on behalf of you

μνείαν ποιούμενος ἐπὶ τῶν προσευχῶν
mention making on(in) the prayers

μου, 17 ἵνα ὁ θεὸς τοῦ κυρίου ἡμῶν
of me, in order that the God of the Lord of us

Ἰησοῦ Χριστοῦ, ὁ πατὴρ τῆς δόξης,
Jesus Christ, the Father of glory.

δώῃ ὑμῖν πνεῦμα σοφίας καὶ ἀποκαλύψεως
may give to you a spirit of wisdom and of revelation

ἐν ἐπιγνώσει αὐτοῦ, 18 πεφωτισμένους τοὺς
in a full knowledge of him, having been enlightened the

ὀφθαλμοὺς τῆς καρδίας [ὑμῶν,] εἰς τὸ
eyes of the heart of you, for the

εἰδέναι ὑμᾶς τίς ἐστιν ἡ ἐλπὶς τῆς
to know you what is the hope of the
–that ye should know

κλήσεως αὐτοῦ, τίς ὁ πλοῦτος τῆς δόξης
calling of him, what the riches of the glory

τῆς κληρονομίας αὐτοῦ ἐν τοῖς ἁγίοις,
of the inheritance of him in the saints,

19 καὶ τί τὸ ὑπερβάλλον μέγεθος τῆς
and what the excelling greatness of the

King James Version

New International Version

us-ward who believe, according to the working of his mighty power, 20 Which he wrought in Christ, when he raised him from the dead, and set *him* at his own right hand in the heavenly *places,* 21 Far above all principality, and power, and might, and dominion, and every name that is named, not only in this world, but also in that which is to come: 22And hath put all *things* under his feet, and gave him *to be* the head over all *things* to the church, 23 Which is his body, the fulness of him that filleth all in all.

believe. That power is like the working of his mighty strength, 20 which he exerted in Christ when he raised him from the dead and seated him at his right hand in the heavenly realms, 21 far above all rule and authority, power and dominion, and every title that can be given, not only in the present age but also in the one to come. 22And God placed all things under his feet and appointed him to be head over everything for the church, 23 which is his body, the fullness of him who fills everything in every way.

Made alive in Christ

2 And you *hath he quickened,* who were dead in trespasses and sins; 2 Wherein in time past ye walked according to the course of this world, according to the prince of the power of the air, the spirit that now worketh in the children of disobedience: 3Among whom also we all had our conversation in times past in the lusts of our flesh, fulfilling the desires of the flesh and of the mind; and were by nature the children of wrath, even as others. 4 But God, who is rich in mercy, for his great love wherewith he loved us, 5 Even when we were dead in sins, hath quickened us together with Christ, (by grace ye are saved;) 6And hath raised *us* up together, and made *us* sit together in heavenly *places* in Christ Jesus: 7 That in the ages to come he might shew the exceeding riches of his grace, in *his* kindness toward us, through Christ Jesus. 8 For by grace are ye saved through faith; and that not of yourselves: *it is* the gift of God: 9 Not of works, lest any man should boast. 10 For we are his workmanship, created in Christ Jesus unto good works, which God hath before ordained that we should walk in them. 11 Wherefore remember, that ye *being* in time past Gentiles in the flesh, who are called Uncircumcision by that which is called the Circumcision in the flesh made by hands; 12 That at that time ye were without Christ, being aliens from the commonwealth of Israel, and strangers from the covenants of promise, having no hope, and without God in the world: 13 But now, in Christ Jesus, ye who sometime were far off are made nigh by the blood of Christ. 14 For he is our peace, who hath made both one, and hath broken down the middle wall of partition *between us;* 15 Having abolished in his flesh the enmity, *even* the law of commandments *contained* in ordinances; for to make in himself of twain one new man, *so* making peace; 16And that he might reconcile both unto God in one body by the cross, having slain the enmity thereby: 17And came and preached peace to you which were afar off, and to them

2 As for you, you were dead in your transgressions and sins, 2 in which you used to live when you followed the ways of this world and of the ruler of the kingdom of the air, the spirit who is now at work in those who are disobedient. 3All of us also lived among them at one time, gratifying the cravings of our sinful nature and following its desires and thoughts. Like the rest, we were by nature objects of wrath. 4 But because of his great love for us, God, who is rich in mercy, 5 made us alive with Christ even when we were dead in transgressions—it is by grace you have been saved. 6And God raised us up with Christ and seated us with him in the heavenly realms in Christ Jesus, 7 in order that in the coming ages he might show the incomparable riches of his grace, expressed in his kindness to us in Christ Jesus. 8 For it is by grace you have been saved, through faith—and this not from yourselves, it is the gift of God— 9 not by works, so that no one can boast. 10 For we are God's workmanship, created in Christ Jesus to do good works, which God prepared in advance for us to do.

One in Christ

11 Therefore, remember that formerly you who are Gentiles by birth and called "uncircumcised" by those who call themselves "the circumcision" (that done in the body by the hands of men)—12 remember that at that time you were separate from Christ, excluded from citizenship in Israel and foreigners to the covenants of the promise, without hope and without God in the world. 13 But now in Christ Jesus you who once were far away have been brought near through the blood of Christ.

14 For he himself is our peace, who has made the two one and has destroyed the barrier, the dividing wall of hostility, 15 by abolishing in his flesh the law with its commandments and regulations. His purpose was to create in himself one new man out of the two, thus making peace, 16 and in this one body to reconcile both of them to God through the cross, by which he put to death their hostility. 17 He came and preached peace to you who were far away and

Greek Interlinear

δυνάμεως αὐτοῦ εἰς ἡμᾶς τοὺς πιστεύοντας
power of him toward us the [ones] believing

κατὰ τὴν ἐνέργειαν τοῦ κράτους τῆς
according to the operation of the might of the

ἰσχύος αὐτοῦ, 20 ἣν ἐνήργηκεν ἐν τῷ
strength of him, which he has operated in –

Χριστῷ ἐγείρας αὐτὸν ἐκ νεκρῶν, καὶ
Christ raising him from [the] dead, and

καθίσας ἐν δεξιᾷ αὐτοῦ ἐν τοῖς ἐπου-
seating [him] at [the] right [hand] of him in the heaven-

ρανίοις 21 ὑπεράνω πάσης ἀρχῆς καὶ
lies far above all rule and

ἐξουσίας καὶ δυνάμεως καὶ κυριότητος
authority and power and lordship

καὶ παντὸς ὀνόματος ὀνομαζομένου οὐ
and every name being named not

μόνον ἐν τῷ αἰῶνι τούτῳ ἀλλὰ καὶ
only in this age but also

ἐν τῷ μέλλοντι· 22 καὶ πάντα ὑπέταξεν
in the coming; and all things subjected

ὑπὸ τοὺς πόδας αὐτοῦ, καὶ αὐτὸν ἔδωκεν
under the feet of him, and ²him ¹gave

κεφαλὴν ὑπὲρ πάντα τῇ ἐκκλησίᾳ, 23 ἥτις
[to be] head over all things to the church, which

ἐστιν τὸ σῶμα αὐτοῦ, τὸ πλήρωμα
is the body of him, the fulness

τοῦ τὰ πάντα ἐν πᾶσιν πληρουμένου.
of the – ²all things ³with ⁴all things ¹filling.
[one]

Chapter 2

Καὶ ὑμᾶς ὄντας νεκροὺς τοῖς παραπτώ-
And you being dead in the tres-

μασιν καὶ ταῖς ἁμαρτίαις ὑμῶν, 2 ἐν
passes and in the sins of you, in

αἷς ποτε περιεπατήσατε κατὰ τὸν αἰῶνα
which then ye walked according to the age

τοῦ κόσμου τούτου, κατὰ τὸν ἄρχοντα
of this world, according to the ruler

τῆς ἐξουσίας τοῦ ἀέρος, τοῦ πνεύματος
of the authority of the air, of the spirit

τοῦ νῦν ἐνεργοῦντος ἐν τοῖς υἱοῖς τῆς
– now operating in the sons of the

ἀπειθείας· 3 ἐν οἷς καὶ ἡμεῖς πάντες
of disobedience; among whom also we all

ἀνεστράφημέν ποτε ἐν ταῖς ἐπιθυμίαις
conducted ourselves then in the lusts

τῆς σαρκὸς ἡμῶν, ποιοῦντες τὰ θελήματα
of the flesh of us, doing the wishes

τῆς σαρκὸς καὶ τῶν διανοιῶν, καὶ
of the flesh and of the understandings, and

ἤμεθα τέκνα φύσει ὀργῆς ὡς καὶ οἱ
were ²children ¹by nature of wrath as also the

λοιποί· 4 ὁ δὲ θεὸς πλούσιος ὢν ἐν
rest; – but God ³rich ¹being in

ἐλέει, διὰ τὴν πολλὴν ἀγάπην αὐτοῦ
mercy, because of the much love of his

ἣν ἠγάπησεν ἡμᾶς, 5 καὶ ὄντας ἡμᾶς
[with] he loved us, even being us
which =when we were

νεκροὺς τοῖς παραπτώμασιν συνεζωοποίησεν
dead – in trespasses quickened [us] with

τῷ Χριστῷ, — χάριτί ἐστε σεσωσμένοι,
– Christ, (by grace ye are having been saved,)

6 καὶ συνήγειρεν καὶ συνεκάθισεν ἐν
and raised [us] with and seated [us] with in

τοῖς ἐπουρανίοις ἐν Χριστῷ Ἰησοῦ, 7 ἵνα
the heavenlies in Christ Jesus, in order that

ἐνδείξηται ἐν τοῖς αἰῶσιν τοῖς ἐπερχομένοις
he might show in the ages – coming on
forth

τὸ ὑπερβάλλον πλοῦτος τῆς χάριτος αὐτοῦ
the excelling riches of the grace of him

ἐν χρηστότητι ἐφ' ἡμᾶς ἐν Χριστῷ
in kindness toward us in Christ

Ἰησοῦ. 8 τῇ γὰρ χάριτί ἐστε σεσωσμένοι
Jesus. – For by grace ye are having been saved

διὰ πίστεως· καὶ τοῦτο οὐκ ἐξ ὑμῶν,
through faith; and this not of you,

θεοῦ τὸ δῶρον· 9 οὐκ ἐξ ἔργων, ἵνα μή
of [is] the gift; not of works, lest
God

τις καυχήσηται. 10 αὐτοῦ γάρ ἐσμεν
anyone should boast. For of him we are

ποίημα, κτισθέντες ἐν Χριστῷ Ἰησοῦ
a product, created in Christ Jesus

ἐπὶ ἔργοις ἀγαθοῖς, οἷς προητοίμασεν
unto works good, which ²previously prepared

ὁ θεὸς ἵνα ἐν αὐτοῖς περιπατήσωμεν.
– ¹God in order that in them we might walk.

11 Διὸ μνημονεύετε ὅτι ποτὲ ὑμεῖς τὰ
Wherefore remember ye that when ye the

ἔθνη ἐν σαρκί, οἱ λεγόμενοι ἀκροβυστία
nations in [the] flesh, the [ones] being called uncircumcision

ὑπὸ τῆς λεγομένης περιτομῆς ἐν σαρκὶ
by the being called circumcision in [the] flesh

χειροποιήτου, 12 ὅτι ἦτε τῷ καιρῷ ἐκείνῳ
made by hand, that ye were at that time

χωρὶς Χριστοῦ, ἀπηλλοτριωμένοι τῆς
without Christ, having been alienated from the

πολιτείας τοῦ Ἰσραὴλ καὶ ξένοι τῶν
commonwealth – of Israel and strangers of(from)
the

διαθηκῶν τῆς ἐπαγγελίας, ἐλπίδα μὴ
covenants – of promise, hope not

ἔχοντες καὶ ἄθεοι ἐν τῷ κόσμῳ. 13 νυνὶ
having and godless in the world. now

δὲ ἐν Χριστῷ Ἰησοῦ ὑμεῖς οἱ ποτε
But in Christ Jesus ye the [ones] then

ὄντες μακρὰν ἐγενήθητε ἐγγὺς ἐν τῷ
being afar became near by the

αἵματι τοῦ Χριστοῦ. 14 Αὐτὸς γάρ
blood – of Christ. For he

ἐστιν ἡ εἰρήνη ἡμῶν, ὁ ποιήσας τὰ
is the peace of us, the [one] having made –

ἀμφότερα ἓν καὶ τὸ μεσότοιχον τοῦ
both one and ²the ¹middle wall –

φραγμοῦ λύσας, τὴν ἔχθραν, ἐν τῇ σαρκὶ
⁴of partition ¹having the enmity, ²in ³the ⁴flesh
broken,

αὐτοῦ 15 τὸν νόμον τῶν ἐντολῶν ἐν
²of him ⁵the ⁷law ⁶of the ⁸commandments ¹⁰in

δόγμασιν καταργήσας, ἵνα τοὺς δύο κτίσῃ
¹¹decrees ¹having abolished, in order ⁴the ⁵two ³he might
that create

ἐν αὐτῷ εἰς ἕνα καινὸν ἄνθρωπον ποιῶν
²in ⁴him[self] ¹into ¹⁴one ¹⁵new ¹⁶man ¹making

εἰρήνην, 16 καὶ ἀποκαταλλάξῃ τοὺς
⁹peace, and might reconcile

ἀμφοτέρους ἐν ἑνὶ σώματι τῷ θεῷ διὰ
both in one body – to God through

τοῦ σταυροῦ, ἀποκτείνας τὴν ἔχθραν ἐν
the cross, killing the enmity in

αὐτῷ· 17 καὶ ἐλθὼν εὐηγγελίσατο εἰρήνην
him[self]; and coming preached peace

ὑμῖν τοῖς μακρὰν καὶ εἰρήνην τοῖς ἐγγύς·
to you the ones afar and peace to the ones near;

King James Version

that were nigh. 18 For through him we both have access by one Spirit unto the Father. 19 Now therefore ye are no more strangers and foreigners, but fellow citizens with the saints, and of the household of God; 20And are built upon the foundation of the apostles and prophets, Jesus Christ himself being the chief corner *stone;* 21 In whom all the building fitly framed together groweth unto a holy temple in the Lord: 22 In whom ye also are builded together for a habitation of God through the Spirit.

3 For this cause I Paul, the prisoner of Jesus Christ for you Gentiles, 2 If ye have heard of the dispensation of the grace of God which is given me to you-ward: 3 How that by revelation he made known unto me the mystery; (as I wrote afore in few words; 4 Whereby, when ye read, ye may understand my knowledge in the mystery of Christ,) 5 Which in other ages was not made known unto the sons of men, as it is now revealed unto his holy apostles and prophets by the Spirit; 6 That the Gentiles should be fellow heirs, and of the same body, and partakers of his promise in Christ by the gospel: 7 Whereof I was made a minister, according to the gift of the grace of God given unto me by the effectual working of his power. 8 Unto me, who am less than the least of all saints, is this grace given, that I should preach among the Gentiles the unsearchable riches of Christ; 9And to make all *men* see what *is* the fellowship of the mystery, which from the beginning of the world hath been hid in God, who created all things by Jesus Christ: 10 To the intent that now unto the principalities and powers in heavenly *places* might be known by the church the manifold wisdom of God, 11According to the eternal purpose which he purposed in Christ Jesus our Lord: 12 In whom we have boldness and access with confidence by the faith of him. 13 Wherefore I desire that ye faint not at my tribulations for you, which is your glory. 14 For this cause I bow my knees unto the Father of our Lord Jesus Christ, 15 Of whom the whole family in heaven and earth is named, 16 That he would grant you, according to the riches of his glory, to be strengthened with might by his Spirit in the inner man; 17 That Christ may dwell in your hearts by faith; that ye, being rooted and grounded in love, 18 May be able to comprehend with all saints what *is* the breadth, and length, and depth, and height; 19And to know the love of Christ, which passeth knowledge, that ye might be filled with all the fulness of God. 20 Now unto him that is able to do exceeding

New International Version

peace to those who were near. 18 For through him we both have access to the Father by one Spirit.
19 Consequently, you are no longer foreigners and aliens, but fellow citizens with God's people and members of God's household, 20 built on the foundation of the apostles and prophets, with Christ Jesus himself as the chief cornerstone. 21 In him the whole building is joined together and rises to become a holy temple in the Lord. 22And in him you too are being built together to become a dwelling in which God lives by his Spirit.

Paul the preacher to the Gentiles

3 For this reason I, Paul, the prisoner of Christ Jesus for the sake of you Gentiles—
2 Surely you have heard about the administration of God's grace that was given to me for you, 3 that is, the mystery made known to me by revelation, as I have already written briefly. 4 In reading this, then, you will be able to understand my insight into the mystery of Christ, 5 which was not made known to men in other generations as it has now been revealed by the Spirit to God's holy apostles and prophets. 6 This mystery is that through the gospel the Gentiles are heirs together with Israel, members together of one body, and sharers together in the promise in Christ Jesus.
7 I became a servant of this gospel by the gift of God's grace given me through the working of his power. 8Although I am less than the least of all God's people, this grace was given me: to preach to the Gentiles the unsearchable riches of Christ, 9 and to make plain to everyone my administration of this mystery, which for ages past was kept hidden in God, who created all things. 10 His intent was that now, through the church, the manifold wisdom of God should be made known to the rulers and authorities in the heavenly realms, 11 according to his eternal purpose which he accomplished in Christ Jesus our Lord. 12 In him and through faith in him we may approach God with freedom and confidence. 13 I ask you, therefore, not to be discouraged because of my sufferings for you, which are your glory.

A prayer for the Ephesians

14 For this reason I kneel before the Father, 15 from whom the whole family of believers[e] in heaven and on earth derives its name. 16 I pray that out of his glorious riches he may strengthen you with power through his Spirit in your inner being, 17 so that Christ may dwell in your hearts through faith. And I pray that you, being rooted and established in love, 18 may have power, together with all the saints, to grasp how wide and long and high and deep is the love of Christ, 19 and to know this love that surpasses knowledge—that you may be filled to the measure of all the fullness of God.
20 Now to him who is able to do immeasura-

[e] Or *from whom all fatherhood.*

Greek Interlinear

18 ὅτι δι' αὐτοῦ ἔχομεν τὴν προσαγωγὴν
because through him ¹we ²have - ⁴access

οἱ ἀμφότεροι ἐν ἑνὶ πνεύματι πρὸς τὸν
- ⁵both by one Spirit unto the

πατέρα. **19** ἄρα οὖν οὐκέτι ἐστὲ ξένοι
Father. Then therefore no more are ye strangers

καὶ πάροικοι, ἀλλὰ ἐστὲ συμπολῖται τῶν
and sojourners, but ye are fellow-citizens of the

ἁγίων καὶ οἰκεῖοι τοῦ θεοῦ, **20** ἐποικοδομη-
saints and members of - of God, having been
the family

θέντες ἐπὶ τῷ θεμελίῳ τῶν ἀποστόλων
built on on the foundation of the apostles

καὶ προφητῶν, ὄντος ἀκρογωνιαίου αὐτοῦ
and prophets, ⁵being ⁶cornerstone ⁷[him]self

Χριστοῦ Ἰησοῦ, **21** ἐν ᾧ πᾶσα οἰκοδομὴ
¹Christ ²Jesus,ᵃ in whom all [the] building

συναρμολογουμένη αὔξει εἰς ναὸν ἅγιον
being fitted together grows into shrine a holy

ἐν κυρίῳ, **22** ἐν ᾧ καὶ ὑμεῖς συνοικοδομεῖσθε
in [the] Lord, in whom also ye are being built together

εἰς κατοικητήριον τοῦ θεοῦ ἐν πνεύματι.
into a dwelling-place - of God in spirit.

Chapter 3

Τούτου χάριν ἐγὼ Παῦλος ὁ δέσμιος
¹of this ¹By reason of I Paul the prisoner

τοῦ Χριστοῦ Ἰησοῦ ὑπὲρ ὑμῶν τῶν
- of Christ Jesus on behalf of you the

ἐθνῶν **2** εἴ γε ἠκούσατε τὴν οἰκονομίαν
nations - if indeed ye heard the stewardship

τῆς χάριτος τοῦ θεοῦ τῆς δοθείσης μοι
of the grace of - God - given to me

εἰς ὑμᾶς, **3** ὅτι κατὰ ἀποκάλυψιν ἐγνωρίσθη
for you, that by way of revelation was made known

μοι τὸ μυστήριον, καθὼς προέγραψα ἐν
to me the mystery, as I previously wrote in

ὀλίγῳ, **4** πρὸς ὃ δύνασθε ἀναγινώσκοντες
brief, as to which ²ye can ¹reading

νοῆσαι τὴν σύνεσίν μου ἐν τῷ μυστηρίῳ
to realize the understanding of me in the mystery

τοῦ Χριστοῦ, **5** ὃ ἑτέραις γενεαῖς οὐκ
- of Christ, which in other generations not

ἐγνωρίσθη τοῖς υἱοῖς τῶν ἀνθρώπων ὡς
was made known to the sons - of men as

νῦν ἀπεκαλύφθη τοῖς ἁγίοις ἀποστόλοις
now it was revealed to the holy apostles

αὐτοῦ καὶ προφήταις ἐν πνεύματι, **6** εἶναι
of him and prophets in spirit, ²to be

τὰ ἔθνη συγκληρονόμα καὶ σύσσωμα καὶ
¹the ¹nations joint-heirs and a joint-body and

συμμέτοχα τῆς ἐπαγγελίας ἐν Χριστῷ
joint-sharers of the promise in Christ

Ἰησοῦ διὰ τοῦ εὐαγγελίου, **7** οὗ ἐγενήθην
Jesus through the gospel, of which I became

διάκονος κατὰ τὴν δωρεὰν τῆς χάριτος
a minister according to the gift of the grace

τοῦ θεοῦ τῆς δοθείσης μοι κατὰ τὴν
- of God - given to me according to the

ἐνέργειαν τῆς δυνάμεως αὐτοῦ. **8** ἐμοὶ
operation of the power of him. To me

τῷ ἐλαχιστοτέρῳ πάντων ἁγίων ἐδόθη
the leasterᵉ of all saints was given

ἡ χάρις αὕτη, τοῖς ἔθνεσιν εὐαγγελίσασθαι
this grace, to the nations to preach

τὸ ἀνεξιχνίαστον πλοῦτος τοῦ Χριστοῦ,
the unsearchable riches - of Christ,

9 καὶ φωτίσαι τίς ἡ οἰκονομία τοῦ
and to bring to light what [is] the stewardship of the

μυστηρίου τοῦ ἀποκεκρυμμένου ἀπὸ τῶν
mystery - having been hidden from the

αἰώνων ἐν τῷ θεῷ τῷ τὰ πάντα κτίσαντι,
ages in - God ¹the - ²all things ²having
[one] created,

10 ἵνα γνωρισθῇ νῦν ταῖς ἀρχαῖς καὶ
in order might be made now to the rulers and
that known

ταῖς ἐξουσίαις ἐν τοῖς ἐπουρανίοις διὰ
to the authorities in the heavenlies through

τῆς ἐκκλησίας ἡ πολυποίκιλος σοφία τοῦ
the church the manifold wisdom -

θεοῦ, **11** κατὰ πρόθεσιν τῶν αἰώνων ἣν
of God, according to [the] purpose of the ages which

ἐποίησεν ἐν τῷ Χριστῷ Ἰησοῦ τῷ κυρίῳ
he made in - Christ Jesus the Lord

ἡμῶν, **12** ἐν ᾧ ἔχομεν τὴν παρρησίαν
of us, in whom we have the boldness

καὶ προσαγωγὴν ἐν πεποιθήσει διὰ τῆς
and access in confidence through the

πίστεως αὐτοῦ. **13** διὸ αἰτοῦμαι μὴ
faith of(in) him.✚ Wherefore I ask [you] not

ἐγκακεῖν ἐν ταῖς θλίψεσίν μου ὑπὲρ
to faint in the afflictions of me on behalf

ὑμῶν, ἥτις ἐστὶν δόξα ὑμῶν. **14** Τούτου
of you, which is glory of you. ²of this

χάριν κάμπτω τὰ γόνατά μου πρὸς
¹By reason of I bend the knees of me unto

τὸν πατέρα, **15** ἐξ οὗ πᾶσα πατριὰ
the Father, of whom every fatherhood

ἐν οὐρανοῖς καὶ ἐπὶ γῆς ὀνομάζεται,
in heavens and on earth is named,

16 ἵνα δῷ ὑμῖν κατὰ τὸ πλοῦτος τῆς
in order he may you according to the riches of the
that give

δόξης αὐτοῦ δυνάμει κραταιωθῆναι διὰ
glory of him by power to become mighty through

τοῦ πνεύματος αὐτοῦ εἰς τὸν ἔσω ἄνθρω-
the Spirit of him in the inward man,

πον, **17** κατοικῆσαι τὸν Χριστὸν διὰ τῆς
to dwell - Christᵇ through -
=that Christ may dwell

πίστεως ἐν ταῖς καρδίαις ὑμῶν, ἐν
faith in the hearts of you, in

ἀγάπῃ ἐρριζωμένοι καὶ τεθεμελιωμένοι,
love having been rooted and having been founded,

18 ἵνα ἐξισχύσητε καταλαβέσθαι σὺν πᾶσιν
in order ye may have strength to apprehend with all
that

τοῖς ἁγίοις τί τὸ πλάτος καὶ μῆκος
the saints what [is] the breadth and length

καὶ ὕψος καὶ βάθος, **19** γνῶναί τε τὴν
and height and depth, and to know ¹the

ὑπερβάλλουσαν τῆς γνώσεως ἀγάπην τοῦ
⁴excelling - ²knowledge ³love -

Χριστοῦ, ἵνα πληρωθῆτε εἰς πᾶν τὸ
²of Christ, in order that ye may be filled to all the

πλήρωμα τοῦ θεοῦ.
fulness - of God.

20 Τῷ δὲ δυναμένῳ ὑπὲρ πάντα ποιῆσαι
Now to the [one] being able beyond all things to do

● This is quite literal!—the apostle coins a word.
✚ See Gal. 2. 16.

King James Version

abundantly above all that •we ask or think, according to the power that worketh in us, 21 Unto him *be* glory in the church by Christ Jesus throughout all ages, world without end. Amen.

4 I therefore, the prisoner of the Lord, beseech you that ye walk worthy of the vocation wherewith ye are called, 2 With all lowliness and meekness, with longsuffering, forbearing one another in love; 3 Endeavouring to keep the unity of the Spirit in the bond of peace. 4 *There is* one body, and one Spirit, even as ye are called in one hope of your calling; 5 One Lord, one faith, one baptism, 6 One God and Father of all, who *is* above all, and through all, and in you all. 7 But unto every one of us is given grace according to the measure of the gift of Christ. 8 Wherefore he saith, When he ascended up on high, he led captivity captive, and gave gifts unto men. 9 (Now that he ascended, what is it but that he also descended first into the lower parts of the earth? 10 He that descended is the same also that ascended up far above all heavens, that he might fill all things.) 11And he gave some, apostles; and some, prophets; and some, evangelists; and some, pastors and teachers; 12 For the perfecting of the saints, for the work of the ministry, for the edifying of the body of Christ: 13 Till we all come in the unity of the faith, and of the knowledge of the Son of God, unto a perfect man, unto the measure of the stature of the fulness of Christ: 14 That we *henceforth* be no more children, tossed to and fro, and carried about with every wind of doctrine, by the sleight of men, *and* cunning craftiness, whereby they lie in wait to deceive; 15 But speaking the truth in love, may grow up into him in all things, which is the head, *even* Christ: 16 From whom the whole body fitly joined together and compacted by that which every joint supplieth, according to the effectual working in the measure of every part, maketh increase of the body unto the edifying of itself in love. 17 This I say therefore, and testify in the Lord, that ye henceforth walk not as other Gentiles walk, in the vanity of their mind, 18 Having the understanding darkened, being alienated from the life of God through the ignorance that is in them, because of the blindness of their heart: 19 Who being past feeling have given themselves over unto lasciviousness, to work all uncleanness with greediness. 20 But ye have not so learned Christ; 21 If so be that ye have heard him, and have been taught by him, as the truth is in Jesus: 22 That ye put off concerning the former conver-

New International Version

bly more than all we ask or imagine, according to his power that is at work within us, 21 to him be glory in the church and in Christ Jesus throughout all generations, for ever and ever! Amen.

Unity in the body of Christ

4 As a prisoner for the Lord, then, I urge you to live a life worthy of the calling you have received. 2 Be completely humble and gentle; be patient, bearing with one another in love. 3 Make every effort to keep the unity of the Spirit through the bond of peace. 4 There is one body and one Spirit—just as you were called to one hope when you were called—5 one Lord, one faith, one baptism; 6 one God and Father of all, who is over all and through all and in all. 7 But to each one of us grace has been given as Christ apportioned it. 8 This is why it*f* says:
"When he ascended on high,
    he led captives in his train
    and gave gifts to men." *g*
9 (What does "he ascended" mean except that he also descended to the lower, earthly regions? 10 He who descended is the very one who ascended higher than all the heavens, in order to fill the whole universe.) 11 It was he who gave some to be apostles, some to be prophets, some to be evangelists, and some to be pastors and teachers, 12 to prepare God's people for works of service, so that the body of Christ may be built up 13 until we all reach unity in the faith and in the knowledge of the Son of God and become mature, attaining the full measure of perfection found in Christ.
14 Then we will no longer be infants, tossed back and forth by the waves, and blown here and there by every wind of teaching and by the cunning and craftiness of men in their deceitful scheming. 15 Instead, speaking the truth in love, we will in all things grow up into him who is the Head, that is, Christ. 16 From him the whole body, joined and held together by every supporting ligament, grows and builds itself up in love, as each part does its work.

Living as children of light

17 So I tell you this, and insist on it in the Lord, that you must no longer live as the Gentiles do, in the futility of their thinking. 18 They are darkened in their understanding and separated from the life of God because of the ignorance that is in them due to the hardening of their hearts. 19 Having lost all sensitivity, they have given themselves over to sensuality so as to indulge in every kind of impurity, with a continual lust for more.
20 You, however, did not come to know Christ that way. 21 Surely you heard of him and were taught in him in accordance with the truth that is in Jesus. 22 You were taught, with

[*f*] Or *God.* [*g*] Psalm 68:18.

Greek Interlinear

ὑπερεκπερισσοῦ ὧν αἰτούμεθα ἢ νοοῦμεν
superabundantly of which we ask   or   we think

κατὰ τὴν δύναμιν τὴν ἐνεργουμένην ἐν
according to the power   -   operating   in

ἡμῖν, 21 αὐτῷ ἡ δόξα ἐν τῇ ἐκκλησίᾳ
us,   to him [be] the glory in the church

καὶ ἐν Χριστῷ Ἰησοῦ εἰς πάσας τὰς
and in Christ   Jesus unto all   the

γενεὰς τοῦ αἰῶνος τῶν αἰώνων· ἀμήν.
generations of the age of the ages: Amen.

Chapter 4

Παρακαλῶ οὖν ὑμᾶς ἐγὼ ὁ δέσμιος
⁷beseech ⁶therefore ⁵you ¹I ²the ³prisoner

ἐν κυρίῳ ἀξίως περιπατῆσαι τῆς κλήσεως
⁴in ⁵[the] Lord ¹⁰worthily ⁸to walk of the calling

ἧς ἐκλήθητε, 2 μετὰ πάσης ταπεινοφροσύνης
of(with) ye were with   all   humility
which called,

καὶ πραΰτητος, μετὰ μακροθυμίας,
and meekness,   with   longsuffering,

ἀνεχόμενοι ἀλλήλων ἐν ἀγάπῃ, 3 σπου-
forbearing one another in love,   being

δάζοντες τηρεῖν τὴν ἑνότητα τοῦ πνεύματος
eager to keep the unity of the Spirit

ἐν τῷ συνδέσμῳ τῆς εἰρήνης· ἓν σῶμα
in the bond   - of peace; [there is] one body

καὶ ἓν πνεῦμα, 4 καθὼς καὶ ἐκλήθητε
and one Spirit,   as   also ye were called

ἐν μιᾷ ἐλπίδι τῆς κλήσεως ὑμῶν· 5 εἷς
in one hope of the calling of you; one

κύριος, μία πίστις, ἓν βάπτισμα· 6 εἷς
Lord, one faith, one baptism·   one

θεὸς καὶ πατὴρ πάντων, ὁ ἐπὶ πάντων
God and Father of all, the [one] over all

καὶ διὰ πάντων καὶ ἐν πᾶσιν. 7 Ἑνὶ
and through all and in all.   ²to ¹one

δὲ ἑκάστῳ ἡμῶν ἐδόθη ἡ χάρις κατὰ
¹But ²each of us was given grace according to

τὸ μέτρον τῆς δωρεᾶς τοῦ Χριστοῦ.
the measure of the gift   - of Christ.

8 διὸ λέγει· ἀναβὰς εἰς ὕψος ᾐχμαλώτευσεν
Where- he says: Having to height he led captive
fore   ascended

αἰχμαλωσίαν, ἔδωκεν δόματα τοῖς ἀνθρώποις.
captivity,   he gave   gifts   -   to men.

9 τὸ δὲ ἀνέβη τί ἐστιν εἰ μὴ ὅτι καὶ
Now the "he   what is it except that also
ascended"

κατέβη εἰς τὰ κατώτερα μέρη τῆς γῆς;
he descended into the lower parts of the earth?

10 ὁ καταβὰς αὐτός ἐστιν καὶ ὁ ἀναβὰς
The descending himself is also the ascending
[one]   [one]

ὑπεράνω πάντων τῶν οὐρανῶν, ἵνα
far above   all   the heavens, in order that

πληρώσῃ τὰ πάντα. 11 καὶ αὐτὸς ἔδωκεν
he might fill - all things. And he gave

τοὺς μὲν ἀποστόλους, τοὺς δὲ προφήτας,
some† apostles,   some†   prophets,

τοὺς δὲ εὐαγγελιστάς, τοὺς δὲ ποιμένας
some† evangelists,   some†   shepherds

καὶ διδασκάλους, 12 πρὸς τὸν καταρτισμὸν
and teachers,   for   the   perfecting

τῶν ἁγίων εἰς ἔργον διακονίας, εἰς
of the saints to [the] work of ministry, to

οἰκοδομὴν τοῦ σώματος τοῦ Χριστοῦ,
building of the body   -   of Christ,

13 μέχρι καταντήσωμεν οἱ πάντες εἰς
until ¹we arrive   -   ²all   at

τὴν ἑνότητα τῆς πίστεως καὶ τῆς ἐπιγνώ-
the unity of the faith and of the full know-

σεως τοῦ υἱοῦ τοῦ θεοῦ, εἰς ἄνδρα τέλειον,
ledge of the Son - of God, at ²man ¹a complete,

εἰς μέτρον ἡλικίας τοῦ πληρώματος τοῦ
at [the] measure of [the] of the fulness -
stature

Χριστοῦ, 14 ἵνα μηκέτι ὦμεν νήπιοι,
of Christ, in order that no more we may be infants,

κλυδωνιζόμενοι καὶ περιφερόμενοι παντὶ ἀνέμῳ
being blown   and being carried round by every wind

τῆς διδασκαλίας ἐν τῇ κυβείᾳ τῶν ἀνθρώ-
- of teaching in the sleight -   of

πων, ἐν πανουργίᾳ πρὸς τὴν μεθοδείαν
men, in cleverness · unto the craftiness

τῆς πλάνης, 15 ἀληθεύοντες δὲ ἐν ἀγάπῃ
- of error, but speaking truth in love

αὐξήσωμεν εἰς αὐτὸν τὰ πάντα, ὅς ἐστιν
we may grow into him in all respects,† who is

ἡ κεφαλή, Χριστός, 16 ἐξ οὗ πᾶν τὸ
the head, Christ,   of whom all the

σῶμα συναρμολογούμενον καὶ συμβιβαζόμενον
body being fitted together and being brought together

διὰ πάσης ἀφῆς τῆς ἐπιχορηγίας κατ'
through every band - of supply according
to

ἐνέργειαν ἐν μέτρῳ ἑνὸς ἑκάστου μέρους
[the] operation in measure of ²one ¹each part

τὴν αὔξησιν τοῦ σώματος ποιεῖται εἰς
²the ³growth ⁴of the ⁵body ¹makes for

οἰκοδομὴν ἑαυτοῦ ἐν ἀγάπῃ.
building of itself in love.

17 Τοῦτο οὖν λέγω καὶ μαρτύρομαι ἐν
This therefore I say and witness   in

κυρίῳ, μηκέτι ὑμᾶς περιπατεῖν καθὼς
[the] Lord, no more you to walk   as

καὶ τὰ ἔθνη περιπατεῖ ἐν ματαιότητι
also the nations walks in vanity

τοῦ νοὸς αὐτῶν, 18 ἐσκοτωμένοι τῇ
of the mind of them, ³having been darkened ²in the
(their)

διανοίᾳ ὄντες, ἀπηλλοτριωμένοι τῆς ζωῆς
⁴intellect ¹being, having been alienated [from] the life

τοῦ θεοῦ, διὰ τὴν ἄγνοιαν τὴν οὖσαν
- of God, through the ignorance -   being

ἐν αὐτοῖς, διὰ τὴν πώρωσιν τῆς καρδίας
in them, on account of the hardness of the heart

αὐτῶν, 19 οἵτινες ἀπηλγηκότες ἑαυτοὺς
of them, who having ceased to care ²themselves

παρέδωκαν τῇ ἀσελγείᾳ εἰς ἐργασίαν
¹gave up   to lewdness for work

ἀκαθαρσίας πάσης ἐν πλεονεξίᾳ. 20 ὑμεῖς
²uncleanness ¹of all in greediness.   ye

δὲ οὐχ οὕτως ἐμάθετε τὸν Χριστόν,
But not so learned   -   Christ,

21 εἴ γε αὐτὸν ἠκούσατε καὶ ἐν αὐτῷ
if indeed ²him ¹ye heard and ²by ¹him

ἐδιδάχθητε καθώς ἐστιν ἀλήθεια ἐν τῷ
¹were taught as   ²is   ¹truth   in   -

Ἰησοῦ, 22 ἀποθέσθαι ὑμᾶς κατὰ τὴν
Jesus,   to put off   you^b as regards the(your)
= that ye put off

569

King James Version

sation the old man, which is corrupt according to the deceitful lusts; 23And be renewed in the spirit of your mind; 24And that ye put on the new man, which after God is created in righteousness and true holiness. 25 Wherefore putting away lying, speak every man truth with his neighbour: for we are members one of another. 26 Be ye angry, and sin not: let not the sun go down upon your wrath: 27 Neither give place to the devil. 28 Let him that stole steal no more: but rather let him labour, working with *his* hands the thing which is good, that he may have to give to him that needeth. 29 Let no corrupt communication proceed out of your mouth, but that which is good to the use of edifying, that it may minister grace unto the hearers. 30And grieve not the Holy Spirit of God, whereby ye are sealed unto the day of redemption. 31 Let all bitterness, and wrath, and anger, and clamour, and evil speaking, be put away from you, with all malice: 32And be ye kind one to another, tenderhearted, forgiving one another, even as God for Christ's sake hath forgiven you.

5 Be ye therefore followers of God, as dear children; 2And walk in love, as Christ also hath loved us, and hath given himself for us an offering and a sacrifice to God for a sweet-smelling savour. 3 But fornication, and all uncleanness, or covetousness, let it not be once named among you, as becometh saints; 4 Neither filthiness, nor foolish talking, nor jesting, which are not convenient: but rather giving of thanks. 5 For this ye know, that no whoremonger, nor unclean person, nor covetous man, who is an idolater, hath any inheritance in the kingdom of Christ and of God. 6 Let no man deceive you with vain words: for because of these things cometh the wrath of God upon the children of disobedience. 7 Be not ye therefore partakers with them. 8 For ye were sometime darkness, but now *are ye* light in the Lord: walk as children of light; 9 (For the fruit of the Spirit *is* in all goodness and righteousness and truth;) 10 Proving what is acceptable unto the Lord. 11And have no fellowship with the unfruitful works of darkness, but rather reprove *them.* 12 For it is a shame even to speak of those things which are done of them in secret. 13 But all things that are reproved are made manifest by the light: for whatsoever doth make manifest is light. 14 Wherefore he saith, Awake thou that sleepest, and arise from the dead, and Christ shall give thee light. 15 See then that ye walk circumspectly, not as fools, but as wise, 16 Redeeming the time, because the days are evil. 17 Wherefore be ye not unwise, but understanding what the will of the Lord *is.* 18And be not drunk with wine, wherein is excess; but be filled

New International Version

regard to your former way of life, to put off your old self, which is being corrupted by its deceitful desires; 23 to be made new in the attitude of your minds; 24 and to put on the new self, created to be like God in true righteousness and holiness.

25 Therefore, each of you must put off falsehood and speak truthfully to his neighbor, for we are all members of one body. 26 In your anger do not sin: Do not let the sun go down while you are still angry, 27 and do not give the devil a foothold. 28 He who has been stealing must steal no longer, but must work, doing something useful with his own hands, that he may have something to share with those in need. 29 Do not let any unwholesome talk come out of your mouths, but only what is helpful for building others up according to their needs, that it may benefit those who listen. 30And do not grieve the Holy Spirit of God, with whom you were sealed for the day of redemption. 31 Get rid of all bitterness, rage and anger, brawling and slander, along with every form of malice. 32 Be kind and compassionate to one another, forgiving each other, just as in Christ God forgave you.

5 Be imitators of God, therefore, as dearly loved children 2 and live a life of love, just as Christ loved us and gave himself up for us as a fragrant offering and sacrifice to God. 3 But among you there must not be even a hint of sexual immorality, or of any kind of impurity, or of greed, because these are improper for God's holy people. 4 Nor should there be obscenity, foolish talk or coarse joking, which are out of place, but rather thanksgiving. 5 For of this you can be sure: No immoral, impure, or greedy person—such a man is an idolater—has any inheritance in the kingdom of Christ and of God. 6 Let no one deceive you with empty words, for because of such things God's wrath comes on those who are disobedient. 7 Therefore do not be partners with them.

8 For you were once darkness, but now you are light in the Lord. Live as children of light 9 (for the fruit of the light consists in all goodness, righteousness and truth) 10 and find out what pleases the Lord. 11 Have nothing to do with the fruitless deeds of darkness, but rather expose them. 12 For it is shameful even to mention what is done in secret. 13 But everything exposed by the light becomes visible, 14 for it is light that makes everything visible. This is why it is said:
"Wake up, O sleeper,
　rise from the dead,
　and Christ will shine on you."
15 Be very careful, then, how you live—not as unwise but as wise, 16 making the most of every opportunity, because the days are evil. 17 Therefore do not be foolish, but understand what the Lord's will is. 18 Do not get drunk on wine, which leads to debauchery. Instead, be

Greek Interlinear

προτέραν ἀναστροφὴν τὸν παλαιὸν ἄνθρωπον
former   conduct   the   old   man
τὸν φθειρόμενον κατὰ τὰς ἐπιθυμίας τῆς
-   being corrupted according to the   lusts   -
ἀπάτης, 23 ἀνανεοῦσθαι δὲ τῷ πνεύματι
of deceit,   and to be renewed   in the   spirit
τοῦ νοὸς ὑμῶν 24 καὶ ἐνδύσασθαι τὸν
of the mind of you   and   to put on   the
καινὸν ἄνθρωπον τὸν κατὰ θεὸν κτισθέντα
new   man   -   ²according to ³God ¹created
ἐν δικαιοσύνῃ καὶ ὁσιότητι τῆς ἀληθείας.
in righteousness and holiness   -   of truth.
25 Διὸ ἀποθέμενοι τὸ ψεῦδος λαλεῖτε
Wherefore putting off the lie   speak ye
ἀλήθειαν ἕκαστος μετὰ τοῦ πλησίον αὐτοῦ,
truth   each man with the neighbour of him,
ὅτι ἐσμὲν ἀλλήλων μέλη. 26 ὀργίζεσθε
because we are of one another members. Be ye wrathful
καὶ μὴ ἁμαρτάνετε· ὁ ἥλιος μὴ
and do not sin;   ²the ¹sun ²not
ἐπιδυέτω ἐπὶ παροργισμῷ ὑμῶν, 27 μηδὲ
¹let ³set on   on provocation of you,   nor
δίδοτε τόπον τῷ διαβόλῳ. 28 ὁ κλέπτων
give ye place to the devil.   The [one] stealing
μηκέτι κλεπτέτω, μᾶλλον δὲ κοπιάτω
no more let him steal, but rather let him labour
ἐργαζόμενος ταῖς ἰδίαις χερσὶν τὸ ἀγαθόν,
working   with the(his) own hands the good thing,

ἵνα ἔχῃ μεταδιδόναι τῷ χρείαν ἔχοντι.
in order he may to share [with] the [one] ²need ¹having
that have
29 πᾶς λόγος σαπρὸς ἐκ τοῦ στόματος
Every ²word ¹corrupt out of the mouth
ὑμῶν μὴ ἐκπορευέσθω, ἀλλὰ εἴ τις
of you let not proceed*,   but if any
ἀγαθὸς πρὸς οἰκοδομὴν τῆς χρείας, ἵνα
[is] good to improvement of the need, in order
that
δῷ χάριν τοῖς ἀκούουσιν. 30 καὶ μὴ λυπεῖτε
it may grace to the [ones] hearing. And do not grieve
give
τὸ πνεῦμα τὸ ἅγιον τοῦ θεοῦ, ἐν ᾧ
the Spirit the Holy - of God, by whom
ἐσφραγίσθητε εἰς ἡμέραν ἀπολυτρώσεως.
ye were sealed for a day of redemption.
31 πᾶσα πικρία καὶ θυμὸς καὶ
All bitterness and anger and
ὀργὴ καὶ κραυγὴ καὶ βλασφημία ἀρθήτω
wrath and clamour and blasphemy let it be
removed
ἀφ' ὑμῶν σὺν πάσῃ κακίᾳ. 32 γίνεσθε
from you with all   evil.   be ye
δὲ εἰς ἀλλήλους χρηστοί, εὔσπλαγχνοι,
And to one another kind,   tenderhearted,
χαριζόμενοι ἑαυτοῖς καθὼς καὶ ὁ θεὸς
forgiving yourselves as   also - God

Chapter 5

ἐν Χριστῷ ἐχαρίσατο ὑμῖν. 5 Γίνεσθε
in Christ forgave you.   Be ye
οὖν μιμηταὶ τοῦ θεοῦ, ὡς τέκνα
therefore imitators - of God, as children
ἀγαπητά, 2 καὶ περιπατεῖτε ἐν ἀγάπῃ,
beloved,   and walk ye   in love,
καθὼς καὶ ὁ Χριστὸς ἠγάπησεν ὑμᾶς
as   also - Christ loved   you
καὶ παρέδωκεν ἑαυτὸν ὑπὲρ ἡμῶν
and gave up   himself on behalf of us
προσφορὰν καὶ θυσίαν τῷ θεῷ εἰς ὀσμὴν
an offering and a sacrifice - to God for an odour
εὐωδίας. 3 Πορνεία δὲ καὶ ἀκαθαρσία
of sweet smell. But fornication and ²uncleanness
πᾶσα ἢ πλεονεξία μηδὲ ὀνομαζέσθω ἐν
¹all or greediness not let it be named among
ὑμῖν, καθὼς πρέπει ἁγίοις, 4 καὶ αἰσχρότης
you, as is fitting for saints, and baseness
καὶ μωρολογία ἢ εὐτραπελία, ἃ οὐκ
and foolish talking or raillery, which things not
ἀνῆκεν, ἀλλὰ μᾶλλον εὐχαριστία. 5 τοῦτο
are becoming, but rather thanksgiving.   this
γὰρ ἴστε γινώσκοντες, ὅτι πᾶς πόρνος
For be ye knowing,   that every fornicator
ἢ ἀκάθαρτος ἢ πλεονέκτης, ὅ ἐστιν
or unclean man or greedy,   who is
εἰδωλολάτρης, οὐκ ἔχει κληρονομίαν ἐν τῇ
an idolater,   not has inheritance in the
βασιλείᾳ τοῦ Χριστοῦ καὶ θεοῦ. 6 Μηδεὶς
kingdom - of Christ and of God.   ²No man
ὑμᾶς ἀπατάτω κενοῖς λόγοις· διὰ ταῦτα
¹you ¹let ²deceive with empty words; because these
of things
γὰρ ἔρχεται ἡ ὀργὴ τοῦ θεοῦ ἐπὶ τοὺς
for is coming the wrath - of God on the
υἱοὺς τῆς ἀπειθείας. 7 μὴ οὖν γίνεσθε
sons   - of disobedience. Not therefore be ye
συμμέτοχοι αὐτῶν· 8 ἦτε γάρ ποτε σκότος,
partakers of them; for ye were then darkness,

νῦν δὲ φῶς ἐν κυρίῳ· ὡς τέκνα φωτὸς
but now light in [the] Lord; as children of light
περιπατεῖτε, 9 — ὁ γὰρ καρπὸς τοῦ
walk ye,   (for the fruit   of the
φωτὸς ἐν πάσῃ ἀγαθωσύνῃ καὶ δικαιοσύνῃ
light [is] in all goodness   and righteousness
καὶ ἀληθείᾳ, — 10 δοκιμάζοντες τί ἐστιν
and truth,)   proving   what is
εὐάρεστον τῷ κυρίῳ, 11 καὶ μὴ συγκοι-
well-pleasing to the Lord, and do not have fellow-
νωνεῖτε τοῖς ἔργοις τοῖς ἀκάρποις τοῦ
ship with the ²works - ¹unfruitful -
σκότους, μᾶλλον δὲ καὶ ἐλέγχετε, 12 τὰ
of darkness, but rather even reprove [them], ²the
γὰρ κρυφῇ γινόμενα ὑπ' αὐτῶν αἰσχρόν
for ¹hidden things ²being done ³by them ¹shameful
ἐστιν καὶ λέγειν· 13 τὰ δὲ πάντα ἐλεγχόμενα
¹it is ²even ⁴to speak [of]; - but all things being reproved
ὑπὸ τοῦ φωτὸς φανεροῦται· 14 πᾶν γὰρ
by the light is(are) manifested; for everything
τὸ φανερούμενον φῶς ἐστιν. διὸ λέγει·
- being manifested ²light ¹is. Wherefore he says:
ἔγειρε, ὁ καθεύδων, καὶ ἀνάστα ἐκ τῶν
Rise, the sleeping [one], and stand up out of the
νεκρῶν, καὶ ἐπιφαύσει σοι ὁ Χριστός.
dead [ones], and will shine on thee - Christ.
15 Βλέπετε οὖν ἀκριβῶς πῶς περιπατεῖτε,
See ye therefore carefully how ye walk,
μὴ ὡς ἄσοφοι ἀλλ' ὡς σοφοί, 16 ἐξαγοραζ-
not as unwise but as wise,   redeem-
όμενοι τὸν καιρόν, ὅτι αἱ ἡμέραι πονηραί
ing the time, because the days evil
εἰσιν. 17 διὰ τοῦτο μὴ γίνεσθε ἄφρονες,
are.   Therefore be ye not foolish,
ἀλλὰ συνίετε τί τὸ θέλημα τοῦ κυρίου.
but understand what the will of the Lord [is].
18 καὶ μὴ μεθύσκεσθε οἴνῳ, ἐν ᾧ ἐστιν
And be ye not drunk with wine, in which is

* That is, " let no corrupt word proceed ... "

King James Version

with the Spirit; 19 Speaking to yourselves in psalms and hymns and spiritual songs, singing and making melody in your heart to the Lord; 20 Giving thanks always for all things unto God and the Father in the name of our Lord Jesus Christ; 21 Submitting yourselves one to another in the fear of God. 22 Wives, submit yourselves unto your own husbands, as unto the Lord. 23 For the husband is the head of the wife, even as Christ is the head of the church: and he is the Saviour of the body. 24 Therefore as the church is subject unto Christ, so *let* the wives *be* to their own husbands in every thing. 25 Husbands, love your wives, even as Christ also loved the church, and gave himself for it; 26 That he might sanctify and cleanse it with the washing of water by the word, 27 That he might present it to himself a glorious church, not having spot, or wrinkle, or any such thing; but that it should be holy and without blemish. 28 So ought men to love their wives as their own bodies. He that loveth his wife loveth himself. 29 For no man ever yet hated his own flesh; but nourisheth and cherisheth it, even as the Lord the church: 30 For we are members of his body, of his flesh, and of his bones. 31 For this cause shall a man leave his father and mother, and shall be joined unto his wife, and they two shall be one flesh. 32 This is a great mystery: but I speak concerning Christ and the church. 33 Nevertheless, let every one of you in particular so love his wife even as himself; and the wife *see* that she reverence *her* husband.

6 Children, obey your parents in the Lord: for this is right. 2 Honour thy father and mother; which is the first commandment with promise; 3 That it may be well with thee, and thou mayest live long on the earth. 4 And, ye fathers, provoke not your children to wrath: but bring them up in the nurture and admonition of the Lord. 5 Servants, be obedient to them that are *your* masters according to the flesh, with fear and trembling, in singleness of your heart, as unto Christ; 6 Not with eyeservice, as menpleasers; but as the servants of Christ, doing the will of God from the heart; 7 With good will doing service, as to the Lord, and not to men: 8 Knowing that whatsoever good thing any man doeth, the same shall he receive of the Lord, whether *he be* bond or free. 9 And, ye masters, do the same things unto them, forbearing threatening: knowing that your Master also is in heaven; neither is there respect of persons with

New International Version

filled with the Spirit. 19 Speak to one another with psalms, hymns and spiritual songs. Sing and make music in your heart to the Lord, 20 always giving thanks to God the Father for everything, in the name of our Lord Jesus Christ.

Wives and husbands

21 Submit to one another out of reverence for Christ.
22 Wives, submit to your husbands as to the Lord. 23 For the husband is the head of the wife as Christ is the head of the church, his body, of which he is the Savior. 24 Now as the church submits to Christ, so also wives should submit to their husbands in everything.
25 Husbands, love your wives, just as Christ loved the church and gave himself up for her 26 to make her holy, cleansing her by the washing with water through the word, 27 and to present her to himself as a radiant church, without stain or wrinkle or any other blemish, but holy and blameless. 28 In this same way, husbands ought to love their wives as their own bodies. He who loves his wife loves himself. 29 After all, no one ever hated his own body, but he feeds and cares for it, just as Christ does the church— 30 for we are members of his body. 31 "For this reason a man will leave his father and mother and will be united to his wife, and the two will become one flesh." *h* 32 This is a profound mystery—but I am talking about Christ and the church. 33 However, each one of you also must love his wife as he loves himself, and the wife must respect her husband.

Children and parents

6 Children, obey your parents in the Lord, for this is right. 2 "Honor your father and mother"—which is the first commandment with a promise—3 "that it may go well with you and that you may enjoy long life on the earth." *i* 4 Fathers, do not exasperate your children; instead, bring them up in the training and instruction of the Lord.

Slaves and masters

5 Slaves, obey your earthly masters with respect and fear, and with sincerity of heart, just as you would obey Christ. 6 Obey them not only to win their favor when their eye is on you, but like slaves of Christ, doing the will of God from your heart. 7 Serve wholeheartedly, as if you were serving the Lord, not men, 8 because you know that the Lord will reward everyone for whatever good he does, whether he is slave or free.
9 And masters, treat your slaves in the same way. Do not threaten them, since you know that he who is both their Master and yours is in heaven, and there is no favoritism with him.

[h] Gen. 2:24. [i] Deut. 5:16.

Greek Interlinear

ἀσωτία, ἀλλὰ πληροῦσθε ἐν πνεύματι,
wantonness, but be filled by [the] Spirit,

19 λαλοῦντες ἑαυτοῖς ψαλμοῖς καὶ ὕμνοις
speaking to yourselves in psalms and hymns

καὶ ᾠδαῖς πνευματικαῖς, ᾄδοντες καὶ
and songs spiritual, singing and

ψάλλοντες τῇ καρδίᾳ ὑμῶν τῷ κυρίῳ,
psalming with the heart of you to the Lord,

20 εὐχαριστοῦντες πάντοτε ὑπὲρ πάντων
giving thanks always for all things

ἐν ὀνόματι τοῦ κυρίου ἡμῶν Ἰησοῦ
in [the] name of the Lord of us Jesus

Χριστοῦ τῷ θεῷ καὶ πατρί, 21 ὑποτασ-
Christ – to God even [the] Father, being

σόμενοι ἀλλήλοις ἐν φόβῳ Χριστοῦ. 22 Αἱ
subject to one another in [the] fear of Christ. The

γυναῖκες τοῖς ἰδίοις ἀνδράσιν ὡς τῷ
wives to the(ir) own husbands as to the

κυρίῳ, 23 ὅτι ἀνήρ ἐστιν κεφαλὴ τῆς
Lord, because a man is head of the

γυναικὸς ὡς καὶ ὁ Χριστὸς κεφαλὴ
woman as also – Christ [is] head

τῆς ἐκκλησίας, αὐτὸς σωτὴρ τοῦ σώματος.
of the church, [him]self Saviour of the body.

24 ἀλλὰ ὡς ἡ ἐκκλησία ὑποτάσσεται τῷ
But as the church is subject –

Χριστῷ, οὕτως καὶ αἱ γυναῖκες τοῖς
to Christ, so also the wives to the(ir)

ἀνδράσιν ἐν παντί. 25 Οἱ ἄνδρες, ἀγαπᾶτε
husbands in everything. The husbands, love ye

τὰς γυναῖκας, καθὼς καὶ ὁ Χριστὸς
the(your) wives, as also – Christ

ἠγάπησεν τὴν ἐκκλησίαν καὶ ἑαυτὸν
loved the church and himself

παρέδωκεν ὑπὲρ αὐτῆς, 26 ἵνα αὐτὴν
gave up on behalf of it, in order that it

ἁγιάσῃ καθαρίσας τῷ λουτρῷ τοῦ
he might sanctify cleansing by the washing of the

ὕδατος ἐν ῥήματι, 27 ἵνα παραστήσῃ αὐτὸς
water by word, in order ²might present ¹he
that

ἑαυτῷ ἔνδοξον τὴν ἐκκλησίαν, μὴ ἔχουσαν
¹to himself ²glorious ³the church, not having

σπίλον ἢ ῥυτίδα ἤ τι τῶν τοιούτων,
spot or wrinkle or any of the such things,

ἀλλ' ἵνα ᾖ ἁγία καὶ ἄμωμος. 28 οὕτως
but in order it might holy and unblemished. So
that be

ὀφείλουσιν [καὶ] οἱ ἄνδρες ἀγαπᾶν τὰς
ought also the husbands to love the

ἑαυτῶν γυναῖκας ὡς τὰ ἑαυτῶν σώματα.
of themselves wives as the of themselves bodies.

ὁ ἀγαπῶν τὴν ἑαυτοῦ γυναῖκα ἑαυτὸν
The [one] loving the of himself wife himself

ἀγαπᾷ· 29 οὐδεὶς γάρ ποτε τὴν ἑαυτοῦ
loves; for no man ever the of himself

σάρκα ἐμίσησεν, ἀλλὰ ἐκτρέφει καὶ θάλπει
flesh hated, but nourishes and cherishes

αὐτήν, καθὼς καὶ ὁ Χριστὸς τὴν ἐκ-
it, as also – Christ the

κλησίαν, 30 ὅτι μέλη ἐσμὲν τοῦ σώματος
church, because members we are of the body

αὐτοῦ. 31 ἀντὶ τούτου καταλείψει ἄνθρωπος
of him. For this ²shall leave ¹a man

[τὸν] πατέρα καὶ [τὴν] μητέρα καὶ
the(his) father and the(his) mother and

προσκολληθήσεται πρὸς τὴν γυναῖκα αὐτοῦ,
shall cleave to the wife of him,

καὶ ἔσονται οἱ δύο εἰς σάρκα μίαν·
and ³shall be ¹the ²two ⁴for ⁵flesh ⁶one.

32 τὸ μυστήριον τοῦτο μέγα ἐστίν, ἐγὼ
This mystery great is, ²I

δὲ λέγω εἰς Χριστὸν καὶ [εἰς] τὴν
¹but say as to Christ and as to the

ἐκκλησίαν. 33 πλὴν καὶ ὑμεῖς οἱ
church. Nevertheless also ye the

καθ' ἕνα ἕκαστος τὴν ἑαυτοῦ γυναῖκα
one by one† each ¹the ²of himself ²wife

οὕτως ἀγαπάτω ὡς ἑαυτόν, ἡ δὲ
so let him love as himself, and the

Chapter 6

γυνὴ ἵνα φοβῆται τὸν ἄνδρα. 6 Τὰ
wife in order that she fears the(her) husband. The

τέκνα, ὑπακούετε τοῖς γονεῦσιν ὑμῶν
children, obey ye the parents of you

ἐν κυρίῳ· τοῦτο γάρ ἐστιν δίκαιον.
in [the] Lord; for this is right.

2 τίμα τὸν πατέρα σου καὶ τὴν μητέρα,
Honour the father of thee and the mother,

ἥτις ἐστὶν ἐντολὴ πρώτη ἐν ἐπαγγελίᾳ,
which is ²commandment ¹[the] ²first with a promise,

3 ἵνα εὖ σοι γένηται καὶ ἔσῃ μακρο-
in order well with thee it may be and thou may- long-
that est be

χρόνιος ἐπὶ τῆς γῆς. 4 Καὶ οἱ πατέρες,
timed(lived) on the earth. And the fathers,

μὴ παροργίζετε τὰ τέκνα ὑμῶν, ἀλλὰ
do not ye provoke to wrath the children of you, but

ἐκτρέφετε αὐτὰ ἐν παιδείᾳ καὶ νουθεσίᾳ
nurture them in [the] discipline and admonition

κυρίου. 5 Οἱ δοῦλοι, ὑπακούετε τοῖς
of [the] Lord. The slaves, obey ye ¹the(your)

κατὰ σάρκα κυρίοις μετὰ φόβου καὶ
²according to ⁴flesh ³lords with fear and

τρόμου ἐν ἁπλότητι τῆς καρδίας ὑμῶν
trembling in singleness of the heart of you

ὡς τῷ Χριστῷ, 6 μὴ κατ' ὀφθαλμοδουλίαν
as – to Christ, not by way of eye-service

ὡς ἀνθρωπάρεσκοι, ἀλλ' ὡς δοῦλοι Χριστοῦ
as men-pleasers, but as slaves of Christ

ποιοῦντες τὸ θέλημα τοῦ θεοῦ ἐκ ψυχῆς,
doing the will – of God from [the] soul,

7 μετ' εὐνοίας δουλεύοντες ὡς τῷ κυρίῳ
with goodwill serving as slaves as to the Lord

καὶ οὐκ ἀνθρώποις, 8 εἰδότες ὅτι ἕκαστος
and not to men, knowing that each man

ἐάν τι ποιήσῃ ἀγαθόν, τοῦτο κομίσεται
whatever he does ¹good thing, this he will get

παρὰ κυρίου, εἴτε δοῦλος εἴτε ἐλεύθερος.
from [the] Lord, whether a slave or a freeman.

9 Καὶ οἱ κύριοι, τὰ αὐτὰ ποιεῖτε πρὸς
And the lords, the same things do ye toward

αὐτούς, ἀνιέντες τὴν ἀπειλήν, εἰδότες ὅτι
them, forbearing the threatening, knowing that

καὶ αὐτῶν καὶ ὑμῶν ὁ κύριός ἐστιν
both of them and of you the Lord is

ἐν οὐρανοῖς, καὶ προσωπολημψία οὐκ
in heavens, and respect of persons not

ἔστιν παρ' αὐτῷ.
is with him.

King James Version

him. 10 Finally, my brethren, be strong in the Lord, and in the power of his might. 11 Put on the whole armour of God, that ye may be able to stand against the wiles of the devil. 12 For we wrestle not against flesh and blood, but against principalities, against powers, against the rulers of the darkness of this world, against spiritual wickedness in high *places.* 13 Wherefore take unto you the whole armour of God, that ye may be able to withstand in the evil day, and having done all, to stand. 14 Stand therefore, having your loins girt about with truth, and having on the breastplate of righteousness; 15And your feet shod with the preparation of the gospel of peace; 16Above all, taking the shield of faith, wherewith ye shall be able to quench all the fiery darts of the wicked. 17And take the helmet of salvation, and the sword of the Spirit, which is the word of God: 18 Praying always with all prayer and supplication in the Spirit, and watching thereunto with all perseverance and supplication for all saints; 19And for me, that utterance may be given unto me, that I may open my mouth boldly, to make known the mystery of the gospel, 20 For which I am an ambassador in bonds; that therein I may speak boldly, as I ought to speak. 21 But that ye also may know my affairs, *and* how I do, Tychicus, a beloved brother and faithful minister in the Lord, shall make known to you all things: 22 Whom I have sent unto you for the same purpose, that ye might know our affairs, and *that* he might comfort your hearts. 23 Peace *be* to the brethren, and love with faith, from God the Father and the Lord Jesus Christ. 24 Grace *be* with all them that love our Lord Jesus Christ in sincerity. Amen.

Written from Rome unto the Ephesians by Tychicus.

New International Version

The armor of God

10 Finally, be strong in the Lord and in his mighty power. 11 Put on the full armor of God so that you can take your stand against the devil's schemes. 12 For our struggle is not against flesh and blood, but against the rulers, against the authorities, against the powers of this dark world and against the spiritual forces of evil in the heavenly realms. 13 Therefore put on the full armor of God, so that when the day of evil comes, you may be able to stand your ground, and after you have done everything, to stand. 14 Stand firm then, with the belt of truth buckled around your waist, with the breastplate of righteousness in place, 15 and with your feet fitted with the gospel of peace as a firm footing. 16 In addition to all this, take up the shield of faith, with which you can extinguish all the flaming arrows of the evil one. 17 Take the helmet of salvation and the sword of the Spirit, which is the word of God. 18And pray in the Spirit on all occasions with all kinds of prayers and requests. With this in mind, be alert and always keep on praying for all the saints.

19 Pray also for me, that whenever I open my mouth, words may be given me so that I will fearlessly make known the mystery of the gospel, 20 for which I am an ambassador in chains. Pray that I may declare it fearlessly, as I should.

Final greetings

21 Tychicus, the dear brother and faithful servant in the Lord, will tell you everything, so that you also may know how I am and what I am doing. 22 I am sending him to you for this very purpose, that you may know how we are, and that he may encourage you.
23 Peace to the brothers, and love with faith from God the Father and the Lord Jesus Christ. 24 Grace to all who love our Lord Jesus Christ with an undying love.

Greek Interlinear

10 Τοῦ λοιποῦ, ἐνδυναμοῦσθε ἐν κυρίῳ
For the rest,† be ye empowered in [the] Lord
καὶ ἐν τῷ κράτει τῆς ἰσχύος αὐτοῦ.
and in the might of the strength of him.
11 ἐνδύσασθε τὴν πανοπλίαν τοῦ θεοῦ
Put ye on the whole armour - of God
πρὸς τὸ δύνασθαι ὑμᾶς στῆναι πρὸς
for the to be able you᷄ to stand against
—so that ye are able . . .
τὰς μεθοδείας τοῦ διαβόλου· **12** ὅτι οὐκ
the craftinesses of the devil; because not
ἔστιν ἡμῖν ἡ πάλη πρὸς αἷμα καὶ σάρκα,
is to us the conflict° against blood and flesh,
—our conflict is not
ἀλλὰ πρὸς τὰς ἀρχάς, πρὸς τὰς ἐξουσίας,
but against the rulers, against the authorities,
πρὸς τοὺς κοσμοκράτορας τοῦ σκότους
against the world rulers - darkness
τούτου, πρὸς τὰ πνευματικὰ τῆς πονηρίας
of this, against the spiritual [hosts] - of evil
ἐν τοῖς ἐπουρανίοις. **13** διὰ τοῦτο
in the heavenlies. Therefore
ἀναλάβετε τὴν πανοπλίαν τοῦ θεοῦ, ἵνα
take ye up the whole armour - of God, in order
that
δυνηθῆτε ἀντιστῆναι ἐν τῇ ἡμέρᾳ τῇ
ye may be able to resist in the day -
πονηρᾷ καὶ ἅπαντα κατεργασάμενοι στῆναι.
evil and all things having wrought to stand.
14 στῆτε οὖν περιζωσάμενοι τὴν ὀσφὺν
Stand ye therefore girding round the loin[s]
ὑμῶν ἐν ἀληθείᾳ, καὶ ἐνδυσάμενοι τὸν
of you with truth, and putting on the
θώρακα τῆς δικαιοσύνης, **15** καὶ ὑπο-
breastplate - of righteousness, and shoe-
δησάμενοι τοὺς πόδας ἐν ἑτοιμασίᾳ τοῦ
ing the feet with readiness of the
εὐαγγελίου τῆς εἰρήνης, **16** ἐν πᾶσιν
gospel - of peace, in all
ἀναλαβόντες τὸν θυρεὸν τῆς πίστεως, ἐν
taking up the shield - of faith, by
ᾧ δυνήσεσθε πάντα τὰ βέλη τοῦ πονηροῦ
which ye will be able ᷄all ᷄the ᷄darts ᷄of the ᷄evil one
τὰ πεπυρωμένα σβέσαι· **17** καὶ τὴν
- ᷄having been equipped ᷄to quench; and the
with fire
περικεφαλαίαν τοῦ σωτηρίου δέξασθε, καὶ
helmet - of salvation take ye, and
τὴν μάχαιραν τοῦ πνεύματος, ὅ ἐστιν
the sword of the Spirit, which° is

ῥῆμα θεοῦ, **18** διὰ πάσης προσευχῆς καὶ
[the] word of God, by means of all prayer and
δεήσεως, προσευχόμενοι ἐν παντὶ καιρῷ
petition, praying at every time
ἐν πνεύματι, καὶ εἰς αὐτὸ ἀγρυπνοῦντες
in spirit, and ᷄to ᷄it ᷄watching
ἐν πάσῃ προσκαρτερήσει καὶ δεήσει περὶ
in all perseverance and petition concerning
πάντων τῶν ἁγίων, **19** καὶ ὑπὲρ ἐμοῦ,
all the saints, and on behalf of me,
ἵνα μοι δοθῇ λόγος ἐν ἀνοίξει τοῦ
in order to me may be given speech in opening of the
that
στόματός μου, ἐν παρρησίᾳ γνωρίσαι τὸ
mouth of me, in boldness to make known the
μυστήριον τοῦ εὐαγγελίου, **20** ὑπὲρ οὗ
mystery of the gospel, on behalf of which
πρεσβεύω ἐν ἁλύσει, ἵνα ἐν αὐτῷ παρ-
I am an in a chain, in order in it I may
ambassador that
ρησιάσωμαι ὡς δεῖ με λαλῆσαι.
speak boldly as it behoves me to speak.
21 Ἵνα δὲ εἰδῆτε καὶ ὑμεῖς τὰ κατ'
Now in order that ᷄may know ᷄also ᷄ye the things about
ἐμέ, τί πράσσω, πάντα γνωρίσει ὑμῖν
me, what I am doing, all things ᷄°will make ᷄¹¹to you
known
Τύχικος ὁ ἀγαπητὸς ἀδελφὸς καὶ πιστὸς
᷄Tychicus ᷄the ᷄beloved ᷄brother ᷄and ᷄faithful
διάκονος ἐν κυρίῳ, **22** ὃν ἔπεμψα πρὸς
᷄minister ᷄in ᷄[the] Lord, whom I sent to
ὑμᾶς εἰς αὐτὸ τοῦτο, ἵνα γνῶτε τὰ
you for this very thing, in order ye may know things
that
περὶ ἡμῶν καὶ παρακαλέσῃ τὰς καρδίας
concerning us and may comfort the hearts
ὑμῶν.
of you.
23 Εἰρήνη τοῖς ἀδελφοῖς καὶ ἀγάπη
Peace to the brothers and love
μετὰ πίστεως ἀπὸ θεοῦ πατρὸς καὶ
with faith from God [the] Father and
κυρίου Ἰησοῦ Χριστοῦ. **24** ἡ χάρις μετὰ
[the] Lord Jesus Christ. - Grace [be] with
πάντων τῶν ἀγαπώντων τὸν κύριον ἡμῶν
all the [ones] loving the Lord of us
Ἰησοῦν Χριστὸν ἐν ἀφθαρσίᾳ.
Jesus Christ in incorruptibility.

---

* Neuter, agreeing with πνεῦμα, not feminine to agree with μάχαιρα.

THE EPISTLE OF

PAUL THE APOSTLE

TO THE

PHILIPPIANS

PHILIPPIANS

1 Paul and Timotheus, the servants of Jesus Christ, to all the saints in Christ Jesus which are at Philippi, with the bishops and deacons: 2 Grace *be* unto you, and peace, from God our Father and *from* the Lord Jesus Christ. 3 I thank my God upon every remembrance of you, 4Always in every prayer of mine for you all making request with joy, 5 For your fellowship in the gospel from the first day until now; 6 Being confident of this very thing, that he which hath begun a good work in you will perform *it* until the day of Jesus Christ: 7 Even as it is meet for me to think this of you all, because I have you in my heart; inasmuch as both in my bonds, and in the defence and confirmation of the gospel, ye all are partakers of my grace. 8 For God is my record, how greatly I long after you all in the bowels of Jesus Christ. 9And this I pray, that your love may abound yet more and more in knowledge and *in* all judgment; 10 That ye may approve things that are excellent; that ye may be sincere and without offence till the day of Christ; 11 Being filled with the fruits of righteousness, which are by Jesus Christ, unto the glory and praise of God. 12 But I would ye should understand, brethren, that the things *which happened* unto me have fallen out rather unto the furtherance of the gospel; 13 So that my bonds in Christ are manifest in all the palace, and in all other *places;* 14And many of the brethren in the Lord, waxing confident by my bonds, are much more bold to speak the word without fear. 15 Some indeed preach Christ even of envy and strife; and some also of good will: 16 The one preach Christ of contention, not sincerely, supposing to add affliction to my bonds: 17 But the other of love, knowing that I am set for the defence of the gospel. 18 What then? notwithstanding, every way, whether in pretence, or in truth, Christ is preached; and I therein do rejoice, yea, and will rejoice. 19 For I know that this shall turn to my salvation through your prayer, and the supply of the Spirit of Jesus Christ, 20According to my earnest expectation and *my* hope, that in nothing I shall be ashamed, but *that* with all boldness, as always, *so* now

1 Paul and Timothy, servants of Christ Jesus,
To all the saints in Christ Jesus at Philippi, together with the overseers[a] and deacons: 2 Grace and peace to you from God our Father and the Lord Jesus Christ.

Thanksgiving and prayer

3 I thank my God every time I remember you. 4 In all my prayers for all of you, I always pray with joy 5 because of your partnership in the gospel from the first day until now, 6 being confident of this, that he who began a good work in you will carry it on to completion until the day of Christ Jesus.
7 It is right for me to feel this way about all of you, since I have you in my heart; for whether I am in chains or defending and confirming the gospel, all of you share in God's grace with me. 8 God can testify how I long for all of you with the affection of Christ Jesus.
9 And this is my prayer: that your love may abound more and more in knowledge and depth of insight, 10 so that you may be able to discern what is best and may be pure and blameless until the day of Christ, 11 filled with the fruit of righteousness that comes through Jesus Christ— to the glory and praise of God.

Paul's chains advance the gospel

12 Now I want you to know, brothers, that what has happened to me has really served to advance the gospel. 13As a result, it has become clear throughout the whole palace guard [b] and to everyone else that I am in chains for Christ. 14 Because of my chains, most of the brothers in the Lord have been encouraged to speak the word of God more courageously and fearlessly.
15 It is true that some preach Christ out of envy and rivalry, but others out of good will. 16 The latter do so in love, knowing that I am put here for the defense of the gospel. 17 The former preach Christ out of selfish ambition, not sincerely, supposing that they can stir up trouble for me while I am in chains. 18 But what does it matter? The important thing is that in every way, whether from false motives or true, Christ is preached. And because of this I rejoice.
Yes, and I will continue to rejoice, 19 for I know that through your prayers and the help given by the Spirit of Jesus Christ, what has happened to me will turn out for my deliverance. 20 I eagerly expect and hope that I will in no way be ashamed, but will have sufficient cour-

[a] Or *bishops.* [b] Or *whole palace.*

ΠΡΟΣ   ΦΙΛΙΠΠΗΣΙΟΥΣ

Chapter 1

Παῦλος καὶ Τιμόθεος δοῦλοι Χριστοῦ
Paul   and   Timothy   slaves of Christ
'Ιησοῦ πᾶσιν τοῖς ἁγίοις ἐν Χριστῷ
Jesus   to all the   saints   in   Christ
'Ιησοῦ τοῖς οὖσιν ἐν Φιλίπποις σὺν
Jesus   -   being   in   Philippi   with
ἐπισκόποις καὶ διακόνοις· 2 χάρις ὑμῖν
bishops   and   ministers: Grace   to you
καὶ εἰρήνη ἀπὸ θεοῦ πατρὸς ἡμῶν καὶ
and   peace   from   God   Father   of us   and
κυρίου 'Ιησοῦ Χριστοῦ.
[the] Lord Jesus   Christ.

3 Εὐχαριστῶ τῷ θεῷ μου ἐπὶ πάσῃ
I thank   the   God   of me   at   all
τῇ μνείᾳ ὑμῶν, 4 πάντοτε ἐν πάσῃ
the remembrance of you,   always   in   every
δεήσει μου ὑπὲρ πάντων ὑμῶν μετὰ
petition of me on behalf of all   you   with
χαρᾶς τὴν δέησιν ποιούμενος, 5 ἐπὶ τῇ
joy   the   petition   making,   over   the
κοινωνίᾳ ὑμῶν εἰς τὸ εὐαγγέλιον ἀπὸ
fellowship of you   in   the   gospel   from
τῆς πρώτης ἡμέρας ἄχρι τοῦ νῦν,
the   first   day   until   the   now,
6 πεποιθὼς αὐτὸ τοῦτο, ὅτι ὁ ἐναρξάμενος
being confident this very thing, that the having begun
[of]   [one]
ἐν ὑμῖν ἔργον ἀγαθὸν ἐπιτελέσει ἄχρι
in   you   work   a good   will complete [it] until
ἡμέρας Χριστοῦ 'Ιησοῦ· 7 καθώς ἐστιν
[the] day of Christ   Jesus;   as   it is
δίκαιον ἐμοὶ τοῦτο φρονεῖν ὑπὲρ πάντων
right   for me   this   to think on behalf of all
ὑμῶν, διὰ τὸ ἔχειν με ἐν τῇ καρδίᾳ
you, because of the to have me[b] in   the   heart
                    =because I have you in the(my) heart,
ὑμᾶς, ἔν τε τοῖς δεσμοῖς μου καὶ ἐν
you,   both in   the   bonds   of me and   in
τῇ ἀπολογίᾳ καὶ βεβαιώσει τοῦ εὐαγγελίου
the defence   and   confirmation of the gospel
συγκοινωνούς μου τῆς χάριτος πάντας
[b]partakers   [2]of me [3]of the [4]grace   [1]all
ὑμᾶς ὄντας. 8 μάρτυς γάρ μου ὁ θεός,
[1]you [2]being.   [2]witness [1]For [4]of me   -   [3]God
                                             [3][is],
ὡς ἐπιποθῶ πάντας ὑμᾶς ἐν σπλάγχνοις
how I long after all   you   in [the] bowels
Χριστοῦ 'Ιησοῦ. 9 Καὶ τοῦτο προσεύχομαι,
of Christ   Jesus.   And   this   I pray,
ἵνα ἡ ἀγάπη ὑμῶν ἔτι μᾶλλον καὶ
in order the love   of you   yet   more   and
that
μᾶλλον περισσεύῃ ἐν ἐπιγνώσει καὶ πάσῃ
more   may abound in full knowledge and all
αἰσθήσει, 10 εἰς τὸ δοκιμάζειν ὑμᾶς τὰ
perception,   for   the   to prove   you[b]   the
                =that ye may prove   things
διαφέροντα, ἵνα ἦτε εἰλικρινεῖς καὶ
differing,   in order ye may sincere   and
              that   be

ἀπρόσκοποι εἰς ἡμέραν Χριστοῦ, 11 πεπληρω-
unoffending in [the] day of Christ,   having been
μένοι καρπὸν δικαιοσύνης τὸν διὰ 'Ιησοῦ
filled [with] [the] fruit of righteousness - through Jesus
Χριστοῦ, εἰς δόξαν καὶ ἔπαινον θεοῦ.
Christ,   to [the] glory   and   praise   of God.
12 Γινώσκειν δὲ ὑμᾶς βούλομαι, ἀδελφοί,
Now [a]to know [b] [2]you   [1]I wish,   brothers,
ὅτι τὰ κατ' ἐμὲ μᾶλλον εἰς προκοπὴν
that the about   me[b] [1]rather   [2]to   [3][the] advance
things
= my affairs
τοῦ εὐαγγελίου ἐλήλυθεν, 13 ὥστε τοὺς
[1]of the [2]gospel   [1]has(ve) come,   so as   the
δεσμούς μου φανεροὺς ἐν Χριστῷ γενέσθαι
bonds   of me [2]manifest [1]in [3]Christ [1]to become
ἐν ὅλῳ τῷ πραιτωρίῳ καὶ τοῖς λοιποῖς
in   all   the praetorium   and   to [2]the [1]rest
πᾶσιν, 14 καὶ τοὺς πλείονας τῶν ἀδελφῶν
[2]all,   and   the   majority   of the brothers
ἐν κυρίῳ πεποιθότας τοῖς δεσμοῖς μου
in [the] Lord being confident in the   bonds   of me
περισσοτέρως τολμᾶν ἀφόβως τὸν λόγον
[2]more exceedingly [3]to dare [4]fearlessly [1]the [5]word
τοῦ θεοῦ λαλεῖν. 15 τινὲς μὲν καὶ διὰ
 -   [6]of God [7]to speak.   Some   indeed even because of
φθόνον καὶ ἔριν, τινὲς δὲ καὶ δι' εὐδοκίαν
envy   and   strife, but some also because good-
of   will
τὸν Χριστὸν κηρύσσουσιν· 16 οἱ μὲν ἐξ
 -    Christ   proclaim;   these[†] from
ἀγάπης, εἰδότες ὅτι εἰς ἀπολογίαν τοῦ
love,   knowing   that for   defence   of the
εὐαγγελίου κεῖμαι, 17 οἱ δὲ ἐξ ἐριθείας
gospel   I am set,   those[†] from   rivalry
τὸν Χριστὸν καταγγέλλουσιν, οὐχ ἁγνῶς,
 -    [2]Christ   [1]announce,   not   purely,
οἰόμενοι θλῖψιν ἐγείρειν τοῖς δεσμοῖς μου.
thinking   [2]affliction [1]to raise to the bonds   of me.
18 Τί γάρ; πλὴν ὅτι παντὶ τρόπῳ,
What then? nevertheless that in every   way,
εἴτε προφάσει εἴτε ἀληθείᾳ, Χριστὸς
whether in pretence or   in truth,   Christ
καταγγέλλεται, καὶ ἐν τούτῳ χαίρω· ἀλλὰ
is announced,   and in   this   I rejoice; yet
καὶ χαρήσομαι· 19 οἶδα γὰρ ὅτι τοῦτό
also I will rejoice;   for I know that this
μοι ἀποβήσεται εἰς σωτηρίαν διὰ τῆς
to me will result   in   salvation through of the
ὑμῶν δεήσεως καὶ ἐπιχορηγίας τοῦ
[1]of you [2]petition and   supply   of the
πνεύματος 'Ιησοῦ Χριστοῦ, 20 κατὰ τὴν
spirit   of Jesus   Christ,   according to the
ἀποκαραδοκίαν καὶ ἐλπίδα μου ὅτι ἐν
eager expectation and hope   of me that in
οὐδενὶ αἰσχυνθήσομαι, ἀλλ' ἐν πάσῃ παρ-
nothing I shall be shamed,   but with all   bold-

• Cf. ver. 27; ch. 2. 19, 20, 23; Eph. 6. 21, 22; Col. 4. 7, 8.

King James Version

also Christ shall be magnified in my body, whether *it be* by life, or by death. 21 For to me to live *is* Christ, and to die *is* gain. 22 But if I live in the flesh, this *is* the fruit of my labour: yet what I shall choose I wot not. 23 For I am in a strait betwixt two, having a desire to depart, and to be with Christ; which is far better: 24 Nevertheless to abide in the flesh *is* more needful for you. 25 And having this confidence, I know that I shall abide and continue with you all for your furtherance and joy of faith; 26 That your rejoicing may be more abundant in Jesus Christ for me by my coming to you again. 27 Only let your conversation be as it becometh the gospel of Christ: that whether I come and see you, or else be absent, I may hear of your affairs, that ye stand fast in one spirit, with one mind striving together for the faith of the gospel; 28 And in nothing terrified by your adversaries: which is to them an evident token of perdition, but to you of salvation, and that of God. 29 For unto you it is given in the behalf of Christ, not only to believe on him, but also to suffer for his sake; 30 Having the same conflict which ye saw in me, and now hear *to be* in me.

2 If *there be* therefore any consolation in Christ, if any comfort of love, if any fellowship of the Spirit, if any bowels and mercies, 2 Fulfil ye my joy, that ye be likeminded, having the same love, *being* of one accord, of one mind. 3 *Let* nothing *be done* through strife or vainglory; but in lowliness of mind let each esteem other better than themselves. 4 Look not every man on his own things, but every man also on the things of others. 5 Let this mind be in you, which was also in Christ Jesus: 6 Who, being in the form of God, thought it not robbery to be equal with God: 7 But made himself of no reputation, and took upon him the form of a servant, and was made in the likeness of men: 8 And being found in fashion as a man, he humbled himself, and became obedient unto death, even the death of the cross. 9 Wherefore God also hath highly exalted him, and given him a name which is above every name: 10 That at the name of Jesus every knee should bow, of *things* in heaven, and *things* in earth, and *things* under the earth; 11 And *that* every tongue should confess that Jesus Christ *is* Lord, to the glory of God the

New International Version

age so that now as always Christ will be exalted in my body, whether by life or by death. 21 For to me, to live is Christ and to die is gain. 22 If I am to go on living in the body, this will mean fruitful labor for me. Yet, what shall I choose? I do not know! 23 I am torn between the two: I desire to depart and be with Christ, which is better by far; 24 but it is more necessary for you that I remain in the body. 25 Convinced of this, I know that I will remain, and I will continue with all of you for your progress and joy in the faith, 26 so that through my being with you again your joy in Christ Jesus will overflow on account of me.

27 Whatever happens, conduct yourselves in a manner worthy of the gospel of Christ. Then, whether I come and see you or only hear about you in my absence, I will know that you stand firm in one spirit, contending as one man for the faith of the gospel 28 without being frightened in any way by those who oppose you. This is a sign to them that they will be destroyed, but that you will be saved—and that by God. 29 For it has been granted to you on behalf of Christ not only to believe on him, but also to suffer for him, 30 since you are going through the same struggle you saw I had, and now hear that I still have.

Imitating Christ's humility

2 If you have any encouragement from being united with Christ, if any comfort from his love, if any fellowship with the Spirit, if any tenderness and compassion, 2 then make my joy complete by being like-minded, having the same love, being one in spirit and purpose. 3 Do nothing out of selfish ambition or vain conceit, but in humility consider others better than yourselves. 4 Each of you should look not only to your own interests, but also to the interests of others.

5 Your attitude should be the same as that of Christ Jesus:
6 Who, being in very nature[c] God,
did not consider equality with God
something to be grasped,
7 but made himself nothing,
taking the very nature[d] of a servant,
being made in human likeness.
8 And being found in appearance as a man,
he humbled himself
and became obedient to death—
even death on a cross!
9 Therefore God exalted him to the highest place
and gave him the name that is above every name,
10 that at the name of Jesus every knee should bow,
in heaven and on earth and under the earth,
11 and every tongue confess that Jesus Christ is Lord,
to the glory of God the Father.

[c] Or *in the form of.* [d] Or *the form.*

Greek Interlinear

ρησία ὡς πάντοτε καὶ νῦν μεγαλυνθήσεται
ness as always also now shall be magnified

Χριστὸς ἐν τῷ σώματί μου, εἴτε διὰ
Christ in the body of me, whether through

ζωῆς εἴτε διὰ θανάτου. 21 ἐμοὶ γὰρ
life or through death. For to me

τὸ ζῆν Χριστὸς καὶ τὸ ἀποθανεῖν κέρδος.
- to live [is] Christ and - to die [is] gain.

22 εἰ δὲ τὸ ζῆν ἐν σαρκί, τοῦτό μοι
But if - to live in [the] flesh, this to me

καρπὸς ἔργου, καὶ τί αἱρήσομαι οὐ
[is] fruit of [?my] work, and what I shall choose not

γνωρίζω. 23 συνέχομαι δὲ ἐκ τῶν δύο,
I perceive. But I am constrained by the two,

τὴν ἐπιθυμίαν ἔχων εἰς τὸ ἀναλῦσαι καὶ
²the ³desire ¹having for the to depart and

σὺν Χριστῷ εἶναι, πολλῷ γὰρ μᾶλλον
²with ¹Christ ¹to be, for by much [this is] rather

κρεῖσσον· 24 τὸ δὲ ἐπιμένειν τῇ σαρκὶ
better; - but to remain in the flesh [is]

ἀναγκαιότερον δι' ὑμᾶς. 25 καὶ τοῦτο
more necessary on account of you. And this

πεποιθὼς οἶδα, ὅτι μενῶ καὶ παραμενῶ
being I know, that I shall and continue
confident remain

πᾶσιν ὑμῖν εἰς τὴν ὑμῶν προκοπὴν καὶ
with all you for the ⁴of you ³advance ¹and

χαρὰν τῆς πίστεως, 26 ἵνα τὸ καύχημα
²joy ⁴of the ³faith, in order the boast
that

ὑμῶν περισσεύῃ ἐν Χριστῷ Ἰησοῦ ἐν
of you may abound in Christ Jesus in

ἐμοὶ διὰ τῆς ἐμῆς παρουσίας πάλιν
me through - my presence again

πρὸς ὑμᾶς.
with you.

27 Μόνον ἀξίως τοῦ εὐαγγελίου τοῦ
Only ²worthily ¹of the ²gospel -

Χριστοῦ πολιτεύεσθε, ἵνα εἴτε ἐλθὼν καὶ
³of Christ ¹conduct in order whether coming and
yourselves, that

ἰδὼν ὑμᾶς εἴτε ἀπὼν ἀκούω τὰ περὶ
seeing you or being I hear the con-
absent things cerning

ὑμῶν, ὅτι στήκετε ἐν ἑνὶ πνεύματι,
you, that ye stand in one spirit,

μιᾷ ψυχῇ συναθλοῦντες τῇ πίστει τοῦ
with one soul striving together in the faith of the

εὐαγγελίου, 28 καὶ μὴ πτυρόμενοι ἐν
gospel, and not being terrified in

μηδενὶ ὑπὸ τῶν ἀντικειμένων, ἥτις ἐστὶν
no(any) by the [ones] opposing, which is
thing

αὐτοῖς ἔνδειξις ἀπωλείας, ὑμῶν δὲ
to them a proof of destruction, but of you

σωτηρίας, καὶ τοῦτο ἀπὸ θεοῦ· 29 ὅτι
of salvation, and this from God; because

ὑμῖν ἐχαρίσθη τὸ ὑπὲρ Χριστοῦ, οὐ
to you it was given - on behalf of Christ, not

μόνον τὸ εἰς αὐτὸν πιστεύειν ἀλλὰ καὶ
only - in him to believe but also

τὸ ὑπὲρ αὐτοῦ πάσχειν, 30 τὸν αὐτὸν
- on behalf of him to suffer, the same

ἀγῶνα ἔχοντες οἷον εἴδετε ἐν ἐμοὶ
struggle having which ye saw in me

Chapter 2

καὶ νῦν ἀκούετε ἐν ἐμοί. 2 Εἴ τις
and now hear in me. ²If [there ³any
is]

οὖν παράκλησις ἐν Χριστῷ, εἴ τι
¹therefore comfort in Christ, if any

παραμύθιον ἀγάπης, εἴ τις κοινωνία
consolation of love, if any fellowship

πνεύματος, εἴ τις σπλάγχνα καὶ οἰκτιρμοί,
of spirit, if any compassions and pities,

2 πληρώσατέ μου τὴν χαρὰν ἵνα τὸ
fulfil ye of me the joy in order that the
that

αὐτὸ φρονῆτε, τὴν αὐτὴν ἀγάπην ἔχοντες,
same thing ye think, the same love having,

σύμψυχοι, τὸ ἓν φρονοῦντες, 3 μηδὲν κατ'
one in soul, the one thinking, [doing] by
thing nothing way of

ἐριθείαν μηδὲ κατὰ κενοδοξίαν, ἀλλὰ τῇ
rivalry nor by way of vainglory, but -

ταπεινοφροσύνῃ ἀλλήλους ἡγούμενοι ὑπερ-
in humility ¹one another ²deeming sur-

ἔχοντας ἑαυτῶν, 4 μὴ τὰ ἑαυτῶν ἕκαστοι
passing themselves, not ²the ³of them- ¹each ones
things selves

σκοποῦντες, ἀλλὰ καὶ τὰ ἑτέρων ἕκαστοι.
²looking at, but ³also ⁴the ⁵of ¹each ones.
things others

5 τοῦτο φρονεῖτε ἐν ὑμῖν ὃ καὶ ἐν
This think ye among you which also [was] in

Χριστῷ Ἰησοῦ, 6 ὃς ἐν μορφῇ θεοῦ
Christ Jesus, who in [the] form of God

ὑπάρχων οὐχ ἁρπαγμὸν ἡγήσατο τὸ εἶναι
subsisting ²not ³robbery ¹deemed [it] the to be

ἴσα θεῷ, 7 ἀλλὰ ἑαυτὸν ἐκένωσεν μορφὴν
equal with God, but himself emptied ²[the] form
things

δούλου λαβών, ἐν ὁμοιώματι ἀνθρώπων
³of a slave ¹taking, ²in ¹likeness of men

γενόμενος· καὶ σχήματι εὑρεθεὶς ὡς
¹becoming· and ²in fashion ¹being found as

ἄνθρωπος 8 ἐταπείνωσεν ἑαυτὸν γενόμενος
a man he humbled himself becoming

ὑπήκοος μέχρι θανάτου, θανάτου δὲ σταυροῦ.
obedient until death, and death of a cross.

9 διὸ καὶ ὁ θεὸς αὐτὸν ὑπερύψωσεν
Wherefore also - God ²him ¹highly exalted

καὶ ἐχαρίσατο αὐτῷ τὸ ὄνομα τὸ ὑπὲρ
and gave to him the name - above

πᾶν ὄνομα, 10 ἵνα ἐν τῷ ὀνόματι Ἰησοῦ
every name, in order in the name of Jesus

πᾶν γόνυ κάμψῃ ἐπουρανίων καὶ ἐπιγείων
every knee should of heavenly and earthly
bend [beings] [beings]

καὶ καταχθονίων, 11 καὶ πᾶσα γλῶσσα
and [beings] under the earth, and every tongue

ἐξομολογήσηται ὅτι κύριος Ἰησοῦς
should acknowledge that ²Lord ¹Jesus

Χριστὸς εἰς δόξαν θεοῦ πατρός.
¹Christ [is] to [the] glory of God [the] Father.

King James Version

Father. 12 Wherefore, my beloved, as ye have always obeyed, not as in my presence only, but now much more in my absence, work out your own salvation with fear and trembling: 13 For it is God which worketh in you both to will and to do of *his* good pleasure. 14 Do all things without murmurings and disputings: 15 That ye may be blameless and harmless, the sons of God, without rebuke, in the midst of a crooked and perverse nation, among whom ye shine as lights in the world; 16 Holding forth the word of life; that I may rejoice in the day of Christ, that I have not run in vain, neither laboured in vain. 17 Yea, and if I be offered upon the sacrifice and service of your faith, I joy, and rejoice with you all. 18 For the same cause also do ye joy, and rejoice with me. 19 But I trust in the Lord Jesus to send Timotheus shortly unto you, that I also may be of good comfort, when I know your state. 20 For I have no man likeminded, who will naturally care for your state. 21 For all seek their own, not the things which are Jesus Christ's. 22 But ye know the proof of him, that, as a son with the father, he hath served with me in the gospel. 23 Him therefore I hope to send presently, so soon as I shall see how it will go with me. 24 But I trust in the Lord that I also myself shall come shortly. 25 Yet I supposed it necessary to send to you Epaphroditus, my brother, and companion in labour, and fellow-soldier, but your messenger, and he that ministered to my wants. 26 For he longed after you all, and was full of heaviness, because that ye had heard that he had been sick. 27 For indeed he was sick nigh unto death: but God had mercy on him; and not on him only, but on me also, lest I should have sorrow upon sorrow. 28 I sent him therefore the more carefully, that, when ye see him again, ye may rejoice, and that I may be the less sorrowful. 29 Receive him therefore in the Lord with all gladness; and hold such in reputation: 30 Because for the work of Christ he was nigh unto death, not regarding his life, to supply your lack of service toward me.

3 Finally, my brethren, rejoice in the Lord. To write the same things to you, to me indeed *is* not grievous, but for you *it is* safe. 2 Beware of dogs, beware of evil workers, beware of the concision. 3 For we are the circumcision, which worship God in the spirit, and rejoice in Christ Jesus, and have no confidence in the flesh.

New International Version

Shining as stars

12 Therefore, my dear friends, as you have always obeyed—not only in my presence, but now much more in my absence—continue to work out your salvation with fear and trembling, 13 for it is God who works in you to will and to do what pleases him.

14 Do everything without complaining or arguing, 15 so that you may become blameless and pure, children of God without fault in a crooked and depraved generation, in which you shine like stars in the universe 16 as you hold out[e] the word of life—in order that I may boast on the day of Christ that I did not run or labor for nothing. 17 But even if I am being poured out like a drink offering on the sacrifice and service coming from your faith, I am glad and rejoice with all of you. 18 So you too should be glad and rejoice with me.

Timothy and Epaphroditus

19 I hope in the Lord Jesus to send Timothy to you soon, that I also may be cheered when I receive news about you. 20 I have no one else like him, who takes a genuine interest in your welfare. 21 For everyone looks out for his own interests, not those of Jesus Christ. 22 But you know that Timothy has proved himself, because as a son with his father he has served with me in the work of the gospel. 23 I hope, therefore, to send him as soon as I see how things go with me. 24 And I am confident in the Lord that I myself will come soon.

25 But I think it is necessary to send back to you Epaphroditus, my brother, fellow worker and fellow soldier, who is also your messenger, whom you sent to take care of my needs. 26 For he longs for all of you and is distressed because you heard he was ill. 27 Indeed he was ill, and almost died. But God had mercy on him, and not on him only but also on me, to spare me sorrow upon sorrow. 28 Therefore I am all the more eager to send him, so that when you see him again you may be glad and I may have less anxiety. 29 Welcome him in the Lord with great joy, and honor men like him, 30 because he almost died for the work of Christ, risking his life to make up for the help you could not give me.

No confidence in the flesh

3 Finally, my brothers, rejoice in the Lord! It is no trouble for me to write the same things to you again, and it is a safeguard for you. 2 Watch out for those dogs, those men who do evil, those mutilators of the flesh. 3 For it is we who are the circumcision, we who worship by the Spirit of God, who glory in Christ Jesus, and

[e] Or *hold on to.*

Greek Interlinear

12 Ὥστε, ἀγαπητοί μου, καθὼς πάντοτε
So as,   beloved   of me, as   always

ὑπηκούσατε, μὴ ὡς ἐν τῇ παρουσίᾳ
ye obeyed, not as in the presence

μου μόνον ἀλλὰ νῦν πολλῷ μᾶλλον ἐν
of me only but now by more rather in

τῇ ἀπουσίᾳ μου, μετὰ φόβου καὶ τρόμου
the absence of me, with fear and trembling

τὴν ἑαυτῶν σωτηρίαν κατεργάζεσθε· 13 θεὸς
¹the ²of yourselves ⁵salvation work out;   ¹God

γάρ ἐστιν ὁ ἐνεργῶν ἐν ὑμῖν καὶ τὸ
²for   is the [one] operating in you both the

θέλειν καὶ τὸ ἐνεργεῖν ὑπὲρ τῆς εὐδοκίας.
to will and the to operate on behalf of the(his) goodwill.

14 πάντα ποιεῖτε χωρὶς γογγυσμῶν καὶ
All things do ye without murmurings and

διαλογισμῶν, 15 ἵνα γένησθε ἄμεμπτοι καὶ
disputings,   in order that ye may be blameless and

ἀκέραιοι, τέκνα θεοῦ ἄμωμα μέσον
harmless, children of God faultless in the
                                      midst of

γενεᾶς σκολιᾶς καὶ διεστραμμένης, ἐν
a generation crooked and having been perverted, among

οἷς φαίνεσθε ὡς φωστῆρες ἐν κόσμῳ,
whom ye shine as luminaries in [the] world.

16 λόγον ζωῆς ἐπέχοντες, εἰς καύχημα
a word of life holding up, for a boast

ἐμοὶ εἰς ἡμέραν Χριστοῦ, ὅτι οὐκ εἰς
to me in [the] day of Christ, that not in

κενὸν ἔδραμον οὐδὲ εἰς κενὸν ἐκοπίασα.
vain   I ran nor in vain laboured.

17 Ἀλλὰ εἰ καὶ σπένδομαι ἐπὶ τῇ θυσίᾳ
But   if indeed I am poured out on the sacrifice

καὶ λειτουργίᾳ τῆς πίστεως ὑμῶν, χαίρω
and service of the faith of you, I rejoice

καὶ συγχαίρω πᾶσιν ὑμῖν· 18 τὸ δὲ αὐτὸ
and rejoice with ²all ¹you;   and the same

καὶ ὑμεῖς χαίρετε καὶ συγχαίρετέ μοι.
also ye rejoice and rejoice with me.

19 Ἐλπίζω δὲ ἐν κυρίῳ Ἰησοῦ Τιμόθεον
But I hope in [the] Lord Jesus ²Timothy

ταχέως πέμψαι ὑμῖν, ἵνα κἀγὼ εὐψυχῶ
⁴shortly ¹to send ³to you, in order I also may be of
                            that   good cheer

γνοὺς τὰ περὶ ὑμῶν. 20 οὐδένα γὰρ
knowing the con-   you.   For no one
        things cerning

ἔχω ἰσόψυχον, ὅστις γνησίως τὰ περὶ
I have likeminded, who genuinely ²the ¹con-
                                   things cerning

ὑμῶν μεριμνήσει· 21 οἱ πάντες γὰρ τὰ
²you ¹will care for;   the   for all ²the
                                          things

ἑαυτῶν ζητοῦσιν, οὐ τὰ Χριστοῦ Ἰησοῦ.
²of them- ¹seek, not the of Christ Jesus.
selves   things

22 τὴν δὲ δοκιμὴν αὐτοῦ γινώσκετε, ὅτι
But the character of him ye know,   that

ὡς πατρὶ τέκνον σὺν ἐμοὶ ἐδούλευσεν
as ²a father ¹a child³[serves] ⁵with ⁶me ⁴he served

εἰς τὸ εὐαγγέλιον. 23 τοῦτον μὲν οὖν
in the gospel.   This one - therefore

ἐλπίζω πέμψαι ὡς ἂν ἀφίδω τὰ περὶ
I hope to send ²whenever ³I see ⁴the ⁵con-
                                   things cerning

ἐμὲ ἐξαυτῆς· 24 πέποιθα δὲ ἐν κυρίῳ
⁶me ¹immediately; but I trust in [the] Lord

ὅτι καὶ αὐτὸς ταχέως ἐλεύσομαι. 25 Ἀναγ-
that ²also ¹[my]self ⁴shortly ³I will come. ²neces-

καῖον δὲ ἡγησάμην Ἐπαφρόδιτον τὸν
sary But ¹I deemed [it] ⁸Epaphroditus ⁷the

ἀδελφὸν καὶ συνεργὸν καὶ συστρατιώτην
⁹brother ¹⁰and ¹¹fellow-worker ¹²and ¹³fellow-soldier

μου, ὑμῶν δὲ ἀπόστολον καὶ λειτουργὸν
¹⁴of me, ¹⁵and ¹⁶of you ¹⁸apostle ¹⁷and ¹⁹minister

τῆς χρείας μου, πέμψαι πρὸς ὑμᾶς,
¹⁸of the ¹⁹need ²⁰of me, ²¹to send ²²to ²³you,

26 ἐπειδὴ ἐπιποθῶν ἦν πάντας ὑμᾶς, καὶ
since   ²longing after ¹he was ³all ⁴you, and

ἀδημονῶν, διότι ἠκούσατε ὅτι ἠσθένησεν.
[was] being because ye heard that he ailed.
troubled,

27 καὶ γὰρ ἠσθένησεν παραπλήσιον θανάτῳ·
For indeed he ailed coming near to death;

ἀλλὰ ὁ θεὸς ἠλέησεν αὐτόν, οὐκ αὐτὸν
but - God had mercy on him, ¹not ²him

δὲ μόνον ἀλλὰ καὶ ἐμέ, ἵνα μὴ λύπην
¹and only but also me, lest grief

ἐπὶ λύπην σχῶ. 28 σπουδαιοτέρως οὖν
on grief I should have. More eagerly therefore

ἔπεμψα αὐτόν, ἵνα ἰδόντες αὐτὸν πάλιν
I sent him, in order that seeing him again

χαρῆτε κἀγὼ ἀλυπότερος ὦ. 29 προσδέχεσθε
ye may and ²I ¹less grieved ³may be. Receive ye
rejoice

οὖν αὐτὸν ἐν κυρίῳ μετὰ πάσης χαρᾶς,
therefore him in [the] Lord with all joy,

καὶ τοὺς τοιούτους ἐντίμους ἔχετε, 30 ὅτι
and - ²such ones ³honoured ¹hold ye, because

διὰ τὸ ἔργον Χριστοῦ μέχρι θανάτου
on ac- the work of Christ ²as far as ³death
count of

ἤγγισεν παραβολευσάμενος τῇ ψυχῇ, ἵνα
¹he drew exposing the(his) life, in or-
near   der that

ἀναπληρώσῃ τὸ ὑμῶν ὑστέρημα τῆς πρός
he might fill up ¹the ²of you ³lack - ⁴toward

με λειτουργίας.
⁵me ⁴of service.

Chapter 3

Τὸ λοιπόν, ἀδελφοί μου, χαίρετε ἐν
For the rest, brothers of me, rejoice ye in

κυρίῳ. τὰ αὐτὰ γράφειν ὑμῖν ἐμοὶ μὲν
[the] Lord. ²The ³same things ¹to write to you for me indeed

οὐκ ὀκνηρόν, ὑμῖν δὲ ἀσφαλές.
[is] not irksome, but for you safe.

2 Βλέπετε τοὺς κύνας, βλέπετε τοὺς
Look [to] the dogs, look [to] the

κακοὺς ἐργάτας, βλέπετε τὴν κατατομήν.
evil workmen, look [to] the concision.*

3 ἡμεῖς γάρ ἐσμεν ἡ περιτομή, οἱ
For we   are the circumcision, the
                                  [ones]

πνεύματι θεοῦ λατρεύοντες καὶ καυχώμενοι
²by [the] Spirit ³of God ¹worshipping and boasting

ἐν Χριστῷ Ἰησοῦ καὶ οὐκ ἐν σαρκὶ
in Christ Jesus and ²not ³in [the] ⁴flesh

* The apostle uses a " studiously contemptuous paronomasia "
(Ellicott). He does not use περιτομή, the proper word for " circumcision ", " as this, though now abrogated in Christ, had still
its spiritual aspects."

King James Version

New International Version

4 Though I might also have confidence in the flesh. If any other man thinketh that he hath whereof he might trust in the flesh, I more: 5 Circumcised the eighth day, of the stock of Israel, *of* the tribe of Benjamin, a Hebrew of the Hebrews; as touching the law, a Pharisee; 6 Concerning zeal, persecuting the church; touching the righteousness which is in the law, blameless. 7 But what things were gain to me, those I counted loss for Christ. 8 Yea doubtless, and I count all things *but* loss for the excellency of the knowledge of Christ Jesus my Lord: for whom I have suffered the loss of all things, and do count them *but* dung, that I may win Christ, 9 And be found in him, not having mine own righteousness, which is of the law, but that which is through the faith of Christ, the righteousness which is of God by faith: 10 That I may know him, and the power of his resurrection, and the fellowship of his sufferings, being made conformable unto his death; 11 If by any means I might attain unto the resurrection of the dead. 12 Not as though I had already attained, either were already perfect: but I follow after, if that I may apprehend that for which also I am apprehended of Christ Jesus. 13 Brethren, I count not myself to have apprehended: but *this* one thing *I do*, forgetting those things which are behind, and reaching forth unto those things which are before, 14 I press toward the mark for the prize of the high calling of God in Christ Jesus. 15 Let us therefore, as many as be perfect, be thus minded: and if in any thing ye be otherwise minded, God shall reveal even this unto you. 16 Nevertheless, whereto we have already attained, let us walk by the same rule, let us mind the same thing. 17 Brethren, be followers together of me, and mark them which walk so as ye have us for an ensample. 18 (For many walk, of whom I have told you often, and now tell you even weeping, *that they are* the enemies of the cross of Christ: 19 Whose end *is* destruction, whose God *is their* belly, and *whose* glory *is* in their shame, who mind earthly things.) 20 For our conversation is in heaven; from whence also we look for the Saviour, the Lord Jesus Christ: 21 Who shall change our vile body, that it may be fashioned like unto his glorious body, according to the working whereby he is able even to subdue all things unto himself.

who put no confidence in the flesh—4 though I myself have reasons for such confidence.

If anyone else thinks he has reasons to put confidence in the flesh, I have more: 5 circumcised on the eighth day, of the people of Israel, of the tribe of Benjamin, a Hebrew of Hebrews; in regard to the law, a Pharisee; 6 as for zeal, persecuting the church; as for legalistic righteousness, faultless.

7 But whatever was to my profit I now consider loss for the sake of Christ. 8 What is more, I consider everything a loss compared to the surpassing greatness of knowing Christ Jesus my Lord, for whose sake I have lost all things. I consider them rubbish, that I may gain Christ 9 and be found in him, not having a righteousness of my own that comes from the law, but that which is through faith in Christ—the righteousness that comes from God and is by faith. 10 I want to know Christ and the power of his resurrection and the fellowship of sharing in his sufferings, becoming like him in his death, 11 and so, somehow, to attain to the resurrection from the dead.

Pressing on toward the goal

12 Not that I have already obtained all this, or have already been made perfect, but I press on to take hold of that for which Christ Jesus took hold of me. 13 Brothers, I do not consider myself yet to have taken hold of it. But one thing I do: Forgetting what is behind and straining toward what is ahead, 14 I press on toward the goal to win the prize for which God has called me heavenward in Christ Jesus. 15 All of us who are mature should take such a view of things. And if on some point you think differently, that too God will make clear to you. 16 Only let us live up to what we have already attained.

17 Join with others in following my example, brothers, and take note of those who live according to the pattern we gave you. 18 For, as I have often told you before and now say again even with tears, many live as enemies of the cross of Christ. 19 Their destiny is destruction, their god is their stomach, and their glory is in their shame. Their mind is on earthly things. 20 But our citizenship is in heaven. And we eagerly await a Savior from there, the Lord Jesus Christ, 21 who, by the power that enables him to bring everything under his control, will transform our lowly bodies so that they will be like his glorious body.

4 Therefore, my brethren dearly beloved and longed for, my joy and crown, so stand fast in the Lord, *my* dearly beloved. 2 I beseech Euodias, and beseech Syntyche, that they be of the same mind in the Lord. 3 And I entreat thee also, true yokefellow, help those women which

4 Therefore, my brothers, you whom I love and long for, my joy and crown, that is how you should stand firm in the Lord, dear friends!

Exhortations

2 I plead with Euodia and I plead with Syntyche to agree with each other in the Lord. 3 Yes, and I ask you, loyal yokefellow,[f] help these

[f] Or *loyal Syzygus.*

Greek Interlinear

πεποιθότες, 4 καίπερ ἐγὼ ἔχων πεποίθησιν
[1]trusting, even though I having trust

καὶ ἐν σαρκί. Εἴ τις δοκεῖ ἄλλος
also in [the] flesh. If any [2]thinks [1]other man

πεποιθέναι ἐν σαρκί, ἐγὼ μᾶλλον·
to trust in [the] flesh, I more:

5 περιτομῇ ὀκταήμερος, ἐκ γένους Ἰσραήλ,
in circumcision eighth day, of [the] race of Israel,

φυλῆς Βενιαμίν, Ἑβραῖος ἐξ Ἑβραίων,
[the] tribe of Benjamin, a Hebrew of Hebrew [parents],

κατὰ νόμον Φαρισαῖος, 6 κατὰ ζῆλος
according [the] law a Pharisee, by way of zeal
to

διώκων τὴν ἐκκλησίαν, κατὰ δικαιοσύνην
persecuting the church, according righteousness
to

τὴν ἐν νόμῳ γενόμενος ἄμεμπτος. 7 ἀλλὰ
- in [the] law being blameless. But

ἅτινα ἦν μοι κέρδη, ταῦτα ἥγημαι διὰ
what were to me gain, these I have [2]on ac-
things deemed count of

τὸν Χριστὸν ζημίαν. 8 ἀλλὰ μενοῦν γε
- [3]Christ [1]loss. But nay rather

καὶ ἡγοῦμαι πάντα ζημίαν εἶναι διὰ
[2]also [1]I deem [3]all things [4]loss [5]to be on account of

τὸ ὑπερέχον τῆς γνώσεως Χριστοῦ Ἰησοῦ
the excellency of the knowledge of Christ Jesus

τοῦ κυρίου μου, δι᾽ ὃν τὰ πάντα
the Lord of me, on ac- whom - all things
count of

ἐζημιώθην, καὶ ἡγοῦμαι σκύβαλα ἵνα
I suffered loss, and deem [them] refuse in order
that

Χριστὸν κερδήσω 9 καὶ εὑρεθῶ ἐν αὐτῷ,
Christ I might gain and be found in him,

μὴ ἔχων ἐμὴν δικαιοσύνην τὴν ἐκ νόμου,
not having my righteousness the [one] of law,

ἀλλὰ τὴν διὰ πίστεως Χριστοῦ, τὴν
but the [one] through faith of(in) Christ,[*] [1]the

ἐκ θεοῦ δικαιοσύνην ἐπὶ τῇ πίστει,
[2]of [4]God [3]righteousness [based] on - faith,

10 τοῦ γνῶναι αὐτὸν καὶ τὴν δύναμιν
- to know[d] him and the power

τῆς ἀναστάσεως αὐτοῦ καὶ κοινωνίαν
of the resurrection of him and [the] fellowship

παθημάτων αὐτοῦ, συμμορφιζόμενος τῷ
of sufferings of him, being conformed to the

θανάτῳ αὐτοῦ, 11 εἴ πως καταντήσω εἰς
death of him, if [some]how I may attain to to

τὴν ἐξανάστασιν τὴν ἐκ νεκρῶν. 12 Οὐχ
the out-resurrection - from [the] dead. Not

ὅτι ἤδη ἔλαβον ἤ ἤδη τετελείωμαι,
that already I received or already have been perfected,

διώκω δὲ εἰ καὶ καταλάβω, ἐφ᾽ ᾧ
but I follow if indeed I may lay hold, inasmuch as

καὶ κατελήμφθην ὑπὸ Χριστοῦ Ἰησοῦ.
also I was laid hold of by Christ Jesus.

13 ἀδελφοί, ἐγὼ ἐμαυτὸν οὔπω λογίζομαι
Brothers, [1]I [2]myself [1]not yet [2]reckon

κατειληφέναι· ἐν δέ, τὰ μὲν ὀπίσω
to have but one thing [3]the [5]on one [4]behind
laid hold; [I do], things hand

ἐπιλανθανόμενος τοῖς δὲ ἔμπροσθεν ἐπεκ-
[1]forgetting [3]the [2]on the [6]before [5]stretching
things other

τεινόμενος, 14 κατὰ σκοπὸν διώκω εἰς
forward to, according to a mark I follow for

τὸ βραβεῖον τῆς ἄνω κλήσεως τοῦ θεοῦ
the prize of the above calling - of God

ἐν Χριστῷ Ἰησοῦ. 15 Ὅσοι οὖν τέλειοι,
in Christ Jesus. [2]As many [1]there- [are]
as fore perfect,

τοῦτο φρονῶμεν· καὶ εἴ τι ἑτέρως
[2]this [1]let us think; and if anything otherwise

φρονεῖτε, καὶ τοῦτο ὁ θεὸς ὑμῖν ἀποκα-
ye think, even this - God to you will

λύψει· 16 πλὴν εἰς ὃ ἐφθάσαμεν, τῷ
reveal: nevertheless to what we arrived, by the

αὐτῷ στοιχεῖν. 17 Συμμιμηταί μου
same to walk. Fellow-imitators of me

γίνεσθε, ἀδελφοί, καὶ σκοπεῖτε τοὺς οὕτω
be ye, brothers, and mark the [ones] thus

περιπατοῦντας καθὼς ἔχετε τύπον ἡμᾶς.
walking as ye have [2]an example [1]us.

18 πολλοὶ γὰρ περιπατοῦσιν οὓς πολλάκις
For many walk [of] whom often

ἔλεγον ὑμῖν, νῦν δὲ καὶ κλαίων λέγω,
I said to you, and now also weeping I say,

τοὺς ἐχθροὺς τοῦ σταυροῦ τοῦ Χριστοῦ,
the enemies of the cross - of Christ,

19 ὧν τὸ τέλος ἀπώλεια, ὧν ὁ θεὸς
of whom the end [is] destruction, of whom the god [is]

ἡ κοιλία καὶ ἡ δόξα ἐν τῇ αἰσχύνῃ
the belly and the glory in the shame

αὐτῶν, οἱ τὰ ἐπίγεια φρονοῦντες. 20 ἡμῶν
of them, the the earthly things thinking. of us
[ones]

γὰρ τὸ πολίτευμα ἐν οὐρανοῖς ὑπάρχει,
For the citizenship in heavens is,

ἐξ οὗ καὶ σωτῆρα ἀπεκδεχόμεθα κύριον
from where also [1]a Saviour [1]we await Lord

Ἰησοῦν Χριστόν, 21 ὃς μετασχηματίσει τὸ
Jesus Christ, who will change the

σῶμα τῆς ταπεινώσεως ἡμῶν σύμμορφον
body of the humiliation of us [making it]
conformed

τῷ σώματι τῆς δόξης αὐτοῦ, κατὰ τὴν
to the body of the glory of him, according to the

ἐνέργειαν τοῦ δύνασθαι αὐτὸν καὶ ὑποτάξαι
operation of the to be able him[b] even to subject
=of his ability

Chapter 4

αὐτῷ τὰ πάντα. 4 Ὥστε, ἀδελφοί μου
to him[self] - all things. So as, brothers of me

ἀγαπητοὶ καὶ ἐπιπόθητοι, χαρὰ καὶ
beloved and longed for, joy and

στέφανός μου, οὕτως στήκετε ἐν κυρίῳ, ἀγαπητοί.
crown of me, so stand in [the] Lord, beloved.

2 Εὐοδίαν παρακαλῶ καὶ Συντύχην
[2]Euodia [1]I beseech and [3]Syntyche

παρακαλῶ τὸ αὐτὸ φρονεῖν ἐν κυρίῳ.
[1]I beseech [4]the [5]same thing [2]to think in [the] Lord.

3 ναὶ ἐρωτῶ καὶ σέ, γνήσιε σύζυγε,
Yes[,] I ask also thee, genuine yoke-fellow,

King James Version

laboured with me in the gospel, with Clement also, and *with* other my fellow labourers, whose names *are* in the book of life. 4 Rejoice in the Lord always: *and* again I say, Rejoice. 5 Let your moderation be known unto all men. The Lord *is* at hand. 6 Be careful for nothing; but in every thing by prayer and supplication with thanksgiving let your requests be made known unto God. 7And the peace of God, which passeth all understanding, shall keep your hearts and minds through Christ Jesus. 8 Finally, brethren, whatsoever things are true, whatsoever things *are* honest, whatsoever things *are* just, whatsoever things *are* pure, whatsoever things *are* lovely, whatsoever things *are* of good report; if *there be* any virtue, and if *there be* any praise, think on these things. 9 Those things, which ye have both learned, and received, and heard, and seen in me, do: and the God of peace shall be with you. 10 But I rejoiced in the Lord greatly, that now at the last your care of me hath flourished again; wherein ye were also careful, but ye lacked opportunity. 11 Not that I speak in respect of want: for I have learned, in whatsoever state I am, *therewith* to be content. 12 I know both how to be abased, and I know how to abound: every where and in all things I am instructed both to be full and· to be hungry, both to abound and to suffer need. 13 I can do all things through Christ which strengtheneth me. 14 Notwithstanding, ye have well done, that ye did communicate with my affliction. 15 Now ye Philippians know also, that in the beginning of the gospel, when I departed from Macedonia, no church communicated with me as concerning giving and receiving, but ye only. 16 For even in Thessalonica ye sent once and again unto my necessity. 17 Not because I desire a gift: but I desire fruit that may abound to your account. 18 But I have all, and abound: I am full, having received of Epaphroditus the things *which were sent* from you, an odour of a sweet smell, a sacrifice acceptable, well pleasing to God. 19 But my God shall supply all your need according to his riches in glory by Christ Jesus. 20 Now unto God and our Father *be* glory for ever and ever. Amen. 21 Salute every saint in Christ Jesus. The brethren which are with me greet you. 22All the saints salute you, chiefly they that are of Cesar's household. 23 The grace of our Lord Jesus Christ *be* with you all. Amen.

It was written to the Philippians from Rome by Epaphroditus.

New International Version

women who have contended at my side in the cause of the gospel, along with Clement and the rest of my fellow workers, whose names are in the book of life. 4 Rejoice in the Lord always. I will say it again: Rejoice! 5 Let your gentleness be evident to all. The Lord is near. 6 Do not be anxious about anything, but in everything, by prayer and petition, with thanksgiving, present your requests to God. 7And the peace of God, which transcends all understanding, will guard your hearts and your minds in Christ Jesus.

8 Finally, brothers, whatever is true, whatever is noble, whatever is right, whatever is pure, whatever is lovely, whatever is admirable —if anything is excellent or praiseworthy— think about such things. 9 Whatever you have learned or received or heard from me, or seen in me—put it into practice. And the God of peace will be with you.

Thanks for the gifts

10 I rejoice greatly in the Lord that at last you have renewed your concern for me. Indeed, you have been concerned, but you had no opportunity to show it. 11 I am not saying this because I am in need, for I have learned to be content whatever the circumstances. 12 I know what it is to be in need, and I know what it is to have plenty. I have learned the secret of being content in any and every situation, whether well-fed or hungry, whether living in plenty or in want. 13 I can do everything through him who gives me strength.

14 Yet it was good of you to share in my troubles. 15 Moreover, as you Philippians know, in the early days of your acquaintance with the gospel, when I set out from Macedonia, not one church shared with me in the matter of giving and receiving, except you only; 16 for even when I was in Thessalonica, you sent me aid again and again when I was in need. 17 Not that I am looking for a gift, but I am looking for what may be credited to your account. 18 I have received full payment and even more; I am amply supplied, now that I have received from Epaphroditus the gifts you sent. They are a fragrant offering, an acceptable sacrifice, pleasing to God. 19And my God will meet all your needs according to his glorious riches in Christ Jesus.

20 To our God and Father be glory for ever and ever. Amen.

Final greetings

21 Greet all the saints in Christ Jesus. The brothers who are with me send greetings. 22All the saints send you greetings, especially those who belong to Caesar's household.

23 The grace of the Lord Jesus Christ be with your spirit.

Greek Interlinear

συλλαμβάνου αὐταῖς, αἵτινες ἐν τῷ εὐαγ-
help them, who ²in ⁴the ⁵gos-
γελίῳ συνήθλησάν μοι μετὰ καὶ Κλήμεντος
pel ¹struggled with ³me with both Clement
καὶ τῶν λοιπῶν συνεργῶν μου, ὧν
and the remaining fellow-workers of me, of
whom
τὰ ὀνόματα ἐν βίβλῳ ζωῆς. 4 Χαίρετε
the names [are] in [the] book of life. Rejoice ye
ἐν κυρίῳ πάντοτε· πάλιν ἐρῶ, χαίρετε.
in [the] Lord always; again I will say, rejoice.
5 τὸ ἐπιεικὲς ὑμῶν γνωσθήτω πᾶσιν
The forbearance of you let it be known to all
ἀνθρώποις. ὁ κύριος ἐγγύς. 6 μηδὲν
men. The Lord [is] near. ²Nothing
μεριμνᾶτε, ἀλλ᾽ ἐν παντὶ τῇ προσευχῇ
¹be ye anxious but in everything – by prayer
about,
καὶ τῇ δεήσει μετὰ εὐχαριστίας τὰ
and – by petition with thanksgivings the
αἰτήματα ὑμῶν γνωριζέσθω πρὸς τὸν
requests of you let be made known to –
θεόν. 7 καὶ ἡ εἰρήνη τοῦ θεοῦ ἡ
God. And the peace – of God –
ὑπερέχουσα πάντα νοῦν φρουρήσει τὰς
surpassing all understanding will guard the
καρδίας ὑμῶν καὶ τὰ νοήματα ὑμῶν
hearts of you and the thoughts of you
ἐν Χριστῷ Ἰησοῦ. 8 Τὸ λοιπόν, ἀδελφοί,
in Christ Jesus. For the rest, brothers,
ὅσα ἐστὶν ἀληθῆ, ὅσα σεμνά, ὅσα δίκαια,
whatever are true, whatever grave, whatever just,
things things things
ὅσα ἁγνά, ὅσα προσφιλῆ, ὅσα εὔφημα,
whatever pure, whatever lovable, whatever well-spoken
things things things of,
εἴ τις ἀρετὴ καὶ εἴ τις ἔπαινος, 9 ταῦτα
if any virtue and if any praise, these things
λογίζεσθε· ἃ καὶ ἐμάθετε καὶ παρελάβετε
consider ye; which ²both ¹ye ²learned and ye received
things
καὶ ἠκούσατε καὶ εἴδετε ἐν ἐμοί, ταῦτα
and ye heard and ye saw in me, these
πράσσετε· καὶ ὁ θεὸς τῆς εἰρήνης ἔσται
practise; and the God – of peace will be
μεθ᾽ ὑμῶν.
with you.

10 Ἐχάρην δὲ ἐν κυρίῳ μεγάλως ὅτι
Now I rejoiced in [the] Lord greatly that
ἤδη ποτὲ ἀνεθάλετε τὸ ὑπὲρ ἐμοῦ φρονεῖν·
al- at one ye revived the on behalf me to think;
ready time of
= now at length =your thought for me;
ἐφ᾽ ᾧ καὶ ἐφρονεῖτε, ἠκαιρεῖσθε δέ.
as to which indeed ye thought, but ye had no opportunity
11 οὐχ ὅτι καθ᾽ ὑστέρησιν λέγω· ἐγὼ
Not that ²by way of ³lack ¹I say; ²I
γὰρ ἔμαθον ἐν οἷς εἰμι αὐτάρκης εἶναι.
¹for learned in what I am ²self- ¹to be.
conditions sufficient
12 οἶδα καὶ ταπεινοῦσθαι, οἶδα καὶ περισ-
I know both to be humbled, and I know to

σεύειν· ἐν παντὶ καὶ ἐν πᾶσιν μεμύημαι,
abound; in everything and in all things I have been
initiated,
καὶ χορτάζεσθαι καὶ πεινᾶν, καὶ περισ-
both to be filled and to hunger, both to
σεύειν καὶ ὑστερεῖσθαι. 13 πάντα ἰσχύω
abound and to lack. ²All things ¹I can do
ἐν τῷ ἐνδυναμοῦντί με. 14 πλὴν καλῶς
in the [one] empowering me. Nevertheless ²well
ἐποιήσατε συγκοινωνήσαντές μου τῇ θλίψει.
¹ye did having partnership in ²of me ¹the ²affliction.
15 οἴδατε δὲ καὶ ὑμεῖς, Φιλιππήσιοι, ὅτι
And ²know ¹also ¹ye, Philippians, that
ἐν ἀρχῇ τοῦ εὐαγγελίου, ὅτε ἐξῆλθον
in [the] of the gospel, when I went out
beginning
ἀπὸ Μακεδονίας, οὐδεμία μοι ἐκκλησία
from Macedonia, not one ²me ¹church
ἐκοινώνησεν εἰς λόγον δόσεως καὶ λήμψεως
¹shared with in matter of giving and receiving
εἰ μὴ ὑμεῖς μόνοι, 16 ὅτι καὶ ἐν
except ye only, because indeed in
Θεσσαλονίκῃ καὶ ἅπαξ καὶ δὶς εἰς τὴν
Thessalonica both once and twice to the
=to my need
χρείαν μοι ἐπέμψατε. 17 οὐχ ὅτι ἐπιζητῶ
need to me⁶ ye sent. Not that I seek
τὸ δόμα, ἀλλὰ ἐπιζητῶ τὸν καρπὸν
the gift, but I seek the fruit
τὸν πλεονάζοντα εἰς λόγον ὑμῶν. 18 ἀπέχω
– increasing to account of you. I have
δὲ πάντα καὶ περισσεύω· πεπλήρωμαι
But all things and abound; I have been filled
δεξάμενος παρὰ Ἐπαφροδίτου τὰ παρ᾽
receiving from Epaphroditus the things from
ὑμῶν, ὀσμὴν εὐωδίας, θυσίαν δεκτήν,
you, an odour of sweet smell, a sacrifice acceptable,
εὐάρεστον τῷ θεῷ. 19 ὁ δὲ θεός μου
well-pleasing – to God. And the God of me
πληρώσει πᾶσαν χρείαν ὑμῶν κατὰ τὸ
will fill every need of you according to the
πλοῦτος αὐτοῦ ἐν δόξῃ ἐν Χριστῷ Ἰησοῦ.
riches of him in glory in Christ Jesus.
20 τῷ δὲ θεῷ καὶ πατρὶ ἡμῶν ἡ δόξα
to the Now God and Father of us [be] the glory
εἰς τοὺς αἰῶνας τῶν αἰώνων· ἀμήν.
unto the ages of the ages: Amen.
21 Ἀσπάσασθε πάντα ἅγιον ἐν Χριστῷ
Greet ye every saint in Christ
Ἰησοῦ. ἀσπάζονται ὑμᾶς οἱ σὺν ἐμοὶ
Jesus. ⁵greet ⁶you ¹The ²with ³me
ἀδελφοί. 22 ἀσπάζονται ὑμᾶς πάντες οἱ
⁴brothers. ⁵greet ⁶you ¹All ²the
ἅγιοι, μάλιστα δὲ οἱ ἐκ τῆς Καίσαρος
³saints, but most of all the ones of ¹the ²of Cæsar
οἰκίας.
³household.
23 Ἡ χάρις τοῦ κυρίου Ἰησοῦ Χριστοῦ
The grace of the Lord Jesus Christ
μετὰ τοῦ πνεύματος ὑμῶν.
[be] with the spirit of you.

King James Version   New International Version

THE EPISTLE OF
PAUL THE APOSTLE
TO THE
COLOSSIANS

COLOSSIANS

1 Paul, an apostle of Jesus Christ by the will of God, and Timotheus *our* brother, 2 To the saints and faithful brethren in Christ which are at Colosse: Grace *be* unto you, and peace, from God our Father and the Lord Jesus Christ. 3 We give thanks to God and the Father of our Lord Jesus Christ, praying always for you, 4 Since we heard of your faith in Christ Jesus, and of the love *which ye have* to all the saints, 5 For the hope which is laid up for you in heaven, whereof ye heard before in the word of the truth of the gospel; 6 Which is come unto you, as *it is* in all the world; and bringeth forth fruit, as *it doth* also in you, since the day ye heard *of it,* and knew the grace of God in truth: 7As ye also learned of Epaphras our dear fellow servant, who is for you a faithful minister of Christ; 8 Who also declared unto us your love in the Spirit. 9 For this cause we also, since the day we heard *it,* do not cease to pray for you, and to desire that ye might be filled with the knowledge of his will in all wisdom and spiritual understanding; 10 That ye might walk worthy of the Lord unto all pleasing, being fruitful in every good work, and increasing in the knowledge of God; 11 Strengthened with all might, according to his glorious power, unto all patience and longsuffering with joyfulness; 12 Giving thanks unto the Father, which hath made us meet to be partakers of the inheritance of the saints in light: 13 Who hath delivered us from the power of darkness, and hath translated *us* into the kingdom of his dear Son: 14 In whom we have redemption through his blood, *even* the forgiveness of sins: 15 Who is the image of the invisible God, the firstborn of every creature: 16 For by him were all things created, that are in heaven, and that are in earth, visible and invisible, whether *they be* thrones, or dominions, or principalities, or powers: all things were created by him, and for him: 17And he is before all things, and by him all things consist: 18And he is the head of the body, the church: who is the beginning, the firstborn from the dead; that in all things he might have the preeminence. 19 For it

1 Paul, an apostle of Christ Jesus by the will of God, and Timothy our brother,
2 To the holy and faithful brothers in Christ at Colosse:
Grace and peace to you from God our Father.*

Thanksgiving and prayer

3 We always thank God, the Father of our Lord Jesus Christ, when we pray for you, 4 because we have heard of your faith in Christ Jesus and of the love you have for all the saints—5 the faith and love that spring from the hope stored up for you in heaven, and which you have already heard about in the word of truth, the gospel 6 that has come to you. All over the world this gospel is producing fruit and growing, just as it has been doing among you since the day you heard it and understood God's grace in all its truth. 7 You learned it from Epaphras, our dear fellow servant, who is a faithful minister of Christ on our[b] behalf, 8 and who also told us of your love in the Spirit.
9 For this reason, since the day we heard about you, we have not stopped praying for you and asking God to fill you with the knowledge of his will through all spiritual wisdom and understanding. 10And we pray this in order that you may live a life worthy of the Lord and may please him in every way: bearing fruit in every good work, growing in the knowledge of God, 11 being strengthened with all power according to his glorious might so that you may have great endurance and patience, and joyfully 12 giving thanks to the Father, who has qualified you[c] to share in the inheritance of the saints in the kingdom of light. 13 For he has rescued us from the dominion of darkness and brought us into the kingdom of the Son he loves, 14 in whom we have redemption,[d] the forgiveness of sins.

The supremacy of Christ

15 He is the image of the invisible God, the firstborn over all creation. 16 For by him all things were created: things in heaven and on earth, visible and invisible, whether thrones or powers or rulers or authorities; all things were created by him and for him. 17 He is before all things, and in him all things hold together. 18And he is the head of the body, the church; he is the beginning and the firstborn from among the dead, so that in everything he might have the supremacy. 19 For God was pleased to have

[a] Some MSS add *and the Lord Jesus Christ.* [b] Some MSS read *your.* [c] Some MSS read *us.* [d] A few late MSS add *through his blood.*

ΠΡΟΣ ΚΟΛΟΣΣΑΕΙΣ

Chapter 1

Παῦλος ἀπόστολος Χριστοῦ Ἰησοῦ διὰ
Paul an apostle of Christ Jesus through

θελήματος θεοῦ καὶ Τιμόθεος ὁ ἀδελφὸς
[the] will of God and Timothy the brother

2 τοῖς ἐν Κολοσσαῖς ἁγίοις καὶ πιστοῖς
to the in Colossae saints and faithful

ἀδελφοῖς ἐν Χριστῷ· χάρις ὑμῖν καὶ
brothers in Christ: Grace to you and

εἰρήνη ἀπὸ θεοῦ πατρὸς ἡμῶν.
peace from God Father of us.

3 Εὐχαριστοῦμεν τῷ θεῷ πατρὶ τοῦ
We give thanks – to God Father of the

κυρίου ἡμῶν Ἰησοῦ [Χριστοῦ] πάντοτε
Lord of us Jesus Christ always

περὶ ὑμῶν προσευχόμενοι, **4** ἀκούσαντες
²concerning ¹you ¹praying, having heard

τὴν πίστιν ὑμῶν ἐν Χριστῷ Ἰησοῦ
the faith of you in Christ Jesus

καὶ τὴν ἀγάπην ἣν ἔχετε εἰς πάντας
and the love which ye have toward all

τοὺς ἁγίους **5** διὰ τὴν ἐλπίδα τὴν
the saints because of the hope –

ἀποκειμένην ὑμῖν ἐν τοῖς οὐρανοῖς, ἣν
being laid up for you in *the* heavens, which

προηκούσατε ἐν τῷ λόγῳ τῆς ἀληθείας
ye previously in the word of the truth
heard

τοῦ εὐαγγελίου **6** τοῦ παρόντος εἰς ὑμᾶς,
of the gospel – coming to you,

καθὼς καὶ ἐν παντὶ τῷ κόσμῳ ἐστὶν
as also in all the world it is

καρποφορούμενον καὶ αὐξανόμενον καθὼς
bearing fruit and growing as

καὶ ἐν ὑμῖν, ἀφ᾽ ἧς ἡμέρας ἠκούσατε
also in you, from which day ye heard
= the day on which

καὶ ἐπέγνωτε τὴν χάριν τοῦ θεοῦ ἐν
and fully knew the grace – of God in

ἀληθείᾳ· **7** καθὼς ἐμάθετε ἀπὸ Ἐπαφρᾶ
truth; as ye learned from Epaphras

τοῦ ἀγαπητοῦ συνδούλου ἡμῶν, ὅς ἐστιν
the beloved fellow-slave of us, who is

πιστὸς ὑπὲρ ὑμῶν διάκονος τοῦ Χριστοῦ,
¹a ²on behalf ¹you ²minister – ²of Christ,
faithful of

8 ὁ καὶ δηλώσας ἡμῖν τὴν ὑμῶν ἀγάπην
the also having shown to us ¹the ²of you ³love
[one]

ἐν πνεύματι.
in spirit.

9 Διὰ τοῦτο καὶ ἡμεῖς, ἀφ᾽ ἧς ἡμέρας
Therefore also we, from which day
= the day on which

ἠκούσαμεν, οὐ παυόμεθα ὑπὲρ ὑμῶν
we heard, do not cease on behalf of you

προσευχόμενοι καὶ αἰτούμενοι ἵνα πληρω-
praying and asking *in order* ye may be
that

θῆτε τὴν ἐπίγνωσιν τοῦ θελήματος αὐτοῦ
filled the full knowledge of the will of him
[with]

ἐν πάσῃ σοφίᾳ ·καὶ συνέσει πνευματικῇ,
in all wisdom and understanding spiritual,

10 περιπατῆσαι ἀξίως τοῦ κυρίου εἰς
to walk worthily of the Lord to

πᾶσαν ἀρεσκείαν, ἐν παντὶ ἔργῳ ἀγαθῷ
all pleasing, in every work good

καρποφοροῦντες καὶ αὐξανόμενοι τῇ
bearing fruit and growing in the

ἐπιγνώσει τοῦ θεοῦ, **11** ἐν πάσῃ δυνάμει
full knowledge of God, with all power

δυναμούμενοι κατὰ τὸ κράτος τῆς δόξης
being empowered according to the might of the glory

αὐτοῦ εἰς πᾶσαν ὑπομονὴν καὶ μακρο-
of him to all endurance and long-

θυμίαν, μετὰ χαρᾶς **12** εὐχαριστοῦντες τῷ
suffering, with joy giving thanks to the

πατρὶ τῷ ἱκανώσαντι ὑμᾶς εἰς τὴν μερίδα
Father – having made ²fit ¹you for the part

τοῦ κλήρου τῶν ἁγίων ἐν τῷ φωτί·
of the lot of the saints in *the* light;

13 ὃς ἐρρύσατο ἡμᾶς ἐκ τῆς ἐξουσίας
who delivered us out of the authority

τοῦ σκότους καὶ μετέστησεν εἰς τὴν
of *the* darkness and transferred into the

βασιλείαν τοῦ υἱοῦ τῆς ἀγάπης αὐτοῦ,
kingdom of the Son of the love of him,

14 ἐν ᾧ ἔχομεν τὴν ἀπολύτρωσιν, τὴν
in whom we have *the* redemption, the

ἄφεσιν τῶν ἁμαρτιῶν· **15** ὅς ἐστιν εἰκὼν
forgiveness of the sins; who is an image
(our)

τοῦ θεοῦ τοῦ ἀοράτου, πρωτότοκος πάσης
of the God – invisible, firstborn of all

κτίσεως, **16** ὅτι ἐν αὐτῷ ἐκτίσθη τὰ
creation, because in him were created –

πάντα ἐν τοῖς οὐρανοῖς καὶ ἐπὶ τῆς
all things in *the* heavens and on the

γῆς, τὰ ὁρατὰ καὶ τὰ ἀόρατα, εἴτε
earth, the visible and the invisible, whether

θρόνοι εἴτε κυριότητες εἴτε ἀρχαὶ εἴτε
thrones or lordships or rulers or

ἐξουσίαι· τὰ πάντα δι᾽ αὐτοῦ καὶ εἰς
authorities; – all things through him and for

αὐτὸν ἔκτισται· **17** καὶ αὐτός ἐστιν πρὸ
him have been created; and he is before

πάντων καὶ τὰ πάντα ἐν αὐτῷ συνέστηκεν,
all things and – all things in him consisted,

18 καὶ αὐτός ἐστιν ἡ κεφαλὴ τοῦ σώματος,
and he is the head of the body,

τῆς ἐκκλησίας· ὅς ἐστιν ἀρχή, πρωτότοκος
of the church; who is [the] firstborn
beginning,

ἐκ τῶν νεκρῶν, ἵνα γένηται ἐν πᾶσιν
from the dead, in order ⁴may be ²in ³all
that

αὐτὸς πρωτεύων, **19** ὅτι ἐν αὐτῷ εὐδόκησεν
¹he ⁵holding the because in him ⁴was well
first place, pleased

587

King James Version

pleased *the Father* that in him should all fulness dwell; 20And, having made peace through the blood of his cross, by him to reconcile all things unto himself; by him, *I say*, whether *they be* things in earth, or things in heaven. 21And you, that were sometime alienated and enemies in *your* mind by wicked works, yet now hath he reconciled 22 In the body of his flesh through death, to present you holy and unblameable and unreproveable in his sight: 23 If ye continue in the faith grounded and settled, and *be* not moved away from the hope of the gospel, which ye have heard, *and* which was preached to every creature which is under heaven; whereof I Paul am made a minister; 24 Who now rejoice in my sufferings for you, and fill up that which is behind of the afflictions of Christ in my flesh for his body's sake, which is the church: 25 Whereof I am made a minister, according to the dispensation of God which is given to me for you, to fulfil the word of God; 26 *Even* the mystery which hath been hid from ages and from generations, but now is made manifest to his saints: 27 To whom God would make known what *is* the riches of the glory of this mystery among the Gentiles; which is Christ in you, the hope of glory: 28 Whom we preach, warning every man, and teaching every man in all wisdom; that we may present every man perfect in Christ Jesus: 29 Whereunto I also labour, striving according to his working, which worketh in me mightily.

New International Version

all his fullness dwell in him, 20 and through him to reconcile to himself all things, whether things on earth or things in heaven, by making peace through his blood, shed on the cross.
21 Once you were alienated from God and were enemies in your minds because of your evil behavior. 22 But now he has reconciled you by Christ's physical body through death to present you holy in his sight, without blemish and free from accusation—23 if you continue in your faith, established and firm, not moved from the hope held out in the gospel. This is the gospel that you heard and that has been proclaimed to every creature under heaven, and of which I, Paul, have become a servant.

Paul's labor for the church

24 Now I rejoice in what was suffered for you, and I fill up in my flesh what is still lacking in regard to Christ's afflictions, for the sake of his body, which is the church. 25 I have become its servant by the commission God gave me to present to you the word of God in its fullness—26 the mystery that has been kept hidden for ages and generations, but is now disclosed to the saints. 27 To them God has chosen to make known among the Gentiles the glorious riches of this mystery, which is Christ in you, the hope of glory.
28 We proclaim him, counseling and teaching everyone with all wisdom, so that we may present everyone perfect in Christ. 29 To this end I labor, struggling with all the energy he so powerfully works in me.

2 For I would that ye knew what great conflict I have for you, and *for* them at Laodicea, and *for* as many as have not seen my face in the flesh; 2 That their hearts might be comforted, being knit together in love, and unto all riches of the full assurance of understanding, to the acknowledgment of the mystery of God, and of the Father, and of Christ; 3 In whom are hid all the treasures of wisdom and knowledge. 4And this I say, lest any man should beguile you with enticing words. 5 For though I be absent in the flesh, yet am I with you in the spirit, joying and beholding your order, and the stedfastness of your faith in Christ. 6As ye have therefore received Christ Jesus the Lord, *so* walk ye in him: 7 Rooted and built up in him, and stablished in the faith, as ye have been taught,

2 I want you to know how strenuously I am exerting myself for you and for those at Laodicea, and for all who have not met me personally. 2 My purpose is that they may be encouraged in heart and united in love, so that they may have the full riches of complete understanding, in order that they may know the mystery of God, namely, Christ,[e] 3 in whom are hidden all the treasures of wisdom and knowledge. 4 I tell you this so that no one may deceive you by fine-sounding arguments. 5 For though I am absent from you in body, I am present with you in spirit and delight to see how orderly you are and how firm your faith in Christ is.

Freedom from human regulations through life with Christ

6 So then, just as you received Christ Jesus as Lord, continue to live in him, 7 rooted and built up in him, strengthened in the faith as you

[e] Some MSS read *know the mystery of God, even the Father, and of Christ.*

πᾶν τὸ πλήρωμα κατοικῆσαι 20 καὶ δι'
¹all ²the ³fulness to dwell and through
αὐτοῦ ἀποκαταλλάξαι τὰ πάντα εἰς αὐτόν,
him to reconcile – all things to him[?self],
εἰρηνοποιήσας διὰ τοῦ αἵματος τοῦ σταυροῦ
making peace through the blood of the cross
αὐτοῦ, δι' αὐτοῦ εἴτε τὰ ἐπὶ τῆς γῆς
of him, through him whether the on the earth
things
εἴτε τὰ ἐν τοῖς οὐρανοῖς. 21 Καὶ ὑμᾶς
or the things in the heavens. And you
ποτε ὄντας ἀπηλλοτριωμένους καὶ ἐχθροὺς
then being having been alienated and enemies
τῇ διανοίᾳ ἐν τοῖς ἔργοις τοῖς πονηροῖς,
in the mind by the(your) works – evil,
22 νυνὶ δὲ ἀποκατήλλαξεν ἐν τῷ σώματι
but now he reconciled in the body
τῆς σαρκὸς αὐτοῦ διὰ τοῦ θανάτου,
of the flesh of him through the(his) death,
παραστῆσαι ὑμᾶς ἁγίους καὶ ἀμώμους
to present you holy and blameless
καὶ ἀνεγκλήτους κατενώπιον αὐτοῦ, 23 εἰ
and irreproachable before him, if
γε ἐπιμένετε τῇ πίστει τεθεμελιωμένοι
indeed ye continue in the faith having been founded
καὶ ἑδραῖοι καὶ μὴ μετακινούμενοι ἀπὸ
and steadfast and not being moved away from
τῆς ἐλπίδος τοῦ εὐαγγελίου οὗ ἠκούσατε,
the hope of the gospel which ye heard,
τοῦ κηρυχθέντος ἐν πάσῃ κτίσει τῇ
– proclaimed in all creation the
ὑπὸ τὸν οὐρανόν, οὗ ἐγενόμην ἐγὼ
under the heaven, of which ¹became ¹I
Παῦλος διάκονος.
¹Paul a minister.
24 Νῦν χαίρω ἐν τοῖς παθήμασιν ὑπὲρ
Now I rejoice in the(my) sufferings on behalf of
ὑμῶν, καὶ ἀνταναπληρῶ τὰ ὑστερήματα
you, and fill up the things lacking
τῶν θλίψεων τοῦ Χριστοῦ ἐν τῇ σαρκί
of the afflictions – of Christ in the flesh

μου ὑπὲρ τοῦ σώματος αὐτοῦ, ὅ ἐστιν
of me on behalf of the body of him, which is
ἡ ἐκκλησία, 25 ἧς ἐγενόμην ἐγὼ διάκονος
the church, of which became I a minister
κατὰ τὴν οἰκονομίαν τοῦ θεοῦ τὴν
accord- the stewardship – of God –
ing to
δοθεῖσάν μοι εἰς ὑμᾶς πληρῶσαι τὸν
given to me for you to fulfil the
λόγον τοῦ θεοῦ, 26 τὸ μυστήριον τὸ
word – of God, the mystery –
ἀποκεκρυμμένον ἀπὸ τῶν αἰώνων καὶ
having been hidden from the ages and
ἀπὸ τῶν γενεῶν — νῦν δὲ ἐφανερώθη
from the generations — but now was manifested
τοῖς ἁγίοις αὐτοῦ, 27 οἷς ἠθέλησεν ὁ
to the saints of him, to whom ¹wished –
θεὸς γνωρίσαι τί τὸ πλοῦτος τῆς δόξης
¹God to make known what [is] the riches of the glory
τοῦ μυστηρίου τούτου ἐν τοῖς ἔθνεσιν,
– mystery of this among the nations,
ὅς ἐστιν Χριστὸς ἐν ὑμῖν, ἡ ἐλπὶς τῆς
who is Christ in you, the hope of the
δόξης· 28 ὃν ἡμεῖς καταγγέλλομεν νου-
glory; whom we announce warn-
θετοῦντες πάντα ἄνθρωπον καὶ διδάσκοντες
ing every man and teaching
πάντα ἄνθρωπον ἐν πάσῃ σοφίᾳ,
every man in all wisdom,
ἵνα παραστήσωμεν πάντα ἄνθρωπον
in or- we may present every man
der that
τέλειον ἐν Χριστῷ· 29 εἰς ὃ καὶ κοπιῶ
mature in Christ; for which also I labour
ἀγωνιζόμενος κατὰ τὴν ἐνέργειαν αὐτοῦ
struggling accord- the operation of him
ing to
τὴν ἐνεργουμένην ἐν ἐμοὶ ἐν δυνάμει.
– operating in me in power.

Chapter 2

Θέλω γὰρ ὑμᾶς εἰδέναι ἡλίκον ἀγῶνα
For I wish you to know how great a struggle
ἔχω ὑπὲρ ὑμῶν καὶ τῶν ἐν Λαοδικείᾳ
I have on behalf of you and the [ones] in Laodicea
καὶ ὅσοι οὐχ ἑόρακαν τὸ πρόσωπόν μου
and as many as have not seen the face of me
ἐν σαρκί, 2 ἵνα παρακληθῶσιν αἱ καρδίαι
in flesh, in order ⁴may be ¹the ²hearts
that comforted
αὐτῶν, συμβιβασθέντες ἐν ἀγάπῃ καὶ εἰς
²of them, being joined together in love and for
πᾶν πλοῦτος τῆς πληροφορίας τῆς
all riches of the full assurance of the
συνέσεως, εἰς ἐπίγνωσιν τοῦ μυστηρίου
of under- for full knowledge of the mystery
standing,
τοῦ θεοῦ, Χριστοῦ, 3 ἐν ᾧ εἰσιν πάντες
– of God, of Christ, in whom ²are ³all
οἱ θησαυροὶ τῆς σοφίας καὶ γνώσεως
⁴the ¹treasures ²of wisdom ⁷and ⁸of knowledge
ἀπόκρυφοι. 4 Τοῦτο λέγω ἵνα μηδεὶς
⁵hidden. This I say in order no one
that

ὑμᾶς παραλογίζηται ἐν πιθανολογίᾳ. 5 εἰ
²you ¹may beguile with persuasive speech. if
γὰρ καὶ τῇ σαρκὶ ἄπειμι, ἀλλὰ τῷ
For indeed in the flesh I am absent, yet in the
πνεύματι σὺν ὑμῖν εἰμι, χαίρων καὶ
spirit ²with ³you ¹I am, rejoicing and
βλέπων ὑμῶν τὴν τάξιν καὶ τὸ στερέωμα
seeing ²of you ¹the ³order and the firmness
τῆς εἰς Χριστὸν πίστεως ὑμῶν.
of the ²in ³Christ ¹faith ⁴of you.
6 Ὡς οὖν παρελάβετε τὸν Χριστὸν
As therefore ye received – Christ
Ἰησοῦν τὸν κύριον, ἐν αὐτῷ περιπατεῖτε,
Jesus the Lord, in him walk ye,
7 ἐρριζωμένοι καὶ ἐποικοδομούμενοι ἐν αὐτῷ
having been rooted and being built up in him
καὶ βεβαιούμενοι τῇ πίστει καθὼς ἐδιδάχ-
and being confirmed in the faith as ye were

King James Version

abounding therein with thanksgiving. 8 Beware lest any man spoil you through philosophy and vain deceit, after the tradition of men, after the rudiments of the world, and not after Christ. 9 For in him dwelleth all the fulness of the Godhead bodily. 10And ye are complete in him, which is the head of all principality and power: 11 In whom also ye are circumcised with the circumcision made without hands, in putting off the body of the sins of the flesh by the circumcision of Christ: 12 Buried with him in baptism, wherein also ye are risen with *him* through the faith of the operation of God, who hath raised him from the dead. 13And you, being dead in your sins and the uncircumcision of your flesh, hath he quickened together with him, having forgiven you all trespasses; 14 Blotting out the handwriting of ordinances that was against us, which was contrary to us, and took it out of the way, nailing it to his cross; 15*And* having spoiled principalities and powers, he made a shew of them openly, triumphing over them in it. 16 Let no man therefore judge you in meat, or in drink, or in respect of a holyday, or of the new moon, or of the sabbath *days:* 17 Which are a shadow of things to come; but the body *is* of Christ. 18 Let no man beguile you of your reward in a voluntary humility and worshipping of angels, intruding into those things which he hath not seen, vainly puffed up by his fleshly mind, 19And not holding the Head, from which all the body by joints and bands having nourishment ministered, and knit together, increaseth with the increase of God. 20 Wherefore if ye be dead with Christ from the rudiments of the world, why, as though living in the world, are ye subject to ordinances, 21 (Touch not; taste not; handle not; 22 Which all are to perish with the using;) after the commandments and doctrines of men? 23 Which things have indeed a shew of wisdom in willworship, and humility, and neglecting of the body; not in any honour to the satisfying of the flesh.

New International Version

were taught, and overflowing with thankfulness. 8 See to it that no one takes you captive through hollow and deceptive philosophy, which depends on human tradition and the basic principles of this world rather than on Christ. 9 For in Christ all the fullness of the Deity lives in bodily form, 10 and you have this fullness in Christ, who is the head over every power and authority. 11 In him you were also circumcised, in the putting off of your sinful nature, not with a circumcision done by the hands of men but with the circumcision done by Christ. 12 In baptism you were buried with him and raised with him through your faith in the power of God, who raised him from the dead.

13 When you were dead in your sins and in the uncircumcision of your sinful nature, God made you alive with Christ. He forgave us all our sins, 14 having canceled the written code, with its regulations, that was against us and that stood opposed to us; he took it away, nailing it to the cross. 15And having disarmed the powers and authorities, he made a public spectacle of them, triumphing over them by the cross.

16 Therefore do not let anyone judge you by what you eat or drink, or with regard to a religious festival, a new moon celebration, or a sabbath day. 17 These are a shadow of the things that were to come; the reality, however, is found in Christ. 18 Do not let anyone who delights in false humility and the worship of angels disqualify you for the prize. Such a person goes into great detail about what he has seen, and his unspiritual mind puffs him up with idle notions. 19 He has lost connection with the Head, from whom the whole body, supported and held together by its ligaments and sinews, grows as God causes it to grow.

20 If you died with Christ to the basic principles of this world, why, as though you still belonged to it, do you submit to its rules: 21 "Do not handle! Do not taste! Do not touch!"? 22 These are all destined to perish with use, because they are based on human commands and teachings. 23 Such regulations indeed have an appearance of wisdom, with their self-imposed worship, their false humility and their harsh treatment of the body, but they lack any value in restraining sensual indulgence.

Rules for holy living

3 If ye then be risen with Christ, seek those things which are above, where Christ sitteth on the right hand of God. 2 Set your affection on things above, not on things on the earth. 3 For ye are dead, and your life is hid with Christ in God. 4 When Christ, *who is* our life, shall appear, then shall ye also appear with him in glory. 5 Mortify therefore your members which are upon the earth; fornication, uncleanness, inordinate affection, evil concupiscence, and covetousness, which is idolatry: 6 For which things' sake the wrath of God cometh on the children of dis-

3 Since, then, you have been raised with Christ, set your hearts on things above, where Christ is seated at the right hand of God. 2 Set your minds on things above, not on earthly things. 3 For you died, and your life is now hidden with Christ in God. 4 When Christ, who is your life, appears, then you also will appear with him in glory.

5 Put to death, therefore, whatever belongs to your earthly nature: sexual immorality, impurity, lust, evil desires and greed, which is idolatry. 6 Because of these, the wrath of God

Greek Interlinear

θητε,   περισσεύοντες   ἐν   εὐχαριστίᾳ.
taught,   abounding   in   thanksgiving.

8 Βλέπετε   μή τις ὑμᾶς ἔσται ὁ συλαγωγῶν
Look ye   lest ²anyone ⁴you ¹there - ³robbing
                                shall be

διὰ   τῆς   φιλοσοφίας   καὶ   κενῆς   ἀπάτης
through -   philosophy   and   empty   deceit

κατὰ   τὴν   παράδοσιν   τῶν   ἀνθρώπων,   κατὰ
accord- the   tradition   -   of men,   according to   ing to

τὰ   στοιχεῖα   τοῦ   κόσμου   καὶ   οὐ   κατὰ
the   elements   of the   world   and   not   accord-
                                              ing to

Χριστόν·   9 ὅτι   ἐν   αὐτῷ   κατοικεῖ   πᾶν
Christ;   because in   him   dwells   all

τὸ   πλήρωμα   τῆς   θεότητος   σωματικῶς,
the   fulness   of the   Godhead   bodily,

10 καὶ   ἐστὲ   ἐν   αὐτῷ   πεπληρωμένοι,   ὅς
and   ye are   in   him   having been filled,   who

ἐστιν ἡ κεφαλὴ   πάσης   ἀρχῆς   καὶ   ἐξουσίας,
is the   head   of all   rule   and   authority,

11 ἐν   ᾧ   καὶ   περιετμήθητε   περιτομῇ
in   whom   also   ye were   with a
                  circumcised   circumcision

ἀχειροποιήτῳ   ἐν   τῇ   ἀπεκδύσει   τοῦ   σώματος
not handwrought by   the   putting off   of the   body

τῆς   σαρκός,   ἐν   τῇ   περιτομῇ   τοῦ   Χριστοῦ,
of the   flesh,   by   the   circumcision   -   of Christ,

12 συνταφέντες   αὐτῷ   ἐν   τῷ   βαπτίσματι,
co-buried   with him   in   the   baptism,

ἐν   ᾧ   καὶ   συνηγέρθητε   διὰ   τῆς   πίστεως
in   whom   also   ye were co-raised   through   the   faith

τῆς   ἐνεργείας   τοῦ   θεοῦ   τοῦ   ἐγείραντος
of(in) the   operation   -   of God   -   raising

αὐτὸν   ἐκ   νεκρῶν·   13 καὶ   ὑμᾶς   νεκροὺς
him   from [the]   dead;   and   you   dead

ὄντας   τοῖς   παραπτώμασιν   καὶ   τῇ   ἀκρο-
being   in the   trespasses   and   in the   uncir-

βυστίᾳ   τῆς   σαρκὸς   ὑμῶν,   συνεζωοποίησεν
cumcision   of the   flesh   of you,   he co-quickened

ὑμᾶς   σὺν   αὐτῷ,   χαρισάμενος   ἡμῖν   πάντα
you   with   him,   forgiving   you   all

τὰ   παραπτώματα·   14 ἐξαλείψας   τὸ   καθ'
the   trespasses;   wiping out   ¹the   ²against

ἡμῶν   χειρόγραφον   τοῖς   δόγμασιν   ὃ   ἦν
¹us   ¹handwriting   -   in ordinances   which   was

ὑπεναντίον   ἡμῖν,   καὶ   αὐτὸ   ἦρκεν   ἐκ
contrary   to us,   and   ²it   ¹has taken out of

τοῦ   μέσου,   προσηλώσας   αὐτὸ   τῷ   σταυρῷ·
the   midst(way),   nailing   it   to the   cross;

15 ἀπεκδυσάμενος   τὰς   ἀρχὰς   καὶ   τὰς
putting off   the   rulers   and   the

ἐξουσίας   ἐδειγμάτισεν   ἐν   παρρησίᾳ,
authorities   he exposed [them]   with   openness,

θριαμβεύσας   αὐτοὺς   ἐν   αὐτῷ.
triumphing [over]   them   in   it.

16 Μὴ   οὖν   τις   ὑμᾶς   κρινέτω   ἐν   βρώσει
²Not   ³there-   ⁴any-   ⁵you   ¹let ⁶judge   in   eating
       fore   one

καὶ   ἐν   πόσει   ἢ   ἐν   μέρει   ἑορτῆς   ἢ
and   in   drinking   or   in   respect   of a feast   or

νεομηνίας   ἢ   σαββάτων,   17 ἅ   ἐστιν   σκιὰ
of a new moon   or   of sabbaths,   which   is(are)   a
                                                       things

τῶν   μελλόντων,   τὸ   δὲ   σῶμα   τοῦ   Χριστοῦ.
of things   coming,   but the   body [is]   -   of Christ.

18 μηδεὶς   ὑμᾶς   καταβραβευέτω   θέλων   ἐν
²No one   ⁴you   ¹let ³give judgment   wishing   in
                                      against   [to do so]

ταπεινοφροσύνῃ   καὶ   θρησκείᾳ   τῶν   ἀγγέλων,
humility*   and   worship   of the   angels,

ἃ   ἑόρακεν   ἐμβατεύων,   εἰκῆ   φυσιούμενος
³things   ²he has   ¹intruding into,   in vain   being puffed up
which   seen

ὑπὸ   τοῦ   νοὸς   τῆς   σαρκὸς   αὐτοῦ,   19 καὶ
by   the   mind   of the   flesh   of him,   and

οὐ   κρατῶν   τὴν   κεφαλήν,   ἐξ   οὗ   πᾶν
not   holding   the   head,   from whom   all

τὸ   σῶμα   διὰ   τῶν   ἁφῶν   καὶ   συνδέσμων
the   body   ⁴by means   ²the   ¹joints   ³and   ⁵bands
             of   (its)

ἐπιχορηγούμενον   καὶ   συμβιβαζόμενον   αὔξει
¹being supplied   ²and   ³being joined together   will grow

τὴν   αὔξησιν   τοῦ   θεοῦ.
[with] the   growth   -   of God.

20 Εἰ   ἀπεθάνετε   σὺν   Χριστῷ   ἀπὸ   τῶν   στοι-
If   ye died   with   Christ   from   the   ele-

χείων   τοῦ   κόσμου,   τί   ὡς   ζῶντες   ἐν   κόσμῳ
ments   of the   world,   why   as   living   in [the] world

δογματίζεσθε·   21 μὴ   ἅψῃ   μηδὲ   γεύσῃ   μηδὲ
are ye subject to   Do not   touch   nor   taste   nor
[its] decrees:

θίγῃς,   22 ἅ   ἐστιν   πάντα   εἰς   φθορὰν
handle,   which   is(are)   all   for   corruption
           things

τῇ   ἀποχρήσει,   κατὰ   τὰ   ἐντάλματα   καὶ
in the   using,   according to the   injunctions   and

διδασκαλίας   τῶν   ἀνθρώπων;   23 ἅτινά   ἐστιν
teachings   -   of men?   ¹which   ²is(are)
                              things

λόγον   μὲν   ἔχοντα   σοφίας   ἐν   ἐθελοθρησκείᾳ
²a repute ³indeed   ¹having   of wisdom   in   self-imposed
                                               worship

καὶ   ταπεινοφροσύνῃ   καὶ   ἀφειδίᾳ   σώματος,   οὐκ
and   humility   and   severity   of [the] body,   not

ἐν   τιμῇ   τινι   πρὸς   πλησμονὴν   τῆς   σαρκός.
in   ¹honour   ¹any   for   satisfaction   of the   flesh.

Chapter 3

Εἰ   οὖν   συνηγέρθητε   τῷ   Χριστῷ,   τὰ
If   therefore ye were co-raised   -   with Christ,   the
                                                       things

ἄνω   ζητεῖτε,   οὗ   ὁ   Χριστός   ἐστιν   ἐν
above   seek,   where   -   Christ   ¹is   ²at

δεξιᾷ   τοῦ   θεοῦ   καθήμενος·   2 τὰ   ἄνω
⁴[the] right   -   ⁵of God   ³sitting;   the   above
[hand]   things

φρονεῖτε,   μὴ   τὰ   ἐπὶ   τῆς   γῆς.   3 ἀπεθάνετε
mind ye,   not   the   on   the   earth.   ye died
                  things

γάρ,   καὶ   ἡ   ζωὴ   ὑμῶν   κέκρυπται   σὺν
For,   and   the   life   of you   has been hidden   with

τῷ   Χριστῷ   ἐν   τῷ   θεῷ·   4 ὅταν   ὁ   Χριστός
-   Christ   in   the   God;   whenever   -   Christ

φανερωθῇ,   ἡ   ζωὴ   ἡμῶν,   τότε   καὶ   ὑμεῖς
is manifested,   the   life   of us,   then   also   ye

σὺν   αὐτῷ   φανερωθήσεσθε   ἐν   δόξῃ.
with   him   will be manifested   in   glory.

5 Νεκρώσατε   οὖν   τὰ   μέλη   τὰ   ἐπὶ
Put ye to death   therefore   the   members   -   on
                                    (your)

τῆς   γῆς,   πορνείαν,   ἀκαθαρσίαν,   πάθος,
the   earth,   fornication,   uncleanness,   passion,

ἐπιθυμίαν   κακήν,   καὶ   τὴν   πλεονεξίαν   ἥτις
desire   bad,   and   -   covetousness   which

ἐστιν   εἰδωλολατρία,   6 δι'   ἃ   ἔρχεται   ἡ
is   idolatry,   because which   is coming   the
               of things

* Ellicott supplies "false". Cf. ver. 23.

King James Version

obedience: 7 In the which ye also walked some-time, when ye lived in them. 8 But now ye also put off all these; anger, wrath, malice, blasphemy, filthy communication out of your mouth. 9 Lie not one to another, seeing that ye have put off the old man with his deeds; 10And have put on the new *man*, which is renewed in knowledge after the image of him that created him: 11 Where there is neither Greek nor Jew, circumcision nor uncircumcision, Barbarian, Scythian, bond *nor* free: but Christ *is* all, and in all. 12 Put on therefore, as the elect of God, holy and beloved, bowels of mercies, kindness, humbleness of mind, meekness, longsuffering; 13 Forbearing one another, and forgiving one another, if any man have a quarrel against any: even as Christ forgave you, so also *do* ye. 14And above all these things *put on* charity, which is the bond of perfectness. 15And let the peace of God rule in your hearts, to the which also ye are called in one body; and be ye thankful. 16 Let the word of Christ dwell in you richly in all wisdom; teaching and admonishing one another in psalms and hymns and spiritual songs, singing with grace in your hearts to the Lord. 17And whatsoever ye do in word or deed, *do* all in the name of the Lord Jesus, giving thanks to God and the Father by him. 18 Wives, submit · yourselves unto your own husbands, as it is fit in the Lord. 19 Husbands, love *your* wives, and be not bitter against them. 20 Children, obey *your* parents in all things: for this is well pleasing unto the Lord. 21 Fathers, provoke not your children *to anger*, lest they be discouraged. 22 Servants, obey in all things *your* masters according to the flesh; not with eyeservice, as menpleasers; but in singleness of heart, fearing God: 23And whatsoever ye do, do *it* heartily, as to the Lord, and not unto men; 24 Knowing that of the Lord ye shall receive the reward of the inheritance: for ye serve the Lord Christ. 25 But he that doeth wrong shall receive for the wrong which he hath done: and there is no respect of persons.

New International Version

is coming.*ᶠ* 7 You used to walk in these ways, in the life you once lived. 8 But now you must rid yourselves of all such things as these: anger, rage, malice, slander, filthy language. 9 Do not lie to each other, since you have taken off your old self with its practices 10 and have put on the new self, which is being renewed in knowledge in the image of its Creator. 11 Here there is no Greek or Jew, circumcised or uncircumcised, barbarian, Scythian, slave or free, but Christ is all, and is in all.

12 Therefore, as God's chosen people, holy and dearly loved, clothe yourselves with compassion, kindness, humility, gentleness and patience. 13 Bear with each other and forgive whatever grievances you may have against one another. Forgive as the Lord forgave you. 14And over all these virtues put on love, which binds them all together in perfect unity.

15 Let the peace of Christ rule in your hearts, since, as members of one body, you were called to peace. And be thankful. 16 Let the word of Christ dwell in you richly as you teach and counsel one another with all wisdom, and as you sing psalms, hymns and spiritual songs with gratitude in your hearts to God. 17And whatever you do, whether in word or deed, do it all in the name of the Lord Jesus, giving thanks to God the Father through him.

Rules for christian households

18 Wives, submit to your husbands, as is fitting in the Lord.

19 Husbands, love your wives and do not be harsh with them.

20 Children, obey your parents in everything, for this pleases the Lord.

21 Fathers, do not embitter your children, or they will become discouraged.

22 Slaves, obey your masters in everything; and do it, not only when their eye is on you and to win their favor, but with sincerity of heart and reverence for the Lord. 23 Whatever you do, work at it with all your heart, as working for the Lord, not for men, 24 since you know that you will receive an inheritance from the Lord as a reward. It is the Lord Christ you are serving. 25Anyone who does wrong will be repaid for his wrong, and there is no favoritism.

4 Masters, give unto *your* servants that which is just and equal; knowing that ye also have a Master in heaven. 2 Continue in prayer, and watch in the same with thanksgiving; 3 Withal praying also for us, that God would open unto

4 Masters, provide your slaves with what is right and fair, because you know that you also have a Master in heaven.

Further instructions

2 Devote yourselves to prayer, being watchful and thankful. 3And pray for us, too, that God may open a door for our message, so that we

[f] Some early MSS add on those who are disobedient.

Greek Interlinear

ὀργὴ τοῦ θεοῦ· 7 ἐν οἷς καὶ ὑμεῖς
wrath — of God; in which indeed ye

περιεπατήσατέ ποτε, ὅτε ἐζῆτε ἐν τούτοις·
walked then, when ye lived in these things;

8 νυνὶ δὲ ἀπόθεσθε καὶ ὑμεῖς τὰ πάντα,
but now ¹put ²away ⁴also ³ye — all things,

ὀργήν, θυμόν, κακίαν, βλασφημίαν, αἰσχρο-
wrath, anger, malice, blasphemy, a-

λογίαν ἐκ τοῦ στόματος ὑμῶν· 9 μὴ
buse out of the mouth of you; not

ψεύδεσθε εἰς ἀλλήλους, ἀπεκδυσάμενοι τὸν
lie ye to one another, having put off the

παλαιὸν ἄνθρωπον σὺν ταῖς πράξεσιν
old man with the practices

αὐτοῦ, 10 καὶ ἐνδυσάμενοι τὸν νέον τὸν
of him, and having put on the new man

ἀνακαινούμενον εἰς ἐπίγνωσιν κατ' εἰκόνα
being renewed in full knowledge according [the]
to image

τοῦ κτίσαντος αὐτόν, 11 ὅπου οὐκ ἔνι
of the [one] creating him, where ⁴have no place

Ἕλλην καὶ Ἰουδαῖος, περιτομὴ καὶ
¹Greek ²and ³Jew, circumcision and

ἀκροβυστία, βάρβαρος, Σκύθης, δοῦλος, .
uncircumcision, barbarian, Scythian, slave, .

ἐλεύθερος, ἀλλὰ πάντα καὶ ἐν πᾶσιν
freeman, but ³all things ²and ¹in ⁴all

Χριστός. 12 Ἐνδύσασθε οὖν, ὡς ἐκλεκτοὶ
¹Christ ²[is]. Put ye on therefore, as chosen ones

τοῦ θεοῦ ἅγιοι καὶ ἠγαπημένοι, σπλάγχνα
— of God holy and having been loved, bowels

οἰκτιρμοῦ, χρηστότητα, ταπεινοφροσύνην,
of compassion, kindness, humility,

πραΰτητα, μακροθυμίαν, 13 ἀνεχόμενοι ἀλ-
meekness, long-suffering, forbearing one

λήλων καὶ χαριζόμενοι ἑαυτοῖς, ἐάν τις
another and forgiving yourselves, if anyone

πρός τινα ἔχῃ μομφήν· καθὼς καὶ ὁ
²against ⁴anyone ¹has ²a complaint; as indeed the

κύριος ἐχαρίσατο ὑμῖν οὕτως καὶ ὑμεῖς·
Lord forgave you so also ye;

14 ἐπὶ πᾶσιν δὲ τούτοις τὴν ἀγάπην,
²over ⁴all ¹and ³these things the love,

ὅ ἐστιν σύνδεσμος τῆς τελειότητος. 15 καὶ
which is [the] bond — of completeness. And

ἡ εἰρήνη τοῦ Χριστοῦ βραβευέτω ἐν ταῖς
²the ³peace — ⁴of Christ ¹let ¹rule in the

καρδίαις ὑμῶν, εἰς ἣν καὶ ἐκλήθητε
hearts of you, to which indeed ye were called

ἐν ἑνὶ σώματι· καὶ εὐχάριστοι γίνεσθε.
in one body; and thankful be ye.

16 ὁ λόγος τοῦ Χριστοῦ ἐνοικείτω ἐν
²The ³word — ⁴of Christ ¹let ¹indwell in

ὑμῖν πλουσίως, ἐν πάσῃ σοφίᾳ διδάσκοντες
you richly, in all wisdom teaching

καὶ νουθετοῦντες ἑαυτούς, ψαλμοῖς ὕμνοις
and admonishing yourselves, in psalms[,] hymns[,]

ᾠδαῖς πνευματικαῖς ἐν τῇ χάριτι ᾄδοντες
[and] ²songs ¹spiritual with — grace singing

ἐν ταῖς καρδίαις ὑμῶν τῷ θεῷ· 17 καὶ
in the hearts of you — to God; and

πᾶν ὅ τι ἐὰν ποιῆτε ἐν λόγῳ ἢ ἐν
every- whatever ye do in word or in
thing

ἔργῳ, πάντα ἐν ὀνόματι κυρίου Ἰησοῦ,
work, all things [do] in [the] name of[the] Lord Jesus,

εὐχαριστοῦντες τῷ θεῷ πατρὶ δι' αὐτοῦ.
giving thanks — to God [the] through him.
Father

18 Αἱ γυναῖκες, ὑποτάσσεσθε τοῖς
The wives, be ye subject to the(your)

ἀνδράσιν, ὡς ἀνῆκεν ἐν κυρίῳ. 19 Οἱ
husbands, as is befitting in [the] Lord. The

ἄνδρες, ἀγαπᾶτε τὰς γυναῖκας καὶ μὴ
husbands, love ye the(your) wives and not

πικραίνεσθε πρὸς αὐτάς. 20 Τὰ τέκνα,
be bitter toward them. The children,

ὑπακούετε τοῖς γονεῦσιν κατὰ πάντα,
obey ye the(your) parents in all respects,

τοῦτο γὰρ εὐάρεστόν ἐστιν ἐν κυρίῳ.
for this well-pleasing is in [the] Lord.

21 Οἱ πατέρες, μὴ ἐρεθίζετε τὰ τέκνα
The fathers, do not ye provoke the children

ὑμῶν, ἵνα μὴ ἀθυμῶσιν. 22 Οἱ δοῦλοι,
of you, lest they be disheartened. The slaves,

ὑπακούετε κατὰ πάντα τοῖς κατὰ σάρκα
obey ye in all respects ¹the ²accord- [the]
(your) ³ing to flesh

κυρίοις, μὴ ἐν ὀφθαλμοδουλίαις ὡς
¹lords, not with eyeservice as

ἀνθρωπάρεσκοι, ἀλλ' ἐν ἁπλότητι καρδίας
men-pleasers, . but in singleness of heart

φοβούμενοι τὸν κύριον. 23 ὃ ἐὰν ποιῆτε,
fearing the Lord. Whatever ye do,

ἐκ ψυχῆς ἐργάζεσθε ὡς τῷ κυρίῳ καὶ
from [the] soul work ye as to the Lord and

οὐκ ἀνθρώποις, 24 εἰδότες ὅτι ἀπὸ κυρίου
not to men, knowing that from [the] Lord

ἀπολήμψεσθε τὴν ἀνταπόδοσιν τῆς κλη-
ye will receive the reward of the in-

ρονομίας. τῷ κυρίῳ Χριστῷ δουλεύετε·
heritance. The Lord Christ ye serve;

25 ὁ γὰρ ἀδικῶν κομίσεται ὃ ἠδίκησεν,
for the [one] doing wrong will receive what he did wrong,

Chapter 4

καὶ οὐκ ἔστιν προσωπολημψία. 4 Οἱ κύριοι,
and there is no respect of persons. The lords,

τὸ δίκαιον καὶ τὴν ἰσότητα τοῖς δούλοις
²the ³just thing ⁴and ⁵the ⁶equality ⁷to the(your) ¹slaves

παρέχεσθε, εἰδότες ὅτι καὶ ὑμεῖς ἔχετε
¹supply ye, knowing that also ye have

κύριον ἐν οὐρανῷ.
a Lord in heaven.

2 Τῇ προσευχῇ προσκαρτερεῖτε, γρηγο-
In the prayer continue ye, watch-

ροῦντες ἐν αὐτῇ ἐν εὐχαριστίᾳ, 3 προσευ-
ing in it with thanksgiving, pray-

χόμενοι ἅμα καὶ περὶ ἡμῶν, ἵνα —
ing together also concerning us, in order —
that

King James Version

us a door of utterance, to speak the mystery of Christ, for which I am also in bonds: 4 That I may make it manifest, as I ought to speak. 5 Walk in wisdom toward them that are without, redeeming the time. 6 Let your speech *be* always with grace, seasoned with salt, that ye may know how ye ought to answer every man. 7 All my state shall Tychicus declare unto you, *who is* a beloved brother, and a faithful minister and fellow servant in the Lord: 8 Whom I have sent unto you for the same purpose, that he might know your estate, and comfort your hearts; 9 With Onesimus, a faithful and beloved brother, who is *one* of you. They shall make known unto you all things which *are done* here. 10 Aristarchus my fellow prisoner saluteth you, and Marcus, sister's son to Barnabas, (touching whom ye received commandments: if he come unto you, receive him;) 11 And Jesus, which is called Justus, who are of the circumcision. These only *are my* fellow workers unto the kingdom of God, which have been a comfort unto me. 12 Epaphras, who is *one* of you, a servant of Christ, saluteth you, always labouring fervently for you in prayers, that ye may stand perfect and complete in all the will of God. 13 For I bear him record, that he hath a great zeal for you, and them *that are* in Laodicea, and them in Hierapolis. 14 Luke, the beloved physician, and Demas, greet you. 15 Salute the brethren which are in Laodicea, and Nymphas, and the church which is in his house. 16 And when this epistle is read among you, cause that it be read also in the church of the Laodiceans; and that ye likewise read the *epistle* from Laodicea. 17 And say to Archippus, Take heed to the ministry which thou hast received in the Lord, that thou fulfil it. 18 The salutation by the hand of me Paul. Remember my bonds. Grace *be* with you. Amen.

Written from Rome to the Colossians by Tychicus and Onesimus.

New International Version

may proclaim the mystery of Christ, for which I am in chains. 4 Pray that I may proclaim it clearly, as I should. 5 Be wise in the way you act toward outsiders; make the most of every opportunity. 6 Let your conversation be always full of grace, seasoned with salt, so that you may know how to answer everyone.

Final greetings

7 Tychicus will tell you all the news about me. He is a dear brother, a faithful minister and fellow servant in the Lord. 8 I am sending him to you for the express purpose that you may know about our circumstances and that he may encourage your hearts. 9 He is coming with Onesimus, our faithful and dear brother, who is one of you. They will tell you everything that is happening here.

10 My fellow prisoner Aristarchus sends you his greetings, as does Mark, the cousin of Barnabas. (You have received instructions about him; if he comes to you, welcome him.) 11 Jesus, who is called Justus, also sends greetings. These are the only Jews among my fellow workers for the kingdom of God, and they have proved a comfort to me. 12 Epaphras, who is one of you and a servant of Christ Jesus, sends greetings. He is always wrestling in prayer for you, that you may stand firm in all the will of God, mature and fully assured. 13 I vouch for him that he is working hard for you and for those at Laodicea and Hierapolis. 14 Our dear friend Luke, the doctor, and Demas send greetings. 15 Give my greetings to the brothers at Laodicea, and to Nympha and the church in her house.

16 After this letter has been read to you, see that it is also read in the church of the Laodiceans and that you in turn read the letter from Laodicea.

17 Tell Archippus: "See to it that you complete the work you have received in the Lord."

18 I, Paul, write this greeting in my own hand. Remember my chains. Grace be with you.

Greek Interlinear

θεὸς ἀνοίξῃ ἡμῖν θύραν τοῦ λόγου,
God may open to us a door of the word,

λαλῆσαι τὸ μυστήριον τοῦ Χριστοῦ, δι᾽
to speak the mystery - of because
Christ, of

ὃ καὶ δέδεμαι, 4 ἵνα φανερώσω αὐτὸ
which indeed I have been in order I may manifest it
bound, that

ὡς δεῖ με λαλῆσαι. 5 Ἐν σοφίᾳ
as it behoves me to speak. In wisdom

περιπατεῖτε πρὸς τοὺς ἔξω, τὸν καιρὸν
walk ye toward the ones outside, ²the ¹time

ἐξαγοραζόμενοι. 6 ὁ λόγος ὑμῶν πάντοτε
¹redeeming. The speech of you always
[let it be]

ἐν χάριτι, ἅλατι ἠρτυμένος, εἰδέναι πῶς
in grace, with salt having been to know how
seasoned,

δεῖ ὑμᾶς ἑνὶ ἑκάστῳ ἀποκρίνεσθαι.
it be- you ²one ²each ¹to answer.
hoves

7 Τὰ κατ᾽ ἐμὲ πάντα γνωρίσει ὑμῖν Τύχικος
²The ²about ⁴me ²all ¹will make ²to you ³Tychicus
things known

ὁ ἀγαπητὸς ἀδελφὸς καὶ πιστὸς διάκονος
the beloved brother and faithful minister

καὶ σύνδουλος ἐν κυρίῳ, 8 ὃν ἔπεμψα
and fellow-slave in [the] Lord, whom I sent

πρὸς ὑμᾶς εἰς αὐτὸ τοῦτο, ἵνα γνῶτε
to you for this very thing, in order ye might
that know

τὰ περὶ ἡμῶν καὶ παρακαλέσῃ τὰς
the concern- us and he might comfort the
things ing

καρδίας ὑμῶν, 9 σὺν Ὀνησίμῳ τῷ πιστῷ
hearts of you, with Onesimus the faithful

καὶ ἀγαπητῷ ἀδελφῷ, ὅς ἐστιν ἐξ ὑμῶν·
and beloved brother, who is of you;

πάντα ὑμῖν γνωρίσουσιν τὰ ὧδε.
¹all ²to you ⁴they will ³the ²here.
make known things

10 Ἀσπάζεται ὑμᾶς Ἀρίσταρχος ὁ
²greets ²you ¹Aristarchus ²the

συναιχμάλωτός μου, καὶ Μάρκος ὁ ἀνεψιὸς
³fellow-captive ⁴of me, and Mark the cousin

Βαρναβᾶ, (περὶ οὗ ἐλάβετε ἐντολάς, ἐὰν
of Barnabas, (concerning whom ye received commandments, if

ἔλθῃ πρὸς ὑμᾶς, δέξασθε αὐτόν,) 11 καὶ
he comes to you, receive ye him,) and

Ἰησοῦς ὁ λεγόμενος Ἰοῦστος, οἱ ὄντες
Jesus the [one] being named Justus, the [ones] being

ἐκ περιτομῆς οὗτοι μόνοι συνεργοὶ εἰς
of [the] circumcision these only fellow-workers for

τὴν βασιλείαν τοῦ θεοῦ, οἵτινες ἐγενή-
the kingdom - of God, who be-

θησάν μοι παρηγορία. 12 ἀσπάζεται ὑμᾶς
came to me a comfort. ²greets ²you

Ἐπαφρᾶς ὁ ἐξ ὑμῶν, δοῦλος Χριστοῦ
¹Epaphras the [one] of you, a slave of Christ

Ἰησοῦ, πάντοτε ἀγωνιζόμενος ὑπὲρ ὑμῶν
Jesus, always struggling on behalf of you

ἐν ταῖς προσευχαῖς, ἵνα σταθῆτε τέλειοι
in the prayers, in order ye may complete
that stand

καὶ πεπληροφορημένοι ἐν παντὶ θελήματι
and having been fully assured in all [the] will

τοῦ Θεοῦ. 13 μαρτυρῶ γὰρ αὐτῷ ὅτι
- of God. For I bear witness to him that

ἔχει πολὺν πόνον ὑπὲρ ὑμῶν καὶ τῶν
he has much distress on behalf of you and the ones

ἐν Λαοδικείᾳ καὶ τῶν ἐν Ἱεραπόλει.
in Laodicea and the ones in Hierapolis.

14 ἀσπάζεται ὑμᾶς Λουκᾶς ὁ ἰατρὸς ὁ
²greets ²you ¹Luke ²the ³physician -

ἀγαπητὸς καὶ Δημᾶς. 15 Ἀσπάσασθε
³beloved ²and ⁴Demas. Greet ye

τοὺς ἐν Λαοδικείᾳ ἀδελφοὺς καὶ Νύμφαν
¹the ³in ⁴Laodicea ²brothers and Nymphas

καὶ τὴν κατ᾽ οἶκον αὐτῆς ἐκκλησίαν.
and ¹the ²at ⁴[the] house ³of her ²church.

16 καὶ ὅταν ἀναγνωσθῇ παρ᾽ ὑμῖν ἡ
And whenever is read before you the(this)

ἐπιστολή, ποιήσατε ἵνα καὶ ἐν τῇ
epistle, cause in order that ²also ³in ⁴the

Λαοδικέων ἐκκλησίᾳ ἀναγνωσθῇ, καὶ τὴν
⁵of [the] ¹church ¹it is read, and the
Laodiceans [one]

ἐκ Λαοδικείας ἵνα καὶ ὑμεῖς ἀναγνῶτε.
⁶of ⁷Laodicea ¹in order ²also ³ye ¹read.
that

17 καὶ εἴπατε Ἀρχίππῳ· βλέπε τὴν
And tell Archippus : Look [to] the

διακονίαν ἣν παρέλαβες ἐν κυρίῳ, ἵνα
ministry which thou receivedst in [the] Lord, in order that

αὐτὴν πληροῖς.
²it ¹thou mayest fulfil.

18 Ὁ ἀσπασμὸς τῇ ἐμῇ χειρὶ Παύλου.
The greeting - by my hand[,] of Paul.

μνημονεύετέ μου τῶν δεσμῶν. ἡ χάρις
Remember ye of me the bonds. - Grace [be]

μεθ᾽ ὑμῶν.
with you.

THE FIRST EPISTLE
OF PAUL THE APOSTLE
TO THE

THESSALONIANS

1 THESSALONIANS

1 Paul, and Silvanus, and Timotheus, unto the church of the Thessalonians *which is* in God the Father, and *in* the Lord Jesus Christ: Grace *be* unto you, and peace, from God our Father, and the Lord Jesus Christ. 2 We give thanks to God always for you all, making mention of you in our prayers; 3 Remembering without ceasing your work of faith, and labour of love, and patience of hope in our Lord Jesus Christ, in the sight of God and our Father; 4 Knowing, brethren beloved, your election of God. 5 For our gospel came not unto you in word only, but also in power, and in the Holy Ghost, and in much assurance; as ye know what manner of men we were among you for your sake. 6And ye became followers of us, and of the Lord, having received the word in much affliction, with joy of the Holy Ghost: 7 So that ye were ensamples to all that believe in Macedonia and Achaia. 8 For from you sounded out the word of the Lord not only in Macedonia and Achaia, but also in every place your faith to God-ward is spread abroad; so that we need not to speak any thing. 9 For they themselves shew of us what manner of entering in we had unto you, and how ye turned to God from idols to serve the living and true God; 10And to wait for his Son from heaven, whom he raised from the dead, *even* Jesus, which delivered us from the wrath to come.

1 Paul, Silas[a] and Timothy,
To the church of the Thessalonians, who are in God the Father and the Lord Jesus Christ: Grace and peace to you.

Thanksgiving for the Thessalonians'
faith

2 We always thank God for all of you, mentioning you in our prayers. 3 We continually remember before our God and Father your work produced by faith, your labor prompted by love, and your endurance inspired by hope in our Lord Jesus Christ.
4 Brothers loved by God, we know that he has chosen you, 5 because our gospel came to you not simply with words, but also with power, with the Holy Spirit and with deep conviction. You know how we lived among you for your sake. 6 You became imitators of us and of the Lord; in spite of severe suffering, you welcomed the message with the joy given by the Holy Spirit. 7And so you became a model to all the believers in Macedonia and Achaia. 8 The Lord's message rang out from you not only in Macedonia and Achaia—your faith in God has become known everywhere. Therefore we do not need to say anything about it, 9 for they themselves report what kind of reception you gave us. They tell how you turned to God from idols to serve the living and true God, 10 and to wait for his Son from heaven, whom he raised from the dead—Jesus, who rescues us from the coming wrath.

Paul's ministry in Thessalonica

2 For yourselves, brethren, know our entrance in unto you, that it was not in vain: 2 But even after that we had suffered before, and were shamefully entreated, as ye know, at Philippi, we were bold in our God to speak unto you the gospel of God with much contention. 3 For our exhortation *was* not of deceit, nor of uncleanness, nor in guile: 4 But as we were allowed of God to be put in trust with the gospel, even so we speak; not as pleasing men, but God, which trieth our hearts. 5 For neither at any time used we flattering words, as ye know, nor a cloak of

2 You know, brothers, that our visit to you was not a failure. 2 We had previously suffered and been insulted in Philippi, as you know, but with the help of our God we dared to tell you his gospel in spite of strong opposition. 3 For the appeal we make does not spring from error or impure motives, nor are we trying to trick you. 4 On the contrary, we speak as men approved by God to be entrusted with the gospel. We are not trying to please men but God, who tests our hearts. 5 You know we never used flattery, nor did we put on a mask to cover up

[a] Greek *Silvanus*.

ΠΡΟΣ ΘΕΣΣΑΛΟΝΙΚΕΙΣ Α

Chapter 1

Παῦλος καὶ Σιλουανὸς καὶ Τιμόθεος
Paul and Silvanus and Timothy

τῇ ἐκκλησίᾳ Θεσσαλονικέων ἐν θεῷ πατρὶ
to the church of [the] Thessalonians in God [the] Father

καὶ κυρίῳ Ἰησοῦ Χριστῷ· χάρις ὑμῖν
and [the] Lord Jesus Christ: Grace [be] to you

καὶ εἰρήνη.
and peace.

2 Εὐχαριστοῦμεν τῷ θεῷ πάντοτε περὶ
We give thanks – to God always concerning

πάντων ὑμῶν, μνείαν ποιούμενοι ἐπὶ τῶν
¹all ¹you, mention making on(in) the

προσευχῶν ἡμῶν, ἀδιαλείπτως 3 μνημο-
prayers of us, unceasingly remember-

νεύοντες ὑμῶν τοῦ ἔργου τῆς πίστεως
ing of you the work – of faith

καὶ τοῦ κόπου τῆς ἀγάπης καὶ τῆς
and the labour – of love and the

ὑπομονῆς τῆς ἐλπίδος τοῦ κυρίου ἡμῶν
endurance – of hope of(in) the Lord of us

Ἰησοῦ Χριστοῦ ἔμπροσθεν τοῦ θεοῦ καὶ
Jesus Christ before the God and

πατρὸς ἡμῶν, 4 εἰδότες, ἀδελφοὶ ἠγαπημένοι
Father of us, knowing, brothers having been loved

ὑπὸ [τοῦ] θεοῦ, τὴν ἐκλογὴν ὑμῶν,
by – God, the choice of you,

5 ὅτι τὸ εὐαγγέλιον ἡμῶν οὐκ ἐγενήθη
because the gospel of us became not

εἰς ὑμᾶς ἐν λόγῳ μόνον, ἀλλὰ καὶ ἐν
to you in word only, but also in

δυνάμει καὶ ἐν πνεύματι ἁγίῳ καὶ
power and in Spirit Holy and

πληροφορίᾳ πολλῇ, καθὼς οἴδατε οἷοι
²assurance ¹much, as ye know what sort

ἐγενήθημεν ἐν ὑμῖν δι᾽ ὑμᾶς. 6 καὶ
we were among you because of you. And

ὑμεῖς μιμηταὶ ἡμῶν ἐγενήθητε καὶ τοῦ
¹ye ²imitators ⁴of us ³became and of the

κυρίου, δεξάμενοι τὸν λόγον ἐν θλίψει
Lord, welcoming the word in ²affliction

πολλῇ μετὰ χαρᾶς πνεύματος ἁγίου, 7 ὥστε
¹much with joy of ³Spirit ¹[the] Holy, so as

γενέσθαι ὑμᾶς τύπον πᾶσιν τοῖς πιστεύουσιν
to become you[b] a pattern to all the [ones] believing
= so that ye became

ἐν τῇ Μακεδονίᾳ καὶ ἐν τῇ Ἀχαίᾳ.
in – Macedonia and in – Achaia.

8 ἀφ᾽ ὑμῶν γὰρ ἐξήχηται ὁ λόγος τοῦ
²from ²you ¹For sounded the word of the

κυρίου οὐ μόνον ἐν τῇ Μακεδονίᾳ καὶ
Lord not only in – Macedonia and

Ἀχαίᾳ, ἀλλ᾽ ἐν παντὶ τόπῳ ἡ πίστις
Achaia, but in every place the faith

ὑμῶν ἡ πρὸς τὸν θεὸν ἐξελήλυθεν, ὥστε
of you – toward – God has gone out, so as

μὴ χρείαν ἔχειν ἡμᾶς λαλεῖν τι· 9 αὐτοὶ
not need to have us[b] to speak anything; ²[them]-
= so that we have no need selves

γὰρ περὶ ἡμῶν ἀπαγγέλλουσιν ὁποίαν
¹for ²concerning ³us ¹they relate what sort of

εἴσοδον ἔσχομεν πρὸς ὑμᾶς, καὶ πῶς
entrance we had to you, and how

ἐπεστρέψατε πρὸς τὸν θεὸν ἀπὸ τῶν
ye turned to – God from the

εἰδώλων δουλεύειν θεῷ ζῶντι καὶ ἀληθινῷ,
idols to serve a God living and true,

10 καὶ ἀναμένειν τὸν υἱὸν αὐτοῦ ἐκ
and to await the Son of him from

τῶν οὐρανῶν, ὃν ἤγειρεν ἐκ τῶν νεκρῶν,
the heavens, whom he raised from the dead,

Ἰησοῦν τὸν ῥυόμενον ἡμᾶς ἐκ τῆς ὀργῆς
Jesus the [one] delivering us from the wrath

τῆς ἐρχομένης.
– coming.

Chapter 2

Αὐτοὶ γὰρ οἴδατε, ἀδελφοί, τὴν
For [your]selves ye know, brothers, the

εἴσοδον ἡμῶν τὴν πρὸς ὑμᾶς, ὅτι οὐ
entrance of us – to you, that not

κενὴ γέγονεν, 2 ἀλλὰ προπαθόντες καὶ
in vain it has been, but having previously and
suffered

ὑβρισθέντες καθὼς οἴδατε ἐν Φιλίπποις
having been as ye know in Philippi
insulted

ἐπαρρησιασάμεθα ἐν τῷ θεῷ ἡμῶν λαλῆσαι
we were bold in the God of us to speak

πρὸς ὑμᾶς τὸ εὐαγγέλιον τοῦ θεοῦ ἐν
to you the gospel – of God in

πολλῷ ἀγῶνι. 3 ἡ γὰρ παράκλησις
· much struggle. For the exhortation

ἡμῶν οὐκ ἐκ πλάνης οὐδὲ ἐξ ἀκαθαρσίας
of us not of error nor of uncleanness

οὐδὲ ἐν δόλῳ, 4 ἀλλὰ καθὼς δεδοκιμάσμεθα
nor in guile, but as we have been
approved

ὑπὸ τοῦ θεοῦ πιστευθῆναι τὸ εὐαγγέλιον
by – God to be entrusted [with] the gospel

οὕτως λαλοῦμεν, οὐχ ὡς ἀνθρώποις ἀρέ-
so we speak, not as ¹men ¹pleas-

σκοντες, ἀλλὰ θεῷ τῷ δοκιμάζοντι τὰς
ing, but God the [one] proving the

καρδίας ἡμῶν. 5 οὔτε γὰρ ποτε ἐν
hearts of us. For neither then with

λόγῳ κολακείας ἐγενήθημεν, καθὼς οἴδατε,
word of flattery were we, as ye know,

οὔτε ἐν προφάσει πλεονεξίας, θεὸς μάρτυς,
nor with pretext of covetousness, God [is] witness,

597

King James Version	New International Version

covetousness; God *is* witness: 6 Nor of men sought we glory, neither of you, nor *yet* of others, when we might have been burdensome, as the apostles of Christ. 7 But we were gentle among you, even as a nurse cherisheth her children: 8 So being affectionately desirous of you, we were willing to have imparted unto you, not the gospel of God only, but also our own souls, because ye were dear unto us. 9 For ye remember, brethren, our labour and travail: for labouring night and day, because we would not be chargeable unto any of you, we preached unto you the gospel of God. 10 Ye *are* witnesses, and God *also*, how holily and justly and unblameably we behaved ourselves among you that believe: 11 As ye know how we exhorted and comforted and charged every one of you, as a father *doth* his children, 12 That ye would walk worthy of God, who hath called you unto his kingdom and glory. 13 For this cause also thank we God without ceasing, because, when ye received the word of God which ye heard of us, ye received *it* not *as* the word of men, but as it is in truth, the word of God, which effectually worketh also in you that believe. 14 For ye, brethren, became followers of the churches of God which in Judea are in Christ Jesus: for ye also have suffered like things of your own countrymen, even as they *have* of the Jews: 15 Who both killed the Lord Jesus, and their own prophets, and have persecuted us; and they please not God, and are contrary to all men: 16 Forbidding us to speak to the Gentiles that they might be saved, to fill up their sins always: for the wrath is come upon them to the uttermost. 17 But we, brethren, being taken from you for a short time in presence, not in heart, endeavoured the more abundantly to see your face with great desire. 18 Wherefore we would have come unto you, even I Paul, once and again; but Satan hindered us. 19 For what *is* our hope, or joy, or crown of rejoicing? *Are* not even ye in the presence of our Lord Jesus Christ at his coming? 20 For ye are our glory and joy.

greed—God is our witness. 6 We were not looking for praise from men, not from you or anyone else.

7 As apostles of Christ we could have been a burden to you, but we were gentle among you, like a mother caring for her little children. 8 We loved you so much that we were delighted to share with you not only the gospel of God but our lives as well, because you had become so dear to us. 9 Surely you remember, brothers, our toil and hardship; we worked night and day in order not be a burden to anyone while we preached the gospel of God to you.

10 You are witnesses, and so is God, of how holy, righteous and blameless we were among you who believed. 11 For you know that we dealt with each of you as a father deals with his own children, 12 encouraging, comforting and urging you to live lives worthy of God, who calls you into his kingdom and glory.

13 And we also thank God continually because, when you received the word of God, which you heard from us, you accepted it not as the word of men, but as it actually is, the word of God, which is at work in you who believe. 14 For you, brothers, became imitators of God's churches in Judea, which are in Christ Jesus. You suffered from your own countrymen the same things those churches suffered from the Jews, 15 who killed the Lord Jesus and the prophets and also drove us out. They displease God and are hostile to all men 16 in their effort to keep us from speaking to the Gentiles so that they may be saved. In this way they always heap up their sins to the limit. The wrath of God has come upon them at last.[b]

Paul's longing to see the Thessalonians

17 But, brothers, when we were torn away from you for a short time (in person, not in thought), out of our intense longing we made every effort to see you. 18 For we wanted to come to you—certainly I, Paul, did, again and again—but Satan stopped us. 19 For what is our hope, our joy, or the crown in which we will glory in the presence of our Lord Jesus Christ when he comes? Is it not you? 20 Indeed, you are our glory and joy.

3 Wherefore when we could no longer forbear, we thought it good to be left at Athens alone; 2 And sent Timotheus, our brother, and minister of God, and our fellow labourer in the

3 So when we could stand it no longer, we thought it best to be left by ourselves in Athens. 2 We sent Timothy, who is our brother and God's fellow worker[c] in spreading the gos-

[b] Or *fully*. [c] Some textual sources read *brother and fellow worker*; others, *brother and God's servant*.

598

Greek Interlinear

6 οὔτε   ζητοῦντες   ἐξ   ἀνθρώπων   δόξαν,
nor   seeking   from   men   glory,

οὔτε ἀφ’ ὑμῶν οὔτε ἀπ’ ἄλλων, 7 δυνάμε-
neither from   you   nor   from   others,   being

νοι ἐν βάρει εἶναι ὡς Χριστοῦ ἀπόστολοι·
able "with "weight" 'to be   as   'of Christ   'apostles;

ἀλλὰ   ἐγενήθημεν   ἤπιοι   ἐν   μέσῳ   ὑμῶν,
but   we were   gentle   in [the] midst   of you,

ὡς ἐὰν τροφὸς θάλπῃ τὰ ἑαυτῆς τέκνα·
as   if   a nurse   should   'the   'of herself 'children;
                                                cherish

8 οὕτως   ὁμειρόμενοι   ὑμῶν   ηὐδοκοῦμεν
so   longing for   you   we were well
                                                pleased

μεταδοῦναι   ὑμῖν   οὐ   μόνον   τὸ   εὐαγγέλιον
to impart   to you   not   only   the   gospel

τοῦ   θεοῦ   ἀλλὰ   καὶ   τὰς   ἑαυτῶν   ψυχάς,
- of God   but   also   'the   'of ourselves 'souls,

διότι   ἀγαπητοὶ   ἡμῖν   ἐγενήθητε. 9 μνημο-
because   'beloved   'to us   'ye became.   ye re-

νεύετε   γάρ,   ἀδελφοί,   τὸν   κόπον   ἡμῶν
member   For,   brothers,   the   labour   of us

καὶ   τὸν   μόχθον·   νυκτὸς   καὶ   ἡμέρας
and   the   toil;   night   and   day

ἐργαζόμενοι   πρὸς   τὸ   μὴ   ἐπιβαρῆσαί τινα
working   for   the   not   to put a burden   any-
                                                on   one

ὑμῶν   ἐκηρύξαμεν   εἰς   ὑμᾶς   τὸ   εὐαγγέλιον
of you   we proclaimed   to   you   the   gospel

τοῦ   θεοῦ. 10 ὑμεῖς   μάρτυρες   καὶ   ὁ
- of God.   Ye [are]   witnesses   and   -

θεός,   ὡς   ὁσίως   καὶ   δικαίως   καὶ   ἀμέμπτως
God,   how holily   and   righteously and   blamelessly

ὑμῖν   τοῖς   πιστεύουσιν   ἐγενήθημεν, 11 καθά-
'to you   'the [ones] 'believing   'we were,   even

περ   οἴδατε   ὡς   ἕνα   ἕκαστον   ὑμῶν   ὡς
as   ye know   how   'one   'each   of you   as

πατὴρ   τέκνα   ἑαυτοῦ   παρακαλοῦντες   ὑμᾶς
a father   children of himself   exhorting   you

καὶ   παραμυθούμενοι 12 καὶ   μαρτυρόμενοι   εἰς
and   consoling   and   witnessing   for

τὸ   περιπατεῖν   ὑμᾶς   ἀξίως   τοῦ   θεοῦ
the   to walk   you^b   worthily   -   of God
=that ye should walk

τοῦ   καλοῦντος   ὑμᾶς   εἰς   τὴν   ἑαυτοῦ
the [one]   calling   you   to   'the   'of himself

βασιλείαν   καὶ   δόξαν.
'kingdom   'and   'glory.

13 Καὶ   διὰ   τοῦτο   καὶ   ἡμεῖς   εὐχαρισ-
And   therefore   also   we   give

τοῦμεν   τῷ   θεῷ   ἀδιαλείπτως,   ὅτι   παρα-
thanks   -   to God   unceasingly;   that   having

λαβόντες   λόγον   ἀκοῆς   παρ’   ἡμῶν   τοῦ
received   '[the] word 'of hearing '[from   'us   'the

θεοῦ   ἐδέξασθε   οὐ   λόγον   ἀνθρώπων   ἀλλὰ
'of God ye welcomed   not   [as] a   of men   but
[it]   word

καθὼς   ἀληθῶς   ἐστιν   λόγον   θεοῦ,   ὃς
as   truly   it is   a word   of God, which

καὶ   ἐνεργεῖται   ἐν   ὑμῖν   τοῖς   πιστεύουσιν.
also   operates   in   you   the [ones]   believing.

14 ὑμεῖς   γὰρ   μιμηταὶ   ἐγενήθητε,   ἀδελφοί,
For ye   'imitators   'became,   brothers,

τῶν   ἐκκλησιῶν   τοῦ   θεοῦ   τῶν   οὐσῶν   ἐν
of the   churches   - of God   -   being   in

τῇ   Ἰουδαίᾳ   ἐν   Χριστῷ   Ἰησοῦ,   ὅτι   τὰ
-    Judæa   in   Christ   Jesus, because 'the

αὐτὰ   ἐπάθετε   καὶ   ὑμεῖς   ὑπὸ   τῶν   ἰδίων
'same   'suffered   'also   'ye   by   the(your) own
things

συμφυλετῶν,   καθὼς   καὶ   αὐτοὶ   ὑπὸ   τῶν
fellow-tribesmen,   as   also   they   by   the

Ἰουδαίων,   15 τῶν   καὶ   τὸν   κύριον
Jews,   the [ones]   'both   'the   'Lord

ἀποκτεινάντων   Ἰησοῦν   καὶ   τοὺς   προφήτας,
'killing   'Jesus   and   the   prophets,

καὶ   ἡμᾶς   ἐκδιωξάντων,   καὶ   θεῷ   μὴ
and   'us   'chasing 'out,   and   'God   'not

ἀρεσκόντων,   καὶ   πᾶσιν   ἀνθρώποις   ἐναντίων,
'pleasing,   and   to all   men   contrary,

16 κωλυόντων   ἡμᾶς   τοῖς   ἔθνεσιν   λαλῆσαι
hindering   us   'to the   'nations   'to speak
=from speaking . . .

ἵνα   σωθῶσιν,   εἰς   τὸ   ἀναπληρῶσαι   αὐτῶν
in order they may   for   the   to fill up   'of them
that   be saved,

τὰς   ἁμαρτίας   πάντοτε.   ἔφθασεν   δὲ   ἐπ’
'the   'sins   always.   But 'came   'on

αὐτοὺς   ἡ   ὀργὴ   εἰς   τέλος.
'them   'the   'wrath   to [the] end.

17 Ἡμεῖς   δέ,   ἀδελφοί,   ἀπορφανισθέντες
But we   brothers,   being bereaved

ἀφ’   ὑμῶν   πρὸς   καιρὸν   ὥρας   προσώπῳ
from   you   for   time   of an hour   in face
                                                (presence)

οὐ   καρδίᾳ,   περισσοτέρως   ἐσπουδάσαμεν   τὸ
not   in heart,   more abundantly   were eager   'the

πρόσωπον   ὑμῶν   ἰδεῖν   ἐν   πολλῇ   ἐπιθυμίᾳ.
'face   'of you 'to see   with   much   desire.

18 διότι   ἠθελήσαμεν   ἐλθεῖν   πρὸς   ὑμᾶς,
Wherefore   we wished   to come   to   you,

ἐγὼ   μὲν   Παῦλος   καὶ   ἅπαξ   καὶ   δίς,
I   'indeed   'Paul   both   once   and   twice
                                                (again),

καὶ   ἐνέκοψεν   ἡμᾶς   ὁ   σατανᾶς.   19 τίς
and   'hindered   'us -   'Satan.   what

γὰρ   ἡμῶν   ἐλπὶς   ἢ   χαρὰ   ἢ   στέφανος
For [is] 'of us   'hope   or   joy   or   crown

καυχήσεως   —   ἢ   οὐχὶ   καὶ   ὑμεῖς   —
of boasting   or   not   even   ye   —

ἔμπροσθεν   τοῦ   κυρίου   ἡμῶν   Ἰησοῦ
before   the   Lord   of us   Jesus

ἐν   τῇ   αὐτοῦ   παρουσίᾳ;   20 ὑμεῖς   γάρ
in(at) the   'of him   'presence?   for ye

ἐστε   ἡ   δόξα   ἡμῶν   καὶ   ἡ   χαρά.
are   'the   'glory   'of us 'and   'the 'joy.

Chapter 3

Διὸ   μηκέτι   στέγοντες   ηὐδοκήσαμεν
Wherefore no longer   bearing up   we were well pleased

καταλειφθῆναι   ἐν   Ἀθήναις   μόνοι,   2 καὶ
to be left   in   Athens   alone,   and

ἐπέμψαμεν   Τιμόθεον,   τὸν   ἀδελφὸν   ἡμῶν
we sent   Timothy,   the   brother   of us

καὶ   συνεργὸν   τοῦ   θεοῦ   ἐν   τῷ   εὐαγγελίῳ
and   fellow-worker   -   of God   in   the   gospel

* ? dignity, authority.

King James Version

gospel of Christ, to establish you, and to comfort you concerning your faith: 3 That no man should be moved by these afflictions: for yourselves know that we are appointed thereunto. 4 For verily, when we were with you, we told you before that we should suffer tribulation; even as it came to pass, and ye know. 5 For this cause, when I could no longer forbear, I sent to know your faith, lest by some means the tempter have tempted you, and our labour be in vain. 6 But now when Timotheus came from you unto us, and brought us good tidings of your faith and charity, and that ye have good remembrance of us always, desiring greatly to see us, as we also *to see* you: 7 Therefore, brethren, we were comforted over you in all our affliction and distress by your faith: 8 For now we live, if ye stand fast in the Lord. 9 For what thanks can we render to God again for you, for all the joy wherewith we joy for your sakes before our God; 10 Night and day praying exceedingly that we might see your face, and might perfect that which is lacking in your faith? 11 Now God himself and our Father, and our Lord Jesus Christ, direct our way unto you. 12And the Lord make you to increase and abound in love one toward another, and toward all *men*, even as we *do* toward you: 13 To the end he may stablish your hearts unblameable in holiness before God, even our Father, at the coming of our Lord Jesus Christ with all his saints.

New International Version

pel of Christ, to strengthen and encourage you in your faith, 3 so that no one would be unsettled by these trials. You know quite well that we were destined for them. 4 In fact, when we were with you, we kept telling you that we would be persecuted. And it turned out that way, as you well know. 5 For this reason, when I could stand it no longer, I sent to find out about your faith. I was afraid that in some way the tempter might have tempted you and our efforts might have been useless.

Timothy's encouraging report

6 But Timothy has just now come to us from you and has brought good news about your faith and love. He has told us that you always have pleasant memories of us and that you long to see us, just as we also long to see you. 7 Therefore, brothers, in all our distress and persecution we were encouraged about you because of your faith. 8 For now we really live, since you are standing firm in the Lord. 9 How can we thank God enough for you in return for all the joy we have in the presence of our God because of you? 10 Night and day we pray most earnestly that we may see you again and supply what is lacking in your faith.

11 Now may our God and Father himself and our Lord Jesus clear the way for us to come to you. 12 May the Lord make your love increase and overflow for each other and for everyone else, just as ours does for you. 13 May he give you inner strength that you may be blameless and holy in the presence of our God and Father when our Lord Jesus comes with all his holy ones.

Living to please God

4 Furthermore then we beseech you, brethren, and exhort *you* by the Lord Jesus, that as ye have received of us how ye ought to walk and to please God, *so* ye would abound more and more. 2 For ye know what commandments we gave you by the Lord Jesus. 3 For this is the will of God, *even* your sanctification, that ye should abstain from fornication; 4 That every one of you should know how to possess his vessel in sanctification and honour; 5 Not in the lust of concupiscence, even as the Gentiles which know not God: 6 That no *man* go beyond and defraud his brother in *any* matter: because that the Lord *is* the avenger of all such, as we also have forewarned you and testified. 7 For God hath not called us unto uncleanness, but unto holiness. 8 He therefore that despiseth, despiseth not man, but God, who hath also given unto us

4 Finally, brothers, we instructed you how to live in order to please God, as in fact you are living. Now we ask you and urge you in the Lord Jesus to do this more and more. 2 You know what instructions we gave you by the authority of the Lord Jesus.

3 It is God's will that you should be holy; that you should avoid sexual immorality; 4 that each of you should learn to control his own body[d] in a way that is holy and honorable, 5 not in passionate lust like the heathen, who do not know God; 6 and that in this matter no one should wrong his brother or take advantage of him. The Lord will punish men for all such sins, as we have already told you and warned you. 7 For God did not call us to be impure, but to live a holy life. 8 Therefore, he who rejects this instruction does not reject man but God, who gives you his Holy Spirit.

[d] Or learn to live with his own wife.

τοῦ Χριστοῦ, εἰς τὸ στηρίξαι ὑμᾶς καὶ
- of Christ, for the to establish you and

παρακαλέσαι ὑπὲρ τῆς πίστεως ὑμῶν 3 τὸ
to exhort on behalf of the faith of you -

μηδένα σαίνεσθαι ἐν ταῖς θλίψεσιν ταύταις.
no one to be drawn by these afflictions.
aside[b]

αὐτοὶ γὰρ οἴδατε ὅτι εἰς τοῦτο κείμεθα·
For [your]selves ye know that to this we are
appointed;

4 καὶ γὰρ ὅτε πρὸς ὑμᾶς ἦμεν,
for even when with you we were,

προελέγομεν ὑμῖν ὅτι μέλλομεν θλίβεσθαι,
we said before to you that we are about to be afflicted,

καθὼς καὶ ἐγένετο καὶ οἴδατε. 5 διὰ
as indeed it happened and ye know. There-

τοῦτο κἀγὼ μηκέτι στέγων ἔπεμψα εἰς
fore I also no longer bearing up sent for

τὸ γνῶναι τὴν πίστιν ὑμῶν, μή πως
the to know the faith of you, lest [some]how

ἐπείρασεν ὑμᾶς ὁ πειράζων καὶ εἰς
[2]tempted [3]you [1]the [one] [4]tempting and in
= the tempter

κενὸν γένηται ὁ κόπος ἡμῶν. 6 Ἄρτι
vain became the labour of us. now

δὲ ἐλθόντος Τιμοθέου πρὸς ἡμᾶς ἀφ'
But coming Timothy[a] to us from
= when Timothy came

ὑμῶν καὶ εὐαγγελισαμένου ἡμῖν τὴν πίστιν
you and announcing good news[a] to us [of] the faith

καὶ τὴν ἀγάπην ὑμῶν, καὶ ὅτι ἔχετε
and the love of you, and that ye have

μνείαν ἡμῶν ἀγαθὴν πάντοτε, ἐπιποθοῦντες
[2]remem- [1]of us [3]good always, longing
brance

ἡμᾶς ἰδεῖν καθάπερ καὶ ἡμεῖς ὑμᾶς,
[2]us [1]to see even as also we you,

7 διὰ τοῦτο παρεκλήθημεν, ἀδελφοί, ἐφ'
therefore we were comforted, brothers, over

ὑμῖν ἐπὶ πάσῃ τῇ ἀνάγκῃ καὶ θλίψει
you on all the distress and affliction

ἡμῶν διὰ τῆς ὑμῶν πίστεως, 8 ὅτι
of us through the [2]of you [1]faith, because

νῦν ζῶμεν ἐὰν ὑμεῖς στήκετε ἐν κυρίῳ.
now we live if ye stand in [the] Lord.

9 τίνα γὰρ εὐχαριστίαν δυνάμεθα τῷ θεῷ
For what thanks are we able - to God

ἀνταποδοῦναι περὶ ὑμῶν ἐπὶ πάσῃ τῇ
to return concerning you over all the

χαρᾷ ᾗ χαίρομεν δι' ὑμᾶς ἔμπροσθεν
joy [with] we rejoice because you before
which of

τοῦ θεοῦ ἡμῶν, 10 νυκτὸς καὶ ἡμέρας
the God of us, night and day

ὑπερεκπερισσοῦ δεόμενοι εἰς τὸ ἰδεῖν ὑμῶν
exceedingly petitioning for the to see of you

τὸ πρόσωπον καὶ καταρτίσαι τὰ ὑστερήματα
the face and to adjust the shortcomings

τῆς πίστεως ὑμῶν; 11 Αὐτὸς δὲ ὁ θεὸς
of the faith of you? Now [him]self the God

καὶ πατὴρ ἡμῶν καὶ ὁ κύριος ἡμῶν
and Father of us and the Lord of us

Ἰησοῦς κατευθύναι τὴν ὁδὸν ἡμῶν πρὸς
Jesus may he direct the way of us to

ὑμᾶς· 12 ὑμᾶς δὲ ὁ κύριος πλεονάσαι
you; and [2]you [1]the [2]Lord [1]make [3]to abound

καὶ περισσεύσαι τῇ ἀγάπῃ εἰς ἀλλήλους
and to exceed - in love to one another

καὶ εἰς πάντας, καθάπερ καὶ ἡμεῖς
and to all men, even as also we

εἰς ὑμᾶς, 13 εἰς τὸ στηρίξαι ὑμῶν τὰς
to you, for the to establish of you the

καρδίας ἀμέμπτους ἐν ἁγιωσύνῃ ἔμπροσθεν
hearts blameless in holiness before

τοῦ θεοῦ καὶ πατρὸς ἡμῶν ἐν τῇ παρουσίᾳ
the God and Father of us in(at) the presence

τοῦ κυρίου ἡμῶν Ἰησοῦ μετὰ πάντων
of the Lord of us Jesus with all

τῶν ἁγίων αὐτοῦ.
the saints of him.

Chapter 4

Λοιπὸν οὖν, ἀδελφοί, ἐρωτῶμεν ὑμᾶς
For the rest therefore, brothers, we ask you

καὶ παρακαλοῦμεν ἐν κυρίῳ Ἰησοῦ, ἵνα
and we beseech in [the] Lord Jesus, in order
that

καθὼς παρελάβετε παρ' ἡμῶν τὸ πῶς
as ye received from us the how

δεῖ ὑμᾶς περιπατεῖν καὶ ἀρέσκειν θεῷ,
it you to walk and to please God,
behoves

καθὼς καὶ περιπατεῖτε, ἵνα περισσεύητε
as indeed ye do walk, in order that ye abound

μᾶλλον. 2 οἴδατε γὰρ τίνας παραγγελίας
more. For ye know what injunctions

ἐδώκαμεν ὑμῖν διὰ τοῦ κυρίου Ἰησοῦ.
we gave you through the Lord Jesus.

3 Τοῦτο γάρ ἐστιν θέλημα τοῦ θεοῦ,
For this is [the] will - of God,

ὁ ἁγιασμὸς ὑμῶν, ἀπέχεσθαι ὑμᾶς ἀπὸ
the sanctification of you, to abstain you[b] from

τῆς πορνείας, 4 εἰδέναι ἕκαστον ὑμῶν
the fornication, [2]to know[a] [1]each one[b] of you

τὸ ἑαυτοῦ σκεῦος κτᾶσθαι ἐν ἁγιασμῷ
[5]the [3]of himself [4]vessel [6]to possess in sanctification

καὶ τιμῇ, 5 μὴ ἐν πάθει ἐπιθυμίας
and honour, not in passion of lust

καθάπερ καὶ τὰ ἔθνη τὰ μὴ εἰδότα
even as indeed the nations - not knowing

τὸν θεόν, 6 τὸ μὴ ὑπερβαίνειν καὶ
- God, - not to go beyond and

πλεονεκτεῖν ἐν τῷ πράγματι τὸν ἀδελφὸν
to defraud in the matter the brother

αὐτοῦ, διότι ἔκδικος κύριος περὶ πάντων
of him, be- [1][the] Lord [1][the] Lord con- all
cause avenger [is] cerning

τούτων, καθὼς καὶ προείπαμεν ὑμῖν καὶ
these, as in- we previously you and
deed told

διεμαρτυράμεθα. 7 οὐ γὰρ ἐκάλεσεν ἡμᾶς
solemnly witnessed. For [2]not [1]called [3]us

ὁ θεὸς ἐπὶ ἀκαθαρσίᾳ ἀλλ' ἐν ἁγιασμῷ.
- [1]God to uncleanness but in sanctification.

8 τοιγαροῦν ὁ ἀθετῶν οὐκ ἄνθρωπον
Wherefore the [one] rejecting [2]not [1]man

ἀθετεῖ ἀλλὰ τὸν θεὸν τὸν καὶ διδόντα
[1]rejects but - God the and giving
[one] in-
deed

τὸ πνεῦμα αὐτοῦ τὸ ἅγιον εἰς ὑμᾶς.
the [2]Spirit [1]of him - [1]Holy to you.

* That is, "to be able"; see note on page xxxviii.

King James Version

his Holy Spirit. 9 But as touching brotherly love ye need not that I write unto you: for ye yourselves are taught of God to love one another. 10And indeed ye do it toward all the brethren which are in all Macedonia: but we beseech you, brethren, that ye increase more and more; 11And that ye study to be quiet, and to do your own business, and to work with your own hands, as we commanded you; 12 That ye may walk honestly toward them that are without, and *that* ye may have lack of nothing. 13 But I would not have you to be ignorant, brethren, concerning them which are asleep, that ye sorrow not, even as others which have no hope. 14 For if we believe that Jesus died and rose again, even so them also which sleep in Jesus will God bring with him. 15 For this we say unto you by the word of the Lord, that we which are alive *and* remain unto the coming of the Lord shall not prevent them which are asleep. 16 For the Lord himself shall descend from heaven with a shout, with the voice of the archangel, and with the trump of God: and the dead in Christ shall rise first: 17 Then we which are alive *and* remain shall be caught up together with them in the clouds, to meet the Lord in the air: and so shall we ever be with the Lord. 18 Wherefore comfort one another with these words.

5 But of the times and the seasons, brethren, ye have no need that I write unto you. 2 For yourselves know perfectly that the day of the Lord so cometh as a thief in the night. 3 For when they shall say, Peace and safety; then sudden destruction cometh upon them, as travail upon a woman with child; and they shall not escape. 4 But ye, brethren, are not in darkness, that that day should overtake you as a thief. 5 Ye are all the children of light, and the children of the day: we are not of the night, nor of darkness. 6 Therefore let us not sleep, as *do* others; but let us watch and be sober. 7 For they that sleep sleep in the night; and they that be drunken are drunken in the night. 8 But let us, who are of the day, be sober, putting on the breastplate of faith and love; and for a helmet, the hope of salvation. 9 For God hath not appointed us to wrath, but to obtain salvation by our Lord Jesus Christ, 10 Who died for us, that, whether we wake or sleep, we should live to-

New International Version

9 Now about brotherly love we do not need to write to you, for you yourselves have been taught by God to love each other. 10And in fact, you do love all the brothers throughout Macedonia. Yet we urge you, brothers, to do so more and more.

11 Make it your ambition to lead a quiet life, to mind your own business and to work with your hands, just as we told you, 12 so that your daily life may win the respect of outsiders and so that you will not be dependent on anybody.

The coming of the Lord

13 Brothers, we do not want you to be ignorant about those who sleep, or to grieve like the rest of men, who have no hope. 14 We believe that Jesus died and rose again and so we believe that God will bring with Jesus those who sleep in him. 15According to the Lord's own word, we tell you that we who are still alive, who are left till the coming of the Lord, will certainly not precede those who have fallen asleep. 16 For the Lord himself will come down from heaven, with a loud command, with the voice of the archangel and with the trumpet call of God, and the dead in Christ will rise first. 17After that, we who are still alive and are left will be caught up with them in the clouds to meet the Lord in the air. And so we will be with the Lord forever. 18 Therefore encourage each other with these words.

5 Now, brothers, about times and dates we do not need to write to you, 2 for you know very well that the day of the Lord will come like a thief in the night. 3 While people are saying, "Peace and safety," destruction will come on them suddenly, as labor pains on a pregnant woman, and they will not escape.

4 But you, brothers, are not in darkness so that this day should surprise you like a thief. 5 You are all sons of the light and sons of the day. We do not belong to the night or to the darkness. 6 So then, let us not be like others who are asleep, but let us be alert and self-controlled. 7 For those who sleep, sleep at night, and those who get drunk, get drunk at night. 8 But since we belong to the day, let us be self-controlled, putting on faith and love as a breastplate, and the hope of salvation as a helmet. 9 For God did not appoint us to suffer wrath but to receive salvation through our Lord Jesus Christ. 10 He died for us so that, whether we are awake or

Greek Interlinear

9 Περὶ δὲ τῆς φιλαδελφίας οὐ χρείαν
Now concerning – brotherly love not need

ἔχετε γράφειν ὑμῖν· αὐτοὶ γὰρ ὑμεῖς
ye have to write to you; for ²[your]selves ¹ye
[for me]

θεοδίδακτοί ἐστε εἰς τὸ ἀγαπᾶν ἀλλήλους·
⁴taught by God ³are for the to love one another;

10 καὶ γὰρ ποιεῖτε αὐτὸ εἰς πάντας
for indeed ye do it toward all

τοὺς ἀδελφοὺς [τοὺς] ἐν ὅλῃ τῇ Μακεδο-
the brothers – in all – Macedo-

νίᾳ. Παρακαλοῦμεν δὲ ὑμᾶς, ἀδελφοί,
nia. But we exhort you, brothers,

περισσεύειν μᾶλλον, 11 καὶ φιλοτιμεῖσθαι
to abound more, and to strive eagerly

ἡσυχάζειν καὶ πράσσειν τὰ ἴδια καὶ
to be quiet and to practise the own and
(your) things

ἐργάζεσθαι ταῖς χερσὶν ὑμῶν, καθὼς ὑμῖν
to work with the hands of you, as ²you

παρηγγείλαμεν, 12 ἵνα περιπατῆτε εὐσχη-
¹we enjoined, in or- ye may walk becom-
der that

μόνως πρὸς τοὺς ἔξω καὶ μηδενὸς
ingly toward the [ones] outside and ²of nothing

χρείαν ἔχητε.
¹need ¹ye may have.

13 Οὐ θέλομεν δὲ ὑμᾶς ἀγνοεῖν, ἀδελφοί,
Now we do not wish you to be brothers,
ignorant,

περὶ τῶν κοιμωμένων, ἵνα μὴ λυπῆσθε
con- the sleeping, lest ye grieve
cerning [ones]

καθὼς καὶ οἱ λοιποὶ οἱ μὴ ἔχοντες
as indeed the rest – not having

ἐλπίδα. 14 εἰ γὰρ πιστεύομεν ὅτι Ἰησοῦς
hope. For if we believe that Jesus

ἀπέθανεν καὶ ἀνέστη, οὕτως καὶ ὁ θεὸς
died and rose again, so also – ¹God

τοὺς κοιμηθέντας διὰ τοῦ Ἰησοῦ ἄξει
¹the ²having slept ³through – ⁴Jesus will
[ones] bring

σὺν αὐτῷ. 15 Τοῦτο γὰρ ὑμῖν λέγομεν
with him. For this to you we say

ἐν λόγῳ κυρίου, ὅτι ἡμεῖς οἱ ζῶντες
by a word of [the] that we the living
Lord, [ones]

οἱ περιλειπόμενοι εἰς τὴν παρουσίαν τοῦ
– remaining to the presence of the

κυρίου οὐ μὴ φθάσωμεν τοὺς κοιμηθέντας·
Lord by no may precede the having slept;
means [ones]

16 ὅτι αὐτὸς ὁ κύριος ἐν κελεύσματι,
be- ²[him]- ¹the ¹Lord with a word of
cause self command,

ἐν φωνῇ ἀρχαγγέλου καὶ ἐν σάλπιγγι
with a voice of an archangel and with a trumpet

θεοῦ, καταβήσεται ἀπ' οὐρανοῦ, καὶ οἱ
of God, will descend from heaven, and the

νεκροὶ ἐν Χριστῷ ἀναστήσονται πρῶτον,
dead in Christ will rise again firstly,

17 ἔπειτα ἡμεῖς οἱ ζῶντες οἱ περιλειπόμενοι
then we the living – remaining
[ones]

ἅμα σὺν αὐτοῖς ἁρπαγησόμεθα ἐν νεφέλαις
to- with them shall be seized in clouds
gether

εἰς ἀπάντησιν τοῦ κυρίου εἰς ἀέρα·
to a meeting of the Lord in air;

καὶ οὕτως πάντοτε σὺν κυρίῳ ἐσόμεθα.
and so always with [the] Lord we shall be.

18 Ὥστε παρακαλεῖτε ἀλλήλους ἐν τοῖς λόγοις
Therefore comfort ye one with – words
another

τούτοις.
these.

Chapter 5

Περὶ δὲ τῶν χρόνων καὶ τῶν καιρῶν,
But concerning the times and the seasons,

ἀδελφοί, οὐ χρείαν ἔχετε ὑμῖν γράφεσθαι·
brothers, ²not ¹need ¹ye have ²to you ⁴to be written;

2 αὐτοὶ γὰρ ἀκριβῶς οἴδατε ὅτι ἡμέρα
for ²[your]selves ³accurately ¹ye know that [the] day

κυρίου ὡς κλέπτης ἐν νυκτὶ οὕτως
of [the] Lord as a thief at night so

ἔρχεται. 3 ὅταν λέγωσιν· εἰρήνη καὶ
it comes. Whenever they say: Peace and

ἀσφάλεια, τότε αἰφνίδιος αὐτοῖς ἐφίσταται
safety, then ³sudden ⁴them ²comes on

ὄλεθρος ὥσπερ ἡ ὠδὶν τῇ ἐν γαστρὶ
¹destruction as the birth pang to the pregnant

ἐχούσῃ, καὶ οὐ μὴ ἐκφύγωσιν. 4 ὑμεῖς
woman,† and by no may they ye
means escape.

δέ, ἀδελφοί, οὐκ ἐστὲ ἐν σκότει, ἵνα
But, brothers, are not in dark- in or-
ness, der that

ἡ ἡμέρα ὑμᾶς ὡς κλέπτης καταλάβῃ·
the day you as a thief should overtake;

5 πάντες γὰρ ὑμεῖς υἱοὶ φωτός ἐστε
for all ye ²sons ³of light ¹are

καὶ υἱοὶ ἡμέρας. Οὐκ ἐσμὲν νυκτὸς
and sons of [the] day. We are not of [the]
night

οὐδὲ σκότους· 6 ἄρα οὖν μὴ καθεύδωμεν
nor of darkness; therefore let us not sleep

ὡς οἱ λοιποί, ἀλλὰ γρηγορῶμεν καὶ
as the rest, but let us watch and

νήφωμεν. 7 οἱ γὰρ καθεύδοντες νυκτὸς
be sober. For the [ones] sleeping by night

καθεύδουσιν, καὶ οἱ μεθυσκόμενοι νυκτὸς
sleep, and the [ones] being drunk by night

μεθύουσιν· 8 ἡμεῖς δὲ ἡμέρας ὄντες
are drunk; but we of [the] day being

νήφωμεν, ἐνδυσάμενοι θώρακα πίστεως καὶ
let us be sober, putting on a breastplate of faith and

ἀγάπης καὶ περικεφαλαίαν ἐλπίδα σωτηρίας·
of love and a helmet hope of salvation;

9 ὅτι οὐκ ἔθετο ἡμᾶς ὁ θεὸς εἰς ὀργὴν
because ²did not appoint ¹us – ¹God to wrath

ἀλλὰ εἰς περιποίησιν σωτηρίας διὰ τοῦ
but to obtainment of salvation through the

κυρίου ἡμῶν Ἰησοῦ Χριστοῦ, 10 τοῦ
Lord of us Jesus Christ, the

ἀποθανόντος περὶ ἡμῶν, ἵνα εἴτε γρηγορ-
[one] having died concern- us, in or- whether we
ing der that

ῶμεν εἴτε καθεύδωμεν ἅμα σὺν αὐτῷ
watch or we sleep ²together ³with ⁴him

603

King James Version

gether with him. 11 Wherefore comfort your-selves together, and edify one another, even as also ye do. 12And we beseech you, brethren, to know them which labour among you, and are over you in the Lord, and admonish you; 13And to esteem them very highly in love for their work's sake. *And* be at peace among yourselves. 14 Now we exhort you, brethren, warn them that are unruly, comfort the feebleminded, support the weak, be patient toward all *men*. 15 See that none render evil for evil unto any *man;* but ever follow that which is good, both among yourselves, and to all *men*. 16 Rejoice evermore. 17 Pray without ceasing. 18 In every thing give thanks: for this is the will of God in Christ Jesus concerning you. 19 Quench not the Spirit. 20 Despise not prophesyings. 21 Prove all things; hold fast that which is good. 22Abstain from all appearance of evil. 23And the very God of peace sanctify you wholly; and *I pray God* your whole spirit and soul and body be preserved blameless unto the coming of our Lord Jesus Christ. 24 Faithful *is* he that calleth you, who also will do *it*. 25 Brethren, pray for us. 26 Greet all the brethren with a holy kiss. 27 I charge you by the Lord, that this epistle be read unto all the holy brethren. 28 The grace of our Lord Jesus Christ *be* with you. Amen.

The first *epistle* unto the Thessalonians was written from Athens.

New International Version

asleep, we may live together with him. 11 There-fore, encourage one another and build each other up, just as in fact you are doing.

Final instructions

12 Now we ask you, brothers, to respect those who work hard among you, who are over you in the Lord and who admonish you. 13 Hold them in the highest regard in love because of their work. Live in peace with each other. 14And we urge you, brothers, warn those who are idle, encourage the timid, help the weak, be patient with everyone. 15 Make sure that nobody pays back wrong for wrong, but always try to be kind to each other and to everyone else.

16 Be joyful always; 17 pray continually; 18 give thanks in all circumstances, for this is God's will for you in Christ Jesus. 19 Do not put out the Spirit's fire; 20 do not treat prophecies with contempt. 21 Test everything. Hold on to the good. 22Avoid every kind of evil.

23 May God himself, the God of peace, sanc-tify you through and through. May your whole spirit, soul and body be kept blameless at the coming of our Lord Jesus Christ. 24 The one who calls you is faithful and he will do it.

25 Brothers, pray for us. 26 Greet all the brothers with a holy kiss. 27 I charge you be-fore the Lord to have this letter read to all the brothers.

28 The grace of our Lord Jesus Christ be with you.

Greek Interlinear

ζήσωμεν.   11 Διὸ   παρακαλεῖτε   ἀλλήλους
¹we may live.   There-   comfort ye   one another
         fore

καὶ οἰκοδομεῖτε εἶς τὸν ἕνα, καθὼς καὶ
and   edify ye   one   the one(other),   as   indeed

ποιεῖτε.
ye do.

12 Ἐρωτῶμεν δὲ ὑμᾶς, ἀδελφοί, εἰδέναι
    Now we ask   you,   brothers,   to know

τοὺς κοπιῶντας ἐν ὑμῖν καὶ προϊσταμένους
the [ones] labouring among you   and   taking the lead

ὑμῶν ἐν κυρίῳ καὶ νουθετοῦντας ὑμᾶς,
of you   in   [the] Lord   and   admonishing   you,

13 καὶ ἡγεῖσθαι αὐτοὺς ὑπερεκπερισσῶς
and   consider   them   most exceedingly

ἐν ἀγάπῃ διὰ ΄ὸ ἔργον αὐτῶν. εἰρηνεύετε
in   love   be- the   work   of them.   Be at peace
      cause of

ἐν ἑαυτοῖς.   14 Παρακαλοῦμεν δὲ ὑμᾶς,
among yourselves.   And we exhort   you,

ἀδελφοί, νουθετεῖτε τοὺς ἀτάκτους, παρα-
brothers,   admonish   the   idle,   con-

μυθεῖσθε τοὺς ὀλιγοψύχους, ἀντέχεσθε τῶν
sole   the   faint-hearted,   hold on to   the
                                         [ones]

ἀσθενῶν, μακροθυμεῖτε πρὸς πάντας.
being weak,   be longsuffering   with   all men.

15 ὁρᾶτε μή τις κακὸν ἀντὶ κακοῦ τινι
See   lest anyone ²evil ⁴instead ⁵evil ²to
                    of

ἀποδῷ, ἀλλὰ πάντοτε τὸ ἀγαθὸν διώκετε
¹returns,   but   always ³the ²good ¹follow ye

εἰς ἀλλήλους καὶ εἰς πάντας.   16 Πάντοτε
in re-   one another   and   in re-   all men.   Always
gard to   gard to

χαίρετε, 17 ἀδιαλείπτως προσεύχεσθε, 18 ἐν
rejoice ye,   unceasingly   pray,   in

παντὶ εὐχαριστεῖτε· τοῦτο γὰρ θέλημα
everything   give thanks;   for this [is]   [the] will

θεοῦ ἐν Χριστῷ Ἰησοῦ εἰς ὑμᾶς.   19 τὸ
of God   in   Christ   Jesus in regard to you.   The

πνεῦμα μὴ σβέννυτε, 20 προφητείας μὴ
Spirit   do not quench,   prophecies   not

ἐξουθενεῖτε· 21 πάντα δὲ δοκιμάζετε, τὸ
despise;   and ²all things ¹prove,   the

καλὸν κατέχετε· 22 ἀπὸ παντὸς εἴδους
good   hold fast;   from   every   form

πονηροῦ ἀπέχεσθε.   23 Αὐτὸς δὲ ὁ θεὸς
of evil   abstain.   And ⁴[him]self ¹the ²God

τῆς εἰρήνης ἁγιάσαι ὑμᾶς ὁλοτελεῖς, καὶ
–   ²of peace may he sanctify you   complete,   and

ὁλόκληρον ὑμῶν τὸ πνεῦμα καὶ ἡ ψυχὴ
entire   of you   the   spirit   and   the   soul

καὶ τὸ σῶμα ἀμέμπτως ἐν τῇ παρουσίᾳ
and   the   body   blamelessly   in(at) the   presence

τοῦ κυρίου ἡμῶν Ἰησοῦ Χριστοῦ τηρηθείη.
of the Lord   of us   Jesus   Christ   may be kept.

24 πιστὸς ὁ καλῶν ὑμᾶς, ὃς καὶ ποιήσει.
Faithful [is] the [one] calling you, ˙ who indeed will do [it].

25 Ἀδελφοί, προσεύχεσθε [καὶ] περὶ
    Brothers,   pray ye   also   concerning

ἡμῶν.
us.

26 Ἀσπάσασθε τοὺς ἀδελφοὺς πάντας
    Greet ye   ²the   ³brothers ¹all

ἐν φιλήματι ἁγίῳ. 27 Ἐνορκίζω ὑμᾶς τὸν
with   kiss   a holy.   I adjure   you [by] the

κύριον ἀναγνωσθῆναι τὴν ἐπιστολὴν πᾶσιν
Lord   ²to be read ¹the(this) ²epistle   to all

τοῖς ἀδελφοῖς.
the   brothers.

28 Ἡ χάρις τοῦ κυρίου ἡμῶν Ἰησοῦ
    The   grace   of the   Lord   of us   Jesus

Χριστοῦ μεθ' ὑμῶν.
Christ   [be] with   you.

King James Version

New International Version

THE SECOND EPISTLE

OF PAUL THE APOSTLE

TO THE

THESSALONIANS

2 THESSALONIANS

1 Paul, and Silvanus, and Timotheus, unto the church of the Thessalonians in God our Father and the Lord Jesus Christ: 2 Grace unto you, and peace, from God our Father and the Lord Jesus Christ. 3 We are bound to thank God always for you, brethren, as it is meet, because that your faith groweth exceedingly, and the charity of every one of you all toward each other aboundeth; 4 So that we ourselves glory in you in the churches of God, for your patience and faith in all your persecutions and tribulations that ye endure: 5 *Which is* a manifest token of the righteous judgment of God, that ye may be counted worthy of the kingdom of God, for which ye also suffer: 6 Seeing *it is* a righteous thing with God to · recompense tribulation to them that trouble you; 7 And to you who are troubled rest with us, when the Lord Jesus shall be revealed from heaven with his mighty angels, 8 In flaming fire taking vengeance on them that know not God, and that obey not the gospel of our Lord Jesus Christ: 9 Who shall be punished with everlasting destruction from the presence of the Lord, and from the glory of his power; 10 When he shall come to be glorified in his saints, and to be admired in all them that believe (because our testimony among you was believed) in that day. 11 Wherefore also we pray always for you, that our God would count you worthy of *this* calling, and fulfil all the good pleasure of *his* goodness, and the work of faith with power: 12 That the name of our Lord Jesus Christ may be glorified in you, and ye in him, according to the grace of our God and the Lord Jesus Christ.

1 Paul, Silas[a] and Timothy,
To the church of the Thessalonians, who are in God our Father and the Lord Jesus Christ:
2 Grace and peace to you from God the Father and the Lord Jesus Christ.

Thanksgiving and prayer

3 We ought always to thank God for you, brothers, and rightly so, because your faith is growing more and more, and the love every one of you has for each other is increasing. 4 Therefore, among God's churches we boast about your perseverance and faith in all the persecutions and trials you are enduring.
5 All this is evidence that God's judgment is right, and as a result you will be counted worthy of the kingdom of God, for which you are suffering. 6 God is just: He will pay back trouble to those who trouble you 7 and give relief to you who are troubled, and to us as well. This will happen when the Lord Jesus is revealed from heaven in blazing fire with his powerful angels. 8 He will punish those who do not know God and do not obey the gospel of our Lord Jesus. 9 They will be punished with everlasting destruction and shut out from the presence of the Lord and from the majesty of his power 10 on the day he comes to be glorified in his holy people and to be marveled at among all those who have believed. This includes you, because you believed our testimony to you.
11 With this in mind, we constantly pray for you, that our God may count you worthy of his calling, and that by his power he may fulfill every good purpose of yours and every act prompted by your faith. 12 We pray this so that the name of our Lord Jesus may be glorified in you, and you in him, according to the grace of our God and the Lord Jesus Christ.[b]

The man of lawlessness

2 Now we beseech you, brethren, by the coming of our Lord Jesus Christ, and *by* our gathering together unto him, 2 That ye be not soon shaken in mind, or be troubled, neither by spirit, nor by word, nor by letter as from us, as that the day of Christ is at hand. 3 Let no man deceive you by any means: for *that day shall not come*, except there come a falling away first, and

2 Concerning the coming of our Lord Jesus Christ and our being gathered to him, we ask you, brothers, 2 not to become easily unsettled or alarmed by some prophecy, report or letter supposed to have come from us, saying that the day of the Lord has already come. 3 Don't let anyone deceive you in any way, for [that day will not come] until the rebellion oc-

[a] Greek *Silvanus*. [b] Or *our God and Lord Jesus Christ.*

ΠΡΟΣ   ΘΕΣΣΑΛΟΝΙΚΕΙΣ Β

Chapter 1

Παῦλος καὶ Σιλουανὸς καὶ Τιμόθεος
Paul   and   Silvanus   and   Timothy

τῇ ἐκκλησίᾳ Θεσσαλονικέων ἐν θεῷ πατρὶ
to the church of [the] Thessalonians in God Father

ἡμῶν καὶ κυρίῳ Ἰησοῦ Χριστῷ· 2 χάρις
of us and [the] Lord Jesus Christ: Grace [be]

ὑμῖν καὶ εἰρήνη ἀπὸ θεοῦ πατρὸς καὶ
to you and peace from God [the] Father and

κυρίου Ἰησοῦ Χριστοῦ.
[the] Lord Jesus Christ.

3 Εὐχαριστεῖν ὀφείλομεν τῷ θεῷ πάντοτε
To give thanks we ought - to God always

περὶ ὑμῶν, ἀδελφοί, καθὼς ἄξιόν ἐστιν,
con- you, brothers, as ²meet ¹it is,
cerning

ὅτι ὑπεραυξάνει ἡ πίστις ὑμῶν καὶ
because ²grows ¹the ²faith ³of you and
exceedingly

πλεονάζει ἡ ἀγάπη ἑνὸς ἑκάστου πάντων
²increases ¹the ²love ³one ⁴of each ⁵all

ὑμῶν εἰς ἀλλήλους, 4 ὥστε αὐτοὺς ἡμᾶς
⁶of you ⁷to ⁸one another, so as us
=so that we ourselves boast

ἐν ὑμῖν ἐγκαυχᾶσθαι ἐν ταῖς ἐκκλησίαις
in you to boastᵇ in the churches
in you

τοῦ θεοῦ ὑπὲρ τῆς ὑπομονῆς ὑμῶν καὶ
- of God for the ¹endurance ²of you ³and

πίστεως ἐν πᾶσιν τοῖς διωγμοῖς ὑμῶν
⁴faith in all the persecutions of you

καὶ ταῖς θλίψεσιν αἷς ἀνέχεσθε, 5 ἔνδειγμα
and the afflictions which ye endure, a plain token

τῆς δικαίας κρίσεως τοῦ θεοῦ, εἰς τὸ
of the just judgment - of God, for the

καταξιωθῆναι ὑμᾶς τῆς βασιλείας τοῦ
to be accounted youᵇ of the kingdom -
worthy
=so that ye may be accounted worthy

θεοῦ, ὑπὲρ ἧς καὶ πάσχετε, 6 εἴπερ
of God, on behalf which indeed ye suffer, since
         of

δίκαιον παρὰ θεῷ ἀνταποδοῦναι τοῖς
[it is] a just with God to repay ²to the
thing   [ones]

θλίβουσιν ὑμᾶς θλῖψιν 7 καὶ ὑμῖν τοῖς
³afflicting ⁴you ¹affliction and ⁴to you ⁵the
                                                [ones]

θλιβομένοις ἄνεσιν μεθ' ἡμῶν, ἐν τῇ
⁶being afflicted ¹rest ²with ³us, at the

ἀποκαλύψει τοῦ κυρίου Ἰησοῦ ἀπ'
revelation of the Lord Jesus from

οὐρανοῦ μετ' ἀγγέλων δυνάμεως αὐτοῦ
heaven with angels of power of him

8 ἐν πυρὶ φλογός, διδόντος ἐκδίκησιν τοῖς
in fire of flame, giving full vengeance to the
                                                [ones]

μὴ εἰδόσιν θεὸν καὶ τοῖς μὴ ὑπακούουσιν
not knowing God and to the not obeying
                              [ones]

τῷ εὐαγγελίῳ τοῦ κυρίου ἡμῶν Ἰησοῦ,
the gospel of the Lord of us Jesus,

9 οἵτινες δίκην τίσουσιν ὄλεθρον αἰώνιον
who ²[the] penalty ¹will pay ⁴destruction ³eternal

ἀπὸ προσώπου τοῦ κυρίου καὶ ἀπὸ
from [the] face of the Lord and from

τῆς δόξης τῆς ἰσχύος αὐτοῦ, 10 ὅταν
the glory of the strength of him, whenever

ἔλθῃ ἐνδοξασθῆναι ἐν τοῖς ἁγίοις αὐτοῦ
he comes to be glorified in the saints of him

καὶ θαυμασθῆναι ἐν πᾶσιν τοῖς πιστεύσασιν,
and to be admired in all the [ones] having believed,

ὅτι ἐπιστεύθη τὸ μαρτύριον ἡμῶν ἐφ'
be- ⁴was believed ¹the ²testimony ³of us ⁵to
cause

ὑμᾶς, ἐν τῇ ἡμέρᾳ ἐκείνῃ. 11 Εἰς ὃ
⁶you, in the day that day. For which

καὶ προσευχόμεθα πάντοτε περὶ ὑμῶν,
indeed we pray always concerning you,

ἵνα ὑμᾶς ἀξιώσῃ τῆς κλήσεως ὁ θεὸς
in or- ²you ¹may ²deem ³of the ⁴calling ¹the ²God
der that   ⁴worthy

ἡμῶν καὶ πληρώσῃ πᾶσαν εὐδοκίαν
³of us and may fulfil every good pleasure

ἀγαθωσύνης καὶ ἔργον πίστεως ἐν δυνάμει,
of goodness and work of faith in power,

12 ὅπως ἐνδοξασθῇ τὸ ὄνομα τοῦ κυρίου
so as ⁷may be glorified ¹the ²name ³of the ⁴Lord

ἡμῶν Ἰησοῦ ἐν ὑμῖν, καὶ ὑμεῖς ἐν
⁵of us ⁶Jesus in you, and ye in

αὐτῷ, κατὰ τὴν χάριν τοῦ θεοῦ ἡμῶν
him, according to the grace of the ¹God ²of us

καὶ κυρίου Ἰησοῦ Χριστοῦ.
³and ⁴Lord Jesus Christ.

Chapter 2

Ἐρωτῶμεν δὲ ὑμᾶς, ἀδελφοί, ὑπὲρ
Now we request you, brothers, by

τῆς παρουσίας τοῦ κυρίου [ἡμῶν] Ἰησοῦ
the presence of the Lord of us Jesus

Χριστοῦ καὶ ἡμῶν ἐπισυναγωγῆς ἐπ' αὐτόν,
Christ and ²of us ¹gathering together to him,

2 εἰς τὸ μὴ ταχέως σαλευθῆναι ὑμᾶς
- the not quickly to be shaken youᵇ

ἀπὸ τοῦ νοὸς μηδὲ θροεῖσθαι, μήτε
from the(your) mind nor to be disturbed, neither

διὰ πνεύματος μήτε διὰ λόγου μήτε
through a spirit nor through speech nor

δι' ἐπιστολῆς ὡς δι' ἡμῶν, ὡς ὅτι
through an epistle as through us, as that

ἐνέστηκεν ἡ ἡμέρα τοῦ κυρίου. 3 μή
¹is come ¹the ²day ³of the ⁴Lord. Not

τις ὑμᾶς ἐξαπατήσῃ κατὰ μηδένα τρόπον·
anyone ²you ¹may deceive by(in) no(any) way;

ὅτι ἐὰν μὴ ἔλθῃ ἡ ἀποστασία πρῶτον
because unless ²comes ¹the ²apostasy ¹firstly

King James Version

that man of sin be revealed, the son of perdition; 4 Who opposeth and exalteth himself above all that is called God, or that is worshipped; so that he as God sitteth in the temple of God, shewing himself that he is God. 5 Remember ye not, that, when I was yet with you, I told you these things? 6And now ye know what withholdeth that he might be revealed in his time. 7 For the mystery of iniquity doth already work: only he who now letteth *will let*, until he be taken out of the way. 8And then shall that Wicked be revealed, whom the Lord shall consume with the spirit of his mouth, and shall destroy with the brightness of his coming: 9 *Even him*, whose coming is after the working of Satan with all power and signs and lying wonders, 10And with all deceivableness of unrighteousness in them that perish; because they received not the love of the truth, that they might be saved. 11And for this cause God shall send them strong delusion, that they should believe a lie: 12 That they all might be damned who believed not the truth, but had pleasure in unrighteousness. 13 But we are bound to give thanks always to God for you, brethren beloved of the Lord, because God hath from the beginning chosen you to salvation through sanctification of the Spirit and belief of the truth: 14 Whereunto he called you by our gospel, to the obtaining of the glory of our Lord Jesus Christ. 15 Therefore, brethren, stand fast, and hold the traditions which ye have been taught, whether by word, or our epistle. 16 Now our Lord Jesus Christ himself, and God, even our Father, which hath loved us, and hath given *us* everlasting consolation and good hope through grace, 17 Comfort your hearts, and stablish you in every good word and work.

3 Finally, brethren, pray for us, that the word of the Lord may have *free* course, and be glorified, even as *it is* with you: 2And that we may be delivered from unreasonable and wicked men: for all *men* have not faith. 3 But the Lord is faithful, who shall stablish you, and keep *you* from evil. 4And we have confidence in the Lord touching you, that ye both do and will do the things which we command you. 5And the Lord direct your hearts into the love of God, and into the patient waiting for Christ. 6 Now we command you, brethren, in the name of our Lord Jesus Christ, that ye withdraw yourselves

New International Version

curs and the man of lawlessness[c] is revealed, the man doomed to destruction. 4 He opposes and exalts himself over everything that is called God or is worshiped, and even sets himself up in God's temple, proclaiming himself to be God.
5 Don't you remember that when I was with you I used to tell you these things? 6And now you know what is holding him back, so that he may be revealed at the proper time. 7 For the secret power of lawlessness is already at work; but the one who now holds it back will continue to do so till he is taken out of the way. 8And then the lawless one will be revealed, whom the Lord Jesus will overthrow with the breath of his mouth and destroy by the splendor of his coming. 9 The coming of the lawless one will be in accordance with the work of Satan displayed in all kinds of counterfeit miracles, signs and wonders, 10 and in every sort of evil that deceives those who are perishing. They perish because they refused to love the truth and so be saved. 11 For this reason God sends them a powerful delusion so that they will believe the lie and 12 so that all will be condemned who have not believed the truth but have delighted in wickedness.

Stand firm

13 But we ought always to thank God for you, brothers loved by the Lord, because from the beginning God chose you[d] to be saved through the sanctifying work of the Spirit and through belief in the truth. 14 He called you to this through our gospel, that you might share in the glory of our Lord Jesus Christ. 15 So then, brothers, stand firm and hold to the teachings[e] we passed on to you, whether by word of mouth or by letter.
16 May our Lord Jesus Christ himself and God our Father, who loved us and by his grace gave us eternal encouragement and good hope, 17 encourage and strengthen you in every good deed and word.

Request for prayer

3 Finally, brothers, pray for us that the message of the Lord may spread rapidly and be honored, just as it was with you. 2And pray that we may be delivered from wicked and evil men, for not everyone has faith. 3 But the Lord is faithful, and he will strengthen and protect you from the evil one. 4 We have confidence in the Lord that you are doing and will continue to do the things we command. 5 May the Lord direct your hearts into God's love and Christ's perseverance.

Warning against idleness

6 In the name of the Lord Jesus Christ, we command you, brothers, to keep away from

[c] Many early MSS read *man of sin*. [d] Some early textual sources read *because God chose you as his first fruits* [e] Or *traditions*.

Greek Interlinear

καὶ ἀποκαλυφθῇ ὁ ἄνθρωπος τῆς ἀνομίας,
and ⁴is revealed ¹the ²man - ³of lawlessness,

ὁ υἱὸς τῆς ἀπωλείας, 4 ὁ ἀντικείμενος
the son - of perdition, the [one] setting against

καὶ ὑπεραιρόμενος ἐπὶ πάντα λεγόμενον
and exalting himself over everything being called

θεὸν ἢ σέβασμα, ὥστε αὐτὸν εἰς τὸν
God or object of worship, so as him in the

ναὸν τοῦ θεοῦ καθίσαι, ἀποδεικνύντα ἑαυ-
shrine - of God to sit,ᵇ showing him-

τὸν ὅτι ἐστὶν θεός. 5 Οὐ μνημονεύετε
self that he is a god. Do ye not remember

ὅτι ἔτι ὢν πρὸς ὑμᾶς ταῦτα ἔλεγον
that yet being with you ²these ¹I used
      things to tell

ὑμῖν; 6 καὶ νῦν τὸ κατέχον οἴδατε,
²you? and now the restraining ye know,
      [thing]

εἰς τὸ ἀποκαλυφθῆναι αὐτὸν ἐν τῷ
for the ²to be revealed ¹himᵇ in the

αὐτοῦ καιρῷ. 7 τὸ γὰρ μυστήριον ἤδη
²of him ¹time. For the mystery ³already

ἐνεργεῖται τῆς ἀνομίας· μόνον ὁ κατέχων
²operates - ¹of lawless- only the restraining
      ness; [there is] [one]

ἄρτι ἕως ἐκ μέσου γένηται. 8 καὶ τότε
just now until ⁴out of ²[the] midst ¹it comes. And then

ἀποκαλυφθήσεται ὁ ἄνομος, ὃν ὁ κύριος
will be revealed the lawless whom the Lord
      one,

['Ιησοῦς] ἀνελεῖ τῷ πνεύματι τοῦ στό-
Jesus will destroy by the spirit of the mouth

ματος αὐτοῦ καὶ καταργήσει τῇ ἐπιφανείᾳ
of him and bring to nothing by the outshining

τῆς παρουσίας αὐτοῦ, 9 οὗ ἐστιν ἡ
of the presence of him, of whom ²is ¹the

παρουσία κατ' ἐνέργειαν τοῦ σατανᾶ ἐν
²presence according operation - of Satan with
to [the]

πάσῃ δυνάμει καὶ σημείοις καὶ τέρασιν
all power and signs and wonders

ψεύδους 10 καὶ ἐν πάσῃ ἀπάτῃ ἀδικίας
of a lie and with all deceit of unright-
      eousness

τοῖς ἀπολλυμένοις, ἀνθ' ὧν τὴν ἀγάπην
in the [ones] perishing, because the love

τῆς ἀληθείας οὐκ ἐδέξαντο εἰς τὸ σωθῆναι.
of the truth they received not for the ²to be saved

αὐτούς. 11 καὶ διὰ τοῦτο πέμπει αὐτοῖς
¹them.ᵇ And therefore ²sends ¹to them

ὁ θεὸς ἐνέργειαν πλάνης εἰς τὸ πιστεῦσαι
- ¹God an operation of error for the ²to believe

αὐτοὺς τῷ ψεύδει, 12 ἵνα κριθῶσιν πάντες
¹themᵇ the lie, in or- ¹⁰may be ¹all
      der that judged

οἱ μὴ πιστεύσαντες τῇ ἀληθείᾳ ἀλλὰ
²the ³not ⁴having believed ⁵the ⁶truth ⁷but
[ones]

εὐδοκήσαντες τῇ ἀδικίᾳ.
⁸having had pleasure - ⁹in unrighteousness.

13 'Ημεῖς δὲ ὀφείλομεν εὐχαριστεῖν τῷ
But we ought to thank -

θεῷ πάντοτε περὶ ὑμῶν, ἀδελφοὶ ἠγαπη-
God always concerning you, brothers having been

μένοι ὑπὸ κυρίου, ὅτι εἵλατο ὑμᾶς ὁ
loved by [the] Lord, because ²chose ³you -

θεὸς ἀπαρχὴν εἰς σωτηρίαν ἐν ἁγιασμῷ
¹God firstfruit to salvation by sanctification

πνεύματος καὶ πίστει ἀληθείας, 14 εἰς
of spirit and faith of(in) [the] truth, to

ὃ καὶ ἐκάλεσεν ὑμᾶς διὰ τοῦ εὐαγγελίου
which also he called you through the gospel

ἡμῶν, εἰς περιποίησιν δόξης τοῦ κυρίου
of us, to obtainment of [the] glory of the Lord

ἡμῶν 'Ιησοῦ Χριστοῦ. 15 "Αρα οὖν,
of us Jesus Christ. So then,

ἀδελφοί, στήκετε, καὶ κρατεῖτε τὰς
brothers, stand, and hold the

παραδόσεις ἃς ἐδιδάχθητε εἴτε διὰ λόγου
traditions which ye were taught either through speech

εἴτε δι' ἐπιστολῆς ἡμῶν. 16 Αὐτὸς δὲ
or through an epistle of us. And ²[him]self

ὁ κύριος ἡμῶν 'Ιησοῦς Χριστὸς καὶ
¹the ³Lord ²of us ⁴Jesus ⁵Christ and

ὁ θεὸς ὁ πατὴρ ἡμῶν, ὁ ἀγαπήσας
the God the Father of us, the [one] having loved

ἡμᾶς καὶ δοὺς παράκλησιν αἰωνίαν καὶ
us and having given ⁶comfort ¹eternal and

ἐλπίδα ἀγαθὴν ἐν χάριτι, 17 παρακαλέσαι
²hope ⁴a good by grace, may he comfort

ὑμῶν τὰς καρδίας καὶ στηρίξαι ἐν παντὶ
of you the hearts and may he in every
      confirm

ἔργῳ καὶ λόγῳ ἀγαθῷ.
²work ³and ⁴word ¹good.

Chapter 3

Τὸ λοιπὸν προσεύχεσθε, ἀδελφοί, περὶ
For the rest pray ye, brothers, con-
      cerning

ἡμῶν, ἵνα ὁ λόγος τοῦ κυρίου τρέχῃ
us, in or- the word of the Lord may run
der that

καὶ δοξάζηται καθὼς καὶ πρὸς ὑμᾶς,
and be glorified as indeed with you,

2 καὶ ἵνα ρυσθῶμεν ἀπὸ τῶν ἀτόπων
and in or- we may be from - perverse
der that delivered

καὶ πονηρῶν ἀνθρώπων· οὐ γὰρ πάντων
and evil men; for ²[is] not ⁴of all men

ἡ πίστις. 3 Πιστὸς δέ ἐστιν ὁ κύριος,
¹the ³faith. But faithful is the Lord,

ὃς στηρίξει ὑμᾶς καὶ φυλάξει ἀπὸ τοῦ
who will confirm you and will guard from the

πονηροῦ. 4 πεποίθαμεν δὲ ἐν κυρίῳ
evil [?one]. And we are persuaded in [the] Lord

ἐφ' ὑμᾶς, ὅτι ἃ παραγγέλλομεν [καὶ]
as to you, that what we charge both
      things

ποιεῖτε καὶ ποιήσετε. 5 Ὁ δὲ κύριος
ye do and will do. And ²the ¹Lord

κατευθύναι ὑμῶν τὰς καρδίας εἰς τὴν
¹may ⁴direct ²of you ⁵the ⁶hearts into the

ἀγάπην τοῦ θεοῦ καὶ εἰς τὴν ὑπομονὴν
love - of God and into the patience

τοῦ Χριστοῦ.
- of Christ.

6 Παραγγέλλομεν δὲ ὑμῖν, ἀδελφοί, ἐν
Now we charge you, brothers, in

ὀνόματι τοῦ κυρίου 'Ιησοῦ Χριστοῦ,
[the] name of the Lord Jesus Christ,

στέλλεσθαι ὑμᾶς ἀπὸ παντὸς ἀδελφοῦ
to draw back youᵇ from every brother

King James Version

from every brother that walketh disorderly, and not after the tradition which he received of us. 7 For yourselves know how ye ought to follow us: for we behaved not ourselves disorderly among you; 8 Neither did we eat any man's bread for nought; but wrought with labour and travail night and day, that we might not be chargeable to any of you: 9 Not because we have not power, but to make ourselves an ensample unto you to follow us. 10 For even when we were with you, this we commanded you, that if any would not work, neither should he eat. 11 For we hear that there are some which walk among you disorderly, working not at all, but are busybodies. 12 Now them that are such we command and exhort by our Lord Jesus Christ, that with quietness they work, and eat their own bread. 13 But ye, brethren, be not weary in well doing. 14And if any man obey not our word by this epistle, note that man, and have no company with him, that he may be ashamed. 15 Yet count *him* not as an enemy, but admonish *him* as a brother. 16 Now the Lord of peace himself give you peace always by all means. The Lord *be* with you all. 17 The salutation of Paul with mine own hand, which is the token in every epistle: so I write. 18 The grace of our Lord Jesus Christ *be* with you all. Amen.

The second *epistle* to the Thessalonians was written from Athens.

New International Version

every brother who is idle and does not live according to the teaching[f] you received from us. 7 For you yourselves know how you ought to follow our example. We were not idle when we were with you, 8 nor did we eat anyone's food without paying for it. On the contrary, we worked night and day, laboring and toiling so that we would not be a burden to any of you. 9 We did this, not because we do not have the right to such help, but in order to make ourselves a model for you to follow. 10 For even when we were with you, we gave you this rule: "If a man will not work, he shall not eat."

11 We hear that some among you are idle. They are not busy; they are busybodies. 12 In the name of the Lord Jesus Christ, we command and urge such people to settle down and earn the bread they eat. 13And as for you, brothers, never tire of doing what is right.

14 If anyone does not obey our instruction in this letter, take special note of him. Do not associate with him, in order that he may feel ashamed. 15 Yet do not regard him as an enemy, but warn him as a brother.

Final greetings

16 Now may the Lord of peace himself give you peace at all times and in every way. The Lord be with all of you.

17 I, Paul, write this greeting in my own hand, which is the distinguishing mark in all my letters. This is how I write.

18 The grace of our Lord Jesus Christ be with you all.

[f] Or *tradition.*

610

Greek Interlinear

ἀτάκτως περιπατοῦντος καὶ μὴ κατὰ τὴν
²idly   ¹walking   and not accord- the
                                    ing to

παράδοσιν ἣν παρελάβετε παρ' ἡμῶν.
tradition which ye received from   us.

7 αὐτοὶ γὰρ οἴδατε πῶς δεῖ μιμεῖσθαι
For [your]selves ye know how it be- to imitate
                                   hoves

ἡμᾶς, ὅτι οὐκ ἠτακτήσαμεν ἐν ὑμῖν,
us,   because we were not idle among you,

8 οὐδὲ δωρεὰν ἄρτον ἐφάγομεν παρά τινος,
nor ²[as] a gift ¹bread ᵃate   ¹from ⁴anyone,

ἀλλ' ἐν κόπῳ καὶ μόχθῳ νυκτὸς καὶ
but by labour and struggle by night and

ἡμέρας ἐργαζόμενοι πρὸς τὸ μὴ ἐπιβαρῆσαί
by day working   for the not to emburden

τινα ὑμῶν· 9 οὐχ ὅτι οὐκ ἔχομεν
anyone of you;   not that we have not

ἐξουσίαν, ἀλλ' ἵνα ἑαυτοὺς τύπον δῶμεν
authority, but in or- ¹our-   ²an ¹we might
               der that selves example give

ὑμῖν εἰς τὸ μιμεῖσθαι ἡμᾶς, 10 καὶ
to you for the to imitate us.   even

γὰρ ὅτε ἦμεν πρὸς ὑμᾶς, τοῦτο παρηγ-
For when we were with you, this   we

γέλλομεν ὑμῖν, ὅτι εἴ τις οὐ θέλει
charged you, that if anyone does not wish

ἐργάζεσθαι, μηδὲ ἐσθιέτω. 11 ἀκούομεν
to work,   neither let him eat. we hear [of]

γὰρ τινας περιπατοῦντας ἐν ὑμῖν ἀτάκτως,
For some   walking   among you idly,

μηδὲν ἐργαζομένους ἀλλὰ περιεργαζομένους·
nothing working   but   working round;

12 τοῖς δὲ τοιούτοις παραγγέλλομεν καὶ
- and to such   we charge   and

παρακαλοῦμεν ἐν κυρίῳ Ἰησοῦ Χριστῷ
exhort   in [the] Lord Jesus Christ

ἵνα μετὰ ἡσυχίας ἐργαζόμενοι τὸν
in or- ¹with ²quietness ¹working   ⁵the
der that

ἑαυτῶν ἄρτον ἐσθίωσιν. 13 Ὑμεῖς δέ,
⁷of them- ⁶bread ⁴they may eat.   And ye,
selves

ἀδελφοί, μὴ ἐγκακήσητε καλοποιοῦντες
brothers, do not lose heart   doing good.

14 εἰ δέ τις οὐχ ὑπακούει τῷ λόγῳ
And if anyone obeys not   the word

ἡμῶν διὰ τῆς ἐπιστολῆς, τοῦτον σημειοῦσθε,
of us through the epistle,   this man mark,

μὴ συναναμίγνυσθαι αὐτῷ, ἵνα ἐντραπῇ·
not to mix with*   him, in or- he may be put
                          der that to shame;

15 καὶ μὴ ὡς ἐχθρὸν ἡγεῖσθε, ἀλλὰ
and yet not as an enemy deem ye [him], but

νουθετεῖτε ὡς ἀδελφόν. 16 Αὐτὸς δὲ
admonish as a brother.   And ⁴[him]self

ὁ κύριος τῆς εἰρήνης δῴη ὑμῖν τὴν
¹the ²Lord - ³of peace may be to you the
                          give   (?his)

εἰρήνην διὰ παντὸς ἐν παντὶ τρόπῳ.
peace   always   in every way.

ὁ κύριος μετὰ πάντων ὑμῶν.
The Lord [be] with ²all ¹you.

17 Ὁ ἀσπασμὸς τῇ ἐμῇ χειρὶ Παύλου,
The greeting - by my hand[,] of Paul,

ὃ ἐστιν σημεῖον ἐν πάσῃ ἐπιστολῇ·
which is   a sign   in every epistle:

οὕτως γράφω. 18 ἡ χάρις τοῦ κυρίου
thus I write.   The grace of the Lord

ἡμῶν Ἰησοῦ Χριστοῦ μετὰ πάντων ὑμῶν.
of us Jesus Christ [be] with ²all ¹you.

---

* Imperative infinitive, as elsewhere (Phil. 3. 16. etc.),

King James Version

New International Version

THE FIRST EPISTLE
OF PAUL THE APOSTLE
TO
TIMOTHY

1 TIMOTHY

1 Paul, an apostle of Jesus Christ by the commandment of God our Saviour, and Lord Jesus Christ, *which is* our hope; 2 Unto Timothy, *my* own son in the faith: Grace, mercy, *and* peace, from God our Father, and Jesus Christ our Lord. 3As I besought thee to abide still at Ephesus, when I went into Macedonia, that thou mightest charge some that they teach no other doctrine, 4 Neither give heed to fables and endless genealogies, which minister questions, rather than godly edifying which is in faith: *so do.* 5 Now the end of the commandment is charity out of a pure heart, and *of* a good conscience, and *of* faith unfeigned: 6 From which some having swerved have turned aside unto vain jangling; 7 Desiring to be teachers of the law; understanding neither what they say, nor whereof they affirm. 8 But we know that the law *is* good, if a man use it lawfully; 9 Knowing this, that the law is not made for a righteous man, but for the lawless and disobedient, for the ungodly and for sinners, for unholy and profane, for murderers of fathers and murderers of mothers, for manslayers, 10 For whoremongers, for them that defile themselves with mankind, for menstealers, for liars, for perjured persons, and if there be any other thing that is contrary to sound doctrine; 11According to the glorious gospel of the blessed God, which was committed to my trust. 12And I thank Christ Jesus our Lord, who hath enabled me, for that he counted me faithful, putting me into the ministry; 13 Who was before a blasphemer, and a persecutor, and injurious: but I obtained mercy, because I did *it* ignorantly in unbelief. 14And the grace of our Lord was exceeding abundant with faith and love which is in Christ Jesus. 15 This *is* a faithful saying, and worthy of all acceptation, that Christ Jesus came into the world to save sinners; of whom I am chief. 16 Howbeit for this cause I obtained mercy, that in me first Jesus Christ might shew forth all longsuffering, for a pattern to them which should hereafter believe on him to life everlasting. 17 Now unto the King eternal, immortal, invisible, the only wise God, *be* honour and glory for ever and ever. Amen. 18 This charge I commit unto thee, son Timothy, according to the prophecies which went before on thee, that thou by them mightest war a good warfare; 19 Holding faith, and a good conscience; which some having put away, concern-

1 Paul, an apostle of Christ Jesus by the command of God our Savior and of Christ Jesus our hope,
2 To Timothy my true son in the faith:
Grace, mercy and peace from God the Father and Christ Jesus our Lord.

Warning against false teachers of the law

3 As I urged you when I went into Macedonia, stay there in Ephesus so that you may command certain men not to teach false doctrines any longer 4 nor to devote themselves to myths and endless genealogies. These promote controversies rather than God's work—which is by faith. 5 The goal of this command is love, which comes from a pure heart, a good conscience and a sincere faith. 6 Some have wandered away from these and turned to meaningless talk. 7 They want to be teachers of the law, but they do not know what they are talking about or what they so confidently affirm.

8 We know that the law is good if a man uses it properly. 9 We also know that law is made not for good men, but for lawbreakers and rebels, the ungodly and sinful, the unholy and irreligious; for those who kill their fathers or mothers, for murderers, 10 for adulterers and perverts, for slave traders and liars and perjurers —and for whatever else is contrary to the sound doctrine 11 that conforms to the glorious gospel of the blessed God, which he entrusted to me.

The Lord's grace to Paul

12 I thank Christ Jesus our Lord, who has given me strength, that he considered me faithful, appointing me to his service. 13 Even though I was once a blasphemer and a persecutor and a violent man, I was shown mercy because I acted in ignorance and unbelief. 14 The grace of our Lord was poured out on me abundantly, along with the faith and love that are in Christ Jesus.
15 Here is a trustworthy saying that deserves full acceptance: Christ Jesus came into the world to save sinners—of whom I am the worst. 16 But for that very reason I was shown mercy so that in me, the worst of sinners, Christ Jesus might display his unlimited patience as an example for those who would believe on him and receive eternal life. 17 Now to the King eternal, immortal, invisible, the only God, be honor and glory for ever and ever. Amen.
18 Timothy, my son, I give you this instruction in keeping with the prophecies once made about you, so that by following them you may fight the good fight, 19 holding on to faith and a good conscience. Some have rejected these and

ΠΡΟΣ   ΤΙΜΟΘΕΟΝ Α
Chapter 1

Παῦλος ἀπόστολος Χριστοῦ Ἰησοῦ κατ'
Paul   an apostle of Christ Jesus accord-
                                     ing to

ἐπιταγὴν θεοῦ σωτῆρος ἡμῶν καὶ Χριστοῦ
a command of God Saviour of us and of Christ

Ἰησοῦ τῆς ἐλπίδος ἡμῶν 2 Τιμοθέῳ
Jesus the hope   of us   to Timothy

γνησίῳ τέκνῳ ἐν πίστει· χάρις, ἔλεος,
a true child in [the] faith: Grace, mercy,

εἰρήνη ἀπὸ θεοῦ πατρὸς καὶ Χριστοῦ
peace from God [the] Father and Christ

Ἰησοῦ τοῦ κυρίου ἡμῶν.
Jesus the Lord   of us.

3 Καθὼς παρεκάλεσά σε προσμεῖναι ἐν
As   I besought   thee to remain   in

Ἐφέσῳ, πορευόμενος εἰς Μακεδονίαν, ἵνα
Ephesus, [I] going   into Macedonia,   in or-
                                       der that

παραγγείλῃς τισὶν μὴ ἑτεροδιδασκαλεῖν
thou mightest certain not to teach differently
charge   persons

4 μηδὲ προσέχειν μύθοις καὶ γενεαλογίαις
nor to pay attention to tales and to ¹genealogies

ἀπεράντοις, αἵτινες ἐκζητήσεις παρέχουσιν
¹unending, which ²questionings ¹provide

μᾶλλον ἢ οἰκονομίαν θεοῦ τὴν ἐν πίστει·
rather than a stewardship of God the in faith:

5 τὸ δὲ τέλος τῆς παραγγελίας ἐστὶν
now the end of the charge   is

ἀγάπη ἐκ καθαρᾶς καρδίας καὶ συνειδήσεως
love out of a clean heart   and conscience

ἀγαθῆς καὶ πίστεως ἀνυποκρίτου, 6 ὧν
a good and faith   unfeigned, from which
                                         things

τινες ἀστοχήσαντες ἐξετράπησαν εἰς
some missing aim   turned aside   to

ματαιολογίαν, 7 θέλοντες εἶναι νομοδιδάσ-
vain talking,   wishing to be   law-

καλοι, μὴ νοοῦντες μήτε ἃ λέγουσιν
teachers, not understanding either what things they say

μήτε περὶ τίνων διαβεβαιοῦνται. 8 οἴδαμεν
nor concerning what things they emphatically assert. we know

δὲ ὅτι καλὸς ὁ νόμος, ἐάν τις αὐτῷ
Now that ¹[is] ⁴good ¹the   ²law, if anyone ¹it

νομίμως χρῆται, 9 εἰδὼς τοῦτο, ὅτι
³lawfully ¹uses,   knowing this,   that

δικαίῳ νόμος οὐ κεῖται, ἀνόμοις δὲ
²for a just ¹law ²is not laid down, but for lawless men
man

καὶ ἀνυποτάκτοις, ἀσεβέσι καὶ ἁμαρτωλοῖς,
and for unruly,   for impious and for sinners,

ἀνοσίοις καὶ βεβήλοις, πατρολώαις καὶ
for unholy and for profane, for parricides and

μητρολώαις, ἀνδροφόνοις, 10 πόρνοις, ἀρ-
for matricides, for menkillers, for fornicators, for

σενοκοίταις, ἀνδραποδισταῖς, ψεύσταις, ἐπιόρ-
paedearsts,   for mensteallers,   for liars,   for per-

κοις, καὶ εἴ τι ἕτερον τῇ ὑγιαινούσῃ
jurers. and if any other thing ¹to the ²being healthful

διδασκαλίᾳ ἀντίκειται, 11 κατὰ τὸ εὐαγ-
⁴teaching ¹opposes, according to the gos-

γέλιον τῆς δόξης τοῦ μακαρίου θεοῦ,
pel   of the glory   of the blessed   God,

ὃ ἐπιστεύθην ἐγώ. 12 Χάριν ἔχω τῷ
which ²was entrusted ¹I.   Thanks I have to the
[with]

ἐνδυναμώσαντί με Χριστῷ Ἰησοῦ τῷ κυρίῳ
[one] empowering me Christ   Jesus the Lord

ἡμῶν, ὅτι πιστόν με ἡγήσατο θέμενος
of us, because ²faithful ³me ¹he deemed putting [me]

εἰς διακονίαν, 13 τὸ πρότερον ὄντα
into [the] ministry,   formerly   being

βλάσφημον καὶ διώκτην καὶ ὑβριστήν·
a blasphemer and a persecutor and insolent;

ἀλλὰ ἠλεήθην, ὅτι ἀγνοῶν ἐποίησα ἐν
but I obtained mercy, because being ignorant I acted in

ἀπιστίᾳ, 14 ὑπερεπλεόνασεν δὲ ἡ χάρις
unbelief,   and superabounded   the grace

τοῦ κυρίου ἡμῶν μετὰ πίστεως καὶ
of the Lord   of us with   faith   and

ἀγάπης τῆς ἐν Χριστῷ Ἰησοῦ. 15 πιστὸς
love   - in Christ   Jesus. Faithful [is]

ὁ λόγος καὶ πάσης ἀποδοχῆς ἄξιος,
the word and ¹of all ²acceptance ¹worthy,

ὅτι Χριστὸς Ἰησοῦς ἦλθεν εἰς τὸν κόσμον
that Christ   Jesus came into the   world

ἁμαρτωλοὺς σῶσαι· ὧν πρῶτός εἰμι ἐγώ·
sinners   to save; of whom first(chief) am   I;

16 ἀλλὰ διὰ τοῦτο ἠλεήθην, ἵνα ἐν
but because of this   I obtained in or- in
                              mercy,   der that

ἐμοὶ πρώτῳ ἐνδείξηται Ἰησοῦς Χριστὸς
me   first   might show forth Jesus   Christ

τὴν ἄπασαν μακροθυμίαν, πρὸς ὑποτύπωσιν
 -   all   longsuffering,   for   a pattern

τῶν μελλόντων πιστεύειν ἐπ' αὐτῷ εἰς
of the [ones] coming to believe on him   to

ζωὴν αἰώνιον. 17 Τῷ δὲ βασιλεῖ τῶν
life eternal.   Now to the King   of the

αἰώνων, ἀφθάρτῳ ἀοράτῳ μόνῳ θεῷ, τιμὴ
ages,   incorruptible invisible only   God, [be]
                                            honour

καὶ δόξα εἰς τοὺς αἰῶνας τῶν αἰώνων·
and glory unto the ages   of the ages:

ἀμήν. 18 Ταύτην τὴν παραγγελίαν παρα-
Amen.   This   -   charge   I com-

τίθεμαί σοι, τέκνον Τιμόθεε, κατὰ τὰς
mit   to thee, child Timothy, according to the

προαγούσας ἐπὶ σὲ προφητείας, ἵνα
preceding ²respecting ³thee ¹prophecies, in order
                                            that

στρατεύῃ ἐν αὐταῖς τὴν καλὴν στρατείαν,
thou   by them   the   good   warfare,
mightest war

19 ἔχων πίστιν καὶ ἀγαθὴν συνείδησιν,
having   faith and a good conscience,

ἥν τινες ἀπωσάμενοι περὶ τὴν πίστιν
which some thrusting away ⁵concerning ⁶the ⁷faith

King James Version   New International Version

ing faith have made shipwreck: 20 Of whom is Hymeneus and Alexander; whom I have delivered unto Satan, that they may learn not to blaspheme.

so have shipwrecked their faith. 20Among them are Hymenaeus and Alexander, whom I have handed over to Satan to be taught not to blaspheme.

Instructions on worship

2 I exhort therefore, that, first of all, supplications, prayers, intercessions, *and* giving of thanks, be made for all men; 2 For kings, and *for* all that are in authority; that we may lead a quiet and peaceable life in all godliness and honesty. 3 For this *is* good and acceptable in the sight of God our Saviour; 4 Who will have all men to be saved, and to come unto the knowledge of the truth. 5 For *there is* one God, and one mediator between God and men, the man Christ Jesus; 6 Who gave himself a ransom for all, to be testified in due time. 7 Whereunto I am ordained a preacher, and an apostle, (I speak the truth in Christ, *and* lie not,) a teacher of the Gentiles in faith and verity. 8 I will therefore that men pray every where, lifting up holy hands, without wrath and doubting. 9 In like manner also, that women adorn themselves in modest apparel, with shamefacedness and sobriety; not with braided hair, or gold, or pearls, or costly array; 10 But (which becometh women professing godliness) with good works. 11 Let the woman learn in silence with all subjection. 12 But I suffer not a woman to teach, nor to usurp authority over the man, but to be in silence. 13 For Adam was first formed, then Eve. 14And Adam was not deceived, but the woman being deceived was in the transgression. 15 Notwithstanding she shall be saved in childbearing, if they continue in faith and charity and holiness with sobriety.

2 I urge, then, first of all, that requests, prayers, intercession and thanksgiving be made for everyone—2 for kings and all those in authority, that we may live peaceful and quiet lives in all godliness and holiness. 3 This is good, and pleases God our Savior, 4 who wants all men to be saved and to come to a knowledge of the truth. 5 For there is one God and one mediator between God and men, the man Christ Jesus, 6 who gave himself as a ransom for all men—the testimony given in its proper time. 7And for this purpose I was appointed a herald and an apostle—I am telling the truth, I am not lying —and a teacher of the true faith to the Gentiles.

8 I want men everywhere to lift up holy hands in prayer, without anger or disputing.

9 I also want women to dress modestly, with decency and propriety, not with braided hair or gold or pearls or expensive clothes, 10 but with good deeds, appropriate for women who profess to worship God.

11 A woman should learn in quietness and full submission. 12 I do not permit a woman to teach or to have authority over a man; she must be silent. 13 For Adam was formed first, then Eve. 14And Adam was not the one deceived; it was the woman who was deceived and became a sinner. 15 But women will be kept safe*a* through childbirth, if they continue in faith, love and holiness with propriety.

Overseers and deacons

3 This *is* a true saying, If a man desire the office of a bishop, he desireth a good work. 2A bishop then must be blameless, the husband of one wife, vigilant, sober, of good behaviour, given to hospitality, apt to teach; 3 Not given to wine, no striker, not greedy of filthy lucre; but patient, not a brawler, not covetous; 4 One that ruleth well his own house, having his children in subjection with all gravity; 5 (For if a man know not how to rule his own house, how shall he take care of the church of God?) 6 Not a novice, lest being lifted up with pride he fall into the condemnation of the devil. 7 Moreover he must have a good report of them which are without; lest he fall into reproach and the snare of the devil. 8 Likewise *must* the deacons *be* grave, not double-tongued, not given to much

3 Here is a trustworthy saying: If anyone sets his heart on being an overseer,*b* he desires a noble task. 2 Now the overseer*b* must be above reproach, the husband of but one wife, temperate, self-controlled, respectable, hospitable, able to teach, 3 not given to much wine, not violent but gentle, not quarrelsome, not a lover of money. 4 He must manage his own family well and see that his children obey him with proper respect. 5 (If anyone does not know how to manage his own family, how can he take care of God's church?) 6 He must not be a recent convert, or he may become conceited and fall under the same judgment as the devil. 7 He must also have a good reputation with outsiders, so that he will not fall into disgrace and into the devil's trap.

8 Deacons, likewise, are to be men worthy of respect, sincere, not indulging in much wine, and

[a] Or *be saved.* [b] Or *bishop.*

Greek Interlinear

ἐναυάγησαν· 20 ὧν ἔστιν Ὑμέναιος καὶ
[1]made ship- of whom is Hymenæus and
wreck;

Ἀλέξανδρος, οὓς παρέδωκα τῷ σατανᾷ,
Alexander, whom I delivered – to Satan,

ἵνα παιδευθῶσιν μὴ βλασφημεῖν.
in or- they may be taught not to blaspheme.
der that

Chapter 2

Παρακαλῶ οὖν πρῶτον πάντων
I exhort therefore firstly of all

ποιεῖσθαι δεήσεις, προσευχάς, ἐντεύξεις,
to be made petitions, prayers, intercessions,

εὐχαριστίας, ὑπὲρ πάντων ἀνθρώπων,
thanksgivings, on behalf of all men,

2 ὑπὲρ βασιλέων καὶ πάντων τῶν ἐν
on behalf of kings and all the [ones] [2]in

ὑπεροχῇ ὄντων, ἵνα ἤρεμον καὶ ἡσύχιον
[3]eminence [1]being, in or- [2]a tranquil [3]and [4]quiet
der that

βίον διάγωμεν ἐν πάσῃ εὐσεβείᾳ καὶ
[5]life [1]we may lead in all piety and

σεμνότητι. 3 τοῦτο καλὸν καὶ ἀπόδεκτον
gravity. This [is] good and acceptable

ἐνώπιον τοῦ σωτῆρος ἡμῶν θεοῦ, 4 ὃς
before the Saviour of us God, who

πάντας ἀνθρώπους θέλει σωθῆναι καὶ εἰς
[3]all [2]men [1]wishes to be saved and [2]to

ἐπίγνωσιν ἀληθείας ἐλθεῖν. 5 εἷς γὰρ
[3]a full [4]of truth [1]to come. For [2]one
knowledge

θεός, εἷς καὶ μεσίτης θεοῦ καὶ ἀνθρώπων,
[1][there one also mediator of God and of men,
is] [4]God,

ἄνθρωπος Χριστὸς Ἰησοῦς, 6 ὁ δοὺς
a man Christ Jesus, the [one] having
given

ἑαυτὸν ἀντίλυτρον ὑπὲρ πάντων, τὸ
himself a ransom on behalf of all, the

μαρτύριον καιροῖς ἰδίοις· 7 εἰς ὃ ἐτέθην
testimony in its own times; for which [1]was
appointed

ἐγὼ κῆρυξ καὶ ἀπόστολος, ἀλήθειαν λέγω,
[1]I a herald and an apostle, [2]truth [1]I say,

οὐ ψεύδομαι, διδάσκαλος ἐθνῶν ἐν πίστει
I do not lie, a teacher of nations in faith

καὶ ἀληθείᾳ. 8 Βούλομαι οὖν προσεύχεσθαι
and truth. I desire therefore [2]to pray

τοὺς ἄνδρας ἐν παντὶ τόπῳ ἐπαίροντας
[1]the [2]men in every place lifting up

ὁσίους χεῖρας χωρὶς ὀργῆς καὶ διαλογισμοῦ.
holy hands without wrath and doubting.

9 Ὡσαύτως γυναῖκας ἐν καταστολῇ κοσμίῳ,
Similarly women in clothing orderly,

μετὰ αἰδοῦς καὶ σωφροσύνης κοσμεῖν
[3]with [4]modesty [5]and [6]sobriety [1]to adorn

ἑαυτάς, μὴ ἐν πλέγμασιν καὶ χρυσίῳ
[2]themselves, not with plaiting and gold

ἢ μαργαρίταις ἢ ἱματισμῷ πολυτελεῖ,
or pearls or raiment costly,

10 ἀλλ' ὃ πρέπει γυναιξὶν ἐπαγγελλομέναις
but what suits women professing

θεοσέβειαν, δι' ἔργων ἀγαθῶν. 11 γυνὴ
reverence, by [2]works [1]good. A woman
means of

ἐν ἡσυχίᾳ μανθανέτω ἐν πάσῃ ὑποταγῇ·
in silence let learn in all subjection;

12 διδάσκειν δὲ γυναικὶ οὐκ ἐπιτρέπω,
but [2]to teach [1]a woman [1]I do not permit,

οὐδὲ αὐθεντεῖν ἀνδρός, ἀλλ' εἶναι ἐν
nor to exercise of(over) a man, but to be in
authority

ἡσυχίᾳ. 13 Ἀδὰμ γὰρ πρῶτος ἐπλάσθη,
silence. For Adam first was formed,

εἶτα Εὔα. 14 καὶ Ἀδὰμ οὐκ ἠπατήθη,
then Eve. And Adam was not deceived,

ἡ δὲ γυνὴ ἐξαπατηθεῖσα ἐν παραβάσει
but the woman being deceived [2]in transgression

γέγονεν· 15 σωθήσεται δὲ διὰ τῆς
[1]has become; but she will be saved through the(her)

τεκνογονίας, ἐὰν μείνωσιν ἐν πίστει καὶ
childbearing, if they remain in faith and

ἀγάπῃ καὶ ἁγιασμῷ μετὰ σωφροσύνης.
love and sanctification with sobriety.

Chapter 3

Πιστὸς ὁ λόγος· εἴ τις ἐπισκοπῆς
Faithful [is] the word: If anyone [2]oversight

ὀρέγεται, καλοῦ ἔργου ἐπιθυμεῖ. 2 δεῖ
[1]aspires to, [3]a good [4]work [1]he desires. It behoves

οὖν τὸν ἐπίσκοπον ἀνεπίλημπτον εἶναι,
there- the bishop without reproach to be,
fore

μιᾶς γυναικὸς ἄνδρα, νηφάλιον, σώφρονα,
of one wife husband, temperate, sensible,

κόσμιον, φιλόξενον, διδακτικόν, 3 μὴ
orderly, hospitable, apt at teaching, not

πάροινον, μὴ πλήκτην, ἀλλὰ ἐπιεικῆ,
an excessive not a striker, but forbearing,
drinker,

ἄμαχον, ἀφιλάργυρον, 4 τοῦ ἰδίου οἴκου
uncontentious, not avaricious, [2]the(his) [3]own [4]household

καλῶς προϊστάμενον, τέκνα ἔχοντα ἐν
[1]well [1]ruling, children having in

ὑποταγῇ μετὰ πάσης σεμνότητος, 5 (εἰ
subjection with all gravity, [1](if

δέ τις τοῦ ἰδίου οἴκου προστῆναι οὐκ
[1]but [2]anyone [3]the(his) [4]own [5]household [6]to rule [2]not

οἶδεν, πῶς ἐκκλησίας θεοῦ ἐπιμελήσεται;)
[4]knows, how [2]a church [3]of God [1]will he care for ?)

6 μὴ νεόφυτον, ἵνα μὴ τυφωθεὶς εἰς
not a neophyte(recent lest being puffed up [2]into
convert),

κρίμα ἐμπέσῃ τοῦ διαβόλου. 7 δεῖ δὲ
[3]judgment [1]he fall in of the devil. And it behoves

καὶ μαρτυρίαν καλὴν ἔχειν ἀπὸ τῶν
also [3]witness [2]a good [1]to have from the [ones]

ἔξωθεν, 7 ἵνα μὴ εἰς ὀνειδισμὸν ἐμπέσῃ
outside, lest [2]into [3]reproach [1]he fall in

καὶ παγίδα τοῦ διαβόλου. 8 Διακόνους
and a snare of the devil. [It behoves] deacons

ὡσαύτως σεμνούς, μὴ διλόγους, μὴ οἴνῳ
similarly [to be] grave, not double-tongued, not [2]wine

πολλῷ προσέχοντας, μὴ αἰσχροκερδεῖς,
[1]to much [1]being addicted, not fond of base gain,

* That is, "cannot"; see note on page xxxviii.

King James Version

wine, not greedy of filthy lucre; 9 Holding the mystery of the faith in a pure conscience. 10And let these also first be proved; then let them use the office of a deacon, being *found* blameless. 11 Even so *must their* wives *be* grave, not slanderers, sober, faithful in all things. 12 Let the deacons be the husbands of one wife, ruling their children and their own houses well. 13 For they that have used the office of a deacon well purchase to themselves a good degree, and great boldness in the faith which is in Christ Jesus. 14 These things write I unto thee, hoping to come unto thee shortly: 15 But if I tarry long, that thou mayest know how thou oughtest to behave thyself in the house of God, which is the church of the living God, the pillar and ground of the truth. 16And without controversy great is the mystery of godliness: God was manifest in the flesh, justified in the Spirit, seen of angels, preached unto the Gentiles, believed on in the world, received up into glory.

4 Now the Spirit speaketh expressly, that in the latter times some shall depart from the faith, giving heed to seducing spirits, and doctrines of devils; 2 Speaking lies in hypocrisy; having their conscience seared with a hot iron; 3 Forbidding to marry, *and commanding* to abstain from meats, which God hath created to be received with thanksgiving of them which believe and know the truth. 4 For every creature of God *is* good, and nothing to be refused, if it be received with thanksgiving: 5 For it is sanctified by the word of God and prayer. 6 If thou put the brethren in remembrance of these things, thou shalt be a good minister of Jesus Christ, nourished up in the words of faith and of good doctrine, whereunto thou hast attained. 7 But refuse profane and old wives' fables, and exercise thyself *rather* unto godliness. 8 For bodily exercise profiteth little: but godliness is profitable unto all things, having promise of the life that now is, and of that which is to come. 9 This *is* a faithful saying, and worthy of all acceptation. 10 For therefore we both labour and suffer reproach, because we trust in the living God, who is the Saviour of all men, specially of those that believe. 11 These things command and teach. 12 Let no man despise thy youth; but be thou an example of the believers, in word, in conversation, in charity, in spirit, in faith, in purity. 13 Till I come, give attendance to reading, to exhortation, to doctrine. 14 Neglect not the gift that is in thee, which was given thee by prophecy, with the laying on of the hands of the

New International Version

not pursing dishonest gain. 9 They must keep hold of the deep truths of the faith with a clear conscience. 10 They must first be tested; and then if there is nothing against them, let them serve as deacons.

11 In the same way, their wives*c* are to be women worthy of respect, not malicious talkers but temperate and trustworthy in everything.

12 A deacon must be the husband of but one wife and must manage his children and his household well. 13 Those who have served well gain an excellent standing and great assurance in their faith in Christ Jesus.

14 Although I hope to come to you soon, I am writing you these instructions so that, 15 if I am delayed, you will know how people ought to conduct themselves in God's household, which is the church of the living God, the pillar and foundation of the truth. 16 Beyond all question, the mystery of godliness is great:
He*d* appeared in a body,
    was vindicated by the Spirit,
  was seen by angels,
    was preached among the nations,
  was believed on in the world,
    was taken up in glory.

Instructions to Timothy

4 The Spirit clearly says that in later times some will abandon the faith and follow deceiving spirits and things taught by demons. 2 Such teachings come through hypocritical liars, whose consciences have been seared as with a hot iron. 3 They forbid people to marry and order them to abstain from certain foods, which God created to be received with thanksgiving by those who believe and who know the truth. 4 For everything God created is good, and nothing is to be rejected if it is received with thanksgiving, 5 because it is consecrated by the word of God and prayer.

6 If you point these things out to the brothers, you will be a good minister of Christ Jesus, brought up in the truths of the faith and of the good teaching that you have followed. 7 Have nothing to do with godless myths and old wives' tales; rather, train yourself to be godly. 8 For physical training is of some value, but godliness has value for all things, holding promise for both the present life and the life to come. 9 This is a trustworthy saying that deserves full acceptance 10 (and for this we labor and strive), that we have put our hope in the living God, who is the Savior of all men, and especially of those who believe.

11 Command and teach these things. 12 Don't let anyone look down on you because you are young, but set an example for the believers in speech, in life, in love, in faith and in purity. 13 Until I come, devote yourself to the public reading of Scripture, to preaching and to teaching. 14 Do not neglect your gift, which was given you through a prophetic message when the body of elders laid their hands on you.

[c] Or *way, deaconesses.* [d] Some MSS read *God.*

Greek Interlinear

9 ἔχοντας τὸ μυστήριον τῆς πίστεως ἐν
having the mystery of the faith with

καθαρᾷ συνειδήσει. 10 καὶ οὗτοι δὲ
a clean conscience. ⁴Also ²these ¹and

δοκιμαζέσθωσαν πρῶτον, εἶτα διακονείτωσαν
²let ⁵be proved firstly, then let them minister

ἀνέγκλητοι ὄντες. 11 γυναῖκας ὡσαύτως
¹irreproachable ¹being. [It behoves]* wives similarly

σεμνάς, μὴ διαβόλους, νηφαλίους, πιστὰς
[to be] grave, not slanderers, sober, faithful

ἐν πᾶσιν. 12 διάκονοι ἔστωσαν μιᾶς
in all things. ²Deacons ¹let ³be ⁴of one

γυναικὸς ἄνδρες, τέκνων καλῶς προϊστάμενοι
⁵wife ⁴husbands, ⁵children ⁶well ¹ruling

καὶ τῶν ἰδίων οἴκων. 13 οἱ γὰρ καλῶς
²and ⁴the(ir) own ³households. For the [ones] ²well

διακονήσαντες βαθμὸν ἑαυτοῖς καλὸν
¹having ministered ⁵position ⁴for themselves ³a good

περιποιοῦνται καὶ πολλὴν παρρησίαν ἐν
²acquire and much boldness in

πίστει τῇ ἐν Χριστῷ Ἰησοῦ. 14 Ταῦτά
faith the [one] in Christ Jesus. These things

σοι γράφω ἐλπίζων ἐλθεῖν πρὸς σὲ
to thee I write hoping to come to thee

τάχιον· 15 ἐὰν δὲ βραδύνω, ἵνα εἰδῇς
shortly; but if I delay, in order thou
that mayest
know

πῶς δεῖ ἐν οἴκῳ θεοῦ ἀναστρέφεσθαι,
how it behoves in [the] of God to behave,
household

ἥτις ἐστὶν ἐκκλησία θεοῦ ζῶντος, στῦλος
which is [the] church ²God ¹of [the] living, pillar

καὶ ἑδραίωμα τῆς ἀληθείας. 16 καὶ
and bulwark of the truth. And

ὁμολογουμένως μέγα ἐστὶν τὸ τῆς εὐσεβείας
confessedly great is the - ²of piety

μυστήριον· ὃς ἐφανερώθη ἐν σαρκί,
¹mystery; Who was manifested in flesh,

ἐδικαιώθη ἐν πνεύματι, ὤφθη ἀγγέλοις,
was justified in spirit, was seen by angels,

ἐκηρύχθη ἐν ἔθνεσιν, ἐπιστεύθη ἐν κόσμῳ,
was pro- among nations, was believed in [the] world,
claimed

ἀνελήμφθη ἐν δόξῃ.
was taken up in glory.

Chapter 4

Τὸ δὲ πνεῦμα ῥητῶς λέγει ὅτι
Now the Spirit ²in words† ¹says that

ἐν ὑστέροις καιροῖς ἀποστήσονταί τινες
in later times ¹will depart from ²some

τῆς πίστεως, προσέχοντες πνεύμασιν
the faith, attending to ²spirits

πλάνοις καὶ διδασκαλίαις δαιμονίων, 2 ἐν
¹misleading and teachings of demons, ²in

ὑποκρίσει ψευδολόγων, κεκαυστηριασμένων
³hypocrisy ¹of men who speak lies, having been branded on

τὴν ἰδίαν συνείδησιν, 3 κωλυόντων γαμεῖν,
the(ir) own conscience, forbidding to marry,

ἀπέχεσθαι βρωμάτων, ἃ ὁ θεὸς ἔκτισεν
[bidding] to foods, which - God created
abstain from

εἰς μετάλημψιν μετὰ εὐχαριστίας τοῖς
for partaking with thanksgiving by the

πιστοῖς καὶ ἐπεγνωκόσι τὴν ἀλήθειαν.
believers and [those] having fully the truth.
known

4 ὅτι πᾶν κτίσμα θεοῦ καλόν, καὶ
Because every creature of God [is] good, and

οὐδὲν ἀπόβλητον μετὰ εὐχαριστίας λαμβαν-
nothing to be put away ¹with ²thanksgiving ¹being
[is]

όμενον· 5 ἁγιάζεται γὰρ διὰ λόγου θεοῦ
received; for it is being sanctified through a word of God

καὶ ἐντεύξεως. 6 Ταῦτα ὑποτιθέμενος
and petition. ²These things ¹suggesting

τοῖς ἀδελφοῖς καλὸς ἔσῃ διάκονος Χριστοῦ
²to the ⁴brothers ²a good ⁵thou ¹minister of Christ
wilt be

Ἰησοῦ, ἐντρεφόμενος τοῖς λόγοις τῆς
Jesus, being nourished by the words of the

πίστεως καὶ τῆς καλῆς διδασκαλίας ᾗ
faith and of the good teaching which

παρηκολούθηκας· 7 τοὺς δὲ βεβήλους καὶ
thou hast followed; but the profane and

γραώδεις μύθους παραιτοῦ. γύμναζε δὲ
old-womanish tales refuse. And exercise

σεαυτὸν πρὸς εὐσέβειαν. 8 ἡ γὰρ σωματικὴ
thyself to piety. - For bodily

γυμνασία πρὸς ὀλίγον ἐστὶν ὠφέλιμος·
exercise ²for ⁴a little ¹is ²profitable;

ἡ δὲ εὐσέβεια πρὸς πάντα ὠφέλιμός
- but piety ²for ³all things ²profitable

ἐστιν, ἐπαγγελίαν ἔχουσα ζωῆς τῆς νῦν
¹is, promise having ⁶life ¹of the ²now
(present)

καὶ τῆς μελλούσης. 9 πιστὸς ὁ λόγος
and of the coming. Faithful [is] the word

καὶ πάσης ἀποδοχῆς ἄξιος· 10 εἰς τοῦτο
and ²of all ⁴acceptance ¹worthy; ²to ²this

γὰρ κοπιῶμεν καὶ ἀγωνιζόμεθα, ὅτι
¹for we labour and struggle, because

ἠλπίκαμεν ἐπὶ θεῷ ζῶντι, ὅς ἐστιν
we have set on ²God ¹a living, who is
[our] hope

σωτὴρ πάντων ἀνθρώπων, μάλιστα πιστῶν.
[the] of all men, especially of believers.
Saviour

11 Παράγγελλε ταῦτα καὶ δίδασκε.
Charge thou these things and teach.

12 μηδείς σου τῆς νεότητος καταφρονείτω,
²No one ¹of thee ³the ⁴youth ¹let despise,

ἀλλὰ τύπος γίνου τῶν πιστῶν ἐν λόγῳ,
but ²a pattern ¹become of the believers in speech,
thou

ἐν ἀναστροφῇ, ἐν ἀγάπῃ, ἐν πίστει,
in behaviour, in love, in faith,

ἐν ἁγνείᾳ. 13 ἕως ἔρχομαι πρόσεχε
in purity. Until I come attend

τῇ ἀναγνώσει, τῇ ·παρακλήσει, τῇ διδασ-
to the reading, ✕ to the exhortation, to the teach-

καλίᾳ. 14 μὴ ἀμέλει τοῦ ἐν σοὶ
ing. Do not be neglectful ¹of the ²in ⁴thee

χαρίσματος, ὃ ἐδόθη σοι διὰ προφητείας
³gift, which was to thee by prophecy
given means of

μετὰ ἐπιθέσεως τῶν χειρῶν τοῦ πρε-
with laying on of the hands of the body

* See verses 7 and 8.
✕ That is, the reading aloud in public worship of the Scriptures
(as nearly always in the N.T.).

King James Version

presbytery. 15 Meditate upon these things; give thyself wholly to them; that thy profiting may appear to all. 16 Take heed unto thyself, and unto the doctrine; continue in them: for in doing this thou shalt both save thyself, and them that hear thee.

5 Rebuke not an elder, but entreat *him* as a father; *and* the younger men as brethren; 2 The elder women as mothers; the younger as sisters, with all purity. 3 Honour widows that are widows indeed. 4 But if any widow have children or nephews, let them learn first to shew piety at home, and to requite their parents: for that is good and acceptable before God. 5 Now she that is a widow indeed, and desolate, trusteth in God, and continueth in supplications and prayers night and day. 6 But she that liveth in pleasure is dead while she liveth. 7 And these things give in charge, that they may be blameless. 8 But if any provide not for his own, and specially for those of his own house, he hath denied the faith, and is worse than an infidel. 9 Let not a widow be taken into the number under threescore years old, having been the wife of one man, 10 Well reported of for good works; if she have brought up children, if she have lodged strangers, if she have washed the saints' feet, if she have relieved the afflicted, if she have diligently followed every good work. 11 But the younger widows refuse: for when they have begun to wax wanton against Christ, they will marry; 12 Having damnation, because they have cast off their first faith. 13 And withal they learn *to be* idle, wandering about from house to house; and not only idle, but tattlers also and busybodies, speaking things which they ought not. 14 I will therefore that the younger women marry, bear children, guide the house, give none occasion to the adversary to speak reproachfully. 15 For some are already turned aside after Satan. 16 If any man or woman that believeth have widows, let them relieve them, and let not the church be charged; that it may relieve them that are widows indeed. 17 Let the elders that rule well be counted worthy of double honour, especially they who labour in the word and doctrine. 18 For the Scripture saith, Thou shalt not muzzle the ox that treadeth out the corn. And, The labourer *is* worthy of his reward. 19 Against an elder receive not an accusation, but before two or three witnesses. 20 Them that sin rebuke before all, that others also may fear. 21 I charge *thee* before God, and the Lord Jesus Christ, and the elect angels, that thou observe these things without preferring one before another, doing nothing by partiality. 22 Lay hands suddenly on no man, neither be partaker of other men's sins:

New International Version

15 Be diligent in these matters; give yourself wholly to them, so that everyone may see your progress. 16 Watch your life and doctrine closely. Persevere in them, because if you do, you will save both yourself and your hearers.

Advice about widows, elders and slaves

5 Do not rebuke an older man harshly, but exhort him as if he were your father. Treat younger men as brothers, 2 older women as mothers, and younger women as sisters, with absolute purity.

3 Give proper recognition to widows who are left all alone. 4 But if a widow has children or grandchildren, these should learn first of all to put their religion into practice by caring for their own family and so repaying their parents and grandparents, for this is pleasing to God. 5 The widow who is all alone puts her hope in God and continues night and day to pray and to ask God for help. 6 But the widow who lives for pleasure is dead even while she lives. 7 Give the people these instructions, too, so that no one may be open to blame. 8 If anyone does not provide for his relatives, and especially for his immediate family, he has denied the faith and is worse than an unbeliever.

9 No widow may be put on the list of widows unless she is over sixty, has been faithful to her husband,[e] 10 and is well-known for her good deeds, such as bringing up children, showing hospitality, washing the feet of the saints, helping those in trouble and devoting herself to all kinds of good deeds.

11 As for younger widows, do not put them on such a list. For when their sensual desires overcome their dedication to Christ, they want to marry. 12 Thus they bring judgment on themselves, because they have broken their first pledge. 13 Besides, they get into the habit of being idle and going about from house to house. And not only do they become idlers, but also gossips and busybodies, saying things they ought not to. 14 So I counsel younger widows to marry, to have children, to manage their homes and to give the enemy no opportunity for slander. 15 Some have in fact already turned away to follow Satan.

16 If any woman who is a believer has widows in her family, she should help them and not let the church be burdened with them, so that the church can help those widows who are all alone.

17 The elders who direct the affairs of the church well are worthy of double honor, especially those whose work is preaching and teaching. 18 For the Scripture says, "Do not muzzle the ox while it is treading out the grain,"[f] and "The worker deserves his wages."[g] 19 Do not entertain an accusation against an elder unless it is brought by two or three witnesses. 20 Those who sin are to be rebuked publicly, so that the others may take warning.

21 I charge you, in the sight of God and Christ Jesus and the elect angels, to keep these instructions without partiality, and to do nothing out of favoritism.

22 Do not be hasty in the laying on of hands, and do not share in the sins of others. Keep yourself pure.

[e] Or *has had but one husband.* [f] Deut. 25:4. [g] Luke 10:7.

Greek Interlinear

σβυτερίου. **15** ταῦτα μελέτα, ἐν τούτοις
of elders. ¹These things ¹attend to, ²in ³these things

ἴσθι, ἵνα σου ἡ προκοπὴ φανερὰ ᾖ
¹be in order of thee the advance clear may
thou, that be

πᾶσιν. **16** ἔπεχε σεαυτῷ καὶ τῇ διδασκαλίᾳ,
to all men. Take heed to thyself and to the teaching,

ἐπίμενε αὐτοῖς· τοῦτο γὰρ ποιῶν καὶ
continue in them; for this doing both

σεαυτὸν σώσεις καὶ τοὺς ἀκούοντάς σου.
thyself thou wilt save and the [ones] hearing thee.

Chapter 5

Πρεσβυτέρῳ μὴ ἐπιπλήξῃς, ἀλλὰ
An older man do not rebuke, but

παρακάλει ὡς πατέρα, νεωτέρους ὡς
exhort as a father, younger men as

ἀδελφούς, **2** πρεσβυτέρας ὡς μητέρας,
brothers, older women as mothers,

νεωτέρας ὡς ἀδελφὰς ἐν πάσῃ ἁγνείᾳ.
younger women as sisters with all purity.

3 Χήρας τίμα τὰς ὄντως χήρας. **4** εἰ δέ
¹Widows ¹honour ¹the ²really ²widows. But if

τις χήρα τέκνα ἢ ἔκγονα ἔχει, μαν-
any widow ²children ²or ²grandchildren ¹has, let

θανέτωσαν πρῶτον τὸν ἴδιον οἶκον εὐσεβεῖν
them learn firstly ²the(ir) ¹own ²household ¹to show
piety to

καὶ ἀμοιβὰς ἀποδιδόναι τοῖς προγόνοις·
and ¹requitals ¹to return to the(ir) forebears;

τοῦτο γὰρ ἐστιν ἀπόδεκτον ἐνώπιον τοῦ
for this is acceptable before --

θεοῦ. **5** ἡ δὲ ὄντως χήρα καὶ μεμονωμένη
God. But the really widow and having been left
alone

ἤλπικεν ἐπὶ θεὸν καὶ προσμένει ταῖς
has set on God and continues in the
[her] hope

δεήσεσιν καὶ ταῖς προσευχαῖς νυκτὸς καὶ
petitions and the prayers night and

ἡμέρας· **6** ἡ δὲ σπαταλῶσα ζῶσα τέθνηκεν.
day; but the living wantonly ¹living ¹has died.
[one]

7 καὶ ταῦτα παράγγελλε, ἵνα ἀνεπίλημπτοι
And these charge thou, in order ²without reproach
things that

ὦσιν. **8** εἰ δέ τις τῶν ἰδίων καὶ μάλιστα
¹they But if anyone ¹the(his) ²own ⁴and ³especially
may be. [people]

οἰκείων οὐ προνοεῖ, τὴν πίστιν ἤρνηται
[his] ¹provides not [for], ¹the ²faith ¹he has
¹family denied

καὶ ἔστιν ἀπίστου χείρων. **9** χήρα
and is ²an unbeliever ¹worse [than]. A widow

καταλεγέσθω μὴ ἔλαττον ἐτῶν ἑξήκοντα
let be enrolled ²not ³less [than] ⁴of years ¹sixty

γεγονυῖα, ἑνὸς ἀνδρὸς γυνή, **10** ἐν ἔργοις
¹having of one man wife, ³by ⁴works
become,

καλοῖς μαρτυρουμένη, εἰ ἐτεκνοτρόφησεν,
²good ¹being witnessed, if she brought up children,

εἰ ἐξενοδόχησεν, εἰ ἁγίων πόδας ἔνιψεν,
if she entertained if ²of saints ²feet ¹she
strangers, washed,

εἰ θλιβομένοις ἐπήρκεσεν, εἰ παντὶ ἔργῳ
if ²being afflicted ¹she relieved, if ²every ¹work
[ones],

ἀγαθῷ ἐπηκολούθησεν. **11** νεωτέρας δὲ
²good ¹she followed after. But younger

χήρας παραιτοῦ· ὅταν γὰρ καταστρηνιάσωσιν
widows refuse; for whenever they grow wanton against

τοῦ Χριστοῦ, γαμεῖν θέλουσιν, **12** ἔχουσαι
- Christ, ²to marry ¹they wish, having

κρίμα ὅτι τὴν πρώτην πίστιν ἠθέτησαν·
judgment because ²the(ir) ³first ⁴faith ¹they set aside;

13 ἅμα δὲ καὶ ἀργαὶ μανθάνουσιν
and at the same time also ²idle ¹they learn [to be]

περιερχόμεναι τὰς οἰκίας, οὐ μόνον δὲ
going round the houses, ²not ¹only ¹and

ἀργαὶ ἀλλὰ καὶ φλύαροι καὶ περίεργοι,
idle but also gossips and busybodies,

λαλοῦσαι τὰ μὴ δέοντα. **14** βούλομαι
speaking the things not proper. I will

οὖν νεωτέρας γαμεῖν, τεκνογονεῖν,
there- younger women to marry, to bear children,
fore

οἰκοδεσποτεῖν, μηδεμίαν ἀφορμὴν διδόναι
to be mistress of ²no ³occasion ¹to give
a house,

τῷ ἀντικειμένῳ λοιδορίας χάριν· **15** ἤδη
to the [one] opposing ²reproach ¹on account of; ²already

γάρ τινες ἐξετράπησαν ὀπίσω τοῦ σατανᾶ.
¹for some turned aside behind - Satan.

16 εἴ τις πιστὴ ἔχει χήρας, ἐπαρκείτω
If any believing has widows, let her relieve
woman

αὐταῖς, καὶ μὴ βαρείσθω ἡ ἐκκλησία,
them, and not let be burdened the church,

ἵνα ταῖς ὄντως χήραις ἐπαρκέσῃ. **17** Οἱ
in or- ²the ²really ⁴widows ¹it may relieve. ²The
der that

καλῶς προεστῶτες πρεσβύτεροι διπλῆς
²well ¹ruling ¹elders ²of double

τιμῆς ἀξιούσθωσαν, μάλιστα οἱ κοπιῶντες
¹⁴honour ¹let ²be ³deemed especially the labouring
⁴worthy, [ones]

ἐν λόγῳ καὶ διδασκαλίᾳ. **18** λέγει γὰρ
in speech and teaching. For says

ἡ γραφή· βοῦν ἀλοῶντα οὐ φιμώσεις,
the scripture: An ox threshing thou shalt not muzzle,

καὶ· ἄξιος ὁ ἐργάτης τοῦ μισθοῦ αὐτοῦ.
and: Worthy [is] the workman of the pay of him.

19 κατὰ πρεσβυτέρου κατηγορίαν μὴ παρα-
Against an elder accusation do not re-

δέχου, ἐκτὸς εἰ μὴ ἐπὶ δύο ἢ τριῶν
ceive, except unless on [the two or three
word of]

μαρτύρων. **20** Τοὺς ἁμαρτάνοντας ἐνώπιον
witnesses. The [ones] sinning ²before

πάντων ἔλεγχε, ἵνα καὶ οἱ λοιποὶ φόβον
³all ¹reprove in ²also ¹the ²rest ²fear
thou, order that

ἔχωσιν. **21** Διαμαρτύρομαι ἐνώπιον τοῦ
⁴may have. I solemnly witness before -

θεοῦ καὶ Χριστοῦ Ἰησοῦ καὶ τῶν
God and Christ Jesus and the

ἐκλεκτῶν ἀγγέλων ἵνα ταῦτα φυλάξῃς
chosen angels in order these things thou guard
that

χωρὶς προκρίματος, μηδὲν ποιῶν κατὰ
without prejudgment, ²nothing ¹doing by way of

πρόσκλισιν. **22** χεῖρας ταχέως μηδενὶ
inclination. ²Hands ¹quickly ²no man

ἐπιτίθει, μηδὲ κοινώνει ἁμαρτίαις ἀλ-
¹lay ²on, nor share ²sins ¹in

619

King James Version

keep thyself pure. 23 Drink no longer water, but use a little wine for thy stomach's sake and thine often infirmities. 24 Some men's sins are open beforehand, going before to judgment; and some *men* they follow after. 25 Likewise also the good works *of some* are manifest beforehand; and they that are otherwise cannot be hid.

6 Let as many servants as are under the yoke count their own masters worthy of all honour, that the name of God and *his* doctrine be not blasphemed. 2And they that have believing masters, let them not despise *them*, because they are brethren; but rather do *them* service, because they are faithful and beloved, partakers of the benefit. These things teach and exhort. 3 If any man teach otherwise, and consent not to wholesome words, *even* the words of our Lord Jesus Christ, and to the doctrine which is according to godliness; 4 He is proud, knowing nothing, but doting about questions and strifes of words, whereof cometh envy, strife, railings, evil surmisings, 5 Perverse disputings of men of corrupt minds, and destitute of the truth, supposing that gain is godliness: from such withdraw thyself. 6 But godliness with contentment is great gain. 7 For we brought nothing into *this* world, *and it is* certain we can carry nothing out. 8And having food and raiment, let us be therewith content. 9 But they that will be rich fall into temptation and a snare, and *into* many foolish and hurtful lusts, which drown men in destruction and perdition. 10 For the love of money is the root of all evil: which while some coveted after, they have erred from the faith, and pierced themselves through with many sorrows. 11 But thou, O man of God, flee these things; and follow after righteousness, godliness, faith, love, patience, meekness. 12 Fight the good fight of faith, lay hold on eternal life, whereunto thou art also called, and hast professed a good profession before many witnesses. 13 I give thee charge in the sight of God, who quickeneth all things, and *before* Christ Jesus, who before Pontius Pilate witnessed a good confession; 14 That thou keep *this* commandment without spot, unrebukeable, until the appearing of our Lord Jesus Christ: 15 Which in his times he shall shew, *who is* the blessed and only Potentate, the

New International Version

23 Stop drinking only water, and use a little wine because of your stomach and your frequent illnesses.
24 The sins of some men are obvious, reaching the place of judgment ahead of them; the sins of others trail behind them. 25 In the same way, good deeds are obvious, and even those that are not cannot be hidden.

6 All who are under the yoke of slavery should consider their masters worthy of full respect, so that God's name and our teaching may not be slandered. 2 Those who have believing masters are not to show less respect for them because they are brothers. Instead, they are to serve them even better, because those who benefit from their service are believers, and dear to them. These are the things you are to teach and urge on them.

Love of money

3 If anyone teaches false doctrines and does not agree to the sound instruction of our Lord Jesus Christ and to godly teaching, 4 he is conceited and understands nothing. He has an unhealthy interest in controversies and arguments that result in envy, quarreling, malicious talk, evil suspicions 5 and constant friction between men of corrupt mind, who have been robbed of the truth and who think that godliness is a means to financial gain.
6 But godliness with contentment is great gain. 7 For we brought nothing into the world, and we can take nothing out of it. 8 But if we have food and clothing, we will be content with that. 9 People who want to get rich fall into temptation and a trap and into many foolish and harmful desires that plunge men into ruin and destruction. 10 For the love of money is a root of all kinds of evil. Some people, eager for money, have wandered from the faith and pierced themselves with many griefs.

Paul's charge to Timothy

11 But you, man of God, flee from all this, and pursue righteousness, godliness, faith, love, endurance and gentleness. 12 Fight the good fight of the faith. Take hold of the eternal life to which you were called when you made your good confession in the presence of many witnesses. 13 In the sight of God, who gives life to everything, and of Christ Jesus, who while testifying before Pontius Pilate made the good confession, I charge you 14 to keep this commandment without spot or blame until the appearing of our Lord Jesus Christ, 15 which God will bring about in his own time—God, the blessed and only Ruler, the King of kings and Lord of lords,

Greek Interlinear

λοτρίαις· σεαυτὸν ἁγνὸν τήρει. 23 Μηκέτι
others't; ³thyself ²pure ¹keep. No longer

ὑδροπότει, ἀλλὰ οἴνῳ ὀλίγῳ χρῶ διὰ
drink water, but ³wine ²a little ¹use on account of

τὸν στόμαχον καὶ τὰς πυκνάς σου
the(thy) stomach and the frequent ⁵of thee

ἀσθενείας. 24 Τινῶν ἀνθρώπων αἱ ἁμαρτίαι
⁴weaknesses. ³of some ⁴men ¹The ²sins

πρόδηλοί εἰσιν προάγουσαι εἰς κρίσιν,
⁴clear ⁵are going before to judgment,
beforehand

τισὶν δὲ καὶ ἐπακολουθοῦσιν· 25 ὡσαύτως
but some indeed they follow on; similarly

καὶ τὰ ἔργα τὰ καλὰ πρόδηλα, καὶ
also the ²works – ¹good [are] clear and
beforehand,

τὰ ἄλλως ἔχοντα κρυβῆναι οὐ δύνανται.
the ³otherwise ¹having ⁴to be hidden ⁵cannot.
[ones] (being)

Chapter 6

Ὅσοι εἰσὶν ὑπὸ ζυγὸν δοῦλοι, τοὺς
As many as are under a yoke slaves, ²the(ir)
[being]

ἰδίους δεσπότας πάσης τιμῆς ἀξίους ἡγείσ-
³own ¹masters ⁵of all ⁷honour ⁶worthy ⁴let them

θωσαν, ἵνα μὴ τὸ ὄνομα τοῦ θεοῦ καὶ
deem, lest the name – of God and

ἡ διδασκαλία βλασφημῆται. 2 οἱ δὲ
the teaching be blasphemed. And ¹the [ones]

πιστοὺς ἔχοντες δεσπότας μὴ καταφρο-
²believing ³having ⁴masters not let them

νείτωσαν, ὅτι ἀδελφοί εἰσιν, ἀλλὰ μᾶλλον
despise [them], because brothers they are, but rather

δουλευέτωσαν, ὅτι πιστοί εἰσιν καὶ
let them serve as slaves, because ⁵believing ⁶are ⁷and

ἀγαπητοὶ οἱ τῆς εὐεργεσίας ἀντιλαμ-
⁸beloved ¹the [ones] ²of the ⁴good service ³receiving in

βανόμενοι.
return.

Ταῦτα δίδασκε καὶ παρακάλει. 3 εἴ
These things teach thou and exhort. If

τις ἑτεροδιδασκαλεῖ καὶ μὴ προσέρχεται
anyone teaches differently and consents not

ὑγιαίνουσιν λόγοις τοῖς τοῦ κυρίου ἡμῶν
to being healthy words the of the Lord of us
[words]

Ἰησοῦ Χριστοῦ, καὶ τῇ κατ' εὐσέβειαν
Jesus Christ, and ¹to the ²accord- ⁴piety
ing to

διδασκαλίᾳ, 4 τετύφωται, μηδὲν ἐπιστά-
³teaching, he has been puffed up, ²nothing ¹under-

μενος, ἀλλὰ νοσῶν περὶ ζητήσεις καὶ
standing, but being diseased about questionings and

λογομαχίας, ἐξ ὧν γίνεται φθόνος, ἔρις,
battles of words, out of which comes envy, strife,

βλασφημίαι, ὑπόνοιαι πονηραί, 5 διαπαρα-
blasphemies, ²suspicions ¹evil, perpetual

τριβαὶ διεφθαρμένων ἀνθρώπων τὸν νοῦν
wranglings ²having been corrupted ¹of men the mind
=of men with corrupted mind

καὶ ἀπεστερημένων τῆς ἀληθείας, νομιζ-
and having been deprived of the truth, sup-

όντων πορισμὸν εἶναι τὴν εὐσέβειαν.
posing ²gain ¹to be the ¹piety.*

6 ἔστιν δὲ πορισμὸς μέγας ἡ εὐσέβεια
But ⁴is ²gain ¹great the ³piety

μετὰ αὐταρκείας. 7 οὐδὲν γὰρ εἰσηνέγκαμεν
¹with ²self-sufficiency;* for nothing we have brought in

εἰς τὸν κόσμον, ὅτι οὐδὲ ἐξενεγκεῖν
into the world, because neither ²to carry out

τι δυνάμεθα· 8 ἔχοντες δὲ διατροφὰς καὶ
³any- ¹can we; but having foods and
thing

σκεπάσματα, τούτοις ἀρκεσθησόμεθα. 9 οἱ
clothings, with these things we will be satisfied. the

δὲ βουλόμενοι πλουτεῖν ἐμπίπτουσιν εἰς
But [ones] resolving to be rich fall in into

πειρασμὸν καὶ παγίδα καὶ ἐπιθυμίας πολλὰς
temptation and a snare and ¹lusts ²many

ἀνοήτους καὶ βλαβεράς, αἵτινες βυθίζουσιν
³foolish ⁴and ⁵injurious, which ⁶cause ⁷to sink

τοὺς ἀνθρώπους εἰς ὄλεθρον καὶ ἀπώλειαν.
– ⁸men into ruin and destruction.

10 ῥίζα γὰρ πάντων τῶν κακῶν ἐστιν
For ⁴a root ²of all – ⁵evils ³is

ἡ φιλαργυρία, ἧς τινες ὀρεγόμενοι
¹the ²love of money,* of which some hankering after

ἀπεπλανήθησαν ἀπὸ τῆς πίστεως καὶ
wandered away from the faith and

ἑαυτοὺς περιέπειραν ὀδύναις πολλαῖς. 11 Σὺ
themselves pierced round ²pains ¹by many. thou

δέ, ὦ ἄνθρωπε θεοῦ, ταῦτα φεῦγε· δίωκε
But, O man of God, these things flee; ¹pursue

δὲ δικαιοσύνην, εὐσέβειαν, πίστιν, ἀγάπην,
²and righteousness, piety, faith, love,

ὑπομονήν, πραϋπαθίαν. 12 ἀγωνίζου τὸν
endurance, meekness. Struggle the

καλὸν ἀγῶνα τῆς πίστεως, ἐπιλαβοῦ τῆς
good struggle of the faith, lay hold on the

αἰωνίου ζωῆς, εἰς ἣν ἐκλήθης καὶ ὡμολό-
eternal life, to which thou wast and didst con-
called

γησας τὴν καλὴν ὁμολογίαν ἐνώπιον
fess the good confession before

πολλῶν μαρτύρων. 13 παραγγέλλω ἐνώπιον
many witnesses. I charge before

τοῦ θεοῦ τοῦ ζωογονοῦντος ' τὰ πάντα
– God the [one] quickening – all things

καὶ Χριστοῦ Ἰησοῦ τοῦ μαρτυρήσαντος,
and Christ Jesus the [one] having witnessed

ἐπὶ Ποντίου Πιλάτου τὴν καλὴν ὁμολογίαν,
in the Pontius Pilate the good confession,
time of

14 τηρῆσαί σε ★ τὴν ἐντολὴν ἄσπιλον
¹to keep ²thee the(this) commandment unspotted

ἀνεπίλημπτον μέχρι τῆς ἐπιφανείας τοῦ
without reproach until the appearance of the

κυρίου ἡμῶν Ἰησοῦ Χριστοῦ, 15 ἣν
Lord of us Jesus Christ, which§

καιροῖς ἰδίοις δείξει ὁ μακάριος καὶ
¹in its/his own times ⁴will show ¹the ³blessed ²and

μόνος δυνάστης, ὁ βασιλεὺς τῶν βασιλευ-
⁴only ⁵Potentate, the King of the [ones] reign-

---

* For order of words see note on John 1. 1.
★ " thee " is the direct object of the verb " charge " in ver. 13:
" I charge . . . thee to keep . . ."
§ The antecedent to this relative pronoun is " appearance ",
not " Jesus Christ ".

King James Version

King of kings, and Lord of lords; 16 Who only hath immortality, dwelling in the light which no man can approach unto; whom *be* no man hath seen, nor can see: to whom *be* honour and power everlasting. Amen. 17 Charge them that are rich in this world, that they be not high-minded, nor trust in uncertain riches, but in the living God, who giveth us richly all things to enjoy; 18 That they do good, that they be rich in good works, ready to distribute, willing to communicate; 19 Laying up in store for themselves a good foundation against the time to come, that they may lay hold on eternal life. 20 O Timothy, keep that which is committed to thy trust, avoiding profane *and* vain babblings, and oppositions of science falsely so called: 21 Which some professing have erred concerning the faith. Grace *be* with thee. Amen.

The first to Timothy was written from Laodicea, which is the chiefest city of Phrygia Pacatiana.

New International Version

16 who alone is immortal and who lives in unapproachable light, whom no one has seen or can see. To him be honor and might forever. Amen.

17 Command those who are rich in this present world not to be arrogant nor to put their hope in wealth, which is so uncertain, but to put their hope in God, who richly provides us with everything for our enjoyment. 18 Command them to do good, to be rich in good deeds, and to be generous and willing to share. 19 In this way they will lay up treasure for themselves as a firm foundation for the coming age, so that they may take hold of the life that is truly life.

20 Timothy, guard what has been entrusted to your care. Turn away from godless chatter and the opposition of what is falsely called knowledge, 21 which some have professed and in so doing have wandered from the faith.

Grace be with you.

Greek Interlinear

ὄντων καὶ κύριος τῶν κυριευόντων, 16 ὁ
ing and Lord of the [ones] ruling, the

μόνος ἔχων ἀθανασίαν, φῶς οἰκῶν
only [one] having immortality, ²light ¹inhabiting

ἀπρόσιτον, ὃν εἶδεν οὐδεὶς ἀνθρώπων οὐδὲ
unapproach- whom ²saw ¹no one ²of men nor
able,

ἰδεῖν δύναται· ᾧ τιμὴ καὶ κράτος αἰώνιον·
²to see ¹can; to [be] and might eternal:
whom honour

ἀμήν. 17 Τοῖς πλουσίοις ἐν τῷ νῦν
Amen. ²the ²rich ⁴in ⁵the ⁶now
(present)

αἰῶνι παράγγελλε μὴ ὑψηλοφρονεῖν, μηδὲ
²age ¹Charge thou not to be highminded, nor

ἠλπικέναι ἐπὶ πλούτου ἀδηλότητι, ἀλλ᾽
to have set on ²of riches ¹[the] uncertainty, but
[their] hope

ἐπὶ θεῷ τῷ παρέχοντι ἡμῖν πάντα
on God the [one] offering to us all things

πλουσίως εἰς ἀπόλαυσιν, 18 ἀγαθοεργεῖν,
richly for enjoyment, to work good,

πλουτεῖν ἐν ἔργοις καλοῖς, εὐμεταδότους
to be rich in ²works ¹good, ²ready to impart

εἶναι, κοινωνικούς, 19 ἀποθησαυρίζοντας
¹to be, generous, treasuring away

ἑαυτοῖς θεμέλιον καλὸν εἰς τὸ μέλλον,
for ²foundation ¹a good for the future,
themselves

ἵνα ἐπιλάβωνται τῆς ὄντως ζωῆς. 20 Ὦ
in or- they may lay the really life. Ο
der that hold on

Τιμόθεε, τὴν παραθήκην φύλαξον, ἐκτρεπ-
Timothy, ²the ²deposit ¹guard, turning

όμενος τὰς βεβήλους κενοφωνίας καὶ
aside from the profane empty utterances and

ἀντιθέσεις τῆς ψευδωνύμου γνώσεως, 21 ἥν
opposing of the falsely named knowledge, which
tenets

τινες ἐπαγγελλόμενοι περὶ τὴν πίστιν
some promising concerning the faith

ἠστόχησαν.
missed aim.

Ἡ χάρις μεθ᾽ ὑμῶν.
- Grace [be] with you.

King James Version

New International Version

THE SECOND EPISTLE

OF PAUL THE APOSTLE

TO

TIMOTHY

2 TIMOTHY

1 Paul, an apostle of Jesus Christ by the will of God, according to the promise of life which is in Christ Jesus, 2 To Timothy, *my* dearly beloved son: Grace, mercy, *and* peace, from God the Father and Christ Jesus our Lord. 3 I thank God, whom I serve from *my* forefathers with pure conscience, that without ceasing I have remembrance of thee in my prayers night and day; 4 Greatly desiring to see thee, being mindful of thy tears, that I may be filled with joy; 5 When I call to remembrance the unfeigned faith that is in thee, which dwelt first in thy grandmother Lois, and thy mother Eunice; and I am persuaded that in thee also. 6 Wherefore I put thee in remembrance, that thou stir up the gift of God, which is in thee by the putting on of my hands. 7 For God hath not given us the spirit of fear; but of power, and of love, and of a sound mind. 8 Be not thou therefore ashamed of the testimony of our Lord, nor of me his prisoner: but be thou partaker of the afflictions of the gospel according to the power of God; 9 Who hath saved us, and called *us* with a holy calling, not according to our works, but according to his own purpose and grace, which was given us in Christ Jesus before the world began; 10 But is now made manifest by the appearing of our Saviour Jesus Christ, who hath abolished death, and hath brought life and immortality to light through the gospel: 11 Whereunto I am appointed a preacher, and an apostle, and a teacher of the Gentiles. 12 For the which cause I also suffer these things: nevertheless I am not ashamed; for I know whom I have believed, and am persuaded that he is able to keep that which I have committed unto him against that day. 13 Hold fast the form of sound words, which thou hast heard of me, in faith and love which is in Christ Jesus. 14 That good thing which was committed unto thee keep by the Holy Ghost which dwelleth in us. 15 This thou knowest, that all they which are in Asia be turned away from me; of whom are Phygellus and Hermogenes. 16 The Lord give mercy unto the house of Onesiphorus; for he oft refreshed me, and was not ashamed of my chain: 17 But, when he was in Rome, he sought me out very diligently, and found *me*. 18 The Lord grant unto him that he may find mercy of the Lord in that day: and in how many things he ministered unto me at Ephesus, thou knowest very well.

1 Paul, an apostle of Christ Jesus by the will of God, according to the promise of life that is in Christ Jesus,
2 To Timothy, my dear son:
Grace, mercy and peace from God the Father and Christ Jesus our Lord.

Encouragement to be faithful

3 I thank God, whom I serve, as my forefathers did, with a clear conscience, as night and day I constantly remember you in my prayers. 4 Recalling your tears, I long to see you, so that I may be filled with joy. 5 I have been reminded of your sincere faith, which first lived in your grandmother Lois and in your mother Eunice, and I am persuaded, now lives in you also. 6 For this reason I remind you to fan into flame the gift of God, which is in you through the laying on of my hands. 7 For God did not give us a spirit of timidity, but a spirit of power, of love and of self-discipline.
8 So do not be ashamed to testify about our Lord, or ashamed of me his prisoner. But join with me in suffering for the gospel, by the power of God, 9 who has saved us and called us to a holy life—not because of anything we have done but because of his own purpose and grace. This grace was given us in Christ Jesus before the beginning of time, 10 but it has now been revealed through the appearing of our Savior, Christ Jesus, who has destroyed death and has brought life and immortality to light through the gospel. 11 And of this gospel I was appointed a herald and an apostle and a teacher. 12 That is why I am suffering as I am. Yet I am not ashamed, because I know whom I have believed, and am convinced that he is able to guard what I have entrusted to him for that day.
13 What you heard from me, keep as the pattern of sound teaching, with faith and love in Christ Jesus. 14 Guard the good deposit that was entrusted to you—guard it with the help of the Holy Spirit who lives in us.
15 You know that everyone in the province of Asia has deserted me, including Phygelus and Hermogenes.
16 May the Lord show mercy to the household of Onesiphorus, because he often refreshed me and was not ashamed of my chains. 17 On the contrary, when he was in Rome, he searched hard for me until he found me. 18 May the Lord grant that he will find mercy from the Lord on that day! You know very well in how many ways he helped me in Ephesus.

624

ΠΡΟΣ   ΤΙΜΟΘΕΟΝ Β

Chapter 1

Παῦλος   ἀπόστολος   Χριστοῦ   Ἰησοῦ   διὰ
Paul   an apostle   of Christ   Jesus through

θελήματος   θεοῦ   κατ'   ἐπαγγελίαν   ζωῆς
[the] will   of God   by way of   a promise   of life

τῆς   ἐν   Χριστῷ   Ἰησοῦ   2 Τιμοθέῳ   ἀγαπητῷ
-   in   Christ   Jesus   to Timothy   beloved

τέκνῳ·   χάρις,   ἔλεος,   εἰρήνη   ἀπὸ   θεοῦ
child: Grace,   mercy,   peace   from   God

πατρὸς   καὶ   Χριστοῦ   Ἰησοῦ   τοῦ   κυρίου
[our] Father and   Christ   Jesus   the   Lord

ἡμῶν.
of us.

3 Χάριν   ἔχω   τῷ   θεῷ,   ᾧ   λατρεύω
Thanks   I have   -   to God, whom   I worship

ἀπὸ   προγόνων   ἐν   καθαρᾷ   συνειδήσει,   ὡς
from   [my] forebears in   a clean   conscience,   as

ἀδιάλειπτον   ἔχω   τὴν   περὶ   σοῦ   μνείαν
unceasingly   I have   ¹the   ²concerning   ³thee   ⁴remembrance

ἐν   ταῖς   δεήσεσίν   μου   νυκτὸς   καὶ   ἡμέρας,
in   the   petitions   of me   night   and   day,

4 ἐπιποθῶν   σε   ἰδεῖν,   μεμνημένος   σου
longing   ²thee   ¹to see,   having been   ³of thee
                           reminded

τῶν   δακρύων,   ἵνα   χαρᾶς   πληρωθῶ,
¹of the   ²tears,   in order   of(with) joy   I may be filled,
                   that

5 ὑπόμνησιν   λαβὼν   τῆς   ἐν   σοὶ   ἀνυποκρίτου
¹recollection   ²taking   ³of the   ⁴in   ⁵thee   ⁶unfeigned

πίστεως,   ἥτις   ἐνῴκησεν   πρῶτον   ἐν   τῇ
⁷faith,   which   indwelt   firstly   in   the

μάμμῃ   σου   Λωΐδι   καὶ   τῇ   μητρί   σου
grand-   of thee   Lois   and [in] the   mother   of thee
mother

Εὐνίκῃ,   πέπεισμαι   δὲ   ὅτι   καὶ   ἐν   σοί.
Eunice,   and I have been   that [it dwells] in   thee.
          persuaded   also

6 Δι'   ἣν   αἰτίαν   ἀναμιμνήσκω   σε   ἀνα-
For   which   cause   I remind   thee   to fan

ζωπυρεῖν   τὸ   χάρισμα   τοῦ   θεοῦ,   ὅ   ἐστιν
the flame [of]   the   gift   of God, which is

ἐν   σοὶ   διὰ   τῆς   ἐπιθέσεως   τῶν   χειρῶν
in   thee   through   the   laying on   of the   hands

μου.   7 οὐ   γὰρ   ἔδωκεν   ἡμῖν   ὁ   θεὸς
of me.   ²not   For   ¹gave   ⁴to us   -³God

πνεῦμα   δειλίας,   ἀλλὰ   δυνάμεως   καὶ   ἀγάπης
a spirit   of cowardice, but   of power   and   of love

καὶ   σωφρονισμοῦ.   8 μὴ   οὖν   ἐπαισχυνθῇς
and   of self-control.   ²not ¹Therefore   ³be ³thou
                                  ashamed [of]

τὸ   μαρτύριον   τοῦ   κυρίου   ἡμῶν   μηδὲ
the   testimony   of the   Lord   of us   nor

ἐμὲ   τὸν   δέσμιον   αὐτοῦ,   ἀλλὰ   συγ-
[of] me   the   prisoner   of him,   but   suffer

κακοπάθησον   τῷ   εὐαγγελίῳ   κατὰ   δύναμιν
ill with   the   gospel   according to [the] power

θεοῦ,   9 τοῦ   σώσαντος   ἡμᾶς   καὶ   καλέσαντος
of God,   of the   having saved   us   and   having called
        [one]

κλήσει   ἁγίᾳ,   οὐ   κατὰ   τὰ   ἔργα   ἡμῶν
¹calling   ¹with a holy, not according to the   works   of us

ἀλλὰ   κατὰ   ἰδίαν   πρόθεσιν   καὶ   χάριν,
but   according to [his] own   purpose   and   grace,

τὴν   δοθεῖσαν   ἡμῖν   ἐν   Χριστῷ   Ἰησοῦ
-   given   to us   in   Christ   Jesus

πρὸ   χρόνων   αἰωνίων,   10 φανερωθεῖσαν   δὲ
before   times   eternal,   but manifested

νῦν   διὰ   τῆς   ἐπιφανείας   τοῦ   σωτῆρος
now   through   the   appearance   of the   Saviour

ἡμῶν   Χριστοῦ   Ἰησοῦ,   καταργήσαντος   μὲν
of us   Christ   Jesus,   ²abrogating   ¹on one
                                    hand

τὸν   θάνατον   φωτίσαντος   δὲ   ζωὴν   καὶ
-   death   ³bringing to   ¹on the   ⁴life   and
                  light   ²other

ἀφθαρσίαν   διὰ   τοῦ   εὐαγγελίου,   11 εἰς   ὃ
incorruption   through   the   gospel,   for which

ἐτέθην   ἐγὼ   κῆρυξ   καὶ   ἀπόστολος   καὶ
²was   ¹I   a herald   and   an apostle   and
appointed

διδάσκαλος·   12 δι'   ἣν   αἰτίαν   καὶ   ταῦτα
a teacher;   for which   cause   also these things

πάσχω,   ἀλλ'   οὐκ   ἐπαισχύνομαι,   οἶδα   γὰρ
I suffer,   but   I am not ashamed,   for I know

ᾧ   πεπίστευκα,   καὶ   πέπεισμαι   ὅτι   δυνατός
whom   I have   and   I have been   that   ²able
    believed,   persuaded

ἐστιν   τὴν   παραθήκην   μου   φυλάξαι   εἰς
¹he is   ⁴the   ⁵deposit   ⁶of me   ³to guard   to

ἐκείνην   τὴν   ἡμέραν.   13 ὑποτύπωσιν   ἔχε
that   -   day.   ²a pattern   ¹Have
                              thou

ὑγιαινόντων   λόγων   ὧν   παρ'   ἐμοῦ   ἤκουσας
of being healthy   words   which   ²from   ³me   ¹thou
                             heardest

ἐν   πίστει   καὶ   ἀγάπῃ   τῇ   ἐν   Χριστῷ
in   faith   and   love   -   in   Christ

Ἰησοῦ·   14 τὴν   καλὴν   παραθήκην   φύλαξον
Jesus;   the   good   deposit   guard

διὰ   πνεύματος   ἁγίου   τοῦ   ἐνοικοῦντος   ἐν
through   Spirit   [the] Holy   -   indwelling   in

ἡμῖν.   15 Οἶδας   τοῦτο,   ὅτι   ἀπεστράφησάν
us.   Thou knowest   this,   that   turned away from

με   πάντες   οἱ   ἐν   τῇ   Ἀσίᾳ,   ὧν   ἐστιν
me   all   the ones in   -   Asia, of whom   is

Φύγελος   καὶ   Ἑρμογένης.   16 δῴη   ἔλεος
Phygelus   and   Hermogenes.   ¹May ⁴give   ⁵mercy

ὁ   κύριος   τῷ   Ὀνησιφόρου   οἴκῳ,   ὅτι
²the   ³Lord   ⁶to the   ⁸of Onesiphorus   ⁷house- because
                                    hold,

πολλάκις   με   ἀνέψυξεν   καὶ   τὴν   ἅλυσίν
often   me   he refreshed   and   the   chain

μου   οὐκ   ἐπαισχύνθη,   17 ἀλλὰ   γενόμενος
of me   was not ashamed [of],   but   coming to be

ἐν   Ῥώμῃ   σπουδαίως   ἐζήτησέν   με   καὶ
in   Rome   ²diligently   ¹he ³sought   ⁴me   ⁵and

εὗρεν·   —   18 δῴη   αὐτῷ   ὁ   κύριος   εὑρεῖν
⁶found;   ¹May ³give   ⁴to him   ²the   ⁵Lord   to find

ἔλεος   παρὰ   κυρίου   ἐν   ἐκείνῃ   τῇ   ἡμέρᾳ·
mercy   from   [the] Lord   in   that   -   day;)

—   καὶ   ὅσα   ἐν   Ἐφέσῳ   διηκόνησεν,
   and what things in   Ephesus   he served,

βέλτιον   σὺ   γινώσκεις.
very well   thou   knowest.

2 Thou therefore, my son, be strong in the grace that is in Christ Jesus. 2And the things that thou hast heard of me among many witnesses, the same commit thou to faithful men, who shall be able to teach others also. 3 Thou therefore endure hardness, as a good soldier of Jesus Christ. 4 No man that warreth entangleth himself with the affairs of *this* life; that he may please him who hath chosen him to be a soldier. 5And if a man also strive for masteries, *yet* is he not crowned, except he strive lawfully. 6 The husbandman that laboureth must be first partaker of the fruits. 7 Consider what I say; and the Lord give thee understanding in all things. 8 Remember that Jesus Christ of the seed of David was raised from the dead, according to my gospel: 9 Wherein I suffer trouble, as an evil doer, *even* unto bonds; but the word of God is not bound. 10 Therefore I endure all things for the elect's sake, that they may also obtain the salvation which is in Christ Jesus with eternal glory. 11 *It is* a faithful saying: For if we be dead with *him,* we shall also live with *him:* 12 If we suffer, we shall also reign with *him:* if we deny *him,* he also will deny us: 13 If we believe not, *yet* he abideth faithful: he cannot deny himself. 14 Of these things put *them* in remembrance, charging *them* before the Lord that they strive not about words to no profit, *but* to the subverting of the hearers. 15 Study to shew thyself approved unto God, a workman that needeth not to be ashamed, rightly dividing the word of truth. 16 But shun profane *and* vain babblings: for they will increase unto more ungodliness. 17And their word will eat as doth a canker: of whom is Hymeneus and Philetus; 18 Who concerning the truth have erred, saying that the resurrection is past already; and overthrow the faith of some. 19 Nevertheless the foundation of God standeth sure, having this seal, The Lord knoweth them that are his. And, Let every one that nameth the name of Christ depart from iniquity. 20 But in a great house there are not only vessels of gold and of silver, but also of wood and of earth; and some to honour, and some to dishonour. 21 If a man therefore purge himself from these, he shall be a vessel unto honour, sanctified, and meet for the master's use, *and* prepared unto every good work. 22 Flee also youthful lusts: but follow righteousness, faith, charity, peace, with them that call on the Lord out of a pure heart. 23 But foolish and unlearned questions avoid, knowing that they do gender strifes. 24And the servant of the Lord must not strive; but be gentle unto all *men,* apt to teach, patient; 25 In meekness instructing those that oppose themselves; if God peradventure will give them repentance to the acknowledging of the truth; 26And *that* they may recover themselves out of the snare of the devil, who are taken captive by him at his will.

2 You then, my son, be strong in the grace that is in Christ Jesus. 2And the things you have heard me say in the presence of many witnesses entrust to reliable men who will also be qualified to teach others. 3 Endure hardship with us like a good soldier of Christ Jesus. 4 No one serving as a soldier gets involved in civilian affairs—he wants to please his commanding officer. 5 Similarly, if anyone competes as an athlete, he does not receive the victor's crown unless he competes according to the rules. 6 The hardworking farmer should be the first to receive a share of the crops. 7 Reflect on what I am saying, for the Lord will give you insight into all this.

8 Remember Jesus Christ, raised from the dead, descended from David. This is my gospel, 9 for which I am suffering even to the point of being chained like a criminal. But God's word is not chained. 10 Therefore I endure everything for the sake of the elect, that they too may obtain the salvation that is in Christ Jesus, with eternal glory.

11 Here is a trustworthy saying:
  If we died with him,
    we will also live with him;
12 if we endure,
    we will also reign with him.
  If we disown him,
    he will also disown us;
13 if we are faithless,
    he will remain faithful,
    for he cannot disown himself.

A workman approved by God

14 Keep reminding them of these things. Warn them before God against quarreling about words; it is of no value, and only ruins those who listen. 15 Do your best to present yourself to God as one approved, a workman who does not need to be ashamed and who correctly handles the word of truth. 16Avoid godless chatter, because those who indulge in it will become more and more ungodly. 17 Their teaching will spread like gangrene. Among them are Hymenaeus and Philetus, 18 who have wandered away from the truth. They say that the resurrection has already taken place, and they destroy the faith of some. 19 Nevertheless, God's solid foundation stands firm, sealed with this inscription: "The Lord knows those who are his," [a] and, "Everyone who confesses the name of the Lord must turn away from wickedness."

20 In a large house there are not only articles of gold and silver, but also of wood and clay; some are for noble purposes and some for ignoble. 21 If a man cleanses himself from the latter, he will be an instrument for noble purposes, made holy, useful to the Master and prepared to do any good work.

22 Flee the evil desires of youth, and pursue righteousness, faith, love and peace, along with those who call on the Lord out of a pure heart. 23 Don't have anything to do with foolish and stupid arguments, because you know they produce quarrels. 24And the Lord's servant must not quarrel; instead, he must be kind to everyone, able to teach, not resentful. 25 Those who oppose him he must gently instruct, in the hope that God will give them a change of heart leading them to a knowledge of the truth, 26 and that they will come to their senses and escape from the trap of the devil, who has taken them captive to do his will.

[a] Num. 16:5.

Greek Interlinear
Chapter 2

Σὺ οὖν, τέκνον μου, ἐνδυναμοῦ ἐν
Thou therefore, child of me, be empowered by

τῇ χάριτι τῇ ἐν Χριστῷ Ἰησοῦ, 2 καὶ
the grace – in Christ Jesus. and

ἃ ἤκουσας παρ' ἐμοῦ διὰ πολλῶν
what thou heardest from me through many

μαρτύρων, ταῦτα παράθου πιστοῖς ἀνθρώ-
witnesses, these commit to faithful men,

ποις, οἵτινες ἱκανοὶ ἔσονται καὶ ἑτέρους
who ²competent ¹will be ³also ⁴others

διδάξαι. 3 Συγκακοπάθησον ὡς καλὸς
²to teach. Suffer ill with* as a good

στρατιώτης Χριστοῦ Ἰησοῦ. 4 οὐδεὶς
soldier of Christ Jesus. No one

στρατευόμενος ἐμπλέκεται ταῖς τοῦ βίου
soldiering is involved ¹with the – ²of life

πραγματείαις, ἵνα τῷ στρατολογήσαντι
²affairs, in order ⁴the ³having enlisted
that [one] [him]

ἀρέσῃ. 5 ἐὰν δὲ καὶ ἀθλῇ τις, οὐ
¹he may And if also ¹wrestles ²any- not
please. one,

στεφανοῦται ἐὰν μὴ νομίμως ἀθλήσῃ.
he is crowned unless ²lawfully ¹he wrestles.

6 τὸν κοπιῶντα γεωργὸν δεῖ πρῶτον τῶν
²the ³labouring ⁴husbandman ¹It be- ⁵firstly ⁷of the
hoves

καρπῶν μεταλαμβάνειν. 7 νόει ὃ λέγω·
⁶fruits ⁸to partake. Consider what I say;

δώσει γάρ σοι ὁ κύριος σύνεσιν ἐν
for ²will give ⁴thee ¹the ³Lord understanding in

πᾶσιν. 8 μνημόνευε Ἰησοῦν Χριστὸν
all things. Remember Jesus Christ

ἐγηγερμένον ἐκ νεκρῶν, ἐκ σπέρματος
having been raised from [the] dead, of [the] seed

Δαυίδ, κατὰ τὸ εὐαγγέλιόν μου· 9 ἐν
of David, according to the gospel of me; in

ᾧ κακοπαθῶ μέχρι δεσμῶν ὡς κακοῦργος,
which I suffer ill unto bonds as an evildoer,

ἀλλὰ ὁ λόγος τοῦ θεοῦ οὐ δέδεται.
but the word – of God has not been bound.

10 διὰ τοῦτο πάντα ὑπομένω διὰ τοὺς
Therefore all things I endure on ac- the
count of

ἐκλεκτούς, ἵνα καὶ αὐτοὶ σωτηρίας τύχωσιν
chosen ones, in or- ³also ¹they ⁴salvation ²may obtain
der that

τῆς ἐν Χριστῷ Ἰησοῦ μετὰ δόξης
– in Christ Jesus with glory

αἰωνίου. 11 πιστὸς ὁ λόγος· εἰ γὰρ
eternal. Faithful [is] the word; if for

συναπεθάνομεν, καὶ συζήσομεν· 12 εἰ
we died with [him], also we shall live with [him]; if

ὑπομένομεν, καὶ συμβασιλεύσομεν· εἰ
we endure, also we shall reign with [him]; if

ἀρνησόμεθα, κἀκεῖνος ἀρνήσεται ἡμᾶς· 13 εἰ
we shall deny, that one also will deny us; if

ἀπιστοῦμεν, ἐκεῖνος πιστὸς μένει, ἀρνή-
we disbelieve, that one ²faithful ¹remains, ²to

σασθαι γὰρ ἑαυτὸν οὐ δύναται. 14 Ταῦτα
deny ¹for ⁴himself ³he cannot. These things

ὑπομίμνησκε, διαμαρτυρόμενος ἐνώπιον τοῦ
remind thou solemnly witnessing before –
[them] [of],

θεοῦ μὴ λογομαχεῖν, ἐπ' οὐδὲν χρήσιμον,
God not to fight with words, for ²nothing ¹useful,

ἐπὶ καταστροφῇ τῶν ἀκουόντων. 15 σπού-
for overthrowing of the [ones] hearing. ¹Be

δασον σεαυτὸν δόκιμον παραστῆσαι τῷ
eager ¹thyself ²approved ³to present –

θεῷ, ἐργάτην ἀνεπαίσχυντον, ὀρθοτομοῦντα
to God, a workman unashamed, cutting straight

τὸν λόγον τῆς ἀληθείας. 16 τὰς δὲ
the word – of truth. – But

βεβήλους κενοφωνίας περιΐστασο· ²τὸ ⁴πλεῖον
profane empty shun; ²to ⁴more
utterances

γὰρ προκόψουσιν ἀσεβείας, 17 καὶ ὁ λόγος
¹for ³they will advance of impiety, and the word

αὐτῶν ὡς γάγγραινα νομὴν ἕξει· ὧν
of them as a canker feeding will have; of
whom

ἐστιν Ὑμέναιος καὶ Φίλητος, 18 οἵτινες
is(are) Hymenæus and Philetus, who

περὶ τὴν ἀλήθειαν ἠστόχησαν, λέγοντες
con- the truth missed aim, saying
cerning

ἀνάστασιν ἤδη γεγονέναι, καὶ ἀνατρέπουσιν
[the] already to have and overturn
resurrection become,

τήν τινων πίστιν. 19 ὁ μέντοι στερεὸς
the ²of some ¹faith. ²the ¹However firm

θεμέλιος τοῦ θεοῦ ἕστηκεν, ἔχων τὴν
foundation – of God stands, having the

σφραγῖδα ταύτην· ἔγνω κύριος τοὺς ὄντας
seal this; ¹knew ²[The] the being
Lord [ones]

αὐτοῦ, καί· Ἀποστήτω ἀπὸ ἀδικίας πᾶς
of him, and: Let stand away from iniquity every-

ὁ ὀνομάζων τὸ ὄνομα κυρίου. 20 ἐν
one naming the name of [the] Lord. ²in

μεγάλῃ δὲ οἰκίᾳ οὐκ ἔστιν μόνον σκεύη
²a great ¹Now ⁴house there is(are) not only vessels

χρυσᾶ καὶ ἀργυρᾶ, ἀλλὰ καὶ ξύλινα
golden and silvern, but also wooden

καὶ ὀστράκινα, καὶ ἃ μὲν εἰς τιμὴν ἃ δὲ
and earthen, and some to honour others

εἰς ἀτιμίαν· 21 ἐὰν οὖν τις ἐκκαθάρῃ
to dishonour; if therefore anyone cleanses

ἑαυτὸν ἀπὸ τούτων, ἔσται σκεῦος εἰς
himself from these [latter], he will be a vessel to

τιμήν, ἡγιασμένον, εὔχρηστον τῷ δεσπότῃ,
honour, having been suitable for the master,
sanctified,

εἰς πᾶν ἔργον ἀγαθὸν ἡτοιμασμένον.
to every work good having been prepared.

22 τὰς δὲ νεωτερικὰς ἐπιθυμίας φεῦγε,
Now the ²youthful ¹lusts ¹flee,

δίωκε δὲ δικαιοσύνην, πίστιν, ἀγάπην,
but pursue righteousness, faith, love,

εἰρήνην μετὰ τῶν ἐπικαλουμένων τὸν
peace with the [ones] calling on the

κύριον ἐκ καθαρᾶς καρδίας. 23 τὰς δὲ
Lord out of a clean heart. – But

μωρὰς καὶ ἀπαιδεύτους ζητήσεις παραιτοῦ,
foolish and uninstructed questionings refuse,

εἰδὼς ὅτι γεννῶσιν μάχας· 24 δοῦλον δὲ
knowing that they beget fights; and ²a slave

κυρίου οὐ δεῖ μάχεσθαι ἀλλὰ ἤπιον
²of [the] ¹it behoves not to fight but gentle
Lord

εἶναι πρὸς πάντας, διδακτικόν, ἀνεξίκακον,
to be toward all men, apt to teach, forbearing,

25 ἐν πραΰτητι παιδεύοντα τοὺς ἀντιδιατι-
in meekness instructing the [ones] oppos-

θεμένους, μήποτε δῴη αὐτοῖς ὁ θεὸς
ing, [if] perhaps ¹may ²them – ¹God
give

μετάνοιαν εἰς ἐπίγνωσιν ἀληθείας, 26 καὶ
repentance for a full knowledge of truth, and

ἀνανήψωσιν ἐκ τῆς τοῦ διαβόλου παγίδος,
they may return out of ¹the ²of the ²devil ¹snare,
to soberness

ἐζωγρημένοι ὑπ' αὐτοῦ εἰς τὸ ἐκείνου θέλημα.
having been by him[.] to ¹the ²of that ¹will.
caught one

* See l. 8.   ✠ That is, of God (the remoter antecedent).

King James Version

New International Version

Godlessness in the last days

3 This know also, that in the last days perilous times shall come. 2 For men shall be lovers of their own selves, covetous, boasters, proud, blasphemers, disobedient to parents, unthankful, unholy, 3 Without natural affection, trucebreakers, false accusers, incontinent, fierce, despisers of those that are good, 4 Traitors, heady, highminded, lovers of pleasures more than lovers of God; 5 Having a form of godliness, but denying the power thereof: from such turn away. 6 For of this sort are they which creep into houses, and lead captive silly women laden with sins, led away with divers lusts, 7 Ever learning, and never able to come to the knowledge of the truth. 8 Now as Jannes and Jambres withstood Moses, so do these also resist the truth: men of corrupt minds, reprobate concerning the faith. 9 But they shall proceed no further: for their folly shall be manifest unto all *men*, as theirs also was. 10 But thou hast fully known my doctrine, manner of life, purpose, faith, longsuffering, charity, patience, 11 Persecutions, afflictions, which came unto me at Antioch, at Iconium, at Lystra; what persecutions I endured: but out of *them* all the Lord delivered me. 12 Yea, and all that will live godly in Christ Jesus shall suffer persecution. 13 But evil men and seducers shall wax worse and worse, deceiving, and being deceived. 14 But continue thou in the things which thou hast learned and hast been assured of, knowing of whom thou hast learned *them;* 15 And that from a child thou hast known the holy Scriptures, which are able to make thee wise unto salvation through faith which is in Christ Jesus. 16 All Scripture is given by inspiration of God, and *is* profitable for doctrine, for reproof, for correction, for instruction in righteousness: 17 That the man of God may be perfect, thoroughly furnished unto all good works.

3 But mark this: There will be terrible times in the last days. 2 People will be lovers of themselves, lovers of money, boastful, proud, abusive, disobedient to their parents, ungrateful, unholy, 3 without love, unforgiving, slanderous, without self-control, brutal, not lovers of the good, 4 treacherous, rash, conceited, lovers of pleasure rather than lovers of God—5 having a form of godliness but denying its power. Have nothing to do with them.

6 They are the kind who worm their way into homes and gain control over weak-willed women, who are loaded down with sins and are swayed by all kinds of evil desires, 7 always learning but never able to acknowledge the truth. 8 Just as Jannes and Jambres opposed Moses, so also these men oppose the truth—men of depraved minds, who, as far as the faith is concerned, are rejected. 9 But they will not get very far because, as in the case of those men, their folly will be clear to everyone.

Paul's charge to Timothy

10 You, however, know all about my teaching, my way of life, my purpose, faith, patience, love, endurance, 11 persecutions, sufferings—what kinds of things happened to me in Antioch, Iconium and Lystra, the persecutions I endured. Yet the Lord rescued me from all of them. 12 In fact, everyone who wants to live a godly life in Christ Jesus will be persecuted, 13 while evil men and impostors will go from bad to worse, deceiving and being deceived. 14 But as for you, continue in what you have learned and have become convinced of, because you know those from whom you learned it, 15 and how from infancy you have known the holy Scriptures, which are able to make you wise for salvation through faith in Christ Jesus. 16 All Scripture is God-breathed and is useful for teaching, rebuking, correcting and training in righteousness, 17 so that the man of God may be thoroughly equipped for every good work.

4 I charge *thee* therefore before God, and the Lord Jesus Christ, who shall judge the quick and the dead at his appearing and his kingdom; 2 Preach the word; be instant in season, out of season; reprove, rebuke, exhort with all longsuffering and doctrine. 3 For the time will come when they will not endure sound doctrine; but after their own lusts shall they heap to themselves teachers, having itching ears; 4 And they shall turn away *their* ears from the truth, and shall be turned unto fables. 5 But watch thou

4 In the presence of God and of Christ Jesus, who will judge the living and the dead, and in view of his appearing and his kingdom, I give you this charge: 2 Preach the Word; be prepared in season and out of season; correct, rebuke and encourage—with great patience and careful instruction. 3 For the time will come when men will not put up with sound doctrine. Instead, to suit their own desires, they will gather around them a great number of teachers to say what their itching ears want to hear. 4 They will turn their ears away from the truth and turn aside to myths. 5 But you, keep your head in all

Greek Interlinear

Chapter 2

Τοῦτο δὲ γίνωσκε, ὅτι ἐν ἐσχάταις
And this know thou, that in [the] last

ἡμέραις ἐνστήσονται καιροὶ χαλεποί·
days ²will be at hand ¹times ¹grievous;

2 ἔσονται γὰρ οἱ ἄνθρωποι φίλαυτοι,
for ²will be – ¹men self-lovers,

φιλάργυροι, ἀλαζόνες, ὑπερήφανοι, βλάσφημοι,
money-lovers, boasters, arrogant, blasphemers,

γονεῦσιν ἀπειθεῖς, ἀχάριστοι, ἀνόσιοι,
²to parents ¹disobedient, unthankful, unholy,

3 ἄστοργοι, ἄσπονδοι, διάβολοι, ἀκρατεῖς,
without natural implacable, slanderers, incontinent,
affection,

ἀνήμεροι, ἀφιλάγαθοι, 4 προδόται, προπετεῖς,
untamed, haters of good betrayers, reckless,
[things/men],

τετυφωμένοι, φιλήδονοι μᾶλλον ἢ φιλόθεοι,
having been pleasure-lovers rather than God-lovers,
puffed up,

5 ἔχοντες μόρφωσιν εὐσεβείας τὴν δὲ
having a form of piety but the

δύναμιν αὐτῆς ἠρνημένοι· καὶ τούτους
power of it having denied: and ²these

ἀποτρέπου. 6 ἐκ τούτων γάρ εἰσιν οἱ
²turn away ¹from. ²of ¹these ¹For are the

ἐνδύνοντες εἰς τὰς οἰκίας καὶ αἰχμαλωτίζ-
[ones] creeping into – houses and captur-

οντες γυναικάρια σεσωρευμένα ἁμαρτίαις,
ing silly women having been heaped* with sins,

ἀγόμενα ἐπιθυμίαις ποικίλαις, 7 πάντοτε
being led* lusts by various, always

μανθάνοντα καὶ μηδέποτε εἰς ἐπίγνωσιν
learning* and never ³to ⁴a full knowledge

ἀληθείας ἐλθεῖν δυνάμενα. 8 ὃν τρόπον
²of truth ²to come ¹being able.* by what way

δὲ Ἰάννης καὶ Ἰαμβρῆς ἀντέστησαν
Now Jannes and Jambres opposed

Μωϋσεῖ, οὕτως καὶ οὗτοι ἀνθίστανται τῇ
Moses, so also these oppose the

ἀληθείᾳ, ἄνθρωποι κατεφθαρμένοι τὸν νοῦν,
truth, men having been corrupted the mind,
= with corrupted mind,

ἀδόκιμοι περὶ τὴν πίστιν. 9 ἀλλ' οὐ
reprobate as to the faith. But not

προκόψουσιν ἐπὶ πλεῖον· ἡ γὰρ ἄνοια
they will advance to more; for the folly
= farther;

αὐτῶν ἔκδηλος ἔσται πᾶσιν, ὡς καὶ
of them very clear will be to all men, as also

ἡ ἐκείνων ἐγένετο. 10 Σὺ δὲ παρηκολού-
the of those became. But thou hast closely
[folly]

θησάς μου τῇ διδασκαλίᾳ, τῇ ἀγωγῇ,
followed of me the teaching, the conduct,

τῇ προθέσει, τῇ πίστει, τῇ μακροθυμίᾳ,
the purpose, the faith, the longsuffering,

τῇ ἀγάπῃ, τῇ ὑπομονῇ, 11 τοῖς διωγμοῖς,
the love, the endurance, the persecutions,

τοῖς παθήμασιν, οἷά μοι ἐγένετο ἐν
the sufferings, which ²to me ¹happened in

Ἀντιοχείᾳ, ἐν Ἰκονίῳ, ἐν Λύστροις· οἵους
Antioch, in Iconium, in Lystra: what

διωγμοὺς ὑπήνεγκα, καὶ ἐκ πάντων με
persecutions I bore, and out of all ¹me

ἐρρύσατο ὁ κύριος. 12 καὶ πάντες δὲ
²delivered ¹the ¹Lord. ²indeed ³all ¹And

οἱ θέλοντες ζῆν εὐσεβῶς ἐν Χριστῷ
the [ones] wishing to live piously in Christ

Ἰησοῦ διωχθήσονται. 13 πονηροὶ δὲ ἄν-
Jesus will be persecuted. But evil men

θρωποι καὶ γόητες προκόψουσιν ἐπὶ τὸ
and impostors will advance to the

χεῖρον, πλανῶντες καὶ πλανώμενοι. 14 σὺ
worse, deceiving and being deceived. ²thou

δὲ μένε ἐν οἷς ἔμαθες καὶ ἐπιστώθης,
But ¹continue in what thou didst and wast assured of,
things learn

εἰδὼς παρὰ τίνων ἔμαθες, 15 καὶ ὅτι
knowing from whom* thou didst learn, and that

ἀπὸ βρέφους ἱερὰ γράμματα οἶδας, τὰ
from a babe ²sacred ³letters ¹thou knowest, [ones]

δυνάμενά σε σοφίσαι εἰς σωτηρίαν διὰ
being able thee to make wise to salvation through

πίστεως τῆς ἐν Χριστῷ Ἰησοῦ. 16 πᾶσα
faith – in Christ Jesus. Every

γραφὴ θεόπνευστος καὶ ὠφέλιμος πρὸς
scripture [is] God-breathed and profitable for

διδασκαλίαν, πρὸς ἐλεγμόν, πρὸς ἐπανόρ-
teaching, for reproof, for cor-

θωσιν, πρὸς παιδείαν τὴν ἐν δικαιοσύνῃ,
rection, for instruction – in righteousness,

17 ἵνα ἄρτιος ᾖ ὁ τοῦ θεοῦ ἄνθρωπος,
in order ⁴fitted ⁵may ¹the – ²of God ³man,
that be

πρὸς πᾶν ἔργον ἀγαθὸν ἐξηρτισμένος.
for every work good having been furnished.

Chapter 4

Διαμαρτύρομαι ἐνώπιον τοῦ θεοῦ καὶ
I solemnly witness before – God and

Χριστοῦ Ἰησοῦ, τοῦ μέλλοντος κρίνειν
Christ Jesus, the [one] being about to judge

ζῶντας καὶ νεκρούς, καὶ τὴν ἐπιφάνειαν
living [ones] and dead, both [by] the appearance

αὐτοῦ καὶ τὴν βασιλείαν αὐτοῦ· 2 κήρυξον
of him and [by] the kingdom of him: proclaim

τὸν λόγον, ἐπίστηθι εὐκαίρως ἀκαίρως,
the word, be attentive seasonably[,] unseasonably,

ἔλεγξον, ἐπιτίμησον, παρακάλεσον, ἐν πάσῃ
reprove, admonish, exhort, with all

μακροθυμίᾳ καὶ διδαχῇ. 3 ἔσται γὰρ
longsuffering and teaching. For there will be

καιρὸς ὅτε τῆς ὑγιαινούσης διδασκαλίας
a time when ²the ³being healthy ⁴teaching

οὐκ ἀνέξονται, ἀλλὰ κατὰ τὰς ἰδίας
¹they will not bear with, but according to the(ir) own

ἐπιθυμίας ἑαυτοῖς ἐπισωρεύσουσιν διδασ-
lusts ²to themselves ¹they will heap up ²teach-

κάλους κνηθόμενοι τὴν ἀκοήν, 4 καὶ ἀπὸ
ers tickling the ear, and ³from

μὲν τῆς ἀληθείας τὴν ἀκοὴν ἀποστρέψουσιν,
¹on ⁴the ⁵truth ²the ⁶ear ¹will turn away,
one hand

ἐπὶ δὲ τοὺς μύθους ἐκτραπήσονται. 5 σὺ
²to ¹on the the ⁴tales ²will be turned aside. ²thou
other

---

* Agreeing with "silly women" (neut. pl.).

King James Version

in all things, endure afflictions, do the work of an evangelist, make full proof of thy ministry. 6 For I am now ready to be offered, and the time of my departure is at hand. 7 I have fought a good fight, I have finished *my* course, I have kept the faith: 8 Henceforth there is laid up for me a crown of righteousness, which the Lord, the righteous judge, shall give me at that day: and not to me only, but unto all them also that love his appearing. 9 Do thy diligence to come shortly unto me: 10 For Demas hath forsaken me, having loved this present world, and is departed unto Thessalonica; Crescens to Galatia, Titus unto Dalmatia. 11 Only Luke is with me. Take Mark, and bring him with thee: for he is profitable to me for the ministry. 12And Tychicus have I sent to Ephesus. 13 The cloak that I left at Troas with Carpus, when thou comest, bring *with thee, but* especially the parchments. 14Alexander the coppersmith did me much evil: the Lord reward him according to his works: 15 Of whom be thou ware also; for he hath greatly withstood our words. 16At my first answer no man stood with me, but all *men* forsook me: *I pray God* that it may not be laid to their charge. 17 Notwithstanding the Lord stood with me, and strengthened me; that by me the preaching might be fully known, and *that* all the Gentiles might hear: and I was delivered out of the mouth of the lion. 18And the Lord shall deliver me from every evil work, and will preserve *me* unto his heavenly kingdom: to whom *be* glory for ever and ever. Amen. 19 Salute Prisca and Aquila, and the household of Onesiphorus. 20 Erastus abode at Corinth: but Trophimus have I left at Miletum sick. 21 Do thy diligence to come before winter. Eubulus greeteth thee, and Pudens, and Linus, and Claudia, and all the brethren. 22 The Lord Jesus Christ *be* with thy spirit. Grace *be* with you. Amen.

The second *epistle* unto Timotheus, ordained the first bishop of the church of the Ephesians, was written from Rome, when Paul was brought before Nero the second time.

New International Version

situations, endure hardship, do the work of an evangelist, discharge all the duties of your ministry. 6 For I am already being poured out as a drink offering, and the time has come for my departure. 7 I have fought the good fight, I have finished the race, I have kept the faith. 8 Now there is in store for me the crown of righteousness, which the Lord, the righteous Judge, will award to me on that day—and not only to me, but also to all who have longed for his appearing.

Personal remarks

9 Do your best to come to me quickly, 10 for Demas, because he loved this world, has deserted me and has gone to Thessalonica. Crescens has gone to Galatia, and Titus to Dalmatia. 11 Only Luke is with me. Get Mark and bring him with you, because he is helpful to me in my ministry. 12 I sent Tychicus to Ephesus. 13 When you come, bring the cloak that I left with Carpus at Troas, and my scrolls, especially the parchments.

14 Alexander the metalworker did me a great deal of harm. The Lord will repay him for what he has done. 15 You too should be on your guard against him, because he strongly opposed our message.

16 At my first defense, no one came to my support, but everyone deserted me. May it not be held against them. 17 But the Lord stood at my side and gave me strength, so that through me the message might be fully proclaimed and all the Gentiles might hear it. And I was delivered from the lion's mouth. 18 The Lord will rescue me from every evil attack and will bring me safely to his heavenly kingdom. To him be glory for ever and ever. Amen.

Final greetings

19 Greet Priscilla[b] and Aquila and the household of Onesiphorus. 20 Erastus stayed in Corinth, and I left Trophimus sick in Miletus. 21 Do your best to get here before winter. Eubulus greets you, and so do Pudens, Linus, Claudia and all the brothers.

22 The Lord be with your spirit. Grace be with you.

[b] Greek *Prisca.*

Greek Interlinear

δὲ νῆφε ἐν πᾶσιν, κακοπάθησον, ἔργον
But ¹be in all things, suffer evil, ²[the] work
sober

ποίησον εὐαγγελιστοῦ, τὴν διακονίαν σου
¹do of an evangelist, ²the ³ministry ⁴of thee

πληροφόρησον. 6 Ἐγὼ γὰρ ἤδη σπένδομαι,
¹fulfil. For I already am being
poured out,

καὶ ὁ καιρὸς τῆς ἀναλύσεώς μου ἐφέστη-
and the time of the departure of me has

κεν. 7 τὸν καλὸν ἀγῶνα ἠγώνισμαι,
arrived. The good struggle I have struggled,

τὸν δρόμον τετέλεκα, τὴν πίστιν τετήρηκα·
the course I have finished, the faith I have kept:

8 λοιπὸν ἀπόκειταί μοι ὁ τῆς δικαιοσύνης
for the rest there is laid up for me ¹the - ²of righteousness

στέφανος, ὃν ἀποδώσει μοι ὁ κύριος
²crown, which ¹will render ⁷to me ¹the ²Lord

ἐν ἐκείνῃ τῇ ἡμέρᾳ, ὁ δίκαιος κριτής,
¹in ²that - ¹³day, ⁴the ⁶righteous ⁵judge,

οὐ μόνον δὲ ἐμοὶ ἀλλὰ καὶ πᾶσι τοῖς
²not ¹only ¹and to me but also to all the [ones]

ἠγαπηκόσι τὴν ἐπιφάνειαν αὐτοῦ.
having loved the appearance of him.

9 Σπούδασον ἐλθεῖν πρός με ταχέως·
Hasten to come to me shortly;

10 Δημᾶς γάρ με ἐγκατέλιπεν ἀγαπήσας
²Demas ¹For ⁴me ³forsook loving

τὸν νῦν αἰῶνα, καὶ ἐπορεύθη εἰς Θεσσαλο-
the now age, and went to Thessalo-
(present)

νίκην, Κρήσκης εἰς Γαλατίαν, Τίτος εἰς
nica, Crescens to Galatia, Titus to

Δαλματίαν· 11 Λουκᾶς ἐστιν μόνος μετ᾽
Dalmatia; Luke is alone with

ἐμοῦ. Μάρκον ἀναλαβὼν ἄγε μετὰ σεαυτοῦ·
me. Mark taking bring with thyself;

ἔστιν γάρ μοι εὔχρηστος εἰς διακονίαν.
²he is ¹for ⁴to me ³useful for ministry.

12 Τύχικον δὲ ἀπέστειλα εἰς Ἔφεσον.
And Tychicus I sent to Ephesus.

13 τὸν φαιλόνην, ὃν ἀπέλιπον ἐν Τρῳάδι
The cloak, which I left in Troas

παρὰ Κάρπῳ, ἐρχόμενος φέρε, καὶ τὰ
with Carpus, coming bring thou, and the

βιβλία, μάλιστα τὰς μεμβράνας. 14 Ἀλέξ-
scrolls, especially the parchments. Alex-

ανδρος ὁ χαλκεὺς πολλά μοι κακὰ
ander the coppersmith ²many ³to me ⁴evils

ἐνεδείξατο· ἀποδώσει αὐτῷ ὁ κύριος κατὰ
¹showed; ²will render ⁴to him ¹the ³Lord according to

τὰ ἔργα αὐτοῦ· 15 ὃν καὶ σὺ φυλάσσου·
the works of him; whom also ²thou ¹guard
²[against];

λίαν γὰρ ἀντέστη τοῖς ἡμετέροις λόγοις.
for greatly he opposed - our words.

16 Ἐν τῇ πρώτῃ μου ἀπολογίᾳ οὐδείς
At the first ²of me ¹defence no one

μοι παρεγένετο, ἀλλὰ πάντες με ἐγκατέ-
²me ¹was beside, but all men ²me ¹for-

λιπον· μὴ αὐτοῖς λογισθείη· 17 ὁ δὲ
sook; not to them may it be reckoned; but the

κύριός μοι παρέστη καὶ ἐνεδυνάμωσέν με,
Lord ²me ¹stood with and empowered me,

ἵνα δι᾽ ἐμοῦ τὸ κήρυγμα πληροφορηθῇ
in or- through me the proclamation might be
der that accomplished

καὶ ἀκούσωσιν πάντα τὰ ἔθνη, καὶ
and ²might hear ¹all ²the ¹nations, and

ἐρρύσθην ἐκ στόματος λέοντος. 18 ῥύσεταί
I was out of [the] mouth of [the] lion. ²will deliver
delivered

με ὁ κύριος ἀπὸ παντὸς ἔργου πονηροῦ
⁴me ¹The ²Lord from every work wicked

καὶ σώσει εἰς τὴν βασιλείαν αὐτοῦ τὴν
and will save to the ¹kingdom ²of him -

ἐπουράνιον· ᾧ ἡ δόξα εἰς τοὺς αἰῶνας
¹heavenly: to [be] glory unto the ages
whom the

τῶν αἰώνων, ἀμήν.
of the ages, Amen.

19 Ἄσπασαι Πρίσκαν καὶ Ἀκύλαν καὶ
Greet Prisca and Aquila and

τὸν Ὀνησιφόρου οἶκον. 20 Ἔραστος
the ²of Onesiphorus ¹household. Erastus

ἔμεινεν ἐν Κορίνθῳ, Τρόφιμον δὲ ἀπέλιπον
remained in Corinth, but Trophimus I left

ἐν Μιλήτῳ ἀσθενοῦντα. 21 Σπούδασον
in Miletus ailing. Hasten

πρὸ χειμῶνος ἐλθεῖν. Ἀσπάζεταί σε
before winter to come. Greets thee

Εὔβουλος καὶ Πούδης καὶ Λίνος καὶ
Eubulus and Pudens and Linus and

Κλαυδία καὶ οἱ ἀδελφοὶ πάντες.
Claudia and ²the ³brothers ¹all.

22 Ὁ κύριος μετὰ τοῦ πνεύματός σου.
The Lord [be] with the spirit of thee.

ἡ χάρις μεθ᾽ ὑμῶν.
- Grace [be] with you.

King James Version

New International Version

THE
EPISTLE OF PAUL
TO
TITUS

TITUS

1 Paul, a servant of God, and an apostle of Jesus Christ, according to the faith of God's elect, and the acknowledging of the truth which is after godliness; 2 In hope of eternal life, which God, that cannot lie, promised before the world began; 3 But hath in due times manifested his word through preaching, which is committed unto me according to the commandment of God our Saviour; 4 To Titus, *mine* own son after the common faith: Grace, mercy, *and* peace, from God the Father and the Lord Jesus Christ our Saviour. 5 For this cause left I thee in Crete, that thou shouldest set in order the things that are wanting, and ordain elders in every city, as I had appointed thee: 6 If any be blameless, the husband of one wife, having faithful children not accused of riot or unruly. 7 For a bishop must be blameless, as the steward of God; not selfwilled, not soon angry, not given to wine, no striker, not given to filthy lucre; 8 But a lover of hospitality, a lover of good men, sober, just, holy, temperate; 9 Holding fast the faithful word as he hath been taught, that he may be able by sound doctrine both to exhort and to convince the gainsayers. 10 For there are many unruly and vain talkers and deceivers, specially they of the circumcision; 11 Whose mouths must be stopped, who subvert whole houses, teaching things which they ought not, for filthy lucre's sake. 12 One of themselves, *even* a prophet of their own, said, The Cretians *are* always liars, evil beasts, slow bellies. 13 This witness is true. Wherefore rebuke them sharply, that they may be sound in the faith; 14 Not giving heed to Jewish fables, and commandments of men, that turn from the truth. 15 Unto the pure all things *are* pure: but unto them that are defiled and unbelieving *is* nothing pure; but even their mind and conscience is defiled. 16 They profess that they know God; but in works they deny *him*, being abominable, and disobedient, and unto every good work reprobate.

TITUS

1 Paul, a servant of God and an apostle of Jesus Christ for the faith of God's elect and the knowledge of the truth that leads to godliness—2 a faith and knowledge resting on the hope of eternal life, which God, who does not lie, promised before the beginning of time, 3 and at his appointed season he brought his word to light through the preaching entrusted to me by the command of God our Savior,

4 To Titus, my true son in our common faith:
Grace and peace from God the Father and Christ Jesus our Savior.

Titus' task on Crete

5 The reason I left you in Crete was that you might straighten out what was left unfinished and appoint[a] elders in every town, as I directed you. 6 An elder must be blameless, the husband of but one wife, a man whose children believe and are not open to the charge of being wild and disobedient. 7 Since an overseer[b] is entrusted with God's work, he must be blameless—not overbearing, not quick-tempered, not given to much wine, not violent, not pursuing dishonest gain. 8 Rather he must be hospitable, one who loves what is good, who is self-controlled, upright, holy and disciplined. 9 He must hold firmly to the trustworthy message as it has been taught, so that he can encourage others by sound doctrine and refute those who oppose it.

10 For there are many rebellious people, mere talkers and deceivers, especially those of the circumcision group. 11 They must be silenced, because they are ruining whole households by teaching things they ought not to teach—and that for the sake of dishonest gain. 12 Even one of their own prophets has said, "Cretans are always liars, evil brutes, lazy gluttons." 13 This testimony is true. Therefore, rebuke them sharply, so that they will be sound in the faith 14 and will pay no attention to Jewish myths or to the commands of those who reject the truth. 15 To the pure, all things are pure, but to those who are corrupted and do not believe, nothing is pure. In fact, both their minds and consciences are corrupted. 16 They claim to know God, but by their actions they deny him. They are detestable, disobedient and unfit for doing anything good.

[a] Or *ordain.* [b] Or *bishop.*

ΠΡΟΣ   ΤΙΤΟΝ
Chapter 1

Παῦλος   δοῦλος   θεοῦ,   ἀπόστολος   δὲ
Paul   a slave of God, and an apostle

'Ιησοῦ   Χριστοῦ   κατὰ   πίστιν   ἐκλεκτῶν
of Jesus Christ   according to [the] faith of chosen ones

θεοῦ   καὶ   ἐπίγνωσιν   ἀληθείας   τῆς   κατ'
of God and full know-   of [the]   -   accord-
              ledge   truth   ing to

εὐσέβειαν   2 ἐπ'   ἐλπίδι   ζωῆς   αἰωνίον,
piety   on(in) hope   life   of eternal,

ἣν   ἐπηγγείλατο   ὁ   ἀψευδὴς   θεὸς   πρὸ
which 'promised   'the 'unlying 'God   before

χρόνων   αἰωνίων,   3 ἐφανέρωσεν   δὲ   καιροῖς
times   eternal,   but 'manifested   'times

ἰδίοις   τὸν   λόγον   αὐτοῦ   ἐν   κηρύγματι
'in [its] own the word   of him   in a proclamation

ὃ   ἐπιστεύθην   ἐγὼ   κατ'   ἐπιταγὴν   τοῦ
which 'was entrust- 'I   accord- [the]   of the
     ed [with]   ing to command

σωτῆρος   ἡμῶν   θεοῦ,   4 Τίτῳ   γνησίῳ   τέκνῳ
Saviour   of us   God,   to Titus a true   child

κατὰ   κοινὴν   πίστιν·   χάρις   καὶ   εἰρήνη
accord- a common faith: Grace   and   peace
ing to

ἀπὸ   θεοῦ   πατρὸς   καὶ   Χριστοῦ   'Ιησοῦ
from   God   [the] Father and Christ   Jesus

τοῦ   σωτῆρος   ἡμῶν.
the   Saviour   of us.

5 Τούτου   χάριν   ἀπέλιπόν   σε   ἐν   Κρήτῃ,
For this reason†   I left   thee in   Crete,

ἵνα   τὰ   λείποντα   ἐπιδιορθώσῃ,   καὶ
in or- the wanting   thou shouldest   and
der that things   set in order,

καταστήσῃς   κατὰ   πόλιν   πρεσβυτέρους,   ὡς   ἐγώ
shouldest appoint in each city elders,   as   I

σοι   διεταξάμην,   6 εἴ   τίς   ἐστιν   ἀνέγκλητος,
'thee 'charged,   if anyone is   unreprovable,

μιᾶς   γυναικὸς   ἀνήρ,   τέκνα   ἔχων   πιστά,
'of one 'wife   'husband, 'children 'having 'believing,

μὴ   ἐν   κατηγορίᾳ   ἀσωτίας   ἢ   ἀνυπότακτα.
not in accusation of profligacy or   unruly.*

7 δεῖ   γὰρ   τὸν   ἐπίσκοπον   ἀνέγκλητον   εἶναι
For it behoves the bishop   'unreprovable 'to be

ὡς   θεοῦ   οἰκονόμον,   μὴ   αὐθάδη,   μὴ
as   of God a steward,   not self-pleasing, not

ὀργίλον,   μὴ   πάροινον,   μὴ   πλήκτην,   μὴ
passionate, not given to wine, not a striker,   not

αἰσχροκερδῆ,   8 ἀλλὰ   φιλόξενον,   φιλάγαθον,
greedy of   but   hospitable,   a lover of good
base gain,   [men/things],

σώφρονα,   δίκαιον,   ὅσιον,   ἐγκρατῆ,   9 ἀντεχ-
sensible,   just,   holy,   self-controlled, holding

όμενον   τοῦ   κατὰ   τὴν   διδαχὴν   πιστοῦ
to   'the 'according to 'the 'teaching   'faithful

λόγου,   ἵνα   δυνατὸς   ᾖ   καὶ   παρακαλεῖν
'word,   in order 'able 'he may both to exhort
         that   be

ἐν   τῇ   διδασκαλίᾳ   τῇ   ὑγιαινούσῃ   καὶ
by   the 'teaching   -   'being healthy   and

τοὺς   ἀντιλέγοντας   ἐλέγχειν.   10 Εἰσὶν   γὰρ
'the [ones] 'contradicting 'to convince.   For there are

πολλοὶ   ἀνυπότακτοι,   ματαιολόγοι   καὶ
many   unruly men,   vain talkers   and

φρεναπάται,   μάλιστα   οἱ   ἐκ   τῆς   περιτομῆς,
deceivers,   specially the ones of the circumcision,

11 οὓς   δεῖ   ἐπιστομίζειν,   οἵτινες   ὅλους
whom   it   to stop the   who   'whole
      behoves mouth,

οἴκους   ἀνατρέπουσιν   διδάσκοντες   ἃ   μὴ
'households 'overturn   teaching   things 'not
                                    which

δεῖ   αἰσχροῦ   κέρδους   χάριν.   12 εἶπέν
'it be- 'base   'gain   'for the   'Said
hoves   sake of.

τις   ἐξ   αὐτῶν   ἴδιος   αὐτῶν   προφήτης·
'a cer- 'of 'them   'an own 'of them 'prophet:
tain one

Κρῆτες   ἀεὶ   ψεῦσται,   κακὰ   θηρία,   γαστέρες
Cretans always liars,   evil   beasts, 'gluttons
[are]

ἀργαί.   13 ἡ   μαρτυρία   αὕτη   ἐστὶν   ἀληθής.
'idle.   This witness   is   true.

δι'   ἣν   αἰτίαν   ἔλεγχε   αὐτοὺς   ἀποτόμως,
For which cause reprove   them   severely,

ἵνα   ὑγιαίνωσιν   ἐν   τῇ   πίστει,   14 μὴ
in or- they may   in   the   faith,   not
der that be healthy

προσέχοντες   'Ιουδαϊκοῖς   μύθοις   καὶ
giving heed   to Jewish   tales   and

ἐντολαῖς   ἀνθρώπων   ἀποστρεφομένων   τὴν
commandments of men   perverting   the

ἀλήθειαν.   15 πάντα   καθαρὰ   τοῖς   καθαροῖς·
truth.   All things [are] clean to the   clean;

τοῖς   δὲ   μεμιαμμένοις   καὶ   ἀπίστοις   οὐδὲν
but to having been   and unfaithful nothing
the [ones] defiled

καθαρόν,   ἀλλὰ   μεμίανται   αὐτῶν   καὶ   ὁ
[is] clean, but 'has(ve) been defiled 'of them 'both 'the

νοῦς   καὶ   ἡ   συνείδησις.   16 θεὸν   ὁμολο-
'mind 'and 'the conscience.   'God   'they pro-

γοῦσιν   εἰδέναι,   τοῖς   δὲ   ἔργοις   ἀρνοῦνται,
fess   'to know, but by the(ir) works they deny [him],

βδελυκτοὶ   ὄντες   καὶ   ἀπειθεῖς   καὶ   πρὸς
'abominable 'being and disobedient and   to

πᾶν   ἔργον   ἀγαθὸν   ἀδόκιμοι.
every 'work   'good   reprobate.

---

* In agreement with " children " (neut. pl.).

King James Version

New International Version

What must be taught to various groups

2 But speak thou the things which become sound doctrine: 2 That the aged men be sober, grave, temperate, sound in faith, in charity, in patience. 3 The aged women likewise, that *they be* in behaviour as becometh holiness, not false accusers, not given to much wine, teachers of good things; 4 That they may teach the young women to be sober, to love their husbands, to love their children, 5 *To be* discreet, chaste, keepers at home, good, obedient to their own husbands, that the word of God be not blasphemed. 6 Young men likewise exhort to be soberminded. 7 In all things shewing thyself a pattern of good works: in doctrine *shewing* uncorruptness, gravity, sincerity, 8 Sound speech, that cannot be condemned; that he that is of the contrary part may be ashamed, having no evil thing to say of you. 9 *Exhort* servants to be obedient unto their own masters, *and* to please *them* well in all things; not answering again; 10 Not purloining, but shewing all good fidelity; that they may adorn the doctrine of God our Saviour in all things. 11 For the grace of God that bringeth salvation hath appeared to all men, 12 Teaching us that, denying ungodliness and worldly lusts, we should live soberly, righteously, and godly, in this present world; 13 Looking for that blessed hope, and the glorious appearing of the great God and our Saviour Jesus Christ; 14 Who gave himself for us, that he might redeem us from all iniquity, and purify unto himself a peculiar people, zealous of good works. 15 These things speak, and exhort, and rebuke with all authority. Let no man despise thee.

2 You must teach what is in accord with sound doctrine. 2 Teach the older men to be temperate, worthy of respect, self-controlled, and sound in faith, in love and in endurance.

3 Likewise, teach the older women to be reverent in the way they live, not to be slanderers or addicted to much wine, but to teach what is good. 4 Then they can train the younger women to love their husbands and children, 5 to be self-controlled and pure, to be busy at home, to be kind, and to be subject to their husbands, so that no one will malign the word of God.

6 Similarly, encourage the young men to be self-controlled. 7 In everything set them an example by doing what is good. In your teaching show integrity, seriousness 8 and soundness of speech that cannot be condemned, so that those who oppose you may be ashamed because they have nothing bad to say about us.

9 Teach slaves to be subject to their masters in everything, to try to please them, not to talk back to them, 10 and not to steal from them, but to show that they can be fully trusted, so that in every way they will make the teaching about God our Savior attractive.

11 For the grace of God that brings salvation has appeared to all men. 12 It teaches us to say "No" to ungodliness and worldly passions, and to live self-controlled, upright and godly lives in this present age, 13 while we wait for the blessed hope—the glorious appearing of our great God and Savior, Jesus Christ, 14 who gave himself for us to redeem us from all wickedness and to purify for himself a people that are his very own, eager to do what is good.

15 These, then, are the things you should teach. Encourage and rebuke with all authority. Do not let anyone despise you.

Doing what is good

3 Put them in mind to be subject to principalities and powers, to obey magistrates, to be ready to every good work, 2 To speak evil of no man, to be no brawlers, *but* gentle, shewing all meekness unto all men. 3 For we ourselves also were sometime foolish, disobedient, deceived, serving divers lusts and pleasures, living in malice and envy, hateful, *and* hating one another. 4 But after that the kindness and love of God our Saviour toward man appeared, 5 Not by works of righteousness which we have done, but according to his mercy he saved us, by the washing of regeneration, and renewing of the Holy Ghost; 6 Which he shed on us abundantly through Jesus Christ our Saviour; 7 That being justified by his grace, we should be made heirs according to the hope of eternal life. 8 *This is* a faithful saying, and these things I will that thou affirm constantly, that they which have be-

3 Remind the people to be subject to rulers and authorities, to be obedient, to be ready to do whatever is good, 2 to slander no one, to be peaceable and considerate, and to show true humility toward all men.

3 At one time we too were foolish, disobedient, deceived and enslaved by all kinds of passions and pleasures. We lived in malice and envy, being hated and hating one another. 4 But when the kindness and love of God our Savior appeared, 5 he saved us, not because of righteous things we had done, but because of his mercy. He saved us through the washing of rebirth and renewal by the Holy Spirit, 6 whom he poured out on us generously through Jesus Christ our Savior, 7 so that, having been justified by his grace, we might become heirs having the hope of eternal life. 8 This is a trustworthy saying. And I want you to stress these things, so that

Σὺ δὲ λάλει ἃ πρέπει τῇ ὑγιαινούσῃ
But ²thou ¹speak things becomes the *being*
　　　　　　　which　　　　　*healthy*
διδασκαλίᾳ. 2 Πρεσβύτας νηφαλίους εἶναι,
teaching.　　Aged men　　²sober　¹to be,
σεμνούς, σώφρονας, ὑγιαίνοντας τῇ πίστει,
grave, sensible, *being* healthy in the faith,
τῇ ἀγάπῃ, τῇ ὑπομονῇ· 3 πρεσβύτιδας
– in love, – in endurance; aged women
ὡσαύτως ἐν καταστήματι ἱεροπρεπεῖς, μὴ
similarly in demeanour reverent, not
διαβόλους, μηδὲ οἴνῳ πολλῷ δεδουλωμένας,
slanderers, nor ²wine ¹by much *having been*
　　　　　　　　　　　　　　　　enslaved,
καλοδιδασκάλους, 4 ἵνα σωφρονίζωσι τὰς
teachers of what is good, in or- they may train the
　　　　　　　　　der that
νέας φιλάνδρους εἶναι, φιλοτέκνους,
young ²lovers of ¹to be, child-lovers,
women [their] husbands
5 σώφρονας, ἁγνάς, οἰκουργούς, ἀγαθάς,
sensible, pure, home-workers, good,
ὑποτασσομένας τοῖς ἰδίοις ἀνδράσιν,
being subject to the(ir) own husbands,
ἵνα μὴ ὁ λόγος τοῦ θεοῦ βλασφημῆται.
lest the word – of God be blasphemed.
6 Τοὺς νεωτέρους ὡσαύτως παρακάλει
The younger men similarly exhort
σωφρονεῖν 7 περὶ πάντα, σεαυτὸν παρ-
to be sensible about all things, ²thyself ¹show-
εχόμενος τύπον καλῶν ἔργων, ἐν τῇ
ing a pattern of good works, in the
διδασκαλίᾳ ἀφθορίαν, σεμνότητα, 8 λόγον
teaching uncorruptness, gravity, ¹speech
ὑγιῆ ἀκατάγνωστον, ἵνα ὁ ἐξ ἐναντίας
¹healthy ²irreprehensible, in or- the of contrary
　　　　　　　　　der that man [the] [side]
ἐντραπῇ μηδὲν ἔχων λέγειν περὶ ἡμῶν
may be put ²nothing ¹having ²to say ¹about ²us
to shame
φαῦλον. 9 Δούλους ἰδίοις δεσπόταις
²bad.　　Slaves to [their] own masters

ὑποτάσσεσθαι ἐν πᾶσιν, εὐαρέστους εἶναι,
to be subject in all things, well-pleasing to be,
μὴ ἀντιλέγοντας, 10 μὴ νοσφιζομένους, ἀλλὰ
not contradicting, not peculating, but
πᾶσαν πίστιν ἐνδεικνυμένους ἀγαθήν, ἵνα
²all ¹faith ¹showing ²good, in or-
　　　　　　　　　　　　　　　　der that
τὴν διδασκαλίαν τὴν τοῦ σωτῆρος ἡμῶν
²the ²teaching – ⁴of the ²Saviour ³of us
θεοῦ κοσμῶσιν ἐν πᾶσιν. 11 Ἐπεφάνη
¹God ¹they may adorn in all things. ¹appeared
γὰρ ἡ χάρις τοῦ θεοῦ σωτήριος πᾶσιν
For ¹the ²grace – ²of God ⁴saving to all
ἀνθρώποις, 12 παιδεύουσα ἡμᾶς, ἵνα
men, instructing us, *in order*
　　　　　　　　　　　　　　　that
ἀρνησάμενοι τὴν ἀσέβειαν καὶ τὰς κοσμικὰς
denying – impiety and – worldly
ἐπιθυμίας σωφρόνως καὶ δικαίως καὶ
lusts ²sensibly ¹and ²righteously ¹and
εὐσεβῶς ζήσωμεν ἐν τῷ νῦν αἰῶνι,
²piously ¹we might live in the now(present) age,
13 προσδεχόμενοι τὴν μακαρίαν ἐλπίδα καὶ
expecting the blessed hope and
ἐπιφάνειαν τῆς δόξης τοῦ μεγάλου θεοῦ
appearance of the glory of the great God
καὶ σωτῆρος ἡμῶν Χριστοῦ Ἰησοῦ, 14 ὃς
and Saviour of us Christ Jesus, who
ἔδωκεν ἑαυτὸν ὑπὲρ ἡμῶν ἵνα λυτρώσηται
gave himself on behalf us in or- he might
　　　　　　　of　　　　　　der that ransom
ἡμᾶς ἀπὸ πάσης ἀνομίας καὶ καθαρίσῃ
us from all iniquity and *might* cleanse
ἑαυτῷ λαὸν περιούσιον, ζηλωτὴν καλῶν ἔργων.
for a people [his] own zealous of good works.
himself possession,
15 Ταῦτα λάλει καὶ παρακάλει καὶ ἔλεγχε
These things speak thou and exhort and reprove
μετὰ πάσης ἐπιταγῆς· μηδείς σου περιφρονείτω.
with all command; ²no one ¹of thee ³let ⁴despise.

Chapter 3

Ὑπομίμνησκε αὐτοὺς ἀρχαῖς ἐξουσίαις
Remind thou them ²to rulers [and] ¹authorities
ὑποτάσσεσθαι, πειθαρχεῖν, πρὸς πᾶν ἔργον
¹to be subject, to be obedient, ²to ⁴every ³work
ἀγαθὸν ἑτοίμους εἶναι, 2 μηδένα βλασ-
¹good ²ready ¹to be, no one to
φημεῖν, ἀμάχους εἶναι, ἐπιεικεῖς, πᾶσαν
rail at, uncontentious to be, forbearing, ²all
ἐνδεικνυμένους πρᾳότητα πρὸς πάντας
¹showing forth meekness to all
ἀνθρώπους. 3 Ἦμεν γάρ ποτε καὶ ἡμεῖς
men.　　For ³were ²then ⁴also ¹we
ἀνόητοι, ἀπειθεῖς, πλανώμενοι, δουλεύοντες
senseless, disobedient, being deceived, serving [as slaves]
ἐπιθυμίαις καὶ ἡδοναῖς ποικίλαις, ἐν κακίᾳ
²lusts ¹and ⁴pleasures ³various, ²in ¹evil
καὶ φθόνῳ διάγοντες, στυγητοί, μισοῦντες
²and ²envy ¹living, hateful, hating
ἀλλήλους. 4 ὅτε δὲ ἡ χρηστότης καὶ
one another. But when the kindness and
ἡ φιλανθρωπία ἐπεφάνη τοῦ σωτῆρος ἡμῶν
the love to man ²appeared ¹of the ²Saviour ³of us

θεοῦ, 5 οὐκ ἐξ ἔργων τῶν ἐν δικαιοσύνῃ
⁴God, not by works – ¹in ²righteousness
ἃ ἐποιήσαμεν ἡμεῖς, ἀλλὰ κατὰ τὸ
¹which ²did ³we, but according to the
αὐτοῦ ἔλεος ἔσωσεν ἡμᾶς διὰ λουτροῦ
of him mercy he saved us through [the] washing
παλιγγενεσίας καὶ ἀνακαινώσεως πνεύματος
of regeneration and renewal ²Spirit
ἁγίου, 6 οὗ ἐξέχεεν ἐφ' ἡμᾶς πλουσίως
¹of [the] which he shed on us richly
Holy,
διὰ Ἰησοῦ Χριστοῦ τοῦ σωτῆρος ἡμῶν,
through Jesus Christ the Saviour of us,
7 ἵνα δικαιωθέντες τῇ ἐκείνου χάριτι
in or- being justified ²by the ¹of that one ²grace
der that
κληρονόμοι γενηθῶμεν κατ' ἐλπίδα ζωῆς
heirs we might accord- a hope of life
become ing to
αἰωνίου. 8 Πιστὸς ὁ λόγος, καὶ περὶ
eternal. Faithful [is] the word, and as to
τούτων βούλομαί σε διαβεβαιοῦσθαι, ἵνα
these I wish thee to affirm in or-
things confidently, der that

King James Version

lieved in God might be careful to maintain good works. These things are good and profitable unto men. 9 But avoid foolish questions, and genealogies, and contentions, and strivings about the law; for they are unprofitable and vain. 10 A man that is a heretic, after the first and second admonition, reject; 11 Knowing that he that is such is subverted, and sinneth, being condemned of himself. 12 When I shall send Artemas unto thee, or Tychicus, be diligent to come unto me to Nicopolis: for I have determined there to winter. 13 Bring Zenas the lawyer and Apollos on their journey diligently, that nothing be wanting unto them. 14 And let ours also learn to maintain good works for necessary uses, that they be not unfruitful. 15 All that are with me salute thee. Greet them that love us in the faith. Grace be with you all. Amen.

It was written to Titus, ordained the first bishop of the church of the Cretians, from Nicopolis of Macedonia.

New International Version

those who have trusted in God may be careful to devote themselves to doing what is good. These things are excellent and profitable for everyone.

9 But avoid foolish controversies and genealogies and arguments and quarrels about the law, because these are unprofitable and useless. 10 Warn a divisive person once, and then warn him a second time. After that, have nothing to do with him. 11 You may be sure that such a man is warped and sinful; he is self-condemned.

Final remarks

12 As soon as I send Artemas or Tychicus to you, do your best to come to me at Nicopolis, because I have decided to winter there. 13 Do everything you can to help Zenas the lawyer and Apollos on their way and see that they have everything they need. 14 Our people must learn to devote themselves to doing what is good, in order that they may provide for daily necessities and not live unproductive lives.

15 Everyone with me sends you greetings. Greet those who love us in the faith.

Grace be with you all.

Greek Interlinear

φροντίζωσιν καλῶν ἔργων προΐστασθαι οἱ
'may take   *of good 'works 'to maintain 'the
thought   [ones]

πεπιστευκότες θεῷ.   ταῦτά ἐστιν καλὰ
'having believed 'God. These things is(are) good

καὶ ὠφέλιμα τοῖς ἀνθρώποις· 9 μωρὰς
and profitable -   to men;   'foolish

δὲ ζητήσεις καὶ γενεαλογίας καὶ ἔριν
'but questionings and genealogies and strife

καὶ μάχας νομικὰς περιΐστασο· εἰσὶν γὰρ
and 'fights 'legal shun thou;   for they are

ἀνωφελεῖς καὶ μάταιοι.   10 αἱρετικὸν
unprofitable and vain.   A factious

ἄνθρωπον μετὰ μίαν καὶ δευτέραν
man   after one and a second

νουθεσίαν παραιτοῦ, 11 εἰδὼς ὅτι ἐξέστραπ-
admonition avoid,   knowing that 'has been per-

ται ὁ τοιοῦτος καὶ ἁμαρτάνει ὢν αὐτο-
verted 'such a man and sins   being self-

κατάκριτος.
condemned.

12 Ὅταν πέμψω Ἀρτεμᾶν πρὸς σὲ
   Whenever I send Artemas to thee

ἢ Τύχικον, σπούδασον ἐλθεῖν πρός με
or Tychicus, hasten to come to me

εἰς Νικόπολιν· ἐκεῖ γὰρ κέκρικα παραχειμά-
in Nicopolis;   for there I have decided to spend [the]

σαι. 13 Ζηνᾶν τὸν νομικὸν καὶ Ἀπολλῶν
winter. Zenas the lawyer and Apollos

σπουδαίως πρόπεμψον, ἵνα μηδὲν αὐτοῖς
urgently send forward, in or- nothing to them
                          der that

λείπῃ. 14 μανθανέτωσαν δὲ καὶ οἱ ἡμέτεροι
may be lacking. And 'let 'learn 'also - 'our [people]

καλῶν ἔργων προΐστασθαι εἰς τὰς ἀναγ-
'of good 'works 'to maintain for - neces-

καίας χρείας, ἵνα μὴ ὦσιν ἄκαρποι.
sary wants, lest they be unfruitful.

15 Ἀσπάζονταί σε οἱ μετ' ἐμοῦ πάντες.
   'greet   'thee 'the 'with 'me 'All.

ἄσπασαι τοὺς φιλοῦντας ἡμᾶς ἐν πίστει.
Greet thou the [ones] loving us in [the] faith.

Ἡ χάρις μετὰ πάντων ὑμῶν.
- Grace [be] with 'all 'you.

King James Version

New International Version

THE

EPISTLE OF PAUL TO
PHILEMON

PHILEMON

Paul, a prisoner of Jesus Christ, and Timothy *our* brother, unto Philemon our dearly beloved, and fellow labourer, 2And to *our* beloved Apphia, and Archippus our fellow soldier, and to the church in thy house: 3 Grace to you, and peace, from God our Father and the Lord Jesus Christ. 4 I thank my God, making mention of thee always in my prayers, 5 Hearing of thy love and faith, which thou hast toward the Lord Jesus, and toward all saints; 6 That the communication of thy faith may become effectual by the acknowledging of every good thing which is in you in Christ Jesus. 7 For we have great joy and consolation in thy love, because the bowels of the saints are refreshed by thee, brother. 8 Wherefore, though I might be much bold in Christ to enjoin thee that which is convenient, 9 Yet for love's sake I rather beseech *thee*, being such a one as Paul the aged, and now also a prisoner of Jesus Christ. 10 I beseech thee for my son Onesimus, whom I have begotten in my bonds: 11 Which in time past was to thee unprofitable, but now profitable to thee and to me: 12 Whom I have sent again: thou therefore receive him, that is, mine own bowels: 13 Whom I would have retained with me, that in thy stead he might have ministered unto me in the bonds of the gospel: 14 But without thy mind would I do nothing; that thy benefit should not be as it were of necessity, but willingly. 15 For perhaps he therefore departed for a season, that thou shouldest receive him for ever; 16 Not now as a servant, but above a servant, a brother beloved, specially to me, but how much more unto thee, both in the flesh, and in the Lord? 17 If thou count me therefore a partner, receive him as myself. 18 If he hath wronged thee, or oweth *thee* aught, put that on mine account; 19 I Paul have written *it* with mine own hand, I will repay *it:* albeit I do not say to thee how thou owest unto me even thine own self besides. 20 Yea, brother, let me have joy of thee in the Lord: refresh my bowels in the Lord. 21 Having confidence in thy obedience I wrote unto thee, knowing that thou wilt also do more than I say. 22 But withal prepare me also a lodging: for I trust that through your prayers I shall be given unto you. 23 There salute thee Epaphras, my fellow prisoner in Christ Jesus; 24 Marcus, Aristarchus, Demas, Lucas, my fellow labourers. 25 The grace of our Lord Jesus Christ *be* with your spirit. Amen.

Written from Rome to Philemon, by Onesimus a servant.

1 Paul, a prisoner of Christ Jesus, and Timothy our brother,
To Philemon our dear friend and fellow worker, 2 to Apphia our sister, to Archippus our fellow soldier, and to the church that meets in your home: 3 Grace to you and peace from God our Father and the Lord Jesus Christ.

Thanksgiving and prayer

4 I always thank my God as I remember you in my prayers, 5 because I hear about your love and faith in the Lord Jesus and your love for all the saints. 6 I pray that you may be active in sharing your faith, so that you will have a full understanding of every good thing we have in Christ. 7 Your love has given me great joy and encouragement, because you, brother, have refreshed the hearts of the saints.

Paul's plea for Onesimus

8 Therefore, although in Christ I could be bold and order you to do what you ought to do, 9 yet I appeal to you on the basis of love. I then, as Paul—an old man and now also a prisoner of Christ Jesus—10 I appeal to you for my son Onesimus,*a* who became my son while I was in chains. 11 Formerly he was useless to you, but now he has become useful both to you and to me.
12 I am sending him—who is my very heart—back to you. 13 I would have liked to keep him with me so that he could take your place in helping me while I am in chains for the gospel. 14 But I did not want to do anything without your consent, so that any favor you do will be spontaneous and not forced. 15 Perhaps the reason he was separated from you for a little while was that you might have him back for good—16 no longer as a slave, but better than a slave, as a dear brother. He is very dear to me but even dearer to you, both as a man and as a brother in the Lord.
17 So if you consider me a partner, welcome him as you would welcome me. 18 If he has done you any wrong or owes you anything, charge it to me. 19 I, Paul, am writing this with my own hand. I will pay it back—not to mention that you owe me your very self. 20 I do wish, brother, that I may have some benefit from you in the Lord; refresh my heart in Christ. 21 Confident of your obedience, I write to you, knowing that you will do even more than I ask.
22 And one thing more: Prepare a guest room for me, because I hope to be restored to you in answer to your prayers.
23 Epaphras, my fellow prisoner for Christ Jesus, sends you greetings. 24And so do Mark, Aristarchus, Demas and Luke, my fellow workers.
25 The grace of the Lord Jesus Christ be with your spirit.

[a] *Onesimus* means *useful.*

638

ΠΡΟΣ ΦΙΛΗΜΟΝΑ

1 Παῦλος δέσμιος Χριστοῦ 'Ιησοῦ καὶ
Paul a prisoner of Christ Jesus and

Τιμόθεος ὁ ἀδελφὸς Φιλήμονι τῷ ἀγαπητῷ
Timothy the brother to Philemon the beloved

καὶ συνεργῷ ἡμῶν 2 καὶ 'Απφίᾳ τῇ
and a fellow-worker of us and to Apphia the

ἀδελφῇ καὶ 'Αρχίππῳ τῷ συστρατιώτῃ
sister and to Archippus the fellow-soldier

ἡμῶν καὶ τῇ κατ' οἶκόν σου ἐκκλησίᾳ·
of us and ¹to the ²at ³house ⁴of thee ⁵church:

3 χάρις ὑμῖν καὶ εἰρήνη ἀπὸ θεοῦ πατρὸς
Grace to you and peace from God Father

ἡμῶν καὶ κυρίου 'Ιησοῦ Χριστοῦ.
of us and Lord Jesus Christ.

4 Εὐχαριστῶ τῷ θεῷ μου πάντοτε μνείαν
I give thanks to the God of me always ¹mention

σου ποιούμενος ἐπὶ τῶν προσευχῶν μου,
²of thee ¹making at the prayers of me,

5 ἀκούων σου τὴν ἀγάπην καὶ τὴν
hearing of thee the love and the

πίστιν ἣν ἔχεις πρὸς τὸν κύριον 'Ιησοῦν
faith which thou hast toward the Lord Jesus

καὶ εἰς πάντας τοὺς ἁγίους, 6 ὅπως
and to all the saints, so as

ἡ κοινωνία τῆς πίστεώς σου ἐνεργὴς
the fellowship of the faith of thee ²operative

γένηται ἐν ἐπιγνώσει παντὸς ἀγαθοῦ τοῦ
¹may in a full of every good thing
become knowledge

ἐν ἡμῖν εἰς Χριστόν. 7 χαρὰν γὰρ
in us for Christ. ⁴joy ¹For

πολλὴν ἔσχον καὶ παράκλησιν ἐπὶ τῇ
²much ³I had and consolation over the

ἀγάπῃ σου, ὅτι τὰ σπλάγχνα τῶν ἁγίων
love of because the bowels of the saints
thee,

ἀναπέπαυται διὰ σοῦ, ἀδελφέ. 8 Διό,
has(ve) been through thee, brother. Wherefore,
refreshed

πολλὴν ἐν Χριστῷ παρρησίαν ἔχων ἐπιτάσ-
²much ⁴in ³Christ ¹boldness ¹having to

σειν σοι τὸ ἀνῆκον, 9 διὰ τὴν ἀγάπην
charge thee the befitting, because - love
of

μᾶλλον παρακαλῶ· τοιοῦτος ὢν ὡς Παῦλος
rather I beseech; such a one being as Paul

πρεσβύτης, νυνὶ δὲ καὶ δέσμιος Χριστοῦ
an old man, and now also a prisoner of Christ

'Ιησοῦ, 10 παρακαλῶ σε περὶ τοῦ ἐμοῦ
Jesus, I beseech thee con- - my
cerning

τέκνου, ὃν ἐγέννησα ἐν τοῖς δεσμοῖς,
child, whom I begat in the(my) bonds,

'Ονήσιμον, 11 τόν ποτέ σοι ἄχρηστον
Onesimus, the [one] then ²to thee ¹useless
(formerly)

νυνὶ δὲ καὶ σοὶ καὶ ἐμοὶ εὔχρηστον,
but now ¹both ²to thee ⁴and ³to me ⁵useful,

12 ὃν ἀνέπεμψά σοι, αὐτόν, τοῦτ' ἔστιν
whom I sent back to thee, him, this is

τὰ ἐμὰ σπλάγχνα· 13 ὃν ἐγὼ ἐβουλόμην
- my bowels: whom I resolved

πρὸς ἐμαυτὸν κατέχειν, ἵνα ὑπὲρ σοῦ
with myself to retain, in order on thee
that behalf of

μοι διακονῇ ἐν τοῖς δεσμοῖς τοῦ εὐαγ-
to me he might in the bonds of the gos-
minister

γελίου, 14 χωρὶς δὲ τῆς σῆς γνώμης
pel, but without - thy opinion

οὐδὲν ἠθέλησα ποιῆσαι, ἵνα μὴ ὡς κατὰ
²nothing ¹I was ²to do, lest ⁴as ⁵by way
willing of

ἀνάγκην τὸ ἀγαθόν σου ᾖ ἀλλὰ κατὰ
¹necessity ¹the ²good ³of ⁴might but by way
thee be of

ἑκούσιον. 15 τάχα γὰρ διὰ τοῦτο ἐχωρίσθη
[being] For perhaps therefore he departed
voluntary.

πρὸς ὥραν, ἵνα αἰώνιον αὐτὸν ἀπέχῃς,
for an hour, in order ²eternally ³him ¹thou mightest
that receive,

16 οὐκέτι ὡς δοῦλον ἀλλὰ ὑπὲρ δοῦλον,
no longer as a slave but beyond a slave,

ἀδελφὸν ἀγαπητόν, μάλιστα ἐμοί, πόσῳ
a brother beloved, specially to me, ²by how
much

δὲ μᾶλλον σοὶ καὶ ἐν σαρκὶ καὶ ἐν
¹and more to thee both in [the] flesh and in

κυρίῳ. 17 εἰ οὖν με ἔχεις κοινωνόν,
[the] Lord. If therefore me thou hast [as] a partner,

προσλαβοῦ αὐτὸν ὡς ἐμέ. 18 εἰ δέ
receive him as me. And if

τι ἠδίκησέν σε ἢ ὀφείλει, τοῦτο ἐμοὶ
any- he wronged thee or owes, ²this ³to me
thing

ἐλλόγα· 19 ἐγὼ Παῦλος ἔγραψα τῇ ἐμῇ
¹reckon; I Paul wrote - with my

χειρί, ἐγὼ ἀποτίσω· ἵνα μὴ λέγω σοι
hand, I will repay: lest I say to thee

ὅτι καὶ σεαυτόν μοι προσοφείλεις. 20 ναί,
that indeed ¹thyself ²to me ³thou owest besides. Yes,

ἀδελφέ, ἐγώ σου ὀναίμην ἐν κυρίῳ·
brother, ²I ³of thee ¹may ⁴have ⁴help in [the] Lord:

ἀνάπαυσόν μου τὰ σπλάγχνα ἐν Χριστῷ.
refresh of me the bowels in Christ.

21 Πεποιθὼς τῇ ὑπακοῇ σου ἔγραψά
Having trusted to the obedience of thee I wrote

σοι, εἰδὼς ὅτι καὶ ὑπὲρ ἃ λέγω ποιήσεις.
to knowing that indeed beyond what I say thou wilt
thee, things do.

22 ἅμα δὲ καὶ ἑτοίμαζέ μοι ξενίαν·
And at the also prepare for me lodging:
same time

ἐλπίζω γὰρ ὅτι διὰ τῶν προσευχῶν
for I hope that through the prayers

ὑμῶν χαρισθήσομαι ὑμῖν.
of you I shall be given to you.

23 'Ασπάζεταί σε 'Επαφρᾶς ὁ συναιχμά-
²greets ³thee ¹Epaphras ⁴the ⁵fellow-

λωτός μου ἐν Χριστῷ 'Ιησοῦ, 24 Μᾶρκος,
captive ⁶of me ⁷in ⁸Christ ⁹Jesus, [also] Mark,

'Αρίσταρχος, Δημᾶς, Λουκᾶς, οἱ συνεργοί
Aristarchus, Demas, Luke, the fellow-
workers

μου.
of me.

25 'Η χάρις τοῦ κυρίου 'Ιησοῦ Χριστοῦ
The grace of the Lord Jesus Christ

μετὰ τοῦ πνεύματος ὑμῶν.
[be] with the spirit of you.

King James Version

New International Version

THE EPISTLE

OF PAUL THE APOSTLE

TO THE

HEBREWS

HEBREWS

The Son superior to angels

1 God, who at sundry times and in divers manners spake in time past unto the fathers by the prophets, 2 Hath in these last days spoken unto us by *his* Son, whom he hath appointed heir of all things, by whom also he made the worlds; 3 Who being the brightness of *his* glory, and the express image of his person, and upholding all things by the word of his power, when he had by himself purged our sins, sat down on the right hand of the Majesty on high; 4 Being made so much better than the angels, as he hath by inheritance obtained a more excellent name than they. 5 For unto which of the angels said he at any time, Thou art my Son, this day have I begotten thee? And again, I will be to him a Father, and he shall be to me a Son? 6And again, when he bringeth in the firstbegotten into the world, he saith, And let all the angels of God worship him. 7And of the angels he saith, Who maketh his angels spirits, and his ministers a flame of fire. 8 But unto the Son *he saith,* Thy throne, O God, *is* for ever and ever: a sceptre of righteousness *is* the sceptre of thy kingdom. 9 Thou hast loved righteousness, and hated iniquity; therefore God, *even* thy God, hath anointed thee with the oil of gladness above thy fellows. 10And, Thou, Lord, in the beginning hast laid the foundation of the earth; and the heavens are the works of thine hands. 11 They shall perish, but thou remainest: and they all shall wax old as doth a garment; 12And as ·a vesture shalt thou fold them up, and they shall be changed: but thou art the same, and thy years shall not fail. 13 But to which of the angels said he at any time, Sit on my right hand, until I make thine enemies thy footstool? 14Are they not all ministering spirits, sent forth to minister for them who shall be heirs of salvation?

1 In the past God spoke to our forefathers through the prophets at many times and in various ways, 2 but in these last days he has spoken to us by his Son, whom he appointed heir of all things, and through whom he made the universe. 3 The Son is the radiance of God's glory and the exact representation of his being, sustaining all things by his powerful word. After he had provided purification for sins, he sat down at the right hand of the Majesty in heaven. 4 So he became as much superior to the angels as the name he has inherited is superior to theirs.

5 For to which of the angels did God ever say,
"You are my Son;
    today I have become your Father*a*"? *b*
Or again,
"I will be his Father,
    and he will be my Son"? *c*
6And again, when God brings his firstborn into the world, he says,
"Let all God's angels worship him." *d*
7 In speaking of the angels he says,
"He makes his angels winds,
    his servants flames of fire." *e*
8 But about the Son he says,
"Your throne, O God, will last for ever and ever,
    and righteousness will be the scepter of your kingdom.
9 You have loved righteousness and hated wickedness;
    therefore God, your God, has set you above your companions
    by anointing you with the oil of joy." *f*
10 He also says,
"In the beginning, O Lord, you laid the foundations of the earth,
    and the heavens are the work of your hands.
11 They will perish, but you remain;
    they will all wear out like a garment.
12 You will roll them up like a robe;
    like a garment they will be changed.
But you remain the same,
    and your years will never end." *g*
13 To which of the angels did God ever say,
"Sit at my right hand
    until I make your enemies your footstool"? *h*
14Are not all angels ministering spirits sent to serve those who will inherit salvation?

[a] Or *have begotten you.* [b] Psalm 2:7. [c] II Samuel 7:14. [d] Deut. 32:43 (Septuagint, Dead Sea Scrolls); Psalm 97:7. [e] Psalm 104:4. [f] Psalm 45:6,7. [g] Psalm 102:25-27. [h] Psalm 110:1.

ΠΡΟΣ ΕΒΡΑΙΟΥΣ

Chapter 1

Πολυμερῶς καὶ πολυτρόπως πάλαι ὁ
¹In many ²and ³in many ways ⁴of old -
θεὸς λαλήσας τοῖς πατράσιν ἐν τοῖς
¹God ²having spoken ³to the ⁴fathers by the
προφήταις 2 ἐπ' ἐσχάτου τῶν ἡμερῶν
prophets in [the] last - days
τούτων ἐλάλησεν ἡμῖν ἐν υἱῷ, ὃν ἔθηκεν
of these spoke to us in a Son, whom he appointed
κληρονόμον πάντων, δι' οὗ καὶ ἐποίησεν
heir of all through whom indeed he made
things,
τοὺς αἰῶνας· 3 ὃς ὢν ἀπαύγασμα τῆς
the ages; who being [the] radiance of the
(his)
δόξης καὶ χαρακτὴρ τῆς ὑποστάσεως αὐτοῦ,
glory and [the] of the reality of him,
representation
φέρων τε τὰ πάντα τῷ ῥήματι τῆς
and bearing - all things by the word of the
δυνάμεως αὐτοῦ, καθαρισμὸν τῶν ἁμαρτιῶν
power of him, ²cleansing - ¹of sins
ποιησάμενος ἐκάθισεν ἐν δεξιᾷ τῆς
¹having made sat on [the] right [hand] of the
μεγαλωσύνης ἐν ὑψηλοῖς, 4 τοσούτῳ
greatness in high places, ²by so much
κρείττων γενόμενος τῶν ἀγγέλων ὅσῳ
¹better ¹becoming ²[than] the angels as
διαφορώτερον παρ' αὐτοὺς κεκληρονόμηκεν
²a more excellent ⁴than ³them ¹he has inherited
ὄνομα. 5 Τίνι γὰρ εἶπέν ποτε τῶν
²name. For to which ¹said he ²ever ¹of the
ἀγγέλων· υἱός μου εἶ σύ, ἐγὼ σήμερον
¹angels· Son of me art thou, I to-day
γεγέννηκά σε; καὶ πάλιν· ἐγὼ ἔσομαι
have begotten thee? and again· I will be
αὐτῷ εἰς πατέρα, καὶ αὐτὸς ἔσται μοι
to him for a father, and he shall be to me
εἰς υἱόν; 6 ὅταν δὲ πάλιν εἰσαγάγῃ
for a son? and whenever again he brings in
τὸν πρωτότοκον εἰς τὴν οἰκουμένην, λέγει·
the firstborn into the inhabited [earth], he says:
καὶ προσκυνησάτωσαν αὐτῷ πάντες ἄγγελοι
And let worship him all angels
θεοῦ. 7 καὶ πρὸς μὲν τοὺς ἀγγέλους
of God. And with re- - the angels
gard to

λέγει· ὁ ποιῶν τοὺς ἀγγέλους αὐτοῦ
he says: The making the angels of him
[one]
πνεύματα, καὶ τοὺς λειτουργοὺς αὐτοῦ
spirits, and the ministers of him
πυρὸς φλόγα· 8 πρὸς δὲ τὸν υἱόν· The
²of fire ¹a flame; but with regard to the Son:
θρόνος σου ὁ θεὸς εἰς τὸν αἰῶνα τοῦ
throne of thee[,] - God[,]*[is] unto the age of the
αἰῶνος, καὶ ἡ ῥάβδος τῆς εὐθύτητος
age, and the rod - of uprightness [is]
ῥάβδος τῆς βασιλείας αὐτοῦ. 9 ἠγάπησας
[the] rod of the kingdom of him. Thou lovedst
δικαιοσύνην καὶ ἐμίσησας ἀνομίαν· διὰ
righteousness and hatedst lawlessness; there-
τοῦτο ἔχρισέν σε, ὁ θεός, ὁ θεός σου
fore ²anointed ³thee, - ⁴God,* ¹the ¹God ⁵of thee
ἔλαιον ἀγαλλιάσεως παρὰ τοὺς μετόχους
[with] oil of gladness above the partners
σου. 10 καὶ· σὺ κατ' ἀρχάς, κύριε,
of thee. And: Thou at [the] beginnings, Lord,
τὴν γῆν ἐθεμελίωσας, καὶ ἔργα τῶν
¹the ²earth ¹didst found, and ²works ³of the
χειρῶν σου εἰσιν οἱ οὐρανοί· 11 αὐτοὶ
¹hands ⁴of thee ⁵are ¹the ⁴heavens; they
ἀπολοῦνται, σὺ δὲ διαμένεις· καὶ πάντες
will perish, but thou remainest; and all
ὡς ἱμάτιον παλαιωθήσονται, 12 καὶ ὡσεὶ
as a garment will become old, and as
περιβόλαιον ἑλίξεις αὐτούς, ὡς ἱμάτιον
a mantle thou wilt roll up them, as a garment
καὶ ἀλλαγήσονται· σὺ δὲ ὁ αὐτὸς εἶ
also they will be changed; but thou the same art
καὶ τὰ ἔτη σου οὐκ ἐκλείψουσιν. 13 πρὸς
and the years of thee will not fail. ²to
τίνα δὲ τῶν ἀγγέλων εἴρηκέν ποτε·
²which ¹But of the angels has he said at any
time:
κάθου ἐκ δεξιῶν μου ἕως ἂν θῶ τοὺς
Sit at [the] right of me until I put the
ἐχθρούς σου ὑποπόδιον τῶν ποδῶν σου;
enemies of thee a footstool of the feet of thee?
14 οὐχὶ πάντες εἰσὶν λειτουργικὰ πνεύματα
²not ¹all ³are they ministering ¹spirits
εἰς διακονίαν ἀποστελλόμενα διὰ τοὺς
²for ¹service ³being sent forth because the
of [ones]

* Articular vocative; see ver. 10.

King James Version

New International Version

Warning to pay attention

2 Therefore we ought to give the more earnest heed to the things which we have heard, lest at any time we should let *them* slip. 2 For if the word spoken by angels was steadfast, and every transgression and disobedience received a just recompense of reward; 3 How shall we escape, if we neglect so great salvation; which at the first began to be spoken by the Lord, and was confirmed unto us by them that heard *him;* 4 God also bearing *them* witness, both with signs and wonders, and with divers miracles, and gifts of the Holy Ghost, according to his own will? 5 For unto the angels hath he not put in subjection the world to come, whereof we speak. 6 But one in a certain· place testified, saying, What is man, that thou art mindful of him? or the son of man, that thou visitest him? 7 Thou madest him a little lower than the angels; thou crownedst him with glory and honour, and didst set him over the works of thy hands: 8 Thou hast put all things in subjection under his feet. For in that he put all in subjection under him, he left nothing *that is* not put under him. But now we see not yet all things put under him. 9 But we see Jesus, who was made a little lower than the angels for the suffering of death, crowned with glory and honour; that he by the grace of God should taste death for every man. 10 For it became him, for whom *are* all things, and by whom *are* all things, in bringing many sons unto glory, to make the captain of their salvation perfect through sufferings. 11 For both he that sanctifieth and they who are sanctified *are* all of one: for which cause he is not ashamed to call them brethren, 12 Saying, I will declare thy name unto my brethren, in the midst of the church will I sing praise unto thee. 13And again, I will put my trust in him. And again, Behold I and the children which God hath given me. 14 Forasmuch then as the children are partakers of flesh and blood, he also himself likewise took part of the same; that through death he might destroy him that had the power of death, that is, the devil; 15And deliver them, who through fear of death were all their lifetime subject to bondage. 16 For verily he took not on *him the nature of* angels; but he took on *him* the seed of Abraham. 17 Wherefore in all things it behooved him to be made like unto *his* brethren, that he might be a merciful and faithful high priest in things *pertaining* to God, to make reconciliation for the sins of the people. 18 For in that he himself hath suffered being tempted, he is able to succour them that are tempted.

2 We must pay more careful attention, therefore, to what we have heard, so that we do not drift away. 2 For if the message spoken by angels was binding, and every violation and disobedience received its just punishment, 3 how shall we escape if we ignore such a great salvation? This salvation, which was first announced by the Lord, was confirmed to us by those who heard him. 4 God also testified to it by signs, wonders and various miracles, and gifts of the Holy Spirit distributed according to his will.

Jesus made like his brothers

5 It is not to angels that he has subjected the world to come, about which we are speaking. 6 But there is a place where someone has testified:
"What is man that you are concerned about him,
or the son of man that you should care for him?
7 You made him a little lower than the angels;
you crowned him with glory and honor
8 and put everything under his feet." [i]
In putting everything under him, God left nothing that is not subject to him. Yet at present we do not see everything subject to him. 9 But we see Jesus, who was made a little lower than the angels, now crowned with glory and honor because he suffered death, so that by the grace of God he might taste death for everyone.

10 In bringing many sons to glory, it was fitting that God, for whom and through whom everything exists, should make the Pioneer[j] of their salvation perfect through suffering. 11 Both the one who makes men holy and those who are made holy are of the same family. So Jesus is not ashamed to call them brothers. 12 He says,
"I will declare your name to my brothers;
in the presence of the congregation I will sing your praises." [k]
13And again,
"I will put my trust in him." [l]
And again he says,
"Here am I, and the children God has given me." [m]
14 Since the children have flesh and blood, he too shared in their humanity so that by his death he might destroy him who holds the power of death—that is, the devil—15 and free those who all their lives were held in slavery by their fear of death. 16 For surely it is not angels he helps, but Abraham's descendants. 17 For this reason he had to be made like his brothers in every way, in order that he might become a merciful and faithful high priest in service to God, and that he might make atonement for the sins of the people. 18 Because he himself suffered when he was tempted, he is able to help those who are being tempted.

[i] Psalm 8:4-6. [j] Or *Originator*. [k] Psalm 22:22. [l] Isaiah 8:17. [m] Isaiah 8:18.

Greek Interlinear

Chapter 2

μέλλοντας   κληρονομεῖν   σωτηρίαν;   2 Διὰ
being about   to inherit   salvation ?   There-

τοῦτο   δεῖ   περισσοτέρως   προσέχειν   ἡμᾶς
fore   ¹it behoves   ⁴more abundantly   ³to give heed   ²us

τοῖς   ἀκουσθεῖσιν,   μήποτε   παραρυῶμεν.
to the   things heard,   lest   we drift away.

2 εἰ   γὰρ   ὁ   δι'   ἀγγέλων   λαληθεὶς   λόγος
For if   ¹the ⁴through   ²angels   ³spoken   ⁵word

ἐγένετο   βέβαιος,   καὶ   πᾶσα   παράβασις
was   firm,   and   every   transgression

καὶ   παρακοὴ   ἔλαβεν   ἔνδικον   μισθαποδοσίαν,
and   disobedience   received   a just   recompence,

3 πῶς   ἡμεῖς   ἐκφευξόμεθα   τηλικαύτης
how   ²we   ¹shall ³escape   ⁴so great

ἀμελήσαντες   σωτηρίας;   ἥτις   ἀρχὴν   λαβοῦσα
⁵neglecting   ⁶a salvation ?   which   ²a beginning   ¹having
received

λαλεῖσθαι   διὰ   τοῦ   κυρίου,   ὑπὸ   τῶν
to be spoken   through   the   Lord,   by   the

ἀκουσάντων   εἰς   ἡμᾶς   ἐβεβαιώθη,   4 συνεπι-
[ones] hearing   to   us   was confirmed,   ³bearing

μαρτυροῦντος   τοῦ   θεοῦ   σημείοις   τε   καὶ
witness with   -   ¹God²   ⁴by signs   ⁵both   and

τέρασιν   καὶ   ποικίλαις   δυνάμεσιν   καὶ
by wonders   and   by various   powerful deeds   and

πνεύματος   ἁγίου   μερισμοῖς   κατὰ   τὴν   αὐτοῦ
³Spirit   ⁴of [the]   ¹by distribu-   according   the   ⁵of him
tions   to

θέλησιν.
²will.

5 Οὐ   γὰρ   ἀγγέλοις   ὑπέταξεν   τὴν
For not   to angels   subjected he   the

οἰκουμένην   τὴν   μέλλουσαν,   περὶ   ἧς
²inhabited [earth]   -   ¹coming,   about   which

λαλοῦμεν.   6 διεμαρτύρατο   δέ   πού   τις
we speak.   But ²solemnly witnessed   ³some-   ¹one
where

λέγων·   τί   ἐστιν   ἄνθρωπος   ὅτι   μιμνήσκῃ
saying: What   is   man   that   thou
rememberest

αὐτοῦ;   ἢ   υἱὸς   ἀνθρώπου   ὅτι   ἐπισκέπτῃ
him ?   or   a son   of man   that   thou observest

αὐτόν;   7 ἠλάττωσας   αὐτὸν   βραχύ   τι   παρ'
him ?   Thou madest ³less   ¹him   ²a little   than

ἀγγέλους,   δόξῃ   καὶ   τιμῇ   ἐστεφάνωσας
angels,   with glory   and   with honour   thou crownedst

αὐτόν,   8 πάντα   ὑπέταξας   ὑποκάτω   τῶν
him,   all things thou subjectedst   underneath   the

ποδῶν   αὐτοῦ.   ἐν   τῷ   γὰρ   ὑποτάξαι
feet   of him.   ³in   the   For ¹to subject[ing]

[αὐτῷ]   τὰ   πάντα   οὐδὲν   ἀφῆκεν   αὐτῷ
²to him   -   ³all things   ⁴nothing   ⁵he left   ⁶to him

ἀνυπότακτον.   Νῦν   δὲ   οὔπω   ὁρῶμεν
⁷unsubjected.   But now   not yet   we see

αὐτῷ   τὰ   πάντα   ὑποτεταγμένα·   9 τὸν   δὲ
³to him   -   ¹all things   ²having been   ²the   ¹but
subjected;   [one]

βραχύ   τι   παρ'   ἀγγέλους   ἠλαττωμένον
⁴a little   ⁵than   ⁶angels   ³having been
made less

βλέπομεν   Ἰησοῦν   διὰ   τὸ   πάθημα   τοῦ
²we see   ¹Jesus   because of the   suffering   -

θανάτου   δόξῃ   καὶ   τιμῇ   ἐστεφανωμένον,
of death   with glory   and   with honour   having been
crowned,

ὅπως   χάριτι   θεοῦ   ὑπὲρ   παντὸς   γεύσηται
so as   by [the]   of God   ³on   ⁴every man   ¹he might
grace   behalf of   taste

θανάτου.   10 ἔπρεπεν   γὰρ   αὐτῷ,   δι'
of ²death.   For it was fitting   for him, because
of

ὃν   τὰ   πάντα   καὶ   δι'   οὗ   τὰ   πάντα,
whom   -   all things   and   through whom   -   all things,

πολλοὺς   υἱοὺς   εἰς   δόξαν   ἀγαγόντα   τὸν
¹⁴many   ¹¹sons   ¹²to   ¹³glory   ⁷leading   ⁴the

ἀρχηγὸν   τῆς   σωτηρίας   αὐτῶν   διὰ
⁵author   ⁶of the   ⁷salvation   ⁸of them   ⁹through

παθημάτων   τελειῶσαι.   11 ὅ   τε   γὰρ
⁹sufferings   ¹to perfect.   the [one] ²both   ¹For

ἁγιάζων   καὶ   οἱ   ἁγιαζόμενοι   ἐξ   ἑνὸς
sanctifying   and   the [ones]   being sanctified [are]   ²of   ¹one

πάντες·   δι'   ἣν   αἰτίαν   οὐκ   ἐπαισχύνεται
¹all;   for   which   cause   he is not ashamed

ἀδελφοὺς   αὐτοὺς   καλεῖν,   12 λέγων·   ἀπαγ-
²brothers   ³them   ¹to call,   saying: I will

γελῶ   τὸ   ὄνομά   σου   τοῖς   ἀδελφοῖς   μου,
announce the   name   of thee   to the   brothers   of me,

ἐν   μέσῳ   ἐκκλησίας   ὑμνήσω   σε·   13 καὶ
in [the] midst   of [the] church   I will hymn   thee;   and

πάλιν·   ἐγὼ   ἔσομαι   πεποιθὼς   ἐπ'   αὐτῷ·
again: I   will be   having trusted   on(in)   him;

καὶ   πάλιν·   ἰδοὺ   ἐγὼ   καὶ   τὰ   παιδία
and   again: Behold[,]   I   and   the   children

ἅ   μοι   ἔδωκεν   ὁ   θεός.   14 Ἐπεὶ   οὖν
whom ²to me   ²gave   -   ¹God.   Since therefore

τὰ   παιδία   κεκοινώνηκεν   αἵματος   καὶ
the   children   has(ve) partaken   of blood   and

σαρκός,   καὶ   αὐτὸς   παραπλησίως   μετέσχεν
of flesh,   ²also   ³[him]self   ⁴in like manner   ¹he shared

τῶν   αὐτῶν,   ἵνα   διὰ   τοῦ   θανάτου
the   same things,   in order   through   the(?his)   death
that

καταργήσῃ   τὸν   τὸ   κράτος   ἔχοντα   τοῦ
he might destroy   the [one]   ¹the   ²might   ³having   -

θανάτου,   τοῦτ'   ἔστιν   τὸν   διάβολον,   15 καὶ
of death,   this   is   the   devil,   and

ἀπαλλάξῃ   τούτους,   ὅσοι   φόβῳ   θανάτου
release   these,   as many as   by fear   of death

διὰ   παντὸς   τοῦ   ζῆν   ἔνοχοι   ἦσαν   δουλείας.
through all   the(ir)   to   ²involved   ¹were   slavery.
[time]   live   in

16 οὐ   γὰρ   δήπου   ἀγγέλων   ἐπιλαμβάνεται,
⁴not   ¹For   ²of course   ³of angels   ⁵he takes hold,

ἀλλὰ   σπέρματος   Ἀβραὰμ   ἐπιλαμβάνεται.
but   of [the] seed   of Abraham   he takes hold.

17 ὅθεν   ὤφειλεν   κατὰ   πάντα   τοῖς   ἀδελφοῖς
Whence   he owed   by all means†   ²to the   ³brothers
(ought)   (his)

ὁμοιωθῆναι,   ἵνα   ἐλεήμων   γένηται   καὶ
¹to become like,   in order   ²a merciful   ¹he might become   and
that

πιστὸς   ἀρχιερεὺς   τὰ   πρὸς   τὸν   θεόν,
faithful   high priest   [in]   the   in regard   -   God,
things   to

εἰς   τὸ   ἱλάσκεσθαι   τὰς   ἁμαρτίας   τοῦ
for   the   to make propitia-   the   sins   of the
tion for

λαοῦ.   18 ἐν   ᾧ   γὰρ   πέπονθεν   αὐτὸς
people.   ²in   ³what   ¹For   ⁴has suffered   ⁵he
[way]

πειρασθείς,   δύναται   τοῖς   πειραζομένοις
being tempted,   he is able   ²the [ones]   ³being tempted

βοηθῆσαι.
¹to help.

King James Version

New International Version

Jesus greater than Moses

3 Wherefore, holy brethren, partakers of the heavenly calling, consider the Apostle and High Priest of our profession, Christ Jesus; 2 Who was faithful to him that appointed him, as also Moses *was faithful* in all his house. 3 For this *man* was counted worthy of more glory than Moses, inasmuch as he who hath builded the house hath more honour than the house. 4 For every house is builded by some *man;* but he that built all things *is* God. 5And Moses verily *was* faithful in all his house as a servant, for a testimony of those things which were to be spoken after; 6 But Christ as a son over his own house; whose house are we, if we hold fast the confidence and the rejoicing of the hope firm unto the end. 7 Wherefore as the Holy Ghost saith, To day if ye will hear his voice, 8 Harden not your hearts, as in the provocation, in the day of temptation in the wilderness: 9 When your fathers tempted me, proved me, and saw my works forty years. 10 Wherefore I was grieved with that generation, and said, They do always err in *their* heart; and they have not known my ways. 11 So I sware in my wrath, They shall not enter into my rest. 12 Take heed, brethren, lest there be in any of you an evil heart of unbelief, in departing from the living God. 13 But exhort one another daily, while it is called To day; lest any of you be hardened through the deceitfulness of sin. 14 For we are made partakers of Christ, if we hold the beginning of our confidence stedfast unto the end; 15 While it is said, To day if ye will hear his voice, harden not your hearts, as in the provocation. 16 For some, when they had heard, did provoke: howbeit not all that came out of Egypt by Moses. 17 But with whom was he grieved forty years? *was it* not with them that had sinned, whose carcasses fell in the wilderness? 18And to whom sware he that they should not enter into his rest, but to them that believed not? 19 So we see that they could not enter in because of unbelief.

3 Therefore, holy brothers, who share in the heavenly calling, fix your thoughts on Jesus, the apostle and high priest whom we confess. 2 He was faithful to the one who appointed him, just as Moses was faithful in all God's house. 3 Jesus has been found worthy of greater honor than Moses, just as the builder of a house has greater honor than the house itself. 4 For every house is built by someone, but God is the builder of everything. 5 Moses was faithful as a servant in all God's house, testifying to what would be said in the future. 6 But Christ is faithful as a son over God's house. And we are his house, if we hold on to our courage and the hope of which we boast.

Warning against unbelief

7 So, as the Holy Spirit says:
   "Today, if you hear his voice,
8   do not harden your hearts
      as you did in the rebellion,
      during the time of testing in the desert,
9   where your fathers tested and tried me,
      and for forty years saw what I did.
10 That is why I was angry with that generation,
      and I said, 'Their hearts are always going astray,
      and they have not known my ways.'
11 So I declared on oath in my anger,
      'They shall never enter my rest.' " [n]
12 See to it, brothers, that none of you has a sinful, unbelieving heart that turns away from the living God. 13 But encourage one another daily, as long as it is called Today, so that none of you may be hardened by sin's deceitfulness. 14 We have come to share in Christ if we hold firmly till the end the confidence we had at first. 15As has just been said:
   "Today, if you hear his voice,
      do not harden your hearts
      as you did in the rebellion." [o]
16 Who were they who heard and rebelled? Were they not all those Moses led out of Egypt? 17And with whom was he angry for forty years? Was it not with those who sinned, whose bodies fell in the desert? 18And to whom did God swear that they would never enter his rest if not to those who disobeyed? [p] 19 So we see that they were not able to enter, because of their unbelief.

A Sabbath-rest for the people of God

4 Let us therefore fear, lest, a promise being left *us* of entering into his rest, any of you should seem to come short of it. 2 For unto us was the gospel preached, as well as unto them: but the word preached did not profit them, not being mixed with faith in them that heard *it.* 3 For we which have believed do enter into rest,

4 Therefore, since the promise of entering his rest still stands, let us be careful that none of you be found to have fallen short of it. 2 For we also have had the gospel preached to us, just as they did; but the message they heard was of no value to them, because those who heard did not combine it with faith. [q] 3 Now we who

[n] Psalm 95:7-11. [o] Psalm 95:7,8. [p] Or *disbelieved.* [q] Many MSS read *because they did not share in the faith of those who obeyed.*

Greek Interlinear

Chapter 3

"Οθεν, ἀδελφοὶ ἅγιοι, κλήσεως
Whence, brothers holy, ²calling

ἐπουρανίου μέτοχοι, κατανοήσατε τὸν
²of a heavenly ¹sharers, consider the

ἀπόστολον καὶ ἀρχιερέα τῆς ὁμολογίας
apostle and high priest of the confession

ἡμῶν Ἰησοῦν, 2 πιστὸν ὄντα τῷ ποιήσαντι
of us[,] Jesus, faithful being to the [one] making

αὐτόν, ὡς καὶ Μωϋσῆς ἐν [ὅλῳ] τῷ
him, as also Moses in all the

οἴκῳ αὐτοῦ. 3 πλείονος γὰρ οὗτος δόξης
household of him. For ²of more ¹this one ⁴glory

παρὰ Μωϋσῆν ἠξίωται καθ᾽ ὅσον πλείονα
³than ⁵Moses ⁷has been by so much as ⁸more
                    counted worthy

τιμὴν ἔχει τοῦ οἴκου ὁ κατασκευάσας
⁶honour ¹has ²the ³house ⁴the ⁵having prepared
          ⁷[than]   [one]

αὐτόν. 4 πᾶς γὰρ οἶκος κατασκευάζεται
⁵it. For every house is prepared

ὑπό τινος, ὁ δὲ πάντα κατασκευάσας
by someone, but ²the [one] ¹all things ³having prepared

θεός. 5 καὶ Μωϋσῆς μὲν πιστὸς ἐν
[is] God. And Moses on one hand faithful in
                                              [was]

ὅλῳ τῷ οἴκῳ αὐτοῦ ὡς θεράπων εἰς
all the household of him as a servant for

μαρτύριον τῶν λαληθησομένων, 6 Χριστὸς
a testimony of the things being spoken Christ
                      [in the future],

δὲ ὡς υἱὸς ἐπὶ τὸν οἶκον αὐτοῦ· οὗ
on the as a Son over the household of him; of
other   whom

οἶκός ἐσμεν ἡμεῖς, ἐὰν τὴν παρρησίαν
a household are we, if ²the ³confidence

καὶ τὸ καύχημα τῆς ἐλπίδος [μέχρι
⁴and ⁵the ⁶boast ⁷of the ⁸hope ¹⁰until

τέλους βεβαίαν] κατάσχωμεν. 7 Διό,
¹¹[the] end ⁹firm ¹we hold fast. Wherefore,

καθὼς λέγει τὸ πνεῦμα τὸ ἅγιον· σήμερον
as says the Spirit – Holy: To-day

ἐὰν τῆς φωνῆς αὐτοῦ ἀκούσητε, 8 μὴ
if the voice of him ye hear, not

σκληρύνητε τὰς καρδίας ὑμῶν ὡς ἐν
harden ye the hearts of you as in

τῷ παραπικρασμῷ κατὰ τὴν ἡμέραν τοῦ
the provocation in the day of the

πειρασμοῦ ἐν τῇ ἐρήμῳ, 9 οὗ ἐπείρασαν
temptation in the desert, when ¹tempted

οἱ πατέρες ὑμῶν ἐν δοκιμασίᾳ καὶ εἶδον
¹the ²fathers ³of you in proving and saw

τὰ ἔργα μου τεσσεράκοντα ἔτη. 10 διὸ
the works of me forty years; where-
                                            fore

προσώχθισα τῇ γενεᾷ ταύτῃ καὶ εἶπον·
I was angry with this generation and I said:

ἀεὶ πλανῶνται τῇ καρδίᾳ· αὐτοὶ δὲ
Always they err in the heart; and they

οὐκ ἔγνωσαν τὰς ὁδούς μου, 11 ὡς
knew not the ways of me, as

ὤμοσα ἐν τῇ ὀργῇ μου· εἰ εἰσελεύσονται
I swore in the wrath of me: If they shall enter

εἰς τὴν κατάπαυσίν μου. 12 Βλέπετε,
into the rest of me. Look ye,

ἀδελφοί, μήποτε ἔσται ἔν τινι ὑμῶν
brothers, lest there shall be in anyone of you

καρδία πονηρὰ ἀπιστίας ἐν τῷ ἀποστῆναι
¹heart ¹an evil of unbelief in the to depart[ing]

ἀπὸ θεοῦ ζῶντος, 13 ἀλλὰ παρακαλεῖτε
from God a living, but exhort

ἑαυτοὺς καθ᾽ ἑκάστην ἡμέραν, ἄχρις οὗ
yourselves – each day, while

τὸ σήμερον καλεῖται, ἵνα μὴ σκληρυνθῇ
the to-day it is being called, lest ¹be hardened

τις ἐξ ὑμῶν ἀπάτῃ τῆς ἁμαρτίας· 14 μέτ-
¹any- ²of ²you by [the] – of sin; ¹shar-
one   deceit

οχοι γὰρ τοῦ Χριστοῦ γεγόναμεν, ἐάνπερ
ers ¹for ⁴of ⁵Christ ²we have if indeed
        the   become,

τὴν ἀρχὴν τῆς ὑποστάσεως μέχρι τέλους
⁵the ⁶beginning ⁷of the ⁸assurance ⁹until ¹⁰[the] end

βεβαίαν κατάσχωμεν. 15 ἐν τῷ λέγεσθαι·
⁴firm ¹we hold fast. In the to be said⁴:
                         – While it is said:

σήμερον ἐὰν τῆς φωνῆς αὐτοῦ ἀκούσητε,
To-day if the voice of him ye hear,

μὴ σκληρύνητε τὰς καρδίας ὑμῶν ὡς
do not harden the hearts of you as

ἐν τῷ παραπικρασμῷ. 16 τίνες γὰρ
in the provocation. For some

ἀκούσαντες παρεπίκραναν; ἀλλ᾽ οὐ πάντες
hearing provoked? yet not all

οἱ ἐξελθόντες ἐξ Αἰγύπτου διὰ
the [ones] coming out out of Egypt through

Μωϋσέως; 17 τίσιν δὲ προσώχθισεν τεσ-
Moses? but with whom was he angry for-

σεράκοντα ἔτη; οὐχὶ τοῖς ἁμαρτήσασιν,
ty years? [was it] with the [ones] sinning,
                                                  not

ὧν τὰ κῶλα ἔπεσεν ἐν τῇ ἐρήμῳ;
of the corpses fell in the desert?
whom

18 τίσιν δὲ ὤμοσεν μὴ εἰσελεύσεσθαι εἰς
and to whom swore he not to enter into

τὴν κατάπαυσιν αὐτοῦ εἰ μὴ τοῖς
the rest of him except to the

ἀπειθήσασιν; 19 καὶ βλέπομεν ὅτι οὐκ
[ones] disobeying? and we see that not

ἠδυνήθησαν εἰσελθεῖν δι᾽ ἀπιστίαν.
they were able to enter because of disbelief.

Chapter 4

Φοβηθῶμεν οὖν μήποτε καταλειπομένης
Let us fear therefore lest ²being left

ἐπαγγελίας εἰσελθεῖν εἰς τὴν κατάπαυσιν
¹a promise⁴ to enter into the rest

αὐτοῦ δοκῇ τις ἐξ ὑμῶν ὑστερηκέναι.
of him ²seems ¹anyone ²of ²you to have come short.

2 καὶ γὰρ ἐσμεν εὐηγγελισμένοι καθάπερ
For indeed we are having had good news even as
                  preached [to us]

κἀκεῖνοι· ἀλλ᾽ οὐκ ὠφέλησεν ὁ λόγος
those also; but ⁴did not profit ¹the ²word

τῆς ἀκοῆς ἐκείνους μὴ συγκεκερασμένος
– ³of hearing those not having been mixed
                                          together

τῇ πίστει τοῖς ἀκούσασιν. 3 Εἰσερχόμεθα
– with faith in the [ones] hearing. we enter

King James Version

as he said, As I have sworn in my wrath, if they shall enter into my rest: although the works were finished from the foundation of the world. 4 For he spake in a certain place of the seventh *day* on this wise, And God did rest the seventh day from all his works. 5 And in this *place* again, If they shall enter into my rest. 6 Seeing therefore it remaineth that some must enter therein, and they to whom it was first preached entered not in because of unbelief: 7 Again, he limiteth a certain day, saying in David, To day, after so long a time; as it is said, To day if ye will hear his voice, harden not your hearts. 8 For if Jesus had given them rest, then would he not afterward have spoken of another day. 9 There remaineth therefore a rest to the people of God. 10 For he that is entered into his rest, he also hath ceased from his own works, as God *did* from his. 11 Let us labour therefore to enter into that rest, lest any man fall after the same example of unbelief. 12 For the word of God *is* quick, and powerful, and sharper than any twoedged sword, piercing even to the dividing asunder of soul and spirit, and of the joints and marrow, and *is* a discerner of the thoughts and intents of the heart. 13 Neither is there any creature that is not manifest in his sight: but all things *are* naked and opened unto the eyes of him with whom we have to do. 14 Seeing then that we have a great high priest, that is passed into the heavens, Jesus the Son of God, let us hold fast *our* profession. 15 For we have not a high priest which cannot be touched with the feeling of our infirmities; but was in all points tempted like as *we are,* yet without sin. 16 Let us therefore come boldly unto the throne of grace, that we may obtain mercy, and find grace to help in time of need.

5 For every high priest taken from among men is ordained for men in things *pertaining* to God, that he may offer both gifts and sacrifices for sins: 2 Who can have compassion on the ignorant, and on them that are out of the way; for that he himself also is compassed with infirmity. 3 And by reason hereof he ought, as for the people, so also for himself, to offer for sins. 4 And no man taketh this honour unto himself, but he that is called of God, as *was* Aaron. 5 So also Christ glorified not himself to be made

New International Version

have believed enter that rest, just as God has said,
"So I declared on oath in my anger,
'They shall never enter my rest.' " *r*
And yet his work has been finished since the creation of the world. 4 For somewhere he has spoken about the seventh day in these words: "And on the seventh day God rested from all his work." *s* 5 And again in the passage above he says, "They shall never enter my rest." *r*
6 It still remains that some will enter that rest, and those who formerly had the gospel preached to them did not go in, because of their disobedience. 7 Therefore God again set a certain day, calling it Today, when a long time later he spoke through David, as was said before:
"Today, if you hear his voice,
do not harden your hearts." *t*
8 For if Joshua had given them rest, God would not have spoken later about another day. 9 There remains, then, a Sabbath-rest for the people of God; 10 for anyone who enters God's rest also rests from his own work, just as God did from his. 11 Let us, therefore, make every effort to enter that rest, so that no one will fall by following their example of disobedience.
12 The word of God is living and active. Sharper than any double-edged sword, it penetrates even to dividing soul and spirit, joints and marrow; it judges the thoughts and attitudes of the heart. 13 Nothing in all creation is hidden from God's sight. Everything is uncovered and laid bare before the eyes of him to whom we must give account.

Jesus the great high priest

14 Therefore, since we have a great high priest who has gone into heaven, Jesus the Son of God, let us hold firmly to the faith we profess. 15 For we do not have a high priest who is unable to sympathize with our weaknesses, but we have one who has been tempted in every way, just as we are—yet was without sin. 16 Let us then approach the throne of grace with confidence, so that we may receive mercy and find grace to help us in our time of need.

5 Every high priest is selected from among men and is appointed to represent them in matters related to God, to offer gifts and sacrifices for sins. 2 He is able to deal gently with those who are ignorant and are going astray, since he himself is subject to weakness. 3 This is why he has to offer sacrifices for his own sins, as well as for the sins of the people. 4 No one takes this honor upon himself; he must be called by God, just as Aaron was. 5 So Christ also did not take upon himself the glory

Greek Interlinear

γὰρ εἰς [τὴν] κατάπαυσιν οἱ πιστεύσαντες,
For into the rest the [ones] believing,

καθὼς εἴρηκεν· ὡς ὤμοσα ἐν τῇ ὀργῇ
as he has said: As I swore in the wrath

μου· εἰ εἰσελεύσονται εἰς τὴν κατάπαυσίν
of me: If they shall enter into the rest

μου, καίτοι τῶν ἔργων ἀπὸ καταβολῆς
of me, though the works ²from ³[the] foundation

κόσμου γενηθέντων. 4 εἴρηκεν γάρ που
⁴of [the] ⁵having come into For he has said some-
world being.⁶ where

περὶ τῆς ἑβδόμης οὕτως· καὶ κατέπαυσεν
con- the seventh [day] thus: And ²rested
cerning

ὁ θεὸς ἐν τῇ ἡμέρᾳ τῇ ἑβδόμῃ ἀπὸ
- ¹God in the ²day - ²seventh from

πάντων τῶν ἔργων αὐτοῦ· 5 καὶ ἐν
all the works of him; and in

τούτῳ πάλιν· εἰ εἰσελεύσονται εἰς τὴν
this [place] again: If they shall enter into the

κατάπαυσίν μου. 6 ἐπεὶ οὖν ἀπολείπεται
rest of me. Since therefore it remains

τινὰς εἰσελθεῖν εἰς αὐτήν, καὶ οἱ πρότερον
[for] to enter into it, and the formerly
some [ones]

εὐαγγελισθέντες οὐκ εἰσῆλθον δι᾽ ἀπείθειαν,
having good news did not enter because disobedience,
preached [to them] of

7 πάλιν τινὰ ὁρίζει ἡμέραν, σήμερον, ἐν
again ²a certain ¹he de- day, to-day, ²in
fines

Δαυὶδ λέγων μετὰ τοσοῦτον χρόνον, καθὼς
³David ¹saying after such a time, as

προείρηται· σήμερον ἐὰν τῆς φωνῆς αὐτοῦ
he has To-day if the voice of him
previously said:

ἀκούσητε, μὴ σκληρύνητε τὰς καρδίας
ye hear, do not harden the hearts

ὑμῶν. 8 εἰ γὰρ αὐτοὺς Ἰησοῦς κατέπαυσεν,
of you. For if ²them ¹Jesus(Joshua) ²rested,

οὐκ ἂν περὶ ἄλλης ἐλάλει μετὰ ταῦτα
²not - ¹concerning ⁴another ³he ²would ⁴after ⁵these
⁴have spoken things

ἡμέρας. 9 ἄρα ἀπολείπεται σαββατισμὸς
²day. Then ²remains ¹a sabbath rest

τῷ λαῷ τοῦ θεοῦ. 10 ὁ γὰρ εἰσελθὼν
to the people - of God. For the [one] having
entered

εἰς τὴν κατάπαυσιν αὐτοῦ καὶ αὐτὸς
into the rest of him also [him]self

κατέπαυσεν ἀπὸ τῶν ἔργων αὐτοῦ,
rested from the works of him,

ὥσπερ ἀπὸ τῶν ἰδίων ὁ θεός. 11 Σπου-
as from the(his) own - God [did]. Let us

δάσωμεν οὖν εἰσελθεῖν εἰς ἐκείνην τὴν
be eager therefore to enter into that -

κατάπαυσιν, ἵνα μὴ ἐν τῷ αὐτῷ τις
rest, lest ³in ⁴the ²same ¹anyone

ὑποδείγματι πέσῃ τῆς ἀπειθείας. 12 Ζῶν
⁴example ³falls - of dis- [⁴is] ⁵living
obedience.

γὰρ ὁ λόγος τοῦ θεοῦ καὶ ἐνεργὴς
For ¹the ²word - ³of God and operative

καὶ τομώτερος ὑπὲρ πᾶσαν μάχαιραν
and sharper beyond every ²sword

δίστομον καὶ διϊκνούμενος ἄχρι μερισμοῦ
²two-mouthed and passing through as far as division
(edged)

ψυχῆς καὶ πνεύματος, ἁρμῶν τε καὶ
of soul and of spirit, ²of joints ¹both and

μυελῶν, καὶ κριτικὸς ἐνθυμήσεων καὶ
of marrows, and able to judge of thoughts and

ἐννοιῶν καρδίας· 13 καὶ οὐκ ἔστιν κτίσις
intentions of a heart; and there is no creature

ἀφανὴς ἐνώπιον αὐτοῦ, πάντα δὲ γυμνὰ
unmanifest before him, but all things [are] naked

καὶ τετραχηλισμένα τοῖς ὀφθαλμοῖς αὐτοῦ,
and having been laid open to the eyes of him,

πρὸς ὃν ἡμῖν ὁ λόγος.⁶
with whom to us [is] the word(account).⁶
= is our account.

14 Ἔχοντες οὖν ἀρχιερέα μέγαν διεληλυ-
Having there- high priest a great having gone
fore

θότα τοὺς οὐρανούς, Ἰησοῦν τὸν υἱὸν
through the heavens, Jesus the Son

τοῦ θεοῦ, κρατῶμεν τῆς ὁμολογίας. 15 οὐ
- of God, let us hold the confession. ²not

γὰρ ἔχομεν ἀρχιερέα μὴ δυνάμενον
¹For ²we have a high priest not being able

συμπαθῆσαι ταῖς ἀσθενείαις ἡμῶν, πεπει-
to suffer with the weaknesses of us, ¹having

ρασμένον δὲ κατὰ πάντα καθ᾽ ὁμοιότητα
been tempted ¹but in all respects† accord- [our] likeness
ing to

χωρὶς ἁμαρτίας. 16 προσερχώμεθα οὖν
apart from sin. Let us approach therefore

μετὰ παρρησίας τῷ θρόνῳ τῆς χάριτος,
with confidence to the throne - of grace,

ἵνα λάβωμεν ἔλεος καὶ χάριν εὕρωμεν
in or- we may mercy and ²grace we ¹may
der that receive find

εἰς εὔκαιρον βοήθειαν.
for timely help.

Chapter 5

Πᾶς γὰρ ἀρχιερεὺς ἐξ ἀνθρώπων
For every high priest ²out of ²men

λαμβανόμενος ὑπὲρ ἀνθρώπων καθίσταται
¹being taken on behalf of men is appointed [in]

τὰ πρὸς τὸν θεόν, ἵνα προσφέρῃ δῶρά
the in re- - God, in order he may offer ²gifts
things gard to that

τε καὶ θυσίας ὑπὲρ ἁμαρτιῶν, 2 μετριο-
¹both and sacrifices on behalf of sins, ²to feel in

παθεῖν δυνάμενος τοῖς ἀγνοοῦσιν καὶ
due measure ¹being able for the [ones] not knowing and

πλανωμένοις, ἐπεὶ καὶ αὐτὸς περίκειται
being led astray, since also he is set round
[with]

ἀσθένειαν, 3 καὶ δι᾽ αὐτὴν ὀφείλει, καθὼς
weakness, and because it he ought, as
of

περὶ τοῦ λαοῦ, οὕτως καὶ περὶ ἑαυτοῦ
concern- the people, so also concerning himself
ing

προσφέρειν περὶ ἁμαρτιῶν. 4 καὶ οὐχ
to offer concerning sins. And ²not

ἑαυτῷ τις λαμβάνει τὴν τιμήν, ἀλλὰ
⁴to him- ¹anyone ²takes the honour, but
self

καλούμενος ὑπὸ τοῦ θεοῦ, καθώσπερ καὶ
being called by - God, even as indeed

Ἀαρών. 5 Οὕτως καὶ ὁ Χριστὸς οὐχ
Aaron. So also - Christ ²not

King James Version

a high priest; but he that said unto him, Thou art my Son, to day have I begotten thee. 6As he saith also in another *place,* Thou *art* a priest for ever after the order of Melchisedec. 7 Who in the days of his flesh, when he had offered up prayers and supplications with strong crying and tears unto him that was able to save him from death, and was heard in that he feared; 8 Though he were a Son, yet learned he obedience by the things which he suffered; 9And being made perfect, he became the author of eternal salvation unto all them that obey him; 10 Called of God a high priest after the order of Melchisedec. 11 Of whom we have many things to say, and hard to be uttered, seeing ye are dull of hearing. 12 For when for the time ye ought to be teachers, ye have need that one teach you again which *be* the first principles of the oracles of God; and are become such as have need of milk, and not of strong meat. 13 For every one that useth milk *is* unskilful in the word of righteousness: for he is a babe. 14 But strong meat belongeth to them that are of full age, *even* those who by reason of use have their senses exercised to discern both good and evil.

New International Version

of becoming a high priest. But God said to him,
"You are my Son;
    today I have become your Father.*u*" *v*
6And he says in another place,
"You are a priest forever,
    just like Melchizedek." *w*
7 During the days of Jesus' life on earth, he offered up prayers and petitions with loud cries and tears to the One who could save him from death, and he was heard because of his reverent submission. 8Although he was a son, he learned obedience from what he suffered, 9 and once made perfect, he became the source of eternal salvation for all who obey him 10 and was designated by God to be high priest, just like Melchizedek.

Warning against falling away

11 We have much to say about this, but it is hard to explain because you are slow to learn. 12 In fact, though by this time you ought to be teachers, you need someone to teach you the elementary truths of God's word all over again. You need milk, not solid food! 13Anyone who lives on milk, being still an infant, is not acquainted with the teaching about righteousness. 14 But solid food is for the mature, who by constant use have trained themselves to distinguish good from evil.

6 Therefore leaving the principles of the doctrine of Christ, let us go on unto perfection; not laying again the foundation of repentance from dead works, and of faith toward God, 2 Of the doctrine of baptisms, and of laying on of hands, and of resurrection of the dead, and of eternal judgment. 3And this will we do, if God permit. 4 For *it is* impossible for those who were once enlightened, and have tasted of the heavenly gift, and were made partakers of the Holy Ghost, 5And have tasted the good word of God, and the powers of the world to come, 6 If they shall fall away, to renew them again unto repentance; seeing they crucify to themselves the Son of God afresh, and put *him* to an open shame. 7 For the earth which drinketh in the rain that cometh oft upon it, and bringeth forth herbs meet for them by whom it is dressed, receiveth blessing from God: 8 But that which beareth thorns and briers *is* rejected, and *is* nigh unto cursing; whose end *is* to be burned. 9 But, beloved, we are persuaded better things of you, and things that accompany salvation, though we thus speak. 10 For God *is* not unrighteous to forget your work and labour of love, which ye have shewed toward his name, in that ye have ministered to the saints, and do minister. 11And we desire that every one of you do shew the same

6 Therefore let us leave the elementary teachings about Christ and go on to maturity. Let us not lay again the foundation of repentance from acts that lead to death, and of faith in God, 2 instruction about baptisms, the laying on of hands, the resurrection of the dead, and eternal judgment. 3And God permitting, we will do so.
4 It is impossible for those who have once been enlightened, who have tasted the heavenly gift, who have shared in the Holy Spirit, 5 who have tasted the goodness of the word of God and the powers of the coming age, 6 if they fall away, to be brought back to repentance, because*x* to their loss they are crucifying the Son of God all over again and subjecting him to public disgrace.
7 Land that drinks in the rain often falling on it and that produces a crop useful to those who farm it receives the blessing of God. 8 But land that produces thorns and thistles is worthless and is in danger of being cursed. In the end it will be burned.
9 Even though we speak like this, dear friends, we are confident of better things in your case—things that accompany salvation. 10 God is not unjust; he will not forget your work and the love you have shown him as you have helped his people and continue to help them. 11 We want each of you to show this same diligence

[u] Or *have begotten you.* [v] Psalm 2:7. [w] Psalm 110:4. [x] Or *repentance while.*

Greek Interlinear

ἑαυτὸν ἐδόξασεν γενηθῆναι ἀρχιερέα, ἀλλ'
²himself ¹glorified to become a high priest, but

ὁ λαλήσας πρὸς αὐτόν· υἱός μου εἶ
the [one] speaking to him: Son of me art

σύ, ἐγὼ σήμερον γεγέννηκά σε· 6 καθὼς
thou, I to-day have begotten thee; as

καὶ ἐν ἑτέρῳ λέγει· σὺ ἱερεὺς εἰς τὸν
also in another he says: Thou a priest unto the
[psalm] [art]

αἰῶνα κατὰ τὴν τάξιν Μελχισέδεκ. 7 ὃς
age according the order of Melchisedec. Who
to

ἐν ταῖς ἡμέραις τῆς σαρκὸς αὐτοῦ δεήσεις
in the days of the flesh of him ⁸petitions

τε καὶ ἱκετηρίας πρὸς τὸν δυνάμενον
⁹both ⁴and ⁵entreaties ¹¹to ¹²the [one] ¹³being able

σώζειν αὐτὸν ἐκ θανάτου μετὰ κραυγῆς
¹⁴to save ¹⁵him ¹⁶out of ¹⁷death ⁶with ⁷crying

ἰσχυρᾶς καὶ δακρύων προσενέγκας καὶ
⁸strong ⁹and ¹⁰tears ¹offering and

εἰσακουσθεὶς ἀπὸ τῆς εὐλαβείας, 8 καίπερ
being heard from(for) the(his) devoutness, though

ὢν υἱός, ἔμαθεν ἀφ' ὧν ἔπαθεν τὴν
being a Son, he ²from ³[the] ⁴he suffered –
learned things which

ὑπακοήν, 9 καὶ τελειωθεὶς ἐγένετο πᾶσιν
¹obedience, and being perfected he became to all

τοῖς ὑπακούουσιν αὐτῷ αἴτιος σωτηρίας
the [ones] obeying him [the] cause ¹salvation

αἰωνίου, 10 προσαγορευθεὶς ὑπὸ τοῦ θεοῦ
¹of eternal, being designated by – God

ἀρχιερεὺς κατὰ τὴν τάξιν Μελχισέδεκ.
a high priest accord- the order of Melchisedec.
ing to

11 Περὶ οὗ πολὺς ἡμῖν ὁ λόγος καὶ
Concern- whom much to us the ¹word⁸ ²and
ing   = we have much to say and hard . . .

δυσερμήνευτος λέγειν, ἐπεὶ νωθροὶ γεγόνατε
⁴hard to interpret ³to say, since dull ye have
become

ταῖς ἀκοαῖς. 12 καὶ γὰρ ὀφείλοντες
in the hearings. For indeed owing⁸

εἶναι διδάσκαλοι διὰ τὸν χρόνον, πάλιν
to be teachers because of the time, ⁴again

χρείαν ἔχετε τοῦ διδάσκειν ὑμᾶς τινα
¹need ¹ye have – ⁵to teach⁴ ³you ⁶someone

τὰ στοιχεῖα τῆς ἀρχῆς τῶν λογίων
the rudiments of the beginning of the oracles

τοῦ θεοῦ, καὶ γεγόνατε χρείαν ἔχοντες
– of God, and ye have become ³need ¹having

γάλακτος, οὐ στερεᾶς τροφῆς. 13 πᾶς
of milk, not of solid food. every

γὰρ · ὁ μετέχων γάλακτος ἄπειρος λόγου
For one partaking of milk [is] without of [the]
experience word

δικαιοσύνης, νήπιος γάρ ἐστιν· 14 τελείων δὲ
of righteousness, for ²an infant ¹he is; but ⁴of mature
men

ἔστιν ἡ στερεὰ τροφή, τῶν διὰ τὴν
²is the ³solid ⁴food, of the because the(ir)
[ones] of

ἕξιν τὰ αἰσθητήρια γεγυμνασμένα ἐχόντων
con- ²the(ir) ³faculties having been ⁴exercised ¹having
dition

πρὸς διάκρισιν καλοῦ τε καὶ κακοῦ.
for distinction ²of good ¹both and of bad.

Chapter 6

Διὸ ἀφέντες τὸν τῆς ἀρχῆς τοῦ Χριστοῦ
Wherefore leaving ¹the ³of the ⁴beginning – ⁵of Christ

λόγον ἐπὶ τὴν τελειότητα φερώμεθα, μὴ
²word ⁶on to – ⁷maturity ⁸let us be borne, not

πάλιν θεμέλιον καταβαλλόμενοι μετανοίας
again ²a foundation ¹laying down of repentance

ἀπὸ νεκρῶν ἔργων, καὶ πίστεως ἐπὶ
from dead works, and of faith toward

θεόν, 2 βαπτισμῶν διδαχῆς, ἐπιθέσεώς τε
God, ²of baptisms ¹of teaching, and of laying on

χειρῶν, ἀναστάσεως νεκρῶν, καὶ κρίματος
of hands, of resurrection of dead persons, and ¹judgment

αἰωνίου. 3 καὶ τοῦτο ποιήσομεν, ἐάνπερ
¹of eternal. And this will we do, if indeed

ἐπιτρέπῃ ὁ θεός. 4 Ἀδύνατον γὰρ τοὺς
²permits – ¹God. For [it is] impossible the
[for] [ones]

ἅπαξ φωτισθέντας γευσαμένους τε τῆς
once being enlightened and tasting of the

δωρεᾶς τῆς ἐπουρανίου καὶ μετόχους
²gift – ¹heavenly and sharers

γενηθέντας πνεύματος ἁγίου 5 καὶ καλὸν
becoming Spirit of [the] Holy and ²[the] good

γευσαμένους θεοῦ ῥῆμα δυνάμεις τε
¹tasting ²of God ¹word and powerful deeds

μέλλοντος αἰῶνος, 6 καὶ παραπεσόντας, πάλιν
of a coming age, and falling away, again

ἀνακαινίζειν εἰς μετάνοιαν, ἀνασταυροῦντας
to renew to repentance, crucifying again

ἑαυτοῖς τὸν υἱὸν τοῦ θεοῦ καὶ παρα-
for them- the Son – of God and putting
selves

δειγματίζοντας. 7 γῆ γὰρ ἡ πιοῦσα
[him] to open shame. For earth – drinking

τὸν ἐπ' αὐτῆς ἐρχόμενον πολλάκις ὑετὸν
¹the ⁸upon ⁹it ²coming ⁴often ³rain

καὶ τίκτουσα βοτάνην εὔθετον ἐκείνοις
and bearing fodder suitable for those

δι' οὓς καὶ γεωργεῖται, μεταλαμβάνει
on ac- whom indeed it is farmed, receives
count of

εὐλογίας ἀπὸ τοῦ θεοῦ· 8 ἐκφέρουσα δὲ
blessing from – God; but bringing forth

ἀκάνθας καὶ τριβόλους ἀδόκιμος καὶ
thorns and thistles [it is] disapproved and

κατάρας ἐγγύς, ἧς τὸ τέλος εἰς καῦσιν.
²a curse ¹near, of which the end [is] for burning.

9 Πεπείσμεθα δὲ περὶ ὑμῶν, ἀγαπητοί,
But we have been concerning you, beloved,
persuaded

τὰ κρείσσονα καὶ ἐχόμενα σωτηρίας, εἰ
the better things and having salvation, if

καὶ οὕτως λαλοῦμεν. 10 οὐ γὰρ ἄδικος
indeed ¹so ¹we speak. For ²not ¹unjust

ὁ θεὸς ἐπιλαθέσθαι τοῦ ἔργου ὑμῶν
– ¹God [is] to be forgetful of the work of you

καὶ τῆς ἀγάπης ἧς ἐνεδείξασθε εἰς τὸ
and of the love which ye showed to the

ὄνομα αὐτοῦ, διακονήσαντες τοῖς ἁγίοις
name of him, having ministered to the saints

καὶ διακονοῦντες. 11 ἐπιθυμοῦμεν δὲ
and ministering. But we desire

ἕκαστον ὑμῶν τὴν αὐτὴν ἐνδείκνυσθαι
each one of you ²the ³same ¹to show

* That is, " ye ought . . . "

649

King James Version

diligence to the full assurance of hope unto the end: 12 That ye be not slothful, but followers of them who through faith and patience inherit the promises. 13 For when God made promise to Abraham, because he could swear by no greater, he sware by himself, 14 Saying, Surely blessing I will bless thee, and multiplying I will multiply thee. 15 And so, after he had patiently endured, he obtained the promise. 16 For men verily swear by the greater: and an oath for confirmation *is* to them an end of all strife. 17 Wherein God, willing more abundantly to shew unto the heirs of promise the immutability of his counsel, confirmed *it* by an oath: 18 That by two immutable things, in which *it was* impossible for God to lie, we might have a strong consolation, who have fled for refuge to lay hold upon the hope set before us: 19 Which *hope* we have as an anchor of the soul, both sure and steadfast, and which entereth into that within the vail; 20 Whither the forerunner is for us entered, *even* Jesus, made a high priest for ever after the order of Melchisedec.

7 For this Melchisedec, king of Salem, priest of the most high God, who met Abraham returning from the slaughter of the kings, and blessed him; 2 To whom also Abraham gave a tenth part of all; first being by interpretation King of righteousness, and after that also King of Salem, which is, King of peace; 3 Without father, without mother, without descent, having neither beginning of days, nor end of life; but made like unto the Son of God; abideth a priest continually. 4 Now consider how great this man *was,* unto whom even the patriarch Abraham gave the tenth of the spoils. 5 And verily they that are of the sons of Levi, who receive the office of the priesthood, have a commandment to take tithes of the people according to the law, that is, of their brethren, though they come out of the loins of Abraham: 6 But he whose descent is not counted from them received tithes of Abraham, and blessed him that had the promises. 7 And without all contradiction the less is blessed of the better. 8 And here men that die receive tithes; but there he *receiveth them,* of whom it is witnessed that he liveth. 9 And as I may so say, Levi also, who receiveth tithes, paid tithes in Abraham. 10 For he was yet in the loins of his father, when Melchisedec met him. 11 If therefore perfection were by the Levitical priesthood, (for under it the people received the law,) what further need *was there* that another priest should

New International Version

to the very end, in order to make your hope sure. 12 We do not want you to become lazy, but to imitate those who through faith and patience inherit what has been promised.

The certainty of God's promise

13 When God made his promise to Abraham, since there was no one greater for him to swear by, he swore by himself, 14 saying, "I will surely bless you and give you many descendants." 15 And so after waiting patiently, Abraham received what was promised.
16 Men swear by someone greater than themselves, and the oath confirms what is said and puts an end to all argument. 17 Because God wanted to make the unchanging nature of his purpose very clear to the heirs of what was promised, he confirmed it with an oath. 18 God did this so that, by two unchangeable things in which it is impossible for God to lie, we who have fled to take hold of the hope offered to us may be greatly encouraged. 19 We have this hope as an anchor for the soul, firm and secure. It enters the inner sanctuary behind the curtain, 20 where Jesus, who went before us, has entered on our behalf. He has become a high priest forever, just like Melchizedek.

Melchizedek the priest

7 This Melchizedek was king of Salem and a priest of God Most High. He met Abraham returning from the defeat of the kings and blessed him, 2 and Abraham gave him a tenth of everything. First, his name means "king of righteousness"; then also, "king of Salem" means "king of peace." 3 Without father or mother, without beginning of days or end of life, like the Son of God he remains a priest forever.
4 Just think how great he was: Even the patriarch Abraham gave him a tenth of the plunder! 5 Now the law requires the descendants of Levi who become priests to collect a tenth from the people—that is, their brothers—even though their brothers are descended from Abraham. 6 This man, however, did not trace his descent from Levi, yet he collected a tenth from Abraham and blessed him who had the promises. 7 And without doubt the lesser person is blessed by the greater. 8 In the one case, the tenth is collected by men who die; but in the other case, by him who is declared to be living. 9 One might even say that Levi, who collects the tenth, paid the tenth through Abraham, 10 because when Melchizedek met Abraham, Levi was still in the body of his ancestor.

Jesus like Melchizedek

11 If perfection could have been attained through the Levitical priesthood (for on the basis of it the law was given to the people), why

---

[y] Gen. 22:17.

Greek Interlinear

σπουδὴν πρὸς τὴν πληροφορίαν τῆς ἐλπίδος
eagerness to   the full assurance of the hope
ἄχρι τέλους, 12 ἵνα μὴ νωθροὶ γένησθε,
unto [the] end, lest dull ye become,
μιμηταὶ δὲ τῶν διὰ πίστεως καὶ μακρο-
but imitators of the through faith and long-
                [ones]
θυμίας κληρονομούντων τὰς ἐπαγγελίας.
suffering inheriting the promises.
13 Τῷ γὰρ Ἀβραὰμ ἐπαγγειλάμενος ὁ
  - For 'to Abraham 'making promise -
θεός, ἐπεὶ κατ' οὐδενὸς εἶχεν μείζονος
'God, since 'by 'no one 'he had 'greater
ὀμόσαι, ὤμοσεν καθ' ἑαυτοῦ, 14 λέγων·
to swear, swore by himself, saying:
εἰ μὴν εὐλογῶν εὐλογήσω σε καὶ πληθύνων
If surely blessing I will bless thee and multiplying
πληθυνῶ σε· 15 καὶ οὕτως μακροθυμήσας
I will multiply thee; and so being longsuffering
ἐπέτυχεν τῆς ἐπαγγελίας. 16 ἄνθρωποι γὰρ
he obtained the promise. For men
κατὰ τοῦ μείζονος ὀμνύουσιν, καὶ πάσης
by the greater swear, and 'of all
αὐτοῖς ἀντιλογίας πέρας εἰς βεβαίωσιν ὁ
'[is] 'to 'contradiction 'an end 'for 'confirmation 'the
them
ὅρκος· 17 ἐν ᾧ περισσότερον βουλόμενος
'oath; wherein 'more abundantly 'resolving

ὁ θεὸς ἐπιδεῖξαι τοῖς κληρονόμοις τῆς
 - 'God to show to the heirs of the
ἐπαγγελίας τὸ ἀμετάθετον τῆς βουλῆς
promise the unchangeableness of the resolve
αὐτοῦ ἐμεσίτευσεν ὅρκῳ, 18 ἵνα διὰ
of him interposed by an in or- through
              oath, der that
δύο πραγμάτων ἀμεταθέτων, ἐν οἷς ἀδύνατον
two 'things 'unchangeable, in which impossible
                    [it was]
ψεύσασθαι θεόν, ἰσχυρὰν παράκλησιν ἔχωμεν
'to lie 'God,ᵇ 'a strong 'consolation 'we may
                    have[,]
οἱ καταφυγόντες κρατῆσαι τῆς προκειμένης
the [ones] having fled to lay hold of the 'set before [us]
ἐλπίδος· 19 ἣν ὡς ἄγκυραν ἔχομεν τῆς
'hope; which as an anchor we have of the
ψυχῆς ἀσφαλῆ τε καὶ βεβαίαν καὶ
soul 'safe 'both and firm and
εἰσερχομένην εἰς τὸ ἐσώτερον τοῦ κατα-
entering into the inner [side] of the veil,
πετάσματος, 20 ὅπου πρόδρομος ὑπὲρ ἡμῶν
where a forerunner on us
                  behalf of
εἰσῆλθεν Ἰησοῦς, κατὰ τὴν τάξιν Μελχισέ-
entered[.] Jesus, 'according 'the 'order 'of Melchise-
                to
δεκ ἀρχιερεὺς γενόμενος εἰς τὸν αἰῶνα.
dec 'a high priest 'becoming 'unto 'the 'age.

Chapter 7

Οὗτος γὰρ ὁ Μελχισέδεκ, βασιλεὺς
For this - Melchisedec, king
Σαλήμ, ἱερεὺς τοῦ θεοῦ τοῦ ὑψίστου,
of Salem, priest - 'God 'of the 'most high,
ὁ συναντήσας Ἀβραὰμ ὑποστρέφοντι ἀπὸ
the [one] meeting Abraham returning from
τῆς κοπῆς τῶν βασιλέων καὶ εὐλογήσας
the slaughter of the kings and blessing
αὐτόν, 2 ᾧ καὶ δεκάτην ἀπὸ πάντων
him, to whom indeed 'a tenth 'from 'all
ἐμέρισεν Ἀβραάμ, πρῶτον μὲν ἑρμηνευ-
'divided 'Abraham, firstly on one being inter-
              hand
όμενος βασιλεὺς δικαιοσύνης, ἔπειτα δὲ καὶ
preted King of righteousness, then on the also
                  other
βασιλεὺς Σαλήμ, ὅ ἐστιν βασιλεὺς εἰρήνης,
King of Salem, which is King of peace,
3 ἀπάτωρ, ἀμήτωρ, ἀγενεαλόγητος, μήτε
without father, without mother, without pedigree, 'neither
ἀρχὴν ἡμερῶν μήτε ζωῆς τέλος ἔχων,
'beginning 'of days 'nor 'of life 'end 'having,
ἀφωμοιωμένος δὲ τῷ υἱῷ τοῦ θεοῦ, μένει
but having been made to the Son - of God, remains
like
ἱερεὺς εἰς τὸ διηνεκές. 4 Θεωρεῖτε δὲ
a priest in the perpetuity. Now behold ye
πηλίκος οὗτος, ᾧ δεκάτην Ἀβραὰμ
how great this man to 'a tenth 'Abraham
[was], whom
ἔδωκεν ἐκ τῶν ἀκροθινίων ὁ πατριάρχης.
'gave 'of 'the 'spoils 'the 'patriarch.
5 καὶ οἱ μὲν ἐκ τῶν υἱῶν Λευὶ τὴν
And 'the 'on one 'of 'the 'sons 'of Levi 'the
[ones] hand
ἱερατείαν λαμβάνοντες ἐντολὴν ἔχουσιν
'priesthood 'receiving ¹¹a commandment ¹⁰have
ἀποδεκατοῦν τὸν λαὸν κατὰ τὸν νόμον,
to take tithes the people accord- the law,
from ing to

τοῦτ' ἔστιν τοὺς ἀδελφοὺς αὐτῶν, καίπερ
this is the brothers of them, though
ἐξεληλυθότας ἐκ τῆς ὀσφύος Ἀβραάμ·
having come forth out of the loin[s] of Abraham;
6 ὁ δὲ μὴ γενεαλογούμενος ἐξ αὐτῶν
'the 'on the not counting [his] pedigree from them
[one] other
δεδεκάτωκεν Ἀβραάμ, καὶ τὸν ἔχοντα
has tithed Abraham, and 'the [one] 'having
τὰς ἐπαγγελίας εὐλόγηκεν. 7 χωρὶς δὲ
'the 'promises 'has blessed. And without
πάσης ἀντιλογίας τὸ ἔλαττον ὑπὸ τοῦ
all(any) contradiction the less 'by 'the
κρείττονος εὐλογεῖται. 8 καὶ ὧδε μὲν
'better 'is blessed. And here on one
                  hand
δεκάτας ἀποθνήσκοντες ἄνθρωποι λαμβά-
'tithes 'dying 'men 're-
νουσιν, ἐκεῖ δὲ μαρτυρούμενος ὅτι ζῇ.
ceive, there on the being witnessed that he
other lives.
9 καὶ ὡς ἔπος εἰπεῖν, δι' Ἀβραὰμ
And as a word to say, through Abraham
=so to speak,
καὶ Λευὶς ὁ δεκάτας λαμβάνων δεδε-
indeed Levi 'the [one] 'tithes 'receiving has
κάτωται· 10 ἔτι γὰρ ἐν τῇ ὀσφύϊ τοῦ
been tithed· for 'yet 'in 'the 'loin[s] 'of
the(his)
πατρὸς ἦν ὅτε συνήντησεν αὐτῷ Μελχισέ-
'father 'he was 'when ·¹⁰met ¹¹him 'Melchise-
δεκ. 11 Εἰ μὲν οὖν τελείωσις διὰ τῆς
dec. If - therefore perfection 'through 'the
Λευιτικῆς ἱερωσύνης ἦν, ὁ λαὸς γὰρ
'Levitical 'priestly office 'was, 'the 'people 'for
ἐπ' αὐτῆς νενομοθέτηται, τίς ἔτι χρεία
'under* 'it has been furnished why yet need
with law,
κατὰ τὴν τάξιν Μελχισέδεκ ἕτερον
[was there 'the 'order 'of Melchisedec 'another
for] 'accord-
ing to

* See note on ch. 9. 15.

King James Version

rise after the order of Melchisedec, and not be called after the order of Aaron? 12 For the priesthood being changed, there is made of necessity a change also of the law. 13 For he of whom these things are spoken pertaineth to another tribe, of which no man gave attendance at the altar. 14 For *it is* evident that our Lord sprang out of Juda; of which tribe Moses spake nothing concerning priesthood. 15And it is yet far more evident: for that after the similitude of Melchisedec there ariseth another priest, 16 Who is made, not after the law of a carnal commandment, but after the power of an endless life. 17 For he testifieth, Thou *art* a priest for ever after the order of Melchisedec. 18 For there is verily a disannulling of the commandment going before for the weakness and unprofitableness thereof. 19 For the law made nothing perfect, but the bringing in of a better hope *did;* by the which we draw nigh unto God. 20And inasmuch as not without an oath *he was made priest:* 21 (For those priests were made without an oath; but this with an oath by him that said unto him, The Lord sware and will not repent, Thou *art* a priest for ever after the order of Melchisedec:) 22 By so much was Jesus made a surety of a better testament. 23And they truly were many priests, because they were not suffered to continue by reason of death: 24 But this *man,* because he continueth ever, hath an unchangeable priesthood. 25 Wherefore he is able also to save them to the uttermost that come unto God by him, seeing he ever liveth to make intercession for them. 26 For such a high priest became us, *who is* holy, harmless, undefiled, separate from sinners, and made higher than the heavens; 27 Who needeth not daily, as those high priests, to offer up sacrifice, first for his own sins, and then for the people's: for this he did once, when he offered up himself. 28 For the law maketh men high priests which have infirmity; but the word of the oath, which was since the law, *maketh* the Son, who is consecrated for evermore.

8 Now of the things which we have spoken *this is* the sum: We have such a high priest, who is set on the right hand of the throne of the Majesty in the heavens; 2A minister of the sanctuary, and of the true tabernacle, which the Lord pitched, and not man. 3 For every high priest is ordained to offer gifts and sacrifices: wherefore *it is* of necessity that this man have somewhat also to offer. 4 For if he were on earth, he should not be a priest, seeing that there are priests that

New International Version

was there still need for another priest to come— one like Melchizedek, not like Aaron? 12 For when there is a change of the priesthood, there must also be a change of the law. 13 He of whom these things are said belonged to a different tribe, and no one from that tribe has ever served at the altar. 14 For it is clear that our Lord descended from Judah, and in regard to that tribe Moses said nothing about priests. 15And what we have said is even more clear if another priest like Melchizedek appears, 16 one who has become a priest not on the basis of a regulation as to his ancestry but on the basis of the power of an indestructible life. 17 For it is declared:

"You are a priest forever,
    just like Melchizedek." [z]

18 The former regulation is set aside because it was weak and useless 19 (for the law made nothing perfect), and a better hope is introduced, by which we draw near to God.

20 And it was not without an oath! Others became priests without any oath, 21 but he became a priest with an oath when God said to him:

"The Lord has sworn
    and will not change his mind,
'You are a priest forever.' " [a]

22 Because of this oath, Jesus has become the guarantee of a better covenant.

23 Now there were many of those priests, since death prevented them from continuing in office; 24 but because Jesus lives forever, he has a permanent priesthood. 25 Therefore he is able to save completely[b] those who come to God through him, because he always lives to intercede for them.

26 Such a high priest meets our need—one who is holy, blameless, pure, set apart from sinners, exalted above the heavens. 27 Unlike the other high priests, he does not need to offer sacrifices day after day, first for his own sins, and then for the sins of the people. He sacrificed for their sins once for all when he offered himself. 28 For the law appoints as high priests men who are weak; but the oath, which came after the law, appointed the Son, who has been made perfect forever.

The high priest of a new covenant

8 The point of what we are saying is this: We do have such a high priest, who sat down at the right hand of the throne of the Majesty in heaven, 2 and who serves in the sanctuary, the true tabernacle set up by the Lord, not by man.

3 Every high priest is appointed to offer both gifts and sacrifices, and so it was necessary for this one also to have something to offer. 4 If he were on earth, he would not be a priest, for there are already men who offer the gifts prescribed by

[z] Psalm 110:4. [a] Psalm 110:4. [b] Or *forever.*

Greek Interlinear

ἀνίστασθαι ἱερέα καὶ οὐ κατὰ τὴν τάξιν
²to arise ³priest and not ⁵accord- ⁴the ⁶order
ing to

'Ααρὼν λέγεσθαι; 12 μετατιθεμένης γὰρ
¹of Aaron ¹to be said(named)?   for ²being changed

τῆς ἱερωσύνης ἐξ ἀνάγκης καὶ νόμου
³the ²priestly office⁴ ⁵of ⁷necessity ⁶also ⁸of law

μετάθεσις γίνεται. 13 ἐφ' ὃν γὰρ λέγεται
⁹a change ¹there ²[he] ³with ⁴whom ¹For ⁵is(are) said
occurs. respect to

ταῦτα, φυλῆς ἑτέρας μετέσχηκεν, ἀφ'
¹these things, ²tribe ³of another ⁴has partaken, from

ἧς οὐδεὶς προσέσχηκεν τῷ θυσιαστηρίῳ·
which no one has devoted himself to the altar;

14 πρόδηλον γὰρ ὅτι ἐξ 'Ιούδα ἀνατέταλκεν
for it is perfectly clear that out of Juda has risen

ὁ κύριος ἡμῶν, εἰς ἣν φυλὴν περὶ ἱερέων
the Lord of us, as to which tribe concerning priests

οὐδὲν Μωϋσῆς ἐλάλησεν. 15 καὶ περισ-
¹nothing ¹Moses ²spoke. And more

σότερον ἔτι κατάδηλόν ἐστιν, εἰ κατὰ
abundantly still quite clear is it, if according to

τὴν ὁμοιότητα Μελχισέδεκ ἀνίσταται ἱερεὺς
the likeness of Melchisedec arises priest

ἕτερος, 16 ὃς οὐ κατὰ νόμον ἐντολῆς
another, who not accord- [the] law ⁵command-
ing to ment

σαρκίνης γέγονεν ἀλλὰ κατὰ δύναμιν ζωῆς
¹of a fleshy has become but accord- [the] power life
ing to

ἀκαταλύτου. 17 μαρτυρεῖται γὰρ ὅτι σὺ
of an indissoluble. For it is witnessed that Thou

ἱερεὺς εἰς τὸν αἰῶνα κατὰ τὴν τάξιν
a priest unto the age according to the order

Μελχισέδεκ. 18 ἀθέτησις μὲν γὰρ γίνεται
of Melchisedec. ⁴an annul- ²on one ¹For ³there
ment hand comes about

προαγούσης ἐντολῆς διὰ τὸ αὐτῆς ἀσθενὲς
of [the] command- because ¹the ⁵of it ⁴weak[ness]
preceding ment of

καὶ ἀνωφελές, 19 οὐδὲν γὰρ ἐτελείωσεν
²and ³unprofitable[ness], for ¹nothing ³perfected

ὁ νόμος, ἐπεισαγωγὴ δὲ κρείττονος ἐλπίδος,
¹the ⁴law, ²a bringing in ³on the of a better hope,
other

δι' ἧς ἐγγίζομεν τῷ θεῷ. 20 καὶ καθ'
through we draw near - to God. And in pro-
which

ὅσον οὐ χωρὶς ὁρκωμοσίας, — οἱ μὲν
portion not without oath-taking, ³the ⁴on one
as (they) hand

γὰρ χωρὶς ὁρκωμοσίας εἰσὶν ἱερεῖς
¹for ²without ⁵oath-taking ⁶are ⁷priests

γεγονότες, 21 ὁ δὲ μετὰ ὁρκωμοσίας διὰ
⁵having the on the with oath-taking through
become, (he) other

τοῦ λέγοντος πρὸς αὐτόν· ὤμοσεν κύριος,
the [one] saying to him: swore [The] Lord,

καὶ οὐ μεταμεληθήσεται· σὺ ἱερεὺς εἰς
and will not change [his] mind: Thou [art] a priest unto

τὸν αἰῶνα· — 22 κατὰ τοσοῦτο καὶ
the age;) by so much indeed

κρείττονος διαθήκης γέγονεν ἔγγυος 'Ιησοῦς.
⁴of a better ⁵covenant ³has become ²surety ¹Jesus.

23 καὶ οἱ μὲν πλείονές εἰσιν γεγονότες
And the on one ²many ¹are ³having become
(they) hand

ἱερεῖς διὰ τὸ θανάτῳ κωλύεσθαι παραμέ-
⁴priests because ¹the ²by death ³to be prevented ⁴to con-
of = being prevented by death from continuing;

νειν· 24 ὁ δὲ διὰ τὸ μένειν αὐτὸν εἰς
tinue; the on the because the to remain himᵇ unto
(he) other of
= because he remains

τὸν αἰῶνα ἀπαράβατον ἔχει τὴν ἱερωσύνην·
the age ²intransmissible ¹has ³the ⁴priestly office;

25 ὅθεν καὶ σῴζειν εἰς τὸ παντελὲς
whence indeed ²to save ¹to ³the ⁴entire
= entirely

δύναται τοὺς προσερχομένους δι' αὐτοῦ
¹he is able the [ones] ¹approaching ⁴through ⁵him

τῷ θεῷ, πάντοτε ζῶν εἰς τὸ ἐντυγχάνειν
- ²to God, always living for the to intercede

ὑπὲρ αὐτῶν. 26 τοιοῦτος γὰρ ἡμῖν καὶ
on be- them. For ¹such ²to us ³indeed
half of

ἔπρεπεν ἀρχιερεύς, ὅσιος, ἄκακος, ἀμίαντος,
⁴was ³a high priest, holy, harmless, undefiled,
suitable

κεχωρισμένος ἀπὸ τῶν ἁμαρτωλῶν, καὶ
having been from - sinners, and
separated

ὑψηλότερος τῶν οὐρανῶν γενόμενος· 27 ὃς
higher [than] the heavens becoming; who

οὐκ ἔχει καθ' ἡμέραν ἀνάγκην, ὥσπερ
has not ³daily ¹necessity, as

οἱ ἀρχιερεῖς, πρότερον ὑπὲρ τῶν ἰδίων
the high priests, firstly on behalf of the(his) own

ἁμαρτιῶν θυσίας ἀναφέρειν, ἔπειτα τῶν
sins sacrifices to offer up, then the [sins]

τοῦ λαοῦ· τοῦτο γὰρ ἐποίησεν ἐφάπαξ
of the people; for this he did once for all

ἑαυτὸν ἀνενέγκας. 28 ὁ νόμος γὰρ
himself offering up. For the law

ἀνθρώπους καθίστησιν ἀρχιερεῖς ἔχοντας
²men ¹appoints ³high priests ⁴having

ἀσθένειαν, ὁ λόγος δὲ τῆς ὁρκωμοσίας
⁴weakness, but the word of the oath-taking

τῆς μετὰ τὸν νόμον υἱὸν εἰς τὸν αἰῶνα
- after the law a Son ¹unto ²the ³age
[appoints]

τετελειωμένον.
¹having been perfected.

Chapter 8

Κεφάλαιον δὲ ἐπὶ τοῖς λεγομένοις,
Now a summary over(of) the things being said,

τοιοῦτον ἔχομεν ἀρχιερέα, ὃς ἐκάθισεν
²such ¹we have a high priest, who sat

ἐν δεξιᾷ τοῦ θρόνου τῆς μεγαλωσύνης
at [the] right of the throne of the greatness

ἐν τοῖς οὐρανοῖς, 2 τῶν ἁγίων λειτουργὸς
in the heavens, ²of the ⁴holy things ³a minister

καὶ ·ῆς σκηνῆς τῆς ἀληθινῆς, ἣν ἔπηξεν
and of the ⁵tabernacle – ⁶true, which ⁷erected

ὁ κύριος, οὐκ ἄνθρωπος. 3 Πᾶς γὰρ
¹the ¹Lord, not man. For every

ἀρχιερεὺς εἰς τὸ προσφέρειν δῶρά τε
high priest for the ²to offer ³gifts ⁴both

καὶ θυσίας καθίσταται· ὅθεν ἀναγκαῖον
⁴and ⁶sacrifices ¹is appointed; whence [it is] necessary

ἔχειν τι καὶ τοῦτον ὃ προσενέγκῃ. 4 εἰ
²to have ³some- ⁴also ¹this which he may offer. If
thing [priest]

μὲν οὖν ἦν ἐπὶ γῆς, οὐδ' ἂν ἦν ἱερεύς,
- there- he on earth, he would not be a priest,
fore were

ὄντων τῶν προσφερόντων κατὰ νόμον
[there] the [ones] offering⁴ ²according to ⁴law
being

offer gifts according to the law: 5 Who serve unto the example and shadow of heavenly things, as Moses was admonished of God when he was about to make the tabernacle: for, See, saith he, *that* thou make all things according to the pattern shewed to thee in the mount. 6 But now hath he obtained a more excellent ministry, by how much also he is the mediator of a better covenant, which was established upon better promises. 7 For if that first *covenant* had been faultless, then should no place have been sought for the second. 8 For finding fault with them, he saith, Behold, the days come, saith the Lord, when I will make a new covenant with the house of Israel and with the house of Judah: 9 Not according to the covenant that I made with their fathers, in the day when I took them by the hand to lead them out of the land of Egypt; because they continued not in my covenant, and I regarded them not, saith the Lord. 10 For this *is* the covenant that I will make with the house of Israel after those days, saith the Lord; I will put my laws into their mind, and write them in their hearts: and I will be to them a God, and they shall be to me a people: 11And they shall not teach every man his neighbour, and every man his brother, saying, Know the Lord: for all shall know me, from the least to the greatest. 12 For I will be merciful to their unrighteousness, and their sins and their iniquities will I remember no more. 13 In that he saith, A new *covenant,* he hath made the first old. Now that which decayeth and waxeth old *is* ready to vanish away.

9 Then verily the first *covenant* had also ordinances of divine service, and a worldly sanctuary. 2 For there was a tabernacle made; the first, wherein *was* the candlestick, and the table, and the shewbread; which is called the sanctuary. 3And after the second vail, the tabernacle which is called the holiest of all; 4 Which had the golden censer, and the ark of the covenant overlaid round about with gold, wherein *was* the golden pot that had manna, and Aaron's rod that budded, and the tables of the covenant; 5And over it the cherubim of glory shadowing the mercy seat; of which we cannot now speak particularly. 6 Now when these things were thus ordained, the priests went always into the first tabernacle, accomplishing the service *of God.* 7 But into the second *went* the high priest alone once every year, not without blood, which he offered for himself, and *for* the errors of the people: 8 The Holy Ghost this signifying, that the way into the holiest of all was not yet made

the law. 5 They serve at a sanctuary that is a copy and shadow of what is in heaven. This is why Moses was warned when he was about to build the tabernacle: "See to it that you make everything according to the pattern shown you on the mountain." *c* 6 But the ministry Jesus has received is as superior to theirs as the covenant of which he is mediator is superior to the old one, and it is founded on better promises.

7 For if there had been nothing wrong with that first covenant, no place would have been sought for another. 8 But God found fault with the people and said:*d*

"The time is coming, says the Lord,
  when I will make a new covenant
with the house of Israel
  and with the house of Judah.
9 It will not be like the covenant I made with
  their forefathers
  when I took them by the hand to lead
    them out of Egypt,
  because they did not remain faithful to my
    covenant,
  and I turned away from them,
                          says the Lord.
10 This is the covenant I will make with the
  house of Israel
  after that time, says the Lord.
I will put my laws in their minds
  and write them on their hearts.
I will be their God,
  and they will be my people.
11 No longer will a man teach his neighbor,
  or a man his brother, saying, 'Know the
    Lord,'
because they will all know me,
  from the least of them to the greatest.
12 I will forgive their wickedness,
  and will remember their sins no more." *e*
13 By calling this covenant "new," he has made the first one obsolete; and what is obsolete and aging will soon disappear.

Worship in the earthly tabernacle

9 Now the first covenant had regulations for worship and also an earthly sanctuary. 2A tabernacle was set up. In its first room were the lampstand, the table and the consecrated bread; this was called the Holy Place. 3 Behind the second curtain was a room called the Most Holy Place, 4 which had the golden altar of incense and the gold-covered chest of the covenant. This chest contained the golden jar of manna, Aaron's rod that had budded, and the stone tablets of the covenant. 5Above the chest were the cherubim of the Glory, overshadowing the place of atonement. But we cannot discuss these things in detail now.

6 When everything had been arranged like this, the priests entered regularly into the outer room to carry on their ministry. 7 But only the high priest entered the inner room, and that only once a year, and never without blood, which he offered for himself and for the sins the people had committed in ignorance. 8 The Holy Spirit was showing by this that the way into the Most Holy Place had not yet been disclosed as

---

[c] Exodus 25:40. [d] Some MSS allow *fault and said to the people.*
[e] Jer. 31:31-34.

Greek Interlinear

τὰ   δῶρα· 5 οἵτινες ὑποδείγματι καὶ σκιᾷ
¹the ²gifts;   who   ³an example ⁴and ⁵a
                                                        shadow

λατρεύουσιν   τῶν   ἐπουρανίων,   καθὼς
⁶serve   of the heavenly things,   as

κεχρημάτισται   Μωϋσῆς   μέλλων   ἐπιτελεῖν
¹has been warned ¹Moses   being about to complete

τὴν σκηνήν·   ὅρα γάρ φησιν,   ποιήσεις
the   tabernacle;   for See[,]   he says, thou shalt
                                                        make

πάντα κατὰ   τὸν   τύπον   τὸν   δειχθέντα
all   according to the   pattern   -   shown
things

σοι ἐν τῷ ὄρει· 6 νῦν δὲ διαφορωτέρας
to thee in the mount;   but now ²a more excellent

τέτυχεν λειτουργίας, ὅσῳ καὶ κρείττονός
¹he has   ministry,   by so indeed ⁴of a better
obtained   much

ἐστιν διαθήκης μεσίτης, ἥτις ἐπὶ κρείττοσιν
¹[as]   ⁵covenant   ³mediator, which ⁷on   ⁸better
¹he is

ἐπαγγελίαις νενομοθέτηται.   7 εἰ γὰρ ἡ
⁹promises   ¹has been enacted.   For if   -

πρώτη ἐκείνη ἦν ἄμεμπτος,   οὐκ ἂν
²first [covenant] ¹that was faultless,   ³would not

δευτέρας ἐζητεῖτο   τόπος.   8 μεμφόμενος
⁵of(for) a ⁴have been ¹place.   finding fault [with]
second   sought

γὰρ αὐτοὺς λέγει·   ἰδοὺ ἡμέραι ἔρχονται,
For   them   he says: Behold[,] days are coming,

λέγει κύριος, καὶ συντελέσω ἐπὶ τὸν
says [the] Lord,   and I will effect over the

οἶκον Ἰσραὴλ καὶ ἐπὶ τὸν οἶκον Ἰούδα
household of Israel and over the household of Juda

διαθήκην καινήν, 9 οὐ κατὰ τὴν διαθήκην
covenant   a new,   not accord- the covenant
                              ing to

ἣν ἐποίησα τοῖς πατράσιν αὐτῶν ἐν
which I made   with the fathers   of them in

ἡμέρᾳ ἐπιλαβομένου μου τῆς χειρὸς αὐτῶν
[the] day taking   me⁰ the hand   of them
          ═when I took

ἐξαγαγεῖν αὐτοὺς ἐκ γῆς Αἰγύπτου, ὅτι
to lead forth them   out [the] of Egypt, because
                         of land

αὐτοὶ οὐκ ἐνέμειναν ἐν τῇ διαθήκῃ μου,
they   continued not in   in the covenant   of me,

κἀγὼ ἠμέλησα αὐτῶν, λέγει κύριος. 10 ὅτι
and I   disregarded them,   says [the] Lord.   Because

αὕτη ἡ διαθήκη ἣν διαθήσομαι τῷ οἴκῳ
this [is] the covenant which I will   with house-
                                  covenant   the   hold

Ἰσραὴλ μετὰ τὰς ἡμέρας ἐκείνας, λέγει
of Israel after those days,   says

κύριος, διδοὺς νόμους μου εἰς τὴν διάνοιαν
[the] Lord, giving   laws   of me into the mind

αὐτῶν, καὶ ἐπὶ καρδίας αὐτῶν ἐπιγράψω
of them,   and on   hearts   of them I will inscribe

αὐτούς, καὶ ἔσομαι αὐτοῖς εἰς θεὸν
them,   and I will be to them for   God

καὶ αὐτοὶ ἔσονταί μοι εἰς λαόν. 11 καὶ
and   they   shall be to me for a people.   And

οὐ μὴ διδάξωσιν ἕκαστος τὸν πολίτην
by no means may they teach each man   the citizen

αὐτοῦ καὶ ἕκαστος τὸν ἀδελφὸν αὐτοῦ,
of him   and each man   the brother   of him,

λέγων· γνῶθι τὸν κύριον, ὅτι πάντες
saying: Know thou the Lord,   because all

εἰδήσουσίν με ἀπὸ μικροῦ ἕως μεγάλου
will know   me from little   to   great

αὐτῶν. 12 ὅτι ἵλεως ἔσομαι ταῖς ἀδικίαις
of them.   Because merciful I will be to the unrighteous-
                                                      nesses

αὐτῶν, καὶ τῶν ἁμαρτιῶν αὐτῶν οὐ μὴ
of them,   and the sins   of them by no means

μνησθῶ ἔτι. 13 ἐν τῷ λέγειν καινὴν
I may   more.   In   the   to say⁰   ' new '
remember   ═When he says

πεπαλαίωκεν τὴν πρώτην· τὸ δὲ παλαι-
he has made old the   first;   and the thing being

ούμενον καὶ γηράσκον ἐγγὺς ἀφανισμοῦ.
made old   and growing aged [is] near   vanishing.

Chapter 9

Εἶχε μὲν οὖν καὶ ἡ πρώτη δικαι-
¹had ²So then ³both ⁴the ⁵first   ordin-
                                          ⁶[covenant]

ώματα λατρείας τό τε ἅγιον κοσμικόν.
ances   of service ²the ¹and ⁴holy place ³worldly.

2 σκηνὴ γὰρ κατεσκευάσθη ἡ πρώτη,
For a tabernacle   was prepared[,]   the   first,

ἐν ᾗ ἥ τε λυχνία καὶ ἡ τράπεζα καὶ
in which ²the ¹both lampstand and the table and
[were]

ἡ πρόθεσις τῶν ἄρτων, ἥτις λέγεται
the setting forth of the loaves,   which is called

Ἅγια· 3 μετὰ δὲ τὸ δεύτερον καταπέτασμα
Holy;   and after   the second   veil

σκηνὴ ἡ λεγομένη Ἅγια Ἁγίων, 4 χρυσοῦν
a taber- the being called Holy of Holies,   ²a golden
nacle [one]

ἔχουσα θυμιατήριον καὶ τὴν κιβωτὸν τῆς
¹having   altar   and the ark   of the

διαθήκης περικεκαλυμμένην πάντοθεν χρυσίῳ,
covenant   having been covered round on all sides with gold,

ἐν ᾗ στάμνος χρυσῆ ἔχουσα τὸ μάννα
in which pot   a golden having   the manna
[were]

καὶ ἡ ῥάβδος Ἀαρὼν ἡ βλαστήσασα
and the rod   of Aaron the budded

καὶ αἱ πλάκες τῆς διαθήκης, 5 ὑπεράνω
and the tablets of the covenant,   ²above

δὲ αὐτῆς Χερουβὶν δόξης κατασκιάζοντα
¹and it   cherubim   of glory overshadowing

τὸ ἱλαστήριον· περὶ ὧν οὐκ ἔστιν νῦν
the mercy-seat;   concern- which there is not now
                    ing   things   [?time]

λέγειν κατὰ μέρος. 6 τούτων δὲ οὕτως
to speak in detail.   These things now thus
                          ═ Now when these things had

κατεσκευασμένων εἰς μὲν τὴν πρώτην
having been prepared⁰ ²into ¹on one ⁴the   ⁵first
been thus prepared   hand

σκηνὴν διὰ παντὸς εἰσίασιν οἱ ἱερεῖς
⁶tabernacle ⁷at all times   ⁸go in   ⁹the ⁸priests

τὰς λατρείας ἐπιτελοῦντες, 7 εἰς δὲ τὴν
¹¹the ¹²services ¹⁰accomplishing,   ²into ¹on the ³the
                                                other

δευτέραν ἅπαξ τοῦ ἐνιαυτοῦ μόνος ὁ
⁴second   ⁵once ⁶of(in) the ¹⁰year   [goes] ⁵the
                                          ⁶alone

ἀρχιερεύς, οὐ χωρὶς αἵματος ὃ προσφέρει
⁸high priest, not without blood   which he offers

ὑπὲρ ἑαυτοῦ καὶ τῶν τοῦ λαοῦ ἀγνοημά-
on be- himself and ¹the ²of the ³people   ⁴ignor-
half of

των, 8 τοῦτο δηλοῦντος τοῦ πνεύματος
ances,   ¹this   ⁴showing   ²the   ³Spirit

τοῦ ἁγίου, μήπω πεφανερῶσθαι τὴν τῶν
-     ¹Holy,⁰   ⁵not yet ⁶to have been   ¹the ²of the
                          manifested

King James Version

New International Version

manifest, while as the first tabernacle was yet standing: 9 Which *was* a figure for the time then present, in which were offered both gifts and sacrifices, that could not make him that did the service perfect, as pertaining to the conscience; 10 *Which stood* only in meats and drinks, and divers washings, and carnal ordinances, imposed *on them* until the time of reformation. 11 But Christ being come a high priest of good things to come, by a greater and more perfect tabernacle, not made with hands, that is to say, not of this building; 12 Neither by the blood of goats and calves, but by his own blood he entered in once into the holy place, having obtained eternal redemption *for us.* 13 For if the blood of bulls and of goats, and the ashes of a heifer sprinkling the unclean, sanctifieth to the purifying of the flesh; 14 How much more shall the blood of Christ, who through the eternal Spirit offered himself without spot to God, purge your conscience from dead works to serve the living God? 15And for this cause he is the mediator of the new testament, that by means of death, for the redemption of the transgressions *that were* under the first testament, they which are called might receive the promise of eternal inheritance. 16 For where a testament *is,* there must also of necessity be the death of the testator. 17 For a testament *is* of force after men are dead: otherwise it is of no strength at all while the testator liveth. 18 Whereupon neither the first *testament* was dedicated without blood. 19 For when Moses had spoken every precept to all the people according to the law, he took the blood of calves and of goats, with water, and scarlet wool, and hyssop, and sprinkled both the book and all the people, 20 Saying, This *is* the blood of the testament which God hath enjoined unto you. 21 Moreover he sprinkled likewise with blood both the tabernacle, and all the vessels of the ministry. 22And almost all things are by the law purged with blood; and without shedding of blood is no remission. 23 *It was* therefore necessary that the patterns of things in the heavens should be purified with these; but the heavenly things themselves with better sacrifices than these. 24 For Christ is not entered into the holy places made with hands, *which are* the figures of the true; but into heaven itself, now to appear in the presence of God for us: 25 Nor yet that he should offer himself often, as the high priest entereth into the holy place every year with blood of others; 26 For then must he often have suffered since the foundation of the world: but now once in the end of the world hath he appeared to put away sin by the sacrifice of himself. 27And as it is appointed unto men once to

long as the first tabernacle was still standing. 9 This is an illustration for the present time, indicating that the gifts and sacrifices being offered were not able to clear the conscience of the worshiper. 10 They are only a matter of food and drink and various ceremonial washings—external regulations applying until the time of the new order.

The blood of Christ

11 When Christ came as high priest of the good things that are already here,[f] he went through the greater and more perfect tabernacle that is not man-made, that is to say, not a part of this creation. 12 He did not enter by means of the blood of goats and calves; but he entered the Most Holy Place once for all by his own blood, having obtained eternal redemption. 13 The blood of goats and bulls and the ashes of a heifer sprinkled on those who are ceremonially unclean sanctify them so that they are outwardly clean. 14 How much more, then, will the blood of Christ, who through the eternal Spirit offered himself unblemished to God, cleanse our consciences from acts that lead to death, so that we may serve the living God!

15 For this reason Christ is the mediator of a new covenant, that those who are called may receive the promised eternal inheritance—now that he has died as a ransom to set them free from the sins committed under the first covenant.

16 In the case of a will,[g] it is necessary to prove the death of the one who made it, 17 because a will[g] is in force only when somebody has died; it never takes effect while the one who made it is living. 18 This is why even the first covenant was not put into effect without blood. 19 When Moses had proclaimed every commandment of the law to all the people, he took the blood of calves, together with water, scarlet wool and branches of hyssop, and sprinkled the scroll and all the people. 20 He said, "This is the blood of the covenant, which God has commanded you to keep." [h] 21 In the same way, he sprinkled with the blood both the tabernacle and everything used in its ceremonies. 22 In fact, the law requires that nearly everything be cleansed with blood, and without the shedding of blood there is no forgiveness.

23 It was necessary, then, for the copies of the heavenly things to be purified with these sacrifices, but the heavenly things themselves with better sacrifices than these. 24 For Christ did not enter a man-made sanctuary that was only a copy of the true one; he entered heaven itself, now to appear for us in God's presence. 25 Nor did he enter heaven to offer himself again and again, the way the high priest enters the Most Holy Place every year with blood that is not his own. 26 Then Christ would have had to suffer many times since the creation of the world. But now he has appeared once for all at the end of the ages to do away with sin by the sacrifice of himself. 27 Just as man is destined to die once,

[f] Some early MSS read *are to come.* [g] Same Greek word as *covenant.* [h] Exodus 24:8.

ἁγίων   ὁδὸν   ἔτι   τῆς   πρώτης   σκηνῆς
⁴holies   ¹way   ¹ºstill   ¹the   ⁹first   ⁸tabernacle

ἐχούσης   στάσιν,   9 ἥτις   παραβολὴ   εἰς   τὸν
¹¹having⁸   ¹²standing,   which [was]   a parable   for   the

καιρὸν   τὸν   ἐνεστηκότα,   καθ'   ἣν   δῶρά
time   –   present,   accord-   which   ²gifts
                                 ing to

τε   καὶ   θυσίαι   προσφέρονται   μὴ   δυνάμεναι
¹both and   sacrifices   are being offered   not   being able

κατὰ   συνείδησιν   τελειῶσαι   τὸν   λατρεύοντα,
in respect   conscience   to perfect   the [one]   serving,
of

10 μόνον   ἐπὶ   βρώμασιν   καὶ   πόμασιν   καὶ
only   on   foods   and   drinks   and

διαφόροις   βαπτισμοῖς,   δικαιώματα   σαρκὸς
various   washings,   ordinances   of flesh

μέχρι   καιροῦ   διορθώσεως   ἐπικείμενα.
²until   ²a time   ⁴of amendment   ¹being imposed.

11 Χριστὸς   δὲ   παραγενόμενος   ἀρχιερεὺς
But Christ   having appeared   a high priest

τῶν   γενομένων   ἀγαθῶν,   διὰ   τῆς   μείζονος
¹of the   ²having come   ²good things,   through the   greater
                                                 about

καὶ   τελειοτέρας   σκηνῆς   οὐ   χειροποιήτου,
and   more perfect   tabernacle   not   made by hand,

τοῦτ'   ἔστιν   οὐ   ταύτης   τῆς   κτίσεως,
this   is   not   of this   –   creation,

12 οὐδὲ   δι'   αἵματος   τράγων   καὶ   μόσχων,
nor   through   blood   of goats   and   of calves,

διὰ   δὲ   τοῦ   ἰδίου   αἵματος   εἰσῆλθεν   ἐφάπαξ
but   the   own   blood   entered   once for
through   (his)   all

εἰς   τὰ   ἅγια,   αἰωνίαν   λύτρωσιν   εὑράμενος.
into   the   holies,   eternal   redemption   having found.

13 εἰ   γὰρ   τὸ   αἷμα   τράγων   καὶ   ταύρων
For if   the   blood   of goats   and   of bulls

καὶ   σποδὸς   δαμάλεως   ῥαντίζουσα   τοὺς
and   ashes   of a heifer   sprinkling   the [ones]

κεκοινωμένους   ἁγιάζει   πρὸς   τὴν   τῆς
having been polluted   sanctifies   to   ¹the   ²of the

σαρκὸς   καθαρότητα,   14 πόσῳ   μᾶλλον   τὸ
⁴flesh   ³cleanness,   by how much   more   the

αἷμα   τοῦ   Χριστοῦ,   ὃς   διὰ   πνεύματος
blood   –   of Christ,   who   through   ²Spirit

αἰωνίου   ἑαυτὸν   προσήνεγκεν   ἄμωμον   τῷ
¹[the] eternal   himself   ³offered   unblemished   –

θεῷ,   καθαριεῖ   τὴν   συνείδησιν   ἡμῶν   ἀπὸ
to God,   will cleanse   the   conscience   of us   from

νεκρῶν   ἔργων   εἰς   τὸ   λατρεύειν   θεῷ
dead   works   for   the   to serve   ²God

ζῶντι,   15 καὶ   διὰ   τοῦτο   διαθήκης   καινῆς
¹[the] living.   And   therefore   ⁴covenant   for a new

μεσίτης   ἐστίν,   ὅπως   θανάτου   γενομένου
⁵mediator   ¹he is,   so as   death   having occurred⁸

εἰς   ἀπολύτρωσιν   τῶν   ἐπὶ   τῇ   πρώτῃ
for   redemption   ¹of the   ²under⁸   ⁴the   ³first

διαθήκῃ   παραβάσεων   τὴν   ἐπαγγελίαν
⁵covenant   ⁶transgressions   ¹ºthe   ¹¹promise

λάβωσιν   οἱ   κεκλημένοι   τῆς   αἰωνίου
⁹may receive   ⁷the   ⁸having been   ¹²of the   ¹³eternal
              [ones]   called

κληρονομίας.   16 Ὅπου   γὰρ   διαθήκη,
¹⁴inheritance.   For where   [there is] a
                                covenant,

θάνατον   ἀνάγκη   φέρεσθαι   τοῦ   διαθεμένου·
⁸[the] death   ¹[there is]   ²to be offered   ⁴of the   ⁵making
              necessity   [one]   covenant;

17 διαθήκη   γὰρ   ἐπὶ   νεκροῖς   βεβαία,   ἐπεὶ
for a covenant   over dead   [? bodies] [is] firm,   since

μήποτε   ἰσχύει   ὅτε   ζῇ   ὁ   διαθέμενος.
never   has it   when   ²lives   ¹the   ¹making
        strength   [one]   covenant.

18 ὅθεν   οὐδὲ   ἡ   πρώτη   χωρὶς   αἵματος
Whence   neither   the   first [covenant]   ²without   ¹blood

ἐγκεκαίνισται.   19 λαληθείσης   γὰρ   πάσης
¹has been dedicated.   For ²having been spoken   ¹every

ἐντολῆς   κατὰ   τὸν   νόμον   ὑπὸ   Μωϋσέως
⁶command-   ²accord-   ¹ºthe   ¹¹law   ⁴by   ⁵Moses
ment⁸   ing to

παντὶ   τῷ   λαῷ,   λαβὼν   τὸ   αἷμα   τῶν
⁸to all   ⁷the   ⁹people,   taking   the   blood   of the

μόσχων   καὶ   τῶν   τράγων   μετὰ   ὕδατος
calves   and   of the   goats   with   water

καὶ   ἐρίου   κοκκίνου   καὶ   ὑσσώπου,   αὐτό
and   ²wool   ¹scarlet   and   hyssop,   ²it[self]

τε   τὸ   βιβλίον   καὶ   πάντα   τὸν   λαὸν
⁸both   ⁴the   ²scroll   ⁵and   ⁷all   ⁶the   ⁷people

ἐρράντισεν,   20 λέγων·   τοῦτο   τὸ   αἷμα   τῆς
¹he sprinkled,   saying: This [is]   the   blood   of the

διαθήκης   ἧς   ἐνετείλατο   πρὸς   ὑμᾶς   ὁ
covenant   which   ²enjoined   ³to   ⁴you   –

θεός.   21 καὶ   τὴν   σκηνὴν   δὲ   καὶ   πάντα
¹God.   ²both   ³the   ⁴tabernacle   ¹And   and   all

τὰ   σκεύη   τῆς   λειτουργίας   τῷ   αἵματι
the   vessels   of the   service   with the   blood

ὁμοίως   ἐρράντισεν.   22 καὶ   σχεδὸν   ἐν
likewise   he sprinkled.   And   ¹almost   ⁷by

αἵματι   πάντα   καθαρίζεται   κατὰ   τὸν   νόμον,
⁸blood   ²all things   ⁶is(are) cleansed   ⁸accord-   ⁴the   ⁵law,
                                        ing to

καὶ   χωρὶς   αἱματεκχυσίας   οὐ   γίνεται
and   without   bloodshedding   there becomes no

ἄφεσις.   23 ἀνάγκη   οὖν   τὰ   μὲν   ὑπο-
remission.   [There was]   therefore   ³[for]   ¹on one   ⁴ex-
           necessity   ²the   hand

δείγματα   τῶν   ἐν   τοῖς   οὐρανοῖς   τούτοις
amples   of the   in   the   heavens   ²by these
           things

καθαρίζεσθαι,   αὐτὰ   δὲ   τὰ   ἐπουράνια
¹to be cleansed,   ¹[them]-   ²on the   ⁸[for]   ⁴heavenly
               selves   other   ⁸the   things

κρείττοσιν   θυσίαις   παρὰ   ταύτας.   24 οὐ
by better   sacrifices   than   these.   not

γὰρ   εἰς   χειροποίητα   εἰσῆλθεν   ἅγια   Χριστός,
For   into   ²made by hand   ⁴entered   ¹holies   ³Christ,

ἀντίτυπα   τῶν   ἀληθινῶν,   ἀλλ'   εἰς   αὐτὸν
figures   of the   true things,   but   into   ²[it]self

τὸν   οὐρανόν,   νῦν   ἐμφανισθῆναι   τῷ   προσώπῳ
¹the   heaven,   now   to appear in   the   presence

τοῦ   θεοῦ   ὑπὲρ   ἡμῶν·   25 οὐδ'   ἵνα   πολ-
–   of God   on behalf of   us;   nor   in order   that often

λάκις   προσφέρῃ   ἑαυτόν,   ὥσπερ   ὁ   ἀρχιερεὺς
he should offer   himself,   even as   the   high priest

εἰσέρχεται   εἰς   τὰ   ἅγια   κατ'   ἐνιαυτὸν
enters   into   the   holies   year by year†

ἐν   αἵματι   ἀλλοτρίῳ,   26 ἐπεὶ   ἔδει   αὐτὸν
with   blood   belonging to others,   since it behoved   him

πολλάκις   παθεῖν   ἀπὸ   καταβολῆς   κόσμου·
often   to suffer   from   [the] foundation   of [the]
                                        world;

νυνὶ   δὲ   ἅπαξ   ἐπὶ   συντελείᾳ   τῶν   αἰώνων
but now   once   at [the] completion of the   ages

εἰς   ἀθέτησιν   τῆς   ἁμαρτίας   διὰ   τῆς   θυσίας
for   annulment   –   of sin   through   the   sacrifice

αὐτοῦ   πεφανέρωται.   27 καὶ   καθ'   ὅσον
of him   he has been manifested.   And   as

ἀπόκειται   τοῖς   ἀνθρώποις   ἅπαξ   ἀποθανεῖν,
it is reserved   –   to men   once   to die,

* It may seem strange to translate a preposition which means
"on" or "over" by "under"; but ἐπί has the meaning of
"during the time of" (see Mark 2. 26; I. Tim. 6. 13).

King James Version

die, but after this the judgment: 28 So Christ was once offered to bear the sins of many; and unto them that look for him shall he appear the second time without sin unto salvation.

10 For the law having a shadow of good things to come, *and* not the very image of the things, can never with those sacrifices, which they offered year by year continually, make the comers thereunto perfect. 2 For then would they not have ceased to be offered? because that the worshippers once purged should have had no more conscience of sins. 3 But in those *sacrifices there is* a remembrance again *made* of sins every year. 4 For *it is* not possible that the blood of bulls and of goats should take away sins. 5 Wherefore, when he cometh into the world, he saith, Sacrifice and offering thou wouldest not, but a body hast thou prepared me: 6 In burnt offerings and *sacrifices* for sin thou hast had no pleasure. 7 Then said I, Lo, I come (in the volume of the book it is written of me) to do thy will, O God. 8 Above when he said, Sacrifice and offering and burnt offerings and *offering* for sin thou wouldest not, neither hadst pleasure *therein;* which are offered by the law; 9 Then said he, Lo, I come to do thy will, O God. He taketh away the first, that he may establish the second. 10 By the which will we are sanctified through the offering of the body of Jesus Christ once *for all.* 11 And every priest standeth daily ministering and offering oftentimes the same sacrifices, which can never take away sins: 12 But this man, after he had offered one sacrifice for sins for ever, sat down on the right hand of God; 13 From henceforth expecting till his enemies be made his footstool. 14 For by one offering he hath perfected for ever them that are sanctified. 15 *Whereof* the Holy Ghost also is a witness to us: for after that he had said before, 16 This *is* the covenant that I will make with them after those days, saith the Lord; I will put my laws into their hearts, and in their minds will I write them; 17 And their sins and iniquities will I remember no more. 18 Now where remission of these *is, there is* no more offering for sin. 19 Having therefore, brethren, boldness to enter into the holiest by the blood of Jesus, 20 By a new and living way, which he hath consecrated for us, through the vail, that is to say, his flesh; 21 And *having* a high priest

New International Version

and after that to face judgment, 28 so Christ was sacrificed once to take away the sins of many people; and he will appear a second time, not to bear sin, but to bring salvation to those who are waiting for him.

Christ's sacrifice once for all

10 The law is only a shadow of the good things that are coming—not the realities themselves. For this reason it can never, by the same sacrifices repeated endlessly year after year, make perfect those who draw near to worship. 2 If it could, would they not have stopped being offered? For the worshipers would have been cleansed once for all, and would no longer have felt guilty for their sins. 3 But those sacrifices are an annual reminder of sins, 4 because it is impossible for the blood of bulls and goats to take away sins.

5 Therefore, when Christ came into the world, he said:

"Sacrifice and offering you did not desire,
　　but a body you prepared for me;
6 with burnt offerings and sin offerings
　　you were not pleased.
7 Then I said, 'Here I am—it is written about
　　me in the scroll—
　　I have come to do your will, O God.' " [i]

8 First he said, "Sacrifices and offerings, burnt offerings and sin offerings you did not desire, nor were you pleased with them" (although the law required them to be made). 9 Then he said, "Here I am, I have come to do your will." He sets aside the first to establish the second. 10 And by that will, we have been made holy through the sacrifice of the body of Jesus Christ once for all.

11 Day after day every priest stands and performs his religious duties; again and again he offers the same sacrifices, which can never take away sins. 12 But when this priest had offered for all time one sacrifice for sins, he sat down at the right hand of God. 13 Since that time he waits for his enemies to be made his footstool, 14 because by one sacrifice he has made perfect forever those who are being made holy.

15 The Holy Spirit also testifies to us about this. First he says:

16 "This is the covenant I will make with them
　　after that time, says the Lord.
I will put my laws in their hearts,
　　and I will write them on their minds." [j]

17 Then he adds:

"Their sins and lawless acts
　　I will remember no more." [k]

18 And where these have been forgiven, there is no longer any sacrifice for sin.

A call to persevere

19 Therefore, brothers, since we have confidence to enter the Most Holy Place by the blood of Jesus, 20 by a new and living way opened for us through the curtain, that is, his body, 21 and since we have a great priest over

[i] Psalm 40:6-8. [j] Jer. 31:33. [k] Jer. 31:34.

Greek Interlinear

μετὰ δὲ τοῦτο κρίσις, 28 οὕτως καὶ
and after this this judgment, so also
ὁ Χριστός, ἅπαξ προσενεχθεὶς εἰς τὸ
- Christ, once having been offered for the
πολλῶν ἀνενεγκεῖν ἁμαρτίας, ἐκ δευτέρου
¹of many ¹to bear ²sins, ²a second [time]

χωρὶς ἁμαρτίας ὀφθήσεται τοῖς αὐτὸν
⁴without ⁵sin ¹will appear ²to the [ones] ³him
ἀπεκδεχομένοις εἰς σωτηρίαν.
⁶expecting for salvation.

Chapter 10

Σκιὰν γὰρ ἔχων ὁ νόμος τῶν
For ⁴a shadow ²having ¹the ²law of the
μελλόντων ἀγαθῶν, οὐκ αὐτὴν τὴν εἰκόνα
coming good things, not ²[it]self ¹the ²image
τῶν πραγμάτων, κατ' ἐνιαυτὸν ταῖς αὐταῖς
of the matters, ⁹every ⁶year† ³by the ⁴same
θυσίαις ἃς προσφέρουσιν εἰς τὸ διηνεκὲς
⁵sacrifices ⁸which ⁷they offer ¹⁰continually†
οὐδέποτε δύναται τοὺς προσερχομένους
¹never ¹can ¹³the [ones] ¹²approaching
τελειῶσαι· 2 ἐπεὶ οὐκ ἂν ἐπαύσαντο
¹¹to perfect; since would not they have ceased
προσφερόμεναι, διὰ τὸ μηδεμίαν ἔχειν
being offered, because of the ²no ⁴to have
ἔτι συνείδησιν ἁμαρτιῶν τοὺς λατρεύοντας
³still ¹conscience ⁵of sins ¹the [ones] ²serving
ἅπαξ κεκαθαρισμένους; 3 ἀλλ' ἐν αὐταῖς
²once ⁴having been cleansed ? But in them [there
ἀνάμνησις ἁμαρτιῶν κατ' ἐνιαυτόν·
is] a remembrance of sins yearly†;
4 ἀδύνατον γὰρ αἷμα ταύρων καὶ τράγων
for [it is] impossible blood of bulls and of goats
ἀφαιρεῖν ἁμαρτίας. 5 Διὸ εἰσερχόμενος εἰς
to take away sins. Wherefore entering into
τὸν κόσμον λέγει· θυσίαν καὶ προσφορὰν
the world he says! Sacrifice and offering
οὐκ ἠθέλησας, σῶμα δὲ κατηρτίσω μοι·
thou didst not wish, but a body thou didst prepare for me;
6 ὁλοκαυτώματα καὶ περὶ ἁμαρτίας οὐκ
burnt offerings and concerning sins not
[sacrifices]
εὐδόκησας. 7 τότε εἶπον· ἰδοὺ ἥκω,
thou wast well Then I said· Behold I have
pleased [with]. come,
ἐν κεφαλίδι βιβλίου γέγραπται περὶ ἐμοῦ,
in a heading of a scroll it has been concerning me,
written
τοῦ ποιῆσαι ὁ θεὸς τὸ θέλημά σου.
- to do[.]ᵈ - God[,]ᵉ the will of thee.
8 ἀνώτερον λέγων ὅτι θυσίας καὶ προσ-
Above saying that sacrifices and offer-
φορὰς καὶ ὁλοκαυτώματα καὶ περὶ ἁμαρτίας
ings and burnt offerings and [sacrifices] sins
concerning
οὐκ ἠθέλησας οὐδὲ εὐδόκησας, αἵτινες
thou didst not wish nor thou wast well which
pleased [with],
κατὰ νόμον προσφέρονται, 9 τότε εἴρηκεν·
accord- law are offered, then he has said:
ing to
ἰδοὺ ἥκω τοῦ ποιῆσαι τὸ θέλημά σου.
Behold I have to doᵈ the will of thee.
come
ἀναιρεῖ τὸ πρῶτον ἵνα τὸ δεύτερον
He takes the first in order the second
away that
στήσῃ· 10 ἐν ᾧ θελήματι ἡγιασμένοι ἐσμὲν
may by which will ²having been ¹we are
set up; sanctified
διὰ τῆς προσφορᾶς τοῦ σώματος Ἰησοῦ
through the offering of the body of Jesus

Χριστοῦ ἐφάπαξ. 11 Καὶ πᾶς μὲν ἱερεὺς
Christ once for all. And ²every ¹on one ¹priest
hand
ἔστηκεν καθ' ἡμέραν λειτουργῶν καὶ τὰς
stands daily† ministering and ³the
αὐτὰς πολλάκις προσφέρων θυσίας, αἵτινες
⁴same ¹often ²offering ⁴sacrifices, which
οὐδέποτε δύνανται περιελεῖν ἁμαρτίας· 12 οὗτος
never can to take away sins; ¹this
[priest]
δὲ μίαν ὑπὲρ ἁμαρτιῶν προσενέγκας
¹on the ⁴one ⁵on behalf of ⁷sins ³having offered
other
θυσίαν εἰς τὸ διηνεκὲς ἐκάθισεν ἐν δεξιᾷ
⁶sacrifice ⁸in - ¹⁰perpetuity ⁹sat at [the] right
[hand]
τοῦ θεοῦ, 13 τὸ λοιπὸν ἐκδεχόμενος ἕως
- of God, henceforth expecting till
τεθῶσιν οἱ ἐχθροὶ αὐτοῦ ὑποπόδιον τῶν
⁴are put ¹the ²enemies ³of him a footstool of the
ποδῶν αὐτοῦ. 14 μιᾷ γὰρ προσφορᾷ
feet of him. For by one offering
τετελείωκεν εἰς τὸ διηνεκὲς τοὺς ἁγιαζ-
he has perfected in - perpetuity the [ones] being
ομένους. 15 Μαρτυρεῖ δὲ ἡμῖν καὶ
sanctified. And ²witnesses ³to us ¹indeed
τὸ πνεῦμα τὸ ἅγιον· μετὰ γὰρ τὸ
¹the ²Spirit ⁴Holy; for after the
εἰρηκέναι· 16 αὕτη ἡ διαθήκη ἣν δια-
to have said· This [is] the covenant which I will
=having said:
θήσομαι πρὸς αὐτοὺς μετὰ τὰς ἡμέρας
covenant to them after - days
ἐκείνας, λέγει κύριος· διδοὺς νόμους μου
those, says [the] Lord· Giving laws of me
ἐπὶ καρδίας αὐτῶν, καὶ ἐπὶ τὴν διάνοιαν
on hearts of them, also on the mind
αὐτῶν ἐπιγράψω αὐτούς, 17 καὶ τῶν
of them I will inscribe them, and the
ἁμαρτιῶν αὐτῶν καὶ τῶν ἀνομιῶν αὐτῶν
sins of them and the iniquities of them
οὐ μὴ μνησθήσομαι ἔτι. 18 ὅπου δὲ
by no means I will remember still. Now where
ἄφεσις τούτων, οὐκέτι προσφορὰ περὶ
forgiveness of these [is], no longer offering concerning
ἁμαρτίας.
[there is]
sins.
19 Ἔχοντες οὖν, ἀδελφοί, παρρησίαν εἰς
Having therefore, brothers, confidence for
τὴν εἴσοδον τῶν ἁγίων ἐν τῷ αἵματι
the entering of the holies in the blood
Ἰησοῦ, 20 ἣν ἐνεκαίνισεν ἡμῖν ὁδὸν
of Jesus, which he dedicated for us[,] a way
πρόσφατον καὶ ζῶσαν διὰ τοῦ κατα-
fresh and living through the veil,
πετάσματος, τοῦτ' ἔστιν τῆς σαρκὸς αὐτοῦ,
this is the flesh of him,
21 καὶ ἱερέα μέγαν ἐπὶ τὸν οἶκον τοῦ
and priest a great over the household -

* The " articular vocative "; cf. 1. 8, 9.

King James Version

over the house of God; 22 Let us draw near with a true heart in full assurance of faith, having our hearts sprinkled from an evil conscience, and our bodies washed with pure water. 23 Let us hold fast the profession of *our* faith without wavering; for he *is* faithful that promised; 24And let us consider one another to provoke unto love and to good works: 25 Not forsaking the assembling of ourselves together, as the manner of some *is;* but exhorting *one another:* and so much the more, as ye see the day approaching. 26 For if we sin wilfully after that we have received the knowledge of the truth, there remaineth no more sacrifice for sins, 27 But a certain fearful looking for of judgment and fiery indignation, which shall devour the adversaries. 28 He that despised Moses' law died without mercy under two or three witnesses: 29 Of how much sorer punishment, suppose ye, shall he be thought worthy, who hath trodden under foot the Son of God, and hath counted the blood of the covenant, wherewith he was sanctified, an unholy thing, and hath done despite unto the Spirit of grace? 30 For we know him that hath said, Vengeance *belongeth* unto me, I will recompense, saith the Lord. And again, The Lord shall judge his people. 31 *It is* a fearful thing to fall into the hands of the living God. 32 But call to remembrance the former days, in which, after ye were illuminated, ye endured a great fight of afflictions; 33 Partly, whilst ye were made a gazingstock both by reproaches and afflictions; and partly, whilst ye became companions of them that were so used. 34 For ye had compassion of me in my bonds, and took joyfully the spoiling of your goods, knowing in yourselves that ye have in heaven a better and an enduring substance. 35 Cast not away therefore your confidence, which hath great recompense of reward. 36 For ye have need of patience, that, after ye have done the will of God, ye might receive the promise. 37 For yet a little while, and he that shall come will come, and will not tarry. 38 Now the just shall live by faith: but if *any man* draw back, my soul shall have no pleasure in him. 39 But we are not of them who draw back unto perdition; but of them that believe to the saving of the soul.

11 Now faith is the substance of things hoped for, the evidence of things not seen. 2 For by it the elders obtained a good report. 3 Through faith we understand that the worlds were framed by the word of God, so that things which are seen were not made of things which do appear. 4 By faith Abel offered unto God a more excellent sacrifice than Cain, by which he

New International Version

the house of God, 22 let us draw near to God with a sincere heart in full assurance of faith, having our hearts sprinkled to cleanse us from a guilty conscience and having our bodies washed with pure water. 23 Let us hold unswervingly to the hope we profess, for he who promised is faithful. 24And let us consider how we may spur one another on toward love and good deeds. 25 Let us not give up meeting together, as some are in the habit of doing, but let us encourage one another—and all the more as you see the Day approaching.

26 If we deliberately keep on sinning after we have received the knowledge of the truth, no sacrifice for sins is left, 27 but only a fearful expectation of judgment and of raging fire that will consume the enemies of God. 28Anyone who rejected the law of Moses died without mercy on the testimony of two or three witnesses. 29 How much more severely do you think a man deserves to be punished who has trampled the Son of God under foot, who has treated as an unholy thing the blood of the covenant that sanctified him, and who has insulted the Spirit of grace? 30 For we know him who said, "It is mine to avenge; I will repay," [l] and again, "The Lord will judge his people." [m] 31 It is a dreadful thing to fall into the hands of the living God.

32 Remember those earlier days after you had received the light, when you stood your ground in a great contest in the face of suffering. 33 Sometimes you were publicly exposed to insult and persecution; at other times you stood side by side with those who were so treated. 34 You sympathized with those in prison and joyfully accepted the confiscation of your property, because you knew that you yourselves had better and lasting possessions.

35 So do not throw away your confidence; it will be richly rewarded. 36 You need to persevere so that when you have done the will of God, you will receive what he has promised. 37 For in just a very little while,

"He who is coming will come and will not be late.

38   But my righteous one[n] will live by faith. And if he shrinks back, I will not be pleased with him." [o]

39 But we are not of those who shrink back and are destroyed, but of those who believe and are saved.

By faith

11 Now faith is being sure of what we hope for and certain of what we do not see. 2 This is what the ancients were commended for.

3 By faith we understand that the universe was formed at God's command, so that what is seen was not made out of what was visible.

4 By faith Abel offered God a better sacrifice than Cain did. By faith he was commended

[*l*] Deut. 32:35. [*m*] Deut. 32:36; Psalm 135:14. [*n*] One early MSS reads *But the righteous.* [*o*] Hab. 2:3,4.

Greek Interlinear

θεοῦ, **22** προσερχώμεθα μετὰ ἀληθινῆς
of God, let us approach with a true

καρδίας ἐν πληροφορίᾳ πίστεως, ῥεραν-
heart in full assurance of faith, having been

τισμένοι τὰς καρδίας ἀπὸ συνειδήσεως
sprinkled [as to] the hearts from ²conscience

πονηρᾶς καὶ λελουσμένοι τὸ σῶμα ὕδατι
¹an evil and having been [as to] body ²water
    bathed the

καθαρῷ· **23** κατέχωμεν τὴν ὁμολογίαν τῆς
¹in clean; let us hold fast the confession of the
    (our)

ἐλπίδος ἀκλινῆ, πιστὸς γὰρ ὁ ἐπαγ-
hope unyieldingly, for faithful [is] the [one] pro-

γειλάμενος, **24** καὶ κατανοῶμεν ἀλλήλους
mising, and let us consider one another

εἰς παροξυσμὸν ἀγάπης καὶ καλῶν ἔργων,
to incitement of love and of good works,

25 μὴ ἐγκαταλείποντες τὴν ἐπισυναγωγὴν
not forsaking the coming together

ἑαυτῶν, καθὼς ἔθος τισίν, ἀλλὰ παρα-
of [our]selves, as custom with some [is], but ex-

καλοῦντες, καὶ τοσούτῳ μᾶλλον ὅσῳ
horting, and by so much more as

βλέπετε ἐγγίζουσαν τὴν ἡμέραν. **26** Ἑκουσίως
ye see ²drawing near ¹the ²day. wilfully

γὰρ ἁμαρτανόντων ἡμῶν μετὰ τὸ λαβεῖν
For sinning us* after the to receive
    =when we sin wilfully   =receiving

τὴν ἐπίγνωσιν τῆς ἀληθείας, οὐκέτι περὶ
the full knowledge of the truth, ²no more ²con-
    cerning

ἁμαρτιῶν ἀπολείπεται θυσία, **27** φοβερὰ
¹sins remains ¹a sacrifice, ²fearful

δὲ τις ἐκδοχὴ κρίσεως καὶ πυρὸς ζῆλος
¹but ²some expectation of judgment and ²of fire ¹zeal

ἐσθίειν μέλλοντος τοὺς ὑπεναντίους.
⁴to consume ³being about the adversaries.

28 ἀθετήσας τις νόμον Μωϋσέως χωρὶς
¹Disregarding ²anyone ¹law ²of Moses ²without

οἰκτιρμῶν ἐπὶ δυσὶν ἢ τρισὶν μάρτυσιν
³compassions ²on [the ⁹two ¹⁰or ¹¹three ¹²witnesses
    word of]

ἀποθνήσκει· **29** πόσῳ δοκεῖτε χείρονος
¹dies; by how much think ye ²of worse

ἀξιωθήσεται τιμωρίας ὁ τὸν υἱὸν τοῦ
¹will be thought ²punishment ³the ⁴the ⁷Son -
worthy   [one]

θεοῦ καταπατήσας καὶ τὸ αἷμα τῆς
³of God ⁵having trampled and ⁴the ⁵blood ⁶of the
    [on]

διαθήκης κοινὸν ἡγησάμενος, ἐν ᾧ ἡγιάσθη,
⁶covenant ⁸common ⁷having by which he was
    deemed, sanctified,

καὶ τὸ πνεῦμα τῆς χάριτος ἐνυβρίσας.
and ³the ⁴Spirit - ⁵of grace ¹having insulted.

Chapter 11

Ἔστιν δὲ πίστις ἐλπιζομένων ὑπό-
Now ²is ¹faith ⁴of things being hoped ⁵[the]

στασις, πραγμάτων ἔλεγχος οὐ βλεπομένων.
reality, ⁶of things ¹[the] proof not being seen.

2 ἐν ταύτῃ γὰρ ἐμαρτυρήθησαν οἱ
by this For ²obtained witness ¹the

πρεσβύτεροι. **3** Πίστει νοοῦμεν κατηρτίσθαι
²elders. By faith we understand ²to have been
    adjusted

---

30 οἴδαμεν γὰρ τὸν εἰπόντα· ἐμοὶ
For we know the [one] having said: To me
    =Vengeance

ἐκδίκησις, ἐγὼ ἀνταποδώσω· καὶ πάλιν·
vengeance,* I will repay; and again:
is mine,

κρινεῖ κύριος τὸν λαὸν αὐτοῦ. **31** φοβερὸν
²will judge [¹The] the people of him. A fearful
Lord   thing [it is]

τὸ ἐμπεσεῖν εἰς χεῖρας θεοῦ ζῶντος.
the to fall in into [the] hands ²God ¹of a living.

32 Ἀναμιμνῄσκεσθε δὲ τὰς πρότερον ἡμέρας,
But remember ye the ²formerly ¹days,

ἐν αἷς φωτισθέντες πολλὴν ἄθλησιν
in which being enlightened ²a much(great) ¹struggle

ὑπεμείνατε παθημάτων, **33** τοῦτο μὲν
¹ye endured ²of sufferings, this on one hand

ὀνειδισμοῖς τε καὶ θλίψεσιν θεατριζόμενοι,
²to reproaches ³both ⁴and ⁵to afflictions ¹being exposed,

τοῦτο δὲ κοινωνοὶ τῶν οὕτως ἀναστρεφ-
this on the ²sharers ³of the ⁵thus ⁴liv-
other   [ones]

ομένων γενηθέντες. **34** καὶ γὰρ τοῖς
ing ¹having become. For indeed in the

δεσμίοις συνεπαθήσατε, καὶ τῇ ἁρπαγὴν
bonds ye suffered together, and ⁴the ¹seizure

τῶν ὑπαρχόντων ὑμῶν μετὰ χαρᾶς
²of the ³possessions ⁴of you ⁵with ⁶joy

προσεδέξασθε, γινώσκοντες ἔχειν ἑαυτοὺς
¹ye accepted, knowing ²to have ¹[your]selves

κρείσσονα ὕπαρξιν καὶ μένουσαν. **35** Μὴ
²a better ¹possession ³and ⁴remaining. not

ἀποβάλητε οὖν τὴν παρρησίαν ὑμῶν, ἥτις
Cast ye away therefore the confidence of you, which

ἔχει μεγάλην μισθαποδοσίαν. **36** ὑπομονῆς
has a great recompence. ¹of endurance

γὰρ ἔχετε χρείαν ἵνα τὸ θέλημα τοῦ
For ¹ye have ²need in order ³the ⁴will -
    that

θεοῦ ποιήσαντες κομίσησθε τὴν ἐπαγγελίαν.
⁴of God ¹having ye may obtain the promise.
    done

37 ἔτι γὰρ μικρὸν ὅσον ὅσον, ὁ ἐρχόμενος
For yet ¹little ¹a very,* the coming [one]

ἥξει καὶ οὐ χρονίσει· **38** ὁ δὲ δίκαιος
will come and will not delay; but the just man

μου ἐκ πίστεως ζήσεται, καὶ ἐὰν ὑπο-
of me by faith will live, and if he

στείληται, οὐκ εὐδοκεῖ ἡ ψυχή ³of me
withdraws, ⁴is not well pleased ¹the ²soul

ἐν αὐτῷ. **39** ἡμεῖς δὲ οὐκ ἐσμὲν ὑποστολῆς
in him. But we are not of withdrawal

εἰς ἀπώλειαν, ἀλλὰ πίστεως εἰς περιποίησιν
to destruction, but of faith to possession

ψυχῆς.
of soul.

4 Πίστει πλείονα θυσίαν Ἄβελ παρὰ
By faith ⁴a greater(? better) ²sacrifice ¹Abel ³than

Κάϊν προσήνεγκεν τῷ θεῷ, δι' ἧς
⁷Cain ⁵offered - ⁶to God, through which

τοὺς αἰῶνας ῥήματι θεοῦ, εἰς τὸ μὴ
¹the ²ages by a word of God, so as† ¹not

ἐκ φαινομένων τὸ βλεπόμενον γεγονέναι.
²out ³things ¹the ²being seen ⁶to have
of appearing thing become.

---

* Cf. our "so so".

King James Version

obtained witness that he was righteous, God testifying of his gifts: and by it he being dead yet speaketh. 5 By faith Enoch was translated that he should not see death; and was not found, because God had translated him: for before his translation he had this testimony, that he pleased God. 6 But without faith *it is* impossible to please *him:* for he that cometh to God must believe that he is, and *that* he is a rewarder of them that diligently seek him. 7 By faith Noah, being warned of God of things not seen as yet, moved with fear, prepared an ark to the saving of his house; by the which he condemned the world, and became heir of the righteousness which is by faith. 8 By faith Abraham, when he was called to go out into a place which he should after receive for an inheritance, obeyed; and he went out, not knowing whither he went. 9 By faith he sojourned in the land of promise, as *in* a strange country, dwelling in tabernacles with Isaac and Jacob, the heirs with him of the same promise: 10 For he looked for a city which hath foundations, whose builder and maker *is* God. 11 Through faith also Sarah herself received strength to conceive seed, and was delivered of a child when she was past age, because she judged him faithful who had promised. 12 Therefore sprang there even of one, and him as good as dead, *so many* as the stars of the sky in multitude, and as the sand which is by the sea shore innumerable. 13 These all died in faith, not having received the promises, but having seen them afar off, and were persuaded of *them,* and embraced *them,* and confessed that they were strangers and pilgrims on the earth. 14 For they that say such things declare plainly that they seek a country. 15 And truly, if they had been mindful of that *country* from whence they came out, they might have had opportunity to have returned. 16 But now they desire a better *country,* that is, a heavenly: wherefore God is not ashamed to be called their God: for he hath prepared for them a city. 17 By faith Abraham, when he was tried, offered up Isaac: and he that had received the promises offered up his only begotten *son,* 18 Of whom it was said, That in Isaac shall thy seed be called: 19 Accounting that God *was* able to raise *him* up, even from the dead; from whence also he received him in a figure. 20 By faith Isaac blessed Jacob and Esau concerning things to come. 21 By faith Jacob, when he was a dying, blessed both the sons of Joseph; and worshipped, *leaning* upon the top of his staff. 22 By faith Joseph, when he died, made mention of the departing of the children of Israel; and gave commandment concerning his bones. 23 By faith Moses, when he was born, was hid three months of his parents, because they saw *he was* a proper child; and they were not

New International Version

as a righteous man, when God spoke well of his offerings. And by faith he still speaks, even though he is dead.

5 By faith Enoch was taken from this life, so that he did not experience death; he could not be found, because God had taken him away. For before he was taken, he was commended as one who pleased God. 6 And without faith it is impossible to please God, because anyone who comes to him must believe that he exists and that he rewards those who earnestly seek him.

7 By faith Noah, when warned about things not yet seen, in holy fear built an ark to save his family. By his faith he condemned the world and became heir of the righteousness that comes by faith.

8 By faith Abraham, when called to go to a place he would later receive as his possession, obeyed and went, even though he did not know where he was going. 9 By faith he made his home in the promised land like a stranger in a foreign country; he lived in tents, as did Isaac and Jacob, who were heirs with him of the same promise. 10 For he was looking forward to the city with foundations, whose architect and builder is God.

11 By faith Abraham, even though he was past age—and Sarah herself was barren—was enabled to become a father because he[p] considered him faithful who had made the promise. 12 And so from this one man, and he as good as dead, came descendants as numerous as the stars in the sky and as countless as the sand of the seashore.

13 All these people were still living by faith when they died. They did not receive the things promised; they only saw them and welcomed them from a distance. And they admitted that they were foreigners and strangers on earth. 14 People who say such things show that they are looking for a country of their own. 15 If they had been thinking of the country they had left, they would have had opportunity to return. 16 Instead, they were longing for a better country—a heavenly one. Therefore God is not ashamed to be called their God, for he has prepared a city for them.

17 By faith Abraham, when God tested him, offered Isaac as a sacrifice. He who had received the promises was about to sacrifice his one and only son, 18 even though God had said to him, "Through Isaac shall your promised offspring[q] come."[r] 19 Abraham reasoned that God could raise the dead, and figuratively speaking, he did receive Isaac back from death.

20 By faith Isaac blessed Jacob and Esau in regard to their future.

21 By faith Jacob, when he was dying, blessed each of Joseph's sons, and worshiped as he leaned on the top of his staff.

22 By faith Joseph, when his end was near, spoke about the exodus of the Israelites from Egypt and gave instructions about his bones.

23 By faith Moses' parents hid him for three months after he was born, because they saw he was no ordinary child, and they were not afraid of the king's edict.

[p] Or *By faith even Sarah, who was past age, was enabled to bear children because she.* [q] Greek *seed.* [r] Gen 21:12.

ἐμαρτυρήθη εἶναι δίκαιος, μαρτυροῦντος ἐπὶ
he obtained to be just, ²witnessing ³over
witness

τοῖς δώροις αὐτοῦ τοῦ θεοῦ, καὶ δι'
⁴the ⁵gifts ⁶of him - ¹God,* and through

αὐτῆς ἀποθανὼν ἔτι λαλεῖ. 5 Πίστει
it having died still he speaks. By faith

Ἐνὼχ μετετέθη τοῦ μὴ ἰδεῖν θάνατον,
Enoch was removed - not to see⁴ death,

καὶ οὐχ ηὑρίσκετο διότι μετέθηκεν αὐτὸν
and was not found because ⁷removed ⁸him

ὁ θεός. 6 πρὸ γὰρ τῆς μεταθέσεως
- ¹God. For before the(his) removal

μεμαρτύρηται εὐαρεστηκέναι τῷ θεῷ· χωρὶς
he has obtained to have been well- - to God; ³without
witness pleasing

δὲ πίστεως ἀδύνατον εὐαρεστῆσαι· πιστεῦσαι
⁴but faith [it is] impossible to be well-pleasing [to God]; ⁵to believe

γὰρ δεῖ τὸν προσερχόμενον [τῷ] θεῷ,
²for ²it ³the [one] ⁴approaching - ⁵to God,
behoves

ὅτι ἔστιν καὶ τοῖς ἐκζητοῦσιν αὐτὸν
⁶that he is and ⁷to the [ones] ⁸seeking ⁹out ¹him

μισθαποδότης γίνεται. 7 Πίστει χρηματι-
²a rewarder ¹becomes. By faith ⁴having been
warned [by

θεὶς Νῶε περὶ τῶν μηδέπω βλεπομένων,
God*] ¹Noah concerning the things not yet being seen,

εὐλαβηθεὶς κατεσκεύασεν κιβωτὸν εἰς
being devout prepared an ark for

σωτηρίαν τοῦ οἴκου αὐτοῦ, δι' ἧς
[the] salvation of the household of him, through which

κατέκρινεν τὸν κόσμον, καὶ τῆς κατὰ
he condemned the world, and ⁵of the ⁶accord-
ing to

πίστιν δικαιοσύνης ἐγένετο κληρονόμος.
⁸faith ⁷righteousness ¹became ²heir.

8 Πίστει καλούμενος Ἀβραὰμ ὑπήκουσεν
By faith ¹being called ²Abraham ¹¹obeyed

ἐξελθεῖν εἰς τόπον ὃν ἤμελλεν λαμβάνειν
³to go forth ⁴to ⁵a place ⁶which ⁷he was about ⁸to receive

εἰς κληρονομίαν, καὶ ἐξῆλθεν μὴ ἐπιστάμε-
⁹for ¹⁰an inheritance, and went forth not understand-

νος ποῦ ἔρχεται. 9 Πίστει παρῴκησεν
ing where he goes(went). By faith he sojourned

εἰς γῆν τῆς ἐπαγγελίας ὡς ἀλλοτρίαν,
in a land - of promise as a foreigner,

ἐν σκηναῖς κατοικήσας, μετὰ Ἰσαὰκ καὶ
in tents dwelling, with Isaac and

Ἰακὼβ τῶν συγκληρονόμων τῆς ἐπαγ-
Jacob the co-heirs of the ³pro-

γελίας τῆς αὐτῆς· 10 ἐξεδέχετο γὰρ τὴν
mise ⁴same; for he expected the

τοὺς θεμελίους ἔχουσαν πόλιν, ἧς τεχνίτης
³the ⁴foundations ²having ¹city, of which ²artificer

καὶ δημιουργὸς ὁ θεός. 11 Πίστει καὶ
³and ⁴maker - ¹God ⁵[is]. By faith also

αὐτὴ Σάρρα δύναμιν εἰς καταβολὴν
²[her]self ¹Sara ³power ⁴for ⁵conception

σπέρματος ἔλαβεν καὶ παρὰ καιρὸν ἡλικίας,
⁶of seed ⁷received even beyond time of age,

ἐπεὶ πιστὸν ἡγήσατο τὸν ἐπαγγειλάμενον.
since ²faithful ¹she deemed the [one] having promised.

12 διὸ καὶ ἀφ' ἑνὸς ἐγενήθησαν, καὶ
Wherefore indeed from one there became, and

ταῦτα νενεκρωμένου, καθὼς τὰ ἄστρα
that too† [he] having died,* as the stars

τοῦ οὐρανοῦ τῷ πλήθει καὶ ὡς ἡ ἄμμος
of the heaven - in multitude and as the ²sand

ἡ παρὰ τὸ χεῖλος τῆς θαλάσσης ἡ
- ³by ⁴the ⁵lip ⁶of the ⁷sea -

ἀναρίθμητος. 13 Κατὰ πίστιν ἀπέθανον
¹innumerable. ⁴By way of ⁵faith ³died

οὗτοι πάντες, μὴ κομισάμενοι τὰς ἐπαγ-
¹these ²all, not having obtained the pro-

γελίας, ἀλλὰ πόρρωθεν αὐτὰς ἰδόντες καὶ
mises, but ³from afar ⁴them ¹seeing ²and

ἀσπασάμενοι, καὶ ὁμολογήσαντες ὅτι ξένοι
⁵greeting, and confessing that ²strangers

καὶ παρεπίδημοί εἰσιν ἐπὶ τῆς γῆς.
³and ⁴sojourners ¹they are on the earth
(? land).

14 οἱ γὰρ τοιαῦτα λέγοντες ἐμφανίζουσιν
For the [ones] ¹such things ²saying make manifest

ὅτι πατρίδα ἐπιζητοῦσιν. 15 καὶ εἰ μὲν
that ²a fatherland ¹they seek. And if on one
hand

ἐκείνης ἐμνημόνευον ἀφ' ἧς ἐξέβησαν,
¹that ²they remembered from which they came out,

εἶχον ἂν καιρὸν ἀνακάμψαι· 16 νῦν
they might time(opportunity) to return; now
have had

δὲ κρείττονος ὀρέγονται, τοῦτ' ἔστιν
on the ²a better ¹they aspire to, this is
other

ἐπουρανίου. διὸ οὐκ ἐπαισχύνεται αὐτοὺς
a heavenly. Wherefore ²is not ashamed [of] ³them

ὁ θεὸς θεὸς ἐπικαλεῖσθαι αὐτῶν· ἡτοίμασεν
- ¹God ⁴God ⁵to be called ⁶of them; ⁷he prepared

γὰρ αὐτοῖς πόλιν. 17 Πίστει προσενήνοχεν
¹for for them a city. By faith ¹has offered up

Ἀβραὰμ τὸν Ἰσαὰκ πειραζόμενος, καὶ
¹Abraham - ²Isaac ²being tested, and

τὸν μονογενῆ προσέφερεν ὁ τὰς ἐπαγγελίας
³the ⁴only begotten ²was ¹the ³the ⁴promises
(his) offering up
[one]

ἀναδεξάμενος, 18 πρὸς ὃν ἐλαλήθη ὅτι
²having undertaken, as to whom it was spoken[.] -

ἐν Ἰσαὰκ κληθήσεταί σοι σπέρμα,
In Isaac shall be called to thee a seed,*
=thy seed,

19 λογισάμενος ὅτι καὶ ἐκ νεκρῶν ἐγείρειν
reckoning that ⁴even ⁵from ⁶dead ¹to raise

δυνατὸς ὁ θεός· ὅθεν αὐτὸν καὶ ἐν
²[was] ³able ¹God; whence ⁶him ⁷indeed ⁵in

παραβολῇ ἐκομίσατο. 20 Πίστει καὶ περὶ
²a parable ⁴he obtained. By faith also ⁴concerning

μελλόντων εὐλόγησεν Ἰσαὰκ τὸν Ἰακὼβ
⁵coming things ³blessed ¹Isaac - ²Jacob

καὶ τὸν Ἠσαῦ. 21 Πίστει Ἰακὼβ
⁴and - ⁶Esau. By faith Jacob

ἀποθνῄσκων ἕκαστον τῶν υἱῶν Ἰωσὴφ
dying ³each ⁴of the ⁵sons ⁶of Joseph

εὐλόγησεν, καὶ προσεκύνησεν ἐπὶ τὸ ἄκρον
¹blessed, and worshipped on the tip

τῆς ῥάβδου αὐτοῦ. 22 Πίστει Ἰωσὴφ
of the rod of him. By faith Joseph

τελευτῶν περὶ τῆς ἐξόδου τῶν υἱῶν
dying ²concerning ¹the ²exodus ³of the ⁴sons

Ἰσραὴλ ἐμνημόνευσεν καὶ περὶ τῶν
⁵of Israel ¹remembered and ²concerning ³the

ὀστέων αὐτοῦ ἐνετείλατο. 23 Πίστει
⁴bones ⁵of him ¹gave orders. By faith

Μωϋσῆς γεννηθεὶς ἐκρύβη τρίμηνον ὑπὸ
Moses having been born was hidden three months by

τῶν πατέρων αὐτοῦ, διότι εἶδον ἀστεῖον
the parents of him, because they saw ²[to be] fine

τὸ παιδίον, καὶ οὐκ ἐφοβήθησαν τὸ
¹the child, and they did not fear the

* This must be understood, as the word always (or at
least generally) has reference to a divine communication.

King James Version

afraid of the king's commandment. 24 By faith Moses, when he was come to years, refused to be called the son of Pharaoh's daughter; 25 Choosing rather to suffer affliction with the people of God, than to enjoy the pleasures of sin for a season; 26 Esteeming the reproach of Christ greater riches than the treasures in Egypt: for he had respect unto the recompense of the reward. 27 By faith he forsook Egypt, not fearing the wrath of the king: for he endured, as seeing him who is invisible. 28 Through faith he kept the passover, and the sprinkling of blood, lest he that destroyed the firstborn should touch them. 29 By faith they passed through the Red sea as by dry *land:* which the Egyptians assaying to do were drowned. 30 By faith the walls of Jericho fell down, after they were compassed about seven days. 31 By faith the harlot Rahab perished not with them that believed not, when she had received the spies with peace. 32And what shall I more say? for the time would fail me to tell of Gideon, and *of* Barak, and *of* Samson, and *of* Jephthah; *of* David also, and Samuel, and *of* the prophets: 33 Who through faith subdued kingdoms, wrought righteousness, obtained promises, stopped the mouths of lions, 34 Quenched the violence of fire, escaped the edge of the sword, out of weakness were made strong, waxed valiant in fight, turned to flight the armies of the aliens. 35 Women received their dead raised to life again: and others were tortured, not accepting deliverance; that they might obtain a better resurrection: 36And others had trial of *cruel* mockings and scourgings, yea, moreover of bonds and imprisonment: 37 They were stoned, they were sawn asunder, were tempted, were slain with the sword: they wandered about in sheepskins and goatskins; being destitute, afflicted, tormented; 38 Of whom the world was not worthy: they wandered in deserts, and *in* mountains, and *in* dens and caves of the earth. 39And these all, having obtained a good report through faith, received not the promise: 40 God having provided some better thing for us, that they without us should not be made perfect.

12 Wherefore, seeing we also are compassed about with so great a cloud of witnesses, let us lay aside every weight, and the sin which doth so easily beset *us,* and let us run with patience the race that is set before us, 2 Looking unto Jesus the author and finisher of *our* faith; who for the joy that was set before him endured the cross, despising the shame, and is set down at the right hand of the throne of God. 3 For consider him that endured such contradiction of sinners against himself, lest ye be wearied and faint in your minds. 4 Ye have not yet resisted

New International Version

24 By faith Moses, when he had grown up, refused to be known as the son of Pharaoh's daughter. 25 He chose to be mistreated along with the people of God rather than to enjoy the pleasures of sin for a short time. 26 He regarded disgrace for the sake of Christ as of greater value than the treasures of Egypt, because he was looking ahead to his reward. 27 By faith he left Egypt, not fearing the king's anger; he persevered because he saw him who is invisible. 28 By faith he kept the Passover and the sprinkling of blood, so that the destroyer of the firstborn would not touch the firstborn of Israel. 29 By faith the people passed through the Red Sea[s] as on dry land; but when the Egyptians tried to do so, they were drowned. 30 By faith the walls of Jericho fell, after the people had marched around them for seven days. 31 By faith the prostitute Rahab, because she welcomed the spies, was not killed with those who were disobedient.[t] 32 And what more shall I say? I do not have time to tell about Gideon, Barak, Samson, Jephthah, David, Samuel and the prophets, 33 who by faith conquered kingdoms, administered justice, and gained what was promised; who shut the mouths of lions, 34 quenched the fury of the flames, and escaped the edge of the sword; whose weakness was turned to strength; and who became powerful in battle and routed foreign armies. 35 Women received back their dead, raised to life again. Others were tortured and refused to be released, so that they might gain a better resurrection. 36 Some faced jeers and flogging, while still others were chained and put in prison. 37 They were stoned;[u] they were sawed in two; they were put to death by the sword. They went about in sheepskins and goatskins, destitute, persecuted and mistreated—38 the world was not worthy of them. They wandered in deserts and mountains, and in caves and holes in the ground. 39 These were all commended for their faith, yet none of them received what had been promised. 40 God had planned something better for us so that only together with us would they be made perfect.

God disciplines his sons

12 Therefore, since we are surrounded by such a great cloud of witnesses, let us throw off everything that hinders and the sin that so easily entangles, and let us run with perseverance the race marked out for us. 2 Let us fix our eyes on Jesus, the Pioneer[v] and Perfecter of our faith, who for the joy set before him endured the cross, scorning its shame, and sat down at the right hand of the throne of God. 3 Consider him who endured such opposition from sinful men, so that you will not grow weary and lose heart.

4 In your struggle against sin, you have not yet resisted to the point of shedding your blood.

[s] That is, Sea of Reeds. [t] Or *unbelieving.* [u] Some early MSS add *they were put to the test.* [v] Or *Originator.*

Greek Interlinear

διάταγμα τοῦ βασιλέως. 24 Πίστει Μωϋσῆς
decree of the king. By faith Moses

μέγας γενόμενος ἠρνήσατο λέγεσθαι υἱὸς
¹great ²having become denied to be said(called) son

θυγατρὸς Φαραώ, 25 μᾶλλον ἑλόμενος
of [the] daughter of Pharaoh, rather choosing

συγκακουχεῖσθαι τῷ λαῷ τοῦ θεοῦ ἢ
to be ill treated with the people - of God than

πρόσκαιρον ἔχειν ἁμαρτίας ἀπόλαυσιν,
for a time to have ⁴of sin ¹enjoyment,

26 μείζονα πλοῦτον ἡγησάμενος τῶν
⁴greater ⁵riches ¹deeming ¹[than] ²the

Αἰγύπτου θησαυρῶν τὸν ὀνειδισμὸν τοῦ
¹⁰of Egypt ³treasures ²the ⁴reproach -

Χριστοῦ· ἀπέβλεπεν γὰρ εἰς τὴν μισθ-
⁴of Christ; for he was looking away to the recom-

αποδοσίαν. 27 Πίστει κατέλιπεν Αἴγυπτον,
pence. By faith he left Egypt,

μὴ φοβηθεὶς τὸν θυμὸν τοῦ βασιλέως·
not fearing the anger of the king;

τὸν γὰρ ἀόρατον ὡς ὁρῶν ἐκαρτέρησεν.
for ¹the ²unseen [one] ²as ¹seeing ¹he endured.

28 Πίστει πεποίηκεν τὸ πάσχα καὶ τὴν
By faith he has made the passover and the

πρόσχυσιν τοῦ αἵματος, ἵνα μὴ ὁ
affusion of the blood, lest the

ὀλεθρεύων τὰ πρωτότοκα θίγῃ αὐτῶν.
[one] destroying ²the ¹firstborns ²should ⁴of them.
touch

29 Πίστει διέβησαν τὴν ἐρυθρὰν θάλασσαν
By faith they went the Red Sea
through

ὡς διὰ ξηρᾶς γῆς, ἧς πεῖραν λαβόντες
as through dry land, which ⁴trial ³taking

οἱ Αἰγύπτιοι κατεπόθησαν. 30 Πίστει
¹the ²Egyptians were swallowed up. By faith

τὰ τείχη Ἰεριχὼ ἔπεσαν κυκλωθέντα ἐπὶ
the walls of Jericho fell having been during
encircled

ἑπτὰ ἡμέρας. 31 Πίστει Ῥαὰβ ἡ πόρνη
seven days. By faith Rahab the prostitute

οὐ συναπώλετο τοῖς ἀπειθήσασιν, δεξαμένη
did not perish with the [ones] disobeying, having received

τοὺς κατασκόπους μετ᾽ εἰρήνης· 32 Καὶ
the spies with peace. And

τί ἔτι λέγω; ἐπιλείψει με γὰρ διηγούμενον
what more may ⁴will fail ²me ¹for ³recounting
I say ?

ὁ χρόνος περὶ Γεδεών, Βαράκ, Σαμψών,
¹the ²time concerning Gedeon, Barak, Sampson,

Ἰεφθάε, Δαυίδ τε καὶ Σαμουὴλ καὶ
Jephthae, ²David ¹both and Samuel and

τῶν προφητῶν, 33 οἳ διὰ πίστεως
the prophets, who through faith

κατηγωνίσαντο βασιλείας, ἠργάσαντο δι-
overcame kingdoms, wrought right-

καιοσύνην, ἐπέτυχον ἐπαγγελιῶν, ἔφραξαν
eousness, obtained promises, stopped

στόματα λεόντων, 34 ἔσβεσαν δύναμιν
mouths of lions, quenched [the] power

πυρός, ἔφυγον στόματα μαχαίρης, ἐδυναμώ-
of fire, escaped mouths(edges) of [the] sword, were em-

θησαν ἀπὸ ἀσθενείας, ἐγενήθησαν ἰσχυροὶ
powered from weakness, became strong

ἐν πολέμῳ, παρεμβολὰς ἔκλιναν ἀλλοτρίων.
in war, ¹armies ²made to yield ³of foreigners.

35 ἔλαβον γυναῖκες ἐξ ἀναστάσεως τοὺς
²received ¹women ⁴by ⁵resurrection ³the

νεκροὺς αὐτῶν· ἄλλοι δὲ ἐτυμπανίσθησαν,
⁴dead ⁵of them; but others were beaten to death,

οὐ προσδεξάμενοι τὴν ἀπολύτρωσιν, ἵνα
not accepting - deliverance, in order that

κρείττονος ἀναστάσεως τύχωσιν· 36 ἕτεροι
²a better ³resurrection ¹they might others
obtain;

δὲ ἐμπαιγμῶν καὶ μαστίγων πεῖραν ἔλαβον,
and ²of mockings ³and ⁴of scourgings ¹trial ¹took,

ἔτι δὲ δεσμῶν καὶ φυλακῆς· 37 ἐλιθάσ-
and more of bonds and of prison; they were

θησαν, ἐπειράσθησαν, ἐπρίσθησαν, ἐν φόνῳ
stoned, they were tried, they were ¹by ²murder
sawn asunder,

μαχαίρης ἀπέθανον, περιῆλθον ἐν μηλωταῖς,
⁴of sword ¹they died, they went about in sheepskins,

ἐν αἰγείοις δέρμασιν, ὑστερούμενοι,
in goatskins, being in want,

θλιβόμενοι, κακουχούμενοι, 38 ὧν οὐκ ἦν
being afflicted, being ill treated, of whom was not

ἄξιος ὁ κόσμος, ἐπὶ ἐρημίαις πλανώμενοι
worthy the world, ²over ³deserts ¹wandering

καὶ ὄρεσιν καὶ σπηλαίοις καὶ ταῖς ὀπαῖς
and mountains and caves and the holes

τῆς γῆς. 39 Καὶ οὗτοι πάντες μαρτυρη-
of the earth. And these all having obtained

θέντες διὰ τῆς πίστεως οὐκ ἐκομίσαντο
witness through the(ir) faith obtained not

τὴν ἐπαγγελίαν, 40 τοῦ θεοῦ περὶ ἡμῶν
the promise, - God ³concerning ⁴us

κρεῖττόν τι προβλεψαμένου, ἵνα μὴ χωρὶς
²better ³some- ¹having foreseen, in or- not without
thing der that

ἡμῶν τελειωθῶσιν.
us they should be perfected.

Chapter 12

Τοιγαροῦν καὶ ἡμεῖς, τοσοῦτον ἔχοντες
So therefore ²also ¹we, ²such ¹having

περικείμενον ἡμῖν νέφος μαρτύρων, ὄγκον
²lying around ⁴us ²a cloud ⁵of witnesses, ¹encum-
brance

ἀποθέμενοι πάντα καὶ τὴν εὐπερίστατον
¹putting away ²every ³and ⁴the ⁵most besetting

ἁμαρτίαν, δι᾽ ὑπομονῆς τρέχωμεν τὸν
⁶sin, through endurance let us run ¹the

προκείμενον ἡμῖν ἀγῶνα, 2 ἀφορῶντες εἰς
⁵set before ⁴us ³contest(race), looking away to

τὸν τῆς πίστεως ἀρχηγὸν καὶ τελειωτὴν
¹the ²of the ⁴faith ³author ²and ⁵finisher

Ἰησοῦν, ὃς ἀντὶ τῆς προκειμένης αὐτῷ
Jesus, who against ¹the ²set before ³him

χαρᾶς ὑπέμεινεν σταυρὸν αἰσχύνης κατα-
²joy endured a cross ²shame ¹de-

φρονήσας, ἐν δεξιᾷ τε τοῦ θρόνου τοῦ
spising, ²at ³[the] ¹and ⁴of the ⁵throne -
right [hand]

θεοῦ κεκάθικεν. 3 ἀναλογίσασθε γὰρ τὸν
⁶of ¹has taken For consider ye ¹the
God [his] seat. [one]

τοιαύτην ὑπομεμενηκότα ὑπὸ τῶν ἁμαρτω-
²such ¹having endured ²by - ³of sin-

λῶν εἰς ἑαυτὸν ἀντιλογίαν, ἵνα μὴ κάμητε
ners ²against ¹himself ³contradiction, lest ye grow
weary

ταῖς ψυχαῖς ὑμῶν ἐκλυόμενοι. 4 Οὔπω
²in the ³souls ⁴of you ¹fainting. Not yet

μέχρις αἵματος ἀντικατέστητε πρὸς τὴν
¹until ³blood ¹ye resisted ²against -

665

King James Version

unto blood, striving against sin. 5And ye have forgotten the exhortation which speaketh unto you as unto children, My son, despise not thou the chastening of the Lord, nor faint when thou art rebuked of him: 6 For whom the Lord loveth he chasteneth, and scourgeth every son whom he receiveth. 7 If ye endure chastening, God dealeth with you as with sons; for what son is he whom the father chasteneth not? 8 But if ye be without chastisement, whereof all are partakers, then are ye bastards, and not sons. 9 Furthermore, we have had fathers of our flesh which corrected *us*, and we gave *them* reverence: shall we not much rather be in subjection unto the Father of spirits, and live? 10 For they verily for a few days chastened *us* after their own pleasure; but he for *our* profit, that *we* might be partakers of his holiness. 11 Now no chastening for the present seemeth to be joyous, but grievous: nevertheless, afterward it yieldeth the peaceable fruit of righteousness unto them which are exercised thereby. 12 Wherefore lift up the hands which hang down, and the feeble knees; 13And make straight paths for your feet, lest that which is lame be turned out of the way; but let it rather be healed. 14 Follow peace with all *men*, and holiness, without which no man shall see the Lord: 15 Looking diligently lest any man fail of the grace of God; lest any root of bitterness springing up trouble *you*, and thereby many be defiled; 16 Lest there *be* any fornicator, or profane person, as Esau, who for one morsel of meat sold his birthright. 17 For ye know how that afterward, when he would have inherited the blessing, he was rejected: for he found no place of repentance, though he sought it carefully with tears. 18 For ye are not come unto the mount that might be touched, and that burned with fire, nor unto blackness, and darkness, and tempest, 19And the sound of a trumpet, and the voice of words; which *voice* they that heard entreated that the word should not be spoken to them any more: 20 (For they could not endure that which was commanded, And if so much as a beast touch the mountain, it shall be stoned, or thrust through with a dart: 21And so terrible was the sight, *that* Moses said, I exceedingly fear and quake:) 22 But ye are come unto mount Sion, and unto the city of the living God, the heavenly Jerusalem, and to an innumerable company of angels, 23 To the general assembly and church of the firstborn, which are written in heaven, and to God the Judge of all, and to the spirits of just men made perfect, 24And to Jesus the mediator of the new covenant, and to the blood of sprinkling, that speaketh better things than *that of* Abel. 25 See that ye refuse not him that speaketh: for if they escaped not who refused him that spake on earth, much more *shall not* we *escape*, if we turn away from him that *speaketh* from heaven: 26 Whose voice then shook the earth: but now he hath promised, saying, Yet once more I shake not the earth only,

New International Version

5And you have forgotten that word of encouragement that addresses you as sons:
"My son, do not make light of the Lord's discipline,
　and do not lose heart when he rebukes you,
6 because the Lord disciplines those whom he loves,
　and he punishes everyone he accepts as a son." [w]
7 Endure hardship as discipline; God is treating you as sons. For what son is not disciplined by his father? 8 If you are not disciplined (and everyone undergoes discipline), then you are illegitimate children and not true sons. 9 Moreover, we have all had human fathers who disciplined us and we respected them for it. How much more should we submit to the Father of our spirits and live! 10 Our fathers disciplined us for a little while as they thought best; but God disciplines us for our good, that we may share in his holiness. 11 No discipline seems pleasant at the time, but painful. Later on, however, it produces a harvest of righteousness and peace for those who have been trained by it. 12 Therefore, strengthen your feeble arms and weak knees. 13 Make level paths for your feet, so that the lame may not be disabled, but rather healed.

Warning against refusing God

14 Make every effort to live in peace with all men and to be holy; without holiness no will see the Lord. 15 See to it that no one misses the grace of God and that no bitter root grows up to cause trouble and defile many. 16 See that no one is sexually immoral, or is godless like Esau, who for a single meal sold his inheritance rights as the oldest son. 17Afterward, as you know, when he wanted to inherit this blessing, he was rejected. He could bring about no change of mind, though he sought the blessing with tears.
18 You have not come to a mountain that can be touched and that is burning with fire; to darkness, gloom and storm; 19 to a trumpet blast or to such a voice speaking words, so that those who heard it begged that no further word be spoken to them, 20 because they could not bear what was commanded: "If even an animal touches the mountain, it must be stoned." [x] 21 The sight was so terrifying that Moses said, "I am trembling with fear." [y]
22 But you have come to Mount Zion, to the heavenly Jerusalem, the city of the living God. You have come to thousands upon thousands of angels in joyful assembly, 23 to the church of the firstborn, whose names are written in heaven. You have come to God, the judge of all men, to the spirits of righteous men made perfect, 24 to Jesus the mediator of a new covenant, and to the sprinkled blood that speaks a better word than the blood of Abel.
25 See to it that you do not refuse him who speaks. If they did not escape when they refused him who warned them on earth, how much less will we, if we turn away from him who warns us from heaven? 26At that time his voice shook the earth, but now he has promised, "Once more I will shake not only the earth but also the

Greek Interlinear

ἁμαρτίαν ἀνταγωνιζόμενοι, 5 καὶ ἐκλέλησθε
'sin 'struggling against, and ye have forgotten

τῆς παρακλήσεως, ἥτις ὑμῖν ὡς υἱοῖς
the exhortation, which 'with you 'as 'with sons

διαλέγεται· υἱέ μου, μὴ ὀλιγώρει παιδείας
'discourses: Son of me, do not make [the] light of discipline

κυρίου, μηδὲ ἐκλύου ὑπ' αὐτοῦ ἐλεγχόμενος·
of [the] Lord, nor faint 'by 'him 'being reproved;

6 ὃν γὰρ ἀγαπᾷ κύριος παιδεύει, μαστιγοῖ
for whom 'loves '[the] Lord he disciplines, 'scourges

δὲ πάντα υἱὸν ὃν παραδέχεται. 7 εἰς
'and every son whom he receives. For

παιδείαν ὑπομένετε· ὡς υἱοῖς ὑμῖν
discipline endure ye; 'as 'with sons 'with you

προσφέρεται ὁ θεός· τίς γὰρ υἱὸς ὃν
'is dealing - 'God; for what son whom [is there]

οὐ παιδεύει πατήρ; 8 εἰ δὲ χωρίς ἐστε
'disciplines not 'a father? But if 'without 'ye are

παιδείας, ἧς μέτοχοι γεγόνασιν πάντες,
discipline, of which 'sharers 'have become 'all,

ἄρα νόθοι καὶ οὐχ υἱοί ἐστε. 9 εἶτα
then bastards and not sons ye are. Furthermore

τοὺς μὲν τῆς σαρκὸς ἡμῶν πατέρας
the - 'of the 'flesh 'of us 'fathers

εἴχομεν παιδευτὰς καὶ ἐνετρεπόμεθα· οὐ
'we had 'correctors and we respected [them]: 'not

πολὺ μᾶλλον ὑποταγησόμεθα τῷ πατρὶ
'much 'more 'shall 'we 'be 'subject to the Father

τῶν πνευμάτων καὶ ζήσομεν; 10 οἱ μὲν
- of spirits and we shall live? 'they 'indeed

γὰρ πρὸς ὀλίγας ἡμέρας κατὰ τὸ δοκοῦν
'for for a few days accord- the seeming ing to thing [good]

αὐτοῖς ἐπαίδευον, ὁ δὲ ἐπὶ τὸ συμφέρον
to them disciplined [us], but he for the(our) profit

εἰς τὸ μεταλαβεῖν τῆς ἁγιότητος αὐτοῦ.
for the to partake of the sanctity of him.

11 πᾶσα μὲν παιδεία πρὸς μὲν τὸ παρὸν
'All 'on 'discipline 'for 'in- 'the 'present one hand deed

οὐ δοκεῖ χαρᾶς εἶναι ἀλλὰ λύπης, ὕστερον
seems not 'of joy 'to be but of grief, 'later

δὲ καρπὸν εἰρηνικὸν τοῖς δι' αὐτῆς
'on the 'fruit 'peaceable 'to the 'through ''it other [ones]

γεγυμνασμένοις ἀποδίδωσιν δικαιοσύνης.
'having been exercised 'it gives back 'of righteousness.

12 Διὸ τὰς παρειμένας χεῖρας καὶ τὰ
Where- 'the 'having been 'hands 'and 'the wearied

παραλελυμένα γόνατα ἀνορθώσατε, 13 καὶ
'having been paralysed 'knees 'straighten ye, and

τροχιὰς ὀρθὰς ποιεῖτε τοῖς ποσὶν ὑμῶν,
tracks straight make for the feet of you,

ἵνα μὴ τὸ χωλὸν ἐκτραπῇ, ἰαθῇ δὲ
lest not the lame be turned 'may 'but aside, be cured

μᾶλλον. 14 Εἰρήνην διώκετε μετὰ πάντων,
'rather. Peace follow with all men,

καὶ τὸν ἁγιασμόν, οὗ χωρὶς οὐδεὶς
and - sanctification, 'which 'without no one

ὄψεται τὸν κύριον, 15 ἐπισκοποῦντες μὴ
will see the Lord, 'observing not(lest)

τις ὑστερῶν ἀπὸ τῆς χάριτος τοῦ θεοῦ,
anyone failing from the grace - of God,

μή τις ῥίζα πικρίας ἄνω φύουσα ἐνοχλῇ
not any root of bitterness 'up 'growing disturb (lest)

καὶ διὰ ταύτης μιανθῶσιν οἱ πολλοί,
and through this 'be defiled the 'many,

16 μή τις πόρνος ἢ βέβηλος ὡς Ἠσαῦ,
not(lest) any fornicator or profane man as Esau,

ὃς ἀντὶ βρώσεως μιᾶς ἀπέδοτο τὰ
who against 'eating 'one gave up the

πρωτοτόκια ἑαυτοῦ. 17 ἴστε γὰρ ὅτι
rights of of himself. For ye know that the firstborn

καὶ μετέπειτα θέλων κληρονομῆσαι τὴν
indeed afterwards wishing to inherit the

εὐλογίαν ἀπεδοκιμάσθη, μετανοίας γὰρ
blessing he was rejected, for 'of repentance

τόπον οὐχ εὗρεν, καίπερ μετὰ δακρύων
'place 'not 'he found, though with tears

ἐκζητήσας αὐτήν. 18 Οὐ γὰρ προσεληλύθατε
seeking out it. For 'not 'ye 'have 'approached

ψηλαφωμένῳ καὶ κεκαυμένῳ πυρὶ καὶ
to [a mountain] and having been with and being felt ignited fire

γνόφῳ καὶ ζόφῳ καὶ θυέλλῃ 19 καὶ
to darkness and to deep gloom and to whirlwind and

σάλπιγγος ἤχῳ καὶ φωνῇ ῥημάτων, ἧς
'of trumpet 'to a sound and to a voice of words, which

οἱ ἀκούσαντες παρῃτήσαντο μὴ προστεθῆναι
the [ones] hearing entreated not to be added

αὐτοῖς λόγον· 20 οὐκ ἔφερον γὰρ τὸ
to them a word; 'not 'they bore 'for the thing

διαστελλόμενον· κἂν θηρίον θίγῃ τοῦ ὄρους,
being charged: If even a beast touches the mountain,

λιθοβοληθήσεται· 21 καί, οὕτω φοβερὸν ἦν
it shall be stoned; and, so fearful was

τὸ φανταζόμενον, Μωϋσῆς εἶπεν· ἔκφοβός
the thing appearing, Moses said: 'Terrified

εἰμι καὶ ἔντρομος· 22 ἀλλὰ προσεληλύθατε
'I am and and trembling; but ye have approached

Σιὼν ὄρει καὶ πόλει θεοῦ ζῶντος,
'Zion 'to mount and to a city 'God 'of [the] living,

Ἰερουσαλὴμ ἐπουρανίῳ, καὶ μυριάσιν
'Jerusalem 'to a heavenly, and to myriads

ἀγγέλων, 23 πανηγύρει καὶ ἐκκλησίᾳ
of angels, to an assembly and a church

πρωτοτόκων ἀπογεγραμμένων ἐν οὐρανοῖς,
of firstborn [ones] having been enrolled in heavens,

καὶ κριτῇ θεῷ πάντων, καὶ πνεύμασι
and 'judge 'to God of all men, and to spirits

δικαίων τετελειωμένων, 24 καὶ διαθήκης
of just men having been made and 'covenant perfect,

νέας μεσίτῃ Ἰησοῦ, καὶ αἵματι ῥαντισμοῦ
'of a 'mediator 'to Jesus, and to blood of sprinkling new

κρεῖττον λαλοῦντι παρὰ τὸν Ἄβελ.
'a better thing 'speaking than - Abel.

25 Βλέπετε μὴ παραιτήσησθε τὸν λαλοῦντα·
Look ye [that] 'not 'ye refuse the [one] speaking;

εἰ γὰρ ἐκεῖνοι οὐκ ἐξέφυγον ἐπὶ γῆς
for if those escaped not 'on 'earth

παραιτησάμενοι τὸν χρηματίζοντα, πολὺ
'refusing 'the [one] 'warning, much

μᾶλλον ἡμεῖς οἱ τὸν ἀπ' οὐρανῶν
more we* 'the 'the [one] 'from 'heavens [ones] '[warning]

ἀποστρεφόμενοι· 26 οὗ ἡ φωνὴ τὴν γῆν
'turning from; of whom the voice 'the 'earth

ἐσάλευσεν τότε, νῦν δὲ ἐπήγγελται λέγων·
'shook 'then, but now he has promised saying:

ἔτι ἅπαξ ἐγὼ σείσω οὐ μόνον τὴν
Yet once I will shake not only the

---

* That is, " much more [shall] we [not escape]"; or, putting it in another way, " much less shall we escape."

King James Version

but also heaven. 27And this *word*, Yet once more, signifieth the removing of those things that are shaken, as of things that are made, that those things which cannot be shaken may remain. 28 Wherefore we receiving a kingdom which cannot be moved, let us have grace, whereby we may serve God acceptably with reverence and godly fear: 29 For our God *is* a consuming fire.

13 Let brotherly love continue. 2 Be not forgetful to entertain strangers: for thereby some have entertained angels unawares. 3 Remember them that are in bonds, as bound with them; *and* them which suffer adversity, as being yourselves also in the body. 4 Marriage *is* honourable in all, and the bed undefiled: but whoremongers and adulterers God will judge. 5 *Let your* conversation *be* without covetousness; *and be* content with such things as ye have: for he hath said, I will never leave thee, nor forsake thee. 6 So that we may boldly say, The Lord *is* my helper, and I will not fear what man shall do unto me. 7 Remember them which have the rule over you, who have spoken unto you the word of God: whose faith follow, considering the end of *their* conversation. 8 Jesus Christ the same yesterday, and to day, and for ever. 9 Be not carried about with divers and strange doctrines: for *it is* a good thing that the heart be established with grace; not with meats, which have not profited them that have been occupied therein. 10 We have an altar, whereof they have no right to eat which serve the tabernacle. 11 For the bodies of those beasts, whose blood is brought into the sanctuary by the high priest for sin, are burned without the camp. 12 Wherefore Jesus also, that he might sanctify the people with his own blood, suffered without the gate. 13 Let us go forth therefore unto him without the camp, bearing his reproach. 14 For here have we no continuing city, but we seek one to come. 15 By him therefore let us offer the sacrifice of praise to God continually, that is, the fruit of *our* lips, giving thanks to his name. 16 But to do good and to communicate forget not: for with such sacrifices God is well pleased. 17 Obey them that have the rule over you, and submit yourselves: for they watch for your souls, as they that must give account, that they may do it with joy, and not with grief: for that *is* unprofitable for you. 18 Pray for us: for we trust we have a good conscience, in all things willing to·

New International Version

heavens." *z* 27 The words "once more" indicate the removing of what can be shaken—that is, created things—so that what cannot be shaken may remain.

28 Therefore, since we are receiving a kingdom that cannot be shaken, let us be thankful, and so worship God acceptably with reverence and awe, 29 for our God is a consuming fire.

Concluding exhortations

13 Keep on loving each other as brothers. 2 Do not forget to entertain strangers, for by so doing some people have entertained angels without knowing it. 3 Remember those in prison as if you were their fellow prisoners, and those who are mistreated as if you yourselves were suffering.

4 Marriage should be honored by all, and the marriage bed kept pure, for God will judge the adulterer and all the sexually immoral. 5 Keep your lives free from the love of money and be content with what you have, because God has said,

"Never will I leave you;
    never will I forsake you." *a*
6 So we say with confidence,

"The Lord is my helper;
    I will not be afraid.
What can man do to me?" *b*
7 Remember your leaders, who spoke the word of God to you. Consider the outcome of their way of life and imitate their faith. 8 Jesus Christ is the same yesterday and today and forever.

9 Do not be carried away by all kinds of strange teachings. It is good for our hearts to be strengthened by grace, not by ceremonial foods, which are of no value to those who eat them. 10 We have an altar from which those who minister at the tabernacle have no right to eat.

11 The high priest carries the blood of animals into the Most Holy Place as a sin offering, but the bodies are burned outside the camp. 12And so Jesus also suffered outside the city gate to make his people holy through his own blood. 13 Let us, then, go to him outside the camp, bearing the disgrace he bore. 14 For here we do not have an enduring city, but we are looking for the city that is to come.

15 Through Jesus, therefore, let us continually offer to God a sacrifice of praise—the fruit of lips that confess his name. 16And do not forget to do good and to share with others, for with such sacrifices God is pleased.

17 Obey your leaders and submit to their authority. They keep watch over you as men who must give an account. Obey them so that their work will be a joy, not a burden, for that would be of no advantage to you.

18 Pray for us. We are sure that we have a clear conscience and desire to live honorably in

Greek Interlinear

γῆν   ἀλλὰ   καὶ   τὸν   οὐρανόν.   **27** τὸ   δὲ
earth   but   also   *the*   heaven.   Now the
[phrase]

ἔτι   ἅπαξ   δηλοῖ   τὴν   τῶν   σαλευομένων
'Yet   once'   declares   ¹the   ²of the things   ⁴being shaken

μετάθεσιν   ὡς   πεποιημένων,   ἵνα   μείνῃ   τὰ
¹removal   as   of things having   in or-   ⁴may   ¹the
been made,   der that   remain things

μὴ   σαλευόμενα.   **28** Διὸ   βασιλείαν   ἀσάλευτος
³not   ⁵being shaken.   Wherefore   ²kingdom   ¹an unshakable

παραλαμβάνοντες   ἔχωμεν   χάριν,   δι'   ἧς
¹receiving   let us have   grace,   through which

λατρεύωμεν   εὐαρέστως   τῷ   θεῷ,   μετὰ
we may serve   ²well-pleasingly   –   ¹God,   with

εὐλαβείας   καὶ   δέους·   **29** καὶ   γὰρ   ὁ   θεὸς
devoutness   and   awe;   for indeed   the   God

ἡμῶν   πῦρ   καταναλίσκον.
of us [is]   fire   a consuming.

Chapter 13

Ἡ   φιλαδελφία   μενέτω.   **2** τῆς
–   ²brotherly love   ¹Let *it* ³remain.   –

φιλοξενίας   μὴ   ἐπιλανθάνεσθε·   διὰ   ταύτης
of hospitality   Be ye not forgetful;   ²through   ³this

γὰρ   ἔλαθόν   τινες   ξενίσαντες   ἀγγέλους.
¹for   ⁴unconsciously†   ⁵some   ⁶entertaining(ed)   ⁷angels.

3 μιμνήσκεσθε   τῶν   δεσμίων   ὡς   συνδεδεμένοι,
Be ye mindful   of the   prisoners   as   *having been* bound
with [them],

τῶν   κακουχουμένων   ὡς   καὶ   αὐτοὶ   ὄντες
of the   *being* ill treated   as   also   [your]selves   being
[ones]

ἐν   σώματι.   **4** Τίμιος   ὁ   γάμος   ἐν   πᾶσιν
in [the] body.   ⁴honourable –   ²marriage   in   all
¹[Let]   ³[be]

καὶ   ἡ   κοίτη   ἀμίαντος·   πόρνους   γὰρ
and   the   bed   undefiled;   for fornicators

καὶ   μοιχοὺς   κρινεῖ   ὁ   θεός.   **5** Ἀφιλάργυρος
and   adulterers   ²will judge   –   ¹God.   ²without love of
money

ὁ   τρόπος,   ἀρκούμενοι   τοῖς   παροῦσιν·
¹[Let]   ³way of   being satisfied   the things   present;
³the   life   ⁴[be],   with
(your)

αὐτὸς   γὰρ   εἴρηκεν·   οὐ   μή   σε   ἀνῶ   οὐδ'
for he   has said: By no means   thee   will I   nor
leave

οὐ   μή   σε   ἐγκαταλίπω·   **6** ὥστε   θαρροῦντας
by no(any)   thee   I forsake;   so as   being of good
means   cheer

ἡμᾶς   λέγειν·   κύριος   ἐμοὶ   βοηθός,   οὐ
us   to say^b: [The] Lord   to me^c [is]   a helper,   not

φοβηθήσομαι·   τί   ποιήσει   μοι   ἄνθρωπος;
I will fear: what   ¹will ²do   ⁴to me   ³man ?

7 Μνημονεύετε   τῶν   ἡγουμένων   ὑμῶν,
Remember   the [ones]   leading   of you,

οἵτινες   ἐλάλησαν   ὑμῖν   τὸν   λόγον   τοῦ
who   spoke   to you   the   word   –

θεοῦ,   ὧν   ἀναθεωροῦντες   τὴν   ἔκβασιν   τῆς
of God,   ²of   ¹looking at   ³the   ⁴result   ⁵of
whom   the

ἀναστροφῆς   μιμεῖσθε   τὴν   πίστιν.   **8** Ἰησοῦς
⁶conduct   imitate ye   the(ir)   faith.   Jesus

Χριστὸς   ἐχθὲς   καὶ   σήμερον   ὁ   αὐτὸς
Christ   ⁴yesterday   ⁵and   ⁶to-day   ¹[is] ²the   ³same

καὶ   εἰς   τοὺς   αἰῶνας.   **9** Διδαχαῖς   ποικίλαις
and   unto   the   ages.   ²teachings   ³by various

καὶ   ξέναις   μὴ   παραφέρεσθε·   καλὸν   γὰρ
⁴and   ⁵strange   ¹Do not be carried away;   for [it is] good

χάριτι   βεβαιοῦσθαι   τὴν   καρδίαν,   οὐ
²by grace   ³to be confirmed   ¹the   ²heart,^b   ³not

βρώμασιν,   ἐν   οἷς   οὐκ   ὠφελήθησαν   οἱ
by foods,   by   which   ⁴were not profited   ¹the

περιπατοῦντες.   **10** ἔχομεν   θυσιαστήριον   ἐξ
²[ones] walking.   We have   an altar   of

οὗ   φαγεῖν   οὐκ   ἔχουσιν   ἐξουσίαν   οἱ   τῇ
which   ⁷to eat   ⁴have not   ⁶authority   ¹the   ²the
[ones]

σκηνῇ   λατρεύοντες.   **11** ὧν   γὰρ   εἰσφέρεται
⁴tabernacle   ³serving.   For ²of what   ¹is brought *in*

ζώων   τὸ   αἷμα   περὶ   ἁμαρτίας   εἰς   τὰ
⁴animals   ¹the   ²blood   ³concerning   ⁵sins   into   the

ἅγια   διὰ   τοῦ   ἀρχιερέως,   τούτων   τὰ
holies   through   the   high priest,   of these   the

σώματα   κατακαίεται   ἔξω   τῆς   παρεμβολῆς.
bodies   is(are) burned   outside   the   camp.

12 διὸ   καὶ   Ἰησοῦς,   ἵνα   ἁγιάσῃ   διὰ
Where-   in-   Jesus,   in order   he might ²through
fore   deed   that   sanctify

τοῦ   ἰδίου   αἵματος   τὸν   λαόν,   ἔξω   τῆς
⁴the(his)   ⁵own   ³blood   ¹the   ²people,   outside   the

πύλης   ἔπαθεν.   **13** τοίνυν   ἐξερχώμεθα   πρὸς
gate   suffered.   So   let us go forth   to

αὐτὸν   ἔξω   τῆς   παρεμβολῆς   τὸν   ὀνειδισμὸν
him   outside   the   camp   the   reproach

αὐτοῦ   φέροντες·   **14** οὐ   γὰρ   ἔχομεν   ὧδε
of him   bearing;   for ¹not   ²we have   here

μένουσαν   πόλιν,   ἀλλὰ   τὴν   μέλλουσαν
a continuing   city,   but   the [one]   coming

ἐπιζητοῦμεν.   **15** Δι'   αὐτοῦ   οὖν   ἀναφέρωμεν
we seek.   Through   him   therefore   let us offer up

θυσίαν   αἰνέσεως   διὰ   παντὸς   τῷ   θεῷ,
a sacrifice   of praise   always   –   to God,

τοῦτ'   ἔστιν   καρπὸν   χειλέων   ὁμολογούντων
this   is   fruit   of lips   confessing

τῷ   ὀνόματι   αὐτοῦ.   **16** τῆς   δὲ   εὐποιίας
to the   name   of him.   But of the   doing good

καὶ   κοινωνίας   μὴ   ἐπιλανθάνεσθε·   τοιαύταις
and   sharing   be ye not forgetful;   ²with such

γὰρ   θυσίαις   εὐαρεστεῖται   ὁ   θεός.   **17** Πεί-
¹for   sacrifices   ²is well pleased   –   ¹God.   Obey

θεσθε   τοῖς   ἡγουμένοις   ὑμῶν   καὶ   ὑπείκετε·
ye   the [ones] leading   of you   and   submit to
[them];

αὐτοὶ   γὰρ   ἀγρυπνοῦσιν   ὑπὲρ   τῶν   ψυχῶν
for they   watch   on behalf of the   souls

ὑμῶν   ὡς   λόγον   ἀποδώσοντες·   ἵνα   μετὰ
of you   as   ²account   ¹rendering*;   in or-   with
der that

χαρᾶς   τοῦτο   ποιῶσιν   καὶ   μὴ   στενάζ-
joy   ³this   ¹they may do   and   not   groan-

οντες·   ἀλυσιτελὲς   γὰρ   ὑμῖν   τοῦτο.
ing;   for profitless   to you   this
[would be].

18 Προσεύχεσθε   περὶ   ἡμῶν·   πειθόμεθα
Pray ye   concerning   us;   ²we are persuaded

γὰρ   ὅτι   καλὴν   συνείδησιν   ἔχομεν,   ἐν
¹for   that   a good   conscience   we have,   ⁴in

πᾶσιν   καλῶς   θέλοντες   ἀναστρέφεσθαι.
⁵all [respects]   ²well   ¹wishing   ³to behave.

* In the future.

King James Version

New International Version

live honestly. 19 But I beseech *you* the rather to do this, that I may be restored to you the sooner. 20 Now the God of peace, that brought again from the dead our Lord Jesus, that great Shepherd of the sheep, through the blood of the everlasting covenant, 21 Make you perfect in every good work to do his will, working in you that which is well pleasing in his sight, through Jesus Christ; to whom *be* glory for ever and ever. Amen. 22And I beseech you, brethren, suffer the word of exhortation: for I have written a letter unto you in few words. 23 Know ye that *our* brother Timothy is set at liberty; with whom, if he come shortly, I will see you. 24 Salute all them that have the rule over you, and all the saints. They of Italy salute you. 25 Grace *be* with you all. Amen.

Written to the Hebrews from Italy by Timothy.

every way. 19 I particularly urge you to pray so that I may be restored to you soon.

20 May the God of peace, who through the blood of the eternal covenant brought back from the dead our Lord Jesus, that great Shepherd of the sheep, 21 equip you with everything good for doing his will, and may he work in us what is pleasing to him, through Jesus Christ, to whom be glory for ever and ever. Amen.

22 Brothers, I urge you to bear with my word of exhortation, for I have written you only a short letter.

23 I want you to know that our brother Timothy has been released. If he arrives soon, I will come with him to see you.

24 Greet all your leaders and all God's people. Those from Italy send you their greetings.

25 Grace be with you all.

Greek Interlinear

19 περισσοτέρως   δὲ   παρακαλῶ   τοῦτο
And more abundantly   I beseech [you]   this

ποιῆσαι,   ἵνα   τάχιον   ἀποκατασταθῶ   ὑμῖν.
to do,   in or-   sooner   I may be restored   to you.
        der that

20 Ὁ   δὲ   θεὸς   τῆς   εἰρήνης,   ὁ   ἀναγαγὼν
Now the   God   -   of peace,   the   having led up
                                        [one]

ἐκ   νεκρῶν   τὸν   ποιμένα   τῶν   προβάτων
out   [the] dead   the   ²shepherd   ³of the   ⁴sheep
of

τὸν   μέγαν   ἐν   αἵματι   διαθήκης   αἰωνίου,
the   ¹great   in (? with)   blood   ²covenant   ¹of an eternal,

τὸν   κύριον   ἡμῶν   Ἰησοῦν,   **21** καταρτίσαι
the   Lord   of us   Jesus,   may he adjust

ὑμᾶς   ἐν   παντὶ   ἀγαθῷ   εἰς   τὸ   ποιῆσαι
you   in   every   good thing   for   the   to do

τὸ   θέλημα   αὐτοῦ,   ποιῶν   ἐν   ἡμῖν   τὸ
the   will   of him,   doing   in   us   the
                                            [thing]

εὐάρεστον   ἐνώπιον   αὐτοῦ   διὰ   Ἰησοῦ
wellpleasing   before   him   through   Jesus

Χριστοῦ,   ᾧ   ἡ   δόξα   εἰς   τοὺς   αἰῶνας
Christ,   to   [be]   glory   unto   the   ages
        whom the

τῶν   αἰώνων·   ἀμήν.   **22** Παρακαλῶ   δὲ
of the   ages: Amen.   And I beseech

ὑμᾶς,   ἀδελφοί,   ἀνέχεσθε   τοῦ   λόγου   τῆς
you.   brothers,   endure   the   word   -

παρακλήσεως·   καὶ   γὰρ   διὰ   βραχέων
of beseeching;   for indeed   through   few [words]

ἐπέστειλα   ὑμῖν.   **23** Γινώσκετε   τὸν   ἀδελφὸν
I wrote   to you.   Know ye   the   brother

ἡμῶν   Τιμόθεον   ἀπολελυμένον,   μεθ'   οὗ
of us   Timothy   having been released,   with whom

ἐὰν   τάχιον   ἔρχηται   ὄψομαι   ὑμᾶς.
if   sooner   I come   I will see   you.

24 Ἀσπάσασθε   πάντας   τοὺς   ἡγουμένους
Greet ye   all   the [ones]   leading

ὑμῶν   καὶ   πάντας   τοὺς   ἁγίους.   Ἀσπάζονται
of you   and   all   the   saints.   ⁶greet

ὑμᾶς   οἱ   ἀπὸ   τῆς   Ἰταλίας.
⁵you   ¹The [ones]   ²from   -   ³Italy.

25 Ἡ   χάρις   μετὰ   πάντων   ὑμῶν.
-    Grace [be]   with   all   you.

671

King James Version

New International Version

THE

GENERAL EPISTLE

OF

JAMES

JAMES

1 James, a servant of God and of the Lord Jesus Christ, to the twelve tribes which are scattered abroad, greeting. 2 My brethren, count it all joy when ye fall into divers temptations; 3 Knowing *this,* that the trying of your faith worketh patience. 4 But let patience have *her* perfect work, that ye may be perfect and entire, wanting nothing. 5 If any of you lack wisdom, let him ask of God, that giveth to all *men* liberally, and upbraideth not; and it shall be given him. 6 But let him ask in faith, nothing wavering: for he that wavereth is like a wave of the sea driven with the wind and tossed. 7 For let not that man think that he shall receive any thing of the Lord. 8A doubleminded man *is* unstable in all his ways. 9 Let the brother of low degree rejoice in that he is exalted: 10 But the rich, in that he is made low: because as the flower of the grass he shall pass away. 11 For the sun is no sooner risen with a burning heat, but it withereth the grass, and the flower thereof falleth, and the grace of the fashion of it perisheth: so also shall the rich man fade away in his ways. 12 Blessed *is* the man that endureth temptation: for when he is tried, he shall receive the crown of life, which the Lord hath promised to them that love him. 13 Let no man say when he is tempted, I am tempted of God: for God cannot be tempted with evil, neither tempteth he any man: 14 But every man is tempted, when he is drawn away of his own lust, and enticed. 15 Then when lust hath conceived, it bringeth forth sin; and sin, when it is finished, bringeth forth death. 16 Do not err, my beloved brethren. 17 Every good gift and every perfect gift is from above, and cometh down from the Father of lights, with whom is no variableness, neither shadow of turning. 18 Of his own will begat he us with the word of truth, that we should be a kind of firstfruits of his creatures. 19 Wherefore, my beloved brethren, let every man be swift to hear, slow to speak, slow to wrath: 20 For the wrath of man worketh not the righteousness of God. 21 Wherefore lay apart all filthiness and superfluity of naughtiness, and receive with meekness the engrafted word, which is able to save

1 James, a servant of God and of the Lord Jesus Christ,
To the twelve tribes scattered among the nations:
Greetings.

Trials and temptations

2 Consider it pure joy, my brothers, whenever you face trials of many kinds, 3 because you know that the testing of your faith develops perseverance. 4 Perseverance must finish its work so that you may be mature and complete, not lacking anything. 5 If any of you lacks wisdom, he should ask God, who gives generously to all without finding fault, and it will be given to him. 6 But when he asks, he must believe and not doubt, because he who doubts is like a wave of the sea, blown and tossed by the wind. 7 That man should not think he will receive anything from the Lord; 8 he is a double-minded man, unstable in all he does.

9 The brother in humble circumstances ought to take pride in his high position. 10 But the one who is rich should take pride in his low position, because he will pass away like a wild flower. 11 For the sun rises with scorching heat and withers the plant; its blossom falls and its beauty is destroyed. In the same way, the rich man will fade away even while he goes about his business.

12 Blessed is the man who perseveres under trial, because when he has stood the test, he will receive the victor's crown, the life God has promised to those who love him.

13 When tempted, no one should say, "God is tempting me." For God cannot be tempted by evil, nor does he tempt anyone; 14 but each one is tempted when, by his own evil desire, he is dragged away and enticed. 15 Then, after desire has conceived, it gives birth to sin; and sin, when it is full-grown, gives birth to death.

16 Don't be deceived, my dear brothers. 17 Every good and perfect gift is from above, coming down from the Father of the heavenly lights, who does not change like shifting shadows. 18 He chose to give us birth through the word of truth, that we might be a kind of firstfruits of all he created.

Listening and doing

19 My dear brothers, take note of this: Everyone should be quick to listen, slow to speak, and slow to become angry, 20 for man's anger does not bring about the righteous life that God desires. 21 Therefore, get rid of all moral filth and the evil that is so prevalent, and humbly accept the word planted in you, which can save you.

672

ΙΑΚΩΒΟΥ ΕΠΙΣΤΟΛΗ

Chapter 1

'Ιάκωβος θεοῦ καὶ κυρίου 'Ιησοῦ
James ¹of God ²and ⁴of [the] Lord ³Jesus

Χριστοῦ δοῦλος ταῖς δώδεκα φυλαῖς ταῖς
⁵Christ ¹a slave to the twelve tribes -

ἐν τῇ διασπορᾷ χαίρειν.
in the dispersion greeting.*

2 Πᾶσαν χαρὰν ἡγήσασθε, ἀδελφοί μου,
All joy deem [it], brothers of me,

ὅταν πειρασμοῖς περιπέσητε ποικίλοις,
whenever ²trials ¹ye fall ²into various,

3 γινώσκοντες ὅτι τὸ δοκίμιον ὑμῶν τῆς
knowing that the approved part ²of you ¹of the
=that which is approved in your faith

πίστεως κατεργάζεται ὑπομονήν. 4 ἡ δὲ
²faith works endurance. - And

ὑπομονὴ ἔργον τέλειον ἐχέτω, ἵνα ἦτε
endurance ²work ¹perfect ¹let it in or- ye may
have, der that be

τέλειοι καὶ ὁλόκληροι, ἐν μηδενὶ λειπόμενοι.
perfect and entire, in nothing wanting.

5 Εἰ δέ τις ὑμῶν λείπεται σοφίας, αἰτείτω
if But any- of you wants wisdom, let him
one ask

παρὰ τοῦ διδόντος θεοῦ πᾶσιν ἁπλῶς
from ¹the ²giving ¹God to all unre-
[one] men servedly

καὶ μὴ ὀνειδίζοντος, καὶ δοθήσεται αὐτῷ.
and not reproaching, and it will be given to him.

6 αἰτείτω δὲ ἐν πίστει, μηδὲν διακριν-
But let him ask in faith, nothing doubt-

όμενος· ὁ γὰρ διακρινόμενος ἔοικεν κλύδωνι
ing; for the [one] doubting is like a wave

θαλάσσης ἀνεμιζομένῳ καὶ ῥιπιζομένῳ.
of [the] sea being driven by wind and being tossed.

7 μὴ γὰρ οἰέσθω ὁ ἄνθρωπος ἐκεῖνος
For let not ²suppose ¹that ²man

ὅτι λήμψεταί τι παρὰ τοῦ κυρίου, 8 ἀνὴρ
that he will any- from the Lord, a man
receive thing

δίψυχος, ἀκατάστατος ἐν πάσαις ταῖς
two-souled, unsettled in all the

ὁδοῖς αὐτοῦ. 9 Καυχάσθω δὲ ὁ ἀδελφὸς
ways of him. But let ⁴boast ¹the ³brother

ὁ ταπεινὸς ἐν τῷ ὕψει αὐτοῦ, 10 ὁ δὲ
- ²humble in the height of him, and the

πλούσιος ἐν τῇ ταπεινώσει αὐτοῦ, ὅτι
rich one in the humiliation of him, because

ὡς ἄνθος χόρτου παρελεύσεται. 11 ἀνέτειλεν
as a flower of grass he will pass away. ⁴rose

γὰρ ὁ ἥλιος σὺν τῷ καύσωνι καὶ ἐξήρανεν
¹For ¹the ²sun with the hot wind and dried

τὸν χόρτον, καὶ τὸ ἄνθος αὐτοῦ ἐξέπεσεν
the grass, and the flower of it fell out

καὶ ἡ εὐπρέπεια τοῦ προσώπου αὐτοῦ
and the comeliness of the appearance of it

ἀπώλετο· οὕτως καὶ ὁ πλούσιος ἐν ταῖς
perished; thus also the rich man in the

πορείαις αὐτοῦ μαρανθήσεται. 12 Μακάριος
goings of him will fade away. Blessed

ἀνὴρ ὃς ὑπομένει πειρασμόν, ὅτι δόκιμος
[the] who endures trial, because ²approved
man

γενόμενος λήμψεται τὸν στέφανον τῆς
¹having become he will receive the crown -

ζωῆς, ὃν ἐπηγγείλατο τοῖς ἀγαπῶσιν αὐτόν.
of life, which he promised to the [ones] loving him.

13 Μηδεὶς πειραζόμενος λεγέτω ὅτι ἀπὸ
²no man ³being tempted ¹Let ⁴say[,] - From

θεοῦ πειράζομαι· ὁ γὰρ θεὸς ἀπείραστός
God I am tempted; - for God ²untempted

ἐστιν κακῶν, πειράζει δὲ αὐτὸς οὐδένα.
¹is of(with) and ²tempts ¹he no man.
evil things,

14 ἕκαστος δὲ πειράζεται ὑπὸ τῆς ἰδίας
But each man is tempted by the(his) own

ἐπιθυμίας ἐξελκόμενος καὶ δελεαζόμενος·
lusts being drawn out and being enticed;

15 εἶτα ἡ ἐπιθυμία συλλαβοῦσα τίκτει
then - lust having conceived bears

ἁμαρτίαν, ἡ δὲ ἁμαρτία ἀποτελεσθεῖσα
sin, - and sin having been
fully formed

ἀποκύει θάνατον. 16 Μὴ πλανᾶσθε, ἀδελφοί
brings forth death. Do not err, ²brothers

μου ἀγαπητοί.
¹of me ¹beloved.

17 Πᾶσα δόσις ἀγαθὴ καὶ πᾶν δώρημα
Every ²giving ¹good and every ²gift

τέλειον ἄνωθέν ἐστιν καταβαῖνον ἀπὸ τοῦ
¹perfect ⁴from above ¹is coming down from the

πατρὸς τῶν φώτων, παρ' ᾧ οὐκ ἔνι
Father of the lights, with whom ²has no place

παραλλαγὴ ἢ τροπῆς ἀποσκίασμα. 18 βου-
¹change ²or ⁴of turning ³shadow. Having

ληθεὶς ἀπεκύησεν ἡμᾶς λόγῳ ἀληθείας,
purposed he brought forth us by a word of truth,

εἰς τὸ εἶναι ἡμᾶς ἀπαρχήν τινα τῶν
for the to be usᵇ ¹firstfruit ¹a certain ²of
=that we should be the

αὐτοῦ κτισμάτων.
²of him ⁴creatures.

19 Ἴστε, ἀδελφοί μου ἀγαπητοί. ἔστω
Know ye, ²brothers ³of me ¹beloved. ¹let be

δὲ πᾶς ἄνθρωπος ταχὺς εἰς τὸ ἀκοῦσαι,
²But every ¹man swift for the to hear,

βραδὺς εἰς τὸ λαλῆσαι, βραδὺς εἰς ὀργήν·
slow for the to speak, slow to wrath;

20 ὀργὴ γὰρ ἀνδρὸς δικαιοσύνην θεοῦ
for [the] wrath of a man ¹[the] righteousness ²of God

οὐκ ἐργάζεται. 21 διὸ ἀποθέμενοι πᾶσαν
¹works not. Wherefore putting away all

ῥυπαρίαν καὶ περισσείαν κακίας ἐν πραΰ-
filthiness and superfluity of evil in meek-

τητι δέξασθε τὸν ἔμφυτον λόγον τὸν
ness receive ye the implanted word the

* See note on Phil. 3.16 in Introduction.

673

King James Version

your souls. 22 But be ye doers of the word, and not hearers only, deceiving your own selves. 23 For if any be a hearer of the word, and not a doer, he is like unto a man beholding his natural face in a glass: 24 For he beholdeth himself, and goeth his way, and straightway forgetteth what manner of man he was. 25 But whoso looketh into the perfect law of liberty, and continueth *therein*, he being not a forgetful hearer, but a doer of the work, this man shall be blessed in his deed. 26 If any man among you seem to be religious, and bridleth not his tongue, but deceiveth his own heart, this man's religion *is* vain. 27 Pure religion and undefiled before God and the Father is this, To visit the fatherless and widows in their affliction, *and* to keep himself unspotted from the world.

2 My brethren, have not the faith of our Lord Jesus Christ, *the Lord* of glory, with respect of persons. 2 For if there come unto your assembly a man with a gold ring, in goodly apparel, and there come in also a poor man in vile raiment; 3And ye have respect to him that weareth the gay clothing, and say unto him, Sit thou here in a good place; and say to the poor, Stand thou there, or sit here under my footstool: 4 Are ye not then partial in yourselves, and are become judges of evil thoughts? 5 Hearken, my beloved brethren, Hath not God chosen the poor of this world rich in faith, and heirs of the kingdom which he hath promised to them that love him? 6 But ye have despised the poor. Do not rich men oppress you, and draw you before the judgment seats? 7 Do not they blaspheme that worthy name by the which ye are called? 8 If ye fulfil the royal law according to the Scripture, Thou shalt love thy neighbour as thyself, ye do well: 9 But if ye have respect to persons, ye commit sin, and are convinced of the law as transgressors. 10 For whosoever shall keep the whole law, and yet offend in one *point*, he is guilty of all. 11 For he that said, Do not commit adultery, said also, Do not kill. Now if thou commit no adultery, yet if thou kill, thou art become a transgressor of the law. 12 So speak ye, and so do, as they that shall be judged by the law of liberty. 13 For he shall have judgment without mercy, that hath shewed no mercy; and mercy rejoiceth against judgment. 14 What *doth it* profit, my brethren, though a man say he hath faith, and have not works? can faith save him? 15 If a brother or sister be naked, and destitute of daily food, 16And one of you say unto them,

New International Version

22 Do not merely listen to the word, and so deceive yourselves. Do what it says. 23Anyone who listens to the word but does not do what it says is like a man who looks at his face in a mirror 24 and, after looking at himself, goes away and immediately forgets what he looks like. 25 But the man who looks intently into the perfect law that gives freedom, and continues to do this, not forgetting what he has heard, but doing it—he will be blessed in what he does. 26 If anyone considers himself religious and yet does not keep a tight rein on his tongue, he deceives himself and his religion is worthless. 27 Religion that God our Father accepts as pure and faultless is this: to look after orphans and widows in their distress and to keep oneself from being polluted by the world.

Favoritism forbidden

2 My brothers, as believers in our glorious Lord Jesus Christ, don't show favoritism. 2 Suppose a man comes into your meeting wearing a gold ring and fine clothes, and a poor man in shabby clothes also comes in. 3 If you show special attention to the man wearing fine clothes and say, "Here's a good seat for you," but say to the poor man, "You stand there" or, "Sit on the floor by my feet," 4 have you not discriminated among yourselves and become judges with evil thoughts?

5 Listen, my dear brothers: Has not God chosen those who are poor in the eyes of the world to be rich in faith and to inherit the kingdom he promised those who love him? 6 But you have insulted the poor. Is it not the rich who are exploiting you? Are they not the ones who are dragging you into court? 7Are they not the ones who are slandering the noble name of him to whom you belong?

8 If you really keep the royal law found in Scripture, "Love your neighbor as yourself," *a* you are doing right. 9 But if you show favoritism, you sin and are convicted by the law as law-breakers. 10 For whoever keeps the whole law, and yet stumbles at just one point, is guilty of breaking all of it. 11 For he who said, "Do not commit adultery," *b* also said, "Do not murder." *c* If you do not commit adultery but do commit murder, you have become a lawbreaker.

12 Speak and act as those who are going to be judged by the law that gives freedom, 13 because judgment without mercy will be shown to anyone who has not been merciful. Mercy triumphs over judgment!

Faith and deeds

14 What good is it, my brothers, if a man claims to have faith but has no deeds? Can such faith save him? 15 Suppose a brother or sister is without clothes and daily food. 16 If one of you

[a] Lev. 19:18. [b] Exodus 20:14; Deut. 5:18. [c] Exodus 20:13; Deut. 5:17.

Greek Interlinear

δυνάμενον σῶσαι τὰς ψυχὰς ὑμῶν. 22 γίν-
being able to save the souls of you. be-
εσθε δὲ ποιηταὶ λόγου, καὶ μὴ ἀκροαταὶ
come ye And doers of [the] word, and not hearers
μόνον παραλογιζόμενοι ἑαυτούς. 23 ὅτι
only misleading yourselves. Because
εἴ τις ἀκροατὴς λόγου ἐστὶν καὶ οὐ
if anyone ²a hearer ³of [the] word ¹is and not
ποιητής, οὗτος ἔοικεν ἀνδρὶ κατανοοῦντι
a doer, this one is like a man perceiving
τὸ πρόσωπον τῆς γενέσεως αὐτοῦ ἐν
the face of the birth of him in
ἐσόπτρῳ· 24 κατενόησεν γὰρ ἑαυτὸν καὶ
a mirror; for he perceived himself and
ἀπελήλυθεν, καὶ εὐθέως ἐπελάθετο ὁποῖος
has gone away, and straightway forgot what sort
ἦν. 25 ὁ δὲ παρακύψας εἰς νόμον
he was. But the [one] having looked into into ²law
τέλειον τὸν τῆς ἐλευθερίας καὶ παραμείνας,
²perfect ¹the – of freedom · and remaining.

οὐκ ἀκροατὴς ἐπιλησμονῆς γενόμενος ἀλλὰ
not ²a hearer ³of forgetfulness* ¹becoming but
ποιητὴς ἔργου, οὗτος μακάριος ἐν τῇ
a doer of [the] work, this one ²blessed ³in ⁴the
ποιήσει αὐτοῦ ἔσται. 26 Εἴ τις δοκεῖ
¹doing ⁵of him ¹will be. If anyone thinks
θρησκὸς εἶναι, μὴ χαλιναγωγῶν γλῶσσαν
²religious ¹to be, not bridling tongue
ἑαυτοῦ ἀλλὰ ἀπατῶν καρδίαν ἑαυτοῦ,
of himself but deceiving heart of himself.
τούτου μάταιος ἡ θρησκεία. 27 θρησκεία
of this one vain the religion. Religion
καθαρὰ καὶ ἀμίαντος παρὰ τῷ θεῷ
clean and undefiled before the God
καὶ πατρὶ αὕτη ἐστίν, ἐπισκέπτεσθαι
and Father ²this ¹is, to visit
ὀρφανοὺς καὶ χήρας ἐν τῇ θλίψει αὐτῶν,
orphans and widows in the affliction of them,
ἄσπιλον ἑαυτὸν τηρεῖν ἀπὸ τοῦ κόσμου.
unspotted himself to keep from the world.

Chapter 2

Ἀδελφοί μου, μὴ ἐν προσωπολημψίαις
Brothers of me, not in respects of persons
ἔχετε τὴν πίστιν τοῦ κυρίου ἡμῶν Ἰησοῦ
have ye the faith of the Lord of us Jesus
Χριστοῦ τῆς δόξης. 2 ἐὰν γὰρ εἰσέλθῃ
Christ[,] of the glory.✝ For if [there] enters
εἰς συναγωγὴν ὑμῶν ἀνὴρ χρυσοδακτύλιος
into a synagogue of you a man gold-fingered
ἐν ἐσθῆτι λαμπρᾷ, εἰσέλθῃ δὲ καὶ πτωχὸς
in ²clothing ¹splendid, and [there] enters also a poor man
ἐν ῥυπαρᾷ ἐσθῆτι, 3 ἐπιβλέψητε δὲ ἐπὶ
in shabby clothing, and ye look on on
τὸν φοροῦντα τὴν ἐσθῆτα τὴν λαμπρὰν
the [one] wearing the clothing – splendid
καὶ εἴπητε· σὺ κάθου ὧδε καλῶς, καὶ
and say: ¹thou ²Sit here well, and
τῷ πτωχῷ εἴπητε· σὺ στῆθι ἐκεῖ ἢ
to the poor man ye say: ¹thou ²Stand there or
κάθου ὑπὸ τὸ ὑποπόδιόν μου, 4 οὐ
sit under the footstool of me, not
διεκρίθητε ἐν ἑαυτοῖς καὶ ἐγένεσθε κριταὶ
did ye dis- among yourselves and became judges
criminate
διαλογισμῶν πονηρῶν; 5 Ἀκούσατε, ἀδελφοί
¹thoughts ¹of evil ?§ Hear ye, brothers
μου ἀγαπητοί. οὐχ ὁ θεὸς ἐξελέξατο
of me beloved. ¹not – ²God ¹Chose
τοὺς πτωχοὺς τῷ κόσμῳ πλουσίους ἐν
the poor in the world rich in
πίστει καὶ κληρονόμους τῆς βασιλείας
faith and heirs of the kingdom
ἧς ἐπηγγείλατο τοῖς ἀγαπῶσιν αὐτόν;
which he promised to the [ones] loving him?
6 ὑμεῖς δὲ ἠτιμάσατε τὸν πτωχόν. οὐχ
But ye dishonoured the poor man. [Do] not
οἱ πλούσιοι καταδυναστεύουσιν ὑμῶν, καὶ
the rich men oppress you, and
αὐτοὶ ἕλκουσιν ὑμᾶς εἰς κριτήρια; 7 οὐκ
they drag you to tribunals ? [Do] not
αὐτοὶ βλασφημοῦσιν τὸ καλὸν ὄνομα τὸ
they blaspheme the good name the
ἐπικληθὲν ἐφ' ὑμᾶς; 8 εἰ μέντοι νόμον
called on on you ? If indeed ²law

τελεῖτε βασιλικὸν κατὰ τὴν γραφήν·
¹ye fulfil ²a royal according to the scripture:
ἀγαπήσεις τὸν πλησίον σου ὡς σεαυτόν,
Thou shalt love the neighbour of thee as thyself,
καλῶς ποιεῖτε· 9 εἰ δὲ προσωπολημπτεῖτε,
²well ¹ye do; but if ye respect persons,
ἁμαρτίαν ἐργάζεσθε, ἐλεγχόμενοι ὑπὸ τοῦ
²sin ¹ye work, being reproved by the
νόμου ὡς παραβάται. 10 ὅστις γὰρ
law as transgressors. For ²[he] who
ὅλον τὸν νόμον τηρήσῃ, πταίσῃ δὲ ἐν
²all ⁴the ⁵law ³keeps, yet stumbles in
ἑνί, γέγονεν πάντων ἔνοχος. 11 ὁ γὰρ
one he has ¹of all ¹guilty. For the
thing, become [one]
εἰπών· μὴ μοιχεύσῃς, εἶπεν καὶ· μὴ
saying: Do not commit adultery, said also: not
φονεύσῃς· εἰ δὲ οὐ μοιχεύεις, φονεύεις
Do murder; now if thou dost not commit adultery, ²murderest
δέ, γέγονας παραβάτης νόμου. 12 οὕτως
¹but, thou hast a transgressor of [the] So
become law.
λαλεῖτε καὶ οὕτως ποιεῖτε ὡς διὰ νόμου
speak ye and so do ye as ²through ⁴a law
ἐλευθερίας μέλλοντες κρίνεσθαι. 13 ἡ γὰρ
¹of freedom ³being about ¹to be judged. For the
κρίσις ἀνέλεος τῷ μὴ ποιήσαντι ἔλεος·
judg- [will unmerci- to the not do(show)ing mercy;
ment be] ful [one]
κατακαυχᾶται ἔλεος κρίσεως. 14 Τί τὸ
²exults over ¹mercy of judgment. What [is] the
ὄφελος, ἀδελφοί μου, ἐὰν πίστιν λέγῃ
profit, brothers of me, if ⁴faith ¹says
τις ἔχειν ἔργα δὲ μὴ ἔχῃ; μὴ δύναται
²any- ⁵to have ⁶works ³but ⁷not ⁸has ? not can
one
ἡ πίστις σῶσαι αὐτόν; 15 ἐὰν ἀδελφὸς
the faith to save him ? If a brother
ἢ ἀδελφὴ γυμνοὶ ὑπάρχωσιν καὶ λειπόμενοι
or a sister ²naked ¹are and lacking
τῆς ἐφημέρου τροφῆς, 16 εἴπῃ δέ τις
of the daily food, ¹and ⁴says ¹anyone

* Genitive of quality: " a forgetful hearer."
✝ That is, taking " the glory " as in apposition to "Jesus Christ";
see Luke 2. 32b.
§ Genitive of quality: " evil-thinking judges."

King James Version

Depart in peace, be *ye* warmed and filled; notwithstanding ye give them not those things which are needful to the body; what *doth it* profit? 17 Even so faith, if it hath not works, is dead, being alone. 18 Yea, a man may say, Thou hast faith, and I have works: shew me thy faith without thy works, and I will shew thee my faith by my works. 19 Thou believest that there is one God; thou doest well: the devils also believe, and tremble. 20 But wilt thou know, O vain man, that faith without works is dead? 21 Was not Abraham our father justified by works, when he had offered Isaac his son upon the altar? 22 Seest thou how faith wrought with his works, and by works was faith made perfect? 23 And the Scripture was fulfilled which saith, Abraham believed God, and it was imputed unto him for righteousness: and he was called the Friend of God. 24 Ye see then how that by works a man is justified, and not by faith only. 25 Likewise also was not Rahab the harlot justified by works, when she had received the messengers, and had sent *them* out another way? 26 For as the body without the spirit is dead, so faith without works is dead also.

3 My brethren, be not many masters, knowing that we shall receive the greater condemnation. 2 For in many things we offend all. If any man offend not in word, the same *is* a perfect man, *and* able also to bridle the whole body. 3 Behold, we put bits in the horses' mouths, that they may obey us; and we turn about their whole body. 4 Behold also the ships, which though *they be* so great, and *are* driven of fierce winds, yet are they turned about with a very small helm, whithersoever the governor listeth. 5 Even so the tongue is a little member, and boasteth great things. Behold, how great a matter a little fire kindleth! 6 And the tongue *is* a fire, a world of iniquity: so is the tongue among our members, that it defileth the whole body, and setteth on fire the course of nature; and it is set on fire of hell. 7 For every kind of beasts, and of birds, and of serpents, and of things in the sea, is tamed, and hath been tamed of mankind: 8 But the tongue can no man tame; *it is* an unruly evil, full of deadly poison. 9 Therewith bless we God, even the Father; and therewith curse we men, which are made after the similitude of God. 10 Out of the same mouth proceedeth blessing and cursing. My brethren, these things ought not so to be. 11 Doth a fountain send forth at the same place sweet *water*

New International Version

says to him, "Go, I wish you well; keep warm and well fed," but does nothing about his physical needs, what good is it? 17 In the same way, faith by itself, if it is not accompanied by action, is dead.
18 But someone will say, "You have faith; I have deeds."
Show me your faith without deeds, and I will show you my faith by what I do. 19 You believe that there is one God. Good! Even the demons believe that—and shudder.
20 You foolish man, do you want evidence that faith without deeds is useless? [d] 21 Was not our ancestor Abraham considered righteous for what he did when he offered his son Isaac on the altar? 22 You see that his faith and his actions were working together, and his faith was made complete by what he did. 23 And the scripture was fulfilled that says, "Abraham believed God, and it was credited to him as righteousness," [e] and he was called God's friend. 24 You see that a person is justified by what he does and not by faith alone.
25 In the same way, was not even Rahab the prostitute considered righteous for what she did when she gave lodging to the spies and sent them off in a different direction? 26 As the body without the spirit is dead, so faith without deeds is dead.

Taming the tongue

3 Not many of you should act as teachers, my brothers, because you know that we who teach will be judged more strictly. 2 We all stumble in many ways. If anyone is never at fault in what he says, he is a perfect man, able to keep his whole body in check.
3 When we put bits into the mouths of horses to make them obey us, we can turn the whole animal. 4 Or take ships as an example. Although they are so large and are driven by strong winds, they are steered by a very small rudder wherever the pilot wants to go. 5 Likewise the tongue is a small part of the body, but it makes great boasts. Consider what a great forest is set on fire by a small spark. 6 The tongue also is a fire, a world of evil among the parts of the body. It corrupts the whole person, sets the whole course of his life on fire, and is itself set on fire by hell.
7 All kinds of animals, birds, reptiles and creatures of the sea are being tamed and have been tamed by man, 8 but no man can tame the tongue. It is a restless evil, full of deadly poison.
9 With the tongue we praise our Lord and Father, and with it we curse men, who have been made in God's likeness. 10 Out of the same mouth come praise and cursing. My brothers, this should not be. 11 Can both fresh water

[d] Some early MSS read *dead*. [e] Gen. 15:6.

Greek Interlinear

αὐτοῖς ἐξ ὑμῶν· ὑπάγετε ἐν εἰρήνῃ,
'to them 'of 'you: Go ye in peace,
θερμαίνεσθε καὶ χορτάζεσθε, μὴ δῶτε
be warmed and filled, 'not 'ye give
δὲ αὐτοῖς τὰ ἐπιτήδεια τοῦ σώματος,
'but 'them the necessaries of the body,
τί τὸ ὄφελος; 17 οὕτως καὶ ἡ πίστις,
what [is] the profit? So indeed – faith.
ἐὰν μὴ ἔχῃ ἔργα, νεκρά ἐστιν καθ'
if it has not works, 'dead 'is by
ἑαυτήν. 18 ἀλλ' ἐρεῖ τις· σὺ πίστιν
itself. But 'will say 'someone: Thou 'faith
ἔχεις, κἀγὼ ἔργα ἔχω· δεῖξόν μοι τὴν
'hast, and I 'works 'have; show me the
πίστιν σου χωρὶς τῶν ἔργων, κἀγώ
faith of thee without the works, and I
σοι δείξω ἐκ τῶν ἔργων μου τὴν πίστιν.
thee will show 'by 'the 'works 'of me 'the 'faith.
19 σὺ πιστεύεις ὅτι εἷς ἐστιν ὁ θεός;
Thou believest that 'one 'is – 'God?
καλῶς ποιεῖς· καὶ τὰ δαιμόνια πιστεύουσιν
'well 'thou doest; also the demons believe
καὶ φρίσσουσιν. 20 θέλεις δὲ γνῶναι,
and shudder. But art thou willing to know,
ὦ ἄνθρωπε κενέ, ὅτι ἡ πίστις χωρὶς
O 'man 'vain, that – faith without
τῶν ἔργων ἀργή ἐστιν; 21 Ἀβραὰμ ὁ
– works barren is? Abraham the
πατὴρ ἡμῶν οὐκ ἐξ ἔργων ἐδικαιώθη,
father of us not by works was justified.

ἀνενέγκας Ἰσαὰκ τὸν υἱὸν αὐτοῦ ἐπὶ
offering up Isaac the son of him on
τὸ θυσιαστήριον; 22 βλέπεις ὅτι ἡ πίστις
the altar? Thou seest that – faith
συνήργει τοῖς ἔργοις αὐτοῦ, καὶ ἐκ
worked with the works of him, and by
τῶν ἔργων ἡ πίστις ἐτελειώθη, 23 καὶ
the works the faith was perfected, and
ἐπληρώθη ἡ γραφὴ ἡ λέγουσα· ἐπίστευσεν
was fulfilled the scripture – saying: believed
δὲ Ἀβραὰμ τῷ θεῷ, καὶ ἐλογίσθη αὐτῷ
And Abraham – God, and it was reckoned to him
εἰς δικαιοσύνην, καὶ φίλος θεοῦ ἐκλήθη.
for righteousness, and 'friend 'of God 'he was called.
24 ὁρᾶτε ὅτι ἐξ ἔργων δικαιοῦται ἄνθρωπος
Ye see that by works 'is justified 'a man
καὶ οὐκ ἐκ πίστεως μόνον. 25 ὁμοίως
and not by faith only. likewise
δὲ καὶ Ῥαὰβ ἡ πόρνη οὐκ ἐξ ἔργων
And also Rahab the prostitute not by works
ἐδικαιώθη, ὑποδεξαμένη τοὺς ἀγγέλους καὶ
was justified, entertaining the messengers and
ἑτέρᾳ ὁδῷ ἐκβαλοῦσα; 26 ὥσπερ γὰρ τὸ
by a way sending [them] For as the
different forth?
σῶμα χωρὶς πνεύματος νεκρόν ἐστιν, οὕτως
body without spirit 'dead 'is, so
καὶ ἡ πίστις χωρὶς ἔργων νεκρά ἐστιν.
also – faith without works 'dead 'is.

Chapter 3

Μὴ πολλοὶ διδάσκαλοι γίνεσθε, ἀδελφοί
'not 'many 'teachers 'Become ye, brothers
μου, εἰδότες ὅτι μεῖζον κρίμα λημψόμεθα.
of me, knowing that greater judgment we shall receive.
2 πολλὰ γὰρ πταίομεν ἅπαντες· εἴ τις
For [in] many [respects] we stumble all; if anyone
ἐν λόγῳ οὐ πταίει, οὗτος τέλειος ἀνήρ,
'in 'word 'stumbles not, . this [is] a perfect man,
δυνατὸς χαλιναγωγῆσαι καὶ ὅλον τὸ σῶμα.
able 'to bridle 'indeed all the body.
3 εἰ δὲ τῶν ἵππων τοὺς χαλινοὺς εἰς
Now if – 'of horses – 'bridles 'into
τὰ στόματα βάλλομεν εἰς τὸ πείθεσθαι
'the 'mouths 'we put for the to obey
=to make them obey us,
αὐτοὺς ἡμῖν, καὶ ὅλον τὸ σῶμα αὐτῶν
them 'to us, and 'all 'the 'body 'of them
μετάγομεν. 4 ἰδοὺ καὶ τὰ πλοῖα, τηλικαῦτα
'we direct. Behold also the ships, 'so great
ὄντα καὶ ὑπὸ ἀνέμων σκληρῶν ἐλαυνόμενα,
'being 'and 'by 'winds 'hard(strong) 'being driven,
μετάγεται ὑπὸ ἐλαχίστου πηδαλίου ὅπου
is(are) directed by a very little helm where
ἡ ὁρμὴ τοῦ εὐθύνοντος βούλεται· 5 οὕτως
the impulse of the [one] steering resolves; so
καὶ ἡ γλῶσσα μικρὸν μέλος ἐστὶν καὶ
also the tongue 'a little 'member 'is and
μεγάλα αὐχεῖ. ἰδοὺ ἡλίκον πῦρ ἡλίκον
great things boasts. Behold how little a fire 'how great
ὕλην ἀνάπτει· 6 καὶ ἡ γλῶσσα πῦρ,
'wood 'kindles; and the tongue [is] a fire,
ὁ κόσμος τῆς ἀδικίας, ἡ γλῶσσα καθίστα-
the world of iniquity, the tongue is

ται ἐν τοῖς μέλεσιν ἡμῶν, ἡ σπιλοῦσα
set among the members of us, – spotting
ὅλον τὸ σῶμα καὶ φλογίζουσα τὸν
all the body and inflaming the
τροχὸν τῆς γενέσεως καὶ φλογιζομένη
course – of nature and being inflamed
ὑπὸ τῆς γεέννης. 7 πᾶσα γὰρ φύσις
by – gehenna. For every nature
θηρίων τε καὶ πετεινῶν, ἑρπετῶν τε
'of beasts 'both and 'of birds, 'of reptiles 'both
καὶ ἐναλίων δαμάζεται καὶ δεδάμασται
and of marine is tamed and has been tamed
creatures
τῇ φύσει τῇ ἀνθρωπίνῃ, 8 τὴν δὲ
by the 'nature – 'human, but the
γλῶσσαν οὐδεὶς δαμάσαι δύναται ἀνθρώπων·
tongue 'no one 'to tame 'is able 'of men;
ἀκατάστατον κακόν, μεστὴ ἰοῦ θανατηφόρου.
an unruly evil, full 'poison 'of death-dealing.
9 ἐν αὐτῇ εὐλογοῦμεν τὸν κύριον καὶ
By this we bless the Lord and
πατέρα, καὶ ἐν αὐτῇ καταρώμεθα τοὺς
Father, and by this we curse the
ἀνθρώπους τοὺς καθ' ὁμοίωσιν θεοῦ
men – 'according to 'likeness 'of God
γεγονότας· 10 ἐκ τοῦ αὐτοῦ στόματος ἐξέρχεται
'having become; out of the same mouth comes forth
εὐλογία καὶ κατάρα. οὐ χρή, ἀδελφοί
blessing and cursing. It is not fitting, brothers
μου, ταῦτα οὕτως γίνεσθαι. 11 μήτι
of me, these things so to be. Not
ἡ πηγὴ ἐκ τῆς αὐτῆς ὀπῆς βρύει τὸ
the fountain out of the same hole sends forth the

677

King James Version

and bitter? 12 Can the fig tree, my brethren, bear olive berries? either a vine, figs? so *can* no fountain both yield salt water and fresh. 13 Who *is* a wise man and endued with knowledge among you? let him shew out of a good conversation his works with meekness of wisdom. 14 But if ye have bitter envying and strife in your hearts, glory not, and lie not against the truth. 15 This wisdom descendeth not from above, but *is* earthly, sensual, devilish. 16 For where envying and strife *is,* there *is* confusion and every evil work. 17 But the wisdom that is from above is first pure, then peaceable, gentle, *and* easy to be entreated, full of mercy and good fruits, without partiality, and without hypocrisy. 18 And the fruit of righteousness is sown in peace of them that make peace.

4 From whence *come* wars and fightings among you? *come they* not hence, *even* of your lusts that war in your members? 2 Ye lust, and have not: ye kill, and desire to have, and cannot obtain: ye fight and war, yet ye have not, because ye ask not. 3 Ye ask, and receive not, because ye ask amiss, that ye may consume *it* upon your lusts. 4 Ye adulterers and adulteresses, know ye not that the friendship of the world is enmity with God? whosoever therefore will be a friend of the world is the enemy of God. 5 Do ye think that the Scripture saith in vain, The spirit that dwelleth in us lusteth to envy? 6 But he giveth more grace. Wherefore he saith, God resisteth the proud, but giveth grace unto the humble. 7 Submit yourselves therefore to God. Resist the devil, and he will flee from you. 8 Draw nigh to God, and he will draw nigh to you. Cleanse *your* hands, ye sinners; and purify *your* hearts, ye doubleminded. 9 Be afflicted, and mourn, and weep: let your laughter be turned to mourning, and *your* joy to heaviness. 10 Humble yourselves in the sight of the Lord, and he shall lift you up. 11 Speak not evil one of another, brethren. He that speaketh evil of *his* brother, and judgeth his brother, speaketh evil of the law, and judgeth the law: but if thou judge the law, thou art not a doer of the law, but a judge. 12 There is one lawgiver, who is able to save and to destroy: who art thou that judgest another? 13 Go to now, ye that say, To day or to morrow we will go into such a city, and continue there a year, and buy and sell, and get gain: 14 Whereas ye know not what *shall be* on the morrow. For what *is* your life? It is even a vapour, that appeareth for a little time, and then vanisheth away. 15 For that ye *ought* to say, If

New International Version

and salt water flow from the same spring? 12 My brothers, can a fig tree bear olives, or a grapevine bear figs? Neither can a salt spring produce fresh water.

Two kinds of wisdom

13 Who is wise and understanding among you? Let him show it by his good life, by deeds done in the humility that comes from wisdom. 14 But if you harbor bitter envy and selfish ambition in your hearts, do not boast about it or deny the truth. 15 Such "wisdom" does not come down from heaven but is earthly, unspiritual, of the devil. 16 For where you have envy and selfish ambition, there you find disorder and every evil practice.

17 But the wisdom that comes from heaven is first of all pure; then peace-loving, considerate, submissive, full of mercy and good fruit, impartial and sincere. 18 Peacemakers who sow in peace raise a harvest of righteousness.

Submit yourselves to God

4 What causes fights and quarrels among you? Don't they come from your desires that battle within you? 2 You want something but don't get it. You kill and covet, but you cannot have what you want. You quarrel and fight. You do not have, because you do not ask God. 3 When you ask, you do not receive, because you ask with wrong motives, that you may spend what you get on your pleasures.

4 You adulterous people, don't you know that friendship with the world is hatred toward God? Anyone who chooses to be a friend of the world becomes an enemy of God. 5 Or do you think Scripture says without reason that the spirit he caused to live in us tends toward envy,[f] 6 but he gives us more grace? That is why Scripture says:

"God opposes the proud,
    but gives grace to the humble."[g]

7 Submit yourselves, then, to God. Resist the devil, and he will flee from you. 8 Come near to God and he will come near to you. Wash your hands, you sinners, and purify your hearts, you double-minded. 9 Grieve, mourn and wail. Change your laughter to mourning and your joy to gloom. 10 Humble yourselves before the Lord, and he will lift you up.

11 Brothers, do not slander one another. Anyone who speaks against his brother or judges him, speaks against the law and judges it. When you judge the law, you are not keeping it, but sitting in judgment on it. 12 There is only one Lawgiver and Judge, the one who is able to save and destroy. But you—who are you to judge your neighbor?

Boasting about tomorrow

13 Now listen, you who say, "Today or tomorrow we will go to this or that city, spend a year there, carry on business and make money." 14 Why, you do not even know what will happen tomorrow. What is your life? You are a mist that appears for a little while and then vanishes. 15 Instead, you ought to say, "If it is

---

[f] Or *that God jealously longs for the spirit that he made to live in us;* or *that the Spirit he caused to live in us longs jealously.* [g] Prov. 3:34.

Greek Interlinear

γλυκὺ καὶ τὸ πικρόν; 12 μὴ δύναται,
sweet and the bitter? Not can,

ἀδελφοί μου, συκῆ ἐλαίας ποιῆσαι ἢ
brothers of me, a fig-tree ²olives ¹to produce or

ἄμπελος σῦκα; οὔτε ἁλυκὸν γλυκὺ
a vine figs? neither ¹salt ⁴sweet

ποιῆσαι ὕδωρ. 13 Τίς σοφὸς καὶ ἐπιστήμων
¹to make ²water. Who [is] wise and knowing

ἐν ὑμῖν; δειξάτω ἐκ τῆς καλῆς ἀναστροφῆς
among you? let him show by the(his) good conduct

τὰ ἔργα αὐτοῦ ἐν πραΰτητι σοφίας.★
the works of him in meekness of wisdom.★

14 εἰ δὲ ζῆλον πικρὸν ἔχετε καὶ ἐριθείαν
But if ²jealousy ³bitter ¹ye have and rivalry

ἐν τῇ καρδίᾳ ὑμῶν, μὴ κατακαυχᾶσθε
in the heart of you, do not exult over

καὶ ψεύδεσθε κατὰ τῆς ἀληθείας. 15 οὐκ
and lie against the truth. ⁴not

ἔστιν αὕτη ἡ σοφία ἄνωθεν κατερχομένη,
³is ¹This - ²wisdom ⁴from above ⁵coming down,

ἀλλὰ ἐπίγειος, ψυχική, δαιμονιώδης· 16 ὅπου
but [is] earthly, natural, demon-like; ²where

γὰρ ζῆλος καὶ ἐριθεία, ἐκεῖ ἀκαταστασία
¹for jealousy and rivalry [are], there [is] tumult

καὶ πᾶν φαῦλον πρᾶγμα. 17 ἡ δὲ ἄνωθεν
and every worthless practice. But ¹the ²from above

σοφία πρῶτον μὲν ἀγνή ἐστιν, ἔπειτα
³wisdom ⁴firstly - ⁵pure ⁶is, then

εἰρηνική, ἐπιεικής, εὐπειθής, μεστὴ ἐλέους
peaceable, forbearing, compliant, full of mercy

καὶ καρπῶν ἀγαθῶν, ἀδιάκριτος, ἀνυπό-
and ²fruits ¹of good, without uncertainty, un-

κριτος. 18 καρπὸς δὲ δικαιοσύνης ἐν
feigned. And [the] fruit ²of righteousness ³in

εἰρήνῃ σπείρεται τοῖς ποιοῦσιν εἰρήνην.
⁴peace ¹is sown for the [ones] making peace.

Chapter 4

Πόθεν πόλεμοι καὶ πόθεν μάχαι ἐν
Whence wars and whence fights among

ὑμῖν; οὐκ ἐντεῦθεν, ἐκ τῶν ἡδονῶν
you? not thence, out of the pleasures

ὑμῶν τῶν στρατευομένων ἐν τοῖς μέλεσιν
of you - soldiering in the members

ὑμῶν; 2 ἐπιθυμεῖτε, καὶ οὐκ ἔχετε·
of you? Ye desire, and have not;

φονεύετε καὶ ζηλοῦτε, καὶ οὐ δύνασθε
ye murder and are jealous, and are not able

ἐπιτυχεῖν· μάχεσθε καὶ πολεμεῖτε. οὐκ
to obtain; ye fight and ye war. not

ἔχετε διὰ τὸ μὴ αἰτεῖσθαι ὑμᾶς· 3 αἰτεῖτε
Ye have be- the not to ask youᵇ; ye ask
cause of
= because ye ask not;

καὶ οὐ λαμβάνετε, διότι κακῶς αἰτεῖσθε,
and receive not, because ²ill ¹ye ask,

ἵνα ἐν ταῖς ἡδοναῖς ὑμῶν δαπανήσητε.
in or- in the pleasures of you ye may spend.
der that

4 μοιχαλίδες, οὐκ οἴδατε ὅτι ἡ φιλία
Adulteresses, know ye not that the friendship

τοῦ κόσμου ἔχθρα τοῦ θεοῦ ἐστιν; ὃς
of the world ¹enmity - ²of God ³is? Who-

ἐὰν οὖν βουληθῇ φίλος εἶναι τοῦ κόσμου,
ever therefore ¹resolves ²a friend ³to be of the world,

ἐχθρὸς τοῦ θεοῦ καθίσταται. 5 ἢ δοκεῖτε
¹an enemy - ²of God ³is constituted. Or think ye

ὅτι κενῶς ἡ γραφὴ λέγει· πρὸς φθόνον
that vainly the scripture says: ⁴to ⁵envy

ἐπιποθεῖ τὸ πνεῦμα ὃ κατῴκισεν ἐν
³yearns ¹The ²Spirit ⁶which ⁷dwelt ⁸in

ἡμῖν; 6 μείζονα δὲ δίδωσιν χάριν· διὸ
⁹you? But ¹greater ²he gives ³grace; wherefore

λέγει· ὁ θεὸς ὑπερηφάνοις ἀντιτάσσεται,
it² says: - God ²arrogant men ¹resists,

ταπεινοῖς δὲ δίδωσιν χάριν. 7 ὑποτάγητε
but to humble men he gives grace. Be ye subject

οὖν τῷ θεῷ· ἀντίστητε δὲ τῷ διαβόλῳ,
there- - to God; but oppose the devil,
fore

καὶ φεύξεται ἀφ' ὑμῶν· 8 ἐγγίσατε τῷ
and he will flee from you; draw near -

θεῷ, καὶ ἐγγίσει ὑμῖν. καθαρίσατε
to God, and he will draw near to you. Cleanse ye

χεῖρας, ἁμαρτωλοί, καὶ ἁγνίσατε καρδίας,
hands, sinners, and purify hearts,

δίψυχοι. 9 ταλαιπωρήσατε καὶ πενθήσατε
two-souled Be ye distressed and mourn
(double-minded).

καὶ κλαύσατε· ὁ γέλως ὑμῶν εἰς πένθος
and weep; the laughter of you to mourning

μετατραπήτω καὶ ἡ χαρὰ εἰς κατήφειαν.
let it be turned and the joy to dejection.

10 ταπεινώθητε ἐνώπιον κυρίου, καὶ ὑψώσει
Be ye humbled before [the] Lord, and he will exalt

ὑμᾶς. 11 Μὴ καταλαλεῖτε ἀλλήλων, ἀδελφοί.
you. Speak not against one another, brothers.

ὁ καταλαλῶν ἀδελφοῦ ἢ κρίνων τὸν
The ¹speaking a brother or judging the
[one] ²against

ἀδελφὸν αὐτοῦ καταλαλεῖ νόμου καὶ κρίνει
brother of him speaks against law and judges

νόμον· εἰ δὲ νόμον κρίνεις, οὐκ εἶ
law; and if law thou judgest, thou art not

ποιητὴς νόμου ἀλλὰ κριτής. 12 εἷς ἐστιν
a doer of law but a judge. One is

νομοθέτης καὶ κριτής, ὁ δυνάμενος
lawgiver and judge, the [one] being able

σῶσαι καὶ ἀπολέσαι· σὺ δὲ τίς εἶ, ὁ
to save and to destroy; ³thou ¹and ²who ⁴art, the

κρίνων τὸν πλησίον;
[one] judging the(thy) neighbour?

13 Ἄγε νῦν οἱ λέγοντες· σήμερον ἢ
Come now the [ones] saying: To-day or

αὔριον πορευσόμεθα εἰς τήνδε τὴν πόλιν
to-morrow we will go into this the city

καὶ ποιήσομεν ἐκεῖ ἐνιαυτὸν καὶ ἐμπορευ-
and we will do there a year and we will

σόμεθα καὶ κερδήσομεν· 14 οἵτινες οὐκ
trade and we will make a profit; who not

ἐπίστασθε τῆς αὔριον ποία ἡ ζωὴ ὑμῶν.
ye know ²of the ³morrow ¹what ⁴the ⁵life ⁶of you
[will be].

ἀτμὶς γάρ ἐστε ἡ πρὸς ὀλίγον φαινομένη,
For ²a vapour ¹ye are - ³for ⁴a little while ⁵appearing,

ἔπειτα καὶ ἀφανιζομένη· 15 ἀντὶ τοῦ
thereafter indeed disappearing; instead of the

★ Genitive of quality : " a wise meekness."

² That is, " the scripture " (as ver. 5).

King James Version

the Lord will, we shall live, and do this, or that. 16 But now ye rejoice in your boastings: all such rejoicing is evil. 17 Therefore to him that knoweth to do good, and doeth *it* not, to him it is sin.

5 Go to now, *ye* rich men, weep and howl for your miseries that shall come upon *you.* 2 Your riches are corrupted, and your garments are motheaten. 3 Your gold and silver is cankered; and the rust of them shall be a witness against you, and shall eat your flesh as it were fire. Ye have heaped treasure together for the last days. 4 Behold, the hire of the labourers who have reaped down your fields, which is of you kept back by fraud, crieth: and the cries of them which have reaped are entered into the ears of the Lord of Sabaoth. 5 Ye have lived in pleasure on the earth, and been wanton; ye have nourished your hearts, as in a day of slaughter. 6 Ye have condemned *and* killed the just; *and* he doth not resist you. 7 Be patient therefore, brethren, unto the coming of the Lord. Behold, the husbandman waiteth for the precious fruit of the earth, and hath long patience for it, until he receive the early and latter rain. 8 Be ye also patient; stablish your hearts: for the coming of the Lord draweth nigh. 9 Grudge not one against another, brethren, lest ye be condemned: behold, the judge standeth before the door. 10 Take, my brethren, the prophets, who have spoken in the name of the Lord, for an example of suffering affliction, and of patience. 11 Behold, we count them happy which endure. Ye have heard of the patience of Job, and have seen the end of the Lord; that the Lord is very pitiful, and of tender mercy. 12 But above all things, my brethren, swear not, neither by heaven, neither by the earth, neither by any other oath: but let your yea be yea; and *your* nay, nay; lest ye fall into condemnation. 13 Is any among you afflicted? let him pray. Is any merry? let him sing psalms. 14 Is any sick among you? let him call for the elders of the church; and let them pray over him, anointing him with oil in the name of the Lord: 15 And the prayer of faith shall save the sick, and the Lord shall raise him up; and if he have committed sins, they shall be forgiven him. 16 Confess *your* faults one to another, and pray one for another, that ye may be healed. The effectual fervent prayer of a righteous man availeth much. 17 Elias was a man subject to like passions as we are, and he prayed earnestly that it might not rain: and it rained not on the earth by the space of three years and six months. 18 And he prayed again, and the heaven gave rain, and the earth brought forth

New International Version

the Lord's will, we will live and do this or that." 16 As it is, you boast and brag. All such boasting is evil. 17 Anyone, then, who knows the good he ought to do and doesn't do it, sins.

Warning to rich oppressors

5 Now listen, you rich people, weep and wail because of the misery that is coming upon you. 2 Your wealth has rotted, and moths have eaten your clothes. 3 Your gold and silver are corroded. Their corrosion will testify against you and eat your flesh like fire. You have hoarded wealth in the last days. 4 Look! The wages you failed to pay the workmen who mowed your fields are crying out against you. The cries of the harvesters have reached the ears of the Lord All-powerful. 5 You have lived on earth in luxury and self-indulgence. You have fattened yourselves in the day of slaughter. 6 You have condemned and murdered innocent men, who were not opposing you.

Patience and suffering

7 Be patient, then, brothers, until the Lord's coming. See how the farmer waits for the land to yield its valuable crop and how patient he is for the fall and spring rains. 8 You too, be patient and stand firm, because the Lord's coming is near. 9 Don't grumble against each other, brothers, or you will be judged. The Judge is standing at the door!

10 Brothers, as an example of patience in the face of suffering, take the prophets who spoke in the name of the Lord. 11 As you know, we consider blessed those who have persevered. You have heard of Job's perseverance and have seen what the Lord finally brought about. The Lord is full of compassion and mercy.

12 Above all, my brothers, do not swear—not by heaven or by earth or by anything else. Let your "Yes" be yes, and your "No," no, or you will be condemned.

The prayer of faith

13 Is any one of you in trouble? He should pray. Is anyone happy? Let him sing songs of praise. 14 Is any one of you sick? He should call the elders of the church to pray over him and anoint him with oil in the name of the Lord. 15 And the prayer offered in faith will make the sick person well; the Lord will raise him up. If he has sinned, he will be forgiven. 16 Therefore, confess your sins to each other and pray for each other so that you may be healed. The prayer of a righteous man is powerful and effective.

17 Elijah was a man just like us. He prayed earnestly that it would not rain, and it did not rain on the land for three and a half years. 18 Again he prayed, and the heavens gave rain, and the earth produced its crops.

Greek Interlinear

λέγειν ὑμᾶς· ἐὰν ὁ κύριος θελήσῃ, καὶ
to say youᵇ: If the Lord wills, both
=your saying:

ζήσομεν καὶ ποιήσομεν τοῦτο ἢ ἐκεῖνο.
we will live and we will do this or that.

16 νῦν δὲ καυχᾶσθε ἐν ταῖς ἀλαζονείαις
But now ye boast in the vauntings

ὑμῶν· πᾶσα καύχησις τοιαύτη πονηρά
of you; all ¹boasting ¹such ⁴evil

ἐστιν. **17** εἰδότι οὖν καλὸν ποιεῖν καὶ
¹is. ¹to [one] ¹There- ⁴good ⁵to do and
knowing* fore

μὴ ποιοῦντι, ἁμαρτία αὐτῷ ἐστιν.
not doing, ¹sin ¹to him ²it is.

Chapter 5

Ἄγε νῦν οἱ πλούσιοι, κλαύσατε
Come now the rich men, weep ye

ὀλολύζοντες ἐπὶ ταῖς ταλαιπωρίαις ὑμῶν
crying aloud over the hardships of you

ταῖς ἐπερχομέναις. **2** ὁ πλοῦτος ὑμῶν
- coming upon. The riches of you

σέσηπεν, καὶ τὰ ἱμάτια ὑμῶν σητόβρωτα
have become and the garments of you moth-eaten
corrupted,

γέγονεν, **3** ὁ χρυσὸς ὑμῶν καὶ ὁ ἄργυρος
have become, the gold of you and the silver

κατίωται, καὶ ὁ ἰὸς αὐτῶν εἰς μαρτύριον
has become and the poison of them for a testimony
rusted over,

ὑμῖν ἔσται καὶ φάγεται τὰς σάρκας
to(against) will and will eat the fleshes
you be

ὑμῶν ὡς πῦρ. ἐθησαυρίσατε ἐν ἐσχάταις
of you as fire. Ye treasured in [the] last

ἡμέραις. **4** ἰδοὺ ὁ μισθὸς τῶν ἐργατῶν
days. Behold[,] the wages of the workmen

τῶν ἀμησάντων τὰς χώρας ὑμῶν ὁ
- having reaped the lands of you

ἀφυστερημένος ἀφ' ὑμῶν κράζει, καὶ αἱ
being kept back from(by) you cries, and the

βοαὶ τῶν θερισάντων εἰς τὰ ὦτα κυρίου
cries of the having reaped ³into ¹the ⁴ears ⁵of [the]
[ones] Lord

σαβαὼθ εἰσελήλυθαν. **5** ἐτρυφήσατε ἐπὶ
⁶of hosts ¹have entered. Ye lived daintily on

τῆς γῆς καὶ ἐσπαταλήσατε, ἐθρέψατε τὰς
the earth and lived riotously, ye nourished the

καρδίας ὑμῶν ἐν ἡμέρᾳ σφαγῆς. **6** κατε-
hearts of you in a day of slaughter. Ye

δικάσατε, ἐφονεύσατε τὸν δίκαιον· οὐκ
condemned, ye murdered the righteous man; not

ἀντιτάσσεται ὑμῖν.
he resists you.

7 Μακροθυμήσατε οὖν, ἀδελφοί, ἕως τῆς
Be ye longsuffering therefore, brothers, until the

παρουσίας τοῦ κυρίου. ἰδοὺ ὁ γεωργὸς
presence of the Lord. Behold[,] the farmer

ἐκδέχεται τὸν τίμιον καρπὸν τῆς γῆς,
awaits the precious fruit of the earth,

μακροθυμῶν ἐπ' αὐτῷ ἕως λάβῃ πρόϊμον
being over it until he receives early
longsuffering

καὶ ὄψιμον. **8** μακροθυμήσατε καὶ ὑμεῖς,
and latter [rain]. Be ²longsuffering ¹also ¹ye,

στηρίξατε τὰς καρδίας ὑμῶν, ὅτι ἡ
establish the hearts of you, because the

παρουσία τοῦ κυρίου ἤγγικεν. **9** μὴ
presence of the Lord has drawn near. not

στενάζετε, ἀδελφοί, κατ' ἀλλήλων ἵνα μὴ
Murmur ye, brothers, against one another lest

κριθῆτε· ἰδοὺ ὁ κριτὴς πρὸ τῶν θυρῶν
ye be behold[,] the judge ²before ¹the ⁴doors
judged;

ἕστηκεν. **10** ὑπόδειγμα λάβετε, ἀδελφοί,
¹stands. ⁴an example ¹Take ye, ²brothers,

τῆς κακοπαθίας καὶ τῆς μακροθυμίας
- ³of suffering ill ⁷and - ⁶of longsuffering

τοὺς προφήτας, οἳ ἐλάλησαν ἐν τῷ
²the ¹prophets, who spoke in the

ὀνόματι κυρίου. **11** ἰδοὺ μακαρίζομεν τοὺς
name of [the] Lord. Behold we count blessed the

ὑπομείναντας· τὴν ὑπομονὴν Ἰὼβ ἠκούσατε,
[ones] enduring; the ²endurance ¹of Job ¹ye heard [of],

καὶ τὸ τέλος κυρίου εἴδετε, ὅτι πολύ-
and ²the ¹end ⁴of [the] Lord ¹ye saw, that ⁴very

σπλαγχνός ἐστιν ὁ κύριος καὶ οἰκτίρμων.
compassionate ²is ¹the ¹Lord and pitiful.

12 Πρὸ πάντων δέ, ἀδελφοί μου, μὴ
²before ²all things ¹But, brothers of me, not

ὀμνύετε, μήτε τὸν οὐρανὸν μήτε τὴν
swear ye, neither by the heaven nor by the

γῆν μήτε ἄλλον τινὰ ὅρκον· ἤτω δὲ
earth nor ¹other ¹any oath; but let be

ὑμῶν τὸ ναὶ ναί, καὶ τὸ οὒ οὔ, ἵνα μὴ
of you the Yes yes, and the No no, lest

ὑπὸ κρίσιν πέσητε. **13** Κακοπαθεῖ τις
²under ¹judgment ¹ye fall. Suffers ill anyone

ἐν ὑμῖν; προσευχέσθω· εὐθυμεῖ τις;
among you ? let him pray; is cheerful anyone ?

ψαλλέτω. **14** ἀσθενεῖ τις ἐν ὑμῖν;
let him sing a psalm. Is weak anyone among you ?

προσκαλεσάσθω τοὺς πρεσβυτέρους τῆς
let him summon the elders of the

ἐκκλησίας, καὶ προσευξάσθωσαν ἐπ' αὐτὸν
church, and let them pray over him

ἀλείψαντες ἐλαίῳ ἐν τῷ ὀνόματι τοῦ
having anointed with oil ın the name of the
[him]

κυρίου. **15** καὶ ἡ εὐχὴ τῆς πίστεως
Lord. And the prayer - of faith

σώσει τὸν κάμνοντα, καὶ ἐγερεῖ αὐτὸν
will heal the [one] being sick, and ²will raise ⁴him

ὁ κύριος· κἂν ἁμαρτίας ᾖ πεποιηκώς,
¹the ³Lord; and if ²sins ¹he ¹having done,
may be

ἀφεθήσεται αὐτῷ. **16** ἐξομολογεῖσθε οὖν
it will be forgiven him. Confess ye therefore

ἀλλήλοις τὰς ἁμαρτίας, καὶ προσεύχεσθε
to one the(your) sins, and pray ye
another

ὑπὲρ ἀλλήλων, ὅπως ἰαθῆτε. πολὺ
on be- one another, so as ye may ²much(very)
half of be cured.

ἰσχύει δέησις δικαίου ἐνεργουμένη.
⁴is ¹strong ¹a petition ²of a ³being made effective.
righteous man

17 Ἡλίας ἄνθρωπος ἦν ὁμοιοπαθὴς ἡμῖν,
Elias ²a man ¹was of like feeling to us,

καὶ προσευχῇ προσηύξατο τοῦ μὴ βρέξαι,
and ²in prayer ¹he prayed - not to rain,
=that it should not rain,

καὶ οὐκ ἔβρεξεν ἐπὶ τῆς γῆς ἐνιαυτοὺς
and it rained not on the earth ¹years

τρεῖς καὶ μῆνας ἕξ· **18** καὶ πάλιν προσ-
¹three and ²months ¹six; and again he

ηύξατο, καὶ ὁ οὐρανὸς ὑετὸν ἔδωκεν καὶ
prayed, and the heaven ¹rain ¹gave and

ἡ γῆ ἐβλάστησεν τὸν καρπὸν αὐτῆς.
the earth brought forth the fruit of it.

* See note on page xxxviii.

King James Version

her fruit. 19 Brethren, if any of you do err from the truth, and one convert him; 20 Let him know, that he which converteth the sinner from the error of his way shall save a soul from death, and shall hide a multitude of sins.

New International Version

19 My brothers, if one of you should wander from the truth and someone should bring him back, 20 remember this: Whoever turns a sinner away from his error will save him from death and cover many sins.

Greek Interlinear

19 Ἀδελφοί μου, ἐάν τις ἐν ὑμῖν πλανηθῇ
Brothers of me, if anyone among you errs

ἀπὸ τῆς ἀληθείας καὶ ἐπιστρέψῃ τις
from the truth and ¹turns ¹anyone

αὐτόν, 20 γινώσκετε ὅτι ὁ ἐπιστρέψας
him, know ye that the [one] turning

ἁμαρτωλὸν ἐκ πλάνης ὁδοῦ αὐτοῦ σώσει
a sinner out of [the] error of way of him will save

ψυχὴν αὐτοῦ ἐκ θανάτου καὶ καλύψει
soul of him out of death and will hide

πλῆθος ἁμαρτιῶν.
a multitude of sins.

King James Version

THE FIRST
EPISTLE GENERAL
OF
PETER

New International Version

1 PETER

1 Peter, an apostle of Jesus Christ, to the strangers scattered throughout Pontus, Galatia, Cappadocia, Asia, and Bithynia, 2 Elect according to the foreknowledge of God the Father, through sanctification of the Spirit, unto obedience and sprinkling of the blood of Jesus Christ: Grace unto you, and peace, be multiplied. 3 Blessed *be* the God and Father of our Lord Jesus Christ, which according to his abundant mercy hath begotten us again unto a lively hope by the resurrection of Jesus Christ from the dead, 4 To an inheritance incorruptible, and undefiled, and that fadeth not away, reserved in heaven for you, 5 Who are kept by the power of God through faith unto salvation ready to be revealed in the last time. 6 Wherein ye greatly rejoice, though now for a season, if need be, ye are in heaviness through manifold temptations: 7 That the trial of your faith, being much more precious than of gold that perisheth, though it be tried with fire, might be found unto praise and honour and glory at the appearing of Jesus Christ: 8 Whom having not seen, ye love; in whom, though now ye see *him* not, yet believing, ye rejoice with joy unspeakable and full of glory: 9 Receiving the end of your faith, *even* the salvation of *your* souls. 10 Of which salvation the prophets have inquired and searched diligently, who prophesied of the grace *that should come* unto you: 11 Searching what, or what manner of time the Spirit of Christ which was in them did signify, when it testified beforehand the sufferings of Christ, and the glory that should follow. 12 Unto whom it was revealed, that not unto themselves, but unto us they did minister the things, which are now reported unto you by them that have preached the gospel unto you with the Holy Ghost sent down from heaven; which things the angels desire to look into. 13 Wherefore gird up the loins of your mind, be sober, and hope to the end for the grace that is to be brought unto you at the revelation of Jesus Christ; 14 As obedient children, not fashioning yourselves according to the former lusts in your ignorance: 15 But as he which hath called you is holy, so be ye holy in all manner of conversation; 16 Because it is written, Be ye holy; for I am holy. 17 And if ye call on the Father, who without respect of persons judgeth according to every man's work, pass the time of your sojourning *here* in fear: 18 Forasmuch as ye know that ye were not redeemed

1 Peter, an apostle of Jesus Christ,
 To God's elect, strangers in the world, scattered throughout Pontus, Galatia, Cappadocia, Asia and Bithynia, 2 who have been chosen according to the foreknowledge of God the Father, by the sanctifying work of the Spirit, for obedience to Jesus Christ and sprinkling by his blood:
Grace and peace be yours in abundance.

Praise to God for a living hope

3 Praise be to the God and Father of our Lord Jesus Christ! In his great mercy he has given us new birth into a living hope through the resurrection of Jesus Christ from the dead, 4 and into an inheritance that can never perish, spoil or fade—kept in heaven for you. 5 Through faith you are shielded by God's power until the coming of the salvation that is ready to be revealed in the last time. 6 In this you greatly rejoice, though now for a little while you may have suffered grief in all kinds of trials. 7 These have come so that your faith—of greater worth than gold, which perishes even though refined by fire—may be proved genuine and may result in praise, glory and honor when Jesus Christ is revealed. 8 Though you have not seen him, you love him; and even though you do not see him now, you believe in him and are filled with an inexpressible and glorious joy, 9 for you are receiving the goal of your faith, the salvation of your souls.
10 Concerning this salvation, the prophets, who spoke of the grace that was to come to you, searched intently and with the greatest care, 11 trying to find out the time and circumstances to which the Spirit of Christ in them was pointing when he predicted the sufferings of Christ and the glories that would follow. 12 It was revealed to them that they were not serving themselves but you, when they spoke of the things that have now been told you by those who have preached the gospel to you by the Holy Spirit sent from heaven. Even angels long to look into these things.

Be holy

13 Therefore, prepare your minds for action; be self-controlled; set your hope fully on the grace to be given you when Jesus Christ is revealed. 14 As obedient children, do not conform to the evil desires you had when you lived in ignorance. 15 But just as he who called you is holy, so be holy in all you do; 16 for it is written: "Be holy, because I am holy." [a]
17 Since you call on a Father who judges each man's work impartially, live your lives as strangers here in reverent fear. 18 For you know that it was not with perishable things such as silver

[a] Lev. 11:14,45; 19:2; 20:7.

ΠΕΤΡΟΥ Α

Chapter 1

Πέτρος ἀπόστολος Ἰησοῦ Χριστοῦ
Peter   an apostle   of Jesus   Christ

ἐκλεκτοῖς παρεπιδήμοις διασπορᾶς Πόντου,
to [the] chosen   sojourners   of [the] dispersion   of Pontus,

Γαλατίας, Καππαδοκίας, Ἀσίας καὶ
of Galatia,   of Cappadocia,   of Asia   and

Βιθυνίας, 2 κατὰ πρόγνωσιν θεοῦ πατρός,
of Bithynia,   according   [the]   of God   Father,
to   foreknowledge

ἐν ἁγιασμῷ πνεύματος, εἰς ὑπακοὴν καὶ
in sanctification   of spirit,   to   obedience   and

ῥαντισμὸν αἵματος Ἰησοῦ Χριστοῦ· χάρις
sprinkling   of [the] blood   of Jesus   Christ: Grace

ὑμῖν καὶ εἰρήνη πληθυνθείη.
to you   and   peace   may it be multiplied.

3 Εὐλογητὸς ὁ θεὸς καὶ πατὴρ τοῦ
Blessed [be]   the   God   and   Father   of the

κυρίου ἡμῶν Ἰησοῦ Χριστοῦ, ὁ κατὰ τὸ
Lord   of us   Jesus   Christ,   the   accord-   the
[one]   ing to

πολύ αὐτοῦ ἔλεος ἀναγεννήσας ἡμᾶς εἰς
much   of him   mercy   having regenerated   us   to
(great)

ἐλπίδα ζῶσαν δι᾽ ἀναστάσεως Ἰησοῦ
²hope   ¹a living   through   [the] resurrection   of Jesus

Χριστοῦ ἐκ νεκρῶν, 4 εἰς κληρονομίαν
Christ   from   [the] dead,   to   an inheritance

ἄφθαρτον καὶ ἀμίαντον καὶ ἀμάραντον,
incorruptible   and   undefiled   and   unfading,

τετηρημένην ἐν οὐρανοῖς εἰς ὑμᾶς 5 τοὺς
having been kept   in   heavens   for   you   the [ones]

ἐν δυνάμει θεοῦ φρουρουμένους διὰ πίστεως
²by   ³[the] power   ⁴of God   ¹being guarded   through   faith

εἰς σωτηρίαν ἑτοίμην ἀποκαλυφθῆναι ἐν
to   a salvation   ready   to be revealed   at

καιρῷ ἐσχάτῳ. 6 ἐν ᾧ ἀγαλλιᾶσθε,
²time   ¹[the] last.   In   which   ye exult,

ὀλίγον ἄρτι εἰ δέον λυπηθέντες ἐν
a little [while]   yet   if   necessary   grieving   by

ποικίλοις πειρασμοῖς, 7 ἵνα τὸ δοκίμιον
manifold   trials,   in order that   the   proving

ὑμῶν τῆς πίστεως πολυτιμότερον χρυσίου
²of you   ¹of the   ³faith[,]   much more precious [than]   ⁴gold

τοῦ ἀπολλυμένου, διὰ πυρὸς δὲ δοκιμαζ-
-   ¹of perishing,   ³through   ⁴fire   ²yet   ⁵being

ομένου, εὑρεθῇ εἰς ἔπαινον καὶ δόξαν
proved,   may be found   to   praise   and   glory

καὶ τιμὴν ἐν ἀποκαλύψει Ἰησοῦ Χριστοῦ·
and   honour   at   [the] revelation   of Jesus   Christ;

8 ὃν οὐκ ἰδόντες ἀγαπᾶτε, εἰς ὃν ἄρτι
whom   not   having seen   ye love,   in   whom   yet

μὴ ὁρῶντες πιστεύοντες δὲ ἀγαλλιᾶσθε
not   seeing   ³believing   ¹but   ye exult

χαρᾷ ἀνεκλαλήτῳ καὶ δεδοξασμένῃ,
with joy   unspeakable   and   having been glorified,

9 κομιζόμενοι τὸ τέλος τῆς πίστεως
obtaining   the   end   of the(your)   faith

σωτηρίαν ψυχῶν. 10 περὶ ἧς σωτηρίας
[the] salvation of [your] souls.   Concerning   which   salvation

ἐξεζήτησαν καὶ ἐξηρεύνησαν προφῆται οἱ
²sought out   ¹ªand   ¹¹searched out   ¹prophets   ²the

περὶ τῆς εἰς ὑμᾶς χάριτος προφητεύσαντες,
⁴con-   ⁵the   ⁷for   ⁸you   ⁶grace   ³[ones] prophesying,
cerning

11 ἐρευνῶντες εἰς τίνα ἢ ποῖον καιρὸν
searching   for   what   or what sort of   time

ἐδήλου τὸ ἐν αὐτοῖς πνεῦμα Χριστοῦ
²made clear   ¹the   ³in   ⁴them   ²Spirit   ³of Christ

προμαρτυρόμενον τὰ εἰς Χριστὸν παθήματα
⁷forewitnessing   ⁸the   ¹⁰for   ¹¹Christ   ⁹sufferings

καὶ τὰς μετὰ ταῦτα δόξας. 12 οἷς
¹²and   ¹³the   ¹⁴after   ¹⁶these   ¹⁵glories.   To whom

ἀπεκαλύφθη ὅτι οὐχ ἑαυτοῖς ὑμῖν δὲ
it was revealed   that   not   to themselves   ²to you   ¹but

διηκόνουν αὐτά, ἃ νῦν ἀνηγγέλη ὑμῖν
they   the same   which   now   were   to you
ministered   things,   announced

διὰ τῶν εὐαγγελισαμένων ὑμᾶς ἐν
through   the [ones]   having evangelized   you   by

πνεύματι ἁγίῳ ἀποσταλέντι ἀπ᾽ οὐρανοῦ,
²Spirit   ¹[the] Holy   sent forth   from   heaven,

εἰς ἃ ἐπιθυμοῦσιν ἄγγελοι παρακύψαι.
into   ¹which   ³long   ²angels   ⁴to look into.
things

13 Διὸ ἀναζωσάμενοι τὰς ὀσφύας τῆς
Wherefore   girding up   the   loins   of the

διανοίας ὑμῶν, νήφοντες, τελείως ἐλπίσατε
mind   of you,   being sober,   perfectly   hope

ἐπὶ τὴν φερομένην ὑμῖν χάριν ἐν
on   ²the   ¹being brought   ⁴to you   ³grace   at

ἀποκαλύψει Ἰησοῦ Χριστοῦ. 14 ὡς τέκνα
[the] revelation   of Jesus   Christ.   As   children

ὑπακοῆς, μὴ συσχηματιζόμενοι ταῖς πρότε-
of obedience,*   not   fashioning yourselves   to the   ²form-

ρον ἐν τῇ ἀγνοίᾳ ὑμῶν ἐπιθυμίαις, 15 ἀλλὰ
erly   ³in   ⁴the   ⁵ignorance   ⁶of you   ¹longings,   but

κατὰ τὸν καλέσαντα ὑμᾶς ἅγιον καὶ
accord-   ¹the   ²having called   ³you   ⁴holy [one]   ⁵also
ing to

αὐτοὶ ἅγιοι ἐν πάσῃ ἀναστροφῇ γενήθητε,
²[your]-   ⁴holy   ⁵in   ¹⁰all   ¹¹conduct   ¹become ye,
selves

16 διότι γέγραπται· [ὅτι] ἅγιοι ἔσεσθε,
because it has been written: -   Holy   ye shall be,

ὅτι ἐγὼ ἅγιος. 17 καὶ εἰ πατέρα
because I [am]   holy.   And   if   ²Father

ἐπικαλεῖσθε τὸν ἀπροσωπολήμπτως κρίνοντα
¹ye invoke [as]   ²the [one]   ²without respect to persons   ¹judging

κατὰ τὸ ἑκάστου ἔργον, ἐν φόβῳ τὸν
accord-   the   ²of each man   ¹work,   ²in   ³fear   ¹the
ing to

τῆς παροικίας ὑμῶν χρόνον ἀναστράφητε,
⁵of the   ⁶sojourning   ⁷of you   ⁴time   ¹pass,

18 εἰδότες ὅτι οὐ φθαρτοῖς, ἀργυρίῳ ἢ
knowing   that   not   with corruptible   silver   or
things,

* Genitive of quality: " obedient children."

King James Version

with corruptible things, *as* silver and gold, from your vain conversation *received* by tradition from your fathers; 19 But with the precious blood of Christ, as of a lamb without blemish and without spot: 20 Who verily was foreordained before the foundation of the world, but was manifest in these last times for you, 21 Who by him do believe in God, that raised him up from the dead, and gave him glory; that your faith and hope might be in God. 22 Seeing ye have purified your souls in obeying the truth through the Spirit unto unfeigned love of the brethren, *see that ye* love one another with a pure heart fervently: 23 Being born again, not of corruptible seed, but of incorruptible, by the word of God, which liveth and abideth for ever. 24 For all flesh *is* as grass, and all the glory of man as the flower of grass. The grass withereth, and the flower thereof falleth away: 25 But the word of the Lord endureth for ever. And this is the word which by the gospel is preached unto you.

2 Wherefore laying aside all malice, and all guile, and hypocrisies, and envies, and all evil speakings, 2 As newborn babes, desire the sincere milk of the word, that ye may grow thereby: 3 If so be ye have tasted that the Lord *is* gracious. 4 To whom coming, *as unto* a living stone, disallowed indeed of men, but chosen of God, *and* precious, 5 Ye also, as lively stones, are built up a spiritual house, a holy priesthood, to offer up spiritual sacrifices, acceptable to God by Jesus Christ. 6 Wherefore also it is contained in the Scripture, Behold, I lay in Sion a chief corner stone, elect, precious: and he that believeth on him shall not be confounded. 7 Unto you therefore which believe *he is* precious: but unto them which be disobedient, the stone which the builders disallowed, the same is made the head of the corner, 8 And a stone of stumbling, and a rock of offence, *even to them* which stumble at the word, being disobedient: whereunto also they were appointed. 9 But ye *are* a chosen generation, a royal priesthood, a holy nation, a peculiar people; that ye should shew forth the praises of him who hath called you out of darkness into his marvellous light: 10 Which in time past *were* not a people, but *are* now the people of God: which had not obtained mercy, but now have obtained mercy. 11 Dearly beloved, I beseech *you* as strangers and pilgrims, abstain from fleshly lusts, which war against the soul; 12 Having your conversation honest among the Gentiles: that, whereas they speak against you as evil doers, they may by *your* good works, which they shall behold, glorify God in the day

New International Version

or gold that you were redeemed from the empty way of life handed down to you from your forefathers, 19 but with the precious blood of Christ, a lamb without blemish or defect. 20 He was chosen before the creation of the world, but was revealed in these last times for your sake. 21 Through him you believe in God, who raised him from the dead and glorified him, and so your faith and hope are in God.

22 Now that you have purified yourselves by obeying the truth so that you have sincere love for your brothers, love one another deeply, with all your hearts.[b] 23 For you have been born again, not of perishable seed, but of imperishable, through the living and enduring word of God. 24 For,

"All men are like grass,
    and all their glory is like the wild flower;
the grass withers,
    and the flower falls,
25 but the word of the Lord stands forever."[c]
And this is the word that was preached to you.

2 Therefore, rid yourselves of all malice and all deceit, hypocrisy, jealousy, and slander of every kind. 2 Like newborn babies, crave pure spiritual milk, so that by it you may grow up in your salvation, 3 now that you have tasted that the Lord is good.

The living stone and a chosen people

4 As you come to him, the living Stone—rejected by men but chosen by God and precious to him— 5 you also, like living stones, are being built into a spiritual house to be a holy priesthood, offering spiritual sacrifices acceptable to God through Jesus Christ. 6 For in Scripture it says:
"See, I lay a stone in Zion,
    a chosen and precious cornerstone,
and the one who trusts in him will never be
    put to shame."[d]
7 Now to you who believe, this stone is precious. But to those who do not believe:
"The stone the builders rejected
    has become the capstone,"[e]
8 and,
"A stone that causes men to stumble
    and a rock that makes them fall."[f]
They stumble because they disobey the message —which is also what they were destined for.

9 But you are a chosen people, a royal priesthood, a holy nation, a people belonging to God, that you may declare the praises of him who called you out of darkness into his wonderful light. 10 Once you were not a people, but now you are the people of God; once you had not received mercy, but now you have received mercy.

11 Dear friends, I urge you, as foreigners and strangers in the world, to abstain from sinful desires, which war against your soul. 12 Live such good lives among the pagans that, though they accuse you of doing wrong, they may see your good deeds and glorify God on the day he visits us.

[b] Some early MSS read *from a pure heart*. [c] Isaiah 40:6-8. [d] Isaiah 28:16. [e] Psalm 118:22 [f] Isaiah 8:14.

Greek Interlinear

χρυσίῳ, ἐλυτρώθητε ἐκ τῆς ματαίας ὑμῶν
gold, ye were redeemed from the vain ⁵of you

ἀναστροφῆς πατροπαραδότου, 19 ἀλλὰ τιμίῳ
¹conduct delivered from but with
[your] fathers, precious

αἵματι ὡς ἀμνοῦ ἀμώμου καὶ ἀσπίλου
blood[,] as of a lamb unblemished and unspotted[,]

Χριστοῦ, 20 προεγνωσμένου μὲν πρὸ κατα-
of Christ, having been foreknown on one from [the]
hand

βολῆς κόσμου, φανερωθέντος δὲ ἐπ' ἐσχάτου
founda- of [the] manifested on the in [the] last
tion world, other

τῶν χρόνων δι' ὑμᾶς 21 τοὺς δι' αὐτοῦ
of the times because of you the ones through him

πιστοὺς εἰς θεὸν τὸν ἐγείραντα αὐτὸν
believing in God the [one] having raised him

ἐκ νεκρῶν καὶ δόξαν αὐτῷ δόντα, ὥστε
from [the] dead and ¹glory; ²to him ¹having given. so as

τὴν πίστιν ὑμῶν καὶ ἐλπίδα εἶναι εἰς
the ¹faith ²of you ²and ⁴hope to be in

θεόν. 22 Τὰς ψυχὰς ὑμῶν ἡγνικότες
God. ²The ²souls ⁴of you ¹having purified

ἐν τῇ ὑπακοῇ τῆς ἀληθείας εἰς φιλαδελφίαν
by – obedience of(to) the truth to ⁹brotherly love

ἀνυπόκριτον, ἐκ καρδίας ἀλλήλους ἀγαπήσατε
¹unfeigned, ⁴from ²[the] heart ²one another ¹love ye

ἐκτενῶς, 23 ἀναγεγεννημένοι οὐκ ἐκ σπορᾶς
²earnestly, having been regenerated not by ⁵seed

φθαρτῆς ἀλλὰ ἀφθάρτου, διὰ λόγου ζῶντος
¹corruptible but incorruptible, through ⁴word ¹[the] living

θεοῦ καὶ μένοντος. 24 διότι πᾶσα σὰρξ
⁴of God ²and ³remaining. Because all flesh [is]

ὡς χόρτος, καὶ πᾶσα δόξα αὐτῆς ὡς
as grass, and all [the] glory of it as

ἄνθος χόρτου· ἐξηράνθη ὁ χόρτος, καὶ
a flower of grass; was dried the grass, and

τὸ ἄνθος ἐξέπεσεν· 25 τὸ δὲ ῥῆμα κυρίου
the flower fell out; but the word of [the] Lord

μένει εἰς τὸν αἰῶνα. τοῦτο δέ ἐστιν
remains unto the age. And this is

τὸ ῥῆμα τὸ εὐαγγελισθὲν εἰς ὑμᾶς.
the word – preached [as good news] to you.

Chapter 2

Ἀποθέμενοι οὖν πᾶσαν κακίαν καὶ
Putting away therefore all malice and

πάντα δόλον καὶ ὑποκρίσεις καὶ φθόνους
all guile and hypocrisies and envies

καὶ πάσας καταλαλιάς, 2 ὡς ἀρτιγέννητα
and all detractions, as newborn

βρέφη τὸ λογικὸν ἄδολον γάλα ἐπιποθήσατε,
babes ⁵the ²spiritual ¹pure ⁴milk ¹desire ye,

ἵνα ἐν αὐτῷ αὐξηθῆτε εἰς σωτηρίαν,
in or- by it ye may grow to salvation,
der that

3 εἰ ἐγεύσασθε ὅτι χρηστὸς ὁ κύριος.
if ye tasted that ²good ¹the ²Lord [is].

4 πρὸς ὃν προσερχόμενοι, λίθον ζῶντα,
to whom approaching, ¹stone ¹a living,

ὑπὸ ἀνθρώπων μὲν ἀποδεδοκιμασμένον παρὰ
by men on one having been rejected ⁵by
hand

δὲ θεῷ ἐκλεκτὸν ἔντιμον, 5 καὶ
¹on the ⁴God ²chosen[,] precious, ³also
other

αὐτοὶ ὡς λίθοι ζῶντες οἰκοδομεῖσθε οἶκος
¹[your]- ²as ⁴stones ⁴living are being built ⁵house
selves

πνευματικὸς εἰς ἱεράτευμα ἅγιον, ἀνενέγκαι
¹a spiritual for ²priesthood ¹a holy, to offer

πνευματικὰς θυσίας εὐπροσδέκτους θεῷ διὰ
spiritual sacrifices acceptable to through
God

Ἰησοῦ Χριστοῦ· 6 διότι περιέχει ἐν γραφῇ·
Jesus Christ; because it is in scripture:
contained

ἰδοὺ τίθημι ἐν Σιὼν λίθον ἐκλεκτὸν
Behold I lay in Sion ⁴stone ¹a chosen

ἀκρογωνιαῖον ἔντιμον, καὶ ὁ πιστεύων
²corner foundation ³precious, and the [one] believing

ἐπ' αὐτῷ οὐ μὴ καταισχυνθῇ. 7 ὑμῖν
on it(him) by no means will be shamed. To you
—Yours

οὖν ἡ τιμὴ τοῖς πιστεύουσιν· ἀπιστοῦσιν
there- ²[is] ¹honour ¹the [ones] ²believing⁺; ⁴to unbelieving
fore ⁴the [ones]

therefore who believe is the honour;

δὲ λίθος ὃν ἀπεδοκίμασαν οἱ οἰκοδομοῦντες,
¹but a stone which ²rejected ¹the [ones] ⁵building,

οὗτος ἐγενήθη εἰς κεφαλὴν γωνίας 8 καὶ
this came to be for head of [the] corner and

λίθος προσκόμματος καὶ πέτρα σκανδάλου·
a stone of stumbling and a rock of offence;

οἱ προσκόπτουσιν τῷ λόγῳ ἀπειθοῦντες,
who stumble at the word disobeying,

9 εἰς ὃ καὶ ἐτέθησαν· ὑμεῖς δὲ γένος
to which indeed they were but ye [are] ²race
appointed;

ἐκλεκτόν, βασίλειον ἱεράτευμα, ἔθνος ἅγιον,
¹a chosen, a royal priesthood, nation a holy,

λαὸς εἰς περιποίησιν, ὅπως τὰς ἀρετὰς
a people for possession, so as ¹the ³virtues

ἐξαγγείλητε τοῦ ἐκ σκότους ὑμᾶς καλέ-
¹ye may tell out ²of the ²out ⁵darkness ⁴you ¹having
[one]

σαντος εἰς τὸ θαυμαστὸν αὐτοῦ φῶς·
called into the marvellous ⁵of him ¹light;

10 οἳ ποτε οὐ λαός, νῦν δὲ λαὸς θεοῦ,
who then not a but [are] a of
[were] people, now people God,

οἱ οὐκ ἠλεημένοι, νῦν δὲ ἐλεηθέντες.
the not having been pitied, but now pitied.
[ones]

11 Ἀγαπητοί, παρακαλῶ ὡς παροίκους
Beloved, I exhort [you] as sojourners

καὶ παρεπιδήμους ἀπέχεσθαι τῶν σαρκικῶν
and aliens to abstain from – fleshly

ἐπιθυμιῶν, αἵτινες στρατεύονται κατὰ τῆς
lusts, which war against the

ψυχῆς· 12 τὴν ἀναστροφὴν ὑμῶν ἐν τοῖς
soul; ²the ²conduct ⁴of you ¹among ⁴the

ἔθνεσιν ἔχοντες καλήν, ἵνα ἐν ᾧ κατα-
¹nations ¹having ⁵good, in order while they
that

λαλοῦσιν ὑμῶν ὡς κακοποιῶν, ἐκ τῶν
speak against you as evildoers, by the
(your)

καλῶν ἔργων ἐποπτεύοντες δοξάσωσιν τὸν
good works observing they may glorify –

θεὸν ἐν ἡμέρᾳ ἐπισκοπῆς.
God in a day of visitation.

King James Version

New International Version

of visitation. 13 Submit yourselves to every ordinance of man for the Lord's sake: whether it be to the king, as supreme; 14 Or unto governors, as unto them that are sent by him for the punishment of evil doers, and for the praise of them that do well. 15 For so is the will of God, that with well doing ye may put to silence the ignorance of foolish men: 16As free, and not using *your* liberty for a cloak of maliciousness, but as the servants of God. 17 Honour all *men.* Love the brotherhood. Fear God. Honour the king. 18 Servants, *be* subject to *your* masters with all fear; not only to the good and gentle, but also to the froward. 19 For this *is* thankworthy, if a man for conscience toward God endure grief, suffering wrongfully. 20 For what glory *is it,* if, when ye be buffeted for your faults, ye shall take it patiently? but if, when ye do well, and suffer *for it,* ye take it patiently, this *is* acceptable with God. 21 For even hereunto were ye called: because Christ also suffered for us, leaving us an example, that ye should follow his steps: 22 Who did no sin, neither was guile found in his mouth: 23 Who, when he was reviled, reviled not again; when he suffered, he threatened not; but committed *himself* to him that judgeth righteously: 24 Who his own self bare our sins in his own body on the tree, that we, being dead to sins, should live unto righteousness: by whose stripes ye were healed. 25 For ye were as sheep going astray; but are now returned unto the Shepherd and Bishop of your souls.

Submission to rulers and masters

13 Submit yourselves for the Lord's sake to every authority instituted among men: whether to the king, as the supreme authority, 14 or to governors, who are sent by him to punish those who do wrong ·and to commend those who do right. 15 For it is God's will that by doing good you should silence the ignorant talk of foolish men. 16 Live as free men, but do not use your freedom as a cover-up for evil; live as servants of God. 17 Show proper respect to everyone: Love the brotherhood of believers, fear God, honor the king.
18 Slaves, submit yourselves to your masters with all respect, not only to those who are good and considerate, but also to those who are harsh. 19 For it is commendable if a man bears up under the pain of unjust suffering because he is conscious of God. 20 But how is it to your credit if you receive a beating for doing wrong and endure it? But if you suffer for doing good and you endure it, this is commendable before God. 21 To this you were called, because Christ suffered for you, leaving you an example, that you should follow in his steps.
22 "He committed no sin,
and no deceit was found in his mouth." *g*
23 When they hurled their insults at him, he did not retaliate; when he suffered, he made no threats. Instead, he entrusted himself to him who judges justly. 24 He himself bore our sins in his body on the cross, so that we might die to sins and live for righteousness; by his wounds you have been healed. 25 For you were like sheep going astray, but now you have returned to the Shepherd and Overseer of your souls.

Wives and husbands

3 Likewise, ye wives, *be* in subjection to your own husbands; that, if any obey not the word, they also may without the word be won by the conversation of the wives; 2 While they behold your chaste conversation *coupled* with fear. 3 Whose adorning, let it not be that outward *adorning* of plaiting the hair, and of wearing of gold, or of putting on of apparel; 4 But *let it be* the hidden man of the heart, in that which is not corruptible, *even the ornament* of a meek and quiet spirit, which is in the sight of God of great price. 5 For after this manner in the old time the holy women also, who trusted in God, adorned themselves, being in subjection unto their own husbands: 6 Even as Sarah obeyed Abraham, calling him lord: whose daughters ye are, as long as ye do well, and are not afraid with any amazement. 7 Likewise, ye husbands, dwell with *them* according to knowledge, giving honour unto the wife, as unto the weaker vessel, and as being heirs together of the grace of life; that your prayers be not hindered. 8 Finally, *be* ye all of one mind, having compassion one of another; love as brethren, *be* pitiful, *be* courteous: 9 Not rendering evil for evil, or railing for

3 Wives, in the same way be submissive to your husbands so that, if any of them do not believe the word, they may be won over without talk by the behavior of their wives, 2 when they see the purity and reverence of your lives. 3 Your beauty should not come from outward adornment, such as braided hair and the wearing of gold jewelry and fine clothes. 4 Instead, it should be that of your inner self, the unfading beauty of a gentle and quiet spirit, which is of great worth in God's sight. 5 For this is the way the holy women of the past who put their hope in God used to make themselves beautiful. They were submissive to their own husbands, 6 like Sarah, who obeyed Abraham and called him her master. You are her daughters if you do what is right and do not give way to fear.
7 Husbands, in the same way be considerate as you live with your wives, and treat them with respect as the weaker partner and as heirs with you of the gracious gift of life, so that nothing will hinder your prayers.

Suffering for doing good

8 Finally, all of you, live in harmony with one another; be sympathetic, love as brothers, be compassionate and humble. 9 Do not repay

[g] Isaiah 53:9.

Greek Interlinear

13 Ὑποτάγητε πάσῃ ἀνθρωπίνῃ κτίσει
Submit to every human ordinance
διὰ τὸν κύριον· εἴτε βασιλεῖ ὡς ὑπερέχοντι,
be- the Lord: whether to a king as being supreme,
cause of
14 εἴτε ἡγεμόσιν ὡς δι' αὐτοῦ πεμπομένοις
or to governors as through him being sent
εἰς ἐκδίκησιν κακοποιῶν ἔπαινον δὲ
for vengeance of(on) evildoers ²praise ¹but
ἀγαθοποιῶν· 15 ὅτι οὕτως ἐστὶν τὸ
of welldoers; because so is the
θέλημα τοῦ θεοῦ, ἀγαθοποιοῦντας φιμοῦν
will – of God, doing good to silence
τὴν τῶν ἀφρόνων ἀνθρώπων ἀγνωσίαν·
¹the – ²of foolish ⁴men ³ignorance;
16 ὡς ἐλεύθεροι, καὶ μὴ ὡς ἐπικάλυμμα
as free, and not ²as ⁴a cloak
ἔχοντες τῆς κακίας τὴν ἐλευθερίαν, ἀλλ'
¹having the ⁵of evil the ³freedom, but
ὡς θεοῦ δοῦλοι. 17 πάντας τιμήσατε,
as ²of God slaves. ²All men ¹honour ye,
τὴν ἀδελφότητα ἀγαπᾶτε, τὸν θεὸν
²the ³brotherhood ¹love, – ¹God
φοβεῖσθε, τὸν βασιλέα τιμᾶτε. 18 Οἱ
¹fear, ²the ²king ¹honour. –
οἰκέται, ὑποτασσόμενοι ἐν παντὶ φόβῳ
House submitting yourselves in all fear
servants,
τοῖς δεσπόταις, οὐ μόνον τοῖς ἀγαθοῖς
to the(your) masters, not only to the good
καὶ ἐπιεικέσιν ἀλλὰ καὶ τοῖς σκολιοῖς.
and forbearing but also to the perverse.
19 τοῦτο γὰρ χάρις εἰ διὰ συνείδησιν
For this [is] a favour if because of conscience
θεοῦ ὑποφέρει τις λύπας πάσχων ἀδίκως.
of God ²bears ¹anyone griefs suffering unjustly.
20 ποῖον γὰρ κλέος εἰ ἁμαρτάνοντες καὶ
For what glory [is it] if sinning and

κολαφιζόμενοι ὑπομενεῖτε; ἀλλ' εἰ ἀγαθο-
being buffeted ye endure ? but if doing
ποιοῦντες καὶ πάσχοντες ὑπομενεῖτε, τοῦτο
good and suffering ye endure, this [is]
χάρις παρὰ θεῷ. 21 εἰς τοῦτο γὰρ
a favour with God. ²to ²this ¹For
ἐκλήθητε, ὅτι καὶ Χριστὸς ἔπαθεν ὑπὲρ
ye were because indeed Christ suffered on be-
called, half of
ὑμῶν, ὑμῖν ὑπολιμπάνων ὑπογραμμὸν ἵνα
you, ²to you ¹leaving behind an example in order that
ἐπακολουθήσητε τοῖς ἴχνεσιν αὐτοῦ· 22 ὃς
ye should follow the steps of him; who
ἁμαρτίαν οὐκ ἐποίησεν οὐδὲ εὑρέθη δόλος
²sin ¹not ¹did nor was ²found ¹guile
ἐν τῷ στόματι αὐτοῦ· 23 ὃς λοιδορούμενος
in the mouth of him; who being reviled
οὐκ ἀντελοιδόρει, πάσχων οὐκ ἠπείλει,
reviled not in return, suffering he threatened not,
παρεδίδου δὲ τῷ κρίνοντι δικαίως· 24 ὃς
but delivered to the judging righteously; who
[himself] [one]
τὰς ἁμαρτίας ἡμῶν αὐτὸς ἀνήνεγκεν ἐν
²the ⁴sins ³of us ¹[him]self ²carried up in
τῷ σώματι αὐτοῦ ἐπὶ τὸ ξύλον, ἵνα
the body of him onto the tree, in order that
ταῖς ἁμαρτίαις ἀπογενόμενοι τῇ δικαιοσύνῃ
– ²to sins ¹dying – ⁴to righteousness
ζήσωμεν· οὗ τῷ μώλωπι ἰάθητε.
²we might live; ¹of ¹by ²bruise ye were cured.
whom the
25 ἦτε γὰρ ὡς πρόβατα πλανώμενοι,
²ye were ¹For ⁴as ³sheep ²wandering,
ἀλλὰ ἐπεστράφητε νῦν ἐπὶ τὸν ποιμένα
but ye turned now to the shepherd
καὶ ἐπίσκοπον τῶν ψυχῶν ὑμῶν.
and bishop of the souls of you.

Chapter 3

Ὁμοίως γυναῖκες, ὑποτασσόμεναι τοῖς
Likewise wives, submitting yourselves to the
(your)
ἰδίοις ἀνδράσιν, ἵνα καὶ εἴ τινες ἀπειθοῦσιν
own husbands, in or- even if any disobey
der that
τῷ λόγῳ, διὰ τῆς τῶν γυναικῶν ἀναστροφῆς
the word, through ¹the ²of ⁴wives ³conduct
the(ir)
ἄνευ λόγου κερδηθήσονται, 2 ἐποπτεύσαντες
without a word they will(may) be gained, observing
τὴν ἐν φόβῳ ἁγνὴν ἀναστροφὴν ὑμῶν.
¹the ²in ³fear ⁴pure ⁵conduct ⁶of you.
3 ὧν ἔστω οὐχ ὁ ἔξωθεν ἐμπλοκῆς
Of whom let it be not ¹the ²outward ³of plaiting
τριχῶν καὶ περιθέσεως χρυσίων ἢ ἐνδύσεως
⁴of hairs ⁵and ⁶of putting ⁷of gold ⁸or ¹⁰of clothing
round(on) [ornaments]
ἱματίων κόσμος, 4 ἀλλ' ὁ κρυπτὸς τῆς
¹¹of(with) ⁹adorning, but ¹the ²hidden ⁴of the
garments
καρδίας ἄνθρωπος ἐν τῷ ἀφθάρτῳ τοῦ
⁵heart ³man in(?by) the incorruptible of the
[adorning]
πραέος καὶ ἡσυχίου πνεύματος, ὃ ἐστιν
meek and quiet spirit, which is
ἐνώπιον τοῦ θεοῦ πολυτελές. 5 οὕτως
before – God of great value. so
γὰρ ποτε καὶ αἱ ἅγιαι γυναῖκες αἱ
For then indeed the holy women –

ἐλπίζουσαι εἰς θεὸν ἐκόσμουν ἑαυτάς,
hoping in God adorned themselves,
ὑποτασσόμεναι τοῖς ἰδίοις ἀνδράσιν, 6 ὡς
submitting themselves to the(ir) own husbands, as
Σάρρα ὑπήκουσεν τῷ Ἀβραάμ, κύριον
Sara obeyed – Abraham, ³lord
αὐτὸν καλοῦσα· ἧς ἐγενήθητε τέκνα
²him ¹calling; of whom ye became children
ἀγαθοποιοῦσαι καὶ μὴ φοβούμεναι μηδεμίαν
doing good and not fearing no(any)
πτόησιν. 7 Οἱ ἄνδρες ὁμοίως, συνοικοῦντες
terror. – Husbands likewise, dwelling together
κατὰ γνῶσιν ὡς ἀσθενεστέρῳ σκεύει τῷ
accord- knowledge as with a weaker vessel the
ing to
γυναικείῳ, ἀπονέμοντες τιμὴν ὡς καὶ
female, assigning honour as indeed
συγκληρονόμοις χάριτος ζωῆς, εἰς τὸ μὴ
co-heirs of [the] grace of life, for the not
ἐγκόπτεσθαι τὰς προσευχὰς ὑμῶν. 8 Τὸ δὲ
to be hindered the prayers of you.ᵇ Now the
τέλος πάντες ὁμόφρονες, συμπαθεῖς,
end[,] [be ye] all of one mind, sympathetic,
φιλάδελφοι, εὔσπλαγχνοι, ταπεινόφρονες,
loving [the] brothers, compassionate, humble-minded,
9 μὴ ἀποδιδόντες κακὸν ἀντὶ κακοῦ ἢ
not giving back evil instead of evil or

King James Version

railing: but contrariwise blessing; knowing that ye are thereunto called, that ye should inherit a blessing. 10 For he that will love life, and see good days, let him refrain his tongue from evil, and his lips that they speak no guile: 11 Let him eschew evil, and do good; let him seek peace, and ensue it. 12 For the eyes of the Lord *are* over the righteous, and his ears *are open* unto their prayers: but the face of the Lord *is* against them that do evil. 13And who *is* he that will harm you, if ye be followers of that which is good? 14 But and if ye suffer for righteousness' sake, happy *are ye:* and be not afraid of their terror, neither be troubled; 15 But sanctify the Lord God in your hearts: and *be* ready always to *give* an answer to every man that asketh you a reason of the hope that is in you, with meekness and fear: 16 Having a good conscience; that, whereas they speak evil of you, as of evil doers, they may be ashamed that falsely accuse your good conversation in Christ. 17 For *it is* better, if the will of God be so, that ye suffer for well doing, than for evil doing. 18 For Christ also hath once suffered for sins, the just for the unjust, that he might bring us to God, being put to death in the flesh, but quickened by the Spirit: 19 By which also he went and preached unto the spirits in prison; 20 Which sometime were disobedient, when once the longsuffering of God waited in the days of Noah, while the ark was a preparing, wherein few, that is, eight souls were saved by water. 21 The like figure whereunto *even* baptism doth also now save us, (not the putting away of the filth of the flesh, but the answer of a good conscience toward God,) by the resurrection of Jesus Christ: 22 Who is gone into heaven, and is on the right hand of God; angels and authorities and powers being made subject unto him.

4 Forasmuch then as Christ hath suffered for us in the flesh, arm yourselves likewise with the same mind: for he that hath suffered in the flesh hath ceased from sin; 2 That he no longer should live the rest of *his* time in the flesh to the lusts of men, but to the will of God. 3 For the time past of *our* life may suffice us to have wrought the will of the Gentiles, when we walked in lasciviousness, lusts, excess of wine, revellings, banquetings, and abominable idolatries: 4 Wherein they think it strange that ye run not with *them* to the same excess of riot, speaking evil of *you:* 5 Who shall give account to him that is ready to judge the quick and the dead. 6 For, for this cause was the gospel preached also to them that are dead, that they might be judged according to men in the flesh, but live

New International Version

evil with evil or insult with insult, but with blessing, because to this you were called so that you may inherit a blessing. 10 For,
"Whoever would love life
   and see good days
must keep his tongue from evil
   and his lips from deceitful speech.
11 He must turn from evil and do good;
   he must seek peace and pursue it.
12 For the eyes of the Lord are on the righteous,
   and his ears are attentive to their prayer,
but the face of the Lord is against those
   who do evil." [h]
13 Who is going to harm you if you are eager to do good? 14 But even if you should suffer for what is right, you are blessed. "Do not fear what they fear[i]; do not be frightened." [j] 15 But in your hearts acknowledge Christ as the holy Lord. Always be prepared to give an answer to everyone who asks you to give the reason for the hope that you have. 16 But do this with gentleness and respect, keeping a clear conscience, so that those who speak maliciously against your good behavior in Christ may be ashamed of their slander. 17 It is better, if it is God's will, to suffer for doing good than for doing evil. 18 For Christ died for your sins once for all, the righteous for the unrighteous, to bring you to God. He was put to death in the body but made alive by the Spirit, 19 through whom also he went and preached to the spirits in prison 20 who disobeyed long ago when God waited patiently in the days of Noah while the ark was being built. In it only a few people, eight in all, were saved through water, 21 and this water symbolizes baptism that now saves you also—not the removal of dirt from the body but the pledge of a good conscience toward God. It saves you by the resurrection of Jesus Christ, 22 who has gone into heaven and is at God's right hand—with angels, authorities and powers in submission to him.

Living for God

4 Therefore, since Christ suffered in his body, arm yourselves also with the same attitude, because he who has suffered in his body is done with sin. 2 As a result, he does not live the rest of his earthly life for evil human desires, but rather for the will of God. 3 For you have spent enough time in the past doing what pagans choose to do —living in debauchery, lust, drunkenness, orgies, carousing and detestable idolatry. 4 They think it strange that you do not plunge with them into the same flood of dissipation, and they heap abuse on you. 5 But they will have to give account to him who is ready to judge the living and the dead. 6 For this is the reason the gospel was preached even to those who are now dead, so that they might be judged according to men in regard to the body, but live according to God in regard to the spirit.

---

[h] Psalm 34:12-16. [i] Or *fear their threats.* [j] Isaiah 8:12.

Greek Interlinear

λοιδορίαν   ἀντὶ   λοιδορίας,   τοὐναντίον   δὲ
reviling   instead of   reviling,   but on the contrary

εὐλογοῦντες,   ὅτι   εἰς   τοῦτο   ἐκλήθητε   ἵνα
blessing,   because   to   this   ye were called in or-
                                        der that

εὐλογίαν   κληρονομήσητε.   10 ὁ   γὰρ   θέλων
blessing   ye might inherit.   For the [one] wishing

ζωὴν   ἀγαπᾶν   καὶ   ἰδεῖν   ἡμέρας   ἀγαθάς,
¹life   ¹to love   and   to see   ²days   ²good,

παυσάτω   τὴν   γλῶσσαν   ἀπὸ   κακοῦ   καὶ
let him   the(his)   tongue   from   evil   and
restrain

χείλη   τοῦ   μὴ   λαλῆσαι   δόλον,   11 ἐκκλινάτω
[his] lips   -   not   to speak^d   guile,   ²let him turn aside

δὲ   ἀπὸ   κακοῦ   καὶ   ποιησάτω   ἀγαθόν,
²and   from   evil   and   let him do   good,

ζητησάτω   εἰρήνην   καὶ   διωξάτω   αὐτήν·
let him seek   peace   and   pursue   it;

12 ὅτι   ὀφθαλμοὶ   κυρίου   ἐπὶ   δικαίους   καὶ
because   [the] eyes   of [the] [are] on   [the]   and
                          Lord   righteous

ὦτα   αὐτοῦ   εἰς   δέησιν   αὐτῶν,   πρόσωπον
[the]   of him [open] to   [the]   of them,   ²[the] face
ears   petition

δὲ   κυρίου   ἐπὶ   ποιοῦντας   κακά.
¹but   of [the]   [is]   [ones] doing   evil things.
        Lord   against

13 Καὶ   τίς   ὁ   κακώσων   ὑμᾶς   ἐὰν   τοῦ
And   who the   harming   you   if   ²of the
        [is] [one]

ἀγαθοῦ   ζηλωταὶ   γένησθε;   14 ἀλλ'   εἰ   καὶ
¹good   ²zealots   ¹ye become ?   but   if   indeed

πάσχοιτε   διὰ   δικαιοσύνην,   μακάριοι.   τὸν
ye suffer   because of   righteousness,   blessed [are ye].   ²the

δὲ   φόβον   αὐτῶν   μὴ   φοβηθῆτε   μηδὲ
¹But   ²fear   ²of them   ²fear ye not   nor

ταραχθῆτε,   15 κύριον   δὲ   τὸν   Χριστὸν
be ye troubled,   ¹but   ²[as] ¹Lord   -   ²Christ

ἁγιάσατε   ἐν   ταῖς   καρδίαις   ὑμῶν,   ἕτοιμοι
²sanctify   in   the   hearts   of you,   ready

ἀεὶ   πρὸς   ἀπολογίαν   παντὶ   τῷ   αἰτοῦντι
always   for   defence   to every one   asking

ὑμᾶς   λόγον   περὶ   τῆς   ἐν   ὑμῖν   ἐλπίδος,
you   a word   concerning   ²the   ²in   ²you   ²hope,

16 ἀλλὰ   μετὰ   πραΰτητος   καὶ   φόβου,
but   with   meekness   and   fear,

συνείδησιν   ἔχοντες   ἀγαθήν,   ἵνα   ἐν   ᾧ
²conscience   ¹having   ²a good,   in order that   while

καταλαλεῖσθε   καταισχυνθῶσιν   οἱ   ἐπηρεάζον-
ye are spoken against   ²may be shamed [by]   ¹the [ones]   ²abusing

τες   ὑμῶν   τὴν   ἀγαθὴν   ἐν   Χριστῷ
[you]   ²of you   ²the   ²good   ²in   ²Christ

ἀναστροφήν.   17 κρεῖττον   γὰρ   ἀγαθοποι-
²conduct.   For [it is] better   doing

οῦντας,   εἰ   θέλοι   τὸ   θέλημα   τοῦ   θεοῦ,
good,   if   ²wills   ¹the   ²will   -   ²of God,

πάσχειν   ἢ   κακοποιοῦντας.   18 ὅτι   καὶ
to suffer   than   doing evil.   Because indeed

Χριστὸς   ἅπαξ   περὶ   ἁμαρτιῶν   ἀπέθανεν,
Christ   once   ²concerning   ²sins   ¹died,

δίκαιος   ὑπὲρ   ἀδίκων,   ἵνα   ὑμᾶς   προσαγάγῃ
a righteous   half of   unrighteous   in or-   ²you   ¹he might
man   ones,   der that   bring

τῷ   θεῷ,   θανατωθεὶς   μὲν   σαρκὶ   ζωοποιηθεὶς
-    to   being put to   on one   in [the]   quickened
    God,   death   hand   flesh[,]

δὲ   πνεύματι·   19 ἐν   ᾧ   καὶ   τοῖς   ἐν
on the   in [the]   in   which   indeed   ²to the   ²in
other   spirit;

φυλακῇ   πνεύμασιν   πορευθεὶς   ἐκήρυξεν,
²prison   ²spirits   ¹going   he proclaimed,

20 ἀπειθήσασίν   ποτε   ὅτε   ἀπεξεδέχετο   ἡ
to disobeying ones   then   when   ²waited   ¹the

τοῦ   θεοῦ   μακροθυμία   ἐν   ἡμέραις   Νῶε
-    ²of God   ¹longsuffering   in   [the] days   of Noe

κατασκευαζομένης   κιβωτοῦ,   εἰς   ἣν   ὀλίγοι,
²being prepared   ¹an ark,⁸   in   which   a few,

τοῦτ'   ἔστιν   ὀκτὼ   ψυχαί,   διεσώθησαν   δι'
this   is   eight   souls,   were   through
                                quite saved

ὕδατος.   21 ὃ   καὶ   ὑμᾶς   ἀντίτυπον   νῦν
water.   ¹Which   ²also   ³us   ⁴figure   ¹now

σῴζει   βάπτισμα,   οὐ   σαρκὸς   ἀπόθεσις
²saves   [even] baptism,   not   ²of [the]   ¹a putting
                          flesh   away

ῥύπου   ἀλλὰ   συνειδήσεως   ἀγαθῆς   ἐπερώτημα
²of [the]   but   ²conscience   ²of a good   ²an answer
filth

εἰς   θεόν,   δι'   ἀναστάσεως   Ἰησοῦ   Χριστοῦ,
toward God,   through   [the] resurrection   of Jesus   Christ,

22 ὅς   ἐστιν   ἐν   δεξιᾷ   θεοῦ,   πορευθεὶς
who   is   at   [the] right   of God,   having gone
                  [hand]

εἰς   οὐρανόν,   ὑποταγέντων   αὐτῷ   ἀγγέλων
into   heaven,   ²being subjected   ²to him   ¹angels

καὶ   ἐξουσιῶν   καὶ   δυνάμεων.
²and   ³authorities   ⁴and   ¹powers⁸.

Chapter 4

Χριστοῦ   οὖν   παθόντος   σαρκὶ   καὶ   ὑμεῖς
²Christ   ¹there-   having   in [the]   ²also   ¹ye
        fore   suffered⁸   flesh

τὴν   αὐτὴν   ἔννοιαν   ὁπλίσασθε,   ὅτι   ὁ
⁴the   ²same   ²mind   ¹arm your-   because the   [one]
                          selves [with],

παθὼν   σαρκὶ   πέπαυται   ἁμαρτίας,   2 εἰς
having   in [the] flesh   has ceased   from sin,   for
suffered

τὸ   μηκέτι   ἀνθρώπων   ἐπιθυμίαις   ἀλλὰ
¹the   ²no longer   ⁴of men   ²in [the] lusts   ¹⁰but

θελήματι   θεοῦ   τὸν   ἐπίλοιπον   ἐν   σαρκὶ
¹¹in [the] will   ¹²of God   ⁴the   ⁴remaining   ⁶in   ⁷[the] flesh

βιῶσαι   χρόνον.   3 ἀρκετὸς   γὰρ   ὁ   παρεληλυ-
⁵to live   ⁴time.   For ⁵sufficient   ¹the ⁶having passed

θὼς   χρόνος   τὸ   βούλημα   τῶν   ἐθνῶν
away   ⁴time ⁷[is]   ³the   ⁴purpose   ⁸of the   ¹⁰nations

κατειργάσθαι,   πεπορευμένους   ἐν   ἀσελγείαις,
⁸to have worked out,   having gone [on]   in   licentiousnesses,

ἐπιθυμίαις,   οἰνοφλυγίαις,   κώμοις,   πότοις
lusts,   debaucheries,   carousals,   drinking
                                bouts

καὶ   ἀθεμίτοις   εἰδωλολατρίαις.   4 ἐν   ᾧ
and   unlawful   idolatries.   While

ξενίζονται   μὴ   συντρεχόντων   ὑμῶν   εἰς
they are surprised   ¹not   ²running with   ²you⁸   to

τὴν   αὐτὴν   τῆς   ἀσωτίας   ἀνάχυσιν,   βλασ-
the   same   -   ²of profligacy   ¹excess,   blas-

φημοῦντες·   5 οἳ   ἀποδώσουσιν   λόγον   τῷ
pheming;   who   will render   account to the
                                    [one]

ἑτοίμως   ἔχοντι   κρῖναι   ζῶντας   καὶ   νεκρούς.
readily   having   to judge   living   and   dead.
= who is ready

6 εἰς   τοῦτο   γὰρ   καὶ   νεκροῖς   εὐηγγελίσθη,
²for   ¹this   ³For   indeed   ⁴to   ¹good news
                          dead men   was preached,

ἵνα   κριθῶσι   μὲν   κατὰ   ἀνθρώπους
in order   ¹they might   ¹on one   according to   men
that   be judged   hand

σαρκί,   ζῶσι   δὲ   κατὰ   θεὸν   πνεύματι.
in [the]   ¹might   ¹on the according   God   in [the] spirit.
flesh,   live   other   to

King James Version

according to God in the spirit. 7 But the end of all things is at hand: be ye therefore sober, and watch unto prayer. 8And above all things have fervent charity among yourselves: for charity shall cover the multitude of sins. 9 Use hospitality one to another without grudging. 10As every man hath received the gift, *even so* minister the same one to another, as good stewards of the manifold grace of God. 11 If any man speak, *let him speak* as the oracles of God; if any man minister, *let him do it* as of the ability which God giveth; that God in all things may be glorified through Jesus Christ: to whom be praise and dominion for ever and ever. Amen. 12 Beloved, think it not strange concerning the fiery trial which is to try you, as though some strange thing happened unto you: 13 But rejoice, inasmuch as ye are partakers of Christ's sufferings; that, when his glory shall be revealed, ye may be glad also with exceeding joy. 14 If ye be reproached for the name of Christ, happy *are ye;* for the Spirit of glory and of God resteth upon you: on their part he is evil spoken of, but on your part he is glorified. 15 But let none of you suffer as a murderer, or *as* a thief, or *as* an evil doer, or as a busybody in other men's matters. 16 Yet if *any man suffer* as a Christian, let him not be ashamed; but let him glorify God on this behalf. 17 For the time *is come* that judgment must begin at the house of God: and if *it* first *begin* at us, what shall the end *be* of them that obey not the gospel of God? 18And if the righteous scarcely be saved, where shall the ungodly and the sinner appear? 19 Wherefore, let them that suffer according to the will of God commit the keeping of their souls *to him* in well doing, as unto a faithful Creator.

5 The elders which are among you I exhort, who am also an elder, and a witness of the sufferings of Christ, and also a partaker of the glory that shall be revealed: 2 Feed the flock of God which is among you, taking the oversight *thereof,* not by constraint, but willingly; not for filthy lucre, but of a ready mind; 3 Neither as being lords over *God's* heritage, but being ensamples to the flock. 4And when the chief Shepherd shall appear, ye shall receive a crown of glory that fadeth not away. 5 Likewise, ye younger, submit yourselves unto the elder. Yea, all *of you* be subject one to another, and be clothed with humility: for God resisteth the proud, and giveth grace to the humble. 6 Humble yourselves therefore under the mighty hand of God, that he may exalt you in due time: 7 Casting all your care upon him; for he careth for you. 8 Be sober, be vigilant; because your adversary the devil, as a roaring lion, walketh

New International Version

7 The end of all things is near. Therefore be clear-minded and self-controlled so that you can pray. 8Above all, love each other deeply, because love covers over a multitude of sins. 9 Offer hospitality to one another without grumbling. 10 Each one should use whatever spiritual gift he has received to serve others, faithfully administering God's grace in its various forms. 11 If anyone speaks, he should do it as one speaking the very words of God. If anyone serves, he should do it with the strength God provides, so that in all things God may be praised through Jesus Christ. To him be the glory and the power for ever and ever. Amen.

Suffering for being a Christian

12 Dear friends, do not be surprised at the painful trial you are suffering, as though something strange were happening to you. 13 But rejoice that you participate in the sufferings of Christ, so that you may be overjoyed when his glory is revealed. 14 If you are insulted because of the name of Christ, you are blessed, for the Spirit of glory and of God rests on you. 15 If you suffer, it should not be as a murderer or thief or any other kind of criminal, or even as a meddler. 16 However, if you suffer as a Christian, do not be ashamed, but praise God that you bear that name. 17 For it is time for judgment to begin with the family of God; and if it begins with us, what will the outcome be for those who do not obey the gospel of God? 18And,
"If it is hard for the righteous to be saved,
    what will become of the ungodly and the
    sinner?" *k*
19 So then, those who suffer according to God's will should commit themselves to their faithful Creator and continue to do good.

To elders and young men

5 To the elders among you, I appeal as a fellow elder, a witness of Christ's sufferings and one who also will share in the glory to be revealed: 2 Be shepherds of God's flock that is under your care, serving as overseers—not because you must, but because you are willing, as God wants you to be; not greedy for money, but eager to serve; 3 not lording it over those entrusted to you, but being examples to the flock. 4And when the Chief Shepherd appears, you will receive the crown of glory that will never fade away.
5 Young men, in the same way be submissive to those who are older. Clothe yourselves with humility toward one another, because,
"God opposes the proud
    but gives grace to the humble." *l*
6 Humble yourselves, therefore, under God's mighty hand, that he may lift you up in due time. 7 Cast all your anxiety on him because he cares for you.
8 Be self-controlled and alert. Your enemy the devil prowls around like a roaring lion looking

Greek Interlinear

7 Πάντων δὲ τὸ τέλος ἤγγικεν.
Now of all things the end has drawn near.

σωφρονήσατε οὖν καὶ νήψατε εἰς
Be ye soberminded therefore and be ye sober unto

προσευχάς· 8 πρὸ πάντων τὴν εἰς ἑαυτοὺς
prayers; before all things – ¹to ²yourselves

ἀγάπην ἐκτενῆ ἔχοντες, ὅτι ἀγάπη
¹love ²fervent ¹having, because love

καλύπτει πλῆθος ἁμαρτιῶν· 9 φιλόξενοι εἰς
covers a multitude of sins; [be] hospitable to

ἀλλήλους ἄνευ γογγυσμοῦ· 10 ἕκαστος καθὼς
one another without murmuring; each one as

ἔλαβεν χάρισμα, εἰς ἑαυτοὺς αὐτὸ διακον-
he received a gift, ²to ³yourselves ¹it ¹minister-

οῦντες ὡς καλοὶ οἰκονόμοι ποικίλης χάριτος
ing as good stewards of [the] manifold grace

θεοῦ· 11 εἴ τις λαλεῖ, ὡς λόγια θεοῦ·
of God; if anyone speaks, as [the] oracles of God;

εἴ τις διακονεῖ, ὡς ἐξ ἰσχύος ἧς χορηγεῖ
if anyone ministers, as by strength which ²supplies

ὁ θεός· ἵνα ἐν πᾶσιν δοξάζηται ὁ θεὸς
– ¹God; in or- in all things ²may be glorified – ¹God
der that

διὰ Ἰησοῦ Χριστοῦ, ᾧ ἐστιν ἡ δόξα
through Jesus Christ, to whom is° the glory
=whose is

καὶ τὸ κράτος εἰς τοὺς αἰῶνας τῶν
and the might unto the ages of the

αἰώνων· ἀμήν.
ages : Amen.

12 Ἀγαπητοί, μὴ ξενίζεσθε τῇ ἐν ὑμῖν
Beloved, be not surprised [at] ¹the ⁴among ⁵you

πυρώσει πρὸς πειρασμὸν ὑμῖν γινομένῃ,
²fiery trial ³for ⁶trial ⁷to you ³happening,

ὡς ξένου ὑμῖν συμβαίνοντος, 13 ἀλλὰ
as a surprising ²to you ¹occurring², but
thing

καθὸ κοινωνεῖτε τοῖς τοῦ Χριστοῦ
²as ³ye share ¹the – ⁴of Christ

παθήμασιν χαίρετε, ἵνα καὶ ἐν τῇ ἀπο-
⁵sufferings ¹rejoice, in order also at the reve-
that

καλύψει τῆς δόξης αὐτοῦ χαρῆτε ἀγαλ-
lation of the glory of him ye may exult-
rejoice

λιώμενοι. 14 εἰ ὀνειδίζεσθε ἐν ὀνόματι
ing. If ye are reproached in [the] name

Χριστοῦ, μακάριοι, ὅτι τὸ τῆς δόξης
of Christ, blessed [are ye], because ¹the – ²of glory

καὶ τὸ τοῦ θεοῦ πνεῦμα ἐφ᾽ ὑμᾶς
⁴and ⁵the(?that) – ⁶of God ³spirit ⁴on ⁵you

ἀναπαύεται. 15 μὴ γάρ τις ὑμῶν πασχέτω
⁷rests. ³Not ¹for ⁴anyone ²of you ³let ⁵suffer

ὡς φονεὺς ἢ κλέπτης ἢ κακοποιὸς ἢ
as a murderer or a thief or an evildoer or

ὡς ἀλλοτριεπίσκοπος· 16 εἰ δὲ ὡς
as a pryer into other men's affairs; but if as

Χριστιανός, μὴ αἰσχυνέσθω, δοξαζέτω δὲ
a Christian, let him not be shamed, but let him glorify

τὸν θεὸν ἐν τῷ ὀνόματι τούτῳ. 17 ὅτι
– God by this name. Because

[ὁ] καιρὸς τοῦ ἄρξασθαι τὸ κρίμα ἀπὸ
the – to begin⁴ the judgment from
[?has come]

τοῦ οἴκου τοῦ θεοῦ· εἰ δὲ πρῶτον ἀφ᾽
the household – of God; and if firstly from

ἡμῶν, τί τὸ τέλος τῶν ἀπειθούντων
us, what [will be] the end of the [ones] disobeying

τῷ τοῦ θεοῦ εὐαγγελίῳ; 18 καὶ εἰ ὁ
the – ²of God ¹gospel? and if the

δίκαιος μόλις σῴζεται, ὁ [δὲ] ἀσεβὴς
righteous man scarcely is saved, ²the – ⁴impious

καὶ ἁμαρτωλὸς ποῦ φανεῖται; 19 ὥστε
³and ¹sinner ⁵where ⁶will ⁷appear ? so as

καὶ οἱ πάσχοντες κατὰ τὸ θέλημα τοῦ
indeed the suffering accord- the will –
[ones] ing to

θεοῦ πιστῷ κτίστῃ παρατιθέσθωσαν τὰς
of God ²to a ²Creator ³let them commit ¹the
faithful

ψυχὰς αὐτῶν ἐν ἀγαθοποιίᾳ.
²souls ³of them in welldoing.

Chapter 5

Πρεσβυτέρους οὖν ἐν ὑμῖν παρακαλῶ
Elders there- among you I exhort
fore

ὁ συμπρεσβύτερος καὶ μάρτυς τῶν τοῦ
the co-elder and witness ¹of the –

Χριστοῦ παθημάτων, ὁ καὶ τῆς μελλούσης
²of Christ ²sufferings. ¹the ²also ⁴of the ⁵being about

ἀποκαλύπτεσθαι δόξης κοινωνός· 2 ποιμάνατε
¹to be revealed ³glory ³sharer : shepherd

τὸ ἐν ὑμῖν ποίμνιον τοῦ θεοῦ, μὴ
¹the ²among ³you ²flock – ³of God, not

ἀναγκαστῶς ἀλλὰ ἑκουσίως κατὰ θεόν,
by way of but willingly accord- God,
compulsion ing to

μηδὲ αἰσχροκερδῶς ἀλλὰ προθύμως, 3 μηδ᾽
nor from eagerness for but eagerly, nor
base gain

ὡς κατακυριεύοντες τῶν κλήρων ἀλλὰ
as exercising lordship over the lots* but

τύποι γινόμενοι τοῦ ποιμνίου· 4 καὶ
¹examples ¹becoming of the flock; and

φανερωθέντος τοῦ ἀρχιποίμενος κομιεῖσθε
appearing the chief shepherd* ye will receive
=when the chief shepherd appears

τὸν ἀμάραντινον τῆς δόξης στέφανον.
the unfading ²of glory ¹crown.

5 Ὁμοίως, νεώτεροι, ὑποτάγητε πρεσβυτέ-
Likewise, younger men, submit yourselves to older

ροις· πάντες δὲ ἀλλήλοις τὴν ταπεινοφρο-
men; and ²to one another – ¹humil-

σύνην ἐγκομβώσασθε, ὅτι ὁ θεὸς ὑπερηφάνοις
ity ¹gird ye on, because – God ¹arrogant men

ἀντιτάσσεται, ταπεινοῖς δὲ δίδωσιν χάριν.
¹resists, but to humble men he gives grace.

6 Ταπεινώθητε οὖν ὑπὸ τὴν κραταιὰν
Be ye humbled therefore under the mighty

χεῖρα τοῦ θεοῦ, ἵνα ὑμᾶς ὑψώσῃ ἐν
hand – of God, in order ²you ¹he may exalt in
that

καιρῷ, 7 πᾶσαν τὴν μέριμναν ὑμῶν
time, ¹all ²the ²anxiety ³of you

ἐπιρίψαντες ἐπ᾽ αὐτόν, ὅτι αὐτῷ μέλει
¹casting on him, because ²to him ¹it matters

περὶ ὑμῶν. 8 Νήψατε, γρηγορήσατε. ὁ
concerning you. Be ye sober, watch ye. The

ἀντίδικος ὑμῶν διάβολος ὡς λέων ὠρυόμενος
adversary of you [the] devil as a lion roaring

* That is, the various spheres assigned to the elders.

King James Version

about, seeking whom he may devour: 9 Whom resist steadfast in the faith, knowing that the same afflictions are accomplished in your brethren that are in the world. 10 But the God of all grace, who hath called us unto his eternal glory by Christ Jesus, after that ye have suffered a while, make you perfect, stablish, strengthen, settle *you.* 11 To him *be* glory and dominion for ever and ever. Amen. 12 By Silvanus, a faithful brother unto you, as I suppose, I have written briefly, exhorting, and testifying that this is the true grace of God wherein ye stand. 13 The *church that is* at Babylon, elected together with *you,* saluteth you; and *so doth* Marcus my son. 14 Greet ye one another with a kiss of charity. Peace *be* with you all that are in Christ Jesus. Amen.

New International Version

for someone to devour. 9 Resist him, standing firm in the faith, because you know that your brothers throughout the world are undergoing the same kind of sufferings.

10 And the God of all grace, who called you to his eternal glory in Christ, after you have suffered a little while, will himself restore you and make you strong, firm and steadfast. 11 To him be the power for ever and ever. Amen.

Final greetings

12 With the help of Silas,*ᵐ* whom I regard as a faithful brother, I have written to you briefly, encouraging you and testifying that this is the true grace of God. Stand fast in it.

13 She who is in Babylon, chosen together with you, sends you her greetings, and so does my son Mark. 14 Greet one another with a kiss of love.

Peace to all of you who are in Christ.

[m] Greek *Silvanus.*

Greek Interlinear

περιπατεῖ ζητῶν τινα καταπιεῖν· 9 ᾧ
walks about seeking whom to devour; whom
ἀντίστητε στερεοὶ τῇ πίστει, εἰδότες τὰ
oppose firm in the faith, knowing the
αὐτὰ τῶν παθημάτων τῇ ἐν τῷ κόσμῳ
same of the sufferings ²in ⁵in ⁶the ⁷world
⁴hings
ὑμῶν ἀδελφότητι ἐπιτελεῖσθαι. 10 Ὁ δὲ
³of you ³brotherhood ¹to be accomplished. ²the ¹Now
θεὸς πάσης χάριτος, ὁ καλέσας ὑμᾶς
God of all grace, the [one] having called you
εἰς τὴν αἰώνιον αὐτοῦ δόξαν ἐν Χριστῷ,
to the ¹eternal ²of him ³glory in Christ,
ὀλίγον παθόντας αὐτὸς καταρτίσει, στηρίξει,
¹[you] ³having [him]self will adjust, confirm,
²a little suffered
σθενώσει, θεμελιώσει. 11 αὐτῷ τὸ κράτος
strengthen, found. To him [is]ᶜ the might
= His is*
εἰς τοὺς αἰῶνας τῶν αἰώνων· ἀμήν.
unto the ages of the ages: Amen.

12 Διὰ Σιλουανοῦ ὑμῖν τοῦ πιστοῦ
Through Silvanus to you the faithful
ἀδελφοῦ, ὡς λογίζομαι, δι᾽ ὀλίγων ἔγραψα,
brother, as I reckon, by a few I wrote,
means of [words]
παρακαλῶν καὶ ἐπιμαρτυρῶν ταύτην εἶναι
exhorting and witnessing this to be
ἀληθῆ χάριν τοῦ θεοῦ, εἰς ἣν στῆτε.
[the] true grace – of God, in which ye stand.
13 Ἀσπάζεται ὑμᾶς ἡ ἐν Βαβυλῶνι
¹⁰greets ¹¹you ¹The ²in ⁴Babylon
συνεκλεκτὴ καὶ Μᾶρκος ὁ υἱός μου.
²co-chosen ⁵and ⁶Mark ⁷the ⁸son ⁹of me.
[? church]
14 ἀσπάσασθε ἀλλήλους ἐν φιλήματι ἀγάπης.
Greet ye one another with a kiss of love.
Εἰρήνη ὑμῖν πᾶσιν τοῖς ἐν Χριστῷ.
Peace to you all the ones in Christ.

---

* Cf. 4. 11 (a statement of fact, not a wish).

695

King James Version

THE SECOND

EPISTLE GENERAL

OF

PETER

New International Version

2 PETER

1 Simon Peter, a servant and an apostle of Jesus Christ, to them that have obtained like precious faith with us through the righteousness of God and our Saviour Jesus Christ: 2 Grace and peace be multiplied unto you through the knowledge of God, and of Jesus our Lord, 3 According as his divine power hath given unto us all things that *pertain* unto life and godliness, through the knowledge of him that hath called us to glory and virtue: 4 Whereby are given unto us exceeding great and precious promises; that by these ye might be partakers of the divine nature, having escaped the corruption that is in the world through lust. 5And besides this, giving all diligence, add to your faith virtue; and to virtue, knowledge; 6And to knowledge, temperance; and to temperance, patience; and to patience, godliness; 7And to godliness, brotherly kindness; and to brotherly kindness, charity. 8 For if these things be in you, and abound, they make *you that ye shall* neither *be* barren nor unfruitful in the knowledge of our Lord Jesus Christ. 9 But he that lacketh these things is blind, and cannot see afar off, and hath forgotten that he was purged from his old sins. 10 Wherefore the rather, brethren, give diligence to make your calling and election sure: for if ye do these things, ye shall never fall: 11 For so an entrance shall be ministered unto you abundantly into the everlasting kingdom of our Lord and Saviour Jesus Christ. 12 Wherefore I will not be negligent to put you always in remembrance of these things, though ye know *them,* and be established in the present truth. 13 Yea, I think it meet, as long as I am in this tabernacle, to stir you up by putting *you* in remembrance; 14 Knowing that shortly I must put off *this* my tabernacle, even as our Lord Jesus Christ hath shewed me. 15 Moreover I will endeavour that ye may be able after my decease to have these things always in remembrance. 16 For we have not followed cunningly devised fables, when we made known unto you the power and coming of our Lord Jesus Christ, but were eyewitnesses of his majesty. 17 For he received from God the Father honour and glory, when there came such a voice

1 Simon Peter, a servant and apostle of Jesus Christ,

To those who through the righteousness of our God and Savior Jesus Christ have received a faith as precious as ours:

2 Grace and peace be yours in abundance through the knowledge of God and of Jesus our Lord.

Making one's calling and election sure

3 His divine power has given us everything we need for life and godliness through our knowledge of him who called us by his own glory and goodness. 4 Through these he has given us his very great and precious promises, so that through them you may participate in the divine nature and escape the corruption in the world caused by evil desires.

5 For this very reason, make every effort to add to your faith goodness; and to goodness, knowledge; 6 and to knowledge, self-control; and to self-control, perseverance; and to perseverance, godliness; 7 and to godliness, brotherly kindness; and to brotherly kindness, love. 8 For if you possess these qualities in increasing measure, they will keep you from being ineffective and unproductive in your knowledge of our Lord Jesus Christ. 9 But if anyone does not have them, he is nearsighted and blind, and has forgotten that he has been cleansed from his past sins.

10 Therefore, my brothers, be all the more eager to make your calling and election sure. For if you do these things, you will never fall, 11 and you will receive a rich welcome into the eternal kingdom of our Lord and Savior Jesus Christ.

Prophecy of scripture

12 So I will always remind you of these things, even though you know them and are firmly established in the truth you now have. 13 I think it is right to refresh your memory as long as I live in the tent of this body, 14 because I know that I will soon put it aside, as our Lord Jesus Christ has made clear to me. 15And I will make every effort to see that after my departure you will always be able to remember these things.

16 We did not follow cleverly invented stories when we told you about the power and coming of our Lord Jesus Christ, but we were eyewitnesses of his majesty. 17 For he received honor and glory from God the Father when the voice came to him from the Majestic Glory, saying

ΠΕΤΡΟΥ Β
Chapter 1

Συμεών   Πέτρος   δοῦλος   καὶ   ἀπόστολος
Symeon   Peter   a slave and   an apostle
'Ιησοῦ   Χριστοῦ   τοῖς   ἰσότιμον   ἡμῖν
of Jesus Christ   ¹to the ²equally   ⁴with
λαχοῦσιν πίστιν   ἐν   δικαιοσύνῃ   τοῦ   θεοῦ
³having   ⁴faith   in   righteousness of God the God
obtained [the]
ἡμῶν   καὶ   σωτῆρος   'Ιησοῦ   Χριστοῦ·
of us   and   Saviour   Jesus   Christ :
2 χάρις   ὑμῖν   καὶ   εἰρήνη   πληθυνθείη   ἐν
Grace   to you anu   peace   may it be multiplied by
ἐπιγνώσει   τοῦ   θεοῦ   καὶ   'Ιησοῦ   τοῦ
a full knowledge - of God and   of Jesus the
κυρίου   ἡμῶν.
Lord   of us.
3 Ὡς   τὰ   πάντα   ἡμῖν   τῆς   θείας   δυνάμεως
As   -   all things to us   the   divine   power
                                     =his divine power has given us all things . . .
αὐτοῦ   τὰ   πρὸς   ζωὴν   καὶ   εὐσέβειαν   δεδωρημένης
of him -   [belong- life and   piety   having given⁹
             ing] to
διὰ   τῆς   ἐπιγνώσεως   τοῦ   καλέσαντος   ἡμᾶς
through the   full knowledge of the [one] having called us
ἰδίᾳ   δόξῃ   καὶ   ἀρετῇ,   4 δι'   ὧν   τὰ   τίμια
to [his] glory and virtue, through which the ³precious
own   things
καὶ   μέγιστα   ἡμῖν   ἐπαγγέλματα   δεδώρηται,
¹and ²very great ³to us ⁴promises   ¹he has given,
ἵνα   διὰ   τούτων   γένησθε   θείας   κοινωνοὶ
in or- through these   ye might ⁴of a divine ⁵sharers
der that   become
φύσεως,   ἀποφυγόντες   τῆς   ἐν   τῷ   κόσμῳ
¹nature,   escaping from ¹the ²in   ⁴the ⁵world
ἐν   ἐπιθυμίᾳ   φθορᾶς.   5 καὶ   αὐτὸ   τοῦτο
⁶by ⁷lust   ³corruption. ⁴also ⁵for this very thing
                                        (reason)
δὲ   σπουδὴν   πᾶσαν   παρεισενέγκαντες
¹But   diligence   ⁴all   ⁵bringing in
ἐπιχορηγήσατε   ἐν   τῇ   πίστει   ὑμῶν   τὴν
supply   in   the   faith   of you   -
ἀρετήν,   ἐν   δὲ   τῇ   ἀρετῇ   τὴν   γνῶσιν,
virtue,   and in -   virtue   -   knowledge,
6 ἐν   δὲ   τῇ   γνώσει   τὴν   ἐγκράτειαν,
and in -   the   knowledge -   self-control,
ἐν   δὲ   τῇ   ἐγκρατείᾳ   τὴν   ὑπομονήν,   ἐν
and in -   self-control -   endurance,   ²in
δὲ   τῇ   ὑπομονῇ   τὴν   εὐσέβειαν,   7 ἐν   δὲ
¹and -   endurance   -   piety,   and in
τῇ   εὐσεβείᾳ   τὴν   φιλαδελφίαν,   ἐν   δὲ
-   piety   -   brotherly friendship, -   and in
τῇ   φιλαδελφίᾳ   τὴν   ἀγάπην.   8 ταῦτα
- brotherly friendship -   love.   these things
γὰρ   ὑμῖν   ὑπάρχοντα   καὶ   πλεονάζοντα
For   ²in you ¹being   and   abounding
οὐκ   ἀργοὺς   οὐδὲ   ἀκάρπους   καθίστησιν
²not ⁴barren ⁵nor   ⁶unfruitful ¹makes ³[you]
εἰς   τὴν   τοῦ   κυρίου   ἡμῶν   'Ιησοῦ   Χριστοῦ
in   ¹the ²of the ³Lord   ⁴of us ⁵Jesus ⁶Christ
ἐπίγνωσιν·   9 ᾧ   γὰρ   μὴ   πάρεστιν   ταῦτα,
⁷full knowledge; for [he] ²not   ¹is(are)   ¹these
              in whom   ⁴present   things.

τυφλός   ἐστιν   μυωπάζων,   λήθην   λαβὼν
²blind   ¹is   being short-sighted, forgetfulness taking
                                       =being forgetful
τοῦ   καθαρισμοῦ   τῶν   πάλαι   αὐτοῦ   ἁμαρτιῶν.
of the   cleansing of the ²in time ³of him ¹sins.
                           past
10 διὸ   μᾶλλον,   ἀδελφοί,   σπουδάσατε
Wherefore rather,   brothers,   be ye diligent
βεβαίαν   ὑμῶν   τὴν   κλῆσιν   καὶ   ἐκλογὴν
²firm   ⁷of you ³the ⁴calling ⁵and ⁶choice
ποιεῖσθαι·   ταῦτα   γὰρ   ποιοῦντες   οὐ   μὴ
¹to make;   for these things doing   by no means
πταίσητέ   ποτε.   11 οὕτως   γὰρ   πλουσίως
ye will fail ever.   For so   ³richly
ἐπιχορηγηθήσεται   ὑμῖν   ἡ   εἴσοδος   εἰς   τὴν
¹will be supplied ²to you the   entrance   into   the
αἰώνιον   βασιλείαν   τοῦ   κυρίου   ἡμῶν   καὶ
eternal   kingdom   of the   Lord   of us   and
σωτῆρος   'Ιησοῦ   Χριστοῦ.
Saviour   Jesus   Christ.
12 Διὸ   μελλήσω   ἀεὶ   ὑμᾶς   ὑπομιμνῄσκειν
Wherefore I will intend always you   to remind
περὶ   τούτων,   καίπερ   εἰδότας   καὶ
concerning these things, though   knowing   and
ἐστηριγμένους   ἐν   τῇ   παρούσῃ   ἀληθείᾳ.
having been confirmed in the   present   truth.
13 δίκαιον   δὲ   ἡγοῦμαι,   ἐφ'   ὅσον   εἰμὶ
And ²right δὲ   I deem [it], so long as† I am
ἐν   τούτῳ   τῷ   σκηνώματι,   διεγείρειν   ὑμᾶς
in   this   τῷ   tabernacle,   to rouse   you
ἐν   ὑπομνήσει,   14 εἰδὼς   ὅτι   ταχινή   ἐστιν
by   a reminder,   knowing that soon   is
ἡ   ἀπόθεσις   τοῦ   σκηνώματός   μου,   καθὼς
the putting off of the tabernacle   of me,   as
καὶ   ὁ   κύριος   ἡμῶν   'Ιησοῦς   Χριστὸς
indeed the Lord   of us   Jesus   Christ
ἐδήλωσέν   μοι·   15 σπουδάσω   δὲ   καὶ
made clear to me;   and I will be diligent δὲ   also
ἑκάστοτε   ἔχειν   ὑμᾶς   μετὰ   τὴν   ἐμὴν
¹always ⁴to have ²you   ³after -   ⁶my
ἔξοδον   τὴν   τούτων   μνήμην   ποιεῖσθαι.
⁷exodus   ⁵the ¹⁰of these things ⁸memory ⁹to cause.
16 οὐ   γὰρ   σεσοφισμένοις   μύθοις   ἐξακολου-
For not   ³having been   ⁴fables   ⁵follow-
              cleverly devised
θήσαντες   ἐγνωρίσαμεν   ὑμῖν   τὴν   τοῦ   κυρίου
ing   we made known to you ¹the ²of the ⁴Lord
ἡμῶν   'Ιησοῦ   Χριστοῦ   δύναμιν   καὶ
⁵of us ⁶Jesus ⁷Christ   ³power   ⁸and
παρουσίαν,   ἀλλ'   ἐπόπται   γενηθέντες   τῆς
³presence,   but   ⁴eyewitnesses ¹having become ²of the
ἐκείνου   μεγαλειότητος.   17 λαβὼν   γὰρ
⁵of that one ⁶majesty.   For receiving
παρὰ   θεοῦ   πατρὸς   τιμὴν   καὶ   δόξαν
from   God [the] Father honour   and   glory
φωνῆς   ἐνεχθείσης   αὐτῷ   τοιᾶσδε   ὑπὸ   τῆς
³a voice ²being borne⁴ ⁵to him ¹such   by   the
μεγαλοπρεποῦς   δόξης·   ὁ   υἱός   μου   ὁ
magnificent   glory :   The   Son   of me   the

697

King James Version

to him from the excellent glory, This is my beloved Son, in whom I am well pleased. 18And this voice which came from heaven we heard, when we were with him in the holy mount. 19 We have also a more sure word of prophecy; whereunto ye do well that ye take heed, as unto a light that shineth in a dark place, until the day dawn, and the daystar arise in your hearts: 20 Knowing this first, that no prophecy of the Scripture is of any private interpretation. 21 For the prophecy came not in old time by the will of man: but holy men of God spake *as they were* moved by the Holy Ghost.

2 But there were false prophets also among the people, even as there shall be false teachers among you, who privily shall bring in damnable heresies, even denying the Lord that bought them, and bring upon themselves swift destruction. 2And many shall follow their pernicious ways; by reason of whom the way of truth shall be evil spoken of. 3And through covetousness shall they with feigned words make merchandise of you: whose judgment now of a long time lingereth not, and their damnation slumbereth not. 4 For if God spared not the angels that sinned, but cast *them* down to hell, and delivered *them* into chains of darkness, to be reserved unto judgment; 5And spared not the old world, but saved Noah the eighth *person*, a preacher of righteousness, bringing in the flood upon the world of the ungodly; 6And turning the cities of Sodom and Gomorrah into ashes condemned *them* with an overthrow, making *them* an ensample unto those that after should live ungodly; 7And delivered just Lot, vexed with the filthy conversation of the wicked: 8 (For that righteous man dwelling among them, in seeing and hearing, vexed *his* righteous soul from day to day with *their* unlawful deeds:) 9 The Lord knoweth how to deliver the godly out of temptation, and to reserve the unjust unto the day of judgment to be punished: 10 But chiefly them that walk after the flesh in the lust of uncleanness, and despise government. Presumptuous *are they*, selfwilled, they are not afraid to speak evil of dignities. 11 Whereas angels, which are greater in power and might, bring not railing accusation against them before the Lord. 12 But these, as natural brute beasts made to be taken and destroyed, speak evil of the things that they understand not; and shall utterly perish in their own corruption; 13And shall receive the reward of unrighteousness, *as* they that count it pleasure to riot in the daytime. Spots *they are* and blemishes, sporting themselves with their own deceivings while they feast with you; 14 Having eyes full of adultery, and that cannot cease

New International Version

"This is my Son, whom I love; with him I am well-pleased." 18 We ourselves heard this voice that came from heaven when we were with him on the sacred mountain.

19 And we have the word of the prophets made more certain, and you will do well to pay attention to it, as to a light shining in a dark place, until the day dawns and the morning star rises in your hearts. 20Above all, you must understand that no prophecy of Scripture came about by the prophet's own interpretation. 21 For prophecy never had its origin in the will of man, but men spoke from God as they were carried along by the Holy Spirit.

False teachers and their destruction

2 But there were also false prophets among the people, just as there will be false teachers among you. They will secretly introduce destructive heresies, even denying the sovereign Lord who bought them—bringing swift destruction on themselves. 2 Many will follow their shameful ways and will bring the way of truth into disrepute. 3 In their greed these teachers will exploit you with stories they have made up. Their condemnation has long been hanging over them, and their destruction has not been sleeping.

4 For if God did not spare angels when they sinned, but sent them to hell,[a] putting them into gloomy dungeons[b] to be held for judgment; 5 if he did not spare the ancient world when he brought the flood on its ungodly people, but protected Noah, a preacher of righteousness, and seven others; 6 if he condemned the cities of Sodom and Gomorrah by burning them to ashes, and made them an example of what is going to happen to the ungodly; 7 and if he rescued Lot, a righteous man, who was distressed by the filthy lives of lawless men 8 (for that righteous man, living among them day after day, was tormented by the lawless deeds he saw and heard)—9 if this is so, then the Lord knows how to rescue godly men from trials and to hold the unrighteous for the day of judgment, while continuing their punishment. 10 This is especially true of those who follow the corrupt desire of their sinful natures and despise authority.

Bold and arrogant, these men are not afraid to slander celestial beings; 11 yet even angels, although they are stronger and more powerful, do not bring slanderous accusations against such beings in the presence of the Lord. 12 But these men blaspheme in matters they do not understand. They are like brute beasts, creatures of instinct, born only to be caught and destroyed, and like beasts they too will perish.

13 They will be paid back with harm for the harm they have done. Their idea of pleasure is to carouse in broad daylight. They are blots and blemishes, reveling in their pleasures while they feast with you.[c] 14 With eyes full of adultery, they never stop sinning; they seduce the unstable;

[a] Greek *Tartarus*. [b] Some early MSS read *into chains of darkness*. [c] Some MSS read *in their love feasts*.

698

Greek Interlinear

ἀγαπητός μου οὗτός ἐστιν, εἰς ὃν ἐγὼ
beloved of me this is, in whom I

εὐδόκησα, — 18 καὶ ταύτην τὴν φωνὴν
was wellpleased,— and this – voice

ἡμεῖς ἠκούσαμεν ἐξ οὐρανοῦ ἐνεχθεῖσαν
we heard ¹out of ²heaven ¹being borne

σὺν αὐτῷ ὄντες ἐν τῷ ἁγίῳ ὄρει. 19 καὶ
³with ⁴him ²being in the holy mountain. And

ἔχομεν βεβαιότερον τὸν προφητικὸν λόγον,
we have more firm the prophetic word,

ᾧ καλῶς ποιεῖτε προσέχοντες ὡς λύχνῳ
to ²well ¹ye do taking heed as to a lamp
which

φαίνοντι ἐν αὐχμηρῷ τόπῳ, ἕως οὗ
shining in a murky place, until

ἡμέρα διαυγάσῃ καὶ φωσφόρος ἀνατείλῃ
day dawns and [the] daystar rises

ἐν ταῖς καρδίαις ὑμῶν· 20 τοῦτο πρῶτον
in the hearts of you; ²this ¹firstly

γινώσκοντες, ὅτι πᾶσα προφητεία γραφῆς
¹knowing, that every prophecy of scripture
=no ... is ...

ἰδίας ἐπιλύσεως οὐ γίνεται· 21 οὐ γὰρ
of [its] own solution not becomes; for not

θελήματι ἀνθρώπου ἠνέχθη προφητεία
by will of man ¹was borne ²prophecy

ποτέ, ἀλλὰ ὑπὸ πνεύματος ἁγίου φερόμενοι
at any but ⁶by ⁵Spirit ⁷[the] ¹being borne
time, Holy

ἐλάλησαν ἀπὸ θεοῦ ἄνθρωποι.
²spoke ⁴from ⁵God ¹men.

Chapter 2

Ἐγένοντο δὲ καὶ ψευδοπροφῆται ἐν
But there were also false prophets among

τῷ λαῷ, ὡς καὶ ἐν ὑμῖν ἔσονται
the people, as indeed among you there will be

ψευδοδιδάσκαλοι, οἵτινες παρεισάξουσιν
false teachers, who will secretly bring in

αἱρέσεις ἀπωλείας, καὶ τὸν ἀγοράσαντα
opinions of destruction,* and ²the ¹having bought

αὐτοὺς δεσπότην ἀρνούμενοι, ἐπάγοντες
²them Master ¹denying, bringing on

ἑαυτοῖς ταχινὴν ἀπώλειαν· 2 καὶ πολλοὶ
themselves swift destruction; and many

ἐξακολουθήσουσιν αὐτῶν ταῖς ἀσελγείαις,
will follow ¹of them ²the ¹licentiousnesses,

δι' οὓς ἡ ὁδὸς τῆς ἀληθείας βλασφημη-
be- whom the way of the truth will be
cause of

θήσεται· 3 καὶ ἐν πλεονεξίᾳ πλαστοῖς
blasphemed; and by covetousness with fabricated

λόγοις ὑμᾶς ἐμπορεύσονται· οἷς τὸ κρίμα
words ²you ¹they will make for the judg-
merchandise of; whom ment

ἔκπαλαι οὐκ ἀργεῖ, καὶ ἡ· ἀπώλεια
of old lingers not, and the destruction

αὐτῶν οὐ νυστάζει. 4 εἰ γὰρ ὁ θεὸς
of them slumbers not. For if – God

ἀγγέλων ἁμαρτησάντων οὐκ ἐφείσατο, ἀλλὰ
²angels ¹sinning not ¹spared not, but

σιροῖς ζόφου ταρταρώσας παρέδωκεν
²in pits ¹of gloom ¹consigning to Tartarus ⁴delivered [them]

εἰς κρίσιν τηρουμένους, 5 καὶ ἀρχαίου
²to ¹judgment ¹being kept, and ²[the] ancient

κόσμου οὐκ ἐφείσατο, ἀλλὰ ὄγδοον Νῶε
³world ¹spared not, but ¹[the] ²eighth man

δικαιοσύνης κήρυκα ἐφύλαξεν, κατακλυσμὸν
¹of righteousness ²a herald ¹guarded, ²a flood

κόσμῳ ἀσεβῶν ἐπάξας, 6 καὶ πόλεις
⁴a world ²of impious men ¹bringing ²on, and ²[the] cities

Σοδόμων καὶ Γομόρρας τεφρώσας
²of Sodom ²and ⁴Gomorra ¹covering [them]
with ashes

καταστροφῇ κατέκρινεν, ὑπόδειγμα μελ-
¹by an overthrow ¹condemned, ²an example ²of men

λόντων ἀσεβεῖν τεθεικώς, 7 καὶ δίκαιον
intending ²to live ¹having set(made), and ²righteous
impiously

Λὼτ καταπονούμενον ὑπὸ τῆς τῶν ἀθέσμων
²Lot *being oppressed ²by ²the ¹of the ¹¹lawless

ἐν ἀσελγείᾳ ἀναστροφῆς ἐρρύσατο· 8 βλέμ-
²in ²licentiousness ¹conduct ¹delivered; ¹in

ματι γὰρ καὶ ἀκοῇ ὁ δίκαιος ἐγκατοικῶν
seeing ¹for and in hear- the righteous dwelling
ing (that) man

ἐν αὐτοῖς ἡμέραν ἐξ ἡμέρας ψυχὴν
among them day after† day ²[his] ⁴soul

δικαίαν ἀνόμοις ἔργοις ἐβασάνιζεν·
²righteous ¹with [their] lawless ³works ¹tormented;

9 οἶδεν κύριος εὐσεβεῖς ἐκ πειρασμοῦ
¹knows★ ¹[the] Lord ²pious men ²out of ⁴trial

ῥύεσθαι, ἀδίκους δὲ εἰς ἡμέραν κρίσεως
²to deliver, ¹unjust men ¹but ²for ¹a day ²of judgment

κολαζομένους τηρεῖν, 10 μάλιστα δὲ τοὺς
⁴being punished ¹to keep, and most of all ³the

ὀπίσω σαρκὸς ἐν ἐπιθυμίᾳ μιασμοῦ
²after ³flesh ²in ⁴lust ²of defilement ☆

πορευομένους καὶ κυριότητος καταφρονοῦντας.
²[ones] going ²and ¹⁰dominion ¹despising.

τολμηταὶ αὐθάδεις, δόξας οὐ τρέμουσιν
²darers ¹Self-satisfied, glories they do not tremble [at]

βλασφημοῦντες, 11 ὅπου ἄγγελοι ἰσχύϊ καὶ
blaspheming, where angels in strength ²and

δυνάμει μείζονες ὄντες οὐ φέρουσιν κατ'
²in power ²greater ²being do not bring against

αὐτῶν παρὰ κυρίῳ βλάσφημον κρίσιν.
them ¹[the] Lord railing judgment.

12 οὗτοι δέ, ὡς ἄλογα ζῷα γεγεννημένα
But these ¹as ⁴without ⁵animals ³having been
men, reason born

φυσικὰ εἰς ἅλωσιν καὶ φθοράν, ἐν οἷς
¹natural for capture and corruption, ²in ³things
which

ἀγνοοῦσιν βλασφημοῦντες, ἐν τῇ φθορᾷ
³they are ¹railing, in the corruption
ignorant [of]

αὐτῶν καὶ φθαρήσονται, 13 ἀδικούμενοι
of them indeed they will be corrupted, suffering wrong

μισθὸν ἀδικίας· ἡδονὴν ἡγούμενοι τὴν
[as] wages of wrong; ²[to be] pleasure ¹deeming ³the

ἐν ἡμέρᾳ τρυφήν, σπίλοι καὶ μῶμοι
⁴in ⁵[the] day ⁴luxury, spots and blemishes

ἐντρυφῶντες ἐν ταῖς ἀπάταις αὐτῶν
revelling in the deceits of them

συνευωχούμενοι ὑμῖν, 14 ὀφθαλμοὺς ἔχοντες
feasting along with you, · ²eyes ¹having

μεστοὺς μοιχαλίδος καὶ ἀκαταπαύστους
full of an adulteress and not ceasing from

---

*Genitive of quality : " destructive opinions."
★That is, " the Lord can deliver "; see note on page xxxviii.
☆Genitive of quality: " defiling lust."

King James Version

from sin; beguiling unstable souls: a heart they
have exercised with covetous practices; cursed
children: 15 Which have forsaken the right way,
and are gone astray, following the way of Balaam *the son* of Bosor, who loved the wages
of unrighteousness; 16 But was rebuked for his
iniquity: the dumb ass speaking with man's voice
forbade the madness of the prophet. 17 These
are wells without water, clouds that are carried
with a tempest; to whom the mist of darkness
is reserved for ever. 18 For when they speak great
swelling *words* of vanity, they allure through
the lusts of the flesh, *through much* wantonness,
those that were clean escaped from them who
live in error. 19 While they promise them liberty,
they themselves are the servants of corruption:
for of whom a man is overcome, of the same is
he brought in bondage. 20 For if after they have
escaped the pollutions of the world through the
knowledge of the Lord and Saviour Jesus Christ,
they are again entangled therein, and overcome,
the latter end is worse with them than the beginning. 21 For it had been better for them not
to have known the way of righteousness, than,
after they have known *it*, to turn from the holy
commandment delivered unto them. 22 But it is
happened unto them according to the true proverb, The dog *is* turned to his own vomit again;
and, The sow that was washed to her wallowing
in the mire.

3 This second epistle, beloved, I now write
unto you; in *both* which I stir up your pure
minds by way of remembrance: 2 That ye may
be mindful of the words which were spoken
before by the holy prophets, and of the commandment of us the apostles of the Lord and
Saviour: 3 Knowing this first, that there shall
come in the last days scoffers, walking after
their own lusts, 4 And saying, Where is the promise of his coming? for since the fathers fell
asleep, all things continue as *they were* from
the beginning of the creation. 5 For this they
willingly are ignorant of, that by the word of
God the heavens were of old, and the earth
standing out of the water and in the water:
6 Whereby the world that then was, being over-
flowed with water, perished: 7 But the heavens
and the earth, which are now, by the same word
are kept in store, reserved unto fire against the
day of judgment and perdition of ungodly men.
8 But, beloved, be not ignorant of this one thing,
that one day *is* with the Lord as a thousand
years, and a thousand years as one day. 9 The
Lord is not slack concerning his promise, as
some men count slackness; but is longsuffering

New International Version

they are experts in greed—an accursed brood!
15 They have left the straight way and wandered
off to follow the way of Balaam son of Beor,
who loved the wages of wickedness. 16 But he
was rebuked for his wrongdoing by a donkey—
a beast without speech—who spoke with a
man's voice and restrained the prophet's madness.
17 These men are springs without water and
mists driven by a storm. Blackest darkness is
reserved for them. 18 For they mouth empty,
boastful words and, by appealing to the lustful
desires of sinful human nature, they entice people who are just escaping from those who live
in error. 19 They promise them freedom, while
they themselves are slaves of depravity—for a
man is a slave to whatever has mastered him.
20 If they have escaped the corruption of the
world by knowing our Lord and Savior Jesus
Christ and are again entangled in it and overcome, they are worse off at the end than they
were at the beginning. 21 It would have been
better for them not to have known the way of
righteousness, than to have known it and then
to turn their backs on the sacred commandment that was passed on to them. 22 Of them
the proverbs are true: "A dog returns to its
vomit," [d] and, "A sow that is washed goes back
to her wallowing in the mud."

The day of the Lord

3 Dear friends, this is now my second letter to
you. I have written both of them as remind-
ers to stimulate you to wholesome thinking. 2 I
want you to recall the words spoken in the past
by the holy prophets and the command given by
our Lord and Savior through your apostles.
3 First of all, you must understand that in
the last days scoffers will come, scoffing and following their own evil desires. 4 They will say,
"Where is this 'coming' he promised? Ever since
our fathers died, everything goes on as it has
since the beginning of creation." 5 But they deliberately forget that long ago by God's word
the heavens existed and the earth was formed
out of water and with water. 6 By water also the
world of that time was deluged and destroyed.
7 By the same word the present heavens and
earth are reserved for fire, being kept for the day
of judgment and destruction of ungodly men.
8 But do not forget this one thing, dear
friends: With the Lord a day is like a thousand
years, and a thousand years are like a day. 9 The
Lord is not slow in keeping his promise, as
some understand slowness. He is patient with

[d] Prov. 26:11.

Greek Interlinear

ἀμαρτίας, δελεάζοντες ψυχὰς ἀστηρίκτους,
sin, alluring ²souls ¹unsteady,

καρδίαν γεγυμνασμένην πλεονεξίας ἔχοντες,
²a heart ³having been exercised ⁴of(in) covetousness ¹having,

κατάρας τέκνα· 15 καταλείποντες εὐθεῖαν
¹of curse ¹children; forsaking a straight

ὁδὸν ἐπλανήθησαν, ἐξακολουθήσαντες τῇ
way they erred, following the

ὁδῷ τοῦ Βαλαὰμ τοῦ Βεώρ, ὃς μισθὸν
way - of Balaam the [son] of who ²[the]
Beor, wages

ἀδικίας ἠγάπησεν, 16 ἔλεγξιν δὲ ἔσχεν
²of wrong ¹loved, and ²reproof ¹had

ἰδίας παρανομίας· ὑποζύγιον ἄφωνον ἐν
of [his] own transgression; ²ass ¹a dumb ⁴with

ἀνθρώπου φωνῇ φθεγξάμενον ἐκώλυσεν
⁴of a man ⁵voice ³speaking restrained

τὴν τοῦ προφήτου παραφρονίαν. 17 οὗτοί
¹the ²of the ²prophet ³madness. These men

εἰσιν πηγαὶ ἄνυδροι καὶ ὁμίχλαι ὑπὸ
are ¹springs ²waterless and mists ²by

λαίλαπος ἐλαυνόμεναι, οἷς ὁ ζόφος τοῦ
²storm ¹being driven, for whom the gloom of the

σκότους τετήρηται. 18 ὑπέρογκα γὰρ
darkness has been kept. For ¹immoderate [words]

ματαιότητος φθεγγόμενοι δελεάζουσιν ἐν
²of vanity ¹speaking they allure by

ἐπιθυμίαις σαρκὸς ἀσελγείαις τοὺς ὀλίγως
[the] lusts of [the] flesh in excesses the [ones] almost

ἀποφεύγοντας τοὺς ἐν πλάνῃ ἀναστρε-
escaping ¹the [ones] ²in ³error ¹liv-

φομένους, 19 ἐλευθερίαν αὐτοῖς ἐπαγγελ-
ing, ³freedom ²to them ¹promis-

λόμενοι, αὐτοὶ δοῦλοι ὑπάρχοντες τῆς
ing, [them]selves ²slaves ¹being

φθορᾶς· ᾧ γάρ τις ἥττηται, τούτῳ
of corrup- for by whom anyone has been to this
tion; defeated, man

δεδούλωται. 20 εἰ γὰρ ἀποφυγόντες τὰ
he has been enslaved. For if having escaped the

μιάσματα τοῦ κόσμου ἐν ἐπιγνώσει τοῦ
defilements of the world by a full knowledge of the

κυρίου καὶ σωτῆρος Ἰησοῦ Χριστοῦ,
Lord and Saviour Jesus Christ,

τούτοις δὲ πάλιν ἐμπλακέντες ἡττῶνται,
yet by these again having been have been
entangled defeated,

γέγονεν αὐτοῖς τὰ ἔσχατα χείρονα τῶν
³have become ⁴to them ¹the ²last things worse [than] the

πρώτων. 21 κρεῖττον γὰρ ἦν αὐτοῖς
first. For better it was for them

μὴ ἐπεγνωκέναι τὴν ὁδὸν τῆς δικαιοσύνης,
not to have fully known the way - of righteousness,

ἢ ἐπιγνοῦσιν ὑποστρέψαι ἐκ τῆς παρα-
than fully knowing to turn from ¹the ²de-

δοθείσης αὐτοῖς ἁγίας ἐντολῆς. 22 συμβέ-
livered ²to them ²holy ²commandment. ²has

βηκεν αὐτοῖς τὸ τῆς ἀληθοῦς παροιμίας·
happened ²to them ¹The ²of the ²true ²proverb:
thing

κύων ἐπιστρέψας ἐπὶ τὸ ἴδιον ἐξέραμα,
[The] dog turning upon the(its) own vomit,

καὶ· ὗς λουσαμένη εἰς κυλισμὸν βορβόρου.
and: [The] washed to wallowing of mud.
sow

Chapter 3

Ταύτην ἤδη, ἀγαπητοί, δευτέραν ὑμῖν
¹This ²now, ³beloved, ²second ²to you

γράφω ἐπιστολήν, ἐν αἷς διεγείρω ὑμῶν
²I write ²epistle, in [both] which I rouse ⁴of you

ἐν ὑπομνήσει τὴν εἰλικρινῆ διάνοιαν,
²by reminder ¹the ²sincere ²mind,

2 μνησθῆναι τῶν προειρημένων ῥημάτων
to remember the ²having been ²words
previously spoken

ὑπὸ τῶν ἁγίων προφητῶν καὶ τῆς τῶν
by the holy prophets and ¹the ²of the

ἀποστόλων ὑμῶν ἐντολῆς τοῦ κυρίου καὶ
²apostles ²of you ¹commandment of the Lord and

σωτῆρος, 3 τοῦτο πρῶτον γινώσκοντες, ὅτι
Saviour, ²this ²firstly ¹knowing, that

ἐλεύσονται ἐπ᾽ ἐσχάτων τῶν ἡμερῶν ἐν
there will come during [the] last of the days ¹in

ἐμπαιγμονῇ ἐμπαῖκται κατὰ τὰς ἰδίας
²mocking ¹mockers ²according to ²the(ir) ²own

ἐπιθυμίας αὐτῶν πορευόμενοι 4 καὶ λέγοντες·
²lusts of them ¹going and saying:

ποῦ ἐστιν ἡ ἐπαγγελία τῆς παρουσίας
Where is the promise of the presence

αὐτοῦ; ἀφ᾽ ἧς γὰρ οἱ πατέρες ἐκοι-
of him? ²from ²which [day] ¹for the fathers fell
= for from the day when . . .

μήθησαν, πάντα οὕτως διαμένει ἀπ᾽
asleep, all things so remains from

ἀρχῆς κτίσεως. 5 λανθάνει γὰρ αὐτοὺς
[the] of creation. For ²is concealed ²them
beginning [from]

τοῦτο θέλοντας ὅτι οὐρανοὶ ἦσαν ἔκπαλαι
¹this wishing* that heavens were of old

καὶ γῆ ἐξ ὕδατος καὶ δι᾽ ὕδατος
and earth by water and through water

συνεστῶσα τῷ τοῦ θεοῦ λόγῳ, 6 δι᾽
¹having been ²by - ²of God ²word, through
held together the

ὧν ὁ τότε κόσμος ὕδατι κατακλυσθεὶς
which the then§ world ²by water ¹being inundated
things

ἀπώλετο· 7 οἱ δὲ νῦν οὐρανοὶ καὶ ἡ
perished· but the now heavens and the

γῆ τῷ αὐτῷ λόγῳ τεθησαυρισμένοι εἰσὶν
earth by the same word ²having been stored up ¹are

πυρὶ τηρούμενοι εἰς ἡμέραν κρίσεως καὶ
²for fire ¹being kept in a day of judgment and

ἀπωλείας τῶν ἀσεβῶν ἀνθρώπων. 8 Ἐν
destruction of the impious men. ²one

δὲ τοῦτο μὴ λανθανέτω ὑμᾶς, ἀγαπητοί,
But ²this let not be concealed you, beloved,
¹thing [from]

ὅτι μία ἡμέρα παρὰ κυρίῳ ὡς χίλια
that one day with [the] Lord [is] as a thousand

ἔτη καὶ χίλια ἔτη ὡς ἡμέρα μία. 9 οὐ
years and a thousand years as ²day ¹one. ²not

βραδύνει κύριος τῆς ἐπαγγελίας, ὥς τινες
¹is ²slow ¹[The] of the promise, as some
Lord (his)

βραδύτητα ἡγοῦνται, ἀλλὰ μακροθυμεῖ εἰς
²slowness ¹deem, but is longsuffering toward

---

* That is, they wish it to be so.
§ This is allowable English : cf. " the then Prime Minister."

King James Version

to us-ward, not willing that any should perish, but that all should come to repentance. 10 But the day of the Lord will come as a thief in the night; in the which the heavens shall pass away with a great noise, and the elements shall melt with fervent heat, the earth also and the works that are therein shall be burned up. 11 *Seeing* then *that* all these things shall be dissolved, what manner *of persons* ought ye to be in *all* holy conversation and godliness, 12 Looking for and hasting unto the coming of the day of God, wherein the heavens being on fire shall be dissolved, and the elements shall melt with fervent heat? 13 Nevertheless we, according to his promise, look for new heavens and a new earth, wherein dwelleth righteousness. 14 Wherefore, beloved, seeing that ye look for such things, be diligent that ye may be found of him in peace, without spot, and blameless. 15And account *that* the longsuffering of our Lord *is* salvation; even as our beloved brother Paul also according to the wisdom given unto him hath written unto you; 16As also in all *his* epistles, speaking in them of these things; in which are some things hard to be understood, which they that are unlearned and unstable wrest, as *they do* also the other Scriptures, unto their own destruction. 17 Ye therefore, beloved, seeing ye know *these things* before, beware lest ye also, being led away with the error of the wicked, fall from your own steadfastness. 18 But grow in grace, and *in* the knowledge of our Lord and Saviour Jesus Christ. To him *be* glory both now and for ever. Amen.

New International Version

you, not wanting anyone to perish, but everyone to come to repentance.

10 But the day of the Lord will come like a thief. The heavens will disappear with a roar; the elements will be destroyed by fire, and the earth and everything in it will be laid bare.*

11 Since everything will be destroyed in this way, what kind of people ought you to be? You ought to live holy and godly lives 12 as you look forward to the day of God and speed its coming.' That day will bring about the destruction of the heavens by fire, and the elements will melt in the heat. 13 But in keeping with his promise we are looking forward to a new heaven and a new earth, the home of righteousness.

14 So then, dear friends, since you are looking forward to this, make every effort to be found spotless, blameless and at peace with him. 15 Bear in mind that our Lord's patience means salvation, just as our dear brother Paul also wrote you with the wisdom that God gave him. 16 He writes the same way in all his letters, speaking in them of these matters. His letters contain some things that are hard to understand, which ignorant and unstable people distort, as they do the other Scriptures, to their own destruction.

17 Therefore, dear friends, since you already know this, be on your guard so that you may not be carried away by the error of lawless men and fall from your secure position. 18 But grow in the grace and knowledge of our Lord and Savior Jesus Christ. To him be glory both now and forever! Amen.

[e] Some early MSS read *will be burned up.* [f] Or *as you wait eagerly for the day of God to come.*

702

Greek Interlinear

ὑμᾶς, μὴ βουλόμενός τινας ἀπολέσθαι
you, not purposing any to perish

ἀλλὰ πάντας εἰς μετάνοιαν χωρῆσαι.
but all men ²to ²repentance ¹to come.

10 Ἥξει δὲ ἡμέρα κυρίου ὡς κλέπτης,
But will come [the] day of [the] Lord as a thief,

ἐν ᾗ οἱ οὐρανοὶ ῥοιζηδὸν παρελεύσονται,
in which the heavens ²with rushing ¹will pass away,
sound

στοιχεῖα δὲ καυσούμενα λυθήσεται, καὶ
and [the] elements burning will be dissolved, and

γῆ καὶ τὰ ἐν αὐτῇ ἔργα εὑρεθήσεται.
[the] and ¹the ²in ⁴it ³works will be
earth discovered.

11 Τούτων οὕτως πάντων λυομένων
²these things ²thus ¹All ⁴being dissolved*

ποταποὺς δεῖ ὑπάρχειν [ὑμᾶς] ἐν ἁγίαις
what sort it be- ²to be ¹you in holy
of men hoves

ἀναστροφαῖς καὶ εὐσεβείαις, 12 προσδοκῶντας
conduct* and piety,* awaiting

καὶ σπεύδοντας τὴν παρουσίαν τῆς τοῦ
and hastening the presence ¹of the –

θεοῦ ἡμέρας, δι' ἣν οὐρανοὶ πυρούμενοι
²of God ¹day, on ac- which [the] being set on fire
count of heavens

λυθήσονται καὶ στοιχεῖα καυσούμενα
will be dissolved and [the] elements burning

τήκεται. 13 καινοὺς δὲ οὐρανοὺς καὶ
melts. But new heavens and

γῆν καινὴν κατὰ τὸ ἐπάγγελμα αὐτοῦ
²earth ¹a new accord- the promise of him
ing to

προσδοκῶμεν, ἐν οἷς δικαιοσύνη κατοικεῖ.
we await, in which righteousness dwells.

14 Διό, ἀγαπητοί, ταῦτα προσδοκῶντες
Wherefore, beloved, ²these things ¹awaiting

σπουδάσατε ἄσπιλοι καὶ ἀμώμητοι αὐτῷ
be diligent ⁵spotless ⁶and ⁷unblemished ⁸by him

εὑρεθῆναι ἐν εἰρήνῃ, 15 καὶ τὴν τοῦ
¹to be found ²in ⁴peace, and ¹the ⁴of the

κυρίου ἡμῶν μακροθυμίαν σωτηρίαν ἡγεῖσθε,
²Lord ⁴of us ³longsuffering ⁵salvation ¹deem,

καθὼς καὶ ὁ ἀγαπητὸς ἡμῶν ἀδελφὸς
as indeed the beloved ²of us ¹brother

Παῦλος κατὰ τὴν δοθεῖσαν αὐτῷ σοφίαν
Paul accord- ¹the ²given ⁴to him ³wisdom
ing to

ἔγραψεν ὑμῖν, 16 ὡς καὶ ἐν πάσαις
wrote to you, as also in all [his]

ἐπιστολαῖς λαλῶν ἐν αὐταῖς περὶ τούτων,
epistles speaking in them concerning these
things,

ἐν αἷς ἐστιν δυσνόητά τινα, ἃ οἱ
in which is(are) ²hard to ¹some which the
understand things,

ἀμαθεῖς καὶ ἀστήρικτοι στρεβλοῦσιν ὡς
unlearned and unsteady twist as

καὶ τὰς λοιπὰς γραφὰς πρὸς τὴν ἰδίαν
also the remaining scriptures to the(ir) own

αὐτῶν ἀπώλειαν. 17 Ὑμεῖς οὖν, ἀγαπητοί,
of them destruction. Ye therefore, beloved,

προγινώσκοντες φυλάσσεσθε ἵνα μὴ τῇ
knowing before guard lest ¹by the

τῶν ἀθέσμων πλάνῃ συναπαχθέντες ἐκπέ-
⁴of the ³lawless ²error ¹being led away with ye fall

σητε τοῦ ἰδίου στηριγμοῦ, 18 αὐξάνετε
from the(your) own stability, ²grow ye

δὲ ἐν χάριτι καὶ γνώσει τοῦ κυρίου
¹but in grace and knowledge of the Lord

ἡμῶν καὶ σωτῆρος Ἰησοῦ Χριστοῦ.
of us and Saviour Jesus Christ.

αὐτῷ ἡ δόξα καὶ νῦν καὶ εἰς
To him^e [is] the glory both now and unto
= His is✝

ἡμέραν αἰῶνος.
a day of age. §

---

* The Greek plurals cannot be literally reproduced in English.

★ See note on I. Pet. 5. 11.

§ ? "An age-lasting (i.e. eternal) day."

King James Version

THE FIRST
EPISTLE GENERAL
OF
JOHN

New International Version

1 JOHN

The word of life

1 That which was from the beginning, which we have heard, which we have seen with our eyes, which we have looked upon, and our hands have handled, of the Word of life; 2 (For the life was manifested, and we have seen *it,* and bear witness, and shew unto you that eternal life, which was with the Father, and was manifested unto us;) 3 That which we have seen and heard declare we unto you, that ye also may have fellowship with us: and truly our fellowship *is* with the Father, and with his Son Jesus Christ. 4And these things write we unto you, that your joy may be full. 5 This then is the message which we have heard of him, and declare unto you, that God is light, and in him is no darkness at all. 6 If we say that we have fellowship with him, and walk in darkness, we lie, and do not the truth: 7 But if we walk in the light, as he is in the light, we have fellowship one with another, and the blood of Jesus Christ his Son cleanseth us from all sin. 8 If we say that we have no sin, we deceive ourselves, and the truth is not in us. 9 If we confess our sins, he is faithful and just to forgive us *our* sins, and to cleanse us from all unrighteousness. 10 If we say that we have not sinned, we make him a liar, and his word is not in us.

1 That which was from the beginning, which we have heard, which we have seen with our eyes, which we have looked at and our hands have touched—this we proclaim concerning the Word of life. 2 The life appeared; we have seen it and testify to it, and we proclaim to you the eternal life, which was with the Father and has appeared to us. 3 We proclaim to you what we have seen and heard, so that you also may have fellowship with us. And our fellowship is with the Father and with his Son, Jesus Christ. 4 We write this to make our[a] joy complete.

Walking in the light

5 This is the message we have heard from him and declare to you: God is light; in him there is no darkness at all. 6 If we claim to have fellowship with him yet walk in the darkness, we lie and do not put the truth into practice. 7 But if we walk in the light, as he is in the light, we have fellowship with one another, and the blood of Jesus, his Son, purifies us from every sin.

8 If we claim to be without sin, we deceive ourselves and the truth is not in us. 9 If we confess our sins, he is faithful and just and will forgive us our sins and purify us from all unrighteousness. 10 If we claim we have not sinned, we make him out to be a liar, and his word has no place in our lives.

2 My little children, these things write I unto you, that ye sin not. And if any man sin, we have an advocate with the Father, Jesus Christ the righteous: 2And he is the propitiation for our sins: and not for ours only, but also for *the sins of* the whole world. 3And hereby we do know that we know him, if we keep his commandments. 4 He that saith, I know him, and keepeth not his commandments, is a liar, and the truth is not in him. 5 But whoso keepeth his word, in him verily is the love of God perfected:

2 My dear children, I write this to you so that you will not sin. But if anybody does sin, we have one who speaks to the Father in our defense—Jesus Christ, the Righteous One. 2 He is the atoning sacrifice for our sins, and not only for ours but also for the sins of the whole world.

3 We can be sure we know him if we obey his commands. 4 The man who says, "I know him," but does not do what he commands is a liar, and the truth is not in him. 5 But if anyone obeys his word, God's love is truly made

[a] Some early MSS read *your.*

ΙΩΑΝΝΟΥ Α

Chapter 1

Ὃ ἦν ἀπ' ἀρχῆς, ὃ ἀκηκόαμεν,
What was from [the] what we have heard,
beginning,

ὃ ἑωράκαμεν τοῖς ὀφθαλμοῖς ἡμῶν, ὃ
what we have seen with the eyes of us, what

ἐθεασάμεθα καὶ αἱ χεῖρες ἡμῶν ἐψηλάφησαν,
we beheld and the hands of us touched,

περὶ τοῦ λόγου τῆς ζωῆς, — 2 καὶ
concern- the word - of life, — and
ing

ἡ ζωὴ ἐφανερώθη, καὶ ἑωράκαμεν καὶ
the life was manifested, and we have seen and

μαρτυροῦμεν καὶ ἀπαγγέλλομεν ὑμῖν τὴν
we bear witness and we announce to you the

ζωὴν τὴν αἰώνιον, ἥτις ἦν πρὸς τὸν
life - eternal, which was with the

πατέρα καὶ ἐφανερώθη ἡμῖν, — 3 ὃ
Father and was manifested to us, — what

ἑωράκαμεν καὶ ἀκηκόαμεν, ἀπαγγέλλομεν
we have seen and we have heard, we announce

καὶ ὑμῖν, ἵνα καὶ ὑμεῖς κοινωνίαν ἔχητε
also to you, in order also ye fellowship may
that

μεθ' ἡμῶν. καὶ ἡ κοινωνία δὲ ἡ ἡμετέρα
with us. indeed the fellowship And - our

μετὰ τοῦ πατρὸς καὶ μετὰ τοῦ υἱοῦ
[is] with the Father and with the Son

αὐτοῦ Ἰησοῦ Χριστοῦ. 4 καὶ ταῦτα
of him Jesus Christ. And these things

γράφομεν ἡμεῖς ἵνα ἡ χαρὰ ἡμῶν ᾖ
write we in order the joy of us may
that be

πεπληρωμένη.
having been fulfilled.

5 Καὶ ἔστιν αὕτη ἡ ἀγγελία ἣν
And is this the message which

ἀκηκόαμεν ἀπ' αὐτοῦ καὶ ἀναγγέλλομεν
we have heard from him and we announce

ὑμῖν, ὅτι ὁ θεὸς φῶς ἐστιν καὶ σκοτία
to you, that - God light is and darkness

ἐν αὐτῷ οὐκ ἔστιν οὐδεμία. 6 Ἐὰν
in him not is none. If

εἴπωμεν ὅτι κοινωνίαν ἔχομεν μετ' αὐτοῦ
we say that fellowship we have with him

καὶ ἐν τῷ σκότει περιπατῶμεν, ψευδόμεθα
and in the darkness we walk, we lie

καὶ οὐ ποιοῦμεν τὴν ἀλήθειαν· 7 ἐὰν
and are not doing the truth; if

δὲ ἐν τῷ φωτὶ περιπατῶμεν ὡς αὐτός
but in the light we walk as he

ἐστιν ἐν τῷ φωτί, κοινωνίαν ἔχομεν
is in the light, fellowship we have

μετ' ἀλλήλων καὶ τὸ αἷμα Ἰησοῦ τοῦ
with each other and the blood of Jesus the

υἱοῦ αὐτοῦ καθαρίζει ἡμᾶς ἀπὸ πάσης
Son of him cleanses us from all

ἁμαρτίας. 8 ἐὰν εἴπωμεν ὅτι ἁμαρτίαν
sin. If we say that sin

οὐκ ἔχομεν, ἑαυτοὺς πλανῶμεν καὶ ἡ
we have not, ourselves we deceive and the

ἀλήθεια οὐκ ἔστιν ἐν ἡμῖν. 9 ἐὰν
truth is not in us. If

ὁμολογῶμεν τὰς ἁμαρτίας ἡμῶν, πιστός
we confess the sins of us, faithful

ἐστιν καὶ δίκαιος, ἵνα ἀφῇ ἡμῖν τὰς
he is and righteous, in order he may us the
that forgive

ἁμαρτίας καὶ καθαρίσῃ ἡμᾶς ἀπὸ πάσης
sins and he may cleanse us from all

ἀδικίας. 10 ἐὰν εἴπωμεν ὅτι οὐχ
iniquity. If we say that not

ἡμαρτήκαμεν, ψεύστην ποιοῦμεν αὐτὸν
we have sinned, a liar we make him

καὶ ὁ λόγος αὐτοῦ οὐκ ἔστιν ἐν ἡμῖν.
and the word of him is not in us.

Chapter 2

Τεκνία μου, ταῦτα γράφω ὑμῖν ἵνα
Little children of me, these things I write to you in order
that

μὴ ἁμάρτητε. καὶ ἐὰν τις ἁμάρτῃ,
ye sin not. And if anyone sins,

παράκλητον ἔχομεν πρὸς τὸν πατέρα,
an advocate we have with the Father,

Ἰησοῦν Χριστὸν δίκαιον· 2 καὶ αὐτὸς
Jesus Christ [the] righteous; and he

ἱλασμός ἐστιν περὶ τῶν ἁμαρτιῶν ἡμῶν,
a propitiation is concerning the sins of us,

οὐ περὶ τῶν ἡμετέρων δὲ μόνον ἀλλὰ
not concerning - ours but only but

καὶ περὶ ὅλου τοῦ κόσμου. 3 καὶ ἐν
also concerning all the world. And by

τούτῳ γινώσκομεν ὅτι ἐγνώκαμεν αὐτόν,
this we know that we have known him,

ἐὰν τὰς ἐντολὰς αὐτοῦ τηρῶμεν. 4 ὁ
if the commands of him we keep. The
ments [one]

λέγων ὅτι ἔγνωκα αὐτόν, καὶ τὰς ἐντολὰς
saying[,] - I have known him, and the commands
ments

αὐτοῦ μὴ τηρῶν, ψεύστης ἐστίν, καὶ
of him not keeping, a liar is, and

ἐν τούτῳ ἡ ἀλήθεια οὐκ ἔστιν· 5 ὃς δ'
in this man the truth is not; but who-

ἂν τηρῇ αὐτοῦ τὸν λόγον, ἀληθῶς ἐν
ever keeps of him the word, truly in

τούτῳ ἡ ἀγάπη τοῦ θεοῦ τετελείωται.
this man the love of God has been perfected.

King James Version	New International Version

King James Version

hereby know we that we are in him. 6 He that saith he abideth in him ought himself also so to walk, even as he walked. 7 Brethren, I write no new commandment unto you, but an old commandment which ye had from the beginning. The old commandment is the word which ye have heard from the beginning. 8Again, a new commandment I write unto you, which thing is true in him and in you: because the darkness is past, and the true light now shineth. 9 He that saith he is in the light, and hateth his brother, is in darkness even until now. 10 He that loveth his brother abideth in the light, and there is none occasion of stumbling in him. 11 But he that hateth his brother is in darkness, and walketh in darkness, and knoweth not whither he goeth, because that darkness hath blinded his eyes. 12 I write unto you, little children, because your sins are forgiven you for his name's sake. 13 I write unto you, fathers, because ye have known him *that is* from the beginning. I write unto you, young men, because ye have overcome the wicked one. I write unto you, little children, because ye have known the Father. 14 I have written unto you, fathers, because ye have known him *that is* from the beginning. I have written unto you, young men, because ye are strong, and the word of God abideth in you, and ye have overcome the wicked one. 15 Love not the world, neither the things *that are* in the world. If any man love the world, the love of the Father is not in him. 16 For all that *is* in the world, the lust of the flesh, and the lust of the eyes, and the pride of life, is not of the Father, but is of the world. 17And the world passeth away, and the lust thereof: but he that doeth the will of God abideth for ever. 18 Little children, it is the last time: and as ye have heard that antichrist shall come, even now are there many antichrists; whereby we know that it is the last time. 19 They went out from us, but they were not of us; for if they had been of us, they would *no doubt* have continued with us: but *they went out,* that they might be made manifest that they were not all of us. 20 But ye have an unction from the Holy One, and ye know all things. 21 I have not written unto you because ye know not the truth, but because ye know it, and that no lie is of the truth. 22 Who is a liar but he that denieth that Jesus is the Christ? He is antichrist, that denieth the Father and the Son. 23 Whosoever denieth the Son, the same hath not the Father: [*but*] he *that acknowledgeth the Son hath the Father also.* 24 Let that therefore abide in you, which ye have heard from the beginning. If that which ye have heard from the beginning shall remain in you, ye also shall continue in the Son, and

New International Version

complete in him. This is how we know we are in him: 6 Whoever claims to live in him must walk as Jesus did. 7 Dear friends, I am not writing you a new command but an old one, which you have had since the beginning. This old command is the message you have heard. 8 Yet I am writing you a new command; its truth is seen in him and you, because the darkness is passing and the true light is already shining. 9 Anyone who claims to be in the light but hates his brother is still in the darkness. 10 Whoever loves his brother lives in the light, and there is nothing in him[b] to make him stumble. 11 But whoever hates his brother is in the darkness and walks around in the darkness; he does not know where he is going, because the darkness has blinded him.

　　12 I write to you, dear children,
　　　　because your sins have been forgiven on
　　　　　　account of his name.
　　13 I write to you, fathers,
　　　　because you have known him who is from
　　　　　　the beginning.
　　I write to you, young men,
　　　　because you have overcome the evil one.
　　I write to you, dear children,
　　　　because you have known the Father.
　　14 I write to you, fathers,
　　　　because you have known him who is from
　　　　　　the beginning.
　　I write to you, young men,
　　　　because you are strong,
　　　　and the word of God lives in you,
　　　　and you have overcome the evil one.

Do not love the world

15 Do not love the world or anything in the world. If anyone loves the world, the love of the Father is not in him. 16 For everything in the world—the cravings of sinful man, the lust of his eyes and his pride in possessions—comes not from the Father but from the world. 17 The world and its desires pass away, but the man who does the will of God lives forever.

Warning against antichrists

18 Dear children, this is the last hour; and as you have heard that the antichrist is coming, even now many antichrists have come. This is how we know it is the last hour. 19 They went out from us, but they did not really belong to us. For if they had belonged to us, they would have remained with us; but their going showed that none of them belonged to us. 20 But you have an anointing from the Holy One, and all of you know the truth.[c] 21 I do not write to you because you do not know the truth, but because you do know it and because no lie comes from the truth. 22 Who is the liar? It is the man who denies that Jesus is the Christ. Such a man is the antichrist—he denies the Father and the Son. 23 No one who denies the Son has the Father; whoever acknowledges the Son has the Father also. 24 See that what you have heard from the beginning remains in you. If it does, you also

---

[*b*] Or *it.* [*c*] Some MSS read *and you know all the truth.*

Greek Interlinear

ἐν τούτῳ γινώσκομεν ὅτι ἐν αὐτῷ ἐσμεν.
By this we know that ⁸in ⁸him ¹we are.

6 ὁ λέγων ἐν αὐτῷ μένειν ὀφείλει καθὼς
The [one] saying in him to remain ought as

ἐκεῖνος περιεπάτησεν καὶ αὐτὸς οὕτως
that [one]⁸ walked also [him]self so

περιπατεῖν.
to walk.

7 Ἀγαπητοί, οὐκ ἐντολὴν καινὴν γράφω
Beloved, ³not ⁴commandment ²a new ¹I write

ὑμῖν, ἀλλ' ἐντολὴν παλαιὰν ἣν εἴχετε
to you, but ²commandment ¹an old which ye had

ἀπ' ἀρχῆς· ἡ ἐντολὴ ἡ παλαιά ἐστιν
from [the] beginning; the ⁸command- - ¹old is
ment

ὁ λόγος ὃν ἠκούσατε. 8 πάλιν ἐντολὴν
the word which ye heard. Again ⁸command-
ment

καινὴν γράφω ὑμῖν, ὅ ἐστιν ἀληθὲς
¹a new I write to you, what is true

ἐν αὐτῷ καὶ ἐν ὑμῖν, ὅτι ἡ σκοτία
in him and in you, because the darkness

παράγεται καὶ τὸ φῶς τὸ ἀληθινὸν
is passing and the ²light - ¹true

ἤδη φαίνει. 9 ὁ λέγων ἐν τῷ φωτὶ
already shines. The [one] saying in the light

εἶναι καὶ τὸν ἀδελφὸν αὐτοῦ μισῶν
to be and the brother of him hating

ἐν τῇ σκοτίᾳ ἐστὶν ἕως ἄρτι. 10 ὁ
in the darkness is until now. The

ἀγαπῶν τὸν ἀδελφὸν αὐτοῦ ἐν τῷ φωτὶ
[one] loving the brother of him in the light

μένει, καὶ σκάνδαλον ἐν αὐτῷ οὐκ ἔστιν·
remains, and offence in him is not;

11 ὁ δὲ μισῶν τὸν ἀδελφὸν αὐτοῦ ἐν
but the [one] hating the brother of him in

τῇ σκοτίᾳ ἐστὶν καὶ ἐν τῇ σκοτίᾳ
the darkness is and in the darkness

περιπατεῖ, καὶ οὐκ οἶδεν ποῦ ὑπάγει,
walks, and knows not where he is going,

ὅτι ἡ σκοτία ἐτύφλωσεν τοὺς ὀφθαλμοὺς
be- the darkness blinded the eyes
cause

αὐτοῦ. 12 Γράφω ὑμῖν, τεκνία, ὅτι
of him. I write to you, little because
children,

ἀφέωνται ὑμῖν αἱ ἁμαρτίαι διὰ τὸ ὄνομα
have been to you the sins on ac- the name
forgiven · (your) count of

αὐτοῦ. 13 γράφω ὑμῖν, πατέρες, ὅτι
of him. I write to you, fathers, because

ἐγνώκατε τὸν ἀπ' ἀρχῆς. γράφω ὑμῖν,
ye have the from [the] I write to
known [one] you,

νεανίσκοι, ὅτι νενικήκατε τὸν πονηρόν.
young men, because ye have overcome the evil one.

14 ἔγραψα ὑμῖν, παιδία, ὅτι ἐγνώκατε
I wrote to you, young because ye have
children, known

τὸν πατέρα. ἔγραψα ὑμῖν, πατέρες,
the Father. I wrote to you, fathers,

ὅτι ἐγνώκατε τὸν ἀπ' ἀρχῆς. ἔγραψα
be- ye have the from [the] I wrote
cause known [one] beginning.

ὑμῖν, νεανίσκοι, ὅτι ἰσχυροί ἐστε καὶ
to you, young men, because strong ye are and

ὁ λόγος τοῦ θεοῦ ἐν ὑμῖν μένει καὶ
the word - of God in you remains and

νενικήκατε τὸν πονηρόν. 15 Μὴ ἀγαπᾶτε
ye have overcome the evil one. Love ye not

τὸν κόσμον μηδὲ τὰ ἐν τῷ κόσμῳ.
the world nor the things in the world.

ἐάν τις ἀγαπᾷ τὸν κόσμον, οὐκ ἔστιν
If anyone loves the world, ²not ¹is

ἡ ἀγάπη τοῦ πατρὸς ἐν αὐτῷ· 16 ὅτι
¹the ²love ³of the ⁴Father in him; because

πᾶν τὸ ἐν τῷ κόσμῳ, ἡ ἐπιθυμία τῆς
all that [is] in the world, the lust of the
which† [is]

σαρκὸς καὶ ἡ ἐπιθυμία τῶν ὀφθαλμῶν
flesh and the lust of the eyes

καὶ ἡ ἀλαζονεία τοῦ βίου, οὐκ ἔστιν
and the vainglory - of life, is not

ἐκ τοῦ πατρός, ἀλλὰ ἐκ τοῦ κόσμου
of the Father, but of the world

ἐστίν. 17 καὶ ὁ κόσμος παράγεται καὶ
is. And the world is passing away and

ἡ ἐπιθυμία αὐτοῦ· ὁ δὲ ποιῶν τὸ θέλημα
the lust of it; but the [one] doing the will

τοῦ θεοῦ μένει εἰς τὸν αἰῶνα.
- of God remains unto the age.

18 Παιδία, ἐσχάτη ὥρα ἐστίν, καὶ
Young children, a last hour it is, and

καθὼς ἠκούσατε ὅτι ἀντίχριστος ἔρχεται,
as ye heard that antichrist is coming,

καὶ νῦν ἀντίχριστοι πολλοὶ γεγόνασιν·
even now ²antichrists ¹many have arisen;

ὅθεν γινώσκομεν ὅτι ἐσχάτη ὥρα ἐστίν.
whence we know that a last hour it is.

19 ἐξ ἡμῶν ἐξῆλθαν, ἀλλ' οὐκ ἦσαν
From us they went out, but they were not

ἐξ ἡμῶν· εἰ γὰρ ἐξ ἡμῶν ἦσαν, μεμενή-
of us; for if of us they were, they would

κεισαν ἂν μεθ' ἡμῶν· ἀλλ' ἵνα φανερω-
have remained with us; but in order it might be
that

θῶσιν ὅτι οὐκ εἰσὶν πάντες ἐξ ἡμῶν.
manifested that they are not all of us.

20 καὶ ὑμεῖς χρῖσμα ἔχετε ἀπὸ τοῦ
And ye an anointing have from the

ἁγίου, καὶ οἴδατε πάντες. 21 οὐκ ἔγραψα
Holy One, and ¹ye ²know ³all. I wrote not

ὑμῖν ὅτι οὐκ οἴδατε τὴν ἀλήθειαν, ἀλλ'
to you because ye know not the truth, but

ὅτι οἴδατε αὐτήν, καὶ ὅτι πᾶν ψεῦδος
because ye know it, and because every lie
—no lie is . . .

ἐκ τῆς ἀληθείας οὐκ ἔστιν. 22 Τίς
of the truth is not. Who

ἐστιν ὁ ψεύστης εἰ μὴ ὁ ἀρνούμενος
is the liar except the [one] denying

ὅτι Ἰησοῦς οὐκ ἔστιν ὁ χριστός; οὗτός
that Jesus not is the Christ? this

ἐστιν ὁ ἀντίχριστος, ὁ ἀρνούμενος τὸν
is the antichrist, the [one] denying the

πατέρα καὶ τὸν υἱόν. 23 πᾶς ὁ ἀρνούμενος
Father and the Son. Everyone denying

τὸν υἱὸν οὐδὲ τὸν πατέρα ἔχει· ὁ
the Son ²neither ³the ⁴Father ¹has; the

ὁμολογῶν τὸν υἱὸν καὶ τὸν πατέρα ἔχει.
[one] confessing the Son ²also ³the ⁴Father ¹has.

24 ὑμεῖς ὃ ἠκούσατε ἀπ' ἀρχῆς, ἐν
²Ye ¹what heard from [the] beginning, in

ὑμῖν μενέτω. ἐὰν ἐν ὑμῖν μείνῃ ὃ ἀπ'
you let it remain. If ⁵in ⁶you ⁴remains ¹what ²from

ἀρχῆς ἠκούσατε, καὶ ὑμεῖς ἐν τῷ υἱῷ
³[the] ³ye heard, ⁸both ¹ye ⁴in ⁵the ⁶Son
beginning

* In a number of places John uses this demonstrative adjective
as a substitute for " Christ " : " the remoter antecedent." See
also John 2. 21.

King James Version

in the Father. 25And this is the promise that he
hath promised us, *even* eternal life. 26 These
things have I written unto you concerning them
that seduce you. 27 But the anointing which ye
have received of him abideth in you, and ye
need not that any man teach you: but as the
same anointing teacheth you of all things, and
is truth, and is no lie, and even as it hath taught
you, ye shall abide in him. 28And now, little
children, abide in him; that, when he shall appear, we may have confidence, and not be
ashamed before him at his coming. 29 If ye
know that he is righteous, ye know that every
one that doeth righteousness is born of him.

New International Version

will remain in the Son and in the Father. 25And
this is what he promised us—even eternal life.
26 I am writing these things to you about
those who are trying to lead you astray. 27As
for you, the anointing you received from him
remains in you, and you do not need anyone to
teach you. But as his anointing teaches you about
all things and as that anointing is real, not
counterfeit—just as it has taught you, remain in
him.

Children of God

28 And now, dear children, continue in him,
so that when he appears we may be confident
and unashamed before him at his coming.
29 If you know that he is righteous, you know
that everyone who does what is right has been
born of him.

3 Behold, what manner of love the Father
hath bestowed upon us, that we should be
called the sons of God: therefore the world
knoweth us not, because it knew him not. 2 Beloved, now are we the sons of God, and it doth
not yet appear what we shall be: but we know
that, when he shall appear, we shall be like him;
for we shall see him as he is. 3And every man
that hath this hope in him purifieth himself,
even as he is pure. 4 Whosoever committeth sin
transgresseth also the law: for sin is the transgression of the law. 5And ye know that he was
manifested to take away our sins; and in him is
no sin. 6 Whosoever abideth in him sinneth not:
whosoever sinneth hath not seen him, neither
known him. 7 Little children, let no man deceive you: he that doeth righteousness is righteous, even as he is righteous. 8 He that committeth sin is of the devil; for the devil sinneth
from the beginning. For this purpose the Son of
God was manifested, that he might destroy the
works of the devil. 9 Whosoever is born of God
doth not commit sin; for his seed remaineth in
him: and he cannot sin, because he is born of
God. 10 In this the children of God are manifest, and the children of the devil: whosoever
doeth not righteousness is not of God, neither
he that loveth not his brother. 11 For this is the
message that ye heard from the beginning, that
we should love one another. 12 Not as Cain,
who was of that wicked one, and slew his
brother. And wherefore slew he him? Because
his own works were evil, and his brother's righteous. 13 Marvel not, my brethren, if the world
hate you. 14 We know that we have passed from

3 How great is the love the Father has lavished on us, that we should be called children of God! And that is what we are! The reason the world does not know us is that it did
not know him. 2 Dear friends, now are we children of God, and what we will be has not yet
been made known. But we know that when he
appears,[d] we shall be like him, for we shall see
him as he is. 3 Everyone who has this hope in
him purifies himself, just as he is pure.
4 Everyone who sins breaks the law; in fact,
sin is lawlessness. 5 But you know that he appeared so that he might take away our sins. And
in him is no sin. 6 No one who lives in him
keeps on sinning. No one who continues to sin
has either seen him or known him.
7 Dear children, do not let anyone lead you
astray. He who does what is right is righteous,
just as he is righteous. 8 He who does what is
sinful is of the devil, because the devil has been
sinning from the beginning. The reason the Son
of God appeared was to destroy the devil's work.
9 No one who is born of God will continue to
sin, because God's seed remains in him; he cannot sin, because he has been born of God. 10 This
is how we know who the children of God are
and who the children of the devil are: Anyone
who does not do what is right is not a child of
God; neither is anyone who does not love his
brother.

Love one another

11 This is the message you heard from the beginning: We should love one another. 12 Do not
be like Cain, who belonged to the evil one and
murdered his brother. And why did he murder
him? Because his own actions were evil and his
brother's were righteous. 13 Do not be surprised,
my brothers, if the world hates you. 14 We know

[d] Or *when it is made known.*

καὶ [ἐν]   τῷ   πατρὶ   μενεῖτε.   25 καὶ
²and   ⁸in   ⁹the   ¹⁰Father ⁸will remain.   And

αὕτη   ἐστὶν   ἡ   ἐπαγγελία   ἣν   αὐτὸς   ἐπηγ-
this   is   the   promise   which   he   pro-

γείλατο   ἡμῖν,   τὴν   ζωὴν   τὴν   αἰώνιον.
mised   us,   the   life   –   eternal.

26 Ταῦτα   ἔγραψα   ὑμῖν   περὶ   τῶν   πλανών-
These   I wrote   to you   concern-   the   leading

things   ing   [ones]

των   ὑμᾶς.   27 καὶ   ὑμεῖς   τὸ   χρῖσμα
⁸astray ¹you.   And   ⁴ye   ¹the   ⁸anointing

ὃ   ἐλάβετε   ἀπ'   αὐτοῦ   μένει   ἐν   ὑμῖν,
²which received   from   him   remains   in   you,

καὶ   οὐ   χρείαν   ἔχετε   ἵνα   τις   διδάσκῃ
and   ⁸no   ⁸need   ¹ye have in order anyone   should
                              that   teach

ὑμᾶς·   ἀλλ'   ὡς   τὸ   αὐτοῦ   χρῖσμα   διδάσκει
you;   but   as   the   ⁸of him   ¹anointing   teaches

ὑμᾶς   περὶ   πάντων,   καὶ   ἀληθές   ἐστιν
you   concerning all things,   and   ⁸true   ¹is

καὶ   οὐκ   ἔστιν   ψεῦδος,   καὶ   καθὼς   ἐδίδαξεν
and   is not   a lie,   and   as   he/it taught

ὑμᾶς,   μένετε   ἐν   αὐτῷ.
you,   remain ye   in   him.

28 Καὶ   νῦν,   τεκνία,   μένετε   ἐν   αὐτῷ,
And   now, little children, remain ye   in   him,

ἵνα   ἐὰν   φανερωθῇ   σχῶμεν   παρρησίαν   καὶ
in or-   if   he is manifested we may   confidence   and
der that

μὴ   αἰσχυνθῶμεν   ἀπ'   αὐτοῦ   ἐν   τῇ   παρουσίᾳ
not   be shamed   from   him   in   the   presence

αὐτοῦ.   29 ἐὰν   εἰδῆτε   ὅτι   δίκαιός   ἐστιν,
of him.   If   ye know   that ¹righteous   ¹he is,

γινώσκετε   ὅτι   καὶ   πᾶς   ὁ   ποιῶν   τὴν
know ye   that   also   every one   doing   –

δικαιοσύνην   ἐξ   αὐτοῦ   γεγέννηται.
righteousness   ⁸of   ¹him   ¹has been born.

Chapter 3

Ἴδετε   ποταπὴν   ἀγάπην   δέδωκεν   ἡμῖν
See ye   what manner of   love   ⁸has given   ⁴to us

ὁ   πατὴρ   ἵνα   τέκνα   θεοῦ   κληθῶμεν,
¹the   ²Father   in order ⁸children   ⁸of God   ¹we may be
                     that   called,

καὶ   ἐσμέν.   διὰ   τοῦτο   ὁ   κόσμος   οὐ
and   we are.   Therefore   the   world   ⁸not

γινώσκει   ἡμᾶς,   ὅτι   οὐκ   ἔγνω   αὐτόν.
¹knows   ⁸us,   because   it knew not   him.

2 ἀγαπητοί,   νῦν   τέκνα   θεοῦ   ἐσμεν,   καὶ
Beloved,   ¹now   ⁸children   ⁸of God ¹we are,   and

οὔπω   ἐφανερώθη   τί   ἐσόμεθα.   οἴδαμεν
not yet   was it manifested   what   we shall be.   We know

ὅτι   ἐὰν   φανερωθῇ   ὅμοιοι   αὐτῷ   ἐσόμεθα,
that   if   he(?it) is manifested like   him   we shall be,

ὅτι   ὀψόμεθα   αὐτὸν   καθώς   ἐστιν.   3 καὶ
be-   we shall see   ⁸him   as   he is.
cause

πᾶς   ὁ   ἔχων   τὴν   ἐλπίδα   ταύτην   ἐπ'
everyone   having   this hope   on

αὐτῷ   ἁγνίζει   ἑαυτὸν   καθὼς   ἐκεῖνος   ἁγνός
him   purifies   himself   as   that one*   ⁸pure

ἐστιν.   4 πᾶς   ὁ   ποιῶν   τὴν   ἁμαρτίαν
¹is.   Everyone   doing   –   sin

καὶ   τὴν   ἀνομίαν   ποιεῖ,   καὶ   ἡ   ἁμαρτία
⁸also   –   ⁸lawlessness ¹does,   and   –   sin

ἐστὶν   ἡ   ἀνομία.   5 καὶ   οἴδατε   ὅτι   ἐκεῖνος
is   –   lawlessness.   And ye know   that   that one*

ἐφανερώθη   ἵνα   τὰς   ἁμαρτίας   ἄρῃ,   καὶ
was manifested in order   –   sins   he might   and
                  that   bear,

ἁμαρτία   ἐν   αὐτῷ   οὐκ   ἔστιν.   6 πᾶς   ὁ
sin   ⁸in   ⁸him   ¹is not.   Everyone

ἐν   αὐτῷ   μένων   οὐχ   ἁμαρτάνει·   πᾶς   ὁ
⁸in   ⁸him   ¹remaining   sins not;   everyone

ἁμαρτάνων   οὐχ   ἑώρακεν   αὐτὸν   οὐδὲ
sinning   has not seen   him   nor

ἔγνωκεν   αὐτόν.   7 Τεκνία,   μηδεὶς   πλανάτω
has known   him.   Little   ⁸no man   ¹let ⁸lead
                      children,   ¹astray

ὑμᾶς·   ὁ   ποιῶν   τὴν   δικαιοσύνην   δίκαιός
⁸you;   the [one] doing   –   righteousness   ¹righteous

ἐστιν,   καθὼς   ἐκεῖνος   δίκαιός   ἐστιν·   8 ὁ
¹is,   as   that one*   ⁸righteous   ¹is;   the

ποιῶν   τὴν   ἁμαρτίαν   ἐκ   τοῦ   διαβόλου
[one] doing   –   sin   ⁸of   ³the   ⁴devil

ἐστίν,   ὅτι   ἀπ'   ἀρχῆς   ὁ   διάβολος   ἁμαρτάνει.
¹is,   because ⁴from   ⁸[the]   ¹the   ²devil   ⁸sins.
                     beginning

εἰς   τοῦτο   ἐφανερώθη   ὁ   υἱὸς   τοῦ   θεοῦ,
For   this   was manifested the   Son   –   of God,

ἵνα   λύσῃ   τὰ   ἔργα   τοῦ   διαβόλου.
in or-   he might   the   works   of the   devil.
der that   undo

9 Πᾶς   ὁ   γεγεννημένος   ἐκ   τοῦ   θεοῦ
Everyone   having been begotten   ⁸of   ³the   ⁴God

ἁμαρτίαν   οὐ   ποιεῖ,   ὅτι   σπέρμα   αὐτοῦ
⁸sin   ²not ¹does, because   seed   of him

ἐν   αὐτῷ   μένει·   καὶ   οὐ   δύναται   ἁμαρτάνειν,
in   him   remains; and   not   he cannot   to sin,

ὅτι   ἐκ   τοῦ   θεοῦ   γεγέννηται.   10 ἐν
because of   –   God   he has been begotten.   By

τούτῳ   φανερά   ἐστιν   τὰ   τέκνα   τοῦ   θεοῦ
this   ⁸manifest   ¹is(are)   the   children   –   of God

καὶ   τὰ   τέκνα   τοῦ   διαβόλου·   πᾶς   ὁ
and   the children of the   devil;   everyone

μὴ   ποιῶν   δικαιοσύνην   οὐκ   ἔστιν   ἐκ
not   doing   righteousness   is not   of

τοῦ   θεοῦ,   καὶ   ὁ   μὴ   ἀγαπῶν   τὸν   ἀδελφὸν
–   God,   and   the not   loving   the   brother
                                              [one]

αὐτοῦ.   11 ὅτι   αὕτη   ἐστὶν   ἡ   ἀγγελία
of him.   Because   this   is   the   message

ἣν   ἠκούσατε   ἀπ'   ἀρχῆς,   ἵνα   ἀγαπῶμεν
which   ye heard   from   [the]   in order we should love
                          beginning, that

ἀλλήλους·   12 οὐ   καθὼς   Κάϊν   ἐκ   τοῦ
one another;   not   as   Cain   ⁸of   ⁸the

πονηροῦ   ἦν   καὶ   ἔσφαξεν   τὸν   ἀδελφὸν
⁴evil one ¹was   and   slew   the   brother

αὐτοῦ·   καὶ   χάριν   τίνος   ἔσφαξεν   αὐτόν;
of him;   and   for the   what   slew he   him ?
               sake of

ὅτι   τὰ   ἔργα   αὐτοῦ   πονηρὰ   ἦν,   τὰ   δὲ
be-   the   works of him   ⁸evil   ¹was(were). but the
cause   [works]

τοῦ   ἀδελφοῦ   αὐτοῦ   δίκαια.   13 μὴ
of the   brother   of him   righteous.   not

θαυμάζετε,   ἀδελφοί,   εἰ   μισεῖ   ὑμᾶς   ὁ
Marvel ye,   brothers,   if   ⁸hates   ⁴you   ¹the

κόσμος.   14 ἡμεῖς   οἴδαμεν   ὅτι   μεταβεβή-
⁸world.   We   know   that   we have re-

King James Version

death unto life, because we love the brethren. He that loveth not *his* brother abideth in death. 15 Whosoever hateth his brother is a murderer: and ye know that no murderer hath eternal life abiding in him. 16 Hereby perceive we the love *of God,* because he laid down his life for us: and we ought to lay down *our* lives for the brethren. 17 But whoso hath this world's good, and seeth his brother have need, and shutteth up his bowels *of compassion* from him, how dwelleth the love of God in him? 18 My little children, let us not love in word, neither in tongue; but in deed and in truth. 19And hereby we know that we are of the truth, and shall assure our hearts before him. 20 For if our heart condemn us, God is greater than our heart, and knoweth all things. 21 Beloved, if our heart condemn us not, *then* have we confidence toward God. 22And whatsoever we ask, we receive of him, because we keep his commandments, and do those things that are pleasing in his sight. 23And this is his commandment, That we should believe on the name of his Son Jesus Christ, and love one another, as he gave us commandment. 24And he that keepeth his commandments dwelleth in him, and he in him. And hereby we know that he abideth in us, by the Spirit which he hath given us.

4 Beloved, believe not every spirit, but try the spirits whether they are of God: because many false prophets are gone out into the world. 2 Hereby know ye the Spirit of God: Every spirit that confesseth that Jesus Christ is come in the flesh is of God: 3And every spirit that confesseth not that Jesus Christ is come in the flesh is not of God: and this is that *spirit* of antichrist, whereof ye have heard that it should come; and even now already is it in the world. 4 Ye are of God, little children, and have overcome them: because greater is he that is in you, than he that is in the world. 5 They are of the world: therefore speak they of the world, and the world heareth them. 6 We are of God: he that knoweth God heareth us; he that is not of God heareth not us. Hereby know we the spirit of truth, and the spirit of error. 7 Beloved, let us love one another: for love is of God; and every one that loveth is born of God, and knoweth God. 8 He that loveth not, knoweth not God;

New International Version

that we have passed from death to life, because we love our brothers. Anyone who does not love remains in death. 15Anyone who hates his brother is a murderer, and you know that no murderer has eternal life in him.

16 This is how we know what love is: Jesus Christ laid down his life for us. And we ought to lay down our lives for our brothers. 17 If anyone has material possessions and sees his brother in need but has no pity on him, how can the love of God be in him? 18 Dear children, let us not love with words or tongue but with actions and in truth. 19 This then is how we know that we belong to the truth, and how we set our hearts at rest in his presence 20 whenever our hearts condemn us. For God is greater than our hearts, and he knows everything.

21 Dear friends, if our hearts do not condemn us, we have confidence before God 22 and receive from him anything we ask, because we obey his commands and do what pleases him. 23And this is his command: to believe in the name of his Son, Jesus Christ, and to love one another as he commanded us. 24 Those who obey his commands live in him, and he in them. And this is how we know that he lives in us: We know it by the Spirit he gave us.

Test the spirits

4 Dear friends, do not believe every spirit, but test the spirits to see whether they are from God, because many false prophets have gone out into the world. 2 This is how you can recognize the Spirit of God: Every spirit that acknowledges that Jesus Christ has come in the flesh is from God, 3 but every spirit that does not acknowledge Jesus is not from God. This is the spirit of the antichrist, which you have heard is coming and even now is already in the world.

4 You, dear children, are from God and have overcome them, because the one who is in you is greater than the one who is in the world. 5 They are from the world and therefore speak from the viewpoint of the world, and the world listens to them. 6 We are from God, and whoever knows God listens to us; but whoever is not from God does not listen to us. This is how we recognize the Spirit*e* of truth and the spirit of falsehood.

God's love and ours

7 Dear friends, let us love one another, for love comes from God. Everyone who loves has been born of God and knows God. 8 Whoever does not love does not know God, because God

[e] Or *spirit.*

Greek Interlinear

καμεν   ἐκ   τοῦ   θανάτου   εἰς   τὴν   ζωήν,
moved   out of   the   death   into   the   life.

ὅτι   ἀγαπῶμεν   τοὺς   ἀδελφούς·   ὁ   μὴ
because   we love   the   brothers;   the [one]   not

ἀγαπῶν   μένει   ἐν   τῷ   θανάτῳ.   15 πᾶς
loving   remains   in   -   death.   Every-

ὁ   μισῶν   τὸν   ἀδελφὸν   αὐτοῦ   ἀνθρωποκτόνος
one hating   the   brother   of him   ¹a murderer

ἐστίν,   καὶ   οἴδατε   ὅτι   πᾶς   ἀνθρωποκτόνος
¹is,   and   ye know   that   every   murderer
= no murderer nas . . .

οὐκ   ἔχει   ζωὴν   αἰώνιον   ἐν   αὐτῷ   μένουσαν.
has not   life   eternal   in   him   remaining.

16 ἐν   τούτῳ   ἐγνώκαμεν   τὴν   ἀγάπην,   ὅτι
By   this   we have known   -   love,   because

ἐκεῖνος   ὑπὲρ   ἡμῶν   τὴν   ψυχὴν   αὐτοῦ
that one*   on behalf of   us   the   life   of him

ἔθηκεν·   καὶ   ἡμεῖς   ὀφείλομεν   ὑπὲρ   τῶν
laid down;   and   we   ought   on behalf of the

ἀδελφῶν   τὰς   ψυχὰς   θεῖναι.   17 ὃς   δ'
brothers   the(our)   lives   to lay down.   Who-

ἂν   ἔχῃ   τὸν   βίον   τοῦ   κόσμου   καὶ   θεωρῇ
ever   has   the   means   of the   world   and   beholds
of life

τὸν   ἀδελφὸν   αὐτοῦ   χρείαν   ἔχοντα   καὶ
the   brother   of him   ²need   ¹having   and

κλείσῃ   τὰ   σπλάγχνα   αὐτοῦ   ἀπ'   αὐτοῦ,
shuts   the   bowels   of him   from   him,

πῶς   ἡ   ἀγάπη   τοῦ   θεοῦ   μένει   ἐν   αὐτῷ;
how   ²the   ³love   -   ⁴of God   ¹remains   in   him?

18 Τεκνία,   μὴ   ἀγαπῶμεν   λόγῳ   μηδὲ   τῇ
Little children,   let us not love   in word   nor   in the

γλώσσῃ,   ἀλλὰ   ἐν   ἔργῳ   καὶ   ἀληθείᾳ.
tongue,   but   in   work   and   truth.

19 ἐν   τούτῳ   γνωσόμεθα   ὅτι   ἐκ   τῆς   ἀληθείας
By   this   we shall know   that   ²of   ³the   ⁴truth

ἐσμέν,   καὶ   ἔμπροσθεν   αὐτοῦ   πείσομεν
¹we are,   and   before   him   shall persuade

τὴν   καρδίαν   ἡμῶν   20 ὅτι   ἐὰν   καταγινώσκῃ
the   heart   of us   that   if   ⁴blames [us]

ἡμῶν   ἡ   καρδία,   ὅτι   μείζων   ἐστὶν   ὁ
³of us   ¹the   ²heart,   that   greater   is   -

θεὸς   τῆς   καρδίας   ἡμῶν   καὶ   γινώσκει
God [than] the   heart   of us   and   knows

πάντα.   21 Ἀγαπητοί,   ἐὰν   ἡ   καρδία
all things.   Beloved,   if   the(our)   heart

μὴ   καταγινώσκῃ,   παρρησίαν   ἔχομεν   πρὸς
does not blame [us],   confidence   we have   with

τὸν   θεόν,   22 καὶ   ὃ   ἐὰν   αἰτῶμεν   λαμβάν-
-    God,   and   whatever   we ask   we re-

ομεν   ἀπ'   αὐτοῦ,   ὅτι   τὰς   ἐντολὰς   αὐτοῦ
ceive   from   him,   because   ²the   ³command-   ⁴of him
ments

τηροῦμεν   καὶ   τὰ   ἀρεστὰ   ἐνώπιον   αὐτοῦ
¹we keep   and   ²the   ³pleasing   ⁴before   ⁵him
things

ποιοῦμεν.   23 καὶ   αὕτη   ἐστὶν   ἡ   ἐντολὴ
¹we do.   And   this   is   the   commandment

αὐτοῦ,   ἵνα   πιστεύσωμεν   τῷ   ὀνόματι   τοῦ
of him,   in order   we should believe   the   name   of the
that

υἱοῦ   αὐτοῦ   Ἰησοῦ   Χριστοῦ   καὶ   ἀγαπῶμεν
Son   of him   Jesus   Christ   and   love

ἀλλήλους   καθὼς   ἔδωκεν   ἐντολὴν   ἡμῖν.
one another   as   he gave   commandment   to us.

24 καὶ   ὁ   τηρῶν   τὰς   ἐντολὰς   αὐτοῦ   ἐν
And   the   keeping   the   command-   of him   in
[one]   ments

αὐτῷ   μένει   καὶ   αὐτὸς   ἐν   αὐτῷ·   καὶ
him   remains   and   he   in   him;   and

ἐν   τούτῳ   γινώσκομεν   ὅτι   μένει   ἐν   ἡμῖν,
by   this   we know   that   he remains   in   us,

ἐκ   τοῦ   πνεύματος   οὗ   ἡμῖν   ἔδωκεν.
by   the   Spirit   whom   to us   he gave.

Chapter 4

Ἀγαπητοί,   μὴ   παντὶ   πνεύματι
Beloved,   ²not   ⁴every   ³spirit

πιστεύετε,   ἀλλὰ   δοκιμάζετε   τὰ   πνεύματα
¹believe ye,   but   prove   the   spirits

εἰ   ἐκ   τοῦ   θεοῦ   ἐστιν,   ὅτι   πολλοὶ
if   of   -   God   they are,   because   many

ψευδοπροφῆται   ἐξεληλύθασιν   εἰς   τὸν
false prophets   have gone forth   into   the

κόσμον.   2 ἐν   τούτῳ   γινώσκετε   τὸ   πνεῦμα
world.   By   this   know ye   the   Spirit

τοῦ   θεοῦ·   πᾶν   πνεῦμα   ὃ   ὁμολογεῖ   Ἰησοῦν
-    of God: every   spirit   which   confesses   Jesus

Χριστὸν   ἐν   σαρκὶ   ἐληλυθότα   ἐκ   τοῦ
Christ   ²in   ³[the] flesh   ¹having come   ⁴of   -

θεοῦ   ἐστιν,   3 καὶ   πᾶν   πνεῦμα   ὃ   μὴ
⁵God   ⁶is,   and   every   spirit   which   not

ὁμολογεῖ   τὸν   Ἰησοῦν   ἐκ   τοῦ   θεοῦ   οὐκ
confesses   -   Jesus   ²of   -   ⁴God   ¹not

ἔστιν·   καὶ   τοῦτό   ἐστιν   τὸ   τοῦ   ἀντιχρίστου,
³is;   and   this   is   the   of the   antichrist,
[spirit] the

ὃ   ἀκηκόατε   ὅτι   ἔρχεται,   καὶ   νῦν   ἐν
which   ye have   that   it is coming,   and   ²now   ¹in
heard

τῷ   κόσμῳ   ἐστὶν   ἤδη.   4 ὑμεῖς   ἐκ   τοῦ
³the   ⁴world   ¹is   ²already.   Ye   of   -

θεοῦ   ἐστε,   τεκνία,   καὶ   νενικήκατε   αὐτούς,
God   are,   little   and   have overcome   them,
children,

ὅτι   μείζων   ἐστὶν   ὁ   ἐν   ὑμῖν   ἢ   ὁ   ἐν
because   greater   is   the   in   you   than   the   in
[one]   [one]

τῷ   κόσμῳ.   5 αὐτοὶ   ἐκ   τοῦ   κόσμου
the   world.   ¹They   ²of   ³the   ⁴world

εἰσίν·   διὰ   τοῦτο   ἐκ   τοῦ   κόσμου   λαλοῦσιν
²are;   therefore   ²of   ³the   ⁴world   ¹they speak

καὶ   ὁ   κόσμος   αὐτῶν   ἀκούει.   6 ἡμεῖς
and   the   world   them   hears.   ¹We

ἐκ   τοῦ   θεοῦ   ἐσμεν·   ὁ   γινώσκων   τὸν
²of   -   ⁴God   ³are;   the [one] knowing   -

θεὸν   ἀκούει   ἡμῶν,   ὃς   οὐκ   ἔστιν   ἐκ
God   hears   us,   [he] who   is not   of

τοῦ   θεοῦ   οὐκ   ἀκούει   ἡμῶν.   ἐκ   τούτου
-    God   hears not   us.   From   this

γινώσκομεν   τὸ   πνεῦμα   τῆς   ἀληθείας   καὶ
we know   the   spirit   -   of truth   and

τὸ   πνεῦμα   τῆς   πλάνης.
the   spirit   -   of error.

7 Ἀγαπητοί,   ἀγαπῶμεν   ἀλλήλους,   ὅτι
Beloved,   let us love   one another,   because

ἡ   ἀγάπη   ἐκ   τοῦ   θεοῦ   ἐστιν,   καὶ   πᾶς   ὁ
the   love   ²of   -   ³God   ¹is,   and   everyone

ἀγαπῶν   ἐκ   τοῦ   θεοῦ   γεγέννηται   καὶ
loving   ²of   -   ³God   ¹has been begotten   and

γινώσκει   τὸν   θεόν.   8 ὁ   μὴ   ἀγαπῶν
knows   -   God.   The [one]   not   loving

οὐκ   ἔγνω   τὸν   θεόν,   ὅτι   ὁ   θεὸς   ἀγάπη
knew not   -   God,   because   -   God   ²love

* See ch. 2. 6, 3. 3, 5, 7.

King James Version

for God is love. 9 In this was manifested the love of God toward us, because that God sent his only begotten Son into the world, that we might live through him. 10 Herein is love, not that we loved God, but that he loved us, and sent his Son *to be* the propitiation for our sins. 11 Beloved, if God so loved us, we ought also to love one another. 12 No man hath seen God at any time. If we love one another, God dwelleth in us, and his love is perfected in us. 13 Hereby know we that we dwell in him, and he in us, because he hath given us of his Spirit. 14 And we have seen and do testify that the Father sent the Son *to be* the Saviour of the world. 15 Whosoever shall confess that Jesus is the Son of God, God dwelleth in him, and he in God. 16 And we have known and believed the love that God hath to us. God is love; and he that dwelleth in love dwelleth in God, and God in him. 17 Herein is our love made perfect, that we may have boldness in the day of judgment: because as he is, so are we in this world. 18 There is no fear in love; but perfect love casteth out fear: because fear hath torment. He that feareth is not made perfect in love. 19 We love him, because he first loved us. 20 If a man say, I love God, and hateth his brother, he is a liar: for he that loveth not his brother whom he hath seen, how can he love God whom he hath not seen? 21 And this commandment have we from him, That he who loveth God love his brother also.

New International Version

is love. 9 This is how God showed his love among us: He sent his one and only Son[f] into the world that we might live through him. 10 This is love: not that we loved God, but that he loved us and sent his Son as an atoning sacrifice for our sins. 11 Dear friends, since God so loved us, we also ought to love one another. 12 No one has ever seen God; but if we love each other, God lives in us and his love is made complete in us.

13 We know that we live in him and he in us, because he has given us of his Spirit. 14 And we have seen and testify that the Father has sent his Son to be the Savior of the world. 15 If anyone acknowledges that Jesus is the Son of God, God lives in him and he in God. 16 And so we know and rely on the love God has for us.

God is love. Whoever lives in love lives in God, and God in him. 17 Love is made complete among us so that we will have confidence on the day of judgment, because in this world we are like him. 18 There is no fear in love. But perfect love drives out fear, because fear has to do with punishment. The man who fears is not made perfect in love.

19 We love because he first loved us. 20 If anyone says, "I love God," yet hates his brother, he is a liar. For anyone who does not love his brother, whom he has seen, cannot love God, whom he has not seen. 21 And he has given us this command: Whoever loves God must also love his brother.

Faith in the Son of God

5 Whosoever believeth that Jesus is the Christ is born of God: and every one that loveth him that begat loveth him also that is begotten of him. 2 By this we know that we love the children of God, when we love God, and keep his commandments. 3 For this is the love of God, that we keep his commandments: and his commandments are not grievous. 4 For whatsoever is born of God overcometh the world: and this is the victory that overcometh the world, *even* our faith. 5 Who is he that overcometh the world, but he that believeth that Jesus is the Son of God? 6 This is he that came by water and blood, *even* Jesus Christ; not by water only, but by water and blood. And it is the Spirit that beareth witness, because the Spirit is truth. 7 For there are three that bear record in heaven, the Father, the Word, and the Holy Ghost: and these three are one. 8 And there are three that bear witness in earth, the spirit, and the water,

5 Everyone who believes that Jesus is the Christ is born of God, and everyone who loves the father loves his child as well. 2 This is how we know that we love the children of God: by loving God and carrying out his commands. 3 This is love for God: to obey his commands. And his commands are not burdensome, 4 for everyone born of God has overcome the world. This is the victory that has overcome the world, even our faith. 5 Who is it that overcomes the world? Only he who believes that Jesus is the Son of God.

6 This is the one who came by water and blood—Jesus Christ. He did not come by water

---

[f] Or *his only begotten Son.*

Greek Interlinear

ἐστίν. 9 ἐν τούτῳ ἐφανερώθη ἡ ἀγάπη
¹is.   By this   was manifested the love

τοῦ θεοῦ ἐν ἡμῖν, ὅτι τὸν υἱὸν αὐτοῦ
- of God in(to) us, because ²the ⁴Son ³of him

τὸν μονογενῆ ἀπέσταλκεν ὁ θεὸς εἰς
- ⁵only begotten ²has sent   - ¹God into

τὸν κόσμον ἵνα ζήσωμεν δι' αὐτοῦ.
the world   in order we might live through him.
                   that

10 ἐν τούτῳ ἐστὶν ἡ ἀγάπη, οὐχ ὅτι
In this   is   the love,   not that

ἡμεῖς ἠγαπήκαμεν τὸν θεόν, ἀλλ' ὅτι
we   have loved   -   God,   but   that

αὐτὸς ἠγάπησεν ἡμᾶς καὶ ἀπέστειλεν τὸν
he   loved   us   and sent   the

υἱὸν αὐτοῦ ἱλασμὸν περὶ τῶν ἁμαρτιῶν
Son of him a propitiation concerning the sins

ἡμῶν. 11 ἀγαπητοί, εἰ οὕτως ὁ θεὸς
of us.   Beloved,   if so   - God

ἠγάπησεν ἡμᾶς, καὶ ἡμεῖς ὀφείλομεν
loved   us,   ²also ¹we   ³ought

ἀλλήλους ἀγαπᾶν. 12 θεὸν οὐδεὶς πώποτε
²one another ³to love. ⁴God ¹no man   ²ever

τεθέαται· ἐὰν ἀγαπῶμεν ἀλλήλους, ὁ θεὸς
¹has beheld· if we love   one another, - God

ἐν ἡμῖν μένει καὶ ἡ ἀγάπη αὐτοῦ
in us   remains and the love   of him

τετελειωμένη ἐν ἡμῖν ἐστιν. 13 Ἐν
¹having been perfected ²in ⁴us   ³is.   By

τούτῳ γινώσκομεν ὅτι ἐν αὐτῷ μένομεν
this   we know   that in him we remain

καὶ αὐτὸς ἐν ἡμῖν, ὅτι ἐκ τοῦ πνεύματος
and he   in us, because ²of ⁴the ⁵Spirit

αὐτοῦ δέδωκεν ἡμῖν. 14 καὶ ἡμεῖς
⁶of him ¹he has given ²us.   And   we

τεθεάμεθα καὶ μαρτυροῦμεν ὅτι ὁ πατὴρ
have beheld and bear witness   that the Father

ἀπέσταλκεν τὸν υἱὸν σωτῆρα τοῦ κόσμου.
has sent   the Son [as] Saviour of the world.

15 ὃς ἐὰν ὁμολογήσῃ ὅτι Ἰησοῦς ἐστιν
Whoever   confesses   that Jesus   is

ὁ υἱὸς τοῦ θεοῦ, ὁ θεὸς ἐν αὐτῷ μένει
the Son - of God, - God in him remains

καὶ αὐτὸς ἐν τῷ θεῷ. 16 καὶ ἡμεῖς
and he   in   - God.   And   we

ἐγνώκαμεν καὶ πεπιστεύκαμεν τὴν ἀγάπην
have known   and   have believed   the   love

ἣν ἔχει ὁ θεὸς ἐν ἡμῖν. Ὁ θεὸς ἀγάπη
which ²has - ¹God in(to) us.   - God ²love

ἐστίν, καὶ ὁ μένων ἐν τῇ ἀγάπῃ ἐν
¹is,   and the remaining in -   love   ²in

τῷ θεῷ μένει καὶ ὁ θεὸς ἐν αὐτῷ
- ³God ¹remains and - God ⁴in   ³him

μένει. 17 Ἐν τούτῳ τετελείωται ἡ ἀγάπη
¹remains.   By this   ²has been perfected ⁻¹love

μεθ' ἡμῶν, ἵνα παρρησίαν ἔχωμεν ἐν
with   us, in order that ²confidence ¹we may have in

τῇ ἡμέρᾳ τῆς κρίσεως, ὅτι καθὼς ἐκεῖνός
the day   of judgment, because as   that one*

ἐστιν καὶ ἡμεῖς ἐσμεν ἐν τῷ κόσμῳ
is   ²also ¹we   ²are   in -   world

τούτῳ. 18 φόβος οὐκ ἔστιν ἐν τῇ ἀγάπῃ,
this.   Fear   is not   in -   love,

ἀλλ' ἡ τελεία ἀγάπη ἔξω βάλλει τὸν
but   - perfect love ²out ¹casts   the

φόβον, ὅτι ὁ φόβος κόλασιν ἔχει, ὁ δὲ
fear, because - fear ²punishment ¹has, and the

φοβούμενος οὐ τετελείωται ἐν τῇ ἀγάπῃ.
[one] fearing has not been perfected in -   love.

19 ἡμεῖς ἀγαπῶμεν, ὅτι αὐτὸς πρῶτος
We   love,   because he   first

ἠγάπησεν ἡμᾶς. 20 ἐάν τις εἴπῃ ὅτι
loved   us.   If anyone says[,]

ἀγαπῶ τὸν θεόν, καὶ τὸν ἀδελφὸν αὐτοῦ
I love   -   God, and ²the ³brother ⁴of him

μισῇ, ψεύστης ἐστίν· ὁ γὰρ μὴ ἀγαπῶν
¹hates, ²a liar ¹he is; for the [one] not loving

τὸν ἀδελφὸν αὐτοῦ ὃν ἑώρακεν, τὸν
the brother of him whom he has seen,   the

θεὸν ὃν οὐχ ἑώρακεν οὐ δύναται ἀγαπᾶν.
³God ²whom ¹he has not seen ¹he cannot   ²to love.

21 καὶ ταύτην τὴν ἐντολὴν ἔχομεν ἀπ'
And this   -   commandment we have from

αὐτοῦ, ἵνα ὁ ἀγαπῶν τὸν θεὸν ἀγαπᾷ
him, in order the loving   -   God loves
       that [one]

καὶ τὸν ἀδελφὸν αὐτοῦ.
also the brother of him.

Chapter 5

Πᾶς ὁ πιστεύων ὅτι Ἰησοῦς ἐστιν
Everyone believing   that Jesus   is

ὁ χριστὸς ἐκ τοῦ θεοῦ γεγέννηται, καὶ
the Christ ²of - ¹God ¹has been begotten, and

πᾶς ὁ ἀγαπῶν τὸν γεννήσαντα ἀγαπᾷ
everyone loving the [one] begetting   loves

τὸν γεγεννημένον ἐξ αὐτοῦ. 2 ἐν τούτῳ
the having been begotten of him. By this
[one]

γινώσκομεν ὅτι ἀγαπῶμεν τὰ τέκνα τοῦ
we know   that we love   the children -

θεοῦ, ὅταν τὸν θεὸν ἀγαπῶμεν καὶ τὰς
of God, whenever - ²God ¹we love   and ²the

ἐντολὰς αὐτοῦ ποιῶμεν. 3 αὕτη γάρ
¹command- ⁴of him ¹we do.   For this
ments

ἐστιν ἡ ἀγάπη τοῦ θεοῦ, ἵνα τὰς ἐντολὰς
is the love   - of in order ²the ³command-
              God, that   ments

αὐτοῦ τηρῶμεν· καὶ αἱ ἐντολαὶ αὐτοῦ
⁴of him ¹we keep; and the commandments of him

βαρεῖαι οὐκ εἰσίν, 4 ὅτι πᾶν τὸ γεγεν-
heavy   are not, because everything - having

νημένον ἐκ τοῦ θεοῦ νικᾷ τὸν κόσμον·
been begotten of - God overcomes the world;

καὶ αὕτη ἐστὶν ἡ νίκη ἡ νικήσασα τὸν
and this   is   the victory - overcoming the

κόσμον, ἡ πίστις ἡμῶν. 5 Τίς ἐστιν
world, the faith of us.   ²Who ¹is

[δὲ] ὁ νικῶν τὸν κόσμον εἰ μὴ ὁ
¹and the overcoming the world except the
[one]

πιστεύων ὅτι Ἰησοῦς ἐστιν ὁ υἱὸς τοῦ
[one] believing that Jesus   is the Son   -

θεοῦ; 6 οὗτός ἐστιν ὁ ἐλθὼν δι' ὕδατος
of God? This   is   the coming through water
                    [one]

καὶ αἵματος, Ἰησοῦς Χριστός· οὐκ ἐν
and blood,   Jesus   Christ;   not by

τῷ ὕδατι μόνον, ἀλλ' ἐν τῷ ὕδατι καὶ
the water only, but by the water and

* See ch. 2. 6, 3. 3, 5, 7. 16.

713

King James Version

and the blood: and these three agree in one. 9 If we receive the witness of men, the witness of God is greater: for this is the witness of God which he hath testified of his Son. 10 He that believeth on the Son of God hath the witness in himself: he that believeth not God hath made him a liar; because he believeth not the record that God gave of his Son. 11 And this is the record, that God hath given to us eternal life, and this life is in his Son. 12 He that hath the Son hath life; *and* he that hath not the Son of God hath not life. 13 These things have I written unto you that believe on the name of the Son of God; that ye may know that ye have eternal life, and that ye may believe on the name of the Son of God. 14And this is the confidence that we have in him, that, if we ask any thing according to his will, he heareth us: 15And if we know that he hear us, whatsoever we ask, we know that we have the petitions that we desired of him. 16 If any man see his brother sin a sin *which is* not unto death, he shall ask, and he shall give him life for them that sin not unto death. There is a sin unto death: I do not say that he shall pray for it. 17All unrighteousness is sin: and there is a sin not unto death. 18 We know that whosoever is born of God sinneth not; but he that is begotten of God keepeth himself, and that wicked one toucheth him not. 19*And* we know that we are of God, and the whole world lieth in wickedness. 20And we know that the Son of God is come, and hath given us an understanding, that we may know him that is true; and we are in him that is true, *even* in his Son Jesus Christ. This is the true God, and eternal life. 21 Little children, keep yourselves from idols. Amen.

New International Version

only, but by water and blood. And it is the Spirit who testifies, because the Spirit is the truth. 7 For there are three that testify:*ᵍ* 8 the Spirit, the water, and the blood; and the three are in agreement. 9 We accept man's testimony, but God's testimony is greater because it is the testimony of God, which he has given about his Son. 10Anyone who believes in the Son of God has this testimony in his heart. Anyone who does not believe God has made him out to be a liar, because he has not believed the testimony God has given about his Son. 11And this is the testimony: God has given us eternal life, and this life is in his Son. 12 He who has the Son has life; he who does not have the Son of God does not have life.

Concluding remarks

13 I write these things to you who believe in the name of the Son of God so that you may know that you have eternal life. 14 We have this assurance in approaching God, that if we ask anything according to his will, he hears us. 15And if we know that he hears us—whatever we ask—we know that we have what we asked of him.

16 If anyone sees his brother commit a sin that does not lead to death, he should pray and God will give him life. I refer to those whose sin does not lead to death. There is a sin that leads to death. I am not saying that he should pray about that. 17All wrongdoing is sin, and there is a sin that does not lead to death.

18 We know that anyone born of God does not continue to sin; the one who was born of God keeps him safe, and the evil one does not touch him. 19 We know that we are children of God, and that the whole world is under the control of the evil one. 20 We know also that the Son of God has come and has given us understanding, so that we may know him who is true. And we are in him who is true—even in his Son Jesus Christ. He is the true God and eternal life.

21 Dear children, keep yourselves from idols.

---

[g] Late MSS of the Vugalte add *in heaven: the Father, the Word and the Holy Spirit, and these three are one. And there are three that testify on earth:*

Greek Interlinear

ἐν τῷ αἵματι· καὶ τὸ πνεῦμά ἐστιν τὸ
by the blood; and the Spirit is the

μαρτυροῦν, ὅτι τὸ πνεῦμά ἐστιν ἡ ἀλήθεια.
[one] bearing be- the Spirit is the truth.
witness, cause

7 ὅτι τρεῖς εἰσιν οἱ μαρτυροῦντες, 8 τὸ
Because three there are the bearing witness, the
[ones]

πνεῦμα καὶ τὸ ὕδωρ καὶ τὸ αἷμα, καὶ
Spirit and the water and the blood, and

οἱ τρεῖς εἰς τὸ ἕν εἰσιν. 9 εἰ τὴν
the three ²in the ³one ¹are. If ²the

μαρτυρίαν τῶν ἀνθρώπων λαμβάνομεν, ἡ
³witness - ⁴of men ¹we receive, the

μαρτυρία τοῦ θεοῦ μείζων ἐστίν, ὅτι
witness - of God ¹greater ¹is, because

αὕτη ἐστὶν ἡ μαρτυρία τοῦ θεοῦ, ὅτι
this is the witness - of God, because

μεμαρτύρηκεν περὶ τοῦ υἱοῦ αὐτοῦ. 10 ὁ
he has borne concern- the Son of him. The
witness ing

πιστεύων εἰς τὸν υἱὸν τοῦ θεοῦ ἔχει
[one] believing in the Son - of God has

τὴν μαρτυρίαν ἐν αὐτῷ. ὁ μὴ πιστεύων
the witness in him. The not believing
[one]

τῷ θεῷ ψεύστην πεποίηκεν αὐτόν, ὅτι
- God ²a liar ¹has made ³him, because

οὐ πεπίστευκεν εἰς τὴν μαρτυρίαν ἣν
he has not believed in the witness which

μεμαρτύρηκεν ὁ θεὸς περὶ τοῦ υἱοῦ
²has borne witness ¹God concerning the Son

αὐτοῦ. 11 καὶ αὕτη ἐστὶν ἡ μαρτυρία,
of him. And this is the witness,

ὅτι ζωὴν αἰώνιον ἔδωκεν ὁ θεὸς ἡμῖν,
that ²life ⁴eternal ³gave - ¹God ⁵to us,

καὶ αὕτη ἡ ζωὴ ἐν τῷ υἱῷ αὐτοῦ
and this the life ²in ³the ⁴Son ⁵of him

ἐστιν. 12 ὁ ἔχων τὸν υἱὸν ἔχει τὴν
¹is. The [one] having the Son has the

ζωήν· ὁ μὴ ἔχων τὸν υἱὸν τοῦ θεοῦ
life; the not having the Son - of God
[one]

τὴν ζωὴν οὐκ ἔχει.
the life has not.

13 Ταῦτα ἔγραψα ὑμῖν ἵνα εἰδῆτε ὅτι
These I wrote to you in order ye may that
things that know

ζωὴν ἔχετε αἰώνιον, τοῖς πιστεύουσιν
²life ¹ye have ²eternal, to the [ones] believing

εἰς τὸ ὄνομα τοῦ υἱοῦ τοῦ θεοῦ. 14 Καὶ
in the name of the Son - of God. And

αὕτη ἐστὶν ἡ παρρησία ἣν ἔχομεν πρὸς
this is the confidence which we have toward

αὐτόν, ὅτι ἐὰν τι αἰτώμεθα κατὰ τὸ
him, that if ²anything ¹we ask according to the

θέλημα αὐτοῦ ἀκούει ἡμῶν. 15 καὶ
will of him he hears us. And

ἐὰν οἴδαμεν ὅτι ἀκούει ἡμῶν ὃ ἐάν
if we know that he hears us whatever

αἰτώμεθα, οἴδαμεν ὅτι ἔχομεν τὰ αἰτήματα
we ask, we know that we have the requests

ἃ ᾐτήκαμεν ἀπ' αὐτοῦ. 16 Ἐάν τις
which we have from him. If anyone
asked

ἴδη τὸν ἀδελφὸν αὐτοῦ ἁμαρτάνοντα
sees the brother of him sinning

ἁμαρτίαν μὴ πρὸς θάνατον, αἰτήσει, καὶ
a sin not unto death, he shall ask, and

δώσει αὐτῷ ζωήν, τοῖς ἁμαρτάνουσιν
he will give to him life, to the [ones] sinning

μὴ πρὸς θάνατον. ἔστιν ἁμαρτία πρὸς
not unto death. There is a sin unto

θάνατον· οὐ περὶ ἐκείνης λέγω ἵνα
death; not concerning that do I say in order

ἐρωτήσῃ. 17 πᾶσα ἀδικία ἁμαρτία ἐστίν,
he should inquire. All iniquity ²sin ¹is,

καὶ ἔστιν ἁμαρτία οὐ πρὸς θάνατον.
and there is a sin not unto death.

18 Οἴδαμεν ὅτι πᾶς ὁ γεγεννημένος ἐκ
We know that everyone having been begotten of

τοῦ θεοῦ οὐχ ἁμαρτάνει, ἀλλ' ὁ γεννηθεὶς
- God sins not, but the [one] begotten

ἐκ τοῦ θεοῦ τηρεῖ αὐτόν, καὶ ὁ πονηρὸς
of - God keeps him, and the evil one

οὐχ ἅπτεται αὐτοῦ. 19 οἴδαμεν ὅτι ἐκ
does not touch him. We know that of

τοῦ θεοῦ ἐσμεν, καὶ ὁ κόσμος ὅλος ἐν
- God we are, and the ²world ¹whole in

τῷ πονηρῷ κεῖται. 20 οἴδαμεν δὲ ὅτι
the evil one lies. ²we know ¹And that

ὁ υἱὸς τοῦ θεοῦ ἥκει, καὶ δέδωκεν
the Son - of God is come, and has given

ἡμῖν διάνοιαν ἵνα γινώσκωμεν τὸν
to us an understanding in order we might know the
that

ἀληθινόν· καὶ ἐσμὲν ἐν τῷ ἀληθινῷ,
true [one]; and we are in the true [one],

ἐν τῷ υἱῷ αὐτοῦ Ἰησοῦ Χριστῷ. οὗτός
in the Son of him Jesus Christ. This

ἐστιν ὁ ἀληθινὸς θεὸς καὶ ζωὴ αἰώνιος.
is the true God and life eternal.

21 Τεκνία, φυλάξατε ἑαυτὰ ἀπὸ τῶν
Little children, guard yourselves from the

εἰδώλων.
idols.

715

THE

SECOND EPISTLE

OF

JOHN

2 JOHN

The elder unto the elect lady and her children, whom I love in the truth; and not I only, but also all they that have known the truth; 2 For the truth's sake, which dwelleth in us, and shall be with us for ever. 3 Grace be with you, mercy, *and* peace, from God the Father, and from the Lord Jesus Christ, the Son of the Father, in truth and love. 4 I rejoiced greatly that I found of thy children walking in truth, as we have received a commandment from the Father. 5And now I beseech thee, lady, not as though I wrote a new commandment unto thee, but that which we had from the beginning, that we love one another. 6And this is love, that we walk after his commandments. This is the commandment, That, as ye have heard from the beginning, ye should walk in it. 7 For many deceivers are entered into the world, who confess not that Jesus Christ is come in the flesh. This is a deceiver and an antichrist. 8 Look to yourselves, that we lose not those things which we have wrought, but that we receive a full reward. 9 Whosoever transgresseth, and abideth not in the doctrine of Christ, hath not God. He that abideth in the doctrine of Christ, he hath both the Father and the Son. 10 If there come any unto you, and bring not this doctrine, receive him not into *your* house, neither bid him God speed: 11 For he that biddeth him God speed is partaker of his evil deeds. 12 Having many things to write unto you, I would not *write* with paper and ink: but I trust to come unto you, and speak face to face, that our joy may be full. 13 The children of thy elect sister greet thee. Amen.

1 The elder,
To the chosen lady and her children, whom I love in the truth—and not I only, but also all who know the truth—2 because of the truth, which lives in us and will be with us forever:
3 Grace, mercy and peace from God the Father and from Jesus Christ, the Father's Son, will be with us in truth and love.
4 It has given me great joy to find some of your children living by the truth, just as the Father commanded us. 5And now, dear lady, I am not writing you a new command but one we have had from the beginning. I ask that we love one another. 6And this is love: that we live in obedience to his commands. As you have heard from the beginning, his command is that you live a life of love.
7 Many deceivers, who do not acknowledge that Jesus Christ has come in the flesh, have gone out into the world. Any such person is the deceiver and the antichrist. 8 Watch out that you do not lose what you have worked for, but that you may be rewarded fully. 9Anyone who runs ahead and does not continue in the teaching of Christ does not have God; whoever continues in the teaching has both the Father and the Son. 10 If anyone comes to you and does not bring this teaching, do not take him into your house or welcome him. 11Anyone who welcomes him shares in his wicked work.
12 I have much to write to you, but I do not want to use paper and ink. Instead, I hope to visit you and talk with you face to face, so that our joy may be complete.
13 The children of your chosen sister send their greetings.

ΙΩΑΝΝΟΥ Β

1 Ὁ   πρεσβύτερος   ἐκλεκτῇ   κυρίᾳ   καὶ
The   elder   to [the] chosen   lady   and

τοῖς   τέκνοις   αὐτῆς,   οὓς   ἐγὼ   ἀγαπῶ   ἐν
to the   children   of her,   whom   I   love   in

ἀληθείᾳ,   καὶ   οὐκ   ἐγὼ   μόνος   ἀλλὰ   καὶ
truth,   and   not   I   alone   but   also

πάντες   οἱ   ἐγνωκότες   τὴν   ἀλήθειαν,   **2** διὰ
all   the   having known   the   truth,   because of
[ones]

τὴν   ἀλήθειαν   τὴν   μένουσαν   ἐν   ἡμῖν,
the   truth   the   remaining   among   us,

καὶ   μεθ’   ἡμῶν   ἔσται   εἰς   τὸν   αἰῶνα.
and   with   us   will be   unto   the   age.

3 ἔσται   μεθ’   ἡμῶν   χάρις   ἔλεος   εἰρήνη
¹will be   ²with   ³us   ⁴Grace[,]   ⁵mercy[,]   ⁶peace

παρὰ   θεοῦ   πατρός,   καὶ   παρὰ   Ἰησοῦ
from   God   [the] Father,   and   from   Jesus

Χριστοῦ   τοῦ   υἱοῦ   τοῦ   πατρός,   ἐν   ἀληθείᾳ
Christ   the   Son   of the   Father,   in   truth

καὶ   ἀγάπῃ.
and   love.

4 Ἐχάρην   λίαν   ὅτι   εὕρηκα   ἐκ   τῶν
I rejoiced   greatly   because   I have   of   the
found [some]

τέκνων   σου   περιπατοῦντας   ἐν   ἀληθείᾳ,
children   of thee   walking   in   truth,

καθὼς   ἐντολὴν   ἐλάβομεν   παρὰ   τοῦ   πατρός.
as   command-   we received   from   the   Father.
ment

5 καὶ   νῦν   ἐρωτῶ   σε,   κυρία,   οὐχ   ὡς
And   now   I request   thee,   lady,   not   as

ἐντολὴν   γράφων   σοι   καινήν,   ἀλλὰ   ἣν
²command-   ¹writing   ⁴to thee   ³a new,   but   which
ment

εἴχομεν   ἀπ’   ἀρχῆς,   ἵνα   ἀγαπῶμεν
we had   from   [the]   in order   we should
beginning,   that   love

ἀλλήλους.   **6** καὶ   αὕτη   ἐστὶν   ἡ   ἀγάπη,
one another.   And   this   is   -   love,

ἵνα   περιπατῶμεν   κατὰ   τὰς   ἐντολὰς
in order   we should walk   accord-   the   command-
that   ing to   ments

αὐτοῦ·   αὕτη   ἡ   ἐντολή   ἐστιν,   καθὼς
of him;   this   ¹the   ²commandment   ¹is,   as

ἠκούσατε   ἀπ’   ἀρχῆς,   ἵνα   ἐν   αὐτῇ
ye heard   from   [the]   in order   ³in   ⁵it
beginning,   that

περιπατῆτε.   **7** ὅτι   πολλοὶ   πλάνοι   ἐξῆλθον
¹ye should walk.   Because   many   deceivers   went forth

εἰς   τὸν   κόσμον,   οἱ   μὴ   ὁμολογοῦντες
into   the   world,   the   not   confessing
[ones]

Ἰησοῦν   Χριστὸν   ἐρχόμενον   ἐν   σαρκί·
Jesus   Christ   coming   in   [the] flesh;

οὗτός   ἐστιν   ὁ   πλάνος   καὶ   ὁ   ἀντίχριστος.
this   is   the   deceiver   and   the   antichrist.

8 βλέπετε   ἑαυτούς,   ἵνα   μὴ   ἀπολέσητε
See   yourselves,   lest   ye lose

ἃ   ἠργασάμεθα,   ἀλλὰ   μισθὸν   πλήρη
[the]   we wrought,   but   ⁸reward   ⁹a full
things which

ἀπολάβητε.   **9** πᾶς   ὁ   προάγων   καὶ   μὴ
¹ye may receive.   Everyone   going forward   and   not

μένων   ἐν   τῇ   διδαχῇ   τοῦ   Χριστοῦ   θεὸν
remaining   in   the   teaching   -   of Christ   ¹God

οὐκ   ἔχει·   ὁ   μένων   ἐν   τῇ   διδαχῇ,   οὗτος
²not   ¹has;   the   remaining   in   the   teaching,   this one
[one]

καὶ   τὸν   πατέρα   καὶ   τὸν   υἱὸν   ἔχει.
²both   ³the   ⁴Father   ⁵and   ⁶the   ⁷Son   ¹has.

10 εἴ   τις   ἔρχεται   πρὸς   ὑμᾶς   καὶ   ταύτην
If   anyone   comes   to   you   and   this

τὴν   διδαχὴν   οὐ   φέρει,   μὴ   λαμβάνετε
-    teaching   brings not,   do not ye receive

αὐτὸν   εἰς   οἰκίαν,   καὶ   χαίρειν   αὐτῷ   μὴ
him   into   [your]   and   ⁴to rejoice   ⁵him   ¹not
house,

λέγετε·   **11** ὁ   λέγων   γὰρ   αὐτῷ   χαίρειν
¹tell ye*;   ²the   ³telling   ¹for   him   to rejoice
[one]

κοινωνεῖ   τοῖς   ἔργοις   αὐτοῦ   τοῖς   πονηροῖς.
shares   in the   ²works   ¹of him   -   ³evil.

12 Πολλὰ   ἔχων   ὑμῖν   γράφειν   οὐκ
⁵Many things   ¹having   ⁴to you   ³to write   ²not

ἐβουλήθην   διὰ   χάρτου   καὶ   μέλανος,   ἀλλὰ
¹I purpose   by means   paper   and   ink,   but
of

ἐλπίζω   γενέσθαι   πρὸς   ὑμᾶς   καὶ   στόμα
I am hoping   to be   with   you   and   ²mouth

πρὸς   στόμα   λαλῆσαι,   ἵνα   ἡ   χαρὰ   ἡμῶν
²to   ¹mouth   ³to speak,   in or-   the   joy   of us
der that

πεπληρωμένη   ᾖ.   **13** Ἀσπάζεταί   σε   τὰ
having been   may be.   ⁷greets   ⁶thee   ¹The
fulfilled

τέκνα   τῆς   ἀδελφῆς   σου   τῆς   ἐκλεκτῆς.
²children   ³of the   ⁴sister   ⁵of thee   -   ⁴chosen.

---

* That is, "do not greet him."

THE

THIRD EPISTLE

OF

JOHN

3 JOHN

The elder unto the well beloved Gaius, whom I love in the truth. 2 Beloved, I wish above all things that thou mayest prosper and be in health, even as thy soul prospereth. 3 For I rejoiced greatly, when the brethren came and testified of the truth that is in thee, even as thou walkest in the truth. 4 I have no greater joy than to hear that my children walk in truth. 5 Beloved, thou doest faithfully whatsoever thou doest to the brethren, and to strangers; 6 Which have borne witness of thy charity before the church: whom if thou bring forward on their journey after a godly sort, thou shalt do well: 7 Because that for his name's sake they went forth, taking nothing of the Gentiles. 8 We therefore ought to receive such, that we might be fellow helpers to the truth. 9 I wrote unto the church: but Diotrephes, who loveth to have the preeminence among them, receiveth us not. 10 Wherefore, if I come, I will remember his deeds which he doeth, prating against us with malicious words: and not content therewith, neither doth he himself receive the brethren, and forbiddeth them that would, and casteth them out of the church. 11 Beloved, follow not that which is evil, but that which is good. He that doeth good is of God: but he that doeth evil hath not seen God. 12 Demetrius hath good report of all men, and of the truth itself: yea, and we also bear record; and ye know that our record is true. 13 I had many things to write, but I will not with ink and pen write unto thee: 14 But I trust I shall shortly see thee, and we shall speak face to face. Peace be to thee. Our friends salute thee. Greet the friends by name.

1 The elder,
To my dear friend Gaius, whom I love in the truth.
2 Dear friend, I pray that you may enjoy good health and that all may go well with you, even as your soul is getting along well. 3 It gave me great joy to have some brothers come and tell about your faithfulness to the truth and how you continue to live according to the truth. 4 I have no greater joy than to hear that my children are living according to the truth.
5 Dear friend, you are faithful in what you are doing for the brothers, even though they are strangers to you. 6 They have told the church about your love. You will do well to send them on their way in a manner worthy of God. 7 It was for the sake of the Name that they went out, receiving no help from the pagans. 8 We ought therefore to show hospitality to such men so that we may work together for the truth.
9 I wrote to the church, but Diotrephes, who loves to be first, will have nothing to do with us. 10 So if I come, I will call attention to what he is doing, gossiping maliciously about us. Not satisfied with that, he refuses to welcome the brothers. He also stops those who want to do so and puts them out of the church.
11 Dear friend, do not imitate what is evil but what is good. Anyone who does what is good is from God. Anyone who does what is evil has not seen God. 12 Demetrius is well spoken of by everyone—and even by the truth itself. We also speak well of him, and you know that our testimony is true.
13 I have much to write you, but I do not want to do so with pen and ink. 14 I hope to see you soon, and we will talk face to face.
Peace to you. The friends here send their greetings. Greet the friends there by name.

718

ΙΩΑΝΝΟΥ Γ

1 Ὁ πρεσβύτερος Γαίῳ τῷ ἀγαπητῷ,
The   elder   to Gaius   the   beloved,

ὃν ἐγὼ ἀγαπῶ ἐν ἀληθείᾳ.
whom I   love   in   truth.

2. Ἀγαπητέ, περὶ πάντων εὔχομαί σε
Beloved,   concerning   all things   I pray   thee
    = that

εὐοδοῦσθαι καὶ ὑγιαίνειν, καθὼς εὐοδοῦταί
to prosper   and   to be in health,   as   ⁴prospers
thou mayest prosper . . .

σου ἡ ψυχή. **3** ἐχάρην γὰρ λίαν ἐρχομένων
³of ¹the ²soul.   For I rejoiced   greatly   coming
thee   = when [some]

ἀδελφῶν καὶ μαρτυρούντων σου τῇ
brothers   and   bearing witness³   of thee   in the
brothers came and bore witness

ἀληθείᾳ, καθὼς σὺ ἐν ἀληθείᾳ περιπατεῖς.
truth,   as   thou   in   truth   walkest.

4 μειζοτέραν τούτων οὐκ ἔχω χαράν, ἵνα
³greater ⁴[than] ²these   ¹I have no   ³joy,   in or-
     der that

ἀκούω τὰ ἐμὰ τέκνα ἐν τῇ ἀληθείᾳ
I hear   –   my   children   ¹in   ²the   ⁴truth

περιπατοῦντα. **5** Ἀγαπητέ, πιστὸν ποιεῖς
¹walking.   Beloved,   faithfully   thou
     doest

ὃ ἐὰν ἐργάσῃ εἰς τοὺς ἀδελφοὺς καὶ
whatever thou workest   for   the   brothers   and

τοῦτο ξένους, **6** οἳ ἐμαρτύρησάν σου τῇ
this   strangers,   who   bore witness   of thee   –

ἀγάπῃ ἐνώπιον ἐκκλησίας, οὓς καλῶς
in love   before   [the] church,   whom   well

ποιήσεις προπέμψας ἀξίως τοῦ θεοῦ·
thou wilt do sending forward   worthily   of God;

7 ὑπὲρ γὰρ τοῦ ὀνόματος ἐξῆλθαν μηδὲν
for on behalf of   the   name   they went forth ²nothing

λαμβάνοντες ἀπὸ τῶν ἐθνικῶν. **8** ἡμεῖς
¹taking   from   the   Gentiles.   We

οὖν ὀφείλομεν ὑπολαμβάνειν τοὺς τοιούτους,
there-   ought   to entertain   –   such men,
fore

ἵνα συνεργοὶ γινώμεθα τῇ ἀληθείᾳ.
in or- ¹co-workers   ¹we may become in the   truth.
der that

9 Ἔγραψά τι τῇ ἐκκλησίᾳ· ἀλλ' ὁ
I wrote   some- to the   church;   but   the
     thing   [one]

φιλοπρωτεύων αὐτῶν Διοτρέφης οὐκ
loving to be first   of them   Diotrephes   not

ἐπιδέχεται ἡμᾶς. **10** διὰ τοῦτο, ἐὰν
receives   us.   Therefore,   if

ἔλθω, ὑπομνήσω αὐτοῦ τὰ ἔργα ἃ ποιεῖ
I come, I will remember ²of him ¹the ²works which he does

λόγοις πονηροῖς φλυαρῶν ἡμᾶς, καὶ μὴ
⁴words   ³with evil ¹prating against ²us,   and   not

ἀρκούμενος ἐπὶ τούτοις οὔτε αὐτὸς
being satisfied on(with)   these   ²neither   ¹he

ἐπιδέχεται τοὺς ἀδελφοὺς καὶ τοὺς
¹receives   the   brothers   and   the

βουλομένους κωλύει καὶ ἐκ τῆς ἐκκλησίας
[ones] purposing he prevents   and   ³out of ²the   ⁴church

ἐκβάλλει.
¹puts out.

11 Ἀγαπητέ, μὴ μιμοῦ τὸ κακὸν ἀλλὰ
Beloved,   imitate not   the   bad   but

τὸ ἀγαθόν. ὁ ἀγαθοποιῶν ἐκ τοῦ θεοῦ
the   good.   The   doing good   ²of   –   ¹God
     [one]

ἐστιν· ὁ κακοποιῶν οὐχ ἑώρακεν τὸν
¹is;   the [one]   doing ill   has not seen   –

θεόν. **12** Δημητρίῳ μεμαρτύρηται ὑπὸ
God.   To Demetrius   witness has been borne   by

πάντων καὶ ὑπὸ αὐτῆς τῆς ἀληθείας·
all   and   by   ²[it]self   ¹the   ³truth;

καὶ ἡμεῖς δὲ μαρτυροῦμεν, καὶ οἶδας
²also   ¹we   ¹and   bear witness,   and   thou
     knowest

ὅτι ἡ μαρτυρία ἡμῶν ἀληθής ἐστιν.
that the   witness   of us   ²true   ¹is.

13 Πολλὰ εἶχον γράψαι σοι, ἀλλ' οὐ
²Many things ¹I had   to write to thee,   but   not

θέλω διὰ μέλανος καὶ καλάμου σοι
I wish ³by means of   ⁴ink   ⁵and   ⁶pen   ¹to thee

γράφειν· **14** ἐλπίζω δὲ εὐθέως σε ἰδεῖν,
¹to write;   but I am hoping ²immediately ³thee ¹to see,

καὶ στόμα πρὸς στόμα λαλήσομεν.
and   ²mouth   ³to   ⁴mouth   ¹we will speak.

15 Εἰρήνη σοι. ἀσπάζονταί σε οἱ φίλοι.
Peace to thee.   ²greet   ³thee ¹The ⁴friends.

ἀσπάζου τοὺς φίλους κατ' ὄνομα.
Greet thou   the   friends   by   name.

King James Version

New International Version

THE

GENERAL EPISTLE

OF

JUDE

JUDE

Jude, the servant of Jesus Christ, and brother of James, to them that are sanctified by God the Father, and preserved in Jesus Christ, *and* called: 2 Mercy unto you, and peace, and love, be multiplied. 3 Beloved, when I gave all diligence to write unto you of the common salvation, it was needful for me to write unto you, and exhort *you* that ye should earnestly contend for the faith which was once delivered unto the saints. 4 For there are certain men crept in unawares, who were before of old ordained to this condemnation, ungodly men, turning the grace of our God into lasciviousness, and denying the only Lord God, and our Lord Jesus Christ. 5 I will therefore put you in remembrance, though ye once knew this, how that the Lord, having saved the people out of the land of Egypt, afterward destroyed them that believed not. 6 And the angels which kept not their first estate, but left their own habitation, he hath reserved in everlasting chains under darkness unto the judgment of the great day. 7 Even as Sodom and Gomorrah, and the cities about them in like manner, giving themselves over to fornication, and going after strange flesh, are set forth for an example, suffering the vengeance of eternal fire. 8 Likewise also these *filthy* dreamers defile the flesh, despise dominion, and speak evil of dignities. 9 Yet Michael the archangel, when contending with the devil he disputed about the body of Moses, durst not bring against him a railing accusation, but said, The Lord rebuke thee. 10 But these speak evil of those things which they know not: but what they know naturally, as brute beasts, in those things they corrupt themselves. 11 Woe unto them! for they have gone in the way of Cain, and ran greedily after the error of Balaam for reward, and perished in the gainsaying of Core. 12 These are spots in your feasts of charity, when they feast with you, feeding themselves without fear: clouds *they are* without water, carried about of winds; trees whose fruit withereth, without fruit, twice dead, plucked up by the roots; 13 Raging waves of the sea, foaming out their own shame; wandering stars, to whom is reserved the blackness of darkness for ever. 14 And Enoch also, the seventh from Adam, prophesied of these, saying, Behold, the Lord cometh with ten thou-

1 Jude, a servant of Jesus Christ and a brother of James,

To those who have been called, who are loved by God the Father and kept by Jesus Christ:

2 Mercy, peace and love be yours in abundance.

The sin and doom of godless men

3 Dear friends, although I was very eager to write to you about the salvation we share, I felt I had to write and urge you to contend for the faith that God has once for all entrusted to the saints. 4 For certain men whose condemnation was written about long ago have secretly slipped in among you. They are godless men, who change the grace of our God into a license for immorality and deny Jesus Christ our only Sovereign and Lord.

5 Though you already know all this, I want to remind you that the Lord [a] delivered his people out of Egypt, but later destroyed those who did not believe. 6 And the angels who did not keep their positions of authority but abandoned their own home—these he has kept in darkness, bound with everlasting chains for judgment on the great Day. 7 In a similar way, Sodom and Gomorrah and the surrounding towns gave themselves up to sexual immorality and perversion. They serve as an example of those who suffer the punishment of eternal fire.

8 In the very same way, these dreamers pollute their own bodies, reject authority, and slander celestial beings. 9 But even the archangel Michael, when he was disputing with the devil about the body of Moses, did not dare to bring a slanderous accusation against him, but said, "The Lord rebuke you!" 10 Yet these men speak abusively against whatever they do not understand; and what things they do understand by instinct, like unreasoning animals—these are the very things that destroy them.

11 Woe to them! They have taken the way of Cain; they have rushed for profit into Balaam's error; they have been destroyed in Korah's rebellion.

12 These men are blemishes at your love feasts, eating with you without the slightest qualm—shepherds who feed only themselves. They are clouds without rain, blown along by the wind; autumn trees, without fruit and uprooted—twice dead. 13 They are wild waves of the sea, foaming up their shame; wandering stars, for whom blackest darkness has been reserved forever.

14 Enoch, the seventh from Adam, prophesied about these men: "See, the Lord is coming with

[a] Some early MSS read *Jesus*.

ΙΟΥΔΑ

1 Ἰούδας Ἰησοῦ Χριστοῦ δοῦλος, ἀδελφὸς
Jude   of Jesus Christ   a slave,   ²brother

δὲ   Ἰακώβου,   τοῖς   ἐν   θεῷ   πατρὶ
¹and of James,   ¹to the ⁴by ⁵God ⁶[the]
                   [ones]   Father

ἠγαπημένοις   καὶ   Ἰησοῦ   Χριστῷ
¹having been loved ²and   ⁵for Jesus   ¹⁰Christ

τετηρημένοις κλητοῖς.   2 ἔλεος ὑμῖν καὶ
⁴having been kept ⁵called.   Mercy   to you   and

εἰρήνη   καὶ   ἀγάπη   πληθυνθείη.
peace   and   love   may it be multiplied.

3 Ἀγαπητοί,   πᾶσαν   σπουδὴν   ποιούμενος
  Beloved,   ²all   ²haste   ¹making

γράφειν   ὑμῖν   περὶ   τῆς   κοινῆς   ἡμῶν
to write to you about   the   common   ²of us

σωτηρίας,   ἀνάγκην   ἔσχον   γράψαι   ὑμῖν
¹salvation, necessity I had   to write to you

παρακαλῶν   ἐπαγωνίζεσθαι   τῇ   ἅπαξ
exhorting   to contend for   ¹the   ²once

παραδοθείσῃ   τοῖς   ἁγίοις   πίστει.   4 παρεισέ-
³delivered   ⁴to the ²saints   ¹faith.   ¹crept

δύησαν   γάρ   τινες   ἄνθρωποι,   οἱ   πάλαι
in   For   ²certain   ¹men,   the [ones] of old

προγεγραμμένοι   εἰς   τοῦτο   τὸ   κρίμα,
having been   for   this   -   judgment,
previously written

ἀσεβεῖς,   τὴν   τοῦ   θεοῦ   ἡμῶν   χάριτα
impious men, ¹the   ⁴of the ³God   ²of us   ⁵grace

μετατιθέντες   εἰς   ἀσέλγειαν   καὶ   τὸν   μόνον
¹making ²a pretext for   wantonness   and   ²the   ¹only

δεσπότην   καὶ   κύριον   ἡμῶν   Ἰησοῦν   Χριστὸν
⁴Master   ⁵and   ⁶Lord   ⁷of us   ⁸Jesus   ⁹Christ

ἀρνούμενοι.   5 Ὑπομνῆσαι   δὲ   ὑμᾶς   βούλομαι,
³denying.   ³to remind   ²-   ⁴you   ¹I purpose,

εἰδότας   ἅπαξ   πάντα,   ὅτι   κύριος   λαὸν
⁵knowing   ¹once   all   that   [the]   ²[the]
                   things,   Lord   people

ἐκ   γῆς   Αἰγύπτου   σώσας   τὸ   δεύτερον
¹out ²[the] ⁴of Egypt   ¹having   in the second place
of   land   saved

τοὺς   μὴ   πιστεύσαντας   ἀπώλεσεν,   6 ἀγγέλους
²the   ⁴not ³believing   ¹destroyed,   ⁴angels
[ones]

τε   τοὺς   μὴ   τηρήσαντας   τὴν   ἑαυτῶν
²and   -   not   having kept   the   ⁵of themselves

ἀρχὴν   ἀλλὰ   ἀπολιπόντας   τὸ   ἴδιον
¹rule   but   having deserted   the(ir)   own

οἰκητήριον   εἰς   κρίσιν   μεγάλης   ἡμέρας
habitation   ²for   ³[the] judgment ⁴of [the] great ¹day

δεσμοῖς   ἀιδίοις   ὑπὸ   ζόφον   τετήρηκεν·
¹bonds   ²in everlasting ⁴under   ⁵gloom   ¹he has kept;

7 ὡς   Σόδομα   καὶ   Γόμορρα   καὶ   αἱ   περὶ
  as   Sodom   and   Gomorra   and   ¹the ²round

αὐτὰς   πόλεις,   τὸν   ὅμοιον   τρόπον   τούτοις,
⁴them   ³cities,   in the   like   manner   to these

ἐκπορνεύσασαι   καὶ   ἀπελθοῦσαι   ὀπίσω   σαρκὸς
committing   and   going away   after   ²flesh
fornication

ἑτέρας,   πρόκεινται   δεῖγμα   πυρὸς   αἰωνίου
¹different, are set forth   an example ⁴fire   ³of eternal

δίκην   ὑπέχουσαι.   8 Ὁμοίως   μέντοι   καὶ
²ven-   ¹undergoing.   Likewise   indeed   also
geance

οὗτοι   ἐνυπνιαζόμενοι   σάρκα   μὲν   μιαίνουσιν,
these   dreaming [ones]   ²flesh   ¹on one   ³defile,
                                            hand

κυριότητα   δὲ   ἀθετοῦσιν,   δόξας   δὲ
¹lordship   ²on the other ³despise,   and   ²glories

βλασφημοῦσιν.   9 Ὁ   δὲ   Μιχαὴλ   ὁ   ἀρχάγ-
¹rail at.   -   But Michael   the   arch-

γελος,   ὅτε   τῷ   διαβόλῳ   διακρινόμενος
angel,   when ²with the ³devil   ¹contending

διελέγετο   περὶ   τοῦ   Μωϋσέως   σώματος,
he argued   about   ¹the   ³of Moses   ²body,

οὐκ   ἐτόλμησεν   κρίσιν   ἐπενεγκεῖν   βλασφημίας,
durst not   ²a judgment ¹to bring on   of railing,

ἀλλὰ   εἶπεν·   ἐπιτιμήσαι   σοι   κύριος.   10 οὗτοι
but   said :   ²rebuke   ³thee   ¹[The] Lord.   these men

δὲ   ὅσα   μὲν   οὐκ   οἴδασιν   βλασφημοῦσιν,
But   what   on one   they know not   they rail at,
      things   hand

ὅσα   δὲ   φυσικῶς   ὡς   τὰ   ἄλογα   ζῷα
what on the   ²naturally   ³as   ⁴the   ⁶without   ⁵animals
things other   reason

ἐπίστανται,   ἐν   τούτοις   φθείρονται.   11 οὐαὶ
¹they understand, by   these   they are corrupted.   Woe

αὐτοῖς,   ὅτι   τῇ   ὁδῷ   τοῦ   Κάϊν   ἐπορεύθησαν,
to them, because in the way   -   of Cain   they went,

καὶ   τῇ   πλάνῃ   τοῦ   Βαλαὰμ   μισθοῦ
and   ²to the ³error   -   ⁴of Balaam   ⁵of(for)
                                           reward

ἐξεχύθησαν,   καὶ   τῇ   ἀντιλογίᾳ   τοῦ   Κόρε
¹gave themselves and ²in the ³dispute   -   ⁴of
up,   Korah

ἀπώλοντο.   12 Οὗτοί   εἰσιν   οἱ   ἐν   ταῖς
¹perished.   These men   are   ¹the   ²in   ³the

ἀγάπαις   ὑμῶν   σπιλάδες   συνευωχούμενοι
²love feasts ⁴of you   ¹rocks   feasting together

ἀφόβως,   ἑαυτοὺς   ποιμαίνοντες,   νεφέλαι
without fear, ¹themselves   ²feeding,   ³clouds

ἄνυδροι   ὑπὸ   ἀνέμων   παραφερόμεναι,   δένδρα
¹waterless ⁴by   ³winds   ²being carried away,   ³trees

φθινοπωρινὰ   ἄκαρπα   δὶς   ἀποθανόντα
¹autumn   without fruit   twice   dying

ἐκριζωθέντα,   13 κύματα   ἄγρια   θαλάσσης
having been uprooted,   ²waves   ¹fierce   ³of [the] sea

ἐπαφρίζοντα   τὰς   ἑαυτῶν   αἰσχύνας,   ἀστέρες
¹foaming up   ³the   ²of themselves   ⁴shames,   ⁵stars

πλανῆται,   οἷς   ὁ   ζόφος   τοῦ   σκότους
¹wandering, for whom the   gloom   -   of darkness

εἰς   αἰῶνα   τετήρηται.   14 Ἐπροφήτευσεν
unto [the] age   has been kept.   ¹prophesied

δὲ   καὶ   τούτοις   ἔβδομος   ἀπὸ   Ἀδὰμ
²And   ³also   ⁴to these men   ⁵[the] seventh   ⁸from   ⁹Adam

Ἐνὼχ   λέγων·   ἰδοὺ   ἦλθεν   κύριος   ἐν
⁶Enoch   saying :   Behold   came   [the] Lord   with

King James Version

sands of his saints, 15 To execute judgment upon all, and to convince all that are ungodly among them of all their ungodly deeds which they have ungodly committed, and of all their hard *speeches* which ungodly sinners have spoken against him. 16 These are murmurers, complainers, walking after their own lusts; and their mouth speaketh great swelling *words,* having men's persons in admiration because of advantage. 17 But, beloved, remember ye the words which were spoken before of the apostles of our Lord Jesus Christ; 18 How that they told you there should be mockers in the last time, who should walk after their own ungodly lusts. 19 These be they who separate themselves, sensual, having not the Spirit. 20 But ye, beloved, building up yourselves on your most holy faith, praying in the Holy Ghost, 21 Keep yourselves in the love of God, looking for the mercy of our Lord Jesus Christ unto eternal life. 22 And of some have compassion, making a difference: 23 And others save with fear, pulling *them* out of the fire; hating even the garment spotted by the flesh. 24 Now unto him that is able to keep you from falling, and to present *you* faultless before the presence of his glory with exceeding joy, 25 To the only wise God our Saviour, *be* glory and majesty, dominion and power, both now and ever. Amen.

New International Version

thousands upon thousands of his holy ones 15 to judge everyone, and to convict all the ungodly of all their ungodly acts they have done in their ungodly way, and of all the harsh words ungodly sinners have spoken against him." 16 These men are grumblers and faultfinders; they follow their own evil desires; they boast about themselves and flatter others for their own advantage.

A call to persevere

17 But, dear friends, remember what the apostles of our Lord Jesus Christ foretold. 18 They said to you, "In the last times there will be scoffers who will follow their own ungodly desires." 19 These are the men who divide you, who follow mere natural instincts and do not have the Spirit.

20 But you, dear friends, build yourselves up in your most holy faith and pray in the Holy Spirit. 21 Keep yourselves in God's love as you wait for the mercy of our Lord Jesus Christ to bring you to eternal life. 22 Be merciful to those who doubt; 23 snatch others from the fire and save them; to others show mercy, mixed with fear—hating even the clothing stained by corrupted flesh.

Doxology

24 To him who is able to keep you from falling and to present you before his glorious presence without fault and with great joy—25 to the only God our Savior be glory, majesty, power and authority, through Jesus Christ our Lord, before all ages, now and forevermore! Amen.

Greek Interlinear

ἁγίαις   μυριάσιν   αὐτοῦ,   15 ποιῆσαι   κρίσιν
saints   ten thousands   of him,   to do   judgment

κατὰ   πάντων   καὶ   ἐλέγξαι   πάντας   τοὺς
against   all men   and   to rebuke   all   the

ἀσεβεῖς   περὶ   πάντων   τῶν   ἔργων   ἀσεβείας
impious   concerning   all   the   works   of impiety

αὐτῶν   ὧν   ἠσέβησαν   καὶ   περὶ   πάντων
of them   which they impiously did and   concerning   all

τῶν   σκληρῶν   ὧν   ἐλάλησαν   κατ'   αὐτοῦ
the   hard things   which   ²spoke   ⁴against   ³him

ἁμαρτωλοὶ   ἀσεβεῖς.   16 Οὗτοί   εἰσιν   γογ-
¹sinners   ¹impious.   These men   are   ¹mur-

γυσταὶ   μεμψίμοιροι,   κατὰ   τὰς   ἐπιθυμίας
murers   ¹querulous,   ²according to   ³the   ⁴lusts

αὐτῶν   πορευόμενοι,   καὶ   τὸ   στόμα   αὐτῶν
⁵of them   ¹going,   and   the   mouth   of them

λαλεῖ   ὑπέρογκα,   θαυμάζοντες   πρόσωπα
speaks   arrogant things,   admiring   faces

ὠφελείας   χάριν.   .
²advantage   ¹for the sake of.

17 Ὑμεῖς   δέ,   ἀγαπητοί,   μνήσθητε   τῶν
But ye,   beloved,   be mindful of   the

ῥημάτων   τῶν   προειρημένων   ὑπὸ   τῶν
words   –   previously spoken   by   the

ἀποστόλων   τοῦ   κυρίου   ἡμῶν   Ἰησοῦ
apostles   of the   Lord   of us   Jesus

Χριστοῦ,   18 ὅτι   ἔλεγον   ὑμῖν·   ἐπ'   ἐσχάτου
Christ,   because they told   you: At   [the] last

τοῦ   χρόνου   ἔσονται   ἐμπαῖκται   κατὰ   τὰς
of the   time   will be   mockers   ²according to   ³the

ἑαυτῶν   ἐπιθυμίας   πορευόμενοι   τῶν   ἀσεβειῶν.
⁴of them-selves   ⁴lusts   ¹going   –   ⁵of impious things.

19 Οὗτοί   εἰσιν   οἱ   ἀποδιορίζοντες,   ψυχικοί,
These men   are the [ones] making separations.   natural,

πνεῦμα   μὴ   ἔχοντες.   20 ὑμεῖς   δέ,   ἀγαπητοί,
²spirit   ¹not   ³having.   But ye,   beloved,

ἐποικοδομοῦντες   ἑαυτοὺς   τῇ   ἁγιωτάτῃ   ὑμῶν
building up   yourselves in the   most holy   ²of you

πίστει,   ἐν   πνεύματι   ἁγίῳ   προσευχόμενοι,
¹faith,   ²in   ⁴Spirit   ³[the] Holy   ¹praying.

21 ἑαυτοὺς   ἐν   ἀγάπῃ   θεοῦ   τηρήσατε,
²yourselves   ³in   ⁴[the] love   ⁵of God   ¹keep,

προσδεχόμενοι   τὸ   ἔλεος   τοῦ   κυρίου   ἡμῶν
awaiting   the   mercy   of the   Lord   of us

Ἰησοῦ   Χριστοῦ   εἰς   ζωὴν   αἰώνιον.   22 καὶ
Jesus   Christ   to   life   eternal.   And

οὓς   μὲν   ἐλεᾶτε   διακρινομένους   23 σῴζετε
some   ²pity ye   ¹[who are] wavering   ²save

ἐκ   πυρὸς   ἁρπάζοντες,   οὓς   δὲ   ἐλεᾶτε
³out of   ⁴fire   ¹seizing,   ·   others   pity

ἐν   φόβῳ,   μισοῦντες   καὶ   τὸν   ἀπὸ   τῆς
with   fear,   hating   even   ³the   ⁴from   ⁵the

σαρκὸς   ἐσπιλωμένον   χιτῶνα.
⁶flesh   ²having been spotted   ¹tunic.

24 Τῷ   δὲ   δυναμένῳ   φυλάξαι   ὑμᾶς
Now to the [one]   being able   to guard   you

ἀπταίστους   καὶ   στῆσαι   κατενώπιον   τῆς
without stumbling   and   to set   [you] before   the

δόξης   αὐτοῦ   ἀμώμους   ἐν   ἀγαλλιάσει,
glory   of him   unblemished   with   exultation,

25 μόνῳ   θεῷ   σωτῆρι   ἡμῶν   διὰ   Ἰησοῦ
to [the] only   God   Saviour   of us   through   Jesus

Χριστοῦ   τοῦ   κυρίου   ἡμῶν   δόξα   μεγαλωσύνη
Christ   the   Lord   of us   [be] glory[,]   greatness[,]

κράτος   καὶ   ἐξουσία   πρὸ   παντὸς   τοῦ
might[,]   and   authority   before   all   the

αἰῶνος   καὶ   νῦν   καὶ   εἰς   πάντας   τοὺς
age   and   now   and   unto   all   the

αἰῶνας·   ἀμήν.
ages: Amen.

723

THE REVELATION OF

St. JOHN the Divine

REVELATION

Prologue

1 The Revelation of Jesus Christ, which God gave unto him, to shew unto his servants things which must shortly come to pass; and he sent and signified *it* by his angel unto his servant John: 2 Who bare record of the word of God, and of the testimony of Jesus Christ, and of all things that he saw. 3 Blessed *is* he that readeth, and they that hear the words of this prophecy, and keep those things which are written therein: for the time *is* at hand.

4 John to the seven churches which are in Asia: Grace *be* unto you, and peace, from him which is, and which was, and which is to come; and from the seven Spirits which are before his throne; 5And from Jesus Christ, *who is* the faithful witness, *and* the first-begotten of the dead, and the prince of the kings of the earth. Unto him that loved us, and washed us from our sins in his own blood, 6And hath made us kings and priests unto God and his Father; to him *be* glory and dominion for ever and ever. Amen. 7 Behold, he cometh with clouds; and every eye shall see him, and they *also* which pierced him: and all kindreds of the earth shall wail because of him. Even so, Amen. 8 I am Alpha and Omega, the beginning and the ending, saith the Lord, which is, and which was, and which is to come, the Almighty. 9 I John, who also am your brother, and companion in tribulation, and in the kingdom and patience of Jesus Christ, was in the isle that is called Patmos, for the word of God, and for the testimony of Jesus Christ. 10 I was in the Spirit on the Lord's day, and heard behind me a great voice, as of a trumpet, 11 Saying, I am Alpha and Omega, the first and the last: and, What thou seest, write in a book, and send *it* unto the seven churches which are in Asia; unto Ephesus, and unto Smyrna, and unto Pergamos, and unto Thyatira, and unto Sardis, and unto Philadelphia, and unto Laodicea. 12And I turned to see the voice that spake with me. And being turned, I saw seven golden candlesticks; 13And in the midst of the seven candlesticks *one* like unto the Son of man, clothed with a garment down to the foot, and girt about the paps with a golden girdle. 14 His head and *his* hairs *were* white like wool, as white as snow; and his eyes *were* as a flame of fire; 15And his feet like unto fine brass, as if they burned in a furnace; and his voice as

1 The revelation of Jesus Christ, which God gave him to show his servants what must soon take place. He made it known by sending his angel to his servant John, 2 who testifies to everything he saw—that is, the word of God and the testimony of Jesus Christ. 3 Blessed is the one who reads the words of this prophecy, and blessed are those who hear it and take to heart what is written in it, because the time is near.

Greetings and doxology

4 John,
To the seven churches in the province of Asia:
Grace and peace to you from him who is, and who was, and who is to come, and from the seven spirits[a] before his throne, 5 and from Jesus Christ, who is the faithful witness, the firstborn from the dead, and the ruler of the kings of the earth.
To him who loves us and has freed us from our sins by his blood, 6 and has made us to be a kingdom and priests to serve his God and Father—to him be glory and power for ever and ever! Amen.

7 Look, he is coming with the clouds,
    and every eye will see him,
    even those who pierced him;
    and all the peoples of the earth will mourn
        because of him.
                    So shall it be! Amen.

8 "I am the Alpha and the Omega," says the Lord God, "who is, and who was, and who is to come, the Almighty."

One like a son of man

9 I, John, your brother and companion in the suffering and kingdom and patient endurance that are ours in Jesus, was on the island of Patmos because of the word of God and the testimony of Jesus. 10 On the Lord's Day I was in the Spirit, and I heard behind me a loud voice like a trumpet, 11 which said: "Write on a scroll what you see and send it to the seven churches: to Ephesus, Smyrna, Pergamum, Thyatira, Sardis, Philadelphia and Laodicea."

12 I turned around to see the voice that was speaking to me. And when I turned I saw seven golden lampstands, 13 and among the lampstands was someone "like a son of man," [b] dressed in a robe reaching down to his feet and with a golden sash around his chest. 14 His head and hair were white like wool, as white as snow, and his eyes were like blazing fire. 15 His feet were like brass glowing in a furnace, and his

[a] Or the *sevenfold Spirit*. *[b]* Daniel 7:13.

ΑΠΟΚΑΛΥΨΙΣ   ΙΩΑΝΝΟΥ

Chapter 1

Ἀποκάλυψις Ἰησοῦ Χριστοῦ, ἥν
A revelation of Jesus Christ, which

ἔδωκεν αὐτῷ ὁ θεός, δεῖξαι τοῖς δούλοις
gave ¹to him – ¹God, to show to the slaves

αὐτοῦ ἃ δεῖ γενέσθαι ἐν τάχει, καὶ
of him things it be- to occur with speed, and
which hoves

ἐσήμανεν ἀποστείλας διὰ τοῦ ἀγγέλου
he signified sending through the angel

αὐτοῦ τῷ δούλῳ αὐτοῦ Ἰωάννῃ, 2 ὃς
of him to the slave of him John, who

ἐμαρτύρησεν τὸν λόγον τοῦ θεοῦ καὶ
bore witness [of] the word – of God and

τὴν μαρτυρίαν Ἰησοῦ Χριστοῦ, ὅσα εἶδεν.
the witness of Jesus Christ, as many as he saw.
things as

3 Μακάριος ὁ ἀναγινώσκων καὶ οἱ
Blessed [is] the [one] reading and the

ἀκούοντες τοὺς λόγους τῆς προφητείας
[ones] hearing the words of the prophecy

καὶ τηροῦντες τὰ ἐν αὐτῇ γεγραμμένα·
and keeping the things ²in ³it ¹having been written;

ὁ γὰρ καιρὸς ἐγγύς.
²the ¹for time [is] near.

4 Ἰωάννης ταῖς ἑπτὰ ἐκκλησίαις ταῖς
John to the seven churches –

ἐν τῇ Ἀσίᾳ· χάρις ὑμῖν καὶ εἰρήνη
in – Asia: Grace to you and peace

ἀπὸ ὁ ὢν καὶ ὁ ἦν καὶ ὁ ἐρχόμενος,
from the being and the was and the [one] coming,
[one] [one who]
=the one who is

καὶ ἀπὸ τῶν ἑπτὰ πνευμάτων ἃ ἐνώπιον
and from the seven spirits which before
[are]

τοῦ θρόνου αὐτοῦ, 5 καὶ ἀπὸ Ἰησοῦ
the throne of him, and from Jesus

Χριστοῦ, ὁ μάρτυς ὁ πιστός, ὁ πρωτότοκος
Christ, the ²witness – ¹faithful, the firstborn

τῶν νεκρῶν καὶ ὁ ἄρχων τῶν βασιλέων
of the dead and the ruler of the kings

τῆς γῆς. Τῷ ἀγαπῶντι ἡμᾶς καὶ λύσαντι
of the earth. To loving us and having
the [one] loosed

ἡμᾶς ἐκ τῶν ἁμαρτιῶν ἡμῶν ἐν τῷ
us out of the sins of us by the

αἵματι αὐτοῦ, 6 καὶ ἐποίησεν ἡμᾶς
blood of him, and made us

βασιλείαν, ἱερεῖς τῷ θεῷ καὶ πατρὶ
a kingdom, priests to the God and Father

αὐτοῦ, αὐτῷ ἡ δόξα καὶ τὸ κράτος
of him, to him² [is] the glory and the might
= his is

εἰς τοὺς αἰῶνας τῶν αἰώνων· ἀμήν.
unto the ages of the ages: Amen.

7 Ἰδοὺ ἔρχεται μετὰ τῶν νεφελῶν,
Behold he comes with the clouds,

καὶ ὄψεται αὐτὸν πᾶς ὀφθαλμὸς καὶ
and ²will see ⁴him ¹every ³eye and

οἵτινες αὐτὸν ἐξεκέντησαν, καὶ κόψονται
[those] who ²him ¹pierced, and ³will wail

ἐπ' αὐτὸν πᾶσαι αἱ φυλαὶ τῆς γῆς.
⁷over ⁸him ⁴all ⁵the ⁶tribes ⁴of the ⁵land.

ναί, ἀμήν.
Yes, amen.

8 Ἐγώ εἰμι τὸ ἄλφα καὶ τὸ ὦ, λέγει
I am the alpha and the omega, says

κύριος ὁ θεός, ὁ ὢν καὶ ὁ ἦν
[the] – God, the [one] being and the was
Lord =the one who is [one who]

καὶ ὁ ἐρχόμενος, ὁ παντοκράτωρ.
and the [one] coming, the Almighty.

9 Ἐγὼ Ἰωάννης, ὁ ἀδελφὸς ὑμῶν καὶ
I John, the brother of you and

συγκοινωνὸς ἐν τῇ θλίψει καὶ βασιλείᾳ
co-sharer in the affliction and kingdom

καὶ ὑπομονῇ ἐν Ἰησοῦ, ἐγενόμην ἐν
and endurance in Jesus, came to be in

τῇ νήσῳ τῇ καλουμένῃ Πάτμῳ διὰ
the island – being called Patmos on account of

τὸν λόγον τοῦ θεοῦ καὶ τὴν μαρτυρίαν
the word – of God and the witness

Ἰησοῦ. 10 ἐγενόμην ἐν πνεύματι ἐν
of Jesus. I came to be in [the] spirit on

τῇ κυριακῇ ἡμέρᾳ, καὶ ἤκουσα ὀπίσω
the imperial* day, and heard behind

μου φωνὴν μεγάλην ὡς σάλπιγγος
me ¹voice ²a great(loud) as of a trumpet

11 λεγούσης· ὃ βλέπεις γράψον εἰς βιβλίον
saying: What thou seest write in a scroll

καὶ πέμψον ταῖς ἑπτὰ ἐκκλησίαις, εἰς
and send to the seven churches, to

Ἔφεσον καὶ εἰς Σμύρναν καὶ εἰς Πέργαμον
Ephesus and to Smyrna and to Pergamum

καὶ εἰς Θυάτιρα καὶ εἰς Σάρδεις καὶ
and to Thyatira and to Sardis and

εἰς Φιλαδέλφειαν καὶ εἰς Λαοδίκειαν.
to Philadelphia and to Laodicea.

12 Καὶ ἐπέστρεψα βλέπειν τὴν φωνὴν
And I turned to see the voice

ἥτις ἐλάλει μετ' ἐμοῦ· καὶ ἐπιστρέψας
which spoke with me; and having turned

εἶδον ἑπτὰ λυχνίας χρυσᾶς, 13 καὶ ἐν
I saw seven ¹lampstands ¹golden, and in

μέσῳ τῶν λυχνιῶν ὅμοιον υἱὸν ἀνθρώπου,
[the] of the lampstands [one] like a son of man,★
midst

ἐνδεδυμένον ποδήρη καὶ περιεζωσμένον
having been clothed to the feet and having been girdled round

πρὸς τοῖς μαστοῖς ζώνην χρυσᾶν· 14 ἡ
at the breasts ²girdle ¹[with] a golden; ¹the

δὲ κεφαλὴ αὐτοῦ καὶ αἱ τρίχες λευκαὶ
²and head of him and the hairs white

ὡς ἔριον λευκὸν ὡς χιών, καὶ οἱ ὀφθαλμοὶ
as wool white as snow, and the eyes

αὐτοῦ ὡς φλὸξ πυρός, 15 καὶ οἱ πόδες
of him as a flame of fire, and the feet

αὐτοῦ ὅμοιοι χαλκολιβάνῳ ὡς ἐν καμίνῳ
of him like to burnished brass as ²in ³a furnace

πεπυρωμένης, καὶ ἡ φωνὴ αὐτοῦ ὡς
¹having been fired, and the voice of him as

* See I. Cor. 11. 20. ★ Anarthrous; see also ch. 14. 14 and John 5. 27. and cf. Heb. 2. 6.

King James Version

the sound of many waters. 16And he had in his right hand seven stars: and out of his mouth went a sharp twoedged sword: and his countenance *was* as the sun shineth in his strength. 17And when I saw him, I fell at his feet as dead. And he laid his right hand upon me, saying unto me, Fear not; I am the first and the last: 18 I *am* he that liveth, and was dead; and, behold, I am alive for evermore, Amen; and have the keys of hell and of death. 19 Write the things which thou hast seen, and the things which are, and the things which shall be hereafter; 20 The mystery of the seven stars which thou sawest in my right hand, and the seven golden candlesticks. The seven stars are the angels of the seven churches: and the seven candlesticks which thou sawest are the seven churches.

2 Unto the angel of the church of Ephesus write; These things saith he that holdeth the seven stars in his right hand, who walketh in the midst of the seven golden candlesticks; 2 I know thy works, and thy labour, and thy patience, and how thou canst not bear them which are evil: and thou hast tried them which say they are apostles, and are not, and hast found them liars: 3And hast borne, and hast patience, and for my name's sake hast laboured, and hast not fainted. 4 Nevertheless I have *somewhat* against thee, because thou hast left thy first love. 5 Remember therefore from whence thou art fallen, and repent, and do the first works; or else I will come unto thee quickly, and will remove thy candlestick out of his place, except thou repent. 6 But this thou hast, that thou hatest the deeds of the Nicolaitans, which I also hate. 7 He that hath an ear, let him hear what the Spirit saith unto the churches; To him that overcometh will I give to eat of the tree of life, which is in the midst of the paradise of God. 8And unto the angel of the church in Smyrna write; These things saith the first and the last, which was dead, and is alive; 9 I know thy works, and tribulation, and poverty, (but thou art rich) and *I know* the blasphemy of them which say they are Jews, and are not, but *are* the synagogue of Satan. 10 Fear none of those things which thou shalt suffer: behold, the devil shall cast *some* of you into prison, that ye may be tried; and ye shall have tribulation ten days: be thou faithful unto death, and I will give thee a crown of life. 11 He that hath an ear, let him hear what the Spirit saith unto the churches; He

New International Version

voice was like the sound of rushing waters. 16 In his right hand he held seven stars, and out of his mouth came a sharp double-edged sword. His face was like the sun shining in all its brilliance. 17 When I saw him, I fell at his feet as though dead. Then he placed his right hand on me and said: "Do not be afraid. I am the First and the Last. 18 I am the Living One; I was dead, and behold I am alive for ever and ever! And I hold the keys of death and Hades. 19 "Write, therefore, what you have seen, what is now and what will take place later. 20 The mystery of the seven stars that you saw in my right hand and of the seven golden lampstands is this: The seven stars are the angels[c] of the seven churches, and the seven lampstands are the seven churches.

To the church in Ephesus

2 "To the angel[d] of the church in Ephesus write:

These are the words of him who holds the seven stars in his right hand and walks among the seven golden lampstands: 2 I know your deeds, your hard work and your perseverance. I know that you cannot tolerate wicked men, that you have tested those who claim to be apostles but are not, and have found them false. 3 You have persevered and have endured hardships for my name, and have not grown weary.

4 Yet I hold this against you: You have forsaken your first love. 5 Remember the height from which you have fallen! Repent and do the things you did at first. If you do not repent, I will come to you and remove your lampstand from its place. 6 But you have this in your favor: You hate the practices of the Nicolaitans, which I also hate.

7 He who has an ear, let him hear what the Spirit says to the churches. To him who overcomes, I will give the right to eat from the tree of life, which is in the paradise of God.

To the church in Smyrna

8 "To the angel of the church in Smyrna write:

These are the words of him who is the First and the Last, who died and came to life again. 9 I know your afflictions and your poverty— yet you are rich! I know the slander of those who say they are Jews and are not, but are a synagogue of Satan. 10 Do not be afraid of what you are about to suffer. I tell you, the devil will put some of you in prison to test you, and you will suffer persecution for ten days. Be faithful, even to the point of death, and I will give you the crown of life.

11 He who has an ear, let him hear what the Spirit says to the churches. He who over-

[c] Or *messengers*. [d] Or *messenger* (and elsewhere in chapters 2 and 3).

726

Greek Interlinear

φωνὴ ὑδάτων πολλῶν, 16 καὶ ἔχων ἐν
a sound waters of many, and having in

τῇ δεξιᾷ χειρὶ αὐτοῦ ἀστέρας ἑπτά,
the right hand of him ³stars ¹seven;

καὶ ἐκ τοῦ στόματος αὐτοῦ ῥομφαία
and out of the mouth of him ⁴sword

δίστομος ὀξεῖα ἐκπορευομένη, καὶ ἡ ὄψις
²two- ³a sharp ¹proceeding, and the face
mouthed(edged)

αὐτοῦ ὡς ὁ ἥλιος φαίνει ἐν τῇ δυνάμει
of him as the sun shines in the power

αὐτοῦ. 17 Καὶ ὅτε εἶδον αὐτόν, ἔπεσα
of it. And when I saw him, I fell

πρὸς τοὺς πόδας αὐτοῦ ὡς νεκρός· καὶ
at the feet of him as dead; and

ἔθηκεν τὴν δεξιὰν αὐτοῦ ἐπ᾽ ἐμὲ λέγων·
he placed the right [hand] of him on me saying:

μή φοβοῦ· ἐγώ εἰμι ὁ πρῶτος καὶ
Fear not: I am the first and

ὁ ἔσχατος 18 καὶ ὁ ζῶν, καὶ ἐγενόμην
the last and the living [one], and I became

νεκρὸς καὶ ἰδοὺ ζῶν εἰμι εἰς τοὺς
dead and behold ³living ¹I am unto the

αἰῶνας τῶν αἰώνων, καὶ ἔχω τὰς κλεῖς
ages of the ages, and I have the keys

τοῦ θανάτου καὶ τοῦ ᾅδου. 19 γράψον
– of death and – of hades. Write thou

οὖν ἃ εἶδες καὶ ἃ εἰσὶν καὶ ἃ
there- [the] thou and [the] are and [the]
fore things sawest things things
which which which

μέλλει γενέσθαι μετὰ ταῦτα. 20 τὸ
(is)are about to occur after these things. The

μυστήριον τῶν ἑπτὰ ἀστέρων οὓς εἶδες
mystery of the seven stars which thou
sawest

ἐπὶ τῆς δεξιᾶς μου, καὶ τὰς ἑπτὰ
on the right [hand] of me, and the seven

λυχνίας τὰς χρυσᾶς· οἱ ἑπτὰ ἀστέρες
¹lampstands – ²golden: the seven stars

ἄγγελοι τῶν ἑπτὰ ἐκκλησιῶν εἰσιν, καὶ
messengers* of the seven churches are, and

αἱ λυχνίαι αἱ ἑπτὰ ἑπτὰ ἐκκλησίαι εἰσίν.
the ²lampstands – ¹seven ⁴seven ³churches ⁴are.

Chapter 2

Τῷ ἀγγέλῳ τῆς ἐν Ἐφέσῳ ἐκκλησίας
To the messenger ¹of the ²in ⁴Ephesus ³church

γράψον·
write thou:

Τάδε λέγει ὁ κρατῶν τοὺς ἑπτὰ
These things says the [one] holding the seven

ἀστέρας ἐν τῇ δεξιᾷ αὐτοῦ, ὁ περιπατῶν
stars in the right [hand] of him, the [one] walking

ἐν μέσῳ τῶν ἑπτὰ λυχνιῶν τῶν
in [the] midst of the seven ²lampstands –

χρυσῶν· 2 οἶδα τὰ ἔργα σου καὶ τὸν
¹golden: I know the works of thee and the

κόπον καὶ τὴν ὑπομονήν σου, καὶ ὅτι
labour and the endurance of thee, and that

οὐ δύνῃ βαστάσαι κακούς, καὶ ἐπείρασας
thou canst not to bear bad men, and didst try

τοὺς λέγοντας ἑαυτοὺς ἀποστόλους καὶ
the [ones] say(call)ing themselves apostles and

οὐκ εἰσίν, καὶ εὗρες αὐτοὺς ψευδεῖς·
are not, and didst find them liars:

3 καὶ ὑπομονὴν ἔχεις, καὶ ἐβάστασας
and ¹endurance ²thou hast, and didst bear

διὰ τὸ ὄνομά μου, καὶ οὐ κεκοπίακας.
be- the name of me, and hast not grown weary.
cause of

4 ἀλλὰ ἔχω κατὰ σοῦ ὅτι τὴν ἀγάπην
But I have against thee that ¹the ⁴love

σου τὴν πρώτην ἀφῆκας. 5 μνημόνευε
²of thee – ³first ¹thou didst leave. Remember

οὖν πόθεν πέπτωκας, καὶ μετανόησον
therefore whence thou hast fallen, and repent

καὶ τὰ πρῶτα ἔργα ποίησον· εἰ δὲ
and the ¹first ⁴works ³do; and if

μή, ἔρχομαί σοι καὶ κινήσω τὴν λυχνίαν
not, I am coming to thee and will move the lampstand

σου ἐκ τοῦ τόπου αὐτῆς, ἐὰν μὴ
of thee out of the place of it, unless

μετανοήσῃς. 6 ἀλλὰ τοῦτο ἔχεις, ὅτι
thou repentest. But this thou hast, that

μισεῖς τὰ ἔργα τῶν Νικολαϊτῶν, ἃ
thou hatest the works of the Nicolaitans, which

κἀγὼ μισῶ. 7 Ὁ ἔχων οὓς ἀκουσάτω
I also hate. The [one] having an ear let him hear

τί τὸ πνεῦμα λέγει ταῖς ἐκκλησίαις.
what the Spirit says to the churches.

Τῷ νικῶντι δώσω αὐτῷ φαγεῖν ἐκ
To the overcoming I will give to him to eat of
[one]

τοῦ ξύλου τῆς ζωῆς, ὅ ἐστιν ἐν τῷ
the tree – of life, which is in the

παραδείσῳ τοῦ θεοῦ.
paradise – of God.

8 Καὶ τῷ ἀγγέλῳ τῆς ἐν Σμύρνῃ
And to the messenger ¹of the ²in ⁴Smyrna

ἐκκλησίας γράψον·
³church write thou:

Τάδε λέγει ὁ πρῶτος καὶ ὁ ἔσχατος,
These things says the first and the last,

ὃς ἐγένετο νεκρὸς καὶ ἔζησεν· 9 οἶδά
who became dead and lived [again]: I know

σου τὴν θλῖψιν καὶ τὴν πτωχείαν, ἀλλὰ
¹of thee the ²affliction ³and ⁴the ²poverty, but

πλούσιος εἶ, καὶ τὴν βλασφημίαν ἐκ
rich thou art, and the railing of

τῶν λεγόντων Ἰουδαίους εἶναι ἑαυτούς,
the [ones] say(call)ing ²Jews ¹to be ¹themselves,

καὶ οὐκ εἰσὶν ἀλλὰ συναγωγὴ τοῦ σατανᾶ.
and they are not but a synagogue – of Satan.

10 μὴ φοβοῦ ἃ μέλλεις πάσχειν. ἰδοὺ
Do not fear [the] thou art to suffer. Behold[.]
things which about

μέλλει βάλλειν ὁ διάβολος ἐξ ὑμῶν
²is about ⁴to cast ¹the ³devil [some] of you

εἰς φυλακὴν ἵνα πειρασθῆτε, καὶ ἕξετε
into prison in order that ye may be tried, and ye will have

θλῖψιν ἡμερῶν δέκα. γίνου πιστὸς ἄχρι
affliction ²days ¹ten. Be thou faithful until

θανάτου, καὶ δώσω σοι τὸν στέφανον
death, and I will give thee the crown

τῆς ζωῆς. 11 Ὁ ἔχων οὓς ἀκουσάτω
– of life. The [one] having an ear let him hear

τί τὸ πνεῦμα λέγει ταῖς ἐκκλησίαις.
what the Spirit says to the churches.

* This, of course, is the prime meaning of the word: whether these
beings were " messengers " from the churches, or supernatural
beings, " angels " as usually understood, is a matter of exegesis.

King James Version

that overcometh shall not be hurt of the second death. 12And to the angel of the church in Pergamos write; These things saith he which hath the sharp sword with two edges; 13 I know thy works, and where thou dwellest, *even* where Satan's seat *is:* and thou holdest fast my name, and hast not denied my faith, even in those days wherein Antipas *was* my faithful martyr, who was slain among you, where Satan dwelleth. 14 But I have a few things against thee, because thou hast there them that hold the doctrine of Balaam, who taught Balak to cast a stumblingblock before the children of Israel, to eat things sacrificed unto idols, and to commit fornication. 15 So hast thou also them that hold the doctrine of the Nicolaitans, which thing I hate. 16 Repent; or else I will come unto thee quickly, and will fight against them with the sword of my mouth. 17 He that hath an ear, let him hear what the Spirit saith unto the churches; To him that overcometh will I give to eat of the hidden manna, and will give him a white stone, and in the stone a new name written, which no man knoweth saving he that receiveth *it.* 18And unto the angel of the church in Thyatira write; These things saith the Son of God, who hath his eyes like unto a flame of fire, and his feet *are* like fine brass; 19 I know thy works, and charity, and service, and faith, and thy patience, and thy works; and the last *to be* more than the first. 20 Notwithstanding I have a few things against thee, because thou sufferest that woman Jezebel, which calleth herself a prophetess, to teach and to seduce my servants to commit fornication, and to eat things sacrificed unto idols. 21And I gave her space to repent of her fornication; and she repented not. 22 Behold, I will cast her into a bed, and them that commit adultery with her into great tribulation, except they repent of their deeds. 23And I will kill her children with death; and all the churches shall know that I am he which searcheth the reins and hearts: and I will give unto every one of you according to your works. 24 But unto you I say, and unto the rest in Thyatira, as many as have not this doctrine, and which have not known the depths of Satan, as they speak; I will put upon you none other burden. 25 But that which ye have *already,* hold fast till I come. 26And he that overcometh, and keepeth my works unto the end, to him will I give power over the nations: 27And he shall rule them with a rod of iron; as the vessels of a potter shall they be broken to shivers: even as I received of my Father. 28And I will give him the morning star. 29 He that hath an ear, let him hear what the Spirit saith unto the churches.

New International Version

comes will not be hurt at all by the second death.

To the church in Pergamum

12 "To the angel of the church in Pergamum write:

These are the words of him who has the sharp, double-edged sword. 13 I know where you live—where Satan has his throne. Yet you remain true to my name. You did not renounce your faith in me, even in the days of Antipas, my faithful witness, who was put to death in your city—where Satan lives.

14 Nevertheless, I have a few things against you: You have people there who hold to the teaching of Balaam, who taught Balak to entice the Israelites to sin by eating food sacrificed to idols and by committing sexual immorality. 15And you have others who hold to the teaching of the Nicolaitans. 16 Repent therefore! Otherwise, I will soon come to you and will fight against them with the sword of my mouth.

17 He who has an ear, let him hear what the Spirit says to the churches. To him who overcomes, I will give some of the hidden manna. I will also give him a white stone with a new name written on it, known only to him who receives it.

To the church in Thyatira

18 "To the angel of the church in Thyatira write:

These are the words of the Son of God, whose eyes are like blazing fire and whose feet are like burnished brass. 19 I know your deeds, your love and faith, your service and perseverance, and that you are now doing more than you did at first.

20 Nevertheless, I have this against you: You tolerate that woman Jezebel, who calls herself a prophetess. By her teaching she misleads my servants into sexual immorality and the eating of food sacrificed to idols. 21 I have given her time to repent of her immorality, but she is unwilling. 22 So I will cast her on a bed of suffering, and I will make those who commit adultery with her suffer intensely, unless they repent of her ways. 23 I will strike her children dead. Then all the churches will know that I am he who searches hearts and minds, and I will repay each of you according to your deeds. 24 Now I say to the rest of you in Thyatira, to you who do not hold to her teaching and have not learned Satan's so-called deep secrets (I will not impose any other burden on you): 25 Only hold on to what you have until I come.

26 To him who overcomes and does my will to the end, I will give authority over the nations—

27 'He will rule them with a rod of iron
        and dash them to pieces like pottery' *e*—
just as I have received authority from my Father. 28 I will also give him the morning star. 29 He who has an ear, let him hear what the Spirit says to the churches.

[e] Psalm 2:9.

Greek Interlinear

'Ο νικῶν οὐ μὴ ἀδικηθῇ ἐκ τοῦ θανάτου
The over- by no will be by the ²death
[one] coming means hurt
τοῦ δευτέρου.
- ¹second.

12 Καὶ τῷ ἀγγέλῳ τῆς ἐν Περγάμῳ
And to the messenger ¹of the ²in ⁴Pergamum
ἐκκλησίας γράψον·
³church write thou:
Τάδε λέγει ὁ ἔχων τὴν ῥομφαίαν τὴν
These things says the having the ²sword -
[one]
δίστομον τὴν ὀξεῖαν· 13 οἶδα ποῦ κατοικεῖς·
¹two-mouthed - ³sharp: I know where thou
(edged) dwellest;
ὅπου ὁ θρόνος τοῦ σατανᾶ· καὶ κρατεῖς
where the throne - of Satan [is]; and thou holdest
τὸ ὄνομά μου, καὶ οὐκ ἠρνήσω τὴν
the name of me, and didst not deny the
πίστιν μου καὶ ἐν ταῖς ἡμέραις Ἀντιπᾶς
faith of me even in the days of Antipas
ὁ μάρτυς μου ὁ πιστός μου, ὃς
²the ²witness ³of me the ²faithful of me, who
ἀπεκτάνθη παρ' ὑμῖν, ὅπου ὁ σατανᾶς
was killed among you, where - Satan
κατοικεῖ. 14 ἀλλ' ἔχω κατὰ σοῦ ὀλίγα,
dwells. But I have against thee a few
things,
ὅτι ἔχεις ἐκεῖ κρατοῦντας τὴν διδαχὴν
be- thou there [ones] holding the teaching
cause hast
Βαλαάμ, ὃς ἐδίδασκεν τῷ Βαλὰκ βαλεῖν
of Balaam, who taught - Balak to cast
σκάνδαλον ἐνώπιον τῶν υἱῶν Ἰσραήλ,
a stumbling-block before the sons of Israel,
φαγεῖν εἰδωλόθυτα καὶ πορνεῦσαι. 15 οὕτως
to eat idol sacrifices and to commit fornication. So
ἔχεις καὶ σὺ κρατοῦντας τὴν διδαχὴν
²hast ²also ¹thou [ones] holding the teaching
τῶν Νικολαϊτῶν ὁμοίως. 16 μετανόησον
of the Nicolaitans likewise. Repent thou
οὖν· εἰ δὲ μή, ἔρχομαί σοι ταχὺ καὶ
therefore; otherwise, I am coming to thee quickly and
πολεμήσω μετ' αὐτῶν ἐν τῇ ῥομφαίᾳ
will fight with them with the sword
τοῦ στόματός μου. 17 'Ο ἔχων οὖς
of the mouth of me. The [one] having an ear
ἀκουσάτω τί τὸ πνεῦμα λέγει ταῖς
let him hear what the Spirit says to the
ἐκκλησίαις. Τῷ νικῶντι δώσω αὐτῷ
churches. To the [one] overcoming I will give to him
τοῦ μάννα τοῦ κεκρυμμένου, καὶ δώσω
of the ²manna - ¹having been hidden, and I will give
αὐτῷ ψῆφον λευκήν, καὶ ἐπὶ τὴν ψῆφον
him ²stone ¹a white, and on the stone
ὄνομα καινὸν γεγραμμένον, ὃ οὐδεὶς οἶδεν
²name ¹a new having been written, which no man knows
εἰ μὴ ὁ λαμβάνων.
except the [one] receiving [it].

18 Καὶ τῷ ἀγγέλῳ τῆς ἐν Θυατίροις
And to the messenger ¹of the ²in ³Thyatira
ἐκκλησίας γράψον·
²church write thou:
Τάδε λέγει ὁ υἱὸς τοῦ θεοῦ, ὁ ἔχων
These things says the Son - of God, the having
[one]
τοὺς ὀφθαλμοὺς [αὐτοῦ] ὡς φλόγα πυρός,
the eyes of him as a flame of fire,
καὶ οἱ πόδες αὐτοῦ ὅμοιοι χαλκολιβάνῳ·
and the feet of him like to burnished brass:

19 οἶδά σου τὰ ἔργα καὶ τὴν ἀγάπην
I know of thee the works and the love
καὶ τὴν πίστιν καὶ τὴν διακονίαν καὶ
and the faith and the ministry and
τὴν ὑπομονήν σου, καὶ τὰ ἔργα σου
the endurance of thee, and the ²works ¹of thee
τὰ ἔσχατα πλείονα τῶν πρώτων. 20 ἀλλὰ
the ¹last more [than] the first. But
ἔχω κατὰ σοῦ ὅτι ἀφεῖς τὴν γυναῖκα
I have against thee that thou permittest the woman
Ἰεζάβελ, ἡ λέγουσα ἑαυτὴν προφῆτιν,
Jezabel, the [one] say(call)ing herself a prophetess,
καὶ διδάσκει καὶ πλανᾷ τοὺς ἐμοὺς
and she teaches and deceives - my
δούλους πορνεῦσαι καὶ φαγεῖν εἰδωλόθυτα·
slaves to commit fornication and to eat idol sacrifices;
21 καὶ ἔδωκα αὐτῇ χρόνον ἵνα μετανοήσῃ,
and I gave her time in order she might
that repent,
καὶ οὐ θέλει μετανοῆσαι ἐκ τῆς πορνείας
and she wishes not to repent of the fornication
αὐτῆς. 22 ἰδοὺ βάλλω αὐτὴν εἰς κλίνην,
of her. Behold[,] I am casting her into a bed,
καὶ τοὺς μοιχεύοντας μετ' αὐτῆς εἰς
and the [ones] committing adultery with her into
θλῖψιν μεγάλην, ἐὰν μὴ μετανοήσουσιν
²affliction ¹great, unless they shall repent
ἐκ τῶν ἔργων αὐτῆς· 23 καὶ τὰ τέκνα
of the works of her; and the children
αὐτῆς ἀποκτενῶ ἐν θανάτῳ· καὶ γνώσονται
of her I will kill with death; and ²will know
πᾶσαι αἱ ἐκκλησίαι ὅτι ἐγώ εἰμι ὁ
¹all ²the ³churches that I am the
[one]
ἐρευνῶν νεφροὺς καὶ καρδίας, καὶ δώσω
searching kidneys and hearts, and I will give
ὑμῖν ἑκάστῳ κατὰ τὰ ἔργα ὑμῶν.
to you each one according to the works of you.
24 ὑμῖν δὲ λέγω τοῖς λοιποῖς τοῖς ἐν
But to you I say to the rest - in
Θυατίροις, ὅσοι οὐκ ἔχουσιν τὴν διδαχὴν
Thyatira, as many as have not the teaching
ταύτην, οἵτινες οὐκ ἔγνωσαν τὰ βαθέα
this, who knew not the deep things
τοῦ σατανᾶ, ὡς λέγουσιν· οὐ βάλλω
- of Satan, as they say: I am not casting
ἐφ' ὑμᾶς ἄλλο βάρος· 25 πλὴν ὃ ἔχετε
on you another burden; nevertheless what ye have
κρατήσατε ἄχρι οὗ ἂν ἥξω. 26 Καὶ
hold until I shall come. And
ὁ νικῶν καὶ ὁ τηρῶν ἄχρι τέλους τὰ
the over- and the keeping until [the] the
[one] coming [one] end
ἔργα μου, δώσω αὐτῷ ἐξουσίαν ἐπὶ
works of me, I will give him authority over
τῶν ἐθνῶν, 27 καὶ ποιμανεῖ αὐτοὺς ἐν
the nations, and he will shepherd them with
ῥάβδῳ σιδηρᾷ, ὡς τὰ σκεύη τὰ κεραμικὰ
²staff ¹an iron, as the ²vessels - ¹clay
συντρίβεται, ὡς κἀγὼ εἴληφα παρὰ
is(are) broken, as I also have received from
τοῦ πατρός μου, 28 καὶ δώσω αὐτῷ τὸν
the Father of me, and I will give him the
ἀστέρα τὸν πρωϊνόν. 29 'Ο ἔχων οὖς
²star ¹the ²morning. The [one] having an ear
ἀκουσάτω τί τὸ πνεῦμα λέγει ταῖς
let him hear what the Spirit says to the
ἐκκλησίαις
churches.

729

King James Version

New International Version

To the church in Sardis

3 And unto the angel of the church in Sardis write; These things saith he that hath the seven Spirits of God, and the seven stars; I know thy works, that thou hast a name that thou livest, and art dead. 2 Be watchful, and strengthen the things which remain, that are ready to die: for I have not found thy works perfect before God. 3 Remember therefore how thou hast received and heard, and hold fast, and repent. If therefore thou shalt not watch, I will come on thee as a thief, and thou shalt not know what hour I will come upon thee. 4 Thou hast a few names even in Sardis which have not defiled their garments; and they shall walk with me in white: for they are worthy. 5 He that overcometh, the same shall be clothed in white raiment; and I will not blot out his name out of the book of life, but I will confess his name before my Father, and before his angels. 6 He that hath an ear, let him hear what the Spirit saith unto the churches. 7And to the angel of the church in Philadelphia write; These things saith he that is holy, he that is true, he that hath the key of David, he that openeth, and no man shutteth; and shutteth, and no man openeth; 8 I know thy works: behold, I have set before thee an open door, and no man can shut it: for thou hast a little strength, and hast kept my word, and hast not denied my name. 9 Behold, I will make them of the synagogue of Satan, which say they are Jews, and are not, but do lie; behold, I will make them to come and worship before thy feet, and to know that I have loved thee. 10 Because thou hast kept the word of my patience, I also will keep thee from the hour of temptation, which shall come upon all the world, to try them that dwell upon the earth. 11 Behold, I come quickly: hold that fast which thou hast, that no man take thy crown. 12 Him that overcometh will I make a pillar in the temple of my God, and he shall go no more out: and I will write upon him the name of my God, and the name of the city of my God, *which is* new Jerusalem, which cometh down out of heaven from my God: and *I will write upon him* my new name. 13 He that hath an ear, let him hear what the Spirit saith unto the churches. 14And unto the angel of the church of the Laodiceans write; These things saith the Amen, the faithful and true witness, the beginning of the creation of God; 15 I know thy works, that thou art neither cold nor hot: I would thou wert cold or hot. 16 So then because thou art

3 "To the angel of the church in Sardis write:

These are the words of him who holds the seven spirits[f] of God and the seven stars. I know your deeds; you have a reputation of being alive, but you are dead. 2 Wake up! Strengthen what remains and is about to die, for I have not found your deeds complete in the sight of my God. 3 Remember, therefore, what you have received and heard; obey it, and repent. But if you do not wake up, I will come like a thief, and you will not know at what time I will come to you.

4 Yet you have a few people in Sardis who have not soiled their clothes. They will walk with me, dressed in white, for they are worthy. 5 He who overcomes will, like them, be dressed in white. I will never erase his name from the book of life, but will acknowledge his name before my Father and his angels. 6 He who has an ear, let him hear what the Spirit says to the churches.

To the church in Philadelphia

7 "To the angel of the church in Philadelphia write:

These are the words of him who is holy and true, who holds the key of David. What he opens, no one can shut; and what he shuts, no one can open. 8 I know your deeds. See, I have placed before you an open door that no one can shut. I know that you have little strength, yet you have kept my word and have not denied my name. 9 I will make those who are of the synagogue of Satan, who claim to be Jews though they are not, but are liars—I will make them come and fall down at your feet and acknowledge that I have loved you. 10 Since you have kept my command to endure patiently, I will also keep you from the hour of trial that is going to come upon the whole world to test those who live on the earth.

11 I am coming soon. Hold on to what you have, so that no one will take your crown. 12 Him who overcomes I will make a pillar in the temple of my God. Never again will he leave it. I will write on him the name of my God and the name of the city of my God, the new Jerusalem, which is coming down out of heaven from my God; and I will also write on him my new name. 13 He who has an ear, let him hear what the Spirit says to the churches.

To the church in Laodicea

14 "To the angel of the church in Laodicea write:

These are the words of the Amen, the faithful and true witness, the ruler of God's creation. 15 I know your deeds, that you are neither cold nor hot. I wish you were either one or the other! 16 So, because you are lukewarm—

[f] Or *the sevenfold Spirit.*

Greek Interlinear

Chapter 3

Καὶ τῷ ἀγγέλῳ τῆς ἐν Σάρδεσιν
And to the messenger ¹of the ²in ⁴Sardis

ἐκκλησίας γράψον·
³church write thou:

Τάδε λέγει ὁ ἔχων τὰ ἑπτὰ πνεύματα
These things says the having the seven Spirits
[one]

τοῦ θεοῦ καὶ τοὺς ἑπτὰ ἀστέρας· οἶδά
– of God and the seven stars: I know

τὰ ἔργα, ὅτι ὄνομα ἔχεις ὅτι ζῆς,
²of ¹the ³works, that a name thou that thou
hast livest,

καὶ νεκρὸς εἶ. 2 γίνου γρηγορῶν, καὶ
and [yet] ²dead ¹thou art. Be thou watching, and

στήρισον τὰ λοιπὰ ἃ ἔμελλον ἀποθανεῖν·
establish the remain- which were to die;
things ing about

οὐ γὰρ εὕρηκά σου ἔργα πεπληρωμένα
for I have not found of thee works having been fulfilled

ἐνώπιον τοῦ θεοῦ μου· 3 μνημόνευε οὖν
before the God of me; remember therefore

ὡς εἴληφας καὶ ἤκουσας, καὶ τήρει
ow thou hast received and didst hear, and keep

καὶ μετανόησον. ἐὰν οὖν μὴ γρηγορήσῃς,
nd repent. If therefore thou dost not watch,

ἥξω ὡς κλέπτης, καὶ οὐ μὴ γνῷς ποίαν
will as a thief, and by no thou at what
ome means knowest

ὥραν ἥξω ἐπὶ σέ. 4 ἀλλὰ ἔχεις ὀλίγα
hour I will come on thee. But thou hast a few

ὀνόματα ἐν Σάρδεσιν ἃ οὐκ ἐμόλυναν τὰ
names in Sardis which did not defile the

ἱμάτια αὐτῶν, καὶ περιπατήσουσιν μετ᾽
arments of them, and they shall walk with

ἐμοῦ ἐν λευκοῖς, ὅτι ἄξιοί εἰσιν. 5 Ὁ
me in white because ²worthy ¹they are. The
[garments] [one]

νικῶν οὕτως περιβαλεῖται ἐν ἱματίοις
vercoming ²thus ¹shall be clothed in ³garments

λευκοῖς, καὶ οὐ μὴ ἐξαλείψω τὸ ὄνομα
¹white, and by no means will I blot out the name

αὐτοῦ ἐκ τῆς βίβλου τῆς ζωῆς, καὶ
f him out of the scroll – of life, and

ὁμολογήσω τὸ ὄνομα αὐτοῦ ἐνώπιον τοῦ
I will confess the name of him before the

πατρός μου καὶ ἐνώπιον τῶν ἀγγέλων
Father of me and before the angels

αὐτοῦ. 6 Ὁ ἔχων οὖς ἀκουσάτω τί τὸ
f him. The [one] having an ear let him hear what the

πνεῦμα λέγει ταῖς ἐκκλησίαις.
Spirit says to the churches.

7 Καὶ τῷ ἀγγέλῳ τῆς ἐν Φιλαδελφείᾳ
And to the messenger ¹of the ²in ⁴Philadelphia

ἐκκλησίας γράψον·
³church write thou:

Τάδε λέγει ὁ ἅγιος, ὁ ἀληθινός, ὁ
These says the holy the true the
things [one], [one], [one]

ἔχων τὴν κλεῖν Δαυίδ, ὁ ἀνοίγων καὶ
aving the key of David, the [one] opening and

οὐδεὶς κλείσει, καὶ κλείων καὶ οὐδεὶς
o one shall shut, and shutting and no one

ἀνοίγει· 8 οἶδά σου τὰ ἔργα· ἰδοὺ
opens: I know of thee the works; behold[,]

δέδωκα ἐνώπιόν σου θύραν ἠνεῳγμένην,
have given before thee a door having been opened,

ἣν οὐδεὶς δύναται κλεῖσαι αὐτήν· ὅτι
hich no one can to shut it; because

μικρὰν ἔχεις δύναμιν, καὶ ἐτήρησάς μου
²a little ¹thou hast power, and didst keep of me

τὸν λόγον καὶ οὐκ ἠρνήσω τὸ ὄνομά
the word and didst not deny the name

μου. 9 ἰδοὺ διδῶ ἐκ τῆς συναγωγῆς
of me. Behold[,] I may [some] the synagogue
(will) give of

τοῦ σατανᾶ, τῶν λεγόντων ἑαυτοὺς
– of Satan, the [ones] say(call)ing themselves

Ἰουδαίους εἶναι, καὶ οὐκ εἰσὶν ἀλλὰ
Jews to be, and they are not but

ψεύδονται· ἰδοὺ ποιήσω αὐτοὺς ἵνα
they lie; behold[,] I will make them in order
that

ἥξουσιν καὶ προσκυνήσουσιν ἐνώπιον τῶν
they shall and they shall worship before the
come

ποδῶν σου, καὶ γνῶσιν ὅτι ἐγὼ ἠγάπησά
feet of thee, and they that I loved
shall know

σε. 10 ὅτι ἐτήρησας τὸν λόγον τῆς
thee. Because thou didst keep the word of the

ὑπομονῆς μου, κἀγώ σε τηρήσω ἐκ
endurance of me, I also ¹thee ¹will keep out of

τῆς ὥρας τοῦ πειρασμοῦ τῆς μελλούσης
the hour – of trial – being about

ἔρχεσθαι ἐπὶ τῆς οἰκουμένης ὅλης, πειράσαι
to come on ²the ¹inhabited [earth] ³all, to try

τοὺς κατοικοῦντας ἐπὶ τῆς γῆς. 11 ἔρχομαι
the [ones] dwelling on the earth. I am coming

ταχύ· κράτει ὃ ἔχεις, ἵνα μηδεὶς λάβῃ
quickly; hold what thou in order no one takes
hast, that

τὸν στέφανόν σου. 12 Ὁ νικῶν, ποιήσω
the crown of thee. The [one] overcoming, I will make

αὐτὸν στῦλον ἐν τῷ ναῷ τοῦ θεοῦ
him a pillar in the shrine of the God

μου, καὶ ἔξω οὐ μὴ ἐξέλθῃ ἔτι, καὶ
of me, and out by no he will [any] and
means go forth longer,

γράψω ἐπ᾽ αὐτὸν τὸ ὄνομα τοῦ θεοῦ
I will write on him the name of the God

μου καὶ τὸ ὄνομα τῆς πόλεως τοῦ
of me and the name of the city of the

θεοῦ μου, τῆς καινῆς Ἰερουσαλήμ ἡ
God of me, of the new Jerusalem –

καταβαίνουσα ἐκ τοῦ οὐρανοῦ ἀπὸ τοῦ
descending out of – heaven from the

θεοῦ μου, καὶ τὸ ὄνομά μου τὸ καινόν.
God of me, and ¹the ²name ⁴of me – ⁵new.

13 Ὁ ἔχων οὖς ἀκουσάτω τί τὸ πνεῦμα
The [one] having an ear let him hear what the Spirit

λέγει ταῖς ἐκκλησίαις.
says to the churches.

14 Καὶ τῷ ἀγγέλῳ τῆς ἐν Λαοδικείᾳ
And to the messenger ¹of the ²in ⁴Laodicea

ἐκκλησίας γράψον·
³church write thou:

Τάδε λέγει ὁ ἀμήν, ὁ μάρτυς ὁ
These things says the Amen, the ⁴witness –

πιστὸς καὶ ἀληθινός, ἡ ἀρχὴ τῆς κτίσεως
¹faithful ²and ³true, the chief of the creation

τοῦ θεοῦ· 15 οἶδά σου τὰ ἔργα, ὅτι
– of God: I know of thee the works, that

οὔτε ψυχρὸς εἶ οὔτε ζεστός. ὄφελον
neither cold art thou nor hot. I would that†

ψυχρὸς ἦς ἢ ζεστός. 16 οὕτως ὅτι
cold thou wast or hot. So because

King James Version

lukewarm, and neither cold nor hot, I will spew thee out of my mouth. 17 Because thou sayest, I am rich, and increased with goods, and have need of nothing; and knowest not that thou art wretched, and miserable, and poor, and blind, and naked: 18 I counsel thee to buy of me gold tried in the fire, that thou mayest be rich; and white raiment, that thou mayest be clothed, and *that* the shame of thy nakedness do not appear; and anoint thine eyes with eyesalve, that thou mayest see. 19As many as I love, I rebuke and chasten: be zealous therefore, and repent. 20 Behold, I stand at the door, and knock: if any man hear my voice, and open the door, I will come in to him, and will sup with him, and he with me. 21 To him that overcometh will I grant to sit with me in my throne, even as I also overcame, and am set down with my Father in his throne. 22 He that hath an ear, let him hear what the Spirit saith unto the churches.

New International Version

neither hot nor cold—I am about to spit you out of my mouth. 17 You say, 'I am rich; I have acquired wealth and do not need a thing. But you do not realize that you are wretched, pitiful, poor, blind and naked. 18 I counsel you to buy from me gold refined in the fire, so you can become rich; and white clothes to wear, so you can cover your shameful nakedness; and salve to put on your eyes, so you can see.

19 Those whom I love I rebuke and discipline. So be earnest, and repent. 20 Here I am! I stand at the door and knock. If anyone hears my voice and opens the door, I will go in and eat with him, and he with me.

21 To him who overcomes, I will give the right to sit with me on my throne, just as I overcame and sat down with my Father on his throne. 22 He who has an ear, let him hear what the Spirit says to the churches."

The throne in heaven

4 After this I looked, and, behold, a door *was* opened in heaven: and the first voice which I heard *was* as it were of a trumpet talking with me; which said, Come up hither, and I will shew thee these things which must be hereafter. 2And immediately I was in the Spirit: and, behold, a throne was set in heaven, and *one* sat on the throne. 3And he that sat was to look upon like a jasper and a sardine stone: and *there was* a rainbow round about the throne, in sight like unto an emerald. 4And round about the throne *were* four and twenty seats: and upon the seats I saw four and twenty elders sitting, clothed in white raiment; and they had on their heads crowns of gold. 5And out of the throne proceeded lightnings and thunderings and voices: and *there were* seven lamps of fire burning before the throne, which are the seven Spirits of God. 6And before the throne *there was* a sea of glass like unto crystal: and in the midst of the throne, and round about the throne, *were* four beasts full of eyes before and behind. 7And the first beast *was* like a lion, and the second beast like a calf, and the third beast had a face as a man, and the fourth beast *was* like a flying eagle. 8And the four beasts had each of them six wings about *him;* and *they were* full of eyes within: and they rest not day and night, saying,

4 After this I looked, and there before me was a door standing open in heaven. And the voice I had first heard speaking to me like a trumpet said, "Come up here, and I will show you what must take place after this." 2At once I was in the Spirit, and there before me was a throne in heaven with someone sitting on it. 3And the one who sat there had the appearance of jasper and carnelian. A rainbow, resembling an emerald, encircled the throne. 4 Surrounding the throne were twenty-four other thrones, and seated on them were twenty-four elders. They were dressed in white and had crowns of gold on their heads. 5 From the throne came flashes of lightning, rumblings and peals of thunder. Before the throne, seven lamps were blazing. These are the seven spirits[g] of God. 6Also before the throne there was what looked like a sea of glass, clear as crystal.

In the center, around the throne, were four living creatures, and they were covered with eyes, in front and in back. 7 The first living creature was like a lion, the second was like an ox, the third had a face like a man, the fourth was like a flying eagle. 8 Each of the four living creatures had six wings and was covered with eyes all around, even under his wings. Day and night they never stop saying:

Greek Interlinear

χλιαρὸς εἶ, καὶ οὔτε ζεστὸς οὔτε ψυχρός,
lukewarm thou art, and neither hot nor cold,

μέλλω σε ἐμέσαι ἐκ τοῦ στόματός μου.
I am ²thee ¹to vomit out of the mouth of me.
about°

17 ὅτι λέγεις ὅτι πλούσιός εἰμι καὶ
Because thou sayest[,] – ²rich ¹I am and

πεπλούτηκα καὶ οὐδὲν χρείαν ἔχω, καὶ
¹ have become rich and ²no ³need ¹I have, and

οὐκ οἶδας ὅτι σὺ εἶ ὁ ταλαίπωρος
knowest not that thou art the [one] wretched

καὶ ἐλεεινὸς καὶ πτωχὸς καὶ τυφλὸς
and pitiable and poor and blind

καὶ γυμνός, 18 συμβουλεύω σοι ἀγοράσαι
and naked, I counsel thee to buy

παρ' ἐμοῦ χρυσίον πεπυρωμένον ἐκ πυρὸς
from me gold having been refined by fire
by fire

ἵνα πλουτήσῃς, καὶ ἱμάτια λευκὰ ἵνα
in or- thou mayest and ²garments ¹white in order
der that be rich, that

περιβάλῃ καὶ μὴ φανερωθῇ ἡ αἰσχύνη
thou mayest and ¹may not be ¹the ²shame
be clothed manifested

τῆς γυμνότητός σου, καὶ κολλύριον
of the ¹nakedness ²of thee, and eyesalve

ἐγχρῖσαι τοὺς ὀφθαλμούς σου ἵνα βλέπῃς.
to anoint the eyes of in order thou
thee that mayest see.

19 ἐγὼ ὅσους ἐὰν φιλῶ ἐλέγχω καὶ
²I ¹as many as love I rebuke and

παιδεύω· ζήλευε οὖν καὶ μετανόησον.
I chasten; be hot therefore and repent thou.

20 Ἰδοὺ ἕστηκα ἐπὶ τὴν θύραν καὶ
Behold[,] I stand at the door and

κρούω· ἐάν τις ἀκούσῃ τῆς φωνῆς μου
I knock; if anyone hears the voice of me

καὶ ἀνοίξῃ τὴν θύραν, εἰσελεύσομαι πρὸς
and opens the door, I will enter to

αὐτὸν καὶ δειπνήσω μετ' αὐτοῦ καὶ
him and I will dine with him and

αὐτὸς μετ' ἐμοῦ. 21 Ὁ νικῶν, δώσω
he with me. The overcoming, I will
[one] give

αὐτῷ καθίσαι μετ' ἐμοῦ ἐν τῷ θρόνῳ
him to sit with me in the throne

μου, ὡς κἀγὼ ἐνίκησα καὶ ἐκάθισα
of me, as I also overcame and sat

μετὰ τοῦ πατρός μου ἐν τῷ θρόνῳ
with the Father of me in the throne

αὐτοῦ. 22 Ὁ ἔχων οὖς ἀκουσάτω τί
of him. The [one] having an ear let him hear what

τὸ πνεῦμα λέγει ταῖς ἐκκλησίαις.
the Spirit says to the churches.

Chapter 4

Μετὰ ταῦτα εἶδον, καὶ ἰδοὺ θύρα
After these things I saw, and behold[,] a door

ἠνεῳγμένη ἐν τῷ οὐρανῷ, καὶ ἡ φωνὴ
having been in – heaven, and the ²voice
opened

ἡ πρώτη ἣν ἤκουσα ὡς σάλπιγγος
– ¹first which I heard as of a trumpet

λαλούσης μετ' ἐμοῦ, λέγων· ἀνάβα ὧδε,
speaking with me, saying: Come up here,

καὶ δείξω σοι ἃ δεῖ γενέσθαι μετὰ
and I will thee things it be- to occur after
show which hoves

ταῦτα. εὐθέως ἐγενόμην ἐν πνεύματι·
these things. Immediately I became in spirit;

2 καὶ ἰδοὺ θρόνος ἔκειτο ἐν τῷ οὐρανῷ,
and behold[,] a throne was set in – heaven,

καὶ ἐπὶ τὸν θρόνον καθήμενος, 3 καὶ
and on the throne a sitting [one], and

ὁ καθήμενος ὅμοιος ὁράσει λίθῳ ἰάσπιδι
the [one] sitting [was] like in appearance ⁴stone ¹to a jasper

καὶ σαρδίῳ, καὶ ἶρις κυκλόθεν τοῦ
²and ²a sardius, and a rain- round the
[there was] bow

θρόνου ὅμοιος ὁράσει σμαραγδίνῳ. 4 καὶ
throne like in appearance to an emerald. And

κυκλόθεν τοῦ θρόνου θρόνους εἴκοσι
round the throne [I saw] ²thrones ¹twenty-

τέσσαρας, καὶ ἐπὶ τοὺς θρόνους εἴκοσι
four, and on the thrones twenty-

τέσσαρας πρεσβυτέρους καθημένους περι-
four elders sitting having been

βεβλημένους ἐν ἱματίοις λευκοῖς, καὶ ἐπὶ
clothed in garments white, and on

τὰς κεφαλὰς αὐτῶν στεφάνους χρυσοῦς
the heads of them ²crowns ¹golden.

5 καὶ ἐκ τοῦ θρόνου ἐκπορεύονται ἀστραπαὶ
And out of the throne come forth lightnings

καὶ φωναὶ καὶ βρονταί· καὶ ἑπτὰ λαμπάδες
and voices★ and thunders; and seven lamps

πυρὸς καιόμεναι ἐνώπιον τοῦ θρόνου, ἅ
of fire [are] burning before the throne, which

εἰσιν τὰ ἑπτὰ πνεύματα τοῦ θεοῦ· 6 καὶ
are the seven Spirits – of God; and

ἐνώπιον τοῦ θρόνου ὡς θάλασσα ὑαλίνη
before the throne as ²sea ¹a glassy

ὁμοία κρυστάλλῳ· καὶ ἐν μέσῳ τοῦ
like to crystal; and in [the] midst of the

θρόνου καὶ κύκλῳ τοῦ θρόνου τέσσερα
throne and round the throne four

ζῷα γέμοντα ὀφθαλμῶν ἔμπροσθεν καὶ
living filling(full) of eyes before and
creatures

ὄπισθεν. 7 καὶ τὸ ζῷον τὸ πρῶτον
behind. And the ²living – ¹first
creature

ὅμοιον λέοντι, καὶ τὸ δεύτερον ζῷον
[was] to a lion, and the second living
like creature

ὅμοιον μόσχῳ, καὶ τὸ τρίτον ζῷον ἔχων
like to a calf, and the third living having
creature

τὸ πρόσωπον ὡς ἀνθρώπου, καὶ τὸ
the(its) face as of a man, and the

τέταρτον ζῷον ὅμοιον ἀετῷ πετομένῳ.
fourth living creature like eagle to a flying.

8 καὶ τὰ τέσσερα ζῷα, ἓν καθ' ἓν
And the four living one by one
creatures,

αὐτῶν ἔχων ἀνὰ πτέρυγας ἕξ, κυκλόθεν
of them having each ²wings ¹six, around

καὶ ἔσωθεν γέμουσιν ὀφθαλμῶν· καὶ
and within are full of eyes; and

ἀνάπαυσιν οὐκ ἔχουσιν ἡμέρας καὶ νυκτὸς
respite they have not day and night

° As so often (see also ch. 1. 19, 2. 10), this verb does not
necessarily connote imminence, but only simple futurity.

★ Or "sounds"; and so elsewhere.

733

King James Version

Holy, holy, holy, Lord God Almighty, which was, and is, and is to come. 9And when those beasts give glory and honour and thanks to him that sat on the throne, who liveth for ever and ever, 10 The four and twenty elders fall down before him that sat on the throne, and worship him that liveth for ever and ever, and cast their crowns before the throne, saying, 11 Thou art worthy, O Lord, to receive glory and honour and power: for thou hast created all things, and for thy pleasure they are and were created.

New International Version

"Holy, holy, holy
is the Lord God Almighty,
who was, and is, and is to come."
9 Whenever the living creatures give glory, honor and thanks to him who sits on the throne and who lives for ever and ever, 10 the twenty-four elders fall down before him who sits on the throne, and worship him who lives for ever and ever. They lay their crowns before the throne and say:
11 "You are worthy, our Lord and God,
to receive glory and honor and power,
for you created all things,
and by your will they were created and
have their being."

The scroll and the Lamb

5 And I saw in the right hand of him that sat on the throne a book written within and on the back side, sealed with seven seals. 2And I saw a strong angel proclaiming with a loud voice, Who is worthy to open the book, and to loose the seals thereof? 3And no man in heaven, nor in earth, neither under the earth, was able to open the book, neither to look thereon. 4And I wept much, because no man was found worthy to open and to read the book, neither to look thereon. 5And one of the elders saith unto me, Weep not: behold, the Lion of the tribe of Juda, the Root of David, hath prevailed to open the book, and to loose the seven seals thereof. 6And I beheld, and, lo, in the midst of the throne and of the four beasts, and in the midst of the elders, stood a Lamb, as it had been slain, having seven horns and seven eyes, which are the seven Spirits of God sent forth into all the earth. 7And he came and took the book out of the right hand of him that sat upon the throne. 8And when he had taken the book, the four beasts and four *and* twenty elders fell down before the Lamb, having every one of them harps, and golden vials full of odours, which are the prayers of saints. 9And they sung a new song, saying, Thou art worthy to take the book, and to open the seals thereof: for thou wast slain, and hast redeemed us to God by thy blood out of every kindred, and tongue, and people, and nation; 10And hast made us unto our God kings and priests: and we shall reign on the earth. 11And I beheld, and I heard the voice of many angels round about the throne, and the beasts, and the elders: and the number of them was ten thousand times ten thousand, and thousands of thousands; 12 Saying with a loud voice, Worthy is the Lamb that

5 Then I saw in the right hand of him who sat on the throne a scroll with writing on both sides and sealed with seven seals. 2And I saw a mighty angel proclaiming in a loud voice, "Who is worthy to break the seals and open the scroll?" 3 But no one in heaven or on earth or under the earth could open the scroll or even look inside it. 4 I wept and wept because no one was found who was worthy to open the scroll or look inside. 5 Then one of the elders said to me, "Do not weep! See, the Lion of the tribe of Judah, the Root of David, has triumphed. He is able to open the scroll and its seven seals."

6 Then I saw a Lamb, looking as if it had been slain, standing in the center of the throne, encircled by the four living creatures and the elders. He had seven horns and seven eyes, which are the seven spirits[h] of God sent out into all the earth. 7 He came and took the scroll from the right hand of him who sat on the throne. 8And when he had taken it, the four living creatures and the twenty-four elders fell down before the Lamb. Each one had a harp and they were holding golden bowls full of incense, which are the prayers of the saints. 9And they sang a new song:

"You are worthy to take the scroll
and to open its seals,
because you were slain,
and with your blood you purchased men
for God
from every tribe and language and people
and nation.
10 You have made them to be a kingdom and
priests to serve our God,
and they will reign on the earth."

11 Then I looked and heard the voice of many angels, numbering thousands upon thousands, and ten thousand times ten thousand. They encircled the throne and the living creatures and the elders. 12 In a loud voice they sang:
"Worthy is the Lamb, who was slain,

[h] Or *the sevenfold Spirit.*

734

Greek Interlinear

λέγοντες·   ἄγιος   ἄγιος   ἄγιος   κύριος   ὁ
saying: Holy[,] holy[,] holy[,] Lord   –

θεὸς   ὁ   παντοκράτωρ,   ὁ   ἦν   καὶ   ὁ   ὢν
God   the   Almighty,   the   was   and   the   being
                          [one who]   [one]
                                                = the one who is

καὶ   ὁ   ἐρχόμενος.   9 Καὶ   ὅταν   δώσουσιν
and   the   coming [one].   And whenever   ²shall give

τὰ   ζῷα   δόξαν   καὶ   τιμὴν   καὶ   εὐχαριστίαν
the   ²living   glory   and   honour   and   thanks
       creatures

τῷ   καθημένῳ   ἐπὶ   τῷ   θρόνῳ   τῷ   ζῶντι
to the   sitting   on   the   throne[,]   to the   living
[one]   [one]

εἰς   τοὺς   αἰῶνας   τῶν   αἰώνων,   10 πεσοῦνται
unto   the   ages   of the   ages,   ⁴will fall

οἱ   εἴκοσι   τέσσαρες   πρεσβύτεροι   ἐνώπιον
²the   ²twenty-four   ³elders   before

τοῦ   καθημένου   ἐπὶ   τοῦ   θρόνου,   καὶ
the [one]   sitting   on   the   throne,   and

προσκυνήσουσιν   τῷ   ζῶντι   εἰς   τοὺς   αἰῶνας
they will worship   the [one] living   unto   the   age³

τῶν   αἰώνων,   καὶ   βαλοῦσιν   τοὺς   στεφάνους
of the   ages,   and   will cast   the   crowns

αὐτῶν   ἐνώπιον   τοῦ   θρόνου,   λέγοντες·
of them   before   the   throne,   saying:

11 ἄξιος   εἶ,   ὁ   κύριος   καὶ   ὁ   θεὸς   ἡμῶν,
Worthy art thou, the   Lord   and   the   God   of us,

λαβεῖν   τὴν   δόξαν   καὶ   τὴν   τιμὴν   καὶ
to receive   the   glory   and   the   honour   and

τὴν   δύναμιν,   ὅτι   σὺ   ἔκτισας   τὰ   πάντα,
the   power,   because thou   createdst   – all things,*

καὶ   διὰ   τὸ   θέλημά   σου   ἦσαν   καὶ
and   on ac-   the   will   of thee   they were   and
        count of

ἐκτίσθησαν.
they were created.

Chapter 5

Καὶ   εἶδον   ἐπὶ   τὴν   δεξιὰν   τοῦ
And   I saw   on   the   right   of the
                          [hand]   [one]

καθημένου   ἐπὶ   τοῦ   θρόνου   βιβλίον
sitting   on   the   throne   a scroll

γεγραμμένον   ἔσωθεν   καὶ   ὄπισθεν,
having been written   within   and on the reverse side,

κατεσφραγισμένον   σφραγῖσιν   ἑπτά.   2 καὶ
having been sealed   with ²seals   ¹seven.   And

εἶδον   ἄγγελον   ἰσχυρὸν   κηρύσσοντα   ἐν
I saw   angel   a strong   proclaiming   in

φωνῇ   μεγάλῃ·   τίς   ἄξιος   ἀνοῖξαι   τὸ
²voice   ¹a great(loud):   Who [is]   worthy   to open   the

βιβλίον   καὶ   λῦσαι   τὰς   σφραγῖδας   αὐτοῦ;
scroll   and   to loosen   the   seals   of it ?

3 καὶ   οὐδεὶς   ἐδύνατο   ἐν   τῷ   οὐρανῷ
And   no one   was able   in   –   heaven

οὐδὲ   ἐπὶ   τῆς   γῆς   οὐδὲ   ὑποκάτω   τῆς
nor   on   the   earth   nor   underneath   the

γῆς   ἀνοῖξαι   τὸ   βιβλίον   οὔτε   βλέπειν
earth   to open   the   scroll   nor to see(look at)

αὐτό.   4 καὶ   ἔκλαιον   πολύ,   ὅτι   οὐδεὶς
it.   And   I wept   much,   because   no one

ἄξιος   εὑρέθη   ἀνοῖξαι   τὸ   βιβλίον   οὔτε
worthy   was found   to open   the   scroll   nor

βλέπειν   αὐτό.   5 καὶ   εἷς   ἐκ   τῶν   πρεσ-
to look at   it.   And   one   of   the   el-

βυτέρων   λέγει   μοι·   μὴ   κλαῖε·   ἰδοὺ
ders   says   to me: Weep not;   behold[,]

ἐνίκησεν   ὁ   λέων   ὁ   ἐκ   τῆς   φυλῆς   Ἰούδα,
⁴overcame   ¹the   ²Lion   –   ³of   ⁴the   ⁵tribe   ⁶Juda,

ἡ   ῥίζα   Δαυίδ,   ἀνοῖξαι   τὸ   βιβλίον   καὶ
the   ⁸root   ⁹of David,   to open   the   scroll   and

τὰς   ἑπτὰ   σφραγῖδας   αὐτοῦ.   6 Καὶ   εἶδον
the   seven   seals   of it.   And   I saw

ἐν   μέσῳ   τοῦ   θρόνου   καὶ   τῶν   τεσσάρων
in [the] midst   of the   throne   and   of the   four

ζῴων   καὶ   ἐν   μέσῳ   τῶν   πρεσβυτέρων
living   and   in   [the]   of the   elders
creatures   midst

ἀρνίον   ἑστηκὸς   ὡς   ἐσφαγμένον,   ἔχων
Lamb   standing   as   having been slain,   having

κέρατα   ἑπτὰ   καὶ   ὀφθαλμοὺς   ἑπτά,   οἳ
²horns   ¹seven   and   ²eyes   ¹seven, which

εἰσιν   τὰ   ἑπτὰ   πνεύματα   τοῦ   θεοῦ
are   the   seven   Spirits   –   of God

ἀπεσταλμένοι   εἰς   πᾶσαν   τὴν   γῆν.   7 καὶ
having been sent forth into   all   the   earth.   And

ἦλθεν   καὶ   εἴληφεν   ἐκ   τῆς   δεξιᾶς   τοῦ
he came   and   has taken   out of   the   right [hand]   of the

καθημένου   ἐπὶ   τοῦ   θρόνου.   8 Καὶ   ὅτε
[one] sitting   on   the   throne.   And when

ἔλαβεν   τὸ   βιβλίον,   τὰ   τέσσερα   ζῷα
he took   the   scroll,   the   four   living
                                              creatures

καὶ   οἱ   εἴκοσι   τέσσαρες   πρεσβύτεροι   ἔπεσαν
and the   twenty-four   elders   fell

ἐνώπιον   τοῦ   ἀρνίου,   ἔχοντες   ἕκαστος
before   the   Lamb,   having   each one

κιθάραν   καὶ   φιάλας   χρυσᾶς   γεμούσας
a harp   and   ²bowls   ¹golden   being full

θυμιαμάτων,   αἳ   εἰσιν   αἱ   προσευχαὶ   τῶν
of incenses,   which   are   the   prayers   of the

ἁγίων.   9 καὶ   ᾄδουσιν   ᾠδὴν   καινὴν
saints.   And   they sing   ²song   ¹a new

λέγοντες·   ἄξιος   εἶ   λαβεῖν   τὸ   βιβλίον
saying: Worthy   art thou to receive   the   scroll

καὶ   ἀνοῖξαι   τὰς   σφραγῖδας   αὐτοῦ,   ὅτι
and   to open   the   seals   of it,   because

ἐσφάγης   καὶ   ἠγόρασας   τῷ   θεῷ   ἐν   τῷ
thou wast slain and   didst purchase   –   to God   by   the

αἵματί   σου   ἐκ   πάσης   φυλῆς   καὶ   γλώσσης
blood   of thee out of   every   tribe   and   tongue

καὶ   λαοῦ   καὶ   ἔθνους,   10 καὶ   ἐποίησας
and   people   and   nation,   and   didst make

αὐτοὺς   τῷ   θεῷ   ἡμῶν   βασιλείαν   καὶ
them   to the   God   of us   a kingdom   and

ἱερεῖς,   καὶ   βασιλεύσουσιν   ἐπὶ   τῆς   γῆς.
priests,   and   they will reign   on(? over)   the   earth.

11 καὶ   εἶδον,   καὶ   ἤκουσα   φωνὴν   ἀγγέλων
And   I saw,   and   I heard   a sound   ²angels

πολλῶν   κύκλῳ   τοῦ   θρόνου   καὶ   τῶν
¹of many   round   the   throne   and   the

ζῴων   καὶ   τῶν   πρεσβυτέρων,   καὶ   ἦν
living   and   the   elders,   and   ⁴was
creatures

ὁ   ἀριθμὸς   αὐτῶν   μυριάδες   μυριάδων   καὶ
¹the   ²number   ³of them   myriads   of myriads   and

χιλιάδες   χιλιάδων,   12 λέγοντες   φωνῇ
thousands   of thousands,   saying   ²voice

μεγάλῃ·   ἄξιός   ἐστιν   τὸ   ἀρνίον   τὸ
¹with a great   Worthy   is   the   Lamb   the
(loud):

* τὰ πάντα = the universe.

King James Version

New International Version

was slain to receive power, and riches, and wisdom, and strength, and honour, and glory, and blessing. 13And every creature which is in heaven, and on the earth, and under the earth, and such as are in the sea, and all that are in them, heard I saying, Blessing, and honour, and glory, and power, *be* unto him that sitteth upon the throne, and unto the Lamb for ever and ever. 14And the four beasts said, Amen. And the four *and* twenty elders fell down and worshipped him that liveth for ever and ever.

to receive power and wealth and wisdom and strength
and honor and glory and praise!"
13 Then I heard every creature in heaven and on earth and under the earth and on the sea, and all that is in them, singing:
"To him who sits on the throne and to the Lamb
be praise and honor and glory and power,
for ever and ever!"
14 The four living creatures said, "Amen," and the elders fell down and worshipped.

The seals

6 And I saw when the Lamb opened one of the seals, and I heard, as it were the noise of thunder, one of the four beasts saying, Come and see. 2And I saw, and behold a white horse: and he that sat on him had a bow; and a crown was given unto him: and he went forth conquering, and to conquer. 3And when he had opened the second seal, I heard the second beast say, Come and see. 4And there went out another horse *that was* red: and *power* was given to him that sat thereon to take peace from the earth, and that they should kill one another: and there was given unto him a great sword. 5And when he had opened the third seal, I heard the third beast say, Come and see. And I beheld, and lo a black horse; and he that sat on him had a pair of balances in his hand. 6And I heard a voice in the midst of the four beasts say, A measure of wheat for a penny, and three measures of barley for a penny; and *see* thou hurt not the oil and the wine. 7And when he had opened the fourth seal, I heard the voice of the fourth beast say, Come and see. 8And I looked, and behold a pale horse: and his name that sat on him was Death, and Hell followed with him. And power was given unto them over the fourth part of the earth, to kill with sword, and with hunger, and with death, and with the beasts of the earth. 9And when he had opened the fifth seal, I saw under the altar the souls of them that were slain for the word of God, and for the testimony which they held: 10And they cried with a loud voice, saying, How long, O Lord, holy and true, dost thou not judge and avenge our blood on them that dwell on the earth? 11And white robes were given unto every one of them; and it was said unto them, that they should rest yet for a little season, until their fellow servants also and their brethren, that should be killed as they *were*, should be fulfilled. 12And I beheld when he had opened the sixth seal, and, lo, there was a great earthquake; and the sun became black as sackcloth of hair, and the moon became as

6 I watched as the Lamb opened the first of the seven seals. Then I heard one of the four living creatures say in a voice like thunder, "Come!" 2 I looked, and there before me was a white horse! Its rider held a bow, and he was given a crown, and he rode out as a conqueror bent on conquest.
3 When the Lamb opened the second seal, I heard the second living creature say, "Come!" 4 Then another horse came out, a fiery red one. Its rider was given power to take peace from the earth and to make men slay each other. To him was given a large sword.
5 When the Lamb opened the third seal, I heard the third living creature say, "Come!" I looked, and there before me was a black horse! Its rider was holding a pair of scales in his hand. 6 Then I heard what sounded like a voice among the four living creatures, saying, "A quart of wheat for a day's wages,[i] and three quarts of barley for a day's wages,[i] and do not damage the oil and the wine!"
7 When the Lamb opened the fourth seal, I heard the voice of the fourth living creature say, "Come!" 8 I looked, and there before me was a pale horse! Its rider was named Death, and Hades was following close behind him. They were given power over a fourth of the earth to kill by sword, famine and plague, and by the wild beasts of the earth.
9 When he opened the fifth seal, I saw under the altar the souls of those who had been slain because of the word of God and the testimony they had maintained. 10 They called out in a loud voice, "How long, Sovereign Lord, holy and true, until you judge the inhabitants of the earth and avenge our blood?" 11 Then each of them was given a white robe, and they were told to wait a little longer, until the number of their fellow servants and brothers who were to be killed as they had been was completed.
12 I watched as he opened the sixth seal. There was a great earthquake. The sun turned black like sackcloth made of goat hair, the whole

[i] Greek *a denarius.*

736

Greek Interlinear

ἐσφαγμένον λαβεῖν τὴν δύναμιν καὶ πλοῦτον
having been slain to receive   the   power   and   riches

καὶ σοφίαν καὶ ἰσχὺν καὶ τιμὴν καὶ
and wisdom and strength and honour and

δόξαν καὶ εὐλογίαν.   13 καὶ πᾶν κτίσμα
glory   and   blessing.   And every creature

ὃ ἐν τῷ οὐρανῷ καὶ ἐπὶ τῆς γῆς καὶ
which ²in - ³heaven ⁴and ⁵on ⁶the ⁷earth ⁸and

ὑποκάτω τῆς γῆς καὶ ἐπὶ τῆς θαλάσσης
⁹underneath ¹⁰the ¹¹earth ¹²and ¹³on ¹⁴the ¹⁵sea

[ἐστίν], καὶ τὰ ἐν αὐτοῖς πάντα, ἤκουσα
¹is,   and – ²in ³them ⁴all things, I heard

λέγοντας· τῷ καθημένῳ ἐπὶ τῷ θρόνῳ
saying: To the [one] sitting on the throne

καὶ τῷ ἀρνίῳ ἡ εὐλογία καὶ ἡ τιμὴ
and to the Lamb the blessing and the honour

καὶ ἡ δόξα καὶ τὸ κράτος εἰς τοὺς
and the glory and the might unto the

αἰῶνας τῶν αἰώνων.   14 καὶ τὰ τέσσερα
ages of the ages.   And the four

ζῷα ἔλεγον· ἀμήν, καὶ οἱ πρεσβύτεροι
living said: Amen, and the elders
creatures

ἔπεσαν καὶ προσεκύνησαν.
fell   and worshipped.

Chapter 6

Καὶ εἶδον ὅτε ἤνοιξεν τὸ ἀρνίον
And I saw when ¹opened ¹the ²Lamb

μίαν ἐκ τῶν ἑπτὰ σφραγίδων, καὶ ἤκουσα
one of the seven seals, and I heard

ἑνὸς ἐκ τῶν τεσσάρων ζῴων λέγοντος
one of the four living creatures saying

ὡς φωνῇ βροντῆς· ἔρχου. 2 καὶ εἶδον,
as with a sound of thunder: Come.   And I saw,

καὶ ἰδοὺ ἵππος λευκός, καὶ ὁ καθήμενος
and behold[,] ¹horse ¹a white, and the [one] sitting

ἐπ᾽ αὐτὸν ἔχων τόξον, καὶ ἐδόθη αὐτῷ
on it having a bow, and ²was given ³to him

στέφανος, καὶ ἐξῆλθεν νικῶν καὶ ἵνα
¹a crown, and he went forth overcoming and in order that

νικήσῃ. 3 Καὶ ὅτε ἤνοιξεν τὴν σφραγίδα
he might And when he opened the ²seal
overcome.

τὴν δευτέραν, ἤκουσα τοῦ δευτέρου ζῴου
–   ¹second,   I heard the second living
creature

λέγοντος· ἔρχου. 4 καὶ ἐξῆλθεν ἄλλος
saying: Come.   And ⁴went forth ¹another

ἵππος πυρρός, καὶ τῷ καθημένῳ ἐπ᾽
²horse[,] ¹red, and to the [one] sitting on

αὐτὸν ἐδόθη αὐτῷ λαβεῖν τὴν εἰρήνην
it was given to him to take – peace

ἐκ τῆς γῆς καὶ ἵνα ἀλλήλους σφάξουσιν,
out the earth and in order ²one ¹they
of   that another shall slay,

καὶ ἐδόθη αὐτῷ μάχαιρα μεγάλη. 5 Καὶ
and ²was given ³to him ⁴sword ¹a great.   And

ὅτε ἤνοιξεν τὴν σφραγίδα τὴν τρίτην,
when he opened the seal – ³third,

ἤκουσα τοῦ τρίτου ζῴου λέγοντος· ἔρχου.
I heard the third living saying: Come.
creature

καὶ εἶδον, καὶ ἰδοὺ ἵππος μέλας, καὶ
And I saw, and behold[,] ¹horse ¹a black, and

ὁ καθήμενος ἐπ᾽ αὐτὸν ἔχων ζυγὸν
the [one] sitting on it having a balance

ἐν τῇ χειρὶ αὐτοῦ. 6 καὶ ἤκουσα ὡς
in the hand of him.   And I heard as

φωνὴν ἐν μέσῳ τῶν τεσσάρων ζῴων
a voice in [the] of the four living
midst   creatures

λέγουσαν· χοῖνιξ σίτου δηναρίου, καὶ τρεῖς
saying: A of of(for) and three
choenix wheat a denarius,

χοίνικες κριθῶν δηναρίου· καὶ τὸ ἔλαιον
choenixes of barley of(for) and ²the ²oil
a denarius;

καὶ τὸν οἶνον μὴ ἀδικήσῃς. 7 Καὶ
⁴and ³the ⁴wine ¹do not harm.   And

ὅτε ἤνοιξεν τὴν σφραγίδα τὴν τετάρτην,
when he opened the ²seal – ²fourth,

ἤκουσα φωνὴν τοῦ τετάρτου ζῴου λέγοντος·
I heard [the] voice of the fourth living creature saying:

ἔρχου. 8 καὶ εἶδον, καὶ ἰδοὺ ἵππος
Come.   And I saw, and behold[,] ²horse

χλωρός, καὶ ὁ καθήμενος ἐπάνω αὐτοῦ,
¹a pale green, and the [one] sitting upon it,

ὄνομα αὐτῷ [ὁ] θάνατος, καὶ ὁ ᾅδης
name to him° – death, and – hades

ἠκολούθει μετ᾽ αὐτοῦ, καὶ ἐδόθη αὐτοῖς
followed with him, and ²was ³to them
given

ἐξουσία ἐπὶ τὸ τέταρτον τῆς γῆς,
¹authority over the fourth [part] of the earth,

ἀποκτεῖναι ἐν ῥομφαίᾳ καὶ ἐν λιμῷ
to kill with sword and with famine

καὶ ἐν θανάτῳ καὶ ὑπὸ τῶν θηρίων
and with death and by the wild beasts

τῆς γῆς. 9 Καὶ ὅτε ἤνοιξεν τὴν πέμπτην
of the earth.   And when he opened the fifth

σφραγίδα, εἶδον ὑποκάτω τοῦ θυσιαστηρίου
seal, I saw underneath the altar

τὰς ψυχὰς τῶν ἐσφαγμένων διὰ τὸν
the souls of the having been on account of
[ones] slain of

λόγον τοῦ θεοῦ καὶ διὰ τὴν μαρτυρίαν
word – of God and on the witness
account of

ἣν εἶχον. 10 καὶ ἔκραξαν φωνῇ μεγάλῃ
which they had.   And they cried ²voice ¹with a
great(loud)

λέγοντες· ἕως πότε, ὁ δεσπότης ὁ ἅγιος
saying: Until when, the Master – holy

καὶ ἀληθινός, οὐ κρίνεις καὶ ἐκδικεῖς
and true, judgest thou not and avengest

τὸ αἷμα ἡμῶν ἐκ τῶν κατοικούντων
the blood of us of the [ones] dwelling

ἐπὶ τῆς γῆς; 11 καὶ ἐδόθη αὐτοῖς ἑκάστῳ
on the earth?   And ²was ³to them ⁴each one
given

στολὴ λευκή, καὶ ἐρρέθη αὐτοῖς ἵνα
²robe ¹a white, and it was said to them in order
that

ἀναπαύσωνται ἔτι χρόνον μικρόν, ἕως
they should rest yet ²time ¹a little, until

πληρωθῶσιν καὶ οἱ σύνδουλοι αὐτῶν καὶ
should be fulfilled also the fellow-slaves of them and

οἱ ἀδελφοὶ αὐτῶν οἱ μέλλοντες ἀποκτέν-
the brothers of them the [ones] being about to be

νεσθαι ὡς καὶ αὐτοί. 12 Καὶ εἶδον
killed as also they.   And I saw

ὅτε ἤνοιξεν τὴν σφραγίδα τὴν ἕκτην,
when he opened the ²seal – ²sixth,

καὶ σεισμὸς μέγας ἐγένετο, καὶ ὁ ἥλιος
and ²earthquake ¹a great occurred, and the sun

ἐγένετο μέλας ὡς σάκκος τρίχινος, καὶ
became black as sackcloth made of hair, and

King James Version

blood. 13And the stars of heaven fell unto the earth, even as a fig tree casteth her untimely figs, when she is shaken of a mighty wind. 14And the heaven departed as a scroll when it is rolled together; and every mountain and island were moved out of their places. 15And the kings of the earth, and the great men, and the rich men, and the chief captains, and the mighty men, and every bond man, and every free man, hid themselves in the dens and in the rocks of the mountains; 16And said to the mountains and rocks, Fall on us, and hide us from the face of him that sitteth on the throne, and from the wrath of the Lamb: 17For the great day of his wrath is come; and who shall be able to stand?

7 And after these things I saw four angels standing on the four corners of the earth, holding the four winds of the earth, that the wind should not blow on the earth, nor on the sea, nor on any tree. 2And I saw another angel ascending from the east, having the seal of the living God: and he cried with a loud voice to the four angels, to whom it was given to hurt the earth and the sea, 3 Saying, Hurt not the earth, neither the sea, nor the trees, till we have sealed the servants of our God in their foreheads. 4And I heard the number of them which were sealed: *and there were* sealed a hundred *and* forty *and* four thousand of all the tribes of the children of Israel. 5 Of the tribe of Juda *were* sealed twelve thousand. Of the tribe of Reuben *were* sealed twelve thousand. Of the tribe of Gad *were* sealed twelve thousand. 6 Of the tribe of Aser *were* sealed twelve thousand. Of the tribe of Nephthalim *were* sealed twelve thousand. Of the tribe of Manasses *were* sealed twelve thousand. 7 Of the tribe of Simeon *were* sealed twelve thousand. Of the tribe of Levi *were* sealed twelve thousand. Of the tribe of Issachar *were* sealed twelve thousand. 8 Of the tribe of Zabulon *were* sealed twelve thousand. Of the tribe of Joseph *were* sealed twelve thousand. Of the tribe of Benjamin *were* sealed twelve thousand. 9After this I beheld, and, lo, a great multitude, which no man could number, of all nations, and kindreds, and people, and tongues, stood before the throne, and before the Lamb, clothed with white robes, and palms in their hands; 10And cried with a loud voice, saying, Salvation to our God which sitteth upon the throne, and unto the Lamb. 11And all the angels stood round about the throne, and *about* the elders and the four beasts, and fell before the throne on their faces, and worshipped God, 12 Saying, Amen: Blessing, and glory, and wisdom, and thanks-

New International Version

moon turned blood-red, 13 and the stars in the sky fell to earth, as late figs drop from a fig tree when shaken by a strong wind. 14 The sky receded like a scroll, rolling up, and every mountain and island was removed from its place.

15 Then the kings of the earth, the princes the generals, the rich, the mighty, and every slave and every free man hid in caves and among the rocks of the mountains. 16 They called to the mountains and the rocks, "Fall on us and hide us from the face of him who sits on the throne and from the wrath of the Lamb! 17 For the great day of their wrath has come, and who can stand?"

144,000 sealed

7 After this I saw four angels standing at the four corners of the earth, holding back the four winds of the earth to prevent any wind from blowing on the land or on the sea or on any tree. 2 Then I saw another angel coming up from the east, having the seal of the living God. He called out in a loud voice to the four angels who had been given power to harm the land and the sea: 3 "Do not harm the land or the sea or the trees until we put a seal on the foreheads of the servants of our God." 4 Then I heard the number of those who were sealed: 144,000 from all the tribes of Israel.

5 From the tribe of Judah 12,000 were sealed,
   from the tribe of Reuben 12,000,
   from the tribe of Gad 12,000,
6 from the tribe of Asher 12,000,
   from the tribe of Naphtali 12,000,
   from the tribe of Manasseh 12,000,
7 from the tribe of Simeon 12,000,
   from the tribe of Levi 12,000,
   from the tribe of Issachar 12,000,
8 from the tribe of Zebulun 12,000,
   from the tribe of Joseph 12,000,
   from the tribe of Benjamin 12,000.

The great multitude in white robes

9 After this I looked and there before me was a great multitude that no one could count, from every nation, tribe, people and language, standing before the throne and in front of the Lamb. They were wearing white robes and were holding palm branches in their hands. 10And they cried out in a loud voice:
   "Salvation belongs to our God,
   who sits on the throne,
   and to the Lamb."
11All the angels were standing around the throne and around the elders and the four living creatures. They fell down on their faces before the throne and worshiped God, 12 saying:
   "Amen!
   Praise and glory
   and wisdom and thanks and honor
   and power and strength

Greek Interlinear

ἡ σελήνη ὅλη ἐγένετο ὡς αἷμα, 13 καὶ
the ²moon ¹whole became as blood, and

οἱ ἀστέρες τοῦ οὐρανοῦ ἔπεσαν εἰς τὴν
the stars – of heaven fell to the

γῆν, ὡς συκῆ βάλλει τοὺς ὀλύνθους
earth, as a fig-tree casts the unripe figs

αὐτῆς ὑπὸ ἀνέμου μεγάλου σειομένη,
of it ²by ⁴wind ³a great(strong) ¹being shaken,

14 καὶ ὁ οὐρανὸς ἀπεχωρίσθη ὡς βιβλίον
and the heaven departed as a scroll

ἑλισσόμενον, καὶ πᾶν ὄρος καὶ νῆσος
being rolled up, and every mountain and island

ἐκ τῶν τόπων αὐτῶν ἐκινήθησαν. 15 καὶ
out of the places of them were moved. And

οἱ βασιλεῖς τῆς γῆς καὶ οἱ μεγιστᾶνες
the kings of the earth and the great men

καὶ οἱ χιλίαρχοι καὶ οἱ πλούσιοι καὶ
and the chiliarchs and the rich men and

οἱ ἰσχυροὶ καὶ πᾶς δοῦλος καὶ ἐλεύθερος
the strong men and every slave and free man

ἔκρυψαν ἑαυτοὺς εἰς τὰ σπήλαια καὶ
hid themselves in the caves and

εἰς τὰς πέτρας τῶν ὀρέων, 16 καὶ
in the rocks of the mountains, and

λέγουσιν τοῖς ὄρεσιν καὶ ταῖς πέτραις·
they say to the mountains and to the rocks:

πέσετε ἐφ’ ἡμᾶς καὶ κρύψατε ἡμᾶς
Fall ye on us and hide us

ἀπὸ προσώπου τοῦ καθημένου ἐπὶ τοῦ
from [the] face of the [one] sitting on the

θρόνου καὶ ἀπὸ τῆς ὀργῆς τοῦ ἀρνίου,
throne and from the wrath of the Lamb,

17 ὅτι ἦλθεν ἡ ἡμέρα ἡ μεγάλη τῆς
because ⁷came ¹the ³day – ²great ⁴of the

ὀργῆς αὐτῶν, καὶ τίς δύναται σταθῆναι;
⁵wrath ⁶of them, and who can to stand ?

Chapter 7

Μετὰ τοῦτο εἶδον τέσσαρας ἀγγέλους
After this I saw four angels

ἑστῶτας ἐπὶ τὰς τέσσαρας γωνίας τῆς
standing on the four corners of the

γῆς, κρατοῦντας τοὺς τέσσαρας ἀνέμους
earth, holding the four winds

τῆς γῆς, ἵνα μὴ πνέῃ ἄνεμος ἐπὶ τῆς
of the earth, in order ²not ³should ¹wind on the
　　　　　　that　　⁴blow

γῆς μήτε ἐπὶ τῆς θαλάσσης μήτε ἐπὶ
earth nor on the sea nor on

πᾶν δένδρον. 2 καὶ εἶδον ἄλλον ἄγγελον
every(any) tree. And I saw another angel

ἀναβαίνοντα ἀπὸ ἀνατολῆς ἡλίου, ἔχοντα
coming up from [the] rising of [the] sun, having

σφραγῖδα θεοῦ ζῶντος, καὶ ἔκραξεν φωνῇ
a seal God of [the] living, and he cried ²voice

μεγάλῃ τοῖς τέσσαρσιν ἀγγέλοις οἷς
¹with a to the four angels to whom
great(loud)

ἐδόθη αὐτοῖς ἀδικῆσαι τὴν γῆν καὶ
it was given to them to harm the earth and

τὴν θάλασσαν, 3 λέγων· μὴ ἀδικήσητε
the sea, saying· Do not harm

τὴν γῆν μήτε τὴν θάλασσαν μήτε τὰ
the earth nor the sea nor the

δένδρα, ἄχρι σφραγίσωμεν τοὺς δούλους
trees, until we may seal the slaves

τοῦ θεοῦ ἡμῶν ἐπὶ τῶν μετώπων αὐτῶν.
of the God of us on the foreheads of them.

4 Καὶ ἤκουσα τὸν ἀριθμὸν τῶν ἐσφραγισ-
And I heard the number of the [ones] having been

μένων, ἑκατὸν τεσσεράκοντα τέσσαρες
sealed, a hundred [and] forty-four

χιλιάδες ἐσφραγισμένοι ἐκ πάσης φυλῆς
thousands having been sealed out of every tribe

υἱῶν Ἰσραήλ· 5 ἐκ φυλῆς Ἰούδα δώδεκα
of sons of Israel: of [the] tribe Juda twelve

χιλιάδες ἐσφραγισμένοι, ἐκ φυλῆς Ῥουβὴν
thousands having been sealed, of [the] tribe Reuben

δώδεκα χιλιάδες, ἐκ φυλῆς Γὰδ δώδεκα
twelve thousands, of [the] tribe Gad twelve

χιλιάδες, 6 ἐκ φυλῆς Ἀσὴρ δώδεκα
thousands, of [the] tribe Aser twelve

χιλιάδες, ἐκ φυλῆς Νεφθαλὶμ δώδεκα
thousands, of [the] tribe Nephthalim twelve

χιλιάδες, ἐκ φυλῆς Μανασσῆ δώδεκα
thousands, of [the] tribe Manasse twelve

χιλιάδες, 7 ἐκ φυλῆς Συμεὼν δώδεκα
thousands, of [the] tribe Symeon twelve

χιλιάδες, ἐκ φυλῆς Λευὶ δώδεκα χιλιάδες,
thousands, of [the] tribe Levi twelve thousands,

ἐκ φυλῆς Ἰσσαχὰρ δώδεκα χιλιάδες,
of [the] tribe Issachar twelve thousands,

8 ἐκ φυλῆς Ζαβουλὼν δώδεκα χιλιάδες,
of [the] tribe Zabulon twelve thousands,

ἐκ φυλῆς Ἰωσὴφ δώδεκα χιλιάδες, ἐκ
of [the] tribe Joseph twelve thousands, of

φυλῆς Βενιαμὶν δώδεκα χιλιάδες ἐσφραγισ-
[the] tribe Benjamin twelve thousands having been

μένοι. 9 Μετὰ ταῦτα εἶδον, καὶ ἰδοὺ ὄχλος
sealed. After these things I saw, and behold[,] ²crowd

πολύς, ὃν ἀριθμῆσαι αὐτὸν οὐδεὶς ἐδύνατο,
¹a much which ²to number it ¹no one ³was able,
(great),

ἐκ παντὸς ἔθνους καὶ φυλῶν καὶ λαῶν
out of every nation and tribes and peoples

καὶ γλωσσῶν, ἑστῶτες ἐνώπιον τοῦ θρόνου
and tongues, standing before the throne

καὶ ἐνώπιον τοῦ ἀρνίου, περιβεβλημένους
and before the Lamb, having been clothed [with]

στολὰς λευκάς, καὶ φοίνικες ἐν ταῖς
²robes ¹white, and palms in the

χερσὶν αὐτῶν· 10 καὶ κράζουσιν φωνῇ
hands of them; and they cry ²voice

μεγάλῃ λέγοντες· ἡ σωτηρία τῷ θεῷ
¹with a great(loud) saying· – Salvation to the God*

ἡμῶν τῷ καθημένῳ ἐπὶ τῷ θρόνῳ καὶ
of us – sitting on the throne and

τῷ ἀρνίῳ. 11 καὶ πάντες οἱ ἄγγελοι
to the Lamb.° And all the angels

εἱστήκεισαν κύκλῳ τοῦ θρόνου καὶ τῶν
stood round the throne and the

πρεσβυτέρων καὶ τῶν τεσσάρων ζῴων,
elders and the four living
　　　　　　　　　　　　　creatures,

καὶ ἔπεσαν ἐνώπιον τοῦ θρόνου ἐπὶ
and fell before the throne on

τὰ πρόσωπα αὐτῶν καὶ προσεκύνησαν
the faces of them and worshipped

τῷ θεῷ, 12 λέγοντες· ἀμήν, ἡ εὐλογία
– God, saying· Amen, – blessing

καὶ ἡ δόξα καὶ ἡ σοφία καὶ ἡ εὐχαριστία
and – glory and – wisdom and – thanks

καὶ ἡ τιμὴ καὶ ἡ δύναμις καὶ ἡ ἰσχὺς
and – honour and – power and – strength

739

King James Version

giving, and honour, and power, and might, *be* unto our God for ever and ever. Amen. 13And one of the elders answered, saying unto me, What are these which are arrayed in white robes? and whence came they? 14And I said unto him, Sir, thou knowest. And he said to me, These are they which came out of great tribulation, and have washed their robes, and made them white in the blood of the Lamb. 15 Therefore are they before the throne of God, and serve him day and night in his temple: and he that sitteth on the throne shall dwell among them. 16 They shall hunger no more, neither thirst any more; neither shall the sun light on them, nor any heat. 17 For the Lamb which is in the midst of the throne shall feed them, and shall lead them unto living fountains of waters: and God shall wipe away all tears from their eyes.

8 And when he had opened the seventh seal, there was silence in heaven about the space of half an hour. 2And I saw the seven angels which stood before God; and to them were given seven trumpets. 3And another angel came and stood at the altar, having a golden censer; and there was given unto him much incense, that he should offer *it* with the prayers of all saints upon the golden altar which was before the throne. 4And the smoke of the incense, *which came* with the prayers of the saints, ascended up before God out of the angel's hand. 5And the angel took the censer, and filled it with fire of the altar, and cast *it* into the earth: and there were voices, and thunderings, and lightnings, and an earthquake. 6And the seven angels which had the seven trumpets prepared themselves to sound. 7 The first angel sounded, and there followed hail and fire mingled with blood, and they were cast upon the earth: and the third part of trees was burnt up, and all green grass was burnt up. 8And the second angel sounded, and as it were a great mountain burning with fire was cast into the sea: and the third part of the sea became blood; 9And the third part of the creatures which were in the sea, and had life, died; and the third part of the ships were destroyed. 10And the third angel sounded, and there fell a great star from heaven, burning as it were a lamp, and it fell upon the third part of the rivers, and upon the fountains of waters; 11And the name of the star is called Wormwood: and the third part of the waters became wormwood; and many men died of the

New International Version

be to our God for ever and ever. Amen!"

13 Then one of the elders asked me, "These in white robes—who are they, and where did they come from?"

14 I answered, "Sir, you know."

And he said, "These are they who have come out of the great tribulation; they have washed their robes and made them white in the blood of the Lamb. 15 Therefore,

they are before the throne of God
  and serve him day and night in his temple;
and he who sits on the throne will spread
  his tent over them.
16 Never again will they hunger;
  never again will they thirst.
The sun will not beat upon them,
  nor any scorching heat.
17 For the Lamb at the center of the throne
  will be their shepherd;
he will lead them to springs of living
  water.
And God will wipe away every tear from
  their eyes."

The seventh seal and the golden censer

8 When he opened the seventh seal, there was silence in heaven for about half an hour.

2 And I saw the seven angels who stand before God, and to them were given seven trumpets.

3 Another angel, who had a golden censer, came and stood at the altar. He was given much incense to offer, with the prayers of all the saints, on the golden altar before the throne. 4 The smoke of the incense, together with the prayers of the saints, went up before God from the angel's hand. 5 Then the angel took the censer, filled it with fire from the altar, and hurled it on the earth; and there came peals of thunder, rumblings, flashes of lightning and an earthquake.

The trumpets

6 Then the seven angels who had the seven trumpets prepared to sound them.

7 The first angel sounded his trumpet, and there came hail and fire mixed with blood, and it was hurled down upon the earth. A third of the earth was burned up, a third of the trees were burned up, and all the green grass was burned up.

8 The second angel sounded his trumpet, and something like a huge mountain, all ablaze, was thrown into the sea. A third of the sea turned into blood, 9 a third of the living creatures in the sea died, and a third of the ships were destroyed.

10 The third angel sounded his trumpet, and a great star, blazing like a torch, fell from the sky on a third of the rivers and on the springs of water—11 the name of the star is Wormwood.*j* A third of the waters turned bitter, and many people died from the waters that had become bitter.

[*j*] That is, Bitterness.

Greek Interlinear

τῷ   θεῷ   ἡμῶν   εἰς   τοὺς   αἰῶνας   τῶν
to the God⁰   of us   unto   the   ages   of the

αἰώνων·   ἀμήν.   13 Καὶ   ἀπεκρίθη   εἰς
ages: Amen.   And   ¹answered   ¹one

ἐκ   τῶν   πρεσβυτέρων   λέγων   μοι·   οὗτοι
¹of   ¹the   ⁶elders   saying   to me: These

οἱ   περιβεβλημένοι   τὰς   στολὰς   τὰς
the   having been clothed   the   ²robes   –
[ones]   [with]

λευκὰς   τίνες   εἰσὶν   καὶ   πόθεν   ἦλθον;
¹white   who   are they   and   whence   came they?

14 καὶ   εἴρηκα   αὐτῷ·   κύριέ   μου,   σὺ
And   I have said   to him: Lord   of me,   thou

οἶδας.   καὶ   εἶπέν   μοι·   οὗτοί   εἰσιν   οἱ
knowest.   And   he told   me: These   are   the

ἐρχόμενοι   ἐκ   τῆς   θλίψεως   τῆς   μεγάλης
[ones] coming out of   the   ²affliction   –   ¹great

καὶ   ἔπλυναν   τὰς   στολὰς   αὐτῶν   καὶ
and   washed   the   robes   of them   and

ἐλεύκαναν   αὐτὰς   ἐν   τῷ   αἵματι   τοῦ
whitened   them   in   the   blood   of the

ἀρνίου.   15 διὰ   τοῦτό   εἰσιν   ἐνώπιον   τοῦ
Lamb.   Therefore   are they   before   the

θρόνου   τοῦ   θεοῦ,   καὶ   λατρεύουσιν   αὐτῷ
throne   –   of God,   and   serve   him

ἡμέρας   καὶ   νυκτὸς   ἐν   τῷ   ναῷ   αὐτοῦ,
day   and   night   in   the   shrine   of him,

καὶ   ὁ   καθήμενος   ἐπὶ   τοῦ   θρόνου   σκηνώσει
and the [one]   sitting   on   the   throne   will spread
[his] tent

ἐπ’   αὐτούς.   16 οὐ   πεινάσουσιν   ἔτι   οὐδὲ
over   them.   They will not hunger   longer   nor

διψήσουσιν   ἔτι,   οὐδὲ   μὴ   πέσῃ   ἐπ’   αὐτοὺς
will they thirst   longer,   neither   not   fall   on   them

ὁ   ἥλιος   οὐδὲ   πᾶν   καῦμα,   17 ὅτι   τὸ
the   sun   nor   every(any)   heat,   because   the

ἀρνίον   τὸ   ἀνὰ   μέσον   τοῦ   θρόνου   ποιμανεῖ
Lamb   –   in the midst   of the   throne   will shepherd

αὐτοὺς   καὶ   ὁδηγήσει   αὐτοὺς   ἐπὶ   ζωῆς
them   and   will lead   them   upon   ²of life

πηγὰς   ὑδάτων·   καὶ   ἐξαλείψει   ὁ   θεὸς
¹fountains   ²of waters;   and   ²will wipe off   –   ¹God

πᾶν   δάκρυον   ἐκ   τῶν   ὀφθαλμῶν   αὐτῶν.
every   tear   out of   the   eyes   of them.

Chapter 8

Καὶ   ὅταν   ἤνοιξεν   τὴν   σφραγῖδα   τὴν
And   whenever   he opened   the   ²seal   –

ἑβδόμην,   ἐγένετο   σιγὴ   ἐν   τῷ   οὐρανῷ
¹seventh,   occurred   a silence   in   –   heaven

ὡς   ἡμίωρον.   2 Καὶ   εἶδον   τοὺς   ἑπτὰ
about a half-hour.   And   I saw   the   seven

ἀγγέλους   οἳ   ἐνώπιον   τοῦ   θεοῦ   ἑστήκασιν,
angels   who   before   –   God   stood,

καὶ   ἐδόθησαν   αὐτοῖς   ἑπτὰ   σάλπιγγες.
and   there were given   to them   seven   trumpets.

3 Καὶ   ἄλλος   ἄγγελος   ἦλθεν   καὶ   ἐστάθη
And   another   angel   came   and   stood

ἐπὶ   τοῦ   θυσιαστηρίου   ἔχων   λιβανωτὸν
on   the   altar   having   ²censer

χρυσοῦν,   καὶ   ἐδόθη   αὐτῷ   θυμιάματα   πολλά,
¹a golden,   and   there was ·to him   incenses   many
(much),

ἵνα   δώσει   ταῖς   προσευχαῖς   τῶν   ἁγίων
in order he will   with the   prayers   of ¹the   ²saints
that   give [it]

πάντων   ἐπὶ   τὸ   θυσιαστήριον   τὸ   χρυσοῦν
²all   on   the   ²altar   –   ¹golden

τὸ   ἐνώπιον   τοῦ   θρόνου.   4 καὶ   ἀνέβη
–   before   the   throne.   And   went up

ὁ   καπνὸς   τῶν   θυμιαμάτων   ταῖς   προσευχαῖς
the   smoke   of the   incenses   with the   prayers

τῶν   ἁγίων   ἐκ   χειρὸς   τοῦ   ἀγγέλου   ἐνώπιον
of the   saints   out of [the] hand of   the   angel   before

τοῦ   θεοῦ.   5 καὶ   εἴληφεν   ὁ   ἄγγελος
–   God.   And   ²has taken   ¹the   ²angel

τὸν   λιβανωτόν,   καὶ   ἐγέμισεν   αὐτὸν   ἐκ
the   censer,   and   filled   it   from

τοῦ   πυρὸς   τοῦ   θυσιαστηρίου   καὶ   ἔβαλεν
the   fire   of the   altar   and   cast

εἰς   τὴν   γῆν·   καὶ   ἐγένοντο   βρονταὶ   καὶ
into   the   earth;   and there occurred   thunders   and

φωναὶ   καὶ   ἀστραπαὶ   καὶ   σεισμός.
sounds   and   lightnings   and   an earthquake.

6 Καὶ   οἱ   ἑπτὰ   ἄγγελοι   οἱ   ἔχοντες
And   the   seven   angels   –   having

τὰς   ἑπτὰ   σάλπιγγας   ἡτοίμασαν   αὐτοὺς
the   seven   trumpets   prepared   themselves

ἵνα   σαλπίσωσιν.   7 Καὶ   ὁ   πρῶτος
in order   they might   And   the   first
that   trumpet.

ἐσάλπισεν·   καὶ   ἐγένετο   χάλαζα   καὶ   πῦρ
trumpeted;   and   there occurred   hail   and   fire

μεμιγμένα   ἐν   αἵματι   καὶ   ἐβλήθη   εἰς
having been   in   blood   and   it Was cast   to
mixed   (with)

τὴν   γῆν·   καὶ   τὸ   τρίτον   τῆς   γῆς
the   earth;   and   the   third [part]   of the   earth

κατεκάη,   καὶ   τὸ   τρίτον   τῶν   δένδρων
was burnt   and   the   third [part]   of the   trees
down(up),

κατεκάη,   καὶ   πᾶς   χόρτος   χλωρὸς   κατεκάη.
was burnt   and   all   ²grass   ¹green   was burnt
down(up),   down(up).

8 Καὶ   ὁ   δεύτερος   ἄγγελος   ἐσάλπισεν·
And   the   second   angel   trumpeted;

καὶ   ὡς   ὄρος   μέγα   πυρὶ   καιόμενον   ἐβλήθη
and   as   ²mountain   ¹a great   ⁴with fire   ³burning   was cast

εἰς   τὴν   θάλασσαν·   καὶ   ἐγένετο   τὸ   τρίτον
into   the   sea;   and   ²became   ¹the   ³third
[part]

τῆς   θαλάσσης   αἷμα,   9 καὶ   ἀπέθανεν   τὸ
²of the   ⁴sea   ⁵blood,   and   ¹⁰died   ¹the

τρίτον   τῶν   κτισμάτων   τῶν   ἐν   τῇ   θαλάσσῃ,
²third   ³of the   ⁴creatures   –   ⁵in   ⁶the   ⁷sea,
[part]

τὰ   ἔχοντα   ψυχάς,   καὶ   τὸ   τρίτον   τῶν
–   ⁹having   ⁸souls,   and   the   third [part]   of the

πλοίων   διεφθάρησαν.   10 Καὶ   ὁ   τρίτος
ships   were destroyed.   And   the   third

ἄγγελος   ἐσάλπισεν·   καὶ   ἔπεσεν   ἐκ   τοῦ
angel   trumpeted;   and   fell   out of   –

οὐρανοῦ   ἀστὴρ   μέγας   καιόμενος   ὡς
heaven   star   a great   burning   as

λαμπάς,   καὶ   ἔπεσεν   ἐπὶ   τὸ   τρίτον   τῶν
a lamp,   and   it fell   onto   the   third [part] of the

ποταμῶν   καὶ   ἐπὶ   τὰς   πηγὰς   τῶν   ὑδάτων.
rivers   and   onto   the   fountains   of the   waters.

11 καὶ   τὸ   ὄνομα   τοῦ   ἀστέρος   λέγεται
And   the   name   of the   star   is said(called)

ὁ   "Ἀψινθος.   καὶ   ἐγένετο   τὸ   τρίτον   τῶν
–   Wormwood.   And   ²became   ¹the   ³third   ³of
[part]

ὑδάτων   εἰς   ἄψινθον,   καὶ   πολλοὶ   τῶν
⁴waters   into   wormwood,   and   many   of the

ἀνθρώπων   ἀπέθανον   ἐκ   τῶν   ὑδάτων   ὅτι
men   died   from   the   waters   because

King James Version

New International Version

waters, because they were made bitter. 12And the fourth angel sounded, and the third part of the sun was smitten, and the third part of the moon, and the third part of the stars; so as the third part of them was darkened, and the day shone not for a third part of it, and the night likewise. 13And I beheld, and heard an angel flying through the midst of heaven, saying with a loud voice, Woe, woe, woe, to the inhabiters of the earth by reason of the other voices of the trumpet of the three angels, which are yet to sound!

12 The fourth angel sounded his trumpet, and a third of the sun was struck, a third of the moon, and a third of the stars, so that a third of them turned dark. A third of the day was without light, and also a third of the night. 13 As I watched, I heard an eagle that was flying in midair call out in a loud voice: "Woe! Woe! Woe to the inhabitants of the earth, because of the trumpet blasts about to be sounded by the other three angels!"

9 And the fifth angel sounded, and I saw a star fall from heaven unto the earth: and to him was given the key of the bottomless pit. 2And he opened the bottomless pit; and there arose a smoke out of the pit, as the smoke of a great furnace; and the sun and the air were darkened by reason of the smoke of the pit. 3And there came out of the smoke locusts upon the earth: and unto them was given power, as the scorpions of the earth have power. 4And it was commanded them that they should not hurt the grass of the earth, neither any green thing, neither any tree; but only those men which have not the seal of God in their foreheads. 5And to them it was given that they should not kill them, but that they should be tormented five months: and their torment *was* as the torment of a scorpion, when he striketh a man. 6And in those days shall men seek death, and shall not find it; and shall desire to die, and death shall flee from them. 7And the shapes of the locusts *were* like unto horses prepared unto battle; and on their heads *were* as it were crowns like gold, and their faces *were* as the faces of men. 8And they had hair as the hair of women, and their teeth were as *the teeth* of lions. 9And they had breastplates, as it were breastplates of iron; and the sound of their wings *was* as the sound of chariots of many horses running to battle. 10And they had tails like unto scorpions, and there were stings in their tails: and their power *was* to hurt men five months. 11And they had a king over them, *which is* the angel of the bottomless pit, whose name in the Hebrew tongue *is* Abaddon, but in the Greek tongue hath *his* name Apollyon. 12 One woe is past; *and,* behold, there come two woes more hereafter. 13And the sixth angel sounded, and I heard a voice from the four horns of the golden altar which is before God, 14 Saying to the sixth angel which had the trumpet, Loose the four angels which are bound in the great river Euphrates. 15And the four

9 The fifth angel sounded his trumpet, and I saw a star that had fallen from the sky to the earth. The star was given the key to the shaft of the Abyss. 2 When he opened the Abyss, smoke rose from it like the smoke from a gigantic furnace. The sun and sky were darkened by the smoke from the Abyss. 3And out of the smoke locusts came down upon the earth and were given power like that of scorpions of the earth. 4 They were told not to harm the grass of the earth or any plant or tree, but only those people who did not have the seal of God on their foreheads. 5 They were not given power to kill them, but only to torture them for five months. And the agony they suffered was like that of the sting of a scorpion when it strikes a man. 6 During those days men will seek death, but will not find it; they will long to die, but death will elude them.

7 The locusts looked like horses prepared for battle. On their heads they wore something like crowns of gold, and their faces resembled human faces. 8 Their hair was like women's hair, and their teeth were like lions' teeth. 9 They had breastplates like breastplates of iron, and the sound of their wings was like the thundering of many horses and chariots rushing into battle. 10 They had tails and stings like scorpions, and in their tails they had power to torment people for five months. 11 They had as king over them the angel of the Abyss, whose name in Hebrew is Abaddon[k] and in Greek, Apollyon.[k] 12 The first woe is past; two other woes are yet to come.

13 The sixth angel blew his trumpet, and I heard a voice coming from the horns[l] of the golden altar that is before God. 14 It said to the sixth angel who had the trumpet, "Release the four angels who are bound at the great river Euphrates." 15And the four angels who had been

[k] That is, *Destroyer.* [l] That is, projections.

Greek Interlinear

ἐπικράνθησαν. 12 Καὶ ὁ τέταρτος ἄγγελος
they were made bitter.　And the　fourth　angel

ἐσάλπισεν·　καὶ　ἐπλήγη　τὸ　τρίτον　τοῦ
trumpeted;　and　⁴was struck　¹the　²third [part]　³of the

ἡλίου　καὶ　τὸ　τρίτον　τῆς　σελήνης　καὶ
⁴sun　and　the　third [part] of the　moon　and

τὸ　τρίτον　τῶν　ἀστέρων,　ἵνα　σκοτισθῇ
the　third　of the　stars,　in order　⁴might be
[part]　　　　　　　　that　darkened

τὸ　τρίτον　αὐτῶν　καὶ　ἡ　ἡμέρα　μὴ　φάνῃ
¹the　²third [part]　³of them　and　the　day　might not appear

τὸ　τρίτον　αὐτῆς,　καὶ　ἡ　νὺξ　ὁμοίως.
the　third [part]　of it,　and　the　night　likewise.

13 Καὶ　εἶδον,　καὶ　ἤκουσα　ἑνὸς　ἀετοῦ
And　I saw,　and　I heard　one　eagle

πετομένου　ἐν　μεσουρανήματι　λέγοντος　φωνῇ
flying　in　mid-heaven　saying　⁵voice

μεγάλῃ·　οὐαὶ　οὐαὶ　οὐαὶ　τοὺς　κατοικοῦν-
¹with a　Woe[,]　woe[,]　woe　to the [ones]　dwell-
great(loud):

τας　ἐπὶ　τῆς　γῆς　ἐκ　τῶν　λοιπῶν　φωνῶν
ing　on　the　earth from　the　remaining　voices

τῆς　σάλπιγγος　τῶν　τριῶν　ἀγγέλων　τῶν
of the　trumpet　of the　three　angels　–

μελλόντων　σαλπίζειν.
being about　to trumpet.

Chapter 9

Καὶ　ὁ　πέμπτος　ἄγγελος　ἐσάλπισεν·
And　the　fifth　angel　trumpeted;

καὶ　εἶδον　ἀστέρα　ἐκ　τοῦ　οὐρανοῦ　πεπτω-
and　I saw　a star　out of　–　heaven　having

κότα　εἰς　τὴν　γῆν,　καὶ　ἐδόθη　αὐτῷ
fallen　onto　the　earth,　and　was given　to it

ἡ　κλεὶς　τοῦ　φρέατος　τῆς　ἀβύσσου.　2 καὶ
the　key　of the　shaft　of the　abyss.　And

ἤνοιξεν　τὸ　φρέαρ　τῆς　ἀβύσσου·　καὶ
he opened　the　shaft　of the　abyss;　and

ἀνέβη　καπνὸς　ἐκ　τοῦ　φρέατος　ὡς
went up　a smoke　out of　the　shaft　as

καπνὸς　καμίνου　μεγάλης,　καὶ　ἐσκοτώθη
smoke　⁴furnace　¹of a great,　and　³was darkened

ὁ　ἥλιος　καὶ　ὁ　ἀὴρ　ἐκ　τοῦ　καπνοῦ
¹the　²sun　²and　²the　air　by　the　smoke

τοῦ　φρέατος.　3 καὶ　ἐκ　τοῦ　καπνοῦ
of the　shaft.　And out of　the　smoke

ἐξῆλθον　ἀκρίδες　εἰς　τὴν　γῆν,　καὶ　ἐδόθη
came forth　locusts　to　the　earth,　and　²was given

αὐτοῖς　ἐξουσία　ὡς　ἔχουσιν　ἐξουσίαν　οἱ
²to them　¹authority　as　⁵have　⁴authority　¹the

σκορπίοι　τῆς　γῆς.　4 καὶ　ἐρρέθη　αὐτοῖς
²scorpions　³of the　⁴earth.　And it was said　to them

ἵνα　μὴ　ἀδικήσουσιν　τὸν　χόρτον　τῆς
in order　they shall not harm　the　grass　of the
that

γῆς　οὐδὲ　πᾶν　χλωρὸν　οὐδὲ　πᾶν　δένδρον,
earth　nor　every　greenstuff　nor　every　tree,
(any)　　　　(any)

εἰ　μὴ　τοὺς　ἀνθρώπους　οἵτινες　οὐκ　ἔχουσιν
except　the　men　who　have not

τὴν　σφραγῖδα　τοῦ　θεοῦ　ἐπὶ　τῶν　μετώπων.
the　seal　– of God　on　the(ir)　foreheads.

5 καὶ　ἐδόθη　αὐτοῖς　ἵνα　μὴ　ἀποκτείνωσιν
And　it was　to them　in order　they should not kill
given　　　　that

αὐτούς,　ἀλλ'　ἵνα　βασανισθήσονται　μῆνας
them,　but　in order　they shall be tormented　²months
that

πέντε·　καὶ　ὁ　βασανισμὸς　αὐτῶν　ὡς
¹five;　and　the　torment　of them　[is] as

βασανισμὸς　σκορπίου,　ὅταν　παίσῃ　ἄνθρωπον.
[the] torment　of a scorpion,　whenever it stings　a man.

6 καὶ　ἐν　ταῖς　ἡμέραις　ἐκείναις　ζητήσουσιν
And in　those days　²will seek

οἱ　ἄνθρωποι　τὸν　θάνατον　καὶ　οὐ　μὴ
¹men　–　death　and　by no means

εὑρήσουσιν　αὐτόν,　καὶ　ἐπιθυμήσουσιν
will they find　it,　and　they will long

ἀποθανεῖν　καὶ　φεύγει　ὁ　θάνατος　ἀπ'
to die　and　²flees　–　¹death　from

αὐτῶν.　7 καὶ　τὰ　ὁμοιώματα　τῶν　ἀκρίδων
them.　And the　likenesses　of the　locusts

ὅμοιοι　ἵπποις　ἡτοιμασμέ·οις　εἰς　πόλεμον,
like　to horses　having been prepared　for　war,

καὶ　ἐπὶ　τὰς　κεφαλὰς　αὐτῶν　ὡς　στέφανοι
and on　the　heads　of them　as　crowns

ὅμοιοι　χρυσῷ,　καὶ　τὰ　πρόσωπα　αὐτῶν
like　to gold,　and　the　faces　of them

ὡς　πρόσωπα　ἀνθρώπων,　8 καὶ　εἶχον
as　faces　of men,　and　they had

τρίχας　ὡς　τρίχας　γυναικῶν,　καὶ　οἱ
hairs　as　hairs　of women,　and　the

ὀδόντες　αὐτῶν · ὡς　λεόντων　ἦσαν,　9 καὶ
teeth　of them · ²as　¹of lions　·were,　and

εἶχον　θώρακας　ὡς　θώρακας　σιδηροῦς,
they had　breastplates　as　²breastplates　¹iron.

καὶ　ἡ　φωνὴ　τῶν　πτερύγων　αὐτῶν　ὡς
and　the　sound　of the　wings　of them　as

φωνὴ · ἁρμάτων　ἵππων　πολλῶν　τρεχόντων
sound　²chariots　³of horses　¹of many　running

εἰς　πόλεμον.　10 καὶ　ἔχουσιν　οὐρὰς　ὁμοίας
to　war.　And they have　tails　like

σκορπίοις　καὶ　κέντρα,　καὶ　ἐν　ταῖς　οὐραῖς
to scorpions　and　stings,　and　³with　¹the　²tails

αὐτῶν　ἡ　ἐξουσία　αὐτῶν　ἀδικῆσαι　τοὺς
³of them　¹the　²authority　³of them　¹[is] to harm　²the

ἀνθρώπους　μῆνας　πέντε.　11 ἔχουσιν　ἐπ'
¹men　¹¹months　¹⁰five.　They have　over

αὐτῶν　βασιλέα　τὸν　ἄγγελον　τῆς　ἀβύσσου,
them　a king　the　angel　– the　abyss,

ὄνομα　αὐτῷ·　Ἑβραϊστὶ　Ἀβαδδών,　καὶ
name　to him·　in Hebrew　Abaddon,　and

ἐν　τῇ　Ἑλληνικῇ　ὄνομα　ἔχει　Ἀπολλύων.
in the　Greek　²[the] name ¹he has　Apollyon.

12 Ἡ　οὐαὶ　ἡ　μία　ἀπῆλθεν·　ἰδοὺ　ἔρχεται
The　²woe　– ¹one(first) passed away;　behold　⁴comes

ἔτι　δύο　οὐαὶ　μετὰ　ταῦτα.
¹yet　²two　³woes　after these things.

13 Καὶ　ὁ　ἕκτος　ἄγγελος　ἐσάλπισεν·
And　the　sixth　angel　trumpeted;

καὶ　ἤκουσα　φωνὴν　μίαν　ἐκ　τῶν　τεσσάρων
and　I heard　¹voice　one out of　the　four

κεράτων　τοῦ　θυσιαστηρίου　τοῦ　χρυσοῦ
horns　of the　²altar　¹golden

τοῦ　ἐνώπιον　τοῦ　θεοῦ,　14 λέγοντα　τῷ
–　before　– God,　saying　to the

ἕκτῳ　ἀγγέλῳ,　ὁ　ἔχων　τὴν　σάλπιγγα·
sixth　angel,　–　having　the　trumpet:

λῦσον　τοὺς　τέσσαρας　ἀγγέλους　τοὺς
Loose　the　four　angels　the

δεδεμένους　ἐπὶ　τῷ　ποταμῷ　τῷ　μεγάλῳ
having been bound at　the　²river　–　¹great

Εὐφράτῃ.　15 καὶ　ἐλύθησαν　οἱ　τέσσαρες
Euphrates.　And　were loosed　the　four

King James Version

angels were loosed, which were prepared for an hour, and a day, and a month, and a year, for to slay the third part of men. 16And the number of the army of the horsemen *were* two hundred thousand thousand: and I heard the number of them. 17And thus I saw the horses in the vision, and them that sat on them, having breastplates of fire, and of jacinth, and brimstone: and the heads of the horses *were* as the heads of lions; and out of their mouths issued fire and smoke and brimstone. 18 By these three was the third part of men killed, by the fire, and by the smoke, and by the brimstone, which issued out of their mouths. 19 For their power is in their mouth, and in their tails: for their tails *were* like unto serpents, and had heads, and with them they do hurt. 20And the rest of the men which were not killed by these plagues yet repented not of the works of their hands, that they should not worship devils, and idols of gold, and silver, and brass, and stone, and of wood; which neither can see, nor hear, nor walk: 21 Neither repented they of their murders, nor of their sorceries, nor of their fornication, nor of their thefts.

New International Version

kept ready for this very hour and day and month and year were released to kill a third of mankind. 16 The number of the mounted troops was two hundred million. I heard their number.

17 The horses and riders I saw in my vision looked like this: Their breastplates were fiery red, dark blue, and yellow as sulfur. The heads of the horses resembled the heads of lions, and out of their mouths came fire, smoke and sulfur. 18A third of mankind was killed by the three plagues of fire, smoke and sulfur that came out of their mouths. 19 The power of the horses was in their mouths and in their tails; for their tails were like snakes, having heads with which they inflict injury.

20 The rest of mankind that were not killed by these plagues still did not repent of the work of their hands; they did not stop worshiping demons, and idols of gold, silver, bronze, stone and wood—idols that cannot see or hear or walk. 21 Nor did they repent of their murders, their magic arts, their sexual immorality or their thefts.

The angel and the little scroll

10 And I saw another mighty angel come down from heaven, clothed with a cloud: and a rainbow *was* upon his head, and his face *was* as it were the sun, and his feet as pillars of fire: 2And he had in his hand a little book open: and he set his right foot upon the sea, and *his* left *foot* on the earth, 3And cried with a loud voice, as *when* a lion roareth: and when he had cried, seven thunders uttered their voices. 4And when the seven thunders had uttered their voices, I was about to write: and I heard a voice from heaven saying unto me, Seal up those things which the seven thunders uttered, and write them not. 5And the angel which I saw stand upon the sea and upon the earth lifted up his hand to heaven, 6And sware by him that liveth for ever and ever, who created heaven, and the things that therein are, and the earth, and the things that therein are, and the sea, and the things which are therein, that there should be time no longer: 7 But in the days of the voice of the seventh angel, when he shall begin to sound, the mystery of God should be finished, as he hath declared to his servants the prophets. 8And the voice which I heard from heaven spake unto me again, and said, Go *and* take the

10 Then I saw another mighty angel coming down from heaven. He was robed in a cloud, with a rainbow above his head; his face was like the sun, and his legs were like fiery pillars. 2 He was holding a little scroll, which lay open in his hand. He planted his right foot on the sea and his left foot on the land, 3 and he gave a loud shout like the roar of a lion. When he shouted, the voices of the seven thunders spoke. 4And when the seven thunders spoke, I was about to write; but I heard a voice from heaven say, "Seal up what the seven thunders have said and do not write it down."

5 Then the angel I had seen standing on the sea and on the land raised his right hand to heaven. 6And he swore by him who lives for ever and ever, who created the heavens and all that is in them, the earth and all that is in it, and the sea and all that is in it, and said, "There will be no more delay! 7 But in the days when the seventh angel is about to sound his trumpet, the mystery of God will be accomplished, just as he announced to his servants the prophets."

8 Then the voice that I had heard from heaven spoke to me once more: "Go, take the

Greek Interlinear

ἄγγελοι οἱ ἡτοιμασμένοι εἰς τὴν ὥραν
angels   - *having been* prepared for the hour

καὶ ἡμέραν καὶ μῆνα καὶ ἐνιαυτόν,
and day and month and year,

ἵνα ἀποκτείνωσιν τὸ τρίτον τῶν ἀνθρώπων.
in or- they should kill the third - of men.
der that [part]

16 καὶ ὁ ἀριθμὸς τῶν στρατευμάτων τοῦ
And the number of the bodies of soldiers of the

ἱππικοῦ δισμυριάδες μυριάδων· ἤκουσα τὸν
cavalry [was] two myriads of myriads; I heard the

ἀριθμὸν αὐτῶν. 17 καὶ οὕτως εἶδον
number of them. And thus I saw

τοὺς ἵππους ἐν τῇ ὁράσει καὶ τοὺς
the horses in the vision and the

καθημένους ἐπ' αὐτῶν, ἔχοντας θώρακας
[ones] sitting on them, having breastplates

πυρίνους καὶ ὑακινθίνους καὶ θειώδεις·
fire-coloured and dusky red and sulphurous;

καὶ αἱ κεφαλαὶ τῶν ἵππων ὡς κεφαλαὶ
and the heads of the horses as heads

λεόντων, καὶ ἐκ τῶν στομάτων αὐτῶν
of lions, and out of the mouths of them

ἐκπορεύεται πῦρ καὶ καπνὸς καὶ θεῖον.
proceeds fire and smoke and sulphur.

18 ἀπὸ τῶν τριῶν πληγῶν τούτων ἀπεκτάν-
From the ³three ²plagues ¹these were

θησαν τὸ τρίτον τῶν ἀνθρώπων, ἐκ
killed the third [part] - of men. by

τοῦ πυρὸς καὶ τοῦ καπνοῦ καὶ τοῦ
the fire and the smoke and the the

θείου τοῦ ἐκπορευομένου ἐκ τῶν στομάτων
sulphur - proceeding out of the mouths

αὐτῶν. 19 ἡ γὰρ ἐξουσία τῶν ἵππων
of them. For the authority of the horses

ἐν τῷ στόματι αὐτῶν ἐστιν καὶ ἐν
¹in ²the ⁴mouth ⁵of them ³is and in

ταῖς οὐραῖς αὐτῶν· αἱ γὰρ οὐραὶ αὐτῶν
the tails of them; for the tails of them

ὅμοιαι ὄφεσιν, ἔχουσαι κεφαλάς, καὶ ἐν
[are] like *to* serpents, having heads, and with

αὐταῖς ἀδικοῦσιν. 20 καὶ οἱ λοιποὶ τῶν
them they do harm. And the rest -

ἀνθρώπων, οἱ οὐκ ἀπεκτάνθησαν ἐν ταῖς
of men, who were not killed by -

πληγαῖς ταύταις, οὐδὲ μετενόησαν ἐκ
plagues these, not even repented of

τῶν ἔργων τῶν χειρῶν αὐτῶν, ἵνα μὴ
the works of the hands of them, in order not
that

προσκυνήσουσιν τὰ δαιμόνια καὶ τὰ εἴδωλα
they will worship - demons and - idols

τὰ χρυσᾶ καὶ τὰ ἀργυρᾶ καὶ τὰ χαλκᾶ
- golden and - silver and - bronze

καὶ τὰ λίθινα καὶ τὰ ξύλινα, ἃ οὔτε
and - stone and - wooden, which ³neither

βλέπειν δύνανται οὔτε ἀκούειν οὔτε
²to see ¹can nor *to* hear nor

περιπατεῖν, 21 καὶ οὐ μετενόησαν ἐκ τῶν
to walk, and they repented not of the

φόνων αὐτῶν οὔτε ἐκ τῶν φαρμακειῶν
murders of them nor of the sorceries

αὐτῶν οὔτε ἐκ τῆς πορνείας αὐτῶν
of them nor of the fornication of them

οὔτε ἐκ τῶν κλεμμάτων αὐτῶν.
nor of the thefts of them.

Chapter 10

1. Καὶ εἶδον ἄλλον ἄγγελον ἰσχυρὸν
And I saw another ²angel ¹strong

καταβαίνοντα ἐκ τοῦ οὐρανοῦ, περιβεβλημέ-
coming down out of - heaven, *having been* clothed

νον νεφέλην, καὶ ἡ ἶρις ἐπὶ τὴν κεφαλὴν
[with] a cloud, and the rainbow on the head

αὐτοῦ, καὶ τὸ πρόσωπον αὐτοῦ ὡς ὁ
of him, and the face of him as the

ἥλιος, καὶ οἱ πόδες αὐτοῦ ὡς στῦλοι
sun, and the feet of him as pillars

πυρός, 2 καὶ ἔχων ἐν τῇ χειρὶ αὐτοῦ
of fire, and having in the hand of him

βιβλαρίδιον ἠνεῳγμένον. καὶ ἔθηκεν τὸν
a little scroll *having been* opened. And he placed ¹the

πόδα αὐτοῦ τὸν δεξιὸν ἐπὶ τῆς θαλάσσης,
²foot ⁴of him - ³right on the sea,

τὸν δὲ εὐώνυμον ἐπὶ τῆς γῆς, 3 καὶ
and the left on the land, and

ἔκραξεν φωνῇ μεγάλῃ ὥσπερ λέων μυκᾶται.
cried ²voice ¹with a as a lion roars.
great(loud)

καὶ ὅτε ἔκραξεν, ἐλάλησαν αἱ ἑπτὰ
And when he cried, ⁴spoke(uttered) ¹the ²seven

βρονταὶ τὰς ἑαυτῶν φωνάς. 4 Καὶ ὅτε
³thunders ⁵the ⁶of them*selves* ⁷voices. And when

ἐλάλησαν αἱ ἑπτὰ βρονταί, ἤμελλον
spoke the seven thunders, I was about

γράφειν· καὶ ἤκουσα φωνὴν ἐκ τοῦ
to write; and I heard a voice out of -

οὐρανοῦ λέγουσαν· σφράγισον ἃ ἐλάλησαν
heaven saying: Seal thou [the] ⁴spoke
things which

αἱ ἑπτὰ βρονταί, καὶ μὴ αὐτὰ γράψῃς.
¹the ²seven ³thunders, and ⁵not ⁶them *thou mayest*
⁷write.

5 Καὶ ὁ ἄγγελος, ὃν εἶδον ἑστῶτα
And the angel, whom I saw standing

ἐπὶ τῆς θαλάσσης καὶ ἐπὶ τῆς γῆς,
on the sea and on the land,

ἦρεν τὴν χεῖρα αὐτοῦ τὴν δεξιὰν εἰς
lifted ¹the ²hand ⁴of him - ³right to

τὸν οὐρανόν, 6 καὶ ὤμοσεν ἐν τῷ ζῶντι
- heaven, and swore by the [one] living

εἰς τοὺς αἰῶνας τῶν αἰώνων, ὃς ἔκτισεν
unto the ages of the ages, who created

τὸν οὐρανὸν καὶ τὰ ἐν αὐτῷ καὶ τὴν
the heaven and the things in it and the

γῆν καὶ τὰ ἐν αὐτῇ καὶ τὴν θάλασσαν
earth and the in it and the sea
things

καὶ τὰ ἐν αὐτῇ, ὅτι χρόνος οὐκέτι
and the things in it, that time ²no longer

ἔσται, 7 ἀλλ' ἐν ταῖς ἡμέραις τῆς
¹shall be, but in the days of the

φωνῆς τοῦ ἑβδόμου ἀγγέλου, ὅταν μέλλῃ
voice of the seventh angel, whenever he is about

σαλπίζειν, καὶ ἐτελέσθη τὸ μυστήριον
to trumpet, even was finished the mystery

τοῦ θεοῦ, ὡς εὐηγγέλισεν τοὺς ἑαυτοῦ
- of God, as he preached [to] the ⁸of him*self*

δούλους τοὺς προφήτας. 8 Καὶ ἡ φωνὴ
¹slaves the prophets. And the voice

ἣν ἤκουσα ἐκ τοῦ οὐρανοῦ, πάλιν
which I heard out of - heaven, again

λαλοῦσαν μετ' ἐμοῦ καὶ λέγουσαν· ὕπαγε
speaking with me and saying: Go thou

λάβε τὸ βιβλίον τὸ ἠνεῳγμένον ἐν τῇ
take the scroll - *having been* opened in the

745

King James Version

little book which is open in the hand of the angel which standeth upon the sea and upon the earth. 9And I went unto the angel, and said unto him, Give me the little book. And he said unto me, Take it, and eat it up; and it shall make thy belly bitter, but it shall be in thy mouth sweet as honey. 10And I took the little book out of the angel's hand, and ate it up; and it was in my mouth sweet as honey: and as soon as I had eaten it, my belly was bitter. 11And he said unto me, Thou must prophesy again before many peoples, and nations, and tongues, and kings.

New International Version

scroll that lies open in the hand of the angel who is standing on the sea and on the land." 9 So I went to the angel and asked him to give me the little scroll. He said to me, "Take it and eat it. It will turn your stomach sour, but in your mouth it will be as sweet as honey." 10 I took the little scroll from the angel's hand and ate it. It tasted as sweet as honey in my mouth, but when I had eaten it, my stomach turned sour. 11 Then I was told, "You must prophesy again about many peoples, nations, languages and kings."

The two witnesses

11 And there was given me a reed like unto a rod: and the angel stood, saying, Rise, and measure the temple of God, and the altar, and them that worship therein. 2 But the court which is without the temple leave out, and measure it not; for it is given unto the Gentiles: and the holy city shall they tread under foot forty *and* two months. 3And I will give *power* unto my two witnesses, and they shall prophesy a thousand two hundred *and* threescore days, clothed in sackcloth. 4 These are the two olive trees, and the two candlesticks standing before the God of the earth. 5And if any man will hurt them, fire proceedeth out of their mouth, and devoureth their enemies: and if any man will hurt them, he must in this manner be killed. 6 These have power to shut heaven, that it rain not in the days of their prophecy: and have power over waters to turn them to blood, and to smite the earth with all plagues, as often as they will. 7And when they shall have finished their testimony, the beast that ascendeth out of the bottomless pit shall make war against them, and shall overcome them, and kill them. 8And their dead bodies *shall lie* in the street of the great city, which spiritually is called Sodom and Egypt, where also our Lord was crucified. 9And they of the people and kindreds and tongues and nations shall see their dead bodies three days and a half, and shall not suffer their dead bodies to be put in graves. 10And they that dwell upon the earth shall rejoice over them, and make merry, and shall send gifts one to another; because these two prophets tormented them that dwelt on the earth. 11And after three days and a half the Spirit of life from God entered into them, and they stood upon their feet; and great fear fell upon them which saw them. 12And they heard a great voice from heaven saying unto them, Come up hither. And they ascended up to heaven in a cloud; and their enemies beheld

11 I was given a reed like a measuring rod and was told, "Go and measure the temple of God and the altar, and count the worshipers there. 2 But exclude the outer court; do not measure it, because it has been given to the Gentiles. They will trample on the holy city for 42 months. 3And I will give power to my two witnesses, and they will prophesy for 1,260 days, clothed in sackcloth." 4 These are the two olive trees and the two lampstands that stand before the Lord of the earth. 5 If anyone tries to harm them, fire comes from their mouths and devours their enemies. This is how anyone who wants to harm them must die. 6 These men have power to shut up the sky so that it will not rain during the time they are prophesying; and they have power to turn the waters into blood and to strike the earth with every kind of plague as often as they want.

7 Now when they have finished their testimony, the beast that comes up from the Abyss will attack them, and overpower and kill them. 8 Their bodies will lie in the street of the great city, which is figuratively called Sodom and Egypt, where also their Lord was crucified. 9 For three and a half days men from every people, tribe, language and nation will gaze on their bodies and refuse them burial. 10 The inhabitants of the earth will gloat over them and will celebrate by sending each other gifts, because these two prophets had tormented those who live on the earth.

11 But after the three and a half days a breath of life from God entered them, and they stood on their feet, and terror struck those who saw them. 12 Then they heard a loud voice from heaven saying to them, "Come up here." And they went up to heaven in a cloud, while their enemies looked on.

Greek Interlinear

χειρὶ   τοῦ   ἀγγέλου   τοῦ   ἑστῶτος   ἐπὶ
hand   of the   angel   the   standing   on

τῆς   θαλάσσης   καὶ   ἐπὶ   τῆς   γῆς.   9 καὶ
the   sea   and   on   the   land.   And

ἀπῆλθα   πρὸς   τὸν   ἄγγελον,   λέγων   αὐτῷ
I went away   toward   the   angel,   telling   him

δοῦναί   μοι   τὸ   βιβλαρίδιον.   καὶ   λέγει
to give   me   the   little scroll.   And   he says

μοι·   λάβε   καὶ   κατάφαγε   αὐτό,   καὶ
to me: Take   and   devour   it,   and

πικρανεῖ   σου   τὴν   κοιλίαν,   ἀλλ’   ἐν   τῷ
it will embitter ²of thee ¹the ²stomach, but   in   the

στόματί   σου   ἔσται   γλυκὺ   ὡς   μέλι.
mouth   of thee   it will be   sweet   as   honey.

10 καὶ   ἔλαβον   τὸ   βιβλαρίδιον   ἐκ   τῆς
And   I took   the   little scroll   out of   the

χειρὸς   τοῦ   ἀγγέλου   καὶ   κατέφαγον   αὐτό,
hand   of the   angel   and   devoured   it,

καὶ   ἦν   ἐν   τῷ   στόματί   μου   ὡς   μέλι
and   it was   in   the   mouth   of me   as   ¹honey

γλυκύ·   καὶ   ὅτε   ἔφαγον   αὐτό,   ἐπικράνθη
¹sweet;   and   when   I ate   it,   ⁴was made bitter

ἡ   κοιλία   μου.   11 καὶ   λέγουσίν   μοι·
¹the ²stomach ³of me.   And   they say   to me:

δεῖ   σε   πάλιν   προφητεῦσαι   ἐπὶ   λαοῖς
It behoves thee   again   to prophesy   before   peoples

καὶ   ἔθνεσιν   καὶ   γλώσσαις   καὶ   βασιλεῦσιν
and   nations   and   tongues   and   ¹kings

Chapter 11

πολλοῖς.   11 Καὶ   ἐδόθη   ·μοι   κάλαμος   ὅμοιος
¹many.   And   was given   to me   a reed   like

ῥάβδῳ,   λέγων·   ἔγειρε   καὶ   μέτρησον   τὸν   ναὸν
to a staff.   saying: Rise   and   measure   the   shrine

τοῦ   θεοῦ   καὶ   τὸ   θυσιαστήριον   καὶ   τοὺς
- of God   and   the   altar   and   the

προσκυνοῦντας   ἐν   αὐτῷ.   2 καὶ   τὴν
[ones] worshipping   in   it.   And   the

αὐλὴν   τὴν   ἔξωθεν   τοῦ   ναοῦ   ἔκβαλε
²court   -   ¹outside   of the   shrine   cast out

ἔξωθεν   καὶ   μὴ   αὐτὴν   μετρήσῃς,   ὅτι
outside   and   ²not   ¹it   thou mayest   because
                                    ¹measure.

ἐδόθη   τοῖς   ἔθνεσιν,   καὶ   τὴν   πόλιν   τὴν
it was given   to the   nations,   and   the   ²city   -

ἁγίαν   πατήσουσιν   μῆνας   τεσσεράκοντα
¹holy   they will trample   ²months   ¹forty-

[καὶ]   δύο.   3 καὶ   δώσω   τοῖς   δυσὶν
and   ²two.   And   I will give   to the   two

μάρτυσίν   μου,   καὶ   προφητεύσουσιν   ἡμέρας
witnesses   of me,   and   they will prophesy   ⁴days

χιλίας   διακοσίας   ἑξήκοντα   περιβεβλημένοι
¹a thousand ²two hundred ³[and] ⁴sixty   having been clothed

σάκκους.   4 οὗτοί   εἰσιν   αἱ   δύο   ἐλαῖαι
[in] sackclothes.   These   are   the   two   olive-trees

καὶ   αἱ   δύο   λυχνίαι   αἱ   ἐνώπιον   τοῦ
and   the   two   lampstands   -   ²before   ⁴the

κυρίου   τῆς   γῆς   ἑστῶτες.   5 καὶ   εἴ   τις
⁴Lord   ³of the ²earth   ¹standing.   And   if anyone

αὐτοὺς   θέλει   ἀδικῆσαι,   πῦρ   ἐκπορεύεται·
²them   ¹wishes   ³to harm,   fire   proceeds

ἐκ   τοῦ   στόματος   αὐτῶν   καὶ   κατεσθίει
out of   the   mouth   of them   and   devours

τοὺς   ἐχθροὺς   αὐτῶν·   καὶ   εἴ   τις   θελήσῃ
the   enemies   of them;   and   if anyone should wish

αὐτοὺς   ἀδικῆσαι,   οὕτως   δεῖ   αὐτὸν
²them   ¹to harm,   thus   it behooves   him

ἀποκτανθῆναι.   6 οὗτοι   ἔχουσιν   τὴν   ἐξουσίαν
to be killed.   These   have   the   authority

κλεῖσαι   τὸν   οὐρανόν,   ἵνα   μὴ   ὑετὸς
to shut   -   heaven,   in order that ²not   ¹rain

βρέχῃ   τὰς   ἡμέρας   τῆς   προφητείας   αὐτῶν,
²may   the   days   of the   prophecy   of them,
¹rain(fall)

καὶ   ἐξουσίαν   ἔχουσιν   ἐπὶ   τῶν   ὑδάτων
and   authority   they have   over   the   waters

στρέφειν   αὐτὰ   εἰς   αἷμα   καὶ   πατάξαι
to turn   them   into   blood   and   to strike

τὴν   γῆν   ἐν   πάσῃ   πληγῇ   ὁσάκις   ἐὰν
the   earth   with   every [kind of] plague   as often as

θελήσωσιν.   7 Καὶ   ὅταν   τελέσωσιν   τὴν
they may wish.   And   whenever   they finish   the

μαρτυρίαν   αὐτῶν,   τὸ   θηρίον   τὸ   ἀναβαῖνον
witness   of them,   the   beast   the   coming up

ἐκ   τῆς   ἀβύσσου   ποιήσει   μετ’   αὐτῶν
out of   the   abyss   ¹will make   ²with   ⁴them

πόλεμον   καὶ   νικήσει   αὐτοὺς   καὶ   ἀποκτενεῖ
⁵war   and   will overcome   them   and   will kill

αὐτούς.   8 καὶ   τὸ   πτῶμα   αὐτῶν   ἐπὶ
them.   And   the   corpse   of them   on

τῆς   πλατείας   τῆς   πόλεως   τῆς   μεγάλης,
the   open street   of the   ²city   -   ¹great,

ἥτις   καλεῖται   πνευματικῶς   Σόδομα   καὶ
which   is called   spiritually   Sodom   and

Αἴγυπτος,   ὅπου   καὶ   ὁ   κύριος   αὐτῶν
Egypt,   where   indeed   the   Lord   of them

ἐσταυρώθη.   9 καὶ   βλέπουσιν   ἐκ   τῶν
was crucified.   And   ¹⁰see   ¹[some] of   ²the

λαῶν   καὶ   φυλῶν   καὶ   γλωσσῶν   καὶ
³peoples   ⁴and   ⁵tribes   ⁶and   ⁷tongues   ⁸and

ἐθνῶν   τὸ   πτῶμα   αὐτῶν   ἡμέρας   τρεῖς
⁹nations   the   corpse   of them   ⁴days   ¹three

καὶ   ἥμισυ,   καὶ   τὰ   πτώματα   αὐτῶν
²and   ³a half,   and   ¹the   ²corpses   ¹of them

οὐκ   ἀφίουσιν   τεθῆναι   εἰς   μνῆμα.   10 καὶ
¹they do not allow   to be placed   in   a tomb.   And

οἱ   κατοικοῦντες   ἐπὶ   τῆς   γῆς   χαίρουσιν
the [ones] dwelling   on   the   earth   rejoice

ἐπ’   αὐτοῖς   καὶ   εὐφραίνονται,   καὶ   δῶρα
over   them   and   are glad,   and   ²gifts

πέμψουσιν   ἀλλήλοις,   ὅτι   οὗτοι   οἱ   δύο
¹they will send   to one another, because   these   -   two

προφῆται   ἐβασάνισαν   τοὺς   κατοικοῦντας
prophets   tormented   the [ones]   dwelling

ἐπὶ   τῆς   γῆς.   11 Καὶ   μετὰ   [τὰς]   τρεῖς
on   the   earth.   And   after   the   ¹three

ἡμέρας   καὶ   ἥμισυ   πνεῦμα   ζωῆς   ἐκ   τοῦ
⁴days   and   ³a half   a spirit   of life   out of   -

θεοῦ   εἰσῆλθεν   ἐν   αὐτοῖς,   καὶ   ἔστησαν
God   entered   in[to]   them,   and   they stood

ἐπὶ   τοὺς   πόδας   αὐτῶν,   καὶ   φόβος   μέγας
on   the   feet   of them,   and   ²fear   ¹great

ἐπέπεσεν   ἐπὶ   τοὺς   θεωροῦντας   αὐτούς.
fell on   on   the [ones]   beholding   them.

12 καὶ   ἤκουσαν   φωνῆς   μεγάλης   ἐκ   τοῦ
And   they heard   ²voice   ¹a great(loud) out of   -

οὐρανοῦ   λεγούσης   αὐτοῖς·   ἀνάβατε   ὧδε·
heaven   saying   to them: Come ye up   here:

καὶ   ἀνέβησαν   εἰς   τὸν   οὐρανὸν   ἐν   τῇ
and   they went up   in   the   heaven   in   the

νεφέλῃ,   καὶ   ἐθεώρησαν   αὐτοὺς   οἱ   ἐχθροὶ
cloud,   and   ⁴beheld   ³them   ¹the   ²enemies

747

King James Version

them. 13And the same hour was there a great earthquake, and the tenth part of the city fell, and in the earthquake were slain of men seven thousand: and the remnant were affrighted, and gave glory to the God of heaven. 14 The second woe is past; *and,* behold, the third woe cometh quickly. 15And the seventh angel sounded; and there were great voices in heaven, saying, The kingdoms of this world are become *the kingdoms* of our Lord, and of his Christ; and he shall reign for ever and ever. 16And the four and twenty elders, which sat before God on their seats, fell upon their faces, and worshipped God, 17 Saying, We give thee thanks, O Lord God Almighty, which art, and wast, and art to come; because thou hast taken to thee thy great power, and hast reigned. 18And the nations were angry, and thy wrath is come, and the time of the dead, that they should be judged, and that thou shouldest give reward unto thy servants the prophets, and to the saints, and them that fear thy name, small and great; and shouldest destroy them which destroy the earth. 19And the temple of God was opened in heaven, and there was seen in his temple the ark of his testament: and there were lightnings, and voices, and thunderings, and an earthquake, and great hail.

12 And there appeared a great wonder in heaven; a woman clothed with the sun, and the moon under her feet, and upon her head a crown of twelve stars: 2And she being with child cried, travailing in birth, and pained to be delivered. 3And there appeared another wonder in heaven; and behold a great red dragon, having seven heads and ten horns, and seven crowns upon his heads. 4And his tail drew the third part of the stars of heaven, and did cast them to the earth: and the dragon stood before the woman which was ready to be delivered, for to devour her child as soon as it was born. 5And she brought forth a man child, who was to rule all nations with a rod of iron: and her child was caught up unto God, and *to* his throne. 6And the woman fled into the wilderness, where she hath a place prepared of God, that they should feed her there a thousand two hundred *and* threescore days. 7And there was war in heaven: Michael and his angels fought against the dragon; and the dragon fought and his angels, 8And prevailed not; neither was their place found any more in heaven. 9And the great

New International Version

13 At that very hour there was a severe earthquake and a tenth of the city collapsed. Seven thousand people were killed in the earthquake, and the survivors were terrified and gave glory to the God of heaven.
14 The second woe has passed; the third woe is coming soon.

The seventh trumpet

15 The seventh angel sounded his trumpet, and there were loud voices in heaven, which said:
"The kingdom of the world has become the
    kingdom of our Lord and of his Christ,
    and he will reign for ever and ever."
16And the twenty-four elders, who were seated on their thrones before God, fell on their faces and worshiped God, 17 saying:
"We give thanks to you, Lord God Almighty,
    who is and who was,
because you have taken your great power
    and have begun to reign.
18 The nations were angry;
    and your wrath has come.
The time has come for judging the dead,
    and for rewarding your servants the
        prophets
and your saints and those who reverence
        your name,
    both small and great—
and for destroying those who destroy the
        earth."
19 Then God's temple in heaven was opened, and within his temple was seen the sacred chest of his covenant. And there came flashes of lightning, rumblings, peals of thunder, an earthquake and a great hailstorm.

The woman and the dragon

12 A great and wondrous sign appeared in heaven: a woman clothed with the sun, with the moon under her feet and a crown of twelve stars on her head. 2 She was pregnant and cried out in pain as she was about to give birth. 3 Then another sign appeared in heaven: an enormous red dragon with seven heads and ten horns and seven crowns on his heads. 4 His tail swept a third of the stars out of the sky and flung them to the earth. The dragon stood in front of the woman who was about to give birth, so that he might devour her child the moment it was born. 5 She gave birth to a son, a male child, who will rule all the nations with a rod of iron. And her child was snatched up to God and to his throne. 6 The woman fled into the desert to a place prepared for her by God, where she might be taken care of for 1,260 days.
7 And there was war in heaven. Michael and his angels fought against the dragon, and the dragon and his angels fought back. 8 But he was not strong enough, and they lost their place in heaven. 9 The great dragon was hurled down

Greek Interlinear

αὐτῶν. 13 Καὶ ἐν ἐκείνῃ τῇ ὥρᾳ ἐγένετο
²of them. And in that - hour ²occurred

σεισμὸς μέγας, καὶ τὸ δέκατον τῆς
¹earthquake ¹a great, and the tenth [part] of the

πόλεως ἔπεσεν, καὶ ἀπεκτάνθησαν ἐν τῷ
city fell, and ²were killed ¹in ¹the

σεισμῷ ὀνόματα ἀνθρώπων χιλιάδες ἑπτά,
¹earthquake ²names ³of men ¹thousands ¹seven,

καὶ οἱ λοιποὶ ἔμφοβοι ἐγένοντο καὶ
and the rest ¹terrified ¹became and

ἔδωκαν δόξαν τῷ θεῷ τοῦ οὐρανοῦ.
gave glory to the God - of heaven.

14 Ἡ οὐαὶ ἡ δευτέρα ἀπῆλθεν· ἰδοὺ
The ²woe - ¹second passed away; behold[,]

ἡ οὐαὶ ἡ τρίτη ἔρχεται ταχύ.
the ²woe - ¹third is coming quickly.

15 Καὶ ὁ ἕβδομος ἄγγελος ἐσάλπισεν·
And the seventh angel trumpeted;

καὶ ἐγένοντο φωναὶ μεγάλαι ἐν τῷ
and there were voices great(loud) in -

οὐρανῷ, λέγοντες· ἐγένετο ἡ βασιλεία
heaven, saying: ²became ¹The ¹kingdom

τοῦ κόσμου τοῦ κυρίου ἡμῶν καὶ τοῦ
²of the ²world of the Lord of us and of the

⁴[the kingdom]

χριστοῦ αὐτοῦ, καὶ βασιλεύσει εἰς τοὺς
Christ of him, and he shall reign unto the

αἰῶνας τῶν αἰώνων. 16 Καὶ οἱ εἴκοσι
ages of the ages. And the twenty-

τέσσαρες πρεσβύτεροι, οἱ ἐνώπιον τοῦ
four elders, - ²before the

θεοῦ καθήμενοι ἐπὶ τοὺς θρόνους αὐτῶν,
¹God ¹sitting on the thrones of them,

ἔπεσαν ἐπὶ τὰ πρόσωπα αὐτῶν καὶ
fell on the faces of them and

προσεκύνησαν τῷ θεῷ, 17 λέγοντες·
worshipped - God, saying:

εὐχαριστοῦμέν σοι, κύριε ὁ θεὸς ὁ
We thank thee, [O] Lord - God the

παντοκράτωρ, ὁ ὢν καὶ ὁ ἦν, ὅτι
Almighty, the [one] being and the was, because
=the one who is [one who]

εἴληφας τὴν δύναμίν σου τὴν μεγάλην
thou hast taken ¹the ²power ⁴of thee - ³great

καὶ ἐβασίλευσας· 18 καὶ τὰ ἔθνη ὠργίσ-
and didst reign; and the nations were

θησαν, καὶ ἦλθεν ἡ ὀργή σου καὶ ὁ
wrathful, and ²came ¹the ²wrath ³of thee and the

καιρὸς τῶν νεκρῶν κριθῆναι καὶ δοῦναι
time of the dead to be judged and to give

τὸν μισθὸν τοῖς δούλοις σου τοῖς προφήταις
the reward to the slaves of thee to the prophets

καὶ τοῖς ἁγίοις καὶ τοῖς φοβουμένοις
and to the saints and to the [ones] fearing

τὸ ὄνομά σου, τοῖς μικροῖς καὶ τοῖς
the name of thee, to the small and to the

μεγάλοις, καὶ διαφθεῖραι τοὺς διαφθείροντας
great, and to destroy the [ones] destroying

τὴν γῆν. 19 καὶ ἠνοίγη ὁ ναὸς τοῦ
the earth. And was opened the shrine -

θεοῦ ὁ ἐν τῷ οὐρανῷ, καὶ ὤφθη ἡ
of God - in - heaven, and was seen the

κιβωτὸς τῆς διαθήκης αὐτοῦ ἐν τῷ
ark of the covenant of him in the

ναῷ αὐτοῦ, καὶ ἐγένοντο ἀστραπαὶ καὶ
shrine of him, and occurred lightnings and

φωναὶ καὶ βρονταὶ καὶ σεισμὸς καὶ
voices and thunders and an earthquake and

χάλαζα μεγάλη.
²hail ¹a great.

Chapter 12

Καὶ σημεῖον μέγα ὤφθη ἐν τῷ
And ¹sign ¹a great was seen in -

οὐρανῷ, γυνὴ περιβεβλημένη τὸν ἥλιον,
heaven, a woman having been clothed [with] the sun,

καὶ ἡ σελήνη ὑποκάτω τῶν ποδῶν αὐτῆς,
and the moon underneath the feet of her,

καὶ ἐπὶ τῆς κεφαλῆς αὐτῆς στέφανος
and on the head of her a crown

ἀστέρων δώδεκα, 2 καὶ ἐν γαστρὶ ἔχουσα,
²stars ¹of twelve, and in womb having,
= being pregnant,

καὶ κράζει ὠδίνουσα καὶ βασανιζομένη
and she cries suffering birth-pains and being distressed

τεκεῖν. 3 καὶ ὤφθη ἄλλο σημεῖον
to bear. And was seen another sign

ἐν τῷ οὐρανῷ, καὶ ἰδοὺ δράκων μέγας
in - heaven, and behold[,] ²dragon ¹a great

πυρρός, ἔχων κεφαλὰς ἑπτὰ καὶ κέρατα
³red, having ²heads ¹seven and ²horns

δέκα καὶ ἐπὶ τὰς κεφαλὰς αὐτοῦ ἑπτὰ
¹ten and on the heads of him seven

διαδήματα, 4 καὶ ἡ οὐρὰ αὐτοῦ σύρει
diadems, and the tail of him draws

τὸ τρίτον τῶν ἀστέρων τοῦ οὐρανοῦ,
the third [part] of the stars - of heaven.

καὶ ἔβαλεν αὐτοὺς εἰς τὴν γῆν. Καὶ
and cast them to the earth. And

ὁ δράκων ἔστηκεν ἐνώπιον τῆς γυναικὸς
the dragon stood before the woman

τῆς μελλούσης τεκεῖν, ἵνα ὅταν τέκῃ
- being about to bear, in order whenever she
that bears

τὸ τέκνον αὐτῆς καταφάγῃ. 5 καὶ
²the ²child ³of her ¹he might devour. And

ἔτεκεν υἱὸν ἄρσεν, ὃς μέλλει ποιμαίνειν
she bore a son[,] a male, who is about to shepherd

πάντα τὰ ἔθνη ἐν ῥάβδῳ σιδηρᾷ· καὶ
all the nations with ¹staff ¹an iron; and

ἡρπάσθη τὸ τέκνον αὐτῆς πρὸς τὸν
⁴was seized ¹the ²child ³of her to -

θεὸν καὶ πρὸς τὸν θρόνον αὐτοῦ. 6 καὶ
God and to the throne of him. And

ἡ γυνὴ ἔφυγεν εἰς τὴν ἔρημον, ὅπου
the woman fled into the desert, where

ἔχει ἐκεῖ τόπον ἡτοιμασμένον ἀπὸ
she has there a place having been prepared from

τοῦ θεοῦ, ἵνα ἐκεῖ τρέφωσιν αὐτὴν
- God, in order that there they might nourish her

ἡμέρας χιλίας διακοσίας ἑξήκοντα.
¹days ¹a thousand ²two hundred ³[and] ³sixty.

7 Καὶ ἐγένετο πόλεμος ἐν τῷ οὐρανῷ,
And occurred war in - heaven,

ὁ Μιχαὴλ καὶ οἱ ἄγγελοι αὐτοῦ τοῦ
- Michael and the angels of him -

πολεμῆσαι μετὰ τοῦ δράκοντος. καὶ ὁ
to make war⁴ with the dragon. And the

δράκων ἐπολέμησεν καὶ οἱ ἄγγελοι αὐτοῦ,
dragon warred and the angels of him,

8 καὶ οὐκ ἴσχυσεν, οὐδὲ τόπος εὑρέθη
and ²prevailed ¹not, not even place was found

αὐτῶν ἔτι ἐν τῷ οὐρανῷ. 9 καὶ ἐβλήθη
of them still in - heaven. And was cast

King James Version

dragon was cast out, that old serpent, called the Devil, and Satan, which deceiveth the whole world: he was cast out into the earth, and his angels were cast out with him. 10And I heard a loud voice saying in heaven, Now is come salvation, and strength, and the kingdom of our God, and the power of his Christ: for the accuser of our brethren is cast down, which accused them before our God day and night. 11And they overcame him by the blood of the Lamb, and by the word of their testimony; and they loved not their lives unto the death. 12 Therefore rejoice, *ye* heavens, and ye that dwell in them. Woe to the inhabiters of the earth and of the sea! for the devil is come down unto you, having great wrath, because he knoweth that he hath but a short time. 13And when the dragon saw that he was cast unto the earth, he persecuted the woman which brought forth the man *child.* 14And to the woman were given two wings of a great eagle, that she might fly into the wilderness, into her place, where she is nourished for a time, and times, and half a time, from the face of the serpent. 15And the serpent cast out of his mouth water as a flood after the woman, that he might cause her to be carried away of the flood. 16And the earth helped the woman; and the earth opened her mouth, and swallowed up the flood which the dragon cast out of his mouth. 17And the dragon was wroth with the woman, and went to make war with the remnant of her seed, which keep the commandments of God, and have the testimony of Jesus Christ.

New International Version

—that ancient serpent called the devil or Satan, who leads the whole world astray. He was hurled to the earth, and his angels with him.
10 Then I heard a loud voice in heaven say:
"Now have come the salvation and the
    power and the kingdom of our God,
    and the authority of his Christ.
For the accuser of our brothers,
    who accuses them before our God day
      and night,
    has been hurled down.
11 They overcame him
    by the blood of the Lamb
    and by the word of their testimony;
they did not love their lives so much
    as to shrink from death.
12 Therefore rejoice, you heavens
    and you who inhabit them!
But woe to the earth and the sea,
    because the devil has gone down to you!
He is filled with fury,
    because he knows that his time is short."
13 When the dragon saw that he had been hurled to the earth, he pursued the woman who had given birth to the male child. 14 The woman was given the two wings of a great eagle, so that she might fly to the place prepared for her in the desert, where she would be taken care of for a time, times, and half a time, out of the serpent's reach. 15 Then from his mouth the serpent spewed water like a river, to overtake the woman and sweep her away with the torrent. 16 But the earth helped the woman by opening its mouth and swallowing the river that the dragon had spewed out of his mouth. 17 Then the dragon was enraged at the woman, and went off to make war against the rest of her offspring —those who keep God's commandments and hold to the testimony of

13 And I stood upon the sand of the sea, and saw a beast rise up out of the sea, having seven heads and ten horns, and upon his horns ten crowns, and upon his heads the name of blasphemy. 2And the beast which I saw was like unto a leopard, and his feet were as *the feet* of a bear, and his mouth as the mouth of a lion: and the dragon gave him his power, and his seat, and great authority. 3And I saw one of his heads as it were wounded to death; and his deadly wound was healed: and all the world wondered after the beast. 4And they worshipped the dragon which gave power unto the beast: and they worshipped the beast, saying, Who *is* like unto the beast? who is able to make war

13 Jesus. 1And the dragon[m] stood on the shore of the sea.

The beast out of the sea

And I saw a beast coming out of the sea. He had ten horns and seven heads, with ten crowns on his horns, and on each head a blasphemous name. 2 The beast I saw resembled a leopard, but had feet like those of a bear and a mouth like that of a lion. The dragon gave the beast his power and his throne and great authority. 3 One of the heads of the beast seemed to have had a fatal wound, but the fatal wound had been healed. The whole world was astonished and followed the beast. 4 Men worshiped the dragon because he had given authority to the beast, and they also worshiped the beast and asked, "Who is like the beast? Who can make war against him?"

[m] Some late MSS read *And I.*

Greek Interlinear

ὁ δράκων ὁ μέγας, ὁ ὄφις ὁ ἀρχαῖος,
¹the ¹dragon - ²great, ⁴the ⁶serpent - ⁵old.

ὁ καλούμενος Διάβολος καὶ ὁ Σατανᾶς,
- being called Devil and the Satan,

ὁ πλανῶν τὴν οἰκουμένην ὅλην, ἐβλήθη
the deceiving the ²inhabited ¹whole, was cast

[one] [earth]

εἰς τὴν γῆν, καὶ οἱ ἄγγελοι αὐτοῦ μετ'
to the earth, and the angels of him with

αὐτοῦ ἐβλήθησαν. 10 καὶ ἤκουσα φωνὴν
him were cast. And I heard ²voice

μεγάλην ἐν τῷ οὐρανῷ λέγουσαν ἄρτι
¹a great(loud) in - heaven saying: Now

ἐγένετο ἡ σωτηρία καὶ ἡ δύναμις καὶ
became the salvation and the power and

ἡ βασιλεία τοῦ θεοῦ ἡμῶν καὶ ἡ ἐξουσία
the kingdom of the God of us and the authority

τοῦ χριστοῦ αὐτοῦ, ὅτι ἐβλήθη ὁ κατήγωρ
of the Christ of him, because ⁶was cast ¹the ²accuser

τῶν ἀδελφῶν ἡμῶν, ὁ κατηγορῶν αὐτοὺς
³of the ⁴brothers ⁵of us, the [one] accusing them

ἐνώπιον τοῦ θεοῦ ἡμῶν ἡμέρας καὶ
before the God of us day and

νυκτός. 11 καὶ αὐτοὶ ἐνίκησαν αὐτὸν
night. And they overcame him

διὰ τὸ αἷμα τοῦ ἀρνίου καὶ διὰ τὸν
be- the blood of the Lamb and because the
cause of   of

λόγον τῆς μαρτυρίας αὐτῶν, καὶ οὐκ
word of the witness of them, and not

ἠγάπησαν τὴν ψυχὴν αὐτῶν ἄχρι θανάτου.
they loved the life of them until death.

12 διὰ τοῦτο εὐφραίνεσθε, οὐρανοὶ καὶ
Therefore be ye glad, heavens and

οἱ ἐν αὐτοῖς σκηνοῦντες· οὐαὶ τὴν
the ²in ³them ¹tabernacling; woe [to] the
[ones]

γῆν καὶ τὴν θάλασσαν, ὅτι κατέβη ὁ
earth and the sea, because ²came down ¹the

διάβολος πρὸς ὑμᾶς ἔχων θυμὸν μέγαν,
²devil to you having ²anger ¹great,

εἰδὼς ὅτι ὀλίγον καιρὸν ἔχει. 13 Καὶ
knowing that ²few(short) ²time ¹he has. And

ὅτε εἶδεν ὁ δράκων ὅτι ἐβλήθη εἰς
when ²saw ¹the ²dragon that he was cast to

τὴν γῆν, ἐδίωξεν τὴν γυναῖκα ἥτις
the earth, he pursued the woman who

ἔτεκεν τὸν ἄρσενα. 14 καὶ ἐδόθησαν
bore the male. And were given

τῇ γυναικὶ αἱ δύο πτέρυγες τοῦ ἀετοῦ
to the woman the two wings of the ²eagle

τοῦ μεγάλου, ἵνα πέτηται εἰς τὴν ἔρημον
- ¹great, in order she might to the desert
      that fly

εἰς τὸν τόπον αὐτῆς, ὅπου τρέφεται
to the place of her, where she is nourished

ἐκεῖ καιρὸν καὶ καιροὺς καὶ ἥμισυ καιροῦ
there a time and times and half of a time

ἀπὸ προσώπου τοῦ ὄφεως. 15 καὶ ἔβαλεν
from [the] face of the serpent. And ²cast

ὁ ὄφις ἐκ τοῦ στόματος αὐτοῦ ὀπίσω
¹the ²serpent out of the mouth of him behind

τῆς γυναικὸς ὕδωρ ὡς ποταμόν, ἵνα
the woman water as a river, in or-
      der that

αὐτὴν ποταμοφόρητον ποιήσῃ. 16 καὶ
²her ²carried off by [the] river ¹he might make. And

ἐβοήθησεν ἡ γῆ τῇ γυναικί, καὶ ἤνοιξεν
²helped ¹the ²earth the woman, and ¹opened

ἡ γῆ τὸ στόμα αὐτῆς καὶ κατέπιεν
¹the ²earth the mouth of it and swallowed

τὸν ποταμὸν ὃν ἔβαλεν ὁ δράκων ἐκ
the river which ³cast ¹the ²dragon out of

τοῦ στόματος αὐτοῦ. 17 καὶ ὠργίσθη
the mouth of him. And ³was enraged

ὁ δράκων ἐπὶ τῇ γυναικί, καὶ ἀπῆλθεν
¹the ²dragon over the woman, and went away

ποιῆσαι πόλεμον μετὰ τῶν λοιπῶν τοῦ
to make war with the rest of the

σπέρματος αὐτῆς, τῶν τηρούντων τὰς
seed of her, the [ones] keeping the

ἐντολὰς τοῦ θεοῦ καὶ ἐχόντων τὴν
commandments - of God and having the

μαρτυρίαν Ἰησοῦ· (18) καὶ ἐστάθη ἐπὶ τὴν
witness of Jesus; and he stood on the

ἄμμον τῆς θαλάσσης.
sand of the sea.

Chapter 13

Καὶ εἶδον ἐκ τῆς θαλάσσης θηρίον
And I saw ²out of ⁴the ³sea ¹a beast

ἀναβαῖνον, ἔχον κέρατα δέκα καὶ κεφαλὰς
²coming up, having ²horns ¹ten and ²heads

ἑπτά, καὶ ἐπὶ τῶν κεράτων αὐτοῦ δέκα
¹seven, and on the horns of it* ten

διαδήματα, καὶ ἐπὶ τὰς κεφαλὰς αὐτοῦ
diadems, and on the heads of it

ὀνόματα βλασφημίας. 2 καὶ τὸ θηρίον
names of blasphemy. And the beast

ὃ εἶδον ἦν ὅμοιον παρδάλει, καὶ οἱ
which I saw was like to a leopard, and the

πόδες αὐτοῦ ὡς ἄρκου, καὶ τὸ στόμα
feet of it as of a bear, and the mouth

αὐτοῦ ὡς στόμα λέοντος. καὶ ἔδωκεν
of it as [the] mouth of a lion. And ²gave

αὐτῷ ὁ δράκων τὴν δύναμιν αὐτοῦ καὶ
⁴to it ¹the ²dragon the power of it and

τὸν θρόνον αὐτοῦ καὶ ἐξουσίαν μεγάλην.
the throne of it and authority ¹great.

3 καὶ μίαν ἐκ τῶν κεφαλῶν αὐτοῦ ὡς
And one of the heads of it as

ἐσφαγμένην εἰς θάνατον, καὶ ἡ πληγὴ
having been slain to death, and the stroke

τοῦ θανάτου αὐτοῦ ἐθεραπεύθη. καὶ
of the death of it was healed. And

ἐθαυμάσθη ὅλη ἡ γῆ ὀπίσω τοῦ θηρίου,
²wondered ¹all ²the ²earth after the beast,

4 καὶ προσεκύνησαν τῷ δράκοντι, ὅτι
and they worshiped the dragon, because

ἔδωκεν τὴν ἐξουσίαν τῷ θηρίῳ, καὶ
he gave the authority to the beast, and

προσεκύνησαν τῷ θηρίῳ λέγοντες· τίς
they worshiped the beast saying: Who

ὅμοιος τῷ θηρίῳ, καὶ τίς δύναται
[is] like to the beast, and who can

---

* αὐτοῦ, of course, may be neuter or masculine—" of it " or
" of him". δράκων being masculine (= Satan), we have kept to
the masculine. But θηρίον is neuter. Yet if it stands for a person,
as ἀρνίον certainly does, then too should be treated, as to the
pronoun, as a masculine. However, not to enter the province of
interpretation, we have rendered αὐτοῦ by " of it", though it
will be seen that αὐτόν (him) is used in ver. 8, τίς (who?) in
ver. 4, and ὅς (who) in ver. 14. See also ch. 17, 11.

King James Version

with him? 5And there was given unto him a mouth speaking great things and blasphemies; and power was given unto him to continue forty *and* two months. 6And he opened his mouth in blasphemy against God, to blaspheme his name, and his tabernacle, and them that dwell in heaven. 7And it was given unto him to make war with the saints, and to overcome them: and power was given him over all kindreds, and tongues, and nations. 8And all that dwell upon the earth shall worship him, whose names are not written in the book of life of the Lamb slain from the foundation of the world. 9 If any man have an ear, let him hear. 10 He that leadeth into captivity shall go into captivity: he that killeth with the sword must be killed with the sword. Here is the patience and the faith of the saints. 11And I beheld another beast coming up out of the earth; and he had two horns like a lamb, and he spake as a dragon. 12And he exerciseth all the power of the first beast before him, and causeth the earth and them which dwell therein to worship the first beast, whose deadly wound was healed. 13And he doeth great wonders, so that he maketh fire come down from heaven on the earth in the sight of men, 14And deceiveth them that dwell on the earth by *the means of* those miracles which he had power to do in the sight of the beast; saying to them that dwell on the earth, that they should make an image to the beast, which had the wound by a sword, and did live. 15And he had power to give life unto the image of the beast, that the image of the beast should both speak, and cause that as many as would not worship the image of the beast should be killed. 16And he causeth all, both small and great, rich and poor, free and bond, to receive a mark in their right hand, or in their foreheads: 17And that no man might buy or sell, save he that had the mark, or the name of the beast, or the number of his name. 18Here is wisdom. Let him that hath understanding count the number of the beast: for it is the number of a man; and his number *is* Six hundred threescore *and* six.

New International Version

5 The beast was given a mouth to utter proud words and blasphemies and to exercise his authority for forty-two months. 6 He opened his mouth to blaspheme God, and to slander his name and his dwelling place and those who live in heaven. 7 He was given power to make war against the saints and to conquer them. And he was given authority over every tribe, people, language and nation. 8All inhabitants of the earth will worship the beast—all whose names have not been recorded in the book of life belonging to the Lamb that was slain from the creation of the world.[n]
9 He who has an ear, let him hear.
10 If anyone is to go into captivity,
    into captivity he will go.
   If anyone is to be killed with the sword,
    with the sword he will be killed.
This calls for patient endurance and faithfulness on the part of the saints.

The beast out of the earth

11 Then I saw another beast, coming out of the earth. He had two horns like a lamb, but he spoke like a dragon. 12 He exercised all the authority of the first beast on his behalf, and made the earth and its inhabitants worship the first beast, whose fatal wound had been healed. 13And he performed great and miraculous signs, even causing fire to come down from heaven to earth in full view of men. 14 Because of the signs he was given power to do on behalf of the first beast, he deceived the inhabitants of the earth. He ordered them to set up an image in honor of the beast who was wounded by the sword and yet lived. 15 He was given power to give breath to the image of the first beast, so that it could speak and cause all who refused to worship the image to be killed. 16 He also forced everyone, small and great, rich and poor, free and slave, to receive a mark on his right hand or on his forehead, 17 so that no one could buy or sell unless he had the mark, which is the name of the beast or the number of his name. 18 This calls for wisdom. If anyone has insight, let him calculate the number of the beast, for it is man's number. His number is 666.

The Lamb and the 144,000

14 And I looked, and, lo, a Lamb stood on the mount Sion, and with him a hundred forty *and* four thousand, having his Father's name written in their foreheads. 2And I heard

14 Then I looked, and there before me was the Lamb, standing on Mount Zion, and with him 144,000 who had his name and his Father's name written on their foreheads. 2And

[n] Or *recorded from the creation of the world in the book of life belonging to the Lamb that was slain.*

Greek Interlinear

πολεμῆσαι μετ' αὐτοῦ; 5 καὶ ἐδόθη αὐτῷ
to make war   with   it ?   And was given   to it

στόμα λαλοῦν μεγάλα καὶ βλασφημίας,
a mouth speaking great things and   blasphemies,

καὶ ἐδόθη αὐτῷ ἐξουσία ποιῆσαι μῆνας
and was given to it   authority to act ²months

τεσσεράκοντα [καὶ] δύο. 6 καὶ ἤνοιξεν
¹forty-two.   And   it opened

τὸ στόμα αὐτοῦ εἰς βλασφημίας πρὸς
the mouth of it in blasphemies against

τὸν θεόν, βλασφημῆσαι τὸ ὄνομα αὐτοῦ
-   God, to blaspheme   the   name   of him

καὶ τὴν σκηνὴν αὐτοῦ, τοὺς ἐν τῷ
and the tabernacle of him, ¹the [ones] ²in -

οὐρανῷ σκηνοῦντας. 7 καὶ ἐδόθη αὐτῷ
⁴heaven ²tabernacling. And it was given to it

ποιῆσαι πόλεμον μετὰ τῶν ἁγίων καὶ
to make   war   with the saints and

νικῆσαι αὐτούς, καὶ ἐδόθη αὐτῷ ἐξουσία
to overcome them, and ²was given ³to it ¹authority

ἐπὶ πᾶσαν φυλὴν καὶ λαὸν καὶ γλῶσσαν
over every   tribe and people and tongue

καὶ ἔθνος. 8 καὶ προσκυνήσουσιν αὐτὸν
and nation. And   ⁷will worship   ⁸him

πάντες οἱ κατοικοῦντες ἐπὶ τῆς γῆς,
¹all ²the [ones] ³dwelling ⁴on ⁵the ⁶earth,

οὗ οὐ γέγραπται τὸ ὄνομα αὐτοῦ ἐν
⁹of ⁸has not been written ¹the ²name of him in

τῷ βιβλίῳ τῆς ζωῆς τοῦ ἀρνίου τοῦ
whom   the scroll   -   of life of the Lamb   -

ἐσφαγμένου ἀπὸ καταβολῆς κόσμου.
having been slain from [the] foundation of [the] world.

9 Εἴ τις ἔχει οὖς ἀκουσάτω. 10 εἴ
If anyone has an ear let him hear.   If

τις εἰς αἰχμαλωσίαν, εἰς αἰχμαλωσίαν
anyone [is] for captivity,   to   captivity

ὑπάγει· εἴ τις ἐν μαχαίρῃ ἀποκτενεῖ,
he goes; if anyone by a sword   will kill,

δεῖ αὐτὸν ἐν μαχαίρῃ ἀποκτανθῆναι.
it behoves him by a sword   to be killed.

Ὧδέ ἐστιν ἡ ὑπομονὴ καὶ ἡ πίστις
Here is   the endurance and the faith

τῶν ἁγίων.
of the saints.

11 Καὶ εἶδον ἄλλο θηρίον ἀναβαῖνον
And   I saw another beast coming up

ἐκ τῆς γῆς, καὶ εἶχεν κέρατα δύο
out of the earth, and it had ²horns ¹two

ὅμοια ἀρνίῳ, καὶ ἐλάλει ὡς δράκων.
like to a lamb, and spoke as a dragon.

12 καὶ τὴν ἐξουσίαν τοῦ πρώτου θηρίου
And ³the ⁴authority ⁵of the ⁶first ⁷beast

πᾶσαν ποιεῖ ἐνώπιον αὐτοῦ. καὶ ποιεῖ
²all ¹it does(exercises) before   it.   And it makes

τὴν γῆν καὶ τοὺς ἐν αὐτῇ κατοικοῦντας
the earth and ¹the [ones] ²in ³it ⁴dwelling

ἵνα προσκυνήσουσιν τὸ θηρίον τὸ πρῶτον,
in or- they shall worship the ⁸beast   -   ¹first,
der that

οὗ ἐθεραπεύθη ἡ πληγὴ τοῦ θανάτου
of which ⁴was healed ¹the ²stroke - ³of death

αὐτοῦ. 13 καὶ ποιεῖ σημεῖα μεγάλα,
of it.   And it does ²signs   ¹great.

ἵνα καὶ πῦρ ποιῇ ἐκ τοῦ οὐρανοῦ
in or- ⁴even ⁵fire ³it ²makes ⁶out of -   ⁷heaven
der that

καταβαίνειν εἰς τὴν γῆν ἐνώπιον τῶν
¹to come down onto the earth before   -

ἀνθρώπων. 14 καὶ πλανᾷ τοὺς κατοι-
men.   And it deceives the [ones] dwell-

κοῦντας ἐπὶ τῆς γῆς διὰ τὰ σημεῖα
ing   on the earth because of the signs

ἃ ἐδόθη αὐτῷ ποιῆσαι ἐνώπιον τοῦ
which it was given to it to do   before   the

θηρίου, λέγων τοῖς κατοικοῦσιν ἐπὶ τῆς
beast, telling to the [ones] dwelling on the

γῆς ποιῆσαι εἰκόνα τῷ θηρίῳ, ὃς ἔχει
earth to make an image to the beast, who has

τὴν πληγὴν τῆς μαχαίρης καὶ ἔζησεν.
the stroke of the sword   and lived [again].

15 καὶ ἐδόθη αὐτῷ δοῦναι πνεῦμα τῇ
And it was given to it to give   spirit to the

εἰκόνι τοῦ θηρίου, ἵνα καὶ λαλήσῃ ἡ
image of the beast, in order ⁴even ⁵might ¹the
that

εἰκὼν τοῦ θηρίου, καὶ ποιήσῃ [ἵνα
²image ³of the ⁴beast, and might make in order
that

ὅσοι ἐὰν μὴ προσκυνήσωσιν τῇ εἰκόνι
as many as might not worship   the image

τοῦ θηρίου ἀποκτανθῶσιν. 16 καὶ ποιεῖ
of the beast should be killed.   And it makes

πάντας, τοὺς μικροὺς καὶ τοὺς μεγάλους,
all men, the small   and the   great,

καὶ τοὺς πλουσίους καὶ τοὺς πτωχούς,
both the   rich   and the   poor,

καὶ τοὺς ἐλευθέρους καὶ τοὺς δούλους,
both the free men   and the   slaves,

ἵνα δῶσιν αὐτοῖς χάραγμα ἐπὶ τῆς
in order they to them a mark   on the
that should give

χειρὸς αὐτῶν τῆς δεξιᾶς ἢ ἐπὶ τὸ
²hand ³of them   - ¹right or on the

μέτωπον αὐτῶν, 17 [καὶ] ἵνα μή τις
forehead of them,   and   lest anyone

δύνηται ἀγοράσαι ἢ πωλῆσαι εἰ μὴ
could   to buy   or to sell except

ὁ ἔχων τὸ χάραγμα τὸ ὄνομα τοῦ
the having the   mark[,] the   name of the
[one]

θηρίου ἢ τὸν ἀριθμὸν τοῦ ὀνόματος
beast or the number of the   name

αὐτοῦ. 18 Ὧδε ἡ σοφία ἐστίν. ὁ ἔχων
of it.   Here ²wisdom ³is. The having
[one]

νοῦν ψηφισάτω τὸν ἀριθμὸν τοῦ θηρίου·
reason let him count the number of the beast;

ἀριθμὸς γὰρ ἀνθρώπου ἐστίν. καὶ ὁ
for ²[the] ¹number ⁴of a man   ³it is.   And the

ἀριθμὸς αὐτοῦ ἑξακόσιοι ἑξήκοντα ἕξ.
number   of it [is] six hundreds [and] sixty-six.

Chapter 14

Καὶ εἶδον, καὶ ἰδοὺ τὸ ἀρνίον
And   I saw, and behold[,] the Lamb

ἑστὸς ἐπὶ τὸ ὄρος Σιών, καὶ μετ' αὐτοῦ
standing on the mount Sion, and with him

ἑκατὸν τεσσεράκοντα τέσσαρες χιλιάδες
a hundred [and] forty-four   thousands

ἔχουσαι τὸ ὄνομα αὐτοῦ καὶ τὸ ὄνομα
having   the name of him and the name

τοῦ πατρὸς αὐτοῦ γεγραμμένον ἐπὶ τῶν
of the Father of him having been written on the

μετώπων αὐτῶν. 2 καὶ ἤκουσα φωνὴν
foreheads of them.   And I heard   a sound

753

King James Version

New International Version

a voice from heaven, as the voice of many waters, and as the voice of a great thunder: and I heard the voice of harpers harping with their harps: 3And they sung as it were a new song before the throne, and before the four beasts, and the elders: and no man could learn that song but the hundred *and* forty *and* four thousand, which were redeemed from the earth. 4 These are they which were not defiled with women; for they are virgins. These are they which follow the Lamb whithersoever he goeth. These were redeemed from among men, *being* the firstfruits unto God and to the Lamb. 5And in their mouth was found no guile: for they are without fault before the throne of God. 6And I saw another angel fly in the midst of heaven, having the everlasting gospel to preach unto them that dwell on the earth, and to every nation, and kindred, and tongue, and people, 7 Saying with a loud voice, Fear God, and give glory to him; for the hour of his judgment is come: and worship him that made heaven, and earth, and the sea, and the fountains of waters. 8And there followed another angel, saying, Babylon is fallen, is fallen, that great city, because she made all nations drink of the wine of the wrath of her fornication. 9And the third angel followed them, saying with a loud voice, If any man worship the beast and his image, and receive *his* mark in his forehead, or in his hand, 10 The same shall drink of the wine of the wrath of God, which is poured out without mixture into the cup of his indignation; and he shall be tormented with fire and brimstone in the presence of the holy angels, and in the presence of the Lamb: 11And the smoke of their torment ascendeth up for ever and ever: and they have no rest day nor night, who worship the beast and his image, and whosoever receiveth the mark of his name. 12 Here is the patience of the saints: here *are* they that keep the commandments of God, and the faith of Jesus. 13And I heard a voice from heaven saying unto me, Write, Blessed *are* the dead which die in the Lord from henceforth: Yea, saith the Spirit, that they may rest from their labours; and their works do follow them. 14And I looked, and behold a white cloud, and upon the cloud *one* sat like unto the Son of man, having on his head a golden crown, and in his hand a sharp sickle. 15And another angel came out of the temple, crying with a loud voice to him that sat on the cloud, Thrust in thy sickle, and reap: for the time is come for thee to reap; for the harvest of the earth is ripe. 16And he that sat on the cloud thrust in his sickle on the earth; and the earth

I heard a sound from heaven like the roar of rushing waters and like a loud peal of thunder. The sound I heard was like that of harpists playing their harps. 3And they sang a new song before the throne and before the four living creatures and the elders. No one could learn the song except the 144,000 who had been redeemed from the earth. 4 These are those who did not defile themselves with women, for they kept themselves pure. They follow the Lamb wherever he goes. They were purchased from among men and offered as firstfruits to God and the Lamb. 5 No lie was found in their mouths; they are blameless.

The three angels

6 Then I saw another angel flying in midair, and he had the eternal gospel to proclaim to those who live on the earth—to every nation, tribe, language and people. 7 He said in a loud voice, "Fear God and give him glory, because the hour of his judgment has come. Worship him who made the heavens, the earth, the sea and the springs of water."

8 A second angel followed and said, "Fallen! Fallen is Babylon the Great, which made all the nations drink the maddening wine of her adulteries."

9 A third angel followed them and said in a loud voice: "If anyone worships the beast and his image and receives his mark on the forehead or on the hand, 10 he, too, will drink of the wine of God's fury, which has been poured full strength into the cup of his wrath. He will be tormented with burning sulfur in the presence of the holy angels and of the Lamb. 11And the smoke of their torment rises for ever and ever. There is no rest day or night for those who worship the beast and his image, or for anyone who receives the mark of his name." 12 This calls for patient endurance on the part of the saints who keep God's commandments and remain faithful to Jesus.

13 Then I heard a voice from heaven say, "Write: Blessed are the dead who die in the Lord from now on."

"Yes," says the Spirit, "they will rest from their labor, for their deeds will follow them."

The harvest of the earth

14 I looked, and there before me was a white cloud, and seated on the cloud was one "like a son of man" *o* with a crown of gold on his head and a sharp sickle in his hand. 15 Then another angel came out of the temple and called in a loud voice to him who was sitting on the cloud, "Take your sickle and reap, because the time to reap has come, for the harvest of the earth is ripe." 16 So he that was seated on the cloud swung his sickle over the earth, and the earth was harvested.

[o] Daniel 7:13.

754

Greek Interlinear

κ τοῦ οὐρανοῦ ὡς φωνὴν ὑδάτων πολλῶν
ut of - heaven as a sound ²waters ¹of many

καὶ ὡς φωνὴν βροντῆς μεγάλης, καὶ
and as a sound ¹thunder ¹of great(loud), and

ἡ φωνὴ ἣν ἤκουσα ὡς κιθαρῳδῶν
he sound which I heard [was] as of harpers

κιθαριζόντων ἐν ταῖς κιθάραις αὐτῶν.
harping with the harps of them.

καὶ ᾄδουσιν ᾠδὴν καινὴν ἐνώπιον τοῦ
And they sing ²song ¹a new before the

θρόνου καὶ ἐνώπιον τῶν τεσσάρων ζῴων
throne and before the four living creatures

καὶ τῶν πρεσβυτέρων· καὶ οὐδεὶς ἐδύνατο
and the elders; and no man could

μαθεῖν τὴν ᾠδὴν εἰ μὴ αἱ ἑκατὸν
o learn the song except the hundred

τεσσεράκοντα τέσσαρες χιλιάδες, οἱ
[and] forty-four thousands. tho

ἠγορασμένοι ἀπὸ τῆς γῆς. 4 οὗτοί εἰσιν
ones] having from the earth. These are

οἱ μετὰ γυναικῶν οὐκ ἐμολύνθησαν·
those] ²with ²women ¹were not defiled;
who

παρθένοι γάρ εἰσιν. οὗτοι οἱ ἀκολουθοῦντες
for ²celibates ¹they are. These the [ones] following [are]

τῷ ἀρνίῳ ὅπου ἂν ὑπάγῃ. οὗτοι ἠγοράσ-
the Lamb wherever he may go. These were

θησαν ἀπὸ τῶν ἀνθρώπων ἀπαρχὴ τῷ
purchased from - men firstfruit the

θεῷ καὶ τῷ ἀρνίῳ, 5 καὶ ἐν τῷ στόματι
to God and to the Lamb, and in the mouth

αὐτῶν οὐχ εὑρέθη ψεῦδος· ἄμωμοί εἰσιν.
of them was not found a lie; ²unblemished ¹they are.

6 Καὶ εἶδον ἄλλον ἄγγελον πετόμενον
And I saw another angel flying

ἐν μεσουρανήματι, ἔχοντα εὐαγγέλιον
in mid-heaven, having ¹gospel

αἰώνιον εὐαγγελίσαι ἐπὶ τοὺς καθημένους
²an eternal to preach over the [ones] sitting

ἐπὶ τῆς γῆς καὶ ἐπὶ πᾶν ἔθνος καὶ
on the earth and over every nation and

φυλὴν καὶ γλῶσσαν καὶ λαόν, 7 λέγων
tribe and tongue and people, saying

ἐν φωνῇ μεγάλη· φοβήθητε τὸν θεὸν
in ²voice ¹a great(loud): Fear ye - God

καὶ δότε αὐτῷ δόξαν, ὅτι ἦλθεν ἡ ὥρα
and give ²to him ¹glory, because came the hour

τῆς κρίσεως αὐτοῦ, καὶ προσκυνήσατε
of the judgment of him, and worship

τῷ ποιήσαντι τὸν οὐρανὸν καὶ τὴν γῆν
the [one] having made the heaven and the earth

καὶ θάλασσαν καὶ πηγὰς ὑδάτων. 8 Καὶ
and sea and fountains of waters. And

ἄλλος ἄγγελος δεύτερος ἠκολούθησεν λέγων·
another angel a second followed saying:

ἔπεσεν ἔπεσεν Βαβυλὼν ἡ μεγάλη, ἣ
Fell[,] fell Babylon the great, which

ἐκ τοῦ οἴνου τοῦ θυμοῦ τῆς πορνείας
of the wine of the anger of the fornication

αὐτῆς πεπότικεν πάντα τὰ ἔθνη. 9 Καὶ
of her has made to drink all the nations. And

ἄλλος ἄγγελος τρίτος ἠκολούθησεν αὐτοῖς
another angel a third followed them

λέγων ἐν φωνῇ μεγάλη· εἴ τις προσκυνεῖ
saying in ²voice ¹a great(loud): If anyone worships

τὸ θηρίον καὶ τὴν εἰκόνα αὐτοῦ, καὶ
the beast and the image of it, and

λαμβάνει χάραγμα ἐπὶ τοῦ μετώπου αὐτοῦ
receives ²a mark on the forehead of him

ἢ ἐπὶ τὴν χεῖρα αὐτοῦ, 10 καὶ αὐτὸς
or on the hand of him, even he

πίεται ἐκ τοῦ οἴνου τοῦ θυμοῦ τοῦ
shall drink of the wine of the anger -

θεοῦ τοῦ κεκερασμένου ἀκράτου ἐν τῷ
of God - having been mixed undiluted in the

ποτηρίῳ τῆς ὀργῆς αὐτοῦ, καὶ βασανισθήσε-
cup of the wrath of him, and will be torment-

ται ἐν πυρὶ καὶ θείῳ ἐνώπιον ἀγγέλων
ed by fire and sulphur before ¹angels

ἁγίων καὶ ἐνώπιον τοῦ ἀρνίου. 11 καὶ
¹holy and before the Lamb. And

ὁ καπνὸς τοῦ βασανισμοῦ αὐτῶν εἰς
the smoke of the torment of them unto

αἰῶνας αἰώνων ἀναβαίνει, καὶ οὐκ ἔχουσιν
ages of ages goes up, and they have not

ἀνάπαυσιν ἡμέρας καὶ νυκτὸς οἱ προσκυ-
rest day and night the [ones] wor-

νοῦντες τὸ θηρίον καὶ τὴν εἰκόνα αὐτοῦ,
shipping the beast and the image of it,

καὶ εἴ τις λαμβάνει τὸ χάραγμα τοῦ
and if anyone receives the mark of the

ὀνόματος αὐτοῦ. 12 Ὧδε ἡ ὑπομονὴ
name of it. ¹Here ²the ⁴endurance

τῶν ἁγίων ἐστίν, οἱ τηροῦντες τὰς
³of the ⁵saints ¹is, the [ones] keeping the

ἐντολὰς τοῦ θεοῦ καὶ τὴν πίστιν Ἰησοῦ.
command- - of God and the faith of Jesus.
ments

13 Καὶ ἤκουσα φωνῆς ἐκ τοῦ οὐρανοῦ
And I heard a voice out of - heaven

λεγούσης· γράψον· μακάριοι οἱ νεκροὶ
saying: Write thou: Blessed [are] the dead

οἱ ἐν κυρίῳ ἀποθνῄσκοντες ἀπ' ἄρτι.
¹the ²in ³[the] Lord ⁴dying from now.
[ones]

ναί, λέγει τὸ πνεῦμα, ἵνα ἀναπαήσονται
Yes, says the Spirit, in order they shall rest
that

ἐκ τῶν κόπων αὐτῶν· τὰ γὰρ ἔργα
from the labours of them; for the work-

αὐτῶν ἀκολουθεῖ μετ' αὐτῶν.
of them follows with them.

14 Καὶ εἶδον, καὶ ἰδοὺ νεφέλη λευκή,
And I saw, and behold[,] ²cloud ¹a white,

καὶ ἐπὶ τὴν νεφέλην καθήμενον ὅμοιον
and on the cloud [one] sitting like

υἱὸν ἀνθρώπου, ἔχων ἐπὶ τῆς κεφαλῆς
a son of man,* having on the head

αὐτοῦ στέφανον χρυσοῦν καὶ ἐν τῇ χειρὶ
of him crown a golden and in the hand

αὐτοῦ δρέπανον ὀξύ. 15 καὶ ἄλλος ἄγγελος
of him sickle a sharp. And another angel

ἐξῆλθεν ἐκ τοῦ ναοῦ, κράζων ἐν φωνῇ
went forth out of the shrine, crying in ¹voice

μεγάλη τῷ καθημένῳ ἐπὶ τῆς νεφέλης·
¹a great to the sitting on the cloud:
(loud) [one]

πέμψον τὸ δρέπανόν σου καὶ θέρισον,
Send(Thrust) the sickle of thee and reap thou,

ὅτι ἦλθεν ἡ ὥρα θερίσαι, ὅτι ἐξηράνθη
because came the hour to reap, because was dried

ὁ θερισμὸς τῆς γῆς. 16 καὶ ἔβαλεν
the harvest of the earth. And ¹thrust

ὁ καθήμενος ἐπὶ τῆς νεφέλης τὸ δρέπανον
¹the ²sitting ³on ⁴the ⁵cloud the sickle
[one]

αὐτοῦ ἐπὶ τὴν γῆν, καὶ ἐθερίσθη ἡ
of him over the earth, and ²was reaped ¹the

* See also ch. 1. 13 and John 5. 27.

King James Version

was reaped. 17And another angel came out of the temple which is in heaven, he also having a sharp sickle. 18And another angel came out from the altar, which had power over fire; and cried with a loud cry to him that had the sharp sickle, saying, Thrust in thy sharp sickle, and gather the clusters of the vine of the earth; for her grapes are fully ripe. 19And the angel thrust in his sickle into the earth, and gathered the vine of the earth, and cast it into the great winepress of the wrath of God. 20And the winepress was trodden without the city, and blood came out of the winepress, even unto the horse bridles, by the space of a thousand and six hundred furlongs.

15 And I saw another sign in heaven, great and marvellous, seven angels having the seven last plagues; for in them is filled up the wrath of God. 2And I saw as it were a sea of glass mingled with fire: and them that had gotten the victory over the beast, and over his image, and over his mark, and over the number of his name, stand on the sea of glass, having the harps of God. 3And they sing the song of Moses the servant of God, and the song of the Lamb, saying, Great and marvellous are thy works, Lord God Almighty; just and true are thy ways, thou King of saints. 4 Who shall not fear thee, O Lord, and glorify thy name? for thou only art holy: for all nations shall come and worship before thee; for thy judgments are made manifest. 5And after that I looked, and, behold, the temple of the tabernacle of the testimony in heaven was opened: 6And the seven angels came out of the temple, having the seven plagues, clothed in pure and white linen, and having their breasts girded with golden girdles. 7And one of the four beasts gave unto the seven angels seven golden vials full of the wrath of God, who liveth for ever and ever. 8And the temple was filled with smoke from the glory of God, and from his power; and no man was able to enter into the temple, till the seven plagues of the seven angels were fulfilled.

16 And I heard a great voice out of the temple saying to the seven angels, Go your ways, and pour out the vials of the wrath of God upon the earth. 2And the first went, and poured out his vial upon the earth; and there fell a noisome and grievous sore upon the men which had the mark of the beast, and upon

New International Version

17 Another angel came out of the temple in heaven, and he too had a sharp sickle. 18 Still another angel, who had charge of the fire, came from the altar and called in a loud voice to him who had the sharp sickle, "Take your sharp sickle and gather the clusters of grapes from the earth's vine, because its grapes are ripe.' 19 The angel swung his sickle on the earth, gathered its grapes and threw them into the great winepress of God's wrath. 20 They were trampled in the winepress outside the city, and blood flowed out of the press, rising as high as the horse's bridles for a distance of 1,600 stadia.[p]

Seven angels with seven plagues

15 I saw in heaven another great and marvellous sign: seven angels with the seven last plagues—last, because with them God's wrath is completed. 2And I saw what looked like a sea of glass mixed with fire and, standing beside the sea, those who had been victorious over the beast and his image and over the number of his name. They held harps given them by God 3 and sang the song of Moses, the servant of God, and the song of the Lamb:
"Great and marvelous are your deeds,
　Lord God Almighty.
Just and true are your ways,
　King of the ages.
4 Who will not fear you, O Lord,
　and bring glory to your name?
For you alone are holy.
All nations will come
　and worship before you,
for your righteous acts have been revealed."
5 After this I looked and in heaven the temple, that is, the tabernacle of testimony, was opened. 6 Out of the temple came the seven angels with the seven plagues. They were dressed in clean, shining linen and wore golden sashes around their chests. 7 Then one of the four living creatures gave to the seven angels seven golden bowls filled with the wrath of God, who lives for ever and ever. 8And the temple was filled with smoke from the glory of God and from his power, and no one could enter the temple until the seven plagues of the seven angels were completed.

The seven bowls of God's wrath

16 Then I heard a loud voice from the temple saying to the seven angels, "Go, pour out the seven bowls of God's wrath on the earth."
2 The first angel went and poured out his bowl on the land, and ugly and painful sores broke out on the people who had the mark of the beast and worshiped his image.

[p] That is, about 200 miles.

Greek Interlinear

γῆ. **17** Καὶ ἄλλος ἄγγελος ἐξῆλθεν ἐκ
²earth. And another angel went forth out of

τοῦ ναοῦ τοῦ ἐν τῷ οὐρανῷ, ἔχων καὶ
the shrine - in - heaven, ¹having ²also

αὐτὸς δρέπανον ὀξύ. **18** καὶ ἄλλος ἄγγελος
¹he ⁴sickle ⁵a sharp. And another angel

ἐξῆλθεν ἐκ τοῦ θυσιαστηρίου, [ὁ] ἔχων
went forth out of the altar, the [one] having

ἐξουσίαν ἐπὶ τοῦ πυρός, καὶ ἐφώνησεν
authority over the fire, and he spoke

φωνῇ μεγάλῃ τῷ ἔχοντι τὸ δρέπανον
¹voice ¹in a great to the having the ²sickle
(loud) [one]

τὸ ὀξὺ λέγων· πέμψον σου τὸ δρέπανον
- ¹sharp saying: Send(Thrust) ⁴of thee ³the ¹the sickle

τὸ ὀξὺ καὶ τρύγησον τοὺς βότρυας τῆς
- ²sharp and gather the clusters of the

ἀμπέλου τῆς γῆς, ὅτι ἤκμασαν αἱ
vine of the earth, because ⁴ripened ¹the

σταφυλαὶ αὐτῆς. **19** καὶ ἔβαλεν ὁ ἄγγελος
²grapes ³of it. And ³thrust ¹the ²angel

τὸ δρέπανον αὐτοῦ εἰς τὴν γῆν, καὶ
the sickle of him into the earth, and

ἐτρύγησεν τὴν ἄμπελον τῆς γῆς καὶ
gathered the vine of the earth and

ἔβαλεν εἰς τὴν ληνὸν τοῦ θυμοῦ τοῦ
cast into the ²winepress ³of the ⁴anger -

θεοῦ τὸν μέγαν. **20** καὶ ἐπατήθη ἡ
⁵of God - ¹great. And ²was trodden ¹the

ληνὸς ἔξωθεν τῆς πόλεως, καὶ ἐξῆλθεν
winepress outside the city, and ³went out

αἷμα ἐκ τῆς ληνοῦ ἄχρι τῶν χαλινῶν
¹blood out of the winepress as far as the bridles

τῶν ἵππων, ἀπὸ σταδίων χιλίων ἑξακοσίων.
of the horses, from ²furlongs ¹a thousand ³six hundred.

Chapter 15

Καὶ εἶδον ἄλλο σημεῖον ἐν τῷ
And I saw another sign in -

οὐρανῷ[,] μέγα καὶ θαυμαστόν, ἀγγέλους
heaven[,] great and wonderful, ¹angels

ἑπτὰ ἔχοντας πληγὰς ἑπτὰ τὰς ἐσχάτας,
¹seven having ²plagues ³seven the last,

ὅτι ἐν αὐταῖς ἐτελέσθη ὁ θυμὸς τοῦ
because in them ¹was finished the ²anger -

θεοῦ. **2** Καὶ εἶδον ὡς θάλασσαν ὑαλίνην
²of God. And I saw as ³sea ¹a glassy

μεμιγμένην πυρί, καὶ τοὺς νικῶντας
having been mixed with fire, and the [ones] overcoming

ἐκ τοῦ θηρίου καὶ ἐκ τῆς εἰκόνος αὐτοῦ
of the beast and of the image of it

καὶ ἐκ τοῦ ἀριθμοῦ τοῦ ὀνόματος αὐτοῦ
and of the number of the name of it

ἑστῶτας ἐπὶ τὴν θάλασσαν τὴν ὑαλίνην,
standing on the ²sea - ¹glassy,

ἔχοντας κιθάρας τοῦ θεοῦ. **3** καὶ ᾄδουσιν
having harps - of God. And they sing

τὴν ᾠδὴν Μωϋσέως τοῦ δούλου τοῦ
the song of Moses the slave -

θεοῦ καὶ τὴν ᾠδὴν τοῦ ἀρνίου, λέγοντες·
of God and the song of the Lamb, saying:

μεγάλα καὶ θαυμαστὰ τὰ ἔργα σου,
Great and wonderful the works of thee,

κύριε ὁ θεὸς ὁ παντοκράτωρ· δίκαιαι
[O] Lord - God the Almighty; righteous

καὶ ἀληθιναὶ αἱ ὁδοί σου, ὁ βασιλεὺς
and true the ways of thee, the king

τῶν ἐθνῶν· **4** τίς οὐ μὴ φοβηθῇ, κύριε,
of the nations; who will not fear, [O] Lord,

καὶ δοξάσει τὸ ὄνομά σου; ὅτι μόνος
and will glorify the name of thee? because [thou]
only

ὅσιος, ὅτι πάντα τὰ ἔθνη ἥξουσιν καὶ
[art] holy, because all the nations will come and

προσκυνήσουσιν ἐνώπιόν σου, ὅτι τὰ
will worship before thee, because the

δικαιώματά σου ἐφανερώθησαν. **5** Καὶ
ordinances of thee were made manifest. And

μετὰ ταῦτα εἶδον, καὶ ἠνοίγη ὁ ναὸς
after these things I saw, and was opened the shrine

τῆς σκηνῆς τοῦ μαρτυρίου ἐν τῷ οὐρανῷ,
of the tabernacle of the testimony in - heaven,

6 καὶ ἐξῆλθον οἱ ἑπτὰ ἄγγελοι οἱ ἔχοντες
and ²came forth ¹the ²seven ³angels - ⁴having

τὰς ἑπτὰ πληγὰς ἐκ τοῦ ναοῦ, ἐνδεδυμένοι
¹the ⁶seven ⁷plagues out of the shrine, having been
clothed [in]

λίνον καθαρὸν λαμπρὸν καὶ περιεζωσμένοι
²linen ¹clean ³bright and having been girdled

περὶ τὰ στήθη ζώνας χρυσᾶς. **7** καὶ
round the breasts [with] girdles ¹golden. And

ἓν ἐκ τῶν τεσσάρων ζῴων ἔδωκεν τοῖς
one of the four living gave to the
creatures

ἑπτὰ ἀγγέλοις ἑπτὰ φιάλας χρυσᾶς
seven angels seven ²bowls ¹golden

γεμούσας τοῦ θυμοῦ τοῦ θεοῦ τοῦ ζῶντος
being filled of(with) anger - of - living
the God

εἰς τοὺς αἰῶνας τῶν αἰώνων. **8** καὶ
unto the ages of the ages. And

ἐγεμίσθη ὁ ναὸς καπνοῦ ἐκ τῆς δόξης
was filled the shrine of(with) smoke of the glory

τοῦ θεοῦ καὶ ἐκ τῆς δυνάμεως αὐτοῦ,
- of God and of the power of him,

καὶ οὐδεὶς ἐδύνατο εἰσελθεῖν εἰς τὸν
and no one could to enter into the

ναὸν ἄχρι τελεσθῶσιν αἱ ἑπτὰ πληγαὶ
shrine until should be finished the seven plagues

Chapter 16

τῶν ἑπτὰ ἀγγέλων. **16** Καὶ ἤκουσα
of the seven angels. And I heard

μεγάλης φωνῆς ἐκ τοῦ ναοῦ λεγούσης τοῖς
a great(loud) voice out of the shrine saying to the

ἑπτὰ ἀγγέλοις· ὑπάγετε καὶ ἐκχέετε τὰς ἑπτὰ
seven angels: Go ye and pour out the seven

φιάλας τοῦ θυμοῦ τοῦ θεοῦ εἰς τὴν γῆν.
bowls of the anger - of God onto the earth.

2 Καὶ ἀπῆλθεν ὁ πρῶτος καὶ ἐξέχεεν τὴν
And ²went away ¹the ²first and poured out the

φιάλην αὐτοῦ εἰς τὴν γῆν· καὶ ἐγένετο
bowl of him onto the earth; and ²came

ἕλκος κακὸν καὶ πονηρὸν ἐπὶ τοὺς ἀνθρώπους
⁴sore ¹a bad ²and ³evil on the men

τοὺς ἔχοντας τὸ χάραγμα τοῦ θηρίου καὶ
- having the mark of the beast and

King James Version

them which worshipped his image. 3And the second angel poured out his vial upon the sea; and it became as the blood of a dead *man:* and every living soul died in the sea. 4And the third angel poured out his vial upon the rivers and fountains of waters; and they became blood. 5And I heard the angel of the waters say, Thou art righteous, O Lord, which art, and wast, and shalt be, because thou hast judged thus. 6For they have shed the blood of saints and prophets, and thou hast given them blood to drink; for they are worthy. 7And I heard another out of the altar say, Even so, Lord God Almighty, true and righteous *are* thy judgments. 8And the fourth angel poured out his vial upon the sun; and power was given unto him to scorch men with fire. 9And men were scorched with great heat, and blasphemed the name of God, which hath power over these plagues: and they repented not to give him glory. 10And the fifth angel poured out his vial upon the seat of the beast; and his kingdom was full of darkness; and they gnawed their tongues for pain, 11And blasphemed the God of heaven because of their pains and their sores, and repented not of their deeds. 12And the sixth angel poured out his vial upon the great river Euphrates; and the water thereof was dried up, that the way of the kings of the east might be prepared. 13And I saw three unclean spirits like frogs *come* out of the mouth of the dragon, and out of the mouth of the beast, and out of the mouth of the false prophet. 14For they are the spirits of devils, working miracles, *which* go forth unto the kings of the earth and of the whole world, to gather them to the battle of that great day of God Almighty. 15Behold, I come as a thief. Blessed *is* he that watcheth, and keepeth his garments, lest he walk naked, and they see his shame. 16And he gathered them together into a place called in the Hebrew tongue Armageddon. 17And the seventh angel poured out his vial into the air; and there came a great voice out of the temple of heaven, from the throne, saying, It is done. 18And there were voices, and thunders, and lightnings; and there was a great earthquake, such as was not since men were upon the earth, so mighty an earthquake, *and* so great. 19And the great city was divided into three parts, and the cities of the nations fell: and great Babylon came in remembrance before God, to give unto her the cup of the wine of the fierceness of his wrath. 20And every island fled away, and the mountains were not found. 21And there fell upon

New International Version

3 The second angel poured out his bowl on the sea, and it turned into blood like that of a dead man, and every living thing in the sea died.

4 The third angel poured out his bowl on the rivers and springs of water, and they became blood. 5 Then I heard the angel in charge of the waters say:

"You are just in these judgments,
    you who are and who were, the Holy One,
    because you have so judged;
6 for they have shed the blood of your saints
    and prophets,
and you have given them blood to drink
    as they deserve."

7And I heard the altar respond:

"Yes, Lord God Almighty,
    true and just are your judgments."

8 The fourth angel poured out his bowl on the sun, and the sun was given power to scorch people with fire. 9 They were seared by the intense heat and they cursed the name of God, who had control over these plagues, but they refused to repent and glorify him.

10 The fifth angel poured out his bowl on the throne of the beast, and his kingdom was plunged into darkness. Men gnawed their tongues in agony 11 and cursed the God of heaven because of their pains and their sores, but they refused to repent of what they had done.

12 The sixth angel poured out his bowl on the great river Euphrates, and its water was dried up to prepare the way for the kings from the east. 13 Then I saw three evil ᵖ spirits that looked like frogs; they came out of the mouth of the dragon, out of the mouth of the beast and out of the mouth of the false prophet. 14 They are spirits of demons performing miraculous signs, and they go out to the kings of the whole world, to gather them for the battle on the great day of God Almighty.

15 "Behold, I come like a thief! Blessed is he who stays awake and keeps his clothes with him, so that he may not go naked and be shamefully exposed."

16 Then they gathered the kings together to the place that in Hebrew is called Armageddon.

17 The seventh angel poured out his bowl into the air, and out of the temple came a loud voice from the throne, saying, "It is done!" 18 Then there came flashes of lightning, rumblings, peals of thunder and a severe earthquake. No earthquake like it has ever occurred since man has been on earth, so tremendous was the quake. 19 The great city split into three parts, and the cities of the nations collapsed. God remembered Babylon the Great and gave her the cup filled with the wine of the fury of his wrath. 20 Every island fled away and the mountains could not be found. 21 From the sky huge hailstones of about

[q] Greek *unclean.*

758

Greek Interlinear

οὺς προσκυνοῦντας τῇ εἰκόνι αὐτοῦ. 3 Καὶ
- worshipping the image of it. And

δεύτερος ἐξέχεεν τὴν φιάλην αὐτοῦ
he second poured out the bowl of him

ἰς τὴν θάλασσαν· καὶ ἐγένετο αἷμα
nto the sea; and it became blood

ὡς νεκροῦ, καὶ πᾶσα ψυχὴ ζωῆς ἀπέθανεν,
as of a dead and every soul of life died,
man,

ὰ ἐν τῇ θαλάσσῃ. 4 Καὶ ὁ τρίτος
he in the sea. And the third
nings

ξέχεεν τὴν φιάλην αὐτοῦ εἰς τοὺς
oured out the bowl of him onto the

οταμοὺς καὶ τὰς πηγὰς τῶν ὑδάτων·
rivers and the fountains of the waters;

αὶ ἐγένετο αἷμα. 5 Καὶ ἤκουσα τοῦ
nd it became blood. And I heard the

γγέλου τῶν ὑδάτων λέγοντος· δίκαιος
angel of the waters saying: Righteous

ἶ, ὁ ὢν καὶ ὁ ἦν, ὁ ὅσιος, ὅτι
rt the being and the was, the holy because
nou, [one] [one who] [one],
= the one who is

αῦτα ἔκρινας, 6 ὅτι αἷμα ἁγίων
these thou judgedst, because [the] blood of saints
things

αὶ προφητῶν ἐξέχεαν, καὶ αἷμα αὐτοῖς
and of prophets they shed, and blood to them

ἔδωκας πεῖν· ἄξιοί εἰσιν. 7 Καὶ ἤκουσα
thou hast to drink; worthy they are. And I heard
given

οῦ θυσιαστηρίου λέγοντος· ναί, κύριε
the altar saying: Yes, [O] Lord

ὁ θεὸς ὁ παντοκράτωρ, ἀληθιναὶ καὶ
God the Almighty, true and

ίκαιαι αἱ κρίσεις σου. 8 Καὶ ὁ τέταρτος
righteous the judgments of thee. And the fourth

ξέχεεν τὴν φιάλην αὐτοῦ ἐπὶ τὸν ἥλιον·
poured out the bowl of him onto the sun;

καὶ ἐδόθη αὐτῷ καυματίσαι τοὺς
and it was given to him to burn -

ἀνθρώπους ἐν πυρί. 9 καὶ ἐκαυματίσθησαν
men with fire. And were burnt [with]

οἱ ἄνθρωποι καῦμα μέγα, καὶ ἐβλασ-
- men heat great, and they blas-

φήμησαν τὸ ὄνομα τοῦ θεοῦ τοῦ ἔχοντος
phemed the name of God the [one] having

τὴν ἐξουσίαν ἐπὶ τὰς πληγὰς ταύτας,
he authority over these plagues,

καὶ οὐ μετενόησαν δοῦναι αὐτῷ δόξαν.
and they repented not to give to him glory.

10 Καὶ ὁ πέμπτος ἐξέχεεν τὴν φιάλην
And the fifth poured out the bowl

αὐτοῦ ἐπὶ τὸν θρόνον τοῦ θηρίου· καὶ
of him onto the throne of the beast; and

ἐγένετο ἡ βασιλεία αὐτοῦ ἐσκοτωμένη,
became the kingdom of it having been darkened,

καὶ ἐμασῶντο τὰς γλώσσας αὐτῶν ἐκ
and they(men) gnawed the tongues of them from

τοῦ πόνου, 11 καὶ ἐβλασφήμησαν τὸν θεὸν
the pain, and they blasphemed the God

τοῦ οὐρανοῦ ἐκ τῶν πόνων αὐτῶν καὶ
of heaven from the pains of them and

ἐκ τῶν ἑλκῶν αὐτῶν, καὶ οὐ μετενόησαν
rom the sores of them, and they repented not

ἐκ τῶν ἔργων αὐτῶν. 12 Καὶ ὁ ἕκτος
of the works of them. And the sixth

ξέχεεν τὴν φιάλην αὐτοῦ ἐπὶ τὸν ποταμὸν
poured out the bowl of him onto the river

τὸν μέγαν Εὐφράτην· καὶ ἐξηράνθη τὸ
- great Euphrates; and was dried the

ὕδωρ αὐτοῦ, ἵνα ἑτοιμασθῇ ἡ ὁδὸς τῶν
water of it, in order might be the way of the
that prepared

βασιλέων τῶν ἀπὸ ἀνατολῆς ἡλίου. 13 Καὶ
kings - from [the] rising of [the] sun. And

εἶδον ἐκ τοῦ στόματος τοῦ δράκοντος
I saw out of the mouth of the dragon

καὶ ἐκ τοῦ στόματος τοῦ θηρίου καὶ
and out of the mouth of the beast and

ἐκ τοῦ στόματος τοῦ ψευδοπροφήτου
out of the mouth of the false prophet

πνεύματα τρία ἀκάθαρτα ὡς βάτραχοι·
spirits three unclean [coming] as frogs;

14 εἰσὶν γὰρ πνεύματα δαιμονίων ποιοῦντα
for they are spirits of demons doing

σημεῖα, ἃ ἐκπορεύεται ἐπὶ τοὺς βασιλεῖς
signs, which goes forth unto the kings

τῆς οἰκουμένης ὅλης, συναγαγεῖν αὐτοὺς
of the inhabited [earth] whole, to assemble them

εἰς τὸν πόλεμον τῆς ἡμέρας τῆς μεγάλης
to the war of the day - great

τοῦ θεοῦ τοῦ παντοκράτορος. 15 Ἰδοὺ
- of God of the Almighty. Behold

ἔρχομαι ὡς κλέπτης· μακάριος ὁ γρηγορῶν
I am coming as a thief; blessed [is] the [one] watching

καὶ τηρῶν τὰ ἱμάτια αὐτοῦ, ἵνα μὴ
and keeping the garments of him, lest

γυμνὸς περιπατῇ καὶ βλέπωσιν τὴν
naked he walk and they(men) see the

ἀσχημοσύνην αὐτοῦ. 16 Καὶ συνήγαγεν
shame of him. And [t]he[y] assembled

αὐτοὺς εἰς τὸν τόπον τὸν καλούμενον
them in the place - being called

Ἑβραϊστὶ Ἁρμαγεδών. 17 Καὶ ὁ ἕβδομος
in Hebrew Harmagedon. And the seventh

ἐξέχεεν τὴν φιάλην αὐτοῦ ἐπὶ τὸν ἀέρα·
poured out the bowl of him on the air;

καὶ ἐξῆλθεν φωνὴ μεγάλη ἐκ τοῦ ναοῦ
and came out voice a great(loud) out of the shrine

ἀπὸ τοῦ θρόνου λέγουσα· γέγονεν. 18 καὶ
from the throne saying: It has occurred. And

ἐγένοντο ἀστραπαὶ καὶ φωναὶ καὶ βρονταί,
there were lightnings and voices and thunders,

καὶ σεισμὸς ἐγένετο μέγας, οἷος οὐκ
and earthquake occurred a great, such as not

ἐγένετο ἀφ' οὗ ἄνθρωπος ἐγένετο ἐπὶ
did occur from when man was on

τῆς γῆς, τηλικοῦτος σεισμὸς οὕτω μέγας.
the earth, such an earthquake so great.

19 καὶ ἐγένετο ἡ πόλις ἡ μεγάλη εἰς
And became the city - great into

τρία μέρη, καὶ αἱ πόλεις τῶν ἐθνῶν
three parts, and the cities of the nations

ἔπεσαν. καὶ Βαβυλὼν ἡ μεγάλη ἐμνήσθη
fell. And Babylon the great was remembered

ἐνώπιον τοῦ θεοῦ δοῦναι αὐτῇ τὸ ποτήριον
before - God to give to her/it the cup

τοῦ οἴνου τοῦ θυμοῦ τῆς ὀργῆς αὐτοῦ.
of the wine of the anger of the wrath of him.

20 καὶ πᾶσα νῆσος ἔφυγεν, καὶ ὄρη
And every island fled, and mountains

οὐχ εὑρέθησαν. 21 καὶ χάλαζα μεγάλη
were not found. And hail a great

* Even in English a city is often personified as feminine.

King James Version

men a great hail out of heaven, *every stone* about the weight of a talent: and men blasphemed God because of the plague of the hail; for the plague thereof was exceeding great.

17 And there came one of the seven angels which had the seven vials, and talked with me, saying unto me, Come hither; I will shew unto thee the judgment of the great whore that sitteth upon many waters; 2 With whom the kings of the earth have committed fornication, and the inhabitants of the earth have been made drunk with the wine of her fornication. 3 So he carried me away in the spirit into the wilderness: and I saw a woman sit upon a scarlet coloured beast, full of names of blasphemy, having seven heads and ten horns. 4And the woman was arrayed in purple and scarlet colour, and decked with gold and precious stones and pearls, having a golden cup in her hand full of abominations and filthiness of her fornication: 5And upon her forehead *was* a name written, MYSTERY, BABYLON THE GREAT, THE MOTHER OF HARLOTS AND ABOMINATIONS OF THE EARTH. 6And I saw the woman drunken with the blood of the saints, and with the blood of the martyrs of Jesus: and when I saw her, I wondered with great admiration. 7And the angel said unto me, Wherefore didst thou marvel? I will tell thee the mystery of the woman, and of the beast that carrieth her, which hath the seven heads and ten horns. 8 The beast that thou sawest was, and is not; and shall ascend out of the bottomless pit, and go into perdition: and they that dwell on the earth shall wonder, whose names were not written in the book of life from the foundation of the world, when they behold the beast that was, and is not, and yet is. 9And here *is* the mind which hath wisdom. The seven heads are seven mountains, on which the woman sitteth. 10And there are seven kings: five are fallen, and one is, *and* the other is not yet come; and when he cometh, he must continue a short space. 11And the beast that was, and is not, even he is the eighth, and is of the seven, and goeth into perdition. 12And the ten horns which thou sawest are ten kings, which have received no kingdom as yet; but receive power as kings one hour with the beast. 13 These have one mind, and shall give their power and strength unto the beast. 14 These shall make war with the Lamb, and the Lamb shall overcome them: for he is Lord of lords, and King of kings: and they that are with him *are* called, and chosen, and faith-

New International Version

a hundred pounds each fell upon men. And they cursed God on account of the plague of hail, because the plague was so terrible.

The woman on the beast

17 One of the seven angels who had the seven bowls came and said to me, "Come I will show you the punishment of the great prostitute, who sits on many waters. 2 With her the kings of the earth committed adultery and the inhabitants of the earth were intoxicated with the wine of her adulteries."

3 Then the angel carried me away in the Spirit into a desert. There I saw a woman sitting on a scarlet beast that was covered with blasphemous names, and had seven heads and ten horns. 4 The woman was dressed in purple and scarlet, and was glittering with gold, precious stones and pearls. She held a golden cup in her hand, filled with abominable things and the filth of her adulteries. 5 This title was written on her forehead:

MYSTERY
BABYLON THE GREAT
THE MOTHER OF PROSTITUTES
AND OF THE ABOMINATIONS OF THE EARTH.

6 I saw that the woman was drunk with the blood of the saints, the blood of those who bore testimony to Jesus.

When I saw her, I was greatly astonished. 7 Then the angel said to me: "Why are you astonished? I will explain to you the mystery of the woman and of the beast she rides, which has the seven heads and ten horns. 8 The beast, which you saw, once was, now is not, and will come up out of the Abyss and go to his destruction. The inhabitants of the earth whose names have not been written in the book of life from the creation of the world will be astonished when they see the beast, because he once was, now is not, and yet will come.

9 "This calls for a mind with wisdom. The seven heads are seven hills on which the woman sits. They are also seven kings. 10 Five have fallen, one is, the other has not yet come; but when he does come, he must remain for a little while. 11 The beast who once was, and now is not, is an eighth king. He belongs to the seven and is going to his destruction.

12 "The ten horns you saw are ten kings who have not yet received a kingdom, but who for one hour will receive authority as kings along with the beast. 13 They have one purpose and will give their power and authority to the beast. 14 They will make war against the Lamb, but the Lamb will overcome them because he is Lord of lords and King of kings—and with him will be his called, chosen and faithful followers."

Greek Interlinear

ὡς ταλαντιαία καταβαίνει ἐκ τοῦ οὐρανοῦ
as a talent in size comes down out of - heaven
ἐπὶ τοὺς ἀνθρώπους· καὶ ἐβλασφήμησαν
on - men; and ²blasphemed
οἱ ἄνθρωποι τὸν θεὸν ἐκ τῆς πληγῆς
- ¹men - God from the plague

τῆς χαλάζης, ὅτι μεγάλη ἐστὶν ἡ πληγὴ
of the hail, because ²great ⁴is ¹the ³plague
αὐτῆς σφόδρα.
²of it ²exceeding.

Chapter 17

Καὶ ἦλθεν εἷς ἐκ τῶν ἑπτὰ ἀγγέλων
And came one of the seven angels
τῶν ἐχόντων τὰς ἑπτὰ φιάλας, καὶ
- having the seven bowls, and
ἐλάλησεν μετ' ἐμοῦ λέγων· δεῦρο, δείξω
spoke with me saying: Come, I will show
σοι τὸ κρίμα τῆς πόρνης τῆς μεγάλης
thee the judgment of the ²harlot - ¹great
τῆς καθημένης ἐπὶ ὑδάτων πολλῶν, 2 μεθ'
- sitting on ²waters ¹many, with
ἧς ἐπόρνευσαν οἱ βασιλεῖς τῆς γῆς,
whom ²practised ¹the ³kings ⁴of the ⁵earth,
fornication
καὶ ἐμεθύσθησαν οἱ κατοικοῦντες τὴν γῆν
and ²became drunk ¹the ²dwelling [on] ³the ⁴earth
[ones]
ἐκ τοῦ οἴνου τῆς πορνείας αὐτῆς. 3 καὶ
from the wine of the fornication of her. And
ἀπήνεγκέν με εἰς ἔρημον ἐν πνεύματι.
he carried away me into a desert in spirit.
καὶ εἶδον γυναῖκα καθημένην ἐπὶ θηρίον
And I saw a woman sitting on ²beast
κόκκινον, γέμοντα ὀνόματα βλασφημίας,
¹a scarlet, being filled [with] names of blasphemy,
ἔχοντα κεφαλὰς ἑπτὰ καὶ κέρατα δέκα.
having ²heads ¹seven and ²horns ¹ten.
4 καὶ ἡ γυνὴ ἦν περιβεβλημένη πορφυροῦν
And the woman was having been clothed [in] purple
καὶ κόκκινον, καὶ κεχρυσωμένη χρυσίῳ
and scarlet, and having been gilded with gold
καὶ λίθῳ τιμίῳ καὶ ·μαργαρίταις, ἔχουσα
and ²stone ¹precious and pearls, having
ποτήριον χρυσοῦν ἐν τῇ χειρὶ αὐτῆς
²cup ¹a golden in the hand of her
γέμον βδελυγμάτων καὶ τὰ ἀκάθαρτα
being filled of(with) and the unclean things
abominations
τῆς πορνείας αὐτῆς, 5 καὶ ἐπὶ τὸ
of the fornication of her, and on the
μέτωπον αὐτῆς ὄνομα γεγραμμένον,
forehead of her a name having been written,
μυστήριον, ΒΑΒΥΛΩΝ Η ΜΕΓΑΛΗ,
a mystery, BABYLON THE GREAT,
Η ΜΗΤΗΡ ΤΩΝ ΠΟΡΝΩΝ ΚΑΙ
The Mother of the Harlots and
ΤΩΝ ΒΔΕΛΥΓΜΑΤΩΝ ΤΗΣ ΓΗΣ.
of the Abominations of the Earth.
6 καὶ εἶδον τὴν γυναῖκα μεθύουσαν ἐκ
And I saw the woman being drunk from
τοῦ αἵματος τῶν ἁγίων καὶ ἐκ τοῦ
the blood of the saints and from the
αἵματος τῶν μαρτύρων Ἰησοῦ. Καὶ
blood of the witnesses of Jesus. And
ἐθαύμασα ἰδὼν αὐτὴν θαῦμα μέγα. 7 καὶ
I wondered ²seeing ³her ⁴[with] ¹wonder ²a great. And
εἶπέν μοι ὁ ἄγγελος· διὰ τί ἐθαύμασας;
²said ³to me ¹the ²angel· Why didst thou wonder?
ἐγὼ ἐρῶ σοι τὸ μυστήριον τῆς γυναικὸς
I will tell thee the mystery of the woman
καὶ τοῦ θηρίου τοῦ βαστάζοντος αὐτὴν
and of the beast - carrying her

τοῦ ἔχοντος τὰς ἑπτὰ κεφαλὰς καὶ τὰ
- having the seven heads and the
δέκα κέρατα. 8 Τὸ θηρίον ὃ εἶδες ἦν
ten horns. The beast which thou wa•
sawest
καὶ οὐκ ἔστιν, καὶ μέλλει ἀναβαίνειν
and is not, and is about to come up
ἐκ τῆς ἀβύσσου καὶ εἰς ἀπώλειαν ὑπάγει·
out of the abyss and ²to ³destruction ¹goes·
καὶ θαυμασθήσονται οἱ κατοικοῦντες ἐπὶ
and ²will wonder ¹the [ones] ²dwelling ⁴on
τῆς γῆς, ὧν οὐ γέγραπται τὸ ὄνομα
⁵the ⁶earth, of whom ²has not been written ¹the ³name
ἐπὶ τὸ βιβλίον τῆς ζωῆς ἀπὸ καταβολῆς
on the scroll - of life from [the] foundation
κόσμου, βλεπόντων τὸ θηρίον ὅτι ἦν
of [the] world, seeing the beast that it was
καὶ οὐκ ἔστιν καὶ παρέσται. 9 ὧδε
and is not and is present. Here [is]
ὁ νοῦς ὁ ἔχων σοφίαν. αἱ ἑπτὰ
the mind - having wisdom. The seven
κεφαλαὶ ἑπτὰ ὄρη εἰσίν, ὅπου ἡ γυνὴ
heads ²seven ³mountains ¹are, where the woman
κάθηται ἐπ' αὐτῶν, καὶ βασιλεῖς ἑπτά
sits on them, and ²kings ¹seven
εἰσιν· 10 οἱ πέντε ἔπεσαν, ὁ εἷς ἔστιν,
²are· the five fell, the one is,
ὁ ἄλλος οὔπω ἦλθεν, καὶ ὅταν ἔλθῃ
the other not yet came, and whenever he comes
ὀλίγον αὐτὸν δεῖ μεῖναι. 11 καὶ τὸ
²a little ³him ¹it behoves ⁴to And the
[while] remain.
θηρίον ὃ ἦν καὶ οὐκ ἔστιν, καὶ αὐτὸς
beast which was and is not, even he
ὄγδοός ἐστιν, καὶ ἐκ τῶν ἑπτά ἐστιν,
²an eighth ¹is, and ²of ³the ⁴seven ¹is,
καὶ εἰς ἀπώλειαν ὑπάγει. 12 καὶ τὰ
and to destruction goes. And the
δέκα κέρατα ἃ εἶδες δέκα βασιλεῖς
ten horns which thou ²ten ¹kings
sawest
εἰσιν, οἵτινες βασιλείαν οὔπω ἔλαβον,
¹are, who a kingdom not yet received,
ἀλλὰ ἐξουσίαν ὡς βασιλεῖς μίαν ὥραν
but ²authority ²as ¹kings ²one ³hour
λαμβάνουσιν μετὰ τοῦ θηρίου. 13 οὗτοι
¹receive with the beast. These
μίαν γνώμην ἔχουσιν, καὶ τὴν δύναμιν
one mind have, and the power
καὶ ἐξουσίαν αὐτῶν τῷ θηρίῳ διδόασιν.
and authority of them to the beast ²they give.
14 οὗτοι μετὰ τοῦ ἀρνίου πολεμήσουσιν
These ²with ³the ⁴Lamb ¹will make war
καὶ τὸ ἀρνίον νικήσει αὐτούς, ὅτι κύριος
and the Lamb will overcome them, because ²Lord
κυρίων ἐστὶν καὶ βασιλεὺς βασιλέων,...
²of lords ¹he is and King of kings, and
οἱ μετ' αὐτοῦ κλητοὶ καὶ ἐκλεκτοὶ καὶ
the with him [are] called and chosen and
[ones]

King James Version

ful. 15And he saith unto me, The waters which thou sawest, where the whore sitteth, are peoples, and multitudes, and nations, and tongues. 16And the ten horns which thou sawest upon the beast, these shall hate the whore, and shall make her desolate and naked, and shall eat her flesh, and burn her with fire. 17 For God hath put in their hearts to fulfil his will, and to agree, and give their kingdom unto the beast, until the words of God shall be fulfilled. 18And the woman which thou sawest is that great city, which reigneth over the kings of the earth.

18 And after these things I saw another angel come down from heaven, having great power; and the earth was lightened with his glory. 2And he cried mightily with a strong voice, saying, Babylon the great is fallen, is fallen, and is become the habitation of devils, and the hold of every foul spirit, and a cage of every unclean and hateful bird. 3 For all nations have drunk of the wine of the wrath of her fornication, and the kings of the earth have committed fornication with her, and the merchants of the earth are waxed rich through the abundance of her delicacies. 4And I heard another voice from heaven, saying, Come out of her, my people, that ye be not partakers of her sins, and that ye receive not of her plagues. 5 For her sins have reached unto heaven, and God hath remembered her iniquities. 6 Reward her even as she rewarded you, and double unto her double according to her works: in the cup which she hath filled, fill to her double. 7 How much she hath glorified herself, and lived deliciously, so much torment and sorrow give her: for she saith in her heart, I sit a queen, and am no widow, and shall see no sorrow. 8 Therefore shall her plagues come in one day, death, and mourning, and famine; and she shall be utterly burned with fire: for strong *is* the Lord God who judgeth her. 9And the kings of the earth, who have committed fornication and lived deliciously with her, shall bewail her, and lament for her, when they shall see the smoke of her burning, 10 Standing afar off for the fear of her torment, saying, Alas, alas, that great city Babylon, that mighty city! for in one hour is thy judgment come. 11And the merchants of the earth shall weep and mourn over her; for no man buyeth their merchandise any more: 12 The merchandise of gold, and silver, and precious stones, and of pearls, and fine linen, and purple,

New International Version

15 Then the angel said to me, "The waters you saw, where the prostitute sits, are peoples, multitudes, nations and languages. 16 The beast and the ten horns you saw will hate the prostitute. They will bring her to ruin and leave her naked; they will eat her flesh and burn her with fire. 17 For God has put it into their hearts to accomplish his purpose by agreeing to give the beast their power to rule, until God's words are fulfilled. 18 The woman you saw is the great city that rules over the kings of the earth."

The fall of Babylon

18 After this I saw another angel coming down from heaven. He had great authority, and the earth was illuminated by his splendor. 2 With a mighty voice he shouted:
"Fallen! Fallen is Babylon the Great!
  She has become a home for demons
  and a haunt for every evil *r* spirit,
  a haunt for every unclean and detestable bird.
3 For all the nations have drunk
  the maddening wine of her adulteries.
The kings of the earth committed adultery with her,
  and the merchants of the earth grew rich from her excessive luxuries."
4 Then I heard another voice from heaven say:
"Come out of her, my people,
  so that you will not share in her sins,
  so that you will not receive any of her plagues;
5 for her sins are piled up to heaven,
  and God has remembered her crimes.
6 Give back to her as she has given;
  pay her back double for what she has done.
  Mix her a double portion from her own cup.
7 Give her as much torture and grief
  as the glory and luxury she gave herself.
In her heart she boasts,
  'I sit as queen; I am not a widow,
  and I will never mourn.'
8 Therefore in one day her plagues will overtake her:
  death, mourning and famine.
She will be consumed by fire,
  for mighty is the Lord God who judges her.
9 "When the kings of the earth who committed adultery with her and shared her luxury see the smoke of her burning, they will weep and mourn over her. 10 Terrified at her torment, they will stand far off and cry:
'Woe! Woe, O great city,
  O Babylon, city of power!
In one hour your doom has come!'
11 "The merchants of the earth will weep and mourn over her because no one buys their cargoes any more—12 cargoes of gold, silver, precious stones and pearls; fine linen, purple,

[r] Greek *unclean.*

Greek Interlinear

πιστοί. **15** Καὶ λέγει μοι· τὰ ὕδατα
faithful. And he says to me: The waters

ἃ εἶδες, οὖ ἡ πόρνη κάθηται, λαοὶ
which thou where the harlot sits, peoples
sawest,

καὶ ὄχλοι εἰσὶν καὶ ἔθνη καὶ γλῶσσαι.
and crowds are and nations and tongues.

16 καὶ τὰ δέκα κέρατα ἃ εἶδες καὶ
And the ten horns which thou sawest and

τὸ θηρίον, οὖτοι μισήσουσιν τὴν πόρνην,
the beast, these will hate the harlot,

καὶ ἠρημωμένην ποιήσουσιν αὐτὴν καὶ
and *having been desolated 'will make 'her and

γυμνήν, καὶ τὰς σάρκας αὐτῆς φάγονται,
naked, and ²the ²fleshes ⁴of her ¹will eat,

καὶ αὐτὴν κατακαύσουσιν [ἐν] πυρί· **17** ὁ
and ²her ¹will consume with fire; –

γὰρ θεὸς ἔδωκεν εἰς τὰς καρδίας αὐτῶν
for God gave into the hearts of them

ποιῆσαι τὴν γνώμην αὐτοῦ, καὶ ποιῆσαι
to do the mind of him, and to make

μίαν γνώμην καὶ δοῦναι τὴν βασιλείαν
one mind and to give the kingdom

αὐτῶν τῷ θηρίῳ, ἄχρι τελεσθήσονται οἱ
of them to the beast, until ⁴shall be accomplished ¹the

λόγοι τοῦ θεοῦ. **18** καὶ ἡ γυνὴ ἣν
¹words – ²of God. And the woman whom

εἶδες ἔστιν ἡ πόλις ἡ μεγάλη ἡ ἔχουσα
thou is the ²city – ¹great – having
sawest

βασιλείαν ἐπὶ τῶν βασιλέων τῆς γῆς.
a kingdom over the kings of the earth.

Chapter 18

Μετὰ ταῦτα εἶδον ἄλλον ἄγγελον
After these things I saw another angel

καταβαίνοντα ἐκ τοῦ οὐρανοῦ, ἔχοντα
coming down out of – heaven, having

ἐξουσίαν μεγάλην, καὶ ἡ γῆ ἐφωτίσθη
²authority ¹great, and the earth was enlightened

ἐκ τῆς δόξης αὐτοῦ. **2** And ἔκραξεν
from the glory of him. And he cried

ἐν ἰσχυρᾷ φωνῇ λέγων· ἔπεσεν ἔπεσεν
in a strong voice saying: Fell[,] fell

Βαβυλὼν ἡ μεγάλη, καὶ ἐγένετο κατοικητή-
Babylon the great, and became a dwelling-

ριον δαιμονίων καὶ φυλακὴ παντὸς
place of demons and a prison of every

πνεύματος ἀκαθάρτου καὶ φυλακὴ παντὸς
²spirit ¹unclean and a prison of every

ὀρνέου ἀκαθάρτου καὶ μεμισημένου, **3** ὅτι
⁴bird ¹unclean ²and ³having been hated, because

ἐκ τοῦ οἴνου τοῦ θυμοῦ τῆς πορνείας
⁸of – ⁷the ⁹wine ¹⁰of the ⁶anger ¹⁰of the ¹¹fornication

αὐτῆς πέπωκαν πάντα ⁴τὰ ἔθνη, καὶ
¹²of her ⁴have drunk ¹all ³the ²nations, and

οἱ βασιλεῖς τῆς γῆς μετ' αὐτῆς ἐπόρνευσαν,
the kings of the earth with her practised
fornication,

καὶ οἱ ἔμποροι τῆς γῆς ἐκ τῆς δυνάμεως
and the merchants of the earth ²from ³the ⁴power

τοῦ στρήνους αὐτῆς ἐπλούτησαν. **4** Καὶ
⁵of the ⁶luxury ¹of her ¹became rich. And

ἤκουσα ἄλλην φωνὴν ἐκ τοῦ οὐρανοῦ
I heard another voice out of – heaven

λέγουσαν· ἐξέλθατε ὁ λαός μου ἐξ αὐτῆς,
saying: Come ye out[,] the people of me[,] out of her,

ἵνα μὴ συγκοινωνήσητε ταῖς ἁμαρτίαις
lest ye share in the sins

αὐτῆς, καὶ ἐκ τῶν πληγῶν αὐτῆς ἵνα
of her, and ²of ³the ⁴plagues ⁵of her ¹lest

μὴ λάβητε· **5** ὅτι ἐκολλήθησαν αὐτῆς αἱ
²ye receive; because ²joined together ⁴of her ¹the

ἁμαρτίαι ἄχρι τοῦ οὐρανοῦ, καὶ ἐμνημό-
³sins up to – heaven, and ⁴remem-

νευσεν ὁ θεὸς τὰ ἀδικήματα αὐτῆς.
bered ¹God the misdeeds of her.

6 ἀπόδοτε αὐτῇ ὡς καὶ αὐτὴ ἀπέδωκεν,
Give ye back to her as indeed she gave back,

καὶ διπλώσατε τὰ διπλᾶ κατὰ τὰ ἔργα
and double ye the double according to the works

αὐτῆς· ἐν τῷ ποτηρίῳ ᾧ ἐκέρασεν
of her; in the cup in which she mixed

κεράσατε αὐτῇ διπλοῦν· **7** ὅσα ἐδόξασεν
mix ye to her double; by what she glorified
things

αὐτὴν καὶ ἐστρηνίασεν, τοσοῦτον δότε
her[self] and luxuriated, by so much give ye

αὐτῇ βασανισμὸν καὶ πένθος. ὅτι ἐν
to her torment and ·rro v. Because in

τῇ καρδίᾳ αὐτῆς λέγει ὅτι κάθημαι
the heart of her she says[,] – I sit

βασίλισσα καὶ χήρα οὐκ εἰμί καὶ πένθος
a queen and a widow I am not and sorrow

οὐ μὴ ἴδω· **8** διὰ τοῦτο ἐν μιᾷ ἡμέρᾳ
by no means I see; therefore in one day

ἥξουσιν αἱ πληγαὶ αὐτῆς, θάνατος καὶ
will come the plagues of her, death and

πένθος καὶ λιμός, καὶ ἐν πυρὶ κατακαυ-
sorrow and famine, and with fire she will be

θήσεται· ὅτι ἰσχυρὸς κύριος ὁ θεὸς ὁ
consumed; because strong [is] [the] Lord – God the

κρίνας αὐτήν. **9** καὶ κλαύσουσιν καὶ
[one] judging her. And ¹will weep ²and

κόψονται ἐπ' αὐτὴν οἱ βασιλεῖς τῆς
²wail ¹over ⁴her ¹the ²kings ³of the

γῆς οἱ μετ' αὐτῆς πορνεύσαντες καὶ
⁴earth ¹⁵the ¹²with ¹⁴her ¹¹having practised and
[ones] fornication

στρηνιάσαντες, ὅταν βλέπωσιν τὸν καπνὸν
having luxuriated, whenever they see the smoke

τῆς πυρώσεως αὐτῆς, **10** ἀπὸ μακρόθεν
of the burning of her, ¹from ²afar

ἑστηκότες διὰ τὸν φόβον τοῦ βασανισμοῦ
¹standing because of the fear of the torment

αὐτῆς, λέγοντες· οὐαὶ οὐαί, ἡ πόλις
of her, saying: Woe[,] woe, the ²city

ἡ μεγάλη, Βαβυλὼν ἡ πόλις ἡ ἰσχυρά,
– ¹great, Babylon the ²city – ¹strong,

ὅτι μιᾷ ὥρᾳ ἦλθεν ἡ κρίσις σου. **11** καὶ
be- in hour came the judgment of thee. And
cause one

οἱ ἔμποροι τῆς γῆς κλαίουσιν καὶ
the merchants of the earth weep and

πενθοῦσιν ἐπ' αὐτήν, ὅτι τὸν γόμον
sorrow over her, because ²the ¹cargo

αὐτῶν οὐδεὶς ἀγοράζει οὐκέτι, **12** γόμον
²of them ¹no one ¹buys ²any more, cargo

χρυσοῦ καὶ ἀργύρου καὶ λίθου τιμίου
of gold and of silver and ²stone ¹of valuable

καὶ μαργαριτῶν καὶ βυσσίνου καὶ πορφύρας
and of pearls and of fine linen and of purple

King James Version

and silk, and scarlet, and all thyine wood, and all manner vessels of ivory, and all manner vessels of most precious wood, and of brass, and iron, and marble. 13And cinnamon, and odours, and ointments, and frankincense, and wine, and oil, and fine flour, and wheat, and beasts, and sheep, and horses, and chariots, and slaves, and souls of men. 14And the fruits that thy soul lusted after are departed from thee, and all things which were dainty and goodly are departed from thee, and thou shalt find them no more at all. 15 The merchants of these things, which were made rich by her, shall stand afar off for the fear of her torment, weeping and wailing, 16And saying, Alas, alas, that great city, that was clothed in fine linen, and purple, and scarlet, and decked with gold, and precious stones, and pearls! 17 For in one hour so great riches is come to nought. And every shipmaster, and all the company in ships, and sailors, and as many as trade by sea, stood afar off, 18And cried when they saw the smoke of her burning, saying, What *city is* like unto this great city! 19And they cast dust on their heads, and cried, weeping and wailing, saying, Alas, alas, that great city, wherein were made rich all that had ships in the sea by reason of her costliness! for in one hour is she made desolate. 20 Rejoice over her, *thou* heaven, and *ye* holy apostles and prophets; for God hath avenged you on her. 21And a mighty angel took up a stone like a great millstone, and cast *it* into the sea, saying, Thus with violence shall that great city Babylon be thrown down, and shall be found no more at all. 22And the voice of harpers, and musicians, and of pipers, and trumpeters, shall be heard no more at all in thee; and no craftsman, of whatsoever craft *he be,* shall be found any more in thee; and the sound of a millstone shall be heard no more at all in thee; 23And the light of a candle shall shine no more at all in thee; and the voice of the bridegroom and the bride shall be heard no more at all in thee: for thy merchants were the great men of the earth; for by thy sorceries were all nations deceived. 24And in her was found the blood of prophets, and of saints, and of all that were slain upon the earth.

New International Version

silk and scarlet cloth; every sort of citron woo and articles of every kind made of ivory, cost wood, bronze, iron and marble; 13 cargoes cinnamon and spice, of incense, myrrh a frankincense, of wine and olive oil, of fine flo and wheat; cattle and sheep; horses and carriage and bodies and souls of men.

14 "They will say, 'The fruit you longed f is gone from you. All your riches and splend have vanished, never to be recovered.' 15 Tl merchants who sold these things and gained the wealth from her will stand far off, terrified at h torment. They will weep and mourn 16 and c out:

'Woe! Woe, O great city,
   dressed in fine linen, purple and scarle
   and glittering with gold, precious ston
   and pearls!
17 In one hour such great wealth has bee
   brought to ruin!'

"Every sea captain, and all who travel by shi the sailors, and all who earn their living fro the sea, will stand far off. 18 When they see tl smoke of her burning, they will exclaim, 'W there ever a city like this great city?' 19 They w throw dust on their heads, and with weeping ar mourning cry out:

'Woe! Woe, O great city,
   where all who had ships on the sea
   became rich through her wealth!
In one hour she has been brought to ruin!
20 Rejoice over her, O heaven!
   Rejoice, saints and apostles and prophet
   God has judged her for the way she treate
   you.' "

21 Then a mighty angel picked up a bould the size of a large millstone and threw it in the sea, and said:

"With such violence
   the great city of Babylon will be throw
   down,
   never to be found again.
22 The music of harpists and musicians, flu
   players and trumpeters,
   will never be heard in you again.
No workman of any trade
   will ever be found in you again.
The sound of a millstone
   will never be heard in you again.
23 The light of a lamp
   will never shine in you again.
The voice of bridegroom and bride
   will never be heard in you again.
Your merchants were the world's great me
   By your magic spell all the nations we
   led astray.
24 In her was found the blood of prophets ar
   of the saints,
   and of all who have been killed on tl
   earth."

Hallelujah!

19 And after these things I heard a great voice of much people in heaven, saying, Alleluia; Salvation, and glory, and honour, and power, unto the Lord our God: 2 For true and

19 After this, I heard what sounded like th roar of a great multitude in heaven shou ing:

"Hallelujah!
   Salvation and glory and power belong to ou
   God,
2 for true and just are his judgments.

Greek Interlinear

καὶ   σηρικοῦ   καὶ   κοκκίνου,   καὶ   πᾶν
and   of silk   and   of scarlet,   and   all

ξύλον   θύϊνον   καὶ   πᾶν   σκεῦος   ἐλεφάντινον
²wood   ¹thyine   and   every   ²vessel   ¹ivory

καὶ   πᾶν   σκεῦος   ἐκ   ξύλου   τιμιωτάτου
and   every   vessel   of   ²wood   ¹very valuable

καὶ   χαλκοῦ   καὶ   σιδήρου   καὶ   μαρμάρου,
and   of bronze   and   of iron   and   of marble,

13 καὶ   κιννάμωμον   καὶ   ἄμωμον   καὶ
and   cinnamon   and   spice   and

θυμιάματα   καὶ   μύρον   καὶ   λίβανον   καὶ
incenses   and   ointment   and   frankincense   and

οἶνον   καὶ   ἔλαιον   καὶ   σεμίδαλιν   καὶ   σῖτον
wine   and   oil   and   fine meal   and   corn

καὶ   κτήνη   καὶ   πρόβατα,   καὶ   ἵππων
and beasts of burden and   sheep,   and   of horses

καὶ   ῥεδῶν   καὶ   σωμάτων,   καὶ   ψυχὰς
and   of carriages   and   of bodies,   and   souls

ἀνθρώπων.   14 καὶ   ἡ   ὀπώρα   σου   τῆς
of men.   And the   fruit   ²of thee ¹of the

ἐπιθυμίας   τῆς   ψυχῆς   ἀπῆλθεν   ἀπὸ   σοῦ,
²lust   ³of the   ⁴soul   went away   from   thee,

καὶ   πάντα   τὰ   λιπαρὰ   καὶ   τὰ   λαμπρὰ
and   all   the   sumptuous   and the   bright
things   things

ἀπώλετο   ἀπὸ   σοῦ,   καὶ   οὐκέτι   οὐ   μὴ
perished   from   thee,   and   no more   by no(any)
means

αὐτὰ   εὑρήσουσιν.   15 οἱ   ἔμποροι   τούτων,
²them   ¹shall they find.   The   merchants   of these
things,

οἱ   πλουτήσαντες   ἀπ’   αὐτῆς,   ἀπὸ   μακρόθεν
the   having been rich   from   her,   ²from   ²afar
[ones]

στήσονται   διὰ   τὸν   φόβον   τοῦ   βασανισμοῦ
¹will stand   because of the   fear   of the   torment

αὐτῆς   κλαίοντες   καὶ   πενθοῦντες,   16 λέγοντες·
of her   weeping   and   sorrowing,   saying:

οὐαὶ   οὐαί,   ἡ   πόλις   ἡ   μεγάλη,   ἡ   περι-
Woe[.]   woe,   the   ²city   –   ¹great,   –   having

βεβλημένη   βύσσινον   καὶ   πορφυροῦν   καὶ
been clothed [with]   fine linen   and   purple   and

κόκκινον,   καὶ   κεχρυσωμένη   ἐν   χρυσίῳ
scarlet,   and   having been gilded   with   gold

καὶ   λίθῳ   τιμίῳ   καὶ   μαργαρίτῃ,   17 ὅτι
and   ²stone   ¹valuable   and   pearl,   because

μιᾷ   ὥρᾳ   ἠρημώθη   ὁ   τοσοῦτος   πλοῦτος.
in one   hour   ²was made   ¹such great   ²wealth.
desolate

καὶ   πᾶς   κυβερνήτης   καὶ   πᾶς   ὁ   ἐπὶ
And   every   steersman   and   ¹every   ²one   ⁴to

τόπον   πλέων   καὶ   ναῦται   καὶ   ὅσοι   τὴν
⁵a place   ³sailing   and   sailors   and as many as   ²the

θάλασσαν   ἐργάζονται,   ἀπὸ   μακρόθεν   ἔστησαν
¹sea   ¹work,   ²from   ¹afar   ²stood

18 καὶ   ἔκραζον   βλέποντες   τὸν   καπνὸν
and   cried out   seeing   the   smoke

τῆς   πυρώσεως   αὐτῆς   λέγοντες·   τίς   ὁμοία
of the   burning   of her   saying: Who(What) [is] like

τῇ   πόλει   τῇ   μεγάλη;   19 καὶ   ἔβαλον
to the   ²city   –   ¹great?   And   they cast

χοῦν   ἐπὶ   τὰς   κεφαλὰς   αὐτῶν   καὶ   ἔκραζον
dust   on   the   heads   of them   and   cried out

κλαίοντες   καὶ   πενθοῦντες,   λέγοντες·   οὐαὶ
weeping   and   sorrowing,   saying: Woe[,]

οὐαί,   ἡ   πόλις   ἡ   μεγάλη,   ἐν   ᾗ   ἐπλούτησαν
woe,   the   ²city   –   ¹great,   by which   ²were rich

πάντες   οἱ   ἔχοντες   τὰ   πλοῖα   ἐν   τῇ
¹all   ¹the [ones]   ²having   ³the   ⁴ships   ²in   ³the

θαλάσσῃ   ἐκ   τῆς   τιμιότητος   αὐτῆς,   ὅτι
⁵sea   from   the   worth   of her,   because

μιᾷ   ὥρᾳ   ἠρημώθη.   20 Εὐφραίνου   ἐπ’
in one   hour   she was made desolate.   Be thou glad   over

αὐτῇ,   οὐρανὲ   καὶ   οἱ   ἅγιοι   καὶ   οἱ   ἀπό-
her,   heaven   and   the   saints   and   the   apost-

στολοι   καὶ   οἱ   προφῆται,   ὅτι   ἔκρινεν   ὁ
les   and   the   prophets,   because   ²judged   –

θεὸς   τὸ   κρίμα   ὑμῶν   ἐξ   αὐτῆς.   21 Καὶ
¹God   the   judgment   of you   by   her.   And

ἦρεν   εἷς   ἄγγελος   ἰσχυρὸς   λίθον   ὡς
⁴lifted   ¹one   ²angel   ³strong   a stone   as

μύλινον   μέγαν,   καὶ   ἔβαλεν   εἰς   τὴν   θά-
²millstone   ¹a great,   and   threw   into   the   sea

λασσαν   λέγων·   οὕτως   ὁρμήματι   βληθήσεται
saying: Thus   with a rush   ²shall be thrown

Βαβυλὼν   ἡ   μεγάλη   πόλις,   καὶ   οὐ   μὴ
¹Babylon   ²the   ²great   ¹city,   and   by no means

εὑρεθῇ   ἔτι.   22 καὶ   φωνὴ   κιθαρῳδῶν
[shall] be   longer.   And   sound   of harpers
found

καὶ   μουσικῶν   καὶ   αὐλητῶν   καὶ   σαλπιστῶν
and   of musicians   and   of flutists   and   of trumpeters

οὐ   μὴ   ἀκουσθῇ   ἐν   σοὶ   ἔτι,   καὶ   πᾶς
by no means [shall] be heard in   thee   longer,   and   every

τεχνίτης   πάσης   τέχνης   οὐ   μὴ   εὑρεθῇ
craftsman   of every   craft   by no means   [shall]
be found

ἐν   σοὶ   ἔτι,   καὶ   φωνὴ   μύλου   οὐ   μὴ
in   thee   longer,   and   sound   of a mill   by no means

ἀκουσθῇ   ἐν   σοὶ   ἔτι,   23 καὶ   φῶς
[shall] be heard   in   thee   longer,   and   light

λύχνου   οὐ   μὴ   φάνῃ   ἐν   σοὶ   ἔτι,   καὶ
of a   by no means   [shall]   in   thee   longer,   and
lamp   shine

φωνὴ   νυμφίου   καὶ   νύμφης   οὐ   μὴ
voice   of bridegroom   and   of bride   by no means

ἀκουσθῇ   ἐν   σοὶ   ἔτι·   ὅτι   [οἱ]   ἔμποροί
[shall] be heard in   thee   longer; because the   merchants

σου   ἦσαν   οἱ   μεγιστᾶνες   τῆς   γῆς,   ὅτι
of thee   were   the   great ones   of the   earth,   because

ἐν   τῇ   φαρμακείᾳ   σου   ἐπλανήθησαν   πάντα
by   the   sorcery   of thee   ²were deceived   ¹all

τὰ   ἔθνη,   24 καὶ   ἐν   αὐτῇ   αἷμα   προφητῶν
²the   ¹nations,   and   in   her   ²blood   ²of prophets

καὶ   ἁγίων   εὑρέθη   καὶ   πάντων   τῶν
⁴and   ⁵of saints   ¹was found   and   of all   the [ones]

ἐσφαγμένων   ἐπὶ   τῆς   γῆς.
having been slain   on   the   earth.

Chapter 19

Μετὰ   ταῦτα   ἤκουσα   ὡς   φωνὴν
After   these things   I heard   as   ²voice

μεγάλην   ὄχλου   πολλοῦ   ἐν   τῷ   οὐρανῷ
¹a great   ²crowd   ²of a much   in   –   heaven
(loud)   (great)

λεγόντων·   ἁλληλουϊά·   ἡ   σωτηρία   καὶ   ἡ
saying: Halleluia: The   salvation   and   the

δόξα   καὶ   ἡ   δύναμις   τοῦ   θεοῦ   ἡμῶν,
glory   and   the   power   of the   God   of us,

2 ὅτι   ἀληθιναὶ   καὶ   δίκαιαι   αἱ   κρίσεις
because   true   and   righteous   the   judgments

765

King James Version

righteous *are* his judgments; for he hath judged the great whore, which did corrupt the earth with her fornication, and hath avenged the blood of his servants at her hand. 3And again they said, Alleluia. And her smoke rose up for ever and ever. 4And the four and twenty elders and the four beasts fell down and worshipped God that sat on the throne, saying, Amen; Alleluia. 5And a voice came out of the throne, saying, Praise our God, all ye his servants, and ye that fear him, both small and great. 6And I heard as it were the voice of a great multitude, and as the voice of many waters, and as the voice of mighty thunderings, saying, Alleluia: for the Lord God omnipotent reigneth. 7 Let us be glad and rejoice, and give honour to him: for the marriage of the Lamb is come, and his wife hath made herself ready. 8And to her was granted that she should be arrayed in fine linen, clean and white: for the fine linen is the righteousness of saints. 9And he saith unto me, Write, Blessed *are* they which are called unto the marriage supper of the Lamb. And he saith unto me, These are the true sayings of God. 10And I fell at his feet to worship him. And he said unto me, See *thou do it* not: I am thy fellow servant, and of thy brethren that have the testimony of Jesus: worship God: for the testimony of Jesus is the spirit of prophecy. 11And I saw heaven opened, and behold a white horse; and he that sat upon him *was* called Faithful and True, and in right-eousness he doth judge and make war. 12 His eyes *were* as a flame of fire, and on his head *were* many crowns; and he had a name written, that no man knew, but he himself. 13And he *was* clothed with a vesture dipped in blood: and his name is called The Word of God. 14And the armies *which were* in heaven followed him upon white horses, clothed in fine linen, white and clean. 15And out of his mouth goeth a sharp sword, that with it he should smite the nations; and he shall rule them with a rod of iron: and he treadeth the winepress of the fierceness and wrath of Almighty God. 16And he hath on *his* vesture and on his thigh a name written, KING OF KINGS, AND LORD OF LORDS. 17And I saw an angel standing in the sun; and he cried with a loud voice, saying to all the fowls that fly in the midst of heaven, Come and gather yourselves together unto the supper of the great God; 18 That ye may eat the flesh of kings, and the flesh of captains, and the flesh of mighty

New International Version

He has condemned the great prostitute
  who corrupted the earth by her adulteries.
He has avenged on her the blood of his
  servants."
3 And again they shouted:
"Hallelujah!
The smoke from her goes up for ever and
  ever."
4 The twenty-four elders and the four living creatures fell down and worshiped God, who was seated on the throne. And they cried:
"Amen, Hallelujah!"
5 Then a voice came from the throne, saying:
"Praise our God,
  all you his servants,
you who fear him,
  both small and great!"
6 Then I heard what sounded like a great multitude, like the roar of rushing waters and like loud peals of thunder, shouting:
"Hallelujah!
  For our Lord God Almighty reigns.
7 Let us rejoice and be glad
  and give him glory!
For the wedding of the Lamb has come,
  and his bride has made herself ready.
8 Fine linen, bright and clean,
  was given her to wear."

(Fine linen stands for the righteous acts of the saints.)
9 Then the angel said to me, "Write: 'Blessed are those who are invited to the wedding supper of the Lamb!' " And he added, "These are the true words of God."
10 At this I fell at his feet to worship him. But he said to me, "Do not do it! I am a fellow servant with you and with your brothers who hold to the testimony of Jesus. Worship God! For the testimony of Jesus is the spirit of prophecy."

The rider on the white horse

11 I saw heaven standing open and there before me was a white horse, whose rider is called Faithful and True. With justice he judges and makes war. 12 His eyes are like blazing fire, and on his head are many crowns. He has a name written on him that no one but he himself knows. 13 He is dressed in a robe dipped in blood, and his name is the Word of God. 14 The armies of heaven were following him, riding on white horses and dressed in fine linen, white and clean. 15 Out of his mouth comes a sharp sword with which to strike down the nations. He will rule them with a rod of iron. He treads the winepress of the fury of the wrath of God Almighty. 16 On his robe and on his thigh he has this name written:

KING OF KINGS AND LORD OF LORDS.

17 And I saw an angel standing in the sun, who cried in a loud voice to all the birds flying in midair, "Come, gather together for the great supper of God, 18 so that you may eat the flesh of kings, generals, and mighty men, of horses

Greek Interlinear

αὐτοῦ· ὅτι ἔκρινεν τὴν πόρνην τὴν
of him; because he judged the ³harlot –

μεγάλην ἥτις ἔφθειρεν τὴν γῆν ἐν τῇ
¹great who defiled the earth with the

πορνείᾳ αὐτῆς, καὶ ἐξεδίκησεν τὸ αἷμα
fornication of her, and he avenged the blood

τῶν δούλων αὐτοῦ ἐκ χειρὸς αὐτῆς.
of the slaves of him out of [the] hand of her.

3 καὶ δεύτερον εἴρηκαν· ἁλληλουϊά· καὶ
And secondly they have said: Halleluia; and

ὁ καπνὸς αὐτῆς ἀναβαίνει εἰς τοὺς
the smoke of her goes up unto the

αἰῶνας τῶν αἰώνων. 4 καὶ ἔπεσαν οἱ
ages of the ages. And ²fell ¹the

πρεσβύτεροι οἱ εἴκοσι τέσσαρες καὶ τὰ
²elders – ²twenty-four ²and ²the

τέσσερα ζῷα, καὶ προσεκύνησαν τῷ θεῷ
⁴four ⁵living and worshipped – God
creatures,

τῷ καθημένῳ ἐπὶ τῷ θρόνῳ λέγοντες·
– sitting on the throne saying:

ἀμὴν ἁλληλουϊά. 5 καὶ φωνὴ ἀπὸ τοῦ
Amen[,] halleluia. And a voice ²from ³the

θρόνου ἐξῆλθεν λέγουσα· αἰνεῖτε τῷ θεῷ
⁴throne ¹came out saying: Praise ye the God

ἡμῶν, πάντες οἱ δοῦλοι αὐτοῦ, οἱ
of us, all the slaves of him, the

φοβούμενοι αὐτόν, οἱ μικροὶ καὶ οἱ
[ones] fearing him, the small and the

μεγάλοι. 6 Καὶ ἤκουσα ὡς φωνὴν ὄχλου
great. And I heard as a sound ²crowd

πολλοῦ καὶ ὡς φωνὴν ὑδάτων πολλῶν
¹of a and as a sound ²waters ¹of many
much(great)

καὶ ὡς φωνὴν βροντῶν ἰσχυρῶν, λεγόντων·
and as a sound ²thunders ¹of strong saying:
(loud),

ἁλληλουϊά, ὅτι ἐβασίλευσεν κύριος ὁ θεὸς
Halleluia, because ²reigned ¹[the] Lord ²the ³God

ἡμῶν ὁ παντοκράτωρ. 7 χαίρωμεν καὶ
¹of us ²the ³Almighty. Let us rejoice and

ἀγαλλιῶμεν, καὶ δώσομεν τὴν δόξαν αὐτῷ,
let us exult, and we will give the glory to him,

ὅτι ἦλθεν ὁ γάμος τοῦ ἀρνίου, καὶ
because ²came ¹the ²marriage ²of the ⁴Lamb, and

ἡ γυνὴ αὐτοῦ ἡτοίμασεν ἑαυτήν, 8 καὶ
the wife of him prepared herself, and

ἐδόθη αὐτῇ ἵνα περιβάληται βύσσινον
it was to her in order she might be ²fine linen
given that clothed [with]

λαμπρὸν καθαρόν· τὸ γὰρ βύσσινον τὰ
¹bright ⁴clean; – for the fine linen ²the

δικαιώματα τῶν ἁγίων ἐστίν. 9 Καὶ
³righteous deeds ⁴of the ⁵saints ¹is. And

λέγει μοι· γράψον· μακάριοι οἱ εἰς τὸ
he tells me: Write thou; blessed the [ones] to ²the

δεῖπνον τοῦ γάμου τοῦ ἀρνίου κεκλημένοι.
¹supper ²of ³marriage ²of ⁴Lamb ³having been
the the called.

καὶ λέγει μοι· οὗτοι οἱ λόγοι ἀληθινοὶ
And he says to me: ¹These – ²words ³true

τοῦ θεοῦ εἰσιν. 10 καὶ ἔπεσα ἔμπροσθεν
– ⁴of God ⁴are. And I fell before

τῶν ποδῶν αὐτοῦ προσκυνῆσαι αὐτῷ.
the feet of him to worship him.

καὶ λέγει μοι· ὅρα μή· σύνδουλός σου
And he says to me: See thou not; ³a fellow- ²of
[do it] slave thee

εἰμι καὶ τῶν ἀδελφῶν σου τῶν ἐχόντων
¹I am and of the brothers of thee – having

τὴν μαρτυρίαν Ἰησοῦ· τῷ θεῷ προσκύνησον.
the witness of Jesus; – ²God ¹worship thou.

ἡ γὰρ μαρτυρία Ἰησοῦ ἐστιν τὸ πνεῦμα
For the witness of Jesus is the spirit

τῆς προφητείας.
– of prophecy.

11 Καὶ εἶδον τὸν οὐρανὸν ἠνεῳγμένον,
And I saw – heaven having been opened,

καὶ ἰδοὺ ἵππος λευκός, καὶ ὁ καθήμενος
and behold[,] ²horse ¹a white, and the [one] sitting

ἐπ᾽ αὐτὸν πιστὸς καλούμενος καὶ ἀληθινός,
on it ²faithful ¹being called and true,

καὶ ἐν δικαιοσύνῃ κρίνει καὶ πολεμεῖ.
and in righteousness he judges and makes war.

12 οἱ δὲ ὀφθαλμοὶ αὐτοῦ φλὸξ πυρός,
And the eyes of him [are as] a flame of fire,

καὶ ἐπὶ τὴν κεφαλὴν αὐτοῦ διαδήματα
and on the head of him ²diadems

πολλά, ἔχων ὄνομα γεγραμμένον ὃ οὐδεὶς
¹many, having a name having been written which no one

οἶδεν εἰ μὴ αὐτός, 13 καὶ περιβεβλημένος
knows except [him]self, and having been
clothed [with]

ἱμάτιον βεβαμμένον αἵματι, καὶ κέκληται
a garment having been in blood, and ²has been
dipped called

τὸ ὄνομα αὐτοῦ ὁ λόγος τοῦ θεοῦ.
¹the ²name ³of him The Word – of God.

14 καὶ τὰ στρατεύματα τὰ ἐν τῷ οὐρανῷ
And the armies the – in heaven

ἠκολούθει αὐτῷ ἐφ᾽ ἵπποις λευκοῖς, ἐνδεδυμένοι
followed him on ²horses ¹white, having been
dressed [in]

βύσσινον λευκὸν καθαρόν. 15 καὶ ἐκ
²fine linen ¹white ³clean. And out of

τοῦ στόματος αὐτοῦ ἐκπορεύεται ῥομφαία
the mouth of him proceeds ²sword

ὀξεῖα, ἵνα ἐν αὐτῇ πατάξῃ τὰ ἔθνη·
¹a sharp, in order with it he may the nations;
that smite

καὶ αὐτὸς ποιμανεῖ αὐτοὺς ἐν ῥάβδῳ
and he will shepherd them with ²staff

σιδηρᾷ· καὶ αὐτὸς πατεῖ τὴν ληνὸν
¹an iron; and he treads the winepress

τοῦ οἴνου τοῦ θυμοῦ τῆς ὀργῆς τοῦ
of the wine of the anger[,] of the wrath –

θεοῦ τοῦ παντοκράτορος. 16 καὶ ἔχει
of God of the Almighty. And he has

ἐπὶ τὸ ἱμάτιον καὶ ἐπὶ τὸν μηρὸν
on the garment and on the thigh

αὐτοῦ ὄνομα γεγραμμένον· ΒΑΣΙΛΕΥΣ
of him a name having been written: KING

ΒΑΣΙΛΕΩΝ ΚΑΙ ΚΥΡΙΟΣ ΚΥΡΙΩΝ.
OF KINGS AND LORD OF LORDS.

17 Καὶ εἶδον ἕνα ἄγγελον ἑστῶτα ἐν
And I saw one angel standing in

τῷ ἡλίῳ, καὶ ἔκραξεν ἐν φωνῇ μεγάλῃ
the sun, and he cried out in ²voice ¹a great
(loud)

λέγων πᾶσιν τοῖς ὀρνέοις τοῖς πετομένοις
saying to all the birds – flying

ἐν μεσουρανήματι· δεῦτε συνάχθητε εἰς
in mid-heaven: Come ye[.] assemble ye to

τὸ δεῖπνον τὸ μέγα τοῦ θεοῦ, 18 ἵνα
the ²supper ¹great – of God, in order
that

φάγητε σάρκας βασιλέων καὶ σάρκας
ye may eat fleshes of kings and fleshes

χιλιάρχων καὶ σάρκας ἰσχυρῶν καὶ σάρκας
of chiliarchs and fleshes of strong men and fleshes

King James Version

men, and the flesh of horses, and of them that sit on them, and the flesh of all *men, both* free and bond, both small and great. 19And I saw the beast, and the kings of the earth, and their armies, gathered together to make war against him that sat on the horse, and against his army. 20And the beast was taken, and with him the false prophet that wrought miracles before him, with which he deceived them that had received the mark of the beast, and them that worshipped his image. These both were cast alive into a lake of fire burning with brimstone. 21And the remnant were slain with the sword of him that sat upon the horse, which *sword* proceeded out of his mouth: and all the fowls were filled with their flesh.

20 And I saw an angel come down from heaven, having the key of the bottomless pit and a great chain in his hand. 2And he laid hold on the dragon, that old serpent, which is the Devil, and Satan, and bound him a thousand years, 3And cast him into the bottomless pit, and shut him up, and set a seal upon him, that he should deceive the nations no more, till the thousand years should be fulfilled: and after that he must be loosed a little season. 4And I saw thrones, and they sat upon them, and judgment was given unto them: and *I saw* the souls of them that were beheaded for the witness of Jesus, and for the word of God, and which had not worshipped the beast, neither his image, neither had received *his* mark upon their foreheads, or in their hands; and they lived and reigned with Christ a thousand years. 5 But the rest of the dead lived not again until the thousand years were finished. This *is* the first resurrection. 6 Blessed and holy *is* he that hath part in the first resurrection: on such the second death hath no power, but they shall be priests of God and of Christ, and shall reign with him a thousand years. 7And when the thousand years are expired, Satan shall be loosed out of his prison, 8And shall go out to deceive the nations which are in the four quarters of the earth, Gog and Magog, to gather them together to battle: the number of whom *is* as the sand of the sea. 9And they went up on the breadth of the earth, and compassed the camp of the saints about, and the beloved city: and fire came down from God out of heaven, and devoured them. 10And the devil that deceived them was cast into the lake of fire and brimstone, where the beast and the

New International Version

and their riders, and the flesh of all people, free and slave, small and great."
19 Then I saw the beast and the kings of the earth and their armies gathered together to make war against the rider on the horse and his army. 20 But the beast was captured, and with him the false prophet who had performed the miraculous signs on his behalf. With these signs he had deluded those who had received the mark of the beast and worshiped his image. The two of them were thrown alive into the fiery lake of burning sulfur. 21 The rest of them were killed with the sword that came out of the mouth of the rider on the horse, and all the birds gorged themselves on their flesh.

The thousand years

20 And I saw an angel coming down out of heaven, having the key to the Abyss and holding in his hand a great chain. 2 He seized the dragon, that ancient serpent, who is the devil, or Satan, and bound him for a thousand years. 3 He threw him into the Abyss, and locked and sealed it over him, to keep him from deceiving the nations any more until the thousand years were ended. After that, he must be set free for a short time.
4 I saw thrones on which were seated those who had been given authority to judge. And I saw the souls of those who had been beheaded because of their testimony for Jesus and because of the word of God. They had not worshiped the beast or his image and had not received his mark on their foreheads or their hands. They came to life and reigned with Christ a thousand years. 5 (The rest of the dead did not come to life until the thousand years were ended.) This is the first resurrection. 6 Blessed and holy are those who have part in the first resurrection. The second death has no power over them, but they will be priests of God and of Christ and will reign with him for a thousand years.

Satan's doom

7 When the thousand years are over, Satan will be released from his prison 8 and will go out to deceive the nations in the four corners of the earth—Gog and Magog—to gather them for battle. In number they are like the sand on the seashore. 9 They marched across the breadth of the earth and surrounded the camp of God's people, the city he loves. But fire came down from heaven and devoured them. 10And the devil, who deceived them, was thrown into the lake of burning sulfur, where the beast and the

Greek Interlinear

ἵππων   καὶ   τῶν   καθημένων   ἐπ'   αὐτῶν,
of horses   and   of the [ones] sitting   on   them,

καὶ   σάρκας   πάντων   ἐλευθέρων   τε   καὶ
and   fleshes   of all   ²free men   ¹both   and

δούλων   καὶ   μικρῶν   καὶ   μεγάλων.   19 Καὶ
slaves   both   small   and   great.   And

εἶδον   τὸ   θηρίον   καὶ   τοὺς   βασιλεῖς   τῆς
I saw   the   beast   and   the   kings   of the

γῆς   καὶ   τὰ   στρατεύματα   αὐτῶν   συνηγμένα
earth   and   the   armies   of them   having been
                                                assembled

ποιῆσαι   τὸν   πόλεμον   μετὰ   τοῦ   καθημένου
to make   the   war   with   the [one]   sitting

ἐπὶ   τοῦ   ἵππου   καὶ   μετὰ   τοῦ   στρατεύματος
on   the   horse   and   with   the   army

αὐτοῦ.   20 καὶ   ἐπιάσθη   τὸ   θηρίον   καὶ
of him.   And   ²was seized   ¹the   ²beast   and

μετ'   αὐτοῦ   ὁ   ψευδοπροφήτης   ὁ   ποιήσας
with   it   the   false prophet   the   having
                                             [one]   done

τὰ   σημεῖα   ἐνώπιον   αὐτοῦ,   ἐν   οἷς   ἐπλάνη-
the   signs   before   it,   by which   he de-

σεν   τοὺς   λαβόντας   τὸ   χάραγμα   τοῦ
ceived   the [ones]   having received   the   mark   of the

θηρίου   καὶ   τοὺς   προσκυνοῦντας   τῇ   εἰκόνι
beast   and   the [ones]   worshipping   the   image

αὐτοῦ·   ζῶντες   ἐβλήθησαν   οἱ   δύο   εἰς
of it;   ⁴living   ⁵were cast   ¹the   ²two   into

τὴν   λίμνην   τοῦ   πυρὸς   τῆς   καιομένης
the   lake   -   of fire   -   burning*

ἐν   θείῳ.   21 καὶ   οἱ   λοιποὶ   ἀπεκτάνθησαν
with   sulphur.   And   the   rest   were killed

ἐν   τῇ   ῥομφαίᾳ   τοῦ   καθημένου   ἐπὶ   τοῦ
with   the   sword   of the [one]   sitting   on   the

ἵππου   τῇ   ἐξελθούσῃ   ἐκ   τοῦ   στόματος
horse   -   proceeding§   out of   the   mouth

αὐτοῦ,   καὶ   πάντα   τὰ   ὄρνεα   ἐχορτάσθησαν
of him,   and   all   the   birds   were filled

ἐκ   τῶν   σαρκῶν   αὐτῶν.
by   the   fleshes   of them.

Chapter 20

Καὶ   εἶδον   ἄγγελον   καταβαίνοντα   ἐκ
And   I saw   an angel   coming down   out of

τοῦ   οὐρανοῦ,   ἔχοντα   τὴν   κλεῖν   τῆς
-    heaven,   having   the   key   of the

ἀβύσσου   καὶ   ἅλυσιν   μεγάλην   ἐπὶ   τὴν   χεῖρα
abyss   and   ²chain   ¹a great   on   the   hand

αὐτοῦ.   2 καὶ   ἐκράτησεν   τὸν   δράκοντα,
of him.   And   he laid hold [of]   the   dragon,

ὁ   ὄφις   ὁ   ἀρχαῖος,   ὅς   ἐστιν   Διάβολος
the ²serpent   -   ¹old,   who   is   Devil

καὶ   ὁ   Σατανᾶς,   καὶ   ἔδησεν   αὐτὸν   χίλια
and   -   Satan,   and   bound   him   a thou-
                                                 sand

ἔτη,   3 καὶ   ἔβαλεν   αὐτὸν   εἰς   τὴν   ἄβυσσον,
years,   and   cast   him   into   the   abyss,

καὶ   ἔκλεισεν   καὶ   ἐσφράγισεν   ἐπάνω   αὐτοῦ,
and   shut   and   ·sealed   over   him,

ἵνα   μὴ   πλανήσῃ   ἔτι   τὰ   ἔθνη,   ἄχρι
in or-   he should·not deceive   longer   the   nations,   until
der that

τελεσθῇ   τὰ   χίλια   ἔτη·   μετὰ   ταῦτα
²are finished   ¹the   ²thousand   ²years;   after these things

δεῖ   λυθῆναι   αὐτὸν   μικρὸν   χρόνον.
it be-   ²to be   ¹him   a little   time.
hoves   loosed

4 Καὶ   εἶδον   θρόνους,   καὶ   ἐκάθισαν   ἐπ'
And   I saw   thrones,   and   they sat   on

αὐτούς,   καὶ   κρίμα   ἐδόθη   αὐτοῖς,   καὶ
them,   and   judgment   was given   to them,   and

τὰς   ψυχὰς   τῶν   πεπελεκισμένων   διὰ   τὴν
the   souls   of the   having been   because of   the
                        [ones]   beheaded   of

μαρτυρίαν   Ἰησοῦ   καὶ   διὰ   τὸν   λόγον
witness   of Jesus   and   because of   the   word

τοῦ   θεοῦ,   καὶ   οἵτινες   οὐ   προσεκύνησαν
of God,   and   who   did not worship

τὸ   θηρίον   οὐδὲ   τὴν   εἰκόνα   αὐτοῦ   καὶ
the   beast   nor   the   image   of it   and

οὐκ   ἔλαβον   τὸ   χάραγμα   ἐπὶ   τὸ   μέτωπον
did not receive   the   mark   on   the   forehead

καὶ   ἐπὶ   τὴν   χεῖρα   αὐτῶν·   καὶ   ἔζησαν
and   on   the   hand   of them;   and   they lived
                                                  [again]

καὶ   ἐβασίλευσαν   μετὰ   τοῦ   Χριστοῦ   χίλια
and   reigned   with   -   Christ   a thou-
                                                sand

ἔτη.   5 οἱ   λοιποὶ   τῶν   νεκρῶν   οὐκ   ἔζησαν
years.   The   rest   of the   dead   did not live [again]

ἄχρι   τελεσθῇ   τὰ   χίλια   ἔτη.   Αὕτη   ἡ
until   were finished   the   thousand   years.   This [is] the

ἀνάστασις   ἡ   πρώτη.   6 μακάριος   καὶ
²resurrection   -   ¹first.   Blessed   and

ἅγιος   ὁ   ἔχων   μέρος   ἐν   τῇ   ἀναστάσει
holy [is]   the [one] having   part   in   the   ²resurrection

τῇ   πρώτῃ·   ἐπὶ   τούτων   ὁ   δεύτερος   θάνατος
-    ¹first;   over   these   the   second   death

οὐκ   ἔχει   ἐξουσίαν,   ἀλλ'   ἔσονται   ἱερεῖς
has not   authority,   but   they will be   priests

τοῦ   θεοῦ   καὶ   τοῦ   Χριστοῦ,   καὶ   βασιλεύ-
-    of God   and   -   of Christ,   and   will

σουσιν   μετ'   αὐτοῦ   [τὰ]   χίλια   ἔτη.
reign   with   him   the   thousand   years.

7 Καὶ   ὅταν   τελεσθῇ   τὰ   χίλια   ἔτη,
And   whenever   are finished   the   thousand   years,

λυθήσεται   ὁ   σατανᾶς   ἐκ   τῆς   φυλακῆς
¹will be loosed   -   ¹Satan   out of   the   prison

αὐτοῦ,   8 καὶ   ἐξελεύσεται   πλανῆσαι   τὰ
of him,   and   will go forth   to deceive   the

ἔθνη   τὰ   ἐν   ταῖς   τέσσαρσιν   γωνίαις   τῆς
nations   -   in   the   four   corners   of the

γῆς,   τὸν   Γὼγ   καὶ   Μαγώγ,   συναγαγεῖν
earth,   -   Gog   and   Magog,   to assemble

αὐτοὺς   εἰς   τὸν   πόλεμον,   ὧν   ὁ   ἀριθμὸς
them   to   the   war,   of whom   the   number

αὐτῶν   ὡς   ἡ   ἄμμος   τῆς   θαλάσσης.   9 καὶ
of them   as   the   sand   of the   sea.   And
[is]

ἀνέβησαν   ἐπὶ   τὸ   πλάτος   τῆς   γῆς,   καὶ
they went up   over   the   breadth   of the   land,   and

ἐκύκλευσαν   τὴν   παρεμβολὴν   τῶν   ἁγίων
encircled   the   camp   of the   saints

καὶ   τὴν   πόλιν   τὴν   ἠγαπημένην·   καὶ
and   the   ²city   -   having been ¹loved;   and

κατέβη   πῦρ   ἐκ   τοῦ   οὐρανοῦ   καὶ   κατέφαγεν
²came   ¹fire   out   -   heaven   and   devoured
down

αὐτούς·   10 καὶ   ὁ   διάβολος   ὁ   πλανῶν   αὐτοὺς
them;   and the   Devil   -   deceiving   them

ἐβλήθη   εἰς   τὴν   λίμνην   τοῦ   πυρὸς   καὶ
was cast   into   the   lake   -   of fire   and

θείου,   ὅπου   καὶ   τὸ   θηρίον   καὶ   ὁ
sulphur,   where [were]   also   the   beast   and   the

---

* Feminine, agreeing with λίμνη, not with the neuter πῦρ.

§ Agreeing, of course, with ῥομφαίᾳ.

King James Version

false prophet *are*, and shall be tormented day and night for ever and ever. 11And I saw a great white throne, and him that sat on it, from whose face the earth and the heaven fled away; and there was found no place for them. 12And I saw the dead, small and great, stand before God; and the books were opened: and another book was opened, which is *the book* of life: and the dead were judged out of those things which were written in the books, according to their works. 13And the sea gave up the dead which were in it; and death and hell delivered up the dead which were in them: and they were judged every man according to their works. 14And death and hell were cast into the lake of fire. This is the second death. 15And whosoever was not found written in the book of life was cast into the lake of fire.

21 And I saw a new heaven and a new earth: for the first heaven and the first earth were passed away; and there was no more sea. 2And I John saw the holy city, new Jerusalem, coming down from God out of heaven, prepared as a bride adorned for her husband. 3And I heard a great voice out of heaven saying, Behold, the tabernacle of God *is* with men, and he will dwell with them, and they shall be his people, and God himself shall be with them, *and be* their God. 4And God shall wipe away all tears from their eyes; and there shall be no more death, neither sorrow, nor crying, neither shall there be any more pain: for the former things are passed away. 5And he that sat upon the throne said, Behold, I make all things new. And he said unto me, Write: for these words are true and faithful. 6And he said unto me, It is done. I am Alpha and Omega, the beginning and the end. I will give unto him that is athirst of the fountain of the water of life freely. 7 He that overcometh shall inherit all things; and I will be his God, and he shall be my son. 8 But the fearful, and unbelieving, and the abominable, and murderers, and whoremongers, and sorcerers, and idolaters, and all liars, shall have their part in the lake which burneth with fire and brimstone: which is the second death. 9And there came unto me one of the seven angels which had the seven vials full of the seven last plagues, and talked with me, saying, Come hither, I will shew thee the bride, the Lamb's wife. 10And he carried me away in the spirit to a great and high moun-

New International Version

false prophet had been thrown. They will be tormented day and night for ever and ever.

The dead are judged

11 Then I saw a great white throne and him who was seated on it. Earth and sky fled from his presence, and there was no place for them. 12And I saw the dead, great and small, standing before the throne, and books were opened. Another book was opened, which is the book of life. The dead were judged according to what they had done as recorded in the books. 13 The sea gave up the dead that were in it, and death and Hades gave up the dead that were in them, and each person was judged according to what he had done. 14 Then death and Hades were thrown into the lake of fire. The lake of fire is the second death. 15 If anyone's name was not found written in the book of life, he was thrown into the lake of fire.

The new Jerusalem

21 Then I saw a new heaven and a new earth, for the first heaven and the first earth had passed away, and there was no longer any sea. 2 I saw the Holy City, the new Jerusalem, coming down out of heaven from God, prepared as a bride beautifully dressed for her husband. 3And I heard a loud voice from the throne saying, "Now the dwelling of God is with men, and he will live with them. They will be his people, and God himself will be with them and be their God. 4 He will wipe every tear from their eyes. There will be no more death or mourning or crying or pain, for the old order of things has passed away."

He who was seated on the throne said, "I am making everything new!" Then he said, "Write this down, for these words are trustworthy and true."

6 He said to me: "It is done. I am the Alpha and the Omega, the Beginning and the End. To him who is thirsty I will give to drink without cost from the spring of the water of life. 7 He who overcomes will inherit all this, and I will be his God and he will be my son. 8 But the cowardly, the unbelieving, the vile, the murderers, the sexually immoral, those who practice magic arts, the idolators and all liars—their place will be in the fiery lake of burning sulfur. This is the second death."

9 One of the seven angels who had the seven bowls full of the seven last plagues came and said to me, "Come, I will show you the bride, the wife of the Lamb." 10And he carried me away in the Spirit to a mountain great and high,

Greek Interlinear

ψευδοπροφήτης, καὶ βασανισθήσονται ἡμέρας
false prophet,   and   they will be tormented   day

καὶ νυκτὸς εἰς τοὺς αἰῶνας τῶν αἰώνων.
and   night   unto   the   ages   of the   ages.

11 Καὶ εἶδον θρόνον μέγαν λευκὸν καὶ
And   I saw   ¹throne   ¹a great   ¹white   and

τὸν καθήμενον ἐπ' αὐτὸν οὗ ἀπὸ τοῦ
the   sitting   on   it   ⁴of   ¹from   ²the
[one]   whom

προσώπου ἔφυγεν ἡ γῆ καὶ ὁ οὐρανός,
²face   ²fled   ¹the ¹earth ²and ⁴the   ²heaven,

καὶ τόπος οὐχ εὑρέθη αὐτοῖς. 12 καὶ
and   a place   was not found   for them.   And

εἶδον τοὺς νεκρούς, τοὺς μεγάλους καὶ
I saw   the   dead,   the   great   and

τοὺς μικρούς, ἑστῶτας ἐνώπιον τοῦ θρόνου,
the   small,   standing   before   the   throne,

καὶ βιβλία ἠνοίχθησαν· καὶ ἄλλο βιβλίον
and   scrolls   were opened;   and   another   scroll

ἠνοίχθη, ὅ ἐστιν τῆς ζωῆς· καὶ ἐκρίθησαν
was   which is [the –   of life;   and   ¹were judged
opened,   scroll]

οἱ νεκροὶ ἐκ τῶν γεγραμμένων ἐν τοῖς
¹the ²dead   by   the   having been   in   the
      things   written

βιβλίοις κατὰ τὰ ἔργα αὐτῶν. 13 καὶ
scrolls   accord-   the   works   of them.   And
    ing to

ἔδωκεν ἡ θάλασσα τοὺς νεκροὺς τοὺς
²gave   ¹the   ²sea   the   dead   –

ἐν αὐτῇ, καὶ ὁ θάνατος καὶ ὁ ᾅδης
in   it,   and   –   death   and   –   hades

ἔδωκαν τοὺς νεκροὺς τοὺς ἐν αὐτοῖς,
gave   the   dead   the   –   in   them,

καὶ ἐκρίθησαν ἕκαστος κατὰ τὰ ἔργα
and   they were judged   each one   according to   the   works

αὐτῶν. 14 καὶ ὁ θάνατος καὶ ὁ ᾅδης
of them.   And   –   death   and   –   hades

ἐβλήθησαν εἰς τὴν λίμνην τοῦ πυρός.
were cast   into   the   lake   –   of fire.

οὗτος ὁ θάνατος ὁ δεύτερός ἐστιν, ἡ
This   ¹the   ²death   –   ²second   ¹is,   the

λίμνη τοῦ πυρός. 15 καὶ εἴ τις οὐχ
lake   –   of fire.   And   if   anyone   not

εὑρέθη ἐν τῇ βίβλῳ τῆς ζωῆς γεγραμ-
was found   ²in   ¹the   ²scroll   –   ²of life   ¹having been

μένος, ἐβλήθη εἰς τὴν λίμνην τοῦ πυρός.
written,   he was cast   into   the   lake   –   of fire.

Chapter 21

Καὶ εἶδον οὐρανὸν καινὸν καὶ γῆν
And   I saw   ²heaven   ¹a new   and   ²earth

καινήν· ὁ γὰρ πρῶτος οὐρανὸς καὶ ἡ
¹a new;   for the   first   heaven   and   the

πρώτη γῆ ἀπῆλθαν, καὶ ἡ θάλασσα
first   earth   passed away,   and   the   sea

οὐκ ἔστιν ἔτι. 2 καὶ τὴν πόλιν τὴν
is not   longer.   And   ²the   ²city   –

ἁγίαν Ἰερουσαλὴμ καινὴν εἶδον κατα-
²holy   ¹Jerusalem   ¹new   ¹I saw   coming

βαίνουσαν ἐκ τοῦ οὐρανοῦ ἀπὸ τοῦ θεοῦ,
down   out of   –   heaven   from   –   God,

ἡτοιμασμένην ὡς νύμφην κεκοσμημένην
having been prepared   as   a bride   having been adorned

τῷ ἀνδρὶ αὐτῆς. 3 καὶ ἤκουσα φωνῆς
for the husband   of her.   And   I heard   ²voice

μεγάλης ἐκ τοῦ θρόνου λεγούσης· ἰδοὺ
¹a great(loud) out of   the   throne   saying: Behold[,]

ἡ σκηνὴ τοῦ θεοῦ μετὰ τῶν ἀνθρώπων,
the tabernacle   –   of God [is] with   the –   men,

καὶ σκηνώσει μετ' αὐτῶν, καὶ αὐτοὶ
and   he will tabernacle   with   them,   and   they

λαοὶ αὐτοῦ ἔσονται, καὶ αὐτὸς ὁ θεὸς
²peoples ¹of him   ¹will be,   and   ²[him]self   –   ¹God

μετ' αὐτῶν ἔσται, 4 καὶ ἐξαλείψει πᾶν
with   them   will be,   and   will wipe off   every

δάκρυον ἐκ τῶν ὀφθαλμῶν αὐτῶν, καὶ
tear   out of   the   eyes   of them,   and

ὁ θάνατος οὐκ ἔσται ἔτι, οὔτε πένθος
–   death   will not be   longer,   nor   sorrow

οὔτε κραυγὴ οὔτε πόνος οὐκ ἔσται ἔτι·
nor   clamour   nor   pain   will not be   longer;

ὅτι τὰ πρῶτα ἀπῆλθαν. 5 καὶ εἶπεν
because the   first things   passed away.   And   ¹said

ὁ καθήμενος ἐπὶ τῷ θρόνῳ· ἰδοὺ καινὰ
¹the [one] ¹sitting   ²on   ²the   throne: Behold   ¹new

ποιῶ πάντα. καὶ λέγει· γράψον, ὅτι
²I make   ¹all things.   And   he says: Write thou, because

οὗτοι οἱ λόγοι πιστοὶ καὶ ἀληθινοί εἰσιν.
these   –   words   faithful   and   true   are.

6 καὶ εἶπέν μοι· γέγοναν. ἐγὼ τὸ ἄλφα
And   he said   to me: It has occurred.*   I [am] the   alpha

καὶ τὸ ὦ, ἡ ἀρχὴ καὶ τὸ τέλος. ἐγὼ
and   the omega, the beginning   and   the   end.   ¹I

τῷ διψῶντι δώσω ἐκ τῆς πηγῆς
¹to the [one] ²thirsting   ⁴will give   out of   the   fountain

τοῦ ὕδατος τῆς ζωῆς δωρεάν. 7 ὁ νικῶν
of the   water   –   of life   freely.   The over-
                                 [one] coming

κληρονομήσει ταῦτα, καὶ ἔσομαι αὐτῷ
shall inherit   these things,   and   I will be   to him

θεὸς καὶ αὐτὸς ἔσται μοι υἱός. 8 τοῖς δὲ
God   and   he   shall be   to me   a son.   But for the

δειλοῖς καὶ ἀπίστοις καὶ ἐβδελυγμένοις
cowardly   and   unbelieving   and   having become foul

καὶ φονεῦσιν καὶ πόρνοις καὶ φαρμακοῖς
and   murderers   and   fornicators   and   sorcerers

καὶ εἰδωλολάτραις καὶ πᾶσιν τοῖς ψευδέσιν
and   idolaters   and   all   the   false [ones]

τὸ μέρος αὐτῶν ἐν τῇ λίμνῃ τῇ καιομένῃ
the   part   of them   in   the   lake –   burning

πυρὶ καὶ θείῳ, ὅ ἐστιν ὁ θάνατος ὁ
with fire and   with   which   is   the   ²death   –
            sulphur,

δεύτερος.
¹second [, shall be].

9 Καὶ ἦλθεν εἷς ἐκ τῶν ἑπτὰ ἀγγέλων
And   came   one   of   the   seven   angels

τῶν ἐχόντων τὰς ἑπτὰ φιάλας, τῶν
   –   having   the   seven   bowls,   the

γεμόντων τῶν ἑπτὰ πληγῶν τῶν ἐσχάτων,
being filled   of(with)   seven   ²plagues   –   ¹last,

καὶ ἐλάλησεν μετ' ἐμοῦ λέγων· δεῦρο,
and   spoke   with   me   saying: Come,

δείξω σοι τὴν νύμφην τὴν γυναῖκα
I will show thee   the   bride[,]   the   wife

τοῦ ἀρνίου. 10 καὶ ἀπήνεγκέν με ἐν
of the   Lamb.   And   he bore away   me   in

πνεύματι ἐπὶ ὄρος μέγα καὶ ὑψηλόν,
spirit   onto   ²mountain ¹a great ²and   ¹high,

καὶ ἔδειξέν μοι τὴν πόλιν τὴν ἁγίαν
and   showed   me   the   ²city   –   ¹holy

* Collective neuter plural; cf. ch. 16. 17.

King James Version

tain, and shewed me that great city, the holy Jerusalem, descending out of heaven from God, 11 Having the glory of God: and her light *was* like unto a stone most precious, even like a jasper stone, clear as crystal; 12And had a wall great and high, *and* had twelve gates, and at the gates twelve angels, and names written thereon, which are *the names* of the twelve tribes of the children of Israel: 13 On the east three gates; on the north three gates; on the south three gates; and on the west three gates. 14And the wall of the city had twelve foundations, and in them the names of the twelve apostles of the Lamb. 15And he that talked with me had a golden reed to measure the city, and the gates thereof, and the wall thereof. 16And the city lieth foursquare, and the length is as large as the breadth: and he measured the city with the reed, twelve thousand furlongs. The length and the breadth and the height of it are equal. 17And he measured the wall thereof, a hundred *and* forty *and* four cubits, *according to* the measure of a man, that is, of the angel. 18And the building of the wall of it was *of* jasper: and the city *was* pure gold, like unto clear glass. 19And the foundations of the wall of the city *were* garnished with all manner of precious stones. The first foundation *was* jasper; the second, sapphire; the third, a chalcedony; the fourth, an emerald; 20 The fifth, sardonyx; the sixth, sardius; the seventh, chrysolite; the eighth, beryl; the ninth, a topaz; the tenth, a chrysoprasus; the eleventh, a jacinth; the twelfth, an amethyst. 21And the twelve gates *were* twelve pearls; every several gate was of one pearl: and the street of the city *was* pure gold, as it were transparent glass. 22And I saw no temple therein: for the Lord God Almighty and the Lamb are the temple of it. 23And the city had no need of the sun, neither of the moon, to shine in it: for the glory of God did lighten it, and the Lamb *is* the light thereof. 24And the nations of them which are saved shall walk in the light of it: and the kings of the earth do bring their glory and honour into it. 25And the gates of it shall not be shut at all by day: for there shall be no night there. 26And they shall bring the glory and honour of the nations into it. 27And there shall in no wise enter into it any thing that defileth, neither *whatsoever* worketh abomination, or *maketh* a lie: but they which are written in the Lamb's book of life.

New International Version

and showed me the Holy City, Jerusalem, coming down out of heaven from God. 11·It shone with the glory of God, and its brilliance was like that of a very precious jewel, like a jasper, clear as crystal. 12 It had a great, high wall with twelve gates, and with twelve angels at the gates. On the gates were written the names of the twelve tribes of Israel. 13 There were three gates on the east, three on the north, three on the south and three on the west. 14 The wall of the city had twelve foundations, and on them were the names of the twelve apostles of the Lamb.

15 The angel who talked with me had a measuring rod of gold to measure the city, its gates and its wall. 16 The city was laid out like a square, as long as it was wide. He measured the city with the rod and found it to be 12,000 stadia*ˢ* in length, and as wide and high as it is long. 17 He measured its wall and it was 144 cubits*ᵗ* thick,*ᵘ* by man's measurement, which the angel was using. 18 The wall was made of jasper, and the city of pure gold, as pure as glass. 19 The foundations of the city walls were decorated with every kind of precious stone. The first foundation was jasper, the second sapphire, the third chalcedony, the fourth emerald, 20 the fifth sardonyx, the sixth carnelian, the seventh chrysolite, the eighth beryl, the ninth topaz, the tenth chrysoprase, the eleventh jacinth, and the twelfth amethyst. 21 The twelve gates were twelve pearls, each gate made of a single pearl. The street of the city was of pure gold, like transparent glass.

22 I did not see a temple in the city, because the Lord God Almighty and the Lamb are its temple. 23 The city does not need the sun or the moon to shine on it, for the glory of God gives it light, and the Lamb is its lamp. 24 The nations will walk by its light, and the kings of the earth will bring their splendor into it. 25 On no day will its gates ever be shut, for there will be no night there. 26 The glory and honor of the nations will be brought into it. 27 Nothing impure will ever enter it, nor will anyone who does what is shameful or deceitful, but only those whose names are written in the Lamb's book of life.

[s] That is, about 1500 miles. [t] That is, somewhat more than 200 feet. [u] Or *high*.

Greek Interlinear

Ἰερουσαλὴμ καταβαίνουσαν ἐκ τοῦ οὐρανοῦ
Jerusalem coming down out of - heaven

ἀπὸ τοῦ θεοῦ, 11 ἔχουσαν τὴν δόξαν
from - God, having the glory

τοῦ θεοῦ· ὁ φωστὴρ αὐτῆς ὅμοιος λίθῳ
- of God; the light of it [was] like to a stone

τιμιωτάτῳ, ὡς λίθῳ ἰάσπιδι κρυσταλλίζοντι·
very valuable, as ²stone ¹to a jasper being clear as crystal;

12 ἔχουσα τεῖχος μέγα καὶ ὑψηλόν,
having ⁴wall ¹a great ²and ³high,

ἔχουσα πυλῶνας δώδεκα, καὶ ἐπὶ τοῖς
having ²gates ¹twelve, and at the

πυλῶσιν ἀγγέλους δώδεκα, καὶ ὀνόματα
gates ²angels ¹twelve, and names

ἐπιγεγραμμένα, ἃ ἐστιν τῶν δώδεκα
having been inscribed, which is(are) of the twelve

φυλῶν υἱῶν Ἰσραήλ. 13 ἀπὸ ἀνατολῆς
tribes of sons of Israel. From east

πυλῶνες τρεῖς, καὶ ἀπὸ βορρᾶ πυλῶνες
²gates ¹three, and from north ²gates

τρεῖς, καὶ ἀπὸ νότου πυλῶνες τρεῖς,
¹three, and from south ²gates ¹three,

καὶ ἀπὸ δυσμῶν πυλῶνες τρεῖς. 14 καὶ
and from west ²gates ¹three. And

τὸ τεῖχος τῆς πόλεως ἔχων θεμελίους
the wall of the city having ²foundations

δώδεκα, καὶ ἐπ' αὐτῶν δώδεκα ὀνόματα
¹twelve, and on them twelve names

τῶν δώδεκα ἀποστόλων τοῦ ἀρνίου. 15 Καὶ
of the twelve apostles of the Lamb. And

ὁ λαλῶν μετ' ἐμοῦ εἶχεν μέτρον κάλαμον
the speak- with me had ²measure ³reed
[one] ing

χρυσοῦν, ἵνα μετρήσῃ τὴν πόλιν καὶ
¹a golden, in order he might the city and
that measure

τοὺς πυλῶνας αὐτῆς καὶ τὸ τεῖχος αὐτῆς.
the gates of it and the wall of it.

16 καὶ ἡ πόλις τετράγωνος κεῖται, καὶ
And the city ²square ¹lies, and

τὸ μῆκος αὐτῆς ὅσον τὸ πλάτος. καὶ
the length of it [is] as much as the breadth. And

ἐμέτρησεν τὴν πόλιν τῷ καλάμῳ ἐπὶ
he measured the city with the reed at

σταδίων δώδεκα χιλιάδων· τὸ μῆκος καὶ
²furlongs ¹twelve ³thousands; the length and

τὸ πλάτος καὶ τὸ ὕψος αὐτῆς ἴσα ἐστίν.
the breadth and the height of it ²equal ¹is(are).

17 καὶ ἐμέτρησεν τὸ τεῖχος αὐτῆς ἑκατὸν
And he measured the wall of it of a hundred

τεσσεράκοντα τεσσάρων πηχῶν, μέτρον
[and] forty-four cubits, a measure

ἀνθρώπου, ὅ ἐστιν ἀγγέλου. 18 καὶ
of a man, which is of an angel. And

ἡ ἐνδώμησις τοῦ τείχους αὐτῆς ἴασπις,
the coping of the wall of it [was] jasper,

καὶ ἡ πόλις χρυσίον καθαρὸν ὅμοιον
and the city [was] ²gold ¹clean(pure) like

ὑάλῳ καθαρῷ. 19 οἱ θεμέλιοι τοῦ τείχους
²glass ¹to clean(pure). The foundations of the wall

τῆς πόλεως παντὶ λίθῳ τιμίῳ κεκοσμημένοι·
of the city ³with ²stone ¹precious ⁴having been
every adorned;

ὁ θεμέλιος ὁ πρῶτος ἴασπις, ὁ δεύτερος
the foundation - first jasper, the second

σάπφιρος, ὁ τρίτος χαλκηδών, ὁ τέταρτος
sapphire, the third chalcedony, the fourth

σμάραγδος, 20 ὁ πέμπτος σαρδόνυξ, ὁ
emerald, the fifth sardonyx, the

ἕκτος σάρδιον, ὁ ἕβδομος χρυσόλιθος,
sixth sardius, the seventh chrysolite,

ὁ ὄγδοος βήρυλλος, ὁ ἔνατος τοπάζιον,
the eighth beryl, the ninth topaz,

ὁ δέκατος χρυσόπρασος, ὁ ἐνδέκατος
the tenth chrysoprasus, the eleventh

ὑάκινθος, ὁ δωδέκατος ἀμέθυστος. 21 καὶ
hyacinth, the twelfth amethyst. And

οἱ δώδεκα πυλῶνες δώδεκα μαργαρῖται·
the twelve gates [were] twelve pearls;

ἀνὰ εἷς ἕκαστος τῶν πυλώνων ἦν ἐξ
respec- ²one ¹each of the gates was of
tively†

ἑνὸς μαργαρίτου. καὶ ἡ πλατεῖα τῆς
one pearl. And the street of the

πόλεως χρυσίον καθαρὸν ὡς ὕαλος διαυγής.
city [was] ²gold ¹clean(pure) as ²glass ¹transparent.

22 Καὶ ναὸν οὐκ εἶδον ἐν αὐτῇ· ὁ γὰρ
And a shrine I saw not in it; for the

κύριος ὁ θεὸς ὁ παντοκράτωρ ναὸς αὐτῆς
Lord - God the Almighty shrine of it

ἐστιν, καὶ τὸ ἀρνίον. 23 καὶ ἡ πόλις
is, and the Lamb. And the city

οὐ χρείαν ἔχει τοῦ ἡλίου οὐδὲ τῆς
not need has of the sun nor of the

σελήνης, ἵνα φαίνωσιν αὐτῇ· ἡ γὰρ
moon, in order they might in it; for the
that shine

δόξα τοῦ θεοῦ ἐφώτισεν αὐτήν, καὶ
glory - of God enlightened it, and

ὁ λύχνος αὐτῆς τὸ ἀρνίον. 24 καὶ
the lamp of it [is] the Lamb. And

περιπατήσουσιν τὰ ἔθνη διὰ τοῦ φωτὸς
²shall walk about ¹the ²nations through the light

αὐτῆς, καὶ οἱ βασιλεῖς τῆς γῆς φέρουσιν
of it, and the kings of the earth bring

τὴν δόξαν αὐτῶν εἰς αὐτήν· 25 καὶ οἱ
the glory of them into it; and the

πυλῶνες αὐτῆς οὐ μὴ κλεισθῶσιν ἡμέρας,
gates of it by no means may be shut by day,

νὺξ γὰρ οὐκ ἔσται ἐκεῖ· 26 καὶ οἴσουσιν
for night shall not be there; and they will
bring

τὴν δόξαν καὶ τὴν τιμὴν τῶν ἐθνῶν
the glory and the honour of the nations

εἰς αὐτήν. 27 καὶ οὐ μὴ εἰσέλθῃ εἰς
into it. And by no means may enter into

αὐτὴ πᾶν κοινὸν καὶ [ὁ] ποιῶν
it every(any) profane thing and the [one] making

βδέλυγμα καὶ ψεῦδος, εἰ μὴ οἱ γεγραμ-
an and a lie, except the having been
abomination [ones]

μένοι ἐν τῷ βιβλίῳ τῆς ζωῆς τοῦ ἀρνίου.
written in the scroll - of life of the Lamb.

King James Version

New International Version

The river of life

22 And he shewed me a pure river of water of life, clear as crystal, proceeding out of the throne of God and of the Lamb. 2 In the midst of the street of it, and on either side of the river, *was there* the tree of life, which bare twelve *manner of* fruits, *and* yielded her fruit every month: and the leaves of the tree *were* for the healing of the nations. 3And there shall be no more curse: but the throne of God and of the Lamb shall be in it; and his servants shall serve him: 4And they shall see his face; and his name *shall be* in their foreheads. 5And there shall be no night there; and they need no candle, neither light of the sun; for the Lord God giveth them light: and they shall reign for ever and ever. 6And he said unto me, These sayings *are* faithful and true: and the Lord God of the holy prophets sent his angel to shew unto his servants the things which must shortly be done. 7 Behold, I come quickly: blessed *is* he that keepeth the sayings of the prophecy of this book. 8And I John saw these things, and heard *them.* And when I had heard and seen, I fell down to worship before the feet of the angel which shewed me these things. 9 Then saith he unto me, See *thou do it* not: for I am thy fellow servant, and of thy brethren the prophets, and of them which keep the sayings of this book: worship God. 10And he saith unto me, Seal not the sayings of the prophecy of this book: for the time is at hand. 11 He that is unjust, let him be unjust still: and he which is filthy, let him be filthy still: and he that is righteous, let him be righteous still: and he that is holy, let him be holy still. 12And, behold, I come quickly; and my reward *is* with me, to give every man according as his work shall be. 13 I am Alpha and Omega, the beginning and the end, the first and the last. 14 Blessed *are* they that do his commandments, that they may have right to the tree of life, and may enter in through the gates into the city. 15 For without *are* dogs, and sorcerers, and whoremongers, and murderers, and idolaters, and whosoever loveth and maketh a lie. 16 I Jesus have sent mine angel to testify unto you these things in the churches. I am the root and the offspring of David, *and* the bright and morning star. 17And the Spirit and the bride say, Come. And let him that heareth say, Come. And let him that is athirst come. And whosoever

22 Then the angel showed me the river of the water of life, as clear as crystal, flowing from the throne of God and of the Lamb 2 down the middle of the great street of the city. On each side of the river stood the tree of life, bearing twelve crops of fruit, yielding its fruit every month. And the leaves of the tree are for the healing of the nations. 3 No longer will there be any curse. The throne of God and of the Lamb will be in the city, and his servants will serve him. 4 They will see his face, and his name will be on their foreheads. 5 There will be no more night. They will not need the light of a lamp or the light of the sun, for the Lord God will give them light. And they will reign for ever and ever.

6 The angel said to me, "These words are trustworthy and true. The Lord, the God of the spirits of the prophets, sent his angel to show his servants the things that must soon take place."

Jesus is coming

7 "Behold, I am coming soon! Blessed is he who keeps the words of the prophecy in this book."

8 I, John, am the one who heard and saw these things. And when I had heard and seen them, I fell down to worship at the feet of the angel who had been showing them to me. 9 But he said to me, "Do not do it! I am a fellow servant with you and with your brothers the prophets and of all who keep the words of this book. Worship God!"

10 Then he told me, "Do not seal up the words of the prophecy of this book, because the time is near. 11 Let him who does wrong continue to do wrong; let him who is vile continue to be vile; let him who does right continue to do right; and let him who is holy continue to be holy."

12 "Behold, I am coming soon! My reward is with me, and I will give to everyone according to what he has done. 13 I am the Alpha and the Omega, the First and the Last, the Beginning and the End.

14 "Blessed are those who wash their robes, that they may have the right to the tree of life and may go through the gates into the city. 15 Outside are the dogs, those who practice magic arts, the sexually immoral, the murderers, the idolaters and everyone who loves and practices falsehood.

16 "I, Jesus, have sent my angel to give you*v* this testimony for the churches. I am the Root and the Offspring of David, and the bright Morning Star."

17 The Spirit and the bride say, "Come!" And let him who hears say, "Come!" Whoever is thirsty, let him come; and whoever wishes, let him take the free gift of the water of life.

[v] Greek *you* (plural).

Greek Interlinear

Chapter 22

Καὶ   ἔδειξέν   μοι   ποταμὸν   ὕδατος
And   he showed   me   a river   of water

ζωῆς   λαμπρὸν   ὡς   κρύσταλλον,   ἐκπορευόμε-
of life   bright   as   crystal,   proceed-

νον   ἐκ   τοῦ   θρόνου   τοῦ   θεοῦ   καὶ   τοῦ
ing   out of   the   throne   –   of God   and   of the

ἀρνίου.   2 ἐν   μέσῳ   τῆς   πλατείας   αὐτῆς
Lamb.   In [the] midst   of the   street   of it

καὶ   τοῦ   ποταμοῦ   ἐντεῦθεν   καὶ   ἐκεῖθεν
and   of the   river   hence   and   thence

ξύλον   ζωῆς   ποιοῦν   καρποὺς   δώδεκα,
a tree   of life   producing   fruits   twelve,

κατὰ   μῆνα   ἕκαστον   ἀποδιδοῦν   τὸν   καρπὸν
accord-   ¹month   ¹each   rendering   the   fruit
ing to

αὐτοῦ,   καὶ   τὰ   φύλλα   τοῦ   ξύλου   εἰς
of it,   and   the   leaves   of the   tree [will be] for

θεραπείαν   τῶν   ἐθνῶν.   3 καὶ   πᾶν   κατάθεμα
healing   of the   nations.   And every   curse
=no curse will be any

οὐκ   ἔσται   ἔτι.   καὶ   ὁ   θρόνος   τοῦ   θεοῦ
will not be   longer.   And   the   throne   –   of God

καὶ   τοῦ   ἀρνίου   ἐν   αὐτῇ   ἔσται,   καὶ   οἱ
and   of the   Lamb   ²in   ³it   ¹will be,   and   the

δοῦλοι   αὐτοῦ   λατρεύσουσιν   αὐτῷ,   4 καὶ
slaves   of him   will do service   to him,   and

ὄψονται   τὸ   πρόσωπον   αὐτοῦ,   καὶ   τὸ
they will see   the   face   of him,   and   the

ὄνομα   αὐτοῦ   ἐπὶ   τῶν   μετώπων   αὐτῶν.
name   of him [will be] on   the   foreheads   of them.

5 καὶ   νὺξ   οὐκ   ἔσται   ἔτι,   καὶ   οὐκ
And   night   will not be   longer,   and   not

ἔχουσι   χρείαν   φωτὸς   λύχνου   καὶ   φωτὸς
they have   need   of light   of lamp   and   of light

ἡλίου,   ὅτι   κύριος   ὁ   θεὸς   φωτίσει   ἐπ᾽
of sun,   because [the] Lord   –   God   will shed light   on

αὐτούς,   καὶ   βασιλεύσουσιν   εἰς   τοὺς
them,   and   they will reign   unto   the

αἰῶνας   τῶν   αἰώνων.
ages   of the   ages.

6 Καὶ   εἶπέν   μοι·   οὗτοι   οἱ   λόγοι   πιστοὶ
And   he said to me: These   –   words [are] faithful

καὶ   ἀληθινοί,   καὶ   ὁ   κύριος   ὁ   θεὸς   τῶν
and   true,   and   the   Lord   the   God   of the

πνευμάτων   τῶν   προφητῶν   ἀπέστειλεν   τὸν
spirits   of the   prophets   sent   the

ἄγγελον   αὐτοῦ   δεῖξαι   τοῖς   δούλοις   αὐτοῦ
angel   of him   to show   to the   slaves   of him

ἃ   δεῖ   γενέσθαι   ἐν   τάχει.   7 καὶ   ἰδοὺ
things it be-   to occur   quickly.   And behold
which hoves

ἔρχομαι   ταχύ.   μακάριος   ὁ   τηρῶν   τοὺς
I am coming quickly.   Blessed [is] the [one] keeping   the

λόγους   τῆς   προφητείας   τοῦ   βιβλίου   τούτου.
words   of the   prophecy   of this scroll.

8 Κἀγὼ   Ἰωάννης   ὁ   ἀκούων   καὶ   βλέπων
And I   John   [am] the [one] hearing   and   seeing

ταῦτα.   καὶ   ὅτε   ἤκουσα   καὶ   ἔβλεψα,
these things.   And   when   I heard   and   I saw,

ἔπεσα   προσκυνῆσαι   ἔμπροσθεν   τῶν   ποδῶν
I fell   to worship   before   the   feet

τοῦ   ἀγγέλου   τοῦ   δεικνύοντός   μοι   ταῦτα.
of the   angel   –   showing   me   me these things.

9 καὶ   λέγει   μοι·   ὅρα   μή·   ²σύνδουλός
And   he tells   me: See thou [do] not;   ²a fellow-slave

σοῦ   εἰμι   καὶ   τῶν   ἀδελφῶν   σου   τῶν
²of thee   ¹I am   and   of the   brothers   of thee   the

προφητῶν   καὶ   τῶν   τηρούντων   τοὺς   λόγους
prophets   and   of the [ones] keeping   the   words

τοῦ   βιβλίου   τούτου·   τῷ   θεῷ   προσκύνησον.
of this scroll: –   ²God   ¹worship thou.

10 Καὶ   λέγει   μοι·   μὴ   σφραγίσῃς   τοὺς
And   he tells   me: Seal not   the

λόγους   τῆς   προφητείας   τοῦ   βιβλίου   τούτου·
words   of the   prophecy   of this scroll;

ὁ   καιρὸς   γὰρ   ἐγγύς   ἐστιν   11 ὁ   ἀδικῶν
²the   ²time   ¹for   ⁴near   ⁵is.   The   [one] unjustly
acting

ἀδικησάτω   ἔτι,   καὶ   ὁ   ῥυπαρὸς   ῥυπανθήτω
let him act   still,   and   the   filthy [one]   let him act
unjustly   filthily

ἔτι,   καὶ   ὁ   δίκαιος   δικαιοσύνην   ποιησάτω
still,   and   the   righteous [one]   ²righteousness   ¹let him do

ἔτι,   καὶ   ὁ   ἅγιος   ἁγιασθήτω   ἔτι.
still,   and   the   holy [one]   let him be hallowed   still.

12 Ἰδοὺ   ἔρχομαι   ταχύ,   καὶ   ὁ   μισθός
Behold   I am coming quickly,   and   the   reward

μου   μετ᾽   ἐμοῦ,   ἀποδοῦναι   ἑκάστῳ   ὡς
of me [is] with   me,   to render   to each man   as

τὸ   ἔργον   ἐστὶν   αὐτοῦ.   13 ἐγὼ   τὸ   ἄλφα
the   work   ²is   ¹of him.   I [am] the   alpha

καὶ   τὸ   ὦ,   ὁ   πρῶτος   καὶ   ὁ   ἔσχατος,
and   the   omega, the   first   and   the   last,

ἡ   ἀρχὴ   καὶ   τὸ   τέλος.   14 μακάριοι   οἱ
the begin-   and   the   end.   Blessed   the
ning   [are]   [ones]

πλύνοντες   τὰς   στολὰς   αὐτῶν,   ἵνα   ἔσται
washing   the   robes   of them,   in or-   ²will be
der that

ἡ   ἐξουσία   αὐτῶν   ἐπὶ   τὸ   ξύλον   τῆς
¹the   ²authority   ³of them   over   the   tree   –

ζωῆς   καὶ   τοῖς   πυλῶσιν   εἰσέλθωσιν   εἰς
of life   and   ²by the   ²gates   ¹they may enter   into

τὴν   πόλιν.   15 ἔξω   οἱ   κύνες   καὶ   οἱ   φαρμακοὶ
the   city.   Outside   the   dogs   and   the   sorcerers
[are]

καὶ   οἱ   πόρνοι   καὶ   οἱ   φονεῖς   καὶ   οἱ
and   the   fornicators   and   the   murderers   and   the

εἰδωλολάτραι   καὶ   πᾶς   φιλῶν   καὶ   ποιῶν
idolaters   and   everyone   loving   and   making

ψεῦδος.
a lie.

16 Ἐγὼ   Ἰησοῦς   ἔπεμψα   τὸν   ἄγγελόν
I   Jesus   sent   the   angel

μου   μαρτυρῆσαι   ὑμῖν   ταῦτα   ἐπὶ   ταῖς
of me   to witness   to you   these things   over(in)   the

ἐκκλησίαις.   ἐγώ   εἰμι   ἡ   ῥίζα   καὶ   τὸ
churches.   I   am   the   root   and   the

γένος   Δαυίδ,   ὁ   ἀστὴρ   ὁ   λαμπρὸς   ὁ
offspring   of David,   the   ²star   –   ¹bright   the

πρωϊνός.
²morning.

17 Καὶ   τὸ   πνεῦμα   καὶ   ἡ   νύμφη   λέγουσιν·
And   the   Spirit   and   the   bride   say:

ἔρχου.   καὶ   ὁ   ἀκούων   εἰπάτω·   ἔρχου.
Come.   And the [one] hearing   let him say: Come.

καὶ   ὁ   διψῶν   ἐρχέσθω,   ὁ   θέλων   λαβέτω
And   the   thirsting   let him   the   wishing   let him
[one]   come,   [one]   take

ὕδωρ   ζωῆς   δωρεάν.
[the]   of life   freely.
water

King James Version

will, let him take the water of life freely. 18 For I testify unto every man that heareth the words of the prophecy of this book, If any man shall add unto these things, God shall add unto him the plagues that are written in this book: 19And if any man shall take away from the words of the book of this prophecy, God shall take away his part out of the book of life, and out of the holy city, and *from* the things which are written in this book. 20 He which testifieth these things saith, Surely I come quickly: Amen. Even so, come, Lord Jesus. 21 The grace of our Lord Jesus Christ *be* with you all. Amen.

New International Version

18 I warn everyone who hears the words of the prophecy of this book: If anyone adds anything to them, God will add to him the plagues described in this book. 19And if anyone takes words away from this book of prophecy, God will take away from him his share in the tree of life and in the holy city, which are described in this book.

20 He who testifies to these things says, "Yes, I am coming soon."

Amen. Come, Lord Jesus.

21 The grace of the Lord Jesus be with God's people. Amen.

Greek Interlinear

18 Μαρτυρῶ ἐγὼ παντὶ τῷ ἀκούοντι
ᵃwitness   ¹I   to everyone   hearing

τοὺς λόγους τῆς προφητείας τοῦ βιβλίου
the   words   of the   prophecy   –   ᵃscroll

τούτου· ἐάν τις ἐπιθῇ ἐπ' αὐτά, ἐπιθήσει
¹of this: If anyone   adds   upon(to) them,°   ᵃwill add

ὁ θεὸς ἐπ' αὐτὸν τὰς πληγὰς τὰς
–   ¹God   upon   him   the   plagues   –

γεγραμμένας ἐν τῷ βιβλίῳ τούτῳ· **19** καὶ
having been written in   this scroll;   and

ἐάν τις ἀφέλῃ ἀπὸ τῶν λόγων τοῦ
if   anyone takes away   from   the   words   of the

βιβλίου τῆς προφητείας ταύτης, ἀφελεῖ
scroll   of this prophecy,   ᵃwill take
            away

ὁ θεὸς τὸ μέρος αὐτοῦ ἀπὸ τοῦ ξύλου
–   ¹God   the   part   of him   from   the   tree

τῆς ζωῆς καὶ ἐκ τῆς πόλεως τῆς ἁγίας,
–   of life   and   out of   the   ᵃcity   –   ¹holy,

τῶν γεγραμμένων ἐν τῷ βιβλίῳ τούτῳ.
of the   *having been*   in   this scroll.
things   written

20 Λέγει ὁ μαρτυρῶν ταῦτα· ναί, ἔρχομαι
  Says   the   witnessing   these   Yes,   I am
    [one]   things: coming

ταχύ. Ἀμήν, ἔρχου κύριε Ἰησοῦ.
quickly.   Amen,   come[,]   Lord   Jesus.

21 Ἡ χάρις τοῦ κυρίου Ἰησοῦ μετὰ
  The   grace   of the   Lord   Jesus [be]   with

πάντων.
all.

---

* Neuter plural; see last clause of ver. 19.